THE PALGRAVE DICTIONARY
OF
TRANSNATIONAL HISTORY

THE PALGRAVE DICTIONARY OF TRANSNATIONAL HISTORY

Edited by

Akira Iriye
Harvard University, USA

and

Pierre-Yves Saunier
Centre National de la Recherche Scientifique, France

palgrave
macmillan

First published 2009 by
PALGRAVE MACMILLAN

Palgrave Macmillan in the UK is an imprint of Macmillan Publishers Limited, registered in England, company number 785998, of Houndmills, Basingstoke, Hampshire RG21 6XS.

Palgrave Macmillan in the US is a division of St. Martin's Press LLC, 175 Fifth Avenue, New York, NY 10010.

Palgrave Macmillan is the global academic imprint of the above companies and has companies and representatives throughout the world.

Palgrave® and Macmillan® are registered trademarks in the United States, the United Kingdom, Europe and other countries.

ISBN-13: 978-1-4039-9295-6
ISBN-10: 1-4039-9295-9

This book is printed on paper suitable for recycling and made from fully managed and sustained forest sources. Logging, pulping and manufacturing processes are expected to conform to the environmental regulations of the country of origin.

A catalogue record for this book is available from the British Library.

A catalog record for this book is available from the Library of Congress.

10 9 8 7 6 5 4 3 2 1
18 17 16 15 14 13 12 11 10 09

Printed in China

Contents

Editorial Board

General Editors

Akira Iriye
Harvard University, USA

Pierre-Yves Saunier
Centre National de la Recherche Scientifique, France

Associate Editors

Jane Carruthers
University of South Africa, South Africa

Donna Gabaccia
University of Minnesota, USA

Rana Mitter
University of Oxford, UK

Mariano Plotkin
Instituto de Desarrollo Económico y Social, Argentina

Patrick Verley
Université de Genève, Switzerland

List of Contributors

Monia Abdallah
École des Hautes Études en Sciences Sociales, France

Phina Geraldine Abir-Am
Brandeis University, USA

Thomas Adam
University of Texas at Arlington, USA

Maude M. Adjarian
University of Arizona, USA

Alexis K. Albion
The World Bank, USA

Carlos Altamirano
Universidad Nacional de Quilmes, Argentina

Sunil Amrith
Birkbeck College, University of London, UK

Irene Anastasiadou
Technische Universiteit Eindhoven, The Netherlands

Gerhard Anders
Universität Zürich, Switzerland

Erik Anderson
Brown University, USA

A. Aneesh
University of Wisconsin-Milwaukee, USA

Peder Anker
Universitetet i Oslo, Norway

Sonia Ashmore
Victoria and Albert Museum, UK

William J. Ashworth
University of Liverpool, UK

Cemil Aydin
University of North Carolina at Charlotte, USA

Tony Ballantyne
Washington University in St Louis, USA

Christopher Balme
Institut für Theaterwissenschaft, Germany

Greg Bankoff
University of Hull, UK

Kelly Bannister
University of Victoria, Canada

Tani Barlow
University of Washington, USA

Thomas Bender
New York University, USA

Jonathan Benthall
University College London, UK

Françoise Berger
Institut d'Etudes Politiques de Grenoble, France

Volker R. Berghahn
Columbia University, USA

Stève Bernardin
Université de Paris 1 – Panthéon Sorbonne, France

Andries Bezuidenhout
University of The Witwatersrand, South Africa

Sanjoy Bhattacharya
University College London, UK

Margaret C. Boardman
Independent scholar, USA

Philip Bonner
University of The Witwatersrand, South Africa

Paolo Brenni
Fondazione Scienza & Tecnica, Italy

John Britton
Francis Marion University, USA

Natalia Brizuela
University of California at Berkeley, USA

Tom Brooking
University of Otago, New Zealand

Tom Buchanan
University of Oxford, UK

Elizabeth Buettner
University of York, UK

Carlos F. Cáceres
Universidad Peruana Cayetano Heredia,
Peru

Melissa L. Caldwell
University of California at Santa Cruz, USA

Robert M. Campbell
Mount Allison University, Canada

David Cantor
National Institutes of Health, USA

Jane Carruthers
University of South Africa,
South Africa

Keith Cartwright
University of North Florida, USA

Youssef Cassis
Université de Genève, Switzerland

Ernesto Castañeda-Tinoco
Columbia University, USA

Luiz A. Castro-Santos
Universidade do Estado do Rio de Janeiro,
Brazil

Richard Cavell
University of British Columbia, Canada

John T. Chalcraft
London School of Economics and Political
Science, UK

Christophe Charle
École Normale Supérieure, France

Charles C. Chester
Brandeis University, USA

Lucy Chester
University of Colorado at Boulder, USA

Mark Cioc
University of California at Santa
Cruz, USA

Patricia Clavin
University of Oxford, UK

Robert Cliver
Humboldt State University, USA

Yves Cohen
École des Hautes Études en Sciences
Sociales, France

G. Daniel Cohen
Rice University, USA

Patrick Cohrs
Yale University, USA

Val Colic-Peisker
RMIT University, Australia

Ken Conca
University of Maryland, USA

Matthew Connelly
Columbia University, USA

Sebastian Conrad
European University Institute, Italy

Sahr Conway-Lanz
National Archives and Records
Administration, USA

Dorota Dakowska
Université de Strasbourg Robert Schuman,
France

Shao Dan
University of Illinois at Urbana-
Champaign, USA

Thomas Richard Davies
University of Oxford, UK

Evan N. Dawley
Harvard University, USA

Simona De Iulio
Université de Strasbourg Robert Schuman,
France

Sarah E. Dedonder
Kansas State University, USA

Mathieu Deflem
University of South Carolina, USA

Luiz Fernando Dias Duarte
Universidade Federal do Rio de Janeiro,
Brazil

Maria Paula Diogo
Universidade Nova e Lisboa, Portugal

Cornelis Disco
Universiteit Twente, The Netherlands

Colin Dival
University of York, UK

Marie-Laure Djelic
ESSEC Business School, France

Kurk Dorsey
University of New Hampshire, USA

Paul J. Dosal
University of South Florida, USA

Rafiqu Dossani
Stanford University, USA

Stephen Dovers
Australian National University, Australia

Jaap Dronkers
European University Institute, Italy

Prasenjit Duara
University of Chicago, USA

Ellen Carol DuBois
*University of California at Los Angeles,
USA*

Laird M. Easton
California State University, USA

Jean-François Eck
*Université Charles de Gaulle – Lille 3,
France*

Andreas Eckert
Humboldt Universität zu Berlin, Germany

Pieter Emmer
Universiteit Leiden, The Netherlands

Clive Emsley
The Open University, UK

Shane Ewen
Leeds Metropolitan University, UK

Stefano Fait
University of St Andrews, UK

Giovanni Federico
European University Institute, Italy

Olivier Feiertag
Université de Rouen, France

Andreas Fickers
*Universiteit Maastricht,
The Netherlands*

Robert Fitzgerald
Royal Holloway, University of London, UK

Laurence Fontaine
*École des Hautes Études en Sciences
Sociales, France*

Barbara A. Frey
University of Minnesota, USA

Harriet Friedmann
University of Toronto, Canada

Peter Fritzsche
University of Illinois, USA

Carlo Fumian
Università degli Studi di Padova, Italy

Ellen Furlough
University of Kentucky, USA

Jonathan Furner
*University of California at Los Angeles,
USA*

Donna Gabaccia
University of Minnesota, USA

Ilya V. Gaiduk
*United Nations Educational, Scientific and
Cultural Organization, Russia*

Oded Galor
Brown University, USA

Karina Galperin
Universidad Torcuato Di Tella, Argentina

Arlette Gautier
Université de Brest, France

Sandra Gayol
*Universidad Nacional de General
Sarmiento, Argentina*

Didier Georgakakis
*Université de Strasbourg Robert Schuman,
France*

David Gerlach
University of Pittsburgh, USA

Karl Gerth
University of Oxford, USA

Michael Geyer
University of Chicago, USA

Jessica C. E. Gienow-Hecht
*Johann Wolfgang Goethe-Universität
Frankfurt/Main, Germany*

Petra Goedde
Temple University, USA

Marisa Gonzaléz de Oleaga
*Universidad Nacional de Educación a
Distancia, Spain*

David Goodman
University of Melbourne, Australia

Timothy Gorringe
University of Exeter, UK

Christopher Goto-Jones
*Universiteit Leiden,
The Netherlands*

Gabriele Gottlieb
Grand Valley State University, USA

Harrison Grafos
University of Pittsburgh, USA

Julie Greene
University of Maryland, USA

Raymond Grew
University of Michigan, USA

Bernd-Stefan Grewe
Universität Konstanz, Germany

J. Bishop Grewell
Political Economy Research Center, USA

Tom Griffiths
*Australian National University,
Australia*

Nicolas Guilhot
Social Science Research Council, USA

Nicolas Guirimand
*Ecole des Hautes Etudes en Sciences
Sociales, France*

Kolleen M. Guy
University of Texas at San Antonio, USA

Jane L. Guyer
Johns Hopkins University, USA

Cindy Hahamovitch
College of William and Mary, USA

Peter L. Hahn
Ohio State University, USA

Jean-Louis Halpérin
École Normale Supérieure, France

Jessica L. Harland-Jacobs
University of Florida, USA

Stephen L. Harp
University of Akron, USA

Christiane Harzig
Arizona State University, USA

Pierre-Cyrille Hautcoeur
*École des Hautes Études en Sciences
Sociales, France*

Johan Heilbron
*Centre National de la Recherche
Scientifique, France*

Hans Heiss
Universität Innsbruck, Austria

Madeleine Herren
*Ruprecht-Karls-Universität Heidelberg,
Germany*

Winton Higgins
University of Technology Sydney, Australia

Neville Hoad
University of Texas at Austin, USA

Dirk Hoerder
Arizona State University, USA

Eri Hotta
Independent scholar, USA

Peter Hough
Middlesex University, UK

Guy Houvenaghel
Université Libre de Bruxelles, Belgium

Elisabeth Hsu
University of Oxford, UK

Madeline Y. Hsu
University of Texas at Austin, USA

Michael Huberman
Université de Montréal, Canada

Tobias Hübinette
Multicultural Centre, Sweden

Jonathan Hyslop
*University of The Witwatersrand,
South Africa*

Akira Iriye
Harvard University, USA

Ruud Janssens
*Universiteit van Amsterdam,
The Netherlands*

Laurent Jeanpierre
*Université Paris XII – Val de Marne,
France*

Alan Jeeves
Queen's University, South Africa

Robert David Johnson
City University of New York, Brooklyn College, USA

Val Marie Johnson
Saint Mary's University, Canada

Dorothy V. Jones
Independent scholar, USA

Guy Julier
Leeds Metropolitan University, UK

Wolfram Kaiser
University of Portsmouth, UK

Hussein Kassim
University of East Anglia, UK

Justin J Kastner
Kansas State University, USA

Jennifer E Keelan
University of Toronto, Canada

Kathleen Kete
Trinity College, USA

Akram F. Khater
North Carolina State University, USA

Anatoly M. Khazanov
University of Wisconsin-Madison, USA

Aysegül Kibaroglu
Orta Dağu Teknik Universitesi, Turkey

Masato Kimura
Bunkyo Gakuin University, Japan

Martin Klimke
Universität Heidelberg, Germany

Jack R. Kloppenburg Jr
University of Wisconsin-Madison, USA

Peter Knight
University of Manchester, UK

Sandrine Kott
Université de Genève, Switzerland

Gary Kroll
State University of New York at Plattsburg, USA

Pedro Krotsch
Universidad de Buenos Aires, Argentina

Glen David Kuecker
Depauw University, USA

Nancy H. Kwak
University of California at San Diego, USA

Nora Lafi
Zentrum Moderner Orient, Germany

Vincent Lagedijk
Technische Universiteit Eindhoven, The Netherlands

Deep Kanta Lahiri-Choudhury
Jamia Millia Islamia, India

Marilyn Lake
Latrobe University, Australia

Nancy Langston
University of Wisconsin-Madison, USA

Solange Lefebvre
Université de Montréal, Canada

Yannick Lemarchand
Université de Nantes, France

Mark Levene
University of Southampton, UK

Harry Liebersohn
University of Illinois at Urbana-Champaign, USA

Marianne Elisabeth Lien
Universitetet i Oslo, Norway

Raphael Liogier
Institut d'Etudes Politiques d'Aix-en-Provence, France

Lisong Liu
University of Minnesota, USA

Tessie P. Liu
Northwestern University, USA

Isabella Löhr
Universität Leipzig, Germany

James Longhurst
University of Wisconsin-La Crosse, USA

Ana Longoni
Universidad de Buenos Aires – CONICET, Argentina

Walton Look Lai
University of The West Indies, Trinidad and Tobago

Emanuelle Loyer
Institut d'Etudes Politiques de Paris,
France

Leo Lucassen
Universiteit Leiden, The Netherlands

Piers Ludlow
London School of Economics and Political
Science, UK

Eithne Luibhéid
University of Arizona, USA

Charles Maier
Harvard University, USA

Michael Makovsky
Bipartisan Policy Center, USA

Erez Manela
Harvard University, USA

Michel Mangenot
Université de Strasbourg Robert Schuman,
France

Patrick Manning
University of Pittsburgh, USA

Peter L. Manuel
City University of New York, John Jay
College, USA

Dominique Marshall
Carleton University, Canada

Jill Julius Matthews
Australian National University,
Australia

Tracie Matysik
University of Texas at Austin, USA

Chloé Maurel
Centre National de la Recherche
Scientifique, France

John Maynard
University of Newcastle, Australia

Cédric Mayrargue
Institut d'Etudes Politiques de Bordeaux,
France

Bruce Mazlish
Massachusetts Institute of Technology,
USA

Sucheta Mazumdar
Duke University, USA

W. Caleb McDaniel
Rice University, USA

Patrick F. McDevitt
State University of New York at Buffalo,
USA

Clay McShane
Northeastern University, USA

Jens Meirhenrich
Harvard University, USA

C. Michael Mellor
Matilda Ziegler Magazine for the Blind,
USA

Karen Merrill
Williams College, USA

Ikechi Mgbeoji
Osgoode Hall Law School, Canada

Alain P. Michel
Université d'Evry-Val d'Essonne,
France

Redner Miklos
Universiteit van Amsterdam,
The Netherlands

Edward Miller
Dartmouth College, USA

Michael B. Miller
University of Miami, USA

William Minter
Africa Focus Bulletin, USA

Tony Mitchell
University of Technology Sydney,
Australia

Gregg Mitman
University of Wisconsin-Madison, USA

Rana Mitter
University of Oxford, UK

Jean-Yves Mollier
Université de Versailles-Saint-Quentin-en-
Yvelines, France

Gijs Mom
Technische Universiteit Eindhoven,
The Netherlands

Fernando Monge
Fundación General de la UNED, Spain

Verónica Montecinos
Pennsylvania State University, USA

Christian Montès
Université Lumière Lyon 2, France

William Moomaw
Tufts University, USA

Jonathan Morris
University of Hertfordshire, UK

Jose C. Moya
University of California at Los Angeles, USA

Michelle Murphy
University of Toronto, Canada

Joseph J. Murray
Mayo Clinic, Norway

Joe Nasr
Independent scholar, UK

Holger Nehring
University of Sheffield, UK

Wing Chung Ng
University of Texas at San Antonio, USA

David Paull Nickles
Office of the Historian, State Department, USA

Abbey L. Nutsch
Kansas State University, USA

Tim Oakes
University of Colorado, USA

David O'Brien
University of Illinois at Urbana-Champaign, USA

Scott O'Bryan
Indiana University, USA

Irene Oh
University of Miami, USA

Gary B. Ostrower
Alfred University, USA

Connie Oxford
State University of New York at Plattsburg, USA

Dominique Padurano
Horace Mann School, USA

Soyang Park
Ontario College of Art And Design, Canada

Karen Hunger Parshall
University of Virginia, USA

Kiran Klaus Patel
European University Institute, Italy

Renaud Payre
Université Lumière Lyon 2, France

Peter Pels
Universiteit Leiden, The Netherlands

György Péteri
Norges Teknisk-Naturvitenskapelige Universitet, Norway

Pascal Petit
Centre National de la Recherche Scientifique, France

Ivan Petrella
University of Miami, USA

Howard Phillips
University of Cape Town, South Africa

Richard Pierard
Gordon College, USA

Jeffrey M. Pilcher
University of Minnesota, USA

Paulo G. Pinto
Universidad Federal Fluminense, Brazil

Claire B. Pitner
Northern Arizona University, USA

Mariano Plotkin
Instituto de Desarrollo Económico y Social, Argentina

David Priestland
University of Oxford, UK

Viviane Quirke
Oxford Brookes University, UK

Marc Raffinot
Université Paris Dauphine, France

Dhruv Raina
Jawaharlal Nehru University, India

Michel Rainelli
Centre National de la Recherche Scientifique, France

Kapil Raj
École des Hautes Études en Sciences Sociales, France

Linda Reeder
University of Missouri, USA

Chris Reid
University of Portsmouth, UK

Pietra Rivoli
Georgetown University, USA

Libby Robin
Australian National University, Australia

Ron Robin
New York University, USA

Philip Robins
University of Oxford, UK

Daniel T. Rodgers
Princeton University, USA

Jonathan Rosenberg
*City University of
New York, Hunter College, USA*

Neal Rosendorf
Long Island University, USA

Jay Rowell
*Centre National de la Recherche
Scientifique, France*

Federico Ruozzi
*Università degli Studi di Modena e Reggio
Emilia, Italy*

Dominic Sachsenmaier
Duke University, USA

Nicole Sackley
University of Richmond, USA

Mark B. Salter
University of Ottawa, Canada

Daniel Sargent
Harvard University, USA

Samir Saul
Université de Montréal, Canada

Pierre-Yves Saunier
*Centre National de la Recherche
Scientifique, France*

**David Schimmelpenninck
van der Oye**
*University of North Carolina at Chapel
Hill, USA*

Oliver Schmidt
*Georg Simmel Center for Metropolitan
Studies, Germany*

Dorothee Schneider
University of Illinois, USA

Johan Schot
*Technische Universiteit Eindhoven,
The Netherlands*

Brigitte Schroeder-Gudehus
Université de Montréal, Canada

Rachel Schurman
University of Minnesota, USA

Giles Scott-Smith
Roosevelt Study Center, The Netherlands

Paolo Scrivano
Boston University, USA

Bruce E. Seely
Michigan Technical University, USA

Milton Shain
*University of Cape Town,
South Africa*

Yaacov Shavit
Tel Aviv University, Israel

Sydney Shep
*Victoria University of Wellington,
New Zealand*

Thomas Shevory
Ithaca College, USA

Hatsue Shinohara
Waseda University, Japan

Christiane Sibille
*Ruprecht-Karls-Universität Heidelberg,
Germany*

Detlef Siegfried
Københavns Universitet, Denmark

Hannes Siegrist
Universität Leipzig, Germany

Suzanne Sinke
Florida State University, USA

Jeffrey Sissons
*Victoria University of Wellington, New
Zealand*

Glenda Sluga
University of Sydney, Australia

Ron P. Smith
*Birkbeck College, University of
London, UK*

Maui Solomon
Independent scholar, New Zealand

Gustavo Sorà
Universidad Nacional de Córdoba, Argentina

Carlotta Sorba
Università degli Studi di Padova, Italy

Nadège Sougy
Université de Neuchâtel, Switzerland

Phia Steyn
University of Stirling, UK

Michael Strangelove
University of Ottawa, Canada

Sarah Strauss
University of Wyoming, USA

Jan Susina
Illinois State University, USA

Kristina Tamm Hallström
Stockholms Universitet, Sweden

Horacio Tarcus
Centro de Documentación e Investigación de la Cultura de Izquierdas en Argentina, Argentina

Hsu-Ming Teo
Macquarie University, Australia

Daya Thussu
University of Westminster, UK

Humphrey Tonkin
University of Hartford, USA

Ian Tyrrell
University of New South Wales, Australia

Eddy U
University of California at Davis, USA

Nicole Ulrich
University of The Witwatersrand, South Africa

Scott Urban
University of Oxford, UK

Jasmien Van Daele
International Labour Office, Switzerland

Erik van der Vleuten
Technische Universiteit Eindhoven, The Netherlands

Lucien van der Walt
University of The Witwatersrand, South Africa

Eric Verdeil
Centre National de la Recherche Scientifique, France

Françoise Vergès
Goldsmiths College, UK

Timothy Verhoeven
University of Melbourne, Australia

Patrick Verley
Université de Genève, Switzerland

Philippe Videlier
Centre National de la Recherche Scientifique, France

Jakob Vogel
Universität Köln, Germany

Penny Von Eschen
University of Michigan, USA

Anne-Catherine Wagner
Université de Paris 1 – Panthéon Sorbonne, France

Adam Walaszek
Uniwersytet Jagielloński, Poland

Kyle Walker
University of Minnesota, USA

Kevin Wamsley
University of Western Ontario, Canada

Stephen Ward
Oxford Brookes University, UK

Deena Weinstein
DePaul University, USA

Kenneth Weisbrode
Harvard University, USA

Blaise Wilfert-Portal
École Normale Supérieure, France

Ara Wilson
Ohio State University, USA

Roberta Wollons
University of Massachusetts at Boston, USA

Aida Yuen Wong
Brandeis University, USA

Laura Elizabeth Wong
Harvard University, USA

Sappho Xenakis
London School of Economics and Political Science, UK

Guoqi Xu
Kalamazoo College, USA

Zhou Xun
School of African and Oriental Studies, UK

Rumi Yasutake
Konan University, Japan

Elliott Young
Lewis and Clark College, USA

Elizabeth Zanoni
Western Michigan University, USA

Thomas Zeiler
University of Colorado, USA

Eduardo Zimmermann
Universidad de San Andrés, Argentina

Introduction

THE PROFESSOR AND THE MADMAN

Borrowing the title of Simon Winchester's novel as the title of this introduction is quite appropriate. Not so much because it would approximately describe the division of roles between the two general editors. Or because this was the very volume that one of us randomly pulled out from the other's bookshelves at the time we tuned the first sketches of this volume. Rather, it is because we want to stress from the start that the making of this volume was not as difficult as the making of the *Oxford English Dictionary* at the end of the 19th century. James Murray had to face many obstacles we have been spared. Making a dictionary is probably easier today than it was just thirty years ago, and a major reason lies in the development of information technologies. We sometimes had an attack of vertigo when we thought about the energy and time that one had to spend during the postal age to invent entries, find contributors, follow up with hundreds of authors and liaise with an editing and publishing team. When we think of how web searches have been complementary to library work when establishing a list of entries or a list of possible contributors, and when we browse the 15,000 e-mails or so that have been generated just by the two of us during the development of this project, we realize how the ability to communicate quickly and cheaply with colleagues from across the globe has been crucial in shaping this endeavour. We also believe that it was an incentive to stretch our editorial suggestions. While you certainly hesitate to send a fourth manuscript or typed letter with editorial comments about a couple of sentences when it takes several weeks to travel back and forth, you do not hesitate to send an e-mail that asks for clarification about a single word or a comma. While you'd tire of chasing an overdue entry by phone at great expense, you now have the ability to swoop down on contributors using Voice over IP software. Somehow, this also makes the standards higher, and we hope to have lived up at least partially to the new claims that are laid on us academics by the possibilities of digital communication.

The use of these possibilities was part of the excitement and pleasure we had in developing this project. But there was something else, where we quite likely touched upon some of James Murray's and other encyclopedia makers' feelings when they worked out their projects. We were starting from scratch without a matrix, without a precedent. There were no 'obvious' entries or contributors that we had to enlist or do without, because of their presence in a previous attempt to do what we were doing. It was definitely not like working on just another edition in a long line of reference volumes on the history of one or another country, or any spin-off from a long series of formatted companions and dictionaries. This provided us with freedom and room for manoeuvre, invaluable possessions if you want to keep a high and even level of commitment and stamina during several years.

This does not mean that we considered we were inventing anything. In the world of knowledge, such a stance is bound to be exposed as a boast at one moment or another. Instead, as historians of the modern age, we simply faced the fact that more and more people were paying attention to the circulations and connections between, above and beyond national polities and societies, from the 19th century to current times. While the history of the modern age had been, more than that of other periods in human history, written from a national perspective, the last twenty years have witnessed the mounting of an explicit challenge to this position, originating from the whole spectrum of the social sciences and the humanities. It was manifest in the growing number of forums, meetings, journals, courses and research projects which addressed the modern world by considering the entangled nature of the different national and local histories.

We saw this trend developing and were ourselves part of it in our fields and specialties. It had many labels, and more have developed since. Some distinguished historians such as Patrick Manning, Jerry Bentley, Chris Bayly and Anthony Hopkins prefer 'world history' to name their concern for cross-cultural and global comparisons and connections. Similarly, a number of people consider that 'international history' is an appropriate way to designate their interest. At the other end of the spectrum, other scholars have coined new terms: Sanjay Subrahmanyam uses the term 'connected histories', Shalini Randeria goes for 'entangled history', Michael Werner and Benedicte Zimmerman have sketched what an 'histoire croisée' would be, David Thelen and his US colleagues have popularized the term 'transnational history' with prompt support from Jürgen Kocka and a host of German colleagues, Bruce Mazlish and Akira Iriye have defended the idea of a 'new global history', while 'shared histories' has taken its cue from people studying the connections between the history of separate ethnic groups. More recently, William Gervase Clarence-Smith, Kenneth Pomeranz and Peer Vries have chosen 'global history' to name the new journal they have been co-editing since 2006. We would not spend a minute disputing the advantages and limits of these and other labels, for we feel those who use them share a

similar interest in what moves between and across different polities and societies. Because of our idiosyncrasies, we just felt that 'transnational history' gave the most faithful indication of what we were trying to do. We are interested in links and flows, and want to track people, ideas, products, processes and patterns that operate over, across, through, beyond, above, under, or in-between polities and societies. Among the units that were thus crossed, consolidated or subverted in the modern age, first and foremost were the national ones, if only because our work addresses the moment, roughly from the middle of the 19th century until nowadays, when nations came to be seen and empowered as the main frames for the political, cultural, economic and social life of human beings.

Both in our research and in our classroom activities, we had the feeling that there did not exist a kind of reference volume that would provide facts and leads as to the shape, content, role and impact of these transnational circulations and connections. This was not available from the existing reference volumes, we thought. The flows of people, goods, ideas or processes that stretched over borders were sidelined or altogether neglected by national dictionaries. Area studies reference volumes also limited their perspective to the area that was studied. World history encyclopedias were mostly organized by national or regional categories, and focused on civilizations while rarely dealing with the relationship among contexts. The time range of world history is so large, from the Big Bang onwards, that the age of nations is just a very brief and recent moment seen from this point of view. Some biographical dictionaries had a wide range but were strictly limited to biographical entries, while the most relevant thematic reference volumes were of course limited by their thematic orientation. Our earliest sketches, and discussion of them with colleagues strengthened our idea that there was room and need for a reference volume that would document the history of connections and circulations in the modern age, from about 1850 to the present.

It was very clear to us from the start that such a project had to be developed by a group of scholars who would share some common dispositions. Discipline or subdiscipline were not discriminating factors, as long as a potential author had a bent for grappling with time and the history of the last 160 years. We sought contributors not only in the discipline of history but also all around the social sciences and humanities rim, from anthropology to economics, theology, linguistics, geography or sociology and the whole range of interdisciplinary studies. But we also imagined that, if the *Dictionary* was to effectively address connections and circulations across polities and societies, it had to be edited and written by people who would be 'transnational' themselves, with regard to their linguistic abilities, their interests and connections with worldwide communities of researchers in their fields, their command of existing literature and, according to our hunch, their personal trajectories. This basic position has found its expression in the list of associate editors and of contributors. However, we were not in search of any politically correct balance of gender, race, ethnicity, countries or continents, and we certainly do not purport to have eliminated biases that are connected to 'wherefrom we write'. Conditions of personal availability, documentation facilities, visibility and command of the English language have also informed our search for contributors and the response of those we have approached. The inequalities of resources throughout the academic world have thus left their mark on this volume, because there are certainly some bright scholars we left aside because we simply did not know them, or because we felt it would be difficult for them to assemble the material from which to write wide-ranging pieces. Last but not least, we were also the complacent victims of our own networks and locations: there is no doubt that the list of

contributors, the headword list and the content of the entries would have been different if this *Dictionary* had been edited, say, by a Latin American historian born/living in China and a Middle Eastern scholar with some experience in Indian universities. We are the first to believe that our historical imagination needs to be enlarged to be able to write transnational history transnationally and we are just looking forward to another such dictionary or encyclopedia, or to a new edition of this one, to add other approaches to our own current attempts. We are pretty sure this will come quite soon as we consider the ongoing development of research and teaching endeavours that endorse a transnational perspective.

Indeed, it may be one of the most salient features of this specific volume that it emerges from a work in progress. Dictionaries and encyclopedias more usually pertain to well established disciplines, and claim to provide an ultimate state-of-the-art survey, whereas many of the entries written for this volume are exploratory to the point that we were tempted to name it the Tentative Dictionary of Transnational History. Inventing the list of entries, identifying possible contributors, was an exciting and difficult task for which we had no previous model or matrix. Accordingly, we established our list of headwords in an attempt to cover the widest possible range of themes for this first foray, leaving comprehensiveness's dreams to lie dormant for a while. We are aware of the gaps that others may recognize in this list: some have been caused by the lack of imagination, curiosity and expertise on our part, and others by the excess of the same at the moment when we trimmed our original list of 1,500 possible entries to establish the framework for a workable volume. We take the blame for both, and consider these flaws an incentive for future endeavours.

The unprecedented nature of this project is also reflected in the contents of the entries themselves. Some subjects may be riper than others, and the content is more 'state of the art'. Other entries are venturing onto new ground, blazing trails that had not been explored as such: they are full of hunches, questions, possibilities, and they focus on the moments and places that are more familiar to their authors. Some other contributors chose the well rounded way, and came up with a piece that will satisfy readers in search of data, facts and figures. Last but not least, while most of the contributors have focused their attention on the development of historical processes, another group have ventured onto more theoretical ground and coped with concepts that have been used to understand such processes, to assess how they have been shaped, appropriated and disputed across borders. It has not been uncommon for entries to eventually take a direction that was not foreseen, and this has always been a pleasure for us as editors. In all these instances, the contributors to this *Dictionary* have been aware that they were just having a first try, and generously offered their insight with the bitter awareness that they could not harness the breadth of literature in various languages and from many disciplinary or subdisciplinary landscapes. Their willingness to expose the range and limits of their expertise has been very generous.

Because of all these limits, this volume is not intended to be canonical. There is no disciplinary brief included in its text, subtext or paratext. We think it is a tool that will be used by scholars to develop their own projects to study other circulations and connections, and to revise or update what has been written in this *Dictionary* about some of these. It is a step, a prop for further research to develop. On the other hand, we do not want to establish a new field or a new subdiscipline, and it is just for the sake of clarity that we have adopted the name of *The Palgrave Dictionary of Transnational History*. We believe the transnational approach to be an angle, a perspective that can be adopted by everyone who wants to address the entangled condition of the modern world and contribute answers to some very specific questions. To summarize, there are three prongs that this volume wants to contribute to. First, the historicization of interdependency and interconnection phenomena between national, regional or cultural spheres in the modern age, by charting the development of projects, designs and structures that have organized circulations and connections through and between them, in an uneven and non-linear way. Second, the advancement of knowledge on neglected or hazy regions of national and other self-contained territorial histories, by acknowledging foreign contributions to the design, discussion and implementation of patterns that are often seen as owing their features to domestic conditions. Third, the understanding of trends and protagonists that are often left on the periphery of national or comparative frameworks; and this leads us to the study of markets, trajectories, concepts, activities and organizations that thrived in-between and across the nations: international voluntary associations, loose transnational ideas networks, diasporas or commodities. Readers and users will be able to tell if this volume delivers on these fronts and on others. But for us, as editors, the contributors to *The Palgrave Dictionary of Transnational History* have made our historical education more complete on all these frontiers. This volume is theirs.

AKIRA IRIYE
PIERRE-YVES SAUNIER

Acknowledgements

Our list of people who have been wonderfully helpful, punctual and conscientious starts with the editorial team. Alison Jones was an enthusiastic publisher when presented with the idea for this volume back in the Spring of 2004 and she has retained the same level of enthusiasm and commitment ever since. It was a pleasure to work with her and her companion in the Palgrave Macmillan offices, Ruth Lefèvre, with whom we have exchanged literally thousands of e-mails on pleasant and not so pleasant subjects throughout the past few years. We know now how important it is to be able to rely on an able publishing team to embark on this kind of long-term endeavour. This also includes people behind the scenes such as Senior Production Editor Phillipa Davidson-Blake and many others whose names we do not know, despite their vital contribution.

The five associate editors who joined us after the initial phase of the project underscore another fundamental requirement of such a project: the pleasure and usefulness of working with colleagues who want to achieve the same goal, and who provide their knowledge, time, wit and energy to do so. Jane Carruthers, Donna Gabaccia, Rana Mitter, Mariano Plotkin and Patrick Verley made us feel part of a community while the seven of us built up the list of entries, looked for contributors and edited the essays received.

Making a dictionary also involves crucial practical tasks: Brian Morrison was a very effective and diplomatic copy editor, who had the additional challenge of mending the English of two non-native speakers in addition to the usual painstaking attention that is expected of copy editors. Piroska Csùri, Karina Iacono and Rosemary Williams translated several pieces from Spanish or French with grace and accuracy, while Susan Curran elaborated the indexes without which no dictionary can exist. Phil Isenberg, Marie-Françoise Cachin and other, anonymous translators also offered their services to our contributors on specific entries. There are many other contributions that need to be acknowledged here, among which we need to single out the input by Michael Geyer and Marilyn Lake, who should have been associate editors and had to withdraw for personal reasons.

A very important moment in the making of this *Dictionary* was the inspirational three-day workshop we were able to organize in the Spring of 2005 with the members of the editorial team. This meeting was funded by the Rockefeller Archives Center in North Tarrytown, New York State, where Norine Hochman, Camilla Harris, Kenneth Rose and Darwin Stapleton were perfect hosts and hostesses.

Throughout the process, a large number of colleagues and friends, some we knew and some we have never met, provided advice, warnings, suggestions, comments or support. They are, in alphabetical order, Arturo Almandoz, Dennis Altman, Chris Arup, Douglas Baynton, Volker Berghahn, Stève Bernardin, Thomas Bender, Denis Bocquet, Paul Boyer, John Braithwaite, Judith Brown, John Chalcraft, Juan Cole, Miriam Cooke, Jasmien van Daele, Michèle Dagenais, Shao Dan, Marie-Laure Djelic, Peter Drahos, Ellen Carol DuBois, Timothy Farnham, Olivier Feiertag, Michael Geyer, Jessica Gienow-Hecht, Pascal Griset, Aaron Gillette, Kristin Hoganson,

Marta Hanson, Roger Hart, Pierre-Cyrille Hautcoeur, John Heilbron, Madeleine Herren, Anthony Hopkins, Braj Kachru, James Kloppenberg, Martti Koskenniemi, Joseph Kinner, Jürgen Kocka, Marilyn Lake, Bruce Lawrence, Mark Levene, Walter K. Lew, Sergio Luzzatto, Gregg Mitman, Verónica Montecinos, Joe Nasr, Holger Nehring, David O'Brien, Scott O'Bryan, Johannes Paulmann, Rosalind Petchesky, Gyury Pétéri, Anne Rasmussen, Annelise Riles, Harriet Ritvo, Daniel Rodgers, Emily Rosenberg, Helen Rozwadowski, Leila Rupp, Johan Schot, Christiane Sibille, Kathryn Sklar, Carlotta Sorba, Darwin Stapleton, George Thomas, Charles Tilly, Humphrey Tonkin, Christian Topalov, Ludovic Tournès, Chantal and Eric Verdeil, Kenneth Weisbrode, Blaise Wilfert, Daniel Wilson and Rumi Yasutake. Some of them are also contributors to this volume, and it is to our contributors in general that we feel most obliged. They coped with our nagging, with our extravagant edits and with our demands for punctuality. Thanks to their labour of love, we have learned so much. Just to write it down at the opening of this volume seems to us an inadequate way to say 'thank you' for all they have done for us. The list of their names, a few pages back, is the roll-call of those who have made our project a reality.

Notes for the Reader

There are always several ways to navigate a dictionary. Most are invented by readers themselves, but the editors can nevertheless provide some guidance. The most obvious is the alphabetical list of entries, mirrored in their arrangement in the volume itself. Thus, headwords have been arranged in alphabetical order, and some appear twice in the case of a complex headword: for instance, the 'GATT and WTO' essay appears under 'G' in the alphabetical arrangement of the volume, but 'WTO and GATT' also appears as a signpost entry under 'W', to direct the reader to the essay itself. Individuals are listed by their family name ('Schwimmer, Rosika'), and books by the first substantive word of their title, for example, under 'Bible' rather than 'The Bible'. When the topic being sought cannot be found in the alphabetical list, the indexes are the place to look. It is fully developed at the end of this volume and allows readers to find the entry which includes or documents the term they are searching for, be it a place name, an individual name, or a topic. 'Automobile', which is not a headword, will thus point to the entries 'assembly line', 'car culture', 'car safety standards', 'industrial organization', 'International Road Federation', 'Toyotism', and 'transportation infrastructures', and perhaps others. Related essays in the *Dictionary* are also cross-referenced at the end of each essay, even when they have not been explicitly mentioned in the body of the essay. Our rationale for cross-referencing entries was, of course, to connect obvious companion and complementary entries (like 'news and press agencies' with 'information society', or 'advertising' with 'marketing'. But we have also tried to suggest hidden or far-reaching connections, that can only be seen after reading the entries; thus we believe it is stimulating to cross-reference 'food' and 'literature', for their methodological hindsight; or to tie 'theatre' with 'kindergarten' and 'organization models' as these three offer detailed views on how some practices and ideas have been exchanged and appropriated; or to suggest that readers of 'League of Nations Economic and Financial Organization' also read 'philanthropic foundations', despite the fact that the financing of the Economic Intelligence Service by the Rockefeller Foundation is not explicitly mentioned in the former article. Cross-references thus give access both to the clusters of substance that group some articles together, and to clusters that we editors have identified at different stages of the editorial process.

Finally, we have provided graphic presentations that may allow readers to find their way into the themes and territories explored by the *Dictionary*. Alphabetical lists and indexes are fine when you know what you are looking for. When you don't, or when you want to get some idea of the general picture, what you need is a kind of map or plan. Ideally, we would have loved to be able to conceive and represent a tangled web of topics, but the result would have been both literally unprintable and unreadable. We eventually came up with a less suggestive but more expressive solution, embodied in the 'tree' diagrams that complete our search tools section. This is an idea we borrowed from our colleagues Victoria de Grazia and Sergio Luzzatto 's *Dizionario del Fascismo* (Turin: Einaudi, 2003) after discussions with them, and that we had used earlier on as a development tool for our headword list. At draft stage, we began by using alphabetically arranged lists, which were useful for launching the whole project and receiving feedback on its usefulness. But when we tried to move towards a final list of entries, development by list was no longer sufficient. Our aim was to cover a wide range of circulatory and connective processes, types and moments, if only to trim the results at a later stage. What we needed were categories within which this development process would take place. In order to open the range of entries, it would have been counterproductive to start from areas, regions, chronological chunks or subdisciplinary fields, and try to imagine entries within those frames. So we started from wide themes, like 'people flows', asking ourselves what the potential headwords were that would appropriately cover the circulations and connections pertaining to people movements between 1850 and today. We imagined some big-picture entries: 'international migration regimes', 'human mobility'; a typology of such movements: 'diasporas', 'labour migrations', 'forced migrations', and from each of these derived a number of entries that grappled with a specific aspect: 'slavery', 'brain drain', 'guestworkers', 'Lebanese Diaspora'. We used the same process for some twenty families/groups of entries, which went from 'places' to 'Planet Earth', trying

to build threads of connected essays within each of them in order to cover our chronological, geographical and thematic range. These families and groups allowed us to distribute the articles amongst the editorial team so that each one could be dealt with and eventually commissioned by the associate editor with the greatest experience or curiosity in that particular field, although several of these groups were eventually handled by several editors. This exercise made it clear that the families/groups allotment was to serve as the basis for building a graphic map of the volume in its final stage. To do so, we have recombined the entries into ten large families. This graphic presentation in the 'tree' diagrams should not be taken literally: these are not Linnaean trees, nor Joshua trees. Some entries are repeated in several of them and their presence in one family or the other is not a consequence of any particular conceptual assignment. Moreover, the presentation of a graphic link between two entries is not an expression of the subordination of one entry to another, nor of an exclusive connection between the two. Our 'tree' merely suggests to the reader that there are gains to be made in reading a number of entries together, just as there was some gain in conceiving, writing or editing them as a cluster. We feel that this will help readers to find their way into the volume, just as we had to find ours.

List of Acronyms

AIDS	Acquired Immune Deficiency Syndrome	ICANN	Internet Corporation for Assigned Names and Numbers
AI	Amnesty International	ISESCO	Islamic Educational, Scientific and Cultural Organization
BBC	British Broadcasting Corporation		
ECLAC	Economic Commission for Latin America and the Caribbean (ECLAC)	IUCN	World Conservation Union
EU	European Union	MBA	Master of Business Administration
GATT	General Agreement on Tariffs and Trade	MSF	Médecins Sans Frontières
GMOs	Genetically modified organisms	NBA	National Basketball Association
HSBC	Hong Kong and Shanghai Banking Corporation Limited	NATO	North Atlantic Treaty Organization
		OPEC	Organization of Petroleum Exporting Countries
IT	Information technology		
ICAO	International Civil Aviation Organization	UCLG	United Cities and Local Government
IATA	International Air Transport Association	UN	United Nations
		UNESCO	United Nations Educational, Scientific and Cultural Organization
IMF	International Monetary Fund		
INGOs	International non-governmental organizations	UPU	Universal Postal Union
IRF	International Road Federation	WTO	World Trade Organization
		WWF	World Wildlife Fund

Tree Diagrams

KEY
- Words in italics refer to a theme, and not to an existing entry.
- Links between entries suggest a relation of complementary nature, but do not exhaust the entanglements of the entries.

1 People flows

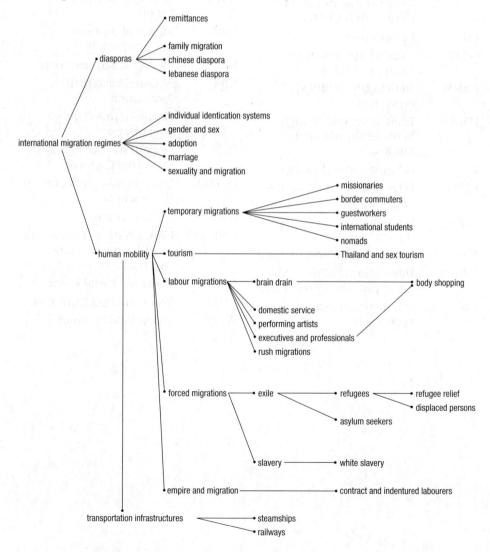

2 World order and disorder

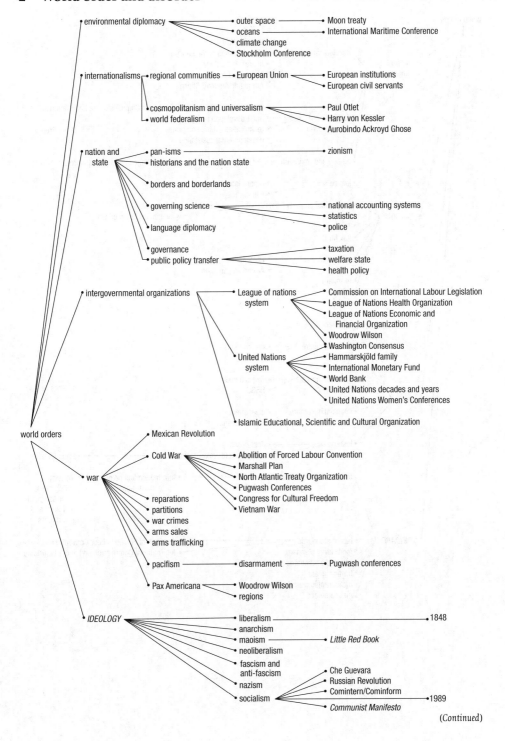

(Continued)

2 World order and disorder (Continued)

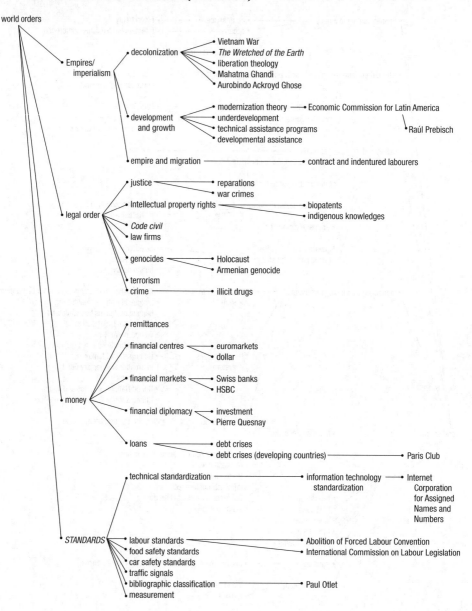

world orders

Empires/imperialism
- decolonization
  - Vietnam War
  - *The Wretched of the Earth*
  - liberation theology
  - Mahatma Ghandi
  - Aurobindo Ackroyd Ghose
- development and growth
  - modernization theory —— Economic Commission for Latin America
  - underdevelopment
  - technical assistance programs
  - developmental assistance
  - Raúl Prebisch
- empire and migration —————— contract and indentured labourers

legal order
- justice
  - reparations
  - war crimes
- Intellectual property rights
  - biopatents
  - indigenous knowledges
- *Code civil*
- law firms
- genocides
  - Holocaust
  - Armenian genocide
- terrorism
- crime —————— illicit drugs

money
- remittances
- financial centres
  - euromarkets
  - dollar
- financial markets
  - Swiss banks
  - HSBC
- financial diplomacy
  - investment
  - Pierre Quesnay
- loans
  - debt crises
  - debt crises (developing countries) —————— Paris Club

STANDARDS
- technical standardization —————— information technology standardization —— Internet Corporation for Assigned Names and Numbers
- labour standards
  - Abolition of Forced Labour Convention
  - International Commission on Labour Legislation
- food safety standards
- car safety standards
- traffic signals
- bibliographic classification —————— Paul Otlet
- measurement

3   Words, sounds, images

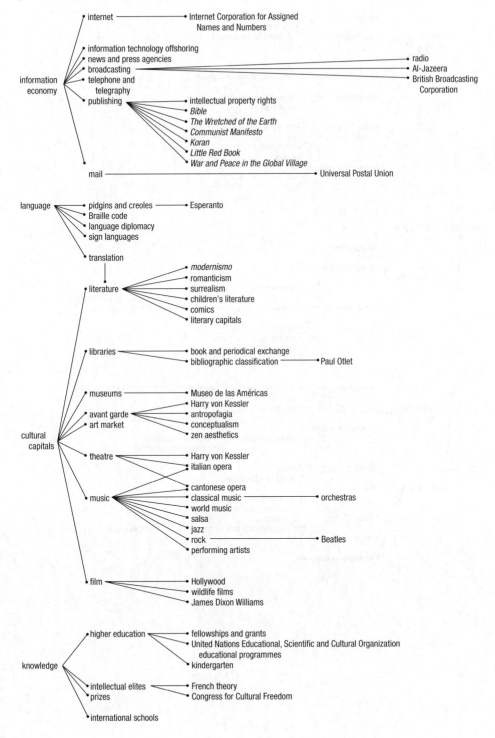

4   Production and trade

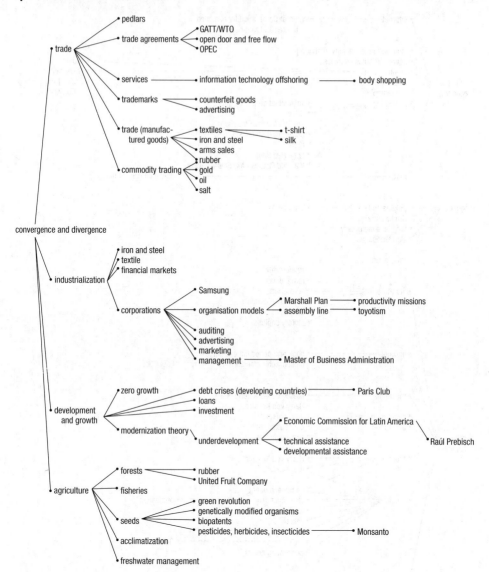

5   Planet Earth

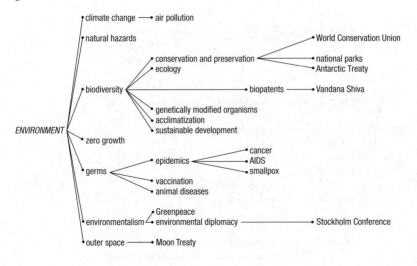

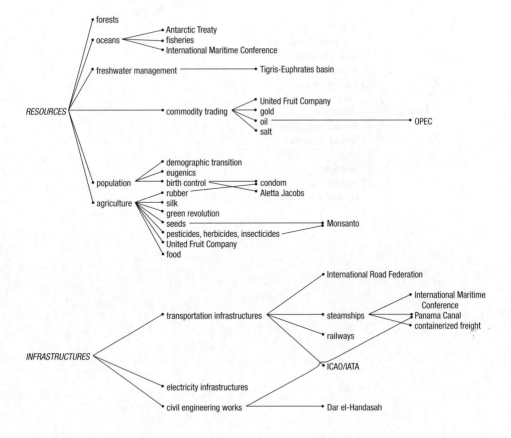

6   Space and time

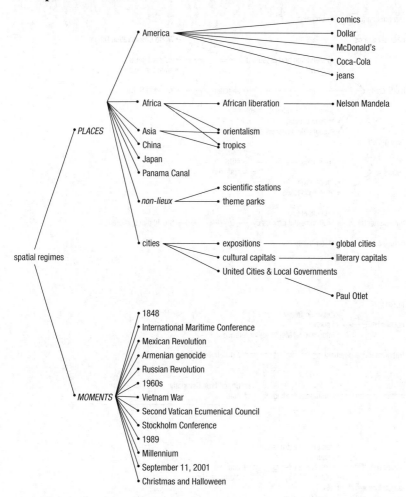

7   Body and soul

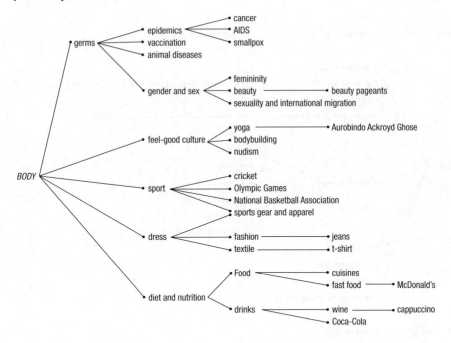

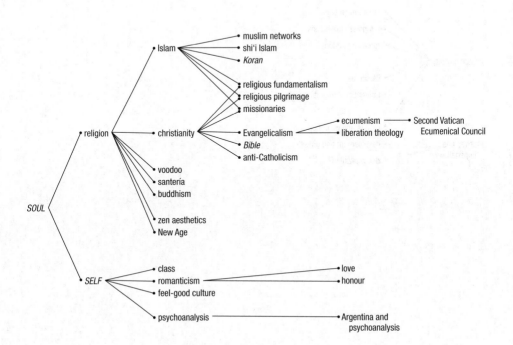

8 Concepts and processes

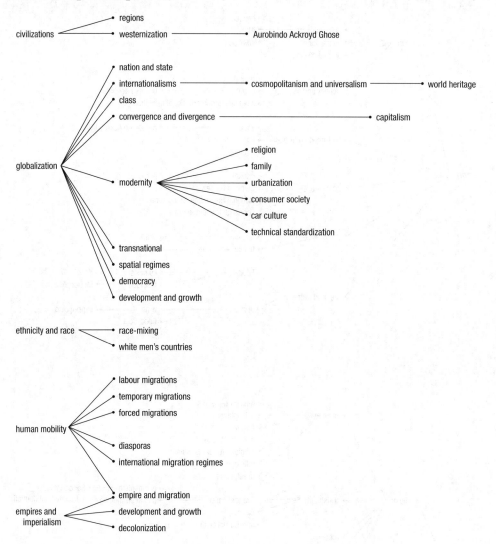

9 Groups and causes

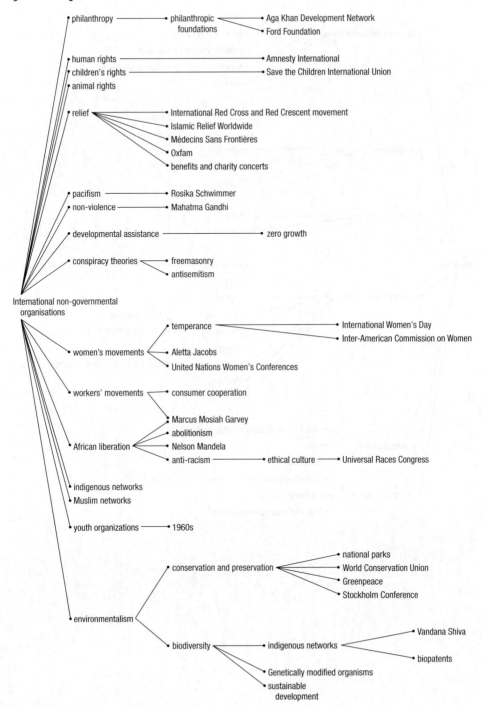

10 Knowledge

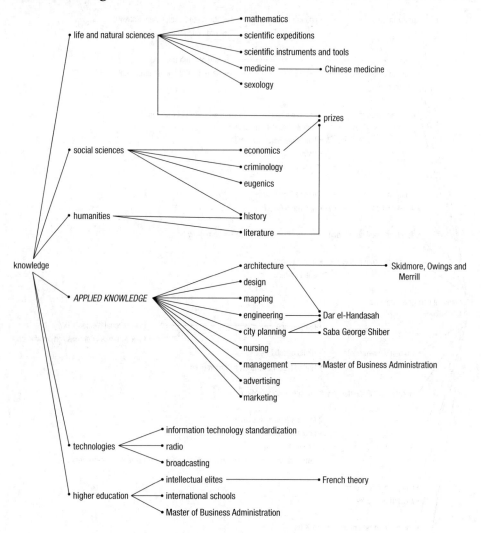

List of Entries

Note: Entries in *italics* are subentries; please refer to the diagrams in the preceding
   section.

1848

From 1848 to 1851 revolutionaries across Europe tried and failed to institute liberal, democratic governments.

The successful toppling of the French monarchy of Louis-Philippe triggered insurrections in one country after another in Northern, Eastern and Southern Europe. Historians in recent years have fruitfully analysed these events side by side and compared their liberal, constitutional, nationalist, and occasionally more socialist and democratic goals. Less attention has been paid to the circulation of ideologies that went along with the movement of political refugees and immigrants across state borders. Yet the resulting network of people and ideas endured long after the revolutions themselves had failed.

Most visible to contemporaries was the exile of leaders whose names were almost synonymous with the movements they inspired, such as Giuseppe Mazzini for the Italian national movement and Louis Kossuth for Hungary. Mazzini (who was already living in exile before 1848 and returned to London thereafter) was admired by English opinion makers like Thomas Carlyle and John Stuart Mill; Kossuth spoke to large cheering crowds in the United States. Yet Mazzini remained an exotic foreigner, and Kossuth ended his speaking tour frustrated over Americans' meagre response to his pleas for arms and money. Far deeper was the impact of German migration on American political culture. Whether or not they left in direct response to the revolution, German workers and intellectuals carried their democratic political culture into utopian ventures, party politics, the anti-slavery campaign, and trade unionism; their newspapers and letters carried political ideals back and forth across the Atlantic.

Radical socialists, exiled after taking part in revolutions, developed a new internationalism. This was particularly true for Karl Marx, who ended up in London in August 1849 after fleeing his native Rhineland and passing through Paris. From his new home, where he stayed until his death in 1883, Marx could use the resources of the British Library, write articles for Charles Dana's *New York Daily Tribune*, get to know British working-class leaders, and meet the European and American socialists who visited the British metropolis. Exiles like Marx were detached from the politics of their adopted countries, but formed an international network that furthered organizations like the First International (International Workingmen's Association), which met in London in 1864. The survivors of the 1848 revolutions learned to look across borders for political allies.

The movement of intellectuals across borders energized the feminist movement during and after 1848. Émigrés like Jeanne Deroin, who was exiled from Paris to London in 1852, and Mathilde Franziska Anneke, who took part in the revolution in Baden (in southwest Germany) and arrived in the United States by 1850, remained active as feminists in their new homes. Margaret Fuller, already abroad as a correspondent for Horace Greeley's *New York Daily Tribune*, sent back enthusiastic reports of the revolutionary republic in Rome and exemplified professional and political activism to the burgeoning American women's movement. For feminists who endured scorn, prison and exile for their belief in universal human dignity, 1848 was an electrifying moment; even after their failure, the revolutions illuminated a community that could aid and inspire them across national borders.

The success or failure of 1848 is usually measured nation state by nation state, and from this viewpoint the individual revolutions disappointed liberals and democrats. From a transnational perspective, however, the outcome looks different. The mid-century revolutions were a watershed in the formation of socialist and feminist alliances that self-consciously looked and worked beyond the limits of state politics, which usually remained hostile to their goals. Whether directly or indirectly, as examples or as agents, the revolutionaries furthered networks of knowledge and action that by the end of the nineteenth century had survived decades of political reaction and returned to define the emancipatory ideals of modern societies.

Harry Liebersohn

Bibliography

Anderson B. S. 2000. *Joyous greetings: the first international women's movement, 1830–1860*. New York: Oxford University Press.

Evans R. J. W. and Pogge von Strandmann H. (eds) 2000. *The revolutions in Europe, 1848–1849: from reform to reaction*. Oxford: Oxford University Press.

Körner A. (ed.) 2000. *1848 – A European revolution? International ideas and national memories of* 1848. Basingstoke: Palgrave Macmillan.

Related essays
1960s; 1989; abolitionism; *Communist Manifesto*; diasporas; exile; human mobility; internationalisms; Italian opera; kindergarten; liberalism; Mexican Revolution; nation and state; Romanticism; Russian Revolution; socialism; women's movements; workers' movements

1960s

The 1960s are commonly remembered as an era of global change, producing an historical caesura, culturally as well as politically. In Italy, France, Germany, Japan, Brazil, Mexico, Great Britain, China, Czechoslovakia, Poland and many other parts of the world, members of the young generation were in revolt against what they regarded as traditional values and conventions, expressing a widening gap between the generations.

However, the outstanding historical characteristic of the 1960s is that they transgressed the ideological fronts of the Cold War. Not only the 'First World' of Western capitalism, but also the 'Second World' of the Communist bloc, and the 'Third World' in Latin America, Africa and Asia were shattered by largely unexpected internal ruptures. In many of these countries, images of protest, generational revolt, countercultural indulgence, sexual liberation, and government repression still circulate in the public memory of those years. The 'Sixties' have therefore become a metaphor for profound social and cultural transformations worldwide based on and spurred by a wide range of transnational processes of exchange.

The roots of the New Left, which shaped and inspired much of the decade's protest movements, were already of transnational origin, uniting activists from Europe and the US in their dissatisfaction with the geopolitical stalemate of the Cold War and its domestic consequences, as well as in the need for a departure from orthodox Marxism and in an active role for intellectuals and the young generation in initiating social change. The civil rights movement in the US at the beginning of the decade was perceived as a particular fulfilment of this desired participatory democracy. Due to the spectacular nature of its actions and its moral implications set in the propaganda battles of the Cold War, it transcended national borders and was formative for various groups of people even outside the US. Its demonstrations, especially, offered protest techniques and models of direct action which would be transported, adopted and recontextualized elsewhere.

Helping this process of transnational diffusion was a globalized media that emerged in the 1960s, which disseminated news and events almost instantaneously to various parts of the globe. A vibrant culture industry also helped spread a transnational youth lifestyle which was predominantly influenced by Anglo-American popular culture. Musicians such as Bob Dylan, The Beatles, The Rolling Stones, and Jimi Hendrix became generational icons and representative of a deep dissatisfaction among the young. At the same time, these cultural items influenced a burgeoning and diverse counterculture (e.g. the 'hippie' movement), which was additionally shaped by artistic traditions such as Dadaism and Situationism, as well as Eastern philosophy and an emerging drug scene.

Intellectually, key thinkers such as E. P. Thompson, C. Wright Mills or members of the Frankfurt School who had inspired the emergence of the New Left at the beginning of the decade were from the mid-1960s on gradually replaced by an increasingly global reception of the works of Herbert Marcuse, Che Guevara, Frantz Fanon and Mao Zedong as well as other socialist/Communist writers deviating from orthodox Marxism. This shift entailed, on the one hand, a greater interest in transcending the spiritual void of modern, affluent industry and the subsequent personal alienation. At the same time, it eventually favoured an anti-colonial and anti-imperialist liberation ideology initiating a revolutionary overthrow of the existing domestic systems and international world order of the Cold War.

Politically, the most significant common denominator, next to university reform on the national level, was the opposition to the war in Vietnam. In the eyes of many activists worldwide, the war was considered an example of the suppression of a national liberation movement and of the promotion of American imperialist interests on a global scale. The anti-war movement thus served as the unifying element among activists worldwide who gathered at international meetings and conferences, creating vibrant personal and institutional networks of dissent.

With the year '1968', these transnational connections of the 1960s reached a perceived climax. The Tet-offensive, the assassination of Martin Luther King Jr and Robert F. Kennedy in the US, the shooting of German student leader Rudi Dutschke, the 'French May' as well as the end of the 'Prague Spring' due to the Soviet invasion of Czechoslovakia all illustrated, especially in the mind of contemporaries, the global dimension of a revolutionary change. In this situation, the affiliations and cross-cultural borrowings between the various national movements had not only developed a transnational lingua franca of protest, but also reached a higher level of intensity and urgency which was further strengthened by the continuing American escalation of the war in Southeast Asia in the early 1970s. As a result, these movements were able to channel a longer history of cultural internationalism they were part of into, among other things, a rapid growth of international NGOs which further gave rise to a global consciousness and the idea of a global community through an enlargement of transnational civil society.

The 1960s were thus a decade during which people from numerous countries established contact, shared ideas, adopted social and cultural practices, and adapted them to their own needs and circumstances. National liberation movements, Black Power, the emergence of the women's and environmental movements, as well as terrorist groups operating internationally, yielded broad-based sociocultural transformations in the following decades in the various domestic systems, while at the same time creating personal and institutional networks which profoundly shaped the transnational sphere for decades to come.

Martin Klimke

Bibliography

Fink C., Gassert P. and Junker D. (eds) 1998. *1968: a world transformed.* Cambridge and Washington, DC: Cambridge University Press.

Marwick A. 1998. *The Sixties: cultural revolution in Britain, France, Italy, and the United States, c.1958–c.1974.* Oxford and New York: Oxford University Press.

Suri J. 2003. *Power and protest: global revolution and the rise of detente.* Cambridge, MA: Harvard University Press.

Related essays

1848; 1989; African Liberation; avant-garde; Beatles; Buddhism; Cold War; drugs (illicit); Guevara, Ernesto ('Che'); higher education; humanities; intellectual elites; liberation theology; *Little Red Book*; Maoism; pacifism; rock; social sciences; *The Wretched of the Earth*; Vietnam War; youth organizations

1989

The year 1989 is associated with the end of the Cold War and a succession of regime changes leading to the democratization of Central and Eastern Europe, which entailed the end of Communist domination in the region and the disintegration of the Soviet Union. Because of the scale and impact of these political changes, 1989 is used as a metaphor designating the triumph of liberal-democratic ideology in Europe or referring to spectacular events such as the fall of the Berlin Wall. However, more than a single event or series of events, 1989 encompasses a number of socially meaningful evolutions with a broader context and significance.

Most publications tend to present the collapse of Communism in national perspective, country by country, each with their detailed chronology. However, in several respects, post-Communist democratization is a transnational phenomenon *par excellence*. First, the events of 1989 represent the convergence of specific political opportunities and social mobilizations already under way: regimes' contestation from the inside, their progressive liberalization and the East–West *détente* facilitated by the Helsinki agreement, German *Ostpolitik* and Gorbachev's *perestroika* policy in the USSR. The fall of Communism sealed the victory of dissident movements (such as *Solidarność* in Poland and *Charta 77* in Czechoslovakia) and their leaders (such as Andrei Sakharov, Václav Havel and Adam Michnik), supported by Western networks comprising intellectuals, radio broadcasting, trade unions, and governmental agencies.

Second, the democratic breakthroughs were characterized by a kind of domino effect: the Round Table between moderate Communist and opposition leaders in Poland from February to April 1989 was followed by semi-democratic elections on 4 June (the day of the Tiananmen Square protest in China), by mass demonstrations during the symbolic funeral of 1956 heroes in Budapest on 16 June, and by the 'velvet revolution' in Czechoslovakia in late autumn. The first visit of Chancellor Helmut Kohl to democratic Poland, celebrating the Polish–German reconciliation, was interrupted by the opening of the intra-German border in Berlin on 9 November, which paved the way for the German unification process. Although the metaphor of 'contagion' appears simplistic, the dynamics of this democratic 'third wave' have puzzled many authors. These events can be understood better when one keeps in mind the connections that existed between the different opposition movements previous to 1989 and, more generally, the emulation and circulation of information during the regime change that was impossible to prevent in the context of liberalization.

Third, 1989 was a crack in the national map of post-1945 Europe. It was a direct challenge to existing states and their territorial dimension and led to a redefinition of national polities. Far from signalling 'the end of history' and the definitive victory of liberal-democratic values in Europe, 1989 and its aftermath also reopened the Pandora's Box of nationalist tensions and territorial conflicts, leading, in a few cases, to war.

Finally, 1989 was the starting point for a broad flow of foreign assistance to democratization. This effort was encouraged by international forums (G7, G24) and coordinated by the European Community which launched its PHARE assistance programme (*Pologne-Hongrie assistance à la restructuration des économies*). Various governmental and non-governmental organisations, such as the US National Endowment for Democracy and private foundations such as Soros, Ford, and the German political *Stiftungen*, joined the movement. Transnational party organisations such as the Socialist or Christian-Democratic International sent their representatives to the region to promote their programmes and search for new partners in the fluid party landscape. These and other 'democracy makers' contributed to the diffusion of institutional and constitutional schemes, as well as principles of pluralism, the rule of law, a market economy, and human rights. However, it became apparent that the visions these foreign organizations were promoting concerning civil society, the nature of regimes or the required speed of privatization could diverge.

Notwithstanding the scale of the breakdown, 1989 was neither a *Stunde Null* nor a *tabula rasa* for transnational cooperation. Ideas not only about human rights, ecology and feminism, but also about monetarism, neoliberalism and the new conservatism, had already penetrated Central and Eastern Europe, owing to intellectual exchanges, scholarships and exile networks. But in 1989 public debates about these ideas became possible.

Dorota Dakowska

Bibliography

Dahrendorf R. 1990. *Reflections on the revolution in Europe*. London: Chatto & Windus.

Elster J., Offe C. and Preuss U. (eds) 1998. *Institutional design in post-communist societies: rebuilding the ship at sea*. Cambridge: Cambridge University Press.

Kenney P. and Horn G.-R. (eds) 2004. *Transnational moments of change: 1945, 1968, 1989*. Lanham: Rowman & Littlefield.

Michnik A. 1990. *La deuxième révolution*. Paris: La Découverte.

Related essays

1848; 1960s; Cold War; convergence and divergence; democracy; developmental assistance; exile; Ford Foundation; grants and fellowships; legal order; management; Master of Business Administration (MBA); neoliberalism; philanthropic foundations; radio; socialism; taxation

A

Abolition of Forced Labour Convention

On 5 June 1957, the International Labour Conference voted almost unanimously to adopt the Forced Labour Convention (C105). With 145 ratifications, it has been one of the most ratified conventions of the International Labour Organization (ILO). This vote ended a highly controversial discussion which began on 24 November 1947 within the Economic and Social Council of the UN (ECOSOC) when the American Federation of Labour (AFL) accused the government of the Soviet Union of practising large-scale forced labour for political and economic purposes.

Four years later (1951), a first joint committee (ECOSOC-ILO) was set up to study thousands of accusations against several countries, mostly European and socialist, for practising 'forced or corrective labour as a means of political coercion or punishment and which [was] also on such a scale as to constitute an important element in the economy of a given country'. In 1953, the very controversial report of this committee insisted that the ILO should develop a new international legal instrument in order to abolish forced labour. The governing body of the Organization placed this topic on the agenda of the 1955 Labour Conference, and a committee was set up to collect additional information and prepare a new convention. This committee submitted two reports (in 1956 and 1957), while questionnaires were sent to governments, and two subsequent conferences hosted fiery debates on the subject.

The first allegations of the AFL were made in 1947, at the beginning of the Cold War. The major American trade union was then fighting a common enemy with the US government: Communism. When it created the International Federation of Free Trade Unions in 1949, with CIA subsidies, the AFL thrust a wedge into the international labour movement organized by the Communist-oriented World Federation of Trade Unions. Both federations would play a very active role in the forced-labour discussion. Within the governing body of the ILO, Philip Delaney, American representative of the workers and AFL member, was the one who constantly pushed the issue, in a clear attempt to use the ILO as a Cold War weapon. He could rely

on the support of David Morse, the American chief director of the ILO, who was close to the direction of the AFL (AFL-CIO after 1955) and – until 1953 – to the Democratic administration of Harry S. Truman. But he could also count on employers' and ICFTU (International Confederation of Free Trade Unions) workers' delegates.

The Convention process had roots that extended beyond this Cold War context, however. Forced labour in concentration camps was a target in the 'human rights decade' that followed World War 2 and the Nuremberg trials. Some NGOs, like the International Committee against the Concentrationary Regime, created by the Frenchman David Rousset and former deported persons in Nazi camps, played a major role in the debates around the Convention, which they conceived as a new episode in the fight against the 'concentration universe'. In a first draft of the Universal Declaration of Human Rights, some delegates had indeed wanted to condemn forced labour explicitly. The UN Human Rights Commission then called upon the ILO's expertise, because of a former ILO Convention on Forced Labour (1930). At that time, though, the question had not been mainly about human rights but about 'colonial rule', and the purpose had not been to abolish political forced labour but to try to encourage the extinction of an excessive economic exploitation of indigenous peoples. During the 1950s discussion on forced labour, this 'old issue' was brought back in, notably by one of the oldest human rights NGOs, the Anti-Slavery League. But most of the discussion was framed by human rights concerns, in continuation of the denunciation of Nazi terror.

The Nuremberg trials had been the acme of the wartime alliance between the US and the Soviet Union, and the Universal Declaration of Human Rights, with its inclusion of social justice, had created a common language that both sides were anxious to control and use. As soon as it became evident that a convention was unavoidable, the representatives of socialist countries insisted on including the economic and social dimension of human rights in a definition of forced labour which could include certain forms of economic exploitation, in particular in underdeveloped countries (as they were then called). Building from the 1951 definition, they worked up this extension of meaning from 1953, and in that respect were able to count on trade unionists of the ICFTU who claimed to defend the interests of world labour. While the US Secretary of State of the Republican administration now resisted the prospect of any proactive international human rights regulation, the American AFL delegate, Delaney, voted in 1956 for a Soviet resolution which included private employers' practices within the jurisdiction of the Convention. The front lines of 1947–53 were turned upside down: beyond the Cold War context, the question of forced labour had been placed on a level of 'universal' concern and could now be voted almost unanimously.

Sandrine Kott

Bibliography

Alcock A. 1971. *History of the International Labour Organisation*. London: Macmillan (now Palgrave Macmillan).

International Labour Conference 2007. *Eradication of forced labour*. Geneva: ILO.

International Labour Organization 1953. *Report of the Ad Hoc Committee on Forced Labour*. Geneva: ILO.

Related essays

abolitionism; Antarctic Treaty; Cold War; Commission on International Labour Legislation; human rights; labour standards; slavery; Stockholm Conference; UN Women's Conferences; war crimes; workers' movements

Abolitionism

Abolitionism, the movement to end slavery, was among the earliest modern transnational social movements. As early as the mid 1700s, European and American abolitionists cooperated to protest slavery in Africa and the Americas. In the 1800s, globalizing forces facilitated thicker anti-slavery networks, enabling the transnational exchange of information and support. Building on these networks, 20th-century abolitionists lobbied organizations like the League of Nations and the United Nations in a campaign that continues today. A transnational history of abolitionism reveals, however, that such networks sometimes hindered abolitionists, whose effectiveness frequently depended on local contingencies.

Organized abolitionism began after the American Revolution, when anti-slavery groups were founded in Philadelphia, London, and Paris and gradual emancipation began in the northern United States. But early abolitionists advocated slave trade abolition, improved slave treatment, the resettlement of manumitted slaves in African colonies, or gradual emancipation – not the immediate abolition of slavery itself. Large emancipations during revolutions in French Saint-Domingue in the 1790s and in South America in the early 1800s owed more to slave resistance and military exigencies than to abolitionism. Abolitionists' main achievement before the 1830s was the abolition of the transatlantic slave trade in 1807 by Britain and the United States, but only British abolition was prompted by mass protest.

In the 1830s, British and American abolitionists, influenced by evangelical religion and political democratization, began advocating immediate emancipation. In 1833, after receiving massive anti-slavery petitions, Parliament abolished British West Indian slavery, compensating owners and apprenticing freedpeople to masters. Further protests ended apprenticeship in 1838, immediately emancipating all slaves. Inspired by British success, abolitionists expanded their networks. Delegations from France, America, and Britain travelled to the West Indies to observe abolition's results. American abolitionists actively sought friendship with British abolitionists, whom they viewed as models and partners. Leading abolitionists on both sides of the Atlantic, including William Lloyd Garrison, Joseph Sturge and Frederick Douglass, crossed the ocean for speaking tours. These tours set precedents, in turn, for numerous trips to Europe by African American abolitionists and former slaves, many of whom became celebrities in Britain in the 1850s. Such Atlantic crossings facilitated correspondence between European and American activists and drew abolitionists into transnational movements for peace, free trade, temperance, women's rights, and political reform.

After 1833, British abolitionists began stressing abolitionism's global dimensions and actively promoted such transnational networks. In 1839, anti-apprenticeship veterans founded the British and Foreign Anti-Slavery Society (BFASS), which in 1840 hosted an international conference in London known as the 'World's Convention'. Over 250 abolitionists from the Caribbean, America and Europe attended. Anglo-American abolitionists dominated the Convention and a sequel in 1843, but delegates heard extensive reports on British emancipation and Islamic slavery in Africa, as well as slavery in Spanish Cuba, Portuguese Brazil, and India. Abolitionists in some countries depended heavily on British aid. In the 1840s French immediatists, harried by official repression, relied on British supporters, who funded French translations of propaganda and initiated a petition campaign in France. American abolitionists also urged Britain to pressure US slaveholders by encouraging free-grown cotton in the British Empire.

Such transnational exchanges led activists to imagine abolitionism as a global movement. When abolition came to France in 1848, Dutch Surinam in 1863, the United States in 1865, Cuba in 1886, and Brazil in 1888, many abolitionists credited a global, British-led campaign. After all, abolitionists as far-flung as Brazil's Joaquim Nabuco, who lived temporarily in London, corresponded with the BFASS. The Spanish Abolition Society, established in 1865, had Anglo-American contacts, and in 1867, Anglo-American, French and Spanish abolitionists convened in Paris to discuss Cuban, Brazilian, and African slavery.

But while abolitionists popularized an image of solidarity, transnational cooperation had uneven results. Economic decline in the British Caribbean undercut free-labour arguments by abolitionists elsewhere. Moreover, abolitionists affiliated with the BFASS were often suspected at home of being British interlopers. Britain deployed diplomatic and naval power to combat illegal slaving after 1807, efforts that intensified after 1840 as Britain searched foreign ships suspected as slavers. Such tactics accelerated abolition in some places while strengthening the perception in the United States and France that abolitionism masked British interests.

Local conditions, moreover, circumscribed abolitionists' political opportunities. Before 1848, state control of public meetings in France forced the cancellation of a planned Anglo-French anti-slavery convention in Paris. It took civil war to demolish American slavery, while Danish and French emancipation required liberal revolutions that abruptly vaulted abolitionists into power. Spanish abolitionists remained marginal until a liberal revolution in 1868, and Cuban emancipation owed less to them than to an anti-colonial rebellion. A Brazilian anti-slavery society with Anglo-American ties was founded in 1880 but languished until the mass migration of slaves from their plantations ignited grassroots protests. Globally, Britain's West Indian model of emancipation prompted by non-violent lobbying remained irreproducible. That model was unique even within the British Empire, since West Indian emancipation had not applied to many Eastern possessions. African slavery outlived the 1800s despite abolitionist protests. European colonialists often outlawed slavery in their protectorates, while simultaneously allowing indigenous institutions to preserve slaveholders' customary rights and permitting African elites to employ forced labour.

Yet 19th-century abolitionists helped shape liberal discourse across borders and successfully stigmatized slaveholding countries as offensive to world opinion. That stigma was formalized in the Berlin Declaration of 1885 and the Brussels Act of 1890, in which the colonial powers pledged to suppress slave trading and work towards abolishing slavery. Admissions that slavery affronted international norms were made partly to justify imperialism as a civilizing mission, a view even abolitionists shared. In 1909, the BFASS merged with the Aborigines Protection Society, underlining abolitionists' basic agreement with the Berlin and Brussels signatories that European powers had an obligation to serve as trustees over less civilized colonial peoples. But the Brussels Act did establish bureaus to collect information on slavery and enabled abolitionists to pressure signatories, as when reformers cooperated at century's end to expose abusive labour practices in the Belgian Congo.

Daunting obstacles nonetheless remained. Many abolitionist movements disbanded or dissipated after achieving emancipation at home. International anti-slavery agreements remained largely promissory and unenforceable since signatories insisted on national sovereignty. In Africa, Latin America, and Asia, abolitionists confronted diverse institutions, from contract labour and debt peonage to concubinage and child trafficking, that were distinct from yet analogous to chattel slavery. Such practices persisted even within putatively anti-slavery empires. Colonial slavery generally lacked legal sanction, but no international mechanisms existed to ensure its extinction.

In the 20th century, however, intergovernmental organizations institutionalized ideals about human rights and offered abolitionists new venues for action. The League of Nations adopted a Convention to Suppress the Slave Trade and Slavery in 1926. Abolitionists, especially British veterans, used League committees on slavery to publicize slavery's persistence in Ethiopia, the Red Sea region, and elsewhere. Most important, the 1926 Convention denounced slavery in 'all its forms', beginning a broadening of terminology that continued under the UN, which adopted a 1956 convention pledging the eradication of 'institutions and practices similar to slavery'. In 1975 the UN created a permanent Working Group on Slavery which met annually to hear reports on progress towards abolition.

Over a century after the 'World's Convention', publicity remained abolitionists' main weapon, but intergovernmental organizations provided unprecedented platforms for collecting and broadcasting information. Yet many states ignored international recommendations, still seeing national sovereignty as inviolate and abolitionism as a British Trojan horse. International bodies often depended for facts on non-governmental organizations, whose objectivity states challenged. Abolitionist tactics also assumed states were sensitive to international pressure, which was often truer of newly independent states who could not enforce abolition than of strong states who could. The dismantling of empires after World War 2 weakened the influence of metropolitan abolitionists in postcolonial states where slavery persisted, while in the West, abolitionists confronted the presumption that slavery was already dead.

The redefinition of slavery to include a host of exploitative practices further complicated abolitionist efforts. As the term 'slavery' became more inclusive, it became harder for abolitionists to estimate progress towards abolition and secure consensus on anti-slavery measures in international organizations. At the UN, slavery became another Cold War battlefield as Communist and capitalist blocs each used expansive definitions of slavery to indict the other's practices. Western nations, for example, attacked Soviet labour camps as slavery while deflecting attention from chattel slavery in their Arabic satellites.

Defining slavery bedevils abolitionists even now, though clear examples still surface in impoverished regions like Mauritania, Sudan, and sub-Saharan Africa. But globalization and the proliferation of international non-governmental organizations have made abolitionism increasingly transnational. Anti-Slavery International (ASI), the direct descendant of the BFASS, adopted its new name in 1990 to reflect its cooperation with local organizations from Niger to Nepal. Yet ASI, like its predecessors, still relies on publicity to pressure states and international groups to suppress slavery. And it faces the old conundrum of how to act transnationally against a wide range of local institutions that are often shielded by or impervious to the sovereignty of nation states.

W. Caleb McDaniel

Bibliography

Blackburn R. 1988. The overthrow of colonial slavery, 1776–1848. London: Verso.

Blackett R. J. M. 1983. Building an antislavery wall: black Americans in the Atlantic abolitionist movement, 1830–1860. Baton Rouge: Louisiana State University Press.

Davis D. B. 2006. Inhuman bondage: the rise and fall of slavery in the New World. Oxford: Oxford University Press.

Miers S. 2003. Slavery in the twentieth century: the evolution of a global problem. Lanham: Rowman and Littlefield.

Related essays

Abolition of Forced Labour Convention; Africa; African liberation; animal rights; Cold War; contract and indentured labourers; criminology; forced migrations; Garvey, Marcus Mosiah; indigenous networks; international non-governmental organizations (INGOs); League of Nations system; pacifism; slavery; temperance; United Nations system; White Slavery; women's movements

Acclimatization

Acclimatization – the introduction of animals and plants to new environments in other parts of the world in the hope that they would thrive – burgeoned in the 19th century and followed on the Enlightenment fascination with collecting exotic animals and discovering economically useful plants. While it has much in common with domestication or naturalization, it is distinct in that the science of acclimatization is predicated on the fact that some biota are easily able to adapt to a different climate or habitat and to survive in circumstances where they have no predators or other pests to control their numbers.

Attempts to acclimatize alien species have had a variety of impacts worldwide. New Zealand provides a very clear case study of how even the environments and landscapes of the last settled and most remote country on earth have been changed. An extraordinary array of more than 1,200 plants and trees, over 500 of which became established, had been introduced deliberately or accidentally to New Zealand by 1900 from all major continents. Gorse, initially a useful wind break, had overrun much of the country by the 1890s. Pinus radiata from California, which grew extraordinarily fast in New Zealand, taking 20–40 years to reach maturity, a much shorter time span than anywhere else, had become ubiquitous by the 1920s as a shelter belt. Then this low quality timber tree became the basis of the government's reforestation programme. Today some 1.6 million hectares are covered in its dark green uniformity. The grey rabbit, as in Australia, proved the most damaging of the acclimatized animal species, eating many high-country farmers out of a living from the 1870s. Plants regarded as useful in Britain often became 'weeds', while animals that provided food and sport became 'pests'. New Zealand was not the only British colony to be irrevocably changed by acclimatization. Australia, with its complex and unique ecology, proved favourable for rabbits, camels, buffalo and many other species, to the detriment of local flora and fauna, some of which have become extinct.

Many of the successful acclimatized species were accidentally introduced – by sealers, whalers, traders and missionaries in their international travels. In New Zealand, this included such notorious European 'weeds' as dock (Rumex crispus) and the Norwegian rat (Rattus norvegicus) which soon overwhelmed the smaller Polynesian rat or kiore (Rattus exulans) and began an assault upon hapless flightless birds. But much of the acclimatization was deliberate, driven by well-intentioned societies established for the purpose from 1861 in countries such as France, Britain, Russia, South Africa, Australia, New Zealand and the United States. It was a global network that included amateurs keen to sample a dish of wombat or eland, farmers intent on improving the land in colonial situations, sportsmen seeking trout-fishing in colonial streams and scientists taking an interest in animal adaptive techniques and behaviour and the study of heredity and evolutionary traits. Many species of animals, fish and plants were translocated with more enthusiasm for enrichment, sport, science and agricultural productivity than consideration for possible future deleterious environmental consequences. Some of the dedication of the societies to transnational exchanges of biota was based on the nostalgic creation of a colonial home that closely resembled the mother country, but more generally the motive was economic. Australian wattles and eucalypts were imported into South Africa to stabilize windblown sand-dunes and to begin a tanning industry. Another arm of the acclimatization initiative was the search for economically valuable plants in remote parts of the world like China and their introduction into Western agriculture, medicine and horticulture.

By the 1920s, as ecological understanding increased, observant botanists, scientists and farmers began to consider that much acclimatization had been unwise. Efforts at biological control of what have become alien invaders have been problematic. Strict border and biosecurity regimes have tried to regulate the circulation of species, but the increasing flow of people, goods and commodities that include animals and plants or carry them unintentionally creates an ongoing battle. Some people have described the current campaign against all non-indigenous species as xenophobic, and there is even fierce resistance from some Cape Town residents to culling the Himalayan tahr that were introduced by Cecil Rhodes in order to 'beautify' Table Mountain.

Acclimatization has both increased and decreased biodiversity. To come back to New Zealand, the result of 200 years of acclimatization is hybrid landscapes with naturalized plants outnumbering natives by 120 to 100. Some 39 million sheep and 10 million cattle graze where only birds once flourished. On the one hand, there are more species in New Zealand than there were before British settlement; but many indigenous species have become extinct and ecosystems irreversibly altered.

Tom Brooking

Bibliography
Crosby A. W. 2004. Ecological imperialism: the biological expansion of Europe, 900–1900. Cambridge: Cambridge University Press.

Lever C. 1992. *They dined on eland: the story of the acclimatisation societies*. London: Quiller.

Star P. 1995. From acclimatisation to conservation: colonists and the natural world in southern New Zealand, 1860–1894. Unpublished doctoral dissertation, University of Otago.

Young D. 2004. *Our islands our selves: a history of conservation in New Zealand*. Dunedin: University of Otago Press.

Related essays

agriculture; animal diseases; biodiversity; Chinese medicine; conservation/preservation; empire; rubber; scientific expeditions; silk; wine

Acquired Immunodeficiency Syndrome (AIDS)

Acquired immunodeficiency syndrome (AIDS) is a medical condition produced by the human immunodeficiency virus (HIV). Transmission occurs primarily through unprotected sexual intercourse and congenitally from mother to child. Needle-sharing intravenous drug users are also at risk. With few symptoms initially, untreated HIV makes its victims eventually vulnerable to opportunistic diseases, particularly tuberculosis. Its slow-developing character, together with the stigma associated with a sexually transmitted, invariably fatal condition, make more difficult effective measures for both prevention and treatment. Like tuberculosis, HIV strikes hardest among society's poorest and most vulnerable populations. Many of the victims are young adults (women face disproportionate risk) but no social group is immune, irrespective of age, sex, or class. First identified among homosexual men in the United States in 1981, HIV was already spreading unrecognized in heterosexual populations of West and Central Africa.

Recent research confirms that HIV originated in a simian immunodeficiency virus (SIV), probably in Cameroon. The jump across the species barrier may have occurred as early as the 1930s, as the disease became transmissible between humans. That development set the biomedical precondition for an epidemic, but favourable socioeconomic circumstances were crucially involved. After a slow start, HIV's initial dispersion was facilitated by the effects of colonialism in West and Central Africa, including new transportation networks, labour migration, and urbanization. Growing globalization eventually permitted the disease to spread across the world with devastating effects, particularly in Africa and the rest of the Third World. With an estimated 38.6 million victims by 2005, HIV/AIDS has become the worst global pandemic since the influenza outbreak of 1918. Worldwide, it is overwhelmingly a disease that afflicts heterosexuals. In North America, for instance, HIV has moved beyond the homosexual community to infect the general population, particularly in poor black and aboriginal communities.

As the global epidemic grew in speed and extent, political and medical responses remained inadequate. Following the first special session of the United Nations General Assembly on HIV/AIDS in 2001, a more coordinated, although still uneven, international campaign began to develop. Even earlier, the uniquely global character and severity of HIV/AIDS received unprecedented institutional recognition in 1996 with the establishment of the Joint United Nations Programme on HIV/AIDS (UNAIDS), the only UN organization devoted to a single disease.

While HIV remains incurable, the Highly-Active Antiretroviral Therapy, using drug combinations in multiple daily doses, turns this killer disease into a chronic condition that can be successfully tolerated for many years. Following from persistent international protests, patent protection that kept drug prices high has been waived or broken, making mass treatment much more affordable, especially in poor countries. These prolonged and ongoing global campaigns were modelled on the early success of gay advocates in the United States during the 1980s and 90s in getting HIV/AIDS onto the research, treatment, and political agendas. Latterly, national activist groups, such as South Africa's Treatment Action Campaign, have successfully fought for lower drug prices and more effective systems to identify victims, prevent congenital transmission, and deliver therapy. Large-scale manufacture of generic versions of the key drugs has helped to make them more available and affordable. Yet, despite the availability of reliable methods to test for infection, relatively few HIV victims know their status and access to therapy remains uneven particularly for the rural poor and child victims.

The consequences of the epidemic extend beyond the immediate effects of the disease itself. There is, for example, the looming crisis associated with the millions of AIDS orphans, growing up uneducated, often homeless and unsocialized, in countries mostly ill-equipped to help them. The recent history of this epidemic demonstrates that existing methods and therapies, if deployed more effectively, have the capability to keep afflicted young adults alive while they raise their children and to prevent millions of new infections. It is also evident, however, that HIV/AIDS will continue to take a heavy toll of people's lives and health for decades to come.

Alan Jeeves

Bibliography

Iliffe J. 2006. *The African AIDS epidemic: a history.* Oxford: James Currey.

Kirp D. and Bayer R. (eds) 1992. *AIDS in the industrialised democracies: passions, politics, and policies.* New Brunswick: Rutgers University Press.

Lewis M., Bamber S. and Waugh M. 1997. *Sex, disease, and society: a comparative history of sexually transmitted diseases and HIV/AIDS in Asia and the Pacific.* Westport: Greenwood.

Related essays

Africa; animal diseases; birth control; cancer; drugs (medical); epidemics; germs; health policy; labour migrations; smallpox; transportation infrastructures; urbanization

Adoption

International adoption, also known as intercountry or transnational adoption, denotes the movement of children for adoption between countries and commonly refers to the global flow of adoptees from the non-Western world to adopters in the West. Although small numbers of children have been exchanged cross-culturally earlier in history, the modern form of international adoption was initiated after the Korean War (1950–53). During the following half-century, at least half a million children from over one hundred different countries in South America, Africa, Asia, Oceania and Eastern Europe were adopted into around 20 Western countries. This migration of children is currently expanding rapidly, with an estimated 30,000 international placements a year.

Transporting large numbers of people intercontinentally began with the emergence of global European empires in the 15th and 16th centuries. Historical precedents for international adoption include the child migration programme of the British Empire which between around 1800 and 1967 shipped out over 100,000 destitute children from Great Britain to foster parents in Canada, South Africa, Australia and New Zealand, the American orphan-train programme which between 1854 and 1929 placed an equal number of orphans from the East Coast with substitute families in the Midwest, and the occasional taking in of indigenous and native children by white settler families in the colonies. This included the tens of thousands of First Nations children in Canada and the US who were placed in white families for adoption throughout the 20th century, and the 'stolen generations' of at least 25,000 Aboriginal children in Australia who between 1900 and 1970 were transferred to the custody of Anglo families. The adoption of children from indigenous and minority populations by white families in Europe's settler colonies is nowadays highly contested and charged, and sometimes branded as ethnocide or cultural genocide as part of an ongoing postcolonial reconciliation process.

International adoption's origins can also be traced back to the refugee movements of European children that took place in connection with World War 1 and World War 2. After World War 1, thousands of Armenian and Austrian children from the disintegrating Ottoman and Habsburg Empires were sent to temporary foster homes in Russia and Greece, and in Switzerland, the Netherlands and the Scandinavian countries respectively. During the interwar years, 20,000 Spanish children were relocated to France, the Soviet Union, Scandinavia, Mexico, Venezuela and Chile at the time of the Spanish Civil War, and an equal number of Jewish children from Nazi Germany, Austria and Czechoslovakia were brought to the UK, Belgium, the Netherlands, Switzerland and Scandinavia. A substantial number of these unaccompanied refugee children never returned to their birth countries after the wars, and were instead adopted by their host families. The same is true for the largest of these temporary placement programmes, namely that involving the 70,000 Finnish children of war who were transported to Sweden during World War 2, of whom almost 10,000 stayed permanently as adoptive or foster children. Finally, at the end of the war, the United States allowed into the country for adoption around 5,000 children from countries like China and Taiwan, Greece, Germany, Italy and Japan, many fathered by American occupation troops.

During the Cold War of the 1950s, American military interventions in Asia and the decolonization process, international adoption became established as a transnational migration phenomenon on a mass scale, particularly in the aftermath of the Korean War. The impetus arouse out of a desire to place the mixed-race children of Korea, mostly fathered by Western soldiers, in the countries that participated in the UN-led anti-Communist coalition, backed by the Korean government and in cooperation with child welfare agencies like the International Social Services. From then on, the movement of unaccompanied children between countries came to be perceived and treated as a child welfare practice rather than as a refugee rescue mission. It was handled by private adoption agencies instead of being organized state-to-state, and made possible by changes in migration and citizenship laws in both the countries of origin and in the receiving countries. It also gradually became an institutionalized legal practice in international, law, included within the 1989 UN Convention on the Rights of the Child, and from 1993 by way of the Hague Convention on Protection of Children and Cooperation in Respect of Intercountry Adoption. Korea's international adoption programme has functioned as a blueprint and model for other countries of origin, while Korean children dominated the field of international adoption until the mid-1990s when children from China and Russia surpassed them in number.

Asia dominated as a supplying continent in the 1950s and 1960s with countries under the American sphere of influence during the Cold War like South Korea, South Vietnam and the Philippines providing the largest numbers of children. The same was true for Latin American countries like Colombia, Brazil, Mexico, El Salvador and Chile, which became involved in the practice after 1970 when international adoption increased dramatically due to a drastic decrease in domestic adoption in the West. In the 1980s, Korea, India, Sri Lanka, Thailand, Peru, Guatemala and Ethiopia became more important as countries of origin, and in the 1990s Eastern European countries like Russia, Ukraine, Belarus, Bulgaria and Romania entered the scene after the fall of Communism. At the same time, China and Vietnam started to become involved with international adoption as a part of their respective opening up to the West, while South Africa, Kazakhstan and Cambodia also increasingly turned up in the global adoption statistics. At the other end, the leading adopting countries have always been the United States and Canada, Australia and New Zealand, Sweden, Norway, Denmark, France, the Netherlands, Belgium, Luxembourg, Switzerland and Germany, while Italy and Spain have appeared as important receivers during recent years. The demographic geography and political economy of international adoption have thus roughly followed the course of globalization as it is usually described for the past half-century.

Several attempts have been made in demographic studies to quantify the volume of global transfers of children for international adoption during given periods. Estimates for the 1980s are 170,000–180,000 for the decade with about 16,268 placements a year, growing to an annual average of 23,857 cases for the early 1990s and 32,295 for the late 1990s. All estimates agree that the United States takes in the most in absolute numbers, perhaps two-thirds of all children, that the Scandinavian countries of Norway, Sweden and Denmark, and nowadays also Spain, are adopting the most per capita, that Korea is the uncontested leading country of origin with 160,000 international adoptees, and that international adoption has been rapidly on the increase since the end of the 1990s. According to the official statistics from the US Citizenship and Immigration Services, formerly the US Immigration and Naturalization Service, a total number of 358,538 children was brought to the United States for international adoption between 1948 and 2004. This could mean an additional 150,000 placements in Europe, Australia and New Zealand, and consequently an estimated global number of something like 500,000 international adoptions between 1948 and 2004.

International adoption highlights political and economic power relations between supplying and receiving countries and problems regarding post- and neocolonialism, and raises issues of gender and race, and questions concerning ethnic identities and national belonging. International adoption is in practice a one-way migration of children from non-Western countries to the West. The Asian children being adopted, especially, have always predominantly been girls, in the case of China over 90 per cent, and minority children are heavily overrepresented, for example Roma children from Bulgaria, indigenous children from India, and Black and Amerindian children from Colombia. Since the migrants are children, normally under the age of 10–12, it is impossible to call these voluntary migrants; they do not exercise any choice or agency over their own destinations or moves. International adoption is primarily demand-driven, and the current dramatic increase reflects a growing infertility rate in Western countries as well as a growing number of single and homosexual adopters, while the supply side is often explained by patriarchal structures and racial and social discrimination in the countries of origin. International adoption has developed into a politically charged and controversial issue in leading supplying countries such as Brazil, Guatemala and India, and Korea, for example, has repeatedly tried to regulate and put an end to the practice ever since the mid-1970s. Finally, adult international adoptees from countries like South Korea and Vietnam have themselves recently started to reach out to each other transnationally, creating diaspora-like networks and resuming connections to their birth countries.

Tobias Hübinette

Bibliography
Kane S. 1993. 'The movement of children for international adoption', *Social Science Journal*, 30, 4, 323–39.
Lovelock K. 2000. 'Intercountry adoption as a migratory practice', *International Migration Review*, 34, 3, 907–49.
Selman P. 2002. 'Intercountry adoption in the new millennium', *Population Research and Policy Review*, 21, 3, 205–22.
Weil R. H. 1984. 'International adoption: the quiet migration', *International Migration Review*, 18, 2, 276–93.

Related essays
childhood; children's rights; diasporas; empire and migration; ethnicity and race; family; refugees

Advertising

Advertising is the act of promoting a product, a brand, a service, or a company by means of paid announcements in the print, broadcasting, or electronic media.

The transnational dimension can be considered a constitutive feature of the history of advertising. Because it is an instrument of commercial action, advertising occupies the intermediate area between production and consumption, or in other words, the third broad sphere of the market which consists of trade and distribution. Advertising is therefore part of the system of commercial transactions; a system which has fostered contacts and confluences among different societies and cultures ever since the first elementary trades took place. And it was in conjunction with the growth of transnational trade in the final decades of the 19th century that the first forms of transnational advertising and the first specialized advertising professions appeared.

Since the end of the 19th century, advertising has acted as a major vehicle for the transnationalization of values, lifestyles, and consumption patterns. The traversing of geographical, political and cultural boundaries has influenced the history of advertising at several levels: firstly, innumerable advertising campaigns have crossed the confines of national markets to promote a particular product among consumers in other countries; secondly, since its beginnings, the advertising industry has sought geographical expansion by creating transnational networks of agencies; thirdly, the expertise and practices of advertising professionals have always been enriched by approaches and perspectives extending beyond national traditions.

Transnational advertising – as an industry and as a set of strategies and messages – is characterized by constant interaction between pressures for standardization imposed by economic exigencies and tendencies toward diversification to match national sociocultural specificities.

As early as the 1920s, and then particularly after the Second World War, the transfer of an advertising message from one national context to another became both a crucial and a controversial problem for advertising professionals. In a world where the revolution in communications and transport seemed to be progressively eliminating geographical and cultural distances, it appeared possible – indeed necessary – to direct a single identical message at consumers in different countries. Following the celebrated example of Esso's campaign, 'Put a tiger in your tank', mounted around the world in the 1960s, attempts were made to communicate with the 'world-consumer' by means of 'universal advertising claims', appropriately translated into the language of each country.

In the course of the 1960s and 1970s, numerous surveys on the reception of standardized campaigns by consumers of differing nationalities revealed the influence of national cultural specificities in the interpretation of messages. Hence, diversification seemed to be the best way to prevent misunderstandings.

In the 1970s, transnational advertising began to shift to a pattern of standardization or semi-standardization. This solution consisted in laying down the campaign's guidelines and central structure, in particular the theme and the claim, and then devising slogans, images and layouts which could be adapted to national contexts. The purpose of pattern standardization was used therefore to 'plan diversity' or to establish a uniform template, various features of which could be adjusted to local circumstances. The problem of adaptation thus arose. It was necessary to reconcile two conflicting needs: retaining the sense of the message, while adjusting the campaign to its reception context. The result of this strategy was the devising of 'multi-domestic' campaigns, consisting of multiple versions of the same model, for example, the television commercials for Ace bleach, which since 1968 have relied on a single basic format – an elderly housewife instructing a younger one on the use of the bleach – while the cast, scenery and dialogues have varied from country to country. The representation of familiar characters and settings, and the elimination of any element alien to the national sociocultural context, responded to a logic of mimicry which sought to overcome consumer resistance to foreign messages and products.

Today, transnational campaigns are characterized by a wide array of solutions, ranging from a maximum of standardization to a maximum of differentiation. Even in the case of global campaigns, however, specific national cultural features are rarely eliminated or ignored. But references to the reception context are restricted to subtle variations and nuances in translation, or changes made to apparently insignificant elements. Advertising reflects the structure of the local, national and worldwide dimensions by producing phenomena of recombination, hybridization and syncretism. Because transnational advertising must cope with the new configuration of markets and cultures, it sometimes exploits the complexity of the new geography of consumption. Increasingly frequent, in fact, are 'glocal' campaigns characterized by the juxtaposition of elements of regional or local folklore with global products and consumption practices: images of windmills in northern China, complete with a soundtrack of festive Chinese music, to promote Coca Cola; young Turkish immigrants depicted playing football in the streets of Berlin by a Nike commercial; Italian peasants singing the praises in Veneto dialect of Kellogg's Corn Flakes, a product entirely extraneous to Italy's dietary habits. In these cases the international character of the brand is no longer dissimulated; the opposition between global and local is deliberately highlighted, and the strength of this strategy resides precisely in the contrast produced by the combination of the local and global dimensions.

The late 19th and early 20th centuries saw the advent of the first organizations specialized in transnational advertising. These were businesses which leased advertising space in the foreign press and also furnished development or translation services, or they were outright advertising agencies with 'foreign departments' engaged in transnational business. In 1899, the J. Walter Thompson advertising agency, founded in 1864 in New York, opened a branch in London in order to encourage British manufacturers to promote their products in the United States. Inauguration of the London office marked the beginning of expansion by the J. Walter Thompson agency into more than 60 countries. During the 1920s and 1930s other American agencies ventured abroad, laying the foundation for the great transnational development of Madison Avenue after the Second World War.

Between the mid-1950s and the end of the 1960s, the largest US agencies began to operate abroad. Proceeding apace with the expansion of the great multinationals (General Motors, Esso, Colgate Palmolive, etc.), the American advertising industry first directed its attention to Europe, Canada and Latin America, and then, from the 1960s onwards, to the Asiatic and African countries. Initially, the agencies opened branches abroad in order to respond adequately to their customers' growth strategies. Subsequently the opportunity to increase turnover by acquiring foreign clients, the prospect of shaking off exclusive dependence on an already saturated American market, and the availability of tax relief on foreign investments encouraged entry into new markets.

Since the end of the 1970s, huge conglomerates consisting of networks of agencies have gained control of the world advertising market. In the new scenario produced by concentration, the supremacy of the American groups was undermined by the advent of Asiatic groups (Dentsu) and European ones (WPP, Publicis). These new groups differ from the first generation of American agency networks not only in their size and their provision of services, which cover the entire range of communication, but also in their endeavour to disguise their origins. Whilst until the 1970s the American provenance of an advertising agency was a signal of competence and professionalism, today the question of geographical provenance has seemingly lost significance because of the composite origin of the capital, personnel and clients of advertising conglomerates. Accordingly, therefore, the new groups seek to present themselves as culturally neutral or cosmopolitan.

In the 1920s, the proliferation of the branches of American businesses and agencies coincided with radical change in the expertise and practices of advertising in Europe and Latin America. The spread of North American advertising theories and techniques was brought about mainly by agencies, but also by the translation of handbooks, training periods in the United States, and meetings and seminars organized by national professional associations. The success of the American model produced strong pressures in all countries for the work of advertisers to be rationalized, and it marked the transition to procedures based on marketing rules.

The Americanization of advertising, however, did not lead to the disappearance of already existing national traditions. The work

organization and methods exported by the United States aroused considerable resistance, criticism, and even hostility among European advertising professionals. The postwar period in Europe saw an outright clash between the 'scientific' approach of American advertising and the 'advertising art' tied to the 19th-century tradition of the poster. The years between the 1950s and the 1970s saw numerous borrowings and fusions between the two models. Similar phenomena are now apparent in China, where the steady advance of Western advertising norms and practices is provoking both the enthusiastic support and the fierce opposition of local practitioners. As global advertising culture is assimilated, some elements are accepted, others rejected, and others adapted, to produce entirely new patterns.

Simona De Iulio

Bibliography

De Mooij M. K. 1994. *Advertising worldwide: concepts, theories and practice of international, multinational and global advertising.* Englewood Cliffs: Prentice-Hall.

Mattelart A. 1990. *L'internationale publicitaire.* Paris: La Découverte.

Mueller B. 2004. *Dynamics of international advertising: theoretical and practical perspectives.* New York: Peter Lang.

Related essays

beauty; cities; consumer cooperation; consumer society; corporations; information economy; marketing; services; sports gear and apparel; trade

Africa

Africa is the second largest and second most populous continent of the world. The origin of the term goes back to the ancient Greek and later Roman classification of the division of the known world into Europe, Asia and Africa (Libya). Medieval geographers continued to rely on this categorization, which took the Nile River as the border between Asia and Africa. In the aftermath of the age of discoveries, European geographers began to refer to the Red Sea, not the Nile, as a border for Africa. Only in the 19th century, together with the development of a continental scheme of world geography, did Africa begin to be conceived of as a continent with distinct characteristics, especially with a black race, that separated it from Europe and Asia. Thus, despite the cultural and ethnic differences between the north and Sub-Saharan Africa, a fact that was especially emphasized by medieval Muslim geographers, a metageographic myth of the African continent became universally accepted during the globalization of Eurocentric knowledge categories.

Africa has always been linked to the rest of the world by various transnational networks, best seen by the fact that the continent has been exposed to all the world diseases. Muslim networks linked Africa not only to the holy cities of Mecca through pilgrimage, but also to Cairo's educational institutions, and to the rest of the world through intra-African or Indian Ocean trade activities. Chinese naval expeditions to Africa during the 15th and 16th centuries illustrate the sea trade routes that linked East Africa to South and South East Asia. The slave trade, European colonial rule and capitalist economic networks created new global connections for Africans. In addition to the dispersal of African peoples in the transatlantic slave trade, transitory black labourers who built railways and other infrastructural projects in the Americas in the second half of the 19th century, African soldiers who fought in both world wars, Africans who worked in European factories after 1945 and the current brain drain of African professionals and academics to the West further connected the continent to the rest of the world. The fact that African students in Europe, together with African Americans and West Indians, played the most prominent role in the emergence of a shared continental African identity illustrates the role of the globalized African diaspora in modern world history. As a result, a shared African identity first emerged in a global/transnational context and was then embraced by the leaders of the rising nationalist movements in different parts of the continent.

The history of Pan-Africanism best illustrates the transnational and global roots of African identity: Pan-Africanism started as a political project calling for the solidarity and potential union of all Africans into a single African federation to which those in the African diaspora could return. More important than its political projects, however, were the movement's cultural achievements, as Pan-Africanism has encouraged and inspired a body of shared literature, artistic projects and historical writings about the African black people in a truly transnational intellectual sphere. Initially, Pan-Africanism was a heterogeneous movement led by intellectuals of African descent in North America and the Caribbean, who thought of themselves as members of a single 'Negro' race. Their focus on the race identity of the Africans reflected the predominant late-19th-century Eurocentric division of humanity into distinct racial, civilizational and continental groups. But by picking race as the primary identity, early Pan-Africanists excluded the lighter-skinned, Arabic-speaking North African populations, who were mostly Muslim, from their vision of unity.

The earliest notions of a Pan-African vision of unity were developed by a wide range of African-American intellectuals, such as Martin R. Delany (1812–85), Alexander Crummell (1822–98) and Edward Blyden (1832–1912), who all shaped the more systematic ideas of African identity and unity in the writings of W. E. B. Du Bois. Their 'negro race' based Pan-Africanism rested in large part on a critique of Western civilization and white-supremacism. The first major international gathering of Pan-Africanist intellectuals was organized in London under the leadership of Henry Sylvester Williams, a London barrister born in Trinidad. The composition of this first Pan-African meeting, which included a dozen representatives from North America (including Du Bois), eleven from the West Indies, five from London, but only four from the actual continent of Africa (one each from Ethiopia, Sierra Leone, Liberia and the Gold Coast) best illustrates the diaspora-centred character of this transnational African-black identity around the turn of the century. Interestingly, before World War I, it was African students in Britain who organized most of the Pan-African intellectual and political activism. They used the name 'Ethiopianism', a pre-World War I movement best depicted in J. E. Casely Hayford's (1866–1930) autobiographical novel Ethiopia Unbound (published in London in 1911). All of these activities aimed at 'race emancipation' while proudly claiming Africa as the 'cradle of civilization'. The political projects of Pan-Africanism became clearer in the First Pan-African Congress, convened by Du Bois in Paris in February 1919, where 50 delegates from Africa, the Caribbean and the United States managed to put forward a proposal for the creation of a new state in Africa based on Germany's former colonies, and asked for the protection of the rights of Africans and those of African descent in the colonies by the League of Nations.

During the interwar period, the Pan-African movement was represented by the growth of the Universal Negro Improvement Association (UNIA) led by Marcus Garvey, a Jamaican immigrant to the United States. At its height in the early 1920s, the UNIA had an estimated 2 million members and sympathizers, and approximately one thousand chapters in 43 countries and territories, becoming the largest black movement in the African diaspora and the most widespread black-led movement in world history. The movement proclaimed 'the inherent right of the Negro to possess himself of Africa' with the goal of establishing a 'Negro independent nation on the continent of Africa' to which all diaspora Africans could return. Even though the UNIA goals exhibited a surprising unawareness of the diversity and multiplicity of African cultures or peoples, it did have some following in Africa, especially in South Africa. In addition to UNIA's activism, cultural ideas emanating from the Caribbean and francophone West Africa in the 1920s and the 1930s, known as *Negritude*, became influential in creating a transnational African-black consciousness. Although it never turned into a formal organization, the Negritude cultural project emerged out of transnational African student groups with a shared colonial background, and was best represented by the achievements of Léopold Sédar Senghor, Aimé Césaire, and Léon-Gontran Damas. Moreover, during the interwar years, Pan-Africanism was strongly influenced by the international Communist movement and Soviet-supported anti-imperialist work. Led by George Padmore, this Comintern-connected Pan-African movement contributed to the international mobility of African nationalists and provided moral and intellectual support for the cause of decolonization. Whether exemplified in Marcus Garvey, Léopold Sengor or George Padmore, these politically active and well-connected diaspora communities contributed immensely to the formation of a new generation of nationalist leaders who challenged Western hegemony with counterclaims about Africa's racial equality, civilizational legacy and the potential for modernization.

World War 2 had a more profound impact on the decolonization of Africa. When the 5th Pan-African Congress gathered in Manchester in 1945, the leadership was handed from the diaspora community to the actual leaders of new nationalism on the African continent such as Kwame Nkrumah. After Nkrumah became the first prime minister of independent Ghana, he declared that 'the independence of Ghana is meaningless unless it is linked up with the total liberation of the African continent'. It was on this mid-20th-century stage, when intellectuals born in Africa took more leading roles in Pan-African thought, that a race-based African identity was challenged in favour of a more geographical, continental idea of African identity and solidarity that included North African Arabs. When postcolonial African leaders such as Nkrumah and Gamal Abdel Nasser of Egypt established the Organization of African Unity (OAU) in 1963, they defined the scope of the organization according to the continental boundaries, though the idea of African unity continued to include those 'blacks' whose ancestors had left the continent as traded slaves. This post-WW2 moment did not also end the involvement of the diaspora immediately, as Du Bois himself died and was buried in Ghana in 1963. Moreover, in the process of decolonization of Africa, especially during the Algerian Revolution, the idea of free Africa turned into a powerful transnational concept, and Pan-Africanist diaspora intellectuals such as Frantz Fanon shaped the content of global postcolonial thought. The Asian-African Conference in Bandung in 1955 became a symbol of this postcolonial moment, which was then followed by the prominent role of African countries in the Non-Aligned Movement.

The OAU did encourage further decolonization of the continent and played a significant role in mediating border disputes. But, in the various Cold War conflicts in Africa, it became highly divided. During the 1970s, the OAU did not play any important role or function in African affairs, when decolonized Africa plunged into problems of nation building and competing ideologies in highly diverse reform experiences. Ironically, it was once again the African-American diaspora of the Black Power movement that emphasized and advocated Pan-Africanism against the background of the conflict-ridden decolonized African continent. While Pan-Africanism today may have lost much of its political influence, it could be said that, for much of the 20th century, the very complex and diverse Pan-Africanist networks played a crucial role in the decolonization of the African continent and in the transnational imagination of both the African diaspora's civil rights movements and national movements on the African continent.

In the aftermath of the Cold War, African intellectuals noted the seeming marginalization and peripheralization of their continent in world affairs, and raised questions as to whether Africa was being de-globalized due to its health crises, economic underdevelopment and lack of leadership. As the place of Africa in the European imagination during the last two centuries connoted various forms of negativity and exoticism, ranging from the Dark Continent of mystery and loot to the underdeveloped and forgotten continent, these images spread to the rest of the world and became confirmed by the image of an underdeveloped continent with a grave health crisis in the last two decades. It was in this post-Cold War context that, paradoxically, the United Nations was led by two secretary-generals of African origin, Boutros Boutros-Ghali and Kofi Annan, in fact overseeing crucial transformations in world affairs. More importantly, the decolonization of South Africa under Nelson Mandela's leadership gave new energy and morale to the continent. This period naturally led to new soul searching among African nations as to how to make the OAU a more effective international organization. In 1993, the OAU began to accept and organize peace-keeping missions on the African continent. In 1994, an African Economic Community was initiated with the very long-term goal of reviving African economies under a free trade zone agreement. In 2002, the OAU was replaced by a seemingly more dynamic and much more ambitious African Union. The African Union currently has 53 member states, and it has all the sub-units and committees that could bring about a further integration of the continent along the lines of the European Union. For example, the African Cup of Nations is a very popular sports event that is followed in all parts of Africa. Recent interest on the part of China in cooperation and investment in Africa has raised new hopes and fears about the future of the continent's economy.

Although the interest of the African diaspora in the affairs of the African continent seems to have diminished compared to the first half of the 20th century, debates about reparations for Africa and the descendants of its slave children for centuries of servitude and colonialism still show common areas of identity, historical consciousness and activism.

Cemil Aydin

Bibliography

Callaghy T., Kassimir R. and Latham R. (eds) 2002. *Intervention and transnationalism in Africa: global-local networks of power.* Cambridge: Cambridge University Press.

Eckert A. 'Bringing the "Black Atlantic" into global history: the project of Pan-Africanism', in Conrad S. and Sachsenmaier D. (eds) 2007. *Competing visions of world order: global historical approaches, 1880s–1930s.* Basingstoke and New York: Palgrave Macmillan, 237–58.

Esedebe P. O. 1994. *Pan-Africanism: the idea and movement, 1776–1991.* Washington, DC: Howard University Press.

Mudimbe V.Y. 1988. *The invention of Africa: gnosis, philosophy and the order of knowledge.* Bloomington: Indiana University Press.

Related essays

abolitionism; Acquired Immunodeficiency Sydrome (AIDS); African liberation; Aga Khan Development Network; anti-racism; brain drain; Comintern and Cominform; conservation and preservation; contract and indentured labourers; convergence and divergence; debt (developing countries); decolonization; development and growth; developmental assistance; developmental taxonomies; diasporas; empire and migration; empires and imperialism; ethnicity and race; evangelicalism; exile; forced migrations; forests; Garvey, Marcus Mosiah; gold; international students; investment; jazz; labour migrations; literature; loans; Mandela, Nelson; missionaries; Muslim networks; national parks; oil; pan-isms; railways; regional communities; regions; reparations; rubber; Santería; slavery; technical assistance; *The Wretched of the Earth*; trade; transportation infrastructures; tropics; United Nations system; voodoo; war; wildlife films; world music

African liberation

African liberation, in the context of this essay, refers to the processes leading to the achievement of political rights by peoples on the African continent and of African descent in the second half of the 20th century.

An even broader definition could extend the time period backward to centuries of resistance to colonial conquest and slavery or forward to the prospect of addressing the legacies of social and economic inequality. But the period following World War 2, encompassing the political independence of almost all African states, the achievements of the US civil rights movement in eliminating legalized racial discrimination, and the end of South African apartheid, constitutes a subject of particular interest not only for African and African diaspora history but also for tracing the emergence of transnational networks.

In some senses the 20th-century history of every African country is intrinsically transnational history. The decolonization process involved interaction between colonizer and colonized, as well as mutual influences among those colonized by the same power. It was also shaped by the evolution of global norms and institutions, interactions between different colonial powers, and Cold War competition. Even in the cases of Liberia and Ethiopia, recognized as independent states before the decolonization era, the *de facto* involvement of outside powers was fundamental.

The subset of African countries that resorted to armed struggle to achieve political rights had particularly strong transnational effects. This included Algeria (1954–62), Eritrea (1961–93), and Western Sahara (1973–). Each of these had significant transnational linkages: witness, for example, the impact of the thinking of Caribbean émigré Frantz Fanon and of the film *Battle of Algiers*. Most prominent, however, were the territories under white-minority or Portuguese colonial rule that defied the trend towards peaceful decolonization in the 1960s. Concentrated in Southern Africa, they included South Africa; South West Africa (Namibia) under South African occupation; Rhodesia (Zimbabwe), ruled by a white-settler regime which declared independence from British rule in 1965; and the Portuguese colonies of Angola, Mozambique, and, in West Africa, Guinea-Bissau and Cape Verde.

Armed struggle began in Angola and South Africa in 1961, in Guinea-Bissau in 1963, in Mozambique in 1964, and in Namibia and Zimbabwe in 1966. From the 1960s into the early 1990s, these struggles and linked

internal resistance to minority rule, particularly in South Africa, were prominent on the agendas of international organizations. They drew in not only the two major Cold War competitors but also many other states. And they evoked an interconnected global network of African solidarity and anti-apartheid organizations that touched every world region.

This network, with a scope shown by the diversity of examples cited in this essay, constituted one of the most significant transnational social movements of the 20th century. It crossed geographic boundaries within and beyond the African continent. It also featured both state and non-state actors and informal personal connections as well as formal ties.

African linkages

Within Africa, transnational linkages included those already established by colonial patterns, particularly in the Southern African region shaped by the mining and migrant-labour complex centred on South Africa, which was of particular interest to international capital. The new networks formed to support independence included continentwide networks as well as those specific to the Southern African region. In 1958, Ghana hosted the first conference of independent African states and the first All African People's Conference, which included representatives from South Africa and South West Africa. The Conferência das Organizações Nacionalistas das Colónias Portuguesas (CONCP), founded in 1961 in Casablanca, Morocco, grouped the movements fighting against Portuguese colonialism. The Casablanca Group of independent states, also formed in 1961, consisted of Morocco, Algeria, Egypt, Ghana, Guinea, and Mali. Preceding the founding of the Organization of African Unity (OAU) in 1963, it stressed support for liberation movements in Southern Africa. The OAU also committed itself to the freedom of the rest of the continent, and established a liberation committee based in Dar es Salaam, Tanzania.

Dar es Salaam was the most prominent meeting place on the continent for African and international support of the Southern African liberation struggles, although its centrality somewhat diminished after the independence of Mozambique and Angola in 1975 and Zimbabwe in 1980. In 1958, Julius Nyerere hosted fellow nationalists from Kenya, Uganda, Nyasaland, and Northern and

Southern Rhodesia in Mwanza, Tanganyika, all six countries then under British rule. The Pan African Freedom Movement for East and Central Africa (PAFMECA) formed then was the predecessor of several later regional groupings. Probably the most critical for the liberation struggles was the Front Line States alliance. This was formed in 1975 with presidents Nyerere of Tanzania and Kenneth Kaunda of Zambia as the nucleus, along with Sir Seretse Khama of Botswana and Samora Machel of the Mozambique Liberation Front (FRELIMO). Later Angola, Zimbabwe, and Namibia also joined the alliance, which featured frequent informal summits as well as a working joint ministerial committee known as the Inter-State Defence and Security Committee.

State links and alliances

Among non-African countries, India not only set an example by its own independence; it was also first in supporting Southern African liberation. It took the lead at the United Nations, raising the issues of the rights of people of Indian descent in South Africa and of South Africa's occupation of Namibia. It was prominent in action on Southern Africa in the Non-Aligned Movement and in the Commonwealth. These commitments were reinforced by personal connections with South African Indians involved in the African National Congress (ANC), and by the memory of Gandhi's links to South Africa. Within the UN secretariat, Indian-born E. S. Reddy played a key behind-the-scenes role as the official in charge of action against apartheid from 1963 to 1984, relating to anti-apartheid groups around the world as well as to governments and liberation movements. In the Commonwealth secretariat, Guyana-born Shridath Ramphal, of Indian descent, kept Southern Africa high on the agenda in his term as secretary-general from 1975 to 1990.

Communist-ruled states, most prominently the Soviet Union, China, the German Democratic Republic, and Cuba, were also central actors in supporting Southern African liberation movements. They provided not only diplomatic support and financial, educational, and medical assistance, but also military training and equipment. Southern Africans travelled to these countries, many learning the languages as well as other skills. African countries such as Tanzania, Congo (Brazzaville), and Angola hosted military trainers as well as civilian personnel from these countries. In most cases, it was party and party-sponsored solidarity associations that were primarily responsible for links to Africa. Among top leaders of these countries, only Fidel Castro gave high personal priority to African issues. But the Soviet involvement in particular was an essential source of support, particularly for the MPLA in Angola, SWAPO in Namibia, and the ANC in South Africa.

In some cases these links benefited from parallel party connections, including the Portuguese Communist Party and particularly the Communist Party of South Africa. But non-Communist liberation movement leaders also regarded the Communist-ruled states as 'natural allies' and were in turn regarded as the legitimate representatives of their movements. Speeches frequently invoked the example of the World War 2 alliance against Nazism.

Also very important in state-level support for the liberation movements, particularly from the early 1970s, were the Nordic countries – Sweden, Norway, Finland, and Denmark. In every aspect but direct military support, these countries were seen by the movements as their most consistent allies. Assistance was provided both directly and through support for international agencies, for the Front Line States, and for anti-apartheid organizations elsewhere in Western Europe. This policy, supported across political party lines, reflected the roles these countries saw for themselves as global citizens, historical links with Southern Africa through missionary connections, and the influence of a cohort of officials and civil society activists who built close ties with liberation movements. Particularly prominent was Swedish Social Democrat Olof Palme, prime minister from 1969 until his assassination in 1986. Southern African liberation became a widely popular cause in the Nordic countries. Leaders such as Eduardo Mondlane of Mozambique, Amilcar Cabral of Guinea-Bissau and Cape Verde, and Oliver Tambo of South Africa were highly respected.

Civil society links

The range of civil society solidarity ties was even greater than that of state involvement, featuring not only specific characteristics in each country but also multiple transnational networks.

The impact of a long history of pan-African ties was particularly significant in the United

States and in the Caribbean, not only in visible rhetorical connections but also in less visible ways. The daily demonstrations at the South African embassy in Washington in 1984–85 mobilized by the Free South Africa Movement coalition, for example, built on the work of the local Southern Africa Support Project. That work was spearheaded by a group of African American women who had helped organize US participation in the Sixth Pan-African Congress in Dar es Salaam in 1974. And their involvement in turn can be traced to the collaboration of the Tanzanian embassy in Washington with groups founded by veterans of the Student Nonviolent Coordinating Committee (SNCC) in 1968 and much influenced by veteran Caribbean revolutionary thinker C. L. R. James.

Other intersecting strands included the international ties symbolized by Paul Robeson and the Council on African Affairs from the late 1930s to the 1950s. Although eclipsed by the McCarthyite campaign against Communist-linked groups, Robeson remained a highly respected figure in activist circles. The non-Communist left and particularly the peace movement was also closely linked to African solidarity. African American pacifist Bill Sutherland, for example, helped spark the formation of the American Committee on Africa by putting US civil rights and peace activists in touch with the ANC's Defiance Campaign in 1952, before moving to Ghana and then to Tanzania. British Anglican cleric Michael Scott, who pled the cause of South West Africans at the United Nations, also linked the peace and African liberation movements.

International church links were also central to building international support for Southern African liberation. This was most dramatically illustrated by the decision in 1969 by the World Council of Churches to provide grants to liberation movements. Although the decision aroused intense controversy in some member churches, it built on a long history of debate about race, as well as the Council's World War 2 support for resistance to Hitler. Western churches were deeply influenced by African leaders such as Eduardo Mondlane of FRELIMO and Z. K. Matthews and Oliver Tambo of the ANC, as well as by the civil rights struggle in the United States.

During the period of widest anti-apartheid mobilization, from the emergence of the United Democratic Front in South Africa in 1983 and Bishop Desmond Tutu's Nobel Prize in 1984 to the London concert for Nelson Mandela in 1988 that was reportedly watched by as many as a billion people, the anti-apartheid movement took on mass proportions, fuelled by global media coverage. Efforts to isolate apartheid economically became serious threats to South Africa's economy. Although not directed by any central organization, this climax was fostered by multiple interconnecting organizational and personal networks crossing national boundaries. South African exiles participated not only as members of South African liberation movements but also through prominent direct roles in anti-apartheid organizations in their countries of exile. The release of Nelson Mandela from prison in February 1990 and South Africa's first non-racial election in April 1994 were global iconic events.

William Minter

Bibliography

Gleijeses P. 2002. *Conflicting missions: Havana, Washington, and Africa, 1959–1976.* Chapel Hill: University of North Carolina Press.

Minter W. 1986. *King Solomon's Mines revisited: Western interests and the burdened history of Southern Africa.* New York: Basic Books.

Omari A. H. 1991. *The rise and decline of the Front Line States (FLS) alliance in Southern Africa: 1975–1990.* Unpublished doctoral dissertation. Dalhousie University, Halifax.

Sellström, T. 1999, 2002. *Sweden and national liberation in Southern Africa.* Uppsala: Nordiska Afrikainstitutet.

Related essays

Mandela, Nelson 1918–

Nelson Mandela is one of the most celebrated political figures of our time. He was arguably the first African politician to acquire a global following and is widely regarded as the greatest African leader in modern history. He spent 27 years in prison, many of them under harsh conditions. However, his authority endured remarkably over generations. His heroic status was a product both of his prominent position within the South African anti-apartheid movement and of his own deliberate efforts to supply a form of quasi-messianic leadership for the movement. Mandela's life and political activities are so appealing for many people in and outside South Africa, because even the most intimate and most oppressive aspects of his experience have become public history.

Mandela's dramatic life delineated the phases of black nationalist politics and anti-apartheid struggle in South Africa from the late 1930s. After a childhood in rural South Africa, Mandela went to Fort Hare, the major higher educational institution for Africans, where he was expelled in 1940 for engaging in a strike action. He subsequently rebelled against an arranged marriage and fled to Johannesburg in 1941. He studied law at Witwatersrand University, where he was exposed to Indian and white students and to radical, liberal, and Africanist thought. He joined the African National Congress (ANC) and in 1944 co-founded the ANC Youth League.

After the Afrikaner National Party had come into power in 1948 and the resulting institutionalization of apartheid, Mandela became one of the key organizers of ANC campaigns against the Nationalists, which soon included non-racial participation in the civil disorder campaigns and alliance with the Communist Party. In 1952 he established the first African law firm in South Africa in partnership with his political colleague, Oliver Tambo. It became a lively centre for Congress political networks, and also contributed to establishing Mandela as an icon of a possible new African world of modernity and freedom, all the more so in that he was one of the first media politicians.

In 1960, in the wake of the Sharpeville massacre and the banning of the ANC, Mandela, who was regularly banned and arrested through the 1950s, decided to go underground, and soon assumed the leadership of the military wing of the ANC. In this capacity he travelled secretly to Tanzania, Ethiopia and other West and North African countries, to seek solidarity and assistance in visits that were his first experience of independent African countries. During these years, Mandela was a core figure in the transformation of the ANC from a nationalist protest movement into a national liberation movement. Mandela and many other ANC leaders were captured. In June 1964, he was sentenced to life imprisonment for sabotage and attempting to overthrow the state through violent revolution.

Mandela's many years in prison steeled and hardened him for the negotiations that lay ahead. He managed to convince radical black-consciousness activists arrested following the Soweto uprising of the advantages of non-racialism and collective discipline. In 1978, to mark his sixtieth birthday, the ANC and the anti-apartheid movement in London launched the first Free Mandela campaign, to be followed by many others, widely supported internationally. In February 1990 President F. W. de Klerk announced Mandela's release and lifted the ban on various liberation organizations. Mandela's authority and his politics of grace and honour, notwithstanding his conservatism, enabled South Africa's relatively peaceful transition to democracy.

Although Mandela had never spent time outside Africa before 1990, he became a truly global figure much earlier. When he was arrested in the early 1960s, there were demonstrations in European capitals and in the United States, a UN Security Council call for amnesty and an all-night vigil in London's St Paul's Cathedral. During his time in prison Mandela accumulated 12 honorary degrees and a range of awards from governments. In 1988, a quarter of a million people assembled in London's Hyde Park at the conclusion of the Free Mandela march to listen to half an hour of readings from Mandela's correspondence with his wife. His face appeared on numerous postage stamps and official sculptures in many corners of the world, so that he described himself quite rightly as 'the world's most famous political prisoner'. When Mandela visited the United States a few months after his release from prison, African American commentators expressed hope that his presence could rekindle the self-confidence of ghetto communities affected by social pathologies and political decay and that he could fill a void which had been left by the deaths of Martin Luther King and Malcolm X.

As the first democratically elected president of South Africa from 1994 to 1999, he devoted much time and energy to reconciliation with former enemies. Although the 'Rainbow Nation' suffered economic crisis and widespread crime, Mandela's positive image remained. Like few other politicians in the world, he represents respect for the freedom to dissent, tolerance and firm convictions.

Andreas Eckert

Bibliography

Beinart W. 2001. *Twentieth-century South Africa*, 2nd edition. Oxford and New York: Oxford University Press.

Lodge T. 2006. *Mandela: a critical life*. Oxford and New York: Oxford University Press.

Related essays

Africa; African liberation; anti-racism; Guevara, Ernesto ('Che'); human rights

Aga Khan Development Network

The Aga Khan Development Network (AKDN) is a transnational umbrella organization for a variety of Ismaili philanthropic enterprises, which spans Europe, North America, Africa, and Asia. It is named after the spiritual leader of the Ismaili community. Aga Khan is the hereditary title of the Imam of the Nizārī Ismāīlī, a sect of the Shi'i Ismaili branch of Islam. Ismailis are members of a transnational community with approximately 20 million followers living in more than 25 countries in Europe, Asia, Africa, the Middle East and North America (at the end of the 1980s; latest available information). Aga Khan III (Sir Sultan Mahommed Shah, 1877–1957) and Aga Khan IV (Prince Karīm Khan, 1936–) were both the heads and instigators of a broad transnational system of philanthropic assistance for Ismaili communities worldwide. Their efforts resulted in the creation of the AKDN. The network focuses on health, education, culture, rural development, institution building and the promotion of economic development, without regard to the faith, origin or gender of those it serves. It includes the Aga Khan University, the Aga Khan Fund for Economic Development, the Aga Khan Trust for Culture, the Aga Khan Foundation, the Aga Khan Health Services, the Aga Khan Education Services, the Aga Khan Planning and Building Services, and the Aga Khan Agency for Microfinance.

In 1899 Ismailis opened their first school in Zanzibar. In the beginning Ismaili schools were run by a teacher who was subordinated to the Mukhi, the local religious leader. In 1905 Aga Khan III presented to his followers a constitution that gave a structure to the evolving educational network. School committees assumed responsibility for the local schools and education boards were appointed by the Aga Khan to administer these schools. By 1943, 43 Aga Khan Schools served 3,062 students in Tanganyika alone. When Tanganyika achieved independence in 1961, the Ismaili communities had about 75 schools serving their community. These schools were important tools to reinforce Ismaili religious values and thus helped sustain Ismaili identity within African society. Parallel to the educational sector, Ismaili communities in East Africa also created their own healthcare facilities. In 1893 the wealthy businessman Sewa Haji responded to the request for help by a British medical officer and provided the funding for the establishment of a hospital in Dar es Salaam. Haji offered his large donation under the condition that the new hospital would bear his name and admit people of all races. By 1961 six Ismaili healthcare facilities operated in Tanganyika. These institutions work with a mix of paid and voluntary service.

To coordinate Ismaili education worldwide, the Aga Khan Education Services (AKES) were established in 1985 in Geneva. This international organization set the standards for schools in Bangladesh, India, Kenya, Kyrgyzstan, Pakistan, Tajikistan, Tanzania, Uganda, and more recently in Afghanistan (see Table 1).

Table 1 Aga Kahn Education Services programmes, 2005

Country	Schools	Students	Teachers
Bangladesh	4	1,162	117
India	82	10,239	416
Kenya	11	5,791	368
Kyrgyzstan	2	441	36
Pakistan	192	36,517	1,601
Tajikistan	3	967	63
Tanzania	5	1,859	136
Uganda	5	1,578	133
Total	304	58,554	2,870

Source: www.akdn.org/agency/akestable.html

Table 2   Aga Khan Health Services, 2005

Category	Pakistan	India	Afghanistan	Kenya	Tanzania
Basic health centres	145	12	17	0	0
Community health centres	6	0	5	0	0
Diagnostic centres	5	2		0	6
Hospitals	4	1	1	2	1
Subtotal	160	15	23	2	7
Nurses	471	169	71	212	159
Doctors	138	47	40	21	40
Outpatient attendances	1,027,585	227,305	154,174	74,343	236,593
Admissions	32,094	7,595	4,000	9,010	6,322

Source: www.akdn.org/agency/akhsproj.html

AKES schools emphasize the education of girls, and provide the poor with greater access to education. AKES also included the Aga Khan University (AKU), which was founded in 1983 in Karachi as the first private autonomous university in Pakistan. AKU is chartered as an international university with the authority to operate programmes and campuses anywhere in the world. It has currently ten teaching sites in seven countries, with a stress on development-oriented programmes.

The Aga Khan Health Services (AKHS) were also established in 1985 in Geneva to create an umbrella organization for the many Ismaili healthcare initiatives worldwide. AKHS provides primary and curative healthcare in Afghanistan, India, Kenya, Pakistan and Tanzania (see Table 2).

In 2005, AKHS controlled 207 healthcare facilities in five countries, and employed 1,082 nurses and 286 doctors who cared for 1,720,000 patients. The sources of funding for these facilities include user fees, the support of Aga Khan, the Aga Khan Foundation, public donations, and grants from development agencies and foundations. The centrepiece of AKHS is the Aga Khan University Hospital in Pakistan with a 654-bed teaching hospital, a medical college, and a nursing school. It provides technical assistance, training, and advanced referral services to the entire Ismaili network of healthcare provision in South Asia and East Africa.

Thomas Adam

Bibliography
Kaiser P. J. 1996. Culture, transnationalism, and civil society: Aga Khan social service initiatives in Tanzania. Westport: Praeger.

Website of the Aga Khan Development Network: www.akdn.org.

Related essays
Africa; Asia; developmental assistance; Ford Foundation; health policy; higher education; Islam; Muslim networks; nursing; philanthropic foundations; philanthropy; religion; Shi'i Islam

Agriculture

Agriculture is the cultivation and harvesting of crops and livestock. It is often juxtaposed with hunting and gathering as the means of feeding and clothing the world's human population. Agriculture began in the Fertile Crescent region of Southwest Asia around 8500 BC. The sedentary and specialized nature of agriculture as a means of food production allowed for the development of modern civilization.

Agriculture changed the nature of the world. Agricultural societies could accumulate possessions because they were not nomadic. Members of agricultural societies could now specialize as inventors, blacksmiths, historians, and in other trades because the basic need of food production was provided by others in society. And agriculture necessitated development of certain technologies that are the basis of civilization. Writing, record keeping, and other advances developed as agricultural societies sought to manage, improve, and tax agricultural output.

For the first ten millennia of its existence, agriculture fomented the problem that it was directed to solve: feeding the human population. With the increased productivity of agriculture, human population grew.

Agricultural production and population seemed locked into a self-catalysing process that evolutionary biologists recognize as the Red Queen Principle. '[I]n this place', declared the queen from Lewis Carroll's *Through the Looking Glass*, 'it takes all the running you can do, to keep in the same place'. Each increase in yield led to another surviving mouth, which produced even more surviving mouths to feed and a need for greater increases in yield. Agriculture and population growth were inextricably linked. But in the last three hundred and fifty years, institutional changes that started in Western Europe led to technological changes and a spread in technology that broke this self-catalysing chain while increasingly expanding the reach of the local farmer's products from first feeding his neighbours, to next feeding his countrymen, to now feeding the world.

Population and agricultural productivity
World population first topped 1 billion around 1804. As 1960 rolled around, it hit 3 billion. In the fall of 1999, the 6 billionth person arrived on planet Earth. The economist Thomas Malthus anticipated this blistering pace in 1798 and questioned whether agriculture could keep up. In *An Essay on the Principle of Population*, Malthus argued that food production grew by an arithmetic progression (1, 2, 3, 4, etc.) but that population grew geometrically (1, 2, 4, 8, etc.) For Malthus, the mathematics of nature meant hungry mouths would always outpace the wheat, milk, and meat required to feed them. If moral constraint and marriage deferment did not provide birth control, only famine and war would keep population in check.

But Malthusian predictions proved false. The link between agricultural productivity and population growth has been cut. Mid-range projections suggest world population will reach just over 9 billion by the year 2050 before levelling off at 11 billion in 2100.

Increased wealth and a shift in inputs from labour to capital in the agricultural arena during the last three and a half centuries are the primary reasons for the tapering population growth. More successful in prediction than Malthus was agricultural historian N. S. B. Gras who predicted in 1925 that 'as increased production brings about greater well-being, as men and women tasting higher things seek even greater cultural heights, there will be everywhere a decline in the birth rate' (Gras, 1925, 200). Wealth improved the educational opportunities for women and caused the opportunity cost of raising children to climb, because an educated woman had to forgo more opportunities to raise children than her less educated predecessors.

While the cost of rearing children rose, the labour benefits of children fell. In 1500, almost four out of every five labourers in England were employed in agriculture. By 1850, the number had declined to one in five. In 2000, it was less than one in 50 (see Figure 1). These declines in demand for agricultural labourers occurred because of technological and institutional changes.

In the 20th century, machines continued to replace animal and human labour. For a better return on investment, a tractor driven by one farmhand could do the job of a dozen horse-drawn ploughs steered by a dozen labourers. The internal combustion engine replaced labourers and lowered the cost of food production. The United States of the 1940s witnessed farm employment decline by 26 per cent. It fell another 35 per cent in the 1950s and another 39 per cent during the 1960s. With agrarian families no longer needing sons to plant and harvest their fields or daughters to winnow the wheat, the need for burgeoning families declined. At the same time, improved contraception gave parents freedom to choose family size without forgoing certain recreational activities. Better survival rates furthered declines in baby making.

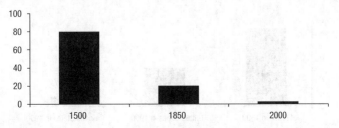

Figure 1 Per cent of English labourers employed in agriculture

While population growth slowed and the agricultural labour force declined, agricultural productivity skyrocketed. Grain represented half of an individual's food basket in 19th-century Europe. Due to the high labour costs of producing wheat, it took 33 minutes for one of the world's most productive workers in 1800 to earn the wages necessary for a pound of bread. One hundred years later, the labour for a pound of bread had fallen to 16 minutes. By 1990, the work time had quartered to four minutes (see Figure 2).

As humanity's hands fed a growing population, its mind improved efficiency. The French worker in 1800 spent five and a half hours on the job to feed his family while today's US labourer devotes just 41 minutes to the same task. A family living in cosmopolitan Berlin, Germany circa 1800 spent almost three-quarters of its budget on food, but the average US family in 2000 spent less than 15 per cent of its budget on food. These changes arose from technologies – better machinery, better irrigation, better pest control, better fertilizer, and better seeds – expanding their reach through improved institutional arrangements in property rights, contracting, and trade.

An agricultural revolution in productivity occurred in the last 350 years because of three factors: technological improvements, institutional incentives for the spread of new and existing technologies, and the transfer of those technologies and institutions around the world.

Technology and agricultural production

Not only did Malthus fail to identify the wealth and technology variables on the population side of the equation, but he ignored the technology and institutional variables on the agricultural production side of the equation. Improvements in irrigation, fertilizer, pest control, machinery, and seeds through breeding were all made well before Malthus' time. Even greater improvements would occur in the 19th and 20th centuries. The spread of these technological advances, catalysed by institutional advances in property and contract, changed the amount of food produced both per acre and per farmer.

Advances in water handling were among the earliest efforts to improve agriculture. Irrigation arose around 5000 BC in the Fertile Crescent of the Tigris and Euphrates rivers, about 3000 years after agriculture began in the same region. Irrigation's impact on agriculture was profound, tripling agricultural productivity on average. While innovations in irrigation stagnated during the Dark Ages, prior innovations spread thanks to institutional changes that brought enlightenment to Europe.

In the 20th century, global innovation ruled again. Industrial dams were built for flood control, electricity, and irrigation. The lining of ditches and drip irrigation reduced agricultural water losses due to evaporation and leakage. Smaller-scale technological changes such as the use of pipes, pumps, and diesel engines were transported to developing nations in Africa and Asia through both international and multinational governmental organizations, including the United States Peace Corps and the United Nations Food and Agriculture Organization, and international non-governmental organizations such as Oxfam International. Larger-scale technological changes in the form of massive dams were sponsored by national governments, often through the development arm of the World Bank. Emigration was a transnational side-effect of dam projects, as new reservoir waters often forcibly displaced peasants living upstream. Dams built with the help of World Bank money in India alone have displaced nearly 1 million people. As the 20th century continued, new advances in biotechnology began to address water scarcity with drought-resistant plants, which after testing and development in the richer countries of the world can be sold in a 21st-century global market that knows fewer and fewer national boundaries.

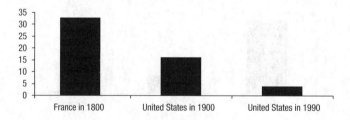

Figure 2   Minutes worked to purchase a pound of bread

Irrigation is only one of a cornucopia of agricultural advances that made life easier and more productive throughout history. Many of the most significant technological advances began to spread in the wake of an agricultural revolution that started in 17th-century Western Europe and has continued into the 21st century. This spread of technologies was inspired by institutional developments involving property rights, contracts, patents, and an expanding globalization of food markets that allowed farmers to capture the benefits of investment in technology.

Fertilizers are a case in point. Fertilizing crops with animal manure existed as far back as the ancient Romans, who probably learned it from earlier farmers of Egypt, Sumer, and Mesopotamia. Pre-industrial Europeans followed the Romans' lead in applying animal manure to fields of crops. In the Middle Ages, the English employed barn-yard manure and marl for improving crop conditions while, across the Atlantic, North American Indians used fish heads for growing maize. But it was the spread of fertilizer and fallowing techniques, and the growing trade in fertilizer that led to astounding increases in productivity.

After spreading throughout Europe, fertilization crossed the Atlantic with the European colonizers. Fertilizers were especially important for surviving the forests of New England's Northeastern Atlantic Coast as the rocky soils made it difficult to plant large plots of land, so higher productivity was needed from the plots that could be planted. The fertilizer trade grew as the new colonists benefited from the close alignment in geographic latitude between North America and Europe. Many of the Old World crops fit perfectly with the similar latitudinal climate and growing seasons of the New World. This synergy promulgated one of the largest agricultural technology transfers that the world has ever seen as colonists from Europe brought their seeds, their technologies, and their institutions to the New World. Notions of property, contract, trade, and common law were reflected in the laws of organization for the new governments of North America, much as they were reflected in the organization of colonies around Oceania. These institutions laid the tracks and sea routes by which the above influx in agricultural varietals and techniques for growing those plants would travel. Extended networks of trade between strangers needed the neutral arbitration and rules of property and contract law to replace local custom, reputation, and kinship ties as enforcers of market agreements to ensure that investments with long time horizons ended profitably.

During the height of New England agriculture from 1830 to 1880, the trade in fertilizer had the side-effect of building a nation almost from scratch. The nitrogen-rich guano created by seabirds off the coast of Peru became such a highly valued fertilizer that by the early 1860s the guano trade constituted about 80 per cent of the Peruvian national government's revenues. It provided the nest in which the modern Peruvian state was hatched. Chinese workers soon poured into Peru to mine the guano from the island rocks where it collected. At the same time, new fertilizers were developing that would replace much of the guano trade. Adding sulphuric acid to bones created the first synthetic fertilizers in the 1840s. As the 20th century shifted agriculture in North America from the Atlantic Coast to the interior plains of Canada and the United States, synthetic fertilizers replaced natural ones in the major agricultural countries and their transport around the world followed the trails blazed by the expanding adoption of private property, contract, and laws blind to a market participant's national origin.

Institutions and agricultural production

The agricultural revolution in productivity that began in the 17th century and that continues today was a revolution in institutions. Nearly every technological improvement in agriculture entailed investments in the future. Changes in property rights, contracts, and the advancement of markets beyond local, regional, and national boundaries provided farmers with the protections needed to make such investments. The increased interaction between merchants of different ethnic backgrounds spread both institutional ideas and a willingness to travel for employment. Drawn by economic opportunities in other lands, migrants sought out work (often in agriculture) beyond their homelands.

Institutions and their spread determined productivity. Without property rights, agricultural entrepreneurs would not invest in technological improvements because no guarantee existed that they would reap the investment in the future that they sewed today. Without markets, farmers would have no reason to invest in feeding more than their immediate families and neighbours. Without contracts, extended markets could not develop because the risks of transporting goods across great distances to trade with strangers could not be managed. Without patents, entrepreneurs had little reason either to research new technologies or to spread the knowledge of the technologies that they did develop. Each technology that increased productivity needed institutions for dissemination.

Property exemplifies the spread of institutions. The spread of private property institutions is first owed to the English where enclosure laws initially passed by the Tudors and later by parliament corralled most of the arable land in England into private property by 1850, with common property lingering on a few pasture lands. As private rights spread, so did agricultural productivity. Improved drainage, liming, fertilizing, crop rotation, selective breeding, and countless other efforts at capital investment all increased where property rights moved from communal to individual. As a consequence, agricultural productivity increased. After other European nations adopted these notions of property, French, German, English, and Dutch colonization spread the ideas to America, India, Australia, Africa, and parts of Southeast Asia. Where the institutions remained after the colonizers left, agricultural prosperity flowered. Where the institutions were rejected, famine often followed.

Immigration and emigration transferred the institutions of property and contract around the world, too. Agricultural prosperity propagated agricultural opportunity, which spurred labourers to travel to new lands where they assimilated the institutional structures of their adopted home. Immigrant children were educated about institutions formally and through osmosis. The Chinese were some of the first labourers to seek opportunity across an ocean, not as colonizers, but as immigrants. After the United States passed the anti-immigrant Chinese Exclusion Act in 1882, the labour ranks of the Chinese were replaced with Japanese labourers crossing the Pacific. In agriculture, they moved from migrant labourers to sharecroppers and soon onto landowning farmers. By 1919, Japanese farmers grew approximately one tenth of the food exported from California. As the Japanese moved out of the ranks of the migrant labourers, they were replaced by Mexican immigrants. The high fertility of California agriculture imported labourers from the world and exported food

to the world. Where immigrants or their children re-emigrated to their homeland, they often returned with a cultural understanding and acceptance of their adopted home's institutions. More often, they chose to remain in their adopted home but exposed their native countries to institutions through trips home, letters, examples of success, and later telephone conversations and the Internet.

The record in exporting institutions has been mixed. Spontaneous, bottom-up generation of institutional adoption has generally thrived while top-down efforts to impose institutions have failed. Efforts to improve agricultural productivity in the developing world top-down first focused on transnational technology transfer. Most often, these efforts ignored diverse conditions in the target country and the benefits of bottom-up localized knowledge. For instance, German efforts at the turn of the 20th century to focus the Togolese in Africa on the cash crop of cotton initially failed to realize that cotton grew better in Togo when interplanted with corn as locals were accustomed to doing. Meanwhile, the Germans upped productivity by educating the Togolese farmer to cultivate with the horse-drawn plough instead of the human hoe, but undermined underlying social structures in the process.

Technology transfer was replaced as the foremost agricultural development strategy in the second half of the 20th century by capacity building, where international aid organizations and multinational governmental organizations sought to inculcate property arrangements and market institutions from the top down. Under the Marshall Plan, mechanized technology was exported to countries like Turkey. Extension of agriculture built on the institutions of private property, contracts, and markets was a key for Western nations in the ideological battle with Communism. Private efforts at technology and institutional transfer accompanied government efforts.

Norman Borlaug, known as the father of the Green Revolution, won the Nobel Peace Prize for bringing high-yield agriculture to the non-Western world. Supported by the Rockefeller Foundation, Borlaug selectively bred plants in Mexico to increase disease resistance and develop dwarf breeds of wheat that expended less energy on growing a tall wheat stalk and more energy on growing the grain kernels that support human life. Borlaug shared his new varietals of grain with India and Pakistan where famine was a regular marker of history. As with the ongoing agricultural revolution of the 17th, 18th, and 19th centuries, the 20th century's Green Revolution was not as much a revolution of new technologies as it was a revolution in spreading old technologies to more and more farmers.

But top-down capacity building often undermined the bottom-up spread of institutions through migration and informal information transfer that had proven successful in the past. High-paying government and development jobs birthed by capacity-building funds absorbed institutional entrepreneurs grown at home and re-immigrating from abroad, leaving few human resources for building institutions from the bottom up. For success, institutions needed retrofitting to local conditions and the imprimatur of being adopted rather than imposed. During the 20th century, multinational corporations arguably had more success building capacity worldwide than multinational development organizations, because the immediate benefits of adopting certain rules demanded by the corporations were clearer to the locals choosing to adapt or adopt.

The failed capacity-building efforts of the 20th century were a response to an apparently successful top-down enterprise: the Communists' effort to destroy property institutions. Marx and Engels wrote, 'the theory of the Communists may be summed up in a single sentence: Abolition of private property'. Through the Soviet Union, the Communists expanded collective agriculture around the world with carrot and stick. In Eastern Europe, Soviet tanks ensured property would not profit in Poland, Romania, and the Baltics. In Vietnam, South America, and Africa, Soviet dollars subsidized the Communist cause. In China and Cuba, ideological synchronicity spurred the collective farm. By deifying the peasant and renouncing the intellectual as well as the providence of institutions, Mao set his nation up for the greatest famine in world history. Ultimately, the Communist efforts collapsed in on themselves or began to accept property. At the same time, failure highlighted the importance of institutions to agricultural productivity.

The expansion of institutions across borders increased food availability. While collective agriculture suffered famine, be it capital-focused as in the Soviet Union or labour-focused as in China, the competing brand of individual, property-focused agriculture offered a bountiful harvest where planted. At the end of the

20th century, agricultural productivity was 64 per cent higher in regions that relied on individualized property rights in land with strong protections for those rights as well as freedom to sell those rights. In contrast, the worst famines in the world were visited upon Communist nations. In the 1930s, millions died in Russia under Stalin. More than 30 million perished during Mao's Great Leap Forward in China.

Conclusion

An integrated global community has continued to increase agricultural productivity. On the supply side, technology, institutional changes, and dissemination of these changes pushed up productivity. On the demand side, reduced barriers to global trade and the opening of markets brought customers a wider array of choices, which increased the demand for different agricultural goods and thus pulled up productivity. The supply side has been more direct in its transnational impact, but the demand side should not be ignored.

Increased world food trade spurred demand-side impacts on agricultural productivity. As world markets for agricultural goods opened and barriers to entry fell during the 20th century, the transfer of agricultural goods across borders increased. This global demand led to improved agricultural productivity in parts of the world where surplus food otherwise would not be grown. Productivity rose as the customer base of farmers spread from their neighbours to consumers on the other side of the planet. This trade improved food security worldwide. At the same time, markets increased the diversity of foodstuffs available as even countries with food surpluses chose to import crop varieties not raised in their own climate from other parts of the world.

In 1950, global grain output stood at 692 million tons harvested from 1.7 billion acres of cropland. By 1992, output had risen 170 per cent to 1.9 billion tons, but the employed cropland only rose to 1.73 billion acres – a 1 per cent increase. Even if that rate of progress fell by half, an area the size of India could revert from agriculture to woodlands or other uses during the first half of the 21st century. Much of this progress was driven by increased demand for grain from an increasingly global market.

Globalization of the agricultural market led to two competing trends regarding transnational food security in the 20th century: mono-cropping and diversification of food sources. An emphasis on specialization increased mono-cropping, which can leave regions that grow mono-crops more vulnerable to devastation by infestation, drought, or other disasters, just like in Ireland's Great Potato Famine of the late 1840s. The expanded marketplace for agricultural goods, however, also spread out this food security risk by diversifying food sources. The advent of refrigerated transport and chemical preservatives allowed food to travel further. The increased distance that foodstuffs could travel provided increased insurance that devastating drought or natural disaster in one region of the world could be overcome through importation of food from another region. The increased yields of mono-cropping allowed one modern farmer to feed 100 other people. Globalization, through increased trade in the last 250 years, diversified the area of the world's food holdings via which humans met their food needs. In this global agricultural market, food production does not determine famine, food distribution does. Thus, it was not mono-cropping that caused the Irish famine, but rather poverty preventing the importation of foodstuffs from elsewhere that led to tragedy.

Finally, the 20th century witnessed a rise in global institutions to negotiate institutional conflicts between regions of the world. The General Agreement on Tariffs and Trade, which was signed in 1947, transmogrified into the World Trade Organization in 1995. This organization established global rules regarding trade barriers and worked to expand market institutions and property protections around the world. Bilateral and multilateral agreements throughout the century also addressed rules about property, contract disputes, and open markets.

The transnational history of agricultural production has been institutions driving and spreading technological innovations, as well as the institutions themselves, to feed a growing populace, with some regions fostering the innovation of technologies via their capital-enhancing institutions and other regions benefiting from those technologies and institutions crossing borders either via free trade or civil society efforts such as those of the Green Revolution.

J. Bishop Grewell

Bibliography

Ausubel J. 2000. 'The Great Reversal: nature's chance to restore land and sea', *Technology in Society*, 22, 3, 289–301.

Braudel F. 1979. *The structures of everyday life: the limits of the possible, vol. 1, civilization and capitalism, 15th–18th century*. New York: Harper and Row.

Easterbrook G. 1997. 'Forgotten benefactor of humanity', *Atlantic Monthly*, 279, 1, 75–82.

Gras N. 1925. *A history of agriculture in Europe and America*. New York: Crofts.

Grewell J. B. and Landry C. J. 2003. *Ecological agrarian: agriculture's first evolution in 10,000 years*. West Lafayette: Purdue University Press.

North D. C. and Thomas R. P. 1973. *The rise of the Western world: a new economic history*. Cambridge: Cambridge University Press.

Related essays

acclimatization; biodiversity; biopatents; Chinese Diaspora; commodity trading; contract and indentured labours; corporations; developmental assistance; food; food safety standards; freshwater management; General Agreement on Tariffs and Trade (GATT) / World Trade Organization (WTO); genetically modified organisms; Green Revolution; labour migrations; Marshall Plan; pesticides, herbicides, insecticides; population; seeds; technical assistance; trade agreements; trade; United Nations system; zero growth

United Fruit Company

A controversial multinational company based in Boston, the United Fruit Company (UFCO) dominated the banana business in Latin America and the United States from its inception in 1899 to 1970.

United Fruit operated a network that stretched across North America, South America, and Europe, with its business affecting even African and Asian countries. With banana plantations, railroads, port facilities, and marketing agents in virtually every country of the Caribbean and all major American ports, UFCO controlled the production and sale of bananas in the Western Hemisphere, with the wealth and power to restrain, eliminate, or absorb competitors. At the peak of its power in 1950, UFCO owned or leased 3 million acres of land, representing 85 per cent of the tropical land suitable for banana cultivation.

UFCO promoted flows and exchanges of capital, technology, managers, workers, and their products across the Western Hemisphere and beyond. The company employed a multinational labor force; it borrowed money from North American and European banks; and it operated shipping lines on both sides of the Atlantic. Its workers spoke English, French, Spanish, Quechua, Maya, and other languages; they worshipped in Catholic, Protestant, Muslim, Jewish, and other faiths; they exchanged ideas, diets, music, cultural values, and social practices that accelerated the pace of globalization in the 20th century.

The transnational nature of United Fruit both conflicted with and promoted the nationalistic sentiments that emerged in Latin America and the Caribbean. United Fruit symbolized the worst aspects of multinational corporate behaviour, a source of the exploitation and poverty common to people who lived in the 'banana republics'. To the nationalists, United Fruit was *el pulpo* (the octopus), a vast enterprise that obstructed their political and economic development. United Fruit merged with AMK-Morrell and became United Brands in 1970. It was renamed Chiquita Brands in 1989 and remains a leader in the banana business.

Paul J. Dosal

Bibliography

Striffler S. and Mark M. (eds) 2003. *Banana wars: power, production, and history in the Americas*. Durham, NC: Duke University Press.

Related essays

agricultural production; containerized freight; indentured and contract labourers; food

Air pollution

Air pollution can be defined as the unintentional introduction into the atmosphere of smoke, dust, fumes, particles or chemicals as side-effects of an otherwise intentional process. While the phrase may be applied to smoke or dust introduced into the atmosphere as a result of non-human action, such as forest fires or volcanoes, this usage is rare and human action is generally implied. The action most often at the root of air pollution is the combustion of fuel for heat, transportation, manufacturing or other productive processes. 'Negative externalities' from these productive processes can become airborne and travel hundreds or thousands of miles through the atmosphere, and can result in immediate or long-term health problems for animals and vegetation alike. Air pollution can also obscure views, settle into water supplies or exposed soil, contribute to complex chemical reactions within the atmosphere or on exposed surfaces, or globally distribute toxic, radioactive, or otherwise undesirable wastes from a localized event or process.

It is this last characteristic of air pollution that is of the most interest when viewing human events from a transnational perspective. Largely invisible to the naked eye and quickly distributed across borders and continents, air pollution is difficult to detect, difficult to trace to its origination point, and particularly difficult to control if those who suffer its ill effects are geographically and politically removed from producers. As air pollution increasingly became an issue of concern in the latter half of the twentieth century, it spawned vast and varied efforts to create international compacts or agreements, settle border disputes, assign blame and litigate liability, all across national boundaries made somewhat meaningless by invisible currents of air.

While human combustion of wood, fossil, and other fuels undoubtedly precedes recorded history, early records of air pollution concerns are scarce, and do not seem to extend past territorial borders. Large urban centres from Beijing to London experienced the ill effects of smoke for most of their histories, but air pollution did not become a pressing national issue until the industrial revolutions of the 19th and 20th centuries, and did not become a significant transnational issue until the 20th.

The most important progenitor of international attempts to control atmospheric pollution is the Trail Smelter case. The culmination of a decades-long dispute between the operators of a lead and zinc smelter in Canada and those who lived under the pall of smoke in the United States, Trail Smelter was the first prominent legal case dealing with transborder pollution. The dispute was finally resolved in 1941 with payments to landowners in Washington state and technological steps to limit and disperse the sulphur dioxide output of the British Canadian smelters.

Sulphur dioxide was also the main culprit in the next major set of events marking the history of transboundary air pollution, this time in Europe. As European industry recovered in the post-World War 2 years, a combination of forces highlighted the importance of air pollution. These forces included increased industrial production, the spread of automobile usage and emissions, the development of new abilities to scientifically measure pollutants, and the emergence of a nascent environmental movement. Scandinavian countries expressed particular concern about acid rain, or the acidification of surface waters by precipitation from atmosphere polluted by sulphur and nitrogen oxide emissions from industrial production in nations to the south. The northern countries first brought up the issue of acid rain at the 1972 United Nations Conference on the Human Environment in Stockholm. The following decade of scientific and diplomatic work contributed to the 1979 Convention on Long-range Transboundary Air Pollution, the first major international agreement to take a regional approach to air pollution issues. Eventually signed by 49 parties, the Convention covers a large part of the globe, centred on the UN Economic Commission for Europe.

Across the Atlantic, the trend towards increased international cooperation set by Europe was being followed, albeit a bit more slowly. The most pressing issues continued to revolve around ore smelters and processors located near national boundaries, rather than the more regional concerns related to acid rain in Europe. Many smelters were located in the arid and sparsely populated American Southwest. Their smoke drifted across the border into Mexico for decades, forming the 'Gray Triangle' area of Arizona and Mexico. The 1983 La Paz agreement marked the first step towards the creation of a joint pollution abatement plan between the US and Mexico. The La Paz agreement preceded further transnational cooperation on these types of matters, including a 1991 acid rain agreement between the US and Canada, a continent-wide framework in 1997's North American Free Trade Agreement, and additional border-region agreements signed in 2002 by the US and Mexico.

The sources of air pollution in the Trail Smelter and 'Gray Triangle' cases were located just miles from international borders, and their pollutants were visible to the naked eye. The industrial producers contributing to acid rain in Europe were regional, their effect was visible, and all parties concerned belonged (eventually) to regional international bodies. But other environmental concerns of the late 20th century were truly global in scope, with causes and impacts far beyond the control of national or regional governments, and depended upon sophisticated technologies to demonstrate their existence, sources and impact.

Ozone is often a part of the ground-level atmosphere as an undesirable component of air pollution and urban smog. But stratospheric ozone is a highly desirable 'shield' against excessive amounts of solar radiation that can damage flora and fauna alike. In the mid-1980s, British scientists published seminal findings arguing that the ozone layer over Antarctica had thinned by more than 50 per cent, producing an immensely large 'hole'. Subsequent research indicated that human activities had increased the amount of chlorine in the atmosphere, particularly as a result of the industrial and commercial use of chlorofluorocarbons (CFCs) as refrigerants and propellants. Human action was determined to be the cause of global atmospheric change, and the 1985 Vienna Ozone Convention was the first attempt to address the problem. The Montreal Protocol of 1987 followed, and was further modified throughout the 1990s. The international response to CFCs is thought to be highly successful, with measurable drops in the rate of increase of CFCs and in the rate of decrease of stratospheric ozone.

The difficulties presented by ozone depletion, however, pale in comparison to the challenges presented by any attempt to respond to global climate change. Beginning in the 1980s, the vast majority – though not always the entirety – of scientists studying global environmental issues argued that human action was introducing increasing amounts of gases into the atmosphere, contributing to increased global retention of solar heat. These 'greenhouse' gases (GHGs), including water vapour and carbon dioxide, are naturally present in the atmosphere and serve to retain heat, but human action was seen to contribute to an increase in these gases and a subsequent increase in global average temperature. This change could portend vast climatic, geophysical, and ecosystem disruption.

Almost all combustion of fuel creates carbon dioxide and other GHGs. Any attempt to limit or control GHGs would require widespread political support, affect almost all human activities worldwide, and rest upon strong scientific support for the anthropogenic causation of GHGs and the possibility of positive results from action. While scientific NGOs such as the Intergovernmental Panel on Climate Change provided a steady stream of evidence supporting the argument for the control of GHGs, the political implications of measures that would require individual nations to control industrial production have made international agreement difficult. The UN has become the main location of attempts to respond to anthropogenic climate change, producing the UN Framework Convention on Climate Change (1992), and the subsequent Kyoto Protocol (1997). These measures are politically contentious in some nations, and their success appears initially limited.

While a narrative of diplomatic efforts to compel or encourage the control of transboundary air pollution might be informative, it does not convey the full range of events and impacts of transnational air pollution. Much of the public interest in global air pollution issues stems from significant scientific findings or global catastrophes, from the discovery of trace amounts of pesticides deposited in the Antarctic, to the 'hole' in the ozone layer, to the disruption in global food supplies (particularly milk from grass-fed dairy cows) in the wake of the Chernobyl meltdown, to the discovery of tetraethyl lead from internal combustion engines present in all of the world's oceans, to images from space showing vast plumes of smoke from forest clearing in the Amazon. Such events serve to pique the public interest, but do not increase the likelihood of successful mediation of disputes over man-made pollution that is unaffected by man-made borders.

James Longhurst

Bibliography
Guruswamy L. 2003. *International environmental law*. St Paul: West Publishing.
Sand P. 1999. *Transnational environmental law: lessons in global change*. The Hague: Kluwer.
Sliggers J. and Kakebeeke W. (eds) 2004. *Clearing the air: 25 years of the Convention on Long-range Transboundary Air Pollution*. New York: United Nations.

Wirth J. 2000. *Smelter smoke in North America: the politics of transborder pollution*. Lawrence: University Press of Kansas.

Related essays
borders and borderlands; car culture; climate change; ecology; environmental diplomacy; environmentalism; food safety standards; intergovernmental organizations; international non-governmental organizations (INGOs); outer space; pesticides, herbicides, insecticides; Stockholm Conference; United Nations system

Al-Jazeera *See* Information Economy

America
The extraordinary transnational appeal of America is one of its most outstanding historical characteristics. The attraction of the ideas of self-government, freedom of religion, and the embrace of universal democratic principles as the nation's foundation transformed the United States of America into a global reference point, both negative and positive, for a plethora of desires, debates and developments. The transnational presence of the US shaped and inspired discussions about political identity, economic success and systems, the role of (civil) religion and democratic missions in various parts of the world. This 'American influence' early on helped create an 'offshore America' (Bright and Geyer), an imaginary space largely disconnected from any direct control by the US. As an intellectual projection, this 'America' had, even well before the foundation of the US, by far transcended its geographical borders, but would reach its greatest worldwide dissemination through the forces of globalization in the course of the 20th century.

A transnational history of the US goes back to its missionary ideology, originating in the Puritan belief of an elected republic with a model character for the world. From John Winthrop ('a city upon a hill') to Ralph Waldo Emerson, the US was understood as an exceptional nation and unique opportunity for the advancement of humankind. The westward territorial expansion of 'New Israel' was interpreted as a symbol of the manifest destiny of America as God's chosen country, where universal civil rights, popular sovereignty, separation of powers and pursuit of happiness were considered guiding principles and a beacon for the world at large. As a product of the European-led globalization of the 17th–19th centuries, the US was part of the larger Atlantic world and could thus spread this democratic mission through a complicated web of cross-cultural exchange and transatlantic commerce, notwithstanding its substantial involvement in the slave trade. With about 65,000,000 people crossing the Atlantic between 1800 and 1914, the immigration waves of the 19th century further extended the diversity and depth of transnational networks and communities tied to the US. In addition, the transportation (railroad) and communication (telegraph) revolutions spurred not only the integration of the continent itself, but also attracted an increasing number of foreign investments in the second half of the century, fostering economic interconnections and the dramatic rise of free-market capitalism. As a consequence, the US economy was thriving and increasingly beginning to reach out for global markets towards the end of the 19th century.

However, it was the 20th century which was to become the 'American century', as Henry R. Luce wrote in 1941, and which was to yield immense consequences for America's outreach. At the end of the 19th century, the US had gradually emerged as a global player, both industrially and politically, and would eventually replace the 'Pax Britannica' with the 'Pax Americana'. In 1902, W. T. Stead in *The Americanization of the World* for the first time detected and exhaustively described the growing influence of the US in other parts of the world: a growing global interconnectedness through commerce, cultural and political exchange. Through World War 1, the US became the strongest economic power with worldwide business interests, continually widening its lead in industrial production. Now a major creditor nation and financial centre, the US began not only to penetrate the European market but also laid the foundations for a liberal market system on a global scale, which it came to dominate after 1945, enabling it to distribute American exports worldwide.

Politically, this search for foreign markets through an open-door policy was accompanied by a final departure from isolationism with the Spanish-American War of 1898,

at a time when the US was already moving from continental to international empire (Caribbean and Eastern Pacific). In this situation, US President Woodrow Wilson's idea 'to make the world safe for democracy' formally lifted the American democratic mission to a global level by supporting internationalism and, at least initially, the creation of supranational governmental bodies such as the League of Nations, although American support for these efforts faltered soon thereafter. At the same time, this internationalist vision was the proclamation of a counterideology against Leninism, and thus foreshadowed as early as in 1917 the ideological division of the world and global power struggle which was to intensify after the World War 2.

World War 2 not only brought the defeat of totalitarian ideologies in Europe with the help of the US intervention, but in its aftermath also the global presence of American occupational troops and military bases, which made America's outreach a physical reality dictated by power politics. In the 1920s American popular culture and consumer goods had already reached Europe and, vice versa, American progressives and social reformers had found inspiration in European models of social policy. After 1945 this cross-pollination proliferated massively, even though in an asymmetrical way, since the geopolitical bipolarity of the Cold War and the race for global influence greatly multiplied the impact of 'America'. Due to the economic and ideological reconstruction of Western Europe under American auspices with the help of the Marshall Plan, a concerted cultural diplomacy effort by the US government, as well as popular demand complementing this official policy, American culture and ideals gradually became an almost unavoidable presence in the world. After the catastrophe of World War 2, the US was largely seen as a successful model democracy which was able to transcend social hierarchies and found its economic representation in a free-market ideology. Culturally, this 'grassroots Americanization' included Hollywood movies, popular music and youth cultures, all of which projected what was perceived as an 'American way of life' of consumerism, convenience and a free and luxurious lifestyle. It was at this historical juncture that American transnational influence, favoured by forces of globalization now qualitatively different in velocity, intensity and extension, started to gain a truly global reach.

To call this global American impact 'Americanization' is, however, misleading, since the term offers multiple meanings. Within the US, its most common usage refers to the naturalization of immigrants coming to America, in other words, their adoption of what are considered American ideals and norms in order to 'become an American'. Outside the US, on the other hand, the term denotes the very export of American goods and values, namely America's transnational impact. 'Americanization' in the latter sense can, broadly speaking, be defined as the transmission of products, institutions, norms, values, customs, modes of behaviour or social practices, as well as symbols, icons and images, which are supposedly or actually adopted from the United States, or in any case perceived to be American. The complexities of this intercultural transfer remain controversial, since the term is frequently burdened with a negative connotation due to an often pejorative historical discourse associating it with an uncritical imitation of American models at the expense of one's own national and cultural identity.

Current research has begun to view American transnational influence as dialogic and tied to larger processes of cultural globalization, interpreting the role of the United States as an 'international phenomenon' and analysing the various ways in which the history of the country has been intertwined with and affected the lives of other people across the world. The influence emanating from the United States is not considered a one-way street or 'cultural imperialism' any more, but rather an outcome of a subtle mutual process of selective adaptation; the result of which would be an amalgam of previous ideas and adapted concepts, which have been adjusted to one's own political and cultural setting. According to this theoretical approach, America as an image, as well as its symbols and myths, has in the course of its existence become part of a transnational lingua franca whose signifiers are widely circulating and whose messages can be decoded worldwide. Thereby, American cultural exports have over time fused into other national histories, becoming a considerable component of local collective memories. In this process of appropriation, however, these cultural items have become recontextualized in a different cultural and linguistic setting.

This amalgamation of supposedly 'American' texts into one's own culture is the reason why these 'offshore Americas' can no longer be controlled by the country of origin. The active role at the receiving end, where constructions of the self and the 'other' are being renegotiated in a 'sign war' of images and references to 'Americanness' (Kaspar Maase) for various purposes (be it class struggle or ironically, even anti-Americanness), is crucial in the process of creative adaptation. Within it, various images, interpretative narratives and selective appropriations of America that have been piling up over the decades can be seen as being historically in competition with each other.

Since national or local cultures are generally constructed through binaries and created through imagined differences between oneself and the 'other', disputes about American influence often reach to the core of identity debates in various parts of the world. In them, America often serves as a projection with which to identify or from which to separate and distance. This is especially true for the decades following the Second World War, when an increasingly globally operating media distributed not only positive images of the US, but also widely transported the internal divisions besetting the country. Particularly the struggle of the civil rights movement as well as the growing internal opposition against America's war in Vietnam fundamentally transformed and damaged the image of the US overseas as a democratic model, guiding spirit and leader of the supposed 'free world'.

The resulting divided perception of the United States and the separation between an 'official' America, which was responsible for racial suppression and the war in Vietnam, and the 'other' America, consisting of countercultures and protest movements opposed to these shortcomings, became the dominating feature of the protest movements of the 1960s/1970s worldwide. Images of the rebellious and critical America experienced a transnational boom in these decades with an extensive appropriation on a global scale, being a further expression of intense mutual relations and an additional degree of American cultural influence in the world. These ambiguous notions massively shaped the reception of the US for decades to come, incorporated dissident voices into the canon of American images to an unparalleled degree and contributed to the spread of a more nuanced and comprehensive image of the US, albeit not free from frequent gross distortions. Anti-Americanism, an ideology and rhetoric of opposition against both what is perceived to be the American model of democracy and liberal capitalism as well as the American influence on the world on a local level, has equally been a consequence of America's transnational impact. In its latest form, it inspired Islamist fundamentalists to blame the US as the sole responsible entity for what they considered wrong with Western modernity, leading them to direct their attacks against the US territory and the American presence in the world. In this setting, the foreign policy of George W. Bush, especially with regard to the Iraq War, is only another example of a power and mission ideology with long-standing roots in American history which nonetheless failed to take into account the complexities and 'soft power' (Joseph Nye) of the transnational perception of the US around the globe.

The variety of the imaginative 'Americas' that emerged in these historical processes stands symbolically for the inextricable link between the central role of the United States' rise as a superpower during the 20th century and the forces of globalization that helped spread its image even further across the globe. The messages transmitted of freedom, independence, consumption and sexuality, as well as critical voices accompanying American popular culture, seem to have come to represent and mould global desires to a previously unmatched degree, causing both agreement and resistance of various kinds. As a result, the complex relationship between Americanization and globalization and its mechanisms on a national level are slowly becoming integral parts of historiographical narratives examining the role of America in the world and the web of its transnational connections.

Martin Klimke

Bibliography

Beck U., Sznaider N. and Winter R. (eds) 2003. *Global America? The cultural consequences of globalization.* Liverpool: Liverpool University Press.

Bright C. and Geyer M. 2002. 'Where in the world is America? The history of the United States in a global age', in Bender T. (ed.) *Rethinking American history in a global age.* Berkeley: University of California Press.

Mazlish B., Chanda N. and Weisbrode K. 2007. *The paradox of a global USA.* Stanford: Stanford University Press.

Pells R. H. 1997. *Not like us: how Europeans have loved, hated and transformed American culture Since World War II.* New York: Basic Books.

Related essays

Coca-Cola

One of the world's best known brand names, the carbonated soft drink Coca-Cola has become an icon of America's economic and cultural globalization. According to the company's 2006 annual report, its product was sold in over 200 countries (a remarkable feat since that year's *World Almanac* only listed 193 countries worldwide). The drink's high international profile has made it a focal point of globalization critics who see Coca-Cola's expansion as a spearhead of a global campaign to homogenize, indeed to liquidate, local tastes and cultures.

John Sythe Pemberton, an Atlanta pharmacist, created the first version of Coca-Cola in the 1880s. Pemberton named his concoction 'French Wine Cola' and sold it at local pharmacies as a 'nerve and tonic stimulant'. After some refinements, including substituting caffeine for wine, Pemberton's business partner Frank Robinson changed the name to Coca-Cola, reflecting two key ingredients, the coca leaf and kola nut. Under the leadership of Asa Candler, who in 1894 had become the sole proprietor of the Coca-Cola company, sales expanded nationally, and by the turn of the 20th century internationally to Hawai'i, Canada, and Mexico.

Coca-Cola's international expansion grew in tandem with America's. The breakthrough for the soft drink (and for American international power) came during World War 2 as Coca-Cola followed American GIs wherever they went. In 1943, the Supreme Commander Allied Forces in Europe, General Dwight D. Eisenhower, requested the shipment of 3 million bottles of Coca-Cola to the European theatre of war. Realizing a unique opportunity, company executives and marketing experts forged a campaign that linked consumption of Coca-Cola to patriotism, freedom, and support for American troops. Americans at home and abroad seemed to imbibe the American way of life with every gulp they took out of the distinctively shaped bottles.

In the postwar period, Coca-Cola became a weapon in the Cold War battles between the United States and the Soviet Union. James Farley, the Chairman of the Board of the Coca-Cola Export Corporation and an ardent anti-Communist, infused advertisements with political messages as he promoted the drink abroad. For the 1952 Olympic Games in Helsinki – Coca-Cola had been sponsoring the Games since 1928 – he shipped 30,000 cases of Coca-Cola in a rebuilt World War 2 landing craft to Finnish shores. Finland had followed a precarious policy of neutrality in the early Cold War; it hosted Soviet troops on its territory and had concluded a security treaty with the Soviets in 1948. Farley's amphibious invasion of a country on the fault-line between capitalism and Communism, even if armed only with a soft drink, suggested the close association between military and cultural weapons in the Cold War.

Critics soon targeted Coca-Cola as a symbol of America's cultural and economic hegemony. In 1949 the French Communist publication L'Humanité accused the American company of 'coca-colonization', suggesting a close alliance between the soft drink's international expansion and what it deemed to be a coercive process of Americanization.

A year later, French Communist parliamentarians proposed a ban on Coca-Cola, warning that the drink posed a potential health threat. In France, as in the US and elsewhere, the company maintained a strict policy of secrecy concerning Coca-Cola's ingredients, thus leaving much room for speculation as to its nutritional composition. Even though the proposal ultimately faltered, the French debate exposed public fears about America's commercial and cultural dominance and concerns about the loss of France's distinctive culinary and cultural identity.

Yet unlike subjects of earlier colonial empires, Europeans consumed this and other American products voluntarily. By the late 20th century, the brand had become a standard staple of a global consumer culture. Even though it faced fierce competition from other soft drink manufacturers, above all its archrival Pepsi-Cola, it still maintained in the international arena its status as a key icon of American popular culture.

Petra Goedde

Bibliography

Keys B. 2004. 'Spreading peace, democracy, and Coca-Cola: sport and American cultural expansion in the 1930s', *Diplomatic History*, 28, 2, 165–96.

Kuisel R. 1991. 'Coca-Cola and the Cold War: the French face Americanization, 1948–1953', *French Historical Studies*, 17, 1, 96–116.

Pendergrast M. 1993. *For God, country and Coca-Cola: the unauthorized history of the great American soft drink and the company that makes it.* New York: Charles Scribner's Sons.

Wagnleitner R. 1994. *Coca-colonization and the Cold War: the cultural mission of the United States in Austria after the Second World War.* Chapel Hill: University of North Carolina Press.

Related essays

America; Cold War; comics; counterfeit goods; diet and nutrition; dollar; drink; drugs (medical); fast food; jeans; Olympic Games; patents; sport; trademarks; wine

Amnesty International (AI)

The London-based Amnesty International (AI) is the largest and best-known voluntary organization campaigning internationally for the defence of human rights. It currently claims a membership of 1.8 million in more than 150 countries. Although the focus of its interests has evolved since its establishment in 1961, the main tenets of its work have not: political impartiality, mobilization of public opinion, and objective research into human rights abuses by states. It has served as a channel for idealism and moral outrage, and a recent study has described Amnesty as a form of 'religionless Christianity' (Hopgood, p. 8).

Amnesty was launched on 28 May 1961, with the publication of an article on 'The forgotten prisoners' in the British *Observer* newspaper. The article, by the barrister Peter Benenson (1921–2005), was syndicated world-wide and elicited a remarkable response from readers. What had initially been envisaged as a year-long campaign on behalf of non-violent 'prisoners of conscience' swiftly evolved into a permanent voluntary organization with branches in many Western European countries. Benenson's charismatic leadership galvanized support amongst lawyers, journalists, students and those from a variety of religious and political backgrounds. He successfully encouraged media interest in the campaign, and was very aware of the power of symbols, such as the now famous 'candle in barbed wire'. The idea that groups of volunteers should 'adopt' political prisoners from across the Cold War divide and the developing world (the 'groups of three') also proved inspirational. Although Benenson was forced to resign in 1967 following a bitter internal conflict, the organization continued to flourish, notably in the United Kingdom, West Germany and Scandinavia. It also became drawn into the emerging international regime for the monitoring and redress of human rights abuses. After Benenson's departure efforts were made to place Amnesty on a more stable bureaucratic basis, and a 'mandate' was devised to determine the conditions under which prisoners might be adopted.

Support for Amnesty was fuelled by the abuse of human rights under military regimes in Greece, Chile and Argentina. During the 1970s Amnesty campaigned strongly against torture and played an influential role in the formulation of the 1984 Convention against Torture. It later extended its remit to cover the issue of 'disappearance', and judicial and extra-judicial killing by the state. Amnesty International was awarded the Nobel Peace Prize in 1977 as a mark of its emerging stature. Probably the most significant development during the 1980s was the growth of a mass membership in the US, where progress had initially been slow. By the mid-1980s AIUSA had 40 per cent of the overall membership and a disproportionate amount of the organization's funds and earning potential.

The end of the Cold War posed fresh challenges for Amnesty. Although it was by no means a creature of the Cold War, Amnesty's work had clearly been moulded by the East–West divide and the myriad conflicts that this spawned in the developing world. Amnesty struggled to adapt to a 'new world order' in which states seductively proclaimed their support for human rights and in which social and economic rights were taking on a new significance. Moreover, Amnesty was increasingly exposed to amicable rivalry from the US-based Human Rights Watch (HRW), which was established in the late 1970s. HRW did not have Amnesty's mass membership and appeared less ponderous in its response to swiftly developing crises. Amnesty was also criticized for being dominated by white, male, middle-class experts. The Senegalese Secretary General Pierre Sané (1992–2001) introduced reforms into Amnesty's organization and working practices, and these met considerable resistance from staff who felt that some of Amnesty's most precious and distinctive characteristics were in danger of being lost. However, Sané's reforms continued under his successor, Irene Khan, who has sought to shift the balance in Amnesty's work between human rights advocacy and impartial research in favour of the former.

Since 1961 AI has both pioneered and defined a new form of international campaigning, while also inspiring the work of many activists at the national level. AI remains a potent 'brand' in international human rights, and its reports and interventions continue to command immense respect.

Tom Buchanan

Bibliography
Buchanan T. 2002. ' "The truth will set you free ...": the making of Amnesty International', *Journal of Contemporary History*, 37, 4, 575–97.
Buchanan T. 2004. 'Amnesty International in crisis, 1966–67', *Twentieth Century British History*, 15, 3, 267–89.

Clark A. M. 2001. *Diplomacy of conscience: Amnesty International and changing human rights norms.* Princeton: Princeton University Press.

Hopgood S. 2006. *Keepers of the flame: understanding Amnesty International.* Ithaca: Cornell University Press.

Related essays
Cold War; exile; human rights; international non-governmental organizations (INGOs); legal order; United Nations system

Anarchism

Although some have found its antecedents in Greek Stoicism and medieval radical Christian sects among other sites, anarchism is an unmistakably modern phenomenon. As an idea, its earliest formulation appeared in the 1790s in the writings of the pioneer English Utilitarian William Godwin, often called the father of philosophical anarchism. Godwin portrayed government not only as unnecessary (because humans were sufficiently rational and cooperative by nature) but also as counterproductive (because its reliance on imposition hindered the development of private judgment and perpetuated ignorance and dependence). Political organization thus should be voluntary and decentralized. Justice should be devoid of punitive elements. Education should foster critical thinking and individual autonomy rather than habits of obedience and respect for authority. Marriage should be replaced by free unions that did not require the sanction of state, church, or family.

During the 1840s these core principles were forged into an ideology that spawned a social movement. Pierre-Joseph Proudhon in France became the first political theorist to label himself an anarchist, explicitly declaring that 'anarchy is order', a dictum that became the source for the circle-A symbol in anarchist graffiti. The state formed part of a broader system of hierarchy and control that Proudhon christened a 'trinity of absolutism', in which government suppressed liberty, capital suppressed labour, and organized religion the spirit. Property such as factories, unoccupied land, or any other type not directly derived from labour was, Proudhon claimed in a famous aphorism, 'theft', maintained only by force or the threat of it. The solution was mutualism, a web of cooperatives among small, independent producers that would undermine and eventually eliminate the appropriation of labour's surplus, profits, interest, and rent. The first anarchist associations indeed appeared among independent artisans such as the watchmakers of the Jura region of France and Switzerland. The 1840s also witnessed the first formulations of individualist anarchism in Max Stirner's book *The ego and its own*, which rejected the state, laws, morality, and any other restraint on individual autonomy.

Although its fundamentals were already set by the middle of the 19th century, anarchism continued to evolve in the following decades. Its dominant economic vision shifted from mutualism to collectivism – which envisioned collectivized property but individual remuneration according to contribution – and later communism, which envisioned the allocation of resources according to need. It acquired, in part through the influence of the ubiquitous Mikhail Bakunin, a revolutionary ethos that Proudhonian mutualism had lacked. And it encompassed a repertoire of seemingly contradictory practices: violent general strikes, insurrections, bombings, and assassinations; and a pacifist ethos that found expression in anti-militarist groups, 'rationalist' schools, musical and theatre troupes, Esperanto leagues, vegetarianism, naturism (nudism), and the pursuit of the 'simple life'.

This set of ideas and practices formed the world's first and most widespread transnational movement organized from below and without formal political parties. The pioneer activism in the Jura region attracted foreign exiles and militants who later spread the movement elsewhere in Europe. By the 1860s it had taken root in the rest of France, Italy, Spain (particularly in Catalonia and Andalusia), Belgium, and to a lesser extent, Central Europe. It later spread to the rest of the Continent and the British Isles, developing particularly strong roots among Ashkenazi Jews, who made up less than 5 per cent of the Russian Empire's population but more than half of its anarchist activists. French, Italian and Spanish migrants took it to Algeria and other areas of European settlement in North Africa. German and Bohemian immigrants played a leading role in its introduction to the United States in the 1870s but by the early 20th century they were outnumbered by Italian and Jewish newcomers. Spanish and Italian militants disseminated it throughout

Latin America. Upper-class students returning from European sojourns introduced it to Japan and China in the early 20th century and returning immigrants from the Americas helped to spread it to the working classes. After World War I, anarchist activism surfaced in much of the rest of Asia and sub-Saharan Africa.

The local intensity of the movement, however, varied much and depended on the density of its external connections. In places where the ideology entered only through commerce in printed material like books and magazines, the diffusion was limited to ideas (with the individualist strains of the ideology predominating) and circumscribed to literary or artistic circles. The addition to these channels of returning students or workers could, as in Japan and China, spread the ideas beyond the literati and forge a social movement. Peripatetic militants added another proselytizing element in many places. But only mass migration and a dense circulation of working-class people could diffuse anarchism not as a set of ideas but as a mass social movement with dedicated structures. And although immigrants from all over Europe participated in this spread, by the early 20th century three specific groups had become the most notorious disseminators of this diasporic anarchism: Italians, Spaniards, and Jews.

Latin America offers an illustrative example of the varying intensities of this transnational movement. Anarchist ideas and even labour organizations could be found in every country of the region. But the movement only engaged a large proportion of the population in regions of heavy European immigration: Cuba, Southern Brazil, Uruguay, and eastern Argentina. And within these regions, it was, as elsewhere, basically an urban phenomenon. By the outbreak of World War I, Buenos Aires had become one of the largest foci of anarchist militancy in the world along with Paris and Barcelona; Santos – the port of São Paulo – and Rosario – another port city in Argentina – were widely known as the 'Barcelonas' of their respective countries.

In these areas of Latin America, in towns and cities of immigration in North America and Europe, and in the southwestern and eastern regions of the latter continent, anarchism developed its fullest manifestation in both ideology and praxis. Ideologically, it included not only the individualist and Tolstoyan strains favoured by bohemians but also the anarchocommunism and syndicalism of the toiling classes. In terms of practice, it promoted and was an important presence in extensive webs of labour unions and federations. And it transcended organized labour to create a veritable subculture marked by meeting places, public celebrations, institutions, theatre, education, an alternative press, their own music and songs, a visual iconography, and even their own lingo.

Ideas, cultural artifacts, practices, and people circulated throughout these sites creating a transnational sociocultural space, an Atlantic anarchism. Through a system of exchanges, anarchist newspapers carried news, letters, messages from people trying to locate kin and comrades, cryptic ones about conspiracies, revolutionary iconography, and pleas for material support for local causes. The same books and pamphlets published and translated by anarchist presses and distributed free or at close to production cost were read by millions from Paris to the 'Paris of the East' (St Petersburg) and that of Caribbean (Havana). The naturalist plays of the Parisian Mirbeau, the Scandinavians Ibsen and Strindberg, and those of scores of working-class amateur authors of various nationalities were being staged from the pampas to the prairies. The iconic image of the 'Chicago Martyrs' (the eight anarchists imprisoned or executed after the 1886 Haymarket Affair) circulated from Budapest to Buenos Aires and São Paulo to San Francisco. Monetary assistance for radical causes flowed throughout all of these foci of the new Atlantic world that the movement of millions of workers had created. And so did thousands of militants whose activism ranged from oratory to terrorism. Most assassinations of heads of state between 1890 and World War I were committed by immigrants, returnees, and wanderers who, collectively, formed a transmigratory group. They were also transnational in that their deeds were meant to avenge perceived injustices committed not against co-nationals, or members of their own ethnic group, but against humanity.

This transnational and anti-nationalist movement began to decline during and after World War I with the advance of nationalism among the working classes, the rising status of the state within the revolutionary left after the Bolshevik Revolution, the democratic left's increasing identification with the proactive or 'welfare' state, and repression in both capitalist and Communist countries. The Spanish Civil War supposedly represented its last stand. But as a set of ideas and to a lesser degree as a social movement, anarchism has proven quite resilient. Radical students resurrected it – quite appropriately since anarchism was always in large part a youth movement – as a non-authoritarian left-wing alternative to communism during the Spring of 1968. It influenced the development of liberation theology in the 1970s. An ideology that throughout the 20th century had been dismissed by Marxists as a premodern relic is being extolled in the 21st as postmodern. Its culturalist critique, once denounced by the proponents of dialectic materialism as soft and 'unscientific', has become the single most important epistemological and ethical source in 'cultural studies', radical feminism and environmentalism, punk rock, the so-called anti-globalization movement (misnamed in the sense that it does not oppose globalization but the terms under which it is being promoted), and in radical arts and the internet.

Jose C. Moya

Bibliography

Guerin D. (ed.) 2005. *No gods, no masters: an anthology of anarchism.* Oakland: AK.
Miller D. 1984. *Anarchism.* London: Dent.
Moya J. C. 2004. 'The positive side of stereotypes: Jewish anarchists in early-20th-century Buenos Aires', *Jewish History*, 18, 1, 19–48.
Woodcock G. 1962. *Anarchism: a history of libertarian ideas and movements.* New York: Meridian.

Related essays

1960s; consumer cooperation; cultural capitals; diasporas; Esperanto; exile; human mobility; information society; liberation theology; nation and state; nudism; police; socialism; students; theatre; workers' movements; youth organizations

Animal diseases

Human concerns about animal diseases go back to the settledness of mankind, the more so as care of domestic animals ensured nutrition and clothing, transmission of energy, wealth, and military weapons for a long time. Starting from the awareness of epidemic diseases being contagious, and based on scientific specification of the animal kingdom in the epoque of the Enlightenment, infectious animal diseases gained a remarkable significance as tracer of transnationalism from the second half of the 19th century. Debates on animal diseases were a constitutive topic in transnational scientific networking (e.g. international veterinary congresses). In addition, the control of border-crossing diseases motivated the foundation of NGOs, international governmental cooperation, and came along with standardization of information transfer, with the extension of health authority administration and trade policy. At the threshold of the 21st century, transboundary animal diseases are even more important, since most of the newly emerging diseases are zoonoses, which are transmittable between humans and animals. As major zoonotic diseases the World Health Organization (WHO) lists anthrax, Severe Acute Respiratory Syndrome (SARS), animal influenza, Bovine Spongeiform Encephalopathy (BSE, also known as mad cow disease), brucellosis, hemorrhagic fevers, hydatidosis, leishmaniasis, leptospirosis, prion diseases, rabies, trematodosis, trypanosomiasis, and tularemia. Cross-species and globally spread illnesses constitute a manifold challenge to inter- and transdisciplinary research by questioning the order of scientific disciplines established in the 19th century. Moreover, the assumed speedup of border-crossing diseases through a more and more globalized food production defies the historical development of control regulations, while the awareness of culturally different traditions in the handling of contacts between animals and humans raises the question of whether transnationalism may include intercultural perspectives.

Referring to animal diseases, transnationalisation was first connected to scientific professionalization and to the establishment of governmental veterinary services in the 18th century. The foundation of the École Vétérinaire de Lyon (France) in 1762 stood at the beginning of the opening of modern veterinary schools in Europe, each of them with a strong focus on Rinderpest (cattle plague). This highly contagious plague, which crossed the continents several times during the 19th century, was regarded as the most dangerous of animal diseases in terms of its mortality as well as relative to economic losses. When a new wave of this plague started in the 1860s, the actions taken coincided with the first era of global govern-ance and liberal internationalism. Whilst railways accelerated the transnational spread of the plague, counteractive measures were also part of transnational networking. In 1863, in an early move of international health cooperation, the first international veterin-ary congress (Hamburg, Germany) discussed measures against the plague. Thenceforward, international meetings followed regularly, creating a border-crossing epistemic scien-tific community, which, in 1906, transformed itself into a permanent committee, and in 1953 into the World Veterinary Association. In the 19th century, these veterinary congresses had a markedly semi-official character, as experts prepared and influenced national legislation and coordination of measures against animal diseases on an international, governmental level. This demonstration of the effectiveness of cross-border cooperation in agriculture, a classic field of domestic pol-icy, was sometimes used as evidence in the contemporary debate on liberal internation-alism (Reinsch, 1909).

Indeed, measures against animal diseases presented a paradigmatic issue at all lev-els of transnationalism. With regard to science, veterinarians participated in the well-organized transnational medical epi-stemic community. Expressed in the estab-lishment of the first chair in comparative medicine in France in 1862, close connections between human and veterinary medicine were supported by the development of bacteri-ology and vaccination, and by the scientific evidence for common diseases among ani-mals and humans. Closely followed by govern-mental representatives, several international congresses against tuberculosis (e.g. Paris, 1885, Paris, 1891, London, 1901) discussed the (given) transmissibility of bovine and human tuberculosis, a problem at the core of public interest. This issue concerned a widespread disease of the 19th century, and many actors, interests and stakeholders were involved. The disease affected sanitary statistics and leg-islations, with the establishment of sanitary offices and the implementation of notifiable disease requirements. In addition, bovine tuberculosis influenced consumption and pro-cessing of meat and milk. In the second half of the 19th century, the transnational element in animal diseases was borne out in the topic's appearance at international meetings, such as statistics conferences and the Congresses of Hygiene and Demography. At the turn of the century, agrarian internationalism was insti-tutionalized, first of all with the foundation of the International Institute of Agriculture in Rome in 1906. This semi-official public inter-national union (transformed into FAO after World War 2) was established by a convention ratified by most of the states in Asia, Europe, Africa and America during the 20th century.

In addition, transnationalism related to ani-mal diseases had (and still has) a strong eco-nomic, political and international background and is deeply mired in international relations and power politics as shown by the develop-ments in the field during the last 150 years. Following the great depression of the 1870s, control of contagious animal diseases gave reasons for import restrictions for animals and meat. As an argument in trade policy, protection against plagues can be found in trade agreements (e.g. the treaty of friend-ship between Belgium and Honduras, 1913), some with duplicating impact through most-favoured-nation clauses. As an element in the global economy, real and pretended fears of animal diseases played a highly controversial role in the European boycott of American pork in the late 19th century. In addition, sanitary control had a decisive role in imperialist pol-icy, as suggested by the 1890s cattle plague that devastated the population of domestic and wild animals in Africa, destroyed the eco-nomic foundation of the indigenous popu-lation, and aggravated imperialist conflicts such as the Herero War of 1904.

In the first half of the 20th century, two world wars challenged the sustainability of transnational networking. Moreover, experiments in the use of virulent animal pathogens aggravated the significance of animal diseases as an instrument of biological warfare. However, global conflicts did not destroy transnational networks substantially. In the area of animal diseases, new developments that had started on the eve of World War 1 continued in the 1920s. During the interwar period, transnational activities concerned protection of wild and exotic animals, the preservation of nature, and border-crossing engagement against vivisection. Agrarian internationalism as part of the global economy consolidated and continued remarkably in three fields. First, under the supervision of the fascist govern-ment in Italy, the International Institute of Agriculture expanded and was a hosting interface for newly founded agrarian stake-holders, many of whom were also interested in animal diseases. Second, in 1921 the French government launched an agreement for the foundation of an international office for epizootics after an outbreak of Rinderpest in Belgium by a transport of infected zebus from India to Brazil through the port of Antwerp. Although the new organization, today's World Organization for Animal Health (OIE), did not hold its first conference till 1928, its politics mirrored the need to establish multilateral forms of control as a requirement for the reduction of import restrictions. Third, animal diseases came onto the agenda of the League of Nations in 1927, at the international economic conference in Geneva. The conference proposed the replacement of sanitarily justified import restrictions by an international agreement. The plan kept a group of experts busy and enforced transgovernmental relations between veterinary offices and transnational contacts between experts and stakeholders. This kind of networking had more success than three poorly ratified conventions that came out of League work. Fourth, consumers' organizations such as the International Co-operative Wholesale Society sustained consumer interests in international trade with agricultural products. Human nutrition and consumers' interests gave animal diseases a growing importance beyond the economic side of agrarian productivity.

After World War 2, the reduction of the agricultural sector in national economies, the introduction of highly efficient industrialized farming, a growing distance between food production and society on one side and an increasing social significance of pets on the other side, orchestrated the gospel of progress. Control of animal diseases became part of a global concept of foreign aid, supported by the United Nations and its special agencies (WHO, FAO). Based on the discovery and production of antibiotics and insecticides, the eradication of contagious animal diseases seemed to define some countries as 'developed' as against more 'backward' ones. The relationship of such a dichotomy to the Cold War is a complex phenomenon that has not been thoroughly investigated.

Transnational cooperation extended through the formation of veterinary public health as an academic discipline after World War 2, integrating veterinary aspects with food hygiene, environmental contamination and public information. The existing transnational network of experts facilitated international standardization processes (e.g. adoption of standard tuberculin by WHO in 1951), enlarged the instruments of disease control and surveillance with the multiplication of regional research institutions, and put forward recommendations addressing especially poor countries.

After the end of the Cold War, animal diseases again indicated a sea change in border-crossing epistemology. In 1989, the first case of Mad Cow Disease (BSE) was reported outside the UK. Instead of zoonotic diseases as a characteristic of livestock-keeping communities, animal diseases now appeared as a result of high-tech food production. Moreover (re-)emerging diseases challenged the concept of defeating diseases by science, technology and development. Since then, zoonoses seem to pose a specific characteristic of the 21st century and a special challenge for transdisciplinary research.

Madeleine Herren

Bibliography

Blancou J. 2003. *History of the surveillance and control of transmissible animal diseases*. Paris: Office International des Epizooties.

Reinsch P. S. 1909. 'International administrative law and national sovereignty', *American Journal of International Law*, 3, 1, 1–45.

Staples A. L. S. 2006. *The birth of development*. Kent: Kent State University Press.

Wilkinson L. 1992. *Animals and disease*. Cambridge: Cambridge University Press.

Related essays

Animal rights

The animal rights movement begins in the 19th century with the establishment throughout Euro-America of animal protection societies. The British Society for the Prevention of Cruelty to Animals (SPCA) was founded in 1824, the French Société

Protectrice des Animaux in 1845, German and Swiss societies in the 1830s and 1840s, and the American SPCA in 1866, each with similar ends. The carter who beat his horse to death in rage or desperation on the streets of Paris, London or New York, the tavern owner who organized cock fighting or cock throwing in the dirt yard of his premises, the drover who led cattle to market without providing them with water and food, these people were the focus of legislation and the attention of middle- and upper-class advocates for animals.

Animal advocacy in the 19th century was tied into a network of bourgeois reform. The British SPCA (the RSPCA from 1840) was founded by philanthropists active in the anti-slavery movement, prison reform, popular education, and Catholic emancipation. Caroline Earle White who organized Philadelphia's SPCA in 1866 came from a wealthy abolitionist family and was herself active in the Women's Christian Temperance Union, the St Vincent's Aid Society for the protection of children, and suffragist circles. Prison reformers, agronomists and public health officials interested in working-class housing were among the French society's supporters. These networks within nation states may not surprise us, primed as we are by Marx's insights. Less well known is the transnational flow of ideas and people which led to a uniformity of approach to the problem of animal abuse.

Henry Bergh, heir to a New York shipbuilding fortune, travelled to London in 1865 to seek out the leaders of the RSPCA and attend its annual meeting. In 1866 he presented a 'Declaration of the Rights of Animals' as preamble to an ASPCA. Caroline White, in turn, sought out Bergh for information on how to establish the Philadelphia society. The founders of the French SPA made specific reference to the British society, and the leadership regularly encouraged its ranks with reports of the RSPCA's successful measures. A universalist outlook was formed through the transnational circulation of news and annual reports. French, British and American reformers together looked down upon the fringes of Europe, at Spain, for example, where bull fighting was practised, and beyond Europe, to North Africa and the Levant. British advocates sought to remedy the plight of animals abroad, founding the Society for the Protection of Animals in North Africa in 1923

and the Brooke Hospital for Animals in Cairo in 1932.

Euro-American ideas about animal protection followed global capitalism. An ebb and flow back from its empires helped to reshape these views for the 20th century. As early as the 1790s Hindu views towards animals were fuelling arguments against meat eating in Britain and France. The spread of vegetarianism in reformist circles in Edwardian England was also placed in the imperial context. Looking ahead, we find Peter Singer explaining how his encounter with vegetarianism (at Oxford) triggered his seminal work Animal Liberation (1975) and Tom Regan crediting his discovery of Gandhi's views with prompting The Case for Animal Rights (1984). Hilda Kean describes well the postcolonial flavour of 'alternative London' in the late 1960s and early 70s with its macrobiotic restaurants like the Hari Krishna offering dahl and brown rice and vegetables to anti-war and other hungry protesters.

Vegetarianism promised spiritual health; it also supposed that animals were to be protected from harm for their own sakes, and not towards the humanist goals of the early animal protection societies. This notion was mooted in anti-vivisection societies founded in Britain, France, Germany, Switzerland, the United States and elsewhere in the last third of the 19th century often as offshoots of established societies for the protection of animals, and primarily by women. Transnational networks are prominent in their histories. White travelled to England to meet with Frances Power Cobbe for advice on organizing an American Anti Vivisection Society (AAVS), which she did in 1883, along with a journal to promote its views. Cobbe, active in campaigns for women's suffrage, the reform of marriage laws, and the opening up of higher education for women, founded the Victoria Street Society for the Protection of Animals liable to Vivisection (VSS) in 1875, the earliest and most important of the anti-vivisection societies. White's associates promulgated the message of the AAVS through contacts in the Women's Christian Temperance Union. Cobbe, herself, became an anti-vivisectionist during a visit to Florence in 1863 where she learned, through an American doctor (a friend of a friend) of experiments being conducted on dogs and other animals by the German physiologist, Moritz Schiff. The prominence of the VSS established it as a crucial reference for French and German societies, with women there too in leadership roles.

Anti-vivisection societies were loosely connected through transnational social circles. An exchange of strategies linked them as well. The objective was to reach a wide audience, which Cobbe's aptly named 1885 pamphlet, 'Light in Dark Places', luridly succeeded in doing, as did Ernst von Weber's 'Die Folterkammern der Wissenschaft' (The Torture Chambers of Science) (1879), a pamphlet which was distributed throughout German-speaking Europe in public spaces such as rail stations and coffee shops. Cobbe and von Weber based their work on details gleaned from old manuals of physiology. In a tactic revisited by direct-action animal rights groups in the late 20th century, others sought to expose the horrors of vivisection by directly infiltrating its laboratories. Louise Lind af Hageby (the English-educated granddaughter of the Chamberlain of Sweden) and Liesa Schartau attended physiology classes in London and published their observations in The Shambles of Science (1903) (which attracted even more attention through the suit for libel which ensued). Elizabeth Blackwell attended Claude Bernard's demonstrations in Paris with the same aims in mind. Sensationalist novels on both sides of the Channel portrayed vivisectors as sexual predators, sadistically causing prostrate animals pain.

Women played a leading role in the movement to protect animals from the excesses of unregulated science but anti-vivisection carried a strong conservative message as well. Euro-rationality was the perceived evil, the cold vivisectionist, its transnational image. The anti-vivisectionist critique of modernity connected it to likeminded movements on the Continent. For some a 'Jewish' attitude towards animals (Schopenhauer) was expressed in both vivisection and kosher butchering. The journal of the German anti-vivisection movement strongly supported the abolition of kosher butchering – a milestone achieved by the Nazis in 1933. The Nazi Animal Protection Laws which protected animals 'for their own sakes' and not on behalf of humanity seem to have attracted little contemporary attention, though resistance to their measures on the part of the occupied French has been reported. British protesters against the export of live animals for slaughter in the 1990s, however, used the images of the death camps to make their points, as did those rallying against slaughterhouses and the use of animals in medical research.

Current thinking about animal rights was inaugurated with Singer's attack on 'speciesism' in Animal Liberation. Dozens of organizations have been formed on the grassroots level to protect animals in the face of global capitalism, with not just Euro-American drug companies and food manufacturers the targets, but Japanese whalers and Inuit hunters. The transnational face of these groups is easy to see in the history of the Animal Liberation Front (ALF), which promotes worldwide direct action against corporate animal abusers. The ALF was formed in England in 1976 and according to its own history, 'migrated' to the United States in the early 1980s. It now claims to have cells of activists in over twenty countries whose activities, though non-coordinated, are credited by the ALF on its website. The history of Greenpeace is instructive in another way. Formed in the 1970s and now claiming 2.5 million members worldwide, in the 1980s it withdrew from a campaign to save Arctic seals when it became clear that the fur trade was crucial to the culture of indigenous peoples. This decision heralded concerns that the defence of wild animals on the part of Western activists was a new imperialism, an eco-imperialism, by placing Western interest in elephants, mountain gorillas, and tigers and the like over the interests of local peoples. Ramachandra Guha's ideas have been the most influential in shaping this critique, offering Indian 'agrarianism', a kind of sustainable growth model which assumes the integration of human and animal life, as an alternative to Western ecocentrism, thus looping the discussion of animal rights back to the human-centred concerns whence it came.

Kathleen Kete

Bibliography

Beers D. 2006. For the prevention of cruelty: the history and legacy of animal rights activism in the United States. Athens, OH: Ohio University Press.

Garner R. 1993, 2004. Animals, politics and morality. Manchester: Manchester University Press.

Kean H. 1998. Animal rights: political and social change in Britain since 1800. London: Reaktion.

Rupke N. (ed.) 1987. Vivisection in historical perspective. London: Croom Helm.

Antarctic Treaty

The Antarctic Treaty, signed by twelve nations
in 1959 and ratified in 1961, is the founding
document of Antarctica's unique political
regime.

Forged in the Cold War era, this remarkable
political text has proven to be a resilient and
evolving instrument for international cooperation. Its main object is to promote the peaceful use of Antarctica and to facilitate scientific
research south of 60° latitude. It distinguishes
between signatory nations, which agree to
the Treaty, and consultative nations which
also actively undertake Antarctic research.
Management is by consensus and every consultative nation has a veto. Forty-five countries have now become parties to the Treaty
(27 of them consultative).

The key provision of the Treaty (Article
IV) neither recognizes nor denies any existing territorial claims to Antarctica. In polar
parlance, such claims are 'frozen'. This political compromise emerged from a period of
escalating national rivalry over Antarctic sovereignty. After 'the Race for the Pole' of the
early 20th century, there was a 'Scramble for
Antarctica' that echoed the famous 'Scramble
for Africa' amongst European powers in the
late 19th century. From the 1920s, commercial whaling intensified along the edges of the
ice and seven nations consistently asserted
territorial claims to sectors of the continent: Argentina, Australia, Britain, Chile,
France, New Zealand and Norway. The United
States established a significant presence in
Antarctica in the interwar period but declined
to make a formal claim, and in 1950 the USSR
announced its renewed interest in Antarctic
exploration. It began to seem that the Cold
War and other conflicts might find their way
to the coldest part of the planet.

In 1948, the US government proposed an
international trusteeship for Antarctica
consisting of the seven claimant states and
the United States. The apparent idealism
of this terra communis was tempered by the
proposal's goal of excluding the Soviet Union
from the power bloc. The claimant nations
rejected the proposal because it required the
renunciation of sovereignty. The Chileans,
however, suggested a compromise (known
as the Escudero Plan) which allowed claims
to be suspended rather than renounced. By
1950 Chile and the US, united by a desire
to exclude the USSR, had agreed on this
revised plan for internationalisation. But a
significant world event was about to change
Antarctic politics.

The International Geophysical Year of
1957–58 (known as IGY) was the biggest scientific enterprise ever undertaken, and the
launching of the Soviet spaceship, Sputnik,
on 4 October 1957 was its most visible
achievement. Building on the tradition of
International Polar Years (held previously in
1882–83 and 1932–33), IGY made a focus of
Antarctica as well as those other regions now
made newly accessible by technology – outer
space and the ocean floor. Nearly 30,000 scientists from 66 nations took part at locations
across the globe. In Antarctica, twelve countries were involved: the seven claimant nations
plus Belgium, Japan, South Africa, the United
States and the USSR. For fifty years the main
motives for Antarctic work had been national
honour and territorial conquest. Now scientific work and international cooperation
became the priorities.

IGY was such a resounding success that it
cried out to be institutionalized. Also, it was
now clear that any management regime for
Antarctica had to include the USSR. Intensive
diplomatic activity following IGY culminated
in a draft for an Antarctic Treaty which incorporated the compromise of the Escudero Plan.
Military activity and testing of any kind of
weapons were prohibited south of 60°, information was to be shared, and inspections of
other nations' bases allowed at any time. In
November 1959, the Antarctic Treaty was
signed in Washington by the twelve nations
that had participated in IGY. Science as a
transnational social system had never before
revealed itself to be so powerful.

The Treaty is augmented by Recommendations adopted at Consultative
Meetings and by two separate conventions
dealing with the Conservation of Antarctic
Seals (1972) and the Conservation of Antarctic
Marine Living Resources (1980). The Treaty
has survived two major challenges since it
entered into force. The first came in 1983

when the United Nations General Assembly considered arguments made by an alliance of Asian and third world nations that the Treaty was a relic of colonialism. Led by Malaysia, the draft UN resolution aimed to build on the Law of the Sea Convention (1982) and the Moon Treaty (1979) by arguing that Antarctica should be managed as the common heritage of humanity. The treaty powers responded with defensive unanimity, insisting that nations had only to accede to the Treaty if they wished to participate in Antarctic affairs.

The other political challenge was precipitated by the oil crisis of the mid-1970s, when Antarctica became regarded as a possible source of fossil fuels. The number of states acceding to the Treaty increased and, in 1988, treaty nations agreed to adopt a Convention for the Regulation of Antarctic Mineral Resource Activities. However, led by Australia and influenced by Greenpeace and other environmental campaigners, treaty nations decided instead to adopt a Protocol on Environmental Protection. Signed in Madrid on 4 October 1991, it declared a fifty-year ban on mining in Antarctica and put into place comprehensive and legally binding measures to protect the Antarctic environment.

Tom Griffiths

Bibliography

Griffiths T. 2007. *Slicing the silence: voyaging to Antarctica*. Sydney and Cambridge, MA: UNSW Press and Harvard University Press.

Pyne S. J. 1986. *The ice: a journey to Antarctica*. Iowa City: University of Iowa Press.

Related essays

climate change; Cold War; conservation and preservation; environmental diplomacy; environmentalism; Greenpeace; legal order; life and physical sciences; Moon Treaty; oceans; oil; outer space; scientific expeditions; scientific stations; United Nations system

Anti-Catholicism

From its inception at the Reformation, hostility towards Roman Catholicism has been shaped by cross-border exchanges of literature, ideas and spokespeople. The English Protestant John Foxe's *Actes and Monuments* (1563), a vivid account of Protestant martyrdom at the hands of an intolerant and vengeful Catholic Church, inspired several imitators in Continental Europe, and was mandatory reading in New England Sunday schools until the 1890s. In the 17th century, another key anti-Catholic text began its long international career: the purported secret constitution of the Order of Jesuits, the notorious *Monita secreta*, which, within decades of its publication in Cracow in 1614, had appeared in 22 editions and seven languages.

The 19th century marked the high point of the international movement against Catholicism. Much of the traffic in books, people and ideas was initially conducted between Protestant nations, with a a growing role for United States Protestants. The purported testimonies of escaped nuns, with their graphic descriptions of sexual corruption and torture in Catholic convents, scandalized and titillated Protestant readers in a range of countries. One such American best-seller, *The Awful Disclosures of Maria Monk*, soon appeared in the United Kingdom, Canada and Australia. The international traffic in anti-Catholic literature then expanded beyond this Protestant channel to encompass majority-Catholic societies, where the ties between Church and state were increasingly coming under attack. A particularly influential author was the French anti-clerical and historian, Jules Michelet, whose denunciation of the power allegedly wielded by the Catholic confessor, *Du prêtre, de la femme et de la famille* (1845), was published in 18 editions in Spain, Great Britain, Belgium, the United States, Hungary and Australia.

By the middle decades of the 19th century, an international anti-Catholic lecture circuit had begun to form. In 1853, the American and Foreign Christian Union invited an Italian renegade priest, Alessandro Gavazzi, who had already won fame as an anti-Catholic orator in England and Scotland, to deliver a series of lectures in the United States as well as Canada. Gavazzi's success as an anti-Catholic orator was mirrored two decades later by another ex-priest, the French-Canadian, Charles Chiniquy. His arrival in Hobart, Tasmania, during his 1878–79 Australian lecture tour, led to street fights between local Protestant and Catholic groups.

Cross-national linkages between opponents of Catholicism were further consolidated in the 19th century by a series of mobilizing events. The most important was undoubtedly the Mortara affair (1858). When Vatican authorities forcibly removed a young Jewish boy, Edgardo Mortara, from his family, on the grounds that he had been secretly baptized as a Catholic, an immense international scandal ensued. Across a range of countries, defenders of the Mortara family shared information and funds in their campaign to have the boy returned. The convocation of the first Vatican Council (1869–70) provided yet another opportunity for an international protest against the allegedly retrograde tendencies of the Church. In October 1869, a French Carmelite monk, Father Hyacinthe, who had abandoned his monastery in protest at what he called Catholicism's alienation from the modern age, received a rapturous welcome in the United States, where he was feted as a second Luther.

Hostility to Catholicism was not confined to Western nations. As the most prominent and well-established Christian group in areas subject to colonial interference or control, Catholic missionaries and their converts were the targets of popular violence throughout the 19th century. However, the anti-Catholic riots which occurred in China, French Indochina and Singapore were motivated by a resentment of Christianity rather than a specific rejection of Catholicism, and did not draw on Western anti-Catholic texts.

In the 20th century, the decline of Protestant–Catholic animosity in many countries, as well as the enactment of the separation of Church and state in majority-Catholic countries such as France (1905) diminished the transnational aspect of anti-Catholicism. Nineteenth-century works dedicated to exposing the alleged depravity of Catholic priests or the purported intrigues of the Jesuits continue to be published, and their international transmission has been facilitated through the Internet. However, anti-Catholicism is no longer a great international crusade.

Timothy Verhoeven

Bibliography
Billington R. A. 1938. The Protestant crusade, 1800–1860: a study of the origins of American nativism. New York: Macmillan.
Clark C. and Kaiser W. (eds) 2003. Culture wars: secular–Catholic Conflict in 19th century Europe. Cambridge: Cambridge University Press.

Related essays
anti-racism; antisemitism; Christianity; conspiracy theories; ecumenism; Ethical Culture; evangelicalism; freemasonry; missionaries; translation; women's movements; workers' movements

Anti-fascism and fascism See Fascism and anti-fascism

Anti-racism

With the identification of 'race prejudice' as one outcome of the growing preoccupation with 'racial difference' in the late 19th century, intellectuals, writers and political activists attempted to understand and explain race prejudice and in some cases to combat it. Racism begot anti-racism. This oppositional stance can thus be traced back to the late 19th century, though the term was not coined until later in the 20th century.

Early critics of racism included champions of British imperialism, who liked to point to the equality of all British subjects, regardless of colour, a claim pressed by Gandhi in South Africa, but increasingly difficult to sustain in the face of the evident unequal treatment of Indians throughout the British world. Chinese and Japanese diplomats also invoked international law to prove the equality of nations.

The sources of anti-racist thought were diverse, including the new anthropological work of Franz Boas and others, that suggested that environment was more important than genetic inheritance in shaping ability and character; religious teachers who insisted on the equality of souls regardless of skin colour; political leaders such as Cuban poet and revolutionary, José Martí, who critiqued what he called 'bookshelf races' and writers, such as the Frenchman, Jean Finot, whose Le préjugé des races was published in 1905 and translated in English in 1906, African-American W. E. B. DuBois (Souls of black folk 1903 and 'Souls of white folk' 1910) and Harvard philosopher, Josiah Royce, whose Race questions was published in 1908.

Royce pointed out that American school children had been taught, for example, that Japanese were a weird people from a weird land, given to boiling criminals in oil and murdering missionaries, yet had since found that Japanese students were courteous and polite, quietly assured of their own superiority. His version of anti-racism cautioned against invoking the authority of science to sanctify prejudice against foreigners and pointed to the fallibility of race judgements. Other critics of race prejudice in the early 20th century included champions of free trade and the movement of peoples, who opposed Exclusion Acts and the erection of other barriers, such as passports, and literacy tests to the mobility of coloured and colonised peoples into self-styled white men's countries across South Africa, North America and Australasia.

Cosmopolitanism was another source of anti-racism. Many critics of race prejudice invoked an imagined Enlightenment tradition of cosmopolitan sympathy that pre-dated and transcended national, racial and religious rivalries and hatreds. In the early 20th century, cosmopolitan clubs were formed by international socialists around the world, inspired, for example, by the English socialist, Tom Mann to promote the international solidarity of the working class as an answer to the racial and national antipathies that increasingly divided workers. The Pan-African Congress of 1900, the conference on Subject Races and Nationalities in 1910 and the Universal Races Congress in 1911, all held in London, were important in circulating ideas, publicizing literature and constructing networks that were crucial to the work of anti-racism.

From the late 19th century, Chinese immigrants and then increasingly all Asians were denied entry to English-speaking settler societies. Initially, Chinese and Japanese diplomats responded to these racist exclusions by insisting on the antiquity of their civilizations or invoking their rights as sovereign nations under international law. Increasingly, however, in the early years of the 20th century, they came to realise that it was their colour, not their civilization, that offended so they reformulated their protests in terms of campaigns to combat racial inequality. In 1919, Japanese delegates to the Versailles Peace Conference lobbied without success to have a racial equality clause inserted in the Covenant of the League of Nations.

Between the wars a range of non-governmental organizations, including the Institut de Droit International and the Federation of League of Nations Unions called for the promulgation of a Covenant of the Rights of Man, enshrining the rights of individuals, without racial distinction. At the end of the Second World War, the ideal of non-discrimination was incorporated into the United Nations Charter and the Universal Declaration of Human Rights in 1948. The renunciation of scientific race thinking, led by Ashley Montagu and others, shaped the work of experts brought together by UNESCO, which published a Statement on Race in 1950 declaring race a social myth that had created 'an enormous amount of damage'.

Postwar anti-racism movements took the form of civil rights activism and revolutionary struggle, often inspired and sustained by the transnational circulation of ideas, strategies, texts such as Frantz Fanon's Wretched of the Earth, and charismatic leaders and singers such as Paul Robeson and Miriam Makeba. An Australian 'Freedom Ride' organized to combat discrimination against Aborigines in New South Wales in 1965 drew inspiration from the example of Martin Luther King in the United States and the struggles against Apartheid in South Africa. Anti-racism also inspired attacks on the policy of assimilationism in favour of, first, integration, then multiculturalism. Some countries passed racial vilification laws. In more recent times the discourse of anti-racism has been mobilized around the world in defence of asylum seekers, refugees and Muslim minorities living in Western communities.

Marilyn Lake

Bibliography

Lake M. and Reynolds H. (eds) 2008. Drawing the global colour line: white men's countries and the international challenge of racial equality. Cambridge: Cambridge University Press.
McKean W. 1983. Equality and discrimination under international law. Oxford: Clarendon Press.

Related essays

Africa; African liberation; America; asylum seekers; cosmopolitanism and universalism; ethnicity and race; eugenics; Gandhi, Mohandas Karamchand; human rights; language diplomacy; League of Nations system; legal order; Mandela, Nelson; pan-isms; race-mixing; The Wretched of the Earth; United Nations system; Universal Races Congress; white men's countries; workers' movements

Antisemitism

Broadly defined as unprovoked and irrational hostility towards Jews, antisemitism, like all forms of prejudice, associates the individual with the perceived characteristics of the group.

The term was only coined in the 1870s by Wilhelm Marr, a one-time German radical. It was used to replace 'Jew hatred' (Judenhetze or Judenhass) which had become outmoded in the 19th century as secularism deemed religious hostility obscurantist and backward. With some justification, antisemitism has been termed 'the longest hatred'. Not only has it existed for more than two millennia, but it extends beyond national borders and is found even where there are no Jews. The Jew was already a classic 'other' or outsider in the pagan world, although scholars disagree on the substance of that antipathy and the extent to which it deserves the appellation 'antisemitism'.

Building upon animosity in antiquity, but with an additional malevolence, Christianity ushered in a period of sustained hostility, driven by the Church Fathers and the Adversus Judaeos tradition. By the late Middle Ages the Jew had attained diabolical status, rooted in the Christian religious imagination. However, from the 15th century there are indications that medieval anti-Judaism was giving way to modern 'racial' antisemitism; by the 18th century anthropological categories were characterizing Jews as having innate and immutable characteristics. These ideas flowered through the 19th century, merging with Darwin's ideas of natural selection and Herbert Spencer's 'survival of the fittest'; in short, the biologization of politics. Houston Stewart Chamberlain defined 'Aryans' and 'Jews' in constant struggle in his major work, Die Grunglagen des XIX. Jahrhunderts (Foundations of the Nineteenth Century, 1899).

In its most extreme form this new conception of politics came to justify war on the Jews. A secular rationale, building on age-old ideas, was provided for an inveterate hatred. The Jew, a rootless, subversive and powerful cosmopolitan, was foreign to the spirit of the people. Whereas in the medieval world, conversion to Christianity had often been possible, new race-based antisemitism, reinforced by organic and romantic notions of the nation, precluded this option. Having an unchangeable nature, the Jew was immutably alien, dangerous and supranational.

Antisemitism entered the public or political arena in the 1870s, with antisemitic movements radiating throughout Europe. In the 1880s a series of International Anti-Jewish Congresses was held against the backdrop of a Europe-wide economic depression, financial scandals, restrictive quotas against Jews in universities and the professions in Russia, and pogroms. The huge waves of identifiable and alien Ostjuden (eastern Jews) entering Central and Western Europe in the late 19th century provoked substantial resentment. Anti-alienism merged with antisemitism from Berlin to Paris. In Vienna, Karl Lueger was elected Mayor on a blatantly antisemitic platform and in Paris, defeat at the hands of the Prussians, financial scandals and clerical concerns at Jewish support for state secularization generated an anti-Jewish backlash culminating in the 'Dreyfus Affair' – named after a young Jewish military officer, Alfred Dreyfus, following his false conviction for spying in 1894. While the affair began in Paris, it rapidly spread across France and beyond.

During the 1890s the Tsarist secret police concocted an infamous forgery, the Protocols of the Elders of Zion. Based on a French political satirical pamphlet compiled in the 1860s against Napoleon III and a German antisemitic novel, Biarritz, written by Hermann Gödsche, the Protocols claimed that Jews had been plotting, in no less than 24 secret meetings, the destruction of Christendom and its replacement with a totalitarian utopia. Initially the Protocols were relatively obscure. However, in the wake of the Russian Revolution and fleeing White Russians during Russia's Civil War, its noxious ideas percolated into the West. Notwithstanding their exposure as a crude forgery by the London Times in 1921, the Protocols attracted an enormous readership. They spread throughout the English-speaking world and were translated into many languages. Of particular interest is the palpable nexus of international antisemitism. By the time Hitler came to power in 1933, some 33 German editions of the Protocols had appeared. By way of example, a trial concerning the Protocols in South Africa in 1934 demonstrated the influence of Hamilton Hamish Beamish, an Irishman and founder of the antisemitic Britons who had spread these canards in England in the early 1920s and was well connected to the underworld of European antisemitism.

Although those focusing on the 'Jewish Question' came largely from the Right, accusations against the Jews as the symbols of modernity and rapacious capitalism were also evident on the Left. Such ideas were easily transferred to the 'new world'. From New York to Sydney, the arrival of large numbers of Eastern European Jews provoked the disapproval of substantial sectors of the population. In parts of Argentina, xenophobia merged with religious hatred, while in outposts of the British Empire the alien newcomer was perceived as an economic competitor and a source of evil. In the United States, nativism merged with antisemitism, characterized by anti-modernism. It had much in common with embryonic *volkisch* nationalism in Germany, far-right exclusivist nationalism in French-speaking Quebec and far-right Afrikaner ethnonationalism in South Africa where the Jews served as a symbol of malevolent capital. *My Lewe en Strewe* (My Life and Struggle), published in 1938 by a South African antisemite, Manie Maritz, illustrated the international connections between those who hated Jews. Maritz employed substantial portions of the *Protocols* and made use of the Canadian publication, *The Key to the Mystery*, a conspiratorial account of Jewish world domination by Adrien Arcand, a close friend of Beamish.

Between the First and the Second World Wars, the 'Jewish Question' was increasingly evident in the new nation states of Central and Eastern Europe. Germany in particular revealed the power of *volkisch* nationalism and fascism, aided and abetted by political and socioeconomic turmoil, culminating in the 'Final Solution', the murder of 6 million Jews.

Antisemitism declined substantially in Western Europe in the wake of the Second World War. But charges of Jewish 'bourgeois individualism' and 'rootless cosmopolitanism' were common in the Soviet Union which directed a powerful anti-Zionist message in the wake of the Six Day War of 1967 in Israel, culminating in its sponsorship in 1975 (together with some Arab states) of a United Nations Resolution condemning Zionism 'as a form of racism and racial discrimination'. The resolution was part of a continuing attempt to delegitimize the Jewish State and to expel Israel from the General Assembly. The Soviet Union and its satellites increasingly published literature with classical anti-Jewish themes, including the use of Christian blood for ritual purposes and the

Jewish world conspiracy. Anti-Zionism was now subsuming antisemitism.

Anti-Zionism and antisemitism are not axiomatically the same. Enmity towards Zionism and the Jewish State is rooted in the Arab–Israeli conflict. However, an analysis of much anti-Zionist rhetoric shows classic anti-Jewish motifs that go beyond the bounds of normal political conflict.

Such language and hostility is relatively new in the Muslim world where hostility towards Jews lacked the sharpness of Christian hatred in the medieval period. But from the 13th century, tension, humiliation and the degradation of Jews begins to characterize Muslim–Jewish relations. European colonialism and its Christian influences further exacerbated the Jewish condition in the Muslim world. Antisemitic calumnies such as the 'blood libel' crept into Muslim discourse amidst the looting, rape and killing of Jews in numerous cities and towns. Arab nationalism and the growth of Islamism in the 20th century exacerbated hostility against a backdrop of Zionist settlement and the complicated question of 'the right to the land'.

A vast anti-Jewish Arabic literature now makes use of texts such as Hitler's *Mein Kampf* and the *Protocols of the Elders of Zion*. Extremist groups such as Islamic Jihad and Hamas have appropriated ideas of a world Jewish conspiracy in what they consider to be a holy war against 'Satanist Zionism'. Such invective takes on the features of delusional Christian antisemitism at its height. Jews are characterised as germs or as a malignant disease and bent on global domination. The levels and rhetoric of this antisemitism go well beyond the sorts of contemporary hostility seen in Western Europe, Russia or even Japan where anti-Jewish discourse has operated despite there being less than one thousand Jews out of a total population of nearly 130 million.

A new form of antisemitism is the denial of the Holocaust in so-called 'revisionist' history. Across national borders it has given birth to a community that brings the far Right together with the Islamists. Its expansion in cyberspace, where antisemitism has burgeoned, has made a great amount of 'hate' material available. It would be foolhardy to expect an 'illness' so deeply entrenched to be entirely eradicated, despite efforts from many quarters, most notably the Catholic Church since the Second Vatican Council in 1965. History has constructed the Jew over centuries. The language, idiom and intensity of hostility have not always been the same, but its extension across borders of empires or nations has been a constant characteristic.

Milton Shain

Bibliography

Laqueur W. 2006. *The changing face of Antisemitism: from ancient times to the present day*. Oxford: Oxford University Press.

Lewis B. 1986. *Semites and anti-Semites: an inquiry into conflict and prejudice*. London and New York: Norton.

Shain M. 1998. *Antisemitism*. London: Bowerdean.

Wistrich R. 1991. *Antisemitism: the longest hatred*. London: Thames Mandarin.

Related essays

anti-Catholicism; anti-racism; Christianity; conspiracy theories; diasporas; ecumenism; ethnicity and race; Holocaust; human mobility; nation and state; religious fundamentalism; Zionism

Antropofagia

Brazilian avant garde is usually considered to have inaugurated at the Modern Art Week in São Paulo in 1922, a landmark event that counted with the participation of intellectuals such as writers Mario de Andrade and Oswald de Andrade, painters Annita Malfatti and Emiliano Di Cavalcanti, and sculptor Vítor Brecheret, among others. This launch – which combined poetry recitals and pictorial exhibitions, and awakened admiration and horror at the same time – set in motion an ensuing process of artistic transformation that unfolded outside the support of the official institutions and the market. Different groups and aesthetics converged in this movement. 'We were never catechized. What we did was carnival', stated Oswald de Andrade some years later; he, together with Mario de Andrade, led the movement.

The concept of 'antropofagia' (anthropophagia) is key to understanding Brazilian avant garde. In 1928 Oswald de Andrade launched the 'Manifesto Antropófago' (Anthropophagist Manifesto) in which he put forth an artistic movement that considered itself descendant of the European avant gardes, while it aimed at rediscovering Brazil, or rather founding a new Brazil. The manifesto reached back to the deglutition

of Father Pero Fernandes Sardinha by aborigines in 1556, designating it as the inaugural event of Brazilian national culture. The metaphor of cultural cannibalism thus formulated freed artists from the burden of imitating European art. It made reference to the devouring of new information and the process of 'cultural digestion' thus provoked that would be capable of assimilating, surpassing (and even nullifying) the ingested product. Already in 1924 Oswald de Andrade had formulated in his 'Manifiesto da Poesia Pau-Brasil' (Manifesto of Brazilwood Poetry) that the Brazilian avant garde had to rest on a double base: the jungle and the school, that is, universal knowledge and the awareness of the specific and particular conditions of local culture, and its singular identity. For him, the shortcomings and deficiencies of Latin American modernity became distinguishing and liberating features, which he defined as practical: experimental, without bookish reminiscences, without supporting comparisons, without etymological investigation, without ontology.

Repressed and forgotten for more than thirty years, the poetics of antropofagia were vindicated in the mid 1950s by the concrete poets, an artistic group that also emerged in São Paulo. One of the group, Haroldo de Campos, proposed that this assimilation of the Brazilian experience into a Brazilian type in its own terms would give the resulting product an autonomous character, and would confer on it the potential of becoming a product for export. Therefore, antropofagia not only implies the deglutition of modern culture produced at the centre, but also a way of actively repositioning oneself with respect to that centre, in a cannibalistic ritual of international cultural relations. The idea of antropofagia was later embraced and popularized by Tropicalism, the Brazilian popular music movement that was born in the 1960s, mixing popular rhythms with experimentalism. Caetano Veloso, one of the undisputed spokespeople of this movement, attested to the protagonists' devouring interest in the Beatles and Jimi Hendrix, mentioning antropofagia as a way to radicalize the exigency of identity, not to elude it.

Brazilian avant garde not only debated with the legitimized and commercial art forms, but also with the conventions of political art and cultural nationalism. It vindicated for itself a radical transforming political dimension, a feature that also distinguishes it from Anglo-Saxon conceptualism. This goal is evidenced by the following fragment from the 1967 'Declaration of the basic principles of the avant-garde', signed by a group of conceptual artists from Rio de Janeiro: 'An avant-garde art cannot be tied down to a given country: it happens in any place, through a mobilization of the available means, with the purpose of changing, or contributing to changing, the conditions of passivity or of stagnation' (quoted in Ramírez 2000, 541–2).

The study of Latin American avant-garde movements contributed crucially to reconsidering, and ultimately leaving behind, the long-standing and traditionally accepted assumptions regarding the diffusion of ideas as a unidirectional process of emanation from the centre towards the periphery. Carlo Ginzburg and Enrico Castelnuovo re-examined the centre/periphery link from a 'polyvalent perspective' and maintained that it was not a relationship of diffusion, rather one of conflict. Beatriz Sarlo, in turn, suggested introducing the concept of 'peripheral modernity', a constellation of locally specific conditions that emerges as a 'culture of mixture' between tradition and cosmopolitanism. Other authors postulate the existence of a shared climate of the era which produces works (and ideas) that flow in forms that are not subordinated to metropolitan canons, thus giving way to similar processes of experimentation in different parts of the world.

Ana Longoni

Bibliography

Aguilar G. 2003. *Poesía concreta brasileña: las vanguardias en la encrucijada modernista.* Rosario: Beatriz Viterbo.

Ginzburg C. and Castelnuovo E. 'Centro e periferia', in VVAA 1979. *Storia dell'arte italiana, Part I.* Turin: Einaudi, 283–352.

Ramírez M. C. et al. 2000. *Heterotopías.* Madrid: Museo Nacional Centro de Arte Reina Sofía.

Sarlo B. 1988. *Una modernidad periférica: Buenos Aires, 1920–30.* Buenos Aires: Nueva Visión.

Related essays

Argentina and psychoanalysis; avant garde; literature; modernismo; music; surrealism; tropics; Westernization

Architecture

In modern times, architecture has always been regarded as a discipline fundamentally transnational. From the 18th century, architects embarked on study tours taking them beyond the boundaries of their own countries; starting with the 19th century, specialized publications began to circulate technical and professional knowledge internationally; and during the 20th century, itinerant exhibitions as well as flows of intellectual emigration contributed to the diffusion of architectural modernism.

While many would argue that the mobility of actors and ideas has always been a prerogative of architectural culture, it is fair to say that architecture acquired a transnational character in coincidence with the increase in travel opportunities. Among the possible examples of this tendency, one is the success during the 19th century of pedagogic systems inspired by a limited number of international models, such as the French *beaux-arts* method: these systems were exported worldwide thanks to the expanded circulation of books and magazines (often lavishly illustrated) but also to the concrete possibility of hiring foreign teachers.

During the 20th century, any aura of internationality surrounding architectural design came to be seen as a positive feature by practitioners and theorists alike. In the 1930s, for example, terms such as 'International Style' (coined after a publication by architectural historians Henry-Russell Hitchcock and Philip Johnson and an exhibition at the Museum of Modern Art in New York) defined a tendency to refer to the same set of aesthetic principles on the part of designers active in Europe, North America, and Japan. While they were more the outcome of the cosmopolitanism of the intellectual elites promoting them, phenomena of this kind were soon accelerated by a significant emigration of architects from Nazi Germany, Fascist Italy, Francoist Spain and, later, the Stalinist Soviet Union to North and South America and also to Africa.

In the postwar years, architectural culture crossed new national borders. For instance, well-established Western designers often received commissions outside Europe and North America which, among other things, were meant to help improve local levels of expertise. It is well known that in 1950 the French-Swiss architect Le Corbusier was called upon by Indian authorities to design the new capital of the state of Punjab, Chandigarh. The presence in India of Le Corbusier and several other foreign professionals (such as Albert Mayer, Matthew Nowicki, Maxwell Fry, Jane Drew, and Pierre Jeanneret) influenced more than one generation of South Asian designers.

The Cold War also played a part in intensifying transnational exchanges, despite a general climate characterized by ideological conflicts and international distrust. Operating within their spheres of political influence, both the United States and the Soviet Union supported programmes favoring the mobility of architects and engineers and the transfer of building technologies. These interactions frequently followed the evolving dynamics of the superpowers' foreign policies. For example, the American firm Skidmore, Owings and Merrill was awarded a number of contracts in the 1950s from the US Department of State and the Armed Forces for civilian and military installations in countries whose governments were close allies of the United States; in the 1970s, the same firm received several commissions in the Persian Gulf area.

At any rate, an inner contradiction seems to inform any notion concerning architecture's transnational nature. In general, this trope is challenged by the apparent contrast between the potential mobility of protagonists and ideas and the general immobility of the actual built work. When realized, in fact, architectures must respond to countless restraints, ranging from space limitations and availability of building material to local bylaws (even though these last may have been defined within common international trends). As Donald McNeill has written, 'while the architects and images travel, the buildings remain fixed within local regulatory systems, financial cycles, aesthetic discourses and histories, and political decision-making processes' (McNeill 2005, 502).

Not surprisingly, architecture's alleged transnational character has often been disputed, in particular during the 20th century. Localist and regionalist tendencies have spread out since the 1920s, in particular in countries peripheral to the main cultural centres of the time; in the late 1940s, movements such as the 'Bay Region Style' engineered a response to what was perceived as a lack of reference to local traditions on the part of the 'International Style' and modern architecture

in general, a reaction which also offers another clue to the increased internationalization of the profession in the mid-century; and in the 1980s, architectural critics such as Kenneth Frampton, Alex Tzonis and Liane Lefaivre coined the term 'Critical Regionalism' in order to plead for an approach to design that valorizes the physical and cultural context within which architectures are built, without at the same time abandoning the supposed progressive nature of modern architecture's legacy.

In recent times, architecture's potential transnational character has been further enhanced by the increased diffusion of jet travel, and by the rising importance of computer-aided design (CAD) and inter-office communication (via the Internet). CAD has contributed to the definition of common design standards while the Internet, by reducing the time for data transmission, has altered the conventional need for 'physical contiguity' between design and building. Furthermore, these technological developments have put transnational communication at the centre of a revolution concerning architectural firms' work organization: in fact, as offices in charge of the same projects are often placed in countries in different time zones, the design process can be organized so as to proceed around the clock.

As a consequence of these transformations, work conception, drawings execution and construction can take place in different locations around the world. This is a major innovation, as design offices no longer need to be situated close to major markets: they rather have to be part of transnational networks relating the world's demand for technologically advanced projects to the availability of skilled yet inexpensive labour in countries such as Mexico, South Korea, the Philippines, Malaysia or Indonesia. This form of globalization concerning architectural practice corresponds therefore to a geographical expansion of the professional market in which education is again playing a decisive role. In the United States, for example, large firms with a carnet of international clients draw on a consistent proportion of the nearly 4,500 students graduating each year from accredited architectural schools: significantly, a number of them are foreigners and their presence undoubtedly contributes to further developing transnational professional relations.

This phenomenon has done nothing more than to reinforce already existing tendencies.

Today, design units with hundreds (and sometimes thousands) of employees dominate the international architectural industry. The headquarters of these firms are mainly located in the United States and, to a lesser measure, in Japan, Australia, and the United Kingdom: their geographical spectrum, however, is often worldwide. For example, between 1967 and 2003 the celebrated British architectural firm Norman Foster and Partners (ranked 27th in the world by fee income) received commissions in 18 countries outside the United Kingdom. In this case, a flaunted transnational attitude has helped boost the practice's status among its competitors: as Donald McNeill has written, the case of Norman Foster and Partners is an example of 'a personalized fame and reputation ... that transcends nationalized professional institutions, client knowledge bases and public discourse' (McNeill 2005, 512).

Contemporary architecture's increased inclination towards transnational operations frequently exposes the profession to yet-to-be-solved problems. One deals with the issue of technology transfer: in fact, systems and procedures developed in one context may not work once they are transferred to others. Today's novelty is that these problems affect not only underdeveloped (or less developed) countries but also developed ones. A recent tendency in the United States has seen a mounting number of developers choosing to outsource important portions of the building work. This also happens when clients draw on non-American designers who resort to technical solutions unfamiliar to the local building industry. In the famous case of the Modern Art Museum of Fort Worth, Texas, designed by the Japanese architect Tadao Ando, after roughly 50 American contractors refused to bid on the job due to the apparent complexity of realizing faultless concrete surfaces as requested by the designer, the Museum's building committee hired a specialized company overseas.

Much emphasis has been placed on the current phenomenon of globalization to explain the transformations that have affected architectural culture in recent years. However, these changes have merely protracted already existing trends: architecture has always lain in an unstable equilibrium between national and transnational cultural and professional attitudes. What is probably new is the rising role played by transnational audiences in the reception of 'iconic' architectures, thanks largely to a wider circulation of information, as is well demonstrated by the worldwide notoriety achieved by works like the Guggenheim Museum in Bilbao, Spain. Phenomena of this kind raise relevant questions not only about the evolution of architectural design but also on how architectural aesthetics will develop in the near future.

Paolo Scrivano

Bibliography

Kentgens-Craig M. 1999. *The Bauhaus and America: first contacts, 1919–1936.* Cambridge, MA and London: MIT Press.

Knox P. L. and Taylor P. J. 2005. 'Toward a geography of the globalization of architecture office networks', *Journal of Architectural Education,* 58, 3, 23–32.

McNeill D. 2005. 'In search of the global architect: the case of Norman Foster (and Partners)', *International Journal of Urban and Regional Research,* 29, 3, 501–15.

Scrivano P. 2001. *Storia di un'idea di architettura moderna: Henry-Russell Hitchcock e l'International Style.* Milan: FrancoAngeli.

Related essays

cities; city planning; design; engineering; exile; expositions; information technology (IT) offshoring; intellectual elites; *non-lieux*; Skidmore, Owings and Merrill; technical assistance

Skidmore, Owings and Merrill

Founded in 1936 in Chicago by Louis Skidmore and Nathaniel Owings, the firm Skidmore, Owings and Merrill (SOM) is among the world's most recognized architectural practices. While not the largest existing design company (in 2003 the magazine *World Architecture* ranked it seventh by fee income), SOM is generally regarded as one with the most marked international profile. Organized in eight offices, five in the US (New York, Chicago, Washington, Los Angeles, and San Francisco) and three abroad (London, Hong Kong, and Shanghai), in 70 years of activity SOM has realized projects in more than 40 countries. The list of realizations includes landmarks such as the Hancock Tower in Chicago (1974) or Canary Wharf in London (1993) and large infrastructures like the Abdul Aziz airport in Jeddah, Saudi Arabia (1981). Whether SOM represents the best example of a truly transnational architectural office, however, remains rather difficult to assert: in fact, only 7 per cent of the more than 1,800 projects elaborated by the firm from 1936 to 1980 were located outside the United States and Canada. SOM owes its worldwide reputation mainly to the notoriety it acquired in the postwar years, when it became one of the major exponents of international modernism in architecture. The Lever House, built in New York in 1952, came to be seen as one of the best examples of corporate building, in particular because it proposed a model, as the architectural historian Henry-Russell Hitchcock wrote in 1961, for 'international reproduction'. SOM's most important contribution to the development of a transnational architectural culture, though, probably relates to the working methodology: in fact, the firm's internal organization became the template for many architectural offices around the world.

Paolo Scrivano

Bibliography
1980. *Skidmore, Owings and Merrill*. New York: SOM.
Adams N. 2006. *Skidmore, Owings and Merrill: SOM dal 1936*. Milan: Electa.

Related essays
architecture; information technology (IT) offshoring; law firms; organization models

Argentina and psychoanalysis

Buenos Aires in Argentina is considered today the 'world capital of psychoanalysis'. What is less well known is the role played by the heterogeneous Argentine psychoanalytic community in the transnational diffusion of psychoanalysis.

In 1942 Spanish émigré Ángel Garma gathered a group of five Argentine and foreign doctors and created the Argentine Psychoanalytic Association (APA), the first one in Latin America to be fully recognized by the International Psychoanalytic Association. The Association not only laid the foundation for the diffusion of psychoanalysis in the country, but also became a centre of dissemination of psychoanalytic practice and ideas throughout Latin America and also in Europe. Psychoanalytic associations in Uruguay, Brazil and Mexico emerged as offshoots of the Argentine association. Analysts from those countries travelled routinely to Argentina for

training while Argentine analysts established themselves there.

Also less well known is the fact that APA analysts played a central role in the reception of British analyst Melanie Klein's (1882–1960) ideas (in the Argentine version) in France and of Jacques Lacan's (1901–81) ideas in Spain. The APA was considered one of the most orthodox 'Kleinian' associations in the world: Argentine analysts kept close contact with Klein and travelled to England for training, psychoanalysis and supervision. In the meantime young French philosopher Willy Baranger established himself in Buenos Aires, where he acquired analytic training and became a very active member of the APA. His (and Swiss-born analyst Enrique Pichon Rivière's) contacts with French analyst Daniel Lagache during the 1950s made possible the publication in Paris of Argentine Kleinian analysts' works (including two books by Ángel Garma) before Klein's own works were available in French translation.

In the 1960s there emerged in Buenos Aires a group of Lacanian analysts led by philosopher / art critic Oscar Masotta (1930–79). Unlike APA analysts, Masotta and most of his followers were not medical doctors. Masotta did not even hold a formal university degree. During the last Argentine military dictatorship (1976–83) Masotta went to Spain as a political exile. There he introduced Lacan's version of psychoanalysis, thus injecting life into the Spanish analytic community which was barely recovering from the long Franco dictatorship. Both the Spanish and the Argentine Lacanian communities recognize Masotta as their 'founding father'. The cycle was closed: it was a Spanish political exile who introduced orthodox Freudian (and Kleinian) psychoanalysis into Argentina, and it was an Argentine political exile who introduced Lacanian orthodoxy into Spain.

Mariano Ben Plotkin

Bibliography
Dagfal A. 'Paris-London-Buenos Aires: the adventures of Kleinian psychoanalysis between Europe and South America', in Damousi J. and Plotkin M. (eds) 2008. *The transnational unconscious: essays in the history of psychoanalysis and transnationalism*. Basingstoke: Palgrave Macmillan.
Plotkin M. 2001. *Freud in the Pampas: the emergence and development of a psychoanalytic*

culture in Argentina. Stanford: Stanford
University Press.

Related essays
cultural capitals; exile; kindergarten;
psychoanalysis

Armenian genocide

The extermination and expulsions of
Armenians from eastern Anatolia in 1915–16,
commonly referred to as the Armenian genocide, was a truly transnational phenomenon.
Taking seriously the transnational dimension
is imperative for making sense of the evolution of the Committee of Union and Progress
(CUP), the ruling party in the Ottoman government, in its destruction policy which
claimed the lives of at least 600,000 victims in
the dying days of the Ottoman Empire.

Three transnational processes are of particular significance: (1) norm diffusion; (2)
regional disintegration, and (3) interstate
war. Each is of immediate relevance for
explaining the twisted path of the Armenian
genocide. The concatenation of these (and
related) processes illuminates the frequently
obscured dynamics of contention within the
beleaguered empire.

Take nationalism. The reception of this
quintessentially Occidental norm, and the
successes of nationalist movements in Italy
and Germany, spurred on the exclusionary
variant of nationalism ('Turkification') pursued by the CUP. Yet the appeal of nationalism
affected not just the CUP, but the Armenian
community (and other subject peoples of the
empire) as well. In some respects, two duelling nationalisms, and the excesses committed by extremists within each movement,
created the background conditions for the
orchestration of a violent, eventually genocidal campaign. The genocide was not provoked by its victims, but the mobilization of
nationalist ideas in Anatolia undoubtedly
shaped the dynamics thereof.

The spillover of military cultural norms
of 'institutional extremism' from Imperial
Germany (where they had first found expression in the destruction of the Herero in South
West Africa, 1904–07), too, left a mark, notably on the genocidal practices of the so-called
Special Organization, a mixed military-CUP
institution. Several German military officers
(although for the most part wary of the cumulative radicalization of CUP policy) advised

the Turkish 3rd Army to deport Armenian
civilians in an attempt to advance the Ottoman
war effort in World War 1. Such final solutions were increasingly appealing in the context of regional disintegration, the second
transnational process that was intractably
associated with the atrocities committed by
Ottomans against Armenians.

The CUP's commitment to rationalization
and centralization – and eventually the ethnic homogenization of the 'Turkish' nation –
promised to stave off the disintegration of
the Ottoman Empire, to ensure the territorial integrity of the state. Borrowed from the
West, it was the Young Turks' (members of
the CUP) solution to the problem of institutional design. The further the declining
empire was pushed out of Europe, the more
visible within it – and targeted – were the
Armenians as a community of 'Others'. It
would be inaccurate, however, to conclude
that extermination rather than centralization was on the Young Turk agenda from the
outset. Inasmuch as elements within the CUP
(particularly those aligned with Talât Paşa,
Bahaettin Şakir, and the Central Committee)
coordinated and perpetrated mass atrocities,
indeed genocide, no a priori blueprint for a
genocidal campaign appears to have existed.
To be sure, this account questions only the
validity of monocausal explanation – not the
responsibility of the Young Turk government
for the atrocities perpetrated against the
Armenians.

If we believe recent scholarship, it was,
above all, the internationalization of the
'Armenian question' that provided the necessary impetus for the cumulative radicalization of CUP ideology, and the consideration,
within the CUP Central Committee, of elimi-
nationist practices. A proximate cause of the
Armenian genocide was World War 1. It transformed latent contention into manifest, violent contention. Significant was the Ottoman
fear that Armenian leaders and their brethren
were colluding with the Entente powers –
Russia, Britain, and France. The spread of
an imperialist norm among these Great
Powers had spawned a brand of interventionism that did its share to radicalize the Young
Turk leadership, contributing to a security
dilemma in the context of which a genocidal
campaign became increasingly desirable. The
vehemence of the CUP's practice of 'absolute
destruction', as we have seen, was owed in
part to German military culture.

The 1915–16 Armenian genocide, we might say, was the result of structured contingency. It was mediated, and affected decisively, by the interplay of several transnational processes. These gave rise to incentives that shaped CUP choices, and thus the causes – and courses – of collective violence in the final days of the Ottoman Empire. Aside from the near-destruction of a stigmatized community, the genocide left an indelible mark on the region. Aside from hastening the rise of exclusionary nationalism – and collective violence – in the Caucasus, where thousands of Armenian survivors had found refuge, the genocide popularized in the post-World War I world the use of massacres and population transfers (cf. CUP deportations of Greeks and Kurds from eastern Anatolia in 1916–17) as means in pursuit of the homogenization of peoples – be they Turkish, Azeri, Georgian, or, indeed, Armeni.

Jens Meierhenrich

Bibliography

Bloxham D. 2005. *The Great Game of genocide: imperialism, nationalism, and the destruction of the Ottoman Armenians*. Oxford: Oxford University Press.

Dadrian V. N. 1993. 'The secret Young-Turk Ittihadist conference and the decision for the World War I genocide of the Armenians', *Holocaust and Genocide Studies*, 7, 2, 173–201.

Hull I .V. 2005. *Absolute destruction: military culture and the practices of war in Imperial Germany*. Ithaca: Cornell University Press.

Karpat K. H. 2001. *The politicization of Islam: reconstructing identity, state, faith, and community in the late Ottoman State*. Oxford: Oxford University Press.

Related essays
diasporas; empires and imperialism; ethnicity and race; forced migrations; genocide; Holocaust; human rights; nation and state; refugees; Westernization; world orders

Arms sales

Arms sales are a substantial and politically sensitive component of international trade, with implications for security, economics and technology transfer, which are subject to regulation by national governments and intergovernmental organisations.

It is common to classify arms into: weapons of mass destruction (nuclear, biological, chemical); major weapons systems (tanks, fighter aircraft, warships, etc); small arms and light weapons; services (those provided by private military companies in Iraq and elsewhere have become increasingly important); and dual-use systems, which have both a civilian and military function. Much military technology is dual use, including the nuclear, biological and chemical technologies and this poses problems of classification. Definitional difficulties and secrecy make measuring the trade problematic. Over the period 2000–04, the Stockholm International Peace Research Institute (SIPRI) estimates that arms exports were around $20 billion a year, in 1990 prices, with the US and Russia accounting for around half the exports. Using a somewhat different definition and measurement procedure, the US Congressional Research Service estimated 2004 agreements to export arms at $37 billion, in 2004 prices, and deliveries at $34 billion; with about 60 per cent going to developing countries: China, India and Egypt being large importers. China is also a significant exporter. The UN introduced a register of conventional arms transfers in 1992, but not all countries report fully.

Because more advanced weapons give a potential advantage to adversaries, restriction on their transfer has been common: in the 8th century Charlemagne declared the death penalty for Frankish merchants selling swords to Vikings. Organized arms production on a large scale, e.g. in naval dockyards and royal arsenals, has a long history; but the modern arms industry dates from the mid 19th century and from the beginning it was global. Nobel's dynamite and cordite, both dual-use systems, were produced in subsidiaries around the world. Technological developments in metals production in the second half of the 19th century were rapidly applied to arms by Krupp in Germany and Armstrong and Vickers in Britain, all of whom relied heavily on foreign sales. Sir Hiram Maxim, an American operating in Europe, sold his guns all over the world. By the beginning of the 20th century there was a dense multinational network of interlinked arms firms and specialized arms merchants, who emulated Krupp, Armstrong and Maxim. George Bernard Shaw's play of 1905, *Major Barbara*, addresses the issues of international arms manufacture as perceived in the early 20th century.

Before the First World War, the thriving international arms trade was largely unregulated, but subsequently many blamed these 'merchants of death' for the war itself. In the interwar period there were a series of inter-governmental initiatives to restrain the arms trade and individual countries began to pass laws regulating arms exports. These were of limited effectiveness. During the Second World War there were vast arms transfers particularly from the US to the UK, initially under lend-lease, and from the US to the Soviet Union. After the Second World War, the arms trade was shaped by the Cold War, particularly in three transnational dimensions. First, each side tried to prevent military technology flowing to the other. In the West this was organized by the Coordinating Committee for Multilateral Export Controls (COCOM) which tried to restrict the transfer of arms and dual-use technologies to Communist countries. Second, each side wanted to ensure that its allies were well armed, because this improved the quality of defence. Third, each side hoped that by providing arms to non-aligned countries they could be aligned a little more closely. The motives at this stage were largely political and transfers were often heavily subsidized.

In the later 20th century, commercial factors became more important. Selling nations hoped to use arms exports to maintain their defence industrial base in the face of fluctuating domestic demand, spread the large fixed costs of developing major weapons systems over more units, and to maintain a technological lead. This was particularly a feature of French policy, where systems were designed with export markets in mind, rather than the needs of the domestic armed forces. Countries buying arms also hoped to acquire technology, and agreements by the exporter to offset the arms sale by purchases from the importer were a common feature of contracts. Arms export contracts are complicated packages that include not just the weapons systems themselves, but munitions, spares and training. They are often paid for by counter-trade, barter (the UK Al Yamamah arms export package to Saudi Arabia is paid for in oil); have associated offsets (e.g. the seller promising to set up production in the buyer country); and may be financed by soft loans from government-supported agencies like the UK Export Credit Guarantee Department. Most governments also have agencies, like the UK Defence Export Services Organisation, to facilitate sales. Evidence on the financial details of arms contracts is scarce. The contract is usually part of a long-term relationship since the weapons will need munitions, spares, upgrades, etc. in the future. A crucial part of the relationship will be whether the supplier is willing to continue supply in time of conflict. Because the market is so competitive, the profitability of arms sales is questionable. In 2003 the French government instructed arms suppliers not to offer products at prices below production cost in order to win contracts. The $3.4 billion 1993 order for 436 Leclerc tanks from the United Arab Emirates (UAE) resulted in a loss of $1.2 billion for France.

Immediately after the Second World War it was common for national arms firms to be almost an extension of the state, and often to be publicly owned. In the later 20th century there has been a trend for the arms firms to become increasingly independent of their national governments, a move that was initially taken to increase the efficiency of weapons production. As competition grows in the international arms market, arms firms become more internationalized and collaborative projects between countries, such as Typhoon/Eurofighter, become more common. Most high-technology industries which require large investments in R&D are concentrated and globalized. This was not the case in the arms industry because of the desire by national governments to protect their national defence industrial base. The SIPRI list of the hundred largest arms-producing firms showed that in 1990 the five largest firms accounted for 22 per cent of the market. This is a very small percentage compared to other high-technology industries: e.g. two companies, Boeing and Airbus, dominate the manufacture of large civil aircraft. The end of the Cold War was followed by a merger wave in the arms industry. Now multinational arms firms operating in a number of countries, like Thales, BAE Systems, EADS, and Lockheed Martin, are starting to appear. In 2003 the five largest firms accounted for 44 per cent of the market. Although concentration has doubled, it is still not high by comparison with similar civilian markets. However, concentration and internationalization create difficulties for governments who can no longer rely on a national defence industrial base.

Increased competition can go along with increased concentration, fewer firms. As competition increases, profit margins fall and the weaker firms are driven out, leaving the remainder to compete more ferociously. Because the US has the largest military R&D budget its weapons tend to be the most technologically advanced and because they are produced in large numbers this gives their manufacturers a cost advantage; hence the US dominance of the arms trade. However, the US tends to impose restrictions on technology transfer and on the use or transfer of the equipment. Thus other suppliers may appear more attractive to importers who fear political and technological dependence on the US.

Arms exports are almost universally regulated by national governments on the basis of certain criteria. A typical set of criteria is given in the 1991 guidelines agreed by the five permanent members of the UN Security Council. These indicate that restrictions on exports are required where the transfer would be likely to: prolong or aggravate an existing armed conflict; increase tension in a region or contribute to instability; introduce destabilizing military capabilities; contravene embargoes or other relevant internationally agreed restraints; be used other than for the legitimate defence and security needs of the recipient state; support or encourage international terrorism; be used to interfere with the internal affairs of sovereign states; or seriously undermine the recipient state's economy. Exports may also be restricted if the transfer has an adverse effect on national security of the exporter or other countries; facilitates internal repression or breaches of human rights; or encourages the proliferation of weapons of mass destruction. These criteria are quite vague and involve subjective judgements. For instance, the European Union (EU) imposed an arms embargo on China after the 1989 Tiananmen Square massacre. During 2003–04 there was a substantial dispute among EU members about whether the embargo should be lifted. Those in favour of lifting it argued that it would help to engage China in dialogue, those against argued that China had not shown sufficient improvements in human rights. In any event, when the embargo was imposed no list of items covered by the term 'arms' had been agreed. Deciding what was covered by the embargo was left to individual EU states, who differed in their interpretation. In addition to national regulation there are a variety of informal multilateral transfer control regimes by supplier countries. These include the Nuclear Suppliers Group, the Australia Group (chemical weapons), the Missile Technology Control Regime, the Wassenaar Arrangement (conventional weapons) and the EU Code of Conduct on arms transfers. There are also more formal agreements like the Treaty on the Non-Proliferation of Nuclear Weapons.

Controls over arms transfers may have unintended consequences. States subject to embargo or control, or who fear that they may be subject to embargo in the future, may develop their own arms industry to produce the weapons that they cannot import. South Africa is an example and the French embargo on Israel also increased the Israeli desire for domestic self-sufficiency. States subject to export controls may also develop weapons of mass destruction to substitute for or to supplement conventional weapons; again Israel and South Africa are examples. As in any industry, high prices and restricted supply encourage new entrants. States that are tightly coupled into the international community may be deterred by the reputational cost of illegitimate transfers. But where the international community has little leverage over a state, it may become a major source of illegitimate supply, while embargoes invariably prompt the development of embargo-busting networks. In addition, there is a large illicit and poorly documented trade in small arms and light weapons as well as an international market for military scientists, particularly those with nuclear expertise. The transnational dimensions of arms sales and of arms traffic are likely to remain a matter of continuing concern.

Ron P. Smith

Bibliography

Sampson A. 1991. *The arms bazaar*. London: Hodder and Stoughton.

Stockholm International Peace Research Institute, annual. *World armaments and disarmament*. Oxford: Oxford University Press.

The Congressional Research Services Reports on arms exports, and other discussion of the arms trade: www.fas.org.

Arms trafficking

Although the legal arms trade has dwarfed the illicit or illegal flow of weapons of war around the world, arms trafficking increased in significance at the end of the 20th century as weapons from this trade fuelled civil wars and concern grew over nuclear terrorism.

The black market in arms has resulted from the use of embargoes and the appearance of national and international laws regulating arms sales. Uncommon before the 19th century, arms trafficking increased as states began to employ embargoes regularly to suppress the slave trade and revolution and to regulate the sale of arms. One of the earliest international arms control agreements was the Brussels Act of 1890, but the First World War and the growing stigma attached to private arms dealers as 'merchants of death' who sought profit out of war increased pressure for further arms control measures. The United Kingdom established a comprehensive licensing system for arms exports in 1921. In the United States, the Neutrality Act of 1935, which established the Munitions Control Board, was the first attempt to regulate the arms trade thoroughly.

Cold War competition between the United States and the Soviet Union fostered a grey market of covert government supply of arms to insurgents. By the 1980s, with the implementation of the Reagan Doctrine, American intelligence agencies were smuggling arms to countries such as Afghanistan, Cambodia, Angola, and Nicaragua. These covert supply networks created opportunities for secondary black markets. For example, Pakistani intelligence agencies diverted a portion of the weapons meant for the muhajideen in Afghanistan and resold them on the black market. The 1970s and 1980s saw another transformation in arms trafficking led by the Soviet Union and South Africa in which embargoed governments switched their illicit acquisitions from the buying of whole weaponry to the transfer of manufacturing technology, which often possessed a dual application for arms making and other production.

Arms trafficking probably reached its peak in the 1980s in reaction to embargoes imposed on Iran, South Africa and Lebanon. The adoption of end-use certificates by governments almost everywhere in the late 1980s turned most of the black market into a grey market of secret or illicit deals with real or nominal government sanction. Virtually any arms transfer could obtain at least superficial government sanction through bribes to states willing to issue fraudulent end-use certificates. Around the same time, arms trafficking received a further boost when a number of developing countries, notably Egypt, Iran, Iraq, Libya, Pakistan, and Syria, increased their efforts to obtain technologies for nuclear and chemical weapons and ballistic missiles. One of the more notorious illicit networks for transferring nuclear technology was run by the Pakistani scientist Abdul Qadeer Khan from the late 1980s until the network was exposed and dismantled in 2003.

Since the 1980s, illicit arms trafficking has become a more prominent source for arms used in civil wars, mostly in the form of small arms and light weapons. The end of the Cold War left large surpluses of these arms available for sale. Late in the Cold War, new producers of small arms emerged in countries such as Israel, China, Brazil, South Africa, and Czechoslovakia. Freer trade also reduced obstacles to illicit arms flows through reduced regulation and oversight. Areas struck by civil war such as Cambodia, Lebanon, the Horn of Africa, and the Afghan–Pakistan border region – where controls on arms flows disappeared – became arms exporters themselves in the 1990s.

By the 1990s, some experts estimated the value of trafficked arms to be second only to that of drugs despite further efforts at international regulation. In 1992, the United Nations implemented a register of conventional arms transfers. Regional arms control efforts included the 1997 Organization of American States Convention on the Illicit Manufacture and Trade in Firearms and the European Union's 1998 Code of Conduct on arms exports. A number of non-governmental organizations such as Human Rights Watch united their efforts to regulate the flow of small arms, the weapons most likely to be used in civil wars and traded illicitly, in an umbrella campaign, the International Action Network on Small Arms.

Sahr Conway-Lanz

Bibliography

Lumpe L. (ed.). 2000. *Running guns: the global black market in small arms.* London: Zed.

Related essays

arms sales; Cold War; crime; drugs (illicit); international non-governmental organizations (INGOs); legal order; war; world orders

Art market

The art market is the current system by which art is traded. It has two main components: Antique (antiques and collectables) and Contemporary. It encompasses luxury items (jewellery, precious plates, antique furniture) and works of art (paintings, drawings, tapestries, engravings, manuscripts). The art market puts into contact many institutions in many countries: museums, auction houses, private galleries, international art fairs (Basel, Cologne) as well as individuals: dealers, collectors, critics, curators and artists. The principal organ of the art market is the system of auctions that can be traced back to antiquity, together with the trading of artistic objects (despite the absence of a formalized and specialized art market). The term 'auctioneers' designates today the experts in charge of organizing public sales, operating under different names in different countries.

It is generally agreed that the principal characteristics of the art market emerged during the French Revolution when the first borders between a work of art and all other human production and art criticism first appeared. But it is only from the second half of the 19th century that the national markets started to interact. The present structures of the art market were now progressively put in place. Competing centres of the market, that did not always coincide with the centres of artistic production like Paris, London and New York, attracted international flows of artists, collectors and dealers who wanted to be where prices and trends were set. There was also a marked increase in the number of museums and fairs, where art from different countries could be shown, sold and bought. Market organs, namely the principal auction houses, began to function as multinational corporations. Sotheby's, created in London in 1733, opened its first New York office in 1955. Listed on the New York stock exchange since 1977, it now counts more than 100 offices around the world. Its rival Christie's, founded in 1766, opened its first overseas office in Rome in 1958 and its New York office in 1977; it now counts more than 110 offices in 42 countries, 16 of these offices carrying out their own auctions. Last but not least, a major evolution was the development of the 'worlds of art'. In the sociological perspective of Howard Becker, 'worlds of art' refers to the social spaces where art was discussed, disputed and priced: international art magazines, private art galleries, art foundations and alternative exhibition spaces developed together with a growingly segmented professional sphere of art experts. The history of the art market of these last 150 years is the history of its globalization. It is linked to the history of the internationalization of business as well as that of the technical and social changes put in place since the second half of the 19th century which marks for example the advent of the methods of displacement on a large scale, the Universal Exhibitions, the democratization of culture, as well as the appearance of easel painting in the artistic domain.

The global model defining the current art market can only be understood through the consideration of these transformations. This global model seems to have integrated all the economic and technical mechanisms of the globalization of transactions. Sparked off by the dematerialization of art-investing financial flows, the number of auctions grew considerably from the mid-1980s and resulted in a considerable increase in the flow of traded items (between 1800 and 1970, 5,000 to 6,000 paintings were publicly traded every year. Today, the number has risen to 50,000). At the same time, a 'deterritorialization' of the market also took place, prompted by a consideration of the differences between national taxations and legislations with regard to works of art. The art market seems to have also adopted the human characteristics of globalization as well in terms of functioning in individual and professional networks and speed in the flow of information (even if what Howard Becker calls 'disinformation' exists, as is the case in all potentially speculative markets).

The painting art market appears to crystallize remarkably and paroxysmally these transformations which marked the end of the juxtaposition of national markets and the birth of a global art market. Preceded by the system of Guilds (during the Middle Ages) and the system of the Academy (after the Renaissance), the new market system placed the trade of painting at the intersection of two fields: the economic field which establishes the monetary value (the price) on the transaction market and the artistic field which determines, according to its own value appraisal, the artistic legitimacy of the work. Therefore, one of the essential characteristics of this system is its foundation on two opposing dynamics: on one hand, the fluid nature of economic transactions and on the other hand, the necessary duration that any legitimization of artistic value implies. Thus, the painting art market connects two opposing temporalities: the short term – *hic nunc* – of the financial markets and the long term of artistic consecration.

Since the early 20th century, the painting art market has been modelled progressively on the structure of the stock exchange. A recent striking feature is that the painting market has been generating all sorts of indexes constructed on the model of stock market indexes, based on reference works and ratings of painters. In 1970 a German specialized magazine, *Capital*, created an indicator of artistic recognition of the one hundred most important contemporary artists called *Kunst Kompass*. Sotheby's also publishes a monthly *Art Index* as an indicator of artistic value. In 1997, Artprice.com was founded in order to collect information from all public sales in the world. Its internet site publishes in real time the indexes of price evolutions of all types of works of art. In the current art market, investors can also acquire parts of an atypical financial product based on 'arts' funds established by banks from a collection of paintings or drawings. Thus, in the same way that banks play the role of museums, museums play the role of banks: 'in the same way that a gold fund is necessary for the public cover of the Bank of France in order to allow circulation of capital and private speculation, the fixed reserve of the museum is necessary in order for the exchange/sign of paintings to function' (Baudrillard, 1972, 142).

However, in the beginning of the 19th century this 'fixed reserve of the museum' only concerned ancient art and 'consecrated art'. It is only during the 19th century that a major reversal takes place: 'art in the midst of its own creation' acquires henceforth its liberty no longer under the regime of the commission, but under the regime of the market. This emancipation from the commission signifies fundamentally an emancipation from the canonical models of art presented in the museums and the salons and, in turn, permits the commercialization of what can be named the 'art of rupture' or 'art of the avant-garde' whose history is inextricably linked with the advent of the 'modern dealer'. This new figure's monopolistic ambition can be exemplified through individuals like Paul Durand-Ruel (1831–1922) for Impressionism, Ambroise Vollard (1868–1939) for Matisse and Gauguin, and Daniel-Henry Kahnweiler (1884–1979) for Cubism. These dealers took charge not only of the survival of these artists but also their media coverage, using cross-national networks of critics and collectors to ensure their artistic consecration. One of the characteristics of this globalized market system therefore appeared: an interchange of roles side by side with the co-existence of an internationalization of the dealer circuit (international networks of galleries, critics) and an internationalization of cultural institutions. The dealer is at the same time critic, collector, curator. The artist is also sometimes entrepreneur, sometimes dealer, collector and/or critic.

The history of the commercialization of the 'art of the avant-garde,' however, is also inevitably linked to the history of the 20th century with its economic crises, but above all with its dark times of war which engendered the exile of numerous artists and collectors to the United States as well as the displacement of numerous works in occupied countries. There was an increased escalation of the numerous transatlantic shifts that had begun at the end of the 1870s. Among the effects of these transatlantic flows are the appearance of the great modern dealers in New York: Samuel Kootz for abstract expressionism who inaugurated as of Christmas 1949 a new sales technique inspired by commercial marketing or Léo Castelli known for his support for the artists of the Pop Art movement. The establishment of New York as a new centre of art from the 1950s was the main consequence of these shifts.

If the recent history of the art market is that of its globalization following on the model of a stock market that delineated its own boundaries amidst a seemingly 'transnational' space, the recent history of the art market is also that of its links to the idea of nation. Indeed, the conception of 'art' as a performative receptacle of the 'genius of the nation', which in addition to its preservation would also actualize its own power, permeates the history of art of the last two centuries. The 'global space' is shaped through and plays around with different national legislations. Despite the globalization of the artistic scene and of the art market, it is acknowledged that the globalization of art, which is accompanied by a universalist discourse, maintains and reproduces the distinctions between 'countries that dictate' and 'countries that follow', in the same way that the globalization of the art market arguably maintains and reproduces the cartography of the world economy. This global art market does not imply necessarily the abolition of the notions of 'centres' and 'peripheries', neither does it imply the elimination of the economic and artistic domination that these notions suppose on a large scale, particularly concerning the North/South axis. The global dimension of the art market is thus not enforced against or without the national variable, but enmeshes with it into the very depths of its mechanisms.

Monia Abdallah

Bibliography

Baudrillard J. 1972. *Pour une critique de l'économie politique du signe.* Paris: Gallimard.

Bertrand-Dorléac L. (ed.) 1992. *Le commerce de l'art de la Renaissance à nos jours.* Besançon: La Manufacture.

Guilbaut S. 1983. *How New York stole the idea of modern art.* Chicago: University of Chicago Press.

Moulin R. 2003. *Le marché de l'art. Mondialisation et nouvelles technologies.* Paris: Flammarion.

Quemin A. 2002. *L'art contemporain international, entre les institutions et le marché.* Paris: Jacqueline Chambon.

Related essays

avant garde; cultural capitals; exile; expositions; financial markets; literary capitals; literature; museums; surrealism; trade; war

Asia

Although the notion of an Asian continent was constructed mostly in European intellectual history to refer to a broad geographical area whose borders were arbitrarily defined, the idea of Asia became a powerful transnational force during the last quarter of the 19th century, inspiring the global imagination of various forms of nationalisms, social movements and diasporas throughout the 20th century.

According to today's predominant geographical construction of the seven continents of the globe, Asia is the largest continent, containing more than half of the world's population. The origin of the term 'Asia' goes back to Ancient Greece, where Asia denoted the areas across the Aegean Sea from Greece, being separated from Africa by the Nile River. Medieval European geographers attributed to the Greeks' view of three continents, Europe, Asia and Africa, a religious connotation by linking each continent with a child of Noah. During the Renaissance period, these early Greek names and the basic continental scheme were given scientific status by geographers and were utilized as an authoritative frame to categorize human societies and their characteristics. In the aftermath of the age of discoveries, geographers suggested new boundaries for Asia; thus the Asia–Africa boundary was set by the Red Sea and the Europe–Asia boundary was changed from the Don River to the Ural Mountains. For example, it was a Swedish military officer of the 18th century, Philipp-Johann von Strahlenberg, who first proposed the Ural Mountains as a border, which was then supported by the intellectuals around Peter the Great's Westernization programme, and gradually embraced by other geographers in Europe. Despite various critiques of these newly suggested borders, the Ural Mountain and Red Sea boundaries set for Asia survived and gained universal acceptance by the late 19th century. More importantly, in the second half of the 19th century, each continent was paired with racial characteristics, identifying Europe as the land of whites, Africa as that of black people and Asia as the land of yellow people. With the gradual invention of the continental imagination of Asia over the centuries, Siberia, Kuwait or Vietnam were then considered part of the same continent of Asia, although separate segments of the imagined Asian continent had very little shared cultural or historical background.

Before the experiences of Eurocentric globalization of the 19th century, various segments of the Asian continent already had transnational and transregional links. The predominantly Muslim parts of West and Central Asia, together with the Muslim populations of South Asia and China, shared various levels of Muslim networks of trade, education, literature and pilgrimage. In fact, these Muslim networks were instrumental in connecting East and South Asia to different parts of the African and European continents. Similar to the networks fostered by Islamic faith and Arabic language, Buddhism and more importantly China-centred Confucianism and Chinese writing culture created powerful networks in East Asia, facilitating the exchange of ideas, goods and human travel in a large region extending from Korea and Japan to India and Southeast Asia. Both the overland silk road and the sea silk road trades further established multiple layers of connectivity among different parts of Asia, linking them to Africa and Europe as well. Yet, until the late 19th century, there was no shared consciousness of being Asian or belonging to a specific continent even among the most active members of these various Asia-wide networks, such as, for example, the Yemeni-originated Hadramaut merchant diaspora in South and Southeast Asia.

During the second half of the 19th century, when the Eurocentric notions of continents, races and civilizations became globalized and spread to different societies in Asia, Asian identity was embraced by individuals and social groups from Turkey and Iran to China and Japan for a multitude of political, social and cultural reasons. Thus, by the turn of the 20th century, Iranian, Turkish, Japanese, Indian, Chinese, or Vietnamese intellectuals would not only perceive themselves as belonging to the same continent, but also believed that they shared similar characteristics of race, history, values and political destiny due to their continental identity. The best indication of how transnational Asian identity became politically and culturally relevant can be seen in the history of Pan-Asian ideology and trends from the 1880s to the 1950s.

The increasing intensity of travel made possible by the 19th-century revolution in transportation and communication technologies, coupled with the spread of Eurocentric categories of knowledge of human geography, became two main pillars of the emergence of Asian identity. Hence, various Buddhist groups in Asia began to travel to other Buddhist lands after they became familiar with the emerging European literature of the history of Buddhism. Thanks to these intra-Asian Buddhist travels and

dialogues, Buddhists from Japan to Sri Lanka contributed to the formation of a modern Buddhist canon and facilitated a new Pan-Asian Buddhist identity that was best reflected in the 1893 Chicago World Parliament of Religions. Similarly, although there already existed premodern Muslim networks, it was only during the mid 19th century that the Muslims of West Asia began to frequently visit, write and read about Muslims in China or Southeast Asia, leading to the formation of a new consciousness about an Asia-centred Muslim world. The new Asian dimension in transnational Buddhist, Confucian and Muslim identities was often defined in relation and response to the European and 'Christian' identity of the imperial powers.

The idea of the solidarity among Asian societies against the perceived threat of Western expansion emerged around the late 1870s, primarily in the Chinese cultural zone of East Asia. Yet, in three decades, the ideal of Asian solidarity and the scope of imagined Asian cooperation expanded to the whole Asian continent. The first Pan-Asianists of the 1880s argued that, although globalization was a positive development that would bring progress and prosperity to Asia, European imperial domination over Asia was preventing Asian societies from benefiting from the blessings of this process. Thus, early Asianists suggested that Asian societies should cooperate with each other first to gain their independence from European colonialism so that ultimately they could achieve higher levels of civilization and progress on their own initiative. When the first Pan-Asianist organization in East Asia, Kôakai (Revive Asia Society) was established in 1880, its members were almost all from China, Korea and Japan. But gradually, new Pan-Asianist organizations included figures from India, West Asia and Southeast Asia. In fact, one of the most important books on Pan-Asianism, The Awakening of the East, was written by a Japanese intellectual, Okakura Tenshin, during his trip to India in 1901, in the context of his conversations with Rabindranath Tagore and other Indian intellectuals of Bengal. The two most famous early Pan-Asian intellectuals, Tenshin and Tagore were both very well connected to the European intellectual trends pessimistic about Western civilization and in search of an alternative in what they considered as Asian spirituality. This underlines the continuing relevance of an Orientalist East–West dichotomy in the reproduction of Asian identity in new political meanings. Early advocates of Asian solidarity also showed interest in the historical achievements of Asian civilizations to counter the narratives of Eurocentric world history, emphasizing that Asia, imagined as a continental unity, contributed immensely to world progress and spirituality, and thus Asians should not be considered racially or civilizationally inferior and in need of the 'civilizing mission' of the European empires.

It is the broader context of responding to the imperial-era European notions of white-race or Western civilizational superiority and their scientific pretensions that made the Russo–Japanese War of 1905 a truly global moment in cherishing a new identity of 'Awakening Asia'. Nationalists from Turkey, Egypt and Iran, to India, Vietnam and China celebrated the Japanese victory as a victory of Asians in general, and a proof that the yellow race and East Asians are not inferior to white-race Europeans. The fact that Turks, Egyptians and Iranians would look to the Japanese and Chinese as fellow Asians in 1905 illustrates the great changes in their transnational consciousness, as only five decades earlier than 1905, West Asian Muslims' views of East Asian societies did not have any Asian identity component.

Although there emerged several Pan-Asianist organizations from the 1880s on, by World War 1 Pan-Asianism became popularized by primarily two ultranationalist organizations of Japan, Genyôsha (The Black Ocean Society, founded in 1881) and its anti-Russian offshoot Kokuryûkai (Amur River Society, founded in 1901), under the charismatic leadership of Tôyama Mitsuru (1855–1944) and Uchida Ryôhei (1874–1937). These two organizations fostered ties with nationalists and intellectuals from Asia, such as Sun Yat-sen of China, Kim Ok-kyun of Korea, Emilio Aguinaldo of the Philippines, Resh Behari Bose and Rabindranath Tagore of India and Abdurreşid Ibrahim of Russia. The idea of Pan-Asianism had many important supporters in East Asia, India, Southeast Asia, and West Asia, and some of these Pan-Asianists expected Japan to take moral leadership by helping other Asian nations against Western imperialism. In fact, many students from India, Vietnam, China and other parts of Asia came to Japan to study and learn an Asian way of rapid modernization exemplified by the Japanese achievements. Yet, the Japanese

government did not officially endorse any Pan-Asian rhetoric in its foreign policy until the mid 1930s.

While Pan-Asianism developed as a strong intellectual current dealing with issues of history, racism and civilizational identity, the practical political projects of Asian solidarity were not supported by any of the state elites. Hence, Pan-Asianism became a discourse to delegitimize the ideology of white-race and European supremacy without having any practical implementation until the 1930s. It also created broader emotions of intra-Asian sympathies, a sort of early third-world consciousness, that allowed Chinese intellectuals to feel closer to the Turkish War for Independence, or Turkish and Iranian nationalists to feel sympathies for Chinese or Indian nationalism. This did not mean that Pan-Asianist figures did not have any programmes of practical cooperation or long term political visions: intra-East Asian trade volumes have always been high, and many Asianists advocated a trans-Asian transportation system extending all the way from Istanbul to Shanghai, Asia-wide banks and development institutions, newspapers, shipping companies and international organizations, but the very fact that they were advocating such grand schemes of cooperation indicates that, in reality, there was not much cooperation in the economic, cultural and political realms on the Asian continent.

The Japanese empire began to utilize a vision of Pan-Asian solidarity during the 1930s, only in the context of its legitimacy crisis in the aftermath of the invasion of Manchuria. Pan-Asianism was used to justify Japanese imperial rule in East Asia as a project of liberation of Asia from Western rule. Japan's call for Asian solidarity under its leadership during the late 1930s showed both the limitations and partial effectiveness of Asian identity in creating political cooperation. While some nationalists in India, Indonesia, China and other areas cooperated with the Japanese efforts, the majority of Asian nationalists underlined the hypocrisy of Japan's declaration of Asian solidarity when the Japanese empire was colonizing large territories in China and Korea.

After Japan's defeat in World War 2, the Japan-centred vision of Asian solidarity was denounced, but the ideal of Asian cooperation and unity continued throughout the Cold War and post-Cold War era. The Bandung Conference of 1955 witnessed renewed, postcolonial calls for Asian solidarity. New post-World War 2 visions of Asian solidarity, associated with the names of Mao Zedong and Jawaharlal Nehru, were generally part of a broader concept of third-world solidarity and included cooperation with the newly independent African countries as well. Since the end of the Cold War, many Asian intellectuals have continued to debate new forms of potential Asian cooperation in a multipolar world where Asia could emerge as a regional power counterbalancing Europe and the United States. There are currently several international organizations, activities and NGOs based on this Asian concept, such as the Asian Development Bank, the Asian Games, the Asian News Network, the Network of Asian Think Tanks, the Asian Football Federation, and so on. For example, international sports associations still use the continent of Asia as a single unit for tournaments and qualifications, and thus countries in two distant parts of Asia, such as Japan and Bahrain, play games with each other regularly despite the geographical distance between their countries. More importantly, the imagined connectivity and unity of a shared Asian culture, or the remnant of exoticism associated with it, are still used by the tourism industry to promote travel to different parts of Asia. For example, the Japanese tourist industry revived a certain level of nostalgic Asian identity in special silk-road tours from the 1970s onwards, while trips to Turkey are being presented as seeing the other end of Asia. Moreover, the recent rise of the Chinese and Korean economies, and the economic dynamism of Association of Southeast Asian Nations (ASEAN) countries, in addition to the already strong Japanese economy, made intra-Asian trade even stronger, and led to new debates on the possibility of an Asian regionalism.

Finally, the concept of Asia appeared in the Asian-American identity of various diaspora communities living the United States. While Asian-American identity was used and recognized, facilitating communication and interactions among various communities originating from different parts of Asia, in reality the stark diversity of Asian-American communities created sharply different diaspora cultures, experiences and organizations in the United States, ranging from Chinese Americans to Americans of Indian, Vietnamese or Korean descent. For all practical purposes, Asians from regions to the west of India, such as Iranians, Kuwaitis, and Pakistanis, do not define themselves as Asian Americans, but tend to identify with the (Caucasian) Middle East racial category. For reasons outlined above, recently many scholars have written about rethinking the 'myth of continents', suggesting that an obsolete Eurocentric concept of Asia should be replaced by more nuanced geographical categories.

Cemil Aydin

Bibliography

Duara P. 2001. 'The discourse of civilization and pan-Asianism', *Journal of World History*, 12, 1, 99–130.

Jansen M. B. 1954. *The Japanese and Sun Yat-sen.* Cambridge, MA: Harvard University Press.

Koschmann V. J. 1997. 'Asianism's ambivalent legacy', in Katzenstein P. J. and Shiraishi T. (eds) 1997. *Network power: Japan and Asia.* Ithaca: Cornell University Press, 83–110.

Lewis M. W. and Wigen K. E. 1997. *The myth of continents: a critique of metageography.* Berkeley: University of California Press.

Related essays

Africa; America; borders and borderlands; Buddhism; Cantonese opera; China; Chinese Diaspora; civilizations; contract and indentured labourers; convergence and divergence; decolonization; developmental taxonomies; empires and imperialism; ethnicity and race; exile; femininity; human mobility; industrialization; international students; Islam; Japan; labour migrations; language diplomacy; modernization theory; Muslim networks; Orientalism; pan-isms; race-mixing; regional communities; regions; religion; tourism; transportation infrastructures; tropics; Westernization; white men's countries; world orders; Zen aesthetics

Assembly line

An assembly line is both a specific working device and a global system of manufacturing. The concept seems simple, but the functioning is complex. Along a conveyor, objects are progressively manufactured by workers posted at specific places with the proper tools to accomplish a defined task. Each one repeats a series of movements while everybody works at the same rhythm. A spot, an action and a schedule are imposed on the workers because the range of operations accomplished in each station has to follow the same timing. It is possible only if all parts are interchangeable, if team discipline is respected, if quality is obtained. The combination of these requirements is a technological and social challenge. It has been applied, adapted or transformed in many ways and in different places for a wide range of productions. It has constantly evolved in ever-changing industrial situations.

In 19th-century America, assembly conveyors were first used for the production of flour in mills or the dismantling of carcasses in slaughterhouses. The working process was later introduced in other manufactures, like brewing, canning industries, foundries or weaponry. An assembly line is relatively easy to use in flow processes where only one product is being worked on. The wheat becomes flour, the animal a carcass, the incandescent metal an ingot or a sheet. It is more complex in tooling or mechanics because different standardized parts have to be assembled with limited time and cost. There are debates concerning the oldest conveyor, but there is no doubt that the Ford Motor Company (FMC) created the first complex assembly line system.

In April 1913 an assembly line was used for the production of Ford's Model T. Conveyors were a way among others – but a mostly efficient one – to meet the crushing demand. First experienced in one workshop, it was swiftly adopted in other departments, and progressively adapted to the final chassis assembly. By Christmas, 191 men worked along the 300-foot line pushing the vehicle along by hand. Sixteen days later, Ford engineers had installed a mechanical line on which the car was carried along an endless chain. As Henry Ford became one of the richest men in the world, his success was attributed to the mechanical working device he adapted to car assembly. The conveyor was the emblem of mass production and the final auto-assembly line became, in the public mind, 'the' assembly line. In fact, Ford combined different types of conveyors adapted to various productive tasks. Most of them were short subassembly lines supplying the final conveyor. Even at the FMC plants, many tasks were still made on static machines. The metaphor of rivulets flowing into streams flowing into a great river was more an image than reality.

Ford's first general assembly line came at the right time in the right place. The manufacturer benefited from the American system of production able to sustain mass production and mass consumption with good quality material, precise machine-tools, an adapted workforce and a receptive market. Henry Ford argued that his complex system of conveyors could handle only a single model. He knew that conveyors did not come alone. Mechanization could step up the production rates only with higher wages to convince the workers and guarantee quality. Ford increased the productivity of his workforce, reduced the cost of fabrication, seduced his customers and sold – up to 1927 – some 15 million Model T cars. Conveyors were not just a technological turning point but a 'lever to move the world'.

Yet this economic revolution was short-lived. Changes in the American consumer's taste and an increase in their purchasing power made the Model T out of date and Ford's assembly line unadapted. In 1923, under the leadership of Albert Sloan, General Motors (GM) passed Ford and took the lead by developing a commercial policy of annual models for each of its multiple brands (Chevrolet, Pontiac, etc) and by inventing a new assembly line system. In 1922, William Knudsen, one of Ford's production wizards, resigned and joined the Chevrolet Division. He did not try to imitate Ford's production system, but reorganized it to accommodate both expansion and change.

GM developed the 'common parts' strategy. The idea was to use identical parts to assemble different cars in order to make economies of scale. The invisible elements of the cars were mass-produced on (classical) subassembly lines. The body components of each specific model were produced using general-purpose machine-tools that could be easily adapted to changing shapes and colours. This was a first radical departure from the Ford idea of single-purpose machine-tools. The body was conceived to be easily assembled, lowering the limits of precision needed for parts to fit. Different versions of the same model could be manufactured alternatively on a conveyor. Thus an attractive variety of scales of cars could be offered at relatively low cost. This was the end of the single and unchangeable mass-produced model. By the time Ford's principles of mass production and global assembly line were known to all, they were obsolete. Management literature often apprehends industrial changes with a gap.

From World War 1 on, the American assembly line experiences and mass production ideas fascinated European industries. But the technologies that were transferred had more to do with the local situation than with what was going on across the Atlantic. In a specific industrial context, it was better not to copy. Assembly line systems were adapted to low volumes and variety. In France, the introduction of assembly lines by Louis Renault in his Billancourt plant was slow, discrete and adapted to the company's culture. Conversely, André Citroën claimed to be the 'French Ford', promoted his modern assembly lines and went bankrupt in 1935. Twenty years were needed by the major automobile producers to master the continuous process of a global assembly line.

Before 1914 the Renault factory was among the first to experience interchangeability and series production. The introduction of Taylor's method of time study caused a major strike against the chronometer (1913), but did not stop the rationalization process. The massive war demand introduced large-scale production and mechanical conveyors for shells, tanks, trucks and automobiles. By 1917, Renault had a staff of competent employees capable of making a rudimentary assembly line work.

In the postwar period, Renault continued to install small manual conveyors but did not consider them as assembly lines because they were not consistent with the Ford model. Aiming at efficiency and profit, these discrete devices were not backward compared to the equipment used by his French competitors. Renault's travail à la chaîne (chain work, the French term for assembly line) was first publicly presented in a 1922 article. It focused on a hand-pushed chassis assembly line which was not very different from what it had been five years before. Journalists give a warped vision of industrial activity.

By contrast, during the next decade Renault's assembly lines were promoted although the process of mechanization was difficult to get right. Frames came out of the line without the complete fittings and the chains were often stopped. In 1929, the inauguration of a new plant was an opportunity to modernize the assembly line system. The final assembly line was a success, and different models could be assembled alternately. However, two structural obstacles were blocking the flow: the composite nature of the body (made out of a wooden skeleton) and the stiffness of body conveyors.

Before World War 2, Renault adopted the 'compact' body for the Juvaquatre model and installed a new automatic chain for glazing. Devices were developed to coordinate conveyors working separately. During German occupation, Pierre Bézier invented the electromechanical head (TEM) thanks to which Renault introduced transfer-machine lines in 1947 and started mass producing the 4 CV engines. A commercial slogan said, 'the chain gets moving again'. With the same idea and different devices, Renault and other European companies had developed specific assembly line systems.

Compared to the Ford model, the Japanese assembly line is often presented as an upside down way of adapting mass production techniques. It indeed emerged from a different starting point. It was not set up to meet high-level production, but to make up for a chronic shortage. Kiichiro Toyoda recommended in 1936: 'There is no way we can adopt the United States method just as it is. The real problem is to make cars inexpensively'. After the defeat of 1945 and under American occupation, the precision knowledge and know-how acquired by Japanese firms in aircraft and naval production were transferred to civilian industries, while engineers used the productivity missions to reconsider American Fordist mass production methods.

Toyota's previous production experiences were adapted by Taïichi Ohno (1912–90). The main idea was to be lean. Kanban (just-in-time) was the first specificity of this conveyor system. It was originally an attempt to reduce the stocks of parts in order to save the cost of their uselessness. The innovation was to invert the order of supply from the bottom up. The production of a component would be launched, not through a top management order, but because this specific part was needed in the workshop. Ohno generalized the practice from the tooling workshops in 1948 to the subcontractors in 1968. The second original idea is autonomization which aims to have a worker work on more than one machine tool at a time, in order to spare the workforce and increase productivity. Ohno later adapted this system to whole assembly lines. The smooth flow of production was allowed by the decomposition of the production process into short steps and limited, independent sections. Ford's metaphor of the river flow was irrelevant here. The third difference concerned time and motion study methods. On the Toyota assembly line this analysis was made in the workshop and not by a centralized bureau. When production volume changed, the standard tasks were immediately redistributed.

The reactivity of all these working devices implied a painstaking study of standard tasks and workers' commitment called Kaïzen activity. It designated the constant, personal contribution of all workers to the increase of quality, the development of productivity and the reduction of costs. Up to the 1970s, through polyvalence of the workforce and improvement of the working process, Toyota's lean assembly line system could cope with a variable growth of volume production.

But this specific adaptation to mass production could not suffice for long. Toyota's assembly line system also had to adapt to the growing variety of models. The second imperative was to be flexible and agile. Conveyors were conceived to be capable of assembling different models. In 1985, Toyota introduced the flexible body line, making it possible to assemble different platforms on any conveyor.

This flexible assembly line system came to a crisis in the beginning of the 1990s, mostly because of growing workforce reluctance. A new line conception was experimented with, where the productive flow was broken through the reintroduction of stocks between independent sections of assembly lines. The humanization of working conditions was obtained through the translation of the hardest activities to robots. The salary system was made more motivating and task rotation was systematized to reduce boredom. At the same time, Toyota externalized and moved off-shore an important part of its assembly lines.

The global assembly lines seem to have disappeared from the industrial countries that invented them. Actually this production system is now international. Items 'made in China' are mostly made elsewhere by international companies that use low-wage countries as the final assembly station of their global production network. The job is moved off-shore but the firms keep most of the profits, until the workshops in Southeast Asia develop their own ways of mass assembly.

Alain P. Michel

Bibliography
Giedion S. 1948. *Mechanization takes command.* Oxford: Oxford University Press.
Hounshell D. A. 1984. *From the American system to mass production, 1800–1932: the development of manufacturing technology in the United States.* Baltimore: Johns Hopkins University Press.
Michel A. P. 2007. *Travail à la chaîne: Renault 1898–1947.* Boulogne-Billancourt: ETAI.
Shiomi H. and Wada K. (eds) 1995. *Fordism transformed: the development of production methods in the automobile industry.* Oxford: Oxford University Press.

Related essays
car culture; containerized freight; corporations; organization models; Toyotism

Asylum seekers

Asylum is a form of protection offered to non-citizens who fear they would be persecuted if they returned to their home country. The term 'asylum' originated from the French word 'asile' that in the Middle Ages referred to a protected place of refuge.

Throughout history, people have migrated en masse from one place to another because their group affiliation (i.e. religious, political, or ethnic) placed them in such danger that leaving one nation state for another became their only alternative. Asylum seekers are currently distinguished from refugees in that asylum seekers tend to migrate alone while refugees move in larger groups. Asylum seekers – like all migrants – must marshal the necessary resources to make their way from one country to another. They are often similar to other migrants in that they, too, seek better economic opportunities and desire reunification with family members living in other nation states. The characterizing feature of asylum seekers is that their motivation for leaving one country for another is based on a fear of persecution. Because fear of persecution distinguishes asylum seekers from other migrants, they are treated as a special category of immigrants under international law and policy.

Since World War 2, the policies and conventions that protect asylum seekers are derived from those created for refugees. The 1951 United Nations Convention Relating to the Status of Refugees and the 1967 United Nations Protocol Relating to the Status of

Refugees serve as the cornerstone of refugee legislation. Nation states that are signatories to the Convention and Protocol are bound to admit asylum seekers based on the refugee definition which includes individuals who, owing to a well-founded fear of persecution for reasons of race, religion, nationality, membership in a social group, or political opinion, are unable or unwilling to return to their country. The United Nations' definition of who gets to claim refugee status determines the procedure for adjudicating asylum claims. The difference between classification as a 'refugee' and as an 'asylee' is circumscribed by legal definitions based on the location of where the application is filed: refugees file their applications prior to entering the country where they seek protection and asylees file after their arrival. Although neither document requires members to provide asylum, there is an explicit prohibition against refoulement – forcible return. Refoulement to the country of origin where one's life or freedom would be threatened is a violation of the spirit and the letter of these documents.

The United Nations cannot force nation states that are signatories to the Convention and Protocol to admit asylum seekers. Instead, nation states decide who may gain asylum and under what circumstances. States capitalize on the vagueness of the term 'well-founded fear' to define persecuted populations. For example, from 1951 to 1980, an overwhelming proportion of asylum seekers who gained entry into the United States came from Communist nation states, reflecting US foreign policy during the Cold War. Since 1985, The United States, Germany, the United Kingdom, and Canada have received the greatest number of asylum applications. While there has been an increase in the number of asylum seekers since the 1970s, there has been a simultaneous decline in the number of asylum applications granted.

States have moved away from policies of awarding permanent asylum towards a commitment to granting temporary protection. Between 1985 and 1995, more than 5 million asylum applications were filed in the industrialized states of Western Europe and North America (with the exception of Mexico). Nearly 1 million of the applications filed are still pending, leaving one-fifth of the asylum-seeking population to await the adjudication of their claims. Although industrial states are reluctant to grant formal asylum status to migrants, they are also unwilling to deport those who claim persecution. Consequently, nation states are granting fewer migrants asylum status, a status which would afford them certain rights and privileges, in particular, those that accompany citizenship status. Therefore, many asylum seekers remain in industrial countries, often as illegal migrants, with limited access to participating in the polity, and with restrictions on their ability to seek and maintain employment that would secure their livelihood in the place where they have sought refuge.

Connie Oxford

Bibliography

Roberts A. 1998. 'More refugees, less asylum: a regime in transformation', Journal of Refugee Studies, 11, 374–95.

Related essays

diasporas; exile; human mobility; intergovernmental organizations; justice; legal order; refugees; remittances

Auditing

Derived from the Latin auditus (hearing) and from the past participle of audire (to hear), auditing can be defined as the methodical examination of a particular aspect of an organization's life in order to improve its operations. Most of the time, an audit is part of a monitoring process in an agency relationship, i.e., when a principal engages another person as his agent to perform a service on his behalf, and the audit is set up to remove the asymmetry of information between the two parties. Our focus here is on financial audit, i.e., the examination by an independent third party of the financial statements of an organization, in order to express an opinion on their truthfulness and fairness and on the reliability of the accounting procedures used. Financial auditing occupies a particular place with respect to other auditing practices, in that it boasts a much longer history than other practices and it provided the model which influenced them.

During the second half of the 19th century the increasing number of limited liability companies in industrialized countries resulted in a growing demand for more reliable accounting information. Due to a series of financial scandals, the progressive separation of ownership from management, as well as government intervention, resulted in institutionalization of financial auditing practices. In the earliest regulations introducing the statutory audit, such as in England (1856) and France (1863), it was supposed to be conducted by shareholders without any special requirement about their qualifications. However, the increasing complexity of accounts and the expertise required by valuation issues rapidly necessitated the intervention of professional auditors. In the early 20th century, in a few countries such as England and Germany where the accounting bodies had already gained a solid legitimacy, statutory auditing became the sole preserve of accounting firms.

On both sides of Atlantic Ocean, the financial and economic crisis of 1929 led to a reinforcement of accounting and auditing regulation. Nevertheless, if Continental European countries developed their own models, the British and the American ones were to become prominent in the 1980s, given the globalization of the financial markets. The economic weight of the USA and the professionalism of their audit firms (which were mainly of British origin) permitted them to play a paramount role in the international harmonization process of accounting and auditing rules.

This harmonization was achieved through the parallel actions of two closely linked organizations, both initiated by the British accounting profession: the International Accounting Standards Committee (IASC), created in 1973 (renamed as the IAS Board – IASB – in 2001), and the International Federation of Accountants (IFAC), created in 1977. Within 25 years, the IASB succeeded in extending its standards all over the world, with the exception of the United States where the standards are defined by the Financial Accounting Standards Board (FASB), although the FASB and IASB are nowadays engaged in a convergence programme. In parallel, through the creation of the International Auditing Practices Committee (renamed as the International Auditing and Assurance Standards Board – IAASB – in 2002), the IFAC encountered a more thorough success, mainly because of the need to rebuild public trust in audit firms and in the functioning of capital markets after the financial scandals of Enron, Arthur Andersen, etc in 2001 and 2002.

These events forged a reinforcement in national legislations pertaining to auditing and an acceleration of the harmonization process. After having adopted the accounting standards promoted by the IASB in 2002, the European Union adopted the international auditing standards defined by the IAASB in 2006. Similarly, most non-European countries have already adopted (or are going to adopt) both sets of standards.

Such harmonization is vital so that capital markets function correctly. High-quality and highly trustworthy audit reports are thus prerequisites but the question is whether these international standards are able to ensure the highest quality of audit. Neither accounting nor auditing are scientific matters, and the setting of standards is the result of decisions subject to political, social, economic and cultural influences. Of course, standards setters are well-known experts but the fact that this standardization process is managed by two international non-governmental organizations which are strongly linked to the four biggest audit firms remains a matter of some concern.

Yannick Lemarchand

Bibliography

Edwards J.-R. 1989. *A history of financial accounting*. London: Routledge.
Power M. 1997. *The audit society: rituals of verification*. Oxford: Oxford University Press.

Related essays

car safety standards; corporations; financial markets; food safety standards; governance; information technology (IT) offshoring; management; national accounting systems; services; technical standardization

Avant garde

The concept originates in the military ambit (the advance guard that ventures into new ground and hostile surroundings), and in the 19th century it was used to label cultural and political radicalism. Only in the 20th century did this word take its most current meaning, when it was increasingly selected to designate the artistic movements that have disturbed the understanding of 'art'.

In his book El objeto del siglo, French historian and psychoanalyst Gerard Wajcman ventures the hypothesis that the status of visuality in the last century lies in the representation of image as absence. Works of art, he says, are objects that think the absent and make it visible. It is not a coincidence that he chooses two critical products of the early avant garde as 20th-century objects: *Bicycle Wheel* (1913) by Marcel Duchamp, and *Black square on a white background* (1915) by Russian suprematist Kazimir Malevich. *Bicycle Wheel* is Marcel Duchamp's first readymade and consists only of a bicycle wheel without its tyre, screwed to the seat of a stool. Mexican writer Octavio Paz defines readymades as anonymous objects that the gratuitous gesture of the artist turns into works of art when he chooses them. Void of their everyday function and out of their original use and context, readymades become empty objects. But rather than random objects, readymades are mostly a gesture, an act that threatens the artistic institution which is forced to accept or reject that object as art, and contradicts the traditional notion of the 'work of art' as a unique, inspired creation performed by the elevated gift of the artist. By signing and declaring a bicycle wheel, a snow shovel or a urinal as a work of art, Duchamp does not create the object, he is merely pointing it out: his is an intellectual, conceptual intervention. Furthermore, Duchamp insists on his attempt to 'aesthetically anaesthetize' readymades: no beauty (or ugliness) justifies his choice. His interest in the chosen object is not aesthetic, but critical. It is not subordinated to visual perception, nor does it allow for aesthetic contemplation.

Black square on a white background is a 'completely naked and frameless icon', an endpoint in his frantic passage from figurative painting to cubism, and then to pure abstraction, which places him at the very edge of representation, at point zero from which painting is to be reinvented. Malevich wrote that he was exhibiting the experience of the absence of an object. What becomes evident in this process of accelerated breakdown of painting into simple geometric forms and basic colours is that visual arts shed their role as representations; they refuse to be or seem to be a window to the world.

These two objects (Duchamp's readymade and Malevich's black square) may be considered starting points for most of the multiple paths that art has trailed and rewritten since then. Both lay bare the constructed condition (the artifice character and the material dimension) of the artistic event, and imply a radical critique of naturalistic or mimetic representation, an anti-idealistic proclamation of the material condition of art. What we call 'art' today is not defined by the intrinsic qualities of a certain object, but responds to its inscription or decoding within a discursive space and an institutional framework. Considering art in terms of a split sphere brings about the idealist risk of falling back on understanding it as universal and ahistorical, and viewing its context as a mere backdrop to which it may or may not be referred. French sociologist Pierre Bourdieu suggests a complex approach to this issue based on the notion of artistic field. He defines it as a socially delimited space, with its own structure and logic, in which different agents (painters, marchands, gallerists, critics, etc.) participate by filling different competing positions, and whose cohesion is granted by their struggle for the specific cultural capital which is disputed in it.

The condition of the artistic field – claims Bourdieu – is its relative autonomy from the pressures exerted on it by external powers. That autonomy is the result of a delimited historical process whose genesis in Western Europe dates back to the mid 19th century, with the passage from a structural subordination of the artistic and literary activity to the dictums of economics and politics (whose domination over cultural producers was direct) to specific forms of validation and legitimacy. This marked the rise of the social figure of the modern professional artist, indifferent to political demands, market trends and moral mandates. Their only rule is that which is specific to their art.

It is worth mentioning that this theoretical approach comes from analysing only the historical experiences of Europe, and that, when it comes to looking into the specific conditions of cultural production in the so-called peripheral societies, it is very difficult to find a system whose regularity and homogeneity compares to the one described by them. In Latin America, economic hardship, political instability, the weakness of the elite cultural market and the frailty of the fabric of artistic and literary institutions, along with their scant autonomy from institutions of power, suggest a very different makeup for the formation of the artistic field, with a different system of autonomy, dependencies and mediations. On the other hand, Bourdieu limits the reach of the notion of field to the national level, which implies a limit and a distortion when it comes to thinking the contemporary processes of production, circulation and reception of artistic expressions. This is not only because the national scale avoids considering the relationships of conflict or inequality between the centre and the periphery, but mostly because of the obvious existence of an international artistic marketplace and the dimensions of international artistic mega-events such as biennial exhibitions, in which the growing presence of the curatorial role weighs on the trend towards the unification of contemporary artistic languages.

Narrating the history of 20th-century art as a succession of trends, styles and movements related by a progression or continuity is an option that is not likely to re-enact the extent of the break avant-garde movements meant, the schismatic effect they had on the understanding of modern art. We suggest thinking about the notion of 'avant garde' not as a set of artistic movements or the procedures that they coined, but rather as those experiences which in certain historical moments produce the expansion, explosion or outburst of the limits of the (relatively) autonomous sphere we define as art; those experiences in which art establishes a relationship with the society, politics or everyday life of people, not in terms of exteriority or autonomy, a discourse about something, but rather from its vanishing or reconnecting points, which threaten the lack of a function and the restricted political nature of art in modern times (i.e., the restriction of politics in art to a matter of language); those experiences which are committed to a non-immanent critical condition, and which claim as their own the ethics-aesthetics, politics-poetics and art-utopia binaries.

Based on this delimitation, we identify three cycles throughout the 20th century that manifest the climates of periods which are marked by crisis or the unrests of capitalism, and in which the peaks of avant-garde intensity can be found.

First, there are the historical avant-garde movements, located between the second and third decades of the 20th century, in the midst of events which shook the world, such as both world wars and the rise of fascism. This period saw the emergence, in Europe and America, of several '-isms', movements or groups which opened – not only in visual arts but also in literature, cinema and drama – a radical challenge to canonical forms, a commitment to experimentation and the questioning of boundaries among genres. In the words of the imagist poet Ezra Pound, 'Make it new', or, as Chilean creationist Vicente Huidobro said, 'invent new worlds'. The inaugural force of the new is committed not only to the invention of new forms and languages, but also to the power of art to transform the bleak conditions of existence. Within this framework, each avant-garde movement defines its characteristic traits in relation to the historical context in which it acts. Thus, Italian futurism will have a political development that will lead it towards fascism, whereas Russian futurism will enthusiastically join the Soviet cause after the triumph of the 1917 Revolution. German Dadaism will keep a sustained, strong political activism, far from the nihilism of the movement's early days in Zürich. The positions of Russian constructivism and productivism will have a different development in the Bauhaus of the Weimar Republic. Likewise, the exiled groups of surrealists in the United States will be linked with the early stages of Abstract Expressionism, whereas in Mexico they will feed on the popular social imaginary of prehispanic roots.

Second, there are the so-called neo-avant-garde movements, born during the postwar era, especially in the 1960s, a period in which an efficient institutional circuit prone to supporting contemporary art consolidated. The broadening of the boundaries of art seemed to have become established, as did the increasingly active role assigned to the audience. After a thirty-year historical hiatus of repression and amnesia, the first avant-garde movements were rediscovered and updated (particularly Duchamp's legacy), in an operation that Hal Foster defines as a 'return' which did not imply a completion of that unfinished project, but, for the first time, a true understanding of it. Neo-avant-garde movements have often been dismissed as illegitimate. Peter Bürger, among others, considers their critical claims inauthentic or doomed to failure in advance, since the historical avant-garde movements' attempts to reconnect art and life (i.e., to overcome the lack of a social function that art is doomed to have in bourgeois society) had already failed. The artistic institutions are now ready to absorb the avant-garde protest, which – although it was an anti-artistic gesture – has come to be regarded as art. Such an absolute challenge loses track of the specific nature of the inscription of some of these artistic movements in the historical situation of the 1960s, characterized by revolutionary and countercultural movements in the so-called Third World countries and later in Europe and the United States, which reactivated the horizon of expectations for a radical change in society. This background becomes evident in movements such as the Situationist International, Viennese Actionism or *Tucumán Arde* (Argentina, 1968). But even in pop art (which is usually interpreted as an art of the exaltation of mass consumerism and the cultural industry) we can explore a critical component. For example, Andreas Huyssen hypothesizes that we may find in these works an attempt to reconnect art to mass popular culture, from which it had split in modernity, while Umberto Eco suggests that pop art is a clever, ironic play on popular culture. Likewise, in conceptualism we may find works which are critical of the artistic institution as well as others which are tautological and self-referential in nature.

Third, there are the post-avant-garde movements. Since the 1980s there has been a debate on the possibility of the rise of new avant-garde movements. In her analysis of the avant-garde Chilean scene during Pinochet's dictatorship, Chilean Nelly Richard draws a line between two alternative models of art and social criticism, and distinguishes the old avant-garde projects – which see art as an articulator of the forces of change – and post-avant-garde projects, which try to plot operations which are capable of altering and subverting the system's logics in actions situated within the micro scale. Conversely, others see post-avant-garde movements as diffuse contemporary movements that socialize knowledge, make resources (many of which were coined by the historical avant-garde movements and the neo-avant-garde movements) available and allow many people (and not just an avant-garde elite) to become a part of the making of new images and languages, as well as their circulation beyond the restricted artistic circles. What used to be an isolated prototype or experiment can nowadays become a collective heritage, a reservoir of socially available resources for a certain social movement.

Ana Longoni

Bibliography

Bourdieu P. 1992. *Les règles de l'art*. Paris: Seuil.

Bürger P. 1974. *Theorie der Avantgarde*. Frankfurt am Main: Suhrkamp.

Eco U. 1968. *La definizione dell' arte*. Milan: Mursia.

Foster H. 1996. *The return of the real*. Boston: MIT Press.

Huyssen A. 1986. *After the Great Divide: modernism, mass culture, postmodernism*. Bloomington: Indiana University Press.

Paz O. 1978. *La apariencia desnuda*. Mexico City: Era.

Richard N. 1994. *La insubordinación de los signos*. Santiago, Chile: Cuarto Propio.

Wajcman G. 2001. *El objeto del siglo*. Buenos Aires: Amorrortu.

B

Beatles *See* **Rock**

Beauty

Both as judgment of others and as self-presentation, human physical beauty is a ubiquitous concern as well as a quotidian practice. But being considered a frivolous and potentially disqualifying preoccupation, serious-minded people only gaze into the mirror in secret. When the subject is taken up thoughtfully, the paucity of analytical and comparative frameworks is immediately apparent. The dilemma of North American Second Wave feminism is a case in point. In recent decades, no other political perspective/social movement has been more successful in bringing the subject to the fore of public debates. Though parodied and often maligned, few discussions of beauty neglect referencing 'a feminist position'. Yet feminist analysis is still in its infancy. Moreover, feminists do not agree. The depths of their disagreement reveal the breadth of the social and philosophical issues involved.

For example, according to best-selling author Naomi Wolf, women in American society today 'are in the midst of a violent backlash against feminism that uses images of female beauty as a political weapon against women's advancement'. '[M]ore insidious than any mystique of femininity yet' – more than motherhood, domesticity, chastity and passivity – '[t]he contemporary ravages of the beauty backlash are destroying women physically and depleting us psychologically. If we are to free ourselves from the dead weight that has once again been made of our femaleness, it is not ballots or lobbyists or placards that women will need first; it is a new way to see' (Wolf 2002, 19).

From this rousing call to consciousness, Wolf proceeds to a perceptive analysis of how normative beauty standards constrain women's public and private choices and limit advancement. Accepting the truth of Wolf's examples, however, does not mean that many or most women would willingly disaffiliate from contemporary beauty culture. Even when women object to its coercive manipulation, they remain loyal to many of its practices. Here feminist historians like Kathy Peiss and others remind us that women helped to create modern beauty culture. Since the 1920s and 30s in urban industrializing societies around the globe – in cities from Tokyo to Paris, from Shanghai to Mumbai, from Berlin to Chicago and New York City – the mass production and dissemination of beauty products has announced a new beauty culture in which both producers (many of them female entrepreneurs) and consumers embraced the language of choice and self-expression. As young women bobbed their hair, smoked cigarettes, painted their lips, wore provocative clothes and sought romantic love, they created a revolution in style – which self-consciously called itself 'modern' and international – that flouted tradition-bound notions of female modesty, respectability, and bodily aesthetics. Variously known as that of 'New Women' or 'Modern Girls', this transnational phenomenon has intrigued historians because of its strong resemblances across vastly different cultures and national/imperial histories.

But if women's pleasures once helped to initiate the now hegemonic engine of fantasy and desire, what went awry with the promise of individual expression and fulfilment? To pose this question is not to blame women for setting in motion the means of their own disempowerment, but to interrogate the psychic and ethical consequences of mass commodification for social life. In other words, if the new beauty culture of the 20th century suggested many non-traditional concepts of personhood and new ways to map individuality, what are the unforeseen or unintended social effects of locating meaning and self formation in the rapid flow of information, images, and resources, that is, in processes that simultaneously constitute markets and identities?

This question, though implicit in many recent feminist critiques of the role of media in propagating beauty culture, has not received adequate attention. Susan Bordo's (1993) influential study of gender and body images, for example, argues that the normal functioning of contemporary commodity culture produces pathological results. In Western capitalist societies where the demand for control instils asceticism while the wealth of goods and temptations encourages hedonism, both anorexia and bulimia must be regarded as exemplary achievements within the logic of the culture. Although her evidence comes primarily from print media, especially from advertising, commodity capitalism itself makes only a fleeting appearance in her analysis. In Bordo's view, the decision to act on oneself – taken as a claim to power – is itself a symptomatic response to a deep-seated mind/body dualism in Western culture, according to which the feminine body is unruly and requires control. In the bitterest of ironies, the most successful assertion of individual will (the curbing of appetite and freedom from desire) is the moment of normative cultural replication.

It is not surprising then that Bordo considers Naomi Wolf's notion of consciousness raising to be ineffective. Bordo and others point out that women cannot simply refuse the 'beauty myth' (once the layers of false ideologies have been cleared away) because the self is not easily detached from or immune to the meaning systems in which it is constituted. Yet feminist scholars like Kathy Davis (1991) suggest, in turn, that Bordo's perspective treats women as 'cultural dopes'. To rescue a sense of agency, Davis enjoins feminists to examine how women deliberate and struggle over what and how they consume. In the specific case of cosmetic surgery, Davis notes that 'the decision itself may become a radical and courageous act' (Davis 1991, 35). The choice may be a 'knowledgeable and rational one, even as it reproduces a complex of power structures that constructs the female body as inferior and in need of change' (1991, 33). Davis's ethnographic approach has the advantage of seeing how women actually negotiate complex mazes of desires and prescriptions to find dignified solutions for themselves. In a parallel nuancing of Naomi Wolf, Davis does not view women as either absolutely inside or outside the 'beauty myth', but as both at the same time.

The strength of Davis's individual-level approach, while more grounded in women's lives, is also the source of its limits. Because Davis's analysis only describes how individuals balance and cope, an individual-level calculus of opportunities and constraints does not build bridges to broader social and cultural analysis of power relations, identity formation of selves, or social replication, as well as social change. As a result, Davis's notion of agency seems unnecessarily truncated. While it is true that consumer capitalism reserves the power to dictate meaning to the corporate few and frustrates those who want entry from the streets, even in our media-saturated and relentlessly commercial world one must not forget that people are still makers of meaning.

Unexpectedly, a longer historical view suggests that the commodification of beauty practices initiated in the 20th century may be more open than previous systems to transformations of bodily meaning. For example, although 19th-century North American and European beauty discourses may have focused obsessively on the features and comportment of wealthy young white women on the verge of the marriage market, this discussion of bodily meaning (whether the fairness of skin or the nobility of carriage indicate a purity of the soul, a virtuous heart or chaste habits) must be seen as an integral part of the broader common language (including laws and science) enforcing class and racial divides. It is often forgotten that phenotypical racism is also a form of aesthetic judgment. The physiognomic fantasy of 19th-century romantic love that hoped to read moral character from physical attraction was dangerous (as well as self-deluding for the beholder) because it was the same hope that drove phrenologists, physiologists and comparative anatomists to try to correlate intelligence with cranial capacities or the slope of the forehead, etc. Genealogically, 19th-century racial sciences built on the politicization of aesthetic judgement by early-18th-century philosophers Shaftesbury and Hutchinson who, responding to the pessimistic Hobbesian assessment of the inherent unruliness of human character, focused on aesthetic appreciation as a realm of disinterested activity in which humans could cultivate moral goodness and hence rule themselves. In the next generation, as Kant, Burke, and Winkelmann wrestled over how to define beauty so as to be worthy of this moral project, a Swiss pastor, Johann Caspar Lavater, claimed to bring aesthetics, science and ethics together by systemizing how to read moral disposition in facial expressions and gestures. Like other Enlightenment claims to science, those of Lavater were as concerned with establishing the credentials and authority of the scientist/ interpreter/connoisseur as they were with establishing the basis of knowledge. Lavater suggested that those trained in his method moved beyond their own embodiment as they discerned (through their superior ability) the true value of those who were consigned only to their bodies. Without consciously understanding his own actions, Lavater contributed to the aesthetic and scientific validation of whiteness (presented here as the universal) established in relation to many 'natives' and 'others' that had begun with colonization and trade in the early modern era.

The transformative potential of the new beauty practices of the early 20th century should be understood against the weight of previous social investments in aesthetic judgement, especially as the latter became the unspoken ethical compass driving scientific measurement and other authoritative ways of knowing that affixed meanings to bodies sorted hierarchically by race, gender, class. Most scholars, however, have underestimated the possibilities of this modernist cultural revolution because they have primarily asked whether the emancipation championed by 'new woman' movements was actually achieved. Because the material effects of style changes rarely spilled over into other aspects of individual lives, scholars have been sceptical of the freedom embraced. Yet, the radical element of commodification may not lie in the actual life choices opened up, but in the destabilization of prevailing methods for regulating bodies and their meanings.

Fashion systems may be disconcertingly indifferent as to whether the meaning they generate emanates from the real, or whether their messages express the attainable, or foster the socially useful. Yet without minimizing this amorality, the complex semiotic logic of commoditized beauty discourse has its social uses. In detaching surface signification from its supposed structural depth, the 20th-century cosmetic industry established new habits: the external body need not always (or inevitably) express the inherent qualities of the soul (or the destinies of organs). Bodies became sites for a plethora of changing messages. This important transformation – and the new habits it inculcated – was not instigated by utopians or militants, but occurred at the seat of power, money, and influence. Such changes at the centre may open the terrain to the initiatives of groups and individuals who use their own bodies as the mode of communication, contestation, innovation and commentary for resignifying and remaking bodily meaning.

To fully appreciate this potential, however, one must not begin with the ready-made language of 'consumer choice' and its prearranged array of meanings. Rather, drawing inspiration from the now-classic analysis of youth subculture developed by the Birmingham School (e.g. Hall and Jefferson, 1976), one needs to ask more anthropological/ ethnographic questions focused on what people do, how they style themselves (with the elements provided by commodity culture), and what they communicate by their self-fashioning. Following the influential work of Judith Butler, students of cultural meaning have asked whether gender binaries are subverted in the crossing and mixing of categories wherein normative beauty signifiers are enacted with the 'wrong' bodies. Yet one does not have to move to the outlandish to chart the contestations over identity and bodily meaning. In African American performance arts, for example, musicians and dancers have explored new bodily expressions that infused their marked bodies with new stories, complex histories and heterodox personal meanings. For many black Americans, the stage offers a space to comment on and to counter deep-seated stereotypes, to present black bodies as lyrical, as agile and intelligent, as imbued with dignity and humanity.

This ethnographic emphasis on bodily performance also helps us navigate the current outcry that Western beauty standards – particularly, the sexualization/exploitation of female bodies – are eclipsing traditional aesthetics and values in all corners of the globe. To be sure, the contents purveyed and the economic practices of global media giants deserve critique – not only for their normative conceptions of gender, sexuality and social roles, but also their ethnocentric and unselfconscious return to earlier colonial and Orientalist tropes. Yet, these outcries rely on the oppositional dualism of earlier anti-colonial discourse which essentializes the people and societies who are cast as vulnerable. They repeat the same problems of human agency discussed earlier. A quick look at the young women and men who parade their self-produced fashion statements around Tokyo's Harajuku station tells us that the situation is more complex.

Harajuku style is famous for its ever changing array of looks that mix unexpected fabrics and shapes, combining them with decontextualized elements of recognizable characters (such as babies, vamps, clowns, cowboys, punks, etc.). As consummate 'bricoleurs', the young participants rely on commodity culture and a media-saturated society to communicate. But not only do the individual creations defy labelling, they are also too ephemeral a product to capitalize upon. Thus Gwen Stefani's hope of launching a clothing line connected to her 2004 hit song 'Harajuku Girls' seemed doomed from the outset to be selling only pale and inadequate imitations because Stefani and her backers have misunderstood the self-subverting nature of these commoditized communications. Moreover, Stefani has tried to promote an 'exotic' appeal – by finding Asian women to pose as Harajuku. Yet, here again, the phenomenon defeats Stefani's orientalizing gaze. In Harajuku creations, it is often the West that is being exoticized and parodied. Thus when Stefani tries to import the style for Western consumption, her project looks like that of a 'straight man' in a joke that Stefani does not understand.

This unique example cautions that understanding the contemporary scene requires some agility. Whereas the vitality of commodity markets needs innovations from 'the streets', before such styles can be capitalized upon and managed commercially the expressive impulse may have already made its statement. Having reclaimed the body, if only momentarily, as a site of communication, the innovators have moved on. Our challenge is to track the messages.

Tessie P. Liu

Bibliography

Bordo S. 1993, reprinted 2003. *Unbearable weight: feminism, western culture and the body*. Berkeley: University of California Press.

Butler J. 2004. *Undoing gender*. London and New York: Routledge.

Davis K. 1991. 'Remaking the she-devil: a critical look at feminist approaches to beauty', *Hypatia*, 6, 2, 21–43.

Hall, S. and Jefferson, T (eds). 1993. *Resistance through rituals: youth subcultures in post-war Britain*. London: HarperCollins.

Miller L. 2006. *Beauty up: exploring contemporary Japanese body aesthetics*. Berkeley: University of California Press.

Modern Girl research group (T. Barlow, M. Y. Dong, U. G. Poiger, P. Ramamurthy, L. M. Thomas and A. E. Weinbaum) 2005. "The Modern Girl around the world", *Gender and History*, 17, 2, 245–94.

Peiss K. 1998. *Hope in a jar: the making of America's beauty culture*. New York: Metropolitan.

Wolf N. 1991, reprinted 2002. *Beauty myth: how images of beauty are used against women*. New York: Morrow.

Related essays
beauty pageants; cosmetic surgery; dress; empires and imperialism; fashion; femininity; gender and sex; honour; Japan; love; Orientalism; tropics; Westernization

Beauty pageants

From drag beauty pageants in the Philippines to agricultural festivals in the US to global media events like the Miss World pageant, beauty pageants perform significant cultural work in a variety of contexts. While the basic elements of the form of the beauty pageant are transnational, the significance of individual pageants is often irreducibly local.

Beauty competitions have a long history. They can be found in a wide variety of social, political and mythological contexts and in many cultural traditions. A famous example from Greek myth is Paris's adjudication of the beauty of the goddesses, Hera, Athena and Aphrodite in the accounts of the prehistory of the Trojan War.

Beauty pageants are now also transnational. Two pageants with global aspirations – the UK-based Miss World pageant, and the US-based and Donald Trump-owned Miss Universe – can accurately be understood as entrepreneurial opportunism in an era of neoliberalism. These two pageants are international – contestants representing nations compete for each title – though transnational in the ways they are organized and financed. They also initially appear to fit a model of globalization as cultural homogenization. But their recent histories suggest a more complex relationship of local, national and global public spheres.

The Miss World pageant scheduled for Kaduna, Nigeria, in 2002 is emblematic. The pageant was moved to London after riots that resulted in 200 fatalities. A Christian journalist, Isioma Daniel, in the Lagos daily, *This Day*, had written that Muhammad would probably have chosen a wife from one of the contestants. His comment exacerbated regional, national and international tensions over the imposition of the death penalty for adultery by a shari'a court on Amina Lawal in Katsina state. An international feminist call for a boycott resulted. Yet the local in this case – shari'a – represented yet another globalizing force, namely Islamism. The pageant, like many other pageants before it, revealed pre-existing political tensions within Nigeria between the predominantly Muslim north and the predominantly Christian and oil-rich south. These tensions go back at least as far as the Nigerian civil war of 1967–70, and beyond that, to the legacy of colonial rule.

The significant work of beauty pageants – the staging of group representation in the flesh – is not only visible in pageants with obvious global reach. Beauty pageants are used by a staggering diversity of constituencies around the world for vastly differing ends. For example, a Miss HIV Stigma-Free pageant is held annually in Botswana – the sub-Saharan Africa country with the highest rates of HIV infection in the world. Contestants appear in evening-wear, and are interviewed by judges. They also appear in 'traditional' Tswana feminine attire. Eligible contestants are either HIV positive themselves or have a close relative who is. As with Miss World contestants, an 'interview' determines 50 per cent of their final scores, but the interview questions are designed to gauge the contestants' knowledge about HIV – its transmission, its symptoms, its prevention and treatment. The majority of the contestants are already HIV/AIDS counsellors.

The pageant is funded through a partnership between a local NGO (The Centre for Youth and Hope), Merck (the pharmaceutical multinational), the Bill and Melinda Gates Foundation and De Beers (the South African diamond monopoly). Even if we simply 'follow the money,' the Miss HIV Stigma-Free pageant is a globalized cultural event. As a form of consumption, the pageant is decidedly national and local. The winner of the pageant is charged with touring Botswana promoting HIV testing and advocating for anti-retroviral treatment. Like many other pageants, this pageant can be understood as the local hijacking of a form from below, taking the popularity of beauty pageants and making the form do other cultural work than the prompting of normative gender fantasy.

Neville Hoad

Bibliography

Banet-Weiser S. 1999. *The most beautiful girl in the world: beauty pageants and national identity*. Berkeley and Los Angeles: University of California Press.

Cohen C., Wilk R. and Stoeltje B. 1995. *Beauty on the global stage: pageants and power*. London and New York: Routledge.

Hoad N. 2004. 'World piece: What the Miss World pageant can teach about globalization', *Cultural Critique*, 58, Fall, 56–81.

Related essays

Africa; Acquired Immunodeficiency Syndrome (AIDS); beauty; benefits and charity concerts; bodybuilding; femininity; gender and sex; prizes; religious fundamentalism

Benefits and charity concerts

Benefits or charity concerts are events in which musical performances are at least in part ostensibly mounted in an attempt to help those in need, mainly by raising funds for them. From their start in early modernity, they have had some transnational elements, initially in the music itself; its style, instruments, composers and/or performers. For example, when the Hungarian Franz Liszt played a concert in Portugal to benefit a Lisbon orphanage in 1845, his repertoire included works by German and Italian composers. Until the later part of the 20th century, the audiences, beneficiaries and mediators (concert hall owners or promoters, for example) of these concerts were local. A complex of economic and technological developments culminating at the start of the 21st century made benefit concerts far more frequent and more transnational.

The rise of the middle class and the increasing affluence of the working classes shifted the musical style played at major benefits. No longer was it the 'classical' music of the elites or non-commercial local folk music, but what is termed today rock or pop music. Created transnationally (British artists reworking American-developed rock 'n' roll – itself an amalgam of European and African musical influences), rock began its spread to other countries in the 1960s.

The first major rock charity concert was the Monterey International Pop Festival held in California on 16–18 June 1967. All of the more than 30 performers, with the exception of the Indian sitar player, Ravi Shankar, were from the US (for example, Jefferson Airplane, Otis Redding, and Jimi Hendrix) and the U.K. (for example, The Who). The beneficiaries were local music programmes and health clinics for the poor, but far less than the $200,000 raised made it to them because 'a bookkeeper absconded with some of the proceeds' (quoted in Morthland). The Concert for Bangladesh held at New York's Madison Square Garden on 1 August 1972 expanded transnationality. Recipients, on the Indian subcontinent, were refugees from the war in what was then called East Pakistan. Proceeds from the show ($243,418.50) were given, after some delay, to the international organization, UNICEF. Performers were from the US (for example, Bob Dylan) and the UK (for example, George Harrison, Eric Clapton), along with Shankar, who instigated the concert. Earnings from the triple-album set and a film augmented the concert's donations. These recordings, since they were heard by those outside the US, created a transnational audience.

Major benefit events in the mid-1980s, Live Aid and the Amnesty International concerts, displayed an even fuller transnationality. Live Aid, addressing the famine in Ethiopia, was held in London and Philadelphia on 13 July 1985. In addition to the combined on-site audience of 162,000, television and radio broadcasts to about 160 countries reached as many as 1.5 billion people. Multinational record companies profited from the release of concert recordings as well as the boost in the performers' record sales. The Amnesty tour, which aimed to assist political prisoners worldwide, played in Western, Communist and Third World countries on five continents in 1988, reaching widely different audiences with different readings of rock music. Beyond British and American rock stars, it included Youssou N'Dour from Senegal – the one distinctively non-Western performer. It also introduced a non-musical commercial sponsor to benefits concerts, a multinational athletic shoe company.

Using the economic and technological approaches of the Live Aid and Amnesty concerts, benefits proliferated. For example, about a month or so after the devastating 26 December 2004 Asian tsunami, there was a raft of them, held independently in Canada, Wales, India, and China, among other countries. The Live8 concert on 2 July 2005, with live performances in Europe, Asia, Africa, Australia and North America, added to television and radio broadcasts the most transnational technological development – streaming the concert over the Internet.

While benefit concerts have responded to a constant need for charitable aid, their recent increase and growing transnationality are functions of the global reach of various technologies, the desire for larger markets by multinational

music and other corporations, and the requirement of celebrities to keep themselves in the increasingly cluttered public eye.

Deena Weinstein

Bibliography
Morthland J. 'Rock festivals', in Miller J. (ed.) 1980. *The Rolling Stone illustrated history of rock & roll*. New York: Random House, 336–8.
Weinstein D. 1989. 'The Amnesty International concert tour: transnationalism as cultural commodity', *Public Culture*, 1, 2, 60–5.

Related essays
Acquired Immunodeficiency Syndrome (AIDS); Amnesty International (AI); classical music; human rights; music; natural hazards; refugees; relief; rock

Bible *See* **Publishing**

Bibliographic classification

Bibliographic classification is the activity of organizing documents (or their representations) so that documents or records with similar characteristics are grouped together in discrete classes. Once the documents in a collection have been classified, proponents argue, the reader may more efficiently identify documents with desired characteristics (e.g., about a particular subject), and may more effectively identify characteristics of interest (by means of browsing systematically ordered lists).

From one point of view, the history of bibliographic classification could be written straightforwardly as an account of the professionalization of a particular set of practices intended to serve library users' needs, and the rationalization of a particular set of principles intended to guide practitioners. The ideal of establishing 'universal bibliographic control' through the global standardization of techniques for describing, organizing, and providing access to the world's recorded knowledge – an ideal first seriously promulgated in the late 19th century – served as the motivation for much of the technical work of library and information scientists through the 20th century, and continues to drive the development of international metadata standards (for digital and multimedia as well as printed resources) in the 21st. At the heart of this system of standards lie classification schemes that define the scope of the classes to which documents are to be assigned and the nature of the hierarchical relationships among those classes. Universal classification schemes (i.e., schemes intended for general application to library materials of all kinds across all subject areas) have come to serve as core components of a global infrastructure that has been strongly facilitative of cross-national flows of information and ideas. Correspondingly, the history of the rise to dominance, since their origins in a 40-year period spanning the 19th and 20th centuries, of the three most widely used universal schemes – the Dewey Decimal Classification (DDC), Library of Congress Classification (LCC), and Universal Decimal Classification (UDC) – is commonly told from a teleological perspective, with little questioning of the benefits that the transnational infrastructure to which they contribute is assumed to bring.

A complementary view of the universal schemes treats them as the objects of (rather than as supports for) circulation, and focuses on explaining the conditions under which some schemes have proven their utility far beyond the boundaries of the contexts in which they were produced, while others have remained purely local in application or have failed even to maintain a lasting local prominence despite their apparent technical advantages. This approach emphasizes the impact not only of aspects of the social, cultural, political, economic, and technological contexts in which classification schemes are developed and promoted, but also of the motivations and intentions of the schemes' developers and promoters. The figures of Melvil Dewey (USA; 1851–1931), an efficiency-conscious entrepreneur, and the more idealistic Paul Otlet (Belgium; 1868–1944) still loom large in the parallel histories of the 'big three' schemes, which are marked by several incidents involving negotiations among rivals that subsequently proved to be crucial turning points. Dewey's initial decision to adopt an innovative notation amounted to a huge advance on existing schemes: decimal fractions expressed in the form of Arabic numerals were easily understood by speakers of different languages, and infinitely hospitable to new subtopics. The advantages of this notation were immediately understood by Otlet and his friend Henri La Fontaine when they began their search for a means of ordering their universal bibliography. Dewey's agreement with Otlet and La Fontaine in the 1890s, that allowed the two Belgians to develop their UDC and base their 'Brussels expansion' on the DDC so long as they refrained from publishing a version in English, was as significant as his subsequent refusal to allow the Library of Congress similarly to model the LCC on the DDC, and as his assistant Dorcas Fellows' refusal in the 1920s to countenance any future convergence between the DDC and the UDC, thereby setting the two schemes off on quite separate trails.

The DDC, LCC, and UDC were all conceived during a period when the objectivity of scientific knowledge was widely assumed, and the positivist certainties of that time are reflected in some of the inflexibilities of the schemes that remain even today. Historians and sociologists have recently begun to emphasize the cultural particularity of any method by which categories are formulated and ordered, and to direct renewed attention to questions about the extent to which it is desirable (or even possible) for designers to adopt a neutral standpoint in the elimination of localized cultural biases from schemes that are used in varied social settings. Resistance to change of the kind that would be required for the reduction of Western, Christian bias in the three major schemes is often met among those for whom the primary purpose of such schemes is to 'save the time of the reader': maintaining integrity of numbers over time (and thus avoiding the need for extensive reclassification) has often been deemed more important than either the traditional ideal that schemes should accurately reflect the state of knowledge at any given time, or the more radical goal of enabling the dynamic representation of multiple culturally specific views of the way the contents of documents (and, ultimately, the universe of knowledge) should be described and organized.

Jonathan Furner

Bibliography

Miksa F. L. 1998. *The DDC, the universe of knowledge, and the post-modern library.* Albany: Forest Press.

Related essays

car safety standards; food safety standards; libraries; measurement systems; Otlet, Paul; technical standardization

Otlet, Paul 1868–1944

Paul Otlet was a key figure in many institutions, organizations and publications of the early 20th century, and for decades pursued projects for the organization of the international scientific and civic spheres.

Otlet's childhood spread over borders. His father, then a prosperous tramways and financial Belgian magnate, travelled extensively. Paul was educated in Paris and Brussels. Working in a Brussels law firm after graduation, he met Henri La Fontaine, with whom he teamed up for a lifetime of international organization work. First, they launched the International Institute of Bibliography (now International Federation for Information and Documentation) in 1895, to develop Melvil Dewey's decimal classification. Subsequently, they collaborated on a complex project to organize international associations of intellectual and scientific elites. Otlet coined the word 'mondialisme' to singularize this project. They initiated, favoured or directed dozens of initiatives, institutions, publications and meetings, including the journal La Vie Internationale (1912), the Office Central des Institutions Internationales (1907, later Union of International Associations) and the Musée Mondial (1910). Resources for this vast effort came from their own funds and from the Belgian industrialist Ernest Solvay, the Carnegie Endowment for International Peace, and the Belgian government. After the First World War, Otlet found himself at odds with the League of Nations he had ardently supported. The League gradually grew hostile to his associative conception of intellectual cooperation, and the institutions he created in Brussels began to wither. Otlet died alone and bitter in 1944. He has been recently rediscovered as a precursor by documentation specialists who have compared his conception of documentation with the Internet, both being based on simultaneous access to small knowledge units no longer bounded by the printed format.

Pierre-Yves Saunier

Bibliography
Rayward W. B. 1975. *The universe of information: the Work of Paul Otlet for documentation and international organisation.* Moscow: VINITI.

Related essays
bibliographical classification; Garvey, Marcus Mosiah; globalization; international non-governmental organizations (INGOs); internationalisms; Jacobs, Aletta; Kessler, Harry von; Schwimmer, Rosika; transnational; United Cities and Local Governments (UCLG); Williams, James Dixon; world federalism

Biodiversity

Biodiversity is often generically defined as the 'variety of life on Earth' – and whether due to or despite of its simplicity, this definition has arguably sufficed for general descriptive purposes to a broad lay public. Yet scientists and conservationists have endowed the term with additional definitions of varying precision. The consequent semantic tension over the word is largely driven by two interrelated problems. First, biodiversity is not strictly speaking about the stuff of life itself (note that before the relatively recent emergence of 'biodiversity', the word 'biota' had long referred to the complete assortment of life in any given region), but rather about the differences between the stuff of life. This leads straight to the second problem: the inherent difficulties of measuring the somewhat ethereal notion of diversity. For how does one go about the practical problem of measuring diversity – particularly when the Earth's living forms confront us with so many gradients of diversity?

The first problem has been largely resolved inasmuch as biodiversity has become widely accepted as referring to both the variety of life and the stuff of life (albeit with the side effect of diminishing the use of 'biota'). The second problem remains unresolved, although scientific debate over 'measuring diversity' has become less of a flashpoint and more of the background noise of biological inquiry. This partly results from the scientific community's broad acceptance of a relatively more rigorous definition of biodiversity, one that establishes a three-tiered hierarchy of diversity: the diversity of ecosystems, the diversity of species, and the diversity of populations and individuals within a single species (commonly called 'genetic diversity' but more precisely referred to as 'allelic diversity'). Some scientists still find this breakdown too simplistic, noting other 'higher' levels of diversity (e.g., landscape and biome diversity) and other types of diversity (e.g., behavioural and functional diversity). Regardless of such reservations, scientists now regularly rely on the term 'biodiversity' in their journal articles, grant applications, and books as shorthand for a distinction between these three levels.

Although different in precision, both the above generic and scientific definitions of biodiversity capture only half of the word's broad connotations. This is because biodiversity – as well as its progenitor 'biological diversity' – were both born within a circle of scientists and conservationists who were becoming increasingly alarmed at a number of threatening planetary trends. Consequently, the etymological origins of the term 'biodiversity' can only be fully understood in the context of the history of conservation practice and conservation thought.

Over the course of the 20th century, the fields of biology and ecology turned away from romantic notions of the 'balance of nature' and toward more dynamic, non-linear models of how organisms interact with their environment. Yet even as scientists found little in the way of biological constancy in their studies, they also discovered that the rates of change in biological and ecological processes had dramatically accelerated since the industrial revolution. This acceleration was due to the apparently ineluctable absorption of the earth's biological productivity for the use of *Homo sapiens*. Within all of the Earth's biomes, from grasslands and forests to deserts and tundra, biological landscapes have experienced an unprecedented degree of anthropogenic alteration – changes that in some cases have led to catastrophic results. On a global scale, for example, scientists have focused on the loss of species, pointing out that human activities have increased rates of species extinction by anywhere between 100 and 1,000 percent compared to normal 'background rates' (i.e., the rate of extinctions on a geologic timescale not including the five major 'mass extinctions' that paleontologists have detected in the fossil record).

A recent terminology

Up until less than two decades ago, scientists and conservationists referred to the general problem of extinction with myriad terms and slogans that ranged from 'endangered species' and 'vanishing wildlife' to 'Bring back the wolf' and 'Save the whales'. The birth of the modern environmental movement is often traced to the 1962 publication of *Silent Spring*, which itself has become another catchphrase (in this case emphasizing the loss of bird species). But none of these disparate labels either caught on or were widely applicable to the loss of various forms of flora and fauna.

This situation changed in the early 1980s with the introduction of the catch-all concept of biological diversity. This term had appeared in the scientific literature as early as 1955 in reference to the development of pisciculture and was used in passing during the 1960s by such noted scholars as the environmental economist John Krutilla (of Resources for the Future) and biologist Raymond Dasmann (of various NGOs and the University of California), both of whom were influential thinkers in the field of international conservation. However, the term did not come to prominence until the 1980 publication of two comprehensive, multi-authored reports emanating from the US federal government that examined environmental issues from an international perspective: *The Global 2000 Report to the President* (viz., Jimmy Carter) and *The Eleventh Annual Report of the Council on Environmental Quality*. A chapter in the former report authored by biologist Thomas Lovejoy, and a chapter in the latter by Elliot Norse and Roger McManus, both used 'biological diversity' in discussing the various anthropogenic threats being identified by scientists and conservationists.

Today, many conservation texts organize these threats into a handful of categories. Although there are multiple permutations of the following listing, six consistent categories can be distilled from the literature: overexploitation, loss of habitat, degradation of habitat, invasive species, climate change, and secondary effects. These threats are often characterized as the 'proximate' causes of biodiversity loss; underlying these proximate causes are the 'root causes' of biodiversity loss that include such phenomena as human population growth, technological change, overconsumption, and affluence.

After the phrase 'biological diversity' became more widely adopted during the early 1980s, the combined version debuted at the 1986 National Forum on BioDiversity. Although credit for coining the term is often attributed to the well-known Harvard biologist Edward O. Wilson, he initially disliked it – but soon came to embrace the term, giving origination credit to the biologist who organized the Forum, Walter Rosen. With thousands in attendance, the Forum attracted significant media attention to the pandemic threats to biodiversity. Notably, all 62 chapters of the subsequent publication of the Forum's proceedings (edited by Wilson under the title BioDiversity) concerned the loss of biodiversity. Thus, from its birth the word connoted an urgent need for conservation.

All but six of the authors of BioDiversity represented US-based institutions, and no doubt the word's origins lie firmly within the US. Yet by the late 1980s, the term 'biological diversity' had been widely adopted by the eclectic body of international conservationists and negotiators who focused on a swath of transborder conservation issues that ranged from 'debt-for-nature' swaps and the establishment of protected areas to the preservation of rare agricultural crops and the attribution of sovereign rights over biological resources. Notably, the same year as the publication of BioDiversity (1988), the United Nations Environment Programme (UNEP) commenced negotiations for a global conservation convention by establishing an 'Ad Hoc Group of Experts on Biological Diversity'. Although the ultimate product of these negotiations would retain the longer title of the 'Convention on Biological Diversity', it would come to be commonly referred to as 'the Biodiversity Convention' (which is discussed in further detail below).

Nonetheless, through to the end of the 1980s 'biodiversity' remained a somewhat obscure expression reserved for the insular conversations of scientists and conservationists. Probably more than anything else, what eventually solidified the term's conservationist identity was the political dispute over the 1992 Convention on Biological Diversity, now more commonly known as the Biodiversity Convention. Concerned about maintaining intellectual property rights over biotechnology, the first Bush administration declined to sign the convention at the 1992 Earth Summit in Rio de Janeiro (President Clinton would sign the Convention in 1993, but the US Senate has yet to ratify it). The refusal to sign provoked clamorous (if short-lived) protests from the conservation community, strong indignation from numerous developed and developing countries, and a good deal of attention from the media – thus giving the word 'biodiversity' a cachet it would likely have taken years to garner otherwise. Consequently, regardless of its scientific definition and use, biodiversity has often been perceived as the 'rallying cry' against the global extinction crisis.

Use of the term has dramatically increased since the 1980s, and 'biodiversity' is now widely employed by physical scientists, social scientists, conservationists, and the media. It is worth noting that approximately four hundred commercially available books have the word biodiversity in their titles – and that at least at one time soon after 2002, the word generated more finds on Google than did 'climate change', 'Beatles', 'George W. Bush', or 'Tiger Woods'. The problem of biodiversity loss has been addressed by investigators in a wide range of academic disciplines, including philosophy, economics, political science, international law, history, geography, linguistics, policy analysis, education, anthropology, chemistry, health, medicine, physics, geology, and, of course, a myriad of subdisciplines in biology (e.g., forestry, ethnobotany, limnology, and genetics).

150 years of multilateral agreements and disagreements

Liberally construed, biodiversity has been a transnational issue since long before the 20th century. Although pre-Westphalian treaties over biological resources – principally fish – focused solely on divvying up rights to fisheries, conservation-oriented measures began to appear in bilateral treaties as early as the mid 19th century. But historians generally point to negotiations between the US and Great Britain (for Canada) over the Pacific fur seal (Callorhinus ursinus) as the first major development toward international law – or at least international standards – for the conservation of biodiversity. These negotiations led to what some consider to be one of the more successful conservation treaties ever to go into force: the 1911 Pacific Fur Seal Treaty. Other international accords over biological resources during this period of the 'dawn of conservation diplomacy' included the 1900 London Convention for the Protection of Wild Animals, Birds and Fish in Africa and the 1902 European Convention Concerning the Conservation of Birds Useful to Agriculture. A seminal agreement was the 1916 Migratory Bird Treaty between the US and Canada, which was extended to Mexico in 1936 and remains in effect today.

Several other conservation-oriented multilateral treaties signed during the interwar period included two conservation treaties on whaling in 1931 and 1937, a 1933 convention on African wildlife (which, unlike the 1900

Convention, garnered a sufficient number of ratifications to come into force), and the 1940 Convention on Nature Protection and Wild Life Preservation in the Western Hemisphere. Although none of these proved effective in enhancing conservation, two important international initiatives occurred in the years immediately following World War 2. First, in 1946, a number of coastal states signed the International Convention for the Regulation of Whaling. Although this convention was intended to enhance sustainable harvesting of whales, parties to the agreement would eventually ban all whaling in 1982 (a decision that took effect in 1986). And in 1948, a large number of countries and conservation organizations established the International Union for the Protection of Nature, now the World Conservation Union (and still denoted somewhat confusingly with the acronym IUCN, which stood for its name from 1956 to 1988). Although faulted through the years for its highly bureaucratic structure, the IUCN was an important early example of cooperation between state and civil society and in a number of ways has been a critical driver of international conservation initiatives – particularly through the publication of its 'Red Lists' of endangered species.

The first major multilateral treaty concerning biodiversity was the Convention on the International Trade in Endangered Species (CITES). The IUCN had called for such treaty as early as 1963, but a final agreement came only in 1973, entering into force in 1975 (and now with 120 member countries). To counter the effects of an international market in wildlife amounting to billions of dollars every year, CITES attempts to impose a worldwide system of trade controls. Distinguishing between various levels of threats, CITES places each endangered species on one of three appendices. Appendix I bans the trade of species whose ability to survive is affected by trade; trade permits are issued for these species only under exceptional circumstances. Appendix II contains species that might become endangered if trade in them is not controlled and monitored. Species are placed in either Appendix I or Appendix II according to a vote among the Conference of the Parties (the member countries of CITES). Individual member countries may at their discretion add species to Appendix III to garner support in enforcing domestic export laws.

Another important multilateral treaty is the Bonn Convention on Migratory Species of Wild Animals (CMS). The origins of this treaty have been traced to a recommendation that came out of the 1972 Stockholm Conference on the Human Environment, but the convention was not signed until 1979 (entering into force in 1983). As with CITES, the CMS works through Appendices that provide various level of protection to individual migratory species. Unlike CITES, however, the CMS has also acted as an umbrella convention for several protocol conventions that have specifically addressed a number of issues, including European bat species, Mediterranean cetaceans, small cetaceans of the Baltic and North Seas, seals in the Wadden Sea, African-Eurasian migratory waterbirds, and albatrosses and petrels.

Throughout the 1970s and 1980s, a growing number of conservation-oriented international non-governmental organizations and foreign aid agencies of the developed world focused on biodiversity conservation projects in the less developed world. At the same time, negotiations over the international control of 'germplasm' or 'plant genetic resources' were taking place under the aegis of the UN Food and Agricultural Organization (FAO). These negotiations concerned the basic question of who 'owns' genetic resources that have been either collected directly from a natural state or modified by human ingenuity. On the one hand, the developing world argued that all genetic resources were the 'common heritage' of mankind, and that the developed world thus had no right to place intellectual property rights (IPRs, which include patents and 'plant breeder's rights') on particular varieties of plants. This practice was seen as particularly egregious in that the original stock often came from the developing world – often in the form of 'landraces' that had been significantly enhanced and modified by traditional farmers. On the other hand, developed countries countered that IPRs provided significant incentives for agricultural enhancement. These negotiations eventually resulted in the formulation of a rare if not unique form of international agreement: the 1984 International Undertaking on Plant Genetic Resources. Opposition to the Undertaking from key countries (viz., the US) and the complex politics behind this nebulous non-treaty made the document more of a position paper than an international agreement. From the perspective of the developing world, however, this may have been just as well – for their position was to take a drastic turn by the end of the decade, particularly in regard to negotiations over the proposed convention on 'biological diversity'.

The Convention on Biological Diversity

The idea of a multilateral treaty focusing on the conservation of biological resources has been traced back to the 1981 General Assembly of the IUCN. But as noted above, focused negotiations over a Convention on Biological Diversity began in 1988, under the auspices of the United Nations Environment Program (UNEP). The original intent was to focus on species conservation and habitat protection, but those basic intentions were soon overwhelmed by a number of other concerns – many of them emanating from the continuing negotiations over the FAO's Undertaking on Plant Genetic Resources. Yet by this point, the developing world's perspective on 'common heritage' had taken a dramatic about-face. This broad policy shift came about due to three principal factors. First was the recognition that species found 'in nature' could be of beneficial and profitable use to the agricultural, pharmaceutical, and biotechnology industries. Second was the recognition that most of the world's species diversity lay in the tropics – and that since developing countries dominated the tropics, it made eminent sense to stake out a strong sovereign claims to those species. The third factor was a strong backlash to the problem of 'biopiracy', an accusation holding corporations accountable for stealing biological specimens from developing nations, modifying them ('modifying them slightly', was a typical refrain), and then using IPRs as a cover to sell them back to developing countries for exorbitant profits. Collectively, these factors led to a new-found perspective on the 'value of nature', with the result that developing countries came to see biodiversity as constituting part of their national patrimony – and not, as before, as the 'common heritage of mankind'. In this regard, it was notable that the 1992 CBD lifted verbatim Principle 21 from the 1972 Stockholm Declaration of the United Nations Conference on the Human Environment:

States have, in accordance with the Charter of the United Nations and the principles of international law, the sovereign right to exploit their own resources pursuant to their own environmental policies, and the responsibility to ensure that activities within their jurisdiction or control do not cause damage to the environment of other States or of areas beyond the limits of national jurisdiction.

Accordingly, the text of the CBD designates biodiversity as 'a common *concern* of humankind' (emphasis added).

In addition to the issue of sovereignty, negotiators from many countries – principally but not exclusively the large block of developing countries – argued that a convention could not solely address biodiversity conservation. To incorporate the additional concerns brought to the negotiating table, the final convention lists three fundamental objectives: 'the conservation of biological diversity, the sustainable use of its components and the fair and equitable sharing of the benefits arising out of the utilization of genetic resources'. To fulfill these broad objectives, the final draft of the convention would pertain to a wide swath of issues – and to understand just how comprehensive the CBD came to be, it is helpful to peruse the titles of the various articles included in the convention (some administrative articles have been omitted):

- Article 6: General measures for conservation and sustainable use
- Article 7: Identification and monitoring
- Article 8: In-situ conservation
- Article 9: Ex-situ conservation
- Article 10: Sustainable use of components of biological diversity
- Article 11: Incentive measures
- Article 12: Research and training
- Article 13: Public education and awareness
- Article 14: Impact assessment and minimizing adverse impacts
- Article 15: Access to genetic resources
- Article 16: Access to and transfer of technology
- Article 17: Exchange of information
- Article 18: Technical and scientific cooperation
- Article 19: Handling of biotechnology and distribution of its benefits
- Article 20: Financial resources
- Article 21: Financial mechanism

That so many contrasting topics could be negotiated into a single non-trade international agreement is nothing short of extraordinary – or at least, it would have been had the convention any teeth. For although most observers would allow that the CBD has significantly raised the international profile of biodiversity conservation, the convention has arguably had little substantive impact in 'on the ground' conservation. Indicative of this is the fact that the only protocol under the CBD has been the 2000 Cartagena Protocol on Biosafety. 'Biosafety' is defined by the CBD secretariat as 'the need to protect human health and the environment from the possible adverse effects of the products of modern biotechnology'. While there are certainly important conservation implications from the use of modern biotechnology, it is notable that the CBD's own definition of biosafety begins with the issue of human health.

One of the more difficult questions regarding implementation of the CBD was how to pay for its implementation. Article 21 on a 'financial mechanism' for the CBD identifies the Global Environment Facility (GEF), a financing mechanism emanating out of the World Bank during negotiations over both the CBD and the Framework Convention on Climate Change (FCCC). Although the GEF has distributed over US$4.5 billion for international biodiversity conservation initiatives throughout the developing world since 1992, many if not most GEF-funded initiatives have received no little criticism for their reputed ineffectiveness.

Border cooperation

Running concurrent with the above multilateral and global initiatives to protect biodiversity, a countless number of formal and informal bilateral conservation initiatives can be found in border areas (for example, an informal survey of the two continental borders of the US identified over thirty such initiatives). The term that is most associated with two countries working together on transborder habitat protection is 'peace park'. Such an idea had been proposed for one of Europe's troubled borders soon after World War 1, but the idea would not come to fruition until 1932 when the US and Canada established the Waterton-Glacier International Peace Park (which the countries had only accomplished after heavy lobbying

by the Rotary Clubs located in nearby towns on either side of the border). Peace parks can now be found on nearly every continent – and given the as yet still peaceful and cooperative Antarctic Treaty System, even the usual exception of Antarctica can be interpreted as somewhat akin to a global peace park.

Ever since the aforementioned 'dawn of conservation diplomacy', civil society actors have played a critical role in protecting biodiversity in the international arena. Two prominent examples of organized transborder coalitions or networks are Great Lakes United (GLU, founded in 1982) and the Yellowstone to Yukon Conservation Initiative (Y2Y, founded in the mid 1990s). Comprised of environmentalists, hunters and anglers, labour unions, community groups and individual citizens from both sides of the US–Canadian border (as well as across US tribal and First Nation boundaries), GLU was formed with the specific objective of strengthening a proposed protocol to the US–Canada Great Lakes Water Quality Agreement. GLU has since grown into an extensive bilateral network focusing on preserving and restoring the Great Lakes-St Lawrence River ecosystem. As one observer noted of GLU, it offered a 'clear and consistent voice' at an intergovernmental negotiating table and 'stands out' as a case study of non-state influence over international negotiations.

Y2Y took a different tack. Instead of focusing on particular intergovernmental diplomatic initiatives, the initiative's early focus was on creating a community between conservationists and scientists on either side of the border. Given the large-landscape requirements of 'flagship species' in the region – most particularly the grizzly bear (Ursus arctos) and wolf (Canis lupus) – participants in Y2Y had long recognized that implementing conservation at a small scale would be insufficient in the long term. Y2Y not only presented a practical way to build a functional network across borders (not only the international border, but also a plethora of state, provincial, tribal, and land agency borders), but offered practical support to conservationists for accessing Internet technologies including email and electronic mailing lists (both only at an inchoate state of use in the region by the mid 1990s). More importantly, in portraying the region as a cohesive biological entity, the Y2Y label attracted both media attention and substantial foundation dollars to the region.

Biodiversity as a transnational challenge

Overall, the concept of 'biological diversity' was inherently transnational long before its contemporary coinage in 1980. And while it remains difficult to assess comprehensively, international cooperation on biodiversity conservation has no doubt led to numerous significant conservation achievements. Yet as many biologists are wont to decry, the successes are vastly outnumbered by the overall failure of the international community to stem the tide of habitat destruction, invasive species, climate change, and other threats to the world's biodiversity. Can the international community – however that be defined – devise the means by which to protect 'what's left' of the world's biodiversity? Despite widespread cynicism over the CBD, that convention nonetheless constitutes a promising start. Regrettably, as with the struggle over the FCCC and its Kyoto Protocol, one of the major impediments to progress has been and remains the intransigence on the part of the United States of America. Without full participation by the world's most powerful state actor, the CBD is unlikely to garner the type of influence it would need to achieve practical implementation of its ambitious agenda.

But of course, US participation in the CBD's bureaucracy hardly constitutes the single ingredient missing from the recipe of global biodiversity conservation. Treacherous as it is to prognosticate over the future of biodiversity, it is probably safe to say that through myriad pathways – be they economic, social, political, demographic, etc – the human impact on the planet will ineluctably increase over the coming century. Conservationists will likely continue to win individual victories in the quest for conservation, but for the most part they simply will have neither sufficient capacity nor adequate knowledge to counter these unfortunate trends at the global scale. Under such a gloomy scenario, perhaps the greatest opportunity for conservation 'action' is indirect – viz., to continue effecting a transformation in how people throughout the various cultures of the world value biodiversity, and in how those values play out in practice. This is not a new call to arms; a transformation in how people value biodiversity – even though it didn't yet carry that label – comprised a critical component of the first effective conservation treaties at the beginning of the 20th century. Ultimately, however, there is no single magic bullet. Indeed, the search for a magic bullet is nothing short of a utopian dream with roughly the same conservation impact of a real bullet. Reflecting the diversity of what it hopes to protect, the international conservation movement will have to adopt myriad approaches in order to protect biodiversity over the course of the 21st century.

Charles C. Chester

Bibliography

Adams W. M. 2004. *Against extinction: the story of conservation*. Sterling, VA: Earthscan.

Chester C. C. 2006. *Conservation across borders: biodiversity in an interdependent world*. Washington, DC: Island.

Dorsey K. 1998. *The dawn of conservation diplomacy: U.S.-Canadian wildlife protection treaties in the progressive era*. Seattle: University of Washington Press.

Le Prestre P. G. (ed.) 2002. *Governing global biodiversity: the evolution and implementation of the Convention on Biological Diversity*. Aldershot and Burlington: Ashgate.

van Heijnsbergen P. 1997. *International legal protection of wild fauna and flora*. Washington, DC: IOS.

Wilson E. O. (ed.) 1988. *Biodiversity*. Washington, DC: National Academy Press.

Related essays

acclimatization; agriculture; air pollution; Antarctic Treaty; biopatents; borders and borderlands; climate; conservation and preservation; ecology; environmental diplomacy; environmentalism; fisheries; forests; General Agreement on Tariffs and Trade (GATT) / World Trade Organization WTO); genetically modified organisms (GMOs); indigenous knowledges; indigenous networks; intellectual property rights; international non-governmental organizations (INGOs); legal order; life and physical sciences; Monsanto; national parks; oceans; pesticides, herbicides, insecticides; seeds; Stockholm Conference; sustainable development; tropics; United Nations decades and years; United Nations system; Vandana Shiva Research Foundation for Science, Technology and Ecology; World Conservation Union (IUCN) and World Wide Fund for Nature (WWF)

Biopatents

Biopatents are utility patents that have been conferred on inventions of novel forms of living organisms and/or their component parts and products.

Though presaged by the development of patent-like 'plant breeders' rights' (PBRs) during the 1960s, the extensive application of utility patents to a wide range of biological materials and substances emerged from the biotechnology revolution of the 1980s. The extension of intellectual property rights (IPRs) to the material basis of life itself has occasioned fierce, international debate over the ethical propriety and the distributional effects of biopatenting in a world characterized by deep economic, social, and scientific inequalities. While business interests now strive to harmonize diverse, national IPR laws in order to facilitate global commercialization of biological inventions, opposition to biopatenting has become a key platform for challenges to corporate-led globalization.

Patents are limited property rights granted to inventors by legal statute. This is an instrumental arrangement intended to provide incentive for innovation. In exchange for public disclosure of a new process or product, inventors are permitted to exclude others from using the innovation (or to license its use for a royalty) for a 20-year period. To be patentable, an invention must be novel, non-obvious, and useful. As early as 1905, plant and animal breeders in the US had sought to have the crop and livestock varieties they developed protected by patents. Breeders of some ornamental crops achieved this goal in 1930, but Congress excluded all food and grain crops from that year's Plant Patent Act because it was deemed inappropriate to confer any form of monopoly control over staples.

As private seed companies in North America and Europe increased their research activities, they pressed their governments to provide some form of IPR protection for their products. During the decade of the 1960s, many European countries instituted PBRs which allowed a breeder to prevent competing companies from selling a protected plant variety. These PBRs were only 'patent-like' inasmuch as farmers were permitted to save and replant seed without paying royalties. Passage of the Plant Variety Protection Act of 1970 in the US generated opposition from farm and social justice advocacy groups who feared the erosion of the genetic commons and the curtailment of free exchange of plant germplasm in research.

Such concerns found expression in a global context as developing nations were asked to institute PBR legislation to protect imported commercial crop varieties while allowing agronomists from the developed North to collect breeding material from their farmers as the freely available 'common heritage of mankind'. Attention to ownership and control of genetic materials was further reinforced in the late 1970s by the emerging promise of recombinant DNA technology.

The corporate push for commodification of life was given considerable momentum in 1980 with the decision issued by the US Supreme Court in Chakrabarty v. Diamond. In that case, the court held that a genetically engineered microorganism was patentable subject matter. Suddenly, novel microbes, plants, animals, and their component parts and products could be protected under the utility patent statutes. The Supreme Court had provided the essential legal scaffolding for the commercial biotechnology revolution.

With the patentability of biotechnological inventions securely established in the US, in-house commitments to genetic research among life sciences and chemical companies soared, as did venture capital investment in biotechnology startup firms. Excitement over the commercial potential of medical, agricultural, and energy applications of the new technologies led to extensive patenting across all levels of biological complexity. In what has been likened to a 19th-century-style land grab, vast tracts of the genescape and its products (e.g., DNA sequences, individual mutations, expressed sequence tags, single nucleotide polymorphisms, proteins, parts of plants, whole organisms, whole classes of organism) have been patented. Not only has genetic material itself been commodified, but the methods and techniques by which it is studied and manipulated are also patentable subject matter and key enabling technologies such as the 'gene gun' and biological vectors for genetic transformation have also been patented.

This pulse of biopatenting has had a variety of implications for various economic sectors and social interests. Although universities and government agencies have also joined the race to stake out ownership of genomes, it is private industry that is the predominant owner of biopatents. Moreover, given continuing consolidation in the life sciences industry, a very narrow set of companies, the so-called Gene Giants (e.g., Monsanto, Dupont, Syngenta, Bayer, Dow), now have a significant degree of control over biotechnology research through the number and quality of the biopatents they hold. There is concern that these companies will use their economic and scientific power to develop technologies that might be privately profitable but are also socially or environmentally problematic.

Such concerns have been most strongly expressed in the agricultural sector where patented, genetically engineered crop varieties have been developed and commercialized on a global scale. Unlike PBR legislation, utility patents on plants do not exempt farmers from compliance with the prohibition on making the invention – that is, they may grow but not save and replant patented seed. Seed companies and their Gene Giant parents firms are aggressively policing the use of patented crop varieties and are systematically enforcing annual purchase of seed. Erosion of the ages-old right to save and resow seed is particularly critical for many small and subsistence farmers in developing countries who simply do not have the resources to buy seed each year.

Extensive contamination of organic and conventional varieties by pollen drift from patented, genetically engineered varieties has introduced profound uncertainties as to who actually owns the product of such genetic drift.

Currently, each nation state constructs its own patent legislation and international enforceability of those diverse patent laws is subject to mutual agreement between countries. However, international structures of governance are now being framed in such a way as to extend the reach of an IPR regime that encompasses biopatents. All members of the World Trade Organization are now required by the TRIPs (Trade-Related Aspects of Intellectual Property Standards) agreement to adhere to a harmonized framework that eliminates much flexibility and mandates imposition of IPRs for biological materials.

Further, while the 1992 Convention on Biodiversity recognizes the contributions of indigenous peoples and farmers and calls for sharing of genetic resources in a fair and equitable manner, it subordinates these considerations to effective protection of intellectual property rights. But the existing IPR regime is unable to reward the collective and time-bound innovation modalities that characterize the generation of useful biological diversity and agronomic and ethnobotanical knowledge by peasant farmers and indigenous peoples. Conversely, it countenances the appropriation and transformation of such material and information by scientists and businesses into patentable products. This asymmetric process has been termed 'biopiracy' by critics, and defended as legitimate 'bioprospecting' by those firms and states with the capacity to engage in the practice.

Recently, the public scientific community has found itself in a position similar to that of farmers and indigenous peoples. Private industry has both the resources and the will to explore the bioscape and to claim property rights over what had, until the Chakrabarty decision, been the public domain. But the proliferation of patents has had some problematic effects. Of particular concern is the apparent lowering of the thresholds for novelty, utility, non-obviousness which some argue has permitted far more patents to issue than is warranted. Increasingly, public scientists have found themselves pressed by thickets of biopatents that constrain their access to biological materials, limit their access to the tools they need, and force them to spend time establishing how much 'freedom to operate' they can carve out for their work. The restrictive licences and covenants and materials transfer agreements that now accompany both public and private research in molecular biology and genetics – as well as the sheer number of biopatents – is feared to be leading to what has been termed a 'tragedy of the anti-commons' in which scientific progress is retarded by the legal and managerial difficulties of reconciling and coordinating different owners' property rights.

For a variety of reasons, biopatents are now generating opposition from a variety of social positions. This resistance is robust, globally distributed, increasingly well-organized, and grounded in a broad range of issues. Such opposition is strongest among farmers, indigenous peoples, and advocacy groups working in the context of a diffuse but powerful social movement that is resisting what has come to be understood as the project of 'corporate globalization'. Biopatents are seen to be the leading edge of that project. Recently, voices from the public science community have raised a parallel, instrumentalist critique in which the fundamental premise for granting biopatents – their ultimate contribution to overall social welfare through technical progress – is called into question.

Jack R. Kloppenburg, Jr

Bibliography

Graf G., Cullen S., Bradford K.,Zilberman D. and Bennet A. 2003. 'The public-private structure of intellectual property ownership in agricultural biotechnology', *Nature Biotechnology*, 21, 989–95.
Heller M. and Heisenberg R. 1998. 'Can patents deter innovation? The anticommons in biomedical research', *Science*, 280, 698–701.
Kloppenburg, J. Jr 2004. *First the seed: the political economy of plant biotechnology, 1492–2000*. Madison: University of Wisconsin Press.

Related essays

agriculture; biodiversity; corporations; ecology; environmentalism; General Agreement on Tariffs and Trade (GATT) / World Trade Organization (WTO); genetically modified organisms (GMOs); Green Revolution; indigenous knowledges; indigenous networks; intellectual property rights; international non-governmental organizations (INGOs); legal order; life and natural sciences; Monsanto; patents; seeds; trademarks; Vandana Shiva Research Foundation for Science, Technology and Ecology

Vandana Shiva Research Foundation for Science, Technology and Ecology

In 1982, Dr Vandana Shiva founded the Research Foundation for Science, Technology and Ecology with headquarters in New Delhi in India. Her role as director has been to produce innovative alternative research from the perspective of the developing world that assists in addressing and solving the world's important ecological issues. Shiva is a far from figurehead leader: the Foundation fulfils her personal vision, and she is a leading writer and speaker in great demand worldwide. This is accomplished through constructing partnerships and by demystifying and clarifying environmental concerns so that local people engaged in grassroots programs can play an active and participative role. For her contributions she has been awarded, among other accolades, in 1993, the Right Livelihood Award (Alternative Nobel Prize).

Born in 1952 to a farmer mother and forester father – both fiercely feminist – in Dehra Dun in the foothills of the Himalaya, Shiva became a scientist. She obtained her PhD in theoretical physics in 1978 at the University of Western Ontario (Canada) and then returned to India to work in the field of interdisciplinary research in science, technology and environmental policy with the Institute of Management, Bangalore. Thereafter she became an environmental activist and since then has investigated issues that impact on the relationships between society and the environment. In this role she has, in turn, created transnational research and community links throughout the world.

The approach of the Research Foundation is committed activism and advocacy based on reputable and careful integrated research. Counterdevelopment arguments that straddle national concerns characterize these efforts, and the empowerment of people at many levels of society are the effect. Within India there is a large following of coordinated grassroots networks, and the transnational reach of Shiva's enormous published output is considerable. She attends a great number of international meetings. She was, for example, a leading figure at the United Nations World Summit on Sustainable Development in Johannesburg in 2002. Her Foundation's influence on the developing world is considerable and she is a major figure in campaigning against biopiracy and privatization of the world's natural resources.

Fundamentally, the Foundation is concerned with agricultural and cultural sustainability. It is not a highly organized hierarchical institution but an informal network with a wide-ranging agenda, that has sought to articulate the environmental concerns of ordinary people wherever they live. Shiva and the Foundation have especially entered the biodiversity arena, with a critical stance on the Green Revolution. arguing that the field needs to include the diversity of cultures and knowledges, not science alone. This has triggered a series of initiatives. An international college for sustainable living, Bija Vidyapeeth, has become part of the growing enterprise, while Shiva has started a movement called Nandanya for collecting and conserving indigenous seeds and for protecting and patenting indigenous knowledge against the 'biopiracy' of capitalist monopolies.

Women are prioritized in this regard, and a movement was launched in 1998 called 'Diverse Women for Diversity'. A dedicated feminist as well as eco-campaigner, Shiva believes that capitalism is a global patriarchy that will destroy small-scale agriculture. Concomitant with this process will be the increasing invisibility of women who are the world's primary food producers and processors, and they require protection from global agribusiness. In the cause of preventing the extinction of this critical economy, the Foundation has not been afraid to tackle international organizations at the highest level. Because of its emphasis on agriculture, it has a stronger foothold in the areas where intensive peasant cultivation is strongest (South Asia) rather than Africa where pastoralism dominates. The Foundation has informal links with other activist organizations that target bodies like the World Bank and the World Trade Organisation and global players have been forced to take Shiva and her Foundation extremely seriously.

Jane Carruthers

Bibliography

Shiva V. (1993) *Ecofeminism*. London: Zed.

Shiva V. (2000) *Stolen harvest: the hijacking of the global food supply*. Cambridge, MA: South End.

Shiva V. (2001) *Water wars: privatization, pollution and profits*. Cambridge, MA: South End.

Related essays

biodiversity; biopatents; ecology; Ford Foundation; genetically modified organisms (GMOs); Green Revolution; indigenous knowledges; Monsanto; philanthropic foundations; seeds; women's movements

Birth control

Birth control is not only an expression used to describe the techniques used to limit fertility, it also designates people and groups who promoted these techniques and the preoccupations that made them desirable. International networks of anarchists and feminists had campaigned for birth control since the end of the 19th century, doctors and experts created family planning clinics and, finally, international organisations and governments (notably that of the United States) conceived methods for controlling population growth. These have been sharply criticized for violating reproductive rights by women's groups since the 1970s.

Contraceptive methods (coitus interruptus, condoms, diaphragms, abortion) have existed for centuries but they only started to be used on a large scale in France after 1750. Other Western countries followed suit between 1870 and 1930. Their adoption caused a sharp reduction in the fertility rate. The shocked reaction of the clergy and natalists along with the adoption of coercive measures prompted protests from neo-Malthusians and anarchists who considered that contraception would diminish the labour supply, thereby raising wages. Charles Drysdale founded the first Neo-Malthusian League in England in 1877; Paul Robin, whom he met in London, created one in France. The French and Dutch movements went beyond economic considerations and were more attentive to the health and freedom of women. The Dutch gynaecologist Aletta Jacobs read about the German gynaecologist Wilhelm Mensinga's improved diaphragm in a medical journal. She tested it on her patients and created the first birth control clinic in 1882. While visiting Europe in the 1910s, Americans Emma Goldman and Margaret Sanger saw in the diaphragm the ideal contraceptive method under women's control that they had been seeking and widely publicized it, notably in Sanger's New York clinic founded in 1916. While in London, Sanger showed the diaphragm to Mary Stopes who promoted its use in England and South Africa.

After the First World War, most associations adopted the term 'birth control' although the phrase 'sexual reform' was used in Germany and Sweden. Voyages, conferences, public meetings and correspondence send the diaphragm and the principles of birth control across the world, notably to India and Japan where women such as Kato Shidzue spread the word.

After 1945, the United Nations created a Population Division that played an essential role in presenting population as a fundamental aspect of national and international development. New associations, which promoted family planning or conscious maternity rather than sexual freedom, were created. Exploiting networks established in the 1930s and the German medical diaspora, Swede Elise Ottesen-Jensen and Margaret Sanger established the International Planned Parenthood Association in 1952. Its goal was to distribute literature and contraceptive products, train personnel and facilitate exchanges between national associations through four regional offices. Through its channels, publications and products (diaphragms and spermicide creams) were exchanged openly or secretly where national legislation prohibited them.

It was during the postwar years that biological contraceptive methods were invented. Margaret Sanger introduced scientist Gregory Pincus to American millionaire Katherine MacCormick, who financed the research for an oral contraceptive that was tested in Haiti and Puerto Rico. At the same time, Austrian Carl Djerassi, who emigrated to the United States and then to Mexico, devised a different formula for the pill. For many, the pill symbolizes women's new power over fertility but, in fact, it is mainly used by Western, and notably French, women because its distribution requires widespread and expensive logistical support.

Among the new nations that emerged from the decolonization movement, India was the first to initiate a family planning programme in 1953, that was based on self-control. The failure of this method led authorities to use intra-uterine devices, vasectomies and, finally, ligatures. In Eastern bloc countries, except the German Democratic Republic, abortion was liberalized in 1955 at the same time as in the Soviet Union. Except in Hungary, birth control was based on self-control followed by abortion if necessary. Trade in contraceptive products developed later; Bulgaria imported pills from Germany and Hungary, intra-uterine devices and condoms from Czechoslovakia, and, after 1980, from Singapore.

In the 1960s, the fear of a Third World demographic explosion was clear and the propagation of contraception took on a worldwide perspective. American foundations led the way, notably the Population Council, propagating intra-uterine devices developed in the interwar years by a German scientist. This method invaded China after the Cultural Revolution. The United States Agency for International Development (USAID) was converted to birth control at the end of the 1960s and financed two-thirds of population international aid to create centres for demographic studies, to carry out population surveys, and for training field personnel in the United States or in other countries that had 'successful' population policies. The United Nations Fund for Population Activities (UNFPA) was created in 1969. All these organizations proposed model population policies,

institutions (the birth control clinic) and contraceptive methods. The pill and intra-uterine devices were offered in areas where medical services were rare and proper sanitary follow-up could not be guaranteed. The reaction of local governments, notably in Africa where leaders favoured population growth, was variable. They were happy to accept the money and the rhetoric that went with it but tried to use it for their own ends. As a result, international agencies linked grants to the adoption of a determined programme to reduce fertility.

In the mid-1970s, the development of simple procedures to sterilize women were taken up in many countries, primarily in Asia and Latin America, but abusive use of them was possible. The United States Committee Against Sterilization Abuse and for Abortion Rights brought to light the continued use of forced sterilization in the US under eugenic legislation passed before 1940, which mirrored Pakistani and Indian experiences. Transnational movements for women's health campaigned against testing of Depo-provera and Norplant (a contraceptive implant) and against a contraceptive vaccine, which could be misused by authoritarian regimes. These movements coalesced at Amsterdam in 1984 and became an international movement in favour of 'reproductive rights'. This term was rapidly taken up in India, South Africa and by coalitions of women from the Third World such as Development Alternatives for Women or the Latin American Network for Reproductive Health And Rights. Because of this massive mobilization, the notion of 'reproductive rights' was adopted by the IPPF and by some American foundations. and, finally, despite opposition from the Vatican, some Muslims and some Latin American countries, it was also endorsed by the United Nations' 1994 Cairo conference on population and development. Henceforth, individuals should have access to safe and reliable contraception outside of state or marital constraint and to quality health services. These demands were taken up in the rhetoric of local and transnational associations, even if the reality is far removed from this ideal.

One of the striking features of recent trends is the internationalization and marketing of contraception. In the 1960s, most populations used traditional methods such as coitus interruptus or periodic abstinence along with condoms and diaphragms. Today, 60 per cent of women between the ages of 15 and 49 use some form of contraception (68 per cent in developed nations and 49 per cent in developing countries): 19 per cent are sterilised, 13 per cent use the pill and an equal percentage an intra-uterine device, 6 per cent traditional methods and 5 per cent condoms. Some developing countries manufacture generic contraceptive products, often with heavy dosages, while others have to import them using grants from the United States, Sweden or Norway. New methods are also promoted. Some associations favour the morning-after pill while attempts to develop a male contraceptive, notably in China, have encountered technical difficulties.

Another recent development is the rise of systematic opposition to birth control and its methods, notably from religious fundamentalists. The Catholic Church has always opposed contraception through encyclicals even though, in some periods or in certain countries, attitudes were more liberal (periodic abstinence or tolerance of contraceptives). John Paul II's papacy, however, hardened the discourse against all contraception. Some Protestant Churches are also intransigent but since 1930 the Anglicans tolerate methods that do not totally end the fertility. This is also the case with most Muslims. Pressure groups have become more virulent in their denunciation, on the web or at international conferences, claiming that intra-uterine devices and the pill are equivalent to abortion. The Republican administrations of Reagan and the Bushes have taken up this crusade, limiting funding to family planning agencies and to the UNFPA, which have had to look to the European Union for necessary resources. The international conference, planned for 2004, was replaced by regional meetings to avoid the protests that it would have entailed. The Objectives for the Millennium that should have mobilized the international community did not mention the right to family planning.

Arlette Gautier

Bibliography
Grossmann A. 1995. *Transforming sex: the German movement for birth control and abortion reform, 1920–1950.* New York and Oxford: Oxford University Press.
Hardon A. 2006. 'Contesting contraceptive innovation: reinventing the script', *Social Science and Medicine,* 62, 614–27.
Segal S. 2003. *Under the banyan tree: a population scientist's odyssey.* Oxford: Oxford University Press.

Related essays
eugenics; Jacobs, Aletta; philanthropic foundations; population; women's movements

Bodybuilding

Defined as 'the feeding and strengthening of the human frame by diet and exercise', the term 'bodybuilding' was coined by Eugene Sandow in 1904. Bodybuilding emerged thanks to advances in science and technology, the most important of which was the camera. From its beginnings it was a transatlantic phenomenon.

Born Friedrich Wilhelm Müller in 1867 in Königsberg, Sandow established bodybuilding as a sport that aestheticized the human body. After early life among circus performers and travelling strongmen, Sandow used photography to highlight the beauty, rather than merely the strength, of his body. Sandow's image, which endorsed products from cigarettes to soap, made him one of the 20th century's first international celebrities.

Sandow's appearance at Chicago's Trocadero Theatre in August 1893, during the Columbian Exposition, helped invigorate the United States' fledging bodybuilding movement. Bernarr Macfadden, a 25-year-old wrestler from the Ozarks who saw Sandow in Chicago, went on to emulate his European idol by posing as a series of classical sculptures in order to edify and titillate British audiences. By 1899, Macfadden returned to the United States and began publishing a monthly, *Physical Culture,* which published photographic and written narratives of readers' physical and moral metamorphoses.

By the 1920s, fitness periodicals had nurtured a robust collection of bodybuilding entrepreneurs, many of them immigrants or ethnic Americans who emphasized the democratic potential of bodybuilding. Instructors like Antone Matysek and Earle Liederman told the readers of *Physical Culture* that working hard in their courses would help endow their working-class bodies with the health and efficiency associated with those of middle-class Americans.

The Great Depression ended the careers of many fitness entrepreneurs, while two bodybuilders vied for hegemony. Charles Atlas, an Italian immigrant born Angelo Siciliano, promised to turn 97-pound weaklings into 'real he-men' without the use of apparatus through isometric contractions. Bob Hoffman, owner of York Barbell Company and publisher of *Strength and Health* magazine, disputed Atlas's claims to have never used weights. Hoffman's approach eventually dominated the 'iron game', as weightlifting enabled men to achieve larger and more muscular physiques than resistance exercises alone.

The internationalized professionalization of bodybuilding came about, in large part, thanks to the efforts of Joe and Ben Weider. Raised in a working-class, Jewish family in Montreal during the Great Depression, elder brother Joe fought anti-Semitism and the limited circumstances of his birth to found a magazine empire which publicized the benefits of strength training to the world. The brothers founded the International Federation of Bodybuilding (IFBB) in 1946, and Ben travelled the globe to promote its contest titles of Mr Olympia (from 1965) and Mr Universe, and to secure Olympic recognition for the sport (accorded in 1998). Though several Mr America and Mr Universe contests coexisted during the 1940s, 50s, and 60s, it was the Weiders' most famous protégé, Arnold Schwarzenegger, who epitomized the heavily muscled aesthetic promoted by professional bodybuilding after World War 2. His Austrian origins attest to the sport's global reach by the 1960s. In the 1970s and 80s, bodybuilding's stars, such as Franco Columbu, Lou Ferrigno, Serge Nubret, and Sergio Oliva, were usually immigrants to the United States, ethnic Americans, or citizens of other countries. By the 1990s, the IFBB was the sport's leading organization, including 160 countries, and the world's fourth-largest sports federation.

The increased global visibility of bodybuilding and the simultaneous impact of second-wave feminism translated into greater acceptance of women bodybuilders in the late 1970s. Photography was again the key: artistic images of female bodybuilder Lisa Lyon helped to normalize women's participation in what had been an all-boys' club. The Ms Olympia contest, founded in 1980 by the IFBB, as well as Schwarzenegger's annual Ms International, attest to the continued transnational appeal of female and male bodybuilding into the 21st century.

Dominique Padurano

Bibliography
Chapman D. L. 1994. *Sandow the Magnificent: Eugene Sandow and the beginnings of bodybuilding*. Urbana and Chicago: University of Illinois Press.
Ernst R. 1991. *Weakness is a crime: the life of Bernarr Macfadden*. Syracuse, NY: Syracuse University Press.
Fair J. D. 1999. *Muscletown USA: Bob Hoffman and the manly culture of York Barbell*. University Park: Pennsylvania State University Press.
Weider J. and Weider B. with Steere M. 2006. *Brothers of iron: how the Weider Brothers created the fitness movement and built a business empire*. Champaign: Sports Publishing LLC.

Related essays
America; beauty; beauty pageants; expositions; feel-good culture; femininity; Olympic Games; prizes; sport

Body shopping *See* **Executives and professionals**

Book and periodical exchange

As information carriers, books and printed artifacts are inherently portable, crossing spatial temporal, linguistic and cultural borders with ease. Historically, resource sharing has been an effective method of extending the global penetration of print, enabling the dissemination of publications unavailable through the usual book trade networks (frequently periodicals) of works otherwise prohibitively expensive and, by default, of non-circulating duplicate copies. Whereas interlibrary loan systems satisfy temporary information needs, formal and informal exchanges, both symmetrical and asymmetrical, have facilitated long-term requirements and shaped transnational knowledge transfer. The decision by the Royal Library of France in the late 17th century to exchange its duplicates for titles in German, English and Chinese marks the formal entry of large institutions into an expanded intellectual and knowledge-brokering arena formerly the unofficial purview of private collectors and learned societies, or the lynchpin of scientific institutions based on the structures and strictures of comparative taxonomy. This was followed in the early 19th century by the establishment of several university consortia in Europe, by the first official governmental exchanges, and then by the formation of an international exchange bureau consequent upon the Brussels conventions of 1886.

The Parisian magician and globetrotter Alexandre Vattemare (1796–1864) is credited with developing the first systemized approach to international publication exchanges. He promulgated the political, economic, social and cultural importance of acquiring and sharing official publications and was applauded as a modern-day humanist in his goal to disseminate knowledge around the world. His extensive travels to European institutions throughout the 1830s and later to the US resulted in creation of the American Library in Paris and the formation of an infrastructure for publication exchange which was adopted by the US Congress in 1840.

From 1834, the Library of Congress was reliant upon book and periodical exchanges to build its collections in keeping with Thomas Jefferson's ideal of a universal library available to all. Shortly thereafter, Vattemare's scheme helped to shape the library's collection development policies and extended the range of international publications. Materials of varied descriptions and languages arrived from Europe, China, Russia, and Turkey, amongst others, exchanged for library duplicates or for US government publications, either in the form of gifts or as supplementary purchases. Initially 25 copies of each US government publication were reserved as stock for trade with foreign countries; later the number rose from 50 to 125. From 1968, the Exchange and Gifts Division of the Library of Congress was responsible for implementing UNESCO's 1958 Convention Concerning the International Exchange of Publications. It is currently engaged in coordinating over 23,000 unofficial exchange agreements in addition to its portfolio of high-profile government-to-government bilateral or executive agreements.

Governments have historically participated in exchange programmes to maintain the necessary specialist information literacy for effective governance. Government-sponsored and non-governmental organizations have coordinated one-way book-aid programmes to countries in transition, but have also instigated exchanges to build libraries and information networks for local, national, and regional development projects, primarily in the areas of literacy, science and technology. Among the key players in this world of information exchange are The British Council, L'Alliance Française, and UNESCO.

The British Council for Relations with Other Countries was established in 1934 as an instrument of cultural propaganda to counter the rise of nazism and fascism. The formation of local British Council libraries as hubs of information was an important aspect in its general scheme to share the best of British cultural endeavour. From its foundation in 1883 as l'Association Nationale pour la Propagation de la Langue Française dans les Colonies et à l'Étranger, the Alliance Française has consistently exported French language, civilization, and culture to the four corners of the globe. Books and periodicals were part of the goods that it spread around. In keeping with its mandate to promote world peace through mutual understanding, one of UNESCO's fundamental goals is the promotion of international exchanges. It offers high-level advice through its multilingual *Handbook on the International Exchange of Publications* and has co-sponsored database projects to ensure the information needs of recipient nations are matched to the appropriate donor-driven programmes. Like many of these ostensibly philanthropic gestures, however, first-world governments and NGOs have frequently been accused of neocolonial motives, implicitly supporting or undermining the political agenda of local authorities.

Today, the development of effective and efficient electronic document delivery systems has reshaped the information exchange landscape. However, the concept of global access to free information is compromised by unequal levels of service infrastructure, particularly for countries in transition, by questions of copyright in the digital domain, and by the profit motives of electronic document aggregators.

Sydney J. Shep

Bibliography

Cole J. Y. 2005. 'The Library of Congress becomes a world library, 1815–2005', *Libraries & Culture*, 40, 3, 385–98.

Einhorn N. R. 1972. 'Exchange of publications', in *Encyclopedia of Library and Information Science*, Vol. 8, New York: M. Dekker, 282–9.

Price P. P. 1982. *International book and library activities: the history of a US foreign policy*. Metuchen and London: Scarecrow.

Tilliette P.-A. 1998. Alexandre Vattemare's international document exchanges and the collection of foreign official publications of the Bibliothèque Administrative de la Ville de Paris: a historian's treasure trove. Paper presented at the IFLA General Conference, Amsterdam [online]. Available: www.ifla.org/IV/ifla64/64intro.htm, accessed 18 December 2007.

Related essays
bibliographic classification; fellowships and grants; governing science; higher education; humanities; information economy; intellectual elites; language diplomacy; libraries; life and physical science; public policy; publishing; social sciences

Border commuters

Border commuters live in one nation state but work in another. Their travel, while short-distance, is international. Border commuters often work in regional economies that pre-date national boundaries. The association of the border with terrorism, crime, or irregular migration can significantly affect their commutes.

In the late 1800s, a transnational labour market already existed along the US-Canada boundary that incorporated border commuting. Detroit advertised the fact that many of its workers lived in Canada in order to attract new business. In the case of the United States and Mexico in the early 20th century, the border historically divided social classes, not national communities. Regardless of nationality, the wealthy lived on the United States side of the border while the poor resided in Mexican border communities. Lower-class workers residing in Nogales, Sonora, commuted daily to Nogales, Arizona, while upper-class Mexicans, including some government officials, lived in Arizona. When partitioning Nigeria from Benin in the late 19th and early 20th century, French and British colonizers divided territories that encompassed the borderlands Shabe Yoruba ethnic community, but failed to demarcate the border firmly. As a result, the Shabe maintained a transboundary economy, with many commuters in informal sector occupations.

Cross-border commuting is significant in both North America and Europe. In 2000, in the cities of Rosarito and Tijuana, Mexico alone, over 27,000 Mexicans reported commuting into the United States to work. Their commutes are aided by programs such as SENTRI, which allows low-risk crossers to use designated commuter lanes. On average, 7,000–8,000 use SENTRI daily to cross the US-Mexico border near San Diego. A similar program, NEXUS, operates along the US-Canada border.

In Europe, cross-border commutes are not limited to European Union member states. In the first quarter of 2006, nearly 180,000 workers commuted regularly to Switzerland, most of them residents of France. Half of all European cross-border commuters live in France; another third reside in Germany, Belgium, and Italy. On the Germany-Netherlands border, commuters from Germany are often Dutch nationals who work, socialize, and send their children to school in the Netherlands while living in Germany.

The frequency of cross-border commuting does not make international boundaries irrelevant. Borders are still often tightened or militarized in response to crises, with profound impacts on border commuters. The United States' immigration restriction legislation of the 1920s affected commuters along both its northern and southern borders. Concern over border inspections may have caused Canadian commuters to choose to migrate permanently to the United States. Increased border security following September 11, 2001, serves as another example of how crises impact frontier workers. In larger cities along the US-Mexico border such as El Paso-Ciudad Juárez, vehicle traffic across the border dropped while pedestrian traffic rose significantly. In 2003, Nigeria took even more drastic measures to combat crime along its border with Benin, closing the border completely for a week. This action effectively closed businesses reliant on cross-border economic activity and stranded some border crossers.

The experiences of border commuters demonstrate both the importance of international boundaries for human mobility and the endurance of regional economic connections across political frontiers. Types of border commuters already vary significantly. In the United States, commuters eligible for SENTRI and NEXUS programmes commute with relative ease while border crossing has become more difficult for others. As economic globalization, political regionalism, and international crises continue to shape the meaning of national borders, the patterns and habits of border commuters will undoubtedly change as well.

Kyle Walker

Bibliography

Bukowczyk J. J. et al. (eds) 2005. *Permeable border: the Great Lakes Basin as transnational region, 1650–1990*. Pittsburgh: University of Pittsburgh Press.

Flynn D. K. 1997. ' "We are the border": identity, exchange, and the state along the Benin-Nigeria border'. *American Ethnologist*, 24, 2, 311–30.

Kada N. and Kiy R. (eds) 2004. *Blurred borders: trans-boundary impacts and solutions in the San Diego-Tijuana border region*. San Diego: International Community Foundation.

Van Houtum H. and Gielis R. 2006. 'Elastic migration: the case of Dutch short-distance transmigrants in Belgian and German borderlands', *Tijdschrift voor Economische en Sociale Geografie*, 97, 2, 195–202.

Related essays

borders and borderlands; crime; European Union (EU); human mobility; individual identification systems; labour migrations; *non-lieux*; regions; September 11, 2001; temporary migrations

Borders and borderlands

Borders usually refer to spatial boundaries between political regimes; more abstractly, they can also refer to cultural symbols that make up identities. Borders divide and unite, delineate and delimit, obstruct and facilitate. Products of the territorialization of states, borders are marks of a state's sovereignty and power in a given space. States' defensive devices along their borders include walls, fences, checkpoints, troops, as well as natural barriers that are difficult to pass.

Borders between countries have attracted the growing interest of historians, who explore the interactions between states, the state and its local communities, as well as the formation of nations and states embroiled in border construction. Though international borders appear as concise lines on maps, they are constructed, negotiated, and contested by different historical agents. The historical processes whereby international borders are drawn or redrawn have practical consequences that can change people's lives, as well as transform communities in the borderlands.

Borderlands usually refer to areas divided and joined by borders, where political, economic and cultural contacts, contestation, or interactions between different forces occur. Territorial borderlands have features different from those areas where there are no borders or border issues. Anthropologists often use borderlands to refer to cultural spaces where conceptual, symbolic, and social markers divide and connect sets of dichotomies, such as Us from Them, old from new, centre from margin, majority from minority, or urban from rural.

The terms 'border' and 'boundary', 'frontier' and 'borderland' are often used interchangeably in English publications. Nevertheless, they are distinct from each other to a certain degree in specialized studies of borderlands. The Frankish word from which 'border' originated, *bord*, literally means the wooden sides of a ship. 'Frontier' has its origins in *frons*, meaning 'in front of'. Boundaries and borders are interchangeable when they refer to dividing lines between peoples and cultures, but borders often refer to the geographical lines on maps, and boundaries are more often used in studies of identity. While frontiers have been popular subjects of inquiry in US history and regarded as an essential element in the pioneering and expansionist past of the country's civilization, in British English the term often refers to remote and rural areas with a negative connotation. Sometimes borderlands are chosen over frontiers in historical studies particularly to avoid the possibly chauvinistic notion conveyed by Frederick Turner's definition of frontiers as 'meeting points between savagery and civilization' or the edging forward of the USA into so-called 'empty land'.

For a variety of reasons, historians of borderlands have yet to develop a comprehensive study on the terms used as equivalents for frontier or borderlands in non-Western contexts. In addition, these scholars have seldom conceptualized borders and borderlands outside the context of American or European history, or West-related colonial studies. For example, there are a variety of terms used as Chinese equivalents for borders and borderlands in different historical settings. Among them, *bian* and *jie* are most used for borders, and *biansai*, *bianchui* or *bianjiang* for both frontier and borderlands. Their connotations were associated with changes in the ruling clans' perception of their relations with people living in China proper during the long imperial era of dynastic changes (3rd century BC – 1912).

Historical and present-day borderlands in our world can be categorized into four types, according to the differences in their re/formation processes, patterns of structures, as well as international/intra-national relations. The four categories do not necessarily exclude each other over time. First are contested and alienated borderlands, where political powers compete over an area, and where there are frequently military violence and ethnic conflicts. In these cases, there is often a lack or an absence of flow of people, goods, and information across borders. Additionally, there is often a disruption of local economic development. Kashmir between India and Pakistan during the second half of the 20th century serves as such an example. Second type includes collaborated and interdependent borderlands, where countries on both sides depend on each other economically and culturally with an unequal or uneven partnership, in either regulated or illegal forms. Border experiences influence the community structure and identity reconfiguration of local peoples who cross borders. Borders between the US and Mexico, China and North Korea, Mongolia and Russia are examples. The third category is made of integrated borderlands, where countries of cultural, economic and ethnic similarities on both sides, which are often strategic allies, keep their borders unrestricted for the purpose of exchanging resources. Examples include the US–Canadian borders and the borders of most European Union countries. Last, there are historical borderlands, where international disputes happened in the past but where recent territorialization of modern states has included the area, either firmly or unstably, under their sovereignty claims, or transformed the area into an independent state; e.g., the areas along China's Great Wall, Northern Ireland, and Singapore after 1965.

Borderland studies in history and anthropology have witnessed development of research on the following four major topics.

The negotiation of borders, the contestation of territory, and the maintenance of sovereignty have been major topics in diplomatic and military history focused on the state. Recent scholarship on cartography (the geobody) and effects of shifting borders on the locale have brought new insights to our understanding of the disparity, or even tension and conflict, between imagined nation and delimitation of state. A state's borders do not necessarily correspond to ethnic, linguistic or cultural boundaries. Border approaches help to analyse the power relations between international forces, state government and local elites, who compete with each other for control over the region. Exemplary works include Winichakul Thongchai's work on mapping Thai nationhood and Laszlo Kürti's book on the place of Transylvania in the Hungarian imagination.

Borders are shifting and crossable. When they cross people and when people cross borders, the ethnic or national identity of borderlanders and border crossers are often transformed. Because of this, the transnational perspective has contributed to our understanding of how border life constructs identities in terms of nationality/citizenship, ethnicity, gender or occupation. They differ from identity construction in other places of the state because a state usually exercises its power to regulate and manage the daily life of the borderlanders with different strategies and policies from those for the inlanders. Stimulating works on the US Southwest include James Brook and Oscar Martinez's cross-disciplinary studies.

Studies of the globalized economic network as well as the expanding labour market across borders also require a transnational approach. Smuggling, human traffic, international organizations and the trade system, as well as the international law of business deserve further studies in the field. Eric Tagliacozzo's volume about the history of smuggling in Southeast Asia illustrates the richness of these aspects. Recent studies on sea borders, a long neglected subfield in border studies, examine economic activities and transport crossing borders in adjacent coastal regions.

Last, borderlands are perceived differently in different temporal or spatial settings. They are also represented by non-physical symbols in literature, arts, and languages. Studies of communication and memories have opened another window to understand the reflections on border experiences. Michael Rösler and Tobias Wendl have illustrated the scholarly side of this, while Gloria Anzaldua built a powerful mix of autobiography and history in *Borderlands/La frontera* (1987).

Historical studies of borderlands show different development patterns in the subfields of US, European, African, and Asian studies. Comparatively, scholars of borderland studies in US, African and European history have developed more conversations with each other than with those in Asian studies.

In the field of US history, topics related to the US–Mexican border have been well explored. Herbert Eugene Bolton's 1921 book, *The Spanish borderlands: a chronicle of old Florida and the Southwest*, has been regarded as the most visible start of 'borderland history' in the field. Bolton and his students called attention to the Hispanic aspect of US frontier history, and explored an alternative approach to Frederick Jackson Turner's foundational narrative of the US frontier. Bolton's students brought this subfield to the attention of other scholars by the 1930s. The popularity of ethnic studies in the social sciences and humanities in the 1950s and the 1960s attracted the interest of scholars to Mexican communities in the United States. During the 1960s through the 1980s, Chicano scholars began to examine racism, discrimination, and exploitation in the US borderlands. A new generation of the Bolton school developed in the 1970s, which examined the Mexican frontier as a historical bridge between Anglo and Latin America, beyond a Hispanic focus and via a transnational perspective. From the 1990s, multilingual materials and cross-disciplinary approach have enabled scholars to examine how US borderland history can contribute to the theorization of borderlands studies and to the studies of general topics such as identity, globalization, immigration, and gender.

Borderland studies in European history have inherited invaluable intellectual treasures for generations of scholars from Lucien Fèbvre's research on the Rhine, regarded as a border between the Teutonic and Gallic worlds, to Peter Sahlins' studies on the shifting relations between states and local society during the historical process of territorialization of modern Spain and France in the Cerdanya valley. Nevertheless, unlike US borderlands history, European studies of borderlands have explored more multiple sites of borderlands in history, covered longer historical periods, and developed multidisciplinary theories and methodologies on contemporary borderlands. The active political, economic, and cultural interactions among European countries through contemporary transborder organizations such as the European Union have also encouraged historians to explore the historical roots of current affairs and problems concerning borders and cross-border activities. In addition, the shifting of borders in recent and present Europe, in particular in Eastern Europe and the areas formerly within the former Soviet Union, provide historians, cultural geographers, political scientists, sociologists, and anthropologists with excellent cases for their research not only on the constructability of nations and identities but also on the management strategies of state machineries in newly formed borderlands that are included in an existing state, as well as on the nationalized territories of historical borderlands that have begun to claim and obtain independent nationhood.

Scholars of African borderlands have joined the historical research trends in the US and European fields, and furthered theoretical discussion on borderlands from the 1980s onward. The national borders in Africa bear obvious marks left by European colonialism: artificiality of border drawing first defined by European treaties, instability of political groupings, as well as the visibility of active international organizations. Through the comparative approach, scholars of African history bring new topics and questions, as well as broader analyses of alternative borderland experiences to the field. Scholars in this field have contributed insightful research on various topics such as similarities in the artificiality of border making between European and African countries, international laws and treaties regarding borders, demarcations of mental space, ecological activities, and the rupturing of cultural space and cross-border ethnic groups.

Borderlands studies in the Asian realm have less communications with US or European scholars. While Western scholars have explored only limited sources of Asian writings on the subject, scholars in Asia have not actively examined or integrated borderland theories or methodology beyond Turner's frontier approach. Scholars working on Asia have studied topics on the edges of Asian empires in premodern history, the cartography of national limits, smuggling across Southeast Asia borders, the legacy of European colonization in Asian borderlands, travel writings, ethnonationalist movements, reconfiguration of the identity of people who live in border regions or across borders, as well as historical relations between communities and institutions across borders. Scholars working on borderlands in East Asia have inherited an academic tradition of combining archival and archaeological methodologies from the evidential research scholarship in the late imperial China. During the past century, Western ethnographic approaches and theories have been more and more influential in East Asian borderland studies. Nevertheless, a lineal framework of a national history has been often adopted in borderlands studies in East Asian countries. Research on borderlands history and ethnography concerning disputable borders or border regions still make a considerable impact on current diplomatic relations among East Asian countries. Within the field of Asian studies, borderlands-related studies do not necessarily employ the terminology of, or adopt theories used in, European and American borderland studies. While the historical study of borderlands in Central Asia is still in formation, geopolitical studies of this area have been closely related to current affairs.

Organizations on borders and borderlands have been established and active in multidisciplinary research, publication, conference organization, as well as policy making during the past half century. Active organizations include the Association for Borderlands Studies, established in 1976 as the Association of Borderlands Scholars in the United States and sponsoring the *Journal of Borderland Studies*; the Center for China's Borderlands History and Geography, within the Chinese Academy of Social Sciences; the Association of European Border Regions; The Nijmegen Centre for Border Research, in the Netherlands; the Centre for Regional and Transboundary Studies in Russia; and the Danish Institute of Border Region Studies. Major international institutions such as the European Union and the Asia-Pacific Economic Cooperation (APEC) sponsor projects and programs concerning borders and borderlands.

Features of borderlands such as 'middle ground', 'contact zone', 'contested space' or 'world in-between' require scholars to take a specific approach to their research subjects. Multilingual materials, multisited archival and fieldwork projects as well as cross-disciplinary methodology have supported many of the recent publications on borderlands. Contemporary globalization does not make human societies a borderless

world. Borderlands are conceived, perceived, and lived similarly or dissimilarly in different regions and eras. While borderland studies provide historians with a vantage point to observe and examine historical changes across national boundaries temporally and spatially, the transnational approach enables borderlands scholars to analyse the dynamic interactions between historical agents in borderlands as well as the social consequences of border making and unmaking.

Dan

Bibliography

Adelman J. and Aron S. 1999. 'From borderlands to borders: empires, nation-states, and the peoples in between in North American history', *American Historical Review*, 104, 3, 814–41.

Baud M. and van Schendel W. 1997. 'Toward a comparative history of borderlands', *Journal of World History*, 8, 2, 211–42.

Chen L. 1897, reprinted 2002. *Lidai choubian lüe* [Strategies of border management]. In *Zhongguo shaoshu minzu guji jicheng*, 11–13. Chengdu: Sichuan minzu chuban she.

McDonald D. (ed.) 2000. *On borders: perspectives on cross-border migration in Southern Africa*. Cape Town: SAMP/Idasa.

Nugent P. and Asiwaju A. I. 1996. *African boundaries: barriers, conduits, and opportunities*. London and New York: Pinter.

Rösler M. and Wendl T. 1999. *Frontiers and borderlands: anthropological perspectives*. New York: Peter Lang.

Truett S. and Young E. 2004. *Continental crossroads: remapping US–Mexico borderlands history*. Durham, NC: Duke University Press.

Wilson T. M. and Donnan H. 1998. *Border identities: nation and state at international frontiers*. Cambridge and New York: Cambridge University Press.

Related essays

Africa; air pollution; arms trafficking; Asia; border commuters; broadcasting; civilization; crime; electricity infrastructures; European Union (EU); genocide; guestworkers; Hollywood; individual identification systems; industrialization; information society; language; legal order; Médecins Sans Frontières (MSF); money; nation and state; national parks; nomads; outer space; partitions; radio; regions; spatial regimes; trade agreements

Braille code

Worldwide acceptance of the raised-dot reading and writing code for blind people, invented in 1824 by the teenage Louis Braille (1809–1852), took many decades. In 1852, braille was accepted at the Asylum for the Blind in Lausanne, Switzerland, the first institution outside France to do so. The first institution in the United States to use braille was the Missouri School for the Blind – in 1854. Still, no deliberate steps to disseminate braille were taken until 1873, when the Vienna Congress of Teachers of the Blind discussed the adoption of a generally acceptable reading and writing system. Indeed, because braille music code was so superior to other tactile systems of music notation, its use spread more quickly than the braille language code.

A barrier to the spread of braille in Europe was that different countries wanted to save space on a page of braille by amending the original code so that the most frequently used letters in their own language were assigned to braille cells with the least number of dots. This difficulty was resolved in 1878 at an international meeting in Paris, the Congrès Universel pour l'amélioration du sort des aveugles et sourds-muets, where a 'strong' majority voted in favour of the general use of the unmodified (French) braille code. In 1870, Great Britain adopted the use of unmodified braille for writing, though not until 1883 did most British schools for the blind use braille. Competition from other popular codes in the United States delayed the full acceptance of braille by many decades. The main competitor, New York Point, which resembled a braille cell on its side, was more widely used than braille well into the 20th century. In an effort to rationalize means of tactile reading and writing, a 'Uniform Type Committee' was set up to determine which of the competing systems was most user-friendly.

Not until 1932 was a uniform braille code accepted by the English-speaking world. It took almost twenty years longer – until 1951 – for the world's Spanish speakers to agree; Brazil and Portugal came to terms the following year. Today, braille is used in almost every country in the world, adapted to almost every known language from Albanian to Zulu.

As a code, braille can stand for virtually anything, including any language (alphabetic or not), just as it can be used for music, mathematics, and computer notation. All that is required is a key to the code. The first adaptations of braille to non-European languages date from the 1870s and were mainly the work of missionaries from Europe and America. The missionaries managed, with various degrees of success, to adapt the braille code to languages with long alphabets, thousands of ideographs, and in Chinese languages, up to six tones. India's multitude of dialects presented such difficulties that, in 1949, India requested a meeting of UNESCO to study the problem at an international level.

International cooperation is still necessary, since most groups do not readily abandon methods that have proven workable over many years. Standardization has also been stimulated by the widespread use of computers to produce and read braille. It is possible that modern braille transcription and embossing technologies will eventually deliver braille to suit the needs of individual readers – at an affordable price. Even paper is no longer vital for braille: "Refreshable braille" uses small pins that move up and down under microchip control to form various dot configurations that may be felt by the fingers. Once the reader has passed his or her fingers over the line, he or she presses a bar, and another new line appears. Such braille displays may increase the availability and popularity of braille, for they allow a blind person to read words displayed on a computer screen, including email, compose and edit documents, translate print documents 'on the fly', and download books online. More than 180 years since its invention, Louis Braille's simple code still efficiently signals its message to the fingertips – in many languages.

C. Michael Mellor

Bibliography

Mellor C. M. 2006. *Louis Braille: a touch of genius*. Boston: National Braille Press.
Mackenzie Sir C. 1954. *World braille usage*. Paris: UNESCO.

Related essays
Esperanto; Internet; language; missionaries; sign language; technical standardization; translation

Brain drain

'Brain drain' is a term used to describe the sustained migration of highly qualified personnel from less developed to more developed countries.

The expression 'brain drain' was first coined by the British Royal Society in the 1950s to describe the outflow of scientists and technologists to the US and Canada. There is no uniform system of recording the number and characteristics of international migrants so it is difficult to measure brain drain precisely. It is clear, however, that the OECD countries, and especially the US, profit through such migration, while many developing countries lose their best human capital. Apart from intakes into the OECD countries, which have over the past decades obtained thousands of doctors, engineers, accountants, academics and scientists from less developed countries, there is a sizeable flow of professionals from the Indian subcontinent to the oil-producing Middle Eastern countries. During the 1980s, due to strong demand in the information technology and other science and technology sectors, brain drain intensified. In addition, the countries with regular immigration intakes have had increasingly selective immigration policies. These have been pursued with most success in Australia, the country with the highest share of foreign-born in high-skilled employment (25 per cent).

Asia and the Pacific are the most significant sources of the highly educated migrants into the OECD countries. The largest drains are from the Philippines, China, India and Korea. More than 75 per cent of Indian emigrants and 53 per cent of Korean emigrants are tertiary educated. In the US in the 1990s, 69 per cent of employer-sponsor visas were issued to persons from India, China, Japan and the Philippines. Iran has also had a substantial brain drain, and so have Pakistan and Taiwan. In the Western hemisphere, the relatively largest brain drain comes from Jamaica and Trinidad and Tobago. In South America, the brain drain champion is Guyana while in the rest of the region the phenomenon is less significant. Anecdotal evidence suggests there is substantial brain drain from the former Soviet Union and Eastern Europe, because of the acute imbalance between highly educated populations and underdeveloped homegrown technology sectors which employ them. Poland, Hungary, the Czech Republic, Estonia and the Balkan States have the biggest brain drains of young tertiary educated people because of high unemployment. As a safety valve for unemployment, brain drain involves the high price of losing the best human capital, as the most talented are most likely to emigrate. However, associating brain drain exclusively with the movement from less developed to more developed countries is a simplification: developmental differential is usually, but not necessarily, present. For example, the drain of scientists with doctoral qualifications from northwestern Europe to the US cannot be attributed to a developmental differential.

The factors that determine brain drain can be classified as 'macrostructural', 'intermediate' and 'individual'. At the macrostructural level, brain drain is caused by economic and developmental differential between countries. The 'intermediate' factors pertain to conditions specific to a particular country at a given time. For example, the Nazi regime in Europe in the 1930s to 1940s caused a brain drain, especially of Jewish intellectuals, to the US, and during the 1980s and 1990s, the crisis and dissolution of Communism prompted the migration of the highly skilled to the West. Many highly skilled people have been forced to leave their homes as a result of war, persecution or civil unrest. Internal imbalances such as the lack of high-level employment opportunities and the lack of meritocratic promotion can also be intermediate causes of brain drain. The third tier of causes is personal: ultimately, the decision to emigrate is made by an individual, upon consideration of personal and family circumstances. On this level, the lack of opportunities translates into an imbalance between expectations and achievements, along with an assessment that emigration would fix this imbalance. Those most likely to emigrate are people with excellent professional records, without family responsibilities, and with networks outside their countries of origin.

The second- and third-tier factors are the best way to explain the current migration of top academics and scientists from Western Europe to the US. Many Western Europeans who further their scientific and academic careers in the US quote the attraction of scientific pre-eminence and the entrepreneurial culture of American universities and research institutes, as well as higher levels of funding for research and development in the United States. Also at play are factors such as high expectations and high mobility of the well-off, and political and cultural closeness between the two regions. According to *Time* magazine, 400,000 European science and technology graduates live in the US. Canadians deem their brain drain to the US to be small but significant. However, skilled migration between advanced countries is often temporary and there may be a gain for everyone involved from the 'brain circulation' and professional cross-fertilisation. In addition, the brain drain from other OECD countries to the US has been compensated for by large intakes of the highly skilled from developing countries.

The outflow from developing countries is a more serious problem, as migrants from these countries are more likely not to return. Seventy-nine per cent of 1990/91 PhD graduates in science and engineering from India and 88 per cent of those from China were still working in the US in 1995, while only 11 per cent of Koreans and 15 per cent of Japanese did. Africa seems to be the hardest hit by brain drain. The UN estimates that between 1960 and 1989, 127,000 African professionals left the continent. According to the International Organization for Migration, Africa has been losing 20,000 professionals each year since 1990. African graduates leave, or fail to return home at the end of their studies at Western universities, and this may be one of the greatest obstacles to Africa's development. There are more African scientists and engineers in the US than on the entire African continent. The biggest migratory flows from Africa are from Ghana, Egypt and South Africa. To fill the expertise gaps created by brain drain, Africa employs up to 150,000 expatriate professionals at a high cost.

The interpretations of the causes and consequences of brain drain are not in unison. Most authors agree that brain drain represents a loss for sending countries, but many see this loss mitigated by potential gains. For example, the sending country can benefit economically through migrant remittances, and culturally and scientifically through a possibility of brain circulation and collaborative projects. *The Economist* emphasizes that the 'whole world benefits' from the 'brightest global talent working at the US universities and high-tech industries'. Some authors emphasize that the migration of highly trained persons to developed countries reflects the incapacity of their countries of origin to employ them to the greatest effect,

and therefore their migration can be viewed as an 'overflow' of brain surpluses rather than a drain. Some take a global rather than a nationalistic position and see the migration of the highly skilled as a positive exchange and inevitable balancing of the global labour market. In contrast, the authors most critical of the brain drain see it as another facet of neocolonial exploitation which widens the developmental gap between the First and the Third Worlds.

Some sending countries have tried to decrease their brain drain. The most drastic example was the closed borders of Eastern European and other Communist countries over the period 1945–89. However, the borders remained more or less porous. It is nearly impossible to stop labour mobility by administrative means if push and pull factors are strong enough. In the increasingly global labour market, the highly skilled remain the most globally connected and mobile.

In a historical perspective, brain drain has increased in magnitude with the increased global mobility of people over the past century and a half, since the development of transportation made long-distance travel possible on a larger scale, combined with an increase in the education levels of populations. Its relevance has grown with the fact that neither land nor financial capital is nowadays the most crucial developmental resource. In the knowledge-based economy, the highly skilled are the crucial resource in global competition. Globalization, with the established global market of talent, brings a new edge to the brain drain/gain dynamic. However, brain drain from the sending countries does not always result in a brain gain to receiving countries: a considerable number of highly skilled migrants from developing countries experience occupational downgrading due to structural barriers, a lack of formal qualification recognition, language and cultural barriers, and discrimination in the labour market. In this case, what occurs is a brain waste.

Val Colic-Peisker

Bibliography

Carrington W. J. and Detragiache E. 1998. *How big is the brain drain?* IMF Working Paper 98/102 [online]. Available: www.imf. org/external/pubs/ft/fandd/1999/06/pdf/ carringt.pdf.

Castels S. and Miller M. 2003. *The age of migration*. Basingstoke: Palgrave Macmillan.

Iredale R. 2001. 'The migration of professionals: theories and typologies', *International Migration*, 35, 5, 7–26.

Mahroum S. 2000. 'Highly skilled globetrotters', *R & D Management*, 30, 1, 23–31.

OECD Observer. 2002. 'The brain drain: old myths, new realities', by Cervantes M. and Guellec D. Directorate for Science, Technology and Industry. *OECD Observer*, May [online]. Available: www. oecdobserver.org/news/fullstory.php/ aid/673/The_brain_drain:_Old_myths,_ new_realities.html.

Portes A. 1976. 'Determinants of brain drain', *International Migration Review*, 10, 4, 489–508.

Related essays

Africa; architecture; executives and professionals; exile; fellowships and grants; higher education; human mobility; intellectual elites; international students; investment; labour migrations; life and physical sciences; oil; remittances; services; social sciences; temporary migrations; transnational

British Broadcasting Corporation (BBC) *See* Broadcasting

Broadcasting

To broadcast means to send out sound and/ or (motion) pictures by means of radio waves through space for reception by the general public.

Broadcasting evolved from prior technologies – the telegraph, the telephone, and wireless (radio) ship-to-shore communication. Services based on these technologies were providing point-to-point and point-to-multipoint communication. The verb 'to broadcast' was adopted to express the idea of scattered, undefined, anonymous dissemination of information on radio waves. It comes from the farmer's way of hand-sowing grain by *casting it broadly*, letting seeds fall where they may. The very nature of radio waves – that is, not to be affected by any political or national boundaries – made them right from the beginning an issue of cross-border negotiation and

legislation. The transnational character of broadcasting therefore calls for a historical contextualisation reflecting the dynamics of a communication tool that reshaped time and space.

The discovery of and subsequent investigation into electromechanical waves by the German physicist Heinrich Hertz in 1886 initiated a phase of intense experimentation that explored the possibilities of wireless communication. The first wireless transmission of a telegraphic message over a distance of five kilometres in 1897 by the Italian inventor-entrepreneur Guglielmo Marconi heralded an era of public enthusiasm about the wonder of 'communicating through the ether' and initiated a worldwide radio amateur movement. Popular journalism surrounded wireless with the aura of technological progress and encouraged boys especially to adventure the secrets of wireless telegraphy and telephony. Radio clubs, national amateur associations and popular magazines testify to the first stage of a 'radio boom' even before the emergence of broadcasting in our modern understanding of the term. It was the Great War that brought an abrupt end to this first phase of the boom, though inaugurating another. The exclusive use of radio frequencies for military purposes in all countries involved in the war not only demonstrated the military and political importance of radio technology in times of crisis, but even more significantly instituted a process of state-controlled use of radio frequencies as means of private or public communication. The concept of broadcasting was the result of 'a concerted effort on the part of big business and government, feeding on the elite public's fear of the masses, to change that vision to the highly centralized, one-way, restricted-access system that is broadcasting' (Hilmes, 2002, 29).

From a transnational historical perspective the process of institutionalization of radio broadcasting after the First World War must be interpreted as a process of national appropriation and social shaping of radio as a broadcast medium. While nearly all states extended their existing authority over the legal regulation of wire communication technologies to radio transmissions (especially the allocation of frequencies), governmental intervention in the institutionalization of broadcasting stations strongly varied from country to country.

Three institutional models emerged, reflecting the political, economic and sociocultural structures of the hosting states: the commercial or private broadcasting model, the national or centralized model, and finally the public service model.

Although these different institutional models resulted in national broadcasting systems with different organizational structures, political agendas and programming, a functional similarity can be stated when it comes to the role of radio as a tool for the construction of national identity. The possibility of creating imagined communities by way of simultaneously shared listening experiences was a central preoccupation in all countries, no matter what institutional form the broadcasting organization had taken. The 'reversion of the public private relationship' (Scannell, 1996, 69) can be described as a structural transformation of the public sphere in a double sense. While national broadcasting institutions or large networks saw radio as a perfect instrument for the transmission of political propaganda, cultural norms and values or basic information to a nationwide audience, radio offered to large populations an unprecedented possibility of medial participation in world affairs and public education beyond the national or governmental spheres.

Till 1930, broadcasting institutions and the radio industry concentrated on the gradual extension of the national radio networks. From 1930 onwards, the main issue became the augmentation of transmitter power. The 'etheric hell' resulting from this crusade of the airwaves became a major challenge for the international regulation of broadcasting. Inspired by the ideals of the League of Nations, 39 countries (among them 25 European, 4 African, 3 American, 5 Asian and 2 countries from Oceania) founded in 1925 the Union Internationale de Radiodiffusion (UIR). The UIR was driven by a humanist ideology, seeing in radio broadcasting an unprecedented instrument for international understanding and the transcending of economic classes, political ideologies and territorial boundaries. In 1926, all members signed a 'gentlemen's agreement' against the illegal and immoral use of radio as an instrument of propaganda. In the ensuing years, several bilateral and international conventions promoting the 'moral disarmament' of the ether have been signed. Despite these noble gestures, the national and sometimes nationalistic instrumentalization of the airwaves for ideological or propagandistic purposes made the frequency plans negotiated by the UIR too often an obsolete undertaking. With the emergence of short-wave stations in the early 1930s a real race for the colonization of the ether took place, followed by the establishment of foreign language services of nearly all big broadcast companies around the world. During the Second World War, the ether mutated into a battlefield of jammed frequencies and 'black broadcasting' – stations pretending to be a domestic broadcaster while deliberately transmitting false reports. Unlike the armed conflict, the war of propaganda knew no 'zero hour' in 1945. Stations like Voice of America, Radio Free Europe and Radio Liberty became backbones in the rising ideological battle between 'West' and 'East' in the Cold War, and transnational broadcasting played a part in the erosion of Communist states in the former Soviet bloc.

The institutionalization of television broadcasting right after the war took place in exactly the same patterns – the ideas about television programming and content followed the proven paths of radio broadcasting. While television can in this respect be described as a 'conservative innovation', the rise of television as the new leading mass medium of home entertainment after the Second World War had a deep impact on both the further development of radio broadcasting and on the structure of the public sphere. The drift of the radio networks' big sponsors to the new attraction of 'tele-vision' caused a regionalization and localisation of the American radio landscape and gave birth to format radio, aiming at specific listener groups and financed by local sponsors. After a certain delay, this structural change of the radio landscape from a national and international space into a regional or local space spread all over the world. Accelerated by the introduction of FM radio from the mid-1950s on, the radio lost its dominant function as a tool of 'high culture' dissemination in Europe and mutated into an important agent of youth culture and so-called Americanization or Westernization of European popular culture.

Parallel to this, television broadcasting established itself as the new leading mass medium with an undeniable national scope. Just as with radio after the Great War, television played a central role in the process of moral recovery in the post-World War 2 crisis of national identity of many countries, offering a unique opportunity to create national spaces of experience, carefully controlled by state authorities and embedded in nationally determined modernization processes. By transmitting conservative moral concepts and by the creation of a new domesticity, television catalysed the stabilization of national culture and identity in the hot era of the Cold War. The politics of national priority, eager to defend national sovereignty over the ether, is symbolized in the different line patterns for black and white television or the different colour television systems that made international programme exchange a costly and tricky business. Without doubt international broadcasting institutions like the Organisation Internationale de Radiotélédiffusion (OIR, founded in 1946) or the European Broadcast Union (EBU, founded in 1950) played an important role in the facilitation of international programme exchanges, but continuous cooperation remained limited to three specific genres: news, sports and music.

Despite the efforts of international organisations in promoting cooperation on broadcasting matters, it was not until the end of the 'public service era' and the international breakthrough of private and commercial television from the early 1980s on that the well protected frontiers of 'television nations' became porous. But the overthrow of the politics of national priority and therefore the beginning of a real era of local and global television broadcasting was the result of private broadcasting competition, not of political motivation nor of cultural visions. The development of satellite broadcasting, inaugurated by the first transatlantic television transmission via the Telstar satellite in 1962, deeply challenged the national television landscapes. While the distribution of programmes in most countries remains terrestrial (via cable net or radio link) and therefore basically national, privatization and commercialization of television broadcasting have spread all over the world. Transnational media conglomerates like Rupert Murdoch's corporations (BSkyB and FOX) and deregulatory media policies have given rise to complex media infrastructures operating simultaneously on a local, regional, national and global level. While political economists interpret this as a new form of media imperialism, cultural theorists emphasize the power of the 'active audience' and underline

the emergence of 'diasporic communities' and 'peripheral visions' (Curran and Park, 2000, 7). Community radio stations in Africa and the local television stations of immigrants in big cities on one side of the coin, transnational news networks (CNN) or global television formats (Who Wants to Be a Millionaire?) on the flip side: even in its digital age, broadcasting reveals its ambivalent nature as both a standardizing and a fragmentizing communication medium. But despite the explosion of satellite television channels and online broadcasting all around the world, detailed comparative schedule analysis has shown that most television programs (and this is even more true for radio programming) on mass channels are not imported but produced nationally. While today the broadcasting industry and technology without doubt do have a transnational character, the audiences remain – at least to a large degree – divided by national cultural and linguistic differences. As many scholarly works in the field of media studies have demonstrated, global formats only 'work' when they are successfully appropriated to national cultures.

Since the first utopian writings on 'speaking through the air' and 'seeing by electricity' in late-19th-century novels, radio and television broadcasting have stimulated people's fantasies about the transcending of space by means of wireless communication technologies. As 'ear' and 'window on the world', radio and television broadcasting have shaped new forms of medial participation and deeply challenged the bourgeois model of the public sphere. Local, national and international circulation of information and their private appropriation have shaped people's worldviews. Incorporating both the possibility of centralistic instrumentalization and democratic diversity of opinion, broadcasting has and will be an arena of political manipulations, competing economic interests, and battles for sociocultural hegemony.

Andreas Fickers

Bibliography

Douglas S. J. 2004. *Listening in: radio and the American imagination.* Minneapolis: University of Minnesota Press.

Curran J. and Park M.-J. (eds) 2000. *De-Westernizing media studies.* London: Routledge.

Hilmes M. 2002. *Only connect: a cultural history of broadcasting in the United States*. Belmont: Wadsworth.

Huth A. 1937. *La radio diffusion: puissance mondiale*. Paris: Gallimard.

Scannell P. 1996. *Radio, television and modern life*. Oxford: Blackwell.

Shohat E. and Stam R. 1994. *Unthinking Eurocentrism: multiculturalism and the media*. London: Routledge.

Smith A. (ed.) 1998. *Television: an international history*. Oxford: Oxford University Press.

Thompson J. B. 1995. *The media and modernity: a social theory of the media*. Cambridge: Polity.

Related essays

al-Jazeera; America; British Broadcasting Corporation (BBC); benefits and charity concerts; borders and borderlands; Cold War; consumer cooperation; cuisines; information economy; intergovernmental organizations; legal order; missionaries; nation and state; Olympic Games; publishing; Second Vatican Ecumenical Council; sport; technical standardization; United Nations Educational, Scientific and Cultural Organization (UNESCO) educational programmes; war; Westernization

British Broadcasting Corporation (BBC)

The British Broadcasting Corporation (BBC) is the world's best-known broadcaster, especially in the field of news and current affairs. In Britain, broadcasting evolved within a public-service framework, with the BBC at its core. From being granted its first Royal Charter in 1927 for radio and starting regular television broadcasts in 1936, the corporation was exempted from commercial pressures, being funded by a licence fee. The BBC frame of public-service broadcasting was adapted in many other countries in Western Europe as well as in Japan and some Commonwealth countries, formerly part of the British Empire.

In addition to its domestic services, the BBC has had an international presence since the inauguration of the Empire Service in 1931 (later BBC World Service radio), which in 2007 was broadcasting in more than 40 languages and reaching around 150 million listeners a week, both directly and through rebroadcasts on local stations. In 1995, drawing on the reputation of the World Service, the BBC launched a 24-hour global television news channel, BBC World, which can be seen in more than 270 million homes across 200 countries. Its international entertainment channel, BBC Prime, has since 1992 offered English-language programming, primarily beamed at Europe. The BBC's other international channels include BBC America, BBC Food and BBC Japan. BBC Worldwide Monitoring, originally created in 1939 as part of the BBC World Service, provides authoritative coverage of political and economic developments around the world and the BBC's website is one of the most widely respected online sources for journalists.

The BBC is also Europe's largest exporter of television programmes through its commercial arm, BBC Worldwide, formed in 1994. BBC has entered into the competitive world media market through a combination of wholly owned channels and joint ventures, with such media conglomerates as Discovery Network.

Daya Thussu

Bibliography

Hilmes M. 2003. 'British quality, American chaos: historical dualisms and what they leave out', *Radio Journal*, 1, 1, 13–27.

Related essays

al-Jazeera; broadcasting; information economy; language; radio

Buddhism

The Buddha was born as Prince Siddhartha (literally 'he who achieves') between the 6th and 5th centuries BC and was brought up in the city of Kapilavastu in the region that is now Nepal, a region culturally dependent on India. A golden youth, the future Buddha decided to become an ascetic and succeeded in finding his own path, which he expounded in a sermon given in Benares, India, that contains the four truths of Buddhism. These are: first, suffering is universal; second, its cause is desire in all its forms; third, desire must be overcome in order to abolish suffering; and fourth, this must be achieved by means of a method, the Eightfold Path, that prescribes a particular ethic and way of life. Buddhism started to expand across Central and South East Asia from the beginning of the Second Century BC, and became in the medieval age the main transnational religion of Asia. After a long period of stagnation, Buddhism has met with renewed transnational success in the last decades.

The image of Buddhism as individualistic, a religion of negation on the level of doctrine and of exclusively personal meditative experience on the level of practice, is tenacious but mistaken. Everything in Buddhism is relative: phenomena, like beings, are conditioned. Only the experience of Nirvana in the Theravada (the 'School of the Elders'), or Bodhi in the Mahayana (the 'great vehicle'), is not conditioned. The emperor Ashoka (304–232 BC), the most powerful emperor in India's history, was a great social reformer. His legend as the prince enlightened by Buddhism, supportive of social equality and respectful of life as a whole including that of animals, still serves as an inspiration for modern Buddhist leaders. These include Buddhadasa Bikkhu from Thailand, who originated the concept of 'dharmic socialism' (dharma being the Buddhist law); the Dalai Lama, who originated the concept of 'universal interdependence'; and the Vietnamese monk Tich Nhath Hanh, who promotes socially engaged Buddhism through the 'Order of Interbeing'. Tich Nhath Hanh, with his radical ecological theories, is today along with the Dalai Lama the main global leader of Buddhism, and both are honorary members of the International Network of Engaged Buddhists (INEB). The INEB, with headquarters in Bangkok and members in 33 countries, was founded in 1989 on the initiative of Sulak Sivaraska, a Thai activist, and Teruo Maruyama, a monk who is a member of the Nichiren Shu (a long established Buddhist pietist movement) and formerly belonged to the Japanese Communist Party.

Buddhism has inspired a range of political and social activities across the world, and especially in the US. Tich Nhath Hanh, a celebrated pacifist, now living in France, fought for equal rights in the US along with Martin Luther King. The other important transnational Buddhist organization is the Buddhist Peace Fellowship (BPF), with headquarters in Berkeley, near San Francisco. Founded by Robert Aitken, whose libertarian, ecologistic and antimilitarist ideas are very close to those of Sulak, this organization is close to the INEB, and Sulak writes regularly in its periodical, Turning Wheel, as do the Dalai

Lama and Tich Nhath Hanh. The BPF is a very active organization, promoting ecology and pacifism and defending human rights. It was involved in the political crisis in Honduras and Nicaragua in 1987. The BPF has a branch concerned with direct social action, the Buddhist Alliance for Social Engagement (BASE), which has introduced courses for students on social engagement, with both theoretical and practical content. The aim is for them to work on campaigns in anti-nuclear pressure groups or ecological associations, or in hospices, following the principles of engaged Buddhism. Another US organization, the Zen Peacemaker Order, was created on the initiative of the Zen monk Bernard Glassman, to consolidate a network of hands-on services for homeless people (of which the New York Greyston Bakery is one of the flagships), with a view to replacing the fragmentary social services provided by the US federal government by a system of positive reintegration into the community. These organizations follow on from the 'beat' movement of the 1960s, when major figures like Jack Kerouac or Allan Ginsberg had a strong interest in Buddhism, while providing an ideological and institutional coherence which was lacking during that period.

The transnational reach of Buddhism goes beyond hands-on activities. The Chinese Communists themselves, after the short-lived attempt during the Cultural Revolution to eliminate all religions, understood the ideological gain to be derived from Buddhism. 'The compassion extolled by Buddhism is aimed at the majority. To destroy, in the interests and towards the happiness of everyone, the evil inflicted on the masses by a small number – there is the true meaning of the compassion and mercifulness of the Buddha' (Zhufeng 1989, 31). One may even find declarations by celebrated Buddhist dignitaries affirming that the Universal Declaration of Human Rights is nothing but a recapitulation of the Lord Buddha's non-violent principles, that is to say non-violation of human dignity and liberty. This interpretation has led to anti-government Buddhist activism in, for example, Burma, with large numbers of militant Buddhists standing up to the army.

Engaged Buddhism itself has come to grapple with the world order, with a critique of 'extreme' capitalism, not on the grounds that it might be contrary to a primordial culture in which Asian identity was rooted, but simply on account of its 'inhumanity', its propensity to exclude the weakest and hence to aggravate suffering. The Asian financial crisis of the 1990s therefore reinforced the position of engaged Buddhism as offering a universal alternative culture – a culture suited to both the Western and the Asian crises, proposing a vision of the world and society that tends to coast between communism and individualism. It represents one of the principal defences against a nationalist 'Asianism' that has spread to Japan and is disturbingly on the increase in Southeast Asian countries such as Malaysia, where it is gradually turning into an anti-Western phobia that verges on a racism against Europeans and Americans and also, more surprisingly, against Jews. Engaged Buddhism is not only a bulwark against 'Asianism' but it is also the kind of Buddhism that is most readily exportable, because of its universalist aspirations and Westernized concepts. This is indeed the form of Buddhism that is expanding in the West. The first Buddhist university in the Western world, the Naropa Institute, was founded in Colorado in 1974. Since then, its programmes have developed towards a 'secularization' of the subjects covered. This idea of a secularized Buddhism is not a category imposed by the researcher, but introduced by Buddhists themselves (as for example in the Dalai Lama's 1997 video *Secular Meditation*, that offers a kind of wisdom and technical principles claimed to be useful for modern people irrespective of all 'religious persuasions'). Sōka Gakkai has gone further with this idea of a secular Buddhism.

Today the Dalai Lama is the iconic figure of engaged Buddhism. He has managed to build on the foundation laid by the engaged Buddhists and at the same time gain acceptance as the Chakravartin, the universal dharmic sovereign, bearer of progressive Buddhist values, conducting a policy of Awakening on a planetary scale. Until the end of the 1980s, the Tibetan cause was very distinct from Buddhist thought. Thereafter we find in the United States and Europe not only publications but also video cassettes aimed at the wider public, dealing with Buddhist concepts of human rights, feminism, engaged Buddhism through social action, psychology and medicine. The Tibetan cause has resulted in a deterritorialization of Tibet, which has become a sort of Utopian land, symbolically present on the whole planet by means of a network of Buddhist centres carrying the names of monasteries in the Himalayas that have been destroyed. It is as if they were the prefectures of this fictive Buddhist State whose governor is the Dalai Lama and whose citizens are Western Buddhists. The Dalai Lama tends to take the lead as the representative authority for westernized Buddhists. He is questioned as to the ethical advisability of such and such a programme of scientific research. His questioners include scientists themselves, who ask about the meaning of their own discoveries and the directions to take for the future. The collective work entitled *Gentle bridges: conversations with the Dalai-Lama on sciences of the mind* (Hayward and Varela 1992) is typical of this intellectual attitude. The scientists engage in self-criticism, almost contrition, as scientists, appealing to the superior insight of the great Lama to guide them on the paths of 'healthy research'. In Asia itself, the Dalai Lama takes the lead in extolling non-violence against violent and oppressive regimes. Aung San Suu Kyi, the Nobel Peace Laureate, takes him as her model in her struggle against the authoritarian Burmese regime. And yet Burmese Buddhism belongs to the Theravada branch (School of the Elders) while the Dalai Lama belongs to the culturally and doctrinally distinct Mahayana or Vajrayana branch (Great Vehicle or Vehicle of Thunder).

Buddhism today, in its different schools and tendencies, is a religious movement fully adapted to cultural globalization, but above all to the values of individual well-being and development that dominate in advanced industrial societies. It has become accepted as ideologically the most coherent and institutionally the best organized component – by contrast with the New Age nexus – of the new 'individuo-global' religiosity, which is characterized on the one hand by ideas of ecological consciousness, sustainable development, global citizenship and humanitarian intervention, and on the other hand by ideas of personal development, solicitude for one's self, the aspiration towards authenticity and the liberation of one's interior world.

Raphaël Liogier

Bibliography

Hayward J. W. and Varela F. 1992. *Gentle bridges: conversations with the Dalai Lama on the sciences of mind*. Boston: Shambhala.

Liogier R. 2004. *Le bouddhisme mondialisé: une perspective sociologique sur la globalisation du religieux.* Paris : Ellipses.

Liogier R. 2009. *La religion post-industrielle: souci de soi, conscience du monde.* Paris: Flammarion.

Venerable Sumano Bikkhu 1987. *Buddhist thought and meditation in the nuclear age.* Nantaburi: Wat Chulapratha Rangsrit.

Zhufeng L. (ed.) 1987. *Zhongguo sheshui zhuyi shiqi de zongjiao wenti* (Religious questions during the Chinese socialist era). Shanghai: Academy of Social Sciences. Extracts translated from the Chinese in Vandermeersch L. 1989. 'Bouddhisme et politique en Asie Orientale', *Problèmes politiques et sociaux,* 603, 3 March.

Related essays

1960s; Asia; Chinese medicine; civilizations; exile; feel-good culture; human rights; New Age; pacifism; religion; universalism and cosmopolitanism; world orders; Zen aesthetics

C

Cancer

The historical study of cancer in transnational perspective is in its infancy: few historians have explored the flows across national borders of this group of diseases. Yet, a growing body of epidemiological research has shown that rates of certain cancers, notably stomach and other gastrointestinal cancers, differ dramatically from country to country, and that migrants (or the children of migrants) from low-risk areas to high-risk areas can be at greater risk of these cancers. For example, rates of colorectal cancer differ significantly among countries, varying by as much as tenfold from low-incidence areas in Asia, Africa, and parts of Latin America, to much higher rates in Northern Europe, New Zealand, Australia, and the United States. Moreover, migrants from low-risk to higher-risk countries experience rapid increases in colorectal cancer risk within the same generation.

Such studies suggest that the history of cancer – or more specifically of certain cancers – should be part of a broader history of transnational migrations. People may carry the disease or a predisposition to the disease across national borders, but its development in the bodies of migrants may, in part, depend on how they adapt to their country of destination, and the type of cancer to which they are subject. Yet, there are no historical studies that systematically explore how such adaptive changes shape rates of cancer in migrant populations, or what such changes tell us about the lifestyles of countries of destination. Nor has there been much to historicize sociological and anthropological insights into how migrants' health beliefs and practices affect their interactions with Western medicine and diseases. Thus, for example, while there is a substantial historical literature on the development of cancer services in France, Germany, Canada, the United Kingdom and the United States from the early 20th century, very little research puts such developments in the context of contemporary migration flows. The result is that we know little about the ways in which immigrant vernacular health traditions intersected with emergent cancer services in these nations. Nor has the history of cancer been used as a lens onto broader processes of social and cultural adaptation and accommodation either in migrant populations or in the native populations with which they come into contact.

The neglect of such issues is particularly striking given the importance of transnational efforts to combat this group of diseases. Organized campaigns against cancer emerged in Europe and North America in the early to mid 20th century. Such campaigns were often nationally based, but they were also sustained by a belief that the science unpinning their efforts was universal, unconstrained by national boundaries, and dependent on the free-flow of knowledge, materials and practices. From such a perspective, the effort against cancer was a worldwide endeavour, research in one part of the world contributing knowledge and techniques that might be applied elsewhere to the eventual solution of the cancer problem. Thus, campaigns against cancer depended on innovations in international postal and telecommunication systems that enabled interchange between scientists and physicians across the world. It was also reliant on the enormous growth of scientific and medical publications, on a transnational trade in the material culture of medicine and science (such as medical and laboratory tools and animals), and on transportation systems that enabled physicians and scientists to travel abroad to learn, hands-on, new techniques and ideas. In the first half the 20th century, physicians and scientists travelled in vast numbers to European cancer institutions; by mid-century the flows tended to focus on the United States, which dominated cancer research from the 1940s, and which accommodated many immigrant scientists and physicians – such as Jewish ones who left Nazi Germany in the 1930s – and who brought their skills and knowledge with them. Thus, if migrant vernacular health traditions intersected in complex ways with the cancer services of their countries of destination, so migrant scientific and medical traditions intersected in complex ways with traditions of science and medicine in their countries of destination, as physicians and scientists adapted knowledge and techniques developed in one country to the circumstances of another.

David Cantor

Bibliography

Cantor D. (ed.) 2007. 'Cancer in the twentieth century', *Bulletin of the History of Medicine*, special issue, 81, 1, Spring.

Lerner B. H. 2003. *The breast cancer wars: fear, hope and the pursuit of a cure in twentieth-century America*. Oxford and New York: Oxford University Press.

Pinell P. 2002. *The fight against cancer: France 1890–1940*. London: Routledge.

Proctor R. N. 1999. *The Nazi war on cancer*. Princeton: Princeton University Press.

Related essays
Acquired Immunodeficiency Syndrome (AIDS); Chinese medicine; drugs (medical); germs; human mobility; life and physical sciences; medicine; scientific instruments and tools; smallpox

Cantonese opera

Cantonese opera is a form of regional musical theatre that emerged in Guangdong, China, during the 18th and the 19th centuries. Based initially in Foshan and later the provincial capital of Guangzhou, itinerant opera troupes travelled across the Pearl River Delta, performing for village communities and entertaining rural visitors to market towns. An urban shift happened toward the end of the 1800s as Cantonese opera captured a growing audience among residents in Guangzhou and nearby British-controlled Hong Kong. At the same time, Cantonese opera followed the footsteps of Chinese migrants who left China in unprecedented numbers. In the early 1900s, Cantonese opera became a vibrant immigrant theatre with regional nodes and networks in different parts of Southeast Asia and North America even as it expanded into a thriving entertainment business in South China.

Troupes organized by actors with the backing of Chinese merchant capital furnished a vital link in the circulation of Cantonese opera overseas. In Singapore, an actors' guild was set up as early as 1857 and the island soon became the most important market for Cantonese opera off the China coast. The early decades of the 20th century saw local Chinese theatre houses playing host regularly to visiting troupes. Actors and musicians further used Singapore as a base for performance circuits connecting the Chinese communities throughout the Malay Peninsula. Singapore was such a viable market that its Cantonese stage groomed some famed performers. Both the comedy specialist Ma Shizeng and the female impersonator Chen Feinong launched their careers in Singapore before they were recruited by the theatre powerhouses in Hong Kong and Guangzhou in the early 1920s. Other notable points on the travelling circuits in Southeast Asia included the Vietnamese Chinese settlement in Saigon-Cholon and the small Cantonese population in an otherwise Hokkien-dominated community in Manila in the Philippines.

In the Americas, the first opera troupe reportedly arrived in San Francisco from South China in 1852, but the financial and logistical arrangements of trans-Pacific crossing were more daunting compared to its counterparts to Southeast Asia. Additional handicaps included widespread prejudice and the enactment of anti-Chinese exclusion laws by the US government starting in 1882. Still, Cantonese opera became a favorite pastime for the immigrant Chinese, especially after they built a permanent theatre house in San Francisco's Chinatown in 1867. Afterwards, more sponsored troupes from South China arrived, and nightly performances were available over extended periods of time. Before the end of the century, some troupes appeared before their compatriots settled elsewhere in California and the Western US, and a few made their way to the East Coast.

Cantonese opera, both at home and abroad, reached a high point around the 1920s. An expansive repertoire, the continuing refinement of arias and acting techniques, a capacity to absorb new elements such as Western musical instruments and the use of stage properties, and the adoption of commercial advertisement led the way in meeting local and more contemporary tastes. The competitive theatre market in South China, the high cost of production, and political instability there, in turn, encouraged more actors to journey overseas. On the North American circuit, San Francisco, New York City and Vancouver emerged as regional anchors, hosting visiting troupes and circulating actors to secondary locations in the US and Canada, as well as Mexico, Peru and Cuba.

Cantonese opera built on – and helped extend – the transnational networks spun by the Chinese immigrants in their global diaspora. Confined to the migrant communities, it was viewed by non-Chinese as exotic and foreign, but without the kind of recognition accorded to Peking opera in the Western world. After the 1940s, Cantonese opera slowly lost its grip among Chinese due to the rise of newer forms of commercial media and popular entertainment. Cantonese opera nonetheless held on to a following among amateur musicians and opera fans. The renewal of Chinese immigration to the West in the late 1900s witnessed a mild revival of Cantonese opera overseas, now performed and enjoyed mostly by members of Chinatown musical societies, as recreation, as part of community gatherings, and as cultural events. Local excitement peaked occasionally when a troupe visited from China and Hong Kong. A number of international performance galas held in Singapore and Guangzhou in the 1990s drew participants from around the world.

Wing Chung Ng

Bibliography

Ng W. 2005–06. 'Chinatown theatre as transnational business: new evidence from Vancouver during the exclusion era', *BC Studies: The British Columbian Quarterly*, 148, 24–54.

Rao N. 2000. 'Songs of the exclusion era: New York Chinatown's opera theaters in the 1920s', *American Music*, 20, 4, 399–444.

Riddle R. 1983. *Flying dragons, flowing streams: music in the life of San Francisco's Chinese*. Westport: Greenwood.

Related essays

Chinese Diaspora; diasporas; empire and migration; femininity; human mobility; Italian opera; music; theatre

Capitalism

Capitalism can refer both to an economic system and a historical epoch defined by that system. Although the term has been used mainly in a European context, and has been an integral part of the development of modern nation states, capitalism has, since its inception, also been a transnational phenomenon. Economists from Marx to contemporary neoliberals have consistently emphasized the universal and transnational nature of the capitalist system, even as most capitalist economies and firms have developed within a national context.

'Capitalist' first appeared in print in 1792, and 'capitalism' in 1854. Karl Marx (1818–83) preferred the terms 'capitalist mode of production' or 'bourgeois society'. He almost never used the term 'capitalism', which first appears in his letters to Russian socialists in 1877. Although they did not use the term 'capitalism', the earliest conscious expressions of capitalist economic principles appear from the late 18th century in the works of Adam Smith (1723–90), David Ricardo (1772–1823) and Jean-Baptiste Say (1767–1832). The classical political economists emphasized free trade among nations and minimal state involvement in the economy. Adam Smith's 'invisible hand', Ricardo's 'law of comparative advantage' and Say's theories concerning market equilibrium, full employment, inflation and diminishing returns remain important economic concepts even today.

Throughout its history, capitalism has undergone repeated transformations, appeared in a variety of national and transnational contexts and been subject to diverse interpretations. Its fundamental principles, however, have remained constant. While commerce and profit have been important aspects of economic life since ancient times, several features distinguish the capitalist economy from its predecessors. One of the most important is private ownership of capital. Capital is defined as money or credit used for the purchase of goods and labour, and also as the materials and fixed assets used in production, such as land, factories and equipment. Capital is an abstract measurement of value calculated in monetary terms. In a capitalist economy, money, especially paper currency, becomes the dominant medium of exchange, and credit, bank loans, private bonds and other financial instruments are developed to provide maximum liquidity and to facilitate the accumulation of capital in the private firm.

Private ownership of goods, land and equipment in capitalist economies has been accompanied by the rise of markets for their exchange. The emergence of relatively free markets for labour, which gradually replaced hereditary guilds and various forms of customary servitude, was crucial to the development of capitalism throughout the world. In capitalist economies, wage labour became the dominant form of employment, transforming the labour relationship into a form of market exchange, a commodity relationship. According to the labour theory of value, the value produced by wage workers provides the capitalist employer with profit in the form of surplus value appropriated by virtue of ownership of the means of production and control of the labour process.

The imperative that a firm must earn a surplus over and above the amount of capital invested in materials, wages, interest and overhead (which Marx defined as the 'law of value') drives firms to increase efficiency and productivity through technological innovation, intensifying the labour process and other measures to increase the efficient use of capital. Market competition (and failure) potentially leads to the concentration of capital in larger firms. Private firms attempt to gain an advantage by establishing cartels and monopolies whenever possible. Such mergers do not eliminate competition, but give the larger firm certain advantages in the marketplace. An economy dominated by non-competitive monopolies would no longer be capitalist.

In addition to private ownership and commodity production, the defining feature of the capitalist firm is control of the production process by the private owner or the owner's agents. This includes decisions concerning hiring and firing, technology, working conditions, the manner in which products are sold and the disposition of the firm's assets. Even without mechanized equipment, the capitalist factory contrasts with 'putting out' arrangements or other systems in which the production process is not concentrated in premises owned and managed by the capitalist.

Historically, capitalism has generally been conceived as a Western European phenomenon, its origins variously dated from the emergence of urban workshops in the 16th century to the industrial revolution of the late 18th century. From its inception, however, capitalism has been a transnational phenomenon and several premodern economies have exhibited capitalist characteristics. While private firms and capitalist economic principles have played an important role in the development of modern nation states, the relationship between national governments and capital, which is potentially stateless, transnational and of dubious loyalty, has been contentious as often as cooperative. Capitalism has also thrived under a variety of political systems, including monarchies and military dictatorships. So long as the state does not violate the principles of private property, competition and free markets for goods, labour and capital, there is no necessary form of state that accompanies a capitalist economy.

In Britain, the rise of capitalism from the 17th century was intimately tied to the imperialist state, as the earliest private fortunes were amassed through overseas commerce based on state-chartered trading monopolies. In the 18th century, China's laissez-faire economy more closely approached the capitalist ideal than many parts of Europe. By that time, China was a highly commercialized and monetized economy. A common feature of capitalist economies in 18th-century Europe, America and Asia was commercialized agriculture. Based on independent farming, sharecropping, manorial estates and even chattel slavery, agricultural production increasingly specialized in cash crops for long-distance markets such as those for cotton and tobacco. Rural workers around the world also participated in 'putting out' arrangements in which households accepted raw materials from wholesale merchants and produced goods for prearranged prices. This was not a fully fledged capitalist arrangement, however, as the merchant did not control the production process and the relationship was based on a commercial exchange rather than wage payments.

Despite similarities in premodern economies around the world, the first dramatic transformation of a capitalist economy occurred in Britain from the early 19th century, when Western capitalism diverged from its Asian counterparts in the industrial revolution. In an effort to reduce production costs, textile capitalists in Britain adopted new production technologies and new sources of power, which greatly increased productivity. The combination of mechanized cotton spinning with steam power gained European and American textile producers a decisive edge in international markets and by 1831, for the first time, Britain was exporting more textile products to China than it imported.

The adoption of new technologies required greater investment of capital, which promoted the development of joint stock companies, bond issues and other financial instruments. The application of the business corporation to industrial manufacturing facilitated the concentration of capital in ever larger and increasingly monopolistic firms. From the late 19th century, large-scale industrial processes and massive corporations came to dominate the world's most developed economies. Electrification and new production techniques, especially in steel and chemicals, both necessitated and facilitated the emergence of monopolistic trusts based on horizontal integration (comprehensive dominance of a particular industry, as in the case of Standard Oil in the United States) or vertical integration (command of an entire production process from beginning to end, as in the case of US Steel). Comprehensive firms engaged in large-scale manufacturing utilizing advanced industrial processes, such as the assembly line, and created an increasingly specialized division of labour leading to the deskilling of industrial work and the demise of the last generalist artisans.

The development of industrial corporations requiring vast amounts of capital also led to the separation of finance and production, with important implications for the nature of the capitalist firm and the role of finance in the global economy. In what is known as 'finance capitalism', manufacturing increasingly came to be dominated by the needs of financial firms providing capital investment through loans and share purchases. This iteration of the capitalist system led to the flourishing of cartels, trusts and transnational corporations from the late 19th century, which invested in all manner of commercial, manufacturing and transportation enterprises on a global scale.

Government responses were contradictory. On the one hand, nation states aggressively pursued advantages in securing overseas markets and sources of raw materials. On the other hand, responding to global economic depressions in the 1870s and 1930s, as well as pressure from voting constituents, governments enacted legislation to restrict financial speculation and the formation of monopolistic trusts. Industrial workers organized to protect their interests, demanding legislation concerning working conditions and collective bargaining. These efforts met with varying degrees of success in different national contexts, but factory laws appeared in Europe, America, China, Japan and many other nations, causing some manufacturers to relocate operations. While the struggle between labour and capital played out on a global stage, capital has always enjoyed greater mobility across national boundaries.

As the global capitalist system evolved in the 20th century, both states and firms changed and adapted. The crisis of the 1930s inspired new economic theories as well as new legislation, often based on John Maynard Keynes' suggestion for a socialization of investment. The Roosevelt administration in the United States, for example, adopted policies to moderate the deleterious effects of financial speculation and monopoly capitalism without fundamentally violating the principles of capitalist economics, leading to a new relationship between transnational capital and national governments.

The 1940s saw the rise of 'mixed economies' characterized by large, transnational firms operating in a context of heightened government regulation, the rise of the 'welfare state' and proactive fiscal policies in the US, Europe and East Asia. The postwar period also saw cautious steps toward international trade agreements and economic institutions under the leadership of the United Nations. The architects of the postwar global economy sought to eliminate the protectionist barriers established from the 1930s, as witnessed by the progressive and uneven development of the GATT/WTO compact.

The rise of the global free-trade regime has been accompanied by a return to classical economics. Keynes' ideas concerning government intervention in the economy were anathema to many theorists and did not go unchallenged for long as proponents of the Austrian school, such as Ludwig von Mises (1881–1973) and Friedrich von Hayek (1899–1992), gained prominence in the postwar years. These 'neoclassical' economists argued that the Great Depression was a product of government intervention rather than market dynamics and called for a return to laissez-faire policies. In the 1970s, the global energy crisis and 'stagflation' (the simultaneous increase of prices and unemployment) intensified interest in neoclassical and neoliberal theory. The neoliberal economists of the Chicago School, such as Milton Friedman (1912–2006), advocated a smaller economic role for government, deregulation and lower corporate taxes, leading to the 'supply-side' economic policies implemented in the US and Britain in the 1980s.

In the waning decades of the 20th century, trends in the evolution of transnational capitalism have remained complex and contradictory. The reform or collapse of socialist economies and the establishment of regional free-trade zones have created a global economy more integrated and more conducive to the free flow of capital, goods and jobs than ever before, leading some to question whether national governments will have any economic role to play in the future. With the consolidation of the European Union and the issuance of a unified Euro currency in 2002, European national borders have practically vanished, at least in economic terms.

Transnational corporations today are better able to seek out new markets, relocate their operations overseas and set standards for employment, working conditions and environmental regulation, even in the face of opposition from states and citizens. At the same time, however, national governments around the world continue to play a major role in shaping economic development, as exemplified by the role of MITI in Japan and state-sponsored Chaebol monopolies in Korea in the 1980s, as well as the stronger role played by governments in China, Africa and Southeast Asia in shaping and guiding their national economies and the role of foreign investment therein. Such developments may well produce new changes in the near future, as competition from late-developing economies, such as China and India, shifts the balance of power away from the North Atlantic.

Robert Cliver

Bibliography

Braverman H. 1998. *Labor and monopoly capital: the degradation of work in the twentieth century*, 25th anniversary edition. New York: Monthly Review.

Chandler A. D. Jr 1977. *The visible hand: the managerial revolution in American business*. Cambridge, MA: Belknap.

Landes D. S. 2003. *The unbound Prometheus: technological change and industrial development in Western Europe from 1750 to the present*, 2nd edition. Cambridge: Cambridge University Press.

Marx K. 1992. *Capital: a critique of political economy*. With an introduction by E. Mandel. New York: Penguin in association with New Left Review.

Osterhammel J. and Peterson N. P. 2005. *Globalization: a short history*. (Geyer D. trans.) Princeton: Princeton University Press.

Pomeranz K. 2000. *The great divergence: China, Europe, and the making of the modern world economy*. Princeton: Princeton University Press.

Wallerstein I. M. 1974. *The modern world-system*. New York: Academic Press.

Related essays
advertising; agriculture; assembly line; auditing; commodity trading; convergence and divergence; corporations; debt crises; development and growth; economics; European Union (EU); financial markets; General Agreement on Tariffs and Trade (GATT) / World Trade Organization (WTO); global cities; industrialization; investment; iron and steel; labour standards; legal order; management; money; nation and state; *non-lieux*; regional communities; socialism; technologies; textiles; trade; transnational; transportation infrastructures; welfare state; workers' movements; world orders

Cappuccino

Coffee has a long transnational history: transplanted between continents, the second most traded global commodity, and subject of numerous cultures of consumption. Yet by the end of the 20th century, 'Italian-style' coffee had conquered much of the developed and developing world.

These beverages are made with shots of espresso, extracted by machines of a type first produced by Achille Gaggia in 1947. Italian postwar urbanization led to a rapid growth in bars serving the short black drink during work breaks. Espresso spread into Southern Europe where machines were easily adjusted to local tastes. Elsewhere, cappuccino, an Italian breakfast drink combining espresso with frothed milk, proved popular due to its theatrical preparation, exotic appearance and 'softer' taste. Longer drinking times encouraged customers to treat coffee bars as leisure venues.

Between the mid-1950s and early 1960s, most machines in the English-speaking world were installed by local entrepreneurs in premises with more 'bohemian' than 'Italian' ambiences. Thereafter they were confined to 'ethnically marked' Italian catering operations as elsewhere in the world. A revival began in the 1980s when the American Speciality Coffee movement championed Italian-style drinks as handcrafted products. The Starbucks chain developed larger, more 'accessible' beverages, serving them in comfortable surroundings to create a '20-minute customer experience' that proved highly popular both in the US and overseas.

This did not simply produce globalization as Americanization. In Asian markets indigenous operators adapted the format to local preferences, while retaining the veneer of Western sophistication. Primary producers benefited from an image-driven imperative for 'fair trade', while Italian machine makers and roasters dramatically expanded their overseas operations. An international speciality coffee community arose, spawning the World Barista Championships, while domestic consumption remained diverse due to the 'drinking out' basis to cappuccino culture.

Jonathan Morris

Bibliography

Schultz H. and Yang D. J. 1998. *Pour your heart into it: how Starbucks built a company one cup at a time*. New York: Hyperion.

Related essays

commodity trading; consumer society; cuisines; drinks; feel-good culture; prizes

Car culture

'Car culture' is a broad phrase that refers to the myriad ways in which use of the automobile since the beginning of the 20th century has shaped social relations, human geographies, national economies, and individual experience around the globe, making the car one of the most defining material artifacts, industrial products, and cultural symbols of the last one hundred years.

Although no country is more associated with the images brought to mind by the term 'car culture' than the United States, the history of cars was transnational from the first. Engineers and entrepreneurs in Great Britain, France, Germany, and the United States developed the automotive idea. Over more than a century, they competed for technical advantage, patents, and sales, participating in a transnational diffusion of knowledge and in technological change that soon after the turn of the 20th century led to the rise of the mass-produced, gasoline-powered, internal-combustion-engine automobile.

Paris was the early centre of automobile production, but by 1910, just two years after Henry Ford introduced the Model T, a United States auto industry centred in the Midwest states had surpassed that of European rivals. Innovations in manufacturing efficiency associated foremost with Ford's company and an increasing availability of gasoline inaugurated an age of reliable and affordable cars for the masses, most expansively in the United States, but eventually also including the wealthy and the middle classes in nations the world over.

Early votaries celebrated the usefulness of the car as a conveyance: it moved you quickly and individually, and it did so reliably over long distances. Soon enough though, idealized images of freedom, escape, travel, romance, and self-expression fuelled the essential pleasure principle long associated with car cultures – and to the marketing of them – across the globe. Thus two intersecting forces drove the transformative and transnational culture of the car that emerged by the middle decades of the 20th century: the economic utility of automobility and the glamour and personal power that consumers often perceived attached themselves to the auto as the most socially visible of products.

Popular images around the world, especially those projected by the globally influential culture industries of the post-World War 2 United States, often celebrated the car as a symbol of youthful excitement, whether in the rock music of Chuck Berry and the Beach Boys or in nostalgic portrayals of drag-racing culture in such movies as *American Graffiti*. The mythic linking of cars with tropes of speed, sexuality, and outlaw heroes was also often a mainstay of postwar European films, including Dino Risi's *Il sorpasso* and Jean-Luc Godard's *Breathless* and *Pierrot le fou*.

Cars have been demonized, too, in particular for their part in the loss of older forms of community life that emphasized social connectedness and locality over individual mobility and speed. Such critiques bemoan suburbanization and the emergence of 'centreless' cities and point to the highway construction booms that took place in industrial nations after World War 2. Even as car ownership rates around the world rose after 1945, unquestioned optimism about the social benefits of the automobile has been comparatively tempered in places like Europe and Japan, where there have been social commitments to mass transit and high-speed railways. In the United States, however, a 'drive-in' culture of the car greatly reshaped the social landscape in the post-1945 years, determining everything from new forms of home design, to the development of the shopping mall and the rise of fast food and the global corporations that produced it.

Cars have often served, moreover, as powerful symbols of national strength for modernizing nations. The manufacture of indigenous automobiles was seen as a form of Communist-bloc resistance to the capitalist West during the Cold War. A boom of private car ownership – known as 'my car-ism' – in Japan during its rapid-growth decades of the 1960s and 1970s seemed evidence of national renewal. And the newly rich in today's marketizing China are rapidly jettisoning their bicycles for cars. Many are alarmed, however, about the prospect of American-style car cultures in the populous nations of China and India in this age of global warming and oil peak.

Scott O'Bryan

Bibliography
Wollen P. and Kerr J. (eds) 2002. *Autotopia: cars and culture*. London: Reaktion.

Related essays
America; assembly line; car safety standards; city planning; Cold War; consumer society; cuisines; fast food; film; Hollywood; International Road Federation (IRF); love; *non-lieux*; oil, transportation infrastructures; rock; spatial regimes; Toyotism; trade (manufactured goods); Westernization

Car safety standards

Car safety standards are the set of norms and rules that define driver, passenger, and pedestrian safety as it concerns automobile usage. As early as the beginning of the 20th century, European and US manufacturers understood the economic stakes inherent in the harmonization of automobile standards and worked on their technical development. In the public sphere, it was not until after the Second World War that the international harmonization of standards took form – giving birth to Europe's and America's recent divergence over how to appropriately negotiate and implement auto standards. In future, the two distinct models of standards negotiation will be shaped by those developing countries representing the most dynamic emerging economies for automakers.

Britain, Germany, Italy, and several European governments have regulated automobile construction since the 19th century. In contrast it would not be until the 1924 National Conference on Street and Highway Safety that similar guidelines for brakes, lights, and anti-skid devices would be introduced in the United States. The notion of automobile standards appeared implicitly at the beginning of the 20th century with the widespread adoption of the front, hood-enclosed engine developed in France by the Panhard Company in 1894, or with the disputes over auto-part licensing and patents that affected early firms like the US-based Ford Motor Company. A scientific community soon became institutionalized around the professional organizations made up of automobile engineers interested in mechanics and automobile design. The Society of Automobile Engineers – now known as the Society of Automotive Engineers, or SAE – envisaged that an exchange of knowledge and know-how would be a means to reduce the cost of automobile parts for small US firms. Considered by some observers to be among the fathers of standardization, Howard E. Coffin served as vice president of Hudson Motor Car Company and assumed the presidency of SAE in 1910. Coffin elevated SAE's stature at both national and international levels. Cross-border exchanges among automobile and engineering representatives of the period's largest companies contributed to this evolution, reflected in early SAE conferences such as the exposition of the European four-wheel brake design by the French engineer Henri Perrot at the 1924 SAE Annual Meeting and the presentation of power steering by the American Francis W. Davis at the 1928 Summer Meeting in Quebec.

In Geneva, the League of Nations housed the Advisory and Technical Committee for Communications and Transit during the interwar period, which initially concerned itself with railroad, maritime, and water transport. The development of the automobile soon moved League officials to branch out into the harmonization of traffic signals and the rights of automobile drivers in various countries. The League's automobile work was again taken up after World War 2 when in May 1947 high-ranking officials at the nascent United Nations foresaw the need for a rational organization of inland transport at the European level; automobile safety formally emerged as a significant UN concern during the 1949 Convention on Road Traffic in Geneva that designated vehicle failures as a principal cause of road traffic accidents. On the basis of a United Nations Economic Commission for Europe (UNECE) Road Transport Committee resolution, Working Party 29 on the Construction of Vehicles (henceforth 'Working Party') was created in

1952 to elaborate the European automobile technical standards for the UNECE Inland Transport Committee. From 1953 on, it brought together in Geneva representatives of governments wishing to negotiate safety regulations characteristic of road vehicles in the presence of non-governmental observers such as the International Organization for Standardization and the International Bureau of Motor Manufacturers. The Italian government's representative Giacomo Pocci presided over the Working Party for 31 years. Pocci began by addressing concerns such as an auto's rear red lights, eventually enlarging the Working Party's regulatory prerogative to cover noise and pollution norms through an international accord called the '1958 agreement'. The accord required a two-thirds vote for UNECE regulations and acceptance of mutual recognition – where one country's regulation is subsequently recognized by another country that is party to the 1958 agreement and vice versa. This work was simultaneously carried out via the then European Economic Community (EEC) rules that were generally developed through informal UNECE and EEC linkages.

As regulations developed by the Working Party came into force in Europe, SAE technical guidelines were criticized as inadequate to protect the safety of auto passengers in the United States: on the one hand, they were voluntary; on the other, they were formulated in the absence of consumer participation and input. In a watershed series of Congressional hearings (1965–66) over the federal government's role in traffic safety, consumer activists such as Ralph Nader demanded strong federal intervention to set new automobile safety standards for manufacturers. In the end, the activists' cause prevailed and legally binding federal motor vehicle safety standards would supersede SAE technical guidelines. Some of the new safety standards, however, were resisted by industry on grounds that they were too technologically advanced for their time, would stifle innovation, or would go against the demands of the marketplace. They also impacted US car imports as foreign manufacturers had to abide by them in order to remain in the US market; some foreign officials denounced the new US standards as protectionist and contrary to international norms such as those set through the Working Party. With American regulators using their own standards and European officials employing

those agreed to in the UNECE, broader standards negotiations increasingly deadlocked. It would not be until 1995 that modification of the 1958 agreement would be seen, allowing former Working Party observers – such as the United States and Canada – to become full voting, contracting parties to the accord. In 1998, the Working Party evolved yet again when Japan joined the 1958 agreement as a full contracting party.

The United States did not sign on to the 1958 agreement, highlighting an important divergence among UNECE members over car safety standards. The US legislation authorizing the issuance of standards mandates that the standards be established through a rule-making process providing manufacturers, consumer representatives, and others with a meaningful opportunity to participate, as well as meeting additional national criteria for safety, performance, cost, and technical feasibility. The US requirements thus diverged from UNECE procedures set under the 1958 agreement, although economic considerations would eventually bring US officials to revisit their role within the Working Party. Links between Japanese and American industry were strengthened during the 1980s, despite the fact that access for American firms to the Japanese market had been slowed by Japan's imposition of technical standards – viewed by some as potential trade impediments. The newly formed Transatlantic Business Dialogue would later denounce such differences in national standards by advocating a reduction in trade barriers linked to the patchwork of national standards regulations; since 1995 it has encouraged US government representatives to join the Working Party in order to advance global harmonization of auto technical standards. The 1958 agreement's mutual recognition principle – which implied a loss of national sovereignty – as well as its two-thirds (compared to unanimous) voting scheme, aroused concerns on the part of American officials in view of its potential impact on the US programme for handling defective vehicles, and they therefore proposed significant changes to the accord. When the contracting parties to the 1958 agreement rejected most of the proposed changes, US officials pressed for a new agreement (signed in 1998) that was predicated on consensus decision making, without mutual recognition as in the 1958 agreement. The new agreement has mitigated for now the divergence over the technical basis for car standards by allowing the United States and others to keep full sovereignty over regulations developed domestically; UNECE standards do not, in other words, automatically supersede national regulations.

Today the 2005 Joint Report on the Roadmap for EU–US Regulatory Cooperation and Transparency states that the EU and US 'are discussing ways to promote a science-based approach to global technical regulations under the United Nations 1998 Agreement'. The '1998 agreement' has thus spurred lively debate among Working Party participants in search of effective science-based rule making: for some it is an indirect attempt to not regulate the most controversial standards as the agreement requires unanimous voting; for others it relies on sound general notions of multilateral governance used within the UN system and other international fora. In any case, questions about how to regulate car safety standards are far from settled. For the Working Party, recently renamed the World Forum for Harmonization of Vehicle Regulations, they will be decided in part by its new developing country members such as China and India.

Stève Bernardin
Harrison Grafos

Bibliography

Thompson G. 1954. 'Intercompany Technical Standardization in the Early American Automobile Industry', *The Journal of Economic History*, 14, 1, 1–20.

Moguen-Toursel M. 2003. 'Strategies of European automobile manufacturers facing Community environmental standards', *Business and Economic History On-Line* [online]. Available: www.thebhc.org/publications/BEHonline/2003/Moguen-toursel.pdf, accessed 12 December 2005.

United Nations 2002. *World Forum for Harmonization of Vehicle Regulations (WP 29): How it works, how to join it*. Document ECE/TRANS/NONE/2002/12. New York and Geneva: United Nations.

Related essays

food safety standards; League of Nations system; measurement; motor industry; technical standardization; traffic signals; United Nations system

Charity concerts and benefits *See* Benefits and charity concerts

Childhood

Childhood is a stage of life between infancy and adulthood, intimately experienced by every human being and different for each child. Yet childhoods are also shaped by cultural attitudes, economic circumstances, social structures, and public policies – all of which change with time. Although recent scholarship has shown the effects of these changes on children, most of that research necessarily concentrates on specific locales. The transnational histories of childhood explore patterns of change across political and cultural divisions. And the dramatic transformations that began in 19th-century Europe make a logical starting point, provided we do not forget that throughout the past two centuries a majority of the world's children have lived in poverty and had but limited experience of these changes.

The challenge of social change

In most of the world (Africa is the notable exception) populations increased significantly in the 17th and 18th centuries and population growth became especially striking in 19th-century Europe, where infant mortality declined and greater numbers could be sustained by more available food and, eventually, by improvements in medicine. With industrialization cities grew larger; and the children in them, lacking their rural roles, troubled sensitive observers who feared that alienated street waifs threatened society itself. Today, 35 of the world's 50 largest cities are in South and Southeast Asia; many, like the megalopolises of the Middle East and South America, are characterized by sprawling slums filled with children. In naturally growing populations, children become a larger proportion of the whole, and in industrial societies families, especially in the middle class, have gradually come to have fewer children. A growing emphasis on the importance of childhood has accompanied these demographic changes.

Increased migration from the European countryside to cities and from Europe overseas brought new strains for families, new hardships and opportunities for their children. Sent to work where families had little influence, children learned to fend for themselves in unfamiliar trades or petty crime.

More adaptable than their elders, they often served as intermediaries in strange cultures and translators of alien languages. A transnational history of childhood must also include the plight of refugees. There were more of them than ever before in the 20th century – in Europe as a result of two world wars and then in Asia and Africa as an effect of civil conflict. Coping with sudden disaster, refugees often take little with them beyond their children and have minimal means to protect them in strange lands or dangerous camps.

These changes in the 19th century led to cries of alarm about the plight of children. Clergy, journalists, and politicians described a moral crisis, radicals issued detailed denunciations, and officials published damning reports. Society responded with more police, hundreds of charities, legislation, and new public agencies. Concern for children won public support for such measures and prompted the state to accept increased responsibility for public health and welfare. Child labour was one of the earliest targets. Industries at the core of industrialization, such as textiles and coal mining, relied on child labour in conditions sufficiently new and horrifying to attract attention. From the 1840s on European governments progressively shortened the hours children could work, raised the age at which they could be employed and sent out inspectors to see that the new regulations were followed. Hardly stringent by later standards, these reforms nevertheless confirmed the principle of government engagement and were followed by others regulating the treatment of children at home and creating special courts to try crimes against children and by them. Such institutional responses proved highly adaptable, spreading from country to country and varying more in effectiveness than form. The laws that urban police enforced increasingly applied to children in working-class slums and, later, immigrant ghettos. Juvenile reformatories, the object of reform movements in Europe and the United States, were established in India in the 1870s. Protestant, Catholic, and Muslim charities proliferated, their accomplishments widely reported and copied; and national parliaments studied each other's social legislation while preparing their own. By the end of the century, those involved in programmes affecting childhood read about each other's work,

visited each other's programmes, and joined professional associations that held international meetings, creating networks that reached farther and grew stronger in the 20th century and disseminated a common conception of childhood needs.

Childhood was most affected, however, by the spread of formal schooling. By the mid 19th century, governments in Europe and the Americas were taking charge of schooling. These varied school systems influenced each other in raising standards. Slowly, ill-equipped schools (the great majority) were replaced and teachers required to meet some standard of qualification. Elementary schools, initially lasting only two or three years, added two or three more and soon continuing in intermediate school became the norm. By the end of the century, most prosperous nations claimed to have a system of universal and free elementary schooling. Formal education had become a competitive standard by which governments demonstrated their progressiveness in Western Europe and North America, Latin America, Japan and a bit later in China.

Leaving home for school became an informal rite and graduation a public one, with the school itself a centre of civic pride. School became a defining element of childhood, and its effects reached beyond the subjects taught. Schools clustered children by age, creating cohorts that cut across sibling ties and remained meaningful years later. Schools institutionalized gender differences, for boys and girls were often kept separate and ostentatiously prepared for men's work or homemaking. Schools enforced a national language and disseminated standards of hygiene, proper conduct, and dress. Expected to teach values, inculcate patriotism, and promote civic virtue, schools treated childhood as the foundation of a nation's future. And schooling was among the clearest indicators of social class; it ended earliest for peasants and workers and extended a few years more for those who would enter the lower professions, with secondary school all but essential for middle-class status. The spread of schooling developed a momentum that continues to this day and stretches from day care to university. Moralists, progressives, and nationalists all embraced the need for universal education. Reports on school systems in other countries served as propaganda for the promotion of education at home. Many graduates of regional schools became teachers themselves, providing the staff for still more schools. Parents in surprising numbers, even in remote areas, accepted that some years of schooling could benefit their offspring. And although classrooms reflect local society and culture, the diffusion of schooling has been truly transnational. Today, there are (often remarkably similar) state schools, religious schools (primarily Muslim, Catholic, and Protestant), even Montessori and Rudolf Steiner schools on every continent.

Cultural concern for childhood

Prominent philosophies and pedagogical theories, from those of Jean-Jacques Rousseau to the present, have explored the nature of a good childhood. A goal of Christian, liberal, and socialist reformers, it became a topic in newspapers, magazines, and sermons and promised a growing commerce in children's clothes, furniture, and toys. As children contributed less to family income and were less likely to be charged with the care of younger siblings, romantic ideas of childhood innocence flourished. Devoted mothers and warm families invoked values dear to the middle class, whose homes featured individual beds, children's rooms, and even nurseries. Principles of privacy, discipline, and self-control served to make childhood a protected, asexual time for forming character.

Child psychology, pedagogy, and paediatric medicine became professional specialties, offering ever-changing advice on how best to achieve the common goal of a childhood that formed responsible adults. Popular manuals and periodicals gave guidance to parents. Novels explored this mythic world and contrasted the evils of poverty and cruel masters. Broadened by universal education, the market for children's literature included magazines and books of general information, fantasy, and religious and patriotic themes. While preserving the child's insulation from unsuitable adult knowledge, it was expected to foster courtesy and cleanliness, obedience and hard work. Nostalgia showed through in stories praising small town and rural life, in the adaptation for children of folk tales once told around peasant hearths, and in toys that evoked earlier eras – costumed dolls, rocking horses, bows and arrows – popular long after their adult models were passé.

Remarkably, this sense of childhood spread wherever there was social change, even where most families remained locked in poverty and well beyond the industrial West.

Anthropological studies broadened horizons by showing that in most societies childhood brings new types of play, assigned chores, changes in dress, and increasingly gendered roles. And the passage out of childhood comes with initiation into women's or men's circles, betrothal, full-time employment, school leaving, or legal rights. These rituals of transition interweave new and old, in Arab societies for example, connecting secular goals to ties of kinship and religion. Finding such parallels, the study of other cultures invites reassessment of Western and American practices, as it did in Margaret Mead's widely cited classic, *Coming of age in Samoa*, published in 1928. The English nanny became an international model, and to be an au pair in another nation is today a recognized form of travel. Women from poorer countries are hired for childcare in every wealthy land, carrying customs and attitudes back and forth across the seas. Adoption has become as transnational as trade, similarly subject to international rules. 'Happy Birthday' is now sung in all major languages; teddy bears and Santa Claus drift far from their origins on a flood of transnational commerce.

Having comparable aspirations and facing similar obstacles, the young of any decade can easily be labelled a distinctive generation with its own values and style, with generational conflict considered inevitable and adolescence a distinctive subculture. Global communications enable the young to share an identity through music and dress, build personal networks by means of Internet and cell phones, imitate the life displayed in films and television, and embrace fantasies based on American and Japanese comics and video games. Mixing music from the United States and Africa, Latin America and Europe, they embrace Hip Hop and Rap to express in local dialects dreams of freedom and a politics of resentment – the essence of globalization in its combination of the intensely local with the global.

Paradoxically, idealization of home life strengthened efforts to supplement and constrain home influences. Schooling often conflicted with what parents taught, and laws allowed social agencies to pry into domestic life and to judge its inadequacies. Adult supervision intruded on the spontaneity of play. Missionary schools and clinics stressed maternal responsibilities, taught ideas of hygiene, and imposed European dress wherever European imperialism reached. Late in the 19th century, movements like the boy scouts sought to inculcate values of valour, self-reliance and discipline feared lost in urban living. In the 20th century churches and political movements (fascist and communist ones most extensively) mobilized boys and girls from 6 to 18 to serve their causes. Especially after World War 1, non-governmental and intergovernmental organizations and professional associations took up the effort to improve childhood around the world. Once again, child labour has been a primary target. The International Labour Organization campaigned against it in the 1930s, and its data collecting continues to expand. Newspapers and NGOs spark outrage at corporations employing children in sweatshops, and globally the employment of children under 15 has gradually declined. Yet we do not really know how many children between 5 and 17 work. Estimates run as high as 240 million (usually not counting migrant agricultural workers), three-fifths of them in Asia, one-third in Africa, one child in five in Latin America.

Innumerable commissions, conferences, and conventions reaffirm belief in the importance of childhood. The League of Nations addressed the rights of the child in the 1920s; the United Nations added a more expansive declaration in 1959 and named 1979 'The Year of the Child'. Its 1989 Convention on the Rights of the Child, signed by more nations in less time than any other UN document, asserted the right of children to freedom of expression, thought, religion, privacy and association. With each round of conferences written standards become more specific and the required national reports more detailed. Scores of publications and hundreds of transnational agencies are now devoted to the welfare of children.

Collectively, these efforts extend well beyond traditional attention to education, nutrition, and welfare. Evidence of an ideal globally recognized and of limited success in achieving it, they have opened further concerns. Some observers fret about a disappearance of childhood, seeing it eroded in wealthy nations by an excess of organized activity, competitive pressure in school, and intrusive media. They see it threatened In poorer lands by famine and disease, conflicts involving child armies in parts of Africa and Asia, sex trafficking in Europe and Asia, and urban gangs and civil strife on every continent. Other reformers argue that children are not so much minors

as citizens and that childhood (long understood as a subcategory in histories of class, family, and gender) has a history of its own. Children, they note, have always passed on to each other ageless mutations of games, rhymes, and songs not taught to them by adults; and children hold political and social views that modify the hopes and prejudices of the society around them. Attracted to idealistic causes demanding sacrifice and ready to oppose authority, the young are catalysts of social change. A stimulus to good works, international agreements, and local reforms, central to questions of identity and social stability, transnational views of childhood are intrinsic to the contention that marks modernity.

Raymond Grew

Bibliography

Pfeffer G. and Kumar D. (eds) 1996. *Contemporary society: childhood and complex order.* New Delhi: Manak.

Stearns P. N. 2006. *Childhood in world history.* London and New York: Routledge.

Stevens S. (ed.) 1995. *Children and the politics of culture.* Princeton: Princeton University Press.

Related essays

1960s; adoption; birth control; children's literature; children's rights; Christmas and Halloween; demographic transition; domestic service; education; health policy; intergovernmental organizations; kindergarten; labour standards; missionaries; National Basketball Association (NBA); public policy; Save the Children International Union; sports gear and apparel; textile; United Nations decades and years; United Nations Educational, Scientific and Cultural Organization (UNESCO) educational programmes; youth organizations

Children's literature

Children's literature, consisting of texts created specifically to be read by or to children or those texts appropriated by children as reading material, is certainly a border-crossing phenomenon; yet the global distribution of children's texts continues to be uneven. The majority of children's texts that travel beyond the country of origin are those originating in Western developed countries and then travelling into less developed areas of the world. Children's literature is strongly rooted in cultural and/or national identity. The role of the child and attitudes and assumptions concerning childhood within society or a specific culture vary significantly over time and geography and are strongly influenced by issues such as race, gender, and the social and economic status of a child. Just as the conditions of childhood vary widely around the world and over history, so do the access to and availability of children's literature.

All cultures have developed collections of children's oral culture: folk tales, animal fables, riddles, and rhymes. In order to establish a print culture of children's literature, a society needs to have a sizeable population that values childhood education and the financial resources to purchase children's books. Folk tales, which were originally adult stories, have circulated orally throughout the world and became some of the first children's texts put into print. The development of children's literature as a publishing field arose in England in the mid 18th century with the growth of the urban middle classes. Some children's literature scholars have suggested that most cultures experience a similar four-step process in the development of children's literature: adaptation of existing adult texts and folklore for children; didactic and educational stories written specifically for children; canonical children's texts; and finally experimental children's texts.

In addition to folk tales, early examples of adult texts that crossed over to children's literature include John Bunyan's The Pilgrim's Progress (1678) and Jonathan Swift's Gulliver's Travels (1726). John Locke recommended Aesop's Fables as appropriate reading for children, while Jean-Jacques Rousseau insisted in Émile (1762) that Daniel Defoe's Robinson Crusoe (1678) be the first and only book in a child's library.

The French historian Paul Hazard proposed a universal republic of childhood in Les livres, les enfants et les hommes (1932), one of the first studies of international children's literature. Hazard believed that the translation and distribution of children's books around the world would foster better understanding and peaceful coexistence. After World War 2, Jella Lepman founded the International Youth Library in Munich, Germany, and the International Board on Books for Young People (henceforth International Board) in 1953 in Zurich, Switzerland, with the goal that international understanding could be achieved through the translation and distribution of children's books inspired by Hazard's text. The International Board still promotes a transnational approach to children's literature through its Hans Christian Andersen Award, which is given every two years to an author or illustrator whose body of work has made a lasting contribution to the world of children, and through the promotion of international children's literature in its journal Bookbird.

Despite the efforts of the International Board and the International Research Society of Children's Literature, the majority of canonical and contemporary children's literature that circulates across borders comes from the cultural centres of Northern Europe and the United States. Children's literature, like other forms of mass culture, while global in distribution, is not international in terms of its origins. In the 19th century, British children's literature tended to dominate the world market. As the British Empire collapsed and the influence of American popular culture expanded, in the 20th century American children's literature joined its English counterparts as the most frequently translated texts. Those texts that are generally seen as the classics of children's literature are primarily from the Anglo-American tradition, including Lewis Carroll's Alice's Adventures in Wonderland (1865), Beatrix Potter's The Tale of Peter Rabbit (1902), Mark Twain's The Adventures of Tom Sawyer (1876), Louisa May Alcott's Little Women (1868–69), or the European folk tales collected by Jacob and Wilhelm Grimm and the literary fairy tales written by Charles Perrault and Hans Christian Andersen. While children's books are increasingly manufactured and printed in Asia and Eastern Europe, authors from English-speaking countries dominate the market. Just as Disney films from the United States dominate the international children's film market, contemporary authors from either the United States or Great Britain, such as J. K. Rowling with her popular Harry Potter series, are the children's writers most frequently translated and read around the world. International children's literature is a lopsided environment where the distribution of British and American children's books are translated and exported to the rest of the world. The countries that export the most children's literature, the United States and Great Britain, also import the least. Children's literature and media, while international, remain a lucrative market dominated by texts in English that are produced by publishers situated in Great Britain and the United States.

Jan Susina

Bibliography

Hazard P. 1932. *Les livres, les enfants et les hommes*. Paris: Flammarion.

Hunt P. (ed) 2004. *International companion encyclopedia of children's literature*. Second edition. London and New York: Routledge.

O'Sullivan E. 2005. *Comparative children's literature*. New York: Routledge.

Pellowski A. 1968. *The worlds of children's literature*. New York: R. R. Bowker.

Related essays

childhood; comics; corporations; film; literature; pacifism; publishing; translation

Children's rights

A category of universal human rights specific to children, in reference to their judicial minority, was fixed in three successive international agreements. Children's entitlements have occupied a privileged place in transnational political cultures of the last two centuries. Their role is important for the history of democracy, not only because they concern the prerogatives of a large group, but also because debates and practices surrounding children's rights have provided at once a refuge, a relay, or a testing ground for the rights of all.

In the 19th century, lawyers and reformists participated in an international movement in favour of the best interests of the child. Isolating children as objects of attention, from their family and community, came partly from the intentions of rising professionals who were establishing childhood as their domain of exclusive competence (paediatricians, social workers, educators). The idea also informed a larger child-saving movement, whose origins can be traced to the rise of romantic notions of children as vulnerable objects of compassion, and children's entitlements figured pre-eminently in Western states' efforts to correct the abuses of capitalism, besides injury in the workplace and help to dependent mothers. Part

of this development was due to the political and intellectual advances of liberalism which attributed, to various and debated degrees, a measure of individuality and freedom to immature citizens. This notion of children's rights was born in close association with the equally liberal idea of citizens attributing to parents the responsibility for their children's education and protection. The tension between these two understandings would be a recurring feature of the history of children's rights.

Associations devoted to child-related issues of an obvious transnational nature were part of the flurry of international institutions from the mid 19th century. International conferences had gathered since 1899 on the 'traffic of children' across borders, resulting in an International Convention on the Traffic of Women and Children in 1910. Children also figured in the preoccupations of international women's groups. Women's challenges to men's authority in families were contributing to the attribution of rights of their own to children and, in 1922, the International Council of Women drafted its own 'Children's Charter'. Finally, the enfranchisement and the unionization of the working class contributed to the promotion of children' rights. There also existed a tradition of child labourers demanding rights for themselves. From 1900, a succession of international labour organizations placed the regulation of child labour amongst their priorities. In industrializing countries, transformations in the economy, by creating a distance between the worlds of fathers and that of children, and by calling for more school training, were helping to spread the idea of children as having their own rights.

The extended warfare of the 1910s–1920s made for the extension of the international means for the protection of soldiers inaugurated by the Red Cross half a century earlier to the protection of children. Faced with unprecedented devastation amongst civilians, many chose to give children of other countries a pre-eminent significance, from anti-slavery campaigners, pacifists, or proponents of friendship with Germany, to churches and trade unions. The war multiplied circumstances that separated children from their families, and in which citizens were called to care for the offspring of others, as if the disruption demanded not only a restatement of the nature of societies' and parents' responsibilities towards children, but also an extension of the responsibility for children to all adults. The notion of children as objects of rights benefited from a wide support in the general population. The extension of political citizenship amongst adults in wartime strengthened the movement, as did the greater involvement of children in public life, from the enlistment of minors to the voluntary work required on the home front.

The war over, national jealousies compromised the implementation of universal ideals, and the patriotic elements present in the campaigns of the war were now threatening to compromise the internationalist ones. Interest in humanitarian actions receded in favour of a renewed attention to domestic problems. Those who attempted to rescue the international movement insisted that children offered the key to future peace, and their hopes turned to the League of Nations, which welcomed all expressions of transnational interests. When the Save the Children International Union (SCIU) succeeded in having its Declaration adopted unanimously by the League's General Assembly, meeting in Geneva in 1924, it became the first universal instrument of human rights of this international body. Five articles stated the requirements for children's health and spirituality, education, protection, the accomplishment of their future responsibilities and their right to be the first to receive relief in times of distress. Thus institutionalized, the temporary arrangements of wartime received a new momentum. The Declaration of 1924, however, did not give children a right to be part of decisions that pertained to them, a fact which contemporary critics already deplored.

Born to address a European situation, the rhetoric of children's rights had a universal aspiration and offered a means to address child welfare in the rest of the world. If the focus on children often served as a way to avoid talking about the political rights of adults in colonies, it nevertheless provided a way to discuss human rights which was impossible within the institutions of the League themselves, which were dominated by colonial governments.

During the Second World War, masses of citizens fought and worked in the name of human rights for all. The conflict over, promises of universal social and economic rights were often translated into domestic programmes directed at children. In Western countries, the public endorsement of the rhetoric of the rights of the young contributed to a certain equalization of the experiences between girls and boys, rural and urban children, aboriginal children and those of European descent, and to a larger autonomy of children within and outside of their families. It also provided a basis to ask for more justice: despite the political expediency that had weakened the programme's universalistic features at the time of their inception, the notion of rights of children helped to maintain an environment where questions of fairness for all remained important. At the same time, the politics of children's rights contained problems that would become important later, such as the tendency to equate freedom and consumption.

After the war, agencies of the UN accepted responsibility for children in distress, unlike the League's Assembly a quarter of century before, which had thought better to leave the task to private agencies. In 1946, when the time came to dissolve the United Nations Relief and Rehabilitation Administration (UNRRA), the UN Assembly allocated the remaining money to a child relief fund, the United Nations International Emergency Fund for Children (UNICEF). The United Nations also harboured the hopes for the rights of all that had mobilized citizens of Allied countries. Adopted in 1948, the Universal Declaration of Human Rights could have made the rights of the child irrelevant, as the secretary of the new Commission on Human Rights (CHR) believed. As early as 1946, the same groups that had supported the Geneva Declaration of 1924 asked the United Nations in vain to update the document. But the matter of children's rights resurfaced in indirect ways: when the time came to put the principles of the Universal Declaration of Human Rights into practice, the topic of children provided the only matter of possible agreement amongst the members of the CHR. During the harshest years of the Cold War, in 1959, the UN Declaration of the Rights of the Child was adopted.

The success of the new Declaration, however, cannot be attributed only to a retrenchment. To its defenders, children called for a specific kind of rights because of their judicial minority: it mentioned explicitly that children needed specific attention because of their 'physical and mental immaturity'. The Declaration now included the principle of state responsibility for the education and welfare of children and for the support of their parents, following recent developments in national welfare states that guaranteed children a minimum of well-being and education; it took a firmer stance against discrimination 'on the grounds of race, colour, sex, language, religion, political or other opinion, national or social origin, property, birth or other status', and added the right to 'a name and nationality'. In addition, the threatening climate of the Cold War enhanced the wish of political leaders to value and educate children, not only to prepare their own countries, but also to predispose the non-aligned countries towards them.

The last forty years have witnessed a rise in the public importance of human rights in general and children's rights in particular. When non-governmental organizations (NGOs) centred on children asked the UN to declare 1979 the International Year of the Child, many inspired by the then recent International Woman's Year, they were acknowledging how the period devoted to the education of each child had increased, as well as the time of their economic dependency. The Year proved very popular amongst member countries and, whereas the UN had initially envisaged a series of practical programmes, a movement to update and strengthen the Declaration of 1959 arose. At the demand of the Polish government, the General Assembly gave the CHR a drafting mandate, a task which the Canadian and Swedish governments helped accomplish thoroughly, together with an NGO founded for this task, Defence for Children International.

The revision movement resulted in part from a criticism of the ideals of development that had informed policies towards ex-colonies after the war, and the attempt to remedy new social problems in the developing countries. The language of human rights in general informed many projects aimed at the uneven economies of developing societies. In addition, from the early 1980s, in the context of the worldwide recession and declining UN budgets, UNICEF was largely responsible for devoting programmes for the South to the survival of children. Once again, its success was helped by the popularity of the theme of children's survival, a fact that many political leaders were eager to use. UNICEF only adopted the language of rights by the mid 1980s: to those weary of the sentimentalism associated with childhood, the notion of rights bore a reassuring seriousness. The agency's considerable expertise in public relations gave a new impetus to the wish to articulate a list of entitlements that would be shared by all cultures and that would be enforceable. The Convention on the Rights of the Child of 1989 is in part the product of its effort, and UNICEF would be especially instrumental in including the notion of the rights to survival and development in the document.

The Convention was also the product of a 1970s movement promoting the freedom of the child, which can be seen as the development of the very ideas present in the Enlightenment. The 'linchpin' of the Convention was the idea that children are autonomous and capable of full participation in society, which had been missing from the two former documents. This tendency had already influenced a series of UN treaties from the 1970s, such as the Guidelines on Refugee Children of 1988 and the Declaration on Foster Placement and Adoption in 1986. Again, this was related to the changing relations of authority between men and women during the last quarter of the 20th century. Finally, with the general rise in standards of living, the resilience of some problems became more of a scandal. In this trend towards more protection, we recognize a tension as old as liberal ideas of childhood.

Since 1991, a Committee on the Rights of the Child has called for twice-yearly government reports in order to monitor national enforcement. The impact of the Convention is impeded by many problems, from bureaucratic slowness to the tendency of many conservative reformists and governments to use the topic of children to diminish their engagement towards the welfare of all. Echoing contradictions present at the SCIU Conference on the African Child of 1931, critics see the notion of children's rights as the new moral face of Western prescriptions for the South, an idea strong enough to serve as a replacement to anti-Communism. At the same time, the unprecedented scale and speed of the Convention's ratification is a sign of the recurring power of childhood to gather transnational efforts and imaginations, while the Convention could have radical implications for claims by the South for a transfer of resources from the North.

Dominique Marshall

Bibliography

Black M. 1996. *Children first: the story of UNICEF, past and present.* Oxford and New York: Oxford University Press.

Marshall D. 'The transnational movements for children's rights and the Canadian political culture: a history', in Miron J. (ed.) 2008. *The history of human rights in post-confederation Canada.* Toronto: Canadian Scholars'.

Veerman P. 1991. *The rights of the child and the changing image of childhood.* Dordrecht, Boston and London: Martinus Nijhoff.

Related essays

Abolition of Forced Labour Convention; animal rights; childhood; Cold War; Commission on International Labour Legislation; human rights; international non-governmental organizations (INGOs); intergovernmental organizations; International Red Cross and Red Crescent movement; labour standards; justice; League of Nations system; liberalism; refugee relief; relief; Save the Children International Union; United Nations decades and years; United Nations system; welfare state; White Slavery; women's movements

China

Since the Mccartney mission to China in 1793, when the Qianlong emperor told the British trade envoy that China had no need for goods from the rest of the world, the prevailing view of the Chinese empire was that it was a world unto itself. Through the 19th century, the wars fought and unequal treaties imposed upon China by the Western powers were justified less by the rhetoric that Chinese were barbarians than that the Chinese perceived foreigners as barbarians; consequently, she could not be dealt with on equal or peaceful terms. Sinocentrism was a key theme in the Fairbank school of Chinese historiography and the renowned scholar Joseph Levenson coined the expression 'Chinese culturalism': that the meaningful world for Chinese was the Confucian-centred universe and nothing of significance mattered beyond the pale of this civilization until the late 19th century.

To be sure, these interpretations are not entirely arbitrary. Historians have celebrated the cosmopolitanism of the Tang dynasty (618–907 AD), and the Mongol, Yuan dynasty (1279–1368) about which we have a record by a European, Marco Polo, in the court of Khublai Khan. Although far less studied, the Yuan empire existed within the much larger Eurasian 'Pax Mongolica'. In contrast, the early modern dynasties of the Ming (1368–1644) and the Manchu, Qing (1644–1911) appear much more Sinocentric. Yet this Sinocentrism was perhaps less an index of the actual involvement of Chinese in transimperial matters than a response to this increasing involvement.

The Ming initially promoted maritime expansion as witnessed by the famous voyages of Zheng He (1405–33), massive projections of the power of the imperial state upon the coastal kingdoms on the Indian Ocean and Arabian Sea. However, the political goal of securing tribute to the Chinese emperor was often accompanied by the expansion of trading opportunities and these voyages were no exception. Meanwhile, Chinese Buddhist pilgrimages continued to circulate cosmological, medical and geographical knowledge – from China through Central Asia, India and Southeast Asia.

The maritime voyages were abruptly stopped in the 1430s. The stoppage has been viewed even by contemporary Chinese intellectuals as a disastrous return to continental, bounded traditionalism. There were, however, more practical reasons to restrict China's maritime activities at this time: as the Ming were fighting an escalating war against the Mongols to the north, the voyages were, in the view of the opposition, far too costly (Dreyer 2006). The successor Manchu or Qing dynasty created a system that engaged several different worlds: with the Russians on the northern frontiers they employed early modern technologies and knowledge; with Central Asian allies, they contracted marriage alliances with the ruling houses, and styled themselves as the reincarnation of Manjusri, the bodhisattva-ruler, so central to Tibetans and Mongols. They succeeded in creating a relatively stable balance of power between the Chinese and the Russian empires that lasted over three hundred years. Sinocentrism cannot capture the diversity of this polity.

Indeed, despite the shift of attention away from the maritime coast, during both the Ming and the Qing, there were substantial Chinese interactions with foreign trade and traders. Much of this was built around the tribute system through which other states and polities in East and Southeast Asia acknowledged the superiority of the Chinese emperor and conducted their relations with China by presenting tribute goods and receiving other goods in turn.

Tribute trade also linked the European trade with the East Asian one. Economic opportunities in the Asian maritime trade were for a long time sufficient to keep most of those involved – even the early-19th-century East Indian Company – vested in the tribute system. Thus China was very much part of the early modern world economy and a superior competitor in that regard until about 1800. This legacy of the tribute system and the accompanying transimperial trade networks lived on long after the system itself collapsed with the Opium Wars (1840–60). The networks of Chinese traders became the conduits for the flow of millions of émigré labourers into the plantations of Southeast Asia and the Americas after the ban on emigration was lifted as a result of Western pressures on the Qing.

With the modernizing reforms of the late Qing (1902–11), there was a flurry of activities associated with nation and state building. Students and professionals were sent to many different parts of the world to study and import Western techniques and practices. The first significant batch of students went to Meiji Japan and their experience there not only shaped their conceptions of modernity but steeled their will to change China. Although they were later profoundly aggrieved by Japanese imperialism in China, this first generation of Japan-returned intellectuals learnt ideas of the Western Enlightenment filtered through the new Japanese terminology and categories which, in many ways, continue to survive in the Chinese language. Subsequent groups went to the West and brought back professional knowledge and technologies in many areas of modern life, whereas radical groups who went to France and the Soviet Union contributed to the Communist movement in China.

Undoubtedly, the most fertile zone of Chinese and global interactions were the Treaty Ports established by Western imperialist powers through the Unequal Treaty System during the 19th century. By the end of the 19th century most major cities with maritime or riverine access were treaty ports. Open to foreign trade, they consisted of settlements and concessions governed by foreign laws and administration – even though the vast majority of the populations in them were

Chinese. Here the Chinese population learned to use and adapt new banking and economic practices, the modern press, educational institutions and political ideologies and strategies of mobilization. Note that the Chinese Communist Party was founded in the French concession in Shanghai in 1921. But while Shanghai has captured the imagination as the node of transnational penetration into China, Hong Kong played an equally important role during much of the 20th century.

Hong Kong, the British colonial bastion of 'free trade' that gave free rein to both European racism and Chinese entrepreneurialism, served as a gateway for knowledge, capital and talent into and out of China from the 19th until the end of the 20th century. The émigré Chinese population, hailing mainly from the south and southeastern coast, fanned out of here to the distant parts of the world, taking Chinese cultural and economic networks with them. The considerable economic success of this population in many Southeast Asian societies was and continues to be a major source of China's transformation. Through their banks and kinship networks in Hong Kong, they made contributions to their home communities, whether through micro-remittances, charities, or major investments. From the early part of the century, different political groups (including the Qing state) competed actively for their loyalty and resources.

There is perhaps no better figure to represent Hong Kong and the Diaspora's role as a major transcultural agency in the emergence of modern China than Sun Yat-sen, the Father of Modern China. Sun was born in South China but spent his most formative educational years in Hong Kong (and Honolulu) which also became the launching pad for his political uprisings to topple the Qing and later, the warlords. For Sun, although Hong Kong was a colony, it represented the promise of a well-ordered modernity and he spent his life seeking to realize it in China. Later, during the Maoist years (1949–79), Hong Kong became still more important as one of the only conduits of information, knowledge, capital, markets and strategic goods from the capitalist world available to the People's Republic of China.

For another twenty years after Deng Xiaoping's 'opening of China', Hong Kong was the international financial centre from which the Chinese Diaspora made the massive investments that propelled the dizzying economic rise of contemporary China. While the industries that mark China's emergence as 'the workshop of the world' are distributed across various urban conglomerations, the Pearl River Delta region – the hinterland of Hong Kong – continues to be among the largest industrial and exporting concentrations in the world. It owes this distinction to the financial, technical, infrastructure and communication services in Hong Kong and the entrepreneurial talents of the southern Diaspora as much as to its own resources.

Two other regions which have emerged as major manufacturing and high-investment clusters are the Yangzi delta and the northeast region around the Bohai sea. Both of these regions have also seen major investments from the Diaspora, the first from Taiwan and Singapore and the second from ethnic Chinese in Korea. These cross-border economic ties have facilitated a vast East Asian cultural region especially as Korean, Japanese and Taiwanese media productions have become hugely popular in China.

Finally, while Chinese products – pre-industrial and industrial – have had an unquestionable impact on the economy of the world, in an age of the peaceful rise of China, it may be pertinent to ask how Chinese culture – or what has been termed 'soft power' – may influence the world. Taking the long view, from the Ming until the present, China's soft power had been considerable, albeit geographically restricted to East and Southeast Asia. The writing system, Confucianism and Chinese cosmology were influential in parts of East Asia –such as Japan – even long after the Japanese had stopped paying tribute. In Southeast Asia, it was the grand power of tribute ritualism through which authority was exercised. In Central Asia, the Qing sought to exercise its suzerainty through shared Buddhist ideas and symbols.

The collapse of the empire together with the Confucian and Buddhist world views among the elites and the state led to a period of intense struggle for power and identity during the first half of the 20th century. When the Communists emerged as the new rulers in 1949, the leaders sought to claim world leadership by presenting an ideology and a path to realize the enlightenment ideals that had allegedly been abandoned by both the old and new (read Soviet Union) imperialist powers. Mao Zedong and Lin Piao generated the 'Three Worlds' theory in which the newly decolonized countries could steer a non-aligned path and ultimately gain socialist justice by following the Chinese revolutionary path where the countryside surrounded and liberated the city. These ideas were very influential in many parts of the world during the Vietnam War. Many African and Asian students came to study in China and often took back revolutionary ideas and mobilization practices to places like Tanzania and Uganda. Moreover, Chinese technical and infrastructural assistance to the African continent which had secured it considerable influence have recently been revived, although under very different auspices.

Meanwhile, in the Diaspora, a new synthesis of Chinese culture was being developed that was more compatible with the liberal capitalist ideology of the United States. Originating in Hong Kong and Taiwan, this postwar culture spread among the Diaspora in Southeast Asia and then to Chinese further overseas and among non-Chinese. An important strand in this culture was the new Confucian movement developed mostly by émigré intellectuals in Hong Kong and Taiwan such as Qian Mu and Du Weiming. This group rehabilitated Confucianism after the fierce denunciations of the 4 May and later Communist movements, as a communally and morally oriented philosophy that was also compatible with market society. These and related ideas of 'Confucian capitalism' became especially widespread with the rise of the East Asian 'tiger economies' in the 1970s and 1980s.

In the realm of mass culture, the phenomenon that caught global attention – other than Chinese food – from the 1970s was the kung fu and martial arts craze popularized originally by Hong Kong cinema and culminating in such artistic productions today as *Crouching Tiger, Hidden Dragon*. While, on the one hand, this popularized Chinese notions of empowered individuality, it also appealed to many masculinist youth groups all over the world. Finally, we should not neglect a form of Chinese religiosity associated with a popular synthesis of Confucianism, Buddhism, Daoism and Western elements. This spiritual smorgasbord covers the gamut from Chinese medicine, *taiqi* and *fengshui* to the more committed universalist, redemptive movements of the Taiwan-based Ciji Buddhist group and the banned Falungong among many others.

At this point, neither the state, nor different groups nor the market has been able to project a universal conception of Chineseness or Chinese civilization. Whether the inevitable further rise of China will generate a sufficient will to subordinate these differences to a single political power or whether the plurality of Chinese cultures will continue to interweave a global culture is one of the most important questions of our future.

Prasenjit Duara

Bibliography
Xianming Chen 2005. *As borders bend: transnational spaces on the Pacific Rim.* Lanham: Rowman and Littlefield.
Dreyer E. L. 2006. *Zheng He: China and the oceans in the Early Ming, 1405–1433.* London and New York: Longman.
Fairbank J. K. 1968. *The Chinese world order; traditional China's foreign relations.* Cambridge, MA: Harvard University Press.
Hamashita T. 1997. 'The intra-regional system in East Asia in modern times' in Katzenstein P. and Shiraishi T. (eds) *Network power: Japan and Asia.* Ithaca: Cornell University Press.
Levenson J. R. 1965. *Confucian China and its modern fate: a trilogy.* Berkeley and Los Angeles: University of California Press.
Naquin S. and Rawski E. 1987. *Chinese Society in the 18th century.* New Haven: Yale University Press.
Pomeranz K. 2000. *The great divergence: China, Europe, and the making of the modern world economy.* Princeton: Princeton University Press.
Tansen Sen 2003. *Buddhism, diplomacy, and trade: the realignment of Sino–Indian relations, 600–1400.* Honolulu: University of Hawai'i Press.

Related essays
America; Asia; Buddhism; Cantonese opera; capitalism; Chinese Diaspora; Chinese medicine; civilizations; classical music; contract and indentured labourers; convergence and divergence; decolonization; development and growth; empire and migration; empires and imperialism; fascism and anti-fascism; femininity; Hong Kong and Shanghai Banking Corporation (HSBC); humanities; industrialization; international students; Japan; kindergarten; labour migrations; language diplomacy; *Little Red Book*; Maoism; modernity; nation and state; open door and free flow; pan-isms; railways; regions; remittances; scientific expeditions; socialism; tourism; trade; transportation infrastructures; Westernization; white men's countries; women's movements; world orders; Zen aesthetics

Chinese Diaspora

China's long history, geopolitical prominence, and varied patterns of migration render the 'overseas Chinese' a rich subject for exploring transnational behaviour and modes of organization.

As early as the third century BC, Chinese travelled overseas as traders, invaders, missionaries, labourers, explorers, imperial emissaries, and petty entrepreneurs. Advancing shipping technologies expanded the geographic reach of 'commuting' Chinese who maintained economic, cultural, family, and political networks that spanned communities scattered through peninsular and island Southeast Asia. By the mid 19th century, identities among overseas Chinese included completely assimilated royal family members in Thailand, the creolized *peranakan* and *baba* of Java and Malacca, leading Filipino nationalists such as José Rizal, and a stream of new arrivals called *xinke*.

Chinese migration accelerated with Europe's colonization of the rest of the world. The expanding reach of capitalism provided unprecedented economic opportunities in regions heretofore largely unconnected to China. Chinese travelled via European routes as both free and coerced workers in the massive population shifts engineered by imperialism's hunger for cheap labourers in North and South America and the Caribbean. In growing numbers, they journeyed to the new cities, plantations, and mines of Southeast Asia where some attained great fortunes and visibility as entrepreneurs and go-betweens on behalf of the colonial elites. Most, however, remained working-class or ran small businesses that provided services such as barbering or cooking, or coordinated the exchange of Chinese goods. They faced the same choices as the earlier generations of Chinese overseas – whether to settle and intermarry locally or to retain family ties in China, depending upon local conditions of tolerance and opportunity although traditional practices of polygamy made it possible for the affluent to do both. The historian Wang Gungwu has described this contingent decision making as essential to Chinese practices of sojourning, or experimental migration.

In the late 19th century, the troubled Chinese government began politicizing its relationship to Chinese overseas by calling upon them to rescue China from corruption, overpopulation, economic stagnation and foreign domination. The new official term, huaqiao or Overseas Chinese, enshrined the supposedly indelible link between homeland and émigrés in a reversal of centuries of previous law which had banned foreign departures and returns. Huaqiao would play key roles in the evolution of 20th-century Chinese republicanism so that the 'Father of Modern China', Sun Yatsen, called them 'Mothers to the Chinese Revolution'. Such honorifics aside, this call to nationalism sometimes contributed to the marginalization of Chinese overseas in their countries of settlement. China's size and the visibility of Chinese in economic sectors fed fears of competition which as early as 1620 periodically ignited violent purges. At the turn of the 20th century, racialization of Chinese as essential foreigners was at the basis of various attempts to exclude their relatively minute numbers from North America. During the post-World War 2 decolonization, newly empowered Southeast Asian nationalists targeted Chinese as suspected agents of an expansionary Chinese empire.

Unlike Sun Yatsen's political party, the Kuomintang, which still relies on US-educated leaders and the assiduous cultivation of foreign support, the Communist leadership of the People's Republic of China (PRC) has been comparatively insular. At the height of anti-Chinese violence in various parts of the world during the 1960s, PRC policy stated that Chinese overseas should either attempt to assimilate in their places of settlement or relocate to China. Emigration from the PRC slowed with the Cold War freeze, although ethnic Chinese from Hong Kong, Taiwan, and Southeast Asia continued their global movements. After the death of Mao in 1976, China reopened its gates. This new outflow of both legal and illegal migrants headed to highly developed economies including older destinations in North America and Australia and, for the first time systematically, Europe. Unlike earlier waves, a higher proportion consists of intellectuals and technically skilled workers, mitigating fears of inassimilable Chinese. Still, the 1998 Jakarta riots and trumped-up prosecution of Wen Ho Lee in the US are potent reminders that Chinese overseas remain feared as economic competitors or fifth-column agents controlled by Beijing. Despite their successes in an ever growing range of places and societies, in the 21st century Chinese overseas still confront both the advantages and the threat of being associated with China's growing international clout and economic influence.

Madeline Hsu

Bibliography
Gungwu W. 2000. *The Chinese overseas: from earthbound China to the quest of autonomy.* Cambridge, MA: Harvard University Press.
Pan L. (ed.) 1999. *The encyclopedia of the Chinese overseas.* Cambridge, MA: Harvard University Press.

Related essays
Asia; Cantonese opera; China; empire and migration; contract and indentured labourers; decolonization; diasporas; human mobility; international students; Lebanese Diaspora; railway; rush migrations; transnational

Chinese medicine

Chinese medical therapies are readily available today, not only in China, Taiwan, and Chinatowns worldwide, but spread out thinly throughout many a society. In kaleidoscopic variation, they are offered on the global health market. Among them belong acupuncture and moxibustion (zhenjiu), Chinese [herbal] medicine (zhongyi or zhongyiyao) based on decoctions, in more or less 'integrated' form with Western biomedicine, the 'integrated' Chinese formula medicines (zhongchengyao) that come in pill and tablet form, and the body techniques of qigong, yangshenggong, and taijiquan as well as anmo and tuina massage.

Anyone studying the learned medical traditions in the Mediterranean, Asia and the Americas will become acutely aware of how constitutive transregional flows of technology, knowledge and people have been over the millennia. Joseph Needham and Paul Unschuld have made hints that the humoral aspects, which are considered so characteristic of Chinese medical learning, may actually represent a knowledge stream that became integral to it due to transregional exchanges in antiquity; and it has been demonstrated beyond doubt that the spread of Buddhism from the 3rd to the 10th centuries not only transformed medieval Chinese medical learning but also led to its export into Japan, Tibet and Korea, providing the seed corn for the medical traditions that nationalism has recently revived. In the 13th century, the Muslim expansion into South and Inner Asia facilitated a knowledge transfer through Arabic sources into the Near East and Europe, with, most prominently, the work by Rahid al-Din (1247–1318). By the late 17th century, several Latin treatises of Jesuit missionaries were published, written in a factual if not admiring tone, sometimes with translations of text excerpts on pulse lore, herbs, needling, and other Chinese medical curiosities. Their knowledge, together with that of physicians of the East India Company, is summarized in monumental works by Engelbert Kaempfer (1712) and Jean-Baptiste Du Halde (1734). In the 18th century, acupuncture repeatedly met with hostility from the professorial rosters of the expanding university medicine in Germany, but the clinicians of the emergent hospital medicine in early-19th-century France, like the renowned René Laennec and Jules-Germain Cloquet, apart from L. V. J. Berlioz and Chevalier Sarlandière, indulged in experimentation with needles (and the newly discovered electricity). While the early modern Chinese medical transfers into Europe were instigated mostly by Europeans, those into insular Southeast Asia and, later, onto the other side of the Pacific, e.g. California, went hand in hand with the several-centuries-long exodus that the mainland experienced from its Southeastern populations. These transfers were effected mainly by Chinese medical practitioners, pharmacists, and merchants working in Chinatowns. Their business, for instance, transformed the Chinese 'ointment worth a thousand' (wanjinyou) into the globally known 'Tiger Balm' with the tiger trademark.

Acupuncture has gained the strongest following in the industrialized countries of the Northern hemisphere. It is practised by at least two different kinds of practitioners: medically and non-medically trained practitioners who consider acupuncture a medical system of its own and medical doctors who use needling as a technique within biomedical care. Among the former belong, for instance, Georges Soulié de Morant who reintroduced acupuncture to France in the 1920s (his

publication dates to 1934) and his followers in the Association Scientifique des Médecins Acupuncteurs de France; J. R. Worseley's 'Five Elements' school founded in the 1970s in Leamington Spa, England (mostly non-medical, many of whom are now members of the British Acupuncture Council); Manfred Porkert's Societas Medicinae Sinensis, founded in 1978 in Munich, Germany (exclusively medical); and practitioners of 'TCM' (traditional Chinese medicine) acupuncture who aim at practising acupuncture as taught in institutions of the People's Republic of China. Associations and schools of the kind each have their own textbooks, journals, and histories. Their practitioners have in common that they use needling for treating a wide range of disorders, from gynaecological problems and pain conditions to mental disorders, or they provide preventive care with needling as an energy booster. Although there is a wealth of anecdotal evidence about the effectiveness of these forms of needling for a wide range of disorders, which can be explained in terms of Chinese medical theory, and although there is research demonstrating its cost-effectiveness in primary care (for instance, for low backache and headache), their efficacy has been proven beyond doubt by only relatively few patient-blinded randomised controlled trials for specific complaints, and no Western biomedical model has yet been found that can explain their wide-ranging effectiveness.

The above acupuncturists practice their trade in highly individualized ways, and appeal mostly to complementary- and alternative-medicine consumers, who, according to some studies, are mostly middle class, and more commonly female. These practitioners grant their clients time to speak about themselves, offer treatment often for weeks and months if not years, and provide lifestyle advice that is grounded in the principles of their Chinese medical theory. They may be of East Asian or Western origin, male or female. Among the latter, many will have learnt acupuncture in Europe or North America, complemented by a brief visit to China. Since the early 1990s, these acupuncturists have been joined by colleagues, mostly of Chinese origin, who practise gradients of 'integrated' Chinese and Western medicine; some only prescribe recipes for decoctions, others only formula medicines, yet others combinations. Most also practise acupuncture. They have Chinese medical degrees but no medical licence issued by their country of residence, and therefore work under cover. Since legislation in Britain basically allows anyone who has the calling to engage in healing, their numbers have rapidly increased in the past two decades. This legislation has also allowed many more white practitioners to actually learn Chinese herbal medicine, as it requires more extensive training than acupuncture courses do. As a result, a wider spectrum of Chinese medicine appears to be available on the British health market. Whether, and if so to what extent, this has resulted in increased levels of health and healthcare remains yet to be seen.

The medical doctors who apply needling as a therapeutic technique within an otherwise biomedical framework make use primarily of its analgesic effects, and research on analgesia has led to a generally accepted physiological model, which is that the irritation that a needle causes in skin tissue leads to the release of body-internal endorphins. Together with epidemiological research, such research presumably led to the categorizing of 'acupuncture' as a complementary therapy that is different from 'traditional Chinese medicine' (a distinction made, for instance, in the report of the House of Lords in 2000), although from a Chinese medical viewpoint such a separation makes no sense. Furthermore, acupuncture conceptualizes bodily processes in ways that can be explained in more mechanistic terms than any other Chinese medical therapy, and this must have worked towards its comparatively greater acceptance among biomedical professionals. This may explain why practices of acupuncture, have been integrated most successfully into pockets of governmentally sponsored institutions of healthcare, even though some are highly idiosyncratic. The Association Française d'Acupuncture founded around 1945, the Deutsche Aerztegemeinschaft für Akupunktur of 1951, and the British Medical Acupuncture Society founded in 1980, with, three years later, its affiliated Acupuncture Association of Chartered Physiotherapists are open to medical acupuncturists of the kind.

In the 1950s and 60s the Chinese Communist government promoted acupuncture for nationalistic reasons as a treatment known to achieve maximal effects with minimal technology: the needle. The Chinese medical expert teams that were sent mostly to countries of the Southern hemisphere, in an era where world socialism was still a vision, generally included among an array of biomedical specialists one acupuncturist. However, neither in India nor Africa has acupuncture gained such a following as in the European and North American complementary- and alternative-medicine markets.

Although official spokespeople (e.g. consuls, experts, team leaders) still speak of acupuncture as the Chinese medical therapy that has most potential to be globalized, the Chinese government has since the 1990s eased trading regulations in respect of 'Chinese formula medicines' to such a degree that, de facto, this appears to be the form of Chinese medicine it most supports. World socialism is no longer high on its agenda. Rather, through its official and semi-official links to partly private, partly governmental corporations, it has become a major player on the global health market, albeit indirectly. Chinese mobility has also altered. Thus, business people trading in formula medicines in Europe and Africa often engage in a star-like or pendulum-like mobility, asserting their presence in multiple places, without however entirely rupturing their connectedness to their homelands. Many come from northeastern China. Few are well-trained TCM practitioners intent on long-term emigration; some have undergone apprenticeship with a parent or relative; most have worked as Western medical paraprofessionals – nurses, lab technicians, pharmacy workers – before retraining as Chinese medical doctors. Many work within corporate structures of motherdaughter firms, with the grandmother in the People's Republic of China, to which go monetary flows from the firms abroad. In this way, trading in Chinese formula medicines feeds into the financial household of the motherland.

As Chinese medical globalisation is currently most rapidly expanding in the highly commodified form of treatment based on formula medicines, which can be purchased over the counter, the meditative practices of qigong and taijiquan are rapidly gaining in popularity. Whereas meditation used to be considered an indispensable aspect of acupuncture and massage, as it replenishes qi (spirit) and thereby ensures a practitioner's therapeutic effectiveness, mercantile forms of meditation are increasingly offered to and practised by the laity, in China and abroad. It appears as though patient demands are currently shaping the market for the globalized forms of an otherwise intrinsically holistic medicine: consumers today engage with it either as a therapeutic quick fix for the body in the medical scene or a as a mindful preventative health and wellness practice.

Elisabeth Hsu

Bibliography

Barnes L. 2005. Needles, herbs, gods, and ghosts: China, healing, and the West to 1848. Cambridge, MA: Harvard University Press.

Bivins R. 2000. Acupuncture, expertise and cross-cultural medicine. Basingstoke and New York: Palgrave Macmillan.

Cochran S. 2006. Chinese medicine men: consumer culture in China and Southeast Asia. Cambridge, MA: Harvard University Press.

Hsu E. and Stollberg S. (eds) 2009. 'Globalising Chinese medicine', Medical Anthropology, special issue.

Related essays

Buddhism; China; Chinese Diaspora; cosmetic surgery; drugs (medical); feel-good culture; Maoism; medicine; missionaries; scientific expeditions; vaccination

Christianity

Counting about 2 billion believers, Christianity is the most widespread religion in the world today. Its historical origins are rooted in the life, teachings, and death of Jesus of Nazareth. After spreading rapidly throughout the Roman empire (notably under the impulse of a non-ethnic understanding of faith), it would become an imperial state religion. In time, it would split into several different denominations: Orthodox Christianity, Roman Catholicism, Protestantism, and various evangelical churches, independent churches, and religious groups claiming inspiration from the Bible. Choosing among Christianity's many transnational issues, this article pays special attention to ultramontanism, the social Gospel, and secularization.

In the 19th century, Catholicism would take a decisive transnational turn. Rome and the papacy would then reaffirm their authority, even Authority itself, against revolutionary movements, first and foremost against the French Revolution. This was expressed specifically in the ideological guise of ultramontanism (from the Latin ultra, beyond, and montes, the mountains, here meaning the Alps). Ultramontanism is founded on moral conservatism and the idea of Catholicism's independence with regard to the various national powers. As the modern age of nation states flourished, the Catholic Church struggled against gallicanism (France), febronianism and josephism (German countries), all proponents of the pre-eminence of the authority of the Assembly of Catholic Bishops over that of the Pope, and of the rights of sovereign states over the affairs of national churches. The Church's struggle received the support of monarchies and conservative circles which stood to gain from the establishment of a universal moral order.

Ultramontanism would triumph with Pope Pius IX (1846–78) who engaged the Holy See in an overt policy favouring Roman centralization and the affirmation of its universality; this policy culminated in the proclamation of the dogma of papal infallibility in 1870 (Vatican Council I) and in the condemnation of the 'errors of modern society' (encyclical Quanta Cura). At the same time, Catholicism was keeping stricter control over the piety of the faithful, by imposing everywhere the same Roman rituals, marked by ceremonial splendour and public displays of devotions. New rituals emerged, imbued with this particular sort of piety and with a concern for anti-modern apologetics. The cult of the Virgin Mary, the mother of Christ, was the heart's core of ultramontanist piety, and it inspired massive pilgrimages to La Salette (1846) and Lourdes (1858) in France or to Fatima in Portugal (1917). The Vatican itself and the holy city of Rome also acted as powerful geographical magnets.

But the heavy trends of modern criticism were gaining ground. A secular project of social justice was mobilizing several groups of Christians across Europe, making them aware of workers' struggles and 19th-century socialist and Marxist theses. The first leaders of social Protestantism were Robert Mac Hall who would found the Popular Evangelical Mission in England in 1872 and Tommy Fallot with his Christian socialism in France (1878). Tommy Fallot was closely related to the economist Charles Gide who sought a third way between liberalism and Marxism and participated actively in the cooperative movement. In the 1860s, more and more Catholics were testifying to the primacy of the principle of social justice over that of charity and striving to evangelize the working masses. The encyclical Rerum Novarum by Pope Leo XIII

(1893) acknowledged social Catholicism and proposed constructive criticism of liberalism, by demanding just wages, state-sponsored protective measures, and associations to defend the rights of workers. With this encyclical, social Catholicism moved into politics. The political parties, social movements, and unions it spawned at the end of the 19th century (such as Christian democracy, Catholic Action – CA) all shared a type of structure combining local, national, and international concerns and drew strength as much from the transnational circulation of ideas as from well-defined 'national' traditions.

This social Christianity served as a matrix for long-term evolution, notably in Catholic circles. Spurred by the criticism of theologians and socially active lay movements, Catholicism launched a period of reform in the wake of the second Vatican Council (1962–65). Radicalization of social struggles in the 1960s ruptured relations between a good number of the lay élite formed by Catholic Action and ecclesiastical authorities. This rupture was visible in the reactions to the publication by Paul VI in 1968 of his encyclical Humane vitae (forbidding chemical birth control). In the postcolonial era, the influence of these broad movements of ideas brought liberation theology onto the scene in non-Western countries. Following Vatican II and its acknowledgement that salvation had a social dimension, the Latin American conference of bishops held in Medellín (1968) appropriated the broad themes which would found liberation theology, above all that of giving priority attention to the economic and social dimensions of salvation, and especially to the poor. In 1972, the father of this current of thought – the Peruvian Gustavo Gutiérrez – would publish his work A theology of liberation, grafting Marxist and communist ideas onto Old Testament and Christian revelation. The movement spread in Europe (René Marlé, Johann-Baptist Metz), in Asia, in Africa, and in India, feeding social and political struggles like the one led by Desmond Tutu in South Africa as well as the daily lives of Christians united in the base-community movement. To these initial options for building solidarity would be added two other forms of resistance to the imperialism of Eurocentric and Western Christianity: alter-globalization and the valorization and reintegration of ancestral cultures into local contextual theologies. These theologies developed through the flow of academic exchange and training, always in tension with established Western forms of thought. Today, countless streams of postcolonial and Third World theologies are flowing both continentally and internationally. Ever since the pivotal years of the Council, the tensions between reformers and conservatives have been very high. Pope John Paul II (1978–2004), who, in 1980, condemned the Marxist dimensions of some of these theologies, would nevertheless make priority attention to the poor a theme of his papacy. This pope from Eastern Europe would also play a crucial role in strengthening the papal role which centralizes transnational aspects of ecclesial practices to the detriment of the process of decentralization begun by Vatican II. Still today, the central ecclesiological debate revolves around the tension between local churches and the universal Church.

Spurred on by the ambitions of social Christianity, both Catholic and Protestant churches were already playing a vital role in the so-called 'volunteer' sector as early as the 19th century in the West (in education, social services and health). After World War 2, in a context where religion was being deinstitutionalized and individualized, religious legitimacy shifted more and more in the direction of social utility. Militancy in providing emergency aid and encouraging development was a driving force in the structures established by the Christian churches (Action Church Together, World Vision, Church World Services, Caritas International, etc.). Liberation theology also had an impact on these foundations. The Dominican Louis Lebret (1897–1966), founder of the journal Économie et Humanisme (1942) and of the Lebret Centre, pioneered the study of development problems and would have a strong influence on Paul VI (as reflected in his encyclical Populorum Progressio). All the organizations mentioned are now active in dozens of countries and define themselves as non-governmental organizations (NGOs) working in the humanitarian and development sector. Emerging in a postcolonial context, this aid work also has a missionary aspect. With the migration of populations over the past 60 years, the great religions have entered into relations made up of both diplomatic alliances (on questions of morals, for example) and competition (to keep and even increase their numbers). Efforts to engage in inter-religious dialogue between

Christian churches and with the other great universal religions have certainly increased in scope. But the rivalry between them is still a big factor. Within Christianity, the Orthodox Church is struggling to protect its Russian domain from the evangelical wave sweeping the world, while national conflicts are causing the expansion of Buddhism into the Christian West in the form of exiled Tibetan monks, not to speak of the recent effects of the migratory movements of Muslims, Hindus, Sikhs, atheists, and Buddhists into Western countries.

Paradoxically, faced with modernization, the world's great religious bodies show a decline in their institutional traditions (religious vocations, ritual practices, community participation, popular devotions), even though they remain strong reference points for culture, spiritual experience and identity. This trend favours the development of transnational and decentralized networks of small churches as well as religious cross-breeding and tends to weaken the influence of the Western version of Christianity. And so the loop has been looped: a remarkable expansion of Christianity occurred in the 18th and 19th centuries due to extensive cross-cultural evangelism carried out by European and North American Protestant and Catholic missionary societies and Russian Orthodox missionaries in Asia. In the 20th century the indigenous churches in Africa, Asia, and Latin America, many of them energized by the dynamism of Pentecostalism, continued these endeavours. So that by the 21st century the numerical strength and influence of the Christian churches in the global South came to equal and even exceed that of those in the global North.

Solange Lefebvre

Bibliography

Jenkins P. 2002, revised edition 2007. *The next Christendom: the coming of global Christianity.* Oxford and New York: Oxford University Press.

Pottmeyer H. J. 1975. *Unfehlbarkeit und Souveränität: die päpstliche Unfehlbarkeit im System der ultramontanen Ekklesiologie des 19. Jahrhunderts.* Mainz: Matthias Grünewald.

Poulat É. 1980. *Une Église ébranlée: changement, conflit et continuité de Pie XII à Jean-Paul II.* Paris: Casterman.

Roof W. C., Jackson W., Roozen C. and Roozen D. (eds) 1995. *The post-war generation and establishment religion: cross cultural perspectives.* Boulder, San Francisco and Oxford: Westview.

Sanneh L. and Carpenter J. A. (eds) 2005. *The changing face of Christianity. Africa, the West, and the world.* Oxford, New York and Toronto: Oxford University Press.

Related essays

anti-Catholicism; antisemitism; Bible; birth control; Buddhism; consumer cooperation; cosmopolitanism and universalism; ecumenism; European Union (EU); liberation theology; international non-governmental organizations (INGOs); Islam; legal order; liberalism; liberation theology; missionaries; nation and state; relief; religion; religious pilgrimage; Santería; Second Vatican Ecumenical Council; workers' movements

Christmas and Halloween

Halloween, celebrated on 31 October, and Christmas, celebrated on and around 25 December (or 7 January in the Eastern Orthodox church), are two of the world's oldest holidays still observed today.

Each has roots in European pre-Christian traditions. Pagan festivities held on 31 October observed the liminal point between the abundance of the harvest and dearth of winter, a day when ghosts and spirits of the dead could make contact with the living. Late December was the pagan winter festival of Yule in Northern Europe, and Roman festivals honouring the winter solstice and the god Saturn. The Christian church overlaid both these sets of festivities with its own feast days. All Saints' (or All-Hallows') and All Souls' days honoured saints and sinners and encouraged the living to pray for the souls of the dead. The twenty-fifth of December was recognized as early as the 4th century as the birthday of Jesus Christ (a symbolic rather than accurate date). The visit of the Three Wise Men was marked 12 days later.

By the medieval period, however, ancient and Christian traditions merged. Festivities continued to be held on the night of All Hallows' Eve (or Hallowe'en), including bonfires, parades and dressing up in costumes, while the next night children were sent door-to-door to sing for 'soul cakes' ('going a-souling'). Christmastime revellers observed the Twelve Days of Christmas from late December to early January, with churchgoing, carolling, dancing, excessive eating and drinking. Both celebrations were de-emphasised after the Reformation, though Christmastime remained a potent religious symbol for both Catholics (who promoted the holiday) and Protestants (who banned it).

The Halloween and Christmas holidays we know today were popularized only in the 19th century. Halloween celebrations made their way to America with European immigration, especially the flood of immigrants from Ireland in the late 1800s, and combined with ethnic and native-American traditions of story telling and fortune telling. The Halloween 'Jack o'lantern,' made from a hollowed-out pumpkin with a carved face, seems to date from this period, after an Irish tradition using turnips. Americans began to dress up in costumes, go house-to-house asking for food or money (later called 'trick-or-treating'), and hold neighbourhood get-togethers on 31 October. By the 20th century, Halloween had become a traditional, secular American holiday.

Christmas was revived in Europe and the United States in the 1800s as a Christian holiday, but with a refocus on family rather than community. Short stories by the American author Washington Irving, and the popular book, A Christmas Carol (1843), by English novelist Charles Dickens, promoted the theme of Christmas as a time for family reunion, a nostalgic occasion for remembering Christian tidings of goodwill and peace on earth, to practice generosity and compassion, and to enjoy and consume large amounts of food and drink. Christmas also became an occasion for gift giving. The poem best known as "Twas the night before Christmas' (1822), by American poet Clement Clarke Moore, popularized the association of Christmas with Santa Claus, a secular figure based on the 4th-century St Nicholas. Santa Claus was depicted as a plump, bearded old man in a red coat trimmed in white, who carried a large sack and rode through the sky on a reindeer-pulled sleigh on Christmas Eve to deliver wrapped gifts to good children in socks or shoes, or under the family Christmas tree. Other cultures adapted this image of Santa Claus (possibly based on a Finnish folk tale) to their own traditional gift-giving figures, such as Father Christmas in England or Père Noël in France.

Today, the celebration of both Halloween and Christmas reaches beyond Western and Christian cultures. By the late 20th century, an aggressive commercial industry in the United States and elsewhere recognized a market for holiday cards, outfits, decorations and foods. Halloween was reintroduced to Europe in its Americanized secular form, and began to be celebrated in many parts of South America, Asia and Australasia. On the evening of 31 October, costumed Halloween partiers, Jack o'lanterns and trick-or-treaters can be found on the streets of New York, London, Hong Kong and Sydney celebrating the holiday in remarkably similar fashion.

In contrast, Christmas celebrations, both religious and secular, continue to display many cultural variations. Mexican celebrations (posadas) begin on 12 December, and involve reenactment of the story of the Nativity and the breaking of piñatas (decorative containers filled with sweets or small toys, suspended in the air so that blindfolded children can break them open with sticks). New Zealanders may decorate their homes with a Pohutukawa tree and hold a backyard barbecue on Christmas Day. Norwegian families gather around the television on Christmas Eve to watch the Christmas specials, while Finns listen to the 'Peace of Christmas' address at noon. While Christmas is still an important religious feast day (and a national holiday) in all Christian countries, its secular and commercial aspects have become more visible. As Christmas festivities have spread outside the Christian world, especially in the burgeoning economies of Asia, they reflect the secular celebrations depicted in the Western media, focused on buying and receiving gifts. The shopping centres of Beijing and Tokyo, decorated with images of Santa Claus and his reindeer, now enjoy heavy business in the weeks leading up to 25 December. These marketed holidays now offer people of all religions on all continents the opportunity to take part in the American or Western lifestyle.

Alexis K. Albion

Bibliography

Dickens C. 1956. A Christmas Carol. New York: Columbia University Press.

Restad P. 1995. Christmas in America: a history. Oxford and New York: Oxford University Press.

Skal D. 2002. Death makes a holiday: a cultural history of Halloween. New York: Bloomsbury.

Cities

When regarded from a world-historical
perspective, competition between cities
assumes the appearance of a potent *perpetuum
mobile* continually spawning new winners and
losers. Even if 'cities' do not compete per se,
the political, economic and cultural actors
who identify with a particular city develop and
promote their cities within an atmosphere of
voluntary, compulsory or imagined competition. Such characteristic traits and aspirations
of a city as the establishment of industry,
economic strength and the diversity of cultural
life represent the playing fields upon which
competition is played out in an ongoing cali-
bration of mythically conceived and inspired
images as well as in a tug-of-war among
measurable economic data, non-measurable
atmospheres as well as comparative rankings.
In the post-Fordist state of today, we have
elevated competition and image politics to
dogmas of neoliberal regional economic policy, attributing critical significance to city
marketing in the planning and development
of urban society.

Traditional city competition

Of course, competition between cities is by no
means a modern invention. The ancient world
was well acquainted with the decades-long
rivalry between cities and city states such as
Athens and Sparta, Rome and Byzantium,
between the metropolises and their satellites.
Political-military feuds between cities and
interurban competition in the arts, in trade
and in innovative products have found their
way into annals the world over. As we know,
Europe's political and economic development
in the early modern era was characterized
by competition among European cities for
prestige and economic progress, as can be
seen in the rise and fall of the Italian city
states, in the competition between Portuguese
and Dutch ports, or in the contest between
German, British and Belgian commercial and
university cities. Competition and cooperation,
which, for example, were the hallmark of
such trading alliances as the Hanseatic
League in Northern Europe, were usually

interwoven on a dialectical basis. Urban
hierarchies took shape, dissolved and, as one
phase succeeded another, gave birth to more
or less dominant metropolises – London in
Shakespeare's time, Manchester as the cradle
of the Industrial Revolution, and Paris in the
19th century.

In the age of nation states and colonial
empires, particularly since the second half of
the 19th century, there has been increasing
evidence of intensified cities competition,
particularly among large cities and metropolises. The dynamic 'new' metropolis that
developed in cities like Berlin, New York and
Chicago and whose chronic fixation on its
own future largely determined its image,
increasingly competed with 'classic' metropolises like Paris, London and Rome with
their well established international reputations
and the allure of their historical legacies.
Economic competition, the intensification and
exchange of manpower and merchandise, and
also the rise of mass culture and incipient
forms of mass tourism catalysed a dynamic
blend of competitive thought, self-marketing
and growing interest in both culturally and
architecturally emblematic urban landscapes.
For many years the European competition
between Paris, London and Berlin – which
was concurrently a mirror of the nation-state
rivalries among the European great powers –
stymied the emergence of a cooperative
metropolitan network and facilitated the rise
of New York as a junior partner of London.

Within this atmosphere it comes as no
surprise that world fairs gained enormous
significance as stages for the presentation of
technological and civilizing achievements,
whereas architecture and urban development
remained proven 'projection and reflection
screens' for the depiction of a city's prestige
both to one's own people and to the world.
This particularly applies to the competing
cities of the industrial age. While the 1854
London World Exhibition in the Crystal Palace
was conceived to embody the promise and
achievements of British ingenuity, the completion of the Eiffel Tower in 1889 pioneered the
concept of technical monuments as reflectors
of international recognition in the modern
industrial city. Other European and American
metropolises copied the French example by
crafting architectural landmarks that always
made their greatest impression from a distance. Preserved by photographs and thus
cheaply and quickly reproducible for daily

newspapers and magazines, our collective memory has stored these landmarks. The early silent films were particularly quick to employ them as symbols of a new world starting around 1900. The camera sweeps across the urban landscape, only to focus in on the city's architectural mainstays. After this first glance at architectural landmarks, the 'moving pictures' then filled the squares, houses and streets with people, personal dramas and clichés. As early as 1923, in his silent film *Paris Asleep* (*Paris qui dort*), René Clair halted time for one day and presented the motif of tranquil, romantic, 'old' Paris as a counterpoint to the frenetic pace of 'new' New York – images that remained characteristic of the way both metropolises were depicted until long after the Second World War. In 1927 Walter Ruttmann's documentary *Berlin: Symphony of a Great City* contrasted the virtually deserted streets of Paris with a mythical snapshot of the pulsating modern metropolis.

As the 19th century drew to a close, such traditional forms of representation as urban planning, architecture and literature were joined by the new mass media – photography and silent films, as well as the rising mass-circulation advertising industry. These media-created images, myths and values loaded the metropolises with new meaning and contributed to an emotional reappraisal and reinvention of the urban ideal. Beginning in the 1930s, the demographic surveys made possible by the rise of the social sciences provided yet another rich source of data. Now it was not only possible to make statistical comparisons but also to employ such surveys as instruments of urban policy.

Cities competition in the post-Fordist age

Perceptions of cities and the evolution of urban societies in the 1950s and 1960s were conditioned by the transformation from the industrial to the service city and the consequences of increasingly global processes. Urban geographers and economic scholars accompany and foment intercity rivalries with rankings and economic forecasts. They are supported by empirical data surveys and also by theoretical debates, not least concerning the perceptual psychology of urban spaces and image research.

Thus urban landscape theoretician Kevin Lynch (1918–84) analysed cities as memorable trademarks. His book *The image of the city* (1959) dealt with the city's visual quality as an overlapping result from the actual *perception* and the *idea* of the city. Employing such concepts as memorability, graphic quality and graphic impact, Lynch underscored his demand to create a 'visual map' of the city. He was concerned less with the outer structural form than with the quality of the image. By contrast, the physical quality of the city takes centre stage in Michael Trieb's study *Stadtgestaltung – Theorie und Praxis* (Urban design – theory and practice, 1974). Trieb postulates that urban design represents the immaterial needs of people in the city. For Trieb, the experiential space – which he views as a kind of 'extract' – is identical to the urban image. In his 1971 book *Wie man seine Stadt verkauft* (How to sell one's city), Roman Antonoff (1934–2003) shows the power an urban image can wield in the development of a city. According to Antonoff, the city is a commodity that must henceforth demonstrate its attractiveness to highly diverse target groups. In order for a city to hold its own in interurban competition, advertising and public relations assume top billing on the municipal agenda. Both as a policy paradigm and as an academic discourse, city marketing first emerged in the United States in the 1970s. It leapt over to the British Isles during the Thatcher era before establishing itself in Continental Europe and elsewhere in the 1990s.

In the meantime, urban geographers and economists had long since been laying the foundations for a worldwide comparison of cities using demographic data. Using the results of the 1930 US Census to isolate the proportion of employees in individual economic areas, the geographer Chauncy D. Harris (1914–2003) localized nine types of cities and developed them into a functional urban classification system in 1943. Refined statistical methods helped to develop classification systems, facilitating comparisons with the prototypical 'standard city'. These systems quickly spread beyond academia. The ranking system of the American business magazine *Fortune*, which started publishing American rankings in 1956 and international rankings in 1957, grabbed attention early on. In the 1960s computer-supported analytic methods allowed for more sophisticated surveys. In 1962, using factor and cluster analysis, British geographer Brian J. L. Berry (b.1934) succeeded in demonstrating an overriding organizational principle and measurable hierarchies within the

American urban system. By relating towns to one another within previously distinct economic and political systems, such systematic screening dovetails with dynamic urban development processes – often at the expense of our awareness of simultaneous and comprehensive cooperative processes occurring between urban entities.

Interurban hierarchies and networks: Debates since 1970

In the 1960s the economic paradigm shift to what was later characterized as a post-Fordist service economy could no longer be ignored. Deindustrialization, economic restructuring and the rise of the service sector went hand in hand with developments that are most familiar under the category of 'globalization': financial markets converged across the world and developments in the transportation and communication sectors accelerated the mobility of capital, merchandise and human beings many times over. As a result, companies and, particularly, the great corporations increasingly found themselves disconnected from individual production sites and traditional production factors. Cities reacted to these trends and sought new avenues toward strengthening local economic development. Earlier industrial regions now positioned themselves as 'postindustrial' areas. Starting in the 1970s, the economically based classification of cities in conjunction with the growing significance of city marketing fed the assumption that cities were units within the dynamics of (global) economic development and that they therefore increasingly behaved like private economic enterprises under competitive pressure. In 1986, in an attempt to address this paradigm, urban and regional planner John Friedmann (b.1926, Vienna) created his 'world city hypothesis', a still controversial but valuable approach. Friedmann describes the structure and function of so-called 'world cities' as the result of a renewed deployment of capital. According to this view, Tokyo's economic position can be ascertained by means of indicators – after all, the Japanese metropolis possesses more headquarters than New York, London and Paris combined. In fact, at the dawn of the 21st century, 9 of the 20 most innovative firms on earth were based there. These 'world cities' are ascribed an internationally significant role that is extricating them from the national urban systems and transferring them onto a new, transnational hierarchical level.

Dutch urban sociologist and economist Saskia Sassen (b.1949) has developed Friedmann's world-city hypothesis and come up with the concept of 'global command capability'. Sassen seeks to explain the concentration of multinational command centres within just a few world cities. Her assumption: while the mobilization of deconcentrated economic activities, which is not least the result of the advanced internationalization of large sectors of the world economy, is dependent on tightly organized and centralized management, multinational headquarters must continue to rely on cooperation with a network of decentralized companies. In conjunction with the world cities and their function as control centres, this approach hints at the existence of a further worldwide network subordinate to the 'world cities' level. Cities such as Frankfurt am Main, Hong Kong, Los Angeles, Paris, San Francisco and Osaka are competing and cooperating with the world cities. Thus the German banking metropolis Frankfurt – while in itself home to fewer than a million people – plays a significant role for the European stock market and will not yield its financial stature to London without contestation.

At the same time, historical urban studies confirm the peculiarities of emergent economic areas. The fact that Europe disperses its ten largest firms to eight locations, while in America eight of the ten most profitable corporations operate out of two large metropolitan areas suffices as evidence for the divergent development patterns in Europe and North America. Peter Hall (b.1932, London) rightly regards the role of European cities such as Brussels, Copenhagen, Stockholm and Vienna as disproportionate to their actual size. Thus capital-city functions coupled with historically developed specializations – e.g., banking in Zürich, fashion in Milan, art in Paris – have given rise to a distinctly 'unhierarchical' urban development pattern in Europe. While Hall characterizes this decentralization and the network idea as a positive 'asset', other urban historians highlight the particularly dense competition that is typical of the European context. Other urban scholars, in turn, challenge the extent to which present-day cities actually still compete, asking whether it might not be more accurate to speak of urban or metropolitan regions that develop in extremely diverse ways.

In 1989 the group of researchers surrounding the French geographer Roger Brunet (b.1931) launched the 'Blue Banana' image – an agglomeration stretching from Birmingham, London, Brussels, Amsterdam, Cologne, Frankfurt and Basel down to Zürich and Milan, which thus encompasses nearly half of all European economic enterprises. A second spatial entity extends along the Mediterranean from Valencia to Barcelona and from there all the way to Milan. Like other subsequent constructs dreamt up by planners and geographers, both the 'Blue Banana' and the Mediterranean crescent known as the 'Sunbelt' represent spatial formations that generously encompass 'established' and 'rising' economic centres. Maximizing the economic power of these constructed spaces is a task for European economic programmes on the basis of the Lisbon Agenda. Overriding urban agglomerations have also been identified in North America – on the east coast, researchers speak of a strip running from Washington, DC in the south, extending to Philadelphia and New York and all the way up to Boston (the 'Megalopolis' identified by Jean Gottman in 1961). On the west coast, they have identified a formation with San Francisco Bay as the dominant core. In addition, there are large cities such as Los Angeles and Chicago, whose spatial expansion is described as urban agglomeration. In characterizing this type of city, Edward Soja has pointed to the restructuring of the Los Angeles area beginning in the 1970s. According to Soja, the coexistence of industrial and service metropolises is a model of success and is a reaction to intensified competition over the preservation and restoration of the city. Against this backdrop it makes sense to assume that renewed rivalries between cities and urban conglomerations will pick up in the near future.

Urban policy decides on a city's attractiveness as well as on establishing industry and support from quasi-government funding. Urban policy courts investors who move from one boom town to the next with their grand projects for new office and retail complexes. Cities become catalysts for economic development. Urban planning is no longer expected to channel growth but rather encourage investment. In the competition over the luring of growth-oriented industries, a city's natural and cultural characteristics are highlighted and enhanced.

Aside from the indicators, a city's image plays an important role in investors' minds. According to Häussermann and Siebel (1993), trade fairs, congresses, sporting events and festivals ('the politics of big events') transmit an excitement that boosts public spirit and identification with the city. Weaker cities, which play a subordinate role in the international competition, are given the opportunity to become visible through media-savvy staging. In a sort of urban doping procedure, cities competition does not just highlight the city itself. Instead, media events impose a prepackaged image upon it. One large city after another has discovered the potential of the artistic and cultural scene as a magnet for investors. Even though Miami has never been regarded as an artistic hotspot, since 2002 the international art scene has been wending its way to 'Art Basel Miami Beach'. In 2006, Singapore touted its first art Biennale, Dubai its goal to build the world's largest library and Hong Kong the construction of a mega-museum project, while cities large and small the world over are hustling to copy the recipe of the metropolises using the means available to them.

Alongside 'festivalization', architecture remains paramount to a city's image. In keeping with this trend, globally active 'starchitects' such as Renzo Piano, Rem Koolhaas and SANAA have been designing haute couture architecture. In the 1990s their colleagues Norman Foster, Santiago Calatrava and Frank O. Gehry catapulted the Basque basket-case of Bilbao to improbable grandeur as an artistic and architectural hub. Today, as in the days when Paris built the Eiffel Tower skyward, the competition for internationally recognizable and ambitious representations of urban prestige – whether in Taipei, Doha or Shanghai – is flourishing.

Future competition and new cooperation

Thus cities competition is taking place on very different levels. Internationally distinct developments and approaches to competitive strategies and benefits have brought forth entirely new types of cities over the last few decades. Concepts such as the 'smart city', the 'intelligent city' or the 'creative city' primarily demonstrate the competitiveness of cities and urban agglomerations that planners and investors are seeking. At the start of the 21st century it is not only the developed-world cities and European metropolises that are competing for a secure future. New competitors are emerging from among the fast-growing megacities in Africa, Asia and South America. The Russian metropolises of Moscow and St Petersburg are being developed into revitalized economic areas, and cities such as Mumbai, Singapore and Hong Kong are strengthening their positions on the international stage. Just what the relationship between cooperation and competition between the new urban types will look like cannot be planned. One thing is likely to remain, however, and that is the permanent integration, recalibration and contestation of urban identity in the ongoing urban development process. Competition always includes multiple intertwined actors who, while they may be bound together in rivalry, are nevertheless compelled to tackle pressing social and economic problems in a spirit of exchange and cooperation.

Oliver Schmidt

Bibliography

Friedmann J. 1986. 'The world city hypothesis', Development and Change, 17, 1, 69–83.

Harvey D. 1989. 'From managerialism to entrepreneurialism: the transformation in urban governance in late capitalism', Geografiska Annaler, Series B, Human Geography, 71, 1, 3–17.

Häussermann H. and Siebel W. 1993. Festivalisierung der Stadtpolitik, Stadten twicklung durch grosse Projekte. Opladen: Westdeutscher.

Jensen-Butler C. et al. (eds) 1998. European cities in competition, Aldershot: Avebury.

Jessop B. 'The narrative of enterprise and the enterprise of narrative: place marketing and the entrepreneurial city', in Hall T. and Hubbard P. (eds) 1998. The entrepreneurial city: geographies of politics, regime and representation, London: John Wiley, 77–99.

Sassen S. 1991. The global city: New York, London, Tokyo. Princeton: Princeton University Press.

Short J., Kim M. and Wells H. 1996. 'The dirty little secret of world cities research: data problems in comparative analysis', International Journal of Urban Research, 20, 4, 697–717.

Ward S. V. 1998. Selling places: the marketing and promotion of towns and cities, 1850–2000. London: E. & F. N. Spon.

Related essays
anarchism; architecture; art market; city planning; cultural capitals; expositions; financial centres; global cities; literary capitals; modernismo; non-lieux; Olympic Games; Skidmore, Owings and Merrill; United Cities and Local Governments (UCLG); urbanization

City planning

Conscious forethought in the laying out of sections of (or indeed entire) cities has been intermittently evident since ancient times. From the mid 19th century, however, the pressures of industrialization and urban growth made more salient the perception in Europe of a common need to plan the development of cities. Baron Haussmann's reshaping of Paris to create grand new boulevards (1853–70) was a key example. This became increasingly known to urban elites, especially after the 1867 Paris Exposition Universelle, and was emulated on a smaller scale in other cities including Brussels, Stockholm and Birmingham. The growing practice of staging open competitions to plan urban extensions following the removal of redundant fortifications also encouraged increasing refinement of planning practice, particularly so in Germany and the Habsburg Empire. British innovations in public health, housing design and community planning, particularly model factory villages, were also important. Britain's economic prowess ensured close attention to these innovations from industrialists and city leaders in continental countries. Hamburg, for example, drew heavily on British practice and employed a British sanitary engineer. The Ruhr manufacturer Alfred Krupp also drew on British ideas about industrial villages following several visits to British factories.

The pace of innovation in both ideas and practice quickened noticeably from about 1890. In Germany, sophisticated zoning mechanisms to regulate land use and density and to facilitate the pooling of land holdings were developed. These innovations soon attracted the interest of urban reformers and professionals, especially so in Britain, the United States and Japan. In each country they contributed, directly though in different ways, to emergent planning practice. In Britain, for example, these German approaches to planning town extensions, reported by visiting reformers and municipal delegations, helped to shape the first town planning legislation in 1909. The already developing American practice of zoning was similarly strengthened by knowledge of German approaches. Japanese planning based its most characteristic feature, land readjustment, on the relevant German legal codes in this period, especially the closely studied Lex Adickes, adopted for Frankfurt in 1902.

An important and widely diffused model was the garden city introduced by the English visionary Ebenezer Howard in 1898. Versions of his book, *To-morrow: A Peaceful Path to Real Reform* were quickly translated into other languages. The Garden City Association founded in Britain in 1899 soon spawned similar bodies in many other countries, beginning in Germany in 1902. By 1913 there was an International Garden City and Town Planning Association (the present International Federation of Housing and Planning).

Urban planning was by 1914 widely recognized as a distinct field of reformist endeavour and technical expertise. The various linguistic neologisms coined to define it: *Städtebau, urbanisme*, town planning, city planning, *toshi keikaku, urbanismo, stedebouw* and so on, suggested distinctive national interpretations. Yet transnational features were integral elements in its emergence, facilitating rapid cross-national learning, synthesis and further innovation. The more gradual and random earlier processes of diffusion increasingly gave way to more systematic mechanisms. The frequency of competitions that were increasingly open to international participation grew, providing an early outlet especially for the careers of French urbanistes such as Léon Jaussely (for example, Barcelona 1904) or Henri Prost (for example, Antwerp 1910). A key role was also played by increasingly frequent discursive events such as international conferences and exhibitions. Most notable was the 1910 London town planning conference of the Royal Institute of British Architects which drew 1,300 delegates, from all parts of the world as well as Britain.

The most powerful European states were also transferring the practice to their colonies. The British, for example, commissioned Sir Edwin Lutyens to plan a new imperial capital for India at New Delhi from 1910. In 1913 the French appointed Henri Prost to undertake the planning work of the protectorate administration in Morocco. These colonial settings, less compromised by indigenous political pressures, were to some extent test-beds for new ideas. This was especially so in the French world, and Morocco's 1913 planning law eventually became one of the bases for France's belated measure of 1919. British (and to a lesser extent American) planners also fostered planning in the more autonomous imperial dominions of Canada and Australia.

These essential characteristics of the international planning movement proved remarkably enduring, despite the disruptive effects of the World War I. Some international linkages were actually intensified by wartime experiences, reflecting solidarity between allies, dispersal of some key individuals and the reconstruction of destroyed cities. Thus Belgian planners, exiled from their occupied country in France, Britain and the Netherlands, gained first-hand new experiences and drew their neighbours into Belgium's reconstruction planning. More generally, although there was some hesitancy in resuming contacts with Germany after 1919, international links soon reappeared. Many newly created states used planning principles to establish identity, facilitate development and foster cohesion. Some (for example, Turkey) hired planners from other countries while others (for example, Finland or Czechoslovakia) used indigenous professionals. Some of the new Central European states also contributed to the emergent movement for 'modern architecture' which appeared during the 1920s. Originating mainly in Weimar Germany, France, the Netherlands, Switzerland and Italy, modernist ideas about the organization of urban space (notably those of Le Corbusier) had long-term international significance for planning. A dedicated organization, the Congrès Internationaux d'Architecture Moderne (CIAM, from 1928), facilitated the spread and adaptation of this movement.

There was some direct contact between the modernists and Soviet planners in the 1920s and 1930s. However, the ascendancy from about 1935 of socialist realist principles in the Soviet Union under Stalin curtailed such links. The rise of fascism in Europe during the 1930s also narrowed the international planning movement. But both trends contributed to a dispersal of individual planners, mainly Jews or those with leftist sympathies. This further spread the latest European planning concepts into other geographical arenas, including Latin America and the future Israel. One of the chief receivers of these émigrés – mainly into educational roles – was the United States which itself became a very important innovator at this time, especially in highways, new settlement and regional planning. The new arrivals began to play some role in these changes, mainly by increasing American knowledge of the principles of European modernism.

World War 2 brought huge destruction of cities in Europe and Japan, creating a major role for planners after 1945. Together with the perceived weaknesses of prewar policies, this ensured that planning would now become deeply embedded in governance. The character of the reconstructions varied between countries, particularly so between Communist and Western states. In the former, socialist realist principles were imposed on the Soviet Union's new client states (though the exact reconstruction of Warsaw's historic core was a notable exception). The typical means by which imposition occurred was to call leading planners from the new Communist states to Moscow for instruction in 'correct' principles. The instructed ones were then expected to insist on the new approaches in their own countries. In some cases Communist exiles from Nazism (such as the German planner Kurt Liebknecht, domiciled since the 1930s in the Soviet Union), were returned to key planning roles in the new regimes. This combination of approaches underpinned such notable planning efforts as the Stalinallee in East Berlin or the MDM complex in Warsaw. Soviet planners only occasionally played direct planning roles in Eastern Europe, for example in Sofia. There were more direct interventions, however, in the new Communist regimes in Asia, for example Beijing from 1949 and, for a longer period, in Vietnam after 1954.

In Western Europe and Japan, the urban planning impact of the other major postwar global power, the United States, was less heavy-handed. The key American concern was to ensure a reconstruction based on democratic capitalism. In planning terms this involved fostering and strengthening Europe's international links, especially now with the United States and other democratic planning examples, particularly Britain. Material assistance through the Marshall Aid programme played a general part in promoting this. However, more efforts were devoted to educating younger European planners, especially from former enemy nations, through scholarship programmes to American universities, sponsored study tours, exhibitions and literature to publicize American approaches.

As the reconstruction was completed, the emphasis everywhere shifted more to urban modernization. After Stalin, the differences between city planning in the Communist bloc and the West became less marked, and more interchange became possible notably in fields such as housing or new towns, where delegations inspected the achievements of the other side. The Communist state of Yugoslavia, pursuing a path relatively independent of Moscow, showed more obvious contact with the West, as seen especially in the uniquely international effort to replan Skopje following the 1963 earthquake.

Emergent common problems, such as planning for the automobile, also strengthened a search for transferable lessons and common approaches. The important 1963 British government report *Traffic in Towns* prepared by Colin Buchanan was symptomatic of this. Following long visits and detailed study Buchanan drew international lessons from the USA and some European countries, principally West Germany. He essentially advocated a variable, synthesized approach, mixing American-inspired major new urban road networks, requiring extensive urban renewal, with the European-, essentially German-inspired environmental areas, where pedestrians had more priority. The report itself exerted an important though far from uniform influence in most major world planning arenas, allowing Buchanan to embark on an international career.

By this time, urban planning was also playing an expanding role in other parts of the world. The last years of British and French colonialism saw planning used more intensively in an attempt to promote economic development and cope with quickening urban growth. This continued as former colonies became independent, with planning now also used to forge national identity, for example in the new post-1948 state capitals of India at Chandigarh, Bhubaneswar and Gandhinagar and the national capital of Pakistan at Islamabad (1958–). Former colonies continued to draw extensively on foreign planning expertise (and financial aid), albeit now from sources beyond the former imperial power. Important in this process were international bodies, particularly the United Nations which first became involved in planning in connection with the resettlement of Palestinian refugees following Israel's creation in 1948. In 1951 a UN office of Housing, Building and Planning was founded, led by the Yugoslav planner Ernest Weissmann. This organization (now incorporated into UN Habitat) played a major role in channelling planning expertise mainly from the West and Communist worlds to countries such as Lebanon, Jordan and Indonesia. It also gave prominence to some planners from less developed countries, notably the Sri Lankan planner and diplomat Oliver Weerasinghe or the Trinidadian Joe Crook (who led the office after Weissmann). Also important in commissioning and funding planning efforts in the developing world, often in conjunction with the UN, were private US agencies, mainly the Ford Foundation. It played a particularly important role in India, sponsoring plans for Delhi (1957–) and Calcutta (1960–), but also elsewhere.

Although these various efforts put Westerners (such as the American Albert Mayer or the Greek Constantinos Doxiadis) into prominent positions, indigenous planning capacity was gradually strengthened in many less developed countries. This was especially evident in Latin America where, following deference to European (especially French) planning expertise before 1939 and American influence thereafter, there was a confident flowering of indigenous modernist planning, particularly at Brazil's new national capital, Brasilia (1956–).

The 1970s and 1980s brought worldwide disappointment with and consequent reactions against modernist planning which were themselves emulated elsewhere. The US anti-freeway movements which began in the late 1950s in California helped inspire and inform similar activism in Europe and beyond. Radical environmental movements which appeared during the late 1960s and 1970s in North America, West Germany and elsewhere also soon began to spread, challenging and helping to shift official planning approaches in many countries. The 1980s also brought a growing reaction against state intervention, initially in the United States and the United Kingdom, emphasizing more market-led or partnership modes of delivering city planning. This approach began to exert a strong international influence, especially but not exclusively in the Anglophone world. Reinforced by the World Bank, it also shifted the emphasis of planning in the developing world. The approach also began to spread much more widely following the almost complete collapse of the Soviet Communist bloc in the late 1980s/early 1990s. In its wake, Western agencies such as USAID and the World Bank promoted the freeing of urban land markets and the development of Western-style land-use zoning in former Communist cities. Though China has remained Communist, its closer engagement with the world market economy, mainly since the 1990s, has been paralleled by equivalent changes in its city planning.

More than ever before, city planning across the world now embraces a common global discourse, of promoting sustainable development which ostensibly combines market-led economic and urban growth with environmental protection. This discourse has grown since the Earth Summit in 1992 and has been widely promoted by international agencies, national governments and local planning actions. Whether the approach really is sufficiently robust to address mounting environmental problems while meeting the huge global aspirations for urban-based material prosperity remains to be seen.

Stephen Ward

Bibliography

Åman A. 1992. *Architecture and ideology in Eastern Europe during the Stalin era: an aspect of Cold War history*. New York and Cambridge, MA: Architectural Foundation/MIT Press.

Home R. 1997. *Of planting and planning: the making of British colonial cities*. London: Spon.

Nasr J. and Volait M. (eds) 2003. *Urbanism: imported or exported? – native aspirations and foreign plans*. Chichester: Wiley.

Ward S. V. 2002. *Planning the twentieth-century city: the advanced capitalist world*. Chichester: Wiley.

Civil engineering works

Civil engineering emerged in the course of
the 18th century as the handmaiden of both
private canal, road and railway companies as well as of modernizing nation states.
A child of industrialization and emergent
nation states, civil engineering was the civilian, 'bourgeois' descendant of a long military
engineering tradition devoted to the construction of fortifications, roads, bridges, and
the conduct of sieges, including tunnelling
and undermining. Like its military predecessor, civil engineering was a practice literally
rooted in the earth. Civil engineers thus cultivated a variety of techniques for surveying;
earth removal; the making of foundations;
and the construction of objects like bridges,
railway lines, dams, shipping locks, tunnels,
and roads.

Civil engineering crystallized around two
basic technological pillars of industrialization and state formation: transportation
infrastructure and water management. At
first the focus was on canals, roads, and rivers. From the 1840s onwards railway construction became a major civil engineering
domain and a new theatre for the public display of civil engineering prowess. In Britain,
daring engineer-entrepreneurs like John
Smeaton, the Stephensons, Thomas Telford,
father and son Brunel and Benjamin Baker
made reputations and fortunes in the process of unifying the newly expanded United
Kingdom by railway lines. Large bridges like
the Britannia Tubular Bridge (1819) or the
Firth of Forth Bridge (1890) drew outlying
regions of the country together and in the
process established civil engineering as an
heroic nation-building enterprise. Elsewhere
in Europe, notably in France and Switzerland,
railroads catapulted the art of tunnel building to literally new heights. The innovative
Mont Cenis Tunnel (1871) was the first trans-
alpine and transnational railway tunnel, soon
followed by the St Gotthard (1881). In France,

the prestigious Corps des Ponts et Chaussées
had abetted the conversion of 'peasants into
Frenchmen' by helping to unify the new
republic with networks of canals, roads and
railways. It was also in France that a vision of
engineering as a learned profession wedded
to the national state gained currency; a vision
that was subsequently discussed and disputed
across borders.

In this 'Age of Imperialism' European powers and the United States were also investing
heavily in their overseas possessions with the
aim of improving prosperity, defensibility
and profitability. As in the home countries,
civil engineering played a crucial role. Roads
and railroads were driven through jungles
and across deserts and savannahs, rivers were
dammed for irrigation and later hydropower,
and seaports were dredged and fitted with
deepwater quays and breakwaters. The colonies, with their challenging environments
and huge geographical scale, not to mention
plentiful supplies of cheap native labour,
often served as laboratories for new civil
engineering approaches which subsequently
revitalized European engineering practices.
The engineering of railways, dams and irrigation systems in Europe and the United States
owed a lot to lessons from concurrent practices in the colonies.

The imperialist world order also encouraged a new look at the world map and new
imaginings about civil engineering projects to
improve imperialist circulation. Prime targets
of such scrutiny were either narrow straits
between headlands, like the Dardanelles or
the Øresund, inviting road and rail bridges
or, alternatively, isthmuses suggesting canals
that would shorten shipping routes. Shipping
was of course especially crucial in the political
economy of imperialism; hence perennially
enticing isthmuses like those of Suez, Corinth
and Panama became foci of civil engineering
speculation. In the 1820s, the idea of a canal
across the Isthmus of Suez had mesmerized
French saint simonian engineers. Three decades later the idea had captured the imagination of the energetic French diplomat,
Ferdinand de Lesseps. Under the aegis of his
international Compagnie Universelle, Suez
became the first major isthmus to be traversed
by a canal (completed 1869). This unique
undertaking not only eliminated the tortuous
voyage to the Orient around the Cape of Good
Hope, but also became emblematic for the

new world-shaping power of transnationally organized civil engineering.

This new supra-national level of organized civil engineering that has been achieved in the 19th and 20th century impacted both on the emerging discipline and on the world. There are three senses in which the new style and scope of engineering produced transnational effects: first, the discipline of civil engineering acquired a new transnational level of circulation and institutionalization, second, the enlarged scope of many engineering projects *nolens volens* produced effects across national borders, and, third, a new style of neo-imperialist civil engineering emerged involving transnational transfers of knowledge, labour and capital.

By the second half of the 19th century, the dynamism of civil engineering increasingly came to depend on the national and transnational circulation of knowledge and persons. Since the Renaissance, itinerant military and building engineers and widely circulated treatises on structures and fortifications (by the likes of Brunelleschi, Da Vinci, Galileo, Simon Stevin) had already been setting the tone. In the 19th century, the institutionalization of national engineering corps, engineering societies and engineering journals dramatically increased the transnational circulation of engineering knowledge. Civil engineering journals regularly reviewed the foreign technical press and engineering societies maintained libraries containing influential foreign engineering texts. In addition major civil engineering works were invariably preceded by 'study tours' abroad in order to draw lessons from the efforts of foreign engineers. The transnational engineering networks built on these written and personal exchanges were augmented by the emergence of a number of permanent transnational engineering forums and institutions dedicated to specific fields of practice or objects of governance. A body like the Central Commission for the Navigation of the Rhine (founded 1815) involved civil engineers from all the riparian Rhine states in the common project of improving and maintaining the Rhine as an international artery of navigation. Likewise, regular four-yearly events like the International Inland Navigation Congresses (from 1885) or the International Road Congresses (from 1908) helped to weld transnational solidarities among civil engineers working in specific fields, at least at the level of exchange of knowledge and experiences.

The second important transnational aspect in civil engineering derives from the extended spatial effects of many civil engineering works. These effects were sometimes intentional but often largely unforeseen. Intentional transnational effects of civil engineering works included the creation of new transportation links by road, rail or water; or the development of border-spanning irrigation, flood-control and hydroelectric schemes. Projects like the canalization of the Columbia or St Lawrence Rivers, the Panama Canal, the Mont Cenis Tunnel, the (English) Channel Tunnel or the Øresund bridge-tunnel – even when realized by a single nation state – were invariably conceived and executed as multinational resources or as links in transnational flows of goods and persons. But most of these projects also had secondary and unintended consequences which often led to complicated international imbroglios. The tragic dessication of (international) Lake Aral as a result of nationalist interests in over-ambitious Soviet Cold-War irrigation schemes is a case in point, as is the environmental degradation in the Eastern Mediterranean basin due to the Nile's reduced burden of silt and nutrients or the protracted German and Swiss struggle with France's post-World War I plans to draw off some 85 per cent of the water of the Upper Rhine into its proposed Grand Canal d'Alsace.

Large civil engineering projects may also be transnational in a third sense, i.e. by virtue of transnational transfers of the knowledge, labour, or capital necessary to build them – even when the projects themselves are firmly situated in national contexts. This was foreshadowed by the peripatetic fortification and drainage engineers of the Renaissance as well as by their Dutch hydraulic engineering descendants of the 17th and 18th century who masterminded drainage and flood-control projects throughout Europe. De Lessep's Compagnie Internationale embodied such transnational transfers, as did the Chinese labour force gathered by the US Army Corps of Engineers to help dig the Panama Canal. The era of the Cold War and postcolonialism involved the superpowers in competitive development schemes that sometimes brought massive transnational transfers of knowledge, capital and labour in the context of civil engineering works, e.g. the Aswan

High Dam in Egypt or various projects carried out in the framework of the Marshall Plan in Europe. These were superseded by large 'development' projects carried out in whole or in part by large transnational engineering firms: projects like Hong Kong International Airport, the Øresund bridge-tunnel linking Sweden and Denmark, or China's Three Gorges Dam are typical of this new mode of transnational civil engineering.

All the projects named, and numerous others not (yet) built, are the material offspring of old and often stubborn imaginings. The enticing transportation prospects offered by straits, isthmuses and proximate reaches of rivers, for example, fired the imaginations of builders even long before adequate technologies were available. As early as 850 AD Charlemagne made the first attempt at connecting the Rhine and the Danube along a route which more than a millennium later would become the Rhine-Main-Danube Canal. The Corinth Canal, completed in 1893 as the 'stepchild' of the Suez and Panama Canals, was the successor of an earlier attempt at the behest of the Roman emperor Nero in 67 AD, who was in turn inspired by even earlier imaginings. With the professionalization of civil engineering in the 19th and 20th centuries and the associated rapid development of excavation and construction technology, many ancient imaginings for the first time began to appear technically feasible and, given the increasing circulation of goods and people, economically and politically desirable as well. This has led to new imaginings, some of which have been executed as others have fallen by the wayside.

In the 19th and 20th centuries, transnational projects have been among the biggest, the most challenging and the most prestigious civil engineering ventures. This is partly because national boundaries have a tendency to respect natural ones (rivers, seas, mountain ranges) and because contiguous seas and rivers are often separated by elevated terrain. Hence, creating links between nations, seas and rivers frequently requires spanning 'insurmountable' physical barriers by means of technologically advanced tunnels, bridges, or canals. This heroic aspect of transnational projects, together with the practical monopoly of civil engineers over the requisite technologies, has transformed imaginings of transnational infrastructure into something like the calling card of the worldwide civil engineering community. Unlike the earlier imaginings of potentates and poets, these latter-day imaginings are firmly anchored in a sense of technological feasibility. However, the more 'impossible' the project, the greater the glory, and this has made it attractive to 'overreach' the state of the art and suggest feasibility where in fact risk and uncertainty rule. This is perhaps an old tradition in civil engineering, but it produces high drama when applied to large transnational projects. The ultimately successful Panama Canal project nearly foundered on the rocks of de Lessep's excessive technological optimism. Other projects like the megalomaniac 'Atlantropa' project to join Europe and Africa, generate hydroelectric power, and lower the level of the Mediterranean Sea by means of a dam across the Strait of Gibraltar never even made it to the design stage, among other things because it never found a stable political base.

This tension between imagination and execution, at first rather informal, but now increasingly mediated by the internationally organized civil engineering profession and a large number of highly expert international engineering companies and contracting firms, has resulted in the permanent circulation of proposals of which a select number are actually executed. 'Atlantropa' and the Bering Strait Bridge remain pipe dreams (or nightmares?) while the St Gotthard Tunnel, the Øresund bridge-tunnel, the Aswan High Dam, the St Lawrence Seaway, and the Channel Tunnel are all realized projects whose hybrid transnational effects will be with us for a long time to come.

Cornelis Disco
Johan Schot

Bibliography

Bukowczyk J. J., Faires N., Smith D. R. And Widdis R. W. 2005. *Permeable border: the Great Lakes Basin as transnational region, 1650–1990*. Pittsburgh: University of Pittsburgh Press.

Katko T., Juuti P. S. And Vuorinen H. S. (eds) 2007. *Environmental history of water: global views on community water supply and sanitation*. London: IWA.

Ley W. 1955. *Engineers' dreams*. London: Phoenix.

Oliver J. A. 2006. *The Bering Strait Crossing: a 21st century frontier between East and West*. London: Information Architects.

Usher A. 1997. *Dams as aid*. London:
Routledge.

Vleuten E. V. D. and Kaijser A. (eds) 2006.
*Networking Europe: transnational infrastructures
and the shaping of Europe, 1850–2000*.
Sagamore Beach: Science History.

Voigt W. 1998. *Atlantropa: Weltbauen am
Mittelmeer; ein Architektentraum der Moderne*.
Hamburg: Dölling & Galitz.

Related essays

developmental assistance; empires and
imperialism; engineering; freshwater
management; International Road Federation
(IRF); investment; nation and state; Panama
Canal; railways; steamships; transportation
infrastructures

Civilizations

Civilization can be defined as a surplus-
extracting, urbanized agromanufactorial and
industrial complex with a large service and
military sector, sharing some overarching
and overriding common ethos. It contains
many different hierarchies, nations, cultures,
societies, communities, sects, ethnicities, and
identities. It is crucially dependent upon a variety of economic, social, political and labour
networks, and is culturally continuously able
to accommodate and induct other elements.
Some definitions of the term have ignored the
essentially composite and inductive nature
of all civilizations; all civilizations are multicultural and multicivilizational mosaics. All
civilizations depend on regional or global
networks that sustain them: civilization as an
exclusive concept is impossible. Earlier definitions of the term 'civilization' have often
ignored its essentially connected nature. For
example, defining civilization as a multiple
city-centred complex, demanding loyalty to
an overriding militaristic, cultural, ethnic, or
religious worldview or as the 'broadest level
of cultural identity' (Samuel Huntington),
is problematic, as this fails to define what
are the constituents of such culture/s or the
similarities and dissimilarities within this
broadest category.

The word 'civilization' comes from Latin
civis, a citizen, and *civilis*, pertaining to the citizen, and in medieval French, *civilisation*. First
used in English around 1704, it gained currency in its present meanings from the later
18th century. Dr Samuel Johnson refused to
include the word in his dictionary, preferring

'civility' instead, although his biographer,
James Boswell, disagreed with him. The word
found particular popularity in the fields of
palaeontology and archaeology during the
second half of the 1800s.

'Civilization' existed as an entry in encyclopaedias until at least the 1960s, albeit apolo-
getically because the two World Wars of the
20th century had undermined the belief in
the efficacy of Western civilization. However,
by 2001 'cities' and variations of 'civil society'
had subsumed the word in many encyclopaedias of social sciences. Nonetheless, the continuing usage of this category or word over
ten years after Huntington brought it into the
limelight again in 1993 in his *The clash of civilizations* resurrects the spectres of imperialism
and religion as the only possible civilizational
identities.

Some of its many usages are: (a) civil and
refined as opposed to 'barbaric' behaviour
(derived from Greek *barbaros* or 'foreign', similar to Sanskrit *barbar* or 'alien speech'); (b) the
process of civilizing or being civilized; (c)
hierarchy and stages of civilization/s, that is,
civilizations in times past such as the Mayan
civilization or different cultures arranged
according to their achievements within a single time period, that is, primitive versus modern; (d) one model of human civilization or
one world that is sufficient for all of us, that
is, the continuous development of human
society and civilization to achieve perfection
or a particular 'modernity'.

European tradition has nurtured the concept of 'high culture', which might include
elements such as fine arts and the opera, and
is different from popular culture (sometimes
used in a pejorative sense but also simply to
mean that which is popular with the majority). The former defines the most refined civilization. Here civilization is indistinguishable
from culture, and reflects the view that civilizations progress through stages to achieve
a particular cultural, political, social, economic, and technological perfection. In this
conceptualization, British and German biological warfare during the First World War,
Auschwitz during the Second World War,
Japanese atrocities in Manchuria, and the
United States' bombing of Hiroshima and
Nagasaki were mere aberrations from a civilizational ideal.

In children's books of the 1980s and 1990s,
there was usually a sketch of evolution of
Homo sapiens changing shape from a dark,

hairy, crouching ape, gradually standing up, to turn into a fair, short-haired, man: Darwin's complex theory of evolution reduced into a one-sided story, and oversimplified (for example, Neanderthal man coexisted with Homo sapiens sapiens). Thus, in the first and second senses of the use of the term, civilization is opposed to barbaric or primitive culture, and is also a process through which primitive people and even popular culture are civilized.

Complementing this view is the notion of hierarchy of civilizations. But, briefly, what defines development and its difference from civilization? Economic markers are as plentiful as technological ones; however, underlying all such strategies of ranking and of categorization is an implicit behavioural judgement regarding refinement. Hierarchy or stages of civilization are problematic because they demand a single model as the end product, that is, they imply a telos: a goal preordained and to be duplicated and striven after; the 'end of history' as Francis Fukuyama calls it. This last concept, liberal democracy as the only civilizational model, echoes 19th-century liberalism, which believed that the technology embodied in the telegraph would make a unified harmonious world. Similarly, contemporary ideas imply that the Internet will produce a global village: one world, one model, and ultimately, a single civilization.

This view of the world increasingly becoming one civilization with flexible boundaries, a world transformed in stages through the telegraph, electronic media, and Internet into a global democratic village, is difficult to match with reality. The quickening pace of time, for example, with the introduction of the International Standard Time based on the Greenwich Observatory for all or most parts of the world by the early 1900s, and the virtual shrinking of space, produced an opposite effect. This is not to suggest a direct causal link between these technologies and emerging differences. Nation states, and not civilization or civilizational progress, were behind the crowning paradox of the late 19th, 20th and 21st centuries, which is that few previous centuries witnessed such large-scale destruction of human and other forms of life by humans all over the world.

If our notion of time and space has telescoped, contradictorily, our statements of difference, civilizational, cultural,

communitarian, sectarian, individual and genetic, have never been starker. Frontiers of nation-state cooperation expanded, forming relatively internally coherent larger blocs with clear economic, military and political objectives, for example, the North Atlantic Treaty Organization (NATO), South Asian Association for Regional Cooperation (SAARC), and the European Union (EU). But there was also relentless definition and redefinition of borders, perhaps, exemplified during the First World War, by not breaking them down but making them more rigid, first on maps, then actually on the ground, as for example, 2000s Afghanistan, Pakistan, India, and Bangladesh, with electrified and barbed-wire fences, shoot-on-sight orders, minefields, and regular exchange of mortar-shells.

Genealogy of 'civilizations'

From at least 1780, Europeans began the enterprise of discovering past civilizations. They claimed to be recovering and preserving those past civilizations (for example, Napoleonic France in Egypt and the East India Company in India) from those very peoples they now ruled and who had lost their past glories, establishing an international traffic in mummies and antiquities, for instance supplying multiplying museums including the National Museum at Kolkata (Calcutta), which has its own Egyptian mummy. Some intellectuals continue to enlist in this glorification of an idealized past, ignoring the realities of the present and the limits of past civilizations. The European of the late 1800s largely viewed civilization as continuous development and social progress and Europe as its apogee, reflecting the ebullience of the second-phase of expansion of the British Empire.

The 1911 Encyclopaedia Britannica recorded under 'civilization': 'when we must speak of a civilization, as that of Egypt,... we must understand thereby a localized phase of society bearing the same relation to civilization as a whole that a wave bears to the Ocean or a tree to the forest'. It cited 'ethnologist' L. H. Morgan, describing prehistoric 'man's progress' from 'bestiality', through Older, Middle, and Later stages of 'Savagery' until laissez-faire and the technological marvels of 1900, which represented the Third or Final Status of civilization.

This view is teleological, linear, and deterministic. It conflates civilization with an Anglo-Saxon definition of modernity; the

European male rising from the crouching ape. It also manufactured a specific concept of civilization in the phase of European imperial expansion to apply to other historical epochs, which then led to the final goal of Western civilization, and justified its mission to 'civilize' most of the world that was, in contrast, uncivilized. Thus, civilization as modernity and as refinement intertwines at the core of the concept of civilization, and can be used by nation states to justify imperial expansion or international military intervention. These early views further emphasized the supposed uniqueness and isolation of European civilization. While there might have been civilizations in other times and other parts, European civilization had reached the point that it had through its own processes of evolution that had nothing to do with other civilizations, other times, or other parts of the world. This leads to the obvious emphasis on exclusivity and difference, and the construction of the 'Other' that was essentially different from the 'civilized', and by implication, European.

Different views of civilizations

In the 19th century, subjugated peoples publicized their own visions of civilizations. This was a reaction to European military, political, linguistic, intellectual, cultural, social and economic onslaughts and their depiction of indigenous past glory and present decay, justifying European rule over much of the globe as the 'white man's burden' (Kipling). The colonized were reacting to European dominance, attempting to explain it, and also to explain their present situation of being ruled over by 'materialistic empires'.

Starting from 1800, Indians such as Rammohan Roy, Aurobindo Ghose, Rabindranath Tagore, Vivekananda, Mohandas Karamchand Gandhi, and Jawaharlal Nehru presented their versions of civilizations, arguing, in some cases, for a spiritual East in opposition to a materialistic West. For example, Aurobindo Ghose viewed the Second World War as a clash between the forces of good and evil, though not in the Christian understanding of these terms, justifying Indian support to the Allies. Nigerian-born Chinua Achebe's *Things fall apart* (1958) and Caribbean-born Jean Rhys's *Wide Sargasso Sea* (1966) revealed the tragedy of colonial displacement, and the experience of being a refugee. Similarly, Manik Bandopadhyay and Rithwik Ghatak,

amongst others, showed how the machine gun and colonial intervention had shattered traditional indigenous worlds, producing a warped modernity where its inhabitants traded their subsistence and socioeconomic freedom for slums and famines.

These tensions were also visible in Japan. Following the Meiji Restoration of 1868, Japan set itself on a path of breakneck modernization, convinced that it must change its fundamental character in order to resist Western encroachment. The writer Fukuzawa Yukichi was instrumental in shaping Japanese attitudes toward 'civilization'. In the last four decades of the 19th century, some 3.5 million copies of his works were printed in Japan, in which he proposed his twin ideas of 'civilization and enlightenment', advocating ideas such as practical learning and individualistic thought over hierarchical social structures, for example, in *Seiyō no Jijō* (*Conditions in the West*, 1867–70). However, his view of 'civilization' was highly Westernized, leading to counter-reactions from other thinkers who worried that some essential quality of Japanese life would be sacrificed in the search for 'civilization'.

The two prevalent views of civilization/s fundamentally contradict each other. The view that civilizations in the religious sense have existed in the past and continue in the present and will expand to 'clash' in the future is contradicted by the view that the most developed form of nation state that ensures the greatest good represents civilization. Civilizationally, it is difficult to distinguish between East and West, North and South, in terms of colonial and neocolonial atrocities, terms which are residues of positional hierarchies: west to whom, east of what?

The 'bestiality of imperialism' (V. I. Lenin)

Everywhere that a particular kind of civilization is forcibly imposed on others by particular nation states, it becomes a form of imperialism, where we find the coexistence of violence with poverty and misery. Colonialism or imperialism rarely disseminated culture but created harsher contrasts to the detriment of indigenous cultures. Some critics of this position have argued that imperialism brought civilization in its wake, leaving behind infrastructures and legacies, but ignoring the fact that colonial cash-crops such as indigo, tea or opium, or the creation of banana republics based on the theory of comparative advantage, retarded industrialization, creating extroverted economic structures vulnerably dependent on global prices. Similarly, bridges, railways, and telegraphs connected the hinterland to port cities, allowing this economy to function. All decolonized nations have been engaged in undoing this so-called 'legacy'. Much of this pseudonostalgia or neoconservatism is found even today, for example, in the work of David Landes. In his The wealth and poverty of nations: why some are so rich and some so poor, Landes speaks of decolonized nations not maintaining their legacy, something echoed in Daniel Headrick's work. The altruism of imperialism is a myth: for example, one of the reasons behind Britain's vigorous championing of abolition of slavery in the 1820s and 1830s was that it had Indian 'indentured' labour, who were slaves by another name.

The resort to violence of the imperial powers also makes it hard to regard their record as one of building 'civilization': examples include Lord Kitchener's 'victory' at Omdurman, Sudan, where he slaughtered over 30,000 dervishes with an early form of the machine gun (the Maxim gun), General Dyer's Jalianwallabagh massacre of unarmed children, women, and men at Amritsar, India, in 1919, and European managers and rubber-plantation workers photographed proudly exhibiting chopped-off hands of other workers in King Leopold's Belgian Congo. Colonial industries like textiles or tea required nimble and soft fingers and depended on child and female labour; European and British plantation owners often stripped, abused, and tortured them. The French, North Americans and the Dutch committed comparable acts of violence in Southeast Asia and South America, and Japanese society went through a process of extreme external and internal repression during the process of modernization and imperial rule over Manchuria in the 1930s and 1940s. Whenever a nation state has employed force under the guise of civilizing other peoples it has not only brutalized those people, but also has, in the process, brutalized itself.

Different civilizations/globalizations?

This does not mean, just because civilization/s is/are difficult to define, that civilizations did not and will not exist. Previous civilizations were at least if not more vibrant than those of the contemporary era. Civilizations were constructed over time though mutual interaction, including the European civilization. Examples of these interactions are numerous: for instance, Hannibal used African elephants in his wars against Rome; the Gandhara style of Greco-Indian sculpture developed after Alexander's contact with India; Roman coins have been found in Kerala, India; and there was Indian contact with Augustus Caesar's Rome. In the religious sphere, Ashoka Maurya's (c. 250 BC) rock-carved edicts are found in Iran, Afghanistan, southern India, and on most major pilgrim routes still in use in India. He spread Buddhism to Sri Lanka, and subsequently, Buddhism spread from Bihar and Bengal to Tibet, Thailand, and much of Southeast Asia. Asian civilizations influenced Europe, as witnessed by the elephant drawn by Matthew Paris in 13th-century Europe; Europe's rediscovery of Greco-Roman learning via Arabia; Bengal and peninsular India's exchanges with Southeast Asia between the 12th and 14th centuries, and then again under British rule, with 19th-century Myanmar, Mauritius, and other countries. Similarly, Dr John Fryer, visiting India and Persia in the 1680s, Dr W. B. O'Shaughnessy, the pioneer of the Indian telegraph system and one of the early compilers of the Indian Materia Medica working with Indian and Anglo-Indian artisans and assistants, Kanai Lal Dey, collaborating with British scientists and doctors, possessing knowledge of both Western chemistry and Indian Ayurveda, and Bhudev Mukherjee, constructing Hindi as the 'national' language of India, all participated in the composite dialogue conveying information from and to the 'east' and 'west'.

The intellectual, social and cultural ferment that seized many parts of the world from 1400 until at least 1830 is astounding in the local, personal, regional and global exchange of ideas and views, and the continuing processes moulding the emergence of different and more unified civilizations, which possibly encountered the limits of their inclusive strategies. But this itself is an exclusionary definition of civilizations, which, if seen as processes and choices, rather than monoliths, continue to reformulate themselves through their experiences at zones or sites of contact.

Hierarchies of civilizations: scientific, technological, and medical Reason

European definitions of civilization, from the 19th century onward, had come to differentiate the fair short-haired Anglo-Saxon from the hairy, crouching 'dark' ape. All roads, in this case racially, led to the European short-haired man and the model of a city-centred democratic industrialized civilization with forms of constitutional and institutional charters, based on a division of power between the executive, the legislative and the judicial, balancing the fragile equation between individual right and the power of the state, and the Church, over its citizenry, a problem facing much of feudal Europe. This model, European thinkers felt, must multiply to constitute the one civilizational arrangement: the end of history, since the perfect idea is established and what remained were the details of practical implementation. To understand this privileging and hierarchy of civilization/s we turn to some of the strategies that underpin the categorizations.

Technologies as civilizational 'markers'

From the 1850s, histories of Science, Technology, and Medicine privileged isolated genius and the European laboratory as the only sites of a sanitized knowledge production. A technological and anthropological understanding of time replaced historical time so that prehistoric tools could be placed alongside those of, for example, present-day Andaman Islanders, and societies were arranged accordingly in the civilizational pyramid that had at its apex Western society symbolizing modernity, development, and technological advancement. Traditional histories ignored and downgraded experience inside and outside the laboratory, the contingent nature of the construction, closure, and replication of an experiment, together with regional and local networks of informants, artisans, instrument makers, intellectuals, collectors, and experts, extra-European and non-metropolitan Europeans, who all joined in the creation of the web of knowledge. Although the centre of the web of the 1700s or 1800s was often an institution like the Royal Society or Kew Gardens, this does not mean the centre stayed there: at various points in time, it moved to different parts of the web, which changed all the time. There was dialogue in different spheres of human activity, often unequal, but the flow of knowledge was not necessarily unidirectional, that is, 'derivative' and only from the West.

The Western laboratory-based narratives of the rise of Western reason, science, technology, and medicine elide these networks of experience, contact, and dialogue. Democracy, hierarchy and bureaucracy were similar composite formulations. The questions now asked are whether the Enlightenment or the Age of Reason, the Kantian, Boylean, Aristotelian Revolutions, the dissection of human bodies, agricultural enclosures in Tudor Britain and agricultural capitalism, Clerk-Maxwell or Lord Kelvin engineered the 'take-off' (to use Rostow's term) of the industrial revolution and Western science, technology and, medicine: the transition debates are a very rich field.

What caused Western industrialization and what were the factors behind the transition from feudalism to capitalism? Though these terms obscured bundles of questions behind what constituted feudalism and capitalism, the classic work on feudal France being by Marc Bloch, they were used to examine the rise of the moneyed professional and industrial urban middle class, through capital-intensive agriculture and rent from land. Moreover, famines, such as the potato famine in Ireland, landlessness, and destruction of subsistence livelihood led to freeing of labour for employment in factories. However, the urban industrialization in Britain was patchy, and the French Revolution did not, as Soboul pointed out, mean the rise of the middle class or industrial development, which proceed at a slower pace than in Britain, indeed as he says there were many Vendées. Contrary to Marx's prediction that because of British imperialism India would industrialize and experience internal revolution, India did not industrialize and is still struggling with a widespread agrarian crisis, partly because of the use of genetically modified seeds distributed by multinational companies, which destroy agricultural cycles while extracting genetic data, emaciating traditional agriculture.

From the 1970s, a school of historians (Gunder Frank, Wallerstein) introduced the notion of metropolis (read Western/developed) and periphery (read non-Western/underdeveloped); we shall use these terms in this sense. South American historiography pointed towards a conjunction between the rise of Western industrialism and the exfoliation and exploitation by the metropolis of the periphery. Varieties of historical fields are rediscovering zones of contact and sites of knowledge production, situated beyond the Western metropolis or laboratory. On the other hand, none can deny the discipline, logical rigour, industry and the celebrated Protestant work ethos described by Weber, and the now well-documented, disparate centres of British industrialization, which permitted women and men to migrate and marry at a later age, allowing for a drop in birth figures leading to greater capital accumulation within a relatively short time. There is a disjuncture therefore between ideas and structural change, differing hegemonies of causation, and different levels at which time and space changed.

World history, modernity, information society or civilizational slush?

The world has changed greatly since 1800. 'Modernity', though represented in the form of Westernization, fundamentally changed the world. The romantic notion that it was the West, or anthropology, that introduced violence in idyllic paradises has been convincingly theoretically and historically challenged. For example, Lévi-Strauss's description of the intrusion of writing, and therefore, of violence into the lives of the Nambikwara, an Amazonian Amerindian people, is used by Jacques Derrida to illustrate the point that violence was always already there, whether through script or through speech. Similarly, 'communalism' or Hindu and Muslim conflict existed in pre-British India. However, it is equally undeniable that the scale and the representation of such local conflict was altered through the colonial experience.

Civilizations are 'imagined communities' on a larger scale, at various points in time 'inventing traditions'. Of course, not all communities are imagined and not all traditions invented. However, any nation state claiming to represent a particular civilization can force the elevation of certain identities over others. For example, there is nothing in common between a Tunisian Muslim and a Bangladeshi Muslim unless they arrive in, for example, France or Germany, and are forced to choose their identities. Similarly, there is nothing that binds a Hindu from the south of India to one in the north except perhaps a commitment to the idea of the nation of India. Secularism, like religion, can be enforced by nation states but it is fundamentally a reflection of freedom of choice as well as a commitment to the secular ideal.

The notion of an 'information society' based on the Internet and telecommunications has some contradictions. As 'technopoles' such as Silicon Valley emerge, they generate technologies duplicated and implemented elsewhere. The notion of such concentration of intellectual force beyond race and class is daily challenged by nation states that have to deal with such diversity, and continuously changing transnational networks of people, information, finance, and commodities. States representing civilizational values, and agreed norms at international forums, are all in jeopardy simply because market expansion controls the logic of nation states.

If civilization is about shared meanings about right and wrong, we have never been further apart than in the present day, but if civilization is read as sharing of globally recognized symbols, institutions, forms, modes of speech, action, dress, politics and consumer goods, then we have been never closer. At the start of this present century, in a polarized world, one might argue that hegemonies of language, communication skills and systems of information have not created new elites in the sense of Old World revolutions but have redistributed power in an entirely new way to privilege corporations of disempowered workers, manipulating and manipulated by the information web.

Deep Kanta Lahiri-Choudhury

Bibliography

Anderson B. 1983. *Imagined communities: reflections on the rise and spread of nationalism.* London: Verso.

Balakrishnan G. 2000. 'Hardt and Negri's Empire', *New Left Review*, 5, September–October.

Barber B. 1996. *Jihad vs. McWorld: how globalism and tribalism are reshaping the world.* New York: Ballantine.

Castells M. 2000. *The information age*, updated edition, 3 vols. Oxford: Blackwell.

Chakrabarti D. K., Singh, R. N., Lahiri-Choudhury, D. K. and Tewari, R. Forthcoming. 'Further thoughts on the Harappan issue in western Uttar Pradesh: sites in the Saharanpur-Muzaffarnagar-Haridwar area', *South Asian Studies*, The British Academy.

Chatterjee P. 1993. *Nationalist thought and the colonial world: a derivative discourse,* 2nd edition. Minneapolis: University of Minnesota Press.

Gluck C. 1985. *Japan's modern myths.* Princeton: Princeton University Press.

Lahiri-Choudhury, D. K. 2004. 'The sinews of panic and the nerves of empire: the imagined states' entanglement with information panic, India, c. 1880–1912', *Modern Asian Studies,* 38, 4, 965–1002.

Raj K. 2006. *Relocating modern science: circulation and the construction of scientific knowledge in South Asia and Europe.* Delhi: Permanent Black.

Related essays
abolitionism; Africa; America; Asia; biopatents; borders and borderlands; capitalism; China; Chinese medicine; Christianity; Cold War; commodity trading; contract and indentured labourers; convergence and divergence; corporations; cosmopolitanism and universalism; democracy; development and growth; developmental taxonomies; dress; empire and migration; European Union (EU); genetically modified organisms (GMOs); Ghose, Aurobindo Ackroyd; globalization; indigenous knowledges; industrialization; information economy; internationalisms; Internet; Islam; Japan; knowledge; liberalism; life and physical sciences; mapping; medicine; modernity; museums; nation and state; Pax Americana; regional communities; regions; religion; Romanticism; slavery; spatial regimes; technologies; telephone and telegraphy; textile; trade; tropics; war; wildlife films; world orders

Ghose, Aurobindo Ackroyd 1872–1950

Aurobindo inspired the Indian *Swadeshi* (indigenous enterprise) and Boycott movement (aimed at foreign goods) between 1905 and 1910. He forged transnational networks, stretching from the Indian regions of Bengal, Madras, Pune, Punjab, and French Pondicherry, to London, Canada, and the United States, and his influence reached as far as Parisian anarchists, and Russian nihilists. Among Aurobindo's political achievements were his insistence that the Indian National Congress adopt the principle of absolute independence, and advocate *Swadeshi* and

the boycott for all India, leading to the split in the Congress party between Moderates and Extremists in 1907. Inspired by the French Revolution, and a brilliant classics scholar, Aurobindo acquired French, Italian, Bengali, and Sanskrit. Sent to England in 1879, he read for the Indian Civil Service examination (ICS) and the Classical Tripos at King's College, Cambridge, passing the ICS examination, but failing the riding test that was required of candidates. The Criminal Investigation Department (CID) arrested him in 1908 in Calcutta, for initiating secret societies that planned assassinations, and imported and distributed bomb-making manuals from Paris. Imprisoned for a year, he was released on the grounds of insufficient evidence. Aurobindo published *Karmayogin,* an English newspaper, in 1909. When the Government moved to arrest him for sedition, he left for French Pondicherry, beyond British authority. Aurobindo then retired from political life to concentrate on yogic spiritualism, refusing offers to rejoin politics, including invitations to preside over the Indian National Congress, though he condemned Nazism and Japanese aggression. His Western admirers saw him as a key figure who could think across artificial boundaries of 'West' and 'East', seeing elements of thinkers such as Marx, Hegel, and Schopenhauer entwined with thought derived from indigenous Indian sources. In turn, Western thinkers such as Michael Murphy and Ken Wilber have been heavily influenced by Aurobindo. Spiritually inspiring, called a prophet and poet of Indian nationalism, Sri Aurobindo, as he became known, never emerged out of the *ashram* (spiritual community) that grew up around him into an international city. Near the *ashram,* the experimental international city of Auroville still exists today with nearly 2,000 members from around the world; it also has a transnational network of support groups called Auroville International.

Deep Kanta Lahiri-Choudhury

Bibliography
Nirodbaran 1990. *Sri Aurobindo.* Pondicherry: Sri Aurobindo Ashram Trust.

Related essays
anarchism; civilizations; consumer society; decolonization; empires and imperialism; Gandhi, Mohandas Karamchand;

Garvey, Marcus Mosiah; Guevara, Ernesto ('Che'); humanities; Kessler, Harry von; knowledge; nationalism; pacifism; Schwimmer, Rosika; terrorism; Westernization; Williams, James Dixon; yoga

Class

The existence of classes is one of the main features of modern societies, reflecting differences in status, power and wealth of the members of these societies. These differences are not unique to some modern societies, but occur in all societies, although form and visibility might vary strongly between modern societies. This existence of classes in all modern societies and their objective and partly subjective commonality is the first reason for transnational relations between the same classes in different societies, although the subjective consciousness of this commonality varies in time. Next to this commonality between classes in all modern societies, more or less members of some classes have developed stronger transnational relations as a part of their construction and self-identification, also depending on the international position of their nation state.

International variation in classes

There are many definitions of social classes, but most refer to differences in status, power and wealth/income, which are related to the occupations of the members of a modern society. Another general term of these differences is social stratification, referring to a layer-like buildup of societal inequality (strata). The early modern political philosophers and scientists (Montesquieu, Pareto) started to compare the social stratifications of various European societies, not only within Europe (France versus England), but also with non-European societies (Persia, China). The initial main aim of these comparisons was to criticize the political, economic or religious situation and inequalities in the thinker's own society. The American Revolution, the French Revolution and the Restoration gave extra impulses to these comparisons of political and social stratification in different societies, especially republican against anciens régimes (for instance de Tocqueville), to understand the new dynamics of society. These cross-national differences in inequality or social strata became also an aspect of 19th-century

modernization and industrialization theories (either authoritarian, liberal or socialist). They referred to both liberalization from the ancien régime (king, nobility, established church, guilds, etc.) and to the development of new economic strata or classes, for instance the capitalist and the labourer class (Karl Marx). According to these frames, modernization and industrialization theories should be applicable more or less to all societies, and thus the strata and classes of these societies should be comparable. Therefore, societies, depending on their development and modernization, should differ in the nature of their social stratification and the amount of mobility between these strata. This should not only be true for European and American societies but also for 'stagnating' Asian societies, like India and China. The cross-national variations in classes and mobility between these strata became important to prove the correctness of the contradictory liberal and socialist modernization theories. The rise of new classes or strata at the end of the 19th century (managerial class, skilled labourers, white-collar middle classes) and the political decline of the last features of the ancien régime after the First World War in most European societies increased further this need for scientific study of strata, classes and the degree of their openness for persons from the lower classes, because they played a significant role in the ideological battles between capitalism, social-democrats, communism and fascism. The study of social stratification and mobility became (and still is) one of the core topics of a new science called sociology. Most studies of classes and strata remain restricted to one or a few national societies in this period (Max Weber is an exception). The American cultural dominance at the end of the Second World War, and the Cold War, intensified the need for comparisons, both between the US and Europe (meritocratic society versus class-ridden societies) and between Communist and capitalist societies. In the 1950s, this need triggered the first scientific cross-national comparisons of classes and mobility between classes. They have since evolved into attempts to build common scales for different societies across the globe.

Looking for universal class scales

Prestige scales are the oldest type of social stratification scales and, perhaps, the best known. Prestige scales refer to the symbolic domain of stratification. The purpose of these scales is to represent 'collective perceptions and beliefs' about the ranking of occupational hierarchies. The usual way to measure these perceptions and beliefs is to ask individuals or experts to rank a number of well-known occupations according to their honorific standing in society. These individual rankings are then combined into one scale: the occupational prestige scale. These types of scales have been built up in various societies since 1950, especially in America, Eastern and Western Europe and in Asia. Despite the differences between these societies, the similarities between these nationally based prestige scales are very large. Donald Treiman (1977) used these highly correlating prestige scales to produce one international prestige scale, which might indicate that the honorific standing of occupations is more or less equal in modern societies with large differences in stage of development, political-economic systems and historical backgrounds. Changes occurring in time in the relative scaling of occupations are smaller than expected if one compares various scales which were constructed in the same society in different decennia. The main problem with these prestige scales is the disagreement regarding the underlying causes of occupational ranking. One stance is that judgments about social standing are sensitive to honorific considerations (for instance based on pre-modern strata) which cannot be equated with socioeconomic factors like income and education, whereas the opposing camp argues that socioeconomic factors, like income and education, play a dominant role in ranking occupational perceptions, and that the prestige scale measures more or less the generalized desirability of occupations.

Socioeconomic stratification scales try to capture the cultural and economic resources connected with occupations. In their simplest but still effective form they represent an averaging of the mean income and educational level of all individuals within an occupation and the projecting of these averages of occupations into one socioeconomic scale. Comparable socioeconomic scales have also been developed in other societies. Based on the same logic Ganzeboom, de Graaf, Treiman and DeLeeuw (1992) have developed an international socioeconomic index, which is applied to many modern societies and is used in many cross-national comparisons, not only by academics but also by international organizations like the Organisation for Economic Co-operation and Development (OECD) to compare educational systems cross-nationally (see PISA-studies, www.pisa.oecd.org).

So the international variation of classes is relatively small. Despite various claims of the dwindling importance of classes in postmodern societies, the empirical proof of that claim has not been more than anecdotal. However, the social and political importance of some classes (unskilled and semi-skilled labourers, small farmers) has declined as a consequence of economic and technological changes, which have undermined their position, while new classes (professionals in the public and service sectors) have been created by the same processes.

International variation in mobility between classes

The first empirical and comparative studies of cross-national variance in mobility ended in the conclusion that the overall pattern of mobility was 'much the same' in Western societies, contrary to the expectation of a huge difference between the US and Europe. These first empirical studies did not distinguish between two possible causes of cross-national variance in vertical mobility. The first cause for a change in intergenerational mobility in a society is the difference between the available positions for older generations and those for the succeeding generations. If, in a society, there are more high-ranking positions available for the younger generation compared to the older generation (due to changes in the socioeconomic development of that society), there is more upward intergenerational mobility, which is structural, because it originates from a change in the structure of occupations. The opposite is true if there are fewer high-ranking positions available for the younger generation compared to the older generation in a society. In that case, there is more downward intergenerational mobility which is also structural because it also originates from a change in the structure of occupations. The second cause for a change in intergenerational mobility is the contrast between two generations in the allocation and selection rules for the attainment of positions in the social stratification, for instance the increased importance of education or the decreased importance of birth. This is called a change in circulation mobility. Both causes of changes in intergenerational mobility can be relevant at the same time and, in studying mobility, one must try to disentangle those two causes. On the basis of this distinction between structural and circulation mobility, it was hypothesized that the latter was basically the same in all industrial societies with a market economy and a nuclear family system (both capitalist and socialist), while the former could be drastically different. Erikson and Goldthorpe (1992) confirmed this by finding basically the same circulation mobility pattern for Western and Eastern Europe, North America, Australia and Japan, rejecting both liberal and Marxist theories on the relation between industrialization and mobility. They also concluded that arguments for culturally caused differentiations in mobility are overstated, although to dismiss cultural influences on mobility entirely would be to go too far (for instance, they found some long-standing effects of the German apprenticeship system). They admit that political intervention (incomes policy, educational reforms) may be a source of cross-national differences in mobility, but without the necessity that this variation should systematically be related to regimes or governments of various types.

Recent studies have found more cross-national variations in circulation mobility. But even in these studies the similarities in the effects of the parental class on their children's educational and occupational attainment are large in comparison with the international variations in these effects. Moreover, these cross-national variations in circulation mobility do not coincide with simple distinctions between capitalist versus communist societies, or the US versus Europe.

Transnational commonality between classes

Given the large commonality of classes in different modern societies, one might expect many transnational aspects in the composition and self-identity of these classes. However, three caveats are necessary.

The first caveat is that one should distinguish between the transnational aspects in the behaviour and culture of individual members of certain classes and the transnational aspects of class itself. This important distinction is analogous to the classical distinction of Karl Marx between the 'Klasse an sich' (class

in itself) and the 'Klasse für sich' (class for itself). Given that most classes are not well organized internationally or are very divided and that international organizations (notably the Socialist Internationals or international labour unions) did not survive nationalism, two world wars, decolonization, the Cold War, and globalization, one can hardly speak of any institutionalized and permanent transnational characteristic of any class in modern society. Only the behaviour and culture of some individual members of certain occupations within classes is becoming more or less transnational. Today a transnational split within many classes and occupations can be found, leaving one part focused on the local or national scene and the other part on a regional or global context.

The second caveat is that changes in the degree of transnational characteristics of classes in a certain nation state depend also on the nation's position within the world system. In the last two centuries the core of the world system has travelled from France via the UK, Germany and the Soviet Union to the US. The latter's core position might be threatened by China and India. The same two centuries have witnessed the rise and decline of open colonialism in Latin America, Asia and Africa, a process which strongly affected the transnational characteristics of class in these colonialized and decolonialized societies. Classes in societies like France and Germany, which lost their central position in the world system, might observe a drastic change in their transnational behaviours and influences, while classes in societies like the Netherlands, which had a semi-peripheral position during these two centuries, observe only a change in the direction of transnational influences (English instead of French as the international language; the US as the cultural point of reference instead of France, Germany or the UK). Classes in colonialized societies like India have experienced a very strong transnational influence by the colonial power on their construction and self-identification, while that influence has waned after their decolonization and might have been partly replaced by transnational influences from other societies, like the US or Russia.

The third caveat is that any claim of an increased transnational character of classes at the end of the 20th century needs precise empirical scrutiny, because anecdotal evidence about classes in a global economy might be misleading and suffer from historical short-sightedness. The few internationally oriented members of the national business elite who get a lot of publicity can hide many nationally oriented members of the same national business elite, who are not so visible or vocal. The increase in the number of foreign-born directors of the major firms of a nation state cannot be equated with a decline of the national business elite, because the former can be just transients while the latter wields the real power in that society. Moreover, the purported newness and increase of the trans-national aspects of class need to be placed in perspective. Before the nationalistic 19th century, universities, churches and nobility were more embedded in a transnational network than their nation state was. The level of inter-national trade before the First World War was higher than for the best part of the 20th century. Evaluation of transnational class devel-opments needs to have a longer time scale that just a few decades or centuries.

Despite a lack of sound empirical studies of the transnational characteristics of classes, I now try to sketch some examples of the chan-ging transnational character of segments or occupations within the upper and middle classes.

Segments of the upper classes: transnational business elites and nobility

During the last two centuries, with the rise of the nation state, many members of the local elites of counties, provinces and regions became members of national elites of that state, as a part of successful nation build-ing. Today one can see a development of a global economy, an increasing popularity of international business schools and the avail-ability of international communication on a large scale. Nevertheless, although rather scarce, research shows that so far there are few indications of the rise of an international business elite. In the boards of executives in countries like France, Germany, Great Britain and the United States the overwhelmingly majority of members of these boards have the same nationality as the countries where these corporations are located. The only exceptions are foreign subsidiaries. Many executives have followed an educational career in their country of birth. This might change in the future, but until today it is very likely that top managers in the core countries of America, Europe and Asia have started in a mainly local

career instead of a global one. However, top managers in the (semi-)peripheral core coun-tries of America, Europe and Asia might start in a mainly global career, but it is debateable whether this is a sign of a global economy or a shift in the power balance within the eco-nomic world system.

Contrary to the case of business elites, European nobilities had long had a stronger transnational dimension that went beyond politics and cross-dynastic weddings. This was obvious during the period before the rise of the nation state, as noble elites built and cherished family ties all across Europe. The rise of the nation state and nationalism decreased this level of transnationalism of the nobles, but until today the European nobility has shown a high degree of transnationalism, compared to other strata. With the de jure or de facto loss of nobilities' separate legal sta-tus and ascribed privileges during the 19th and 20th centuries, a noble title is assumed to have become an irrelevance in gaining an elite position in a modern nation state, because its social and cultural capital has become obso-lete and unproductive. This de facto loss of its ascribed privileges is one of the best examples of a change of the allocation-and-selection rules for attaining positions within the social stratification, needed for a change in circula-tion mobility.

However, studies of the elite positions held by members of Dutch noble families in the 20th century have shown that they still have more elite positions than comparable mem-bers of high-bourgeois families. Moreover, the likelihood of an elite position being held by members of Dutch noble families has barely decreased for different generations of the nobility, also in contrast to the high bour-geoisie (patricians). There are empirical indi-cations that this 'constant noble advantage' is also true for the nobility of other European societies. This advantage of the Dutch nobil-ity in the 20th century contradicts a basic sociological assumption about the changes of the rules for attainment of the highest social classes in modern societies: high positions and professions have become increasingly more open to people with capacities based on their own achievements and less open to persons with only ascribed characteris-tics. The number of potential candidates for elite positions in modern societies has risen strongly, thanks to modernization and dem-ocratization and the ensuing changes in the allocation-and-selection rules. The resulting strong competition for elite positions among the many competitors can make 'old-fashioned' characteristics, like the transnational aspect of noble social and cultural capital, again relevant as an efficient and effective means for selection, while modern characteristics like education only become necessary but not sufficient conditions. The 'outdated' transnational aspect of this noble social and cultural capital has become again an advantage and a productive characteristic in a globalizing world.

Divided occupations of the upper middle classes: professors and lawyers

Professors at national universities are in principle members of two communities. Their first community is their own society. Universities are paid more or less by their government which regulates them more or less. They are supposed to teach in the national language and to study topics which are relevant for their own nation state or important actors within that society. They also serve often as members of important councils, committees and other bodies of the government, political movements, employers and business organizations. Their second community is international scientific networks. They present the results of their studies in international conferences and journals, cooperate or compete with their colleagues from other societies in their research and have to keep in touch with their foreign colleagues to update their knowledge for research and teaching. This dual relationship with the national society and the international community of scientists forces university professors, especially from the smaller or peripheral countries, often to make a choice: either they orient themselves to their own society but have a less strong orientation to the international community of scientists, or they orient themselves to this latter international community but are less visible and useful for national society. The contradictions between this dual membership of professors grew during the 20th century. Universities and sciences have become more internationally oriented because research-oriented firms and enterprises became internationally and multinationally orientated. This globalization changed the nationally based laboratories of research-oriented firms into truly international ones. But this trend meant also that scientists connected with these laboratories were forced to compete on an international basis instead of a national one. The same trend can be seen in those industrial and service sectors which depend heavily on the applied results of science. As a consequence of globalization, the firms of these sectors are no longer fully dependent on the cooperation of universities within the country of their establishment, but they can get these applied results of science from many part of the world, with comparable costs and benefits.

Professors in nation states who have retained their own national languages experience an even stronger contradiction between this dual membership, because of the minority status of their language. We only point here to the fact that this unimportance is not restricted to the scientific sector, but is also true for the industrial, trade and service sectors. The number of publications in international peer-reviewed scientific journals and the number of citations of these publications in the same journals have become important criteria, both for obtaining a slice of the financial resources and for promotion within the academic hierarchy. This decline of their national language can affect the transnational construction and the self-identity of the academically and culturally oriented upper middle classes.

The law has always been strongly connected with that of national states. The main reason for this strong connection is the national state as the source of law making and law enforcement. The monopoly of the state on the use of force and violence, and on taxation, goes together with the importance of the national state in all juridical affairs. This development also focused the activities of most lawyers on the national law, both civil and penal. International law was very weakly developed and in any case not an important part of the juridical system. In the middle of the 20th century, most lawyers who were inscribed as members of the Bar worked as independently established professionals or as partners within a small law firm. These firms had only a small number of non-partner lawyers, mostly freshly recruited from university and still in training on the job. Between these firms and independently established lawyers some division of labour had emerged, however informal and non-public.

During the second half of the 20th century, the importance of European, supranational and international law increased.

This importance grew as a consequence of the rise of the European Union and the globalization of the world economy. The rise of the European Union means that an important part of the civil law is more and more formulated outside the national state by the Union (European Commission, European Parliament). Also, normal lawsuits do not end any longer within the borders of the national state, but can be continued at the European level, often with results which strongly affect the national arena. National European lawyers are forced by this rise of the European Union to include European law and regulations as an important aspect of their juridical activities. But by offering these European services to clients they also meet competition from other European law firms outside their own countries which can offer the same services. Thus as a consequence of the rise of the European Union, national law firms meet more and more competition from other European law firms and one possible answer to this competition is cooperation or even fusion between law firms from different European states.

The globalization of the world economy promoted the rise of multinational firms, and more cooperation or growing fusion between firms from different societies, also outside Europe. This increased the degree of contact between the different juridical systems of different parts of the world and the importance of supranational law (especially trade law). The growing demand for this juridical knowledge also forces law firms to specialize further and to cooperate with law firms in those societies which are important for their clients. The consequence of this internationalization of a part of the activities of national lawyers in big law firms is that their orientation is no longer only directed at the national state but has become divided between the traditional national orientation to national law and the developing international orientation to European and supranational law and on laws of other societies. This decline of the national orientation of a proportion of lawyers will affect the transnational construction and the self-identity of the academically and culturally oriented upper middle classes.

These examples show that there is not a new and clear-cut relationship between class and transnational influences on the social situation and self-identity. Old characteristics might revive and classes and occupations split into a local and an international part. This is not only true for upper- and middle-class occupations, but might also be applicable for occupations of the lower classes, like truck drivers, plumbers (also the non-Polish) and other skilled labour occupations, which have become scarce due to the democratization of non-vocational education.

Jaap Dronkers

Bibliography

Erikson R. and Goldthorpe J. H. 1992. *The constant flux: a study of class mobility in industrial societies*. Oxford: Clarendon.

Ganzeboom H. B. G., Graaf P. de and Treiman D. J. with DeLeeuw J. 1992. 'A standard international socio-economic index of occupational status', *Social Science Research*, 21, 1–56.

Hartmann M. 1999. 'Auf dem Weg zur transnationalen Bourgeoisie', *Leviathan*, 27, 1, 113–41.

Lenski G. E. 1966. *Power and privilege: a theory of social stratification*. New York: McGraw-Hill

Schijf H. J. and van den Broeke-George J. 2004. 'Recruitment of members of Dutch noble and high-bourgeois families to elite positions in the 20th century', *Social Science Information*, 43, 3, 435–75.

Sklair L 2001. *The transnational capitalist class*. Oxford: Blackwell.

Stokman F. N., Ziegler R. and Scott J. (eds) 1985. *Networks of corporate power: a comparative analysis of ten countries*. Oxford: Oxford University Press.

Treiman D. 1977. *Occupational prestige in comparative perspective*. New York: Academic Press.

Classical music

From the mid 19th century to the present day, transnational forces have powerfully affected the course of Western classical music, shaping the creative activities of performers, composers, and performing institutions, along with the experience of listeners. ('Western classical music' here refers to that creative tradition that began in medieval Europe before the year 1000 and continued to evolve over the next several centuries, becoming more harmonically complex and more texturally dense.) The movement of peoples – particularly the flow of composers, conductors, and performers – across state and hemispheric boundaries has significantly shaped the history of Western classical music. In addition, emerging technological developments in the 20th century, especially in the realm of recorded sound, have expanded the outreach of Western classical music. In considering these themes, this essay will focus mainly, though not exclusively, on the musical scene in the United States.

In the 1920s, Aaron Copland, who was destined to become America's most celebrated composer, journeyed to Paris to study composition. The image of the young American working in the French capital under the guidance of the learned Nadia Boulanger, whose knowledge spanned five centuries of Western classical music, is instructive. Copland had gone to France to hone his compositional skill, and under Boulanger's tutelage deepened his understanding of harmony, form, and style. While in Paris, Copland studied the work of an eclectic group of European composers, from Monteverdi to Mahler. In this culturally rich environment, the music of an entire continent became part of his daily life. In France, this Jewish American from Brooklyn met the Russian Igor Stravinsky, studied his music, and claimed later it would influence his own work. Copland encountered another Russian transplant in Paris, Serge Koussevitsky, a gifted conductor who would one day champion his music, and the American also crossed paths with innovative figures like Erik Satie and Darius Milhaud, who were helping to reshape the way composers conceived of their art. Together, the French city and Boulanger's studio served as a musical crossroads, a place where geographic boundaries meant little. For Copland, this overseas experience nourished his creative potential, helping him develop the unique voice that would make him one of the 20th century's leading composers.

Such creative convergences, along with the transplantation of musicians from one place to another, have long influenced the development of composers, performers, and listeners. Serge Koussevitsky, who had enthralled Parisian audiences with his path-breaking programmes in the early 1920s, would leave the French city for Boston in 1924, where as music director of the Boston Symphony for the next 25 years he helped shape the musical culture of a leading ensemble, a major city, and his new country. Russian-born, with a deep commitment to performing contemporary music, Koussevitsky introduced audiences in Boston and beyond to the works of Bartók, Hindemith, Stravinsky, Ravel, Prokofiev, Copland, and others. Whether listeners attended one of his concerts in Boston's Symphony Hall or tuned in to one of his radio broadcasts, the case of Koussevitsky illustrates how a gifted artist – who had left one country for another – could compel a generation of listeners to expand its musical horizons.

Earlier, the contours of American musical life were influenced in a rather different way – by the movement of peoples between German-speaking Europe and the United States. Classical music had long been an intrinsic part of German culture and in the second half of the 19th century and the early years of the 20th, America's developing symphonic tradition was shaped by the employment of German conductors and musicians who played a key role in America's evolving musical life. With their passion for orchestral music, highly trained German musicians – with a propensity to perform the works of Bach, Handel, Mozart, and Beethoven – contributed to the successful establishment of symphony orchestras in cities throughout the country. If one considers the rosters of conductors and the orchestras they led in this period, one is struck by the Germanness of the American symphony orchestra, an institution that played an important cultural role in a society undergoing rapid urbanization. Throughout America, orchestras were typically headed by and comprised mainly (though not exclusively) of Germans, who were thought to possess a unique capacity to produce symphonic music of the highest calibre.

The following list of German conductors and the cities in which they worked evinces the extent to which the German musical tradition was transplanted in urban America during a formative period in the history of classical music in the United States: Carl Bergmann (New York), Leopold and Walter Damrosch (New York), Max Fiedler (Boston), Wilhelm Gericke (Boston), George Henschel (Boston), Ernst Kunwald (Cincinnati), Karl Muck (Boston), Emil Oberhoffer (Minneapolis), Emil Paur (New York and Pittsburgh), Karl Pohlig (Philadelphia), Fritz Scheel (San Francisco and New York), Anton Seidl (New York), Fredrick Stock (Chicago), and Theodore Thomas (New York and Chicago). Moreover, it should be noted that the cultural vitality and sophistication of many a city was tied to the success of its orchestra, and an ensemble's prestige was linked to its capacity to engage German maestros and players.

A key figure in the growth of the American symphony orchestra and, more generally, of classical music in the United States was the German Theodore Thomas, who came to America as a boy in 1845, part of the wave of German immigrants who left Europe for the United States in those years. According to a contemporary, Thomas, who would go on to found the Chicago Symphony Orchestra, was responsible for teaching people 'how to listen to beautiful music from Bach to Richard Strauss' (Levine 1988, 112). By the end of his life, writes historian Lawrence Levine, Thomas 'had a permanent orchestra with a guaranteed budget and the right to concentrate on what he considered the highest forms of musical expression' (ibid., 118–19). And for Thomas, that often meant the music of four German-speaking composers: Bach, Handel, Mozart, and Beethoven, whom he referred to as the 'sons of God' (ibid., 118).

But the Western classical music tradition was not confined to Europe and North America. Indeed, in considering the current international music scene, one is especially struck by the prominence of Asian musicians. Clearly, the influence of Western classical music has radiated outward from Europe and North America to Asia and beyond.

In the case of Japan, interest in Western music stretches back to the late 19th century, an era when Japan's drive to modernize led the country to embrace many facets of Western culture, including music. Thus, Western music would be introduced for pragmatic rather than aesthetic reasons, and in 1878 the government established a department to study

it. Seeking to modernize the educational system, Japanese public schools stopped teaching traditional music in this period, replacing it with music from the West, which was frequently taught by educators from outside Japan. Toward the end of the 19th century, some (though not all) Japanese composers began writing pieces in the Western classical style, and the first symphonic work by a Japanese composer appeared in 1912. The 1920s saw the establishment of the first full-time Japanese symphony orchestra in Tokyo, with Japanese musicians and a Japanese conductor.

According to musicologist Hwee Been Koh (1998), after World War 2, innovative styles in the realm of Western classical music became popular among Japanese composers, whose work was informed by contemporary techniques from Europe and the United States. Indeed, during the postwar American occupation, Takemitsu Tōru (1906–96), who would become Japan's most distinguished composer, listened intensively to recordings of Western classical music, especially the orchestral works of contemporary American composers. And in the 1950s, Tokyo's Toho School of Music provided the young Ozawa Seiji the opportunity to study Western music, particularly conducting and composition. (Significantly, Ozawa's principal teacher at the school, Saitō Hideō, had studied in Germany in the 1920s and 1930s, and upon returning, he would become a mentor for young Japanese musicians.) Ozawa left Japan to continue his training in Europe and North America, studying conducting in France, the United States, and Germany. Ultimately, Ozawa would hold a series of important posts in the United States, culminating in 1973 with his appointment as music director of the Boston Symphony Orchestra. Today, as head of the Vienna State Opera, Ozawa occupies one of the most prestigious posts in all of Western classical music.

The rich history of China's encounter with Western classical music stretches back to the start of the 17th century, when an Italian missionary seeking to introduce Christianity into China presented the emperor with a clavichord. However intriguing the latter event, a more significant development – the emergence of China's first Western symphonic ensemble – occurred three centuries later with the establishment of the Shanghai Municipal Orchestra in 1920. The orchestra's founder and conductor was an Italian pianist, Mario Paci, who had performed in the city the previous year. Though Shanghai had a vibrant traditional music scene, relatively little Western classical music was performed there, a source of dismay for some of the city's thousands of European residents. Mario Paci would fill that gap, having decided Shanghai would be an ideal place to live. After holding auditions for his new ensemble, Paci planned the programmes for the 1920–21 season, which opened with Beethoven's iconic Fifth Symphony. During the orchestra's first season, Paci's audience encountered the music of Grieg, Tchaikovsky, Liszt, Rimsky-Korsakov, and other Western masters. But his listeners were all non-Chinese, a result of discriminatory policies that prohibited the Chinese from entering the Town Hall where the orchestra performed. Paci opposed such policies, realizing they would stunt the orchestra's development and dampen its impact on the city's cultural life. Due partly to his efforts, the ban was lifted in 1925 and growing numbers of Chinese citizens began to attend the concerts, though the orchestra had no Chinese members in this period. Within three years of its founding, a Japanese musicologist called the group the 'best orchestra in the Far East' (Melvin and Cai 2004, 39), and Paci, having introduced Western classical music to a growing number of Chinese citizens, had created an ensemble that would become an important institution in Shanghai's cultural life.

A final theme concerns the technology of recorded sound and its influence on the dissemination of Western classical music. The advent and development of sound recordings and the marketing of celebrated artists has had a powerful impact on listeners and musicians, exposing countless classical music consumers to performances they could not otherwise have heard. Certain milestones in the history of recorded music, which improved the fidelity of recorded sound, should be noted: in 1877, Thomas Edison made the first recordings using a cylinder; in 1888, the gramophone, using flat discs rather than cylinders, was patented; in 1925, electrical recordings allowed for the production of the 78rpm disc; in 1948, the first long-playing microgroove records permitted longer playing time and better fidelity than did 78rpm discs; in 1957, stereophonic records offered more spacious, clearer sound; and in 1983, the compact disc further improved the sonic quality of recorded music.

In the late 19th and early 20th centuries, as singers, instrumentalists, and symphony orchestras began making commercial recordings in Europe and the United States, a growing number of people could encounter the work of distinguished artists. While listeners in major American or European cities were able to hear important performers live, for those living elsewhere, it was difficult to hear leading musicians or celebrated symphonic ensembles on a regular basis. But as the 20th century unfolded, recording companies in Europe and the United States began recording the major works in the Western classical canon, affording increasing numbers of listeners the opportunity to hear pre-eminent musicians and orchestras. Moreover, after 1900, major recording companies in Europe and the United States worked to expand both domestic and overseas markets for their product. As the research of Pekka Gronow (1981, 1983) suggests, as firms in Germany, England, France, and the United States sought to increase record sales around the world, the recording industry became globalized. While it is difficult to identify precisely what portion of this growing export market Western classical recordings comprised, one can say that people outside Europe and the United States were increasingly able to purchase Western classical recordings. In recent decades, listeners throughout the world have become enthusiastic consumers of such recordings.

Today, a reflective concertgoer would recognize that transnational factors continue to shape the contours of Western classical music, informing the experiences of listeners and musicians. Recently, New York audiences were excited to hear the celebrated Chinese pianist Lang Lang play Beethoven's Fifth Piano Concerto with the New York Philharmonic under the direction of the Italian conductor Ricardo Muti. As Lang Lang strode onto the stage to perform this beloved piece by a German composer, one might have pondered the following: he had grown up in Shenyang; he had received his musical training in Beijing and Philadelphia; and he now records for Deutsche Grammophon, a multinational conglomerate that has fuelled his enormously successful global career – a career devoted to performing the music of Bach, Beethoven, Tchaikovsky, and other exemplars of a Western creative tradition that stretches back more than a thousand years.

Jonathan Rosenberg

Bibliography

Day T. 2000. *A century of recorded music: listening to musical history*. New Haven: Yale University Press.

Eppstein U. 1994. *The beginnings of Western music in Meiji era Japan*. Lewiston: Edwin Mellen.

Gronow P. 1981. 'The record industry comes to the Orient', *Ethnomusicology*, 25, 2, 251–84.

Gronow P. 1983. 'The record industry: the growth of a mass medium', *Popular Music*, 3, 1, 53–75.

Horowitz J. 2005. *Classical music in America: a history of its rise and fall*. New York: Norton.

Hwee Been Koh J. 1998. *East and West: the aesthetics and musical time of Toru Takemitsu*. Unpublished doctoral dissertation, Boston University.

Levine L. 1988. *High brow/low brow: the emergence of cultural hierarchy in America*. Cambridge, MA: Harvard University Press.

Melvin S. and Cai J. 2004. *Rhapsody in red: how Western classical music became Chinese*. New York: Algora.

Related essays

Cantonese opera; China: executives and professionals; human mobility; Italian opera; Japan; kindergarten; labour migrations; music; orchestras; performing artists; Westernization

Climate change

The one constant of climate is that it changes. The pattern of these changes has been the subject of speculation and study for perhaps as long as human history. What is new is the study of how human actions have altered the climate in the past and continue to do so at an accelerating rate. These studies are accompanied by attempts to write future climate history by projecting current knowledge about the climate system onto alternative scenarios of future human activity. The history of climate change is both an accounting of what has happened to the climate prior to and during human existence, as well as the process by which natural and anthropogenic climate change have been studied and described.

First, it is important to identify the relationship between weather and climate. Weather is the daily set of meteorological conditions that we experience locally. Local climate is the 40-year average of climate variables, regional and global climate is the 40-year average of the weather variables for a region or spatially averaged for the planet as a whole. Even though there are variations from mean values for temperature or precipitation, these long-term averages convey a sense of place and dictate appropriate agriculture, buildings and even cultural characteristics of entire societies. The variations can also be averaged to arrive at a normal range of weather conditions such as the frequency of heat waves or droughts.

The planetary mechanics theory of ice ages

There is evidence that the Mesozoic era 100 million years ago was significantly warmer than it is today. For the past million years, it appears that the Earth has been subject to several alternating ice ages and interglacial warming periods like our current Holocene that began about 10,000 years ago. The timing of the ice ages and relatively short intermediate warm periods have a frequency of approximately 100,000 years.

The realization that there has been at least one past ice age developed gradually in the 19th century. The German-born Swiss geologist, Jean de Charpentier, studied glaciers and developed the argument in the 1830s for extensive past glaciers to explain the polished bedrock and the appearance of large boulders many kilometres from their place of origin. This contrasted with the traditional view that these marks were evidence of the great biblical flood and supported the model of slow geological processes advocated by Charles Lyell, the Scottish developer of 'Uniformitarianism', a theory rejecting the abrupt changes described in the Bible. Louis Agassiz, a Swiss-born scientist, adduced additional evidence with his *Origins of ice ages* in 1840. Agassiz was also a great palaeontologist but unlike Lyell never accepted Darwinian evolution even after moving to America and becoming the foremost scientist there. By the 1860s, the existence of a past ice age was generally accepted in Europe and North America, but John Muir still met scepticism in his first published paper in 1871 when he proposed that Yosemite Valley in California had been formed by glaciers like those he had seen in Alaska.

Attempts to unravel the mystery of the ice ages in the 19th and early 20th centuries shifted to planetary mechanics. The first to recognize that the Earth's eccentric orbital motion might be related to ice ages appears to have been the French mathematician, Joseph Adhémar, who proposed it in his book, *Revolutions de la mer* in 1842. James Croll, a janitor at the Andersonian College and Museum in Scotland, while browsing in the library after hours, came across Adhémar's book and the updated calculations of the Earth's orbit by the French astronomer Urbain LeVerrier. Having taught himself physics, Croll developed a mathematical theory that the eccentricities in the Earth's orbit would alter the amount of sunlight hitting the Earth's surface. He was also apparently the first to recognize the role of large ice sheets in reflecting sunlight back to space, and the importance of ocean currents, but erroneously concluded that the last ice age had ended 80,000 years earlier, and that ice ages alternated in the Northern and Southern hemispheres.

It remained for a Serbian mathematician, Milutin Milankovitch, to build on Croll's insights and develop a robust mathematical model that gave a quantitative prediction of the frequency of ice ages. Milankovitch, a professor at the University of Belgrade, began his work in 1912 and completed it while in prison during World War I. His insight about the different reflecting properties of oceans and land masses, plus his use of improved orbital calculations by Ludwig Pilgrim, provided what he thought was a final solution to the theory of ice ages. He eventually published a full accounting in 1941 just in time for World War 2 to divert attention from it. In 1970, American chemical oceanographers Wally Broecker and Jan van Donk published evidence from deep seabed sediments that confirmed the predicted 100,000-year Milankovitch cycle, and cast further doubt on the heat-trapping theory of climate. Throughout the 19th and early 20th centuries the planetary mechanics theory of ice ages developed through communication among individual Continental scientists and mathematicians in France and Switzerland and geologists and physicists in England and Scotland. Their

work was refined into an elegant predictive theory by a lone Serbian mathematician. In the 20th century the scale of the research expanded, and recently multinational teams have worked on massive efforts to extract deep ice cores to go back in time. These teams were assembled with deliberate political as well as scientific goals whether it was to maintain cooperation during Cold War tensions, or to cement relationships within a new and fragile European Union. It would take an additional strand of atmospheric research to create a scientifically robust explanation of the onset of the ice ages.

Atmospheric composition and climate – an alternative theory

Having narrowly escaped the guillotine during the French Revolution, the French mathematical physicist, Jean Baptiste Joseph Fourier, published a paper in 1827 in which he posited that the Earth did not lose its absorbed solar heat back to space because clouds and (unknown) gases in the atmosphere absorbed that radiant heat and reradiated it back to the Earth's surface. He likened this to a glass bell jar trapping heat, and this process eventually came to be known as the 'greenhouse effect'. Throughout the 19th century there was intense intellectual competition among leading physical scientists to study heat and electromagnetic radiation, and their work contributed to an understanding of how gases trap radiant heat from the earth and return it to the surface. John Tyndall, an Irish-born Professor of Natural Philosophy, demonstrated that the bulk of the atmosphere made up of oxygen and nitrogen had no effect on the radiant heat from the earth, but that water vapour, carbon dioxide and ozone did. He correctly identified water vapour as the most important heat-trapping gas, and also postulated the urban heat island effect, and contributed to the theory of the motion of glaciers.

The latter part of the 19th century saw a lively dialogue about the nature of the heat balance of the Earth. The American founder of aviation, Samuel P. Langley, a solar physicist, invented the bolometer to accurately measure the incoming energy from the sun in 1878. In 1884 he published a paper in *Professional Papers of the Signal Service* and in 1890 a study of the radiant properties of the atmosphere-free moon that quantified the infrared portion of the solar spectrum. Combing these data with Tyndall's quantitative measurements of radiant heat absorption in the Earth's atmosphere allowed the calculation of the thermal heat balance of the Earth. This task fell to Svante Arrhenius, a Swedish chemist whose chemical rate equation is still in use today, and who won the chemistry Nobel Prize in 1903 for his doctoral research on the electrical conductivity of charged ions in water despite its having received the lowest passing grade.

Arrhenius was convinced that it was the concentration of carbon dioxide, water vapour, ozone and other trace gases that determined just how much heat was retained by the Earth's atmosphere. He conducted painstaking calculations, and published his landmark paper 'On the influence of carbonic acid in the air on the temperature of the ground' in 1896 in the British journal *Philosophical Magazine*. He correctly predicted that warming would be greater in winter, and at higher latitudes, and estimated that if carbon dioxide were doubled, global temperatures would increase by 5–6°C. Arrhenius believed it might be possible to avoid entering another ice age by adding carbon dioxide to the atmosphere by burning more coal, and indeed this would be essential if the world were to avoid catastrophic descent into the next ice age. The Swedish physicist Knut Ångström in 1900 quantitatively measured the absorption of infrared radiation by carbon dioxide, and strongly criticized Arrhenius for overestimating its absorption intensity. Current best estimates suggest that a doubling of carbon dioxide would increase global average temperatures by 2–4.5°C. Ångström was right. Arrhenius had overestimated the 'greenhouse effect', not the last time that charge would be levelled at scientists studying this phenomenon.

Guy S. Callendar, a British steam engineer, became interested in testing the theory of carbon dioxide-driven climate change, and saw that by the 1930s carbon dioxide had increased by an estimated 10 per cent from a poorly verified preindustrial baseline. He collected data from his own home over many years, combined temperature records from many weather stations and examined the modest number of available measurements of retreating glaciers. He found statistically significant increases in Northern hemisphere temperatures, especially in northern

latitudes (consistent with recent findings), and attributed this rise to the increase in carbon dioxide. His initial publication in 1938 was largely dismissed as the work of an amateur. Undeterred, he continued his research and established the basis for the current global system of temperature measurements.

In 1957, Hans Suess and Roger Revelle of Scripps Institution of Oceanography in California published an initially confusing finding about the uptake of atmospheric carbon dioxide released to the atmosphere. Using the new science of dating by radioactive carbon 14, they were able to show that the oceans rather quickly absorbed fossil-fuel-generated carbon dioxide, but nearly as quickly released much of it back to the atmosphere. They also included the observations of California Institute of Technology professor Harrison Brown that carbon dioxide concentrations could increase significantly if fossil fuel combustion continued its rapid rise. In their own calculations, they greatly underestimated the future growth of carbon dioxide emissions or atmospheric concentrations. In concluding, the paper made the now famous statement that humans are conducting a large-scale geophysical experiment that cannot be reproduced. They also paid tribute to the ignored work of Callendar and called augmented global warming from fossil fuel carbon dioxide the 'Callendar effect'.

Creating the new synthetic theory of climate and climate change

Bringing the planetary and atmospheric threads together required a new synthesis in the 20th century. The atmospheric heat trapping alone did not account for the periodicity of the ice ages. While accounting for their periodicity, the planetary mechanics seemed insufficient to account for the large drop in temperature required to bring about an ice age, or to explain the sudden large rise in temperature marking the start of an interglacial warming period. The connection between the two theories grew out of the increase in interest in the possibility suggested by Arrhenius that the addition of heat-trapping gases to the atmosphere from industrial processes might be responsible for significant future warming, and the confirmation of ice age frequency that corresponded to the predicted Milankovitch cycle. Climate research remained the province of individual scientists publishing in journals in Western

Europe and increasingly North America until after the middle of the 20th century when 'Big Science' began to dominate the field. An independent and parallel analysis of climate during the mid to late 20th century was under way in the Soviet Union and later Russia.

Realizing that the complexity of the climate system required coordinated study by atmospheric scientists, oceanographers, terrestrial ecologists as well as meteorologists, glaciologists, solar physicists, and others from the physical and biological and even social scientists, an argument was made to include it on the agenda of the International Geophysical Year (IGY) in 1957–58. IGY drew a total of 67 nations and 80,000 scientists to study the physical properties of the planet from solar radiation to earthquakes, glaciers, ocean currents, the Arctic and Antarctica, weather and climate. This effort to study the physical processes of the Earth was proposed by the International Union of Scientific Unions (National Academies of Science) and organized jointly with the World Meteorological Organization (WMO). The latter is a UN organization founded in 1950 from the pre-existing International Meteorological Organization that dated back to an 1873 Congress of Vienna. Its purpose is to encourage collaborative sharing of data about weather and later climate. IGY mobilized previously unavailable funding for research from governments and stimulated the design of collaborative projects across disciplines and Cold War boundaries. While there had been two 'polar years' in 1882–83 and 1932–33, IGY was the first integrated look at the climate system, the oceans and other global-scale systems and an important shift from traditional individualistic research and analysis to the rise of larger groups of interdisciplinary scientists working together. Large-scale, multidisciplinary national and international teams of scientists have come to dominate climate science.

Just before the IGY began, C. David Keeling, who was a doctoral research student of Harrison Brown, signed on to work as a post-doctoral researcher with Roger Revelle at Scripps. He had developed a highly accurate way to measure the amount of carbon dioxide in the atmosphere. Keeling began his atmospheric measurements at two pure-air sites, the South Pole research station in Antarctica and atop Mauna Loa volcano in Hawai'i. Each of these sites was thousands of miles from contaminating industrial emissions. What resulted were the most important geophysical measurements in history. The monthly averages showed an annual oscillation that was higher in the Northern hemisphere winter, and lower in summer as the relative seasonal rates of plant respiration and photosynthesis affected the atmospheric concentrations. The average concentration for the first full year of 1959 was 316ppm (parts per million), or just over 0.03 per cent. Concentrations in October of 2007 reached 384ppm. Measurements at the South Pole were slightly lower, but the oscillations because of the inverted seasons were exactly out of phase, and because of the lower biomass of plants in the Southern hemisphere the annual oscillations were smaller.

The prospect of predicting or modifying the weather to improve agriculture or as a weapon of warfare captured attention during the 1960s and 70s. In preparation for the first global environmental conference in Stockholm, a report, *Man's impact on the global environment*, was released in 1970. It examined the atmospheric measurements of rising carbon dioxide made by Keeling, and found that it seemed to confirm that future global warming might be of concern.

By the 1980s, new evidence began to provide an answer to the riddle of the ice ages. Drilling down 3km into the ice carries us back in time and allows the measurement of the concentrations of heat-trapping gases in air bubbles trapped in the ice and isotope ratios that are a surrogate of temperature. The initial measurements involved large international teams of Russian, French and American scientists working at the Soviet Vostok, Antarctica site in an attempt at Cold War cooperation. The data from ice cores demonstrated the strong correlation between heat-trapping carbon dioxide, methane and nitrous oxide in the atmosphere, and the temperature of the ice ages and interglacial periods. The data extended back 420,000 years and covered five cycles, each lasting approximately the Milankovitch periodicity of 100,000 years. This record was extended back 650,000 years and two more warming periods at a nearby site by the 17-nation European Project for Ice Coring in Antarctica. The rise and fall of temperature is strongly correlated with carbon dioxide, methane and nitrous oxide, all heat-trapping greenhouse gases. This latter study confirmed that current carbon dioxide levels are 27 per cent higher than at any time in this entire period. The earlier results were first published in the British journal *Nature* in 1985, and the latter work in the American journal *Science* in 2005.

The carbon dioxide concentrations ranged from about 180ppm during the depths of the ice ages to a maximum of 300ppm during the warmer interglacial periods. Today's concentration of 384ppm exceeds any amount ever measured over the past 650,000 years by 27 per cent. A careful analysis found that the carbon dioxide lags the temperature rise by about 800 years during the warming period. This is just about the time needed to begin releasing the vast amounts of carbon dioxide dissolved in the deep oceans. It therefore appears that the Milankovitch cycle triggers global warming when planetary orientation to the sun is optimal. This warming releases carbon dioxide from the ocean surface and eventually from the deep ocean, trapping more heat and giving rise to the rapid acceleration of warming as an ice age abruptly ends within a single millennium. Additional carbon dioxide may be released from plant decay, and methane releases are accelerated from anaerobic decay and from deposits in melting permafrost. These same trapped air samples show an increase in atmospheric concentrations of methane rising abruptly starting in the 19th century from 715ppm to 1,774ppm in 2005. Methane adds to the atmospheric heat trapping until the planetary alignment falls out of favour, and cooling sets in. The cooling allows more carbon dioxide to dissolve in the ocean and slows the rate of decomposition and methane release from soils. A new ice age will begin. Hence both the planetary cycle advocates and the greenhouse backers were partially correct, but it took both aspects to account for the observed periodicity of the climate system.

The possibility of multiple positive and some negative feedback loops began to be realized. Melting snow and ice increased the absorption of solar radiation by dark land and water, which is one reason that high latitudes warm more than the equator. Warmer temperatures evaporated more ocean water and the air could hold more of it because of the higher temperature. This in turn could trap more heat. Of course there are other factors that can affect the climate such as fluctuating solar intensity, volcanic eruptions, deforestation, dust storms, shifts in ocean currents, massive forest fires, and other phenomena. These have been found to have only episodic, short-term influences on the climate.

The advent of satellites and other remote sensing technology has greatly enhanced the ability to monitor the planet and its climate. A global network of over 7,000 weather stations now sends daily high and low temperatures, precipitation and other weather data to central locations where they are combined with sea surface temperature measurements to provide daily and annual regional and global average temperatures. Buoys and ships monitor sea surface temperature and measure ocean currents. Satellites provide observations of sea ice breakups, glacial retreat, atmospheric opacity from dust and aerosol droplets, surface albedo or reflectivity, planetary thermal emissions, and sea levels confirm patterns of climate change. Initially, these observational satellites were derivative from military technology and were mostly launched by the United States and the Soviet Union. Increasingly, European, Japanese and other nations are launching their own satellites to observe the Earth's climate and other natural processes. Over 7,000 surface-based weather stations were first linked in 1992 by research agencies of the US government as the Global Historical Climatology Network. Each locality sends its data directly to a central global location as well as to its national weather agency. The Climatic Research Unit at the University of East Anglia in England has established an alternative sampling system. The historical data collected by these stations over the years have now been compiled to provide a continuous record dating back to the mid 19th century.

As the global data accumulated, the pattern became clear. Following a brief rise from 1900 until 1940, temperatures levelled and actually dropped slightly for 30 years, prompting statements that the Earth was about to enter a new ice age. Then temperatures began soaring up through 2007. Based on major databases in the United States and the United Kingdom, the average global temperature has increased by 0.71°C over the period 1906–2005. Eleven of the twelve warmest years have occurred between 1993 and 2005. Michael Mann and colleagues reported surrogate temperatures going back 1,000 years, demonstrating that the recent rise in temperature is abrupt and greater than the fluctuations observed in prior centuries. Challenges to this work were found not to alter its ultimate message. The small temperature dip at mid century has been shown to arise from sunlight reflected off small droplets of sulphuric acid that are produced downwind from the combustion of sulphur-laden oil and coal. Removing sulphur to reduce acid rain has uncovered the imbedded heat-trapping capability of greenhouse gases. As predicted by theory, the moisture content of the atmosphere has increased with the temperature rise trapping yet more heat.

Beginning in the 1980s, the other tool that began to make an impact on understanding of climate change was the introduction of supercomputers that could simulate the circulation and heat trapping by greenhouse gases, and couple the atmosphere to ocean currents, plants and soils as they absorb and release carbon dioxide. Independent modelling efforts were initiated in the United States, the United Kingdom, within the European Union, Russia, Japan and now China. While part of the impetus for these models originated from attempts to better predict weather or explain ocean currents, they soon outgrew that mission. In fact today, there is some scepticism among many meteorologists that climate change is happening because of human contributions of heat-trapping gases into the atmosphere. They can usually find a micro-explanation for an observed shift in weather patterns rather than attribute them to larger changes in the global climate system. With the advent of very powerful supercomputers it has become possible to incorporate a great deal of the physics, chemistry and biology of the planet as it relates to climate. These models have been verified in that they 'can accurately predict the past'. They are increasingly being used to test future trajectories of heat-trapping gases under different scenarios to see how atmospheric concentrations of greenhouse gases might increase, and how that might affect future temperatures and sea levels. Depending on emission scenario assumptions, future temperatures could rise between 1.5°C and 3.5°C, which would create remarkable changes in natural and agricultural systems as well as affect human health.

In 1983 and again in 1985, groups of climate and biological scientists from American and European universities and independent research centres issued reports on the likelihood that climate change could become a serious problem. In the summer of 1988, at a hearing before a US Senate committee, atmospheric scientist James Hanson from NASA stated that he was 99 per cent certain that climate change was already happening and that within a decade it would be obvious to the man in the street. This began an intense debate over the science of climate change.

Climate change policy

Also in 1988, the United Nations created the Intergovernmental Panel on Climate Change (IPCC) through the World Meteorological Organization and the United Nations Environmental Programme (UNEP). The organization was to produce a report every five to six years on the state of climate science, climate change impacts and adaptation and to identify mitigation options. Physical, natural and social scientists were to be appointed by governments. They were to base their report on existing peer-reviewed scientific literature and were to avoid making prescriptive recommendations. The first report, which was hastily assembled under the chairmanship of the Swedish meteorologist Bert Bolin, was published in 1990, and concluded that it was likely that human release of carbon dioxide and other gases into the atmosphere was responsible for changing the climate. A second report, also chaired by Bolin in 1995, found stronger climate change evidence and the third report chaired by Robert Watson, an English-born American chemist at the World Bank, reported in 2001 evidence of human-induced climate change. The fourth assessment report issued in 2007 under the chairmanship of Rajindra Pachauri, an Indian engineer and economist, stated that it was highly likely with a 90 per cent degree of confidence that observed climate change was due to human actions. The reports also evolve in providing more information: on impacts and adaptation in the second, more economic analysis and mitigation options in the third, and mitigation and equity issues of climate change in the fourth report. The scale and scope of this critical review and assessment of climate change is unprecedented. A rotating body of IPCC participants consists of nearly 2,000 scientists and other technical researchers who spend three years reviewing data, research articles and reports without pay while working in their jobs in academia, government, industry, non-governmental organizations and research institutes. In

October 2007, they shared the Nobel Peace Prize with former US vice president Al Gore.

The IPCC reports influenced governments to negotiate and adopt the 1992 UN Framework Convention on Climate Change that called upon all nations to work to stabilize 'greenhouse gas concentrations in the atmosphere at a level that would prevent dangerous anthropogenic interference with the climate system'. The treaty quickly entered into force and as of 22 August 2007 had 192 nations as parties. In 1997 following the release of the second IPCC report, nations negotiated the Kyoto Protocol that called upon developed countries to reduce their emissions of carbon dioxide and several other heat-trapping greenhouse gases by specified amounts during the period 2008–12. It took until 2005 for enough nations to ratify this agreement for it to come into force. The United States and Australia were the only industrial nations to opt out of the system. As of 6 June 2007, 171 nations had ratified the Protocol. To date relatively little action has been taken to lower the release of heat-trapping greenhouse gases. A key component of future climate history will be how effectively global action can be mobilized and the fossil-fuel economy moderated to reduce dramatically the release of heat-trapping greenhouse gases.

So the synthesis between planetary mechanics and atmospheric heat-trapping theories seems to provide an explanation for both the ice ages and recent warming. If left unchecked concentrations of carbon dioxide could double or triple against preindustrial levels during the 21st century, and raise temperatures as much as they increased coming out of the last ice age. While a few may question whether climate change is human-caused, the discussion has moved on to what can be done to avoid excessive warming. The only possible remedial action is to reduce human contributions of heat-trapping greenhouse gases to the atmosphere, since altering planetary mechanics clearly remains beyond our reach. The science continues to unfold. We await future climate historians' accounts, and the inevitable next ice age.

William Moomaw

Bibliography
Arrhenius S. 1896. 'On the influence of carbonic acid in the air on the temperature of the ground', *Philosophical Magazine*, 41, 237–76. Excerpts available online: http://web.lemoyne.edu/~GIUNTA/Arrhenius.html, accessed 31 January 2008.

Fleming J. R. 1998. *Historical perspectives on climate change*. Oxford and New York: Oxford University Press.

Fleming J. R. 2006. *The Callendar effect: the life and times of Guy Stewart Callendar (1898–1964)*. Boston: American Meteorological Society.

Imbrie J. and Imbrie K. P. 1986. *Ice ages: solving the mystery*, revised edition. Cambridge, MA: Harvard University Press.

Somerville R. et al. 'Historical overview of climate change science', in Solomon S. et al. (eds) 2007. *Climate change 2007: the physical basis of climate change: contribution of Working Group I to the Fourth Assessment Report of the IPCC*, Cambridge and New York: Cambridge University Press, 93–127.

UN Intergovernmental Panel on Climate Change (IPCC) *Assessment reports and special reports; technical papers; methodology reports; supporting material* [online]. Available: www.ipcc.ch/ipccreports/index.htm, accessed 31 January 2008.

Weart S. R. 2003. *The discovery of global warming*. Cambridge, MA: Harvard University Press.

Wilson C. L. and Matthews W. H. (eds) 1970. *Man's impact on the global environment: report of the Study of Critical Environmental Problems (SCEP)*. Cambridge, MA: MIT Press.

Related essays
air pollution; Antarctic Treaty; environmental diplomacy; environmentalism; human mobility; indigenous knowledges; life and physical sciences; mathematics; millennium; natural hazards; scientific expeditions; scientific stations; Stockholm Conference; United Nations decades and years; United Nations system; zero growth

Coca-cola *See* America

Code civil *See* Legal order

Cold War

The Cold War was a bipolar conflict between the Soviet Union and the United States that began shortly after the end of World War 2 and ended with the fall of the Berlin Wall and the collapse of the Soviet Union, in 1989/91. This conflict concerned primarily the geopolitical preservation and extension of two spheres of influence in Europe, Asia, Latin America and Africa. Policy makers in Moscow and Washington defined these spheres of influence by ideological adherence and the question of which belief system – democracy or communism – would prevail in the world.

At the same time, the Cold War represented a multifaceted and transnational phenomenon that affected nearly every single country on the globe in often highly individual ways. The conflict embedded a war about two different *Weltanschauungen*, two ways to organize society, the economy and cultural life, two possibilities to define modernity and to grapple with its most pressing cultural challenge: how to transport a society into modernity and preserve tradition in the face of fundamental change?

The Cold War went hand in hand with the gradual preponderance of ideology as the principal way to delineate the boundaries between East and West. It triggered the forceful transmission of inspirations and artifacts for political ends. It first caused and then halted a massive migration wave from East to West. It forced and inspired governments to define their geopolitical interest in areas that prior to 1947, only few decision makers would have been able to locate on a map.

State interest, geopolitical strategy, economic interest, ideological preconceptions, obsessive self-definition and the continuous challenge of an enemy image dictated the Cold War's contours to an unprecedented degree. Regions and people that had never concerned the European powers or the United States all of a sudden moved into the limelight of the superpowers' geopolitical interest. In Korea and in Indochina the superpowers and their client states fought two relentless wars, the legacy of which still traumatize American society today.

To overthrow unfriendly governments, throughout the Third World both superpowers increased the use of covert action and foreign support. During the latter half of the Cold War, the United States as well as Communist regimes resorted to harnessing and supporting terrorist groups in order to reduce the opponent's influence around the world. In the Islamic world resistance to any

bloc alliance ran high because many Muslims feared the loss of traditional and religious values against the onslaught of secularism, consumerism, and a host of values imported by both the United States and the Soviet Union. As a result, the United States clandestinely supported Islamic movements and promoted religious, anti-secular and anti-socialist values in countries such as Iraq, Syria and Iran; the revolution of 1979 in Iran showed that such action could produce counterproductive results, including profound anti-Western sentiments. Meanwhile the Kremlin became deeply involved in mass terrorism directed against Jews but also at destabilizing the West. In a single year, 1983, East Germany sent AK-47 ammunition worth some $1,877,600 to Lebanon. Airplane hijacking, the bombing of public spaces, kidnappings and assassinations of politicians throughout the Middle East and Western Europe became an attractive alternative to open warfare in the age of nuclear weapons and mutually assured destruction.

Numerous nations in the Third World refused to seek an alignment with either one of the superpowers. Founded in 1955 and headed by Jawaharlal Nehru of India, Josip Tito of Yugoslavia, and Gamal Abdel Nasser of Egypt, the Non-Aligned Movement sought to unite the Third World against great-power-bloc politics, colonialism and any form of foreign aggression or hegemony. Comprising 55 per cent of the Earth's population and close to two-thirds of the member states of the United Nations, the Non-Aligned Movement counted among its members major states such as India, Egypt, Yugoslavia, South Africa, Malaysia, Iran, and, for a period of time, China.

Culture and ideology were the key themes in the battle for the minds of people and the territories they inhabited. As a result, in Europe, Latin America, the Middle East and in Asia, the Cold War privileged culture and cultural relations to an unprecedented degree. Even governments in countries that had formerly not prioritized the support of culture now invested massively in the promotion of high culture. Both superpowers deliberately employed psychological warfare and cultural infiltration to weaken the opponent and its client states on the other side of the Iron Curtain. Never before (and never since) did governments, hegemonic powers, NGOs and private individuals invest as much money, energy, and thought in the promotion of science, political dialogue, the arts, academic exchange and cultural self-presentation. Never again did people living in the United States, the Soviet Union and its client states enjoy so many state-subsidized travel programmes, international perform-ances, cosmopolitan exhibitions and shows as during these decades.

The Cold War both polarized but also linked together two very different continents, Europe and America, geographical areas that for nearly 200 years had viewed each other critic-ally. On both continents, the conflict created its own culture and heroes, its own artistic inspirations and avalanche of artifacts: idols such as James Bond and Yuri Gagarin, films like Star Wars or Admiral Nakhimov. At the same time it drew on cultural connections and pol-itical misgivings originating in the 18th and 19th centuries: materialism vs high culture, populism vs feudalism and so on.

Many developments crucial to mid-20th-century history were not created but rather touched by the bipolar conflict. The post-war development of the oil market with its international conflicts and crises very likely would have been the same without the super-power struggle. Likewise, the history of eco-nomics after 1945 cannot be understood simply as a result of the struggle between socialism and capitalism. The same can be observed in the field of culture: the Cold War played itself out against a background of tremendous global cultural change, a trans-formation that would have occupied people around the world even if there had never been a Cold War. The debate over modern-ity and the need for modernization, the clash between tradition and consumer culture, and the relation between the state, culture and the economy had occupied French, German, Chinese, Japanese and Indian thinkers since the early 1900s. Everywhere around the globe, conservative critics worried over the preservation of traditional values in the face of modernity. But while Europeans had already begun the process of transformation in the interwar period, Middle Eastern and Asian societies, above all China, sought a way to establish themselves as an alternative to 'the European way' and, thus, to avoid the pitfalls of modern society.

Knocking at the door of every single country in 1945, in both Europe and the Third World, modernization provided the ideological propaganda of both superpowers with an unexpected leverage. This is because at the core of the Cold War was an international battle over the meaning of modernity and the process of modernization; the relation-ship between the state and the individual; the organization, control and administration of politics, culture, ideology and the economy; and the place of popular culture in the future of every single country. That battle eventually led to the division of the world and the cre-ation of two distinct spheres of influence.

Of course, the Cold War's significance differed according to region. In Europe, its impact on regional culture was qualita-tive more than quantitative: it shaped exist-ing disputes and developments more than it inspired new trends. In Asia, Africa and the Middle East, its influence was far more quan-titative: it triggered and accelerated processes of modernization by introducing a multitude of new consumer products, organizational structures and political alliances that might otherwise not have occurred. And it encour-aged Third World countries to play the super-powers against one another and demand heavy financial subsidies for their own mod-ernization from their new political friends. For example, when Americans refused to fund the building of the Aswan High Dam in Egypt, the Soviets gladly financed the project, thus accelerating the country's moderniza-tion, and also signed a treaty of cooperation with Nasser. Modernization in Third World countries, then, was directly contingent on the political and ideological engagement of the superpowers.

The Cold War did not inspire this debate over the meaning of modernity and the pro-cess of modernization. But it provided discus-sions, and the ways in which positions were acted out, with a decisive note. Similarly, the debate lent the Cold War an intellectual and cultural depth that turned the superpower disagreements from a geopolitical conflict into a mortal clash of ideologies in which each side saw the other as the incarnation of evil and aggression.

Curiously, in nearly every country East and West of the Iron Curtain as well as in Asia and Africa, the culture of the Cold War in Europe also produced a powerful forum for the expres-sion of critical anti-government tendencies. In other words, the bipolar conflict evoked cultural responses and protests everywhere that were detrimental to the confrontation between the superpowers. In nearly every Western country, the decades after 1945 witnessed protests against American culture and racism, which the United States could never defy. Likewise, popular protest movements in the Communist bloc demanded a more open society and more exchange opportunities with the West. And on both sides of the Iron Curtain people used popular culture to voice their remonstration.

In this respect, the Cold War is not a story of clear-cut winners and losers. For one thing, despite the preponderance of the two superpowers in the Cold War, their client states as well as the members of the Non-Aligned Movement chose a process of cultural adaptation and rejection. Western European consumers, for example, dismissed, changed and reinvented the significance of many US products, stars and movies, ideas and trends. In Eastern Europe, the consummation of popular culture became part of the language of silent protest. Because popular culture bred the lure of capitalism and the language of protest, Warsaw Pact governments remained extremely opposed to it while their countries grew increasingly vulnerable to foreign imports.

Ironically, fostered by technological innovations such as satellite TV, in the end the only artifacts and programmes surviving the Cold War were those that had already been in place in the United States since the 1920s, in Western Europe since the 1950s, in the Third World beginning in the 1960s and 1970s, and that finally arrived in Eastern Europe in the 1990s: films, cartoons, and fashion thrived everywhere once the Wall came down.

This is the paradox of the Cold War: centring on the ongoing debate over how to trigger, modify, and cope with modernity, the bipolar conflict had a profound qualitative effect on the development of culture, ideology, science, politics, the economy and society everywhere. The ideological confrontation between the United States and the Soviet Union led to a cultural cold war which scholars commonly believe the United States won thanks to the lure of popular culture. But early on the Soviets mounted the most powerful and irresistible argument in the battle for the minds of men and women: under Communism, a nation could modernize and, at the same time, preserve its traditional culture. Therefore, the Soviets cherished a great cultural past. Americans did not. Their version of modernization went hand in hand

with the triumph of popular culture and a loss of tradition.

The influx of American popular culture in Europe eventually cemented both the victory as well as the failure of American propaganda: popular culture successfully defeated Communist ideology in most areas of the world, save for China, Korea, and Cuba. But it also defeated any efforts to improve the image of America. Even after their demise, Communist states never lost the argument that Western capitalism threatened traditional values. The United States may have won its 'first' cultural war against the Warsaw Pact states and the global influence of Communism in 1989/91. But it lost the second one, the battle against deeply rooted pessimistic images of American civilization. And while the Cold War is over, the debate over how to define modernity and deal with its challenges continues throughout much of Eastern Europe and the Third World.

Jessica C. E. Gienow-Hecht

Bibliography

Caute D. 2003. The dancer defects: the struggle for cultural supremacy during the Cold War. Oxford and New York: Oxford University Press.

Engerman D. C. 2003. Staging growth: modernization, development and the global Cold War. Amherst: University of Massachusetts Press.

Gaddis J. L. 2005. The Cold War: a new history. New York: Penguin.

Gienow-Hecht J. C. E. 2000. 'Shame on US: cultural transfer, academics, and the Cold War – a critical review', Diplomatic History, 24, 465–94.

Junker D. et al. (eds) 2004. The United States and Germany in the era of the Cold War, 1945–1990: a handbook. Cambridge and New York: Cambridge University Press.

McMahon R. J. 1994. The Cold War on the periphery: the United States, India and Pakistan. New York: Columbia University Press.

Mitter R. and Major P. (eds) 2004. Across the blocs: Cold War cultural and social history. Portland and London: Frank Cass.

Congress for Cultural Freedom; crimes; decolonization; development and growth; developmental assistance; developmental taxonomies; disarmament; displaced persons; economics; empires and imperialism; euromarkets; fellowships and grants; film; forced migrations; governing science; Hollywood; human rights; information economy; information society; intergovernmental organizations; international non-governmental organizations (INGOs); liberalism; life and physical sciences; modernity; modernization theory; North Atlantic Treaty Organization (NATO); oil; outer space; pacifism; partitions; performing artists; philanthropic foundations; police; public policy; radio; Samsung; social sciences; socialism; terrorism; underdevelopment; United Nations system; United Nations Women's Conferences; Vietnam War; war; welfare state; workers' movements; world orders; youth organizations

Comics

In the late 19th century, American newspapers began proposing a 'comic' section including graphic stories. These pages, printed in colour and generally published on Sunday, were designed to entertain the readers, whence the name 'comics' or 'funnies'. Their popularity grew week after week, boosting the sales of the papers and creating artistic vocations. It became a new art form dealing both with narration and drawing. The modern comics are made of a sequence of pictures telling a story and including characters able to talk through specific codes. An international symposium of specialists held in Lucca (Italy) in 1989 decided that the official and global date of birth of the 'comics' would be 1896, when Joseph Pulitzer's New York World published The Yellow Kid and His New Gramophone, a five-panel story with dialogues written in what would be called 'balloons'. The Yellow Kid, by Richard Felton Outcault (1863–1928), was a poor and facetious bald child wearing a yellow shirt, whose adventures in Hogan's Alley delighted ordinary people. The following year, Pulitzer's rival William Randolph Hearst got his own comic stars in his New York Journal: The Katzenjammer Kids by Rudolph Dirks (1877–1968). Within a few years, comics in their purpose and shape became more sophisticated. Early authors produced masterpieces such as Little Nemo in Slumberland by

Winsor McCay (1867–1934) and Bringing up Father by George McManus (1884–1954).

Even if comics are said to have been born in the US, an objective archaeology of the art form shows that graphic narration had its roots in Europe and Asia. Some academics like to refer to the Norman Bayeux Tapestry of 1066, while others prefer to mention 16th-century German manuscripts with their expressive phylacteries. Latin Americans root for the memory of Aztec, or the Maya's Codex, and experts on Japan recall painted rolls from the 12th century. Graphically and chronologically closer are the graphic novels Histoire de M. Vieux-Bois by Rodolphe Töpffer (Switzerland, 1827) or Max und Moritz by Wilhelm Bush (Germany, 1865). This last novel inspired Rudolph Dirks, himself a German émigré, when he created his Katzenjammer Kids. It is indisputable that the US comic strips, based on mass communication, the growing power of US capitalism and the increasing influence of the American way of life, imposed their models and rules on the world. US comic characters and strips travelled quickly: in 1912, El Capitán y los Pilluelos (The Captain and the Kids, another name of the Katzenjammer Kids) was available in Havana (Cuba). In the 1930s it was definitely a global art. The exciting news of the end of the world, first announced in the US by the King Features Syndicate on 7 January 1934, took ten months to get to Italy on the front page of L'Avventuroso (October 1934), and a few month more to reach Spain (in Aventurero by the Hispano Americana de Ediciones, managed by an Italian publisher, 1935). The news hit France in April 1936. Later, the youngsters of Belgrade, Yugoslavia, learned about it, as did those of Warsaw, Poland, and then the colonial readers of De Orient in Batavia, Indonesia. The carrier of such breaking news, space-opera hero Flash Gordon, as he was named, produced in all minds a revolution. The prolific and talented Alex Raymond (1909–56), its creator, also authored a mystery and an exotic series (Secret Agent X-9 and Jungle Jim). Adventures of all sorts opened up new fields. The comics explored unknown territories of the imagination and ceased to be strictly funny.

Comics got specific names in other countries, drawing from their material appearance: bande dessinée insisted on the sequence of pictures in French-speaking countries; fumetti in Italy, for the smoke clouds the balloons suggested; quadradhinos in Portugal and

Brazil emphasized the shape of the picture. In Spain comics were called *tebeos* to remember the first journal dedicated to young people whose title was TBO (1917). In Japan they were called *manga*, with two ideograms for 'whimsical pictures', as far as the concept can be translated, and in Korea *manhwa*. In China the *lianhuanhua* or 'linked pictures' won the favour of a large public. The well-known writer Mao Dun said that these cheap booklets, sold or rented directly on the streets, were read by poor people as well as sons of the bourgeoisie. China had its own paper heroes such as Mr Wang by Ye Qianyu (1907–95) or San Mao by Zhang Leping (1910–92). Early in the 1930s, some Japanese artists formed the New Manga group. One of the characters they created, Fuku Chan, was so popular that the US Army used it in propaganda leaflets dropped on Japan during World War 2.

At that time, heroes were enlisted to win battles. Of course, the most powerful of all were Captain America, Wonder Woman and their friends of the Justice Society of America. A string of superheroes had been born in the wake of the great Superman, brought to life in 1938 in its own comic book: *Action Comics*. Batman came in 1939, Captain Marvel and its *shazam* word in 1940. But classic heroes took up arms too. Flash Gordon himself came back from the far Planet Mongo to help the US Army to beat off an attempted invasion. Tarzan struggled against the Germans in Africa. Terry and the Pirates fought in China with Chiang Kai-shek's troops, under the pencil of Milton Caniff (1907–88), and the author specially created *Male Call* and *Miss Lace* for the Marines. With the victory over Axis forces, American comics had a deep impact on young people in liberated countries, even when they did not embrace America's political ideology. In France, *Vaillant*, published by the Communist Party, was paradoxically the best American-style weekly for children: Les Pionniers de l'Espérance was a kind of Flash Gordon, Wango a kind of Jungle Jim and Yves le Loup a kind of Prince Valiant. Artists fleeing Iberian dictatorships went to work on this periodical: the Spanish Cabrera Arnal who had begun its career with a Disney-like dog, and the Portuguese E. T. Coelho, born in the Azores, who took in charge for a time the character of Davy Crockett. In General Franco's Spain, the epic tale *Tragedia en Oriente* by Jesús Blasco (1919–94), appearing in *Chicos* and brought to Salazar's Portugal through *O Mosquito*, was

very close to the Flash Gordon's framework, just as in Belgium was Blake & Mortimer's *Le Secret de l'Espadon* by Edgar P. Jacobs (1904–87), published in the weekly Tintin.

Comics are a cosmopolitan and transnational art, be it for authors, series or characters' features. The Italian Hugo Pratt (1927–96) brought from Africa American reviews with Milton Caniff's black-and-white stories that the Allied soldiers in occupied Ethiopia lent to teenagers like him. He began his career after the war in Venice, with a Yankee-type superhero, l'Asso di Pique. He then left for Argentina, sold some series in Britain, came back to Europe where his fame grew with a new hero and his breathless adventures throughout the tormented history of the 20th century: Corto Maltese. Lyons, the centre for publication of comic periodicals in World War 2 occupied France, had three big publishing houses of comic books during the 1950s and subsequently: one of them, LUG, printed mostly Italian material (the trapper Blek-le-Roc, the cowboy Tex and the Nevada Ranger Miki); another, Éditions des Remparts, chose American material (Mandrake, The Phantom); the third one, Imperia, specialized in British productions (Battler Britton, X-13, Jim Canada / Dick Daring). Comic heroes often had an international destiny, sometimes attaining the status of classical myths. The very French Astérix, by René Goscinny (1926–77), who spent his youth in Argentina and New York, and Albert Uderzo (b. 1927), the son of Italian immigrants, was translated into near thirty languages, including Classical Latin. One can find it in India and South Africa, in Finland and Australia. Tintin, the Belgian reporter created in 1929 by Hergé (1907–83), was translated into more than fifty languages including Arabic and Hebrew, Turkish and Armenian, Alsatian and Corsican, Welsh and Esperanto. In the People's Republic of China, when it was still a strict Communist state, Tintin (Ding-Ding in Chinese) was printed without permission on bad paper as a little *Lianhuahua*: The Blue Lotus, Tintin in Tibet, and even The Calculus Affair, whose action takes place in a Stalinist-type state under a moustachioed dictator and where the hero baffles the *Cai Po* (Secret Police).

Ideological criticism of the comics can be done in different ways. In Allende's Chile two sociologists wrote *Para leer al Pato Donald* (How to read Donald Duck, 1971) to denounce the war fought by US imperialism against the people's will for change. On the other side, the character of Mafalda, created in Argentina, was a true voice of contestation appreciated in the North and South of the planet. Comics are, in reality, a galaxy of worlds, an infinite and contradictory universe. Comics can even depict tragedy. Art Spiegelman, born in Sweden after World War 2, drew Maus in New York to narrate the Holocaust in Poland. Nakazawa Keiji realized Barefoot Gen (Hadashi no Gen) to represent the bombing of Hiroshima, and was even known in Finland, being the first Japanese manga author in that country. Marjane Satrapi wrote Persepolis in exile to tell the fate of Iran, but in her country the graphic novel is read underground in English or French.

The Italian writer and scholar Umberto Eco said that the comic, a fusion of two forms of expression – the picture and the written word – had produced an autonomous idiom, langage sui generis, that influenced the cinema, painting and even literature. But above all, it brings happiness to the kids worldwide ... whatever their age.

Philippe Videlier

Bibliography

Collective 1972. The art of the comic strip. Zürich: Graphis.

Collective 1980. Histoire mondiale de la bande dessinée. Paris: Pierre Horay.

Collective 2000. Maîtres de la bande dessinée européenne. Paris: Bibliothèque Nationale de France / Seuil.

Marschall R. 1989. America's great comic-strip artists. New York: Abbeville.

Related essays

America; children's literature; Cold War; Japan; literature; translation; war; Westernization

Comintern and Cominform

The origins of the Communist International (Comintern, or the 'Third International') can be found in the split between the majority of Social Democratic (Marxist) parties in the 'Second International' which supported their national war efforts in 1914, and a minority of Social Democrats who opposed war, who included the Bolshevik Vladimir Lenin. In September 1915, an International Socialist Group was founded at the Zimmerwald conference, and this ultimately became the Comintern in March 1919, formalising the split between pro-Soviet 'Communist' and 'Social Democratic' parties. Its goal was the promotion of the world revolution on the Bolshevik model of 1917.

Communist parties were founded most rapidly in Europe – by the end of 1921 they had been founded in all but four countries (Norway, Greece, Ireland and Albania); Communist parties had also been established in Asia (China, Korea, the Dutch East Indies, Iran and Turkey), North America (US, Canada), Australia, New Zealand, Egypt, South Africa and Algeria. By 1927 there were 47 parties and by 1935, 76, but many of these were very small: in 1927 over half of the parties had fewer than 1,000 members and only two, Germany's and Czechoslovakia's, had more than 100,000. The relationship between the central party organs in Moscow and local parties has been the subject of historiographical debate. The opening of Soviet archives in the 1990s has tended to support those who stress the importance of Moscow's control, although the debate continues, and scholars are still examining the interaction between Soviet imperatives and local context.

Even so, all are agreed that Communist parties had to follow the 'line' of the Soviet Communist Party as it zig-zagged between hostility to and accommodation with the 'bourgeois' moderate left. When it was founded, the Comintern's line was uncompromisingly revolutionary. However, in the summer of 1921, after the failure of revolutions in Hungary and Germany, and of Soviet intervention in Poland, Lenin declared that 'united fronts' had to be pursued with non-communist socialists and trade unionists because capitalism had undergone a 'temporary stabilization'. In China and Britain, in particular, close relations with non-communist forces were established.

However, the Bolshevik leadership became convinced that this policy was not working – the failure of the British General Strike in 1926, the nationalist Guomindang's attack on the Chinese Communist Party in 1927, and Stalin's conviction that Western powers were planning an invasion of the USSR, all led the Comintern to change its policy. In February 1928 the leadership argued that capitalism was now in crisis, revolution was necessary and alliances with Social Democrats were unacceptable. The new policy was defined as 'class against class'. Yet the rise of nazism in Germany showed that this policy was not working, and from the early 1930s national Communist parties some-times established informal alliances with Social Democrats against the radical right, occasionally with informal Comintern help. By 1934 Stalin accepted that Communist parties had to create 'popular fronts' with Social Democrats to counter the fascist threat, and appointed the main advocate of this policy, the Bulgarian Georgi Dimitrov, as head of the Comintern, who declared it the official line in February 1935.

The policy had some success, attracting new members to some parties, and popular front governments were established in France, Spain, Chile and Cuba. However, the ultimate goal of the policy – the avoidance of war – was not achieved, and the Comintern's line shifted drastically and embarrassingly, in 1939 endorsing the Nazi–Soviet pact, and in 1941 the war against fascism. From 1941 communists in allied states were expected to be patriotic and support their governments in their war efforts. The dissolution of the Comintern in 1943 was merely the continuation of this approach: the allies had to be assured that Communist parties were not agitating for world revolution, but following the foreign policy of the Soviet Union, which required loyalty to its allies.

With the beginning of the Cold War, Stalin decided to restore a Communist international organization, but, as its name suggested, the Communist Information Bureau (Cominform) founded in 1947 was a less ambitious organization and served the narrower requirements of Stalin's foreign policy more explicitly than its predecessor. It included the ruling parties of Eastern Europe except for the Albanian (to avoid upsetting the Yugoslavs) and the East German (because unification was still expected), together with the French and Italian parties. The Greek party was excluded, as it was involved in civil war and Stalin did not want to upset the West too much. No Asian or African party was invited to join, as Stalin's focus was on the balance of power in Europe. Soon after Stalin's death, in 1955, the Cominform was dissolved, as the embodiment of Stalin's authoritarian realpolitik in his relations with the international communist movement.

David Priestland

Bibliography

Claudin F. 1975. *The Communist movement from Comintern to Cominform.* Harmondsworth: Penguin.

McDermott K. and Agnew J. 1996. *The Comintern: A history of international Communism from Lenin to Stalin.* London: Macmillan (now Palgrave Macmillan).

Rees T. and Thorpe A. (eds) 1998. *International Communism and the Communist International.* Manchester: Manchester University Press.

Related essays
Cold War; Russian Revolution; socialism

Commission on International Labour Legislation

During the Paris Peace Conference in 1919 a special commission was set up to prepare the founding of the International Labour Organization (ILO), a new international organization for the promotion of labour standards worldwide. The Commission on International Labour Legislation was composed of experts from a broad range of disciplines and backgrounds. Focusing on the role of these experts, their trajectories, and the circulation of their ideas across national borders allows for an analysis of non-diplomats as important protagonists in international relations.

The members of the Commission on International Labour Legislation had been invited by the plenipotentiaries to the Peace Conference to advise the official delegates, who did not possess the necessary technical knowledge on labour matters. In 1919, during the immediate postwar euphoria, the idea of transnational labour regulation found fruitful soil. Through establishing uniform labour standards in order to improve working conditions and prevent unfair competition among states, the world leaders attempted to procure universal (social) peace. The Commission on International Labour Legislation, composed of 15 members from nine countries (Unites States, Great Britain, France, Italy, Japan, Belgium, Czechoslovakia, Poland, and Cuba), was a 'meeting point' of internationally renowned labour experts from different backgrounds: university professors, senior officials in government administration, trade unionists and political leaders.

The core members of the Commission knew one another from various international networks in politics, science, or labour administration before they came together in Paris in 1919. The International Association for Labour Legislation (IALL), for example, created in 1900, was a transnational epistemic community of social reformers that exchanged scientific knowledge about labour regulations in industrial countries, legitimized themes for public debate and recommended labour reforms to policy makers. The IALL, but also the Second International and the international trade union movement, were important because they translated new ideas for international social policies. The prewar contacts and activities in these various international networks enabled the members of the Commission on International Labour Legislation to come to concrete results very quickly in 1919 – in contrast to the general peace negotiations, where politicians debated, rather chaotically, on much less well-prepared issues.

Although the ILO founding fathers idealistically believed in creating universal social peace by means of international labour law, a new scientific discipline, the real outcome of the Commission's work was marked by political pragmatism. In the context of the plenary Peace Conference, national premises could not be fully trespassed upon. In developing the structure and the programme of the ILO, at least three major difficulties caused dissension.

Firstly, the problem of state sovereignty. The idea, strongly defended by French and Italian government officials and the international trade union movement, of a supranational 'parliament of labour' that could create binding international labour standards for the national states was thwarted by (especially American) non-interventionists. A compromise was achieved with the creation of a non-binding system of conventions and recommendations.

Secondly, the dominance of national labour traditions. In modelling the ILO's tripartite structure the American trade unions (American Federation of Labor, AFL) tried to minimize government participation. They traditionally did not trust the legislative powers of governmental authorities to improve labour standards and feared the idea of state control. But the Commission felt the obligation to create a framework that would be acceptable to the national parliaments, so finally it was decided that each national delegation to the International Labour Conference would be composed of two government representatives, one employer, and one worker.

Thirdly, the 'political viability' of the ILO programme. While organized labour and private experts, whose expectations ran high in the realm of transnational cooperation, pleaded for the drawing up of a detailed action plan, a general charter with minimum principles was adopted in order to be accepted by as many member states as possible.

The Commission produced a draft constitution of the ILO, which was approved by the Peace Conference and embodied in Part XIII of the 1919 Peace Treaties. The ILO came into being as the first international organization that recognized both trade unions and employers as full-fledged social partners of national governments. The 'invention' of transnational tripartism by the Commission on International Labour Legislation made the ILO a pioneering institution, since tripartite negotiations were hardly institutionalized within the national context at that time.

Jasmien Van Daele

Bibliography

Phelan E. 'The Commission on International Labor Legislation', in Shotwell J. T. (ed.) 1934. *The origins of the International Labor Organization*, Vol. 1, New York, Columbia University Press, 127–98.

Van Daele J. 2005. 'Engineering social peace: networks, ideas, and the founding of the International Labour Organization', *International Review of Social History*, 50, 3, 435–66.

Related essays

Abolition of Forced Labour Convention; cosmopolitanism and universalism; intellectual elites; intergovernmental organizations; international non-governmental organizations (INGOs); labour standards; League of Nations system; Pax Americana; social sciences; workers' movements; world orders

Commodity trading

This term conventionally indicates the collection, storage and exchange of raw materials, agricultural products, basic chemical products: goods which, on the market, are mainly differentiated by their price (according to standardized typologies). Since the mid 19th century the revolution in the fields of transport, goods preservation and communications, along with significant financial and organizational innovations, have globalized the transactions of commodities and, consequently, removed the determination of the price from the place of production.

Large transnational companies (TNCs) have established themselves as leaders in the new international markets. Some of them control very considerable portions of the production and trading of agricultural commodities: 20 companies control the coffee trade, six control 70 per cent of the grain trade, one controls 98 per cent of the production of packed tea. Along with more traditional commodities (such as grain, the trading of which has also been revolutionized), or 'new' raw materials (oil, rubber, fertilizers, etc.), in the last few decades the trade in commodities such as water or blood (plasma) has been developing in specific markets. To the list of the most transnational of commodities could also be added, though their trading is illegal: the trafficking (and smuggling) of human beings.

The reduction in the cost of maritime transport has been one of the most important factors in the creation of a global setting in commodity trading: between 1750 and 1990 the actual cost of overseas transport fell from 298 to 51 (100 = 1910). In real terms, the reduction in the cost of land transport was even more dramatic during the 19th century (90 per cent between 1800 and 1910), while the cost of air transport decreased by 80 per cent between 1930 and 1960, and that of telecommunications by 98 per cent.

This reduction was more marked between 1870 and 1913, while world trade expanded ten times as fast as world production, with a strong increase in the demand for maritime transport. The increase in international trade stimulated an extraordinary rise in the exchange of raw materials: between 1840 and 1893 the amount of traded coal increases by 65 times, and that of grain by 13. Together, the two commodities 'weighed' about half of the total maritime transport tonnage in 1893, as against 20 per cent in 1840. Such dramatic changes inevitably exposed local markets to international competition, especially with regard to agricultural products, which had long been protected by distances and space.

In the 20th century the composition of world trade changed, too: in 1937 the volume of agricultural and raw materials (fuels and non-ferrous metals) exports was still higher than the exports of manufactured goods, while in 1995 it was the other way round. The predominance of manufacturing trade is clearly mirrored in the so-called post-1945 'container revolution', which has completely altered the typology of maritime trade introduced by steam navigation.

The exceptional increase in the volume of commodities that were produced and exchanged was made possible by revolutionary qualitative, organizational and conceptual transformations. The most radical changes concerned the beginning of impersonal market relationships; considerable improvements in sea and rail transport; better safety guarantees (against piracy, for example); product standardization; product packaging; limited liability corporations and oligopoly (in 1909 oligopoly was already the most prevalent form in the tobacco, oil, rubber and raw metal industries); corporate trademarks; in particular, the end of seasonality in agriculture (continuous supplies from the two hemispheres); the emergence of a very small number of places fixing the price of commodities; finally, the creation of a global futures market, not by chance developed in the context of the trading of North American grains within Chicago's Board of Trade (1848).

The American case and the rise of Chicago as the premier world grain market was emblematic. The search for rationalization determined the construction of huge elevators driven by steam (the first appeared in Buffalo, New York state, in 1842), which greatly reduced the loading and unloading time between Midwest trains and ships heading for New York and the Atlantic. The sale in sacks by the single producer to the single trader-middleman was substituted by a preliminary assessment based on quality and then by the separate storing of wheat of similar quality. Thus, wheat of a certain grade could immediately be given a value and became exchangeable in time, that is to say with the future production of grains of the same quality: 'because now a ton of this year's "number 2 spring wheat" was also interchangeable with a ton of next year's, wheat futures trading, options, and the Chicago Board of Trade were born' (Pomeranz and Topik 2006, 187).

The new futures trade opened the way for speculators, who were totally uninterested in buying or selling grains, as well as for the manipulation of the price on the part of speculating traders 'cornering' the market (that is, controlling or owning enough of the available supply of a commodity or security in order to manipulate the price). Famous corners were made by Hutchinson (1888), Leiter (1898), and Patten (1909): regardless of their degree of success, these caused abrupt increases in the price of grains, whose consequences were felt in many areas of the world. Leiter's attempt, for example, contributed to the outbreak of riots in Italy and Spain, which resulted in violent demonstrations causing dozens of casualties.

During the ancien regime the grain trade was characterized by the predominance of small regional markets, considerable difference in seasonal productions, high price volatility, and an endemic recurrence of famines and food riots. During the 19th century the picture transformed radically, thanks to the establishment of a new, integrated world food system: similar consumption models spread all over the world while agriculture, from traditional food producer, changed into supplier of raw materials to the food industry, with a downward trend in both the actual price of grain and its volatility.

In 1815 wheat was an essentially European product; in 1913 it mostly came from North and South America, India, Australia, Russia; in the 18th century wool came from Spain, in the 19th century from Central Europe and, since the beginning of the 20th century, from countries in the Southern hemisphere; in 1905 Japan overtook China in silk exports and also left behind the Mediterranean countries, while the rubber produced in Southeast Asia (Ceylon, Malaysia, Indonesia, Indochina) replaced rubber from the Amazonian region. At the beginning of the 19th century the price of grain was basically fixed in Gdansk, demonstrating the importance of the Eastern European supply area. From the 1860s, instead, Liverpool rapidly became the main port from which grains entered Europe, due to the strong demand of the whole industrial-metropolitan area in northern England as well as to larger and larger imports of American and Russian grain. As from 1868 Liverpool – by then connected to America by telegraph – was equipped for transatlantic grain trade and could receive 5,000-ton ships, soon becoming the most important European grain port, while from 1880 futures began to be traded. The price volatility reduced by one third in 19th-century Europe compared to the

previous centuries. On the other hand, it is possible to demonstrate that, for instance, in mid-19th-century England there was a strong correlation between the negative fluctuations of domestic crops and an increase in ship building – above all in Canada – financed by joint-stock companies.

The traditional importance of geographical distances declined rapidly: the difference in the price of wheat between Odessa and Liverpool, which in 1870 was close to 40 per cent, by 1906 had been almost completely erased, and these cities' grain markets were more integrated than the Liverpool and New York ones. However, for the creation of a real global grain market it was necessary to wait for the integration between the production and trading of wheat (the main staple of the Atlantic world) and rice (the main staple of the Pacific and Indian Ocean worlds, whose consumption was affected by strong dietary preference for some kinds of rice), characterized by the mutual conditioning of their price.

In the mid 19th century there was no integrated rice market yet, but from that time onwards a new kind of consumer appeared, who was willing to consume rice according to its price. A trade in rice futures, similar to the grain futures trade conducted in Chicago, and in Liverpool from 1883 onward, started up in Singapore at the end of the century. The heart of this transformation was India, one of the main producers and exporters of grains (both wheat and rice) in the 19th century. Millions of Indians were too poor not to take price into account in their purchases, and when the price of rice rose, at the end of the 19th century, exports readily increased, while the consumers switched to wheat: 'For the first time, a worldwide market existed in the most basic of commodities, and for the first time – like it or not – the impact of harvests in Saskatchewan was felt in Sichuan, no matter what the local population grew, or ate' (Pomeranz and Topik 2006, 188).

The old regional production system was disrupted also thanks to the appearance, at the end of the 19th century, of new technologies suitable for the transport of highly perishable tropical goods, as was the case with bananas, for the trade of which in 1870 the Boston Fruit Company (from 1899 United Fruit Company) was founded, possessing the largest private merchant fleet at the time, the Great White Fleet.

The new world food system has witnessed the decline of the traditional commercial transnationality, with its myriad middlemen, substituted by the transnationality of a few large corporations (but in which the control of the founding families lasts for a long time, in some cases until today). The main companies that in the 1990s were still dominant in commodity trading – Cargill, Continental Grain, Louis Dreyfus, Bunge and Born, Garnac – began operating in the turbulent mid-19th-century grain market.

Louis Dreyfus's house provides a typical example: from short-range trading by river between France and Germany at mid 19th century to the Mediterranean exchanges between Odessa, Leghorn and Marseille, to overseas trade. Cargill, founded in 1865, is America's largest privately owned firm. As of 2007 it employed 158,000 people in 66 countries and today it is devoted to trading and processing grains, oilseeds, fruit juices, tropical commodities and fibres, meats and eggs, salt and petroleum, livestock feeds, fertilizers and seeds. These companies are often 'invisible giants' with no obligation, as is the case with joint-stock companies, to make public the data necessary for a factual and independent reconstruction of their history and transactions.

The trading of commodities also changed national and regional situations. The 19th-century transformation of guano into a commodity (started in 1842 and monopolized for about twenty years by the London company Antony Gibbs & Sons) – without looking for monocausal and reductive economic explanations – deeply influenced both Peru's public finances and the international relationships in the region. The search for guano spurred the United States to pass the Guano Islands Act in 1856: in the space of ten years about sixty islands, above all in the Pacific Ocean, the so-called 'American Polynesia', were claimed and registered by the Department of State as 'guano islands', while the guano trade launched American trade houses which were destined to rapidly become large TNCs, for example W. R. Grace & Co., which later proved successful in the chemical field. The collection of guano in Peruvian islands also forced some populations in the Pacific to move: the Peruvian and Chilean governments used convicts, indentured Chinese workers, and they kidnapped and enslaved almost all of the populations of Easter Island and Tongareva (Penrhyn, Cook Islands), before international protests stopped this traffic.

The case of plasma sheds light on the most recent commodification phenomena in the field of biological products. By the late 1990s the so-called biologics industry, that controlled the collection, processing and trading of plasma, had a turnover of about US$5 billion a year, but without a central clearing house. Pharmaceutical companies (such as Bayer, which later abandoned this sector) generally relied on their own networks to collect 'raw' plasma, even though there existed intermediary companies. But lately the whole market has radically changed, also thanks to the production, via genetic engineering, of many plasma-related products, such as Factor 8 for haemophiliacs, and it is monitored – after the major scandals exposed in the 1980s – by associations such as the Plasma Protein Therapeutics Association (PPTA).

Trade has been always a vector of transnational behaviours and organizations. But in the last 150 years the exponential quantitative growth of commodity trading, and the process of commodification of many new goods, have affected both the world map of production and the world labour market, centralizing the price-fixing process, backing up the development of TNCs, revamping the global port hierarchy and the ancient entrepôt system. Meanwhile, the availability of old and new goods triggered converging ways of production, trade and consumption, led both by transnational patterns of colonization and by imitative catching up.

Carlo Fumian

Bibliography

Bairoch P. 1997. *Victoires et déboires: histoire économique et sociale du monde du XVIe siècle à nos jours*, 2 vols. Paris: Gallimard.

Bordo M. D., Taylor A. M. and Williamson J. G. (eds) 2003. *Globalization in historical perspective*. Chicago and London: University of Chicago Press.

Federico G. 2005. *Feeding the world: An economic history of agriculture, 1800–2000*. Princeton: Princeton University Press.

Fumian C. 2003. *Verso una società planetaria: alle origini della globalizzazione contemporanea (1870–1914)*. Rome: Donzelli.

Kenwood A. G. and Lougheed A. L. 1999. *The growth of the international economy 1820–2000*. London and New York: Routledge.

McCusker J. J. (ed.) 2006. *History of world trade since 1450.* Farmington Hills: Thomson Gale.

O'Rourke K. H. and Williamson J. G 1999. *Globalization and history: the evolution of a nineteenth-century Atlantic economy.* Cambridge, MA and London: MIT Press.

Pomeranz K. and Topik S. 2006. *The world that trade created: society, culture, and the world economy, 1400 to the present,* 2nd edition. New York and London: M. E.Sharpe.

Related essays

agriculture; Chinese Diaspora; containerized freight; convergence and divergence; corporations; crime; drugs (illicit); financial markets; food; forests; gold; iron and steel; measurement; oil; Pax Americana; railways; rubber; salt; Samsung; seeds; silk; steamships; trade; trade agreements; transportation infrastructures; United Fruit Company; yoga

Communist Manifesto

The *Communist Manifesto* was born as a transnational work. Karl Marx and Friedrich Engels were commissioned to write it by a semi-secret society of German exiles which had created 'correspondence committees' in Paris, Brussels, London and other European capitals, becoming in the 1840s a sort of *avant la lettre* International. Marx and Engels had contributed to the doctrinaire and organizational renewal of the Bund der Gerechten (League of the Just), which under their influence abandoned conspiracy, veered towards political action and changed its name to the Communist League (Bund der Communisten). In its second congress, which gathered in London in 1847, the League commissioned Marx and Engels with the writing of a public programme. Engels had previously written, in Paris, the 'Principles of Communism' to that effect, a sort of political 'catechism' in the traditional question-and-answer format. But Marx, from Brussels, blended Engels' work into a new text, which he gave the manifesto format that earned it its fame, between December 1847 and January 1848. It made its first public appearance in London, in German, under the title *Manifest dei kommunistischen Partei* in February 1848, on the eve of the European Revolution.

Paradoxically, the pamphlet went almost unnoticed then, but in one and a half centuries it has never gone out of print and has been translated into all of the world's languages.

It was first translated into English (1850), Russian (1859), Spanish and French (1872). Many quotes – such as 'Proletarians of all countries, unite!' – have become worldwide mottoes. Between 1871 and 1917, its titled shortened to *Communist Manifesto,* it was disseminated on the wings of the new labourist parties. After the Russian Revolution in October 1917, it became the canonical text of the Communist world, while left-wing thinkers and academics have reworked it endlessly ever since.

Horacio Tarcus

Bibliography

Andréas B. 1963. *Le Manifeste Communiste de Marx et Engels: histoire et bibliographie 1848–1918.* Milan: Feltrinelli.

Related essays

Bible; exile; Koran; Little Red Book; publishing; Russian Revolution; socialism; *The Wretched of the Earth;* translation; workers' movements

Conceptualism

Conceptualism is much more than a specific trend or artistic movement: it is the turn that contemporary art has taken since the 1960s, and which could be defined as a delayed 'Duchamp effect'. The different appropriations and implications of Duchamp's legacy towards an 'anti-retinal painting' (art understood as a device that works as a mental operation, implying the elimination of all visual information and of the conventions of representation) lay out a necessarily self-reflective nature for contemporary art, which lays bare its procedures for construction, puts its dialogues with the history of art on display and reflects critically on its mechanisms of production, circulation and consumption.

According to Benjamin Buchloh, conceptualism implies the subsequent assault on the different dimensions of the artistic object as it was understood until then: its visual aspects (inasmuch as visuality is eliminated and the traditional definitions of representation are displaced), its status as merchandise and its forms of distribution. Along similar lines, Mari Carmen Ramírez identifies conceptualism as a major 20th-century leap in the understanding and production of art (the second most important after the revolution of the historical avant-garde movements), that called obsolete the status and preciousness of the autonomous work of art and transferred the artistic practice from aesthetics to the realm of linguistics. It is not, therefore, one of the many new styles that took place one after the other in postwar art, but a 'strategy of anti-discourse' against the fetishism of art and the systems of circulation and production of the work of art in late capitalism.

In an accelerated, generalized process of experimentation, artists go beyond the bidimensional limits of painting into the object, and even interventions, happenings and spaces. The materiality of the work is also expanded remarkably by incorporating not only ignoble or ephemeral elements (urban trash, organic waste, etc.), but even procedures and devices taken from other disciplines and forms of knowledge (from mathematics to sociology). Any aspect of reality becomes susceptible to being signalled and appropriated as 'art'. The extreme physical fragility of the work, its ephemeral condition, means that more emphasis is laid on the process than the final result.

The word 'conceptualism' was not taken up unanimously throughout the world. Peruvian Juan Acha uses the category of non-objectualism to describe these new artistic experiences, whereas American Lucy Lippard and Argentine Oscar Masotta use the term dematerialization. It is worth mentioning that we are always talking about displacing the emphasis from the object towards the conception and the project, towards the receiver's perceptive, imaginative or creative behaviour. The viewer is no longer in front of the work, and is instead located within the work, which is modified by their presence and participation. Also, their consciousness is modified by their contact with the artistic experience. Even in the most extreme cases, we cannot talk about a full dematerialization, since the written or spoken word is also material.

In recent years, the Anglo-American canonical version of the origins of conceptual art, which circumscribed the movement to its linguistic or tautological trend represented mostly by Joseph Kosuth and the British group Art & Language, has been questioned insofar as it is limited mostly to male artists located in the 'centres'. An exhibit such as 'L'Art conceptuel: une perspective' (Musée d'Art Moderne de la Ville de Paris, 1989) is symptomatic of that limitation. Benjamin Buchloh

has criticized emphatically the organizing criteria of that exhibit. Other versions of conceptual art have established counterpoints with the aforementioned Anglo-American positivist canon of conceptual art and work towards constructing a heterogeneous, off-centred and multicentred model. 'Global conceptualism' highlights not only the early practices generated outside of the centre (in Latin America and Eastern Europe, mostly), but also practices which took place in the United States or Central Europe and were displaced from the canon. A series of international exhibitions, books and anthologies in recent years support a broadening of the perspective on global conceptualism. Clearly, the curatorial operations that Luis Camnitzer, Jane Farver and Rachel Weiss, Mari Carmen Ramírez and others have been carrying out since 1999 (mostly in American museums and universities) have shaken up the canonical narrative of conceptualism, which has become more inclusive.

To this effect, Alex Alberro points out four trajectories in the early days of conceptualism. The first is the self-reflexivity of modernist painting and sculpture that systematically problematizes and dismantles the integral elements of the traditional structure of the artwork. The second trajectory is the 'reductivism' of artwork in a complete dematerialization. The third genealogy of conceptualism is a negation of aesthetic content. And the fourth trajectory is one that problematizes placement.

As early as in 1972, Marchán Fiz pointed out the existence of an 'ideological conceptualism' which aimed at becoming actively involved with 'the real'. He included in this characterization some Spanish (the Catalan Grup de Treball) and Latin American expressions which surfaced in the 1960s and 70s within dictatorships, and which spent as much energy in trying to define the limits of artistic languages as in establishing the relationship between the artistic institutions and ideology and politics.

The peculiar nature of the relationship between this cultural process and the centre(s) lies in what Ramírez calls 'a model of inversion' (inasmuch as the assimilation or conversion of central art on the peripheries is guided by an internal dynamics and the contradictions of the local context), in which politics serves as a starting point to question art as an institution. Thus, Latin American conceptualism differs from the canonical version in its ideological and ethical profile, its will to transform the world through the specificity of its art. Latin Americans do not cling to the idea of art in terms of autonomy. Rather, conceptualism appears as a strategy to expose the limits between art and life, which in that precise historical context were translated as avant garde and revolution. Many of its products go beyond the restricted circulation of the art world and aim at a massive scope.

Ramírez supports its 'precursor nature', distinguishable through its eclectic, heterogeneous (and contradictory) forms, which are not subordinated to metropolitan canons. He refers to three moments: the first, between 1966 and 1974, was restricted to Brazil, Argentina and the community of Latin American artists settled in New York; during the second, between 1975 and 1980, conceptualism expanded to other countries (for instance, Chile's so-called 'avant-garde scene'); and the third is identified by the institutionalization of conceptualism on the subcontinent.

Within this framework, landmarks of the Argentinean avant garde of the 1960s such as Arte de los Medios (1966) and Tucumán Arde (1968) are today recognized as precursors in the history of global conceptualism. The Arte de los Medios (Media Art) collective started out with an 'anti-happening': the invention of an event (a non-existent 'happening') that many mass media outlets reported, thanks to the information disseminated in fake news releases, doctored photographs, false testimonies, etc. The circle closed when the artists denied the news, revealing not only the obvious fact that the media lie, but also an idea which was advanced for its time: that they construct reality. In 1968, Tucumán Arde (Tucumán Burns) was a collective work by avant-garde artists in Rosario and Buenos Aires, direct heir to 'Arte de los Medios', which aimed at drawing public attention to the crisis that struck a province of the north of Argentina and at refuting the doctored information issued by the state on the situation, through a complex operation that included on-site research by the artists, in which they resorted to multiple means, as well as a massive incognito campaign, and the exhibition of the materials they produced on the premises of the unions that opposed the military regime. Government pressure interrupted the exhibition in Buenos Aires and brought about the dissolution of this radicalized avant-garde movement.

In contrast to the Anglo-American version of conceptualism, that has directed its criticism towards the institutionalized artistic world, Latin American conceptualism targeted the public sphere. It did not insist on emphasizing the limits of the modern notion of autonomous art. Latin American conceptualist artists were claiming neither a place for themselves in the artistic establishment, nor a recognition of their peripheral condition, but something much more daring: they wanted, by overflowing it, to question the very statute of art.

Ana Longoni

Bibliography

Alberro A. and Stimson B. 1999. *Conceptual art: a critical anthology.* Cambridge, MA and London: MIT Press.

Buchloh B. 2004. *Formalismo e historicidad: modelos y métodos en el arte del siglo XX.* Madrid: Akal.

Camnitzer L., Farver J. and Weiss R. 1999. *Global conceptualism: points of origin, 1950s–1980s.* Flushing, NY: Queens Museum of Art.

Marchán Fiz S. 1972. *Del arte objetual al arte del concepto.* Madrid: Akal.

Related essays

antropofagia; avant garde; literature; modernismo; theatre

Condom

Although the condom has been in use since at least the 16th century and has been fashioned from such materials as linen and stitched sheep intestine ('lambskin'), the latex condom occupies an important place in modern history as an international commodity of the industrializing world, an effective prophylactic for transnational public health advocates, and a controversial contraceptive device.

After American Charles Goodyear vulcanized rubber in 1839 and patented the rubber condom in 1844, companies like the British E. Lambert and Sons soon became worldwide producers. Early sheet rubber condoms like the UK's 'Paragon' (1891) were unattractively thick, but in 1919, American Frederick Killian developed a hand-dipped natural latex version that was thinner, odourless, cheaper than most lambskin, and lasted three to five years.

Despite more effective production techniques, condoms connoted illicit sex and faced strong opposition from some quarters. The Catholic Church argued that all contraceptive devices were against 'the law of God and nature' (Pope Pius XI, 1930), and pronatalist Americans, Britons, and Germans (among others) opposed personal prophylaxis into the early 20th century. It was not until the explosion of sexually transmitted infections during World War I – particularly among American GIs – that more governments began acknowledging the importance of practical preventive measures. By World War 2, both Allied and Axis governments were issuing condoms to their troops and encouraging soldiers to 'put it on before you put it in' (US). In short, the global movement of troops triggered a worldwide escalation in sexually transmitted infections, which in turn adjusted sexual mores and condom use, at least temporarily.

After 1945, non-governmental organizations, intergovernmental organizations, and bilateral aid programs enthusiastically endorsed condoms in the developing world. Ansell International, a condom producer now owned by Dunlop Australia, became the largest supplier to the United States Agency for International Development for use in developing nations. The International Planned Parenthood Federation (IPPF) encouraged advertising agencies to share marketing techniques in Thailand, Iran, and Ghana, and companies like Lipton and Union Carbide participated in the government-subsidized condom programme in India; the Rockefeller, Ford, and Asia Foundations also assisted with distribution in the developing world. In the early 1960s, American and Japanese companies dominated international condom sales and standards, together exporting over 14,000 kilos of condoms to Peru in 1963 and sending expert advisors to South Koreans building their own condom factory in 1964. Overall, however, inadequate supplies of disposable condoms and the inconvenience of 'wash and reuse' condoms undermined use in many countries during the 1960s: aid workers preferred sterilization and intrauterine devices for their low price and efficiency, while women increasingly chose the pill for the privacy and control it afforded them. The condom was neither the prophylactic nor contraceptive method of choice.

The HIV/AIDS epidemic changed this. National governments had already begun savvier campaigns to manage international sexually transmitted infections transmission, as in the case of Thailand which distributed condoms at Cambodian refugee camps in the 1970s. After HIV/AIDS hit in the 1980s, Thailand started a much-praised 100% Condom Program (1991) targeting both sexually transmitted infections and HIV seroprevalence in the sex industry. The incurable nature of HIV/AIDS, along with the lack of any known vaccine and the inaccessibility of treatment in many parts of the world, brought the condom into unprecedented favour. The IPPF tripled condom supplies to Africa from 1987 to 1990, and the World Health Organization, United Nations Population Fund, and US Agency for International Development together delivered 258 million condoms to that continent by 1990. The Dutch received the European Health Award for its 'Have safe sex or no sex' campaign (1993) openly displaying a condom and including homosexual couples, and organizations like the Society for Women and AIDS in Africa, the Joint United Nations Programme on HIV/AIDS, and the Female Health Company promoted the new female condom in the late 1990s, rejoicing in women's increased control over disease prevention.

Today condoms continue to be internationally produced and marketed, with 8 to 10 billion male condoms being made annually. Production has largely shifted from the West to Asia and Central America, and brands like Durex (UK) and Carter-Wallace's 'Trojans' (US) have become household names around the world. Heated debates continue about appropriate use and distribution, and some programmes like the five-year American Presidential Emergency Plan for AIDS Relief (2004) controversially allocated the lion's share of its US$15 billion budget to abstinence over condom or other prophylactic education in the developing world.

Nancy H. Kwak

Bibliography
Mindel A. (ed.) 2000. *Condoms*. London: BMJ Books.

Related essays
Acquired Immunodeficiency Sydrome (AIDS); birth control; developmental assistance; family; Ford Foundation;

intergovernmental organizations; international non-governmental organizations (INGOs); philanthropic foundations; population; rubber; war

Congress for Cultural Freedom

The purpose of the Congress for Cultural Freedom (CCF) was to build a transnational network of anti-Stalinist intellectuals and scholars for the cause of defending freedom of thought and expression. Its inaugural meeting was held during 26–29 June 1950 in the Titaniapalast, a cinema in West Berlin, and soon afterwards it established a permanent secretariat in Paris. In the late 1960s it was revealed first via the New York Times that the CCF had received large-scale funding from the Central Intelligence Agency, and the resulting scandal forced many original members to resign and its name to be changed to the International Association for Cultural Freedom (IACF). Grants from the Ford Foundation sustained the IACF for several more years, but in 1979 it too was closed down, its mission no longer clear.

From the Paris secretariat the CCF functioned through various associated national bodies (such as the American Committee for Cultural Freedom and the British Society for Cultural Freedom). Its political outlook was centre-right/centre-left, and in its promotion of an anti-Communist consensus it opposed neutralism in the West as much as Soviet repression in the East. It was also predominantly a transatlantic network, with the main goal being to establish strong bonds between European and American intellectuals. Of the 21 nationalities represented at the inaugural conference, only two were non-European. However, greater attention was given to developing contacts in the Third World from the late 1950s onwards due to the strategic impact of decolonization. Between 1951 and 1966 the CCF organized major conferences and seminars in Bombay, Rangoon, Mexico City, Tokyo, Ibadan, Canberra, Cairo, Khartoum, Freetown, Dakar, Manila, Montevideo, Nairobi, and Kuala Lumpur.

The CCF's importance as a transnational institution, and its lasting legacy, stem largely from two sources. Firstly, there was its structural power as a well-funded organizer among the postwar intelligentsia. Alongside the conferences and book publications, great emphasis was placed on creating and sponsoring high-quality scholarly journals in several different countries. The aim was to use the journals as a means to attract and maintain an intellectual community sympathetic to the central principles of the CCF. Significantly, these publications generally sought to avoid direct intellectual combat with left-wing and Communist detractors, with editorials choosing instead a middle-ground position and a mix of political analysis and cultural review essays ensuring a broader public appeal. Most notorious was Encounter in London, but other prominent titles in the Congress stable were Preuves (France), Tempo Presente (Italy), Der Monat (Germany), Cuadernos (Spain), Quest (India), Quadrant (Australia), and Soviet Survey (later Survey). Some, such as Minerva and China Quarterly, are still in print.

Secondly, in the context of the Cold War, there was the role of the CCF as a normative institution. This is particularly evident in its support for the End of Ideology hypothesis. Emerging in the mid-1950s from the combined work of Frenchman Raymond Aron and the Americans Daniel Bell, Edward Shils, and Seymour Martin Lipset, the End of Ideology position claimed that politics should no longer be defined as a contest between rival ideological movements of the right or the left. Instead, the common forces of industrialization were causing both democratic capitalist and authoritarian collectivist systems to adopt similar methods of socioeconomic, technocratic management. The CCF promoted the view that the increasing application of scientific methods to social problems needed to be assessed, especially in terms of their success, efficiency, and implications for democracy, individuality, and freedom. This effectively shifted the debate away from simplistic observations on East–West competition, thereby claiming greater scholarly merit and opening up a dialogue with a wider audience. The CCF's Future of Freedom conference held in Milan in September 1955, at which Aron, Bell, and Shils participated, was the headline event in this movement. It was followed by seminars in Europe, Africa, and East Asia that focused on the relevance of these developments for the newly independent, industrializing states in Asia and Africa.

Giles Scott-Smith

Bibliography
Coleman P. 1989. *The liberal conspiracy: The Congress for Cultural Freedom and the struggle for the mind of postwar Europe.* New York: Free Press.
Grémion P. 1995. *Intelligence de l'anticommunisme: Le Congrès pour la Liberté de la Culture à Paris 1950–1975.* Paris: Fayard.
Scott-Smith G. 2002. *The politics of apolitical culture: The Congress for Cultural Freedom, the CIA, and postwar American hegemony.* London: Routledge.
Stonor Saunders F. 1999. *Who paid the piper? The CIA and the cultural cold war.* London: Granta.

Related essays
capitalism; Cold War; Comintern and Cominform; decolonization; European Union (EU); Ford Foundation; governance; governing science; humanities; intellectual elites; North Atlantic Treaty Organization (NATO); Pax Americana; philanthropic foundations; Pugwash Conferences; social sciences; socialism; Westernization; world orders

Conservation and preservation

Early scientific conservation ideas about vegetation and climatic change strove to control nature without destroying the basis for human subsistence and future use. The earliest uses of the word 'conservation' dating back to 1490 concerned official responsibilities for rivers, sewers and forests. 'Conservation' was one of the ways that the Graeco-Islamic traditions of thinking about nature were transformed by the scientific revolution, and became philosophies of governance. Although natural philosophy was concerned with the conservation of matter and energy, 'conservation' was more commonly used for technical management of public goods, especially water and forests, by the state in the long term. 'Preservation' concerned romantic or nostalgic ideas about restoring nature's 'balance' (often the preindustrial landscape in Europe) and was seldom the focus of state initiatives.

Concern in Britain about deforestation dated back to John Evelyn (1664), but forest estates and forestry practice remained largely in private hands until the 19th century. By contrast, in France the state led a vigorous forest conservancy initiative (following the French Forest Ordinance of 1669), containing the seeds of 'wise use' conservation ideas that shaped much transnational forestry education and practice for the next two centuries. British imperialism, which grew rapidly from 1847, developed practical conservation in the crucible of Indian forests. Education in forestry was led by French and German forestry schools. Towards the end of the 19th century Oxford and Yale also became major players.

The great 19th-century idea about scientific conservation linked anthropogenic deforestation with other losses and changing climatic conditions. The German scientific traveller, Alexander von Humboldt, observed in 1849 that by felling trees which cover the tops and sides of mountains, men in every climate prepare at once two calamities for future generations – the want of fuel and the scarcity of water. The American diplomat, George Perkins Marsh, who also travelled widely in Europe in the course of his work, took this further, showing how physical geography could be modified by human action. *Man and Nature* (1864) brought together his observations about the disappearance of forests from New England and Italy, and the erosive consequences of changing the face of the earth from a 'sponge' into a 'dust heap'. Marsh considered the whole forest, not just the products of immediate use to humanity. His ideas about 'physical geography' included concern for wildlife, watersheds and intangible forest values. Preservationists and conservationists alike heeded his words.

William Schlich, one-time head of Indian forestry, in his influential *Manual of Forestry* (1889), commented on the direct and indirect value of forests to the economy that the former chiefly through their produce, and the latter through the influence which they exercise upon climate, the regulation of moisture, the stability of the soil, the healthiness of a country and allied subjects. Conservation was a 'contract with nature', philosophically tied to capitalism, industrialism and modernity, in a deal whereby conservation was provided in exchange for sustained, long-term yield.

Tropical Indian forest regions were experimental training grounds for transnationalism. Indian foresters established New Zealand's first forest service in 1876 and one in Mauritius in 1880. By 1882, requests had also been received from Ceylon, Cyprus and the Cape Colony, and Indian foresters continued to head forest authorities emerging in the early 20th century (for example, Kenya 1902;

Nigeria 1903; Gold Coast 1909; Sierra Leone 1911; Uganda 1917) and Forest Commissions in various Australian states from 1918 to 1921. Tropical environments revealed more quickly than elsewhere the potential for destruction and desiccation caused by European-style 'development', and, as Richard Grove has argued, provided a crucible for conservation thinking from the 17th and 18th centuries, some of which transferred via India back to Europe and North America.

In the United States, the progressive conservationist, Gifford Pinchot, defined 'conservation' as the opposite of 'waste', distinguishing it from 'preservation'. Pinchot trained at Yale, but also studied at the national French forestry school in Nancy, before founding the United States Forest Service in 1905. Pinchot also established the Conservation League of America (CLA) in 1908 to provide popular support for 'progressive development' through the wise use of natural resources, especially water and timber. Pinchot's claim to have originated the term 'conservation' is disputed, but he did make it popular, and distinct from the preservationist thinking of other growing groups such as the Sierra Club. While preservationists fought for wild country (by definition, outside the economy), the CLA was concerned with professional and government conservation of economically valuable resources.

Progressive conservation was readily translated elsewhere in the world, and Pinchot's philosophy was highly influential in Canada, South Africa and Australia. The idea of sustained yield was important not just in forests but also in fisheries and increasingly in the management of game (later wildlife). In Canada, like the Pacific northwest, forestry, fisheries and game management often went together. 'Wise use' conservation applied to soil in southern Africa, and was part of progressive agricultural practice, where the veldt was seen as analogous to forest.

The idea of the state being responsible for conservation (whether it was forests, water, fisheries or game) was a key legacy of Pinchot, and his friend and President, Theodore Roosevelt. The United States 'federal' model was much discussed even where states took major responsibilities for natural resource management, such as in Australia and Canada. An example of progressivism applied to water management was that of the American, Elwood Mead, who was the foundation chairman of the State Rivers and Water Supply Commission in Victoria, Australia in 1907. Mead advocated higher-yielding uses of water and land, as well as dams to ensure reliable supply, and built a bureaucracy to lead these initiatives.

Preservation, by contrast, was typically the province of community and amateur natural history groups with local concerns. It was usually less transnational in reach, but a notable exception was the international 'preservationist' campaign run largely by amateur ornithologists that led to the closing of plumage markets in New York in 1913 and London in 1914.

Wildlife was a central conservation concern in places where its commercial value was high, such as Canada and Africa. By the end of the 19th century the value of wildlife in Africa was increasingly derived not so much from animal products, as from their status as 'game' for recreation. Sporting hunting was increasingly reserved for wealthy European and American foreigners. While in England, Germany and Sweden game was managed and defended against poaching by wealthy private owners (including Royalty), the state took responsibility for game reserves in places like the Transvaal. Such reserves protected wildlife from subsistence hunters and also from diseases such as Rinderpest. In Canada, the Great Depression of the 1930s forced greater state efforts for wildlife preservation, driven by the interests of the local poor, rather than the foreign rich. The beaver and muskrat preserves established in Quebec, Ontario, Manitoba and Saskatchewan provided unemployment relief in the 1930s and 40s, and were rationalized by the notion that the availability of wildlife for trapping might reduce the rising costs of Aboriginal welfare. Wildlife conservation tended to be advocated by ecologists and other biologists, rather than foresters, and in Canada, the Oxford trained ecologist, Charles Elton, was influential.

In the southwestern United States, Aldo Leopold (trained at the Yale forestry school) developed a philosophy about co-managing the conservation of forests and the preservation of wildlife, especially wolves. He also worked to restore eroded farming land in Wisconsin, and this was the subject of essays in Sand County Almanac (1949). In 'Thinking like a mountain', Leopold urged his readers to take the broad perspective of the mountain itself, and go beyond the squabbling between deer-hunters and foresters, each of whom sought to conserve only what they needed.

In the 1930s 'dustbowl' events struck both the central United States and large swathes of southeastern Australia, dramatically defining 'limits' to agricultural development. Soil conservation science was recognized as crucial to the prevention of erosion and gullying in South Africa as well. F. E. Kanthack, Director of Irrigation at the Cape, made a passionate speech to the South African Association for the Advancement of Science in 1908 about gully erosion in which he called for an extension of Pinchot's progressive forest conservation to include the veldt. In Australia, the literary biologist, Francis Ratcliffe, who trained under Julian Huxley at Oxford at the same time as Charles Elton, was one of the major advocates of soil conservation through his powerful popular book, Flying fox and drifting sand: the adventures of a biologist in Australia (1938). Judge Leonard Stretton, in his Royal Commission into the major fires of 1939 in southeastern Australia, recognized the conservation of forests, soil and water as interrelated concerns, in his term 'The Inseparable Trinity'.

Forests have remained central to ideas about conservation. Very long-term 'officialdom' is needed to support their requirements for 40 years and longer between yields – even up to 400-year cycles in New Zealand, for sustaining slow-growing Podocarps. As forestry became an entrenched arm of the state, long-term management styles became increasingly out of step with new developments in environmental thinking in the latter half of the 20th century. An environmental revolution in the 1970s across much of the Western world redefined relations between people and forests. Borrowing preservationist ideas from European and North American Romantic traditions, many 'eco-activists', working outside the structures of the state, argued that the intrinsic value of nature was higher than its utilitarian value, and argued for the preservation of 'old growth' forests. New Age thinking also brought a greater appreciation of contemplation – looking at nature without destroying it – rather than consumption, echoing earlier moves in the 1930s and 40s away from hunting wildlife to photography and observation. Some environmentalists took the extreme view that plants, animals and landscapes had 'moral standing'. The environmental revolution

gave 'preservation' an international platform as never before. Groups like Greenpeace have since the 1970s engaged actively on the international stage over such issues as whaling, international fisheries and the question of mining in Antarctica.

The World Conservation Strategy of 1980 was, however, still primarily economic in focus, concluding that conservation of living resources was needed to preserve genetic diversity, to maintain essential ecological processes, and to ensure the sustainable use of species and ecosystems. It aimed to ensure stocks of plants and animals, and clean air, water and soil for human use in the future. Since the 1990s, influenced by the Brundtland Report, Our Common Future (1987), the value of nature to disadvantaged peoples has become better acknowledged in the global environmental agenda. Forests, water and common lands provide crucial subsistence for some of the world's poorest peoples. In the 1960s and 70s, the Australian Conservation Foundation (ACF) concentrated its efforts on 'kangaroos' and 'the Great Barrier Reef', ignoring industrial needs such as oil and fossil fuels. The ACF also overlooked the plight of Aboriginal people, despite an active contemporaneous social movement for indigenous land rights. Two decades later, indigenous and green activism was pursued as a joint purpose. 'Nature' was no longer isolated from society and economy, and the conservation agenda reflected this. Nor was it just the province of government. Large corporate international groups such as the Nature Conservancy Council and World Wide Fund for Nature have increasingly worked to preserve biodiversity through philanthropic support, not just by lobbying governments, but by paying for conservation initiatives from private funds.

In the 21st century, forests, wetlands and increasingly, production landscapes are being 'conserved' as biodiversity increasingly becomes accounted for as part of the economy. Central to the idea of ecosystem services (or what the environment provides that makes life possible, including clean water, fresh air and shelter) are sciences like conservation biology that measure environmental change and assess how environments provide that service. Gretchen Daily defined 'ecological services' as including 'production' (food, pharmaceuticals, fibre, energy, industrial products and genetic resources), 'regeneration' (cycling and filtration), 'stabilization' (saving coasts, mountains and river banks from erosion), and 'life-fulfilling processes' (aesthetic beauty – but in the 'eye of the beholder', not intrinsic worth). She also included 'preservation' – but defined it as 'future options' such as 'new goods and services awaiting discovery'. This new 'conservation' is still measured in Western scientific terms.

The recent discovery of anthropogenic global warming reinforces the economic side of ecological services, and this may become the most 'transnational' form of conservation yet. Potentially, international carbon trading could take the idea of the 'whole environment' into the ultimate 'private sector', the stockmarket.

Libby Robin

Bibliography
Beinart W. 2003. The rise of conservation in South Africa: Settlers, livestock and the environment 1770–1950. Oxford: Oxford University Press.
Carruthers J. 1995. The Kruger National Park: a social and political history. Pietermaritzburg: University of Natal Press.
Daily G. 1999. 'Developing a scientific basis for managing Earth's life support systems', Conservation Ecology, 3 (online).
Grove R. H. 1995. Green imperialism: colonial expansion, tropical island edens and the origins of environmentalism 1600–1860. Cambridge: Cambridge University Press.
Loo T. 2006. States of nature: conserving Canada's wildlife in the twentieth century. Vancouver: UBC Press.
Marsh G. P. 1864. Man and nature or physical geography as modified by human action. New York: Scribner.
Rajan S. R. 2006. Modernizing nature: forestry and imperial eco-development 1899–1950. Oxford: Clarendon Press.
Robin L. 1998. Defending the Little Desert: the rise of ecological consciousness in Australia. Melbourne: Melbourne University Press.

Related essays
acclimatization; Antarctic Treaty; biopatents; climate change; ecology; empires and imperialism; environmental diplomacy; environmentalism; fisheries; forests; Green Revolution; Greenpeace; indigenous knowledges; national parks; New Age; philanthropic foundations; sustainable development; tropics; wildlife films

Conspiracy theories

A conspiracy theory is a belief, usually regarded as unfounded, that there is a malign, hidden agenda to history, coupled with a conviction that the official version of events is mistaken. To date, most research into this form of popular political belief has focused solely on national examples (particularly American and European ones), but conspiracy thinking is now widespread in many other regions, and in recent decades it has begun to identify transnational organizations as the evil enemy, creating a form of pop sociology of globalization. At the same time, however, the popular panics that conspiracy theories create often play their part within local political struggles.

Although there has been a long history of speculation in classical and European history about intrigue, assassination and plotting, until the 18th century this was mainly confined to rumours about small-scale Machiavellian conspiracies within the inner circles of power. Periodic episodes of witch crazes and anti-Semitism swept through medieval and Renaissance Europe, but it was only with the Enlightenment and the French Revolution that recognizably modern conspiracy theories began to emerge. They were characterized by a belief that the whole course of history – not just an isolated event here or there – was being manipulated by a secret cabal of evil plotters, whose ambitions reached beyond national borders towards global domination. The emerging theories of a hidden agenda to world history were not necessarily the mark of irrational paranoia, but were inspired by an Enlightenment refusal to accept Providence or coincidence as the explanation for the unfolding of events. In the case of the French Revolution, for example, many refused to accept that the people had spontaneously risen up seemingly without leaders because of nebulous factors such as poverty or hunger, arguing instead that the events had been planned by groups of radicals such as the *philosophes* or secret societies such as the Bavarian Illuminati. However, it has been argued that with the development of the social sciences in the late 19th century it is no longer entirely rational to believe in the idea that small groups of plotters can manipulate the course of global history.

The other major reason for the emergence of recognizably modern conspiracy theories in the late 18th century was the increasing interconnectedness of an international literate public with the rapid growth of print culture. Thus fears about the Bavarian Illuminati were not limited to their native Germany (where the society had been disbanded by the authorities by 1788), but spread throughout Europe with the publication in France of the Abbé Barruel's Memoirs of the history illustrating Jacobinism (1798) and in Scotland of John Robison's Proofs of a conspiracy (1797), both of which alleged that the Illuminati and other Masonic secret societies had plotted the overthrow of the ancien régime. These conspiracy rumours quickly transferred to the United States, fuelling fears that the fledgling republic was in grave danger from a vast, coordinated group of external plotters.

Although the Illuminati myth is a striking example of a new style of conspiracy theory that seemed to transcend national borders, it is important to note that the particular meaning and political functions of such theories are often much more local. In the United States, for example, wild claims about the existence of an Illuminati plot were promoted by the New England preachers partly in order to bring the faithful back into line and thereby reaffirm the clergy's local importance as community leaders, at a historical moment when their authority was diminishing. These scare stories were also used by the Federalist party as a way of insinuating that their opponents (Thomas Jefferson's anti-Federalists) were in league with insidious, foreign forces. Indeed, it is arguable that most conspiracy theories about the vast global secret designs of alien enemies – up to the middle of the 20th century, at any rate – are more accurately thought of not as spontaneous outbursts of popular paranoia, but deliberately manipulated moral panics that serve to promote the vested interests of particular power groups by scapegoating vulnerable minorities. Other examples of demonological scares about global conspiracies that are put to local political uses include the way that conspiratorial fears about subversive Jesuit plots served to unite the disparate forces of the Left in France in the 19th century; or the cynical manipulation by elite factions within the Republican party of Senator McCarthy's popular anti-Communism in order to further their own political agenda. The Protocols of the Elders of Zion, the document forged by the Russian secret police in the 1890s that supposedly laid out the secret plans of Jewish leaders for the takeover of the world, created the most famous and influential conspiracy theory of the 20th century. Despite being quickly proven a hoax, the Protocols has been put to many different uses within the broad umbrella of anti-Semitism, being published, for example, not only in Czarist Russia and Hitler's Germany but also by Henry Ford in the 1930s; it also circulated among radical black nationalists in the United States in the 1990s, and is still a popular book within the Arab world.

Although the fears that conspiracy theories name are often international, deterritorialized threats to the way of life or even the very existence of the proponent's community, their underlying social function is to bolster a sense of group and often national identity precisely by imagining it under threat. Be they Catholics, Masons, Jews, Communists, white supremacists, or shape-shifting reptoid aliens, the accusation often made against the conspirators in the kind of countersubversive demonology that repeatedly erupted in Europe and the United States in the 19th and 20th centuries was that they secretly swore allegiance to alien and typically transnational powers (the Pope, the Grand Master of the Masonic lodges, the international Communist Party, and so on). Likewise the rhetoric of conspiracy has often served to create and confirm an ideology of national exceptionalism, the belief (most prominent in the case of the United States, but also apparent elsewhere) that one's nation has a special destiny, any deviation from which must have been caused by a deliberate and usually foreign plot to derail the course of history.

In the last half-century (and most notably since the 1990s) a raft of new conspiracy fears has emerged that focuses specifically on transnational institutions, in particular the United Nations, the European Union, the Council on Foreign Relations, the Bilderberg group, and the Trilateral Commission, organizations that are often lumped together in the conspiracy rhetoric under the umbrella terms 'the Illuminati' or the 'New World Order'. These conspiracy theories have become common currency on the Internet and in global popular culture, but they have their roots in a specific convergence within American history of anti-Communism and Protestant evangelicalism that has slowly been gaining ground since the 1960s. The underlying source of fears about transnational organizations is a premillennialist prophecy interpretation of the Book of Revelation, in which the rise of the Antichrist and the subsequent plunge towards End Times will see the loss of national sovereignty.

Over and above the specific evangelical prophecy interpretation that lies behind these contemporary transnational conspiracy fears is an increasingly widespread but often vague perception that the lives of individuals are more than ever controlled by large, unseen and malign forces. Many contemporary conspiracy theories have moved away from the more focused populist demonology of the 19th and early 20th centuries. Instead they characterize organizations, systems and technologies as all-pervasive plots, in effect calling up the spectre of a conspiracy that doesn't have obviously identifiable conspirators. It has been argued therefore that these newer conspiracy fears that are omnipresent on the Internet and provide the lifeblood of many Hollywood thrillers are a displaced expression of concerns about the globalization of the economy and the attendant inability of individuals (and even individual nations) to make sense of or control the sweeping changes that affect the lives of ordinary citizens. Conspiracy theories are thus a flawed but powerful explanatory framework for a socioeconomic situation that is marked by causal ambiguity and a pervasive sense of unspecific risk. In short, the operating principle of both contemporary conspiracy theory and neoliberal globalization is that everything is ultimately connected. It is important to recognize, however, that there are conspiracy fears in the present not just about the processes of globalization but also – in the case of the conspiracy-infused rhetoric of Islamic fundamentalism – about the forces of cosmopolitanism and modernity.

The specifically American, premillennialist version of conspiracy theories about transnationalism has now been exported in a diffused form around the world through the dominance of US mass entertainment, with international cinematic blockbusters such as Independence Day, Conspiracy Theory, and The DaVinci Code. Alien conspiracy theories such as those portrayed in the globally successful television series The X-Files might well be the perfect scare story for a post-Cold War world, since the enemy evoked is not tied to a specific national threat but is nevertheless feared as both immanent and imminent. The kind of dedicated conspiracy theorist typified by hard-core X-Files fans or Kennedy assassination buffs belongs to a global community of armchair sceptics who often share a post-1960s automatic distrust of the official version of events. Despite the prominence of these forms of globalized conspiracy culture (conspiracy theory, it has been said, is the gossip of the global village), there are also many other local versions of conspiracy rumours that provide an expression of a sense of perplexed victimhood at the hands of vast, transnational forces, coupled with a desire to see these forces as not merely structural and inevitable but the product of specific, malign agency, whether human or supernatural. Anthropologists conducting field work, for example, have discussed the turn to conspiracy-infused shamanic practices in South Korea as a way of making sense of the devastating changes brought about by the economic strictures imposed upon the country by the IMF; or the use of 'occult cosmologies' by the Christian minority in Indonesia to account for what they regard as the unseen powers of globalist Islam and state bureaucracy. Yet if conspiracy theory has been used to frame popular thinking about the centrifugal effects of globalization in a host of local contexts, it has also served to create a cohesive sense of community among diasporic populations. In the case of Algeria, for example, one of the ways that the dispersed, international community of Algerians in exile comes together – both in person and on the Internet – is through the sharing and debating of gossip, rumour, speculation and conspiracy theory.

Peter Knight

Bibliography

Cubitt G. 1993. *The Jesuit myth: conspiracy theory and politics in nineteenth-century France.* Oxford: Clarendon Press.

Hofstadter R. 1967. *The paranoid style of American politics and other essays.* New York: Vintage.

Knight P. 2000. *Conspiracy culture: from the Kennedy assassination to 'The X-Files'.* London: Routledge.

Melley T. 2000. *Empire of conspiracy: the culture of paranoia in postwar America*. Ithaca: Cornell University Press.

Pipes D. 1996. *The hidden hand: Middle East fears of conspiracy*. New York: St. Martin's.

Robins, R. and Post J. 1997. *Political paranoia: the psychopolitics of hatred*. New Haven: Yale University Press.

Silverstein P. 2004. 'An excess of truth: violence, conspiracy theorizing and the Algerian civil war', *Anthropological Quarterly*, 75, 4, 643–74.

West H. and Sanders T. (eds). 2003. *Transparency and conspiracy: ethnographies of suspicion in the New World Order*. Durham, NC: Duke University Press.

Related essays

anti-Catholicism; antisemitism; capitalism; evangelicalism; financial markets; freemasonry; globalization; information economy; nation and state; revolution; transnational; United Nations system

Consumer cooperation

Consumer cooperation, the provision of consumer goods and services through collectively owned and managed private institutions, emerged in most European countries and the Americas from the mid 19th century, and became a global movement over the course of the 20th century. The European origins of consumer cooperatives drew upon self-help societies that found new expression within early 19th-century socialism, political reform, and cooperatives. One cooperative, the Society of Equitable Pioneers in Rochdale, England (founded 1844) proved particularly important for the subsequent development of the international consumer cooperative movement. The creators of the Rochdale cooperative included Owenite workers who believed in retaining profits from their labour, weavers displaced by new production methods, and ex-Chartists committed to political democracy. The Rochdale Pioneers advocated practical means to achieve a just social and economic order, and envisioned sequential cooperative activities. Profits from the consumer cooperative would fund cooperative production; consumer cooperatives would sell items produced cooperatively. The Rochdale model proved attractive and proliferated within the British Isles. English cooperatives formed the first wholesale society in Manchester in 1863

to buy goods on behalf of local cooperatives, and created the first national cooperative organization, the Co-operative Union, in 1869. The Union spread the Rochdale model through education, publications, and meetings. Over time, cooperative principles developed and practised by the Rochdale Pioneers evolved and guided cooperators worldwide: open membership; democratic control; dividend on purchases; limited interest on capital; political and religious neutrality; cash trading; and promotion of education.

The Rochdale cooperative system provided a compelling model of practical economic initiative combined with social and educational goals. Success bred imitation and adaptation. Consumer cooperatives inspired by Rochdale spread across Europe during the second half of the 19th century and later around the world, as did other cooperative forms (credit, housing, banking, farm and insurance societies). Cooperatives gained recognition and survived in competitive economies as international modes of communication accelerated. Steam travel, the electric telegraph, cheaper newspapers and other publications made it easier for people in different countries to share ideas, report on activities, and meet to discuss cooperative activities. Advocates of cooperation journeyed to each other's countries and subscribed to cooperative newspapers. Reformers Victor-Aimée Huber and Édouard Pfeiffer visited British cooperatives in the 1850s and 1860s and returned to found cooperatives in German states. H. C. Sonne, a pastor who subscribed to a British cooperative newspaper, introduced the Rochdale system of consumer cooperation to Denmark in the 1860s, as did a professor in Finland who learned about Rochdale in the press and founded the first cooperative there. Cosmopolitan intellectuals and professionals organized consumer cooperatives in Russia; Kharkov's cooperative sold items produced by British cooperatives after its director visited Britain. Other transnational cooperative forms proliferated from the late 19th century. Savings and credit cooperatives gained strength in Germany and Central Europe; cooperative People's Banks multiplied in Italy, Belgium, and Argentina.

Networks of people and institutions drew upon 'old world' experiences to introduce consumer cooperation beyond Europe from the late 1850s. British immigrants founded the first Australian consumer cooperative in 1859, and one in Nova Scotia shortly thereafter that was the first of dozens created in Canadian mining and industrial communities. In the United States, British immigrants created a consumer cooperative in Philadelphia with bylaws obtained directly from Rochdale. During the 1870s–1880s, the Knights of Labour established thousands of consumer cooperatives in the US and Canada, as did the Patrons of Husbandry (Grange) farmers' movement. Agrarian and urban communities of Finnish migrants formed cooperatives selling agricultural and household supplies.

Similar transnational patterns obtained in South America and Asia. German and French refugees from the Franco-Prussian War established the first consumer and bakery cooperative in Argentina. A Brazilian cooperative federation founded in 1907 for growing, processing, and marketing coffee maintained an agency for European distribution in Belgium, and a representative of Italian consumer cooperatives toured Brazil seeking direct relations between Brazilian and Italian cooperatives in 1912. Cooperation reached Japan after a newspaper article introduced the Rochdale system in the 1870s, and civil servants and workers later founded consumer cooperatives. Social activist Kagawa Toyohiko visited European cooperatives after World War 1 and returned to organize them in Japan. Knowledge about consumer cooperatives also traveled with colonial administrators and colonists through imperial space. The British actively promoted cooperation in their empire and introduced laws on cooperation modelled on English legal structures. France, Holland, and Belgium also established consumer and marketing cooperatives within their empires, as did the United States in the Philippines.

The transnational context for consumer cooperation expanded through the growing acceleration of working-class militancy coupled with the rise of socialism. From the 1880s, the labour movement and international socialism forged networks fostering militancy and political efforts. In this context, socialists re-evaluated older concerns about cooperation's association with liberal self-help and potential reformism. Cooperators also questioned the tenet of political neutrality. By the turn of the century, consumer cooperatives closely aligned with socialist and labour organizations flourished. In Belgium, consumer cooperation was a fully integrated part of socialism and labour activism and considered as one of the 'three pillars of socialism'. The Belgian model inspired cooperators elsewhere who travelled there for advice much as earlier cooperative enthusiasts travelled to Rochdale.

The strength of consumer cooperation before and after World War 1 was also due to the proliferation of national cooperative unions. These provided institutional cohesion, a national press, and regular congresses attended by representatives from other national cooperative organizations. Activists in national organizations served as spokespersons for the movement, and represented it to their respective governments. National movements struggled with different visions of cooperation's goals and purposes. Religious divisions split the Belgian, German, Italian, and Austrian movements, divergent interests between farmers and workers fragmented Danish cooperation, and politics undermined national cooperative unity in Finland, Poland, and France. Sweden owes its persistent strength in part to its social, political and institutional unity within one organization founded in 1889.

One institution where cooperators debated cooperation's forms and purposes was within the International Cooperative Alliance (ICA) founded in 1895 with headquarters in London (now in Geneva). The first international congress met at London, where 207 delegates represented cooperative organizations in 11 mostly European countries, with observers from Russia, Argentina, and India. The ICA held triennial congresses, regular meetings, promoted and regularized cooperative principles, fostered the circulation of ideas and practices, and represented the cooperative movement within other international organizations. While the ICA initially promoted all forms of cooperation, its 1910 congress established the ascendancy of consumer cooperation as a means toward a new economic and social system, one where 'consumer sovereignty' would influence production and redistribute profits based on purchases rather than share capital.

The ICA's institutional structures created mechanisms for the circulation of people, cooperative forms and principles on a transnational scale. Regular congresses in different countries hosted sectional international committees that included banking, insurance, wholesaling, and women's guilds. Exhibitions depicting the range of cooperative products and services often accompanied congresses. The ICA's secretariat and research department distributed materials to cooperators around the world. The ICA's monthly *Review of International Co-operation* conveyed ideas and practical information, complementing other writing about the cooperative movement in journals such as *Annals of Collective Economy* founded in 1908 by French socialist Edgard Milhaud, and publications on cooperation by intellectuals such as Charles Gide and Beatrice Potter Webb.

The transnational circulation of ideas and information about consumer cooperation operated across different scales. National consumer cooperative organizations published regular newspapers, as did many regional and larger consumer cooperative societies. Journals from national cooperative movements, such as the British Co-operative Union's *Co-operative Review*, also enjoyed transnational circulation. The Cooperative League of the USA's journal, *Consumers' Cooperation*, published essays provided by the ICA on cooperative endeavours across the globe, along with news of cooperatives in small American towns. During the early 1940s, some 50 cooperative newspapers and magazines in Argentina reported on international cooperation and published translated materials.

The cooperative movement promoted education in cooperative principles and practical methods of cooperative business for international constituencies. The Cooperative College located at Holyoake House, Manchester, taught (and continues to teach) the history of the movement and ideals and principles of cooperation to cooperators from many nations, along with educational initiatives founded in the early to mid 20th century at universities and training schools for cooperative managers in France, Brazil, Mexico, Japan and elsewhere. Transnational cooperative educational endeavours on regional and international levels also attracted students, cooperative administrators, and groups of cooperators. Manuals for directors and members of local cooperative societies circulated ICA materials covering practical administrative information and cooperative principles. Radio broadcasts and later film also spread transnational news of cooperation. Vacation centres and a cooperative flag and holiday provided activities and unifying symbols for constituencies across national boundaries and furthered the movement's transnational principles and character. The 1896 congresses of the ICA adopted a rainbow flag to symbolize cooperative unity in diversity and the power of enlightened progress. In 1923 the ICA institutionalized 'International Cooperative Day' in July, a time for cooperative festivities that continued into the 21st century.

The internationalization of the cooperative movement posed opportunities as well as challenges. Consumer cooperation initially emerged stronger from World War 1. During the war, consumer cooperatives helped governments ensure food distribution, promoted rationing, and provided postwar relief. The heightened interest in cooperation after the war resulted in a surge of members. Yet even as consumer cooperation weathered the economic shoals of the interwar period, it confronted changing consumer desires and new transnational forms of retailing such as chain stores. National cooperative organizations encouraged mergers of older stores carrying a narrow range of staple foodstuffs into larger regional societies and adopted the COOP brand to compete with new commercial forms of capitalist commerce.

Interwar politics also posed challenges. Despite the recognition by cooperation and socialism of their mutual interests in 1910, the relationship between them remained vexed well into the 20th century. The Russian Revolution and the Soviet government's nationalization of cooperatives in the 1920s and 1930s raised fundamental questions about cooperation's economic and political neutrality. The greater challenge to cooperatives in the interwar period, however, came from hostile fascist and Nazi regimes that destroyed or absorbed cooperatives in Austria, Germany, Italy, Czechoslovakia, Spain and Japan. The ICA vigorously protested these actions and aided besieged cooperators. In the politicized context of the 1930s, the ICA created a committee to review the key principles of the Rochdale system. Its report, presented at the ICA congress held during the 1937 Paris Exposition, claimed that 'political and religious neutrality' was one of the seven principles, although not one required for admission to the ICA. The 1937 congress also passed a resolution for peace and encouraged assistance for cooperators in Spain. In 1939, when Spanish cooperators crossed the Pyrenees after the fall of Barcelona, the French cooperative movement received and housed them. While the meaning of 'neutrality' continued to inspire heated debate within the movement, the ICA included representatives from capitalist, socialist, and Communist countries throughout the Cold War era.

Two major themes characterize the transnational dimensions of the consumer cooperative movement following World War 2. First, the cooperative movement became truly international, in large part due to its relevance within transnational institutional networks promoting economic development outside Europe and North America. By 1960, the number of non-European countries represented in the ICA outnumbered European ones for the first time due to the proliferation of cooperatives in Africa, Asia and Latin America. The Central Cooperative Institute in Moscow translated work on cooperation into multiple languages and trained cooperative administrators from Eastern Europe, India, Indonesia, Mongolia, Ghana and Nigeria in the 1960s. The expanding system of international aid included the promotion of cooperation. The ICA's close relationship with the United Nations led to partnerships with UN agencies on international development projects. One UN body, the International Labour Office (ILO), whose first director had been the French cooperator and moderate socialist Albert Thomas, maintained an Advisory Committee on Cooperation that arranged seminars and provided technical assistance for cooperatives worldwide. In 1965, the ILO and the ICA promulgated what was in essence a 'Cooperative Charter' for developing countries that entailed education and training, financial aid, and responsibility for creating cooperatives in developing countries. The ILO established cooperative colleges and training centres in Europe, North America, and Japan that educated students from Africa and Asia, often with UNESCO funding. The ICA's Development Fund, created in 1954, provided technical assistance, information, specialized training, and educational programmes for purchasing, distribution, and credit cooperatives in Africa, Asia, and the Indian subcontinent. National movements also promoted development, as with the Norwegian cooperative movement's assistance programme in

The Gambia. Consumer cooperatives grew in conjunction with these efforts and benefited from government subsidies and legal advantages.

Second, the rapidly changing business and commercial practices of large-scale capitalist enterprises and multinational corporations challenged cooperators to increase the scale and scope of their operations, modernize their business methods, and sharpen the focus on training and research to remain economically viable in the fiercely competitive conditions of a capitalist global economy. The post-1945 proliferation of large-scale capitalist supermarkets and department stores with extensive advertising budgets required technical expertise, mergers of local and regional consumer cooperatives and the integration of retail and larger-scale wholesale societies. The French cooperative movement, for example, consolidated all cooperative forms and federations in 1968. The national federation (FNCC) promoted intra-cooperative mergers and modernization after many French cooperatives underwent structural crises and bankruptcy during the 1970s. In France and elsewhere, strong demand for consumer durables and well designed products that appealed to consumer-oriented lifestyles called for rethinking consumer cooperation's historic focus on thrift and necessities. By the 1980s, the FNCC's cooperative stores included 'hypermarkets', supermarkets, and non-food consumer cooperatives.

The ICA promoted the concentration and integration of cooperatives on a transnational scale, and its research section offered seminars and publications on modern marketing, advertising, and business techniques. Successful transnational integration included the Scandinavian Wholesale Society (NAF, founded 1918) which maintained branch offices across the globe, and the International Cooperative Petroleum Alliance (ICPA) founded by the ICA in 1945 to counter multinational oil industries and provide oil and services to cooperatives. By 1970 the ICPA comprised over 40 member cooperatives from 20 countries, operated a processing plant in The Netherlands, and drilled for oil in Libya. The ICA also encouraged 'zonal integration' to foster larger integrated markets and economic concentration. National cooperative unions in Common Market countries founded the European

Community of Consumer Cooperatives (EUROCOOP) in 1957 to represent consumer coops in the EEC and coordinate relations among consumer, wholesale and producer cooperatives. In 2007, it represented the interests of consumer cooperatives within the European Union and their 22 million consumer-members in 17 European countries. The most significant action taken by the ICA to foster regional zones of cooperative coordination took place at the 1992 ICA Congress in Tokyo. There the ICA introduced a new decentralized global and transnational regional structure with offices in Africa, the Americas, Asia and the Pacific, and Europe. Administrative structures include a regional assembly that formulates policies and elects a chairperson to represent the region on the ICA board. The new ICA structures created large international and transnational bodies encompassing cooperative sectors: consumer cooperatives, banking, health, housing, insurance, tourism, and producers' cooperatives. The growing scale and scope of consumer and other forms of cooperation raised concerns among some cooperators about the movement's historical emphasis on democratic participation, and in 1995 the ICA revised its cooperative principles to strengthen cooperative democracy.

The consumer cooperative movement has enjoyed a resurgence in the 21st century, in large part because it has adapted to new economic circumstances, and advanced its historic emphasis on unadulterated food, fair trade, and a democratic participatory ethos. The consumer cooperative movement continues to embrace and refine principles and practices that came to define consumer cooperation – community self-reliance, democratic governance, profits returned to consumers rather than corporations, and economic justice. These serve as inspiration and model for a dynamic international cooperative movement of over 800 million people. Robert Owen's 1830 claim that 'The-co-operator is necessarily a cosmopolite; his principles are of a character not provincial, not national, not continental, but universal: he claims and owns a relationship to the world, viewing all men as his brethren; and regarding, with a tender concern, the interests and well-being of others' remains alive in the 21st century.

Ellen Furlough

Bibliography

Birchall J. 1997. *The international co-operative movement*. Manchester: Manchester University Press.

Furlough E. and Strikwerda C. 1999. *Consumers against capitalism? Consumer cooperation in Europe, North America, and Japan, 1840–1990*. Lanham: Rowman & Littlefield.

Watkins W. 1970. *The International Co-operative Alliance, 1895–1970*. London: International Co-operative Alliance.

Related essays

anarchism; capitalism; Cold War; consumer society; cosmopolitanism and universalism; expositions; food; human mobility; intergovernmental organizations; international non-governmental organizations (INGOs); socialism; technical assistance; trade; translation; United Nations system; women's movements; workers' movements

Consumer society

New terms abound to describe and define the politics, economics, and culture of using commodities to create individual and collective identities. Because these terms are often used interchangeably and imprecisely, this entry begins by defining and differentiating the key terms before discussing their application.

The term 'consumption' is as vague as its antonym, 'production'. 'Consumption' refers to the selection and use of goods and services and the individual and social consequences. Until the late 20th century, 'consumption' was a minor subject, especially compared to the politics, economics, and social history of production. The rise of mass production, mass media, mass culture and urbanization, as well as the development of social and cultural history, led scholars across disciplines to focus on consumption not simply as the natural end of production but rather as the partner or even the progenitor of production through the creation of new needs and desires. Because all people in all places 'consume', this term lacks historical, spatial, and cultural specificity. Scholars now use more focused terms such as 'consumerism', referring to the consumption of branded, mass-produced commodities and the orientation of social life and discourse around such commodities.

The term 'consumerism' is used synonymously with 'consumer culture'. In contrast, 'consumer society' suggests not merely pockets of consumerism or consumer culture in an otherwise largely agricultural or proto-industrial country but rather the spread of such lifestyles centred on consumption to the majority of the population. Thus the more restrictive term 'consumer society' generally applies to levels of consumerism seen in Western Europe and America in the decades after World War 2, in Japan in the 1960s, Korea and Brazil in the 1970s and 1980s, and former Communist countries in Eastern Europe in the 1990s. However, scholars have identified consumerism in major trading cities and colonial outposts around the globe such as Mexico City, São Paulo, Istanbul, Beirut, Seoul, Tokyo, and Shanghai by the early twentieth century.

These definitions are especially problematic when applied to entire countries with huge populations, wide regional variation, and vast inequality such as India, China, and Brazil. China is a good example of this. By some measures, regions such as the Shanghai-Yangzi Delta and Pearl River Delta already approach per capita levels of disposable income, exposure to mass consumer goods, and availability of mass media required for consumer society. But levels of inequality in cities have widened dramatically, resulting in an extreme range of consumption from desperate poverty to unprecedented wealth. China is, for instance, expected to become the number one market for luxury brands by 2015. Despite the development of 'consumerism' in cities across China, one would not label the country a 'consumer society' without major qualifications.

Until recently, the study of consumer society and consumerism has focused on Western Europe and North America. Although the origins of consumerism have been linked to countries as diverse as the Netherlands and China as well as in eras stretching back to classical antiquity, scholars generally focus on the 18th-century spread of luxury goods and the ways their consumption reinforced or challenged social hierarchies. The spread of such goods was directly linked to European imperial expansion and the introduction of novelty goods such tea, sugar, coffee, tobacco, china, and spices. As these goods became more widely available, a growing bourgeois commercial class used them to signify and solidify their social standing. In 18th-century England, generally regarded as the birthplace of consumer society, new manufacturing techniques began mass-producing luxury goods, driving down their costs and widening the circle of those that could afford them. At this point, we encounter a critical issue in the secondary literature: did excess production force merchants to invent new ways to stimulate demand or did production follow demand? Did a 'consumer revolution' precede, accompany, or follow the better studied 'industrial revolution'? Historians no longer take demand as an automatic consequence of supply.

The initial historiographical emphasis on England inventing 'consumer society', and the post-World War 2 United States perfecting it, was misleading. Such an approach neglected the transnational origins of mass consumption. It also failed to explain the indigenous foundations in non-Western contexts. Middle and East Asian countries, for instance, had consumer cultures in court and elite circles for centuries. In Tokugawa Japan (1600–1868), regional rulers (daimyo) were required to maintain residences in their domains as well as in Edo/Tokyo. A nationwide infrastructure developed to supply the vast entourages making their way back and forth, culminating in the city itself, where rulers and their emulators engaged in conspicuous consumption. As with Europe, early modern Middle and East Asian countries saw consumption of one-time luxuries gradually spread down the social hierarchy.

Western imperialist expansion in the late 19th century did introduce or develop key aspects of mass consumerism. Colonies became the destination of mass-produced goods ranging from chemical and textile products to cigarettes, soap, and toothbrushes. New print media supported by advertising multiplied commodity spectacles, which placed objects on display for visual entertainment, and allowed their transmission across social classes, regions, and countries. As in European and American consumer cultures, these commodity spectacles, which informed people of a new universe of mass-produced, branded products and stimulated the desire for their consumption, included fashion shows, newspaper and magazine advertising, movie houses, dance halls, department stores, museums, and industrial product exhibitions. In East Asia, such spectacles were introduced by the first decades of the 20th century through imperialist-controlled treaty ports.

In the decades before World War 2, nascent consumer cultures around the globe became deeply linked to modern ideas of the nation state. The simple market presence of 'imports' became politicized as representations of imperialism and the loss of national sovereignty. China had a multidimensional social movement that promoted the consumption of 'national products' and the avoidance of 'foreign products' through sumptuary laws, frequent anti-imperialist boycotts, gender norms, and nationalistic commodity spectacles. Indian nationalists also attempted to nationalize consumption during the *swadeshi* (belonging to one's own country) and non-cooperation movements (1904–08, 1920–22). Likewise, the United States, Japan, Ireland, Korea, Britain, France, Germany, Nigeria, and Spain, among other countries, also experienced such popular movements with varying intensity in nation-making projects from late colonial times to the present. Since the 1990s, the rapid international spread of neoliberal 'globalization' through the WTO, IMF, and World Bank has greatly reduced or eliminated tariffs, ensuring the mass consumption of imports and reviving a sensitive political and cultural issue worldwide.

Japan has supplied a heavily studied model of high-speed growth by suppressing consumption. From the start of the Korean War in 1950 to the oil crisis of 1973, Japan's GNP grew at an average of 10 per cent a year. The Japanese model featured heavy state involvement in economic planning, environmental degradation, and, above all, an emphasis on production and export-led growth at the expense of domestic consumption. By the early 1960s, mass consumerism emerged with the formation of a new urban middle class comprised of nuclear families. Subsequent decades witnessed similar phenomena in Korea and the three other 'Asian Tigers' (Taiwan, Hong Kong, and Singapore), namely high growth rates and the establishment of new consumer societies.

Consumerism re-emerged in China. In 1978, Deng Xiaoping initiated the depoliticization of daily life and economic reforms with growth rates on par with Japan's earlier record levels. The Chinese state has staked its legitimacy on economic growth, encouraging citizens to consume, a shift in attitudes and policies toward consumerism embodied in the improbable popular 1980s Communist Party slogan: 'to get rich is glorious'. By 2005, Chinese officials were alarmed by the high import rates and began to shift the economy from Japanese-style reliance on exports toward domestic consumption-driven growth. Policies designed to boost consumption include phasing out the household registration system, permitting the establishment of private lending companies, accelerating urbanization, and deregulating the financial sector to facilitate consumer borrowing.

Growing environmental awareness raises important questions about the sustainability of consumerism and 'consumer society'. The consequences are not clear but are certainly worrying if consumerism spreads from the estimated 100 million middle-class consumers living in major Chinese cities to secondary cities and villages across the countryside. The same would be true in India. What will happen as consumers in developing countries 'catch up' in per capita consumption of energy and other commodities? New strains on world resources and ecological catastrophe may challenge accepted notions of consumerism based on individual, acquisitive rationality and, indeed, may challenge the economic and political organization of the world.

Karl Gerth

Bibliography

Gerth K. 2003. *China made: consumer culture and the creation of the nation.* Cambridge, MA: Harvard University Press.

Glickman L. B. (ed.) 1999. *Consumer society in American history: a reader.* Ithaca: Cornell University Press.

de Grazia V. and Furlough E. (eds) 1996. *The sex of things: gender and consumption in historical perspective.* Berkeley: University of California Press.

Brewer J. and Trentman F. (eds) 2006. *Consuming cultures, global perspectives: historical trajectories, transnational exchanges.* Oxford: Berg.

Related essays

advertising; art market; avant garde; beauty; capitalism; car culture; China; civilizations; commodity trading; development and growth; drink; fashion; feel-good culture; film; food; Ghose, Aurobindo Ackroyd; information society; Japan; love; marketing; modernization theory; Pax Americana, Westernization; zero growth

Containerized freight

Containerized freight is the transport system made possible by the seamless circulation of commodities between truck, rail, and ship resulting from the consolidation of multiple cargoes into one standardized unit, normally a 20- or 40-foot steel container.

Prior to containerization's advent, cargo moved break-bulk. This method was labour intensive, slow, and expensive. Door-to-door service was not possible, because fragmented cargo prevented linkage between transport nodes, such as ports and rail terminals, and the producer and consumer of goods. Several ocean carriers undertook global freight's rationalization after World War 2. In the 1950s, they experimented with containerization, which proved effective at connecting all parts of the transport chain. Unitization produced time and cost efficiency by reducing handlers of cargo. Before containers, for example, it took 12,000 labour-hours to unload a 10,000-ton vessel; with containers it takes 750 labour-hours to unload 20,000 tons of cargo. These improvements transformed transportation. By 1969 there were 115 container ships, with a capacity of 70,000 containers. These numbers are dwarfed by today's volume. The world shipped 266,337,242 container units in 2004. Carrying 90 per cent of the world's cargo, there are approximately 18 million containers circulating trade routes. In 2004, nearly 29 million units flowed through United States ports, with Los Angeles-Long Beach being most active with 8,638,987 units in 2003. Most of this commerce comes from China, which produces 75 per cent of the world's shoes and toys, and 30 per cent of its electronics. China exported 8,776,889 units in 2004, mostly to United States markets.

Containerized freight's transnational system consists of three interacting networks: physical, logistical, and regulatory. The physical network consists of the system's equipment. It includes trucks, railroads, and ships, as well as terminal, storage, and repair facilities. The network also involves forklifts, chases, cranes, and cargo holds designed for the particular needs of standardized containers. Docks and terminals are built to leverage containerization's advantages. In some cases, such as Sydney's Botany Bay, huge port facilities are constructed strictly for containerized freight. Storage depots are uniquely designed for rapid entrance and departure of the container within congested urban spaces. As containers can be anywhere in the world, a logistical network exists for their management. This network also requires universal standards for tracking the transnational flow of containers. The use of powerful computers is essential for the management of 18 million containers circulating the world's multitude of depots, production facilities, ports, trucks, railroads, and ships. It is a phenomenal logistical task, one that can have significant impact on the global economy. An upsurge in an economy, for example, can cause structural problems as containers flow to the boom area from every corner of the world, causing scarcity in other markets and subsequent disruptions to trade. Finally, the transport system has a transnational regulatory network. It consists of international agreements and treaties that establish standards for equipment, rates, documentation, customs procedures, and security. The regulatory network mediates the tense and contradictory distinctions between the prerogatives of the nation state and the needs of transnational trade.

Containerized freight is a factor fundamental to if not causal of globalization. Flexible capital accumulation's transnational production and assembly depends on containerized freight to deliver parts from any production point in the world. Without containerization, 'just-in-time' production would not be possible, as container ships represent floating warehouses of assembly parts produced in facilities throughout the world. Manufacturers like General Motors and retailers like Wal-Mart are largely shaped and defined by the transportation network created by containerized freight.

As a tightly coupled system, containerized freight does not adapt well to disruptions within its links and nodes. Unlike the Internet or an electrical grid, diverting from blocked paths within the system is a slow, complicated, and expensive exercise. If a port shuts down because of a natural disaster, labour action, or terrorist event, the impact on the entire system can be significant. With continued expansion of global trade, the transnational system will need to devise innovative solutions to these structural weaknesses.

Glen David Kuecker

Bibliography

Bonacich E. and Wilson J. 2008. *Getting the goods: ports, labor, and the logistics revolution.* Ithaca: Cornell University Press.

Levinson M. 2008. *The box: how the shipping container made the world smaller and the world economy bigger.* Princeton: Princeton University Press.

Van Den Burg G. 1975. *Containerisation and other unit transport.* London: Hutchinson Benham.

Related essays
commodity trading; industrialization; railways; steamships; technical standardization; technologies; Toyotism; trade; trade (manufactured goods); transportation infrastructures

Contract and indentured labourers

Together with slavery, peonage, and serfdom, indentured labour, or indentured servitude, has been described as a form of unfree labour. The term has sometimes also been used interchangeably with 'contract labour', though some have described it as just one form of contract labour, with the implication that some forms of contract labour were 'freer' than others. While the terminology surrounding its usage has not always been consistent, we can clearly define its main features and its place in labour history. Indenture involved the voluntary surrender by the labourer, for a specified period of time, of their freedom to leave their designated job; breach of which promise involved some form of legally approved penal sanction. They were to receive in exchange specified wages and other benefits. This arrangement may be embodied in a formal written contract, enforceable in the host country's courts, or it may be informally arranged and governed by 'custom'. The proposed duration of service has varied from one year to ten years. Ambiguities surrounding the term 'voluntary recruitment', and disparities between formal contractual obligations and treatment of labourers in some destinations, resulted in its classification as a form of unfree labour.

Indenture arose with the settlement of British North America and the West Indian islands in the 17th century, and was generally used in the English colonies as a mechanism by which the plantations in the US South and the West Indies arranged for a steady flow of labour from the British Isles. Later on the period of service was extended beyond the plantation and involved various types of labour obligation in the mid-Atlantic colonies. During this period of the indenture system, this form of immigration was basically an extension of the pattern of work arrangements employed in Britain itself, and recognized by the master–servant legislation in Britain, so that emigration for work in the colonies was an extension of the British labour market. This form of labour fell into disuse on the US South and West Indian plantations by the late 17th century, as enslaved Africans became the primary source of labour in the tobacco, rice and sugar plantations. Early American indenture arose out of the dual need for workers and voluntary settlers in an underpopulated colonial settlement environment. In its day-to-day operation, there was no sense of an abrupt transition from one code of rules to another, even if on occasion there were instances of excessive exploitation of individuals, as often happened in the West Indies.

The revival of indenture in the 19th century was more global in its relevance (see Table 1). It was the result of an acute global labour shortage arising in two distinct regions of the tropical world during the Industrial Revolution. One was the tropical plantation previously cultivated by African slaves (West Indian islands; Mauritius in the Indian Ocean), the other was the hitherto autonomous parts of the tropical world which had never been exposed to African slavery, but which found themselves in this century being annexed into the expanding European imperial economies (Southeast Asia, Southern Africa or the Pacific Islands of Fiji and Hawai'i). As the need for raw materials and agricultural products grew larger in the metropolitan market, the expansion of production in the tropics followed accordingly. In those areas where the end of slavery had resulted in the withdrawal of much labour from the market (West Indies), or in those areas where slavery continued but the end of the slave trade had reduced regular supplies of slave labour (Cuba), the shortage was felt more acutely. Still, all areas of the expanded tropical orbit of European imperialism generated their own local versions of the tropical agricultural boom and its consequent need for labour.

Because European migrations in the 19th century were voluntary, self-financed, and destined for the temperate (and industrializing) areas of settlement, most of the indentured migrants in this period were non-Europeans – Indians and Chinese above all, but also Javanese, Pacific Islanders and Japanese, and even a few thousand from the older groups of European and African workers. In regions close to the source of migrant workers (Southeast Asia), indentured and free seasonal migration coexisted. In Malaya, indentured Indian labour was numerically larger than free as long as the sugar estates were the principal recruiters; when rubber cultivation took precedence over sugar after 1900, free Indian migrants predominated. By contrast, in regions physically distant from the migrants (Latin America and the Caribbean, the Indian Ocean – Mauritius, Reunion – and Pacific Fiji, indentured immigration predominated, since workers had to rely on recruiting agents – which could be government-sponsored Emigration Agencies or private entrepreneurs and shippers – to subsidize or pay their transportation costs.

Wherever indenture developed in the 19th century it tended to be mainly in the sugar industry, where global production leapt from 300,000 tons in 1790 to 10 million tons in 1914. The expanding British Empire, while relying on the indentured labour of many nationalities, relied principally on Indian indentured labour. This was true of the Malayan sugar industry, but not of Queensland (Australia), which relied on Pacific Islander labour. Indian labour remained within the British Empire, and only went elsewhere under special arrangements (the French and Dutch Caribbean, Reunion). The non-British sugar-producing countries of the 19th century recruited Chinese indentured labour (Cuba, Peru); in the case of Hawai'i, the Chinese were later joined by Japanese and Pacific Islanders, and even Madeirans. British and Dutch destinations tried to maintain gender ratios of 13 to 25 per cent female, but non-British destinations recruited primarily men. The British and Dutch generally had free or subsidized repatriation options in their indentured contracts (at least for the Indians), while the others did not.

Sugar was the main global industry employing imported indentured labour in the 19th century, but not all large sugar-producing countries resorted to it. Java and the Philippines relied primarily on domestic labour. (In 1894 Java produced 552,667 tons of sugar – twice as much as the British West Indies – while the Philippines produced above 191,277 tons.) Brazil (275,000 tons in 1894) relied solely on its Black labourers, slave and ex-slave. In the Caribbean region, middle-sized producers Puerto Rico and Barbados relied mainly on their own workers (white campesinos and Black ex-slaves in the case of the former, ex-slaves in the case of the latter).

Not all indentured labour was destined for the sugar industry. Coffee plantations in Malaya, cocoa in Trinidad, bananas in Jamaica, rubber in Malaya, all used the indentured labour of Indians, alongside free and postindenture labourers. The guano deposits in Peru (Chinese), and the mines and railways of the British Empire (Chinese in Transvaal gold mines; Indians in Kenya/Uganda railroad construction) became destinations for indentured labourers. In Singapore, South Indian indentured labourers worked in public works projects, building roads, railways, bridges, canals and wharves until 1910, when the practice was officially banned.

Finally, it should be noted that through most of the 19th century, 'free' British labourers at home, like 'unfree' indentured labourers in the colonies, could also be legally imprisoned for breach of labour obligations under the British master–servant legislation. This was made illegal after 1875, but the laws remained in place for the colonies until the formal abolition of indenture in 1917. Within the USA, the courts were largely opposed to the notion of applying penal sanctions to labour contracts by the early 19th century, but the practice of importing labour already under contract was not made illegal until the Alien Contract Labour Law of 1885 (the Foran Act).

Contract labour of sorts is still found among migrant workers to the US, although the main features of classic indenture (impounding of wages to repay passage money; penal sanctions for breach of contract; physical binding of labourers to specific jobs for fixed terms) would seem to have disappeared. The oppressive conditions under which foreign migrant workers from the Indian subcontinent and Southeast Asia – many of them female – work in the Arab Gulf States today have often been compared to indentured servitude, but it is not clear whether the undoubted human rights

Table 1   Key data on migration of indentured and contract labourers, 1820s to 1930s

Nationality of migrants	Destination	Dates	Numbers	Subtotals
Indian	*Slave and ex-slave societies*			
	British Guiana	1838–1917	238,861	
	Trinidad	1845–1917	149,623	
	Jamaica	1845–1915	38,595	
	Other British West Indies	1856–95	11,152	
	Mauritius	1834–1910	455,187	
	Reunion	1826–82	74,854	
	French Caribbean	1853–89	79,089	
	Dutch Guiana	1873–1916	34,503	
	Non-slave societies			
	East Africa	1895–1922	39,437	
	Natal	1860–1912	152,932	
	Fiji	1878–1917	61,015	
	Total indentured			**1,335,248**
	South and Southeast Asia		Mainly free seasonal, many indentured	
	Malaya	1844–1910	1,754,000 (249,800 indentured)	
	Ceylon		2,321,000	
	Burma		1,164,000	
	Total Indian			**5,239,000**
Chinese	*Slave and ex–slave societies*			
	British Caribbean	1853–84	18,587	
	French Caribbean	1859–60	2,250	
	Dutch Guiana	1853–74	2,979	
	Cuba	1847–74	138,156	
	Peru	1849–74	117,432	
	Mauritius	1843–51	850	
	Reunion	1845–46	1,350	
	Non–slave societies			
	Tahiti	1864–65	1,100	
	Transvaal	1904–10	63,938	
	Queensland	1848–58	5,950	
	Hawai'i	1852–1900	34,309	
	Total indentured			**386,901**
	South and Southeast Asia		Mainly free, many indentured	
	Malaya Straits	1881–1915	5,750,000	
	Philippines	1876–1901	325,000	
	Siam	1876–1901	310,000	
	Sumatra, Java	1876–1901	86,000	
	Total Chinese			**6,471,000**
Pacific Islanders	Peru	1862–63	3,470	
	Queensland	1863–1904	62,795	
	Fiji	1863–1914	27,334	
	Hawaii	1863–1914	2,444	
	Total indentured			**96,043**

Continued

Table 1 Continued

Nationality of migrants	Destination	Dates	Numbers	Subtotals
Africans	British Caribbean	1834–67	39,332	
	Reunion	1848–61	37,200	
	French Caribbean	1854–62	19,500	
	Total indentured			96,032
Japanese	Peru	1898–1923	20,168	
	Hawai'i	1868–99	65,034	
	Total indentured			85,202
Europeans	British Caribbean	1835–81	40,966	
	French Caribbean	1840s	1,180	
	Dutch Guiana	1855–60s	480	
	Hawai'i	1878–99	13,401	
	Total indentured			56,027
Javanese	Dutch Guiana	1890–1939		33,000
North Americans	British Caribbean	1840–67		1,842
	Grand total (excluding South and Southeast Asia)			2,090,295

Sources: Northrup (1995), Appendix A; Engerman (1986).

violations which occur there would fall under the term 'indenture' as we have described it, where the existence of a contract containing clauses in contravention of normal labour practice, and the acceptance by the local court system of such contracts as legally valid, are indispensable features.

Walton Look Lai

Bibliography

Engerman S. 1986. 'Servants to slaves to servants: contract labour and European expansion', in Emmer P.C. (ed.) *Colonialism and migration: indentured labor before and after slavery*. Dordrecht: Nijhoff, 263–94.

Helly D. (ed.) 1993. *The Cuba Commission Report: a hidden history of the Chinese in Cuba. The original English language text of 1876*. Baltimore: Johns Hopkins University Press.

Look Lai W. 1993. *Indentured labor, Caribbean sugar: Chinese and Indian migrants to the British West Indies, 1838–1918*. Baltimore: Johns Hopkins University Press.

Northrup D. 1995. *Indentured labour in the age of imperialism, 1834–1922*. Cambridge and New York: Cambridge University Press.

Tinker H. 1974. *A new system of slavery: the export of Indian labour overseas, 1830–1920*.
London and New York: Oxford University Press.

Related essays
agriculture; commodity trading; domestic service; empire and migration; food; guestworkers; human mobility; international migration regimes; labour standards; oil; railways; rubber; slavery; temporary migrations; tropics; wine; workers' movements

Convergence and divergence

The terms 'convergence' and 'divergence' are used in rather different senses by economists, political scientists and historians. Economists use them to mean the widening or narrowing of divergences among countries with regard to macroeconomic aggregates such as GNP. Such convergence/divergence often relates to integration with the international market, and price convergence among different countries is often taken as a criterion of such integration. This 'economic' interpretation is, to a degree, deterministic: convergence results from flows of exchange in goods or the necessities of production (labour, capital, technology), and is more or less powerful depending on how far the local economy is integrated with the international economy. For political scientists, by contrast – and for French regulatory economists – 'convergence' refers to processes which increase similarities between modes of organization and macroeconomic, macrosocial and macropolitical processes, such processes being further related to concepts such as 'models' or 'regimes'. Historians tend to feel uneasy with such all-embracing concepts and prefer to address the question on a narrower basis: convergence or divergence in approaches to industrialization, policies, economic institutions, etc. There is little common ground between these approaches; case studies show that they have no fixed relationship and that while there may be some signs of convergent evolution in the long term, the periodization of structures and practices is very different in the different disciplines.

Convergence among industrialized countries and integration with the international economy (1850–1930)

The economist's approach, based on comparing the relative advancement of levels of development, has only a limited significance if applied over a long period, because it involves measuring the differences among groups of countries whose membership does not necessarily remain constant throughout the period in question. Statistical studies always apply a predetermined framework based on geographical units, which may be either continents (as in the work of Angus Maddison, 1998) or countries whose present boundaries are anachronistically backdated. For example, does it make any sense to talk about a bloc of 'Eastern countries' before 1945? Such sweeping categorizations do not in the least guarantee that there will be any similarities in the structure and development of the countries concerned.

Statistical findings have their limits; it is more enlightening to consider processes, or the relative positions of countries in the international economy. The international division of labour determines positioning in the international system. At the end of the 19th century this division was very simple: the European industrialized countries exported mainly manufactured products and imported mainly raw materials. Conversely, the primary exporting countries exported only a very limited number of manufactured products. W. Arthur Lewis (1978) aroused some controversy by calculating the terms of Great Britain's trade between 1870 and 1913: he concluded that the interests of primary exporters were subordinate. The way the two groups fitted into the international economy exacerbated the difference between them while encouraging convergence within each group. Countries that found themselves in similar situations would tend to react in similar ways owing both to the reactions of economic actors and to deliberate policy decisions: the end result would be transnational imitation.

This line of argument, however, takes no account of the very substantial drop in the global transport costs of bulky products in the 1880s, which enabled the industrialized countries to obtain primary products at ever decreasing prices that were not matched by a decrease in the price of exports. Thus Lewis's simple typology cannot adequately account for divergent evolution between the two groups and therefore does not prove the existence of a quasi-mechanical process which impoverished primary exporters while enriching the industrialized nations. In any case, the group of 'primary exporting countries' was not homogeneous. Towards the end of the 19th century it included both underdeveloped countries and rich countries with high growth rates (see Table 1).

There is a great difference between the typology of countries at the beginning of the 20th century and the one that might apply today. The former classification depended on the position of each country in the international economy, which did not necessarily coincide with its geographical situation. Thus the positions of Argentina, Canada and Australia converged, whereas Romania and Bulgaria fell into the 'poor primary exporters' group. By the end of the 20th century, however, modes of integration favoured convergence among neighbouring countries in the same geographical region. As in any typology, some aspects resist classification or fall between groups: thus Japan or Russia were industrializing but remained poor; Brazil fell between the two groups of primary exporters; and the United States, the biggest industrial power, was itself a primary exporter.

The group consisting of poor primary exporters with low growth rates was poorly integrated with the international economy: in 1913 Africa and Asia, with a population roughly twice as large as that of Europe (excluding Russia), were responsible for 15 per cent of world exports as against Europe's 55 per cent. This low level of integration restricted convergence within the group.

'New' countries, with a population largely drawn from Europe, producing chiefly raw materials for export, enjoyed a high standard of living but were very vulnerable to adverse circumstances and financial instability. Their internal situation depended on developments in the industrialized countries who bought from them. Fluctuations were exacerbated by the fact that their prosperity depended on the price of their principal export – which was often unstable because the demand was inelastic and many buyer countries were heavily indebted and shaken by repeated financial crises. The methods used to regulate the gold standard, which kept the economies of the industrial heartlands stable, had an alarming knock-on effect on heavily indebted countries with trade-reliant economies. Moreover, the fact that economic, financial and political decision makers, both in the new countries and in the old industrialized nations, were aware of this structural interdependence encouraged copycat behaviour and self-fulfilling prophecies, ensuring that the whole group of new nations suffered equally from crises in trade and finance. This favoured convergence among them.

Economic and social convergence were also perceptible among capitalist industrial societies. This does not mean that differences among them were unimportant; rather that we should pay attention to the structural similarities that underlay traditional differentiating factors. Such factors were obvious in the social sphere – Germany's 'social state' as compared with paternalism elsewhere, for example – and in the structure and workings of corporations – big American corporations, as described by the historian Alfred Chandler, as opposed to small family businesses, German cartels or Japanese zaibatsu. But this should not obscure the fact that the leading markets – goods, money, labour – were managed in more or less the same way everywhere. Recent historians have paid a good deal of attention to this kind of convergence. Early-20th-century Japanese undertakings managed their labour forces in much the same way as European and American corporations. Researchers have also tended to play down differences among banking

systems, such as the traditional contrast between the specialist British bank and the all-purpose Continental variety seen, for example, in Germany and Austria, where banks and industries developed a form of symbiosis (what Hilferding called 'financial capital'). Similarly, historians have stressed resemblances in the way economies were financed, in the identities of major borrowers (governments and companies involved in infrastructure, transport or heavy industry), and in the omnipresent self-financing nature of undertakings. If there were differences it was rather in the morphology of the system: for example, whether or not the same undertaking acted as both a merchant bank and a deposit taker, or whether these functions were distributed among a number of banks within the same group.

These resemblances were the outcome of exchanges among economic actors and of conscious imitation, leading to convergence among companies and national economies whose similarities would have been much less marked a century earlier. Although massive labour movements – from Europe to the United States, for example – did not lead to any noticeable convergence in salary levels, the similarities were reinforced by flows of capital. The banks that organized the financing of infrastructure and industry in newly industrialized countries tended to transpose and adapt the structures of their home countries. Where the capitalists led the engineers followed, applying and adapting new forms of technology, new forms of organization, and new ways to solve production problems. Trade flows unified consumer structures and encouraged industrialists to think in terms of international markets. Much 19th-century trade growth can be accounted for by exchanges within the same industry, among industrialized countries with similar socioeconomic structures.

The impact of the 1914–18 war thoroughly shook up the hierarchies of development and industrialization, but at the same time it fostered the convergent evolution of institutions, economies, policies and social structures. Government intervention increased, the labour market became more rigid and leading industrialists were empowered to organize some sectors of the economy. The governments of the belligerent nations had forced manufacturers to gear production to the needs of war, while

Table 1 Per capita GNP (1990 US$) in 1913

Poor primary exporters		Rich primary exporters		Industrialized countries	
Peru	1,037	Australia	5,505	United States	5,307
Brazil	839	New Zealand	5,178	Great Britain	5,032
China	688	Argentina	3,797	Germany	3,833
Egypt	508			France	3,452

Source : Maddison (1998)

intervening in labour relations to ensure that overexploitation of workers did not trigger strikes in the armaments industry. This government interference lessened with the coming of peace, but certain sectors of the economy remained rigidly organized and labour conflicts turned into politicized three-way struggles from which governments could no longer hold aloof.

These convergent processes continued to operate in the 1920s within each of the three groups of countries (poor primary exporters, rich primary exporters, industrialized countries). To some extent the convergence was the result of deliberate political and financial decisions, and of the cartelization of industrial markets. Similarities among 'new' countries with increasingly trade-dependent economies were accentuated by their vulnerability to an international market that was becoming steadily more unfavourable as supplies – of corn, meat or coffee – outstripped demand; their indebtedness grew as they strove to bridge ever widening trade gaps and service pre-existing debts in a hostile environment where long-term capital was both scarce and costly. They were the first victims of the crisis.

The great divergence (1930–1980)
The crisis of the 1930s was universally seen as proof of the failure of a liberal capitalism that had imposed no self-regulation on the markets. Leading politicians and economists were unanimous on this point, at the very time when the crisis was forcing markets everywhere to impose voluntary regulation: ideological representations fused with political ones. The priority of every government was to reduce unemployment, and this continued after the Second World War, when all other objectives (trade balance, price stability, balanced budgets) were sacrificed in favour of preventing another depression and securing full employment. Ton Notermans (2000), who describes this consensus as

'social-democratic' and sees it as the root of the welfare state, explains it as an attempt to ensure that governments and social partners – employers and employees – contributed in their different ways towards the attainment of common goals. Growth and employment were treated as macroeconomic objectives managed by governments, whereas inflation, from 1945 onwards, was identified as a microeconomic problem to be dealt with by the social partners: hence the appearance of incomes policies. By contrast, Notermans argues, the 'liberal consensus' of the 1920s, and later of the 1980s, saw price stability as the macroeconomic objective to be managed by governments while the labour market was left to the social partners. Here we certainly find an element of structural convergence among the policies of all the developed countries.

But it was precisely at this juncture, with a high level of interventionism and a proliferation of economic and social policies, some geared to the moment, others structural, that the highest degree of divergence was possible: in levels of intervention, in the ranking of objectives, in the interaction of social and economic factors. Convergent thinking did not necessarily produce uniform practices.

Reactions to the shock of the Depression differed according to the economic standing of each country and the political convictions of its rulers. Reactions among the primary exporting countries were sharply opposed. The more developed ones responded by abandoning the export-led growth model and espousing a policy of industrialization predicated on the internal market (Brazil, Argentina, Chile). This change could stimulate growth, but it assumed a greater degree of political control, relying on the support of the middle classes and going against the interests of the former ruling class (the great exporting landowners). Latin American governments undoubtedly copied each other's policies so that their economies became aligned; the change of direction was not so easy for democratic countries such as Australia or New Zealand. Meanwhile, it was, however, the poor primary exporters that bore the brunt of the crisis so that their economies stagnated or regressed, generating a problem of 'underdevelopment' that was already worrying economists by the late 1940s. In the industrialized countries, political choices and national characteristics created diverging path dependencies. Retrospective observers often claim to detect in the 1930s the first signs of a growing divergence between liberal 'Anglo-Saxon' capitalism and the illiberal capitalism of countries such as Germany or Japan, or the corporatist capitalism characteristic of small countries. The United States and Great Britain subsequently embraced greater regulation by the market, even when it came to financing the economy or to monetary policy – tendencies that became more marked after the war. Both government and industry tried to attract external finance by issuing negotiable securities on very active markets nourished by an abundance of available capital both national and international. However, whereas Britain had a comprehensive welfare state, Americans were driven by the near-absence of state pensions and health insurance to make their own personal savings. Existing American savings were not destroyed by war inflation, which meant that capitalized pension schemes could operate and stimulate business on the financial markets. Though the London market received a generous share of this capital, the United States was now the only nation on earth that could absorb all the international capital that came seeking an investment. This meant that the Americans did not need to support their banking system by printing money, which in turn meant greater price stability. Monetary policy consisted in manipulating interest rates on a free money market, rather than confining the banks within a regulatory system that curbed loan volumes, as happened in France.

By contrast, the priority of Germany and Japan in the 1930s was growth in preparation for war, using the banking system as a lever. Thus they treated banking as a tool for developing industry, rather than as an industry in its own right with its own approach to financial operations. To prevent inflation, therefore, the government had to exercise strict control over labour, commodities and money flows, and closely organize all sectors of the economy. Concentration of undertakings also made it possible to maximize the profitability of sectors depending on selections between specific areas of the economy. After the Second World War, outcomes were largely determined by path dependency despite American efforts to encourage market models in both countries. Leading economic actors and politicians distrusted them; financial markets had ceased to exist; the liquid assets of both banks and private individuals had been destroyed by inflation, followed by the creation of new currencies supported by American aid. Hence the only way to inject finance was by overdraft. The relatively even distribution of incomes in both Germany and Japan discouraged the accumulation of savings that would revive the money market, while the destruction of liquid assets forced the adoption of joint retirement schemes. This does not mean, however, that Japan's developing financial market was a mere imitation of Wall Street, because it was essentially an interbank market. To prevent such 'overdraft economies' from sliding into inflation, it was necessary to develop a set of characteristics that observers in the 1960s began to refer to as the 'Rhine model' or 'Japanese model'. Canny specialization in goods for the export market stimulated internal growth and created surpluses to support the currency on the external money market. The Rhine model was predicated on heavy expenditure on research and development and a highly trained workforce able to produce high-value-added goods with prices that were slow to adjust to demand, which in turn meant that wages could be kept high. The model also required good labour relations, bolstered by high wages and government regulation. This model was successful because it harnessed sociopolitical attitudes to economic ends; that is, the economy was well embedded in society. In other words, the constituent elements of the Rhine and Japanese models were well integrated with one another, to excellent effect – producing higher growth rates than in the US or Britain – so that they set the standard to which others aspired.

This state of affairs was complicated by other, divergent factors. For example, Peter Katzenstein (1985) has shown how far the relative sizes of countries determined their differing reactions to the crises of the 1970s.

Big countries responded by imposing protectionism and interfering with market mechanisms. The US developed a brand of protectionism that did not involve tariffs but imposed 'voluntary' limits on (e.g.) imports from Asia. Medium-sized countries, such as Japan, Germany and France, were more interventionist, with policies aimed at long-term structural adaptation to external change. Such policies were feasible because these countries had deliberately opened their economies to trade and so could exercise some degree of control over the international economy. Former colonialist powers made up for lost empires by increasing their dependence on external trade. By the mid 1980s the US, whose foreign trade had stayed level at some 7–8 per cent of its output for many years, was exporting over 20 per cent of its industrial production.

By contrast, the smaller European countries, which depended heavily on world markets, could not play the protectionist card; moreover, their high dependency on external trade made it impossible for them to reorganize their output so as to impose a kind of selective protectionism by the back door. Ever since the 1930s they had responded to external shocks by adjusting their economic, social and political structures in a framework that was basically corporatist. Switzerland, for example, had a concentrated system of economic interest groups represented by powerful associations; its intensive cartelization enabled it to sell its products more dearly at home in order to sell more competitively abroad (as is done by the pharmaceutical firms), while its sustained political bargaining and ideology of social partnership were deployed to avert damaging internal disputes.

Post 1980: back to convergence?

Various attempts to establish the statistics of diverging or converging levels of development in the post-1980 world, using such indicators as GNP or per capita income, have produced differing results. Some authors think that the developing countries have converged with the advanced industrialized countries; others insist that divergence is increasing. This contradiction is due to the fact that the former are looking at a stable group of what were developing countries in the 1970s; their average level of macroeconomic development has progressed solely thanks to their status as newly industrialized or oil-producing

countries. Globally, it is true, the number of poor countries has diminished; but the difference between the ten poorest and ten richest countries has increased enormously since 1980. The big change is not in the general distribution – which is difficult to map in any case – but in the hierarchy among groups of countries. Per capita output in the US remained stable between 1980 and 1996 (at about four times the world average), and so did that of the European Community, which, independent of its geographical expansion, maintained a growth rate about 3.2–3.3 times higher than the world average. The most important changes were the advance of Japan and the newly industrialized Asian countries, and the decline of Latin America and Africa. The late 1990s and the start of the new millennium were marked by a number of differing trends: recovery in the US, a slowdown in Japan, advances by a few Latin American countries after the 2000/01 debt crisis, and very rapid growth in India and China. It is hard to discern any overall direction in this.

As a process, most economists tend to describe convergence in terms of structures and economic policies tending to align themselves on the Anglo-American capitalist model. They consider that the societies and economies of the advanced industrialized countries resemble one another far more at the dawn of the 21st century than they did twenty or thirty years ago, thanks to a reduction in government interference; more market regulation; a decline in the welfare state and in redistributive social engineering (witness the spread of mutual retirement funds and their impact on the capitalization of insurance and private banking schemes); and a tendency for production to be financed by the money markets rather than the banks. A number of developments have contributed to this result. The poor performance of the economies previously seen as models for the rest – Germany and Japan – the resurgence of the American economy in the 1990s, and the free circulation of capital have encouraged convergence in socioeconomic organization, policies and ideologies. The reunification of Germany, which included monetary unification at a highly unrealistic, politically inspired rate of exchange, slowed growth, boosted unemployment and destroyed the social consensus inherited from the regulated liberalism of the postwar years. Belief in the Rhine/Japanese model was finally shattered by the stagnation of the Japanese economy post 1990. Meanwhile the corporatism of the smaller European countries has become less and less compatible with attitudes in the European Union: this applies not only to EU member states but also to Switzerland, which is more or less compelled to align itself with the EU in many respects.

In point of fact, empirical studies are few and far between and always lag behind recent developments. Although new economic paradigms began to appear in the 1980s, it was not until the 1990s that the tendency to converge on the Anglo-American model became evident, and even so, very substantial differences remain at the dawn of the 21st century. Many researchers and politicians see globalization as a process of convergence because it reduces the political autonomy of individual countries. This, however, is to some extent contradicted by studies showing a correlation between the ratio of exports to GDP and the importance of public expenditure: increased government control is a response to globalization. Researchers can argue in two ways. For one group, the convergence factors are objective and economic, chief among them the mobility of capital and goods. The impact of changes in the volume and size of such exchanges cannot, in this view, be palliated by national policy. Capital gravitates towards the most auspicious location: thus competition among firms gives way to competition among countries to attract firms and investments directly from abroad by offering specific advantages and light regulation. The countries with the most accommodating fiscal and legal regimes will become the new models, resulting in a regulatory race to the bottom. The second group argues that the principal agent of convergence is ideology: politicians are increasingly espousing the same, liberal creed and believe that there can be no salvation beyond it. They cannot, however, ignore specific national characteristics and traditions, because neither the population at large nor the economic actors can be easily induced to give them up. Politicians therefore have to compromise between those traditions and what they see as the exigencies of current global trends. This contradiction is shown up, for example, by the difficulties a country like France has in regulating the labour market and the functioning of the welfare state. How far this ideological convergence can go will depend on the extent of agreement or disagreement among the economists and international institutions who shape economic ideologies. Apart from a few mavericks, economists have in fact been joining the liberal mainstream since the 1980s, forming what can be called, or symbolized by, the 'Washington Consensus'.

Globalization, however, is not so much a universal or multilateral phenomenon as a process of integration that works mainly through regional groups. The Common Market, now the European Union, pointed the way, and regional common markets have proliferated since the 1980s: ALENA, MERCOSUR, ASEAN. Such regionalization has been a conscious attempt to ward off globalization, but it has also proved to be a powerful aid to structural convergence among the countries in each 'market'. At the outset politicians did not really know whether they were heading for divergence or convergence. They probably anticipated the former, since – in Europe at least – they had set up an arsenal of resources for preventing the gap between the poorest and richest countries from widening. Later developments showed that joining the European Union did indeed help close the gap (assuming that this was the result of joining the EU and not of compensatory policies); above all, it encouraged the development of transnational networks among both public and private actors.

It is dangerous to try to identify trends over a very short period, or based on developments that did not begin to emerge until the 1990s. There do seem to be powerful factors promoting convergence, both structural and developmental, and they are likely to be further emphasized in the long term by increasing globalization. But the emergence of two new industrial giants, China and India, with path dependencies quite different from the Anglo-American model could be seen, on the contrary, as a factor for divergence. The Washington Consensus and the policies of the IMF, which were responsible for crises such as the one that hit Asia in 1998, are now being seriously challenged, even amongst the leaders of international organizations. Countries that have taken a different path, as Argentina has since 2001, have done rather better. Finally, geopolitical changes are likely to re-present the problem in entirely different terms in the years to come. The one-way prophecies – of convergence or divergence – that have showered on us for the last 150 years are far from exhausting the diverse potential of our pasts, presents, and futures.

Patrick Verley

Bibliography

Crouch C. and Streeck W. (eds) 1997. *Political economy of modern capitalism: mapping convergence and diversity.* London and Thousand Oaks: Sage.

Drezner D. W. 2001. 'Globalization and policy convergence', *International Studies Review*, 3, 1, 53–78.

Hollingsworth J. R. and Boyer R. (eds) 1997. *Contemporary capitalism: the embeddedness of institutions.* Cambridge: Cambridge University Press.

Katz H. C. and Darbishire O. 2000. *Converging divergences: worldwide changes in employment systems.* Ithaca: ILR Press / Cornell University Press.

Katzenstein P. J. 1985. *Small states in world markets. industrial policy in Europe.* Ithaca and London: Cornell University Press.

Lewis W. A. 1978. *Growth and fluctuation, 1870–1913.* Hemel Hempstead and Boston: Allen & Unwin.

Maddison A. 1998. *Monitoring the world economy, 1820–1992.* Paris and Washington, DC: OECD.

Notermans T. 2000. *Money, markets and the state: social democratic economic policies since 1918.* Cambridge: Cambridge University Press.

O'Rourke K. H. and Williamson J. G. 1999. *Globalization and history. the evolution of the 19th Century Atlantic economy.* Cambridge, MA: MIT Press.

Shonfield A. 1965. *Modern capitalism: the changing balance of public and private power.* Oxford: Oxford University Press.

Streeck W. and Yamamura K. (eds) 2001. *The origins of nonliberal capitalism: Germany and Japan in comparison.* Ithaca and London: Cornell University Press.

Related essays

1989; agriculture; class; commodity trading; corporations; debt crises; development and growth; Economic Commission for Latin America and the Caribbean (ECLAC); economics; European Union (EU); financial markets; industrialization; International Monetary Fund (IMF); labour standards; modernization theory; neoliberalism; public policy; regional communities; Samsung; taxation; trade; trade (manufactured goods); trade agreements; underdevelopment; welfare state; Washington Consensus; workers' movements

Corporations

Transnational corporations are large-scale businesses whose core activities span national borders. They administer and coordinate the international movement of capital, goods, technology and management, and exercise a significant influence on the world economy and individual nation states. International trade grew alongside the rise of civilization. Nonetheless, the origins of the transnational corporation are associated with the expansion of world trade from the early 17th century onwards, and they are closely identified with the business strategies and organizational forms that emerged in the 19th century.

Frequently used interchangeably, alternative terms for the transnational corporation (TNC) can cause confusion. On other occasions, analysts use these terms to make distinctions. 'Multinational enterprise' (MNE) and 'multinational corporation' (MNC) suggest a firm that operates in many national venues, but it may in practice refer to a firm with only two main bases of operation (the term 'transnational' more accurately covers both possibilities). While 'multinational enterprise' or 'transnational enterprise' (TNE) may include varied types of ownership, size and structure, 'multinational corporation' or 'transnational corporation' may indicate a firm that is incorporated, large-scale, and managerial. The United Nations employs the term 'transnational corporation', and founded the United Nations Centre on Transnational Corporations (UNCTC) in 1973.

A company with only a sales subsidiary overseas would not normally be classified as a TNC. Overseas or 'host' economies are differentiated from the nation that is 'home' to the company headquarters or the main business. There is, however, no convenient yardstick with which to distinguish core activities, given overlap between all activities, and the vital capacity of companies to adapt over time. There are no agreed criteria for the percentage of overseas ownership, employees or sales that are needed before any business can be deemed a transnational. It may be more insightful to focus instead on international business strategies, economic benefits, market power, political influence, or corporate accountability. How we consider the TNC, as the key organization of international business, will inevitably affect our interpretation of the contemporary world economy and its history.

Trading companies were leaders in international business activities before 1914, and they frequently developed into large-scale business groups. They were both a cause and response to the rapid growth in international trade. Through their specialist knowledge and experience of overseas markets, they undertook banking and insurance, and invested in primary products and manufacturing. TNCs engaged in civil engineering; public utilities and mining were also prominent. From the 1920s onwards, but more obviously from the 1950s, manufacturing began to dominate company investment overseas, initially by US corporations in Western Europe. By the 1980s, US, European and Japanese manufacturers were investing in the economically leading regions of North America, Western Europe and East Asia. In following decades, the service industries became increasingly internationalized, and cross-border mergers and acquisitions emerged as a commonplace of international business strategy.

The transnational or multinational enterprise was identified for the first time as a business enterprise with distinctive characteristics or strategic objectives in the 1960s. Therefore, historians commonly apply the concept of transnational enterprise in order to understand the development of the international economy from the 19th century onwards, during a time when the concept was unknown. The economists who conceived the term of multinational and then transnational enterprise wanted to explain why firms might abandon the exporting of goods or services for foreign direct investment (FDI). International business consists of trade in either manufactures or services, or the costly and organizationally difficult task of providing goods or services at an overseas location through an act of FDI. International business theory argues that each successful TNC has organizational capabilities or advantages in resources, management, knowledge, products or technology that are compensation for the disadvantage of being 'foreign'. Moreover, the national business system of the home economy has a determinant influence on these capabilities, and, as a result,

countries are leaders in particular industries or clusters of related industries. The national business system includes diverse factors, from location-specific market mechanisms to formative institutions such as government. TNCs may additionally gain from host economy factors, notably nearness to consumers, or cheaper labour, and from the very fact of being transnational, most obviously through greater returns to scale. International business theory was initially used to explain the dominance of US manufacturers in the postwar decades, and critics have posed a number of questions. Can we properly understand the global service sector by using a TNC model that emphasizes the advanced capabilities in technology and organization associated with manufacturing? Is this model applicable to the strategies of TNCs from industrializing as well as the economically advanced nations of North America and Western Europe? Is the concept of an integrated, managerial enterprise transferring capabilities from the home base in one direction to subsidiaries justified by the historical evidence? Lastly, does the weight placed on the original capabilities of the main 'home' company underestimate the very transnationality of the TNC in explaining its success and impact?

Economic historians have a long tradition of writing on the growth of the international economy. They tended to portray the international economy as operating outside each individual national economy, seeing trade as a consequence of unsymmetrical factor advantages generated by national developments. Business historians began to investigate the distinct phenomenon of the TNC in the 1970s, but debates since the 1990s have brought new perspectives. Globalization trends implied that the importance of the TNC's home market was declining, while cross-border presence and transactions were a growing source of competitive advantage. If the integrity of the nation state was being undermined, not least because of footloose international capital, so too was the notion of the TNC that simply replicated mini-versions of its home base operations and management overseas.

The study of transnational history challenges over-reliance on the nation state as the fundamental unit of analysis, and questions ethnocentric interpretations of worldwide change that are weighted to the 'role of the West'. It follows that nation states, having distinct institutions and cultures, are not an historical given or constant. Nor are TNCs. Nation states were formed from the 19th century onwards, contemporaneously with the growth of international business and the emergence of TNCs. Rather than focusing on how nation states shaped business systems and international business, we must consider how TNCs affected the development of political entities, for example 19th-century Borneo or Southern Africa, or 20th-century Iran and Guatemala. Many of the tendencies currently associated with contemporary globalization can be found in the internationalization of the world economy before 1914 and again in the immediate postwar decades. The focus on national-level factors glosses over the diversity of business systems within nations, and overlooks the impact of international forces. The stress on determinant national institutions or national cultures, as the bases for national business systems, precludes the possibility of change, which must derive from either internal differences or external influences. National-level analysis, therefore, may direct attention to sources of institutional, organizational and economic stability and away from sources of change. It may prevent a fuller understanding of complex factors, national and international, and how they interrelate with each other over time. As units of analysis, TNCs operate simultaneously in specific locales and across borders. They provide a means of exploring the interplay of international and national factors that depends on neither the nation nor the state, while not being separate from them.

Global history has been associated with World Systems Theory, in which the rise of capitalism from the 16th century marks an historical discontinuity. Europe and the West more generally changed the world by developing capitalism as a transformative international system, which could exist separately from political entities. Chartered companies at first and then TNCs had a vital role in these developments. Nonetheless, while influential, TNCs were themselves influenced by events. Considerable changes in the organization and commercial activities of TNCs over time reveal their ability to remain central to the international system and individual national economies. The capitalism of the 19th century did form an international system with notable characteristics, such as a preference for markets, free trade, and capital mobility. Nations could, however, mediate the impact of trade and FDI, and TNCs had to adjust to the overlapping realities of an international system and national varieties of capitalism.

Furthermore, international business activity was led by Britain before 1939, and subsequently by the US. The leading economies in North America, Western Europe or Japan continue to account for the majority of TNCs. In other words, the global economic map has never been flat, and the dominance of specific nations or regions has been a major driver of internationalization. The transfer of capital, goods, technology and management by TNCs validates, to an important extent, ideas based on the 'rise of the West'. Modernity brought dominance, rivalry and inequality between nation states, and illustrated too a pathway of development. But World System Theory ignores, for example, the multilateral effects of international interaction on the West, the continued contribution of Arab, Indian and Chinese merchants, and the influential arrival of the Japanese TNC. The dominance of particular nations, economic internationalization, state formation and modernization were coterminous. For example, the Japanese government did strengthen its position by encouraging the imitation of Western methods, but there were also a series of adaptations in management, production and technology. In other words, there were varieties of modernity and industrialization processes, as well as examples of dominant practice, and divergence was an automatic partner of convergence. The Japanese cotton industry in the 19th century purchased spinning technology from British engineering companies; by the late 1920s, it was selling its breakthroughs in weaving. Japanese businesses, reliant on US expertise after 1945, emerged in turn as the architects of internationally influential managerial systems in the 1980s.

The international economic system had underlying structures that determined the flow of trade and FDI. In the 19th century, the role of TNCs was shaped by the dominance of Europe as a source of capital, technology and manufactures, and by the relationship of Europe to Asia, Latin America and Africa as locales for primary products and investment. The strengthening of European nation states was associated after 1870 with economic rivalry, and with the pursuit of imperialism in Asia and Africa. The existence of multinational empires causes difficulties for the phrase 'transnational history'. On the other hand, empires were an extension of the power of nation states, and the policies and opportunities of TNCs, most notably in the form of trading companies, were vital to the process of colonization. We have to account for the political entities of empires as well as nations in order to understand the historical role of TNCs, while simultaneously acknowledging that the international economic system had its own dynamics, as witnessed by the involvement of TNCs in Latin America. The emergence of the US to economic pre-eminence and the geopolitics of the Cold War, after 1945, were another example of underlying structures that shaped the international economy.

In order to explain the historical characteristics and impact of the TNC, we need to look at a wide variety of influences, including global, regional-international, imperial, national, and regional-local factors. There will, too, be market- or industry-level factors, which can have international as well as national scope. Debates in transnational history have not yet greatly influenced the business history of the TNC, but could be effectively used to explore one of the key organizations of the international system.

Robert Fitzgerald

Bibliography

Chandler A. and Mazlish B. 2005. *Leviathans: multinational corporations and the new global history*. Cambridge: Cambridge University Press.

Fitzgerald R. 2008. *Corporation: rise of the global company*. Cambridge: Cambridge University Press.

Jones G. 2005. *Multinationals and global capitalism*. Oxford: Oxford University Press.

Smith C., McSweeney B. and Fitzgerald R. (eds) 2007. *Remaking management: between global and local*. Cambridge: Cambridge University Press.

Wilkins M. 1970. *The emergence of multinational enterprise*. Cambridge, MA: Harvard University Press.

Wilkins M. 1974. *The maturing of multinational enterprise*. Cambridge, MA: Harvard University Press.

Wilkins, M. 1989. *The history of foreign investment in the United States to 1914*. Cambridge, MA: Harvard University Press.

Related essays

advertising; auditing; capitalism; commodity trading; development and growth; empires and imperialism; financial markets; gold; industrialization; information technology (IT) offshoring; investment; iron and steel; management; marketing; organization models; publishing; rubber; Samsung; services; taxation; technologies; trade; trade (manufactured goods); trade agreements; transnational; United Fruit Company; world orders

Cosmetic surgery

In the 19th century, a number of surgeons in the United States and Europe created a new medical genre: cosmetic or aesthetic surgery performed on bodies free of all pathologies, congenital anomalies and functional handicaps. Progress in anaesthesiology, antisepsis and asepsis had transformed operating standards in surgery, making it safer and less painful. The first cosmetic surgery was performed in the United States in 1881, but it was only between World Wars 1 and 2 that plastic surgery gained its autonomy from the specialized fields of otorhinolaryngology, orthopaedics, and general surgery. At that time, the idea of formally structuring the field of plastic surgery on a national level developed in the United States before spreading to Europe. The American Association of Plastic Surgery was founded in 1921, and mostly gathered surgeons specialized in reconstructive surgery and rarely in cosmetic surgery. The American Board of Plastic Surgeons was later created in order to distinguish quacks from real surgeons. A new association, the American Society of Plastic Reconstructive Surgery, soon appeared to cater for those surgeons not admitted into this elitist Board, in order to accommodate the larger number of surgeons willing to practise plastic surgery. France was the first nation to follow this organization pattern (Société Française de Chirurgie Réparatrice Plastique et Esthétique, 1931), with England in second place just after World War 2. Cosmetic surgery continued to develop independently in both these countries without any real interchanges, each national group laying claim to the discovery of new techniques. This atmosphere of competition did not deter Dr Maurice Coelst, a Belgian otorhinolaryngologist, from gathering surgeons from around the world in order to publish a plastic surgery review (1931). He also organized in 1936 in Brussels the first international Congress on Plastic, Reconstructive and Cosmetic Surgery.

Whereas World War 2 allowed for the emergence of new surgical possibilities (particularly skin grafts and antibiotic therapy) which vastly increased the use and popularity of cosmetic surgery, it also slowed the development of cosmetic surgery in its civil and aesthetic aspects. But Nazis used it to heighten their Aryan looks, and Resistance movements to make wanted faces unrecognizable. The end of the war brought unexpected fame to cosmetic surgery when Nazis on the loose sought refuge in Argentina and changed their identity using face lifts. The war also created a meeting point for surgeons caring for those wounded in battle, in particular as in London after the Blitz or in Algeria after the Allied landing, thus favouring international discussions. These discussions gravitated around a group of surgeons who would later go on to shape the field of cosmetic surgery, the British surgeon McIndoe, the New Zealander Gillies, the Americans Converse and Vilray P. Blair, or again the Frenchmen Dufourmentel and Merle d'Aubigné. From the end of the war, the field of plastic surgery was on the rise again on a national level (British Association of Plastic Reconstructive and Aesthetic Surgeons in 1946, Société Française de Chirurgie Plastique, Reconstructive in 1952). In 1955, surgeons practising plastic surgery and representing about 41 nations joined forces to form the International Confederation of Plastic Reconstructive and Aesthetic Surgery and held the first international plastic surgery congress.

From the 1950s and 1960s, a network of cross-referencing women's magazines proposed new standards for feminine beauty and life, which largely contributed to the spread of the idea that beauty could be improved by specific products and techniques, even outside high society. Many of the readers of these magazines were middle-class women. The appearance of the mini-skirt in the 1960s, which soon became an emblem of female liberation, brought legs covered with varicose veins to the forefront, and this soon became an aesthetic issue. The medical community quickly proposed a solution, with new hygiene standards and specific therapies. A prophylactic medical approach to varicose veins developed, alongside the more invasive curative surgical techniques. Jeans and hot pants, the successors to the mini-skirt, similarly put more pressure on the concept of the ideal female form, and opened new avenues for cosmetic surgery and medicine, including liposuction or abdominoplasty.

By the end of the 20th century, the cosmetic surgery market had become more lucrative and competitive. Whilst the well-off continue to turn to the most prestigious surgeons (American, British and French), the growth of less expensive cosmetic-surgery vacations in emerging markets (Brazil, Mexico, Tunisia and Morocco) is on the rise. Some seaside resorts enhance this mix of sun and beauty with a drop of technique in the mix: almost every year, that of Puerto Vallarta welcomes the International Annual Symposium of Plastic and Aesthetic Surgery to strengthen its reputation and place in the market.

Nicolas Guirimand

Bibliography

Gilman S. L. 1999. *Making the body beautiful: a cultural history of aesthetic surgery*. Princeton: Princeton University Press.

Guirimand N. 2005. 'De la réparation des "gueules cassées" à la "sculpture du visage": la naissance de la chirurgie esthétique en France pendant l'entre-deux-guerres', *Actes de la Recherche en Sciences Sociales*, 156–157, March, 72–87.

Haïken E. 1997. *Venus envy: a history of cosmetic surgery*. Baltimore: Johns Hopkins University Press.

Related essays

1960s; beauty; bodybuilding; dress; fashion; feel-good culture; femininity; gender and sex; jeans; medicine; war

Cosmopolitanism and universalism

Universalism assumes a universal knowledge, morality and salvation that can overcome particularist exclusion posed by different nations and cultures to achieve universal good. The term 'cosmopolitanism' originated from the Greek, *kosmopolitês*, meaning 'citizen of the world' and is a moral and sociopolitical paradigm that has envisioned different ideas of transnational community throughout history. These terms can be used as synonyms so long as they point to a possibility of attaining universal humanity and the transnational community across different religions, languages and cultures. But they are used as antonyms when universalism slips into intolerance and associates itself with imperialistic ventures of domination that defies the cosmopolitan ideals of inclusion and diversity.

The interaction and contestation of these two ideals lie at the core of transnational development of modern world history over the last few centuries. Many religions in the world such as Christianity, Hinduism, Islamism, Judaism and Confucianism also propose universalism, whose respective teachings and doctrines of a universal human nature, moral duties, and rules of social organization have laid the cultural foundation of countries in Europe, the Middle East, Asia, and Africa. From the late 18th century, the idea of the Enlightenment became the most influential universalist idea that reshaped the world across cultures and nations. It enabled the flowering of modernity in Europe and later in America. To its protagonists the Enlightenment was conceived as a cosmopolitan force that promoted the idea of liberty across nations by opposing the constricting allegiances of religion, class, and the state. The expansion of the advanced industrial nations in Europe into other parts of the world also meant the spreading of the universal ideals of the Enlightenment from the 16th to the 21st century. The intolerant and violent nature of European expansionism, however, caused serious political and cultural resistance from people in colonies against a Eurocentric and chauvinistic universalism that lacked cosmopolitan characteristics. As the era of imperialism and the ideological contestation of the Cold War came to an end towards the close of the 20th century, new reflections on indigenous cultural traditions and the universalisms of the formerly colonized territories seem to have re-emerged as the former colonial subjects strive to redefine their identity and promote voluntary unity among themselves in the new world order after the Cold War.

The single most powerful idea of universalism that shaped the modern era has been Enlightenment thought, the idea of which was that through reason human beings could usefully apply knowledge to achieve happiness. According to the Enlightenment thinkers, reason is a universal part of human nature that could be developed equally across

cultures and that all nations could eventually achieve the same degree of progress. When that happened the human species would have eliminated all superstitions, irrationalities and the prejudices that drive men apart, and mankind would finally achieve a peaceful and liberal social order. Immanuel Kant was a major thinker of the 18th century who advocated such universalist ideas and the belief in a peaceful cosmopolitan future through action based upon a universal morality. The industrial revolution provided the economic basis for the idea of the Enlightenment to prosper in the minds of the emerging bourgeois citizens and helped move towards a new era of liberal civil society. The bourgeois civil revolution in Europe as symbolized by the French Revolution in 1789 was instigated by the ideas of the Enlightenment. These quickly spread to other parts of Europe, America and beyond in the following centuries with the spreading effects of the industrial revolution everywhere.

The imperialistic venture that was begun concomitantly by Europeans was a natural result of capitalist development achieved through the industrial revolution, where Enlightenment universalism came to underpin their assertion of the 'civilizing mission' over the rest of the world. The assurance that this would bring about progress in 'backward' nations, however, involved a great deal of violence and intolerance. In particular, the universal and liberal values of the Enlightenment were not applied to all equally, as the subjects of the colonized territories were discriminated against. This double standard caused huge anxiety in those who became objects of the civilizing mission, inclining them to perceive the universalist message as empty ideology.

Some historians equate the history of capitalist globalization driven by Eurocentric universalism with the development of cosmopolitan history. This force did increase the interactions among cultures which were normally segregated and closed to outside influences. However, the violent nature of such forces cast a deep shadow over the history of the cosmopolitanism of the era. At the other end of the spectrum of cosmopolitan thoughts of the Enlightenment, cosmopolitan morality motivated some conscience-driven citizens to oppose slavery and racism, as well as encouraging colonized people to empower themselves against colonialism with the ideas of liberty and universal rights that the Enlightenment had promoted. Enlightenment thinkers had indeed used cosmopolitanism as a paradigm against the constricting allegiances of religion, class, and the state. Due to the struggle of indigenous people, as well as campaigns endorsing universal equity and justice, European slavery of Africans, which started in the 16th century, was gradually abolished in different places from the end of the 18th century through to the late 19th century. Opposition to racism and racial segregation became a universal ethos of the modern world through the demise of colonialism across the globe throughout the period after World War 2. The five decades of the policy of apartheid in South Africa finally ended in 1994 thanks to indigenous opposition and the support of the international community who were opposed to anachronistic policies of racial segregation.

The major achievement of universalist and cosmopolitan ideals in the 20th century was the establishment of the League of Nations and the United Nations following the two world wars. They embodied the ideals of the transnational cosmopolitan community that Immanuel Kant had discussed in *Idea for a universal history from a cosmopolitan point of view* (1784) and *Perpetual peace* (1795). He advocated cosmopolitan thinking while dealing with the issues of universal morality, prosperity, and world peace. The origins of the League of Nations and the United Nations can be traced back to the Westphalian system of states in the 17th century based on a limited and exclusive club of nations. The cosmopolitan effort to cooperate among nations through common law for international security and economic development has been manifested through various organizations affiliated with the UN. For instance, the International Criminal Court, set up in 2002, provides the means to establish a form of universal justice against individuals who might have committed genocide, other crimes against humanity, or war crimes, as defined by international agreements. It developed through dealing with war crimes in the former Yugoslavia in 1993 and Rwanda in 1994 and has become an important avenue for international justice where judicial systems of nation states fail.

Socialism was one powerful universalist ideal that challenged the globalizing Western capitalist thrust and imperialism that emerged at the turn of the 20th century and influenced the independence struggle of the colonized world. Karl Marx and his supporters originally started out from Europe in the mid 19th century and spread its international influence from the late 19th century through expanding the sphere of influence from London to Peking and from Libya to Cuba. Socialists claimed that imperialism was the peak of capitalism in its transnational development and that it perpetuated exploitation and alienation of working people across all nations. Socialist universalism is a part of the legacy of the Enlightenment and is based on a materialist theory of human history that foresees a universal path of class struggle and revolution in the advanced capitalist economies. As capital is transnational in nature, class struggles and revolutionary projects also required transnational perspectives and practices to consolidate the gains of an internationalizing economy and to find the political means to defeat the defenders of capital.

Thus socialists and communists established transnational socialist organizations (i.e. the First International, the Second International, and the Comintern) and supported other socialist revolutions throughout the first half of the 20th century. As much as capitalism turned into imperialistic ventures, this counterproject, however, was also involved in a significant degree of violence and intolerance in both domestic and transnational terrains. The Stalinist period in the USSR, the Khmer Rouge in Cambodia and the Cultural Revolution in China produced an immense human toll, and the Soviet Union became involved in expansionist ventures in neighbouring territories. This elucidates the danger inherent in universalisms, as seen in the cases of the 'civilizing mission' of imperialists and the state violence of 'socialism'. Universalism in this case was an ideal that these derivative projects of the Enlightenment did not live up to.

In the last half of 20th century cosmopolitanism was often defined against extreme allegiances to nation, race and ethnos. Cosmopolitanism has been a frequently discussed theme in the context of dealing with issues such as the rights of asylum seekers and immigrants, as well as with racism and nationalism in the new phase of globalization. The international conventions on the right to asylum approved by a United Nations conference in 1951 reflect the cosmopolitan efforts of the international community to help those whose liberties and lives are under threat due to their race, religion, or political opinion. All nations are under an obligation to grant asylum to those political refugees according to this convention.

In advanced industrial societies, cosmopolitanism has become a part of the new civil consciousness with regard to issues of refugees and immigrants (including those without documentation). It is based on the recognition of the nature of a transnational world in an age when political instability in the world continues, developed nations continue to need immigrant labour, and people have become increasingly mobile in search of better economic opportunities. The 1999 French Debré Law that imposed hardship on immigrants and those without rights of residence troubled a section of French society that had promoted cosmopolitan ideals such as tolerance, openness and hospitality throughout the 20th century. In South Korea, the idea of a homogenized nation whose definition of Koreanness often relied on ethnic oneness and a defensive nationalism was challenged by the influx of foreign workers of different nationalities and ethnic backgrounds after 1993. Some emergent cosmopolitan citizens in Korea have criticized the Industrial Trainee System, a government policy that has facilitated an influx of workers from Nepal, Pakistan, Mongolia, and other less developed Asian countries into Korea but also gave generous leeway to Korean employers to exploit them, contrary to the universal rights of workers and cosmopolitanism. In their search for a new national identity, Korean elites and the public began to contemplate the significance of cosmopolitanism as a counterbalancing power to parochial nationalism and racism.

Cosmopolitanism has increasingly been a matter of concern for policy makers and educators in those world industrial centres whose primary concerns have become sustainable multicultural societies. The idea of multiculturalism derives from the concern that the cultures of different ethnic and religious groups must be respected and tolerated in a multiethnic society. All ethnic groups are encouraged to interact peacefully with each other without being forced to assimilate into one singular national culture. The United Kingdom, Canada and Australia have adopted such multiculturalism as government policy. For instance, 'Britishness' has been favoured as a term to discuss the national identity of the United Kingdom, which reflects the multicultural nature of the society better than

the term 'Englishness', which represents only the dominant group. Affirmative action in the United States was adopted in the 1960s in an effort to tackle racial discrimination rooted in society and is based on the belief that inclusion and diversity would make social equality and security more enduring.

With increasing strength, the activities of many NGOs and their transnational associations or networks have built on a belief in a universal humanism when dealing with various issues such as humanitarian relief, human rights, workers' rights, the environment, and freedom of expression. At the core of these transnational actions there is the cosmopolitan ideal of the free association of people without conforming to restrictive forms of identity and national borders in order to achieve humanitarian goals. The International Red Cross, for instance, is an early example of such an NGO that aims to ensure human dignity regardless of national, religious, ethnic difference and class or political opinion. Its voluntary, non-governmental and independent activities are regulated by an international federation and are recognized by international humanitarian law.

The Cold War, driven by the polarized and divisive universalist ideals of market-centred liberalism and socialism, seemed to have ended with the collapse of the Berlin Wall and the subsequent fall of the USSR at the end of the 1980s. This also seemed to be the end of the age of the grand universalist ideals and paradigms. However, the subsequent era of globalization centred on the US model of a liberal market economy and driven by multinational corporations has become a new universalist imperative that has created much anxiety in the rest of the developing world. The world faces the question of how to dissolve the mistrust and conflict between cultures and nations in order to construct a peaceful world community and let cosmopolitan societies flourish in every corner of the globe. The transnational ideal of cosmopolitanism is impossible to conceive of without a certain level of belief in universal ethics, rights, and reason which, however, requires careful reflection on the dangers of intolerance that can counteract a plural development of society.

So yang Park

Bibliography
Anderson A. 'Cosmopolitanism, universalism, and the divided legacies of modernity',

in Cheah P. and Robbins B. (eds) 1998. *Cosmopolitics: thinking and feeling beyond the nation.* Minneapolis and London: University of Minnesota Press.

Beck U. 2006. *The cosmopolitan vision (Der kosmopolitische Blick, oder, Krieg ist Frieden, 2004),* trans. Cronin C. Cambridge and Malden: Polity

Vertovec S. and Cohen R. (eds) 2002. *Conceiving cosmopolitanism: theory, context, and practice.* Oxford: Oxford University Press.

Related essays
abolitionism; African liberation; anti-racism; antisemitism; asylum seekers; Buddhism; capitalism; Christianity; civilizations; conspiracy theories; consumer cooperation; democracy; diasporas; empire and migration; empires and imperialism; Ethical Culture; ethnicity and race; freemasonry; globalization; Hammarskjöld family; human rights; humanities; indigenous knowledges; internationalisms; Islam; justice; Kessler, Harry von; knowledge; labour migrations; labour standards; League of Nations system; legal order; liberalism; modernity; nation and state; nomads; Pax Americana; religion; socialism; transnational; underdevelopment; United Nations system; Universal Races Congress; Westernization; women's movements; workers' movements; world federalism; world orders

Counterfeit goods

The Organization for Economic Cooperation and Development (OECD) defines counterfeiting as 'unauthorized representation of a registered trademark carried on goods identical or similar to goods for which the trademark is registered, with a view to deceiving the purchaser into believing that he/she is buying the original goods' (1988). While the practice itself may be ancient, it was not until the second half of the 19th century, when industrial property rights were first formulated, that the exact nature of counterfeiting began to be defined as a consequence of the struggle to suppress it. Quite a number of infringements of intellectual property rights come under the general umbrella of 'counterfeiting': not only trademarks as such, but any illegal production and distribution of a product protected by an intellectual property right, e.g. copyright.

In the 19th century, soaring production as a result of industrialization, together with increased trading volumes in ever widening markets, led to a great increase in counterfeiting, which was further stimulated by a rapid decline in product quality as a result of mass production, and by downward pressure on prices as manufacturers vied for a share of the mass market. All sectors were affected, including luxury goods: textile designs were copied over and over again; the names of famous watch and clock makers were ruthlessly taken in vain. But counterfeiting also affected everyday consumer goods such as medicines, developed by pharmacists who complained bitterly as they realized their products were being copied. France, which was among the first countries to specialize as the result of an international division of labour in the production of high-added-value goods with prestigious labels, was also among the first to introduce effective countermeasures with laws passed as early as 1824 and 1857.

A number of French industrialists, realizing the comparative ineffectiveness of court action in preventing the counterfeiting of their products, banded together to defend themselves against such unfair competition. Pharmacists were in the van, signing the foundation charter of a manufacturers' union towards the end of the 19th century. This union was international almost from the outset: bilateral agreements were signed with first Germany, then Russia, the United States, Greece, Portugal, Peru and Austria – all countries which imported French pharmaceuticals.

In the 20th century, counterfeiting became big business, riding on the back of mass consumerism. Copies of both finished and semi-finished products (toys, computers, automobile and aeroplane spare parts) flooded the market. In the 1960s, when Western Europe was invaded by mass consumption, counterfeiting went international and fraud was conducted through highly structured, well informed networks with solid financial backing, using commercial channels with links to organized crime. It was a structure that encouraged regional specialization, as in Asia, where by the 1980s the counterfeiting of watches, computers and cosmetics was centred in Taiwan; of textiles and leather goods, in Korea; of computers, toys and precision instruments, in Hong Kong or Japan; of pharmaceuticals, in India, Indonesia or

Pakistan. In the Mediterranean world, fine leatherwork, luggage and textiles were copied chiefly in Morocco, Greece or Turkey; Italy specialized in silk and leather goods. From the 1980s onwards, as trade was liberalized and customs barriers removed, counterfeiting increased yet again, but so did the drafting of new rules to repress it and control the circulation of goods. While some countries introduced their own criminal sanctions, the struggle was also conducted on the international level.

In 1986 the European Community issued a regulation which prohibited the sale of obvious counterfeits of trademarked goods, but did not extend to infringements of patents or the copying of designs or models. The situation worldwide remains very unsatisfactory. Anti-counterfeiting measures are part of the general regulation of world trade and their effectiveness depends very closely on the negotiating powers of the World Trade Organization (WTO). The 1994 Trade Related Intellectual Property Standards (TRIPS) (Marrakech) agreement introduced anti-counterfeit measures as part of the WTO regulations. After canvassing opinion among its member states, in June 2003 the World Intellectual Property Organization (WIPO) set up a consultative committee on the enforcement of intellectual property rights. All states have an interest in resisting the proliferation of counterfeit products, especially as WTO statistics indicate that their share of world trade increased from 3 per cent in 1990 to over 5 per cent in 1995. The rapid conversion of a number of controlled economies into market economies has further stimulated the production and consumption of counterfeit goods and calls for further endeavours to repress counterfeiting at global level.

Nadège Sougy

Bibliography
Beltran A., Chauveau S. and Galvez-Behar G. 2001. *Des brevets et des marques: une histoire de la propriété industrielle.* Paris: Fayard.
Comité Colbert 1997. *Communication sur les effets des produits de contrefaçon dans l'industrie française.* Paris: Comité Colbert.
International Chamber of Commerce 1996. *Industrial property protection in East Asia.* London: ICC Commercial Crime Services.
Union des Fabricants pour la Protection Internationale de la Propriété Industrielle et Artistique 2005. *Rapport contrefaçon et criminalité organisée*, 3rd edition. Paris: Union des Fabricants. [Also online] Available: www.unifab.com/index. php?page=publications&lang=FR, accessed 14 January 2008.

Related essays
borders and borderlands; consumer society; crime; drugs (medical); General Agreement on Tariffs and Trade (GATT) / World Trade Organization (WTO); industrialization; intellectual property rights; patents; pedlars; publishing; sports gear and apparel; textiles; trade; trade (manufactured goods); trade agreements; trademarks

Creoles and pidgins *See* **Pidgins and creoles**

Cricket

Cricket is a bat-and-ball game developed by the English leisure classes in the 17th and 18th centuries. The first set of written rules dates from 1727.

Cricket began to take its modern form in the Marylebone Cricket Club (MCC) rules of 1788. The first international cricket matches occurred in 1859 when an English team organized by Fred Lillywhite toured the United States and Canada. The legalization of overhand bowling in 1864 ushered in the truly modern game. The MCC first served as the unofficial governing body for the sport internationally; today, the International Cricket Council (ICC) oversees the game. The ICC grew out of the Imperial Cricket Conference (founded in 1909) with England, Australia and South Africa as members. (India, New Zealand and the West Indies joined in 1926, followed by Pakistan in 1953.)

Cricket was an integral part of the so-called 'games revolution' of the 19th century. When Queen Victoria ascended to the throne of the United Kingdom in 1837, 'sport' referred exclusively to hunting and fishing and 'games' were largely the province of children and schoolboys. By the turn of the 20th century, sport and games were central to the self-perception of the British as a unique people.

Games also gave Britain's far-flung empire a common language and culture, while providing a vehicle through which the British could culturally instruct their imperial subjects in the codes of 'proper', that is British, behaviour. These same imperial subjects used the games to challenge British notions of superiority by playing them in unique ways or simply trying to beat the English at their own game. Thus, cricket in the empire both functioned as a way to unite British subjects through shared competition and simultaneously worked to divide them along a number of different fault-lines, notably those of class, age, and gender.

Beginning in the Victorian era, cricket tours were meant to sow imperial goodwill, strengthen bonds of loyalty and act as festivals of English civilization. These great occasions often did just that, although there were also moments of tension. Traditionally, the fiercest rivalry was found in the 'Ashes' – that is, a Test series between Australia and England. The name dates from 1882 when following the first Australian Test victory on English soil, the Sporting Times ran a faux obituary which solemnly announced: 'In Affectionate Remembrance of ENGLISH CRICKET, which died at the Oval on 29 August, 1882. Deeply lamented by a large circle of Sorrowing Friends and Acquaintances, R.I.P. N.B. – The body will be cremated, and the Ashes taken to Australia.'

Perhaps the low point in the history of Test cricket came in the Australian summer of 1932/33 when an English touring side employed a new form of bowling attack (dubbed 'bodyline bowling' by the Australian press) in a desperate attempt to neutralize the bat of a young Australian named Don Bradman. The sportsmanship of the attack was a matter of some debate and indeed led to charges of poor sportsmanship. Although initially declared legal and sportsmanlike by the MCC, bodyline bowling was declared illegal after a West Indian team (possessing sufficiently fast bowling to render the tactic dangerous) employed the attack against the MCC in the English summer of 1933. This incident caused an international uproar and marked the end of unquestioned English leadership of cricket.

The International Cricket Council is still dominated by England and former British colonies, but the ICC now has over 30 associate member nations and over 50 affiliated member nations, many of which were never part of the empire. While Test cricket continues to be played, it has arguably been surpassed in popularity by one-day cricket and especially one-day internationals (ODIs), which began in 1971. These games, as the name suggests, are completed in a single day, in contrast to full Tests which are scheduled for five days and can frequently end in draws because they are not completed in the allotted time. Both Test matches and ODIs continue to excite tremendous interest and partisanship among national fans.

Patrick F. McDevitt

Bibliography
Beckles H. and Stoddart B. (eds) 1995. *Liberation cricket: West Indies cricket culture.* Manchester: Manchester University Press.

Guha R. 2002. *A corner of a foreign field: the Indian history of a British sport.* New Delhi: Picador.

Mangan J. A. 1981. *The games ethic and imperialism; aspects of the diffusion of an ideal.* Cambridge: Cambridge University Press.

Related essays
civilizations; empires and imperialism; sport; sports gear and apparel; Westernization

Crime

Crime is a label given to socially deviant action or expression that is believed to harm any being or object other than the perpetrator or the perpetrator's property. Deviance can be considered criminal both when victims or their property are directly harmed and clearly identifiable, or when its effects have no obvious victims and the harm is perceived as a more general ill produced by the behaviour.

It is a matter of debate whether some acts are intrinsically criminal, or whether judgement on the definition of any act as a crime is fundamentally contingent on the sociopolitical and historical context in which such judgements are made, as well as the circumstance and reasons for the act. Acts considered to be criminal in one time and place may not be in another. Delineation of 'crime' can typically be expected to reflect the notions of harm and fairness held by a society and embodied in its laws. Equally, the degree of interchange between societal sentiment and official values concerning the constitution of crimes may be anticipated to vary according to time, place, and the specific context of state–societal relations in question.

Internationally, state policies against crime tend to be dominated by conservative approaches to the subject. Conservative approaches are largely supportive of restrictive definitions of crime that limit its interpretation to acts or behaviour stipulated as such by a state's laws. Their efforts therefore focus on providing assessments of the motivations of the criminal and means of combating such activity. More radical criminological perspectives strive to explain why a particular act has been criminalized, highlighting the sociopolitical functions of crime labelling and their connection with the state and its various mechanisms and efforts aimed at societal governance.

Whether an act that is not legally defined as criminal is to be considered as such is a particularly politically sensitive issue when the act is perpetrated by the state itself. The notion of a criminal state has evolved with gathering momentum since the end of World War 2, strengthened by international agreements that have accompanied a concerted attempt to construct an international normative regime on state-perpetrated crimes (war crimes, crimes against humanity, crimes against peace, and the countermeasures that can be taken by the international community in response to such crimes). Nevertheless, because of the nature of international public law, states will only consider themselves and their citizens liable to prosecution with regard to international agreements to which they have acceded and in some cases (e.g. the US) only if in addition the agreement has been incorporated into the state's domestic criminal law through a specific legislative act.

Restrictive and more abstract interpretations of what constitutes a crime minimize the risk of cross-cultural differences in labelling an act a crime. Thus, if a harmful effect is directly attributable to an act or behaviour and no information about the actor, motivation or ultimate end of the action is known, cross-societal consensus is likely to be maximized that the act constitutes a crime. The more that is known about the social context of a harmful act – the perpetrator and the perpetrator's motives, the ultimate social effects of the act – the more obviously political and differentiated become interpretations of whether or not the act constitutes a crime. It is important to recognize, however, that the use of the language of crime and attendant discussion of its rationalities may itself be viewed as an indication of a particular politicocultural standpoint.

The relationship of sociopolitical context to an understanding of the meaning of 'crime' is particularly important when norms and laws on crime are transposed from one such context to another. When they occur, such transpositions can have far-reaching politicocultural outcomes (problematic, positive, or both, depending on one's perspective), especially with regard to relations between states and their societies. In recent years, the promotion of common anti-crime agendas in the international arena has provided numerous examples of the domestic political potency of attempts to change laws and influence popular beliefs about what constitutes 'crime' (and how it should be combated). In the fields of human rights, the environment, and financial regulation (to mention just a few), the experience of member states of the European Union in harmonizing their laws – often introducing new categories of crime as well as new rights and obligations for the member state and their citizen – provides ample evidence of the contentious domestic politics which have been stimulated by the expectations and demands such efforts have fed.

Apart from the obstacles of normative differences that have hindered attempts to unify definitions of crime across political borders and within them, understanding the significance of crime and what is perceived to constitute crime in different places is also made harder due to the inherent problems of comparative empirical research into crime rates amongst different states and regions. Varying trends of crime reporting and levels of policing and interdiction efficiency mean that the relative scale of specific crime rates between countries can be hard to verify.

The history of crime and transnational crime in particular is difficult to write, partly because of the difficulty in accurately recording such activities, and partly because of continual developments in the meaning of both crime and of national borders.

Although less commonly acknowledged, peace, as well as war, is believed to stimulate intrastate transnational crime. Scarcity imposed by wartime conditions may fuel black-market trade, in anything from consumer essentials to luxury products. The arrival of peace can also lead to problems of crime, from acts committed by decommissioned and often traumatized men returning from battle, to the flooding of light weapons onto the international black market following the weakening of border controls of states newly at peace. In this latter category, it is of particular note that the end of the Cold War (1989–90) has widely been interpreted as the stimulus behind a wave of transnational crime, including the smuggling of luxury goods to the relatively deprived states of Eastern Europe and Russia, and the launch of a wave of legitimately and illegitimately cascading weaponry onto international and regional arms markets as a result of the 'peace dividend'. The flow of such illicit traffic was aided by the collapse of police and judicial institutions in the former Communist states at that time.

Perhaps the most notable form of transnational crime that has evolved over the course of the 20th century as a legal concept is that of organized crime. When the legal term 'organized crime' was first applied in the 1920s, it referred to types of smuggling activities which had long been engaged in but which were increasingly being clamped down on by state authorities (in the case of weapons) or were being newly prohibited (such as drugs) and were therefore novel commodities to be trafficked in this way (the object of traffic or illegal interest has demonstrated consistent diversification over time). Stemming first from a number of bilateral and multilateral agreements, then becoming the subject of international conventions, 'organized crime' and its component crimes have developed into a significant theme of international cooperation and were a particularly prominent topic of concern on international agendas during the 1990s (until being overtaken by the challenge of terrorism in late 2001).

Each illicit good and service has its own history of criminalization and control, particular to specific geographical areas as well as overlapping them. On the European Continent, for example, concern about transnational smuggling of weapons to independence movements fighting the Ottoman Empire had provided the stimulus for international conferences seeking to clamp down on cross-border traffic during the late 1800s. With regard to international efforts to stem illicit transnational drug flows, Western governments had been pressed to take action in the 1920s due to public alarm at overproduction by drug manufacturers and consequential massive diversions from legal supply channels. International treaties were subsequently agreed in 1925 and 1931, which were effective in reducing the flow from legal drug manufacturers to illicit markets, but also heralded the birth of clandestine factories that sprang up to fill the demand for suppliers, particularly when the League of Nations began to implement enforcement procedures for these conventions in the early 1930s. While it was nowhere near the proportions it would achieve in the second half of the 20th century, illicit drug traffic already displayed its competency in worldwide mobility and connections.

In the mid 20th century, international cooperation against a variety of illegal activities subsumed within the catch-all category of 'organized crime' emerged parallel to the struggle to combat Mafia activity in Italy and the US. Recent international agreements have promoted the broader conceptualization of organized crime, focusing more on illicit transnational commercial groups and goods subject to illicit trade. In international policy, 'organized crime' has been used to refer to a wide range of activities including illicit-drugs trafficking, trafficking in people, trafficking in weapons, and smuggling people and consumer goods (such as cigarettes and cars), as well as the laundering of the proceeds of such activities. A series of defining characteristics of organized crime was drawn up by the World Ministerial Conference on Organized Transnational Crime in 1994, including inter alia the collective use of violence, intimidation or corruption, with the aim of earning profit or of controlling territories or markets, and which may include the laundering of illicit proceeds. These groups may be structured hierarchically and may cooperate with other transnational criminal groups, but neither is strictly necessary. The UN Convention against Transnational Organized Crime (2000) upheld a similarly broad conceptualization of organized crime. Despite the rising concerns, considerable ambiguity and division has remained apparent with regard to the meaning of the term and, consequently, to the implementation of approaches to combat it.

Since 1989, concern has largely shifted focus from the combatting of individual groups active in certain states, to connections between organized crime networks internationally. In particular, numerous international conferences have demanded cooperative state action to repel the perceived assault on the integrity of Western markets and states by the influx of illicit goods and finance, and/or especially when these may also be being used to provide terrorist groups with revenue. Many governments and experts have asserted that a transnational component has become integral to most organized criminal trade, which in turn requires the construction and implementation of a concerted international counter-response to the problem. It is assumed that organized crime seeks to maximize its operational opportunities and minimize the risks posed by law enforcement. The 'balloon effect' (where, facing a clampdown by a country's law-enforcement agencies, organized criminal traffic simply displaces itself to another jurisdiction) has been a continual bane to efforts to crush organized crime internationally. Thus it is argued by some experts that there needs to be an effective equal distribution of the risk of organized crime amongst different states via policy and policing harmonization on the issue.

Closer approximation of, or moves to harmonize state laws against crime internationally have been a relatively recent step, in contrast to a longer history of agreements by which states mutually recognized their different criminal laws and came to arrangements about how extradition of suspected criminals could thus take place. International police cooperation began to be institutionalized in the early 1920s with the launch of an International Criminal Police Commission, the forerunner of INTERPOL, which emerged in 1956. In the second half of the 20th century, a system of bilateral treaties (Mutual Legal Assistance Treaties, or 'MLATS') began to emerge, providing a formal framework in which extradition requests and information cooperation between the investigators and prosecutors of different states could be regularized. The insufficient exchange of intelligence within and between states nevertheless continues to be cited as the greatest internal challenge to the effectiveness of such international and regional countercrime efforts.

Over recent years, then, organized criminal activity has graduated to being seen as a global, rather than a mere national threat, as a consequence of the opportunities offered by the lowering of economic and political barriers in 1989, the establishment of new, weak democracies, and increases in trade and global communications networks. As evident in statements made within UN Congresses on the Prevention of Crime in the 1970s and 1980s, however, such perceptions also preceded the collapse of Communist regimes in 1989. While the difficulties of measuring transnational crime trends and evaluating related threat assessments have remained considerable, scholarly attention has been able to focus with more substantive results on providing histories of international criminalization trends and the evolution of international norms and agreements regarding different forms of cross-border traffic.

Sappho Xenakis

Bibliography

Andreas P. and Nadelmann E. 2006. *Policing the globe: criminalization and crime control in international relations.* Oxford: Oxford University Press

Cherif Bassiuoni M. and Vetere E. (eds) 1998. *Organized crime: a compilation of UN documents, 1975–1988.* Ardsley: Transnational.

McLaughlin E. and Muncie J. (eds) 2001, 2003. *The Sage dictionary of criminology.* London: Sage.

Savona E. 1995. 'Harmonizing policies for reducing the transnational organized crime risk', *Transcrime Working Paper,* 2. Trento: University of Trento.

United Nations 2000. *UN Convention Against Transnational Organized Crime* [online]. Available: www.uncjin.org/Documents/ Conventions/dcatoc/final_documents_2/ convention_eng.pdf, accessed 16 January 2008.

Vlassis D. and Williams P. 2001. *Combating transnational crime: concepts, activities and responses.* London: Frank Cass.

Related essays

arms trafficking; commodity trading; counterfeit goods; criminology; drugs (illicit); drugs (medical); European Union (EU); genocide; justice; legal order; police; terrorism; trademarks; war crimes; white slavery; women's movements

Criminology

Criminology, the study of crime and criminals, has been characterised by the transnational exchange of ideas through books and congresses since its emergence in Europe during the 18th-century Enlightenment. Until that period Western society tended to understand crime in terms of sin. The perception of humans as rational beings, making decisions and acting through choice, together with an increasing aversion to the public infliction of pain in the hope of deterring others fostered debate about crime and punishment among 18th-century jurists, philosophers and philanthropists.

The new attitudes towards crime were encapsulated in Cesare Beccaria's *On Crime and Punishment*. First published in Italy in 1764, this pamphlet was rapidly translated into all major European languages and became the seminal text for what is known as classical criminology. The idea was to replace the complex legal practices of the old regime with a legitimate criminal justice system based on equality before the law and rational punishments that were proportionate to the crime committed and designed to deter. This, in turn, linked with the move towards the creation of penitentiaries; by the end of the 18th century, and particularly in the 1830s and 1840s, this generated international visits by government agents and philanthropists to study the most effective practices employed in other countries. The first international congresses on penitentiaries were held in 1846 and 1847 in Frankfurt and Brussels respectively.

Classical criminology also fed into the legal changes wrought by the French Revolution and other new legal codes established in the late 18th and early 19th centuries. But in the early 19th century the belief that events and social relations might be studied by employing methods derived from the natural sciences gave rise to positivist criminology. The statistics of crime and criminals, which began to be collected and collated with increasing sophistication by European states, figured significantly here. Adolphe Quetelet, a Belgian, and André-Michel Guerry, a Frenchman, were the first that sought to draw meaning from the criminal statistics. Their work was translated, widely circulated and, together with similar analyses, was discussed and debated at a variety of national and international meetings of philanthropic reformers, medical experts, statisticians and others.

It was, however, only in the last quarter of the 19th century that criminology, or criminal anthropology as it was initially called, emerged as an academic discipline in its own right and began to hold international congresses in its own name. The key figure here was the Italian doctor Cesare Lombroso who moved positive criminology to a new theoretical level with his concept of the born criminal. Lombroso's *Criminal Man* (sometimes translated as *Delinquent Man*) was published in 1876. He argued that crime was not so much the result of individual choice but more brought about by the pathological temperament of the criminal. The individual criminal, he maintained, was dominated by his or her physiological nature; criminality was to be found principally among those individuals in whom primitive instincts remained and could be recognised, at least by experts.

Lombroso's ideas had a wide circulation. *Criminal Man* went through several new editions and was greatly expanded, and the translations and précis in circulation were not always a clear reflection of Lombroso's current thinking. The book sparked heated debate at the Second International Congress of Criminal Anthropology held in Paris in 1889. Much of this debate appears to have been national posturing, particularly between the rival Italian and French delegations. The French took a much more sociologically based approach that emphasised the roles of environment, economic situation and nurture as the causes of criminal behaviour. The clash in Paris led the Italian school to boycott the third congress held in Brussels in 1890. But the sociological perspective struck a chord with people working in the field elsewhere and who were beginning to see a need for penal systems that, rather than taking a particular crime as the focus for the kind of sentence handed down by the courts, shifted their policies towards a consideration of the individual offender.

In the same year that the French and Italians clashed publicly in Paris, Franz von Liszt, the head of an institute of criminology in Berlin, founded the International Union of Penal Law. The Union was decidedly transnational, drawing its leadership and membership from across Europe. It sponsored research, held frequent congresses and, with some success, urged the reform of criminal law along what it considered to be modern lines, reflecting, in particular, the sociological thrust of criminological thinking.

Transnational debate continued into the new century. In Europe much of this was the result of men like Liszt and his successors. In the English-speaking world also there was a tremendous boost from the translation and publication of a large number of continental European works, following an initiative, in 1909, by the American Institute of Criminal Law and Criminology. During the interwar years many international congresses became the principal preserve of practitioners and when the Nazis came to power the atmosphere could become poisonous. The

11th International Prison and Penitentiary Congress held in Berlin in 1935 was a notable instance with squabbles over whether votes should be taken by delegate (which would have given the large number of German participants an automatic majority) or by participant state. The discourse was often similar, and a large number of liberal democracies shared Nazi views on the sterilization of certain offenders, but overall the perspectives and outcomes of policy were markedly different.

After the Second World War, the statistics of criminal offending began to rise across the developed world. From the mid-1950s the rise became steep and dramatic. This gave a new impetus to academic debate on the aetiology of crime, much of which was conducted across national boundaries in conference rooms and in print. These developments were linked with the role of critical analysts of society and policy making that was publicly assumed by many academic social scientists during the 1960s. New Deviancy Theory and New Criminology were both developed during the 1960s and early 1970s. The former emphasised the ways that interaction between individuals and law enforcement agents could in itself generate behaviour labelled as 'deviant'. The latter sought a theoretical framework for understanding crime in the context of a radical political critique of the inequalities and the other social factors that appeared to generate criminal offending. While the former originated largely in the United States and the latter in Britain, the ideas were taken up and explored elsewhere. So too was the Neo-Conservative Criminology that emerged in the United States during the 1980s as a counter to liberal and radical theories and that emphasised technocratic rationality and traditional norms and values. In addition to the theoretical developments, there were significant shifts in the focus of study: historians were sucked into the area; victims became subjects for attention as much as the perpetrators of offences; and there was a move away from unspoken assumptions that prioritised male actors to a more nuanced approach, giving full recognition to gender issues.

All of these developments took place on an international stage though relatively few of the participants conducted comparative research across national boundaries – there was a general recognition that legal categories of criminal offences, differing from state to state, could make comparisons particularly difficult. It was, overwhelmingly, the fora of debate and exchange that were transnational. Increasing numbers of criminological journals began to appear, and while few included 'international' in their titles – International Criminal Justice Review is exceptional – virtually all accepted articles from different national contexts. It was much the same with associations of criminologists. The American Society of Criminology had long seen itself as international; in 2000, a European Society was formed with an annual conference drawing wide participation in both delegates and subject matter. The International Association for the History of Crime and Criminal Justice, established in the mid-1980s, is unique in having 'international' in its name.

In the last 30 years of the 20th century crime became highly political in the Western world with politicians on both the left and the right seeking to outdo each other by playing the populist card of promising to be tougher on criminals and the causes of crime. Governments funded criminological research, often very generously. And, as they had always done, they looked out for what appeared to work in other national contexts and sought to adapt it to their own. The growth of criminal activity that crossed national frontiers – most obviously drugs and people trafficking, and forms of terrorism – brought governments and criminal justice practitioners together to provide common approaches. Interpol, which originated in the 1920s, appeared on the surface to be an ideal institution to manage transnational policing and develop an 'applied criminology'. Moreover, Interpol was the result of different national police institutions coming together to discuss matters of common interest, and was not the creation of an international treaty. But national sensibilities and differences in national legal systems have always acted as a brake on cooperation. In the 1990s the European Union established Europol to manage transnational policing in Europe, but jurisdictional problems existed even within the EU, and the institution has never extended its remit much beyond intelligence gathering.

Clive Emsley

Bibliography

Bierne P. (ed.) 1994. *The origins and growth of criminology: essays on intellectual history, 1760–1945*. Aldershot: Dartmouth.

Fattah E. A. 1997. *Criminology: past, present and future: a critical overview*. Basingstoke: Macmillan (now Palgrave Macmillan).

Nye R. A. 1976. 'Heredity or milieu: the foundations of modern European criminological theory', *Isis*, 67, 335–55.

Related essays

individual identification systems; statistics; terrorism

Cuisines

Cuisines offer some of the most obvious and seemingly fixed markers of authentically local and unique cultural groups. But cuisine is also an important marker and conduit for globalization. Even thousands of years ago, seeds, grains, food vessels and cooking implements circulated the globe. Attention to the movement of cuisines sheds important light on how societies interact, how identities and cultural authenticity are created and presented, and ultimately how global processes work and their impact on the world's societies.

Despite the pervasive nature of global forces, not every cuisine enjoys the same degree of global mobility. Nor does every cuisine enjoy the status of being recognized and consumed by people throughout the world. Only some cuisines can be called 'global cuisines'. Many factors influence which cuisines emerge as 'global cuisines'.

France and Italy, for example, were two of the primary centres of intellectual, artistic, and technological development; their citizens created standards for every aspect of daily life, including cuisine, that were prized and emulated by citizens of other countries around the world. In Russia during the 18th and 19th centuries, French cuisine was privileged as the ultimate mark of refinement, and French chefs were imported to Russia to provide authentic French food for the nobility.

The status of French cuisine as a global cuisine was further cemented by France's empire-building projects. Already by the 18th century, France was actively imposing its political and economic might throughout the world, and the relocation of French bureaucrats ensured the simultaneous dispersion of French cuisine throughout Africa and Asia. At the same time, one consequence of France's empire-building activities was the incorporation of foreign ingredients and dishes into French cuisine, even as these foreign tastes were occasionally refined to fit with mainstream French preferences. Similar processes of culinary integration are apparent in England. One of the consequences of England's role in the global slave trade, its move into the Caribbean, and its long history of global trade with Asia and India was that foods such as tea and sugar were introduced into England from abroad. Today England is probably most distinguished by its tea-drinking culture.

Population migration is another means by which certain food cultures have attained recognition on the global stage. The physical relocation of population groups from one country to another has been accompanied by the relocation of their culinary traditions, and the predominance of some food cultures as global cuisines depends on the size and dispersal of diaspora communities as well as their commitment to maintaining cultural traditions. To some extent, the relocation of culinary traditions is a product of cultural nostalgia, such as with Indian immigrants to the United Kingdom or Silicon Valley who attempt to retain connections with their homeland and assuage a sense of homesickness by shopping in Indian grocery stores and eating in Indian restaurants. For members of other immigrant groups, the relocation of people and their culinary traditions has not been exclusively for personal reasons of nostalgia or cultural continuity, but rather has also afforded opportunities for becoming integrated into the local economies of their new host countries. Perhaps the most obvious example of the coupling of social and economic integration is that offered by Chinese cuisine. As Chinese immigrants spread throughout the world, setting up restaurants was often one of the most effective ways for them to establish themselves culturally and financially in their new homes and to earn money that they sent back to support relatives in their home country.

In still other cases, the cultural distinctiveness of cuisines becomes muted, especially as immigrant populations become assimilated into, or even become the majority in, their host countries. During the 19th and early 20th centuries, the westward migration of Central and Eastern Europeans to North America and South America facilitated the movement of food traditions based heavily on sausages, cabbage, and potatoes. Over time, as members of this population have become integrated into their new homelands and reproduced themselves socially and biologically, their food habits have become established as local cuisines. The American Midwest, home to large numbers of Central European immigrants and their descendants, is known for the pleasures of bratwurst, sauerkraut, and beer. Mexican and other Latin American cuisines are showing similar tendencies in North America, although in other parts of the world they are still marked as being culturally distinct.

Processes of industrialization facilitated the emergence of another type of global cuisine based less on individual ingredients than on techniques of food preparation and storage. Industrialization was part of a larger set of modernizing trends that swept the globe during the late 19th and early 20th centuries. Industrial food production rested on principles of hygiene, safety, efficiency, and convenience. The application to food of industrial techniques of cleaning, processing, and preservation for long-term storage resulted in a generic cuisine in which foods existed in cans, jars, bottles, and other types of packaging. Qualities of freshness and individuality were replaced by attributes such as consistency, conformity, and predictability. The fact that factory-produced foods were packaged for long-term storage ensured that they were appropriate to be shipped to markets throughout the world, thus making canned and bottled foods another form of global food culture.

A related type of global cuisine is fast food. Fast-food purveyors aim to provide food quickly, cheaply, and efficiently. The United States is usually credited with being the home of fast food in the 1940s and 1950s with the emerging popularity of hamburger restaurants (McDonald's in particular), diners, the Automat, and standalone vending machines, among other food services, that offered customers on the go a quick snack or even a full meal. In many parts of the world at this time, the rise of fast-food culture coincided with the growing importance of car culture and long-distance driving. Fast-food restaurants are now a mainstay of service centres along highways in the United States and elsewhere.

Yet even as presumably American foods such as hamburgers and soft drinks are held up as the ubiquitous symbols of a global fast-food cuisine, each food culture has its own idea of what constitutes 'fast' food. For Russians, fast food is called 'fast hands' and signifies anything that can be prepared and eaten quickly and with a minimum of fuss. By contrast Japanese fast food includes a wide variety of items that are sold from mini-markets or the ubiquitous vending machine: soft drinks, beer, potato chips, dumplings, and even sushi. Yet fast food as a global phenomenon existed long before industrial capitalism. In China, sidewalk stalls and walkup storefronts selling dumplings and noodle dishes and located along travel routes, such as at railway stations and street corners, not only preceded fast-food chains, but also provided menu items that have subsequently been assimilated into the offerings of fast-food chains such as McDonald's.

Since the 1950s, global capitalism has become an increasingly important medium by which some culinary traditions, and not others, become distributed throughout the world and elevated to the status of 'global cuisines'. In some cases, the movement of capital itself – money, labour, knowledge, and the physical means of production – across borders has facilitated the spread of particular culinary systems. Transnational food corporations such as McDonald's, Coca-Cola, and other food-processing companies rely on the global market to expand their businesses and increase profits. The result is the appearance of McDonald's and its competitors throughout the world, a development that some critics have lamented as an imperialist process that has effectively eliminated cultural distinctiveness and replaced local cuisines with a single, homogenized cuisine. More generally, the circulation of global capital has also facilitated the distribution and availability of a wide variety of ethnic cuisines throughout the world, so that it is now possible to enjoy Brazilian cuisine in Asia, South African cuisine in the Netherlands, and Indonesian cuisine in Germany. The trajectories of these travelling cuisines are diverse, as are the values attached to them. For instance, North American and European cuisines have travelled south to Africa and east across Eurasia, where they have become celebrated as markers of status and capitalist modernity. Middle Eastern and Asian cuisines, by contrast, have travelled north and west to Russia, Europe, and North America, where they are valued for their association with 'the exotic'. Other travelling cuisines embody the values of particular political and economic systems as they move across spaces that are more symbolic than geographic, as in the case of 'socialist' and 'capitalist' foods that have crossed the borders separating formerly state-socialist societies like Poland and East Germany from their non-socialist neighbours.

In other cases, participation in the global economy has created both a new class of consumers who travel the world to experience regionally distinct culinary traditions, and a new form of culinary geography in which food cultures are mapped onto the physical topography of the world. The purpose of this culinary tourism is to experience geographic difference through culinary difference. A variant of these trends is that of travelling foods that leave their places of origin and migrate around the world via commodity chains. Commodity chains also emphasize the personal relationships that are created at the different steps of the production, distribution, and consumption cycle: for instance, relationships among farmer, market seller, buyer, factory worker, shipping agent, grocery store seller, customer, and family. This emphasis on interconnectedness creates a sense of shared cultures and relationships among individuals who come from radically different backgrounds and live in places geographically distant from each other. Fair-trade products such as coffee and fresh vegetables are among the most well-known foods that move through commodity chains. British and French consumers who buy Kenyan green beans affirm a sense of connection with Kenyan growers and pickers. This circulation of food through multiple nodes in the global network also increases its aesthetic and economic value. For instance, the value of blue-fin Tuna for the Japanese sushi industry is enhanced by the multiple relationships through which the fish pass after being caught by American fishermen along the northeast coastal states of Maine and Massachusetts, then purchased by Japanese sushi buyers, shipped to Tokyo where they are regraded and cut by Japanese sushi chefs, and then either sold in Japanese restaurants to Japanese customers or shipped back to the United States and sold in American restaurants.

In still other cases, global capitalism has encouraged the development of particular global cuisines through media technology. Advances in telecommunications and in both technological and linguistic literacy – especially the global spread of English language fluency – have coincided with the growing popularity of television shows, cookbooks, and other literature devoted to food. Chefs, food critics, and food scholars have emerged as new cultural brokers, and their audiences can tune in from around the world via satellite and the Internet. These new technologies have catapulted regional food practices onto a global stage. For instance, the entertainment value of the *Iron Chef* television game show (broadcasted in such places as Asia, the US, Canada, the United Kingdom, Australia, Israel, and Scandinavia) introduced Japanese food habits, although not necessarily an identifiably Japanese cuisine, to a worldwide audience. Similar trends are apparent with the distribution of cooking shows hosted by American, British, French, and Italian chefs, among many others, who have introduced both regional cuisines from their own countries and foreign cuisines to a global audience. In many ways, the global consumption of print, television, and electronic media is generating a form of cuisine that is defined as 'global' not because it is associated with a culturally distinct culinary tradition but rather because it is presented and disseminated to a global audience via global media technology.

What 'global cuisines' have in common is both recognition and popularity among a global audience. Although specific culinary content and heritage are important in some cases, in other cases what matters is the extent to which certain food systems are available to consumers throughout the world. Ultimately, it is the issue of mobility – of food cultures, consumers, and technology – that has the greatest impact on which cuisines become elevated to the status of 'global cuisines'.

Melissa L. Caldwell

Bibliography

Bestor T. C. 2000. 'How sushi went global', *Foreign Policy*, 121, November–December, 54–63.

Freidberg S. 2004. *French beans and food scares: culture and commerce in an anxious age*. Oxford and New York: Oxford University Press.

Mankekar P. 2002. '"India shopping": Indian grocery stores and transnational configurations of belonging', *Ethnos*, 67, 1, 75–98.

Mintz S. W. 1986. *Sweetness and power: the place of sugar in modern history*. Harmondsworth and New York: Penguin.

Pilcher J. M. 1998. *¡Que vivan los tamales!: food and the making of Mexican identity*. Albuquerque: University of New Mexico Press.

Watson J. L. (ed.) 1996. *Golden arches East: McDonald's in East Asia*. Stanford: Stanford University Press.

Wilk R. R. (ed.) 2006. *Fast food / slow food: the cultural economy of the global food system*. Lanham: Altamira.

Wilk R. R. 2006. *Home cooking in the global village: Caribbean food from buccaneers to ecotourists*. Oxford: Berg.

Related essays

car culture; Chinese Diaspora; commodity trading; corporations; diasporas; diet and nutrition; domestic service; drink; empires and imperialism; fast food; feel-good culture; food; food safety standards; human mobility; McDonald's; tourism

Cultural capitals

A cultural capital is any urban area which is marked by a certain amount of converging evidence of being a centre of attraction and structural power for a certain domain of cultural activity, or even – in the case of the most important centres during certain periods – for a wide range of cultural activities. Any town may have, gain or lose the status of a cultural capital as a result of general changes in principles of symbolic production and recognition; or with changes in the cultural sphere involved, or in power relationships among dominant towns, or in transnational cultural relationships. The strength of a cultural capital depends on the closeness of its relationship with its regional, national or international hinterland: how much it can attract, how much it can export. The exponential increase in transnational relationships over the last three centuries has increased both the influence of cultural capitals generally and competition for the title among an ever growing number of towns. Because research to date has focused almost exclusively on the West, I have been compelled to take my examples from that region; but it is probable that comparable examples could be found in the Arab world (Cairo) and in Asia (Delhi, Peking, Calcutta, etc.).

A rapid review of the main contenders for the title of 'cultural capital' shows that the list did not change much between 1750 and 1850, while a major shakeup took place in the second half of the 19th century. As new nations strove to shake off old hegemonies, a series of new claimants emerged: in Germany, Munich and Berlin; in Italy, Milan and Florence (and later Rome); in Austria-Hungary, Vienna and her competitors, Budapest and Prague; in Russia, St Petersburg and Moscow were bitter rivals for primacy in the Slav world, each offering a different definition of 'genuine Russian culture'. In America, New York was incontestably the first aspirant to the title, but the United States had no one obvious 'centre' and the civic pride of elites in other cities produced a number of weighty challengers towards the end of the century, such as Chicago and San Francisco. The other continents, one after another, followed this lead: through the 19th and 20th centuries the capitals of Mexico, Brazil and, a little later, Argentina set out to dazzle the rest of the country with substantial monuments of culture, often imitating European models, such as academies, opera houses, universities, ambitious newspapers and journals and publishing houses. The dawn of political emancipation in colonial (or semicolonial) Africa, Asia and Oceania was often presaged by the emergence of would-be cultural capitals, the scene of more or less harmonious contact between imported European culture and a local culture hesitating between adherence to tradition and appropriation of imported modernity. The transfer of Japan's capital from Kyoto to Tokyo in 1868, as the country opened itself to Western influences, typifies this importation of European models. Another, very different manifestation of the same culture shock is exemplified by the tension in Chinese cities between European concessions and native quarters.

The heyday of the 'cultural capital', from c. 1830 to c. 1930, produced a twofold reaction. On the one hand, the magnetic attraction of big cities, including (political and economic) capitals, became steadily stronger. This attraction became institutionalized as networks of publishing houses, secondary and higher education establishments, exhibitions, touring theatre productions, newspapers, travellers and tourists were created to dispense an ever more lavish cultural output to an ever increasing and more varied audience. On the other hand, as audiences became more varied, with different expectations and different capacities of appreciation, the cultural products served up to them became more specialized and so cultural production became fragmented, mirroring general changes in society, culture and urban development as well as the contrasting strategies employed by producer groups unequally affected by all these changes. As a result, certain cultural capitals acquired an unprecedented prominence, though Paris, London and Rome always maintained their conspicuous dominance at the head of the table. Milan, for example became a byword for opera after the decline of Naples in the 1820s. Leipzig, in Central Europe, remained the capital of German publishing and the fountainhead of erudition. By 1914 Berlin, capital of the Reich since 1871, had universities and scientific academies whose attraction was felt as far afield as the United States, and a greater number of museums and theatres than any other city could boast, putting the city on a par with Paris and London. London, though it could not rival Paris's monopoly of national academic, literary and artistic life, was undoubtedly the capital of English literature and theatre, the indispensable reference point from Toronto to Montreal, from New York to the other great American cities, from the Cape to Melbourne and Sydney.

The chief frontiers between cultural capitals faithfully reflected linguistic differences, but music and the visual arts could transcend such boundaries with relative ease, enabling Paris, for example, to exercise an influence far beyond its 'natural' cultural hinterland. Paris, for Walter Benjamin the 'capital of the 19th century' and for Patrice Higonnet 'the capital of the world', is, as a cultural capital, unique in the duration of its national and transnational influence and the magnetic pull it exercised over the most diverse cultural areas and domains. The educational side of this – the universities and other institutions of higher education, the Museum of Natural History, etc. – was already attracting students and scholars from all over Europe by the 1830s and, by the end of the century, from all over the world. On their return home they helped foster the mythic cult of Paris and spread the gospel of French language,

thought and literature. Over the same period Paris became the centre of the European, and later also the American, art market, and attracted ever more exotic colonies of artists. The Impressionists, Symbolists, Cubists, as well as the more traditional painters, all included a substantial number of foreign artists; indeed, the so-called 'Paris school' of the 1920s did not include a single native French painter. Paris's École des Beaux-Arts also educated substantial numbers of foreign architects, and Haussmann's town-planning ideas were espoused as far afield as Madrid, Buenos Aires and Bucharest. Even in the realm of music and opera – in which Paris had not been particularly prominent since 1789, tending rather to import from neighbouring countries – towards the end of the 19th century 'French', which really meant 'Parisian', works arose as a bulwark against the influence of Wagner and the Italians. This music was exported all over the world, as is shown by the frequent performances of French operas, comic operas and operettas everywhere from Vienna and Berlin to London, Rio, Buenos Aires and even Japan.

This concentration of talents and this ever widening influence had an objective underpinning: the revolution in transport, the spider's web spread of railways through France, and from France to other countries, facilitated the exchange of cultural products and travel by intellectuals, elites and artists, particularly in order to visit the great exhibitions. The greatest of these exhibitions gave Paris a chance to pose regularly as the international capital of culture, entertainment and business (50 million visitors in 1900). Secondly, the French capital had always received lavish cultural subsidies from government, far more so than London or even the German capitals. The Revolution set up the Louvre as an important reference for the great museums that were being founded or extended at the turn of the 19th century. It helped to establish a canon of artists from both the recent and the more distant past and a hierarchy of national 'schools'; it regulated the flow of art objects from capital to capital. The Paris Opéra, rebuilt at enormous expense under the Second Empire and generously subsidized – unlike Covent Garden or La Scala – attracted musicians and singers from all over Europe and created an instant international reputation for new works, despite the chauvinistic French distrust of all things Wagnerian.

Touring performances by the Comédie Française and star actors from other Parisian theatres performed to fascinated audiences in London, Germany, Central Europe and, later, North and South America. People in far-flung corners of the world came to know about this cultural life thanks to the expansion and diversification of the Parisian press and the space it devoted to the sort of impassioned literary and aesthetic debates that gave foreign readers the feeling that they were participating in a perpetually lively cultural forum. French avant-garde movements such as Naturalism, Symbolism and Surrealism were imitated everywhere, from Munich, Berlin and Brussels to Rio, from London and Prague to St Petersburg.

Another reason for the transnational importance of Paris was the close connection between its cultural life and major political changes which, by their violence and abruptness, fascinated artists and intellectuals from other countries that – except for the USA and Switzerland – were ruled by monarchic or aristocratic, often authoritarian, regimes, at least up to the 1920s. Students came to Paris in large numbers from countries such as Russia, Greece and Romania, not only to receive an advanced scientific education and gain qualifications not open to them at home (e.g. Russian Jews), but also to breathe the air of liberty and equality. Paris's transnational importance also made itself felt in countries, capitals or among people who called down imprecations on a city they saw as a sink of moral turpitude, decadence and political excess – cries that became particularly insistent after the political crises of 1793, 1848 and 1871. But these denunciations of Paris, these attempts to counter its influence, were in themselves acknowledgements of the city's centrality throughout the long 19th century.

The dominance of Paris started to decline at the turn of the century, along with the retreat of the French language before the advance of English and the rapid rise of the United States as a great power. New cultural capitals that had drawn their inspiration from Paris were now seeking emancipation, affirming their autonomy and identity through the assertions of their own national 'schools'. The French tendency towards centralization had stifled innovation and encouraged xenophobia in many Parisians, making them more reluctant to embrace the artists of the

avant-garde: increasingly, such artists – Neo-impressionists, Fauvists and Cubists among others – had to gain recognition abroad before they could hope for it in France. It may well have been only thanks to the Allied victory in 1918 that Paris did not lose what remained of its international cultural empire well before World War 2. Defeat in the Great War weakened the influence of emerging cultural capitals in Germany and Russia as those countries turned in on themselves, while Vienna lost its cosmopolitan appeal and America slid towards isolationism – a concatenation of circumstances which enabled Paris to retain its pre-eminence as a world cultural centre for another twenty years.

In the mid 20th century the role of cultural capitals in transnational exchange became rather uncertain. Two world wars, followed by the Cold War, cut off some national cultures, and their cultural capitals, from the outside world: thus Rome under the Fascists, Berlin under the Nazis, St Petersburg (Leningrad) and Moscow under the Communists, and Madrid and Barcelona under Franco. Culture was so subjected to political ends that the reaction isolated many cultural capitals from what had been very intense spheres of influence. Very many representatives of the kind of Italian, German, Spanish or Russian culture that was still open to the rest of the world were living as exiles in other capitals: Russian exiles in Weimar Berlin, anti-fascist intellectuals in Paris; anti-Nazi and Jewish exiles, expelled from Germany after 1933, in Paris, London, New York or California in the 1930s and 1940s.

Since the 1950s cities have continued to aspire to the status of international capitals of culture. Those already mentioned have been joined by a number of major American and Asian cities: New York as the new capital of modern art, San Francisco of the 'counter-culture', Los Angeles of mass culture; Bombay with its film industry. But the hierarchy, and even the cultural function, of such centres have been profoundly changed by new factors. The advent of electronic media, and the adoption, even in Europe, of the American out-of-town campus model for universities and major scientific research centres, have leached a number of cultural functions away from even the greatest cities. High scientific culture now resides in ever less visible networks: the Internet, international journals, decentralized and specialized conferences, festivals, temporary exhibitions. Traditional written, book-based culture is in decline along with the arts as formerly defined; to be replaced by standardized, and to an extent denationalized, forms of mass culture such as blockbuster films, American and Japanese cartoons, recorded music, etc. All this is undermining the national and international importance of cultural capitals. Rather, we now have global cities, less strongly linked than formerly with the political and civic functions of cultural capitals. The old cultural capitals, with their transnational pretensions, are increasingly turning into living museums for the delectation of mass tourism.

Christophe Charle

Bibliography

Casanova P. 2004. *The world republic of letters*. Cambridge, MA: Harvard University Press.

Charle C. 1998. *Paris fin de siècle, culture et politique*. Paris: Seuil.

Charle C. and Roche D. (eds) 2002. *Capitales culturelles, capitales symboliques: Paris et les expériences européennes, XVIIIe–XXe siècles*. Paris: Publications de la Sorbonne.

Higonnet P. 2002. *Paris capital of the world*. Cambridge, MA and London: Harvard University Press.

Joyeux-Prunel B. 2004. 'Nul n'est prophète en son pays: l'internationalisation des avant-gardes artistiques (1855–1914). Unpublished doctoral dissertation, Université de Paris I.

Karady V. 'Student mobility and Western universities: patterns of unequal exchange and the European academic market, 1880–1939', in Charle C., Schriewer J. and Wagner P. (eds) 2004. *Transnational intellectual networks: forms of academic knowledge and the search for cultural identities*. Frankfurt and New York: Campus, 361–99.

Nicolet C., Ilbert R. and Depaule J.-C. (eds) 2000. *Mégapoles méditerranéennes: géographie urbaine rétrospective*. Paris, Aix and Rome: Maisonneuve et Larose, Maison méditerranéenne des sciences de l'homme and École française de Rome.

Schorske C. E. 1979. *Fin-de-siècle Vienna: politics and culture*. New York: Knopf.

Related essays

Argentina and psychoanalysis; art market; avant-garde; Cantonese opera; city planning; comics; conceptualism; exile; expositions; fashion; film; global cities; higher education; Hollywood; intellectual elites; international students; Italian opera; jazz; language; libraries; literary capitals; literature; modernismo; museums; music; performing artists; philanthropy; publishing; Romanticism; salsa; social sciences; spatial regimes; surrealism; theatre; tourism; translation; world orders

D

Dar al-Handasah

Dar al-Handasah (DaH) (Shair and Partners) is a multidisciplinary consulting firm working in the fields of engineering, architecture, planning, environment and economy.

DaH (in Arabic: the House of Engineering) has more than 4,000 employees. Headquartered in Beirut, Cairo and London, it has local offices in 84 countries. The firm was created in 1956 by five partners of Lebanese and Jordanian-Palestinian origin, four of them full-time professors at the American University of Beirut.

DaH is a global firm with deep roots in the Middle East. It was one of the first consultancy firms in the Middle East to be established according to the American model of partnership, while most local firms remained familial businesses. It grew on commissions in Kuwait and later, Saudi Arabia. There, oil was providing governments with high revenues, but projects in infrastructure and urban development were hampered by shortages in the local skilled labour force. DaH's success and expansion were not unique. Various consulting and contracting companies led by Lebanese, Palestinians, Jordanians and later Egyptians were able to draw on the Gulf markets' rise, some of these being groups split from the original DaH.

The next step in the expansion of DaH was towards Africa. Thanks to the oil boom, Nigeria and Algeria became in the 1970s two of its most profitable clients, with DaH planning and supervising the construction of new towns and infrastructure devoted to oil exploitation (Sokoto in Nigeria or Hassi Messaoud in Algeria). Later on, DaH expanded towards other African oil countries like Mozambique and Angola, and from the 1990s, to Asian countries, where it has been, for instance, in charge of master-planning Astana, the new capital city of Kazakhstan. Nevertheless, DaH's presence in the rising markets of Asia remains weak. Meanwhile, the reversal in oil price led to weakening in the oil states' economy. The recent trend towards liberalization resulted in new commissions for firms like DaH: local private groups investing in large developments and tourism as well as international organizations like the UNDP or the World Bank are now among DaH clients. Subsequently, DaH expanded much beyond the usual scope of Middle Eastern firms. In the 1980s, DaH had established the Dar Group, which bought a number of American and European firms active in Eastern Asia, America and Europe. According to the 2004 *Engineering News-Record* ranking, it is the number one consulting firm for the Middle East and one of the leaders in Africa.

While a global firm, DaH remains strongly rooted in the Middle East: its chairman, Dr Kamal Shair, and its main shareholders and partners originate and live in that region. DaH staff also include many Arabs, largely Lebanese. Mostly trained in Western or Western-style local universities, highly regarded as professionals, multilingual (in Arabic, English and often French), they illustrate the fact that being global is not adverse to remaining local. Local doesn't mean here being limited to one country but playing on various levels of identity and belonging, as well as actively participating in various networks, through and in spite of national borders.

Pan-Arabism seems to have been no explanation for access to the markets. But the deep knowledge of political leaders, administrations and business milieus that DaH's managers have been able to gather over time certainly helps. Dr Shair himself was involved in Jordanian politics as a Senator, and is a board member in various institutions. In Africa, DaH was able to rely on the Lebanese diaspora.

In Middle Eastern countries where public administrations, because of budget limitations, have difficulty in retaining their skilled professionals and therefore lack continuity in their vision, a firm like DaH not only works as a one-shot consultant. Thanks to its continued activity in the region, it acts like a kind of professional memory.

Thus, one cannot consider DaH only as a Trojan horse of an American or Western professional and liberal ideology, though of course it is. Its cultural role is more complex because of the ties it maintains in Middle Eastern cities and countries, and beyond.

Eric Verdeil

Bibliography

Ghosn R. 2005. 'Le secteur privé dans l'urbanisme des pays en voie de développement. Une étude de cas: Dar El Handasah', *Villes et territoires du Moyen-Orient*, 1 [online]. Available: www.ifporient. org/IMG/pdf/Article_ghosn.pdf, accessed 13 December 2006.

Debt crises

A sovereign debt crisis arises when a sovereign state cannot repay its debts to foreign lenders. Whereas a private debtor can be made bankrupt or pursued through the courts, a state cannot be held to account by a higher authority if it refuses to pay up. In a few instances, creditor states, or states whose subjects are creditors, have tried to obtain payment of interest, or repayment, by force. But in such cases financial interests were always subordinated to political ends, as when Spain, Britain and France intervened in Mexico in 1861 (followed by French military intervention in 1863), when Britain seized control of Egypt in 1882, and when French and Belgian troops occupied the Ruhr in 1923. Such action tended increasingly to be greeted by international howls of protest. Evolving international law implicitly assumed that states could not use force on one another for financial ends. Governments were all the less inclined to take this to heart because most creditors were savers prepared to take higher risks by lending to peripheral states in return for higher rates of interest; moreover, the securities might have changed hands since they were issued in London or Paris. After the Second World War, however, lenders were no longer private individuals but other states (the Paris Club) or banks (the London Club). Sometimes, governments or international organizations would lend to a poor country as a form of development aid, and so were reluctant to demand repayment if the borrower got into difficulties; at other times, governments would be reluctant to take diplomatic, let alone military, action in support of a creditor bank, since this would be repugnant to both the international community and public opinion.

Transnational systemic crises

When a sovereign state is unable to repay a foreign creditor, a crisis ensues which is not simply budgetary but also macroeconomic. The mechanics of this crises originate in the debtor nation's balance of payments. Such nations are usually financially insecure and do not borrow in their own currency: they have to seek international liquidity in order to service the debt. The debts incurred by the American Treasury in the last decades of the 20th century were very much the exception, because the international status of the dollar produced an apparent 'deficit without tears' which did not seem to threaten any sort of crisis. Otherwise, if the country does not have a trading surplus the debt can only be serviced by further borrowing. If this refinancing arrangement breaks down, the result will be a cessation of payments, a currency and cash crisis and an attempt to redress the trade balance by reducing imports, which triggers an internal economic crisis. This sudden contraction of the debtor country's imports may even rebound on the dominant economies by shutting off vital export outlets. This happened to the US in the early 1930s, faced with balance-of-payments crises in Latin America, Canada and Australia.

Thus debt crises, which have been recurrent since the early 19th century (see Table 1), do not necessarily affect only the most heavily indebted countries, but they do affect the most financially unstable ones. They occur chiefly in times of global economic slowdown after a period of strong capital exports, or during or immediately after a war. They are not inevitable, indeed they are rather exceptional: only about 13 per cent of total international loans to sovereign states between 1820 and 1939 ended in a suspension of payments.

If the loan is spent on non-productive sectors such as the army, this will not facilitate repayment, and if the country's economy cannot stand the budgetary strain, it will be caught in a vicious circle whereby the lion's share of each new loan goes on servicing the previous ones. This happened to the Latin American countries which borrowed to help their struggle for independence in the 1820s, and to finance innumerable boundary disputes with their neighbours throughout the 19th century; likewise to the Ottoman Empire, whose struggle to escape dissolution through the action of centrifugal forces induced it to enlarge its military capacity far beyond what was sustainable by its then current economic development. Central Europe faced the same situation in the late 1920s, particularly when German towns and provinces borrowed in order to develop their urban and social structures.

Contemporaries in the 19th and 20th centuries always tended to attribute such crises to misuse of borrowed funds by irresponsible or even corrupt governments,

Table 1   Main periods of sovereign debt crisis and principal countries concerned

1825–1840	Newly independent Latin American countries, Spain
1873–1880	Ottoman Empire, Egypt, Spain, Mexico, Peru
1890–1895	Argentina, Portugal, Brazil.
World War 1 and aftermath	Russia, Turkey, Mexico
1930–1950	Germany, Latin America, Central Europe
1980–1990	Mexico, Brazil, Argentina, Poland
1997–2000	Southeast Asia, Russia, Argentina

without attaching any blame to lenders who might have incorrectly assessed the risks. Thus the international financial crisis of 1931 was immediately blamed – especially in France – on a deliberate wrecking strategy by German governments endeavouring to throw off the burden of reparations, which were duly cancelled by the Lausanne conference in 1932.

Such circumstantial explanations cannot account for the continued recurrence of debt crises, especially as they also affect countries that use their loans to finance sound development projects. Analysis shows that sovereign debt crises are in fact systemic and essentially transnational, probably arising from the mismatch between the situations of lending and borrowing countries, and the time lag between the decision to borrow, the decision to invest, the growth resulting from the investment and its impact on the trade balance. If a lending country experiences an economic slowdown or financial crisis, this will be passed on to, and have a far more drastic impact on, the more peripheral borrower; this impact then rebounds on other countries that are either geographical neighbours or are similarly placed internationally. Moreover, these crises reveal a good deal about the transnational dynamics of the world economy, from the 1860s up to at least the 1980s. This is a complex mechanism which works at the intersections between national economic frontiers and the multiple flows of capital, goods and information that structure international markets. In this context, debt crises could be viewed as short-term dysfunctions, or alternatively as snapshots of the world economy. Probing a little deeper, they could be said to correspond historically to phases in the long-term globalization of the world economy. Certainly the sovereign debt crises of the 1890s, 1930s and 1980s can be interpreted in this light.

The Argentine crisis of 1890

In the 1880s Argentina could be seen as a 'new' country enjoying extensive immigration from Europe and rapid development: from 1870 to 1890 the annual growth in GDP averaged 5.8 per cent, compared with 2 per cent in Britain and 4 per cent in the United States (as calculated by Angus Maddison). Its contribution to international trade focused on large-scale temperate agricultural exports, animal products including wool, and, a little later, wheat. But to export these products required infrastructure – railways, ports – and the financing of agricultural development through regional lending banks. Therefore the country – both the Confederation and the provinces – was thirsty for capital. To lenders, Argentina looked like another United States in the making, and this naturally inspired confidence. The only drawbacks were that about 40 per cent of new loans went to service previous debts, and that incessant conflicts, including a war with Paraguay, had provoked the issue of lavish quantities of inflationary paper pesos. The Argentine Congress had, however, vowed to restore the monetary situation, and in 1883 it successfully restored the peso to gold convertibility.

British savers were all the more eager to subscribe to Argentine loans in that investment opportunities at home had been scanty since the economic slowdown of the 1870s, and demand even from the United States had slackened. Interest rates were low, a fact that encouraged the Argentine government to borrow and to convert previous loans. Capital imports swelled rapidly from 1885, half being used to service the ever growing debt and the equally fast-growing trade deficit. The latter was due to the fact that foreign capital was spent not only on industrial equipment but also on consumer goods (home production being limited), whereas exports did not increase because the results of investment had not yet worked through the system.

The economic situation worsened rapidly: the peso was taken off the gold standard in 1885, leading to twofold monetary circulation and more inflationary paper issues. This actually suited the large landowners who monopolized power in the country, since they profited from the gap between gold and paper currency. They exported in gold, paid their workers in paper and repaid their bank loans with more paper, while the banks refinanced themselves with foreign gold. Their profits rose accordingly, while the buying power of the ordinary Argentinean fell. By 1889 the situation was worrying: capital imports had fallen from 248 million gold pesos to 154 million, whereas the trade deficit had risen to 42 million and debt servicing to 60 million. And this happened just as Europe was becoming increasingly reluctant to refinance the debt.

By 1885, the economy of Britain, and indeed of Europe, was recovering, and investment in industry triggered a rush on mining securities. The financial bubble swelled further in France in 1888, and subsequently in Germany. Baring and Murietta, the banks which specialised in Argentine funds, could no longer place their securities and became bogged down. The stock-market situation changed in Paris and Berlin in 1889, and in New York and London in 1890. Credit became tighter in London as the Bank of England put up its lending rate. At this point the usual sequence clicked in as measures to mitigate the crisis in Britain rebounded brutally on peripheral countries that exported raw materials.

As the Bank of England acted to safeguard its reserves by raising interest rates, credit became dearer; with a range of knock-on effects. As usual, British imports of raw materials were the first to suffer because they were more expensive to finance, merchants and manufacturers had enough stocks to last several months, and forecasts were bleak. Faced with a dramatic drop in exports and unable to procure international capital to service its debts or to borrow more money, the Argentine government was forced to suspend payments. There was an immediate knock-on effect on other economically fragile countries: revolution and bankruptcy in Portugal and Brazil, a coup d'état in Chile and a financial crisis in Italy. The crisis spread to Uruguay as Argentinean funds were withdrawn.

Meanwhile, Britain was again suffering from deflation owing to the increased cost of borrowing. As imports fell, all primary exporting countries were affected, being forced to adjust their trade balances by reducing imports of manufactured products. This hit British exporters, which meant most manufacturers. Output remained stagnant for several years, depressing raw materials imports, so international prices were kept low even after Europe began to recover. Thus Argentina's external situation remained bad although its internal economy had been reformed, the English banks had reached agreement with the Argentine government, and railway investments had opened up new areas to the plough, leading to a huge increase in wheat exports. But while volumes were large, prices were low, and the trade balance did not become positive until the late 1890s, by which time foreign investments from London had resumed and lenders were regaining confidence in the Argentine economy.

This debt crisis can be seen as one stage in a cycle of heavy investment in infrastructure by a primary exporting country, which is likely to be heavily indebted because its principal sources of finance are foreign markets and it cannot finance its own expenditure, both because it lacks the resources and because the government does not want to extort cash from the wealthy landowners whom it chiefly represents. The time lag between developments affecting the lender's and the borrower's economy explains why recurring financial crises at the centre disrupt the refinancing of international debt just at the time when the debtor countries are least able to do without it. Eventually, the attempts of the Bank of England to safeguard the gold standard had a wider and more durable effect on debt crises in peripheral countries.

Sovereign risk and international financial crisis in the 1930s

The international financial crisis of 1931 highlights the centrality of sovereign debt to developments in the world economy, and hence to the Great Depression of the 1930s. As one country after another defaulted on its payments in 1931, the domino effect swiftly spread the effects worldwide. The crisis began, as always, at the periphery. In November 1930 Brazil, hard hit by the collapse in raw materials prices after the 1929 crash, defaulted on its foreign debt. Most of the other Latin American states, except Argentina, followed suit in early 1931. The effect on American and British banks was devastating. It was only guarantees from the US Treasury that prevented the Central American countries and Canada from going bankrupt. Meanwhile, in summer 1931 the crisis spread to Central and Eastern Europe. The spark that ignited the economic gunpowder was the collapse in May of Austria's leading bank, the Kredit Anstalt, owing to the sudden cutback in international capital in the first half of the year. International floating funds in Europe totalled US$12 billion at the end of 1930, but only half that by June 1931. This international run immediately weakened all the Central European banks that had based their domestic loans on foreign deposits. This is a perfect illustration of how the transnational mechanisms of international money markets impact on domestic markets: 1931 was a classic case. It was this process that spread the crisis to Hungary, and especially Germany, in early June 1931. The German crisis culminated in July with the collapse of the Danat Bank.

The German banking crisis of summer 1931 was undoubtedly the epicentre of the international financial crisis insofar as it produced a default on the payment of German reparations. The flight from Germany of short-term foreign capital upset the fragile equilibrium of German payments, after trade surpluses had already been sharply reduced by the collapse of world trade as debtor countries slashed imports, and by the erection of protectionist barriers (the US introduced the Smoot-Hawley tariff in summer 1930). On 20 June 1931, Hoover proposed a moratorium on all intergovernmental payments, including German reparations (of course) but also France's and Britain's war debts to the US. Accordingly, in August all sovereign transfers stemming from German reparations were suspended – an unprecedented situation in international law. This was followed by an agreed standstill in repayments by the Reichsbank to the leading American and British private banks.

It is difficult to overestimate the impact of this default by Germany, the world's leading international debtor at the time. The reparations question lay at the heart of the crisis. The Dawes Plan (1924), and still more the Young Plan (1929), had made a large proportion of reparations tradeable by placing it, in the form of private bonds, on all the world's great financial marketplaces. In fact reparations contributed powerfully to, and even led, the international crisis of confidence, because a large number of international loans had been made by German cities and provinces in the wake of the Dawes and Young issues. The trade in reparations, originally intended as a way of depoliticizing intergovernmental transfers, had precisely the opposite effect in 1931: it created an intense politicization of the whole international financial scene. This explains why no cooperative efforts by international finance, even those conducted under the aegis of the Bank for International Settlements, were able to restore confidence or stem the crisis.

Finally, it was the series of international defaults in the first half of 1931 that was directly responsible for Britain's going off the gold standard on 19 September. Britain's invisible exports had been seriously damaged by her heavy involvement with debtor countries, both in Latin America and in Central Europe, which now suspended payments. The Bank of England had to draw increasingly on its reserves to finance Britain's persistent trade deficit; this undermined international confidence in the continued convertibility of sterling. When sterling was devalued most of the world's currencies followed suit, including, in 1933, the US dollar. The international sovereign debt crisis had led to a worldwide crisis in the international monetary system as each nation rallied to 'monetary nationalism' and the defence of its own currency.

The crisis of the 1980s

Between 1982 and 1986 eighteen countries, chiefly Latin American states with medium-sized per capital GDP, were forced to suspend payments. Apart from Poland, the biggest defaulters were Mexico, Brazil, Argentina and Venezuela. Ironically, the most heavily indebted countries – the poorest – avoided defaulting thanks to the rescheduling of their debts by foreign governments and international organizations.

Mexico, Brazil and Argentina had borrowed heavily throughout the 1970s. The first two of these countries had then been in a promising way of development, with much higher growth rates than Western countries. Brazil had pursued a policy of 'industrialization by import substitution' (IIS). Owing to the importance of the public sector since the 1930s, not only in infrastructure and heavy industry but also in manufacturing and services, productive investment had produced a high demand for capital on the part of the government, which had consequently become progressively indebted. The country then embarked on the final 'substitution' – industrial equipment and high-tech – which required particularly strong investment but promised only long-term profitability. In the early 1980s things were looking good, with a favourable trade balance. But this kind of industrialization has its downside: it inflates public borrowing, which in Brazil's case led to refinancing problems and galloping inflation. Mexico's policies were similar, but its financial situation was less tight owing to the high price of its oil exports, which eased the budget and produced a trade surplus.

Although other countries were performing less well, lending banks saw the whole region in an equally rosey light and concluded that its development potential was excellent. Accordingly, the military governments of Argentina and Chile espoused economic liberalism to the point of deindustrialization, consigning numerous firms to oblivion. Nonetheless many Westerners considered this a healthy, American-inspired attempt to reduce the public presence in the productive sector.

These Latin American countries had called on Western banks to finance their projects, and in the 1970s this suited the banks very well. The recent slowdown in growth had produced a superabundance of capital while reducing the demand for it. As internal investment became less profitable, Western companies had cut back, preferring to invest in the financial market, thus further increasing the supply of capital. Meanwhile, the oil-producing countries were investing their profits in Western banks, creating still more liquidity.

Banks, therefore, were ready to welcome Latin American borrowers and offer them very favourable interest rates, especially as, convinced that international organizations would not abandon the countries concerned if they got into financial difficulties, they underestimated the risks. The borrowers were equally sanguine, because the burden of debt was lightened by the ubiquitous inflation of the 1970s. Few, if any, bankers were worried that short-term loans (six to nine years) were being given for much longer-term projects, and were thus dependent on continual refinancing. Nor did anyone worry that interest rates were variable. Such easy borrowing increased instability. Countries blithely increased imports; internally they were awash with cash, producing substantial inflation; and the accumulation of exchange reserves in central banks encouraged overvaluation of the currency, with painful results.

When the 1979 oil shock put the brakes on Western economies and the US changed its economic policy, Latin America was plunged into crisis. The 1980s were a hard time for industry in the most advanced industrialised countries; even when recovery came, it was fuelled by the tertiary economy rather than by industry. Imports from primary exporting countries, which depended heavily on advanced industrial activity, declined. Primary exporters tried to stabilize their tottering trade balances by exporting still more, bringing prices down. In consequence they had to cut back savagely on imports: Brazil's lost 34 per cent in value and 56 per cent in volume between 1980 and 1985. Countries that had no oil, and were forced to import it, were particularly hard hit. This produced a severe internal economic crisis as unemployment soared, purchasing power plummeted, inequality of income became more rampant and governments, starved of cash, cut back their social spending.

This budgetary crisis coincided with a drop in refinancing and a steep rise in the cost of international credit. While Poland's default in 1980 had little impact, that of Mexico in 1982 induced the banks to refuse all new loans, extending the crisis to every Latin American country. By 1983 the capital transfer balance was negative throughout the region. To compound the effect, the liberalization of capital movements encouraged rich Latin Americans, losing confidence in their own countries, to export their capital to the US.

In 1980 the American government decided to crush inflation by embarking on a restrictive monetary policy with high interest rates. Economic stagnation did nothing to bring down these rates, because the policy was combined with budgetary stimulation which led to a recovery in 1983. America's trade and budget deficits were financed by attracting foreign capital, principally from Europe and Japan. Interest rates had to remain high. At the same time, deflation considerably increased the cost of servicing the Latin American debt, especially as interest rates on existing loans were adjusted to reflect the new situation: the real average rate, which had been negative (averaging −5.3 per cent between 1972 and 1980) rose to an average of 14.6 per cent between 1981 and 1987. The influx of foreign capital into the US also raised the price of the dollar, making dollar debts even more expensive. This induced the Americans to try to reduce their trade deficit by bringing in protectionist measures, making it harder still for countries to acquire dollars in order to service their debts.

Finally, while the Latin American countries that were thus plunged into debt crises may have had their own particular vulnerabilities – since the Asian economies remained immune – the changes wrought in the international regulatory system by the dominant power's attempts to support its own economy further increased the shock to the peripheral states.

Conclusion

From the last quarter of the 19th century to the present, the world economy has been profoundly affected by periodic sovereign debt crises. The knock-on effect on the world at large has been due to truly transnational mechanisms whereby the policies of sovereign states are enmeshed with the dynamics of international markets to affect trade balances and currency exchanges. This means that sovereign debt crises can paralyse international exchange in the short, and sometimes even in the medium, term. In the long term, however, they contribute to the process of globalization, which has left as profound a mark on this period as economic nationalism.

The crises of the 1980s led to a structural transformation of the international financial system. At the same time, national financial systems tended to converge on a global economic model. This created a new framework within which financial innovations – such as the commercialization of debt – were able to proliferate. As a result, by the 1990s the distinction between the public and private domains had become very blurred. In the last analysis, these changes account for the complexity of late-20th-century crises and the powerful domino effect which characterized them.

Olivier Feiertag
Patrick Verley

Bibliography

Eichengreen B. 1992. *Golden fetters: the gold standard and the Great Depression, 1919–1939*. Oxford: Oxford University Press.

Heyde P. 1998. *Das Ende der Reparationen: Deutschland, Frankreich und der Youngplan, 1929–1932*. Paderborn: Shöningh.

Marichal C. 1989. *A century of debt crises in Latin America: from independence to the Great Depression, 1820–1930*. Princeton: Princeton University Press.

Suter C. 1992. *Debt cycles in the world economy: foreign loans, financial crises and debt settlements, 1820–1990*. Boulder, San Francisco and Oxford: Westview.

Tirole J. 2002. *Financial crises, liquidity and the international money system*. Princeton and Oxford: Princeton University Press.

Related essays

agriculture; convergence and divergence; debt (developing countries); development and growth; financial diplomacy; financial markets; International Monetary Fund (IMF); investment; loans; Paris Club; trade; trade (manufactured goods); trade agreements; Washington Consensus; World Bank; world orders

Paris Club

The Paris Club (PC) is an informal body for restructuring the public debts to public creditors. Jean-Claude Trichet, a former President of the PC, once stated that the PC 'is a non-institution mixing Latin imagination with Anglo-Saxon pragmatism' (*Le Monde*, 7 January 1986). The PC held its first meeting in 1956 for Argentina. Before this meeting, the restructuring of debts occurred on an ad hoc basis, witch poses problems of coordinating the creditors for sharing the burden of debt restructuring. Since 1956, every meeting of an indebted government with its public creditors has been held in Paris, the French Treasury acting as a technical secretariat.

Nineteen countries are members of the PC as of 2008, and some others take part occasionally, when they are significant creditors of the country. They discuss the reference doctrine, trying to stick to financial orthodoxy in order to protect their taxpayers' money. The rules of the game resulting from the discussions are presented as agreements of the G8 although all members of the PC are not members of this group.

An agreement with the International Monetary Fund is a prerequisite for a government to meet with its PC creditors. The role of the PC is to find a suitable agreement between a government and its public creditors.

The PC follows a set of rules and principles:

- The case of each country is considered separately.
- At the first meeting of the PC the 'cutoff date' is defined and is not changed in subsequent PC 'treatments' (see below). Credits granted after this cutoff date are not subject to future rescheduling or cancellation. The cutoff date is intended to help in restoring access to credit.
- The PC agreement is a framework agreement. It has to be later ratified on a bilateral basis to become effective.

The founding principles are consistent with the idea that a debt crisis arises because of liquidity problems, but that the country is likely to be solvent in the long run: the debt is expected to be eventually repaid in full. This idea may be relevant for emerging countries, but proved to be debatable in the case of Low Income Countries. Most of these went to the PC not just once, but several times (Senegal 14 times), meaning that they faced structural problems and, in some cases, insolvency.

Initially, the only possibility was rescheduling (paying later), usually with some penalty. The G8 meeting in Toronto in 1988 broke with the orthodoxy by allowing the PC to provide some debt relief (about one third of eligible debt service) according to three equivalent schemes (menu option). Afterwards, different 'treatments', each named for the place where the annual G8 meeting has been held, have been set up for Low Income Countries. The share of debt relief has been steadily increased. Since Naples (1994), the PC may deal with the debt stock as a whole, and not only with the service due in some specific year.

The role of the PC is likely to decline, because of the decrease of public bilateral lending. Most developed countries no longer make loans to poor countries, just grants. The new lenders to Low Income Countries, like China and India, are not members of the PC. This tendency could be temporarily offset if debt relief was to be extended to countries that are market borrowers, as it has been the case for Nigeria in 2005. A new, very prudent, 'Evian' approach has been set up for such cases.

Under heavy political pressure, the flexibility of the PC proved to be rather high. Egypt and Poland in 1991, and Iraq in 2004 have been granted generous debt relief by the PC for political reasons.

Because of the improvement in their fiscal situation in the early 2000s some emerging countries (Brazil, Algeria, Russia, etc.) are asking the PC to allow them to repay their debt early. Moreover, the governments of emerging countries are increasingly borrowing from markets, mostly domestic. The process of sovereign debt restructuring becomes trickier, as seen during the Argentinean debt crisis (2001), leaving no room for the PC.

Marc Raffinot

Bibliography

Lawson D. 2004. *Le Club de Paris: sortir de l'engrenage de la dette*. Paris: L'Harmattan.

Rieffel L. 2003. *Restructuring sovereign debt: the case for ad hoc machinery*. Washington, DC: Brookings Institution.

UNCTAD 2001. *The conversion of Paris Club debt: procedures and potential*. Geneva: United Nations Conference on Trade and Development.

Zerah D. 1992. *Économie financière internationale: les interventions du Trésor*. Paris: Études de la Documentation Française.

Related essays

debt crises (developing countries); development and growth; International Monetary Fund (IMF); loans; underdevelopment

Debt crises (developing countries)

Developing countries' debt could be defined as the debt of the entire nation to foreigners. As most problems arise because of the public debt of those countries, we will focus on the public external debt (or sovereign debt). Moreover, we will focus on debt crises, which occur when a country does not repay its debt. Nevertheless it should be clear that some developing countries do successfully manage their foreign liabilities and do not experience any debt crisis: money borrowed from abroad may be used in an efficient way (China, India, Bangladesh, and Bhutan belong to this category). When a government does not consider repaying the debt, one should distinguish between default (not repaying) and repudiation (refusing to acknowledge the claim). Cases of repudiation are indeed very rare (Russia 1918, Democratic Kampuchea 1975), even when a state disappears (USSR, Yugoslavia, Czechoslovakia, etc.). On the other hand, developing countries became indebted even before they were already independent states. Latin American states, for instance, borrowed for financing the independence wars. Haiti became indebted to France to gain independence.

In the 19th century, the repayment of sovereign debt was enforced by all means, including military ('gunboat' diplomacy). As many emerging countries did borrow to finance wars, the relationship between debt and military operations was very close. Enforcement of debt contracts was often considered more important than the national sovereignty of debtors. It sometimes became an excuse for colonization. This limited sovereignty implied the right of creditors to repay themselves by levying taxes. For instance, in 1881 the debt crisis of the Ottoman Empire resulted in the creation of a 'Public Debt Administration' under the lead of a consortium of foreign creditors, to oversee part of the Ottoman economy and use the supervised revenues to repay the debt.

Since World War 2, international law has been based on a very restrictive definition of the assets of indebted states that may be seized in case of default. In practice, the pressure that the creditor may exert on a defaulting state is limited to stopping the supply of more loans. Pressures exerted on a defaulting government are supposed to result in losses, so that the government may prefer repaying. For this system to be effective, tight coordination among creditors has to be in place. The International Monetary Fund (IMF) is widely seen as a coordinating body, but its coordination efforts are not likely to be successful when there are diverging interests. Moreover, it has been shown that the threat to stop future loans acts as a potential tax and can reduce the incentive of the debtor country to invest or to reform in order to increase its income (debt overhang).

A major debt crisis occurred in 1982 when Mexico announced that it was not likely to repay its foreign debt. The tightening of monetary policy in the US resulted in a dramatic increase in interest rates, and in a slowing down of economic activity (and in the exports of Latin American countries), prompting the crisis. For seven years, creditors insisted that the debt should be repaid in full, and the IMF imposed structural adjustment programmes in order to restore the solvency of the indebted countries, although capital was flowing out of those countries. The Paris Club was only allowed to reschedule (postpone) the debt servicing. It became rapidly evident that this strategy was bound to fail. It resulted in a large decrease in investment and growth, as well as in an increase of poverty. To avoid major losses, banks began to trade their debts at discount prices, giving birth to a secondary market for developing countries' debt.

Since 1988–89 dramatic steps have been taken. The idea that debt could be repaid in full has been given up, and some kind of debt reduction was recognized as unavoidable. The theory of debt overhang shows that, in certain circumstances, a debt reduction may improve the situation of the defaulting country, and even lead to an increase in repayments, thus being also beneficial for the creditor. Debt relief has been achieved in different ways for emerging countries and for low-income countries (LICs). The bulk of the external debt of developing and emerging countries, excluding Europe and countries of the former USSR (US$2,003 billion in 2000) is owed by emerging countries (US$772 billion by Latin America and US$657 by Asian developing countries). In 1982, this large debt of emerging countries was a threat to the international financial system. In sharp contrast, African debt was only US$270 billion in 2000 (about the same amount as Brazil alone). Moreover, emerging countries owed their debt to private lenders and LICs to public institutions.

For emerging countries, debt relief has been granted under 'market terms', meaning that creditors should agree to the terms. The Brady initiative of 1989 (named after N. Brady, Secretary of the Treasury of the United States) proposed to banks a securitization (exchanging their debts for bonds) with a discount, but with better prospects of repayment. Banks were at first reluctant but agreed under US Treasury pressure, recognizing certain fiscal advantages. The secondary market in the debt made possible innovative ways of reducing the debt, for instance buying assets with discounted debt (debt equity swaps). It also made it possible for speculators to buy discounted debt, expecting a decrease of the discount, and even to try to have it be repaid in full (vulture funds) by suing the government. Loans to emerging countries resumed but resulted in a new crisis (Mexico 1994).

Further debt crises occurred (Asia 1997, Russia 1998, Turkey 2000, Argentina 2001, etc.). The causes of these crises differed. The 'traditional' crisis happened when a country was running low foreign currency reserves. 'New' types of crises happened because creditors expected the debt not to be repaid and withdrew their money suddenly, resulting in the crisis that was expected, even if 'fundamentals' were sound (self-fulfilling crises).

These crises did not result in debt relief. Under the lead of the IMF, rescue packages were provided, jointly and with hard conditionality. This proved unsatisfactory, leading to high losses in the income of the debtor countries. Two proposals may be considered to ease the resolution of such crises. The first one, made by the IMF, would be to pass a bankruptcy law at the international level to protect the defaulting states and share the burden of debt relief in an orderly way. This would be a way of tackling the problem of the debt owed to the private markets, which is not easy to renegotiate due to the lack of an institution like the Paris Club (for debts to foreign governments) or the London Club (for debts to banks). The second proposal would be to have a real lender of last resort at the international level. The IMF does not play this role, because its shareholders oppose money creation by the Fund, outside limited amounts of Special Drawing Rights (SDRs). The idea would be the prevention of crises, which would be much more cost-effective than acting after a crisis has occurred.

For LICs, debt relief has been advocated since as early as 1976. 'Debt crises' for these countries are somewhat different from emerging countries' crises, characterized by huge outflows of capital and negative transfers. When LICs do not repay their debt, they face a progressive decrease of foreign loans, but for most of them, transfers remain positive because of grants.

After the G8 meeting in Toronto (1988), some reduction of debt servicing was provided to LICs, reaching an agreement with the Paris Club. The share of debt relief increased and was extended to the entire (bilateral) debt stock (Naples 1994). Moreover, in 1996 the international financial institutions launched a Highly Indebted Poor Countries (HIPC) Initiative. This initiative was aimed at providing debt relief in order to lower the debt to sustainable levels. Under pressure from international civil society, debt relief was made faster and more generous under the Enhanced HIPC Initiative (1999). Most bilateral creditors agreed to cancel their remaining debt to the HIPCs. Conditions were attached to this debt relief (sound economic policies and a poverty alleviation strategy) in order not to waste the money that has been freed. The HIPC initiative was supposed to restore the sustainability of the debt. The G8 changed this objective and committed itself to total multilateral debt relief for a broader set of poor countries at its 2005 meeting in Gleneagles (Multilateral Debt Relief Initiative, MDRI). This aims at correcting the previous unfairness in the distribution of debt relief. Nevertheless, basically, debt relief amounts to providing grants to countries that are indebted, sidelining those that have managed their budgets prudently. Under MDRI, most low-income countries will benefit from a nearly complete relief of their multilateral debt, provided they reach an agreement with the IMF. This has been delayed in some countries by social unrest, conflicts or political fragility.

Beyond its economic dimension, debt has always been used as a means of exerting political pressure. In the 20th century, this did not completely disappear, but the increasing debt relief illustrates a certain power of the (poor) debtors, backed by international civil society. This might also encourage some middle-income countries to be harder with their creditors: Argentina succeeded in reducing its private foreign debt by 70 per cent in 2005. Furthermore, the large debt relief that has been eventually granted to LICs could be considered by not-so-poor countries as a signal of being granted debt relief. Nigeria in 2005 negotiated such a favourable treatment, and the Paris Club (very carefully) opened the door to such a possibility ('Evian treatment').

Some parts of civil society are pushing for a total writing off of the debt of developing countries. Many arguments support this view. A part of the debt may be labelled 'odious', meaning that it has been incurred without democratic approval, sometimes against the interest of the population. Moreover, from an ethical point of view, it seems difficult to justify repaying the debt if it is likely to result in worsening the welfare of the poorest. Nevertheless, it is difficult to imagine how this could be institutionalized: which body could decide which loan is odious, or which country should be considered unable to repay out of ethical concerns? The main problem is that any doubt on repayment will deter potential creditors from lending. As debt relief means that the country will not be able to borrow in the future, debt cancellation is rejected by emerging countries. It is naturally welcome by most low-income countries, as they are already excluded from the international financial markets. Nevertheless, such a total debt writeoff for poor countries would not be entirely good news. As debt is basically a contract, it would render it difficult to build new relationships based on a contractual framework. Poor countries would then depend only on grants, which could result in more dependence because grants depend on the goodwill of donors. Moreover, the amounts granted are likely to be lower than those that could be borrowed. And there are typically profitable opportunities even in very poor countries that could be financed by loans. One may wonder if those countries will resist the temptation of using their new 'debt-less' status to incur new debt from countries like China or India.

The emerging-countries debt scene is changing quite fast at the beginning of the 21st century. Governments of emerging countries borrow more and more from their own domestic financial markets. Some of them have repaid the IMF and the Paris Club early (Argentina, Brazil), in order to recover some room for manoeuvre. Moreover, governments of some emerging countries have been able to raise funds from foreigners in their domestic currencies, which implies a reduction in the risks incurred. Asian countries have increased their reserves of foreign currencies to unprecedented levels, in order to prevent any recurrence of balance-of-payment crises. All these changes may well sound the knell of the financial system designed at the end of WW2.

Marc Raffinot

Bibliography
Bougouin A.-S. and Raffinot M. 'The HIPC Initiative and poverty reduction', in Cling J.-P., Razafindrakoto M. and Roubaud F. (eds) 2003. *New international poverty reduction strategies*, London and New York: Routledge, 239–64.

Boyer R., Dehove M. and Plihon D. 2004. *Les crises financières*. Rapports du CAE, 50. Paris: Documentation Française.

Cohen D. and Portes R. 2003. *Crises de la dette: prévention et résolution*. Rapports du CAE, 43. Paris: Documentation Française.

Eichengreen B. and Lindert P. (eds) 1989. *The international debt crisis in historical perspective*, Cambridge, MA and London: MIT Press.

Marichal C. 1988. *Historia de la deuda externa de América Latina*. Madrid: Alianza América.

Obstfeld M. and Rogoff K. 1996. *Foundations of international macroeconomics*. Cambridge, MA and London: MIT Press.

Raffinot M. 2000. 'Économie politique de la dette: pouvoir, normes et dépendance', *Économie et société*, Série P, 8, août, 115–41.

Related essays
debt crises; development and growth; financial diplomacy; financial markets; industrialization; International Monetary Fund (IMF); investment; legal order; loans; Paris Club; taxation; underdevelopment; Washington Consensus; World Bank

Decolonization

Decolonization is a historical process in which colonial powers transferred institutional and legal control over the territories and dependencies they had occupied to indigenously based, formally sovereign nation states. Western empires occupied around three quarters of the world by 1900. In a few cases, such as China and Iran, even the countries that were never completely colonized regarded their struggle for autonomy against foreign powers as anti-colonial struggles. Therefore decolonization means not only territorial independence for one nation or community but also a process in which a relationship based on respect for national sovereignty, justice and autonomy is established with foreign powers. Decolonization was an inherently transnational process on the part both of the colonizing powers and of the colonized. For the former, changing global norms affected the attitude of individual powers toward their colonies, forcing them into letting go of their empires. For the latter, the rapidly increasing number of decolonized nations in the postwar world encouraged the remaining colonized peoples to struggle further for liberation.

The search for independence in colonies in Asia, Africa, the Caribbean and Pacific Islands began to be successful during the interwar period and flourished after the Second World War. Earlier, America had gained independence from Britain at the end of the 18th century and subsequently Latin America became independent as the Spanish and Portuguese empires collapsed.

Causes and context

The exploitative nature of colonialism created anti-colonial resistance among the people of most colonized nations. Forms of both random and organized struggle occurred virtually everywhere. The Boxer Uprising in China (1899–1901), the 1857 Rebellion in India, the 1919 March First Movement in Korea, the 1931 Senussi Uprising in Libya, and the mid-20th-century Mau Mau Uprising in Kenya are a few examples of such struggles. Yet these struggles, despite their geographical distance from each other, did not exist in a vacuum, but rather reflected the increasingly transnational nature of anti-colonial discourse. A prime example of this for many colonial peoples was Japan's victory over Russia in 1905, which was seen all over the world as a historical event that challenged the confidence of the Western colonial powers and provided momentum for decolonization. Techniques used by one colonized people could be applied by another, bypassing the control of the colonizing powers: the May Fourth demonstrations in Beijing in 1919, protesting the treatment of China at the Paris Peace Conference, consciously echoed the March First anti-Japanese protests in Korea earlier that year. Yet the Paris Peace Conference also provided one of the most powerful transnational ideas, the right of national self-determination that was proclaimed by President Woodrow Wilson, and was welcomed by international society, enhancing the mood for emancipation. The League of Nations established at the end of the war aimed to mediate this process, although its efforts amounted to redistribution of the colonies from the defeated powers to the victors. During the Second World War many of the colonies of the Old Powers of Europe were overrun by Axis forces in North Africa and in Southeast Asia. However, Wilsonian ideas had enough impact on colonized peoples that the colonizing powers were forced to recognize new forms of identity in them. The United Nations, established after the Second World War, actively crystallized many of the ideals of the decolonization era into a vision for perpetual peace among nations in the world, championing the right of national self-determination, as well as the rights of the oppressed. For instance, UN General Assembly Resolution 1514 was adopted as a Declaration on the Granting of Independence to Colonial Countries and Peoples on 14 December 1960. Eighty-nine countries including major colonial powers voted in favour. The UN General Assembly in 2000 also adopted Resolution 55/146 that declared 2001–10 the Second International Decade for the Eradication of Colonialism. The Soviet Union and the United States, which emerged as new hegemonic powers from the early 20th century, were also initially seen as forces for decolonization to the degree that they opposed European imperialism.

Forms

Decolonization involved a long period of development rather than a single historical event, and the ideas which underpinned it were not confined to any one nation state. The end came in both comparatively peaceful ways and also through bloody revolt or war launched by the colonized. India's independence was indebted to many decades of non-violent struggle led by Gandhi which invited violent oppression by the British occupying forces (although other Indian independence activists did endorse violence).

Gandhian non-violence, however, became a powerful rallying-call to protest movements across the world, providing a weapon that enabled the colonized to declare their own moral superiority over the violence used by their rulers. Notably, Kwame Nkrumah in Ghana and Kenneth Kaunda in Zambia led successful independence movements following the tactics of non-violence after 1947. However, after 1954, the colonized in Asia and Africa began to accept the need for violence as a strategy after the mounting colonial violence in Algeria, the example of the Vietnamese defeat of France, and the rise of new forms of imperialism. The formerly pacifist Nkrumah was one who shifted his emphasis to justifying violence for emancipation.

One notable voluntary transnational formation that emerged from decolonization was the association of sovereign independent states known as the Commonwealth under the British Crown, more recently just the Commonwealth. This organization, mostly consisting of former British colonies, has few formal obligations between members, and Britain no longer has any formal leadership role within it (although the Queen is its head). Nonetheless, it has for over half a century become a powerful voice for certain values that the participating states feel are central to their shared legacy. In particular, abandoning democracy has been the only recent grounds for suspension from the Commonwealth (Pakistan, Zimbabwe and Fiji are among the states thus sanctioned). The Commonwealth has been regarded as a remarkably successful way of dealing with the colonial legacy in an egalitarian way, so much so that at least one state, Mozambique, with no British colonial connections, has joined it.

However, decolonization is a more complex process than mere territorial decolonization and concerns matters of economic, political and cultural decolonization. Many postcolonial societies have suffered from political, cultural and psychological legacies of colonialism which caused a dependency complex in relation to the former colonial powers. Thus, the characteristics of colonization, as Homi Bhabha has pointed out, lie in the fact of hybridization and the complex interrelations between politics, cultures, and the economies of the colonizer and colonized, which make the decolonization process more than a simple removal of the 'foreign' power.

Major ideological instruments and visions

Decolonization came to the fore as an international political phenomenon because of the rise of nationalism, an empowering and enabling force for many colonized people in the struggle against imperialism. The indigenous elites and the would-be leaders of their future independent nations supported nationalism in order to mobilize all anti-imperialist forces against the occupying power. Jawaharlal Nehru and Mahatma Gandhi in India, Ho Chi Minh in Vietnam, and Jomo Kenyatta in Kenya were powerful nationalist leaders who led independence movements, and who drew on each other's ideas.

In many cases this anti-imperial nationalism was not the product of one national tradition, but rather a highly transnational interaction of indigenous cultural traditions, Western education, and radical social ideas such as socialism and communism. The European idea of civilization, in its extreme Eurocentric forms, assumed the superiority of its own and the absence or inferiority of the others'. Challenges to those claims of civilizational superiority came from both Europe (e.g., Civilization on trial [1948] by Arnold Toynbee) and the colonies, helping to provide intellectual justification for the move to decolonization. The latter reflected values and civilizations of their own in order to present an alternative to those of the West. The ideals of the East (1904) by Okakura Tenshin, writings on 'new history' by Liang Qichao, Song offerings (1913) and The home and the world (1916) by Rabindranath Tagore, the teachings on non-violent resistance of Mahatma Gandhi, and the Négritude movement of Léopold Senghor and Aimé Césaire promoted this idea of 'other civilization'. Decolonization was also often instigated by the ideas of liberalism held by indigenous leaders educated in the West. They became equipped with liberal ideals of 'humanity' and modern technology that were useful in the battle against the West's domination. Another idea that sought to break down the nation state's boundaries, socialism, also served as a major instrument for decolonization of oppressed nations, for instance, in China, Vietnam, Cuba, and Angola among other societies. Marx's egalitarianism and denunciation of capitalism led Lenin to formulate a comprehensive criticism of imperialism which he regarded as the highest stage of capitalism and a source for a war among capitalists and capitalist nations. The idea of Third World solidarity against imperialism created a cosmopolitan impetus among the oppressed people that reinforced the decolonization movement. The Bandung Conference of 1955 provided a powerful public face for the newly independent nations to oppose the rising neocolonialism of the United States and the Soviet Union as well of as the remaining imperial powers.

In 1917 the Communist revolution in Russia and the 1918 proclamation of national self-determination by the US President Woodrow Wilson brought powerful new transnational political ideologies to the fore. Both countries claimed to oppose old European imperialism and rose as superpowers during the Second World War, which ended in the defeat of the late-coming imperial powers such as Germany and Japan. As hegemonic powers in the polarized post-1945 world, they also acted as intervening forces in the affairs of other sovereign nations in pursuit of international expansion of market liberalism or socialism. The United States mediated the transition of the old colonial order to a new order which shaped the former colonies of Europe and Japan in Asia, Africa, Latin America, and the Caribbean, advocating market liberalism as universal means to prosperity and freedom for all, and also competing with the socialist Soviet Union. The latter initially encouraged and supported independence movements in colonial territories, offering economic, military, and ideological assistance to countries such as Vietnam, Nicaragua, and Congo. But it soon expanded forcibly to annex all the colonial territories of the Russian empire, including Central Asia.

Legacies of decolonization and neocolonialism

Decolonization continues to create political instability in postcolonial societies because of the long-lasting legacies of colonialism and also the fact that the formerly colonized societies were not always well prepared when independence was won. This political instability is often characterized by intercommunal conflicts involving different religious and ideological beliefs. Indeed, it has been observed that European colonialism in Asia and Africa created new categories of people by utilizing pre-existing systems of castes or tribes in order to govern effectively and also to establish their power through a policy of divide and rule. For instance, Britain's division of electoral constituencies along religious lines in India during its colonial rule deepened communal tensions that seriously affected the unity of postcolonial South Asian society. The large-scale immigration that Britain facilitated from China and India to work on plantations and mines in Southeast Asia, the Caribbean and Africa also left long-lasting ethnic strife between the indigenous population and late-coming immigrant groups. The process of decolonization tended to be dominated by patriarchal nationalists who subordinated claims of justice and equality of women or other subaltern groups to the nationalist claim, as in the cases of the long-silenced 'military sexual slave women' in Korea. The nationalism of these newly established countries also often tended to follow the trajectory of the previous colonial powers in establishing a new nation state through militarizing boundaries and becoming involved in frontier expansionism, as can be seen in the activities of China, India, Iraq, and Indonesia in relation to Tibetans, Kashmir, the Kurds and East Timorese respectively. The hope of decolonization as a means to transnational solidarity between countries with a shared history of a struggle for freedom has often been crushed by indigenous regimes which perpetuate the colonial social system in postcolonial society and exploit their own people by suppressing their democratic will.

The spirit of Third World solidarity and non-alignment represented by the Bandung Conference seems to have been lost through territorial disputes among the member nations, such as the conflict between India and China in 1962, and the end of the Cold War in 1989. However, the economic rise and political empowerment of the formerly colonized nations in Asia, including the 'Asian dragons' of East Asia (South Korea, Taiwan, Singapore), a process beginning in the 1960s but which also encompasses the rise of China and India through the 1980s and 1990s, presents a new phase of decolonization as these formerly colonized countries increasing their global standing and their transnational reach in terms of prestige and influence. This has given hope to the other once-colonized nations in Asia and Africa which have been searching for models of development and autonomy to overcome the devastating legacies of centuries of subjugation and colonialism.

'Neocolonialism' is the term that refers to the informal economic ties and financial and military dependencies that postcolonial societies continue with their former colonial powers and the dominance of colonial culture and values in newly independent states. Many formally sovereign Third World countries have been trapped by debt, alien institutions and cultural dependency well after territorial independence. So much so, that this indicates an instance of 'empire without colonies' as Kwame Nkrumah called it, meaning the new world order under the United States. As Duara has noted, 'the era of decolonization may be over, but the pains of the transition have found their way into the new era of globalization' (Duara 2004, 17).

Soyang Park

Bibliography

Duara P. (ed). 2004. *Decolonization: perspectives from now and then*. London and New York, Routledge.

Young R. 2001. *Postcolonialism: an historical introduction*. Oxford: Blackwell.

Related essays

1960s; Africa; African liberation; Asia; Chinese Diaspora; civilizations; class; contract and indentured labourers; Cold War; debt crises (developing countries); democracy; development and growth; developmental assistance; diasporas; empire and migration; empires and imperialism; ethnicity and race; exile; film; financial diplomacy; higher education; international migration regimes; liberalism; literature; loans; Maoism; nation and state; non-violence; partitions; patents; socialism; technical assistance; *The Wretched of the Earth*; United Nations system; Vietnam War; war; Washington Consensus; Wilson, Woodrow; women's movements; world orders

---

The Wretched of the Earth

Published in the context of the war of national liberation in Algeria, the Bandung conference (1955), and the Cuban revolution, *The Wretched of the Earth* instantly became the manifesto of Third World revolutions. In 1960, Frantz Fanon (1925–61) learned that he had leukaemia and rushed to write a book that would summarize his thought and clarify his view of political emancipation. Jean-Paul Sartre accepted an invitation to write the preface.

In *The Wretched of the Earth*, Fanon revisited central aspects of liberation in a colonial situation. In the first chapter, 'Concerning violence', Fanon went further in his analysis of the primary role of violence in colonialism. The colonial world was a 'world cut in two' whose foundations were racism, brutality, and the repression of all forms of native culture. Against such violence, Fanon defended a counter-violence and argued that the struggle for emancipation not only implied the individual's participation in the collective fight for freedom but also, for each, the necessity to violently expunge from themselves the complex of inferiority produced by colonialism: 'At the level of individuals, violence is a cleansing force', Fanon wrote, for violence 'frees the native from his inferiority complex and from his despair and inaction'. Then Fanon turned to the question of the vanguard class and concluded that the peasantry was the true revolutionary class. The 'country people as a whole remain disciplined and

altruistic' whereas those colonized in the cities had adopted the 'Western values' of individualism and egotism. Country life was 'evocative of a confraternity, a church, a mystical body of belief at one and the same time'. In another chapter, 'The pitfalls of national consciousness', Fanon, who had observed the corruption and betrayal of revolutionary ideals in independent African countries, warned his readers. To prevent the emergence of similar deceptions, a programme of political education was necessary in which 'we ought to uplift the people; we must develop their brains, fill them with ideas, change them and make them into human beings'. In the chapter 'On national culture', Fanon advocated as well a cleaning process from the colonial legacy of all forms of cultural expression: poetry, music, dance, theatre, literature, pottery. The mission of national culture was to reveal to the public the 'existence of a new type of man'. 'Every culture is first and foremost national', he wrote. In his last chapter, 'Colonial war and mental disorders', Fanon presented cases of Algerians or Europeans who, caught in the violence of colonial war, displayed mental disorders. The conclusion was a call to 'brothers' and 'comrades' to forfeit the desire for Europe, to abandon the temptation for an 'obscene caricature' of history and to start a 'new history of Man'.

The millenarian tone of his text, as in 'The last shall be first', its construction of a redemptive group, the peasants, leading the people who 'march proudly in the great procession of the awakened nation', its repeated use of terms such as those of purification, decadence, moral values, mark *The Wretched of the Earth* as a messianic text. The book was quickly translated into English and other languages, making it some kind of a blueprint for Third World emancipation. Fanon's insights about the consequences, psychic and material, of colonial violence, heavily indebted to Aimé Césaire's *Discourse on colonialism*, served to remind Europe of its responsibility in the enslavement and the subjugation of non-European peoples.

Françoise Vergès

Bibliography

Alessandrini A. (ed.) 1999. *Frantz Fanon: critical perspectives*. London and New York: Routledge.

Macey D. 2000. *Frantz Fanon: a life*. London: Granta.

Read A. (ed.) 1996. *The fact of blackness: Frantz Fanon and visual representation*. London: ICA.

Related essays
African liberation; Bible; *Communist Manifesto*; decolonization; democracy; developmental taxonomies; justice; Koran; nation and state; socialism; underdevelopment; Westernization

Democracy

Conventional understandings of democracy – still usefully defined as rule 'of the people, by the people, for the people' (Abraham Lincoln, US President, 1861–65) – are profoundly linked to the conception that the relevant political community is the nation state. It is generally accepted that the 'people' in question are enfranchised national citizens ruling themselves collectively through rules and rights enforced by modern states exercising sovereignty over a bounded territory. This conception holds for both formalists, defining democracy minimally in terms of the existence of multiparty elections leading to a change of government, and substantivists, who demand evaluation of the depth and breadth of citizenship, the quality and inclusiveness of democratic participation, and raise issues of ethnicity, exclusion, and socioeconomic inequality. The same notion informs most theories of direct democracy, in which citizens engage in political decision making directly through referenda and participation in assemblies, on the one hand, and theories of indirect or representative democracy, in which citizens periodically elect 'the best' to take political decisions on their behalf, on the other. The national framework also dominates conventional explanatory theory. Structuralists searching for fundamental background conditions conducive to democracy – whether through modernization, economic development, education and the like with Seymour Lipset, or through fundamental shifts in the power of different social classes à la Barrington Moore locate the substance of democratic politics within the national political community, emergent or full-blown. Structuralism shares this fundamental premise with more recent theories stressing the power of human agency, contingency, institutional design and elite pacts in shaping democratic outcomes in particular

national settings, exemplified by Guillermo O'Donnell's and Philip Schmitter's work. These different theories, even those paying attention to 'external' factors, such as foreign occupation, the world economy, diplomatic pressure, conditionality and the like, presuppose that democracy is made or unmade in a political community coterminous with the national state.

These visions are underpinned by a pervasive nationalist historiography, authorized and supported by the considerable resources of the modern state itself, which conceives history itself in terms of a narrative of the emergence of national states since the 18th century. On this basis, the history of 'the West' since the 16th century can be presented as involving the steady march of democratic progress, while conquest, empire, genocide, slavery, and capitalism are relegated to the epiphenomenal. In this context, it is unremarkable that political scientists regularly present their students with a list of nation states, asking which are democratic, which less so, and proposing an analysis premised on the notion of the discrete and in principle autonomous development of national political communities.

In an age of 'globalization' and transnationalism, the limits of this vision are perhaps more readily perceived than before. The central problem with this conception is its narrow notion of the limits and boundaries of *rule* on the one hand, and *the people* on the other. Uncontroversially, rule in democracy is exercised by, over, and for, the people. Few would dispute that in general terms, this implies that those who rule are also the ruled, hence the unremarkable notion of democracy as collective self-rule. The close identification of rulers and ruled is resolutely confirmed by the felicitous phrase 'rule of the people', which simultaneously implies rule exercised *by* the people as well as rule exercised *over* the people, wherein 'the people' are one and the same entity. The key questions become, therefore, 'what is rule?' and 'who are the people?' Here the nationalist framework supplies a ready set of answers. Rule refers to the decisions of the government, exercising power through the apparatus of the modern state, embedded in a national political community successfully claiming a monopoly of the legitimate use of force in a particular territory. The people are the set of national citizens within this political community in whom sovereignty resides.

But the definition of both 'rule' and 'people' need not be solely restricted to those of the normatively laden nationalist imaginary. These definitions must be unbound. Since at least the 14th century in English one important meaning of 'rule' has been, as the *Oxford English Dictionary* has it, 'control, government, sway, dominion'. Rule in this sense is not necessarily coterminous with national boundaries, and does not necessarily emanate from formally constituted national governments linked to a state apparatus. Indeed, the notion of rule in this sense, especially that of dominion, is much more closely linked to the history of empires and imperialism, polities tending to incorporate the peoples of many nations, a history only formally terminated in the decades following World War 2. Forms of transnational rule, indeed, far from involving something new under globalization, approximate much more closely the historical norm over millennia. The original Latin meaning of the word *imperium* referred to the legal right of a Roman magistrate to exact obedience and enforce the law over those subject to his authority. The first *imperatores* were those Roman generals possessed of martial virtue who imposed dominion and law on barbarian lands and peoples. In this sense, rule and dominion has not implied the national model and need not do so in general.

Even after the old, multinational European and Asian empires had been eclipsed, during what Eric Hobsbawm called the short 20th century (1917–89), the notion of the 'age of nation states' may fall rather short in characterizing the forms of rule at stake under the Cold War, superpower rivalry, military interventions, global economy, and different kinds of empire building, conducted under opposed ideologies of communism and free-market capitalism. An important tradition from Lenin to André Gunder Frank analysed these conditions in terms of neocolonialism and economic dependency. Third Worldism drew attention not just to the economy, but issues of transnational culture and direct domination, especially racial hierarchy. Others have made productive use of a more political notion of empire: it has been persuasively argued, for example, that the very condition of global power during these years, fulfilled only by the Soviet Union and the United States, was the achievement of rule over vast numbers in a territory of continental scale via an ideological principle which could incorporate peoples of many nationalities, immigrants or not.

With the demise of the Soviet Union, in the unipolar (US-based) or Triadic (US-EU-Japan-based) world of the 1990s and 2000s, Antonio Gramsci's notions of hegemony and *direzione* have been developed in critical international relations theory, notably by Robert Cox, in order to understand forms of transnational power linked at various levels to the economy, culture, and the state. Rule in these productive formulations is not conceived simply in the sense of the repressive, direct, and exposed capacity of A to impose his/her will over B against resistance. Hegemony is also a form of moral and intellectual leadership involving the shaping of conditions and structures, including the institutions of 'civil society' – the media, schools, churches and so on – in ways which set the terms in which individuals, groups and states attempt to pursue goals and forge policies. In some respects, as Michel Foucault extensively explored, political subjects are produced under these conditions, and sites of apparent autonomy are authorized. Arguably, however, decision making continues to matter, not just because individuals and groups are purposeful and not simply dupes, but also because command posts in international institutions, such as the IMF, the World Bank and so on, and in powerful states such as the United States, are occupied by a transnational elite, whose members take decisions which work to shape the increasingly neoliberal, global structures within which groups and individuals are forced to operate in their attempts to make meaningful choices. Military force, client states, and since 2001, the language of an endless 'war on terror' play important roles in enforcing this profoundly undemocratic transnational order.

However 'rule' is conceptualized, therefore, there is no reason in principle why it should only be conceived in terms of an idealized and restricted model of national governments ruling over their own national citizens. This is to confuse legitimate rule and authority – normative judgements – with analytical judgements respecting the exercise of rule, sway and dominion. The notion of 'the people', therefore, can hardly be rather arbitrarily restricted to national citizens within a bounded territory. This is to mistake a particular vision of who comprises the relevant political community for the actual community of all those involved in rule or subjugated by it. This latter group is precisely a political community, in that its members hold a political relation in common – perhaps above all other more substantive and visible commonalities and commitments. It is precisely the conflation of national belonging, political community, the state, and a given territory, a conflation rooted in the nationalist imaginary, which produces an analytical blind-spot in regard to this really-existing political community across national, ethnic and territorial boundaries. Indeed, in order that the 'rule of the people' in the double-sense noted above make logical sense, it must denote all of those persons subject to the various forms of control, hegemony, sway, dominion and government at stake in rule. Any derogation from this exercise of 'rule by the people' through the exception of certain categories of people from the right to participate in decision making, whether on grounds of nation, race, civilization, geography, gender, ethnicity, education, economic characteristics, or age, should properly be construed as anti-democratic.

Indeed, far from nurturing democracy, the European empires and their settler colonial offshoots of the last half-millennium established political communities based on the principle of one group of people ruling over others – whether those others were conceived as racial or Oriental inferiors, benighted souls to be uplifted, children in the tawdry pedagogy of progress and civilization, or simply noncitizens to be repressed and exterminated. European fascism – whether in Germany, Italy or Spain – and totalitarianism (in the Stalinist Soviet Union) brought some of these colonial principles home to the metropole.

New approaches to the notion of democracy would do well to take proper account of this transnational historical and theoretical context, to unbind often rather narrow conceptions of 'rule' and 'people', and think in terms of democratic politics above, between and below the conventional categories bequeathed by the nationalist imagination. While really-existing democracies are said to be increasingly minimalist, formalistic, out of touch, and choiceless, especially in the context of global neoliberalism, it is hardly surprising that the early 21st century world is witnessing a resurgence of religious and communal politics, and various forms of nativism and culturalism. But the notion of rule of, by and for the people is almost certainly too polysemic, and too politically explosive to be successfully sutured to the depoliticizing World Bank-style design of elite-crafted technocratic good governance, and popular struggles in the name of democracy, will continue.

John T. Chalcraft

Bibliography

Cox R. 1987. *Production, power, and world order: social forces in the making of history.* New York: Columbia University Press.

Danzinger J. N. 2007. *Understanding the political world: a comparative introduction to political science,* 8th edition. New York: Pearson, Longman.

Harriss J., Stokke K. and Törnquist O. (eds) 2004. *Politicising democracy: the new local politics of democratisation.* Basingstoke: Palgrave Macmillan.

Lipset S. M. 1959. 'Some social requisites of democracy: economic development and political legitimacy', *American Political Science Review,* 53, 1, 69–105.

Mehta U. S. 1999. *Liberalism and empire: a study in 19th century British Liberal thought.* Chicago: Chicago University Press.

Moore B. Jr 1966. *Social origins of dictatorship and democracy: lord and peasant in the making of the modern world.* Boston: Beacon.

O'Donnell G. and Schmitter P. C. 1986. *Transitions from authoritarian rule: tentative conclusions about uncertain democracies.* Baltimore: Johns Hopkins University Press.

Rueschemeyer D., Huber Stephens E. and Stephens J. D. 1992. *Capitalist development and democracy.* Chicago: Chicago University Press.

Related essays

civilizations; class; development and growth; empires and imperialism; exile; financial diplomacy; governing science; historians and the nation state; information society; intellectual elites; liberalism; nation and state; neoliberalism; Pax Americana; *The Wretched of the Earth;* transnational; underdevelopment; women's movements; world orders

Demographic transition

The evolution of economies over most of human history was marked by Malthusian stagnation. Technological progress and population growth were miniscule by modern standards and the average growth rate of income per capita was even slower due to the offsetting effect of population growth on the expansion of resources per capita. In the past two centuries, however, the pace of technological progress increased significantly in association with the process of industrialization. Various regions of the world departed from the Malthusian trap and experienced a considerable rise in the growth rates of income per capita and population. The increasing role of human capital in the production process in the second phase of the Industrial Revolution triggered a demographic transition, liberating the gains in productivity from the counterbalancing effects of population growth. The decline in population growth spanned across borders and the associated advancement in technological progress and human capital formation paved the way for the emergence of the modern state of sustained economic growth.

The growth of world population was sluggish during the Malthusian epoch, creeping at an average annual rate of about 0.1 per cent over the years 0–1820. The Western European takeoff along with that of the Western offshoots (i.e., United States, Canada, Australia and New Zealand) brought about a sharp increase in population growth in these regions. The world annual average rate of population growth increased gradually, reaching 0.8 per cent in the years 1870–1913. The takeoff of less developed regions and the significant increase in their income per capita generated a further increase in the world rate of population growth, despite the decline in population growth in Western Europe and the Western offshoots, reaching a level of 1.92 per cent per year in the period 1950–73. Ultimately, the onset of the demographic transition in less developed economies in the second half of the 20th century, reduced population growth to an average rate of 1.63 per cent per year in the period 1973–98.

The demographic transition in Western Europe occurred towards the end of the 19th century. A sharp reduction in fertility took place simultaneously in several countries in the 1870s, resulting in about 30 per cent decline in fertility rates within a 50-year period. Over the period 1875–1920, crude birth rates declined by 44 per cent in England, 37 per cent in Germany, and 32 per cent in Sweden and Finland. A decline in mortality rates preceded the decline in fertility rates in most of Western Europe. The decline in

fertility outpaced the decline in mortality and brought about a decline in the number of children who survived to their reproductive age. A similar pattern has characterized mortality and fertility decline in less developed regions. Infant mortality sharply declined and total fertility rate over the period 1960–99 plummeted from 6 to 2.7 in Latin America, from 6.14 to 3.14 in Asia, and more moderately from 6.55 to 5.0 in Africa.

The decline in infant and child mortality

The decline in infant and child mortality that preceded the decline in fertility in many developed countries, with the notable exceptions of France and the US, has been a favourable explanation for the onset of the decline in fertility. Nevertheless, this viewpoint appears inconsistent with historical evidence. While it is highly plausible that mortality rates were among the factors that affected the *level* of fertility throughout human history, historical evidence does not lend credence to the argument that the decline in mortality accounts for the *reversal* of the positive historical trend between income and fertility.

The mortality decline in Western Europe started nearly a century prior to the decline in fertility and was associated initially with increasing fertility rates in some countries. In particular, the decline in mortality started in England in the 1730s and was accompanied by a steady increase in fertility until the 1820s. The significant rise in income per capita apparently increased the desirable number of surviving offspring and thus, despite the decline in mortality rates, fertility increased significantly. The decline in fertility during the demographic transition occurred in a period in which this pattern of increased income per capita (and its potential effect on fertility) was intensified, while the pattern of declining mortality (and its adverse effect on fertility) maintained its course in the 140 years that preceded the decline in fertility. The reversal in the fertility patterns in Western European countries in the 1870s suggests therefore that the demographic transition was prompted by a different universal force.

Furthermore, most relevant from an economic point of view is the cause of the reduction in net fertility (i.e. the number of children reaching adulthood). The decline in the number of surviving offspring that was observed during the demographic transition is unlikely to follow from mortality decline. Mortality decline would have led to a reduction in the number of surviving offspring if, implausibly, individuals were risk-averse with respect to the number of surviving offspring more than with respect to their own consumption, and if sequential fertility were modest.

The rise in the level of income per capita

The rise in income prior to the demographic transition has led researchers to argue that the demographic transition was triggered by its asymmetric effects on households' income and on the opportunity cost of raising children. Becker argues that the rise in income induced a fertility decline because the positive income effect on fertility was dominated by the negative substitution effect that was brought about by the rising opportunity cost of children. Similarly, he argues that the income elasticity with respect to investment in children's education is greater than that with respect to the number of children, and hence a rise in income led to a decline in fertility along with a rise in the investment in each child.

This theory suggests that the timing of the demographic transition across countries in similar stages of development would reflect differences in income per capita. However, the decline in fertility occurred in the same decade across Western European countries that differed significantly in their income per capita. In particular, in 1870, on the eve of the demographic transition, income per capita in Germany, Sweden, and Finland was only 57 per cent, 48 per cent and 36 per cent respectively of that in England – the richest country in Western Europe. The simultaneity of the demographic transition across Western European countries that differed significantly in their income per capita suggests that the high level of income reached by Western Europeans countries in the post-Malthusian regime had a limited role in the demographic transition.

The rise in the demand for human capital

The gradual rise in the demand for human capital in the second phase of industrialization, and its close association with the timing of the demographic transition, has led researchers to argue that the increasing role of human capital in the production process induced households to increase investment in the human capital of their offspring, leading to the onset of the demographic transition. Galor and Weil argue that the acceleration in the rate of technological progress increased the demand for human capital in the second phase of the Industrial Revolution. The increase in the demand for human capital brought about two effects on population growth. On the one hand, the rise in income eased households' budget constraints and provided more resources for the quality as well as the quantity of children. On the other hand, it induced a reallocation of these increased resources toward child quality. In the early stages of the transition from the Malthusian regime, the effect of technological progress on parental income dominated, and the population growth rate as well as the average quality increased. Ultimately, further increases in the demand for human capital induced a reduction in fertility, generating a decline in population growth along with an increase in the average level of education.

This theory suggests that a universal acceleration in technological progress raised the demand for human capital in the second phase of the Industrial Revolution and generated a simultaneous increase in educational attainment and a fertility decline across Western European countries that differed significantly in their levels of income per capita. The effect of the rise in the demand for human capital on the reduction in the desirable number of surviving offspring was magnified via its adverse effect on the desirability of child labour. Moreover, it was reinforced by improvements in health and life expectancy and their positive effect on the return on investments in children's human capital. Interestingly, international trade and its differential effects on the demand for human capital in developed and less developed countries had an asymmetric effect on the timing of the demographic transition across these regions, expediting the transition in developed countries and delaying it in less developed countries. Consistent with the theory, the growth rates of income per capita among these Western European countries were rather similar during their demographic transition, ranging from 1.9 per cent per year over the period 1870–1913 in the UK, 2.1 per cent in Norway, 2.2 per cent in Sweden, to 2.9 per cent in Germany. Moreover, the demographic transition was associated with a significant increase in schooling.

The decline in the gender gap

The rise in the demand for human capital and its impact on the decline in the gender gap in the last two centuries could have reinforced a demographic transition and human capital formation. Galor and Weil argue that technological progress and capital accumulation complemented mental-intensive tasks and substituted for physical-intensive tasks in industrial production. In light of the comparative physiological advantage of men in physical-intensive tasks and women in mental-intensive tasks, the demand for women's labour input gradually increased in the industrial sector, decreasing monotonically the wage deferential between men and women. In early stages of industrialization, wages of men and women increased, but the rise in females' relative wages was insufficient to induce a significant increase in women's labour force participation. Fertility, therefore, increased due to the income effect that was generated by the rise in men's absolute wages. Ultimately, however, the rise in women's relative wages was sufficient to induce a significant increase in labor force participation. It increased the cost of child rearing proportionally more than households' income, generating a decline in fertility and a shift from stagnation to growth.

The old-age security hypothesis

The old-age security hypothesis has been proposed as an additional mechanism for the onset of the demographic transition. It suggests that in the absence of capital markets that permit intertemporal lending and borrowing, children serve as an asset that permits parents to transfer income to old age. The process of development and the establishment of capital markets reduce this motivation for rearing children, contributing to the demographic transition. However, evidence shows that in the pre-demographic transition era wealthier individuals, who presumably had better access to credit markets, had a larger number of surviving offspring, raising some doubts about the significance of this mechanism.

Concluding remarks

The demographic transition has been a prime force in the transition from stagnation to growth. The rise in the demand for human capital in the second phase of industrialization brought about significant reductions in population growth, enabling economies to convert a larger share of the fruits of factor accumulation and technological progress into growth of income per capita.

Oded Galor

Bibliography

Becker G. S. 1981. *A treatise on the family.* Cambridge, MA: Harvard University Press.

Caldwell W. J. 1976. 'Toward a restatement of demographic transition theory', *Population and Development Review,* 2, 321–66.

Clark G. and Hamilton G. 2006. 'Survival of the richest', *Journal of Economic History,* 66, 707–36.

Doepke M. 2004. 'Accounting for fertility decline during the transition to growth', *Journal of Economic Growth,* 9, 347–83.

Galor O. and Moav O. 2002. 'Natural selection and the origin of economic growth', *Quarterly Journal of Economics,* 117, 1133–92.

Galor O. and Weil D. N. 1996. 'The gender gap, fertility, and growth', *American Economic Review,* 86, 374–87.

Galor O. and Weil D. N. 2000. 'Population, technology and growth: from the Malthusian regime to the demographic transition and beyond', *American Economic Review,* 110, 806–28.

Maddison A. 2001. *The world economy: a millennia perspective.* Paris: OECD.

Related essays

birth control; childhood; development and growth; family; industrialization; trade

Design

Design is a term that denotes both the processes of shaping artifacts for serial reproduction – from transportation, furniture and interiors to fonts, websites, corporate identity and branding programmes – and their eventual material and visual outcome. Its transnational movement therefore involves the coursing of ideas through, for example, the internationalization of educational models or the publication of design theories as well as through the dissemination of products via exchange or display.

The internationalization of design coincided with its identification as an imperative for securing national wealth. The Great Exhibition of the Works of Industry of All Nations of 1851 is invariably invoked as the watershed to this. Held in London, this event featured 13,000 exhibits from around the world. The public were, for the first time, able to view and compare the strengths and weaknesses of different nations' industrial output in a direct manner. There followed a century of almost annual World Fairs or International Exhibitions. These served both to reinforce national styles and disseminate new design languages as well as to present the material culture of imperial territories in Latin America, Africa or East Asia. International Exhibitions were therefore key locations through which design ideas flowed between Europe and the rest of the world. However, the adaptation of European and American products to non-Western contexts and the influence of the latter on design styles in the West – beyond the decorative arts – remain little researched.

The success of these International Exhibitions precipitated the foundation of national museums of decorative arts in the UK, Germany, Austria and France with a remit to encourage standards in design and stimulate their respective economies. Collecting and display policies were invariably influenced by the writings of John Ruskin and William Morris. They were critical of commercially led industrial manufacture, in terms both of the alienating effects of labour and of the shoddiness of its output. Instead, they championed the dignity of highly skilled craftsmanship. Therefore these museums exhibited historical examples of the decorative arts alongside contemporary industrial products. Schools of design, often attached to these museums, emulated this mixture in their approach. Thus the central debate in design between art and industry was carried across Europe. The resultant emergence of European Art Nouveau in the late 19th century is evidence of the transnational character of design education and thinking. Its national variations drew on local decorative traditions, sharing these with a commitment to modern technologies.

An important agent in the transference of design ideas during this period was Hermann Muthesius. Appointed as cultural attaché to the German embassy in London in 1896, he spent six years investigating and reporting on aspects of British design. His studies, and in particular his enthusiasm for William Morris and the Arts and Crafts movement, later influenced the Deutscher Werkbund (German Work Federation) which he instigated in Munich in 1907. This state-sponsored association of architects, designers and industrialists itself had a direct influence on the foundation of the Bauhaus in 1919. This art school functioned as an international focus for modernist designers. Apart from its core German teaching staff, the Bauhaus benefited from the input of the Hungarian artist László Moholy-Nagy, the Swiss artist and designer Max Bill and the Dutch exponent of De Stijl, Theo Van Doesburg. El Lissitsky, the versatile Russian, was also important in forging transnational links between exponents of Modernism. He travelled regularly across Europe, establishing close relationships between Dada artists in Düsseldorf, members of De Stijl in the Netherlands and the Bauhaus.

The rise of Nazism and the dissolution of the Bauhaus in 1933 gave further impetus to the internationalization of Modernism. Max Bill had already returned to Switzerland, but was joined by typographic designer Jan Tschichold in 1933. They were both instrumental in the development of the so-called 'International Typographic Style' that favoured san-serif typefaces, the use of white space and asymmetrical layouts. Subsequently Adrian Frutiger designed the typeface 'Univers' in 1956, while fellow Swiss Max Miedinger designed 'Helvetica' in 1957. These, and their derivations, became accepted on a worldwide scale.

Other Bauhaus teachers such as Gropius, Breuer and Mies van der Rohe moved on to the USA by the late 1930s. An exhibition at New York's Museum of Modern Art in 1932 had clearly established Modernism as the 'International Style' (the name of the exhibition itself). The subsequent arrival of these modernists in the USA contributed to the style's global diffusion.

Totalitarianism not only contributed indirectly to the internationalization of design ideas through turning key figures into political refugees. Even within nationalistic totalitarian regimes, frequent transferences of international design ideas took place. Taking inspiration from the success of the America's Model T Ford, Hitler ordered the development of the KdF-Wagen, a family-size car designed to run at up to 100kph on Germany's new autobahns. This appeared in prototype form in 1936 and was also to be known as the Volkswagen – the people's car. Its stream-lined styling was, however, a development from Hans Ledwinka's T97, created for the Tatra company in Czechoslovakia. In the postwar era, countries of the Soviet bloc also adopted the concept of an affordable, family-size vehicle, although their overall design was adapted from conceptions of American saloons (limousines), but in a greatly reduced size. Hence the Trabant was manufactured in East Germany from 1957 and the Zaporozhet in the USSR from 1960.

While the USSR had largely been resistant to modernist design during the Stalinist era, the integration of Eastern European economies within the Soviet bloc in the postwar years ensured greater exchange of design styles. The dominant architectural ideology was outlined by the notion of 'Socialist in content, national in style'. However, the Khrushchev Thaw of 1958 to 1964 saw the importation of Czech furniture, lighting and glass and Polish products into the USSR, bringing with them a more modernist vocabulary. By the 1960s, in its controlled turn towards an accommo-dation of consumerism, Soviet bloc design began to emulate Western products and fash-ion. Meanwhile, beyond state-controlled sys-tems, 'do-it-yourself' in dress and home décor allowed individuals to express an even more cosmopolitan outlook.

The 1960s also saw a loosening of national design boundaries in the West, not least within the counterculture movement. The emergence of a critical position amongst some Italian designers and studios – such as Ettore Sottsass and Superstudio – in the face of growing consumerism, led them to develop design concepts that challenged and over-turned traditional commercial approaches. They enjoyed close connections with other European design groups such as Archigram in London. This so-called 'Anti-Design' or 'Radical Design' movement reached its apogee through its exhibition at New York's Museum of Modern Art in 1972. Meanwhile, the coun-tercultural ambitions of American designers were more focused on developing design that encouraged self-sufficiency, environmental activism and Third World development. The publication of Victor Papanek's book *Design for the Real World* in 1971 had a profound glo-bal impact in this respect. Subsequently pub-lished in 21 languages, it became one of the world's most widely read books on design.

Commercially driven design became increasingly globalized from the 1980s. The stock market flotation of some design consultancies or their tying up with glo-bal advertising and media conglomer-ates allowed firms such as Wolff Olins, Fitch, Ideo and Addison to establish offices throughout the developed world. They were then able to exploit emergent global markets for design, particularly in the retail, cor-porate identity and packaging sectors. The growth of information technology usage with Computer Aided Design (CAD) facilities also meant that products could be developed between design studios in different parts of the world. This would bring together dif-ferent forms of know-how and ensured that local market knowledge could be exploited. Global brands would then be nuanced into local contexts.

Conversely, while targeting an export mar-ket, post-World War 2 Japanese design often included easily recognizable national fea-tures in its products. Hence, for example, the 1956 Canon VT Rangefinder camera incorpo-rated the geometry of Japanese pagodas and the colouring of martial arts clothing. Thus, international product design typologies were adjusted, appropriating stereotypical national imagery for global consumption.

The 1990s saw the emergence of urban centres as creative nodes on a global stage. Cities such as Singapore, Palo Alto, Milan and Barcelona benefited from an intense con-centration of design activity. Some global companies such as Samsung and Ford set up major design studios in London, seeing the cosmopolitanism of the city as a strategic resource. Indeed, the development of the 21st-century notion of 'creative cities', and therein 'creative quarters', became an increasingly standard feature of the planning and policy initiatives of city authorities. Alongside this, cities used modern design – such as urban furniture, lighting or signage – to distinguish and brand themselves. Almost uniformly, the objects of design were mobilized to commu-nicate an idea of modernity and difference.

Guy Julier

Bibliography

Calvera A. and Mallol M. 1999. *Historiar desde la periferia*. Barcelona: University of Barcelona.

Greenhalgh P. 1988. *Ephemeral vistas*. Manchester: Manchester University Press.

Margolin V. 2005. 'A world history of design and the history of the world', *Journal of Design History*, 18, 3, 235–43.

Related essays
1960s; advertising; architecture; avant garde; cities; city planning; consumer society; cultural capitals; exile; expositions; modernity; museums; Samsung; services

Development and growth

Economic development is a multifaceted term conveying the idea of improvement of the human condition. It is a broad indicator of collective well-being, understood to include, inter alia, the increase of material welfare resulting from the greater importance of manufacturing and services relative to agriculture, constant resort to more efficient technology, higher productivity per unit of labour, elimination of poverty, availability of productive employment, and fairness in income distribution. Extending beyond the strictly economic domain, it implies the amelioration of the standard of living. Removal of social barriers, greater fluidity between classes, opportunity to alter or abandon traditions, capacity to influence demographic conditions, eradication of disease, lengthening of life expectancy, higher educational standards, more leisure time, and democratization are facets or byproducts of economic development. It is associated with the idea of progress and the struggle against backwardness and obscurantism. Economic growth is a narrower term, synonymous with the enhancement in material wealth of a society. It can be measured by the rise of the gross national product (GNP) and the gross domestic product (GDP). It can also take into account other indicators, such as per capita production (to verify if change in aggregate output outpaces population growth), sustained rise in average income or gains in productivity (a ratio of the volume of output relative to inputs) more likely to be achieved in industry than in agriculture.

Economic growth may or may not translate into economic development. In developed countries, the connection is relatively close. In less developed countries (LDCs), it is more tenuous. Growth without development is possible, in the sense of an increase in the volume of production coupled with the absence of concomitant change in the structures of production, social conditions, and the institutional framework. The phenomenon of resource-based economies experiencing a rise in production and exports of primary commodities unaccompanied by the transformations understood as development is common. The reverse does not hold in practice, although it may be conceivable in theory. Economic development is not a feature of nongrowing economies. Improvement is unlikely if it amounts to redistribution of scarcity. Raising the standard of living requires economic growth, but economic growth has to be accompanied by the reduction of poverty and social inequality for economic development to occur.

Economic development and economic growth are processes embedded in the international context. They have a transnational dimension since they originate in conditions and result in interactions that cross state borders without necessarily involving state action. Internationality and transnationality gained added prominence after 1945 as the decolonizing world took up the challenge of development. Standard economics assumed that growth theory drawn from the experience of Western industrial countries had universal validity. Yet, observation of socioeconomic structures made such claims difficult to substantiate. The underdeveloped parts of the world were not simply less advanced on a continuum of development, they represented a specific category. They underdeveloped by becoming sources of primary products, captive markets, and often political appendages. The very essence of the developed economies and their hold over the world's markets, resources and knowhow precluded the reproduction of Western patterns of development in the non-Western world. Transnationality was accentuated in the 1990s with the adoption of the 'basic needs' philosophy by international agencies. As state structures in the less developed countries disintegrated and development economics became practically synonymous with humanitarian assistance, the extragovernmental approach gained favour and nongovernmental organizations were thrust to the forefront. The advance of transnationality was mainly a corollary of the dysfunction of states and institutions in the less developed world, but international agencies continued to be subject to the overwhelming influence of developed countries.

Growth and development in history

Growth and development are recent phenomena. Stagnation or minimal change have been the lot of humanity for most of its past. Maddison estimated world GDP in 1990 US dollars to be $102.5 in the year 0, $116.8 in 1000, $694.4 in 1820 and $33,726 in 1998. Corresponding GDP per capita was $444, $435, $667 and $5,709. GDP grew at a composite average annual rate of 0.01 between the years 0 and 1000, 0.22 from 1000 to 1820, and 2.21 from 1820 to 1998. Growth of composite average annual GDP was null between 0 and 1000, 0.05 from 1000 to 1820, and 1.21 from 1820 to 1998. After millennia of inertness, world GDP was multiplied by 300 and per capita GDP by 13 in the last thousand years. Despite periodic setbacks, the long-term trend for GDP and per capita GDP was upward. According to Bairoch, the GNP index in Europe rose from 30 in 1835 to 60 in 1870, 90 in 1895 and 120 in 1910 (1900 = 100).

Acceleration everywhere was accompanied by a growing differential between higher rates in developed countries (Western Europe, European-peopled countries, Japan) and lower rates in LDCs (Eastern Europe, Latin America, Asia, Africa). During the 19th century, disparities in GNP per capita between developed and less developed areas of the world widened and the 'North'/'South' dichotomy solidified as the colonial system expanded to include most non-Western areas. Highlighting the international and transnational character of the process, the fact that the most developed countries were the ones most related to LDCs through trade and finance was not coincidental to the expanding spread between them.

Although growth can be based on increasing productivity in agriculture (e.g. Denmark), it is historically associated with industrialization. Mechanical production and use of new sources of energy offer the most scope for gains in productivity. Sustained growth and industrialization got under way in the latter part of the 18th century when production and productivity leaped forward, never to return to their original levels. Both sustained growth and machine-based manufacturing were novel. Industrialization was the outcome of an intertwining of national, international and transnational factors. Its appearance in England resulted from a spontaneous combination of favourable conditions, including the availability of internal and foreign markets, increased agricultural surplus, rising average income, efficient means of transportation, availability of coal, inventions, etc. It was fortuitous, not the application of policy.

The rise of industrial production in England had a profound universal impact. The country's peculiar circumstances provided the impetus. Preindustrial England was already the leading commercial power in the world, at the hub of thriving trade between Europe, Asia and North America. The repercussions of its industrialization affected the rest of the world in a lasting way. Although industrialization emerged in a geographically circumscribed environment, it was from the start internationally cast. Since England needed raw materials, food, markets and investment opportunities to employ profits amassed, it was propelled outward to integrate more parts of the world into its economic system and seek complementarity. Those areas that could not compete by industrializing were pressed to specialize in primary products.

Belgium was the next to embark on industrialization. In France and Germany, industrial production was aided by protective tariffs. Large German banks financed expansion and concentration of German firms. Foreign borrowing and customs walls assisted nascent American and Russian industry, while state support mitigated the absence of protection in Japan. Russia did not fully industrialize until Soviet state control and planning spurred transformations. The British model has not proved reproducible, the conjunction of factors that made it possible not being available elsewhere. What emulation early industrializers practised became less and less appropriate with the passage of time. In contrast with the British experience, subsequent industrialization has relied to varying degrees on the state, culminating in the Soviet model and its myriad replicas in the developing world. Its aim has been less imports, reliance on the national market and greater self-sufficiency. In all respects, the trend has been away from transnationalism. Even export-led industrialization by East Asian countries in the 1980s and 1990s involved state intervention and protected national markets.

Industrialization furthered the division of the world. It confirmed the developed status of the few countries that achieved it. Others were relegated to the ranks of underdeveloped, less developed or developing countries.

Success has largely eluded their efforts. Unlocking the mystery of industrialization has been a prime objective for most LDCs. The internal structural legacy of prior integration in a world market dominated by the developed countries and continued ties with that market have not helped. History reveals a multitude of scenarios for growth and development. Economic thought attempted to give them a theoretical grounding.

Theories of growth and development

'National income' and the increase thereof were the main object of Adam Smith's *An inquiry into the nature and causes of the wealth of nations* (1776). Division of labour and specialization were viewed as the source of the rise of productivity and the root of economic growth. The 'invisible hand' of the market led investments to the most profitable employment. In turn, profits generated investment, leading to increased productive capacities, economies of scale, income and growth. Although Smith's motivation was the national interest, his perspective was international. He reflected the historical experience of Great Britain for whom foreign trade was a cornerstone of its enrichment and its power. International commerce was the engine of growth and the source of national prosperity. Exports extended the national market, stimulated production, induced higher productivity by means of more efficient allocation of resources, promoted full employment and increased national revenue.

The classical economists made their mark in the first half of the 19th century. They believed growth to be a result of 'accumulation' (capital formation or investment) and the latter to be dependent on profits and saving. David Ricardo's concern was the maintenance of the stream of profits on which he predicated growth. The volume of profits was in inverse proportion to that of wages, themselves determined by the price of food (subsistence costs of labour). Unlike capital and labour, the third factor, land, was constant. Since the quantity of arable land was limited, the price of food could only rise, pushing wages upward, depressing profits, stifling investment and bringing growth to a halt. The spectre of diminishing returns hung like a pall over the economy. The 'stationary state' would be reached as profits and investments fell to zero. To Thomas Malthus, the widening gap between limited food supplies and rising population led to 'overpopulation' and catastrophic famines. Ricardo was less fatalistic. Food could be purchased abroad in exchange for manufactures. In fact, based on comparative advantage, foreign trade and the international division of labour were indispensable to growth. Projecting specialization on a global scale, this free-trade model made England the 'workshop of the world', with other countries providing primary products and markets.

Neoclassical theory emerged in the latter part of the 19th century. Like their classical forerunners, neoclassical models of growth were based on factors of production. The neoclassical theory of international specialization was provided by Eli Hecksher and Bertil Ohlin. Ricardo's comparative-advantage theory rested on a single variable factor (wages or cost of labour) to explain international specialization. It was developed to include changes in other factors, such as land and capital. Labour productivity was taken to be the same in all countries but availability of factors differed, leading to dissimilar relative factor prices, international trade and specialization. The policy implications of the multifactor endowment theory were convergent with those of the comparative advantage model. Countries with abundant labour supplies were urged to concentrate on labour-intensive activities, such as raw materials, leaving manufactured goods to capital-rich countries.

Classical and neoclassical economists posited that growth occurred over the long term, despite unevenness and periodic interruptions. It became a pressing problem during the Depression of the 1930s, giving rise to Keynesian economics. John Maynard Keynes recognized that, left to operate freely, markets tended toward stagnation and unemployment. He sought to pump-prime faltering economies, beset with massive unemployment and operating below their full capacity, by stimulating aggregate demand through deficit spending and state intervention. Keynesian theory envisioned output and employment in the framework of a national or 'closed' economy. But it could be applied to an 'open' economy wherein a positive balance of foreign trade represented an addition to aggregate demand, and a negative balance implied lower national income.

Macromodelling deriving from the Keynesian and classical traditions was undertaken by Roy F. Harrod and Evsey Domar in the late 1940s. They were no more optimistic than Keynes about the market's capacity to generate growth, capital formation and employment. The Harrod-Domar growth model focused on one input or factor of production, capital. Economic growth or increased output required new investment representing net additions to capital stock. The source of investment was saving. The greater the unconsumed proportion of national income, the higher the rate of growth of the GNP. Harrod and Domar provided formulae to quantify the relationship. In this theory of value, capital formation was the key element and increase of national saving and investment the means to achieve it. As in other 'trickle-down' models, development was conceived as starting with accumulation of capital, percolating into the economy and eventually reaching labour through more employment opportunities and higher wages.

Although Keynesianism was better suited to advanced economies, where supply can quickly respond to increased demand, Ragnar Nurkse, Jan Tinbergen and Simon Kuznets extended the Harrod-Domar theory to the less developed economies. It inspired the preparation of Five-Year Plans, such as India's Second Plan that was put into effect from 1953 to 1957. In 1960, Walt W. Rostow affirmed that all economies underwent five stages. A single path led to development. The key prescription involved the raising of the rate of investment from 5 per cent to 10 per cent, then to 20 per cent of GNP. If the propensity to save was low, foreign transfers (investment, loans, grants) should make up the difference. References to history notwithstanding, Rostow's scheme was an ahistorical and atemporal abstraction assuming that Britain's experience can be reproduced. In 1956, Robert Solow gave the Harrod-Domar growth model a neoclassical orientation and a more positive stamp. His version included diminishing returns but offset the tendency by introducing an independent exogenous variable, technological change. Acting as an external shock or 'residual' factor unaccounted for by established theory, it made growth possible and state intervention superfluous.

The capital-centred theories of growth equated development with growth. They described features of economic growth but did not explain why they emerged in some countries but not in others. That growth presupposes higher investment is a truism. What needed to be determined were the reasons investment came about in the first place. The theories were better adapted to already developed countries than to developing economies where setting the process in motion is the main challenge. Nor was it demonstrated that investment was the key precondition for growth. Moreover, the theories' assumption that injections of capital produced similar results in developed and less developed economies derived from the premise that their historical experiences were similar. Refutation of Ricardian reasoning came from those for whom the apparently neutral universalist trappings of comparative-advantage analysis were but a thin cover for British interests. Specialization and international division of labour put the world at the service of the British economy. Free play of the market and unrestricted trade opened all markets to British exports. No country would be able to industrialize in the face of Britain's more advanced industries and cheaper goods. All would be locked in the status of raw materials suppliers to Britain and consumers of British products. Contrary to classical economists' unspoken assumption of a level playing field, Britain's early lead rendered it impossible for late-starters to adopt similar methods. In the 1840s, Friedrich List brought to light tensions within the world economy which classical economics ignored. Unabashedly taking the nation to be his unit of analysis, he advocated government intervention and protective tariffs to defend new industries (later dubbed 'infant industries') from foreign competition, in the early stages.

Karl Marx concurred with the classical economists on the labour theory of value and the unsustainability of economic growth. But he looked for the source of falling profit rates not in rising wages or diminishing supplies of land and food, but in the increasing proportion of constant capital (machinery) relative to variable capital (labour from which surplus value, or profits, is extracted). Marx conceived of economic development and growth as corollaries of the spread of capitalism, whether home-grown or imposed from outside.

The distinction between economic development and economic growth arose out of historical experience. At first, it was not thought necessary to elaborate analytical tools suited to the context of less developed economies. In so far as they were considered specific, their needs were attributed to poor factor endowment, narrowness of markets or lack of opportunity for free individual choice by economic agents. However, applied to LDCs, where allocation of resources by market mechanisms remained embryonic, where 'rationality', 'utility' and 'profit' were not understood in the same light as in developed countries, growth theory was found wanting. The institutional framework and the socio-cultural background had to be put in place. Theories of economic growth also assumed the stability of structures, whereas development had to engender structural change, in particular the increase of the share of the industrial and service sectors, relative to agriculture, in terms of total output and employment.

Growing awareness of fundamental differences between developed and developing countries led to the search for understanding of development per se. In an article published in 1943, Paul Rosenstein-Rodan may be said to have launched development economics. Economic development became an acute concern in the context of decolonization, the quest for improved living conditions in the former colonies, and Cold War rivalry between East and West for hearts and minds in the 'Third World' (an expression coined in 1952).

Balanced strategies of growth were advocated but unbalanced growth also had proponents. Rosenstein-Rodan, and later Nurkse, promoted industrialization as the way to quickly raise income in less developed countries. Balanced growth rested on heavy outlays in overhead, mainly by the state, and simultaneous creation of a network of complementary industries fostering inter-industry demand. It tended toward self-sufficiency, sacrificing specialization and international comparative advantage to preserve internal equilibrium. Below-optimum-size plants could lead to dispersal of effort and imported capital-intensive technology was costly. Strategies of unbalanced growth proceeded from the premise that change occurred discontinuously or in fits and starts, as a result of bottlenecks, shortages, tensions and disproportions in the economic context. Imbalance and disequilibrium were a normal and permanent state.

Albert Hirschman preferred unbalanced growth and stressed that installing advanced technology in LDCs induced dynamic backward and forward linkages. The push-pull mechanism was vertical, rather than horizontal, as in balanced-growth models. Unbalanced-growth strategies were ambitious, usually built around nuclei of heavy industry, even megaprojects. They relied on leading or showcase industries, and greater resort to foreign markets. Weakness of linkages, excess size, deficiencies in management or adverse international conditions could jeopardize such strategies. Both balanced- and unbalanced-growth strategies are industry- and urban-biased; neither paid much attention to agriculture.

The concept of dual societies conveyed the dichotomy between indigenous and imported socioeconomic structures within the same entity. W. Arthur Lewis elaborated the two-sector model of development. The starting point was the existence of 'surplus labour' in the traditional subsistence sectors where productivity was low and underemployment widespread. Labour whose marginal productivity was nil could be considered in excess and transferable without loss to more productive occupations in the modern capitalist sectors. With labour abundance preventing wage levels from rising significantly, profits would grow and the modern sectors expand according to the classical mechanisms of capital accumulation, saving and investment. Lewis envisaged a gradualist or sequential development pattern in which modern production displaced the premodern economy.

Several propositions of the model have not been borne out. Labour migrating from the countryside to the city does not necessarily find employment. Marginalization and mushrooming shantytowns speak aloud of urban unemployment, in part because the modern sectors are capital-intensive and require quantities of labour that are both limited and skilled. Job creation has not proved commensurate with capital formation, however modest the latter may have been. In fact, surplus labour is more manifest in cities than in the countryside where harvests give rise to seasonal full employment. Nor was it clear why investment would continue if wages, hence consumption, stagnate. Recognition that capital formation and investment were not sufficient to obtain growth led to examination of unexplained factors ('residuals') like technology, knowledge, entrepreneurial skills, sociological factors or the political environment. Hollis B. Chenery extended the Lewis model during the 1970s to give due weight to the organization of production, consumption patterns, social transformations, demographic changes and international pressures.

Marxist thinking on development was renewed by the international-dependency paradigm whose exponents (Raúl Prebisch, Osvaldo Sunkel, Celso Furtado, Samir Amin, André Gunder Frank, and others) portrayed underdevelopment as a condition created by outside domination and exploitation, a state distinct from lack of development due to internal causes or isolation. Underdevelopment of the 'periphery' was the direct counterpart of the development of capitalism at the 'centre'. Dualist analyses were incorrect because sectors considered as traditional in underdeveloped economies were also integrated into the world system. Dependency theorists rejected the Ricardian notion of comparative advantage and the free trade policies it justified. They were part and parcel of the process of unequal exchange which impoverished the periphery and shackled it to specialization in low-value primary products. Decolonization had not severed the relationship of subordination since neocolonial ties continued to bind ex-colonies tightly to former metropoles. A hierarchical world system perpetuated underdevelopment and precluded development in dependent countries. Underdevelopment was a consequence of externally imposed dependence, not insufficient investment and resource allocation. Imitation of the historical experience of the developed countries of the centre was the wrong prescription. Development required socialism or state capitalism, including external and internal structural change, a New International Economic Order altering the international division of labour, inward-looking or self-centred growth strategies, concentration on the internal market, protection of 'infant industries' or outright disconnection from the world market, nationalization, planning, state-run production and import-substituting industrialization (ISI).

LDCs following the capital-intensive ISI path eventually ran balance-of-payments deficits which increased foreign borrowing. When the United States raised interest rates in the 1980s, a debt crisis ensued, putting the developing world at the mercy of the International Monetary Fund (IMF), the World Bank and the Paris and London clubs of lenders. At the same time as supply-side laissez-faire orthodoxy undid Keynesian policies in the West, it ascribed underdevelopment to state intervention, protection and limitations on free markets. The diagnosis became part of the 'Washington Consensus'. Under the aegis of the British and US governments, a return to neoclassical economics and supremacy of the market were the order of the day. Privatization, end of planning, dismantling the public sector, deregulation, liberalization, correction of price 'distorsions', drastic cutbacks in public spending, free scope to foreign investment in order to raise the rate of capital formation and opening of national markets to imports were 'conditionalities' demanded by international agencies as part of 'stabilization', 'debt restructuring' and 'structural adjustment'.

The record of the newly industrialized countries (NICs) of East Asia was touted as proof that export-led industrialization outclassed ISI, a neoliberal interpretation which downplayed the predominance of pragmatism over doctrinal and ideological dogma, and neglected the fact that ISI, tight protectionism, restrictions on foreign investment, government intervention, planning, centralized industrial policy and public spending on physical and human capital were vital to the NIC policy mix. The role of foreign borrowing was ignored until the financial crises of the late 1990s suddenly brought it to light, raising doubts about the stability of export-led development strategies.

Reversible growth, elusive development

In the 1950s and 1960s, economic growth was registered in developing countries but it was offset by a rise in population, failure of redistributive mechanisms, incomplete restructuring of the economy, or insufficient sociopolitical change. By the 1970s and 1980s, even growth was compromised, as developing economies crumbled under the weight of mounting foreign indebtedness, soaring interest rates and lower exports due to a severe slowdown in the developed countries. Many LDCs suffered a contraction of GNP, absolute impoverishment and social dislocation. Some experienced regression to premodern forms of barter and the status of subsistence economies. Consonant with the neoliberal market-supremacy outlook, 'structural adjustment' policies prompted removal of governmental redistributive mechanisms, lowered living standards, marginalized substantial segments of the population and favoured the return of famines and diseases previously under control. Deepening inequalities within countries combined with widening disparities between developed and underdeveloped countries.

Arduous during the 1950s and 1960s, growth and development ceased to be attainable objectives for many LDCs in subsequent decades. Preventing collapse seemed more realistic. Macroeconomic planning having proved ineffectual, it became urgent to bypass state structures and downplay the 'top down' approach in order to cater to the 'basic needs' of the poorest of the poor, if only to ensure survival. The World Bank discovered 'human development', 'social equity', 'civil society' and the virtues of small-sized projects. Lending priorities changed from infrastructural projects aimed at maximizing GNP to immediate redressal of poverty and satisfying primary necessities such as food, clothing and shelter. In the 1990s, development economics came to resemble a combination of large-scale relief work and the promotion of local self-help schemes.

The shift to 'basic needs' was an ad hoc emergency measure to forestall catastrophe by keeping body and soul together. Recent 'endogenous' growth theory adjusts the traditional approach by allowing for maintenance of the rate of returns through private and public expenditure in human capital, infrastructure and higher productivity. Technological change ceases to be exogenous and state intervention is legitimated, but sociopolitical structural transformations are not considered. Institutional factors are attracting attention. Former World Bank chief economist Joseph Stiglitz, a Keynesian, explicitly advocates an active role for the state in order to correct market imperfections, but 'human development' remains a heterodox notion held at bay by officially sanctioned doctrine.

Afterthoughts

Historical explanations of growth and development reveal the multiplicity of paths, models and strategies. Diversity and heterogeneity are major features of processes simultaneously characterized by twists and turns, occasional successes and frequent failures. Generalizations are tentative at best and laden with caveats. Economic theory points to the inherent tendency for marginal returns to diminish, reducing investment and causing long-term decline in the rate of growth. Too often growth is accounted for by falling back on the deus ex machina of 'residuals'. No all-encompassing theory of economic development has yet been devised and none has been validated by success in overcoming underdevelopment. Sluggish, occasionally negative, growth rates remain the lot of most less developed countries. In this sense too, the problems of growth and development are not bound by national borders.

Samir Saul

Bibliography

Bairoch P. 1976. *Commerce extérieur et développement économique de l'Europe au XIXe siècle*. Paris: Mouton.

Baran P. 1957. *The political economy of growth*. New York: Modern Reader Paperbacks.

Chang H.-J, 2002. *Kicking away the ladder: development strategy in historical perspective*. London: Anthem.

Denison E. F. 1967. *Why growth rates differ: postwar experience in nine Western countries*. Washington, DC: Brookings Institution.

Maddison A. 2001. *The world economy: a millennial perspective*. Paris: OECD.

Verley P. 1997. *L'échelle du monde: essai sur l'industrialisation de l'Occident*. Paris: Gallimard.

Related essays

agriculture; capitalism; Cold War; convergence and divergence; debt crises; debt crises (developing countries); developmental assistance; developmental taxonomies; Economic Commission for Latin America and the Caribbean (ECLAC); economics; empires and imperialism; industrialization; information technology (IT) offshoring; International Monetary Fund (IMF); investment; League of Nations Economic and Financial Organization; modernization theory; national accounting systems; Paris Club; population; Prebisch, Raúl; technologies; trade; trade (manufactured goods); trade agreements; underdevelopment; urbanization; Washington Consensus; World Bank

Developmental assistance

Developmental assistance refers to transfers of capital or services in the form of grants or concessional loans from developed to developing countries for the principal purposes of promoting economic development and raising living standards.

Since the 1950s, these transfers have been facilitated by a complex transnational network of institutions and programmes. These programmes administer official developmental assistance (ODA), either in the form of bilateral aid (government-to-government assistance) or multilateral aid, assistance provided by international bodies such as the United Nations (UN). Developmental assistance also includes aid to and through non-governmental organizations (NGOs).

Until the 1940s, missionary boards and a few foundations were the only international organizations focused on 'poor relief' and 'rural reconstruction' in world areas deemed 'backward'. The colonial powers devoted their energies to extracting resources from their colonies, not advancing them economically. The British Colonial Development and Welfare Acts of 1929 and 1940 did introduce the idea of development to colonial administration. However, after the war, assistance from the new International Bank for Reconstruction and Development (World Bank) and Organization for European Economic Cooperation (OEEC) focused on rebuilding Europe and Japan.

In 1948, calls began for 'developing the underdeveloped areas'. NGOs such as Church World Services, Civil Service International, and Oxfam turned from European relief to development in Asia, Africa, and Latin America. Private foundations, particularly the Ford and Rockefeller Foundations, bankrolled development projects in Asia. By 1950, the United States, the United Kingdom, France, and the Netherlands, along with the UN and its specialized agencies, the UN Children's Fund (UNICEF) and the Food and Agriculture Organization (FAO), had all entered the development field.

Four geopolitical trends drove concerns for development. First, the tabulation of comparative national poverty statistics by the UN yielded the discovery that two-thirds of the world was 'underdeveloped'. Second, newly decolonized nations such as India and Indonesia placed economic development at the top of their national agendas. Third, former colonialists sought to influence their former possessions by establishing bilateral aid programmes. Finally, the Cold War generated fears (particularly within the United States) that developing nations would join the Soviet bloc if not helped along the capitalist path by developmental assistance. The Cold War rationale hardened after 1955 when the USSR inaugurated its own development assistance programme and China embarked on an ambitious development scheme.

Early developmental assistance projects focused on technical assistance. In 1949, US President Harry S. Truman launched the Point IV programme to transfer American scientific and industrial knowledge to developing nations. The UN created the Expanded Programme of Technical Assistance (EPTA), a network of foreign experts and field offices in developing countries. By 1956, EPTA provided 2,300 experts from 77 governments to 103 nations and territories. Despite the global traffic of development workers, developmental assistance had yet to become a professional field and ideas still circulated informally.

Economists from developing nations criticized the technical assistance approach. The greatest obstacle to development, they argued, was not a shortage of skills but a shortage of capital. The World Bank, the US, and the UK had been supplying limited soft loans for specific improvement projects. In 1953, developing nations called for a Special UN Fund for Economic Development (SUNFED) that would make annual US\$400–\$500 million block grants that developing nations could use for national industrialization plans. SUNFED was rejected by the United States, the largest donor country in the 1950s, and by its European allies on three grounds: funding exceeded what wealthy nations were willing to give; national development plans struck US officials as socialistic; and SUNFED moved assistance from bilateral aid, where donor nations could impose strings, to the UN, an organization dominated by the developing nations.

The chorus for SUNFED persisted among an expanding group of newly decolonized nations, and US officials determined they needed alternate mechanisms for multilateral capital aid. In 1959, they set up a Development Assistance Committee within the OEEC and in 1960, remade it into the Organization for Economic Cooperation and Development (OECD). Its new mission was to promote world economic development. The US also took the lead in establishing the International Development Association (IDA) within the World Bank to provide very soft loans to developing nations. Together, the creation of OECD and IDA encouraged European donors (along with Japan and Canada) to share the aid burden within multilateral institutions led by the United States.

In the early 1960s, developed and developing nations alike believed that developmental assistance would soon yield dramatic returns. The UN designated the 1960s to be 'the United Nations Development Decade', in which the gap between rich and poor countries would be closed by having wealthy countries contribute 1 per cent of their national incomes to raise the average GNP of developing nations by 5 per cent annually. These targets reflected the dominant 'takeoff' theory of development: large, short-term capital injections would raise a poor nation's growth rates enough to spark an economic takeoff into 'self-sustaining' growth.

Spurred by such promises, governments and international organizations created a plethora of new aid institutions. UK Prime Minister Harold Wilson declared 'war on want' and formed the Ministry of Overseas Development. US President John F. Kennedy established the US Agency for International Development (USAID) and launched the volunteer Peace Corps and the Alliance for Progress, a ten-year programme of aid to Latin America. Between 1961 and 1964, Canada, France, Germany, Japan, Norway, the Netherlands, and Sweden also established ministries to manage their official aid programmes. Within the United Nations, developing nations pressed successfully for the UN Conference on Trade and Development (UNCTAD), the UN Industrial Development Organization (UNIDO), and the UN Development Programme (UNDP), which expanded on and subsumed the EPTA. These institutions, as well as OECD and FAO, devoted expanding resources to promoting industrialization, food production, and agricultural development.

As institutions grew, so too did the professionalization of the field. In the 1960s, development economics and planning became academic and professional fields with marked career paths and settled bureaucratic systems. Planning became the central device by which national and international institutions doled out aid. Planning occurred at the national level, buoyed by the proliferation of national planning commissions and the IDA's decision to favour a country approach to aid

where nations made loan requests in terms of comprehensive economic plans. Planning for regional integration also directed the decisions of the new regional development banks – the Inter-American Development Bank (1959), African Development Bank (1964), Asian Development Bank (1966), and the Caribbean Development Bank (1970).

Between 1960 and 1970, wealthy nations devoted an average of 0.4 per cent of their GNPs to ODA, and 70 poor countries met the target growth rates of the 'development decade'. Yet, the wealth gap between the most and least developed countries widened. High growth failed to raise the living standards of most of the world's poor. The Pearson Commission, a UN panel assessing the decade's progress, disavowed 'instant development' and argued for redoubling efforts in a second development decade. Others were more critical: assistance had failed because growth-obsessed experts had ignored poverty; aid had become a Cold War weapon; and structural inequalities plagued global capitalism. In 1974, developing nations within the UN demanded a New International Economic Order (NIEO) in which the poor 'global South' held more control over foreign investment. NIEO failed, but the World Bank, stewarded by new chairman Robert McNamara, announced it would prioritize the 'basic needs' of the world's poorest 800 million people. World Bank and UN funding was directed toward new public health, population control, and nutrition initiatives.

During the 1970s, ODA increased in real terms but declined as a relative share of donor nations' GNPs. Despite the growth of multilateral institutions, bilateral aid continued to dominate the field. The most dramatic change in ODA was in the relative role of the United States. Where the US provided 43.8 per cent of ODA in 1960, by 1980 its contributions had declined to 23.4 percent. Western European nations and Japan now provided 47.5 and 17.5 per cent, respectively.

For developing nations, the 1980s and 1990s were decades of crisis, restructuring, and divergence. The shakeup began in 1982, when several Latin American nations failed to meet their debt obligations. Although precipitated by structural changes and a slowdown in the world economy, the debt crisis gave ammunition to a burgeoning movement that charged developing nations with profligacy and demanded a return to 'market forces' and fiscal discipline. The vogue for planning had waned by 1980, and the collapse of the Soviet bloc in 1989 would further discredit state-led development. In their place, neoliberal economists and the new conservative US and UK leaders, Ronald Reagan and Margaret Thatcher, pushed for privatization and tied assistance to policy reforms in countries seeking aid. The IDA and the International Monetary Fund imposed spending reductions, trade liberalization, and economic deregulation. While UN experts remained generally more sceptical of neoliberalism, its acceptance by major donor nations and the World Bank cemented what became known as the Washington Consensus.

The push for privatization accelerated an emerging trend in which newly industrializing countries (NICs), such as South Korea and Taiwan, forged dynamic economies and moved away from developmental assistance, while others nations remained deeply impoverished. In the 1980s and 1990s, the NICs enjoyed access to private investment through international investment banks. Mexico and Brazil recovered from the crises of the 1980s, and once state-managed economies such as India and China used economic reforms to spark industrial booms. Struggling nations, particularly in sub-Saharan Africa, which confronted AIDS, drought, famine, war, and negative growth, continued to rely almost exclusively on ODA.

Development institutions also faced new critiques of their practices. A transnational feminist network publicized serious gender disparities in development and demanded projects to improve women's working conditions, access to credit, and property ownership. With support from the UN Decade of Women (1975–86) and the UN Development Fund for Women, the 'women in development' movement gained ground. Simultaneously, environmental groups questioned the environmental impact of development projects. After the 1992 Rio Earth Summit, aid institutions made 'sustainable development' a new criterion for developmental assistance. Still other critics condemned the entire 'development industry'. Tracts like Graham Hancock's *Lords of poverty* (1989) and Michael Maren's *The road to Hell* (1997) characterized aid as big business, one that prioritized the interests of governments, the World Bank, NGOs, and their overpaid experts over those of the world's poor. Moreover, the politics of aid lined the pockets of corrupt officials and governments with billions of dollars.

Developmental assistance has become an increasingly large and complex industry, and complexity has yielded competing interest groups. The many subfields of aid have generated their own transnational advocacy networks of international NGOs, national groups, foundations, and intergovernmental bodies. Yet, the size of the field has also encouraged the growth and funding of smaller, more experimental NGOs. Criticism of expert-led development has swung the pendulum back toward 'participatory development', ceding greater control to local people and organizations. Still, the politics of aid continues to generate controversy. Projects in the world's top ODA recipients since 2002, Iraq and Afghanistan, have been plagued by accusations of incompetence and corruption.

By the turn of the century, the influence of multilaterals UNDP and IDA had declined. In 2006, the World Bank's contribution to the poorest nations amounted to only 7 per cent of the aid received from 230 international aid agencies. Although the US, Japan, UK, France, and Germany continue to dominate the field, Scandinavian nations and the European Union have entered the field in earnest.

As the people and institutions involved in developmental assistance look to the future, they confront persistent poverty and global divergence. A central question for this century will be whether the Washington Consensus of economic liberalization can yield sustainable growth and poverty reduction throughout the globe.

Nicole Sackley

Bibliography

Führer H. 1996. *The story of official development assistance*. Paris: Organization for Economic Cooperation and Development.

Jolly R., Emmerij L., Ghai D. and Lapeyre F. 2004. *U.N. contributions to development thinking and practice*. Bloomington: Indiana University Press.

Schmidt H.-I. and Pharo H. (eds) 2003. Special issue on European development policy, *Contemporary European History*, 12, 4, 387–546.

Related essays

Africa; Aga Khan Development Network; agriculture; Asia; birth control; brain drain; capitalism; China; Christianity;

civil engineering works; civilizations;
Cold War; debt (developing countries);
decolonization; development and growth;
developmental taxonomies; economics; food;
Ford Foundation; governance; governing
science; industrialization; intergovernmental
organizations; International Monetary Fund
(IMF); international non-governmental
organizations (INGOs); loans; missionaries;
modernization theory; neoliberalism;
Oxfam; philanthropic foundations; relief;
sustainable development; technical assistance;
The Wretched of the Earth; transportation
infrastructures; underdevelopment; United
Nations decades and years; United Nations
system; United Nations Women's Conferences;
Washington Consensus; World Bank

Developmental taxonomies

The notions of development and underdevelopment appeared with the breakdown
of European colonial empires, after the
Second World War. It is true that the idea of
'backward', uncivilized, uneducated societies
accompanied the colonial mission to civilize,
justifying the destruction of non-European
techniques and practices, but the notion of
a mission to develop, which took form in the
United States of America, rested on the notion
of an underdeveloped society. The word
'development', which combined the Hegelian
concept of history, the Darwinist concept of
evolution and Marx's theory of laws of historical process that obeys a similar process
to natural laws, then acquired a new dimension. Its authors sought to indicate a rupture
with colonial imperialism. In his inaugural
speech on 20 January 1949, US President
Harry S. Truman pronounced the 'old imperialism' dead and declared: 'We must embark
on a bold new program for making the benefits of our scientific advances and industrial
progress available for the improvement and
growth of underdeveloped areas'. Industrial
development was necessary because it was
the key to 'prosperity and peace' since 'poverty was a threat (to poor people) and to more
prosperous areas', Truman explained.

The division of the world into developed
and underdeveloped territories became a
familiar device. The terms came to indicate
moral, political, cultural and economic
phases of development on a scale where the
top was occupied by countries of the 'West',
set as models to reach and emulate. They have
served to organize the world into neat and
easily understandable territories and have
encouraged thinking of history and economy in linear terms. The scale, whose criteria of hierarchy have been regularly revised,
answers to the logic of 'development' still
understood in terms of numbers and of Gross
National Product growth, where poverty is
seen purely as income deprivation. In the
decades following World War 2, the notion
provided a frame of reference in the struggle
against the policies developed by the Soviet
Union for political and economic emancipation. Though inspired by the same trust in
industrial development, the Soviet Union and
the US differed on the role of the state and of
the individual. The Soviet Union saw the state
as the principal actor whereas the US argued
that freedom of the individual and the market
were the essential factors of development.

Overnight, newly independent countries
became 'underdeveloped countries' (that is,
all the countries that did not belong to the
West and were not under Soviet influence, i.e.
two-thirds of the world) lacking the human
and technical resources to develop and thus,
in need of aid. The rhetoric of development
received important help from economists
such as Walt Whitman Rostow with its theory of 'stages of economic growth', which
posited that there existed a global process of
development, which was linear and progressive. New states with economies at the bottom of the scale, because their progress had
been hindered by European colonialism, were
told by international institutions to embrace
free-market economic policies and American
ideas about freedom. US philanthropic foundations put forward programmes devised
to train, advise, and guide local initiatives,
which came to depend entirely for their
funding, training and recognition on these
programmes.

Inevitably, the word 'development' came
to imply a favourable change, from worse
to better, inferior to superior and acquired
a positive meaning, but it also inevitably
reminded two-thirds of countries of what
they were not. Human society was likened to
a biological organism, with different parts
corresponding to the different institutions,
themselves predicated on the affirmation
of hierarchical order as a requisite to social
stability and continuity. The division of the
world into developed and underdeveloped
countries rested on a logic that presumes the

universality of economics with its premise of scarcity. 'Scarcity' was given a technical meaning: the wants of humans are infinite, their means are limited, but the latter can be improved (thank to technical solutions). Underdeveloped countries should therefore acquire the technical means to defeat scarcity. In 1952, French economist Alfred Sauvy invented the term 'Third World' to challenge this logic. The term harked back to the 'Third Estate' of the French Revolution, the 'ignored, despised, exploited' people who did not seek more wealth but the end of privileges and a just and more equal world. Third World countries belonged neither to the 'Communist' nor to the 'Western' world, Sauvy argued; their existence was marginalized by the Cold War principle of organizing the world into two opposing blocs. Their needs were singular and had to be answered with their singularities in mind. However, Sauvy's notion soon lost its political dimension and became a synonym for 'underdeveloped'.

For decades, the mapping of the world obeyed a binary logic imposed by the Cold War where the US blamed poverty on unequal access to the free market and the Soviet Union blamed it on imperialism. When the United Nations published the first *Report on the World Social Situation* in 1952, it described 'existing social conditions' but its pragmatic concerns were overshadowed by the general credo of all-out industrialization and Gross National Product growth. There was however no agreement among researchers and observers on the causes of underdevelopment. Was it a legacy of colonialism? The corruption of post-colonial elites? The new forms of imperialism? The dependency of non-European economies on Western-led multinationals? The logic of unequal development? There was a quest for a unifying principle as well as a quest for a more 'human-centred' conceptualization of development. The collapse of the Soviet Union and the emergence of new regional economic powers (India, China) led to a renewed discourse on development. The 1980s were termed by many the 'lost decade for development' with the policies of 'structural adjustment' led by the International Monetary Fund and the World Bank.

Critics of the notions of developed/underdeveloped countries and of the policies that followed explored the assumptions embedded in its programmes, pointing to blindspots, stereotypes, and marginalization of non-European knowledge and techniques. With the publication of the path-breaking volume by Ester Boserup, *Women's role in economic development* (1979), the invisibility of women's roles was challenged and 'gender and development' became an important subdivision of development policies. Environmentalists, demographers, sociologists, and anthropologists all provided their own critique of development. Philosophers and cultural critics questioned the idea of a single and universal way to progress, exploring the ways in which groups had invented their own forms of moral economy and of protecting the environment, and constructed an alternative view of what constituted poverty and needs. In the 1980s and 1990s, terminologies were changed: the term 'underdeveloped' was generally replaced by the seemingly less freighted term 'less developed', although the idea of a hierarchy was still clearly embedded in it. In addition, the emergence of newly industrializing countries (NICs), particularly the 'dragon' economies of East Asia (Taiwan, Hong Kong, South Korea, Singapore) meant that a new term had to be found for a developmental model that had not been shaped in the West, leading to discussions of an 'Asian Developmental Model' in the early 21st century, of which China is considered to be the leading test case.

Also in the 1980s, economist and Nobel Prize winner Amartya Sen, with the philosopher Martha Nussbaum, proposed the conceptual framework of 'capability' for evaluating social states in terms of human welfare. Functional capabilities or 'substantial freedoms', such as the ability to live to old age, engage in economic transactions, or participate in political activities, were construed as freedoms that people have reason to value, instead of utility or access to resources. The theory has been highly influential in development policy where it has shaped the evolution of the human development index (HDI), has been much discussed in philosophy and is increasingly influential in a range of social sciences. Yet, the vocabulary of development/underdevelopment with its inevitable assumption of a universally applicable road to 'progress' continues to influence the ways in which the world is understood and the future defined in terms of material fulfilment. It has pervasively spread these assumptions, setting up a global agenda of 'catching-up'. Though the contours of the notion are now blurred and its goal as a socioeconomic endeavour has been highly criticized and considered by many to have failed, the success of its rhetoric implies that it continues to shape policies and representations. The use of the word with caveats and restrictions paradoxically denotes its enduring power.

Françoise Vergès

Bibliography

Arndt H. W. 1978. *The rise and fall of economic growth: a study in contemporary thought.* Chicago: Chicago University Press.

Kothari U. (ed.) 2005. *A radical history of development studies.* London: Zed.

Latouche S. 2005. *Paradigms lost: an exploration of post-development.* London: Zed.

Related essays

civilizations; Cold War; convergence and divergence; development and growth; developmental assistance; Ford Foundation; International Monetary Fund (IMF); modernization theory; national accounting systems; philanthropic foundations; population; technical assistance; underdevelopment; Westernization; World Bank; zero growth

Diasporas

At the core of most recent studies of diasporas is the issue of identities. By looking at the identities of persons dispersed around the globe, scholars seek to escape a linear research paradigm that focuses on national territories. In studies of diasporas, 'identities' become deterritorialized through international migrations and global communication systems.

The phenomenon we today call diaspora has existed since Antiquity. It originated in Greek ($\delta\iota\alpha\sigma\pi\circ\rho\alpha$) and referred to Greek migration and colonization in the Eastern Mediterranean after 800 BC; diaspora later became primarily associated with the dispersion of Jews. Since the 1960s and 1970s it has also been used to describe African, and then Irish, Italian, Armenian, Chinese, Sikh and other migrations. For historians of migration the concept of diaspora no longer depends on a sharp distinction between voluntary and forced movements. Even in the emigration of Jews from Eastern Europe in the late 19th century, one finds considerable exercise of choice. The Irish provide a particularly complicated and controversial example

of diaspora. Was this a forced migration of exile (as Kerby Miller supposes) or motivated by the search for work (as Donald Akenson suggests)?

Gabriel Sheffer, William Safran, Robin Cohen and others have sought to define diasporas in order to capture their complexity. Cohen describes nine features of diaspora: dispersion to two or more places; an expansion in search of work, trade or colonial ambitions; a collective memory or myth about the homeland; maintenance of connection between the dispersed and their purported home; a return movement; a strong ethnic group consciousness sustained over time; a troubled relationship with host societies; a sense of empathy and solidarity among co-ethnics across nations; and the possibility of a creative, enriching life in tolerant host countries. When scholars detect at least some of these features, they now tend to identify migrants as a 'diaspora'.

A typology

Cohen has also proposed a typology of diasporas – the 'classical' Jewish diaspora, victim diasporas, labour diasporas, merchant diasporas, imperial diasporas and cultural diasporas. But he and most other scholars acknowledge that historical diasporas typically exhibit characteristics of more than one type.

Victim diasporas

The classic 'victim diasporas' were formed by the Jewish dispersion (after 586 BC) and the relocation, via the slave trade, between the 16th and 19th centuries, of 9.5 million from Africa to European colonies in the Americas. Causes of expulsion changed over time. In the 17th and 18th centuries Protestant refugees (Puritans, Mennonites, Old Lutherans, Anabaptists) numbered among English- and German-speaking emigrants to America. Swedish (Janssonists) and Norwegian Quakers (Haugeans) left their countries somewhat later.

Nineteenth-century Europe generated waves of individual political refugees. Participants in Polish national uprisings – conspirators, revolutionaries, religious groups, militaries, civilians, and men and women avoiding imprisonment or massacre – fled to the West. Sometimes huge masses of people fled countries as the result of political turmoil (as was the case of Tibetans after 1959). In the 20th century millions of refugees escaped from persecution and wars, or were expelled, resettled, or forced into slave labour. For example, in the years 1940–41 'elements socially dangerous and anti-Soviet' were deported from former Polish lands or from the Volga region into the interior of the USSR. Some of them had no chance to return from Siberia, 'the world's biggest prison', or from Kazakhstan. In other cases states expelled minorities in the name of modernization: such was the fate of Greeks in Kemal Attatürk's Turkish Republic (1923) and of Bulgarian Turks in Bulgaria in 1989. After the formation of the state of Israel in the year 1948 many Palestinians formed one of the most recent and active modern diasporas. Palestinians know the events as Al-Nakbah (a catastrophe), clearly pointing at the associated trauma. After the Cuban revolution an entire sociopolitical class left the island. This was also the case in Cambodia (after 1975), Afghanistan (since 1980), Uganda (1972). The diaspora of Hmong, people who originated in China and who in the 19th Century fled to Indochina, supplies another example. Those Hmong who settled in Thailand were able to preserve their culture and adapt. The ones who reached Laos and Vietnam, in the 1960s and 1970s engaged in the Vietnam War. After 1975, Hmong who had fought against Communists abandoned their villages, fleeing to refugee camps in Thailand, or to the US. As this suggests, the search for a place of refuge abroad often invigorated ethnicity and nationality among the victims of persecution.

Labour diasporas
Labour diasporas are probably the most common of modern diasporas. Most migrating Chinese were indentured labourers or workers in the Malayan Peninsula and other British colonies. Hindu people in the 19th and early 20th centuries migrated within the British Empire as labourers. When Great Britain banned slavery, North and East Indian workers travelled to the Caribbean, Fiji, South and East Africa (where they constructed railway lines) and to Malaya, Burma, Mauritius, and Hong Kong. By 1917 approximately 1,5 million South Indians (people originating in the Indian Peninsula, an area spreading from today's Pakistan to Bangladesh, and from Nepal to Sri Lanka and the Indian islands) had worked abroad for five to ten years. They called the system of indentured

labour *narak* – hell. After Indian independence, in new political and economic contexts, Indians continued to migrate to Great Britain, Canada, and the US.

Massive labour migrations from Europe created shorter-lived diasporas. In the 18th century, the Kingdom of Prussia recruited farmers, craftsmen and skilled workers from the West. Between the years 1763 and 1800 Tsarina Catherine II opened the South of Russia for German settlement. English, Irish, Scottish, and German indentured servants travelled to the New World. But the largest labour migrations responded to 19th-century Western industrialization. The movements of migrants from Central and Eastern Europe, Greece, Italy, Spain, and Portugal shared many features. Poles and Italians constituted two especially significant labour diasporas. People from Polish partitioned lands participated in two massive intercontinental migration systems – the Euro-Atlantic and the Russian-Siberian. Those from Italy connected northern and southern Atlantic systems. In both regions, rural populations had long been familiar with the idea of migration as a solution to everyday problems. Migrations, often circular, became a way of coping with harsh realities.

People from particular regions chose specific destinations, often separating by skills. For example, textile workers from Biella (Piemonte) immigrated to Paterson, New Jersey, while construction workers went to southern and eastern France. Inhabitants of the Podhale region in Poland travelled to Hungary and the US while people from the north of Mazowsze chose Germany, Brazil, and the United States. Diasporas were small enclaves of settlements linked through family relationships and networks of communication. They did not connect a Poland or an Italy to the Americas but villages to a few destinations. Identities were local, not national.

Trade diasporas
As it had since Antiquity, trade also led to diaspora formation. In the 18th and 19th centuries, Greek merchants and entrepreneurs formed communities in the Ottoman Empire, Egypt, Austria and Russia. In the Middle East in particular Greeks perceived themselves as people living on the borderlands, who served as a bridge between West and East. They nurtured dual identities, feeling equally comfortable as Westerners and Easterners. The

Chinese have a very long history of diaspora in the Pacific and Indian Ocean region. In the 17th and 18th centuries Chinese merchants formed vibrant colonies in Southeast Asia, as part of family initiatives, without approval from the Chinese authorities. In the 19th century Chinese formed communities in Penang after the British established their rule there in 1768, and a few years later in Singapore.

Imperial diasporas
In order to control, supervise, and exploit colonized territories, the Dutch, French, Spanish, Portuguese, and British sent military and civil personnel abroad, forming imperial diasporas. Others followed in search of careers. In the process, Spanish and Portuguese settlers sometimes experienced creolization, but, liberated from European ruling centres, their connections with the Iberian Peninsula remained strong even until today (as recent large migrations of Argentineans to Spain illustrate).

Millions of empire-building Englishmen settled across the globe. In 1890, 1.5 million people born in Great Britain lived in Canada, Australia, New Zealand and South Africa. It is estimated that 40 per cent of British colonials returned home, a fact which raises the question of whether, or for how long, overseas British considered themselves British or underwent identity transformation. Analysis of the Irish suggests interesting conclusions: whereas in the US immigrants sustained and demonstrated their ethnic identity and culture, in the other British colonies and dominions they identified with the British diaspora. The Polish diaspora provides another example: in 1909 approximately half a million Poles lived in the Russian Empire as voluntary labour migrants working as high-ranking specialists, technical personnel, inspectors, and skilled industrial workers. A 'Polish colony' even existed in Harbin, Manchuria. Part of the Polish diaspora, these people might simultaneously be viewed as part of the Russian imperial diaspora. Sikhs could also become imperial auxiliaries (for the British, as 'servants of the Raj' in Asia and Africa).

The impact of diasporas
Diasporas in the countries of settlement
Receiving societies frequently exhibited hostility towards newcomers, making discrimination an integral part of diaspora experience. The traumatic experience of discrimination

encouraged stronger ties with the homeland and co-ethnics abroad. For labour diasporas, workplace hostility reinforced such dynamics. Aliens' jobs were almost always inferior and underpaid. Native-born workers insulted immigrants. Working-class racism was particularly intense in France, Switzerland, the US, and Australia. The newcomers were blamed for workplace problems and strike failures. Trade unions demanded immigration restriction. In the US, supervising personnel often belonged to groups that had arrived earlier and had succeeded in establishing themselves. More recent immigrants realized they were not accepted. Migrants faced discrimination outside workplaces as well. Nativist movements first arose in the US in the 1840s, directed toward Catholic immigrants, Irish in particular. But racially motivated hate especially affected Asians, and Chinese, Japanese, and Sikh labour diasporas. After the 1882 US Chinese Exclusion Act, Chinese workers could not enter the US. In 1907 a gentlemen's agreement halted immigration of Japanese. A year later Canada signed a similar agreement. Nonetheless, racial violence continued. In 1934 hostility against Japanese erupted in Brazil. During World War 2 those living on the coast were resettled to the interior, and violence continued after the war (in March 1946) as well. During World War 2 anti-Japanese hysteria in the US resulted in the internment of first- and second-generation Japanese immigrants. In independent Malaysia (after 1957) non-Malay populations (Chinese, Hindu, and Sikhs) also experienced discrimination. In 1958 in Manchester, Great Britain, tensions erupted, when Sikhs wearing turbans were forbidden to drive buses. Hostility against them was also observed in the United States after September 11, 2001.

Europeans were not exempt from discrimination. In the late 1930s, building his *Estado Novo* in Brazil, President Getúlio Vargas turned against immigrant enclaves that maintained their cultural distinctiveness. In 1938 Brazilians feared that Germany, Italy and Poland would deal with Brazil in the same way the Nazi Reich had claimed Czechoslovakia's Sudeten Germans. Because of the aggressive rhetoric of European countries of origin, Poles and Italians in Brazil faced repression from the host state.

After World War 2, Displaced Persons (DPs) from Central and Eastern Europe settling in

Canada, Australia and the US faced similar problems. DPs for a long time had to work as unskilled workers, irregardless of education or previous social position. In the 1950s in Cleveland, Ohio, three former Hungarian generals, who in Europe had fought against the Soviets, worked as common labourers. The later fate of Hmong and Vietnamese diasporas was far worse; as former agrarian workers, their chances for upward mobility were extremely limited. What has certainly mattered is the way that discrimination, violence, and hatred have encouraged the consolidation of diasporas.

Creativity in diaspora

Paradoxically, however, migrant diasporas functioning in multicultural societies can also simultaneously enrich and inspire cultural creativity. Among other things, diasporas provide migrants with opportunities to define and formulate their historical experiences in new ways. Without their diasporas many national cultures and identities would be very different. The first Bible printed in the Armenian language appeared in Amsterdam, in the Armenian community there. When Russia banned Lithuanian publications in the Latin alphabet, émigrés filled the gap. In the year 1898, 18 newspapers in Lithuanian were published in the US and East Prussia. Fully one-seventh of all Lithuanian books published between 1547 and 1904 appeared in the United States. Thanks to institutions functioning abroad after World War 2 (be it in Paris, London, Rome, New York or Toronto or Edmonton), Polish and Ukrainian cultures developed in directions that were foreclosed in their homelands. Today, books for Kurdish children, which now are distributed in Kurdistan, are translations from Swedish, and printed abroad by members of the diaspora. Similarly, the William Merlaud-Ponty high school in Dakar (established in French Senegal to educate the young African intelligentsia) became the place where young men from all over West Africa met and (in French) developed the ideology of négritude. Graduates who returned to their regions became leaders of Africa's postwar national movements. Emigrants have thus not only contributed to the expansion and wealth of the countries where they settled but have also had a significant impact on the culture, arts, and ideas of their native countries.

Diasporas change the homeland

Diasporas have very significant social, material, and cultural consequences for the areas left behind. The homelands of 19th-century labour migrants – whether in rural Hungary, Italy, Spain, or Portugal – were transformed materially and psychologically through contacts with migrants. Return migrants brought savings and elements of new material culture. In Europe village houses that looked more modern were often called 'American' ones. Diasporic communities supported relatives and clansmen in many ways. The most significant were financial assistance, money orders, and cash mailed from the US or brought by returnees. Villages became increasingly dependent on migrations. Today, some regions of Poland fully depend on people's work abroad (for example, those from the Siemiatycze region whence people go to work in Brussels); identical networks are known for contemporary Sikh labour migrations. About 8 million Filipinos are overseas, and each day more than 2,500 people leave the islands, generating yearly (2002) $6.23 billions; returnees bring with them even more. Both the Polish and the Philippine economies rely on their diasporas. In the past, the same was true of Italy and the Iberian Peninsula.

Diasporas even influenced gender roles in the villages. Women (in Italy, Portugal, Poland and elsewhere) who took care of households while their husbands went away, became more independent and gained more authority within the households. This local expression of labour diasporas was important precisely because it developed within the privacy of the family.

Return and circulation were not uncommon, even in the past. Of 4.8 million Chinese who left China between 1876 and 1901, 4 million returned. Seasonal (agricultural) workers regularly returned to the Polish or Italian lands. Approximately 30 per cent of Poles who had left for the United States before World War 1 returned to their native country. Among Italians, returns were estimated at least at the level of 50 per cent, among Greeks they were higher. From the Latin American countries too a considerable number of Italian men and women returned to Europe. Returns to Spain are estimated at the level of 50 per cent.

Ideological commitments to the homeland were equally important, even when actual returns were planned but never fulfilled. New

World returns to Africa (Sierra Leone, Nigeria, Liberia) were few but for the African diaspora, Ethiopia (a country from which there were very few emigrants until recently) became a symbol of the homeland, and was constantly referred to as such in Afro-American and Afro-Caribbean culture. When in the 20th century Afro-American culture experienced a renaissance, and such slogans as 'Black is beautiful' were propagated, the idea of return to Africa became popular. Although this idea of return was not new (in the 18th century Thomas Jefferson talked about it, and in 1816 the American Colonization Society organized settlements of free Afro-Americans in Liberia), it was Marcus Garvey who first transformed ideas of return into a movement. The ships he purchased transported returnees to an imagined African homeland.

The parallels to Zionism are obvious. Beginning in the late 19th century European Jews abandoned the goal of assimilation to support a political movement to return to Zion. Its founder, Theodor Herzl, functioned effectively in German and French culture, and was not familiar with Jewish rites and religion, but once shocked by the Dreyfus Affair (1894–95), he devoted himself to Zionism. When anti-Semitism again rose in Europe, Zionist ideology gained followers. The Zionist movement originated in diaspora and during a period of 50 years brought six aliyah (waves of Jewish immigrants from diaspora) to Palestine, eventually in 1948 establishing the state of Israel.

In other ways, too, diasporas engage in struggles for independence of their homelands, real or imagined. In the 19th century, Greek patriots took shelter on the British-occupied Ionian Islands and created ideological centres in Vienna, Paris, and Odessa, while planning revolution in Greece. One of the most long-lasting, active and complex influences on homeland politics was the Italian political diaspora, dating back at least to 1799. Italian nationalist exiles took la via d'esilio (the way of exile) to France, Switzerland, England, building a form of diaspora nationalism and fighting for the unification of Italy. In 1843 Giuseppe Garibaldi formed his Italian Legion in Uruguay. Giuseppe Mazzini, who envisioned a united Italy independent from the old regimes, became the icon of this diaspora. Young Italy groups formed in France, Switzerland, Argentina, Uruguay, Brazil, and United States.

One of the most recent examples of a diaspora's influence on the politics of the homeland is the activity of Sikhs. The anti-British, revolutionary Gadr movement in the years 1913–14 originated in San Francisco. Subsequently, Sikhs tried to mount an uprising in India. Khalistan, the imagined and mythical homeland of Sikhs, reappeared as a homeland in the diaspora in 1950s and 1960s, but it was only after the Punjabi crises of the 1980s and the Indian army's attack on the Golden Temple in Amritsar that a worldwide diaspora again played an active political role, using all available means – force and terrorism included. The World Sikh Organization and the International Sikh Youth Federation were formed by the Sikh diaspora after the crises of 1984. Kurds, too, dispersed since the 19th century, have mobilized politically. Recently, that diaspora's involvement in Kurdistan has become more dynamic. In 1995 a Kurdistan Parliament-in-Exile was organized in The Hague (the Netherlands) for Kurds from all parts of Kurdistan and its diaspora. Kurdish professionals from the diaspora work in the autonomous part of northern Iraq, serving their compatriots. Returned migrants – from Benito Mussolini in Italy to Vaira Viķe-Freiberga, elected in 1999 as the president of Latvia, and Hamid Karzai, president of Afghanistan – have often become leaders of their homelands.

Diasporic identities

While diasporas are generally associated with the politics of nationalism, the identities of diasporas have been more complex and have changed over time. Diasporas of 19th-century peasants had village identities. In some villages people read Polish, Slovak, Croat or Hungarian publications and, by the late 19th century, boasted a genuinely national spirit; in others, the inhabitants were completely indifferent to national issues. Similarly, few 19th-century people of the Apennine Peninsula saw themselves as Italians, and only very few participated in the national unification movement. They shared a spirit of region-based campanilismo. This spirit was transplanted in the process of emigration. The migration activists who fought for the unification of Italy (Risorgimento exiles) had but a minor influence on diasporic villagers. Deep within their hearts, migrants still belonged to their villages, towns, or 'private homelands'. Abroad, immigrants longed for their private homelands, but they began to discover translocal links (stronger in the case of diasporas originating in Asia; but faster in the case of Europeans). Some social scientists argue that migrants came to be aware of a national identity only through a diaspora's change in cultural environment.

To exist as cultural groups, emigrant communities had to retain a collective memory of a homeland or to create a new memory. These collective memories and myths are key elements of diasporas. Armenians claim they descend from Haik, and Mount Ararat is their symbol. Lebanese link themselves to ancient Phoenicians and Sikhs to Khalistan. A diasporic press was crucial to such myth making. Nationalist intellectuals among the labour migrations often moved from countries of first asylum to other, distant destinations, spreading nationalist ideas. The efforts of middle-class migrants to foster a national identity co-existed with the local spirit of a Polish village or Italian *paese*. In the 19th century political leaders of the Polish emigrant communities emphasized the political and cultural role of the diaspora and discussed the way Poles abroad should behave. In America a split between religionists and nationalists did not divide the community; rather, immigrants turned to nationalistic ideals and developed a strong sense of national identity. By the time of World War 1 many labour diasporas supported nationalist political activities at home. While Italian workers in France, Belgium and Argentina became strongly anti-fascist, those in the US welcomed Mussolini's successes. In diaspora, German pro-Nazi organizations (for example, in Misiones, La Pampa, Argentina) also supported Hitler's regime. *Volksdeutsche* in Central and Eastern Europe sympathized with it as well.

Demonstrating ethnonational pride became one of a diaspora's chief expressions of solidarity. Irish St Patrick's Day originated in 1737 in Boston. Poles in New York did not hold a Pulaski Day parade until 1937. For identical reasons, Italian-Americans also began celebrating Columbus Day. The aim of all such festivities is to demonstrate links with homelands and with other dispersed members of nations and, at the same time, to prove loyalty and contributions to host societies. They document double, but not contradictory, identities. Similarly, the Vietnamese communities in Warsaw, Poland and in Australia celebrate Tet and Moon festivals, thus stressing their association with the homeland. Brazilians in New York City or Newark, New Jersey celebrate the carnival and Brazilian Independence Day. Jamaicans in the US and Great Britain or Cape Verdeans celebrate their Independence Days. Across many types of diasporas, and many particular times and places, then, the characteristics of diasporas appear and reappear, allowing scholars to understand migration and culture as phenomena that stretch across national boundaries as well as fostering nationalism.

Adam Walaszek

Bibliography

Akenson D. H. 1995. 'The historiography of English-speaking Canada and the concept of diaspora: a skeptical appreciation', *Canadian Historical Review*, 76, 3, 377–409.

Cohen R. 1997. *Global diasporas: an introduction*, Seattle: University of Washington Press.

Ember M., Ember C. R. and Skoggard I. (eds) 2004. *Encyclopedia of diasporas: immigrant and refugee cultures around the world*, Vols 1, 2. New York and Boston: Kluwer Academic/Plenum.

Gabaccia D. R. 2000. *Italy's many diasporas*. Seattle: University of Washington Press.

Miller K. A. 1985. *Emigrants and exiles: Ireland and the Irish exodus to North America*. Oxford and New York: Oxford University Press.

Safran W. 1991. 'Diasporas in modern societies: myths of homeland and return', *Diaspora*, 1, 83–99.

Tatla D. S. 1998. *The Sikh diaspora: the search for statehood*. Seattle: University of Washington Press.

Walaszek A. (ed.) 2001. *Polska diaspora*. Kraków: Wydawnictwo Literackie.

Related essays

Diet and nutrition

Nutrition is the science of the processes by which foods are taken in and assimilated by a living organism, and their relation to growth, body maintenance and health. Diet involves a selection of foods intended to achieve a particular outcome, such as good health, weight loss or the prevention of particular diseases.

Nutrition science involves the study of the impact of various diets on health and growth, while a diet is generally based on a theory about the relation between food intake and the human organism. Such theories are often, but not always, based upon nutritional science.

Ideas of the relationship between diet and health are ancient, and have followed different trajectories in various parts of the world. The science of nutrition is a much more recent phenomenon that emerged in Europe towards the end of the 18th century. The establishment of nutrition as a modern science took place around 1840, when the investigation of the chemistry of food was linked to animal physiology in a systematic fashion.

The establishment of nutrition as a modern science is closely related to the rise of the modern nation state and the rise of modern laboratory science. During this period, states in different parts of the world began to intervene, both in science and in people's diet, and took a systematic interest in the health of their citizens. As a link between health and diet was already assumed, it was in the interest of states to define what constitutes an adequate diet. This became the driving force, especially in Europe, for research in chemistry, physiology and the emerging physiological chemistry which laid the foundation of modern nutrition science.

The early approach to nutrition focused on the energy-providing components of the diet. The history of nutrition science is generally associated with the achievements of 19th century scientists in chemistry and physiology. German chemist Justus Liebig is a key figure who focused on the role of nitrogen-rich foods (meats and legumes) for energy and muscle growth from the 1840s onwards. At his laboratory in Giessen, he measured and analysed the foods consumed by the animal, and the products exhaled and excreted. His quantitative assessment of the relation between input and output, especially in relation to physical work, remained central to nutrition science throughout most of the 19th century,

and attracted great interest from those who were keen to secure a physically strong labour force. Liebig established a distinction between nitrogenous and non-nitrogenous foods, arguing that only the former could support work and muscle growth. Hence, he embraced protein as a superior nutrient, and meat as an essential source of it. Although Liebig's theories were soon criticized and his scientific importance remains contested, his influence on the public understanding of nutrition and diet was deep and far-reaching. This is due, in part, to his commercial promotion of meat extract as a substitute for meat (see below).

Liebig's commercial success, as well as his impact on public understandings of nutrition, reflect the concerns of his time. Military planners in Europe recognized the need to provide soldiers with a diet that matched their needs, and needed advice on how to compose a standard ration. Chemists and physiologists were called upon, and Liebig recommended meat as an essential component of the soldiers' diet. However, providing fresh meat to soldiers in battle was unpractical and often not feasible, as armies needed foods that were not only nutritious, but also light to carry, compact and easy to preserve. Liebig's chemical analyses inspired the idea that the nutritious element of meat could be extracted. An extract of meat in the form of 'meat biscuits' was supplied to the French soldiers during the Crimean War, while Florence Nightingale recommended meat extract in the form of 'beef tea' for wounded British soldiers.

In Britain, as well as on the Continent, the interest in nutrition was linked to social reform, and the feeding of the urban poor became a political concern. Jacob Moleschott, a German physiologist and Liebig's contemporary, saw nutrition as an integral part of humanist philosophy, as he aimed to improve the material condition of man. Others linked nutrition to the strength of nations, associating the consumption of meat to imperial powers' geopolitical supremacy. Despite the increased interest in meat products in Europe, consumption was limited as meat was in short supply. Liebig suggested that cattle herds in the European colonies could meet the European demand, and invited entrepreneurs to develop a commercial production of beef extract. A new business venture was set up extracting meat juice from the flesh of South American cattle, and in 1865, 'Liebig's extract of meat' appeared on the European market. The meat extract was an immediate success, and the company soon established agencies in the US, Mexico, Venezuela, Brazil, Chile, Java and many European countries. The product appeared to solve many of the challenges of the time: it demonstrated the potential application of science in the service of humanity, as well as the commercial potential of scientific research. It suited the needs of military planners as it could easily be reconstituted to make a soup to feed large armies, while for social reformers, it seemed to alleviate political crises as it helped in feeding the urban poor. Finally, it brought convenience and flavour to recipes, and was quickly adopted as an essential ingredient in the domestic sphere.

The nutritive value of the meat extract was grossly overstated, and critics soon argued that it lacked the basic elements of nutrition. This forced the company to reformulate its marketing strategy, and soon they played down nutritional claims as they turned from nutrition to domestic science for testimonials. Yet, the hint as to its health benefits remained part of the promotion for many years.

Liebig's extract of meat was a truly transnational endeavour, with implications for the farming practices of a large area of South America. Advertisements for Liebig's cattle extract appeared in Europe and North America as well as in colonies in Southeast Asia and Africa. Soon it was challenged by the Swiss Maggi company which launched a cheap substitute for meat extract in 1886. Later, in 1908, Maggi introduced the bouillon cube, or what is now known as the 'Maggi cube', which remains today an indispensable part of the local cuisine in many parts of West Africa.

After the turn of the 20th century, nutrition science took a new turn as animal experiments revealed the vital importance of other components of the diet than those that had hitherto been known. These components, which could not by synthesized by the human body, were called 'vitamines' in 1912. In the following years, vitamin research became a key focus, while scientific authority shifted from Germany to Britain and the United States. The new understanding of nutrition has been described as a qualitative approach, as opposed to the quantitative approach of the earlier era. Unlike the energy-providing nutrients (fats, carbohydrates, proteins), vitamins are unstable chemical components and some are easily destroyed through cooking and preservation. The successive discovery of the vitamins and of essential amino acids underscored, for the first time, the nutritional importance of fresh food (fruit, milk, green vegetables) as essential components of a healthy diet.

The outbreak of the First World War (1914–18) placed diet and nutrition on the political agenda, demonstrating the enhanced interest in nutrition in times of war. In Britain and Germany, the nutritional quality of wartime diets became for the first time a political concern, and scientists were enlisted to make food policy. In Britain, novel research on vitamins and curative measures in cases of deficiency were applied in outbreaks of beriberi and scurvy among British troops. Such experiences, in turn, encouraged the awareness of vitamins, and led to an increase in many European countries in the use of fresh foods, such as fruits, milk and vegetables.

In Japan, dietary reforms had reached the Imperial Navy in the 1880s as a result of outbreaks of beriberi. Suspecting that it might be caused by protein deficiency, the head of the Bureau of Medical Affairs of the Navy (who had studied at a medical school in London) suggested a shift to a diet comparable to that of the British Navy, which was richer in proteins. Although the idea of a link between beriberi and protein was incorrect, the measure proved to be effective. This marks the beginning of a shift from a Japanese to a Western-style diet in the Japanese army and navy. Dishes served in cheap Western-style restaurants served as the inspiration for the hybrid Japanese-Western dishes that were incorporated gradually in the early 20th century. After 1918, Chinese-Japanese dishes were also included. The emphasis on Western-style and Chinese food continued throughout the 1930s and served as a uniform and standardized compromise in a situation marked by distinct regional cuisines. The popularity of the army and navy soon made the dishes popular among the Japanese public as well, and had a lasting impact on Japanese eating habits.

In the 1920s and 1930s the establishment of international committees consolidated knowledge of nutrition and diet on a transnational scale. The initiatives of the League of Nations were particularly important in setting dietary standards and in encouraging national authorities to take responsibility for diet and public health. Such initiatives were strengthened in the 1940s when nutrition science became consolidated as a discipline in its own right.

The League of Nations was also instrumental in placing global nutritional problems on the political agenda. In Britain, reports from the 1930s on the nutritional conditions among the colonized reflected a heightened concern with nutrition, especially in Africa. The reports spurred a scientific interest in sociocultural aspects of diet as well. Especially through the works of Audrey Richards, a cross-disciplinary field which would later become nutritional anthropology emerged. Many of the problems and complexities identified in the 1930s reappeared many decades later, and have been addressed in the context of development studies.

In the 1960s and 1970s, protein became the focus of attention again, now in relation to malnutrition in the developing world. Partly due to what appears today as an overestimation of the human need for protein, protein deficiency was identified as a global nutritional problem, and seen as the cause of diseases associated with food shortage, such as kwashiorkor. Malnutrition due to food shortage became a global political issue, and spurred worldwide agricultural innovations known as the 'Green Revolution'. A shift towards high-yielding seeds, irrigation, fertilizers, pesticides and farm machinery spread in countries such as Mexico, India, Turkey and the Philippines.

Since the 1970s, global health problems due to undernutrition have been rivalled by health problems due to overnutrition. The shift in nutritional advice from 'eat more' during the first decades of the 20th century, to 'eat less' during the last decades reflects the emergence of obesity as a global health problem of epidemic proportions. This is due to an increased intake of energy-dense, nutrient-poor food with high levels of sugar and saturated fats, combined with a sedentary lifestyle. A World Health Organization (WHO) estimate indicates that more than 1 billion adults are overweight, while at least 300 million of them are clinically obese. Since the 1980s, childhood obesity has risen at an alarming rate, and poses a particular challenge. The problem was first identified in the US, where the prevalence of overweight among children and adolescents nearly doubled between the early 1970s and the 1990s. Since then, the problem has accelerated in Europe as well, where one in four children across the EU are classified as overweight or obese. An epidemic has also been identified in Australia, and among parts of the population in the Middle East, parts of Asia and the Pacific and South America. At the turn of the 21st century, the estimated number of overweight people in the world matched, for the first time, the number of undernourished people, at 1.1 billion each.

Obesity increases significantly the risk of many chronic diseases such as cardiovascular disease, type-2 diabetes and certain cancers. In Europe, it is estimated that six out of the seven most important risk factors for premature death relate to how we eat, drink and move. The epidemic growth of obesity has been associated with overabundance on the food supply side, and what have been referred to as 'obesogenic' environments. These involve a very competitive food market in which advertising and value adding are key strategies to generate sales of food that are often high in sugar and/or fat content.

Obesity represents a new and challenging sort of epidemic, as its prevention cannot be achieved through a focus on a single causal factor. Rather, it must be addressed on multiple levels, by government, food companies, healthcare providers, and schools as well as by individuals. Consequently, the efforts to combat obesity transcend both national and institutional boundaries. The World Health Organization and the EU have launched international strategies to curb the epidemic. However, as recommendations and structural measures geared towards making people eat less oppose the interests of commercial actors in food business, they have been contested at various levels. Thus, obesity represents a huge political challenge as it calls for the joint cooperation of science, food business, and health policy intervention at both a national and a transnational scale.

Marianne Elisabeth Lien

Bibliography

Brantley C. 2002. *Feeding families: African realities and British ideas of nutrition and development in early colonial Africa*. London and Portsmouth, NH: Heinemann.

Cwiertka K. J. 2002. 'Popularizing a military diet in wartime and postwar Japan', *Asian Anthropology*, 1, 1–30.

Kamminga H. and Cunningham A. 1995.
  The science and culture of nutrition,
  1840–1940. Amsterdam: Rodopi.
Nestlé M. 2002. *Food politics: how the food*
  industry influences nutrition and health.
  Berkeley: University of California Press.

Related essays
advertising; agriculture; Coca-Cola;
commodity trading; cuisines; developmental
assistance; drink; empire and migration;
empires and imperialism; fast food; food;
food safety standards; Green Revolution;
health policy; League of Nations Health
Organization; life and physical sciences;
McDonald's; nation and state; population;
trade; war

Disarmament

Disarmament, also referred to as arms
control or arms limitation, involves the
reduction or elimination of armaments possessed by sovereign states as well as by non-
state entities.

Since armament is considered one of the
most basic prerogatives of a nation, few
countries are willing to give it up voluntarily, believing, as the ancient Romans did,
that 'if you want peace, prepare for war'.
Nevertheless, there is a long history of disarmament negotiations and agreements
among states, which constitutes an important
aspect of international history. The subject
becomes a theme in transnational history
when movements have developed across
national boundaries to promote arms control. Such movements reflect a determination
to reshape the international order, away from
power politics and toward a world without
wars. There have been significant instances
where nations have reduced their armaments,
whether voluntarily or against their will,
because of these transnational pressures.

A transnational history of disarmament
would have to go back at least to early modern
Europe when the Religious Society of Friends
(Quakers), Mennonites and other religious
organizations called upon all nations to treat
one another peacefully and desist from acts
of war. Their pleas mostly went unheeded,
but their message spread from Europe to
North America and eventually to all parts of
the world where various religions (such as
some Hindu and Buddhist sects) had a long
tradition of non-violence, and others (notably

Confucianism) had held the military in low
esteem. In the second half of the 19th century, as technological innovations were making wars more and more destructive, peace
societies in various countries became strong
advocates of arms control. Some of them,
such as the Universal Peace Union founded
in the United States in 1866, sought to coordinate their activities with their counterparts
elsewhere. Women were particularly notable
in the movement to limit the use of dangerous weapons. The Inter-Parliamentary Union
(established in 1888) and the International
Peace Bureau (1892) were among transnational
organizations that stressed the codification
of international law, international arbitration, and disarmament as essential requirements for a peaceful world order. Before the
First World War, arguably the most transnationally connected of arms control advocates were socialists. The second Socialist
International, organized in 1889, frequently
brought together workers' representatives
from various parts of the world, and they collectively vowed never to support their governments' wars.

Although all such efforts proved ineffectual in preventing a world war from erupting
in 1914, transnational efforts for peace and
arms control did not disappear altogether.
Even during the war, for instance, a number
of women from the United States and Europe
established the Women's International
League for Peace and Freedom, which was followed during the 1920s by other transnational
organizations to promote disarmament.
Indeed, the unprecedented catastrophe of
the Great War generated, in its wake, a large
number of both intergovernmental and
non-governmental organizations dedicated
to the pursuit of peace and disarmament.
The League of Nations is the most obvious
example of the former, and the International
Federation of League of Nations Societies of
the latter. Several transnational advocacy
groups were particularly active on behalf of
the movement to ban the use of biological
and chemical weapons, and their efforts were
a major factor in the conclusion of a treaty,
negotiated at the Washington conference of
1921–22, to the same effect. This conference
also was notable because it limited the respective sizes of the navies of the United States,
Britain, Japan, France, and Italy. Although
the negotiations for, and the conclusion of,
the naval limitations agreement were in the

hands of these states' official representatives, it should not be forgotten that both the League of Nations and international non-governmental organizations (the Inter-Parliamentary Union was the most notable example in this connection) actively supported the treaty and agitated for additional disarmament initiatives. The Geneva convention of 1925, prohibiting the use of poison gas, resulted from such pressures, as did the convening of the Geneva disarmament conference in 1933 that was preceded by a worldwide campaign organized by the International Federation of League of Nations Societies, the International League for the Rights of Man and Citizenship, and other groups.

Despite such promising beginnings, neither armament nor use of destructive weapons could be controlled, and the Second World War proved to be almost ten times as destructive, measured by the number of casualties, as the First. The war did, however, result in a major disarmament programme: demilitarization of Germany and Japan. The victorious powers (the United States, the Soviet Union, China, Britain and France) made themselves custodians of postwar arms control by designating themselves permanent members of the United Nations Security Council, the idea being that they would function as the world's police force and that all other countries' armaments would either remain limited or be altogether abolished. While demilitarization of Germany and Japan belongs in the realm of international, rather than transnational, history, it is important to keep in mind that its success was in part dependent on the presence in these countries of active peace movements that were also connected to disarmament advocacy groups in victorious countries. These organizations, many of which had existed since the 1920s, actively supported the United Nations as the best hope for achieving arms control, especially with regard to nuclear weapons.

The extensive use of nuclear, biological and chemical weapons during the war impressed disarmament advocates with the need to focus their efforts on the abolition, or at least limitation, of such armaments. Led by eminent scientists such as Albert Einstein and Robert Oppenheimer, the Federation of Atomic Scientists (established in the United States in November 1945) warned the world of the danger of nuclear war and called upon all countries to establish an international regime to control weapons of mass destruction. Even during the 1950s, when the Cold War, rather than international cooperation to undertake disarmament, defined world order, individuals and organizations in the United States, Canada, Britain, Germany, Japan and elsewhere (including newly independent countries such as India) became actively engaged in movements to limit nuclear arms. They argued that the escalating arms race would not only imperil world order but would also endanger the natural environment as unrestricted tests for more and more destructive weapons polluted the atmosphere and poisoned water resources. Some of these movements were organized by socialist and Communist parties, in Europe, Asia, and elsewhere, but others were far less partisan and more truly transnational. Typical was the Pugwash Conferences on Science and World Affairs, an association of prominent scientists from around the world that spearheaded the movement and provided the impetus for collaboration between American and Soviet nuclear scientists to help their respective governments work out specific arrangements for a verifiable programme of weapons restriction. Due in large part to the efforts of this and other organizations (such as the Women's International League for Peace and Freedom, Women Strike for Peace, established in the United States in 1961, and the Japan Committee for the Abolition of Atomic and Hydrogen Bombs, created in the wake of an international conference in Hiroshima in 1955), the 1960s produced some important arms control measures, including the partial nuclear test-ban treaty of 1963 and the nuclear non-proliferation treaty of 1968. In the 1970s, when the nuclear powers negotiated an agreement to limit their respective arsenals and to prohibit altogether the development and possession of anti-ballistic missiles, scientists from those countries played a pivotal role as technical experts, assisting their governments in the dismantling of certain categories of weapons.

A major landmark at the end of the 20th century was the treaty to ban anti-human landmines that was signed by most countries in the world (though not yet by the United States or China). The chief impetus for this achievement came from a non-governmental organization, the International Campaign to Band Landmines, which was founded in

1992 to persuade governments to negotiate such an agreement. More recently, there has been much interest in establishing transnational demilitarized areas. For instance, the Association of Southeast Asian Countries (ASEAN) has declared Southeast Asia a nuclear-free zone, indicating that the nations in the region would not manufacture, introduce or use nuclear weapons in the region. A strong citizens' multinational movement preceded such a development, and similar movements have resulted in the declaration of nuclear-free zones in the South Pacific, southern Africa and other parts of the globe.

Despite such successful instances of disarmament, there are more weapons in various countries' possession today than in any other period in history. Transnational networks for arms control have had to contend with the seemingly unstoppable spread of all types of weapons throughout the world. At bottom is disagreement as to the nature of international relations. If they are viewed as being in a constant state of anarchy, each state pursuing its own interests and using whatever means are available to achieve its ends, disarmament amounts to committing suicide, or else entrusting national security and international order to some untested faith in the morality of nations. 'Realists' who argue this way have insisted that international order can only be maintained through power, in particular some power equilibrium, and, therefore, that it is foolish to undertake disarmament that may disrupt the balance and may make another war more, rather than less, likely. Disarmament advocates have pointed to some successful instances of collective disarmament and argued that, even if minimal military force might be necessary for the protection of national security and the maintenance of world order, nations have a tendency to go beyond that level and use the quantity and quality of their weapons as a measure of prestige. That, according to proponents of disarmament agreements, would not ensure peace but, on the contrary, make the world that much more unstable. Equally important, they argue that excessive armament shifts a nation's resources away from its essential needs such as economic development, education and social welfare. The whole world would become more impoverished if people everywhere were less educated, less fed and clothed, and less inclined to interact economically and culturally with one another. Put this way, the history of disarmament is nothing less than that of humankind's perpetual debate concerning the nature of man and society. The debate will continue so long as there remain nations as the key units of human association.

More than nations are involved, however, in the story of disarmament, for many non-state groups have also been armed. Traditionally, families, religious communities and commercial associations acquired arms in self-defence, and political dissidents and revolutionaries created their own military units. Pirates, gangsters and other illicit groups were likewise armed. As modern states steadily established their authority, and as international agreements came to control illicit activities across national boundaries, weapons, especially those that were expensive to manufacture, came to be monopolized by sovereign states. Even so, private armies with their own arsenals never disappeared. Their activities took place across borders, and in recent decades they may, if anything, have begun to increase in number and scale. This is one area where disarmament movements have failed to produce notable gains.

In 2004, the United Nations' 'high-level panel on threats, challenges and change' noted that, along with 'economic and social threats, including poverty, infectious disease and environmental degradation', interstate conflict, internal conflict, nuclear, radiological, chemical and biological weapons, terrorism, and transnational organized crime posed the most serious threats to humankind. All these categories of threat have to do with armaments, whether undertaken by states or amassed by private armies and terrorist groups. Thus, promoting arms control among states and disarming non-state bodies remain among the most urgent transnational objectives today.

Akira Iriye

Bibliography
DeBenedetti C. 1980. *The peace movement in American history.* Bloomington: Indiana University Press.
Evangelista M. 1999. *Unarmed forces: the transnational movement to end the Cold War.* Ithaca: Cornell University Press.

Taylor R. 1988. *Against the Bomb: the British peace movement, 1958–1965*. Oxford: Oxford University Press.

Wittner L. S. 1993. *One world or none: a history of the world nuclear disarmament movement through 1955*. Stanford: Stanford University Press.

Related essays

arms trade; arms trafficking; Cold War; environmentalism; international non-governmental organizations (INGOs); League of Nations system; legal order; non-violence; pacifism; Pugwash Conferences; United Nations decades and years; United Nations system; war; *War and Peace in the Global Village*; women's movements; world orders

sponsoring conferences and research on such issues as the transition from military to civilian economies and dealing with the fate of nuclear weapons in the former Soviet states. In 1995, the Pugwash Conference met in Hiroshima, a reminder of the use of atomic weapons. In that year, the organization and its president, Joseph Rotblat, received the Nobel Peace Prize for the organization's efforts to diminish the part played by nuclear arms in international politics and in the longer run to eliminate such arms.

The Pugwash Conference was not the first non-governmental organization (NGO) to win the Nobel Peace Prize; Amnesty International did so in 1977. Pugwash did, however, foreshadow the dramatic growth of NGO influence after 1970.

Robert David Johnson

Bibliography

Dyson F. 1992. *From Eros to Gaia*. New York: Pantheon.

Related essays

Amnesty International (AI); Cold War; disarmament; Greenpeace; international non-governmental organizations (INGOs); International Red Cross and Red Crescent movement; Islamic Relief Worldwide; life and physical sciences; Médecins Sans Frontières (MSF); Oxfam; pacifism; prizes; Save the Children International Union; United Cities and Local Governments (UCLG); war

Pugwash Conferences

The Pugwash Conferences – named for the Nova Scotia city which hosted the original conferences in 1957 – have championed nuclear disarmament and peaceful resolution of international crises.

The genesis of the non-governmental organization came from a 1955 resolution by Albert Einstein, Bertrand Russell, and nine other scientific and intellectual luminaries. The signatories called for 'distasteful limitations of national sovereignty' to avoid any superpower war, which they feared inevitably would escalate and involve nuclear weapons. Accordingly, they resolved, 'In view of the fact that in any future world war nuclear weapons will certainly be employed, and that such weapons threaten the continued existence of mankind, we urge the governments of the world to realize, and to acknowledge publicly, that their purpose cannot be furthered by a world war, and we urge them, consequently, to find peaceful means for the settlement of all matters of dispute between them' (Russell-Einstein Manifesto of 9 July 1955).

Pugwash conferences have met annually since 1957. Twenty-two scientists from ten countries attended the first conference; gatherings now attract between 150 and 250 people. To facilitate free exchange of ideas, invitees attend in their private capacity, not as representatives of their governments or organizations. After the fall of the Soviet Union, the organization redefined its purpose,

Displaced persons

While displaced persons received particular attention following the Second World War their experience fits into a longer history of forced displacement by wars, armed conflicts and state-engineered population policies.

The term 'displaced persons' (abbreviated as 'DPs') first referred to people who had been forced to leave their country during the war and came under Allied military control in 1944–45. Displacement represented a temporary category, and the Allies planned to quickly return DPs to their home countries. In this sense they differed from refugees, who because of political, racial, religious or other persecution became recognized as permanently dislocated individuals. The distinction arose, in part, through the difficulty of repatriating people to Soviet-controlled countries following the war.

Of the roughly 14 million displaced persons concentrated in Germany, the majority came from Eastern Europe. This figure does not include German expellees (the so-called *Volksdeutsche*), who were also driven west as part of this massive dislocation. Some DPs had been forced laborers who were shipped westward during the war to work for the Nazi economy. Jews comprised a special category of displaced persons; having survived the Holocaust, they had no place to move until the establishment of Israel in 1948. The postwar situation in countries like Poland, Hungary and Czechoslovakia proved unwelcoming to the return of their former Jewish inhabitants. In addition, the fear of being inundated by refugees left many countries unwilling to accept large numbers of DPs. Displaced persons who were unwilling or unable to return home had little option but to remain in the camps.

At the war's end the Western zones of Germany held from 6 to 7 million DPs and similar estimates existed for the Soviet zone. Military officials administered these camps, some of which were former concentration or prisoners of war camps, until October 1945 when the United Nations Rehabilitation and Relief Administration (UNRRA) took over control. The UNRRA had expanded the number of camps in Western occupational zones from 227 to over 733 by June 1947. A handful of camps also existed in Austria (21) and Italy (8). By the end of 1945 most DPs had returned home, so that only 737,375 people continued living under UNRRA care. Yet, as political, ethnic and anti-Semitic persecution persisted in Eastern Europe, the number of DPs began to rise again in early 1946.

A multilayered social, political and economic life developed in the camps. In Jewish camps recovery from the Holocaust left many physically and psychologically unable and unwilling to work. Camps, rather than local businesses, employed the majority of DPs who did work. Jewish DPs also had very high birth rates. Displaced persons became effective political organizers. Many Jewish DPs actively supported the Zionist programme to create a Jewish state in Palestine. Likewise, resistance to Soviet repatriation became a critical political struggle in the camps. Hundreds of thousands of Ukrainians, Poles and others refused to

return to Soviet territory, mostly from fear of ethnic and political persecution. While US soldiers forcibly repatriated some DPs in 1945, this policy shifted as a result of burgeoning Cold War tensions. Between 1947 and 1951, DPs from Baltic countries, Poland and Ukraine were permitted to emigrate in large numbers to Canada, Australia, the United States and Israel.

More recent conflicts have continued to uproot civilians, often as part of specific political and military objectives. The war in Vietnam displaced millions during ongoing fighting from the 1950s to the 1970s. While some Vietnamese moved for ideological reasons or fear of persecution, others were forced to leave by bombing campaigns and local skirmishes. During the 1990s the ethnic cleansing in the former Yugoslavia, which targeted ethnic groups for expulsion, and the mass killing of Tutsis in Rwanda, forced millions into flight. In 2003 more than 20 million people were listed as displaced across the world. Many of them remain within their own country as internally displaced persons. This status partially reflects the international community's attempts to challenge ethnic cleansing by forcing targeted civilians to remain or immediately return to their country, but simultaneously leaves those displaced without the protection, resources and political pressure necessary to resolve their plight.

David Gerlach

Bibliography

Wyman M. 1998. *DPs: Europe's displaced persons, 1945–1951*, 2nd ed. Ithaca: Cornell University Press.

Related essays

Armenian genocide; Cold War; diasporas; empire and migration; forced migrations; genocide; human mobility; international migration regimes; partitions; population; refugee relief; refugees; war

Divergence and convergence See Convergence and divergence

Dollar

The dollar is a currency unit utilized by several countries such as the United States, Canada, Australia, New Zealand and

Hong Kong although it is predominantly a unit of American currency. Since its first actual coinage in 1794, the dollar had been linked with gold. Accompanying the rise of American power in the late 19th and 20th centuries, the dollar became a key currency in the world economy, establishing its international significance.

In the late 19th century, large American companies such as the General Electric Company and the Standard Oil Company expanded their business to overseas markets in Latin America and East Asia. This so-called 'dollar diplomacy' in the later era of President William Howard Taft (1909–13) was symbolic of the transnational business activities emerging at that time. The dollar became an international currency along with the pound sterling after World War 1. American bankers such as Thomas Lamont played an important role in the rebuilding of the European economy through dollar-denominated lending to Germany during the 1920s. The Allied victory in World War 2 made the dollar the main currency under the General Agreement on Tariffs and Trade (GATT), International Monetary Fund (IMF) and World Bank regime. During the 1950s, many countries throughout the world attempted to tie the dollar to their foreign currency reserves. The dollar was so highly valued as a currency that it circulated even in the Communist countries of the Soviet Union and Eastern Europe. In the 1960s, excess supply brought about its devaluation as the US economy was buffeted by growing competition from Japan and West Germany alongside balance of payments difficulties at home. On 15 August 1971, President Richard Nixon declared the suspension of the dollar's direct linkage to the gold standard, in an effort to revive the American economy. Under the current floating-rate system, the dollar continues to be the most powerful currency in the world and it has even assumed a role as a 'quasi-currency' in such Central and South American countries as Argentina and Mexico.

Masato Kimura

Bibliography

Kindleberger C. P. 1981. *International money: a collection of essays*. London: George Allen & Unwin.

Related essays

Coca-Cola; comics; euromarkets; financial diplomacy; financial markets; International Monetary Fund (IMF); jeans; loans; money; World Bank

Domestic service

Past and present, domestic service is numerically one of the most important employment categories for women.

Working in domestic service usually means crossing regional and national as well as class and cultural borders. Though often considered a premodern and preindustrial type of work, this form of (mostly female) employment generates profoundly modern transnational experiences. All cultures know some labour form by which women move (temporarily) into servitude. It provided an acceptable, if not a respectable form of employment for lower-class women, leaving class and gender structures untouched. Being hired out relieved the stem family of another mouth to feed, added some small income and implied learning a trade (though it was never called such) – to cook, to clean, to do farm chores (slaughtering, preserving fruit, raking corn) or to run a household.

Although work in domestic service often brought exploitation and abuse, it was not beyond control and regulation. Servants could seek out better or more suitable employment by changing positions. A good reputation, experience on the job and the quality of work performed could enable a servant to find better employment, which meant better pay, shorter work hours, some degree of privacy, and, most of all, respect from the employer. However, overwork, being thrown out of job without notice and left with no place to go, sexual harassment and unwanted pregnancy were, through all times and regions, work-related risks and hazards.

Work in domestic service was and is a type of employment readily available for women; a woman willing to work in domestic service can always assume she will find a job. Conversely, modernizing, 'Western' societies, where other forms of gainful employment for women are available, experience 'servant crises', meaning the bourgeois housewife – unsuccessfully seeking domestic help for the price she is willing to pay – is experiencing a crisis. She may have to look beyond the hegemonic group to find a person willing to work as a domestic. Thus migration and 'otherness' become integral elements of domestic servitude.

Though for some women migration was a necessary means to find employment in domestic service, for others domestic service was a vehicle to facilitate migration in search of a better livelihood. During the century of mass migration from Europe to North America, the 1830s to the 1930s, women migrating alone in search of work were a minority. In the 1850s, when women constituted a small majority among migrants from Ireland, many of them who ventured out alone knew that they could always find employment as domestics. Often referred by friends from home, living-in with a family from their own ethnic group and religion seemed to be an ideal first employment for female newcomers.

But not only the 'new world' was attractive for adventurous women, making use of the traditionally acceptable type of female employment to seek out new and strange places, or to liberate themselves from confining home circumstances. Paris, London, Berlin, Vienna, and the Netherlands were attractive places for women from the European periphery. While Bohemian women reigned supreme in Vienna kitchens, thus impacting on a national Austrian cuisine, the male English butler rarely left the English cultural space. The English nanny, however, travelled widely, signifying professionalism and class distinction for the employer. Which ethnic group occupied the domestic service niche originally depended on migration patterns and systems, later utilized in stereotypes. Female-informed networks supported female migration; agencies helped in locating placements.

Today's migration into domestic service proceeds along similar lines under accelerated conditions of transportation and communication. The incentives are similar. In the early 1990s, Castle and Miller, in their study on international migration, outlined four major trends in migration patterns: globalization, acceleration, differentiation and feminization. The agency of women migrating into domestic service is at the core of all of these trends. Massive restructuring processes in agriculture and (proto-)industrial production in 'Third World' and newly industrialized countries (NICs) on the one hand and increased employment of women in professional, well paying and highly demanding jobs in industrial countries on the other have created a world-encompassing supply and demand relationship for women willing to work in domestic service. The occupation considered premodern and in decline 20 years ago remains in great demand, and the demand is rising.

New migration systems of domestic workers have emerged from historical relations (such as colonialism); from specific immigration policies (such as live-in-caregiver programmes in Canada, foreign domestic workers programmes in Hong Kong); from employment agencies (like those contracting Muslim Malayan women to work in the Gulf states), and from personal networks and referrals. The largest system engages the various labour-exporting and labour-importing countries in Asia and the Gulf states. Within this migration system some countries are at the same time sending and receiving people. It has been estimated for the late 1980s that up to 1.7 million women migrated within that system. A second system provides European households with domestic labour. Women who migrate from the former colonies to Britain and France often find domestic service their only employment option; women from neighbouring Eastern and Central European countries provide household service, mainly in the form of char work in Germany and Austria. Most recently, Spain began to attract women from Latin America; and middle-class women in Italy and Greece rely on service from migrants from Albania, Ethiopia, and Somalia. A lively migration network also exists between the Philippines and Italy. A third system feeds into the North American labour market, drawing from the Philippines, the Caribbean and Latin America (especially the Dominican Republic, Jamaica, El Salvador, Guatemala and Mexico). Though Latin America and Africa experience female out-migration, internal migrations from rural to urban areas, or from the urban outskirts into (white) middle-class city households are more common. In South Africa in the late 1990s domestic service is the fifth largest source of formal employment.

Women who leave home to work in domestic service today are no longer single or unattached. Often they leave children, husbands and parents behind. Though family networks may provide the necessary care for children, they also depend on the financial support from women working abroad. Transnational motherhood creates severe pressures for migrant women. To provide a better education for their children, support ageing parents and create security (through home ownership) for their own retirement are important incentives. Legal frameworks (as in Canada) that allow sponsorship of family-member immigrants are another incentive. Whether domestic workers become pioneers in migration networks depends on the legal framework of their migration. Providing household services in Berlin coming from Poland may take the form of seasonal labour making use of a tourist visa, whereas working in Hong Kong or in the Gulf states, return migration is implied by law. Migration to Canada may turn into permanent settlement. But even here the transnational social space the women create may facilitate return in old age.

Statistical information on women migrating into domestic service is notoriously difficult to obtain. Not only do many women migrate clandestinely, government agencies have shown little interest in reporting on an aspect of the labour market they consider insignificant. This seems to be a particularly inadequate analysis when one considers the volume of remittances made by women working abroad and their impact on homeland development. In the last decade, remittances have emerged as the second largest source of external funding in some developing countries. The gendered analysis of remittances has become a research issue for INSTRAW (the United Nations International Research and Training Institute for the Advancement of Women).

The question remains whether migration into domestic service is a mechanism not only to overcome economic/financial difficulties of the household but also to surpass individual limitations and gendered constraints. In deciding to migrate, women exercise considerable agency; whether they can turn waged work into an empowering experience depends on the legal framework, employment conditions and support received when claiming better working conditions or respectful treatment. During the past decade feminist advocacy and self-help groups have stirred public attention in order to rectify exploitative working conditions and racial discrimination. Former domestic workers also move into other sectors of the service industry (nursing, geriatric care). Since there is an ever growing demand for these services and since this type of work is very much structured by the race-gender

system, the feminization of global migration will continue.

Christiane Harzig

Bibliography

Anderson B. 2000. *Doing the dirty work? The global politics of domestic labour.* London: Zed.

Ehrenreich B. and Russell Hochschild A. (eds) 2002. *Global woman: nannies, maids, and sex workers in the new economy.* New York: Henry Holt.

Fauve-Chamoux A. (ed.) 2004. *Domestic service and the formation of European identity: understanding the globalization of domestic work, 16th–21st centuries.* Bern: Peter Lang.

Harzig C. 2006. 'Domestics of the World (Unite?): labor migration systems and personal trajectories of household workers in historical and global perspective', *Journal of American Ethnic History.*

Related essays

childhood; contract and indentured labourers; cuisines; diasporas; empire and migration; family; gender and sex; human mobility; labour migrations; nursing; remittances

Dress

Dress is what we wear, but it is also a broad concept with many tacitly understood meanings. It may be defined as clothing in general, an outer covering, or more specifically as a one-piece woman's garment made up of a bodice and skirt. Dress can be a complete style of clothing such as a national dress or a coded uniform costume such as military or religious dress. It may be made of almost any material from animal or even fish skin to vegetable and synthetic fibres and other materials such as metals and plastics. It may be a plain garment or an elaborately and symbolically decorated one such as the costumes shown in portraits of Queen Elizabeth I of England. It may be fashioned from an uncut, unsewn length of cloth and wrapped around the body in the manner of an Indian sari or dhoti, or it may be the product of complex cutting and tailoring. Yet, simplicity of construction does not imply simplicity of meaning, as Gandhi recognized with his deliberate replacement of Western dress with the hand-woven dhoti, or as represented by the values imbued in the Muslim woman's hijab or veil, both used symbolically in the global political arena. Essentially these are strips of cloth, but they have also been saturated with cultural and political meanings. Furthermore, dress can incorporate more than clothing: hairstyle, ornament and accessories can be an essential part of individual clothing styles.

In recent years, the academic study of dress has moved from the precise study of the stylistic changes of mainly elite clothing to a broader cultural and historical approach, and this has been reflected in museum displays and collecting policies, such as the Victoria and Albert Museum's 1995 exhibition, 'Street Style'. Earlier historical approaches which tended to record the historical evolution of dress have been expanded by more inclusive examinations of material culture including clothing, often following the model of ethnography. Recent studies of dress have considered the political and economic relationships between Western and non-Western cultures as embodied in dress, and also deconstructed the myth that dress in the latter is somehow immutable. Besides the essential and patient persistence of detailed, object-based studies, dress is now also discussed more broadly in terms of its part in the formation of social identity and cultural practices. New ethnographies of clothing reflecting contemporary preoccupations with 'identity' and 'authenticity' have analysed contemporary cultures in terms of textiles and dress. Recognizing the cultural and economic role of dress, a more eclectic cohort of scholars such as sociologists and geographers have also become students of dress and fashion systems. The study of subcultural, non-elite dress styles has become a source of modern dress folklore and has been reflected in fashionable dress, such as the Italian designer Gianni Versace's (1946–97) use of a 'punk' safety pin, associated with deliberately torn and dishevelled street clothing which itself symbolically rejected commercial fashion, on a glamorous and expensive evening gown in 1994.

The description of 'national costume' was one aspect of the construction of cultural hierarchies through clothing, based on the assumption that every social group or class could be identified by the way it dressed. Traditional, or 'ethnic' costumes, often very localized, also represented community and continuity as garments, techniques for making them and modes of wearing them were passed from one generation to the next. In the late 18th and early 19th centuries, interest in regional dress and other forms of folklore such as fairy tales was developed by the new discipline of ethnology, the development of printing technology that made the imagery of 'folk customs' widely available, and emerging nationalist movements across Europe. In many countries, changing ways of life have now reduced the making of these garments to small groups of people anxious to preserve their material and cultural traditions, and wearing of these garments to festivals and deliberately preserved rituals, such as traditional weddings in parts of Slovenia for example. 'National' dress has also been promoted throughout the world to appeal to the tourist industry as forms of both material and cultural consumption, and performers such as dancers, or musicians on the 'world music' circuit often dress according to the expectations of their audiences. Scholars have recently been examining the evolution of localized dress forms in response to global pressures towards uniformity.

Nevertheless, while local, or 'ethnic', dress may be considered the opposite of international fashion, it is not necessarily as unchanging as once supposed; change and the incorporation of new materials and motifs is now considered to indicate a live and versatile culture. Yet the idea of 'ethnic' dress has also historically been appropriated by governments wishing to develop 'national' or 'folk' costumes for political reasons, as in 17th-century Russia where the wearing of European dress was punished. In contrast, governments have also prohibited 'national' dress in attempts to indicate their modernity. Peter the Great subsequently ordered the wearing of French fashions at the Russian court; Westernization and secularization of dress was one of the reforms introduced to Turkey by Mustafa Kemal Atatürk (1881–1938) in his reforms of the 1920s and 30s. There was a particular emphasis on headwear, with hats replacing the male fez and turban, and women's veils were abolished.

As the development of mass markets and faster communications were perceived as a threat to traditional and local ways of life including dress, there were efforts to describe and preserve national dress for both cultural and political reasons. In Meiji Japan traditional court dress was considered Chinese-inspired and effeminate and in 1870 was temporarily replaced by the compulsory wearing of European costume. Yet, within twenty years, a revival of nationalistic sentiment allowed the return of the kimono. Dress 'traditions' have also been artificially constructed, revived and conserved as with the development of a stylized 'Scottish' dress and the cult of tartan in 19th-century Scotland or the promotion of a peasant-like 'folk' costume in Nazi Germany, mythologizing both the role of women and the German past. In the present-day Himalayan kingdom of Bhutan, citizens are required to wear in public a national dress which was introduced in the 17th century, in order to preserve a sense of tradition and national identity in the face of globalizing pressures.

The growth of mass tourism has encouraged both the reinventions of traditional dress and non-Western fashion production systems. The tourist's search for local authenticity has led to both commercialization, stereotyping and pure invention, as in the case of *aloha* apparel in Hawai'i, which was developed by Chinese tailors using Japanese kimono fabrics in the 1920s and 30s. It has also, paradoxically, led to the fashionable rediscovery of traditional costume such as the sudden popularity of Indian folk dress among wealthy Delhi women in the late 20th century or the reworking of the traditional kaftan by contemporary Moroccan designers. Furthermore, in recent years a number of fashion entrepreneurs have played on cultural nostalgia by reappropriating and aggressively marketing 'traditional' forms of dress as global brands. The Shanghai Tang company's reinvention for a global market of the prerevolutionary Chinese *cheung sam* as a garment of ethnic chic, sold in appropriately retro-chic interiors vaguely evocative of old Shanghai, Burberry's classic British, or Ralph Lauren's classic American clothing are examples of this synthetic construction of authenticity.

During historical periods of colonial expansion, European dress, imbued with its own hierarchical codes, was presented by a self-appointed foreign elite as the norm to be emulated by the colonized, with particular emphasis on the covering of the naked body to indicate in material terms the arrival of civilization. In pre-independence India, during the period of the British Raj, dress codes were introduced by the British for civil servants and even the public appearance of the native princes. These were intended to indicate 'civilizing' influences and to maintain symbolic

social distance between rulers and ruled. Yet recent studies have shown the inadequacy of the binary model of Western/non-Western when clothing styles are examined in relation to lived cultures. In 19th-century Jamaica, for instance, women's dress was not indigenous but the product of borrowings from a wide variety of outside cultures; 'traditional' attire is often hybrid and sometimes recent. In addition a European-based form of global dress has developed, but often with its own local variation and sometimes connected to world fashion. In early-21st-century Tokyo, young men and women borrow essentially Western subcultural clothing vocabularies, using words such as 'punk', 'goth' or 'hip-hop', to create distinctively Japanese styles of dress.

Dress can also be a uniform, a potent signifier as well as a means of identification. Often survivals from long obsolete fashions, ceremonial dress and the ritualized uniform clothing of political, religious and military leaders indicate identity, power and rank, from Pope to acolyte, general to private soldier. As a form of functional clothing, a uniform can, alternatively, have the practical attributes of work or sports wear, or indicate social distinction – in the case of servants' dress, or visibility in the case of police, firefighters or other emergency services. A uniform can distinguish work from leisure or school from home; it may be an obligatory occupational marker, or, in the case of the business suit, tacitly provide a universally understood, transnational, dress code. In a broader sense of the word, uniform can be the expectation of cultural conventions of dress considered appropriate to status, occasion or gender. The gradual erosion of such conventions is epitomized by the evolution of blue jeans from work clothes to a global uniform promoted by international fashion brands. This apparent expression of personal consumption choices had a paradoxical parallel in Communist China where another kind of blue cotton uniform came to represent state control over individual clothing.

A surprising survival of ritual clothing that has become something of a global convention, the white wedding dress, evolved in a period of expanding affluence in Victorian Britain. This dramatic if impractical garment continues to be worn, often with increasing ritual extravagance, and often 'inappropriate' design, at odds with the virginal symbolism of its white fabric, perhaps as a symbolic bulwark against the growing number of marriage failures. It is also part of the costume of a ceremonial situation in which the defence of national traditions and the search for a formatted image of universal love can be played out together. In Japan, where Shinto or Buddhist wedding ceremonies, in full 'traditional' Japanese dress, are often accompanied by a Western, even Christian ceremony, the bride and groom wear (usually rented) conventional white wedding gown and morning suit.

Theories of fashion based on the idea that dress norms and fashion innovation either 'trickle down' from elite social groups or 'upwards' from the 'street', may need to be considered more laterally and cross-culturally at a historical moment when national boundaries and cultures have been significantly permeated by large-scale migration and diaspora. There is currently a tendency both to the homogenization of dress and also to a continual revitalization of clothing traditions as clothing codes are exchanged and renovated. The penetration of both French and British couture by Japanese fashion designers in the late 20th century arguably had a profound effect on the cut of clothes, for instance. At a more popular level, the close association of clothes and popular music such as Hip-Hop has created transnational constituencies or markets for associated youth wear. Thus dress is, as it always has been, functional, evocative, contentious, and a crucial and active part of cultural and economic life.

Sonia Ashmore

Bibliography
Breward C. 2003. *Fashion.* Oxford: Oxford University Press.
Eicher J. B. (ed.) 1995. *Dress and ethnicity: change across space and time.* Oxford: Berg.
Kuchler S. and Miller D. 2005. *Clothing as material culture.* Oxford: Berg.
Maynard M. 2004. *Dress and globalisation.* Manchester: Manchester University Press.
Niessen S., Leshkowich A. M. and Jones C. 2003. *Re-orienting fashion: the globalisation of Asian dress.* Oxford: Berg.
Tarlo E. 1996. *Clothing matters: dress and identity in colonial India.* London: Hurst.
Taylor L. 2002. *The study of dress history.* Manchester: Manchester University Press.

Related essays
1960s; beauty; civilizations; cosmetic surgery; femininity; jeans; love; modernity; music; nation and state; silk; sports gear and apparel; textiles; tourism; tropics; T-shirt; Westernization; world music

Drink

Drink is any ingested liquid – tea and coffee, wine and beer, spirits and soft drinks, water and fruit juices. Consumption of liquid is a basic need of all humans. The human body cannot function without replenishing fluids. It is this urgent necessity that gives drink a special status. Drink has the paradoxical quality of being both ordinary and special: a simple food item to be consumed with a meal, it is also widely used as a means of changing human mood or consciousness. The caffeine, alcohol, and sugar included in many drinks give them the quality of a recreational or medicinal drug. As a result, drink often has multiple meanings connected to life and death, health and pollution, purity and spirituality, conceptions of order and disorder. Drink choices typically reveal social distinctions of age, sex, status, culture and even occupation among humans.

Water

There is only one drink that is absolutely essential to life: water. While water exists in the natural environment in various states, it is a relatively fragile beverage, easily contaminated. It is unwieldy and heavy, not easily packed or transported. For these reasons, most societies, even if they did not grant open access to water, appear to have recognized a 'Right of Thirst'. This assumption of a 'Right of Thirst' resulted in two different visions of drinking water: as a public good provided and assured by the state and as a private good marketed commercially.

Since the 19th century, most nation states and their citizens have approached drinking water as simultaneously a public and private good. Pressures from urbanization and population growth, on the one hand, and new forms of agricultural and industrial demands, on the other, decreased the quality and quantity of available drinking water. By the early 19th century in Europe and North America, the contamination and odour of urban water led all but the very poor to search for alternatives, including beer or wine or private water delivery. Public health concerns with cholera outbreaks and other water-borne epidemics led many national governments to take over responsibility for water delivery in the late 19th century.

State interest in the management of drinking water did not eliminate private commerce in water. It was one thing to identify and eliminate pathogens in the water supply, it was a very different thing to alleviate public fear and deliver a beverage whose taste, smell, and appearance were palatable. Decentralized water sale and delivery continued to exist in most urban, industrialized centres. At the same time, there emerged a new trade in waters. Water was an element of health in most systems of medicine around the globe. In Europe, medical professionals believed in the health benefits of mineral waters from particular springs or sources. Therapeutic benefits were conveyed through the water, whether taken internally or externally, but results could only be achieved on-site. By the mid 19th century, educated European and American clients were taking advantage of new transport networks to travel for waters as part of therapeutic regimes. Saline waters were prescribed for their purgative effects; chalybeate waters containing iron were prescribed for their tonic and restorative properties; sulphur waters were prescribed for problems of the skin and complexion; still others were said to cure gout and rheumatism.

Advances in chemistry in the Atlantic world made it possible to 'reduce waters' and isolate their mixture of compounds. Many physicians resisted the implication of this new research: that these medicinal waters had qualities or a peculiar 'life' that could exist off-site. Entrepreneurs, however, embraced the new concept and began to bottle spring water to sell in pharmacies. Shifts in understanding about what constituted a contaminant and reliance on technology, as opposed to the senses, to define what was objectionable contributed to greater government oversight of these private water supplies by the turn of the century. Declaring the supply of spring water a 'public interest', the French government developed a system of legal permits for bottling natural mineral water. Vittel and Perrier were the first sanctioned suppliers of natural mineral water. Other countries in Europe as well as in North and South America quickly followed with their own oversight of private suppliers.

By the mid 20th century, annual global production climbed to several hundred million bottles. The revolution in the market, however, came in 1968 when Vittel introduced the first plastic bottle. Individuals could now take their own private water supply with them throughout their daily routine. New categories of bottled water, including spring water and specially formulated, 'enhanced' drinking water, began to attract a global consumer base of wealthy, educated consumers – much like the consumer base that made 'taking the waters' fashionable in the 19th century. The lure of water from sources believed to be far from urban contaminants remains strong. This preference for commercially bottled and marketed water has grown in the developed world where, ironically, the drinking water is clean, relatively inexpensive, and readily available.

Water as a private good, however, has not eliminated a transnational commitment to the 'Right of Thirst', particularly in developing nations where neither the quality nor quantity of clean drinking water can be assumed. As a result of urbanization, the number of communal water sources worldwide is decreasing. Concern over the poor state of water provisioning has led to the United Nations Committee on Economic, Social and Cultural Rights to formulate a modern version of the 'Right of Thirst' that seeks to create a human right to water that would entitle everyone to sufficient, safe, affordable water for personal and domestic use. Communities in the developing world have led these efforts, in part, because of a tendency in recent decades by government and private entrepreneurs to approach water as a purely economic resource. The United Nations efforts are a response to these concerns over whether purely private markets can adequately manage a shared, global resource.

Alcoholic beverages

Historically, the term 'drink' has been understood in the much narrower sense to mean alcoholic beverage. Beverage alcohol has been ingested in one form or another for much of recorded human history, offering an alternative to water. Only Pacific Islanders and some indigenous tribes of North America appear to have not produced naturally fermented alcoholic beverages until European exploration and colonization introduced 'drink'. Beverages containing ethanol – the drug substance at the base of all 'drink' – were widely available in much of the world prior to the age of European exploration in the

15th century. Given their antiquity and geographic distribution, it is perhaps not surprising to find a wide range of variation in behaviour and belief accompanying alcohol around the world.

All societies have developed some form of escape from the material and social difficulties of life. Drink, in the form of alcohol beverages, has often served that purpose. Regardless of geography or epoch, people appear to take pleasure in the sociability surrounding fermented drinks. It can form a part of rituals of reciprocity and social exchange. At other times, it offers relief from the monotony (and sometimes dangers) of water consumption. In extreme cases, drink has been used to release people from ordinary inhibitions, such as those that prevent acts of aggression or violence. Alcohol appears frequently, for example, in memoirs of soldiers or of those responsible for perpetrating genocide in the 20th century. Unlike water, alcoholic beverages have been more frequently used to earn wealth or display social prestige, French wines, such as champagne, eventually becoming the worldwide status symbol par excellence for much of the 20th century. Yet, drink can also be a central part of religious duty, far removed from market relations, sealing a covenant between god(s) and man.

Most societies make distinctions between 'good' alcoholic drinks and 'bad'. Alcoholic beverages have been promoted for therapeutic usages, particularly in the treatment of diseases of the digestive organs and the cardiovascular system. Some 'good' drinks are believed to serve as a conduit for access to a spiritual realm, others as a material manifestation of cultural superiority. With the rise of colonialism, the nation state, and global capital, 'good' and 'bad' beverages were increasingly defined in terms of what was 'traditional' and 'authentic' culturally and what was introduced from 'outside'. One writer in modern Buganda, Africa, for example, contrasts native banana-wine, which he sees as an unproblematic drink regardless of the frequency and quantity consumed, with dangerous foreign, distilled drinks, such as whisky.

Many of the world's alcoholic beverages are highly localized, dependent on the availability and abundance of a particular cereal, fruit, root, or tree sap. The vast majority of naturally fermented beverages have, historically, remained bound to their immediate production area. Mexican pulque, for example, is made from the sap of the maguey cactus. Viscous and slightly acidic, pulque, like many drinks made with fermentable saps and juices, is at best a regional beverage. Poor Mexicans commonly consumed pulque until the 1940s. Susceptible to spoilage and bound to a particular set of localized tastes, it is not easily marketable on a larger scale. Distilled beverages, in particular, retain this localized character and when exported have caused social and physical harm. These beverages offer little in the way of nutrients while at the same time deliver a high concentration of ethyl alcohol that is quickly absorbed into the blood stream. Widely expanding markets for these 'exotic' distilled beverages, such as rum and whisky, during European imperial expansion had sometimes devastating effects on aboriginal populations in America, Asia, Australia.

Beer is also a highly localized drink, brewed from whatever is found in great quantity – corn, rice, millet, sorghum, manioc, or wheat. Estimates from areas of West Africa in the late 20th century, for example, where the staple food was sorghum and domestic brewing thrived, suggested that half the annual grain consumption was in the form of beer. Those beers that have most successfully moved into markets beyond their local brewing area have been modelled on the pilsner lagers that revolutionized the brewing industry in the 19th century. Originating in Bohemia, Bavaria and the Baltic coast, these lighter, refreshing beers found mass markets with the ever growing working-class populations of industrial Europe and North America. One key to the eventual global success of the new beers was their longevity. English firms, catering to colonial markets, developed brews into a commodity that could withstand long ocean journeys with no climate control. The McEwan firm, for example, developed India Pale Ales, a warm maturation ale that was a success in colonial markets in the Pacific. By the mid 19th century, German immigrant brewers (Miller, Coors, Stroh, Schlitz, and Pabst) in the United States had similarly innovated with cold maturation lagers that would eventually become popular throughout the Americas where cold drinks were preferred. With the advent of commercial refrigeration and pasteurization, these products could survive long journeys and move beyond local and regional markets as well.

Throughout the late 19th and early 20th centuries, beers were marketed mainly to men as part of a fraternal culture of bars, cafes, and icehouses and as a wholesome means for enhancing strength. The Irish firm, Guinness, with a near-monopoly on the island, sought to expand export markets in the early 20th century through a worldwide marketing campaign that revolved around the phrase 'Guinness is Good for You'. The beverage was promoted as much as a health-giving, restorative beverage as it was a recreational drink. Health claims aside, beer was increasingly popular as a recreational drink, linked to a culture of organized and professional sports. The fact that it was a beer company that became the keeper of the compendium of sporting excellence with the launching of The Guinness Book of World Records in 1955 attests to this linkage. The book was originally issued as part of an advertising campaign, but quickly became a recognized global resource for recording and legitimizing records of achievements.

The trend in the 20th century was toward large-scale commercial breweries. From the 1950s, the global beer market was increasingly dominated by a number of beverage conglomerates. American and European firms tended to dominate. This meant that home brewing and domestic distilling worldwide slowly declined as large, corporate breweries at the international level lured customers away from home brew and shifted drinking tastes. The one exception to the American and European dominance on the global market is Singha from Thailand, which is a standard beverage on the menu of Asian restaurants. Today, the brewing and distilling industry is characterized by two main trends: first, at a global level, major mergers between large groups of breweries and, second, at a regional level, the revival of small and medium-sized breweries developing a variety of products whose characteristics are linked to local tastes and traditions. Known as 'microbreweries', these small-scale producers have found a niche primarily with affluent consumers.

Arguably the most transnational of drinks is wine. Historians have suggested that patterns of consumption and the subsequent spread of wine production were linked to the symbolic requirements of many religious cultures, which facilitated circulation of wine as a global commodity. Wine can be made by fermenting the juice of any fruit, but the most successfully globally marketed wine is based on grapes. Today those grapes are almost exclusively V.vinifera, a hybrid developed in France in the early 20th century and subsequently transplanted around the world. Wine and V.vinifera grape vines are cultivated and consumed in a variety of forms, from distilled alcohols, which are relatively uniform, to fermented drinks with remarkable variations.

Two central processes characterized the fortunes of viticulture and the wine trade in the 19th century. These were the spread of various fungal and insect parasites to Europe from North America, and the introduction and expansion of viticulture in new areas of the globe, most notably Australia and the Americas. By the beginning of the 20th century, viticulture and wine production had become truly global in scale. The industry was often plagued by crises of overproduction with short-term collapses in prices. A widening consumer base could not absorb the flow of wines from around the world. In an attempt to solidify their image as a quality producer and stem fraudulent practices at home and abroad, the French developed a system of legal classifications known as Appellation d'Origine Contrôlée (AOC) and other 'Old World' producers followed. While the worldwide demand for lower-priced country wines declined, wines that could benefit from the prestige of classification and demarcation increased their market share. Buyers of these wines tend to embrace nuances in the finished product that are said to be produced by the physical characteristics of the growing site and local production techniques (terroir).

Caffeinated beverages

Tea, coffee and chocolate were part of an early modern 'hot drink revolution' in Europe that had a global impact. All three have been, at one time or another ingested for their medicinal benefits, including as an early cure for venereal disease. Chinese medical manuals referenced tea as a cure for various inflammations, such as tumours and abscesses, and aliments of the bladder. Coffee was prescribed to lessen the desire for sleep and aid with digestion. Similarly, in more recent years, chocolate has been identified as a possible anti-depressant. Caffeine gives these beverages similar impacts on the body, including the potential of being habit-forming if not addictive.

Coffee is a global commodity and its importance to the world economy cannot be overstated. It is one of the most valuable primary products in world trade, in many years second only to petroleum in dollar value. Its cultivation, processing, trading, transportation, and marketing provide employment for 5 million people worldwide. Coffee is crucial to the economies and politics of 50 exporting countries – led by Brazil, Colombia, Indonesia, and the Ivory Coast. For these countries, exports of coffee account for a substantial part of their foreign exchange earnings (in some cases over 80 per cent). Prices remain relatively stable due to the London-based International Coffee Organization, which coordinates prices for exporting countries.

By the middle of the 18th century, the Middle East and Southeast Asia were the world's principal coffee-consuming regions. One hundred years later it had become the breakfast beverage of choice on the European Continent and increased demand led to the global expansion of coffee cultivation. Today, it is the North Americans who are the world's largest consumers of coffee while Latin America provides the bulk of the world's coffee supply, supplemented by African coffees from Côte d'Ivoire, Ethiopia, and Uganda. Seattle is the American capital of coffee, having given birth in the 1970s to a cafe or 'Latte' culture exported worldwide by Starbucks. This 'coffee culture' rests on a level of uniformity and a fast-food-style service. Yet, in those countries with great coffee traditions of their own, such as Italy, Germany, and Scandinavia, there has been a renewed interest in the pleasures of varieties of quality coffee. Specialty coffee beans, marketed much like wines, stress the commodities' geographic origins and qualities, such as aroma, body, richness. Marketing campaigns have made gourmet coffee a status symbol. It is now possible to find good coffee in every major city of the world, from London to Sydney to Tokyo.

Tea, too, has emerged as a global commodity. It may be the most culturally significant transnational beverage. It was in China that the plant emerged as a marketable commodity, and tea was largely traded in Asia until the first trade links with Europe were established in 1557 by the Portuguese. Great Britain was the last of the early modern maritime powers to break into the Chinese and East India trade routes. Britain, and eventually its colonies,

took to tea drinking. By the 18th century, tea was sold in specialized tea shops, such as Twinings in London, steadily supplied by the trade monopoly held by the British East India Company. Tea became a staple not only in England but also in its vast colonial empire. Tea trade was particularly strong in Britain's holdings in North America. The only way for colonists to buy tea was through the British East India Company, which delivered to ports in Boston, New York, and Philadelphia, future centres of American rebellion. The colonists ultimately rebelled against taxes such as the one on tea. Tea cultivation in India flourished under British rule in the 19th century when the great English tea-marketing companies were founded and production mechanized. British rule would turn India into a major global supplier of tea. Today India is listed as the world's leading producer, well ahead of China.

By 1850, tea had become a global commodity. Each year ships would race from China and India, from Ceylon and Indonesia to ports around the globe for auction. Throughout the British and former British colonies, tea took on a new significance as part of the backlash against the copious amounts of alcohol available on the market and what was perceived as an increase in drunken and disorderly carousing by professed Christians and the 'natives' whom they ruled over. Members of temperance societies promoted tea or 'teetotaling' as an alternative to strong drink, particularly the spread of distilled beverages. By the end of the 19th century, tea was linked with healthy living.

The health message linked with tea became more pronounced in the 20th century. The battle for market share between huge European and American manufactures, such as Lipton and Twinings, led to investment in new research on the benefits of tea consumption. Recent findings suggests that tea may prove beneficial in combatting heart disease and warding off certain cancers. To satisfy the worldwide demand for teas as well as a taste for stronger, more pungent beverages, plantations were established in parts of Africa. Large tea plantations can be found in Natal, then Nyasaland (now Malawi), and finally in Kenya, which today supplies approximately 50 per cent of the British market. The teabag, introduced outside of North America in the 1960s, has catered to a worldwide desire for convenience and uniformity. Made up mainly of black tea, these are the preferred brew worldwide. In recent decades, however, green tea has begun to gain market share because many consumers, particularly in the wealthy industrial nations, regard it as healthier. With the development of smaller specialty tea companies, many selling direct to retailers or over the Internet, consumers have unprecedented access to a wide range of teas from around the world.

Soft drink

There has been a phenomenal rise in the number of manufactured 'soft' drinks consumed around the globe in the last thirty years. Any drink that is not hard liquor can be considered a soft drink although in contemporary usage we tend to use the term to refer to a sweet, carbonated beverage. Many commercial sugar-based beverages were first developed around the mid to late 19th century although weak ales and fruit-flavoured drinks (lemonades) were available almost a century earlier. If the popularization of coffee and tea constituted a hot-beverages revolution, one can talk today of a cold-drinks revolution.

Consumption of soft drinks emerged from the general concern with health that also made mineral and sparkling water popular. Originally flavours were added to naturally sparkling water and sold in pharmacies. Eventually, manufacturers perfected the technique of infusing plain water with carbonic gas to mimic sparkling water. Tonics were then made with a plethora of ingredients, including the African kola nut. Kola tonics along with coca wines were sold as nerve stimulants in both Europe and the United States at the end of the 19th century. These medicinal tonics were prescribed mainly to a wealthy clientele and some, such as Vin Mariani, became widely prescribed throughout the Atlantic world.

The variety of soft drinks, as both tonics and refreshments, kept pace with European maritime expansion and the growth of capitalist markets. Citrus juices, originally used by sailors to prevent scurvy on long sea voyages, became increasingly important ingredients in soft-drink manufacturing. Ginger beers and ginger ales as well as a variety of fruit ciders emerged from global exchanges of flora. While soft drinks have diverse origins, it was American manufacturers who turned soft-drink consumption into a worldwide

phenomenon. Many of the early American soft drinks were sold for medicinal purposes.

It was not until the 1960s and the initial mass popularity of Coca-Cola that cold, non-alcoholic bottled drinks began to constitute a substantial proportion of the total number of drinks consumed worldwide. The cold-beverage revolution, however, was not the exclusive purview of Americans. Most countries in Europe and North America with an interest in overseas trade expanded their soft-drink industry in the 20th century. While many European companies shipped essentials supplies from the parent country, US soft-drink manufacturers tended to work with merchants who were already involved in trade and might take up the task of mixing and local bottling. Although international brands, such as Coca-Cola and Canada Dry, took over a substantial share of the market, their savvy, expensive marketing campaigns could serve to stimulate demand and encourage the growth of a market for local soft drinks, particularly with young people. In recent decades, many soft drinks have been promoted as part of a healthy diet, returning the soft-drink industry back to its origins as provider of a health tonic. Low-calorie soft drinks and vitamin-infused sports drinks, promoted as part of a health-conscious lifestyle, have revived dormant markets and created new ones. Soft drinks are now said to be one of the most widely sold manufactured products in the world.

Kolleen Guy

Bibliography

Barrows S. and Room R. (eds) 1991. *Drinking: behavior and belief in modern history.* Berkeley: University of California Press.

Evans J. C. 1992. *Tea in China: the history of China's national drink.* New York: Greenwood.

Goubert J.-P. 1988. *The conquest of water: the advent of health in the industrial age* (trans. Wilson A.). Oxford: Polity.

Marshall M. (ed.) 1979. *Beliefs, behaviors & alcoholic beverages: a cross-cultural survey.* Ann Arbor: University of Michigan Press.

Salzman J. 2006. 'Thirst: a short history of drinking water', *Yale Journal of Law & the Humanities*, 17, 3, 94–121.

Unwin T. 1991. *Wine and the vine: an historical geography of viticulture and the wine trade.* London: Routledge.

Drugs (illicit)

The production, distribution and consumption of drugs, defined as cultivated or man-made substances purporting to bring about alterations in the mental and physical state of the individual, are timeless activities. Such activities are most infamously associated with such drugs as cannabis, cocaine and heroin. However, a range of other cultivated crops, like coffee and tobacco, though often socially perceived as more benign, are broadly comparable. The other main type of drug group, mass-produced psychotropic drugs, is much younger, being only around four decades old in its mass form. It is only over the last century that systematic attempts have been made to introduce an international regime restricting the availability of such substances. In spite of these considerable efforts, the illicit drugs trade is estimated to be worth anywhere between US$50 billion and US$500 billion per year.

Man's temptation to consume toxins is as old as mankind itself. It is therefore no surprise to learn that the cultivation of narcotic drugs is a practice thousands of years old. Opium was traditionally grown in areas like south and west Asia, and to a lesser extent in the Balkans. The coca plant was closely identified with the Andean countries of Bolivia and Peru. The production of qat (a.k.a. khat) was associated with southern Arabia, notably Yemen, and the Horn of Africa. Cannabis and its associated products, like hashish and marijuana, were the most geographically diverse of the main cultivated drugs in their origins, being produced in such disparate places as Afghanistan, Colombia, Lebanon and Morocco. For most of their history, such drugs were consumed in their raw or near raw state, with the refining of narcotics simple in process, and confined to such activities as the lancing of opium poppies or the drying and rolling of hashish and marijuana. Such drugs were then consumed, mostly through smoking or ingestion, for a wide range of purposes, including recreational, medicinal and ritualistic use.

As the properties of such drugs became better known, a thriving trade built up. The centres of Western trading powers grew to know such narcotics, and used them for similar purposes as those in the producing areas. The opium derivative of laudanum became extensively used as a legally available analgesic in places like 19th-century Europe. The hallucinogenic properties of opium were celebrated through the creative art of the likes of the poet Samuel Taylor Coleridge. Drugs and trade became an instrument of state interest, power and subjugation, notably in the triangular relationship between Britain, China and India in the 19th century. Britain fought two wars with the waning Chinese state, popularly referred to as the first and second 'Opium Wars', over the issue of access to Chinese markets for opium grown in India and controlled by Britain.

Scientific and medical innovation in Western Europe in the last quarter of the 19th century led to a more sophisticated approach to drugs production. The natural properties of imported drugs could be harnessed in a way that maximized the effect of their transformative nature. It was during this time that such drugs as cocaine and heroin emerged. The quantitative abuse of drugs, notably in China, and the qualitative impact of new drugs, dovetailing with the temperance values of some late-century social reformers, like Gladstone, helped to ignite a movement for the formal restriction of such products. In the 1890s and 1910s, the mature states of Western Europe adopted procedures for restricted, professional-based access to the new drugs of the day, now redefined in socially acceptable terms as pharmaceutical products. The domestic regulation of the sector had been added to the rapidly growing list of functional activities that states properly carry out.

It was not long before this trend towards internal, state-based regulation and proscription became replicated at the international level. The Ten Year Agreement of 1907, which restricted the flow of Indian opiates to China, the first of its kind, became an influential model for the rest of the century. It was arguably the emergence of the US, with its broader embrace of prohibition, as a powerful advocate for the proscription of drugs that was to transform the international atmosphere. The US used the embryonic multilateralism of early-20th-century diplomacy to provide an impetus for growing regime building and norm diffusion on drugs. This effort first worked in an ad hoc fashion, spawning in quick succession the 1909 Shanghai Opium Commission, the first international meeting to address drugs problems, and the 1911/12 Hague Opium Conference. By the 1920s the US had set about establishing a more systematized approach to the control of drugs on the international stage. With the 1931 Convention for Limiting the Manufacture and Regulating the Distribution of Narcotic Drugs, this aim had been realized.

The next fifty years would see the extension and more rigorous application of this newly created international anti-drugs regime. Further international conventions consolidated the existing body of international law (1961), and extended it to include psychotropic substances (1971) and illicit trafficking (1988). The international supervisory machinery for the scrutiny and regulation of drugs production, which emerged in the 1920s, was eventually consolidated into the International Narcotics Control Board, which remains in place today. During this regime-building process, the reservations and vested interests of a dozen or so independent, producer states, ranging from Bolivia through Iran to Thailand, were swept aside. Not all narcotics have been brought within the remit of such international norms, however. Though debilitating in its short-term effects, and detrimental to the development of a modern economy, the consumption of qat in Yemen has grown to become a mass-consumption, national pastime, beloved of virtually Yemen's entire social hierarchy. This activity has not been successfully interfered with, arguably because of its geographical limitations, far away from the advanced, industrialized countries, from which global norms emerge in codified form.

In spite of or perhaps because of these extensive efforts to build international norms and practical machinery to restrict the consumption of now illicit drugs, the trade in such substances continued to grow, owing to a combination of innovation in transportation, the emergence of iconoclastic youth cultures and simple economics. The advent of motorized freight transport and later intercontinental aircraft travel promoted the mass movement of goods, of which drugs was one among many.

The newly established illicit status of a range of drugs increasingly drew the interest of organized criminal activity, conscious of the high margins that could be garnered from the production, trafficking and distribution of such substances. For example, criminal networks in Turkey, Lebanon, Italy and France colluded during the 1960s to produce refined heroin from opium poppy grown in Turkey. This criminal nexus became immortalized in the movie, The French Connection, released in 1971.

It was during the 1960s and the early 1970s that a mass consumer market began to emerge for highly addictive substances like heroin. Pull as well as push factors were responsible for this development. A large and persistent heroin market based on the intravenous consumption of the drug grew quickly in parts of the eastern seaboard of the US, centred on New York. This trend of hard-drug abuse, with a short lead time, was subsequently witnessed in Western Europe, notably Britain, in the 1970s and 1980s, and in the Russian Federation in the 1990s. Hard drugs increasingly went hand in hand with social status. While cocaine continues to be regarded as a drug of affluence, heroin abuse has increasingly been associated with working-class 'sink' estates, whether in Glasgow or south Tehran. Criminal activity to fund heroin dependence is perceived to be responsible for more than half of the crimes committed in contemporary Britain. Significant health problems have emerged, both because of the unregulated adulteration of the raw drug, and the secondary effects of shared syringes and the unsanitary conditions in which drugs are consumed. Persistent intravenous drug use has become associated with such serious conditions as human immunodeficiency virus (HIV) and hepatitis B.

Richard Nixon, elected president of the US in 1969, made drugs one of the top priorities of his newly installed administration. The precedent of a state-led war against drugs, with foreign policy ramifications, had been established. A more explicit version of this strategy would be adopted under the Clinton and two Bush presidencies in the 1990s and 2000s. A congressional certification process was introduced according to which US foreign relations with key countries was indexed to their policies and performance on the drugs issue. Illicit drugs became a privileged functional area of federal policy in the US, with a dedicated and well resourced law enforcement arm, the Drugs Enforcement Agency, a so-called 'drugs czar' to direct policy, and the adoption of battlefield jargon in the pursuit of 'a war against drugs', both at home and abroad. This war acquired a de facto operationalization in 'Plan Colombia', aimed at rooting out that country's cocaine drugs networks, and then literally a fully fledged war in Afghanistan since 2001, which was in large part about preventing opiate production.

The surging expansion of the international drugs market also embraced psychotropic drugs. Popularized through the hippy culture of the 1960s, which regarded Lysergic acid diethylamide (LSD) as a medium to a higher state of consciousness, amphetamines became the synthetic drug of choice in the 1970s and 1980s. However, it has only been over the last two decades that a mass market in synthetics has emerged through the advent of rave drugs like 'ecstasy'. Manufactured in liberal-regime states like Holland, and freely available throughout Western Europe, ecstasy is no longer a marginal drug, but one which has become a routinized part of the all-night club scene. Such clubbing drugs have spread to the islands of Western youth culture around the world, from Turkey's Aegean resort towns to the beaches of Thailand and Bali, and are increasingly being embraced by usually wealthy, indigenous, Westernized youth in such places.

As the drugs 'problem' has persisted and indeed grown more extensive, so attitudes towards it have been re-examined. The supply-side preoccupation of states, that dominated the period between the 1920s and the 1980s, and which put a premium on law-enforcement-related responses, has softened. The UN General Assembly Special Session (UNGASS) on illicit drugs in June 1998 was a reflection of the evolution of thinking. The meeting placed an unprecedented emphasis on demand-side related issues, like public education, the health-related consequences of hard-drug abuse and the need to take detoxification and rehabilitation seriously by making appropriate resources available. Medium- and long-term targets were introduced within which to address and to try to reduce long-term drug abuse, and the UN membership formally signed up to the policy.

The involvement of many states in UNGASS was nominal, either because they are not perceived to have a serious domestic problem, or because they do not have the state capacity effectively to address the issue. Moreover, it is doubtful if, in spite of this policy recalibration, resources are being shared equitably between the supply and demand sides of the strategy. What is even more clear is that the radical end of the demand-side lobby has failed to win the debate over more controversial issues, such as those bundled together under the phrase 'harm reduction'. This approach seeks to contain the effects of the abuse through a range of pragmatic responses. These stretch from pharmacologists checking the content of 'ecstasy' pills for clubbers, through to the provision of a free needle exchange and so-called 'shooting galleries', where intravenous users can inject drugs in safe and secure surroundings. Such practical responses have been introduced in Holland and Switzerland respectively, while other countries, notably Sweden, remain implacably opposed to such steps. By and large the US too, as the single most important driver of policy, remains hostile to any moves that may be perceived as condoning the mass consumption of illicit substances.

Philip Robins

Bibliography

Courtwright D. T. 2001. *Forces of habit: drugs and the making of the modern world.* Cambridge, MA: Harvard University Press.

Davenport-Hines R. 2001. *The pursuit of oblivion: a global history of narcotics, 1500–2000.* London: Weidenfeld & Nicolson.

Goodman J., Lovejoy P. E. and Sherratt A. 1995. *Consuming habits: drugs in history and anthropology.* London: Routledge.

McAllister W. B. 2000. *Drug diplomacy in the twentieth century.* London: Routledge.

Musto D. F. 1999. *The American disease: origins of narcotic control.* Oxford and New York: Oxford University Press.

Related essays

1960s; crime; health policy; intergovernmental organizations; legal order; temperance; United Nations system

Drugs (medical)

The Industrial Revolution, and the growing prosperity that followed, created vast markets for medicines in Europe and North America. This, and the scientific knowledge and technical capabilities developed there, turned the West into a hub of drug discovery.

Although the developing world has continued to provide it with sources of material and inspiration for drugs, the so-called 'diseases of civilization' have become the main focus of drug research and development, while those affecting poorer countries have suffered from relative neglect.

Medicinal plants have always played a part in the treatment of disease, but it was only at the beginning of the 19th century that the first active principle was extracted from a plant. It was the narcotic principle of opium, extracted from the Chinese poppy, which is alkaline and forms salts with acids. It was later named 'morphine'. The isolation and identification of other plant alkaloids, many of them from tropical regions of the European empires, followed. These included emetine from ipecacuanha root for dysentery, and quinine from cinchona bark for malaria. The presence of malaria in Southern Europe as well as in the tropics led pharmaceutical businesses to begin the large-scale processing of cinchona bark and other plants. Not only did they manufacture the drugs, but they also developed the chemical expertise necessary for selecting suitable material. Demand for quinine was high, and supplies difficult to obtain, therefore attempts were made to synthesize it. It was one such attempt, by the British chemist William Perkin, which led to the first artificial dye, mauveine, and to the synthetic dyestuffs industry. Because of favourable economic and political conditions, it reached considerable size in Germany.

Efforts were also made to prevent diseases using vaccination. Louis Pasteur's demonstration on a young Alsatian boy, who had been bitten by a rabid dog, and was saved by his new vaccine, caused a sensation. He therefore obtained funds from an international public subscription to create an institute in Paris that was named after him. The Pasteur Institute was founded in 1888, and inspired other medical research institutions, for instance Robert Koch's Institute for Infectious Diseases in Berlin, and the Lister Institute in London. The discovery of diphtheria antitoxin by Emil von Behring and his Japanese colleague Kitasato Shibasaburō at the Koch Institute in 1891 stimulated pharmaceutical firms into producing vaccines and antitoxins. Many of these firms also became involved in the manufacture of other biological remedies, such as organ and glandular extracts. However,

chemotherapy, rather than biotherapy, would become the dominant approach to therapy in the 20th century. The father of chemotherapy was Paul Ehrlich, one of Koch's former assistants, who developed Salvarsan, a 'magic bullet' capable of attacking the micro-organism responsible for syphilis without killing its human host. Shortly after its discovery, the First World War interrupted supplies of German imported drugs, justifying the abolition of German patent rights, and encouraging the production of synthetic drugs in countries at war with Germany.

However, other than a few successes against tropical diseases caused by protozoa, for instance Plasmaquin and Atebrin against malaria, in the interwar period chemotherapy appeared to fail its early promise. Nevertheless, there were important achievements in replacement therapy, against deficiency diseases caused by a lack of vitamins or hormones. In this area, the most significant developments occurred in Britain and North America. The word 'vitamin' was coined by a Polish chemist, Casimir Funk, when he was a guest worker at the Lister Institute in 1912. The Institute later became involved in a study of rickets in postwar, famine-stricken Vienna, which led to the identification of the antirachitic factor, vitamin D. By the 1930s most of the other vitamins had been isolated, their structures worked out, and their chemical synthesis realized. In the field of hormones, important milestones included the isolation of the active principle of the thyroid gland by E. C. Kendall at the Mayo Clinic in Rochester, Minnesota, in 1919; the extraction of the pancreatic hormone insulin, by F. Banting, J. J. R. Macleod, C. Best and J. B. Collip at the University of Toronto in 1922; and the characterization of steroid hormones by various researchers in the 1920s and 1930s.

Meanwhile, the search for chemical agents to treat bacterial infections continued, especially at Bayer, now part of the German chemical group IG Farben, where it was modelled on Ehrlich's earlier work. In 1932, Bayer's director of research in experimental pathology, Gerhard Domagk, carried out experiments in mice infected with streptococci using a red dye, Prontosil rubrum. He found that the animals treated with the compound survived, whilst the controls died. By 1935, clinical trials were under way, and the results of Domagk's experiments were published. The study of Prontosil was taken up by numerous centres, including the Pasteur Institute. There, Ernest Fourneau's team showed that Prontosil was broken down in the body, and that its active principle was, in fact, the colourless compound sulphanilamide. Because it had been known for a long time, it could not be patented. Hence other drugs, all based on the sulphanilamide molecule, soon followed. Septoplix was launched in 1936 by Rhône-Poulenc, which had a collaborative arrangement with Fourneau. M&B 693, which became famous for curing Winston Churchill from pneumonia during the Second World War, was developed in 1937 by the British subsidiary of Rhône-Poulenc, May & Baker.

At the start of World War 2, the production of sulpha-drugs was therefore well under way outside Germany. Nevertheless, as had been the case in the Great War, supplies of other German synthetic drugs, including Plasmaquin and Atebrin, were once again interrupted. When the conflict extended from Europe to the Far East, this might have created difficulties for the Allies. However, projects to synthesize novel anti-malarials had begun even before the Japanese attack on Pearl Harbor in December 1941. Cooperative research programmes were initiated in order to pool British and American scientific knowledge and technical expertise. Because of a rumour that adrenal cortical extracts were being administered to German aircraft pilots to enable them to fly at high altitudes, they included compound E (later known as cortisone), as well as anti-malarials. By 1942, the programme to produce penicillin in large quantities for the treatment of war wounds, and to find a synthetic route to its manufacture, dominated the Allies' cooperative ventures in pharmaceuticals.

The impact of penicillin on drug discovery in the second half of the 20th century was immense. The penicillin industry that emerged from the war included newcomers from the fermentation industries, whose expertise contributed to the growth of the new biotechnology in the 1970s, and from countries like Japan. Penicillin was soon followed by streptomycin, the first effective chemotherapeutic treatment for tuberculosis, and by other antibiotics. They appeared to spell the end of infectious diseases. Together with the great vaccination campaigns, they help to explain the optimism and faith in modern medicine that reigned in this period. At the same time, they put pressure on the new national health services, leading to an increase in public expectations, and to spiralling drugs bills.

The American pharmaceutical sector, and to some degree its British counterpart, had emerged victorious from the war. In contrast, the German drug industry had been beaten. The links between German industry and Hitler's regime led to the dismantling of IG Farben. German biologists, tainted by their association with eugenics, were for a time excluded from the international scientific community. This compounded the effects of emigration of Jewish scientists in the 1930s, and later led to a need for researchers as well as companies to catch up with developments abroad.

The period following the Second World War saw an explosion in the numbers of new drugs being developed and marketed. Some of them had their origins in wartime projects, but many others were the product of increased investments in pharmaceutical and biomedical research, and of the mass market for drugs created by national health services. They have extended across all therapeutic classes, from anti-inflammatories, to drugs for heart disease and cancer. Following the discovery in the early 1950s of sources of steroids in plants such as the Mexican wild yam, of therapeutic properties in Rauwolfia serpentina (Indian snakeroot: for hypertension), and Catharanthus rosea (Madagascar periwinkle: for leukaemias and lymphomas), there was also renewed interest in plants as potential sources of drugs.

However, by 1975, the pace of innovation had begun to slacken. The new biotechnology has benefited from this, tapping into public anxieties about the end of the 'age of optimism'. However, the extent to which it has fulfilled its early promise has been questioned. Hence, in the last decades of the 20th century, the disillusion with modern medicine has created a growing interest in non-Western medical traditions (such as Chinese and Indian medicine). Coupled with the expansion of the generic drugs industry, this may alter the balance between the developed and the developing world, not only in terms of drug discovery, but also in terms of the diseases being targeted. However, it is unlikely that this will happen without intervention from the governments concerned, for the history of drug discovery in the 20th century is also one of growing interdependence between the industry and the state.

Viviane Quirke

Bibliography

Le Fanu J. 2000. *The rise and fall of modern medicine*. London: Abacus.

Liebenau J., Higby G.J. and Stroud E.C. (eds) 1990. *Pill peddlers: essays on the history of the pharmaceutical industry*. Madison: American Institute of the History of Pharmacy.

Quirke V. 2008. *Collaboration in the pharmaceutical industry: changing relationships in Britain and France, ca 1935–1965*. London and New York: Routledge.

Sneader W. 1985. *Drug discovery: the evolution of modern medicines*. Chichester: John Wiley.

Weatherall M. 1990. *In search of a cure: a history of pharmaceutical discovery*. Oxford: Oxford University Press.

Related essays

Acquired Immunodeficiency Syndrome (AIDS); Chinese medicine; counterfeit goods; diet and nutrition; drugs (illicit); epidemics; germs; indigenous knowledges; League of Nations Health Organization; life and physical sciences; medicine; indigenous networks; scientific expeditions; sexology; tropics; vaccination; war

E

Ecology

Ecology originates from the Greek words *oikos*, meaning house or habitat and *logos*, meaning discourse. The term was first used by the German biologist Ernst Haeckel in 1866. Haeckel defined ecology as an economy of nature: the study of all relationships of the animal with its inorganic and organic environment.

Ecology is used widely, and in many different circumstances, making the term difficult to define. Haeckel's definition is one of many accepted definitions for ecology. Sir Hans Krebs defines ecology as the study of relationships of organisms with their environment, or the study of interactions that determine the distribution and abundance of organisms. Paul Duvigneaud defines ecology as the science of relationships between living things and their environment, or a science of complex, functional biological systems called ecosystems. According to Robert Barbault, ecology is the study of ecosystems opening into a wide field, ranging from physiology to biogeography.

Ecology is a science which uses elements from other natural sciences to describe the basic functioning of the natural world. From biology, ecology takes the study of nature and the living cover of the earth including plants, animals, and bacteria which are organized by laws. From physics, ecology borrows systems theory, and from chemistry, ecology looks at the reactions which control the cycling of elements in the biosphere. Ecology's use of elements of many different sciences makes it an effective discipline of study for management of natural resources.

Ecology began and evolved concurrently but independently in several countries. The unique environments within these countries helped focus their ecological development. An history of ecology dates back to the earliest developments of ecological theory in the mid-1800s. Development of ecology and the ecosystems concept stems from the natural sciences in the 18th and 19th centuries. Scientists in different regions of the world worked separately to build ecological theory. Ecology did not take on a transnational theme until the environmental crises of the 1960s forced scientists and society alike to realize the importance of collaboration in solving pressing environmental concerns facing the world today.

From the early to mid-1900s two groups of botanists studied the ecology of plant communities from different viewpoints. Europeans studied the composition, structure, and distribution of plant communities. At the same time, Americans studied succession, or the development of plant communities. Both plant and animal ecology developed separately between America and Europe until American biologists demonstrated the interrelation of animal and plant communities as a biotic whole.

Breakthroughs in ecological theory occurred as scientists laboured independently to create a theoretical framework for ecology separate from the other natural sciences. In 1920, August Thienemann, a German freshwater biologist, introduced the concept of trophic or feeding levels. According to Thienemann, food's energy is transferred through a series of organisms from producers up to several levels of consumers. Also during the 1920s American A. J. Lotka, and Italian V. Volterra created mathematical foundations for population studies. These studies led to experiments on the interactions of predators and prey, competition between species, and population regulation. Lotka in 1925, and Volterra in 1926, simultaneously but independently proposed a predator-prey model, which consists of a pair of equations used to describe the interactions of two species: one a predator and the other its prey. Today, the model is known as the Lotka-Volterra model, and continues to be the basis of many models used to analyse population dynamics. C. E. Elton, an English animal ecologist, further developed Thienemann's concept of trophic levels in 1927. Elton came up with the concept of ecological niches, which describe organisms' habitats. By the 1930s, ecology became more widely used by scientists in England and the United States. During this decade, Americans E. Birge and C. Juday developed the concept of primary production, or the rate at which food energy is generated, or fixed, by photosynthesis. In 1934, G. F. Gause, a Russian scientist, presented the theory of competitive exclusion, which declares that no two species can inhabit the same niche in any single community. Gause tested competitive exclusion in the lab in a test-tube environment containing yeast cells and protozoa. R. L. Lindeman of the United States developed the trophic-dynamic concept of ecology in 1942. Lindeman's concept describes the flow of energy through an ecosystem.

The trophic-dynamic ecosystem marks the arrival of modern ecology. Modern ecology uses the ecosystem as a conceptual base. An ecosystem is a functional unit containing interacting organisms and all parts of the environment in a given area. The trophic-dynamic concept of ecosystem refers to the flow of energy through the system using trophic or feeding levels which transfer the energy from food through organisms. Ecosystems contain both living or biotic and non-living or abiotic components through which nutrients and energy flow. The ecosystem concept combines plant and animal ecology with population dynamics, behaviour, and evolution.

Ecology's progression as a science was temporarily stalled in the 1940s by World War 2. The war not only halted ecology's progress, but also led to the loss of trained professionals, laboratories, and equipment. After the war, the ecological sciences were set aside as countries struggled with more pressing societal needs. Coordinated, transnational acquisition of ecological theory did not begin until the 1960s.

Ecology's acceptance into mainstream science and society came during the environmental crises of the 1960s. Previously, the ecological sciences were concerned with the interactions between organisms and the terrestrial or marine environment. Limited attention was given to interactions of the planetary environment with the biosphere. Ecology in the 1960s began to stress these interactions. For example, ecologists discussed the close relationship between climate and life on earth. At this time, the idea emerged that ecology heralded a view of nature that countered cultural and economic norms accepted by Western societies. Ecology held that human civilizations, especially technologically advanced civilizations, fell outside of the limitations and laws of nature.

Environmental crises leading to widespread recognition of ecology occurred on an international scale. Academic studies warning of the consequences resulting from violations of natural limits were accompanied by a series of environmental disasters. In 1966, a pit-heap collapsed in Aberfan, South Wales leaving 144 dead and reminding people of the hazards of abandoned land and pollution. In 1967 the oil tanker, *Torrey Canyon*, spilled 875,000 barrels of crude oil off the southwest coast of England. The blowout on a Union Oil Company platform off of the coast of Santa Barbara, California allowed 200,000 gallons of crude oil to rise to the surface of the ocean in 1969. Other events occurring in nations around the world added momentum to an increasing awareness of ecology for management of the earth's natural resources.

The world responded to these crises through efforts embodied in international conferences and organizations. As the international community realized the consequences of environmental problems facing the globe, nations began to work together to develop solutions. The UNESCO Conference on Use and Conservation of the Biosphere in 1968 embodies one step to solve these problems. The conference concluded that action must be taken immediately to prevent irreversible environmental deterioration on a global scale. Since the conference, scientists have worked to better understand the consequence of human impact on the global ecosystem.

By the 1960s and 1970s, several countries established national ecological societies to discuss important ecological questions and support ecological research. In 1967, the International Association for Ecology (INTECOL) was established to address important ecological questions on a global scale. INTECOL's first International Conference of Ecology took place in The Hague in 1974. The conference was a success. Today INTECOL is known for its conferences, and many national ecological societies are highly supportive of INTECOL. In recent years conferences have been organized in conjunction with the national society of the host country.

Various ecological non-profit organizations have emerged on the international scene within the past few decades as well. For example, The Society for Ecological Restoration (SER) International was founded in 1987, with a mission to promote ecological restoration in order to sustain the diversity of life on Earth and re-establish an ecologically healthy relationship between nature and culture. SER has members in 37 countries working to achieve its mission. Members communicate with one another through conferences, journals, restoration networks, websites, newsletters, and e-bulletins, which enhance communication and exchange of information among member countries.

Ecology has become part of the international agenda in a number of ways. In 2001, UN secretary-general Kofi Annan ordered the start of the Millennium Ecosystem

Assessment in response to growing human demand on ecosystems around the world. The Millennium Ecosystem Assessment was created to address a gap in understanding of issues like species extinction, climate change, and pollution. The results of the assessment were supposed to help decision makers by providing scientific information discussing the consequences of ecosystem change for the population's health as well as options for responding to ecosystem changes. The report, which contained the work of nearly 1,400 experts from 95 countries, came out in 2005. The assessment found that human activities are degrading 60 per cent of the planet's ecosystem. The Millennium Ecosystem Assessment provides a baseline for society to measure the successes and failures of future policies and actions.

Ecology became an adjunct of the environmental movement. The subject now symbolizes both a scientific discipline and an ethic or responsibility to the Earth.

The phrase 'age of ecology' emerged on the first Earth Day in 1970. The age of ecology represents hope that the ecological sciences will be able to save the planet. Ecology, however, has not fulfilled the hopes of many. The ecological sciences could not find a clear, convincing standard in nature to appease the public. Instead, the concept broke down into many subfields. Ecology has fragmented into the work of ecosystematists, populationists, biospherians, theoretical modellers, forest and range managers, agroecologists, toxicologists, limnologists, and biogeographers. The subfields of ecology pinpoint different issues as the greatest threat to the Earth. Populationists, for example, insist that the greatest threat to the Earth is human fertility. The diversity of the ecology movement is not surprising due to the scale of ecological problems facing human society today.

Claire B. Pitner

Bibliography

'About SER', Society for Ecological Restoration International [online]. Available: www.ser.org/about.asp, accessed 22 June 2006.

'Change in the global ecology and the future of development', The America's Intelligence Wire, Jakarta [online]. Available: www. thejakartapost.com, accessed 15 May 2006.

'Ecosystem assessment provides baseline', Millennium Ecosystem Assessment [online].

Available: www.millenniumassessment.org/en/Article.aspx?id=60, accessed 15 May 2006.

Faurie C., Ferra C., Médori P. and Dévaux J. 2001. Ecology: science and practice. Paris: Balkema.

Kormondy E. J. and McCormick J. F. (eds) 1981. Handbook of contemporary developments in world ecology. Westport: Greenwood.

Lévêque C. 2003. Ecology: from ecosystem to biosphere. Enfield, NH and Plymouth: Science Publishers.

'Overview', The International Association for Ecology [online]. Available: www.intecol. net/about/sub_012.html, accessed 22 June 2006.

Roussopoulos D. 1993. Political ecology: beyond environmentalism. Montréal: Black Rose.

Related essays

acclimatization; air pollution; biodiversity; climate change; conservation and preservation; environmental diplomacy; environmentalism; forests; indigenous knowledges; intellectual elites; intergovernmental organizations; international non-governmental organizations (INGOs); life and physical sciences; outer space; population; sustainable development; zero growth

Economic Commission for Latin America and the Caribbean (ECLAC)

ECLAC is an organization for regional cooperation, one of several created by the United Nations Economic and Social Council (ECOSOC). Originating in 1948 as the UN Economic Commission for Latin America (ECLA), ECLAC added 'the Caribbean' to its purview in 1984. Since its inception, the United Nations has taken the position that regional economic cooperation is the preferred approach to economic development, as contrasted to reliance on exclusive economic blocs. Indeed, the emergence of exclusive economic blocs was seen as one of the causes of World War 2 and regional economic cooperation a prescription for postwar economic recovery. It was under these circumstances that ECLA, the predecessor to ECLAC, was founded in 1948 as a United Nations economic commission comparable in function to the Economic Commission for Europe (ECE) and the Economic Commission for Africa (ECA). ECLA's original purview included not only Latin American countries but also the United States, Canada and several European countries such as France, Portugal, the Netherlands, Spain, and the United Kingdom. The main purpose of ECLA was 'to promote economic development through concerted actions, including technical cooperation'. The head office was located in Santiago, Chile. The most influential intellectual leader of ECLA's general secretaries was Raul Prebisch, an Argentinean economist who conceived of the 'Singer-Prebisch theory'. Prebisch also served as Secretary General at the United Nations Council on Trade and Development (UNCTAD), from 1964.

Today, ECLAC, which is composed of 41 member countries and seven non-independent Caribbean territories as associate members, has as its objective the promotion of transnational economic activities and technical cooperation between Latin America, the US, Europe, and other regions and countries. In addition to its applied work, ECLAC conducts theoretical research on such issues as import substitution industrialization (ISI) theory as well as the gathering of statistical data in its analysis of Latin American economy and society.

The Great Depression, a consequence of the crash of the New York stock market in October 1929, seriously damaged capitalist economies throughout the world, including those in Latin American economies. Lasting a decade, the scope and significance of the Great Depression was not anticipated by most economists, with the notable exception of John Maynard Keynes. National economic policy responded to the crisis by reconsidering the need to manage economies more directly; no longer was the so-called automatic adjustment mechanism of the free market system, as articulated by Adam Smith in the late 18th century, in favour. The gold standard endorsed by the United Kingdom also came into question. Each government became more likely to manage domestic economic activities for the purpose of promoting rapid economic recovery and to ensure longer-term economic sustainability.

In the international arena, the League of Nations and the International Chamber of Commerce conducted several World Economic Conferences in order to address and resolve the serious, worldwide economic problems that characterized the 1930s. Although there were some positive

discussions through these forums in favour of international cooperation, leading to the establishment of the United Nations after World War 2, on the whole they were unable to generate the recovery of the world economy. Exclusive regional economic groupings, such as the Sterling Bloc which strictly managed foreign exchange rates and trade, were formulated by European countries, a countervailing trend away from collaborative thinking about the need for new economic policies.

In the post-World War 2 era, organizations like the United Nations identified such exclusive economic blocs as one of the causes of World War 2. In response, and with recognition of the need to promote rapid economic recovery, regional economic cooperation was promoted. ECLA's establishment in 1948 is one example of this. A principal influence on ECLA was the intellectual leadership provided by Raul Prebisch, a major international economist who was heavily influenced by John Maynard Keynes. Prebisch sought to clarify how Latin American countries could reduce their trade barriers by enlarging exports; his thinking was embraced by Keynesian economists and Central European institutionalists who strongly supported such leadership for promoting ECLA's activities. Prebisch and others were of the opinion that government had a unique responsibility to rebuild the national economy. Such thinking coincided with then-current thinking that strong and large governments were required in order to solve the serious problems of the day.

Based on policy prescriptions promoted by ECLA, each Latin American government was encouraged to set a policy to eliminate overdependence on foreign trade, to improve the trade balance, and to create employment opportunities in order to absorb a rapidly growing labour force. In particular, governments imposed duties on imported goods to protect domestic industries. In terms of the latter, such policies were based on efforts to protect infant industry; for example, in 1958, Argentina raised the rate of duties by 141 per cent and Brazil by 88 per cent. Moreover, governments were encouraged to improve the social infrastructure for transportation, telecommunications and electricity, and establish semi-governmental basic industries. Examples included subsidized manufacturing industries and government-supported financial sectors providing credit to major industries. In accordance with such policies, governments also participated in the management of selected private companies. Overall, Latin American countries produced a high economic growth of 5.4 per cent (average annual compound growth) over the period 1950–73. Economic growth in Latin America declined from 1973 to 1998: 4.8 per cent for 1973–80, 1.5 per cent for 1980–89 and 4.0 per cent for 1989–98.

ECLAC encouraged several diversified styles of development and promotion of export goods for Latin American countries. During the 1970s, the fundamental conditions of the world economy had drastically changed. First, there occurred the strong resource protectionism of oil-producing countries, as represented by OPEC. Such thinking was chronicled by publications triggered by the Club of Rome report on energy resources, which was written in 1968. A second example of change concerned the issue of how to cope with the worldwide stagflation caused by increasing production costs. A third factor was the emergence of several Asian economies such as South Korea, Taiwan, and Singapore, each accomplishing high-speed economic growth through heavy reliance on their export-oriented industries. Taken as a whole, these factors raised questions about the validity of the 'Singer-Prebisch Theory'. Through the 1970s, the average growth rate of Latin American countries was relatively low and there were huge gaps between oil-producing countries such as Venezuela and others such as Argentina and Peru. This gap was complicated in particular for those countries possessing few resources and their accumulation, at this time, of large financial deficits and foreign debt. Each government, having been positioned as a main actor according to the 'Singer-Prebisch Theory', could not cope with stagflation, financial deficits and the resulting debt crisis.

Through the 1980s, the main task of ECLAC was to overcome, through promotion of economic growth, the serious debt crisis adjustment. ECLAC introduced a neoliberal model based on the Washington Consensus; this allowed the International Monetary Fund (IMF) and World Bank to initiate economic reform. Taking an overview, the model was composed of three major programmes, as follows: (1) opening the Latin American market to the world economy through trade liberalization and foreign direct investment; (2) limiting the intervention of governments in their economies through privatization of the financial sector, well-balanced budgets and tax reforms, and (3) increasing the role of market mechanisms, hand-in-hand with resource distribution, deregulation and liberalization of finance. In this neoliberal model, the role of each government was lessened and reforms were based on market mechanisms. The private sector, as a result, became a driving force for economic growth.

These reforms succeeded in the reduction of foreign debt and promotion of sustainable economic growth. The averaged annual economic growth rate in Latin America was 3.2 per cent through the 1990s. As a result, these economies came into the spotlight as a new market for foreign direct investment. The amount of foreign direct investment in Latin America reached US$77.3 billion in 1999, growing from US$12.5 billion in 1992. The share of agricultural goods in exports from Latin America stood at 13.6 per cent in 2000, decreasing from 29.0 per cent in 1980 (percentages are of the total value of 'free on board' (FOB) export of goods). Crude oil's share drastically dropped from 28.1 per cent to 12.5 per cent during the same period. On the other hand, the share of manufactured goods increased from 17.9 per cent to 58.2 per cent by 2000. Trade liberalization and privatization increased the amount of exports and imports.

It is possible to conclude that from the viewpoint of macroeconomics ECLAC's goals, based on the 'Singer-Prebisch theory', had been realized not by larger but by smaller-scale government activity. This irony notwithstanding, the neoliberal model gave rise to serious problems, as follows: (1) enlargement of income differences in the workforce; (2) increasing unemployment and

Table 1   Manufacturing products as % of GDP

Region	1960	1970	1980	1990	2000	2005
East Asia	16	24	28	34	n/a	n/a
Latin America	21	25	25	25	18	9

Source: World Bank 2007. World Development Indicators. WDI Online.

Table 2   Latin America: share of manufacturing
sector in GDP, 1950–1990 (percentages)

	1950	1980	1990
Argentina	21.4	25.0	21.6
Brazil	23.2	33.1	27.9
Chile	20.6	21.4	21.7
Colombia	17.2	23.3	22.1
Mexico	17.3	22.1	22.8
Peru	16.7	20.2	18.4
Venezuela	10.2	18.8	20.3
Central America*	11.5	16.5	16.2
LATIN AMERICA	18.4	25.4	23.4

Note: *Includes the five countries of the Central American
   Common Market (CACM).
Source: ECLAC, Statistical Yearbook for Latin America and the
   Caribbean, 1991 and data from the ECLAC Statistical
   Division. Figures for 1950 are expressed in 1970 prices;
   those for 1980 and 1990, in 1980 prices.

social costs accompanying rapid economic reform, and (3) visible class differences. After the end of the Cold War, globalization facilitated by the information technology revolution accelerated the movement to one huge market based on capitalism, thus accentuating the gap between winners and losers. ECLAC must now address the challenge of thinking anew about changing production patterns as balanced against social equality. In other words, the question of how to overcome 'structural heterogeneity', a key concept which ECLA identified as a characteristic of Latin American society in the 1950s, has come into the spotlight once again.

Building on the organizational framework of ECLAC, established in 1948, the institutional structure added, as of 1951, a subregional headquarters in Mexico City to cover Central America. Since the 1960s, ECLAC has established six offices in various cities such as Buenos Aires and Brasilia, and three research institutes: (1) Center for Latin American Database of Economy and Society (CLADES); (2) Latin American and Caribbean Institute for Economic and Social Planning (ILPES), and (3) Latin American Demographic Center (CELADE). The Research Division of ECLAC issues several periodical journals such as Economic Survey of Latin America and other specific reports. These publications are of high quality and of indispensable use to researchers engaged in comparative analysis of Latin American countries.

In summary, the contributions of ECLAC are threefold: (1) analysis of economic and social problems faced by Latin America and the Caribbean since the 1940s, analysis that has been creatively shaped by the 'Singer-Prebisch theory'; (2) the establishment of a statistical database on Latin American economies that has deepened empirical understanding and theoretical research on the past, present, and future direction of the socioeconomic development of this world region, and (3) despite several conflicts and disputes between past and former ECLAC members, the promotion of transnational intellectual exchange and collaboration between Latin America, the Caribbean, and North America and Europe based on the goal of easing perpetual political friction based on Latin America's nationalism and misunderstanding of other world areas.

Masato Kimura

Bibliography

Nurkse R. 1953. *Problems of capital formation in underdeveloped countries*. Oxford: Basil Black and Mott.

Stallings B. and Peres W. 2000. *Growth, employment, and equity: the impact of the economic reforms in Latin America and the Caribbean*. Washington, DC: Brookings Institution.

United Nations, ECLA 1962. 'The economic development of Latin America and its principal problem', *Economic Bulletin for Latin America*, 7, 1, Santiago, Chile: ECLAC.

United Nations, ECLA 1966. *A basic guide to the Commission and its secretariat*. Santiago, Chile: United Nations.

United Nations, ECLAC 2001. *Preliminary overview of the economies of Latin America and the Caribbean*. Santiago, Chile: United Nations.

Williamson J. 1997. 'The Washington Consensus revisited', in Emmerij L. (ed.) *Economic and social development into the XXI century*. Washington, DC: International Development Bank.

Related essays
convergence and divergence; debt crises; debt crises (developing countries); development and growth; industrialization; intergovernmental organizations; investment; League of Nations Economic and Financial Organization; modernization theory; neoliberalism; Prebisch, Raúl; regional communities; technical assistance; trade; trade agreements; underdevelopment; United Nations system; Washington Consensus

Prebisch, Raúl 1901–86

Raúl Prebisch was an Argentine economist and international public servant known for defining the dependent relationship between developed and developing countries in terms of the 'centre–periphery' structure. He made explicit contributions to an understanding of the world economy as a system.

Born in San Miguel de Tucumán, Argentina, he graduated from the University of Buenos Aires in 1922. He majored in Economics and was strongly affected by the approach of John Maynard Keynes. While professor of political economy, University of Buenos Aires (1925–48), he served as the first governor of the Central Bank of the Republic of Argentina from 1935 until 1943. During his career as executive secretary to what was then the United Nations Commission for Latin America (ECLA) from 1948 until 1962, Prebisch developed his famous theory, the Singer-Prebisch thesis, in 1950. There, he insisted that the 'centre–periphery' relationship between developed countries that export industrial goods, and developing countries that export primary goods, represents an asymmetrical trade relationship that is unfavourable to the latter. During the 1960s, his theory was embraced and further elaborated into a theory of dependency by many economists.

At the United Nations Council on Trade and Development (UNCTAD), where he served as secretary-general after 1964, Prebisch urged developed countries to repeal and reduce their trade barriers by enlarging the exports of developing countries. His theory was applied to South American countries from the 1950s until the 1970s but underwent criticism in the 1980s because several East Asian countries succeeded in achieving rapid economic growth not by exporting primary goods based on Prebisch's theory, but by cultivating export-oriented manufacturing industries. Prebisch's theory has been in decline in the field of development economics, but his approach has been consistent with the analysis of transnational economic relations, most notably as articulated by Immanuel Wallerstein's world-system theory.

Masato Kimura

Bibliography
Dosman E. J. 2006. *Raúl Prebisch: Power, principle, and the ethics of development*. Buenos Aires: IDB-INTAL.

Related essays
convergence and divergence; development and growth; developmental taxonomies; economics; Hammarskjöld family; intergovernmental organizations; modernization theory; national accounting systems; Quesnay, Pierre; underdevelopment; United Nations system; Washington Consensus

Economics

Economics has strengthened its claims to universality as well as the cosmopolitanism of its practitioners for well over a century. No other social science has influenced the affairs of so many states and peoples or even aspired to. Economists analyse the shifting boundaries between governments and markets and offer advice on how to configure or reconfigure them. This professional mission has placed economists at the intersection of the academic, political and business worlds. Their ideas are reflected in the contemporary international trade and financial systems. Diplomacy and national security also bear this profession's marks. The advance of globalization, pivoted on market competitiveness and efficiency, further broadened the professional jurisdiction of economists. Even areas in which economists had not ventured before are conforming to the dictums of their trade. A telling illustration is the closer relationship between economics and emerging jurisprudence, as global norms supplant national legal traditions. The law and economics movement now counts with several international and regional associations to promote neoclassical economics in legal education, theory and practice around the world.

As the appeal of Marxism and other variants of socialism was mounting in the 1870s, modern economics emerged, supplanting political economy pioneered by Adam Smith a century earlier. The new economics was the product of a transnational convergence. Important early figures of this so-called Marginalist revolution included the English William S. Jevons, the French Léon Walras and the Austrian Carl Menger. Its success in legitimating claims to scientific objectivity, a hallmark of the neoclassical paradigm, elevated the stature and authority of economics, with enduring consequences for the professional values and identity of economists.

In the eyes of its detractors, however, neoclassical analysis has only the appearance of scientific rigour. It attempted to imitate 19th-century physics, but could not explain or even confirm regularities the way the laws of physics do. Critics see class and gender biases instead of neutrality, a preference for efficiency over equality, and inadequate explanations of historically or geographically specific economic realities. Others contest the concept of an instrumentally rational, egocentric and autonomous homo economicus. The idealization of markets, others say, has been more crucial to the global expansion of capitalism than to improvements in human well-being.

These unresolved disputes within economics have persisted, even in periods of significant doctrinal agreement. The Keynesian Consensus, once widely accepted in rich and poor countries alike, contended that government intervention was necessary to combat economic decline and mass unemployment, serious problems during the interwar period. Before Keynes, orthodox economists saw unfettered markets as the royal road to prosperity. After the stagflation of the 1970s, Keynesianism declined and free market economics regained prominence.

Pendulum swings notwithstanding, nations test the assumed advantages and limitations of economic ideas as they respond to major economic crises and other transnational processes. Thus the spread of hegemonic paradigms is accompanied by redefinitions, adaptations – and rejections – in different parts of the world.

The United States became the centre of world economics after succeeding England as the core of world capitalism. Today, economists born or residing in the United States produce the most prestigious economic theories and methods; publishing in their top academic journals is considered a clear indication of high competence; their centres of economics education have enrolled generations of economics students from all over the world; and most foreign and native economists secure careers in exclusive professional circles if trained in their best universities. Although the fluid territoriality of economics can be best understood from a de-centred viewpoint, the Anglo-American tradition remains so dominant that historians of economics rarely venture elsewhere. The transnational history of economics, in which a rich variety of national and regional schools of thought and professional practices are properly represented, is still uncharted ground.

The image of economics as a universal science has been successfully disseminated through professional associations and training institutions thanks in part to its allegedly apolitical disciplinary discourse, articulated in abstract generalizations and models. The role of textbooks as transmission vehicles has been crucial. Samuelson's 1948 *Economics* is credited with facilitating the adoption of a common language: it merged the Keynesian focus on market failures with the neoclassical stress on market virtues.

Since the early 19th century, the largest professional associations have contributed to the international circulation of economic ideas. As the presence and activities of these organizations grew, so did transnational professional exchanges. The large, prestigious Econometric Society (founded in 1930) promotes the idea that well-specified methodological and epistemological rules have universal validity, although its own regional chapters have developed somewhat distinctive styles.

The PhD is now the sine qua non of professionalism in economics. Doctoral programmes, at the top of a well-guarded hierarchy of prestige, refine and perpetuate disciplinary conventions. Technically demanding standards of excellence and diminished attention to sociopolitical and other contextual variables are characteristic of the Americanization of world economics. In Milton Friedman's famous

1974 pronouncement: 'There is ... only good economics and bad economics'.

The soaring rate of foreign students in doctoral programmes in the United States has cemented transnational networks and increased uniformity. Doctoral programmes in other countries emulate US models, but are also flexible in accommodating local needs and constituencies.

Public and private patronage foster the propagation of neoclassical economics, supplementing the parsimony of its methods. During the Cold War, academic exchanges and scholarship programmes helped discredit socialist doctrines and anti-capitalist rhetoric. In the 1950s, for example, the University of Chicago began nurturing economic orthodoxy in Latin America, with funds from the US government and philanthropic foundations. Within a few decades, the professional landscape of several countries was transformed, and the Chicago connection has retained its importance. Regional or global geopolitical considerations also reshaped economics in Korea and Eastern Europe.

Governments in developing countries finance graduate education of their economics students in universities abroad to enhance prestige and credibility in international negotiations. 'Money Doctors' – and coercive measures – persuade some poor countries to adopt economic principles consistent with wealthy creditors' preferences. The World Bank and the International Monetary Fund (IMF), for sixty years bastions of orthodox economic policy models, curb resistance to marketization with their authoritative publications, economics training, lending programmes, and the many thousands of economists employed as consultants and itinerant experts.

In the 1980s and 1990s, the blueprint for privatizing and liberalizing post-socialist and developing economies was summarized in what is known as the 'Washington Consensus'. International conferences, popular and scholarly publications back the spread of market ideas and reforms, often funded by private think-tanks and foundations. Financial institutions and international investors, with much to gain from the opening of previously regulated economic systems, also promote market orthodoxy, helping entice conversions to pro-market economics in countries reluctant to abandon protectionism. The Washington Consensus, supported by many renowned economists, is often criticized for its social and environmental costs. Lately, a few illustrious economists have joined the sceptics of 'market fundamentalism', adding strength to transnational networks of anti-globalization scholars, experts and activists.

It should be noted that the transfer of economic knowledge follows unanticipated routes; it does not always flow directly from dominant countries. Consider that Germany, not just England, shaped economics in Japan and several European countries around the turn of the 20th century. The early cohorts of American economists also studied in Germany, and the founders of American institutionalism borrowed from the German Historical School to create their branch of heterodoxy, popular until the inter war years. Consider also Chile's unexpected prominence in the global revival of market economics. The neoliberal policies of Chile's Chicago Boys preceded Thatcherism and Reaganomics.

American institutionalism shared a critical stance toward neoclassical doctrines with Latin American structuralism. The latter, which flourished in the 1950s and 1960s, also had affinity with state-led industrialization formulas devised by Central European economists earlier in the century. Another instance of unanticipated transnational contacts occurred in the 1930s and 1940s, when the flow of European émigrés – several stellar mathematicians among them – strengthened formalism in American economics. The ideological and demographic make-up of the profession has been reconfigured by other waves of exiles and by the relocation of illustrious economists: the Argentine Prebisch, the Canadian Currie, the Indian Sen, and the cosmopolitan Stanley Fischer. Keynes's visits to and his students' influence in the United States were enormously consequential.

The United Nations system was a major conduit for transferring economic ideas in the postwar period. Thanks to the diffusion of Keynesianism, macroeconomic models and planning were then the rage. The heyday of Third World attempts to redraw the map of economics followed decolonization and new alliances among developing countries in the 1960s and 1970s. They inspired various forms of economic nationalism and the elaboration of modes of analysis more suited to their own history and circumstances. Against the background of a lingering Cold War, theoretical rivalries among orthodox and heterodox economics produced a range of interpretative nuances in the field. The East Asian industrialization model encouraged numerous inter-regional contacts that rekindled development theorizing in the 1970s and 1980s. In the 1990s, global exchanges were renewed by experts in 'transitional economies'.

Today, the international elite of the profession seems drawn to emulate the American way and marginalize dissenters. Nevertheless, national differences remain in rhetoric and intellectual traditions. Feminist and environmental economics, postmodernist approaches and other heterodoxies have challenged the discipline's mainstream, which is itself becoming less homogeneous, partly because of overtures to neighbouring disciplines. Perhaps another intractable global crisis will force a new disciplinary realignment. In any event, the continuous influx of talented foreign economists to the United States may end up redefining Americanization.

Verónica Montecinos

Bibliography

Augello M. M. and Guidi M. E. L. (eds)
2001. *The spread of political economy and the professionalisation of economics.* London and New York: Routledge.

Coats A. W. (ed.) 1997. *The post-1945 internationalization of economics.* Durham, NC and London: Duke University Press.

Daunton M. and Trentmann F. (eds) 2004. *World of political economy: knowledge and power in the nineteenth and twentieth centuries.* Basingstoke and New York: Palgrave Macmillan.

Related essays

capitalism; Cold War; convergence and divergence; debt (developing countries); development and growth; developmental assistance; developmental taxonomies; Economic Commission for Latin America and the Caribbean (ECLAC); exile; financial diplomacy; higher education; industrialization; intellectual elites; intergovernmental organizations; International Monetary Fund (IMF); League of Nations Economic and Financial Organization; legal order; modernization theory; national accounting systems; open door and free flow; Pax Americana; philanthropic foundations; Prebisch, Raúl; social sciences; socialism; trade agreements; transnational; underdevelopment; Washington Consensus; World Bank; world orders; zero growth

Ecumenism

Ecumenism is a modern movement that is concerned with the essential unity and renewal of the Christian church, the solidarity and cooperation of the churches, and their common witness and action in and for the world. The term is derived from the Greek word *oikoumene*. In the New Testament it meant the Roman Empire or 'the whole world' and gradually it came to refer to the whole church or Christendom in its entirety.

This entirety was challenged by the estrangement of several regional churches along the centuries, from Eastern (Greek) churches to Protestant denominations that blossomed in early modern times. Because the New Testament taught the unity of the church, the Roman Catholic (RC) position was that this oneness was found through the Petrine succession, but the other churches were unwilling to accept papal authority. However, beginning in the 18th century, various European and North American Protestant churches launched a worldwide missionary outreach. This endeavour among non-Christian peoples forced them to consider anew the prayer of Jesus in John 17 that all who believed in Him would be one so that the world might believe as well. As a result, cooperation in missionary work, beginning with the German Pietists and the Moravian missions, quickly gathered steam. In India the missionaries of various denominations began meeting as early as 1825 to promote fellowship and exchange ideas and by mid-century they were discussing ways to overcome denominational divisions and achieve unity, a process that occurred elsewhere in Asia as well. Over time national Christian councils were formed in India, China, and Japan. A variety of interdenominational endeavours (such as the Evangelical Alliance formed in 1846) and missionary conferences in Britain and Germany addressed the topic of cooperation and unity. This was capped by the 'Ecumenical Missionary Conference' in New York in 1900 which used the term 'because the plan of campaign which it proposes covers the area of the inhabited globe'. Several youth organizations also promoted world evangelism and greater unity. These forces came together at the World Missionary Conference in Edinburgh in 1910, which in spite of its global focus was a meeting of Western church and mission leaders. As its main objective was fostering global cooperation in proclaiming the Gospel, a 'continuation committee' headed by John R. Mott, the foremost ecumenist of the day, was formed to carry out the vision. The Protestant unity forged at Edinburgh collapsed in World War I but was revived in the postwar period with the creation of the International Missionary Council (IMC) in 1921. At its conferences in Jerusalem (1928) and Madras (1938) representatives of the 'younger' churches played a more prominent role and more emphasis was placed on the indigenous churches and their expansion.

Two other ecumenical streams appeared in the 1920s and 1930s. 'Life and Work', inaugurated at a conference in Stockholm in 1925, focused on the social outreach of the church and its role in the political context. 'Faith and Order', inaugurated at a meeting in Lausanne in 1927, addressed the more knotty issues of the church's confession of faith, its ministry, the sacraments, and the unity of Christendom. Both groups met again in 1937 – at Oxford and Edinburgh respectively – refined their visions, and agreed that a World Council of Churches (WCC) should be formed to carry out the process of greater church unity. Delegates from some of the Orthodox churches attended these various meetings, thus broadening the ecumenical vision from that of the Protestant missionary movement. An advisory conference was held in Utrecht in 1938 to define the basis of membership and the constitution of the WCC, but the coming of World War 2 delayed any action. Finally, at the Amsterdam assembly in 1948 the WCC formally came into existence. The WCC established its headquarters in Geneva and carried on a wide-ranging programme to further the cause of church unity, including an assembly held every six or seven years in a different part of the world. In 1961 the IMC merged with the WCC. Protestant evangelicals, wary of the theological inclusiveness of the WCC, developed their own ecumenical structure based on united effort in world evangelism. This began with a large congress in Berlin in 1968 and reached its peak at the first International Congress on World Evangelisation in Lausanne in 1974 and a second congress in Manila in 1989. A parallel enterprise was the World Evangelical Alliance, formed in 1951, which focused on linking evangelical organizations. Both conciliarists and evangelicals engaged in extensive efforts to promote their understandings of unity. Some people in both groups did not see these as incompatible and were willing to work together on issues of common interest.

Although many in the Orthodox community participated in conciliar ecumenism, Roman Catholics were unwilling to do so. However, the Second Vatican Council (1962–63) saw a significant change in the attitude of this church. The Decree on Ecumenism (1964), reflecting Pope John XXIII's own strong feelings on the matter, called for the restoration of unity among all Christians and acknowledged that the differences among the Christian communions contradicted the will of Christ, scandalized the world, and damaged the cause of preaching the Gospel to every creature. It went on to identify Catholic principles on ecumenism, encouraged Catholics to take an active and intelligent part in the work of ecumenism by engaging in dialogue with others, and called for cooperation with others to relieve such current afflictions as famines, natural disasters, poverty, and unequal distribution of wealth. Through this all believers in Christ would be able to learn how they might understand each other better and esteem each other more, thereby smoothing the road to the unity of Christians.

Several moves developed from these premises: in 1965 Pope Paul VI and Eastern Orthodox Patriarch Athenagoras met and issued a common declaration that expressed regret for the harsh and offensive statements of past generations and retracted the mutual sentences of excommunication that had occurred. Subsequent declarations of common christological faith were signed by the Pope (as Bishop of Rome) and the Patriarchs of some of the Eastern Orthodox churches re-establishing fraternal relations. In 1995 John Paul II issued the encyclical Ut unum sint, a major papal statement on ecumenism. He declared ecumenism to be 'an organic part' of the church's life and work that should pervade it all. He identified several areas in need of fuller study before a true consensus of faith could be achieved, including the relationship between Scripture and Tradition, the Eucharist, ordination, the Magisterium of the church, and the place of the Virgin Mary. The basic problem of the primacy of the papacy clearly remained untouched.

To carry on ecumenical conversations with other bodies, a Pontifical Council for Promoting Christian Unity was appointed, and some important dialogue documents were produced such as the joint declaration with the Lutheran World Federation on 'Justification' that affirmed the same doctrine could be legitimately be expressed in different formulations, and the statement on 'Evangelisation, Proselytism and Common Witness' adopted in a dialogue with 'Some Classical Pentecostal Denominations and Leaders'. Catholics also participated with other groups in prayers for Christian unity.

Some successful attempts occurred at uniting various Protestant denominations, such as the United Church of Canada, the Uniting Church in Australia, the Church of South India, and the Church of North India. More noteworthy are the efforts at global cooperation among specific denominations, such as the Lambeth Conferences of the bishops of the Anglican communion, the World Alliance of Reformed Churches, the Baptist World Alliance, the World Methodist Council, the Lutheran World Federation, and numerous others. These bodies have no power to interfere in the life of local or national bodies, but they assist in coordinating the efforts of their church constituencies. They are known collectively as Christian World Communions, and their general secretaries hold low-key meetings annually to discuss issues of common interest. Some in the WCC regard them as undermining the effort to achieve church unity.

The term 'ecumenism' is generally not applied to the larger area of interreligious dialogue, although some would contest this. The major example of such an endeavour is the 'World Parliament of Religions' that was held in Chicago in 1893, and the jubilee observance a century later, renamed the 'Parliament of World Religions'. These brought together representatives from the major world religions to discuss issues of mutual concern, and the 1993 meeting adopted a declaration calling for an end to religious conflicts, the arms race, environmental destruction, and gender discrimination. In this regard, the Vatican II Declaration on the Relation of the Church to Non-Christian Religions (1965) is noteworthy for its repudiation of the charge of deicide against the Jews and for its affirmation of God's continuing love for the Jewish people. It also urged Christians to enter with prudence and charity into discussions and collaboration with members of other religions and to acknowledge, preserve and encourage the spiritual and moral truth found among non-Christians. It further noted that the church has a high regard for Muslims. The WCC appointed a sub-unit to pursue dialogue with people of living faiths that held a consultation in 1990. It issued a report on religious plurality that recognized the 'mystery of salvation' in men and women of other religions and called on Christians to respect their religious convictions and to admire the things which God had accomplished and continues to accomplish in them through the Spirit.

Richard Pierard

Bibliography

Desseaux J. 1983. Vingt siècles d'histoire oecuménique. Paris: Cerf.

Fitzgerald T. 2004. The ecumenical movement: an introductory history. Westport: Praeger.

Kinnamon M. and Cope B. (eds) 1997. The ecumenical movement: an anthology of key texts and voices. Geneva: WCC Publications.

World Council of Churches 1954–2005. A history of the ecumenical movement, 3 vols. Vol. 3, 1968–2000. Briggs J., Oduyoye M. and Tsetsēs G. (eds) 2004. Geneva: WCC Publications.

Related essays

antisemitism; Buddhism; Christianity; cosmopolitanism and universalism; evangelicalism; internationalisms; Islam; missionaries; religion; Second Vatican Ecumenical Council; youth organizations

Electricity infrastructures

During the 20th century, the supplying of electricity became a transnational force in several ways. First, in the realm of ideas, the planning of transnational electricity systems intertwined with broader ideas of regional integration. Since the 1920s electrical integration has been ideologically linked to the creation of interdependency, joint prosperity and peace, especially in Europe. Second, international organizations promoting infrastructure were among the earliest and most successful experiments in global community building. The electricity supply sector produced its own international organizations after 1920, hosting structural interactions between individuals and organizations from across the world. Finally, on a purely material level, economies and societies were electrically interconnected. Some cross-border links date from the early decades of the 20th century, but electrical integration was more systematically pursued only in the century's second half. These developments were far from homogeneous or smooth. They resulted in asymmetrical patterns of interconnection and collaboration even within the most advanced regional power pools.

If electricity became a connecting force only in the 1910s and 1920s, this is in part due to the sector's internal development. Systems to supply electricity to the public had been established since the early 1880s. However, using low-voltage distribution (typically 110 or 220 volts) these had an economic reach of only a few kilometres. They were inner-city or even village systems. Relative power losses decrease with increasing transport voltages, and the introduction and diffusion of medium-voltage transmission (often 10 kilovolts) in the 1890s increased the transmission range to some 30–50 kilometres, enabling an increase of supply areas and scaling up of power stations. Several of such increased power systems grew to cross national borders. Most important for our topic, however, is the notion of interconnecting power stations in a power pool, using still higher transmission voltages (often higher than 50 or 100 kilovolts). This notion of power pools was much debated in the 1910s. Well-advertised advantages included integrating distant lignite or hydropower plants into the system; allocating production to those power stations in the pool producing cheapest at any given time; and mutual provision of backup capacity in case of breakdowns within the pool. These promises inspired projects for national as well as transnational power pools.

Electricity and ideas of regional integration

The notion of transnational electricity systems first entwined with emerging ideas of regional integration in interwar Europe. Engineers evoked political notions of a pan-European Union in their thinking about electricity supply; simultaneously, functionalist politicians embraced electrical integration as a practical, 'technical' alternative to the troublesome 'high politics' road to European integration. Both groups enthusiastically debated how transnational electricity networks could make the energy of Europe's unevenly distributed coal fields and hydropower sites available to all its countries. Moreover, this process would create electrical interdependencies that would secure peace better than any political treaties on paper. Like railroads in the 19th century and information and communication technologies networks today, electrical interconnection promised cooperation, prosperity and peace. By the early 1930s several engineers were proposing all-European power grids fed by hydropower plants in Scandinavia and the Alps. Meanwhile the League of Nations discussed electrical integration in the context of a wider scheme for European public utilities.

While the promises of electrical cooperation boosted functionalist thought on regional integration, in reality such collaboration remained rather limited. Until the 1940s, the competing idea of creating national power pools ensuring national energy independence proved stronger. The idea of regional electrical integration gained a coercive character when Nazi Germany, too, sought to integrate an envisaged Neuropa by electric power networks, by which occupied territories' energy resources would feed Germany's war economy.

In postwar Europe promises of prosperity and peace via electrical integration re-emerged, although the functionalist ideology was often downplayed relative to the promise of sectoral efficiency gains of cooperation and concerns to create large markets for projected nuclear power plants. Still, electrical integration remained an important concern to political bodies working for regional integration. The United Nations Economic Commission for Europe (UNECE, 1947), the Organization for European Economic Co-operation (OEEC, 1948), and the Council of Mutual Economic Assistance (COMECON, 1949) all included electricity supply in their regional integration efforts.

In the 1990s, neoliberal thinking strengthened interlinked notions of regional and electrical integration: regional markets require transnational networks. The European Union includes electricity in its Trans European Network programme to forge economic, social and territorial cohesion (1992). In comparable phrasing, the Economic Community of West African States (ECOWAS) set up a West African Power Pool (WAPP, 1999) to achieve 'physical integration by means of infrastructures'. A similar constellation of ideas led the South African Development Community

(SADC) to establish the South African Power Pool (SAPP, 1995), the Association of South East Asian Nations (ASEAN) to plan an ASEAN power grid (1998), and the NAFTA countries to set up the North American Energy Working Group (NAEWG, 2001) to 'enhance North American energy trade and interconnections', including electricity.

International organizations

A different type of transnational force is global community building through the work of international organizations. In the history of international organizations, infrastructure-related organizations count among the earliest and most successful examples. Electricity-related organizations emerged rather late, as did the field of electrotechnical science.

Prior to World War I, the main organizations fostering coherence and community in the electricity supply world were electrical equipment manufacturers and leading national electrotechnical engineering bodies such as the American Institute of Electrical Engineers (AIEE, 1884; renamed IEEE in 1963) and its German counterpart, the Verein Deutscher Elektrotechniker (1893). In 1906 these and others founded the first international organization in the field, the International Electrotechnical Commission (IEC). Based in London (and later in Geneva), the IEC codified technical standards, definitions and symbols. By 1914 it had produced several lists of terms and symbols; since 1938 it has published the multilingual International Electrotechnical Vocabulary, which currently comprises some 20,000 terms. Today the IEC associates experts from industry, government, academia, test labs and others from over 130 member or affiliated countries.

In the interwar years several international organizations were added. The broadest of these was the London-based World Power Conference (WPC, 1923; later renamed World Energy Conference and World Energy Council), serving as a 'non-commercial, non-aligned' forum to discuss the world's energy questions, including electricity. Its first congress (1924) attracted some 1,700 delegates from 40 countries; by the 1990s it associated member committees in nearly a hundred countries. Again, members included representatives from power companies and electrotechnical manufacturers, but also policy makers, academic researchers, and user organizations.

Specifically focusing upon electric power exchanges, the International Council on Large Electric Systems (CIGRE, 1921) was set up as a platform 'to develop and distribute knowledge' related to electricity generation and high-voltage transmission. Today it links over 4,000 individual and collective members in some 80 countries. The International Union of Producers and Distributors of Electrical Power (UNIPEDE, 1925) was established by the electrotechnical industries of Italy, France and Belgium, but quickly gained more members. It prime task was the study of problems of efficiency and operation and to promote the electrotechnical industry. It included non-European members, but focused mainly on Europe. In 1999 UNIPEDE merged with the European lobby group Eurelectric (1990). Also the International Energy Agency (1974), founded in response to the first oil crisis, includes primarily European countries among its 26 industrialized members.

Electrical integration and fragmentation

The earliest cross-border interconnections linked producers and consumers or individual utilities on different sides of the border, rather than interconnecting power pools or countries. These include a hydropower system in the bi-national town of Rheinfelden, which expanded into Germany and Switzerland from 1898, and a transmission line across the US-Canadian border at the bi-national Niagara Falls in 1901. Many such rather local projects followed in the next decades. From 1916, subnational power pools in Eastern Denmark and Southern Sweden were linked by a submarine cable.

Structural attempts for regional electrical integration took off from the 1950s and 1960s. However, its asymmetrical and incomplete nature puts the transnational dimension of electricity into critical perspective. Electricity trade is generally dwarfed by the domestic production of individual countries. According to US Energy Information Administration statistics in 2004, transnational power flows worldwide only amounted to about 3 per cent of net domestic production, meaning that an overwhelming 97 per cent of electricity flows circulate within national borders. Moreover, transborder power exchange developed a regional scope only in 'Europe' (here including former COMECON countries) and 'Eurasia' (the former Soviet countries). There, virtually all countries participated in regional power pools. In 2004 'European' exports amounted to some 312 terawatt hours (TWh), constituting about 9 per cent of net domestic production. The figures for 'Eurasia' were 83 TWh and 6 per cent, following a significant decline in the 1990s.

In 2004 significant transborder power flows existed in the Americas, but these were completely dominated by a few bilateral exchanges. These include US imports from Canada (33 TWh) and the Paraguayan yields of the giant bilateral hydroelectric power projects at Itaipú (1984) and Yaciretá (1995), which were almost completely exported (45 TWh) to Brazil and Argentina respectively. Transnational power exchanges in the Middle East and Asia remain negligible. In Africa exports rapidly increased in the last decade following the creation of several regional power pools mentioned above; compared to domestic production, however, they remain minor.

Regional electrical integration was relatively successful only in Europe, but a closer look reveals ruptures even there. European electrical integration typically proceeded in distinct mesoregional blocks. The OEEC set up the Union for the Coordination of Production and Transport of Electricity (UCPTE, 1951; currently UCTE) to arrange multilateral electricity exchanges, but only for Western Europe. The COMECON set up its own regional power pool, the Interconnected Power System of the Central Dispatch Organization (IPS/CDO, 1962), The IPS/CDO synchronized and cooperated with a third pool, the USSR United Power Systems (UPS). Simultaneously, utilities in the Nordic countries – where Nordic economic integration still counted as a viable alternative to Western European integration – set up their own Nordic electric power collaboration called Nordel (1963). French, Spanish and Portuguese utilities established the Union Franco-Ibérique pour la Coordination de la Production et du Transport de l'Électricité (UFIPTE, 1963). Italian, Austrian, Yugoslavian and Greek utilities too established their own cooperation (SUDEL, 1964).

UFIPTE and SUDEL coordinated networks which operated synchronously with the UCPTE, of which they became full members in the 1980s. Nordel, which currently coordinates the best integrated power pool in the world, did not join the UCPTE. However, it did develop an intensive collaboration with UCPTE members through submarine high-voltage direct current power cables (which do not require system synchronization). After 1989 the Central Eastern European IPS/CDO was dissolved. Several members disconnected from the successor to the USSR network and synchronized with the UCPTE network instead, culminating in the so-called Trans-European Synchronously Interconnected System (TESIS, 1995). The former Soviet system continued as a separate international power pool as former Soviet republics gained independence. Here several countries were caught in a dilemma. The Baltic republics of Latvia, Estonia, and Lithuania, for instance, chose electrical disconnection from the USSR system as a key arena to achieve national independence in the late 1980s. Later they found their power exports to Russia too valuable to lose, and continued to cooperate, while slowly exploring collaboration to the North and West.

Electrical integration thus proves a deeply political phenomenon. In terms of power flows, it is still much less important than (sub)national electricity circulation. However, recent transnational blackouts suggest that economies and societies have nevertheless become electrically interdependent, albeit in an unexpected way. Breakdowns may cascade through interconnected systems across national borders. In the 'Northeast blackout' of 2003, a failure in Ohio caused a power outage for some 50 million Americans and 10 million Canadians. In the same year, a failing Swiss-Italian cross-border line plunged some of Switzerland and almost the entire Italian peninsula into darkness. In November 2006, a power failure in northern Germany cascaded through the network as far as Morocco and Croatia. Experts expect more such failures to occur in the coming years.

Vincent Lagendijk
Erik van der Vleuten

Bibliography

Cardot F. (ed.) 1987. *1880–1980: un siècle d'électricité dans le monde: actes du premier colloque international d'histoire de l'électricité.* Paris: Presses Universitaires de France.

Hughes T. P. 1983. *Networks of power: electrification in Western society 1880–1930.* Baltimore: Johns Hopkins University Press.

Lagendijk V, 2008. Electrifying Europe: the power of Europe in the construction of electricity networks. Unpublished doctoral dissertation, Eindhoven University of Technology, Eindhoven.

Lagendijk V. 'High voltages, lower tensions: the interconnections of Eastern and Western European electricity networks in the 1970s and 1980s', in Bussière E., Dumoulin M. and Schirmann S. (eds) 2006. Milieux économiques et intégration européenne au XXe siècle: la crise des années 1970 de la conférence de La Haye à la veille de la relance des années 1980. Brussels: Peter Lang, 137–65.

Trédé M. (ed.) 1992. Électricité et électrification dans le monde: Actes du deuxième colloque international d'histoire de l'électricité. Paris: Presses Universitaires de France.

Van der Vleuten E. and Kaijser A. (eds) 2006. Networking Europe: transnational infrastructures and the shaping of Europe 1850–2000. Sagamore Beach: Science History Publications.

Related essays
borders and borderlands; broadcasting; European Union (EU); intergovernmental organizations; international non-governmental organizations (INGOs); Internet; League of Nations system; mail; pan-isms; radio; railways; regional communities; regions; technical standardization; telephone and telegraphy; transportation infrastructures; world orders

Empire and migration

'Empire' describes a wide variety of hegemonic territorial conquests that produce flows of people, goods, and ideas across frontiers. Prior to the making of the modern nation state, the boundaries of contiguous kingdoms and empires remained fuzzy. Nomads circulated across boundaries, peasants fled war from one kingdom to another. However, the analytical value of the term 'empire' (without dynastic appellation) as a conceptual category for the study of history emerged in its relationship to the nation state, defined by territorial sovereignty and the elimination of fuzzy boundaries. After the formation of modern nation states, empire was embedded in two sets of geopolitical relationships: its economic and political relationship with a specific nation state; and the simultaneous control that empire exercises, in the name of the sovereign nation state, over colonies and their peoples.

The sovereign-territory-based nation state, originating as a historical form in Western Europe, rested on processes of mapping and fencing off borders culminating in state-controlled points of entry and departure of peoples and goods. Policed borders were sustained by the political, military and financial institutions of the state. Crucially, the nation state framed legal systems defining nationality, citizenship, and property rights. Definition of 'the nation' marked off the included and the excluded peoples, those of the nation, and those who did not 'belong'. These legal definitions of citizenship made the visa-stamped passport of the 20th century the single most important document in the migrant's life. The nation state recast empire, for both are imbued with transnational and global capital. Migration in the age of national borders began a distinctive chapter in the history of the transnational world.

It is possible to distinguish three periods in this new era. The first, from the 1830s to the 1920s, marks a period when both voluntary and indentured global migrations reached new levels and colonial empires inaugurated controlled transnational migration of their subjects. The period from the 1920s to the 1940s marked the end of the plantation-culture migration and restrictions on migrations in areas such as the US. This was a period of capital contraction due to the worldwide economic depression, which affected both empire and trajectories of migration. These were also the beginnings of decolonization. The last period, commencing from the 1940s to the present, marks the end of formal political controls of empire with decolonization, but the uneven world that empire made continues to shape the trajectories of transnational migrations. This essay focuses on the first and the last period, when the world was remade through the processes of massive migrations.

In the post-1750 period Europe looked to Asia and Africa for new imperial possessions. As the European powers withdrew from the Americas, parts of Mexico were formally annexed by the US, and Central and Caribbean America became part of its informal empire of 'Manifest Destiny'. By the 20th century, the British empire was the largest in terms of population and territory controlled, followed by the French, Dutch, Spanish,

Portuguese, Belgian, Italian, American and Japanese empires. The British colonies of South Africa, Australia and New Zealand, used as white penal colonies, became white settler colonies while local peoples were disenfranchised. Some states were controlled by conflicting imperial interests: Somalia, on the strategic entryway to Suez, was controlled by England, France, Italy and Ethiopia. Different areas of China were controlled by various European, American and Japanese imperial interests, but the entire country was not directly subject to the colonial control of any one imperial power. British and French dominion extended over much of the Middle East, while the 'Great Game' between Tsarist Russia and Great Britain divided Central Asia.

As the combined economic and political power of the global North, empire was able to assert its model of capitalist modernization on a global scale. But the lived experience of modernization was uneven and unequal in different parts of the globe. The political structure of Asian and African colonies, while drawing on the legacies and institutions developed during the colonization of the Americas, were not settler colonies. At the political level, the colonial administrators from metropolitan centres ran local government in hierarchical systems of exclusions. At the economic level, the colonial agricultural and manufacturing systems were reorganized and integrated into the demands of global capital. Resources of the colonies were redirected in the interests of the colonial power to flow to the metropolitan centre or to other parts of empire. Limited social expenditures by the colonial state in crucial spheres of the essential ancillaries of modernization such as institutions of higher learning, scientific and medical research, infrastructure construction, healthcare and primary education over time produced ever greater levels of divergence between the various colonial and the metropolitan worlds. Some colonies, like French West Africa, for example, had fewer than 0.47 per cent of school-age children entering school in 1938, while in contemporary France, school education was free and universal.

Secondly, the colonized were de jure subordinate to the colonial state which controlled all sorts of aspects of life ranging from where the 'natives' could live in their own land, which educational and recreational facilities they could enter, and so on, to outright apartheid and the Code de l'indigénat. The colonized were not de facto citizens of the metropolitan nation state and therefore did not have the same privileges, protections and passports throughout empire. The distinguishing feature of migration under empire was racialization of migrants both at the point of origin and at the point of arrival. Ideas of 'race', evolving during colonization of the Americas and the African slave trade, acquired global salience in the 19th century with the development of 'scientific' racism just at the time when modern colonial empires were extending dominion over vast numbers of people in Asia and Africa. Colonized populations were now marked off as biologically and racially 'different' from the denizens of the metropolitan core and, as relevantly, also from each other. Hierarchies of race and hierarchies of difference became pivotal factors in migrant lives with state-mandated exclusions/inclusions, miscegenation laws, citizenship, and property rights.

The concomitant rise of colonial empires and migration

From the 1830s to the 1920s, expansion of colonial empires furthered asymmetrical economic relationships. Raw materials for industry, and food, goods and beverages for industrial workers of the global North expanded plantation economies in the South. Transnational migration patterns diverged. In the global North migrants left rural sectors for more rapidly industrializing sectors within Europe or the Americas or fled from political inequality in new nation states, as did the Jews from Eastern Europe and Russia. In the global South, the major trajectory of transnational migration was within the tropical zone to plantations and mines, with very limited numbers moving to North America and Europe. Migrations in the global South, from the 1830s to the 1920s, can be viewed under three rubrics: the self-financed trading communities, forced migrants, and labour migrants.

Trading communities in Asia and Africa, with activities ranging from those of packpedlars, retailers and small-time money lenders to those of entrepreneurs, multinational bankers and industrialists emerged as partners in empire, largely building on precolonial trade and migration patterns. Merchants from Fujian and Guangdong in China, Chettinad and Gujarat in India, and Arab Hadrami had trading communities throughout the Indian Ocean that extended into the Pacific at one end and the Mediterranean at the other. Other long-distance networks, such as those of the Sindhis and Parsees, stretched throughout Central Asia overland into China, Russia and Syria, and then under empire extended into the Pacific and the Atlantic. Senegalese (Togotalan) merchants ranged from west to central and east Africa, and major Omani slave and ivory traders like Tippu Tipp linked the east coast to the Belgian Congo. Lebanese Christian merchants, one of the major trading groups in the Ottoman empire, spanned the globe by the early 20th century from South Africa to the Andes. These trading-community migrations included annual and multi-year sojourns alongside permanent settlement.

Transnational migration was a collective family decision. The percentage of women migrating depended on marital status, land-holding, and whether local social cultural practices included polygyny. If the husband owned land, the wife's labour in sustaining the family farm and keeping the husband's share, providing care of the elderly and raising his children was too vital to allow for her migration. In systems with polygyny, the husband could take a secondary wife with him or marry a local woman where he lived, and return home to reclaim status, including burial in the lineage land. Women migrating with their husbands tended to be from landless and land-poor families. Out-migration of women from smallholder cultivation economies, where the men intended to return, was comprised primarily of single women, widows, and the wives of merchants and wealthier migrants. For married working women, their earnings were not controlled by them but by the male head of household and portions were remitted back. Some women did run independent businesses. But for the majority of trading communities, ranging from the Indians in Malaya and Uganda to the Syrians, Lebanese and Chinese in the US, the wives of small merchants, migrant pack-pedlars and grocery-store owners kept businesses going with their unpaid labour.

At the other end of the economic scale, empire increased transnational migrations through forced migrations, penal labour and transfer of prisoners of war. The Dutch brought Chinese, Indians, Sinhalese and Malays to Cape Town and took East Africans and Bengalis to Java as part of the 18th-century slave trade. Chinese bonded labour was recruited for construction and ship-repair from Australia to St Helena. The East India Company brought several hundred Cantonese to St Helena in the period from 1806 to the 1820s, to work as gardeners, mechanics and builders, including on the infrastructure for Napoleon's exile. Many stayed and married emancipated slaves. Today, 25 per cent of the St Helena population is of Chinese origin.

The hegemonic power of empires increased forced migrations and created a patchwork of racialized communities throughout the globe. Between 1820 and 1873, when the convict migration system ended, over 250,000 people were shipped within the British empire. Besides Australia, convict workers from India, China, and Madagascar were taken to British colonies in Malaya, Sumatra, Mauritius, and the Andaman Islands. Over 10,000 Indians were sent to Burma, and 25,000 along with several thousand Chinese to Singapore, Penang and Melaka. Prisoners of war were everywhere. The last Mughal emperor and empress, exiled to Burma (1858), died there, while Thebaw, the last Burmese king, queen and court were packed off to western India (1885). When the border between British India and Afghanistan was drawn (1893), Afghan Pathans on the wrong side of the border ended up in Guyana. Several thousand Boer prisoners were sent to Sri Lanka while others were sent to Bermuda. Between 1854 and 1922, the French banished 22,000 Parisian socialists and Kabyle Berber nationalists out to Melanesian New Caledonia.

However, the most significant impact of empire on migration came with abolition of slavery (1807) and eventual emancipation (1833) in the British empire. This transformed the existing patterns of African and Asian migrations in volume and direction. While African forced migrations to the Americas did not cease until 1850, British emancipation decrees intensified trans-American Afro-Caribbean migrations. Former slaves, denied living wages and conditions little changed since slavery, moved to other colonies. By 1835, of the 22,359 Trinidadian slaves, only 8,000 stayed, others moving to labour in Central American plantations, railway and canal construction. To supplement Afro-Caribbean labour on plantations, empire turned to Asian sources. The collapse of dynastic empire – Mughal, Qing and Ottoman – accompanying wars of colonial conquest, economic restructuring, domestic rebellions, and religious strife, dislocated millions from Lebanon to Japan. The coolie trade, a generic term for Asian labour, became dominant. All of Asia produced large migrant labour pools with labour arrangements ranging from indenture contract or credit ticket to wage labour. Populous China and India provided the most migrants. Between 1846 and 1940, transnational Asian migration numbers are estimated to have been around 48–52 million.

The great arc of sugar plantations extending from Suriname-Guyana and Cuba in the Atlantic to Mauritius and Reunion in the Indian Ocean were primary destinations. Each new surge in world demand for sugar, tea, coffee, palm oil, bananas and rubber brought more lands under plantation culture, and with it the need for more labour. Plantation culture spread to the Pacific Islands from Fiji to Hawaii where disease and labour recruitment had decimated local populations. New crops were introduced to meet world markets: rubber for the automobile industry brought the Brazilian plant to plantations in Indonesia, Malaya, Sri Lanka, and Vietnam. US agrobusiness transformed the Asian banana, a food crop for Caribbean slaves, into megaplantations shaping the economy and politics of the Central American states. Brazil's coffee plantations drew around 190,000 Japanese. Italy transformed Somalia with over one hundred banana plantations and moved Bantu labour in from Tanzania, Mozambique and Malawi. Demand for tin to line and waterproof tea-chests, tinned palm oil from Malaya and Nigeria for machine lubrication, and tinned foods for the soldiers in wars of empire meant more tin mines in Malaya, Sumatra, Thailand. Some 200,000 Chinese worked in these mines. The Nigerian tin mines of Jos drew southern Igbo migrants. Diamond and gold mines in British South Africa operated by recruiting labour from Mozambique. Soil depletion in the American South cotton plantations drove the market for guano fertilizer. Recruiters brought 100,000 Chinese coolies and 3,500 Easter Islanders to the guano mines of Peru. Along with several hundred Mayan Indians from the Yucatan, 125,000 Chinese were brought to work Cuba's sugar cane fields between 1847 and 1874. And when the American colonies stretched from the Atlantic to the Pacific after 1898, Puerto Ricans were brought to Hawai'i to join Chinese, Japanese and Filipino plantation labour.

Empire managed labour by residential segregation according to 'race'. Diversity of food cultures, language, and social and religious practices of the workers were amplified into hierarchies of pigmentocracy and the residential 'plantation pyramid' from Fiji to Guyana to Hawai'i. Interracial relationships brought social sanctions. Mines and towns throughout empire from Indonesia to South Africa operated with the 'pass' and 'quarter' and township systems limiting internal travel and residential locations. The only meeting points between the different peoples of empire were the small businesses started predominantly by the Chinese and Indians who became shopkeepers and moneylenders when their labour contracts ended. For the local communities, dislocated by empire and new migrant labour, these small businesses were the most visible faces of empire and exclusion. The owners were also the first victims of racial antagonisms, economic nationalism, and exclusion.

Empire shaped transnational settlements through the management of quotas of female labour for plantations and miscegenation laws. In non-plantation areas of the US and Canada, successive restrictive regulations from 1875 onwards curtailed entry of Asian females and males. Similar Asian-exclusion laws were passed in New Zealand (1881) and Australia (1901). When planters and colonial officials found that men extended term-contract labour services if they had families with them, and that women workers on plantations doing the same jobs as men could be paid lower rates, active female recruitment began. Emigration quotas to plantations ranged from 25 to 40 women per 100 men. The Japanese government negotiated similar terms for female migration. Indian-labour-dominant plantations on Fiji, Malaya, Mauritius, Guyana, and Japanese-labour-dominant plantations in Hawai'i, Brazil, and Peru had larger numbers of permanent settlers. Colonial ordinances sometimes restricted male, but not female, migration. British Malaya (1929) stopped Chinese male, but not female, labour leading to feminization of migration.

Outside plantations and family shops, women worked as domestics and nannies, known as *ayahs* and *amahs*. The trend towards

Asian domestics started early. Chinese *amahs* and Indian *ayahs* could be found throughout empire. including the metropolitan centres. In 1855, one study found 200 Indian *ayahs* fending for themselves in London slums after employment ended. 'Chinese Emmas' lived riverside at Lower Shadwell. Today, Asian female domestic workers constitute one of the largest groups in transnational labour. Sex work, then and now, was another major arena of women's work. The expansion of male-labour-dominant industries of mining, railway construction and transportation brought worldwide increase in sex work from London to New York to Buenos Aires and Johannesburg. Workers from China, Mexico and Peru in the gold- and silver-mining towns of the American West, Chinese and Javanese sex workers in the mining towns of Malaya, and Indian women in Burma would have had much in common with prostitutes from Lesotho working in South Africa's gold and diamond mines of the Rand. Most worked under indenture or contract. These 'private sector' sex workers replicated imperial arrangements. Military procurement of local women to work as prostitutes to service soldiers existed throughout empire. A system of registered sex workers serving military barracks developed throughout British India, to protect British soldiers from venereal disease. During World War 2, over 200,000 women from Japan, Korea, Taiwan, Indonesia, the Philippines, Burma and Thailand were sent to serve as 'comfort women' at overseas Japanese military camps. Today, Japan has over 100,000 sex workers from the Philippines and Thailand while thee oil-rich Gulf Emirates and Saudi Arabia have large numbers of Filipino and South Asian sex workers. The connections between military bases and sex workers continue most notably around the more than two hundred American military bases throughout the world.

Colonial demand for roads and railways, harbours and docks for the transportation and export of commodities produced transported labour across imperial lines. The US Transcontinental Railroad (1864–69) employed 10,000 Chinese, many imported directly from China. Japanese and Indians built railways in the resource-rich but labour-poor Pacific Northwest in the 1910s. Chinese labour moved to Texas and the southwest United States for railway construction in the recently acquired expansions of the American empire,

where they met up with some 20,000 Mexican workers recruited for the railway. Between 1850 and 1880, more than 55,000 Mexican workers had migrated to the southwest US to work in what had been Mexican territory. Construction of the Ugandan railroad (1899–1901) relied on 38,000 Indians from Gujarat and the Punjab. The British West African railway moved thousands of workers from Lagos to the then Gold Coast and Sierra Leone; each construction post of the Sierra Leone railroad cost 545 deaths and 'invalidity'.

Intensified colonial expansion and trade brought sailors and soldiers into migration streams. Tens of thousands of lascars, Indian, Chinese, Malay, Arab, Yemeni, Somali, Filipino, and Pacific Islander seamen came to England and America. Some abandoned ship, and became part of working-class settlements in port cities. Imperial might was backed by the 'martial races' of Ghurkhas from Nepal and Sikhs from Punjab from the 1840s onwards. The British Indian army numbered 1.3 million in World War 2, and 2.5 million in World War 2. British East African troops fought in Burma while Burmese troops fought in France. Fascist Italy recruited 40,000 Somalis for the 1935–36 invasion of Ethiopia. Like the seamen, servicemen did not always return 'home'. The first Punjabi immigrants to British Columbia (1897) and California (1899) arrived after stints in the British army and Hong Kong police. Soldiers from the Maghreb, including 173,000 Algerians, served in the World War 1 French forces, as thousands more did in World War 2. Declared 'surplus to requirements' after 1919, most were repatriated, but others started Maghrebi communities in France.

The legacies of empire

A second pattern of migration commenced with the end of World War 2, amidst decolonization and formation of new nation states. At the founding of the UN (1945), there were 50 nations; today there are 192. The birth of nations, dismantling of colonial control, and revolutions were, and are, bloody affairs. Refugees became the first major group of transnational migrants in 1945–50; some 50 million people moved from one nation to another, including 14 million people between India and Pakistan. Refugees continue to be a very large group among transnational migrants. The UNHCR (June 2007) estimates there are almost 10 million refugees, with an additional 20.8 million people living as internally displaced peoples, some of whom will join transnational migration flows. Very poor refugees cannot afford to move to distant lands permanently unless sponsored through refugee migration and family reunification programmes. Before 1975, there were some 300,000 Vietnamese living outside Vietnam, mostly in France. When some 3 million Vietnamese left after 1975, most settled in the US, sponsored through refugee programmes.

Decolonization was a deeply contested process, and the result of nationalist struggles which also gave rise to ideologies defining the new nation and its peoples. Colonial policies of racialization assumed new vicious forms of exclusion marking off the rights of 'sons of the soil' versus 'others'. Transnational colonial migrants became targets in Fiji, Indonesia, Myanmar, Malaya, Vietnam, Sri Lanka, Uganda, Kenya, Guyana and other locations. Without rights in lands they had lived and worked on for decades they migrated again. Return to ancestral lands left decades ago was impossible. These were the 'twice migrants', Uganda- Indians in the UK and the US, Indo-Fijians in British Columbia, Hoa (Sino-Vietnamese) in Paris and Los Angeles, Indo-Guyanese in New York and Sri Lankan Tamils in Toronto. Some came as refugees, with little to call their own. Others moved with transferable economic and social resources. East African Indians invested in the undervalued periurban American hotel-motel industry. Fifty per cent of all lodging properties in the US today are owned by Asian-Indians, many with an East African connection.

Lastly, and perhaps most unexpectedly, for the architects of *bracero* and 'guestworker' policies, these labourers became permanent settlers. Underdevelopment and incomplete modernization of the global South, exacerbated by the cutbacks in social expenditures through Structural Adjustment Programmes (SAPs), created pools of migrants for the global North. Cheap blue-collar labour was required to rebuild postwar Europe, and the expanding North American agro-industry. As in the case of plantation labour, recruitment was from within each empire's sphere of influence. *Bracero* programmes brought millions of Mexicans to the US, Algerians and Moroccans to France, Koreans and Chinese to Japan, Pakistanis and Indians to Britain, and Italians, Greeks and Turks to Germany.

Conditions of farm work remained akin to the experiences of contract workers on plantations, with exorbitantly priced credit tickets, lower wages than promised, and travel papers and passports held by the employer. Today there are almost 3 million farm workers employed in the US, 77 per cent of whom were born in Mexico. Schooling, as on the plantation, remains limited. Children work with parents. Life expectancy of farm workers is 49 years, while the national average is 75 years. Everywhere, able-bodied men were the first targets of recruitment and the assumption was this would be migrant contract labour without settlement rights. But a new, culturally diverse working class began to form instead. South Asians currently represent about 5.3 per cent of the population of England. In Germany, 3.4 per cent of the population is of Turkish origin; almost 10 per cent of France's population is Muslim. One in eight people in the US is of Hispanic origin.

Another unanticipated group of post-imperial migrants came from ranks of professional and technical white-collar workers brought to sustain the welfare-state health programmes initiated after the 1950s and 1960s. From Britain's National Health Services (NHS) to Johnson's 'Great Society' project in the US, health services for ageing inner cities, collapsing mining towns, and growing suburbia faced inadequate numbers of medical personnel. While working conditions and wages were poorer for immigrants than those for Europeans and Euro-Americans, they were many times better than those in the decolonized South. Thousands of Caribbean and Filipino nurses, and Indian, Pakistani, Taiwanese and Filipino doctors were recruited. By 1965 there were 18,000 Indian doctors in England alone. In the US today, 1 in every 20 doctors is of Indian origin. In 2002, the WHO found that there were over 250,000 Filipino nurses working in the US, the UK and other developed countries. High proportions of professionals from the global South in scientific research units and in engineering corps are common. The sum total of these initiatives has contributed to an unexpected cultural and racial diversity of the global North, a reality for which national populations raised within the ideological frames of the homogenous nation state are poorly prepared. The Migration Policy Institute notes that currently there are 175–200 million migrants worldwide, and that 1 out of every 35 people on Earth is an international migrant. By the end of the decade, the foreign-born population of the US will surpass 14.7 per cent. Empire has come home, and it is not yet the end of the imperial impact on migration.

Sucheta Mazumdar

Bibliography

Cohen R. (ed.) 1995. *The Cambridge survey of world migration*. Cambridge: Cambridge University Press.

Kikumura-Yano A. 2002. *Encyclopedia of Japanese descendants in the Americas*. New York: Rowan and Littlefield.

Pan L. (ed.) 1998. *The Encyclopedia of the Chinese overseas*. Singapore: Chinese Heritage Center.

Lal B. V. (ed.) 2006. *The Encyclopedia of the Indian Diaspora*. Honolulu: University of Hawai'i Press.

Related essays

Africa; agriculture; childhood; Chinese Diaspora; commodity trading; decolonization; diasporas; displaced persons; domestic service; empires and imperialism; ethnicity and race; executives and professionals; exile; family; food; forced migrations; genocide; gold; guestworkers; human mobility; indentured and contract labourers; international migration regimes; labour migrations; Lebanese Diaspora; marriage; nation and state; nomads; nursing; pedlars; pidgins and creoles; railways; refugees; remittances; rubber; scientific expeditions; slavery; Thailand and sex tourism; United Fruit Company; white men's countries; White Slavery

Empires and imperialism

Empire is one of the most powerful transnational political formations. The term is highly disputed, with a variety of societies from the world of the ancient Aztecs to the economic power of the modern financial markets described as an 'empire' of sorts. The term 'imperialism' is more explicitly modern, but it used to describe phenomena varying from the classic colonial land-grabs of the mid 19th century to the hegemonic power of institutions such as the World Bank. Certain phenomena tie together definitions of both 'empire' and 'imperialism', however.

The underlying definition in both terms is an idea about power. The examination of power relationships generally helps to distinguish meaningful uses of the term 'empire' or 'imperialism' from thoughtless ones. For instance, critics of the European Union have sought to paint it as a new empire, crushing free nations beneath its will. Yet this definition will not serve: ultimately, an association of freely associating states with a right of withdrawal cannot be termed an empire. At its heart, the definition of empire is an entity, usually a state, but not always so, that has the power to dominate, whether militarily, financially, or even culturally, over other such states or societies. This does not mean that the weaker parties are without power of their own: few empires can operate without some level of collaboration from the colonized. However, the balance of power is clearly uneven and not freely given on the part of those subjected to empire.

Empires in the modern world

The emergence of the modern world saw a variety of competing ideas of empire coexist. 'Traditional', territorially based contiguous empires, such as Russia and China, found themselves alongside 'modern' empires, the products of smaller European countries who found that a combination of technological advance and ideological unity propelled them into territorial expansion in areas geographically remote from the metropole. Yet both of these formations had many things in common, allowing them to be classed as empires. In particular, the dominant states within the empire gave themselves the right to absorb neighbouring peoples, and created the cultural context that justified this sort of absorption. However, the emergence of the idea of modern nationalism led to different responses from different empires.

In the 19th century, the spread of nationalism was intimately connected to the rise of a particular type of empire: the European model of a metropolitan state with a wide periphery, much of which was at a geographical distance. This model did not, for the most part, enslave pre-existing 'nations' as later nationalist rhetoric would imply; instead, it confronted and defeated a rather different model of empire, the land-based, cultural assimilative empire. The development of a metropolitan/periphery distinction helped to stimulate the idea of uniqueness that lies within nationalism: by means of the metropole's geographical separation from its empire, which in turn stimulated racial and cultural separation, ideas of a separate destiny were easier to nurture. Notions of nationhood were developed in conditions of relative stability for the British and French, even though the forging of Great Britain in 1707 had been highly politically controversial at the time. In addition, it was notable that one of the major imperial crises for the United Kingdom (as the country became known after unification with Ireland in 1801) was in the part of its empire that was geographically most contiguous and culturally similar: Ireland. In contrast, the rulers of the Russian and Austro-Hungarian empires in the 19th century made few attempts to create ruling identities that were nationally bounded in nature, instead drawing on premodern identities including shared religious observance (Holy Russia). This made them transnational, in the sense that their identities were not just imperial, but did not acknowledge the nation state as the defining polity which they either had to coalesce around, or else suppress. By definition, the idea of the nation, which demanded its own bounded state, was at odds with the idea of an empire, which encompassed many different peoples (not all self-defining as 'nations') in a hierarchical relationship. The contradictions inherent in this balancing act were, in a sense, best managed by the more 'traditional' empires. Qing China, for instance, was able to use terms such as 'suzerainty' to conceal the fact that many states (such as Kokand in Central Asia, or Annam in contemporary Vietnam) that nominally accepted Chinese overlordship were in fact essentially autonomous. The Austro-Hungarian empire came to a variety of local arrangements, which looked deeply inconsistent with each other when viewed from the top down, to allow varying degrees of self-definition and determination among its subject peoples.

However, the overall trend in empires from the mid 19th century onward was toward the model pioneered by Britain and France, with Germany arriving late on the scene. For these countries, there was a self-defeating flaw in the ideology that they brought to their colonies. The British and the French defined themselves in terms of nationhood, and defined the strength of the state in large part as lying in an essentially non-hierarchical, modern vision of how the state should operate. It was inevitable that this set of ideas should be transmitted to

the colonized, and that the latter would find it less and less convincing that a state model that was deemed appropriate for their conquerors should be denied to them. In this way, the ideology of imperialism, and nationalism inflected by anti-imperialism, both struggled over the course of the 20th century in a transnational context in which empires and colonized learned from each other, and moved forward over the corpses of the 'traditional' empires which had either died by 1919 or else, as in the case of the USSR, metamorphosed under a different name.

Modern imperialism and its discontents

Imperialism is a more explicitly modern phenomenon: it is an ideology, and in many ways similar to the other ideological products of the modern age such as nationalism and socialism. Rather than a phenomenon of action, like empire, imperialism is a product of a worldview, in which certain realities, whether economic, racial, or cultural, permit the domination of other subject groups or states by a more powerful one.

Imperialism is a powerful and essentially transnational phenomenon. Imperialist states must deny the agency of other nations to colonize them. Yet its analysis is more difficult in one sense than that of ideologies such as fascism, communism, or nationalism. The latter are, for the most part, self-aware and self-declared: people declared themselves, at various points in time, to be fascists, communists, or nationalists. Except for a very short period in Victorian Britain, very few actors explicitly termed themselves 'imperialists', or at least, not with a positive connotation. This means that the analysis of transnational imperialism has to take place in large part through a mirror: in other words, an examination of the tremendous power of anti-imperialist thought to shape understandings of imperialism over the past two centuries.

Anti-imperialism was, after all, in the late 19th and early 20th centuries, the form through which much of the nationalism in colonized, non-Western societies was expressed, and in doing so, nationalists made use of a clearly transnational mode of thought. The Leninist definition of imperialism also became influential during this period: this was imperialism as a form of primarily economic exploitation that derived from the inevitable failure of capitalism to find adequate domestic markets. However, this proved insufficient on its own to explain the dynamic of that era between anti-imperialism and non-European nationalism. The term 'anti-imperialism' remains powerful even after the ending of the era of territorial empire, and it has been revived in the post-Cold War global environment as a means of resisting a perceived hegemonic social and political order.

Anti-imperialism was one of the most powerful strains of thought in the non-Western world in the late 19th and early 20th centuries. Much of the language and terminology in which it was discussed emerged from political discussions in the metropole. The idea of imperialism as an ideological phenomenon emerged as a clear province of discussion in the late 19th century. Marxist thinkers, most notably Lenin, became dominant in this field, despite influence from non-Marxists such as J. L. Hobson, who argued in 1902 that imperialism was largely a product of the need for private capital to find markets outside the home country, and as such, was a means of increasing capitalist exploitation. While the circumstances of the early 20th century made it most obviously a critique of the establishment and exploitation of formal territorial colonies by the European powers, this was not the only channel for anti-imperialist sentiment.

Some of the earliest critics of British imperialism came from within the metropole. For instance, Hobson's argument was not so much a condemnation of imperialism per se, but rather an argument against the inefficiency of its practice as he saw it used in reality. The emergence of the British Labour Party in the early 20th century also brought opposition to empire more fully into the mainstream of metropolitan politics, but it still fell short of an outright, fully theorized, position of opposition to the structures of empire. Radicalization of the idea of anti-imperialism moved further with the Bolshevik Revolution of 1917 and the establishment of a Soviet state. The desire to harness anti-imperialism as a driving force for the new Soviet Union shaped the development of the Comintern, the foreign policy instrument of the USSR which aimed to foment revolution outside the USSR's borders. Initially, the rulers of the new state hoped that this would be a relatively swift process, but even when this proved not to be the case, the Comintern developed a significant role as a sponsor of

anti-imperialist feeling in the non-European world.

Imperialism, Marxism, and transnational thought in the colonial world

Unsurprisingly, the notion of anti-imperialism had particular significance in the colonial world of the early 20th century. One of the societies in which the Marxist-Leninist interpretation of anti-imperialism was particularly influential was China. The Chinese Communist Party (CCP) was founded in 1921, and drew heavily on the atmosphere of the largely anti-traditional May Fourth Movement, and the closely associated New Culture Movement which shaped much radical thinking in China in the early years of the Republic (1912–49). The Communist Party was by no means unique in seeking to use opposition to the imperialist presence in China as part of its political message. From the Opium Wars of the mid 19th century onwards, China's political elites had considered foreign encroachment in the form of extraterritoriality, lack of tariff autonomy, and outright colonial occupation, to be a grave political crisis, and sought means to oppose it. At the grassroots level, the incursion of traders, soldiers, and missionaries into the interior of China allowed anti-foreign feeling to thrive. The introduction of Western thought provided a new means for those elites to conceptualize China's place in the world in the early 20th century, and nationalism explicitly shaped around the idea of opposition to imperialism emerged at around that time. The arrival of the Republic after the 1911 Revolution paved the way for a nationalist politics based on opposition to 'warlordism without, imperialism within'. This formulation expressed what nationalists of all persuasions felt were the two major problems facing China: political division that made a mockery of the republic, and imperialist aggression that prevented unity. The Chinese Nationalist Party (Guomindang) led by Sun Yat-sen until his death in 1925 was one of the primary vehicles for anti-imperialist sentiment in China, and the Nationalist government established by Chiang Kai-shek in 1928 made the recovery of Chinese sovereignty a key part of its platform. However, it regarded imperialism as a threat because of the dominant world order which allowed an unequal status to different states, rather than because imperialism was the inevitable product of the move toward capitalism. While not denying the economic significance of imperialism, the Nationalists did not theorize the term in great detail.

Anti-imperialism was given a much more explicitly Marxist economic definition by the CCP. This definition was heavily influenced by the Comintern advisors to the party, who encouraged a definition of imperialism which stressed the need of national capitalist elites to seek to exploit colonies and other smaller nations. Anti-imperialism, in the CCP definition, demanded the overthrow of these exploitative structures so that China could achieve self-determination, and it drew on Soviet models whose attraction was their (supposed) universal validity well beyond the confines of any one nation state. The works of Bukharin, Stalin, and Lenin were translated and propagated by CCP members as a means of promoting the anti-imperialist strategy as part of a Communist programme, and an understanding of imperialism, defined in Leninist terms, was an essential part of the training for membership of the party after 1925. After the split with the Nationalists in 1927, the CCP's need to compromise their definition of anti-imperialism was significantly lessened, and it became a vigorously argued part of their agenda, along with class warfare.

The nationalist movement in French Indochina was also significantly influenced by a transnational, Marxist definition of anti-imperialism. By the mid 1940s, the leading independence movement, the Viet Minh, led by Ho Chi Minh, was dominant in the struggle against French and then Japanese colonialism in the region. Elsewhere in the colonial world, the establishment of Communist parties allowed a discourse of anti-imperialism to spread, for instance, after the establishment of the South African Communist Party in 1921, which from the 1940s was allied with the African National Congress.

Marxist influence was widely felt in anti-colonial struggles around the world in the early 20th century. However, the specifically Marxist-Leninist definition of anti-imperialism as a key stage in the class struggle was not shared by all such movements of the era. For instance, the Indian struggle for independence against the British was marked by various strands of thought which, once again, claimed universal validity beyond any one nation state, including secular socialism (exemplified by Nehru and the Congress Party), countermodern pacifism (Gandhi), and from the 1940s, a drive for a separate Muslim state, as well as radical and moderate communal variants. While an Indian Communist Party existed from 1921, and had significant influence, particularly among intellectuals, it was not the dominant shaper of anti-imperialism during the period, although its position was aided by radicalization caused by the Bengal famine of 1943. While Gandhi, for instance, regarded economic exploitation as a crucial element for the rallying of anti-imperialist feeling, his response was not Leninist, but rather anti-industrial (a return to localized production) and based on moral suasion (for instance, civil disobedience expressed through the breaking of laws on salt production). Gandhi's programme for the Congress Party in India, while gathering immense moral authority, was never wholly accepted by nationalists throughout India, yet even among those who turned to other forms of anti-British opposition, the use of a strictly Marxist definition of anti-imperialism was the province of a relative minority.

The contrast between developments in India and China, ostensibly both agrarian countries suffering from the effects of imperialism (albeit in different forms), suggests one reason for the inadequacy of a purely Marxist/Bolshevik analysis of what defined anti-imperialism, despite its 'scientific' claims to transnational validity. Perhaps the Marxist definition's greatest problem was its concentration on economic exploitation over issues of culture. Naturally, the distortions in social development caused by the economic exploitation of imperialist powers was a significant part of the power of the concept of anti-imperialism, as the boycotts of Western goods in India and China in the interwar period show. Yet the issues of nationhood and racism, treated by many Marxists as relatively incidental to the wider issues of economic exploitation, in fact loomed rather larger in the minds of many of the most potent anti-imperialist movements, as they epitomized the essentially exploitative power relationship that lay inherent within empire. Essentially, therefore, the classic Marxist analysis fell short because it sought to define anti-imperialism as being in some way forced to deviate to take account of nationalism, rather than accepting nationalism, ironically, as a primary product of a transnationally inflected anti-imperialism in its own right.

The Japanese empire in Asia during the early 20th century perhaps best shows how the language of transnational, anti-imperialist nationalism could be used in the service of exploitative imperialism, rather than in resistance to it. Japan's imperialism, from the late 19th century onward, was fuelled by a mutually contradictory pair of ideologies, one declaring that Japan was uniquely fitted through racial destiny to rule in Asia, the other, a conviction that it had a duty to liberate its colonized neighbours (China and the countries of Southeast Asia) from Western imperialist rule. The recipe that the Japanese military offered for the latter, namely the replacement of Western imperialism with Japanese, was hypocritical in the extreme. Nonetheless, the willingness of pan-Asian thinkers, starting with Okakura Tenshin, to develop the definitionally transnational idea that 'Asia is one' sparked interest among many nationalist intellectuals of the area across borders, notably Tagore in India and Sun Yat-sen in China. Pan-Asian thought, a variant of anti-imperialist nationalism based on the idea of an 'Asian' identity that crossed borders and cultures, was a prime example of a powerful anti-imperialist stream that owed little to the economic determinants of the Marxist version, not least since one of its primary exponents, Japan, was an economic exploiter in the most classic sense, but which drew on the positing of transnational links.

The imperialism of anti-imperialist actors

Also worth noting is the disparity between the language and behaviour of the two major anti-imperialist powers of the prewar era. Accusations of being an imperialist power were always particularly hurtful to the United States, which used its own liberation from empire (the British empire of the 18th century) and its assistance to other nations seeking self-determination as a central part of its identity. The country defined anti-imperialism as a moral and cultural issue more than an economic one. Yet the radicalization of politics in one of the US's immediate neighbours, Mexico, was shaped by Marxism at least in part defined in opposition to the perceived economic imperialism of the United States, and which allowed the government of Lázaro Cardenas (1934–40) to institute a radical policy of land redistribution. In general, Latin American revolutions (such as that in Cuba in 1959) have used opposition to US imperialism as a means of gaining support, and have used ideas of a Latin American solidarity beyond the confines of one particular country to boost it (using icons such as Simón Bolívar, for instance). The USSR has frequently been in support of such movements. Yet the latter's own explicit anti-imperialism was belied by its retention of Tsarist territorial acquisitions in, and further incursions into Ukraine, Central Asia and the Baltic states, as well as the maintenance of a ring of satellite states during the Cold War, whose economic relationship to the USSR certainly fitted the classic Leninist definition of exploitation.

The postwar world was marked by the process of decolonization, and by the 1970s, there were very few formal colonies left in the world. Nonetheless, the Cold War was marked by a continuing usage of anti-imperialism as a source of legitimacy by the great Communist powers, the USSR and China. Mao Zedong's model of anti-imperialist struggle took on particular vigour during the 1950s and 1960s as China sought to portray the USSR as a once-revolutionary state now backsliding into revisionism and stagnation. The two Communist superpowers found themselves in direct competition for the adherence of global parties and Communist states, and while the USSR succeeded for the most part in retaining the support of the European parties, the Chinese model made much more inroad into the Third World. While there was evidence of Chinese involvement in particular conflicts, notably in Korea (1950–53), much of the reality failed to match the rhetoric. However, the willingness of China to portray itself as the mentor of a new transnational grouping, the Third World, to newly liberated states meant that it played a particularly powerful role in development in areas outside its traditional sphere of influence, such as Africa, where it helped develop healthcare and railway infrastructure, and India, where the Naxalite peasant movement took its inspiration from Mao.

One of the most long-lasting anti-imperialist conflicts of the Cold War era, the war in Vietnam, provided one of the most prominent opportunities for both Soviet and Chinese rhetoric of Third World liberation. However, it also showed up the unbridgeable contradictions in the way in which each state used the term. After the defeat of the French in 1954 and the subsequent division of Vietnam into a Communist North and non-Communist South, the government of the North under Ho Chi Minh began to undermine the southern regime as part of the former's project of national reunification. The fact that the southern government was a dictatorship with relatively little public support enabled the USSR and China, however, to portray the struggle for reunification not just as a nationalist movement, but one that was symbolic of a wider, supranational form of anti-imperialism aimed at the United States. However, the Vietnamese government never fully trusted the Chinese, and from the late 1960s, broke off their alliance with the Chinese partly out of fear that Mao Zedong's state was seeking to establish a version of a more traditional East Asian order in which Vietnam would be seen as a secondary state within China's orbit. China's anti-imperialist credentials were further wrecked during its unsuccessful 1979 incursion into Vietnamese territory, which was quickly repulsed. Meanwhile, the USSR's own credibility as an anti-imperialist power had been damaged in the early Cold War because of its invasions of Hungary (1956) and Czechoslovakia (1968), and became yet more vulnerable in 1979 when the Soviet Union invaded Afghanistan because it perceived the country as a destabilizing influence on its borders.

Empire and imperialism in a postcolonial age?

The ending of the classic territorial empires has not ended the usefulness of the term 'imperialism'. The ending of the Cold War gave rise to concern about the way in which seemingly rational and neutral international bodies might in fact embody norms that entrenched the hegemonic power of one country, in particular the United States, with regard to the autonomy of states to defend their borders, set up trade barriers, or define human rights in their own terms. Ironically, the collapse of the Soviet Union allowed the circumstances for anti-imperialism, used primarily but not exclusively in an economic sense, to re-emerge as a term of critique. The breakdown of the bipolarity of the Cold War structure meant that the competition for global values had now changed to an effectively unipolar world, where increasingly globalized economic and geopolitical structures (such as the World Bank, World Trade Organization, and International Monetary Fund) now threatened

to dominate. Anti-globalization movements and sentiments frequently use the language of anti-imperialist struggle to express themselves in the present era.

Rana Mitter

Bibliography

Etherington N. 1982. 'Reconsidering theories of imperialism', History and Theory, 21, 1, 1–36.

Hardt M. and Negri A. 2000. Empire. Cambridge, MA: Harvard University Press.

Hobson J. A. 1948 [1905]. Imperialism: a study. London: Allen and Unwin.

Howe S. 2002. Empire: a very short introduction. Oxford: Oxford University Press.

Hunt M. H. 1996. The genesis of Chinese Communist foreign policy. New York: Columbia University Press.

Lenin V. I. 2002 [1916]. Imperialism: the highest stage of capitalism. New York: Pathfinder Press.

Related essays

Asia; capitalism; China; civil engineering works; civilizations; Cold War; Comintern and Cominform; corporations; cosmopolitanism and universalism; decolonization; development and growth; empire and migration; exile; financial diplomacy; Gandhi, Mohandas Karamchand; Garvey, Marcus Mosiah; General Agreement on Tariffs and Trade (GATT) / World Trade Organization (WTO); governing science; International Monetary Fund (IMF); internationalisms; liberalism; Maoism; modernity; nation and state; nonviolence; pan-isms; Pax Americana; railways; regional communities; religion; telephone and telegraphy; The Wretched of the Earth; transportation infrastructures; Universal Races Congress; Vietnam War; Westernization; white men's countries; wildlife films; women's movements; World Bank; world orders

Engineering

The transnational perspective on the community of engineers, which is presented in this article, proposes an interpretation of its internal relationships by taking into account both the dynamics of the centres as theoretical and organizational models, and the active role of the peripheries in appropriating – which in this instance implies interaction, change, adaptation – these same models.

Circulation of knowledge, through the travel of people, print material, ideas or objects, has historically been structured by asymmetric relationships, and technological culture partakes of this historical tradition. During the Middle Ages and the Renaissance, the constitution of a corpus of technical knowledge, expertise and common goals, which crystallized in the publication of technical treatises, was built on personal networks of artisans, stonemasons, architects and engineers, who travelled and exchanged correspondence. The exchange of scientific and technical knowledge was clearly enhanced by the growing number of periodicals circulating in Europe from the mid 17th century, usually linked to scientific and technical societies. On the other hand, the social recognition of the role of technical knowledge and practices envisaged as cognitive forms grew during this period. This is the characteristic which distinguished Europe from the rest of the world, in particular from China and the Islamic world, in which despite their strong technical tradition 'understanding' and 'acting' remained separated, the former being part of the domain of the sage and the latter of the artisan. During the 18th century, the increasing levels of specialized knowledge led to the definition of the profile of the modern European engineer, whose professional identity relied primarily on a specific and exclusive body of expert knowledge which differentiated engineering from other skills. However, this general notion of engineering encompasses distinct historical contexts, in particular, economic and political, the former corresponding to the period of affirmation of industrialization, the latter to the enhancement of the authority of the state.

By defining the Anglo-Saxon and the Continental paradigms, Britain and France became role models. On the British side, the model developed in a context characterized by the existence of a strong civil society; a less imposing and more decentralized state; a job market linked to private industrial initiative; informal training of engineers (workshopculture and hands-on training), and the recognition of the role and individual prestige of the inventor (engineer)-entrepreneur through market mechanisms such as patents. In turn, the Continental model was characterized by a strong intervention by the state in economic affairs, the state becoming itself an economic agent and main employer, especially in

public works. In this context, engineers had to be formally trained according to a selective and rigid academic system, which normally opened up a much sought-after career in the civil service.

The British model was adopted in the United States, a society whose economic and political characteristics were similar to those of Britain, and in the British colonial possessions, in particular in India, first through the action of engineers in imperial territories, and afterwards through the training of local elites in accordance with the model of the colonizer.

In Continental Europe the French model prevailed. The *Grandes Écoles*, in particular, the *École Nationale des Ponts et Chaussées* (1747), the *École Nationale Supérieure des Mines* (1778) and the *École Polytechnique* (1794) became the paradigm of academic training together with the professional organization of French engineering, which required an academic professional title. The French model was also the main reference for the Portuguese, Spanish and, naturally, French colonies, during both colonial and postcolonial periods.

In this context, some questions deserve particular attention: (i) a considerable number of engineering students and even European engineers went to Paris to complete or complement their training, predominantly in institutions for higher education, but also in industrial plants; (ii) this training was funded by national official institutions, which saw in this training abroad an easy way of embedding among their technical elites and in their technological structures the *avant garde* knowledge generated in the centre(s); (iii) following the return to their native countries and endowed with a technological culture acquired abroad, engineers aimed at responding to local challenges, namely the modernization of their respective countries; (iv) this process led to a consolidation of a transnational professional culture, which mirrored itself in peer-based networks.

From the 1860s onwards the French paradigm gradually lost its dominance. On the one hand, the German model of *Technische Hochschulen*, increasingly dedicated to the practical training of engineers to enter the private sector, became particularly appealing to the industrial agendas of European peripheries; on the other, despite local differences and for reasons not exclusively academic and professional, local schools in the peripheries earned recognition and in some cases competed directly with foreign educational models. Finally, the growing specialization in engineering and the participation of engineers in increasingly more diversified fields, led to a proliferation of centres of expertise, a phenomenon initiated in the 19th century as exemplified by the Freiberg Mining Academy or the Swiss Polytechnic School, but which intensified in the 20th century. In this context, the growing influence of the United States of America is particularly relevant.

Following World War 2 and especially with the Marshall Plan, the United States of America clearly became the reference for the engineering community all over the world. The missions of European engineers in the United States made them familiar with the American team research in laboratories, with new methods of production and new forms of management, which together with the competitiveness of the American economy and globalization dislocated the reference for engineering outside European borders. The American model became the paradigm of excellence in engineering, both for Europe and for the developing world.

However, in spite of distinct local, regional and national models and asymmetric relationships, a unifying rhetoric remained: engineering as a tool serving progress and prosperity, and the engineer as the pivotal actor of modernity. The almost messianic character of the engineer, anchored in a Saint-Simonian tradition and easily developed in a technology-driven society, is a distinctive professional mark, shared by all engineers: 'The engineer is a superior being', claimed the President of the American Society of Civil Engineers in 1895.

Despite the diversity of paradigms, European countries used the know-how of their engineers to establish their own rhythms of industrialization, first through railways and telegraphs, at the end of the 19th century, and then throughout the whole industrial fabric. Through engineering, European nations confronted each other in relation to their colonial possessions, especially following the Berlin Conference in 1885, and the imposition of effective occupation of overseas territories (the Portuguese case is an excellent example). The efficiency and creativity of engineers provided the basis for both the American and the Soviet nationalistic and expansionist rhetoric during the Cold War. In various ways, engineering, patriotism and modernization became the backbone of nationalism in former colonies such as those in South America (for instance the concept of Ordem e Progresso in Brazil and of Patria in Mexico, both founded on an engineering-minded basis), Africa (for instance the Maghreb, where local engineers affirmed their status by being one of the main artisans of independence), and Asia (the cases of India and Japan). A variety of solutions was adopted, both in time and space, ranging from continuity through local technical elites trained in the former colonizing countries, to confrontation with former patterns imposed by colonizers, and the adoption of alternative models aimed at minimizing the tension between local culture and foreign technological models. Just three brief examples: in Tunisia, engineers confronted the former colonial French power but they kept the professional structure inherited from the colonial period; in India, local techniques played a key role in Ghandi's rhetoric of independence, but at the same time colonial/Western technology is a powerful tool for Indian development (see, for instance the case of the Indian Institute of Technology in information technology); in Japan the Wakon Yosai ('Japanese spirit and Western technology') is still perceived as one of the main characteristics of Japanese modernization.

From the mid 20th century, the increasing power of multinationals and globalization changed deeply the world market which affected engineering. However, the question to engineers was rather a matter of scale than of substance, since working abroad was part and parcel of their professional tradition: Renaissance engineers circulated from patron to patron; 17th-century military engineers were frequently contracted by foreign courts; in the nineteenth century French, British and Dutch engineers often served the state or private companies in public works, industry and teaching. In imperial European countries, a large number of engineers made a career in the colonies benefiting from a kind of experience which, in the postcolonial era, constituted an important professional asset.

By intervening increasingly in borderline areas between technology and the management of human and material resources on a planetary scale, engineering is today a tentacular profession whose geographical limits and fields of application are widespread and of diffused contours.

In contemporary society, often referred to as the 'knowledge society' and the 'information society', the role of technology is omnipresent. It controls resources, legitimizes discourses on modernity, ensures the reliability of decisions and 'domesticates' the risks inherent in technological development.

As a specific field of expertise, engineering and engineers face the major challenge of keeping their disciplinary territory and perpetuating the iconic role which they have traditionally played in society.

Maria Paula Diogo

Bibliography

Cardoso Matos A., Diogo M. P., Gouzevitch I. and Grelon A. (eds) 2007. *The professional identity of engineers. historical and contemporary issues*, Lisbon: Colibri.

Fox R. and Guagnini A. 1993. *Education, technology and industrial performance in Europe: 1850–1939*. Cambridge: Cambridge University Press.

Gouzevitch I., Grelon A. and Karvar A. (eds) 1995. *La formation des ingénieurs en perspective: modèles de référence et réseaux de médiation: XVIIIe – XXe siècles*. Rennes: Presses Universitaires de Rennes.

Kranzberg M. (ed.) 1986. *Technological education – technological style*. San Francisco: San Francisco Press.

Related essays

civil engineering works; Cold War; developmental assistance; gold; higher education; industrialization; information technology (IT) offshoring; intellectual elites; Marshall Plan; modernity; nation and state; organization models; productivity missions; railways; salt; technical assistance; technical standardization; technologies; telephone and telegraphy

Environmental diplomacy

The term 'environmental diplomacy' refers to all governmental and non-governmental negotiations that lead to transboundary agreements, arbitrations, and judicial precedents designed to protect the world's natural and living resources from overexploitation or pollution. This includes all transnational efforts to preserve species, habitats, and biodiversity, eliminate acid rain and greenhouse gases, ban toxic wastes and nuclear contaminants, reduce the world's dependence on fossil fuels, and the like.

In the past, foreign and colonial ministries in Europe and the United States conducted most of the negotiations and produced most of the major environmental agreements, with the League of Nations and United Nations (UN) serving as secondary forums. Since 1972, the United Nations Environment Programme (UNEP), headquartered in Nairobi, Kenya, has served as the world's most important centre for handling transnational environmental issues. Many countries responded to the establishment of UNEP by creating separate environmental ministries empowered to negotiate and oversee transnational agreements (the United States is a major exception). UNEP was established in the wake of the United Nations Conference on the Environment, held in Stockholm, Sweden in 1972, when the 'acid rain' problem was high on the diplomatic agenda. Twenty years later, when UNEP sponsored the United Nations Conference on Environment and Development (or '1992 Earth Summit') in Rio de Janeiro, Brazil, the main focal points of discussion were 'global warming', 'biodiversity', and 'deforestation'.

Non-governmental organizations (NGOs) have been more active in environmental negotiations and treaty making than in most other arenas of diplomacy. Historically, the British-based Society for the Preservation of the Wild Fauna of the Empire (or 'Faunal Society'), founded in 1903, has been one of the most powerful of the early NGOs. Because many of its most prominent members were big-game hunters or ex-hunters with close ties to the British Foreign and Colonial offices, detractors dubbed them 'penitent butchers'. Penitent or not, the Faunal Society largely determined the direction of conservation policies in colonial Africa and India until 1945. The efforts of Paul Sarasin (Switzerland) and P. G. van Tienhoven (Netherlands) to create a pan-European lobby group were stymied by World War 1 and World War 2, but Sir Julian Huxley finally fulfilled their dreams with the founding of the International Union for the Protection of Nature in 1948, renamed the International Union for the Conservation of Nature and Natural Resources (IUCN) in 1956 and renamed anew the World Conservation Union in 1991. Along with its sister organization, the Worldwide Fund for Nature (or World Wildlife Fund, as it is known in the Anglo-American world), it remains a powerful force in the formulation of conventions to protect endangered habitats and species. Aside from the World Conservation Union and the Worldwide Fund for Nature, UNEP works day to day with hundreds of lesser-known local, national, regional, and international NGOs on a variety of environment-related issues worldwide.

The best source for the complete texts of modern environmental treaties is the multivolume work, International Protection of the Environment: Treaties and Related Documents, edited by Bernd Rüster, Bruno Simma, and Michael Bock (Dobbs Ferry, New York: Oceana Publications, 1983–present). This series includes more than fifteen hundred environmental conventions, treaties, accords, court decisions, amendments, and intergovernmental directives that have been signed since 1750. Only around sixty agreements were signed before the 20th century; most were negotiated after 1900, with an acceleration after 1970. Many are simple bilateral treaties and side-agreements designed to regulate a shared natural resource or mitigate a shared pollution problem. Fishing treaties, transboundary air and water agreements, and nuclear-energy regulations are the most common of these simple accords. Others are complex conventions that involve many countries and include vast tracts of land, ocean, or air. Treaties that protect migratory species, or ban the use of chlorofluorocarbons (CFCs), or control greenhouse gases are all examples of these more complex multilateral accords.

Environmental conventions and treaties can be subdivided into seven overlapping categories: (1) the protection of flora and fauna (especially migratory animals) on land; (2) the safeguarding of rivers, lakes, and groundwater, as well as freshwater organisms; (3) the safekeeping of marine systems (oceans, seas, coastlines) and marine life; (4) restraints on the discharge of pollutants into the atmosphere, water systems, and soil; (5) regulations related to the manufacturing, transport, and use of chemicals for industrial and military purposes; (6) controls over the use of nuclear materials for peaceful and military purposes; and (7) general guidelines and judicial decisions regarding the transboundary responsibilities and liabilities of governments.

Flora and fauna protection has been a major concern of environmental diplomacy since the late 19th century, when the invention of powerful new rifles and imperial expansion led to the extinction of the passenger pigeon and the quagga, and the near extinction of the American buffalo and many other hunted species. The earliest treaties, notably the Convention for the Preservation of Wild Animals, Birds, and Fish in Africa, signed in London in 1900, and the Convention for the Protection of Migratory Birds, signed between the United States and Great Britain (on behalf of the Dominion of Canada) in 1916, read more like international hunting accords than conservation agreements, since they were designed primarily to protect high-value prey rather than preserve animal habitat. Subsequent treaties of importance – such as the Convention Relative to the Preservation of Flora and Fauna in their Natural State, signed in London in 1933, and the Convention on Nature Protection and Wild Life Preservation in the Western Hemisphere, signed in Washington, DC in 1940 – focused on the creation of national parks in Africa, South Asia, and the Americas as habitat protection sites. More recently, the trend has been toward global accords, notably the Convention on Wetlands of International Importance especially as Waterfowl Habitat, signed in Ramsar, Iran in 1971, and the Convention on the International Trade in Endangered Species of Fauna and Flora (CITES), signed in Washington, DC in 1973.

The safekeeping of watery regions, along with their living resources (the 'fisheries'), has also been a primary concern of coastal and maritime governments over the past century, especially after the invention of sophisticated nets and traps, long lines, harpoon guns, and modern factory ships led to the overexploitation of many hunted species. The conservation record is spottier for oceans and seas (and for some large lakes) than for riverine habitats because the marine world belongs to the global commons and is thus beyond the control (coastlines aside) of any government. International efforts to protect the cod fisheries in the North Atlantic failed, as did later efforts to protect haddock, halibut, salmon, and tuna, largely due to the 'the fisherman's dilemma': any fish that a fisherman leaves in the ocean for purposes of propagation most likely just land in the net of a less conservation-minded rival. A rare bright moment came with the Convention between the United States, Great Britain, Russia, and Japan for the Preservation and Protection of Fur Seals, signed in Washington, DC in 1911, which was designed to regulate the fur seal harvest around the Pribilof islands. This treaty, however, was only possible because the Pribilofs belonged to Alaska, and the US government was willing to work with the other powers to end the major cause of the stock depletion: pelagic sealing. The three major whaling conventions of the 20th century – the Convention for the Regulation of Whaling (signed in Geneva in 1931), the International Agreement for the Regulation of Whaling (signed in London in 1937), and the International Convention for the Regulation of Whaling (signed in Washington, DC in 1946) – were more typical of marine treaties. Not only did they fail to reverse the decline of whale populations, they may actually have made matters worse by lending the slaughter an aura of legitimacy and respectability. The whaling business began to collapse in the 1960s not because of the whaling treaties but because by then there were too few whales left in the Antarctic to justify the chase.

International efforts to control air, water, and soil pollution, as well as attempts to regulate chemicals and nuclear materials, have had mixed results. The Treaty Banning Nuclear Weapon Tests in the Atmosphere, in Outer Space and under Water (the 'Partial Test Ban Treaty'), signed in Moscow in 1963, while not normally viewed as an environmental treaty, greatly reduced the amount of strontium-90 and other radioactive pollutants in the atmosphere. Another success story is the Convention for the Protection of the Ozone Layer, signed in Vienna in 1985. Championed by the US government, it phased out the use of CFCs ('freon') in refrigerants, styrofoam, spray cans, and other products, after scientists discovered that these chemicals were dangerously thinning the ozone layer. The industrialized nations, however, have repeatedly failed to address the twin problems of acid rain and global warming caused by the industrialized overdependence on fossil fuels. The Convention on Long-range Transboundary Air Pollution, signed in Geneva, Switzerland in 1974, has proven to be an ineffective tool of environmental management, largely because many Western democracies, former Eastern bloc countries, and newly industrializing states have been reluctant to put restraints on their economic growth. Similarly, the Kyoto Protocols, designed to reduce greenhouse gas emissions, have failed to solve the global warming problem, partly due to resistance to their implementation in the US and Australia but also in part due to the broad exemptions that the protocols give to China and India.

The Stockholm and Rio conferences were instrumental in laying out general principles and global frameworks for future environmental negotiations. The most important declaration to emerge from the Stockholm conference was Principle 21: 'States have, in accordance with the Charter of the United Nations and the principles of international law, the sovereign right to exploit their own resources pursuant to their own environmental policies, and the responsibility to ensure that activities within their jurisdiction or control do not cause damage to the environment of other States or of areas beyond the limits of national jurisdiction'. Similarly, the Rio conference delegates laid out a comprehensive roadmap for the ensuing twenty years, known as Agenda 21, which stated in part: 'integration of environment and development concerns and greater attention to them will lead to the fulfilment of basic needs, improved living standards for all, better protected and managed ecosystems and a safer, more prosperous future. No nation can achieve this on its own; but together we can – in a global partnership for sustainable development'. The choice of the number 21 at both Stockholm and Rio was no accident: the UN was signalling the centrality of environmental issues to the 21st century.

Environmental diplomacy tends to suffer from several interrelated weaknesses. First, while environmental damage is often easily detected (species extinction, ozone depletion, forest death, and the like), the exact causes of the destruction often elude researchers for decades. The absence of reliable data, and the resulting difficulty in achieving a scientific consensus, can slow the treaty-making process: all too often, an agreement comes too late to save the species, resources, or habitat that it was designed to safeguard. Second, effective protection of the environment often requires far-reaching and painful choices in national economic policies. In the interest of reaching a domestic and international consensus, negotiators often utilize vague and ambiguous textual phrases. While these negotiating practices often smooth the path toward implementation, they can also undermine a treaty's efficacy by providing wriggle-room for government regulators and the affected industries. Third, international agreements must be ratified and implemented at the national level. National governments, however, are often reluctant to apply stringent environmental rules, especially if these rules impose restraints on economic growth. As a result, some treaties exist only on paper. Finally, though international law is binding upon the signatories, there is no effective way to enforce transboundary agreements except moral persuasion and voluntary arbitration (and in some cases the International Court of Justice). All too often, countries ratify a treaty and then flout one or more of its stipulations, safe in the knowledge that international reprisals are rare. Still, the field of international environmental law is growing side-by-side with the field of environmental diplomacy, as can be seen by the successful conclusion of the Fur Seal, Trail Smelter, Lac Lanoux, Icelandic Fisheries, and many other precedent-setting arbitrations and adjudications over the past century.

Mark Cioc

Bibliography

Benedick R. E. 1991. *Ozone diplomacy: new directions in safeguarding the planet.* Cambridge, MA: Harvard University Press.

Darst R. G. 2001. *Smokestack diplomacy: cooperation and conflict in East–West environmental politics.* Cambridge, MA: MIT Press.

Dorsey K. 1998. *The dawn of conservation diplomacy: U.S.–Canadian wildlife protection treaties in the progressive era.* Seattle: University of Washington Press.

McCormick J. 1989. *Reclaiming paradise: the global environmental movement.* Bloomington: Indiana University Press.

Susskind L. E. 1994. *Environmental diplomacy: negotiating more effective global agreements.* Oxford and New York: Oxford University Press.

Tolba M. 1998. *Global environmental diplomacy: negotiating environmental agreements for the world, 1973–1992.* Cambridge, MA: MIT Press.

Wirth J. D. 2000. *Smelter smoke in North America: the politics of transborder pollution.* Lawrence: University Press of Kansas.

Related essays

air pollution; biodiversity; climate change; conservation and preservation; disarmament; ecology; environmentalism; fisheries; forests; freshwater management; indigenous knowledges; intergovernmental organizations; international non-governmental organizations (INGOs); national parks; oceans; Stockholm Conference; sustainable development; World Conservation Union (IUCN) / World Wide Fund for Nature (WWF)

Environmentalism

Dictionaries typically define environmentalism as advocacy for the preservation of the natural environment, most particularly from the effects of pollution. Although useful and accurate within the bounds of its brevity, such a working definition belies not only the intricate history of environmentalism, but also the fact that it has entailed significant transnational aspects for many decades.

Previous to the 1960s, the field of psychology had used the word 'environmentalism' under a different guise, one that was at times tied to certain political ideologies and has since transmogrified into 'environmental determinism'. Origins of the current usage of the word are commonly correlated to either one of two particular events: the publication of Rachel Carson's *Silent Spring* in 1962 and the first Earth Day in 1970. No few historians have relied on these particular dates to distinguish environmentalism from an older 'conservation movement' that had arisen during the last half of the 19th century. According to this perspective, the conservation movement had focused on 'green' issues of natural resource and wildlife conservation – a movement that had matured into a distinctive if not prominent feature of a handful of mid-20th-century Western societies. Environmentalism, in contrast, brought the 'brown' issues of toxic poisons into a national and international limelight.

This chronological distinction between the conservation and environmental movements has been considered both semantic (it depends on how broadly one defines environmentalism) and important (it identifies the significant ramifications of an intellectual 'paradigm shift' on law and policy). While this latter interpretation cannot be outrightly dismissed, taking the more chronologically expansive perspective will better illuminate the transnational character of environmentalism. For notwithstanding ancient roots to environmental thinking, it is probably fair to argue that the transnational roots of environmentalism reach back to the Enlightenment, an era marked by the advancement of scientific methodologies and by the adoption of science as a way of understanding the world. The Enlightenment saw not only dramatic growth in natural history (the basic empirical observation and recording of what exists out there in 'Nature'), but also a flourishing interest in scientific exploration across the globe's inchoate borders. Of those who set out to record the world during this period, the archetype was the Prussian Alexander von Humboldt. Although relatively obscure today, his accounts of his travels through South America at the dawn of the 19th century would eventually grant him status as the era's pre-eminent man of science. Along with many of his peers, von Humboldt not only fostered the somewhat haphazard development of various protoecological concepts, but also put forth a mode of thinking about the interrelatedness of Nature that would become a staple of environmentalism.

Yet Nature's wholeness was only one pillar of the origins of environmentalism. Another important pillar was erected by the clergyman Thomas Malthus, a well recognized figure in environmental history who consciously detracted from the pandemic optimism of the Enlightenment. Known today as the father of demography, Malthus's very name symbolizes pessimism over the relationship between food resources and human population. Although Malthus did not travel widely like von Humboldt, his work was global in perspective and comparative in approach.

These two broad perspectives – the interrelatedness of Nature and pessimism regarding man's ability to ruin it – appear in what is widely accepted to be the first environmental tract: *Man and Nature: or, physical geography as modified by human action*. Published in 1864 by the polymath scholar, linguist, and diplomat George Perkins Marsh, the book presciently identified a now-familiar suite of environmental threats to species, forests, water, and deserts. Notably, the book's gloomy portents were provoked by extensive land degradation that Marsh directly observed not only in his home state of Vermont, but during his travels around the Mediterranean.

Three years after the publication of *Man and Nature*, the US would purchase the territory of Alaska from Russia. This purchase marked a seminal moment in the history of transnational environmentalism, for it set the stage for a decades-long controversy over utilization of the Pacific fur seal from their rookeries on the Pribilof Islands (which were included in the Alaska purchase). Throughout the textured history of this conflict, a critical factor was the role of non-governmental actors – what we would call 'civil society' today – in advocating for the species' protection. This advocacy took many forms, at times generating significant animosities among those who were advocating for the seal's protection. Thus, whether described as between preservationists and conservationists, between cooperators and protestors, or between 'dark green' and 'light green' advocates, contemporary internecine debates in the environmental community were all prefigured in this one early controversy.

In Europe, non-governmental advocates played a prominent role in the establishment of two early international treaties: one on African wildlife (1900) and one on birds important to agriculture (1902). In 1903 a group of British aristocrats established the Society for the Preservation of the Wild Fauna of the Empire, which would have a significant influence on the course of species conservation in Europe and Africa over the course of the century. Known today as Fauna & Flora International, the group was in the vanguard of early European involvement in international environmental affairs. Also within Europe, a 1909 International Congress for the Protection of Nature eventually led to the 1913 establishment of a Consultative Commission for the International Protection of Nature, a body that dissipated with the onset of World War 1. Although the idea resurfaced in the late 1920s, coalescing in 1934 as the International Office for the Protection of Nature, it would soon share a similar fate to its predecessor with the onset of World War 2.

Back on the other side of the Atlantic, the US had looked to Mexico to sign an international treaty for the protection of migratory birds as early as the first decade of the 20th century. But with civil war making Mexico a dubious partner at best, conservationists turned instead to Canada. The result was a 1916 Convention for the Protection of Migratory Birds, which entailed the significant effect of endowing the US federal government with the lawful authority to oversee bird conservation across the country – and thus constituted an early environmental victory by bird conservation advocates in both countries. In 1936, a similar treaty was signed with Mexico, although this one included game mammals within its purview. Five years later, the conservationists' agenda expanded dramatically when the US and six Latin American countries signed the Convention on Nature Protection and Wild Life Preservation in the Western Hemisphere. Despite the fact that 12 other countries would sign on before the summer of 1941, the onset of World War 2 ensured that the 'Western Hemisphere Convention' would share the same fate as its European counterparts.

Despite the dampening effects of World War 2, environmentalism would resurface with at least three signature events before the end of the 1940s. First, 12 countries signed the International Convention for the Regulation of Whaling in 1946. Although two multilateral treaties in the 1930s had sought some level of protection for whales, it was only this treaty that would eventually lead to significant conservation gains for cetaceans. Second, in 1948, 18 countries, seven international organizations, and 107 national organizations would come together to form the International Union for the Preservation of Nature (IUPN) – a hybrid organization that gave voting powers to both governments and non-governmental organizations. The third event occurred in 1949 with the United Nations Scientific Conference on Conservation and Utilization of Resources at Lake Success, New York. While the IUPN held a side-meeting there, the formal contributions by over 500 participants at the UN meeting ranged across a much broader swath of resource issues, including forests, land, water, minerals, and energy.

While the 1950s commenced with a new European convention for the protection of birds, the decade would conclude few notable developments in international protection of the environment. Nonetheless, the 1956 publication of *Man's role in changing the face of the Earth* provided a significant indication of where environmentalism was heading. The result of a symposium bringing together many of the era's key thinkers on natural resource issues – recall that the phrase "environmental issues" did not yet exist – the symposium addressed not only a range of conservation issues in Asia, Africa, Europe, and North America, but also covered various aspects of pollution – including a section on the 'Ecology of wastes'.

Although participants at the 1955 symposium included such notable intellectuals as Carl Sauer, Lewis Mumford, and Clarence Glacken, these names remain recognizable only among fairly specialized audiences – and none of them would become strongly associated with environmentalism. In contrast, during the 1960s a number of prominent thinkers would become intimately associated with the advent of the 'new' environmentalism, most significantly the aforementioned Rachel Carson. Yet she was hardly alone; three other notable environmentalists were Paul Ehrlich (who focused on the issue of overpopulation), Barry Commoner (who focused on the ill effects of human high technology), and Ralph Nader (who, despite being more associated with consumer protection issues, also strongly advocated for environmental protection). While all four of these individuals focused on the amelioration of US environmental problems, many of their writings incorporated an international perspective that helped generate widespread concern over environmental problems.

During this time period, concern over international environmental issues led to separate planning efforts on either side of the Atlantic Ocean for an international conference on the environment. These efforts merged to form the 1968 Intergovernmental Conference of Experts on the Scientific Basis for the Rational Use and Conservation of the Resources of the Biosphere, commonly known as the Biosphere Conference. The conference's organizers deliberately avoided the potentially inflammatory topics of policy and advocacy in favour of the role of scientific knowledge in solving environmental problems. As such, the conference has most often been associated with the establishment of UNESCO's Man and the Biosphere Programme and the internationally popular idea of a 'biosphere reserve' (although this latter idea would only be articulated three years after the conference). Yet the Biosphere Conference did play a significant role in swaying the UN General Assembly to endorse the idea of an overtly political global conference on environmental issues. After a tremendous amount of preparatory work, this came about with the 1972 Stockholm Conference on the Human Environment.

The Stockholm Conference was significant for two primary reasons. First, it demarcated the drastically different perspectives on environmental issues emanating from the 'global North' and the 'global South'. Efforts to find compromise between the two perspectives led to the essential concept, if not the label, of 'sustainable development' (this being 15 years before the phrase became the shibboleth promulgated by the World Commission on Environment & Development). Second, Stockholm opened the floodgates of international environmentalism. A deluge of transnational activism has since surged across the environmental spectrum, with a growing number of environmental organizations advocating on issues ranging from biodiversity, desertification, and air pollution to climate change, stratospheric ozone depletion, and the transboundary shipment of hazardous substances. One of the more recognizable of these organizations was incorporated the same year as Stockholm, emanating out of the Canada-based 'Don't Make a Wave Committee' that had sent a ship – The Greenpeace – to protest against US nuclear testing in the Aleutian Islands in 1971. Today, the iconic image of a Greenpeace zodiac boat manoeuvring between whales and harpooners lies at one end of the spectrum of NGO activities; far at the other end lie groups such as the World Resources Institute, which conduct research and disseminate information in the hopes that it will sway decision makers and public opinion. In between lie a vast number of NGOs – and, importantly, 'transnational advocacy networks' – conducting multifarious forms of environmental advocacy.

Since Stockholm, one can discern a general trend within transnational environmentalism to expand the purview from a focus on particular regional or issue-specific problems to a focus on more global environmental challenges. Biodiversity is emblematic of this trend. Only a year after Stockholm, the international community signed the Convention on the International Trade of Endangered Species (CITES), a treaty that would become widely recognized despite the fact that it dealt with only one of many threats to biodiversity. Six years later, the 1979 Bonn Convention on Migratory Species would take a broader approach, but again limited itself to a small portion of the wide panoply of biodiversity issues. It was only with the 1992 Convention on Biological Diversity (CBD) that the international community (only a handful of states did not sign the CBD) would declare

its intentions to protect biodiversity in a comprehensive manner.

The same trend is evident with atmospheric issues. In 1979, for instance, a large number of European and North American countries signed the Convention on Long-Range Transboundary Air Pollution. Considered one of the most significant atmospheric conventions ever negotiated, it nonetheless was generally limited to ameliorating the problem of acid rain. In the 1980s, the international community would focus on the problem of the deterioration of the ozone layer due to the release of chlorofluorocarbons (CFCs) and related compounds. Although this treaty was global in terms of its effects, the focus was primarily on eliminating the use of such materials in the developed world while preventing their expansion in the developing world. It would only be in the next decade that an international atmospheric convention would come about that would be truly global in scope: the 1992 Framework Convention on Climate Change (FCCC). Over the course of its establishment, through the continued negotiations leading up to the 1997 Kyoto Protocol, and up to the present day, the FCCC has been the nexus of a far-reaching global debate between varied countries, international organizations, nongovernmental actors, and a host of complex coalitions within each of these sectors.

While this trend in transnational environmentalism from the particular to the general is discernible from a bird's eye view, it should not be overinterpreted as a diminution of the particular. Indeed, there has been no small amount of backlash to 'high-level' international environmental negotiations, and many in both the governmental and civil-society sectors have chosen to eschew such global 'agreements to agree' for more local, tangible projects. This became particularly evident at the 2002 World Summit on Sustainable Development (WSSD), which was formally conducted as a ten-year review of the UN Conference on Environment and Development (the 1992 'Earth Summit' held in Rio de Janeiro, Brazil, where both the CBD and FCCC had originally been opened for signature along with three other international instruments). WSSD focused on enhancing the role of both civil society and the private sector, and promoted the idea of 'Type II agreements' between governments and these other actors. Despite the fact that such agreements hardly constituted anything novel on the international landscape, WSSD did serve to underscore an implicit admission by the world's governments that they alone did not have the capacity to solve the globe's myriad environmental ills. A more cynical perspective on WSSD held that 'Type II agreements' only enhanced the capacity of governments to spread the blame for the Earth's woes. No doubt, WSSD has provoked strong cynicism over the potential of environmentalism, the growing pervasiveness of which is accused of being inversely proportional to its effectiveness.

But even as there is good reason to be sceptical of how much environmentalism has improved the environment, such scepticism must face the counterfactual: what would the world now look like if the social phenomenon of transnational environmentalism had never arisen? While we can never know, we can glimpse how different the world might have become by summarizing the above history of transnational environmentalism as a series of five distinct stages. The first stage came in the first half of the 20th century, when a number of governments and advocates began to understand that effective natural resource management often transcended the influence of domestic authority. The second stage came with new multilateral environmental institutions of the post-World War 2 world, which demonstrated that such broad-scale cooperative efforts could maintain institutional viability over the long term. The 1972 Stockholm Conference marked the beginning of the third stage, in which a common conception of the goals of transnational environmentalism became pervasive through multiple societal sectors within and between numerous developed countries (albeit ominous to numerous developing countries). Fourth, the 1992 Earth Summit marked the high point in hopes and expectations over what the international community might achieve in order to 'save the Earth'. Finally, although an assessment of the fifth stage most assuredly comes from a non-historical perspective, WSSD may have signalled a transition of environmentalism toward a complex web of applied and 'grounded' initiatives to solve environmental problems.

While numerous variations on these five stages can be found in the extensive literature on transnational environmentalism, collectively they indicate that the social phenomenon of environmentalism has had a significant – if ultimately inadequate – effect in protecting the 'global environment'. In this regard, over the past decade a sizeable number of scholars have developed a variety of methodological approaches to assessing the effectiveness of 'international environmental regimes'. Not unexpectedly, the results of these investigations have indicated that varying levels of 'effectiveness' have been achieved by different regimes. But perhaps most notable in this literature is the increasingly consistent theme of complex governance. As already pointed out, non-governmental actors have long driven the amorphous and constantly changing agenda of transnational environmentalism; at the same time, governments retain those sovereign powers that, contrary to premature claims of 'governance without government' in a borderless world, directly shape humanity's effects on the biophysical world. Although these two perspectives were once commonly interpreted as contradictory, scholars now generally regard them as complementary. Consequently, understanding transnational environmentalism has to a large degree become a matter of discerning amongst the diversity of interactions – ranging from outright rebellion to poorly disguised cooptation – that occur between non-governmental actors and governmental decision-making authorities.

Charles C. Chester

Bibliography

Breitmeier H., Young O. R. and Zürn M. 2006. *Analyzing international environmental regimes: from case study to database.* Cambridge, MA: MIT Press.

Caldwell L. K. 1996. *International environmental policy: from the twentieth to the twenty-first century,* third edition. Durham, NC: Duke University Press.

Dauvergne P. 2005. *Handbook of global environmental politics.* Cheltenham and Northampton, MA: Edward Elgar.

Dorsey K. 1998. *The dawn of conservation diplomacy: U.S.–Canadian wildlife protection treaties in the progressive era.* Seattle: University of Washington Press.

Holdgate M. 1999. *The Green Web.* London: Earthscan.

McCormick J. 1995. *The global environmental movement.* New York: John Wiley.

Keck M. E. and Sikkink K. 1998. *Activists beyond borders: advocacy networks in international politics.* Ithaca: Cornell University Press.

Wapner P. 1996. *Environmental activism and world civic politics.* Albany: State University of New York Press.

Related essays

acclimatization; air pollution; biodiversity; car safety standards; climate change; conservation and preservation; consumer society; ecology; environmental diplomacy; forests; freshwater management; Greenpeace; international non-governmental organizations (INGOs); intergovernmental organizations; national parks; New Age; oceans; outer space; pesticides, herbicides, insecticides; population; scientific expeditions; Stockholm Conference; United Nations system; wildlife films; World Conservation Union (IUCN) / World Wide Fund for Nature (WWF); world orders; zero growth

Epidemics

Epidemics – especially in their expanded form as pandemics – have long been classic examples of transnational phenomena. While an epidemic – an unusually high prevalence of a lethal infectious disease – is primarily confined to one area or country, it is not uncommon for it to spill over to adjoining regions, across national boundaries. If this process spreads the disease even more widely, through a whole continent or even across oceans to the entire globe, the term 'pandemic' becomes appropriate.

To attain epidemic levels, most diseases require a minimum concentration of previously uninfected people living in close proximity to each other; for it to spread to neighbouring territories requires a degree of contact, usually via exploration, trade, migration, flight or a military campaign. In human history such conditions were rare until agriculture took root and settled communities developed. Consequently, epidemics began to appear in recorded history only once towns had developed and long-distance movement had become more frequent.

Even then, for a long time the relatively slow nature of such movement meant that few epidemics grew into pandemics – in the 2,000 years before 1800 there were only seven major recorded instances of this: the Antonine Plague, the Plague of Cyprian and the Plague of Justinian in the Near East and along the Mediterranean coast in the second, third and sixth centuries AD; the 'Black Death' of bubonic/pneumonic plague across Asia, the Middle East, North Africa and Europe from the 14th century; the spread of a cluster of Old World diseases like smallpox, measles, typhus and malaria to the Americas from late in the 15th century – and the passage of syphilis in the opposite direction in return – and the recurrent waves of smallpox carried around the world by sea from the 16th century.

However, the introduction of quicker forms of travel in the 19th century, especially with the advent of steam, and the consequent acceleration and expansion of human movement around the globe significantly facilitated the evolution of pandemics out of local epidemics. The occurrence of seven pandemics in just 200 years after 1800 bears clear testimony to this fact.

Modern pandemics

The earliest of these 'modern' pandemics, that of cholera, was spread from that disease's endemic 'home' in deltaic Bengal to the rest of India by the campaigns of British troops across the subcontinent from 1817, and from there by sea and land to Asia, East Africa, Europe and North America during the next two decades. Between 1840 and 1910 five more pandemic waves of cholera spread, following similar paths of infection from India; in several of them, pilgrims going on hajj to Mecca or returning from there were major carriers of the disease.

In the case of yellow fever, the advent of faster sea travel in the 19th century only hastened processes which had already caused several pandemic surges of this disease in the previous 150 years. From the Caribbean where it had taken root in the 17th century after being brought there from West Africa aboard slave-ships, yellow fever was repeatedly spread by traders and refugees to North and South America from 1741 onwards, and even, on occasions, to the Iberian Peninsula. At its greatest extent, in 1878, it raged simultaneously in Havana, Memphis and Madrid, claiming thousands of lives.

In comparison, bubonic plague, taking full advantage of the steamship revolution of the late 19th century, easily outran yellow fever. Reaching Hong Kong in 1894 after germinating in south-west China for 40 years, it swept around the world from there in less than a decade, breaking out in ports on every continent. Between 1894 and 1901 cities as far apart as Mumbai, Alexandria, Oporto, San Francisco, Sydney, Buenos Aires and Cape Town all experienced outbreaks of this flea- and rat-borne disease. Finally peaking in about 1907, this pandemic ebbed during World War 1, revived briefly in its wake and then slowly petered out over the next 20 years.

To steamship technology and increased sea-traffic as an effective means of turning epidemics into pandemics, World War 1 added the concentration and transportation of young men on a scale without precedent in world history, providing circumstances tailor-made for infectious diseases to thrive. In this situation, typhus flourished among soldiers in the trenches of Europe and the Middle East, while a new strain of influenza was able to sweep around the world with deadly effect thrice in 18 months during 1918–19 from its probable place of origin in Kansas, USA. Only remote islands like St Helena and Tristan da Cunha escaped infection by this so-called 'Spanish' flu, the greatest and swiftest pandemic in global history, before it burned itself out, leaving more than 50 million people dead, in other words over 2.5 per cent of the earth's population. Though a return of the 'Spanish' flu was predicted, subsequent influenza pandemics, in 1957, 1968 and 1977, caused but a fraction of their predecessor's mortality.

By World War 2, such had been the improvement in the military's monitoring and prevention of infectious diseases that only one disease, polio, attained pandemic status and, even then, at a relatively low level. From a focus of the disease in the Middle East, Allied soldiers carried it back to their respective homes in the Northern and Southern Hemispheres where, between 1942 and 1945, a number of outbreaks occurred. There it remained entrenched until the 1950s, triggering fears of a global pandemic each time it erupted. A sign that fresh innovations in transport could speed up and extend the transmission of epidemic disease even further is evident from the fact that, when the polio virus was carried to Malta in 1942, it did so aboard an overnight flight from Egypt.

Such speedy movement of infected people by air increasingly became the dominant means by which infectious diseases were transmitted during the next 60 years. In the case of the first phase of the HIV/AIDS pandemic in the early 1980s, it was critical in turning what had been a burgeoning but localized epidemic in East and Central Africa into a pandemic which spanned the world within five years. In 2003 Severe Acute Respiratory Syndrome (SARS) showed how a far more easily communicable disease could threaten to become pandemic by crossing the globe literally overnight.

Transnational responses to pandemics

While pandemics are inherently transnational in character, from the 19th century onwards the responses which they drew from governments and the medical profession became increasingly so too, as the inadequacy of narrowly national countermeasures was recognized. Thus, in the 1890s epidemic outbreaks with the potential to spread transnationally prompted neighbouring states to send in their own scientists to investigate the disease with a view to containing it at the point of outbreak. For instance, the bubonic plague outbreak in Hong Kong in 1894 saw research teams from France and Japan arrive there to try and identify the cause. Within weeks, two of these scientists, the rivals, Alexandre Yersin from France and Kitasato Shibasaburō from Japan, both claimed to have done so. When the disease spread to Mumbai two years later, scientific teams from Britain, France, Germany, Russia and Egypt descended on the city to probe the disease and its mode of transmission further, with no little success.

When doctors did come up with an effective antidote, in keeping with their commitment to help the sick across-the-board, this was readily spread across national boundaries. The earliest example of this in the 19th century was vaccination against smallpox. Within ten years of Edward Jenner reporting its efficacy in England in 1796, it was being used as a preventive measure all around the world by both allies and foes of Jenner's nation. Indeed, in 1803 the king of Spain even commissioned an expedition to visit every Spanish colony in the Americas and Asia to vaccinate his subjects. Vaccination is the most striking example of the globalization of an effective countermeasure to a widespread epidemic.

Similar therapeutic or preventive breakthroughs against such diseases during the next 200 years were adopted all around the world as quickly – Haffkine's anti-plague vaccine in the late 1890s, Salvarsan against syphilis from the 1910s, quinacrine compounds against malaria from 1934, the 17-D vaccine against yellow fever from 1939, the anti-typhus vaccine from 1942, sulfonamides and antibiotics against a host of infectious bacterial diseases from the 1940s, DDT against insect-borne malaria and yellow fever in the same decade, polio vaccines from the mid 1950s and AZT and Nevirapine against HIV in the late 1980s and the 1990s.

Medical altruism is not the only reason for the existence of such a list, of course. Manufacturing the drugs mentioned for sale worldwide became big business in the 20th century, stimulating the creation of an increasingly transnational pharmaceutical and insecticide industry from the 1930s. This escalating process underpinned the rise to multinational status of firms like Burroughs Wellcome, Bayer, Merck, Parke-Davis, Ciba-Geigy, Roche and Pfizer.

However, dealing with epidemics and pandemics transnationally was not limited just to a search for specific therapies and preventives. The emergence of epidemiology as the scientific study of epidemics was a parallel international response to epidemics. Tellingly, the first body formally constituted to do this in 1850, the Epidemiological Society of London, was originally to be named the Asiatic Cholera Society. From its origin in Britain, epidemiology spread to Continental Europe and North America. The first academic departments in that discipline were established at Johns Hopkins University in Baltimore in 1919 and at the London School of Tropical Hygiene and Medicine in 1928, before spreading to European-style medical schools overseas in the 1940s and 1950s.

Even more overtly transnational in approach were the attempts made to coordinate individual countries' quarantine measures which had long been the standard response in Europe to the threat of infection from abroad. Beginning with a meeting in Paris in 1851 in the shadow of a cholera pandemic, eleven international sanitary conferences were held over the next half-century in a bid to lay down uniform quarantine procedures and set up an international notification system for outbreaks of three dread diseases, cholera, yellow fever and, after 1894, plague. While the states of Europe were best represented at each of these conferences, delegates from the Ottoman Empire, Persia, China, Japan and the USA attended most of the later conferences,

giving these an increasingly global character. The 1903 conference sought to put the ad hoc steps which flowed from these conferences onto a more sustained footing, and called for the creation of a permanent international health bureau which, consequently, was set up in 1907 as the Office International d'Hygiène Publique in Paris.

In addition to consolidating and standardizing the existing quarantine measures of its members, the Office kept them abreast of the latest knowledge on epidemic diseases and acted as a clearing-house for news about epidemic outbreaks around the world. Within five years it had 41 members – only half of them European states – and by 1926 this figure had risen to 65. By then its international epidemic reports, drawing on its own sources and those of kindred health bureaux in Singapore, Washington and Alexandria, were being sent out weekly by telegram.

With one exception – the League of Nations Health Organization established in 1921 – these kindred health bureaux were regional in focus and, consequently, less transnational in character. Even so, an association like the Pan-American Sanitary Organization (established in 1902 in immediate response to a fresh outbreak of an epidemic of yellow fever) spanned both North and South America in a bid to counter the spread of epidemics in the region. For its part, though it lacked the membership of several major countries for political reasons, the League of Nations Health Organization's engagement with epidemics was avowedly transnational as it sought to fill gaps in the global epidemic monitoring and notification network of the Office International d'Hygiène Publique. Occasionally, the former went beyond this, seeking not only to coordinate campaigns against typhus in the new states of Eastern Europe and against cholera in China in the 1920s, but also to provide drugs and insecticide, those staples in transnational biomedicine's arsenal.

After World War 2, the League's Health Organization – and the International Office d'Hygiène Publique too – were incorporated into the new World Health Organization (WHO, founded in 1948) which continued many of their transnational functions, but on an extended and increasingly global scale. Its creation of a Global Influenza Surveillance Network in 1952 is a good example of this. Coordinating transnational campaigns against epidemics and assisting states materially so as to try and prevent such epidemics from turning into pandemics loomed very large on its agenda from its inception. As a result of its crusades, three epidemic diseases, smallpox, polio and malaria, were either wholly eradicated from the world or significantly controlled in the 1960s and 1970s. The comprehensive UNAIDS programme, created in 1996 out of the World Health Organization's initial Global Programme on AIDS, is the most recent example of its global response to existing pandemics, while its endeavours to stifle the emergence of a new H5N1 influenza pandemic since 1997 demonstrate its preventive zeal against potential pandemics.

Nor were public organizations the only bodies to take up the cudgels against epidemic diseases across national boundaries. Through its International Health Board (set up in 1913) non-governmental organizations like the American Rockefeller Foundation energetically (and often unilaterally) pursued biomedical intervention with funds and personnel between the world wars to eradicate epidemics like malaria and yellow fever in South America, Europe and Africa. In more recent times, the fear of a devastating pandemic conjured up by AIDS, as the pace of globalization grew, called forth large-scale private funding in the developed world to support projects aimed at checking the disease where it was at its most rampant. Of these, the Gates Foundation's Global Health Programme (established in 2000) and the private-public Global Fund to Fight AIDS, TB and Malaria (established in 2002) have been the most prominent to date. Transnational in conception, composition and contribution, this Global Fund's very name epitomizes the two-sides-of-the-same-coin relationship between epidemics and transnationality in modern history, and also hints at the way in which countering this lethal duo has, in response, itself generated greater transnationality since 1850.

Howard Phillips

Bibliography

Goodman N. M. 1971. *International health organizations and their work*. Edinburgh & London: Churchill Livingstone.

Harrison M. 2004. *Disease and the modern world, 1500 to the present day*. Cambridge: Polity.

Kiple K. F. (ed.) 1993. *The Cambridge world history of human disease*. Cambridge: Cambridge University Press.

McNeill W. H. 1979. *Plagues and peoples*. Harmondsworth: Penguin.

Ranger T. and Slack P. (eds) 1992. *Epidemics and ideas: essays on the historical perception of pestilence*. Cambridge: Cambridge University Press.

Watts S. 1997. *Epidemics and history: disease, power and imperialism*. New Haven and London: Yale University Press.

Related essays

Acquired Immunodeficiency Syndrome (AIDS); corporations; diet and nutrition; drugs (medical); forced migrations; germs; health policy; human mobility; intergovernmental organizations; League of Nations Health Organization; life and physical sciences; medicine; pesticides, herbicides, insecticides; philanthropic foundations; relief; religious pilgrimages; slavery; smallpox; steamships; transportation infrastructures; United Nations system; vaccination; war

Esperanto

Esperanto, a constructed language intended for communication between people with different mother tongues, was launched in Warsaw in 1887 by Lazar Ludwik Zamenhof (1859–1917), an ophthalmologist.

Zamenhof, having experienced anti-Semitism, believed language differences were a root cause of ethnic hostilities. He based his language (published under the pseudonym 'Dr Esperanto', meaning 'one who hopes') on the vocabulary and semantics of European languages, but used grammatical principles akin to those of the so-called isolating languages, in which invariable lexical elements are ordered to create meaning. His was not the first attempt at a 'universal' or 'international' language: such efforts came to prominence in the 17th century, with 'philosophical' languages based on systems for classifying concepts, such as that of John Wilkins (1614–1672), secretary of the Royal Society. Creation of an easily learned and readily used international language had particular appeal in the late 19th century, when an emergent middle class with limited language education had time and money for tourism and business travel and a growing interest in the world. Volapük, created by Johann Martin

Schleyer (1831–1912), attracted considerable, though short-lived, public interest when published in 1880. Like Esperanto, it was based on existing languages, and may have inspired Zamenhof's project.

A constructed language is a mere project until it is used. Zamenhof sought to create an active and living community that would take charge of the language. He corresponded widely with would-be adherents, and the language rapidly gained popularity in Russia and beyond. The year 1889 saw the first local Esperanto society (in Nuremberg, Germany) and the first periodical in Esperanto. Initially the language was used mostly for written correspondence: it was not until 1904 that the first international gatherings of Esperantists took place. In 1905 the first World Esperanto Congress was held in Boulogne-sur-Mer, France; such meetings, each year in a different country, have continued ever since, generally attracting 2,000 or more participants.

To expand the language, Zamenhof almost immediately began translating literary works, including Shakespeare's Hamlet (1894), works by Goethe and Schiller, and the entire Old Testament. Soon Esperanto was used for commercial and professional activities. Despite calls for reform, most Esperantists remained attached to the original Esperanto, though a reformed version, Ido, emerged around 1907 and attracted a small following. As the 20th century began, the language moved beyond Europe, for example to the United States (the World Esperanto Congress took place in Washington in 1911) – and to Japan and China, where it was associated with modernization and left-wing causes.

From Switzerland, the Universal Esperanto Association (founded 1908) assisted in reuniting family members separated by World War I. Later the language caught the attention of the League of Nations, but French intervention prevented its further consideration. Popular in the labour movement, Esperanto gained an immediate following in the USSR, but in the Stalinist purges of the 1930s its leaders were condemned to death or exile. Between the wars, Esperanto grew in expressivity and flexibility, generating a large literature of original and translated works, periodicals, radio broadcasts, and so on. A petition presented to the United Nations after the war with almost a million signatures resulted in a 1954 UNESCO resolution declaring Esperanto in accord with the aims and ideals of that organization. After Stalin's death (1953), Esperanto's popularity grew in Russia and Eastern Europe, primarily because it allowed ordinary citizens to have personal contact with people abroad. A similar desire stimulated interest in such countries as Iran, Cuba, and China.

Since the 1970s, Esperanto has been increasingly recognized as a phenomenon worthy of serious study, with courses and programmes available in some universities. While the collapse of socialism in Eastern Europe weakened formal organizational structures, the Internet has made it easier to learn and use Esperanto, and it has experienced a sharp rise in popularity recently. It is unlikely to dislodge languages like English and Spanish as languages of transborder contact, but as it permits communication on a level playing field, and while its users maintain a readily navigable network, it is likely to continue to have a lively following.

Humphrey Tonkin

Bibliography
Eco U. 1995. The search for the perfect language. Oxford and Cambridge, MA: Blackwell.
Janton P. 1993. Esperanto: language, literature, and community. Albany: State University of New York Press.
Tonkin H. (ed.) 1997. Esperanto, interlinguistics, and planned language. Lanham: University Press of America.

Related essays
anarchism; antisemitism; Braille code; broadcasting; consumer cooperation; intergovernmental organizations; international non-governmental organizations (INGOs); language; League of Nations system; pidgins and creoles; radio; sign language; socialism; translation; United Nations system; universalism and cosmopolitanism; workers' movements

Ethical Culture
Founded in 1876 by the German-born Jewish-American philosopher Felix Adler as an alternative to conventional religions, Ethical Culture promoted ethics as the foundation for meaningful private and social life in a modern and seemingly secular world. In Adler's view, religion no longer convinced a modern public of its moral guidelines, yet individuals still sought the moral

orientation and social functions conventional religions had once provided. While it catered in its earliest years to a largely secularized Jewish community, Adler and his colleagues understood ethics as a universal language that could transcend cultural and religious difference. Thus it took consideration of 'universal humanity' as its common starting point.

Although conceptually universal at its inception, Ethical Culture only gradually realized a transnational project. The movement extended itself first beyond its New York City roots into other US cities such as St Louis, Philadelphia, and Chicago in the 1880s, before making connections abroad. With common language traditions, the US movement shared an intellectual orientation with several long-standing free-thinker movements in Great Britain, most notably the South Place Ethical Society, itself a product of 18th-century religious dissenters. When Adler, who had spent several years studying philosophy in Germany, returned to Berlin in 1892, he participated in the founding of the German Society for Ethical Culture. Together these three groups formed the core of what came to be the International Union of Ethical Societies (sometimes also referred to as the International Ethical Union), inaugurated in Zürich in 1896. Although the first meeting of the International Union of Ethical Societies consisted almost exclusively of participants from Germany, Switzerland, Austria, Britain, and the US, chapters eventually grew not only in other European countries but in Japan, India, and New Zealand as well.

As an international organization, Ethical Culture was most active in the decades before World War I. The International Union of Ethical Societies maintained a very loose structure that, as indicated in its first formal constitution of 1906, survived financially on voluntary contributions. The organization's primary purpose, according to its constitution, was 'to assert the supreme importance of the ethical factor in all the relations of life – personal, social, national, and international, apart from all theological and metaphysical considerations'. Its secondary tasks aimed largely to facilitate intellectual exchange between individuals and groups of diverse national backgrounds for the sake of furthering the pursuit of ethical understanding. To this end, it sponsored or co-sponsored multiple international meetings which aimed to foster transnational activism and intellectual exchange, including a 1908 meeting on moral education, from which the idea for the 1911 Universal Races Congress arose.

Not surprisingly, Ethical Culture routinely met up with limits to its governing conception of 'universal humanity'. Already at its first international meeting, tensions arose regarding the relationship of shared universal principles to the specificity of local political activism. An especially perplexing challenge confronted members in the context of the Universal Races Congress, at which participants sought to balance respect for cultural difference with commitments to concepts of universal humanity, universal moral norms and education, and universal paths of political-economic development. In the domestic realm, local branches contended with particularist challenges to conceptions of universal humanity. World War I tore definitively at the fabric of Ethical Culture and its universalist commitments. While some individual participants objected on all fronts to the war in the name of universal humanity and a moral command to love the nearest and most distant neighbour, others – from all participating countries – sought moral languages with which to justify defensive war and the protection of local communities.

Ethical Culture continues to exist today in many cities throughout the United States, as does the South Place Ethical Society in London. The German Society for Ethical Culture, conversely, was briefly coopted by National Socialism in 1933 before finally folding in 1936. Founded in 1952, the International Humanistic and Ethical Union has resumed the project of the International Union of Ethical Societies to provide a global network for non-confessional moral action and thought.

Tracie Matysik

Bibliography

Groschopp H. 1997. *Dissidenten: Freidenkerei und Kultur in Deutschland*. Berlin: Dietz.

MacKillop I. D. 1986. *The British Ethical Societies*. Cambridge: Cambridge University Press.

Matysik T. 2008. *Reforming the Moral Subject: Ethics and Sexuality in Central Europe, 1890–1930*, Ithaca, NY: Cornell University Press.

Radest H. D. 1998. *Felix Adler: an Ethical Culture*. New York: Lang.

Related essays
anti-racism; cosmopolitanism and universalism; development and growth; freemasonry; modernity; modernization theory; pacifism; religion; Universal Races Congress; women's movements; workers' movements; Zionism

Ethnicity and race

Since the 1960s there has been an ongoing discussion on definitions of race and ethnicity. Most approaches within social science assume that race and ethnicity are socially and politically, as well as culturally and historically constructed modern phenomena. In other words, they are phenomena that vary significantly across time, place and culture, though ultimately they rest on 'supra-individual processes', such as formations of a group boundary, social segregation, and the creation of racial hierarchies in terms of the 'in-group' and the 'other'. A growing number of scholars in recent years have also shown that the phenomena that underlie ideas of race are widespread in the modern world, and transcend nation-state boundaries, even when they are used to shore up ideas of national identity: they can be found across boundaries between Europe and North America, to Latin America, China, Singapore and so on. In the contemporary world, 'race' and 'ethnicity' have been used interchangeably to justify biological, social and cultural differences, and to defend individual and group rights.

The origins of 'race' as a discourse lie in European ideas of scientific modernity in the 19th century. During this period, the advance of Western imperialism in the non-European world, combined with a new interest in scientific categorization and taxonomy, led thinkers to construct pseudoscientific hierarchies of 'race' that were defined by allegedly biological characteristics. The Social Darwinism of Herbert Spencer became the best known of the systems of thought that underpinned this new categorization of racial difference. In these categorizations, the white race was generally placed at the top, and the African races at the bottom, with Asians placed in the middle. Ideas of 'racial purity' persisted into the early 20th century, with eugenic campaigns for breeding out 'inferior' members of the population popular with figures on the European left as well as right (in Britain, both H. G.

Wells and Winston Churchill were advocates of it). However, the term's association with Nazi Germany resulted in 'race' becoming a controversial term in the West after World War 2, although its assumptions have persisted in many Western societies up to the present day. Recent scholarship tends to view 'race' as a cultural construct which does not exist in biological reality.

Ethnic groups on the other hand are held to exist and be meaningfully categorizable, and 'ethnicity' has become an important issue in public and academic discourse across the world. The term only emerged in the English language in 1953, and has been defined by Glazer and Moynihan as 'the condition of belonging to a particular group'. Based on Max Weber's argument that blood ties were crucial to the members of ethnic groups, Van den Berghe in his 1978 *Ethnic phenomenon* went on to claim that ethnicity was an 'extended kinship' based on 'common descent and shared blood', and endogamy and territory were some of the key elements that define ethnic boundaries. According to him, race was a 'special marker' of ethnicity. Contrary to Van den Berghe's view, in a more recent work, Michael Banton's ethnicity entry in the *Encyclopedia of nationalism* (1981) suggests that there exists a complex and ambiguous relationship between race and ethnicity. Deriving from the 'us–them' dichotomy proposed by anthropologist Fredrick Barth in 1969, Banton argues that while biological differences are central to racial discourse, group identity is what defines ethnicity. Banton's view has led a growing number of social scientists to separate 'race' and 'ethnicity' as two separate terms.

The separation however does not solve the problem. Today, racial tension and racial prejudice continue to be a cause for ethnic conflict in many societies. Social groups are still being divided into biological units, and in parts of the world these imagined biological differences are being used to legitimize ethnic cleansing and genocide. The myth of race has not disappeared. On the contrary, in many countries, for instance China, it is still an integral part of contemporary discourse, where a prejudice towards coloured people is evident in everyday life.

Transnational links and comparisons: 'Chinese' and 'Jews'

In China, the influence of racial ideas of identity demonstrates the importance of 'race' as a means of defining a transnational idea of 'China' since overseas Chinese and ethnic Chinese outside the boundaries of the nation state itself are effectively brought into the wider definition of the 'nation' through the use of race as a binding factor. While this is not unprecedented among other ethnicities (for instance, overseas Indians), it is perhaps among the Chinese that the idea of race and ethnicity as markers is most clearly and explicitly used as a means of creating transnational identity that draws on the diaspora.

In China to the present day, as Frank Dikötter demonstrates, '"Chineseness" is seen primarily as a matter of biological descent, physical appearance and congenital inheritance' (Dikötter 1997, 1) Biological distinctions have been frequently used as a marker for ethnic differences. Minzu is the Chinese word used for both ethnicity and race, as well as for nation. It was first conceptualized in 1903 and was used by modernizing reformers to promote symbolic boundaries of blood and descent. The Chinese minzu, according to the reformers, was a political unit based on a group of people called 'Chinese', who were bound together by imagined blood ties, kinship and descent. 'Common blood' was viewed as the greatest force of nationalism, which surpassed cultural, gender, regional and class differences. European discourse on race was appropriated and Darwinian evolutionary theories were deployed to support the myth of 'a biologically pure origin'. At the same time folk notions of patrilineal descent were reconfigured into 'scientific' racial discourse. The ethnic 'Han' became the 'Chinese', who were represented as the descendants of the Yellow emperor, thus the 'yellow race'. The cultural identity of the 'Han' was replaced by the racial identity of the 'yellow race'; national struggle was viewed in terms of racial war between the 'yellows' and the 'whites'. Yet the battle was now essentially between groups of people and not defined as being between territorial nation states.

Traditionally marginalized groups such as the peasants, women and the uneducated had been recruited into the army of the 'yellows', and became members of the homogenous 'in-group'. At the same time there was also produced a racialized new 'other' such as Blacks and Jews. Previously viewed as a cultural and religious group, the Jews were reimagined by the modernizing reformers in China as a 'race': they were all descendants of Abraham who could trace their biological ancestry back to the Semites, and therefore were a 'historically white race'. Standing in symbolic contradistinction to the 'historically yellow race' – the Chinese in this case – Jews acted as a constitutive outsider, who embodied all the negative as well as positive qualities which were feared or desired, and various social groups in China could thus project their own anxieties onto this 'other'.

The use of racial categories such as the 'Jews' was central to many thinkers of modern China in the construction of the 'self' – the Chinese group identity. Just as 'Chineseness' was believed to be rooted in every part of the body, the differences in the Jews were marked in their physical appearance: from their face, to their eyes, their noses and their skin colour. Such biological differences determined cultural stereotypes: 'the money-grabbing Jew', 'the canny Jew', 'the untrustworthy Jew', 'the smart Jew' and so on. Although these representations corresponded to European anti-Semitic images of the Jews, they were however being endowed with indigenous meanings. They were an intrinsic part of a network of symbolic relations, in which the 'Jew' played a contradictory and ambiguous role: while the 'stateless Jew' became a warning for racial extinction, the 'rich Jew' or the 'powerful Jew' became an inspiration, a model of a 'new people' in China.

In the course of the 20th century, definitions of the Jews were constantly being reconfigured according to the social and political climate within China: the 'Jew' could either be a nationalist or an imperialist, a filthy capitalist or an ardent communist, a committed revolutionary or a spineless loser. In other words, anything which is not Chinese is Jewish, at the same time as anything which is Chinese is also Jewish; anything which the Chinese aspire to is Jewish, at the same time anything which the Chinese despise is Jewish. These definitions bore little relation to the reality – there had been a very small Jewish presence in China and less social encounter than there had been in Europe. They have however helped to shape the identity of millions of people in China. As such, this was a powerful example of how a nationalist struggle for identity looked beyond its own national symbols for cohesion.

Indonesia in Southeast Asia, as argued by Anthony Reid, is 'a nation created consciously, with a new language, a founding myth, and a whole identity that dates from no earlier than the start of the 20th century' (Chirot and Reid 1997, 20–1). It was more a 'civic' nationalism than a 'blood' nationalism, as was the case with China, or in Europe. R. E. Elson calls the creation of 'Indonesian race' a 'new and strange concept'. The term 'Indonesian' was initially a racial category. It first emerged in the 1850s, as George Windsor Earl in his essay 'On the leading characteristic of the Papuan, Australian, and Malayu-Polynesian nations' (1859) attempted to classify the people of the so-called 'Indian Archipelago' as the 'brown races'. This was legitimized by works of writers such as Logan, Kean and so on, and 'Indonesian' came to represent all indigenous people living in a territory of what rapidly became the Dutch East Indies. However, in the first two decades of the 20th century, a specific ethnic and racial identity of 'Indonesianness' was constructed by Indonesian intellectuals themselves – many of them were students in the Netherlands – as a part of the processes of the region's struggle for independence from the Dutch colonization. The notion of 'Indonesian fellow countrymen' first emerged amongst them, providing them with a sense of solidarity and giving them a 'common origin', although they were of different ethical, cultural, social and religious backgrounds. It was amongst this group of students that the terms 'Indonesia' and 'Indonesians' were first used to describe a unified national consciousness on the part of Indonesians themselves. Although in principal anyone loyal to a common anti-Dutch cause was seen as an Indonesian, the Indonesian Chinese and those born of mixed-race marriages – Eurasians – remained marginalized. They served as the ultimate scapegoat, the 'other' in an attempt to construct an Indonesian 'self'. The Chinese were constantly portrayed as 'middlemen', who had driven out all competitors, and 'fatten on the necessities of people', thus hated by both the Dutch and the native people. The Eurasians, on the other hand, were thought to have been derided by 'pure blood' Dutchmen and were thus the target of jealousy from 'pure' Indonesians. It was warned by some nationalists that 'within a short time ... the land of the Javanese will fall into the hands of Europeans, Chinese and Arabs' (Darmo Kondo, 13 November 1918, Overzicht van de Inlandsche en Maleisch-Chineesche pers, 46/1918). In 1918, an anti-Chinese riot

in Kudus resulted in the destruction of 43 homes and five deaths of local Chinese. Such incidents, as well as general anti-Chinese sentiment, led many Indonesian Chinese to feel a closer attachment to China – which came to be viewed as their 'homeland' from the late 19th century in the wake of the nationalistic movement in China – and many of them became increasingly nationalistic and supported that movement. Such action further induced anti-Chinese feelings in Indonesia. Some argued that the Chinese, by keeping close ties with their native land, were attempting to take over Indonesia. In 1927, with the establishment of Partai National Indonesia, it was stated that only those belonging to the 'Indonesian nation' could be enrolled as full members, while those of mixed blood, such as Indonesian Chinese and Eurasians, could aspire only to associate membership. The latter's effort to modernize Indonesia were often unappreciated and served as a source of suspicion. As one Javanese journalist wrote: 'We value your efforts, but you are still Chinese'. As racial and ethnic tension persists in Indonesia to the present day, there is no guarantee that the 'blood' definition will not come to the fore in the future, as some Indonesians are demanding.

Contrary to the civic form of nationalism in Indonesia, the National Socialist government in Germany, however, used blood as the basis of its racism against the Jews, Gypsies and other racial groups in Europe, which led to their physical extermination in the latter years of the Second World War. Although hostility towards Jews existed in the Middle Ages, not only in Germany but also in other parts of Europe, hostility to the racial group defined as 'Semites' was then a recent development. It only emerged in the 19th century. As suggested by George M. Kren, it grew out of the process of trying to construct the self-image of the German character following the Napoleonic Wars, 'an image essentially the product of middle class'. The Jews served as the ultimate anti-image of German middle-class virtues which emphasized a spiritual or inner quality rather than the material one. The Jews were depicted as dishonest, money-loving, rootless, avaricious and with bad taste, but above all they lacked the German's reverence for the higher things in life. The famous nationalist historian Heinrich von Treitschke further attacked the Jew for his foreignness, for being cosmopolitan and for his 'un-Germanness'. These representations of 'the Jew' were often endowed with racial and biological connotations. Race as a scientific concept had increasingly become important in the latter part of the 18th century. Aspects of physical appearance such as skin colour and cranial measurements were used to differentiate the Jews from the Germans. Ethnologist Friedrich Max Müller, on the other hand, also suggested that Aryan language was also a common German expression and thus a 'racial soul'. As result the Jew was viewed as innately inferior, with inferior physical features and language, who was immoral and parasitic. Gobineau's anthropological work *Essay on the inequality of human races* (1854) was used to legitimize the notion of a superior German race. It is interesting to note that in his attempt to create a superior German race, which was said to possess energetic intelligence, courage, physical force, perseverance, and a sense of utility that was broad and far-sighted, Gobineau also constructed the inferior black and yellow races in contrast. While Gobineau's 'black man' was portrayed as physically powerful, filled with strong desires, wildly imaginative, and having little capacity for thought, the 'yellow man', according to him, was physically lethargic and tending to obesity, emotionally apathetic, generally mediocre, and lacking in imagination, but having a dogged practical sense geared to the simple fulfilment of narrow material desires.

The old tradition of anti-Semitism was conflated with the scientific notion of race, which led to the argument that the 'inferior blood' of the Jew could corrupt the good blood of the Aryan, and lead to the ruin of the German nation; thus the Jewish blood must be eliminated. Chamberlain's *The foundations of the 19th century* (1910) interpreted history in terms of a Darwinian notion of racial struggle, and he argued that the basic dynamic of history consisted in the inevitable battle between the Teutons (Germans) and the Jews. Popular novels such as Arthur Dintner's novel *Sin against the blood* (1918) and the booklet *The Protocols of the Elders of Zion* (1903) – which became popular in Germany during World War I – further enforced the danger of the Jews and led many to believe that the Jews and other racially inferior groups must be expelled from the country or be exterminated. During the Hitler period, the Jewish danger became a central issue of Nazi propaganda. The

Nuremberg laws in 1935 led to the exclusion of anyone of Jewish descent from German public life. This laid the foundation for a more vigorous, systematic and widespread persecution of Jews in the following years, beginning first in 1938 in Austria and then spreading throughout many other parts of Europe, especially after the outbreak of World War 2. The persecution eventually ended in the mass killing of Jews, Gypsies and Slavs.

Even if one may argue that what the genocide of Jews, Gypsies and Slavs was partly based on a utopian vision of racially pure Europe, the notion of racial contamination based on blood is however not uniquely European. A similar motif also found anti-Negro or anti-Chinese racism in America in the late 19th century and early 20th century. The very definition of an 'American' in the 19th century was exclusionary: it viewed an American not only as a republican, committed to the principles of liberty, equality and self-government, but also as a 'white'; at the same time it viewed the Native Americans as a 'foreign nation', and the African slaves were regarded as non-human. The Civil War deepened the racial divide and induced racial fear amongst the white population. The influx of Chinese coolies into California from the 1850s became also seen by some as a 'real threat' to America. In parts of America, the 'Negro question' shifted to the 'Chinese question', and a number of anti-Chinese movements took place. This eventually led to the Chinese exclusion law in 1882, and subsequent immigration laws which allowed only whites to become full-fledged members of the American nation, and marked Asian immigrants, Latinos, African Americans, and Native Americans as outsiders. Anti-Chinese and anti immigration laws help to legitimize popular racist discourse in America in the years to follow. The image of the 'yellow peril', rooted in Gobineau's image of the 'yellow race', haunted popular American imaginations. While believing the West was being overpowered and surrounded by an irresistible dark force of the East – much like today's anti-terrorist discourse – many feared that through sexual contact, the blood of 'Chinese opium addicts' would contaminate the American blood, and poison the American race. The sexual danger was one of the most potent aspects of anti-Chinese discourse. In the following years, a number of Hollywood films centred on the theme, depicting the image of 'evil China man' as a rapist, and Chinatown as an underworld full of opium addicts, pimps and fallen women. These films perpetuated a widespread fear of the yellow Chinese amongst the general American populations. The fear of racial degeneration also served as an important argument for introducing anti-drug policy in America. Some even argued that the Chinese were trying to take the revenge on the West: after China had been reduced to a state of chaos by opium, the Chinese now tried to poison the white people through sexual contacts with that very substance. The Dangerous Drug Act in 1920 meant the 'Chinaman' was not only 'evil' but also a 'criminal'. Besides the Chinese, the African Americans and the Latinos were also depicted as drug fiends, whereas the Native Americans were said to be prone to alcohol problems. Habitual use of drugs became viewed as a disease or addiction, which was thought to be hereditary and could be passed down from one generation to another. As it was with race, so drugs became colour-coded: opium became a 'yellow drug', cannabis became a 'black drug' whereas coca was a 'Latino drug'. Although in the course of time, the danger of yellow peril and opium seems to have become no longer an issue in America, the 'war on drugs' is continuing. In the aftermath of 9/11, the Bush administration has waged a new 'war on terror'. Although ideology seems to be at the centre of this war, in many ways, the issue of race continues to play a part.

The myths of race carries on; they form an intrinsic part of the politics of identity in which one group's power, privilege and status are based on the exclusion of other groups. Although images and representations of the 'other' might transmute from negative to positive or from 'inferior' to 'superior', their real object remains – that is to act as a distant mirror in the construction of the 'self'. This 'other' may be anybody, from the 'Jew', to the 'Muslim', the 'black', or the 'homosexual', but the attempt to draw racially defined boundaries between people has been, and still is, an important part of many contemporary cultures and societies.

Xun Zhou

Bibliography

Aarim-Heriot N. 2003. *Chinese immigrants, African Americans, and racial anxiety in the United States, 1848–82.* Urbana and Chicago: University of Illinois Press.

Chirot D. and Reid A. (eds) 1997. *Essential outsiders: Chinese and Jews in the modern transformation of Southeast Asia and Central Europe.* Seattle: University of Washington Press.

Dikötter F. 'Introduction', in Dikötter F. (ed.) 1997. *The construction of racial identity in China and Japan,* London: Hurst.

Elson R. E. 2005. 'Constructing the nation: ethnicity, race, modernity and citizenship in early Indonesian thought', *Asian Ethnicity,* 6, 3, 145–60.

Glazer N. and Moynihan D. P. 1975. *Ethnicity: theory and experience.* Cambridge: Cambridge University Press, 1.

Kren G. M. 1960. 'Race and ideology', *Phylon,* 23, 2, 167–77.

Mosse G. L. 1978. *Toward the Final Solution: a history of European racism.* New York: H. Fertig.

Xun Z. 2001. *Youtai: Chinese perceptions of the 'Jews' and Judaism.* London: Routledge/Curzon.

Related essays

America; antisemitism; empire and migration; empires and imperialism; eugenics; femininity; Hollywood; Holocaust; missionaries; nation and state; Nazism; performing artists; population; race-mixing; Westernization; white men's countries; wildlife films; workers' movements

Eugenics

The logo of the Third International Congress of Eugenics, held in New York in 1932, defined eugenics as 'the self direction of human evolution'. Negative eugenics was concerned with the elimination of inheritable diseases and malformations and involved prenuptial certificates, birth control, selective abortion, sterilization, castration, immigration restriction and, in Nazi-occupied Europe, involuntary 'euthanasia'. Positive eugenics would instead encourage the propagation of desirable characteristics via tax incentives for 'fit parents', assortative mating, cloning, and germline engineering.

The term 'eugenics' was coined in 1883 by Sir Francis Galton (1822–1911), after the Greek εὐγενής, meaning 'wellborn'. Galton mistakenly assumed that all traits are passed down unaffected from our ancestors ('law of ancestral heredity') and envisioned eugenics as a naturalistic religion antagonistic to Christianity. An extreme version of this theory, called *Ahnenerbe* ('ancestral inheritance'), which described individual life as the epiphenomenon of perpetual bloodlines, was deployed by Heinrich Himmler to justify his plans for a New European Order.

Traces of this erroneous understanding of genealogies in terms of genetic continuity were evident in the writings of Nietzsche, Ernst Haeckel, the most influential German popularizer of evolutionary theory, American biologist Charles Davenport, who held that predispositions to social deviance were inherited from 'ape-like ancestors', and British biostatistician R. A. Fisher, who once (1929) remarked that, if King Solomon's line was not extinct, he was 'in the ancestry of all of us, and in nearly equal proportions, however unequally his wisdom may be distributed'. A similar combination of Eternal Recurrence – human beings as expressions of the immortal germplasm – and natural teleology of history – biology as destiny – stamped their positions.

Similar convictions informed Cesare Lombroso's theory of atavism and those of various Social and Racial Darwinists, animal breeders and pedigree researchers. Among them was the American psychologist Herbert Goddard, who authored a study of hereditary feeble-mindedness. *The Kallikak Family* (1912), based on patently manufactured data, proved so influential on both sides of the Atlantic that the German translation (1914) was reprinted in 1933. Other genealogical studies stressed the linkage between folk hereditarian beliefs about the transmission of patrimonial and biological inheritance and the religious notion of the inheritability of sins, concurring to foster notions of evolutionary throwbacks and of populations as bundles of lineages, together with the equation of genealogical perpetuation with social distinction.

Most early eugenicists were raised in deeply religious families and, between 1907 and 1940, eugenics laws were only promulgated in those countries where Puritan, Pietistic and Calvinist denominations were stronger. In fact, religious affiliations and the heterogeneity of Western cultures led to different styles of eugenics. The rediscovery of Mendelian laws, August Weismann's experiments on inheritability, T. H. Morgan's gene theory and the publication of Wilhelm Johannsen's seminal scientific review 'The Genotype conception of heredity' (1911), established the new orthodoxy of genetic research. 'Germplasm' (reproductive tissues) and 'somatoplasm' (non-reproductive tissues) were distinct and separate. In Romance and Far Eastern countries, the prevalent interpretation was that the distinction between soma and germplasm did not imply the one between germplasm and environment. Accordingly, medical researchers focused on external, physiochemical mutagenic factors, rather than on differential genetic predispositions and hereditary transmission, which had strong eugenic implications. Given these conflicting allegiances, it was inevitable that the large Italian and French delegations attending the first and second international eugenics congresses (London 1912, New York 1921) would criticize those scholars who posited the existence of biologically distinct human groups with differential disease susceptibility.

The tenor of most of the papers presented at the first International Congress of Social Eugenics, held in Milan in 1924, made it clear that Latin eugenicists had opted for hygienism, social medicine and pro-natalism. They urged greater caution before drawing conclusions from a limited sample of data on inheritance transmission. On that occasion, Russian biologist N. K. Kol'tsov juxtaposed the unnecessary timidity of Italian eugenicists with the hasty determination of American eugenicists.

In 1929, while Eugene Gosney and Paul Popenoe's *Sterilization for Human Betterment*, extolling the achievements of Californian eugenicists, was being translated into German and would soon become an important source of inspiration for European race hygienists, Corrado Gini, a world-famous Italian demographist and eugenicist, and Mussolini's confidant, presided over the second Italian Congress of Genetics and Eugenics in Rome. This international meeting was attended by race hygienists Alfred J. Mjoen (Norway), Eugen Fischer and Fritz Lenz (Germany), who hoped to persuade Mussolini to become the saviour of the white race's genetic pool. However, Mussolini's conception of totalitarian demography privileged quantity over quality, and did not regard the genetic enhancement of the Italian stock as a priority. Gini himself decried the determinism, racialism, and coerciveness of the American and 'Germanic' eugenics proposals. Lenz's dispirited comment in the *Archiv für Rassen- und Gesellschaftsbiologie* was that whenever the subject of eugenics was brought up at the Italian congress, it was only to stigmatize it.

This rift, aggravated by comparable contrasts between North American and Latin American eugenicists that had emerged at the 1927 Pan-American Eugenics Conference in Havana, led, in 1934, to the creation of the short-lived Latin Federation of Eugenics. Its first and last congress, held in Paris in 1937, restated the strong commitment to ameliorative social reforms, public hygiene, and the Hippocratic/Galenic ethos of compassionate care.

Fragmented and with its credibility increasingly eroded, the international eugenics movement was on the wane already in the late 1920s, so that mainline eugenics gave way to 'reform eugenics', family planning and population control, characterized by a greater emphasis on environmental factors, voluntary sterilizations, birth control, the rational management of human resources, and the repudiation of an overtly racist language. This tactic made eugenics far more palatable and effective: if the impact of nurture was so important, then children should only be raised in healthy home environments. In order to redress nature's essential randomness and synchronize biological and socioeconomic processes, irresponsible citizens unable to meet the challenges of modern society could be forced, blackmailed, or cajoled into accepting sterilization or castration. Neo-Malthusianism replaced biological determinism, and the Hardy-Weinberg theorem (1908), which demonstrated that sterilizing or segregating the 'mentally unfit' would not appreciably reduce the incidence of 'feeble-mindedness', was now deemed irrelevant.

Consequently, by the early 1930s, eugenics sterilisations programmes were in full swing. Following the moral panic generated by the Great Depression, few families were prepared to put up with the social protection of what was perceived to be a disproportionate number of dependent people. It was argued that under exceptional circumstances, basic rights could be withheld and that social services should only be granted to those whose social usefulness and biological capability were certain. Consequently, the international political climate proved very receptive to the arguments of those prominent American, German, and Swedish jurists who agreed that personal and social rights were culturally and historically relative legal fictions or superstitions, their existence depending, to a large extent, on the majority's willingness to uphold them. Enlightened governments were expected to foster virtues and restrict personal rights for the sake of communal rights and civic responsibility.

This led to the paradoxical result that involuntary sterilizations and confinements were almost exclusively carried out in the most advanced and progressive democracies, the only exception being Nazi Germany. Most such laws would only be repealed in the late 1960s and 1970s. By contrast, in those same years, legislators and jurists in Latin, Eastern European, East Asian, and developing countries, as well as in Holland and Britain, objected to selective breeding, involuntary sterilization, the assault on the notion of free will, and the linear extension of natural laws into the social sphere. Eugenics and the marriage between bureaucratic rationality and scientism did not resonate with every local repertoires of values and symbols.

After World War 2, the transnational eugenics movement was forced underground by the popularity of the human rights discourse, and pro-eugenics journals and organizations adopted new names. But eugenics never died out. While some eugenicists espoused the aims of Planned Parenthood and addressed questions of population quantity, celebrated scientists at the 1962 CIBA-sponsored London conference and 1998 UCLA 'Engineering the human germline' symposium advocated programmes of involuntary sterilization, human cloning, and genetic enhancement. Meanwhile, Singapore adopted incentives to support assortative mating among college graduates and voluntary sterilization among the poor and, in 1995, the Chinese 'Maternal and Infant Health Law' urged premarital certification of a healthy constitution, mostly targeting ethnic minorities and the rural population.

Western societies themselves are on the verge of a eugenics revival in the form of reprogenetics, germline engineering, and cloning, a trend which is indirectly reinforced by the courts' recognition of wrongful birth and wrongful life claims, by the commodification of healthcare, by the diffusion of testing for genetic predispositions, and by the rhetoric of genetic responsibility, involving new forms of discrimination and exclusion.

Stefano Fait

Bibliography

Kerr A. and Shakespeare T. 2002. *Genetic politics: from eugenics to genome.* Cheltenham: New Clarion.

Kevles D. J. 1985. *In the name of eugenics: genetics and the uses of human heredity.* New York: Knopf.

Stock G. and Campbell J. (eds) 2000. *Engineering the human germline.* Oxford: Oxford University Press.

Related essays

antisemitism; birth control; childhood; civilization; criminology; diasporas; ethnicity and race; health policy; human mobility; human rights; intellectual elites; life and physical sciences; medicine; Nazism; philanthropic foundations; population; race-mixing; religion; statistics; white men's countries

Euromarkets *See* **Financial markets**

European civil servants

The social history of civil servants and their emergence as guardians of the state is inextricably linked to the building of the modern state. If the existence of a stable European civil service is today taken as a given, a civil service independent of the nation state is a contradiction in terms. How was this constitutive tension overcome throughout the history of the European institutions? The advent of a hybridized transnational social group composed of something more than a juxtaposition of civil servants representing their national styles and interests was both a conflictual and an uncertain process. It was only with the progressive consolidation of the European Economic Community (EEC) and the drafting of a solid legal status for European civil servants in the late 1960s that an institutional framework favourable to integrative social processes and practices came into being, thereby making possible the construction of specific and partially denationalized group identity.

The immediate postwar years were marked both by a proliferation of competing projects for European cooperation and by the apogee of strong and legitimate state bureaucracies which made the very idea of a supranational civil service nearly unthinkable. The Organization for European Economic Cooperation (OEEC) created in 1948 to coordinate the administration of Marshall funds and the creation of the Council of Europe in 1949 mobilized and employed national civil servants well before the European Coal and Steel Community (ECSC) and the EEC. The jump from a career in national civil services to these organizations was largely determined by the administrative structure and career opportunities for civil servants in each country. Civil servants specialized in finance tended to gravitate to the OEEC, while career diplomats favoured the Council of Europe. These first European careers were therefore largely determined by national contexts, all the more so in that a specific 'European' professional training was still in its infancy. The initial mission of the College of Europe in Bruges (1949) was not primarily directed to filling the less than five hundred positions in the embryonic European institutions. Aspiring civil servants continued to prefer national educational paths. It was only in 1955 that reflection began about specific institutions and curricula to 'create' the new European civil servant.

The success of the Treaty of Rome and the relative marginalization of competing European organizations meant that a number of administrators employed by the OEEC continued their careers in Community organizations. However, this circulation of personnel was still largely determined by national factors, with German and Dutch civil servants moving frequently to the EEC while their French counterparts predominantly returned to the national civil service or moved to the private sector. In the other direction, a generation of young French civil servants without prior international experience entered the new institutions after 1958 as a response to their relative marginality in national administrations. If the national diversity of personnel fuelled the debate on status, professional qualities and administrative models, the previous experience of many administrators in competing organizations also added to the uncertainty about adequate administrative forms.

Nowhere was the institutional and sociological heterogeneity more visible than in the recurrent debates on the status of and recruitment procedures for personnel. It only found its final conclusion in 1968, with the unified codification of the Community civil service. The debate opposed two visions: a flexible contractual arrangement largely inspired by other intergovernmental organizations and private enterprise, and a specific legal status based on competitive exams and lifetime employment.

The administrative personnel of the ECSC was recruited on a contractual basis, centred primarily on political and national patronage. Jean Monnet showed little interest in the creation of a new statute. According to close advisors, Monnet was influenced by the human resource management of the Dutch firm Philips and sought, through generous pay packages, to attract not only national civil servants, but also managers from industry. For Monnet, the new 'European' was not first and foremost a civil servant. However, the inducements were not enough for private-sector managers, and national civil servants formed the backbone of the ECSC administration. A more 'statist' model was promoted by Monnet's successor, René Mayer, and by Jacques Rueff at the Court of Justice in Luxembourg. Derived in particular from the French administrative tradition, the objective was to 'create a corps of national civil servants for whom nationality is synonymous with supranationality' (Conrad 1992, 64).

These opposing visions coexisted in the new Communities created in 1958. Without a consensus, the rapid administrative growth (over a thousand positions in less than a year) of the new institutions was based on pragmatic contractual arrangements. But the rapid turnover of qualified personnel was considered a serious preoccupation as early as 1966. Civil service status was finally pushed through in 1962 for the EEC, but the issue remained hotly debated as some national governments were averse to relinquishing control over careers. However, the fusion of the Community executives in 1967 brought new urgency and concluded in the creation of unified civil service status throughout the entire Community in 1968.

The increased institutional stability and a meritocratic civil service limiting political and national patronage made careers independent from national civil services possible, thereby creating preconditions for an autonomous transnational space. However, if the institutional framework favoured the denationalization of the European civil service, it is not by itself sufficient to explain why the European civil service became a highly integrated transnational social group rather than a mere juxtaposition of civil servants of different national origins bringing with them their own national representations and administrative practices.

National origins have of course not completely disappeared from the career paths of European civil servants, and in particular for the most senior positions. If the unwritten rule of 'flagged' positions has become less prevalent in recent years, national governments still have a say in some strategic appointments. Furthermore, the administrative and political configuration of each member state continues to influence the social and political profile of national civil servants who embark on European careers, and their chances of promotion within the European civil service. It is for example more difficult for a director-general to be promoted if affiliated to the political opposition in his country of origin, and the objective chances of attaining positions in certain sectors remain largely linked to nationality. Since 1958, the headship of the Directorate-General (DG) Agriculture has always been occupied by a French national, while Germans have tended to occupy the position of director-general in DG Competition.

Socialization and professional training also play a role in maintaining national differences as initial training is still largely carried out by national institutions. A number of prestigious and highly integrated programmes such as those of the College of Europe or a number of elite Masters programmes have emerged, but less than 10 per cent of Bruges graduates enter the European civil service and they represent less than 10 percent of 'A' grade civil servants. Furthermore, despite being administered directly by the European Union, the process of recruitment by competitive exams does not completely avoid questions of nationality, as national university curricula, language skills, and the promotion of candidates from new Member States underrepresented in the administration reintroduce nationality.

Even if national administrative cultures are less pronounced than often claimed, national origins remain perceptible in day-to-day practice: attitudes to hierarchy, organization and functioning of the cabinets of commissioners, career expectations and strategies testify to their resilience. Moreover, informal social or political networks are often constructed around nationality, even if not exclusively, and these informal ties tend to aggregate persons into multinational yet segmented groups reproducing national stereotypes of affinities such as the North/South divide, or more recently the cleavage between old and new Member States.

Despite this persistence of nationality, there has been a general trend to an increasingly integrated and autonomous space which is quite far from the pessimistic prognosis of those like Michelmann (1978) who predicted an implosion of the institution under the weight of national rivalries. This acculturation processes came partly from the neutralization of national monopolies in European policy sectors. The cabinets of commissioners catered for national diversity and the same attention was paid to national plurality among top officers in each directorate. The commissioner, the director-general and the deputy director-general had to be of different nationalities. More generally, the complex institutionalized system of decision making and the culture of compromise erected barriers to outside interference, and thereby encouraged the denationalization of issues under consideration. This institutional closure has tended to denationalize debates and replace them with internal turf wars among DGs: Competition vs Regional Policy; Foreign Relations vs Development; Internal Markets vs Social Affairs, for example.

In addition to these dynamics of denationalization, one can identify a complex process giving shape to an increasingly cohesive transnational community. The reflexive definition of European civil servants as a social group led to the emergence of a distinct group identity through the creation of images and discourses defining the idealized figure of the European civil servant. This process can be observed in internal documents and discourse (newsletters, speeches, memoirs and biographies) which place emphasis on the independence, unique skills and multinational dispositions which sets the group apart from national civil servants. Strong and active trade unions (30 per cent of the personnel) also contributed to forging group identity by pushing for improved pay and working conditions and defending their legal status through participation in personnel committees, or during the strikes which have punctuated the history of the European civil

service from the 1950s until the civil service status reform of 2004. The emergence of this group identity has thus produced powerful effects of self-censorship with regard to any action potentially construed as nationally biased.

This never ending process of community building is not limited to the definition of group identity, values and visions. It is underpinned by the creation of specific resources. Over time, the possession of European institutional capital, accumulated through a succession of positions, has superseded nationally based political and administrative resources. Nearly 60 per cent of directors-general nominated since 1996 have spent the major part of their careers in Brussels and 44 per cent previously occupied a position in a commissioner's cabinet. Before the 1980s, less than a third of directors-general had had a predominantly European career, nearly none had cabinet experience and nominations mostly resulted from the 'pitchforking' of top national civil servants directly to the highest positions in the European civil service (Georgakakis and de Lassalle 2007, 43). A successful career in the EU increasingly implies a euphemization of nationality, and the accumulation of varied professional experiences within European institutions has become an essential resource. Speaking of his director-general Alexander Schaub, former Commissioner van Miert said that it was impossible to tell he was German, thereby exemplifying the more general trend of the creation of a relatively autonomous denationalized transnational social and institutional space of European civil servants.

Didier Georgakakis
Michel Mangenot
Jay Rowell

Bibliography

Abélès M. and Bellier I. 1996. 'La Commission européenne: du compromis culturel à la culture politique du compromis', *Revue Française de Science Politique*, 46, 3, 431–56.

Conrad Y. 1992. 'La CECA et la situation de ses agents', in *Annuaire d'histoire administrative européenne*, 4, Baden-Baden: Nomos.

Georgakakis D. and de Lassalle M. 2007. 'Genèse et structure d'un capital institutionnel européen: les très hauts fonctionnaires de la Commission européenne', *Actes de la Recherche en Sciences Sociales*, 166–167, 38–53.

Georgakakis D. forthcoming. 'Civil servant unions and social construction of the European civil service: sociological perspectives on Eurocrats' identities', *Journal of European Integration*.

Hooghe L. 2001. *The European Commission and the integration of Europe: images of governance*. Cambridge, Cambridge University Press.

Mangenot M. 2008. *De l'État à l'Europe: les hauts fonctionnaires français aux origines des institutions européennes*. Strasbourg: Presses Universitaires de Strasbourg.

Michelmann H. 1978. 'Multinational staffing and organisational functioning in the Commission of the EEC', *International Organization*, 32, 2, 477–96.

Scheinman L. 1966. 'Some preliminary notes on bureaucratic relationships in the European Economic Community', *International Organization*, 20, 4, 750–73.

Related essays

class; diasporas; empire and migration; European institutions; European Union (EU); executives and professionals; Hammarskjöld family; intergovernmental organizations; language; nation and state; pan-isms; regional communities

European institutions

The European Union is the product of nearly sixty years of institutionalized and supranational integration within Western Europe. It traces its origins back to the European Coal and Steel Community (ECSC) established in 1952 but it has expanded dramatically since its start. A Community of six, dealing exclusively with the management of two limited (if important) sectors of the economy has grown into a Union of 25 involved in a huge array of policy areas. While the basic quartet of institutions at its heart still bears some resemblance to the bodies established to run the ECSC, the EU's institutional structure has had to expand and become significantly more complex so as better to manage the vastly increased workload of the Union.

The idea of European unity was not new in 1950. The notion had been much discussed in interwar Europe, contemplated by both sides during World War 2 itself, and identified by many as a crucial element in Europe's postwar recovery. From 1947 it had also acquired a very powerful external sponsor in the shape of the United States. And in the context of the early Cold War there were even stronger incentives than before for European states to maximize their influence by cooperating closely. But it was only with the announcement on 9 May 1950 of the Schuman Plan – made public by the French foreign minister Robert Schuman, but largely devised by Jean Monnet, the head of the French planning authority – that a formula was identified that could transform a widely debated idea into a functioning reality.

Crucial to the Schuman Plan's success were its purpose, timing, proposed institutional structure and membership. As far as the first of these was concerned, the plan put forward by the French foreign minister combined short-term economic utility with long-term political potential. It thus promised immediately to solve the problems which France's steel industry seemed likely to face as the postwar controls on its German rival were progressively abolished, by establishing a neutral European authority to control the whole sector. But given the centrality of coal and steel to any war effort and the way in which rivalry between France and Germany had been at the heart of tension within Europe since the late 19th century, the establishment of joint institutions, irrevocably linking the coal and steel production of the two countries, could also justifiably be seen as a way of making war between France and Germany impossible and of starting a process of Franco–German reconciliation. Similarly the timing of the plan was well judged. The crisis of the French steel industry was sufficiently urgent to spur Paris into determined action, and the Federal Republic of Germany, its key potential partner, was still a new enough and weak enough state eagerly to appreciate any gesture of friendship from France. The balance of the institutional structure was also highly appropriate: strong enough to be able to complete its task of controlling the coal and steel industries credibly but not so strong as to alarm member states unduly. Additionally, the membership was big enough to matter (in addition to the key Franco–German pairing, Italy, the Netherlands, Belgium and Luxembourg took part) but not so large as to be unwieldy. Crucially, the British, who had always mistrusted far-reaching European cooperation, decided not to take part.

Quite how important each of these factors had been was soon to be demonstrated when an ambitious successor plan to the ECSC, the proposed European Defence Community (EDC) collapsed after being rejected by the French National Assembly in August 1954. The EDC was just too ambitious, its purpose – that of creating a European army – scaring as many as it attracted, its timing was suspect since the Cold War threat diminished greatly after Stalin's death in 1953, its institutions posed too great a threat to national sovereignty and its membership seemed inappropriate. In the military sphere as opposed to the economic, the presence of the British was seen as more vital so as to counterbalance the potential dominance of the Germans. The UK's refusal to join the EDC was thus much more damaging than its decision to opt out of the ECSC.

Momentum was rapidly regained, however, with the start in 1955 of the negotiations that were to lead to the creation of the European Economic Community (EEC). This once again found the right combination of purpose, timing, structure and membership. Thus it appealed to some as a purely economic project, a common market designed to consolidate and build upon the boom in intra-European trade that was already fuelling the continent's postwar recovery. But to others, economic integration was merely a stepping stone to much further-reaching political union, whether designed to address the relative powerlessness of individual European countries in a superpower-dominated world or to consolidate the peace and stability of the region. A wide coalition could thus rally behind the same treaty text. The timing was also propitious. Enough time had elapsed for the French government which had allowed the defeat of the EDC to lose office, but the disappointment felt by many at the fall of the EDC was still alive enough for them to rally behind the new European cause. At a crucial point in the negotiations, the Anglo-French humiliation at Suez may also have encouraged those who sought a mechanism to restore European power. The institutional structure was well balanced, moreover. The same basic quartet of institutions that had been at the heart of the ECSC was imitated, but in the light of the fears about rampant supranationalism caused by the EDC debacle, the mechanisms of national control (primarily the Council of Ministers) were reinforced at the expense of the supranational authorities. The European Commission created in 1958 was thus much less powerful than its predecessor, the High Authority of the ECSC, had been. And the membership again included all six of the ECSC member states – thereby offering commercial access for each to the booming German economy – but excluded the ever-sceptical British. The UK had briefly been involved in the negotiations but had quickly left, thereby greatly facilitating the task of reaching consensus amongst the remaining participants.

The new Community enjoyed a highly successful first decade of operation. The European economy continued to boom and the new institutions, which worked better than most had anticipated, were widely credited with helping underpin the continent's growing prosperity. In 1961 and again in 1967 the success of the EEC was underlined when Britain, Ireland, Denmark and Norway, all of whom had initially chosen to stay aloof from the integration process, submitted belated applications. They were not initially successful, as their path to membership was blocked by French President Charles de Gaulle, but the mere fact that they went on trying to enter confirmed the extent to which the EEC was seen as outperforming the European Free Trade Association (EFTA) to which all the applicants except for Ireland belonged. Throughout these years, however, the EEC remained a relatively narrow body, both in terms of countries directly involved and in policy scope. Most the EEC's early activity was centred upon the establishment and operation of a customs union amongst the six member states and upon the creation of an ambitious Common Agricultural Policy (CAP) designed to support Europe's still substantial population of farmers.

From the 1970s this began to change dramatically. The most obvious transformation was that of the Community's membership. In 1973 Britain, Ireland and Denmark finally joined. The Norwegians did not accompany them after rejecting EEC membership in a referendum. Then in 1981 the Greeks acceded, followed five years later by Spain and Portugal. The Six of the 1960s had become the Twelve. In 1995 the total then rose to 15, as Sweden, Finland and Austria joined. All had not felt able to join earlier because of their neutral status, but saw this barrier removed once the Cold War came to an end in 1990. And in 2004 a further ten members entered, mainly from the former Soviet Bloc. They were Poland, Hungary, the Czech Republic,

Slovakia, Slovenia, Latvia, Lithuania, Estonia, Cyprus and Malta. Two more states – Bulgaria and Romania– entered in 2007 and several other countries, notably Turkey, have made known their desire to follow. The size of the EU has thus expanded vastly from the six Western European countries that had formed the ECSC and early EEC.

Equally crucial, however, has been the expansion in the Community's range of activities. The customs union and the CAP of the 1960s still exist, but they have gradually been flanked with monetary policies (culminating in the launch of the single currency in 2002), environmental policies, competition policies, redistribution policies designed to provide financial support for the less affluent parts of the Union, cooperation on justice and home affairs (including cooperation on immigration, visas, cross-border security, etc.), and efforts to establish foreign-policy cooperation. This broadening of the agenda reflects in part the changed circumstances in which the EC/EU has found itself. Its efforts to devise cooperative mechanisms in the monetary field, for instance, arose largely in response to the collapse of the global Bretton Woods monetary system. Also important has been the arrival of new member states, each with different policy priorities. Redistribution, for instance, became much more central to the EC's activities after the first and second enlargements had brought a number of much poorer regions into the Community. And in some cases European activity in one policy area has created pressures for further action elsewhere. Thus the 1980s drive to establish a single market, unencumbered by time-consuming border controls, obliged member states to begin much greater cooperation in order jointly to control immigration and cross-border crime.

The growing complexity of the Union both in terms of membership and activity has also necessitated a number of alterations in its institutional structure. The first big change occurred in the 1970s with the establishment of the European Council – a forum which brought together the leaders of each of the member states at least once every six months – and the move to direct elections for the European Parliament. This was followed by a succession of new treaties in the 1980s and 1990s, each of which formalized the expansion of the Community agenda, and modified the details of the Community's legislative process so as to enable the larger and more complex EC/EU to go on functioning. One of these, the Maastricht Treaty signed in 1992, also formally introduced the name European Union. Throughout these changes, however, the basic pattern of EU activity has remained recognizably that pioneered by the ECSC and early EEC decades before. Thus much of the EU's activity still involves the establishment of a body of European law, initially proposed by the European Commission, but then debated and discussed by both the European Parliament and, crucially, the Council of Ministers. This last, composed of ministerial representatives of all of the member states, always has the final say. The implementation of this law is then overseen by the European Commission and where necessary the European Court of Justice. For all the vast transformation of the membership, agenda and institutional balance of the EC/EU which has occurred, the debt to the methods first devised by Monnet and others in the 1950s and 1960s remains strikingly high.

The EU has in many ways been a remarkable success story. It has pushed the integration of Europe both economically and politically to a level unmatched elsewhere in the world. It has had an important transformative effect both on the way that politics and diplomacy are conducted within Europe and on the continent's standing elsewhere. The EU's collective clout within global trade negotiations is an obvious example of this last. It has also made it much easier for all Europeans to holiday, study, work and live in parts of the EU other than those where they were born. But for the purposes of this volume it is important to note that the process of European integration has always been pushed forward primarily by its political leaders acting collectively, rather than a phenomenon arising spontaneously out of popular involvement. As a result, there has always been a danger that integration might go further and faster than some of the wider European population could easily accept – a danger which seemed particularly real after the French and Dutch referendums rejecting the proposed European constitution in 2005. One of the challenges that the EU confronts in the early years of the 21st century is therefore that of re-engaging with its citizens and rekindling that popular enthusiasm for European unity which characterized the earlier years of the process.

Piers Ludlow

Bibliography

Dinan D. 2004. *Europe recast: a history of European Union*. Basingstoke: Palgrave Macmillan.

Dinan D. 2006. *Origins and evolution of the European Union*. Oxford: Oxford University Press.

Milward A. 1992. *The European rescue of the nation state*. London: Routledge.

Loth W. (ed.) 2001. *Crises and compromises: the European project 1963–1969*. Baden-Baden: Nomos; Brussels: Bruyant.

Ludlow N. P. 2006. *The European Community and the crises of the 1960s: negotiating the Gaullist challenge*. London: Routledge.

Middlemas K. 1995. *Orchestrating Europe: the informal politics of European Union 1973–1995*. London: Fontana.

Related essays

Cold War; European Union (EU); intellectual elites; iron and steel; Marshall Plan; nation and state; pan-isms; Pax Americana; police; regional communities; trade agreements

European Union (EU)

The European Union (EU) was created in its current constitutional form with its pillar structure and this name in the Maastricht Treaty (1992), although it has since been modified by the treaties of Amsterdam (1997) and Nice (2000). It developed out of the European Communities (EC) – now its first pillar. They in turn resulted from the institutional merger in 1967 of the three 'core Europe' organizations, the European Economic Community (EEC) and Euratom formed in 1957–58 and the European Coal and Steel Community (ECSC) created in 1951–52. Despite its supranational features like the supremacy of European over national law and the role of the European Commission and the European Parliament in the policy-making process, most contemporary historians have discussed the origins and evolution of the EU from an often implicitly realist perspective: as an international organization dominated by the member states in which the major treaty revisions and policy making are controlled by national governments in the European Council of heads of governments and state formed in 1974 and institutionalized in the Single European Act (1987), and in the Council of Ministers. However, from an economic, not the dominant diplomatic history perspective, Alan S. Milward has even framed the origins of early

'core Europe' integration as the attempt by the national governments of the six founding member states, France, Italy, the Federal Republic of Germany, Belgium, Luxembourg and the Netherlands, to 'rescue the European nation state' by Europeanizing some of its welfare state functions in the ECSC and the EEC, thus also substituting for a peace treaty with Germany which was never signed after World War 2.

Political science and sociological research on the EU has long since overcome the extremely state-centric analysis espoused by Andrew Moravcsik with his liberal intergovernmentalist study of 'grand bargains'. It is widely acknowledged that national governments still play a crucial role in decision making in the enlarged EU of 27 member states (2007). At the same time, most observers emphasize the EU's complex constitutional character with many supranational features which invites comparisons with European federal states like Germany, Belgium and Switzerland or, for that matter, the United States as a federal political system rather than with intergovernmental international organizations. The EU's institutional setup is highly complex with 'horizontal' interaction between the Commission, which has retained the exclusive formal right to initiate legislation, the Council, and the European Parliament, which has acquired substantial (co-)decision-making powers in many policy fields. At the same time, 'vertical' relations link the supranational EU level not only with the member states, but also with regions and local authorities which have increased decision-making powers resulting from widespread nation-state decentralization, and enhanced interest in EU legislation and participation in consultative deliberation as in the Committee of the Regions. Some scholars have thus characterized the EU as 'multi-level governance': a political system with a complex institutional setup and decision making involving and linking various levels. 'Governance' in turn refers to the increased tendency for political decision making to be characterized – as at the nation-state level – by predominately informal network-type mechanisms of consultation, coordination and often consensus-oriented decision making involving a substantial number of different actors; importantly, not just member states and supranational institutions, but also partially transnationally constituted societal actors such as political parties, formal business associations and trade union organizations, informal business networks like the European Round Table of Industrialists (ERT) and a large number of non-governmental public interest groups. In fact, the European Commission in its White Paper on European Governance (2001) emphasized especially the importance of such 'civil society' actors for optimizing policy outcomes and legitimizing the policy process through wide consultation with non-traditional transnational societal actors with a justifiable claim to represent significant sections of EU society.

In view of these contemporary debates about the nature of the EU, its origins and evolution in postwar (Western) Europe also appear in a very different light and the state-centric notions of intergovernmental bargaining of 'national interests' as conceptually very underdeveloped and inadequately capturing only one – albeit important – dimension of the process of European integration, that is, decision making at the centre. A new generation of contemporary historians of the EU now advocate conceptualizing European integration as the closely linked trends of the evolution of a complex political system and of transnational societal integration and 'Europeanization'. In this perspective, (a) the politics and decision making of the present-day EU have always been shaped to a greater or lesser extent by partially transnationally constituted actors, not just member-state governments – the more interesting question concerning the internal constitution, activities and influence of different types of actors and how their roles have changed over time and differed according to the policy field concerned; (b) supranational policy making and legal integration in turn have fostered the deepening of the formal organization of transnational actors, as when the political parties revamped their European-level organizations in the 1970s; encouraged the formation of new transnational actors, especially those growing out of the new social movements in the 1970s which played an important role in the development of new policy agendas and EU-level powers in fields like environmental policy and women's rights; and facilitated the transformation of these actors' collective identities and political claim making, directed increasingly at the European, not just the national level of government; and (c) the slow formation of a transnational European

society which has been much facilitated by EU-level policies such as freedom of movement and educational exchange programmes, for example. European society formation extends to such phenomena as growing social contacts across borders, changing collective identities with a growing European allegiance despite popular criticism of EU institutions, and the intensified institutional competition and cross-border transfer of policy solutions and cultural practices.

Transnationally networked actors actually played a crucial role as early as during the formation of the ECSC, following upon the declaration by French Foreign Minister Robert Schuman on 9 May 1950. Neofunctionalist accounts of European integration by Ernst B. Haas and others claimed that transnational actors were relevant mainly through their cooperation with the new supranational institutions, the ECSC High Authority and the European Commission. Yet they focused exclusively on those actors' formal organization at the European level and showed no interest in why and how the European institutions were formed in the first place. Historian Walter Lipgens argued that federalist ideals developed in the European resistance movements during World War 2 guided the formation of 'core Europe', but he was unable to demonstrate causal links between federalist ideas and political decision making. In fact, other more informally transnationally networked actors were much more effective in influencing the agenda of supranational functional economic integration with political objectives. By 1950 this only seemed possible without the United Kingdom as British governments had a strong preference for intergovernmental cooperation and refused to participate in sectoral or horizontal economic integration which could endanger existing Commonwealth trading links. In particular, transnationally networked Christian Democrats, who had established high-level secret contacts involving leading politicians like Konrad Adenauer and Georges Bidault, colluded in advancing the 'core Europe' project. Their cross-border party cooperation created social capital, especially trust, within the network, which the Christian Democrats could invest in steering intergovernmental negotiations when they were in power alone or in coalitions in all six founding member states of the ECSC at the time of Schuman's declaration. This transnational network pushed strongly for the exclusion of Britain (described by Bidault and Pierre-Henri Teitgen in a meeting with German Christian Democrats as France's real 'eternal enemy'), a supranational institutional setup and sectoral integration, later supporting its extension to horizontal economic integration in the EEC customs union.

At the same time, informal transatlantic policy networks, partly centred around Jean Monnet, who had drafted the plan for a coal and steel pool, played an important role during the negotiations in defining the ECSC's anti-trust policy and thus established the outlines of a European-level competition policy which could draw upon indigenous European intellectual traditions, especially ordoliberalism (emphasizing especially the need for the state to create a secure legal order to guarantee free competition), but was also influenced by US anti-trust policy. The creation of the ECSC in turn created what historical institutionalists call 'path-dependency'. The self-exclusion of Britain, encouraged by the Christian Democratic-led governments' wish to allow supranational economic integration, not least to bring about Franco–German reconciliation, was precedent-setting and was followed by the British decision against participating in the customs union in 1955. Without the geographically limited 'core Europe' integration in the 1950s, however, the EEC's institutional setup would hardly have been characterized by the same degree of supranationalism and important policies like the Common Agricultural Policy (CAP) would never have developed in the same way as they did in the 1960s.

Transnationally constituted actors have also played a crucial role in EU politics since the formation of the EEC. In the 1960s, for example, the agricultural policy network bringing together farmers' interest groups and protectionist-minded agricultural ministries played a central role in shaping the CAP to avoid faster modernization of the sector as originally foreseen by the European Commission. At the same time, an expert community of lawyers and economists in the European Commission, national economics ministries and universities succeeded in shaping the EEC's competition policy broadly in line with ordoliberal preferences, which was completely contrary to the official French policy under President Charles de Gaulle. From the 1970s onwards,

the European Commission also facilitated the formalization of transnational links of new social movements by organizing European-level conferences and involving their representatives in policy advisory functions, encouraging them to direct their political claims at the EC level. This in turn made it much easier for the Commission to develop initiatives even in fields like environmental policy where no EC competence at all existed at the time, before one eventually came into being in 1987, followed by the introduction of majority voting for environmental policy in 1992. Even more importantly, the oil crisis and the subsequent period of 'Eurosclerosis' with low growth, high inflation, rising budget and state debts and unemployment in all EC member states motivated European business leaders to extend their cooperation and political engagement beyond the limited activities of their EC-level associations like UNICE (now called Business Europe). The ERT then played a crucial role in the early 1980s in cooperation with the European Commission and some member states like Britain in promoting the '1992' programme for a Single Market that would abolish the massive remaining nontariff barriers after the customs union had been fully implemented in mid 1968. This very informal network also set the agenda in the mid 1990s for the intergovernmental 'Bologna process' geared towards streamlining European higher education systems not least to facilitate mobility and allow European business to recruit the best personnel from across the EU and beyond.

The growth of policy networks of different kinds, often involving state and non-state actors in informal opinion formation and decision-making processes, has encouraged some political scientists to characterize EU governance as 'network governance'. In any case, transnational actors have played a crucial role in such networks that can fulfil different functions from agenda setting to facilitating policy implementation. Importantly, the EU legal framework has also eased the growth of transnational structures and social communication from business activities in the internal market, political cooperation between parties, foundations and think-tanks to networks of higher education institutions, integrated study programmes and student exchanges. The density of social contacts has for the most part not reached the level of nation-state social integration, although language barriers have become less important resulting from the widespread use of English. In the 19th century, however, the same was true of territories like Italy and Germany where social contacts were initially much more regional and only became denser at national level in the process of nation-state integration. It is also clear that the social integration within the EU as a whole has become less restricted to elites than in the early postwar period and is much more advanced than globally, with the partial exception of some non-European migrant communities. The social integration in Europe has not resulted exclusively from the legal and political framework of the present-day EU. Worker migration from Southern Europe to Northern Europe, which began in the late 1950s, for example, was controlled by national governments and included people from countries outside of the EEC like Portugal and Spain. Social processes of transnationalization have extended beyond the EU in other ways, too. The European Free Trade Association (EFTA) founded in 1959–60, for example, also impacted on cross-border business activities by creating a free-trade zone which especially facilitated the economic and social integration of Scandinavia from the 1960s onwards. The present-day enlarged EU has developed more and more into the economic, political and legal centre of gravity in Europe, however. It has exercised crucial functions of spreading legal and political norms and institutional arrangements to prospective member states in Eastern and Central Europe, preparing the eastern enlargement of 2004. More recently, its role has been extended in the context of the European Neighbourhood Policy (ENP) involving countries in Southeastern Europe and the Near East which may never, or at least not for some time, become full members of the EU. Societal actors like foundations, for example, have played a crucial role in this larger process which has often been described as Europeanization, or with a less elegant, but now more precise term, EU-ization.

In these different ways, the history of the present-day EU should be treated not merely as the institutionalized intergovernmental bargaining of 'national interests'. Such a state-centric rational-choice framework ignores other crucial dimensions of European integration such as the formation of a complex political system in which the member states have continued

to play a fundamentally important role, but are neither as purposeful nor as cohesive as realist diplomatic history and rational-choice social science accounts of the EU would have it. More importantly, this supranational political system is characterized by dense transnational political networks with strong involvement of non-state actors that shape policy making in important ways, possibly even justifying the description of EU politics as 'network governance'. Beyond the preoccupation with the supranational centre and policy making in 'Brussels', moreover, the process of European integration has also encouraged the slow formation over time of a fragmented, but increasingly recognizable transnational European society.

Wolfram Kaiser

Bibliography

Gehler M., Kaiser W. and Leucht, B. (eds) 2008. *Netzwerke im europäischen Mehrebenensystem: von 1945 bis zur Gegenwart / Networks in European multi-level governance: from 1945 to the present.* Vienna: Böhlau.

Haas E. B. 2004 [1958]. *The uniting of Europe: political, social, and economic forces 1950–57.* Notre Dame: University of Notre Dame Press.

Kaiser W. 'Transnational Western Europe since 1945: integration as political society formation', in: Kaiser W. and Starie P. (eds) 2005. *Transnational European Union: towards a common political space.* London: Routledge, 17–35.

Kaiser W. 'From state to society? the historiography of European integration', in Cini M. and Bourne A. K. (eds) 2006. *Palgrave advances in European Union studies.* Basingstoke: Palgrave Macmillan, 190–208.

Kaiser W. 2007. *Christian Democracy and the origins of European Union.* Cambridge: Cambridge University Press.

Kaiser W., Leucht B. and Rasmussen M. (eds) 2008. *The history of the European Union.* London: Routledge.

Lipgens W. 1982. *A history of European integration,* Vol. 1: 1945–1947. Oxford: Clarendon.

Milward A. S. 1992. *The European rescue of the nation-state.* London: Routledge.

Moravcsik A. 1998. *The choice for Europe: social purpose and state power from Messina to Maastricht.* London: UCL Press.

Evangelicalism

Evangelicalism is a Christian movement, originally Western, which spread worldwide in the course of the 20th century. By 2000 it was estimated to have between 400 and 500 million followers. Its dynamism, talent for expansion and organizational methods have made it a major example of transnational religion.

While any kind of Christianity can be loosely described as 'evangelical', Evangelicalism represents a particular approach to Christian living predicated on the idea of Christian 'rebirth'.

The origins of the movement lie in the unending ramifications of 16th-century Protestantism. While Evangelicalism is intrinsically Protestant, however, it has defined itself in opposition to other Churches which its followers consider too traditional, too hierarchical, or insufficiently dynamic. Its direct ancestry is to be sought in the great revivals of the 18th and 19th centuries (particularly in the United States), some of which sprang directly from existing Christian Churches while others remained on the fringe. North American-based Evangelicalism as we know it today has grown out of two religious currents that originally arose in England: Baptism, as initially preached in the early 17th century by John Smyth while in exile in Amsterdam; and Methodism, inspired by the 18th-century Anglican clergyman John Wesley. In the 19th century Baptism and Methodism flourished in both rural and newly industrializing areas of Britain and, above all, the United States; they also spawned missionary societies, sending out preachers to 'evangelize' not only Continental Europe but also Western colonies overseas.

Evangelicalism is not easy to define exactly. The movement is neither unified nor centralized, but has numerous representatives even within Churches that do not describe themselves as evangelical. Some salient characteristics do, however, emerge: a focus on the Bible, the Cross, and conversion; and militancy. Evangelicals lay great stress on unmediated access to and daily reading of the Bible, which is to be understood in its literal sense as a handbook for Christian living. The figure of Christ is central, while the Cross symbolizes the hope of new life and the way of human salvation. Great stress is laid on conversion: 'You are not born Christian, you become a Christian', the saying goes. Conversion is a deeply personal experience which transforms the life of converts: through adult baptism they are 'born again', and there is a sharp division between their former and present lives, constituting a new identity. Evangelicals are militantly committed and zealous proselytes: having wholeheartedly embraced conversion, they incline towards religious activism. They feel the need to exhibit their faith outside their own fold, while bringing as many other people as possible within it.

At the beginning of the 20th century two significant lines began to stand out on this vast canvas: Pentecostalism and fundamentalism. It is widely accepted that the first manifestations of Pentecostalism were witnessed in America in 1901 and 1906. The movement lays great stress on the centrality and effective intervention of the Holy Spirit, especially through the granting of gifts (healing, prophecy, speaking in tongues, etc.). Religious observance tends to be flamboyant, with an eager expectation of miracles. Pentecostalism spread to Latin America in the first decade of the 20th century and to Africa some ten years later, and it put on another spurt of growth in the 1970s, making it the most rapidly expanding movement within Evangelicalism. Fundamentalism is another early 20th-century American movement, a reaction against modernism characterized by a literal reading of the Bible, a premillenarian eschatology (Jesus will return before the thousand-year reign of the Saints), and a deliberate self-isolation from the rest of society. Fundamentalists did not develop a 'global' strategy until the 1970s.

It could be said that Evangelicalism is intrinsically transnational: it is not centralized, it encourages open exchange and it aspires to universalism. Its presence worldwide can be explained in terms of both diffusion and appropriation.

The diffusion is partly due to the labours of numerous American and European missionaries sent out to found new Churches in virgin territory; but some of it is the work of international preachers heading their own ministries. The latter may organize huge open-air meetings – in sports stadiums, for example – attended by tens, or even hundreds, of thousands of people. The most zealous of these preachers have been at work for decades, particularly in the Third World: for example, the Americans Billy Graham and T. L. Osborn, and the German Reinhard Bonnke. There are even worldwide evangelization movements based in the United States: for example, the 'Discipling A Whole Nation Ministries' (founded 1985) and the 'AD 2000 & Beyond Movement' (1989). These movements have released a flood of material objects (bibles, brochures, religious books, cassettes, DVDs) together with symbols, rules for Christian living and organizational models. Evangelicals are also involved in humanitarian action and development aid, but see these as tools for evangelization: for example, World Vision, an NGO set up by an American pastor in 1950 which is chiefly known for its sponsoring of children.

Evangelicals have always made copious use of modern communications, from the books and pamphlets of the 19th century to radio, television and the Internet. The 1950s saw the rise of the televangelists – TV preachers, programme presenters or even owners of TV channels whose popularity depends precisely on their exploitation of the televisual medium. Among the most famous names are the Americans Pat Robertson, who founded the Christian Broadcasting Network in 1960, and Jimmy Swaggart. Some of these programmes are subsequently broadcast on cable or even national networks worldwide, particularly in the Southern hemisphere.

As Evangelicalism spread outwards from its origins through the 20th century, it was continually reinterpreted, reinvented and adapted to local conditions. The Evangelical Churches acquired new meanings as they penetrated new territories; moreover, many groups originally established by missionaries have matured into autonomous local Churches not all of which are closely bound to their parent body. Some Evangelical Churches are purely local, without links to any outside structure. At times, internal schisms have produced competing groups. Many of these movements are purely local, having started by imitating new, imported religious ideas and then adapted them to fit their immediate context.

These processes of appropriation and localized reinvention were of major importance in the success of Evangelicalism. Churches founded by American or European missionaries were already going native in the early 20th century; the rapid growth seen in Latin America from the 1970s, and in sub-Saharan Africa from the 1980s, was led by local Churches and local pastors. Examples are the Universal Church of the Kingdom of God (Brazil), the Redeemed Christian Church of God (Nigeria) and the Yoido Full Gospel Church (Korea).

Most worldwide Evangelical networks are still more or less controlled from the USA, but currents of influence now run both ways. A considerable number of Evangelical movements in the Southern hemisphere are committed to re-Christianizing the West and were setting up missionary centres in major Western cities by the end of the 20th century. The principal Evangelical association is the World Council of Churches. A historic first meeting took place in London in 1846, but it was not until 1951 that the alliance itself was created in Lausanne by Christians from 21 countries, partly in opposition to the World Ecumenical Council founded in Amsterdam in 1948. Thus it can be seen that the expansion of Evangelicalism is not necessarily part of a process of global Americanization or homogenization. Although much of its background lies in American culture, and it is to an extent controlled by American leaders, the movement has been continually re-created as it has spread to and been appropriated by other societies.

Questions have often been raised as to possible links between Evangelicalism and US foreign policy. Some have seen the spread of the movement as part of an American anti-Communist strategy, particularly in Latin America since the Second World War, while others insisted on the fact that worldwide armed interventions by US forces often brought missionaries in their wake. Probably this was a case of reciprocal benefit rather than organized cooperation: independence and autonomy have always been at the heart of Evangelicalism.

Since the 19th century Evangelicalism has established itself as a dynamic Christian movement which has contributed significantly to the worldwide spread of Christianity, most notably since 1950. It exhibits all the contradictions of transnational religious activity: the instinct of self-isolation and openness to outside influence; the urge to break with the past and the urge to reinvent it; strong local links and awareness of belonging to a worldwide community; diversity and universalism.

Cédric Mayrargue

Bibliography

Corten A. and Marshall-Fratani R. (eds) 1998. *Between Babel and Pentecost: transnational Pentecostalism in Africa and Latin America.* London: Hurst.

Cox H. 1994. *Fire from Heaven: the rise of pentecostal spirituality and the reshaping of religion in the twenty-first century.* Reading, MA: Addison-Wesley.

Fath S. (ed.) 2004. *Le protestantisme évangélique, un christianisme de conversion.* Turnhout: Brépols.

Noll M. A. 1994. *Evangelicalism: comparative studies of popular Protestantism in North America, the British Isles, and beyond, 1700–1990.* Oxford and New York: Oxford University Press.

Related essays

adoption; Africa; Bible; broadcasting; childhood; Christianity; cosmopolitanism and universalism; ecumenism; internationalisms; missionaries; new man; Pax Americana; radio; relief; religion; religious fundamentalism; translation; world orders

Executives and professionals

Executives and professionals working for transnational corporations or development programmes on temporary work assignments outside their country of origin are the most mobile and transnational part of the global population. Their number has been steadily rising, although it is extremely difficult to be specific: there may be as many as hundreds of thousands, even millions, depending on the categories of individuals one chooses to include.

Economic expansion and the globalization of capitalist business are led by a mobile technomanagerial elite. Expatriate executives and professionals are part of the fast-growing migration of skilled transients. In terms of frequency and ease of movements, these organizational flows of expatriates are different from flows of settler migrants: for the former, who represent the highly paid elite, often headhunted by international recruitment agencies, the world is indeed borderless, and their transnational circulation is virtually unhindered. They are usually company transferees who disseminate managerial and technical corporate knowledge within the office networks of corporations, as the corporations expand their operations across borders. Intra-company transfers account for an increasing portion of the total flow of skilled workers. Such transfers ensure the effective use of human resources and facilitate the business expansion of multinational corporations. This most often happens in oil and gas production and other primary-resources exploitation industries. Executives and professionals, who staff global movements of capital and fit into Sklair's definition of a 'transnational capitalist class', usually find these transfers beneficial for the development of their professional careers. Transfers between companies are also common.

Apart from direct foreign investment, international development and aid programmes are another important vehicle of the mobility of this group. The growth of transnational corporations as vehicles of global capitalism has been accompanied by the increased presence of NGOs, usually headquartered in the West, which involve transnational flows of researchers, medical professionals, engineers and managers. NGOs' executives and professionals who work on developmental, humanitarian, scientific and other non-profit projects can be seen as part of the development of the 'global civil society'. Transnational executives and professionals may also work for intergovernmental organizations (IGOs) of global governance, usually within the UN. There are other significant groups of professionals on expatriate assignments through government and non-governmental sectors, such as diplomats, journalists, artists and academics.

The growing presence of these persons is especially noticeable in the 'world cities', where the headquarters of multinational corporations, as well as of transnational NGOs and IGOs, are located. They can also be found in various sites in developing countries where aid and developmental projects take place, as well as in oil-producing countries.

The expatriate migration of executives and professionals privileges Westerners from English-speaking countries, as they are native speakers of the global lingua franca. However, most multinational corporations promote diversity in recruitment and target personnel from 'non-traditional backgrounds' (Sklair 2001, 161–2), and most NGOs are equal opportunity employers looking for staff from under-represented countries. A large majority of transnational executives and professionals are men, not only because of the gender division of labour where men dominate highly paid sectors of the labour markets – national as well as transnational – but also because of the general gender division of roles in society, where women find it harder to lead an itinerant lifestyle for longer periods because of their parenting and family care role. Many women follow their male partners on their expatriate assignments as 'trailing spouses'.

The social and cultural impact of transnational executives and professionals on their host environments, especially in developing countries, is understudied. Expatriates often live in segregated compounds that minimize contact with the host culture and society. This is more likely to be the case with the staff of transnational business firms, while governmental and IGO/NGO staff often mix with the local society as part of their role and mandate. Therefore, transnational businesses may have significant economic effects on host societies, but executives and professionals on non-profit projects are likely to have social and cultural impacts. Whether such impact is Westernization pure and simple or rather a more balanced cultural cross-fertilization and 'cosmopolitanization' depends on the type of role that they perform.

Val Colic-Peisker

Bibliography

Sklair L. 2001. *The transnational capitalist class.* Oxford: Blackwell.

Tzeng R. 1995. 'International labor migration through multinational enterprises', *International Migration Review*, 29, 1, 139–54.

Related essays

auditing; body shopping; brain drain; class; contract and indentured labourers; corporations; developmental assistance; diasporas; domestic service; empire and migration; engineering; global cities; gold; grants and fellowships; Hammarskjöld family; higher education; human mobility; intellectual elites; intergovernmental organizations; international non-governmental organizations (INGOs); international schools; labour migrations; language; life and physical sciences; nursing; oil; performing artists; philanthropic foundations; race-mixing; social sciences; temporary migrations; transnational; United Nations Educational, Scientific and Cultural Organization (UNESCO) educational programmes; Quesnay, Pierre; United Nations system; Westernization; Williams, James Dixon

Body shopping

Body shopping refers to the recruitment across international borders of software professionals on work visas.

Firms recruit software professionals in India, for example, and contract them out for short-term projects in the United States. Programmers stay on the payroll of their local company but provide services for an overseas corporate client. In the late 1990s, recruitments from India were more than 50,000 a year.

There are three important characteristics of body shopping. The first is its relative universality, or its universal use in a diversity of unrelated industries. Programmers are quickly deployed and transferred among aviation, financial services, healthcare, insurance, pharmaceuticals, technology, shipping, apparel, animation, accounting, Internet services, and the military. Second, programmers are higher-earning but lower-cost labour. While annual contracts fetch good incomes, the receiving company economizes on long-term benefits – social security, retirement contributions, health insurance, and unemployment insurance. Third, body shopping is analogous to the application of the just-in-time (JIT) techniques developed by Japanese firms in the 1970s. Body-shopping firms help companies to reduce costs by flexibly scheduling the supply of software professionals only for the length of time needed. During inactive periods, when programmers were between assignments, many consulting companies in the 1990s cut their pay by as much as 75 per cent. Evidently, the flexibility of the just-in-time system demanded immense flexibility from workers. Culturally, workers displayed a complex nationalist orientation. While they lived out their dream of American life brought from home, they also felt alienated and critical residing in the United States. The lives of programmers displayed a continuous nostalgia for the 'other' nation; that is, they missed India while in the United States and longed for American life when they went back to India.

A. Aneesh

Bibliography
Aneesh A. 2006. *Virtual migration: the programming of globalization.* Durham, NC: Duke University Press.

Related essays
America; brain drain; class; diasporas; executives and professionals; information technology (IT) offshoring; labour migrations; services; spatial regimes; temporary migrations; welfare state

Exile

Although it is difficult to unravel the motivations that lead to human migration, a distinction is often made between economic migration and political migration. Often referred to as 'exile', these movements are characterized by dramatic departures, an obsession with the lost motherland, and the intense and reactive human dynamics of an exiled community. Still, contemporary exiles are not refugees who are driven from their homes. When the Huguenots fled France due to religious persecution under Louis XIV, or when the opponents of Napoleon III's coup d'état left France, their exile was a choice to fight oppression from abroad. By contrast, the 1951 Geneva Convention defines refugees as those forced to leave their homelands because of race, religion or sociopolitical affiliation. An exiled individual is a particular kind of refugee, and exile is a more selective phenomenon, limited to militants, union leaders, journalists, artists, professional politicians, and all those who conceive of their exile as a form of political activity. Nevertheless, political exiles were not necessarily involved in politics prior to their departure and they are sociologically more diverse than most political elites. Exile itself can politicize a life.

Although exile existed before the modern age, as witnessed by the many forms of banishment practised by ancient societies, modern exile is not merely a form of spatial distancing but, also, of deep and lasting estrangement. It is a by-product of the modern international political economy, established along with the progressive building of nation states, the rationalization of the State, and the nationalization of politics and societies. The 19th-century flowering of nationalisms, 20th-century decolonization, including world wars and the rise of totalitarianism, gave birth to new groups of refugees and political exiles, from the Polish nationalists who gathered in Paris after the Warsaw Insurrection of 1831 to the Arab elites dispersed throughout Europe and North America in the second half of the 20th century.

Nor has exile received 'good press': for Marx, himself an exile, it was 'a school of scandal and mediocrity', and a training ground for failure, as suggested by the dismal fates of such emblematic exiles as White Russians after 1917, the anti-Franco forces after 1938, or the Eastern European opponents of the Communist regimes of the post-1945 era. A strongly negative shadow has been projected onto contemporary exile, discrediting it as a useless form of agitation plagued with petty in-fighting. Ever since, exiles have resisted being labelled as 'émigrés' (or 'émigrants'), a term referring to the counter-revolutionary exile of French monarchists after 1789.

Still, exiles were often successful. Norwegian, French, Dutch or Belgians exiles returned to their homelands as guardians of national honour and as dedicated opponents of Nazi Germany. Their exile and political activity against the regimes in power in their countries of origin were effective. The new political space constructed in exile is now receiving the attention of scholars. The French political scientist Stéphane Dufoix has coined the term 'exopolity', to emphasize the double bind experienced by exiles: accepting the break with the homeland, they maintained continuity with it by creating national political movements abroad.

In their claim to be the genuine guardians of national sovereignty, the true voice of the people, exiled movements often distinguished between state and nation. Loyalty to the nation justified their acts: exiles claimed to embody the principle of national destiny, defended from abroad against a vicious regime at home and, sometimes also, against national diasporas that did not identify with their struggles. The relationship between exiles and the larger diasporic communities is crucial and creates a subtle typology. Historic diasporic communities did not necessarily welcome the new potential 'leaders' exile brought their way. For example, the Italian-American diaspora did not embrace the opinions of the anti-fascist exiles of the 1930s.

The need to demonstrate their loyalty to the nation explains why exiles often seemed locked into a separate time and space. The exile removed them from national space while time stood still for them after departure, making changes in the homeland difficult to perceive. This explains difficulties experienced by exiles when returning home after a long absence abroad: they discovered a place that was very different from the painful image they had learned to live with.

To re-establish political legitimacy, exiles had to explain their departures. Each group had its founding event: the Reichstag Fire for the German exiles of the 1930s, the Prague Coup for the Czechs. Exiled communities scrupulously commemorated these events, not only to remind those in the homeland of the initial crime but also to distinguish exiles from the larger diasporas, thereby facilitating recognition by foreign governments or the international community. Meanwhile subgroups within exiled communities typically engaged in ferocious competition for recognition. It was sometimes an internal struggle (as witnessed among the French supporters and opponents of General de Gaulle in the United States during the Second World War). Such competition also took place in the international arena: the impact of Czech, Polish or 'Yugoslavian' exiled leaders on the Versailles peacemakers in 1919 is clearly established. Identified by the Allied powers as the genuine voice of the oppressed peoples of the Austro-Hungarian Empire, they lobbied effectively for the establishment of new Central European countries. Exopolities have operated both within the nation and across national borders. Exiles from a given land often scattered throughout different host countries. There is, for instance, a very visible Cuban anti-Castro community in Florida, but also in Spain and France. These communities interact with the Florida one in both cooperative and conflictual ways.

Despite their deep, even sublimated, identifications with the lost homeland, exiles' experience and exposure to a different society can lead to cultural and political metamorphosis. Return home can become occasions for transfers, with exiles acting as translators and brokers. At least three types of transfers were operating during the 19th and 20th centuries.

First, the acquisition or the completion of a revolutionary culture in exile, especially through the interaction with other exiled groups. This was the case in the 1830s and 1840s, when the European exiled communities mingling in Paris formed a propitious matrix for the expansion of the revolutionary ideas of 1848. Karl Marx's final transition to communism took place in this setting. In Paris from 1843 to 1845, Marx was very much part of the revolutionary bohemia and was a protagonist of exiled German discussion groups and French political 'levellers' circles inspired by the thought of Gracchus Baboeuf. While this exiled bohemia was the training ground for the political leaders of the 1848 European revolutions, a large proportion of 20th-century revolutionaries were also shaped into the politics of exile. Many Chinese students became critical intellectuals during their exile in Japan, like Sun Yatsen, or in France for the following generation that included Zhou Enlai. Emancipated from the link with the state that was postulated by the Chinese learned tradition, they perceived themselves as revolutionary and nationalist leaders.

This transfer of the national idea as a revolutionary weapon might eventually have been the largest transfer resulting from political exile in the modern age. In the name of anti-imperialism, there were many who learned the discourse of the nation in colonial metropolises. Funnelled by imperial migrations, Ho Chi Minh and several future Khmer Rouge leaders studied in France, and repatriated in Vietnam and Cambodia a revolutionary creed painted with national colours they had adapted from Lenin and the Bolsheviks as much as from the epic narratives of the French Revolution and the Commune. The major Algerian nationalist movement, Messali Hadj's Étoile Nord Africaine, was created in Paris in 1926 with the assistance of the Communist Party, which was anxious to open an anti-colonial front in the class struggle. This revolutionary nationalism of European origin, adapted to colonial lands, often gave birth to virulent postcolonial nationalisms, as in Algeria.

Those who had left the country may also, on their return, bring back democratic culture on the soles of their shoes. This was typical of returns that followed long dictatorial stints. Whether Francoist, Salazarist or Communist, long-term authoritarian regimes were often followed by a democratic transition phase, a critical conjuncture that was propitious for returned exiles to contribute to shaping the new order. In like manner, the exiles of the 1930s and 1940s prepared the way for the westernization of European elites in the postwar period, the reconstruction that followed the war being such a critical conjuncture rich of possibilities and openings for the exiles to have their say. Recruited by the American war effort between 1940 and 1945, many European exiles built solid relationships with American political, military, and business elites, thereby forging a consensus of opinion between themselves and the American interventionists, particularly those in the newly created war agencies. Accordingly, the changes that took place in postwar Europe cannot be understood merely as 'Americanization', but rather as an instance of transatlantic cultural transfer that occurred within the framework of a community of shared values forged in the 1930s and 1940s. Many individual trajectories attest to the fact that the exile of European elites in the United States was an important factor in the deployment of major narratives of the postwar era: the Americanization of Europe; anti-communism; the modernization of socialism; the construction of Europe.

In light of the fervent national loyalty proclaimed by exiles, it is paradoxical that exile contributed both to the exportation of the national ideology, and to the internationalization of politics and culture. In the 20th century the United States was a centre of this internationalization in large part due to the diverse groups of exiles it had welcomed, not always in the most disinterested manner. The process of cultural and political transfer does not preclude the possibility that the US strategically engaged with exiles. Certainly, during the Cold War, it supported and financed Eastern European exiles much as it gave support to Latin American exiles, a policy that can also be understood as foreign policy writ small.

Emmanuelle Loyer

Bibliography

Dufoix S. 2002. *Politiques d'exil: Hongrois, Polonais et Tchécoslovaques en France après 1945*. Paris: PUF.

Fey I. and Racine K. (eds) 2000. *Strange pilgrimages: exile, travel, and national identity in Latin America, 1800–1990s*. Wilmington: SR.

'Les États-Unis et les réfugiés politiques européens, des années 1930 aux années 1950', *Matériaux pour l'histoire de notre temps*, 60, October–December 2000.

Traverso E. 2004. *La pensée dispersée: figures de l'exil judéo-allemand*. Paris: Léo Scheer.

Related essays

1848; 1989; Argentina and psychoanalysis; *Communist Manifesto*; decolonization; democracy; diasporas; empire and migration; empires and imperialism; fascism and anti-fascism; governing science; humanities; intellectual elites; kindergarten; nation and state; social sciences; surrealism; temporary migrations; Westernization

Expositions

Since the mid 19th century cities around the world have regularly played host to huge fairs drawing participation from many different countries, as well as private business and industrial interests and often various nongovernmental and intergovernmental organizations. Variously called 'great exhibitions', *expositions universelles*, and 'world's fairs' in Great Britain, France, and the United States, the three countries that for many years were the most frequent hosts, these gatherings normatively created vast mini-cities in or near their host metropolises. These international expositions have drawn, in many cases, millions of visitors over the course of several months or more, attracted to grandly scaled national and private-enterprise pavilions, re-creations of exotic locales, examples of the latest technologies and popular entertainments. Over the past two decades these great exhibitions have increasingly attracted historians' attention as a transnational phenomenon, as evidenced by the excellent *Historical dictionary of world's fairs and expositions, 1851–1988*, edited in 1990 by John Findling and Kimberly Pelle.

International expositions fall broadly into two categories. The first is the more familiar multithemed fair, which includes displays and pavilions on a wide variety of arts, sciences, manufactures, culture, and the like, mounted by participating countries and organizations. The second is more tightly focused on a single theme or several related themes. For example, in 2006–07 Thailand hosted an International Horticultural Exposition that featured contributions by 30 countries from Asia, Europe, North and South America, and Africa. Moreover, while the majority of expositions have sought to achieve a global scope, drawing on participants from all over the world, some have been regionally focused (such as the various Pan-American Expositions held in the US during the first quarter of the 20th century). But the rubric is a broad one: the Bureau of International Exhibitions, an intergovernmental organization which oversees the planning and holding of these events, defines a fair in its Convention as international 'when more than one state takes part in it'.

The international exposition as it developed from the mid 19th until the mid 20th centuries was a product, indeed an avatar of modernity. The phenomenon developed within the context of mass industrialization, 19th–20th-century intensification of exchanges and connections, and its paradoxical consort, nationalism. From the vantage point of the early 21st century, the international exposition in its heyday might seem at once quaintly naïve and sinister. However, the history of these expositions and their offspring embodies many of the most dramatic and contentious elements of international history over the past two centuries, with many ongoing tensions: nationalism versus internationalism; racism and a sense of cultural superiority versus a genuine desire for intercultural awareness; a concomitant cultural imperialism and hybridization/creolization; edification versus commercialism; and spurring tourism for some while satisfying wanderlust for many without leaving one's home country or even city.

World's fairs and expositions revelled in the civilization-altering potential of industry, science, technology and engineering as they provided a venue for advertising national or regional wares (the German left-wing cultural theorist Walter Benjamin decried world's fairs as pilgrimage sites devoted to the commodity fetish). International expositions offered the opportunity for nations at the apex to trumpet their power and dominance, including over subject peoples, as well as for rising nations to seek to introduce themselves to the established powers and their peoples on their own terms.

Origins of expositions: market fairs

The international exposition has its deepest roots in the regularly scheduled market fairs of antiquity and the medieval period. The Egyptians, Greeks and Romans were among the many cultures that held fairs and festivals combining merchant activity and entertainment, two hallmarks of the modern world's fair. What would become France was a leading force in perpetuating trade fairs in the centuries following the decline of Rome. By the 15th century Parisian fairs had some international participation; in the 17th century French fairgoers could purchase such exotic products as chocolate and china ware.

The French Revolution brought to power a series of governments that saw the fairs' potential for propaganda and edification. The 1798 Paris Exposition Publique des Produits de l'Industrie Française, conceived by the French revolutionary regime, set the tone in crucial ways for the world's fairs to come. It featured a mix of the martial and manufactures; it sang the praises of 'progress' as a universal aspiration; it was conceived and convened by the state for solemn, edifying purposes, but it could not keep out a strain of raucous revelry. While this fair and several subsequent ones in France during the early 19th century were purely Gallic in character, in the 1840s French planners originated the idea of mounting an international exposition with universal participation, which had an explicit element of Saint Simonian utopianism: one writer, an adherent of the philosophy, called for both *expositions universelles* and the construction of the Suez Canal in order to facilitate the free worldwide movement of goods. But it was the British who would first fully realize this grand ambition.

Fair revolution: the 'Crystal Palace Exhibition'

The British had been holding their own arts and industry exhibitions since the 18th century, a trend that befitted the world's first industrialized nation. The 1851 London

'Great Exhibition of the Works of Industry of All Nations', often referred to as the 'Crystal Palace Exhibition' after the immense, iconic cast-iron and glass structure that housed the fair, is rightly considered the first true international exposition. Organized by a Royal Commission and with the strong official support of Prince Albert, Queen Victoria's spouse (and the Commission's titular leader), the 1851 London Exhibition took the exposition to a new level, with the issuance of invitations to participate in 'the friendly competition' to all of the nations in existence at the time. No fewer than 34 sovereign countries accepted the invitation and implicit challenge; they combined with the subject states and regions of several imperial participants, not least of which Britain herself, to make the Crystal Palace Exhibition a truly worldwide convocation. In the middle of the 19th century Great Britain was the world's foremost economic and naval power, with a global scope and commitment to free trade. Unsurprisingly, a key focus of the Royal Commission organizers, who included active public servants such as Prime Minister Lord John Russell, was trade, with the confident expectation that foreign visitors would deem British goods best in side-by-side comparisons and buy them over the wares of other countries.

However, despite economic motives behind the fair, just as important was that the Crystal Palace Exhibition established a template for dreams of global fraternity. In his 'First Address to the Delegates of the Human Race Met at the World's Fair in the Crystal Palace', the utopian socialist Robert Owen used the occasion of the exhibition to proclaim, 'For the delegates of the human race thus to meet ... is the first great step towards the everlasting peace of nations; it will prepare the world to understand and receive the principles of universal union, and to create the desire for universal brotherhood'. Many subsequent expositions would explore variants on this theme, even as they offered at the same time paeans to imperialism, Anglo-Saxon or Western racial dominance, and national and martial virtues of host countries and contributing guests. Modernity has been complicated, and the fairs have been a fair reflection of that complexity.

Expos and international organization

There have been over one hundred international expositions since the Crystal Palace Exhibition.

Britain, France and the United States would be the foremost hosts. Nonetheless, these fairs have been held all over the world, for example from New York to Paris to Sydney to Guatemala City to Nanking (Nanjing) to Montréal to Osaka. As of this writing, Turkey is the first state to bid to host 'Expo 2015'. Until 1928, international expositions were organized on an ad hoc basis; any nation or indeed city could choose to play host, which sometimes led to unseemly struggles, such as the three-way battle among San Francisco, San Diego and New Orleans over where to hold an exposition in honour of the recently completed Panama Canal – eventually, San Francisco and San Diego worked out a compromise that gave a major fair to the former and a lesser but still impressive one to the latter, while New Orleans, lacking the deep pockets of the two West Coast cities, was forced to bow out altogether.

By the early 20th century states began discussions on a governing body; the first such conference took place in Germany in 1912, and a preliminary protocol was drafted. But World War 1 intervened, and the issue of establishing an appropriate bureaucracy did not arise again until well into the 1920s. The establishment in 1928 of the Bureau International des Expositions (BIE), based in Paris, brought a measure of order to the scheduling of international expositions and the arbitration of disputes among contenders for hosting fairs. However, on occasion major exhibitions such as the 1964–65 New York World's Fair were mounted without the sanction of the BIE, to the enduring annoyance of the organization – indeed, the BIE's website pointedly omits the 1964–65 New York fair from its official historical list of international exhibitions.

Beyond Britain: new hosts, ever grander spectacles

During most of the latter half of the 19th century, the main national rivalry on the world's fair turf was waged between Great Britain, pioneer of the international exhibition and of course the world's wealthiest and most imperially extensive state, and France, culturally pre-eminent but perennially envious and anxious about her status in relation to Britain. But 'smaller' countries also played ball. Belgium, flush with land, wealth and ambition as it gained control over the Congo and opened a major shipping facility in Antwerp, made a splash in 1885 with a large-scale exposition in that port city; Belgium would hold other exhibitions in later decades, including Liège in 1905 and Brussels in 1910, 1935 and again in 1958.

But Belgium's 1885 fair was dwarfed by the Brobdingnagian Chicago Exhibition of 1893, in which the United States announced itself as a strong third force in the contest for grandest world's fairs. Henry Adams, staggered by the size and grandeur of the Chicago fair, succinctly posed the question about America's future development as 'How long and how far?'. Henceforth Britain would effectively recuse herself from the competition with a series of more modestly scaled exhibitions, leaving the French and the Americans to mount ever more stunning fairs in an ongoing display of one-upmanship. This competition lasted into the 1930s; only the advent of World War 2 ended the rivalry for good. While European world's fairs in the 19th and early 20th centuries were ordinarily held in capital cities, the seats of national power and culture, from an early point American fairs were held around the country by cities such as Philadelphia, Chicago and St Louis seeking to establish or reinforce their metropolitan status vis-à-vis other US cities. During the 20th century, the American site approach would become more common around the world, with many fairs held in non-national capitals, for example, in Barcelona in 1929, Osaka in 1970 and Brisbane in 1988.

The dark side of expos

Many scholars have properly stressed the role international expositions have played in justifying colonialism, codifying and encouraging racism, and stoking nationalism. For example, at the 1889 Paris Exposition Universelle the French set up a series of re-created villages drawn from around their empire, in which native Senegalese, Indochinese and New Caledonians, among others, were placed in tableaux vivants to go about their ostensible quotidian business before crowds of gawking visitors; the effect was that of a human zoo. Egyptian scholars visiting the Paris fair were angered and embarrassed at the Egypt exhibit, set up to resemble a chaotic Cairo bazaar, when they walked through the door of a building façade of a 'mosque', only to find themselves in a coffee house complete with dancing girls and whirling dervishes. These sorts of potted anthropology exhibit showed up in numerous

fairs for decades; and indeed the British, the Belgians, and the French would devote entire expositions to empire and colonialism in 1924–25, 1930 and 1931 respectively (the US was among the colonial powers contributing to the Paris fair).

Nationalist chest-beating, an ongoing phenomenon at world's fairs, reached a crescendo with the German pavilion at the 1937 Paris Exposition Internationale des Arts et Techniques dans la Vie Moderne, designed by Hitler's architect Albert Speer: a stark neoclassicist rectangular structure, well over 50 metres tall, marble-clad and topped with a huge bronze swastika-bearing eagle. The pavilion was set directly across from that of Nazi Germany's arch-rival the USSR, which built its own bombastic structure; as war loomed in the near future, the fair's rather Panglossian stated objective as set forth in its programme pamphlet was 'to be a meeting place for harmony and peace by not only striving to promote economic exchange between peoples but also the exchange of ideas and friendship'. The 1958 Brussels exposition was a veritable festival of US–Soviet Cold War rivalry in which the central motif was the huge 'Atomium', a steel molecule over 100 metres tall, ostensibly meant to symbolize peaceful atomic energy but inadvertently driving home the omnipresent threat of superpower thermonuclear war and the destruction of human civilization.

Expos as agents of optimism, aesthetics and arrival

But to monofocus on colonialism, racism and nationalism is to miss the series of ingenuous attempts that many fair organizers and participants were making to come to grips with a world that was at once far smaller and more complex than in earlier human epochs. The 1893 Chicago World's Columbian Exposition, for example, was rife with exhibits infected with 'scientific' racism toward blacks and Amerindians; yet it was also the site of the first meeting of the World Congress of Religions, which brought together as at least nominal equals representatives from ten faith traditions, including Judaism, various Christian denominations, Islam, and Buddhism. One could properly decry the racial and ethnic hierarchies on display at the 1889 and 1900 Paris Universelles and the colonialism that undergirded them. Yet among the many visitors to the ethnographic displays, with their

Oceanic and African arts and crafts, were Paul Gauguin, Pablo Picasso, and Henri Matisse, who were captivated and transformed by the aesthetic power of what they viewed, and who in turn took Western art in a new and globalized direction. The Museum of Modern Art in New York City, itself the site of two world's fairs, provides stark evidence of the cultural dialogue sparked by international expositions, in the form of Picasso's seminal 'Les Demoiselles d'Avignon', two of whose visages have been transmogrified by the artist into African tribal masks. As one writer has put it, 'Without the African mask there might well have been no cubism; without imperialism there would have been no African masks for the cubists to look at' (Greenhalgh 1988, 221). Indeed, the fairs were spurs to the establishment of numerous lasting museums and displays, such as the Victoria & Albert Museum in London, the Museum of Science and Industry in Chicago, and the Musée des Arts d'Afrique et d'Océanie in Paris (recently incorporated into the new Musée du Quai Branly). And the very same 1937 Paris exposition that featured the duelling Nazi and Soviet pavilions as a prelude to renewed world war was also host to the World Documentation Congress, where representatives from 31 member nations of the International Institute for Documentation met to discuss the possibility of a global documentation network, at which author H. G. Wells, a key popularizer of the idea of a 'world brain' universal knowledge compendium, was the star speaker.

Additionally, non-Western countries that sought to establish their status as 'progressive' or modern, or as significant players on the world stage, saw a golden opportunity to make their case, both by contributing pavilions and exhibits to fairs and by hosting fairs themselves. For example, from even before the 1868 Meiji Restoration onward Japan has consistently been among the most enthusiastic participants in international expositions. With its fair pavilions and, later, hosted expositions, Japan sought, with variable success, to drive home an image of modernization, Westernization on Japanese terms, martial and imperial power, and after defeat in World War 2 and reconstruction, a commitment to peace, prosperity and better living through technology. The Japanese government placed the nation's first official exhibits on display at the 1867 Paris Exposition Universelle; with succeeding fairs Japan's pavilions became increasingly elaborate. At the 1910 Japan-British Exhibition, held in London to celebrate the strategic alliance between the two maritime powers, displays drove home Japan's recently consolidated status as a major, imperial power and a technologically modern society. In the late 1930s, a Japan at war in Asia depicted itself as both ultramodernist (at the 1937 Paris Exposition) and possessing a proud and ancient heritage (at the 1939 New York World's Fair). In the aftermath of Hiroshima and the US occupation, Japan's exhibits took on a tone of reassurance that the nation's considerable energy was being channelled toward benign ends, as exemplified by the Japanese pavilion at the 1964–65 New York World's Fair, which offered up to visitors electron microscopes, ultra-high-speed motion-picture cameras, and a seemingly endless array of consumer goods, many actually for sale. And a half-decade later, the Japan World Exposition at Osaka dedicated itself explicitly to Progress and Harmony for Mankind, in case anyone had missed out on the message that the Land of the Rising Sun was now on the side of the angels.

Mexico was another of many non-Western states that saw world's fairs as attractive presentation venues. During Porfirio Diaz's rule from 1877 to 1910 Mexico contributed numerous displays to expositions, most notably at Paris in 1889, where the national pavilion aimed to overturn the rampant image of a lawless and violent country in favour of a rapidly modernizing and stable 'promised land', with an eye toward attracting both international investment and large-scale immigration from Northern Europe – even as the pavilion's design was an ersatz Aztec palace, itself a reflection of proud, non-European nationalism. Postrevolutionary Mexico would continue using world's fairs to make public statements, stressing for example national renewal at Rio de Janeiro in 1922, in the wake of a decade of bloodshed, or defending the revolution's accomplishments and legacy, currently under attack in some international quarters, at the 1929 Seville exposition. Much later, at the 1970 Osaka Exposition, the Mexican pavilion's eleven visually stunning, huge, specially commissioned murals (measuring some 20 by 30 feet each) would proclaim the prowess of Mexico as a centre of modern artistic excellence. It is fair to ask how receptive audiences were to these sorts of attempts at international public relations and image making; but the central point is that the emerging states themselves perceived the value of world's fairs and made use of them for their own purposes.

National and international progress and modernity and the technologies that enabled them were for over a century a central motif of international expositions. From the displays of huge steam engines and small but potent sewing machines at the 1851 Crystal Palace exhibition to the first public demonstration of nuclear fusion at the 1964–65 New York World's Fair, the wonders of the present and the promise of a better tomorrow were touted to exposition visitors. A certain tower designed by the French architect Gustave Eiffel, erected for the 1889 Paris exposition, demonstrated the very latest techniques in high-quality steel manufacture and precision-engineering tolerances that made possible the following century's explosion of skyscraper architecture (a quarter-century later, the Eiffel Tower would serve once again as a literal beacon of modernity when it was used to transmit the first global wireless time synchronization signal). The telephone, the Ferris Wheel, and broadcast television are but a few of the marvels introduced at international expositions in the 19th and 20th centuries. Related to these technologies were icons of modernity, both permanent and ephemeral, constructed for various international expositions – for example the Eiffel Tower and the Seattle Space Needle versus the 1939–40 New York World's Fair's famous Trylon and Perisphere, with the 1964–65 New York World's Fair's Unisphere, still standing today but set in the midst of a neglected public park, occupying a forlorn middle ground. Despite a brief life span, one of the most architecturally influential structures ever built for an exposition was the gracefully austere German pavilion at the 1929 Barcelona fair, designed by the visionary Ludwig Mies van der Rohe, which codified the International Modern aesthetic that would dominate building design for better or worse for decades to come.

Expos and the making of modern popular culture

One of the most important dimensions of the international exposition was its central role in the development of national and global popular culture, which ironically would in turn play an equally central role in the ultimate marginalization of the exposition concept.

While the earliest exhibitions were intended first and foremost to edify and to spur trade, it was clear that the public was interested in being entertained as well – which would increase the likelihood of fairs recouping their operating costs. Belly dancers were among the notable attractions at the Paris 1889 and Chicago 1893 fairs, as well as Buffalo Bill Cody and his Hippodrome (officially at the Paris fair, next door to the Chicago fair). The Chicago Columbian Exposition's 'Midway Plaisance', a congeries of popular entertainments and exhibits, provided the template for the modern American amusement park, for example Coney Island's famed Luna Park which opened in 1904. For several decades the popular-culture elements were segregated from the higher-toned pavilions in the manner of Chicago's Midway from the gleaming Beaux Arts 'White City'. However, by the early 1900s, the wall of separation at world's fairs between high- and popular-culture exhibits broke down, so that for example the 1904 St Louis (Missouri) exposition's planners formally incorporated the Midway exhibits into the core of the exposition itself.

Unsurprisingly, American fairs became especially adept in weaving together the popular entertainment and edification aspects of expositions, as anyone could attest who rode the General Motors-sponsored Futurama ride at the 1939–40 New York World's Fair, with its stunning glimpse ahead via elaborate miniatures of the world two decades hence. Rides like the Ferris Wheel and Futurama and national and 'native' pavilions would in turn provide much of the inspiration for Walter Elias Disney, who constructed his eponymous theme parks first in Anaheim, California and, more elaborately, in Orlando, Florida (and subsequently in France, Japan and China). Disney's studio designed several pavilions and rides for the New York 1964–65 World's Fair, most enduringly, the Pepsi Pavilion's 'It's a Small World After All', which was then reopened at Disneyland, where it remains a popular attraction over four decades later. On a somewhat more modest scale, the international cultural influence of world's fair displays can be seen in, for example, the European theme parks that celebrate the American Wild West, such as Germany's Pullman City, which comes complete with bison, American Indians and Mexican mariachi bands; and Japan's proliferating theme parks which offer small-scale re-creations of European countries such as the

Netherlands, Italy and Spain. And of course we must not forget Las Vegas, which offers up eye-popping, only slightly smaller-than-life versions of the New York City skyline, the Eiffel Tower, and the bell tower of Venice's Basilica of San Marco, as well as would-be competitor Macau, whose Venetian Macao Resort Hotel proudly boasts three canals versus only one at the Las Vegas Venetian.

The fate of the fair?

But with proliferating Disney Worlds, increased access to international communications and travel, and a widespread loss of the faith in 'progress' that had been so embedded in the rationale of the international exposition, the question of these fairs' continued relevance and utility arose, never to be satisfactorily addressed. If one could inexpensively fly to Orlando, Anaheim, Paris, Tokyo, Las Vegas or Macau at one's convenience to take in exposition-like exhibits and rides (and gamble to boot in the case of the latter two), why wait for the officially sanctioned fairs at multiyear intervals? To be sure, cities around the world still vie to serve as hosts, and urban planners and politicians still see potential benefits – Brisbane, for example, improved both its infrastructure and its international profile as the result of its 1988 fair. China clearly views its hosting of the 2010 Shanghai exposition, along with the 2008 Beijing Summer Olympics, as an important element in that country's recasting of its international image as a stable, prosperous, forwarding-looking land. The Bureau International des Expositions continues to field numerous host-city applications for future fairs. The international exposition, over a century and a half old at the time of this writing, will doubtless persist into the distant future. Given the very different cultural, political and technological landscape from even fifty years ago, however, it is doubtful that the exposition will ever be able to recapture a large portion of its earlier transnational cultural and political significance.

Neal Rosendorf

Bibliography

Burris J. P. 2002. Exhibiting religion: colonialism and spectacle at international expositions, 1851–1893. Charlottesville: University of Virginia Press.

Çelik Z. 1992. Displaying the Orient: architecture of Islam at 19th-century world's fairs. Berkeley: University of California Press.

Galopin M. 1997. Les expositions internationales au XXe siècle et le Bureau International des Expositions. Paris: L'Harmattan.

Geppert A. C. T., Coffey J. and Lau T. International exhibitions, expositions universelles and world's fairs, 1851–2005: a bibliography [online]. Available: www.csufresno.edu/library/subjectresources/specialcollections/worldfairs/ExpoBibliography3ed.pdf, accessed 1 November 2007.

Greenhalgh P. 1988. Ephemeral vistas: the expositions universelles, great exhibitions and world's fairs, 1851–1939. Manchester: Manchester University Press.

Lockyer A. 2000. Japan at the exhibition, 1867–1970. Unpublished doctoral dissertation, Stanford University.

Rydell R. 1987. All the world's a fair: visions of empire at American international expositions, 1876–1916. Chicago: Chicago University Press.

Tenorio-Trillo M. 1996. Mexico at the world's fairs: crafting a modern nation. Berkeley: University of California Press.

Related essays
architecture; cities; city planning; consumer cooperation; cosmopolitanism and universalism; cultural capitals; empires and imperialism; humanities; intergovernmental organizations; internationalisms; Japan; modernity; museums; music; nation and state; nursing; Olympic Games; public policy; religion; rubber; technologies; theme parks; tourism; trade; trade (manufactured goods); welfare state; Westernization; world orders; yoga

F

Family

Families scattered across national borders existed long before the 19th century – and indeed predated any modern manifestation of the 'nation' itself – yet they evolved to develop historically specific economic, social, and emotional contours that might involve ongoing contact or, alternatively, attenuated or ruptured family relationships.

Migrants before and during the late 1800s were, in general, less likely to remain in close contact with kin staying behind than those who left later, and maintaining ties depended upon the circumstances of their journeys as well as upon class. Forced migrations, in particular those of enslaved Africans sent to America, involved a complete rupture with family left behind. Indentured Indian labourers who replaced slave labour on plantations in the Caribbean or went to work in South Africa and Southeast Asia also largely lacked the ability to remain actively linked with kin at home. Few Indians returned after their labour contracts ended, instead staying on to form new communities in Trinidad, Natal, Fiji, and other colonies within the British Empire. In an era when the cost and speed of transport often precluded or limited further travels, such economically disadvantaged migrants worked to form new families where they had settled, mainly with those of the same ethnicity. Creating new family formations was thus central to the process of shaping diasporas and their relationships with other groups residing in the areas of settlement.

For migrants who had greater freedom (and the financial means) to make choices, however, settlement abroad might range from brief sojourns to longer-term stays to permanent residence. Such families had the capacity along with practical motives to perpetuate ties with kin living far away. Several examples from Europe's upper classes include royal, noble, merchant, and banking families – the Rothschilds providing an obvious case – in which blood relatives were spread across borders yet remained part of a family network through ongoing interlinked political or economic interests and the luxury of access to all means of travel and communication then available.

Britain's middle-class empire builders also illustrate forms of family dynamics that, albeit historically specific and predicated upon socioeconomic status, nonetheless bore some resemblance to those of many other globally dispersed kin groups between the 19th century and the present. Many Britons opting for life in the Empire emigrated permanently to settler colonies, but others engaged in circular migration that involved comings and goings between metropole and colony. This pattern applied to the families of colonial officials, army officers, and businessmen in parts of the Empire like India that were envisioned as places where Europeans sojourned temporarily as opposed to settled permanently. Indian careers were frequently chosen on an informed basis: young men (and the women they married) from families already connected with the subcontinent were considerably more likely to take the decision to live and work far from home themselves. In many cases, they had been born in India and sent back to Britain as young children to attend school while their parents stayed overseas and paid sporadic visits on leave. Colonizers' offspring in Britain lacked a 'normal' nuclear family life for much of their childhood and youth. Boarding schools, the extended family (especially grandparents, aunts, and uncles), and paid guardians all might serve in loco parentis, while relationships with mothers and fathers were enacted on a long-distance basis.

Such families illustrate how historical portrayals that collapse an understanding of 'family' with that of 'household' inevitably fail to illuminate, let alone explain, the wider meanings and practices of family life, and this was particularly true for imperial families. Parental roles came to be played by a wide circle of kin and non-kin alike. Lengthy separations led to attenuated ties between parents and children in some cases, yet distances were bridged by sending letters, photographs, and other gifts by post as well as by the steamships that periodically brought parents home after three-week journeys. Such lifestyles might wreak emotional havoc on Britain's colonizers, but this failed to prevent many children from perpetuating a multi-generational pattern of overseas life in which time in the colonies alternated with time (and ultimately retirement) at home.

As this example illustrates, class status and incomes that enabled occasional travels back and forth as well as the available means of communication – postal and steamship services – account for the forms that transnational family life took between the late 1800s and the end of empire in the mid-1900s. Moreover, India's transient British colonial community also highlights how transnational families acquired specific contours through migrants' gender. British women were far outnumbered by British men in India, yet they were central to the reproduction of families as 'European' as opposed to 'Eurasian' at a time when mixed-race sexual relationships – once common and relatively tolerated – fell into increasing disrepute. Transnational families involved complex gender dynamics, as the following cases explore in greater detail. Whether or not men or women went abroad or remained at home, their lives were decisively shaped by family activities that criss-crossed national borders.

Although histories of international migration often argue it to have been a predominantly male phenomenon, persons who left their homeland for a period of time – or indeed a lifetime – abroad included women as well as those who embarked as part of larger family groupings. In some cases – such as in rural regions of Portugal – families did indeed conform to a pattern in which 'men migrated' and 'women waited'. Like their forebears, young men sought work in other parts of Europe or in Brazil to earn wages that enhanced family finances and status within an underdeveloped agricultural economy at home. Most periodically returned to marry, have children, and retire, although some left permanently. Until the later 20th century, Portuguese women mainly stayed behind, raising children in their husbands' absence and becoming 'widows of the living' for protracted periods. Transnational labour opportunities and circular migration thus drew entire families into their orbit regardless of whether individual members moved or stayed put.

This example shares many features in common with that of Bangladeshi, Pakistani, and Indian men who travelled to Britain to work after the Second World War. Like Portuguese men, many embarked overseas on the basis of relatives having already paved the way, heading for destinations where they knew they could draw upon the resources and moral support of kin when seeking jobs and housing. At the outset, few women made the journeys themselves. South Asian men were among the many migrant groups entertaining the 'myth of return', understanding their time overseas as a temporary better-paid interlude that would enable the family to advance back home. Remittances, meanwhile, were invested in the purchase of small plots of land or in building new houses. In the Sylhet district of Bangladesh, the proliferation of 'Londoni' houses attested to the earnings of men working in England, while in rural Portugal 'casas francesas' were inhabited by families (both nuclear and extended) supported by those absent in France. Such families were habitually split as migratory members led dual lives, returning as often as finances and work obligations allowed.

Despite these instances that support a rendition of male-dominated migration histories, women nonetheless participated both as single women and as wives. More Irish women than Irish men left their homeland during most decades between the 1870s and the present. Some went to England or Scotland, but the vast majority embarked permanently for the United States. Ireland's land inheritance system – whereby property was passed to only one son – fuelled the exodus of male and particularly female siblings, with the latter able to find work in America's textile mills or as domestic servants. Departing Irish women may have been unmarried, yet they nevertheless emigrated as part of extended family networks. As in the predominantly male migrant stories noted above, they were involved in chain migration patterns that relied on support from and ongoing contact with siblings, cousins, aunts, and uncles who had left previously. Irish emigrant women were highly valued for the remittances they sent home, rendering them key players in transnational family networks in multiple ways.

Although the gender contours of the Irish case were somewhat unusual when compared with other groups in the later 19th and the first half of the 20th century, recent decades have witnessed migration becoming increasingly feminized in many other contexts as well. The demand for domestic servants (in addition to sex workers) in affluent countries has led to substantial migration flows of Filipina women to Japan and Hong Kong, Mexican women to the United States, Indonesian and Sri Lankan women to the Gulf States, and Portuguese women to France – to name but several possibilities. Such women worked to support a range of kin in their countries of origin: they financed siblings' education; they helped parents; and they supported their own children who lived with their grandparents during their time abroad. Such women's international work could be temporary or – if permitted by the host society – involve permanent stays, whereby they have often attempted to send for those, particularly children, initially left behind.

Family reunification accounts for a considerable portion of transnational migration flows during the past several decades. Nations like Britain and France that once permitted residents of their former colonies to settle in the early postwar period gradually acted to restrict primary migration – in part in response to changing labour markets and in part due to racist responses to newcomers. In the 1960s and 1970s, immigration restriction laws largely curtailed legal channels of unskilled immigration from non-European countries. Paradoxically, however, such regulations encouraged persons already resident to bring family members over quickly in order to 'beat the ban', in the case of Britain. Many men (and some women) who had once envisioned their time in Europe as temporary effectively rendered their presence increasingly permanent once spouses and children arrived as well. Indeed, in the wake of a series of immigration controls, family reunification has been responsible for augmenting ethnic minority communities after other forms of legal migration – at least, for non-elites lacking sought-after skills – became largely closed off. Furthermore, it can work to limit intermarriage with other groups, for instance in the case of Muslims who often arrange marriages with kin in Bangladesh or Pakistan who then join spouses in Britain.

In this context, 'myths of return' once widely entertained have altered as communities have become more settled. With both nuclear and extended family life – in all that this economically and emotionally entails – a possibility within the host society, migrants and their descendants may retain ties with those in their countries of origin, yet these have often weakened over time. 'Londoni houses' and 'casas francesas' may well become occupied by distant kin, or alternatively sit empty for protracted periods until their owners return for brief vacations or possibly in old age.

Compared with the later 19th century, many members of transnational families today enjoy far greater opportunities to retain links with their own, or their forebears', countries of origin and kin residing there. In place of costly weeks-long journeys by steamship or letters which took close to a month to reach their recipients, migrants now have access to relatively cheap flights, faster postal delivery, the telephone, and the Internet in their quest to remain in contact and maintain affective relations. As in the past, however, their circumstances continue to be characterized by infinite variety, structured by their cultural backgrounds, individual priorities, class status, and the national spaces between and in which they move, making any uniform picture of the transnational family impossible to paint.

Elizabeth Buettner

Bibliography

Brettell C. 1986. *Men who migrate, women who wait: population and history in a Portuguese Parish.* Princeton: Princeton University Press.

Brown J. 2006. *Global South Asians: introducing the modern diaspora.* Cambridge: Cambridge University Press.

Bryceson D. and Vuorela U. (eds) 2002. *The transnational family: new European frontiers and global networks.* Oxford: Berg.

Buettner E. 2004. *Empire families: Britons and late imperial India.* Oxford: Oxford University Press.

Sharpe P. (ed.) 2001. *Women, gender, and labour migration: historical and global perspectives.* London: Routledge.

Walter B. 2001. *Outsiders inside: whiteness, place and Irish women.* London: Routledge.

Related essays

childhood; class; contract and indentured labourers; diasporas; domestic service; empire and migration; executives and professionals; family migration; forced migrations; gender and sex; Hammarskjöld family; human mobility; Internet; labour migrations; mail; marriage; race-mixing; sexuality and migration; steamships; telephone and telegraphy

Family migration

Theoretical assertions about the newness of transnationalism as lives lived simultaneously in more than one nation are easily dismissed by historical studies of migration. But how long could and did mobile families actually maintain those ties?

Take the case of just one ordinary family from Italy. In 1881, Pietro B was a newly married man with a pregnant wife. The son of a peasant in a Po Valley village, he had moved to the industrializing city of Torino without finding secure work. With family obligations looming, he, along with many other men from this region, left Italy in search of work. He was among the minority who headed to the US.

But in New York City, too, Pietro experienced difficulties finding work. Worse, his wife died while he was abroad. By 1885, he was back in Torino and the return promised to be a permanent one. He quickly found a new wife, Felicita. The couple found housing and Pietro found constantly changing work as a janitor. Six more children arrived between 1888 and 1906. Pietro B's pay was small but his children stayed in school long enough to learn to read and write. As they reached maturity, boys and girls sought work in Torino's retail shops and emerging auto industry. The eldest boys proved as restive as their father, however. By 1910, two had travelled to France in search of temporary work; one did his military service in North Africa during Italy's war with Libya in 1911. Now approaching 60 years, Pietro B lost a job as a sextant in a church after quarrelling with the priest. Convinced (rightly, it developed) that another war threatened, Pietro did not want to lose sons to a draft or to death: they were his guarantee of support in retirement.

In 1912, Pietro's three oldest sons went to New York. Then, with the end of World War 1, Pietro, Felicita and the remaining children (including Pietro's oldest daughter) followed, accompanied by two sons- and daughters-in-law and two grandchildren. Also accompanying the group was a young woman who had agreed, sight unseen, to marry one of the brothers already in the US. The marriage took place in Lower Manhattan. The reunited family then relocated to a small town north of the weaving town of Paterson, New Jersey, where many immigrants and former industrial workers from northern Italy already worked. Family photographs celebrating its reunification and several new marriages with picnics and bottles of imported wine quickly gave way to fierce family quarrels. When Pietro B died, the family began to split into warring factions.

Particularly hard-hit by the family tensions was one of the older sons, Giuseppe B, whose new wife-by-arrangement, Maria, was constantly homesick. The marriage was an unhappy one, and Maria's unhappiness persisted even after one of her brothers joined her in New Jersey. Her behaviour became increasingly bizarre after the birth of her first son, Louis; for long intervals she stopped speaking, straining relations with all her in-laws still further. Hoping for a cure, Giuseppe decided to return to Italy. But the relocation to Torino in the early 1920s proved a disaster. Giuseppe could not find a job and Maria again fell silent after the birth of a second child, Felix. Back to the US travelled the troubled family.

This time, Giuseppe B refused to return to New Jersey. For the rest of the 1920s, he occasionally sent his oldest son Louis to live with his mother while he, Maria, Felix and Remo (born in 1926) boarded in the homes of a shifting series of friends in the New York borough of Queens. Maria's illness worsened, and in 1929 she was diagnosed a catatonic schizophrenic and institutionalized. During the Great Depression, Giuseppe worked occasionally as a mechanic or dishwasher; his search for boarding situations to guarantee the care of his young sons without depending on relatives or an orphanage resulted in constant changes in residence. After Felicita died in the 1930s, Giuseppe began again to communicate with his younger siblings and with his brother-in-law in New Jersey. But he had almost no contacts with his older siblings. Indeed, some were never even to learn of the birth of Remo.

As war again threatened in Europe, Giuseppe B and his younger brother made an unusual decision. Hoping to raise their own food and ultimately to purchase land, they moved their families to rural upstate New York to work as tenant farmers. Giuseppe tried unsuccessfully to raise chickens and vegetables for a French friend (and former landlord), a chef in a Westchester County country club. Giuseppe's nephew ultimately reaped some benefit from the move: as a dairy farmer's son in the 1940s, he was exempt from the wartime draft. Giuseppe's sons instead all quickly enlisted. And only two returned.

When Maria also died, still institutionalized, in 1944, Giuseppe married again, this time to an English-speaking widow in a small, rural town. Expecting his sons to support him, he left the chicken farm to live with her. With help from his former brother-in-law in New Jersey, Giuseppe also sponsored the migration of a distant cousin from Italy, hoping that his youngest son Remo would agree to marry her when he returned from his service in the US Navy. Remo refused. He and Louis also refused to support their father. And they signed away their rights to the small piece of Po Valley farmland they inherited from their mother. Giuseppe's sons seemed determined to cut all ties to Europe and to the older generation. Not so some of their New Jersey cousins: the last arrival in this familial chain-migration arrived in New Jersey in 1956.

But the transatlantic story of Giuseppe's branch of the family was also not quite over. A decade after Giuseppe died in 1956, his youngest son Remo – the father of three daughters who grew up knowing nothing of their New Jersey relatives – divorced. His remarriage to a German woman began two decades of yearly trips to Bavaria, Austria and northern Italy. Remo's eldest daughter would study European languages, and as a peripatetic academic not only live in Italy, Germany and France but reconnect with her New Jersey cousins after Remo's death in 1997. Together, the cousins of the B family pieced together the story of a century of European and American familial connections recounted here.

Donna Gabaccia

Bibliography

Bailey S. L. and Ramella F. 1988. One family, two worlds: an Italian family's correspondence across the Atlantic, 1901–1922. New Brunswick: Rutgers University Press.

Liu H. 2005. The transnational history of a Chinese family: immigrant letters, family business, and reverse migration. New Brunswick: Rutgers University Press.

Related essays

diasporas; family; Hammarskjöld family; human mobility; marriage; transnational

Fascism and anti-fascism

Fascism is commonly defined as nationalist, militarist, corporatist, anti-democratic, anti-socialist and anti-bolshevik. Its origins are usually traced to the political movement that began in Italy at the end of the First World War, under Benito Mussolini, while the interwar period is regarded as the apogee of fascism. Of course, fascism also featured in a number of European and New World states, including Nazi Germany and Falangist Spain. By the 1930s, there were fascist organisations of varying influence in constitutionally liberal states, including France, Australia, Britain, Hungary, Romania, and Yugoslavia, and noticeable intellectual variants of fascism in Japan and China. Anti-fascism had its roots in the struggle against fascism, and comprised a wide range of left-wing or democratic political positions in all of these places. Anti-fascists were often motivated by Communist and socialist reform programs on an international scale. As a censored form of oppositional politics, anti-fascism was by nature transnational, its agents forced to campaign from outside their own state borders. In the Italian case, for example, anti-fascism originated among exile communities in Paris in the 1920s.

The study of both fascism and anti-fascism has traditionally been conducted within the framework of nation states, specifically European, even when comparative analyses have encouraged the examination of similarities, and differences between national trends. However, the few implicitly transnational studies that have been attempted, and the evidence offered by national studies, indicate at least three possible areas in the study of fascism and anti-fascism for which a transnational perspective is most relevant.

The first is the study of the role of diasporas. In the Italian case, the Fascist government formulated a foreign policy that cultivated support for its programmes among diaspora communities as a way of exerting influence abroad. Historians have exposed the transnational links between fascists and anti-fascists respectively, as far as Australia. There, local Italian supporters of fascism marched openly in parades commemorating the First World War, while anti-fascists focused their efforts on the building of a Casa d'Italia, opened in Melbourne in 1938, with the mission of promoting opposition to Mussolini and fascism more generally.

The second, related area, is the study of organizational and institutional links between fascist and anti-fascist movements in a range of nation states and established through individuals and associations. In the 1930s, the Italian ambassador to Britain, and organizations such as the special Italian School in London, attempted to forge a fascist consciousness among the expatriate middle classes. New historical work is being done on the links between fascist governments in Europe and Muslims and some Arab countries, and the legacy of that influence in local political movements and ideas. Gerd-Rainer Horn has described the transnational patterns in the 1930s, when 'in the face of a common enemy, despite widely dissimilar political cultures and governments ranging from liberal democracies to fascist dictatorships, the left was able to develop a unifying language across national frontiers' (Horn 1996, 14). The most obvious examples of transnational links in the history of interwar fascism and anti-fascism occur in the Spanish Civil War (1936–39), where international involvement set up the forces of fascism – Italy, Germany, and Spain – against those of anti-fascism – socialists, Communists, and anarchists, and the Soviet Union. The study of internationally minded anti-fascist volunteers is common to this history. More recently, Judith Keene has described the foreigners – White Russians, members of the Romanian Iron Guard, and the Joan of Arc Company from France and North Africa – who crossed into Western Spain to support the fascist forces. Other examples of these transnational organisational links include, on the one hand, the pro-fascist Axis alliance formed in the Second World War between Germany, Italy, and Japan, and, on the other hand, the military coalition of anti-fascists from around the Italian/Yugoslav border region created for reasons of expediency and ideological commitment to anti-nationalism. Indeed, in Europe, a critical dimension of intellectual anti-fascism was the ideal of a united Europe.

The third strand of the historical examination of both fascism and anti-fascism as transnational phenomena traces the spread of fascist and anti-fascist ideologies and cultural forms. It includes the spread of anti-fascist ideals, as well as fascist terminology and its aesthetics. For example, the concept of the charismatic leader – whether the British Mosley, the Italian Mussolini, or the Spanish Franco – and the symbols of the blackshirt and the *fasces* were transmitted across national borders. Susan Sontag has famously defined a core fascist aesthetic, which emphasized monumental and mass obeisance to the hero, the rendering of movement in grandiose and rigid patterns, and the choreographed unity of the polity. Whether the fascination of fascism should be understood in terms of the primal psychological appeal of this aesthetic – which was certainly not shaped by national structures and processes alone

– or in some more transnational framework remains open to consideration. Certainly, while there was no fascist movement in China as such, there was a vogue for fascism as a method of political progress that developed in the context of thriving Chinese trade relations with Germany. Chinese republicans (many of them foreign-educated) in general responded well to German national socialism and its emphasis on nationalism, militarism and mass mobilization, modernization and industrialization. The Chinese (who declared war on Germany in 1941) took from fascist Germany 'a model for a modern army and war economy'. In Japan, Germany's interwar and wartime ally, the New Order Movement drew on an intellectual fascination with the West and studied connections with Germany to develop a Japanese version of fascism. This intellectual idealism also emphasized the nationalist aspirations of fascism, and its anti-liberal and anti-Marxist tendencies. Japanese intellectuals developed the notion of an Oriental or community that might be revived as an economic as well as cultural form. Indeed, historians have noted the similarities in the interwar emergence of leisure and welfare institutions across East and West, such as the fascist *dopolavoro*, catering for a new mass politics. What has not been explored is the interwar role of the League of Nations as a site where various national interests and influences intersected, whether through personal connections or institutional circumstances.

As this brief outline makes clear, the possibilities of a transnational perspective on fascism and anti-fascism lie in establishing the links between individuals, institutions, and ideas across national borders. They promise a redefinition of the nature of fascism, and of the significance of anti-fascism in a variety of thematic and spatial contexts.

Glenda Sluga

Bibliography

Baldoli C. 2003. *Exporting fascism*. Oxford: Berg.
Bosworth R.1996. *Italy and the wider world*.
  London: Routledge.
De Grand A. 2005. '"To learn nothing and
  to forget nothing": Italian socialism and
  the experience of exile politics, 1935–1945',
  Contemporary European History, 14, 4, 539–58.
Horn G.-R. 1996. *European socialists respond to
  fascism: ideology, activism and contingency in
  the 1930s*. Oxford: Oxford University Press.

Fashion

Fashion, as opposed to 'dress', has been defined as having stylistic connotations linking it to terms such as behaviour, way of life and social standing. Thus, 'fashion', while materially ephemeral, can be considered an aspect of the cultural and social construction of the self, something perfectly understood and exploited by the media of advertising and the fashion press. Although commonly associated with an elite model of fashion 'leaders' centred in Western fashion capitals, recent literature has also emphasized that the concept of 'fashion' is not limited to Western capitalist societies. Recently new forms of Western-style fashionable dress have evolved which are associated with the porous map of global commerce and stateless world of branded fashion goods. Furthermore, international fashion has in a sense transcended national boundaries as, instead of being produced through a network of local skills, it now tends to be produced in the developing world for consumption among the more affluent citizens of the 'developed' world, and promoted by fashion media with global reach.

In one sense, fashion has always had an international infrastructure since fashionable clothing has often relied on a world trade in raw materials such as cotton, silk and dyestuffs. Indian trade textiles dating from the Roman period have been found in Egypt and probably of much earlier date in the Middle East. Well before the British colonial period, India produced textiles specifically for the Southeast Asian market and later established a textile trade with Africa. The luxury garments of Europe were historically the final stage of a journey along the silk roads crossing Central Asia which brought ideas as well as textiles from China and other parts of Asia to Europe. Fashionable dress has thus been historically linked with the political and economic power structures expressed in international trade, including the institution of slavery upon which the cotton trade depended.

In terms of modern clothing markets, early forms of mass-producing, promoting and selling fashion often followed the 'trickle down' model of mass-market tastes with aspiration in clothing following the lead of socially exclusive and wealthy elites. In fashion terms this was reflected in the supremacy of French haute couture, which evolved specific defining rules about the production and dissemination of the products of its industry. Such national labelling is deceptive: aristocratic French clothing had paragon status in Europe long before the 19th century, but it was the British-born Charles Frederick Worth (1826–95) who, from the late 1850s, established the model of the designer-led Parisian fashion house with an international clientele. Until the late 20th century, Paris effectively dominated Western-world fashion trends with much of the world's fashion industry devoted to copying or interpreting its latest styles such as Christian Dior's New Look launched in 1947. Paris remained internationally influential and exclusive and depended upon on a local labour force of skilled seamstresses or *petites mains*. However, during the 1960s and 70s in Britain particularly, the expansion of a younger and less reverent cohort of consumers with a greater sense of individualism, as well as a new generation of trained fashion designers, contributed to the development of clothing styles which neither took Paris as their starting point nor accepted the perceived monotony of mass-produced clothing provided by chain stores, evocative of the Fordist production line. Anti-fashion, or 'trickle up', became significant in the formation of fashion tastes. Many individuals adopted elements of global clothing forms, inspired by greater mobility, the habit of world travel and symbolic rejection of the capitalist marketplace. Other cities like New York, with a local manufacturing base and affluent consuming public, offered more relaxed, casual garments as well as high-style clothing. Cinema, and especially Hollywood, has also had an international impact on fashion, partly through the direct involvement of designers such as Elsa Schiaparelli who designed glamorous costumes for screen stars like Mae West in the 1930s, or Ralph Lauren, whose wearable, androgynous look for Diane Keaton as *Annie Hall* (1977) was widely copied. A study of cowboy dress has suggested that American cowboys modified their dress inspired by their screen image.

The ever increasing cost of haute couture and greater affluence and mobility of the average fashion-buying public led to alternative models of fashion production and consumption, although essentially based on the industrialized and democratized production and distribution of clothing developed through the 20th century. The speed of modern communications and production of 'fast fashion' by mass-market clothing companies such as Zara (Spanish) or H&M (the Swedish company Hennes and Mauritz) have meant that previously universally recognised (Western) fashion stereotypes such as the 'little black dress' may have been superseded by more global, ephemeral and highly coded differences in, say, the cut of a pair of jeans. By the early 21st century, couture houses, with only a very small number of customers able to afford their clothes, have become the creative motor of a system of luxury brands experiencing a contradictory relationship between the need to maintain an image of exclusivity and a desire to compete in global mass markets. Ironically, many competitors in this fashion and luxury goods market are at present owned by a handful of holding companies such as Louis Vuitton Moet Hennessy (LVMH) and Pinault Printemps Redoute (PPR), both French-based. Following the lead of Coco Chanel in the early 20th century, their international fashion niche has become increasingly supported by diffusion of relatively cheaper ranges of garments as well as licensed ranges of cosmetics, perfumes and other branded commodities which, although not cheap, are nonetheless within reach of a far wider range of consumers worldwide and have become part of the international airport economy.

By the end of the 20th century, the clothing and fashion industry had become part of a global movement of capital associated with a shifting hierarchy of fashion cities such as Paris, London, and New York, and the linking of fashion businesses to transnational corporations. The fashion industry has become increasingly international and diffuse as cities on different continents, most recently in Asia, compete for creative kudos and commercial advantage in a competitive world fashion arena, often driven by the need to develop and sustain an infrastructure of textile and clothing production. Increasingly similar fashion media promote the formation of global tastes and their consumption in the form of fashionable clothing and lifestyles. Condé Nast's *Vogue* is published in 19 countries, including Brazil, Mexico, five Asian countries and India from late 2007; *Elle* magazine, based in Paris, has comparable global coverage. It has been suggested that transnational companies create and control a virtual 'world' as imaginary model and market for their mass-produced products, thereby developing a new form of colonial rhetoric. Yet, while fashion may have become democratized, offering a dress style of global similarity such as blue jeans, T-shirts or 'trainer' shoes with their own constructed hierarchies of desirability and fashionability, its actual making often depends upon the maintenance of global social inequality. Fashion brands, heavily promoted as offering the possibility of personal self-expression through consumption, have sought global reach through international markets but are increasingly underpinned by the production of fashion garments by poorly paid workers in the developing world.

The traces of these new commodity flows can be hard to map, due to the speed and diffuseness of financing and the practice of widespread subcontracting. Companies like Nike, which dominates the world athletic shoe market and has effectively transformed that once functional item into a fashion accessory, disperse financial risks and are relatively invisible in the networks of production. The shift in production bases has also occurred at the expense of workers' jobs in parts of the world which industrialized earlier, particularly in Western Europe and the United States. Recent studies of fashion production have addressed both labour conditions and local fashion networks in Asia, Africa and elsewhere which have developed in spite of the global dominance of international companies, partly because of their exclusion for economic reasons. In a world less obviously demarcated by clearly defined national or business units, where cultural identity is no longer inevitably linked to nation states, a wide variety of goods have been assumed under the label of 'fashion'. While high-profile brands now appear to be the key to international fashion, whether at the luxury couture level or with more popular labels such as Benetton, Gap, Diesel or Nike, recent commentators have reminded us that we need to look past these highly visible style surfaces to find more subtle and varied examples of fashionable dress.

Sonia Ashmore

Bibliography

Breward C. 2003. *Fashion*. Oxford: Oxford University Press.

Brydon A. and Niessen S. (eds) 1998. *Consuming fashion: adorning the transnational body*. Oxford: Berg.

Maynard M. 2004. *Dress and globalisation*. Manchester: Manchester University Press.

Rabine L. 2002. *The global circulation of African fashion*. Oxford: Berg.

Wilson L. 2001. 'American cowboy dress: function to fashion', *Dress*, 28, 40–52.

Related essays

art market; beauty; cosmetic surgery; cultural capitals; dress; femininity; film; global cities; Hollywood; labour standards; literary capitals; publishing; silk; sport; sports gear and apparel; textiles; T-shirt; Westernization; Zen aesthetics

Fast food

'Fast food' refers to a form of standardized restaurant chain, pioneered in the United States, which has come to symbolize American global influence.

McDonald's, the archetypical brand, boasts that an identical hamburger with fried potatoes and Coca-Cola can be purchased at any of its more than 23,000 stores around the world. Critics denounce this standardization as a threat to the diversity of local cultures, while the product itself is seen as an unhealthy cause of a global obesity epidemic. Anthropologists have emphasized the varying reactions to fast food whereby global products have been transformed to fit into local culinary cultures.

The fast food industrial model seeks to achieve profits through high volume sales of standardized, low-cost foods. Beginning in the 1920s, the first US hamburger chain, White Castle, made an ethnic food of questionable hygiene seem respectable to middle-class diners by serving it in sparkling clean, fairy tale surroundings. Richard and Maurice McDonald pioneered the efficient kitchens of modern fast food in 1948, and a few years later, Ray Kroch began franchising the system. Hamburger University, founded in 1961 to maintain uniform standards within the chain, now has branch campuses in England, Germany, Japan, and Australia.

Fast food triggered diverse reactions as US chains spread around the world.

McDonald's opened restaurants in Canada, Japan, Australia, and Western Europe in the late 1960s and early 1970s, followed by Latin America, Asia, and the former Communist bloc in succeeding decades. To avoid criticism of 'cultural imperialism', the chain established local sources of supply and gave franchise holders considerable autonomy. McDonald's also adapted to local dietary preferences; for example, religious restrictions in India forced the substitution of Vegetable McNuggets for hamburgers. Contrary to the downscale associations of fast food in the United States, these restaurants often became the preserve of relatively affluent diners. When the chain came to Japan in 1971, it appealed primarily to young people eager for Western fashions, yet subsequent generations grew up with McDonald's and no longer considered it to be foreign. What many Asian customers appreciated most were such seemingly trivial experiences of Americanization as the democracy of everyone waiting in the same line and the novelty of clean public restrooms.

Nevertheless, McDonald's eventually became a focus for anti-American protests. Immigration restrictions in the United States inspired an assault on one Mexico City restaurant, while the French sheep farmer José Bové became a celebrity after demolishing another in the town of Millau. The most serious blow to McDonald's public relations was self-inflicted, when the company sued two British environmental activists for libel in 1994. Dave Morris and Helen Steel had distributed a pamphlet accusing the company of abuses ranging from tropical deforestation to underpaying employees. The so-called McLibel case humiliated the company, for although the court ultimately found the defendants guilty of some instances of libel, many of their accusations turned out to be true.

Fast food has also been held responsible for a spectacular growth in the number of overweight people around the world. The incidence of obesity began to climb in the United States in the late 1970s, and within two decades a full third of the population weighed at least 20 per cent more than what doctors considered optimum. Nor was this trend limited to McDonald's homeland; by the end of the century, 15–20 per cent of Western Europeans were significantly overweight, and in Eastern Europe the figure rose to 40–50 per cent. A documentary film called *Super Size Me* sensationalizing the health risks of fast food won widespread acclaim around the world.

Yet McDonald's greatest challenge has come from local competitors offering rival versions of fast food. For example, Nando's, a Mozambican chicken franchise specializing in spicy Peri Peri sauce, spread first to South Africa, then crossed the Indian Ocean to Australia, where it inspired numerous imitators. In Hong Kong, purveyors of Chinese-style fast food have regained 70 per cent of the market from international hamburger chains.

Jeffrey M. Pilcher

Bibliography

Fantasia R. 1995. 'Fast food in France', *Theory and Society*, 24, 201–43.

Schlosser E. 2002. *Fast food nation: what the all-American meal is doing to the world*. London: Penguin.

Watson J. (ed.) 1997. *Golden arches east: McDonald's in East Asia*. Stanford: Stanford University Press.

Related essays

America; Coca-Cola; comics; cuisines; diet and nutrition; empires and imperialism; food; food safety standards; jeans; labour standards; McDonald's; salt; technical standardization; Westernization

Feel-good culture

The early 1960s saw the beginnings of a quiet revolution, a silent transformation of values which has broadened out since the 1980s as 'feel-good culture'. Ronald Ingelhart, commenting on successive phases of the World Values Survey since the 1970s, has distinguished three types of values. First, traditional values, derived from a world dominated by the traditional religions. Second, materialist or security values, typical of industrial societies at the stage of their construction and development, as in the case of Europe or the United States until the end of the first half of the 20th century. These values are associated with the maintenance of law and order, the struggle against price increases, the pursuit of economic growth, support for the armed forces, priority in education given to optimizing an individual's economic potential (in the law, medicine and so forth), and finally an emphasis on scientific, technical and industrial progress.

The values that have emerged since the 1960s in advanced industrial – otherwise known as 'postindustrial' – societies, identified by Ingelhart as the values of postmaterialism or well-being, are associated with the following: the expression of individual will, the growth of autonomy, harmony with the environment, the quest for a fulfilling profession, participation in democratic politics, the criticism of science and technology as impersonal, emphasis on well-being rather than maximizing economic gain, tolerance of marginal forms of behaviour such as homosexuality, interpersonal trust, setting a high value on the 'authentic' and the 'natural'. The goals are happiness, personal growth, sustainably agreeable sensations.

This imperative of well-being may be observed in every domain of social life. In medicine, everything must be done to reduce pain, at least as much as curing the disease, so that even the moment of death is considered to be undignified unless the patient is enabled not to suffer. The fact of feeling good assumes an objective significance, that of a physical well-being which leads sometimes to the cult of the perfect body, and to the quest for the best possible material conditions; but it also assumes a subjective significance. Increasingly, people opt for dieting, they become addicted to gym or martial arts, they submit to thalassotherapy, health cures, courses of *shiatsu* (Japanese massage) or spiritual retreats. Some businesses organize sessions in energetic massage, relaxation or sophrology for their staff. More or less fantastic systems of psychic therapy abound, from psychoanalysis for the more rational to karmic psychology, which is held to restore individual happiness by means of 'working on the psychic blockages of former lives'. Thus the values of well-being run into a thoroughgoing culture of well-being, and even into a multifaceted industry providing consumer goods and services.

This transformation of values and life priorities is becoming the dominant culture in advanced industrial societies, but has so far affected only very partially the poorer countries and those beginning to industrialize. However, this culture is gradually becoming accepted as the criterion for a better life even by the least privileged who have as yet no access to the goods and services of well-being.

The notion of well-being is not restricted to the individual level but has expanded to include also a concern for global well-being and harmony, expressed for instance in the ecological and humanitarian movements. Individual narcissistic preoccupations are justified, implicitly or explicitly, by the idea of a non-egoistic commitment to the whole world. Conversely, interventions on a global scale, such as humanitarian action, are justified by the idea of restoring a balance that has advantages for the self-fulfilment of individuals. Feel-good culture may therefore be interpreted in the context of a new orthodoxy that has been called 'individuo-globalism'. Moreover this doctrine of individuo-globalism is also reproduced and disseminated through channels that are religious in a stricter sense, such as New Age and Buddhism.

Raphaël Liogier

Bibliography

Ingelhart R. 1977. *Silent revolution: changing values and political styles Among Western publics*. Princeton: Princeton University Press.

Liogier R. 2004. *Le bouddhisme mondialisé: une perspective sociologique sur la globalisation du religieux*. Paris: Ellipses.

Liogier R. 2007. *La religion post-industrielle: sur l'individuo-globalisme*. Paris: Entrelacs.

Related essays
bodybuilding; Buddhism; China; consumer society; environmentalism; Japan; modernity; New Age; nudism; psychoanalysis; relief; religion; salt; yoga; Zen aesthetics

Fellowships and grants

Fellowships and grants are means to achieve border-crossing mobility as well as to promote project-based transnational cooperation of researchers, artists, and professionals. In academia, arts, and the professions (as well as handicrafts), learning and research abroad have a history reaching back to antiquity. However, it was the nation states and the philanthropies of the modern and late-modern era that came to pursue deliberate policies to promote such mobility and cooperation in a sustained and large-scale manner. The general objective of international fellowships and funding programmes has been to secure, for citizens and/or foreign nationals, access to and the appropriation of new knowledge, new technologies, and new ideas not readily available where the need seems to be greatest. Throughout the modern era, an increasing number of institutions encouraged the mobility of scholars and professionals in order to bring about the dissemination of knowledge and 'best practices' across national boundaries. Such ambitions have characterized the activities of major philanthropies such as the Rockefeller and Ford Foundations, as well as a number of modern, publicly funded scholarship and exchange programmes in the fields of education, research, and culture. Governments did not lag much behind private philanthropy in realizing the benefits of international studies and research. By the early 1930s, the governments of Belgium, Canada, China, Czechoslovakia, France, Germany, Hungary, Italy, and Switzerland offered international scholarships to advanced students and young scholars from among their own nationals. Contrary to what might be expected, these practices not only survived into the Cold War era, but, after an initial setback, even gathered momentum.

This widespread use of fellowship programmes should not, however, lead us to believe that there has ever been anything like an even distribution of either the opportunities offered by or the actual use of international grants and fellowships among the different countries. Rather, the geography of grant giving and grant receiving has tended to follow the changing regional and global hierarchies of economic power, socioeconomic dynamism, scientific-technological capabilities, and cultural influence and hegemony. The strongest transnational pull in the field of international fellowships has been exercised by countries of significant power and dynamism in these regards. The high international reputation of the Rhodes Scholarship after 1902, the ascendancy to global significance of the Rockefeller or Ford Fellowships between the wars and after World War 2 or, again, the popularity in East Central Europe of the German DAAD Fellowships (or, during the Cold War era, the dominant position in the same region of scholarships to the Soviet Union) should be seen not merely as reflections of regional or global power, but also as deliberate projections of imperial and/or hegemonic ambitions. Indeed, international fellowship and exchange programmes constitute one of the most powerful means of creating and sustaining informal empires via generating transnational elites culturally, socially and politically receptive and sympathetic towards cosmopolitan agendas.

International fellowships and grants had, by the interwar years, come to belong to the most important infrastructures, enabling and promoting transnational tendencies in academic, professional, and cultural life. Transfers of knowledge, ideas, and organizational and political know-how constitute a very important part of these tendencies. Just as important are, however, other consequences of this impressively growing and more and more regular traffic across national boundaries in various creative fields.

Studies and research conducted in foreign places foster not only better understanding among the intelligentsia of different countries and cultures, but they also give rise to networks of social bonds that enhance and cement the transnationalism of the modus operandi of these fields. Fellows returning to their countries bring with them new standards in and new horizons on their fields and keep these latter open and receptive to 'foreign' ways of doing science (or art), 'foreign' agendas of creative activity and 'foreign' norms of evaluation of performance. Indeed, the tendency is that international fellowships and collaboration based on international grants have promoted, if not the 'universalism', at least the transnationalism of the various fields of creativity and the professions. The achievements of Hungarian biochemistry, Soviet physics, or Czech surrealist art of the former century cannot be fully understood without proper consideration of the intensely transnational nature of these fields and of the transnational networks within which these 'national communities' of practitioners operated.

While in common usage 'fellowship' tends to be treated merely as meaning a grant, it is in fact a much more complex and many-sided term. A Fellow is not simply a grantee but someone who gets affiliated with the funding institution. Although in most cases such an affiliation is for a limited period of time, as a distinction (an item in the Fellow's CV) it will last forever. Depending on the status of the particular institution within the hierarchies of academia, profession, or arts, the bestowal of such a fellowship carries with it not only cash but also, and sometimes more importantly, symbolic capital (reputation).

This capital is reproduced by the rigorous procedures of peer review attendant on the election of Fellows. Both grants and fellowships are gained under competition in which candidates and their project proposals are evaluated by leading experts in their fields. In this respect, grant-based fellowships are rather similar to fellowships (memberships) of learned and professional societies (academies). International Fellows affiliated with leading research institutions, with leading philanthropies (such as the Rockefeller, Ford, or MacArthur Foundations), with the Institutes for Advanced Study, etc., are members of the transnational elite of their fields. They are not only adherents of an internationalist ethos in their work but also carry the weight and have the status and prestige to assert such values in their domestic (national) environment.

György Péteri

Bibliography

Curti M. 1963. *American philanthropy abroad: a history.* New Brunswick: Rutgers University Press.

Gemelli G. and Macleod R. (eds) 2003. *American foundations in Europe: grant-giving policies, cultural diplomacy and trans-Atlantic relations, 1920–1980.* Brussels: PIE / Peter Lang.

Schaeper T. J. and Schaeper K. 1998. *Cowboys into gentlemen: Rhodes Scholars, Oxford, and the creation of an American elite.* Oxford and New York: Berghahn.

Schmidt O. 1999. *Civil empire by co-optation: German-American exchange programmes as cultural diplomacy, 1945–1961.* Unpublished doctoral dissertation, Harvard University.

Related essays

1989; class; cosmopolitanism and universalism; executives and professionals; higher education; humanities; intellectual elites; International Road Federation (IRF); international schools; life and physical sciences; performing artists; philanthropic foundations; public policy; social sciences; surrealism; white men's countries

Femininity

Femininity refers to behaviour and ideas associated with womanliness or normative female sexuality, separable from women's anatomical sex. As intersexuals, men and women can all possess femininity, so historically the organization of this quality is quite diverse. Particularly in the transnational movement of ideas, practices and habits, conflicts occur over how feminine normality is to be understood and enforced. Thus it is important to explore femininity as such in relation to political spatialities or regions. In light of current Pacific Area politics and commodity flows it is illuminating to see questions of femininity via regional politics among Tokyo, London, New York, Shanghai and Beijing rather than, for instance, Buenos Aires, Mexico, Madrid, Paris and Washington.

Events in Tokyo, London, Washington, Shanghai and Beijing lay at the bottom of one crisis that erupted over the question of who definitively owned normal femininity in the period of colonial modernity (circa 1842–1937). The power of transnational capital to transform states and rewrite interregional trade relations accelerated in the mid 19th century, when Britain, the United States and other imperialists sought to marketize China and Japan and assimilate the Korean peninsula into a new region named the Far East (now East Asia). The Japanese Imperial Meiji state rose and the Chinese Qing dynasty devolved to a weak form of republicanism. As the United States accelerated its empire building in the Pacific, a subimperialism emerged in which the Japanese state and corporate entities seized territory, markets and labour on the China mainland, Taiwan, Okinawa, Korea and other traditional Chinese suzerainties.

During the 18th and 19th centuries, jingxi theatre in China and kabuki theatre in Japan had inspired widely accepted social norms of femininity in this part of Asia. The gender of onnagata, for instance, refers to Japanese male actors' theatrical performance of femininity in the 18th century, and to the fact that throughout the 19th century, civilized female performance of femininity and male impersonation of women conformed to identical codes. In these same centuries, Chinese norms of cultivated femininity stressed two elements: interiority and the power of passionate emotion, qing. This style of femininity was canonized and naturalized in widely performed stories starring a hero and a heroine, a scholar and an educated beauty, who share a qing femininity.

Elites in the Far East came into contact with English social biological theories of femininity in two ways. First, many educated men travelled to Europe or the United States (later to Tokyo) and learned firsthand about evolution of the species, sexual selection theory, advances in surgery, hygiene, anatomical science and so on. The modernists they encountered saw femininity as an outgrowth of physiological libido, and thus a driver of evolutionary social and national progress. Asians educated abroad accepted such European ideas as truthful. Second, missionaries and adventurers to East Asia, both women and men, entered colonizable space armed with enthusiastic blueprints for emancipating and civilizing Asian erotic and domestic life. They believed that they knew Nature's plan for all societies because they knew modern science. Scientific principles and social theory, they held, offered liberation to ancient, oppressive states and backward peoples.

Contention broke out early in Chinese cultural circles over which dramatic performance of femininity was normative – that of an emerging, internationalistic female movie star or of male-impersonated, jingxi heroines. As a defensive measure, anti-imperialist nationalists of the 1890s had already moved jingxi performance from popular venues into teahouses, where they set about to rework the national culture through dramatic performance. This elite male, homosocial preference for masculine femininity rested on the belief that actually female sexual expression was not feminine: femininity is not a quality in women's bodies or a healthy instinctual expression of erotic desire. Rather, femininity is a cultivated form of artistic expression.

Two events repositioned femininity into the sex of women – the rise of a new film culture and the acceleration of colonial modern flows of ideas, commodities, styles and people throughout the re-regionalizing space of the new East Asia. Under pressure of economic imperialism, modernism and the new media, enlightened women and men challenged the male performance of femininity. They pointed to a 'natural' female performance of femininity in the international media that was beginning to centre Hollywood globally and link the Hollywood system to Tokyo, Shanghai, Beijing, Seoul and other emergent markets. The moving picture, like the modern printing press, underwrote a large-scale transvaluation of erotic and aesthetic values, including a modernist association that linked anatomical sex, normative femininity, and performance styles in Asia, as in Europe and America.

In the second event, Chinese, Korean and Japanese connoisseurs, colonialists, students, merchants, artists, professionals and military (not to mention overseas Chinese and itinerant Japanese throughout Southeast Asia) brought a torrent of Japanese translations of European enlightened ideas to Chinese readers. Because Chinese students found Japanese easier to learn than European languages, Japanese became one major conduit of new ideas, including theories about who owned generic femininity. It was a translation event of massive proportions. A surprisingly large readership supported particularly publications on sexuality, femininity and natural-social evolutionary theory in the book market. Japanese-to-Chinese scientific sexual theory, along with the emergent avant-garde spoken theatre, informed audiences who were already absorbing norms of femininity in silent-film culture through Clara Bow, Colleen Moore, Ri Koran, Theda Bara, Ruan Lingyu, Hu Die and other globally known stars.

As a consequence, there emerged an 'international', enlightened feminine look and performance style that was considered natural rather than artificial, and which rejected the older masculine aesthetic. Of course, for women to acquire the international look cost money. The cosmetics, cigarettes, clothing styles, education and élan associated with new femininity had a clear class bias. Still, it is obvious in studies of female workers that the aspiration to these allegedly natural forms of femininity and feminine self-expression was not confined to the elite classes. Wherever civilized, enlightened European, American and Japanese women of any class went to populate the new empires, they brought with them the idea that femininity is the natural expression of female sexual physiology. For their part, nationalist transnational corporations like Japanese manufacturer Nakayama Taiyodo pioneered colonial, 'Chinese' forms of commercial femininity, as did American companies like Pond's and Cutex.

Throughout the 1920s and 30s, the political avant garde and left-wing artists challenged grosser forms of sexualized commercial images. A politicized critique of mass-mediated, movie-star femininity could be found throughout East Asia among anarchists, communists, feminists, middle-class reformers and religious figures. Nonetheless, during the interwar years (1919–37) two central figures – the female factory worker and urban middle-class modern girl – reshaped styles of femininity to cohere around the desire for capitalist commodities. This acquisitive, middle-class, urban and commodity-focused feminine style would lead, at the close of the Pacific war (1937–45), to an impasse in the Chinese social revolution. By then a significant historical transition was complete. The nationalist icon and world-renowned performer of female roles in nationalist jingxi, Mei Lanfang, bequeathed femininity to younger, female players. A symptom of this critical shift is illustrated by the contemporary complaint that Mei Lanfang was a homosexual, and that male impersonator femininity and homosexuality itself were, in a revolutionary age, 'feudal leftovers'. Although it is regularly argued in the Western media and among some Chinese feminist ideologists that the Chinese revolution made women into men or denied the femininity of women, this is incorrect. More accurately, revolutionary aesthetics would sever the modernist link between eroticism and femininity, just as it would delink sexuality and masculinity.

During the Cold War, the Maoist Revolution exuberantly forwarded an official femininity rooted in the rustic village peasant styles and in Soviet Russian Bolshevik fashion, feminine figures whose large hands, muscled arms and prominent breasts romanticized the productive femininity of liberated working women. The earlier association of women's sexuality with commercial commodities was demonized in the Great Proletarian Cultural Revolution (GPCR, 1966–76), although the right of women to claim femininity in their bodies did not change. In fact, some Maoist feminine poses resembled politically cleansed silent-movie star photo images. The GPCR promoted a range of balletic political stories like 'The White Haired Woman' and 'Red Detachment of Women' that offered women's femininity with two opposing aspects: the female rape victim on the one hand and eroticized militant avenger on the other. By the late Cold War period, a crisis of masculinity emerged along with a charge that politics had emasculated men, in great part because it caused insufficient femininity of women. The writing of postrevolutionary memoirists like Jung Zhang rested uneasily on this perceived crisis of femininity, voiced by Zhang Xianliang in his hit novel, *Half of man is woman*. The alleged deficiencies of femininity and masculinity were resolved, in the end, as regnant neotraditionalism not just at the level of personal identity, but in the new domestic commodity markets and the marriage market, as well.

Transnational styles of Communist femininity originated from diverse and contiguous places. The importation of Communist Russian advisors, films, high-art conventions, and styles of clothing and language in the 1950s had offered a European socialist tradition of labour femininity. Soviet fiction and the translation of the Russian masters into Chinese injected a strong romanticism (and provided a facsimile of the bourgeois women's style for readers who had never seen or travelled in a capitalist country with an existing bourgeoisie). Other elements of mass media in the socialist period included popular films from India and other points in Asia. Resurgent interest in Chinese rural art forms, which had begun early in the 1940s, and the saucy ingénue and pedagogue Li Shuangshuang, who teaches her cadre husband a thing or two about commune management, exhibits an unmistakably socialist feminine posture.

In fact, one could interpret Cultural Revolution aesthetics as a nationalist Chinese effort to surpass the USSR Communist bloc iconography, philosophy and ideology. And in a final interesting twist to this socialist transnational flow, the Cultural Revolution's fiery and vengeful peasant heroines and iron-like feminine martyrs shuffled off the old, sadomasochistic stories about the anti-Japanese war period, and leaped into United States so-called Second Wave feminist iconography in the late 1960s. Speaking bitterness emerges transformed in this era, as post-Maoist 'consciousness raising'. Socialist notions of femininity across the Communist world had previously been mocked, maligned and tarred with being 'masculine'. This Cold War tactic allowed the capitalist bloc countries to claim not just a vision of femininity as hyperfeminine but also the complement of the hyperfeminine style, the hypermasculine man. (Just think John Wayne.) At the same time in the socialist bloc, as the case of China makes clear, femininity had been redefined as a physical, balletic performance of liberation. Sexuality was sublated into a statist idea that femininity is compassionate service to the society through labour and social service to the dispossessed, a code that remains in play to this very day.

The ongoing rise of China as a significant element of the world capitalist economy is a central fact. Globalization is a term used to understand the impact of the two-decade-old rise of China in relation to US imperialist policies of containment, re-regionalization and now a global war on terror, tailored to expand its military footprint. The greatest human migration in history is sending vast labour pools from rural areas in China to continental urban sites, and from China to every part of the world. As the world's greatest factory, Chinese urban areas are importing style even as China exports its own. Any current understanding of femininity in today's globalized world, then, should stress two factors. First, the movement of corporate giants into the production of femininity is a potential reformatting of the body. Chinese and Japanese cultural markets are now as entranced as Americans are with the phenomenon of the medically altered physical body, exemplified in the transsexual, whose presence – among other things – raises the question of how femininity is instilled into a body that is anatomically female. Body alteration will continue to affect male and female bodies at medical, social (i.e. sovereignty and citizenship), market, cultural and media levels. Second, although disputes over copyright and ownership of style and fashion are real, what is occurring in China now is an obsessive recoding of femininity as money. Much of the world is being tugged toward Asian modes of postdevelopment capitalist culture. What began as a ploy to gain market penetration is flowering into a massive, uneven, yet globally commodified femininity. In the international sex markets, transnational movies, digital games and cartoon art, and in the transnational knowledge informatics regarding genetic, social, medical, hormonal, sexual production of femininity, we confront future changes of unimaginable dimensions.

Tani Barlow

Bibliography

Barlow T. 2004. *The question of women in Chinese feminism*. Durham, NC: Duke University Press.

Barlow T. et al. 2005. 'The modern girl around the world: a research agenda', *Gender & History*, 17, 2, 245–94.

Barlow T., Ito R. and Sakamoto H. (eds)
2008. *The modern girl and colonial modernity
in East Asia* (in Japanese). Tokyo: Iwanami
Shoten.

Chou K. H. 1997. Staging revolution:
actresses, realism and the New Woman
Movement in Chinese spoken drama and
film, 1919–1949. Unpublished doctoral
dissertation, New York University.

Isaka M. 2002. 'The gender of *onnagata* as
the imitating imitated: its historicity,
performativity, and involvement in the
circulation of femininity', *Positions: east
asia cultures critique*, 10, 2, 245–84.

Pun N. 2005. *Made in China: subject, power and
resistance in a global workplace*. Durham, NC:
Duke University Press.

Sato B. H. 2003. *The new Japanese woman:
modernity, media, and women in interwar
Japan*. Durham, NC: Duke University Press.

Yeh C. 'The female impersonator as the
national cultural symbol of Republican
China', in Croissant D., Mostow J. and Yeh
C. (eds) 2008. *Performing nation*, Leiden:
Brill.

Related essays

beauty; Cantonese opera; China; consumer
society; dress; empires and imperialism;
fashion; film; gender and sex; Hollywood;
honour; Japan; language; language
diplomacy; love; Maoism; missionaries;
new man; performing artists; sexuality
and migration; theatre; translation;
Westernization; women's movements

Film

What is film? Moving images: two-dimensional
artificially created images constructed by
capturing objects in motion in real time on
photographic celluloid, which are then strung
together onto reels and flashed at a regular
high velocity before the light shining through
a projector, such that they produce the illusion of continuity.

Film as an intrinsic transnational artefact

Devices such as the magic lantern dating back
well into late-18th-century and 19th-century
experiments aimed at presenting sequential images in phantasmagoria spectacles as
well as the much-in-vogue vaudeville, popular melodrama and the illustrated lecture are
the main precursors to film as it developed
concurrently in Germany, France, the US and
the UK in the last decades of the 19th century. Film spread globally with a speed quite
unprecedented for a new art form. Screenings
were held within months of the first presentation of sequential images – through the kin-
etoscope in the form of private viewings (1891,
although commercially released in 1894)
and the short public screenings through the
cinématographe (1895) – throughout Eastern
Europe and Russia, East Asia, the Indian
subcontinent, Australia, and Latin America,
underlying the medium's operation across
national borders.

During the first 15 years of its existence,
film went from being moving snapshots of a
few seconds to ten-minute-long shorts, but
was still a medium closer to a visual spectacle
than to storytelling. It would not be until the
development of feature length (a term borrowed from vaudeville, where 'feature' referred to the main attraction in that day's
programme), and with/through it the expansion into narrative and eventually specifically cinematic narratives – executed through
a language and conventions particular to
cinema – around 1910, that film would become a large-scale business although there
are earlier, isolated features. One of the
earliest feature-length films is the Australian
The Story of Kelly Gang, dating back to 1906.
During this first decade the national origin of
film production companies was irrelevant, as
reels were sold to exhibitors and screened as
novelties regardless of their nationality, circulating as commodities with the advantage,
at the time, of their silent nature. National
film industries, in this sense, evolved well before the notion of national cinemas.

Film is the primordial industrial art form
of the 20th century, one of the key urban
exponents of industrial modernity, notably as it was part of the redistribution and
reorganization of time that took place in
urban centres with the definition of 'free
time' opening the way for mass leisure activities. The history of film is in tension between
the assessment of national traditions and the
narrative of national histories of film, and
the need to consider its rise and development
within a context of metropolitan expansion
in a cross-national web of circulating cultural
products. This entry will try to use the first
approach to emphasize the second.

If the flaneur is one of the emblematic
figures of urban life, strolling through the
shockwaves of the cityscape, film allowed the

flaneur the possibility of continuing to leisurely wander without even having to walk: mobility in immobility, including that across borders. City dwellers in the US in the 1920s were fascinated with Robert Flaherty's feature films which documented life elsewhere – whether in the Arctic or on a Samoan island in the South Seas – bringing urbanites another time and space without the need to be mobile. Film opened up precisely that possibility of being elsewhere without moving: be it by travelling to faraway lands – which the 1920s and 1930s explosion of ethnographic films granted; or by inhabiting, for the length of the film's duration, the fantasy worlds offered in the first experimental films which coalesced in the 1920s and 1930s, concurrently with the emergence of the documentary genre, but which had been explored since the medium's origins – Melies' 1902 *Voyage to the Moon* would attest to the forthcoming possibilities that experimental film would explore beginning in the 1920s; or by staying close to home, entering the privacy of those near and known, but always, also far off. Voyeurism is thus intrinsic, conceptually, to film, where the pleasure gained watching others is offered as the prime mode of entertainment, making Hitchcock's *Rear Window* a masterful parody of the medium. All film spectators are engaged in some form or other of the tourist's gaze. This clue as to the intrinsic transnational characteristics of film can give us our cue to survey some aspects of film history in the last hundred years.

Flashed so quickly in the dark: a brief transnational history of film

Until World War I, France, Italy and Denmark dominated the film market worldwide. The outbreak of the war would turn the tables and gave the US leeway to become the main producer and distributor of films, developing and controlling the nascent industry as it became increasingly difficult for the European films to reach the markets. This coincided with the rapid move of most production companies in the US to the Los Angeles suburb of Hollywood and the vertical integration of the industry into studios which proliferated in the late 1910s and early 1920s and then consolidated into some seven studios which, since the end of the 1920s, have shared the control over the monumental enterprise. Branches of these studios – Fox, Paramount, Samuel Goldwyn among others – were opened up outside of the US to control the local markets. In the latter half of the 1920s, Hollywood films took up 80 per cent of the market in, for example, Brazil.

The 1920s saw the development of various leading genres: animation, comedy and documentary, genres which very much configured the studio system in Hollywood, made it possible to export its production to the main urban venues in the Europe, Latin America, the Near East and East Asia to develop its model of vertical integration. Other countries had strong film industries as well, but none with the far-reaching force that the Hollywood studios already had by then. Japan was, during this period, the country with the largest feature film production, but this was not part of an international distribution as the films were marketed only nationally. 'National cinemas' was already at that time the term used to refer to those cinemas which were not Hollywood-produced – although at times following Hollywood modes of narrative structure as well as of production – thus pointing, indirectly, to both the historically transnational nature of the Hollywood film industry, as well as to its early thrust as an empire of the audiovisual medium which, by the late 1920s made up 85 per cent of films shown worldwide, despite the fact that in 1919, 90 per cent of films had been French.

In the meantime, the introduction of synchronized sound dialogue into film in Warner Bros' *The Jazz Singer* in October 1927 had changed the cinematic experience forever. The advent of sound temporarily set back Hollywood's rise as audiences worldwide demanded dialogues in their own languages. Thus if the sudden Babel-like explosion of languages on the screen – 'the language of cinema is universal' – attested once again to the inherent transnational quality of cinema from its historical and material origins, it was also very quickly appropriated as it consolidated the strength of the studio system, systematizing and generating yet more conventions in film language. The musical emerged worldwide as a consequence of sound synchronization. By 1931 the first and very successful Hindi sound film had been made, which unleashed the astounding Bollywood phenomenon: the largest number of films produced and consumed in the world today are the lavish productions from Mumbai (formerly

Bombay) and the rest of India, exported mainly to Asia and the Middle East also with enormous success.

World War 2 changed the configuration not only of film production, sending a number of directors and actors into exile – mainly Europeans who moved to Hollywood – but also of film viewing and distribution as the most important international film festival was created during those years. The Cannes International Film Festival, still considered today the most prestigious film event in the world, was established in 1939, as a response to the growing intervention of the Italian fascist state in the Venice Film Festival at the time. Due to France's declaration of war on Germany a few months after the creation of the festival, it did not take off until 1946. The festival's growth into the limelight of non-Hollywood cinema, together with the creation in 1951 of the *Cahiers du Cinema*, configured film culture such that, if the US – epitomized by Hollywood – would represent the colonization and globalization of the film world, France – epitomized by Cannes and *Cahiers* – would become the staunch supporter of 'world cinema' and 'art house cinema'. This postwar film culture, very much supported and fashioned by venues such as Cannes and *Cahiers*, led to the decade of auteur cinema. Both national and global at the same time, the auteur emerged as the figure that, organized film according to her/his very personal style and thus led film out of discussions of communal belonging. It is also, interestingly, the decade when sex divas – Brigitte Bardot, Gina Lollobrigida, Sophia Loren – took over the screen, and their iconicity, which quickly spread on a global scale, can be seen as another element of both a certain return to Europe as the seat of film culture as well as of its attempt to organize it by at the same time erasing and underlining film's national and cultural specificity.

The cinema that emerged in the 1960s in the aftermath of the Cuban Revolution, the Algerian War, left-wing revolutions and the decolonizing of the Third World was marked, on the one hand, by displacement – in the form of exile, migration, diaspora and political refugees – and on the other hand, by the emergence of Third and Revolutionary Cinema practices. The overall aim was to challenge the vertical modes of film production and the colonization of the global film market by American cinema and to use film as a political and aesthetic instrument towards the decolonization of the mind. Gillo Pontecorvo's *The Battle of Algiers*, which premiered at the Venice Film Festival in 1966, is a landmark for these cinemas, and a key film in the transnational revolutionary potential and ideal of cinema. A year before, in 1965, Glauber Rocha presented, in Genoa, his radical proposition for decolonized cinema, 'An aesthetics of hunger'. He called for the need to acknowledge and reflect on the violence that had befallen the cultural and political life of Latin Americans, and the need to make of hunger – lack, poverty – an aesthetic and political stand instead of attempting to produce 'beautiful', 'perfect' films emulating a supposed First World standard. Rocha called for 'a cinema of the future', for 'an anti-symphony of sound and image'. Fernando Solanas and Octavio Getino argued in their 'Towards a Third Cinema' manifesto (1969) that film until then had been just another consumer good, dealing with effect and not cause. Third Cinema called for films of 'decolonization', also stressing from the very beginning that art had been a way in which to mesmerize the masses, instead of being used as a pedagogical and communicative tool for decolonization (the very aim of their 1968 *La hora de los hornos* which was shown in underground venues). As an apparatus for and of the market, film had belonged, they argued, to 'The System'. With the birth of a 'new man' through the emergence of 'masses on the worldwide revolutionary plane', and a tricontinental film project – Asia, Africa and Latin America – calling for collaborations across national boundaries, film would become a communal and transnational endeavour. Meant to generate ties that would resist and eventually subvert the colonial and neocolonial structure of the world economy, film, as part of this world economy, would be liberated. The same year Cuban Julio García Espinosa in his statement on film, 'Towards a revolutionary cinema', attempted to conceptualize the role and place of film within a revolutionary state and its importance as both a pedagogical instrument as well as an audiovisual binder in the relationship between culture and the state. He called for an 'imperfect cinema' that would on the one hand find in those who struggle its audience, themes and problems and on the other hand break free from Hollywood's demand for technical and narrative perfection. For this the Cuban state had organized the famous ICAIC (Instituto Cubano del Arte e Industria Cinematográficos) headed by García Espinosa. The belief in a tricontinental revolution via the figures of Franz Fanon, Che Guevara and Ho Chi Minh influenced the discourse and practice of these and other Third World film makers like Ousmane Sembene, Ohmar Khlifi, Med Hondo and Ruy Guerra as they chronicled struggles of liberation in their early films of the 1960s and 1970s.

The displacement that the wars of liberation generated brought about another radical change in film production as subjects were forced out of their homelands, either through the routes of political exile and asylum or through the channels of mass migrations. Black British cinema and British Asian cinema of the 1950s through to the 1980s, and Beur cinema in France of the 1980s are a prime example of this. They offered reflections on the in-between place of displaced and migrating subjects for whom nation is an ever more complex configuration and for whom the out-of-place and out-of-context condition allows for a critical approach to the naturalized category and affect of 'home', generating as well a critique of national cinemas. This, together with observations on the subaltern condition and discrimination experienced by these subjects, make up the poetics and politics of many of these productions. Exploring mainly the tense integration into metropolitan life of the second generation of North African immigrants that grew up in the housing projects on the outskirts of some of France's main cities, Beur cinema as a cinema of community identification and protest emerged from the social conflicts of the 1970s and 1980s. A play on the French word for Arabic (arabe) and at the same time a reference to Berbers – the main ethnic group among the Algerian immigrant community – and to the French word for butter (beurre), Beur stresses both integration and alienation. Mehdi Charef's film Miss Mona (1987), where a young beur pickpocket befriends an ageing transvestite, retraces – as many Beur films do – the Parisian geography, drawing over the emotive landscape of that most cinematic of cities, a transgressive and racially fraught mediascape. Despite its combative edge and activist history, Beur cinema, like many of these multicultural endeavours in other countries, is completely dependent upon and a participant in French film-making institutions. In a more conservative and commercial form, the logo for Panamax Films – a US production and distribution company with an output deal with Lion's Gate Films – which reads, 'There are 40 million Latinos in the United States. We make movies for them', stresses the institutional rootedness of these displaced cinemas. Film has, in these instances, as the epitome of the non-place, served as the imaginary homeland of these displaced communities or as one of the sites for reflecting on complex racial, ethnic, religious and gendered contentions and assumptions.

The 1990s brought about a new configuration of production, distribution and consumption in the film industry. Non-Hollywood films – yet box-office hits – are frequently coproduced by companies from as many as nine countries, as Walter Salles' Motorcycle Diaries exemplifies (Argentina, the US, Cuba, Germany, Mexico, the UK, Chile, Peru, France 2004). It is perhaps not a random example, given that the film presents the spectator with Ernesto Guevara's early years before becoming the 'Che' and being claimed as the model for the 'new man' that Third Cinema, and revolutionary proponents in the Third World at large, would call forth as the promise of a true international revolution. The fact that Salles is Brazilian would be an unimportant detail.

The 2007 Golden Globe Awards could serve as a case study for the uncontrollable transnational status of current cinema: Clint Eastwood's Letters from Iwo Jima winning the award for Best Foreign Language Film, and Babel, directed by Mexican Alejandro González Iñárritu, taking the prize for Best Motion Picture. The mobility of directors, and their ability to produce successful films both 'at home' and abroad – in and out of context, one might be tempted to say – could be characterized by Mexican Alfonso Cuarón's move from his 2001 box-office-smashing worldwide success with Y tu mamá también, made in Mexico in Spanish, to his more recent success, Children of Men, a Japanese, US and British coproduction. The instantaneous worldwide release – epitomized by the simultaneous opening of The Matrix Revolutions on 5 November 2003 in more than one hundred countries at 1400 Greenwich Mean Time – which can be seen as a future distribution model for the film industry, happens only to some films from particular types of global capital configurations. This model follows, and even exacerbates, the model of capitalism run riot, although it also builds on the global allure of fandom in the 1950s model of stardom.

Film and the nation

The return, since the 1980s, to the use of geographically confining taxonomies to organize and market non-Hollywood films – the New Argentine cinema of the late 1990s, New Taiwanese cinema of the early to late 1990s, New African cinema of the 21st century – bears the irony that these films are the product, to a large degree, of an international film-festival circuit – Sundance, Venice, Rotterdam, Cannes, Toronto – which has been instrumental in ensuring the very existence of these films, sponsoring, among other things, funding opportunities in the form of grants, residencies, labs, and very crucially, multinational coproductions. Thus, the new national or continental cinemas are, in general, coproductions by companies of far-ranging, historically disparate cultural settings and specificities.

The nation and its wars have been intricately connected to film. Although during its first decade film production companies and their films were not assigned or identified with nationalities – reels were sold to exhibitors and screened as 'novelties' – the transition and development of narrative form marks this encounter. D. W. Griffith's *Birth of a Nation* (1915) is one of the first landmarks in this triumvirate. But one could say that cinema followed war very closely from its very conception: the Spanish American War (1898), which deeply changed the shape of the postcolonial world at the dawn of the 20th century, contemporaneously with the emergence of film, was documented in film only a couple of years after the first public screenings of the *cinématographe*. Film in its materiality bears witness to the world and to history and yet has not always been able to offer itself as document. Most notably, film was not able to really show the World War 2 concentration camps, only allude to them, thereby marking a point of inflection in the medium, where war would become either a spectacle or the machine which would, through its power of expulsion, force peoples into migration. The changes in film culture in the post-World War 2 years thus bring to the forefront the question of the intricate relationship between film and 20th-century war. Whether one thinks of the émigrés who left Europe during World War 2 and flocked to Hollywood, affecting that cinematic landscape, or of the Gulf War (1991), so heavily intertwined with the possibility of it existing in real time in an audiovisual format and becoming, as war, an audiovisual landscape, the connection between cinema and war has marked the history of the medium. Jean-Luc Godard's immense video project *Histoire(s) du cinema* (1988–98) makes use of that bond, turning it into its guiding concept.

The acme of the relationship between nation and cinema would be when film served many a totalitarian regime as an aid in the formation of national subjects. It was in the 1920s and 1930s that film was used – not for the first time, but on a massive scale – as a tool for propaganda and direct ideological interventions and the manufacture of consent. In the aftermath of the Russian Revolution, the Cultural Revolution first, followed by the consolidation of Socialist Realism, made clear that the new Soviet state that emerged in the aftermath of the Russian Revolution would be at the forefront of the use of film for propaganda. German National Socialism would soon follow in this use of film. It is estimated that there were 1,100 films made between 1933 and 1945 in Germany. Audiovisual technologies and techniques were key to the development and implementation of National Socialism. Mussolini openly quoted Lenin in repeating his famous dictum that 'film is our strongest weapon', although the Italian fascist state would not begin the systematic use of the medium until 1933, when it became obligatory to show one Italian film for every three non-Italian. Not officially linked to a particular state, the films made under the Marshall Plan, or European Recovery Program, after World War 2, in an overtly pedagogical form and tone called for a free and democratic continent ready to embrace its Western – i.e. non-Communist – brothers on a journey down the lane of consumer culture.

To refer to film in terms of national cinema binds a cultural practice to a geopolitical setting as well as to an understanding of cultural production which still in the 21st century would be subjected by and to the nation state. The warring nation states in the aftermath of World War 2 could only with difficulty be thought of as the connective force in cultural production. For if, as Hannah Arendt observed during the war years, the displaced person or refugee had become the new citizen of the world, as well as the vanguard of the people, cultural poetics, practices and products would also articulate configurations and constellations beyond the confines of the nation.

This deterritorialized state of the motion picture is not a recent phenomenon but rather belongs to its very origin. As Epicurean philosophy would have it, film, being an emanation from the surface of bodies which were objects of perception, has, in one of its uses – even before inhabiting its 1905 meaning as motion picture – made reference to migration, displacement and travel and therefore also, in this sense, to the paradox of representation, embodying in presence an absence. Film's other etymological history points to membranes, coatings, pellicles, laminas, veils and hazes, whereby at the root of film such as the late 19th century came to know it is found, as well, the concept of separation and distance as it covers masks, cases, sheaths. Film, therefore, as the industrialized art form of the 20th century, is predicated on the illusion of meetings and encounters of differing times, spaces, subjects and objects moving beyond and across themselves and the borders which contain and confine them.

Natalia Brizuela

Bibliography

Ezra E. and Rowden T. (eds) 2006 *Transnational cinema: the film reader*. London and New York: Routledge.

Getino O and Solanas F. 1969. 'Hacia un tercer cine', *Tricontinental*, 13, Havana.

Hjort M and MacKenzie S. (eds) 2000 *Cinema and nation*. London and New York: Routledge.

Naficy H. 2001. *An accented cinema: exilic and diasporic filmmaking*. Princeton: Princeton University Press.

Rocha G. 2006. *O século do cinema*. São Paulo: Cosac Naify.

Salles Gomes P. E. 1980. *Cinema: trajetória no subdesenvolvimento*. Rio de Janeiro: Paz e Terra.

Staiger J. and Gomery D. 1979. 'The history of world cinema: models for economic analysis', *Film Reader*, 4, 35–44.

Stam R. and Shohat E. 1994. *Unthinking Eurocentrism: multiculturalism and the media*. London and New York: Routledge.

Related essays

consumer cooperation; decolonization; diasporas; empire and migration; exile; Russian Revolution; Guevara, Ernesto ('Che'); Hollywood; literature; Marshall Plan; nation and state; new man; *non-lieux*; performing artists; prizes; temporary migrations; *The Wretched of the Earth*; theatre; war; Westernization; wildlife films; Williams, James Dixon; world orders

Williams, James Dixon c. 1877–1934

The career of film pioneer James Dixon Williams across three decades and four continents must be traced through four different national historiographies, each interested only in his moment on their territory. This scholarly isolationism, and the absence of any known archive of his papers, means that the extent to which he was an innovator of commercial practices for the global film industry remains speculative. His American obituary may have underestimated his influence: 'Had Williams been more of an executive and less the promoter he might have revolutionized the industry's set-up' (*Variety*, 4 September 1934).

Born in West Virginia in the late 1870s, Williams, known as 'J.D.', worked first in live theatre and then as one of the earliest travelling picture showmen. Reaching the far edge of the continent, he established a number of storefront picture houses in the North West and Canada. Then he continued moving west. He arrived in Sydney in 1909 where he began acquiring, then building, increasingly palatial picture theatres. Employing scientific management techniques, he concentrated the theatres geographically in the 'block system' and introduced cheap ticket prices and the continuous picture show. By 1912, his company controlled a circuit of 15 picture theatres and amusement complexes throughout Australasia. It ran five film exchanges, had agents in London and America and a distribution outlet in China.

J.D. had a passionate commitment to the possibilities of film as the new medium of entertainment and instruction for the mass of ordinary people, and a clear vision of how to bring the picture business into an intimate relation with daily life. He knew that making quality pictures took huge amounts of money, which could only be provided by a world market. But, in turn, quality pictures would realise their full power and destiny within such a world market. In a business of cutthroat competition, he understood that the future belonged to the efficient and the consolidated. In 1913 he engineered a complex amalgamation with his chief competitors and became the dominant partner in what was called 'the Combine' – the distribution and exhibition company Union Theatres/Australasian Films, which stood as a colossus dominating the national moving-picture field for decades, and still exists in hybrid form today. He took this ideal of a vertically integrated and monopolistic enterprise with him to the United States after a falling out with his Australian partners around 1913.

In 1917 he returned to commercial notice as the founder, with Thomas L. Tally, of the First National company. As its general manager, he plunged headlong into American film industry politics, stopping the previously irresistible rise of Paramount. He forged First National into a production/exhibition combine and one of the most powerful film companies in the US. In 1922, *Motion Picture News* listed him as one of the twelve greatest people in the motion picture industry, but by the end of that year he was pushed to resign from First National over policy differences. At this point he dropped out of American film history and the trail again goes cold until 1925, when he re-emerged, this time as a British film producer: founder and managing director of British National Pictures. In 1926, he bought a 40-acre site and began to develop a huge super-studio – a British Hollywood – at Elstree.

His aim seems to have been the same as it had been 14 years earlier in Australia, and then in America: to foster the possibilities of film as the pre-eminent modern medium of instruction and entertainment. On the basis of his transnational experience, he encouraged a pan-European rather than narrowly nationalistic film industry and developed a scheme for multilanguage film production. He proposed the formation of an Academy of Motion Pictures with a teaching staff, preferably attached to Oxford or Cambridge University. He wanted to rationalize the highly fragmented British film industry and develop the size of the available market in order to finance quality production. For a third time, he put the strategy of the Combine into play, but he lost control of the resulting British International Pictures in 1927. Thereafter, until his death in 1934, he engaged in intercontinental film distribution, still seeking, in his own words, 'a film conversation between nations instead of the present Hollywood monologue'.

Jill Matthews

Bibliography
Higson A. and Maltby R. (eds).1999. 'Film Europe' and 'Film America': cinema, commerce and cultural exchange 1920–1939. Exeter: Exeter University Press.
Matthews J. J. 'Modern nomads and national film history: the multi-continental career of J D Williams', in Curthoys A. and Lake M. (eds) 2006. *Connected worlds: history in a trans-national perspective*. Canberra: ANU ePress.

Related essays
executives and professionals; film; Garvey, Marcus Mosiah; globalization; Hammarskjöld family; historians and the nation state; Hollywood; Kessler, Harry von; Quesnay, Pierre; Schwimmer, Rosika; Shiber, Saba George

Financial centres

The organization of global finance is strongly hierarchical: a few big financial centres handle operations that are huge in comparison with those pursued in smaller places. The activity of these centres is also disproportionate in terms of other economic indicators: stock-market or exchange operations, especially where derivatives are concerned, can involve sums of money several times greater than the GNP of even the largest countries. The resulting international capital flows can be big enough to help integrate a worldwide financial market, but they may also cause currency exchange crises, or financial crises capable of destabilizing the economy of whole regions, as happened with the Asian crisis of 1997 and the subprime crash of 2007. Financial centres can also bring big advantages – in terms of both money and power – to the countries where they are situated.

Definition

A financial centre is a town or city where financial actors organize or carry out financial transactions and deal with the ensuing payments. These operations may involve a range of different professions: modern banks, for example, receive deposits and make loans (clearing banks), but also manage savings and organize financial operations such as stock issues (investment banking). Stock markets aim to create the optimal match between supply and demand for listed securities, i.e. to offer dealers maximum liquidity (thanks to fast, easy transactions) combined with openness (security and transparency of operations). Insurance companies offer protection against life's uncertainties, but also represent, along with other actors such as pension funds, a repository for long-term savings. Central banks regulate interest rate fluctuations and lay down rules for their operations. Audit and accounting firms, rating agencies, financial journals and other purveyors of financial information generate or certify information about borrowers, without which no financial system can be made to work.

All these elements are always to be found, in some form or other, in big modern financial centres, but that was not always the case. In the past, a financial centre might well concentrate on a limited number of activities while ignoring others. Some actors, such as central banks or rating agencies, did not originally exist, or did so in a different form. Most analyses, however, stress the interdependence of all these activities and operators, leading to externalities that encourage the concentration of financial activity in a small number of centres.

Thus the importance of a financial centre can be gauged from the number or range of its operators and from the volume of operations. However, the term 'financial centre' tends rather to evoke an area over which the centre exercises some form of control. In terms of economic geography, a major financial centre will control financial activity over a very wide area; a smaller one may exercise national, regional or purely local influence, and the levels fit together, like concentric circles, as a result of the crystallization of nation states which culminated in the 19th/20th centuries, whereby regional centres became subject to national centres, which in turn were dependent on international centres. In this article we shall look only at major centres of international importance.

History

A recognizable hierarchy of financial centres can be observed as far back as the Renaissance, if not farther. Fernand Braudel drew attention to a historical succession of supranational economies centring first on Italy (Venice and Genoa), then on the Low Countries (Antwerp followed by Amsterdam), and finally on London, which assumed world leadership in the 19th century. This straightforward list brings out the interdependence of international trade and finance: the first major financial centres were great ports at the heart of international commerce. There may be a time lag, however: Amsterdam's commercial importance began to decline at the beginning of the 18th century, whereas its financial decline was a consequence principally of the French Revolution, when many Dutch financiers left for exile in London.

London, as a financial centre, was notable by the mid 19th century not only for the extent of its financial activity but also for the diversity, or specialization, permitted by its size. The merchant banks, led by Rothschild and Barings, specialized in international finance, the acceptance of commercial papers and government borrowing. Overseas banks used London as a base for controlling business activities mainly within the Empire: they had 132 overseas agencies in 1860, 739 in 1890. The big clearing banks took deposits and made loans chiefly in Britain, though they gradually acquired networks covering other countries. By then London was probably what it still is today: the only centre which included every branch of financial activity and was active throughout almost the entire world. It was because Paris could not equal this level of international trade that in the first half of the 19th century it failed to develop a market for short-term loans and discounting, particularly international acceptance. However, the Paris stock market grew rapidly under the Second Empire, mainly (like London) on the back of railway securities, a solid public debt and banking shares; and as the stock market grew, so did the banking system, including banks with large international networks and investment banks of a global reach. In Europe – particularly Austria, Spain and Italy – and in Latin America, French banks (particularly Crédit Mobilier and Rothschild) even outstripped English ones, although the latter dominated a much larger geographical area coterminous with the British Empire and with British commerce.

The Franco–Prussian war of 1870 and the subsequent rise of Berlin as a European centre weakened Paris and seemed to threaten even the pre-eminence of London. The development of Berlin's universal banks, on the model of Belgium's Société Générale and Paris's Crédit Mobilier, cast doubt on the superiority of the British model, particularly its high degree of specialization in financial activities. The involvement of the big German banks extended to most of the industries of Central Europe and Italy. Nevertheless the German financial market remained difficult of access and regional banks remained powerful, preventing Berlin from attaining the international prominence of London or Paris. Moreover, London was busy reinventing itself through a series of mergers that eventually produced the 'Big Five' (originally deposit takers but diversified by 1918) which were to dominate world banking between the wars: proof that the versatility of leading financial actors can swiftly make any facile typology obsolete.

After the First World War there was some reshuffling among leading financial centres. Germany was decimated by hyperinflation and Berlin lost its international dimension as the country became dependent on American dollar loans before espousing autarchy in the 1930s. Paris made huge losses on its overseas portfolio (particularly its Russian assets) and was sapped by inflation up to 1926; despite the attempts at collective organization, it never regained its prewar role. London retained a symbolic pre-eminence that was strengthened by Britain's return to the gold standard in 1925. This gave the Bank of England considerable weight in the monetary reorganization of Central Europe in the 1920s, but at the price of strained relations with Paris. London, however, no longer had the means to back up its policies: Britain could not now invest overseas on the same scale as in the 1890s. The new leader was New York, now the fulcrum of both worldwide capital exports and world financial dealing, with acceptance and stock-market transactions rivalling those of London, banks that to an extent lacked the international dimension but were expanding rapidly, and a stock market that became a global point of reference even if it kept its eyes mostly on the national economy. The world financial crisis of 1930–32 may have started in Europe, but it was intensified and extended worldwide by the banking crisis in the United States, which in turn stemmed partly from the German commitments of New York banks. The dominance of US capital in Latin America chained that region to the financial destiny of those same New York

banks, a chain that was to remain in place for many years. The pre-eminence of Wall Street made it a model for the development of financial systems throughout the world. The Glass-Steagall Act of 1933, intended to regulate and monitor – but also to restrain and partition – financial activity, was inspired by Jeffersonian thinking – isolationist, decentralizing, anti-finance – rather than on emergent Keynesian doctrines. It was imitated throughout the world in the 1930s and 1940s.

Hostility to financial markets and the way they clustered around a small number of major, transnationally minded centres had long antecedents. Towards the end of the 19th century a number of countries had taken steps to protect the financial autonomy of particular regions or localities: for example, the cooperative, mutual, and public banks movement in Germany, Italy, France and even Britain and the US. This trend was reinforced by a tendency towards state control during the First World War and the conflictive financial upheavals that followed (reparations, war debts, competitive monetary reorganization in the 1920s), but it did not succeed in overturning the notion that international capital markets were more efficient. The great crisis nonetheless fostered and legitimized such feelings of hostility, leading to a shrinking back within national borders and a collapse in the international importance of major financial centres.

War, financial crisis and inward-turning national economies may have weakened the great financial centres, but they tended to strengthen the smaller ones which were capable of finding their own niches. This applied in particular to Switzerland, which became a worldwide leader in the management of private wealth thanks to the two wars and the hosts of refugees they produced. But this activity was not so closely woven with the world economy as it had been earlier, when the bankers of Brussels or Geneva directly financed the trams and the electricity industry of many European countries. Apart from the discreet nudges administered by the Bank for International Settlements (though this was based in Basle, rather than Geneva or Zürich), Swiss financiers did not greatly contribute to the recovery of international finance. This happened – once again – in London, beginning in the 1950s.

The resurgence of London started with the rise of the Eurodollar market – the making of deposits, then loans, and finally stock issues in dollars, but in London, among financial dealers from many countries. London bankers would take dollar deposits from anyone, anywhere (from Soviet Russians to Arab oil sheikhs via just about every big Western exporter), and use them to lend to multinationals, or anyone else who wanted dollars, which were convertible into a wide range of other currencies once European convertibility had been restored in 1958. This market developed because Britain made a choice that was quite unprecedented for a country of its size: it ceased to insist on the autonomy of its national financial system. Even more than in the 19th century, London became the preferred rendezvous and business platform of all the big world banks, which used London to conduct innumerable operations that had nothing to do with Britain. This success was bolstered by the fact that other European countries continued to insist on exchange controls and foster financial chauvinism throughout the 1960s, and sometimes long after. It was further amplified when the London stock market opened up to increased competition after the Big Bang of 1986.

One by one, other leading countries followed London's lead, producing a massive liberalization of financial activity. New York remained pre-eminent, but continued to concentrate on its own national economy – although the nature of that economy implied global responsibilities, which were assumed mainly via the International Monetary Fund (IMF) and the World Bank. New York took a further step forward in the 1980s, but never became as 'international' as London. The great Continental centres, Paris and Frankfurt, were slow to liberalize both their stock markets and their banking systems (not until 1984 for Paris; the late 1990s for Berlin), and remained Europe-oriented. Meanwhile, for the first time, Asian centres attained worldwide prominence, starting with Tokyo in the late 1970s: its banks occupied all the top rankings in the 1980s, although in the 1990s its stock market and its banks embarked on a long and painful decline. Tokyo was followed by Singapore and, in particular, Hong Kong, which supplied the region with stock-market and business finance services until the emergence of Shanghai.

At the dawn of the 21st century, a number of factors seemed likely to reinforce the dominance of the biggest financial centres.

Stock markets turned themselves into public companies and embarked on an orgy of alliances and takeovers, while some of the biggest banks – most notably HSBC and Citigroup – aimed to become truly global. The ultimate outcome of this strategy remains to be seen; for the time being, banking consolidation, in both Europe and the US, continues to be mainly regional. Euronext, a merger between the stock markets of Paris, Brussels, Amsterdam and Lisbon, and subsequently with the New York Stock Exchange, has not yet succeeded in centralizing market activity in New York (or, for that matter, Paris); rather it remains an alliance of national stock markets with a degree of interoperability and some shared centralized systems (computerized listings and deliveries). Increased centralization may actually stimulate the formation of new, national stock markets, or strengthen smaller ones, by encouraging banks – and still more, stock markets – to adopt a cavalier attitude towards smaller businesses and offer them a poorer quality of service. Governments may also intervene in the belief that listing national companies on national (or, for the EU, European) stock markets represents a strategic advantage. Nonetheless, ever larger proportions of the world's savings are now being managed by funds located in London and New York that impose their rules on borrowers worldwide. Government equity funds (from Norway, Qatar, Bahrain, China, etc.), which were front-page news quite recently, will probably not make such a difference, because most of them are managed in the same centres and subject to the same news.

There is one process that is more important than the location of pension funds, banks or stock markets: the harmonization of international accounting standards currently being pursued by the leading British and American audit firms, and quietly imposed everywhere (e.g. in Europe by the European Commission itself). It will further strengthen the American and British financial centres, which already apply these standards and accept the financial theory behind them – which is not the case in countries such as Japan, Germany or France, where they are being enforced. The most notable instance is the adoption of valuation at market value instead of net book value. That these rules may be found uncongenial is shown by the fact that some companies have withdrawn their listings from the New York stock exchange just for that reason.

Explanations

What are the reasons behind this concentration of finance and financial actors? One possibility is that capital now has to be redistributed on a large scale: if some parts of the world have capital surpluses and others have not, a financial centre may prove a useful intermediary. Loans to emerging countries, which may prove highly profitable, are the classic example. However, while such loans were indeed massive, and centralized, in the 19th century, nowadays capital flows into emerging countries are not necessarily channelled through financial centres; they may be injected directly by multinationals or international organizations such as the World Bank, or through local stock exchanges (such as Shanghai or Kuala Lumpur). The role of financial centres is rather to offer a complex set of services to borrowers and savers over a wide area. In the 19th century the hierarchy of financial centres doubtless reflected the hierarchy of global economic geography – European centre, European periphery, and a wider non-European periphery, for the most part colonial. Nowadays it depends rather on the ability to offer competitive financial services to firms and investors in rich countries worldwide, and political domination is no longer the deciding factor.

The reasons behind the emergence or development of a financial centre are well known, but the reasons for the hierarchy of such centres are still disputed, and have probably changed over time. It is essential that the host country – still more the host city – should be at an advanced stage of economic development, more because this guarantees the availability of a highly qualified workforce than because it guarantees a steady flow of savings. Until 1914 – perhaps until 1960 – most financial centres were the capital cities of leading capital-exporting countries, but this is no longer true, at least in the US and Britain, where international, rather than national, savings are processed and reallocated. The importance of a skilled workforce, together with experience and reputation, makes financial centres strongly path-dependent. This applies in particular to London, which has kept its pre-eminence through all the vicissitudes of modern history.

It has been suggested that suitable legislation is a precondition for a flourishing financial centre, and it is possible that in the current, highly competitive environment, moderate capital taxation and pro-business legislation may indeed prove advantageous. Hong Kong is one example. Historically, a liberal attitude towards modern businesses and markets was certainly helpful, but such an attitude generally followed, rather than preceded, the emergence of such centres: this is clear from the chronology of liberalization as regards, for example, limited-liability companies or futures transactions. In this, Britain preceded other European countries by only a few years. On the other hand, surveillance by a regulator is also a sine qua non of confidence among operators. All in all, their preference would probably be for rigorous self-regulation, monitored by governments that can offer an effective legal system and head off deviations from the strait and narrow. This is what happens in London, where the stock market has always been essentially self-regulating, and the Bank of England and the other big banks have jointly guaranteed the stability of the banking system without substantial interference from the Treasury, even during interventionist periods such as the 1950s and 1970s. The United States had no central bank up to 1913 – a fact which, according to some commentators, has restrained the country's financial development by allowing financial crises to get thoroughly out of hand – but this did not prevent the emergence of New York as a financial centre, any more than it restricted development in Switzerland, which did not acquire a national bank until 1907. To sum up, if governments influence the relative standing of financial centres it is not so much by means of financial regulation as by direct intervention in the financing of the economy. It was such intervention that severely restricted the importance of Paris, and reduced that of London before the latter turned to international business in the 1950s. In particular, the development of financial systems attributing less importance to markets, focusing rather on national banks and the organized allocation of credit, did a good deal during the so-called *trente glorieuses* (the thirty years following the end of World War 2) to slow the internationalization of numerous economies and with it, the creation of large financial centres.

Until recently it appeared that no financial centre could succeed internationally unless the currency of its host country also played an international role (and vice versa). The florin, for example, had a pre-eminence in the 18th century far surpassing that of the Dutch economy; under the Second Empire the dominance of the franc led to the emergence of the Latin Monetary Union (1865) and plans for a universal currency; and in the heyday of the gold standard (from 1873) sterling, seconded by the franc, assumed a global importance that strengthened London as a financial centre. Similarly, the rise of the dollar went hand in hand with the rise of New York, or at least its rise to international importance after 1900, and even more so after 1920. However, the current position of London – or Hong Kong or, more recently, Shanghai – shows that a financial centre can flourish on the back of the leading global currency even if it has no control over the monetary policy which governs that currency. The same seems to be true of political dominance, which used to closely parallel monetary dominance. In the 19th century, the zone of influence of a financial centre would be more or less coterminous with the political and commercial ambit of its host country. Thus the primary recipients of capital exports and banking developments from London were the British Empire and other countries with European settlers; those from Paris went primarily to Continental Europe and the Mediterranean region. Nowadays political influence seems less important to the success of financial centres: the major ones are no longer necessarily the capital cities of big capital exporters (indeed, since the 1990s the US has been the world's biggest borrower), and private capital flows are no longer harnessed to political ends as they were before 1914, when they financed the national debts of Russia, Italy and the Ottoman Empire.

Consequences

Is the political and economic impact of financial centres positive or negative? Within individual countries they are often accused of steering economic policy in their preferred direction, to the detriment of the rest of the economy. Even before the First World War, London and Paris were suspected, and accused, of exporting capital that was needed by the national economy, and in the 1920s the London markets were blamed for sterling's return to prewar parity, which was damaging to industry – as Keynes argued. As early as the 1900s, the growing importance of Wall Street led to accusations that the big banks and insurance companies were creating monopolies or abusing their powers, and the eventual result was regulation; similar perceptions led to regulations during the New Deal, the 1950s and, more recently, the Sarbanes-Oxley Act (2002).

The real reason for such accusations is the concentration of power in big financial centres. Although there is no reason to believe that the finance industry is more likely than others to push its own interests in the centres of political power, it may do so more effectively, because this very concentration inevitably creates links between financiers and governments (who often borrow from them). Moreover, financial actors are mobile: any threat to their business, or their profits, may induce them to emigrate, as the Amsterdam bankers emigrated to London after the Napoleonic invasion, and some Paris brokers emigrated to Brussels in 1893 after a law was passed curbing their activities.

If there is a risk that financial centres may abuse their dominant position, there is also a risk that the centralization of finance, together with the expansion of leading centres, may prevent smooth, decentralized economic development by destroying local networks for the distribution of credit. To balance these drawbacks (which in any case are not proven), financial centres offer advantages to the host economy. In the first place, finance, like other service industries, generates revenue, which may make an important contribution to the balance of payments – as it does in Britain, America and Hong Kong. The concentration of the finance industry in a few major centres even suggests that the latter may profit from a monopoly position vis-à-vis other countries, which would explain why those other countries are so keen to develop financial centres of their own. Moreover, a concentration of high-quality financial services and support services may stimulate other industries in the host country.

At international level, financial centres help keep international capital markets working efficiently, but also maintain their hierarchy: they impose rules and regulations on borrowers and lenders from every country, and apply their own values in order to classify nations in terms of solvency and credibility. In the 19th century the big banks were already developing sophisticated methods of ranking government borrowers, and rating agencies such as Moody's started publishing their listings after the First World War. As we have seen, this hierarchy led to the definition of zones of influence, with countries in intermediate position – such as the Ottoman Empire or Mexico – becoming bones of contention between financiers from a number of different countries. Nowadays the hierarchy covers the whole spectrum of financial centres – which are all in major first-world countries, though this may shortly change with the rise of Bahrain and Shanghai – and excludes the rest of the world, particularly emerging economies whose rapid development calls for international finance and external resources. The same rules now tend to apply to all the financial communities in the leading centres as they vie with each other to produce innovative services. Most countries have to conform to the dominant values (or fashions) of the big financial centres if they want to tap the international financial market. From this point of view, financial centres contribute also to global inequality.

Pierre-Cyrille Hautcoeur

Bibliography

Cassis Y. 2006. *Capitals of capital: a history of international financial centres 1780–2005.* Cambridge: Cambridge University Press.

Coste P. 1932. *La lutte pour la suprématie financière: les grands marchés financiers.* Paris, London and New York, Paris: Payot.

Jones G. 1990. *Banks as multinationals.* London: Routledge.

Kindleberger C. P. 1974. *The formation of financial centers.* Princeton: Princeton University Press.

Michie H. 1992. *The City of London: continuity and change, 1850–1990.* Basingstoke: Macmillan (now Palgrave Macmillan).

Reed H. C. 1981. *The preeminence of international financial centers.* New York: Praeger.

Robert R. (ed.) 1994. *Offshore financial centres.* Aldershot: Ashgate.

Sassen S. 2001. *The global city: New York, London, Tokyo.* Princeton: Princeton University Press.

Related essays

conspiracy theories; cultural capitals; development and growth; electricity infrastructures; empires and imperialism; euromarkets; financial diplomacy; financial markets; global cities; Hong Kong and Shanghai Banking Corporation (HSBC); International Monetary Fund (IMF); investment; literary capitals; loans; Quesnay, Pierre; railways; services; Swiss banks; trade; war; World Bank

Financial diplomacy

Financial diplomacy means the partial or total integration of international financial relations into the conduct of foreign policy. This may be by direct exercise of the finance weapon, i.e., by granting a loan to a foreign state subject to certain conditions which may relate either to the trade of the beneficiary or more generally to its social and economic policy. Alternatively, the conditions may affect its foreign policy, including diplomacy and defence. They may even bear on internal matters such as modes and political orientations of governments. But financial diplomacy may also assume a more indirect form: a demand for conditioned access to the borrower's money market, including licences for foreign banks to operate in the borrower's territory; control of capital outflows including direct investment and the repatriation of profits from trade and industry; or compulsory technical assistance, with financial consultants appointed to supervise and guide not only the borrower's monetary policy, but its taxation and budget as well.

All these forms of financial diplomacy, which are often applied simultaneously, are aimed at enabling one sovereign state to impose financial constraints on the policies of another sovereign state in order to further the general aims of its foreign policy. Seen in that light, financial diplomacy raises the question of how much autonomy is possessed by actions and actors on the international economic scene vis-à-vis the policies of individual states. Are the dynamics of the international financial market entirely constrained by the workings of intergovernmental power politics? Or do they arise, intrinsically, from specific motives such as the drive for maximum profit, which may not coincide at all with so-called national interests? These questions have been central to the history of international financial relations since the discipline first emerged in the 1960s, and they are inseparable from the issue of imperialism. Currently they are stimulating fresh debate about the historical mechanics of globalization. It may be that financial diplomacy is not, as has often been suggested, an inevitable consequence of the political supremacy of the nation state in the field of international relations; rather, since the last third of the 19th century it has been the Trojan Horse that has introduced the practices, standards and values of the market onto the international scene.

The era of financial diplomacy can be said to have begun in the late 1860s, when European governments, as the 'world's bankers', set up international agencies to assume control of the finances of bankrupt peripheral states. Tunisia (1868), Egypt (1878), the Ottoman Empire (1881) and Greece (1898) were in turn subjected to 'international financial commissions' imposed to ensure payment of arrears on the national debt by sequestering the proceeds of indirect taxation. This meant that the debtor country's finances were managed by a permanent international authority backed by a substantial bureaucracy. These commissions were directly answerable to representatives of the country's foreign creditors, acting hand in glove with the governments concerned – chiefly those of Britain, France, Germany, Austria and Italy.

There can be no doubt that these pre-1914 international commissions were essentially imperialist. Indeed, the concept of imperialism, then just emerging from the pens of Hobson, Hilferding and Lenin, thrived mightily on the back of this new development in international relations. Examples of the mingling of finance and politics increased steadily between the late 19th century and the First World War. Loans to Russia in particular, but also to Japan, Turkey, Serbia, Greece and Argentina, mobilized the forces of financial diplomacy. Collaboration between governments and the banks of the world's leading financial centres (London, Paris, Berlin, New York) increased steadily, as is well attested by the archives of the Bank of England, Rothschild's or Morgan – and of Crédit Lyonnais, the Deutsche Bank, the Banque de l'Union Parisienne and the Ottoman Bank. The trend was fostered by the then current atmosphere of growing military rivalry and alliances among major powers. Financial diplomacy could also contribute powerfully to colonialism, as in the cases of Tunisia and Egypt. It could even substitute for colonialism, as witnessed by the US's 'dollar diplomacy' in Central America and Asia.

Thus the early 20th century can be seen as the golden age of financial diplomacy. But it was a complex mechanism, and the 'finance weapon' was difficult to deploy. At that time the power of a government rested almost entirely on its authorization of prospective foreign loans: the Treasury might agree to such a loan, or it might not. The authorization might be a statutory process, as in France or Germany, or an informal one, as in Britain or the US. Either way, the financiers retained considerable freedom of action. Though accusations of collusion between international bankers and government imperialists were frequent, such collusion was not the norm. Competition among bankers in the lender country was one reason. Another was the primacy of profit. The real engine of financial diplomacy was the international flow of capital. The reverse, however, is not true. It was the rapid worldwide growth of capital during this period, rather than imperial rivalry however intense, that made it the golden age of financial diplomacy.

Even before 1914 this growth of capital was marked by the appearance of financial actors, rules and practices that were genuinely transnational. International financial commissions appeared along with the forerunners of the present international monetary organizations. Their legal nature – part private, part public – was unprecedented. They served as nurseries for the first generation of international financial experts, the 'money doctors' as they were called after the French liberal economist Jean-Gustave Courcelle-Seneuil had spent ten years (1852–62) sorting out the finances of Chile. They also helped to develop principles and standards as part of a transnational doctrine: 'strong money and sound finance'. In the 1900s the very incarnation of this doctrine was the American money doctor Edwin W. Kemmerer, whose name was inseparable from dollar diplomacy until the early 1930s. Starting as monetary advisor to the American mission to the Philippines in 1903, Kemmerer went on to travel the world for thirty years, doctoring money anywhere from Latin America to southern Africa, from Poland to China and Turkey.

The First World War put an abrupt end to this growth of transnational capital and thereby profoundly changed the ways of financial diplomacy. The suspension of the gold standard led to all international capital flows being brought under government control. In practice, they were mostly controlled by national issuing banks. During the war years, it was through their accounts, or those of commercial banks subject to exchange controls, that all international settlements deriving from trade among allies, or with neutrals, had to pass. This turned them into leading actors in the game of international finance, whereas before 1914 they had intervened only occasionally and through market operators, under the banner of 'mutual assistance' among issuing banks. The war acted as a laboratory for the newborn idea of international monetary cooperation, which became the major form of financial diplomacy throughout the 20th century.

Government control of international financial relations remained the norm until the dismantling in the 1980s of exchange controls which – up to 1971 at least – had safeguarded the gold exchange standard on which the century's international monetary system had rested. The idea of using certain key currencies alongside gold was not actually new. Sterling had had that role before 1914. What was new was the competition among convertible currencies to assume the same role. The First World War had propelled international financial relations into the era of managed money. And as Keynes pointed out in The economic consequences of the peace, the inevitable result was that financial relations became politicized. The putting of reparations at the heart of the Treaty of Versailles was an expression of this new reality which, along with the problem of indebtedness among allies, weighed so heavily on international relations in the 1920s. The wave of monetary stabilizations in the 1920s provides a perfect illustration.

In Austria (1923), Germany (1924), Hungary (1925) and, even more, Poland (1927) and Romania (1929), attempts at monetary stabilization depended on the availability of international credit, which brought the banks – and first and foremost, the central banks – into what Jean-Baptiste Duroselle called the 'diplomatic machine'. Montagu Norman, governor of the Bank of England, Benjamin Strong, president of the Federal Reserve, and Émile Moreau, governor of the Banque de France, were very conscious of this status, as were Lamont of the Morgan Bank, Finaly of the Banque de Paris et des Pays Bas, and Monnet of Blair and Co. Also involved in this financial diplomacy was the finance committee of the League of Nations, which was very soon being denounced as a tool of 'financial imperialism' wielded by the Bank of England. Another consequence was the foundation, in 1930, of the Bank for International Settlements – although this was founded with the precise aim of turning the ever looming problem of reparations into a commercial transaction, thereby removing it from the sphere of intergovernmental politics.

The global financial crisis that started in 1931, followed by the Second World War, led to governments assuming total control of international capital flows. In such a context it is hard to speak in terms of financial diplomacy. Monetary transfers demanded by Nazi Germany as 'occupation indemnities', or loans granted on the lend-lease system by the United States, were not acts of diplomacy but acts of war.

After 1945, however, financial diplomacy reappeared in a different context: international monetary cooperation and intergovernmental financial institutions such as the IMF and the World Bank, the Organization for European Economic Cooperation (OEEC), the European Payment Union (EPU), and the monetary committee and EEC governors' committee. The Bretton Woods agreement led to a period of 'sterling-dollar diplomacy' which reflected the changed power relationship between Britain and the US at the end of the war. The development and implementation of the Marshall Plan were likewise part of the international outlook of the Cold War. The negotiation of international loans through the EPU and/or IMF to enable debtor nations to balance their budgets also depended on the exercise of financial constraint by the creditors, who subjected the loans to explicit or implicit economic policy conditions: witness West Germany in 1951, France in 1957–58 and Britain and Italy in the 1960s.

Financial diplomacy changed profoundly in the 1970s. The close of the era of decolonization brought a new factor into international relations: the mechanisms of aid and cooperation between 'North' and 'South'. Soviet intervention in Africa and Asia in the 1970s and 1980s was another factor. More recently, the Chinese presence in Black African countries such as Nigeria and Sudan, to the detriment of international organizations such as the World Bank, has been another token of the new reality. But in all these cases the crushing inequality between donor nations and debtor nations has loaded the dice. It is hard to speak of financial diplomacy in such situations. It is rather a sort of neocolonialism.

Another thing that has profoundly affected the practice of financial diplomacy is the changing nature of international financial markets. The privatization of international capital flows has quickly and effectively removed them from government – and central bank – control. The exponential growth of the eurodollar in the 1970, feeding chiefly on the wealth of oil-exporting countries, is a perfect illustration. This development has helped to transform the mechanisms of traditional financial diplomacy. Instead of direct government control we have control by the markets and by international organizations whose nature is complex and whose diplomatic efficiency remains unproven. This new state of affairs is well illustrated by the international financial pressure brought to bear on France, for example, in the difficult days of 1981–83, when she had to face both the draconian conditions laid down by the central bank of Saudi Arabia and 'routine' visits from the IMF.

Thus it can be seen that the financial constraints imposed in the 20th century in the name of international monetary cooperation – as they had been before 1914 in the name of imperialism – are more than just an extension of nation-state power-politics into the realm of financial relations. The transnational mechanisms at work in the area of financial diplomacy have undoubtedly contributed to the trend towards convergence – in practices, standards and doctrines – of national financial systems. They also give a long view – from 1860 to 1914 and from the 1920s to the present – of a dynamic of capital expansion which is now reaching its triumphant culmination as it becomes truly and completely 'global'.

Olivier Feiertag

Bibliography

Bussière E. and Feiertag O. (eds) 1999. 'Banques centrales et convergences monétaires en Europe (1920–1971)', Histoire, Économie et Société, 18, 4, 715–36.

Flandreau M. (ed.) 2003. Money doctors: the experience of international financial advising 1850–2000. London and New York: Routledge.

Rosenberg E. 1999. Financial missionaries to the world: the politics and culture of dollar diplomacy, 1900–1930. Cambridge, MA: Harvard University Press.

Related essays

debt crises; debt crises (developing countries); decolonization; democracy; developmental assistance; empires and imperialism; financial markets; international loans; International Monetary Fund (IMF); investment; League of Nations Economic and Financial Organization; nation and state; public policy; Quesnay, Pierre; taxation; technical assistance; war; World Bank; world orders

Quesnay, Pierre 1895–1937

The French Pierre Quesnay can be seen as the perfect incarnation of the transnational civil servant type who appeared on the international relations scene between the two world wars. He followed the career of an international financial expert, in tune with the emergence of international institutions that characterized the 20th century. He was at the heart of the transnational financial dynamics of the period and their interaction with the national – or nationalist – attitudes and the new international situation that emerged from the First World War.

Quesnay studied under the economist Charles Rist, who recognised his brilliance, and in 1919 served in Budapest and Vienna, first as France's assistant representative on the Allied Commission for Austria, and from 1920 on the Reparations Commission. From 1922 to 1925 he was one of the principal architects of the financial recovery of Austria steered by the Finance Committee of the League of Nations. He then joined the general commissariat of the League of Nations in Vienna, and forged lasting friendships with many members of the new class of international monetary experts, including Harry Siepmann, Per Jacobsson and Jean Monnet. From 1925 to 1926 he was in Geneva as a member of the League of Nations Economic and Financial Section, then directed by Arthur Salter, and with such members of the finance committee as Henry Strakosch and Otto Niemeyer. At this time he also made the acquaintance of Montagu Norman, the governor of the Bank of England.

In June 1926 he was recalled to Paris, where the new governor of the Banque de France, Émile Moreau, appointed him as the Bank's head of economic studies. In collaboration with Rist as deputy governor, Quesnay designed and negotiated most of the international aspects of the stabilization of the franc (1926–28), liaising with Benjamin Strong of the Federal Reserve Bank of New York and monitoring the difficult relationship with the Bank of England. He took part in the international drive to stabilize the currencies of Poland and, in particular, Romania. He was also asked to consider the persistent question of the final payment of reparations. He acted as secretary to the committee of experts meeting in Paris in 1929 whose deliberations led to the Young Plan and the founding of the Bank for International Settlements. He exercised considerable influence at the conferences at The Hague, Rome and Baden-Baden which established the Bank's charter.

Quesnay, with the support of Moreau and Monnet (and despite opposition from Schacht) was appointed managing director of the Bank for International Settlements and presided at its formal establishment in Basel in 1930. Assisted by a team of experts, notably Jacobsson, he immediately assumed overall responsibility for the Bank's principal functions: as trustee for intergovernmental payments under the reparations system, and as a 'club of central banks' and centre for international monetary cooperation. As the architect of the attempt to stabilize the Spanish peseta in 1930 he worked closely with the Banque de France. When the world plunged into financial crisis in 1931, Quesnay established the Bank for International Settlements, seconded by most central banks, as an international lender of last resort. But his initiative was swamped by the extent of the crisis and frustrated by the rise of monetary nationalism. Until his death – he died in an accident in 1937 – Quesnay struggled unsuccessfully against the global economic depression and strove to restore 'monetary internationalism' by stabilizing exchange rates as well as the legal framework for international settlements.

Despite this failure, Quesnay's career highlights the importance of the transnational mechanisms at work in international financial relations between the two world wars: not just experts and international financial institutions, but also national central banks whose uneasy collaboration was essential to the operation of the gold exchange standard. Quesnay and others first asked the question of how transnational financial settlements ought to be made; they did not find a lasting

solution, but neither – from the end of World War 1 to the present – has anybody else.

Olivier Feiertag

Bibliography

Feiertag O. 'Pierre Quesnay et les réseaux de l'internationalisme monétaire en Europe (1919–1937)', in Dumoulin M. (ed.) 2004. *Réseaux économiques et construction européenne au XXe siècle*, Brussels: PIE-Peter Lang, 331–49.

Related essays

debt crises; economics; executives and professionals; financial diplomacy; financial markets; Hammarskjöld family; League of Nations Economic and Financial Organization; loans; Pax Americana; reparations; Shiber, Saba George

Financial markets

Financial markets include both market actors whose activities consist in issuing and placing of new securities and thus, in particular, to financing new investments – the primary market – and organized exchanges on which existing securities (principally bonds and shares) are traded – the secondary markets which ensure that investments retain long-term liquidity. These two parts of the market interact since the secondary market determines and publicly advertises prices, which then become a yardstick for fixing terms and conditions for issues on the primary market, including unlisted shares and debts in general.

Financial market analysts attach great importance to secondary markets. A (secondary) financial market is said to be integrated if the price of any particular securities is the same in all parts of that market, and particularly if two identical securities, both of which are subject to competition and arbitrage (buying in one place and selling in another), are traded at the same price whatever the location and whoever the traders. In such a free competitive market, two identical investment plans ought to be granted the same financial conditions (on the primary market), generating an optimal correspondence between savings and investments (i.e., only the best investment projects are financed). To gauge the integration of a financial market, a historian will look first at published prices and information about issuers. Such information is provided chiefly by stock exchanges.

The history of financial markets and the trade in negotiable securities is chiefly based on a study of the financial press and stock-market and firms' archives. The existence of highly integrated financial markets covering the whole of Western Europe can be traced back to the 18th century, especially as regards the British and French national debts, a substantial share of which was held by Dutch capitalists.

In the 19th century an ever larger number of cities created organized stock markets, and the resulting deluge of published prices can be used to track the integration of financial markets on a range of geographical scales. Increasing numbers of transactions and improved communications (from telegraph to telephone, stock markets being among the first to adopt both) promoted market integration by permitting direct arbitrage on an ever growing number of securities listed on more than one market, and indirect arbitrage on thousands of others. Public debts and bonds issued by the big railway companies accounted for the majority of multilisted securities throughout most of the century, though their numbers were swelled by big mining companies, banks and certain industrial firms. Paradoxically, this integration was international rather than national, insofar as numbers of securities listed on regional markets remained very limited, and their issuers were too small to attract the big trading banks, who found meatier fare on the international loan markets. From 1818, when France started raising big loans for the liberation of her territory, truly international financial operations grew at an unprecedented rate. Russia, the Ottoman Empire, Italy and Argentina could issue securities simultaneously in London, Paris and Berlin – and Brussels or Amsterdam – depending on the investment, and also the diplomatic, climate. From 1850 onwards the development of the railways generated enormous international capital flows over and above the ever increasing volumes of government borrowings. By the end of the century, yearly foreign issues accounted for several percentage points of the GDP of the leading European nations; in Britain's case this rose to 10 per cent in the decade leading up to the First World War. In 1913 Britain's stock of foreign stocks was worth more than her entire GDP

(she held some 40 per cent of international long-term assets); and almost the same could be said of France, Belgium, Switzerland and the Netherlands, while the capitalization of foreign securities listed in Paris and London was even higher (up to twice GDP).

The primary market for these international securities was originally sustained by private bankers with international connections, e.g. the Rothschilds in Paris, London, Vienna and Naples; the Barings in England; and Hope in Amsterdam. Gradually their place was usurped by deposit banks who could place investments within their own networks, such as France's Crédit Lyonnais or Société Générale. They organized massive increases in capital exports from England, France and Belgium at the end of the century, leading to unprecedented levels of international integration. They were accused of favouring government issues, or foreign issues in general, to the detriment of investment in national industries. More systematically, the primary markets were accused of dividing markets into a centre (in Western Europe) and a periphery: people on the periphery were denied access to capital unless they accepted the conditions laid down by the centre, and the result was far from the ideal allocation that integrated markets were supposed to produce. 'Peripheral' countries had to offer higher interest rates than 'safe' issuers (starting with the British crown!); the difference (the 'risk premium') corresponded to the default risk that subscribers had to accept. The risk assessment was based not only on the objective characteristics of the borrower (their indebtedness and various measures of their repayment capacity), but also on the opinions and prejudices of the lender: for example, British investors tended to look with disfavour on any country which had never been a British colony. The guarantees demanded from borrowers – securities to be issued in the currency of a central country, adherence to the gold standard, openness to trade, strict budget controls, etc. – might help them to establish sound economic policies, but in difficult circumstances they might equally become harassing constraints that could actually encourage default, as happened in the 1880s in particular. Moreover, such guarantees tended to debar the poorest parts of the world – in Asia or Africa – from access to capital. In fact, this first wave of financial globalization was not as idyllic, nor as effective, as is sometimes claimed. It imposed its hierarchy on the entire world and reinforced existing zones of influence.

Between the two world wars a number of factors contributed to dividing financial markets along national boundaries, and also to calling into question their capacity to evaluate and provide finance at national level. This was due partly to wartime restrictions on capital movements, and partly to the fact that leading nations adopted diverging tax and monetary policies and put obstacles to international capital flows, making arbitrage more difficult and sometimes destabilizing. The result was a general loss of international integration among financial markets, although the limits of exchange controls and a continued open access to the American market still allowed some substantial flows (e.g. American loans to Germany in the 1920s). This came to an end with the European exchange-rate crisis of 1931 and the coming of the Great Depression. At the same time, the role of secondary (stock) markets in national finances came under suspicion: whereas such markets had worked too well in the late 1920s and had generated much speculation (especially in New York), they were now accused of provoking the crisis. Nowadays the consensus is that the markets only 'contributed' to the crisis through runs on the banks and the collapse of loan guarantees, but at the time a good many governments – and the public opinion – believed that stricter regulation of financial markets was a necessity. Such regulation strengthened the role of banks and public authorities in financial decision making at the expense of the markets, reinforcing a trend that had begun with the rise of the great banks in the 19th century. Banks and public authorities allocated credit in accordance with administrative procedures that took no account of the markets and probably helped reduce their integration. The Second World War saw increased public intervention in all the belligerent nations, further accentuating the trend. When the war ended, the financial markets were definitely playing second fiddle. Big firms were covering most of their investments out of retained profits, and some of them, especially in Europe and Latin America, were nationalized; the banks (some of them also under government influence) provided the lion's share of other requirements. The demand for securities from private savers also fell as benefits were dealt out by social security systems. And at international level, the flow of money was largely controlled by governments: reconstruction aid was followed by development aid and then direct investment by multinationals. Keynesian economic theory was opposed to the free circulation of capital, since this would weaken the ability of governments to pursue the policies of their choice.

Gradually the situation changed. Governments – with Britain's in the van – came round to the idea of separating their internal monetary policies from their control of the monetary and financial system, and from the late 1950s the eurodollar market was left to its own devices. Thus deregulated, that market dealt first in dollar bank loans, and then in bonds. It included banks from many countries which were thus enabled to conduct operations which would have been impossible nationally, particularly American banks tied hand and foot by Regulation Q (put in place by the 1933 Glass-Steagall Act which was repealed in 1980). In the 1960s/1970s the eurodollar market was international, intensely competitive and lightly supervised, managing transactions so massive that they destabilized the fixed-exchange-rate system agreed at Bretton Woods. This led to the rapid propagation of a global change: instead of the triple alliance of fixed exchange rates, independent monetary policies and restrictions on the international flow of capital, the new combination consisted of flexible exchange rates, independent policies and free capital flows. This did not apply, however, to the European Union, which opted for progressive monetary integration culminating in 1999. Before that date it already imposed on its members restrictions on the free circulation of capital (initially), and (after 1985) on the de facto independence of their monetary policies (except for Germany, which provided the anchor to the whole system).

Under this new international regime the organized financial markets regained the preponderance they had enjoyed in the 19th century. They set the price of assets and the cost of debt, imposing worldwide constraints on issuers. The actions of big institutional investors – pension funds, life insurance companies, and more recently, private equity funds – affect all current and potential investors, and they have also taken control of numerous companies: in France, for example, it is thought that foreign institutional investors own about half the shares in the big companies that constitute the CAC 40. Even governments (with the probable exception of the US) are scarcely able to influence these constraints. They leave room for substantial monetary flows, particularly towards the American Treasury bonds market, which has enough liquidity and enough depth to attract capital from all over the world, especially from fast-growing economies such as those of China and other parts of Asia. Indeed, financial integration has reached such a pitch that a country's investments can be durably dissociated from its savings, the difference being borrowed or loaned on the international market.

The organized markets, presumed to be neutral locations for such operations, become part of the problem: the way they are organized is a subject of debate insofar as they can affect the successful conclusion of operations, efficient arbitrage and the occurrence of crises. As in the 19th century, organizations which were originally very different (centralized like the Paris stock market, decentralized like the Nasdaq) tend to converge. Technical innovations (e.g. listing systems, delivery systems, complex futures and options transactions) have spread rapidly, as have regulations – particularly in Europe, under pressure from the European Commission. Unlike in the 19th century, however, stock markets are now companies. They may compete with one another, or they may merge or cooperate: thus Euronext was created in 2000 by merging the stock markets of Paris, Amsterdam and Brussels, and was later extended to include Lisbon and the London LIFFE; in 2007 Euronext was taken over by the New York Stock Exchange. The hierarchy of stock markets reflects the distribution of financial power worldwide: London is the international market par excellence, New York the financial capital of the world's only remaining superpower; both have benefited from liberal policies since 1980. Tokyo, which reached the world top rank around 1990, declined for a long decade after that, owing to massive indebtedness among companies that had lost value after their growth forecasts had been revised downwards; in Europe, competition hotted up between Euronext and Berlin. Behind these mighty markets, in the 1990s and particularly after the fall of the Berlin Wall, stock markets proliferated even in small countries, where they symbolized progress and modernity: Kuala Lumpur or even Ulan Bator proposed securities worldwide. The fluctuations on these emerging markets bear witness to surges of enthusiasm alternating with fits of distrust of financial organizations or loss of confidence in economic growth forecasts.

These changes have taken place in an atmosphere of confidence in free markets approaching that which prevailed during the Belle Époque. Although, as in those earlier years, markets are still regularly hit by financial crises, to which emerging markets are particularly vulnerable (Mexico in 1994; Southeast Asia in 1997), such crises do not seem to weaken the underlying framework. Nevertheless, a good many economists have voiced grave doubts about the preponderance of financial markets in modern economies, pointing out that their price-making efficiency is not strong enough to prevent numerous speculative deviations from the 'fundamentals', which in turn means that the markets cannot be trusted to channel capital effectively into the best investments at either national or international level. Nor does specialization necessarily lead to stability. Moreover, markets are not neutral; rather they tend to establish rigid hierarchies, especially as regards access to information. Small businesses, and indeed small countries, are subject to sterner constraints (first and foremost, on their access to credit) and are more vulnerable to crises. This is leading to demands both for international regulation of financial markets and for the construction of financial systems in which other organizations will be used to counterbalance the weight of the markets.

Pierre-Cyrille Hautcoeur

Bibliography

Carnevali F. 2005. *Europe's advantage: banks and small firms in Britain, France, Germany, and Italy since 1918.* Oxford: Oxford University Press.

Cassis Y., Feldman G. D. and Olsson U. (eds) 1995. *The evolution of financial institutions and markets in 20th century Europe.* Aldershot: Scolar.

Eichengreen B. 1996. *Globalizing capital: A history of the international monetary system.* Princeton: Princeton University Press.

Flandreau M. and Zumer F. 2004. *The making of global finance 1880–1913.* Paris: OECD.

Hautcoeur P.-C. and Gallais-Hamonno G. (eds) 2007. *Le marché financier français au 19e siècle.* Paris: Publications de la Sorbonne.

Kindleberger C. P. 1984. *A financial history of Western Europe*. London: George Allen & Unwin.

Obstfeld M. and Taylor A. 2004. *Global capital markets: integration, crisis and growth*. Cambridge: Cambridge University Press.

Related essays

cities; conspiracy theories; convergence and divergence; corporations; debt crises; debt crises (developing countries); euromarkets; financial centres; financial diplomacy; information economy; investment; loans; Pax Americana; railways; telephone and telegraphy; trade; urbanization; world orders

Euromarkets

Euromarkets (occasionally called 'xenomarkets') are markets on which banks deal in a currency other than their own. For example, eurodollars are dollars held by banks outside the United States. The prefix 'euro' refers to the fact that such deposits first appeared in Europe in around 1955. The origins of the eurodollar are traceable partly to the Cold War, when the USSR (in particular) desperately needed international liquidity – dollars – but did not want to hold them in the United States. The rise of the dollar as an international currency encouraged companies worldwide to hold dollar cash reserves, and banks to ask for dollars on deposit. Some countries decided that such deposits did not need to be so closely regulated as deposits in the national currency because they did not affect the internal money supply. This produced a very liberal loan market, particularly in comparison with the prevailing heavy postwar regulation. On top of that, America's Regulation Q (put in place by the 1933 Glass-Steagall Act) set a ceiling on the interest rates payable on bank deposits and so savers looked for more attractive rates elsewhere. Similarly, eurobonds benefited from an equalization tax imposed in 1963 on interest payable on foreign issues placed in the US.

London played a key role in the development of euromarkets. Eurodollar loans, still negligible in 1958, rose to US$25 billion in 1968 and US$130 billion in 1973. At that time London accounted for almost 80 per cent of the market, which was still largely controlled by London branches of foreign banks – mostly American, but also some French, Japanese and German. By 1975 there were 243 such subsidiaries in London.

While the main incentive for the development of euromarkets was the avoidance of national regulations, their development also helped to weaken those same regulations by providing both borrowers and lenders with alternatives to nationally regulated solutions. The logical outcome of euromarkets was the liberalization of capital movements. They undoubtedly represented one nail in the coffin of the Bretton Woods fixed-exchange-rate scheme, which assumed that central banks were capable of controlling exchange rates; this they could only do if they could control capital flows, at least in the short term.

At present, the term 'euromarket' is less often employed, since lending in a currency other than that of the borrower or lender has now become commonplace.

Pierre-Cyrille Hautcoeur

Bibliography

Bakker A. F. 1996. *The liberalization of capital movements in Europe: the Monetary Committee and financial integration, 1958–1994*. Dordrecht: Kluwer.

Kerr, I. M. (ed.) 1984. *A history of the Eurobond market: the first 21 years*. London: Euromoney.

Schenk C. 1998. 'The origins of the Eurodollar Market in London, 1955–1963', *Explorations in Economic History*, 35, 2, 221–38.

Related essays

dollar; financial centres; financial markets; loans; Swiss banks

Fisheries

Although an established global industry the development and importance of fisheries is overlooked by many historians, disregarded as a parochial coastal trade. This is disappointing, since fisheries epitomise many aspects of man's relationship with the maritime world and the environment: the congruence between occupation and community; the projection of power and national identity; the construction and appropriation of scientific knowledge; and the development of international institutions to ameliorate conflict and engender development. Most importantly, fisheries offer a history of our exploitation of a global commons that has conditioned national jurisdiction over marine resources. The current status of world fisheries demands transnational perspectives: if they are to provide meaningful insights, so must historical accounts.

The growth of production

The figure illustrates the growth of fisheries production since the mid 19th century, the data from 1950 collected by the United Nations Food and Agriculture Organisation (FAO) being more reliable.

Modernization began in the mid 19th century, but was most fully realised after World War 2. Production of about 2 million tonnes in 1850 had grown nearly fivefold by 1913, doubling again by 1938. Landings from capture fisheries grew by some 3.3 per cent annually between 1950 and 2000: sustained, if not sustainable, growth. This era also saw the rise of aquaculture. Aquaculture's postwar 'blue revolution' brought a radical and technologically sophisticated departure from traditional fish cultivation, lowering prices, improving quality, and establishing new international markets. Aquaculture

production grew by some 9 per cent per annum from 1950, and remains the world's fastest growing food sector.

Fisheries development was uneven. Japan, the USSR, Atlantic Europe, and North America dominated world fisheries by the late 1930s. Fisheries in Latin America, Oceania, Africa, and most Asian states were modest in scale and influence. The table shows that the Northern dominance of fisheries was broken after 1950.

African fisheries, negligible before World War 2, exceeded those of North America by the late 20th century, aided by the latter's relative decline. Europe's contribution diminished even though production increased threefold. Asia emerged as the world's foremost fishing region, responsible for some two-thirds of production and some 85 per cent of fisheries employment. In Latin America, Chilean and Peruvian industrial fisheries accounted for the majority of expansion. Growth, however, was achieved at a price: in *The state of world fisheries and aquaculture 2000*, FAO estimated that 75 per cent of resources were fully exploited, overexploited, depleted or recovering in 1999.

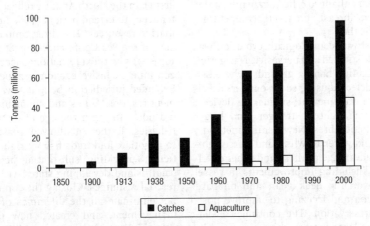

Figure 1   World fish production 1850–2000

Table 1   Distribution of world fisheries production 1950–2000 (% of total)

Region	1950	1960	1970	1980	1990	2000
Africa	6.2	6.8	6.3	5.6	5.1	5.0
Asia	36.6	43.8	39.7	51.0	49.3	61.7
Europe	33.0	23.8	20.5	19.8	21.2	13.1
Latin America & Caribbean	3.4	13.9	25.9	14.8	16.1	14.7
North America	20.3	11.3	7.4	8.2	7.7	4.6
Oceania	0.4	0.4	0.4	0.7	0.8	0.9

Fishing effort

Growth was underpinned by continued expansion in fishing effort, in terms of capital employed and its sophistication. Britain epitomized the first industrialization of fishing. Improved transport established a demand for fresh fish in growing urban markets. While initially satisfied by sailing trawlers, intensive exploitation of nearer North Sea grounds demanded longer, more distant voyages. The solution was the steam trawler, the first of which was launched in 1881. Independent of wind and tide, these could fish distant waters more intensively using larger gears. Inshore herring fisheries were also revolutionized by steamboats. These vessels epitomized an emerging technological regime, subsequently augmented by the development of suitable internal combustion engines, and was quickly replicated in other countries, extending as far as Japan (1908) and China (1912). Through the interwar period European trawler fleets extended their operations north to Iceland and the Barents Sea, and also south to Spain and Portugal, the Mediterranean, Adriatic, and Black Sea. Advances in vessel design were complemented by improved trawl designs that further enhanced efficiency, while radios kept fishers abreast of markets, competitors, and the weather.

The postwar technological revolution was more sophisticated and pervasive. Navigation aids helped find fishing grounds, where fish could be detected using echo sounders developed from wartime anti-submarine devices. Nets became lighter, stronger, and larger with synthetic fibres. New fishing methods, such as mid-water trawling and purse seining took advantage of these and other developments, including improvements in vessel design, hydraulic deck gear, and onboard refrigeration and freezing to improve postharvest preservation. The continued evolution of the large factory ship, pioneered by Japan and the USSR in the 1930s, extended the global range of the world's fishing nations. Many developing economies, unencumbered by antiquated fleets, were able to adopt these advances wholesale. Synthetic nets, motors, and fibreglass and ferrocement hulls offered artisanal fishers similar scope to revolutionise production.

Overfishing and the Law of the Sea

T. H. Huxley's address to the 1883 London Fisheries Exhibition declared the main commercial fisheries inexhaustible and their regulation pointless. Sadly, this was not true then or since, as the 'tragedy of the commons' unfolded through unfettered competition for shared resources. The current status of world fisheries resources demonstrates that ideal natural resource management policies are easier to design than implement, although the exercise is no longer considered futile.

The contraction of the commons drew inspiration from President Truman's 1945 proclamation, which declared the United States' entitlement to exclusive jurisdiction over all resources on, within, or beneath its continental shelf, including the right to establish fisheries conservation zones. Chile and Peru quickly established 200-mile maritime zones in 1947, in part to protect fisheries and whaling. Ecuador followed in 1951. In Northern Europe, where fisheries limits had been more intensely contested, Iceland extended its fishery limit from three to four miles in 1950, and again to 12 miles in 1958, provoking the first 'cod war' with Britain. Further extensions to 50 miles in 1972 and 200 miles in 1975 prompted further conflicts. Britain's failure to defend mare liberum in the North Atlantic reflected a wider tendency to extend national jurisdiction over marine resources. The three United Nations Law of the Sea Conferences (1958, 1960, and 1973–77) saw the international acceptance of 200-mile exclusive economic zones (EEZs). Extended jurisdiction bought new management responsibilities and opportunities, but did not extinguish the age of distant water fisheries. Rather, it allowed coastal states to negotiate and trade fishing rights, in particular providing substantial benefits for small island developing states with few terrestrial resources. Closing the commons did not eliminate all the dilemmas of fisheries management, and created new problems, particularly with respect to high seas and transboundary resources. It has, though, seen greater control of world fisheries resources flow to less developed economies where their economic and social significance is greatest.

The monitoring and management of commercial fisheries engendered the formation of a network of regional fisheries organizations providing scientific advice (such as the International Council for the Exploration of the Sea, established 1902), international coordination (such as the Asia-Pacific Fishery Commission, established 1948), and the design and implementation of management strategies (such as the Inter-American Tropical Tuna Commission, established 1950). Coordinated by the FAO, the role of regional fisheries bodies has been tempered by continued problems of the incongruent interests of members, occasionally with spectacular and catastrophic consequences.

Postwar advances in fisheries science and management were not sufficient to prevent overfishing and, on occasion, the collapse of major fisheries. North Sea herring was historically the world's most important and contested fishery. Intensive fishing caused the Southern North Sea fishery to collapse in the mid 1950s, intensifying pressure on stocks elsewhere in the ecosystem. Although various factors underpinned the eventual closure of North Sea herring fisheries in 1977, the North East Atlantic Fisheries Commission's failure to convince member states to adhere to scientific advice to limit fishing ensured that the tragedy of the commons relentlessly unfolded. Fishing recommenced in 1983 once stocks had recovered. Not all fisheries were similarly fortunate. Overfishing, combined with overoptimistic stock assessments, poor stock recruitment, and discarding of undersized fish, resulted in the moratorium imposed on Atlantic Canada's cod fisheries in 1992. The collapse ultimately cost thousands of jobs that, like the cod, have not returned.

While fisheries management was once an obscure technical endeavour, it became more visible and politicized as environmental non-government organizations (NGOs) made overfishing a key campaigning issue. While US policies addressed dolphin by-catches during tuna harvesting as early as 1972, it did not become an international cause célèbre until NGOs brought it to international attention. The ability of NGOs to establish the cause of sustainable fisheries in the public domain was facilitated by the absence of strong countervailing fishing industry organizations, in strong contrast to the role of agriculture's multinationals. The most interesting development has been the joint initiative by Unilever and the World Wildlife Fund in 1997 to establish the Marine Stewardship Council, an independent body certifying the sustainability of fisheries and fish commodities. It remains unclear whether marine fisheries can attract and retain similar levels of public sympathy to whales and other marine mammals.

International exchange

International trade in fisheries resources has honourable historical precedents. In the modern period, trade in Northwest and Northeast Atlantic cod and herring, and trade in canned fish (especially Pacific salmon), were exceptional. Postwar increases in fisheries trade, which exceeded the growth of output, are attributable to a combination of technological and market factors, as well as to the decline in many European and North American fisheries. The humble fish finger's ubiquity reflects the triumph of fishing and processing technology, as well as the marketing strength of multinational food processors and retailers, who now exert a dominant influence over the fisheries supply chain.

Two developments – fishmeal production and aquaculture – exemplify the postwar transformation of fisheries trade, in which less developed economies exported fisheries commodities to the North. Redundant Californian fishmeal equipment was illegally installed in Peru in 1953, owing to the guano trade's control over fisheries resources. Production and exports grew so rapidly Peru had saturated the world fishmeal market by 1960, a market driven by industrial poultry and pig farming. Peru, together with Chile, remains the world's largest producer of fishmeal and fish oil, representing a huge flow of resources from the southern oceans to markets in Europe, Asia, and North America. Vietnam's development as an exporter of farmed fisheries commodities represents a second key stream in modern fisheries development. Shrimp is the most important aquaculture product and traded fisheries commodity. Vietnamese production was about 200 tonnes in 1976; by 2000 it was some 100,000 tonnes, and Vietnam was the fifth largest shrimp exporter.

However, fisheries trade has been a two-edged sword: while providing a livelihood for fishers in developing countries, it has raised significant issues about the sustainability of fisheries development, food security, and the livelihoods of producers. Conflicts over tariffs and other barriers to trade, and control of the fish food chain, are likely to become more acute given the limits to further growth in fisheries production.

Towards a transnational history of fisheries

The scope for a transnational history of fisheries remains considerable in an arena dominated by national perspectives. There are many challenges in overcoming the short-comings in our understanding of fisheries development, particularly with respect to developing economies, international institutions, and the role of multinational corporations. The most pressing assignment may be to overcome the view of fisheries and those for whom they constitute a livelihood as marginal and insulated from modernity, a view at variance with the development of globally integrated fisheries markets. If world fisheries are in crisis, then there is a strong case for a detailed understanding of the underlying historical dynamics of fisheries development to appreciate how we arrived at this sorry state.

Chris Reid

Bibliography

Butcher J. G. 2004. *The closing of the frontier: a history of the marine fisheries of Southeast Asia c. 1850–2000.* Singapore: ISEAS.

Holm P., Starkey D. J. and Smith T. D. (eds) 2001. *The exploited seas: new directions for marine environmental history.* St. John's: International Maritime Economic History Association.

Ibarra A. A., Reid C. and Thorpe A. 2000. 'The political economy of marine fisheries development in Peru, Chile and Mexico', *Journal of Latin American Studies,* 32, 2, 503–27.

Sahrhage D. and Lundbeck J. 1992. *A history of fishing.* Berlin: Springer.

United Nations Food And Agriculature Organization 2000. *The state of world fisheries and aquaculture 2000.* Rome: FAO.

Related essays

conservation and preservation; drink; environmentalism; food; food safety standards; forests; freshwater management; international non-governmental organizations (INGOs); oceans; trade; United Nations system

Food

Food, which underlies all human institutions, permeates every aspect of material and cultural life. Agriculture and livestock rearing, together with hunting, fishing and foraging, are the necessary interface between humans and the rest of nature (locally known as eco-systems or bioregions). Tastes, ingredients, and techniques of preservation, storage and cooking are foundations of cultures, and familiar foods are one of the most intimate ways that individuals identify with large collectivities. Food therefore offers a lens to observe social organization and cultures at every scale, from domestic to global.

The key to transnational history of food is the lengthening across political borders of food supply chains, which follow the stages of transformation from field to mouth. In contrast to international trade, which measures categories of commodities crossing borders, supply chains create very different perceptions. Thus, trade figures do not reveal the criss-crossing of borders by ingredients of a composite food, such as cheese imported to make a frozen pizza shipped to another country (or back to the original country). The history of transnational food sectors has also involved movements of people (as farmers, food workers, and cultural cooks and eaters) and capital (investing in land, transportation, and commercial infrastructures). The mutual relations connecting lands in far-flung parts of the world are revealed by tracing supply chains wherever they lead.

Two of the first transnational supply chains began in the second half of the 19th century. Wheat seeds were adapted to climates and soils in regions where the plant was introduced for the first time in the Americas, Australia and southern Africa. Then it was shipped to new industrial mills and sent to shops or bakeries in England and other parts of Europe. Cattle were herded across vast open plains in North and South America, then fattened in feedlots near industrial slaughterhouses (pioneered in Chicago), and transported in refrigerated railcars and ships to butchers across the Atlantic. A century later, after several reconfigurations, wheat and beef chains have become elaborated into networks including specific varieties, and many other crops and animal products, to become ingredients for a proliferating array of complex edible commodities in supermarkets and fast-food outlets.

Widening the geographical scope of food systems has always depended on stable rule. Ancient Rome organized far-flung shipments of wheat across the Mediterranean, and complex rice markets developed in ancient China. Imperial stability always faltered when agriculture itself reached the limits of sustainability, for instance with salination of soils through irrigation in ancient Mesopotamia. Relocalization of food systems was part of revival after collapsed empires, for instance in feudal Europe. Whatever the extent or nature of rule, until less than 200 years ago governments took security of domestic food supplies as a matter of utmost importance, and political power usually rested on control over land and agricultural production. Only when Britain triumphed over colonial rivals in the early years of the 19th century, enforcing rules of trade on a world scale, was it possible for governments to rely on imports of staple foods.

Two changes anticipated the rise of a world wheat market in the second half of the 19th century. First, colonial imports (sugar, tobacco, opium, and tea, as well as the older spice trades) had changed diets in Europe. Second, a significant wheat trade had previously emerged in the 16th century between Eastern and Western Europe. Although both were disrupted by the Napoleonic Wars – leading to significant changes in European agriculture, such as sugar beets to replace colonial cane sugar imports – they anticipated key features of the global agrifood system that emerged in the late 19th century. New relations of production (social and ecological) were brought into existence by specialized export production, and diets changed in response to transnational food markets.

Pillars of the transnational food economy

Emergence of a transoceanic wheat economy between 1870 and 1914 marked a profound departure whose implications continue to unfold. Impetus for the first transnational food market came from Britain in the 1840s. As demand for commercial foods exploded among the burgeoning populations of English towns and cities, urban populations changed their ideas about what to eat as they lost touch with traditional cuisines based on the produce of local farms and gardens, and on the 'coarse grains' (oats, rye, barley) eaten by the lower classes. Organized working-class movements began to demand higher wages to support a better standard of living, according to the cultural ideas of the time. They aspired to eat the food of the rich – wheat and beef. At the same time, governments urged the poor to eat potatoes, an unfamiliar food from the Andean region of South America. This succeeded only in Ireland, where potatoes became associated with a colonized population. Then in the years after 1845 a potato blight led starving Irish to flee to England (as well as abroad) – while wheat continued to be shipped to England – where they became an underclass accepting conditions so far resisted by English workers.

Trade and migration at once reduced pressures on the food supply of industrializing England, and created two of the four pillars to support a transnational food system. In 1846, under pressure from an emerging class of capitalists who wanted to keep wages low by lowering food prices, the British Parliament abolished protective grain tariffs (called Corn Laws), thus removing the main blockage to imports of wheat. This opened the borders of the world's largest market and made it possible within one generation for massive specialized wheat and cattle regions to emerge, which transformed indigenous farming, hunting and herding regions into 'neo-European' landscapes in the Americas and elsewhere. The transoceanic supply chains of wheat and beef were part of the dominance of Europe over the world economy; regional markets in rice or maize (the grains of Asian and American early civilizations) were not comparable in scale or depth.

Emigration complemented the opening of borders to imports. Many individuals were forced to emigrate by poverty or deportation for petty crimes; others were encouraged by elites fearing social unrest; still others sought a better life in the colonies. Some of them became commercial family farmers in colonies of 'new settlement'. Although immigrants from many European countries were to join them in 'homesteading' lands offered by governments in Canada, the United States, Australia, New Zealand, southern Africa, and Argentina, these European migrant farmers constituted an imperial diaspora defining wheat and beef as the primary food staples in the emerging transnational food system.

The two remaining pillars of a transnational food system were land and finance. The United States, Canada, Australia, New Zealand, and Argentina (and contiguous regions) were created as export wheat and beef regions by emerging states which seized lands by force from indigenous peoples, surveyed them into grids, offered blocks of land of vast dimensions by European standards and recruited settlers from England and other parts of Europe. These same expanding states borrowed on emerging capital markets, in which investment in railways anticipated profits from carrying settlers from Europe and wheat and beef in the opposite direction. These settlers were unlike peasants in Europe because they depended entirely on specialized farming of commercial crops. Their vulnerabilities in the ecological and social conditions of neo-Europes guaranteed that they would supply emerging markets and secure newly settled territories for expanding national states.

Transnational trajectories

The world wheat market that emerged after 1870 laid the foundation for an industrial food system which eventually came to include most of the world's crops and livestock, and to displace most traditional farming systems Family farms in neo-Europes displaced capitalist farms in England by exploiting their own family labour and 'mining' the fertility of virgin lands. Paradoxically, family farms promoted industrialization of flour mills, by supplying the variety needed by large operations with steel rollers (invented in the 1880s), which provided white flour to urban markets.

Industrial mills joined canning factories (inspired by earlier military purchases), while the new sciences of chemistry and genetics changed farming and food processing. Chilled railcars and ships, and industrial meat packing and giant grain silos were invented in the 1880s. Thus the transformation of food into edible commodities that survive storage and shipping began with wheat and beef. Yet extension of industrial processes to other crops, and displacement of local farming systems in Continental Europe and across the world, would await new technologies that arose half a century later, and within the framework of highly national agricultural policies after two world wars and collapse of the first world food market.

Industrialization of a transnational agrifood sector has been interpreted through two related tendencies. 'Appropriation' is the process by which profit-seeking enterprises reduce those elements of farming subject to nature. Thus, machines replace horses and oxen for drawing ploughs, and of course humans (also natural beings) for labour. Machinery in turn requires that fields be adapted to single crops and that the plants themselves be bred to specifications of machines. Such changes account for much of the measured increase in productivity of field crops. Thus wheat yields in the 1930s in the United States and Canada increased partly because when horses were no longer needed, pasture and hay could be converted to commercial crops such as wheat. The price of tractors and later machines, however, was dependent on fossil fuel. This was compounded by loss of manure from horses, which was partly replaced by industrial nitrogen, also made from fossil fuels. Single crops were more vulnerable to pests, especially with increasing genetic uniformity, leading to use of pesticides also derived from fossil fuels. Since that beginning, industrialization has grown in mutual if erratic relationship with single-crop fields of increasing scale. Later appropriation of this kind displaced mixed agroecosystems and village farming cultures; for instance, the 'Green Revolution' of 1970s India replaced not only animals but also more complex mixed-cropping systems with specialized, mechanized production of rice.

After World War 2, government research, which had supplemented selection and breeding done by farmers, began to replace it in laboratories, especially but not only in the US. A key step in this process was the widespread introduction of hybrid maize in the 1950s – which has been called the 'second agricultural revolution'– and which provided commercial feedstuffs for full industrialization of livestock production. Government advice to farmers (called 'extension') promoted hybrid seeds, which must be bought each year rather than saved to replant next season. Farmers thus became dependent on industrial machines, chemicals, and even seeds, even as they retained formal independence. Even formal independence was threatened when genetic technologies (along with information technologies) became the leading edge of technological change in the 1990s. Agriculture became an important arena for genetic research companies, linking the sector to pharmaceuticals. Corporations had created direct contracts with farmers, incorporating instructions with packages of seeds and chemicals, thus paving the way for a drastic reduction of government advice to farmers, and increasing their integration with industrial corporations.

The second tendency is 'substitution'. This is the process by which food industries reduce their dependence on the variability of natural ingredients. They create denatured categories, such as starches, sweeteners and fats, some derived from plants but others created without them in laboratories. The search for durability led to new processes (high heat) and substances (preservatives) which created foods impossible to create in domestic kitchens. Industrial changes began with meat packing in Chicago (along with standard grades and bulk handling of wheat), which dissolved individual cows, bags of wheat and identities of farmers into 'rivers of wheat' and 'tides of flesh'. Industrial systems created standard products, identified by 'grades' suitable for transnational market demands.

Margarine offers a microcosm of industrial food as a whole. Marketed as a healthy alternative to butter, margarine was a novel substance created through industrial techniques designed for substitutable fats. However intense was breeding of dairy cattle, butter could not compete with the efficiencies achieved when manufacturers could buy any available fat in the world. At first margarine was produced in the US to use cheap industrial by products of meat packing (lard) and textiles (cottonseed oil). As the industry grew, in the 1920s it introduced Asian soybeans into North America to ensure a steady oil supply. Soybean oil had to compete with other globally sourced oils, such as tropical palm oil. The new soy sector created its own byproduct, soybean meal, which became in the 1950s one of the two raw materials (along with hybrid maize) of a new feedstuffs industry, which in turn supplied the Concentrated Animal Feeding Operations (CAFOs) of the 1980s. CAFOs have become one of the most dynamic – and contested – transnational food sectors of the late 20th and early 21st centuries.

Industrial food production, which has gone through several phases of transnational growth, changed the nature of cooking and eating. In the 19th century substitution began with manufacture of home or handicraft foods, such as biscuits. First sold in barrels, they attracted rats which were one of many new safety problems arising with industrial foods. Industrial biscuits were sponsored by the British government to supply the navy, but then provided the basis for private industries, such as Warburton's and Kellogg's, which dominated national markets for a century. Pasteurization of milk was an early instance of government requirements that led to industrial dairies, taking advantage of the possibilities for large-scale operations opened by growing urban markets

and local rail networks. Canning, another new technology made possible by advances in chemistry, created paradoxical outcomes; while Kraft and other industrial giants offered mass-produced commodities, home canning was also made possible by mass production of vacuum bottles, offering households new possibilities for self-provisioning. Although home gardening and preservation became even more important when world markets collapsed in the two world wars and 1930s world depression, the overall trajectory towards industrial cuisine resumed in the 1950s, this time within an intensely national framework. Industrial food became transnational again in the 1980s, with deepening and widening of supply chains to all products and all parts of the world. As supermarkets and fast-food chains grew in size, geographical reach and power, they streamlined supply chains across the globe. Using electronic technologies, corporate supply chains began to monitor increasingly dense webs of subcontractors for every sort of food product, from shrimp aquaculture to 'ethnic' spice mixes.

While refrigerated railcars and ships had allowed chilled meat to cross the Atlantic in the 1880s, only in the mid 20th century did freezing technologies reached more deeply into commercial and daily life. Frozen foods, which started with simple crops and meats, soon included complete meals. Both grew in tandem with freezers in stores and homes. As technological investments came to favour increasing scale, supermarkets gained advantages despite relative inconvenience of distance and self-service. Daily life after 1950 became reorganized around appliances and private automobiles. 'TV dinners' could be prepared quickly in electric (later microwave) ovens and eaten while entertained by another appliance. As food became more durable, that is, less subject to weather in its availability or to decay in storage and transport, a modern homogeneous cuisine arose, based on complex industrial meals. Beginning in the 1960s, fast-food franchises selling hot meals further standardized industrial cuisines, and in the 1990s supermarkets regained the initiative at the expense of manufacturing companies by offering 'own brand' ingredients and prepared meals. By the mid 1990s, fast-food chains were introducing standard meals worldwide, and supermarkets were beginning to displace street markets and to contract with selected farmers to supply fresh products to specified standards under intense controls.

Although industrial cuisine undoubtedly solved long-standing problems of inadequate supply, its nutritional risks came into policy focus late in the 20th century. Traditional cuisines had survived for millennia by achieving some measure of sustainability with regard to human health and agroecosystems. They consisted of a starchy staple (grain or root), protein (often beans and lentils) and the wide variety of flavour- and vitamin-giving plants typical of specific cuisines – such as the 'three sisters' of maize, beans and squash indigenous to the Americas, complementary fish and rice paddy farming in Asia, and early polycultures of wheat, chickpeas, olives, and wine in the Mediterranean and Aegean. Industrial foods broke the links and changed nutrition. Industrial foods offer a vast array of composite foods according to what marketing specialists determine that consumers desire. Some evidence exists that without cultural guides to taste, individuals fall back on biological desire for sweetness, fats, and salt, predispositions which were useful to foragers in deciding what was good to eat; thus, industrial cuisines offer what focus groups reveal decultured consumers as liking: sugars, fats, and salt. The desire for white bread and meat of English workers in 1870 has transmuted into a desire for 'junk food' throughout the world. As industrial food corporations targeted growing urban consumer markets in the so-called developing world in the 1970s and 80s, obese populations there as well as in rich countries came to equal those affected by undernutrition. In 2003, the World Health Organization declared this industrially inflected 'nutrition transition' to be a global epidemic.

Food regimes: cycles of transnational reorganization

A linear account misses two major interruptions and restructurings since 1870. Each transition included major government controls over food, from agriculture to final consumption. Food regime is the name for each in a sequence of stable, transnational complexes, which include regional specialization, dominant crops and livestock, class/production relations, patterns of plenty and want, and cuisines. The two food regimes of the past century and a half corresponded to accepted world leadership by Britain and the US, respectively over the periods 1870–1914

and 1947–73. The transitions between food regimes and hegemonic governance were equally prolonged. The contours of a third food regime remain unclear, but seem likely to reflect not only explicit attempts at intergovernmental regulation of agriculture and food safety by the World Trade Organization, but even more private regulation of supply lines by transnational supermarkets and other agrifood firms.

The food regime of 1870–1914 affected the conduct and outcomes of both world wars in 1918 and 1945. Several contradictory factors underpinned the dominant story of specialized commodity regions and homogenized food cultures. Settler agriculture led to class and racialized hierarchies. Settler farming throughout the British Empire, including a former colony, the United States, can be understood as part of an imperial diaspora. Although many Eastern and Southern Europeans entered into migrant settler schemes after 1870, most adapted to the language and cultures of empire. Even major exporting nations which were never part of the British Empire, such as Argentina, came to have elite cultural attachments to Britain. Once World War 1 was under way, international agreements against civilian blockades were jettisoned, and the imperial supplies organized through British hegemony shifted the advantage decisively against Germany. As a result, Germany secured its land-based food empire in Eastern Europe as part of its strategy in the first stages of World War 2. While crucial to Great Power wars, imperial diets remained restricted to the European settler states; other colonies of all the powers were expected to feed themselves. While colonial farming systems and cuisines incorporated plants and animals from distant regions of the world, such as Asian bananas and African coffee in South America, and American chilis and maize in Asia and Africa, colonial food systems remained local.

Between the wars, global economic crisis began with world wheat markets. Trade collapsed in 1925, anticipating the general crisis which began in 1929 (the Great Depression). Until World War 2, governments took a major role in rationing food and intervened directly in agricultural markets. In settler countries, the crisis profoundly affected the huge classes of specialized, commercial family farmers dependent on exporting their crops, and farmers mobilized politically. In the United States, which was to become the new hegemonic power, farmers were one of three groups allied in the 1930s New Deal. US farm programmes instituted an unprecedented form of subsidy based on government guarantees of a price above a notional market price. This created massive 'surpluses' of wheat and other commodities, which the US government acquired, and which required import controls and disposal outside of 'normal' markets. US commitment to this farm policy overrode postwar plans for intergovernmental regulation of transnational agrifood relations (the proposal for a World Food Board, defeated in 1947), and rendered powerless the new Food and Agriculture Organization of the United Nations.

Distribution of 'surplus food' became key to transnational food relations after 1945 and created a national framework for the deepening of industrialization. Non-market food distribution was accomplished domestically through the first (and enduring) US welfare programme of Food Stamps and internationally through Food Aid, which transferred massive quantities of wheat, soya, and other crops through negotiated arrangements in soft currencies. First conceived for support of the Allies in World War 2 and for postwar Marshall Aid, this 'food aid' to industrializing countries of Africa, Asia, and Latin America became key to a US-centred food regime. On one side it extended wheat and beef (and then the whole array of industrial) cuisines to new areas, from Japan to Colombia to Nigeria. Within two decades, food import dependence was widespread among formerly self-sufficient countries. The declared 'World Food Crisis' of 1973–74 was precipitated by the sudden end of surpluses (for a variety of reasons, including Soviet purchases after decades of isolation) and tripling of prices. Governments borrowed heavily to pay for expensive commercial food imports, bills which were compounded by soaring energy costs.

Transnational restructuring resumed dramatically in the 1980s. Livestock had paved the way. Beneath the apparently national organization of meat and dairy markets in the 1950s and 60s, a transnationally integrated sector emerged through industrial feedstuffs and chemicals. At first focused on North America, Europe and Japan, after 1980 this extended to indebted governments in the so-called developing world. Pressure to refinance debts led one government after another to abandon national food distribution programmes and farm policies in favour of promoting food exports. Land and labour shifted from domestic food to fresh fruits and vegetables, feed and meat, aquaculture, and even cut flowers, to serve a transnational consuming elite in global cities. This elite, after food safety scandals and fears about new technologies, from hormones in beef to genetic engineering, offered a growing market for foods with guarantees of quality in relation to health, ecology and sometimes social justice and animal welfare. In the 1990s, a new system of controls under rubrics such as 'traceability' were introduced by intergovernmental agencies and some governments. However, deadlock over safety and quality standards between exporting countries and the European Union has shifted these controls in practice to private corporations, especially supermarkets, which increasingly regulate complex relations with consumers, manufacturers, shippers, and farmers and other participants in supply chains.

The deepening and widening of supply chains threatens to evict from the land the last peasantries on earth, also threatening loss of genetic diversity of traditional food crops (landraces) and linking food to emerging issues of climate change and fossil energy depletion. As some of the displaced formed new diasporas, they increased availability of traditional cuisines in global cities. Like 'organic', cultural cuisines came to be commodified as 'ethnic' commodities in supermarkets and fast-food franchises. Yet countermovements arose in response, which were also transnational. Via Campesina, an organization of small farmers from many countries formed in 1992, advocates 'food sovereignty' – a form of transnational connection based on diversity. In 2001 the Slow Food Foundation for Biodiversity was formed with the goal of supporting and helping to connect farmers and artisans making foods typical of their regions. The two movements, plus the European Union's policy of paying farmers for environmental services (called 'multifunctionality'), could converge. Instead of elite refusal of industrial ('fast') foods in favour of expensive artisanal foods, these three initiatives offer renewed income and status to farmers and small processors as well as renewed attachment of eaters to their agricultural habitats. In settler countries, where new diasporas are changing the cultural mix, it is possible to discern the outlines of a creative transnational food system based on diversity of tastes, cooks, and gardeners, adapting crops and culinary techniques from many regions, just as those of Europe were adapted in the 19th century. Myriad innovations connecting farmers to cooks and discerning (but not necessarily rich) eaters are part of a transnational movement of 'locavores', which, like organic and cultural cuisines, have influenced supermarkets to find local suppliers even as organic and other quality commodities become transnationally organized. The play between two types of transnational food system continues.

Harriet Friedmann

Bibliography
Arraghi F. 1995. 'Global de-peasantization, 1945–90', *Sociological Quarterly*, 36, 2, 337–68.
Cohen R. 1997. *Global diasporas: an introduction*. Seattle: University of Washington Press.
Counihan C. 1984. 'Bread As world: food habits and social relations in modernizing Sardinia', *Anthropological Quarterly*, 57, 2, 47–59.
Cronon W. 1991. *Nature's metropolis: Chicago and the Great West*. New York: Norton.
Friedmann H. 'From colonialism to green capitalism: social movements and the emergence of food regimes', in Buttel F. H. and McMichael P. D. (eds) 2005. *New directions in the sociology of international development*, Amsterdam: Elsevier, 227–64.
Goodman D., Sorj B. and Wilkinson J. 1987. *From farming to biotechnology: a theory of agro-industrial development*. Oxford: Basil Blackwell.
Goody J. 1982. *Cooking, cuisine and class: a study in comparative sociology*. Cambridge: Cambridge University Press.
Popkin B. M. 2002. 'The shift in stages of the nutritional transition in the developing world differs from past experiences!', *Public Health Nutrition*, 5, 1A, 205–14.

Related essays
acclimatization; advertising; agriculture; animal rights; assembly line; biopatents; capitalism; car culture; commodity trading; consumer cooperation; consumer society; corporations; cuisines; development and growth; diasporas; diet and nutrition; drink; empire and migration; empires and imperialism; fast food; financial markets; food safety standards; General Agreement on Tariffs and Trade (GATT) / World Trade Organization (WTO); intergovernmental organizations; genetically modified organisms (GMOs); Green Revolution; human mobility; labour standards; marketing; Marshall Plan; Monsanto; Pax Americana; pesticides, herbicides, insecticides; salt; seeds; spatial regimes; trade; United Nations system; urbanization; war; world orders

Food safety standards

Food safety standards address how farmers, manufacturers, distributors, retailers, and consumers should produce, process, label, transport, handle, and prepare food so that it is safe to eat. From technical prescriptions issued by international organizations and national governments, to norms of practice adopted by businesses and individuals, food safety standards affect global health as well as international trade. During the last 150 years, food safety standards have both resolved and fuelled transnational problems.

Historically, governments have led the way in the formulation of food safety standards. Legislative bodies in nation states engage in food safety policy making to set forth what ought to be done to reduce the risk of foodborne illness. For example, a century ago the United States (US) Congress adopted the Federal Meat Inspection Act (1906); this policy, although not the first in the US, legislatively established food safety standards for domestic meat companies as well as foreign firms seeking to export meat products to the US. Through the authority granted by similar legal enactments, governments and regulatory agencies craft specific regulations and directives. For example, in 1989 the supranational European Union issued a regulatory directive regarding 'use-by' dates for highly perishable prepackaged foods.

Non-government actors have affected the international food trade throughout history. During the mid 19th and early 20th centuries, technological advancements (e.g., refrigeration) and age-old preservation practices (e.g., the salting of food) became de facto standards that helped ensure the safety of chilled and frozen food shipped over long distances (e.g., from South America to Europe). Today, private-industry food safety standards, enforced through supply-chain audits, facilitate the global movement of food.

Food safety standards address biological, chemical, and physical hazards. Biological hazards include – but are not limited to – bacteria, viruses, and parasites. While virtually all hazards may appear in all countries, the risks associated with them may be viewed differently across borders. These differences can affect international relations. Cultural differences often come into play in transnational disputes over food safety. For example, during the late 19th century, global trade quarrels arose regarding trichinosis (a human disease caused by consuming undercooked, parasite-contaminated pork). Culturally accepted risk management standards (i.e., the thorough cooking of pork) in Great Britain paved the way for relieving trade concerns; British consumers were content to eat cooked pork. However, elsewhere – in Continental Europe – consumers' preference for raw pork contributed to trade tensions. More recently, philosophical differences over genetically modified foods have affected agricultural trade relations between, for example, North America and Europe.

Food safety standards are typically adopted to protect public health, but international trade officials recognise that such standards can sometimes be disguised barriers to trade. In light of this problem, national governments have signed the World Trade Organization Agreement on the Application of Sanitary and Phytosanitary Measures (1995, the SPS Agreement). This agreement recognises the sovereign right of nation states to protect health but also provides a framework for ensuring that food safety standards do not pose arbitrary, discriminatory, or scientifically unjustifiable trade restrictions. National governments decide the levels to which they seek to protect health from disease threats; these are known as their Appropriate Levels of Protection. Under the agreement, Appropriate Levels of Protection and the regulations adopted to achieve them must be consistently applied, non-discriminatory, and not more trade-restrictive than necessary. With a view to promoting transnational harmonization in the food trade, the SPS Agreement also acknowledges three scientific bodies responsible for developing food, animal, and plant health standards for international trade. Of the three, the Codex Alimentarius Commission develops international food safety standards for human health.

The predecessor of the modern-day Codex Alimentarius – the Codex Alimentarius Austriacus – was developed during the late 19th century in the Austro-Hungarian Empire; it was a collection of food descriptions and standards for a wide spectrum of foods and food products. True to this heritage, today's Codex Alimentarius Commission (created in 1963) seeks to develop food standards and guidelines for dual purposes – to protect the health of consumers and to facilitate international trade. Delegates from national governments participate in Codex committee work, thereby helping draft food safety standards and guidelines for sundry areas of the world food system – from fresh fruits and vegetables, to foods derived from biotechnology, to food labelling, to infant formulas, to name just a few. Increasingly, the Codex Alimentarius Commission recognizes the value of input provided by international non-governmental organizations, which may apply for non-voting 'observer status'. The Codex Alimentarius Commission invites advice and assistance from non-governmental entities, many of which offer unique technical competence on food standards or represent specific aspects of public opinion. The SPS Agreement, Article 3 of which specifically mentions the Codex Alimentarius Commission, has raised the profile and importance of Codex committee work.

In the context of international trade, food safety standards are applied to products coming from nation states defined by geopolitical boundaries. However, and especially in large exporting countries such as Brazil and Canada, governments may identify smaller, subnational regions or zones. Today, leaders in food safety thinking increasingly advocate focusing on regions and particular commodity supply chains – not just nation states – when applying food safety standards. This allows for a transnational approach to the agricultural and food trade by focusing on regional and supply-chain realities across borders, rather than merely the political boundaries that separate nation states.

Over the last 150 years, governments have adopted standards to address many food safety problems: food adulteration, misleading food labels, false therapeutic claims, wartime food safety concerns, standards of identity and quality, and the scientific discovery of new hazards, to name a few. Today, international food safety standards are based on formal risk assessments and rely on such risk management tools as Hazard Analysis and Critical Control Point (HACCP) systems. First developed in the 1960s, HACCP is a preventive approach to food safety that, within the food safety regulatory community, has enjoyed worldwide appeal. By 1993, the European Union, the Codex Alimentarius Commission, and the US National Advisory Committee on Microbiological Criteria for Foods had adopted similar HACCP principles. However, the precise implementation of these principles has since differed across regulatory regimes. In the US, HACCP has been mandated for certain segments of the food system (e.g., juice, seafood, and meat and poultry industries). However, even in industries for which HACCP is not mandatory, companies frequently implement HACCP systems out of a motivation to improve food safety and meet customer demands. International standard-setting organizations such as the Codex Alimentarius Commission have not always provided specific implementation details. In 2003, the Commission updated its general guidelines for applying HACCP, emphasizing that the application of HACCP may vary among food operations.

Despite the absence of surveillance data to accurately estimate the worldwide burden of foodborne illness, the World Health Organization emphasises that cases of foodborne disease occur daily in all countries from the most to the least developed. In selected developed countries, an estimated one in four people annually contract food poisoning; more specifically in the US, it is estimated that as many as 5,000 deaths annually are attributable to foodborne illness. Food safety standards will continue to evolve as new technologies arise, new foods are developed, and new hazards are recognized.

Ana M. Douthit
Justin J. Kastner
Abbey L. Nutsch

Bibliography

Griffith C. J. 2006. 'Food safety: where from and where to?', *British Food Journal*, 108, 1, 6–15.

Caswell J. A. and Hooker N. H. 1996. 'HACCP as an international trade standard', *American Journal of Agricultural Economics*, 78, 3, 775–9.

Related essays

agriculture; animal diseases; car safety standards; corporations; diet and nutrition; food; General Agreement on Tariffs and Trade (GATT) / World Trade Organization (WTO); genetically modified organisms (GMOs); information technology (IT) standardization; international non-governmental organizations (INGOs); technical standards; trade

Forced migrations

Forced migrations, while historically conditioned, have been a recurring and perhaps constant phenomenon in human history. The earliest chronicles convey tales of refugees from natural disaster, expelled communities, resettled communities, and the enslaved. The Hebrew Bible conveys tales of the great flood of Noah's time, of the enslavement and resettlement of the Hebrews by the Egyptian and Babylonian states. Passages of the Shih Ji of Han China tell of Yellow River floods and their devastation, and of the expulsion of defeated parties from early Chinese kingdoms.

The term 'forced migration', while commonly invoked in academic discussion of slavery and refugees, has yet to achieve a clear, technical definition. In this entry, a broad framework is proposed to encompass most of the historical phenomena that arguably qualify as both migratory and forced. The framework takes the form of a typology in three stages: expulsion, voyaging, and resettlement. At the first and most central stage, forced migration is the expulsion of people from their homeland either by natural forces or by human forces. The natural phenomena include flood, famine, earthquake and epidemic; the human forces include the actions of families, communities, ethnic groups, and states. In addition, expulsion depends on interactions of natural and human forces, as when those displaced by famine encounter robbery and enslavement.

The second and third stages of forced migration consist of the movement of expelled persons through unfamiliar regions and their settlement in a region of destination. For both of these stages, the question is whether the forced migrants are able to regain the initiative: whether they travel as free migrants or under coercion in their journey from home, and whether they are free or coerced in settling. Thus refugees from natural disasters and persons expelled by families or states have commonly been able to travel and settle on their own initiative. But for slaves and for subject ethnic groups, it was often the case that they were transported under guard or under lock and key, and that they were settled in places and under conditions determined by state or private authorities.

Forced migration is generally accompanied by high mortality at all three stages, but especially at the initial stage of expulsion. The high mortality came from natural causes (floods, earthquakes, epidemics), from social causes (massacres and warfare), and also from the human and natural hazards of travel. An extreme case is that of genocidal killing in the homeland and flight by those who can get away.

The main patterns of forced migration have been enslavement, natural disasters, expulsion of groups from localities, and forced resettlement by imperial powers. Of these, enslavement has been most consistently documented. One should distinguish, however, between *forced migration* (the seizure and transportation of captives) and *forced labour* (the exploitation of those held in slavery). The two processes, while inextricably linked, are quite different.

Slavery, emancipation, nationhood, and genocide, 1850–1945

Up until 1850, the principal instance of forced migration had been the pairing of enslavement and slavery – of forced migration and forced labour. Africans especially were sent to the Americas, to other Old World destinations, and held within Africa. From 1850 forced migration both declined and expanded. The anti-slave-trade movement grew in the Atlantic and spread steadily to other regions. Yet during the 19th century the forced migration of slaves expanded in parts of the Americas (Brazil and Cuba), in many parts of Africa, and in lands bordering the Mediterranean to the Indian Ocean. Slave trade was almost fully interrupted at the end of the century, but the abolition of forced migration did not end forced labour. Despite the abolition of slave trade in the US and British territories after 1808, slavery continued until 1838 in British territories, 1865 in the US, and until 1888 in Brazil. In Africa, European conquerors at the end of the 19th century systematically abolished slave trade but not corvée labour, and they generally declined to emancipate slaves, allowing forced labour to continue for several decades.

The balance of forced and voluntary migration changed sharply in about 1850. The beginning of safe and dependable steamship travel encouraged the dramatic expansion of voluntary and contract migration, especially from the 1840s, for millions who left the densely populated areas of Europe, South Asia, and East Asia to travel, predominantly, to the Americas and Southeast Asia. Ironically but not accidentally, this great expansion in voluntary movement across frontiers coincided with the development of stronger national states, firmer national boundaries, and the expansion of empires governed by the great powers.

Nineteenth-century emancipation brought the granting of rights of citizenship to slaves and, in Europe, to serfs (in 1848 for Austria and Prussia; in 1861 for Russia), and to Jews and Romani previously restricted by law. Yet these moves toward emancipation opened the door to another sort of forced migration. An ideology of racial categorization and racial hierarchy arose, partly in response to innovative biological thinking of the era. In its social function, this ideology provided a reason for marginalizing those who were just gaining rights of full participation in society. This reasoning of racial hierarchy gave new justification for forced resettlements that had already been taking place – the expulsion of Amerindians in the US and of Algerians under French rule from their homes, the resettlement of Jews under Russian rule in the Pale, and displacement of Kurds by various powers. Forced and voluntary migration mixed with each other, with floods and famines, and with imperial expansion in what Mike Davis has called 'Victorian Holocausts'.

Colonial occupation of Africa, 1890–1910, generated flight by conquered African populations. Perhaps most extreme was the Herero War of 1904–05 in German Southwest Africa, where the German military pursued a genocidal response to a rebellion, and drove most surviving Herero north into Angola. The Ottoman Empire responded to Armenian nationalism during World War I with a policy of forced relocation from eastern Armenia to Mesopotamia, resulting in a far larger number of mass killings and large-scale flight. Nineteenth-century Russian policies, including Jewish displacement and Siberian exile of dissident individuals and groups, had their sequel in Soviet-era forced migration of Kurdish and Chechen ethnic groups as well as the exile of Baltic and Ukrainian individuals considered anti-Soviet.

Anti-black racism and anti-Semitism appeared to be entering a slow decline in the 1920s, until the rise of Nazi Germany brought ethnic and racial discrimination to an unprecedented level of restriction, expulsion, and then full-scale genocide. Forced migration and massacre reached a global peak in almost every theatre of World War 2 but concentrated in Eastern Europe. Postwar realization of the scale of this oppression brought near-universal denunciation of such practices, but did not bring to an end either their causes or consequences. Research continues into the balance of state action and vigilante assault in the killings and expulsions of World War 2.

Forced migration since 1945

In the aftermath of the horror of the Holocaust and the other mass killings of World War 2, the United Nations formed and adopted both a declaration of human rights and a convention opposing genocide in 1948, and created the United Nations High Commission for Refugees in 1950. But the hope that forced migration could be ended by mutual agreement proved illusory.

The great wave of decolonization from 1946 into the 1980s led to formation of new sovereignties and sometimes new borders. The 1947 flight and expulsion across the hastily defined boundary between India and Pakistan killed many thousands and displaced millions, and each stage of decolonization brought more conflicts and refugees. Since this process took place in the atmosphere of the Cold War confrontation of the US and the Soviet Union, the United Nations underwent political struggles over who could be defined as a refugee. The United States, where many refugees wished to settle, developed increasingly elaborate and restrictive distinctions between economic and political migrants as devices to limit immigration.

Natural disasters, though they had never been absent as a cause for forced migration, became especially prominent in the late 20th century. A series of great famines in Africa beginning in 1967, powerful earthquakes in Guatemala, Iran, and elsewhere, and the Indian Ocean tsunami of 2004 are only the most obvious examples. The effect of the hurricane-induced 2005 flooding of New Orleans was outstanding in that, because it was in the US, the waves of disruption brought by the forced migration of the city's inhabitants were unusually well documented. The transnational dimension of the latter disaster – the dispersal of the city's thousands of Mexican immigrants, many of them undocumented – confirmed that the policing of national borders had become a factor in the response to natural calamity.

The recurring tendencies to resolve national conflicts by identifying certain groups as pure citizens of the nation and others as impure threats to the nation led to a mixture of expulsion and genocidal killing. Such waves of killing in Cambodia (1973), Rwanda (1994), and Bosnia (1995) confirmed that genocide might recur despite the horrors it brought.

Slavery, finally, reappeared in the public eye. While enslavement was everywhere illegal, acts of enslavement took place wherever moral scruples were lacking and profits were to be made. Slavery lost its importance in agricultural production, but it continued in domestic service and it expanded in sexual slavery, as young males and especially females were transported and exploited to meet the demands of an affluent clientele.

Forced migration thus continues as a factor in human society, not only as a result of natural disasters that drive people from their homes, but because groups of people decide, for a shifting range of reasons, to expel neighbors or to resettle others forcibly. It is surely important that the United Nations has facilitated the articulation of a global consensus opposing the various sorts of forced migration and offering aid to refugees. But it appears that the very largest forced migrations have taken place within the past century, so it is unlikely that we have escaped our history of association with this phenomenon.

Patrick Manning

Bibliography

Bates K. 1999. *Disposable people: new slavery in the global economy*. Berkeley: University of California Press.

Davis M. 2002. *Late Victorian Holocausts: El Niño famines and the making of the Third World*. London: Verso.

Mann M. 2005. *The dark side of democracy: explaining ethnic cleansing*. Cambridge and New York: Cambridge University Press.

Prunier G. 1995. *The Rwanda crisis: history of a genocide*. New York: Columbia University Press.

Related essays
Abolition of Forced Labour Convention; abolitionism; antisemitism; Armenian genocide; Cold War; decolonization; displaced persons; empire and migration; empires and imperialism; ethnicity and race; exile; genocide; Holocaust; natural hazards; refugees; relief; slavery; White Slavery; women's movements

Ford Foundation *See* Philanthropic foundations

Forests

Forests are bounded by biophysical patterns and processes rather than by state borders. Particular trees grow in particular ecological sites, not within undifferentiated global spaces. Yet the influences of forests – political, geographic, ecological, and social – are transnational, crossing the boundaries of specific sites and local ecologies. For centuries, the movement of forest products has influenced the migrations of people, ideas, and goods across political borders. Colonialism accelerated the pace of deforestation, as forest communities across the globe were transformed into a collection of resources exported out of a given region to feed the demands of distant markets. Yet even as colonialism led to intensified deforestation and global climate change, it also shaped the roots of modern environmental concern, by providing 'a context in which those on the periphery could witness and think critically about such change' (Sutter 2003, para 4).

Important as colonialism has been in shaping forest practices across the globe, deforestation has a much longer history, stretching back for at least 14,000 years. As Michael Williams argues in *Deforesting the Earth* (2003), before the colonial era, deforestation was largely a function of agricultural clearing and growth in human populations, not trade in timber products. Nevertheless, it is the flow of timber products that has shaped transnational exchanges of trade, knowledge, and peoples. In Southeast Asia, for example, trade and associated rain forest deforestation began in the first century, when an extensive trade in ceramics began, linking ports throughout Southeast Asia with the interiors of rainforests. The forest products trade helped create new governance structures and relations between peoples. The upland rainforests were beyond the administrative control of the royal courts, which had to establish new exchange relationships with the forest villages in the interior. Expanding sea trade in the modern world intensified the demands on forests across the globe and helped to link European and Asian centres of power. As European nations depleted their forests, they turned to Asia for shipbuilding materials, particularly lightweight woods from Asian rainforests. As early as the 17th century, the Dutch began negotiating contracts with Javanese rulers for access to teak forests, and commercial timber extraction became widespread in the 19th century. From the 1850s on, Burma, Thailand, and much of the lowland Philippines were being intensely harvested.

Even with new trade relations, forest peoples were often able to retain their distinctive identities and cultural practices. The power of the precolonial state was limited in forests, and local communities maintained substantial autonomy. In particular, precolonial forests were usually explicitly gendered spaces, and forests were of fundamental economic and cultural importance to the lives of women. Forests provided the foods that sustained families with protein, minerals, and vitamins lacking in grains, and women collected those forest foods. Forests provided the fodder that sustained the small livestock that women usually tended, and fuel food for cooking and heating. Forests provided habitat for the medicinal plants that women collected, developing intricate cultural practices in the process.

With the professionalization of forestry in the 19th century, women lost many of their customary rights to forest access, and the diversity of forest life that sustained these uses also diminished. As colonial foresters transformed complex forest communities into professionally managed forests, the diversity of women's work vanished in the forests, as did the traditional tenure rights that gave women access to forests. With the increasing growth of sustained-yield forestry, 'working forests' had room only for timber – not for medicinal plants, mushrooms, firewood, fish and insects and herbs. 'Working forests' became the province of 'working men': of loggers, professional foresters, and corporate accountants. In the process, women lost many of their customary rights to forests, and women were increasingly defined as peripheral to the concerns of forestry.

Changing tenure relations structured these changes in access to forests. Across the world, it is a reasonable generalization to state that, before the 18th century, most forests were traditionally some form of common property, with no single person owning all the rights to a forest. Unlike agricultural fields, which were often private property in many cultures, forests had broader – but not unrestricted – access. Customary tenure systems traditionally regulated access to common property resources. Women's work was critical in shaping forests under these customary tenure regimes, through gathering, fishing, and other activities that altered forest disturbance processes and plant communities. In turn, even as women changed forests, forests changed women as well, affecting their family's health, welfare, and food. While customary tenure regimes were not necessarily equitable toward women, women did have important access to forest resources under these tenure systems.

The links between women and forests were often invisible to the cadre of professional foresters who followed colonial powers around the world. By the 19th century, with the deterioration of customary tenure systems under colonial regimes of taxation and land allocation, forests lost many of their traditional protections from overuse. Professional foresters saw the forests being depleted, and being almost completely ignorant of the complex tenure systems that had traditionally regulated access to the forest, they made the erroneous conclusion that the problem was the customary tenure systems – not the breakdown of these tenure systems. In an effort to slow the deterioration of forests that resulted from the deterioration of tenure systems, colonial powers called on a new generation of technically trained foresters who attempted to use forest science, quantification, and conservation laws to slow forest destruction. Ironically, these attempts at forest conservation ignored the root causes of depletion, and so the result was often increased exploitation, accompanied by a centralization of decision making that often led to ecological simplification and a failure to protect forest

resources or communities dependent on forests, particularly women.

With the growing power of the state, statutory tenure codes were drawn up by centralized governments, reflecting the values and interests of the state. Power shifted from those who knew the land to those who knew the law. As James C. Scott argues, 'state simplifications such as maps, censuses, cadastral lists, and standard units of measurement represent techniques for grasping a large and complex reality; in order for officials to be able to comprehend aspects of the ensemble, that complex reality must be reduced to schematic categories' (Scott 1998, 76–7). For tax purposes, German foresters had to figure out a way to measure standing timber, and the most efficient and accurate way to do so was to legislate that the only legal forest was the measurable, regulated forest. Throughout Europe, then India and the Americas, the state simplified forests and land tenure systems to make forests easier to tax, regulate, and ultimately control.

For all the chaos sparked by 19th-century state interventions in forests, colonial foresters encountered new ecologies, cultures, and politics, and those encounters constrained the practices and colonial forestry and transformed scientific practices. For example, federal foresters in the United States were trained in European silviculture, but their experiences in British India and the Philippines had profound influences on their forestry practices in America. As Sutter shows, 'many important American conservationists, from Elwood Mead to Hugh Hammond Bennett, had a surprising amount of international and/or imperial conservation experience, and the activities of federal conservation agencies reached well beyond U.S. borders throughout the twentieth century' (Sutter 2003, para 14). Richard Tucker, in *Insatiable Appetite*, reveals how the Philippines shaped the American forest history, 'for it was there that U.S. foresters and timber firms learned the methods of systematic tropical logging ... The Philippines became a stage that showcased the tropical foresters' great gamble with technological and political power' (Tucker 2000, 364).

In the decades following World War 2, global timber trade shifted toward the South. Net deforestation in the temperate developed world declined to almost zero, while nearly 555 million hectares in the Southern hemisphere have been harvested. Increasing protections on forests in the Northern hemisphere have been accompanied by a shift toward the South, not by a decrease in wood consumption. With this has come industry consolidation, loss of jobs, increase in chipping and pulping, intensive capital investments, and significant ecological changes brought about by the massive planting of eucalyptus and pinus radiata plantations in places as diverse as Brazil, Chile, New Zealand, and Southeast Asia (Carrere and Lohmann, 1996). Reforestation has a complex history, growing from agro-forestry projects composed largely of fruit-bearing species such as olives, palms, coffee, cocoa, and apples. Teak and eucalyptus began to be planted in the 19th century as a response to depletion of oak in Europe. Nevertheless, extensive industrial tree plantations in the South are a 20th-century invention, established as a result of overexploitation of native forests for wood. Their justification was the discourse of environmentalism. Yet plantations were a way of responding to problems brought about by the prevailing economic model without addressing their underlying causes: rising demand, decreasing access, and changing climate. Plantations have also had severe social consequences, for they have often been used as a means of colonizing indigenous groups and dispossessing villagers from common lands.

The rising power of postcolonial, transnational organizations such as the Food and Agriculture Organization (FAO) of the United Nations and environmental non-governmental organizations has transformed environmental discourses and forestry practices. Melissa Leach and James Fairhead have argued that global non-governmental and governmental organizations have 'systematically exaggerated' forest loss in West Africa, with profound effects on African peoples, blaming them for deforestation which they have not caused (and which may well not exist).

Enormous changes are now happening in global forestry. Increased fibre production, the shift of industry to the South, the devolution of forest control from centralized states to local communities, the increased preservation of Northern lands accompanied by increased deforestation in Southern lands – all these have the potential to transform not just forests, but also the local communities that directly depend on those forests, and the global community as well.

Nancy Langston

Bibliography

Carrere R. and Lohmann L. 1996. *Pulping the South: industrial tree plantations and the world paper economy*. London: Zed Books.

Fairhead M. and Leach J. 1996. *Misreading the African landscape: society and ecology in a forest-savanna mosaic*. Cambridge and New York: Cambridge University Press.

Grove R. 1995. *Green imperialism: colonial expansion, tropical island Edens, and the origins of environmentalism, 1600–1860*. Cambridge and New York: Cambridge University Press.

Guha R. 2001. 'The prehistory of community forestry in India,' *Environmental History*, 6, 2, 213.

Scott J. C. 1998. *Seeing like a state: how certain schemes to improve the human condition have failed*. New Haven: Yale University Press.

Sutter P. 2003. 'Reflections: What Can U.S. environmental historians learn from non-U.S. environmental historiography?', *Environmental History*, 8, 1, 31. [Also online] Available: www.historycooperative.org/journals/eh/8.1/sutter.html, accessed 3 February 2007.

Tucker R. 2000. *Insatiable appetite: the United States and the ecological degradation of the tropical world*. Berkeley: University of California Press.

Williams M. 2003. *Deforesting the Earth: from prehistory to global crisis*. Chicago: University of Chicago Press.

Related essays

acclimatization; agriculture; air pollution; biodiversity; climate change; conservation and preservation; drink; ecology; environmentalism; fisheries; governing science; international non-governmental organizations (INGOs); oceans; rubber

Free flow and open door *See* Open door and free flow

Freemasonry

Originating in early modern Britain, Freemasonry spread worldwide to become one of the most far-reaching and successful fraternities in history.

The brotherhood emerged out of the world of medieval stonemasons' guilds, from which it drew its organizational structure, symbols, and practices. The local unit of Masonic organization is the lodge; as a lodge,

Freemasons perform rituals that teach them to 'build' themselves into better men and treat one another as brethren. Members participate in convivial gatherings and practice mutual assistance. In 1717, the first grand lodge was founded in London to monitor the activities of existing lodges and oversee the creation of new lodges; grand lodges were established in Ireland in 1725 and Scotland in 1736.

During the 18th century, Freemasonry spread from the British Isles to the Continent and to the burgeoning empires of the European powers. Three mechanisms were responsible for the brotherhood's diffusion: military lodges attached to army regiments, overseas provincial grand lodges set up by metropolitan grand lodges, and the processes of migration. By the mid 18th century, lodges had been set up in Bengal, Turkey, the Caribbean, and throughout North America. Thereafter, Freemasonry spread everywhere Europeans assumed direct political control or established themselves informally through trade. The late 19th century witnessed the formation of independent grand lodges in Canada, Australia, and New Zealand. By the interwar period, Freemasonry was advancing across Africa to such an extent that the Grand Lodge of England established provincial grand lodges in Nigeria, East Africa, Rhodesia, and Ghana. As in the British case, Freemasonry took root in Dutch, French, Spanish, and American spheres of influence.

Freemasonry's success is reflected not only in the proliferation of its lodges, but also in the emergence of many 'appendant bodies', such as the Royal Arch, Knights Templar, and the Order of the Eastern Star, which have a basis in Freemasonry but are not governed by Masonic grand lodges. Moreover, Freemasonry served as an organizational model for countless other fraternal organizations including the Independent Order of Odd Fellows and the Orange Order. The brotherhood was especially popular and influential during the golden age of American fraternalism from the 1870s through the mid 20th century.

Freemasonry is at once a transnational and a national organization. Its ideology and many of its functions fundamentally operate across national and cultural boundaries. Born during the Enlightenment, the brotherhood promotes an ideology of fraternal cosmopolitanism characterized by toleration and inclusiveness, belief in the universal family of man, a sense of global citizenship, affection and sociability,

and benevolence. Membership requirements are minimal: according to Freemasonry's *Constitutions*, originally published in London in 1723, candidates must be 'good and true Men, free-born and of a mature and discreet Age' and believe in a supreme being. The *Constitutions* also forbid the discussion of politics and religion in lodge meetings. Freemasonry thus aims to become 'the Centre of Union, and the Means of conciliating true Friendship among Persons that must have remain'd at a perpetual Distance' as James Anderson wrote in his The *ancient constitutions* in 1731. Masonic ideology remained remarkably consistent over time – whether from the 18th century or the 20th, Masonic sermons, speeches, handbooks, and periodicals celebrate Freemasonry's ability to bring men together in a spirit of toleration and brotherly love. By the 19th century, such texts were also keeping their audiences well informed about global Masonry and thus the wider world.

Not surprisingly, a tension between Freemasonry's inclusive ideology and its members' exclusive practices has characterized the brotherhood from its beginnings, particularly in colonial settings. Eighteenth-century lodges included men of various religious, racial, social, and political backgrounds, but Freemasonry was a predominantly white, Protestant, respectable organization by the early 19th century. As a result, excluded groups began testing Freemasonry's claim to be 'of all Nations, Tongues, Kindreds, and Languages', and British Freemasons found themselves in the midst of heated debates over the admissibility of free blacks, Parsis, Hindus, and other interested constituencies. Metropolitan grand lodges ultimately ruled that representatives of such groups could not be excluded, and by the late 19th century they were entering lodges in significant numbers, especially in India. Though blackballing candidates on the basis of their religion or race undoubtedly continued to mark the practice of Masonry at the local level, membership in Freemasonry did encourage men of all backgrounds to think of one another as brothers.

Freemasonry facilitated transnational linkages and movements not only through its ideology, but also through its functions. Over time, as lodges were founded across the globe, Masons constructed a vast, multi-layered network. Provided he could prove his membership in the brotherhood (either by producing a certificate or demonstrating his knowledge of handgrips, passwords, and rituals), any Mason had access to the network. He could use it to establish new relationships, fulfil recreational and spiritual needs, seek employment, and receive assistance in almost any part of the world. At a public ceremony in 1896, a Scottish Grand Lodge officer made note of Freemasonry's transnational functions when he described belonging to the brotherhood as 'a passport in all parts of the globe'. Indeed, every node of the Masonic network – the individual Mason, local lodge, provincial grand lodge, grand lodge – worked to encourage a sense of global fraternity and facilitate members' movements around the world. For example, during the second half of the 19th century, British and Canadian lodges developed schemes to assist the migration of British Freemasons and their dependents to British Columbia. Meanwhile, on the other side of the empire, the District Grand Lodge of Madras assisted Masons who were stranded in India make their way to cities throughout the Indian Ocean region.

Efforts by Masons to think and move across borders continued in the 20th century. A number of so-called 'Anglo-Foreign lodges' were founded in London to encourage linkages and movements. For example, Argentine Freemasons and British Masons with interests in Argentina gathered in the Anglo-Argentine Lodge during the early decades of the century. An International Masonic Club was set up in London in 1903. The interwar period witnessed the founding of several Masonic organizations designed to bring Masons of different nations together. European Masons set up an International Bureau for Masonic Affairs (1902) and a Masonic International Association (1921), the latter founded 'to extend to all members of the human family the bonds of fraternity, which unite Freemasons the world over' according to the Builder Magazine of April 1922.

At the same time, the brotherhood has existed very comfortably within – and indeed buttressed – the framework of nations. Since the early 19th century, when the British grand lodges eliminated a clause in the Constitutions that protected the Masonic membership of political rebels, British Freemasonry has expected, and in fact encouraged, members to express loyalty to the state. Freemasonry has also played a role in independence movements that led to the emergence of new nations, as in the case of Latin America. Freemasons' contributions to the decolonization movements of the 20th century remain unexplored.

Moreover, Freemasonry's bureaucracy is organized primarily along national lines. Grand lodges, such as the Grand Lodge of the Philippines or the Grand Orient of Belgium, oversee local lodges within national borders (though some nations like the United States and Australia have state grand lodges). Much like nations, grand lodges determine which other grand lodges they recognize as legitimate, or 'regular', thereby allowing their members to visit their subordinate lodges. Grand lodges that recognize one another are said to be 'in amity' and exchange 'fraternal correspondence' and official representatives (just as nations have ambassadors).

Various differences – national, religious, racial, generational – have stood in the way of Freemasonry's ability to realize fully its goal of cosmopolitan fraternalism and create truly supranational Masonic organizations. For example, British, American, and other 'English-speaking' Freemasons refused to participate in the Masonic International Association in 1921 due to a dispute over an 1878 decision on the part of the Grand Orient de France to allow atheists to join the brotherhood. Another serious schism that persists to this day is the dispute over the legitimacy of Prince Hall Masonry, founded by African-American Freemasons who were excluded from lodges in the 19th-century United States. Meanwhile, the Masonic world is irreparably split over the Co-Masonry movement, which encourages women's full and equal participation in Freemasonry. For these and other reasons, most nations (or states) have several grand lodges vying for legitimacy and members. Freemasonry's future as a cosmopolitan institution thus remains uncertain.

Jessica L. Harland-Jacobs

Bibliography

Harland-Jacobs J. 2007. *Builders of empire: Freemasons and British imperialism*. Chapel Hill: University of North Carolina Press.

Jacob M. 2006. *The origins of Freemasonry: facts and fictions*. Philadelphia: University of Pennsylvania Press.

Jacob M., Burke J. M., Beachy R. and Bullock S. C. 2000. 'Forum: exits from Enlightenment', *Masonic Routes*, 33, 2, 251–79.

Melton J. 2001. *The rise of the public in Enlightenment Europe*. Cambridge: Cambridge University Press.

Related essays
conspiracy theories; cosmopolitanism and universalism; empires and imperialism; Ethical Culture; temperance; voodoo; women's movements; workers' movements; youth organizations

French theory

'French theory' is a term that was coined in the literature departments of North American universities to refer to a varied range of theoretical positions that are associated with some of the great names of French intellectual life of the last third of the 20th century, principally Michel Foucault, Jacques Derrida, Gilles Deleuze and Jean-François Lyotard.

Even though the different orientations of the so-called French theory, trends that tend to be grouped together under the labels of postmodernism and post-structuralism, could not be considered the expressions of one and the same philosophical school or theory, there are some elements common to the principal authors of this intellectual constellation that bring them together. Born between 1924 and 1930, Lyotard, Deleuze, Foucault and Derrida were exposed to, and were formed within, the same philosophical and cultural frames of reference, from phenomenology and the French version of the philosophy of existence – represented by Jean-Paul Sartre and Maurice Merleau-Ponty – to the intellectual revolution of structuralism, psychoanalysis, and, finally, the rediscovery of Nietzsche.

The rise of structuralism, which talked of signs, codes, and laws of structure, not only marked the decline of existentialism in French intellectual culture, it also anticipated some of the themes of post-structural thinking, such as the theme of the 'death' of the subject as the source of meaning and, consequently, the 'death' of the author as the source of the meaning of the text. In the rediscovery of Nietzsche as a paramount thinker, the interpretation that Heidegger, the other philosopher essential for French theory, presented of the author of *Thus spoke Zarathustra* was crucial. For the thinkers of French theory Nietzsche is the critic *par*

excellence of occidental metaphysics and is considered an antidote against Hegel, who was seen as the culmination of the metaphysics that centred on the predominance of theoretical reason, *logos*. Nietzscheanism, likewise, also constitutes a central element of postmodern radicalism, a radicalism that is no longer tied to the idea of social or political revolution but rather to the exercise of transgression. The radicalist sensibility of French theory is exercised in terms of local strategies and struggles, in situated subversions, and oftentimes in the subversion of reading, that is, textual subversions.

The 'family likeness' that is observed among the thinkers of French theory is further due to the presence of some common themes in their works, even though they may not be spelled out the same way. One example would be the theme of the crisis or death of the classical idea of the modern subject – be it individual or collective – as founding category of knowledge, of discourses or of historical action. Another theme, which found its most explicit expression in Lyotard's essay *The postmodern condition*, is the demise of the philosophies of history or, to put it in Lyotard's own words, the crisis of the great narratives. With this formula, Lyotard heralded the loss of all intellectual or scientific credit that bore down on all different visions of the historical process, visions that had, from the 18th century on to the 20th, provided modern thinkers with a hermeneutics of the meaning of history, and of the end that was leading its path.

In North American universities the work of Foucault, though considered controversial, attracted the interest of philosophers and historians. The work of Derrida, in contrast, stirred up, first and foremost, the field of literary criticism. It was precisely through the field of literary studies that French theory made its entrance into North American academe. In 1966, when French structuralism was at its zenith, Johns Hopkins University in Baltimore organized a colloquium on 'The Language of Criticism and the Sciences of Man' where various French invitees participated, among them Derrida. There commenced a long journey for the above mentioned positions throughout the humanities of North American academic life, a journey that has not concluded yet. In its trajectory through the campus,

'French theory' upset the establishment of various disciplines, in particular that of literary criticism, which had been attracted by the strategy of reading texts called deconstruction.

Carlos Altamirano

Bibliography

Cusset F. 2003. *French theory*. Paris: La Découverte.

Descombes V. 1986. *Modern French philosophy*. Cambridge: Cambridge University Press.

Merquior J. G. 1986. *From Prague to Paris*. London: Verso.

Related essays

higher education; humanities; intellectual elites

Freshwater management

Water is a resource vital to various aspects of human survival for which there is no substitute. It ignores political boundaries, fluctuates in both space and time, and has multiple and conflicting demands on its use. Less than 1 per cent of the world's freshwater is usable in a renewable fashion, and riverine ecosystems are endangered virtually everywhere by the overuse and misuse of these limited freshwater resources. More than half of the world's major rivers are heavily polluted and/or drying up in their lower reaches because of overuse. During the past century, the world population has tripled, and water use has increased sevenfold. And water is intimately linked to health, agriculture, energy and biodiversity.

Some 1.1 billion people lack access to improved water supply and 2.4 billion to improved sanitation. Water-related diseases are a growing human tragedy, killing more than 5 million people each year. Some 60 per cent of all infant mortality worldwide is linked to infections, most of them water-related. Almost 70 per cent of all available freshwater is used for agriculture. It takes an enormous amount of water to produce crops: one to three cubic metres to yield just one kilo of rice, and 1,000 tons of water to produce just one ton of grain. Current global water withdrawals for irrigation are estimated at about 2,000 to 2,555 km3 per year. Poor irrigation and drainage practices have led to saline buildup in about 30 million hectares of the world's 240 million hectares of irrigated land. A combination of salinization and waterlogging affects another 80 million hectares.

Hydropower is the most important and widely used renewable source of energy; it represents 19 per cent of the world's total electricity production. There are now about 45,000 large dams in operation worldwide. Built to provide hydropower and irrigation water and to regulate river flow to prevent floods and droughts, they have had a disproportionate impact on the environment. Collectively, they have inundated more than 400,000 km² of mostly productive land – an area the size of California. Fully one fifth of the world's freshwater fish are now either endangered or extinct. Millions of people have been displaced by dams, and moved to other rural and urban areas.

Politics of transboundary water resources

Effective freshwater management is imperative for both humankind and nature. Freshwater management is, however, complicated by the international character of many freshwater resources. Water flows across any two sets of interests including legal or political boundaries. Transboundary water disputes occur whenever demand for water is shared by any sets of interests, be they political, economic, environmental or legal. Thus, transboundary waters share certain characteristics that make their management especially complicated, most notable of which is that these basins require a more complete appreciation of the political, cultural, and social aspects of water.

There are 263 transboundary rivers that cross the political boundaries of two or more countries. The Cold War terminating in the 1990s marked a significant increase in the number of transboundary rivers. These international basins cover about 45 per cent of the land surface of the earth, contain about 40 per cent of the world's population, and account for approximately 60 per cent of global river flows. A total of 145 nations include territory within international basins.

The vital role of water for human beings and development has received worldwide attention. Through the activities of intergovernmental and non-governmental organizations from the beginning of the 1970s, much emphasis was placed on the global status of water, namely water scarcity in absolute terms, and a lack of access to clean water and sanitation; and some specific regions of the world such as the Middle East and North Africa were identified as the scarcest regions with shared surface and groundwater resources between two or more countries. Under such striking developments, water was picked up as a sensational issue by the popular press. And, scholarly interest joined them. There is an ongoing debate among scholars from various fields of science on the issue of management and utilization of water resources, as well as on the likelihood of a conflict that would be a result of the worsening situation of water supply and demand. In the debate one can delineate basically three groups of scholars and experts.

Proponents of the first school of thought, namely the 'realists' such as Naff, Matson and Lowi, argue that disputes over water distribution in major watersheds, the Middle East in particular, are likely to lead to conflicts since there are striking asymmetries among the riparians in terms of resource and power endowments. In their contention, it is highly unlikely that cooperative outcomes could be achieved in such river basins since the upstream riparian, having regard to its advantageous position, would not be motivated to come to terms with the downstream riparians. Further, they assert that cooperation is likely only when it serves the interests of a dominant power (which implies the upstream riparian in most cases) that takes the lead in creating cooperative arrangements and enforces compliance to its rules. This literature describes water both as an historic and a future cause of interstate warfare.

Realist arguments proved to be less insightful for the major river systems in the Middle East, namely the Nile and the Tigris-Euphrates. That is, even the most 'powerful' riparians in these two river systems, Egypt and Turkey respectively, have not engaged in any kind of coercive practices to date. Quite to the contrary, they tend to ameliorate their cooperative postures, which are in accordance with the rising necessity for efficient and equitable allocation and management practices in the water sector both at national and basin-wide levels. Water wars literature has proved to be short-sighted in its analysis pertaining to the sustained cooperation in the Nile Basin. The ongoing success story of cooperation in the Nile Basin, namely the Nile Basin Initiative, which became a formal cooperation process in 1999, grew out of six years of intense technical and scientific cooperation, and has been supported by high-level political commitment. The realists disregard this process.

Proponents of the second school of thought, namely the 'liberal international political economists', assert that, despite the dramatically worsening regional water balance in the Middle East, water has not been the source of a hot conflict over the last forty years simply because of the fact that the governments of the region managed to substitute water with cheap imported food staples ('virtual water') through international trade. Political economists like Allan believe that, by means of reallocation of water resources at the national level by shifting the major emphasis from irrigation, which is the most consumptive user, to domestic and industrial uses, countries compensated for the overall deficiencies in agricultural production by importing foodstuffs. This situation is likely to continue for the foreseeable future.

Proponents of the third school of thought, namely the 'institutionalists', assume that water-related disputes are more likely to lead to political confrontations and negotiations short of violent conflict. In their reasoning, water wars are highly unlikely in transboundary rivers, while there are still real concerns over the equitability of distribution. In their contention, the core of any water crisis is clearly national water-planning policy, which is a potential cause of instability but also the basis for solutions. They emphasize that water-related disputes are a consequence of, rather than a catalyst for, deteriorating relations between states. Moreover, institutionalists reject the hypothesis of upstream riparian unilateralism because such an argument does not take into account the complex political and economic interrelationships among the riparian states. Further, institutionalists claim that water-war scenarios are misleading and mask the complexity of water resource management at the national as well as international level. Institutionalists point out that there has been a significant trend towards collaboration, and with Beschorner they underscore small-scale confidence-building measures such as cooperation on the exchange of hydrological data, flood forecasting, joint hydroelectric power and water-recovery ventures.

International water law

International water law comprise three sources: the bilateral and multilateral treaties concerning international watercourses; the customary international law which evolves through the efforts of the international organizations in the codification of the water law; and the legal framework doctrines which develop through a process of claim and counterclaim between riparians along a transboundary river. There is a huge number of treaties: the United Nations Food and Agriculture Organization (FAO) has identified more than 3,600 treaties relating to international water resources dating between 1805 and 1984.

The majority of these treaties deal with some aspect of navigation. Since 1814, approximately 300 treaties have been negotiated which deal with non-navigational issues of water management, flood control or hydropower projects, or allocations for consumptive or non-consumptive uses in international basins However, international customary water law could only go as far as providing some universal principles and major guidelines, namely the 'principles' and 'norms' of the institutions which are to be built for effective management and allocation of troubled waters. For instance, among the general principles set forth in the UN Convention on the Law of the Non-Navigational Uses of International Watercourses (1997) are those of 'equitable utilization', the 'obligation not to cause significant harm', the general 'obligation to cooperate', and the 'obligation to exchange hydrologic and other relevant data and information on a regular basis'. Those principles certainly provide useful references for the riparians of the disputed regions striving to conclude agreements, yet they have to be operationalized and institutionalized through the 'rules' (rights and obligations) of specific regimes.

Integrated water resources management

Water has certainly become a high-priority issue in the strategies of key international organizations such as the UN and its specialized agencies as well as non-governmental organizations such as the World Water Council (1996) and the Global Water Partnership (1996). These non-governmental organizations were established as think-tanks by the water professionals, water policy experts and water managers from private and state institutions. They are not a product of grassroots movements. The approach of international agencies to water resources took a significant turn at the beginning of the 1990s. The material accrued by the key figures of these agencies reflects the transition from the 'old agenda' of emphasizing water supply augmentation to a 'new agenda' that requires sustainable, environmentally sensitive use of water resources. All these developments during the 1990s initiated a new paradigm in the last years of the decade, that of Integrated Water Resource Management (IWRM) which has become a concept and strategy for policy change in the water sector, taking over from the traditional understanding and practice of water resources development mainly directed at policy and institutional changes on a national and subnational level. IWRM is a process which promotes the coordinated development and management of water, land and related resources in order to maximize the resultant economic and social welfare in an equitable manner without compromising the sustainability of vital ecosystems.

The current consensus on IWRM is the result of a reorientation after a century of development in which the water sector was faced with a number of serious problems. The water sector expanded during the last century in the industrialized countries and from the 1960s onward in the developing countries by augmenting the supply of water for the various increasing uses. Although IWRM is bringing forward approaches which include participation, consultation and inclusive political institutions, it still remains as a vague concept received with much reluctance by the developing world. Thus, some of the principles of IWRM remain subject to continued debate in the international discussion context, particularly along the North-South line, while others receive redefinition and different emphasis by individual states or other actors.

Aysegül Kibaroglu

Bibliography

Allan J. A. 1996. 'The political economy of water: reasons for optimism but long term caution', in Allan J. A. (ed.) *Water, peace and the Middle East*. London: IB Tauris, 75–133.

Beschorner N. 1992. 'Water and instability in the Middle East', *Adelphi Paper*, 273.

Kibaroglu A. 2002. *Building a regime for the waters of the Euphrates-Tigris river basin.* London, The Hague and New York: Kluwer Law International.

Lowi M. 1993. *Water and power.* Oxford: Oxford University Press.

McCaffrey S. C. 2001. *The law of international watercourses: non-navigational uses.* Oxford: Oxford University Press.

Naff T. and Matson R. 1985. *Water in the Middle East: conflict or cooperation.* Boulder: Westview.

Shiklomanov I. A. 1993. 'World fresh water resources', in Gleick P. H. (ed.) *Water in crisis: a guide to the world's fresh water resources.* Oxford: Oxford University Press.

Wolf A. 1998. 'Conflict and cooperation along international waterways', *Water Policy*, 1, 2, 251–65.

Related essays

agriculture; civil engineering works; drink; fisheries; forests; Green Revolution; intergovernmental organizations; legal order; oceans; Tigris-Euphrates basin; world orders

Tigris-Euphrates basin

Being one of the vital freshwater resources in the Middle East, the Tigris and Euphrates rivers constitute a single transboundary watercourse system. They are linked not only by their natural course when merging at the Shatt-al-Arab, but also by the man-made Thartar Canal connection between the two rivers in Iraq.

Turkey, Syria and Iraq are the three major riparians of the Tigris-Euphrates river system. Annual mean flow of the Euphrates is 32 billion cubic meters per year (bcm/year). Approximately 90 per cent of the mean flow of the Euphrates is drained from Turkey,

whereas the remaining amount of 10 per cent originates from Syria. As for the Tigris and its tributaries, the average total discharge is determined as 52 bcm/year. Turkey contributes approximately 40 per cent of the total annual flow, whereas Iraq and Iran contribute 51 per cent and 9 per cent, respectively

The water question emerged on the regional agenda when the three riparians initiated major development projects. From the 1960s Turkey and Syria have had ambitious plans to develop the waters of the river system for energy and irrigation. Iraq has also initiated schemes extending the irrigated area. The uncoordinated nature of these supply-led developments, together with inefficient and ineffective policy and management, continue to be the principal causes of water imbalance in the Tigris-Euphrates river basin.

From the early 1960s to the 1990s attempts were made to foster dialogue and information exchange through a series of technical water negotiations. But the intransigent positions of the riparians have led to their suspension, stressing the need to create new cooperative transnational framework that includes other development issues such as technological infrastructure, agriculture, trade, industry, and health and environmental matters.

Aysegul Kibaroglu

Bibliography

Kibaroglu A. 2002. *Building a regime for the waters of the Euphrates-Tigris river basin.* London, The Hague and New York: Kluwer.

Related essays

borders and borderlands; freshwater management

G

Gandhi, Mohandas Karamchand
See **Non-violence**

Garvey, Marcus Mosiah 1887–1940

Marcus Garvey is recognized today as the charismatic leader of the largest Black Nationalist movement ever mobilized in the United States. His capacity to influence a massive grassroots following which spread rapidly across the globe before mass media technology remains unprecedented. His own wide travels as a young man throughout the Caribbean, Central America and Europe where he witnessed firsthand the horrific oppression of black people undoubtedly impacted upon his later political directive. He was a powerful and inspiring speaker, published an influential weekly newspaper The Negro World and established an effective global network of information and inspiration that was far-reaching and enduring.

The end of World War I witnessed an erosion of colonialist imperialist power. Oppressed peoples in India, Egypt and Ireland found voice and mounted campaigns for freedom proclaimed on the foundation of 'self determination'. Garvey founded the Universal Negro Improvement Association (UNIA) in Jamaica in 1914. Moving to the United States in 1916 his organization experienced phenomenal growth particularly at grassroots level where his message of race pride had an astonishing impact.

The organization strove for American, African, West Indian, Canadian, Australian Aborigines and South and Central American black people to realize they faced common obstacles. At the height of its power in the mid-1920s the UNIA had successfully established chapters in 41 countries with millions of followers. Garvey was able to draw people from diverse and differing cultural backgrounds to an organization with a common aim. A Federal Bureau of Investigation report in 1919 revealed that Garvey's office in Harlem was attracting oppressed peoples from all manner of backgrounds, indeed 'international radical agitators, including Mexicans, South Americans, Spaniards, in fact black and yellow from all parts of the globe who radiate around Garvey' (Hill, 1983, 495) This worldwide network of information was achieved by sending out agents to spread his message, and many who undertook this task were black seamen. This global maritime network was the transmitter of political ideology that crisscrossed the world sea lanes.

In Africa, the Garvey doctrine was received with elation. Kenyan nationals devoured The Negro World and memorized its contents before setting off and running into the interior with Garvey's message. In Australia, Aborigines working on the Sydney docks came into contact with black mariners and received Garvey's message of self-determination and race pride with open arms. They were originally part of a UNIA branch operational in Sydney from 1920 until 1924 but eventually formed their own organization, the Australian Aboriginal Progressive Association, to combat enforced oppression.

Establishing the Black Star shipping line in 1919 heralded the zenith and then rapid decline of the UNIA movement. Within a year the company owned three ships and everywhere the black owned and operated ships sailed they were met by enthusiastic supporters. By 1922 the company had to suspend operations, 'a victim of white businessmen who sold it decrepit vessels at inflated prices'. (Levine, 1993, 128) The venture, lawyer Henry Lincoln Johnson noted, 'was a loss in money but it was a gain in soul' (Levine, 1993, 128). Similarly the UNIA conventions made a global impression. The first convention was staged at Madison Square Garden in New York 1920. Some 25,000 members attended representing 25 countries and four continents.

The British, French and United States governments perceived Garvey as a threat and instigated means to undermine Garvey and the UNIA. The Negro World was targeted by colonial governments as seditious literature and they blocked its circulation. The movement was also hampered by damaging press from rival groups like the NAACP led by W. E. B Du Bois.

Garvey was gaoled in 1923 on trumped-up mail fraud charges. He was released in 1927, deported from the USA and never allowed to return. Garvey continued on in Jamaica and later England but he and his movement were only a shadow of what they had been. He died in London in 1940 aged 52.

John Maynard

Bibliography

Hill R. (ed.) 1983. The Marcus Garvey and Universal Negro Improvement Association Papers Vol. 1. Berkeley: University of California Press.

Levine L. 1993. *The unpredictable past –
explorations in American cultural history*. New
York: Oxford University Press.

Martin T. 1976. *Race first*. Dover, MA: Majority
Press.

Maynard J. 2005. '"In the interests of our
people" – the influence of Garveyism on
the rise of Australian Aboriginal political
activism', *Aboriginal History*, 29.

Stephens M. 1998. 'Black transnationalism
and the politics of national identity: West
Indian intellectuals in Harlem in the age of
war and revolution', *American Quarterly*, 50, 3.

Related essays

Africa; African liberation; diasporas;
empires and imperialism; ethnicity and
race; forced migrations; indigenous
networks; pan-isms; slavery; steamships;
transportation infrastructures; white men's
countries; workers' movements

Gender and sex

Gender as a term designating a constructed
social form of difference, as distinct from the
term sex (as a biological form of difference),
was first articulated in the middle of the 20th
century. Previously, within the English language and since the 18th century, the term
'sex' as a noun instead referred capaciously
to male and female bodily and behavioural
differences, as well as to sexual desire and to
sex acts. Sex, in this capacious sense, offered
a dense conjuncture for the interpretation
of transnational processes of colonialism, of
slavery, of production and consumption, of
citizenship and its others, as well as of questions about the ontological status of human
variation.

Sexual relations, their racialization, and
the status of potential progeny from sexual
encounters were ongoing concerns of empire
builders, especially when attempting to
demarcate and regulate colonial and enslav-
able subjects around the world. For example,
chattel slavery, as an Atlantic world configuration, rested on laws that established a maternal inheritance of enslavement, which in turn
were used to render enslavability a biological
feature of a particular group of humans designated as black. In metropoles and colonies
alike, laws concerning miscegenation, policies about concubinage, and the regulation of
citizenship of children born of sexual encounters across the lines of colonial difference

were important features of European colonial
regimes in the 19th century.

By the mid 19th century, evolutionary
thought fostered a reformulation of the problem of sex for colonial regimes in terms of
time, civilization and modernity. In this
reformulated colonial imaginary, the status
of women and their relationship to 'tradition'
and 'modernity' was deployed as a recurring
mark of a region's level of historical and civilizational development. As abstract generalities, colonial understandings of sexuality
and racialization worked in concert to designate bourgeois elites as more highly evolved,
civilized, and sexually dimorphic, and at the
same time to mark women, within this formation, as the site of 'tradition'. The sexual-
ization of colonized or subjugated peoples
in this colonial imaginary, in turn, tended to
emphasize promiscuity, underdevelopment,
and increased homology between males
and females, thereby explaining the hard
labour both women and men did, or might
be forced to perform as enslaved or colonized
persons. In India under British colonialism,
for example, struggles over age-of-consent
laws deployed discourses of civilization,
colonial modernity, and cultural tradition,
all of which took sex as a ground for struggles between colonial and local elites. In the
Congo, for another example, colonial regimes
reconstrued multiple-partner family forms as
backwards and oppressive 'polygamy' against
the hegemonic norm of heterosexual modern
marriage. In California, white Methodist missionary women joined in calls to police the
sexual relations of Chinese women, including
the status of second wife.

Sex also figured in the transnational production of differential labour. Physical labour
by females in colonial regimes could be a sign
of savagery, at the same time that industrialization, by the early 20th century, increasingly enrolled women as the ideal nimble
and cheaper labourers on assembly lines. In
the United States, the physical agricultural
labour performed by Omaha women became
a justification for the Dawes Act of 1887, which
sought to assimilate and modernize gender
norms of labour as well as property relations.
As industrialized production took hold at
different sites in the form of mining, plantation economies or garment factories, gender relations were typically transformed. For
example, Asante men and women negotiated
transformations in marriage relations and

sexed divisions of labour inaugurated by the establishment of cocoa production in the early 20th century. Likewise relations to consumption – to makeup, mass-produced clothing, cigarettes, soap and other commodities increasingly available across borders – helped to craft new transposable hegemonic figures of the modern, urban woman. The figures of the 'modern girl' and 'new woman', for example, with varieties expressed in Beijing, Mexico, Tokyo, St Petersburg, Paris or New York, were gendered tropes of capitalist formations as well as of newly emergent Communist state projects.

In the early 20th century, the problem of governing modern 'sex' – in terms of reproduction, race, and sexuality – was channelled through the international and hegemonic movement of eugenics, which took the form of regimes of segregation (as in Jim Crow United States), criminalization, incarceration, or even genocide (as in Nazi Europe). At the same time, sex (meaning here, still, the capacious male/female distinction) as a basis for demarcating uneven citizenship was increasingly challenged and overturned in law as states began to grant women suffrage. At the same time, national and transnational women's movements politicized questions of sex, citizenship and eugenics more generally.

By the mid 20th century, the status of 'sex' itself underwent radical material transformation through (1) the transnational distribution of mass-produced commodified contraceptives such as the pill and intrauterine device (IUD); (2) the development of hormone treatments and surgeries that could dramatically alter the sex attributed to bodily diversity; (3) the rise of genetic formulations of biological variations for sex and race that decentred physiognomy; (4) the establishment of new forms of governmentality that accompanied decolonization, and (5) a Cold War that targeted fertility and women's status in labour force and education as manipulable components of national economic development regimes, particularly in decolonizing nations. The material malleability of sex in the second half of the century, both in terms of the body and in terms of population control, was a feature of the establishment of the new term 'gender'.

Before mid-century 'gender' was a grammatical term, most often used by linguists. In the 1950s, doctors at Johns Hopkins School of Medicine in the United States who sought to develop medical protocols to manage ambiguously sexed infants first deployed the term 'gender' to indicate the social expression of masculinity and femininity. Feminists, particularly feminist anthropologists and sociologists, then picked up the term in the 1970s, to name the social construction of gender as distinct from the biological realm of sexed difference. 'Gender' as a term, however, proliferated most expansively in the 1980s and 1990s, not through feminist circuits but through institutions, such as the World Bank and United Nations, as well as the broader and more diverse postcolonial development industry.

Uneven economic development generated by colonial and postcolonial forms of dispossession and accumulation not only called upon 'gender' as a governable term, but also constituted changes in the phenomena it named. Thus, gender also figures in the late-20th-century emergence of globalized flexible production, where export-processing zones characteristically drew on single, young women as the ideal workforce, a workforce that could be characterized as cheap, docile and disposable, thereby reconstituting women as the prototypical figure of a new highly insecure transnational working class. Transnational circuits of domestic workers also made possible the careers of bourgeois professional women who could purchase cheap gendered labour from abroad, thereby establishing new arrangements of stratified reproduction and remittances that unevenly distributed childrearing across space as well as class.

The linking of women to levels of evolutionary development in the late 19th and early 20th centuries was largely replaced by the linking of gender and levels of economic development in the late 20th century. A focus on women as subjects of supranational governance was inaugurated in the 1975 with the UN Decade of Women, and in the decades that followed gathered steam as 'gender mainstreaming', a production of emergent neoliberal forms of governance. The travels of the term 'gender' were also shaped by its enrolment in Bills of Rights and constitutions drafted in this period, as in South Africa. Gender also mutated as the NGO became the primary form for feminist organizing. This reworking of gender – as a term of governance, social science, and politics – took place as it shuttled between local and transnational feminist and non-feminist NGOs in the growing development industry. The ubiquity of 'gender' as an enunciation within transnational governance lost much of the earlier sharp distinction between the social and the biological, instead becoming a new capacious term that encompassed all sexed phenomena with the exception of sexuality. For example, the term gender as indicating both biological and socially shaped phenomena can be found in many late-20th-century transnational and national health programmes about women's health. The proliferation of gender, as an English-language term, underscores the hegemonic positions of both the earlier English empire and later American imperialism characteristic of the late 20th century.

The translatability of gender has been uneven as it has circulated and been deployed in other languages by feminists and others. As a neologism within English, historical equivalents in other languages typically do not exist, and thus gender is translated and circulated through the creation of new neologisms or through its use in the English form. The friction-filled circulation of gender through development projects and its untranslatability into such terms as jins in Arabic, Shehui xingbie ('social sex') in Chinese, or korn in Swedish, draws attention to the historical specificity of this articulation of human difference. What these diverse terms demonstrate is the variety of languages in which the mid-20th-century English separation between the social (gender) and biological (sex), as well as between sex and other forms of human variation, has been refused in favor of linguistically capacious or local terms.

As gender travelled and expanded, sex as a term of politics and identity far from disappeared. Sex-acts as a concern of transnational politics were profoundly shaped by the global Human immunodeficiency virus (HIV) epidemic in the last two decades of the 20th century, resulting in the emergence of sex-acts and sexuality as central targets of development and transnational public health projects, resulting in a recent globalization of the 'facts of life'. The intensification of attention to sex in transnational public health has been accompanied by many reconfigurations of how sexual identities were named and problematized. Transnational processes, including new media, diasporic communities, migration, and flows of global capital shaped by Western hegemony, resulted, for example,

in new forms of sex tourism, new national regulations of non-normative sexuality (to restrict it as in the United States and Iran, or to recognize it as in Canada or Spain), as well as new local articulations of sexual identity and lifeworlds. For example, local 'gay' and 'lesbi' identities crafted in 1970s Indonesia were non-identical to Western identifications, and yet were synergistically connected by transnationally produced media. Sex, gender and sexuality have been, and continue to be, relationally connected and distinctly politicized articulations of difference where questions of subjectivity and personhood meet with and shape transnational conjunctures and movements.

Michelle Murphy

Bibliography

Bergeron S. 2004. *Fragments of development: nation, gender and the space of modernity*. Ann Arbor: University of Michigan Press.

Boellstorff T. 2005. *Gay archipelago: sexuality and nation in Indonesia*. Princeton: Princeton University Press.

Chow E. N.-L., Zhang N. and Wang J. 2004. 'Promising and contested fields: women's studies and sociology of women/gender in contemporary China', *Gender & Society*, 18, 161–88.

Hunt N. R. 1991. 'Noise over camouflaged polygamy, colonial morality taxation, and a woman-naming Crisis in Belgian Africa', *Journal of African History*, 32, 3, 471–94.

Mehrez S. 2007. 'Translating gender', *Journal of Middle East Women's Studies*, 3, 1, 106–27.

Sinha M. 1995. *Colonial masculinities: the 'manly Englishman' and the 'effeminate Bengali' in the late 19th century*. Manchester and New York: Manchester University Press.

Stoler A. L. 2002. *Carnal knowledge and imperial power: race and the intimate in colonial rule*. Berkeley: University of California Press.

Widerberger K. 1998. 'Translating gender', *Nordic Journal of Women's Studies*, 6, 2, 133–8.

Related essays

Acquired Immunodeficiency Syndrome (AIDS); beauty; birth control; bodybuilding; class; consumer society; cosmetic surgery; domestic service; dress; empire and migration; empires and imperialism; ethnicity and race; eugenics; family; femininity; guestworkers; health policy; human mobility; industrialization; labour migrations; marriage; modernity; new man; Olympic

Games; performing artists; population; race-mixing; remittances; sexology; sexuality and migration; slavery; sports gear and apparel; temporary migrations; Thailand and sex tourism; translation; United Nations decades and years; United Nations Women's Conferences; White Slavery; wildlife films; women's movements

General Agreement on Tariffs and Trade (GATT) / World Trade Organization (WTO)

Over the past 60 years, the General Agreement on Tariffs and Trade (GATT) and later the World Trade Organization (WTO) have played the important economic role of promoting the expansion of free international trade. The GATT was created in 1947 in order to put an end to the commercial warfare that had characterized the 1930s. Notwithstanding the protectionist context that prevailed during the Great Depression, greater cooperation in the form of bilateral trade policy slowly developed under the influence of US Secretary of State Cordell Hull, as illustrated by the passing in 1934 of the US Reciprocal Trade Agreements Act, whereby the United States conceded tariff reductions to its trading partners in exchange for reciprocal concessions. A second important step was the organization of negotiations with the United Kingdom during World War 2. Article VII of Lend-Lease Act (1941) engaged the two countries to set down in writing new principles for the building of a new postwar trading system.

The main principles underlying this system were the elimination of discriminatory treatment in international trade, and the reduction of both tariffs and trade barriers. The general goal was to stimulate, with the help of additional domestic measures, production and employment together with trade and consumption of goods. Discussions between the transatlantic negotiators began in late 1943 and went on till December 1945, ending in a declaration, 'Proposals for Consideration by an International Conference on Trade and Employment', whose outcome in February 1946 was the creation of the United Nations Conference on Trade and Employment. The new body held its first session in October of the same year. Eighteen countries were initially involved in the negotiations, with a view to founding the International Trade Organization (ITO) and entering agreements on trade policy that would preclude restrictive business practices, prompt greater employment, and liberalize international investment. In Geneva, 23 countries entered a round of negotiations that resulted in trading rules that were binding for their governments with respect to foreign trade policies. The negotiations involved large tariff cuts, and 45,000 tariff concessions had been agreed on when they came to an end on 30 October 1947. Negotiations on the ITO charter began in November 1947, leading in March 1948 to a draft agreement for the creation of the organization. However, the charter required ratification by national legislatures. In the United States, the Truman administration never submitted ITO to Congress for approval, and in 1950 the government announced it definitely would not seek ratification. Enacted at the Geneva Round, the GATT was adopted as a temporary measure, but it did not become a permanent institution until its transformation into the WTO on 1 January 1995.

The GATT was an agreement, not an organization, so GATT signatories are contracting parties. Their objectives, as stated in the Preamble, are not free trade but 'raising standards of living, ensuring full employment and a large and steadily growing volume of real income and effective demand, developing the full use of the resources of the world and expanding the production and exchange of goods'. These objectives can be reached 'by entering into reciprocal and mutually advantageous arrangements directed to the substantial reduction of tariffs and other barriers to trade and to the elimination of discriminatory treatment in international commerce'. As a de facto organization, the GATT was member-driven and ruled by consensus.

The GATT was basically a set of rules: contracting parties apply most-favoured-nation (countries accord each other the lowered tariffs that the other contracting parties receive) treatment and tariff concessions to other nations whereas unfair trade (discrimination, dumping, and subsidies) is prohibited. Nonetheless, the GATT was also a forum for negotiations: multilateral trade negotiations ('rounds') were organized with a view to liberalizing international trade between contracting parties. From 1947 to 1951, three rounds of multilateral trade negotiations took place in Geneva (1947), Annecy (1949) and Torquay (1951). Five more rounds followed: the Dillon Round (1960–61), the Kennedy

Round (1964–67), the Tokyo Round (1973–79), the Uruguay Round (1986–94), and the Doha Round (2001–06). The outcome of the eight rounds was a gradual extension of the GATT in several respects: the number of participating countries (increasing from 23 in 1947 to 125 in 1994); the topics covered by the negotiations (shifting from tariff barriers to a large variety of non-tariff barriers); the extent of international trade (from goods only to goods and services); and institutional reform (with the founding of the WTO). This enlargement explains the growing difficulties encountered over time and the increasing length of every new round. From a club of industrialized countries under the leadership of the United States, the GATT had become in the 1980s a forum where the United States, the European Community, Japan, and the developing countries defended their national interests.

The first rounds took place in a world where tariffs were the main barriers to international trade: negotiations focused on reducing tariffs, between an increasing number of contracting parties (62 in the Kennedy Round). The Kennedy Round was the first to deal with non-tariff issues, such as anti-dumping measures. The Tokyo Round involved 102 contracting parties, and the agenda encompassed not only tariff reductions, but also non-tariff barriers and revisions of GATT articles. During the negotiations, the less developed countries demanded that GATT rules be improved so as to promote development. The final results included new tariff reductions, several codes concerning non-tariff barriers, and industry-specific agreements (for dairy products, meat and aircraft). However, no agreement was reached on some products (agriculture, textiles) and on any special and differential treatment for developing countries. By the early 1980s, the structure of world trade was drastically different from that prevailing in the 1950s, and the Uruguay Round had to cope both with new issues (intellectual property, services) and old ones (agriculture and subsidies, textiles and protection of developed countries). The Uruguay Round was the most ambitious trade negotiation: involving 125 countries, it covered almost all areas of trade, and its agenda also included institutional reform of the world's trading system and the establishment of the WTO. New issues in the Uruguay Round were numerous: several GATT articles were revised, leading to what became known as GATT 1994, and the final act comprised 27 agreements, the most important being the General Agreement on Trade in Services (GATS), the Trade-Related Intellectual Property Rights (TRIPs) and the Sanitary and Phytosanitary measures (SPS) agreements. The Uruguay Round succeeded in implementing new tariff cuts, staged a very difficult attempt to reintegrate international trade of agricultural products into common GATT law, planned the liberalization of trade in textiles, set timetables for future negotiations in several areas (the so-called 'built-in agenda'), and created the WTO.

The main differences between the GATT and the WTO are purely formal, as the GATT remains an agreement within the WTO. But the WTO is a novel organization on numerous points: first, its scope is drastically larger, as it includes services and intellectual property rights. Second, after China's accession to membership in 2001, 97 per cent of international trade is now covered by agreements negotiated by WTO members. The WTO has introduced an important innovation by creating a procedure for settling disputes between members, managed by the Dispute Settlement Body (DSB), an important improvement over the procedure that existed under the GATT. Dispute settlement is a touchstone of the multilateral trading system, ensuring that members' commitments negotiated within WTO agreements are binding. The whole procedure involves different stages: bilateral consultations between members, submission of the dispute to a panel, a possible appeal heard by the Appellate Body – composed of seven permanent members with recognized standing in the field of law and international trade – before submission for approval to the DSB. The DSB either accepts or rejects the appeal, rejection being possible only if achieved by consensus. The defendant is required to follow the recommendations of the panel report or the Appellate Body report. If it does not comply after a 'reasonable period of time', the plaintiff may ask the DSB for permission to impose trade sanctions. In a few cases, like the 'hormone-beef' dispute between the USA and the European Union, trade sanctions did not bring about compliance with recommendations. Moreover, the plaintiff could not apply trade sanctions. This loophole in the procedure explains the fact that Mexico has proposed the creation of a 'market for trade sanctions' in which a member could sell its rights to retaliate to a third member in exchange for a negotiated benefit. On the whole, however, dispute settlement has been a significant success: at the end of 2005, 335 cases had been submitted to the DSB.

Like the GATT, the WTO is also an arena for rounds. The built-in agenda of the Uruguay Round involved negotiations in several fields, like agricultural and services trade, and the opening of a new round was a subject submitted to several Ministerial Conferences (which are scheduled to meet at least once every two years). The opening of a new round involves, first, a negotiation on the agenda between the members. In May 1998, the European Union asked for a round on a vast array of topics, with other countries, like India and Pakistan, being more reluctant. The discussion of a possible agenda was the purpose of the Seattle conference in November–December 1999. However, the conference was a complete failure: for the first time, street demonstrations were organized by non-governmental organizations and trade unions, the WTO being charged with being at the heart of the globalization process. The official meetings also began to resemble a battlefield: the Ministerial Conference was unable to reach a consensus in several areas, especially agriculture. The latter saw a clash of opinions between the USA and the European Union and the Cairns Group which called for a true liberalization of agricultural trade. A similar dispute took place about the place of developing countries in world trade, as the governments and public opinion of these countries had become more and more dubious about the positive effects of the Uruguay Round on their economies. For the very first time since World War 2, the conference ended with no declaration.

The fourth Ministerial Conference held in Doha, in November 2001, led to the opening of a new round, known as the Doha Development Agenda, the deadline for negotiations being 1 January 2005. The agenda was very ambitious, ranging from agriculture and services to non-agricultural tariffs, trade and the environment, WTO rules (anti-dumping and subsidies), investment, competition policy, government procurement, and intellectual property. The emphasis was placed upon issues raised by developing countries. The ministerial declaration reaffirmed the role of international trade in the promotion of economic development, recognizing the vulnerability of the least-developed countries within the global economy. The purpose of the fifth Ministerial Conference held in Cancun in September 2003 was to assess progress in the negotiations on these different subjects, but it failed. The conference witnessed the birth of a new informal coalition of developing countries, the G20, headed by Brazil, China, Argentina, India and South Africa, violently opposed to US and European agricultural subsidies. If agriculture was the main subject uniting the G20, several other issues, raised in the 1996 Singapore Ministerial Conference, namely international investment, competition policy, government procurement and exchange facilitations, were also rejected by developing countries. The agenda of the round approved in Doha was de facto no longer relevant, nor was the initial deadline, postponed to 2006. The sixth Ministerial Conference, held in Hong Kong in December 2005, was also unsuccessful, despite the efforts of Director-General Pascal Lamy: the very long Ministerial Declaration and its six annexes clearly indicate that negotiations on trade between 150 countries are becoming impossible.

If the WTO can be considered a success from the viewpoint of international trade governance, owing to the dispute settlement procedure, it is now facing drastic difficulties in promoting greater trade liberalization and in modifying the rules that were approved in the Uruguay Round.

Michel Rainelli

Bibliography

Graz J.-C. 1999. *Aux sources de l'OMC: La Charte de La Havane 1941–1950.* Geneva: Droz.

Irwin D. A. 1995. 'The GATT in historical perspective', *American Economic Review*, 85, 2, 324–8.

Macrory P. F. J., Appleton A. E. and Plummer M. G. (eds) 2005. *The World Trade Organization: legal, economic and political analysis.* Heidelberg: Springer.

Related essays

agriculture; biodiversity; biopatents; capitalism; counterfeit goods; development and growth; food; food safety standards; higher education; intellectual property rights; internationalisms; legal order; patents; technical standardization; textiles; trade; trade (manufactured goods); trade agreements; underdevelopment; United Nations system; world orders

Genetically modified organisms (GMOs)

The term, 'genetically modified organisms', or GMOs, refers to human alteration of an organism's genotype or phenotype through the use of recombinant DNA (rDNA) or other molecular biological techniques. The techniques that form the basis for modern methods of genetic engineering include tissue cell culture, protoplast fusion, monoclonal antibodies, and embryo transfers. While these methods can be used to alter genes within a particular plant or species, their scientific, environmental, and social significance lies in the fact that they have also made it possible to transfer genes *across* species in ways that would not likely occur in nature.

Recombinant DNA (or 'gene splicing') was first developed in the San Francisco Bay area labs of Herbert Boyer, a biochemist at the University of California-San Francisco, and Stanley Cohen, a professor of medicine at Stanford University, in 1973. The commercial potential of this discovery was immediately evident, and very shortly a rash of 'biotechnology startup' companies engaged in pharmaceutical, medical, and agricultural research appeared on the scene and a number of multinational chemical, energy, and pharmaceutical corporations began investing. These firms were attracted by the notions that rDNA techniques could be used to produce pharmaceuticals faster and more cheaply, that crop scientists could take genes from one species and insert them into another to introduce particular traits, and that human health could be enhanced through gene therapy. Indeed, as the former CEO of Monsanto, John Hanley, explained, 'The parameters of what genetic engineering could mean, even in those days, were so broad, so wide and so deep, that it just seemed a foregone conclusion that if one mastered genetic engineering, one would be at the forefront of the development of new products' (author interview, 2006).

The first commercial applications of genetic engineering were in the medical and pharmaceutical areas and included such products as genetically modified insulin and a genetically engineered human growth hormone. In the 1980s, GMOs began to be developed for use in agriculture: the first US regulatory approval was given in 1990 to a recombinant form of chymosin, an enzyme used in cheese production; and in 1993, the US government approved bovine somatotropin, a genetically engineered growth hormone that stimulates cows to produce more milk. The first genetically engineered crops firms introduced into the market were GM cotton (1995) and GM corn and soy (1996). Thanks to the push for regulatory approval and the intensive marketing efforts of transnational corporations such as Monsanto, Dupont, and Syngenta, farmers planted GM crops – mainly corn, soy, cotton and canola – on approximately 102 million hectares of land in 2006. Over half of this acreage was in the US. Despite industry claims that GMOs have the potential to solve a wide range of agricultural problems, such as low yields or crop sensitivity to drought, the two most heavily deployed agricultural biotechnologies are those that confer herbicide tolerance on plants so that they will not be harmed by chemical herbicides such as Monsanto's Roundup® or AgrEvo's Liberty®; and those that render plants pest-resistant by using a natural insecticide (*Bacillus thuringiensis*, or Bt) previously used exclusively by organic farmers. The fact that the biotechnology industry has incorporated Bt genes into its seeds has generated concern within the sustainable agriculture community that organic farmers will lose one of their few natural protections against pests, when pest populations evolve a resistance to Bt.

It is impossible to understand the strong commercial interest in GMO research and development without a concomitant understanding of the changes states have made in their intellectual property rights regimes. Beginning in the 1970s, a number of countries, led by the United States, began strengthening their intellectual property protection over the genetic transformation of living organisms, through 'plant breeders' rights' legislation and patent law. In 1980, the US Supreme Court made the landmark ruling (in *Diamond v. Chakrabarty*) that genetically engineered microorganisms are legally patentable if they meet the standard criteria of novelty, utility, and non-obviousness. In 1998, the European Union extended its patent regime after a long struggle with civil society organizations. These changes created a powerful incentive for firms to invest in genetic engineering since their genetic transformations would be protected as private property. Since the 1990s, the US government has used its economic and political influence in the World Trade Organization (WTO), other multilateral fora, and bilateral negotiations to pressure other countries to strengthen their intellectual property rights regimes and to create intellectual property infrastructures commensurate with that of the US. Many countries have committed themselves to implementing the minimum standards of intellectual property rights protection specified in the 'Trade Related Aspects of Intellectual Property' (TRIPs) agreement under the WTO in order to secure trade access.

In response to developments in the science, business, and ownership of GMOs, concerned scientists, activists, farmers, indigenous peoples, and others have created a transnational social movement to try to stop the global spread of GMOs and the related expansion of intellectual property rights. The roots of this transnational social movement reach back to the 1960s and the plethora of social movements that emerged around environmental issues, nuclear power, appropriate technology, social justice, and world hunger. The two networks that have been most active in transnational organizing around GMOs are the anti-genetic engineering network, associated with a number of European organizations (e.g., the German Green Party, Greenpeace International, Friends of the Earth), North American organizations (e.g., Foundation on Economic Trends), and a few organizations in other countries; and the global 'seeds' network, which is most closely associated with the Rural Advancement Fund International, or RAFI (subsequently renamed ETC Group) and Genetic Resources Action International (GRAIN). Activists in the anti-genetic engineering network have primarily concerned themselves with the public health and environmental risks of GMOs, such as 'species jumping' to human beings and other living things, and the social and ethical issues raised by intervening in living organisms with such a powerful set of tools. The 'seeds' network has tried to prevent loss of genetic diversity in the 'gene-rich' global South; called attention to increased corporate control of the seed sector; and sought to thwart industrialized countries' efforts to establish stronger intellectual property regimes worldwide. Although these two networks came to focus on GMOs through distinct pathways, they share many concerns and organize together on many issues.

The most significant achievement of the anti-GMO movement to date has been the shift it has generated in European public opinion, retailer behaviour, and public policy toward GMOs. In the late 1990s, activists successfully turned public opinion in Europe against GMOs and mobilized European consumers to pressure the continent's major food processors and supermarket chains to stop using and selling foods made with GM ingredients. Activists also pushed the EU to establish a de facto moratorium on new GM crop approvals from 1999 to 2004, which imposed an enormous economic cost on the agricultural biotechnology industry.

A major lightning rod for anti-GMO activists has been the issue of 'biopiracy', or Northern corporations' practice of taking knowledge or living material (plants, seeds, medicines) originating in the global South, and seeking to patent it as their private property. Examples include efforts by the US-based company, RiceTec, to patent Basmati rice, and the WR Grace Company's efforts to patent an anti-fungal product derived from Neem, a tree whose medicinal uses have been used for millennia in India. In 2005, after a protracted battle with Southern and Northern activists, the European Patent Office overturned the patent awarded to Grace, signalling a major victory for the global anti-genetic engineering movement.

The deployment of Genetic Use Restriction Technologies (GURTs) has represented another major focus of conflict. Colloquially known as 'Terminator technology', GURTs are a class of genetic engineering technologies that allow companies to build intellectual property protection directly into the seed. The most controversial type of GURTs (known as V-GURTS) produce seeds whose offspring are sterile, preventing farmers from replanting seeds from previous harvests. Another type (T-GURTs) introduces traits that are triggered only when specific proprietary chemicals are applied. Activists refer to GURTs as 'suicide seeds' and argue that they threaten the lives and livelihoods of millions of people who depend on seed saving; Monsanto and other biotechnology firms defend these technologies on the grounds that they have a right to protect their intellectual property and argue that their use is a matter of farmer choice. In 1999, RAFI and other activist groups began to organize around Terminator technologies, and in 2000, this transnational coalition helped convince the Parties to the UN Convention on Biological Diversity to adopt a moratorium on Terminator seeds. Nonetheless, the Terminator battle is likely to continue, given the strong incentive agricultural biotechnology companies have to protect their intellectual property rights.

Rachel Schurman

Bibliography

Charles D. 2001. *Lords of the harvest: biotech, big money, and the future of food.* Cambridge, MA: Perseus.

Schurman R. and Munro W. 2007. *Making biotech history: how social activists changed the course of agricultural biotechnology.* Minneapolis: University of Minnesota Press.

Wright S. 1994. *Molecular politics: developing American and British regulatory policy for genetic engineering, 1972–1982.* Chicago: University of Chicago Press.

Related essays

agriculture; biodiversity; biopatents; civilizations; corporations; environmentalism; food; General Agreement on Tariffs and Trade (GATT) / World Trade Organization (WTO); Greenpeace; indigenous knowledges; indigenous networks; intellectual property rights; legal order; life and physical sciences; Monsanto; patents; pesticides, herbicides, insecticides; seeds; Vandana Shiva Research Foundation

Genocide

The term 'genocide' made its first public appearance in 1944, in the book, *Axis rule in Occupied Europe,* by international lawyer, Raphael Lemkin. Combining the Greek *genos*, meaning 'race' and the Latin *cide*, indicating killing, Lemkin produced a neologism to describe 'a coordinated plan of different actions aiming at the destruction of the essential foundations of the life of national groups, with the aim of annihilating the groups' (Lemkin, 1944, 79). Himself a Polish Jewish refugee from the Nazis, Lemkin perceived their destructive urge aimed at various peoples across Europe, not only his own. The impetus to combat genocide thus paradoxically came out of Nazism's predatory activity; one whose defeat and future prevention lay, according to Lemkin, in its outlawing at the international level.

Though Lemkin had been lobbying the League of Nations in prewar years for a treaty of this kind, his great achievement was in gaining the ear of the victorious Allies at a time when the UN was in embryonic form. The term 'genocide' was used briefly in the context of the International Military Tribunal to try Nazi war criminals at Nuremberg, before being firmly embodied in international law in the UN Genocide Convention of 1948, of which Article II refers to 'acts committed with intent to destroy in whole, or in part, a national, ethnical, racial or religious group'. Though elements of Lemkin's original formulation were lost, the core principle remains as testimony to the efforts of this singular individual. That said, equally significant was the complete failure of the UN, in following decades, to respond to the rising global incidence of genocides. Not until after the Cold War were efforts made to remedy this situation. Even then, the main emphasis was on punishment, not prevention. An ad hoc tribunal was created at The Hague, to try those involved in atrocities in the former Yugoslavia, more particularly Bosnia-Herzegovina, in the period 1991–95. A second followed, in the form of the Arusha tribunal (in Tanzania), to try leaders from the radicalized Hutu regime in Rwanda who, in 1994, had attempted to exterminate the minority Tutsi.

The latter case, alongside that of the destruction of European Jewry, between 1941 and 1945, commonly referred to as the Holocaust, is usually considered an uncontested example of genocide. So, too, for most scholars, though not without political controversy, is the attempted destruction of the Ottoman Armenians in 1915–16. It is significant, however, that there continues to be no expert consensus as to an exact definition, or what examples fall within its scope. Nor can Lemkin be treated as an absolute guide. The assumed fixity of victim groups in given preordained categories is particularly unsatisfactory in an era when group identity is acknowledged as considerably more elastic. The Convention's rubric also fails to consider the possibility that a group without biological attributes can still be imagined to have an existence and vitality by a genocide's perpetrators. The destruction in Stalinist Russia, of those categorized as Class 1 'kulaks' for instance, in the course of the 1929–32 collectivization programme, is a case in point.

What this example, too, might suggest is the importance of psychological projection by the perpetrators onto 'groups' who are perceived as threatening the integrity, security or agenda of state and dominant society. This does not exclude the possibility of actual threat though in the most severe cases the danger is much more likely to be imagined than real. Targeted groups with a notably transnational profile would appear to be particularly vulnerable. In the face of the Nazis, for instance, it was not only Jews, the diasporic community par excellence, but also Roma (gypsies) who were key victims: in the latter case, with proportionally devastating losses among their European numbers (the Jewish death toll was between 5 and 6 million out of an estimated 11 million, that of the Roma not less than half a million out of 2 million or more). This is neither to deny that the main thrust of the Nazi 'final solution' was against Jews nor to suggest Jewish and Roma transnationality were alike. Nevertheless, what also stands out about Jewish Holocaust and Roma Porrajmos ('devouring') taken together, is not simply the relentless exterminatory assault on these entirely non-threatening communities by a racially obsessed and fantasy-driven Hitlerism but the degree to which other European nationalists were simultaneously willing to collaborate with, or pursue their own independent genocides against them, or other ethnic groups. What this might suggest, in more general terms, is the narrow limits within which modern states can tolerate difference, especially in periods of acute stress.

Genocides very often occur during a crisis of war, when a leadership fears that state survival may be in doubt and blames an alleged fifth column. This was the fate of some 1 million Ottoman Armenians in the First World War, deported and then destroyed by the Ittihadist regime. The fact that a main part of the Armenian population straddled the Ottoman-Russian border region, while a sizeable minority acted in overseas-orientated middleman trading roles in towns and cities across the empire, heightened regime anxieties that Armenian allegiances lay with the Allies, at a juncture when the latter were attempting to crush the empire. By the same token, a commercial, outward-looking, increasingly Anglophone profile of Tutsi in early 1990s Rwanda (not to say the existence of Tutsi in several neighbouring countries, including Burundi where their elites were politically and militarily powerful), incited majority Hutu suspicion and hatred against them when second-generation, mostly Tutsi Rwandans invaded the country from Uganda. The ensuing war, destabilization and breakdown of an internationally brokered power-sharing agreement helped pave the way for a crisis of state during which, in just a hundred days, over 800,000 mostly Tutsi Rwandans were exterminated, out of a total population of 8 million.

To imply that the causes of genocide boil down to an urge for patriotic or peasant revenge against urbane, cosmopolitan 'outsiders' is, however, to overstate the case. Jews, Armenians and Tutsi have been as integral to the broader societies of which they are part as those who have denounced them. Labelling someone an 'outsider' often tells us more about the fevered cultural political mindset of the accuser than it does about the accused. By the same token, essentially territorially stable 'indigenous' communities may find themselves unwittingly metamorphosed into exposed, transnational ones by nation-building projects from which they have been excluded or marginalized. As an example, Kurds, an ethnographically complex but by the 20th century majority set of peoples in Ottoman eastern Anatolia and beyond, were cast instead as 'problem' minorities as a result of the post-1918, internationally sanctioned splitting of the region primarily between Turkey and Iraq. A minority across further borders, especially in Iran, Kurds have suffered repeated mass killing, at the hands of the Ottoman successor states, culminating in Saddam Hussein's Anfal campaign of 1987–88. As in many other cases, here, too, such violence has engendered mass refugee flights across borders and the paradox of a genuinely diasporic Kurdish community which identifies itself increasingly in 'national' terms. When one factors in other communities who have suffered atrocity in the transition from polyethnic Ottoman empire to much more monocultural and homogenized nation states, we begin discerning a pattern at work. In relation to Suryaya (Syriac-speaking Christians) and Greeks in addition to Kurds and Armenians in the empire's Anatolian range, Christian Serbs and Croats, Albanian, Bosnian and other Muslim muhajirs (refugees) in its former Balkan domains, in each instance, genocide has been an apparent way station en route from redundant empire to modern nation state.

An alternative argument might focus instead on an imperialism more specifically associated with the rise of the West and hence transnational movements of peoples and capital across the globe (most particularly from Europe to the neo-Europes of the Americas, Africa and the antipodes). European settlement leading to cycles of resistance from indigenous peoples and then to explosions of settler genocide against them was already a prevalent feature of the Western 'advance' in North America from the 1600s. A new paroxysm of this type of violence was more widespread at *fin-de-siècle* as the competing hegemonic powers sought to ensure direct or indirect control of remaining regions of the planet yet unabsorbed into the global market. The post-1945 genocidal violence we associate with, for instance, Indonesia's invasion of East Timor, Communist China's actions in Tibet, Bangladesh's onslaughts on its Jumma peoples in the Chittagong Hill Tracts, or Burma's against its Karen, Shan and other hill communities, could be seen as latter-day examples of this trend. If these cases suggest the dangers of internal colonialism, however, each might equally be seen as a consequence of state attempts to firmly delineate international boundaries, leaving indigenous populations adrift from their historic habitus and fighting for their very lives.

If this would again bring us back to the nation state as prime culprit, an alternative Communist, primarily Soviet state model presents no exemption from the general rule. Exterminatory violence against Caucasian peoples which had been a hallmark of pre-1914 Tsarism was vastly ratcheted up under Stalinism. Largely confabulated fears of Crimean Tatars or Chechens as part of some pan-Islamic or pan-Turkic conspiracy again suggest continuity across the revolutionary divide, while the ethnic cleansing of other, including Polish, Baltic, and Korean populations from regions which straddled borders, albeit within a larger landscape of Soviet mass murder, also offers similarities with post-Ottoman Turkish consolidation. The fact that a Stalinist 1941 assault on its diaspora German population had an even more transnational dimension in the end-of-war expunging of longstanding German communities from across post-Axis Eastern Europe, also has the added piquancy of Western Allied sanction.

Contemporary scholarship keenly debates whether ethnic cleansing such as this constitutes genocide, often through a comparative approach. It has been slower, however, to analyse the underlying zonal, regional or transnational attributes of the phenomenon. This omission is noteworthy given that the effect of genocide across borders can be sufficiently destabilizing that neighbouring countries have on occasion intervened to stop it. Vietnam, for instance, invaded an ostensibly fraternal Communist Cambodia in 1978 to put an end to the 'auto-genocide' perpetrated by its Khmer Rouge regime. India, in 1971, similarly invaded East Pakistan (Bangladesh) in part to halt the mass refugee flows provoked by West Pakistan's exterminatory campaign against a region clamouring for independence. Tanzania's invasion of Idi Amin's Uganda in 1979 is another case in point.

Genocide's transnational characteristics thus have often precipitated a wider crisis for an international community which, at least in principle, is duty-bound to respond to infractions of its Convention. Against that principle, however, is the practice of international relations, as predicated both on the existence of a global political economy of nation states and on the sovereignty of each. Add the hegemonic realities of power in the world both during and after the Cold War and it is little wonder that genocides, according to some scholars running at nearly one a year on average in post-1945 decades, have not elicited effective international action up to and including the crisis in Darfur.

Awareness of genocide itself often has come through the advocacy of transnational victim groups. The impact of Holocaust consciousness worldwide has been particularly profound but this in turn leaves a range of threatened indigenous peoples including Papuans of Irian Jaya, Nuba of Sudan, the Yanomani of Amazonia, heavily dependent on global, transnational movements for justice to act as their advocates. The creation of the International Criminal Court in 2002 may provide a further guarantee that international law is there to protect them, as Lemkin would have sought. In practice, with nation-statism the political cornerstone of internationalism, the possibility of genocide, including against transnational minorities, remains high.

Mark Levene

Bibliography

Chalk F. and Jonassohn K. 1990. *The History and Sociology of Genocide*. New Haven: Yale University Press.

Harff B. and Gurr T. R. 1996. 'Victims of the state: genocides, politicides and group repression from 1945 to 1995', in Jongman A. J. (ed.) *Contemporary genocides: causes, cases, consequences*. The Hague: CIP-Gegevens Koninklijke Bibliotheek, 33–58.

Lemkin R. 1944. *Axis rule in occupied Europe*. Washington, DC: Carnegie Endowment for International Peace.

Levene M. 1998. 'Creating a modern 'zone of genocide': the impact of nation and state formation on eastern Anatolia, 1878–1923', *Holocaust and Genocide Studies*, 12, 3, 393–433.

Related essays

antisemitism; Armenian genocide; borders and borderlands; decolonization; diasporas; displaced persons; empires and imperialism; forced migrations; Holocaust; indigenous networks; intergovermental organizations; justice; legal order; nation and state; Nazism; nomads; socialism; United Nations system; war; war crimes; world orders

Germs

The story of germs – from the elaboration of disease-causation theories to the development of disease-control programmes – features many transnational themes. Germs are ubiquitous, microscopic organisms capable of causing disease. The English word 'germ' comes from the Latin verb 'to sprout', a reference to the elusive seeds of disease. During the last 150 years, these metaphorical and literal 'seeds of disease' have exerted public health and economic influence both within and across nation-state boundaries. During the same period of time, and through transnational exchanges, experiences, and collaborations, scientists and regulators have come to better understand germs and control their spread. Over a century ago, scientists used a variety of terms to describe germs: chemical poisons, ferments, degraded cells, fungi, bacteria, and parasites. Today scientists classify specific organisms capable of causing specific diseases; these include bacteria, viruses, fungi, and parasites. Improved microbiological understanding has led to worldwide improvements in public health and preventative medicine, but germs continue to move easily across borders in short periods of time; looking to the future, international scientific and regulatory collaboration will remain critical to understanding and controlling germs.

Accounting for disease: the world wrestles with the germ theory of disease

In the middle of the 19th century, confusion about disease causation abounded. Competing hypotheses included, but were not limited to, a belief in miasms – volatile, noxious products of organic decomposition in the earth. Under certain, mysterious circumstances, these miasms could supposedly produce an 'epidemic influence'. Upon inhalation, they could cause disease. In 1854, epidemiologist William Farr proposed that miasmatic diseases were diffusible through air or water and could produce fevers derived from either (1) the human body or animal matter or (2) the earth or plant matter. Early public health pioneers Edwin Chadwick and Florence Nightingale reportedly espoused the miasmatic theory, and as late as 1872 some British medical officers of health persisted in their miasmatic beliefs. Other competing disease-causation theories included the notion that living organisms generated spontaneously from the environment and could inflict disease upon healthy individuals. The zymotic theory of disease held that chemical ferments produced by filth could spontaneously generate under the appropriate atmospheric conditions. These mid-19th-century ideas of disease causation often – but not always – developed in an international context in which scientists learned from one another. For example, William Farr, while British, studied medicine in Continental Europe, later returning to London. Similarly, the Briton Florence Nightingale – whose first name signals her Italian birthplace – learned from and applied her international experiences; following her tenure of service in the Crimea (where she saw at first hand the pathogenic nature of germs in unsanitary, wartime conditions), she championed sanitation. In some cases, efforts to bring together international scientists did not work so well; for example, in 1864, John Gamgee sought to bring together British and Continental European veterinarians to discuss the cause, spread, and control of livestock diseases; however, at his international veterinary congress, only two from Great Britain, including himself, actually attended.

During the second half of the 19th century, a new concept of disease causation – the germ theory of disease – began to enjoy circulation throughout the world. The germ theory of disease consisted of two related ideas: (1) animal and human diseases were caused by specific micro-organisms, which were widely dispersed in the environment; and (2) germs could not spontaneously generate, but always came from a previous case of the exact same nature. Between 1865 and 1895, Western medicine in particular experienced an intense debate about this hypothesis. The initial promoters of the germ theory of disease faced a difficult task in persuading those who already strongly embraced other views. The daunting task involved convincing doubters that 'undetectable' organisms existed in the atmosphere. For many, the invisibility of these germs presented a stumbling block; these supposedly widely dispersed, disease-causing organisms could not be seen, smelt, or felt. Persuasion came in part through visualization offered by the microscope. Scientists sought to detail the true identity of pathogenic agents (i.e., agents capable of producing disease) and explain how they were part of the natural order of the earth. Disciples of the germ theory began to see the world differently – as a place where air, soil, and water harboured micro-organisms. Those who believed in the germ theory placed a great deal of faith in the world of scientific investigation. Previously, physicians had based their diagnoses solely on the behaviour of the afflicted individual. The advocates of the germ theory believed that laboratory medicine would play a crucial role in accurate diagnosis as well as aid in uncovering the unknown world of microbes. Thus laboratory work initiated in the 1850s and 1860s dealt mainly with microscopic evaluations, test-tube cultures, and animal experimentation. Together, these three provided the potential evidence to demonstrate the true nature of 'germs'. Despite experimental evidence, some sceptics of the germ theory were not persuaded. In their view, laboratory experimentation did not accurately portray real-life situations. Even among its believers, the germ theory was not fully accepted; they, as well as other sceptics in the medical community, demanded more experimental evidence.

A considerable number of experimental studies involving germs occurred during the second half of the 19th century; these scientific contributions, made by scientists from different countries, helped usher in Western medicine's acceptance of the germ theory of disease. By discrediting spontaneous generation, Louis Pasteur's famous swan-flask experiments in France provided a firm foundation for the germ theory of disease. However, many other scientists – including, but not limited to, German physician Robert Koch, French physician Casimir Davaine, English physician John Burdon Sanderson, German pathologist Rudolph Virchow, and German botanist Ferdinand Cohn – helped clarify the link between microbes and disease. Rudolph Virchow demonstrated that an intestinal worm, Trichina spiralis (later renamed Trichinella spiralis), could via uncooked pork enter the human digestive track, where it went on to affect other parts of the body. This observation showed that it was possible for an entire biological system to be affected by a single germ, and it provided more insight into the microbe/host relationship. Additional evidence for the germ theory emerged not from the laboratory, but from the operating room. British surgeon Joseph Lister, acquainted with Pasteur's experimental observations, investigated the cause of post-surgical infections. Lister concluded that post-surgical survival hinged on the destruction of bacteria in the wound and, to prevent future bacterial growth, the immediate application of dressing to the wound. Lister also pioneered the successful use of carbolic acid as an antiseptic spray for the surgical theatre. Lister's work helped lay the foundation for modern surgery. While British, Lister credited scientists from other countries (e.g., the Hungarian Ignaz Semmelweis) for paving the way for his contribution to the control of germs. As in the middle of the 19th century, during the second half of the century scientists continued to exchange ideas across national borders. For example, the germ-theory notion that specific micro-organisms caused specific diseases prompted microbiologists in the United States, Great Britain, and Germany to exchange specimens and narratives to ascertain if there were etiological differences between American and English versions of the disease hog cholera; scientists based in Berlin were sent cultures to help settle the matter.

The actual phrase 'germ theory of disease' came into popular usage around 1870. The germ theory gained popularity among scientists until setbacks occurred in the latter part of the 19th century. The first setback occurred when investigators discovered germs on the bodies of healthy individuals; some had difficulty believing that germs were the direct cause of disease because of a symbiotic relationship occurring between microbes and people. Others questioned animal inoculation experiments because it was not yet possible to separate pathogenic organisms in blood from the blood itself; some argued that another chemical substance – not a pathogenic microorganism – in the inoculum was responsible for disease. Robert Koch's work on anthrax in 1876 provided the crucial evidence that was needed to resolve many of the objections. Significantly, anthrax was the first disease to which scientists could link a specific organism. Koch had identified the disease-causing agent as *Bacillus anthracis*. Koch also showed the life cycle of *B. anthracis* to have two biological forms. The mature bacillus was not capable of survival after the death of its host but produced spores capable of surviving the most extreme conditions. This finding helped to further explain why anthrax was confined to certain areas and appeared and disappeared spontaneously. The spores remained in the soil and matured only in the appropriate environmental conditions. His demonstration of two biological forms of anthrax confirmed work by Ferdinand Cohn, who described bacterial spores. After 1880, there was a growing acceptance that most disease germs were bacteria. The success of laboratory experiments erased doubts in many minds. The germ theory established that germs did exist, but left open other questions concerning their pathogenic mechanisms. The germ theory also offered insights into many clinical and industry observations. John Tyndall, an Irish philosopher, explained that the time between introduction of the agent into the culture medium and time of multiplication was equivalent to the latency period (the time between a patient being exposed and experiencing the onset of symptoms) observed by doctors. By identifying fermenting organisms, experiments conducted by Pasteur helped explain the processes of making wine and beer. In the biological world, the germ theory enabled the demonstration that microbes did not need a male and a female to reproduce; they were capable of replication by budding, dividing, or producing spores.

From a transnational perspective, countries and continents differed in the degree to which they embraced the germ theory of disease. Adoption of the germ-theory concept came in part through international exchanges. Most successful research in the field of bacteriology occurred in France and Germany under the guidance of Pasteur and Koch, respectively. Scientists from other countries, including the United States and Japan, travelled to Europe to learn from these two founders. By 1891, the germ theory had been accepted in Japan because of the determination of Kitasato Shibasaburō; there, the germ theory became the foundation for government public health programmes. Kitasato had studied under Robert Koch for six years prior to founding Japan's successful medical institution – the Kitasato Institute of Infectious Disease. The cross-continental collaborations involving scientists in Europe, Japan, and the United States helped advance the germ theory from debatable hypothesis to an almost-universally accepted scientific fact. By the close of the 19th century, the germ theory of disease had been assimilated into scientific discourse worldwide, albeit to varying degrees. Among scientists there was little doubt that specific micro-organisms sometimes caused disease; in that sense, the germ theory had been accepted. Nevertheless, some medical officials still doubted that the actions of micro-organisms in laboratory settings could explain their activity in the real world. While the spread of the germ theory helped many countries improve their approach to disease control, doubts about the theory persisted.

The dissemination and understanding of 'germs'

Planetary political phenomena, including imperialism and colonialism, at times frustrated the adoption of germ-theory views. This was the case in parts of India during the late 19th century. In 1896, the bubonic plague was detected in Calcutta. Many speculated that the disease had spontaneously arisen due to extreme filth in the city. If true, this speculation would refute conclusions – made by scientists in Europe, North America, and Japan – that diseases were caused by specific micro-organisms. At the start of the outbreak, leading medical practitioners had limited experience in diagnosing or treating the plague. However, a previous outbreak had occurred in Hong Kong and scientists were able to identify the plague bacillus. Many medical officials felt bacteriological evidence was not enough to support diagnosis. Eventually, Dr. Nasserwanji Surveyor suggested that the plague could be diagnosed by the presence of the plague bacillus without one ever actually observing a symptomatic patient. Throughout the outbreak, medical officials could not determine the underlying cause of the plague. Many felt that the plague was not due to a specific bacillus, but still merely a result of filth. By late 1896, William Simpson, the (British) Health Officer to Calcutta, joined surgeon-major Robert Cobb in arguing that the plague had been introduced into Calcutta following the return of two travellers from Bombay. Simpson and Cobb cited both symptomatic and bacterial evidence. However, a separate Calcutta committee consisting of some laypersons doubted Simpson's and Cobb's diagnosis. Controversy over Simpson's and Cobb's analysis, which was rooted in the germ theory of disease, appears to have stemmed as much from colonial politics as from *bona fide* scientific disagreement; since being hired as Health Officer over an Indian candidate, Simpson had been labelled as insensitive to the cultural, physical, climatic, and religious circumstances of India. Debates continued, but eventually control measures were adopted; among other things, these included sanitation programs targeted at filthy areas of the city. Some disagreed over where precisely the bacterium was harboured, but by the conclusion of the outbreak most believed in the germ theory of disease. As in India, elsewhere the advancement and assimilation of the germ theory did not eliminate debates about diseases and their cause. For example, Drs Frank Billings and Daniel Salmon in the US conferred with scientists in Germany as the two bickered over what caused hog cholera.

Chinese medicine offers a useful lens for revealing differences regarding the understanding of germs. Chinese medicine viewed disease differently than did Western medicine. Pulmonary tuberculosis provides one example. Leading thinkers in Western medicine concluded that this disease was caused by a pathogenic microbe. In contrast, Chinese medicine coined the term 'wasting disease' and attributed it to an exhaustion of an internal organ or a possession disorder caused by bad spirits or worms. A barrier of terminology arose between the Western and Chinese medical communities. At the end of the 19th century, only a few Chinese officials were willing to abandon their beliefs and promote Western medicine. Meanwhile, missionary doctors – primarily Protestants – spent time in China encouraging acceptance of the germ theory. Textbooks from, for example, the London Missionary Society provided Western theories of medicine in Chinese. However, the missionary doctors sometimes had difficulty communicating the tenets of Western theories of medicine. Emphasis on Western medicine intensified following the Chinese revolution of 1911. After the revolution, many young practitioners were sent to Japan to learn Western medicine. The practitioners incorporated a new vocabulary of disease which helped to bridge Chinese and Western medicine. After 1920, descriptions of disease revealed who in China had embraced Western medicine and who had not abandoned their cultural heritage. For some Chinese medical practitioners, modern medicine did not imply Western medicine; for them, it was possible to incorporate some new insights of modern medicine into Chinese practice. In this manner, the germ theory was interpreted and incorporated into Chinese medicine in several different ways. The germ theory's assimilation in China helped in the successful rebuilding of traditional Chinese medicine.

Irrespective of countries and scientists adopting (or not adopting) the germ theory of disease, germs have exerted influence through international trade channels. For example, in 1865 cattle plague struck Great Britain following the importation of infected livestock through the English port of Hull. Cattle plague is an infectious, viral disease of cattle also known as Rinderpest. The momentous cattle plague events that ensued in Britain during 1865–67 occurred as the likes of Pasteur and Koch were still early on in their research careers. Scientists and regulators circulated varying hypotheses regarding the cause of the Rinderpest incursion. Like other early opponents of the germ theory, some felt that laboratory discoveries were not applicable to occurrences in the natural environment. New legislation, adopted in 1867 for contagious animal diseases, signalled an idea gaining ever-increasing currency in the British livestock-raising community – the importation theory of disease. This theory, detailed by historian Michael Worboys, held that epidemics like that of Rinderpest stemmed largely from human error. Significantly, the importation theory of disease signalled a shift in focus – from attention to causative microbes to a preoccupation with the livestock economy and regulatory controls. Proponents of the theory noted that increased speed of transportation facilitated the transport to other countries of infected but asymptomatic cattle. Upon arrival at ports, cattle (such as those aboard the shipment that arrived into Hull in 1865) were in the shedding phase of infection. Advocates of the importation theory of disease felt that disease was spread by close animal contact, extreme compactness of cattle markets, and farms containing the favourable conditions for transmission. In some ways, this theory paralleled the germ theory of disease. Both were attempts to explain disease events. In the germ theory, the agents were germs, the system was the body, and the process was infection; under the importation theory of disease, the agents were infected animals, the system was the livestock economy, and the process was importation.

Germs under control?

As scientists and regulators have advanced in their understanding of germs, new immigration policies, international trade standards, vaccines and medicinal technologies, and public health programmes have emerged. Many problems, including drug-resistant germs and vector-borne diseases, persist in today's increasingly mobile global society.

In the late 19th century, the efficiency and availability of transportation rapidly increased. Individuals were no longer confined to their home area; they were able to travel the world. With this freedom of travelling came the spread of germs from one location to another. Much of the late 19th century witnessed the application of quarantine and sanitary measures to control germs transported by immigrants. Border and port policies often fuelled perceptions about 'germs' and their culpable carriers. For example, as immigrants poured into American seaports, some in the United States began to oversimplify the attribution of such problems as overcrowding, city slums, filth, and disease; they blamed immigrants. While some were also preoccupied with a fear of blending languages and cultures, many focused on the unwelcome travellers that did indeed

sometimes accompany the immigrants. These unwelcome travellers were silent voyagers – namely, germs that could spread infectious disease among people. Unfortunately, immigrants were stigmatized according to the country from which they came and the diseases which they supposedly harboured. More often than not, the perceived threat was far greater than the actual threat.

The advent in the 20th century of air transportation also played a role in the spread of disease-causing germs. Much like travelling by train in the 19th century, an infected but asymptomatic individual can today board an airplane, land in a different country, become deathly ill, and spread disease to another population of people. Affected, germ-carrying individuals may feel perfectly well, produce no symptoms, and continue to go about their daily activities; when travelling, these persons provide the necessary conditions for the survival and transport of pathogens. The risks posed by rapid travel and communication of germs represent a pressing policy issue for public health officials. As scientists experienced in the 19th century, the naked eye cannot detect these microscopic causes of disease; micro-organisms – germs – can evade the best border security mechanisms. Today, air travel can aid in the dispersion of vector-borne bacteria, viruses, and parasites among cities, countries, and continents. Examples of diseases spread between continents include that of West Nile Virus. West Nile Virus was first described in an eastern country in Africa, but then spread to many other regions throughout the world. This specific disease affects both humans and animals and results from contact with its primary vector, the mosquito. West Nile Virus illustrates the capability of some diseases to move across borders through movement of the vector itself.

The development of vaccines accelerated as scientists worldwide became more familiar with germs. While the first vaccine was developed 200 years ago using the cowpox virus (which helped confer immunity to smallpox), by the 20th century vaccines were in use for a host of diseases including rabies, typhoid fever, plague, and diphtheria. The story of vaccine development is replete with transnational controversy (e.g., in 1930 when the French physician Albert Calmette, at the request of a Lübeck laboratory, sent his already successful tuberculosis vaccine to Germany, where it was implicated in the deaths of scores of German children; in fact the children had received a version of Calmette's vaccine that had been contaminated in a German laboratory). Notwithstanding controversy, vaccines have for the last 150 years been increasingly incorporated into public health programmes. In the United States a century ago, the bacterium *Corynebacterium diphtheriae* caused fever, coughing, and death from a paralyzing toxin; by the 1990s, and owing to diphtheria vaccination programmes, only three cases were being reported each year. Many vaccination programmes have extended across borders. Transnational campaigns by such groups as Rotary International have helped distribute polio vaccines worldwide; polio has been eliminated from the Western hemisphere, and global eradication is a realistic goal.

The development of antibacterial drugs ushered in a new era of fighting infectious disease; modern research on antibiotics began with the discovery of penicillin in 1928 by the Scottish scientist Alexander Fleming. In the past there have been diseases localized to certain regions of the globe, but today drug-resistant diseases are arising spontaneously in other parts of the world. Germs are now mutating and developing mechanisms to survive outside the body. Drug-resistant germs have become more common, making it harder to combat bacterial infections. Both developed and developing countries have experienced problems with antibiotic resistance. Today there is a short list of antibiotic-resistant bacteria; unfortunately, as bacteria adapt to new interventions, the list of resistant 'germs' may continue to grow.

Both within and across borders, vector-borne diseases have historically posed significant problems. Improved understanding of vector-borne diseases has helped national governments and international agencies develop eradication programmes centred on germ carriers – including mosquitoes, lice, ticks, and mites. Such programmes have often proven effective but short-lived; this has resulted in the re-emergence of some diseases. For example, during the middle of the 20th century, the Pan American Health Organization sought to control yellow fever by eradicating the mosquito *Aedes aegypti* from many Central and South American countries. This campaign successfully hedged against the spread of so-called 'tropical diseases'; however, the mosquito eradication programme was discontinued in the United States in the 1970s, contributing to a re-emergence of the disease-carrying mosquito in North, South and Central America.

Micro-organisms can be spread via people, animals, water, insects, plants, and food. Indeed, there are numerous ways that germs travel across borders. Germs are biological phenomena the movement of which demands transnational regulatory attention. Globalization of the agricultural and food trade has justifiably fuelled concerns about germs and triggered some relevant cases of regulatory attempts. Food-borne pathogens including, but not limited to, *E. coli* O157:H7 and *Salmonella* have received the attention of such groups as the World Health Organisation. During the 20th century, three international scientific organizations were created and commissioned to develop standards and guidelines to guard against the transnational spread of germs in agricultural and food products. These include the World Organization for Animal Health (animal disease), the International Plant Protection Convention (plant disease), and the Codex Alimentarius Commission (food safety). Through international cooperation, conferences, and exchanges, scientists and regulators can heed the lessons of history and work to solve problems related to 'germs'.

Sarah E. DeDonder
Justin J. Kastner
Abbey L. Nutsch

Bibliography

Andrews B. J. 1997. 'Tuberculosis and the assimilation of germ theory in China, 1895–1937', *Journal of the History of Medicine*, 52, 1, 114–57.

Beck R. W. 2000. *A chronology of microbiology in historical context*. Washington, DC: ASM.

Brock T. D. 1988. *Robert Koch: a lifetime in medicine and bacteriology*. Madison: Science Tech.

Sedgwick W.T. 1901. 'The origin, scope and significance of bacteriology', *Science*, 13, 317, 121–8.

Sutphen M. P. 1997. 'Not what, but where: bubonic plague and the reception of germ theories in Hong Kong and Calcutta, 1894–1897', *Journal of the History of Medicine*, 52, 1, 81–113.

Tomes N. 1998. *The gospel of germs*. Cambridge, MA: Harvard University Press.

Worboys M. 1991. 'Germ theories of disease and British veterinary medicine, 1860–1890', *Medical History*, 35, 308–27.

Worboys, M. 2000. *Spreading Germs: Disease Theories and Medical Practice in Britain, 1865–1900*. New York: Cambridge University Press.

Related essays
Acquired Immunodeficiency Syndrome (AIDS); animal diseases; Chinese medicine; epidemics; food; food safety standards; gold; health policy; intellectual elites; League of Nations Health Organization; medicine; missionaries; nursing; philanthropic foundations; scientific instruments and tools; smallpox; vaccination

Ghose, Aurobindo Ackroyd *See* Civilizations

Global cities

A global city, or world city, is where the local meets the global. Whereas a city used to be the focal point of a region, a global city is less connected to the hinterland, and more part of an international network. Global cities are a phenomenon in which the role of the nation state is less important, and worldwide, a number of cities experience a similar type of expansion.

Originally, a major characteristic of a global city was the number of inhabitants. Rome was probably the first city with a million inhabitants. Constantinople in the Middle Ages and Beijing in the early modern period might have equalled Rome. London in the 19th century increased in population from 1 million in 1800 to 4.5 million by 1900. New York overtook London after 1900, with 3.5 million inhabitants in 1898 and 7.45 million in 1940. After 1950, the fastest-growing cities were predominantly in the developing world. In 1960, 9 out of the 19 largest cities were there; by 2000, it was 50 out of the 66 largest cities. There are now 16 cities worldwide with more than 10 million inhabitants.

Patrick Geddes was one of the first authors to write about global cities – or world cities as he named them. In his book on urban planning, *Cities in Evolution* (1915), he focused on the functions of the city and not on the number of inhabitants. Geddes saw world cities as cities that had a disproportionate role in world politics and business. In his definition, world cities were centres of trade and banking, politics, mass media, and education. In 1966, Peter Hall in his *World Cities* built on Geddes' definition and added aspects like professional activities in medicine, law, and technology; consumption; and, art, culture, and entertainment.

To define global cities, sociologist Saskia Sassen focuses on international production and information networks. Within these cities, she sees a clear segregation between an elite of financial and information managers and a group of low-income workers, which can compete with labourers in low-wage countries. According to Sassen, this dichotomy is reflected in the outlay of the global cities, with high investments in business centres and a lack of resources in the low-income neighborhoods. She sees this development also in the relation between a rich global city and the country it is located in, with fewer services and facilities. Often the low-income workers in a global city are immigrants. Culture is represented at different levels: corporate culture is part of an international business management style, linked sometimes to highbrow culture; while in the low-income neighborhoods lowbrow cultures from around the world meet. When in the low-income neighborhoods the various cultures become localized – or defined as 'other' – immigrant and local culture might clash violently.

Sassen has also pointed out that global cities contribute to a process of 'denationalization'. Through globalization the nation state becomes less relevant as an institution of organization or identification. Sassen sees this development in combination with 'informal citizenship', referring to individuals who are part of a community without formal membership. Examples of 'informal citizens' are the 'anti-globalists', who attend international conferences to protest the policies of world leaders; students from different nations studying at renowned universities, or illegal immigrants who live for many years in urban communities.

There is much debate on the definition and characteristics of a global city. Scholars generally agree that a global city must play multiple roles, that it should be part of an international network. To this extent, the number of inhabitants per se is less significant. Other elements that could define a global city include influence in world affairs because of the presence of the headquarters of an important international organization, such as the United Nations headquarters in New York, NATO headquarters and the European Commission in Brussels, or the European Central Bank in Frankfurt. An advanced communication system, including Internet access, fibre optics networks, wireless networks, and cellular phone networks is also seen as important. A global city has to have various means of transportation, ranging from bus services, train, light rail, to a subway, in combination with freeways. International airports and rail stations have a crucial role since even with international electronics networks, face-to-face meetings remain important in international business life. In the West, global cities have a large immigrant population, whereas elsewhere in the world a global city has a substantial number of expatriates, mostly working in foreign businesses. A global city also has an active and attractive cultural life, with museums, opera, a philharmonic orchestra, a film festival, theatre, popular music, and one or more universities. A final category that adds to the global standing of a city is the presence of major media outlets, such as the BBC, Le Monde, the New York Times, Asahi Shimbun, or Frankfurter Allgemeine Zeitung.

With so many elements influencing the definition of the concept of a global city, it is no surprise that there are many different lists of global cities. The Globalization and World Cities Study Group & Network at Loughborough University in the United Kingdom has drawn up its own list, with a focus on financial and business services. In its view, there are three categories of global cities, with an additional group of candidates for the shortlist. At the highest level they mention cities such as London, Paris, New York, and Tokyo. Chicago, Frankfurt, Hong Kong, Los Angeles, Milan, and Singapore are included in this group as well. At the second level we find cities such as San Francisco, Sydney, Toronto, Zurich, Brussels, Madrid, Mexico City, São Paulo, Moscow, and Seoul. The third level includes, but is not limited to, the cities of Amsterdam, Boston, Jakarta, Johannesburg, Melbourne, Taipei, Bangkok, Beijing, Rome, Shanghai, Prague, Santiago, Istanbul, Montréal, and Buenos Aires. The concept of global city is a fluid one, not just in its definition, but also as to when a city achieves the status or loses it. When Argentina went through an economic and political crisis from 1999 to 2002, Buenos Aires was not considered to be a global city anymore.

Although global cities are a global phenomenon, there are regional differences. In the West, declining numbers of inhabitants, because of suburbanization, can undermine the status of a city. Some cities try to regain or improve their status through urban regeneration, attracting tourism, and increasing revenue. In the 1990s, cities in East Asia along the Pacific Rim attracted workers because of substantial economic growth for over a decade. In this case, urban planning became the major challenge for city governments. In Africa and South America, the growth of cities was characterized by poverty driving people to cities, where they ended up in shanty towns. In its 2005 Report on the State of World Cities, the United Nations Human Settlements Programme (UN-HABITAT) warns that in Latin America there is much poverty, an increasing gap between rich and poor (even during economic growth), much crime and violence (including the highest rate of sexual violence worldwide), and an increasing lack of trust in public government (in spite of a decline in corruption). Sub-Saharan Africa also has an increasing urban population, without economic growth. The UN report stresses the point that there is also increasing poverty and homelessness in North America and Europe.

Ruud Janssens

Bibliography

Burgess R., Carmona M. and T. Kolstee (eds) 1997. The challenge of sustainable cities: neoliberalism and urban strategies in developing countries. London: Zed.

Clark D. 1996. Urban World/Global City. London: Routledge.

Hall P. 1966. The world cities. London: Weidenfeld and Nicolson.

Sassen S. 1991. The global city: New York, London, Tokyo. Princeton: Princeton University Press.

Related essays
architecture; art market; cities; city planning; class; commodity trading; cultural capitals; executives and professionals; financial centres; literary capitals; literature; trade; urbanization

Globalization

One could start from the sheet of paper stuck up in the window of the shop around the corner the other day: 'Today nothing is spared by globalization, not even the baguette'. In order to explain the price rise of this familiar French breadstick to grouchy customers, my baker used 'globalization' as a contemporary factor and the underlying cause behind the skyrocketing price of wheat and cereals. Just like him, leaders and simple citizens alike have resorted to such an interpretative scheme in the last thirty years, after the terms 'global' and 'globalization', hardly new even then, began their march both to the headlines and to small talk in the middle of the 1980s.

To keep the grip these terms seemed to offer on the current state of our worldly affairs, their users mostly insisted on the break in intensity and nature that was at play in the last decades in terms of interconnection, dependence, convergence, homogenization and fragmentation of human societies and polities on this planet. Just like my baker, they were not very receptive to powerful voices that very early on had warned about the *longue durée* aspects that were incorporated into current patterns. Roland Robertson, Immanuel Wallerstein, Olivier Dollfus, Kevin O'Rourke, Jeffrey Williamson or Anthony King's caveats failed to remind the baker that cereals have been traded over long distances for centuries; that the grain market was 'cornered' from the late 1880s, with speculations in the futures trade on the Chicago market causing prices to rise in Europe; that the baguette is but one juncture in the historical and anthropological history of bread as a staple food of humankind; or that the culture of cereals has expanded and contracted throughout history through acclimatization, random journeys or conquest.

When we embarked upon the project of this Dictionary, one of our aims was to act as go-betweens, as it were, for the baker and the social theorists who unsuccessfully tried to urge commentators and citizens alike to identify the ways in which the global pasts of our world were incorporated within its present, rather than asserting its 'newness'. We were also keen to bring firsthand historical material to the growing choir of scholars who have stressed that not everything transnational or even long-distance is global. Many if not most of the connections and circulations that cross national borders do not embrace the whole planet, they do not by nature add to the interdependence or integration of the world, nor do they connect to integration processes regardless of circumstances of birth.

In other words, and for probably similar empirical reasons, we shared the concerns that Frederick Cooper had expressed in his 2001 paper. This historian of Africa identified three questions that were left unasked by the prophets and Cassandras of globalization: newness (about the historical depth of interconnection); comprehensiveness (the evolving linking and delinking operated by the circulations in play), and operation (the specificity of the structures that make connections and circulations work). He called for modest but effective ways to analyse processes, networks and social fields that crossed borders by focusing on these empirical questions. Such a contract had been signed up to by a significant number of historians in the past and clearly does foot the bill for what we call the transnational perspective. The firsthand study of connections and circulations by historians of all trades offers a genuine opportunity to engage the globalization discourse with our picks and shovels: sources and material. Picking up from Cooper's leads, this entry will sketch the possible contribution of a transnational perspective on history to the study of globalization.

Cycles, waves, processes: the timing of globalization

Periodization is the bread and butter of historians, and it stays central as they try to have their say within the globalization discussion. Part of their contribution has to deal with the very long term: the questions about the age of the world system ('500 or 5000 years?', asked Frank and Gills provocatively in 1993) have been pushed backwards and forwards by such proposals as Christopher Bayly's (2004) ideal-type chronologizing of 'archaic', 'proto', 'modern' and 'postcolonial' globalization, while world historians or geographers have scrutinized 'human webs' that started to thrive with the colonization of the planet by homo sapiens. Such developments have been possible because of firsthand research that could be mobilized to chart and map circulations and connections of and about goods, ideas, germs, people, capital, with the result that past interconnections and interdependencies, especially those which were not centred around Europe or the Atlantic world, are now more familiar and prevent us from teleological readings of current trends and patterns. The stakes appear to be not so much to tunnel through the past to read the origins of what our times have called globalization, as to identify the manifold configurations that have been seen as high points of integration and interconnection at other times.

A similar possibility is opened up by the development of firsthand research on circulations and connections in the modern age. The most widely accepted chronologies have been developed within the general attempt to 'root' our current situation and forecast a possible future, and are embedded within two major frames: on one hand, the desire to assess the good and evil sides of globalization, and on the other, a focus on the economic aspects that have been central in the perception of 'our' globalization. The most classical formulation is the one inspired by the work of Jeffrey Williamson, that has produced a narrative articulated in three episodes as he contested the 'newness' of globalization together with the views that erected the turn of the 15th and 16th centuries as a landmark. Focusing on the 'open economy forces of trade and mass migrations', Williamson (1996) identified economic performance and convergence as the key criteria to assess globalization. His first phase, between 1850 and 1914, was when globalization began. Its expansion was cut short by a deglobalization phase from 1914 to 1950, as national economies turned outside-in, to thrive again from 1950 until the peak of the late 20th century. Some others have proposed a slightly different periodization, like the French economist Charles Albert Michalet who claims to build from a wider range of economic data as he charts three configurations of *mondialisation* ('international' from the 19th century until the 1960s, 'multinational' from then on to the 1980s, and 'global' ever since), each one being characterized by the prominence of a different kind of economic material (goods, services, investments or capital). But Williamson's narrative has become the basis of a canon, endorsed by the World Bank (who shifted the time frames to 1870–1914, 1914–45 and 1945–80) or popularized by expressions like 'first globalization'.

In a recent article, Adam McKeown has engaged this periodization by stressing that it was built mostly from North Atlantic data and focused on a model of development bounded in time and space. Using the example of migrations, McKeown has suggested that the portrait of the first globalization left two of the biggest world frontiers out of the picture, that is Northern and Southeast Asia. He also underlines that the depiction of 1914–45 as

a moment of deglobalization was only possible by a camouflage of the 1920s and their impressive record of economic convergence and migrations. Following up on his suggestion to pick up from different flows and different regions, reconstructing the connections and circulations across borders can effectively contribute to consideration of a wider world, which is the least one can expect when studying globalization. Considering non-economic flows certainly puts the canonical chronology in a different light. Though immigration quotas restricted some kinds of migration in the Atlantic world, refugees' and seasonal workers' movements did not come to a halt, and even increased, while the sea transportation of Asian pilgrims to Mecca peaked in the late 1920s. The interwar years were a crucial moment of connections and circulations in both the social and natural sciences, when both conceptual and organizational definitions were exchanged, translated and appropriated across borders to shape the development of scientific research, policies and institutions. Even the 1930s, the hard core of 'deglobalization' according to the master narrative, saw almost unprecedented cross-fertilization in the worlds of science, especially with the departure of Italian, Spanish or German artists, scientists and thinkers. Similarly, those who linked across borders to defend a cause or an interest in the arts, politics or social activism did not abruptly stop doing so during the interwar years. The renationalization of the world, which presumably brought about economic deglobalization, also triggered an impressive range of new flows and links (if only in relation to public policies to cope with the Depression), while existing ones did not vanish in a snap.

Existing and current research to document the history of circulations and connections, of which only a fraction is presented in this volume, should ultimately lead to reconsideration of the master narrative's periodization. They should support and expand the idea that connections and circulations, and their contribution to fostering convergence and divergence, homogeneity and difference, were at the core of the history of the modern age in a constant fashion. Christopher Bayly, working from existing scholarship, has gone some way in insisting on this aspect for the period 1780–1914. His work is especially powerful in stressing how much two of the most salient aspects of the modern age, the strengthening of the nations and the development of circulations and connections of all sorts, were intertwined variables of an equation rather than two elements in a zero-sum game. Besides being a clue that the 'first globalization' is a fragile typification, the connections and circulations he has identified do not cease abruptly after 1914.

But what about the lesson that periodizations are ultimately supposed to deliver, that is the assessment of change over time? Is this just to be jettisoned in favour of a blunt and dull recognition that the modern age has been nothing but a space of flows, at best ebbing and rising but deprived of any order, or conversely the steady expansion of a single, core capitalist system that integrated the rest of the planet in the connections and circulations it generated? This is when the master narrative periodization should be kept in mind to provide a first clue, and returns with a vengeance. Just like today, there have been several moments in the modern age where protagonists were keen to predict a period of unprecedented change and the advent of a new global age, while former epochs were frozen into 'a past of borders, isolation and stasis' (McKeown 2007, 220). Every teacher of a class on the history of globalization has probably played the quotation game, mixing anonymized citations from Karl Marx, Ulysses S. Grant, Kenichi Ohmae, Jean Charles de Sismondi, Aurobindo Ackroyd Ghose, Thomas Friedman, Wendell Wilkie, Johann Wolfgang von Goethe, Édouard Glissant or Manuel Castells (among the famous) and Carl Ritter, William Stead, King Kalakaua, Élisée Reclus, Max Nordau, Alexander Supan or Guillaume de Greef (my favourite underdogs). When informed about the whos and whens, students are both amused and amazed by how repetitive are the consciousness of what has recently been called the time-space compression, and the assertion of a move toward a world culture, economy or society. They are also intrigued by the lexicological invention that has been demonstrated to create appropriate neologisms in different languages (like the French mondialité which was used in early-20th-century Belgium). A subsequent batch of contradictory quotes about the delinking and unmaking of planetary connections usually helps to bring home the idea that there has been a long contest throughout the modern age over the direction, impact and value of connections and circulations. The canonical periodization not only derives from a

focus on economic circulations in the North Atlantic world, it is also an inscription of the personal and collective feelings that turned out to be dominant (but not exclusive) at different moments of the attempts to capture or define the order of the world: the description of a world united by technologies is a striking common feature between the contemporary observers who felt they were living in a 'great acceleration' in the 1890s or the 1990s, while commentators of the late 1930s lumped the interwar years into a dark and gloomy whole to explain to themselves how their world had fragmented and bumped into a wall.

Moreover, such visions were in large part prescriptive and should be read as exhortations to go with the grain and catch the wind of a shrinking or expanding world system. There are no reasons to be satisfied with encoding these visions into our own understanding of the past, and the painstaking reconstruction of connections and circulations should help us imagine other periodizations while we explore the making and unmaking of economic and non-economic flows in order to document how circulations and connections between societies and polities have framed the very existence of these. It might ultimately tell us more about the business of history, that is the assessment of change, than to try telling 'when globalization began', walking backwards or forwards with what we call our globalization as a focal point. If we want to narrate the world's pasts in an age of globality, we must not work backwards and fall prey to the self-fulfilling prophecies of this very age.

What makes connections work?

If so, the current diagnosis of 'globalization' would thus have to be read with the hindsight of previous moments where other such prescriptive narratives were developed in the context of universal hubris, including the writing of 'universal histories'. Beyond the scope of this volume are world and space views that were defended in the context of the Chinese empire, the protagonists of dar al-islam in Caliphate times, the Iberian monarchy or the Tokugawa dynasty. But a transnational perspective suggests that there is profit in considering the range of projects and protagonists that have been at work, engineering connections and circulations with some universal aspirations in the background in the last 150 years. This includes both wide and modest designs powered by national governments (Old and New 'American Century' blueprints, late-19th-century plans by 'Cosmopolitan King' Kalakaua of Hawai'i or current worldviews in sections of Chinese business and government), political ideologies (the Revolution mantra or the different strands of communism) or private agencies (the Rockefeller Foundation's schemes for a 'free trade of ideas'), as well as individual hankerings for contributing to developing norms, standards, as well as other forms of conversation where what was at stake was to dispute what was or should be universal. Recovering the agency of these projects requires us to work from firsthand material, and to take a deep look into the 'structures necessary to make connections work', in Cooper's words.

This volume has understood 'structures' in a very catholic sense. The steamship, the freight container, the symphony orchestra, the news agency, the publishing house, submarine or terrestrial power cables, the international non-governmental organization are such structures. Their detailed study may seem a bit dry, but it has the potential to disclose the logics and order of circulations. This clearly calls for extensive historical investigation. For example, it is not satisfactory to draw on the existence of international associations or non-governmental organizations to assert the existence of a global civil society. The analysis of their printed output, such as conference proceedings or campaign material, does not give access to the debates and discussions about their programmes and activities, nor to their spatial extension or how they got along with other existing groups with similar goals, nor to the way they organize the circulation of information and funds within their flock. To get at what makes the connections of such an organization work, one needs to dive into personal correspondence, outsiders' comments and archives of the organization, to access what shapes the above-water part of the iceberg, that is the public face of campaigns, conferences and publications. The transnational perspective is about the operation and agency of the structures at work across borders. Only then can one assess their 'global' reach and aim.

The search for circulatory regimes

Just as the exploration of different kinds of flows offers a different insight into the periodization of globalization and the question of its newness, the study of circulations also provides the opportunity to consider its comprehensiveness and the limits of interconnections between the different parts of the world. The fact that transnational circulations and connections are not global by nature seems to be obvious. While the non-ubiquitous characteristics of flows and ties have often been discarded in both celebratory and critical accounts of globalization, there is a growing concern to recover the extent, direction and order of flows and ties. Several of the contributors to this volume, with very different disciplinary or research track records, have come up with a suggestion to make sense of connections and circulations they research and record over the last 150 years. The proposal is to focus on the structural but dynamic, specific orders that organized, directed and empowered flows and networks of goods, people, ideas, projects or capital. This does not boil down to a desire to reconnect these flows to the identification of metaprocesses such as capitalism, imperialism or ideological and religious universal aspirations, and the proposal is much more modest than a suggestion to rethink and expand the world-system theory. Everything that crosses a border is not bound to go global, and there are circulations and connections that have had major impact despite their very limited spatial reach (think of the complex processes of comparison, emulation and rejection that have taken place between the polities and societies of Japan and China, or Germany and France). Beyond the specific experiences that are encapsulated in the Dictionary entries, we believe that the study of circulatory regimes or configurations, and of their concatenation over time, is a promising way to capture historical developments of circulations and connections in their multiscalar instantiations. I am not sure whether what we mean by 'regimes' or 'configurations' has been inspired by the definitions of these two notions by John Ruggie and Stephen Krasner in international relations theory or Norbert Elias in sociology respectively, but this is not the right place to linger on this theoretical dimension. What we are trying to identify are sets of structures and practices with durable effects on the orientation, extent and impact of circulations and connections. A circulatory regime or configuration might be identified by the following characteristics:

- the existence of individual and collective actors – 'regime makers' – who invest time, energy and resources (social, economic, or cultural) in the establishment, maintenance and use of connections made to circulate specific items beyond the limits of their polities and societies;
- the formation of intertextual (reading, translation, quotation) and interactional (visits, correspondence, formal and informal organizations) communities, which can be used as resources for action by every member of these communities;
- the establishment of long-term and relatively stable patterns of interactions between mutually identified protagonists that take part in connections and circulations (these interactions pertaining to a range of possibilities, i.e., from competition to cooperation);
- the agreement of these protagonists and actors on a common language that is the basis of further agreements, disagreements and misunderstandings around notions, categories, processes, worldviews that are discussed and disputed among themselves;
- the purposive development of projects, trajectories, aspirations and institutions able to establish connections, nourish circulations and orient them in specific directions;
- the production of a finite, differentiated and uneven landscape where the status of a region (be it a place, an institution, an individual or collective protagonist and actor) is tied in with its role and place in the circulatory regime or configuration.

Establishing the circulatory configurations that have succeeded, vied with each other or cohabited in time and space would allow us to assess the orders that have presided over the spatial extension of connections and circulations, and to map the changing intensity, contractions and dilatations of the latter. This does not presuppose the existence of a single and comprehensive system of circulations, but takes it for granted that different systems have unfurled in interaction with each other, while some regions may have been left out of the picture. Again, such a concern will be familiar to those who have paid attention to the work of our colleagues in sociology or anthropology who have tried to make sense of

the problems they had to deal with when they tried to grasp people, artifacts, projects or ideas that stretched across national borders. According to their affiliations, some have used the terms 'transnational system' while others go for 'transnational social field' to name their tools. While we would certainly all insist on the specific value and reach of these different labels, they have nevertheless all been triggered by a common search for order in the 'space of flows', a desire to recover the degree of autonomy of circulations and connections, and a wish to recover the agency, projects and resources of historical actors. Behind these different proposals, though in different degrees, is the desire to disassemble the seeming singleness and comprehensiveness of globalization, and to establish the historical basins of convergence and divergence that were created in order to build or fight interdependence and interconnection among polities and societies. The multiscalar methodology that is increasingly proposed and used by scholars from a wide range of disciplines to study transnational processes enhances such possibilities, as the idea is more and more to study formations, circulations, networks that cut across social spheres usually encoded in our perception of nested scales (the local, the national, the global). The study of circulatory configurations fits within this concern, as it does not start from the local or the global or the national to wonder about the 'impact' of one on the other, but rather picks up from connections and circulations that defy the conception of nested scales because their structures and protagonists most often simultaneously make use of resources and positions that are usually ascribed to one of these levels. As documented in this Dictionary, the study of the circulatory configurations at work during the last 150 years suggests that none of them has embraced the whole planet in its conception or operation, and that connections and circulations do not work 'from' one level 'to' the others.

Conclusion

If a transnational historical perspective can contribute to the discussions about the whens and wheres of globalization, it is likely because it ultimately proposes a hands-on approach to what is said to characterize globalization. Interdependence, interconnection and their expansion, deepening or speeding up are said to be its trademarks. Because it stresses the study of connections and circulations, the transnational approach is very much concerned with what make them work, and accordingly allows us to identify their individual and collective protagonists. It is not a metahistory of tropes, discourses and processes (Westernization, development, the adventure of humankind) as 'big picture' history sometimes turns out to be. When it deals with the global, it is to consider projects, designs, aspirations that boasted or concealed a global perspective and implemented it through a mechanics of a sort: an organization, a community, a wire. When it deals with the universal, it is to reconstruct the practical struggles between different definitions of possible universals, definitions which were embodied in institutions, printed material, technical norms, individual behaviours and group ethos. Such a passion for nuts, bolts and pipes might seem trivial to those who love to juggle with imperialism, capitalism, revolution, modernization, secularism, post-Fordism or other metaprocesses and concepts. But by enlisting such processes and concepts as connected circulatory regimes on their own, the modest study of circulatory systems helps pinpoint the goals and resources of specific regimes and regime makers that have tried to control existing connections and circulations, or to establish new ones, sometimes with hankerings for a general and ubiquitous extension in space and society. Ultimately, this empirical dimension might be what makes the transnational approach valuable for students of globalization.

Pierre-Yves Saunier

Bibliography

Bayly C. A. 2004. *The birth of the modern world 1780–1914: global connections and comparisons.* Oxford: Blackwell.

Cooper F. 2001. 'What is the concept of globalization good for? An African historian's perspective', *African Affairs*, 100, 399, 189–213.

Grataloup C. 2007. *Géohistoire de la mondialisation: le temps long du monde.* Paris: Armand Colin.

Hopkins A.G. (ed.) 2002. *Globalization in world history.* New York: Norton.

Hopkins A.G. (ed.) 2006. *Global history: interactions between the local and the universal.* Basingstoke and New York: Palgrave Macmillan.

Mattelart A. 1999. *Histoire de l'utopie planétaire: de la cité prophétique à la société globale.* Paris: La Découverte.

McKeown A. 2007. 'Periodizing globalization', *History Workshop Journal*, 63, 1, 218–30.

Williamson J. G. 1996. 'Globalization, convergence, and history', *Journal of Economic History*, 56, 2, 277–306.

Related essays

acclimatization; civilization; contract and indentured labourers; convergence and divergence; cosmopolitanism and universalism; exile; food; history; human mobility; life and physical sciences; Otlet, Paul; Pax Americana; philantropic foundations; public policy; refugees; religious pilgrimage; social sciences; spatial regimes; trade

Gold

Gold is a precious metal that is sold and accepted worldwide, because of its convertibility into money depending only on its purity. This made gold an ideal object for trade and smuggling, too. Due to its indestructibility, gold was considered a guarantee for the validity of currencies, but since the end of the gold exchange standard in the 1970s it has become a commodity among others and an object of international speculation.

The 1849 gold rush in California paved the way for an age of gold. When the news of the gold finds arrived on the East coast and in Europe, thousands of men went to the newly discovered gold fields to make their fortune. This also caused a large influx of gold seekers from Mexico and South America, and some twenty thousand Chinese. The gold rush was an international event with tremendous economic consequences. Within three years the world's annual gold production rose from an estimated 77 tons a year to 280 tons in 1852. This flood of gold underwrote a big increase in international trade during the 1850s. Many contemporaries expected that the price of gold, fixed in London since 1717 at £ 3.17.10½d per ounce, would fall because of a surplus of gold, but this did not happen as more money became available to the financial markets and was thus pumped into the world economy.

Individual prospectors who had been less successful in California started to seek for gold in other countries. In 1850, the Australian gold finds attracted some 370,000 immigrants, mainly from the British Isles. About 80 per cent of the Australian gold was refined and sold in London by the five members that formed the London gold market: N. M. Rothschild, Mocatta & Goldschmid, Sharps & Wilkins, Pixley & Able and Samuel Montagu. For the next 150 years, these five bullion houses and banks held a daily meeting to fix the gold price, which from then on was the basis for the global gold trade.

Once the alluvial deposits of gold were exhausted, the age of the individual prospector was over. The gold ores had then to be mined and this needed much more knowledge and money than most of the gold seekers could afford. Mining corporations or bigger enterprises took over the exploitation of the precious metal. The prospectors had short comebacks with the gold rushes in Alaska and in Eastern Siberia on the Aldan river in 1924/25, but most of the gold produced from the end of the 19th century already came from industrial mining.

The biggest gold finds ever had been made at the Witwatersrand in South Africa in the 1880s. A third of the gold ever mined came from the South African mines. Johannesburg's mining houses dominated the world's gold production throughout the following century. From 1910 until the late 1970s they yearly produced up to two thirds of the world's new gold, often more than 1,000 tons. The geological conditions entailed a different organization of mining, based on professional mining and an enormous capital to run a mine. The mines on the Witwatersrand profited from the experience acquired in Kimberley where a diamond rush had occurred a decade before. The profits from the diamond mines and the miners from this area provided an ideal start for the new industry. Very quickly the magnates of the diamond mines (Eckstein, Rhodes, Robinson, Barnato, Albu) also gained control over the major gold mines and formed the mining houses. They were backed by the financial markets in London, Paris and Berlin. Europe provided about 85 per cent of the needed investments. Even at an early stage about £500,000 had to be invested in a new mine. This huge inflow of capital and outflow of profit were further transnational effects of the gold finds.

Migration was a second and long-term effect of the gold industry at the Rand. For the development of mines, professionals like English and Welsh miners as well as American engineers were attracted by higher wages. But the bigger part of the workforce came from the so-called 'natives' from the neighbouring colonies and countries. In order not to compete for workers and thus raise the wages, the mining houses formed the Chamber of Mines which organized the recruiting of the migrant workers on behalf of the mines. For about eight decades, the Witwatersrand Native Labour Association (Wenela) yearly provided more than 100,000 workers for the mines of the Rand from the regions formed by the actual states of Mozambique, Malawi, Tanzania, Zambia, Angola, Namibia and Botswana. This hard and very dangerous way of earning a bit of money helped the migrant workers to cope with insufficient harvests, unpredictable droughts and deprivation of their livestock. Young men used their small wages to buy cattle as a bride-prize and thus gained independence within their kraal (settlement). The migrant work thus had an enormous economic and social impact on distant communities due to the long absence and disappearance of many men, the income and independence of young men, and the spread of diseases (up to AIDS in our day).

As the gold price was fixed by the gold standard, the mines did not have to compete on a world market for gold, but they could sell any amount of gold. This enabled them to coordinate their know-how and to develop the mining technologies together. The high wages for the mining experts and European miners and the rising costs of deep-level mining made them limit the wages of the black labour force and exclude them from better-paid jobs which were reserved for white workers only. This 'colour bar' was erected and became a law with the Mines and Work Act in 1911. As long as the gold standard existed, any increase of black workers' wages was kept out of the discussion.

The rise in the world's gold production in the 19th century, to 11,000 tons, compared to the 800 tons produced in the 18th century, made most states establish the gold standard to assure the validity of their currency. During the First World War, most countries dropped the gold standard, which was re-established by Great Britain in 1922 and finally dropped in 1931 as a consequence of the economic depression. But the City of London and the pound sterling had lost their leading role in world economy; the gold price was now set by the USA and fixed as a part of the

New Deal in 1934 at $35 an ounce. After the Second World War, the world currency system of Bretton Woods can be summarized as being a system based on a gold exchange standard, maintained by the reserve bank of the leading economies in the Western world. The so-called Gold Pool (the US, Great Britain, France, Italy, West Germany, the Netherlands, Belgium and Switzerland) tried to guarantee this gold price by intervening on the London gold market by buying and selling parts of their national gold reserves. But the international demand for gold and the speculation on a rising gold price became so strong in the 1960s that the London market finally started a two-tier system, with an open market for non-monetary gold and another one reserved for monetary gold. Before this, the London market had functioned more as a distributor for South African gold production than as a marketplace. In 1968, as a result of increasing pressure on the gold price, the London Gold fixing operation at Rothschild's remained shut for two weeks. This enabled the three leading Swiss banks (Swiss Bank Cooperation, Swiss Credit Bank and Union Bank of Switzerland) to immediately establish an own gold market for physical gold in Zürich. They convinced the South Africans and four years later also the second biggest gold producer, the Soviet Union, to sell their gold via Zürich instead of London. This new alliance worked very well, as the Swiss banks had built up a transnational network with local bullion dealers in markets all around the world. From 1968, about three quarters of the physical gold passed through the Zürich market. The Swiss supplied not only the jewellers and industry of Italy and West Germany, but also held a strong position in the Middle East and Asia.

In 1971, the US government also dropped the gold exchange standard and four years later allowed its citizens to buy gold. Although greatly expected, an American rush did not occur. But the price of gold rose to some $100 an ounce and made gold mining more profitable than ever. The exploitation of gold started wherever gold had been discovered before, but so far had not been worth mining, from Madre de Dios in Peru to Bougainville in Papua New Guinea.

The new futures market became another important factor in the gold market. The New York Commodity Exchange (COMEX) and Chicago's International Monetary Market (IMM) made it possible for the mines to sell their gold forward when prices were high, and for buyers like jewellers to protect themselves against increasing gold prices. The futures market was primarily a virtual market, as in fact very little gold was really delivered. The gold market now became the playground for speculators. Futures offered a cheap way of getting into gold without the embarrassment of delivery and storage. Economically, gold altered its character from a monetary metal to a commodity, from something to hoard into an object of speculation. The global telecommunication networks facilitated a non-stop market for gold from Hong Kong via Zürich/London to New York. Since the late 1970s, all these markets and their prizes have been closely linked and profits from arbitrage have become difficult to realise.

Beside the reserve banks, many private hoarders have also been attached to gold. The more unstable the political and social conditions were, the more people tended to invest in gold; the scope ranged from African dictators, Gulf families who made a fortune from petroleum to the Egyptian and Indian farmer who saved the profit of a good harvest in gold.

Gold's high price in relation to its weight and size made it an ideal object for smuggling. People distrusting their government brought their savings to the vaults of Swiss banks, often in gold. In 1980, an estimated 40 per cent of the world's annual production was smuggled into other countries after passing through the London and Zürich markets. The biggest gold consumer in 20th century was India where about a quarter of the world's yearly gold production was bought by hoarders. Despite the Gold Import Act of 1946, which prohibited the import of bullion, India took the biggest part of the physical gold. Gold smugglers were organized in another transnational network, in syndicates driven from Beirut and Dubai. To meet the demand their dhows brought the gold onto the Indian Ocean, where it was transhipped on fishing boats from Bombay (Mumbai). Further gold was smuggled via Singapore to Indonesia; smaller lots were brought to India and Pakistan by thousands of migrant workers in the Gulf region. During the military conflicts in Indochina, a lot of gold also went into this region, with which the 'Boat People' from Vietnam paid for their transport.

Gold was also used in dentistry, mainly in wealthy countries like Sweden or West Germany with a generous system of health insurance. Despite the high prices, the electronic industry also consumed a greater part of the newly produced gold from the late 1970s onwards.

However a major quantity of gold was used for jewellery. In opposition to Western countries, in the Middle East and most Asian regions, the value of the jewellery depended not on the quality of the handicraft but on the gold's high purity. In many non-European cultures, gold was a traditional bride-gift that expressed not only the social standing of the bride's family, but which gave her (limited) economic security especially when she was left by her husband. When in January 1980 the gold price rose to US$800 an ounce, a great amount of jewellery between Beirut and Hong Kong was smelted down into bullion, brought to Zürich on night-flights and sold the next day. Even hoarders in countries far away from the financial centres were thus affected by the world gold price.

Bernd-Stefan Grewe

Bibliography

Bernstein P. L. 2000. *The power of gold: the history of an obsession*. New York: John Wiley.

Feinstein C. H. 2005. *An economic history of South Africa*. Cambridge: Cambridge University Press.

Gold Survey. London: Consolidated Gold Fields Ltd (1967–89), Gold Fields Mineral Service (since 1989) [online]. Available: www.gfms.co.uk, accessed 30 April 2007.

Vilar P. 1976. *A history of gold and money, 1450–1920*. London: New Left Books.

Weston R. 1983. *Gold: a world survey*. New York: St. Martin's.

Related essays

Africa; Chinese Diaspora; commodity trading; contract and indentured labourers; executives and professionals; financial centres; financial markets; germs; guestworkers; International Monetary Fund (IMF); labour migrations; money; rush migrations; salt; Swiss banks; temporary migrations

Governance

Governance implies transparency and accountability. The concept is used in many contexts: corporate governance, public governance, non-profit governance (for non-government organizations), electronic (or digital) governance (the use of the Internet to offer services by or information about government; not to be confused with Internet governance: the shared roles of government, private sector, and civil society in the development of the Internet), or clinical governance (offering services and accountability in the context of healthcare services). Governance is also used in a more abstract context. Political scientists like James Rosenau and Thomas G. Weiss used the term 'global governance' to describe an international political system without a central power. Governance in this context is more about international cooperation among national governments, international institutions, non-government organizations, and sometimes even individuals based on shared interests and international law.

Originally governance meant just the act of governing, stressing administration more than politics. In recent years, however, governance as a concept not only applies to wielding power, but is also about the interaction between government and other institutions and civilians in a society. Key concepts within this context are the public good, transparency, the rule of law, and the active participation of civilians in their society. Governance also depends on and determines the legitimacy of a regime.

Internationally, it is notably the World Bank and the United Nations that have built upon the concept of governance, often preferring the term 'good governance'. From the early 1990s onward, after years of failed efforts at development aid, 'good governance' was seen as a way to be more successful in improving life in many parts of the world. Development aid, either given directly to governments or used as an investment to support local initiatives, regularly resulted in sustaining the political and economic systems that had created the original problems. 'Good governance' meant to the World Bank an end to arbitrary policy making, unaccountable bureaucracies, unenforced or unjust legal systems, the abuse of executive power, a civil society unengaged in public life, and widespread corruption. The World Bank, in cooperation with the United Nations, tries to introduce 'good governance' in the countries that borrow its money to improve their economy.

A complication with the demand for 'good governance' is that it is hard to determine what exactly the quality of governance is. Both the World Bank and the United Nations Development Programme use the concept of 'indicators' when they analyse the quality of governance in a certain country. An example of the complexity of the use of indicators is the 'corruption' indicator. Since corruption can only be positively identified when people get caught, 'successful' corruption will never be registered. Consequently, the corruption indicator tends to be unreliable. Researchers at the World Bank have devised a system with 350 variables to determine the quality of governance.

Another transnational aspect of governance has to do with major corporations. After the financial crisis in Asia in the second half of the 1990s and incidents in the early 2000s, when companies either went broke (like Enron or Worldcom) or ended up in financial troubles (like Parmalat in Italy or the Dutch-based international supermarket chain Albert Hein/Ahold), investors, suppliers, employees and national governments wanted more transparency regarding company policies. To regain the public's trust, companies emphasized corporate governance, in which the strategic goals of the company, the risks of a business strategy, the ethics of the company (or how its stays within legal bounds), and an independent audit of the company's finances had to be guaranteed.

Although there is not a concerted international effort in relation to corporate governance, initiatives to support corporate governance are taken at different levels, and in many countries. National governments have been concerned about the consequences of bad business practices for individual investors. They either support self-regulation of companies, like the Kodex of best practices formulated by the commission led by Gerhard Cromme (2002) in Germany, or legislation like the Sarbanes-Oxley Act (2002) in the United States. Investors have become more powerful, since small, individual investors have been partly replaced by more powerful institutional investors, like banks, insurance companies, mutual funds and pension funds. Finally, there are now only four major firms that control the audit market internationally – Ernst & Young, Deloitte, PricewaterhouseCoopers, and KPMG – and through their powerful position contribute to setting the standards for corporate governance.

Ruud Janssens

Bibliography

Clarke T. 2004. *International corporate governance: a comparative perspective.* London and New York: Routledge.

Healey J. & Robinson M. 1994. *Democracy, governance and economic policy: Sub-Saharan Africa in comparative perspective.* London: Overseas Development Institute.

Hyden G. (ed.) 2004. *Making sense of governance: empirical evidence from 16 developing countries.* Boulder: Lynne Rienner.

Kaufmann D., Aart K. and Massimo M. 2005. 'Governance matters IV: governance indicators for 1996–2004', *World Bank Policy Research Working Paper,* 3237 [online]. Available: http://worldbank.org/wbi/governance/pubs/govmatters4.html

World Bank 1994. *Governance: the World Bank's experience.* Washington, DC.

Related essays

auditing; democracy; developmental assistance; financial markets; governing science; intergovernmental organizations; international non-governmental organizations (INGOs); legal order; United Nations system; world orders

Governing science

Michel Foucault has suggested that, in the 18th century, a new relation was established between politics as a practice and politics as a knowledge, resulting in a shift from an 'art of government' to a 'political science'. From that moment on, power has consisted in mastering things rather than in imposing laws. To the structures of sovereignty was added 'governmentality', a body of knowledge and techniques governments mobilized to steer the behaviour of the people, mostly through the administrative apparatus. These governing sciences are uncertain and blurred objects. They have not crystallized into organized institutions like other academic disciplines, through periodicals, textbooks, treaties or professional organizations. They sum up practical knowledges or know-hows incorporated in regulatory instruments directed at the population, rather than being the implementation of a seam of political theory. To the extent that these bodies of knowledge do not pertain to logics rooted in sovereignty, then the notion of a border, that touchstone of sovereignty, is of no epistemological value in addressing these governing sciences. These bodies of knowledge have their roots within and without state boundaries. Cameral sciences (*Cameralwissenschaft*) were thus an object of emulation among 18th-century German states from as early as 1720. Not only did governing sciences circulate, they were defined and shaped through this process of circulation.

National or local governments, individual brokers, professional and scholarly groups, and intergovernmental organizations have been major actors in such flows, as they tried to organize and control them.

A first instance of these circulations had to do with the training of the governing elites. At the end of the 19th century American students and scholars travelled to Europe, most notably in Germany and Great Britain, and the institutional faith of the German historical school of economics subsequently imbued American universities and the 'progressive movement'. Some training institutions for governing elites were taken as models abroad, of which the most famous has been the London School of Economics and Political Science (1895). In Paris, the École Libre des Sciences Politiques explicitly referred to the London School project as it tried to train 'republican gentlemen' to staff the French higher administration in the early 20th century. US Ivy League universities also emulated the British institution, and their schools of government and law schools have ultimately become the major training institutions for national governing elites worldwide, with a special appeal for South and Latin American ones.

Sciences of government have also been produced and exchanged through the study of foreign practices. This included the study of administrations. Delegations from Meiji Japan thus came to Europe in the early 1870s to find new ways to administer their police, and eventually selected the Parisian *Préfecture de police* system to implement in Japan.

Public policy transfers have also been the opportunity their administrative apparatus and implicit norms to travel. When American scholars and officials studied public works, urban planning, collective transportation or sewer systems in the late 19th century, they also soaked up the practical know-how used to discipline the beneficiaries and users of these public endeavours.

Forms of institutional imitation must be mentioned among the vectors for the circulation of governing sciences. Institutional crises or post-conflict situations were especially propitious to such circulation, as was the case after World War 2 when institutional forms from the occupying countries were pushed onto German and Japanese local and national institutions.

Scholarship has also contributed to the circulation of knowledge about government. As scientific language allows one to move away from national paradigms, because of its claim to universal relevance, the scientific versions of governing knowledges have vouched for the neutrality of their tenets regarding politics. Statistics were one of these scientific versions. Alain Desrosières has insisted on the hybrid character of this science of government, a mix of administrative practice (with the establishment of systems to record and publish statistics) and scientific work (with the production and circulation of mathematic tools to winnow the collected data). As conferences on statistics multiplied in the middle of the 19th century, statistics was among the first governing sciences to travel with its full-fledged toolbox of norms and standards to rationalize state control over populations and their evolution. Social sciences came a bit later, as their original focus was on inventing practical means to achieve social peace, notably through the establishment of new institutions and policies, and the improvement of existing ones. French social economy Le Play style, the German Verein für Sozialpolitik, British Fabians and Northern American social reform movements took part in a conversation about practical solutions to restore or establish social stability, while participants also included their Japanese or South American counterparts. Last but not least, juridical science also delivered: subdisciplines such as comparative law spread knowledge of different national administrative regimes, while also establishing a field where the hierarchy of their value was fiercely disputed. Followers of international law formalized an international political order which materialized in the interwar period with the League of Nations and its implicit and explicit standards for good government, and they would have a high hand in establishing the pattern of the European institutions after the Second World War.

Governing sciences do not float freely, and their circulation is not symmetric between the different actors that have a hand in it. This is a prerequisite for transactions to take place, establishing the conditions under which governing sciences are exchanged, appropriated or imposed. Two differing interpretations of these transactions are usually at odds: one of them finds the transnational matrix in the power relations between nation states while the other pays attention to the autonomy of groups of actors with specific resources and interests, irreducible to their national characteristics. These two approaches can be considered as the two poles of a scale on which transactions can be qualified according to their degree of coercion.

Colonialism or imperialism established the context of coercive transactions. As far as colonialism is concerned, a genuine colonial science was constructed in the first half of the 20th century, with intense cross-observation between the French and British institutions in charge of training the civil servants for their respective empires. In the interwar period, this science of colonial administration was at the heart of a competition between France and Great Britain as to the management of the territories under League of Nations mandates. Some of the governing know-hows that were developed in imperial contexts were subsequently brought back to the motherland with senior civil servants when empires rolled back. Housing, immigration and cultural policies in France received an enduring stamp from such 'backfiring' during the 1960s and 1970s.

A bipolar world set the frame of competitive transactions. This was the case in the postwar period, with the conflict between totalitarian and democratic states during the Cold War. Then, major ideological oppositions guided the transactions. Governing sciences were instrumentalized in this competition as a result, as both sides tried to convey the sense that their administration and government style and substance worked out best. During the 1930s, the international congresses of administrative science were a battlefield where a lot of heat was generated about the role of the leader or the content of administrative methods, while research and scholarship in Europe and the United States was absorbed in defending one or the other conception of governmentality.

Finally, knowledge played a major role in situations where coercion was apparently less intense. One thinks of the diffusion of directions or public policy instruments by intergovernmental organizations or experts. Organizations such as the OECD and the World Bank have contributed to this cognitive harmonization in areas ranging from employment to pensions policies. They have structured communities of experts who have elaborated solutions with a claim to be universal. This was especially clear for new health policies developed within the networks of health economists supported by the OECD in the 1980s. Stanford University economist Alan Enthoven was the emblematic figure in this movement. He advised the Reagan administration about the establishment of health maintenance organizations before exporting his expertise to Great Britain, the Netherlands or France. In all these instances, the reform of public health policies and administrations marked a shift away from the public sphere, and identified healthcare with a quasi-market.

Chronologically speaking, one can locate four configurations by which different streams of scholarship retained substantial power to define what 'good government' was, thus laying claim to be 'the' science of government.

Political economy, the 'science of liberalism', got stronger at the end of the 18th century and all through the 19th century. It was the backbone of German cameral sciences, epitomized by Johann Heinrich Gottlob von Justi (1717–71), with their specialized police, public finance and administration branches. As the liberal gospel spread through the fabric of journals, correspondence, translations and conferences that thrived during the 19th century, so there spread the notion that the market was a natural presence which needed to be preserved. Government institutions, according to political economy, must understand these economic operations in their intimate and complex nature. This being done, it should respect them, so that politics is equipped with a precise knowledge of society and the market. Accordingly, a science of government would be that derived from the understanding and respect of scientific laws that were said to govern markets.

Later in the 19th century, political economy's supremacy was called into question by the contradictions of the liberal state, whose realms of intervention had not ceased to expand. Administration was more and more complex. Building from the premises of cameral sciences, and keen to distinguish itself from the discipline of law, a science of administration or administrative science was sketched out to handle this complexity. Its early thinkers, such as the Americans Woodrow Wilson or Frank Goodnow, insisted it was a technical and rational knowledge, separate from politics, and it was successfully heralded as the ultimate science of government. According to the First International Conference on Administrative Science (1910), it should develop an understanding of social facts, a perfect knowledge of the mentality of individuals, and a just appreciation of their conception of discipline and order. Top of the list of the new credo's tenets were the expansion of the executive branch of government and the rationalization of administrative tasks. A coalition of political scientists and administrators created a vibrant transatlantic community that made the new science a shared frame in Europe and North America during the interwar period.

After World War 2, economics asserted itself as the prominent science of government, bringing about new forms of governmental legitimacies and expertise. It suggested a reorganization between the political, economic and social realms. The state had a legitimate role in the regulation of society, that broke away from the self-regulating and natural market. Beyond the mere economic sphere, planning and forecasting became central aspects of the new scientific conception of government and administration, with a growing role for higher civil servants and specialized government departments. The new doctrine, that had been sketched out in the 1930s, crystallized into the cooperation between US and British war administrations. It spread into Africa, Asia and South or Latin America on the wings of bilateral US technical assistance (the Marshall Plan, the Point IV Program) and multilateral or regional programmes, most notably through the installation of 'development administration' as a type of administrative and governmental organization and knowledge tailored to third-world countries.

From the 1980s, these conceptions came under fire from supporters of New Public Management, which suggested revamping the relationship between civil servants and elected officials to the advantage of the latter, restructuring the administration by means of autonomous agencies created out of the civil service realm, and fostering a new conception of the administered, now conceived of as customers. Indicators were among the new instruments to be used for a rational management of government, while administration should be geared towards the reduction of public expenses, with the different administrative agencies competing for this achievement. New Public Management included a specific transnational dimension as it suggested that local and national administrations should be able to learn from one another across borders: benchmarking was the key to this mutual awareness. Intergovernmental organizations quickly caught up with this idea, that seemed a smooth and soft path to convergence and integration. First applied in EU employment policy in the late 1990s, it became the spine of European policies in 2000 when the Council of the European Union adopted the Open Method of Coordination, whose keywords are 'indicators', 'guidelines', 'timetables', 'benchmarks' and 'mutual learning'.

As standards, indicators and norms get generalized in the conduct of public policies, at the prompting of actors and institutions whose trajectories and designs stretch across national, regional and local governments, public government and administration takes on a more technical style and substance. A new relationship between power and knowledge, in other words a new governmentality, is taking shape under our eyes.

Renaud Payre

Bibliography

Desrosières A. 1993. *La politique des grands nombres*. Paris: La Découverte.

Dezalay Y. and Garth B. 2002. *The internationalization of palace wars: lawyers, economists, and the contest to transform Latin American States*. Chicago: Chicago University Press.

Foucault M. 1978, 'La "governementalità"', *Aut-Aut*, 167–168, 12–29. Reprinted in Foucault M. 1994. *Dits et Écrits*, Vol. 3, Paris: Gallimard, 635–57.

Ihl O., Kaluszynski M. and Pollet G. (eds) 2003. *Les sciences de gouvernement*. Paris: Economica.

Rueschmeyer D. and Skocpol T. (eds) 1996. *States, social knowledge, and the origins of modern social policies*. Princeton: Princeton University Press.

Stolleis M. 1998. *Histoire du droit public en Allemagne: droit public impérial et science de la police, 1600–1800*. Paris: PUF.

Westney E. 1987. *Imitation and innovation. the transfer of Western organizational patterns to Meiji Japan*. Cambridge, MA: Harvard University Press.

Related essays
book and periodical exchange; civilizations; convergence and divergence; democracy; economics; empires and imperialism; European Union (EU); forests; governance; health policy; higher education; intellectual elites; intergovernmental organizations; international students; legal order; liberalism; nation and state; Pax Americana; police; public policy; social sciences; statistics; technical assistance; welfare state; Westernization

Grants and fellowships *See* Fellowships and grants

Green Revolution
The Green Revolution refers to the efforts of scientists and policy makers to meet the growing food needs of an exploding global population by using natural gene selection to create new plants hybrids adaptable to a variety of climates. The Green Revolution is divided into two distinct phases. The first phase began in Mexico in the 1940s with the creation of new, high-yielding, light-sensitive corn and wheat hybrids. The second phase of the Green Revolution began in the 1980s when Green Revolution institutional structures began to address socioeconomic and environmental dislocations created by the spread of Green Revolution hybrids. The Green Revolution is institutionalized in the Consultative Group in International Agricultural Research (CGIAR). Its international research centres have trained over 8,000 researchers working in 80 different countries. Its budget accounts for approximately 4 per cent of total worldwide public funding for agricultural research. Its current mission is based on five key goals: increasing productivity, integrating natural resource management, preserving biodiversity, improving national policies, and building capacity.

The impetus of the Green Revolution was US Vice President Henry Wallace's official state visit to Mexico in 1941. Wallace, a third-generation owner of the hybrid seed company Pioneer

Hi-Breed and publisher of the popular *Wallace Farmer's Almanac*, was interested in agricultural projects that would help Mexico lower its wheat and corn imports. In 1943, the Rockefeller Foundation signed a formal agreement with the Mexican Department of Agriculture to provide funding for a Mexico Field Office whose mission was to increase the yield per acre of corn and beans. The office was located at the Mexican National College of Agriculture in the Mexico City suburb of Chapingo. It was headed by J. George Harrar (who later became Rockefeller Foundation president, 1961–72). By 1950, an investment of $1.5 million dollars had produced eight new hybrid corn stocks and Mexican corn production increased by 8 per cent. Successful new corn hybrids led to new research on wheat, bean sorghums and soybeans.

Between 1959 and 1963, the Rockefeller Foundation's Mexico Field Office operations were internationalized. Funding expanded beyond the scope of the Mexican government and the Rockefeller Foundation to include the Ford Foundation, the US Agency for International Development (USAID), the United Nations Development Program (UNDP) and the Inter-American Development Bank (IDB). A new scientific international non-governmental agency named the International Centre for the Improvement of Maize and Wheat (CIMMYT) was formed to coordinate all research experiments.

In the late 1960s and 1970s, population experts were particularly concerned that the growing populations of India and Pakistan faced mass starvation. CIMMYT's chief wheat agronomist Norman Borlaug made arrangements with local, state, and national governments to export high-yielding, semi-dwarf wheat hybrid seeds to these countries. His seeds had been developed in high and low altitudes in the Mexican states of Sonora and Toluca. They were insensitive to light and therefore adaptable to a wide variety of climates. In his efforts to export the seeds from Mexico to Asia, Dr Borlaug encountered a variety of political and logistical difficulties. This included a prolonged delay due to bureaucratic regulation at the US–Mexico border, transit problems through Los Angeles in the midst of the Watts Riots, and near destruction due to a war between India and Pakistan. Between 1969 and 1970, he succeeded in planting approximately 6 million hectares of Mexican semi-dwarf wheat hybrid seeds in Pakistan and 14 million hectares in India. In 1970, Dr Borlaug was awarded the Nobel Peace Prize for his work.

In 1968, in an effort to generate greater public awareness, the Rockefeller Foundation sponsored an international symposium on 'Strategy for the Conquest of Hunger'. Research from this conference highlighted that the global population would add an additional 2 billion people between 1965 and 1990. Experts underscored the urgent need to globalize efforts to transfer Green Revolution hybrids. In May 1971, these efforts were institutionalized with the creation of CGIAR. Its founding membership included 28 national governments and international non-governmental organizations (INGOs).

CGIAR's mission was to provide administrative support and management reviews to the four existing international agricultural research centres. These included: (1) CIMMYT in Mexico for maize and wheat; (2) the International Centre For Tropical Agriculture (CIAT) in Colombia for rice, bean, forage grasses and cassava; (3) the International Rice Institute (IRRI) in the Philippines for rice; and (4) the International Institute of Tropical Agriculture (IITA) in Nigeria to study the special foods and ecosystems related to Africa. Each individual international centre remained responsible for conducting its own research and facilitating the exchange of information between national agricultural research programs. (E.g., CIMMYT coordinated information between the Mexican and Indian government agricultural agencies regarding wheat and maize issues.)

In the 1970s, the number of international centres within CGIAR grew from four to 16. New research focused on plants in the tropics and semi-arid tropics, roots and tubers, livestock and pastures, cereals, and legumes. By the mid-1970s, work had expanded to genetic resources, plants in dry areas, and West African rice.

The second phase of the Green Revolution began in the 1980s as CGIAR reacted to criticism that its work was creating serious political, socioeconomic, cultural, and environmental dislocations. From the outset, Dr Borlaug's transfer and promotion of high-yielding Mexican wheat varieties over native plants such as lentils and rice had caused controversy. In 1969, during the first year's harvest in Kerala, India, hungry protesters had rioted against a switch from rice to wheat. Borlaug had argued that high-yield strains of indigenous plants simply did not exist and his Mexican wheat varieties were the best way to

fight starvation. In his opinion, wheat cultivation could produce the most food calories and it could be grown in nearly all environments with little pesticide.

Critics denounced the transfer of a whole new technology focused on producing plants with the highest yield possible. Some decried wheat as a Western crop that used enormous quantities of water and fertilizer. The only way to meet these demands was by developing new irrigation systems and using organic or chemical fertilizers. Organic fertilizers required large livestock herds that ate a considerable portion of the harvest and chemical petroleum fertilizers destroyed the environment. Others protested that there was pressure on Third World governments to pass policies that gave wheat farmers relatively high prices for their product, created special credit programmes for wheat farmers, and promoted the distribution of insecticides, weed killers and machinery manufactured in developed countries.

To address these criticisms, CGIAR expanded its membership to include developing nations. These new members were influential in modifying CGIAR's budget and objectives. CGIAR's mission was redefined as being to 'increase sustainable food production in the developing countries in such a way that the nutritional level and general economic well-being of the poor are improved'. New emphasis was placed on protecting biodiversity, land, and water. In the 1990s, CGIAR's mission was further expanded to agroforestry and forestry, living aquatic resources, and natural resources management.

CGIAR also changed its position on pesticides. The original wheat varieties introduced by Dr Borlaug that relied heavily on pesticides and fertilizers were replaced with more productive CIMMYT varieties. These require little or no pesticide as they have been selected for their durable built-in resistance to disease and pests and their efficient use of soil nutrients, water and sunlight. Today, these new hybrids account for approximately 80 per cent of global production of wheat and maize germ plasm. More than 75 per cent of the developing world's wheat area (excluding China) has been planted to semi-dwarf wheat developed by CIMMYT and its national agricultural research partners.

CGIAR's success in transferring its hybrid varieties has generated strong criticism that the Green Revolution is responsible for reducing biodiversity. The 1992 Rio Treaty, signed by 189 countries, promoted a global debate on this topic. It was argued that varieties developed through gene selection were susceptible to new diseases and pathogens and this could lead to a global crop failure. Centuries-old genetic varieties had mutations that could prevent such a catastrophe. In response, CGIAR expanded its commitment to the categorization and preservation of genetic plant material. CGIAR and its international research centre partners house one of the world's largest collections of plant genetic resources and make this available to researchers around the world. CIMMYT's Wellhausen-Anderson Plant Genetic Resources Centre provides long term storage for close to half a million seed samples including more than 6,000 endangered farmer-developed maize varieties. CIMMYT research has also helped to rescue numerous samples held in seed banks throughout Latin America and at the National Seed Storage Laboratory in the United States. Its International Wheat Information System (IWIS) has set global standards by providing computerized data to researchers worldwide on 1.5 million genotypes of bread wheat, durum wheat and triticale.

Currently, Green Revolution scientists are working on expanding Quality Protein Maize (QPM) experiments based in Africa. Maize is a major staple for the poor in African countries. Regular maize provides protein but lacks adequate levels of two essential amino acids, lysine and tryptophan. Based on ongoing natural gene-selection experiments started at CIMMYT in the 1960s, these two proteins were added to QPM.

In the 1990s, CIMMYT teamed with SG 2000, a joint programme sponsored by the Carter Center and the Sasakawa Africa Association. In 1990, a formal QPM research and development programme was initiated in Ghana. In 1992, SG 2000 agronomists released an improved QPM from Obatanpa, Ghana. From 1996 to 2001, phase one of the QPM project was based on this variety. Seeds were transferred to Mozambique, Uganda, Benin, Togo, Mali, Burkina Faso, Nigeria, and Ethiopia. Following the acquisition of additional funding from the Nippon Foundation of Japan, phase two was initiated in 2002 at research stations in Harare, Zimbabwe and Nairobi, Kenya. In 2006, SG 2000 estimated that there were between 800,000 and 1,000,000 hectares of QPM planted in sub-Saharan Africa. An additional 400,000 hectares of commercial QPM hybrids have also been successfully grown in China, India, Brazil, Mexico, and Central America. In 2006, several other philanthropic foundations initiated new, well-funded agricultural programmes in Africa. The Gates and Rockefeller Foundations jointly invested $150 million in projects that will finance farmers and agricultural distribution and produce high-yielding seeds. In a separate project focused on sustainable development, the Soros Foundation allocated $50 million to support the distribution of fertilizers and construction of schools and clinics. The goal of this project is to assist African farmers to transition from subsistence farming to productive market-oriented farming.

The Green Revolution has been controversial and it continues to force changes in centuries-old agricultural traditions. Green Revolution scientists and policy makers have encouraged the use of conventional hybridization methods, new financing methods, and new distribution systems. These changes in agriculture are occurring at the same time that biotechnology is also having a significant impact on modernizing agriculture. By definition, the two processes are separate and distinct. Biotechnology research is patented and conducted by private corporations such as Monsanto. Research relies on DNA splicing to create new genetically modified organisms (GMOs). Green Revolution experiments continue to be based on natural gene selection.

Margaret C. Boardman

Bibliography

Brown L. R. 1970. *Seeds of change: the Green Revolution and development in the 1970s.* New York: Praeger for the Overseas Development Council.

Conway G. 1997. *The doubly Green Revolution: food for all in the 21st century.* London: Penguin.

Dil A. (ed.) 1997. *Norman Borlaug on world hunger.* San Diego: Bookservice International.

Pearse A. C. 1980. *Seeds of plenty, seeds of want: social and economic implications of the Green Revolution.* Oxford and New York: Oxford University Press.

Perkins J. H. 1997. *Geopolitics and the Green Revolution: wheat, genes, and the Cold War.* Oxford: Oxford University Press.

Stakman E. C., Bradfield R. and Mangelsdorf
P.C. 1969. *Campaigns against hunger.*
Cambridge, MA: Harvard University Press.

Related essays
acclimatization; agriculture; biodiversity;
developmental assistance; food; Ford
Foundation; forests; genetically modified
organisms (GMOs); international non-
governmental organizations (INGOs);
Monsanto; pesticides, herbicides,
insecticides; philanthropic foundations;
population; remittances; seeds; sustainable
development; technical assistance

Greenpeace

Formed by American and Canadian anti-
nuclear activists living in Vancouver in the
late 1960s and early 1970s, Greenpeace is noteworthy for its innovative use of non-violent
direct action campaigns to garner media
attention for environmental issues. By 2004
Greenpeace International had offices in 40
countries, a gross income of €158.5 million,
and 2.7 million financial supporters.

Greenpeace began as the Don't Make a
Wave Committee, an organization founded in
1969 by four Americans living in Vancouver,
Irving and Dorothy Stowe and Jim and Marie
Bohlen, to stop the American nuclear weapons
testing on the Alaskan island of Amchitka.
All four were veterans of the American peace
movement and brought to the Committee
the Quaker notion of bearing witness and
Gandhi's philosophy of non-violent resistance. Concepts from popular ecology, the
counterculture movement, and the New Left
also influenced the early and contentious
development of the organization.

In 1971 the Committee attempted to sail
two ships to Amchitka to bear witness to the
test. Whilst neither *Greenpeace*, a renamed fishing vessel, nor a second ship, *Greenpeace Too*,
reached the island, their provocative voyages
brought media attention to the organization
and its cause. The voyages demonstrated the
effectiveness of non-violent direct action
when combined with a savvy media campaign
and suggested the possibility of an organisation of environmental and peace activists.

After much debate, members of the
Committee transformed it into a permanent
environmental organization renamed the
Greenpeace Foundation. The new chairman,
Ben Metcalfe, organised a 1972–73 campaign

against French nuclear testing on the South
Pacific island of Moruroa, employing a combination of international protests and efforts
to sail to the island from New Zealand. Led
by David McTaggart, the voyages each ended
in encounters with the French. In the first
encounter, a French naval vessel collided
with *Greenpeace III*, while during the second
encounter, French commandos boarded the
vessel and assaulted those on board. The
campaign resulted in the formation of new
national Greenpeace offices and may have
contributed to the French government's decision to end atmospheric nuclear testing on
Moruroa. It also marked the beginning of
French hostility towards Greenpeace which
climaxed on 10 July 1985, when, in response
to protests against underground nuclear
testing on Moruroa, French agents deto-
nated two bombs on the Greenpeace vessel
The Rainbow Warrior while it was docked in
Auckland harbour, killing photographer
Fernando Pereira.

Following the Moruroa campaign, Robert
Hunter assumed leadership and moved
Greenpeace towards issues of ecology and
animal rights. In 1975 Greenpeace embarked
on an anti-whaling campaign that resulted
in a dramatic encounter with Soviet whalers off the California coast and a subsequent
increase in the prominence of the organization. Critics argue that some of Greenpeace's
animal rights operations, such as the 1976
effort to stop the Canadian harp seal hunt,
ignore the cultural and economic needs of
indigenous and working-class peoples.

As Greenpeace grew during the late 1970s,
so did the tensions between the Vancouver
international headquarters and its loosely
affiliated national offices. In 1979, using these
divisions as well as the financial difficulties of
the head office as leverage, McTaggart orchestrated a restructuring of Greenpeace. The new
Greenpeace International, headquartered in
Amsterdam, operated as a hierarchical and
centrally organized entity reminiscent of a
multinational corporation. National offices
were obligated to send a percentage of their
funds to Greenpeace International and to
follow its directives.

Though often employing more mainstream
tactics such as scientific reports, Greenpeace
International continued to engage in direct
action. However, Greenpeace International
has limited such campaigns to those it considers winnable and consistent with its 'brand

image'. Greenpeace International campaigns have included opposition to ozone-layer-damaging chemicals, protests against ocean dumping, support for the preservation of Antarctica, and the publication of a global warming report.

Erik D. Anderson

Bibliography

Bohlen J. 2001. *Making waves: the origins and future of Greenpeace*. Montréal and London: Black Rose.

Pearce, F 1996. 'Greenpeace: storm-tossed on the high seas', in Bergesen O. and Parmann G. (eds) *Green Globe Yearbook 1996*. Oxford: Oxford University Press, 73–80.

Zelko F. forthcoming. *'Make it a Green Peace': the history of an international environmental organization*. Lanham: Rowman & Littlefield.

Related essays

Amnesty International (AI); biodiversity; climate change; ecology; environmental diplomacy; environmentalism; Gandhi, Mohandas Karamchand; international non-governmental organizations (INGOs); Islamic Relief Worldwide; Médecins Sans Frontières (MSF); non-violence; oceans; Oxfam; pacifism; Pugwash Conferences; Save the Children International Union; Stockholm Conference; sustainable development

Growth and development *See* Development and growth

Guestworkers

'Guestworker', a translation of the German, *Gastarbeiter*, was a euphemism for the roughly 30 million workers who travelled from Europe's periphery to its centre after World War 2. The term is now used widely to describe workers – whether in the US, the Middle East or the Pacific Rim – who are admitted on fixed-term or revocable work visas to do work that is often dangerous, dirty or just ill-paid.

Critics of guestworker programmes have likened their status to slavery but guestworkers are recruited and paid for their work (except in the most abusive cases). They send remittances home; and, usually, can return home at any time. As voluntary labour migrants, guestworkers have far more in common with indentured labourers. The essential difference is that indentured labourers were usually encouraged to settle at the end of their indenture; guestworkers are prized for their deportability.

The practice of importing workers on fixed-term, government-approved contracts was a response to the resurgence of indentured servitude and high rates of international labour migration in the 19th century. Temporary contract labour schemes were designed to maintain high levels of low-wage immigrant labour while placating anti-immigrant sentiment. So, for example, in the early 20th century, after an outcry among white settlers in Queensland about sugar planters' importation of Kanakas (Pacific Islanders) as cane-cutters, the newly unified Commonwealth of Australia expelled the Kanakas, proclaimed Australia for Whites Only, but allowed the sugar planters to reimport them on fixed-term contracts. Prussia did the same with Polish farm workers after 1890 and South Africa cycled Southern African gold and diamond miners in and out of the country on a seasonal basis.

This first phase in the history of guestworker programmes ended with the Great Depression but wartime demands for labour began the next phase, which lasted for about three decades and involved far more nations and migrants, and far greater state involvement. In the US, the federal government imported hundreds of thousands of Mexicans and British West Indians to harvest crops and take other essential war jobs. The Mexican Bracero Program ended in controversy in 1964 but, at its peak, growers recruited half a million Braceros a year. The smaller, privately run West Indian programme continues today. Contracts negotiated by US, Mexican, West Indian and British officials seemed to protect workers but conditions deteriorated rapidly, and guestworkers who contested violations of their contracts were deported. In Europe, in contrast, conditions tended to improve over time because guestworkers laboured, not just in agriculture, but also in highly unionized industries such as mining, construction, and manufacturing. Still, as guestworkers' numbers grew in Europe and as they brought their families to join them, their presence generated growing controversy, which resulted by the mid-1960s in the end of large guestworker programmes in Europe as well.

The oil shocks of 1973 dealt Europe's programmes their death blow but gave birth to

Asian guestworker schemes. In this third phase, temporary labour migrants moved in very large numbers from oil-importing nations in Asia – the Philippines, India, Pakistan, Bangladesh, and Sri Lanka – to booming oil-exporting nations like those in the Middle East and to Indonesia. These programmes were so large that they resulted in majority foreign work forces in at least four countries. These late-20th-century guestworker programmes have much in common with earlier schemes. But while still supplying workers for dirty, dangerous and difficult work, they also recruit engineers, nurses, doctors, mechanics, and, more recently, computer systems analysts. Guestworker programmes have also become feminized through 'the Maid Trade'. Sending governments now exhibit greater enthusiasm for the idea of exporting their citizens as contract workers. Paradoxically, even as sending nations play a larger role in charting the paths labour migrants follow, they exert less influence on the conditions under which their nationals live and work. Conditions for modern guestworkers remain abysmal.

Cindy Hahamovitch

Bibliography

Castles S. and Miller M. J. 1998. *The age of migration: international population movements in the modern world*, 2nd ed. New York: Guilford.

Hahamovitch C. 2003. 'Creating perfect immigrants: guestworkers of the world in historical perspective', *Labor History*, 44, 1, 69–94.

Parrenas R. S. 2001. *Servants of globalization: women, migration, and domestic work*. Stanford: Stanford University Press.

Related essays

body shopping; brain drain; contract and indentured labourers; domestic service; empire and migration; film; gold; human mobility; international migration regimes; labour migrations; marriage; nursing; oil; remittances; temporary migrations; white men's countries

Guevara, Ernesto ('Che') 1928–67

The US magazine *Time* has listed Ernesto ('Che') Guevara one of the hundred most important people of the 20th century. The son of upper-class Argentines who trained to be a doctor, Guevara was born in 1928. Influenced by Marxist tracts and the poverty that he witnessed on a 1952 journey throughout South America, he endorsed violent revolution as the solution to Latin America's problems. In 1953, Guevara travelled to Guatemala, where President Jacobo Arbenz's land reform programme had generated furious opposition from the United States.

Guevara travelled from Guatemala to Mexico, where he met Fidel Castro; he was one of four non-Cubans to participate in the military campaign that concluded with Castro as Cuba's new leader. Che's personal courage and tactical skillfulness proved critical in the guerrilla campaign to oust Fulgencio Batista. Despite his image as a Bohemian intellectual, Guevara exercised power ruthlessly when he contributed to the establishment of a brutal internal security apparatus. Che was less effective in economic matters. In 1959, Castro placed him in charge of land reform; in early 1961, he also became minister of industry. But the lost access to the US market combined with Che's rigidly collectivist policies led to a sharp downturn: between 1961 and 1963, the sugar harvest fell by nearly 50 per cent by value.

Che's greatest impact, however, came in international affairs. During the early months of Castro's regime, he pushed for a closer alliance with the Soviet Union, and he helped negotiate the stationing of Soviet nuclear missiles in Cuba. After the peaceful resolution of the Cuban Missile Crisis, Che grew alienated from the Soviets; he increasingly embraced a revolutionary nationalism focused on Asia, Africa, and Latin America. In the mid 1960s, Che traveled to Zaire to assist leftist rebels battling the corrupt, pro-US regime of Mobutu Sese Seko; in 1967, he was captured and killed in Bolivia, in a joint operation of the Bolivian army and the CIA. In some ways, the manner of death was fitting for a man who never recognized political boundaries – an Argentine who played a key role in the Cuban revolution, fought in Africa, and then died in one of South America's poorest countries.

Guevara's death made him a martyr among leftist intellectuals worldwide: French philosopher Jean-Paul Sartre termed him 'the most complete human being of our age' (García and Solar 2000, 198). The cult of Che intensified on the thirtieth anniversary of his death, in 1997, after the discovery of his remains. Memorialized on baseball caps, bandannas, and especially T-shirts containing prints of Alberto Korda's photograph of him, Che symbolized anti-Establishment dissent, protest against globalization, or simple cultural trendiness. This Che revisionism peaked in 2004, with the film The Motorcycle Diaries, in which Mexican heartthrob Gael García Bernal portrayed Che as an iconoclastic rebel, a Latin American version of Jack Kerouac.

Chilean novelist Ariel Dorfman had rallied on Che's behalf following the revolutionary's death. To Dorfman, Che's transnational status was central to his lasting appeal: 'Perhaps in these orphaned times of incessantly shifting identities and alliances, the fantasy of an adventurer who changed countries and crossed borders and broke down limits without once betraying his basic loyalties provides the restless youth of our era with an optimal combination, grounding them in a fierce center of moral gravity while simultaneously appealing to their contemporary nomadic impulse' (Dorfman 1999). The writer Paul Berman had a less optimistic view: 'Che was an enemy of freedom, and yet he has been erected into a symbol of freedom. He helped establish an unjust social system in Cuba and has been erected into a symbol of social justice. He stood for the ancient rigidities of Latin-American thought, in a Marxist-Leninist version, and

he has been celebrated as a free-thinker and a rebel' (Berman 2004).

With the Castro era now passing and Cuban archives possibly becoming open to scholars, perhaps a third image of Che will soon emerge.

Robert David Johnson

Bibliography

Berman P. 2004. 'Should we love Che Guevara?', Slate, 24 September [online]. Available: http://slate.com/id/2107100/, accessed 20 January 2008.

Dorfman A. 1999. 'Che Guevara', Time, 14 June [online]. Available: www.time.com/time/time100/heroes/profile/guevara01.html, accessed 20 January 2008.

García F. and Solar O. (eds) 2000. Che: images of a revolutionary. London: Pluto.

Vargas Llosa A. 2005. 'The killing machine: Che Guevara, from communist firebrand to capitalist brand', New Republic, 11 July.

Related essays

1960s; Africa; Cold War; exile; film; Gandhi, Mohandas Karamchand; Little Red Book; Mandela, Nelson; Mexican Revolution; Russian Revolution; socialism; The Wretched of the Earth; T-shirt; world orders

H

Halloween and Christmas See
Christmas and Halloween

Hammarskjöld family

The significance of Dag Hammarskjöld, second secretary-general of the United Nations, is known to most students of international affairs. Less well-known is the degree to which he was a product not only of his single-minded commitment to international peace and justice, but of a family that transcended the narrow nationalism haunting pre-1914 Europe.

Dag's father, Hjalmar Hammarskjöld (1862–1953), headed an aristocratic household that took *noblesse oblige* seriously indeed. The elder Hammarskjöld combined an unapologetic loyalty to his own country with an appreciation of Sweden's participation in the larger community of nations (he took the word 'community' literally). Trained as an international lawyer, he served for a time as a diplomatic envoy, eventually joining The Hague Arbitration Tribunal and, later, the Permanent Court of International Justice. He also held civil service posts and, after 1918, remained a provincial governor for more than two decades.

Hjalmar's most notable service, however, was as his country's prime minister. From 1914 to 1917, he helped to preserve Sweden's neutrality amid the carnage of World War I. He believed neutrality would protect Swedish interests, but he also believed it would allow Sweden to champion international legal principles that might help prevent another catastrophic war. Only a strict adherence to the rule of law, he claimed, would protect smaller countries from the revolutionary forces unloosed by modern industrialism and nationalism.

Hjalmar and his wife, the former Agnes Almquist, raised four children. Where Hjalmar was stern and politically elitist, Agnes was warmhearted, generous, and unapologetically democratic. Together they instilled in their children the importance of integrity and service. Agnes's strongly humanistic religion, reflected in Dag's book, *Markings*, also contributed to that sense of service.

Little wonder that three of their four sons had international affiliations. Their oldest, Bo (1891–1974) emulated his father's entry into Sweden's civil service and eventually held posts in two of Sweden's major international corporations. Ake Hammarskjöld (1893–1937) even more closely paralleled his father's career, getting a law degree before heading, as had Hjalmar, to The Hague where Ake became secretary-general of the Permanent Court of International Justice. Only writer and journalist Sten (1900–1972), their third son, literally stayed at home.

It was Hjalmar and Agnes's youngest son, Dag (1905–61), who became an icon of 20th-century internationalism. Dag studied economics under John Maynard Keynes, then received his doctorate at the University of Stockholm. Like his father, he also received a law degree before entering the Swedish civil service. During the Second World War, he simultaneously chaired neutral Sweden's central bank board of governors and served as permanent under-secretary of the finance ministry. During the early Cold War, he gravitated toward foreign affairs, joining the foreign ministry and becoming president of the OEEC in 1950.

It was, of course, at the United Nations (UN) where Dag made his most important contributions. As the Cold War intensified, neither the US nor the USSR wanted a strong or independent secretary-general. After the Soviets more or less forced Norway's Trygve Lie to surrender the post of secretary-general in 1953, both superpowers misjudged in accepting Dag Hammarskjöld as a 'safe' compromise candidate to succeed Lie. In fact, as secretary-general, Hammarskjöld charted an aggressively independent course. No UN official since 1945 did more to restate the principle of an impartial international civil service.

Hammarskjöld reinvigorated the organization with imaginative diplomatic initiatives, from securing the release of American pilots held in China following the Korean War, to his support for Canadian Lester Pearson's 1956 proposal to create UN peace-keeping units. Perhaps his greatest triumph was in what he did not do. Anger over his efforts to dispatch UN Blue Helmets to the Congo in 1960 led Soviet Premier Nikita Khrushchev to demand Hammarskjöld's resignation. In one of the most memorable speeches in UN history, the secretary-general rejected Khrushchev's demand, pledging to serve the weak, not just the great powers. He courageously preserved his office from almost certain evisceration.

True to his family ideals, he had energized internationalism. He gave his life for these ideals when an air crash ended his efforts to settle the Congo crisis in 1961. For this and more, he received the 1961 Nobel Peace Prize posthumously. In reality, the prize honoured his family.

Gary B. Ostrower

Bibliography

Hammarskjöld D. 1964. *Markings*. New York: Knopf.

Urquhart B. 1972. *Hammarskjöld*. New York: Harper and Row.

Related essays

class; cosmopolitanism and universalism; executives and professionals; family migration; Gandhi, Mohandas Karamchand; Garvey, Marcus Mosiah; intergovernmental organizations; internationalisms; justice; Kessler, Harry von; Quesnay, Pierre; Schwimmer, Rosika; United Nations system; Williams, James Dixon

Health policy

Health policy encompasses diverse techniques of government to improve the health of populations – ranging from quarantine and mass vaccination, to the generation of health statistics, the construction of medical facilities, and health education. A striking feature of the history of health policy – neglected, until recently – is the role of transnational networks, exchanges and connections in fostering the development of both national and intergovernmental health policies.

The dramatic cholera epidemics that swept Europe between 1830 and 1847 provoked the beginnings of intergovernmental cooperation in public health. A series of eleven international sanitary conferences took place between 1851 and 1903, to coordinate international information and policies on quarantine regulations and the containment of outbreaks of disease. The first International Sanitary Convention eventually took effect in 1892, and led to the establishment of a permanent international health organization: the Office International d'Hygiène Publique, in Paris.

Underlying these conferences, however, was the development of an increasingly transnational medical profession. The professionalization, specialization, standardization, and centralization of medical knowledge during the 'long' 19th century underpinned the intergovernmental sanitary conferences. Disputes between governments at the sanitary conferences often stemmed from disputes between scientists, arguing across borders in circulating medical journals and at meetings, and in debates over the causation of diseases like cholera and over their treatment. The scientific knowledge produced in European colonies figured particularly prominently in informing international health policy, as tropical medicine emerged as a transnational discipline with its own set of assumptions, conventions and a distinctive body of knowledge.

International cooperation in health policy built upon transnational medical debates. So, too, did the development of voluntary organizations concerned with health and sanitary policy. The 19th century saw many missionary groups embrace the results of medical research, taking an increasingly active role in devising their own health policies for colonized societies. At times their ambitions were not just transnational but universal – Florence Nightingale's 'gaze' ranged from the Crimea to India. Yet missionaries often came up against alternative and competing universalisms: other religious and secular visions of health, healing and policy. Perhaps the most prominent expression of religiously informed humanitarian concern with health policy was the International Red Cross, founded by Henri Dunant in 1863 with the mission of 'civilizing' – not preventing – war. Yet the Red Cross was itself established through the signing of the first Geneva Convention, in 1864, by 12 governments at a diplomatic conference. The relationship between intergovernmental and voluntary organizations, on the one hand, and between international organizations and national governments, on the other, is not easy to demarcate.

This multiplicity of national and international, public and private organizations characterizes the history of health policy in the first half of the 20th century, a period which saw significant growth in the range of both international and transnational institutions concerned with health and welfare.

The period after the First World War saw a flourishing of such connections in the field of health policy. The trend is epitomized by the founding of the League of Nations in 1919. In 1920, a League committee on 'Social and General Questions' was established, the concerns of which ranged from the condition of refugees, to the opium trade and the 'traffic in women and children', all decidedly transnational issues. Health policy quickly became one of the League's responsibilities. It convened expert commissions of enquiry on subjects ranging from tuberculosis to biological standardization; its work on nutritional and anti-malarial policies was particularly innovative. Although the League had initially confined its interest to Europe, and particularly Eastern Europe, Asia and Africa soon became important areas of concern for the organization. It established an epidemiological surveillance station in Singapore in 1925.

Throughout its life, the League of Nations Health Organization had a close working relationship – intellectual, institutional, and financial – with the Rockefeller Foundation. Following the early work of the Rockefeller Sanitary Commission for the Eradication of Hookworm Disease from the southern states of the US, the Foundation established its International Health Division in 1913. This division played a role in war relief during the World War 1, and went on to launch research-driven public health campaigns in Europe, Latin America, South Asia, and China, targeting yellow fever, malaria, and tuberculosis, as well as developing medical education. The Rockefeller Foundation stood at the heart of new transnational networks of medical research and training, linking Eastern Europe to China and India. The more critical histories of the Rockefeller Foundation's health work have interpreted it as facilitating the global expansion of American capital. Others have highlighted, by contrast, the relative autonomy of the Foundation's experts from political pressures and motivations.

The Second World War was a watershed in the history of health policy. New technologies – the insecticide DDT, new vaccines, and the development of anti-biotic drugs – transformed the bounds of the possible. New organizations emerged to take responsibility for health policy. Out of the remains of the League of Nations and the emergency wartime humanitarian organization grew plans for a new international order. These plans culminated in the design of the United Nations and its specialized agencies, many of which were concerned with aspects of health policy – the World Health Organization, the United Nations Children's Fund, and the Food and Agriculture Organization, amongst others.

On the whole, the three decades following the Second World War saw a shift from transnational towards international health. The WHO was much more an intergovernmental organization than the League of Nations Health Organization had been. The WHO's annual assembly was made up of representatives of national ministries of health; independent 'experts' were given less autonomy that they had possessed in the League's health organization. The WHO offered its services, its expertise and its resources to national governments, as instruments towards national development. Nevertheless, the WHO continued to build upon and foster transnational connections in the making of health policy: this can be seen in the many scholarships WHO funded, allowing health professionals from different parts of the world to train together. It is evident, too, in the example of the Indian malariologists who toured Burma and Indonesia, advising on health policy, or of the young American epidemiologists from the Centers for Disease Control who staffed the ultimately successful smallpox eradication campaign in South Asia.

For much of the 1950s and 1960s, there was consensus on what we might call modernism in health policy: a belief in using simple technology on a mass scale, channelled primarily through states. Health policy increasingly took the form of targeted 'campaigns' – against malaria, against yaws, against smallpox. The near-universality of this approach suggests the extent of policy transfer across borders in this period.

This approach had many successes – for example, the great diminution in levels of malaria, by the early 1960s – but also began to run into difficulties. Drug resistance, a lack of medical infrastructure, and the persistent diseases of poverty in the developing world raised questions about whether health policy could be so narrow as to exclude questions of a social and economic nature. At the same time, there was a general shift towards prioritizing population control over health policy, partly as a result of pressure from transnational networks, including the Population Council, the Ford Foundation and the International Planned Parenthood Federation.

A sense of disappointment and failure hung over international health policy, notwithstanding the successful eradication of smallpox. The failure of malaria eradication, in particular, haunted the WHO. Partly as a result of this, the 1970s saw a revival of transnational activism in the field of public health, in a way that echoed the experience of the early 20th century. It was in this period, then, that some of the changes historians associate with contemporary globalization began to affect health policy: the increasing influence of transnational 'civil society'; an increasingly global locus of political concern; faster and more extensive electronic communication.

The formation of the International Baby Food Action Network signalled the emergence of this new kind of activism, which was part of a broader Western concern with humanitarian disasters in the Third World, beginning with the Biafra crisis. In the early 1970s, a number of groups of consumers and citizens in Europe and North America expressed concern over the challenge to health policy posed by the aggressive marketing of breast-milk substitutes in the Third World. By 1979, numerous such campaigning groups from around the world had come together to form the Network, exerting pressure on international organizations, on their own governments, and on corporations. Some have seen in such transnational campaigns echoes of the humanitarian movements of the 19th century – and, indeed, they are open to the same criticisms as their predecessors: charges of paternalism and Western dominance.

The emergence and rapid spread of the human immunodeficiency virus (HIV) posed grave new challenges for health policy in the 1980s. The disease, in its spread, was quintessentially transnational: it took hold along routes of long-distance trade, travel and migration, throughout eastern and southern Africa, and in parts of Asia. Indeed, the initial recognition of the epidemic linked North American gay communities, Haiti and West Africa in a 'geography of blame', an example of moral panic about globalization. Initial responses to the epidemic reverted quite strongly to national and international approaches: many states attempted to reinforce national boundaries, with the compulsory testing and exclusion of migrants. The role of the United Nations and other international organizations became increasingly important by the late 1980s in making states face up to the epidemic. The UN served as a repository of epidemiological information, as a forum for debating policies, and as a source of monetary assistance.

Yet just as the epidemic spread along the contours of unequal transnational relationships – political, economic, social – so its recognition and diagnosis revealed the extent of transnational connections in medical research, training and epidemiology. As John Iliffe (2006) has shown in his masterly history of the African acquired immuno deficiency syndrome (AIDS) epidemic, professional connections and networks allowed African researchers to make a central contribution to studying the epidemiology of heterosexually transmitted HIV. A picture of the virus's origins and transmission emerged from the connection between many local studies, communicated through specialist journals, the press and, increasingly, the Internet.

Perhaps what is most striking, however, is the rapidity with which HIV/AIDS became an issue for transnational activism, with literally thousands of meetings, conferences, protests, reports and campaigns bringing together diverse NGOs – religious and secular; local and transnational – often led by organizations like Médecins Sans Frontières and Oxfam. At the same time, national governments and international organizations like the World Bank and WHO have, themselves, worked increasingly closely with transnational institutions, both private pharmaceutical corporations and large corporate charitable foundations, and with NGOs themselves. The relationship between transnational, international and national actors grows more complex. In recent years, transnational networks of NGOs have mounted campaigns that invoke international agreements (the emergency provisions of international intellectual property law) to pressure national governments to provide anti-retroviral treatment to patients infected with HIV, if need be by asserting national sovereignty over the rights of transnational corporations.

The formation of People's Health Assembly, first convened in 2000, marks a formal institutionalization of the kind of transnational health activism that began in the 1970s, and is a fitting conclusion, perhaps, to this sweep through the transnational history of health policy. Self-consciously styled as an alternative, or at least as a complement, to the World Health Assembly made up of nation states and their representatives, the People's Health Assembly (www.phmovement.org/en) claims to be a transnational, rather than an international, network of health activists, demanding the right to have their say in shaping health policy in the future. It seems clear that the transnational dimensions of health policy are more important than ever; yet, paradoxically, the ultimate goal of so many transnational networks remains that of changing national health policies.

Sunil Amrith

Bibliography

Amrith S. 2006. *Decolonizing international health: India and Southeast Asia, 1930–1965*. London: Palgrave Macmillan.

Farmer P. 1996. *Infections and inequalities: the modern plagues*. Berkeley: University of California Press.

Hutchinson J. 1996. *Champions of charity: war and the rise of the Red Cross*. Boulder: Westview.

Iliffe J. 2006. *The African AIDS epidemic: a history*. Oxford: James Currey.

Murard L. and Zylberman P. 'French social medicine on the international public health map in the 1930s', in Rodriguez-Ocaña E. (ed.) 2002. *The politics of the healthy life: an international perspective*. Sheffield: European Association for the History of Medicine and Health Publications.

Packard R. 1997. 'Malaria dreams: postwar visions of health and development in the Third World', *Medical Anthropology*, 17, 3, 279–96.

Weindling P. (ed.) 1995. *International health organizations and movements, 1919–39*. Cambridge: Cambridge University Press.

Related essays

Acquired Immunodeficiency Syndrome (AIDS); cancer; epidemics; germs; intergovernmental organizations; international non-governmental organizations (INGOs); League of Nations Health Organization; League of Nations system; Médecins Sans Frontières (MSF); medicine; philanthropic foundations; population; public policy; relief; smallpox; transfers; vaccination

Herbicides, insecticides, pesticides *See* Pesticides, herbicides, insecticides

Higher education

The notion of higher education, used today to refer to the ever extending range of third-level education institutions, still maintains however, the university as its focal point. Even though its historical origins may not be obvious, its common use in North America – product in large measure of that continent's varied range of third-level institutions – has come to be a common way of referring to the university as it takes into account the variety, in terms both of structures and prestige, that characterizes this level of education.

The first universities emerged in 12th-century Italy and France. However, their regional character is evident if one takes into consideration the mobility of students, professors and the institutions themselves, as well as the use of a common language such as Latin. The historical relevance of the university as an institution is clearly demonstrated by the rapid expansion of at least two institutional models to almost all regions of medieval Europe: the Bologna model, based on the power of the students, and the Paris model, centred on the power of the faculty. With the consolidation of modern states, however, universities gradually acquired an increasingly national character. The evolution of the Western university as a space for the concentration of knowledge runs parallel to the gradual centralization of the states during the *ancien régime* and the later conformation of national states. The prestige of the universities was related to their monopoly in awarding degrees and to the honorific tradition that these titles incarnated. However, it was only in the 19th century that universities came to monopolize intellectual and scientific activities, which until then had developed, to a great extent, independently of them. The creation of universities, which in great measure responded to the necessities of the evolving states, was not an exclusively medieval European phenomenon: the Confucian Academies in China as well as the University of Al Azhar in Egypt were institutions of more than a thousand years' standing that fulfilled similar functions. The economic and political hegemony of the Western world after the 16th century, however, contributed to the extension of the Western model of higher education.

Birth of the research university

One fundamental characteristic that marked the history of the university up until the 19th century was a permanent call for autonomy with respect to the established powers, particularly the Papacy and royal power. The research-centred 'modern university' arose with the foundation of the University of Berlin by Wilhelm von Humboldt in 1810. Philosophically rooted in late-18th-century German idealism and Romanticism, this intellectual and political creation – itself to some degree a cultural reaction to the military defeat and economic backwardness of Prussia vis-à-vis France – later had important consequences when it was considered as an ideal model in other countries. The modern university developed around the concept of *Bildung*, conceived as a general education that simultaneously included instruction in philosophy, arts and sciences, the latter conceptualized as *Wissenschaft*, that is, pure and disinterested knowledge. The tension inherent in this conception of knowledge, unified around philosophy but at the same time closely related to culture, language and the national state, created a conflict with respect to the high epistemological and cultural aspirations this notion expressed. One fundamental component in the new conception of the university was the so-called *Lehrfreiheit* and *Lernfreiheit*, the freedom to teach and to learn, which served as the base of the Humboldtian and post-Humboldtian university. This was a clear challenge to national states or cross-national institutions like the Catholic Church, which claimed that the search for truth and knowledge was subject to requirements belonging in the spiritual ream.

The new definition of the university – which has been hegemonic up until very recent times, when it had to confront new challenges to its identity – emerged in a conjuncture of decadence and impoverishment of traditional university definitions, a decline that became manifest around the end of the 18th century in various European countries. This crisis, for example, led to a reform of the Scottish universities, whose system of chairs brought about the blossoming of numerous disciplines. Nonetheless, the Scottish pattern did not have lasting consequences in spite of its influence on the English and North American institutions. In contrast, the influence of the Humboldtian university was predominant not only in Great Britain, but also in France. This was due, above all, to its impact on the reforms that followed the creation of the Napoleonic university, whose professional and centralized character later served as a referent for different national university systems. The Humboldtian arrangement also had a significant, though not exclusive, impact on the creation of Tokyo University at the end of the 19th century, an institution which in turn exercised its influence in Eastern Asia, especially in China and Korea.

Nevertheless, the Humboldtian way had its most significant repercussions in the later history of higher education. North American universities made it into a model, and following World War 2, exerted their direct or indirect influence on almost all regions of the planet. The 'research university' emerged as the result of the reception of cultural and academic models that ensued from a generalized preoccupation with the quality of higher education and, even more importantly, the role assigned to science in the universities. The particularities of this process of circulation of institutional ideals consisted in the creative adaptation of research activities to the already established academic structures of general studies that had been inherited from the Anglo-Saxon tradition.

The mid 19th century brought a growing preoccupation with the quality of higher education in North America, the outcome of which was the enactment of the Morrill Land Grant Colleges Act of 1862. This piece of legislation promoted, through land donations, the creation of new institutions of higher learning that were associated with the economic and social development of local communities. At the same time the Humboldtian model exercised its influence almost simultaneously through scholars and scientists for whom the European, and in particular the German, university served as a referent and a model to follow. With the establishment of its Graduate School in 1876, the Johns Hopkins University inaugurated the model of a 'modern university' with regard to the institution's relation to the production of knowledge. The graduate school was the product of a creative adaptation of the legitimizing principles of the German university to traditional academic structures in order to develop the North American institution. The so-called 'research university' thus surged up from a process of hybridization of structures. This paradigm was later imitated by other American universities with the purpose of claiming their legitimacy as prestigious and academically distinguished institutions.

In contrast to the Continental European model, the development of higher education in the United States followed the logic of the market. It was founded on the confidence placed in the virtues of competition, public opinion and civil society as the means of resolving problems related to the quality of the educational system. This brought a systemic differentiation from the European organization, in particular from the French and German versions, whose pretensions to uniformity – though in different ways – were based on state control.

Pilgrim's progress: the research university and its journeys

From the mid 19th century on, the North American influence became manifested incipiently either through the direct transfer of the North American model by way of religious missions, as occurred in China, Korea and other regions, or indirectly through the process of syncretic reception, as happened in some Latin American countries. Nonetheless, the international impact of the North American type of university was moderate until the 1920s when the colonial models of higher education – especially those introduced in Africa and the Orient by France and England – started to weigh less. This North American presence in the Middle East was exemplified by the American University of Beirut (AUB). Currently linked to the State University of New York, with origins going back to 1866 as a college directed by Protestant missionaries, the AUB built up significantly in the 1920s, to the extent of upsetting the French authorities. The American University in Cairo was founded in 1919, with its main focus on training the local elite in Western values, and the North American conception of universities gained ground in the Arabian Peninsula during the same period.

This impact was also felt in Europe itself during the interwar period. This was not so much through the creation of branches of American institutions in Europe (though a number of 'French-American' learning institutions did emerge, for example), but mostly through American support for European institutions of higher learning. Triggered by a desire to sustain and orient European reconstruction after World War 1, a number of private American organizations, most notably the Rockefeller Foundation and its satellites, developed a range of programmes which had a lasting impact on the European university. Their grant-in-aid programmes for institution building supported many medical schools (Brussels in Belgium, University College London, Lyon in France), research institutes in public health (schools or institutes of hygiene in Belgrade, Warsaw, Budapest, London) or social science research

and teaching institutions (London School of Economics, Deutsche Hochschule für Politik, economic research institutes in Scandinavia and Western Europe). At the same time, many European scholars were offered fellowships to spend some time teaching or studying in US universities. Once back home, many of them used their experience to change the organization of their own universities, while the circumspection toward the US system this acquaintance had generated with some others was the flip side of these increased transatlantic circulations.

Following World War 2, this impact of the North American institutional system was accentuated, and some see the second half of the 20th century as a moment of an 'Americanization of higher education' in the world. This trend was not simply a consequence of the growing North American economic and political protagonism. The international diffusion of values and structures since the 1950s has also been in tune with the predominance of an episteme based on the hegemony of structural-functionalism as a theory and interpretive framework of the role of the university in society, and on the conception of the university as functional to the needs of society, based on the adoption of modernization and order, more than on political or cultural critique, something which would have led to a conception of a politically committed university. This latter conception prevailed in Latin America and in other places in the 1960s.

In Europe, a number of research centres not directly related to universities and mainly focused on economics and the social sciences were established, often with support from US philanthropic foundations. They arose from the need to consolidate European unity and were connected with important politicians of the region who favoured this aim. They also sought to improve the level of democracy and at the same time strengthen an Atlanticist conception of relations between Europe and North America in the context of the Cold War. North American foreign policy in the educational field after the Second World War can also be seen in other Cold War flash points. This was the case in Korea, where North American educational policy had an enormous influence both on the structure of education and the values it transmitted after the occupation in 1945. The influence of foundations such as the Rockefeller Foundation was significant in specific regions such as Latin

America in the 1950s, although this in large measure depended on government instability, the continuity of public policies and the institutional strength or otherwise of existing universities.

The growing North American influence was favoured by the collapse of the colonial structures, in particular those of Great Britain and France, whose educational policies were different in structural terms, but not in their aspiration of educating an intermediate sector of their colonial administration systems. Incidentally, members of this same administrative sector would later play a significant role in the independence movements of the colonies. At the same time, during the decades that followed World War 2, and within the context of the Cold War, the Soviet Union impacted strongly – be it directly or indirectly – by exporting a system of higher education both in Eastern Europe and in countries that were undergoing a process of decolonization and revolutionary change, as in the cases of Cuba and the People's Republic of China.

In the mid 1960s different sociodemographic factors contributed to transforming the old elitist model of the university into what came to be called the university of the masses. The impact of the rise in enrolment on traditional university patterns resulted in the introduction of a new wave of reforms in academic structures as well as the diversification of the institutional offer, addressing for example the need for a stronger link between universities and labour markets. The role of education in economic development thus got strengthened, which then led to the establishment of techniques for educational planning. The determination to plan the higher-education offer according to the needs arising from the sphere of production became customary both in Europe and in recently industrialized countries. Such a convergence regarding ways to conceive the place of higher education within a wider economic and social landscape sowed the seeds for further conversations on the organization of higher education.

Simultaneously, the emerging student movements also exerted their influence on the process of university reforms. The student unrest originally born in Berkeley, California was followed up by the French May '68, as well as by other movements in different parts of the world. The appearance of the university as a political force in the arena of cultural politics became almost universal. Different countries of Latin America, Africa, the Middle East and East Asia became the stage for movements that had later consequences for the meaning of the university as a political and cultural agent. At the same time, and particularly in North America, this process opened the door to the creation of new disciplines and research themes, and to the establishment of new centres and departments dedicated to comparative and interdisciplinary approaches to cultural, gender, and ethnic studies, whose impact on the disciplinary divisions of the social sciences has been considerable. Established disciplines like Oriental studies were shaken by such upheavals. New groupings were sketched, like the so-called area studies which were orientated towards the study of other regions and countries, pre-empting the development of cultural studies which would have an undeniable impact on the structural-functionalist framework, shifting it towards a more interpretative comprehension of the social. These new tendencies modified the framework of disciplines which had consolidated itself at the end of the 19th and start of the 20th centuries and also had a role in the increasing interest in minorities, a development in which gender theory played an important role.

These developments not only occurred in the sphere of ideas but also had a role in the necessity to develop a more interdisciplinary approach to social problems, and this had obvious consequences for the academic organization of universities. To these developments new themes, epistemological in causes and consequences, can be added; the critiques of the Newtonian model from a perspective of non-linearity and complexity caused a crisis in determinism and gave rise to ideas based more on probability. Changes in the field of social science thus tended to give rise to a modification in the traditional division between the natural and the social and human sciences which had prevailed until the middle of the 20th century.

Shifting values?

From the 1980s on it is possible to observe a crisis in higher education and a turn towards the market. The crisis of the welfare state, growing unemployment and fiscal deficits, together with the rise of conservative parties into power in Europe and in the US, provided the conditions for a transition from state-financed universities to budget restrictions and financial accountability in almost all countries of the world. Thus, there has been a shift from a policy founded on the a priori compromise with educational expansion based on planning to the emergence of the state as an evaluator, aiming at strengthening the autonomy of educational institutions and processes. Paradoxically, the control over educational results was strengthened, while the mercantilization of education and the orientation towards the institutional market were accentuated. Quality, accountability and evaluation became the new mantras of a higher education ever more plural, complex and diversified in terms both of the quality of provision and the social and cultural origin of its students.

The new information and communication technologies generated the conditions for an increasing internationalization of higher education through the increase of mobility of students, professors, institutions and programmes. The spectacular growth of enrolment at the international level and the development of new private universities in different regions, in particular in East Asia, Eastern Europe and some Latin American countries, add complexity to the present configuration of higher education. The current process of globalization is being realized by way of varying forms of delocalization and deterritorialization of higher education. These include the establishing of university branches abroad (the French Sorbonne in Abu Dhabi being a recent attempt to counter US universities' presence in the Middle East), the franchising of institutions and programmes and the introduction of online services, often linked to corporations. A salient example is the success, in Europe just as in other regions of the world, of the US Master of Business Administration (MBA) postgraduate model, which is reorienting the values and orientation of higher education, by way of a growing focus on market and businesses values at this level of education. On the other hand, these developments involve a questioning of national frontiers at the same time as raising questions of quality and the validity of degrees in the context of constant growth in the kinds and levels of quality of higher education as it expands throughout the world. The unequal nature of this growth has led to an increasing resort to rankings of institutions and programmes (most notably the Academic Ranking of World Universities by the Jiao Tong University of Shanghai). This ranking, in which the industrialized nations usually dominate, is used worldwide by educational leaders and policy makers to identify lags or claim success. This phenomenon is giving rise to new forms of dependency in the development of higher education. This crossing of frontiers has played an important role in Southeast Asia and various African countries, as well as to a lesser degree in Latin America. North America, Great Britain and Australia have been the driving forces behind this process, in which the English language has played a fundamental role.

The inclusion in the General Agreement on Trade in Services (GATS) of education as a globally tradeable service is in harmony with this existing transnationalizing trend, a process that nonetheless reinforces the inequalities between North and South. Simultaneously, however, one can observe the formation of programmes of educational integration at the regional level, which tend to strengthen the competitive capacity of educational systems. The Bologna Agreement of 1999 among the countries of the European Union that projected the establishment of a European Higher Education Area for regional exchange as well as the attunement of academic structures, curricula, and degrees, however, remains an adaptive response to the new transnationalizing processes of higher education.

Within the framework of the so-called 'knowledge-based society', the formation of a 'world system of higher education' that is ever more interconnected and interdependent creates new challenges that call into question the traditional 'idea of the university' from which the modern university arose. The old disciplinary paradigms, just like their self-referentiality in terms of the criteria of truth and academic legitimacy, are now in crisis at a time when the institutional formats in which disciplines had reproduced and multiplied experience the disappearance of the boundaries that distinguished the university with respect to the state, society and the market. These tendencies in turn call into question the present hegemony and legitimacy of the aspiration of the modern 'idea of the university', an ideal that, on the other hand, had never been fully realized.

Pedro Krotsch

Bibliography

Altbach P. 2007. *Tradition and transition: the international imperative in higher education.* Center for International Higher Education, Chestnut Hill, Boston College and Rotterdam: Sense.

Gemelli G. 2003. *American foundations in Europe: grant giving policies, cultural diplomacy and trans-Atlantic relations 1920–1980.* Brussels: Peter Lang.

Gibbons M., Limoges C., Nowotny H., Schwartzman S., Scott P. and Trow M. (eds) 2001. *La nueva producción del conocimiento: la dinámica de la ciencia y la investigación en las sociedades contemporáneas.* Barcelona: Pomares-Corredor.

Kerr C. (1994) *Troubled times for American higher education: the 1990s and beyond.* Albany: State University of New York Press.

Levine A. (ed.) 1993. *Higher learning in America: 1980–2000.* Baltimore: Johns Hopkins University Press.

Musselin C. 2007. *La longue marche des universités françaises.* Paris: Presses Universitaires de France.

Perkin H. 'The historical perspective', in Clark B. (ed.) 1984. *Perspectives on higher education: eight disciplinary and comparative views.* Berkeley: University of California Press, 17–55.

Related essays

1960s; book and periodical exchange; China; class; consumer cooperation; decolonization; economics; educational programmes; European Union (EU); fellowships and grants; humanities; intellectual elites; international students; Japan; kindergarten; life and physical sciences; Master of Business Administration (MBA); mathematics; missionaries; modernity; Muslim networks; nation and state; Orientalism; philanthropic foundations; scientific expeditions; services; social sciences; tropics; United Nations Educational, Scientific and Cultural Organization (UNESCO); Westernization; women's movements; youth organizations

Historians and the nation state

This article is concerned with the erratic fortunes of the nation state as an expository tool for understanding the past. The nation state dangles between the exalted position of primary unit of historical inquest, and, conversely, its dismissal as a politically laden obstruction to meaningful scholarship. A confluence of intellectual critiques of many different ideological persuasions has both challenged and championed the nation state's pallor over history. The purpose of this brief survey is to identify the symbiotic ties between historians and the nation state, explain the timing of the onslaught of critical scholars from both right and left, and finally to predict the future of this conceptual framework.

History and the nation state

From its very inception in the mid 19th century and through the first half of the 20th century, the modern discipline of history cultivated a comfortable, perhaps incestuous relationship with the nation state. The primary preoccupation of professional historians was the conduct of inquests on national origins and their spatial manifestations. Historians wavered and weaved their way through many variations of the origin of the species of the nation state. Up until the mid 20th century historians assumed that nation states were entities with roots dating back to antiquity, although the nature of those roots was a point of contention between two major schools: primordialists and essentialists.

Primordialism – the assumption that nation states were organic entities and indispensable components in the development of human civilization – dominated historical scholarship throughout the late 19th century. Having accepted the axiomatic assumption on the organic nature of nation states, primordialists concentrated on charting an evolutionary trajectory, from prenational kinship networks to full-blown nation states. The only significant challenge to the primordial school came from perennialists who were troubled by the sweeping analogy between nations and the biological origin of species. Perennialists argued that the phenomenon of nation state was a permanent and recurring historical manifestation. From antiquity through modern times, and in all societies, including non-Western societies, the nation state had existed and flourished. The task of the historian was that to sift through the layers of archaeological evidence and uncover the nation state in all its chronological and cultural variations (Smith 2004).

For the most part, historians – both primordialists and essentialists – methodically ignored those who could not be shoe-horned into the nation state. Civilizations and societies that did not support the paradigm elicited little interest as they offered no insight for a profession wedded to a dominant paradigm. Non-nation entities were at best a backdrop and supporting cast for understanding the triumphant efflorescence of the nation state.

The horrors of the World Wars initiated the first major rethinking of such imbedded assumptions. The spectre of national excess and blood letting in the name of nations encouraged a group of critical historians to question the nation state's imposition on a disciplined understanding of the past. History stood accused of a complicit relation with the nation state, in particular its compartmentalization of the world into intransigent and mutually suspicious political silos as well as the effacement of forms of remembering beyond the rigid contours of nationalism.

The most prominent of these historians was Elie Kedourie whose 1960 treatise on nationalism left an indelible mark on contemporary scholarship. Kedourie denounced nationalism and the nation state as pathologies driving the modern world's most virulent tragedies. This allegedly baneful creation of poets and political cynics fostered myths of blood and kinship that eventually led to horrific excesses. History's attempts to legitimize the historical origins of the nation state were, in Kedourie's view, unadulterated quackery. The nation state was first and foremost a conscious decision of contemporaries to spread a political mantle of collective identity over a given territory. Despite claims of authenticity and a common heritage – language or ethnic origin, for example – the historical rhetoric of its promoters were myths, at best. Nation states were, he explained, 'a determination of the will' rather than a historical inevitability. Nation states according to Kedourie were politically repressive and the source of most of the violent shockwaves of modern times.

Modernists and the nation state

By the late 1970s the interrogation of the nation state had moved from periphery to centre-stage. Building upon the scholarship of Kedourie and others, these scholars were first and foremost modernists. Their scholarship sought to prove that nation states were inventions of modern times: self-defined territorial and social constructions of recent human imagination. Spanning numerous disciplines, modernists challenged the contention of strong and documentable ethnocultural origins of nation states. Modernists discovered the rise of the nation state in the wake of an 18th-century political and social rupture in the Western world. The premodern period – feudalistic and entangled in a web of irrelevant kinship networks – offered no meaningful insight for understanding the rise of the nation state.

Eric Hobsbawm, one of the primary progenitors of the modernist movement, offered the notion of 'invented traditions', in the eponym 1983 volume co-edited with Terence Ranger. The viability of the nation state, Hobsbawm argued, hinged upon creating a protocol of an invented past, the mass-manufacturing of national symbols, and the empowering of a mythology transformed into historical fact by complicit historians. Although the nation state was an eminently modern project, its promoters sought its naturalization by retrospectively rooting it in the past. The nation, then, was not an essential or primordial entity; it was, in fact, a artificial production of pseudo-history implying continuity with the past.

Most surveys of nation states and history credit the anthropologist and philosopher Ernest Gellner with a particularly sharp disentanglement of nationalism and historic origins. Nation and state, he argued, were not inevitably 'destined for each other'. In the renowned 1995 'Warwick debates' with his student, Anthony Smith, Gellner rejected Smith's argumentation that nations were rooted in a premodern 'ethnie' which Smith defined as 'a named population sharing a collective proper name, a myth of common ancestry, shared historical memories', derived in one way or another from an 'association with a specific "homeland"' (Smith 2004). Gellner, by contrast, argued that states did not necessarily have 'navels' and umbilical cords connecting them to the historical life line of national origin. In fact, he claimed, state and nation could exist independently of each other; the reason for their conflation was instrumental and modern rather than historic.

Gellner did not dispute the presence of primordial roots; in some cases they did, indeed, exist. His argument was that such historical pedigrees were fortuitous, exceptional, and largely irrelevant for understanding the rise of this powerful entity. Beginning in the 18th century the disruptive forces of market economies and attendant social mobility – not historic roots – created the globe-spanning, European-dominated community of nation states. In other words, the nation state was a product of, and an instrumental device for, hastening and solidifying modernization. At times the nation state reflected primordial origins, at times the roots were figments of the imagination. Both historic fact and fiction were merely the backdrop to an inherently modern project that destroyed the privileges of premodern elites and the parochialism of their peasants.

Benedict Anderson added an important corrective to the work of Hobsbawm and Gellner. Rather than invention or fabrication Anderson's Imagined Communities (1991) preferred using the moderate nomenclature of imagined communities, the idea being that the rise of the nation state was a creative process rather than a foisting of false consciousness upon an unwitting community. In fact, Anderson argued that all communities larger than villages of face-to-face contact (and perhaps even these) are imagined. Measuring the authenticity of collective identities was a meaningless exercise; their viability rested upon the manner in which they were imagined. Relying heavily on Karl Deutsch's definition of the nation state as 'a community of complementary habits of communication', Anderson argued that a nation state could only exist if its adherents had the technological, political and cognitive capacity to created an abstract, territorially rooted community of strangers.

As opposed to the unbounded cosmic horizons of the Church or the contained ethnic enclave, the nation state of the modernists was a subjectively defined political community. Moreover, these territorial entities were the creation of modernity and its attributes. The ability to imagine the nation state was due to the interaction between an inherently capitalistic technology of communications (print), the spread of vernacular languages as instruments of both administrative centralization and social interaction, and the widespread desire for a sense of order and belonging that had dissipated with the loosening hold of religion and feudalism. The rapid rise of the nation state may have fed upon an opaque sense of common historical roots. But whether these common grounds were constructed or rooted in historical reality did not make the nation more or less real than its alternatives – all communities were imagined. In fact, the measuring stick of authenticity belonged to the province of antiquarianism rather than rigorous scholarship. The consciousness of nationhood, Anderson argued, was the result of the democratization of literacy and an attendant technology which allowed enterprising elites to produce and disseminate visions of community despite and perhaps due to the erosion of premodern forms of identity.

Postnationalism

These creative exercises in uncovering the modern dimensions of nationhood did not, by any means, represent the last word. Such interrogations swiftly elicited significantly more radical attempts to indict the nation state for its falsehoods and chart the collateral damage of its grand historical narrative. The fact that the 1980s were the starting point for the interrogation of the nation state was anything but happenstance. This period witnessed the coming of age of seemingly incompatible groups of politically diverse intellectuals in the West whose common ground was a profound disillusionment with the nation state of their times. Chronic energy shortages, military and foreign policy debacles, recurring domestic and political crises, rampant political scandals and the visibility of an impoverished class all induced a broad consensual disenchantment with the traditional Western national state.

History's entangled ties with the nation state, according to postnationalist scholars, was anything but a creative intellectual exercise; it involved a harsh and unrelenting repression of alternatives to this dominant imaginary enterprise. The overbearing nation state – with its emphasis on external divisions, on the one hand, and unrelenting internal uniformity, on the other – employed history to write out other forms of collective identity created by the hybridizing exchanges of people, ideas, and goods across and within national borders. The nation state had monopolized the historical imagination by 'naturalizing' its foundational myths, projecting this fabricated past into the present, and, by implication, into the future too. History occluded recognition of hybrid political, economic, and social trends. Beholden to the nation state, historians created a grand narrative of monolithic qualities while effacing the presence of competing social frameworks.

The most dominant and vocal critics of the nation state go even a step further, positing the nation state as a lethal weapon in the hands of a sinister coalition of racist empire builders and historian-collaborators.

Critics from the right identified the crisis of the nation state as stemming from a liberal hijacking of the nation's political agenda, governmental micromanagement, and the infusion of contested notions of social justice into the national arena. Driven by a deep resentment of the social welfare state and its attempt to control the power of social and market forces for a partisan version of the common good, a coterie of highly resonant public intellectuals indicted the nation-state-as-welfare-state as a 'soft variation of totalitarianism' (Reinhard 1996).

This basically neoliberal tradition argued that the traditional nation state was a redundant and hence, harmful feature in a world predicated upon the free flow of both goods and ideas. The contemporary post-World War 2 nation state, they argued, reified a sense of narrow intellectual horizons and endorsed a species of social border control that hindered the spread of both globalized enterprise and universal moral values. This much maligned entity appeared to be particularly unsuited for managing a globalized economic regime based upon the free flow of commodities, information, and moral values.

The post-World War 2 harnessing of the powers of the state to fund nationally endowed regimes of social welfare was anathema. Detaching the state from ideological interventionism in the private sphere, and politically motivated regulatory constraints in the public sphere, represented the ultimate goal of this neoliberal inquest. Hence, these critics envisioned a minimalist national entity, primarily committed to maximizing borderless entrepreneurial freedom.

Somewhat paradoxically the neoliberal criticism valorized the American version of the nation state. Claiming that the historical American state had been temporarily suspended by World War 2, the New Deal, and their aftermath, they argued for resurrection and the purging of the latter-day welfare state. With its minimalist government, aggressive promotion of universal values, and the endorsement of open, porous frontiers in the realm of knowledge, commerce and people, an idealized version of the American nation state represented an exception to the allegedly decrepit archetype of the mid 20th century. A laissez-faire American democracy – wedded to transnational and unfettered exchanges – contrasted with the Old World insularism and stagnation associated with the nation state.

Promoting the American version of the nation state, with minimal government and open-door policies in both the economic and political spheres, lay at the basis of this paradigm. The historiographic promotion of American exceptionalism offered the proposition that a pristine American national experience has produced a set of universal values for maintaining order in a transnational world and offered a working alternative to the classical nation state. This American version of the nation state stood, therefore, at the end of history.

With the rise of postmodernist scholarship in Western academia, such neoliberal post-nationalism was both complemented and confronted by a significantly different postcolonialist critique. Postcolonialists argued that the symbiotic relationship between state and history had discredited beyond repair the integrity of historical inquiry. History's empowerment of grand narratives of national grandeur had diminished – if not annihilated – alternative narratives of popular sovereignty, while serving the interests of the powerful and rapacious few. In fact, postcolonialists claimed that the nation state had contaminated history to such a degree that it had become a useless tool for retrieving the past.

Hopelessly wedded to narratives of national grandeur, and resistant to any critical inquiry of their disciplinary practices, historians allegedly promoted a perniciously false and exclusive narrative of origins. Postnationalists accused historians of having arbitrarily ordained the nation state as the singular discursive framework for the creation of collective identities. Historians promoted an exclusive national-identity template at the expense of all alternatives forms of remembering. They compliantly and ruthlessly produced a politically restrictive understanding of society as a set of territorialized enclosures governing well defined, mutually exclusive social and political entities. A past governed by the paradigm of the nation state valorized enclosure and ignored anything beyond the uniform, all-encompassing national narrative.

Rather than offering an objective, scientifically based chronicling of events past, history sanctioned and promoted the transformation of heterogeneous, assimilative identities into boundaried national entities, where the phobic fear of an encroaching, pernicious Other encouraged the uncritical endorsement of an exclusive collective identity. 'Once the boundary is beaten back and troops posted around the perimeter', postnationalist Nigel Harris has explained, 'the state undertakes to colonise all within, to drill all the inhabitants who find themselves trapped behind the fence with an invented common inheritance of loyalty, supposedly to a common culture or way of life, but in practice to a particular state' (Harris 1982, 24).

History – as a discipline dedicated to discovering the gestation and the evolution of collective self-consciousness within a well defined territory – had effaced the local and the integrative. History had invented, fabricated, and promoted an insular identity intolerant of diversity and permeable social interactions. Thus, according to Paul Gilroy – whose epochal The Black Atlantic (1993) remains one of the finest critiques of traditional history making, the nation state perpetuated and fostered a false consciousness of insular and integrative national cultures.

History's methodological and cognitive limitations provided additional pressure points for the postnationalist interrogation. Focusing on the craft's addiction to narrative as well as its rejection of theory, critics pronounced history as being resistant to any meaningful intellectual soul-searching. The discipline of history, they argued, perpetuated a static and obsolete scientific protocol. Born during the 19th century's rise of national self-consciousness and scientific self-consciousness, history was immutably committed to a culture of logical positivism and an unreflective, empirical collection of facts. Such exercises in fact-collection were, in turn, wedded to a simplistic, linear understanding of time and an evolutionary model of societal development from primitive protonationalism to the modern nation state. The embrace of this Victorian mode of empiricism and the attendant rejection of theory precluded any meaningful self-examination of the underlying assumptions of the profession. History appeared terminally infected by its intellectually narrow parameters and its commitment to one singular form of identity formation.

In assessing the allegedly statist addiction of history, critics have at times assigned the most heinous developments in Western culture and society to this hapless discursive framework. Racism, Social Darwinism, and the rise of fascism were, according to prominent postnationalists, but a few of the iniquities born out of history's intimate relationship with the nation state. Authoritarianism, in particular its two ugly offspring of fascism and communism, are allegedly the tragic result of the overbearing relationship between nationhood and complicit historians. The weltering of Third World nationalism, such as Hindu extremism, is tied, too, to the contamination of porous and tolerant authentic cultures with the disease of the nation state. The vector, postcolonialists argue, has been Western-style history. History, therefore, was not a useless form of knowledge; it was, in fact, a lethal weapon. Hence the task of the postnationalist, to use Prasenjit Duara's felicitous (1995) phrase, was to rescue the past from the nation.

Having relinquished hope for the fostering of alternative forms of identity by means of a disciplined historical construction of the past, postnationalists have retreated to the enclaves of theory and the borderlands of identity politics. The theories offered for the advancement of the postnationalist cause are cutting-edge. One very prominent example is borderland theory, an attempt to expose how stifling discursive regimes, such as the nation state, can be undermined by resurrecting the plethora of individual identities thriving in the unregulated borderlands of imagination. Borderland theory offers an unbounded discursive space in which the hierarchies of inclusion and exclusion, centre and periphery, are replaced by a ceaseless, individualized exchange of meanings and identities that challenge overarching tropes such as the nation state. Borderlands foster a liberating confusion of identities that undermine the discriminatory regimes of nation histories.

The key obstacle to the fostering of such capacious practices of remembering are, according to these theorists, the professional historians who have transformed their craft from a broad all-encompassing focus on the individual and local to a stifling promotion of territorially bound collective identities.

Thus, the primary role of the postnationalist is to discredit the historian-collaborator and, instead, redeem the fractured alternatives to nation-centred perspectives.

Polycentrism

Such harsh indictments of history and the nation state have not gone unchallenged. In fact, sceptical critics of the postnationalist impulse come in a variety of ideological colours. United by misgivings concerning the sweeping denouncement of the nation state and the alleged complicity of historians, the critics of postnationalism are best described as polycentrists.

Polycentrism rejects overblown representations of the monopolistic nation state by charting the thriving existence of multiple identities alongside and within the collective territorially bound nation state. In fact, polycentrists claim that for a host of reasons the nation state was never as intolerant of diversity as its critics claimed. Attacks on nation-oriented historiography assume that its practitioners are hopelessly ensnared by a rigid version of national history. In actual fact, historical representations of the nation state, they claim, have been a project in motion. Quoting Ernst Renan's famous 1882 lecture, they posit the nation as 'a daily plebiscite' forever adjusting its agenda in response to a host of competing interests and identities bounded by, but not imprisoned in, the territorial state. Their interrogation of the nation state is, therefore, somewhat more tolerant of discursive frameworks of territorial identity and less dismissive of the analytical tools of history.

By promoting an unreflective and at times empirically suspect demonization of the nation state, postnationalism stands accused of contributing to the mystification and hardening of 'inequalities and oppressions' whose origins lie outside of the nation state. According to the polycentrist view, the excommunication of the nation state from our understanding of the past, accompanied by the valorization of individualized forms of remembering, promotes new forms of erasures and other, no less tendentious understandings of the past. A historical acknowledgement of the nation state does not necessarily valorize this entity; it merely recognizes its existence. In the hands of scholars who have been able to deconstruct its Eurocentricity, its capitalist underpinnings, and all of its other faults, the history–nation-state nexus even offers crucial tools for its own interrogation.

Polycentrists – such as David Hollinger, John Keane, and Thomas Bender, to mention but a few – have contended that nation is first and foremost a discursive framework encompassing a wide-ranging and often contradictory amalgam of social and political developments unbeholden to any unifying territorial paradigm. The rise of individual rights which has accompanied the rise of the nation date has in fact made visible entire constituencies – religious minorities and women, to name but two obvious examples – who under the arbitrary frameworks of prenationalist frameworks were invariably invisible.

If anything, the nation state has procreated rather than negated alternative and capacious understandings of the past. To be sure, the subject matter of historical scholarship and its methodology are intertwined with the nation state. However, under the illusory uniform framework of the nation state lie thick, intertwining layers of competing paradigms, espousing multiple and contradictory notions of self-awareness, collective loyalty and even conflicting comprehensions of the idea of the nation state.

Polycentric historiography of the nation state advocates a decentring rather than an effacement of the powerful presence of states, empires, and attendant forces of urbanization, industrialization, and global conquest. Decentring the nation within history is quite different from its erasure. Recognizing and by implication neutralizing the nexus of history and nation state – in particular the construction of the Western nation state as the only genuine site of historical development – entails revision rather than the purging of historical scholarship from an understanding of the past.

Polycentrists acknowledge that Western historians did indeed create problematic bonds between professional history making and the nation state: the construction of modern civilization as tied to, and derived from, a uniquely European nationalism being the most obvious example. Yet, the argument that historical scholarship is hopelessly and immutably ensnared in this Gordian knot is belied by recent scholarship. A multifaceted history recognizing the robust presence of the nation state is not necessarily a deadly recipe for 'a politics of blood'. In fact, as recent scholarship of the United States suggests, it may lead to 'acceptance and even celebration of difference'. Contemporary polycentrist historiography posits the nation state in a world of overlapping, rather than mutually exclusive 'imagined communities' and acknowledges that the nation state functions as a well honed 'weapon of the weak' and not only as the coercive tool of the powerful few.

While polycentrism is usually identified with the vital centre, one may argue that latter-day Marxist scholarship belongs to this category too. Contemporary Marxist historiography and its derivatives accept the nation state, albeit as a necessary evil. It was, after all, the universal suffrage of the Western version of the nation states that ushered the masses into its historical construction. Class consciousness could flourish only after the nation state had eclipsed traditional barriers of status and deference.

Marxist historiography faults postnationalists for transforming the basically salutary interrogation of the nation state into a glib ignorance of class-based collective forms of identity existing within and sustained by national identities. The postnationalist preoccupation with fractured identity politics has, according to Marxists, induced a pernicious and historically slanted blindness to its social dynamics. Among the pasts erased by the rejection of a historical acknowledgment of multiple identities within the nation state is the obliteration of a revolutionary phase in national movements in which national self-consciousness served as a primary launching pad – however imperfect – for addressing class inequities.

For both Marxists and others, privileging the expository framework of the nation state does not necessarily entail a blinkered understanding of the past. Moreover, the transnational movement of people, ideas, and commerce has not negated but, rather, enriched our understanding of the nation state. Beyond the intellectually suspect idea of an exclusive historical paradigm of the nation state resides an intellectually capacious history, in which different ways of understanding the past overlap rather than eclipse each other.

In fact, polycentrists have argued that postnationalism is far from a liberating force. The cultural landscape of the postnationalist is cluttered with a deluge of identities without any galvanizing common denominator. Paradoxically, the centrifugal identity politics espoused by postnationalists leads to an indiscriminate equalizing of minutiae that obscures, and in fact, rejects a synthesis of common values of any shape or form. Such fracturing, far from redressing past iniquities, creates a pool of free-flowing unrelated causes with no capacity for generating change.

The future of the nation state

Such attempts to relegitimize the nation state are by no means universally acclaimed. Any attempt to valorize the nation state strikes a prominent body of scholars as anachronistic. In the final analysis, Arjun Appadurai explains in Modernity at Large (1996), unchecked waves of immigration, new technologies of communication and economic globalization have transformed the nation state into a redundant appendage. In an age in which supranational organizations such as the European Union appear to have eclipsed the nation state, and at a time when the world's most powerful nation states extol their multiculturalism rather than their unique, historically derived characteristics, the fortunes of the nation state appear to be receding. Nationalism appears now only on the periphery. Marginal and extreme separatist movements – such as those of the Basques or the Tamil Nadu – appear to be manifestations of a dying nationalist cause. Many contemporary national crises – such as the Palestinian conflict – have their roots elsewhere, religion being the obvious motor behind most latter-day crises.

Such dismissals of the nation state are, however, premature and overtly judgmental. In fact, detractors of the nation state invariably seem concerned with its ethical dimensions rather than its viability. For all of its intellectual incisiveness, the odes to a moribund nation state are hopelessly ensnarled with philosophical and ideological condemnation of its moral qualities.

Triumphant declarations of the nation state's sharp hegemonic decline – as a domestic force or in the international arena – are, as well, derived from a selective reading of historical data. Even at its historic pinnacle, the nation state existed alongside paradigms of multiple identities, global flows, and subregional entrenchments. Despite its autocratic and totalitarian excesses, the nation state regularly tolerated – through benign neglect or deliberate policy – the transcending of national affiliation, an exchange with hybrid cultures, and a level of personal expression that never existed in prenational communities. In fact, the subversion of national borders by diasporadic communities – Jews, Chinese and South Asians, to mention but a few – flourished at the very height of nation states.

As for the moral argument against the nation state, it too, is breathtakingly oblivious to the liberatory qualities of this entity. Despite protestations to the contrary, the nation state is more often than not the weapon of the weak rather than a blunt tool of the oppressor. In actual fact, the primary victim of weakened or dissolved nation states is the subaltern subject of the postnational discourse.

Thus, Kwame Appiah argues, the United States is a contemporary example of how a nation state can tolerate and encourage multiple, emancipatory identities. Many Americans, Appiah observes, have strong patriotic feelings about the United States precisely because it has enabled them to cultivate ostensibly competing identities, 'to choose who they are and to decide, too, how central America is in their chosen identity' (Appiah 1997, 633). It is perhaps time to recall Tom Nairn's truism that the nation state, like most human phenomena, is Janus-faced: a harsh oppressive force in some instances, and a liberating force in others.

Finally, the dismissal of the contemporary nation state as overwhelmed by interlocking tidal waves of postmodern plurality and globalization has not affected everyday cognition, either. In fact, as Michael Billig suggests, 'banal nationalism' still rules in the consciousness of everyday life, even in the ostensibly postnationalist West. While at a superficial level it may seem that in the absence of acute crises, nationalism fades into the background, Billig argues that nationalism exists at all times in less visible, but quite powerful forms. Far from being a peripheral or outmoded ideology, the nation state continues to dominate both our historical and contemporary consciousness. Billig suggests that people do not forget their nationalism. Instead, nationalism is routinely channelled into our consciousness through such banal means as sporting events, street naming, the framing of media events, and, of course, everyday language in which the nomenclature of national belonging is indelibly embedded. 'Nationalism, far from being an intermittent mood in established nations, is the endemic condition' (Billig 1995, 6). Despite misgivings – moral, epistemological or otherwise – the nation state remains a powerful and omnipresent sociological phenomenon.

Ron Robin

Bibliography

Appiah K. A. 1997. 'Cosmopolitan patriots', Critical Inquiry, 23, 3, 617–39.

Billig M. 1995. Banal nationalism. London: Sage.

Dirlik A. 1997. The postcolonial aura: Third World criticism in the age of global capitalism. Boulder: Westview.

Harris N. 1982. Of bread and guns. Harmondsworth:Penguin.

McNeill W. H. 1986. Polyethnicity and national unity in world history. Toronto: University of Toronto Press.

Ostrom V. 1987. The political theory of a compound republic. Lincoln: University of Nebraska Press.

Reinhard W. (ed.) 1996. Power elites and state building: the origins of the modern state in Europe. Oxford: Clarendon.

Smith A. D. 2004.The antiquity of nations. Cambridge: Polity.

Related essays

borders and borderlands; cosmopolitanism and universalism; globalization; higher education; history; humanities; Kessler, Harry von; nation and state; regions; transnational; Williams, James Dixon

History

The term 'transnational history' has been closely associated with work in American history from the 1990s. The new approach explicitly concerned the movement of peoples, ideas, technologies and institutions across national boundaries. It was related to, but not the same as global history. 'Transcultural history' or 'intercultural relations' were competitor terms but practitioners considered these as too vague for use in elucidating cross-national connections. The 'transnational' label enabled scholars to recognize the nation's importance while at the same time contextualizing its growth. Advocates generally distinguished their work from comparative history too. Nevertheless, they concluded that comparative and transnational approaches could be complementary to one another.

Though the research project was relatively new in the 1990s, the term 'transnational' was older in legal, historical and sociological discourse. It was used in the 1970s, for example, to describe the activities of multinational corporations, and non-governmental organizations and social movements, and the English term's origins can be traced further back to a seminal 1916 essay, 'Transnational America', on multicultural influences in the United States by radical intellectual Randolph Bourne. Historians, however, have treated the term in different ways and have produced a longer tradition of transnational historiography than can be identified either with the current movement or Bourne's intellectual agenda.

Without the benefit of the label, progenitors of and influences upon transnational history could be detected in the 19th century. In the work of German historicism, idealist philosophers aspired ultimately to synthesize all historical knowledge and to establish laws of historical evolution. From the 1820s, Leopold von Ranke built upon this idealist tradition and sought to use 'scientific' methods of assessing evidence to produce 'universal history'. By the 1870s, scientific historians in England, France, and the United States as well as Germany had taken up Ranke's dreams. In Britain, introduction of the scientific method was accompanied by a search for broad themes that was in part an application of the idea of universal history. Imperial historiography dealt with the transnational diffusion of British institutions and the comparative political development of societies of Anglo-Saxon origin.

Efforts to unite the strands of scientific historical inquiry on comparative and imperial history underpinned the early work, beginning in Paris in 1900, of what became the International Committee of the Historical Sciences (CISH). A group of mostly French and German historians saw that comparative study was 'a path toward historical synthesis'. They held further international conferences, but the World War shattered hopes for a universalist synthesis and focused attention on nationalist rivalries. After 1919, many scholars urged renewal of the 19th-century ideals. The agency of this re-establishment was the American Historical Association. In 1923 the International Committee was formed under American leadership with money from the Rockefeller Foundation. The Committee

continued (except for a World War 2 interruption), sponsored internationally focused research, and held further congresses. At the same time a new stream of influence developed from Marc Bloch, the celebrated French scholar who founded, along with Lucien Febvre, the *Annales* journal. At the 1928 CISH Congress, Bloch showed how comparative approaches worked best when dealing with case studies subject to mutual influences. This approach came close to the future transnational angle. Though dealing with prenational periods, the *Annales* pioneered forms of cross-cultural and regional history greatly influenced by geography that inspired later transnational historians to develop similar models.

Meanwhile, traditions of transnational writing continued in the United States, a nation acutely aware of its European origins, however modified subsequently. Imperial perspectives on American colonial history mutated post-World War 2 into the study of Anglo-American political and cultural influences with the founding of the Institute for Early American History and Culture. A transnational perspective also appeared in the 1930s, with Herbert Bolton's hemispheric analysis of 'Greater America'. While this approach to Hispanic-American history became unfashionable from the 1950s, its basic precepts later influenced the new borderland studies by the 1980s.

Conditions within American higher education also encouraged broad surveys of European and Western civilization from the 1920s. Thus did historians such as C. J. H. Hayes depict European societies in transcontinental perspective. The changing political conditions of the end to American formal isolationism and the beginnings of the Atlantic alliance then produced a new wave of transnational approaches in the 1950s. Yet these attempts suffered from increasing historical specialization. American historians ceased to pay much attention to European history, whilst European scholars resented Americanist efforts to interpret European history from a Western Hemisphere perspective. It was not just nationalist historiography that intervened to block such transnational moves. The Cold War did too. When Robert R. Palmer and French scholar Jacques Godechot presented the idea of an Atlantic history at the Rome Conference of CISH in 1955, Soviet and other left-wing scholars denounced the idea as NATO for historiography. The same confluence of ideological problems with the trend toward historical specialization doomed the UNESCO-sponsored history of the world. This broadly intercultural effort produced both a journal, the first *Journal of World History*, and a six-volume synthetic history. Louis Gottschalk's contributed volume was typical: its sweep was too general to be more than a compendium of interesting information. By the 1960s William H. McNeill and Leften Stavrianos championed 'World History' self-consciously, but World History as it developed professedly sought connections between civilizations, not nations, and reached much further back in time.

Adding to a parochial trend within modern history was the flowering of social history in the 1960s, which helped to weaken the transnational perspective, except in a few select areas. One was the work of historians such as David Brion Davis, who linked slavery to capitalism and modern humanitarian sensibilities in the era of the American Revolution. Though modified Marxism encouraged such transnational perspectives, these had been assimilated to different national historiographical traditions, as seen in the empiricist influences on English Marxism. A promising development in the 1980s was postcolonial studies, which reconnected transnational approaches to formerly peripheral fields of research, especially those concerning race and gender. Women or black activists who were historically not fully integrated into nation states as citizens often found leverage in cross-national activities. So too did their historians, starting with the work of activist scholar W. E. B. Du Bois on African American history in world historical perspective in the 1930s. A landmark study reflecting postcolonial themes was Catherine Hall's *Civilising Subjects* (2002), which showed how imperial experiences shaped national identity.

A self-conscious transnational agenda for historians, linked to a specific research programme first came into being in 1989–91 and was discussed in a 1991 forum in the *American Historical Review*. The new movement was the product of both intellectual and political causes, including desires to synthesize the fragmented scholarship of social history, and to introduce cultural perspectives on diplomatic history. Also influential was the changing world historical situation. The collapse of the Soviet Union and a perception of what

was being labelled as 'globalization' led historians to question the efficacy of nation-state analysis. The years 1992–2002 saw institutionalization of the approach within American historiography. In 1992 the *Journal of American History* devoted a special issue to 'internationalizing' American history. The journal's editor, David Thelen, also organized a seminar on transnational history at the International Institute of Social History, Amsterdam, in 1998, and published the participants' work as another special issue in 1999. Meanwhile, Thomas Bender and the Organization of American Historians began a wider project to internationalize American history. A series of conferences held at La Pietra in Florence, Italy, led to *Rethinking American History in A Global Age* (2002), with contributions by La Pietra participants. This book has become the standard introduction to American transnational history. Simultaneously, new transnational work appeared on migrations, diasporas, and many other topics.

Despite deep-rooted intellectual influences, the transnational turn of the 1990s was new in its research programme of treating the nation state as one of a series of historical actors, and in the depth and self-consciousness of its agenda. Moreover, the momentum existed for the first time to institutionalize the intellectual transformations of globalization into new perspectives within the historical profession. Concerns over the consequences of growing transnational interdependence have produced new political configurations encouraging transnational views. Thus the inception of the European Community enhanced interest in European Studies, with new journals where transnational topics were explored. However, while university curricula have begun to reflect transnational approaches, curriculum development has not proceeded very far in the Anglo-American world. Historians still widely consider that scholars need a deep grounding in one geographical field, and those (often national) specializations, linked also to language capabilities, have restricted the practice of transnational history thus far.

Ian Tyrrell

Bibliography

Bender T. (ed.). 2002. *Rethinking American history in a global age*. Berkeley: University of California Press.

Erdmann K. D. 2005. *Toward a global community of historians: the International*

Historical Congresses and the International Committee of Historical Sciences, 1898–2000. Oxford and New York: Berghahn Books.

Hall C. 2002. Civilising Subjects: metropole and colony in the English imagination 1830–1867. Cambridge/Chicago: Polity/University of Chicago Press.

Thelen D. (ed.) 1999. 'The nation and beyond: transnational perspectives on United States History', Journal of American History, special issue, 86, December.

Tyrrell I. 1991. 'American exceptionalism in an age of international history', American Historical Review, 96, October, 1031–55, 1068–72.

Related Essays

historians and the nation state; humanities; mathematics; new man; Pax Americana; philanthropic foundations; social sciences; transnational

Hollywood

When in 1923 a colossal sign reading 'Hollywoodland' was erected as a billboard for an upscale real-estate development in the Los Angeles area by the owner of the LA Times, Hollywood was not only already part of the city of Los Angeles but also housed dozens of film studios which were producing the vast majority of US cinema at the time and had already given birth to some of the classics of film historiography. The real-estate venture was brought to a halt with the 1929 stock-market crash and appropriately now stands as the eternal empty signifier of the allure of celluloid lives. The history of the sign's emergence concentrates a number of axes which configure film history's Hollywood, past and present: place as elsewhere; visibility; the gaze; the appeal and glamour of heavenly outposts; mark and symbol; and last, but not least, electricity. An announcement of a dream that can only be like a flashy highlight of an extreme self-referential narcissism, Hollywood – and film – is that sign. David Lynch's Lost Highway (1997), Mulholland Drive (2001) and Inland Empire (2006) have traced, uncannily and ironically, this history.

Probably both Hollywood's proximity to Central and South America as well as its characteristic as both the epitome of the US and the quintessential melting pot helped configure in the films there produced a fascination with, desire and need for elsewhere.

Symptoms were the early 1914 contract signed by the California-based Mutual Film Corporation with General Francisco Villa for the making of the lost The Life of General Villa – which helped finance his last battles in the Mexican Revolution and which included a clause for re-enactment of battle scenes; one of the four parts of Babel (2006) – a multinational production anchored with Paramount, directed by Mexican Alejandro González Iñárritu – where a Mexican nanny crosses the border into Mexico taking with her the two American children she cares for and is unable to return; Orson Welles' Touch of Evil (1958) – which for many film historians closes the film noir cycle – and its story of police corruption in a Mexican border town where Welles himself, playing Hank Quentin, a corrupt US police officer, famously said 'I don't speak Mexican'. Hollywood's fascination with the South border is only one of the manifestations of its migrating soul.

By the same token, Hollywood became, from early on, the land of promise in the motion picture world for many. Two years after the Mutual Film Corporation signed a contract with Pancho Villa, it signed up the young 27-year-old British comedian, Charles Chaplin, who quickly became one of the most internationally recognized actors of the 20th century. That in 1961, when the Cuban revolutionary state formed the ICAIC (Instituto Cubano del Arte e Industria Cinematográficos) which sponsored a project known as cine móvil – film screenings in remote rural areas of the island, bringing film to many Cubans for the first time through mobile units – and that one of the films always screened during these events was one of Chaplin's Hollywood films, Modern Times (1936), further stresses the ever present migrating Hollywood, as well as the ideological potentialization and reconfiguration opened up by commodity circulation. A number of Hollywood's most important directors, cinematographers and actors arrived from abroad, especially between the mid 1920s and the early 1950s, underlining the non-place trait of Hollywood: Alfred Hitchcock, Michael Curtiz, Jacques Tourneur, Max Ophüls, Karl Freund, Ernst Lubitsch, Greta Garbo, Marlene Dietrich, Joseph von Sternberg, Ingrid Bergman, Fritz Lang, Hedy Lamarr, even the brief stay of the Russian Sergei Eisenstein. This flooding of foreign talent which continues through to the present has consistently privileged certain areas of the world and excluded others, most notably

Africa, the Middle and East Asia. To this human traffic is added now the slow but solid rise of transnationally owned film companies which finally have made of Hollywood more of an imaginary – and highly nostalgic place – than the centre of film production.

Between the 1930s and the early 1960s the reasons for these flows of people, funds and films were often political – although not all the time: the sheer number and volume of both films and people that Hollywood manages does not allow for generalizations. Some of these attempts were a failure in practical terms. At the height of the studio system and in the midst of World War 2, after the explosive success of *Citizen Kane* (1941), Orson Welles was sent by RKO studio – at the suggestion of millionaire Nelson Rockefeller who was both Assistant Secretary of State for Latin American Affairs and a stockholder in RKO, as well as close friends with Welles – to Latin America as cultural ambassador. Welles' post was part of the US Good Neighbor Policy, a programme whose objective was to cultivate better relations with Central and South America, thus promoting a better image of US foreign policies. As part of the Good Neighbor Policy, Welles would make a film on an archetypical Brazilian theme – the Carnival in Rio de Janeiro. Other Hollywood films from the war and postwar period that used Latin America as a setting – *Down Argentine Way* (1940), *Notorious* (1946), *Latin Lovers* (1953) – miserably misrepresented and exoticized Central and South America as they attempted to build alliances for an anti-Communist continent. Welles' unfinished project, *It's All True*, was deemed a failure in great part for the opposite reasons: the awareness, realist-intent and unglamorous Brazil that his reels were displaying did not go down well with either the Hollywood studio executives or the Washington politics that triggered them initially, and RKO quickly put an end to the film's financial backing.

Nevertheless, the record of successful connections and circulations to and from Hollywood between the 1930s and 1960s seems to outnumber the list of mishaps. In the years prior to World War 2, with the rise of German National Socialism and the increasing anti-Semitism, and the apparently infinite possibilities that Hollywood offered, many European directors, actresses and actors fled to California with its promise of freedom, not having lost entirely the allure of adventure that had marked its beginnings. Conrad Veidt, Eric Pommer, Billy Wilder, and Max Ophüls are some of the most salient names of this migration. Many critics have argued that out of this migration was born film noir, the most Hollywood of moods if ever there was one, much influenced by, in particular, the expressionist talent of émigré Fritz Lang. Considered by some a genre or style, and by others a cycle, phenomenon, movement or series, this retrospectively Hollywood type was the consequence of a transnational circulation and recodification of cultural goods. Influenced by the German Expressionist mode of lighting and focus on the mise-en-scène, and in this sense also by German and Spanish 16th- and 17th-century Baroque painting, propelled by the literary hardboiled crime and detective fiction epitomized by writers like Dashiell Hammett, and at the same time imbued with conventions appropriated from gangster films, social-problem pictures, and classic 1930s melodramas as well as French poetic realist films by directors Jean Renoir, Jean Vigo, Marcel Carne and Julien Duvivier among others, the film noir classics go from John Huston's *Maltese Falcon* (1941) to Orson Welles' *Touch of Evil* (1958). Nostalgic, bitter, and highly stylized, these films are often set in Los Angeles, thus adding, through this self-referentiality, an empty self-reflexivity and uncanny feel to the films. Los Angeles – which, by the 1940s, and still today, is Hollywood – was already the site for failed fantasy, the location of the American dystopia. Ridley Scott's 1982 *Bladerunner*, set in a decrepit 2019 Los Angeles, is one of the most perfect neo-noirs to return to some of the classic tropes, and also attests to the paradoxical international and transnational quality of Hollywood in particular and cinema in general and the hyper-real, replica and dreamlike quality of place, industry and affect.

Those were also the years of the consolidation of genre as the Hollywood trademark, and that some of Hollywood's genres found their afterlife in other lands speaks not only to the always changing form of the rules and formulas of genre – always different from itself, never quite itself – but also to the allure and control that Hollywood films have had globally and to the changing perception that in particular Europe had of Hollywood cinema in the years after the war, in part due to the strong presence of non-American talent involved in the Hollywood film industry before the war.

The French critics / film makers both inside and outside the *Cahiers du cinema* nucleus, with their *politique des auteurs* (the polemical debate on the concept of auteurism) praised Hollywood directors – Howard Hawks, John Ford, Anthony Mann, George Cukor, Orson Welles, Alfred Hitchcock – as some of the first true auteurs in a drastically paradoxical reading of genre, the studio system and Hollywood. The Western, which could be the most American of genres, underwent a remarkable transformation in the 1960s. Revolving around the universal theme of the solitary man fighting the law, Hollywood's classic Westerns had as their other central figure the seemingly irreplaceable and unique landscape of the American West – precisely the same vast and seemingly infinite landscape that first attracted the Easterners fleeing to Hollywood. Its Italian renaissance disguised its rapid decline: Hollywood had produced 130 Western features in 1950 and by 1960 had dropped to 28, before the rise of the Italian 'spaghetti' western. The migration of Hollywood stars to Rome – notably Clint Eastwood – helped in this cultural translation. Sergio Leone's 'spaghetti' westerns – *A Fistful of Dollars* (1964), *The Good, the Bad and the Ugly* (1966), *Once Upon a Time in the West* (1968) – though only a handful of the 300 Westerns made in Italy in the 1960s, are landmarks in the genre. The same decade saw the appropriation and socialist transformation of this popular Hollywood genre by state-controlled film studios in East Germany with the production of films like the 1966 *Die Söhne der großen Bärin* (Sons of the Great Bear) and the 1968 *Spur des Falken* (Trail of the Falcon).

But Hollywood's exporting capacities and reverberations in national cinemas had started early on. Hollywood quickly came to be analogous with large-scale, big-budget film making, as well as with conventions which, regulating films, made them easily sellable in markets outside their domestic sphere due to their decipherability. Akin to the American film factory, Bollywood – the conflation of Bombay (now Mumbai) and Hollywood, coined by the West in the 1980s – now produces more films per year than the US. Since the enormous success of the first Hindi sound film in 1931, a specific genre has been overwhelmingly popular not only on the Indian subcontinent, but in East Asia and the Middle East as well. 'Bollywood films' refer mainly to the singing-dancing-action Hindi films, although the term is used imperfectly to refer sweepingly to the whole film production in India. A mixture of epic, melodrama, romance and musical, the unequivocal coded conventions, the immense South Asian diasporic community and the multilanguage production of 'Bollywood films' have channelled their wide appeal. The originality of Bollywood films lies not in their plots or narratives but rather in their complex song-and-dance routines which Hollywood musicals have never been able to imitate despite many attempts. Audience consumption is one of the main differences between Bollywood films and Hollywood musicals in that in the former audiences interact with the screen – either by clapping, hissing, laughing, or even storming out of the movie theatre to then return – making the experience of them much closer to cinema's origin as spectacle and part of vaudeville attractions. Bollywood continues with the conception of a cinema of attractions. Lavish sets and a tight star system are some of the main characteristics elaborating the popularity of these films. 'Hindi films', as which this industry is also referred to, are studio productions receiving no state funding, churning out features in over twelve languages. During the 1970s and 1980s, and for a 15-year period, the song-and-dance films were replaced, in popularity, by the action, 'angry young man' films that were produced in the Hindi film industry. By the 1990s the song-and-dance extravaganzas returned to being the all-time favourite, and even diasporic Indian film makers have made, at the dawn of the 21st century, Bollywood-type musicals which have been commercially successful at the international box offices – such as Mira Nair's *Monsoon Wedding* (2002) or Gurinder Chadha's *Bride and Prejudice* (2004).

One also needs to mention Nigeria's multimillion-dollar film industry, which produces over two hundred 'home videos' per month. It is considered the third largest film industry after those of the US and India, and is colloquially referred to as 'Nollywood'. Nollywood is, more accurately, a video movie industry which grew out of the frustrating costs of film making and the popularization of video in the 1980s and the spread of digital technologies in the last decade. In this case it is just the name which has been transferred, for 'Nollywood' films share none of the production or distribution structures of Hollywood. Nollywood has also thus come to stand for sheer volume.

The US and India are the only two countries in the world where 95 per cent of box-office sales come from their respective domestic film industries. The highly protectionist film policies in play in India since partition have not allowed for Hollywood films to be marketed successfully there. Sony Pictures, Walt Disney and Warner Bros have recently started to produce 'Bollywood films' in India. If 'Bollywood' took from Hollywood, initially, its name, it is now Hollywood that is mimicking Bollywood, for despite some rare exemplary successes of Hollywood films in India, Hollywood's American, English-language films do not stand a chance in competition with the local production. Are the Hollywood-produced Bollywood films American or Indian? Hollywood, a recent article stated, by joining Bollywood instead of conquering it with its own products – as has been standard practice – 'has gone native'. What, exactly, is American about Hollywood?

Natalia Brizuela

Bibliography

Anger K. 1975. Hollywood Babylon. San Francisco: Straight Arrow.

Bordwell D. and Thompson K. 1985. The classical Hollywood cinema: film style and mode of production to 1960. New York: Columbia University Press.

Kindem G. (ed.) 1982. The American movie industry. Carbondale: Southern Illinois University Press.

Sarris A. 1969. The American cinema: directors and directions 1929–1968. New York: Dutton.

Sklar R. 1975. Movie made America: a social history of American movies. New York: Random House.

Related essays

America; Asia; borders and borderlands; executives and professionals; exile; femininity; film; Mexican Revolution; orchestras; Pax Americana; performing artists; war; Westernization; world orders

Holocaust

The Holocaust, a word of Greek origin meaning 'sacrifice by fire', designates the systematic campaign undertaken by Nazi Germany to destroy Jewish life in Europe during World War 2 (1939–45). Although the Nazis targeted other groups including political opponents, allegedly genetically defective people, and Gypsies, the war against the Jews was conducted with ruthless thoroughness. By the end of World War 2, the Nazis had murdered nearly 6 million Jews, two thirds of the Jewish population of Europe. The Holocaust thus also designates the particularly Jewish aspect to the horrors of the world war: the creation of legally binding racial categories to distinguish Jews, the reliance upon collaborators throughout Europe to seize and murder Jews, the determination to kill all Jews, men, women, and children. Finally, the Holocaust designates the intellectual difficulty in understanding how such a murderous event could have taken place and in representing it in history and memory. It is important to remember that historical interest in the Holocaust is relatively recent. The centrality of the Holocaust in contemporary intellectual life is itself a historical product, but no less significant for being so.

Historians debate whether the Nazis pursued with ruthless single-mindedness the physical destruction of the Jews. Fanatical anti-Semites, including Adolf Hitler, the leader of the Nazi Party, spoke frequently about murder and extermination. Anti-Semitism was central to the worldview of the National Socialists who regarded political revival in biological terms. They believed that the regeneration of the German body politic required the destruction of 'unworthy' and alien elements. As alleged agents of social and national decomposition, Jews were regarded as particularly dangerous enemies. Accordingly, after coming to power in 1933, the Nazis promulgated anti-Semitic legislation, in which Jews were regarded as biologically distinct from Germans. However, the idea of murdering hundreds of thousands of German Jews or millions of European Jews remained unimaginable until a series of increasingly radical intermediate steps had been taken. In the years after 1933, National Socialists in the government and in local positions of power in large part agreed on policies to exclude Jews from German civil and economic life. The 1935 Nuremberg race laws deprived German Jews of citizenship and outlawed marriage or sexual relations between Germans and Jews. Jewish businesses had been largely expropriated by the time of the nationwide pogroms the Nazis organized in November 1938.

The majority of German and Austrian Jews were able to escape their tormentors before the onset of World War 2. The majority fled to the United States and to the British mandate in Palestine, but thousands only managed to leave the Third Reich by emigrating to unfamiliar countries such as Bolivia and Haiti. As a result, Jewish communities were transplanted around the world, particularly in Latin America.

Once Nazi Germany began its war against Europe in 1939, more far-reaching demographic ambitions could be realized. The Nazis envisaged a three-pronged policy of settling and resettling German colonists in an expanded German empire, evacuating ethnic Slavs out of German territory and/or exploiting their labour, and removing Jews. Germany's military victories in the first two years of the war had the paradoxical effect of postponing long-range deportation of Jews while steadily increasing the number of Jews under German occupation. This set the stage for 'final solutions' which advanced from deportation to Madagascar in 1940 to deportation somewhere in the Soviet Union in 1941. Finally, after Germany's invasion of the Soviet Union in June 1941, dreams of empire and a new German order created conditions for the physical destruction of Jews. Special killing units carried out the mass shootings of Jewish civilians in the Soviet Union in 1941 and 1942 while Germany's security service organized the deportation of the rest of Europe's Jews under German control in the years 1942–44. The vast majority of deported Jews were murdered in death camps; only a minority were selected for slave labour. The percentage of European Jews seized varied from country to country and depended on various factors including ideological inclination, bureaucratic organization, and Germany's military presence. A well organized, but ideologically disinterested civil administration in the Netherlands, for example, facilitated the deportation of most Dutch Jews. By contrast, the Italians, Nazi Germany's erstwhile allies, actively obstructed the seizure of Jews. But everywhere German efforts to deport Jews relied on local collaborators, police officials, and railway employees, a historical legacy of complicity that remains highly charged and intellectually relevant.

It is difficult to imagine a satisfying answer to why the Nazis targeted the Jews with such relentless energy and how they carried out mass murder over a period of four years. The Holocaust stands for a larger inadequacy of historical explanation. In this way, it is a central part of the postwar intellectual legacy. However, the Holocaust has become a fundamental object of analysis only since the 1970s. At first, historians and other commentators stressed the uniqueness of the Holocaust which was not unrelated to justifications for the existence of the state of Israel. The intentions of the Nazis to seize every Jew on the Continent are indeed extraordinary. But since the end of the Cold War and the genocides in Yugoslavia (1991–95) and Rwanda (1994), the Holocaust has been studied more profitably in comparative frameworks. At the same time, the Holocaust is widely regarded as a European, rather than simply a German crime. It now forms the basis of a pan-European identity which is rooted in the recognition of the wide complicities of the recent past. Finally, the Holocaust has become one way to think through the suffering of others. A genuinely global historical datum, the Holocaust has created connections of empathy around the world.

Peter Fritzsche

Bibliography

Bigsby C. 2006. *Remembering and imagining the Holocaust: the chain of memory*. Cambridge: Cambridge University Press.

Browning C. R. 2004. *The origins of the Final Solution: the evolution of Nazi Jewish Policy, September 1939 – March 1942*. Lincoln, NE: University of Nebraska Press.

Friedlander S. 1997–2007. *Nazi Germany and the Jews*, 2 vols. New York: HarperCollins.

Levy D. and Sznaider N. 2006. *The Holocaust and memory in the global age* (Oksiloff A. trans.). Philadelphia: Temple University Press.

Related essays

antisemitism; ethnicity and race; fascism and anti-fascism; forced migrations; genocide; Nazism; nomads; war crimes; Zionism

Hong Kong and Shanghai Banking Corporation Limited (HSBC)

'The world's local bank!' The advertising slogan used in recent years by HSBC, the London-based banking group, somewhat accurately describes a major characteristic of this bank from its very beginnings in 1865.

HSBC is one of the very few survivors of financial institutions variously known as

Colonial and Foreign banks, overseas banks, or, more recently, British multinational banks. These banks were British, insofar as their capital and management were British and their registered office usually in London, but their sphere of activity was in the British Empire or elsewhere abroad. Most of them were founded during the second third of the 19th century, starting in Australasia, Canada and the West Indies before expanding to India, China and the Far East, Latin America, the Middle East, and Africa. Their goal was to finance trade with the region in which they were established and to obtain exchange facilities. They also offered financial services in regions often lacking in banking infrastructure, thus winning a clientele from the well-off members of the local community.

The establishment of the Hong Kong and Shanghai Banking Corporation followed this pattern, offering facilities to the business communities of the China coast. The bank also issued banknotes and acted as banker to the Hong Kong government. The bank opened an office in Shanghai within a few months of its foundation and soon expanded to Japan, India, the Philippines, Singapore, Burma, Thailand, Indochina, as well as the United States (San Francisco and New York) and France. It had 22 branches outside the United Kingdom by 1890, and 32 by 1913. Unlike most British overseas banks, the bank's head office was in Hong Kong, the London office having a supervisory function and being directly involved in international financial operations. The bank played a pioneering role in the Chinese government loans, as well as the Japanese loans, issued in London between 1895 and 1914, benefiting from its knowledge of the Far Eastern business, its relationships in the City, and the support of the Foreign Office, owing to the political nature of a number of these loans.

Like all British overseas banks, the Hong Kong and Shanghai Banking Corporation remained specialized in a single geographical area. Mainly for regulatory reasons, in the first place the opposition from the Bank of England, the integration between overseas banks and domestic banks proceeded very slowly. During the 1950s, consolidation took place at regional level, with the Hong Kong and Shanghai Banking Corporation acquiring the Mercantile Bank in 1959, the British Bank of the Middle East in 1960, and a controlling interest in Hang Seng Bank in 1965.

The bank reached a new dimension in the last decades of the 20th century. In 1980, it acquired 51 per cent of Marine Midland Banks Inc. of New York (100 per cent in 1987) and, after being organized in 1991 under a new holding company, HSBC Holdings Plc, it acquired the Midland Bank, one of Britain's 'Big Four', in 1992, thus becoming one of the world's largest banks. It continued to grow in the following decade, through strategic acquisitions in various parts of the world, most notably the Republic New York Corporation and its European subsidiary Safra Republic Holdings in 1999, and Crédit Commercial de France (CCF) in 2000.

More than any other bank, HSBC exemplifies the transnational nature of modern banking and finance, in terms of worldwide presence (more than 10,000 offices in 83 countries in 2007) and business operations (retail banking, investment banking, and private banking on a global scale) – a position resulting from its origins as a British colonial bank, the strategic decisions of its management and the opening of the world economy.

Youssef Cassis

Bibliography

Jones G. 1993. *British multinational banking 1830–1990*. Oxford: Oxford University Press.

King F. H. H. 1987–91. *The history of the Hong Kong and Shanghai Banking Corporation*, 4 vols. Cambridge: Cambridge University Press.

Related essays

China; empires and imperialism; financial centres; financial markets; loans; Swiss banks; trade

Honour

Most modern languages possess a word for the concept of honour or one of its equivalents. Beyond the apparent universality of the concept itself are overall trends governing its content and the changes it underwent. In the course of the 19th and 20th centuries specifically, ideas about honour and status shifted to depend more on personal achievements and less on birthright privilege.

In Europe, North America, Latin America and Africa – especially in sub-Saharan Africa – male honour was defined in terms of proper education, economic independence, patriarchal authority, honesty and good manners. In contrast, in the case of women, honesty, kindness, work and cunning were considered increasingly important qualities, even though male control over women, and women as sexual property, remained at the core of the modern definition of female honour. Virginity and chastity were apparently valued everywhere and by people of all classes. Many cross-border factors like colonization and the expansion of universal religions favour the spread, through conversion and/or adoption, of these gendered conceptions of honour. The fact that, overall, women's reputation depended on their sexual conduct and on their conduct in private life, while the reputation of men was judged by their honest conduct in economic matters and public affairs, brought very real political consequences, such as the exclusion of women from the citizenry.

Challenges to one's honour were handled in different ways by different segments of society. In general, males were deemed responsible for the honour of their womenfolk. Nonetheless, women could also respond to an insult by verbally or physically attacking their aggressor or by turning to the courts. The relationship between honour and violence can be non-existent, as in contemporary Bedouin societies, or it can be very intense. An example of the latter was the result of transnational circulations. Among the elites of Europe, America and Latin America notions of honour generally operated outside the normal legal system. The duel was the typical form of defence of one's honour, and the only form of legitimate violence. This practice, which originated in Italy at the beginning of the modern era and was propagated to almost the whole continent in the course of the centuries, evolved from a crude and very violent act into a kind of ritualized and stylized violence restricted by specific rules that were observed based on the consent of the parties. By the end of the 19th century and the beginning of the 20th century, the code of the duel became more genteel, as no more blood, brutal gestures or deaths were expected. In certain places and in particular in the south of Latin America this code was imported directly from Europe at the end of the 19th century. The end of civil wars, the remarkable economic growth and advances in communications facilitated the circulation of information and of people. Reports filed by foreign correspondents posted in Europe – a system that was inaugurated by the principal Latin American newspapers at the beginning of the 20th century – allowed the Latin American male audience to get acquainted with, follow, and eventually imitate the combats of their European peers. The educated elites of the Río de la Plata, for example, were reading the manuals of duelling published in Europe. Others, during their long stays on the Old Continent, witnessed duels in the Bois de Boulogne in Paris, and brought back to their home country renowned professors of fencing. The elites of the New World moreover thought that the duel was the purest form of defence of one's honour, and that its practice was one of the clearest symbols of belonging to the upper class. As such, the duel united the integrants of this class, joined them in an international community of honourable men and separated them from the rest of their co-citizens.

Sandra Gayol

Bibliography

Caulfield S., Chambers S. and Putnam L. (eds) 2005. *Honour, status and law in modern Latin America*. Durham, NC and London: Duke University Press.

Iliffe J. 2005. *Honour in African history*. Cambridge: Cambridge University Press.

Spierenburg P. (ed.) 1998. *Men and violence: gender, honour and rituals in modern Europe and America*. Columbus: Ohio State University.

Stewart F. H. 1994. *Honour*. Chicago: University of Chicago Press.

Related essays
class; femininity; love; marriage

Human mobility

Throughout history, men and women have voluntarily and involuntarily moved between neighbouring regions, distant lands, or between continents to pursue life-course projects for themselves and their children. They crossed cultural and political borders as well as natural obstacles in the process.

Whether internal or international, migration received little attention from scholars before the 20th century. Then, under the hegemony of nation-state ideology, people were said to possess fixed national identities; they could not move without uprooting or even damaging themselves and without becoming traitors to their homelands. If they did move, they were said to settle in 'ethnic' enclaves whose cultures were considered inferior to that of the receiving state. Economic historians, aware of worldwide trade and of the transnational reach of economic sectors, like cotton plantations and cloth factories, studied movements of products rather than of the men and women who produced them. Everyday language as well as research designs treated mobile slaves, contract workers, and free migrants as different categories, associating the former with passivity, the indentured with depravity, and the latter with free will and initiative. This classification repeated the Black–Brown–White racialization of political discourse.

Around 1900, sociological studies of immigrants in North America focused on immigrants as problems and paupers. National polemics about emigration focused on human capital and potential soldiers. The first major quantitative study of international migration appeared in the 1920s (Willcox and Ferenczi, 1929, 1930). Only after 1960 – as nation-state ideology came under scrutiny – did more scholars study human mobility, first, with an emphasis on the Atlantic World, then emphasizing 'developing countries', and finally in continent-specific as well as globally integrative approaches. Scholars shifted from emphasizing state-imposed constraints to analysing human agency, emphasizing differences in migration according to gender and age. They connected internal and cross-border migrations and recognized the ubiquity of migration and its constituent role in societal change. Scholarship focused on labour migration systems before 1914, refugee generation in the first half of the 20th century, the impact of decolonization in the second postwar era, and new migration systems emerging since 1960. These themes are now outlined here.

Migration systems before 1914

In the Euro-Atlantic World, migrations resumed in 1815 after the caesura of the Napoleonic Wars. They intensified at the mid-19th century. In the Afro-Atlantic World, the slave trade, formally abolished in 1815, lasted into the 1870s. In the tropical and subtropical colonized parts of the world, the continuing demand for cheap and controllable labour led to the institution of a contract labour system in British-controlled India in 1838 and a parallel intensification and globalization of the existing system of bound labour in China. Free Chinese and Indian migrants moved along the same routes and to North America. In Tsarist Russia, the abolition of serfdom in 1861 increased mobility. From the southern German-language regions, an eastbound settler family migration targeted agricultural lands in southern Siberia.

By the mid-19th century, four intercontinental migrations systems operated – the Euro- or White Atlantic one, the Afro- or Black Atlantic, the Asian system of indentured labour and the Russo-Siberian system. Slave trading continued in the Indian Ocean. Within Europe and North America, rural–urban migrations resulted in massive growth of cities. The worlds of migrants, slaveholders and capitalists were increasingly entwined everywhere. For example, consumption of goods produced by forced and free migrant men and women entered European and North American households as cotton dresses, tropical fruits, spices, coffee and tea.

Agricultural settler migrations to North America notwithstanding, labour migrations accounted for the largest numbers in the century before 1914: 2 million in the transatlantic slave migrations, 50 million out of Europe (of which perhaps 7 million returned), 32–50 million in the Asian system of free and contract migrations, and 10 million towards trans-Caspian and Siberian destinations. In the slave and contract labour regimes, women accounted at most for one-third of the migrants. Buyers and employers considered them weak even though in many cultures of origin they did the agricultural labour. In the so-called free migrations, women accounted for roughly 40 per cent of the migrants. Building intergenerational communities and procreation depended on the presence of women.

In the second half of the 19th century, European agriculturalists from the East and the South migrated to the United States and to Canada as well as to Australia, South Africa, Algeria and other African destinations. The settlement of fertile plains displaced local populations; the introduction of machinery resulted in worldwide overproduction of grain and collapsing prices. In consequence, ever larger numbers of peasants left their smallholds to earn their living in North America's factories, making this an age of proletarian mass migrations. Italian migrants, who sought wage incomes and acceptable receiving cultures, expanded their moves to South America and to New York's and Montréal's labour markets, thus integrating the South and North Atlantic migration systems into one macroregion. Neither Brazilian plantation agriculture after the abolition of slavery in 1888 nor US industrialization at the time of Taylorization would have occurred without the mass migrations. Migrations associated with plantations created 'many-cultured' (culturally complex but hierarchically structured) societies and supplied European consumers with food, facilitating rapid population growth.

In Asia, new migrations developed after Japan's US-enforced opening to Western influences in 1853 and the Meiji period's centralization and industrialization, as well as after the increased accessibility of the Chinese Empire imposed by the (mainly) British warfare of the 1840s and 1850s to gain control of ports and to permit sale of opium. Direct British rule over India after 1858, on the other hand, did not change migratory practices. European access and economic domination were facilitated by the opening of the Suez Canal in 1869. Japan's industrialization, financed by its peasantry, resulted in a rural exodus towards Japan's expanding cities, to North America, and other destinations. Agrarian expansion to the subtropical Ryukyu islands and to the northern Hokkaido involved millions. Indentured men and women from India were moved through the British Empire and beyond; after their indenture ended, they often stayed, either freely or because their employers refused to pay for their return. They formed communities, especially in the Caribbean and East Africa. Chinese men, mainly from the four southern provinces, moved for cultural and economic reasons, usually without women. Their enclaves comprised the Southeast Asian Chinese diaspora, which had originated in the mid-17th century, Hawai'i, and the Pacific Coast of the Americas. Within the Chinese Empire, major settlement migrations from the mid-19th century brought peasant families to the lands of the Mongol and Manchurian peoples. Between 1911 and 1931 alone, at least 15 (and possibly as many as 50) million migrants reached Manchuria. With the division of the remaining independent regions of Africa among Europe's imperial powers in the 1880s, white colonizer settlers moved into North, West, and East Africa.

Dislocation and forced labour were imposed on the resident peoples. Finally, in the 1920s, when agricultural settlement was once again advocated in the White Atlantic, the rural exodus accelerated, which from the mid-19th century had contributed to Europe's urbanization. Under the impact of mechanization and concentration, families in North America left the recently settled agricultural regions for urban agglomerations.

By 1914, Europe's imperial expansion ended and industrialization in the Atlantic World had been achieved. Thus the need for immigrant or forced labourers, skilled or unskilled, male or female, declined. In Europe, the growth of mining and industry created sufficient jobs for rural surplus populations. Internal migrations supplanted the transatlantic mobility. The US began to draw on Mexican working men and women when needed and expelled them when not needed. Racist policies in North America had legally excluded migrants from Asia from the 1880s, but, pursuing their life projects, tens of thousands circumvented these regulations. Others changed destinations and, after 1900, moved to Mexico and Peru.

Refugee generation, forced labour, and apartheid in the first half of the 20th century

Towards the end of the 19th century, the dissolution of the Ottoman Empire in the eastern Mediterranean and the expansion of Japan in Asia accelerated. Called the apogee of the nation states, this period was in fact, the apogee of the worldwide power of Europe's multiethnic empires as well as the beginning of United States imperialism. The Habsburg, Hohenzollern, Windsor, and Romanov empires all contained many peoples with one group elevating itself to 'nation' and imposing its language and culture on the others. The 'nationals' had better access to educational, political, and economic resources than the 'minorities'. The combination of interimperial competition and struggles against imperial control and for self-determination was a major cause of World War 1 in Europe. In Asia, war resulted from Japanese expansion: the annexation of Chinese islands including Taiwan, a major victory over Russian forces in 1905, and the annexation of Korea in 1910. Millions of so-called surplus Japanese people were sent to settle in the newly acquired territories. During World War 1, both France and

Britain brought Indian, Chinese, and Indo-Chinese men as labourers and soldiers to Europe. Nationalist movements then ended the regime of indentured labour between 1917 and the early 1930s.

From the 1880s, Western Europe's well integrated Jewish diaspora encountered increasing anti-Semitism while, in Eastern Europe, pogroms occurred. European apartheid was the result. Two million left the Russian 'pale of settlement' for Europe's large cities and for North America. A small number went to Palestine in a kind of pilgrimage, aliyah, to the spiritual centre. During and after the Holocaust in the regions under Nazi Germany's control, large numbers fled. When Israel was established as a state in 1948, this refugee movement in turn created Palestinian Muslim refugees who, over time, would number hundreds of thousands and, with their children, millions.

Nationalism's corollary, the superiority of one group over another, acerbated policies of exclusion of non-white migrants and imposed new regimes of forced labour on 'lesser peoples'. When Australia and South Africa achieved Dominion status in the British Empire in 1901 and 1910, a 'white Australia' policy was designed to exclude migrants from Asia needed for Queensland's plantations. The white South African government also increased segregation, expelling Chinese workers, restricting Africans to reserves with poor soil ('homelands'), circumscribing the space of Indian migrants and their descendants, and prohibiting mixed marriages. There, apartheid was fully established by 1950.

In Germany, with the declaration of war in 1939 and the need for workers, some 7 million Eastern European men and women were transported from occupied territories into labour camps. After the end of the war in 1945, millions attempted to return home; hundreds of thousands of others, as 'displaced persons', were permitted to migrate to the United States, Canada, and Australia. In the Soviet Union, wartime destruction and subsequent civil war, the collectivization of agriculture and the resulting famines, as well as the intensification of industrialization including the establishment of new mining towns and industrial centres, mobilized tens of millions – mostly involuntarily. Under Stalin, labour controls began in 1928 and a passport and workbook system was introduced. In this case, people disaffected by the political regime were sent to labour camps. Figures vary from 2.3 to 20 million at the height of the system, in 1941. While the Nazi system ended in 1945, the Stalinist one lasted to the mid-1950s, and the South African forced labour to the end of apartheid, 1989–94.

Chauvinist nationalisms and the resulting ravages of the two world wars made Europe the major refugee-generating region. Ethnocultural and racist antagonisms, fanned by nationalist elites, led to an 'un-mixing' of peoples, later cynically called ethnic 'cleansing'. In the Balkans, where both the Habsburg and the Ottoman Empires ceded territories to new states defining themselves by 'national' group, centuries of interspersed settlement had established multi-ethnic and multireligious societies of Orthodox Christian, Catholic, and Muslim. Most new 'nation states' had mixed populations and 'their' minorities became even more oppressed than under the imperial governments. After 1918, populations were 'exchanged' between Greece and Turkey and in the Balkans and Northwestern Europe as intercultural settlements were divided by new national borders. The process was repeated under Fascist, especially Nazi expansion: large numbers of Polish people were expelled and East European German-origin people resettled; after 1945 borders were again redrawn and again moved over people rather than allowing people to cross borders as they pleased.

In Asia, under Japanese expansion and during the wars, large numbers of refugees, in particular in China and Korea, moved within their respective regions. Korean workers were forced to move to Japan. Japanese men expanded throughout what the government called the Greater East Asia Co-Prosperity Sphere. Plans for the migration of Japanese peasants to Manchuria could not be executed when people refused to go there. Auxiliary workers from many ethnicities were moved over long distances to support military activities or build infrastructures, with lasting consequences. First, the wartime suspension of colonizer administration led to immediate demands for independence. In the South Asian subcontinent, self-government brought partition into a predominantly Hindu India and a predominantly Muslim West and East Pakistan in 1947. By 1951, some 14.5 million people had been unsettled, crossed the borders, and hoped for resettlement. Elsewhere, independence was achieved after long struggles and new forms of migration emerged. Finally, the United States and Canada, in view of their military alliance with China, abolished Chinese and, later, Asian exclusion from their immigration law, opening the opportunity, at first miniscule, for transpacific mobility.

Throughout the wars of the twentieth century, the mobilization of tens of millions of soldiers, their aggressive crossing of borders and their life in occupied territories produced involuntary cultural exchanges and new cultural hierarchies, increasing ethnonational antagonisms. From sexual violence against women as well as from consensual unions in occupied territories, 'mixed' children were born, often unwanted in their own societies. Some voluntary consorting led to marriages between US soldiers and Asian as well as European women, who returned with their husbands to form the nuclei of post-World War 2 immigrant communities.

Migration from the depression of the 1930s to decolonization in the 1950s

Voluntary migration declined globally after the beginning of the Great Depression in 1929. A little noticed corollary was the decrease of return migration and increasing family formation abroad. Thus, women began to account for the majority of migrants (at first of roughly 52 to 48 per cent). Industrialization of Europe's societies reduced transatlantic migrations; the exclusion of Asians from North America reduced transpacific ones. The war-related unsettling of peoples resulted in migration that was only minimally voluntary and the high levels of mobility after the wars, 1918–21 and 1945–50, were of brief duration. When reconstruction stabilized the war-ravaged economies in the late 1940s, people reduced their outbound migration strategies. The rigorously drawn border between East and West and, after 1949, between the People's Republic of China and other parts of Asia slowed migration across these lines to almost zero.

Wars also seriously weakened the former colonizer states' global reach and, after World War 2, many colonized societies demanded independence. When refused, they initiated unsettling, refugee-generating armed liberation struggles. After the achievement of independence, reverse migrations brought colonizer personnel back to the countries of origin and, in some cases, large numbers

of settlers (from French Algeria and Dutch Indonesia), plantation owners, as well as merchants and traders. The latter had lived for generations in the colonies and were culturally creole; whites or mixed-race persons had been mentally socialized in colonial settings, with corresponding identities. In some cases, colonial auxiliary troops and administrators were also transported to the metropole. Though sometimes called 'repatriation', these movements involved creole white colonials and non-white auxiliaries who left their home for an unknown (former) national 'homeland'. These movements ended in the aftermath of independence of Vietnam and of the Portuguese African colonies in 1975. Such reorganization of societies across the globe reduced migrations for a while. New patterns of migration developed after this restructuring of global political relations and in response to a fundamental shift in governance and new terms of trade. With internal warfare and political misrule added, the states of the Southern Hemisphere – in fact a territory that includes three-quarters of the earth's surface, and extends southward from the Mediterranean, the Caribbean and Rio Grande, and the Himalayas – became the major refugee-generating region of the world in the latter part of the 20th century.

New migration systems since the 1960s

Beginning as early as the 1950s, new migration systems developed across the world. The transatlantic system was replaced by two South–North labour migration systems: from Southern Europe and subsequently decolonized North Africa to Western and Northern Europe and from Mexico and the Caribbean, and subsequently other South American societies, to the United States and, to a lesser degree, to Canada. In both regions additional male and increasingly female labour was needed. From the 1980s on, Europe became a socioeconomic region of immigration. In several Latin American states the US government's support for right-wing refugee-generating regimes created a reservoir of northbound involuntary migrants. The pull of opportunity structures and the push of political regimes combined. In the year 2000, migrants in North America accounted for 8.6 per cent of the population, in Western Europe for 6.1 per cent; in other regions of the world (special cases excluded) the percentage was lower.

The gradual decline of racism in the white Atlantic World also ended Asian exclusions in Anglo North America but quota systems continued to advantage white European-origin newcomers. Canada, in the early 1960s, and the US, in 1965, changed immigrant admission policies to systems based on individual qualifications. These reflected the early phases of deindustrialization and the emergence of a 'knowledge-based economy'. Since many Asian societies – or the urban sections of them – had high levels of educational achievement, a new transpacific migration system brought more people by the mid-1980s from Asia than from Europe to Anglo North America. 'Points' and 'preference' systems for visas did provide for family migration or reunion, encouraging new community formation. The migrations bound for Anglo North America became multicultured and multicoloured. With the change to service economies and under the continued gender-based division, labour migrations also became increasingly feminized. Both Canada and the United States developed integrative policies of pluralism or multiculturalism.

A new, third major labour-attracting region after 1970 was comprised of the oil-producing economies of the Persian Gulf region. First, technicians came from industrialized Western countries; second, administrative personnel came from India's many cultures; finally, workers came from surrounding societies – Palestinians, Egyptians, Yemeni – and from further away. The 1.7 million 'guest workers' of 1975 increased to 3 million by 1980. Independent entrepreneurs from Pakistan and India came with their families. Finally, the rising wealth in the oil-producing societies created demand for domestic personnel, and women began to arrive from Indian Ocean societies and from as far as the Philippines as well as from Somalia and other African societies disrupted by internal conflicts. For domestics living with family employers, legal protections are minimal. Acculturation is not wanted, all workers have to depart when their temporary visas expire.

The world where income and standards of living are high is separated from the Southern migrant-sending societies by migration controls that have been called 'global apartheid'. (Richmond, 1994). Worldwide, Western-imposed terms of trade and rigorous control of southern borders are intended to prevent entry of women and men from the poorer

societies whose efforts to improve their life chances otherwise resemble those of Europe's 19th-century America-bound migrants. The change from industrial to service economies results in a predominance of women among the migrants; the change to knowledge-based economies results in recruitment of highly qualified men who may migrate with their families. Male industrial workers, the majority of 19th-century migrants and the majority of those in the southern reservoirs of labour are still needed but in smaller numbers. Demand for domestics (said to be unskilled), for caregivers (expected to provide emotional comfort to children and the elderly), and for (trained) nursing personnel mobilizes millions of women worldwide and especially in the Philippines, Bangladesh, Somalia, and West Africa. Unlike factory jobs, these positions require intimate contact between migrants and resident employers. The raising of infants and children devolves from 'mothers of the nation' onto 'foreign' women of different colour of skin in receiving societies and onto networks of female relatives in the sending societies who care for the migrant women's children. On the sending side, 8 million Filipinos and Filipinas (or 22 per cent of the state's working-age population) labour in some 160 countries abroad and their remittances accounted for 12 per cent of the state's GNP in 2005. On the receiving side, Canada has developed as special immigration category that permits such women to acquire citizenship and bring in family members.

Rural–urban migrations in Central and South America, Africa, and Asia now also result in rapid urbanization but migration often ends in shantytowns on the cities' fringes. Frequently, the cost of innovation and industrialization is politically allocated to weak social groups – to workers through low wages and to peasant families through low returns on labour. In China, living conditions in the countryside produced vast out-migrations, estimated at 150 million in 2005, with projections as high as 360 million by 2025. At the self-selected destinations, this so-called 'floating population' acquires neither rights of residence nor legal remedies against exploitation. As in multilingual India, migrants congregate in linguistic and cultural enclaves since most do not speak Mandarin or English, the languages of intercultural communication in the two societies. Other rapidly industrializing societies, such as South Korea, Vietnam, and Brazil, also experience vast internal migrations. External migration from the People's Republic of Chinas, Hong Kong (till 1997), or Taiwan to North America or other parts of the world thus account for only a tiny fraction of total migrations.

In civil-war- or violence-ravaged societies – Latin American in the 1980s, Africa in the 1990s – refugee mobility is directed towards camps rather than towards jobs or urban fringes. Since men wage war or are forced to do so, most of those fleeing are women and children. The vast majority of 'Third World' refugees stay within the region of origin; only a tiny minority reaches Northern job- and security-providing societies. Refugee admission to the highly developed North, sometimes criticized as too lax, is on the contrary extremely restrictive. The UN High Commissioner for Refugees is permitted by treaty to deal only with refugees crossing international borders.

Perspectives

To the voluntary labour migrations of the 19th century, 20th-century politics has added unprecedented numbers of refugees. Good governance that would permit satisfactory lives in the state or macroregion of origin is not being achieved. Global imbalances of military, economic, and political power as well as intrastate mismanagement, ethnopolitical conflict, and the destructiveness of male 'war-lords' combine to destroy life chances. New fundamentalisms as regards ethnic identity (for example former Yugoslavia, Nigeria), as regards religion (Muslim, Christian, Jewish, Hindu), or as regards economic doctrine (neoliberalism) continue to force people into involuntary migration. Natural and human-made environmental deterioration also forces millions to move, whether in the Sahel-zone of Africa or on the desert fringes of China. Rising ocean levels would force populations of the Pacific islands and of the below-sea-level Dutch regions to depart. Huge infrastructural projects, like dams and water reservoirs, and the fast expansion of urban fringes cause developmental displacement and further mobility. Policies and politicking as well as corruption and malplanning displace tens of millions as reports by both the World Bank and the United Nations Development Fund indicate. Migration is unlikely to disappear any time soon; it will remain a constant source of conflict, change and accommodation in the 21st century.

Dirk Hoerder

Bibliography

Appleyard R.T. (ed.) 1988. *International migration today*, two vols. Paris: Unesco.

Bade K. J. 2003. *Migration in European history*, trans. Brown A. Oxford: Blackwell.

Cohen R. (ed.) 1995. *The Cambridge survey of world migration*. Cambridge: Cambridge University Press.

Gungwu W. (ed.) 1997. *Global history and migrations*. Boulder: Westview.

Hoerder D. 2002. *Cultures in contact: world migrations in the second millennium*. Durham, NC: Duke University Press.

Northrup D. 1995. *Indentured labor in the age of imperialism, 1834–1922*. Cambridge: Cambridge University Press.

Okpewho I., Davis C. B. and Mazurui A. A. (eds) 1999. *The African diaspora: African origins and new world identities*. Bloomington: Indiana University Press.

Richmond A. 1994. *Global apartheid: refugees, racism and the new world order*. Toronto, New York and Oxford: Oxford University Press.

Skeldon R. 1992. 'International migration within and from the East and Southeast Asian region: a review essay', *Asian and Pacific Migration Journal*, 1, 1, 19–63.

Willcox W. F. and Ferenczi I. 1929, 1931. *International migrations*, 2 vols. New York: National Bureau of Economic Research.

Related essays

adoption; agriculture; China; climate change; contract and indentured labourers; decolonization; domestic service; empire and migration; empires and imperialism; ethnicity and race; executives and professionals; family; family migration; food; forced migrations; international migration regimes; Japan; labour migrations; marriage; money; nation and state; natural hazards; nursing; oil; pan-isms; performing artists; population; race-mixing; refugees; remittances; sexuality and migration; slavery; steamships; temporary migrations; tourism; urbanization; war; white men's countries; Zionism

Human rights

The concept of human rights, an important feature of Western European and North American politics since the 18th century, has become increasingly salient within international politics since the end of the Second World War. Many successful campaigns during the 19th and early 20th centuries had mobilized opinion around specific issues and abuses. However, the idea that human rights were universal, and that the behaviour of states towards their citizens should be governed by enforceable codes of conduct, was still not widely accepted. In this regard, the passage of the Universal Declaration of Human Rights (UDHR) by the General Assembly of the United Nations (UN) on 10 December 1948 should be seen as a seminal moment. The declaration set in motion a slow and hesitant process, held back for many decades by the impact of the Cold War, towards the eventual emergence of human rights as a 'hegemonic political discourse' (Donnelly, 2001, 38) within modern world politics. This process picked up speed during the 1970s, and developed even more rapidly following the end of the Cold War. Accordingly, a human rights 'regime' has evolved that consists of internationally agreed standards of behaviour (expressed in treaties and conventions), a variety of monitoring agencies, and some forms of legal redress. This regime has been both supported and extended by a burgeoning culture of domestic and transnational non-governmental organizations (NGOs). However, events since the end of the Cold War – notably the genocidal conflicts in Rwanda and Bosnia, and the restrictions placed on individual freedoms following the '9/11' attacks in the United States – suggest that the rise of human rights is by no means remorseless or inevitable.

The forerunners of the modern human rights movement can be found in the 19th century, notably in the campaigns against slavery, for female emancipation, for the rights of children, and for workers' rights. Such movements were transnational in scope and were often inspired as much by religious morality as by abstract conceptions of human rights. Apart from the latter case they drew their support primarily from the middle classes. Many of these campaigns continued their work into the 20th century, despite the vicissitudes of war and revolution: witness the constant succession of international declarations and conventions relating to the rights of women and children since 1918. There was, however, no movement for universal human rights prior to the Second World War. Such campaigns were essentially concerned with discrete issues and, indeed, sometimes at odds with each other. Socialist advocates of workers' rights were hostile to 'bourgeois' feminism and liberalism, while supporters of national self-determination clashed with socialist internationalists. Moreover, when the term 'human rights' was employed it was by no means politically neutral. The French League of the Rights of Man, established in 1898 at the height of the 'Dreyfus Affair', was associated with the left in the polarized politics of the Third Republic. Despite the achievements of the League of Nations or the International Labour Office after 1919, notably in the sphere of minority and workers' rights, the attempts by lawyers André Mandelstam and Antoine Frangulis to introduce resolutions on universal human rights to the League and other international bodies made scant progress amidst the hypernationalism of the early 1930s. Hence the significance, in both symbolic and practical terms, of the 1948 UDHR.

Any concept of 'human rights' posits the existence of inalienable and indivisible attributes of humanity. These broadly fall into three categories: civil and political rights (including religious rights), social and economic rights, and group rights (such as the right to national self-determination). There has been considerable debate as to whether the rights defined in the UDHR and related documents are essentially 'Western' in origin, or whether they are, in fact, intrinsic to other cultural and religious traditions. A 1947 UNESCO survey of the views of 70 noted scholars and intellectuals (including Mahatma Gandhi, Jacques Maritain and Aldous Huxley) claimed to detect certain rights 'implicit in man's nature' across cultures and religions. In form, at least, the UDHR owed much to previous statements such as the American Declaration of Independence (1776) and the French Declaration of the Rights of Man and the Citizen (1789). In content, however, the UDHR went far beyond these classic assertions of freedom from despotic rule, to include insights derived from 19th-century socialism, feminism and, to a degree, nationalism. It is apparent, therefore, that conceptions of 'human rights' have developed over time and that they are by no means immutable. Any agreed statement is bound to reflect the values and mores of societies at any given moment, as well as a compromise between different approaches, cultures and traditions. 'Human rights' are, therefore, normative, and represent a benchmark for just and dignified relations between citizens and states. Hence, according to its preamble, the UDHR was envisaged as a 'common standard of achievement for all peoples and all nations'. This appeal to universality was a novel development in international politics and represented a challenge to the longstanding sovereign rights of states to manage their own internal affairs.

The postwar moment in human rights

During the closing stages of World War 2 the victorious Allies were unusually susceptible to considerations of human rights in their planning for the postwar world. President Franklin D. Roosevelt's 'Four freedoms' speech of January 1941 had envisaged 'a world founded upon' freedom of speech and worship and freedom from want and fear. For their part, Britain and the Soviet Union were also amenable to the rhetoric of liberal internationalism and human rights, although both, in practice, had profound reservations. The shared desire to punish fascist aggression created an opening in which traditional concerns of state sovereignty were briefly overridden. There was, for instance, an unprecedented attempt to hold the rulers of Germany and Japan to account at the Nuremberg and Tokyo war crimes tribunals of 1946–48. A commitment to 'fundamental human rights' was also enshrined in the Charter of the UN, although the same document precluded the UN from intervening in matters 'which are essentially within the domestic jurisdiction of any State' without the approval of the Security Council. The founding conference of the UN invited a Human Rights Commission (HRC) chaired by Eleanor Roosevelt to draft an 'international bill of rights'.

The UDHR was principally the work of the French jurist René Cassin, Lebanese Christian academic Charles Malik, Chinese philosopher P. C. Chang, and the Canadian UN official John Humphrey. After almost two years of discussion within the HRC and other UN committees, the UDHR was eventually passed by 48–0 in the General Assembly. Eight states (principally the Soviet Union and its allies, plus South Africa and Saudi Arabia) abstained. Its 30 articles dealt in turn with political and civil liberties, social and economic rights, and the duties and obligations that such rights entailed. Article 28 stated that everyone was entitled to a 'social and international order' within which these rights could be 'fully realized'. With hindsight the UDHR can be hailed as a remarkable achievement, all the more so given the rapid intensification of Cold War tensions during this period. Even so, it should be noted that the Declaration was non-binding, and that there was as yet no indication of how it might be implemented. In many respects the UDHR represented merely an aspiration as human rights were still routinely abused and neglected in the dictatorships of Southern Europe, in the European colonial empires, in apartheid South Africa, and in the emerging Communist regimes of Eastern Europe. Moreover, there was little immediate prospect of the international order favourable to human rights envisaged in Article 28.

The Cold War

The impact of the Cold War greatly impeded the development of human rights at the international level for almost two decades after the signing of the UDHR. Neither side wished to give up the benefits of state sovereignty in favour of an intrusive regulatory regime. The Soviet Union largely ignored the Declaration, while claiming to champion the social and economic rights enshrined in it. The USA criticized the lack of political freedoms within the Soviet bloc, but the demands of *realpolitik* led it to ignore similar oppression by its own allies in Latin America and the Middle East. States with poor human rights records such as Portugal, Greece and Turkey were even allowed to join the North Atlantic Treaty Organization (NATO). In an influential 1979 article the American academic and diplomat Jean Kirkpatrick argued that pro-Western dictatorships were essentially different from Soviet 'totalitarian' regimes. Human rights, therefore, were not allowed to interfere with state interests. Hence, in May 1972, during their Moscow summit, President Richard Nixon and the Soviet leader Leonid Brezhnev recognized that ideological differences should not be allowed to preclude improvements in bilateral relations.

Despite the lack of superpower interest, slow progress was made towards the implementation of the UDHR, although at the cost of abandoning the principle of indivisibility. Two separate treaties were eventually concluded in 1966: the International Covenant on Civil and Political Rights (ICCPR) and the Covenant on Economic, Social and Cultural Rights (CESCR). However, it was a further ten years before sufficient numbers of states ratified the treaties for them to come into effect. (The USA did not ratify the ICCPR until 1992, and even then with numerous reservations. It still has not ratified the CESCR.) A Human Rights Committee of 18 experts was established to monitor compliance with the ICCPR, and a similar committee for the CESCR was set up in 1985. In both cases, however, the obligation for enforcement of the treaties remained with individual states. Far more rapid progress was made at the regional level, notably within Western Europe, where the European Convention for the Protection of Human Rights and Fundamental Freedoms (ECHR) was signed in 1950 under the auspices of the Council of Europe. The major Western European states supported the Convention, but with some ambivalence. For instance, Britain initially excluded its colonial territories, while France did not ratify the ECHR until 1974. Even so, the rapid development of the ECHR's associated institutions demonstrated how an effective mechanism for devising norms of behaviour and monitoring their observance could be achieved. A European Court of Human Rights sat at Strasbourg from 1959, and from 1966 allowed individual petitions. This became the model for the Inter-American Court of Human Rights that sat in Costa Rica from 1979.

One further significant development during this period was the emergence of NGOs which were able to challenge governments effectively at an international level. A group of NGO 'consultants' had been present at the founding of the UN, although their exact role in the framing of the Charter and the formation of the Human Rights Commission is disputed. From the 1950s two significant organizations sought to channel concerns over human rights within the legal profession. The US-based International Commission of Jurists (ICJ) was founded in 1952 following the abduction and execution of the anti-Communist West German lawyer Dr Walter Linse by East German agents. The

organization survived damaging revelations in 1967 that it had received secret funding from the Central Intelligence Agency (CIA). The British-based JUSTICE, which was founded in 1957 and which became the British branch of the ICJ, deliberately sought to investigate abuses of human rights across the Cold War divide. Amnesty International (AI), which, like JUSTICE, was founded by the British barrister Peter Benenson, represented a different approach. From its creation in 1961, Amnesty aimed to mobilize international public opinion in support of 'prisoners of conscience' and soon established a worldwide profile and membership. The award of the Nobel Peace Prize to AI in 1977 not only recognized the value of its work but also marked the growing seriousness with which the international community regarded the issue of human rights. Amnesty's campaign against state torture from 1972 onwards was influential in the conclusion of the 1984 Convention against Torture. This convention was underpinned by a separate committee and, in an important innovation, a roving 'Special Rapporteur'.

Carter, Helsinki and the European Community (EC)

During the 1970s Western governments and politicians began to give far greater weight to the question of human rights. This development is particularly associated with the presidency of Jimmy Carter (1977–81) who used human rights to provide a new legitimacy to US foreign policy after the trauma of Vietnam. Carter appointed a high-profile advocate of human rights, Patricia Derian, to the post of Assistant Secretary of State, and the State Department was required to submit annual reports on human rights in countries that were in receipt of US aid. On occasion, Carter's administration acted to cut arms supplies to the more egregious offenders such as the military dictatorships in Guatemala and Argentina. However, it should be noted that the basis of a human rights bureaucracy within the State Department had been laid during the previous Ford administration. Moreover, human rights were also being promoted from the late 1960s by the EC, which saw them as the basis for a democratic 'European' identity in its dealings with the USSR and Eastern Europe. Western European populations were increasingly sensitive to the abuses of human rights whether in Greece during the military junta of 1967–74 or in Chile, following the coup d'état of General Augusto Pinochet in 1973. Moreover, many Western politicians had come to see that human rights presented the West with a powerful political lever over the Soviet Union at a time when the Communist world was increasingly seeking to pursue détente and improved economic relations. In 1974, for instance, the Jackson-Vanik congressional amendment stipulated that US trading relations with the Soviet Union could only be normalized when Soviet citizens (especially Jews and other minorities) had the freedom to emigrate.

The most significant development in the field of human rights during the 1970s was arguably the 'Helsinki Process', which represented the first occasion on which human rights were institutionalized as norms within international relations. The Conference on Security and Cooperation in Europe (CSCE), which was concluded at Helsinki in August 1975, brought together the USA, the USSR and 33 other European states. It was initially seen as something of a success for the Soviet Union, which secured acceptance of the existing borders within Europe as well as the promise of future cooperation in science and technology. In return, however, the Soviets and their allies had been forced to concede a commitment to 'respect for human rights and fundamental freedoms' as one of ten basic principles for relations between participating states. In addition, one of the four 'Baskets' (or chapters) of further measures entailed a commitment to cooperation in the humanitarian field. The Soviets mistakenly believed that this agreement, like the UDHR, could be ignored: in fact, the Helsinki Accords emboldened critics of the Communist regimes (such as the Czechoslovak 'Charter 77') who now felt able to call their governments to account. In turn, these movements stimulated a new wave of NGOs in the West, of which the best-known was Human Rights Watch (HRW),

The 1980s

During the 1980s increasingly assertive human rights campaigners came into conflict with conservative Western governments conducting a new – and final – phase in the Cold War. After a slow start Amnesty International developed rapidly in the USA from the mid 1970s onwards, and by the 1980s the US branch (AIUSA) represented 40 per cent of the organization's worldwide membership. The high profile of AIUSA was confirmed in 1988 by its organizing of a world tour by leading rock stars, backed by the sports company Reebok. In the same year the various 'watch' committees were united under the US-based Human Rights Watch. HRW, which received financial support from institutions such as the Ford Foundation, brought a new level of professional research and political advocacy to human rights campaigning, and also clashed with the US administration when its initial focus on Eastern Europe extended to encompass America's allies within its own hemisphere. There were also significant developments on the regional level, such as the signing of the 1981 African Charter on Human and People's Rights by the states of the Organization of African Unity.

In both the United States and Britain, the right-wing, neoliberal governments of President Ronald Reagan (1981–89) and Prime Minister Margaret Thatcher (1979–90) took a hard line on domestic human rights while often turning a blind eye to friendly repressive regimes. Thatcher's brand of populist conservatism reclaimed the question of 'freedom' for the political right wing, by asserting the right to work (against striking trade unionists) or the right to purchase social housing from local authorities. The general air of intolerance of dissent and non-conformity within Britain radicalized the legal profession and gave rise to the movement Charter 88 (knowingly and somewhat pretentiously named after Charter 77) which called for a written constitution. In international politics the principal arena of conflict was in Central America where US-backed regimes in El Salvador and Guatemala were in conflict with leftist guerrillas, while in Nicaragua the Reagan administration provided support to the insurgent 'Contra' rebels against the revolutionary Sandinista government. The administration was often locked in conflict with human rights NGOs over alleged violations of human rights, and accused its critics of being politically motivated. However, there were also signs that the administration was becoming more savvy in handling such criticisms and responsive to the greater public interest in human rights. In 1988, for instance, the USA finally ratified the 1948 UN Convention on Genocide. In 1990 the Bush administration (1989–93) skilfully used Amnesty International's (later withdrawn) allegations of Iraqi atrocities during the invasion of Kuwait to build support for the Gulf War of 1990–91.

After the Cold War

The collapse of the Communist regimes in the Soviet Union and Eastern Europe in 1989–91 gave rise to talk of a 'new world order' within which human rights would, at last, take the central place that many had hoped for after 1945. Indeed, there is no question that human rights came to play a very central role in both international and domestic politics from 1989. The machinery for monitoring and promoting human rights was greatly expanded, notably with the creation of the office of UN High Commissioner for Human Rights after the 1993 Vienna world conference (a post held with great distinction by the former Irish President Mary Robinson in 1997–2002). Moreover, an International Criminal Court was finally established in 1999, albeit with very circumscribed powers, to deal with allegations of crimes against humanity. NGO activity also greatly increased, and human rights considerations were embedded in all aspects of international governance such as relief work, peacekeeping and post-conflict processes of reconciliation. There have been many notable examples of the growing salience of human rights. For instance, improvements in human rights have been an essential condition for the absorption of post-Communist states into the EU and NATO. There was a particularly telling moment in October 1998 when the former Chilean dictator Pinochet was arrested while visiting Britain and detained for 17 months pending his possible extradition to Spain. Although he was finally allowed to depart on grounds of ill-health, the episode showed that chronic abusers of human rights could no longer expect to find an untroubled haven in the democratic states.

However, the conflicts in Rwanda (1994) and Bosnia (1992–95) offered a stark reminder of the failure of the current human rights regime to prevent genocidal atrocities. Moreover, the Bush administration's response to the 9/11 attacks, from the Patriot Act to the seemingly limitless detention without trial of al-Qaeda suspects at Guantánamo Bay, as well as the degradations inflicted on Iraqi prisoners at Abu Ghraib prison, showed that powerful states were still willing to curb – or even disregard – human rights when it suited their interests. The use of the defence of human rights as a justification for NATO to wage war on Serbia over Kosovo in 1999, and then for the US-led 'Coalition of the willing' to overthrow Saddam Hussein in 2003, raised uncomfortable questions as to the degree to which force could and should be used to achieve human rights objectives. Michael Ignatieff, for instance, detected a new era of American imperialism and global hegemony 'whose grace notes are free markets, human rights and democracy' (Ishay 2004, 288–9). Amnesty International's stinging denunciation of Guantánamo Bay as 'the gulag of our time' (Guardian, 26 May 2005) restored an essential critical distance between advocates of human rights and the state.

The most important – and complex – issue since the end of the Cold War has been the rise of a 'globalized' world economy and the associated developments in communications and travel. This brought both benefits and immense challenges for the promotion of human rights. The political agenda became ever more transnational, with the rise of issues of pressing global concern such as climate change, health and poverty. Moreover, while a small number of states such as North Korea and Burma remained largely beyond international purview, most states now paid at least lip-service to their international human rights obligations. In addition, the rise of 'ethical' investment and consumption placed greater pressure on multinational companies to improve the rights of their workers. The 'anti-globalization' movement, with its demonstrations against free trade in Seattle (1999), Genoa (2001) and elsewhere, showed how human rights issues could be central to a new, international protest movement. At the same time, however, global competition and trade drove down wages, accelerated damage to the environment in the developing world and weakened traditional bastions of workers' rights such as the trade unions. Poverty, in turn, increased the allure of Europe and North America for many in Latin America, Africa and the Far East. The rights of migrant workers and asylum seekers within the developed world became an urgent concern for human rights activists, but also a focus for the intolerant, populist politics of Jean-Marie Le Pen (in France) and Jörg Haider (in Austria). Therefore, in the 21st century the somewhat neglected social and economic aspects of the UDHR seemed likely to take on ever greater significance.

Conclusion

The increasing centrality of human rights within international politics since World War 2 has been brought about by a potent mixture of state interest, the setting of legal norms through the UN and other international agencies, NGO activism and individual idealism. The failure to secure the peace after World War 1 and, above all, the bitter experience of World War 2 spurred on the pursuit of a new world order based on respect for universal human rights. The advent of the Cold War meant that this goal was initially unattainable. However, progress was made at the regional level during this period, as well as in the development of single-issue regimes (in areas such as women's rights and racial equality). The Cold War also saw the emergence of genuinely transnational NGOs, committed to confronting the abuse of human rights and promoting new norms of international behaviour. The Helsinki Process demonstrated that the promotion of human rights could be pursued through international agreements between states, and that such agreements may well have unforeseen consequences.

Since the end of the Cold War concerns for human rights have become a central, normative issue within world politics, enshrined in numerous treaties and conventions. However, a degree of caution is justifiable. It has often been remarked that the state is at the same time the leading defender of and the leading threat to human rights, and it could be argued that little has changed in this regard. Hence, states will continue to advance human rights primarily when it conforms to their interests. Moreover, the 'War on Terror' since 2001 demonstrated that human rights may well lack popular support when the security of the individual and the state is perceived to be under threat. For all of the achievements in the legal sphere since 1945, the promotion of international human rights remains an incomplete project.

Tom Buchanan

Bibliography

Donnelly J. 2001. *Universal human rights in theory and practice*, 2nd ed. Ithaca: Cornell University Press.

Dunne T. and Wheeler N. J. (eds) 1999. *Human rights in global politics*. Cambridge: Cambridge University Press.

Glendon M. A. 2002. *A world made new: Eleanor Roosevelt and the Universal Declaration of Human Rights*. New York: Random House.

Halliday S. and Schmidt P. (eds) 2004. *Human rights brought home*. Oxford and Portland: Hart.

Ishay M. R. 2004. *The history of human rights*. Berkeley: University of California Press.

Keck M. E. and Sikkink K. 1998. *Activists beyond borders: advocacy networks in international politics*. Ithaca: Cornell University Press.

Sellars K. 2002. *The rise and rise of human rights*. Sutton: Stroud.

Thomas D. C. 2001. *The Helsinki effect*. Princeton: Princeton University Press.

Related essays

Abolition of Forced Labour Convention; abolitionism; African liberation; Amnesty International (AI); animal rights; asylum seekers; benefits and charity concerts; Buddhism; children's rights; Cold War; cosmopolitanism and universalism; Ford Foundation; indigenous knowledges; indigenous networks; international non-governmental organizations (INGOs); International Women's Day; justice; legal order; Mandela, Nelson; Oxfam; Pax Americana; philanthropic foundations; Save the Children International Union; September 11, 2001; slavery; United Nations system; United Nations Women's Conferences; war crimes; women's movements; world orders

Humanities

The core practice of the humanities is a 'learned habit of attention to textual detail'. Such work was thought to be embedded in an intellectual tradition that was 'given, absolute, to be mastered' (Grafton and Jardine, 1986, xiv). In time that assumption would coexist uneasily with a critical stance toward authority. For most of modern history the method of the humanities has been positivist, deriving from the philological tradition of scholarship in classical and literary studies. The academic humanities represent an extension and transformation of Renaissance Humanism, a vocation that adhered to a set of (supposedly) universal and superior values. This idealized understanding persists, but it was diluted over the course of the 20th century as the humanities became a discipline that focused on the acquisition and demonstration of a technique of scholarship. The transition from humanism to the humanities in Europe (with specific help from the Enlightenment, which pushed God into the background) secularized knowledge, establishing the terms of the incorporation of the humanities into the core of the modern university, though the ideal of the secular university remains contentious in some places.

It was not until after World War 2 that the humanities in Europe and the United States became entirely enclosed in academe, and not until the end of the century elsewhere. Until then the intellectual work of the humanities – examining the historical forms of cultural expression, making aesthetic and moral judgments, and critically examining truth claims – was carried on outside of the academy by writers, called 'intellectuals' after that word came into circulation in the wake of the Dreyfus Affair (1898) in France. The very territory or compass of the humanities varies by nation, as does the general rubric to which these clusters of disciplines are referred. Although the word humanities has, as already indicated, a long European lineage, it tends to be used mostly in American universities, where it emerged, more or less as a catch-all category for those arts and sciences disciplines that were neither sciences nor social sciences. The disciplines that in the United States are referred to collectively as 'the humanities' would in Britain be called the 'arts' disciplines, and in France the reference would be lettres.

Universities, nation states and the humanities

Contrary to common assumption, modern academic scholarship in the humanities, as embodied in classical and comparative philology, preceded the natural sciences in taking academic form and establishing the disciplinary vocation characteristic of university life. They also imbibed the spirit of nationalism, and were associated with the project that made modern nation states. These new disciplines were established on a national basis, in national universities, such as the University of Berlin (1810) or the Russian system of higher education. Later in the 19th century, this European model was exported to the United States, with the founding the The Johns Hopkins University (1876), and to Asia, with the creation of American-sponsored universities in China (Peking, 1899, and Sichuan, 1901) or the German-style universities in Japan (Tokyo).

There was a persistent tension between the cosmopolitanism inherent in the humanistic enterprise and the nation state that sponsored the university and asked of its humanities departments the legitimation of a national high culture. The academic humanities became less cosmopolitan than the older 'Republic of Letters' had been. Although universalistic in sharing a historicist interest in the culture and texts of the classical world, humanist scholars tended, especially in Germany, to funnel that culture into their own projects of making and legitimating distinctive national cultures. There were many tensions in the European emergence of humanistic scholarship: some epitomized in the cross-observation between France and Germany. Indeed, one can say that German humanistic scholarship (neuhumanismus), associated with the individual creativity and character-defining culture of Bildung that formed men, was defined in part against the materialism of French Enlightenment notions of civilization. The powerful philological methods developed by 19th-century German scholars were resisted in French universities for fear that they would undermine France's self-proclaimed role as the custodian of European literary life. The flip side of this use of the humanities was that scholars in Germany and elsewhere often played the card of international scholarly competition to extract imperial funds. Perhaps one should not be surprised that the director of the dig at Pergamon, the spectacular results of which are displayed in Berlin, was an employee of the German Foreign Ministry.

If the humanities as an academic practice emerged in the 19th-century European university, both the university and its disciplines gradually integrated other parts of the world. Again there were tensions. The acceptance of modern disciplinary practices in China at the turn of the 20th century was marked by great unease. These European models were not eagerly sought. But the combination of the new Imperial University in Japan and that nation's success in the Sino–Japanese War convinced the Chinese that incorporation of Western scholarship and science was a matter of survival in a world dominated by this new mode of knowledge production. This engagement with Western scholarly practices had a price, nearly discrediting China's own tradition cultivating classical knowledge to form scholar officials.

Broadly speaking, the European humanistic self-understanding was formed partly in contrast to the Orient, or what the Orient was supposed to represent – decay as opposed to Western progress. Conversely, Asian scholars tended to frame intellectual culture as an East (spiritual) / West (material) contrast. Such was the case with India's Rabindranath Tagore, the first Asian awarded a Nobel Prize in literature (1923), and China's Liang Qichao, the scholar, writer, and leader in the democracy movement who was the first Chinese member invited in 1923 to join PEN, the international writers' group.

Founded as they were on the base of civic humanism and classical ideals of virtue (deriving from Latin *vir*, meaning 'man' and the root also of 'virile' and 'virility'), the humanities were a masculine discipline preparing students for masculine public roles until the 20th century, when the classical republican tradition exhausted itself. It was an education for leadership, an ideal most fully realized in England, least so in the United States. Until the 1890s, an Atlantic-wide international class of intellectuals and high public officials shared a humanistic lingua franca based on knowledge of classical languages and culture that would dissolve with the proliferation of specialized knowledges, electives, and useful knowledge in the curriculum of higher learning, most evident in the United States.

By the end of the 19th century something distinctive about the humanities had become evident. Theodore Merz, the British author of the four-volume *History of European Thought in the Nineteenth Century* (1903–14), observed that in scientific thought 'national differences were gradually disappearing'. By contrast, while what he called philosophical thought was becoming international, he pointed out that it still carried traces of the 'narrower limits of national or local interests or of special schools'. This parochialism was keeping 'philosophical literatures apart'. One can say of the 20th century that the university and the disciplines that find their homes there are at once nationalist and internationalist. While the humanities in particular are regarded as custodians expected to manage the transmission of the specific national culture across the generations, there was over the century an increasing interest in and realization of the international circulation of scholars and knowledge, and one important measure of scholarly excellence of a nation's universities became its appeal to foreign scholars and students.

International congresses

The decades from roughly 1860 through 1940 witnessed a veritable explosion of international congresses and conferences, in all fields of knowledge and human activity. Some were one-time events, but most continued their existence in a sequence of meetings of varying length. Organization was the order of the day, and the humanities were active participants in this development – in roughly three phases. The first, between 1860 to 1890, was often associated with the organization of new areas of knowledge into proto-disciplines, with archaeology and history, including the history of art, ethnography, linguistics, and orientalist studies leading the way. The spirit of the next phase was imbued with a new sense of a more compact world, woven together by new means of communication. It was assumed that communication among the educated classes would bring forth a sense of brotherhood, international understanding and peace, an aspiration that was also behind the later development of academic exchanges. About 60 per cent of the international congresses and conferences organized between 1840 and 1937 took place between 1890 and 1930. In 1908, at the Third International Congress of Philosophy, meeting in Heidelberg, there were hopes that philosophy as a discipline would sustain a culture that would include various people from different states. and that international congresses would deepen the solidarity of nations. To make this point, an American commentator observed that Germans were treating French participants with impressive grace, even though the anniversary of the German victory over France in Sedan fell on the opening day. The Germans graciously even omitted the usual celebration of the day. Such sentiments were rehearsed regularly by humanities assemblies and journals.

Many of the international congresses in the humanities were held in conjunction with international expositions. The most important instance was the Paris Exposition of 1900, which hosted a large number of congresses. The event itself was less important than what it stimulated: for many disciplines, including philosophy and history, the experience prompted the establishment of regular congresses at various intervals. But there were still ad hoc congresses at some expositions, and after Paris 1900, the most important was the International Congress of Arts and Sciences that was part of the Universal Exposition of St Louis in 1904. The Congress was organized with grand ambition by Hugo Munsterberg, a German psychologist who taught in Germany and the United States. It was to contribute to the unification of knowledge, a Hegelian aspiration that suited the host city, for St Louis had sustained a significant community of philosophical Hegelians in the final third of the 19th century.

Munsterberg shared the optimism of his generation that international exchanges and communication would foster peace and progress, but his agenda for the Congress went beyond that. He believed that the challenge facing the 20th century was to overcome 'mere heaping up of disconnected, unshaped facts'. He thought that this could not be 'dealt with otherwise than by the combined labour of all nations and all sciences'. Only then would humankind discover the 'fundamental conceptions that bind together all the specialistic results' (Haines and Jackson, 1947, 209). For the humanities he planned histories of literature, art, religion, and language. Methods and epistemology were the focus of Munsterberg, but a synthesis on these issues was not reached by the 500 participants, quite unbalanced in respect to internationalist representation with too many Americans and Germans. James Bryce, the English historian, statesman and diplomat – and participant – thought the Congress had made an important contribution to peace and international understanding, but he made no claim that any of the serious intellectual work Munsterberg had unrealistically anticipated had been accomplished.

That was typical of the era of congresses. Few of the international congresses achieved much of intellectual substance as far as synthesis was concerned, but many participants agreed that a shaping of differences justified the meetings. Even inconclusive results were better than not meeting at all. In 1930, the American philosopher Ralph Barton Perry characterized the conferences as a happy fellowship of irreducible differences.

International organization

If the hope of the humanist internationalists was to bring harmony to the competition among nations, that competition and the wars it produced played havoc with the internationalism of the congresses and other forms of international organization of the humanities. While small nations, like Norway, were able to reach out to restore intellectual cooperation in a bilateral way after World War I, the division between Germany and its Central European allies and the Western Europeans stood in the way of a full recovery of prewar intellectual relations. The creation of the International Union of Academies (IUA), established in Paris in the shadow of the creation of the League of Nations, forced the issue. The founding nations included France, Great Britain, the Netherlands, Norway, Denmark, Italy, Greece, Poland, Russia, and Japan. Germany and its allies were noticeably absent. One of the founders, Sir F. G. Kenyon, president of the British Academy, explained the problem in his presidential address of 1920. He described his position as moderate, opposed to those who would bar any scholarly relations with Germany in the future. But there was a sticking point for him. A manifesto supporting Germany's war aims had been signed by 93 German scholars. It was, complained Kenyon, as scholars that they signed but it was as scholars that they failed in their obligations. They had, according to Kenyon, affirmed the truth of these government justifications without investigating them, which he called a crime against scholarship. While he did not ask for an apology, he hoped that there would be some suggestion of regret, even reconsideration. Without that, he insisted, there could be no reconciliation. Only in 1926 were Germany and Austria integrated into this community of scholars, at the insistence of American delegates.

The League of Nations had also spawned another and somewhat different international organization – the League of Nations Committee on Intellectual Cooperation, which met for the first time in 1922. Unlike the IUA, which was an organization of organizations, the Committee on Intellectual Cooperation connected more directly with scholars by establishing national committees of its own. It was a direct forerunner of UNESCO, created in 1945 with the founding of the United Nations and now the sponsor of 190 national committees.

The greatest accomplishment of the international organizations and meetings of humanists was not the resolution of scholarly questions of method or substantive interpretations of the past or texts or works of art. Rather it was collaboration in expanding the research technologies available to scholars of all countries: indexes, dictionaries, translations and the like.

Political crisis, exile, and new directions

As the 1920s passed into the 1930s the crisis of the Great Depression and the emergence of anti-democratic governments of the right and left seriously weakened the internationalism of the prewar decades and the 1920s. There was a distinct decline in humanistic internationalism in the nationalistic 1930s, but there were also efforts to form intellectual ties that would advance a Euro-American ambition for an anti-fascist alliance. The United States and some Latin American countries – under the auspices of the Pan-American Union, which established a Division of Intellectual Cooperation in 1924 and received US government 'Good Neighbor Policy' funding beginning in 1938 – organized conferences that brought together humanists from both hemispheres, with philosophers among the most active. The philosophers were proud of holding a conference in Haiti. They should have been proud: invitations and participation at international conferences rarely went beyond Europe, though after World War 1 Japan became an active participant in international humanities organizations. After World War 2, with US activities in Latin America before and during the war something of a model, international intellectual exchange in the humanities was incorporated into the strategic objectives of the United States and the USSR, morphing into an aspect of diplomacy, cultural diplomacy.

In 1934, the American philosopher Ernest Nagel perceived that the Eighth International Congress of Philosophy, meeting in Prague, felt the weight of the social, spiritual, and intellectual issues pressing upon European politics and culture even in those sessions devoted to 'pure' philosophy. He found the absence of Russia very conspicuous, and deemed the appearance of Professor Reichenbach, formerly of Berlin, as spokesman for Turkey ironical as well as dramatic. The German philosopher's representative circumstance of exile amounted to a personification of the crisis. Yet this very condition and the combat of ideologies drew particular attention to the contributions of the positivist philosophers of the Vienna Circle at the Prague meeting. European events, Nagel thought, had made apparent the 'bitter consequences of loose speculation', and that produced a welcome for the school's rigour and commitment to the sufficiency of the scientific method. Perhaps, Nagel reflected, many would realize that the 'only road to salvation' was the 'myopic dissection of logical problems' (Nagel, 1934, 589–91). This speculation anticipated a move after the war, particularly in the Anglo-American world, toward a focus on scientific rigour in the humanities and social sciences. The positivist method may have been reductionist, but for that very reason it promised universal truths that might tame the century's ideological combat and actual wars.

The rise of European fascism and a murderous anti-Semitism produced a diaspora of European scholars in the social sciences as well as in the humanities that has never been adequately mapped. The most thoroughly studied destination has been the United States, where, as the historian Carl Schorske recalled, speaking of the impact on his generation coming of age in the 1940s, they 'made intellectuals out of young academics by broadening our horizons and multiplying our awareness of the ... implications of ideas – philosophic and literary as well as social and political' (quoted in Charle et al., 2004, 61). But the case of Reichenbach in Turkey suggests that the impact might have been much broader. Not only was Reichenbach working in Turkey in the 1930s, but it was in Istanbul that Erich Auerbach wrote one of the great classics of literary study, *Mimesis: the representation of reality in Western literature* (1946). It was also there that Auerbach and Leo Spitzer began the conversations that culminated in the postwar blossoming of the discipline of comparative literature.

There was in the 1940s and 1950s a longing for universalism. With the mushroom cloud of the Atomic Bomb on people's minds, there was worldwide acclaim for a travelling photographic exhibition mounted at New York's Museum of Modern Art that insisted upon the oneness of 'The Family of Man'. At the same time humanist scholars seeking to reunite the world that had been split between the Allies and Axis powers, and in the Cold War divide between the United States and the USSR, were looking for harmony in some combination of 'Nationalism, Internationalism, and Universality in Literature', as the hope was naively phrased in the title of an article published in the *Journal of Aesthetics and Art Criticism* in 1946. UNESCO, which in 1949 established the International Council for Philosophy and Humanistic Studies, had the same hopes. The preamble of its constitution posited that 'since wars begin in the minds of men, it is in the minds of men that defences of peace must be constructed'. It was 'ignorance of each other's ways and lives [that] has been a common cause' of the mistrust among peoples that 'too often' has 'broken into war' (Evans, 1965, 38). Of course, the conundrum faced by those with such aspirations was how to preserve and respect cultures and make of them a universalism – to say nothing of moderating the state power and militarism of the contending superpowers.

Academic exchanges

At the beginning of the 20th century European and American universities, and the modern Asian universities in Japan and China, established a number of faculty and student exchange programmes and library exchanges of books and journals. Perhaps the first exchange of scholarly materials was organized by the 19th-century French historian and statesman François Guizot, who initiated an exchange that brought 70,000 books from the United States to France, and 100,000 French books went in the other direction. Early in the 20th century many of the world's national (and university) libraries made explicit decisions to become international in their holdings, generally acting in advance of the actual scholarship being produced, which remained national in orientation longer.

Humans make ideas and the social networks they form are perhaps the most effective carriers of ideas. Some of these networks were informal, casually constructed out of social life, but at the end of the 19th century, prompted by a sense that new developments in transportation and communication had made the world smaller, European and American universities initiated formal bilateral agreements for exchange professorships. In 1905 the University of Berlin established the Theodore Roosevelt chair for a visiting American professor. Harvard University and Columbia University created a parallel Kaiser Wilhelm II chair, and the first faculty crossed the Atlantic the next year. While phrased in the language of peace and mutual understanding, it is clear that these were gestures made by the two fastest rising new empires. German scholars also helped establish modern academic disciplines and universities in Japan, while the United States did the same in China. In 1909, the Sorbonne, Columbia and Harvard established an exchange of faculty in the field of medieval literature.

France had a very large impact on the development of modern universities in Latin America, especially Brazil. In 1910, an exchange agreement was put in place between France, Brazil and Argentina, and a year later Oliveira Lima offered the first course on Brazilian literature in Paris. Over the course of the first half of the 20th century a very large number of French humanities scholars, including some of the most distinguished humanists, such as Gustave Glotz, Lucien Febvre and Paul Hazard, spent time in Argentina or Brazil, either through exchanges or cooperative programmes of various sorts. Paris also established many exchanges with the smaller nations of Europe, such as Sweden and Belgium, and mostly humanists participated in them. In these and other exchanges, Paris was the preferred destination for scholars in *lettres*, while more scientists went to Berlin. Professors from the US tended to divide in equal numbers, roughly half going to Berlin and Paris respectively. There were no such exchanges between Paris and Berlin, however, until 1926. From that year to 1939 there were exchanges, but almost all the participants were scientists, not humanists – though some notable French humanists did go, including Raymond Aron. Russians, too, were scholarly travellers after 1890, and the traffic was two-way, especially after the Russian Revolution, when the philosopher John Dewey was impressed by the commitment to experimental education and appalled by the political indoctrination and philosophical narrowness he saw there.

At mid-century for the humanities 'international' still effectively meant European. Indeed, the discipline of comparative literature at its founding searched for the 'essential unity of European culture' (Bernheimer 1995, 40). Oddly, in practice this internationalization actually reinforced nationalist outlooks, and the Eurocentric practice limited the cosmopolitanism in literary studies that would emerge only at the end of the century. When the Modern Language Association's international bibliography was initiated in 1922, it covered English, American, German, and Romance language literatures. In 1955, Eastern European languages were added, and in the 1960s African, Latin American, and Asian listings were added. By the end of the century, history, literature, musicology and art history moved beyond the nationalist origins of the humanities disciplines to a global perspective. This vastly expanded the archive of human art and experience, and the humanities disciplines incorporated transnational perspectives into their methodologies. Finally, at the beginning of the 21st century the humanities disciplines live up to their designation, their scope and significance encompassing the whole of humanity. In the new century the humanities have come closer than ever before to the expansiveness imagined but not attained by the 18th-century Enlightenment. This humanistic vision points toward the hope expressed by Alain Locke, a leader of the Harlem Renaissance early in the 20th century: 'culture-goods, once evolved, are no longer the property of the race or people that originated them. They belong to all who can use them; and belong most to those who can use them best' (quoted in Posnock, 1998, 11).

Thomas Bender

Bibliography

Bernheimer C. 'Bernheimer Report', In Bernheimer C. (ed.) 1995. *Comparative literature in the age of multiculturalism.* Baltimore: Johns Hopkins University Press, 39–48.

Charle C. 1996. *Les intellectuels en Europe au XIX siècle: essai d'histoire comparée.* Paris: Seuil.

Charle C., Schriewer, J. and Wenger J. (eds) 2004. *Transnational intellectual networks.* Frankfurt and New York: Campus.

De A. 2004. *International understanding and world peace, 1919–1957.* Unpublished doctoral dissertation, CUNY Graduate Center, New York.

Evans L. H. 1965. 'The humanities and international communication', PMLA, 80, 2, 37–42.

Grafton A. and Jardine L. 1986. *From humanism to the humanities.* Cambridge, MA: Harvard University Press.

Haines G. and Jackson F. H. 1947. 'A neglected landmark in the history of ideas', *Mississippi Valley Historical Review,* 34, 2, 201–20.

Nagel E. 1934. 'The Eighth International Congress of Philosophy', *Journal of Philosophy,* 31, 22, 589–601.

Posnock R. 1998. *Color and culture: Black writers and the making of the modern intellectual.* Cambridge, MA: Harvard University Press.

Related essays

book and periodical exchange; China; civilizations; class; Cold War; cosmopolitanism and universalism; cultural capitals; exile; expositions; fellowships and grants; Garvey, Marcus Mosiah; higher education; historians and the nation state; history; intellectual elites; intergovernmental organizations; international non-governmental organizations (INGOs); internationalisms; Japan; knowledge; League of Nations system; literature; mathematics; museums; music; nation and state; Orientalism; Otlet, Paul; pan-isms; scientific expeditions; social sciences; Westernization; yoga

I

Indentured and contract labourers
See **Contract and indentured labourers**

Individual identification systems

Governments have always had an interest in determining, defining, and managing the populations under their control. Systems of individual identification provide each citizen or resident with a unique identifier, connected to information to determine nationality, status, benefits, or anomalies, and most often expressed through a form of personal identification (ID card, smart card or passport) and a database. To secure the integrity of frontiers and borders, social services, cultural identity, and economic growth, governments aim to both know and control the population which resides in, works in, accesses benefits in, visits and leaves the national territory. In times of emergency, war, or totalitarian rule, identification systems have been crucial in the management of large national populations. In addition to birth certificates, national or social insurance numbers, and driver's licences, the modern passport is the crucial foundational individual identification system.

Early forms of individual identification systems were diplomatic credentials, passes for international couriers, and sea-passports which identified the allegiance of ships and their crews. The three main forms of pre-national identification systems were diplomatic or special status (i.e. religious), agents of violence (i.e. military identification and sea-passports or letters of marque), and health passports (i.e. certifications of good health or freedom from the plague). Commercial or scholarly travellers also carried letters from sovereigns or associates. Identification in the pre-national era depended upon personal relations, the bearer of the letter, and broad physical descriptions. States were constrained in issuing these documents by their inability to manage information.

Only later did modern 'population states' develope the ability to manage the individual identities of large numbers of citizens. At the end of the 18th and beginning of the 19th century France, Germany, and the Austro-Hungarian Empire began to develop national identity systems but these remained fragmentary and decentralized. By mid-century France, Britain, and the Austro-Hungarian Empire recorded births, deaths, crimes, and illness in local offices but did not collate the data centrally. French anti-vagrancy laws made it a criminal offence to be without an identity document; German states often had similar residence, travel and work permits. European countries experimented with national identification documents, and governments simplified the administration of colonies through individual identification documents. Identity cards were issued in Egypt, India, Algeria, South Africa and other colonial possessions. They allowed the colonial official to differentiate and control what was viewed as a racially homogenous 'mass'. However, for the most part, passports were not necessary for cross-border movement in the 19th century, and (outside of Germany with its extremely restrictive domestic passes and work permits), no identification documents were needed for national movements. The non-domestic circulation of labour and tourists operated with local documentation – passports were often simply official letters by consulate or foreign ministry officials, which had no bearing on nationality or residence. During the massive migrations of population within Europe and towards North America in the late 19th and early 20th centuries, identification happened briefly at frontiers: the chief concern of American immigration inspectors, for example, was the physical and moral health of prospective immigrants, not their name, number, or status.

The First World War saw an explosion of identity documents, and bureaucratic attempts to harness population information in preparation for total war. The primary transnational identification system, the passport, originated in the post-World War 1 era. It was a solution to the problem of refugee populations and the disintegration of the Austro-Hungarian and Ottoman Empires. It was not until 1922 that the League of Nations agreed on an international form of the passport. Although it was hoped that the passport would not be necessary for longer than five years, this temporary solution became indispensable to the control of modern mobility. Almost immediately, fraud became a central issue, which spawned new forms of international police cooperation. The British National Insurance number and American Social Security number were introduced in the mid-1930s to track personal contributions to welfare programmes, but there was wide-scale and enduring popular resistance to widening the functions of such identification numbers. After fading during the interwar years, ration cards, military identification cards, and national registration cards were reintroduced at the start of World War 2. In both Britain and America, greater interrelations were made between databases to manage the male population able to complete military service, which required the management of birth, service, death, and health records. The Nazi state, and some of its occupied territories including the Vichy regime, used national identity cards which bore a racial description to facilitate their deportation of Jewish and Gypsy populations during the Second World War. During and after the war, as the bureaucratic abilities of governments increased, states were increasingly capable of controlling national population movement (both inwards and outwards) through identification systems.

Two notorious examples of the use of identification systems for the control of domestic populations were the Soviet Union and South Africa. The Soviet Union utilized an internal passport which indicated permission for travel or residence within the various states of the USSR, also indicating nationality. South Africa used an identity card with fingerprints and denoting identity and race to support the apartheid system. While the Soviet system has collapsed the South African system continues to use a centralized database of biometric information although it no longer records race. The majority of countries now have some sort of national identification system, although the degree to which data are centralized varies greatly.

Approximately 100 countries currently have mandatory national identification cards. ISO 8710 defines the standard for contemporary identity cards, while the International Civil Aviation Organization (ICAO Document 9303) determines the standards for passports and other travel documents. Egyptian identity cards are unlaminated cardboard bearing a photograph and information, whereas Côte d'Ivoire, Malaysia, Hong Kong and South Africa all use RFID (non-contact radio frequency identification) smart-card technology which couples biometric information in their identity cards. The American army has used identity cards to ascertain and monitor population movements in their occupation efforts in Iraq.

National identification systems are now more than government records of identity; they are interconnected databases with biometric information – data which measures the human body for purposes of identification and authentication. Schemes such as explicit national ID cards, as in France and Germany, indicate nationality, citizenship and residence. Despite resistance to a national identity card in the United States, the Real ID Act standardizes state-issued driver's licences and makes those augmented documents required for air travel or access to federal services (and mandates a digital photograph and signature on each document). All US states must also agree to share this data with all other US states. Both the new American 'Lincoln visa' and the US-VISIT programme require a digital photograph and fingerprints that are checked at the border and stored by Department of Homeland Security officials. The United Kingdom has progressed further in this direction of control, as the government now proposes to introduce a controversial national ID card scheme. Although an integrated national registry database has been withdrawn, a national DNA database is now in full operation. DNA samples may be taken from any individual arrested by police, without their consent, regardless of whether DNA is related to the offence, and the data will be retained regardless of the outcome of the charge.

Contemporary identification systems also extend beyond the national state. The exchange of international civil aviation passenger information is also representative of a new 'assemblage' of identification systems, by which is meant a non-centralized system comprised of different elements which have nonetheless a controlling or policing effect on the population. In 1995, the Schengen Accord required the construction of the Schengen Information System. European governments may now access entry/exit and visa information, and details of outstanding criminal warrants for all citizens and visitors to Schengen countries. The expansion of the 'war on terror' has led to an intensification of this interchange of intelligence between countries as demonstrated by the American programmes of extraordinary rendition, illustrated by the case of Canadian Maha Arar and German Khaled el-Masri. Passenger manifests and CIA watch-lists are not integrated, but intelligence sharing between national governments has the effect of creating a dispersed assemblage of control and identification.

Since the emergence of modern bureaucracies in the mid-19th century, tensions have grown between the desire of the state to control and know its mobile population, the ability of the state to manage vast amounts of data, and the value afforded privacy and civil rights. Individual identification systems are most often and most extensively used to identify, define, and manage anomalous or putatively dangerous populations, such as migrants and foreigners. As the ability of state bureaucracies increases, they are able to include more and more individuals and more and more information in these systems of power/knowledge.

Mark B. Salter

Bibliography

Caplan J. and Torpey J. (eds) 2001. *Documenting individual identity: the development of state practices in the modern world*. Princeton: Princeton University Press.

Foucault M. 2004. *Sécurité, territoire, population: cours au Collège de France 1977–1978*. Paris: Seuil.

Salter M. B. 2003. *Rights of passage: the passport in international relations*. Boulder: Lynne Rienner.

Torpey J. 2000. *The invention of the passport: surveillance, citizenship and the state*. Cambridge: Cambridge University Press.

Related essays
border commuters; empire and migration; human mobility; international migration regimes; League of Nations system; nation and state; police; population; refugee relief; refugees; technical standardization; terrorism; travel and tourism; war; welfare state; white men's countries; workers' movements

Indigenous knowledges

Indigenous knowledge, also referred to as the traditional knowledge of indigenous peoples, has no universally agreed definition. It is not a concept uniformly held by all indigenous peoples and is problematic to generalize, especially within Eurocentric frameworks. Although commonly discussed in the singular, the plural (knowledges) better acknowledges the diversity across different communities and cultural groups.

The term has been variously defined and vigorously debated across academic/non-academic and indigenous/non-indigenous perspectives. Understandings vary and are highly dependent on the specific cultural context and application. For example, while Western-trained philosophers and political scientists debate whether indigenous knowledge even constitutes a form of knowledge, the indigenous knowledge of Inuit peoples (called Inuit Qaujimajatuqangit in Inuktituk) is actively sought by environmental scientists and policy makers on Arctic wildlife, environmental contaminants, and climate change. Instrumental conceptions of indigenous knowledges often underlie commercial interest in specific applications, such as use of the medicinal plant knowledge of indigenous peoples in identifying new medicines from nature – a practice known as 'bioprospecting' undertaken by some Western-trained scientists working in concert with the herbal, biotechnology and pharmaceutical sectors.

Beyond instrumental and reified notions is an understanding of indigenous knowledges as complex *systems* that arise from indigenous cosmologies and are based on indigenous epistemologies. In this understanding, indigenous knowledges refer to the intergenerational accumulation of the collective stories, experiences, practices, genealogies, legends, mythologies, customs, laws, lore, spiritual teachings, wisdom, values and knowledge that have been passed down from one generation of indigenous peoples to the next. Indigenous knowledge systems share the commonly held belief that there is an interdependence and holistic relationship existing between the physical and spiritual worlds. Integral to these belief systems is that the physical and spiritual well-being of present and future generations is dependent upon maintaining the physical and spiritual health and vitality of the environment in which they live. Indigenous knowledges are generally understood as collective in nature and usually, although not exclusively, utilized and practised for the benefit of the wider group. Knowledge may be utilized for the benefit of individuals or groups within the collective who are recognized by the collective as having authority to do so. Indigenous knowledges emerge from specific lands and traditions. Although 'traditional' in the sense of having evolved and matured over time and thus gained legitimacy as a characteristic or attribute of the peoples concerned, indigenous knowledges are not seen as limited in time or space but continually evolving and responding to the modern world. Regarded in this way, indigenous knowledges may be seen as dynamic, collectively held, intergenerational by nature, and generally used for the benefit of the collective and authorized individuals or groups within the collective.

The quest to understand and precisely define what is and what is not 'indigenous knowledge' is a recent phenomenon that raises a number of challenges. To a large degree, pressure to understand and define indigenous knowledges has been driven externally by at least three transnational trends. The first is increasing globalization of markets and movements of goods across national borders as a result of multilateral trade agreements, such as the 1994 Agreement on Trade-Related Aspects of Intellectual Property Rights administered by the World Trade Organization. The second is increasing connectivity and global access to improved communication, transportation and information technology, aiding the formation of transnational indigenous coalitions and networks, and contributing to organizational ability and more effective assertion of collective interests and rights. The third is the global transition to an 'information society' and 'knowledge-based economy', and escalating multistakeholder interest in intellectual property protection mechanisms for securing commercial rights to intellectual know-how. Collectively, these driving forces have contributed to a significant increase in the appropriation and commodification of some aspects of indigenous knowledges, which has catalysed international calls for protecting indigenous knowledges and associated land, resource, cultural heritage and human rights of indigenous peoples.

While the most dramatic gains in institutionalizing indigenous rights to indigenous knowledges in the international arena have occurred over the last couple of decades, the foundations of this progress began over a century ago. The first organized international movements of indigenous peoples date back to around 1900 in North America and Scandinavia, but more stable international networks of 'first peoples' did not come into being until the 1970s.

The first United Nations agency to directly acknowledge and address the problems faced by indigenous peoples was the International Labour Organization. Work beginning in the 1920s led to the adoption in 1957 of the Indigenous and Tribal Peoples Convention 169, the first international standard specifically devoted to indigenous rights. The Convention was revised in 1989 and, although limited in scope, is viewed as a key international legal instrument on indigenous rights to self-determination, cultural and spiritual values, practices and institutions. Subsequent United Nations agreements such as the 1976 International Covenant on Civil and Political Rights and the 1997 International Covenant on Economic, Social and Cultural Rights also include the rights of self-determination and cultural development. Calls for the protection of indigenous knowledges are integrally linked with self-determination since knowledge appropriation and commodification tend to be viewed not only as potential intellectual property issues, but as more broadly related to human and land rights. Framing indigenous knowledges as intellectual property is more a reflection of Eurocentric institutions than of indigenous communities. Indeed, for many indigenous peoples, the so-called 'protection' of their knowledge systems within an intellectual property legal framework is antithetical.

A pivotal event in 1977 was the first presentation by indigenous peoples at the international level to the United Nations. The Special Rapporteur of the United Nations Sub-commission on Prevention of Discrimination and Protection of Minorities conducted an investigation during the 1970s into the discrimination faced by indigenous peoples. As a result, the United Nations established a Working Group on Indigenous Populations in 1982, which heightened awareness of the importance of indigenous issues and led to two key accomplishments – the United Nations Draft Declaration on the Rights of Indigenous Peoples in 1994, and the establishment of a Permanent Forum on Indigenous Issues in 2000. The Declaration addresses the rights of indigenous peoples in respect of self-determination, culture and language, land and resources, environment and development, intellectual and cultural property, indigenous law and treaties and agreements with governments, among other things. The Declaration was adopted by the United Nations General Assembly in 2007. The Permanent Forum on Indigenous Issues was established by the United Nations Social and Economic Council to serve as an advisory body to the Council on indigenous issues related to economic and social development, culture, the environment, education, health and human rights.

Issues of legal protection, permission, credit and economic compensation for use of indigenous knowledges became subjects of contentious international debate at the intersection of international environmental and human rights law by the early 1990s, largely stimulated by the concerted bioprospecting efforts of academic-industrial partnerships seeking novel medicinal or other compounds of commercial value. Bioprospecting has been endorsed by some conservationists and ethnoscientists as a strategy for halting deforestation of tropical forests based on the rationale that biologically diverse ecosystems provide novel genetic resources that may lead to new scientific discoveries for social and economic gain, thus forests are more valuable if left intact. Others have raised ethical and legal concerns about the negative impacts of commercial bioprospecting on indigenous communities and ecosystems.

The International Society of Ethnobiology was the first to explicitly recognize the inextricable links between biological and cultural diversity through the Declaration of Belém (1988). In 1990 the Society called for specific implementation measures to protect the intellectual property rights of indigenous peoples through the Kunming Action Plan and establishment of the Global Coalition for Biological and Cultural Diversity. An initial activity of the Global Coalition was to organize 'The Earth Parliament', the principal venue for indigenous and traditional peoples at the 1992 United Nations Earth Summit in Rio de Janeiro. The Convention on Biological Diversity (1992) was a major outcome of the Earth Summit, calling on signatory nations to undertake measures for conservation and sustainable use of biodiversity, and equitable sharing of its benefits. Article 8(j) of the Convention (In-situ conservation) underscores specific obligations to respect, preserve and maintain the knowledge, innovations and practices of indigenous and local communities, promote their wider application with the approval and involvement of the traditional holder, and encourage the equitable sharing of the benefits arising from use. Since 1998, the Ad hoc Working Group on Article 8(j) has been a key body in furthering international understanding and debate on issues related to indigenous knowledges. As a response to both Article 8(j) and Article 15 (Access to genetic resources) of the Convention, the Bonn Guidelines on Access to Genetic Resources and Fair and Equitable Sharing of the Benefits Arising out of their Utilization were developed in 2002 as a voluntary measure to assist countries in establishing legislative, administrative or policy measures for access to genetic resources and associated traditional knowledge as well as equitable sharing of benefits from use.

In 1998, the World Intellectual Property Organization began to examine intellectual property issues in relation to indigenous knowledges through a fact-finding mission and establishment of an Intergovernmental Committee on Intellectual Property and Genetic Resources, Traditional Knowledge and Folklore. The Committee is currently discussing draft provisions for the enhanced protection of indigenous knowledges and traditional cultural expressions against misappropriation and misuse. A growing number of examples exist in which indigenous peoples have employed intellectual property laws, such as copyright and trademark, for protecting certain aspects of indigenous knowledge and cultural heritage. However most legal analyses conclude that the Western intellectual property system is unlikely to adequately meet indigenous peoples' needs for protection from misappropriation, and sui generis protections are required.

Since the mid 1990s, significant effort has been invested in developing non-legal mechanisms of protection, such as codes of ethics and research guidelines, to complement legal regimes. Increasingly, indigenous communities themselves are developing written protocols and guidelines based on their customary traditions and practices to promulgate expectations for research and other activities in or related to their communities. The International Society of Ethnobiology completed a Code of Ethics in 2006 that represents an international consensus achieved over a decade of discussion by indigenous and non- indigenous scholars and practitioners on ethical and equitable principles and practices for research involving indigenous peoples. The Code promotes collaboration based on mutual respect and mutual benefit, and recognizes the importance of indigenous community-level processes and decision-making structures as a basis for engagement on indigenous knowledges and cultural heritage.

Kelly Bannister
Maui Solomon

Bibliography

Battiste M. and Henderson J. (S.) Y. 2000.
 *Protecting indigenous knowledge and heritage: a
 global challenge*. Saskatoon: Purich.

Dutfield G. 2000. *Intellectual property rights,
 trade and biodiversity*. London: Earthscan.

International Society of Ethnobiology 2006.
 *International Society of Ethnobiology Code
 of Ethics* [online]. Available: http://ise.
 arts.ubc.ca/global_coalition/ethics.php,
 accessed 31 January 2008.

Laird S. (ed.) 2002. *Biodiversity and traditional
 knowledge: equitable partnerships in practice*.
 London: Earthscan.

Posey D. and Dutfield G. 1996. *Beyond
 intellectual property: toward traditional
 resource rights for indigenous peoples and local
 communities*. Ottawa: IDRC.

Smith C. and Ward G. 2000. *Indigenous cultures
 in an interconnected world*. Vancouver: UBC.

Related essays

biodiversity; biopatents; conservation
and preservation; drugs (medical);
environmentalism; human rights;
indigenous networks; intellectual property
rights; intergovernmental organizations;
knowledge; language; United Nations
system

Indigenous networks

Indigenous networks are relations of
political alliance and cultural exchange
between peoples who define themselves as
indigenous. Both the terms 'people' and
'indigenous' are, however, highly contested.
Many state governments have opposed the
official use of the term 'peoples' because
'peoples' have been accorded the right to
self-determination under the International
Covenant on Civil and Political Rights and
the International Covenant on Economic,
Social and Cultural Rights. The term 'indigenous' has meanings derived from use
within two transnational discursive fields –
one exposing and seeking acknowledgement for histories of colonial oppression,
the other defending the endangered ways
of life of tribal and subsistence-based cultures.
These fields of postcolonial indigeneity and
eco-indigeneity have, since the early 1990s,
come to overlap to a considerable extent
and today both serve to legitimize the political and cultural struggles of indigenous
networks against the hegemony of nation

states and the international order that they
uphold.

The first significant transnational indigenous networks were formed in the Americas,
the Arctic and the South Pacific in the early
1970s. In 1971, George Manuel, a member of
Canada's Shushwap tribe and President of
that country's National Indian Brotherhood,
accompanied a government delegation to
New Zealand and Australia that sought comparative information on indigenous political
representation. Upon his return, Manuel set
in motion plans for a conference of indigenous peoples that would include representatives from Canada, the United States,
Australia, New Zealand, Colombia, Guyana,
Norway, Finland, Sweden and Denmark. A
preparatory meeting was held in 1974, and
the following year, in Canada, the World
Council of Indigenous Peoples was launched.
Also in 1974, frustrated at their inability to
get treaties recognized by the United States
Government, the American Indian Movement
called a meeting of over 5,000 indigenous people from the Americas and the South Pacific.
One of the outcomes of this meeting was the
formation of the International Indian Treaty
Council. Both soon gained consultative status with the United Nations Economic and
Social Committee. It has been estimated that
some 35 million indigenous people became
directly and indirectly linked through these
federations in the 1970s and 1980s.

In addition, two further transnational
organizations – the Inuit Circumpolar
Conference and the Consejo Indio de Sur
América / Indian Council of South America
(CISA) – had gained consultative status at
the UN by 1985. The first Inuit Circumpolar
Conference took place in 1977, following an
invitation issued at the 1975 meeting of the
World Council of Indigenous Peoples. The
meeting was attended by indigenous representatives from Canada, Greenland and
Alaska (Inuit from the former Soviet Union
joined after 1989). By 1990, this conference
could claim to represent more that 150,000
Inuit. The early regional significance of
the CISA was eclipsed by a massive grassroots mobilization across North, Central
and South America opposing celebrations
marking 400 years since Columbus' 'discovery' of the continent. In June 1990, a major
conference attended by over 300 indigenous
representatives from countries across the
Americas was held in Quito, Ecuador. This

meeting, organized by the Confederation of Indian Nations of Ecuador, the national Organization of Indian People of Colombia and the South and Meso-American Indian Information Centre, was a turning point for transnational indigenous protest in the Americas.

Beyond these regional conferences and meetings, the most significant focus of indigenous political networks has been the United Nations Working Group on Indigenous Populations, formed in 1982. The annual conferences of the Working Group were occasions at which a truly global sense of indigenous identity was created, both through formal participation within the meetings and by networking around them. As membership increased from an original 30 delegates to over 1,000 by the year 2000, the range of indigenous organizations attending greatly expanded, stretching the definition of 'indigenous'. The early dominance of delegations from the Americas gave way to increasing protagonism from Asia and Africa. This expansion of the Working Group was accompanied by a shift in the dominant meaning of 'indigenous'; originally a term for colonized peoples, it increasingly referred to peoples living close to 'mother earth'. In 2002, after seven years of debate within the Working Group and at workshops held in Copenhagen, Santiago and Geneva, a Permanent Forum on Indigenous Issues was established within the United Nations. This Forum enabled, for the first time, direct indigenous participation at the UN.

The role of indigenous forums in facilitating informal transnational networking has been as significant as their officially defined functions. This informal networking has, since the mid-1990s, been greatly enhanced and extended through the use of the internet as both an archive and medium for the exchange of ideas. In 1984, in response to a request from the World Council of Indigenous Peoples, the Centre for World Indigenous Studies was established in Toronto, Canada. In 1992 the Centre began the Fourth World Documentation Programme, one of the earliest web-based archives of documents relating to indigenous politics. In addition to this programme, the Centre has facilitated research on indigenous issues and operated a Forum for Global Exchange, encouraging transnational dialogue between indigenous peoples.

One of the most respected of the many indigenous internet organizations is NativeWeb, a non-profit organization that began in 1994. The searchable database of this site is massive and is extensively used by indigenous groups. Indigenous peoples also use this site to advertise events and share ideas and resources. By the year 2000, NativeWeb was hosting over fifty selected indigenous sites from peoples based mainly in the Americas. The internet also became a powerful tool for indigenous networks during the 1994 Zapatista rebellion in Chiapas, Mexico. It enabled a transnational reach for the Zapatista message of opposition to neoliberal globalization across the Americas and Europe. While most indigenous people in Chiapas did not have access to computers, leaders and supporters, some based in universities, were able to translate local concerns into a global campaign. Members of the Zapatista National Liberation Army were also able to send messages of support to protestors in the Netherlands, Italy and the United States. In 1996, the internet was used by Zapatistas and their supporters to set the agenda for a meeting held in Chiapas that brought together 3,000 activists from forty countries in opposition to neoliberal capitalism.

Transnational indigenous networks are also relations of contemporary cultural exchange. Indigenous film makers, for example, have, since the mid-1980s, shown their works at festivals and workshops in North and South America. Beginning in 1986, the Latin American Council on Indigenous Peoples' Film and Video organised festivals and training seminars in Mexico, Brazil, Venezuela, Peru, Bolivia, Guatemala and Chile. In Montreal, Canada, indigenous film making was promoted by the ImagineNative film and Media Arts Festivals and, in New York, the annual Pacifika Festival brought together indigenous film makers from throughout the Pacific.

Such exchanges of contemporary culture have been accompanied by efforts to protect the traditional knowledge of indigenous peoples from commercial exploitation. In 1993, in the year designated by the UN as 'International Year for the World's Indigenous Peoples', Maori tribal representatives convened a conference on the cultural and intellectual property rights of indigenous peoples. This conference was attended by over 150 delegates from 14 countries, including indigenous delegates from Japan (Ainu), Australia, Cook Islands, Fiji, India, Panama, Peru, Philippines, Suriname, the USA and New Zealand. In a document known as the Mataatua Declaration (the host tribes belonged to the Mataatua Federation) the conference declared that in exercising their right to self-determination, indigenous peoples 'must be recognised as the exclusive owners of their cultural and intellectual property'. Since this conference the notion that indigenous peoples may be able to copyright culture has been widely debated, and states have been prompted to review copyright legislation.

The protection of indigenous knowledge is also one of the main aims of the International Indigenous Forum on Biodiversity, formed in 1996. This Forum is a transnational network of indigenous representatives and activists organised around the Convention on Biological Diversity, an international convention that recognises traditional resource and knowledge rights. In April 2006, indigenous activists linked to the Forum and the Indigenous Women's Biodiversity Network protested their exclusion from full participation at the 8th Conference of Parties to the Convention of Biological Diversity in Brazil.

Shared concerns about neoliberal economics, the protection of cultural property and biodiversity are now at the cutting edge of transnational indigenous politics, reflecting a significant shift in the focus of indigenous networks away from colonialism and towards a more global ecopolitics. As this shift occurs, the lack of gender balance in earlier networks has been highlighted and challenged by women's groups critical of male leaders who are thought to have been too willing to join national and international structures. In confronting the power of nation states, transnational indigenous women's networks in particular have emphasized the importance of preserving and strengthening their grassroots connections. Ultimately, it is from these that transnational networks draw their sustenance and derive their influence.

Jeffrey Sissons

Bibliography
Niezen R. 2003. *The origins of indigenism: human rights and the politics of identity.* Berkeley: University of California Press.
Sissons J. 2005. *First peoples: indigenous cultures and their futures.* London: Reaktion.

Related essays
biodiversity; ecology; empires and imperialism; Ethical Culture; film; freemasonry; indigenous knowledges; intellectual elites; intellectual property rights; Internet; nation and state; United Nations decades and years; United Nations system; women's movements; workers' movements; youth organizations

Industrialization

'Industrialization' can be used to mean either the 'birth' of industry – as in 'new' countries such as Argentina, Australia, Canada, New Zealand and, to a lesser extent, the United States – or, as often, the adaptation of older forms such as protoindustries into modern forms characterized by mechanization and concentration of labour in disciplined factories. It is a gradual process involving the growth of the industrial and services sectors at the expense of agriculture; it is impossible to put a date on its 'completion'. As for 'deindustrialization', the term is deceptive because it is often used to mean not a decline in industry but a growth in industrial productivity so rapid, by comparison with services, that output continues to soar despite a continual drop in the workforce.

There is no commonly accepted yardstick for industrialization. If the criterion is the distribution of the working population, this will place undue emphasis on unproductive areas of the economy and will focus on national societies, glossing over regional disparities. For example, Germany and France in the 1900s were highly industrially 'advanced' nations but with overwhelmingly rural, indeed peasant, societies. If the criterion is industry's contribution to GDP, the result is not much more satisfactory, though it correlates strongly with key development indicators such as per capita GDP. The criterion of per capita consumption of major commodities such as coal, electricity, oil, cotton or steel tends to overemphasise the industrialization of countries such as Britain that are, or were, heavily dependent on the industries that produced those commodities.

The best measure of industrialization is the change from a preindustrial economy to an industrial one where not only is the industrial sector dominant, but where the whole economy is enmeshed with it. Thus a crisis in one of the major industries will have a knock-on effect on all the others, on services, and even on agriculture – as happened in the 1930s in both the advanced industrialized countries and the primary exporting countries. In other words, assessing the degree of industrialization means measuring the interdependence of activities in, and the relative homogeneity of, the economic area concerned. This will generally be the nation, to which all other macroeconomic indicators refer.

Entangled scales

The historiographic tradition that arose with the birth of the nation state, and the statistical approach aimed at ranking nation states and developing their policies, have always taken the nation as the framework for their assessments of economic activity, even if the nation itself comprised a number of discrete units (e.g., the United Kingdom or the 19th-century German and Austro-Hungarian empires). Paradoxically, however, the process of industrialization should rather be assessed on a regional scale, with an eye on its cross-national features.

Industrial development was in fact a regional process, spreading out from more or less concentrated loci of development that specialized in a single industry. If, as in Europe and some Asian countries, this meant a transformation of previous cottage industries, the result could be that regions that had formerly combined such industries with agriculture became solely agricultural, leading to increased regional inequality. The industrial geography of the whole country would change as work became divided on a national scale, or adapted to the international environment. Thus, for example, the cotton weavers of Bengal in the mid 19th century were hit by competition from Lancashire, just as Bombay was reacting to a shortage of cotton during the Wars of Secession by developing its own mechanized industry, while the home textile weavers in the centre and south of India were largely unaffected by both developments because the country was still so poorly integrated. Thus it makes little sense to talk about 'the industrialization of India' without taking account of regional differences. Similarly, historians who think nationally often argue that Germany, Italy and America were slow to industrialize (mid 19th century). In fact, New England had big textile factories at an early date, and its machine industry was more highly mechanized than any in Europe,

producing more machines in greater variety; but this was a regional phenomenon within a poorly integrated national framework. As for Germany, there is not much point in talking about 'German' industrialization before Germany even existed as a country (pre-1871), even if the process of integration had already begun with the Zollverein and the ensuing monetary unification: industrial development took place within a number of different political units (Prussia, Saxony, Swabia, Bavaria, etc.) under the protection of their respective sovereigns. Even after unification, German industrialization continued to focus on a multiplicity of industrial loci each following its own particular developmental path.

Regional processes often interacted with transnational ones. On the small scale the map of Europe in the 19th century or in the 1950s shows how industrial areas ignored frontiers. One zone extended from northern France through Belgium to the Rhineland and Westphalia; another from Alsace to northwestern Switzerland; almost contiguous to it, another running from southern Switzerland to the Dauphiné and the Lyon and Saint-Etienne basins, which could even be extended to include northern Italy; yet another from Berlin via Saxony to Bohemia or even Upper Silesia, which until 1918 was split between the German and Austro-Hungarian empires. Some of these cross-border industrializations were the result of geological chance (e.g., the coalfield that stretches from northern France across Belgium and into Germany), but most of them can be traced back to the persistence of European political configurations that originated at the beginning of the 19th century – Napoleon's Europe, in fact – and to action by entrepreneurs and investors. This transnationalism was fostered by networks of information, solidarity and intermarriage among entrepreneurial and banking families: between northern France and Belgium, between Basle and Mulhouse, between the northern USA and Canada, between neighbouring Latin American countries or, in Asia, among Chinese businessmen wherever they might establish themselves.

It would be wrong for analysts to make rigid distinctions between these infra- or transnational relationships and national boundaries: the two were complementary, but operated on different levels. In the 19th century most nations sealed off their territories behind customs barriers which by

1870 (except in the case of Great Britain) had become strongly protectionist. This national isolationism was still more pronounced in the 1920s, when monetary instability accentuated exchange difficulties, and under- or overvaluation of currencies either encouraged export industries or penalized them, as in Britain. Changing frontiers and changing alliances cut off channels that had arisen from previous economic complementarities, cut off firms from their markets and redefined the international division of labour in ways that were not always favourable to industrialization. The dissolution of the Austro-Hungarian empire forced industrialists in the new countries to reorganize their sources of supply and markets in the new political context, which did not always take account of economic complementarities. In the 1930s the policy of monetary blocs created a range of very different environments for potential industrialization. From the 1920s to the 1950s, and again after 1971, floating or volatile exchange rates, curbs on international payments, and the overvaluation of certain currencies were barriers to transnational industrial development, causing delocalization that clearly revealed the importance of national boundaries to markets and employment legislation, tax legislation, etc. Since 1980 the growing internationalization of production has promoted industrialization in Asia, under the spell of sourcing strategies and procurement efforts in low-cost countries. But this globalization, or rather trend towards global uniformity, has done nothing to suppress differences between nations; it has merely exploited them.

Industrialization: a single process, a national process or a transnational process?

Early historians of industrialization mostly adopted a technological approach. Nineteenth-century historians called it 'the industrial revolution', as if it were a single, homogenous phenomenon, everywhere the same: the same machines, the same processes, and the same impact on the organization of labour – whether we are referring to the 19th-century factory system or to 20th-century mass production and scientific organization of labour – and on society. Industrialization, in fact, was a process that simply repeated itself in a series of waves, starting with the early industrializers (Britain, Belgium, France) and going on to the late industrializers (Germany and the US,

followed by Italy, Russia and Japan), with some new departures in and after the First World War (Brazil, Argentina, India, etc.), and concluding with the newly industrialized countries (NICs) of Asia – first the 'dragons', then the 'tigers'.

This approach reduces the problem of accounting for industrialization to a simple question of chronology – at what time a particular country adopted the technology, and thence how technology was transferred from country to country. In fact, such transfers did not involve slavishly copying an existing 'industrialization': technologies were not adopted, but rather appropriated and adapted. This process was to an extent transnational. It depended on the mobility of technical and financial experts (such as engineers employed by companies with foreign capital), and might be politically inspired (thus American engineers set up the Soviet automobile industry in the 1930s because a country that held aloof from European politics did not constitute a rival, unlike the German engineers who were at work in the 1920s); it could also be seen as a token of solidarity among expatriates, or citizens of a particular country living outside its borders. The transfer of European know-how to the United States was largely due to emigration. The clothing industry was brought by Jewish immigrants from Central Europe; brewing came with the Germans.

It is significant that no historian uses the term 'industrial revolution' to refer to the 20th century – to the industrialization of Brazil, Korea or Taiwan, for example. It is obvious that such a technological approach is inapplicable and that the industrialization of NICs is not the same process as the industrialization of Britain or the US; in fact the differences are greater than the similarities. Historians of the 19th century had already realized that Britain was a unique case rather than a model for subsequent imitation. Britain's industrialization was unique because it was the first, because it was concentrated on just a few industries and just a few parts of the country, because rapid mechanization triggered a massive exodus from the countryside and a high social cost (poor working conditions, poor housing, sickness, poverty), and because it was powered by coal rather than water.

From the 1930s to the 1950s historians produced a plethora of regional and national histories of industrialization; some worked on particular industries. It was not until 1962 that Alexander Gerschenkron (1962), a specialist in the history of Russia and the USSR, noted the vast differences between industrialization in his own area and industrialization in Britain, and attempted to rationalize those differences by postulating a progressive divergence from an original model.

The Gerschenkron approach

Gerschenkron tried to safeguard the notion of a homogenous process, postulating that industrialization could have taken place in all countries at the same time, were it not that many of them were 'backward' owing to economic, social, political or cultural factors. This meant that specific approaches or institutions were needed to make up for this structural backwardness: government, merchant banks, foreign capital and technology, rapid development of heavy industry.

Gerschenkron's analysis contrasted early and late industrializers. He described the very rapid development of Russian industry – the fastest in the world – from 1890 to 1914. The Russian government was heavily involved in this industrialization, starting in the 1850s with the steel industry in the Urals; it financed the building of its railways by borrowing on Western financial markets. Foreign banks, firms and entrepreneurs were also actively involved, such as the French specialists who got involved in the mechanical engineering industries in the Moscow region (notably the Schneider company, supported by the Banque de l'Union Parisienne).

These characteristics are not necessarily found, however, in other late industrializers. The Japanese government opted for a policy of Western-style modernization and industrialization, which it financed by squeezing taxes out of the peasantry. It set up firms which in the 1880s were sold off to the private sector. It systematically encouraged technology transfer from advanced industrialized countries, bringing in engineers to train Japanese workers. France created a military arsenal; English firms provided textile machinery and the technological, commercial and financial know-how required to exploit it. However, neither the Japanese government nor Japanese firms borrowed heavily from abroad and they never allowed foreign banks, businessmen or technicians to seize control over the economy. The money came not from foreign banks but from traditional trading houses which became the nuclei of industrial, banking and business

conglomerates – quite a different structure from that of Western companies and groups. Industrialization began with consumer industries serving the internal Japanese market before exports began. The steel and ship-building industries developed later, filling the gap left by the disappearance of British exporters from Asia during the First World War. Thus Japanese industrialization incorporated and adapted foreign elements within an existing economic framework which was advanced enough to easily absorb them.

Germany and the United States do not fit Gerschenkron's criteria very closely. Heavy industry did develop very quickly from the 1870s onwards, but it was preceded by growth in consumer industries. The inclusion of these countries, commonly identified as 'late industrializers', distorts the interpretation. It makes degrees of industrialization difficult to measure objectively, leading to a variety of judgments on the results.

Gerschenkron's viewpoint, and his insistence on the importance of government action, were conditioned by the era in which he lived. The industrialization of Soviet Russia was seen at the time as a tremendous success: it had continued unabated through the crisis of the 1930s on a basis of centralized planning; it had started upstream with heavy industry, used this as a basis to construct infrastructure, and only then turned its attention to consumer goods. It offered a new model, the Soviet way, which was to prove very attractive to a number of Third World countries after the Second World War. This was sort of an extreme instance of Polanyi's 'Great Transformation': the market-oriented management of commodities, labour and money had such catastrophic consequences that the government had to take charge, re-embedding the economy in state-oriented management.

Although they have not always proven true in practice, Gerschenkron's theories remain highly influential, even as regards instances of 20th-century industrialization which he never considered – e.g., Brazil in the 1930s – or which took place after his work was completed. The role played by government is, obviously, a major factor in categorization. All over the world this role increased between the 1930s and the 1970s and subsequently tended to diminish; but it remained fundamental even in the most liberal countries that have a monetary, budgetary, customs and industrial policy and a form of economic diplomacy. It goes without saying, then, that governments had a key role in every instance of 20th-century industrialization. We need to take this general trend into account whenever we try to judge how far government was involved in the process of industrialization. In Latin America, for example, this involvement was very heavy. So it was, notoriously, in Japan, through the Ministry of Industrial Trade and Industry (MITI); but it was also a deciding factor in the industrial success of South Korea.

While the role of government was essential in terms of policy and the direction given to industrialization, imitation was also a factor, particularly within the major world regions. Political choices were influenced by knowledge of how industrialization had proceeded in neighbouring countries which had structural similarities or previous experience that had created path dependencies. Imitation might also be drawn from a wider geographical area, particularly if there was a strong political bias. When Fidel Castro took power in Cuba, he tried to develop heavy industry on the Soviet model before falling back on a reorganization of the fast-collapsing sugar cane industry. Also ideologically inspired was Algeria's attempt to prioritize heavy industry, which was costly and created few jobs at a time when the country was still short of capital and affected by rapid population growth. Current research is focusing on the relevance of political regimes to industrialization, and to development in general. The conclusion is often that democracy favours industrialization. Sometimes, however, the opposite is true. Latin American industrialization in the 1930s depended on strong governments that could force through a total and rapid change of direction; Brazil's success in this field sparked off imitation in other countries.

Similarly, foreign banks and firms, whose importance has grown worldwide, have generated instances of transnational imitation. Foreign decision makers tend to exaggerate the similarities between the economies of different parts of the world and so their actions foster such similarities. Thus English and American banks lent heavily to Latin American governments in the 1970s although the situations and economic policies of Brazil, Argentina, Mexico and Chile were actually very different. To most concerned Westerners in the 1970s, the whole of Latin America looked very promising owing to its strong growth rates in the 1960s and the prospect of rapid industrialization – in Brazil and Mexico, for example – at a time when Western economies were beginning to slow down. In fact, Chile's growth was weak and in Argentina the new military regime was 'liberalizing' the industrial base by destroying the public sector, whose presence was essential to infrastructure, heavy industry and consumer industries; it also throttled small businesses which, having previously been supported by the national banks, had no access to foreign capital. The crisis of the 1980s hit the entire area, by contagion and because Western decision makers lumped all these countries together; the 1980s became the 'lost decade' of Latin America. The International Monetary Fund (IMF) compounded the problem by imposing identical structural adjustments on countries whose structures were in fact very different.

The inductive approach of the developmental economists

In the 1960s and later, Hollis Chenery and Moises Syrquin (1975) and a few other scholars did some empirical research comparing a set of economic, social and demographic variables across developing countries in order to detect the differences in their approaches to industrialization. Previous studies, chiefly by historians, had started from the supply side: technology, production factors (workforce, training of the workforce, availability of capital, circulation of capital, investment rates) and prices (industrialization was either fundamentally labour-intensive or fundamentally capital-intensive, depending on wages and interest rates); these economists favoured a demand-based categorization, considering what proportion of demand came from the internal market and what from exports. Thus we have two opposing models for industrialization: 'import substitution' (predicated on growth in the internal market) and 'export-led'. In both cases, however, the core of the analysis will be the interaction between internal and external markets and the transnational flows that ensue (see Table 1).

In Mexico from 1950 to 1975, industrial growth depended on the growth in internal demand and on import substitution; exports played no part. In Korea and Taiwan, by contrast, exports quickly became a motor, but early industrialization also depended on internal demand and import substitution. In Japan the development took place gradually after the Second World War. The recovery

Table 1   Sources of growth in manufacturing output 1914–75

Country	Period	Average annual growth rate (%)	Domestic demand expansion (% of total)	Export expansion (% of total)	Import substitution (% of total)	Changes in input-output coefficients (% of total)
Korea	1955–63	10.4	57	12	42	−11
	1963–70	18.9	70	30	0	0
	1970–73	23.8	39	62	−3	2
Taiwan	1956–61	11.2	35	28	25	12
	1961–66	16.6	49	44	2	5
	1966–71	21.1	35	57	4	4
Japan	1914–35	5.5	70	33	5	−8
	1955–60	12.6	76	12	−3	15
	1960–65	10.8	82	22	0	−4
	1965–70	16.5	74	18	−1	9
Mexico	1950–60	7.0	72	3	11	14
	1960–70	8.6	86	4	11	−1
	1970–75	7.2	81	8	3	8

Source: Chenery H. B. 1980. 'Interactions between industrialization and exports', *American Economic Review*, 70, 2, 284.

depended on the internal market; Japan was not a big exporter before the 1970s, and products were piloted on the internal market before any attempt was made to sell them abroad.

An older example of industrialization by import substitution is 19th-century America, which benefited from a rapid increase in population, including many people with sufficient income to create a dynamic demand for manufactured goods. Imported foreign goods were gradually replaced by American-manufactured ones, which flourished under the protection of inordinately high customs barriers; however, this import substitution had only a limited effect insofar as the country had a low degree of openness and so its dependency rate was also low. Although the US has been the most advanced of industrialized countries since the end of the 19th century, the proportion of manufactured products in its exports remained low until the 1920s; thus exports did little to stimulate industrial growth until the last quarter of the 20th century, the degree of openness remaining very low. Internal growth remained so rapid that external markets were not required to take up the slack.

In countries with a greater degree of openness, where the internal market was originally fed by imported manufactured products, this model became an import substitution model requiring high tariff barriers and an internal demand sufficient to absorb output. This assumes that inequalities of income are not excessive, so that a large proportion of the population – the middle class and even some of the lower – is available as a source of dynamic demand.

Choosing between these two approaches means espousing different policies in different economic situations and in structurally different economic contexts, and often in different ideological and political environments; as a result, countries in different parts of the world may end up following the same route to industrialization. There are two ways of looking at this question, and they are not necessarily contradictory: either internal structures incline the country towards one of the possible policies, or initial political choices, often based on imitation, influence structures and accentuate their resemblance. Regional organizations such as ASEAN and MERCOSUR have reinforced this zoning effect.

In the 1930s, under the impact of the crisis, the countries of Latin America tended to follow the path of import substitution. Previously they had had a high degree of openness and their livelihood had depended on exporting one or more primary products. When markets for such products became saturated in the 1920s, this, combined with government subsidies for production, led to catastrophe once the crisis began to bite. To face up to the crisis in the coffee market, the new government of Brazil – a dictatorship – decided on a complete reversal of economic policy, based on industry rather than agriculture. This assumed a change of political support, from the oligarchy of the planters to the middle classes. The government sealed the frontiers, supported internal investment by printing money, and, to avert inflation and a plunge in the exchange rate, imposed controls on prices, exchange and the movement of capital. The state took over from private initiative. These policies were reinforced after the Second World War by the ideological support they received from the economic theorists of the United Nations Economic Commission for Latin America (ECLA). Gradually they shifted import substitution towards heavy industry and more complex technology: Brazil succeeded in this in the 1970s before the onset of crisis in the next decade. These policies, and their selective imitation within the region, produced structural similarities between Brazil, Argentina and Mexico: in particular, a very large public sector, extending into industry, commerce and banking; a very large service and administrative sector; an enormous national debt; and a high rate of structural inflation. The snag with this model of industrialization was inequality of income, which kept a large part of the population in poverty and unable to consume manufactured goods. It started to sag in the 1980s, still more in the 1990s, when these countries settled for 'technological activism' with a strong focus on R&D to encourage local innovation. Here we perceive the influence of new theories of endogenous growth.

The same line of development, from simple consumer goods to complex products, can be discerned in the export-led industrialization of certain Asian countries. The first manufactured goods were simple, requiring little investment and suited to local consumption by an impoverished population. The goods sold cheaply because wages were low; they were easy to export, thanks to the general reduction of tariff barriers in the second half of the 20th century, whereby, for a time, the industrialized countries did not protect their markets against competition from, e.g., Korea. The United States supported this trend, accepting exports from these countries for political reasons – to combat the contagion of communism – and American industrialists started to relocate. American textile manufacturers decided that they could compete with Japanese firms if they had their goods produced in Hong Kong. Very soon, however,

the markets of the industrialized countries started to protect themselves not through tariffs but by imposing, e.g., technical or health-and-safety curbs on imports and voluntary limits on exports. Government influence was also very strong, but the common characteristics of these new industrial countries were poles apart from those of Latin America: a high export rate, a smaller public sector (although state-owned enterprises were omnipresent in heavy industry and equipment/infrastructure), a smaller service sector and a low national debt. Nor did these Asian countries suffer severely from the financial crisis of the 1980s. The limitations of the model emerged in the 1990s, as gains in productivity and technological progress began to slow, probably due to a lack of investment in human resources, while worldwide demand for traditional products such as clothing began to show signs of saturation.

Thus different routes to industrialization generate differing economic and social structures which mesh with them and create path dependencies. This makes a change of direction difficult. The reckless liberalization of the Argentine economy in the 1970s proved catastrophic, shattering the industrial fabric and slashing GNP. The unsubtle policies of the IMF, indiscriminately applying the criteria of the British or American economies, also produced some abrupt collapses in the late 1990s as the crisis spread from country to structurally dissimilar country – Thailand, Russia, Argentina. The progressive integration of the international economy, which by the beginning of the 21st century was based less on multilateralism than on the formation of a number of regional groupings worldwide, favours transnational developments: a multiplicity of intersecting intrazonal flows – often within the same multinational company – and policies that tend to converge within a single macroeconomic and import control framework.

Patrick Verley

Bibliography

Berend I. and Ranki G., 1982. *The European periphery and industrialization 1780–1914.* Cambridge: Cambridge University Press.

Chenery H. B. and Syrquin M. 1975. *Patterns of development 1950–1970.* London: Oxford University Press for the World Bank.

Gerschenkron A. 1962. *Economic backwardness in historical perspective: a book of essays.* Cambridge, MA: Belknap.

Johnson C. 1982. *MITI and the Japanese miracle: the growth of industrial policy, 1925–1975.* Stanford: Stanford University Press.

Krueger A. and Osser F. (eds) 1985. *Export oriented development strategies.* Boulder: Westview.

O'Brien P. K. 1986. 'Do we have a typology for the study of European industrialization in the 19th century?', *Journal of European Economic History,* 15, 2, 291–333.

Pollard S. 1981. *Peaceful conquest: the industrialization of Europe 1760–1970.* Oxford: Oxford University Press.

Trebilcock C. 1981. *The industrialization of the Continental powers.* London: Pearson.

Related essays

agriculture; assembly line; borders and borderlands; capitalism; convergence and divergence; debt crises; development and growth; developmental taxonomies; diasporas; Economic Commission for Latin America and the Caribbean (ECLAC); empire and migration; engineering; European Union (EU); financial markets; International Monetary Fund (IMF); investment; iron and steel; Japan; modernization theory; neoliberalism; organization models; Prebisch, Raúl; public policy; regional communities; regions; Samsung; services; socialism; taxation; technologies; textile; trade; trade (manufactured goods); underdevelopment; Washington Consensus; welfare state; World Bank

Information economy

Although the phrase 'information economy' may have a late-20th-century ring to it, the idea of an economy based on trading of information has a very long history, going back to antiquity. In addition to well-established official systems of communication, spurred by trade and cultural interchanges between imperial powers, informal networks of travellers and traders have existed for more than two millennia, as in between the Graeco-Roman world and North Africa, Arabia, India and China. Information also travelled the Silk, the Gold, the Slave and the Tortoise roads that crisscrossed different regional systems.

Communication technologies were crucial in the establishment of European domination of the world during the era of modern colonial empires. The new technologies of the 19th century 'shattered traditional trade, technology, and political relationships, and in their place they laid the foundations for a new global civilisation based on Western technology' (Headrick 1981, 177). If trains and ships facilitated the movement of manufactured products from one part of the world to another, fibre optics, satellites and the Internet can now trade information instantly across the globe, though the volume, value and velocity of this transaction is historically unprecedented.

The Industrial Revolution in Western Europe, founded on the profits of the growing international commerce encouraged by colonization, gave a huge stimulus to the commodification of information. Among European countries, Britain, with its supremacy in undersea cables and a prominent role in expansion of telegraphy, played a crucial part in creating an information economy. Britain's domination of the sea routes of international commerce was to a large extent due to the pre-eminence of its navy and merchant fleet, a result of pioneering work in the mapping out of naval charts by the great 18th-century explorers, enabled also by the determination of longitude based on the Greenwich Meridian. Technological advances such the development of the iron ship, the steam engine and the electric telegraph all contributed to an emerging global communication network.

An institutionalized information economy started to emerge within the British Empire, stimulated by the growth of trade and investment which required a constant source of reliable data about trade and economic affairs. Access and control of information was also central for maintaining political alliances and military security. As European empires grew in their political and economic power, waves of populations from the continent migrated to distant shores of the dominions, creating and sustaining a growing popular demand for news from relatives at home and abroad. Such traffic also revolutionized postal communication, leading in 1875 to the establishment of the Universal Postal Union in Berne, to harmonize international postal rates and to recognize the principle of respect for the secrecy of correspondence.

Radio as wireless communication

After the first radio transmissions of the human voice in 1902, radio communication became increasingly important. One reason for this was that radio equipment was comparatively affordable and could be produced and sold as a mass object. It was the United States and corporations based there that were first to exploit the commercial potential of the new medium. The US government was keen to support radio as it believed that if developed extensively, radio could be used to undercut the huge advantages of British-dominated international cable links. Since radio waves did not respect geographical borders, it was difficult to control this new medium of transnational communication. However, international mechanisms, concerning who should allocate radio frequencies and how, soon entered diplomatic parlance as radio's potential strategic and commercial value was becoming apparent. At the 1906 International Radiotelegraph Conference in Berlin, governments from 28 countries – including Britain, Germany, France, the US and Russia – debated radio equipment standards and procedures to minimize interference. The great powers imposed a regime of radio frequency allocation, allowing priority to the country that first notified the International Radiotelegraph Union (IRU) of its intention to use a specific frequency.

As worldwide radio broadcasting grew, stations that transmitted across national borders had, in accordance with an agreement signed in London in 1912, to register their use of a particular wavelength with the IRU. However, there was no mechanism for either assigning or withholding slots; it was a system of first come, first served. As a result the companies or states with the necessary capital and technology gained control over the limited spectrum space, to the disadvantage of less developed countries. Two types of national radio broadcasting emerged: in the US, the Radio Act of 1927 confirmed its status as a commercial enterprise, funded by advertising, while the British Broadcasting Corporation, founded in 1927, as a non-profit, public broadcasting monopoly, provided a model for many other European countries. As the strongest voice in the World Radio Conference in Washington in 1927, private companies helped to write an agreement that allowed them to continue developing their use of the spectrum, without regard to possible signal interference for other countries. By being embodied in an international treaty, these provisions took on the character of 'international law', including

the principle of allocating specific wavelengths for particular purposes. A major consequence of this conference was to reinforce US and European domination of the international radio spectrum. However, it was the newly formed Soviet Union which became the first nation to exploit this new medium for international broadcasting: the first public broadcast to be recorded in the history of wireless propaganda was by the Council of the People's Commissars, of Lenin's historic message on 30 October 1917.

Political implications of global information flows

During World War 1, the power of radio was quickly recognized as vital to the management both of public opinion at home and of propaganda abroad, directed at allies and enemies alike. Recognizing the ideological and strategic importance of broadcasting, the Russian Communists skilfully deployed the radio to promote their cause of socialist revolution internationally. By the time the Nazis came to power in Germany in 1933, radio broadcasting had become an extension of international diplomacy. Until World War 2 radio in the US was known more for its commercial potential as a vehicle for advertisements rather than a government propaganda tool, but after 1942, the year the Voice of America (VOA) was founded, the US government made effective use of radio to promote its political interests – a process which reached its high point during the decades of the Cold War.

By the late 1960s, Moscow Radio was the world's largest single international broadcaster – between 1969 to 1972 it broadcast more programme hours than the United States. In addition, it used more languages – 84 – than any other international broadcaster. Soviet broadcasts helped shape news media organizations in many Eastern European countries as well as Communist nations of the global South, but had very little impact in the West, in contrast to the popularity of Western broadcasts in the Eastern bloc. Radio Moscow was no match for Western broadcasters in terms of the power of its transmitters and the availability of broadcasting outlets outside the Communist world. The key instruments of US international broadcasting – the official VOA and the American Forces Network, as well as the two major clandestine stations, Radio Liberty and Radio

Free Europe – were all state-funded. VOA operated a global network of relay stations to propagate the ideal of 'the American way of life' to international listeners. The nodal points in this worldwide network linked to the control centre in Washington included relay stations in Thailand, the Philippines, Sri Lanka, Morocco, Greece, Botswana, Liberia, West Germany, Britain and Belize, to cover the entire globe.

With the establishment of its Russian language unit in 1946, the BBC World Service played a key part in the Cold War through its strategically located global network of relay stations. These included: stations on Ascension Island and on Antigua, on Cyprus, in Oman, the Seychelles, Singapore and Hong Kong. Other Western stations such as Deutsche Welle and Radio France International (RFI) also contributed to the war of words. RFI, particularly strong in the former colonies of France, had two main relay stations – in Gabon and French Guiana – and also leased transmitting facilities from commercial Radio Monte Carlo in Cyprus to broadcast to the Middle East. As one study of Cold War propaganda noted: 'The weapons used in the propaganda war were the same on both sides, with one difference. Both sides broadcast to the world, but the Communist side had few listeners. The difference was the weapon of defence: the Russians used jamming; the West used free communication' (Nelson 1997, xiv).

With the disintegration of the Soviet Union and the collapse of the Communist bloc, Western propaganda outfits were struggling for a role and the funding for public diplomacy was constantly declining – by 2001, it consisted of less than 4 per cent of the US government's overall international affairs budget. Despite the growing importance of television in implementing the foreign-policy agenda, the US Congress had reduced the budget for international broadcasting. However, the attacks of 11 September 2001 in New York and Washington revived the need for public diplomacy, the main aim of which then became to understand the roots of anti-Americanism, especially among Arab and Muslim countries. During the US invasion of Afghanistan in October 2001, Washington launched the round-the-clock Coalition Information Center, to manage news flow, later upgraded into a permanent Office of Global Communications, to coordinate

public diplomacy. In 2002, an Arabic-language popular music and news radio station, Radio Sawa ('Radio Together'), aimed at a younger Arab audience, was launched and Radio Farda ('Radio Tomorrow' in Persian) began transmitting into Iran. In 2004, the Middle East Television Network – al-Hurra (Arabic for 'The Free One') started broadcasting from Springfield, Virginia, as well as from bureaus in the Middle East, funded by the Broadcasting Board of Governors, a US federal agency that supervises all non-military international broadcasting. Other transnational information channels such as the Arab news network al-Jazeera and the pan-Latin American TV channel Televisora del Sur ('Television of the South', Telesur) based in Venezuela have emerged to challenge the US version of world events.

Institutional and commercial engines for global information economy

The end of the Cold War prompted a new discourse on international information, with the focus of debate shifting from news and information flows to such areas as global telecommunication and transnational data flows. The Paris-based Organization for Economic Co-operation and Development (OECD) and the International Telecommunication Union (ITU) were becoming increasingly important fora for discussions of transnational information flows.

The availability of new information technologies such as direct-broadcasting satellites, fibre optics and microcomputers coupled with the growing convergence between information and informatics – the combination of computer and telecommunication systems, traditionally dealt with as separate entities – made it essential to re-examine global information flows in the light of technological innovations. With the demise of the Soviet system the public ownership of state information assets was rapidly replaced by the new mantra of privatization. As more and more countries embraced market 'reforms' and new markets in Eastern Europe and the former Soviet Union emerged, a particular version of the information economy, increasingly integrated into a privatized global communication infrastructure, was promoted. The 'time–space compression' that new technologies encouraged made it possible for media and telecommunication corporations to operate in a global market, part of a planetary neoliberal capitalist system. Trading information was a central feature of this digitally connected globe. The ability to move all forms of data via the Internet revolutionized international information exchange. In the digital age, information processing became far cheaper and faster, as global traffic in digitized data – images, moving pictures, text and sounds – increased exponentially. Combined with the rapid growth in computing capacity and concomitant reduction in costs, the convergence of computing and communication technologies opened up potential for unprecedented global interconnectedness through the Internet.

Such changes would not have been possible without a global institutional shift towards the marketization of information. The privatization of communication and information industries became a major development of the 1990s, accelerated by the liberalization of global trade, under the auspices of the General Agreement on Tariffs and Trade (GATT). The processes of liberalization, deregulation and privatization in the communications and media industries combined with new digital information and communication technologies enabled a quantum leap in information industries. The new information and communication technologies helped create a global communication infrastructure based on regional and global satellite networks, used for telecommunications, broadcasting and, increasingly, electronic commerce. At the same time and more broadly there was a shift from a state-centric view of communication to one governed by the rules of the free market, reflecting policy changes among major powers and multilateral organizations, such as the ITU.

In the past, information technologies were primarily managed by governments, with a few powerful states shaping the information agenda. For most of the 20th century, the state was the main provider of national telecommunications infrastructure and equipment, and regulator of international traffic. In the 1990s, the state monopolies of Post, Telegraph and Telecommunication (PTTs) were forced to give ground to private telecommunication networks. Pioneered in the US and followed by the UK, this shift affected telecommunications globally, leading to the rapid privatization of PTTs – especially in the field of Internet services – across the world.

Regulating the information economy

Regulating information providers within such a neoliberal environment emerged as a major challenge for multilateral institutions. From the founding of the International Telegraph Union in 1865, regulation of international telecommunication was the subject of multilateral accord, setting common standards for telecommunication networks across the globe as well as prices for access to and use of these networks. These conventions were based upon the principles of national monopoly and cross-subsidization, so that national telecom operators could keep the costs affordable for small users by subsidies from international telephony revenues.

New technological innovations, such as computing and fibre-optic cables, and the increasing blurring of the distinction between the transmission of voice and data made possible by these new technologies, challenged the old models of regulation. In addition, as telecommunication traffic increased, so did the demand from transnational corporations for the reduction of tariffs for international services. They opposed national monopolies, arguing that a competitive environment would improve services and reduce costs. Following the US-UK model of liberalization, even the generally pro-regulation European Union relented. Martin Bangermann, European Union Commissioner for Telecommunications, conceded in his 1994 report that liberalization was 'absolutely crucial' and that the European Commission had 'got to push organizational restructuring of telecoms operators to prepare for privatization' (quoted in Venturelli 1998, 134). The liberalization of the communication sector was considerably strengthened with the creation in 1995 of the World Trade Organization (WTO), with stricter legal mechanisms for enforcing international trade agreements. The WTO was set up with a clear agenda for privatization and liberalization: 'The fundamental cost of protectionism stems from the fact that it provides individual decision makers with wrong incentives, drawing resources into protected sectors rather than sectors where a country has its true comparative advantage. The classical role of trade liberalisation, identified centuries ago, is to remove such hindrances, thereby increasing income and growth' (WTO 1998, 38). Accordingly, the WTO counselled countries that dismantling barriers to the free flow of information was essential for economic growth. It was even implied that it was not possible to have significant trade in goods and services without a free trade in information. The importance of a strong communication infrastructure as a foundation for international commerce and economic development was increasingly emphasized by such other international organizations as the ITU, the World Bank and the UN Development Programme (UNDP).

The 1995 General Agreement on Trade in Services (GATS), the first multilateral, legally enforceable agreement covering trade and investment in the services sector, had a profound impact on creation of a global information economy. The services sector encompasses financial services (including banking and administration of financial markets), insurance services, business services (including rental and leasing of equipment), market research, computer services, advertising, communication services (including telecommunication services – telephone, telegraph, data transmission, radio, TV and news services). The most significant component of this agreement, the GATS Annex on Telecommunications, demanded, among other things, that foreign and national telecom suppliers must be treated equally. This had a huge effect on the globalization of the information economy as powerful telecoms – mostly based in the North – could now operate around the world, unhindered by national regulatory constraints. Telecommunications plays a dual role as a communications service, as well as as the delivery mechanism for many other services and is one of the largest and fastest-growing service sectors: by 2004, the overall network-generated revenue globally had reached US$1.3 trillion (UNCTAD 2005).

The year 1997 was particularly significant for the globalization of the information economy. Under the aegis of the WTO, three major international agreements were signed which had profound impact on global trade in information services: in February, 69 WTO countries agreed a wide-ranging liberalization of trade in global telecommunication services. A month later, an agreement was reached to eliminate all import duties on information technology products (which include computers and communication hardware, software, and services) and in December, 102 countries agreed to open up their financial services sector, covering more than 95 per cent of

trade in banking, insurance, securities and financial information, to greater foreign competition. The globalization of financial services, especially banking and insurance, which has contributed substantially to the emerging global electronic economy, would not have been possible without such agreements which provided the privatized international telecommunication networks with the ability to transmit data across borders unhindered by national regulators.

These WTO agreements were the logical culmination of a process that had its origins in the 1980s debates about transborder data flows (TDF). The Southern countries, concerned that such technological innovations as the integrated services digital networks would make it possible for a huge amount of data to be instantly transferred in or out of their territories, wanted to discuss the implications of this for their sovereignty within the UN. However, at US insistence the debate was moved to the OECD, in essence shifting the argument from being one about national sovereignty to one about trade in global information through electronic networks. The 1985 OECD declaration on TDF was unambiguous about the need to dismantle regulations on international movement of data, arguing that the TDF would enhance access and exchange of international data and information-related services. Since then, even the term 'transborder data flows' has been gradually allowed to fall into disuse, to be replaced by phrases with a more contemporary ring to them, such as 'information trade'.

Since 1990, more than 150 countries have introduced new telecommunication legislation or modified existing regulation, while the percentage of international telephone traffic open to the market has grown exponentially. Recognizing the change, the ITU abandoned its traditional role in pursuance of a communication agenda set by the world's most powerful nations and the telecommunication corporations based in them. One indication of this was that, following the 1998 OECD Ministerial Conference on electronic commerce, the ITU began to play a leading role among international organizations in the development of electronic commerce, particularly through standardization activities and working with developing countries, where the goal was to promote global connectivity and participation in the global information society.

US foreign policy saw the creation of such a society as a critical factor for the success of electronic commerce, which required a partnership between the private and public sectors, with the private sector playing the dominant role. The policy of liberalizing the global telecommunication system was greatly influenced by the 1996 Telecommunications Act, which transformed the industry within the US, facilitating the expansion of private US telecommunication corporations such as AT&T to operate globally. These US-based corporations have in turn played a leading role in pushing the WTO and the ITU to further liberalize global communication. Always a champion of free trade, the United States wants to further reduce the role of its state regulatory mechanisms. The Federal Communications Commission saw its role changing from 'an industry regulator to a market facilitator', promoting competition in the international communications market. The information economy received a further boost during the World Radiocommunication Conferences in Istanbul in 2000 and in Geneva in 2003, which further liberalized global communication infrastructure and spectrum harmonization to enable satellite systems to deliver mobile voice and high-speed broadband services.

Trading information globally

The free-market ideology and the new international trading regime that it produced have encouraged the free flow of capital across a borderless world. Concerns about transborder data flows and their impact on national sovereignty have been replaced by the race to embrace the global electronic marketplace. The information technology revolution has also created a global 'outsourcing' service industry, in which developing countries such as India have excelled.

The deregulation and liberalization of the communication sector was paralleled in the media industries and, in conjunction with the new communication technologies of satellite, cable and digital and mobile delivery mechanisms, created a global marketplace for media products, making it imperative for media conglomerates to plan their strategies in a global context, with the ultimate aim of profitable growth through exploiting economies of scope and scale. The process of vertical integration in the media industries to achieve this aim has resulted in the concentration of media power in the hands of a few large transnational corporations,

undermining media plurality and democratic discourse. With deregulation and the relaxation of cross-media ownership restrictions, media and information corporations have broadened and deepened their existing interests through a wave of mergers and acquisitions.

Integration, from content origination through to delivery mechanisms, has enabled a few conglomerates to control all the major aspects of mass media: newspapers, magazines, books, radio, broadcast television, cable systems and programming, films, music recordings, video cassettes and online services. With the revolution in digital distribution a range of new revenue-earning opportunities has surfaced as the media and telecommunications sectors intersect globally. The expanding bandwidth, coupled with the rapid globalization of fixed and mobile networks, as well as the digitization of content and growing use of personal computers worldwide, have considerably helped global media and communication conglomerates to capitalize on emerging markets and experiment with new media products. The global trade in cultural goods (films, television, printed matter, music, computers) almost tripled between 1980 and 1991, from US$67 billion to US$200 billion, and has grown at a rapid pace with the liberalization of these sectors across the world. The global market value of cultural and creative industries has been estimated at US$1.3 trillion and is rapidly expanding. According to the 2005 UNESCO report on International Flows of Selected Goods and Services, between 1994 and 2002, international trade in cultural goods – largely dominated by a few Western nations – increased from US$38 billion to US$60 billion, with the United States being the leading exporter of cultural products.

The availability of mobile Internet access amounts to a telecommunication revolution, opening up new revenue streams for selling music, games, gambling, adult content, video and personalization services to consumers worldwide. As more mobile handsets become capable of playing video, TV brands are migrating to what has been called the 'fourth screen' – after cinema, TV and PC. The 'e-corporations' operating in a 'net-centric world' cut businesses free of their geographic moorings so that increasingly, global trade in computer software, entertainment products, information services and financial services is taking place using the Internet. The technological and organizational structures of the so-called 'webonomics' have contributed to what Manuel Castells has called a global 'informational economy'. 'The rise of the informational, global economy', he writes, 'is characterized by the development of new organizational logic which is related to the current process of technological change, but not dependent upon it. It is the convergence and interaction between a new technological paradigm and a new organizational logic that constitutes the historical foundations of the informational economy' (Castells 2000, 164).

Daya Thussu

Bibliography

Castells M. 2000. *The information age: economy, society and culture, Vol. 1: The rise of the network society*, 2nd edition. Oxford: Blackwell.

Hale J. 1975. *Radio power: propaganda and international broadcasting*. London: Paul Elek.

Headrick D. 1981. *The tools of empire: technology and European imperialism in the 19th century*. Oxford and New York: Oxford University Press.

Nelson M. 1997. *War of the black heavens: the battle of Western broadcasting in the Cold War*. Syracuse, NY: Syracuse University Press.

Organization for Economic Cooperation and Development 1985. *Declaration on transborder data flows* (Press/A(85) 30), 11 April. Paris: OECD.

United Nations Conference on Trade and Development 2005. *Information economy report 2005: E-commerce and development*. Geneva: UNCTAD.

Venturelli S. 1998. *Liberalizing the European media: politics, regulation and the public sphere*. Oxford: Oxford University Press.

World Trade Organization 1998. *Annual report 1998*. Geneva: WTO.

Related essays

al-Jazeera; British Broadcasting Corporation (BBC); broadcasting; Cold War; conspiracy theories; democracy; development and growth; financial centres; financial markets; General Agreement on Tariffs and Trade (GATT) / World Trade Organization (WTO); information technology (IT) offshoring; information technology (IT) standardization; Internet; mail; nation and state; news and press agencies; Pax Americana; radio; services; spatial regimes; telephone and telegraphy; trade; Universal Postal Union (UPU); war

Al-Jazeera

Since its launch in 1996, the Qatar-based pan-Arabic 24/7 news network al-Jazeera has redefined journalism in the Arab world and provided viewers globally with an alternative source of information from a news-rich arena. Media coverage of the 'war on terror' catapulted al-Jazeera into the position of an international broadcaster, whose logo can be seen on television screens around the world, challenging the Anglo-American domination of news and current affairs in one of the world's most geopolitically sensitive areas. In the wake of 9/11, al-Jazeera broadcast the videotapes of Osama bin Laden, the self-styled leader of al-Qaeda, and when the US forces started bombing Afghanistan in 2001, it was the only television network on the ground to provide live coverage. During the 2003 US invasion of Iraq, al-Jazeera's English-language website, launched at the time of Operation Iraqi Freedom, became a favourite source for journalists, activists and others interested in the conflict, providing an alternative perspective on the progress of the war.

One reason the network has reached such acceptance is the professional nature of its output – the core of its multinational staff have experience of working for the BBC, which pioneered the idea of pan-Arabic television news in 1994 with its BBC Arabic service – a joint venture with the Saudi-owned Orbit. The service was abandoned in 1996 after disagreement between the BBC and the Saudi government over editorial matters. The BBC's loss was Qatar's gain. At the time of its launch, the Emir of the Gulf state provided US$140 million with the aim of making the network self-sufficient in five years. However, this has not materialized. Given the political tenor of its output, the channel has found it difficult to attract transnational advertisers, raising questions about its long-term financial viability. To broaden its reach, in 2006 the network launched an English-language version of al-Jazeera – al-Jazeera English – with simultaneous broadcasts from four key centres – Kuala Lumpur, Doha, London and Washington.

Daya Thussu

Bibliography

Miles H. 2005. *Al-Jazeera: How Arab TV news challenged the world*. London: Abacus.

Information technology (IT) offshoring

The offshoring of services is now over thirty
years old. The work began with the offshoring of software services in the 1970s from the
United States to India, Ireland and Israel. In
each country, the initial work and its organization differed. In Ireland, software was
localized by American firms for European
markets. In Israel, software product maintenance and R&D were undertaken by American
firms. India's software industry was begun
by local firms who exported programmers to
American shores to help on-site maintenance
of hardware and software systems.

Since then, there have been dramatic
changes in the size, scope and depth of work
undertaken in these countries. Israel's software industry currently generates export revenue of US$2.5 billion a year and Ireland about
US$4 billion. Their current growth rates are
in line with industry growth rates of about
7 per cent per year. The Irish software industry employs 25,000 engineers and the Israeli
software industry employs 35,000 engineers.

India's is a more dramatic story. For the fiscal year ended March 2007, it generated US$23
billion in export revenue, or 4.3 per cent of
global IT services expenditure. A further
US$8 billion in export revenue was earned
from IT-enabled services such as call centres and back-office work. As of March 2007,
the industry employed 1.25 million people in
software and IT-enabled export services. The
US is the largest export market, with a 68 per
cent share, followed by Europe at 23 per cent.
Exports have grown at an average of 34 per
cent annually for the last decade.

Given its growth and current size, we shall
focus on India for the rest of this article. The
Indian software story is little understood, in
part because its clients are firms rather than
retail consumers. The Indian software industry caters to firms' needs in IT services, which
include simpler work such as deploying hardware and software, training and system maintenance, but also more complex work such as
integrating different pieces of product and

custom software into a working system and a
range of outsourced managed services, such
as email, network management, accounting, research and development and customer
care. Software services, a US$475bn industry
worldwide, is a larger field than that of software products. Globally, software products
had sales of US$206bn in 2006.

The Indian software success is particularly
interesting because it is a rare case of services rather than manufactured goods being
exported from a developing country. Also
unusual is that it happened in custom software
rather than product software (software written for general use): most software-exporting
countries develop product software. The third
unusual thing is that IT is considered one of
the most difficult items to export due to the
requirement of staying regularly updated
with rapidly changing customer requirements
and the ability to respond quickly to the latest
technological changes. These have tended to
deter technology-oriented service exports, as
documented by Hobday (1995).

The first software exporter in India was
TCS which was founded in 1968 to serve the
in-house data-processing requirements of the
Tata industrial group. In 1969, it began offering data-processing services to outside clients on a Burroughs mainframe and became
Burroughs' exclusive India sales agent in 1970.
In 1974, Burroughs, attracted by the India cost
advantage, asked TCS to install its system
software at Burroughs' clients' offices in the
US. Thus started the export business termed
'body shopping', i.e., the export of programmers for assignments typically lasting a few
months. The Indian firms did little other than
recruiting, while the overseas client decided on
the work for the programmers. They initially
focused on systems installation and maintenance. Later, they did 'conversion' of clients'
existing applications software into (primarily)
IBM-compatible versions. By 1980, the industry had export revenue of US$4 million, shared
by 21 firms, of which TCS and a sister-firm
accounted for 63 per cent (Heeks 1996, 88).

As Table 1 shows, the industry grew substantially after 1984 when the number of firms
grew from 35 to 700 by 1990. This was enabled
by three factors. First, the Indian government,
after a period of hostility to the private IT sector, turned around and announced the New
Computer Policy in 1984. This substantially
reduced import tariffs (on hardware from 135
per cent to 60 per cent, and on software from

Table 1   Growth of the Indian software industry 1980–2007

Year	Total exports (US$m)	No. of firms	Average revenue per firm (US$)	Average revenue per employee (US$)	Share of top 8 firms (%)	Average revenue per firm excluding top 8 firms (US$)
1980	4.0	21	190,476	16,000	90.0	30,769
1984	25.3	35	722,857	18,741	78.0	206,148
1990	105.4	700	150,571	16,215	65.0	53,309
2000	5,287	816	6,479,167	32,635	38.3	4,734,406
2003	8,600	3,031	2,837,347	33,076	64.8	1,711,214
2007	23,000	N/A	N/A	N/A	N/A	N/A

Notes:
1. Year refers to the fiscal year ending 31 March of that year, e.g., 2007 refers to the period 1 April 2006 – 31 March 2007.
2. Figures are for software only and do not include IT-enabled services such as call centres.

Sources: Heeks (1996); Nasscom (2004, 2007)

100 per cent to 60 per cent), reallowed wholly owned foreign firms for exports and (in separate legislation), exempted all export income from tax in 1985. Second, the workstation with its sophisticated graphics and numerical computational capabilities was introduced in the mid 1980s. The workstation, unlike the PC which had been introduced a few years earlier, had the capacity for standalone programming for the mainframe and could run small business applications. Third was the widespread adoption of Unix as the standard operating system for workstations and mainframes from the mid 1980s. (We term these latter two developments the U-W standard.) The U-W standard enabled programmers to develop programs on any workstation in a common language (C), whereas earlier programmers needed to work on specific mainframes and write programs in the language of that mainframe supplier. Thanks to the U-W standard and reduced tariffs, it became economic to write programs in India.

A foreign firm, Texas Instruments (TI) was the first to do so, setting up a wholly owned subsidiary in Bangalore for software product development. Although several multinationals and Indian firms followed TI's lead in attempting to develop product software in India, they did not succeed. TI's legacy lay in two other directions. First, it showed that a team of programmers working in India could do the same work as the team overseas, though at lower cost. Second, it showed the advantages of Bangalore, most importantly of being located close to the largest pool of engineers (the four southern states, Karnataka, Andhra Pradesh, Tamil Nadu and Kerala produce 52 per cent of India's engineering graduates). TCS

was the first firm to apply TI's offshore model to the Indian strength of writing custom software. TCS pioneered the first complete custom software project for an overseas client done remotely, thus giving birth to a new way of working. Termed the 'remote project management model', it generated large new-firm entry. It was to remain the industry's mainstay for the next two decades. It also played to Bangalore's strengths as a programmer base and enabled it to gain market share over the leader, Mumbai. Whereas in 1980, none of the top eight software exporters were from Bangalore and even by 1990, TI was the only Bangalore firm in the list (the rest were Mumbai-based firms), by 2000, there were two Bangalore firms on the list and Bangalore firms made up a quarter of the industry's exports.

In the 1990s, India went through major reforms. Apart from tariff reductions, a key reform was that firms were allowed to spend their export dollars on opening offices overseas, thus giving them access to more firms, particularly the middle-sized firms, and enabling them to offer both remote and proximate support – which was valuable for the larger clients. In the 1990s, an important technological change led to another paradigm shift for the custom software industry. Variously termed the 'digital age' or the 'information age', it consisted of two components: the PC replaced the workstation as both the vehicle for programming and, through creating networks of computers, became the vehicle for applications delivery for small businesses (large businesses continue to use mainframes for data management and use the PC only as a user interface). This allowed many more corporate users than before to directly access applications software. Second, the costs of transmitting information fell, particularly towards the end of the 1990s.

The digital age had two fundamental impacts. First, it revolutionized the conversion of service flows into stocks of information, making it possible to store a service. For example, a legal opinion that earlier had to be delivered to the client in person could now be prepared as a computer document and transmitted to the client by email or, better yet, encoded into software. Easy storage and transmission allowed for the physical separation of the client and vendor as well as their separation in time. It also induced the separation of services into components that were standardized and could be prepared in advance (such as a template for a legal opinion) and other components that were customized for the client (such as the opinion itself) or remained non-storable. Taking advantage of the possibility of subdividing tasks and the economies that come with a division of labour, this reduced costs by offering the possibility of preparing the standardized components

with lower-cost labour and, possibly, at another location. The second fundamental impact was the conversion of an increasing number of non-information service flows into information service flows. For example, sampling of tangible goods by a buyer visiting a showroom is increasingly being replaced by virtual samples delivered over the Internet. Once converted to an information flow, the service may also then be converted into a stock of information, as noted earlier, and subjected to the above mentioned forces of cost reduction through standardization of components and remote production. Thus, by enabling transmission and storability, the digital age enabled the offshoring of services. As transmission costs continued to fall after 2000, even non-storable services, such as call centre services, could be offshored.

Whereas earlier, India's software industry was restricted to preparing custom software programs, the digital age enabled the offshoring of what are termed 'managed services' or 'business process outsourcing', i.e., functions such as bookkeeping, payroll and customer

Table 2　Comparing IT work done in the US and India in common time frames

| Work type → | US | | India | |
	More complex	Less complex	More complex	Less complex
Upto 1970	In-house IT) support (mainly conversion work	OS; software support for IT firm		EDP
1971–80	Applications; EDP	In-house IT support	In-house IT support (mainly conversion work); EDP	OS; software support for global IT firm
1981–90	Systems integration (hardware with systems); EDP	Applications; OS; Unix conversion work	Off-site conversion work and applications development; in-house product development by MNEs	On-site conversion work; applications development
1991–2003	Consulting, systems integration (software); managed services	Applications; web services	Large applications; development projects; engineering services; web services; in-house product development by MNEs	On-site conversion (including Y2K) work; website maintenance

Acronyms:
EDP Electronic data processing;   MNEs Multinational enterprises;   OS Operating system
Y2K Year 2000 work to convert old mainframe applications software containing two-digit year codes to four-digit codes

Source: Author's compilation

care are part of an ever increasing list of services that may now be offered remotely. Thus, a large new industry has been opened up to offshoring. As in custom software, India is already the developing world's largest supplier of managed services to developed countries.

Several scholars and policy makers have questioned the sustainability of India's IT-enabled sector. Of course, the record over the past three decades speaks for itself, but their critiques and some new issues need to be addressed. Their reasons for claiming future unsustainability are: the absence of domestic markets from which to acquire domain skills, lack of intellectual property (IP) protection, small firm sizes, migration of skilled IT professionals to developed countries, lack of R&D in universities and industry, limited involvement of a skilled diaspora and the lack of clusters. It turned out that these factors were not industry 'killers' but took the industry in a particular direction. For example, lack of learning from the domestic market and migration forced the industry to restrict the work to programming rather than higher-end work such as system design and integration. Similarly, the absence of venture capital discouraged startups but left large, well capitalized firms unaffected. The lack of venture capital and R&D, non-involvement of the diaspora and weak IP laws discouraged software product development but did not affect the custom software industry. A bigger challenge is the quality of the labour force. This is generally unnoticed due to the high growth in the industry's employment. But it hides issues of quality. According to Nasscom (2000), only 27 per cent of the IT workforce has an undergraduate or graduate degree in computer sciences or electrical engineering. Despite this, the industry has thrived. The credit must go to private enterprise. In the early days, when the government imposed high tariffs on imports, the industry responded by exporting programmers. When tariff walls were lowered, the work shifted to India. With the advent of the Internet, the industry expanded the scope of work to include business process work. It is particularly remarkable that the industry, even when the government was hostile, managed to keep up with the work done in the US and other developed countries, albeit with a lag of about a decade. This is shown in Table 2.

Since 2004, the industry has headed in the direction of providing higher value-added services. Recent reforms, especially in telecommunications, venture capital, and enabling access by domestic firms to overseas markets have changed the direction of the industry significantly, moving it toward higher-value services such as managed services, software product development and R&D. For instance, the world's largest contract IT R&D firm is now an Indian firm, Wipro. Looking ahead, outsourcing of software services to India remains a growth industry, entering its fourth decade. This is likely to be bolstered by a greater presence of multinationals, clusters, diaspora involvement and access to risk capital. Only poor education puts growth at some risk.

Rafiq Dossani

Bibliography

Dossani R. 2004. 'Origins and growth of the IT industry in India', Working paper, Asia-Pacific Research Center, Stanford University.

Heeks R. 1995. *India's software industry*. New Delhi: Sage.

Hobday M. 1995. *Innovation in East Asia: the challenge to Japan*. Cheltenham: Edward Elgar.

Ministry of Human Resource Development 2001. *Technical Education Quality Improvement Project of the Government of India*. New Delhi: Ministry of HRD.

Nasscom various years. *The IT industry in India*. New Delhi: Nasscom.

Schware R. 1992. 'Software industry entry strategies for developing countries: a "walking on two legs" proposition', *World Development*, 20, 2, 143–64.

Related essays
architecture; body shopping; development and growth; information economy; information technology (IT) standardization; intellectual property rights; Internet; law firms; legal order; services; technologies; temporary migrations; trade agreements

Information technology (IT) standardization
Information technology (IT) refers to digital electronic means of managing and communicating information; its standardization applies to the tangible 'hardware' involved, the 'software' that drives it, and the means whereby digital information is communicated across distance.

The first digital computers appeared in the early 1940s. They were enormous, expensive and high-energy machines custom-built for government departments, and military and scientific establishments. Standardization only became relevant after several technological breakthroughs (especially the replacement of vacuum tubes with transistors) vastly increased the power of computers while reducing their size and expense. These innovations led to the development of microprocessors from the 1970s. The rapid pace of technological development, which still characterizes the hardware industry, has meant that proprietary and industry standards (rather than national and international ones) have dominated it. IBM's 1981 launch of its affordable personal computer, IBM PC 5150, did not bring any decisive change in this situation. Proprietary standards governed (and largely still govern) the manufacture of all components going into the successive generations of IBM 'clones' and 'compatibles', which have in turn invaded millions of homes and workplaces around the world.

Formal standardizers have found a greater role in the production of software, even though market leaders (especially Microsoft since the 1980s) have dominated this sector too, and have thus been able to assert many proprietary standards, not least in operating systems. Standardizers have nonetheless been able to make their mark in important IT applications, for instance in the 1980s, when they introduced standards to enforce an open system on emerging electronic funds transfers (EFT), including automatic teller machines (ATMs), in the face of banks' attempts to protect their individual market shares by developing proprietary networks. Another early example of software standardization to protect the public interest came in cartography ('digital mapping'), which allowed for a free exchange of topographical data.

By the late 1980s governments and standards bodies alike undertook a generalized quest for Open Systems Interconnection (OSI) by way of standardized protocols for the 'seamless' exchange of digital information, such as medical data, between remote terminals. At this time both the International Organization for Standardization (ISO) and the International Electrotechnical Commission (IEC) were raising the profile of international standards as such, and national IT standards quickly stimulated – then gave way to – international ones published by these bodies.

Software – far more than hardware – has offered the major business opportunities in 'the information society', since software has proliferated with computer applications, and it enjoys the protection of copyright. In the 1990s standardizers (such as the USA's Institute of Electric and Electronic Engineers Computer Society, IEEE) began to apply quality management standards to software-development projects. ISO in turn produced a special version of its ISO 9000 series (ISO 9000–3) covering the development, supply and maintenance of software.

From the 1950s through to the 1980s, various universities and corporations worked on developing computer networks that could span long distances. Many 'protocols' – a kind of standard – were required to allow remote computers to 'interface', and so become 'interoperable'. Ad hoc interest groups, which were unincorporated and worked informally, developed these protocols, which functioned as de facto standards. Even after the emergence of today's Internet in 1986, and its wider public availability from 1993–94 with the launch of the World Wide Web (WWW), the earlier ad hocery and informality have remained, despite the incorporation of a transnational umbrella organization, the Internet Society (ISOC) in 1992.

Under ISOC's authority, the Internet Engineering Task Force, in consultation with the Internet Engineering Steering Group, publishes international standards – many of the documents still coded with the original prefix, 'RFC' (Request for Comments) – which can in turn be appealed to the Internet Architecture Board. ISOC and these subsidiaries also cooperate with their counterparts in ISO/IEC and the ITU (see below).

The WWW was developed largely at the European Organization for Nuclear Research (CERN) which – in cooperation with the Massachusetts Institute of Technology and other bodies – formed the World Wide Web Consortium (W3C) in 1994. The W3C is another transnational body that takes charge of the Web's development, including promulgating its enabling standards. The three standards crucial to upholding wide public access the Web are those that underpin the Uniform Resource Identifier (URI), the HyperText Transfer Protocol (HTTP), and the HyperText Markup Language (HTML).

Developments in computer applications, the Internet and the WWW since the early 1990s have changed the way many people, institutions and businesses function around the world, for example in the spread of e-commerce, e-business and online education. The increasingly used term 'information and communication technologies' (ICT) witnesses to a vital integration of formerly discrete technological areas, and the need for standards bodies to reorganize themselves and to cooperate more closely with each other in order to develop standards in aid of interoperability, security and privacy, and an equitable global spread of the benefits of 'the information society'.

In 1993 the International Telegraphic Union (ITU) restructured into three sectors, one of which, the ITU Telecommunication Standardization Sector (ITU-T) had 2,700 current 'recommendations' (standards) by 2006. The ITU has also provided the secretariat for UN efforts to address 'the digital divide' – the skewed distribution of access to ICT within and between countries – especially in the World Summit on the Information Society in 2003 and 2005. This engagement runs parallel with ITU's sister organization, ISO's development of a standard for social responsibility.

Winton Higgins
Kristina Tamm Hallström

Bibliography

Jakobs K. (ed.) 2000. *Information technology standards and standardization: a global perspective.* Hershey: Idea Group Publishing.

Schmidt S. and Werle R. 1998. *Coordinating technology: studies in the international standardization of telecommunications.* Cambridge, MA: MIT Press.

Related essays

car safety standards; food safety standards; information technology (IT) offshoring; international non-governmental organizations (INGOs); Internet; Internet Corporation for Assigned Names and Numbers (ICANN); mapping; patents; technical standardization; technologies; telephone and telegraphy

Insecticides, herbicides, pesticides See **Pesticides, herbicides, insecticides**

Intellectual elites

Transnational history is a particularly fruitful approach to be employed in the study of intellectual elites. As we know, the traditional 'diffusion model' whereby ideas and doctrines (scientific theories, political ideologies, cultural trends) were simply disseminated from the West – Europe and the United States – to the rest of the world has been superseded in recent years by new perspectives on worldwide knowledge creation. It is now recognized that original currents of thought were often profoundly modified in the process of adaptation and generalization in their new settings. In fact, as stated by Chris Bayly (2004), the emergence of hybrid bodies of learning and linked networks of scientists and intellectuals, rather than a one-directional transmission of ideas, seems a better way of describing this process.

Two consequences arise from this recognition: one, the history of this process is not just a record of how ideas originated in one place and were received in others; on the contrary, history is also being made precisely in the movement between different regions of the world, that is, the process of transition is a historical process of knowledge creation. Secondly, this process of transit, of hybridization of knowledge, is effected by specific social forms: intellectuals, writers, scientists, policy makers and academics, and their international networks, conferences, journals, and books. The study of global intellectual elites is the study of these social forms of intellectual interconnection that make possible the creation of new knowledge.

This particular interconnection has always implied an inevitable tension between the two poles of global or transnational and local influences. Far from being ever resolved, the tension between the local and the global became a common feature in the emergence and consolidation of intellectual elites all over the world. This interplay can be interpreted as a tension between certain sociological or historical forces – local or transnational – or as an epistemological issue: universalistic or particularistic claims on the validity of knowledge. On the one hand, intellectual elites can reflect an ever present aspiration to the universal validity of knowledge over particularistic claims; moreover – even more frequently in the non-European world – local intellectual elites resort to international references as a source of legitimacy and prestige in their milieu. On the other, national academic traditions, local practices, and singular cultural characteristics generate localized conditions for knowledge production and the emergence of persistent claims for 'national' sciences, ideologies, or cultural manifestations (Charle et al. 2004). In the realm of the social sciences and the humanities, these claims were reinforced by the demands that the processes of state and nation building pressed on local intellectual elites to contribute to the strengthening of national identities through their disciplines, or, as Thomas Bender has illustrated, in the dilemma between a global epistemic community and the role of academics and intellectuals in their local, shared public culture.

We can differentiate between three types of intellectual elites in which this tension is clearly visible: scientific and academic communities; state technical elites and policy makers; politically motivated intellectuals and writers.

The internationalization of science and academic life

The process of institutionalization and professionalization of academic disciplines in the modern university has been closely connected to the transnational circulation of ideas, theories, models, and individuals.

Scientific missions, international conferences, exchange programmes, grants and joint research projects, specialized journals; all these have been the channels of interaction for academic elites, and crucial elements in the institutionalization and professionalization of academic disciplines. Transnational mobility, however, can also be a debilitating factor, when the emigration of a scientific elite results in the loss of a unifying framework, as exemplified in the decline of the Austrian School of economics in the interwar years.

The history of science and of academic institutions provides an abundant record of such interactions: the spread and adaptation of Darwinism in the non-European world, tropical medicine in Brazil and Cuba, biomedics in the Andean republics, German historical economics and its influence in the United States, and more recently French historiography and American anthropology and sociology in Latin America, have all been fields in which local elites have had a 'recourse to internationality' (Charle et al. 2004, 21), both as a source of professional legitimacy and as a common discourse.

Nevertheless, this search for a common transnational paradigm was constantly challenged by the demands posed by national identities and national scientific cultures. The emergence of the research university as a locus of knowledge creation coincided in time with the consolidation of the nation state and, above all, with public concerns about the role of the state in preserving national cultures and national identities. Thus, local intellectual elites were called upon to put their knowledge to the task: sciences and academic disciplines were also tools for a better understanding of national realities and an instrument for their improvement. Intellectual elites in the non-European world thus developed what Mauricio Tenorio described as a 'stereophonic' approach to scientific modernity: global or transnational paradigms called upon to interpret national problems, as exemplified by the obsessions with race in the emerging Latin American social sciences.

World War 1 represented the culmination of this duality: European nationalistic conflicts exploding at the pinnacle of scientific internationalism. By the early 1920s, a disappointed Latin American social scientist (José Ingenieros) wrote to philosopher Henri Bergson, president of the League of Nations Commission Internationale de Coopération Intellectuelle, that 'the international organization of science has been severely hurt by the xenophobic passions aroused by war, nationalism and imperialism'. Efforts made under the auspices of the League of Nations, such as the cited Commission, or the Institut International de Coopération Intellectuelle, were doomed from this perspective. Only time and the replacement of the generation of scientists and academics involved in the corruption of the scientific ethos by nationalism would allow the re-emergence of genuine intellectual and scientific solidarity. However, despite the pessimistic climate of the interwar years, new forms of scientific cooperation gradually emerged.

The international circulation of people, of texts and objects of scientific research, and transnational ways of financing research are now common features of the contemporary 'scientific field', and give shape to a very specific form of transnationality: an international market for research and higher education with a strong bias for certain fields of knowledge and the predominance of English as its language. In the field of the social sciences, economists perhaps best embody these trends: economics is today a profoundly transnational field, socialized in increasingly homogeneous programmes dominated by American universities, and, as Verónica Montecinos and John Markoff have shown, the consequences of this go well beyond the walls of academia.

Transfers of social technology

Just as the institutionalization of scientific and academic disciplines included a transnational component, the development of new areas of state intervention in social and economic matters gave birth to internationally linked state technical elites, a process that coincided in time – from the late 19th century onwards – and had obvious connections with the process of scientific globalization. In what E. P. Hennock described as 'the transfer of social technology', i.e., the international adaptation of social institutions or specific pieces of legislation related to the new social questions, an intense transnational movement of social reform initiatives and innovative public policies connected like-minded state officials, academics and journalists in such fields as labour legislation and arbitration of labour disputes, welfare and protection of children, social insurance, unemployment, housing, city planning, public health, prison reform, poverty relief, and many others. Therefore, the creation and circulation of this new 'social knowledge', the foundation of many modern social policies, was also deeply influenced by its international dimension. To copy, modify, and adapt policies from one country to another was mostly what these elites were involved in. In Europe, German social security was perhaps the most notable case of an influential model imitated despite national rivalries; between Europe and the United States, the multiple examples studied by Daniel Rodgers reveal a recurrent 'Atlantic crossing' of projects and individuals; in countries or regions of recent settlement, the willingness to experiment with new social policies was quickly adopted by reformist elites, in admiration of the ambitious initiatives developed in Australia and New Zealand. In many Latin American countries, the reference to an international precedent was the best way to overcome ideological objections: the backing of the 'civilized world' for a reform initiative was the best guarantee its proponents could offer.

Technical cooperation soon expanded far beyond social reform. Agriculture, education, or judicial institutions were all fields in which networks of experts and specialists operated as channels for the circulation of knowledge, connected through a web of facilitating institutions: intergovernmental committees, international conferences, state-appointed investigative commissions (frequently promoting a modern Grand Tour to the places in which new developments were being implemented); well informed local journalists, who chronicled other countries' policies.

Structural state reform has become the contemporary equivalent. Again, national circumstances and globalization shape the agenda of state technical elites, both in the process of imitation and adaptation of certain policies and in the strategies of implementation chosen by each country. Philanthropic foundations, NGOs, national and transnational agencies, consultants, think tanks and international law firms develop what have been described as 'cosmopolitan scholarly strategies in and around the state': the use of international credentials, expertise and connections to build capital that can be reinvested in the domestic public arena. The rise of what Jorge Domínguez called Latin American 'technopols' illustrate how frequently this technocratic expertise legitimized by international connections has led to political ascendancy.

An 'International of spiritual life'

We can identify another type of internationalization of intellectual elites: the expansion of philosophical, political and economic ideas with worldwide reach, from the Enlightenment onwards, a topic that has inspired a good deal of Western intellectual historiography. As an example, James Kloppenberg has brilliantly presented the creation of a transatlantic community of discourse in philosophy and political theory by two generations of progressive and social-democratic American and European intellectuals, between 1870 and 1920. Similar studies trace the ways in which publicists from the French Third Republic or the Spanish Restoration inspired hundreds of Latin American writers, politicians and journalists in similar communities of political discourse.

Again, World War 1 is a watershed: nationalisms fractured intellectual life and shattered the ideal of a universal republic of letters. Julien Benda's *Trahison des clercs* (1928) amply illustrated the feelings of disillusion and bitterness raised by that traumatic experience. Nevertheless, the interwar years fostered the gradual emergence of new intellectual solidarities and forms of cooperation. On a more pragmatic level, institutions such as the already mentioned Institut International de Coopération Intelllectuelle, and the Conféderation Internationale des Travailleurs Intellectuels (1923) developed forms of cooperation reflecting common professional interests, for instance, the protection of intellectual property rights of writers, artists and intellectuals. But they also fostered a new kind of internationalism as an answer to ideological radicalization, the rise of fascisms and political persecutions. A new international solidarity based not on the traditional, working-class internationalism but on the idea of the defence of the spiritual rights of a universal intellectual class, an *Internationale des esprits*. In a sense, the ideological inspiration for this movement was the international expansion of a certain model of cultural action: the republican intellectual as the flagship of a rational humanism opposed to the threat of political totalitarianism. This metapolitical project was channelled through a number of international institutions: L'Association Internationale des Écrivains pour La Défense de la Culture (1934); the PEN Clubs (1921), and several international committees of writers, artists, and journalists in aid of the victims of fascism in Spain or Italy. Cases of emigration to Latin America of Italian scientists and intellectuals persecuted by Mussolini´s 'racial laws', or Republican émigrés during and after the Spanish Civil War, and their strategies of settlement in the host societies are examples of the ways in which this culture of anti-fascist intellectual mobilization forged a new international solidarity.

At the turn of the new century, a new movement of solidarity arises across all national boundaries, paradoxically, to challenge globalization. New forms of communication give rise to electronic networks of writers, artists, and intellectuals in general, connecting them with activists and militants all over the world. Anti-globalization movements and calls for a new 'cosmopolitan social democracy' are thus the latest form in which transnationality shapes intellectual life. It remains to be seen how the new global intellectual elites face the challenge of integrating the transnational and the local, the professional and the civic, in order to reconcile the ideals of global scientific, technological and economic development with local cultural values.

Eduardo Zimmermann

Bibliography

Bayly C. A. 2004. *The birth of the modern world 1780–1914: global connections and comparisons.* Oxford : Blackwell.

Bourdieu P. 2002. 'Les conditions sociales de la circulation internationale des idées', *Actes de la recherche en sciences sociales,* 145, 3–8.

Charle C., Schriewer J. and Wagner P. (eds) 2004. *Transnational intellectual networks: Forms of academic knowledge and the search for cultural identities.* Frankfurt and New York: Campus.

Dezalay Y. and Garth B. G. 2002. *The internationalization of palace wars: lawyers, economists, and the contest to transform Latin American states.* Chicago: Chicago University Press.

Fogarty J. 'Social experiments in regions of recent settlement: Australia, Argentina and Canada', in Platt D. C. M. (ed.) 1989. *Social welfare 1850–1950: Australia, Argentina and Canada compared.* London: Macmillan (now Palgrave Macmillan).

Gingras Y. 2002. 'Les formes spécifiques de l'internationalité du champ scientifique', *Actes de la recherche en sciences sociales,* 141–142, 31–45.

Klausinger H. 2006. '"In the wilderness": emigration and the decline of the Austrian School', *History of Political Economy,* 38, 617–74.

Trebitsch M. 'Organisations internationales de coopération intellectuelle dans l'entre-deux-guerres', in Wolikow S. and Bleton-Ruget A. (eds) 1998. *Antifascisme et nation: les gauches européennes au temps du Front Populaire,* Dijon: EUD.

Related essays

civilizations; class; Commission on International Labour Legislation; cosmopolitanism and universalism; cultural capitals; developmental assistance; economics; engineering; eugenics; European civil servants; exile; expositions; fascism and anti-fascism; fellowships and grants; French theory; governing science; Hammarskjöld family; health policy; higher education; history; humanities; intellectual property rights; intergovernmental organizations; international non-governmental organizations (INGOs); international schools; Kessler, Harry von; knowledge; law firms; legal order; liberalism; literature; Master of Business Administration (MBA); nation and state;

pan-isms; philanthropic foundations; prizes; public policy; publishing; Quesnay, Pierre; Romanticism; social sciences; transnational; welfare state; women's movements

Intellectual property rights

The history of intellectual property is embedded in the institutional revolution, the media revolution, the reader revolution, and industrialization and scientification; terms which refer to a dramatic social and cultural shift which took place in Western societies in the 19th century. Between 1750 and 1900, the production, reproduction and use of books, works of art and music rose to ever greater heights. Simultaneously there was a tendency towards temporarily protecting knowledge, achievements and symbols by means of copyrights, patents and trademarks, in the competition for scientific, political and cultural power. Modern liberal societies, states and nations increasingly had to deal with who was entitled to publish, exploit and receive literary and artistic works, which were cultural goods, political goods and commodities all at the same time; and how the rights of disposal over commercially utilized, new technical knowledge and trademarks ought to be regulated. Where this problem was settled by the legal standards and doctrines of the individual state and the nation, there arose the second question of what was to be done outside the national monopoly on rights and, vice versa, how foreign works ought to be handled, exploited and appropriated on home ground. For reasons of space the present article focuses on the history of literary and artistic property and leaves aside both the history of inventor and patent rights and the history of trademarks and branding.

Intellectual property between nationalization, transnationalization and internationalization in the 19th century

Once cultural goods came to be exchanged in significant quantities between different states, and among different legal, cultural and linguistic areas, modern constitutional states endeavoured to create national and international regulations for the rights of disposal and their handling. Inevitably, states had to actively include enterprising and culturally aware publishers and authors in these processes of negotiation and legislation, who stressed the necessity for international agreements. Thus, the development of intellectual property, copyright and author rights was determined, firstly, by the diffusion and reception of cultural works; secondly, by the different linguistic, cultural and scientific areas of reference for producers, exploiters and the public, which were not necessarily covered by the nationally defined areas; and thirdly, by the newly established international institutions and legal standards for protecting intellectual property, which were negotiated and implemented by heterogeneous networks of states, professional and civil society actors.

The term 'intellectual property' was established between 1750 and 1850 in the states of Europe, North America and South America, and spread worldwide in the course of the late 19th and the 20th centuries. Modern intellectual property law is a bundle of individual rights, which has developed in secular, market economies and liberally organized societies. As politics, the economy, society and culture became nationalized and legalized, intellectual property rights became a fundamental institution of national culture. The national cultural cartel regulated the relations between the different bodies responsible for national culture and the public in terms of ownership, that is to say as a relationship between an owner with strong exclusive rights and third parties. Intellectual property law was meant to guarantee and standardize the rights of authors, publishers, theatre companies, performing actors, the public and the state to act in scientific, cultural and social competition and to provide all cooperation in the production, dissemination and reception of culture and knowledge on a secure contractual foundation. Thus, the related laws were formulated as a more or less comprehensive and exclusive bundle of the individual rights of disposal and exclusion. The tendency to assign an exclusive right to authors in developing and processing their work has a long cultural tradition. In 19th-century Anglo-Saxon law, for example, this bundle of rights primarily comprised the right to copy, to sell and to disseminate the work. Copyrighting helped to protect the author or the holder of the rights against unauthorized reprinting or performance. Intellectual property law also regulated the balance between private and collective intellectual property rights by restricting the term and contents of private ownership of intellectual property rights for the benefit of public, national and state interests.

The state and national coding of intellectual property law began to intensify from the 1790s onwards. The national state, as a guarantor of exclusive rights, acquired the function of creating a permanent balance between individual and private handling rights on the one hand and corporate and public handling and control rights on the other. As a legislator, the state established the cultural, social and legal regulations for producing, disseminating and using culture, moderated the cultural cartel of the elites and created a balance among protection standards negotiated on a transnational level, national interests and national law. Extensive nationalization of education, tuition and science enabled the state to become an influential and, in many connections, a monopolistic producer and user of culture and knowledge in its own right. As a modern cultural state, it exclusively pursued its own user interests, which could potentially come into conflict with the interests of private and international intellectual property rights.

As state and legal areas in Europe ceased to be congruent with linguistic and cultural areas and while intellectual works were handled beyond states, customs and legal boundaries, protecting native authors and publishers from unauthorized reprinting abroad became a considerable challenge for efficient national copyright law. Therefore, from the middle of the 19th century onwards, authors, composers and publishers increasingly pushed for an interstate and international alignment of intellectual property and for acknowledgement of their individual author rights outside their own country.

An early attempt to solve this problem involved bilateral trade agreements; these determined, predominantly from the middle of the 19th century onwards, mutual acknowledgement of copyrights and protection from reprinting between different European states. The first multilateral interstate agreements were concluded in linguistically homogeneous but politically splintered areas such as pre-national Germany and pre-national Italy in 1832, 1837 and 1840. In both regions, the authors and original publishers of the Northern states wished thereby to be protected against reprinters in the 'South'. However, these bilateral and multilateral agreements were restricted to the short term

and their implementation was uneven. Thus it became increasingly urgent from the middle of the 19th century onwards to introduce long-term, universal legal standards which covered the greatest area possible on a European level. In 1886, these efforts resulted in the Berne Convention, a multilateral contract system for the protection of copyrights.

The Berne Convention firstly established an internationally negotiated standard for the protection of intellectual property rights, which used a so-called principle of home treatment in order to put foreign and home authors on a legal par with each other within the association of states. By harmonizing national and international law, authors and exploiters were ensured binding rights above and beyond national boundaries and security for all cross-border trade.

The founding members of the Berne Union were predominantly culture-exporting states with a high level of cultural and scientific production, such as Great Britain, France, Germany, Belgium and Switzerland. They had a special interest in ensuring the remuneration of their cultural economies. In stark contrast to the Berne Union, the USA and multicultural and multilingual empires, such as Austro-Hungary and Russia, tended rather to receive cultural works from foreign authors and generally reprint and translate the works of foreign holders of rights without the authors concerned earning any royalties.

The internationalization of intellectual property law in the form of multilateral contract definitions remained necessarily dependent on close coordination with the national legislation and jurisdiction of the member states, because the international rules of law could only become effective when ratified and implemented in national law. However, the willingness of member states to align their national laws of protection internationally was an acknowledgement of the intercultural processes of exchange.

The states thus boosted the scope of their national rights by expanding the area of legal protection to cover the entire territory of the Berne Union, but at the same time handed over parts of their function in institutionalizing culture to an international administrative union. Consequently, they triggered considerable dynamics to align national copyrights which, in spite of the First and Second World Wars and the significant political, social and scientific crises of the 20th century, remained comparatively stable and have influenced national legal and cultural politics until the present day.

The achievement of the Berne Convention was due largely to the initiative and involvement of non-state actors such as writers, scientists, artists, musicians, publishers and lawyers. Organized in national and international interest groups and trade associations, they held congresses and campaigned from the 1850s onwards for cross-border acknowledgement of copyrights by the national and international public. In this sense, the Berne Convention not only benefited the national creators of culture by internationalizing their cultural property rights and thus improving their chances of surviving in scientific, social and cultural competition, but it also created structures which made international cooperation between states and non-state actors possible. This widely established international cooperation led to an inclusion of social groups in interstate relations and to a boosting of transnational actors from culture and science. Intercultural processes of exchange and interconnection in the creation, publication, dissemination and reception of cultural works thus became enshrined in law and institutionalized across borders with the help of transnational legal standards. In the age of the global dominance of European imperialism, these legal and cultural regulations were also spread with considerable pressure throughout India, China, the Middle East and parts of Africa.

International and transnational governance of intellectual property in the 20th century

The international cooperation and interest politics of authors, publishers and states were continued in the 20th century with repeated revisions of the Berne Convention. A comparable international convention for the protection of copyrights was also established for the American Continent. Under the auspices of the Pan-American Union, the Convention of Montevideo (1899) formulated a legal standard for the protection of copyrights for the majority of American states, which, in contrast to the Berne Union, followed the Anglo-Saxon legal copyrighting tradition and the specific regional interests of the (South) American states as predominantly culture-importing states. Since the Berne Union, despite its universalistic self-conception, essentially

remained a Western European-centred cultural cartel existing abruptly side by side with the Pan-American copyright agreement, initial attempts were made after 1918 to harmonize these two decisively transnational legal standards. International governmental organizations played an important role, in particular the League of Nations and its Institute for Intellectual Cooperation (and later UNESCO). They convened state and non-state actors (writers, composers, artists, publishers and lawyers) in order to negotiate globally applicable standards for the protection of copyrights. UNESCO's initiative led to the adoption of the World Copyright Agreement in 1952, which made fewer protection provisions than the Berne Convention and therefore was preferred by developing and socialist countries. The tendency towards giving international organizations authority to administer, negotiate and extend the protection of intellectual property continued increasingly from the 1960s onwards.

The different traditions and threads of internationalizing intellectual property were brought together at the end of the 1960s into the World Intellectual Property Organization (WIPO). Today, as a suborganization of the UN, it represents worldwide the idea that the original creators of works that are protected against copying have a right to economic profit as well as moral rights. However, many critics feel that it actually represents the interests of international media companies and pharmaceutical concerns more than the wishes of writers, artists, scientists, and the public. Since the 1980s, copyrights have been aligned in the European states within the framework of the European Union's guidelines. Worldwide, the World Trade Organization (WTO) and the Agreement on Trade-Related Aspects of Intellectual Property Rights (TRIPs), which it administers, have been in effect since 1994 to standardize and implement intellectual property rights in accordance with trade-related objectives.

In developing countries, protests have been developing since the 1960s against the expansion and worldwide introduction of Western-style copyright standards. They have deplored richer countries' disenfranchisement, oppression and exploitation of economically poorer nations and greater regions by using intellectual property law to block access to knowledge and certain cultural creations. In many cases, moreover, they claim their collective rights have been ignored and appropriated by foreigners aided by private intellectual property law. There is also criticism on the part of creators of culture and users in the First World who thrive on the creative opportunities offered by new technologies and search for alternative forms of institutionalizing and organizing culture beyond an individualized and owner-based understanding of intellectual property rights. They are fighting against the criminalization of a participatory understanding of culture, stressing the exchange, borrowing and transfer of cultural works and ideas as a motor for creativity and innovation in modern societies.

Isabella Löhr
Hannes Siegrist

Bibliography
Alford W. P. 1995. *To steal a book is an elegant offense: intellectual property law in Chinese civilization.* Stanford: Stanford University Press.

Davies G. 1994. *Copyright and the public interest.* Weinheim: VCH.

Geller P. E. 2000. 'Copyright history and the future: what's culture got to do with it?', *Journal of the Copyright Society of the USA,* 47, 209–64.

Kornicki P. 1998. *The book in Japan: a cultural history from the beginnings to the nineteenth century.* Leiden: Brill.

Ladas S. P. 1975. *Patents, trademarks and related rights: national and international protection.* Cambridge, MA: Harvard University Press.

May C. N. 2000. *A global political economy of intellectual property rights: the new enclosures?* London and New York: Routledge.

Ricketson S. 1987. *The Berne Convention for the protection of literary and artistic works: 1886–1986.* London: Centre for Commercial Law Studies, Queen Mary College, University of London.

Siegrist H. 'Geschichte des geistigen Eigentums und der Urheberrechte. Kulturelle Handlungsrechte in der Moderne', in Hofmann J. (ed.) 2006. *Wissen und Eigentum.* Bonn: Bundeszentrale für politische Bildung, 64–80.

Related essays
biodiversity; biopatents; counterfeit goods; genetically modified organisms (GMOs); indigenous knowledges; indigenous networks; information economy; intellectual elites; intergovernmental organizations; international non-governmental organizations (INGOs); Internet; League of Nations system; legal order; literature; music; nation and state; patents; publishing; Romanticism; theatre; trade; trademarks; translation; United Nations system; Vandana Shiva Research Foundation

Inter-American Commission on Women

In 1928 in Havana, Cuban and US feminists together pressured the Pan-American Union to establish a women's rights division. The Inter American Commission of Women / *Comisión Interamericana de Mujeres* (IACW/CIM), became the first transnational women's rights body centred outside of Europe and the first official intergovernmental women's organization (with representatives formally appointed by participating governments). In the 1930s, the IACW/CIM succeeded in getting its parent organization to pass an intergovernmental treaty ensuring independent nationality for wives. In the 1940s, IACW/CIM leadership passed out of the hands of US women and into those of Latin American feminists. The Commission also survived its host institution to become a division of the newly formed Organization of American States in 1948.

Given the collapse of European-based international feminist organizations, and the Cold War preoccupation of the US delegation, veterans of the IACW/CIM provided most of the leadership for women's rights in the early years of the United Nations, notably the successful campaign to establish a Commission on the Status of Women answerable directly to the UN Economic and Social Council. Former IACW/CIM president, Minerva Bernardino of Santo Domingo, served as chairwoman of this Commission from 1953 through 1955. The concentrated efforts of the UN during the Decade of Women (1975–85) somewhat overshadowed the IACW/CIM. But in 1994, the organization reasserted its pioneering role in setting intergovernmental women's rights policy by securing passage through the Organization of American States of a legally binding Inter American Convention on the Prevention, Punishment and Eradication of Violence against Women, which preceded by one year similar action by the UN.

Ellen Carol DuBois

Bibliography
Stoner K. L. 'In four languages but with one voice: division and solidarity within Pan American feminism, 1923–1933', in Sheinin D. (ed.) 2000. *Beyond the ideal: pan Americanism in inter-American affairs.* Westport: Praeger, 79–94.

Related essays
Abolition of Forced Labour Convention; Cold War; health policy; intellectual property rights; International Civil Aviation Organization (ICAO) and International Air Transport Association (IATA); pan-isms; United Nations decades and years; United Nations system; United Nations Women's Conferences; women's movements; World Conservation Union (IUCN) / World Wide Fund for Nature (WWF)

Intergovernmental organizations (IGOs)

Intergovernmental organizations (IGOs) are standing bodies or institutions created through formal agreements between states, whose respective governments constitute the organization's membership. Intergovernmental organizations, as identified from the early 19th century onward, may be distinguished from international congresses and treaty systems by their maintenance of permanent secretariats which perform implemental and often advisory functions for the organization. The United Nations and its precursor, the League of Nations, represent by far the largest intergovernmental organizations established to date, although almost a thousand intergovernmental organizations have come into existence over the past two centuries. Some intergovernmental organizations are open to all states, while others restrict their membership by interest or region. Their roles vary widely from coordinating technical functions to creating international policy to organizing peacekeeping forces.

The exponential growth in the number and scope of IGOs speaks to the persistence of the belief that permanent organizations are necessary to peacefully manage the shared interests of the growing number of nations on the planet. The proliferation of IGOs does not, of course, attest to their individual efficacy. IGOs with universal membership answer to nearly two hundred member governments, who rarely express unanimity in their views. The requisites of intergovernmental compromise and consensus thus make for heavy, slow-moving operations. IGOs remain, nonetheless, important points of intergovernmental contact. Each one of these behemoths is a multilateral forum that strives to keep member states engaged in some form of dialogue with each other.

Coming of age: a compact history of IGOs

The earliest example of a modern IGO is generally recognized as the Central Commission for the Navigation of the Rhine, established at the Congress of Vienna in 1815. While the Rhine Commission was made up mostly of German-speaking states, the Superior Council of Health, founded in Constantinople in 1838, already had a membership which spanned Ottoman and European states. In the 19th century, IGOs such as the International Telegraphic Union and Universal Postal Union came into existence as governments found that international cooperation was required in order to effectively manage these new forms of interstate trade and communication. In other cases, humanitarian and state interests intertwined when breakthroughs in epidemiology showed that the public health was an issue that transcended national boundaries, spurring the creation of transnational health organizations. The benefit of international legal cooperation was also gaining recognition. Following the Hague Peace Conference in 1899, the International Court of Arbitration was established to mediate disputes between states as well as other parties. The total number of intergovernmental bodies grew slowly at first, gaining momentum towards the end of the 19th century, by which point at least eleven IGOs had been established.

Awareness of the growing interdependence of national concerns was tragically compounded by the First World War, which was sparked by regional conflict that ignited a worldwide conflagration. Upon the conclusion of the war, the Treaty of Versailles established the League of Nations to facilitate the resolution of future conflicts in a peaceful manner. The League's creation in 1919 represented the largest intergovernmental endeavour yet, though US President Woodrow Wilson failed to bring his own country into the organization he helped to conceive. The League fostered the development of a number of specialized international organizations, which focused on technical, as opposed to political cooperation. Both pre-existing and newly formed intergovernmental institutions were brought into the League structure. They included the Permanent Court of International Justice (PCIJ), a Health Organization, the International Labour Organization (ILO), the International Committee on Intellectual Cooperation (ICIC) and the International Institute of Agriculture (IIA). IGOs being created around new technologies also developed outside of the League of Nations structure soon after the First World War. The International Commission for Air Navigation, set up in 1919, and the International Consultative Committee for Long-Distance Telephony are examples of such bodies.

Although the League, which had never been as strong as it was hoped, had largely collapsed by the outbreak of the Second World War, some of its technical agencies such as the ILO, the Health Organization, the Central Opium Board, and the League's transport and economic agencies continued to function at a minimal level, making temporary headquarters in North America. In 1946, when the League was officially dissolved, the United Nations system replaced and expanded upon the League's powers and responsibilities. With a membership that included the United States, the United Nations (UN) came to represent the world's largest intergovernmental organization. Much as the League had drawn international bodies which predated it into a formal relationship with the League, many IGOs that came through the Second World War or were formed after it were drawn into the orbit of the new UN system. The League's Health Organization and the ILO were brought in, as were the PCIJ, the IIA and the ICIC. The latter provided the foundation for the International Court of Justice (ICJ), the Food and Agriculture Organization of the UN (FAO) and the United Nations Educational, Scientific and Cultural Organization (UNESCO), respectively.

In the aftermath of the Second World War, new IGOs were formed to address the disastrous humanitarian situation in Europe. The United Nations Relief and Rehabilitation Administration (UNRRA), which later became the United Nations High Commission for Refugees (UNHCR), was established in 1943 in order to resettle European refugees, and the Provisional Intergovernmental Committee for the Movement of Migrants from Europe, now the International Organization for Migration (IOM), was founded in 1951 to orchestrate the logistics of postwar migrations. In order to provide food, clothing and healthcare for European children, the United Nations International Children's Emergency Fund (UNICEF) was established in 1946.

While humanitarian relief was the immediate focus of IGO attention after the war, the recent memory of Nazi genocide led to the articulation of universal human rights in the preamble to the UN Charter. In 1946, a Human Rights Commission was established in the UN's Economic and Social Council and, in 1948, the landmark Universal Declaration of Human Rights was approved, although the Soviet bloc, South Africa and Saudi Arabia abstained from voting on it. The UN's engagement with human rights exemplified IGO struggles to develop and promote universal norms or values while upholding the commitment to respect states' sovereignty. The UN's own Human Rights Commission lost much authority as it became apparent that states sitting on or leading the Commission were openly violating human rights at home. A separate Human Rights Council with stricter election standards was eventually established (2006) in an attempt to restore UN credibility in the field.

After World War 2, the overall responsibilities allotted to IGOs in terms of international law, finance, health, and food and agriculture grew considerably. The creation of UNESCO was one remarkable example of governments' commitment to cooperate not only around technical matters, but also on topics like school textbooks, which touched closely on issues of national identity. It was in part because of culture and education's relation to national identity that the formation of an IGO around these topics was so potentially interesting and conflict-laden. Less controversial organizations responsible for economic and financial cooperation and assistance or trade had already been created at the 1944 United Nations Monetary and Financial Conference held at Bretton Woods, New Hampshire. They included the International Bank for Reconstruction and Development (IBRD), the General Agreement on Tariffs and Trade

(GATT), and the International Monetary Fund (IMF). The IBRD was established as one of the five institutions composing what came to be known as the World Bank. The General Agreement on Tariffs and Trade, which emerged from Bretton Woods, became the World Trade Organization (WTO) in 1995.

The state of IGOs: representation and expansion

The organizations developed or remodelled by the Allied powers during and after the Second World War owe much of their current structure to the balance of world power as it appeared in late 1945. Like the League of Nations, the new UN bodies were not the product of universal consultation, but a system conceived among the war's victors. Axis power visions for regional and global organization had been dismantled in defeat and their new governments were eventually drawn into the postwar system. As the Cold War heated up, Soviet-bloc countries formed international organizations of their own, such as the Council for Mutual Economic Assistance (COMECON), which functioned from 1949 to 1991. Requiring unanimous agreement for all decisions and heavily influenced by Moscow, COMECON nonetheless exemplified another stream of states' proclivity to form intergovernmental organizations. The Non-Aligned Movement, which kicked off at Bandung in 1955, also anticipated permanent intergovernmental cooperation among its members, which failed, however, to materialize as concretely as hoped, relying instead on provisional secretariats in the home country of the chairman.

The common feature of all IGOs is, of course, their foundation on the basic unit of the nation state. Varied concepts of nation have influenced the formation of IGOs, just as they have influenced the shape of nations, especially new ones. American, British and French policy makers designing the League of Nations debated the criteria for nationhood and membership particularly as it should be applied to the inhabitants of the defeated empires. Control over these lands and populations was redistributed in the form of League mandates which were organized according to limited Eurocentric perceptions of the concerned groups' history, religion and race, and then ranked according to their estimated capacity for self-determination. Only twenty years after these new, protonational boundaries were imposed, however, war set the

world map open to further redefinition. So it was little wonder that the questions of who had the right to speak for whom in IGOs only multiplied with their scope and scale.

Representation at IGOs was not always restricted to government representatives, of course. Some IGOs, like the International Labour Office (ILO), the International Committee on Intellectual Cooperation (ICIC), the International Union for the Conservation of Nature (IUCN) and UNESCO have a history of including non-governmental representatives in their decision making. The ILO, founded on respect for the rights of workers, requires that one worker and one employer represent their country alongside two government-appointed representatives. The interwar ICIC based its decisions on the votes of prominent intellectuals considered representatives of their countries, though not necessarily their governments. This practice was adopted by the ICIC's successor, UNESCO, although the individual status initially attributed to those sitting on UNESCO's executive board was phased out as it became clear that executive board members were also representing their governments at UNESCO's General Conference, making the private and governmental stances nearly indistinguishable.

The cast of characters populating IGOs continued, nevertheless, to diversify, albeit largely in terms of governmental representation. As the rate of decolonization accelerated after World War 2, the attention of IGOs shifted from the rebuilding processes in Western Europe to the agenda of emerging states. The UN, which had taken over administration of what remained of the League's mandate system, became a site for international discussions of decolonization and national independence movements. The phenomenon of decolonization tested and reshaped the IGO community and generated normative pressures that helped to shape states in areas ranging from education and energy policies to their very constitutions. Offering states the possibility of quasi-democratic representative status on the global level, the IGO system lent incentive to groups to assert their independence in state form. This phenomenon was not entirely welcomed by the imperial powers which had established the intergovernmental system. North African attempts to discuss their independence agendas before the UN General Assembly and Security Council, for example, were opposed by France and the US, but achieved recognition, nevertheless, with support from future members of the Non-Aligned Movement, in an early instance of developing countries successfully building alliances through IGO mechanisms.

The so-called Third World gained considerable ground in IGOs during the 1960s and 1970s. In 1960 alone, 16 new African states joined the UN. The increased presence of African, Arab, and Asian states shifted IGO attention to the concerns of the developing world, ranging from the need for better models of development to the recognition of cultural heritage and diversity. By the mid 1970s, a host of IGOs had redirected their agendas towards development. After the first United Nations Decade for Development concluded (without having reached its goals) in 1970, UNESCO, for example, scaled up efforts to direct world attention to the need for more human-focused development policies that took account of different cultures. In order to boost recognition of the relationship between culture and economic development, and to assert its own relevance, UNESCO declared 1988–97 the Decade for Culture and Development and developed programmes to 'protect' cultural diversity. This general shift in IGO concerns – from humanitarian relief, to development, to culture and development – particularly the latter, further demonstrated the growing influence of the postcolonial states in the IGO system once so clearly dominated by European and North American powers. These states, which had initially provided the greatest backing for universal IGOs, in turn began to re-examine the relevance of their IGO involvement.

The significance of IGOs to their various member states and the people living in those states has varied dramatically. Membership in IGOs has often meant recognition and increased international leverage in global affairs for smaller states. On the other hand, critical elements of member states have vilified IGOs as encumbering and unnecessary attachments, particularly when IGOs take decisions opposed by the home government. The US, UK and Singaporean governments actually withdrew from UNESCO (in 1984, 1985 and 1986, respectively), in response to the organization's support for a New World Information and Communication Order, which looked to the opposed governments like an attempt to limit the amount of negative

news reporting allowed about developing countries. The withdrawal from UNESCO also reflected conservative sentiment in the US and UK that IGOs like UNESCO had become corrupt and anti-Western. Though both the UK (1997) and the US (2003) returned following organizational reform at UNESCO and political realignments at home, the damage to UNESCO's programmes and reputation was considerable. Bodies like the UN Security Council and the World Bank have tried to avoid alienating more powerful states by simply being less democratic in their division of power. Rather, they have allotted voting power to member states according to the scale (albeit an archaic one in the case of the Security Council) of global might and wealth. Going on the theory that some nations are more equal than others, this strategy has kept the major players engaged.

Slowly but surely, new IGOs have continued to develop in response to globally recognized issues. Of particular note are those focused on women and on the environment. After World War 2, many environmental concerns were treated within disarmament conferences concerned with the wholesale destruction of the human environment through nuclear warfare. The International Whaling Commission, founded in 1946, and the International Union for the Protection of Nature – later the IUCN – founded in 1948, however, were early examples of IGOs specifically focused on environmental protection. The inauguration of the United Nations Environment Programme (UNEP) in 1973, which followed the 1972 United Nations Conference on the Human Environment, marked a more advanced stage in intergovernmental recognition of the seriousness of environmental concerns. Women's rights experienced a similar breakthrough in 1975, when the United Nations First World Conference on Women called for the establishment of the United Nations Voluntary Fund for the Decade for Women. Established in 1976 and known as UNIFEM, the organization was set up to improve the living standards of women in developing countries, placing women's empowerment and gender equality at the centre of its efforts.

Structural issues: recurring themes in the world of IGOs

For all their diversity, IGOs face certain common structural issues. While the advantages and disadvantages of being founded upon and ultimately responsible to national governments have already been touched upon, other recurring issues of fundamental importance include the definition of an IGO's role or purpose and its structure; its location, language and secretariat; and its character and relationships with other entities.

The functions and the goals of IGOs are usually laid out in their founding agreement, constitution, charter or covenant. IGOs such as the UN have a broad mandate to maintain peace, while other, technical or functional IGOs pursue peace, or at the very least, improved relations between member states through missions in particular fields. As these IGOs have matured and the international climate has changed, however, they have reinterpreted their mandates in order to stay viable, as did UNESCO by shifting its emphasis to development and culture in the 1970s. IGOs compete with each other for territory, moving in to fill gaps left by other organizations. In this manner, both the OECD and World Bank moved into the field of education, in which neither initially specialized. Administrative styles, too, have changed, as UN bodies try to demonstrate their efficiency by applying 'results-based management' techniques to their activities and turn to private management consultancies to guide their reforms.

IGOs remain deeply hierarchical in their administration, with authority entrenched at headquarters. The locations of these headquarters reveal much about the power and history behind the organizations. Certainly, no other European city yet compares with Geneva as a centre for international organizations, a role begun with the establishment of International Red Cross headquarters there in 1864, and solidified by the arrival of the League of Nations in 1920. There are, to be sure, other IGOs headquartered in Paris, Vienna, Rome, Brussels and London, established through the invitation and support of the respective governments, which gain prestige and influence as the host nation. For instance, no one familiar with UNESCO headquarters in Paris and UNDP headquarters in New York could deny the strong local influences upon the working culture of either organization. Headquarters location is also deeply symbolic. The establishment of UN headquarters in New York and those of the IMF and World Bank in Washington, for example, marked not only a new stage of US engagement in international

affairs, but interrupted the traditional positioning of IGOs in Western Europe. It did not, however, alter the fact that the headquarters of universal-membership IGOs remained exclusively in Western centres of power. It has been easy to criticize this aspect of IGOs and at the same time hard to imagine them moving from the monumental headquarters and practical conveniences which these cities offer the organizations and government missions. IGOs do have various categories of field offices in countries and regions around the world where their programmes are executed, but most of the leadership and critical decision-making organs remain in Europe and the US. The positioning of UNEP (1972) and UN HABITAT (1978) headquarters in Nairobi, therefore, have stood out as exceptional gestures towards the decentralization of IGO authority.

Like the positioning of headquarters, the official and working languages of IGOs also reflect the balance of power and the history of their founding. The six official languages of the UN reflect the languages of the permanent members of the Security Council (English, French, Russian, Chinese), and also include Arabic and Spanish. The inclusion of Chinese, which was long the official language of a single member state (represented by Taiwan from 1949 to 1971), perhaps best represents the symbolic weight of official languages. UNESCO shares the UN's six official languages, but the FAO has five official languages (English, French, Spanish, Arabic and Chinese), the WTO three (French, English and Spanish) and the OECD two (English and French). While IGOs maintain a variety of symbolic official languages, the choice of the actual working languages is more significant. English and French are standard, although the IMF and World Bank use only English. In all cases, staff members are expected to be fluent in at least one of the working languages, though none is the official language of more than a handful of member states. While the use of English and French reflects the colonial history through which these languages came to predominate in transnational communication, it also represents a pragmatic decision that facilitates communication. It remains, nevertheless, a conundrum that the very critical work of these IGOs is executed through what is at best a second language for the majority of secretariat officers.

By definition, all IGOs maintain permanent secretariats staffed by international civil servants, sworn to serve the interest of the organization. While the secretariat is, in theory, a neutral, functional unit, the hiring and advancement of international civil servants is an undeniably political process motivated not only by the organizations' attempts to maintain a balanced distribution of nationals from the member states, but also by states' lobbying to place their candidates in influential positions. For high-level positions, which entail considerable diplomatic privileges and remuneration, it is no secret that candidates require the support of strategically important member states. Considerable challenges naturally arise if the leader of an organization later opposes the government to which he or she owes their position. Political obligations within secretariats are rarely so clear, however, and officers operate through networks of multilateral influence to manage the bureaucratic and diplomatic processes which at once define and confound the work of IGOs.

Another element crucial to the functioning of IGOs is the presence of non-governmental organizations (NGOs). The development and activities of IGOs are closely tied to their relationships with NGOs, which often play important roles in translating issues of transnational concern directly to the level of intergovernmental policy. IGOs such as the UN and UNESCO have institutionalized this intersection of state and civil-society interests by granting NGOs consultative status and even housing them on IGO premises. The symbiotic relationship between IGOs and NGOs is furthered when IGOs subcontract work to NGOs, which varies from running refugee camps to maintaining public relations, tasks which NGOs can often perform more effectively and inexpensively than bureaucratically encumbered IGOs. Another area in which civil-society partnerships have emerged are public–private partnerships, in which large corporations fulfil their corporate social responsibility agendas by working with IGOs to carry out specific projects that lie within the mandate of the organization, but cannot be financed or managed without extrabudgetary resources.

Though universal-membership IGOs linked to the League and UN systems have occupied centre-stage in studies of IGOs, considerable attention is turning to the potential of limited-membership organizations to be more effective than their larger cousins. Membership in these organizations is restricted to those states meeting certain regional, cultural or economic requirements, to name a few distinguishing factors of organizations like the European Union (EU), the Organization of the Islamic Conference (OIC), L'Organisation Internationale de la Francophonie (OIF) and the Organization for Economic Cooperation and Development (OECD). These intergovernmental structures define themselves in terms that distinguish their member states from others, giving them an exclusive character which fundamentally separates them from bodies striving for universal membership. They nevertheless work closely with universal-membership organizations in order to reinforce international cooperation around their interests. The EU stands out among these limited-membership IGOs for its degree of regional cooperation, which has become so deeply integrated that it approaches the status of a supranational authority.

In conclusion, IGOs remain a category of organizations generating high global expectations, but weighed down by awkward structures and protocols. While criticized for failures ranging from ineffectiveness to corruption, IGO achievements, such as persisting through the Cold War and facilitating cooperation around health, culture and the environment, attest to their continued usefulness as mechanisms for sustaining intergovernmental cooperation around global concerns.

Laura Elizabeth Wong

Bibliography

Barnett M. and Finnemore M. 2004. *Rules for the world: international organizations in global politics*. Ithaca: Cornell University Press.

Hoggart R. 'UNESCO and NGOs: a memoir', in Willetts P. (ed.) 1996. *The conscience of the world: the influence of non-governmental organisations in the U.N. System*, Washington, DC: Brookings Institution, 98–115.

Iriye A. 2002. *Global community: the role of international organizations in the making of the contemporary world*. Berkeley: University of California Press.

Kennedy P. 2006. *The Parliament of Man: the United Nations and the quest for world government*. London: Allen Lane.

Schiavone G. 1993. *International organizations: a dictionary and directory*. London: Macmillan (now Palgrave Macmillan).

Sluga G. 2006. *The nation, psychology and international politics, 1870–1919*. Basingstoke: Palgrave Macmillan.

Taylor P. and Groom A. J. M. (eds) 1977/1978. *International organizations: a conceptual approach*. London: Frances Pinter; New York: Nichols.

Related essays

Abolition of Forced Labour Convention; Acquired Immunodeficiency Syndrome (AIDS); arms sales; arms trafficking; birth control; book and periodical exchange; broadcasting; car safety standards; children's rights; city planning; climate change; Cold War; Comintern and Cominform; Commission on International Labour Legislation; conservation and preservation; consumer cooperation; crime; decolonization; developmental assistance; disarmament; displaced persons; drugs (illicit); Economic Commission for Latin America and the Caribbean (ECLAC); economics; electricity infrastructures; environmental diplomacy; environmentalism; epidemics; European civil servants; European Union (EU); expositions; financial diplomacy; fisheries; food safety standards; freshwater management; General Agreement on Tariffs and Trade (GATT) / World Trade Organization (WTO); genocide; germs; governance; Hammarskjöld family; health policy; human rights; humanities; indigenous networks; intellectual property rights; International Civil Aviation Organization (ICAO) and International Air Transport Association (IATA); international migration regimes; International Monetary Fund (IMF); international non-governmental organizations (INGOs); International Women's Day; internationalisms; investment; Islamic Scientific, Educational and Cultural Organization (ISESCO); justice; language; language diplomacy; League of Nations Economic and Financial Organization; League of Nations Health Organization; League of Nations system; legal order; loans; music; nation and state; national accounting systems; neoliberalism; North Atlantic Treaty Organization (NATO); oceans; Organization of Petroleum Exporting Countries (OPEC); pan-isms; Paris Club; patents; Pax Americana; police; population; public policy; radio; railways; refugee relief; regional communities; relief; services; sign languages; slavery; smallpox; Stockholm Conference; sustainable development; telephone and telegraphy; traffic signals; translation; transnational; transportation infrastructures; United Nations decades and years; United Nations Educational, Scientific and Cultural Organization (UNESCO) educational programmes; United Nations system; United Nations Women's Conferences; Universal Postal Union (UPU); vaccination; war crimes; Washington Consensus; women's movements; workers' movements; World Bank; World Conservation Union (IUCN) / World Wide Fund for Nature (WWF); world federalism; world heritage; world orders

International Civil Aviation Organization (ICAO) and International Air Transport Association (IATA)

The International Civil Aviation Organization and the International Air Transport Association, the first a specialized agency of the UN, the second a trade association performing regulatory functions, are twin pillars of the regime that has governed the air transport sector since the end of the Second World War. Both have contributed to the industry's spectacular postwar development. Linked since their creation, the closeness of their relationship is symbolized by the proximity of their global headquarters in Montréal.

Between the wars, aviation had been governed by two regional systems. One was based on the Paris Convention (1919), to which 38 states, mainly in Europe and Asia, adhered; the other on the pan-American Treaty of Havana (1928), signed by 21 states including the US. Both ICAO, which superseded these organizations, and IATA, the successor to the interwar International Air Traffic Association, find their origins in the 1944 Chicago Conference. Delegates were brought together at the invitation of the US to decide global principles and rules for commercial aviation as part of President Roosevelt's ambition to achieve lasting worldwide peace through structured international cooperation. Although delegates failed to agree a multilateral system for the economic regulation of the industry, a number of agreements were finalized, the most important of which was the Convention on International Civil Aviation (the 'Chicago Convention'), signed by 52 states. The first article of the

Convention, which enshrined the principle of absolute sovereignty, formed the cornerstone of the bilateral system that has regulated international aviation since the 1940s. The air services agreement signed by the US and Britain ('Bermuda I') in 1946, wherein the two governments set down the terms on which designated carriers from the two states could operate services between their respective territories, provided the template for subsequent bilateral accords, which multiplied thereafter.

Though the Chicago Convention created ICAO and entrusted it both with responsibility for developing 'the principles and techniques of international air navigation' and with fostering 'the planning and development of international air transport', the organization has been more successful with respect to the (first) technical aim than the (second) economic objective. Economic issues are discussed periodically within the organization, but regulation of commercial aviation remains in the power of governments, and in Europe in that of the European Union.

On the technical side, the ICAO secretariat under the direction of the Council maintains and updates the 18 annexes to the Convention that lay down standards and recommended practices, covering such subjects as personnel licences, airworthiness, security, and customs and immigration facilities. Commanding wide international assent, the adoption of these provisions has ensured high standards of safety and an almost complete absence of technical barriers to the provision of international air services. Respect for sovereignty is safeguarded since standards agreed within ICAO are promulgated as regulations by aviation authorities in the signatory states, while individual governments retain the power to impose more restrictive measures. Regulations are national, and enforced by national authorities, who decide whether an aircraft is airworthy, impose requirements on flight and cabin crew, regulate aviation infrastructure, and license air transport operators.

A global organization open to world airlines from states eligible for ICAO membership, IATA was formed in Havana in April 1945 after delegates to the Chicago conference decided that setting tariffs would be better managed by airlines than governments. The stipulation in 'Bermuda I' that the tariffs

charged on services between the contracting states should be those agreed within IATA, subject to the approval of both governments, became a standard provision of bilateral agreements worldwide. For thirty years, air fares across the globe were decided at biannual IATA tariff conferences and enforceable by law. A compliance department was responsible for detecting breaches and prosecuting airlines that stepped out of line, not only with respect to tariffs, but also quality of service, as exemplified by the infamous 'IATA sandwich'. Its tariff arrangements attracted the charge that IATA was effectively a cartel. The organization was forced into a retreat in the late 1970s, when challenged by US authorities to 'show cause' as to why it should continue to be exempted from US anti-trust law. It responded by reforming its rules. It introduced two categories of membership so that airlines could choose whether or not to participate in tariff conferences and it altered its internal decision-making processes.

IATA has made a major contribution to the development of international aviation by 'bringing order out of chaos, co-ordinating and synchronising the polyglot airlines', and forging 'the services of the world's airlines into an integrated world transport system' (Sampson 1984, 93). In providing a forum for discussion of issues of interest to its membership and performing technical functions through a series of standing committees, IATA has largely fulfilled its founding aims of promoting safe, regular and economical air transport, providing means for collaboration among air transport enterprises, and cooperating with ICAO.

Even if it no longer controls tariffs, IATA's influence remains significant. It would not be possible for a passenger to purchase a single set of tickets in one currency for a journey involving several airlines without IATA's clearing-house facility, which ensures that each airline receives the fraction of the fare owing to it. As well as continuing to provide the apparatus for multi-airline ticketing, IATA coordinates the complex network of interlocking airline schedules for each summer and winter season. The rates that governments approve under the terms of their bilateral agreements are still largely those discussed and agreed within IATA. Since the Association reformed its tariff procedures, there has been significant competition on discounted fares, subject to conditions that limit their availability and flexibility, but for both airlines and regulatory authorities the agreed IATA rate remains an important benchmark, particularly in regard to the fully flexible fare which many business passengers still require.

Both ICAO and IATA have expanded significantly since their formation. ICAO welcomed the newly independently states of Africa and Asia in the 1950s and 1960s. The Soviet Union, meanwhile, joined in 1970. IATA's membership swelled similarly as a result of decolonization. Also, though originally an association of international scheduled carriers that was concerned over significant periods to limit the opportunities for non-scheduled companies, membership is now open to its former competitors. Both ICAO and IATA have demonstrated great flexibility in responding to new challenges, whether technological, regulatory, political or environmental, and even with the development of powerful regional actors, such as the European Union, retain their centrality as genuinely global forums for governments and airlines.

Hussein Kassim

Bibliography

Naveau J. 1989. *International air transport in a changing world*. Brussels: Bruyland; London and Boston: Martinus Nijhoff.

Sampson A. 1984. *Empires of the sky: the politics, contests and cartels of world airlines*. London: Hodder & Stoughton.

Sochor E. 1991. *The politics of international aviation*. Iowa City: University of Iowa Press.

Staniland M. 2003. *Government birds: air transport and the state in Western Europe*. Boulder: Rowman & Littlefield.

Related essays

Amnesty International (AI); car safety standards; food safety standards; Greenpeace; human mobility; inter-governmental organizations; international non-governmental organizations (INGOs); International Red Cross and Red Crescent movement; Oxfam; Pugwash Conferences; Save the Children International Union; technical standardization; transportation infrastructures; United Cities and Local Governments (UCLG); United Nations system; world orders

International Maritime Conference 1853

The Brussels International Maritime Conference of 1853 is commonly considered a watershed event in triggering global understanding of ocean-surface phenomena.

Maritime trade and naval operations grew considerably during the early 19th century, as imperial and economic competition increased demands for safe, efficient and speedy navigation. New developments included better meteorological and oceanographic support in order to escape bad weather, gales and loss of ships and cargoes. Beginning in 1839, Matthew Fontaine Maury (1806–73), head of the US Naval Observatory, compiled all available meteorological and oceanographic data, using the logbooks of US Navy and later merchant ships. The resulting charts of surface currents and winds were provided to merchant captains in exchange for more data, resulting in gains in punctuality, speed and safety. First published in 1847, the charts were improved annually; after 1850 they were completed by the edition of *Explanations and Sailing Directions*. Such documents, called 'Pilot Charts', immediately became popular among shipmasters and owners since they shortened sailing journeys by many days. This first databank for environmental maritime parameters was nevertheless far from comprehensive. Not only were there missing data, but Maury quickly became convinced that an understanding of maritime weather required knowledge of continental meteorology, requiring international cooperation among national navies and merchant marines. He diagnosed the need for international standardization of tools, measurements and parameters among countries using different measurements, calendar organization and naval agendas. Maury began to pursue such cooperation with the result that the British government called upon US authorities to organize an international meeting.

Initially, Maury wanted to hold a global weather conference encompassing both oceanic and continental meteorology. Because of the lack of agreement among continental US meteorologists, Maury in 1851 launched a call for delegates to join an oceanic conference (to be held in Western Europe). He originally arranged for the conference to be held in France, a powerful nation with maritime interests, independent of British influence. The French had devised standards like the new metric-unit system (length, distance and volumes), new temperature units (°C = degrees Celsius), and a system for measuring tides. In addition, the French Minister of the Army and Navy, Dominique-François Arago (1786–1853), was a scientist (with expertise in astronomy and physics). But the turmoil of the post-1848 years in France made it impossible for Arago to arrange the conference in France, and Maury soon explored other options. He approached the Prussian scientist and explorer Alexander von Humboldt (1769–1859) and the Belgian mathematician Adolphe Quetelet (1796–1874). Belgium was a small country with great maritime history, major harbours and a developed maritime trade. Quetelet was also familiar with the project to establish a world meteorological organization. He was the director of the Royal Belgian Observatory in Brussels and Secretary of the Royal Academy of Sciences of Belgium. An astronomer, mathematician, statistician and economist, Quetelet had – as one of the few European members of the US National Institution for the Promotion of Sciences – been in touch with Maury since the early 1850s.

The conference Quetelet organized took place in Brussels in August 1853, under the aegis of the Royal Observatory and with the government's patronage. Quetelet arranged to have the conference occur at the same time as the First International Congress of Statistics, when 126 delegates from 26 countries were expected. In June 1853, Maury's last call for delegates included the information that the merchant ships of the participating countries were entitled to purchase the *Wind and Current Charts* issued by 'his' Naval Office in Washington.

The conference did not proceed without hiccups. The British government reluctantly answered the invitation, and British delegates skipped the first day of the conference, while the Danish representative did not show up before its last session. The delegates met from 23 August until 8 September. They reached an agreement on parameters to be observed (i.e. magnetic variation of the earth, sea currents, winds, clouds, rain, barometric pressure, temperature – air, water surface and depth – and seawater density). They discussed the instruments to be used and the system to record observations: each parameter found its place in a specially designed logbook in which additional phenomena could be declared. Standardization of tools and methods was to be the foundation for equalizing the quality of the measurements and making them perfectly comparable from one country and one part of the oceans to another. One of the consequences was the adoption of the Beaufort scale for measuring wind force. The conference issued a 126-page scientific report (prepared by Maury), an abstract of log samples and instructions for recording observations and measurements at sea. These and the minutes of the conference were sent to delegates and their governments within three weeks.

Immediately after the conference, participating countries began to contribute to data collection and were able to use US Naval Observatory documents to improve the routing of their fleets. The British, the most active maritime nation of the time, estimated in 1854 that the annual savings for their commerce would amount to US$10 million. The conference changed not only navigation, but also the professional roles of sailors: beginning with the navies of the participating countries, and quickly spreading throughout the world, officers took on the role of assistant scientists, providing measurements and observations in uniform logbooks. This progressively led to the building of a gigantic database of environmental parameters. Instead of constructing the first steps toward world meteorology, as Maury had wished, conference participants instead laid the foundation of modern oceanography.

Guy Houvenaghel

Bibliography

Houvenaghel G. ' Belgium and the early development of modern oceanography. Including a note on A. F. Renard', in Sears M. and Merriman D. (eds) 1980. *Oceanography: the past.* Berlin, Heidelberg and New York: Springer, 667–81.

Williams F. L. 1963. *Matthew Fontaine Maury: scientist of the sea.* New Brunswick: Rutgers University Press.

Related essays

Abolition of Forced Labour Convention; climate change; environmental diplomacy; life and physical sciences; mapping; measurement; oceans; statistics; steamships; Stockholm Conference; trade (manufactured goods); transportation infrastructures; United Nations Women's Conferences

International migration regimes

The movement of people has always been shaped by formal and informal rules, whether by (gendered) family strategies, institutional dynamics (career migration) or state legislation. Sometimes these rules aimed at restricting the movement of men and women, whereas otherwise migration was stimulated and left relatively free. In this entry I will mainly restrict myself to formal rules and use the term 'regime' to identify historical sets of regulations, specified in time and space.

Although commonly used in the past, by around 1860 most European countries (with the exception of Russia and the Ottoman Empire) as well as the United States had abolished passports and most migrants were more or less free to cross international borders. The relatively free Atlantic migration regime lasted until World War 1, when states started monitoring migrants from other countries and guarding their borders. Many believe that the involvement of national states in regulating migration then increased across the 20th century, creating a highly restrictive migration regime, with the US South (West), Southern Europe, Southeast Asia (Indonesians and Filipinos in Malaysia) and Japan as magnets of illicit movement.

Questioning the 'Golden age of migration', 1850–1914

The first regime that I deal with here is the well known era of free migration between the middle of the 19th century and the beginning of the First World War in the Atlantic. Although many of the Europeans who crossed the Atlantic in the second half of the 19th century were more or less free to leave their countries of birth and to enter the Americas, both in the North and in the South, they constitute only part of the migration story. At least six caveats should be made, as follows.

(1) The national states making up the so-called 'Concert of Europe' after 1815 were initially highly interested in migration and attempted to control and monitor 'foreigners', usually for political reasons and fear of revolutions. In addition, the early modern mercantilist tradition of restricting the exit of subjects persisted in some German states. Finally, states increasingly tried to keep out poor and destitute migrants by regulating the movement of alien 'vagrants' throughout Europe. The Habsburg Monarchy and German states (before the Unification of 1870) also monitored labour migrants in an effort to limit the burdens of poor relief. They demanded that working-class migrants carry official identification papers from their sending community, guaranteeing they were entitled to poor relief there. Belgian and Dutch authorities also insisted on some sort of identification for foreign labourers. In England, the Poor Law gave local authorities the power to send back internal migrants – notably the Irish – who applied for assistance.

(2) In the US, racism and nativism worked to restrict migration even in the 19th century. From 1819 onwards the federal government tried to reduce immigration by the various passenger acts, and in the 1830s US consular agents abroad were instructed to report on the alleged shovelling out of paupers by European states. Whereas Europeans were more or less free to choose their destination in the US, people from Asia increasingly faced restrictions. Chinese migrants were portrayed and racialized as the 'yellow peril', associated with coolie labour. Opposition started in the American West, during the 1850s Gold Rush, when European settlers protested against what they saw as unfair competition from Chinese workers. After 1882, the US barred the immigration of Chinese labourers (and after 1885 barred all contract labourers). The exclusion of the Chinese had a strong racist undertone and many Americans feared that the 'white race' would be overwhelmed by people of colour who were regarded as inferior. Racism, eugenics and social Darwinism joined forces and soon formed a powerful ideology in the white settler colonies, from America to South Africa and Australia, keeping coloured migrants out. As a result most Asian migrants either moved within colonial empires (30 million Indian who migrated temporarily to Southeast Asia or the Caribbean) or within Asia (30 million Chinese moving to Northern Asia). This racialized discourse soon touched Europeans too. By the 1880s in the US, concerns about the racial 'quality' of Eastern and Southern European immigrants fuelled a nativist movement that resulted in the Immigrant Restriction Acts of 1917 and 1924. The racialization and then restriction of European immigrants was closely related to their (perceived) status on the labour market.

(3) Migration within colonial empires, such as the British, French, Dutch and Portuguese was also heavily regulated. In general,

colonial subjects were not allowed to enter the colonial 'motherland' and were subjected to all sorts of coercive limitations when they wanted to move within the empire. The best known example is that of the Indian and Chinese coolies who partly replaced African slaves – as well as European indentured labour – in the second half of the 19th century, especially in the Caribbean (West Indies, Surinam, Haiti and Cuba), Mauritius, Natal and Fiji. But also within Asia, above all in the Southeast, migrants were not entirely free to move and often treated harshly in the regions where they were put to work. In fact, in the absence of a formal indenture system the bulk of the 30 million Indians who went to Southeast India and Ceylon were bonded in one way or another. The Kangani system in Malaya, the Maistry system in Burma or the Tundu system in Ceylon used debt and advances to tie down labourers to particular employers through the mediation of the labour contractors. Similar developments were under way in South Africa after the discovery of diamonds (Kimberley 1867) and gold (Witwatersrand 1886), where mine owners, backed up by the state, subjected ten thousands of black and Asian miners to a highly oppressive and restricted migration regime from the 1880s onwards. At the same time (neo)colonial links could foster migration to the core of the empire, as in the case of the Philippines. With the country occupied by Americans after a short war with Spain in 1898 it was stipulated that Filipinos were American nationals (not citizens) and therefore could enter the United States, until the Philippines became independent in 1946. This colonial backward linkage would become especially important in the process of decolonization after World War 2.

(4) Even migration between the colonial motherland and its colonies was highly regulated. Great Britain and France forced citizen criminals to move to penal colonies. Some 160,000 British convicts, sentenced for petty crimes such as vagrancy, were sent to Australia between 1788 and the 1860s. They were joined from the 1820s onwards by some 750,000 assisted migrant labourers under the auspices of the Colonial Office. Fearing migrants from China and the Pacific, from the 1860s onwards Australian authorities increasingly selected Europeans on the basis of occupation, religion, literacy, age, gender and familial status. This racist attitude towards the Chinese laid the foundation of the 'White Australia' policy, which developed under pressure of the labour movement, and by 1900 closed off migration from the Pacific Islands and China. Until the 1940s the official policy was to reserve Australia to free white British migrants. Apart from the exclusion of the Chinese in the US, comparable restrictions against Asian contract labour were imposed in British Columbia and New Zealand. Assisted migration to the colonies also included millions of European soldiers who left for the colonies: the French in North Africa (Algeria and Morocco) and Indochina, the British in India and South Africa, and various Europeans (mostly Dutch, German and Swiss) in the Dutch East Indies. Often disregarded in accounts of such movements are the millions of Russians who colonized Siberia in the period 1800–1914, most of whom were coerced in some way by the Imperial government.

(5) The freedom to migrate abroad did not extend to all. Especially in Russia a feudal system still bound an overwhelmingly peasant population to their villages. Even after the abolition of serfdom in 1861, obstacles to free movement remained considerable. Russia required internal passports for moves of more than 30 kilometres, and applications increased between 1860 and 1920, from 1.3 to 9 million. The Siberian frontier also attracted some 10 million migrants between 1880 and the 1920s. Still, compared with Western Europe the small percentage of the peasant population who actually moved over longer distances (5 per cent in 1900) is striking.

(6) Conclusions about migration regimes in the long 19th century need to take into account both Asia and Europe, both Atlantic and Pacific movements. In the second half of the 19th century in Asia two similar systems emerged which attracted equally large numbers of migrants as in the Atlantic: one in North Asia (Eastern Siberia, Manchuria and Japan), and one in Southeast Asia (the Dutch East Indies, Burma, Siam). From the 1850s onwards these Asian systems were firmly linked to the Atlantic by the process of economic globalization. Although in all three systems migrants were relatively free, as we have seen coercion seems to have been more important in the Southeast Asian case, not least because of the power exercised by European colonial rulers. After 1870, the streams became clearly compartmentalized

and segmented under the influence of racial taxonomies, through which European migrants predominantly remained within the Atlantic realm and some specific white settler colonies in the Pacific and South Africa, whereas the bulk of the Asian (especially Indian, Chinese) migrants moved within Asia. Only a small fraction of the total number of Asian migrants entered the Atlantic orbit, mostly as indentured workers in the Caribbean and Latin America.

Migration systems and the two world wars

The racialization of Asian migrants coincided with the growing aversion of organized labour in the US and Western Europe against foreign workers and led to a wave of restrictionist measures, during and immediately after the First World War. Although some countries, such as Argentina, the Netherlands and France still welcomed migrants until the 1930s, and the US turned a blind eye to the immigration of some 400,000 Mexicans in the 1920s, overall by 1918 a clear regime change had taken place. States increasingly and openly controlled or at least monitored migrants entering their territories and the legal and social distance between natives and foreigners became greater than ever before. At the same time subjects from the colonies who had acquired a legal right to enter the colonial 'motherland', like Algerians and Moroccans in France in 1914 (and thus became de facto citizens), were often subjected to a much greater monitoring and discriminatory treatment than the actual foreigners.

The change to a more restrictive migration regime is not so much explained by the war itself, as by developments in state formation and nation building. The most important factor was the increasing involvement of the central state in the social and economic domain. Whereas the 19th-century nation state had largely contented itself with basic tasks such as providing protection (police and army), education (schools), infrastructure and communication (roads, canals, postal service), the increasing democratization from 1850 onwards put great pressure upon the state to intervene in social and economic matters as well. Crucial was what became known in Europe as the 'social question' in the second half of the 19th century: the miserable condition of the working classes, represented by unions and political parties, from the left

but also the centre of the political spectrum. One of the areas in which states, especially in Western Europe, became more active was the provision of unemployment benefits, insurances for disabled persons and pensions for war veterans. Even in the United States, where the state was less willing to take over welfare arrangements from unions or other organizations, the idea that the state was responsible for the moral and material well-being of its citizens took root.

Within Europe these developments culminated during World War 1 in a rapid growth of the state in the social domain and the extension of democratic rights to the working class. With millions of men mobilized, fighting and dying in the trenches, unions and socialist parties had a strong bargaining position, as labour was scarce and strikes, especially in war-related industries, unwelcome. The establishment of a state-run system of welfare benefits made the issue of citizenship much more salient and resulted in demands from organized labour and others to draw a clearer line between citizens and foreigners in the national labour market or even to exclude immigrants altogether. In many cases this sociopolitical dynamic was reinforced by racist notions of some migrants' inferiority, as in the US, or by fear of foreign political extremists, especially in 1918 when Europe saw many revolutionary movements. In the US, where the discussion on the restriction of immigration from Europe had started already in the 1880s, and culminated in establishment of the Dillingham Commission in 1907, the quota laws of 1921 and 1924 greatly reduced the immigration from Southern and Eastern Europe. This policy change was not only supported by right-wing nativists and conservative unionists (such as the American Federation of Labor, AFL), but also by progressive intellectuals who were deeply influenced by eugenic ideas and demanded a restriction of the immigration from Southern Europe, because in their view these immigrants were largely illiterate and physically and morally unfit to become good American citizens.

During and immediately after World War 1 the changing character of the state also became apparent in other ways. As ethnocentric nationalism developed into the core feature of state building various states took to ethnic cleansing, either to exchange populations or kill them. Well known examples include the mass relocation and subsequent killing of hundreds of thousands of Armenian citizens by the Turks and the massive population exchange between Turkey and Greece in the early 1920s. Warring states, especially Germany, Russia and France, moreover, used their powers to mobilize soldiers from the colonies, both in Africa, India and Indochina, to fight or work behind the lines, or to force captured soldiers and other foreigners to work in factories and in agriculture.

When the borders had been redrawn and the refugee crisis gradually resolved in the first half of the 1920s, the laissez-faire era seemed to return, but very soon it became clear that the free migration era was over for good. Not only because of the emerging welfare states in the Atlantic, but also because of the global economic crisis from the 1930s onwards, most states became increasingly protectionist. Finally the relatively free migration regime was ended by the emergence of totalitarian regimes in Europe (Germany, Italy), Russia and Asia (Japan). This became especially visible when German Jews started to flee their country from 1933 onwards. Whereas their coreligionists from Russia had earlier faced few bars to entering countries like the US, France, Germany and Great Britain, German Jews in the 1930s were confronted with severe restrictions abroad. Both Western Europe and the Americas followed a very restrictive policy and tried to admit as few as possible. The interference of states with migration increased massively during the Second World War when dictatorial states like Nazi Germany and Russia under Stalin and fascist Japan used their powers to move millions of people: either to kill them (like the Jews and Gypsies), to put them to work in labour camps and factories, to use them as soldiers or to resettle entire populations for various nationalist, racist, and political reasons. Finally, when the war ended unprecedented numbers of refugees and displaced persons were scattered over Europe, creating a refuge crisis that outstripped the one after the Great War.

Restructuring migration regimes

The era after the Second World War was itself a period of dramatic, large scale and usually forced population movements, both in Europe and Asia. Whereas in Eastern Europe emigration to the Western world was severely restricted (apart for Jewish citizens in certain periods), in the Western part of Europe

the thirty years of continuous economic growth and prosperity, between 1945 and the mid 1970s, constituted a contradictory interlude. Although nation states introduced strict migration controls and reinstituted or expanded welfare provisions, they also unconsciously paved the way for a huge permanent settlement of newcomers, both from other European nations as well as from Asia, the Caribbean and Africa. Germany received millions of German-speaking refugees from Eastern and Southeastern Europe and later on newcomers from Russia who could prove a German ancestry, the so-called *Aussiedler*. Other Western European states faced the demographic consequences of their colonial pasts. In 1950 an unexpected influx of colonial immigrants arrived in the United Kingdom from the West Indies, India and Pakistan (and later on East Africa and Bangladesh); the Netherlands saw the arrival of Eurasians from Indonesia and later of former slaves and indentured labourers from Surinam; to France came ex-colonials from Algeria, Morocco, Indochina and West Africa. They were followed by 'guestworkers' from Southern Europe, North Africa and Turkey who sought work in Northwestern European countries. Whereas the colonial migrants came unexpectedly, most guestworkers (predominantly, but not exclusively, men) were invited. Against all expectations, they stayed on and called for their families when in the 1970s the economic growth finally came to a halt. This unexpected mass settlement of guestworkers, predominantly from non-European countries, was regarded as undesirable by the receiving states. Due to what is now known as the 'liberal paradox', they were however forced to accept these newcomers: having entered liberal democracies and welfare states guestworkers had built up both legal and social rights, which laid the basis of a permanent stay and the right to bring over their families. Thus millions of Turks and Moroccans, to mention the most important groups, settled permanently in Scandinavia, Germany, Austria, France, Belgium and the Netherlands. Although most states had tried to prevent permanent settlement from the 1970s onwards some 10 per cent of Europe's total population in 2000 was foreign-born.

Japan, too, rose from its ashes in a spectacular way after 1945, but it solved its demand for labour only partly by importing it. Japan turned to the offspring of Korean and Taiwanese migrants who had entered the country during the period of the empire. A second source was female labour. In contrast to Western Europe, Japanese women were mobilized on a large scale, so that immigration of foreigners, which was resisted for ethnocentric reasons, could be avoided. After 1980, however, foreign immigration, both legal and illegal, rose – with the bulk coming from nearby Asian countries.

In the US the temporary work scheme for Mexican migrants, the Bracero Program that started off in 1942, rekindled a migration from Latin America temporarily suspended in the 1930s that continues until today. With the end of the Bracero system in 1964 and the imposition of visa quotas on Mexico, increasing numbers entered the country illegally or overstayed their visas; still most found work and many stayed on permanently, helped by occasional legislative amnesties and employers' demand for temporary work visas in agriculture. Even draconian restrictive measures did little to stem the tide; their chief effect was not to deter migrants but to discourage migrants from returning home – the costs of re-entering had become much too high.

The American 1965 Immigration Act facilitated large-scale legal immigration that marked the end of the quota acts of the 1920s. There was a sharp upswing in Asian (especially Chinese and Indian) migrants to the US, Canada and Australia. Finally American's military involvement in Asia (Korea, the Philippines, Vietnam, Laos, Cambodia) engendered migrations somewhat similar to the postcolonial movements in Europe. Both the refugees generated in these areas and the women who marry American military personnel make these migrations more female-dominated than most of the Europe-bound postcolonial migrations.

A third major attraction pole (besides Western Europe and North America) was the Persian Gulf, where the booming oil industry increased the wealth of the population and simultaneously stimulated the demand for both industrial and service sector workers, men and women, most of whom came from Asia (India, Pakistan) and East Africa. The difference with Europe and the America's was that these guestworker programmes lacked the surrounding welfare state and humanitarian agreements that influenced Europe. Migrants in the Gulf had virtually no rights and could be expelled when deemed necessary. Finally the Asian Tigers, such as Hong Kong, Taiwan, South Korea, Malaysia and Singapore attracted large numbers of migrants from surrounding Asian countries.

Contemporary developments and the effects of globalization

During the last decades of the 20th century most Western countries (including Australia) have become very restrictive towards non-Western migrants, but with important differences. Whereas Western Europe (which through the enlargement of the European Union draws Eastern Europeans legally), tries to keep out non-Europeans, Spain and Italy are confronted with massive illegal migration from Africa, but also from Asia and Eastern Europe. Much like the US, both countries allow foreigners to work and at times organize mass legalisations of formerly illegal residents. A third type of migration system is represented by Canada and to some extent the United Kingdom and the US, where immigration as such is primarily seen as an economic stimulus. In order to attract those who fit best in the labour market, Canada developed a selective points system that puts a premium on skills and education – a principle that was already used by British dominions and South Africa after World War 2.

Comparing the relatively laissez-faire 19th century regimes (1870–1914) governing migration with those in today's world (1965–90), interesting differences become apparent. Notwithstanding ongoing globalization, transport and communication revolutions, the relative volume of current world migrations (measured as the crossing of national boundaries) is probably somewhat lower than a century ago. A mix of migration controls, the inability of people in the poorest part of the world population to migrate, and the unexpected effects of welfare state systems, produces this result. At the same time, inequalities between poorer and richer parts of the world have grown. Finally the number of women migrants, who nowadays account for more than half of the migrants, has substantially increased. And even when they stay put, they are important, because they force men to return and engage in circulatory systems, especially in Asia. Another interesting aspect of female migration is the globalization of care and service work (servants, nannies, nurses, prostitutes), making it possible for women from poorer parts of the world

(Asia, Eastern Europe and Latin America) to work in countries with a great demand for low-paid work in gendered sectors of the labour market.

For centuries and long before the Industrial Revolution international migrations were at the core of economic development. Migrations have survived and continued under a wide variety of regimes to govern human movement and are unlikely to cease, even under the most restrictive of regimes.

Leo Lucassen

Bibliography

Fahrmeir A. et al. (eds) 2003. *Migration control in the North Atlantic world: the evolution of state practices in Europe and the United States from the French Revolution to the Inter-War period.* Oxford and New York: Berghahn.

Gozzini G. 2006. 'The global system of international migrations, 1900 and 2000: a comparative approach', *Journal of Global History*, 1, 1, 321–41.

Hoerder D. 2002. *Cultures in contact: world migrations in the second millennium.* Durham, NC and London: Duke University Press.

Lucassen J. and Lucassen L. (eds) 1997. *Migration, migration history, history: old paradigms and new perspectives.* Bern: Peter Lang.

Manning P. 2005. *Migration in world history.* London and New York: Routledge.

McKeown A. 2004. 'Global migration 1846–1940', *Journal of World History*, 15, 2, 155–89.

Moch L. P. 2003. *Moving Europeans: migration in Western Europe since 1650.* Bloomington: Indiana University Press.

Zolberg A. 2006. *A nation by design: immigration policy in the fashioning of America.* Cambridge, MA and New York: Harvard University Press and Russell Sage Foundation.

Related essays

agriculture; anarchism; Chinese Diaspora; contract and indentured labourers; decolonization; displaced persons; domestic service; empire and migration; empires and imperialism; ethnicity and race; eugenics; exile; forced migrations; globalization; gold; guestworkers; health policy; human mobility; individual identification systems; labour migrations; marriage; money; oil; police; population; railways; refugee relief; refugees; rubber; rush migrations; temporary migrations; transnational; war; welfare state; white men's countries; workers' movements; world orders

International Monetary Fund (IMF)

The International Monetary Fund (IMF, or the Fund) is an organization which has overseen global financial stability since its establishment under the Bretton Woods accords of 1944. By promoting monetary cooperation among its 184 member countries, which it annually surveys to determine the economic health and prospects of each, the IMF provides a structure for the freer flow of money, goods, and services across borders that, in turn, promotes employment and growth and combats poverty worldwide. Facilitating financial stability, the IMF works with nations and non-state entities to foster official and transnational transactions in the global economy, with a decidedly American, free-market bent. Because of its overweening economic strength after the Second World War, the United States managed to make the Bretton Woods system an instrument for its objectives of reducing barriers to trade and finance around the globe and compelling adoption of its open-door policy, which, by the end of the Cold War, would be entrenched in the process of globalization. But while the ideology leaned toward America, so did the non-governmental power of the Fund. IMF advisors, from the outset of the Fund, emerged as third-party professionals who intervened in countries around the world with technical economic assistance. By doing so, they participated in the transnational financial networks that grew after World War 2.

From its inception, the IMF has influenced the course of the global economy by, above all, providing the necessary regulatory mechanism for world finance. Its roots lay in Great Depression-era protectionism and financial autarchy when nations curbed imports, failed to stabilize exchange rates, and used the gold standard to devalue currencies. The proliferation of national trade and monetary controls during the 1930s led to a deflationary spiral that shrank demand, incomes, and employment. This global crisis, linked to the belief that the precipitous decline in international commerce had propelled nations toward World War 2, led leaders to convene at Bretton Woods, New Hampshire (USA), under the auspices of the United Nations Monetary and Financial Conference. Twenty-nine countries agreed to Articles of Agreement creating the IMF and International Bank for Reconstruction and Development (World Bank), which took effect on 27 December 1945. The actual operations of the IMF began on 1 March 1947. The goal was to relieve the world of national economic restrictions and, while safeguarding domestic employment and growth, allow market mechanisms to prevail in the world economy.

Negotiations regarding the scope and purpose of the IMF occurred mainly through talks between the United States and Great Britain, and their respective spokesmen, namely Harry Dexter White of the US Treasury Department and British economist John Maynard Keynes. They argued not over the need for financial regulation, for both White and Keynes staunchly supported government intervention and intergovernmental collaboration in the world economy. Rather, Keynes understood that the declining status of his country, especially in the face of rising American hegemony and the crisis of deflation in Britain, demanded that he protect British fortunes by promoting economic growth through a vigorous, activist IMF. He determined to end the gold standard and create a new currency. For his part, and along the lines of US free-trade ideology, White preferred to encourage price stability by restricting the authority of the IMF and pushing for a multilateral approach that veered in the direction of laissez-faire rather than Keynesian-style management of economies. In essence, the big issue centred on whether the IMF would become the world's central bank, with an ability to create new reserves of money that would boost international liquidity (Keynes' plan), or whether it would serve as a more limited borrowing mechanism (the White position). Worried about deflation, Keynes demanded that creditor nations, like the United States, assume more of the burden of correcting balance-of-payments problems by importing more goods from debtor countries. Fear of inflation drove White to counter that responsibility for a payments imbalance lay with the debtor nations.

Because of the sheer power and wealth of the United States at the end of World War 2, White prevailed, although the Keynesian approach of taxation and currency devaluation remained in effect. Headquartered in Washington, DC, the IMF followed (and adheres to to this day) a policy of controlling inflation through a fixed, limited pool of national currencies. Each IMF member contributed to a fund, according to a quota system calculated on their size and ability to pay, by payments in gold and a currency that could be converted into gold. This latter requirement elevated the dollar as the dominant currency of the world since it was the only money that central banks would convert from gold at the time. From the pool of quota subscriptions, the IMF made loans needed to stabilize nations experiencing economic problems; that is, when there was a 'fundamental disequilibrium' that demanded currency devaluation. Each member nation could also withdraw one-quarter of its subscription to address its own difficulties and could request additional funds when necessary. The higher the quota in the IMF, the higher the amount of money the country could borrow. Thus, America, with the biggest quota, remained the most powerful entity in the Fund.

That structure played to American strengths. The IMF was designed to alleviate payments imbalances by discouraging nations from resorting to deflationary measures to avoid depression but there were limits on the loan policy. With the US Treasury monitoring the IMF, the Fund tried to ensure that no nation would run into a deep debt. Rules required that a country pay back its IMF debt within five years after it exercised its 'special drawing rights', but most loans were called in earlier. Furthermore, the United States guided the IMF's ideology in the direction of ending exchange controls and currency blocs (such as the British sterling system) as well as protectionist barriers to trade. Finally, policy decisions made in the IMF were based on weighted voting, rather than a procedure of one country, one vote. The 'weight' derived from the size of the quota in the Fund account, and thus the US held predominant power. Harry Dexter White became the American representative to the IMF, but in the absence of a permanent director in 1946, he served, essentially, as the manager of the Fund in its first year before Belgian Camille Gutt took the helm. There has never been an American managing director but an unwritten agreement prescribes that a European runs the IMF while an American heads the World Bank. Thus, the advanced industrial nations, and specifically the United States and Europe, dictate the course of the IMF.

Since World War 2, just as it reformed the international capitalist economy, the IMF itself underwent reforms due in particular to globalization, the addition of new members from the Soviet bloc and the Third World (which expanded the original membership of 44 countries at the IMF's inception), and the rapid transformation in capital and commercial markets. One major crisis came in 1971, when the Nixon administration decided to unpeg the dollar from the established, fixed exchange rate of US$35 per ounce of gold. By doing so, the United States led the world toward floating exchange rates, where currencies fluctuated according to market demands. This monumental change, many experts believe, prompted the rapid expansion of globalization, as private institutions and even individuals started to buy and trade more freely than before in the world economy. Closing the 'gold window,' therefore, boosted the power of transnational players in the global financial system. These adaptations, however, also planted the Fund more firmly in the grounds of neoliberal, capitalist ideology and practices. That has earned the organization criticism from around the world, but especially from developing nations struggling to meet American (and European) free-market demands.

Opposition became evident as the Cold War ended in the late 1980s and then blossomed with the anti-globalization movement from 1999 onward, much of it centred on Third World development. The framers of the original Articles of Agreement at Bretton Woods had ruled out any attempts to distinguish between groups of members in terms of wealth, and thus a phrase offered by the Indian delegation alluding to special assistance for the underdeveloped nations was vetoed. Development, however, would become a major issue, especially by 1963, when IMF membership shot up from 68 to 101 countries. Critics charged that the IMF, and thus the US, favoured military dictatorships, which granted benefits to corporations, over socialist-leaning nations and leaders, who demanded consideration for democratic values, labour rights, and human rights. Throughout Latin America in the late 1970s to the mid-1990s, severe debt caused by skyrocketing inflation appeared to be a systemic issue. Such criticism launched a debate over whether economic stability was a precursor to democracy, as argued by the IMF, or vice versa, as stated by the opposition.

The dissent became especially pronounced during the debt crisis of the 1980s. The Fund required members who sought loans or the reduction or forgiveness of an overdue IMF credit, to raise taxes and undertake other fiscally burdensome measures under so-called 'austerity programmes' to balance their budgets. This meant that governments, particularly in the developing world, would cut back welfare programmes, subsidies, development projects and other social spending popular with citizens and deemed essential to fighting poverty. Some associate these austerity measures with a decline in living standards, and raising taxes in a weak economy actually contradicted Keynesian prescriptions. The IMF came under repeated attack for its rigidity that, ironically, worsened balance-of-payments problems.

Furthermore, examples emerged in which IMF austerity programmes backfired, worsening the debt positions of Third World nations and, thus, aggravating poverty. For instance, Malawi followed IMF and World Bank advice regarding national 'structural adjustment' of its economy from the early 1980s. This included trade liberalization and privatization of state-owned enterprises. The results placed the struggling nation on a sounder fiscal basis, but critics also blame a famine in 2002 on such austerity measures. Likewise, budget restrictions in Argentina, which had been a model of IMF reform during the 1990s, caused such hardship that by 2001, the nation's economy collapsed. The Menem administration had devalued the peso in the early 1990s in order to bring rampant inflation in line. This worked, and foreign investment poured into the country as the flow of European finance, in particular, soon dominated Argentina's banking sector. Privatization of the nation's resources also occurred. But austerity measures chipped away at public spending to the extent that the government cut health and education programmes. When the economic crisis hit, Argentina defaulted on its IMF loan repayments. A leftist administration righted the economic ship but not before the Fund's reputation was further stained by failure.

Because of its uneven record in alleviating poverty and its role in worsening economic problems, the IMF and its sister organization, the World Bank, became targets of dissent especially in Latin America, and to a lesser extent Africa. Austerity programmes and lending policies actually provoked such rancour that hostility against the IMF helped elect leftist and populist governments in Latin America. While the Fund might have been a victim of political grandstanding, it also became a representative of the inequities of American free-market policies and of the process of globalization. Critics charged the Fund with an inability to prevent crisis; the IMF seemed able only to step in with a harsh solution. Also, the record shows that over one hundred countries have suffered a banking collapse since 1980, and the blame rested, in part, on IMF ideology and practices.

Still, scholars also view the IMF's role as essential to maintaining economic health and, since the early 1990s, to easing conflict around the world. IMF officials are viewed as political actors who can use stabilization policies to prevent the use of arms. For instance, Fund technical assistance created a central banking system in the Balkans in 2000 that worked to overcome the exclusionary banks of Bosnian Muslims, Croats, and Serbs. In this way, IMF economists provided professional assistance, yet another way that the Fund became a transnational force. This raises new challenges for the IMF regarding its accountability to regions, nations, and peoples on nearly all issues of economic governance.

Thomas W. Zeiler

Bibliography

Black S. *Life and debt*. Documentary film. New York: New Yorker Video, 2001.

James H. 1996. *International monetary cooperation Since Bretton Woods*. Washington, DC: International Monetary Fund.

Vines D. and Gilbert C. L. 2004. *The IMF and its critics: reform of global financial architecture*. Cambridge: Cambridge University Press.

Related essays

debt crises; debt crises (developing countries); democracy; developmental assistance; developmental taxonomies; dollar; Economic Commission for Latin America and the Caribbean (ECLAC); economics; financial centres; financial diplomacy; financial markets; industrialization; intergovernmental organizations; investment; League of Nations Economic and Financial Organization; loans; money; neoliberalism; Pax Americana; taxation; trade; trade agreements; underdevelopment; United Nations system; Washington Consensus; World Bank

International non-governmental organizations (INGOs)

'Non-governmental organizations' (NGOs) is a phrase that developed after 1945 in the ambit of the United Nations agencies, to name all that was not a mere element of the governmental systems of member nations. This definition by default was pushed into the Charter during the UN San Francisco Conference by the civic groups' representatives included as consultants to the official US delegation. According to Article 71 of the UN charter, the UN Economic and Social Council (ECOSOC) was allowed to 'make suitable arrangements for consultation with non-governmental organizations which are concerned with matters within its competence'. The term became part of the vocabulary used by groups who wanted to develop a working relationship with the UN, UNESCO and the other intergovernmental agencies that adopted the Article 71 terminology. Even groups that have thrived under a distinct legal tradition, such as the Catholic groups which have adopted the status of private International Catholic Organizations as defined by articles 321–329 of the 1983 Code of Canon Law, are eager to call themselves non-governmental organizations. There are several characteristics that make these organizations of importance for those who try to follow circulations and connections across national units: their programmes, their partnerships, their memberships, their funding, their aspirations, all of which frequently extend beyond one country. International non-governmental organizations (INGOs) that share one or several of these characteristics are the subject of this entry.

The previous generation of intergovernmental organizations, which had no specific mechanism to deal with such bodies, had called them 'semi-private' 'voluntary' or 'unofficial' organizations, though the phrase 'non-government organizations' was used in the early 1920s by some labour activists connected to the International Labour Office and the International Association for Labour Legislation. These groups have had other terms to describe themselves, such as 'international associations', or from the late 1970s 'transnational associations', while their name flagged words such as 'union', 'conference' or 'council'. But they progressively adopted the UN denomination in their public presentation and working vocabulary, especially from the 1970s when it rang true with some groups' intention to distinguish themselves from governments and from intergovernmental organizations. Nevertheless, the 1945 terminology quickly broke up into a myriad of subcategories. Acronyms flourished to match the variety of organizational forms, memberships, and purposes, such as GRINGOs (government-regulated and initiated NGOs), GONGOs (government-industrial NGOs), BINGOs (business-organized NGOs) or DONGOs (donor-industrial NGOs).

Social science researchers have contributed to this abundance, creating ad hoc typologies to study particular questions and aspects. 'Transnational advocacy networks', 'global social movements', 'issue networks', 'transnational activism', 'principled issue movements', 'transnational coalitions' are some types which have been distinguished from 'international non-governmental organizations'. Despite this flourishing cottage industry of labels, the recent explosion of scholarship has focused on a very limited chronological range (mostly from the late 1970s onwards), and on a limited number of 'blazing' fields and groups (development, human rights, environment, humanitarian relief) at the expense of NGOs in sports, business or disputable moral causes. The formidable expansion of this field of study, which has created its own forums with journals like Voluntas, has not yet explored the breadth of its variety. Monographs are still scarce, and studies are very much focused thematically and chronologically. Together with Margaret Keck and Kathryn Sikkink, Sidney Tarrow is among the few social scientists to engage with historical transnational voluntary organizations from the early 19th century, while Steve Charnowitz and Akira Iriye are the only ones who have recently attempted to grasp the development of voluntary groups from the 19th to the 21st centuries, expanding previous overviews such as Lyman Cromwell White's International non-governmetnal organisations (1951) or Francis Stewart Lyons's Internationalism in Europe (1963). This entry will adopt such a catholic spirit for its chronological and typological extension.

Another salient common feature of the literature about voluntary organizations is the teleological or millennarian statement that the growing number of these different organizations attests to a quasi-linear march towards world society since the beginning of the modern age. Some underscore the role of non-governmental organizations as handmaidens of globalization, others stress their activity as a resistance to the latter, most view INGOs as 'good' in nature, and by and large few detract from the idea of a trend towards 'global civil society' fostered by non-governmental organizations.

INGOs scholarship is still, by many aspects, very close to the home-made glorious founding narratives which INGOs themselves have produced. One aspect of this immature character is that all researchers in the field are elaborating upon the data of the Union of International Associations (UIA), without acknowledging that this international association, a creation of Paul Otlet and Henri La Fontaine in 1907, has been an active protagonist of international voluntary organizing, that it developed its statistical perspective retrospectively for the 19th century, and that its categories are framed by its cooperation with the League of Nations, and later with the UN ECOSOC NGO committee.

There are a number of studies which have elaborated detailed tables and charts from UIA data. Though it still suffers from some statistical fallacies because of the absence of a reflection on UIA data and typology, the study by Boli and Thomas is the most complete, and offers stimulating charts and graphs on the chronological, thematic and geographical evolution of non-governmental organizations since 1875. For this entry, lest it should fall into a mere paraphrasing of their explorations, it may be enough to stress the overall numerical expansion of INGOs, though non-linear and uneven, the geographical focus of headquarters in a limited number of cities (Paris, Brussels, London, New York, Geneva), or the growing importance of non-Western countries' nationals in INGOs' memberships and in the creation of new INGOs. This essay will, instead, assume an exploratory dimension and focus on two aspects of the modern history of voluntary organizations, among so many which have attracted the attention of researchers.

Charts and faces

INGOs have mostly been studied for their discourse, impact or programmes but rarely for their mode of operation. We know very little about the historical evolution of their financial situation, staffing, or organizational culture. While a comprehensive view is far from possible here, the focus will be on organizational lines and personnel.

Membership of INGOs has been and is still mediated by national lines in most cases. National sections or branches have been created as a convenient way to manage membership and funding, and as an acknowledgement of the importance of the national in voluntary action, both as a scene and as a target. This national character was also dictated by the existing legal frameworks for private and voluntary activities. Belgium was the first nation to create a legal status for international associations (1919), before the Council of Europe presented its member states with a European Convention on the Recognition of the Legal Personality of International Non-Governmental Organizations (Convention No. 124, 1986). Some voluntary groups have tried to breach this organizational nationalism, and the Women's International League for Peace and Freedom imagined a 'world section' in 1924, with some of its leaders fancying it would be a 'psychological laboratory' to disconnect national affiliations. But the national-branches plan was the basic scheme that was promoted by international organizers such as Paul Otlet and Henri Lafontaine, and even recent groups have overwhelmingly developed along national lines. Accordingly, it is national sections that are represented in the governing bodies of INGOs, and the 'one member / one vote' principle that governs their life has often turned out to be 'one national section / one vote'. This feature has established the national dimension as a central aspect of international associations' politics. Many of the conflicts that straddled their life, be they of professional, ideological or conceptual origin, were mediated through national lines, or at best had to overlap with them. Accordingly, INGO politics was often stemmed from or dressed as national rivalries as attested by famous Shenanigans within the Fédération Internationale de Football Association (FIFA) and International Olympics Committee (IOC). One of these struggles for national domination of INGOs took place in the 1930s and opposed US civic groups, that wanted to seize international societies' imagination, to the Nazi government, which sought to capture their apparatus. The battle raged on several fronts: the International Criminal Police Commission, the International Union of Local Authorities, the International Institute of Administrative Sciences, or the International

Union for the Scientific Investigation of Population Problems. Both sides won, it can be said, but one victory was more durable than the other. This contest developed in the open field, but mostly in the dull areas of agenda control, fixation of membership fees, board meetings or nominations to executive and honorary positions. The governance mechanisms of voluntary groups became weapons for both sides.

Since the middle of the 19th century, the inner life of voluntary groups, international or other, has extensively been moulded over the general framework of parliamentary regimes, with a distinction between a legislative branch (assembly) and an executive branch (council/committee) topped with a collegial leadership (board). There has been a number of variations on this scheme, though it remains unclear whether this matrix was equally successful among the groups which were bolstered by the Eastern Bloc during the Cold War, or among the voluntary groups which emerged in Africa or Asia more recently. Catholic organizations have maintained some links with the church hierarchic organization that balanced the democratic factor, and so did Muslim relief groups which are financed by the Saudi monarchy or the Sudanese state. Within this wide framework, the informal political, professional or cultural networks that are crystallized in a given organization have given birth to different organization cultures. During the interwar years, for example, organizations with a large membership among Continental European socialist parties and political personnel, like the International Union of Local Authorities, followed the rule of majority opinion to take their decisions, while the architects, civil servants and city planners of the International Garden Cities and Town Planning Federation relentlessly sought compromise and consensus.

Very often, the coming of age of voluntary groups went hand in hand with incremental changes in organization. A classic pattern was the evolution from sporadic to regular meetings, which solidified informal networks of individuals with a similar interest or purpose, followed by the creation of a 'permanent committee' to organize these meetings, and later by the establishment of a regulated governance system with elected officers. This was especially true in scientific groups which began to expand from the 1850s after initial gatherings during World

Fairs, like the Congress of Statistics. But some groups lived for years under the charismatic leadership of an energetic individual and founder, such as Frances Willard for the World's Women's Christian Temperance Union (WWCTU) in the late 19th century, Jean-Marie Bressant at the United Towns Organization from the 1950s to the 1980s or Abdallah Suleyman al'Awad at the Islamic African Relief Agency (1981). These examples attest to more autocratic rules for internal discussion and decision making.

The governance question often crystallized around the issue of headquarters. Creating a headquarters was an act of faith in the cause defended by the organization (e.g. the project of a 'Women's Temple' for WWCTU), but also a strong organizational, intended designed to hold the community together and manifest its presence to the world. It was no accident that, in the 1920s, more and more organizations created their headquarters in Geneva: three international associations were located in the Swiss city in 1919, and 60 in 1930. The IWLPF with its *Maison Internationale* in 1919 and the International Council of Nurses in 1925 were among those who saw increased opportunities for international understanding from a location in neutral Switzerland, and from the propinquity to the League of Nations or the International Labour Office's officers and national delegations. But the establishment of headquarters also signified the affirmation of a central power inside the association, at the expense of regional or national sections (Amnesty International or the second version of Greenpeace being instances of centralized decision making and operations). This made the central secretariat formula a favourite device for those who wanted to push a cosmopolitan or internationalist agenda within a given association. The location of such a secretariat was a matter of national or cultural prominence, and an important element as to the inward and outward perception of the group. Discussions about the location of the secretariat was one of the reasons behind the 1928 split plotted by Continental European housing reformers who left the International Federation of Garden Cities and Town and Country Planning (with headquarters in London), to create the International Housing Association with a secretariat in Frankfurt (Germany). Discussions about headquarters creation and site led to heated discussions, all the more so since these groups were often living on a shoestring, with conferences and congresses being major sources of funding.

The creation or the expansion of headquarters included the question of a permanent staff, and the uneasy relationship between volunteers and paid staff. The process of change was not linear, but in the early days, management tasks were often performed by members themselves, possibly people with independent resources such as Christiane Reinmann at the International Council of Nurses. She was the society's secretary from 1925, and contributed to the group finances from her own funds as well as by her unpaid labour. Solutions were also found by employing staff who were paid part time or full time by some political group or governmental agency with which the voluntary group was associated, as in the Brussels-based International Institute of Administrative Sciences that relied on Belgian civil servants from the Department of the Interior in the 1920s–30s. But the workload increased with the growth of the associations, with the need for field agents when they began to develop specific programmes 'out there', or with the growing cooperation with funding agencies that required accountability and full time availability. The professionalization process often began with the hiring of clerical and publications personnel, and opened breach in the social fabric of the voluntary groups. Julia Henderson, secretary of the International Planned Parenthood Federation from 1970, spent a lot of energy in talking with key volunteers so they accepted both professionalization and the growing importance of the London (global headquarters) paid staff over voluntary regional directors and committees. More recently, such a transition was especially challenging in humanitarian relief organizations that constructed their organizational culture around the cameo of the dedicated voluntary activist. For instance at Médecins Sans Frontières or Médecins du Monde, where the number of logistical and administrative staff grew at the expense of health volunteers when these organizations expanded the size and budget of their operations during the 1990s. A specialized labour market has appeared: it is now a familiar profile, that of the expatriated or local field worker who commutes between short-term contracts for different NGOs in the same region or country, or that of the managing officer who switches from Médecins Sans Frontières to CARE. This is but the latest aspect of a long history where voluntary organizations interacted continuously with one another, through cooperation or competition mechanisms.

A field of international non-governmental organizations?

The world of ideals is not an ideal world, and voluntary societies have been competing for members, funds, recognition and territory in the very name of the cause they defend. In the middle of the 19th century, national and transatlantic abolitionist societies split over the question of immediate or incremental abolition of slavery. More widely, the endorsement of programmes, values and activities by the newest societies willingly contrasted with those from older groups in the field. The history of women's organizations at the turn of the century thus looks like a chain reaction: the International Council of Women was created in 1888 following the conclusion that issue-oriented groups (temperance, abolitionism, socialism, peace) were not giving due place to women and to women's problems. The International Woman Suffrage Alliance took shape in 1904 as the Council was deemed too shy about suffrage, and the Women's International League for Peace and Freedom was born of the imagination of some women who wanted to oppose the Great War while the Alliance leaders had decided to suspend activities and follow their respective national loyalties. Similarly, the foundation of Médecins Sans Frontières in 1971 resulted from a disagreement with the neutral attitude of the International Committee of the Red Cross (ICRC) during the Biafra conflict. The whole 'sans frontierism' repertoire and values have, for a long time, explicitly been defined against ICRC practices. Competition has also contributed to shape relationships between voluntary associations that share a field of action with different geographical, cultural, religious or ideological affiliations. They often end up in competing for non-elastic resources, be it funding, members, recognition or even beneficiaries. Competition can be severe, as witnessed by attempts by some Muslim relief organizations to get exclusive access to Muslim beneficiaries in African or Asian terrains since the 1990s, a communitarism they justify by the attempts of

some Christian NGOs to cure, care...and convert. On a lighter note, there have been a lot of comments on the 'logo wars' that saw relief organizations competing to plant their flag or show their branded apparel in front of TV cameras, during the Yugoslavia and the Rwanda crises of the 1990s. The increasing number of NGOs on emergency relief terrains has certainly sharpened the elbows: the Save the Children Fund and the ICRC were alone in Ethiopia in 1935–36, while there were 43 NGOs in Bangladesh in 1972, and 120 around the Great Lakes during the Rwanda civil war of 1994–95. But competition was already the order of the day during 19th-century world fairs when scientific groups competed for conference opportunities, or during the 1930s when the scarcity of financial resources led to disputes on congress locations and the 'proper' affiliation of members between organizations with similar audiences. Such rivalries surfaced in intergovernmental arenas during the Cold War years. There were continuous battles between the blocs to include or expel non-governmental organizations from consultative status at ECOSOC, such as when the boycott of Russian representatives in July 1950 gave the Western side the opportunity to downgrade the International Organization of Journalists (based in Czechoslovakia). Voluntary societies sometimes instrumentalized this conflict to get prominence over a neighbouring group.

But this sense of competition did not radically alter the common feeling that voluntary societies were some sort of a global avant garde, an elite group of 'people of good will' bonded by brotherhood or sisterhood ties. The fact that it was quite common to belong to several international voluntary societies, especially in the 19th century when professional or issue specialization was not so developed, facilitated both competition and cooperation. Competition itself suggested that coordination was a solution that would allow for peaceful coexistence. A range of solutions were imagined to manage the latter, from the geographical or intellectual division of labour to the creation of informal or formal mechanisms. Thus in the 1920s and 1930s, the International Union of Local Authorities and the International Institute of Administrative Sciences had agreed that the latter would leave municipal administration out of its. Many other 'non-governmental Yaltas' have taken place among INGOs. In the 1920s, the different women's societies held meetings to coordinate their conference schedule, and joint conferences were not rare even among feuding groups, especially in the 1930s when members could not afford to attend two conferences in a row. Merger, the ultimate coordination device, was also a solution that was contemplated to solve conflicts that were seen as financially and intellectually perilous. The International Council of Women and the International Woman Suffrage Alliance contemplated it several times during the 1920s, but the Alliance refused for reasons of 'pace and temper', a diplomatic way to say the Council was deemed too conservative. More recently, the United Towns Organization and the International Union of Local Authorities have merged into a new organization, United Cities and Local Governments, after half a century of confrontation to monopolize the representation of municipal urban governments.

It is no accident that this last merger was strongly supported by the United Nations and its specialized agencies, who wanted a single candidate for possible partnership. Convergence among non-governmental organizations owed a good deal to the gentle pressure of funding and partner agencies. This has been made obvious by evolutions in the relief field for a couple of decades, following some earlier attempts in relation to development aid in the 1960s. National governments and intergovernmental organizations (such as the European ECHO or the UN High Commission for Refugees) have recently massively farmed out their emergency aid to INGOs, coupling their funding with requests for accountability, norms and, sometimes, obedience. Sierra Leone (1998) and later West Timor for the UN, Afghanistan operations for the US government, have been places where the integration of NGOs into governmental operations has been pushed quite far. The confusion that reigned during the Rwanda crisis and on other 1990s scenes was a crucial reason for non-governmental relief groups to participate in this quest for norms and standards. Ad hoc programmes have been created to foster this convergence and coordination with more or less directivity, such as Parinac for the UN High Commission for Refugees, InterAction for US-based international development and humanitarian non-governmental

organizations, or the Sphere Project (1997), which documents minimum standards in disaster response. The latter has been accepted by part of the NGO community and by concerned United Nations agencies. The production of the now famous *Sphere handbook* (2000, revised in 2004) has nevertheless been contested, and other NGOs, mostly but not exclusively French, launched their own 'quality programme' in 1999. Private givers have also been keen to request increased efficiency from the organizations they aided. Thus the Spelman Fund of New York (a by-product of the Rockefeller Foundation) pushed for the creation of a joint secretariat and common information services for several international associations in Brussels, and succeeded in 1938, despite the fact that the project's growth was interrupted by World War 2.

But there is more to the history of coordination and convergence than the weight of external pressure in recent times. Cross-observation among voluntary groups was part of the original culture of these groups, as suggested by the reproduction of charters and statutes among different families of organizations (e.g. the International Council of Nurses got its name, its personnel and its first constitution from the International Council of Women). The establishment of coalitions and councils of non-governmental organizations has extensive precedents. Early in the 20th century, Belgian international organizers Otlet and Lafontaine, with their Union des Associations Internationales, wanted to coordinate the action and programmes of the bunch of international associations they had created or rallied. Catholic groups held their first Conference of International Catholic Organizations in 1927, well before the Holy See gave them recognition in 1953. Making international associations' contributions to the League of Nations' different committees more effective was the reason for the creation of several coalitions during the interwar period, especially among women's and welfare organizations. Practical issues also called for coordination, and a 'Fédération des Institutions Internationales semi officielles et privées établies à Genève' was created in Geneva in 1929, to lobby for tax exemptions and access to League of Nations operations. The United Nations and its specialized agencies more openly incited INGOs to get together. The 1948 creation of the Conference of Non-Governmental Organizations in Consultative Relationship with the United Nations (CONGO) has been an important step to associate NGOs with the UN committees and working groups. Many more regional, specialized, religious or opportunistic federations have been established in the last decades: International Council of Voluntary Agencies (1962), International Cooperation for Development and Solidarity (CIDSE, 1967), Islamic Coordination Council (*maglis al-tansiq al-islami*, 1986), International Islamic Council for Da'wa and Relief, Caritas Internationalis, Forum for African Voluntary and Development Organizations.... Together with the narrative of competition, this long history of federations, coalitions and organization among voluntary agencies underscores a bottom line: these groups are part of a field where they take inspiration and positions from one another, and this field is in constant tension with the international system to gain some degree of autonomy.

Conclusion

The historical study of international non-governmental organizations, as foreseen by Ian Tyrrell in a 1991 *American Historical Review* article, is a rich seam for historians who want to adopt a transnational perspective. Existing scholarship has brought food for thought in three of the directions that these may want to follow. During the last two centuries, from informal networks to organized bodies, these groups have been making and unmaking the threads of interdependence and interaction between polities and societies across borders. Ironically, they acted as globalizers or regionalizers even when they wanted to fight globalization or regionalization, as recently illustrated by the anti-globalization movement. They also have been crucial in the construction of national societies and polities, by showcasing differences and similarities, and by fostering cross border conversations which shaped social, professional, cultural and political aspects of national life. Also, they are historical objects in their own right, which have invented forms of action, of governance, of dedication, in their attempt to do away or cope with national differences and pressures and their frequent – but not ominous – aspiration to some universal.

But there is still a long way to go, beyond a narrative of moral righteousness,

linear development, splendid isolation and millenarist accomplishment that limits our understanding of the operation and role of INGOs. Historical depth is one of the solutions to these flaws of 'third sector' scholarship. History makes us realize that 'new domains' of INGO activity have infact been framed by generations of activism, organizational work and campaigns. The range of INGOs' activities has expanded and shrunk unevenly, and there is something to be gained from considering together the different fields which have impelled new dynamics in the space of INGOs: abolitionism/temperance/social reform/feminism from the first half of the 19th century, where a large part of the current repertoire of INGOs was created (the boycott, the petition, the conference...); human rights and development as a powerhouse of geographical expansion and interaction with intergovernmental organizations since the 1950s; environmental groups of the 1960s with, their aggressive media strategy science in the middle of the 19th century, where the congress and its rituals were invented; or humanitarian relief from the from the early 20th century, with the aspiration to define a human solidarity in the face of fear, disease and catastrophes. All these contexts have operated as vortices which aspired to and inspired changes. The history of specific INGOs, needs to be written by taking into account these concatenating configurations. As historians and fellows social scientists take this high road, and reconstruct INGOs strife and cooperation, together with their ties with political parties, religious institutions, national governments, intergovernmental organizations, corporations or philanthropic foundations, they will also establish their role and impact. The resulting picture, that emerges in numerous entries of this volume, underscores that INGOs are more than 'the conscience of the world': they have been making and unmaking our modern world, for better and for worse

Pierre-Yves Saunier

Bibliography

Boli J. and Thomas G. (eds) 1999. *Constructing world culture: international nongovernmental organizations since 1875*. Stanford: Stanford University Press.

Charnowitz S. 1996. 'Two centuries of participation: NGOs and international governance', *Michigan Journal of International Law*, 18, 2, 183–286.

Dauvin P. and Siméant J. 2002. *Le travail humanitaire: les acteurs des ONG du siège au terrain*. Paris: Presses de Sciences Po.

Iriye A. 2002. *Global community: the role of international organizations in the making of the contemporary world*. Berkeley: University of California Press.

Keck M. E. and Sikkink K. 1998. *Activists beyond borders: advocacy networks in international politics*. Ithaca: Cornell University Press.

Mabille F. 2002. *Approches de l'internationalisme catholique*. Paris: L'Harmattan.

Rasmussen A. 1995. *L'Internationale Scientifique 1890–1914*. Unpublished doctoral dissertation, École des Hautes Études en Sciences Sociales, Paris.

Willetts P. (ed.) 1996. *The conscience of the world: the influence of non-governmental organisations in the UN system*. Washington, DC: Brookings Institution.

Related essays

Abolition of Forced Labour Convention; abolitionism; Acquired Immunodeficiency Syndrome (AIDS); adoption; Amnesty International (AI); animal rights; anti-racism; birth control; children's rights; Congress for Cultural Freedom; conservation and preservation; consumer cooperation; cosmopolitanism and universalism; counterfeit goods; criminology; cultural capitals; developmental assistance; disarmament; ecumenism; environmental diplomacy; environmentalism; eugenics; expositions; forests; freemasonry; Garvey, Marcus Mosiah; global cities; globalization; Green Revolution; Greenpeace; health policy; history; human rights; humanities; indigenous networks; information technology (IT) standardization; intellectual elites; intellectual property rights; intergovernmental organizations; International Civil Aviation Organization (ICAO) and International Air Transport Association (IATA); International Red Cross and Red Crescent movement; International Road Federation (IRF); internationalisms; Islamic Relief Worldwide; labour standards; League of Nations system; legal order; life and physical sciences; mathematics; Médecins Sans Frontières (MSF); music; nudism; nursing; oceans; Olympic Games; Otlet, Paul; Oxfam; pacifism; philanthropic foundations; population; psychoanalysis; publishing; Pugwash Conferences; railways; relief; salt; Save the Children International Union; social sciences; statistics; technical standardization; temperance; transnational; United Cities and Local Governments (UCLG); United Nations Educational, Scientific and Cultural Organization (UNESCO) educational programmes; United Nations system; United Nations Women's Conferences; Vandana Shiva Research Foundation; women's movements; workers' movements; World Conservation Union (IUCN) / World Wide Fund for Nature (WWF); world heritage; world orders

International Red Cross and Red Crescent movement

The International Red Cross and Red Crescent Movement is the leading humanitarian network. It includes the International Committee of the Red Cross (ICRC) and the International Federation of Red Cross and Red Crescent Societies (IFRCS), both based in Geneva, as well as 183 National Societies. It has surmounted various crises in its history to become widely recognized as a non-confessional global force for help, compassion and restraint. It is a unique institution in that its activities are authorized by intergovernmental conferences, and the National Societies are auxiliaries to their respective governments, yet it is guided by overriding principles of neutrality and independence.

The Swiss businessman Henri Dunant happened to be present at the bloody battle of Solferino in northern Italy in 1859. After helping to care for the wounded of both sides, he published in 1862 his appeal for a new humanitarian organization, *A Memory of Solferino*, and succeeded in forming a committee, soon to become the ICRC after international meetings in Geneva in 1863–64 and the ratification of the first Geneva Convention. A red cross on white background (reversing the Swiss flag) was chosen as a single protective emblem, and national committees were formed for the relief of military wounded. The choice of emblem helped in the global expansion of the Movement, but became an irritant as early as 1876 during the Serbian war, when memories of the Crusades provoked some Turkish soldiers to attack those wearing it. A year later the Committee reluctantly gave permission to the Ottoman Empire to use a crescent instead of a cross. The ICRC continued to use the red cross only, but now some 32 National Societies use the crescent emblem, and in 1983 the words Red Crescent were finally included in the name of the 'League' (as the Federation was known until 1991). This dilution of the principle of a single emblem has caused problems ever since, especially with Israel, but they have been partly resolved by the adoption of an additional distinctive emblem in 2005, the 'red crystal'.

The ICRC has remained custodian of the Geneva Conventions, which were gradually developed and eventually reformulated in 1949 to cover warfare at sea, prisoners of war and civilians under enemy control, and later supplemented by Additional Protocols in 1977, covering international and non-international conflicts.

The ICRC became highly active as a neutral intermediary during World War 1, not only providing medical aid but also visiting prisoners of war, calling for improvements in conditions of detention, and helping to trace captured military personnel. In 1919, in the aftermath of the War, the Federation was founded under the driving force of the American Red Cross, as a loose union of National Societies from which the defeated belligerents were initially excluded. The ICRC has always treasured its independence and has remained a Swiss private institution with informal links to the Swiss State (though recently with many non-Swiss employees). Its cooperation with the Federation was initially sporadic, and the dual structure of the Movement has caused continual confusion. In general, the ICRC has been concerned more with war and civil strife, and the Federation more with natural disasters, but there have been substantial overlaps. Since 1997, with the Seville Agreement, an integrated strategy for the Movement and for division of labour between its components has improved cooperation.

The Second World War was a severe test for the Red Cross. The Federation moved its headquarters from Paris to Geneva. The ICRC persuaded all parties to the conflict to extend the provisions of the Geneva Conventions to civilians of enemy nationality who were on unfriendly territory and had been arrested only because of their nationality. This protection was not extended to civilians of enemy nationality on occupied territory, such as Poland, so that the victims of Nazi concentration camps remained without protection. Though the ICRC in Geneva had information about the Nazi genocide of the Jews in 1942, they decided that they were not legally authorized to take action in internal matters, and that speaking out might make it more difficult for them to continue their work for prisoners of war held by Germany. Pressure from the Swiss government, and the location of Geneva on the border of German-occupied France, no doubt influenced the decision. A historian of the ICRC concludes that some leading Swiss figures in the ICRC of the day 'were more narrow nationalists than universal humanitarians' (Forsythe, 2005, 187). In the late 1980s, the ICRC opened its archives to historians and it later expressed regret for its timidity during World War 2 on this issue.

In 1965, the Fundamental Principles of the Red Cross were proclaimed: Humanity, Impartiality, Neutrality, Independence, Voluntary Action, Unity and Universality. There followed some specially challenging crises. The Nigerian civil war of 1967 to 1970 faced the ICRC with its gravest emergency since 1945, and resulted in a huge increase in its budget. Fourteen employees paid with their lives. The principle of neutrality was called into question when at first it organized intensive airlifts of relief aid into secessionist Biafra, thereby allowing the rebels to strengthen their resistance, but in 1969 it changed its policy and decided to cooperate with the Federal authorities, reverting to the discreet approach that it made its hallmark. Some young French doctors' dissatisfaction with the ICRC over the issue of getting food aid into Biafra was a major incentive towards the foundation of Médecins Sans Frontières (MSF) (Doctors Without Borders) in 1971.

A major turning point in the Red Cross's history was the evaluation report commissioned from Donald Tansley, a Canadian development official, and published in 1975. It included blunt criticism of organizational weaknesses. Its recommendation that coordination within the Movement should be improved was only gradually implemented. But one of the eventual outcomes of the Tansley report, together with competition from new agencies such as MSF and Oxfam, was a trend towards greater openness on the part of the ICRC. By the 1990s, the ICRC had become as sophisticated in dealing with the media as any other agency. It has continued to distinguish itself from campaigning organizations for human rights such as Amnesty International. It has stressed its need for confidential dealings with governments and armies, and has generally abstained from rhetoric – adhering to the unsentimental position that conflict is sadly a historical constant, and that institutions are needed to moderate its human toll. Much of its work, for instance on negotiating ceasefires or prisoner exchanges, requires discretion and patient confidence building.

The ICRC has been deeply involved in most humanitarian crises since the Nigerian civil war. In one of its main tasks, dissemination of respect for humanitarian values, international humanitarian law and the red cross and red crescent emblems, it has perhaps not had enough support from world leaders. In May 1992, when the ICRC was the only foreign agency left in Sarajevo, the capital of Bosnia-Herzegovina, one of its delegates, Frédéric Maurice, died as a result of an apparently deliberate attack on a Red Cross convoy bringing medical supplies to the beleaguered city, and the ICRC was forced to leave. Some international protest followed, but it was muted. A few commentators at the time pointed out that if the red cross emblem, with its unique and legally grounded message of protection as well as neutrality, promoted through a century of successful marketing as a 'logo', could be affronted without provoking universal outrage, there was not much hope that newer emblems such as those of the UN and European Commission would easily acquire the respect they needed. Since then, working for any agency in a war zone has become more dangerous. After the beginning of the war in Iraq in 2003, a number of ICRC staff members were killed – the most serious attack being by car-bomb against its Baghdad delegation in October 2003 – and it had to reduce its activities there.

Though the ICRC has expanded somewhat from its classical mandate to include, for instance, public campaigning against landmines, it has remained highly conscious of its unique legal mandate – both an advantage and a constraint. The Federation, by contrast, has embraced wide variety just like its national components. The American Red Cross, founded in 1881 by Clara Barton, became the USA's leading homeland emergency response organization, including the organization of blood donorship, but its overwhelming emphasis has been on assisting co-nationals rather than engaging with international aid

as a priority. Other National Societies have developed special expertise in locally prevalent natural disasters, such as earthquakes in Iran. Increasingly the National Societies of the developed world have engaged directly with National Societies in poorer countries to bring aid to the most vulnerable.

Jonathan Benthall

Bibliography

Benthall J. and Bellion-Jourdan J. 2003. *The Charitable Crescent: politics of aid in the Muslim world.* London: IB Tauris, Chapter 3.

Forsythe D. P. 2005. *The humanitarians: the International Committee of the Red Cross.* Cambridge: Cambridge University Press.

Moorehead C. 1998. *Dunant's dream: war, Switzerland and the history of the Red Cross.* London: HarperCollins.

Related essays

Greenpeace; health policy; intergovernmental organizations; international non-governmental organizations (INGOs); Islamic Relief Worldwide; justice; Médecins Sans Frontières (MSF); natural hazards; Oxfam; Pugwash Conferences; relief; United Cities and Local Governments (UCLG); war; war crimes; youth organizations

International Road Federation (IRF)

The International Road Federation (IRF) was founded in 1948 by several large, international American and English companies in the road construction and automobile industries.

Although explicitly global in its scope, the IRF must be understood against the background of the postwar reconstruction of Europe. Its first three regional bureaus were in Washington, London and Paris (soon to be followed by a fourth, in Geneva).

From there, the IRF campaigned to spread American road construction knowledge and equipment through a global network of engineers and employees of the founding companies. A combination of effective lobbying and American marketing techniques, such campaigns were new to European road builders. Annual conferences and two periodicals, *Road International* (a glossy journal with a fascination for large technical projects such as the Panamerican Highway, the Pan African Highway and the Pan Arabian Highway) and a newsletter, World Highways, supported the building of this network.

In Europe, IRF competed with the much older PIARC (Permanent International Association of Road Congresses, also known as Association International Permanente des Congrès de la Route, AIPCR, in French-speaking countries). Founded in 1909 after a 1908 conference organized by the French government the PIARC had, prior to the Second World War, organized large triennial conferences where representatives of national, regional and local governments (and some road-building companies) sought consensus on everything from purely technical problems and methods of counting road traffic to issues of road financing and management.

In 1945, the American government refused to rejoin PIARC, arguing that the association should try to become an advisory member of the Economic Commission for Europe of the United Nations. IRF officials, with their excellent contacts within the American government, quickly achieved this advisory status. With Marshall Plan funds for road and bridge building, as well as for building hotels to accommodate a growing number of American tourists to Europe, IRF managed to become an important factor in European debates about investing in road building or public transport. Consciously applying modern techniques of marketing and publicity, the IRF style of lobbying contrasted sharply with that of the civil servants of the PIARC, and with their verbatim reports of committee meetings in their Bulletin de l'AIPCR.

IRF was especially influential in postwar technical knowledge transfers. Beginning in 1949 it offered a Fellowships Training Program that sent engineers from all over the world to universities in England and the United States. Most popular was Yale University and its 'Traffic Engineering' programme, founded in 1943. By the end of the 1960s, 500 students from 83 countries had been Fellows in the program. Traffic Engineering courses, according to an IRF commemorative brochure, formed the basis of an 'elite corps of highly-trained road administrators, ministers and directors throughout the world'.

In Europe, the British Road Federation, founded in 1934, was among the earliest members of IRF. Remarkably, the Dutch 'Stichting Weg' (Road Foundation, founded in 1946) was among the earliest members,

despite strong PIARC presence in the country. But whereas IRF soon predominated in Great Britain, France and the Scandinavian countries, the Dutch PIARC managed to maintain its dominance. Although Dutch road engineers and civil servants complained that PIARC conferences focused on exporting knowledge towards developing countries, the local PIARC representative kept sending engineers to Yale. The IRF thus played a crucial role, either directly or indirectly, in the 'Americanization' of the debate about postwar road networks in Europe and many other regions in the world.

In the 1960s PIARC and IRF began to organize common activities, from putting on conferences to delivering experts to EEC advisory committees. In 1962 the French PIARC president André Rumpler became director-general of IRF. Some countries continued to see IRF as too commercial. But IRF and PIARC are today well-accepted partners and advisors of national and transnational governments, despite organizing separate conferences.

Gijs Mom

Bibliography

Hamer M. 1987. Wheels within wheels: a study of the road lobby. London and New York: Routledge & Kegan Paul.

International Road Federation. n.y. [1997]. Fifty years of service, 1948–1997. Geneva: IRF.

Michelet P. 1061. Les transports au sol et l'organisation de l'Europe. Lausanne: Imprimeries Réunies.

Mom G. and Filarski R. 2007. De mobiliteitsexplosie. Zutphen: Walburg Pers.

Related essays

car culture; car safety standards; civil engineering works; fellowships and grants; infrastructures; intergovernmental organizations; international non-governmental organizations (INGOs); Mashall Plan; technologies; tourism; transportation; United Nations system

International schools

Giving a definition of an 'international school' is rather a difficult undertaking, as many different kinds of schools claim to be 'international'. Some of them offer a bilingual curriculum or reinforced foreign language courses; some of them enrol pupils of different nationalities; others have agreements with schools in foreign countries, or prepare their students for international diplomas.

A common feature point is that all international schools were created for a small social elite. The oldest ones, most appreciated by members of the aristocracy and of the upper class, were the Manoir at Lausanne and the Rosey at Rolle (Switzerland), the college of Sion at São Paulo (Brazil) or the École des Roches in French Normandy; all of them were created at the end of the 19th century and the turn of the 20th century, and have always had a cosmopolitan recruitment. Later in time, new international schools were founded for the children of high-ranking civil servants working for international organizations. One school opened in 1924 in Geneva for the League of Nations staff's children; another one opened in 1947 in New York to serve the United Nations Organization. The fast development of private international schools from the 1960s appears as a consequence of the growing number of expatriates from the private sector.

An homogenizing pattern is at work. In 1968 an International Baccalaureate Programme was established by a private foundation in Geneva, 'to provide students with a balanced education, to facilitate geographic and cultural mobility and to promote international understanding'. By 2006, its spinoff, the International Baccalaureate Organization, worked with 1,855 schools in 124 countries and offered its programmes to over 200,000 students aged 3 to 19 years. Member schools are quite free to choose their own teaching methods. But the overall pattern is closer to the Anglo-Saxon than to the Latin educational tradition. Every school insists on foreign language courses, courses are often delivered in English, while a lot of time is devoted to personal accomplishments and socializing. Children attending those institutions are brought into an educational and cultural environment which explicitly aims at fostering a new culture. Curriculum and parallel activities such as foreign exchanges or participation in the Model United Nations in the Hague put a special emphasis on mobility, adaptation and other values pertaining to the social origins and profiles of the targeted children. The transnational education they receive often reflects the cultural diversity of their own families. It also includes an ethical dimension, with a stress on peace,

understanding, and an 'open door/free flow' capitalist-friendly rhetoric.

Nevertheless, international schools rather maintain segregation from the society where they are settled. Their curriculum and timetable are specific, a lot of teachers are foreign, and they end up creating extraterritorial training centres amidst national systems of education. Children are constantly reminded that they are different, and learn how to recognize their own social group, the new transnational upper middle class, and to value their own special characteristics. This type of education gives the pupils access to a wider range of universities at home and abroad, and provides them with more social opportunities, especially on the marriage and job markets.

International schools generally recruit both expatriate children and local children whose parents want to prepare them for the global labour market, though recruitment patterns are influenced by some national attitudes. In France, for example, international schools are reserved for 'internationally mobile' families, with a strong presence of foreign expatriates. In several Northern European and Latin American countries, local families are the major customers of international schools. The latter scarcely intend to prepare their children for international mobility. They are lured by a desire to assert and enhance their membership in national social elites. Be that as it may, the growing number of international schools all over the world proves the growing importance, in the upper and the middle classes, of international assets and international skills as a source of power.

Anne Catherine Wagner

Bibliography

Almeida A.M.F. and Nogueira M. A. (eds) 2002. *A escolazação das elites: um panorama internacional de pesquisa*. São Paulo: Editora Vozes.

Wagner A. C. 1998. *Les nouvelles élites de la mondialisation*. Paris: PUF.

Weenink D. 2005. *Upper middle-class resources of power in the education arena: Dutch elite schools in an age of globalisation*. Unpublished doctoral dissertation, Amsterdam School for Social Science Research.

Related essays
class; cosmopolitanism and universalism; executives and professionals; family;

fascism and anti-fascism; higher education; international students; language

International students

According to the United Nations Educational, Scientific and Cultural Organization (UNESCO) definition, international (or 'foreign') students are persons 'enrolled in an institution of higher education in a country or territory in which he/she is not a permanent resident'.

Early student mobility was regional, contributing to the formation of distinctive regional cultures. Japan sent students along with its envoys to Tang Dynasty China (618–907). They returned to Japan with the advanced Tang legal system, literature, architecture, Confucian classics, and denominations of Buddhism, thus strengthening the cultural ties between China and Japan. After 1850, the numbers of international students rose along with modern transportation, the expansion of European and American empires, and the accelerated transmission of goods and ideas across nations and oceans. Soon, large numbers of Indians studied in Britain. The US and European intrusion into Japan in the mid-19th century stimulated the Japanese government to send students to Western countries who later led Japan's historic Meiji reform (1868–1912). In the last decades of the 19th century, many young Americans sought postgraduate education overseas – for example, in economics in Germany or medicine in Switzerland. They forged the 'transatlantic progressive connections' that empowered social reforms in the US.

As it developed its educational and research facilities after World War 1, the US replaced Europe as the most important destination for international students. In 1922, among the 8,357 foreign students in the United States, 2,506 were from Asia, 1,425 from Latin America, and 1,379 from Europe. The end of World War 2 restructured the flow of international students toward competing Cold War centres in the USSR and the US. Competition between the two camps for international youth encouraged deeper involvement of governments in international student exchanges. For example, the US passed the Fulbright Act of 1946 and the Information and Education Exchange Act of 1948.

The number of international students worldwide had increased tremendously and represented around 2 per cent of all in higher education institutions in the post-World War 2 world. According to UNESCO reports, the number almost doubled every decade, from 108,000 in 1950 to 238,000 in 1960, then to 508,811 in 1970 and more than a million in the 1980s. The proportion of female international students increased from 18.5 per cent in 1962 to 23 per cent in 1973. The distribution of the fields that international students chose for their study had generally been stable over these decades, with a preponderance in the arts and sciences. Around 80 per cent of international students went to developed countries, with the US as the largest host country. The imbalance in student flows often aroused heated discussions of a 'brain drain' from developing countries. While development theorists portrayed education in developed countries as good and necessary for transferring critical development knowledge and technology from the West, dependency theorists emphasized how international education sustained the dependency of developing countries on the West.

The end of the Cold War contributed to growing international student mobility. The number of exceeded 1.7 million in 2000 and was predicted to reach 8 million by 2025. Host countries modified their immigration policies, facilitating international students' change of residence status to solve the shortage of skilled labour migrants. For example, the US introduced the H-1B temporary work visa in the early 1990s and increased the number of such visas in a bid for highly skilled international students. After 2001, foreign students in Australia could apply for permanent resident visas based on their skills, without work experience or being sponsored by an Australian employer and without having to return to their home country to apply. At the same time, countries that sent international students, such as China and India, made efforts to compete for skilled workers by encouraging return migration of students from abroad. In the future, there remains a challenge as to how to enhance student mobility as well as creating a better environment for 'brain circulation' and international cultural exchanges.

Lisong Liu

Bibliography

Davis T. M. 2003. *The atlas of student mobility.* New York: Institute of International Education.

Barber E. G. et al. (eds) 1984. *Bridges to knowledge: foreign students in comparative perspective*. Chicago: University of Chicago Press.

Related essays
brain drain; China; Chinese Diaspora; decolonization; exile; fellowships and grants; higher education; intellectual elites; international schools; Japan; language diplomacy; Master of Business Administration (MBA); temporary migrations; youth organizations

International Women's Day

International Women's Day (IWD) exemplifies transnational historical processes. This worldwide feminist holiday was instigated in one place, institutionalized in another, and has shifted meanings many times in the century since its inauguration.

In 1908 the Women's National Committee of the Socialist Party of the USA called for an annual women's protest day, in part to challenge the recent successes of non-socialist suffragists at mobilizing wage-earning women. Two years later, the Second International Conference of Socialist Women internationalized the holiday. In 1911 the fire at the Triangle Shirtwaist Company in New York City killed 146 young women and added yet another dimension of meaning to the day. Starting in 1913, IWD was observed on 8 March, its date ever since.

In Russia in 1917, an IWD demonstration in St Petersburg sparked the protests that led to the abdication of the Tsar. In the decades after the Bolshevik Revolution, IWD was celebrated in Communist countries as the official holiday honouring working women's contributions. US women rediscovered IWD when they travelled to Cuba and China in the 1960s, and women's liberation groups organized an IWD celebration in Berkeley, California in 1969 and more widely the next year, celebrating the revolutionary contributions of women around the world. By action of the US Congress in 1981, IWD became National Women's History Week (later Month) in the United States, gaining national legitimacy but losing its international character.

IWD continues to be observed around the world, and continues to provide occasions for women to gather together to take important political stands. On 8 March 1979 in Tehran, just after the establishment of the Islamic Republic, Iranian women demonstrated in favour of their rights and against the repression that was beginning to fall on their sex.

Ellen Carol DuBois

Bibliography
Kaplan T. 1975. 'On the socialist origins of International Women's Day', *Feminist Studies*, 11, 1, 163–71.

Related essays
Christmas and Halloween; consumer cooperation; millennium; socialism; United Nations decades and years; women's movements

Internationalisms

The most common sense of internationalism today rests on the idea that nations need to cooperate with each other for peace in the community of the world. The major internationalist forces that dominated the world from the 16th century until the mid 20th century, however, were under the shadow of an imperialism where a few advanced industrial nations in the West occupied the world and identified the interest of all nations with their own. Socialist internationalism, which also spread globally across Asia, Africa, and Latin America, was a major impetus to create a transnational alliance of those who opposed such an imperial order and the expansion of capitalism as well as nourishing the independence struggle of the non-Western world in many different forms and directions. In the post-1945 period, the United States-led market liberalism and the Soviet-led socialist force came to constitute bipolar hegemonic powers which exercised a powerful transnational force. Meanwhile, the transnational solidarity among newly independent nations in Asia and Africa against the old and new imperialisms was manifested through the Bandung Conference in Indonesia. This presented a fresh form of an alternative internationalism to the imperialist internationalism that created a feeling of solidarity developed through their common struggle against colonialism. Most importantly, a consensus for multilateral intergovernmental organizations gained strong impetus through the devastating experiences of the world wars in an effort to ensure perpetual peace in the international arena, which culminated in the establishment of the League of Nations and the United Nations. Over the last few decades, a transnational network of non-governmental organizations (NGOs) and their activities to implement the universal ideas of humanitarianism, justice and peace across the borders of nation states has been burgeoning globally and brought about an era of new civil- society-driven internationalism which interacts with and counters other global forces of internationalism.

Imperialism

Imperialism formed a powerful transnational force that shaped the world from the 16th century into the 20th century. In nature, imperialism was however a mode of nationalism where a few nations identified the interest of all nations with their own. The imperialism begun by European nations such as Portugal, Spain, Britain, and France was further developed by other late-coming colonial powers such as the United States, Germany and Japan which achieved more advanced industrial, commercial, and military power than other nations. At the core of the political and economic practices of annexation of remote territories and the expansion of empires lies an idea of modernity and the colonial ideology of a 'civilizing mission' propagated by the colonialists. Their transnational ventures were both exploitative and transformative: these changed the ways of life of almost every corner of the globe from Africa to Asia, the Caribbean, and Oceania throughout the centuries. The internationalism driven by these forces also meant that all the continents of the world were absorbed into the capitalist industrial world system created by a few nations in the West, and the sovereignty and autonomy of those colonies were suppressed.

The 'Greater East Asia Co-prosperity Sphere' advocated by Japan during the Pacific War is a rare case of an anti-Western imperialist internationalist ideology: however, it ultimately became a short-lived colonial ideology in practice. Japan emerged as a new hegemonic power in the region from the end of the 19th century and advocated 'Asia for the Asians' in order to create a common 'Co-prosperity Sphere' among Asian nations free of Western influence but under its control. This for a short period motivated Asians to think of themselves as Asians rather than as colonial subjects or through their own traditional categories. The remarkable success of Japan after the Meiji restoration, and the long suffering endured by many Asians under Western imperialism, resulted in many Asians endorsing this idea and temporarily deferring their own nationalist aspirations. However, the subsequent brutality and the hardship inflicted by Japan in the territory it occupied led many Asians to become disillusioned by Japan's role. The first modern indigenous transnational 'internationalist' idea created by Asians defining themselves as Asians collapsed with Japan's downfall.

Socialist internationalism

Close to the beginning of the 20th century, a major group of opponents to a globalizing capitalism and imperialism felt the need to form a transnational collaboration beyond national boundaries to fight for the oppressed at the international level. In particular, the social and international ideals of socialism as expounded by Karl Marx nourished not only the struggle of the working classes in the Western metropoles but also the struggle for independence in the colonial regions. The First International of the socialist movement was founded in 1864 and focused on European colonialism within Europe such as the British presence in Ireland and the Russian occupation of Poland in particular. The Second International, which was formed in 1889, was mainly concerned with Russian and Austro-Hungarian relations with other European nations. It was also the historical moment when the socialists had to refine Marxist theories on nationalism and multinational empires. At their 1896 conference, they officially endorsed the right of national self-determination in opposition to capitalist colonial expansionism. Through the Third International (also called the Comintern), Lenin reaffirmed the right of self-determination of oppressed nations, a line which initially was opposed by other Marxists who endorsed a doctrine that denounced nationalism as a bourgeois attribute. The anti-nationalist tendency of international socialism however became a recurrent issue that was in conflict with revolutionary nationalism in many colonized nations. Socialist internationalism has become a marginalized force in world politics, especially after the fall of the Berlin Wall and the collapse of the USSR. However, the Socialist International, as reconstituted after World War 2, inherited the legacy of the Second International and has a worldwide organization of hundreds of social-democratic, labour, and democratic socialist parties from all continents that seek to coordinate efforts to establish democratic socialism. The internationalist legacy of opposing capitalist hegemony lives on and converges in the recent global network of the anti-globalization movement where heterogeneous elements of socialist, social-democratic, anarchist, ecosocialist, and anti-corporate globalization groups have converged. In the case of the ubiquitous anti-war groups, including the Stop the War Coalition, a wide spectrum of left-wingers constitutes the steering committees. This was first set up in Britain to oppose the United States invasion of Afghanistan in 2001 and launched formidable demonstrations in major cities around the world against the invasion of Iraq in 2003.

Third World internationalism

A larger picture of the transnational history of the globe before 1945 seems to present a one-way process from the West to the Rest due to the domination of the world colonial order. However, other transnational forces and influences did flow the other way. The opposition to European imperialism and racism created new transnational categories that people in the non-Western part of the world could use and explore. Muslims in India, for instance, campaigned against the abolition of the Turkish Ottoman Sultanate in the Khilafat movement which was based on the notion of a world-wide *umma*, or community of Muslims. This was initially a transnationally focused action by Muslims to influence British government policy on behalf of religious sovereignty in Turkey but became part of the Indian independence movement. A sense of solidarity among the colonized and their resistance movements developed through their decolonization struggles and the threat of new imperialism in the postwar era. The Bandung Conference consolidated the spirit of Third World internationalism among the newly independent nations in Asia and Africa. The emergence of the new superpowers, the United States and the USSR, and their divisive forces made this movement a new alternative that counterbalanced the continual domination of the international scene by Western nations through cooperative resistance. Delegates from 29 nations including Egypt, India, Indonesia, and China, covering almost half of the world's population, participated in this conference. The conferees announced their solidarity against any form of imperialism or racism and pledged themselves to promote economic and cultural cooperation among Third World nations. Many of the participants joined the 'Non-Aligned Movement' established in 1961 to avow their distance from both the United States and the Soviet Union during the Cold War. This alliance, however, became obsolete because of conflicts among the member nations, such as the border struggle between India and China in 1962, and also the end of the Cold War towards the end of 1980s.

Multilateral internationalism

Through the experience of two world wars and rapid decolonization, the old and newly independent nations felt the need for multilateral cooperation among nations to sustain peace in the world. The multilateral intergovernmental organizations such as the League of Nations (after the First World War) and the United Nations (after the Second World War) were born in this context of international cooperation. With a consensus that wars and colonialism were the products of global competition among nations for more markets, the League of Nations focused on international and collective security through peaceful means. The United Nations, which succeeded the League of Nations, has expanded to 192 member states (as of early 2008) and has become a global association of governments, cooperating in international law, international security, economic development, and social equity. The UN has championed the right of the oppressed and self-determination for colonized territories to help ensure that the voices of indigenous peoples are heard. The first step in asserting an internationalist value by the League of Nations and the United Nations was to restrict the right of states to use force as they pleased. These bodies existed, in part, to restrain the hitherto unrestricted powers of the nation state. By asserting the existence and importance of universal values, as represented in such documents as the United Nations Declaration of Human Rights (1948), these bodies have strengthened the ability of transnational groups to intervene against the state from below, by allowing appeals to these international bodies from minorities, and from above, by encouraging scrutiny of the conduct of member states.

The European Union (EU), consisting of 27 European states as of 2007, and the African Union (AU), consisting of 56 African states, are examples of regional intergovernmental unions. These aim to facilitate cooperation, encourage economic prosperity and improve the welfare of member nations through inter-governmental frameworks. The European Union has been particularly successful in creating a transnational economic frame-work that has handed over many planning and regulatory powers to common European institutions. Gradual moves towards common foreign and defence policies have also meant a shift in power from individual member nations to the EU as a transnational organization.

Global network of NGOs

The late 20th century saw the rise of NGOs, and their global networks have also become a growing form of grassroots internationalism, or a civil-society-based transnational social movement. These NGOs raise and deal with a wide range of issues such as human rights, women's rights, the environment, poverty, and global economic and political justice across international borders. Many of these NGOs began developing along the edges of the activities of already established inter-national organizations such as the UN agen-cies, but operated through closer links to local grassroots populations. The International Red Cross, Amnesty International, Oxfam, Friends of the Earth, and Focus on the Global South are a few examples of such successful international NGOs. Among those, Amnesty International campaigns for international human rights, protected by the Universal Declaration of Human Rights and other inter-national human rights standards. Its research and action across borders are based on the principle of impartiality and independence from any government, religious organization or political party. It presses states to open up their judicial records to scrutiny and in doing so restrains the ability of the state to oppress its own citizens.

NGOs not only work on humanitarian relief in the post-disaster context and on conflict resolution. International fora focusing on intellectual dialogue among leaders and citi-zens across the world regarding global issues show a new emergence of transnational ini-tiatives. For instance, the State of the World Forum (SWF) founded in 1995 is an NGO and has provided an international platform for leaders, citizens and institutions of the world to connect across a multiplicity of disciplines in order to create cross-sectoral dialogue and a more sustainable global civilization. It holds conferences, promotes collaboration among leaders and convenes multiple spin-off organisations to produce relevant action. The World Social Forum (WSF) is another successful international social forum that promotes discussions among citizens across the world with a particular interest in just-ice in the international terrain. WSF is an initiative by transnational civil societies that focuses on finding an alternative model of globalization to those proposed by multi-national corporations. The WSF was held in 2001 in the Brazilian city of Porto Alegre and has developed to hold multiple regional social fora around the world rather than one cen-tralized forum. Among its activities was the campaign against the American pre-emptive war on Iraq in 2003. The remarkable devel-opment of information and communica-tion technology and the World Wide Web over the last few decades has revolutionized transnational networking among people and societies. As forces of globalization posed by multinational corporations become stronger, the resistance and cooperation among trans-national civil societies have also prospered. For instance, a transnational coalition, the Anti-Globalization Movement, has made the World Trade Organization a major target, criticizing it for promoting free-trade policies which allegedly favour the rights of corpora-tions over the rights of international workers and undermine national laws protecting the environment, endangered species and cap-acity building of the Third World.

Religious internationalism

Religious internationalism is a powerful transnational force that is underpinned by the long-established spiritual authority and international institutions of many world religions, in particular Christianity, Islam and Judaism, and the sense of unity among believers across the nations. For instance, the World Council of Churches (WCC), the Roman Catholic Church, the Organization of the Islamic Conference and the World Jewish Congress have provided international contacts among their believers across national boundaries. Many religious authorities have a powerful international standing and exert their power on issues that matter to their religious principles and practices. Their mis-sionary practices and internationalism have always crossed national boundaries. In this context, the case of Christian organizations has shown an interesting transnational development. For instance, the foundation of the Roman Catholic Church was originally European but now has a stronger base in Africa, the Caribbean, and Latin America with more believers in the Third World than in Europe and America. Pope John Paul II was able to mobilize his international standing, the organization of the Church and a network of believers worldwide to confront what he saw as the dangers of Communism, contraception, dictatorship, materialism, and unrestrained capitalism. His support for grassroots protesters in Poland, for instance, played an important role in the collapse of the Soviet Union. The solidarity among believers of the same religion has been powerfully manifested in the protests in the early 21st century by Islamic nations against the war on Iraq and the Danish press's contentious satires on the Prophet Muhammad in 2006.

Very much with us today, the spirit of internationalism has increasingly become a significant part of contemporary state and citizen practices in the metropolitan centres of the world, particularly in dealing with the issues of asylum seekers, foreign immigrant workers and ethnic minorities. These movements often represent the local construction of a cosmopolitan civil society which resists parochial nationalism and racism and promotes fairness, tolerance, and openness towards others. They stand in contrast to the rise in nationalisms worldwide which was also a phenomenon of the post-Cold War period.

Soyang Park

Bibliography
Cheah P. and Robbins B. (eds) 1998.
  *Cosmopolitics: thinking and feeling beyond
  the nation.* Minneapolis and London:
  University of Minnesota Press.
Goldmann K., Hannerz U. and Westin C.
  (eds) 2000. *Nationalism and internationalism
  in the post-Cold War era.* London: Routledge.
Iriye A. 2002. *From nationalism to
  internationalism.* London: Routledge.
Iriye A. 2002. *Global community: the role of
  international organizations in the making of the
  contemporary world.* Berkeley: University of
  California Press.
Kant I. 1963 [1784]. *Idea for a universal history
  from a cosmopolitan point of view.* Translated
  by Beck L. W. in *From Immanuel Kant: On
  history.* New York: Bobbs-Merrill.
Klein N. 2000. *No logo.* London:
  HarperCollins/Flamingo.
Nation R. C. 1989. *War on war: Lenin, the
  Zimmerwald Left, and the origins of Communist
  internationalism.* Durham, NC: Duke
  University Press.
Navari C. 2000. *Internationalism and the state in
  the twentieth century.* London: Routledge.

Related essays
1848; anarchism; anti-racism; Christianity; civilizations; Cold War; Comintern and Cominform; *Communist Manifesto*; cosmopolitanism and universalism; decolonization; ecumenism; empires and imperialism; Ethical Culture; European Union (EU); globalization; Hammarskjöld family; humanities; intergovernmental organizations; international non-governmental organizations (INGOs); Islam; justice; League of Nations system; nation and state; new man; Otlet, Paul; pan-isms; Pax Americana; regional communities; religion; United Nations system; Universal Races Congress; Westernization; white men's countries; workers' movements; world federalism; world orders; Zionism

Internet

The Internet, also known as the Net, is a publicly accessible global network of diverse computer networks that exchange all forms of digital communication and data.

The most common applications associated with the Internet are electronic mail (email), search engines, and the World Wide Web (Web). Also of growing political and social significance is the use of the Internet for telephony, video conferencing, and amateur videography and journalism. The Internet significantly increases the communicative capabilities of individuals and can be said to have democratized access to international communication. All its transnational implications flow from the increased communicative freedom it provides to Internet users – a freedom of speech and ease of digital exchange within and across boarders that has proven difficult to control.

The Internet had its beginning in the late 1960s as part of the United States Department of Defense's Advance Research Projects Agency (ARPA) initiative to create a robust and reliable computer network, ARPANET. In the early 1970s ARPA researchers Robert Kahn and Vinton Cerf began work on transforming ARPANET (a single network) into a system that could connect not just many computers but also many diverse computer networks and expand in size indefinitely. Their solution was the TCP/IP software protocol, developed with the aid of collaborators from an international networking community. When ARPANET completed its transition to TCP/IP in 1983 the Internet was born.

In 1992 the US National Science Foundation announced its intention to withdraw from funding the main 'backbone' (physical connection) of the American Internet. This in turn fostered the growth of commercial Internet service providers (ISPs), the largest of which is America Online (AOL). By 1993 the Internet's commercialization was well under way as the business sector established early forms of electronic commerce and online retail.

A combination of investor speculation and media hype culminated in the infamous stock-market bubble that burst in 2000, when an estimated US$1.75 trillion in value evaporated from 280 publicly traded Internet companies. Economists now acknowledge that the Internet plays a substantial role in a globalized market system. The commercialization of the Internet also gave local businesses access to global niche markets. In this and many other areas of life, the Internet had inadvertently transformed the local into the transnational. A wide range of laws governing areas such as taxation, obscenity, trade, libel, trademarks, and intellectual property had to be redrawn to accommodate the Internet's easy violation of national borders.

Coinciding with commercialization was the beginning of a massive migration onto the Internet by the general population. The rapid adoption of the Internet was facilitated by affordable desktop computers and the invention of the Web by Tim Berners-Lee. Lee developed a graphical interface (browser) for the Internet and released the first public version in 1991. Eric Bina and Marc Andreessen released an improved browser called Mosaic in March 1993. Mosaic was quickly named the 'killer application of the Internet' by the global business press and was soon copied by Netscape's Navigator and Microsoft's Internet Explorer. The Web itself is based on a system for sharing information, also pioneered by Lee, called hypertext. Web browsers translate the hypertext markup language (HTML) into typographical features such as bold or italics and, far more importantly, allow users to create links between any two documents within the Internet. It is HTML which enables users to 'surf' across countless documents and other forms of digital files. In essence, Lee invented a transnational language for communicating connections between ideas and objects.

By the mid-1990s lawsuits between European governments and Internet service providers such as America Online highlighted how the Internet violated local mores surrounding content regulation. In 1996 Claudia Nolte, a member of the German parliament, called on the United Nations to establish international standards for censoring pornography and neo-Nazi material within the Internet. Today the notion of an international body regulating Internet content is seen as naive. There are substantial technical and legal barriers to the centralized control of information flows across the Internet. The Internet's ability to transmit money, information, goods, and services across borders continues to both facilitate and complicate transnational relations.

Such implications of the Internet are also seen in the phenomenon of offshore gambling. By the late 1990s various nations had proposed or enacted legislation regulating gambling via the Internet, often with negligible effect. The legal status of online gambling in many countries remains uncertain, and offshore Web sites are in wide use by businesses seeking to evade prosecution. Legislators often claim that offshore gambling operations which make use of the Internet are a haven for organized crime, fraud, and money laundering. In an age of transnational governance, the Internet often renders local laws ineffective.

In 1999 Shawn Fanning created a file-sharing program called Napster and the age of digital piracy began in earnest. Napster was eventually shut down by legal action in 2001 and then resurrected as a legitimate commercial service. Napster was followed by a series of programs that facilitate the illegal exchange of songs, movies, video games, software, books, and other digital products. The direct exchange of digital files between Internet users (known as peer-to-peer) is proving to be exceedingly difficult to control through either technical or legal solutions. The international harmonization of intellectual property laws is seen by some government and industry representatives as a solution to the problem of property rights within the Internet. Yet there is considerable doubt as to whether or not such harmonization is possible or potentially effective in limiting digital piracy. Piracy, child pornography, organized crime, terrorist organizations, hacking, hate-speech, and other forms of unlawful behaviour continue to flourish on the Internet.

In 1994 the Zapatista movement of indigenous Mexican peasants demonstrated that the Internet would play a role in bringing local political struggles to the attention of the international community. Supporters of the Zapatistas created a global network of online activists and gained international sympathy for their fight for indigenous rights. Today the Internet is used extensively for promoting transnational social networks which bring together non-government organizations and grassroots movements.

As a result of the use of the Internet for political and social activism the local is increasingly intertwined with the national and transnational. Yet the Internet's communicative freedom carries with it certain contradictions. Western corporations develop software that allows repressive regimes to censor Internet communication (although with only limited effectiveness). The transnational flow of information across the Internet also leaves Western corporations beholden to foreign nations. In 2005 the American Internet company Yahoo handed over information to Chinese police that led to a ten-year sentence for the journalist Shi Tao. In the same year Microsoft closed down a Web site at the request of the Chinese government. American Internet companies regularly censor their Web sites and online discussion forums to appease other governments and gain access to foreign markets.

In an era when supranational institutions repeatedly bypass national governments, the Internet has emerged as a crucial tool for new forms of mass political action. In 1999 a meeting of the World Trade Organization (WTO) in Seattle, Washington State was disrupted by activists who used new forms of online independent journalism to document police brutality against protestors and communicate an alternative perspective of the protest and the WTO's agenda to the global press. Perhaps the epitome of the Internet's transnational implications was seen on 15 February 2003, when between 6 and 10 million people gathered in the streets of cities around the world to protest the American invasion of Iraq. The event took place in over 60 countries and was coordinated via the Internet through the use of Web sites and email. The impact of the protest is uncertain, but it did demonstrate that the Internet can be used to coordinate mass events on a global scale.

As political and economic power shifts to transnational organizations the online community has responded with innovative uses of the Internet to organize and express opposition against corporate global hegemony. By 2006 the word 'boycott' occurred over 74,000,000 times on the Web. The new level of expressive freedom found within the online community suggests that the Internet is emerging as a new form of public sphere where both collaboration and resistance flourish.

It is now taken for granted by consumers that cell phones, cameras, laptops, desktop computers, video game consoles, televisions, and personal digital assistants come equipped with the ability to connect to the Internet, a feature that is being extended to a wide variety of consumer goods from cars to refrigerators. Whether in coffee shops, classrooms, offices or airplanes, there is an expectation that individuals will not only be able to connect to the Internet, but that they will be able to do so for free. As of September 2005, approximately 960 million people were using the Internet across the globe.

Michael Strangelove

Bibliography

Abbate J. 1999. *Inventing the Internet*.
  Cambridge, MA: MIT Press.
Strangelove M. 2005. *The empire of mind: digital piracy and the anti-capitalist movement*.
  Toronto: University of Toronto Press.

Related essays

benefits and charity concerts; higher education; indigenous networks; information economy; intellectual property rights; internationalisms; Internet Corporation for Assigned Names and Numbers (ICANN); Koran; libraries; mail; non-lieux; *War and Peace in the Global Village*

Internet Corporation for Assigned Names and Numbers (ICANN)

The Internet Corporation for Assigned Names and Numbers (ICANN) was established by the United States in 1998 to take over the management of the Internet's domain name systems. Initially formed as a private sector non-profit organization, ICANN now controls the addressing system which appoints operators of the Internet's two-letter country code suffixes (such as '.ca' for Canada), and coordinates the assignment of distinct domain names (such as 'www.strangelove.com'). ICANN also formally establishes and coordinates the technical standards which ensure the Internet's interoperability. Between 1968 and 1998 these tasks were almost single-handedly performed by Jonathan Bruce Postel, an engineer with the US Department of Defense's Advanced Research Projects Agency.

Although the Internet is seen as non-hierarchical and beyond control, ICANN commands ultimate control over the technical standards behind the Internet, standards that determine both communicative freedom and censorship and surveillance capabilities. Theoretically, ICANN has the ability to disrupt a country's Internet presence. It could do so by deleting the country's domain name from the Internet (it is noteworthy that this did not happen to Iraq during the second Gulf War). Now that an enormous volume of communication flows over the Internet, and as electronic commerce is now an integral part of most nations' economies, ICANN's central control over the Internet's addressing system has become a thorn in the side of many governments. On 30 June 2005, the United States Commerce Department announced its intention to retain control over ICANN indefinitely.

Unilateral control of the Internet represented a reversal of earlier policy. It was a matter of public record that Washington planned to grant ICANN autonomy by 2006. Unfortunately, this was a period of unparalleled unilateralism by the Bush administration. Just prior to the release of a United Nations report on the need for shared transnational control of ICANN, Washington opted for retaining control. ICANN would remain firmly in the control of the United States government. The editorial pages of the American press almost uniformly reported that this was a wise decision, but even among America's closest allies there was dissent against such a unilateral move.

ICANN's current position recognizes that countries have 'sovereignty concerns' over the control each of their own country's domain name, but significant voices in the foreign policy field, such as the journal *Foreign Affairs*, have declared the new US position as unsustainable in the long term. It is all but certain that as the Internet becomes a vital resource for commerce, culture, and national security, nations will devise a technical alternative to an American-controlled domain-naming system. While any such alternative Internet addressing systems would jeopardize the Internet's interoperability, one can see how nations might place such concerns in a secondary position to their own demands for sovereign control of what they consider to be their virtual territory.

ICANN is only one among numerous contradictions that surround the Internet. In what is a highly decentralized global communication system we find a central authority under the control of one nation. As a source of uniform technical standards ICANN may eventually evolve into a multilateral intergovernmental organization or its transnational influence may diminish as other countries establish parallel naming and addressing systems.

Michael Strangelove

Bibliography
Cukier K. N. 2005. 'Who will control the world? Washington battles the world', *Foreign Policy*, 84, 6, 7–13.

Related essays
empires and imperialism; information economy; Internet; nation and state; Pax Americana; technical standardization

Internet Corporation for Assigned Names and Numbers (ICANN) *See* Internet

Investment

'Transnational investment' is not a common expression. It is a reminder of the headway the term 'transnational' still has to make as an operational concept. Preference for the term 'foreign investment' is revealing of the empirical difficulties of attempting to single out the transnational variety of investment. Statistics, official and privately produced, do not distinguish transnational from other international investment.

'Foreign direct investment' (FDI) designates the opening of branches or the acquisition of companies or controlling positions in companies abroad. It typifies transnational investment. But bonds (i.e. debt securities issued by governments) are registered as part of 'foreign portfolio investment' alongside other non-controlling investment in the equity and debt instruments of private corporations. Disentangling transnational company debentures from international government bonds would require reframing the working categories in the field of foreign finance, where the main divide has been between investment seeking managerial control and investment in search of revenue.

From a historical point of view, a narrow definition of transnationality (whereby governments and states are not involved) would exclude purchase by foreigners of a state's long-term bonds and short-term Treasury bills, more than half of pre-1914 foreign investment in the world, most of transfers from 1945 to the early 1950s and a considerable part of present-day inflow of capital in the US. Borrowing by states from sources outside of their borders would belong to the international, but not the transnational, category. Transnational investment would then be understood as acquisition of shares and debentures by foreign nationals in a country's privately owned companies.

A wider definition of transnationality, where at least one actor in an international interaction is not an agent of a government, would have less restrictive consequences and be more in keeping with usage. Leaving out state-to-state loans and grants, it would consider all other transfers of capital between countries to be transnational. In 2004, private investment corresponded to 97 per cent of the total US foreign asset position. Most foreign investment would qualify as transnational. The present entry refers to transnational investment in this sense.

Economists and historians have pondered the determinants of foreign investment and their effects on initiator and destination economies. On a microeconomic level, the attraction of higher interest rates, better returns on capital and asset diversification have been identified as motives of the individual investor for directing savings abroad. Whether such decisions have been validated by positive results, proved to be bad investments or suffered from adverse circumstances, such as bankruptcies or repudiations, has been the subject of investigation.

From a macroeconomic point of view, scrutiny of the reasons capital flowed outward have given rise to explanations ranging from normal allocation of resources by free play of the market to insufficient investment opportunities due to slow growth at home. The latter explanation is sometimes rendered in the notion of 'surplus' capital or capital unemployed because inequalities in income distribution and low purchasing power induce 'underconsumption' of goods produced but not bought, leading to economic slowdown and stagnation. Collective consequences of foreign investment have been and continue to be debated. Was capital put to optimal use, increasing national income and stimulating external trade by developing the economies of partners, or was it diverted from investment in the national economy? Was it hurting the home countries' international balance of payments by the flow outward or helping it by the flow inward of revenue from interest and dividends earned abroad? Debate has been intense about the effects of foreign investment on host economies. Did it contribute to development or to drainage of wealth toward outside beneficiaries, structural distortions, dependency and underdevelopment?

Cross-national lending was originally associated with the rise of modern states and their need to raise armies, wage war or pay war-related indemnities. Starting in the latter part of the Middle Ages, Italian and Dutch bankers granted loans to English monarchs, while German bankers lent to the Spanish crown and to the Papacy. The most successful were the Rothschilds who emerged in the early part of the 19th century, making their fortune by lending to European states and acting as intermediaries for British government subsidies to Continental allies during the Napoleonic wars. Transfers from private sources to government end-users continues to this day in the form of loans raised on the international market and credit extended by financial institutions.

Private borrowing on the international market appears in the 19th century in the shape of bonds issued by firms – e.g. railroad companies – to increase their capital base or acquire means to conduct their business. Such lending has not abated. Private foreign investment implies advancing funds to finance a company operating away from home with the expectation of profit or in the hope of gaining control of the company.

Private investment abroad is more precocious than private lending. In its primitive form, it began with partnerships to finance maritime ventures overseas. Later chartered companies – e.g. the East India Company – mobilized the resources of many partners to engage in exclusive trade in faraway lands. They are the remote ancestors of Europe-based firms which came to prominence in the 19th century. Transnational corporations (TNCs) are the latest and most common form of transnational investment.

Transnational investment really got under way in the 19th century when non-European states borrowed in Europe to finance infrastructure development and foreign companies raised capital on European financial markets. Savings provided a ready source to be tapped, while the birth of the limited liability company and the division of ownership by means of shares mobilized resources in a new direction. Capital-rich European countries had less need for foreign investment than non-European countries in the process of modernization and, in some cases, industrialization. Cross-border capital movements tended to be unidirectional, from Europe outward. The flow of capital from the 1850s to 1914 was unprecedented. Volume of foreign investment in 1913 was almost 5 per cent of the gross national product of source countries, an apex never again equalled. Nine tenths of capital exported in the world came from Western Europe. Great Britain's share of accumulated foreign stock was about 41 per cent, France's 20 per cent, Germany's 13 per cent, with Belgium, the Netherlands and Switzerland jointly having claims on 13 per cent.

Enriched by trade even before the 19th century, then by revenue drawn from industrial production, Great Britain was the leading provider of capital to the outside world. London was the hub of international finance, the pound a universally accepted currency and the gold standard the guarantor of international monetary stability. In the half-century preceding 1914, British subjects channelled two thirds of national savings outside their country. In 1914, one third of assets they held were foreign. Their external holdings represented 1.5 times gross domestic product (GDP) and three fifths of Europe's assets abroad. France was the world's second exporter of capital before 1914. The Paris financial market ranked next to London's. At the turn of the century, one third to one half of French savings went into foreign securities. Independent countries, especially the US, received 60 per cent of British foreign investment, the rest going to the Empire. In 1914, over 60 per cent of France's long-term investments were in Europe, Russia alone drawing 25 per cent.

Nearly three quarters of capital exported from Europe financed the building of infrastructures (railroads, tramways, the Suez and Panama canals, ports, telegraph lines) – often related to foreign trade and the export of raw materials to industrial economies – and social overhead (municipal services such as water purification, gas lighting). A tenth was invested in mining, with the rest devoted to banking, industry, agricultural plantations and stock farming.

The pre-1914 heyday of transnational investment was interrupted by the First World War. Foreign assets were liquidated to pay for the war; portfolios depreciated; debts were repudiated by insolvent states. Major realignments occurred then. Europe became a net international debtor, while the US became an international creditor, even the leading source of capital flows in the world. New York's rapid rise as a financial centre put it on a par with London. Contrasting with the 19th century, the interwar period was marked by inflation and currency fluctuations, making long-term investment decisions difficult. Capital flows tended to be short term. Following the Wall Street crash of 1929, securities prices plunged, while massive selloffs drove down the value of assets. Exchange controls established during the Depression further discouraged transnational investment, until the Second World War brought about the breakdown of the international economy.

International economic relations were reconstituted after 1945 as the Bretton Woods system restored stable currencies and fixed exchange rates. With Europe engaged in reconstruction, the US was the only source of available capital. US predominance was as complete as Western Europe's had been before 1914. At first, transfers were government-to-government. Private investment by Americans resumed as European economies recovered. It never stopped going to resource extraction in Latin America and the Middle East. US investment rose substantially in Canada during the 1950s. It then poured into Western Europe when the

Common Market was formed. In the 1950s, 70 per cent of net long-term private flows originated in the US.

At the end of the 1960s, the postwar economic boom showed signs of exhaustion and investment conditions changed dramatically. Mounting US budget deficits, expansion of the money supply and increasing quantities of privately created Eurodollars weakened the dollar, bringing down the Bretton Woods system and leaving exchange rates to float. Western Europe and Japan became sources of investment, next to the US. Fuelled by the recycling of 'petrodollars' in the 1970s and deregulation of Western capital markets in the 1980s, capital flows expanded considerably. Aggregate amounts grew tenfold during the last two decades of the 20th century. The stock of external assets and liabilities of the 14 leading industrial countries nearly tripled between 1983 and 2001 relative to their GDP. During the 1970s, developing countries were recipients of numerous loans extended by foreign banks until the burden of debt drove them to bankruptcy and brought lending to a halt.

Most transnational investment since the 1960s has occurred among developed countries, a pattern very different from that of the pre-1914 era when orientation was North-South. While outflows continued from the US, European and Japanese capital flowed into the US. Not only was the US again a net capital importer, it was the world's leading debtor, as it had been in 1914. The value of American-owned stock of foreign assets, including all types of investment, rose from 43 per cent of US GDP in 1989 to 89 per cent in 2005. Aggregate value of stock of foreign assets in the world amounted to half of global GDP. In the 1990s, enormous volumes of mobile portfolio capital sought profitable employment. Rushing into developing countries, they could withdraw at a moment's notice, as they did from Mexico in 1994 and East Asia in 1997, leaving both in the throes of financial crises.

A notable aspect of transnational investment was the rise of FDI. Prominent in US transnational investment since the end of the 19th century, it expanded spectacularly during the 1960s. European and Asian companies are now active practitioners of FDI. The proportion of FDI in capital flows has risen regularly worldwide; it represented a third of the total at the end of the 1990s. Direct investment is practised mainly by corporations. Its role in promoting integrated capitalist world production makes it a key agent of transnationalism.

Samir Saul

Bibliography

Dunning J. H. 1970. *Studies in international investment.* London: George Allen & Unwin.

Kindleberger C. P. 1987. *International capital movements.* Cambridge: Cambridge University Press.

Saul S. 2006. *Has financial internationalization turned into financial globalization?* Globalization Working Papers 06/2. Hamilton: Institute on Globalization and the Human Condition.

Siebert H. (ed.) 1991. *Capital flows in the world economy.* Tübingen: Mohr.

Related essays

capitalism; convergence and divergence; corporations; debt crises; economics; ecumenism; empires and imperialism; euromarkets; financial centres; financial diplomacy; financial markets; globalization; industrialization; international loans; International Monetary Fund (IMF); open door and free flow; remittances

Iron and steel

More than for any other industrial products, the production and the distribution of iron and steel took place against the regional and then worldwide background of material, financial and political constraints. Of crucial importance was the intervention of the states, the international political context with rearmament moments and wars, various economic crises, the exporting capacity of producing countries, the emergence of new national competitors and ongoing technological innovations and the growth of replacement products. After the Second World War, this trade fell under the liberalization movement of world trade until the crisis of the 1970s. Since then, there have been important tensions and crises on the world iron and steel market.

International trade in steel experienced a formidable explosion, much more than that of iron and steel making, soaring after the middle of 19th century, from a negligible part of the production marketed out of the producing countries to nearly 45 per cent nowadays. This very strong growth was accompanied by a widening of production areas (five major producing countries at the beginning of the century, 20 in 1950, and 80 in the 1980s) which led to total globalization of the iron and steel trade, although for a long time much of this was regional in scale.

After 1815, the European iron and steel market opened with English metallurgical products. Traditional steels (crucible iron) disappeared thanks to Britain's new, low-cost production technology (the puddling process), but the innovation took a long time to be adopted on the Continent, mainly for financial reasons. The production of iron and steel remained little marketed outside national borders until the middle of the 1860s.

New inventions (the Bessemer converter, 1855 and the Siemens-Martin process, 1865) upset the world market: whereas steel had until then been an expensive product, manufactured in small quantities (world production 1848: 70,000 tons), its expansion became phenomenal (600,000 tons in 1867, 10 million tons in 1877). Thereafter, a new process, the Thomas process (1878) further increased the quality of the steel, whose uses seemed unlimited. Its production moved from small factories to modern integrated units, concentrated in coal areas near large consumption markets, mostly connected to the sea (via a river system).

Technologies were widely shared between Great Britain and the Continental European countries, primarily France, Germany and Belgium, which had the main European coal mines. However, for the middle of the 19th century one can speak of hegemonic British domination in the world market (1.6 million tons sold in 1866) thanks to its great technological advance, to very low raw material costs, and to early agreements between producers. Britain's productivity and low prices compared favourably with those of its European or American competitors.

After 1880 another phase of the competition started, and British advantages were steadily reduced (see Figure 1). Until the end of the 1870s, European (French, Belgian, German) and American exports had remained unimportant, because British products were cheaper (by as much as 50 per cent). In 1881, Great Britain exported 3.8 million tons of iron and steel, representing 47 per cent of its total production. The period between 1870 and 1895 saw the progressive emergence of Germany as an exporter. Whereas this country had occupied a negligible place until then because of the very high profit

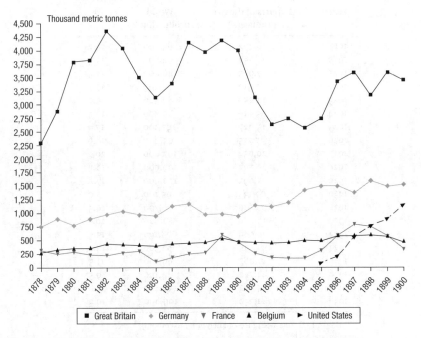

Figure 1   Iron and steel exports of the five major producers 1878–1900

Source: Duncan (1961)

margins it sought to make, the abolition of the Zollverein (German Empire Customs Union) led to declining prices, and German exports went from 241,000 tons in 1871 to 1.1 million in 1881. However, the Americans remained importers because of their high price levels.

Between 1895 and 1913, the British share of steel exports quickly declined, and Great Britain even became a net importer (approximately 200,000 tons in 1880, more than 2 million tons in 1913). The evolution of German and American trade in iron and steel was diametrically different. During the 1890s crisis, German exports increased considerably, exceeding 5 million tons in 1913. The United States also became a main exporter (almost 3 million tons in 1913), while its imports fell. These changes reflected declining price levels: from the 1890s onwards, American and German prices fell to the same level as British ones, sometimes even lower.

At the beginning of the 20th century, demand was high and supply followed: 30 million tons in 1900, 100 million tons during the war. But the marketed share remained modest (5 per cent on average), because of a rather general protectionism, a retention of iron and steel products by the industrialized countries for their own development, and also relatively weak prices of current steels which made them not very competitive at long distances. Therefore trade was organized on a regional scale.

The First World War changed the situation through globalization of supply (see Table 1). In spite of the intensification of manufacturing, European countries still had to import from the United States (until then, the transatlantic trade had remained very small, US sales being especially directed towards other countries of the Americas). It was the first fundamental upheaval in the organization of steel markets.

Steel markets used to be organized on a national scale, with the installation of single sales counters, parallel to the general trend toward a national economic concentration movement. Before the First World War there were also bilateral agreements among European countries, but it was due to private

Table 1   Iron and steel exports (thousand metric tonnes) of the five major producers as a percentage of world production 1913–1938

Year	Exports of the five producers*	World production**	%
1913	16,472	85,900	19.2
1920	11,452	74,700	15.3
1921	7,985	46,000	17.4
1922	12,510	70,700	17.7
1923	12,250	80,400	15.2
1924	13,136	80,400	16.3
1925	15,637	92,100	17.0
1926	17,715	95,000	18.6
1927	20,652	102,000	20.2
1928	20,732	109,900	18.9
1929	21,093	120,900	17.4
1930	17,133	95,100	18.0
1931	13,619	69,700	19.5
1932	10,086	49,800	20.3
1933	10,589	68,100	15.5
1934	12,015	82,500	14.6
1935	11,482	99,700	11.5
1936	11,742	124,100	9.5
1937	15,662	135,400	11.6
1938	11,330	109,800	10.3

* USA, UK, Germany, France and Belgium-Luxembourg
** Crude steel
Sources: Duncan (1961) for exports; Stahl-Zentrum (2005/06) for world production

initiatives that these agreements succeeded. The interwar period saw their apogee.

In 1926 the International Steel Trust (ISC) between Germany, France, Belgium and Luxembourg was signed. Quickly associate members were added: Austria, Hungary, Czechoslovakia (1927), and then the Steel Export Association of America (1928). The objective was to regulate production by creating quotas for each country and preparing the constitution of transnational common sales agencies. With the world economic crisis, the ISC was broken up, but a new agreement was signed as early as 1932. It was much more flexible and divided the export markets, and was followed by price agreements.

The general rise of European iron and steel production in the interwar period turned the European Continent into the first world exporter, with its share of exported production reaching 10 per cent. However, competition for raw material supplies grew, and there was a strong expansion of the products of the USSR and Japan, as well as the development of new producers in the Commonwealth (Australia, India, South Africa and Canada).

After the Second World War, there were problems of restructuring of the iron and steel industry, but it expanded greatly, thanks to the growth of consumer societies in Europe and to a major technological breakthrough, continuous casting, which spread under the Marshall Plan, and Europeans made a vigorous entry into the flat-products market; 200 million tons were produced in 1950 and 700 million tons in 1973–74. From the beginning of the century, the steel world production had increased by more than twentyfold. The growth opportunities seemed unlimited.

However, the distribution of iron and steel production and their trade changed. New producers developed their own steel industry (Norway and the Netherlands) while others renovated theirs (Italy). The British consolidated their position during the conflict. Competition was revived by these changes. With the rebuilding and the progressive development of the newly independent countries, the consumption of steel still grew apace, on average 6 per cent, from 1950 to 1974.

Steel was at the heart of the construction of the European Community. In 1951, the European Coal and Steel Community replaced the private initiatives of the interwar period.

Even if the British did not join, the explosion of the demand for steel because of the Cold War ensured stability for all European exporters until the end of 1960. The share of marketed steel production increased from 10.7 per cent in 1950 to 23.9 per cent in 1974, and the share of Western Europe in world steel trade was almost 70 per cent in 1950, and then decreased to 50 per cent in 1969.

Until the 1960s, the steel trade continued on a regional scale, Europe, North America and East Asia accounting for two thirds of the total. An increase in the Western European share of steel exchanges from 60 per cent to 75 per cent was made within this regional framework. The world trade still consisted of various parts, little connected with one another.

After 1974, the growth in steel consumption began to abate (an annual growth rate of 1.1 per cent on average), with a period of slowing down (1980s) followed by one of acceleration (1990s). These cyclic fluctuations were the principal cause of tension in the international market (see Figure 2). With the entry onto this market of more and more producing countries (Brazil, South Korea and others) and economic stagnation, these tensions were transformed into open conflicts.

In the 1980s–1990s, there were restructuring crises in the old producing countries, with the emergence of the minimills technology and the strength of Third World production. These new producers, selling their products in their national markets with difficulty, sought to sell abroad, using dumping techniques, which upset already precarious market balances. Other threats appeared, including that from Japan (trying even harder to export, after the oil crisis), the Eastern countries (focused on external markets), and with outsiders like Australia or Spain, as well as the dynamic area of Brescia in Italy (with small but formidable producers). This caused a ruthless battle, affecting the international strategy of all the great groups involved. To fight dumping, the European steel industrialists gathered within Eurofer, for more effective action by the Brussels authorities.

On the whole, from the 1980s, we see a profound change of balances and strength ratios on a worldwide scale. The former large producers were in decline, and newcomers took over. A very strong reinforcement of the globalization of iron and steel products trade began, which has not been countered since.

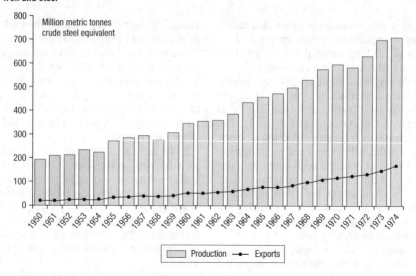

Figure 2 World trade in steel products 1950–1974
Source: International Iron And Steel Institute 1980. *Steel Statistical Yearbook*

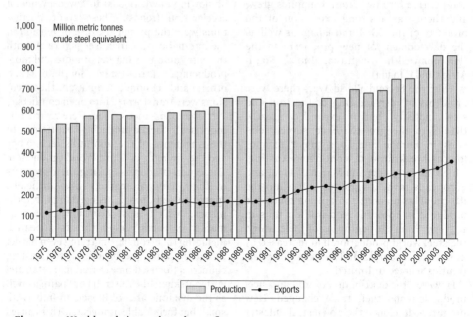

Figure 3 World trade in steel products 1875–2004
Source: International Iron And Steel Institute 2006. *World Steel in Figures*

However, the intraregional commercial share was reinforced over the 1980–92 period.

The steel trade quickly increased from 1980, and then slowed down from 1985 to 1989 (140 million tons in 1980, 175 million tons in 1992), because of strong increases in Chinese and American imports and due to demographic growth (see Figure 3). An increasingly strong share of steel consumption is part of international trade (28.5 per cent in 1985, 42 per cent in 2004). After the end of the 1990s (the Asian economic crisis), the producers have called for protective measures for their national markets because of falling prices and financial losses through to 2001. The irregularity of the international steel market during such a dynamic time also led to a sometimes excessive optimism on the part of producers, who launched ambitious programmes of expansion with significant consequences for world capacities, especially during periods of less dynamism.

Since 2002, the prices of iron and steel products have increased considerably because of an auspicious economic situation, high energy prices and especially thanks to the enormous and increasing demand from China. If the Asian growth and that of Eastern Europe continue, this tendency will not change any time soon. But the fast development of Chinese exports (350 million tons in 2005) may lead to new 'steel wars' in the future. However, transnational cooperation can avoid them. The Organization for Economic Cooperation and Development (OECD) Steel Committee gathers countries accounting for 81 per cent of world steel production and 86 per cent of world steel trade (in 2006). It is today the central organization of all international negotiations for the iron and steel market.

Françoise Berger

Bibliography

Allen R. 1979. 'International competition in iron and steel, 1850–1913', Journal of Economic History, 39, 4, 911–37.

Burn D. 1961. Economic history of steelmaking, 1867–1939: a study in competition. Cambridge: Cambridge University Press.

Baumier J. 1981. La fin des maîtres de forges. Paris: Plon.

Duncan B. 1961. Economic history of steelmaking, 1867–1939: a study in competition. Cambridge : Cambridge University Press.

International Iron and Steel Institute. Annual. Steel Statistical Yearbook and World Steel in Figures. Brussels: The Institute.

Mueller H. 2002. Consensus and conflict in the steel market. Working Paper 02-1. Kingston, RI: Institute for the Study of International Aspects of Competition, University of Rhode Island.

Stahl-Zentrum. 2005/06. Statistische Jahrbuch der Stahlindustrie. Düsseldorf: Stahl-Zentrum.

Nations unies, Commission économique pour l'Europe 1994. Changements structurels dans la consommation et le commerce de l'acier. New York and Geneva: United Nations.

Related essays
commodity trading; industrialization; literature; Marshall Plan; nation and state; productivity missions; regions; rubber; salt; technologies; trade; trade (manufactured goods); trade agreements

Islam

Islam is one of the major religious systems in the contemporary world with 1.2 billion followers spread throughout the globe. The major sectarian division in the Muslim world is between Sunni and Shi'i Islam, 85 per cent of the Muslims being Sunnis and almost all the remaining 15 per cent Shi'is. The Shi'is constitute the largest Muslim community in Iran (90 per cent), Iraq (61 per cent), Azerbaijan, Bahrain and Lebanon. Both Sunni and Shi'i Islam are crossed by mystical trends, which are collectively known as Sufism (tasawwuf). The ritual and textual traditions that constitute Sufism are organized into Sufi orders, the more important ones being the Qadiriyya, Rifa'iyya, Shadhiliyya, Khalwatiyya and the Naqshbandiyya, which connect various local communities under the guidance of charismatic shaykhs. The master/disciple (murshid/murid) relation that the Sufi shaykhs establish with their followers is the normative model for power relations in the Sufi communities.

The largest demographic concentration of Muslims happens in South Asia (India, Pakistan and Bangladesh), which has a Muslim population of circa 420 million. The country with the largest Islamic population is Indonesia, with 190 million Muslims. In the second half of the 20th century, migrations allowed the constitution of expressive Muslim communities in Western Europe and the Americas. There are 5 to 6 million Muslims in the US, 5 million in France, 3 million in Germany, 1.6 million in the United Kingdom and 900,000 in the Netherlands. There are also large Muslim communities in Argentina and Brazil, with 1 million Muslims each, as well as in Suriname (20 per cent of the population).

Muslim missionary work, which intensified and amplified its scope after the 19th century, has been linked to movements of religious reform or to Sufism. In the last three decades certain Islamic regimes, such as those of Saudi Arabia and Iran, have sponsored missionary work in order to spread their religious ideology. While certain Sufi orders, such as the Khalwatiyya and the Naqshbandiyya, and Islamic reform movements are very active trying to present Islam to non-Muslim populations in Africa, Europe and the Americas, most of the Muslim missionary work aims to spread a particular interpretation of Islam among the already existing Muslim communities. Muslim transnational organizations tend to be bounded by linguistic, ethnic or cultural factors. Therefore, Fetullah Gülen is very active in Turkey, Central Asia, Albania, Kosovo, Bosnia and the Turkish immigrant communities in Europe and North America, while the Tabligh Jamaat is present in India, Bangladesh and Pakistan, as well as among South Asian diasporas in Europe and the US.

The Islamic doctrine affirms that all Muslims are equals and united in a universal community of the faithful, the umma. While the umma is not a territorial concept, its historical destiny is seen as linked to dar al-islam, the territories under Muslim rule within which Muslims can move freely in search of knowledge and in pilgrimage. In principle the concept of dar al-harb, the territories against which war is lawful, was applied to lands ruled by non-Muslims, but in practice it was applied to Muslim territories under rulers of distinct sectarian affiliations as well. Defensive wars to protect the umma against threats by non-Muslim powers were doctrinally defined as jihad (effort in the cause of God) and seen as a religious obligation.

According to the doctrine of hijra (migration), Muslims living under non-Muslim rule also had the obligation to immigrate to the territories of dar al-islam if they were not free to practise their religion. This doctrine gave a religious character to the large flux of Muslim immigrants and refugees that left the Balkans for the Ottoman Empire after the independence of Serbia, Bulgaria and Romania in the second half of the 19th century. The presence of these displaced Muslims, together with the demands for protection and alliance against the European military expansion that were directed to the Ottoman Sultan by Muslim rulers in Africa and Asia, fostered the emergence of a pan-Islamic consciousness by the end of the 19th century.

Movements of religious reform, usually framed as the restoration of the 'original' message of the prophetic revelation, periodically happened in the Muslim communities from the beginnings of Islam. Such movements had their scope limited by the social, cultural and sectarian differences among the various Muslim communities. This picture changed with the emergence of a pan-Islamic consciousness that amplified the effects of the movements of religious reform. This phenomenon is linked to the colonial occupation or imperialist influence of the European powers over Muslim societies, which created similar situations of political, economic and social subordination throughout the Muslim world. These religious changes are also connected to the introduction of new communication technologies, such as the printing press, and technologies of mass transportation, such as rail and the steamboat, which allowed faster and larger circulation of texts and pilgrims. The introduction of new instruments of cultural governance, such as the modern school system, allowed a larger number of people to have direct access to the written text of the Qur'an.

The main movement of religious reform in the second half of the 19th century was the Salafiyya, which preached the restoration of the original message of Muhammad as a way to regenerate Islam, eliminating the additions and superstitions that were seen by the Salafis as the cause of its decline as a civilization. The main figures of the Salafiyya were the Iranian Jamal al-Din al-Afghani (1839–1897), the Egyptian Muhammad 'Abdu (1849–1905), and the Syrian Rashid Rida (1865–1935). These thinkers called for a reform in Islam in order to reconcile reason and faith, and allow Muslim societies to incorporate the cultural framework that enabled the technological development of the European societies. Their writings circulated among the intellectual elites of the Muslim world and influenced many local movements of religious reform from Morocco to India.

The political potential of Islam as a force of resistance against European colonialism became part of the pan-Islamic consciousness after events such as the Sufi-based revolt led by shaykh 'Abd al-Qadir (1832–47) against the French occupation of Algeria. The successful fight of the Mahdiyya (1881–98) against the British and their Egyptian allies in Sudan and the resistance of the Sanusiyya Sufi order against the Italians in Libya (1911–32) enhanced the appeal of Islamic forms of anti-colonial resistance. In 1928 Hasan al-Banna, a schoolteacher in Ismailiyya, Egypt, founded the society of the Muslim Brothers (al-Ikhwan al-Muslimun). Al-Banna preached the necessity of a 'Muslim state' for freeing Muslim societies from European colonialism and its local allies. He defined the Muslim state as a political entity committed to the implementation of the shari'a (Islamic law) as its main instrument of governance. The ideas of the Muslim Brothers spread among the educated middle class of professionals and bureaucrats and they became the main model for Islamic activism throughout the Middle East.

In the 1960s and 1970s groups linked to the ideology of political Islam emerged as the main channel of opposition to the authoritarian states imbued with secular nationalist ideology in most of the Muslim world. During this period there was a movement towards the radicalization of Muslim political activism. This trend was best expressed in the writings of Sayyid Qutb (1906–66), the ideologue of the Egyptian branch of the Muslim Brothers under Nasser's rule. Qutb called for jihad against the secular state, but also against society itself, for he considered that Muslim societies had fallen into a state of ignorance (jahiliyya) of the tenets of Islam.

While the Islamic militancy inspired by the Muslim Brothers was directed towards the nation state, the transformation of the tribal resistance against the Soviet invasion of Afghanistan into an Islamic jihad with the support of the US, Saudi Arabia and Pakistan from 1979 to 1989 internationalized its ideological horizon and political objectives. Also, the Islamic Revolution of 1979 in Iran created a model of political action emulated by Sunni and Shi'i militant groups throughout the Islamic world. However, despite the efforts of Iran in exporting its revolution, cultural and sectarian differences, as well as the growing influence of the conservative Islamic regime of Saudi Arabia, prevented its reproduction elsewhere. The challenges created by local movements animated by an internationalized Islamist ideology forced many authoritarian regimes in the Muslim world to liberalize their political system, as in Jordan, or to 'islamize' it, as in Egypt.

During the 1990s the project of islamization of society through the conquest of the state declined as a factor of political mobilization in the Muslim world, being substituted by a discourse focused on the moral reform of the individual as the base for the construction of a 'true' Islamic society. This development led to the emergence of a plurality of options, trajectories and demands in the religious universe of Islam, which is reflected in the intellectual elaboration of a 'liberal Islam' by thinkers such as the Iranian Abdulkarim Soroush and the Syrian Muhammad Shahrur. The dynamics of political Islam developed along two divergent lines: its more violent trends became a fully globalized phenomenon after September 11, 2001, through the confrontation of militant and terrorist groups, such as the Al-Qaida, with American imperial and military expansion on a global scale. On the other hand, the arrival in power of the AK party in Turkey signalled the emergence of Islamic political parties linked to civil society or grassroots social movements that aim for power through participation in democratic or liberal elections on a national scale.

Paulo G. Pinto

Bibliography
Eickelman D. and Piscatori J. 1996. *Muslim politics*. Princeton: Princeton University Press.
Hourani A. 1970. *Arabic thought in the liberal age 1798–1939*. Oxford: Oxford University Press.
Kepel G. 2004. *Fitna: guerre au coeur de l'Islam*. Paris: Gallimard.
Salvatore A. and Eickelman D. 2004. *Public Islam and the common good*. Leiden: Brill.

Related essays
Aga Khan Development Network; Buddhism; Christianity; cosmopolitanism and universalism; decolonization; empires and imperialism; evangelicalism; intellectual elites; internationalisms; Islamic Scientific, Educational and Cultural Organization (ISESCO); Islamic Relief Worldwide; Koran; millennium; missionaries; Muslim networks; nation and state; New Age; pan-isms; refugees; regional communities; religion; religious pilgrimage; Santería; September 11, 2001; Shi'i Islam; terrorism; voodoo

Islamic Scientific, Educational and Cultural Organization (ISESCO)

The Islamic Scientific, Educational and Cultural Organization – ISESCO – was set up by the Organization of the Islamic Conference (OIC) and began its activities in

1982. Its headquarters are in Rabat, Morocco. It aims to strengthen and promote cooperation among Muslim states in the fields of education, science, culture and communication, and tries to achieve a certain level of Islamic cultural internationalism, with the final goal of contributing to world peace and security. Although these goals are almost the same as the goals of UNESCO, ISESCO emphasizes the Muslim cultural legacy and identity in its work by referring to the 'framework of the lofty and perennial Islamic values and ideals' and hoping to 'safeguard the features and distinct characteristics of the Islamic civilization'. Moreover, it includes 'Islamic identity' of Muslims living in non-Muslim-majority areas as one of its goals. Like its umbrella organization, the OIC, ISESCO uses three official languages, Arabic, English and French. As of January 2008, ISESCO had 51 member states. From 1991 to the present, ISESCO has been led by its director-general, Dr Abdulaziz Othman Altwaijri.

Muslim societies have historically had multiple cultural, economic and religious networks, which facilitated transnational ties in and between the broader Euro-Asian and African continents. But there was no conception of an idea of a united Muslim civilization or 'Muslim world' before the globalization of the 19th century. Ironically, the emergence of the idea of a united Muslim civilization in the late 19th century was also accompanied by the division of the Muslim world into colonial zones and separate nationalities. There emerged more than fifty Muslim-majority nation states, while millions of Muslims became citizens of other nation states as minorities. It is striking to note that, during the era of decolonization and the post-World War 2 world order, there were no major transnational or international Muslim organizations. Many Muslim nations joined the United Nations system and worked with other Muslim nations within that context. It was only in 1969, in response to an arson attack on the Muslim holy sites in Jerusalem, that Muslim majority states came together to establish an intergovernmental organization, the OIC, in order to address shared problems and concerns. It was as part of OIC that a UNESCO-type intergovernmental Islamic cultural organization, ISESCO, was established in the early 1980s.

In many ways, ISESCO's activities have confirmed or paralleled the international cultural cooperation activities of the UN system, with a more focused attention to the Islamic world and Muslims in Europe and America. Its action plans and activities include many of the same activities as those of UNESCO, UNICEF and the UN (mostly in cooperation with them) such as the promotion of education, science, technology and literacy, children's rights, cultural values and diversity, and intercultural understanding. ISESCO also aims to achieve a unification of the Islamic cultures, as part of the broader goal of the harmony of world cultures. However, ISESCO assumes that there is already a shared legacy of Islamic civilization, and focuses on issues and areas that are specific to Muslim societies, such as dialogue among different Islamic schools of jurisprudence, discussion of ethics in science from Islamic faith perspectives, coordination and consultation among Muslim organizations in Europe and America, cultural activities in the West with regard to the image of Islam, and representation of Islamic civilization in various venues for dialogues of civilizations conducted at conferences and symposiums. ISESCO, like the OIC, conceives of the Islamic world both as a cooperation of various Muslim-majority nation states and as a universal civilization whose essence transcends the particularities of each nation state.

Despite its numerous activities, ISESCO is much less well known than UNESCO or UNICEF throughout the Muslim world. It has only two regional offices, one in United Arab Emirates and one in Tehran. More importantly, it does not have permanent representatives or cultural ambassadors from Muslim countries in its headquarters. Post-September 11 developments, especially increasing hostility towards Muslims in Europe and America, seem to have created a global transnational space for the actions of ISESCO's work, especially those dealing with the image of Islam, the dialogue of civilizations and the situation of Western Muslims. Hence, despite ISESCO's previous lack of popularity in the Muslim world, its activities might become more relevant for public opinion and the intellectual life of transnational Muslim community and networks.

Cemil Aydin

Bibliography
ISESCO website: www.isesco.org.ma, accessed 15 November 2006.

Khan S. S. 2001. *Reasserting international Islam: a focus on the Organization of the Islamic Conference and other Islamic institutions.* Oxford: Oxford University Press.

Related essays

civilizations; cosmopolitanism and universalism; intergovernmental organizations; internationalisms; Islam; Muslim networks; regional communities; United Nations Educational, Scientific and Cultural Organization (UNESCO) educational programmes; United Nations system

Islamic Relief Worldwide

Islamic Relief is the largest and probably the most respected Islamic relief and development agency in the world. It was founded in 1984 by Dr Hany El-Bana, then an Egyptian medical student in Birmingham, England, after he visited refugee camps in Sudan.

Islamic charity in the broad sense has a history as old as that of Islam itself, entrenched in the institutions of *zakat* (mandatory alms) and *waqf* (the Islamic charitable foundation). But leaving aside the 32 Red Crescent National Societies, which are non-denominational, and such atypical organizations as the Edhi Foundation, launched in 1951 in Pakistan, or the Aga Khan Foundation, launched in 1967 in Switzerland, Islamic NGOs in the modern sense date back to the late 1970s. They result from the convergence of two historical movements: first, the rise and diversification of NGOs, including Faith-Based Organizations, and second, the 'Islamic resurgence'.

Political controversy, especially since 9/11 and the Al-Aqsa Intifada in Israel-Palestine, has dogged the Islamic NGOs that originated in the Gulf or in the United States. The United States government's charges against them of complicity in terrorist financing, though poorly substantiated, were so unselective as to cause many of them to shut down, downsize, or have recourse to cash transfers. Islamic Relief, however, like some other Islamic charities in the United Kingdom such as Muslim Aid, largely avoided these problems. No doubt the sympathetic policies of the British government and its Charity Commission were helpful, as well as the precedent of organizations such as Christian Aid, which decided thirty years earlier to eschew missionary activity and concentrate on relief and development. Unlike some of the Gulf-based Islamic charities, which (like many Christian charities) propound mixed religious and welfare aims, Islamic Relief soon decided to eschew proselytism – even the building of mosques. Whereas many older interpretations of the quranic rules concerning the distribution of *zakat* had restricted it to Muslim beneficiaries, Islamic Relief relied on the view that it should go to the neediest. By embracing non-discrimination, Islamic Relief opened the door to cooperation with government agencies and with non-Muslim NGOs.

For the first three years since its foundation, Islamic Relief operated from a tiny room in a student hostel in Birmingham. It gradually developed the traditions of *zakat*, *Qurbani* (annual festive sacrifice) and the holy month of Ramadan as professional fund-raising opportunities. In 1986, it produced a documentary film on hunger in Africa and war in Somalia. In 1989, after some years of negotiation, it was registered with the Charity Commission. Rapidly expanding, in 1990 and 1991 it raised two sums of £250,000, for an earthquake in Iran and floods in Bangladesh. In 1996 – a foretaste of issues that were to hit Islamic charities later – it was attacked by the French newspaper *Le Figaro* concerning its programmes in Bosnia, but it extracted an out-of-court settlement and an apology.

By 2006, Islamic Relief Worldwide's annual expenditure had reached over £40 million and it had fund-raising or operational branches in 33 countries. In the previous year it was elected a member of United Kingdom's Disasters Emergency Committee, which coordinates joint fund-raising through the media, and its UK manager appeared on television to represent all the British NGOs after the Indian Ocean tsunami. Such integration into the international aid system did not protect its representative in Gaza from being held by the Israeli authorities for 21 days in May 2006 and deported, on no convincing evidence of misconduct.

Islamic Relief has stood out against more conservative Muslim organizations in, for instance, challenging significant forms of discrimination against women. A notable video film it produced during the Bosnian war sought to dispel the popular prejudices that often stigmatized women victims of rape. Yet its success has rested firmly on Islamic values, such as a special concern for orphans and refugees. It has also mobilized international support for Islamic charities as a whole through leadership of the Humanitarian Forum.

Jonathan Benthall

Bibliography

Benthall J. and Bellion-Jourdan J. 2003. *The Charitable Crescent: politics of aid in the Muslim world*. London: I.B. Tauris.

Benthall J. 2006. 'Islamic aid in a north Malian enclave', *Anthropology Today*, 22, 4, August, 19–21.

Related essays

Aga Khan; international non-governmental organizations (INGOs); International Red Cross and Red Crescent movement; Islam; Médecins Sans Frontières (MSF); Muslim networks; natural hazards; Oxfam; Pugwash Conferences; relief; religion; Save the Children International Union; September 11, 2001

Italian opera

Opera – a musical genre that unifies music and words – has been a nomadic phenomenon since its origins. It started in Italy at the beginning of 17th century, and imposed itself during the following century as an essential element of court life and aristocratic form of entertainment in all the European countries, both Catholic and Protestant.

By the mid 1700s, a cultural world had already been created around the Italian operas, from Naples to St Petersburg, from Lisbon to Vienna. This was an Italian-speaking world, dominated by Italian or Italian-trained composers, by travelling troupes of Italian origin, by directors and managers coming from Italy. The diffusion of the genre also led to the propagation of an architectural model, the so-called baroque *sala all'italiana*, and large theatres often designed by Italian architects that spread well beyond Europe.

More than an Italian musical 'colonialism', this success can be linked to opera's versatility and ability to adapt to different social and cultural contexts. On the one hand, a precocious codification of literary and musical conventions originated clearly recognizable textual and musical formats which allowed for adaptations to new situations, audiences and expectations. On the other hand, the rapid consolidation of a modern and dynamic production and distribution structure, based on the mobility of *impresarios* and troupes, also suited different markets.

Opera spread considerably between the 18th and 19th centuries. Behind its regular Italian façade, it constantly adapted and expanded in a variety of forms, while nomadic and versatile Italian composers adapted their compositions to the taste and the customs of the public, as Giuseppe Verdi (1813–1901) did in Paris or Gaetano Donizetti (1797–1848) in Vienna.

During the 19th century, the Italian opera spread out to the other continents. At the end of the 1800s it arrived in Asia as a sophisticated expression of European culture. The first Verdi operas were presented in Japan in 1887, whilst from the beginning of the 1900s the Italian 'belcanto' spread rapidly through a network of new musical schools. But it was in the Americas that the genre would meet its fate. The first New York Italian Opera House opened in 1833 and from 1847 many travelling companies began to visit all parts of the different states with some success. Opera was a real craze in Latin America where it was identified as a European product which carried notions of progress, steeped in romantic culture and patriotic ideals. Among the Italian political immigrants exiled in Latin America, especially after the 1848 revolution, there were also composers and performers, to such an extent that opera became a synonym of republican liberalism. Emulating the Italian context, forms of naturalization of the Italian opera that integrated events from pre-Colombian history or native mythology soon assumed the decisive character of national symbols in Argentina as in Chile. Later, from the end of the 19th century, this Latin American success became an opportunity for business and transoceanic opera cartels were created that performed in Italian and Latin American theatres. This expansion took place when the attraction of the Italian opera in Europe declined, while other forms of musical nationalism became popular in many countries. The Théâtre des Italiens in Paris closed and the Royal Italian Opera in London notably decreased its activity. In the meantime, the major companies crossed the ocean to the new world, and composers like Giacomo Puccini (1858–1924) and Pietro Mascagni (1863–1945) assigned the *premières* of their works to Latin American theatres. Even Toscanini (1867–1957) began his long career as an orchestra conductor in Brazil, and a few years later opened the golden US age of Italian opera that was embodied by the tenor Enrico Caruso.

Nineteenth-century Italian opera is a form of art in which the modern hierarchical distinction between high and low culture occurred surprisingly late. As the century progressed, an increasing dichotomy developed between translated versions and those in the original language. The former, and especially the individual arias, became part of popular culture, whilst the latter became an exclusive status marker.

From the beginning of the 1930s the phenomenon of the Italian opera reached its historical low. The post-tonal languages of contemporary music radically altered the singing registers which operas had always been based on. Other languages, in particular that of the cinema, inherited the narrative and communicative patrimony of melodrama. The increasingly global world of opera was associated with the preservation of the great 19th-century opera repertoire. Today, it has been defined as a 'living museum' that keeps a secular tradition alive in all corners of the world.

Carlotta Sorba

Bibliography

Bianconi L. and Pestelli G. (eds) 1998. *The history of Italian opera*. Chicago: University of Chicago Press.

Preston , K. 1993. *Opera on the road: traveling opera troupes in the United States, 1825–60.* Urbana: University of Illinois Press.

Rosselli J. 1984. *The opera industry in Italy from Cimarosa to Verdi: the role of the impresario*. Cambridge: Cambridge University Press.

Rosselli J. 1990. 'The opera business and the Italian immigrant community in Latin America (1820–1930): the example of Buenos Aires', *Past and Present*, 127, May, 155–82.

Related essays

1848; Cantonese opera; classical music; cultural capitals; exile; music; nation and state; orchestras; performing artists; rock; Romanticism; salsa; theatre; world music

IUCN and WWF *See* World Conservation Union (IUCN) / World Wide Fund for Nature (WWF)

J

Jacobs, Aletta *See* **Women's Movements**

Japan

Modern Japan has been profoundly shaped by its transnational contexts, while at the same time herself shaping these contexts. In most narratives of national history, the forceful opening of the country on behalf of Commodore Perry and his 'black ships' in 1853 serves as the almost mythical point of departure signaling Japan's entry into the world. The powerful imaginary of 'opening' has in turn produced the notion of premodern Japan as a country unto itself, entirely sealed off from the rest of the world. As an ideological foundation of the modernization project of the late 19th century, the discourse on the 'closed country' (*sakoku*) located the causes for what was perceived as the country's backwardness in the isolationist regime of the Shogunate.

The Tokugawa Era (1600–1868) was indeed characterized by a policy of strict regulations and limitations of outward interactions. Catholic missionaries who had started to spread Christianity and artifacts of European culture (most notably, guns) in the 16th century were now driven out by the Japanese Shogun. European ships were not allowed to land on the archipelago, and castaway fishermen were prohibited from returning. Most notably, commercial interaction with the European powers was limited to one Dutch vessel a year allowed entry at the port of Nagasaki.

Recent scholarship, however, has done much to subvert this image of seclusion, not only by stressing the impact of artifacts and knowledges conveyed through the Dutch trade. More importantly, is has become clear to what extent interactions and commerce within East Asia continued to flourish. The government entertained formal relationships within a Japan-centred tribute system with Korea, Ezo, and the Ryûkyû islands, while goods and ideas continued to pour in from China through private trade. The system of maritime prohibitions, typical of the age and the region, was part of Japan's attempt to assert its place vis-à-vis China, and official relationships to the Qing court were broken off. These restrictions notwithstanding, the 18th century was a period of close cultural entanglement with the Chinese world. The notion of seclusion, then, was partially constructed in retrospect; and indeed the very term 'closed country' (*sakoku*) was a neologism of the 19th century, gaining popular acceptance at a time when Japan's modernization drive was under way.

The Meiji Restoration in 1868 then initiated a feverish era of social reform under the pressures of Western imperialism and the geopolitical constraints of the time. As the Imperial Charter Oath famously phrased it, 'Knowledge shall be sought throughout the world'. As a consequence, an influx of goods, ideas, and people from Europe and the United States set in that contributed to a fundamental transformation of Japanese society. The Westernization craze in the 1870s, in particular, was the context in which many areas of social practice were revolutionized. The Gregorian calendar, a Western school system, modern sciences, but also a conscript army, cylinder hats, and gender separation in public baths were introduced in an effort to turn Japan into a 'modern' country.

The appropriation of things Western took many forms and happened on different levels, but from the start the government took an active part in it. In 1872 a group of high-ranking government officials under the leadership of Iwakura Tomomi set out for an 18-month tour to the United States and Europe. The significance of this study tour (the concomitant aim of revision of unequal treaties was not successful) is underscored by the fact that important government decisions were halted until the return of the delegation. The government then began to hire foreign experts (*oyatoi gaikokujin*) who were expected to establish institutions and forms of knowledge that were considered advanced and enlightened. They included the German Erwin von Bälz, who was instrumental in institutionalizing Western medicine, the American zoologist Edward S. Morse, the Italian artists Antonio Fontanesi and Edoardo Chiossone (who painted the emperor), the German Jacob Meckel whose military reforms are sometimes credited with Japan's victory over China in 1895, and Ludwig Riess who helped transform the various traditions of studying the past into the academic discipline of History. In the opposite direction, large numbers of students were sent to Western Europe and the United States with the intention of replacing the foreign experts upon return. The reciprocal mobility of experts and students, too, drew on Shogunate (bakufu) precedent in the 1860s, although the quantity and impact of this interaction was now of a different quality.

Philosopher and reformer Fukuzawa Yukichi, in a famous phrase, gave expression to the Westernization drive of Meiji Japan with his call to 'leave Asia' and enter the 'civilized' world of the modern West. It is interesting to note that this preoccupation with the 'West' was reciprocated, in the United States, England and France in particular, with a fad for things Japanese. The most significant examples are Japanese wood-block prints, flowing into Europe after the World Exhibition in Vienna in 1873, profoundly influencing painters like van Gogh and Monet and thus contributing to the emergence of modernity in the arts. It is just as important to recognize, however, that the Japanese modernization project was not only oriented towards, and influenced by, the 'West', but drew on resources in the region as well. Good examples are the neologisms that were coined to translate the concepts of the European social sciences but were frequently based on the vocabulary of ancient Chinese texts. In more general terms, the refashioning of Japan as 'modern' not only was predicated on appropriations of Western ideas and institutions, but at the same time needs to be seen against the backdrop of interactions in East Asia.

Japanese colonialism is a case in point. According to the ideology of the time, Japan's colonial conquest was a means both to exhibit power status and to transmit what Japan had learned from the West to the less 'civilized' neighbors in the region. Frequently, however, the colonies were more than areas of supposedly benevolent intervention, or objects of exploitative politics; rather, they were seen as large testing grounds for – sometimes competing – Japanese visions of modernity. The puppet state of Manchukuo, in particular, from the late 1920s served the function of a laboratory of social reform in which the colonial state experimented with labour politics, interventions in the economy, city planning and urbanism. It is clear that the older interpretation of colonialism as an appendix to Japanese history needs to be complemented by insights into the formative and reciprocal relationships between metropole and colonial periphery.

In the first half of the 20th century, the expansionist move into East Asia continued. This was true for migration, as Korea and later Manchuria replaced Hawai'i and California as the principal targets of outward mobility and as locations of diaspora Japaneseness. After the United States, influenced by the discourse of the 'yellow peril', closed its borders to Japanese immigrants provisionally in 1907 and almost entirely in 1924, the government designated the neighbouring colonies as the sites of Japanese settlement. Even though the migration programme in 1936 that aimed at sending 5 million people to Manchuria ultimately failed, nevertheless more than 320,000 Japanese actually settled in Manchuria, frequently organized in farm villages in which they experimented with new forms of ownership and cultivation in an attempt to implement alternative, agrarian forms of Japanese modernity.

The construction of Japan in East Asia, driven by the pan-Asian ideologies that had emerged since the 1890s, continued through the war years. The imperialist drive into the Asian mainland and Southeast Asia was legitimized as a war of liberation from the yoke of European colonialism. As the war increasingly required the total mobilization of the population, the empire needed to grow more inclusive as well. Supported by a discourse that perceived Japan in essence as a 'mixed nation', the incorporation of colonial populations – in particular in Taiwan and Korea – was intensified with inauguration of the so-called kôminka politics of forced (and highly asymmetrical) assimilation from 1937.

The American occupation after defeat in 1945 has usually been described as a Japanese reconversion to the 'West'. Political scientist Maruyama Masao spoke of a 'third opening' of the country, after those of the 16th and the 19th centuries, thus equating transnational ties within East Asia with 'closing' the country; democratic reforms (kaikaku) and 'opening' the country to the West (kaikoku) were seen as almost interchangeable strategies. Under the occupation, the effects of social reforms, of the new constitution and the myriad aspects of cultural exchange reached deep into Japanese society. The postwar years were characterized by a principal orientation towards the United

States, in the framework of the dichotomies of the Cold War and institutionalized through trade flows and the security treaty. 'Asia', by contrast, was relegated to the margins of a discourse that now, differently from during the war years, posited Japan as a homogenous nation.

This has begun to change since the 1990s. The end of the Cold War, the death of Emperor Hirohito, and the breakdown of the monopoly of the Liberal Democratic Party all contributed to the sense that an era had come to an end. In the context of, and as a reaction to, globalization, regional ties re-emerged, and Japan again began 'homing in on Asia'. This is not to say that interactions with Europe and the Americas ceased – the current vogue of *sushi* restaurants and Japanese cartoons (*manga*) in the 'West' suggests the contrary. But trade with the neighbouring countries surpassed commercial exchange with the United States in 1993 for the first time, and the products of Japanese popular culture found ready markets and audiences in Korea, Taiwan, and Singapore after prohibitions of cultural imports from Japan had been abolished. At the same time, Asia emerged as a factor in Japanese politics and society as well. In the field of memory, in particular, the voices of former victims – and of those who claim to represent them – have clamoured for a hearing and have fundamentally changed the dynamics of how the past of the nation is negotiated in Japan. At the beginning of the third millennium, Japan continues to be profoundly shaped by its transnational interactions – and the logic of national self-assertion, of the rhetoric of uniqueness so prominent in Japan, is itself best understood in the context of cross-border exchanges and entanglements.

Sebastian Conrad

Bibliography

Howland D. R. 2002. *Translating the West: language and political reason in 19th-century Japan.* Honolulu: University of Hawai'i Press.

Miyoshi M. and Harootunian H. D. (eds) 1993. *Japan in the world.* Durham: Duke University Press.

Oguma E. 1998. '*Nihonjin*' no kyôkai: Okinawa, Ainu, Taiwan, Chôsen shokuminchi shihai kara fukki undo made. Tokyo: Shinyôsha.

Sansom G. B. 1950. *The Western world and Japan: a study in the interaction of European and Asiatic cultures.* New York: Alfred A. Knopf.

Toby R. 1991. *State and diplomacy in early modern Japan: Asia in the development of the Tokugawa bakufu.* Stanford: Stanford University Press.

Westney E. D. 1987. *Imitation and innovation: the transfer of Western organization patterns to Meiji Japan.* Cambridge, MA: Harvard University Press.

Young L. 1998. *Japan's total empire: Manchuria and the culture of wartime imperialism.* Berkeley: University of California Press.

Related essays

America; Asia; assembly line; China; city planning; Cold War; convergence and divergence; corporations; diasporas; dress; empire and migration; empires and imperialism; ethnicity and race; exile; expositions; financial markets; germs; globalization; history; human mobility; humanities; industrialization; international students; labour migrations; language diplomacy; liberalism; medicine; modernity; museums; nation and state; organization models; pan-isms; population; public policy; regional communities; regions; reparations; Samsung; silk; temperance; tourism; Toyotism; trade; trade (manufactured goods); war; Westernization; white men's countries; world orders; Zen aesthetics

Jazz

From its origins in the overlapping diasporas of Africa and the Americas, as an art form grounded in improvisation and innovation, jazz has always confounded national boundaries. The origins of jazz have long been contested, but whether insisting on the primacy of the Caribbean basin city of New Orleans as the birthplace of jazz, or noting other significant tributaries, critics can agree that jazz was born of a fusion of African and European elements, all mediated through numerous migrations across and within the Caribbean and the Americas. Indeed, W. C. Handy's jazz standard 'St Louis Blues' combines ragtime syncopation with a 16-bar bridge written in the *habanera* or 'Spanish Tinge' rhythm, as well as the standard 12-bar blues with which the song is more commonly associated. Underscoring the transnational conditions of the production and distribution of jazz, 'St Louis Blues' was first recorded with lyrics in 1917 by the Ciro's Club Coon Orchestra, a group of black American artists appearing in Britain.

This cultural hybrid had international appeal. It travelled to Europe with African American soldiers during World War 1, finding audiences in the cosmopolitan cities of Paris, Berlin, and London. For modern writers and artists, jazz epitomized a spirit of rebellion against self-destructive militarism and nationalism. In the US and Europe, the visceral impact of syncopated music became synonymous with the physical and emotional liberation from the strictures and provincialism of late Victorian society. Even such classical music composers as Igor Stravinsky Darius Milhaud and George Gershwin explicitly used jazz syncopation.

American jazz troupes criss-crossed Europe during and after the war. In the summer of 1914, Louis Mitchell and his Southern Symphonist Quintet opened in London and would return to London and travel though England and Scotland over the next two years. In 1919, Will Marion Cook's 'The Syncopates' crossed the Atlantic along with the New Orleans-born soprano saxophonist Sidney Bechet. Among the African American soldiers who chose to remain in Europe after demobilization were members of The Harlem Hellfighters – volunteers in New York's 15th Heavy Foot Infantry Regiment. In Paris, clubs such as Le Grand Duc, run by Eugène Jacques Bullard, the first black combat pilot who had flown for France during the war, transformed the Montmartre district. The jazz scene of Paris and other European cities received a boost from the circulation of jazz records and touring by American jazz musicians. Such musicians as Louis Armstrong and Duke Ellington, who toured Europe during the 1930s, along with hundreds of others over the next decades, often found the European tours more lucrative and audiences more appreciative than those in the United States.

By World War 2, jazz big bands, and the danceable swing music they featured, had become the popular music of choice for several generations of American and European youth, promoted by national mass communications industries of phonograph recordings, film and radio. The war facilitated the further export of swing through military bands; and postwar American occupations had a lasting influence on jazz. The Japanese jazz scene had begun as early as the 1920s, powered by American visitors and especially, immigrants from the US-occupied Philippines, and developed in the dance halls and jazz cafes of Osaka, Yokohama, and Kobe. As in Germany, jazz was banned during World War 2, but took off in popularity during the subsequent US occupation and the Korean War, as American and Japanese musicians mingled; many musicians had served in the armed forces, or performed on tours for the troops. Jazz remains highly popular in Japan, promoted by a younger generation of musicians associated with the 'Jazz Restoration' of the 1980s and 1990s, including drummers Kobayashi Yōichi and Osaka Masahiko, and many Japanese performers work outside of Japan. Other contemporary jazz musicians such as Okuda Atsuya have fused jazz with Zen minimalism and Japanese instruments.

Latin jazz was invigorated in the 1940s when trumpeter Dizzy Gillespie and pianist and arranger Stan Kenton combined the rhythms of Afro-Cuban music with jazz big band ensembles and solo improvisation. Gillespie had met arranger Mario Bauzá in the Cab Calloway Orchestra in the late 1940s. Bauzá introduced Gillespie to the Cuban *conguero* (Conga player in a Yoruba tradition) Luciano 'Chano' Pozo. As percussionist with the Gillespie big band, Chano Pozo co-wrote with Gillespie the Afro-Cuban jazz classic 'Manteca'. Another Cuban *conguero*, Mongo Santamaría, worked with the American vibraphonist Cal Tjader, and Afro-Latin mambo dance music was represented by such artists as Celia Cruz, Tito Puente, Tito Rodrigues, and Machito and His Afro-Cubans. Bossa Nova, a fusion of Brazilian samba and jazz, was created in the late 1950s out of a fusion of jazz and Afro-Brazilian samba by Brazilians Antonio Carlos Jobim and João and Astrud Gilberto. Tenor saxophonist Stan Getz recorded with Jobim and the Gilbertos.

At the same time, Argentinean-born Astor Piazzolla revolutionized the classic tango by incorporating jazz and classical elements and creating *Nuevo tango*. Piazzolla spent most of his childhood in New York City, but travelled between New York and Argentina between 1937 and 1955, when he returned to Buenos Aires to form the Octeto Buenos Aires. Composing with musicians including Gerry Mulligan and Al Di Meola, Piazzolla gained recognition throughout Europe and the United States. His transnational influence was further facilitated by his residency in Italy during Argentina's military dictatorship from 1976 to 1983.

During the early 1960s, Duke Ellington heard the South African pianist and composer

Abdullah Ibrahim (Dollar Brand) playing in a club in Zürich and produced Ibrahim's debut album. Over the next decades, during which he was mainly in exile from apartheid South Africa, Ibrahim toured Europe and the United States, eventually returning to the post-apartheid Republic of South Africa in the mid 1990s. Ibrahim has brought his distinctive fusion of the stylings of jazz innovators such as Ellington, Thelonious Monk and others with the rhythms and melodies of his upbringing in South Africa to audiences the world over.

The profoundly transnational origins and circulation of jazz lend an ironic quality to the characterization of jazz as 'America's music'. There is much truth to this view of jazz as an American art form. But to suggest that jazz is a quintessential expression of American identity, as trumpeter Wynton Marsalis, documentary film maker Ken Burns and others have done, tends to obscure the past and continuing dynamism of jazz as a music that crossed numerous national and cultural boundaries.

The idea that jazz was not only unique, but that it epitomized American ideals of freedom became axiomatic during the Cold War era as the Voice of America broadcaster Willis Conover introduced jazz to audiences behind the Iron Curtain and throughout the decolonizing world. When Conover's 'Music USA' was launched over short-wave radio in January 1955, a flood of mail came in from Europe, Africa, Asia, the Middle East, and from behind the Iron Curtain. In 1955, the programme reached an estimated 30 million people in 80 countries, a number that would triple over the next decade. Through Conover's broadcasts, jazz developed in deep and vibrant clandestine subcultures throughout the Soviet Union and Eastern Europe, in cities from Moscow and Leningrad to Prague and Warsaw. New generations of writers and artists, such as Václav Havel, Umberto Eco, and countless others found inspiration in jazz, as evidenced in the Czech novelist Josef Škvorecký's The Bass Saxophone (1978). When jazz musicians toured Eastern bloc countries in the 1960s and 1970s under the auspices of the State Department, they encountered deeply knowledgeable fans.

Ironically, the US State Department was a catalyst for the further internationalization of jazz, when beginning in 1956 Dizzy Gillespie and his big band toured the Middle East, South Asia, and Brazil. Over the next two decades, the State Department sent hundreds of jazz – and later gospel, soul and blues – musicians on tours throughout Africa, the Middle East, Eastern Europe and the Soviet Union, South America, and Asia. While the State Department hoped to showcase American modernism at its finest and to counter global charges of US racism by promoting black American musicians, the musicians themselves promoted civil rights, and above all, sought out local musicians for informal sessions and creative exchanges. The collaborations that resulted from these encounters were represented in such releases as Duke Ellington's Far East Suite (1963) and Soul Call (1966) and Dave Brubeck's Jazz Impressions of Eurasia. While in India in 1958, the pianist Brubeck accompanied Abdul Jaffra Khan, the acclaimed sitar player. On his final State Department tour in 1972, Duke Ellington and his band played with Mulatu Astatqé, whose compositions fused traditional Ethiopian music and jazz.

In 1978, while performing at the Bombay Jazz Festival, along with trumpeter Clark Terry and jazz musicians from India, Japan and Europe, saxophonist Sonny Rollins declared that 'jazz is really an international music'. From his calypso-inspired jazz standard 'St Thomas' to his many international tours, and his personal study of Zen philosophy, Rollins's career and experience demonstrated the global impact and resonances of jazz. Trumpeter Don Cherry, who had performed with 'Free Jazz' innovator Ornette Coleman, frequently toured overseas, promoting 'World Music' at jazz festivals. Cherry experimented with musics from China, Japan, Brazil, India, Tibet, Bali, and North Africa, and developed expertise on the Brazilian berimbao and the Balinese gamelan. Rollins and Cherry are among the countless musicians who have contributed to the ongoing evolution of jazz as a global musical language.

Today, as debates rage on about the origin and character of jazz, and cities around the globe from Mumbai to Prague host international jazz festivals, irony abounds in the fact that jazz remains more popular in many countries than it is in the United States.

Penny Von Eschen

Bibliography
Atkins E. T. 2001. Blue Nippon: authenticating jazz in Japan. Durham, NC and London: Duke University Press.

Fernández R. A. 2006. *From Afro-Cuban rhythms to Latin jazz*. Berkeley: University of California Press.

Shack W. A. 2001. *Harlem in Montmartre: a Paris jazz story between the Great Wars*. Berkeley: University of California Press.

Von Eschen P. 2004. *Satchmo blows up the world: jazz ambassadors play the Cold War*. Cambridge, MA: Harvard University Press.

Related essays

America; classical music; Cold War; cultural capitals; diasporas; music; orchestras; performing artists; radio; salsa; Santería; voodoo; war; World Music; Zen aesthetics

Jeans

Blue jeans symbolized the emerging international youth culture of the post-World War 2 period. They evolved from rugged work clothes in the 19th-century American West to rebellious symbol in the 1950s and 60s to designer fashion in the 1980s. By the turn of the 21st century blue jeans had achieved universal appeal, transcending class, age, and gender differences to become an integral part of a globalized wardrobe. Yet they still maintained their mythical status as icons of American culture.

Contrary to popular assumptions, blue jeans were not invented by Levi Strauss, the Bavarian immigrant turned wholesaler in gold rush California. The earliest references to a heavy cotton-wool blend fabric called serge de Nîmes (later called denim) date from the 16th century. Around the same time a similar fabric was produced in Genoa, Italy, and used for heavy-duty sailor pants. This fabric came to be known in France and England by the French name for Genoa, Gênes (later Jeans). Yet until Levi Strauss introduced them to the American West and outfitted them with the characteristic rivets around openings and pockets in the 1870s, jeans were a little known commodity in textile manufacturing.

Until World War 2, manufacturers marketed blue jeans and denim overalls primarily to US farmers, cowboys, and other workers. In the 1950s, young working- and middle-class men began wearing jeans as physical markers of social and cultural protest against middle-class respectability and its grey flannel suit standard. Blue jeans acquired iconic status among youth with the 1953 motion picture *The Wild One*, starring Marlon Brando

as the leader of a raucous motorcycle gang, followed in 1955 by *Blackboard Jungle* with Vic Morrow as a high-school delinquent. That same year, James Dean wore jeans, a white T-shirt, and a windbreaker in the movie *Rebel Without a Cause*. Unlike Brando and Morrow, who depicted working-class rebels, Dean portrayed the high-school-aged son of middle-class parents in a solidly middle-class environment. Dean's character Jim Stark discarded his suit and tie along with his willingness to conform to his parents' middle-class expectations. The movie associated the business suit with effeminacy; jeans with male prowess, personal integrity, and a will to act.

Blue jeans entered the global marketplace as part of the export of American movies, music, and popular culture in the post-World War 2 era. European youth in particular embraced the new fashion along with jazz, rock and roll, and new forms of dance. American popular culture offered an escape from the stifling, tradition-bound, and nationalist norms prescribed by the older generation. Yet the new form of dress also made these youths easily identifiable targets of conservative critics of Americanization who associated jeans and American fashion with juvenile delinquency.

The generational battles over blue jeans spread to the Eastern bloc and thus became part of the Cold War conflict. In East Germany, in particular, authorities equated jeans with Western materialism, political dissidence, and criminal behaviour. Ironically, the efforts of socialist states to undercut the wearing of jeans facilitated their acceptance among conservative anti-Communists in the West. Much like jazz, blue jeans evolved from counterculture to mainstream culture. Rather than breaking with American tradition, as they had in the 1950s, they became part of that tradition. In the international arena blue jeans now signified Americanization.

As blue jeans became part of an androgynous wardrobe in the 1960s and 70s – by then women bought between 30 and 40 percent of all jeans – fashion designers discovered them as a versatile commodity that could be stylized for an international middle- and upper-class clientele. Advertisers began to mix ambiguous sexualized imagery and gender bending with standard American myths of freedom and the rugged American West. By the turn of the 21st century, blue jeans thus epitomized the fundamental contradictions of the global marketplace: they were seen as

both individualist and conformist, materialist and idealist, cosmopolitan and rustic.

Petra Goedde

Bibliography

Gordon B. 'American denim: blue jeans
and their multiple layers of meaning', in
Cunningham P. and Voso Lab S. (eds) 1991.
Dress and popular culture. Bowling Green:
Bowling Green State University Popular
Press, 31–7.

Kroes R. 'American empire and cultural
imperialism: a view from the receiving
end', in Bender T. (ed.) 2002. *Rethinking
American history in a global age.* Berkeley:
University of California Press, 295–313.

Poiger U. G. 2000. *Jazz, rock, and rebels: cold
war politics and American culture in a divided
Germany.* Berkeley: University of California
Press.

Sullivan J. 2006. *Jeans: a cultural history of an
American icon.* New York: Gotham.

Related essays

1960s; America; Cold War; dress; fashion;
jazz; rock; textiles; T-shirt; Westernization

Justice

Justice in international affairs is the quality
of fairness. It finds expression through equitable legal institutions, actions directed
toward peace, and the affirmation of human
rights.

It would be difficult to overestimate the
importance of the concept of justice in international affairs. No matter what the cultural
or political background of the various nation
states, justice is seen as a foundational virtue
that can serve as both a goal to be sought and
a guide for actions to attain that goal. The
struggle to take this concept, which has for
centuries been at the heart of philosophical
thought and argument, and give it meaning
in a world of contending nation states has
been long and arduous. The problem lies in
defining the subject for whom justice is to
be sought. How that subject is defined will
affect how justice itself is defined, and that, in
turn, will affect what steps are to be taken to
achieve that goal. An emphasis on individual
human beings as the subject of justice gives
quite a different result from an emphasis on
the state, and if the emphasis is shifted from
the state to the international community as a
whole, the outcome is different yet.

Philosophers have not found a solution to
this problem that can command widespread
assent, nor have they been able to agree on
exactly what justice is. Where they end up in
their discussions depends on where they start,
whether from a utilitarian, a Kantian, an idealist, or some other base. It has been left to
non-specialists such as government officials,
diplomats, international civil servants, military leaders, and concerned private citizens
to work through the conceptual and institutional difficulties and provide ways for justice
to have a transnational presence. This has
meant taking broad generalities regarding the
desirability of justice, and giving those generalities specific content and sometimes a specific institutional base. Thus the statement in
the preamble to the Covenant of the League of
Nations (1919) about achieving international
peace and security, 'by the maintenance of
justice and a scrupulous respect for all treaty
obligations' was given an institutional means
of operation through the establishment of
the Permanent Court of International Justice
at The Hague in The Netherlands in 1922.
Similarly, the general statement in the United
Nations Charter (1945) about settling international disputes 'in conformity with the principles of justice and international law' was
given a definite place in international affairs
through the establishment that same year of
the International Court of Justice, also at The
Hague, where the content of those 'principles
of justice' could be worked out.

These are examples of the way that the
concept of justice has been brought out
of the realm of discussion into the messy,
sometimes violent, give-and-take of everyday life on the international plane. In these
examples, justice has been linked to international law. This linkage gives a transnational presence to justice and provides it
with an institutional vehicle through which
that presence can be felt. Further, linking
justice and law to these two international
courts gives one answer to the subject-
problem mentioned earlier. The subject of
justice in this instance is the state. States
and only states can bring disputes to the
International Court of Justice, and the same
was true for its predecessor, the Permanent
Court of International Justice. In their various dealings with each other, and especially
in their disputes with each other, the states
of the international system have, since the
end of the First World War, been able to seek

justice in a court of law, first through the Permanent Court, and, since 1945, through the International Court. That the states have frequently preferred bullying and balancing tactics – with war as a common result – does not negate the fact that other means have been available where contending concepts of justice could be thrashed out. The confusion that results when justice becomes not a standard to be administered by an impartial body, but a prize to be seized in rhetorical battle can be seen in the exchanges between the Allied and Associated Powers and the delegates of Germany following the latter's defeat in World War 1.

The fighting had been brought to a close in November 1918 on the basis of an agreement in which the concept of justice occupied a central position. Justice was to be the basis of arrangements that would not only restore peace to the world but would ensure the continuance of that peace far into the future. Reliance was placed on US President Woodrow Wilson's many inspiring references to justice in his wartime speeches. But when it came to drawing up a treaty that would give practical expression to this Wilsonian ideal – an ideal that was agreed on by all parties – inspiration was not enough. Confident in their ideas of justice, the Powers drew up a treaty that the German representatives promptly decried for its lack of justice and for putting might 'in place of right'. There the matter stood so far as definitions of justice were concerned since, in 1918, there was no transnational institution that could resolve the issue.

Of particular interest in this case is the fact that all the parties involved in these negotiations agreed on one thing: the peace to come must be based on justice. Without justice, peace would be little more than a pause between fighting as aggrieved states attempted to remedy what they saw as an unjust state of affairs. This, as it turned out, is exactly what happened some 20 years after the peace treaty was signed at Versailles in 1919 with the outbreak of World War 2. The renewal of war, despite last-ditch efforts to avoid it, is a powerful demonstration of the way that peace in the international system depends on some agreed-upon definition of the concept of justice as well as agreement on ways to remedy a situation felt to be unjust.

The belief that such an agreement was not only possible but that it had been reached was behind the establishment of the League of Nations in 1919. That same belief undergirds the United Nations, established in 1945. The provisions of the United Nations Charter are designed to maintain peace by creating equitable international arrangements, and providing ways for those arrangements to be adjusted to the changing international situation. Thus the linkage of the transnational goals of peace and justice is given both institutional expression and a means of operation in the United Nations through its organs such as the General Assembly and the Economic and Social Council, and through associated agencies such as the International Labour Organization and the World Health Organization.

The United Nations organization had scarcely got under way when its provisions for peace and justice were brought to a test. The Korean War (1950–53) was the result of members of the United Nations attempting to restore peace to the Korean peninsula after North Korean troops crossed an internationally recognized dividing line into South Korea. At issue was the question of what means should be used to achieve justice in international arrangements. Had the Charter outlawed the unilateral use of force to achieve that end, or was the Charter just another list of laudable but impractical goals? For Trygve Lie, the first secretary-general of the United Nations, the answer was obvious. If the unilateral pursuit of justice were to become the norm, warfare would be perpetual, and justice, however defined, would disappear. Lie spoke for many when he said that a collective response to enforce the Charter was essential in this first serious test of its provisions.

The political complications of the Korean situation are beyond the scope of this entry. What is important here is to note the transnational aspects of this defense of the link between peace and justice in the international system. The unspoken assumption was and is that a just peace is the ideal international condition, one that benefits each individual state as well as the system as a whole. But the transnational aspects of this linkage between peace and justice go further. If a just peace were to be achieved, not only states but also individual human beings would benefit, and they would benefit in ways that would transcend or take no account of national borders. In that ideal condition, people would be able to pursue their individual goals and live out their lives without fear that international tensions might at any moment plunge them into war.

With this reference to individual human beings we come to the third linkage that gives justice a transnational presence. A link between justice and human rights is now added to the links of justice and law and justice and peace. Here the intended subject of justice is quite clearly the human person, no matter where that person is living and no matter whether dealt with in an individual or collective capacity. In an international system where the emphasis has traditionally been on the nation state's unchallenged freedom of action within its own borders, this shift of emphasis to individual human beings carries obvious risks. At the least it can create tension if a state's treatment of its citizens is perceived to be so unjust as to call for international comment, and perhaps international action. But if international action to uphold the link between justice and human rights should become the norm, the whole system could be in danger, based as it is on the sovereign state as the basic unit of international organization.

Because they are aware of this threat, the states of the international system have been slow to move toward the enforcement of international human rights standards. They have agreed, in principle, that any attempt to give the concept of justice an international presence must include not only the maintenance of peace and the establishment of legal institutions, but also a firm commitment to human rights. Thus they have been willing to sign on to the many human rights declarations, resolutions, and treaties that have, since the end of the Second World War, issued from the UN General Assembly or from UN-sponsored conferences. Implementation is another matter. They have insisted that implementation is wholly within their sovereign prerogatives. To give authoritative weight to this claim, they can fall back on one of the oldest principles of the present international system, that of non-interference in a state's internal affairs. As Article 7 of the UN Charter puts it, 'Nothing contained in the present Charter shall authorize the United Nations to intervene in matters which are essentially within the domestic jurisdiction of any state.'

Revulsion at egregious offenses against human rights, plus increasing pressure from private individuals and non-governmental organizations are gradually softening this attitude. The establishment of the European Court of Human Rights (1953), the Inter-American Court of Human Rights (1979), and the International Criminal Court (2002) are signs of this change. Here are institutions for mediating disputes about human rights implementation, and in some cases for bringing offenders to trial. The connection between justice and human rights is affirmed by the existence of these courts. And, as their proceedings and opinions become part of ongoing discussions of international affairs, the link between justice and human rights will be strengthened.

Justice and law. Justice and peace. Justice and human rights. Through these linkages the transnational principle of justice has been provided with ways to become a vital presence in international affairs. Whether those ways will be used, is a question for each generation to answer.

Dorothy V. Jones

Bibliography

Jackson R. 2000. *The global covenant: human conduct in a world of states.* Oxford: Oxford University Press.

Jones D. V. 2002. *Toward a just world: the critical years in the search for international justice.* Chicago: University of Chicago Press.

Nardin T. and Mapel D. R. (eds) 1992. *Traditions of international ethics.* Cambridge: Cambridge University Press.

Politis N. 1943. *La morale internationale.* Neuchâtel: La Baconnière.

Related essays

Ethical Culture; human rights; intergovernmental organizations; internationalisms; League of Nations system; legal order; pacifism; *The Wretched of the Earth*; United Nations system; war; war crimes; Woodrow, Wilson; world orders

K

Kessler, Harry von 1868–1937

Called by W. H. Auden the most cosmopolitan man who ever lived, Count Harry von Kessler played an important role before the First World War in the international art scene and after the war as a spokesman for pacifism and reconciliation.

Born in Paris to a German father and an Anglo-Irish mother, Kessler was educated in France, England, and Germany. As a university student he discovered Nietzsche and befriended Eliszabeth Förster-Nietzsche, becoming an important supporter of the Nietzsche Archive. Inheriting a fortune upon his father's death, Kessler hoped to join the diplomatic service. While waiting in Berlin for a position to open up, he became interested in the emerging modern art and literature of the 1890s, eventually joining the board of *Pan*, the most influential modernist journal in Germany. On behalf of *Pan* Kessler travelled frequently to Paris and London to solicit the work of such writers and artists as Paul Verlaine, William Morris, and the Belgian architect and designer Henry van de Velde. Through his connections Kessler was able to obtain for van de Velde the post of director of the school of arts and crafts in Weimar, the forerunner of what would become the Bauhaus. When his application to join the diplomatic service was finally rejected in 1902, Kessler joined van de Velde as director of the grand ducal museum of arts and crafts there in Weimar.

Under the leadership of van de Velde and Kessler the 'New Weimar' became a flourishing centre of aesthetic modernism in Imperial Germany. Kessler put on important exhibitions featuring modern French, English, and German artists. In 1903 he helped found the German Artists League, an umbrella organization designed to protect and support modern artists in Germany. Due to the opposition of conservative circles in Weimar and of Kaiser Wilhelm II, he was forced to resign his post in 1906 but nevertheless continued to sponsor modern artists. His patronage of Aristide Maillol launched the French sculptor's career. He introduced the English theatre visionary Gordon Craig to Germany, and his sponsorship of English book design helped revolutionize German publishing as well. In 1906, at a time of growing tension between Germany and Great Britain, Kessler drafted two public letters that were published in newspapers in both countries, signed by prominent German and British cultural figures, expressing mutual admiration and peaceful sentiments. Other transnational endeavours of the prewar years included his effort to build a monument to Nietzsche for which he created an international committee of writers and artists. In 1914 his ballet *The Legend of Joseph*, written with Hugo von Hofmannsthal, opened in London and Paris, danced by the Ballets Russes and composed by Richard Strauss.

Despite his international sympathies, Kessler proved an ardent supporter of the German war effort, serving principally on the Eastern front. In 1916 he was sent to Switzerland as an attaché to organize cultural propaganda but with a secret mission of feeling out the possibilities of a separate peace with France. He increasingly began to criticize the leadership of Imperial Germany and to express an interest in pacifism. Upon the defeat of Germany, he was therefore prepared to support the new Weimar Republic. After a brief stint as ambassador to Poland, he returned to Germany to help organize the Democratic Party. In response to Wilson's League of Nations, he drafted a plan for a genuinely transnational world organization where international bodies such as unions and cartels of producers and consumers would supervise the world economy and ease international tensions. With this proposal Kessler became a leading figure in the German pacifist movement. During the Ruhr crisis he undertook a number of diplomatic missions to England and France on behalf of the German government. He also embarked upon extensive lecture tours in America in 1923 and 1924, explaining the German position. After a serious illness in 1925, he dedicated himself to his famous Cranach-Presse. The Nazi seizure of power forced him into exile where he died in 1937. His most enduring work is the diary he kept from 1880 to 1937, one of the greatest ever written.

Laird M. Easton

Bibliography

Easton L. M. 2002. *The Red Count: the life and times of Harry Kessler*. Berkeley: University of California Press.

Related essays

cosmopolitanism and universalism; design; Garvey, Marcus Mosiah; internationalisms;

Kindergarten

The kindergarten is a diasporic institution, global in its identification and local in its execution. While we all understand the kindergarten in some ways, it inevitably reflects the culture and values of its location. Kindergarten, in this essay, is narrowly defined as the institution originating in Germany in the mid 19th century, based on Friedrich Froebel's theory of child development. It began as a specific programme of instruction, brought out of Germany by trained teachers who believed in and taught the original codified system. The example of the kindergarten, with its popularity and wide dissemination, provides an ideal opportunity to show how one idea was diffused globally, separated from its original context, and transformed in each setting by local needs.

The kindergarten movement began in Germany with Friedrich Froebel (1782–1852), an educator and visionary figure in the study of early childhood development. Rejecting religious beliefs about the inherent sinfulness of children, Froebel declared that children were essentially good, that a child's will should not be broken but shaped. He divided the process of early education between birth and age six into discrete stages of physical and mental development. For each stage, he devised special exercises, materials, 'gifts', and 'occupations', which consisted of objects and games carefully designed to teach specific skills and moral lessons. Suspecting that parents were not capable of giving the child the necessary education and discipline, but believing also that the child was not ready for school, he sought an institutional alternative suited to the 'wealth, abundance, and vigour of the inner and outer life' of childhood. His solution was the Kindergarten, or 'children's garden', where the child could be with peers, outside family restraints, yet in a protected environment.

In the years following the German revolution in 1848, educators familiar with Froebel's ideas fled to Britain and the United States and the countries of Western Europe, where the kindergarten remained a small movement dominated by an intellectual coterie of Froebel's German disciples. Within a relatively short period in the latter decades of the 19th century, however, the kindergarten spread with astonishing rapidity around the world. By World War 1, the kindergarten was a standard feature of education systems in both the modern and developing nations throughout Asia, Africa, and the West. The questions raised by this phenomenon are central to current discourses regarding the influences of Western culture on national identities globally: has Western education been a form of imperialism or colonialism; what is the importance of education in the creation of citizenship and national identity; what are the processes of cultural borrowing by which ideas are diffused and transformed and, most centrally, how do we understand the hybridized result?

Although Western institutions such as the kindergarten have flowed freely from west to east and from north to south, the accompanying presumed ideologies of individualism, Christianity, and democratic liberalism have not necessarily accompanied these institutions. On the contrary, examples of kindergartens outside the West reveal the power of local culture, politics, and nationalism to separate the kindergarten from its original context. Local educators transformed, or recontextualized, the kindergarten in accordance with local needs and practices and, simultaneously, were drawn into contact with international organizations, movements, and ideas. Moreover, the kindergarten did not always flow from the West to other nations. It was also borrowed among non-Western nations, disconnected entirely from its origin in the West.

The kindergarten travelled internationally in several ways. The first method was through direct contact with the ideas. After 1848, German educators, including political refugees Bertha Ronge, Margarethe Schurz and Baroness von Marenholtz-Bülow who had worked with Froebel, brought the ideas to England, the United States, and Western Europe in the late 19th century. In these locations, the kindergartens remained German-language schools for the small communities of German exiles. It would take time for the idea to be recognized by local educators and adapted to the language, values, and cultural practices of the kindergarten's new homes. In the United States, kindergarten pioneers Susan Blow and William T. Harris in St Louis became acquainted with the German educators and were eager to introduce the kindergarten to American schools, as a way of bringing it into wider use. They were public school teachers, and naturally wanted to incorporate the kindergarten into the public schools. There and elsewhere, it was seen as a socializing institution. Sensitive to parents' complaints about the 'Germanness' of the immigrant version, they opened the first Americanized public kindergarten in 1873 where instruction was in English and references to German culture were replaced with familiar American songs, folk stories, and games. Moreover, the original Froebelian idea of free play was modified to reflect the American parents' demands for early reading instruction.

Secondary acquisitions were those models taken from kindergartens that had already gone through a process of transformation. As an illustration, members of the Japanese government, including Minister of Education Tanaka Fujimaro, travelled to the United States in 1871 where they observed the nascent St Louis model. In a flurry of Westernization after the Meiji Restoration of 1868, the Japanese also borrowed books, desks, pencils, and other material objects of American schooling along with the kindergarten idea. Drawing on the Americanized model, Japanese educators established the first private kindergarten in Kyoto in 1875, and the next year founded the first national kindergarten training school attached to the Tokyo Women's Normal School. Similarly, in 1883, Australian educators enthusiastically imported the more established Americanized (not British) kindergarten as their model. Once adopted, these models were similarly indigenized to conform to local norms.

From kindergarten training schools in France, the United States, and Britain, new kindergarten teachers also included Protestant and Catholic missionaries who would bring the kindergarten to Asia, Africa, and Latin America, either attached to colonial governments or as agents of independent Christian missionary agencies. In some instances, the presence of the missionaries played an oppositional role in the establishment of government-sponsored kindergartens. As an illustration, Ottoman Turkey, deeply engaged in nation building, attempted to inculcate a unifying national identity through education by applying a one-language policy and regulating Muslim religious stories and moral lessons. Christian education was banned among Muslims, allowing the government to embrace the modern ideas of child development while distancing itself from what were perceived as divisive teachings and political activism brought by missionaries who supported the Christian minorities.

In unique cases, the kindergarten was coopted both to create national identity and to preserve it. As early as 1899, kindergartens were established in pre-statehood Palestine as the site for teaching the secular Zionism that would form the values and nationalism essential to settlement. Educating boys and girls alike, secular kindergartens replaced religious schools. Idealistic teachers sought to unify immigrant children using modernized Hebrew to teach Jewish history, and celebrated holidays and festivals newly created to commemorate and embed the Settlement of Palestine. In a different environment of extreme oppression, during the long period of Poland's partition and occupation from 1772 to 1918, the kindergarten was used subversively to teach Polish language and culture as a form of resistance against the various occupying governments of Russia, Germany, Austria, and Prussia. Along with the Catholic Church, the kindergarten served as a location for the preservation of Polish language, history, and culture until Poland's independence.

Finally, tertiary acquisitions were those models twice removed from the original. In China, the kindergarten was borrowed from Japan rather than from the West. The Chinese preferred to adopt the Japanese version, which they saw as already adapted to a Confucian social order. It was easier to borrow the Japanese model than to attempt translating Western texts and institutions. In another case, the Communist Vietnamese government borrowed the post-Tsarist model from Russia for political reasons, rejecting the French colonial model in their midst. Whether in missionary or colonial settings or as welcomed acquisitions, clearly the subtext of the kindergarten curriculum was not only to nurture and enhance the natural stages of child development, but also to support core national values.

As a function of language and the traditions of activism, the international organizations of the kindergarten movement were located in the West. The Froebel Institute in Chicago, along with other American and British centres, trained the kindergarten leaders who in turn trained others in Western and non-Western settings. Linked through journals and newsletters, the international movement, composed predominantly of women, refined and debated the details of Froebelian pedagogy and practice and kept in touch with the work of kindergartners 'abroad'. Froebel's *Mother Play* and other texts were translated and disseminated widely, linking the international, indigenized kindergartens to the movement's theoretical origins. Among American missionaries committed to education along with evangelism, many remained connected to the Western educationists through regular communication and travel.

In summary, the kindergarten spread from the West, producing a complex global discourse on the child, education, psychology, and a newly evolving science of child rearing and child development. In this respect, educators who adopted the kindergarten, even those distancing themselves politically from the West, were linked to a global community of modern pedagogy. On the other hand, despite the kindergarten's Western origin, in each instance the kindergarten became a local institution. In the end, the kindergarten took on an identity and function of its own in each national setting, unevenly connected to the rest of the world by a belief in the kindergarten idea, and always conventionalized as a comfortable neighbourhood school.

Roberta Wollons

Bibliography

Altbach P. and Kelly G. P. 1978. *Education and colonialism*. Harlow and New York: Longman.

Brosterman N. 1997. *Inventing kindergarten*. New York: Harry N. Abrams.

Ross E. D. 1976. *The kindergarten crusade: the establishment of preschool education in the United States*. Athens, OH: Ohio University Press.

Shapiro M. 1983. *The child's garden: the kindergarten movement from Froebel to Dewey*. University Park: Pennsylvania State University Press.

Wollons R. (ed.) 2000. *Kindergartens and cultures: the global diffusion of an idea*. New Haven: Yale University Press.

Related essays
1848; childhood; children's rights; exile; femininity; language diplomacy; missionaries; nation and state; organization models; theatre; United Nations Educational, Scientific and Cultural Organization (UNESCO)

educational programmes; Westernization; women's movements; Zionism

Knowledge

Theories of science and the transmission of scientific knowledge have undergone substantial revision and reworking over the last three decades. Different perspectives, theories and bodies of scholarship have more specifically revised the topos of the exchange or the circulation of scientific knowledge between India, for instance, and Europe over the last three centuries, providing a platform from which to explore such phenomena in other regions of the non-Western world. Modernization theory is founded on the premise that modern science is one of the constituents of modernity itself that encroaches upon and invades the domain of the traditional sciences of non-Western societies. Modern science is contrasted with these traditional sciences, a science whose growth, it is argued, was arrested for a number of social and cultural reasons. One version of the standard tale suggests that the rate of expansion of the dominion of modern science was curtailed by resistance posed by persisting premodern forces within these societies in transition. There are several cognate versions, sharing a number of tropes. These have been challenged from a variety of theoretical perspectives in sociology proper, sociology of science, and postcolonial history and theory.

Theories of multiple modernities and transmodernity have opened up a discussion of non-Western forms of knowledge that is not anchored in the standard binaries of tradition–modern, Eastern–Western, primitive–advanced etc. The first of two underlying assumptions of theories of modernity and modernization considered modernization to be a process of the global diffusion of Western civilization – this assumption was contested, especially by scholars such as Shmuel Eisenstadt, Wolfgang Schluchter or Björn Wittrock in a *Daedalus* special issue in 1998, and subsequently by many others. It had been supposed that the expansion of modernity and the global diffusion of the institutions, structure and culture of modernization would eliminate differences among nations and civilizations. The persistence of differences was explained in terms of the endurance of premodern factors. However, the non-emergence of a single modern civilization implied that the cultural codes of modernity were reshaped by the codes of the societies that were exposed to new external and internal challenges, inaugurating multiple modernities. The recognition of the multiplicity of modernities inspired the study of non-Western societies with a new social theory, while avoiding the pitfalls of the previous approaches.

The idea of transmodernity relates to that of multiple modernities, and arises from the understanding that the centrality of Europe is just two centuries old. Consequently, elements of non-Western societies that escaped the clasp of Western modernity became the foci for the resurgence of potentialities thus far blinded by Western culture and modernity. Dussel advances the thesis that 'modernity's recent impact on the planet's multiple cultures (Chinese, Southeast Asian, Hindu, Islamic, Bantu, Latin American) produced a varied "reply" by all of them to the modern "challenge"' (Dussel 2002, 221). The cultural horizon where these novel renewals erupt, Dussel calls the multicultural moment of transmodernity. Modernization theory thus appears as a technology for managing the world system, while its critique in the Latin American world and South Asia is limited by Eurocentrism since it is located within a system of cultural production that defines itself with respect to the disciplinary boundaries as established in the West. This led postcolonial theorists such as Dipesh Chakrabarty to make a case for 'provincializing Europe', which in effect requires a re-reading of the modern European canon in order to reveal the parochialism of the Western academic imagination.

Furthermore, the diversity of disciplinary renewals produced by an intersecting set of intellectual concerns has generated a particularly fruitful conjuncture of postcolonial theory, feminist theory and post-Kuhnian science studies. Postcolonial studies have disclosed the close interaction between the European and non-European sciences, revealing the causal relations between the processes of European expansion and the growth of modern science and technology. Consequently, new spaces open up for interrogating modernization and development theory, and for challenging prevalent models of the expansion and diffusion of European sciences and technology. A polycentric model of the growth of several scientific traditions in interaction with each other replaces the script of modern science as a cultural universal. The accompanying table heuristically contrasts the distinction between the Eurocentric and another version of postcolonial theory of science in terms of the theory of history, the theory of science, and the underlying theory of transmission (see Table 1).

There are features common to the range of postcolonial standpoints. The production of scientific knowledge, on the one hand, is viewed from a contextualist perspective across the frames. This is further evident in the uniform opposition to Eurocentrism in theory. The genre of social history has played a very important role in destabilizing the Eurocentric study and theorization of history. The sociology of scientific knowledge highlighted the distributed nature of the process of knowledge production, argued for the socially embodied nature of scientific knowledge and thereby brought into the field of visibility a variety of actors hitherto invisible to the gaze of the historian or sociologist. In fact, this is one of the three radicalizing strains in our conception of science that Sandra Harding refers to in her Is science multicultural? (1998). The social studies of science have pushed along several directions over the last couple of decades, some of which have given cause for controversy. A new direction that is increasingly being pursued moves the question away from epistemology and cultural practices, to divergent geographies of knowledge, or 'spatially oriented histories of scientific thought and practice'. This translates into a concern with spatial contexts or microgeographies of places where science is pursued, such as the city, the region and the nation, the 'local environment in which ... practitioners carry out their tasks' (Naylor 2005, 1).

Table 1 The distinction between Eurocentric and postcolonial theories of science

Constitutive elements	Eurocentric theory	Postcolonial theory
Theory of history	Isolationist	Multicultural
Theory of science	Transcendent	Contextual
Theory of transmission	Arrow of influence points eastward	Multidirectional arrows of influence constituting a network

We now address the question about what counts as 'knowledge' in the Indian philosophical tradition. One construction of the Indian philosophical tradition presents it as either purely metaphysical or mystical. David Zilberman argued that traditionally in Indian civilization philosophy enjoyed the status of a 'system of culture'. This shifts the standard essentialization of Indian philosophy as other-worldly, in the opposite direction where it occupies the centre of culture. This approach runs into the possibility of conflating Indian civilization with Hinduism at whose core are the Hindu systems of philosophy, to the exclusion of other equally significant systems such as Buddhism, Jainism, Islam and the other heterodox systems. The important feature of this characterization is the assertion that these are not religious philosophies, since philosophical concerns were never coupled with the personal devotion or the lack of it of the philosophers. Thus reckoning with the differences between the literary production of Western and Indian philosophical texts, the latter being more technically oriented than discursively reflective, the essential difference resided in that Indian philosophical systems 'can be understood as a constituent of objective reality, rather than as an abstract mental reflection upon it' (Zilberman 1988, 3). Similarly, P. T. Raju argues that the aims of Indian philosophy included not merely the love of wisdom, but more importantly the life of wisdom, and in that sense philosophy of action is a central theme in the tradition. Approaching Indian philosophy from the perspective of religious thought is then inadequate, and it should be possible to look at the schools of philosophy functioning within an extended geographical cosmopolis.

The comparative method

Most often cross-cultural dialogue between philosophical traditions has been set within the frame of the Western philosophical tradition which provides a vocabulary and a grammar within which to apprehend or translate the Indian philosophical tradition. The weight of traditions, disciplines and theories inherited from ancient, medieval and early modern commentators shapes any exploration of what the Indian traditions consider knowledge to be. A number of factors shaped the encounter of 17th-century Europeans with Indians. Firstly,

the Europeans lived in a world of 'signs and correspondences', whilst the Hindus and Muslims 'operated within a substantive theory of objects and persons' (Cohn 1997, 18). The spectacles through which the English viewed the divinely created world meant that it was apprehended through the senses and comprehended empirically. In invading India, Cohn contends, Europeans had unwittingly encroached upon the native epistemological space which they believed could be grasped through translation by establishing correspondences. This shaped their encounter with the languages of treaties and philosophical systems of India and subsequently their reception and translation.

Beyond the deep hermeneutic problem that underpins any project in translation or commentary, there are conceptual barriers that separate Indian philosophy from Western philosophy. But these barriers were erected by formulations that became philosophically institutionalized, and portrayed not just Western philosophy but Western thought as intellectual, discursive, abstract, theoretical, axiomatic-deductive and Indian philosophy and Indian thought as intuitive, experiential, pragmatic and computational. In these binaries of the history of ideas the Indian philosophical tradition was constructed as guided by practical goals as well as aiming at transforming human existence.

Two contemporary Indian philosophers, Matilal and Mohanty, dedicated themselves to the task of demolishing these barriers and the latter suggests that the goals of Western and Indian philosophy frequently cross each other, in the sense that Western philosophy has a practical side to it, just as Indian philosophy has theoretical components. To our generation this may seem, to employ a usage common among mathematicians, 'intuitively obvious', but the weight of intellectual and cultural institutions had prevented earlier generations from seeing through this point. Further, an issue that needs to be addressed is that Indian philosophy itself is internally quite diverse and large constructions of systems such as Indian philosophy collapse the internal distinctions between the different streams that comprise the Indian philosophical tradition. Thereby the 'Indian philosophical tradition' often collapses to what Western philosophy has classified as Hindu, Buddhist or Jaina philosophies. In Western accounts of Eastern philosophy the term itself comes to connote either Indian or Chinese or

Japanese philosophy – the one to the exclusion of the others.

It is relevant here to refer to a concrete dialogue organized between the Centre for Advanced Research in Phenomenology (Pittsburgh) and the Indian Council of Philosophical Research (New Delhi), two organizations devoted to philosophical research. Close to two decades ago they jointly organized a conference on Western phenomenology and Indian philosophy. A critical review of the conference questioned the modality of the encounter. The principal objection was that Western phenomenology with its sophisticated technical apparatus was permitted to face a 'diluted ideality called Indian philosophy' that would have been lacking a coherent technical apparatus. An effective encounter, it was felt, could have been organized in terms of an encounter between two philosophical systems belonging to the two traditions in order to ensure a conceptual sharing of technical concerns at the appropriate systemic levels. Even in well intentioned dialogues, attention is not often paid to the systemic levels at which the dialogue is organized.

The comparative method emerged in the early half of the 19th century as an antidote to Eurocentrism, though it was founded on the idea of correspondences between different cultural or civilizational systems. How was the comparative method employed in the study of Indian philosophy or knowledge systems? Despite the differences, 'Orientalism' appears as a shorthand for the 'imperial sociology of knowledge' (Pinch 1999, 390–3). Colonialism, as postcolonial scholarship has detailed for us, produced 'complicated forms of knowledge that Indians had constructed but were codified and transmitted by Europeans' (Cohn 1997, 16).

The comparative method developed out of several strains of European thought that included technologies for the textual construction of a history of Europe, which were now extrapolated to the study of India. The European preoccupation with the 'origin of things' was reflected in the questions and technologies of comparative history that included the collection and classification of texts and languages in the hope of establishing original versions of texts, pure languages and a chronology. In this manner the comparative method through its power of classification facilitated the control of variety and

difference. The linearity of the comparative narrative was oriented either forward as was done in the case of European history, or as hurtling down from a pristine authentic past as was suggested by some Europeans and Indian scholars – the discovery of the pure versions, it was contended, would reverse this degeneration. Consequently, the production of new dictionaries altered the languages of the region and thus altered radically the access to the past by future generations of both Europeans and Indians.

This brings us to the point whether postcolonial scholarship will ever be able to access the past as 'undistorted' by the experience of colonialism or the encounter with the West. In fact, as suggested by Sheldon Pollock in 2000, postcolonial scholarship has ignored the social history of knowledge on the eve of colonialism, which in a way reinforces the perspective that colonialism certainly marked the end of the Sanskrit episteme and thereby changed the rules for the generation of knowledge on the subcontinent. There are two simple presuppositions at stake. Outside the cultural encounter between East and West one could as well ask in the European context what the writings of the ancient Greeks would have meant without the works of the Arab commentators on those texts. Further, we can then ask whether even a Western philosopher can access ancient Western philosophy in terms that are unmediated by two millennia of history. The Indian philosopher Matilal rejected the objection that 20th-century attempts to articulate the ideas of the ancients were futile. On the contrary, while the motivations of philosophers from different periods and cultures might differ, there were important philosophical questions and puzzles that continued to be of contemporary relevance, including 'the problem of knowledge and its criteria, the problem of perception and the status of the external world' (Matilal 1986, 2).

It stands to reason that the problem of the origins of knowledge is central in the Western philosophical tradition and has been addressed differently, e.g., by rationalists who foreground reason and empiricists who foreground science. But the Sanskrit tradition has no equivalents for either of these terms. In which case, how do we transit from the discussion of 'knowledge' in one system to another, when there are differences in some essential conceptions? On the contrary, the concern of the Indian philosophers pivoted around the question whether perception was the only means of acquiring valid knowledge or whether inference was also a valid instrument for the acquisition of knowledge. The term 'perception' does not in this tradition map onto merely sensory perceptions, but includes the perception of the self and its qualities. The epistemological vocabularies in the two traditions are comprised of terms considered synonymous, but which actually denote different concepts.

The comparative method emerges as indispensable for philosophers attempting to render one tradition comprehensible in the language and vocabulary of another. The task for the philosopher is to ascertain the nature of the philosophical enterprise, and the relevance of the comparison of ideas and theories to the philosophical goal of studying 'things-in-themselves'. Mohanty argues that comparative philosophy is an unavoidable enterprise for cultural amphibians rendering one tradition in terms of another or translating from one language into another. But then one must ask what philosophy is – is it about things-in-themselves or about the comparison of ideas, concepts and theories? According to Mohanty, comparative philosophy is a second-order discipline, as a result of which it falls short of genuine philosophy. It nevertheless serves the important role of liberating philosophers from dogmatically inhabiting their own traditions and thereby of freeing philosophy itself.

Mohanty identifies four ways in which the enterprise of comparative philosophy is undertaken. The first he calls intellectualist, and the engagement is initiated when a philosophical tradition A is perplexed by some problems that seeks a solution, and turns to philosophical tradition B in the hope of being enriched by it or being aided in arriving at a solution. The down side of this engagement is that votaries of tradition A may tend to view the tradition as possessing a solution to all problems. The second path is that of the wisdom seeker, and this path is characterized by an asymmetry. Indian philosophy is portrayed as mystical and a blind eye is turned to the analytical or logical or epistemological components or traditions in Indian philosophy. In like manner, Indian philosophers studying Western philosophy have paid little attention to the Christian mystics or the Gnostics. In this manner a particular construction of Indian philosophy is reproduced on both sides of the East–West philosophical divide. The third modality is that of supplementation. The programme of supplementation is prompted by the desire to fill perceived gaps and vacancies in one tradition by importing the missing components from another tradition. The problem then is that this filling up may not be tantamount to assimilating the imported components into the deficit tradition. Finally, I suspect we have the purely philosophical modality, that Mohanty and Matilal are themselves committed to, which is the project of 'recognizing how a different tradition realizes a quite different possibility not envisaged in one's own' (Mohanty 2001, 89).

Epistemological encounters

The foregoing discussion on the comparative approach seeks to point out that the discourse on the character of knowledge in the Indian tradition is really a social-epistemological one, and may throw some light on the similarities between the conception of knowledge in the Indian tradition and the insights emerging from the sociology of scientific knowledge. Zilberman's investigations commenced with a comparative elaboration of the notion of epistemology in Indian theories of knowledge and the Western tradition(s). This examination was prompted by his understanding that analogy was a central problem in modern philosophy of science, language and phenomenon, and that Indian philosophy provided some very interesting insights. This intellectual journey is similar in spirit to that of Matilal and Mohanty, despite their different cultural or philosophical orientations.

The contemporary study of classical Indian philosophy, Matilal informs us, is oriented towards two problematics. One deals with the historical reconstruction of classical views, and the second is the more contemporary project of critically examining similar modern views. The dialogue about knowledge that Matilal sets up at a relevant systemic level is between the Nyaāya, Miīmaāmsa and Sautrāntika schools on the one hand and the Cartesian philosophers on the other, with a concern to contrast the relationship between doubt and true knowledge. Even in the Indian tradition knowledge is seen as a product of a process prompted by doubt and hence the latter is the precursor of knowledge. Thus in the Nyaāya tradition doubt is the 'harbinger of knowledge and certainty' (Matilal

1986, 98). But this uncertainty must in turn be based on a few certainties. There must be certainty about the existence of the subject about which there is uncertainty. Hence, 'uncertainty or doubt gets formulated only in the background of some certainty of another kind ... to be able to doubt is to be able to concede some minimal knowledge about something' (Matilal 1986, 99). The notion of doubt founded around a central core of some existential certainty leading onto knowledge is entrenched in the Nyāaya tradition and this could be used by Matilal to subject the Cartesian tradition to investigation and scrutiny.

In the Nyaāya argument the process set in motion by doubt produces as an end result a decision or certainty (nirnaya). The end-product takes the form of a mental episode called pramā (a knowledge episode), a process whereby the cognitive episode (jnana) to strike the truth transforms it into a knowledge episode (pramā). The immediate point worth noting is that a belief stands out as knowledge when it is connected with the fact believed; or else it remains a true belief but not knowledge. Thus for beliefs to stand in as knowledge they must be based on correct pramāna.

One of the correct means of knowing was sabda or verbal testimony. In other words verbal testimony serves as a correct pramaāna when it generates knowledge in an appropriate hearer provided the speaker is an apta – a trustworthy person, be it a sage or a barbarian (mlechha), or from sacred or secular origins. The testimony of a trustworthy person is of two kinds, that relate to either perceptible or imperceptible objects. Consequently, the problem of the origin of knowledge in the Indian tradition is not merely linked up with the epistemological task of formulating the criteria for the validation of belief to become knowledge but as much with the establishment of trust among knowledge seekers so that the utterances and claims of these seekers can be appropriately judged. This brings us squarely into the domain of social epistemology in the Western tradition.

Zilberman was particularly disposed to the perspective of the social dimensions of knowledge though he approached the problematic differently. In his The birth of meaning in Hindu thought, his focus was on the sociological presuppositions of Indian epistemology and formal logic. In attempting to explicate the sense in which Hindu systems of thought constitute epistemic disciplines, Zilberman was aspiring to reform the whole idea of philosophy, as the object for a new science what he called 'science of philosophies'. Put differently, Indian philosophy offered a categorical framework for metaphilosophy. The ssadadarsanas, or the several systems of Indian philosophy, were not to be viewed as different philosophical systems but as part of the categorical apparatus that would be required in the making of philosophy as an object of the science of philosophy.

An interesting feature is that the conjuncture produced by the linguistic turn in philosophy and the social turn in philosophy of science has occasioned the sorts of projects that are being discussed. In the 1980s, this conjuncture marks the end of a philosophical project through its century-long attempt to become more scientific. Secondly, in the domain of the sciences, the recognition of the normative constitution of science rendered it an object of investigation of a second-order discipline such as the science of culture. In the circumstance where philosophy is drawn towards science, it itself becomes the object for a second-order science.

However, while making this case for metaphilosophy, it is necessary to reckon with the absence of connection between science and philosophy in the Indian tradition. The inability of those elements of anticipation that could have led to the germination of science led Zilberman to propose that Indian philosophy could never produce a science. Surely when taken literally, ample historical evidence would disqualify Zilberman's claim. Nevertheless, when read metatheoretically, it could be taken to mean that a good metatheory does not always generate a good science. And here too the recent history of logical positivism would stand out as testimony to the point being made.

Returning to the discussion of knowledge in the Indian tradition, we must address the question of authority and what comes to be counted as knowledge. A historian of science who raised the issue in the Marxist tradition was Debiprasad Chattopadhyaya. He arrived at the opinion quite contrary to that of Zilberman, namely that the only discipline in the ancient Indian world that could be counted as a science was medicine, which benefited from the methodological interventions of the philosophical schools such as that of the Nyaāya. The fruitful possibilities within the tradition were nipped in the bud by the gradual domination of idealist thought and the obstacles posed by the caste hierarchy of Indian society. Zilberman's radical thesis then is not so distant from Chattopadhyaya's thesis, but the former attempts to limit the sociological reduction of philosophical activity to the caste organization of Indian society. As pointed out earlier in the essay, Zilberman considers Indian philosophy to be a unique, system-generating factor of Indian civilization. If that be the case then the structure of Indian philosophical thought contributed to the growth and development of Hindu social organization rather than the other way round.

This exploration of the term 'knowledge' in the Indian tradition identifies several points of contrast of the theory of knowledge in India from a broadly defined Western philosophical tradition, just as what is discussed here is within the broadly defined Sanskritic tradition of Indian philosophy. While recognizing that any current dialogue between Western and Eastern philosophy will take place in a Western language, Western philosophical categories take precedence in the dialogue and define the terrain of the dialogue. But having said that, the two central concerns of Indian philosophy according to a modern Indian interlocutor, discussed here, are the reconstruction of classical views and critically examining modern perspectives. One such modern perspective is that of social epistemology that addresses the social dimensions of knowledge or rational belief. It is here that we find an axis of intersection between Western epistemology and its Indian counterpart. Social epistemology or social theory reflexively examines the conditions under which it theorizes about what counts as knowledge; it potentially is metatheoretically oriented as well. These two dimensions, it is summarily argued, are of significance in Indian theories of knowledge, and attempts have been under way to orient epistemological engagement in metatheoretic directions within the rubric of not merely comparative philosophy but philosophy proper.

Dhruv Raina

Bibliography

Chattopadhyaya D. 1979. *Science and society in ancient India.* Calcutta: Research India Publications.

Cohn B. S. 1997. *Colonialism and its forms of knowledge: the British in India.* Oxford: Oxford University Press.

Dussel E. 2002. 'World-system and transmodernity', *Nepantla: Views from the South,* 3, 2, 221–44.

Matilal B. K. 1986. *Perception: an essay on classical Indian theories of knowledge.* Oxford: Oxford University Press.

Mohanty J. N. 2001. *Explorations in philosophy: essays by J. N. Mohanty* (Gupta B. ed.). Oxford: Oxford University Press.

Naylor S. 2005. 'Introduction: historical geographies of science – places, contexts, cartographies', *British Journal of History of Science,* 38, 1, 1–12.

Pinch W. R. 1999. 'Same difference in India and Europe', *History and Theory,* 38, 3, 389–407.

Zilberman D. B. 1988. *The birth of meaning in Hindu thought.* Dordrecht: Reidel.

Related essays

Asia; Chinese medicine; civilizations; humanities; indigenous knowledges; Koran; life and physical sciences; modernity; modernization theory; Orientalism; religion; scientific expeditions; technologies; tropics; Westernization; yoga

Koran

The Koran or, in a more faithful transliteration of the Arabic, Qur'an is the collection of the divine revelation received by Prophet Muhammad between 610 and 632. It was first transmitted orally, and the organization of the definitive edition of the Koran was done in the 7th century. The Koran provided legal, moral and religious norms and values, as well as paradigms and metaphors, which were adapted to local cultural contexts by the religious and legal specialists. This cultural elite allowed the Islamic world to maintain a degree of civilizational unity beyond the cultural, social and political differences that existed between the various Muslim communities.

The introduction of the printing press and modern school education in the Muslim world in the late 18th and early 19th centuries, by European missionaries and colonial powers, who were soon joined by the modernizing efforts of the Ottoman and Egyptian governments, fostered a new process of textualization of the Koran, beginning with an edition of the

Koran printed in Istanbul in 1877. The Koran printed in the official press in Bulaq, Egypt, in 1924 became the model for all the other editions until the second half of the 20th century, when Saudi editions acquired a 'canonical' status. The growing rates of literacy and the mass production of Korans allowed a larger parcel of the Muslim population to have direct access to the quranic text, in Arabic or vernacular translations. Since the Middle Ages there had been translations of the Koran into literary languages, such as Persian and Turkish, but the greater demand for the sacred text allied with a renewed Muslim missionary impulse in Africa and South Asia fostered its translation into various vernacular languages during the 19th and 20th centuries.

Modern conceptions of knowledge influenced the new frameworks of textual interpretation linked to reform movements in the Muslim world, such as the Salafiyya. Late-19th-century Muslim thinkers, such as Muhammad 'Abduh or Rashid Rida, saw the meaning of the revelation as something encoded in the written text of the Koran and accessible through the rational analysis of its linguistic content. Therefore there was an expansion of the production and circulation of interpretations of and commentaries on the Koran beyond the circle of religious specialists, leading to a fragmentation of doctrinal consensus and religious authority throughout the Muslim world.

The rise of political Islam in the 20th century was accompanied by the objectification of the Koran as the source of norms, values and examples for both the social order and individual behaviour. The Koran also provided a web of shared categories and metaphors that were used by the various Islamic movements to give cultural depth to their political program and enhance their capacity of recruiting adepts. For example, the confrontation between Moses and the Pharaoh narrated in the Koran was used by Islamist groups in Egypt and in Iran to define the sacred nature of their fight against the secular state during the 1970s and 1980s. Since the 1990s Sufism and liberal Islam, as well as radical Islamic militancy, have gained force as frameworks of interpretation of the Koran which compete by using various communication media, such as television, radio and the press, to spread their message.

Towards the end of the 20th century, new technologies widened even more the access of Muslims to the quranic text: it can be browsed on the internet or on a CD-ROM; individuals can join an internet-based discussion group or pose questions by telephone or e-mail to religious scholars who have TV religious shows or Islamic webpages, thus enhancing the relevance of the Koran as a wellspring of inspiration and solutions to individual and collective issues. The establishment of English, together with Arabic, as the language of the internet webpages and printed publications devoted to interpretation of the Koran shows how it articulates an arena of transnational cultural debates and disputes. Furthermore, the objectification of quranic verses as religious markers on commodities, such as car-stickers or wall calendars, allowed their incorporation as source of meaning and identity in the individualized spaces and ordinary activities of everyday life. Therefore, the role of the Koran as a shared reference to the various social and cultural universes that constitute the Muslim world has been enhanced in the last decades, but nowadays it rather articulates an enlarged arena of cultural debates and disputes than hierarchized spheres of religious consensus and authority.

Paulo G. Pinto

Bibliography

Berque J. 'The Koranic text: from revelation to compilation', in Atiyeh G. (ed.) 1995. *The book in the Islamic world*. Albany: SUNY Press.

Eickelman D. 'Mass higher education and the religious imagination in contemporary Arab societies', in Atiyeh G. (ed.) 1995. *The book in the Islamic World*. Albany: SUNY Press.

Starrett G. 1995. 'The political economy of religious commodities in Cairo', *American Anthropologist*, 97, 1, 51–68.

Stenberg L. 1996. *The Islamization of science*. Lund Studies in the History of Religion, Vol. 6. Lund: Lunds Universitet.

Related essays

Bible; *Communist Manifesto*; Internet; Islam; knowledge; language; Little Red Book; missionaries; Muslim networks; religion

L

Labour migration

Labour migration, the movement of people in search of work, has been the dominant form of transnational migration in the modern era.

The desire to find steadier and better-paying work has motivated millions of men and women annually to move across continents and regions. Labour migrants are considered to be acting voluntarily, but their decision to leave and the circumstances of their migration often bear the hallmarks of involuntary departure in search of survival. Most have also been considered transient workers, although in many cases the migration has turned into permanent settlement in a new country.

Experts from economics, sociology and history distinguish labour migration from other forms of migration. For economists labour migration is part of a world system of flexible flows of capital and labour. This approach validates migration as a way to increase market efficiency in the distribution of labour. Other social scientists and historians of transnational labour migration concentrate on social changes among migrants and in their host societies.

Labour migrations have always followed the trajectory of economic development in different parts of the world but three major factors accelerated the migration of labour after the mid 19th century. First, the years before 1850 marked the end of slavery, opening additional labour markets for individual migrants. Second, the availability of reliable and cheap modes of transportation made the movement of large numbers of workers safe, predictable and affordable. Third, legal and political prohibitions against the free movement of people gradually diminished in many countries.

Two major streams of transnational labour migration dominated in the period between 1850 and the second decade of the 20th century. Europeans migrated within and out of Europe, especially to North and South America. A second stream, about equal in size, took workers from China and India to other parts of Asia, Eastern and Southern Africa and to the Americas. (A third set of long-distance movements that took place mostly within China and Russia were not transnational.) Transnational movements often accompanied contemporaneous migrations within countries or regions.

The 19 million workers who moved from their homelands in China and the 29 million who left India to move overseas and to Southeast Asia between 1845 and 1940 worked as plantation workers, miners, seamen, railroad workers and service workers. In some places these migrants succeeded slaves (in the Caribbean, for example); elsewhere they were part of the emergence of large-scale agricultural economies (such as in the rubber plantations of Southeast Asia and sugar cane growing in the Caribbean, Hawaii and Fiji). In some countries the labour migrants propelled industrialization and modernization, building railroads in Uganda and the United States, or working in mines in South Africa and Peru. The majority of transnational migrants from China and India in this period migrated under contract or had their travel financed through middlemen. Most returned home after their contracts ended.

The largest labour migration of the late 19th and early 20th century departed Europe for the Americas. Between 55 and 58 million Europeans left between 1846 and 1940, 65 per cent of them for North America. Virtually all these migrants came as free labourers and the great majority financed their own journey (though often with the help of family). The United States' industrializing economy, in particular, attracted workers on many levels of skill and, as a result, immigrants to the United States and Canada were more likely to stay than migrants to virtually any other area in the world. Latin America attracted mainly Europeans from Southern and Southwestern Europe, while until the 1890s the majority of European labour migrants to North America came from Western and Central European regions; thereafter emigration to the US originated mainly in Eastern and Southern Europe. Within North America, the migrants from Asia and Europe converged on the West Coast of the United States, where a virulent anti-Asian movement pushed for racial exclusion laws which curtailed the migration of Asians to the United States after 1882. As in China and India, transnational migration occurred in tandem with a transcontinental and regional migration within Europe.

Both the Asian and the European-American migrations mobilized mainly young men, but migrants from Europe were more likely, in the long run, to bring their families with them.

Family migration aided permanent settlement and promoted economic and social stability in the destination country. Settlement and family migration was easier for Europeans in part because these immigrants were not contract labourers and also had the right to move and settle freely in their new home.

During the period from 1914 to about 1950 the character of transnational labour migration changed. Large-scale warfare disrupted long-existing movements. Voluntary labour migration declined because of economic depression, stricter exit controls (from Russia, for example) and increased entry controls (in most of Europe and North America). Countries alleviated wartime labour shortages through contract labour and forced migration from neighbouring countries. For example, the United States allowed Mexican agricultural labour to be brought in after 1916 and again after 1940, whereas Nazi-ruled Europe and Stalinist Russia used forced labourers from Eastern and Central Europe. A mixture of incentives and force pushed migrants from Korea to Japan and from Japan into Manchuria during the same period. Asian migration in Southern and Southeast Asia was less affected by wartime developments.

Economic expansion, the disintegration of European overseas colonial empires, and the gradual opening of Europe, Australia and North America to immigrants from Asia and Africa characterized labour migration after 1945. Working-class immigrants from postwar Europe formed the first wave of postwar labour migrants to traditional countries of immigration in the United States, Canada, Australia and Argentina. Contract workers from Mexico and the Caribbean (braceros) met North American labour needs in agriculture. The independence of India and Caribbean and African nations stimulated labour migration to Great Britain and later to France. The Netherlands and to a lesser degree Portugal and Italy followed, turning, in the 1960s, from countries of emigration into countries of immigration. For the most part, however, Northern European countries filled labour shortages by importing contract workers from other parts of Europe and the Mediterranean. These so-called guest workers (Gastarbeiter) came from Italy, Greece, Portugal, Yugoslavia, Turkey and North Africa; they were nominally contract labourers, but over time earned the right to stay or even gained citizenship under various provisions. By the 1970s this turned

a labour migration of transient single males into a family migration.

Labour migrants have historically been employed in agriculture, industrial and low-level service occupations. In some colonial economies such as Burma or South Africa, colonial authorities also promoted the migration of the skilled and educated to perform specific supervisory or professional tasks as teachers, mid-level administrators or supervisors in factories and mines. Since the 1960s growing numbers of highly educated labour migrants have crossed borders in search of more remunerative and rewarding specialized work. Information technology, engineering and medical care are fields in which the highly educated formed the so-called 'brain drain' of migrants from rigidly structured, less developed to more varied and flexible labour markets. Some of these professional labour migrants entered their new destinations with limited-time labour contracts but many soon became permanent residents who settled with their families.

The social consequences of transnational migrations for the migrants, the home and the receiving societies have varied over time. Countries with a high percentage of permanent emigrants (Ireland, Norway, Southern Italy, Lebanon) were profoundly affected: their societies and economy showed little dynamic development before World War 2, and their economies depended on migrants' remittances. Many other countries profited in a more dynamic way from the back and forth of labour migration. Urbanization, more varied social and economic opportunities for women, and business expertise were connected to the experiences of transnational migrants in capitalist economies and more open societies. Acknowledging the importance of labour migrants for their societies, many countries' legal and social systems incorporated the temporary labour migration of its young people by granting citizenship rights to migrants, and accepting transnational marriages, for example. In the second half of the 20th century, some countries such as the Philippines, nations in the Caribbean and Mexico have made numerous adjustments in naturalization and property laws to acknowledge the large group of labour migrants among their nationals.

The strength of labour migrants' ties to their country of origin also depended on the welcome they received at their destination.

Especially in Southeast Asia and Africa, host societies, under the direction of colonial powers, segregated labour migrants from majority populations in racially and ethnically separate neighbourhoods long after migrants turned into permanent immigrants. But within neighbourhoods and economic niches change occurred over time. South Asian labourers turned into small merchants and later professionals in Uganda and South Africa; Chinese plantation workers merged with an older Chinese merchant class in Southeast Asia; Japanese turned from agricultural labourers into hotel keepers and merchants in Hawaii and California. European labour migrants in the Americas and Australia also faced segregation during their initial years, but within one or two generations segregation and discrimination diminished greatly and social mobility was high.

In the 19th century, transnational migration of craft and industrial workers in Europe and the Americas was closely connected to the emergence of a labour movement which derived its strength from the international experience and mobility of its members. In Europe and North America, socialist and anarchist movements and many unions were transnational from the beginning. In countries of immigration where permanent settlement was encouraged, immigrants could also shape political life through membership in unions or political parties. Politicians who had begun as immigrant workers rose to prominence in the United States, Canada and Australia. When migrants arrived as contract labourers, political integration was blocked and citizenship often impossible. This meant political exclusion and invisibility for the immigrant generation among Indians in South Africa, Asians and Mexicans in the United States and Chinese in much of Southeast Asia. Continued segregation made some labour migrants, such as Chinese in the North American West, targets of political violence and expulsion.

From the mid 19th to the mid 20th century most transnational labour migrants were men. Women remained at 'home' or migrated only regionally. Male dominance was and is especially pronounced among workers who migrate under contract and work in agriculture, construction and heavy industry. Chinese labour migrants had a female to male ratio of 1:100 in Latin America; Indian migrants were only between 15 per cent and 30 per cent female during the late 19th and early 20th century. After 1920 a more balanced ratio came to prevail as laws in countries of immigration began to give preference to those entering for the sake of presumably 'family unification' over unskilled workers. A majority of immigrants to the United States have been female almost every year since the 1930s. While women who entered under family unification provisions were not primarily motivated by the search for wage work, they often became part of an immigrant workforce in the host economy as industrial, agricultural and service workers. As labour market opportunities for women migrants expanded worldwide, a largely female stream of labour migrants also poured into the Middle East, Western Europe, Japan and North America from India, the Philippines and from Eastern Europe. These female immigrants found places as nannies, healthcare workers and sex workers. There has also been a significant migration of female nurses from Korea, Africa and the Caribbean to Great Britain and North America since the 1950s.

Labour migration – always an important factor in international economic development – has become recognized as a motor for globalization in the 21st century. Most countries have been reluctant to translate this insight into effective migration and integration policies, for their insights about global labour mobility conflict with their desire to protect employment and social cohesion among their citizens. Ongoing tensions divide the needs of labour markets, the strategies of labour migrants, and the politics of immigration around the world.

Dorothee Schneider

Bibliography

Bade K. 2003. *Migration in European history.* Oxford and Malden: Blackwell.

Hoerder D. 2002. *Cultures in contact: world migrations in the second millenium.* Durham, NC and London: Duke University Press.

McKeown A. 2004. 'Global migration 1846–1940,' *Journal of World History*, 15, 2, 155–89.

Related essays
agriculture; border commuters; brain drain; Chinese Diaspora; contract and indentured labourers; diasporas; domestic service; empire and migration; family; family migration; forced migrations; gender and sex; guestworkers; human

mobility; international migration regimes; marriage; nursing; Panama Canal; railways; remittances; rush migrations; slavery; temporary migrations; workers' movements

Labour standards

The odd couple of economics and humanitarianism has guided discussion on the need for and effects of international labour standards since the 19th century. Economic and moral positions have been as often complementary as competing. The basic moral arguments, found in the international movement to end slavery and late-20th-century boycotts of goods produced by child labour, have melded with the basic economic position that, because of market failure, there exist positive externalities to fixing standards about the nature of work – when it can be done, by whom, and under what conditions. These externalities include a better educated, healthier, and more productive labour force.

The origins of the modern movement to fix international standards are generally ascribed to Robert Owen (1818), although this has been contested. Others give paternity to Charles Hindley (1833), a British manufacturer and Member of Parliament. Regardless of origin, many European contemporaries recognized that national laws to regulate child labour and hours of work would be toothless in the absence of multilateral standards because international competition would undo their effectiveness in a race to the bottom. Because of these pressures, international accords made little headway before the establishment of the International Labour Organization. That said, 19th-century debates about the viability of international labour standards merit attention because they foreshadow 21st-century concerns.

Beginning in 1870, a series of international conferences, with representation mainly from Europe and occasional North American input, met to establish uniform standards. There were two types: the more numerous conferences run by social reformers and trade unionists, and meetings organized by states. Belgium and Switzerland, small open countries, hosted many of the meetings of social activists. At these conferences, leading reformers from France (Arthur Fontaine), Germany Ludwig Joseph (Lujo Brentano), and the United States (Richard Ely) came together in an epistemic community that led to the creation of the International Association for Labour Legislation (IALL) in Paris in 1900. The meetings served to collect and diffuse information on national rules and regulations, exposing industries and countries that had inferior work conditions. But when it came to implementation social reformers were limited to moral suasion only. Labour-sponsored conferences were equally unsuccessful. The International Trade Union Congress held in Paris in 1886 condemned the 'action of certain English capitalists' who had moved their factories to France because of its lower wages and inferior working conditions but, when called upon to standardize regulations, British labour balked in fear of losing market share. There was a strong belief that labour in rich countries could do better by collective bargaining than by international settlement. They could trade off higher wages against unprotected working conditions; they saw danger in leaving part of this equation in the hands of some distant third party. This was the attitude of Samuel Gompers in the United States, but the argument resonated across Europe.

The Berlin conference of 1890 was typical of state-led initiatives to standardize national labour laws. Organized by Germany, the conference had more to do with Bismarck's geopolitical ambitions than his interest in the well-being of workers around the world. The outcome was predictable. Even the developed countries with the most advanced labour standards could not find common ground. Representatives of the United Kingdom did not want to follow Germany's lead, wanting to protect the British legal tradition of leaving to (adult) workers and firms the right and obligation to fix their own employment arrangements. Southern European states, like Italy, saw Berlin as a forum to dictate to poorer countries a set of labour standards that would preserve richer countries' market share. As today, developing countries decried this manoeuvre as protectionism. At the Berne conference of the IALL in 1906 there was general agreement on the prohibition of night work for women; there was also partial agreement to limit the content of phosphorous in matches, but the United States refused to ratify this standard claiming that Japan, its chief competitor, had opted out. Like many of the later directives of the International Labour Office (ILO), the resolutions of state-run conferences had not much impact on actual legislation at the national level.

The failure of multilateralism provoked states to negotiate bilateral labour accords. Social and political changes lay behind discussions. The concept of citizenship was in flux before 1914 and many of the agreements about accident compensation and pensions sought to establish the obligations of states to nationals and alien residents within their borders. But there was an economic aspect as well. Many of the signatories had high tariff protection and had signed most-favoured-nation agreements with major trading partners. The labour accords served as a side clause that strengthened bilateral commercial ties – in the same fashion that the late-20th-century North American Free Trade Agreement contained side clauses on labour and the environment. The Franco–Italian labour treaty of 1904 became an integral part of the trade agreements between the two countries that put an end to a decade-long trade war. France, seeking to maintain the effective level of protection it provided to its own nationals, initiated negotiations. Italy had no history of labour legislation and, because the percentage of eligible voters was low, government leaders needed the French initiative to go around the vested interests of the Italian business elite who opposed labour reform. The agreement gave Italian workers in the hexagon the same level of benefits that French workers received, and in exchange the Italian government introduced in the peninsula some measures of the more advanced French labour legislation. The Franco–Italian accord was the most extensive of its kind and it was heralded as a model of future negotiations linking trade and domestic labour policy. World War 1 put a temporary end to such experiments.

The ILO, established in 1919, benefited from many of the discussions and experiments of the pre-1914 years. The early transnational movement which lacked resources and authority had transformed itself into an international organization with a professional research branch. The interwar period saw continuity with the past, the chief concerns being the length of the working day and the work week and other employment conditions. In its first two decades 67 conventions were passed, but ratifications by individual nations were uneven. Passed in 1919, Convention 6, which limits the night work of young persons, has been ratified by 59 countries. These include Brazil (1934) and India (1921), but exclude Canada, the United Kingdom and the United States. Given political rivalries and the deepening depression, conventions after 1930 met with even less success. Convention 33, the minimum age convention for non-industrial employment (1932), has been ratified by 25 countries.

After World War 2 the ILO modified its tactics. It distinguished between two types of standards: those that dealt with processes (the right to work and freedom of association, most notably) and those that dealt with outcomes (hours of labour and the like). The former which harkened back to early humanitarian arguments became known as core standards. The intent was to remove this set of standards from economic debates on labour costs and trade. Here the ILO achieved gains with the new member states that joined the organization in the wake of decolonization and political change in Eastern Europe. Since 1957, 167 countries have signed on to Convention 33 that calls for the abolition of forced labour.

Despite these gains, debates on the role and legitimacy of international labour standards have been renewed vigorously during the wave of globalization of the late 20th century. The arguments, albeit more sophisticated, are not much different from what they were one hundred years earlier. Labour in developed countries has called for tighter labour standards in the developing world because they believe that inferior standards give certain countries a competitive advantage, while employers in richer countries argue that international competition necessitates lower labour standards across the globe. But newly developing countries claim that their comparative advantage has to do with their abundance of labour and not their inferior labour standards. In any event, it is not for the developed world to dictate standards elsewhere. If globalization is left to run its course and raise income levels, then newly developing countries will establish their own standards, just as the developed world did before 1914. The failure of the ILO, according to some, to address these competing pressures has led to initiatives to tie labour standards to multilateral trade agreements negotiated by the WTO. There has as well been a return to humanitarian arguments in favour of international standards. If history is any guide, labour standards improve when economic and moral arguments are combined.

Michael Huberman

Bibliography

Brown D. K. 2001. 'Labor standards: where do they belong on the international trade agenda?', *Journal of Economic Perspectives*, 15, 2, 89–112.

Follows J. 1951. *Antecedents of the International Labour Organization*. Oxford: Oxford University Press.

Huberman M. 2004. 'Working hours of the world unite? New international evidence of worktime, 1870–1913', *Journal of Economic History*, 64, 4, 964–1001.

International Labour Organization. 2005. *Rules of the game: a brief introduction to international labor standards*. Geneva: ILO Publications.

Related essays

Abolition of Forced Labour Convention; car safety standards; childhood; children's rights; Commission on International Labour Legislation; convergence and divergence; fashion; food safety standards; industrialization; social sciences; sports gear and apparel; technical standardization; trade; welfare state; workers' movements

Language

Language has been described as the characteristic that most clearly differentiates human beings from other species. Human language is conveyed through auditory or visual signs that are arbitrary in nature. These signs (sounds, written marks, or, in the case of sign languages, gestures) are articulated into systems ('languages') that are made to carry meaning through application of certain rules of usage (grammar, syntax etc.) by their users. These rules are productive: they enable utterances that may be entirely new but that are comprehensible because they apply rules and words that already exist. All languages change and develop over time, in response to the internal needs of, and external influences on, particular communities, and they spread or retreat as these communities expand their influence or decline. Interactions among communities often take linguistic form and thus the transnational flow of language, and resistance to that flow, can illuminate transnational interaction generally. Many linguistic systems exist in the world today; others have died out, often leaving no trace.

Language and community

Language can be regarded as a social phenomenon. Some see speech as a form of social bonding, developed not so much to convey information as to establish community. Not only is language productive (see above), but it also allows us to describe things distant in time or space and to define and use abstractions. It reinforces a sense of community through the sharing of knowledge and experience and through repetition of stories and other forms of performance, creating a kind of collective memory. Shared linguistic norms and practices are a defining characteristic of a speech community – a community that may be coterminous with a language or may use a particular variety of a language, distinguishing it from neighbouring communities that use a different variety, or dialect. In some parts of the world, distinguishing one language from another is problematic, because each small community uses a language variety only slightly different from the next, but significantly different from the variety at the other end of what is known as a dialect string or dialect continuum. The establishment of a language as a separate entity may be political rather than linguistic: we recognize Norwegian and Danish as separate languages even though they are largely mutually comprehensible, and Chinese as a single language even though there are forms of Chinese that are mutually incomprehensible.

Language is closely related to ethnic and national identity. When languages are in contact, they influence one another structurally, bringing about language change through lexical borrowings and the like. Over time the relative standing of languages changes as people use more than one language in the home, for example, or choose to raise their children in the language of their adopted community or the language carrying most prestige. Changes in relative standing lead to language shift, in which one language declines as another spreads by expanding its domains of use. Often this process is assisted by education or employment policies. Thus French has gained in prestige and currency in Quebec over the past thirty years as the provincial government has enacted legislation favouring its use, but its influence has declined in Belgium in this same period as Dutch speakers have insisted on equal treatment for their language. It is not necessarily the case that the use of a single language in a community, rather than multiple languages, results in feelings of solidarity, nor that multilingualism automatically divides. Indeed, linguistic diversity may have the effect of promoting social and economic inclusion for all members of the community.

Modern societies have at their disposal two distinct modes of communication, the one spoken and the other written, governed by different rules. Writing systems (based sometimes on arbitrary signs for sounds, sometimes on representation of ideas) allow the recording of information over time and its conveyance across space. Writing serves as a memory system, allowing us to record information for our own use, make lists, develop systems of accounting, and preserve religious and literary texts. Without writing, and its dissemination through paper and printing (and, today, through electronic communication) the institutions of the modern state – legal systems, schools, universities, tax collection, and the like – would be inconceivable. Because written text endures and is widely disseminated, its inherent conservatism fosters linguistic standardization and the emergence of standard national languages linked to centres of power.

We associate the 18th century with the emergence of nationalism and its link to language, but the linkage seems to emerge from medieval Europe, at least as early as Dante Alighieri (1265–1321), who urged the development of a standardized Italian literary language in his De Vulgari Eloquentia (1304–07), or Martin Luther (1483–1546), whose decision to use Saxon, the precursor of High German, for his translation of the Bible enhanced cultural unity in Germany long before political unity arrived. In Florence the Accademia della Crusca (1585) and in Paris the French Academy (1634) were founded to assist in standardizing and preserving their respective languages. These efforts accompanied a growing interest in the advancement of national literatures. The resulting print communities – communities of readers grouped around a common core of literary and religious texts and contributing to a print economy by buying texts and by borrowing from circulating libraries – created and sustained such forms as novels, a largely 18th-century invention, and newspapers.

The nationalist movements of the 18th and 19th centuries saw language and nationhood as near allied. The German Johann Gottlieb Fichte (1762–1814) advanced a theory of national identity and national education rooted in the possession of a common national language, while Johann Gottfried Herder (1744–1803) saw German folk poetry as the true expression of the people, looking behind the expanding industrialization of his own time to the spirit of Germany, much as, for example, Elias Lönnrot (1802–84) did for the Finnish spirit in the collection of Finnish-language folk poetry that he wove into the continuous 'epic' Kalevala (1835). In the United States, Noah Webster (1758–1843) compiled his American Dictionary of the English Language with its distinctive American version of English. Still today language is regarded by many as an important imperative in national unity, for example in the United States (with its 'English Only' movement) and in France. By contrast, the revival of minority languages and establishment of language rights is central to political movements promoting regional autonomy on the basis of ethnicity.

Although the apparatus of the expanding print culture in the various emergent nations in the early modern age was largely in the hands of entrepreneurs, their efforts, combined with those of educational and cultural institutions as well as governments, constituted a form of national policy promoting the national language and encouraging exclusion of regional languages with no political base. As early as the 16th century, the English and French monarchies took measures for the establishment of a single official language. Following the Revolution (1789), French was seen as the language of civil liberties, and its promotion as a unifying force through the educational and legal systems drove regional languages to the margins. But it was overseas and overland expansion that took the languages of expanding states to distant parts, as overland imperial expansion did for Russian and Chinese, and the brief advances of Japan in the 20th century expanded Japanese.

Language policy varied from colonizer to colonizer. French policy favoured the integration of native elites into French culture, while the British developed systems of indirect rule that encouraged acquisition of English by local elites but promoted local languages for the rest. In the territories that became the United States, Canada, Australia, and New Zealand, local populations were subjugated and exterminated, and immigrant or enslaved populations assimilated, leading to the expansion of English (but to some degree its localization) and marginalization or elimination of indigenous languages. In Spanish America intermarriage and integration with the local Indian populations led to the dominance of the Spanish language, maintained (though in somewhat diverging forms) when the countries of Latin America gained independence – though hundreds of indigenous languages have survived and are today the focus of revival efforts in several countries. In Paraguay, Guaraní now shares with Spanish the status of official language. The Russian Empire, firmly established by Peter the Great (1682–1725), expanded throughout the following two centuries, bringing Russian with it. Stalin pursued a similar policy of russification in the Soviet Union, marginalizing regional languages, but these languages regained dominance in the newly independent states (often with a latinized alphabet replacing the old Cyrillic one) and in some measure within the Russian Federation itself. In Korea under the Japanese occupation (1910–45), use of the Korean language was forbidden in schools and in business. While imperial bureaucracies and educational systems tended to reinforce the use of standard written language, the local use of imperial languages by non-native speakers in oral situations often produced divergence from the norm. Independence led to the formation of in-country standard forms different from those of the colonizing power, as happened over time in the US – and in Spanish-speaking America, where today there is considerable lexical and phraseological variation from country to country, and extensive variation of accent, though the various forms of Spanish remain mutually comprehensible. The same is true of Portuguese in Brazil and in the other former Portuguese possessions.

In postcolonial Africa, where boundaries drawn by colonial powers in the 19th century seldom follow ethnic or linguistic lines, a lack of alternatives has necessitated retention of the languages of the colonizers in many countries, though some efforts have been made to modernize and institutionalize African languages. Most successful has been Tanzania and Kenya's promotion, alongside English, of Swahili, a trade language widely distributed in East Africa as a second language.

Post-apartheid South Africa has replaced its old policy of English/Afrikaans bilingualism by raising nine African languages to official status, but the complexity of the resulting language policies has tended to strengthen English as a lingua franca. Political independence from the European powers in African countries did not eliminate their commercial, educational and cultural dependency on the former home countries, and accordingly the use of European languages continues among the elites. English is seen as the language of technology and of access to a globalized world, and its use is even expanding in the former French and Portuguese colonies.

There are instances of quite radical realignment of languages for newly developing states. Bahasa Indonesia, the official language of Indonesia, was fashioned out of the old trading language of Malay. Hebrew was revived as a spoken secular language by Eliezer Ben-Yehuda (1858–1922), who was born in Lithuania, studied in Paris and emigrated to Palestine. It eventually became the language of the State of Israel. Other instances of language planning (as the field is known) include the adoption of the Latin alphabet and of European vocabulary in Turkish in the 1920s and 1930s under that country's reforming president Kemal Atatürk, and shifts among the Arabic, Cyrillic and Latin alphabets in the countries of Central Asia. All countries, and many institutions within those countries, have their language policies: they recognize certain languages and not others, and dictate language use or language choice in government offices, the courts, or education. The provision of interpretation services in hospitals or in courts, or the choice of which languages to teach in schools, also constitute language policy. Occasionally such policies are articulated; often they are unarticulated and simply happen through custom or inadvertence.

Sometimes language policies are put into effect through successful claims of language rights. The idea that one has a right to use one's own language in a given setting and the related idea that groups or communities have language rights have a relatively short history, and language rights are often derived from other rights, such as rights to free expression, to a fair trial, or to vote. The Final Act of the Congress of Vienna (1815) was the first international treaty to give limited recognition to rights of ethnic or linguistic (as opposed to religious) minorities. The Austrian Constitutional Law of 1867 went further, allowing ethnic minorities in the Austro-Hungarian Empire 'an absolute right to maintain and develop their nationality and their language', including its use as medium of instruction in schools. After World War I, peace treaties, conventions developed under the auspices of the League of Nations, and various national constitutions recognized minority rights, including linguistic rights. The United Nations Charter (1945) recognized 'respect for human rights and for fundamental freedoms for all without distinction as to … language … '. The Universal Declaration of Human Rights (1948) did the same, but in the Declaration language rights can only be inferred from the expression of other rights dependent upon language. The Council of Europe's European Charter for Regional or Minority Languages, in its preamble, calls for 'the protection of the historical regional or minority languages of Europe' and upholds 'the right to use a regional or minority language in private and public life'.

Languages of the world

Given the difficulty of defining a language, it is hard to assess how many languages exist today, but most experts put the figure at between 6,000 and 7,000 (excluding the numerous sign languages used by the deaf). The field is dominated by a small number of major languages; most languages in the world are spoken by a few thousand speakers at most, and the vast majority have no writing systems. In 1786, Sir William Jones posited the existence of a vast Indo-European family of languages extending from Sanskrit in India through the Middle East (by way of Persian) to most of Europe. Jones was one of several comparative philologists who identified families of languages of similar structure and lexicon that supposedly developed through contact between peoples and through migration, followed by periods of relative isolation from one another. Though language families are less easy to discern in areas of settled isolation, scholars have divided the world's languages into some thirty 'families'. Other classification systems include area approaches, in which languages in a given region are shown to have similar traits, and typological classifications, in which languages displaying similar characteristics (primarily grammatical)

but clearly separated from one another are grouped for comparative purposes.

While we tend to identify a given language with a given geographical area, many languages occupy shared space. Bilingualism may be individual (each individual speaks both languages, perhaps to a varying degree) or societal (within a given community or geographical area two languages are used, but by different people). In fact, most people in the world regularly use more than one language to some degree. Modern patterns of migration have brought hundreds of languages together in many major cities across the world; in the United States and Britain, for example, immigrant children in urban schools use dozens, even hundreds, of different languages in their homes. Such mingling of languages has been common in urban life, and in many cases in rural life too, since the beginning of history. In modern times, redrawing of national boundaries through conquest or international agreement may isolate speakers of a given language from the linguistic centre; for example, the reduction of Hungary's boundaries following World War I produced Hungarian-speaking minorities in Yugoslavia, Romania and Czechoslovakia.

Because languages (or rather their speakers) compete for territory and influence, and because there is overlap among languages, some scholars discern a single world-wide linguistic system, arranged in a hierarchy of influence, with languages of purely local currency at the bottom, languages of national or regional influence in the middle, and major languages with international reach at the top. English has the broadest international reach, but Mandarin Chinese is most spoken as a native language. The reason for the current prestige of English is mostly economic and political: languages rise and fall in the hierarchy, as is clear, for example, from the rise and decline of Assyrian in the ancient Middle East, Greek in the Eastern Mediterranean, and Latin in Western and Southern Europe. A similar shift can be seen in the use of German as a scholarly language or French as a diplomatic language. A century ago German was widely used in such fields as archaeology and medicine, but today most major scholarly journals publish in English. As for diplomacy, until the peace conference following World War I and the Treaty of Versailles (1919), which was redacted in French and English, French was the dominant diplomatic language, but at Versailles English was used alongside French, and English and French became the working languages of the League of Nations. Major documents appeared in both languages, and consecutive interpretation was employed in debate. Today, English has largely eclipsed French as the world's diplomatic language.

Although the League of Nations used consecutive interpretation, simultaneous interpretation was first used at the 1928 annual conference of the International Labour Organization, with equipment devised by the Boston department store owner Edward Filene (the patent was later acquired by IBM). At the Nuremberg Trials after World War 2, at which four languages were used, it was employed systematically: interpreters in booths listened to interventions delivered through microphones in the courtroom and simultaneously interpreted them into the other languages used. Aided by this system, the United Nations General Assembly adopted five 'official' languages (the four languages of the Allies – English, French, Russian and Chinese – plus Spanish), while preserving French and English as 'working' languages and as the languages of the Secretariat. The official languages eventually became working languages. Arabic was added in the 1970s. Today the General Assembly works in six languages with full interpretation and translation services.

When Belgium, France, Italy, Luxembourg, the Netherlands, and West Germany founded the European Coal and Steel Community (1952), the four languages of these states (Dutch, French, German, Italian) were accorded equal status, an arrangement continued when the organization became the European Economic Community (EEC, 1958) on the grounds that EEC decisions had to be available in the official legal languages of the member states. When Britain, Denmark and Ireland joined (1973), English and Danish were added, and the pattern has been followed ever since. By 2007 the European Union (EU) consisted of 27 countries using 23 languages (including three writing systems) and supporting an immensely complicated translation and interpretation system, the world's largest. Despite holding formally to the principle of language equality, in practice the EU has developed informal ways of conducting its business without using all languages. As with the United Nations, the formal language arrangements endure for reasons of prestige rather than communication and persuasion. In practice, English is emerging as the EU's dominant language of informal exchange and general administration.

If the world's languages constitute a vast system, its gatekeepers are those with a command of more than one language, serving as mediators of information across language lines. There are several forms of what some scholars call interlingualism, the crossing of language boundaries. They include translation, where a text or utterance in one language is rendered in a second (oral translation is generally known as interpretation); language learning, where an individual acquires a language through extended exposure or through a teacher; the use of a constructed language; and the use of language technology. Many of these interlingual situations are inherently unequal. Native English speakers are often at an advantage in transnational communication because others feel obliged to use English rather than their native languages, and the financial costs of interlingualism are borne unequally. Language learning is a significant part of most educational systems, with the burden falling mostly on communities whose languages lack wide circulation: schools in English-speaking countries spend less time and money per pupil on language instruction than schools elsewhere, though as English gains wider currency more children come to school with a rudimentary knowledge of the language. With the invention of computers, linguists began exploring ways of translating texts by machine. Today, computers can translate certain highly specialized material with considerable accuracy, and can recognize and apply basic rules of grammar and syntax, but the complexity of contextual meaning in even simple human utterances cannot be readily translated by machines. Computers are valuable aids to human translators since they can store and easily access dictionaries and formulaic phrases required in the translation of legal and diplomatic documents.

Language, previously limited by geography and technology, is becoming less and less dependent on location and medium. Invention of the telegraph and development of the Morse Code were the first steps in conveying written language instantaneously over distance by means of electronic impulse, i.e. in virtual rather than written form. Later the telephone expanded this capability beyond written to spoken language. Radio and television followed the telephone, and in our own day the invention and popularization of the computer has allowed the instantaneous conveyance of both written and spoken language and also its instantaneous dissemination. The recording of spoken language in film and on tape commodified spoken language in ways resembling the commodification of written text in books and newspapers. These advances have eroded the classic differences between written and spoken language, increasing the ephemeral nature of the first (for example e-mail vs paper correspondence) and the enduring quality of the second (speech can be recorded and preserved) – and allowing for the dissemination and exportation of both. Although the capital investment required for development and expansion of the new technologies favours the stronger languages over the weaker, such organizations as Microsoft have helped advance regional and local languages by 'localization' of software to take into account differing writing systems, diacritics, spelling, and the like.

English

The continued hold of the European languages, and especially English, on the world economy and the huge market in English-language-based cultural products (films, television programming, videogames) have led many scholars to see this worldwide market as evidence of continued linguistic imperialism, one element in the globalization of English and marginalization of other languages to the advantage of the United States and other English-speaking countries; but others point to the widening competitive use of English by non-native speakers. Others remind us how quickly language preferences can change – as instanced by the recent rapid decline of Russian in Eastern Europe, and by the fact that, despite government promotion, French and German appear to be steadily losing ground transnationally. As the principal language of transnational communication, English has consolidated its position as the major language of trade and technology, of education and science, and of culture and cultural products. It also serves as a lingua franca in some multilingual countries, sometimes in varieties markedly different from those employed in Britain or the US (causing scholars to speak of world Englishes rather than global English). David Graddol identifies three types of English speakers: first-language speakers for whom English is the first or only language, second-language speakers with a command of the language who use it in particular contexts (a common condition in India, the Philippines, Israel, and many African countries, and increasingly among the elite in Europe and the Americas), and a third and growing category of learners of English as a foreign language (in 2006, Graddol put this number at 1.1 billion). First-language speakers are now in a minority: for most users of the language, English is not the native language. The teaching of English in schools across the world now exceeds the teaching of any other language, perhaps of all other languages combined. However, regional languages remain strong and in some cases are growing stronger – for example in China with a huge population that is increasingly linguistically unified, in the Americas where Spanish is widely used across national borders, and in the Arab countries where standard Arabic is increasingly used in regional mass communication (for example on the news channels al-Jazeera, founded in 1996, and al-Arabiya, founded in 2003). The percentage of English texts on the world wide web is declining as other languages, such as Chinese and Spanish, emerge as Internet languages.

Though the growth of English would appear to favour English-speaking countries, the decline in foreign-language learning in those countries, prompted by perceptions of the apparent dominance of English, has a potentially negative effect on national defence, on international marketing, and, above all, on the sophisticated transnational understanding of the cultures, customs and beliefs of other countries. Most of the world realizes that to adapt and prosper in today's environment requires a knowledge of more than one language.

Humphrey Tonkin

Bibliography

Anderson B. 1983. *Imagined communities: reflections on the origin and spread of nationalism.* London and New York: Verso.

Coulmas F. (ed.) 1997. *The handbook of sociolinguistics.* Oxford and Malden: Blackwell.

Crystal D. 1997. *The Cambridge encyclopedia of language.* Cambridge and New York: Cambridge University Press.

Edwards J. 1995. *Multilingualism*. London and New York: Penguin.

Graddol D. 1997. *The future of English?* London: British Council.

Graddol D. 2006. *English next*. London: British Council.

Skuttnabb-Kangas T. and Phillipson R. (eds) 1995. *Linguistic human rights*. Berlin and New York: Mouton de Gruyter.

Tonkin H. and Reagan T. (eds) 2003. *Language in the 21st century*. Amsterdam and Philadelphia: John Benjamins.

Related essays

al-Jazeera; Braille code; British Broadcasting Corporation (BBC); broadcasting; class; cultural capitals; empires and imperialism; Esperanto; European civil servants; European institutions; higher education; Hollywood; indigenous knowledges; international schools; language diplomacy; League of Nations system; literature; missionaries; nation and state; pan-isms; patents; pidgins and creoles; publishing; radio; regions; sign languages; translation; transnational; United Nations system; Westernization; world orders

Language diplomacy

This term refers to the use of language as a tool for conducting and/or altering relations between different national groups, within the context of both traditional and cultural diplomacy. The intentional spread of languages to enhance foreign relations was not new to the 19th and 20th centuries. Latin served as a medium of communication among the literate few during Europe's Middle Ages, and numerous states in Asia adopted Chinese writing in order to facilitate relations both with China's successive ruling dynasties and with each other. However, because of the close identification between a particular language and modern nation state, language itself became a matter of national policy, and thus also a potential diplomatic tool. Historically, there have been three main categories: type one, in which the study of a particular national language is promoted in order to improve the global position of the nation associated with that language; type two, in which foreign national languages are studied in order to better understand or interact with the governments or citizens of other nations; and type three, in which a particular vocabulary is adopted for primarily defensive purposes in the conduct of foreign relations.

The first type, in which state-run or supported institutions have taught national languages overseas, is perhaps the most familiar. Although it is related to 19th- and 20th-century linguistic imperialism, whereby an imperial power taught its national language to subject populations, it differs in that it seeks to promote peaceful relations between equally sovereign nations rather than to dominate colonized groups. A prime example is the Alliance Française, an institution established in Paris on 21 July 1883 as 'a national association for the spread of French in the colonies and overseas', according to its founding document. Those who created the Alliance saw it as a weapon in a linguistic war between French, English, and German that reflected the imperial conflicts of the period. However, when English emerged victorious, especially after World War 2, the Alliance focused more on promoting French as the medium of French literature, film, and culture. Throughout its existence, the Alliance has employed soft power in the practice of French cultural diplomacy.

From its creation, the Alliance linked state and non-state actors in the pursuit of national objectives. Founded by both officials and private citizens, it received funding from the French Ministry of Culture, relied upon government approval for its continued existence, and embodied the *mission civilisatrice* (civilizing mission) upon which the French empire was based. At the same time, it depended entirely upon non-French individuals and groups around the world in order to carry out its mission. In the United States, Americans with an interest in French language and culture, and in improving French–American relations, established the first local chapters in 1885 in New York and Louisiana, and by 1902 there were 33 local committees and one national union. These groups were completely independent from the parent office in Paris as they planned activities ranging from lectures to courses to film screenings. Thus the Alliance has long had the support of the French government but it has functioned as a transnational network of like-minded individuals. The same is true of organizations such as the Goethe-Institut and the British Council, which employ language diplomacy for Germany and the UK, respectively.

In the second type, governments and NGOs promote the study of foreign languages in order to learn more about other nations, often those perceived as threats. While foreign languages are often learned to meet military or intelligence objectives, this type is devoted to the conduct of diplomatic relations. For example, during the 19th century, China's Qing Dynasty felt a growing danger from the Western powers. To meet this challenge, it needed a corps of diplomats and others with knowledge of the Western nations to effectively manage relations with the foreigners. Since language training was essential to this effort, in 1861 the Qing established an institute for the purpose of educating Chinese officials in Western languages and began sending Chinese to study overseas. During the 1980s and 1990s, the government of the People's Republic of China launched a similar effort when it required schools at all levels to teach English, and made funds available for bringing foreign teachers of English to China. This sparked the growth of educational networks composed of Chinese and foreign schools, and foreign NGOs dedicated to international education. These networks have created constituencies with a strong interest in promoting good relations between China and the United States in particular.

This type can also be seen in the US government's efforts to promote the study of Russian, Chinese, Spanish, and other languages. The government required people with a knowledge of the Russian language and of the Soviet Union to fight the Cold War, but in 1950 few Americans had these skills. Therefore it provided funding for universities to establish area studies centres and programmes through Title VI grants from the Department of Education, and supported language study with Foreign and Area Studies (FLAS) fellowships. Private groups, such as the Ford and Rockefeller Foundations, and the universities themselves provided additional funding to maintain and expand these initiatives. Although the end of the Cold War in 1989 altered the rationale behind these programmes, they have continued to operate and train individuals both to work for the US government or the non-profit sector.

Finally, the second type manifests in the spread of a lingua franca. Following the end of World War 2 English emerged as what scholar Abram de Swaan has termed the global 'hypercentral language'. As a result of the long-term pre-eminence of Britain and the United States, English has become the most used language for international relations. For example, even though the constitution of the European Union requires the use of all member languages in its proceedings, English has become the primary language of operation, with the previous language of international diplomacy, French, filling a secondary role. Although nations and private citizens have not abandoned their national languages in domestic usage, they have adopted English in order to better function in the global arena.

The third type differs from the other two because it relies primarily upon the discursive functions of language. It appeared in 19th-century East Asia, where Western imperial powers replaced the China-centred system of regional politics and trade with a developing discourse of international law, and forced regional states to adopt an alternative model of international relations.

Chinese official Lin Zexu attempted to use Western concepts of sovereignty to gain an advantage over the British as early as the 1840s, but Japan more thoroughly adopted the discourse of international law in its dealings with both the Western powers and with its neighbours. After the Meiji Restoration (1868), Japan's leaders both internalized the concepts of international law via translation and used the original Western words to establish and maintain sovereign control over their territory. This implied that Japanese diplomats learned foreign languages in order to interact with their Western counterparts, but adopting this specific terminology boosted the fulfilment of the Japanese government's ambitious foreign policy. Japan legitimized itself as an imperial power by employing international legal norms in its negotiations with China after the First Sino–Japanese War (1894–95), and by explaining its colonization of Taiwan and Korea through the internationally accepted discourses of liberation, civilization, and sovereignty.

By the end of the 19th century, Chinese officials and scholars saw the essential utility of this new discourse of diplomacy, and they turned initially to Japan for instruction. Over the next several decades, thousands of Chinese went to study in Japan in order to master the terms of modern international relations through their Japanese translations. In fact, because Chinese and Japanese share the same written characters, many of the words used in Japan were either Chinese in origin or earlier Chinese translations from Western languages. Regardless, Chinese students learned Japanese in the process, but that was merely a means to the acquisition of a specific vocabulary and discourse. By the middle of the 20th century, Chinese diplomats successfully used this language of diplomacy to negotiate treaties that guaranteed the return of China's tariff autonomy and recognition of China's sovereignty over most of the Qing Dynasty's former territory. A particular national language provided the medium of communication, but the power to influence foreign relations came in part from China's participation in a shared discursive system where words and concepts did matter more than the language itself.

Evan N. Dawley

Bibliography

de Swaan A. 2002. *Words of the world: the global system*. Cambridge: Polity.

Dubosclard A. 1998. *Histoire de la Fédération des Alliances Françaises aux États-Unis (1902–1997): l'Alliance au Cœur*. Paris: L'Harmattan.

Dudden A. 2005. *Japan's colonization of Korea: discourse and power*. Honolulu: University of Hawai'i Press.

Liu L. 1995. *Translingual practice: literature, national culture, and translated modernity – China, 1900–1937*. Stanford: Stanford University Press.

Related essays

Asia; China; European civil servants; film; Ford Foundation; higher education; intergovernmental organizations; international students; Japan; language; legal order; libraries; literature; nation and state; pan-isms; philanthropic foundations; regions; translation; world orders

Law firms

Law firms are partnerships between several lawyers. Their appearance in the 18th century was an exception to the solo practice of advocacy. An Anglo-American formula had emerged during the 19th century and the first half of the 20th century, before big law firms expanded widely after the Second World War and became important actors in shaping legal norms in the business world.

The first law firms can be identified among English solicitors at the end of the 17th century. While the barristers exclusively worked solo, the junior branch of the legal profession had admitted partnerships, perhaps imitating businessmen. Some solicitors' firms, like Freshfields, had their roots in 18th-century associations between two partners, often father and son. Those English firms worked with the business world. A handful of small – and often temporary – attorneys' firms were created in New York early in the 19th century, to work with English solicitors, banks and ship companies. The Cravath firm of Wall Street began as a partnership between two brothers in 1832. In the late 19th century, 70 firms with five or more lawyers had thrived in other large US cities and the 'Cravath system' had created the profile of the stipended associate. In Europe, the numerous urban German *Rechtsanwälte* seem to have been the first to develop, also as family partnerships. Such evolution was also manifest in Switzerland, in Austria, in Denmark and in Sweden, whereas it proved inconceivable in countries like France, Italy or Spain. Thus, the first European law firms seem to have germinated into Protestant ethics, Jewish juridical networks and areas of dense interaction between lawyers and businessmen. One must wait till 1939 in Italy and 1954 in France to see legal associations among lawyers. Earlier, American lawyers like the Coudert brothers had had to rely on minor and non-regulated professions in France, the business agents (*agents d'affaires*), then the legal counsels (*conseils juridiques*) to create partnerships.

After 1945, English and American law firms expanded to compete with the in-house lawyers of long-range corporate companies. Two Chicago lawyers created Baker & McKenzie in 1949 with two other associates and soon the firm had branches in South America and Europe. The rule limiting the number of partners to 20 was abolished in England in 1967. This growth took different forms: increases in associates over partners, creation of branches in cities of federal countries (national law firms are rather recent in the US or in Germany), installations of quasi-franchised outfits in many countries, and mergers of law firms from different countries. Since the 1980s, a merger-mania has given birth to megafirms with more than 100 partners: Linklaters, Clifford Chance, Allen & Overy in London, Shearman & Sterling, Finley & Kumble, Hyatt (a chain of legal clinics) in the United States. The movement soon reached Canada and Australia, and on the European continent quite recently it has spread to Germany, France, Switzerland, Belgium, the Netherlands and the Scandinavian countries, while more modest law firms have developed in Spain or Italy. With the participation of Australian or Canadian law firms, the Anglo-American model and firms swarmed in Cairo – a centre of international commercial arbitration – and in Asia. Multinational law firms have coexisted with domestic firms in Hong Kong since the 1970s, and now they exist in the rest of China (with foreign licensed firms and private Chinese ones), and in Singapore with about 100 law firms, some indigenous with less than ten partners, others related to English, American or Australian big firms. This form of organization is also familiar in South Korea or Malaysia, as well as in India and Japan, but on a lesser scale. Though concentration does not reach the levels of the accounting field and its Big Four – which are now delivering legal services – law firms have by now woven a wide network where they share resources and push for the development of worldwide standards in business law.

Jean-Louis Halpérin

Bibliography

Abel R. L. 1989. *American lawyers*. Oxford and New York: Oxford University Press.

Dezalay Y. and Garth B. G. 1996. *Dealing in virtue: international commercial arbitration and the construction of a transnational legal order*. Chicago: University of Chicago Press.

Pritchard J. 1992. *Law firms in Europe*. London: Legalease Europe.

Related essays
auditing; governance; legal order

League of Nations Economic and Financial Organization

The Economic and Financial Organization (EFO) was the collective name given the economic and financial agencies of the League of Nations.

EFO evolved considerably in structure and mission during the 25 years it sought to facilitate the coordination of the world's economy. It undertook pioneering work in the collection and dissemination of economic and, to a lesser extent, financial data. Consequently, part of its work could be characterized as intergovernmental in character and the materials EFO collected remain among the most widely cited source of materials used to measure the performance of the interwar economy. But the policy dimension of EFO's work which evolved after 1920 was more transnational in its operation and in its preoccupation with integrating the world economy. This transnational dimension ensured the longevity of EFO's contribution to the content and context of economic and financial relations in the 20th century.

When the League was founded in 1919, no real thought was given to economics. This reflected the widespread conviction that national governments should play but the most minimal role in the management of the national and international economy. In capitalist countries, the nation state was expected to return to the role of 'night-watchman' and international coordination, when it was necessary, should be led by independent central banks. This conviction was typified by the efforts to reconstruct the gold standard in the 1920s and the self-righting properties assigned to the gold-standard 'system'. The League was expected to keep its nose out of financial and economic affairs. Statesmen, bankers and economists all feared the potential anarchy that might be unleashed by allowing an international organization, with an expressed commitment to open debate, to attempt to resolve sensitive issues of economic and financial policy.

But by 1920 rising levels of inflation, the end of the worldwide postwar boom and the economic difficulties faced by Central and Eastern Europe all illustrated the world economy was not likely to right itself. More sustained international cooperation was needed. The officials of the League, supported by Britain and France, might have been the prime movers in this drive for greater international cooperation, but pressure exerted by transnational communities of bankers and big business were also key elements, although the central banks remained suspicious of League involvement.

EFO was created by establishing a new wing of the League secretariat known as the Economic and Financial Section. Its remit was intended to pacify the concerns of nations and banks, and seemed harmless enough: to collate economic statistics so that everyone could see and compare what was happening to national economies and within the international economy as a whole, although some states already regarded this as an affront to their national autonomy. In this early form, the Economic and Financial Section had neither the authority nor the means to formulate policy recommendations.

But from the outset, officials of the Economic and Financial Section became one of the most proactive groups in the League, arguing for an expanded technical institution, with intergovernmental and expert committees that would have the means and power to develop and advocate particular policies to member and non-member states. The League's successful intervention in the currency crises of Central and Eastern Europe bolstered their claim, and by 1923 the section had its way. EFO's scope was expanded with the creation of two intergovernmental committees: the Economic Committee and the Financial Committee. In 1927 came the next significant step when the US, the world's new economic powerhouse, agreed to participate in its work, nominating representatives to the Economic and Financial Committees and maintaining close links with the director of the Economic and Financial Section, the Briton Sir Arthur Salter. In 1931 the section itself was divided in two and new directors appointed: the Italian Pietro Stoppani became director of the Economic Section, and the Briton Alexander Loveday was put in charge of the Financial Section.

These further subdivisions were a sign that EFO was continuing to grow in size and ambition, and the transnational dimension to its work was an essential part of this process. In 1927 and 1933 EFO supported two huge World Economic Conferences whose participants included representatives from over sixty national governments and key non-governmental organizations including trade unions, employers' organizations and economic think tanks, to discuss an agenda that ran to over 25 pages in length. Topics included: tariffs and trade, monetary stability, public works, primary production and poverty. Although the conferences failed to produce any lasting political agreements, to reduce the rising levels of international protectionism for example, they were vitally important in establishing the agenda for future international economic cooperation. They gave all parties the opportunity to appreciate the challenges before individual national economies and how these related to the performance of the international economy.

A further layer to EFO's work came from the special subcommittees, which revealed the most transnational aspect of its work. The subcommittees were notionally created to address single issues, although in reality they could perform a multiplicity of functions. The committees comprised members from the Economic and Financial Committees and nominated experts from universities, central banks, and business both big and small. A good example was the 1931 committee on the Gold Delegation, led by J. L. A. Trip, the governor of the Dutch Central Bank, which included Feliks Mylnarski, Professor of Economics in Warsaw and the Vice-Governor of the Central Bank of Poland, Oliver Sprague, Professor of Banking and Finance at Harvard University, the hugely influential Professor of Economics at Stockholm University, Gustav Cassel, and, the driving force behind the group, Henry Strakosch, a financier who had represented South Africa and Britain at the League and who had very close contacts with the Bank of England.

The transnational network of economists who worked for EFO reads like a *Who Was Who* of leading economists in the 20th century. It includes highly respected contemporary economists, like the Austrian Gottfried Haberler (whose pioneering study on *Prosperity and depression* was published by the League in 1937), as well as men who became famous in later years: the Dutch economists Jan Tinbergen and Tjalling Koopmans, and the Briton James Meade (all were awarded the Sveriges Riksbank Prize in Economic Sciences in Memory of Alfred Nobel), and future leaders of key economic institutions including Per Jacobsen (director of the International Monetary Fund), and Jean Monnet, an architect of the EEC.

Equally important in helping to forge an international network of economic and financial expertise was EFO's path-breaking Economic Intelligence Service (EIS). The fact that EFO devolved part of its original responsibility to collate economic and financial data to this separate agency was a sign both of EFO's growth and of the importance of these data to the wider world. Aside from its commonly cited *Annual report on the general economic situation*, EFO's publications included the *Statistical yearbook of the League of Nations*, the *Monthly bulletin of statistics*, *Money and banking*, the *Review of world trade* and the *World economic survey*. Many of these series were taken up by the United Nations after 1946.

But it would be a mistake solely to see EFO as a super-sized think tank. It is clear that EFO sought to use its expertise to encourage nation states to recognize that the boundaries between the national and international economy were contingent and best left porous. While the peacekeeping activities of the League lurched from crisis to crisis in the 1930s, EFO's political activities sought to advance cooperation on a range of pressing issues, including the impact of clearing agreements, the utility of the gold standard, the effects of protectionism (good and bad), the causes of the Great Depression and the means by which another might be averted.

Behind the scenes EFO made an important contribution to a number of economic and monetary international negotiations, including the 1936 Tripartite Stabilization Agreement. It also urged Britain, France and the United States to exploit EFO as a means to reinternationalize the economies of the 'rogue states' of Germany, Italy and Japan. In 1940 a slimmed-down EFO moved to the Institute for Advanced Study at Princeton. In common with most of the 'technical' agencies of the League, EFO carried on working throughout the war. Although in public the United States administration went to great lengths to ensure the 'new' United Nations was not associated with the 'failed' League, in private the US drew widely on EFO's intelligence and its personnel. Economic and financial cooperation was now top of the agenda for postwar reconstruction and the reshaping of international relations. EFO's intellectual and political legacy played a significant role in the creation of organizations intended to coordinate economic and financial policy in the Bretton Woods agreements of 1944 and in the UN.

Patricia Clavin

Bibliography

Clavin P. and Wessels J.-W. 2005.
  'Transnationalism and the League of Nations: understanding the work of its Economic and Financial Organization', *Contemporary European History*, 14, 4, 465–92.
Pauly L. 1998. *Who elected the bankers? Surveillance and control in the world economy*. Ithaca: Cornell University Press.

Related essays

economics; financial diplomacy; financial markets; General Agreement on Tariffs and Trade (GATT) / World Trade Organization (WTO); intergovernmental organizations; International Monetary Fund (IMF); League of Nations system; philanthropic foundations; Quesnay, Pierre; statistics; Swiss banks; trade; United Nations system; World Bank

League of Nations Health Organization

The success of a temporary Epidemic Commission, which was authorized by the League to contain the diseases that had spread in Eastern Europe and the Soviet Union in the early 1920s, resulted in the establishment of the League of Nations Health Organization (LNHO) at the Fourth Assembly in September 1923.

The LNHO had two major organs. The Health Committee, usually meeting twice a year, was comprised of about 15 specialists, who did not necessarily represent any government. The Health Section, a permanent secretariat in Geneva, served as an intermediary to coordinate activity between experts and various institutions. Ludwik Rajchman, a Polish medical doctor, served as director of the Health Section (1923–39), and his outstanding leadership was indispensable for its growth.

Since the work of the LNHO had a highly technical and scientific character, nonmember states, including the US and Japan, also participated in its activities. For instance, even after its official withdrawal from the League in 1933, Japan continued to contribute to the LNHO's operating costs and sent a delegate to the Health Committee, and some Japanese specialists contributed technical reports. The LNHO enjoyed relative autonomy from the main body of the League due to the technical nature of its work and its considerable financial independence, due in large part to Rockefeller Foundation subsidies, which covered almost a third of its annual budget. This grant in aid financed the Epidemiological Intelligence Service and the medical interchange programme that brought Latin American, North American, European and Asian public health personnel into contact with public health methods and organization in other regions and continents.

The LNHO was involved in numerous activities. The Epidemiological Intelligence Service, which was the forerunner of the organization, continued throughout this period, by collecting data and disseminating information in its *Weekly Epidemiological Report* and *Weekly Fasciculus of the Eastern Bureau*. The

Eastern Bureau – set up in Singapore in 1925 to function as a branch office of the LNHO – communicated by telegraph with ports and health administrations covering the vast region from the Near East to East Asia.

The LNHO launched several important efforts in standardization, such as the standardization of mortality statistics, and a unified notation of blood groups: the O, A, B, AB system that was agreed upon in 1927. One of its most significant achievements was the establishment of standards for biological agents such as Insulin and vitamins. After several years of work involving experts, administrators, industries, and laboratories, the LNHO set the standard for these agents. The Health Committee then proposed an intergovernmental conference on biological standardization. It was held in October 1935 with delegates from 24 countries, including the US and Japan, and the delegates agreed to authorize the standard as a form of international convention. Furthermore, the LNHO created the system of supplying standard samples from the National Institute for Medical Research in London, which stored them, to designated national control centres in 34 countries.

In the field of social medicine, deteriorating working conditions brought about by the Great Depression facilitated cooperation between the LNHO and the International Labour Organization, which led to the study of nutrition and housing conditions and resulted in widely read publications such as the *Nutrition Report of the League of Nations* (1937).

The LNHO published numerous reports on disease, health conditions, and health education, regarding conditions in many different areas. In total, more than a thousand authors contributed to LNHO reports covering more than 70 countries and regions. The LNHO also provided technical assistance. For instance, in China the LNHO helped to establish the public health service and carried out anti-epidemic programs from the late 1920s. In Greece, the LNHO collaborated with the Greek government to reorganize the public health service. As F. P. Walters, a historian of the League, once noted, the LNHO was 'the most successful' of the League's affiliated organizations, building up a dense network of expertise beyond the boundaries of any one nation.

Hatsue Shinohara

Bibliography

League of Nations Health Organization 1945. 'Bibliography of the technical work of the Health Organization of the League of Nations', *Bulletin of the Health Organization*, 11.

Weindling P. (ed.) 1995. *International Health Organizations and Movements, 1918–1939*. Cambridge: Cambridge University Press.

Related essays

diet and nutrition; health policy; intergovernmental organizations; International Red Cross and Red Crescent movement; League of Nations Economic and Financial Organization; League of Nations system; medicine; philanthropic foundations; relief; technical assistance; technical standardization; vaccination

League of Nations system

When we examine the record of the League of Nations through an intergovernmental or interstate perspective, we are compelled to reach the conventional conclusion that the League failed in its original and primary task of promoting peace. There can be no more convincing evidence for this conclusion than the outbreak of World War 2. However, an alternative review of the League's history – especially one taking into account the League's influence on the development of transnational activities and relations – affords a fresh outlook on the role of the international organization in shaping world order. Among its successes, the League was involved in numerous efforts which invited non-state actors such as individuals and NGOs to its discussions, and the aims and scope of certain of the League's policies, most notably in social, humanitarian and cultural fields, well transcended national interests and concerns.

The Central Administrative Agency

The main organs of the League were the Council and the Assembly, which were composed exclusively of representatives of member governments. In addition to the Council and the Assembly, the League also created auxiliary committees and organizations, and, most importantly, a permanent secretariat. The former included the Financial and Economic Committees, the Organization for Communication and Transit, and so on. Some of the auxiliary organizations invited individuals to their official discussions to secure their neutrality and impartiality. For instance, the Mandates Commission that was to study the annual reports of mandate areas and to observe their conditions was composed of individuals rather than of government representatives so that it could avoid political intervention from the countries that were in charge of the territories.

The secretariat created a body of civil servants whose main task was to attend to the daily workings and administrative matters of the League. These employees were supposed to act within constitutional limits defined by the League Covenant, while the Assembly and Council determined their working provisions. However, since they were assured permanency of their position to a degree, and coherence of policy was both necessary and desirable, they were occasionally able to draft policies and influence decision making within their respective areas of expertise and/or authority.

At its zenith in 1931, the League had 707 staff members who were employed by the secretariat. The representation of the secretariat members was heavily Western, but there were also personnel from Asian and Latin American countries. Additionally, the League also permitted individuals from non-member states to work at the secretariat, and in 1930, for instance, there were 34 employees from the US out of a total secretariat staff of 658. The secretariat staffs were expected to act fairly and independently of national interests, aiming for the overall improvement and betterment of the world and the conditions of its inhabitants. The League noted that what was ideally required for an international servant was the simultaneous maintenance of 'global' as well as 'national' loyalty.

The creation of the Central Administrative Agency under the auspices of the League signified the birth of a key and core entity which was entitled to address issues on behalf of humanity as a whole, and to identify itself as the sole international organization whose jurisdiction and scope of activities could likely surpass national concerns and help orient the energies of the community of nations instead towards more global and universal concerns. The League, with its gravity, permanency and universality, served as a positive asset for further transnational development.

Social and humanitarian activities

The rise of new issues required better and more efficient coordination between the League, national governments, and other, private organizations. This resulted in increasing calls for the League's more active involvement and leadership in the social and humanitarian fields.

When the issue of refugees emerged in September 1921, the League asked Frijthof Nansen of Norway, who had been successful in the task of repatriation of war prisoners, to take the post of High Commissioner. Due to budget considerations, the League was not willing to take full responsibility for relief efforts, and its role as a result was largely confined to coordination of relief and settlement efforts carried out by private agencies such as the International Red Cross and the Save the Children Fund. However, Nansen and his office were successful in setting the standard for a legal definition of refugees, thereby enabling the issuing of 'Nansen passports', which were accepted under international agreement as the equivalent of national passports.

The control of the opium traffic was another matter of global concern during this era. To address the issue, the League set up the Advisory Committee on Traffic in Opium and other Dangerous Drugs, which played a role in bringing about the Geneva Convention of 1931. It limited the production of narcotic drugs to medical and scientific needs. Both official and unofficial delegates sat on the Opium Committee, but the private 'assessors', who otherwise enjoyed authority similar to that conferred upon official delegates, could not vote.

Private groups were also involved in children's and women's issues to a significant degree. Private organizations including the International Alliance of Women, the International Council of Women, and the All Asian Conference of Women presented to the League their positions and opinions on the nationality of married women and legal equality between men and women. In 1931, the League officially asked these groups to form a consultative committee. Both the Traffic in Women and Children Committee and the Child Welfare Committee invited NGOs to their discussions; these NGOs included the International Federation of Girls' Friendly Societies, International Women's Associations and others. Attention given to the issues of the protection of children and traffic in women well illustrates 'an example of an outside organization being put under the League auspices', as noted in the League's official history, Ten Years of World Cooperation.

The 'League of Minds'

The International Committee on Intellectual Cooperation (ICIC) was established in May 1922 to facilitate the exchanges of ideas, culture and thought across national boundaries. The Committee invited the cooperation of notable scholars of the time such as Henri Bergson, Marie Curie, and Sigmund Freud. The French government set up and sponsored the International Institute of Intellectual Cooperation in Paris to serve as an executive organ of the ICIC. It launched various important efforts: the improvement of conditions for intellectual professions; the establishment of the concept and handling of copyrights; the fostering of international dialogue among intellectuals; and the strengthening of the League's initiatives for promoting the cause of peace. In short, the ICIC sought to create a 'League of Minds', as it was aptly described by Paul Valéry. The ICIC invited the setting up of National Committees in each country with the intended function of their serving as liaison offices between the ICIC and national institutions of the press, universities, and museums. National Committees on their part held a General Conference of the National Committee of Intellectual Cooperation. In 1937, 39 National Committees participated in such a gathering. In addition, regional initiatives were undertaken in the form of inter-Baltic and inter-American conferences. The relationship was strong enough that, after Japan's official withdrawal from the League, the Japanese National Committee maintained its relationship with the ICIC.

In the meantime, the Information Section of the League secretariat had also been engaged in efforts to educate, enlighten, and inform the general public about the League by publishing general information materials such as the Essential Facts about the League of Nations or How to Make the League of Nations Known and to Develop the Spirit of International Cooperation. The Information Section conducted a survey on how information about the League was disseminated in various countries. Additionally, the League published and sold official documents, technical reports, and general information literature. Three non-member states (the US, Germany and Japan) were among the most regular purchasers of League literature.

When we think of a 'League of Minds' we should also note the private initiatives that followed the prewar movement for the establishment of a league of nations. After the League was founded, those who were involved in the movement realized that the organization would not be successful unless they continued their efforts and were able to secure public support. In Great Britain, the growth of the League of Nations Union was quite vigorous, as evidenced by the popularity of its journal, Headway, which enjoyed a circulation of 100,000 subscriptions in 1930. It not only engaged in educational efforts to publicize the idea of the League with the collaboration of schools and churches, but also proclaimed its support for certain policies of the League, notably disarmament and the Geneva Protocol of 1924. Similar associations were active in other nations as well. Although the United States, for example, did not join the League, the League of Nations Association, the Woodrow Wilson Foundation and the Foreign Policy Association were actively involved in promoting intellectual discussions and educational activities about the organization in the country. In the 1930s these groups sponsored a model League Assembly for students. The League of Nations Association of Japan published periodicals, sponsored lectures and students' essay contests, and in May 1932 boasted a membership of some 12,000 – including 5,600 students – well distributed in both urban and rural areas. The association declared itself Japan's peace group in the 1920s, although like almost all Japanese civilian associations of the era, it gradually came to support more militaristic policies during the 1930s.

The League of Nations Associations of various countries established a small international headquarters in Brussels, with 20 national organizations participating in 1921 and 35 by 1924, although these associations never combined their efforts in any significant and tangible manner. However, the League of Nations Associations' activities served as a window through which members learned about major developments at the League, as well as in the world at large. It should also be noted that communication channels existed between the National Committee of the ICIC and the League of Nations Association in some countries, demonstrating the existence of complex networks emerging from and revolving around the League.

Toward a future League

General conditions around the globe became adverse for the League towards the end of the 1930s. While the international situation deteriorated and economic conditions did not recover from the effects of the Great Depression, the League's inability to cope with these challenges was conspicuous. Under the circumstances, it was natural and inevitable for the League to both raise and face questions regarding reconsideration of its policy priorities and orientations. The outcome was the Report of the Special Committee on the Development of International Cooperation in Economic and Social Affairs that was issued on 22 August 1939. It became widely known as the Bruce Report, named after its framer, Stanley M. Bruce, an Australian delegate at the League. The report proposed a shift of League policy from collective security, disarmament, and peaceful settlement of disputes to a greater emphasis on social, economic and humanitarian matters. In the 20 years of its activities there was emerging a recognition among the League officials that improvement of individual well-being was a step toward peace, and that the League should play a more decisive and active role in attending to this goal.

It will be fair to conclude that at least as far as social, humanitarian, and cultural affairs were concerned, the League was quite successful and effective in promoting transnational and global interests and concerns, and in developing a compound network among international organizations, national governments, private groups, and individuals.

Hatsue Shinohara

Bibliography

Aufricht H. 1966. Guide to League of Nations publications: a bibliographical survey of the work of the League, 1920–1947. New York: AMS.

Clavin P. and Wessels J. 2005. 'Transnationalism and the League of Nations: understanding the work of its Economic and Financial Organisation', Contemporary European History, 14, 4, 465–92.

Pemberton J. 2002. 'New worlds for old: The League of Nations in the age of electricity', Review of International Studies, 28, 311–36.

Ranshofen-Werheimer E. F. 1945. International secretariat: a great experiment in international administration. Washington, DC: Carnegie Endowment for International Peace.

The League of Nations in Retrospect: Proceedings of the Symposium. 1983. Berlin: Walter de Gruyter.

Walters F. P. 1952. A history of the League of Nations, Vols 1, 2. London: Oxford University Press.

Related essays

children's rights; Commission on International Labour Legislation; diet and nutrition; disarmament; drugs (illicit); electricity infrastructures; forced migrations; human rights; humanities; individual identification systems; intellectual elites; intellectual property rights; intergovernmental organizations; international non-governmental organizations (INGOs); International Red Cross and Red Crescent movement; internationalisms; Kessler, Harry von; language; League of Nations Economic and Financial Organization; League of Nations Health Organization; marriage; music; nation and state; refugees; relief; Save the Children International Union; technical statdardization; traffic signals; transportation infrastructures; vaccination; Wilson, Woodrow; women's movements; world orders

Lebanese Diaspora

After 1880, peasants from Lebanon (then part of the Ottoman Empire) began to leave for the Americas. By World War 2 some 400,000 men and women had left their villages and towns. Their scattering produced a predominantly mercantile diaspora.

As labour migrants, Lebanese peasants sought to sustain a comfortable quality of life in the face of a stagnating economy, a fast-growing population, and limited opportunities. Most planned to travel overseas temporarily to gather money before returning home to live as wealthy peasants. With limited resources and skills most chose a life of trade in the mahjar (the lands of immigration). Thus, in Brazil in the 1930s 90 per cent of all pedlars were of Lebanese background. In Australia limited language skills and discrimination against the Lebanese immigrants shifted most of them toward hawking goods in the countryside of New South Wales and Victoria. In New York, about 40 per cent of immigrant Lebanese women worked as pedlars and their male counterparts worked in that same trade at double that percentage.

Most immigrants found work through a compatriot or relative who supplied them with the stuff of itinerant peddling (buttons and lace, thread and needles, crosses and mementoes from the 'Holy Land'), and integrated them into the trading network. Other immigrants had only heard of a person, either back in Lebanon or while crossing the Atlantic, to look for in the *mahjar*. Once established in their new communities by purchase of an urban dry goods store immigrants provided conduits for yet later arrivals, creating a network that linked immigrants with relatives and friends who had remained behind.

This network, more than a unilateral connection between Lebanon and the *mahjar*, was a complex matrix of social and economic relations that tied Mexico City to Rio de Janeiro as well as to Lebanon. Lebanese immigrants in Senegal around the turn of the 20th century sent family members to Brazil to establish a trading network between the two countries. Similarly, the Lebanese in Cuba and the Caribbean shuttled back and forth to Florida in an effort to benefit from commerce between the two areas. In addition to travel and correspondence, Arabic newspapers published in North and South America after 1890 provided another layer to that matrix. News of globally dispersed communities, announcement of products imported from one area into another, requests for commercial contacts, and news of relocation, marriage or death thickened the links in this network of immigrants.

Similar networks continued to draw Lebanese immigrants after World War 2. What changed over time were the countries of destination and the religious makeup of the persons leaving Lebanon. Between 1890 and World War 1 most – but not all – immigrants were Christians. After World War 2 and through the 1970s, tens of thousands of Shi'a Muslims from Lebanon went to West Africa and Central America rather than to earlier destinations, although trade remained their primary occupation. After the start of the Lebanese civil war in 1975, and for the following 30 years, close to 1.5 million immigrants left Lebanon. More than

half went to the oil-rich Gulf countries, and most were professionals in search of salaried employment rather than trade.

After 125 years of immigration, there are today five times more individuals of Lebanese descent outside Lebanon than in the country itself. In Brazil alone there are an estimated 2–3 million, and in the US the number is around 500,000 while the number in Senegal is a modest 30,000. Regardless of when immigrants left or where they are, many maintained a link with Lebanon. Travel to Lebanon, cultural and religious organizations, and institutions such as the Lebanese League and the Ministry of Immigrants have allowed many immigrants and their descendants to maintain a fluctuating relationship with Lebanon.

Akram F. Khater

Bibliography
Hourani A. and Shehadi N. 1992. *The Lebanese in the world*. London: I.B. Tauris.
Khater A. 2001. *Inventing home: emigration, gender, and the middle class in Lebanon, 1870–1920*. Berkeley: University of California Press.

Related essays
Chinese Diaspora; diasporas; empire and migration; executives and professionals; human mobility; pedlars; religious pilgrimage

Legal order
The concept of transnational legal order is ill-defined and includes aspects of public international law, international private law, comparative law and the law of transnational commercial and financial transactions. It differs from the concept of public international law or the law of nations since it is not limited to nation states but includes non-state law-making actors and institutions transcending the boundaries of nation states. In legal theory the concept of legal order is usually implicitly presupposed. The term legal order or legal system does not figure prominently in Anglo-American publications but German, French, Spanish and Italian dictionaries and study books often refer to *Rechtsordnung, ordre juridique, ordenamento jurídico* or *ordinamento giuridico*, which is primarily defined in terms of efficacy, unity, coherence and comprehensiveness. In its conventional sense the term

legal order refers to the rules of codified or customary law formulated and applied by specialized bodies such as organizations and tribunals. Sociologically it may also pertain to a domain of specific social interaction like private commercial transactions or humanitarian activism. In order to appreciate the contested and heterogeneous processes that have shaped conceptions of transnational legal order throughout history it is necessary to sketch the complex interrelations between institutions and social actors in various domains of interaction.

The notion of transnational legal order is historically and geographically contingent. It emerged as a political project in the second half of the 19th century in Europe and it was from the very beginning inextricably connected with the colonial expansion of European powers and American-European economic and cultural hegemony. From such a perspective transnational legal order is neither an abstract principle nor the *telos* of history but rather a contested idea transmitted by individuals and groups in the pursuit of careers and designs. Several historical periods can be distinguished in which the vision of transnational legal order was transformed or reconfigured. The first one encompasses the second half of the long 19th century, between the 1860s and 1914. The second one is the interwar period between 1918 and 1939. The third one is the time between 1945 and the 1980s, while the fourth phase covers the time since the end of the Cold War.

The 19th century: the formation of cosmopolitan social movements

The prefix 'trans' presupposes the existence of an imagined national realm. In the course of the 19th century the model of the nation state became fully consolidated in Europe. Territorial boundaries were equated with the boundaries of the nation, a people sharing a common national identity usually defined in ethnic, genealogical, linguistic and cultural terms. Of course, nationalism and state formation had been long-term processes but in the 19th century they became paradigmatic shaping cosmopolitan ideas about the transcendence of national boundaries to an unprecedented degree.

Internal consolidation and unification by means of the bureaucratic state apparatus and nationalist ideology were connected to the colonial expansion of the European powers in Africa and Asia and the colonization of North America by the US. For example, a range of conferences of scientific associations and governments during the 1870s and 1880s, many of them sponsored by the Belgian King Leopold II, laid the legal foundation for the total colonization of Africa agreed upon at the Berlin conference in 1885. Even formally sovereign states such as the newly independent Latin American countries and the Ottoman Empire were economically and politically dominated by the US and the European colonial powers by the end of the 19th century. Recent scholarship argues that colonial expansion was not peripheral to the project of establishing universal global legal order: on the contrary, the colonial encounter and its consequences have shaped conceptions of public international law, the theory of comparative law and even international private law from the very beginning.

Rapid industrialization and urbanization in many parts of Europe and North America necessitated the legal regulation of increasing communication and trade across state boundaries (e.g. the International Telegraph Union 1865 and the General Postal Union 1874). The legal regulation of cross-border flows of goods, money, persons and information led to the formation of a class of legal experts who promoted a more encompassing concept of transnational legal order than that of postal and customs agreements. In the 1860s lawyers from different European countries formed professional associations, organized conferences and founded scientific journals with the aim of carving out a separate identity for the new scientific disciplines of international law and comparative law. They distanced themselves from the doctrine of natural law and embraced legal positivism, a doctrine that recognized only positive law codified in legislation or treaties between nation states. Hence, they advocated the gradual codification of universal legal principles in order to further international peace. The first academic bodies promoting these aims were created: the Société de Législation Comparée in 1869, the Institut de Droit International and the International Law Association, both in 1873. The first international law journal, the *Revue de Droit International et de Législation Comparée*, was founded in 1868 and around the turn of the century the first chairs in international law were established at European universities.

Due to the increase in transnational relations these experts were in high demand, setting up law firms, facilitating arbitration between states and exporting legal knowledge such as the French *Code civil* and the German civil code.

These lawyer-activists, however, were not the only internationalist social movement at the time. A whole range of groups and movements had emerged in the late 18th century as one of the consequences of the formation of the modern public sphere in Europe and the Americas dedicated to the advancement of transnational legal order. The most important of these were the abolitionist movement striving to ban slavery, and the peace movement. The latter was associated with radical politics and utopian goals such as the abolishment of war and the establishment of a world government. Governments preferred to deal with the more moderate project of regulating warfare, which led to the establishment of the International Red Cross and a series of treaties (Geneva Convention 1864 and the Hague Conventions 1899 and 1907). These conflicting early attempts at advancing the concept of a cosmopolitan legal order aimed at limiting state sovereignty formed the reference point for subsequent attempts at codifying and standardising international law.

The interwar period: institutionalizing global legal order

The period between the two World Wars is characterized by explicit attempts to institutionalize a global legal order. This process of institutionalization was bifurcated: governments, the peace movement and the academic bodies tried to establish a system of collective security and the rule of law in Europe, on the one hand, while colonial rule in Africa and Asia became more entrenched, on the other. The legitimacy of colonial rule depended to a large degree on the concept of global legal order as it had been developed by positivist legal science since the second half of the 19th century.

The idea of a global legal order, which had been advanced by activists and academics both in Europe and the US since the second half of the 19th century, gained wider currency after World War I. At the 1919 Paris peace conference it was decided to establish the League of Nations called for by US President Wilson. It was the first international organization with a mandate to regulate the relations between nation states and represented a new type of subject of international law that limited absolute state sovereignty. The League's ambitious goals were disarmament, the prevention of war, the settlement of international disputes and welfare. In spite of the demise of this new system of collective security in the 1930s, the utopian vision of a universal legal system with the League of Nations as global law-making and law-enforcing institution was realized in many respects during the 1920s.

Institutionalization of a global legal order was also reflected in the creation of the Permanent Court of International Justice (PCIJ) and ambitious efforts to codify international law, projects that had been on the agenda of the peace movement and internationalist lawyer-activists since the end of the 19th century. The PCIJ was the first international court with universal jurisdiction concerning disputes between states and operated between 1921 and 1940. The various institutions of the League and a number of expert bodies were engaged in countless attempts to codify existing rules of international law and to formulate new ones in a 'frenzy of law-making' (Grewe 2000, 603) between 1920 and the 1930s, especially in the areas of arms control and international communications and transportation. However, most of these efforts, particularly in the sphere of arms control, were thwarted by the insistence of governments on state sovereignty and particularistic policies.

The establishment of international bodies and the codification of international law have to be seen in the context of theories of international law developed after World War I. The science of international law expanded considerably in the interwar period: new academic journals were founded, a growing number of monographs were published and international law became better established at the universities. The 1920s were characterized by the revival of natural law conceptions, which postulated the concept of universal mankind or cosmopolitan world society first advanced by French and German Enlightenment thinkers. These theories constituted an attempt to overcome the legal positivist view that the sovereign state was the ultimate source of international law.

This cosmopolitan vision of a global legal order based on natural law was, in spite of its apparently universal character, primarily a project advanced by social movements and governments in North America and Europe. The idiom of inclusiveness and peace continued to be coupled with the legitimization of colonialism and European supremacy. The only difference was the emphasis put on the duty of colonial powers to protect the interests of the 'native' populations and the 'development' of colonial territories. This shift is best exemplified in the mandate system of the League of Nations. Article 22 of the Covenant of the League of Nations stipulated that the German colonies and the Ottoman territories in the Middle East 'which are inhabited by peoples not yet able to stand themselves under the strenuous conditions of the modern world' should be placed under the tutelage of 'advanced nations' as 'mandatories on behalf of the League of Nations'.

Many historians of international law make much of differences between the mandate system and the legal theories of the 19th century that denied 'savage' and 'primitive' populations full legal rights, arguing that the mandate system marked the beginning of the end of colonialism. Such a teleological reading fails to recognize that the League's concern for the welfare of 'natives' was not new: since King Leopold II's appropriation of the Congo Basin at the Berlin Conference in 1885 it had been common to mask colonial exploitation with altruistic rhetoric. Nor was it unique since colonial administration in general was influenced by ideas about 'welfare' and 'development' in the interwar period. Especially the British and the French developed the notion of 'colonial development' in the 1930s by which they sought to take the welfare of the population into account while aiming at maximizing the profit for the metropolitan centre. Hence, the utopian vision of a global legal order continued to exclude 'those who have a different complexion or slightly flatter noses', as Joseph Conrad put it in Heart of Darkness, by means of a 'standard of civilization' that relegated large parts of mankind to an inferior position vis-à-vis the colonial powers in Europe and North America.

1945–80: codification and the rise of the Third World

The project of institutionalizing a global legal order and a system of collective security was revived after World War 2. On 26 June 1945 representatives of fifty countries signed the Charter of the United Nations (UN). The lofty goals of the UN, to 'save succeeding generations from the scourge of war' and to 'reaffirm faith in fundamental human rights', reflected the prevalent idealism after the war and echoed the rhetoric of its predecessor, the League of Nations. The UN, however, had a more efficacious organisational setup and, more importantly, enjoyed the support of the two new hegemonic powers, the US and the Soviet Union, although their ideological antagonism soon overshadowed the work of the UN. A new international court, the International Court of Justice (ICJ), was established in The Hague to adjudicate disputes between states. Postwar reconstruction and development fell under the mandate of the World Bank and the coordination of monetary policies was overseen by the International Monetary Fund (IMF), both established one year earlier at the Bretton Woods conference.

The academic bodies, which had proved to be instrumental in the advancement of ideas about international legal order before and after World War 1, were re-established after 1945 and became very active in the codification of international law within the UN framework. The International Law Commission was probably the most influential organization, drawing up proposals for codification and lobbying for functionally differentiated treaty regimes in all legal domains. Other bodies such as the International Institute for the Unification of Private Law (UNIDROIT) and the UN Commission on International Trade Law (UNICTRAL) actively pursued projects to uniform and codify the norms of international private law and trade law. The work of these organizations contributed to the project of codifying and developing the rules of international law by means of treaties between states.

An important area for the development of a transnational legal order affording rights to entities other than governments proved to be the codification of human rights law. The Universal Declaration of Human Rights of the UN General Assembly in 1948, the covenants on Civil and Political Rights and Economic, Social and Cultural Rights (both 1966, entry into force 1976) and the European Convention on Human Rights (1950) were declared and signed by states but they served as important resources for transnationally operating individuals and groups who challenged state sovereignty during the 1980s and 1990s and became participants in law making within the UN framework.

The new universalistic movement towards a global legal order was based on functionalist differentiation and regional integration. The former was based on the assumption that separate agencies with limited mandates should deal with specific issue areas such as health, trade, development, human rights and the economy. The architects of the UN system hoped that conflicts between these organizations could be minimized by defining their respective fields of intervention. Functionalist differentiation was matched by regional integration. In Western Europe the European Economic Communities (EEC) was created with the objective to ensure political stability among its members by means of economic cooperation and development. Furthermore, economic development was seen as an important defence against the challenge posed by Communism. Anticommunism influenced also the establishment of other regional organizations such as the Organization of American States (OAS) and the Association of South East Asian Nations (ASEAN). These regional organizations have the potential to function as nuclei for the codification of regional legal orders but so far only the European Union is regarded as a regional legal order in its own right. The project of a socialist international law was abandoned with the demise of the Soviet Union.

The assumptions about the connection between economic development, political liberalism and cooperation between nation states were heavily influenced by the modernization paradigm, the idea that all nation states could follow a unilinear progressive trajectory towards development and welfare by reforming society. The modernization paradigm influenced the export of legal reform from the US to developing countries, especially in Latin America. This movement, known as 'law and development', blossomed during the 1960s and the early 1970s and constituted an attempt to reform developing societies by means of translating superior legal knowledge from the US into national legislation. 'Law and development' was heavily criticized for being ethnocentric, based on simplistic notions about social change, and serving the political agenda of the US, and disappeared in the mid-1970s. It would resurface in the 1990s when notions about law as an instrument for social change ('good governance') became popular again. Socialism,

in turn, shaped legislation in countries under Soviet influence although there was no particular emphasis on law as an instrument for social change due to ideological reasons.

The competition between the US and the Soviet Union affected the decolonization process in general during the 1960s and 1970s when most colonial territories achieved their independence and joined the UN. By the late 1970s membership in the UN had risen to about 160 member states and the newly independent countries formed the majority in the UN. The decolonization process transformed international relations: for the first time in history, international law making was not dominated by the European and North American countries. In the 1970s the new member states, called the Third World by contemporaries, were able to overcome the Cold War ideological antagonism and used their majority in the UN General Assembly to redefine their legal relationships with the industrialized world by passing resolutions on the creation of the New International Economic Order (NIEO) and the independence of colonial countries and peoples in 1974. These resolutions reflected the confidence of the newly independent states and their desire to secure economic self-determination by legal means. In an attempt to create new institutions sympathetic to their cause the Third World countries established the UN Conference on Trade and Development (UNCTAD) and the UN Development Programme (UNDP). The Third World movement for the codification of this new order lost much of its momentum when the effects of the debt crisis in the late 1970s triggered economic decline in most developing countries. When neoliberalism emerged as the new economic and political paradigm in the 1980s, attempts to codify rights to development and economic self-determination were by and large abandoned in favour of the new 'structural adjustment' policies of the World Bank and the IMF with their emphasis on economic deregulation and non-legal arrangements.

Since the 1980s: transnational legal pluralism and US hegemony

Economic globalization, the advent of neoliberalism and the end of the Cold War had far-reaching consequences for the transnationalization of law and ways to conceptualize it. Organizations such as the World Bank, the European Union, the World Trade

Organization and the UN operate much more autonomously and their law-making activities affect individuals to a much greater extent than before. This development is particularly conspicuous in developing countries with a weakened state apparatus where public services are often provided by international organizations and foreign non-governmental organizations (NGOs). NGOs have proliferated since the 1980s and acquired considerable influence on law-making, especially in the areas of human rights, indigenous peoples' rights and environmental protection. The growing influence of NGOs on international law making is especially conspicuous with regard to the expansion of international criminal justice during the 1990s. The international tribunals that have been established since the 1990s are the result of intense lobbying by a coalition of mainly Western NGOs such as Amnesty International and Human Rights Watch and a group of determined international lawyers. Other private actors like transnational corporations and law firms have also become active actors in the development of international private law, commercial law and national law reform, especially in developing countries.

It is hotly debated whether the growing influence of transnationally operating civil rights groups and the proliferation of institutions of global and regional governance indicate the development of a cosmopolitan legal order. Three current trends, however, seem to undermine the teleological perspective of a gradual evolution of transnational legal regimes towards a global unified, coherent and efficient legal system. The first trend is deformalization, the growing importance of flexible and informal networks and regimes with regard to global governance. Second, there is a tendency towards fragmentation, the increasing division of international regulation into specific fields, and transnational legal pluralism, the co-existence of different legal orders at the transnational level. The third trend is the disengagement of the US from the consensual multilateralism of the UN system and the continued importance of unilateralism and bilateralism outside the UN framework.

The shift towards deformalization is reflected in the growing importance of 'soft law', non-binding rules, 'gentlemen's agreements' and technical standards such as the International Organization for Standardization (ISO) norms.

Deformalization characterizes especially the dealings of Northern donor agencies with the governments in the South. Since the 1980s the World Bank and the IMF have been imposing conditions for their financial support to developing countries, known as 'structural adjustment'. In exchange for financial support governments have to reduce government expenditure, conduct multiparty elections and deregulate the economy according to neoliberal economic theory. Both organizations are at pains to point out that these conditions merely reflect the intention of the borrowing government to implement certain reform measures and do not constitute legally binding obligations.

Fragmentation and legal pluralism have become more conspicuous since the 1980s. Many new tribunals and dispute settlement bodies have been established, resulting in a proliferation of legal forums with often overlapping claims for jurisdiction. Furthermore, non-state actors such as international organizations, transnational corporations and NGOs exacerbate fragmentation by producing their own rules, which in practice often take precedence over international and national law. Within the context of European integration a regional legal order is in the process of formation. Legal pluralism is one of the consequences since the relations between national legal systems, European law and international law are indeterminate and have to be established in a complex interplay between national and European institutions. The trend towards fragmentation and legal pluralism is further intensified by the rise of transnational commercial law. Since the 1980s there has been a dramatic increase in transnational commercial arbitration, resulting in the development of a new body of law. This law is a very heterogeneous mix of elements of national contract law and lex mercatoria, an autonomous non-national body of law regulating transnational economic transactions. The transnational character of commercial arbitration, however, does not preclude the influence of national law. Transnational commercial transactions have become dominated by large Anglo-American law firms and US law has become the law of choice in many commercial disputes.

The Americanisation of international private law is only one of the aspects of the diffusion of law made in the US. Legislative reforms in developing and post-Communist countries often draw on legal knowledge originating in the US, especially in the fields of constitutional reform and foreign investment. 'Alternative dispute resolution', a set of techniques for the extra-legal settlement of disputes, and the new 'law and development' are also mainly US products. Another aspect of US hegemony is the partial withdrawal of the US from multilateral treaty regimes and the UN system: the US refrained from joining a number of international treaties such as the statute of the International Criminal Court, the Kyoto Protocols, the Mine Ban Treaty and the Law of the Sea Convention. Of course, unilateralism and a preference for bilateral agreements are not limited to the US and will continue to compete with the multilateral UN system.

In conclusion it appears that the utopian vision of a cosmopolitan legal order formulated by the lawyer-activists of the Institut de Droit International and the International Law Association in the 19th century continues to exert its influence on academics and policy makers although deformalization, legal pluralism and US unilateralism seem to indicate much more ambivalent and undirected processes of transnationalization of law.

Gerhard Anders
Miklos Redner

Bibliography

Anghie A. 2005. *Imperialism, sovereignty and the making of international law.* Cambridge: Cambridge University Press.

Benda-Beckmann F., Benda-Beckmann K. and Griffiths A. 2005. *Mobile people, mobile law: expanding legal relations in a contracting world.* Aldershot: Ashgate.

Dezalay Y. and Garth B. 1996. *Dealing in virtue: international commercial arbitration and the construction of a transnational legal order.* Chicago: University of Chicago Press.

Dezalay Y. and Garth B. (eds) 2002. *Global prescriptions: the production, exportation, and importation of a new legal orthodoxy.* Ann Arbor: University of Michigan Press.

Grewe W. G. 2000. *The epochs of international law.* Berlin and New York: Walter de Gruyter.

Jessup P. C. 1956. *Transnational law.* Yale Law School, Storrs Lectures on Jurisprudence. New Haven: Yale University Press.

Koskenniemi M. 2002. *The gentle civilizer of nations: the rise and fall of international law 1870–1960.* Cambridge: Cambridge University Press.

Mattei U. 2003. *The European codification process: cut and paste.* The Hague: Kluwer Law International.

Related essays

Abolition of Forced Labour Convention; abolitionism; air pollution; arms trafficking; biodiversity; biopatents; car safety standards; *Code civil*; Cold War; Commission on International Labour Legislation; corporations; cosmopolitanism and universalism; counterfeit goods; debt crises (developing countries); decolonization; democracy; developmental assistance; developmental taxonomies; disarmament; empires and imperialism; environmental diplomacy; European institutions; European Union (EU); financial diplomacy; financial markets; food safety standards; General Agreement on Tariffs and Trade (GATT) / World Trade Organization (WTO); genetically modified organisms (GMOs); genocide; governance; governing science; higher education; human rights; industrialization; information technology (IT) offshoring; information technology (IT) standardization; intergovernmental organizations; International Monetary Fund (IMF); international non-governmental organizations (INGOs); Internet Corporation for Assigned Names and Numbers (ICANN); justice; language diplomacy; law firms; League of Nations system; loans; modernization theory; neoliberalism; oceans; Otlet, Paul; pacifism; patents; refugees; regional communities; relief; technical standardization; telephone and telegraphy; trade agreements; trademarks; transnational; underdevelopment; United Nations system; Universal Postal Union (UPU); war; war crimes; World Bank; world orders

Code civil

The words *Code civil* are commonly used for all codifications of private law in modern times. The Bavarian *Codex civilis* (1756) is perhaps the first specialized collection with this title, but the French Napoleonic Code (1804) remains the best known code, because of its wide circulation.

In France and outside France, the *Code civil* was, during the 19th century, a revolutionary symbol and a useful tool for conservative states. It combines the confirmation of civil equality, secularized marriage, and a right of property liberated from feudal duties with an authoritarian frame for the family (limits to divorce, strong paternal power, inferior rights for illegitimate children) and a liberty to contract under state control. Outside France, the Code civil was, first, imposed in the European annexed or client territories of the French Empire. After 1815, though rejected by the nationalist movements in Germany, the French text was voluntarily upheld in Rhineland, Geneva, the principality of Lucca and the part of Poland under Russian rule. This adoption is generally interpreted as a liberal choice made by the local upper class or by a nation subjected to a foreign monarch, as in Poland. The choice of the Belgians to keep the Code civil after independence (1830) was also a reaction against the Dutch. Moreover, the Code civil has been imitated in Europe (Swiss cantons since 1819, Romania and Italy in 1865, Portugal in 1867, Spain in 1889), in North America (Louisiana from the 1808 Digest to the Livingstone Code in 1825, Quebec with the Code civil du Bas-Canada in 1866) and in most Latin American states (one of the first examples is the Code of the Mexican State of Oaxaca in 1828). In these cases, the model is transported into other social contexts as a kind of talisman, a ready made tool for the modernization of the law of property and obligations, without the political message about civil marriage (unknown in South America until the laws of Juarez in Mexico, 1857–59), or even equality (in Louisiana and in Peru, slavery was maintained for several years after the introduction of a civil code). This exportation of French legal culture was rather successful in Belgium and in the Rhineland, Catholic countries where divorce became possible. It failed in the face of ancestral customs, as epitomized by the vigour of local succession laws in Romania or Latin America.

At the turning point between the 19th and 20th centuries, the Code civil lost its cross-national appeal because of the competition with new codifications. Such were the German Civil Code of 1896, whose introduction in 1900 ended the use of the Napoleonic Code in the Rhineland, and the 1907 Swiss Code that replaced the Code civil in Geneva. The failure at that time of the Civil Code draft which French law professor Gustave Émile Boissonade wrote for Japan is often interpreted as a sign of the decline of the French model. But the Japanese Code (1898) was nevertheless a combination of German and French rules, for example about liability matters. And with colonization, the Code civil was introduced in Africa and in Indo-China for colonists and a few indigenous people who renounced their domestic law. After independence, French rules about property and obligations were often maintained with some amendments, family law being in most cases regulated by separate Codes. The Egyptian Code (1948) is, in Islamic countries, a model for the mixture of French inspiration and Koran-based directions. In more recent times, French law expertise has been important in the writing of the Civil Code of Vietnam (1995–96). Some professors in China are interested in the French model while they prepare drafts for a Civil Code. The new Civil Codes of the Netherlands (1992) and Quebec (1994) are now competing with the French Code, and Romania has preferred to use legal experts from Quebec for its new Code. All in all though, the Code civil has been amalgamated in various ways with the legal traditions of more than half of the countries of the world.

Jean-Louis Halpérin

Bibliography

Halpérin J.-L. 2006. The French Civil Code. London: Cavendish.

Maillet J. 1970. 'The historical significance of French codifications', Tulane Law Review, 44, 4, 681–92.

Wieacker F. 1995. A history of private law in Europe with particular reference to Germany. Oxford: Clarendon.

Related essays

agriculture; civilization; empire; legal order; marriage; Westernization

Liberalism

Liberalism, as both a political philosophy and a political tradition, accords primacy to liberty as a political value: mankind is naturally free and autonomous. Consequently, liberals contend that any restrictions of an individual's liberty must be justified. In particular, government is justified only to the extent that it secures the liberty of citizens. A corollary is that governments should sustain a position of neutrality about the meaning and content of the good life: value is subjective and plural.

As a distinct political philosophy, liberalism took shape during the European Enlightenment, particularly in England with the 'classical liberalism' of John Locke (1632–1704), who was concerned about the scope of governmental interference permissible in the newly emerging nation states. Locke argued powerfully for limited government, and tied political liberty to economic liberty. From the 18th century to the present day, liberals have insisted that there is a close (even essential) connection between liberty and property: a free-market system based on private property has become seen as the embodiment of liberty. In the 18th and 19th centuries, when the Englishman John Stuart Mill (1806–73) penned his classic 'On Liberty', liberalism was one of the dominant topics that defined a trans-European intellectual culture and political philosophy. Building on Locke's ideas about a social contract that laid the basis for limited government, Rousseau (1712–78, France) and then Kant (1724–1804, Germany) transformed the nature of liberty itself. Rather than being content with the 'negative' conception of liberty found in Locke (being *free from* external restraints), Rousseau and Kant (and then Mill) were more interested in a 'positive' sense of liberty (being *free to* be self-directed or autonomous).

Early on in the transnational history of liberalism, it was the idea of negative liberty that seemed most contagious. One of the harbingers of the so-called 'Indian Renaissance', Raja Ram Mohun Roy (1777–1833), for example, argued that the traditional practice of *seti* (self-immolation) contradicted women's individual dignity. He also argued that censorship by the British authorities in India contradicted local rights of freedom of speech and press. In a manner that would become a familiar pattern in the assimilation of liberal ideas in the 'non-Western' world, Roy bolstered his arguments by appealing to their affinity with indigenous intellectual traditions, such Vedanta Hinduism, although his scholarship on the Vedantas was seen as unorthodox by some of his peers. Later, in the 20th century, following the thought of Jawaharlal Nehru (1889–1964), Indian liberalism took a turn away from individualism and towards communalism.

However, conceptions of positive liberty, particularly as expressed by the British neo-Hegelians of the late 19th and early 20th centuries, were of special interest to thinkers in non-European contexts. In Japan, for example, Thomas Green's (1836–82) emphasis on autonomy qua liberty was engaged by the Zen-influenced philosophers of the Kyoto School, which formed around the eminent philosopher Nishida Kitarô (1870–1945). Controversially, the Kyoto School challenged the central liberal notion of an atomic, self-sufficient individual as the essential political actor: they interpreted and interrogated the concept of autonomy in an expansive sense, giving it a quasi-religious meaning closer to self-actualization. Whilst remaining controversial because of its alleged associations with Imperial Japan's militant anti-Westernism (and anti-liberalism), the Kyoto School is certainly the most influential school of philosophy in modern Japan.

Ostensibly liberal traditions in other non-European countries have also sought to challenge atomistic conceptions of the individual. In the postwar years, liberal movements in parts of Africa and Asia (especially in India and Japan) have attempted to reorient the locus of liberalism's doctrine of freedom around more organically communal notions of the self, which were seen as more faithful to local, indigenous beliefs and traditions. The postwar Japanese constitution, for instance, contains articles that appear to limit individual rights and freedoms 'to the extent that they do not interfere with the public welfare' (Articles 12 and 13), and individualist parties in post-independence India have tended to lose out to more communally oriented parties. However, the most influential theoretical postwar statements of liberalism, such as those by the American philosopher John Rawls (1921–2002), make little or no mention of these and other transnational currents, leading to persistent charges that liberalism is actually a Western ideology. Conversely, the field of 'postcolonial liberalism', wherein Duncan Ivison invites mainstream liberal political theorists and practitioners in the West to provide space within the theoretical mainstream for the intervention of indigenously developed conceptual schemes and political structures that emphasize communal rather than individual freedoms, has been criticized for stretching the central tenets of liberalism beyond breaking point. In addition, the emphasis on individualistic moral egalitarianism (especially at the international level) has been linked with accusations of moral relativism and a renewed attention to cosmopolitanism and so-called 'cosmopolitics'.

Leaving aside the transnational contagion (and controversial elasticity) of liberalism as a philosophy, it is its emphasis on free trade that has made it impossible to confine liberalism within national boundaries. Paradoxically, the rapid, colonial expansion of Europe around the globe was fuelled by the drive to establish free-trade zones: liberalism appears inherently pregnant with attempts to render national borders permeable, and it should be located at the heart of the phenomenon of globalization. The result, however, is that the historical experience of many nations outside Europe and North America defines liberalism as part of the colonial legacy of 'Western modernity'. Indeed, for many critics, the experience of an imperial or 'illiberal liberalism' in the postcolonial world is deeply contradictory. Hence, although a number of Asian nations might be considered to have joined a regime of liberal states since 1945 (India, Japan, South Korea, Taiwan), the troubling colonial legacy has not been forgotten and debates about the ongoing salience of 'Asian values' as alternatives to (or sometimes as varieties of) liberalism continue.

In large parts of Africa, the significance of liberalism has less to do with abstract legal or political rights and more to do with economic inequalities, both in domestic as well as in international terms. A number of influential voices from the continent have argued that the transnational liberal regime should shift its emphasis from laissez-faire and tolerance of inequality towards an acceptance of economic intervention in the interests of the structurally underprivileged. However, in some places, liberalism's focus on domestic political rights has been vital, and liberal political movements that emphasize the inalienable dignity of the individual have provided voices of resistance against prejudice and tyranny. The South African Liberal Party, for example, fought against apartheid for 15 years, until it was outlawed in 1968, at which point a number of its members became extrapolitical activists.

Throughout the Cold War, the coherence of a US-centred, liberal regime (the 'capitalist bloc') became the subject of significant strategic interest and importance. Arguably starting with Woodrow Wilson's liberal agenda for the League of Nations in 1918, liberal ideals became enshrined in a number of Cold War international institutions (such as Bretton Woods and GATT), NGOs and intergovernmental organisations such as the UN. Intellectuals in the US, sparked by a controversial article by Michael Doyle in 1983, started to argue that such transnational liberalism could actually prevent war. Citing Kant's idea of 'perpetual peace', Doyle argued that it was an iron law that liberal democracies would not go to war against each other. With a few contested exceptions, Doyle has been proven correct. In recent years this argument has been extended to claim that a transnational liberal regime serves to stabilize the international system and hence to perpetuate the dominance of the US as the world's solitary superpower: according to this argument transnational liberalism mitigates against the natural 'realistic' tendency of the international system towards a balanced distribution of power.

At the end of the Cold War, the liberal regime took on a new character when Francis Fukuyama famously declared that the world had reached the 'end of history', arguing that liberalism had become the only viable political ideology after the defeat of Communism. Fukuyama has been widely criticized, particularly by participants in the 'Asian values' debate, and the terrorist strike of September 11, 2001 has been interpreted by some commentators as demonstrating that Fukuyama's conclusions are at best premature. In fact, the relationship between Islam and liberalism remains hotly contested, in both philosophical and institutional terms, just as does the relationship between liberalism and many of the world's other major religions, such as Confucianism and Buddhism. Whilst it appears to provide a defence for those oppressed by social, racial or gender discrimination, liberalism appears less able to protect the economically disadvantaged. As liberalism has travelled around the globe and entered into dynamic relationships with many other systems of thought, one of its greatest challenges continues to be how and whether it can respect and accommodate them, rather than clash against them or simply tolerate them.

Christopher Goto-Jones

Bibliography

Cheah P. 2003. *Spectral nationality: passages of freedom from Kant to postcolonial literatures of liberation*. New York: Columbia University Press.

Doyle M. 1983. 'Kant, liberal legacies, and foreign affairs', parts 1 and 2, *Philosophy and Public Affairs*, 12, 3 and 4, 205–35, 323–53.

Ivison D. 2002. *Postcolonial liberalism*. Cambridge: Cambridge University Press.

Mehta U. 1999. *Liberalism and empire: a study in nineteenth-century British liberal thought*. Chicago: Chicago University Press.

Related essays

anarchism; Asia; capitalism; civilizations; Cold War; cosmopolitanism and universalism; empires and imperialism; fascism and anti-fascism; General Agreement on Tariffs and Trade (GATT) / World Trade Organization (WTO); human rights; Japan; knowledge; Maoism; modernity; modernization theory; nation and state; Romanticism; socialism; trade agreements; Westernization; Zen aesthetics

Liberation theology

Liberation theology emerged in Latin America in the 1960s partly as a response to situations of poverty and oppression but also to complex ideological factors which included Catholic Action (an organization of lay Catholics seeking to influence wider society) and its slogan 'See, Judge, Act', the Second Vatican Council, a rapprochement between Christianity and Marxism, and the 'pedagogy of the oppressed' of Paolo Freire (an influential Brazilian theorist of education). The language of 'liberation' drew on the anti-colonial struggles of the previous decade, which in turn drew on an ancient (and in part biblical with the Exodus episode) discourse of struggle for freedom. The second conference of Latin American bishops at Medellín (Colombia) in 1968 was an important moment where these patterns coalesced in a structured movement at the continental scale.

The classic statement of this phase of liberation theology was Gustavo Gutiérrez's *A theology of liberation* (1972), quickly translated into every European language. Gutiérrez argued that theology was a second step, reflection on action. Marx's eleventh thesis on Feuerbach was certainly in the background. He was concerned to oppose the privatization of religion and to insist that both sin and faith were social realities. The struggle for a just society was seen as part of salvation history.

Liberation theology grew, therefore, in a context of opposition, and some of its most brilliant exponents were murdered, especially in El Salvador. It moved away from a narrow focus on the Exodus, developed its own systematic theology, and defined itself polemically against European political theology. The focus on class struggle gave way, in the 1990s, to an increasing awareness of the need to take the role of culture seriously. Meanwhile, this theology boomeranged back to Europe, and had a role in the British churches' *Faith in the city* report (1984), a response to the impact of neoliberal economics.

At the same time, and coming from rather different contexts, black theology and feminist theology emerged in the United States. Both were concerned with the issue of rights, and they challenged racial and gender hegemonies. Latin American theology was rather slow to pick up on these movements. Feminist theology, which is part of the much broader women's movement, has affected every church and brought concrete results in many, most notably in the shape of women's ordination. Everywhere, but perhaps especially in Asia and Africa, it has challenged patriarchal stereotypes. Its power to shape and change culture is therefore greater than most other forms of liberation theology.

Black theology, growing out of the civil rights movement, but much more polemical than Martin Luther King, has been an important source for anglophone African theology. In South Africa it contributed to the anti-apartheid struggle where the Kairos document (1985) was a milestone in theological opposition. Francophone African theology, whose best-known spokesman is Jean-Marc Éla, is theoretically more sophisticated and engages with Frantz Fanon and the whole critique of colonialism.

In Asia the issue of culture was foregrounded from the start. In Korea, Minjung theology made its appearance in the 1970s, appealing not only to biblical sources but to the traditional Korean category of *han*, the sense of oppression together with the determination to resist it. Liberation theology therefore mutated into traditional Korean categories. Black theology has been an important source for Indian Dalit theology, which challenges caste oppression. In Sri Lanka the Jesuit Aloysius Pieris has developed a highly creative Asian liberation theology, which begins with Asian religiousness. Asian poverty has both a peasant and a monastic form and must be understood as liberative in the context of capitalist culture. Asian theology is a 'christic apocalypse' of the non-Christian struggle for liberation and involves a baptism in the Jordan of Asian religiousness. What Christianity brings to Asian religions is consciousness of the incompatibility of God and Mammon and an awareness of the unbreakable covenant between God and the poor. These themes had been prominent in the writings of Latin American theology, most notably with Hinkelammert's indictment of transnational corporations.

The fall of the Socialist bloc in the 1980s has conducted Latin American theology to a revision of some of its socialist principles, while its support of dependency theory has also faltered. New global issues were also slow to emerge: because liberation theology began with class struggle it was slow to take account of the environment, an area where more formal university-based theology proceeded it. By 1990, however, it had addressed this, perhaps unsurprisingly, in Brazil where Leonardo Boff applied liberation theology to the ecological crisis. Last but not least, the Vatican also tried to curb the movement with the appointment of conservative bishops in Latin American countries.

Despite this the beating core of liberation theology has kept its momentum: some of its proponents embraced the cause of indigenous movements as in the Mexican regions of Chiapas or Oaxaca, which involved them in a new cross-border network of alliances and connections. Liberation theology has now embraced transgender issues, where the most creative exponent is the Argentine theologian Marcella Althaus-Reid. When the time came to defend Jon Sobrino, a Salvadorian theologian attacked by the Vatican, the International Theological Commission of the Association of Third World Theologians put together a book to argue about the continuous need to 'get the poor down from the cross' (2007). Though it claimed to gather voices from the whole of the Third World, the overwhelming majority of the contributors came from Latin and South America.

Timothy Gorringe

Bibliography
Rowland C. (ed.) 1999. *The Cambridge companion to liberation theology*. Cambridge: Cambridge University Press.

Related essays
African liberation; Christianity; development and growth; missionaries; modernization theory; Second Vatican Ecumenical Council; *The Wretched of the Earth*; women's movements

Libraries

Ptolemy of Alexandria once assumed it was possible to collect all written forms of human knowledge together in a single library, thereby symbolically perpetuating Alexander the Great's vision of universality. The explosion of information in the 19th century facilitated by post-Enlightenment educational and scientific imperatives and disseminated through global networks of printing and publishing rendered the library a far more complex institution. The elite libraries of church, state, university and aristocrat became specialist libraries serving the interests of emerging nationhood, the restructuring of knowledge, the intellectual property rights of the academy, the philanthropic ideals of governments and individuals, and the didactic and/or recreational values and needs of a widening reading public. As the bastion of literacy, power, and culture, the library represented, at least in the humanist ideology of the West, the civilizing potential of man, preserving and making accessible his intellectual offspring across space and through time.

Library history has hitherto focused primarily on individual institutional histories and/or biographies of the great institutional heroes. Little work has been done on the fluid boundaries between institutions epitomized by the inherent portability of print objects and their complex chains of ownership, the transnational and transcultural migration of collections and their formative influence on readers, writers, and knowledge systems, the impact of collection diaspora, or the way in which publishers, booksellers, and library suppliers have shaped the structure of library collections, and thus the activities of library users, over time.

The mid to late 19th century was a watershed in the development of libraries. Private collectors and private subscription libraries competed with new circulating libraries in the form of rate-based public libraries, mechanics' institutes, workingmen's clubs, and other socially oriented or public-service-related organizations. A proliferation of self-help manuals promoting individual, social, political, economic and cultural advancement underpinned and popularized the democratization of knowledge. Travel writing and popular fiction brought the world into the reading room and into the home, as did magazines, newspapers, and periodicals. At the same time, bibliographic control of a nation's printed output, legislated through legal-deposit provisions and regulated through copyright, meant many national libraries and national bibliographies were increasingly synonymous with the creation of national identity, achieved through the institutional organization and canonization of its national literature. As such, libraries as centres of political power were instrumental in creating and perpetuating hegemonic ideology, reinscribing and reflecting a nation's image back to itself. The domestic and international circulation of library materials as well as the creation of exchange programmes and loan agreements for exhibition and use further reinforced imperialist ideologies and the project of cultural expansionism. Moreover, because many libraries were more concerned with the bibliographic control of their monograph collections, rather than popular print media such as educational texts, newspapers, pamphlets, posters and other ephemera, they were complicit in privileging the book as the primary vehicle of knowledge transmission and cultural formation. Libraries became the gatekeepers of information and collective memory, regulating their readers in the form of collection acquisition policies, rules and regulations, and the shaping and monitoring of the spaces of reading.

One national institution which originally resisted this trend was the Library of Congress. Originally founded in 1800 as a legislative library to serve the needs of congressmen, it carried forward Thomas Jefferson's vision of a free access, universal library, sustained Jefferson's own encyclopedic collecting habits through international exchanges, and later justified its international collection development policies by promoting the information needs of new immigrants and by encouraging the civic duty of all responsible Americans – now citizens of the world. Philanthropists such as Andrew Carnegie (1835–1919) considered the library to be a tool for social equity. Funding 2,509 spaces of reading as well as the training of professional librarians, he left a distinctive worldwide legacy. By 1956, the Carnegie Corporation financially underwrote the American Library Association's landmark Public Library Standards project. The British Council, the United Nations Educational and Scientific and Cultural Organization (UNESCO), and the International Federation of Library Associations (IFLA) have carried on and extended Carnegie's ideological work, bringing the printed word to the world in the form of international projects devoted to establishing and maintaining libraries and their related infrastructure, particularly for countries in transition in Asia and Africa. But books and libraries have never been their sole brief. By 1978, for example, The British Council owned and maintained 125 libraries, administered book-aid and literacy programmes, provided global information and bibliographical services, encouraged professional exchanges, scholarships, and education, offered specialist courses in librarianship and information science, promoted book exports, and acted as the overseas arm of the British Library. In Ethiopia during the 1980s, the British Council entered the local political arena by facilitating education about famine relief and drought reconstruction, providing specialist medical training for Ethiopian doctors, technicians and students, and doubling their emphasis on English-language acquisition as a passport to democratic reform and future economic and political stability. The Council's 'printed word policy' was a self-avowed form of cultural and educational propagandism arising out of the 1930s interwar anxiety about the rise of fascism, the erosion of parliamentary democracy, and the destruction of civilization. It has variously been accused of neocolonialism, cultural imperialism, and cultural invasion, and currently runs an aggressive marketing campaign to promote the UK culture industries.

During the postwar period, UNESCO implemented its policy of peace through global understanding by means of the worldwide establishment of libraries and information networks in member states of the United Nations, in less developed countries and, through the International Committee for the Blue Shield, in countries needing assistance in war reconstruction. The assumption remains that freedom of knowledge informing freedom of speech are the twin pillars of democracy and democratic reform. UNESCO has also demonstrated significant international leadership by formulating and implementing various manifestos on subjects ranging from public and school libraries to preservation management of records and archives, from intellectual property issues to its flagship General Information Programme / Programme Générale d'Information (PGI) and its Memory of the World initiative. UNESCO supports the activities of IFLA as well as the International Council on Archives, and is a key partner in the International Council on Museums (ICROM) and the International Council on Monuments and Sites (ICOMOS). UNESCO's widening brief reflects the contemporary redefinition of libraries as organizations facilitating the two-way flow of information, whether it be embodied in books, electronic documents, monuments, cultural artifacts, or memory. Founded in Scotland in 1927, the International Federation of Library Associations now boasts over 1,800 member associations in over 150 countries. This global reach has resulted in a coordinated approach to library and information service provision, including guidelines for best practice and infrastructure development. Members meet and work through its six core activities programmes hosted by national libraries or other related institutions around the world, its 45 special interest sections, its annual conference, its quinterly journal, and its quarterly monograph publication.

In the wake of new institutional paradigms, today's libraries along with archives and museums are now part of a cultural triumvirate of memory institutions whose global reach continues to be achieved through digitization and computer-mediated information networks. A new dream of universalism is embodied in the concept of libraries without walls, that is, digital collections in which computer networks foster global access to knowledge. UNESCO's Memory of the World Programme and Register (www. unesco.org), Project Gutenberg (www.gutenberg.org), The Way Back Machine (www.archive.org), even Wikipedia (www.wikipedia.org) are only a few examples of major international, collaborative or social participation projects which aim to preserve and deliver global knowledge to a global audience. At the same time, the practice of cultural piracy and privateering has resulted in a flurry of legislation to protect tangible and intangible cultural heritage property from crossing national borders. Censorship, always an unquiet partner in the formation of libraries, has expanded to embrace the regulation

of cultural polity as in the US Patriot Act of 2001/2005. And, while both a physical and virtual Bibliotheca Alexandrina rises from the ashes of its ancient Egyptian namesake, the erasure of cultural memory in the form of libricide continues, whether it be the burning of the National Library of Sarajevo, or the looting of the National Library of Baghdad. The symbolic power of libraries is ever present; the goal of universal knowledge remains a utopic dream of Western culture.

Sydney J. Shep

Bibliography

Cole J. Y. 2005. 'The Library of Congress becomes a world library, 1815–2005', Libraries & Culture, 40, 3, 385–98.

Coleman S. J. Jr 2005. 'The British Council and UNESCO in Ethiopia: a comparison of linear and cyclical patterns of librarianship development', Library History, 21, 121–30.

Coombes D. 1988. Spreading the word: the library work of the British Council. London and New York: Mansell.

Jacob C. and Treves J. A. 1997. 'Bibliotheca Alexandrina: towards the encyclopedism of the 21st century', Diogenes, 45, 83–5.

Knuth R. 2003. Libricide: the regime-sponsored destruction of books and libraries in the twentieth century. Westport: Praeger.

Oram R. W. 2005. 'Ebb and flow: the migration of collections to American libraries: a report', Libraries & Culture, 40, 2, 145–8.

Related essays

bibliographic classification; book and periodical exchange; humanities; intellectual property rights; intergovernmental organizations; Internet; language diplomacy; literature; museums; nation and state; Otlet, Paul; philanthropic foundations; philanthropy; publishing; United Nations Educational, Scientific and Cultural Organization (UNESCO) educational programmes

Life and physical sciences

The biological, physical, and chemical sciences evolved as autonomous disciplines in institutional settings such as universities that often had a pronounced national context. However, the opening of university education to foreign nationals, especially in Western Europe in the last quarter of the 19th century, meant that even in universities, each discipline became an arena for transnational encounters between the teaching staff of a leading scientific country and students from scientifically less advanced countries, for example in the flocking of Russians and Americans to German, Swiss, French, or British universities. Along these lines, the growing importance of the various national Associations for the Advancement of Science (e.g. British, French, German, American) and major scientific anniversaries, such as Louis Pasteur's 70th jubilee in 1892, also provided opportunities for transnational encounters, as foreign scientists were routinely invited to attend, while many countries were also represented by delegations of scientific societies. However, rivalries between the scientifically advanced European nations often meant that scientific controversies followed national lines, such as those between French and German chemists and bacteriologists. Indeed, prior to World War 1, transnational patterns in science were usually limited to a quest for better educational and scientific opportunities (e.g. the careers of Sophia Kovalevskaia (1850–91) in Germany, France, and Sweden or Albert Einstein (1879–1955) in Switzerland, the Austro-Hungarian Empire, Germany, and the US).

After World War 1, the support of research became more explicitly national with the establishment of National Research Councils during World War 1 in the UK, Canada, the US, among other countries. Such national forces were further reinforced by interwar American isolationism, and conformity of major countries, to pursue influence in the international arena in non-overlapping areas (the British Commonwealth, the French colonies and dominions, or the Western hemisphere of the Americas). At the same time, under the influence of the newly founded League of Nations, which promoted peace and cooperation especially in areas connected to public health, new transnational ventures were established, especially after Locarno. Cross-national funding of research also started on a large scale with transatlantic funding by philanthropic foundations, most notably the Rockefeller Foundation (hereafter RF), which established a European office after World War 1 in Paris and scouted for investment opportunities in basic science all over the newly reconstituted Europe, but also in the UK and the US, initially aiming at 'making the peaks higher'.

The rise of ideologies with a transnational impact, such as communism and fascism, greatly added to this constellation of forces, in the 1930s. While the RF's transnational activities focused on the ultra-elite of the most promising as well as the already proven scientific minds, the central place of science in Marxism, and science-favourable policies on the part of the Communist Soviet Union caused many left-leaning scientists (among other intellectuals) from various countries to visit it often, collaborate, and even work there. The arrival of a large Soviet delegation headed by chief ideologue Nikolai Bukharin at the 2nd International Congress for the History of Science in London in 1931 was treated at the time, and later, as a major event. Throughout the 1930s, the Soviet Union focused on supporting Communist parties and fellow travellers in various countries, via organizational structures such as the Comintern, while sponsoring transnational solidarity in cultural and artistic circles around the concept of class, as overriding prevailing divisions of race and nation. Communist ideology had a great transnational impact on science at the level of cultural politics or the flow of ideas, as for example in J. D. Bernal's book *The social function of science* (1939) which became the best-known argument for the compatibility of science and communist ideas. By contrast, fascist ideology and policies had a transnational impact on the circulation of scientific human resources, since its racial discriminatory policies and totalitarian suppression of political dissent forced many scientists to emigrate, while scrambling to find positions in any country they could, from the next-door UK to the farther-away US and even the remote New Zealand and South America. The territorial conquests by fascist countries, culminating with the large-scale occupation of many nations by the Axis countries in World War 2, further displaced many scientists from Spain, Italy, France, Central and Eastern Europe.

This combination of transnational forces in the 1930s further intersected with new scientific opportunities that increasingly transcended the disciplinary boundaries between the life and physical sciences. For example, the quest for solving the 'secret of life' emerged as a paramount scientific challenge that required both transdisciplinary research programmes and transnational science policies. Thus, between 1934, when the problem of protein structure became soluble in principle, via X-ray diffraction, and 1962, when the Nobel Prize was awarded to the first two efforts to achieve a good approximation of that goal, the bulk of transdisciplinary and transnational efforts revolved around research programmes and science policies focused on the problem of protein structure.

After World War 2, especially from the late 1940s, transdisciplinary and transnational efforts had also begun to include Deoxyribonucleic acid (DNA) structure, in response to mounting evidence that DNA might well be the sole genetic material. By the late 1950s, these efforts began to include Ribonucleic acid (RNA), which emerged as a key functional intermediary between DNA and proteins. In 1963, the needs of the then new field of molecular biology, emerging at the interface of life and physical sciences, were recognized when leading scientists agreed to form interlocking structures in Europe: a European Molecular Biology Laboratory (EMBL), a European Molecular Biology Council (EMBC) and a European Molecular Biology Organization (EMBO) were modelled on the already existing Conseil Européen pour la Recherche Nucléaire (CERN), established in the early 1950s. Though it took over a decade to launch EMBL in 1974, EMBL, EMBO, and EMBC have since become central to this field, especially in Europe.

Transdisciplinary issues at the interface of life and physical sciences

A key reason for the success of transnational movements at the interface of life and physicochemical sciences was the fact that they intersected with transdisciplinary changes within science, or a parallel system for discrediting the power of prevailing disciplinary boundaries, hierarchies, and barriers to communication within the scientific order itself. The impetus for transdisciplinary interactions across the life and physicochemical sciences came largely from research on protein structure, research that proved the inherent limitations of institutionalized disciplines such as biology, physics, and chemistry for solving major scientific problems such as the 'secret of life' or how precise molecular structures, soluble via the application of a variety of physicochemical techniques (e.g. the ultracentrifuge, electrophoresis, chromatography, X-ray diffraction, electron microscopy) might

shed light on key biological functions such as respiration, or reproduction.

The formulation of the problem of protein structure as the major challenge of the day in the late 1930s depended upon the theoretical recognition, from the mid 1920s, that proteins were true macromolecules, not colloidal systems, or aggregates of small particles; upon experimental innovations in X-ray diffraction, that made that technique suitable for complex biological macromolecules after 1934; and upon a reorientation of the historical relationship between life and physical sciences, away from hierarchical reductionism and toward complementary parity. All these transdisciplinary trends converged with transnational trends in 1931, at two international congresses, the Centennial Meeting of the British Association for the Advancement of Science (BAAS) and the Second International Congress for the History of Science, both held in London.

The Centennial Meeting in 1931 was the best-attended BAAS meeting ever. Many addresses dwelled on the relationship between biological and physical sciences. Sir Frederick Gowland Hopkins, President of the Royal Society, a 1929 Nobel Laureate for the discovery of vitamins, and the Dunn Professor of Biochemistry at Cambridge University, extolled biology as the promising 'science of life' while denigrating physics as the 'science of death' (Abir-Am 1985, 400). These messages were diffused widely because of the international presence at the BAAS Centennial.

The impact of the BAAS rhetoric on 'biology and physics' was reinforced by, the Second International Congress for the History of Science (ICHS) in July 1931. It was a media sensation, due to the dramatic impact of the Soviet delegation's unexpected arrival, by air, as a last-moment decision by Stalin. The drastic message conveyed by the delegations had both a transdisciplinary and a transnational component. The Soviet speaker Boris Zavadovsky denounced reductionism (or the hierarchical ordering of scientific disciplines as reducible to the presumably more basic physical sciences) as a reflection of the contradictions of international capitalism, while further advocating the complementarity of biological and physical sciences in the liberated science of the future.

A young generation of ideologically sensitive British scientists including J. D. Bernal, J. B. S. Haldane, L. Hogben, and J. Needham, were much impressed. A year later, some of them set out to explore the ramifications of new relationships between physics and biology, so forcefully advocated at the 1931 international congresses, as part of a new transdisciplinary research agenda, eventually coming to focus on the problem of protein structure by the mid 1930s. The controversy over protein structure in the mid and late 1930s, revolving around the transdisciplinary agendas of avant-garde British scientists, soon acquired transnational dimensions.

The internationalization of the problematique of the changing relationship between life and physical sciences from 1931 was further reinforced by several international conferences held in Paris, Klampenborg (Denmark), London, and Cold Spring Harbor (USA). But the main force sustaining the transnational and transdisciplinary reconfiguration of the relationship between life and physical sciences was the Rockefeller Foundation, especially its Division of Natural Sciences. RF's role is illustrated below by looking at the experiences and practices of some among the scientists who emerged as key RF grantees, and shapers of the restructuring of the relationship between life and physical sciences.

The transnational agenda of the Rockefeller Foundation

Transnational scientific cooperation received a great boost from RF's policy of encouraging the circulation of both human resources – i.e. fellowships to young scientists to study in another country for six months to two years; and direct financial investments or research grants, initially given to well-established scientists in Europe and the US. After a reorganization in the late 1920s and early 1930s, RF's Division of Natural Sciences under Warren Weaver began to focus on encouraging an actual transfer of techniques from physical to biological sciences. This agenda revolved around the problem of protein structure, a problem which required a wide spectrum of physicochemical techniques while promising a precise solution for key biological mechanisms such as respiration and reproduction; as well as around RF's self-acquired role in coordinating a transnational network of research projects in the UK, the US, Sweden, Denmark, among other countries. The RF's actions in stimulating interaction in science can be captured through the intense experience of half a dozen key RF grantees who shaped science

policy and statesmanship, before and/or after World War 2.

Herman J. Muller (1890–1967) was an American-born member of the founder group of cytogenetics at Columbia University during the 1910s (the so-called 'Fruit fly group'). Muller anticipated the integration of biology with physics and chemistry as early as 1922, and advocated it strongly especially after his discovery of X-ray-induced mutations in 1927, a discovery for which he received the Nobel Prize in 1945. During the 1930s, Muller conducted research in Germany, the Soviet Union, and the UK, while supplying geneticists there with both rare mutants and radiation techniques for producing such mutants. The RF paid Muller's salary during his stays in both the UK and the US, and was instrumental in his Indiana University appointment in 1944. Muller alerted scientists to the danger posed to science by totalitarian regimes in Germany and the Soviet Union. In the 1950s, he emerged as a major critic of atomic testing, arguing that damage from such testing adversely affects the genetic legacy of humankind. Muller's scientific activities in the US, Russia, Germany, Denmark, and the UK, in sharing mutants and cytogenetic techniques, advocacy for physicochemical approaches to the problem of the gene, and safeguarding of the genetic legacy of humankind influenced many scientists at the interface of the life and physical sciences, including Niels Bohr, Max Delbruck, Salvador Luria, and James Watson, among others.

A Russian-born Canadian citizen who became naturalized in France, Louis Rapkine (1904–48) was a biochemist at the Institute of Physico-Chemical Biology in Paris, an interdisciplinary private institute supported by both the Rothschild and the Rockefeller Foundations in the interwar period. Rapkine's research was sponsored by the Rockefeller Foundation, as part of a group grant, starting in the mid 1920s and continuing until his premature death in 1948. After 1941, Rapkine coordinated scientific missions on behalf of Free France, in London and New York, where French scientists who escaped Vichy were settled and critical equipment for French science was acquired, especially after the end of World War 2. He maintained close contacts with RF officers, who often took his advice as a scientist who moved with great ease across France, England, the US, and Canada.

Andreas Querido (1913–) is a Dutch-born Professor of Endocrinology at Leiden University's Medical School. Querido has had a spectrum of unique transnational experiences: in the US, as a Rockefeller Fellow, he spent the academic year 1936–37 at The Johns Hopkins Medical School and 1949–50 at Harvard Medical School; in France, he spent the academic year 1938–39 at the Pasteur Institute in Paris. During World War 2 he served as a doctor at a 'model' concentration camp, Teresienstadt, in the Czech Republic, which needless to say, had many transnational dimensions with Nazi Germans running the camp with forced labour from many European countries, while trying to impress delegations of the International Red Cross. In 1962–63, Querido served as an advisor on health policy in Dutch New Guinea, and as a Rockefeller Fellow worked in India and Indonesia, among other developing countries.

Leó Szilárd (1904–64), a Hungarian-born physicist turned biologist, went to pursue research in Germany but left on the very day Hitler assumed power. After he took out patents in the UK on controlling chain reactions, he moved to the US where he persuaded Einstein to sign a letter to President Roosevelt alerting him to the necessity to build an atomic bomb prior to Hitler obtaining one. After World War 2, Szilárd moved to biology, as part of the Phage Group, spending a large part of his time as a roving science advisor in the US and Europe. He was among the earliest proponents of EMBL, modelled on CERN, and also became a founding member of the Salk Institute in La Jolla, California. His habit of systematically collecting data on research by others, and interacting with many scientists due to his roving scientific advisory missions, greatly influenced the post-World War 2 interface of life and physical sciences, in terms of ideas (e.g. negative feedback on genetic regulation) and new institutions and political activism (advocating against the use of the atomic bomb). Szilárd was a quintessential transnational scientist whose career stretched over numerous countries, ranging from Hungary, Germany and the UK to the US, Switzerland, and France.

Max Delbrück (1906–81), born and trained in quantum physics in Germany, did post-doctoral studies and assumed a Rockefeller Fellowship in Bristol, UK and in Copenhagen, Denmark, where he became an ardent disciple of Niels Bohr and decided to follow the latter's suggestion of extending the complementarity principle from physics to biology. Following several years as a junior scientist at the Kaiser Wilhelm Institute in Berlin, Delbrück obtained a Rockefeller Fellowship to explore genetics at Caltech (1937–39). Upon the outbreak of World War 2, RF helped him obtain a position at Vanderbilt University. His 1943 collaboration with Luria led to his sharing the 1969 Nobel Prize. After joining Caltech in 1947, Delbruck transformed it into a transnational centre of phage research, especially in the immediate post-World War 2 period. Though he contributed to the creation of new institutes of genetics in post-World War 2 Germany, his main transnational contribution was to import the Copenhagen spirit from Denmark to the USA, as well as from physics to biology, while serving as the prime mover of the Phage Group.

Transnational aspects of post-World War 2 scientific discovery: the case of DNA structure

Post-World War 2 legacies such as a great increase in the science budget, the creation of new and/or the revival of old agencies for the sponsorship of basic research, such as the National Science Foundation (NSF) and National Institutes of Health (NIH) in the US; the Conseil National pour la Recherche Scientifique (CNRS) in France; the Medical Research Council (MRC) in the UK; the promotion of transdisciplinary flows of human resources and techniques along the managerial lines of the atomic bomb project; and large-scale commitments of aid to the economies of European allies, such as the Marshall Plan, all created a new scale of transnational exchanges. American scientists were able to attend numerous conferences overseas; visit European laboratories more frequently and for longer durations; host European scientists in their laboratories and invite them frequently to conferences in the US; and even lure them with job offers. The new agencies also enabled Europeans to purchase American-made laboratory equipment and scarce supplies such as nuclear isotopes, not available elsewhere, to the effect that transatlantic exchanges became a necessary part of the scientific activity. This post-World War 2 legacy is particularly well illustrated in the case of the discovery of DNA structure in 1953, in itself a turning point in the relationship of the life and physical sciences. The argument can be made that the ultimate success went to those most able and willing to engage in transnational activities, such as visiting the largest number and variety of science centres, and collecting the widest ensemble of pertinent data.

Indeed, when the discourse on life and physical science, totally focused on protein structure until the mid-1940s, came to include DNA in the late 1940s, transnational forces came to impact upon the work on both protein and DNA structure – the key research problems at the interface of the life and physical sciences. Perhaps the best-known aspect pertains to the US State Department's refusal of a passport to Linus Pauling (1901–94), then a leading structural chemist from Caltech, due to unfounded suspicions that he was a Communist, during the McCarthy era. Pauling, who had the habit of making undiplomatic public statements, was invited to give the keynote address at a Royal Society Conference on Protein Structure in London in May 1952. A year earlier, Pauling and his collaborators had published a series of papers announcing the discovery of two configurations (the alpha- and gamma-helix) of fibrous proteins, thus making a big step in solving the long-puzzling problem of protein structure. In addition to being the first discovery of important motifs of protein structure Pauling's discovery further refuted a previous effort by a British team in 1950.

Transdisciplinary considerations loomed large in this case, since it revealed that the British team, led by veteran physicist, W. L. Bragg, had focused on X-ray crystallography – a physical technique he had coinvented in the 1910s, but ignored quantum chemistry. But the transnational dimension should not be missed. In 1951–52, as the British remained obsessed with their ability, or increasingly the lack of it, to keep up with the two superpowers, a triumph by an American in a scientific territory long considered a British possession thus served as a reminder of British vulnerability. W. L. Bragg's determination not to be anticipated by Pauling again played a crucial role in the events leading to the discovery of DNA structure early in 1953.

Ironically, Pauling's inability to arrive in London in May 1952 to lecture on his discovery had greater ramifications for the work on DNA structure. Pauling was able to circumvent the ban on his passport by hosting a large meeting on protein structure at his home institution, Caltech, in September 1953, funded by the Rockefeller Foundation, who had known many of the invitees for two decades or so. Those who could not get a US visa, most notably Bernal and Hodgkin, who were leading protein structure scientists and supporters of Communist countries, went instead to Moscow where Bernal received the Lenin Prize. Hodgkin lectured in China and India numerous times, thus further illustrating the transnational dimensions of research at the interface of life and physicochemical sciences.

Many scientists expressed the opinion that had Pauling been allowed to travel in May 1952, he would have seen the famous X-ray photo of form B of DNA, obtained just at that time by Rosalind Franklin in the Biophysics Unit at King's College, London. Pauling's inability to see the DNA photos in London, due to transnational tensions in mid 1952, was a key element in his failure to propose a correct structure for DNA, though many other factors also played a role. By contrast, a remarkable British–American cooperation was evident in the research on the bonds between DNA bases, pursued by Alexander Todd in the Department of Chemistry at Cambridge University in UK and Waldo Cohn at Oak Ridge National Laboratory in the US, who supplied Todd with a variety of isotopes, then available only in national laboratories operated by the US Atomic Energy Commission, that were needed to prove the bonds.

Transnational constraints also shaped the role of other key players in the DNA saga. Franklin's DNA photos were taken in London from fibres produced by R. Signer at the University of Berne, Switzerland and by E. Chargaff at Columbia University in the US. Chargaff, a quintessential European, had a unique profile: in the interwar era he quit a sequence of countries including Austria, Germany, and France, due to the rise of fascism, but maintained an extensive transnational correspondence with colleagues in many countries. At Columbia University since 1935, Chargaff continued to dream of European science and culture. He spent a sabbatical in 1949 in Stockholm, Sweden, while also exploring various opportunities in Europe, especially in Switzerland and Scandinavia. In 1952, in connection with the Congress of Biochemistry in Paris, Chargaff lectured in the UK, France, and Switzerland on his discovery of base-ratios in DNA. Hence, it is ironic that Chargaff proved unable to engage in collaborative work with either European or American scientist interlocutors. Conceivably, the distance between Europe and America in the immediate post-World War 2 era became too wide to bridge via fleeting lecture trips to Europe, or pre-World War 2 sentimental memories that had since been displaced for the Europeans by World War 2 horrors. Chargaff's transnational mind remained out of phase with world history: he dreamed of a Europe that no longer existed, remaining reluctant to admit that America, which he twice tried to leave, was the best place for science after World War 2. No wonder his pioneering DNA work got lost in the context of such an existential, transnational dilemma of one's identity, both national and scientific.

By contrast, members of the young generation of the Phage Group in the US, such as Gunther Stent and James Watson, sent to Europe on postdoctoral fellowships in 1950, made better use of their transnational adventures. Following a year at the University of Copenhagen's Department of Biochemistry, Stent secured a job at the University of California at Berkeley, as well as another postdoctoral year at the Pasteur Institute in Paris where he became a lifelong friend and collaborator of Eugene Wolman, a leading microbial geneticist. Another major accomplishment stemming from his postdoctoral fellowship in Copenhagen was his marriage to a Scandinavian. Watson, in his turn, accompanied their Danish host, biochemist Herman Kalckar, to a scientific conference in Naples' famed Stazione Zoologica, Italy where he was inspired by DNA photos shown by Maurice Wilkins of King's College, London, who substituted for his Director John Randall, then on one of many transnational trips that heads of large laboratories conducted at the time. After transferring his American postdoctoral fellowship from Denmark to the UK so as to do structural rather than biochemical studies of DNA, Watson compensated for belonging to a laboratory that did not work on DNA by foraging after clues to DNA in a remarkable transnational fashion, travelling frequently to Switzerland, France, Italy, and various parts of the UK, in addition to conducting correspondence and meetings with his American colleagues. Of particular use was the combination of informal communication via correspondence with the American Alfred Hershey, then at Cold Spring

Harbor Laboratory in New York; his oral communication with two young American scientists in England, Peter Pauling and Jerry Donohue; and finally, his prolonged oral exchanges with the British Maurice Wilkins and Francis Crick.

To the extent that other DNA workers were less able to pursue so many transnational contacts, then, the collection of scientific intelligence determined to a large extent who could and would make the discovery of DNA structure. Pauling (and Luria) were among those on whom travel restrictions were placed by the Cold War context; Chargaff's sentiments toward Europe were too complex to focus solely on DNA; Randall travelled widely to the US and Europe but had little time for actual research; while Franklin, who sought advice in France and the UK, yet did not interact with most Americans, who did crucial work on DNA, such as Chargaff, Hershey, or Pauling, though she did communicate with Pauling's collaborator, Robert Corey. In a similar manner, the solution of the mRNA function in 1961, by two teams, each composed of nationals of three to five countries, also testifies to the centrality of transnational exchanges and experimental practices at the interface of the life and physical sciences not only before World War 2 but also during the Cold War, or shortly after the launching of *Sputnik*.

Following the end of the Cold War, a new era of transnational encounters known nowadays as globalization continues to affect the interface of the life and physical sciences, most notably via transnational ventures in the biotech industry, the applied phase of molecular biology that focused on new medical and agricultural products. Biotech began to take off in the late 1970s, spiking in the early 1980s and again in the early 1990s, crashing in the early 2000s, and taking off again these days, in a wide variety of countries, including not only the US, the UK, France, Switzerland, Germany, Sweden, but also Japan, India, and Israel. At the time of writing (May 2007), a mega-conference on biotech known as BIO-IT is being held in Boston, with 20,000 participants from numerous countries. The Governor of Massachusetts has just announced a US$1 billion initiative to lure transnational business to Boston (*Boston Globe*, 6–8 May 2007). Thus, the 21st century is well poised to surpass the 20th century in its quest for transnational ad/ventures on an ever-larger scale.

Pnina Geraldine Abir-Am

Bibliography

Abir-Am P. G. 1985. 'Recasting the disciplinary order in science: a deconstruction of rhetoric on "biology and physics" at two International Congresses in 1931', *Humanity and Society*, 9, 388–427.

Abir-Am P. G. 'The strategy of large versus small scale investments: the Rockefeller Foundation's international network of protein research, 1930–1960', in Gemelli G. (ed.) 2001. *American Foundations and large scale research*. Bologna: Clueb, 71–90.

Crawford E., Shinn T. and Sorlin S. (eds) 1993. *Denationalizing science: the international context of scientific practice*. Dordrecht: Kluwer.

Fleming D. and Bailyn B. (eds) 1969. *The intellectual migration, Europe and America, 1930–1960*. Cambridge, MA: Harvard University Press.

Gemelli G. (ed.) 2000. *The 'Unacceptables': American Foundations and refugee scholars between the two world wars*. Brussels: Presses Interuniversitaires Européennes.

Krige J. 2000. 'NATO and the strengthening of Western science in the post-Sputnik era', *Minerva*, 38, 1, 81–108.

Schroeder-Gudehus B. 1978. *Les scientifiques et la paix: la communauté scientifique internationale au cours des années 20*. Montréal: Presses de l'Université de Montréal.

Strasser B. J. and de Chadarevian S. (eds) 2002. 'Molecular biology in post-war Europe', *Studies in History and Philosophy of Biological and Biomedical Sciences*, special issue, 33c.

Related essays

Acquired Immunodeficiency Syndrome (AIDS); antisemitism; book and periodical exchange; brain drain; Cold War; diet and nutrition; disarmament; ecology; environmentalism; epidemics; exile; fascism and anti-fascism; higher education; humanities; intellectual elites; mathematics; Nazism; philanthropic foundations; Pugwash Conferences; social sciences; socialism; vaccination; world orders

Literary capitals

Over the last two centuries the world's literary system has been dominated by a few tens of thousands of authors and a few hundred publishers, concentrated in less than a dozen major cities which constitute the poles and foci of literary output that dictate the acceptability of genres, books and authors. In fact literature, including 'world' literature, depends on a way of thinking and being that is specifically urban. Major metropolitan centres house the greatest numbers of publishers, newspapers and reviews, professional organizations and public institutions with an interest in literature. They are the inescapable focus for all authors and would-be authors who write, or aspire to write, in the metropolitan language. Any transnational history of literature has to take account of this inescapable dimension of literary life.

The concentration just described depends basically on the size and wealth of the metropolis. Paris, London, New York each dominated the literary world for a time because they were great cities with a leisured social class that constituted a readymade, competitive market for the book trade. If publishers and booksellers enjoyed a competitive advantage from being in a metropolis – a dynamic local market, a centralized travel network and access to technical expertise – the same was true of authors. An author living in London or New York had publishers and other authors on his or her doorstep and could attend the right salons, rubbing shoulders with critics who could make or break a literary reputation. Moreover, living in the metropolis gave access to the irreplaceable cultural material represented by the metropolis itself. Paris, as a centre of power and therefore a hotbed of (hi)story, has served as the setting for works of fiction since the 17th century: an inexhaustible vein of drama, narrative and poetry is mined by such writers as Eugène Sue, Honoré de Balzac, Gustave Flaubert and Émile Zola. Like Dickens's novels in the mid 19th century, or *Bridget Jones* in the late 20th, the worldwide success of these French novels derived from their location in the fictionalized metropolis.

If a literary metropolis, the capital of a literary language, can do so much for authors, it can do just as much for critics, academics and readers. A critic working for the celebrated *Revue des deux mondes* in (say) 1890 was sure of a large and prosperous Parisian readership, but also benefited from the amazing international circulation of a review which recommended itself to the elites of Europe and America thanks to the cultural status of the French language, and even more to Paris's reputation as a city where literature was really important. Such a critic could expect to be read from Argentina to Rome, from Madrid to Brussels or Washington, and this could give him or her considerable power to make or break authors, introduce them to the world or consign them to oblivion. Now, at the dawn of the 21st century, books with a potentially limited readership depend on the immense power exercised worldwide by, e.g., the *New York Review of Books*, or in London's sphere of influence by *The Times Literary Supplement*.

Literary capitals also house the publishers who publish the largest numbers of translations. In most cases a translation requires substantial investment; the translator has to be paid, and the time taken to produce the book has to include the time it takes to translate. Equally, the best translators are usually to be found in the metropolis, because it is there that they can earn a decent living. In the 19th century, translators working from German into French were not to be sought on the frontier between the two languages, in Strasbourg or Nancy, but in Paris, where one would find, for example, Hoffmann's translator Loève-Veimars, and later Henri Albert, the first to translate Nietzsche's complete works.

Once this trend towards the concentration of publishing and writing capital has established itself, it is likely to be self-perpetuating, since participants would converge wherever success seemed most likely. This explains why the hierarchy of world literary capitals has changed so little in two hundred years. It also leads to the literary capital imposing its will on the periphery through a kind of economic and symbolic violence against all aspiring authors. What Balzac's provincial hopeful, Lucien de Rubempré, suffered in the early 19th century in his attempts to succeed in the capital was much like the experiences of postcolonial Black African writers in English. If a social group does exist outside the capital, and throws up some aspiring authors, the literary salvation of such authors – unless they are content to drag out an obscure existence without readers and most likely without a publisher or even a 'worthwhile' subject – will depend on their ability to play according to the capital's rules, either by going there or by insinuating themselves into one of its networks. From Jean-Jacques Rousseau (Geneva) to Salman Rushdie (India); from Maurice Barrès (Lorraine) to John Coetzee (South Africa); from T. S. Eliot (Missouri) to Ngugi wa Thiong'o (Kenya); from Henri Michaux (Belgium) to Rubén Darío (Nicaragua), the

author from the provinces has always had the same sort of relationship with the capital, whether that capital be Paris or London, Rome or Madrid: there they are educated, there they write in the language of the metropolis (and of which the metropolis is the capital), there they find a publisher, and there they will receive what awards the capital is pleased to bestow. Such authors will be without status in their own countries (and elsewhere) until they have gained it in the capital. Authors already living in the capital, or with access to networks directly connected to it, such as the Parisian dramatists of the 1850s and the literary New Yorkers of the late 20th century, have a decisive advantage over their rivals.

Thus the polarization of literature by capitals has imposed on every literary language a fundamentally unequal literary set of relationships which governs its internal workings. But capitals also attract numerous authors from different language areas who are not necessarily anxious to sever their literary roots. The years that Rubén Darío spent in Paris (1890s) were crucial to his work; for Ernest Hemingway, one of the most brilliant of the 'lost generation', a sojourn in Paris proved to be a turning point in his international career. When the Futurists set out in the 1900s to revolutionize aesthetics, they knew that if they were ever to spread the revolution outside their home city of Milan they would have to conquer London and Paris, which they attempted to do through a series of happenings and manifestos. Such capitals may occasionally act as refuges from political persecution, but they are above all efficient, dynamic literary workshops, and a place where strangers to the prevailing literary language come to seek aesthetic or institutional solutions to their own problems. To come to a literary capital can be a kind of pilgrimage – with the returned pilgrim proudly bringing home a little of the 'capital' so abundant in the metropolis – or a way of keeping up with the literary Joneses by learning the aesthetics, the organization, and the very language where aesthetics and organization appear to best advantage; or a kind of geographical and literary triangulation, whereby a little input from a dominant, but distant world capital can be used to offset the oppressive, because proximate, dominance of the regional capital: if one is from Valparaiso, Paris may seem less oppressive than Madrid; if from St Louis, London may weigh less heavy than New York.

World literary capitals can, in fact, offer outsiders a range of strategies for profiting from their visits.

Thus a literary capital may establish authors' reputations, subjugate them, perhaps even alienate them. But they are also hotbeds of invention and strategy: dominant, overpowering, devouring, they are nonetheless subject to transformation through the initiative and inventiveness of the people they attempt to absorb, and this is an indispensable element in their cultural dynamic.

Blaise Wilfert-Portal

Bibliography

Casanova P. 2004. *The world republic of letters.* Cambridge, MA: Harvard University Press.

Charle C. and Roche D. 2002. *Capitales culturelles, capitales symboliques: Paris et les expériences européennes, XVIIIe–XXe siècles.* Paris: Publications de la Sorbonne.

Giordano V. (ed.) 2002. *Linguaggi della metropoli.* Naples: Liguori.

Sassen S. 1991. *The global city: New York, London, Tokyo.* Princeton: Princeton University Press.

Vandamme S. 2005. *Paris, capitale philosophique.* Paris: Odile Jacob.

Related essays

Argentina and psychoanalysis; art market; cities; cultural capitals; exile; fashion; global cities; literature; *modernismo*; publishing; religious pilgrimage; surrealism; translation

Literature

The Harry Potter books unite all the world's children in enthusiasm for a single mythology. Amitav Ghosh admits us to the world of India through the medium of English. Giant publishing houses extend their activities worldwide. French postcolonial authors and theorists conquer America. Gao Xingjian, writing in Mandarin from his Paris apartment, wins the Nobel Prize. Second-generation Turkish immigrants inject a powerful new vein into German literature. Quietly but unmistakably, as the 21st century opens, literature is going global, or to put it another way, postnational. After the age of balkanization, when the literatures of the nations withdrew into mutually hostile camps; after the age of imperialism, when the colonial adventure exported certain national literatures worldwide along with their languages,

genres and canons, comes the age of literary interbreeding, hybridization, and unfettered circulation.

The above is a rather complacent description of the current situation, and at least three criticisms of it can be made. First, it is not at all clear that nationalism and imperialism have vanished or been transcended in modern world literature. Secondly, worldwide bestsellers are no new phenomenon; nor are migrant or multicultural authors, or arguments over the positive or negative consequences of the international trade in cultural objects. Finally, the fact that, thanks to the book trade, works of literature, and the huge output of criticism and literary theory that accompanies them, circulate freely among nation states and/or national languages has not prevented the emergence of 'national' literatures; indeed, such literatures have been emerging alongside 'world' literature for a century and a half. If we look more closely at how the world literary system has functioned and developed since its birth in the 18th century, we should be able to see beyond these apparent contradictions and gain a fresh insight into present conditions.

Republic or empire? Literary capital from the centre to the periphery

In what follows, I use 'literature' to refer to what has been accepted as literature since the mid 18th century, first in Europe and subsequently in America: poetry, drama, fiction and, later, autobiography, that is (normally) published texts with a claim to aesthetic qualities as verbal art. In that sense, 'literature' is now what Franco Moretti calls 'a planetary system'. Literary works, books and reputations travel all over the globe: the Somali author Nuruddin Farah is read worldwide, and French creole literature is discussed as much in Los Angeles and Paris as in Martinique. Universities worldwide teach and research foreign literature. Much new writing in traditional genres is from places very far, and very different, from those that engendered them: Nigerians, South Koreans, Chileans or Algerians may write in the tradition of Dickens, Balzac or Thomas Mann. Publishers produce catalogues, develop complex capitalistic structures and global strategies, and open windows on the world, such as the Frankfurt Book Fair. The Nobel Prize for Literature, known and esteemed the world over, has been awarded to authors from an ever increasing diversity of nations, including in recent years Nigeria, Egypt, China, Turkey and South Africa. As these ties of literary interdependence extend further round the world, from writing to reading via interpretation and critical approbation, it becomes meaningful to suggest that any work, any author, any reading experience, should now be considered as 'world literature'. By this I do not mean a corpus, or a new canon, but a context.

In reality, however, this worldwide system is neither as cosmopolitan nor as interbred as one might suppose. Works that circulate in their original versions are more or less limited to the list of global languages compiled by Abram de Swaan, and the only works that can really transcend their own linguistic sphere and travel all over the world are those written in the 'supercentral' language, English. Outside universities and university libraries, the diffusion of books written in languages of the 'second circle' (i.e., those with over 100 million speakers, such as Russian, Chinese, Arabic, Spanish, French and German) drops like a stone. English/other-language bilingualism is very common; bilingualism involving two of these second-rank languages is much rarer. As for works in 'third circle' languages, they scarcely circulate at all.

Translations, which include most of the works that circulate and attract international interest, are subject to the same threefold compartmentalization. A vast, and ever increasing, number of translations are from English; a substantial minority from the five second-rank languages (French, German, Spanish, Italian and Russian), and a very small minority from other languages. Western-style literature is spreading across the world as economic prosperity enables 'peripheral' areas to develop a new internal market (witness the recent explosion in book production in Mandarin or Hindi), but this spread has not had much effect on global literary circulation, which is still monopolized by a small number of languages.

On the other hand, English-speaking countries show little interest in translations of foreign literature. In the 1990s fewer than 5 per cent of literary works published in the UK were translations; in the US the figure was 3 per cent. The percentages are higher in countries whose languages belong to the 'second circle': 14 per cent in France, 18 per cent in Germany and 20 per cent in Spain. At the centre of the literary world the situation is plain: the more translations from a language, the fewer translations into it. The high rates of translation into European languages, and in European countries, are due to their publishing structure: a publisher tapping a rich national market can afford to translate foreign works with expensive translation rights. Not all countries or languages share this advantage. Bi- or multilingual developing countries such as Algeria or India do not translate many works into local languages, because competition from the old imperial language is too strong. In Africa translation into local languages is almost non-existent. Moreover, if a publisher is not well resourced the effect on quality can be disastrous: translations tend to be hasty, virtually uncorrected and small in number, confined to a few bestsellers. If you can only afford to translate a few works, you will naturally go for canonical works that pose the lowest financial risk.

Thus the world's literary system is asymmetric, unequal and hierarchical. This is nothing new: Franco Moretti has shown that the same was true to a lesser degree in the early 19th century, based on comparative statistics for the circulation of novels, the key genre in the global spread of the Western European model. Even at that time, literary circulation depended heavily on the entrepreneurial spirit of publishers, and on bestsellers scorned by highbrow critics: most literary translations and exports were of, e.g., adventure stories by Fenimore Cooper or Captain Marryat, love stories by Paul de Kock, and mystery stories by Eugène Sue. The core of the international literary system was the abundant and efficient output of works in the core countries of France and England. This core was an efficient exporter, its output being translated into all the European languages, but it imported few works even from its own periphery – Germany, Scandinavia, Russia, North America, Italy – and virtually nothing from the margins – Spain, Eastern Europe, South America. These regions were peripheral for two reasons: their own literary output was seldom translated at the centre or in other parts of the periphery; and their publishing industries were weak, limiting both their capacity to export to the centre and their capacity to import from the centre, with the ensuing obligation to accept what was doled out to them from the centre. Hence, in the mid 19th century, and for that matter in the mid 20th, the world literary system consisted of a centre, which exported massively but was shamelessly protectionist; an inner periphery which exported on a small scale but imported on a huge one; and an outer periphery which was doubly isolated, incapable of exporting and limited in what it could import. This spatial asymmetry was, and remains, temporal as well: on the periphery, central works are not received until much later, so the periphery always lags behind modernity.

The difference between this system, which lasted until the First World War, and the system we have at the beginning of the 21st century is that the competition inherent in the earlier configuration, between the domains of English and of French literature, was won unequivocally by the English camp, but at the cost of a partial shift to the other side of the Atlantic, with London relegated to a secondary role. The number of players increased steadily, as literature – in the Western meaning of the word – spread more widely as a cultural activity. This worldwide dissemination can be mapped using the flagship genre of modern literature, the novel. American literature burst on the world with James Fenimore Cooper and Nathaniel Hawthorne; Russian literature was read and discussed in the West starting with Pushkin in the 1820s. The first Japanese writer to produce Western-style novels was Natsume Sōseki in the early 20th century – just when the Japanese university was inventing the idea of a Japanese national literature. In Qing China, at the end of the 19th century, Western novels were being translated – some of the translators' names, such as Lin Shu and Yan Fu, are still well known – and educated Chinese were beginning to write their own, seeing novel-writing as part of China's drive for modernization. Literary Bengal entered the world stage with the award of the Nobel Prize to Rabindranath Tagore in 1913. Last – after World War 2 and usually after independence – came the novelists of the new African nations, Wole Soyinka in Nigeria, Nuruddin Farah in Somalia, and also V. S. Naipaul, representing the last frontier of Western poetics in the West Indies.

The structural inequality of the world's literary system does not end there. To rise to the top of the tree, access to English is not enough, as the situation of Kenyan or Nigerian writers shows. The language statistics in the Index translationum, often used as a basis for discussion, and even the statistics on 'national literature' used to assess degrees of openness to foreign literature, are really abstractions concealing very concrete and radical power relationships. All of the languages and literatures concerned were and are polarized around culturally hyperactive literary capitals such as London, Paris, New York, Leipzig, Berlin, Munich, Milan, Madrid, Chicago, Los Angeles, etc., depending on period. Thus for over two centuries, the real masters of the world's literary systems have been the publishers, critics, academics, and authors whose family, social or physical situation is in one of these centres, and who are introduced at an early stage to its social rules, commercial and ideological expectations, and cultural fashions. And their mastery is consolidated by the fact that their symbolic dominance enables them to impose what is really just one form of expression, born of a series of lucky historical chances, as the very expression of whatever is modern, beautiful and universal.

Nation versus empire

Throughout the history of the world literary system, the centre, which puts its seal of approval on authors, makes reputations and guides careers, has chosen freely among candidates for admission by requiring them to conform as closely as possible to the arrangements and projects of the metropolitan elites who dominate the cultural system 'governed' by the capital concerned. From 1850 to 1880 Paris was the capital of bourgeois theatre and exported it worldwide. Anybody who wanted to practise this genre had to produce 'well-made plays', which meant Paris-style plays; anyone who did not, be he Ibsen or Strindberg, was shown the door, whatever his reputation in other circles. Similarly, anyone seeking recognition in Moscow, the political and cultural capital of the Soviet empire, in the age of socialist realism had to renounce any kind of aesthetic predilection that could be labelled 'bourgeois'. When the works of Antonio Fogazzaro and Gabriele d'Annunzio were translated into French in the 1890s, the guardians of Paris's temple of culture had them altered, cut and even rewritten, because one of those guardians, the critic and publisher Ferdinand Brunetière, had decreed that they were 'unreadable', too 'Italian' and 'too harsh for a French ear'. To be published in Paris, in reviews or by publishers who could give their authors access to the entire French-speaking world, one had to accept a set of unwritten and arbitrary rules imposed by censors whose power derived from their positions in the institutions of the literary 'centre'. More recently, Nuruddin Farah and Kateb Yacine chose to write in the colonial language and were accordingly accepted by the corresponding literary capital, but also suffered acutely from the schizophrenia thus imposed on them by history and geopolitics which involved them in a never ending succession of 'contradictory mismatches'. For the last two centuries, anyone who succeeds in gaining access to the literary world through the centre has had to bow to its unwritten laws; in other words, any candidates for assimilation have to do what the centre wants and accept its forms and standards.

But even these expected forms and standards will not necessarily produce an author who, despite his foreign-sounding name, is accepted by the centre. As Jean Cassou remarked in 1924, in the *Nouvelle Revue Française*, 'we ask foreigners to surprise us, but only in the way we tell them to, as if their role was to serve not their own race, but our pleasure'. Peripheral authors wishing to succeed in the centre, which by definition does not 'need' them, have to find the correct distance which will make them assimilable but also leave them enough distinctiveness to attract a publisher. Without this permissible degree of distinctiveness there would be no point in accepting an author from some far-flung location who would not stand out in an already crowded market. Vikram Seth, an Indian who holds degrees from Oxford and Stanford, returned to India to write novels such as the bestseller *A suitable boy* (1993), transposing to an Indian setting the very familiar and very European techniques of the 19th-century dynastic novel. This was hailed as a triumph by London critics, a sort of literary revanche for the loss of empire: an Indian writing in the tradition of Jane Austen and Dickens! By combining the exotic appeal of geographical remoteness with the most threadbare conventions of the European novel, he turned an outworn art form into a sales pitch midway between inarticulate nostalgia and reassuring familiarity.

Those who do not seek such remoteness, or cannot achieve it, risk becoming invisible. If there is one thing worse than being exploited by the centre, it is not being exploited by the centre, because then one is literarily dead. Charles Ferdinand Ramuz, from the Vaud district of Switzerland, remained invisible to Parisians up to 1914 because he was trying to write what he thought French publishers and reviews expected from a Parisian author. As he explained in *Questions* (1935), he was too off-beat – Swiss, Protestant, provincial – to easily find a place in the metropolis, and so he had to break away to reconstitute himself as 'different'. He became what he had not been previously, an 'authentically' Vaudois author. A similar experience awaited Ngugi wa Thiong'o of Kenya, and the poets and dramatists of the late-19th-century Irish Renaissance – Yeats, Synge, Padraic Colum, George Moore – not to mention Elias Lönnrot, who set himself up as a Finnish author in the 1830s. Not dissimilar were the German writers Goethe, Herder and Möser when they declared themselves representatives of 'German art' in contradistinction to the omnipotence of French. In each case, an author oppressed by the paradoxical dominance of a literary or artistic metropolis, either too untypical to become truly 'central' or reluctant to assimilate, decided instead to be radically different. They wanted to show they could exist without recognition from the metropolis, but hoped to gain that recognition subsequently by staging an organized secession from the centre and creating a world of their own, with its own standards, its own rules, its own works and its own public.

If such a secession was to succeed it required access to at least some of the advantages of metropolitan literature: a language that could reach a substantial number of people, a publishing industry that could put the author's works into circulation, and a range of genres that could challenge comparison with the metropolitan output. And – though this aspect is not unconnected with the preceding – a belief in this literature and its ability to produce works that may constitute a symbolic capital. Ramuz, for example, espoused the idea of regional literature in order to justify his secession and turn his provinciality to account, but like others in similar situations, he came up against the huge difficulty of creating, or tapping, a common and recognizable stock of linguistic, lexical, historical and landscape motifs.

Hence any secessionist must start by inventing a past which never really existed. Sometimes they face the very practical task of inventing a kind of language in which local authors can write the stories, poems and plays of their dreams. Elias Lönnrot, writing in Finland in the 1830s, had to invent a new literary language, based on rural dialects yet with an extensive lexicon and capable of adaptation to such forms as novels, poetry and theatre – but also a language known for previous literary achievements, so that authors hesitating between languages might be induced to select it. Similarly, in 20th-century Nigeria both before and after independence, authors were faced with the task of inventing a peculiarly Nigerian literature. The task fell upon Daniel Olorunfemi Fagunwa, who in the 1930s transcribed the tales and legends of his people, in Yoruba, but in the form of a Western, printed book. At one and the same time he was inventing a literary language, establishing stories and characters who could be used in further stories, and making a bold attempt to create a reading public.

This deliberate revolution in values has a precise historical origin, though it has been played out over the two-and-a-half-century history of the worldwide literary system, in various locations on the literary periphery. It was in the latter half of the 18th century that pioneering authors from the periphery first attempted to impose a literature of which they were both authors and masters, defying the literary sophistication required by the literary centre of the time – Paris and the royal court at Versailles – and rejecting a literature that claimed to be based on a universal poetics based in its turn on reason. Against this literature, such authors as James Macpherson (Scotland) in the 1760s, Johann Jakob Bodmer (Switzerland) in the 1750s, Paul Henri Mallet (working in Copenhagen) and many others set literatures which emanated, or were claimed to emanate, from barbarian peoples: the Edda, Ossian's *Fingal*. Whole corpuses of texts were constituted, invented and/or reconstructed precisely because their rustic origin, simplicity of form and epic register offered an alternative to the literature of Paris. Johann Gottfried Herder, educated in Königsberg, provided a systematic conceptualization of this attempted revolution in his *Reflections on the philosophy of the history of mankind* (1784–91): the value of a literature does not depend on its proximity to the dominant, and would-be universal, culture, but on its difference from that culture and on its authenticity, which derives wholly from the people. The closer that people is to nature, the more vigorous its literature, and the truest literature is to be found in the songs of the peasantry.

National literatures were invented through a process of comparison and coalition which went far beyond national limits. The most potent aid to that invention was the combination of Ossianism with German revolutionary fervour: Herder adored Ossian; Klopstock imitated Milton; Gottfried Bürger, inventor of the German ballad, took his inspiration from Thomas Percy's *Reliques of ancient English poetry*. This folk poets' international banded together against the dominance of psychological and philosophical literature written in French. By 1800, the Scottish-German movement had spread over all Europe: Russians and Italians, Welsh and Swiss responded with equal fervour.

A similar process took place in Norway in the 1850s, when Ibsen started collecting the folksongs of western Norway as a basis for a kind of popular theatre that would establish him as the national dramatist. But he also imported the methods and techniques of Parisian theatre so as to give a modern colouring to the ancient themes he claimed to be dramatizing. As a result, his works were fêted in Norway as typically Norwegian, in Germany as typically Nordic, and in other European capitals as avant-garde. Much the same could be said of the 'Irish Renaissance' (c.1890–1930), which again began by constituting a corpus of folk literature, followed by the creation of a literary language, the assimilation of foreign works and the affirmation of a national aesthetic which would conquer the local market before exporting itself worldwide. In point of fact, however much these literary secessions, these inventions of a national literature, claimed to express the authentic spirit of some people or other, they were all in principle international: to make their mark, new literary nations had to band together; they had to import foreign literature, translate it and take inspiration from it; in order to fight the centre they had to do what was being done at the centre, only better; they had to prove that their national languages were rich and flexible enough to express the greatest products of the human mind – to become world languages.

Not all attempts at literary secession were similarly successful – far from it. The Kenyan Ngugi wa Thiong'o began by writing in English before independence, under the name of James Ngugi; this made him look like a typical literary product of the British Empire, trying to insinuate himself into the literature of the centre, meaning the literature of the colonial power. He wrote a series of works – in English – about Kenyan history and identity, bringing in the great events of the history of his own people, the Kikuyu. He was in fact trying to construct a literary and cultural history for Kenya – for Africa – which he then tried to teach at the university. But he very soon came up against serious shortcomings in the school and university system, illiteracy, and the authoritarian regime of Kenyatta, who refused to recognize any kind of intellectual autonomy and could and would not give any effective support to the constitution of a Kenyan national reading public, even if it read English. Unlike the Norwegian romantics, the Weimar Germans and the Meiji Japanese, Ngugi wa Thiong'o enjoyed no real government support and was not backed by a solid process of nation building. Indeed, all these attempts at subverting the literary centre, by turning its own best practice against it, were more than literary revolutions aiming at cultural particularism: they were part of the process of founding a nation, and if such nations needed their own original literatures, they needed a great many other things as well.

From national literature to world literature

This process of literary inter-nationalization – international production of literary nationalities – has been going on for two centuries but is still far from complete. And it is this process which explains the highly nationalized structure of the world literary system, and even conditions our cultural perception of the world.

The translation statistics used to assess literary circulation are all national, calculated either from accessions to copyright libraries or from figures and declarations supplied by publishing houses with professional structures that are equally 'national'. This, along with the fact that publishers, like any other business, have to have a nationality (which will be that of their registered office), means that published works will inevitably be assigned to some nation or other. Similarly, all literary imports and exports go through a legal process including copyright, publishers' judicial rights, translators' rights and payment terms for all concerned. In other words, they are treated as intellectual property under the Berne Convention, which was first drawn up in 1886 as a precept of international law, and became almost universal as different national copyright laws converged (with general acceptance of the Franco-German model for the professional and legal regulation of all aspects of authorship and publication), guaranteeing respect for the copyright of both national and foreign authors.

The intellectual and symbolic organization of the bookselling trade has evolved in a similar way. The idea that literature had to be national, first expounded in works of aesthetics and criticism from Herder to Mme de Staël and from Matthew Arnold to Hippolyte Taine, gradually became fixed to the point where it determined the structure of the book trade. We now take it for granted that books – in bookshops, in university reading lists, in publishers' catalogues – will be classified according to their (presumed) nationality. Collections of foreign literatures, which have existed in Europe and the US since the end of the 19th century, sound the death knell of 'literature' and its replacement by 'literatures': our literary perceptions have been, effectively, nationalized. It is possible to talk about half-breeds and hybrids, but these are always cultural hybrids, as if no mingling can taint the pure and constant essence of national culture, and as if all authors were doomed to act as the vehicles of pre-existing cultural entities.

In fact, all those involved in the circulation of literature carry a national label. Transnational studies may talk in terms of mediators or cross-border agents, who dwell apparently in a sort of supranational limbo; but no translator, publisher, press critic, professor of foreign literature, or any other agent of international literary circulation has ever been thus removed from the national framework. When Loève-Veimars, a German diplomat in French service, translated Hoffman in the 1830s it was because he wanted to be a French author, contributing something to French literature, which he considered to be unduly averse to the fantastic. When Japanese professors in the 1890s used imported French and German methodologies to constitute a national literature, they did it as employees of the Imperial University and for the glory of Imperial Japan. Similarly, translation into Hebrew, in the 1930s and subsequently, was an indispensable aid to affirming Hebrew as an international language, and Hebrew literature as a universal literature which could transcribe the great works of Western literature. Cross-border agents are not at all cosmopolitan or internationalist by nature; they are far more likely to act as the invisible stokers of some national literary juggernaut.

Thus we can see that the shaping dynamic of world literature over the last three centuries has been an inseparable combination of nationalization and globalization. National literatures have been invented by authors who felt themselves to have been marginalized and so decided to secede from literatures that had been imposed by social elites determined to mobilize culture in support of their bid for power, or by the governments that emerged in part from that same bid. This proved to be a powerful and effective model and, from the formal viewpoint, astonishingly creative; it spread, through imitation, competition and circulation, to almost every part of the world as new regions developed social groups and institutions capable of assimilating it. For the last two centuries, in fact, the globalization of literature, sustained by a power struggle among national literatures, has been structurally unequal and has consisted in the worldwide spread of literality nationalization.

Literary circulation may give the impression of annihilating cultural difference. In its current manifestation, however, it is just as likely to perpetrate literary inequality and literary nationalities, and to invent frontiers within which such nationalities can be identified. Literary circulation, in fact, is not only international but also transnational: it is constantly in motion, it crosses frontiers, activates frontiers, and may even create them.

Blaise Wilfert-Portal

Bibliography

Apter E. 2006. *The translation zone: a new comparative literature.* Princeton: Princeton University Press.

Bourdieu P. 2002 [1990]. 'Les conditions sociales de la circulation internationale des idées', *Actes de la Recherche en Sciences Sociales*, 145, 3–8.

Casanova P. 2004. *The world republic of letters.* Cambridge, MA: Harvard University Press.

Moretti F. 1998. *Atlas of the European novel: 1800–1900.* London and New York: Verso.

Moretti F. 2000. 'Conjectures on world literature', *New Left Review*, 1, January/February, 54–68.

Pym A. 2000. *Negotiating the frontier: translators and intercultures in Hispanic history.* Manchester: St Jerome.

Thiesse A.-M. 1998. *La Création des identités nationales.* Paris: Seuil.

Wilfert-Portal B. 'Des bâtisseurs de frontières: traduction et nationalisme culturel en France, 1880–1930', in Lombez C. and von Kulessa R. (eds) 2007. *De la traduction et des transferts culturels*, Paris: L'Harmattan.

Related essays

antropofagia; art market; avant garde; children's literature; comics; cultural capitals; globalization; humanities; intellectual property rights; language; modernity; nation and state; prizes; publishing; Romanticism; translation; Westernization

Little Red Book *See* Maoism

Loans

International loans are as old as finance itself. Loans were granted by foreigners in the Middle Ages to finance wars, ransoms (or war reparations) on the one hand, and long-distance trade on the other hand. These loans were granted from a point of view of profit, even if the lenders were also guided by political considerations and tried obtaining advantages beyond simple refunding.

In the 19th century, international loans developed in the form of bank loans, or by issuing bonds on the principal financial market, the London market. The interest rate on the London market was the reference for lenders and borrowers in the entire world. Emerging countries (the United States, Russia, Argentina, Australia, for instance) borrowed on this market. The idea that special conditions should be granted to the emerging countries, or to the colonies, was totally unknown. On the contrary, as is still the case today for the emerging countries, it was considered that the interest rate should be higher for countries perceived as risky (interest rates include a risk margin or 'spread').

This 'first globalization' ended with the great crisis of 1929, which led to an almost complete standstill of capital flows at the international level. It took rather a long time to settle an agreement between creditors and defaulting states. For this reason, private international loans were not resumed before the 1970s. In order to provide some financing of reconstruction (of Europe and Japan) and development, a public system was put in place at Bretton Woods (1944). The International Bank for Reconstruction and Development (the World Bank) was the main institution for providing international public loans, but regional development banks were also set up. These new public institutions were aimed at financing public infrastructures in order to attract private capital.

Moreover, a big share of international loans is granted to governments. These sovereign loans are a special category because there is no collateral and no legal system able to enforce decisions against a sovereign state. In this case, theory shows that an indebted government would repay only if the loss incurred in the case of default exceeds the debt service. This applies to the total debt service, and for this reason implies that every single creditor should carefully monitor the increase of the debt in order to keep it below the threshold of default (provided that the relevant information is available on time). To cope with risks, loans at the international level are often provided by a pool of banks ('syndicated loans').

After the independence of African countries in the 1960s a new category of loans was launched: 'concessional' loans. The idea was to provide loans to poor countries at low interest rates, with a significant grace period and a long duration (up to fifty years). Specialized agencies were created to manage this kind of loan, namely the International Development Association (IDA, a subsidiary of the World Bank), but also specialized 'windows' in national or regional development banks. Although economic theory shows that the profitability of such investments would be higher in poor countries because of a lack of capital, it was recognized that the poor countries would have special difficulties in repaying their debts. These loans are rather close to grants, although some amounts have to be repaid.

Economic theory shows that financial markets do not work like textbook markets but are likely to result in the exclusion of some proportion of the would-be borrowers because of an asymmetry of information. This is the case in the international financial market. Emerging countries may borrow huge amounts from private lenders at market rates with a spread. Their main problem is to keep access to the financial market because they repay their debt by new borrowing. In order to do so, they have to maintain a high level of credibility to persuade lenders that they will be able to repay in full. Any sign of potential problems results

in an increase of the spread, and the debt may become unsustainable. On the other hand, low-income countries are usually excluded from the private market. They may just borrow relatively small amounts from specialized institutions, on very soft conditions. Difficulties in repaying are then linked to the poor institutional framework, not to the debt as such. More and more, foreign financing of these countries is made up of grants. Nevertheless, even poor countries have access to private loans if they are able to provide some collateral (like oil-producing countries borrowing against their future oil revenue).

A striking feature about international loans is their cyclical way of functioning. International lending has experienced successive periods of fast growth followed by periods of collapse. After the Latin American debt crisis of 1825–50, a boom in international lending occurred from 1850 to 1873. After a new crisis (1874–80), international loans resumed, with a strong increase in the years following the World War 1, until the 1929 crisis. International loans increased again after World War 2, and especially in the 1970s because of a blend of an abundance of liquidities at the international level (petrodollars), sharp competition among banks, low interest rates, and growth in Gross Domestic Product and in exports of developing countries fuelled by sustained growth in OECD countries. This resulted in high profits made by banks (also because of favourable fiscal devices in emerging countries), loan pushing and eventually overborrowing. Some of these features were again to be observed in 2006.

Kindleberger has shown that this cyclical movement typically consists of three phases. The story begins with a fad, because some new event changes the expectations of returns to investors (discovery of mines, new technology, financial innovation, increase in the price of a commodity, etc.). A boom results because of the gregarious behaviour of investors, leading to high profits and speculation (mania, bubble). After some time, a crash occurs when some incident undermines confidence. Then panic follows, as every investor wants their money back. This generally results in losses for lenders (as, for instance in the 1930s, or after 1982). Nevertheless, after some time, the same process starts again. The delay is sometimes quite long (as after the 1929 crisis), but in some other cases it is surprisingly short.

This gives rise to the question of the rationality of lenders, since in retrospect investors seem rather shortsighted, or driven by 'animal spirits' (Keynes). In a review of Lissakers' book (Lissakers 1991, back cover), Dornbusch notes that 'Sovereign risk irresistibly attracts banks as honey attracts bees'. Nevertheless, the case for 'irrationality' has been challenged by theorists, who have shown that in some cases a bubble may result from the rational behaviour of investors (if expectations are arrived at by observing the expectations of other investors) in a context of uncertainty.

This apparent absence of memory can be explained in some other ways. The form of each crisis differs, either because of the instruments, or because of the countries concerned. For instance, before the 1994 Mexican crisis, debt was not supposed to be a problem because most of it was made up of bonds, not of bank loans as in 1982. Before the Asian crisis of 1997, investors were confident because the international debt of Asian countries was private, not public as in the former Mexican crisis. The competition among lenders may also be an explanation for the 'overlending' during the 1970s. Empirical work comparing the spreads on the loans and returns has shown that lenders are generally unable to correctly forecast the risks taken, as happened before the 1929 crisis.

A major problem for international loans to develop in a more orderly manner is the lack of a suitable institutional framework for international debts. Bank regulations improved with the Basle Agreements (1988). Nevertheless, a problem arises because a big share of international loans is created by the issuing of bonds, not by banks. In case of default, banks may reach an agreement through the London Club. On the other hand, it has proved difficult to reach an agreement with private lenders, and when a partial agreement is made, to avoid free-rider problems (bondholders suing the government to get full repayment). The introduction of Collective Action Clauses (CAC, giving the opportunity to a qualified majority of bondholders to impose an agreement with the debtor) in some debt contracts may be a way to facilitate the resolution of problems. But it does not resolve the problems arising from the existence of different types of creditors, including domestic banks and bondholders.

Marc Raffinot

Bibliography

Cardoso E. A. and Dornbusch R. 'Foreign private capital flows', in Chenery H. and Srinavasan T. N. (eds) 1989. *Handbook of development economics*, Vol. 2. Amsterdam: Elsevier, 1387–1439.

Eichengreen B. and Portes R. 1988. 'Foreign lending in the interwar years: the bondholders' perspective', *Institute of Business and Economic Research Working Papers*, 8856, University of California at Berkeley.

Kindleberger C. 1978. *Manias, panics, and crashes: a history of financial crises*. New York: Basic Books.

Lissakers K. 1991. *Banks, borrowers and the Establishment: a revisionist account of the international debt crisis*. New York: Basic Books.

Sgard J. 2002. *L'Économie de la panique: faire face aux crises financières*. Paris: La Découverte.

Suter C. 1992. *Debt cycles in the world-economy: foreign loans, financial crisis and debt settlements, 1820–1990*. Boulder, San Francisco and Oxford: Westview.

Related essays

convergence and divergence; debt crises; debt crises (developing countries); development and growth; financial centres; financial markets; International Monetary Fund (IMF); Paris Club; World Bank

Love

Feelings of love – the bliss, euphoria, optimism and exhilaration associated with the early stages of love, passion, or infatuation – are universal to all human beings in that their physiological causes can be identified. How individuals and societies express, interpret and act on the meaning of these feelings, however, is culturally specific. 'Romantic love' as a grounded and expanding system of explicated beliefs has cultural, political and economic dimensions that allow us to examine the transnational dimensions of love.

Historical studies of love in Europe used to insist on the exceptionalism of Western romantic love without questioning its cross-cultural origins. In these accounts, ideals of love appeared out of nowhere and were spread by male troubadours in the Languedoc region of southern France. Zeldin, however, has argued for the Arabic or Islamic origins of these discourses. The troubadour tradition originated in Mecca and Medina at the beginning of the Muslim era (622 CE), when new Greek music was fused with traditional Bedouin strains and songs were composed about love instead of war. Newly articulated ideals about love flourished in the court of Haroun al Rashid in Baghdad. They crossed over into Moorish Spain, subsequently spreading via the Reconquista as well as musical interchanges along the Franco-Spanish border until they took root in 12th-century France and evolved from there.

From at least the 18th century onwards, the European discourse of romantic love expanded well beyond Europe. In many places, it changed the acceptable criteria for choosing life partners so that 'love' became the socially sanctioned reason, even if it whitewashed more mercenary motivations. In this sense, European romantic love may be said to have become transnational. Countless versions of romantic love may be found in various cultures around the world. But the notion that lifelong partnerships should ideally be made on the basis of individual choice as a result of emotional and sexual attraction, without the intervention of family or state institutions, and that all other unions are somehow inferior – this system of belief has gradually become a norm or an aspiration in many countries and civilizations.

This discourse became transnational firstly through the globalizing effects of European imperialism. Tapan Raychaudhuri has examined how, through colonial rule, romantic love and notions of consensual marriage gained ground among the gentry classes in Bengal during the second half of the 19th century. The hierarchical mentalities of 'culture' and 'civilization' produced by colonialism privileged what was a relatively recent (and by no means ubiquitous) Western romantic practice over those of indigenous cultures. This was supported by British legislation concerning widowhood, sati, and child marriage. Secondly, by the late 19th and early 20th centuries, this particular discourse of romantic love was disseminated through the global spread of modern consumerism and cultural production: through the romanticization of commodities and the commodification of romance in film, popular literature, advertising, and the leisure and hospitality industries.

Illouz has shown that the American transition from courtship to dating played a crucial role in this process. Dating depended on practices of consumption and new technologies of transport and mass-market entertainment. It taught men and women to commodify each other as well as the experience of 'romance', which was split from 'love'. Romance had an exchange value in dating, one reinforced by advertising which romanticized as well as glamorized consumer goods, so much so that romance eventually came to refer to consumption practices: boxes of chocolates, red roses, romantic candlelight dinners, cruises at sunsets. As the 20th century progressed, sexual activity became part of dating, not because it was expected or because it had been 'bought', but because consumption reinforced the message that dating was about pleasure and the goal of romance was happiness. Thus a commercialized mass-market romantic culture framing contemporary understandings of love has become transnational, shaped by new technologies, communications systems and advanced consumer capitalism, fed by transnational publishing, media corporations, sophisticated marketing and international distribution. Romantic love is not merely a private, interpersonal concern; it is a transnational political and economic issue.

Hsu-Ming Teo

Bibliography

Illouz E. 1997. Consuming the romantic utopia: love and the cultural contradiction of capitalism. Berkeley: University of California Press.

Raychaudhuri T. 2000. 'Love in a colonial climate: marriage, sex and romance in nineteenth-century Bengal', Modern Asian Studies, 34, 2, 349–78.

Teo H. 'The Americanisation of romantic love in Australia', in Curthoys A. and Lake M. (eds) 2006. Connected worlds: history in transnational perspective. Canberra: ANU E Press, 171–92.

Zeldin T. 1994. An intimate history of humanity. New York: HarperCollins.

Related essays

America; beauty; consumer society; empires and imperialism; film; Hollywood; honour; jeans; marriage; sexuality and migration; Westernization

M

Mail

Mail refers to the physical communication of written, physical items (such as letters, notices, bills) typically distributed through a Public Postal Operator (PPO). Also referred to as 'post', it has been integral to political economic and international development. The concept of mail, its purpose, and its primary agents have changed over time. Mail has an uncertain future, its public character in competition with an emerging private character in the face of globalization, alternate technologies, and the gradual privatization of its agents and functions.

The evolution of mail tracked society's evolution and cross-border development. Its organized origins as official or government mail lie in the Egyptian, Persian, Chinese, and Roman empires. An instrument of authority and control over extended distances and colonies, it communicated political orders and decrees and collected information and taxes. The word 'mail' refers to the bag containing letters (French *malle* meaning box or trunk) and 'post' was derived from Latin for position or placing (of the postal or horse relay spots). A more distinctly commercial mail developed with the rise and interaction of city states, which (like guilds and universities) initiated inter-city mail systems. Mail during much of European history was privately operated by the house of Thurn and Taxis. Starting as a 13th-century Italian city service, Thurn und Taxis grew into the official and integrated mail system of the Holy Roman Empire. It employed 20,000 messengers in a postal monopoly for over 400 years, and extended from the Baltic to the Adriatic and from Poland to Gibraltar. The Napoleonic Wars and the rise of the modern nation state saw the nationalization of mail and its absorption into the state system as PPOs.

Mail moved from an elite to a mass system through the 19th and 20th centuries. It balanced social and economic dimensions, as it tracked the evolution of capitalism and democracy. Mail served the growth of capitalism by extending the market geographically, both domestically and internationally. Rowland Hill's postal reforms in England (1840) brought universalization, simplification and rapid expansion of the mail, as it was reconceptualized as part of a prepaid, inexpensive, and uniform price system (penny post). The leading commercial nations then internationalized the free flow of cross-border mail (1874) via the creation of the Universal Postal Union (UPU), which has managed the international mail system to the present. These developments accelerated commercial relations to a considerable extent particularly in the 'new lands' (North America, Australasia), where the mail played a critical role in nation building and advancing the frontiers of modernization and capitalism. Postage stamps themselves expressed this, as in American stamps' depiction of the Pony Express, the locomotive, and the national movement across the Mississippi. These developments also reflected and contributed to the extension of democracy. An increasingly educated, literate and engaged population insisted on access to inexpensive and reliable mail. This allowed the wide and easy circulation of ideas and debates in notices, circulars, newspapers and periodicals. This function is well exemplified in newspaper names (such as *Daily Mail*, *Washington Post*) where letters played a key role. The modern mail system was enormously successful and consequential, and evolved into the largest retail operation in the world with the largest number of employees (after the military and agriculture). Typically subsidized as a free or inexpensive service, mail became a 'public good', guaranteed through states' commitment (domestically and internationally) to the universal service obligation to provide a regular, accessible and low-cost mail service to all its citizens. Mail volumes tracked the growth of the economy and the rise in household education and income, as exemplified in North America. Canadian mail volumes doubled during the postwar boom (1948–70) and doubled again by the early 1990s. The United States is the greatest per capita user of mail – over 400 units annually (the world figure is 68). Volumes grew 50-fold from 1890 to 2000, from 4 billion to over 200 billion units. International mail has grown to nearly 10 per cent of total volumes.

The 'public' concept of mail is currently changing slowly but inexorably to a 'private', competitive and commercial one, under the impact of dramatic changes in communications technology, the success of neoliberal ideology, and the acceleration and impact of globalization. Technological developments generated complexity as well as competing communications alternatives and the digital economy (fax, email, computer banking). Neoliberalism delegitimized many of the public services, including the public character of the postal sector. This led to the liberalization and the deregulation of mail, and the commercialization of the PPOs (the Dutch and German Posts are semi-privatized). Globalization accelerated competitive commercial pressures on the mail sector and international organizations – the European Union and the World Trade Organization, as well as regional associations like NAFTA – directed states to open up their service markets to international trade. The European Union plans for a free mail market by 2009.

Mail is an important component of the infrastructure underpinning international activity and the growing service economy. Changes in air and maritime transport cut shipping costs, leading to private opportunities and growth in international mail. Globalization stimulated trade in services, of which infrastructural activities like international mail are significant. While the importance of the traditional 'letter' declines, postal services are of continuing importance to business activity. International mail is growing faster than domestic mail, and the globalized postal environment is dominated by private US firms like FedEx and UPS and semi-privatized PPOs like the Dutch (TNT) and German (DHL) Posts.

The concept of mail as a 'public good' has slowly but surely been replaced by its conceptualization as a communications commodity no different from others. Governments have looked at mail differently, in the face of rising deficits as well as alternate forms of mail organization (privatization) and public communications (email, electronic transfer). The concept of the 'mail' has narrowed and the idea of the universal service obligation seems to be less compelling politically – not surprisingly, as the primary agents of the sector are increasingly private. A structural asymmetry exacerbates this development. Over 80 per cent of mail can be categorized as 'business' mail, while less than 20 per cent of mail can be categorized as 'social' mail or personal letters. Business mail is in turn dominated by 500 or so large customers in each country. This mail is especially amenable to digitization and electronic transmission, giving operational and ideological resonance to the idea that mail is basically an economic commodity.

Mail currently faces a highly political and uncertain future. Cassandra-like predictions about its demise have proved to be somewhat overstated and the mail sector remains reasonably healthy albeit uncertain. The mail sector generates over 440 billion letters annually (including 7 billion international units), or 1.2 billion units a day. The rate of change of mail volumes has peaked but will continue to grow with the economy. This activity employs over 5 million people in 700,000 post offices, and postal market coverage is over 96 per cent. However, aggregate statistics obscure a structural asymmetry. The leading 28 industrialized countries generate over 80 per cent of the domestic and over 70 per cent of the international mail. Per capita mail per year in industrialized countries is 30 times that of the rest of the world (405 vs 14), as mail usage is directly related to economic and educational development. The number of people served by post offices is 45,000 in non-industrialized vs 5,000 in industrialized countries. Only 20 per cent of Africans enjoy home mail delivery and 20 per cent have no delivery at all.

Mail's current discourse has an ironic public/private ideological divide. Industrialized countries – with the more developed and utilized mail system – increasingly see mail as an economic commodity and support its liberalization, deregulation and privatization. The less advanced countries – with an underdeveloped mail sector – defend the idea of mail as a public good and the universal service obligation. The former advance their case via corporations and through the World Trade Organization (WTO) and international agencies dominated by the private sector. The latter articulate their position via states and through their enormous majority in the UPU.

A further irony is that mail likely has a reasonably healthy future. It survived and expanded even as new communications technologies appeared: the telegraph (long since gone), the telephone (influence peaked) and the fax (no longer an issue). Per capita mail usage remains steady despite the email explosion. The latter helped expand the communications market, dominating it only in certain segments. Physical and electronic communications serve different functions, enjoying complementarities that feed off each other. Mail has developed 'hybrid' products that combine physical and electronic features and services. Recent research indicates that the more prosperous, educated and 'wired' the household, the more mail it receives and generates. Significant parts of the marketplace and households prefer physical (paper) communication. Direct marketing and delivery of Internet purchases are enormous markets. Social issues like employment, integration of small-town and rural communities, development in the Less Developed Countries and public service issues, as well as tradition and a continuing public sense of its reliability and security, give mail ongoing resonance and a role in social and economic life. However, its long-term qualitative significance remains uncertain, as it undergoes an epochal transition from a public, state-dominated world and discourse to a globalized environment dominated by the private sector and neoliberal ideology.

Robert M. Campbell

Bibliography

Campbell R. M. 2002. *The politics of postal transformation: modernizing postal systems in the electronic and global world*. Montréal: McGill-Queen's University Press.

Campbell R. M. 1994. *The politics of the post: Canada's postal system from public service to privatization*. Peterborough, ON: Broadview.

Jimenez L. 2006. Is there a future for mail? Pitney Bowes presentation to United States Postal Rate Commission, Washington, DC, 22 February.

Related essays

diasporas; General Agreement on Tariffs on Trade (GATT) / World Trade Organization (WTO); globalization; governance; information economy; internationalisms; Internet; nation and state; neoliberalism; services; telephone and telegraphy; trade; Universal Postal Union (UPU)

Management

'Management' is a ubiquitous term today, so widely used as in fact to lose meaning. The term suggests layers of references and associations that need to be deciphered.

Historically, the emergence of the notion of management and its progressive institutionalization reflect the intersection of three main developments – the spread of the modern belief in science; the progress of bureaucratization and the profound corporate reinvention of American capitalism at the turn of the 20th century. By the end of World War 2, management was a set of practices and tools and an emergent body of knowledge associated with a few institutions of socialization and professionalization. The core was clearly in the United States with little impact on the rest of the world. Things changed, however, after World War 2, when the scope and the nature of management evolved progressively. Firstly, management became transnational. Secondly, management turned from a set of practices and a body of knowledge sustained by a few institutions into a transnational ideology or structuring frame. Management gave way to managerialization. Management knowledge and tools are increasingly seen as a common reference frame and language, across borders, over and beyond the boundaries of what used to be differentiated spheres of social and human life. Management, furthermore, becomes globally a dominant socialization frame for future elites, whether economic or political, or even for elites from the non-profit sector.

The turn of the 20th century saw a profound reinvention of American capitalism. A merger wave on a historically unprecedented scale led to the reorganization of most industries as oligopolies. Large firms were built from an aggregation of many small ones and those integrated giants were incorporated. The emergent joint stock companies were often associated with dispersed ownership and the separation between ownership and control was a consequential outcome. Owners stepped out of day-to-day decision making, leaving the space to salaried decision makers – or managers as those came to be called. The new industrial or service 'monsters' required new tools and techniques making it possible to plan, coordinate and control in spite of size.

Management became a job and was progressively professionalized. Business schools were set up across the country and became important actors of this professionalization. Later on, from the 1930s on, consultants, the press and professional associations would further strengthen and institutionalize management as a quasi-profession. Together with management and its development as an activity came the structuration of an intellectual field vying through time for the status of a scientific field. In the early years, both the influence of the bureaucratic model and the scientific impulse were strongly felt. Bureaucratic principles were adopted and adapted to the large American private firm, while technicians and engineers pondered on the 'scientific management' of the production process. In his *The principles of scientific management*, Frederick Taylor in 1911 set out to 'prove that the best management is a true science, resting upon clearly defined laws, rules and principles as a foundation' (Taylor 1911, introduction).

Needless to say, management in this sense defined and carried a masculine world and imprint. Management was the new progressive project, reflecting the modernist dream of an absolute control over matter. Rational human beings could access and master the information and the tools needed to maximize the collective good and induce progress, both for the firm and for society at large. Starting in the 1950s, new challenges and opportunities emerged for management.

The context was a unique geopolitical situation where the United States had reached superpower status. That country then projected into the (Western) world insolent wealth and power and the connection was often made to the peculiarities of American managerial capitalism. American political authorities in fact constructed management as a geopolitical weapon. In the words of Paul Hoffman, a high-ranking Marshall Plan official, the United States should 'fight the Communist party line with the American assembly line'. On the other side of the Atlantic, in Europe, chaos, destitution and crisis reigned. This soon also implied dependence when the United States launched a major aid programme around the Marshall Plan and associated initiatives. As a consequence, the desire to imitate encountered the wish to project – and management became an object of export/import between the United States and many countries in Europe and beyond. Productivity missions, where Europeans 'discovered' American capitalism and more particularly management, expert visits and exchanges all played a part in the progressive acculturation. From the 1960s on, the internationalization of American firms and service providers took over as a major diffusion channel. Of even more significance in the longer term, though, one should mention the progressive structuration of a management education field in Europe starting in the 1950s. This structuration set itself in direct continuity to Marshall Plan-related initiatives and was financed in part by private American foundations, such as the Ford Foundation. Incidentally, the first President of the Ford Foundation was Paul Hoffman.

The transnational expansion of management reached Europe and Japan first. With the fall of the Berlin Wall, though, a similar process and similar mechanisms opened up new frontiers – and management went East (in the broad sense of the term). While management spread as sets of tools and practices, the intellectual and scientific sphere around 'management knowledge' also expanded and matured significantly during this period. Here again, the reach became progressively global. Originally American journals became global references and targets for scholars, professional associations (both scientific and administrative such as the AACSB – American Association of Collegiate Schools of Business) entered internationalization paths. Locally or regionally, initiatives to structure the field of management knowledge were deployed and multiplied. The number of business schools exploded everywhere, the MBA (Master of Business Administration) went from being a uniquely American degree to a global label or 'licence to manage'; regional associations and conferences were set up; journals were launched and English imposed itself as the lingua franca of this intellectual and scientific community.

The diffusion of management as sets of tools and practices and associated institutions and bodies of knowledge thus marked the second half of the 20th century. Progressively, the organization of economic activity has come to be profoundly influenced all around the world. In the meantime, management has become increasingly depoliticized, in appearance at least. When management emerged, at the end of the 19th century in the United States, it was a tool of power for decision makers without ownership rights. They used this tool in their interactions with both labour and shareholders. After World War 2, management was clearly construed and constructed as a geopolitical weapon. Management would bring wealth and prosperity to battered countries, it was assumed. Wealth and prosperity would keep Communism at bay.

Since then, though, the evolution has clearly been towards claims of neutrality and scientific 'purity'. Management on the whole presents itself as preoccupied only with efficiency questions, not power issues. This neutral posture has probably significantly contributed to the broadening appeal of management and its universalist ambitions. The progress of management in the past twenty years or so has reinforced and has been reinforced by the transnationalization of our economies and societies, the success almost everywhere of marketization and neoliberal ideas and the triumph of science. All organizations, including state administrations, universities, cultural or health sector organizations are reinventing themselves using models from the private business sector. Hence, management is spreading into many spheres of social life, which had until then been governed according to different logics. Undeniably, this is having a profound impact. Management tools and knowledge even spread to institutions like the Church, marriage, the family. The individual him/herself should manage him/herself, his/her career, love and sexual life, family relationships, self-presentation...Bookstores are full of 'self-management' books and guides.

Management undeniably has become an institution, in the profound sense of a stabilized cognitive frame. As an institution, it plays out furthermore at the transnational level with a profound impact on the most unexpected corners of the world and on the most surprising sides of our lives. As an institution, a stabilized structuring frame, management is becoming less and less discussed and contested. In fact, it is more and more transparent to the actors themselves and has an air of taken-for-grantedness. The progress of management education all around the world is important here as a powerful socialization mechanism. Elite formation across the world increasingly implies some training in management, in one form or another – and this is true for elite formation in general not merely for the training of economic elites. This confirms that the posture of neutrality is nothing more than that – a posture. From a simple power tool, management has turned into a 'regime of practices', an 'hegemonic' or 'disciplinary' discourse, in the words of Michel Foucault.

Marie-Laure Djelic

Bibliography

Djelic M. L. 1998. Exporting the American model. Oxford: Oxford University Press.

Djelic M. L. and Sahlin-Andersson K. (eds) 2006. Transnational governance. Cambridge: Cambridge University Press.

Gemelli G. 1998. The Ford Foundation and Europe (1950s–1970s). Brussels: European Interuniversity Press.

Sahlin-Andersson K. and Engwall L. (eds) 2002. The expansion of management knowledge. Palo Alto: Stanford University Press.

Sklar M. 1988. The corporate reconstruction of American capitalism. Cambridge and New York: Cambridge University Press.

Taylor F. 1911. The principles of scientific management. New York: Harper Bros.

Related essays

class; Cold War; corporations; Ford Foundation; higher education; language; Marshall Plan; Master of Business Administration (MBA); organization models; Pax Americana; philanthropic foundations; productivity missions

Mandela, Nelson *See* African Liberation

Maoism

Maoism, like Marxism, does not have a single clear definition, and has gone well beyond the specific precepts of its originator, China's long-time ruler Mao Zedong (1893–1976). However, it is generally associated with movements that seek to use the peasantry to engage in revolutionary liberation, and which stress violent confrontation and direct participation rather than representative governance. In its stress on the peasantry's role and its enthusiasm for grassroots participation, it differentiates itself from classic Marxism or the Bolshevik coup that took over Russia in 1917. Particularly during the Cold War, it had considerable impact beyond China as a system of political action.

The height of Maoism's transnational value was in the 1950s and 1960s, when its principles appeared to many, particularly in the newly decolonized world, to provide a convincing alternative to Western capitalism and Soviet communism. Defence Minister Lin Biao in 1965 issued the important policy statement 'Long Live the Victory of People's War!', an encouragement to peoples around the world who were still colonized either territorially or economically to use Mao's revolutionary thought as a means of liberation. Although the statement was addressed to particular countries, including Indonesia and Turkey, the thrust of the argument was highly subversive of the nation state as the vehicle through which such societies would be liberated. First, an explicitly class-based rhetoric was used, in which it was implied that the proletariat and peasantry of all societies had aims, best expressed through the tenets of Maoism, which bound them in common, and in distinction from the bourgeois and capitalist classes of their own societies. This was not, of course, that far removed from the revolutionary sentiments of the early Bolsheviks, but by the Cold War, the USSR's quest for territorial security had effectively made it a new empire, preventing its message of Third World liberation from being fully convincing. In contrast, Maoist rhetoric attempted to use anti-colonialism as a bond between China and other recently decolonized societies, suggesting that a bloc that transcended national boundaries, but with China as its exemplar, was a meaningful Third Way within the Cold War. Many intellectuals in the West also found Maoism an inspiring force for the definition of a new politics, with Mao's influence being particularly strong in France.

This strategy was not wholly convincing, as the 1962 Sino–Indian War showed that traditional territorial disputes could still trump claims of Third World harmony. However, Maoist ideas did provide new alliances all over the Third World. Chinese technical assistance, linked with ideas of self-reliance, contributed to the building of the important TanZam (Tanzania Zambia) railway in 1970–75. In India, that country's long-simmering political crisis gave rise to a set of new, extraparliamentary peasant movements in various regions, but most notably West Bengal. These groups, collectively known as Naxalites, demanded a peasant revolution, and encouraged violent action against landlords to promote it. They explicitly acknowledged the contribution of Maoism to their philosophy, with some stating that 'China's Chairman is our Chairman', and stressing this link over their national bonds with India. However, the combination of violence and transnational peasant bonding proved unsustainable, and the Naxalite movement faded by the mid 1970s. Maoist beliefs that peasant unity went across national boundaries also shaped the most devastating agrarian revolution of the 20th century, the Khmer Rouge regime under Pol Pot (Saloth Sar), which ruled Cambodia from 1975 to 1978. Pol Pot, who had come to Beijing to seek advice from Mao when still an insurgent in the Cambodian jungle, was told by Mao to deal with the cities first; Mao indicated that his problems had come from ignoring this idea. Pol Pot, however, took this principle far further than Mao had ever done, emptying the cities completely, and turning the entire country into a vast slave-labour agricultural commune. In this way, Cambodian Maoism become more extreme than the original. In the 1980s, Maoism reached Latin America. Peru was racked by an armed guerrilla movement called the Shining Path (Sendero Luminoso), led by a mysterious Comrade Gonzalo (Abimael Guzmán), and which committed many violent atrocities in its struggle to mobilize the countryside against the government. In the post-Cold War era, however, Maoism, like other forms of Marxism, has fallen from favour. With its emphasis on violence and self-sufficiency, Mao's thought has fewer powerful adherents in an era that is both more globalized and more consumerist.

Rana Mitter

Bibliography

Mitter S. 1977. *Peasant movements in West Bengal: their impact on agrarian class relations since 1967*. Cambridge: Department of Land Economy, University of Cambridge.

Short P. 1999. *Mao: a life*. London: Hodder and Stoughton.

Related essays

China; decolonization; developmental assistance; empires and imperialism; Little Red Book; nation and state; socialism; technical assistance; terrorism; transportation infrastructures; workers' movements

Little Red Book

'Little Red Book' refers to an anthology of quotations attributed to Mao Zedong.

The compilation of Mao's sayings, which drew upon earlier publications, was most influential during the late 1960s and early 1970s. After the Bible, the Little Red Book still is the second most printed text in the world. More than 1 billion copies have been published – mainly in Chinese but also in more than 30 additional languages. The book functioned as the core text for the Cultural Revolution and many transnationally oriented Maoist movements in developing and industrialized societies.

In the English language, the title 'Little Red Book' is taken from the vinyl plastic cover, in which most versions appeared. Alternative connotations are 'Chinese Bible', 'Mao Bible', and especially 'Quotations From Chairman Mao' – a direct translation of the official Chinese title ('Mao zhuxi yulu'). Most probably defence minister Lin Biao initiated the original compilation of the Little Red Book, which was first published as an army handbook in 1964. Two years later, from the beginning of the Cultural Revolution onwards, the book became a study guide for the masses. By 1968 at least 720 million Chinese copies had been printed, and ownership became mandatory for Chinese citizens.

The most common editions of the Little Red Book contain – depending on the specific edition – about 427 aphorisms that are typically five to 15 lines in length. The work is loosely structured into 33 chapters, which were supposed to provide a comprehensive overview of Mao Zedong's thought. Among the Little Red Book's most influential parts were modifications of established socialist doctrines. Very important for the Red Guards and their international sympathizers was the idea that changes in human nature do not merely result from changing material conditions but have to be achieved in addition to socioeconomic revolutions. Other central passages define positive nationalism as the struggle against the foreign and domestic enemies of socialism. According to the Little Red Book, national liberation movements conducted by socialists are inseparably connected with proletarian internationalism, which is why they differ from 'tribal' kinds of nationalism propounded by imperialist or reactionary forces. Reflecting the fallout with the Soviet Union, the book tends to depict China as the new leader of a transnational socialist revolution.

In line with this agenda, the Little Red Book not only came to be envisioned as a political guidebook for Chinese citizens but also as the textual fundament of a worldwide movement. Between 1966 and 1972, the Chinese government's Foreign Language Press published bilingual editions or translations into 33 languages of Communist, Western and Third World societies. For example, editions in Russian, Hungarian, Serbian, Spanish, French, English, German, Arabic, Thai, Arabic, Persian and Hindi were printed in China and then disseminated. In many countries independent reprints of the Little Red Book appeared in addition to these publications. In the United States, for instance, the first edition of the Little Red Book was published as a Bantam paperback in 1967.

The international influence of the Little Red Book paralleled the national and transnational topographies of Maoism. For example, around the time of 1968 the book was very prominent among transnational student groups in Western societies. Also the Albanian government under Enver Hoxha promoted the Little Red Book until the end of the Mao era. Furthermore, the work was – and partly continues to be – influential among rebel groups such as the Khmer Rouge in Cambodia, the Shining Path in Peru, or the Maoist guerrillas in Northeast India as well as Nepal.

During the mid-1970s the Little Red Book was no longer an international bestseller – its transnational rise and decline paralleled the work's evolution in China. In the People's Republic the iconic status of the Little Red Book started to wane during the political consolidation period after 1971 and dropped sharply after the death of Mao Zedong five years later. Starting from the late 1970s, the Chinese government under Deng Xiaoping discouraged its further circulation, even though replicas were published during the centenary of Mao's birth in 1993.

Dominic Sachsenmaier

Bibliography
Han O. L. 2003. 'Sources and early printing history of Chairman Mao's "Quotations"', *Antiquarian Book Review*, 9.

Related essays
Bible; China; *Communist Manifesto*; Koran; Maoism; socialism; *The Wretched of the Earth*; translation; workers' movements

Mapping

The maps we usually come across in our everyday lives are nationally framed – for instance, weather maps, or maps in newspapers – leading us to conceive of the nation as the fundamental unit for building maps depicting larger areas and even the whole globe. This idea is shored up by another commonly held belief that cartography is primarily a form of political discourse aimed at acquiring and maintaining power. The history of mapping, however, urges us to nuance these received notions. Maps from the earliest times, and in almost all cultures where they existed, have been conceived of as a representation either of spaces of real or potential power, control or negotiation for princes, merchants and traders, or of universal and religious space, or yet again as directional aids for travellers, pilgrims and navigators – in other words as objects which represent spaces beyond the world of the actors concerned. All these varieties of maps were made from information, or pictorial representations, garnered from travellers, pilgrims and merchants or their contacts in other parts of the world which were the result of a negotiation as to what information was to be represented on the map, and how. In their making too, maps have often been, and as we shall see, still are, transnational. This implies that the representations, scales, conventions, instruments and practices that go into mapping and map making, albeit locally specific, also circulate across the spaces that are mapped and across which the maps themselves circulate. An essential tension between national interests and transnational methods then characterizes mapping.

Maps began to gain increasing importance in the early modern world. They accompanied imperial conquest and began to find new uses in the administration of newly conquered territories. The use of indigenous spatial and social knowledge was crucial to the mapping process. This is all the more true of large-scale maps made in the wake of European expansion and territorial possession across the globe. Thus, the first maps of New Spain drawn in the 1580s, the *Relaciones geográficas*, were largely the result of Amerindian expertise. They were meant to define, control and make visible the Spanish empire and as such became a template for future representations of early modern imperial space. Even Chinese imperial maps of the 16th century have been shown to be the result of the circulation of maps and map-making practices across the Eurasian landmass.

An excellent example of the circulation and the coming together of representations, techniques and practices from across empires is James Rennell's (1742–1830) map of India published in 1783. This is the first detailed map of so vast a territory made by the British. Rennell, himself a hydrographer and coastal surveyor, brought in techniques of marine surveying, together with various data from the geographical manuals of the Mughal empire and from military route surveys, which he then projected onto a French map of South Asia, made by the renowned French map maker, Jean-Baptiste Bourguignon d'Anville (1697–1782). Curiously, it was Rennell's mapping of India that provided the impetus for setting up the Ordnance Survey of Great Britain and Ireland from 1800 onwards.

This, however, does not imply that the same procedures, or scales, were appropriated across the world. Quite to the contrary: although the French had a half-century lead on the British in national territorial mapping and had developed the repeating circle specifically for accurate triangulation, the Ordnance Survey developed its own instrument – the altazimuth theodolite, far more unwieldy than the former and requiring its own procedures and protocols for use and conversion of readings into mapping data. Similarly, the plane table, in wide use in the Austro-Hungarian Empire since the 18th century, was not used in Britain until the early 20th century although it was a standard instrument of the Survey of India, a British colonial institution. The same holds true of scale: different regions of the same country were mapped on different scales until well into the 20th century. Standardization, an essentially transnational activity, is then crucial to the success of mapping as an operation.

From the early 19th century, new uses for maps developed – as instruments for civil administration and for military strategy, as well as a means of defining interstate boundaries and settling wars – always the result of the circulation of information and negotiations between states or empires. Already in 1783, much time was taken up during the negotiations leading up to the Treaty of Paris in mapping the line that would henceforth separate Canada from the United States. Subsequent treaties have almost always had a cartographic component, sometimes including historical maps, to elucidate the respective claims. Furthermore, the mapping of boundaries cannot be reduced to simply tracing static lines of demarcation: it often also involves mapping the activities of borderland communities and their rights with respect to resources on either side of the boundary, such as the use of grazing lands, rivers, roads and other lines of communication. Determining and agreeing upon these aspects are typically transnational and international activities. The Anglo–Afghan Treaty of 1875, the Anglo–Tibetan Border Treaty of 1904, or the Sino–Pakistan Border Treaty of 1963 are good examples.

The creation and endemic instability of Afghanistan and of the northwestern frontier of what is now Pakistan is also in part the failed attempt to identify and map a 'scientific' frontier to bound an artificially created buffer state between the British and Russian empires in Asia in the latter half of the 19th century. Indeed, Britain, perceiving Russia's *Drang nach Osten* as a direct threat to its interests in India, sought to create a large buffer zone covering Tibet, Afghanistan and large parts of Central Asia. In order to do this, they sought to map this vast no-man's land to which they had no direct access. Between 1863 and 1885 no less than 15 native Indians were to crisscross Tibet and Eastern Turkistan, measuring their paces which had been carefully regulated to always measure 31½ inches, rendering 2,000 paces equivalent to a mile (1,750 yards). All the data collected by these men, codenamed 'Pundits', were published over the years in learned journals and computed into a highly detailed map of the Transhimalaya which allowed the British to invade Tibet in 1904.

The exploration of the terrae incognitae in the course of the 19th century provides some of the most spectacular examples of the transnational encounter and intercourse involved in field surveys, the backbone of mapping. Partly in order to colonize sub-Saharan Africa and partly in order to determine its geography and the source of the Nile, for instance, a number of European expeditions were organized from the 1850s. That of Richard Francis Burton (1821–1890) and John Hanning Speke (1827–1864) is one of the best known and certainly the most dramatic – the latter shot himself just before a public showdown with the former in 1864 concerning their identification of the origin of the great river. At the bottom of the controversy lay the perceived reliability of their respective 'native' informants, Arabs for Burton and Ugandan tribespeople for Speke.

The history of mapping commonly ends at the end of the 19th century, and has demonstrated the importance of the map in the creation and maintenance of the core ideologies of European expansion and imperialism. The revolutionary changes in cartographic technology, the sheer amount of scattered material and its inaccessibility owing to the strategic nature of cartographic information, together with the fact that the military, social and environmental agencies which hold the data are notorious for selective reporting and political posturing, make the writing of a 20th-century history of map making a daunting challenge. We are tempted to think that with the recent rise of computer-assisted mapping and remote-sensing techniques, human intervention is now limited to purely technical manipulation and that the transnational aspects of mapping have all but disappeared. This vision is, however, highly deceptive, for the collection and processing of relevant primary data necessarily continue to rely heavily on fieldwork as well as on the circulation of data and practices between different professions, mapping techniques and governmental and commercial organizations and learned societies. Fiercely competitive nationalism and changing strategic alliances between various nations all through the 20th century have curiously reinforced the transnationalization of the circulation networks of cartographic information and mapping techniques. For instance, contemporary topographic mapping emerged through the circulation and competition between different cultures of land-surveying and aerial-mapping techniques in the first four decades of the 20th century. And, although present-day relief mapping, including the 3-D depiction of buildings, relies massively on photogrammetry, the input of artists as model makers has been shown to be crucial to Allied military model making during World War 2. This is also true of route, boundary and hydrographical maps. Or again, the construction of a precise geodetic grid for US intercontinental ballistic missile delivery systems during the Cold War depended on World War 2 German cartographic records, civilian mapping and satellite geodesy.

In addition, in the course of the last decades a number of novel mapping enterprises have emerged, for instance to map international migration, weather patterns, or global warming. In each case, it is easy to see how the very nature of the objects only strengthened the transnational nature of mapping.

Kapil Raj

Bibliography

Monmonier M. and Woodward D. (eds) 2002. 'Exploratory essays: history of cartography in the twentieth century', *Cartography and Geographic Information Science*, special issue, 29, 3.

Mundy B. 1996. *The mapping of New Spain: indigenous cartography and maps of the Relaciones geográficas*. Chicago: Chicago University Press.

Prescott J. R. V. 1978. *Boundaries and frontiers*. London: Croom Helm.

Raj K. 2007. *Relocating modern science: circulation and the construction of knowledge in South Asia and Europe, 1650–1900*. Basingstoke and New York: Palgrave Macmillan.

Related essays
borders and borderlands; empires and imperialism; information technology (IT) standardization; measurement; oceans; scientific expeditions; scientific instruments and tools; technical standardization

Marketing

Marketing is a set of analytical, strategical and tactical activities that a company undertakes in order to launch and maintain a product or a service in the market. Marketing practices such as market research, product management, pricing, distribution and promotion are related to the marketing philosophy which implies that companies have to orientate their activities toward consumer needs, habits and expectations.

Because its very essence is concerned with the relationship between producers and consumers, marketing thought has always been an intrinsic element of the commercial exchange process. It began, however, to be formalized and practised shortly after the turn of the 20th century, when shifts in the balance between supply and demand pushed companies to give more attention to trade and distribution.

Marketing abroad is not a recent phenomenon. Cross-cultural trade has existed ever since the early contacts between communities foreign to each other occurred. However, the use of marketing devices beyond national borders appeared at the beginning of 20th century, as a consequence of the growth of international trade and of the effort to rationalize export operations.

Throughout its history the key questions in marketing have always been concerned with the opportunity to employ a uniform strategy in all targeted countries: is it possible to adopt the same product, the same price, the same channels of distribution, the same advertising everywhere? Or is it necessary to change or adapt them according to national, political, economic and sociocultural conditions?

During the first half of the 20th century, a pragmatic approach, oriented toward the adaptation of only a few commercial tools, such as branding and advertising, dominated marketing activities beyond national boundaries. Since the 1960s, transnational marketing issues have become a crucial matter of marketing thought and the debate about standardization and diversification of marketing strategies has divided marketing academics and practitioners. In 1962, Ernest Dichter, founder of motivational research, claimed that modernization was a driving force behind a general convergence of tastes, desires, and consumers' choices, leading to the inevitable birth of 'world-customers'. In 1968, in the *Harvard Business Review*, Robert Buzzell, another leading figure in this field, argued, 'There are significant opportunities for cost reduction via standardization in a global marketing strategy.'

Instead, experts in market research warned against the risks of the uniformization of marketing decisions. In particular, in-depth studies of the European market, being the main target of American businesses during the postwar years, showed that it was more opportune to adjust marketing strategies and tactics to each country.

In practice, at that time, transnational marketing remained predominantly a contextual activity. Even when most multinational corporations tried to coordinate their plans and to have a coherent identity across different countries, they would customize variables of the marketing mix – not so much product and distribution as price and promotion – to fit national market differences. At the end of the 1960s, the then president of Philip Morris, George Weissman, declared that, 'Until we achieve "One World", there is no such thing as international marketing, only local marketing around the world.'

Nevertheless, since the 1980s, some marketing theorists have advised multinational companies to focus more on analogies across national boundaries and less on differences. In 1983, the economist Theodor Levitt wrote that new communication technologies were irrevocably homogenizing consumer needs and desires around the world. In Levitt's opinion, firms should give up the 'multidomestic' approach and cease to tailor their marketing operations to suit national contexts. Instead, companies should become 'global' like Coca-Cola, Revlon and McDonald's and take advantage of economies of scale by standardizing products, prices, distribution and advertising across all countries.

These arguments have contributed to consolidating the perception of marketing as a steamroller that crushes customs and traditions rooted in national cultures. In fact, since the 1960s, critical analysts have denounced the worldwide diffusion of a monoculture founded on a standardized array of practices and values promoted by large multinational companies. Based on this interpretation, marketing managers are responsible for a process of cultural homogenization: people everywhere are induced to demand the same goods and feed their imaginations with the same themes and symbols. To quote the pamphlet No Logo by the Canadian journalist Naomi Klein: 'The branded multinationals may talk diversity, but the visible result of their actions is an army of teen clones marching – in "uniform", as the marketers say – into the global mall. Despite the embrace of polyethnic imagery, market-driven globalization doesn't want diversity; quite the opposite. Its enemies are national habits, local brands and distinctive regional tastes.'

With this view then, marketing for transnational brands and products is the most eloquent expression of commercial universalism. It is alleged that not only does marketing flatten culture into worshipping commodities as well as producing excessive waste, but it is one of the principal causes of the erosion of national and local traditions.

However, since the 1980s, transnational marketing practices have been oriented towards strategies which exclude the extreme options of total standardization and total diversification. Different companies adopt different solutions. Moreover, according to different products and brands, they may choose both highly decentralized and highly centralized approaches within their organizations. The combination of a centralized common strategic marketing framework with local decisions and executions produces a wide range of solutions. 'Think global, act local' has become the motto for many companies that aspire to enlarge their market beyond national boundaries. Current transnational marketing practices are extremely diversified: one goes from the highly standardized orientation of perfume and cosmetic companies such as L'Oréal to the pattern-standardization strategies of many multinational food corporations, such as Nestlé, to the localized solutions of press and media publishers such as Condé Nast.

Today, while the different environments within which the marketing plan is implemented are not ignored, and the strategies and tactics adopted can be radically different, the overall principles of marketing are quite the same worldwide. From around 1960 onwards, the 'marketing management' school of thought has, in fact, created a uniform approach that has dominated marketing practice in the United States and in many other countries.

During the 1930s many behavioural scientists, among them the aforementioned Austrian, Ernest Dichter, moved from Europe to the US, introducing a more rigorous analysis of consumer needs and choices. This migration played an important role in the emergence of a new 'marketing era' characterized by a consumer-driven approach to production. Nonetheless, since the 1960s, the normative approach to marketing has been established by US academics and practitioners.

The main concepts of this approach, such as the sequence analysis/planning/control, the marketing mix and the '4Ps' (product, place, price, promotion) were formulated in 1967 by Philip Kotler in the handbook, Marketing Management. It was translated into 20 languages and is still the most widely used text in graduate schools of business throughout the world. Since the 1960s, national professional reviews, training periods in the United States, and workshops organized by national professional associations have encouraged the dissemination of the marketing management approach among European and Latin American businesses. An important role has been played by US and European multinational companies such as Procter & Gamble and Unilever in the rationalization of marketing activities among their different branches.

Since the end of the 1980s, as entire blocs of nations have moved toward market-based systems, there has been a still further spread of marketing management education and application. In Central and Eastern Europe the number of secondary-level schools offering marketing management courses has risen exponentially, and the MBA degree is now the largest single field of study for graduate programme applications in China.

Since the 1990s, the most significant sign of academic transnationalization in marketing has come less from educational programmes than from the remarkable increase in the number of international scholars who have enriched marketing knowledge with new theories, concepts and findings. Until the 1980s, the clear majority of contributors in marketing thought were US natives and were at work in US institutions. Today, the overall picture has changed substantially; internationally related scholars now constitute a majority of the total number of contributors in marketing literature. In the last decades, innovative theories and models have emerged in Europe within the fields of industrial and service marketing. The presumed universality of the conception of marketing as business management technology based on an economic rationale is being questioned by new paradigms. These paradigms consider marketing as a social process and propose to refound the discipline, giving more importance to the relationship of consumers as individuals and taking into account the social responsibilities of marketing operations.

Simona De Iulio

Bibliography

Douglas S. P. and Wind Y. 1987. 'The myth of globalization', *Columbia Journal of World Business*, 22, 19–29.

Levitt T. 1993. 'The globalization of markets', *Harvard Business Review*, 3, 91–102.

Related essays
advertising; auditing; consumer cooperation; consumer society; corporations; exile; Master of Business Administration (MBA); National Basketball Association (NBA); services; social sciences; trade; translation

Marriage

To use the word 'marriage' is to unleash a host of assumptions about a societal institution which exists in a wide variety of forms. The union of an adult man and woman is one, but polygynous unions, same-sex partnerships, and common law marriages offer other alternatives. The relationship between marriage and migration varies substantially.

Some individuals migrate in order to marry – marriage migration is one of the most common forms of mobility. Others migrate to avoid marriage, for example in cases where a potential spouse escapes an arranged marriage. Spouses sometimes migrate voluntarily to join their partners but at other times women are coerced. Some spouses use migration to end a marriage, through outright desertion or through lengthy separations that break the marital bond. Spouses may migrate to fulfil what they perceive to be marital duties, such as earning wages that will support the family, or providing household services and care.

Other individuals marry in order to migrate. Among the so-called 'picture brides' who went from Japan to North America at the turn of the 20th century were many progressive individuals who wanted a new life in a new location. At its extreme marriage migration includes those who participate in fraudulent marriages (sometimes for money) in order to evade immigration law.

Conversely, people may marry in order to avoid migration, a strategy favoured by young adults whose parents seek their participation (and wages) in a family migration endeavour. Migration can also transform an 'unmarriageable' person (e.g. an older widow with children) into a desired potential spouse in a new location. Some people seek better marriage opportunities through migration, a strategy that plays into the uneven sex ratios of migrant populations, for example. But then there are the individuals who find that marriage eludes them because of migration. The interplay of marriage and migration remains one that scholars of transnational circulations can plumb to much greater depths.

Economics and law
Marriage typically entails economic and political roles. Migration policies often try to regulate both of these functions, allowing entry to spouses but not workers, for example, meaning a 'dependent' immigrant could engage in unpaid domestic work or family business support, but not work for wages. Alternatively, a country may admit migrant workers, but forbid them to marry or to bring spouses. Both types of policies increased in the late 20th century as the scale of women migrating across borders for remunerative work increased. Even 150 years ago, however, there were many women migrating for employment opportunities, and married women weighed

the wage-earning and wage-saving economic roles they could fill if they joined spouses in new locations. In more recent times, as women have become the majority in some migrant streams, it is sometimes husbands who arrive as dependants. To become a key breadwinner due to migration often appears as a positive for either men or women, though to different degrees. Likewise, scholars often colour the shift to dependants negatively, particularly for men. These evaluations affect return rates, transnational linkages, and identity more generally.

When one spouse migrates to work for a period of time in another land, the remaining spouse may also become part of the migration circuit, sometimes changing economic roles by becoming more independent in supporting the household, or adopting new consumption patterns based on remittances. When transnational ties link many individuals in a particular place, these economic roles may shift for all. The meaning of dowries or other marriage exchanges may change. One might not need a dowry to wed in a new location because of the scarcity of potential spouses, or one might earn more and hence have a larger dowry and up the ante for those who did not migrate.

Nations articulate their ideals of inclusion and exclusion, often based on race or ethnicity as well as culture and sexuality, in policies about whether migrants may marry, reunify with spouses who live elsewhere, or recruit spouses, as well as in how they handle current citizens who marry those from other lands. Where marital regimes differ, states may judge some marriages but not others to be legitimate. Conflicts over arranged marriages in contrast to 'love matches' appear in many jurisdictions. This results in much closer scrutiny of certain marriages at the time of entry than may exist for others.

Marriages of people from different countries create transnational ties on various levels from the familial to the regional to the global. Policies of family reunification that go beyond spouses – bringing in parents, children, siblings, and other relatives – mean that individual marriages may have long-lived consequences for migration chains. Some scholars discuss these policies under the rubrics of dependent citizenship or marital citizenship.

In the past, liberal theories of political individualism rooted in the European Enlightenment clashed with patriarchal assumptions that citizenship followed the husband as head of the household, a clash that sometimes meant women became stateless upon marriage. This has been the target of different campaigns by voluntary organizations of women at the turn of the 21st century. Yet conversely, women in many cultures represent the nation, or carry the role of cultural conservators, and hence their migration receives more intensive scrutiny than that of men. Policies to protect women in transit from problems related to migration are commonly related to ideas about morality.

From the anti-White Slavery measures (that limited a woman's ability to join her betrothed in the US at the turn of the 20th century) to the requirement that Filipinas receive training in their rights before joining a prospective spouse overseas at the turn of the 21st century, states have sought to mitigate some of the automatic disadvantages that newcomers may face, but at the same time have supported a legal structure that has tended to place women in citizenship and visa categories of dependence.

Global connections and chronologies

Who would be an appropriate spouse? What roles do spouses play? These questions take on new meaning in a transnational context. It appears that the cartographies of desire shifted in the course of the late 20th century sufficiently for significant numbers of people, especially men from industrialized nations of the North, to have sought spouses from other parts of the world. Leaving aside cross-border marriage among the European aristocracies, there had been many marriages across borders in the century before, but most were between those of similar ethnic and regional origins – sending for or going back for a spouse. Ethnic endogamy, marriage to those of like group, remains strong. Foreign-bride sites on the Internet attest, however, to the demand for difference, or to a different perception of nationality by the late 20th century. Being male or female in a particular locale creates cultural capital on the virtual marriage market, much as it did in the many letters and classified ads which recruited spouses over a hundred years ago. In this exchange, notions of 'modern' and 'traditional' collide in interesting and occasionally tragic ways. Scholars disagree strongly on how to evaluate transnational images of gender roles.

In the 20th century, the military brought many young adults into contact across borders. Both World War 1 and World War 2 sparked relationships, some of which could become marriages with official recognition, and others which military authorities quashed, often based on racial prejudice. Shifting ideas of suitable spouses for European and North American men relate at least in part to the images of women created by such liaisons. Military wives, especially those from Asia and the Pacific, suffered from the assumed taint of sex work, meaning a long-term campaign to prove their respectability.

The changes that take place in cultural perceptions and cultural practices over time illustrate some of the effects migration brings to marital life. When migrants enter a culture that places emphasis on monogamy, or conversely on concubinage, they may shift perceptions of what spouses can and should do, of what masculinity and femininity within marriage means. The evaluation of married women leaving spouses and children behind to engage in paid work (especially housework and childcare) elsewhere typically has different connotations from the migration of married men for better job opportunities, either in the past or today. Those perceptions may result in legal or economic shifts and in new definitions of marriage that entwine on many levels in transnational space. Because scholarship on transnational marriage and migration remains limited it offers many opportunities for future research.

Suzanne Sinke

Bibliography

Bao J. 2005. *Marital acts: gender, sexuality, and identity among the Chinese Thai Diaspora*. Honolulu: University of Hawai'i Press.

Charsley K. and Shaw A. 2006. 'South Asian transnational marriages in comparative perspective', *Global Networks*, 6, 4, 331–44.

Constable N. 2003. *Romance on a global stage: pen pals, virtual ethnography, and 'mail order' marriages*. Berkeley: University of California Press.

Ehrenreich B. and Hochschild A. R. (eds) 2003. *Global woman*. New York: Metropolitan.

Reeder L. 2003. *Widows in white: Sicilian women and mass migration, 1880–1930*. Toronto: University of Toronto Press.

Sinke S. M. 'The International marriage market: theoretical and historical perspectives', in Hoerder D. and Nagler J. (eds) 1995. *People in transit*. Cambridge and New York: Cambridge University Press, 227–48.

Suzuki N. 'Filipina Modern: "Bad" Filipino women in Japan', in Miller L. and Bardsley J. (eds) 2005. *Bad girls of Japan*. Basingstoke and New York: Palgrave Macmillan, 158–210.

Yuh J. Y. 2002. *Beyond the shadows of Camptown: Korean military brides in America*. New York: New York University Press.

Related essays
diasporas; domestic service; forced migrations; gender and sex; guestworkers; honour; human mobility; international migration regimes; labour migrations; League of Nations system; love; remittances; war; White Slavery; women's movements

Marshall Plan

After World War 1, the United States shied away from formal political connections to Europe. Following World War 2, in contrast, the power vacuum caused by Germany's total defeat, combined with the perceived threat of Soviet expansionism, pulled the United States into a more permanent role in continental affairs.

In spring 1947, advisors to US President Harry Truman decided that rebuffing the Communist threat required stabilizing the Western European economy. Key European political and economic leaders, such as Ernest Bevin in Great Britain and France's Jean Monnet, had reached a similar conclusion. At Harvard University's 1947 commencement address, Secretary of State George C. Marshall announced the administration's response to the problem. US policy, according to Marshall, would be 'directed not against any country or doctrine but against hunger, poverty, desperation and chaos' – though the initiative would 'permit the emergence of political and social conditions in which free institutions can exist'. The Secretary of State also indicated that 'governments, political parties, or groups which seek to perpetuate human misery in order to profit therefrom politically or otherwise will encounter the opposition of the United States' (Marshall

1947). While the European Recovery Program theoretically offered aid to any European nation, it was, from its inception, a Cold War measure.

The Marshall Plan faced two major obstacles – one domestic, one international. Domestically, because it involved the power of the purse, the initiative required approval from Congress. Republicans had seized control of both houses in the 1946 elections, and GOP conservatives, along with a few like-minded Democrats, contended that the foreign aid package would subsidize European leftists and bankrupt the US Treasury. Senator George Malone spoke for the group in dismissing the measure as an 'amazingly brazen and preposterous scheme for a world-wide redistribution of wealth' that would allow the 'socialistic European governments' to undermine American capitalism. H. Alexander Smith marvelled at how his Republican colleagues 'cannot seem to realize that the type of socialism' existing in postwar Great Britain or Scandinavia 'is hardly even a distant cousin to Russian communism' (Johnson 2005, 22–4). In the event, Smith and more powerful, like-minded internationalist colleagues on the Foreign Relations Committee – chairman Arthur Vandenberg and World War 2 veteran Henry Cabot Lodge II – worked behind the scenes with the administration to shepherd the Bill to passage. Vandenberg, who also consulted with key French and British leaders as the Bill proceeded through Congress, suggested minor tweaks, such as slightly reducing the duration of the funding. These changes did not affect policy in any substantive way; and, with the fiction of congressional oversight preserved, both houses easily approved the aid. The vote set a precedent: two decades would pass before Congress seriously challenged executive control of policy toward Europe.

Internationally, the task confronting recipients of Marshall Plan assistance was enormous. The region needed to recover not only from World War 2 but also from the Depression and even the effects of World War 1. The Western European states targeted by the programme all faced inflationary pressure that threatened to radicalize the middle class. Popular demands existed throughout the region for an improved standard of living after the deprivations of the previous 15 years. Nationalist pressures threatened to disrupt intraregional trade, as had occurred

in the 1930s. And because of a dramatic decline in their foreign commerce, most European nations had large trade deficits with the United States. US economic assistance represented not a departure from but instead an affirmation of decisions already made. Key policy makers in the United States, Britain, and (to a lesser extent) France had already concluded that the region's future depended on more robust economic collaboration. As Jean Monnet explained during the war, the small size of European nations made it impossible to ensure economic and social prosperity.

All nations in the Soviet bloc ultimately declined the offer; so too did neutral Finland, which feared antagonizing its powerful neighbour. Because of its pro-Nazi sympathies during World War 2, Spain was not invited to participate in the programme. Around $13.2 billion in US aid thus went to Austria, Belgium, Denmark, France, Greece, Iceland, Ireland, Italy, Luxembourg, the Netherlands, Norway, Portugal, Sweden, Switzerland, Turkey, West Germany, and the United Kingdom. In the process, the Marshall Plan helped to create an institutionalized pattern of economic interdependence among the nations of Western Europe. While Western Europe's economy recovered impressively by the early 1950s, foreshadowing more than a decade of steady growth, historians have debated the Marshall Plan's economic impact, especially since US restrictions prevented most recipient governments from maximizing the aid's economic benefit. Western European nations benefited not simply from an infusion of outside assistance but also from increased intraregional cooperation. And Western Europe's export market particularly experienced a dramatic surge between 1946 and 1951. French exports, for instance, increased from US$850 million in 1946 to US$4.25 billion (in 1984 dollars) in 1951; the comparable figures for West Germany were US$280 million (1946) to US$3.5 billion (1951).

While the direct economic effect of the Marshall Plan is, therefore, debateable, its political impact is not. The aid effectively substituted for a formal peace settlement between the West and Germany, setting the stage for the reintegration of West Germany into Western Europe. Nearly US$1.4 billion in Marshall Plan funds went to Germans from the British, French, and American zones, where, as of early 1947, overall industrial production registered at just 24 per cent of the 1938 level. The subsequent German participation in the Marshall Plan provided another step in restoring German self-rule, with or without Soviet consent. From the perspective of Soviet leader Josef Stalin, the Marshall Plan and West Germany's political and economic rehabilitation signalled the capitalist powers' intent to encircle the Soviet Union. He responded by consolidating the Soviet sphere of influence, imposing Stalinist regimes on the remaining Eastern European states that had not come under full Communist control.

Hungary was the first nation to suffer. The postwar coalition government, headed by the Smallholders' Party, struggled to implement an economic reform package, its task hampered by a hyperinflationary collapse of the Hungarian currency. The Communists and their allies, meanwhile, presided over the cabinet ministries that controlled the police and the army. In 1947, Soviet officials falsely charged the Smallholders' secretary-general with plotting to overthrow the regime and orchestrated the party's removal from government. Shortly thereafter, Communist leader Mátyás Rákosi, a committed Stalinist, became the new prime minister. Using a law banning statements that could be interpreted as hostile to the democratic order or the country's international esteem, Rákosi's government denounced opposition politicians as 'anti-democratic', and then imprisoned, exiled, or killed them. By 1949, Hungary was a one-party state with a Soviet-style constitution. In Czechoslovakia, the coalition government of President Eduard Beneš, which was evenly divided between Communists and non-Communists, also maintained some flexibility in the months before Marshall's Harvard address. When the US offer of aid initially came, the Czech cabinet, including its Communist members, unanimously voted to accept. Stalin immediately summoned Beneš and Foreign Minister Jan Masaryk to Moscow. After he informed them that continued Soviet friendship depended on Czechoslovakia rejecting Marshall Plan aid, the cabinet reversed its decision; back in Prague, Masaryk famously said he had gone to Moscow as the minister of a free state and was returning as Stalin's slave. In a separate conversation, the Soviet leader ordered Klement Gottwald, head of the Czech Communist Party (KSČ), to prepare for a coup. With the KSČ's electoral support waning, Stalin abandoned hope that the Communists, the largest party in the 1946 elections, would assume power by popular vote. In February 1948, the KSČ executed its coup; several days later, Foreign Minister Masaryk was discovered dead, having fallen from his apartment window.

The division of Europe and the integration of West Germany into the West could very well have occurred without the Marshall Plan. But the initiative also set the stage for more ambitious economic structures that crossed national boundaries, such as the European Coal and Steel Community (ECSC), which established common industrial policies in France, Germany, Italy, and the Low Countries. Jean Monnet, who had previously served as deputy secretary-general of the League of Nations, gushed that the new organization, which was founded in 1951, gave the first impression of the Europe to come. Between 1953 and 1958, steel production in the six nations increased by 42 per cent; trade among the ECSC members soared. This performance, in turn, intensified the political and economic momentum toward even further economic integration, which culminated in creation of the EU and establishment of a common European currency.

Robert David Johnson

Bibliography

Johnson R. D. 2005. *Congress and the Cold War.* Cambridge and New York: Cambridge University Press.

Marshall G. C. 1947. 'Commencement address at Harvard University', 5 June [online]. Available: www.usaid. gov/multimedia/video/marshall/ marshallspeech.html, accessed 20 January 2008.

Milward A. 1984. *The reconstruction of Western Europe, 1945–51.* Berkeley: University of California Press.

Schain M. (ed.) 2001. *The Marshall Plan: fifty years after.* Basingstoke and New York: Palgrave Macmillan.

Related essays

Cold War; European institutions; European Union (EU); film; iron and steel; management; organization models; productivity missions; regional communities; technologies; trade; world orders

Master of Business Administration (MBA)

The Master of Business Administration (MBA) is probably today the postgraduate degree with the most global impact. The MBA is a 'licence to manage' and a label broadly recognized around the world.

The MBA emerged in the United States at the turn of the 20th century as a two-year postgraduate programme where students enrolled straight after three or four years of college. In the background, the corporate transformation of American business suggested that management should become a 'profession' and even a 'science'. The progress of the MBA in the United States before 1945 came together with the emergence of management consultancy and the birth of a business press. These developments reinforced each other and structured a field of professionalized management. In the 1950s, the MBA came to be harshly criticized; student bodies and curricula were of low quality and faculty members were not research-oriented. American business schools reacted, reaching for academic respectability. They built permanent faculties, fostered research and publication, created PhD programmes in business studies and strengthened curricula.

At the same time, the MBA became an object of exportation. A one-year MBA opened at INSEAD in Fontainebleau, France, in 1959; a two-year programme at the IESE in Barcelona in 1964 and in both cases the Harvard Business School was involved. Early versions of an MBA came to the London and Manchester Business Schools during the 1960s. This was, in fact, only the slow start of a global diffusion process that intensified from the 1980s onwards. Business schools and MBA programmes sprouted up everywhere in the world. In Europe alone, around 400 business schools opened in the late 1980s. There was resistance but education systems progressively transformed themselves to allow for local versions of the MBA – even Oxford and German universities were eventually converted!

The spread of MBA programmes does not seem perfectly coupled with transformations in corporate governance. The progress of market logics, multinational firms and foreign capital naturally all play a role. However, the spread of the MBA can be documented in countries with very different business systems. In Eastern Europe, the fall of the Berlin Wall marked the beginning of a rush. American universities and non-profit organizations worked with local universities to develop management training programmes – including MBAs. Financing came from large American foundations (Mellon or Ford). The European Union also jumped in, but to a lesser extent. And a few private donors realized major investments – the case of George Soros is worth mentioning here. The spread to Asia was also striking. By 2002, 62 Chinese universities had obtained from the state the right to deliver an MBA. Even in Africa, the forgotten continent of globalization, MBA programmes are flourishing today. From South Africa to Ethiopia, Zimbabwe, Egypt or the Gulf states, getting an MBA seems to be the way to go for local elites.

MBAs around the world still exhibit diversity although global diffusion comes together with powerful homogenizing pressures. Accreditation bodies such as the AACSB (American Association of Collegiate School of Business) play a role here. They have gone international and spread around their criteria, practices and processes. The ranking business that emerged in the 1980s around MBA programmes also has an impact while the predominant role of American academia in the development of management knowledge and texts has further reinforced standardization in curricula and contents. Language, finally, is important – MBA programmes around the world are partially if not fully in English. Recently, criticisms surfaced again, some echoing old debates: MBAs are too detached from practice, research is too academic, there are too many MBAs around and business schools share in the responsibility of recent business scandals. The MBA will have to adjust, possibly quite significantly, but altogether it is here to stay.

This, potentially, has important consequences. The global spread of the MBA carries with it a progressive homogenization, across the world, of models of economic elite production and reproduction. This homogenization is bound to be reflected at the helm of corporations – increasing the possibility of 'global corporations' at least at the managerial level. Even in developing countries, research seems to show that the spread of MBA programmes and graduates implies conformity across cultures to dominant (Western) leadership paradigms. The progress of the MBA is an expression but also a driver of current globalization – it is a category through which a transnational class of leaders is being produced and reproduced.

Marie-Laure Djelic

Bibliography

Daniel C. 1998. MBA: the first century. Lewisburg: Bucknell University Press.

Engwall L. and Zamagni V. (eds) 1998. Management education in historical perspective. Manchester: Manchester University Press.

McKenna C. 2006. The world's newest profession. Cambridge: Cambridge University Press.

Mellahi K. 2000. 'Western MBA education and effective leadership values in developing countries: a study of Asian, Arab and African MBA graduates', Journal of Transnational Management Development, 5, 2, 59–73.

Sklar M. 1988. The corporate reconstruction of American capitalism, 1890–1916. Cambridge: Cambridge University Press

Related essays

1989; advertising; class; corporations; higher education; language; management; marketing

Mathematics

Mathematics has evolved over its four millennia of recorded history as an area of abstract inquiry and as a language through which to understand and interpret nature.

As a language, in particular, it can be learned; its rules can be embraced and shared by those with sufficient fluency. As a lingua franca of nature, moreover, mathematics has the peculiar quality of being both grounded in and, to some extent, transcendent of time and place. Following the rise of the nation state in the 19th century – but even as early as the medieval period in European history, which witnessed the movement and development of mathematical knowledge from the Greco-Roman world through the medieval Islamic lands and back into the Latin West – this transcendence has facilitated the transportation of mathematical ideals and ideas across culturally and politically determined borders.

As the construct of the nation state began to result in a new geopolitical reality in the 19th century, emerging states increasingly embraced the cultural standards of those states with which they hoped to compete effectively. Relative to mathematics, the mid-century trendsetters were the German states and particularly Prussia, which, following the Napoleonic Wars, had enacted a series of educational reforms that had produced a strong university system geared not merely toward the imparting of received knowledge but toward both the production of new knowledge and the training of future researchers. In this new Prussian system, high-level teaching and research defined the university faculty's mission, and in mathematics, programmes developed around the notion of the graduate seminar at the universities in Königsberg and Berlin and later in Göttingen and elsewhere that produced stunning new mathematical results and brilliant young mathematical researchers. In the context of their shared research ethos, the members of this new generation of German mathematicians self-consciously created a mathematical profession through their support of a specialized society, the Deutsche Mathematiker-Vereinigung (founded in 1890), as well as of new research-level journals like the Mathematische Annalen (founded in 1869) for the effective communication of results.

Taken as a model, this had come to define individual, national mathematical research communities in settings as diverse as Japan, Spain, and the United States by the early decades of the 20th century. It made natural the transnational communication of mathematical research and the increasing conviction among mathematicians that personal and national reputation was established in an international arena. As early as the late 1860s, mathematical output was perceived as growing so quickly that a reviewing journal, the Jahrbuch über die Fortschritte der Mathematik, was founded to survey and report on the latest mathematical literature transnationally; beginning in 1898, publication of the Encyklopädie der mathematischen Wissenschaften further codified the state of the transnational mathematical research endeavour. Supplementary to these initiatives, new research-level journals such as the Swedish-based Acta Mathematica (1882 to the present) and the Rendiconti del Circolo matematico di Palermo (1887 to the present) were created explicitly as transnational publication venues aimed at uniting mathematicians in the different, then fast-evolving national mathematical communities. By 1897, the first International Congress of Mathematicians (ICM) had brought together some 208 mathematicians from 15 European countries as well as from the United States to Zürich, Switzerland to impart their mathematical insights not just in print but in person.

The second ICM three years later in Paris further underscored the transnational nature of mathematical research when the German mathematician, David Hilbert, challenged the world's mathematicians with 23 open problems intended meaningfully to shape a transnational mathematical research agenda in the opening decades of the 20th century. Hilbert's address – which produced deep results in the mathematical areas of foundations, algebraic number theory, geometry, and analysis – was echoed a hundred years later in 2000 when the Clay Mathematics Institute in Cambridge, Massachusetts announced its seven Millennium Prize Problems. As the latter two initiatives suggest, mathematicians, regardless of their mother tongue, have come to share both a mathematical language and an appreciation of what constitutes important research. That shared recognition further manifested itself, at least symbolically, in the establishment of the Fields Medal in recognition of the mathematical work judged 'the best' worldwide. Since the first Fields Medal presentations in 1936, some 48 mathematicians from China, Finland, France, Germany, Italy, Japan, New Zealand, Norway, the former Soviet Union, Sweden, the United Kingdom, and the United States have won the award.

Mathematics, however, has not been immune to the broader political forces at work internationally. Following the Paris ICM in 1900, three more ICMs were held at four-year intervals in Heidelberg, Rome, and Cambridge, England, respectively, but the ICM planned for 1916 in Stockholm was ultimately cancelled due to World War 1. After the war, political tensions continued to run so deep, especially between some French and German mathematicians, that the ICMs as well as attempts to establish a viable International Mathematical Union (IMU) were adversely affected. In 1920, the first postwar ICM was held in Strasbourg, a city wrested from France during the Franco–Prussian War and returned to French control only following World War 1. However, mathematicians from the former Central Powers were barred both from attending the meeting and from membership in the IMU after its founding in 1920,

despite the strong conviction on the part of mathematicians from the United States, the United Kingdom, and elsewhere that political hatchets should be buried in the postwar era. This exclusionary policy also cast a political shadow over the ICMs held in Toronto in 1924 and in Bologna in 1928, although the IMU had officially lifted the membership restrictions in 1926 – as Germany joined the League of Nations. By 1932 and the occasion of the second Zürich ICM, the IMU had ceased to exist largely as a consequence of international politics.

Transnational communication and cooperation among individual mathematicians continued without this more formalized manifestation of their internationalization. For example, as early as 1909 and following the establishment of Boxer Indemnity Scholarships, Chinese students pursued advanced mathematics at major universities in the United States and returned to China both to continue their own mathematical research and to establish mathematical centres on the Western model. After the founding in Princeton in 1930 of the Institute for Advanced Study, moreover, Chinese mathematicians joined mathematicians from the United States, Europe, and elsewhere in this unique setting for the promotion of original research. Transnational cooperation and influence were also evident in the late 1920s and 1930s in the support of mathematical research institutes in both Paris and Göttingen by the Rockefeller Foundation's International Educational Board. Although located in France and Germany, respectively, these institutes were to serve as magnets to attract mathematicians, regardless of nationality, who were interested in and capable of pursuing cutting-edge research.

The rise of National Socialism in Germany and the strengthening of Japanese imperial impulses in the 1930s, however, resulted in the outbreak of World War 2 in both the European and the Pacific theatres as well as in the severing of many transnational lines of communication. For example, the reviewing journal, *Zentralblatt für Mathematik*, which had been founded in 1931 by Otto Neugebauer and edited by him until 1938, suffered a severe blow when Nazi policies resulted in the resignation of almost the entire editorial board. The war, however, also prompted the transnational migration especially of Jewish mathematicians to England, South

America, Turkey, the United States, and elsewhere. The influx of these mathematicians into new national venues both boosted and expanded mathematical activity in the new host nations.

Following the close of the war in 1945, efforts were soon mounted afresh to re-establish a formal international structure for the mathematical community. The new IMU, which emerged in the early 1950s, had by the early 1960s assumed leadership in coordinating both the selection of Fields medallists and the organization of the ICMs, two of the most visible symbols of the transnational nature of the present-day mathematical endeavour. The IMU has also proved instrumental in promoting transnational exchange and interaction through its sponsorship, beginning in 1953, of symposia in different national venues on specialized mathematical topics and through its maintenance of a *World directory of mathematicians* (first published in 1958).

Since the 1960s, the transnational structures and impulses – as outlined above and which developed beginning in the 19th century – have continued to strengthen. Collaborations of two and sometimes more mathematicians from two and sometimes more countries are now commonplace as a glance at reviewing journals like *Zentrallblatt* or the *Mathematical Reviews* (founded in 1940) reveals. Mathematical meetings, even meetings of national mathematical societies, are, in fact, international affairs that routinely draw significant numbers of participants from abroad. Research journals, regardless of where they are home-based, call on transnational bodies of referees to judge papers submitted by mathematicians from around the world. As a body of knowledge and as a language of science, mathematics largely transcends national boundaries, even though international politics may affect the social structures characteristic of its professionalization.

Karen Hunger Parshall

Bibliography

Lehto O. 1998. *Mathematics without borders: a history of the International Mathematical Union.* New York: Springer.

Parshall K. H. and Rice A. C. (eds) 2002. *Mathematics unbound: the evolution of an international mathematical research community, 1800–1945.* Providence: American Mathematical Society; London: London Mathematical Society.

Siegmund-Schultze R. 2001. *Rockefeller and the internationalization of mathematics between the world wars.* Basel: Birkhäuser.

Related essays

economics; exile; fellowships and grants; higher education; historians and the nation state; history; international migration regimes; international students; knowledge; life and physical sciences; philanthropic foundations; psychoanalysis; prizes; social sciences; war

McDonald's

McDonald's, the world's largest fast-food chain, with over 30,000 restaurants in 118 countries by 2007, has become a lightning rod for debates about globalization and cultural homogenization. Critics have used McDonald's as a metaphor for the global spread of American cultural and economic power since the Second World War. Others have regarded the rise of McDonald's as a manifestation of economic modernization.

Founded by two brothers in suburban Los Angeles in 1937, McDonald's began its national expansion in the 1950s under the management and later ownership of Ray Kroc. By the 1960s McDonald's restaurants could be found on the outskirts of most metropolitan areas in the United States. The first restaurants outside the US opened in Canada and Puerto Rico in 1967, followed by the first European franchise in the Netherlands in 1969.

The global impact of McDonald's has been twofold. First it served as a model for post-industrial business culture. Ray Kroc did not invent the concept of a fast-food restaurant, nor did he invent the concept of rationalization. Yet he expanded the principles of rationalization from the primary and secondary sector of the economy to the service sector. McDonald's thus represents the culmination of rationalization, first identified by Max Weber and applied to industrial production by Henry Ford and Frederick Winslow Taylor in the early 20th century. Ford's invention of the assembly line revolutionized industrial production. Taylor, in turn, advocated the optimization of worker productivity through the scientific analysis of the mechanics of a worker's every move on the job. McDonaldization, as George Ritzer has termed it, emerged out of Fordism and Taylorism by applying these principles not only to the food business, but also to areas as diverse as retailing, education, childcare, healthcare, travel, and leisure. The essential elements of McDonaldization, according to Ritzer, are efficiency, calculability (the emphasis on quantifiable aspects of products sold), predictability (service and product are the same everywhere), and control through technology.

Secondly, McDonald's has become a symbol for the globalization of consumer culture. Hamburgers and French fries are now available in most parts of the world and international travellers do not have to adjust their palates to the local flavours of exotic places. However, according to some observers McDonald's sold more than food. It sold a way of life associated with America; it sells cosmopolitanism; yet, as some critics charged, it also sold a homogenized and deterritorialized global culture that was devoid of any local identity. These critics adopted Max Weber's view that rationalization restricts the importance of charisma and of individually differentiated conduct. For that reason McDonald's became a frequent target for anti-globalization and anti-American protests in the late 1990s and early 2000s. Protesters associated the presence of McDonald's in their neighborhoods with the negative domestic economic and social consequences of modernization. They feared the destruction of local entrepreneurship and community structures in the face of powerful international corporations.

Yet its association with modernization also served as McDonald's biggest asset. In Asia, for instance, customers frequently cited exemplary sanitary standards, the predictability of food choices and quality, and the professional courtesy of the staff as major benefits of the restaurant chain. These customers associated eating at McDonald's with American culture, yet researchers found little indication that the presence of these restaurants undermined indigenous cultures. Instead, they found that McDonald's engaged in a process of localization and hybridization. Franchises adapted to local culinary and service preferences, while communities in turn emulated some of McDonald's innovations in other settings.

McDonald's has become the foremost emblem of the fusion between business and cultural globalization. Its American origins have also fostered a sense in the world that globalization is intimately connected to or even synonymous with Americanization. At the same time anthropologists and sociologists have seen in the worldwide proliferation of McDonald's the resilience and adaptability of local cultures to global change.

Petra Goedde

Bibliography
Ritzer G. 2004. *The McDonaldization of society*. Revised edition. London: Pine Forge.
Schlosser E. 2002. *Fast food nation: the dark side of the all-American meal*. New York: Harper Perennial.
Watson J. (ed.) 1997. *Golden arches East: McDonald's in East Asia*. Stanford: Stanford University Press.

Related essays
assembly line; Coca-Cola; comics; consumer society; diet and nutrition; fast food; food; jeans; organization models; Pax Americana; Westernization

Measurement

Pick up a ruler, any ruler, and ponder how those lines came to be where they are or, similarly, how the temperature scale on a thermometer came into being. If you start questioning the credibility of those lines, an array of practices dependent upon such scales also comes into question. If you then decide to trace the history of its particular evolution the ground gets even shakier, and a long chain of social negotiation, national rivalries and frequently arbitrary decisions appear.

We live in a world dominated and sculpted by measurement systems. From the moment you go to work by a form of transport to the time you turn off the lights at night, an assortment of activities functioning and defined by forms of measurement have been used (and taken for granted). Such systems require agreement and uniformity including, for example, 'time' itself, filling your car with fuel, the dimension of your shoes, units of energy, the size of a loaf of bread, the Indian rupees or Argentinean pesos in your pocket, and the weight of a packet of pasta.

All measurement systems depend upon standards and the scientific enterprise pursued to create them is termed 'metrology'. To have a standard requires a quantitative embodiment of some parameter – a unit by which that standard is to be measured, and a value that is the numerical quantity of the unit. To illustrate this consider the following example. The standard of electrical resistance is the length of wire, and the unit that measures this standard is the ohm, which has the dimensions of a velocity. Consequently the value of the ohm is a certain proportion of the speed of light.

Creating measurement systems

Modern systems of measurements cross the boundaries of countries and cultures. This transnational element is, historically speaking, a recent phenomenon, with past systems characterized by a multitude of units used both within a country and across the globe. As we shall see, an array of factors has driven the universalization of measurement systems over the last two centuries. Frequently, the establishment of measurement systems has required standards that appear neutral and devoid of social interests. To found such seeming objectivity often disguises the historical work that has gone into their creation and the interests that were involved in their production – from commerce and imperialism to nationalism, revenue collection, consumption and industry.

Measurement systems demand agreement. But this obvious statement is highly problematic. Who has the authority to define such systems? What is the rationale for their basis? How do you reproduce such measures through time and space?

Once agreement has been established the system becomes 'black-boxed' and all the arguments, negotiation, labour, hardware and interests that have gone into its creation disappear. However, the work does not stop there – the system of measurement needs to be sustained by an intricate network of instruments, institutions and policing. Consider the work and money that needs to be done just to maintain 'time' – based upon the rotation of the earth's axis – a journey that isn't quite 24 hours. With the formalization of global time zones and national standard bureaus armed with expensive atomic clocks, such agreement can be maintained. But, then, what is an atomic clock? This costly device, which keeps better time than the rotation of the earth (the fundamental standard of time), is based upon the oscillation in an atom between its nucleus and the surrounding electrons. Thanks to this contrivance, global

time and everything that relies upon it, for example the Internet, remains synchronized.

Over the last three or so decades historians and sociologists have revealed that the creation and circulation of measurement systems takes a great deal of luck, arbitrary decisions, institutional backing, recognizable expert authority, national rivalries and money.

It has been argued, amongst others, that forms of measurement have been conceived to enforce authority in the workplace, to deflect weakness from unpopular bureaucracies, to secure and ease the flow of commerce, and improve the efficiency and seeming equitability of tax collection. Historically the evolution of public and increasingly international measures has been seen as legitimated by an enlightened quantifying spirit. Beginning with the standardization of metrology (weights and measures) and progressing into the 19th century, an array of measurement systems born from an ever increasing division of specialist sciences, technological contrivances and products of commerce has globally penetrated national boundaries.

To reiterate: the emergence of global forms of measurement is a relatively recent phenomenon. In the West there was an array of competing systems of weights and measures until the 19th century and even into the 20th century. The situation was just as varied within national boundaries – with the measurement and weighing of goods predominantly defined locally. Indeed the state of affairs was such that some regions literally had hundreds of variations. Within this context the work of the Polish historian of metrology, Witold Kula, is particularly useful. Kula has demonstrated that prior to the establishment of the metric system in Europe, concrete concepts such as the finger, foot and ell (elbow) were in everyday use. They had no abstract, standardized denomination, and accounting for the weight or measure of a commodity was a qualitative process that varied from region to region (and indeed within regions). It was a process suited to small communities and local markets. Consequently, making measures accountable to a centralized source of social authority was extremely difficult.

Gradually these predominantly anthropomorphic measures were replaced by abstract public measures. Standardized measurement came also to be seen during the course of the 18th century and especially the 19th century as part of a process moving towards precision. A system of measurement requires trust. Over the last two centuries, precision has become central to this trust, which in turn has bred a flock of experts to ensure such objectivity. The 'precision' of measurement systems has not only been pursued as a foundation for objectivity, but also as a moral value.

The requirements of increased trade and the fiscal demands of the ruling authority fuelled the march toward a regular form of metrology. As we have noted, measures originally gained their meaning (and practice of gauging) from the local understanding of the object being assized. However, the proper functioning of an emerging integrated national market required a reduction in the diversity of weights, measures and containers. In short, with the increasing spread of trade such urgency took on a national and then global dimension.

Historically there are much earlier non-European examples of kingdoms and dynasties attempting to standardize their own weights and measures. For instance, the Qin Dynasty, after unifying China around about 221 BC, attempted to standardize the region's weights and measures, while in South Asia (what we now know as India) during the reign of Chandragupta Maurya (320–293 BC) there was an attempt to enforce a well-defined and regularized system of weights and measures. However, the move toward a global system arrived much later and emanated from Europe.

One impetus towards standardizing weights and measures came from the fiscal demands of the ruling authority. A uniform system of taxation meant accounting for foreign and domestic customary variations in weights, measures and containers. Not surprisingly this could be a tiresome, complicated and time-consuming process. As a result of this, and of course of rapidly expanding trade, the diversity of metrological practices, containers and packaging came increasingly under pressure to simplify.

Attempts to reform measurement systems, however, were met with a great deal of local hostility. In all these instances measurement, as such, was not the primary issue; rather, it was the fact it was a royal, dynastic or state-defined version, increasingly alienated from the object being gauged, and being implemented over local versions that really rattled dispersed communities. Everyday folk may have been suspicious of state or crown approaches to quantification but they themselves lived by their own version, dominated by a local notion of the 'just measure'. To have national (let alone international) standardized abstract measures requires a legitimating form of knowledge, the agencies to enforce it, and a process of regional education. The interesting issue is not diversity in measurement, but rather when diversity was seen to be a problem.

Legislating for a system of regularized weights and measures was one thing, but making containers to strict specifications – i.e. all the same – was another. The technology, skills and sheer cost in manufacturing standardized casks (or packaging in general) were simply not available prior to the 19th century. This problem haunted all 18th-century attempts at imposing accurate measures like, for example, that of the bushel in Britain. How could a village turner or cooper correctly calculate and build an accurate representative of a bushel? What materials should be used and what should the relation be between circumference and outer body? How could the vessel be made to avoid tampering and how should the grain be poured into the vessel?

Local communities were used to and happy with their own measures, which raises a paradox. To appear fair the measurement system involved in production, trade, consumption and taxation should be universally used and governed by a set of standards equitably applied. However, to impose such measures required illiberal methods that often trampled on the rights and practices of local communities.

Accompanying the growth of European power and the expansion of the region's reach, combined with increased commerce and expanding markets during the second half of the 18th century, weights and measures were increasingly made accountable to an abstract standard separated from people's everyday lives and work. This argument is neatly summarized by Theodore Porter: 'Informal measurement was inseparable from the fabric of these relatively autonomous communities. It broke down with the intrusion of more centralised forms of power – both political and economic – with the relatively private domain of communal life' (Porter 1995, p. 223). The people that most frequently suffered from metrological standardization were those excluded from wealth and some form of institutional power. The uncertainty of measures often aided those in positions of weakness while the standardization of measures tended to aid traders, manufacturers and the ruling authority. Greater regularization and centralization were accompanied by increased abstraction – the antithesis to localism and diversity. To legitimate this abstraction and make it appear real required an accompanying form of reason that appealed to a notion of objectivity (and equity).

The metric example

Today, partly as a result of commercial globalization and growth in science, over 95 per cent of the world uses the metric system. The only countries that remain outside the system are the United States of America, Liberia and Burma. The current metric form was formalized at the General Conference on Weights and Measures in 1960 and is known as the International System of Units (SI, from the French *Système International*). The base units of this system are the metre (length), kilogram (mass), second (time), ampere (electrical current), Kelvin (thermodynamic temperature), mole (amount of substance) and candela (luminous intensity).

The colonization of the metric system really accelerated from 1850 when it started to become absorbed throughout much of Europe, Latin America and elsewhere. In 1875 most of the world's industrial countries (apart from Britain) signed the Treaty of the Meter. This created an International Bureau of Weights and Measures that still manages and monitors the SI. The body periodically puts out an official SI brochure and publishes an established academic journal entitled *Metrologia*. As well as distributing copies of the system throughout the world, it also revises it when new technology invites an improvement in the precision of the units. The establishment of this classification and coordination took years of conflict and negotiation. An endeavour to introduce standardized global measures of electrical current was also pursued in the 19th century. In 1861 at the first International Electrical Congress in Paris scientists and industrialists worked to agree upon a system. It was not till 1904, however, that a permanent institution – the International Electrotechnical Commission

(IEC) – was set up to monitor and regulate such measures.

The story of the metric system, in particular, sheds light upon the clash of two of the 19th century's leading world powers, namely, France and Britain. Measurement systems took on an added contentious meaning within a competing context of commercial, imperial, scientific and military conflict. The British Imperial and French metric systems were both fuelled by an 18th-century drive to radically reduce the huge diversity of weights and measures both within their own boundaries and, increasingly, the world.

What, then, is the foundation of the first truly transnational form of measurement? The basis of the metric system was the Earth or, more precisely, one ten-millionth of the distance from the Equator to the North Pole. The work to find this unit was conducted by two French astronomers, Jean-Baptiste-Joseph Delambre and Pierre-François-André Méchain, and took seven years, beginning in 1792. Using a one-second pendulum, measurements were taken between Dunkerque, at the northern tip of France, and Barcelona in Spain. It was hoped this rational and seemingly neutral basis would at a moment crush the estimated 250,000 different units of weights and measures in France. 'This diversity', writes Ken Alder, 'obstructed communication and commerce, and hindered the rational administration of the state' (Alder 2002, pp. 2–3).

This effort arose from a 'rational' attempt to smash the French Old Regime's political economy and provide a more precise, simple and efficient tool to ease the flow of commerce and everyday exchange. The new system was an endeavour to base weights and measures upon a natural standard, which was part of a wider revolutionary movement to create social laws as solid and equitable as laws of nature. This is an aim that has been quite common in the history of metrology – from passages in the Bible to the French Revolution and beyond, we find sermons on standards of measurement being one of the principal foundations of justice. To achieve this perception of equity based on a natural unalterable standard requires all the labour and social elements of compromise and negotiation to be erased.

Even in France it was not till the mid-19th century that the metric system was permanently and legally established after years of hostile opposition and compromise using alternative systems. French revolutionary authority seriously underestimated the disruption that trying to establish its new measurement system would have on everyday lives.

Certainly the adverse impact it had in France intensified opposition in Britain to the French abstract measurement system. But this does not mean that there was not a push for greater uniformity across the Channel. In 1742 an anonymous Gentleman of the Royal Society was struck by the diversity of supposed standard weights and measures kept in the various London locations, which were meant to hold the original authoritative ones. A few years later Lord Crayford's Select Committee report on Weights and Measures was published (1758) – followed by a second report the following year. Its contents centred upon the inadequacy of current legislation and the weak process of enforcement. Although attempts were made to act on the committee's resolutions, the Bills that were subsequently introduced were so late in the session that they failed.

One problem militating against the standardization and enforcement of weights and measures was the vast array of legislation that allowed exemptions. The locally informed and therefore haphazard nature of legislation till this point was thwarting what the Crayford Committee termed 'the Principles of Uniformity'. The committee concluded, 'in order effectually to ascertain and enforce uniform and certain Standards of Weight and Measures to be used for the future, that all the Statutes relating thereto should be reduced into one Act of Parliament; and all the said Statutes now in being, subsequent to the Great Charter, repealed'. But it was precisely because communities were so devoted to local measures that Members of Parliament couldn't agree on authorizing a system that overturned such a highly charged context. This was a problem amplified across the globe.

In Britain the work of the Crayford Committee and numerous early 19th-century attempts finally culminated in the Imperial system of weights and measures in 1824. The new metrology was aimed at reaching a balance between scientific objectives, practical requirements and commercial reception – an aim neatly captured by the term 'practical objectivity'. The implementation of French-style abstraction to overcome localism and diversity was considered too dangerous to be made the evangelical basis of a new British and Imperial metrology. It had to be consistent, recognizable, and simple in the sense of being easily understood and enforceable. Exactness was a negotiation of all these boundaries. Unlike the French metric system, which was now perceived in Britain as having been an expensive failure and commercial disaster, the 1824 solution was a pragmatic compromise. The customary practices and use of old measures were considered far too deeply ingrained to be simply replaced at a stroke – as had been demonstrated by the disastrous French experience. As the precision instrument maker, Jessie Ramsden, had observed in 1792 while investigating the standard for proof spirit: 'To retain the present value of Proof, will, no doubt, have many advantages: it will prevent that confusion which always happens in commerce, when any change of value, or denomination, of merchandise takes place.' The new Imperial weights and measures took the most widespread and everyday consistent standards in use, and simplified them into a coherent system. The key imperative of the Act was to ensure as little disruption to the commercial environment as possible.

By the Victorian period hostility to the French system had become ever more closely linked to nationalism, with a stout defence of the British Imperial system based on 'pyramidology'. The House of Commons Select Committee of 1862 on the subject of measurement unanimously recommended the adoption of the metric system, which, in turn triggered a hostile reaction. During the 1860s British scientists conducted a survey of ancient Egyptian monuments to reveal the basis of God's units of length and mass. Their findings, especially those of the respected astronomer Piazzi Smith, were used to validate the British system – as if the yard had some divine origin traceable to ancient monuments.

British imperialism also had a transnational impact with the yard, foot and pound still currently the official units in the United States. By contrast, after many apocalyptic predictions, Britain went partly metric in 1971, moving to decimal currency. However, although most manufacturing in Britain today is in metric and though children learn this measurement system at school, the country has still not totally converted to the system: opposition to it is still prevalent, particularly among the anti-EU and anti-euro constituency. Switching to a new measurement system is costly and complicated. The disruption to United States domestic commerce, for example, has been deemed too problematic to merit change. Meanwhile, in much of Europe the switch to a single currency has had a disruptive impact, generating much anti-European sentiment.

In conclusion, measurement systems make the external world understandable and stable. They are held together by a sequence of historical decision making, and a string of transnational institutions, instrumentation, money and enculturation. Consider more closely the role of instruments. To export measurements across time and place requires trustworthy instruments uniformly calibrated – from, say, a simple ruler, thermometer, barometer, and hydrometer to the atomic clock we looked at earlier or a device for measuring car emissions. Alexandre Mallard captures many of the issues when he writes, 'metrological principles are immersed in a legal universe; manufacturers are controlled; markets are organized for the instruments as well as for the standards; administrative intervention is submitted to regular procedural schemes of action; users are inventoried and periodically visited; and inspectors are taught the virtues of precision and conformity' (Mallard 1998, p. 577).

Today the level of metrological robustness is a product of how well the measurement system is inscribed within instrumentation and the extent of the latter's diffusion. For example, a multitude of devices are used in the market to facilitate transnational exchange, while much of the scientific body of knowledge is held together by measuring instruments calibrated to the internationally accepted form of measurement. In turn, as we have seen, this requires a chain of worldwide institutions used to police and ensure the stability of such systems. Once general agreement has been institutionalized and taken for granted, such measurement systems allow both goods and 'knowledge' to be transported across nations, cultures, mountains and oceans. When one

buys a TV, a prefabricated panel or a jet fighter, measurement systems of all sorts come with them. Joseph O'Connell nicely captured this idea when he wrote about the military equipment that the US Navy sold to Kuwait in the early 1990s. 'By the spring of 1990, Kuwait had purchased not only the airplanes from the US Navy, but also the volt and a host of dimensional, time interval, and other standards as well. The airplanes were simply the most visible components of the whole package' (O'Connell 1993, p. 164).

William J. Ashworth

Bibliography

Alder K. 'A revolution to measure: the political economy of the metric system in France', in Wise M. N. (ed.) 1997. *Values of precision*, Princeton: Princeton University Press, 39–71.

Ashworth W. J. 2003. *Customs and Excise: trade, production and consumption in England 1640–1845*. Oxford, Oxford University Press.

Kula W. 1986. *Measures and men*, trans. Szreter R. Princeton: Princeton University Press.

Latour B. 1987. *Science in action: how to follow scientists and engineers through society*. Cambridge, MA: Harvard University Press.

Mallard A. 1998. 'Compare, standardize and settle agreement: on some usual metrological problems', *Social Studies of Science*, 28, 4, 571–601.

O'Connell J. 1993. 'Metrology: the creation of universality by the circulation of particulars', *Social Studies of Science*, 23, 1, 129–73.

Porter T. 1995. *Trust in numbers: the pursuit of objectivity in science and public life*. Princeton: Princeton University Press.

Schaffer S. 'Metrology: metrication and Victorian values', in Lightman B. (ed.) 1997. *Victorian science in context*, Chicago: Chicago University Press, 438–74.

Related essays

car safety standards; empires and imperialism; food safety standards; information technology (IT) standardization; nation and state; prizes; scientific expeditions; scientific instruments and tools; spatial regimes; taxation; technical standardization; trade; traffic signals; transportation infrastructures

Médecins Sans Frontières (MSF)

Médecins Sans Frontières (MSF or Doctors Without Borders) is the leading independent humanitarian agency supplying emergency medical services to conflict and natural disaster zones and combating epidemic disease in developing countries, with a budget of €460 million in 2004. Conspicuously French in its origins, it expanded to become genuinely international, and in 1999 it was awarded the Nobel Peace Prize.

MSF was founded in 1971 in the aftermath of the Nigerian Civil War, during which Bernard Kouchner and some other young French doctors became dissatisfied with the reticent approach of the International Committee of the Red Cross in protecting secessionist Biafra from what they saw as attempted genocide. Ever since, MSF has set itself the complementary task of *témoignage*, bearing witness to inhumane behaviour, and in its earlier years it was seen as an *enfant terrible* among aid agencies. MSF was originally conceived as providing a pool of expatriate doctors on short contracts to assist established agencies. It gradually became more professional and engaged publicity experts, and in 1987 it was nominated as a 'major national cause' in France. Meanwhile in 1979, a typically Parisian schism arose when Kouchner and some associates, unable to persuade their MSF colleagues that a hospital ship should be sent to the China Sea to pick up Vietnamese refugees (then known as Boat People), split off to found a rival organization, Médecins du Monde, which also went on to develop an international presence.

Whether or not the founders of MSF were subliminally influenced by the name of the long-running television stunt-game Jeux Sans Frontières, founded six years earlier, the word *sans-frontiérisme* crept into the French language and has since inspired other professions. However, when new MSF sections were founded in the early 1980s, these were initially seen as extensions of the French mother organization. Divergences of policy and ideology soon arose, and in 1985 MSF-France unsuccessfully sued MSF-Belgium to try to stop it using the MSF trademark and logo. A more pacified expansion began in the early 1990s.

In 2006, MSF-International consisted of 19 sections, of which five – those of Belgium, France, Holland, Spain and Switzerland – were operational centres. Its coordination office was in Geneva. Unlike most European NGOs, which have tended to follow the geographical circuits of the colonial past, MSF has consciously deviated from these: the Australian section, for instance, was an offshoot of MSF-France, and the British section grew out of the more reserved MSF-Holland.

MSF has sought, through minimizing any dependence on institutional funding, to entrench its fierce independence of spirit, and its determination not to be coopted by government interests. In 1985, MSF-France was the only international agency to leave Ethiopia in the course of disagreement with government policies such as forced resettlement. After the 2003 Indian Ocean tsunami, MSF decided to put a limit on raising funds earmarked for its relief as it felt unable to spend them constructively – a principled decision but not popular with all other aid agencies. In 2006 after the victory of Hamas in the Palestinian election, MSF spoke out against the 'hypocritical' proposal that governmental aid for Palestine should be diverted through UN agencies and NGOs.

In the early years, MSF seemed like a gadfly on the back of the Red Cross, but it inherited the Dunantist values of non-confessionalism, impartiality and neutrality, and a mutual respect grew between the two movements. MSF has been medically innovative, for instance in developing diagnostic tools and clinical services in very poor areas. Critical of the wider humanitarian scene and somewhat aloof from all NGO consortia, MSF has also been rigorously self-critical and has avoided becoming an ossified bureaucracy. In a policy review process conducted in 2005–06, it debated the balances to be struck between emergency medicine and a public health mission linked to *témoignage*; between an overarching global identity and the principle of 'subsidiarity'; and between traditional volunteering and local capacity building. The importance of an organization combining effective action on the ground with a willingness to speak out in the international arena was not in doubt.

Jonathan Benthall

Bibliography

Benthall J. 1993. *Disasters, relief and the media.* London: IB Tauris, 124–39.

Vallaeys A. 2004. *Médecins Sans Frontières: la biographie.* Paris: Fayard.

Weissman F. (ed). 2004. *In the shadow of just wars: violence, politics and humanitarian action*. London: Hurst.

Related essays

developmental assistance; health policy; human rights; intergovernmental organizations; international non-governmental organizations (INGOs); International Red Cross and Red Crescent movement; medicine; natural hazards; refugee relief; relief; war

Medicine

Medicine has historically been a central concern in societies across the globe. Issues of life, good health and death have affected individuals and human communities on a consistent basis, causing them to strive for healthiness, to prolong life and to delay death. Medicine, widely defined, has had an important place in all such calculations and has, therefore, been an imbedded feature of societal workings and negotiations.

We should here avoid a simplistic definition of medicine. It was by no means merely representative of a specific set of practices and cures, associated with what is often referred to as scientific medicine, mainstream biomedicine or allopathy. Instead, it accommodated a range of other healing traditions, providing access to an array of pharmacology-, herb-, mineral-, animal- and faith-based products; indeed, items sanctified through religious ceremonies were – and continue to be – accepted as being important medicinal objects in several societies across the world.

The supply of medicine, which is best defined as a product or service that was intended to improve health and retain healthiness, involved several providers. While there can be little doubt that the expansion of state-sponsored health services developed hand in hand with efforts at expanding and consolidating political power (as in European colonial possessions in the 19th century), it would be foolhardy to assume that government agencies monopolized the production and dissemination of medical knowledge (this generalization about the frequently circumvented powers of the state can be said to be true of all administrative and geographical contexts). If anything, the state-sponsored health services had to compete with a dynamic, multifaceted medical marketplace, which was extremely difficult to regulate at the best of times. Patients and their families, the paying customers who kept the marketplace ticking over as they searched for cures for all sorts of ailments, played an active role in shaping the nature and intensity of supply. It is important to remember that patients could pick and choose from a range of available remedies, services and practitioners, and it was (and is) not unknown for more than one medicinal product to be used at any point in time. All these trends suggest that the picture on the ground was very complex, involving many more actors in the dissemination of medicinal regimes than some state-centric historical accounts have assumed.

Viewed from this perspective, a truly transnational history of medicine has to be viewed from multiple perspectives. At one level, we have to acknowledge that most nation-oriented and state-centric histories – a genre which has tended to predominate in studies dealing with almost every region of the globe – tend to simplistically assume that a relatively small number of people, based usually in the capitals of different nation states, were able to design policies and then implement them (sometimes with the use of force, but often through public relations exercises). Such histories tend to ignore regional variations in medical provision and the attitudes of the public towards the health delivery systems available in specific localities. In fact, these historiographical trends have caused the importance of the medical marketplace to be downplayed, if not completely ignored, in many geographical and temporal contexts – private practitioners, in such analyses, have generally been presented as hand-maidens of those in charge of running the supposedly unified levers of the state.

An important corrective to all these trends has been provided in the works of social history of medicine, which study a society's complex attitudes towards an integral part of day-to-day living in great detail. While historians like Roy Porter have shown us how unhappiness with state-sponsored medical services generally led patients to investigate and use the alternatives provided by private practitioners, scholars like Harold Cook have described how, contrary to standard historical understandings of nation-oriented therapeutic regimes, this was often achieved by crossing national borders (the thriving Dutch trade with the East Indies was, for example, a direct consequence of the great demand for exotic medical products, many of which commanded princely prices across the markets of Europe).

Such scholarship also forces us to recognize the important point that the medical marketplace was always based on an eclectic group of private practitioners, who, in turn, remained dependent on a thriving market for medicinal raw materials and medical instruments. This trade was deeply transnational in nature, both before and after the consolidation of European colonialism in Asia, Africa and the Americas. It is for example instructive to remember that the European East India Companies were generally unwilling to let national borders and claims of territoriality made by local potentates affect their extremely profitable trading business in medicinal products. This was business conducted with an understanding of the porous nature of borders and the possibility of buying over powerful political allies; such trade in the 17th, 18th and 19th centuries was diverse and rich, surprisingly unrestrained by the nationalistic impulses that led to the clearer demarcation of borders of colonial possessions in the second half of the 19th and early 20th centuries.

Interestingly, while the organization, extension and communication of laboratory- and hospital-based medical research, which is widely regarded as having been the cornerstone for the institutionalization of scientific medicine, was, at one level at least, deeply marked by the nationalism characterising the 19th and 20th centuries (and attendant nationalist calculations), it was also surprisingly transnational on another plane. Research into disciplines like tropical medicine did not, as is now increasingly accepted, flow only within national spaces (the metropolitan centres) or in one direction (from the metropole to the periphery); we are now being told about the construction of knowledge at several sites, as ideas developed in one region were tested in another and then often implemented elsewhere. Nationalism and national borders could not constrain exchanges of medical ideas nor, indeed, attempts at innovating and re-adapting medical technologies, strategies or products (research into all manner of vaccines in the 19th century is a prime example, as this was often spurred on not only by communications in a range of widely read publications, but also by a spate

of local political, institutional and financial requirements). Tropical medicine gives us further clues about such complex processes. Here medical ideas constantly flowed in all directions, especially in a situation where specialized knowledge of the climatic and geographical conditions marking specific localities was used to justify adaptations of metropolitan medicine and medical theories. These trends are, for instance, particularly marked in relation to assessments concerning the nature, cause and effects of ailments like 'malaria', 'cholera' and smallpox during the 19th century – characterized by indecision and disagreement, such assessments were frequently linked to specific local environmental conditions like atmospheric humidity, aridity, wind and rain patterns, and, not least, individual constitutions and so-called 'civilizational markers'. Strikingly, the influence of these ideas would regularly transcend national and imperial borders, as a range of publications – formal medical journals or locally printed pamphlets and books (which would often get reported in metropolitan medical publications) – which had been brought out in a variety of locales, transmitted region-specific explanations for the causation and cure of diseases. This knowledge ended up becoming part of a transnational bank of knowledge, as countless articles and editorial correspondence within learned medical journals attest – local examples from British India, imperial possessions across other parts of Asia or Africa, or, indeed, the Americas would often be put forward in defence of particular arguments about disease aetiology, which, in turn, would spur new debates and discussions (the pages of 19th- and early 20th-century editions of journals like The Lancet, the British Medical Journal and the Indian Medical Gazette, for example, richly illustrate the existence of a plethora of medical ideas, their enthusiastic communication across territorial boundaries and, not least, the utilization of local case studies to put forward arguments about all manner of epidemic diseases). The local and the transnational were thereby linked in myriad, often unexpected, ways.

It is equally significant that new knowledge developed in imperial possessions was often reimported back into the imperial metropoles, even if this act of reception was downplayed by politicians and bureaucrats keen to underline the civilizing nature of their rule, which, they often claimed, was the result of the transmission of their national scientific and technological expertise. Researches carried out in the so-called imperial peripheries into 'tropical' diseases like malaria were a good case in point – this information was often transferred back into teaching and research institutions located within imperial metropoles, which then proceeded to offer training in the ways in which ailments in the hot, colonial climates could be best tackled (particularly by the European ruling elite, who were tasked with the goal of surviving the tropics and civilizing its territories).

Indeed, one cannot help but feel that the time has come for a major reassessment of the complexities attending the creation of medical knowledge, which was generally much more multisited and collaborative than has been recognized till now by historians; their transnational dissemination and impact is also worthy of detailed examination. Robert Koch, for instance, had a far greater impact on the 19th-century sanitary practices of some British Indian provinces than the ideas and formulations of his extremely outspoken British scientific competitors – a complexity frequently ignored by historians unable or unwilling to move away from nation-centric models of analysis, dependent on notions about the ideological hegemony of a small group of people over society at large; an argument that appears to smack of an Orientalist ideology of a bygone era.

Similar issues also come up in relation to the second half of the 20th century, which was a period that witnessed the independence of numerous ex-colonial territories. These nation states were often fiercely protective of their borders and domestic policy, even as their leaders embarked on projects intended to increase social justice and access to health, education and employment services. However, the problem was that these efforts at developing new welfare states were frequently compromised by political and bureaucratic corruption. Therefore, when we go beyond the veil of rhetoric, it becomes obvious that urban–rural, class and gender imbalances in relation to access to medical services remained rampant during this period, even if the contours of inequitable distribution moved around. In the republic of India, for instance, the development of a new system of parliamentary democracy ensured that the constituencies of the most powerful politicians in federal and provincial government received the most generous resource allocations for the development of state-funded health delivery systems. This, in turn, created a situation where the influence of the medical marketplace remained undiminished, as a variety of cures were provided by Tibetan, homeopathic, unani, ayurvedic and faith healers, each of whom drew on a combination of local, national and international suppliers of raw materials and goods.

We cannot, of course, claim that political borders set up by national governments were irrelevant. They certainly were meaningful on one plane of operation. International bargains down the ages about trade agreements, in relation to medicinal drugs and medical technologies, like those negotiated by the European East Indian Companies with Asian and African potentates in the 17th, 18th and 19th centuries, as well as all the ones put into place on bilateral and multilateral bases in the latter half of the 20th century, highlight the need for a historical assessment of the influence of political factors on the spread of medicines and medical technologies. Indeed, the introduction of regional public health and medical policies (like those negotiated by agencies such as the World Health Organization and UNICEF with different national governments across the globe) shows that national units and their priorities were significant agents in the circulation of medical policies or products, even where these were widely presented as being cutting-edge and beneficial by a variety of international actors. Medical policies that are negotiated at and by WHO eventually put an emphasis on this: they impose, maintain, initiate or regulate the circulation of medical goods of all sorts through, beyond, under or above national limits (from monitoring to standard setting).

At the same time, an assessment of medical practice shows that these national territorial borders were less rigid than is often assumed, as traders, medical practitioners, health agencies, patients and the civilian targets of organized public health campaigns were able to determine the demand and supply of medical products. Examples abound, but the multifaceted instances of the many national immunization campaigns that underpinned the global smallpox eradication programme heralded by the WHO from the 1960s onwards are a good case in point. A variety of actors, both official and civilian, were able to affect the implementation of medical policies and technological choices, so much so that the smallpox eradication campaign is best seen as a complex amalgam of international, national and local projects; each of these was affected by myriad political, financial and social calculations, some of which were deeply rooted in local conditions whilst also being marked by interregional administrative negotiations. Seen from this perspective, the experiences of health agency personnel and patients alike were frequently transnational in nature, as they were generally based on the import and exchange of medical products, ideas and practices from across national territories and distributive centres; a detailed examination of this dynamism in the choice and servicing of medical requirements holds out the possibility of showing us how human societies have never allowed themselves to be completely constrained by political boundaries or, indeed, national or international political calculations and policies. Human experiences are necessarily complex and this truism is powerfully highlighted in the range of (often competing and sometimes paradoxical) societal responses to the identification, marketing and acceptance of medicine.

Sanjoy Bhattacharya

Bibliography

Arnold D. 1993. *Colonizing the body: state medicine and epidemic disease in nineteenth century India*. Berkeley: University of California Press.

Bhattacharya S., Harrison M. and Worboys M. 2005. *Fractured states: smallpox, public health and vaccination policy in British India, 1800–1947*. New Delhi/London: Orient Longman/Sangam.

Bynum W. F. 1994. *Science and the practice of medicine in the nineteenth century*. Cambridge: Cambridge University Press.

Greenough P. 1995. 'Intimidation, coercion and resistance in the final stages of the South Asian smallpox eradication campaign, 1973–1975', *Social Science and Medicine*, 4, 5, 633–45.

Packard R. M. 1997. 'Malaria dreams: postwar visions of health and development in the Third World', *Medical Anthropology*, 17, 3, 279–96.

Related essays

drugs (medical); empire and migration; germs; higher education; League of Nations Health Organization; smallpox; tropics; vaccination

Mexican Revolution

The revolution that wracked Mexico from 1910 until at least 1920 was a fundamentally parochial affair. No grand ideology undergirded the calls to arms, unlike the Russian revolution that broke out while the Mexicans were still slaughtering each other (at least 1.5 million perished, double the number of deaths during the US Civil War). Indeed, V. I. Lenin was so unimpressed by the upheaval in Mexico that he did not write a single word on the topic. Still, there would be an ultimate, tragic connection between the Mexican and Russian revolutions via Leon Trotsky's fatal sojourn in post-revolutionary Mexico from 1936–40 as an escapee from Stalin's purges – but not from Stalin's will to murder.

Yet the Mexican Revolution can and must be seen in a transnational context. Although its causes were local and The Cause parochial, it was nonetheless one of a series of outbreaks of revolutionary change that swept across three continents in the first two decades of the twentieth century. Aside from the Chinese revolution of 1911, preceded by the 1900 Boxer Rebellion and the Russian revolution of 1917, with the 1905 revolution as its antecedent, there was the Persian (Iranian) Constitutional Revolution of 1905–11 and the Turkish Revolution of 1908–09, which was followed in the early 1920s by the Kemalist revolution under Ataturk. Like most of these other revolts, the Mexican Revolution saw the ultimate establishment of an authoritarian regime. Indeed, the Mexican revolution can in some ways be seen as template for many subsequent 20th century Latin American uprisings in its harnessing of popular discontent in the service of oligarchic or dictatorial rule. And to be sure, while leading Mexican revolutionaries made few if any universalist claims, their struggle did influence regional figures such as the Peruvian political leader Víctor Raúl Haya de la Torre and Augusto Sandino in Nicaragua.

Additionally, while the causes of the revolution might have been local, Mexico was caught up in international political and economic cross-currents that profoundly affected the course of the revolution. The greatest external influence was, unsurprisingly, the United States, the hovering giant to the north, which had wide-ranging business interests in Mexico, including oil, the "black gold" that was of increasing economic and strategic importance. The US threw its support in favor of particular aspirants to power, occupied Vera Cruz when it disapproved of a coup, and launched a military "punitive expedition" against the revolutionary leader Pancho Villa after Villa's bloody raid on a New Mexico border town in 1916. But influence in Mexico was a potential prize for the US's competitors, particularly Britain, which had its own oil interests in the country, and likely future adversaries Germany and Japan, especially once the Great War broke out in Europe. The most infamous episode was of course the Zimmerman Telegram affair of 1917, in which the German foreign minister proposed to the Mexican government an alliance in the event of German-US war, with Mexico to receive in return the lost territories of Texas, New Mexico, and Arizona. What is often forgotten is that Zimmerman encouraged the Mexicans to invite Japan to adhere as well to the proposed alliance. In fact, Japan had significant economic operations as well as thousands of émigrés in Mexico, and at one point sent a battleship to Mexico to protect Japanese interests, which caused considerable consternation in the United States. In any event, neither Japan nor Mexico embraced the German plan – the Japanese prime minister denounced it publicly in no uncertain terms. But the telegram, leaked by British intelligence, was a bombshell that helped propel the US into World War I. (As an odd aside, the US government apparently conscripted several Japanese-Americans to pose as representatives of the Japanese government in an unsuccessful attempt to poison Pancho Villa – they were able to achieve entrée because Villa wanted weapons and other support from Japan.)

But we must not limit our transnational analysis of the Mexican Revolution to the traditional themes of war, peace, and power politics. Another World War I-related transnational phenomenon was the exodus into Mexico of thousands of American men seeking for various reasons to evade the draft. Some were political radicals, including communists and anarchists, who brought their ideas with them and sought to participate in the Revolution; many more simply loitered in city and town squares to evade US military service, the real-life progenitors of Fred C. Dobbs in the novel and film The Treasure of Sierra Madre. At the same time, thousands of Mexicans fled north into the US seeking relief from the violence as well as work.

Prior to the descent of the "slackers" on revolutionary Mexico came a "Who's Who" of American journalists, including John Reed, Lincoln Steffens, and Jack London. Reed and Steffens sang the revolution's praises from a leftist perspective, London was more jaundiced; all of them helped to turn a bloody national affair into an epic of global prominence.

A key, long-term transnational outcome of the Revolution was the extraordinary artistic output it spurred, and the degree to which the internecine conflict imbued the art and inspired artists who would achieve world-wide fame. Painter Magdalena Carmen Frida Kahlo Calderón credited the passions and issues of the Revolution as her inspiration for joining the Communist Party as a teenager. Mexico's great muralists Diego Rivera, David Siqueiros and José Clemente Orozco were all deeply affected by the Revolution, with Rivera and Siqueiros waving the banner of the struggle and Orozco horrified by the bloodshed (years later Siqueiros, whose left-wing passion curdled into Stalinism, would lead an unsuccessful machine gun assault on Trotsky's Mexico City home several months before an assassin buried an ice pick in the Old Bolshevik's head; after a stint in prison he spent time in exile at Pablo Neruda's home in Chile).

But as much as artists worked to mythologize the revolutionary struggle and its leaders, they arguably pale in long-term significance in comparison with the efforts of Hollywood, that unparalleled mythologizer and global disseminator of images. In fact, arguably the longest-term transnational impact of the Mexican Revolution can be discerned in the American film industry's seemingly endless fascination with the conflict and its aftermath. During the fighting, there was a synergistic relationship between Hollywood and the leaders Pancho Villa and Venustiano Carranza, who allowed US movie makers to record their exploits. In fact, Villa actually signed an exclusive contract with the Mutual Film company, which according to at least one account included a proviso that executions were to be held during the day for the sake of better lighting. Over the succeeding decades Hollywood would return repeatedly and profitably to revolutionary Mexico. To name but a few: Viva Villa! in 1934, improbably featuring the hulking Wallace Beery as Pancho Villa; the aforementioned 1948 Treasure of the Sierra Madre, directed by John Huston and starring Humphrey Bogart in one of his signature roles; Marlon Brando in the title role (and heavy "brown-face" makeup) in the 1952 production, *Viva Zapata*, about the exploits of Emiliano Zapata, the foremost hero of the Mexican Revolution; perhaps the greatest (certainly the bloodiest) Western of all time, Sam Peckinpah's 1969 *The Wild Bunch*; the 1971 Sergio Leone film *A Fistful of Dynamite* (technically Italian, but with American film stars James Coburn and Rod Steiger); and most recently, the 2003 HBO production *And Starring Pancho Villa as Himself* (the company's most expensive film thus far), dramatizing Villa's contractual relationship with Mutual, which resulted in the 1914 release, *The Life of General Villa*.

Within Mexico, the spirit of the 1910–20 conflict was kept alive by the paradoxically-named Institutional Revolutionary Party, which ruled the country without effective opposition until the late 1990s. But outside Mexico, it was Hollywood, more than any Mexican cultural or political effort, that preserved the memory and mythologized the Western Hemisphere's bloodiest single conflict of the past two centuries.

Neal Rosendorf

Bibliography

Brown J. C. 1993. *Oil and revolution in Mexico*. Berkeley: University of California Press.

Katz F. 1981. *The secret war in Mexico: Europe, the United States and the Mexican Revolution*. Chicago: Chicago University Press.

Knight A. 1986. *The Mexican Revolution*, 2 vols. Cambridge: Cambridge University Press.

de Orellana M. 2004. *Filming Pancho Villa: how Hollywood shaped the Mexican Revolution*, transl. John King. New York: Verso.

Richards M. D. 2004. *Revolutions in world history*. London and New York: Routledge.

Rochfort D. 1998. *Mexican muralists: Orozco, Rivera, Siqueiros*. San Francisco: Chronicle.

Related essays

1848; 1989; anarchism; exile; film; Hollywood; oil; Pax Americana; Russian Revolution; surrealism; war

Migration and empire *See* Empire and migration

Migration and sexuality *See* Sexuality and migration

Millennium

A millennium is the passage of a thousand years. As a measured point on the calendar, millennia occur at different times in human history according to different calendars – Christian, Jewish, Islamic, Hindu, Chinese, Japanese, or Buddhist, to name a few. But as a human experience, the advent of the millennium across cultures and religions has been accompanied by beliefs about the imminent transformation of the world – by apocalyptic predictions and joyous celebrations, by both fear and hope. A millennium can, then, be defined as a chronological moment in time as well as a transnational concept of religious, cultural, psychological and even political and technological significance. The symbolic power of this concept is most clearly reflected in the shared global moment of the Year 2000 as the dawning of the third millennium.

The versatile meaning of the millennium is part of the dispute over the correct date when millennia actually begin. This debate took on importance in the 1990s with the planning of millennium celebrations, the growing interest in millennial studies (looking back at how those in the past have managed millennial moments) and general reflection on the past thousand years and the thousand years to come.

According to the commonly recognized Gregorian calendar the third millennium did not officially begin until 1 January 2001. Using the Western religious counting system adopted by Pope Gregory XIII in the 16th century, the year 1 AD marks the year Jesus Christ was born (in the absence of a year zero). The period from Jesus' birth through 1000 AD therefore constituted one millennium, and, as most scholars and scientists pointed out, New Year's Eve 2000 marked the end of the second.

The majority of the Earth's population, however, celebrated the new millennium at the dawn of the year 2000. Commentators acknowledged the accuracy of the Gregorian calendar, but argued for the greater symbolism of watching the date roll over from nines to zeroes. American anthropologist Stephen Jay Gould interpreted the millennium date debate as one between high and low culture – with low culture winning out. As widespread planning for Year 2000 celebrations proceeded, Gould saw it as a sign that popular culture had successfully dominated the global marketplace. 'The old guard... may pout to their heart's content', Gould wrote, 'but the world will rock and party on January 1, 2000' (Gould 1997). Some who argued for millennial festivities for 2001, such as British science fiction author Arthur C. Clarke and Australian Prime Minister John Howard, were labelled spoilsports and 'party poopers'.

The debate between the 2001 and the 2000 celebrants highlights the fact that defining the millennium is more complicated than simply choosing a date on the calendar. The millennium is certainly, for example, an important religious concept. In the Christian Bible, the millennium is cited in the Book of Revelations as the prophesy of a post-apocalyptic period of a thousand years of peace and justice when Christ will establish his kingdom on earth (the Second Coming). This period will be followed by a final battle between Christ and Satan when God will resurrect all human beings and judge them, sending the righteous to Paradise and the evil to Hell for eternity (the Last Judgment). Christian belief of the millennium (or millennialism) has differed greatly over time, in both interpretation of the Apocalypse and Second Coming as literal or merely figurative (Christ's rule occurs in the heart, not on earth), and in opinions on how and when the millennium will start.

Historians in the 1990s hotly disputed whether the period around the year 1000 was recognized as a time of Christian millennial significance. Some scholars argued that apocalyptic fever ran rampant across the European continent. Peasants stopped planting crops, gave away their possessions, and abandoned their families to make pilgrimages to Jerusalem in both wonderment and terror at the approach of Second Coming or the Apocalypse. Other scholars challenged the evidence supporting these claims, noting that most peasants in the 10th century were not even aware of the calendrical date, and that apocalyptic anticipation was no more a feature of medieval Europe in the year 1000 than at any other time. Expectations of an eschatological date occurred periodically throughout the medieval period, and have usually marked the end of each century up to the modern day.

In fact, the concept of the millennium as a set of ideas about the destiny and destruction of the world (or millenarianism) can be found in many different belief systems, from the religions of Islam and Hinduism to Babylonian and Native American cultures. Common to all these systems are beliefs about a time when there is the cessation of evil and human suffering, regeneration and the creation of an ideal age of harmony and earthly perfection. This shared conception of the millennium is evident in the transnational and cross-cultural acceptance of the symbolism of the Year 2000 as a pivotal moment in history, an opportunity for renewal or the gateway to destruction.

Some millenarian thinking surrounding 2000 was religiously based, though not necessarily Christian. Particularly noted were the violent activities of certain apocalyptic groups. In 1993, dozens of members of an apocalyptic Christian sect called the Branch Davidians were killed in a fire at their compound in Waco, Texas, after a siege against US federal agents trying to investigate possible criminal activities inside the compound. In 1995, leaders of the Japanese Aum Shinrikyō sect released nerve gas in a subway station in Tokyo, Japan, in an apparent attempt to fulfil apocalyptic prophesies. In 1997, members of a religious group called Heaven's Gate committed mass suicide near San Diego, California, believing their souls could escape the coming Apocalypse by hitching a ride on a giant spaceship carrying Jesus that had been hiding in the wake of Comet Hale-Bopp. People attending millennium celebrations in US and European cities, and in the Middle East, were warned of the potential for attacks by Islamist terrorists.

Most people's attitudes toward the third millennium were more secular than religious. New technological developments, such as the creation of nuclear weapons, certainly influenced apocalyptic visions. But the ecological, environmental and demographic changes witnessed by the 20th century also shaped conceptions of what the destruction of the world might look like. Beginning in the 1970s, studies began to make projections for the future based on already evident trends showing stresses on population, resources, and the environment. In 1980, the Council on Environmental Quality's Global 2000 Report to the President was released in the United States, predicting a poorer, more crowded world in which greater material output would not be able to keep up with population growth, global hunger and disease.

Millennial anxiety was also triggered by fear of technological calamity when the clocks rolled over into 2000, due to a glitch in early computer program design. Corporate and government studies, as well as media speculation, cautioned that if the Y2K (Year 2 kilo/thousand) problem, or millennium bug, caused date-related computer programs to operate incorrectly, critical industries, financial markets and government functions might stop working. The consequences could be catastrophic. The press warned of malfunctioning missile and air transportation systems (planes would fall from the skies); disruption of electrical, gas and telecommunication services; delays in gasoline production and distribution; and the breakdown of banking and other financial services, plunging the world into a global recession. In preparation, some people in the West began to stock up on fresh water and canned goods.

World leaders tried to channel this millennial anxiety into millennial hope. Just as Y2K had the potential for disaster, it offered an opportunity for earthly salvation – or at least some improvement. On the international level, the period surrounding 2000 saw a number of efforts to galvanize the community of nations into action on issues of global concern.

At the United Nations Fourth World Conference on Women in 1995, delegates adopted the Beijing Declaration committing the international community to the advancement of women, and a Platform for Action to improve women's lives in such areas as health, education, decision making and through legal reforms. In the late 1990s, many nations signed the Kyoto Protocol, an amendment to the United Nations International Treaty on Climate Change, agreeing to mandatory limits on their carbon dioxide and other greenhouse gas emissions. In September 2000, the largest gathering of world leaders in history adopted the United Nations Millennium Declaration, committing member states to an action plan for ending poverty and inequality, improving education, reducing HIV/AIDS, safeguarding the environment, and protecting people from deadly conflict and violence.

These global partnerships all rested on a broad consensus that, at the end of the 20th century – with the Cold War tensions left behind and the hope of the millennium ahead – there could exist a new paradigm for social transformation. As the American rock band R.E.M. sang, 'It's the end of the world as we know it, and I feel fine'.

On the national level, heads of state also tried to foster a sense of positive change with the coming of the new millennium. US President Bill Clinton urged Americans not to fear the Year 2000 but to recognize its potential and prepare for it by building 'a bridge to the 21st century' with new social policies. A number of millennium projects focused literally on building tangible structures, in recognition of the country's achievements as it looked to embark upon a new era: the Millennium Monument in Beijing (a huge sundial-shaped building to welcome the 21st century to China); the Millennium Dome and Millennium Wheel in London (respectively the largest single-roofed structure and observation wheel in the world); the World Peace Bell in Newport, Kentucky (the largest swinging bell in the world, inaugurated at the dawning of the year 2000).

Many millennial celebrations incorporated emblems of hope that were more symbolic. In Capetown, Nelson Mandela, the prominent anti-apartheid activist and former President of South Africa, passed a millennium flame from the old to the young at a millennium party on Robben Island where he had been imprisoned during apartheid for more than two decades. In South Korea, just south of the demilitarized zone, an enormous bell, fashioned in part from a melted-down Russian helmet, Israeli rifle and a piece of a US warship, rang at midnight. In Berlin, German revellers packed the road running through the Brandenburg Gate that was once blocked off the by the Berlin Wall. In the city of Bethlehem in Israel, which had come under Palestinian control in 1995 in accordance with the Oslo Peace Accords, the Year 2000 arrived on the wings of two thousand doves released on the stroke of midnight. Different nations thus embraced the millennium as an opportunity to express their national potential.

Different religions also acknowledged the turn of the millennium as globally significant. In Vatican City, thousands crowded into St Peter's Square to hear Pope John Paul II issue his first blessing of the new millennium at the stroke of midnight. For those following religious or ceremonial calendars, used by about two thirds of the world's population by the end of the 20th century, neither of the years 2000 or 2001 were millennial dates. Nonetheless, notable non-Christian millennium celebrations took part in Indonesia, Japan, across

India, in Jordan, Egypt and Israel – though not in Saudi Arabia, where celebrations were banned. The Dalai Lama, however, led Hindu and Buddhist monks in singing hymns of devotion on the banks of the River Ganges.

With the Year 2000, therefore, the concept of the millennium included many concepts: religious belief (Christian and non-Christian); environmental degradation and regeneration; technological disaster; global partnership to address shared global concerns; national healing – and many others. The multifaceted and multicultural nature of this concept found powerful expression in the worldwide celebrations of the symbolic changeover in date from 1999 to 2000. Spreading westward across the globe in a continuing 24-hour circuit from Micronesia to Samoa, live television coverage of the festivities brought the entire planet into the new millennium at the same time. This dramatic, globally shared experience of the millennial moment provided yet another defining feature of the current conception of the millennium: globalization.

Alexis K. Albion

Bibliography

Claggett H. (ed.). 1999. *The 21st Century*. New York: H. W. Wilson.

Gould S. J. 1997. *Questioning the Millennium: a rationalist's guide to a precisely arbitrary countdown*. New York: Harmony.

Landes R., Gow A. and Van Meter D. (eds) 2003. *The apocalyptic year: religious expectation and social change, 950–1050*. Oxford: Oxford University Press.

Related essays

Christianity; Christmas and Halloween; climate change; developmental assistance; environmentalism; Islam; New Age; religion; terrorism; underdevelopment; United Nations Women's Conferences

Missionaries

Missionaries have been some of the most pervasive, powerful and persistent protagonists in the long story of globalization. Christian missionaries did perhaps more to unify the Roman Empire than any other single group after the Roman army. Expanding from either marginal parts of the world (such as Palestine or Ireland) or from the power base of a state religion, Christian missions not only provided basic ingredients of the identity of 'Europe' as such, but a globally dominant time frame as well – 'Anno Domini'. While it is debateable whether the first six or seven centuries of Islamic jihad can be defined as 'missionary' – but see below – the spread of Islam undoubtedly helped to construct the early modern consciousness of Christian Europe through the Crusades, the reconquest of Spain, and the Ottoman Empire's expansion until the 16th century. For the proper interpretation of the missionary contribution to transnational modern history, however, it is more urgent to consider the term 'mission' in its contemporary usage, connect it to the historical prominence of Christian missions since the early modern period, its immersion in the spread of modernity, and the extent to which such 'civilizing missions' have become characteristic of any modern attempts to spread a religious message.

Having a 'mission' implies perceiving a lack or deficit among the people towards whom the mission is directed, and moving 'out there' to rectify that lack. That means that mission is not necessarily restricted to something religious: bombers fly missions, French bureaucrats are *en mission*, even anthropologists (usually thought to embody the opposite of missionaries) were once, in the 1960s, sent on a mission to Thailand for military research in the US Department of Defense's employ. Mission, therefore, not only implies the bringing of a message (or bombs) but also the gathering and taking away of the intelligence needed to bring this message. Missionary work is, in other words, not restricted to a specific type of traveller: a missionary perspective was, at least, a staple of most European travellers' diets from the early modern period onwards. Only rarely did anyone venture out from Europe without perceiving that the countries visited lacked the most vital human civilities, even if not all those travellers agreed that it was a European's duty to transfer those civilized competences to others. Interestingly, certain Christian missionaries made up the most striking exceptions to this rule – the Jesuits who, under Matteo Ricci, adopted the civilization of the Chinese literati around 1600 being the most obvious and prominent example.

The historical prominence of missionaries from Europe, however, makes it both inevitable and dangerous that stereotypes about Christian missionaries predominate in scholarly reflections on the missionary contribution to transnational history. Twentieth-century anthropologists, in particular, have contributed to the description of Christian missionaries as exemplary colonialist indoctrinators trampling over every cultural difference they happened to encounter – partly because this stereotype made anthropologists themselves look like people driven by an essentially harmless curiosity. The historical ethnography of Christian missions of the past three decades, however, has shown that this radical separation between Europeans who came to learn about strange customs, and Europeans who only came to impose their own creed, cannot be maintained. Even when missionaries were driven by the urge to convert the heathen, they could rarely do so without learning from these heathens as well.

This becomes immediately obvious once one considers the primary role of Christian missionaries in generating conditions for global communication. Faced with the need to preach the Gospel, Christian missionaries quickly outnumbered all other Europeans in the field of translating, codifying and standardizing non-European languages. Because learning a language implies learning cultural competences, missionaries also had to learn to cope with the power differences that are expressed in them and in the relationships between languages (especially where some languages, such as Latin, were thought to be more sacred and powerful than others) in their notation and translation, and therefore also in the conversations entered into on that basis (see Rafael 1988). On the one hand, all colonial relationships require a language of command, and the dictionaries, grammars and vocabularies of colonial power were most often provided by Christian missionaries. On the other, the indeterminacies of meaning not only gave missionaries much trouble in translation, but often provided their potential converts with a certain, sometimes subversive, liberty of meaning. The example of language alone is sufficient to show that missionaries were dependent on the people to be converted as mediators and translators of their concerns – in some case, to such an extent that they depended more on the future converts' hospitality than on the mission's spiritual persuasions or material attractions. Where missionaries were more dependent on the might of the state – usually, the colonial state – to make people listen to their preaching, this state itself often could not find

purchase among the people to be converted without the prior conversations and translations set in motion by the missionaries. Missionaries, therefore, were some of the prime mediators of the inequalities of communication and interaction that connected different parts of the globe to each other.

The proximity of Christian missionaries to European colonial rule implies that it is impossible to separate the missionary movement from broader processes of propagating modern forms of life, and that Christian and secular 'conversions' usually went hand in hand in the 19th and 20th centuries. Missionaries were pivotal in the process of professionalizing ethnology and anthropology, and therefore stood at the basis of the way in which people all over the globe started to reconceptualize 'tradition' and 'modernity'. In a country like India, the rise of a notion of secular literature is directly connected to the opposition against Christian missions from Hindu or Muslim circles. Missionaries, again, codified and spread the languages by which groups of people came to invent their current ethnic identities. Above all, Christian missionaries spread notions of proper bodily comportment, dress, hygiene, modes of speech, working habits, gender relations, and agriculture that were often only arbitrarily related to the Christian message, but that copied the European civil context of Christianity. In this sense, Christian missionaries provided an indispensable complement to the European colonizing effort (see Comaroff and Comaroff 1991, 1997).

Even if much Christian missionizing was more of a 'conversion to modernities' (van der Veer 1996), the use of 'modernity' in the plural should remind us of the specificity of the missionizing act. Missionary modernities were usually formed around a specific technology of self and an emphasis on the formation of new persons. In contrast to, for instance, colonial administrators, who conceived human otherness usually in terms of the classification and control of essential territorial or racial differences, Christian missionaries usually based their representations and transformations of the 'other' people they encountered in an assimilationist attitude, which effectively meant that they defined human otherness as something to be left behind, after conversion, in a future past. This focus on personal transformation – not least through the new convictions and practices of the converts themselves – generated a relative autonomy of Christian missions from the practices of colonial administration. While it would be wrong to say this also implied a relative autonomy from colonial rule, it does point out that in many cases, missionary education and examples provided colonized peoples with some of the first models of ways to attain independence from colonial rule.

This already took place during the earliest moments of the Christian/colonial encounter: the converts of Mayan and Inca descent in colonized South and Meso-America, for example, already helped to reconfigure the historical narrative of the Spanish American conquest so that they could claim an original revelation of the Christian message received among indigenous groups before the coming of the Spaniards. Such conversion stories could, at times, be asserted against the arbitrary racial violence of the Spanish *conquistadores* themselves – often helped by the early anthropological accounts of missionaries like Bartolomeo de las Casas. While it would, on the one hand, be silly to reduce anti-colonial consciousness to the spread of Christianity, it is, on the other, crucial to realize that in the 19th and 20th centuries, few anti-colonial movements were not influenced by Christian missions – whether in terms of adopting the Christian message of the potential equality of all true believers against the colonizers, or in terms of resisting the Christian message as a prime example of colonial imposition and indoctrination. Especially from the mid 20th century onward, this could also result in forms of reverse Christian mission: not only did a considerable number of European Christian missionaries come back to find that their Christians in South America or Africa were more Christian than the secularized public at home, they increasingly brought back viewpoints and doctrines of mission – liberation theology, messages of social and physical healing, or forms of Pentecostal fervour – that, it seemed, were now lacking in the 'original' homeland from which the Christian missionaries had departed. The extreme case of reversed mission is that former missionary centres are sometimes declared to be in need of preachers from a former mission area – epitomized in the (admittedly rare) case of the Vatican endorsing the need to send priests from the Third World into, say, the Netherlands.

A perhaps even more important development is that non-Christian religions have, in a number of cases, increasingly adopted practices modelled on modern civilizing missions in the attempt to spread their religion's messages. The Vishwa Hindu Parishad, for example – an organization for proselytizing right-wing Hinduism founded in the 1960s – copied the social development effort among 'backward' castes of Christian missions in India, while extending it to poor Hindus in the South Asian diaspora. Another, perhaps more significant example is provided by Islamic missions to West Africa since the late 20th century that not only employ both Egyptian and Libyan but also Malian or Senegalese teachers of Arabic and the Koran in *madrasas*, but join them with explicit attempts towards development aid – not just modernizing Islamic education away from the older model of Koran schools, but coupling it to, for example, community development by building wells. The popularity of much Islamic missionizing today – a factor usually disregarded by the Western press – lies in the fact that many of its organizations (such as Lebanese/Syrian Hizbollah, but also the Afghan Taliban) invest considerable energy in projects similar to those of late-20th-century Christian missions: community participation, grassroots development, and Islamic forms of 'liberation theology'. Finally, the rapid mediatization of Christian missions – on the model of the televised revival meeting of American Pentecostalism – is paralleled in other religions' missionary efforts by the rise of TV imams, a thriving Islamist radio- and cassette-sermon industry, and Hindu nationalist film making. Thus, our contemporary transformations of 'civilizing missions' are no longer the exclusive prerogative of a once globally dominant Christianity, and this shows that the need of spreading a religious message is, more often than not, coupled to an equally pressing need to spread a kind of sacred (but paradoxically also secular) civility. Whenever they desire to also secure secular sovereignty for these civilities, all religious missions will turn to, and rely on, violence.

Peter Pels

Bibliography

Comaroff J. and Comaroff J. L. 1991. *Of revelation and revolution, Vol. 1: Christianity, colonialism and consciousness in South Africa*. Chicago: Chicago University Press.

Comaroff J. L. and Comaroff J. 1997. *Of revelation and revolution, Vol. 2: the dialectics of modernity on a South African frontier.* Chicago: Chicago University Press.

Rafael V. L. 1988. *Contracting colonialism: translation and Christian conversion in Tagalog society under early Spanish rule.* Ithaca and London: Cornell University Press.

Veer P. van der (ed.) 1996. *Conversion to modernities: the globalization of Christianity.* New York and London: Routledge.

Related essays

anti-Catholicism; Bible; childhood; Chinese medicine; Christianity; civilizations; decolonization; empires and imperialism; evangelicalism; health policy; higher education; Islam; kindergarten; language; liberation theology; medicine; modernity; music; religion; scientific expeditions; temperance; temporary migrations; translation; youth organizations

Modernismo

The Nicaraguan poet Rubén Darío (1867–1916) – born Félix Rubén García Sarmiento – is considered the father of *modernismo*, a literary movement that renewed Hispanic letters at the turn of the 19th century, endowing it with a vitality and voluptuousness it had not enjoyed for 400 years. Even if it is usually associated with poetry, its impact on prose was equally significant. Its reach, partly due to Darío's relentless travels as a correspondent and later as a diplomat in Chile, Argentina, Spain, France, Central America and Mexico – among other places – extended to all countries in Hispanic America and also to Spain. Beyond its notorious aesthetic relevance, *modernismo* was crucial in reconfiguring the cultural relations between Latin America and Spain on the one hand, and the Hispanic world and the United States on the other. It asserted the cultural independence and even pre-eminence of Latin America over Spain, and reversed the old pattern as innovation was now carried from the former colonies to the mother country. *Modernismo* is also linked to Hispanism, a transatlantic cultural program seeking to unify Hispanic America and Spain, which Darío formulated and promoted in order to counter the growing political, ideological and material influence of the United States and Great Britain, increasingly perceived as a threat by Latin American

intellectuals. Darío's tireless journeys and his fluid contacts with writers and thinkers all around the Hispanic world made him the point of connection between the Spanish-speaking intelligentsia.

Even though some critics signal the appearance of Martí's *Ismaelillo* (1882, New York) as the starting point of *modernismo*, it is generally agreed Darío's *Azul* (1888, Chile) marked the decisive break. As in the case of Martí – the other funding figure of the movement, who spent an important part of his literary life as a chronicler in New York – Darío developed his aesthetics through a personal experience of modernity and metropolitan life while he resided in Santiago de Chile, Buenos Aires, Madrid and Paris. His cosmopolitan poetics, heavily indebted to the French Parnassians for their doctrine of art for art's sake and to the Symbolists for their musical conception of poetry, was more fully realized in *Prosas profanas* (Buenos Aires, 1896). This work condenses the most emblematic features of the movement. It boldly explores new meters, accentual patterns and strophic forms, giving fresh life to ossified verses such as the alexandrine and the hendecasyllable. It emphasized style, beauty and formal perfection, embracing a resolute aestheticism in rejection of the centrality of utilitarian and materialistic values in modern bourgeois society at the time of Latin American incorporation in the global economy. Against positivism, it asserted intuition and the senses, welcoming the erotic and the occult. To transcend a daily life perceived as vulgar and massified by capitalism, it stressed the exotic and the aristocratic, abounding in far-removed geographies and luxurious objects, places and creatures such as swans, pearls, palaces, and pheasants.

Acclaimed all around Latin America and Spain (Juan Valera was one of the first to celebrate Darío's novelty), Darío was also criticized for what writers such as the Uruguayan Rodó regarded as an excessive artificiality. Partly as a response, his next books – *Cantos de vida y esperanza* (1905, Madrid) and *Canto errante* (1907, Madrid) – displayed a more mature and intimate conception of poetry, and engaged explicitly with history and politics.

Encompassing all the Spanish-speaking world, *modernismo* attracted writers of diverse national origins and its centre of activity shifted, mostly following Darío's course.

What is considered the first generation of the movement (from its beginning to around 1896) included, besides Darío, the Cubans Martí and Casal, the Mexican Gutiérrez Nájera, and the Colombian Asunción Silva, all born north of the equator. When by 1896 all but Darío were dead, Buenos Aires and Montevideo became the new capitals of *modernismo* and a second generation of writers joined him: among others, the Argentinian Lugones, the Uruguayans Rodó, Herrera y Reissig and Delmira Agustini, the Bolivian Freyre and the Mexican Amado Nervo. In Spain, *modernismo* affected figures such as the brothers Machado, Juan Ramón Jiménez and Valle-Inclán. When Darío moved to Paris, where he spent his last 15 years, Mexico replaced Buenos Aires as the axis of the movement. *Modernismo* faded away in the second decade of the 20th century.

Karina Galperin

Bibliography

Aching G. 1997. *The politics of Spanish American 'modernismo': by exquisite design.* Cambridge: Cambridge University Press.

Rama J. 1970. *Rubén Darío y el modernismo.* Caracas: Universidad Central de Venezuela.

Ramos J. 2001. *Culture and politics in nineteenth-century Latin America.* Durham, NC and London: Duke University Press.

Related essays

America; antropofagia; avant garde; conceptualism; information society; Kessler, Harry von; language; literature; Romanticism; surrealism

Modernity

Transnationalism and modernity are clearly linked, and modernity has been perhaps the single most powerful transnationally transmitted idea in the era since 1800. While regions and nations have clashed and cooperated, the vast majority of those conflicts, particularly in the 20th century, were essentially about modernity, its meaning, and how it might be dealt with. This stems, in large part, from the ultimate dominance of the nation state during that era. Among the defining characteristics of the nation state are the desire to maintain a self-aware, non-hierarchically defined citizenry deriving its legitimacy from the people themselves, within a territorially sovereign unit. The assumptions behind the

nation state are, then, essentially modern, meaning that the rise of the nation state and the dominance of the modern mentality have developed in tandem with each other.

The development of modernity in the Western world was underpinned by a set of assertions, many of which are still powerful today, about the organization of society. Most central was the idea of 'progress' as the driving force in human affairs. Philosophers such as Descartes and Hegel ascribed to modernity a rationality and teleology, an overarching narrative, that suggested that the world was moving in a particular direction – and that that direction, overall, was a positive one. There were several drivers of progress. One was the idea that dynamic change was a good thing in its own right: in premodern societies, the force of change was often feared as destructive, but the modern mindset welcomed it. In particular, an acceptance and enthusiasm for progress through economic growth, and later, industrial growth, became central to the development of a modern society. Particularly in the formulation of the Enlightenment of the 18th century, the idea of rationality, the ability to make choices and decisions in a predictable, scientific way, also became crucial to the ordering of a modern society.

Modernity also altered the way in which members of society thought of themselves. Society was secularized: modernity was not necessarily hostile to religion, but religion was confined to a defined space within society, rather than penetrating through it. (This was ironic, considering that many of modernity's assumptions, such as a teleological view of progress and a breakdown of hierarchy, are clearly Christian in derivation.) The individual self, able to reason, was now at the centre of the modern world. At the same time, the traditional bonds that the self had to the wider community were broken down; modern societies did not support the old feudal hierarchies of status and bondage, but rather, broke them down in favour of equality, or at any rate, a non-hierarchical model of society.

Above all, societies are modern in large part because they perceive themselves as being so: self-awareness ('enlightenment') is central to modernity and the identities that emerge from it, such as nationhood. Yet this has led the West, in particular, into a misconception particularly powerful during the

19th century: that is, one of drawing far too strong a distinction between its own 'modern' values and those elsewhere in the world. China, for instance, showed many features over thousands of years that shared assumptions of modernity long before the West had a significant impact there. China used a system of examinations for entry to the bureaucracy from the 10th century CE, a clearly rational and ordered way of trying to choose a power elite, at a time when religious decrees and brute force were doing the same job in much of Europe. At the same time, China started to develop an integrated and powerful commercial economy, with cash crops taking the place of subsistence farming. It is clear that many aspects of 'modernity' were visible earlier and more clearly in China than in Europe.

Nonetheless, China before the mid 19th century also shows why the emergence of modernity in Europe did have certain important features that were not shared by other systems of thought, in this case, Confucianism. China did not, during that time, develop powerful political movements that believed in flattening hierarchies; Chinese thinkers did not stress the individuated self as a positive good in contrast to the collective, although there was a clear idea of personal development to become a 'gentleman' or 'sage'; nor, overall, did it make the idea of a teleology of forward progress central to the way it viewed the world: rather, history was an attempt to recapture the lost golden age of the ancients, and rather than praising innovation and dynamic change in its own right, premodern China developed highly sophisticated technology and statecraft while stressing the importance of past precedent, and of order. As for economic growth, while the later dynasties saw a comfortable accommodation by the state with the idea of commerce, the concept of economic growth as a good in its own right was not as central to the premodern Chinese mindset as it was to the type of modernity that emerged in Europe.

Yet ideas of modernity have always been fluid and hybrid: no one society or country has captured all of its complexities. Very broadly, one could describe the 19th century as the era of the confrontation between a particular type of Western-derived modernity and pre-existing worldviews (Islamic, Confucian), which encountered modernity primarily through imperialism, whereas the 20th century was one where modernity was adapted, hybridized and reflected back at the West as part of a process of resistance and adaptation by the colonized.

It may seem paradoxical that nationalism is so central to discussing the interaction between modernity and transnationalism. Yet the ideology of nationalism, based on the idea of the nation as the defining vehicle of political and social organization, has in fact been one of the most powerful forces for cross-border, cross-cultural social change in the past two centuries, based on a set of assumptions that come from the mindset of modernity (including an idea of teleological progress and breakdown of hierarchies). Nationalism's power derives from the fact that, while it claims legitimacy from a set of supposedly uncontested, solid facts about the group that defines itself as a 'nation', it is in fact a highly flexible concept which regularly redraws political, cultural, and even national boundaries to serve purposes which may be in constant flux. The term 'nation' has been used in a very particular way in the modern era. The early modern era in Europe saw an increasing movement away from sources of legitimacy based on either religious or inherited authority, and a greater prominence of the individuated self, with inherent and inviolable rights of its own. In this context, the political formation that became known as 'the nation' grew powerful. Central to its self-definition was the idea of 'the people' as its source of legitimacy. It rejected earlier, hierarchical forms of social relationship, suggesting that all members of the nation were equal (although over time, differing factors such as race and sex were used to make essentially arbitrary distinctions about who would count as part of 'the people'). Different forms of the nation have existed over the past two centuries, including ones that defined it variously in civic, ethnic, racial, and linguistic terms. A key aspect of nationhood, which differentiates it from other characteristics such as class, is that it must be self-aware. Although nations frequently claim a long and primordial history for themselves, they can only meaningfully be analysed as nations when they consciously understand themselves in those terms: this is reflected in the term 'nation' itself, which derives from the past participle of the Latin verb *nasci*, meaning 'to be born'. The idea of birth, or often, rebirth, stands central to the way in which nationalism defines its political terms. The stress on progress, self-awareness, individuation within a wider body, and citizenship based on the legitimacy of the people make the idea both modern and, in the supposed universality of its applicability, transnational. For instance, the central ideas of the French Revolution, of 'liberty, equality, fraternity', gave a powerful impetus to the formation of nationalism well beyond France itself, leading Thomas Jefferson to say 'Every man has two countries: his own and France'.

However, the power of modernity lay in large part in its ability to conceal the non-European elements in its construction which lay below or across the often arbitrarily drawn boundaries of the nation state. Among the most powerful elements of modern thought in Europe was its ability to maintain the idea that its own genesis and construction were profoundly different from those of other societies. In part, this was because of a desire to create a profound distinction between Western European politics and that of other societies, particularly in the 19th century, when imperialist ideology became important. Yet in many ways, the attributes of modernity – particularly self-awareness and its associated sense of anti-hierarchy – were drawn from a pre-existing religious tradition, in which birth and rebirth were crucial. While Christianity was clearly one source of this concept (having also provided the cultural grounding for the teleology of progress that underlies the long-standing definition of modernity), the idea of enlightenment and self-awareness emerged much earlier as part of Buddhist thought, and in the centuries after Christ, developed another path defined by Islam. Because of its particularistic nature, the most strongly Eurocentric understandings of modernity have found it hard to acknowledge their cross-cultural roots – yet they are there.

Modernization is not the same as modernity: the former is a process (and a highly contested one at that), and the latter is a mindset. Modernization, in one form or another, occupied the minds of rulers across the globe in the era of decolonization. However, the greatest sign of success of the assumptions of modernity is that they sparked a variety of reactions from peoples who encountered the concept first, often through imperial aggression, both within Europe and without. Rather than seeking an alternative political framework to that with which they had been confronted, peoples around the globe drew on the heady power of the idea of 'modern' ideas of nation, race, citizen, and so forth to shape themselves politically. Particularly notable was the spread of the idea of nationhood to two non-European areas of the world, Asia and Latin America. The most immediately successful Asian modernization was found in Japan. The country had faced its major crisis from imperialism a decade after the Opium Wars in China (1839–42, 1856–60), when the American Commodore Matthew Perry arrived with his 'black ships' in Edo (Tokyo) Bay. The demands of the Americans for refuelling rights in Japan provoked a major political crisis, which ended with the overthrow of the ruling Tokugawa shoguns in 1868. The elite which replaced the shoguns made the decision that Japan would be reconstituted as a modern nation state, modelled in particular on Germany and France. Among the elements of the Japanese nationalism created as part of the so-called Meiji Restoration were the move to a citizen army (arms had formerly been the province of the elite only), universal education, and also, more controversially, the acquisition of territorially non-contiguous colonies.

Japan was relatively unusual in Asia, in that it was one of the few countries (Siam being another) which was not colonized or semi-colonized by Europe in the late Victorian era. Other countries had different experiences. India was wholly colonized, with imperial control becoming stronger after the Uprising of 1857, and Korea was annexed (1910) by another Asian power, Japan. China was in a more unusual situation. Its size and instability meant that the imperial powers did not choose to take it over wholesale, but rather left its imperial dynasty (until 1911) and then its successor Republic (until 1949) to rule the country, while mandating preferential trade tariffs and extraterritoriality (i.e. legal immunity) for foreigners covered by treaty rights. Yet all these societies based their resistance to imperialism on tenets which were clearly modern in their inflection (even when they drew on 'traditional' thought), and which clearly, and often consciously, shared assumptions and tactics drawn from each other across the borders of the fledgling nations. The May Fourth nationalist demonstrations in Beijing in 1919 were inspired by the March Thirtieth demonstrations held in Seoul earlier that year. In the 1920s, the Chinese patriotic journalist Zou Taofen wrote long essays about Gandhi's non-violent protest movement, analysing whether its tactics were appropriate for the case of China. They were also about much more than nationhood: Chinese debates of the May Fourth era about whether 'science and democracy' could save China, and Gandhian strictures about the links between *swadeshi* and *swaraj* (self-production and self-rule) went to the heart of how a culturally hybrid modernity could be defined.

Overall, changing ideas of how modernity could be defined proved themselves both capable of reaching out to provide transnational influence, as well as retreating into a self-defined isolation that denied the cross-border matrix that had created them in the first place. This can be marked by the way in which, in the Cold War, two dominant models of Enlightenment-influenced modernity (Western capitalism and Soviet Marxism) were contested by a variety of non-European societies who sought modernity on their own terms, even while trying to find the model that would fit such a description. In retrospect, it was perhaps East Asia that was most successful in finding different ways of defining that alternative modernity. During the high Cold War, Japan managed to reach economic superpower status while bucking many of the trends of the free-market orthodoxy espoused in the Anglo-American West. Less noticed, but equally suggestive, were the 'Asian dragons' – South Korea, Singapore, Taiwan, and Hong Kong – which also flouted economic orthodoxy to protect their economies and eventually liberalize. The greatest challenge, however, has come from the East Asian Model espoused by reform-era China (1978 onward). In its rapid growth to become an economic giant, China has combined accepting some of modernity's assumptions (citizen body, self-awareness) with rejecting others (there is little progress or intention of progress toward empowerment of the individual in a political sense).

Rana Mitter

Bibliography

Bayly C. A. 2004. *The birth of the modern world 1780–1914: global connections and comparisons*. Oxford: Blackwell.

Taylor C. 1989. *Sources of the self: the making of the modern identity*. Cambridge: Cambridge University Press.

Related essays

capitalism; China; civilizations; consumer society; convergence and divergence; cosmopolitanism and universalism; decolonization; design; development and growth; dress; empires and imperialism; Ethical Culture; exile; historians and the nation state; Japan; knowledge; liberalism; literature; missionaries; modernization theory; museums; nation and state; *non-lieux*; religion; religious fundamentalism; rush migrations; socialism; spatial regimes; Westernization

Modernization theory

Modernization theory was the name given to a rather coherent set of novel ideas and proposals that emerged in the United States after World War 2 on the development of the under-industrialized countries and newly independent but agrarian societies.

Its main proponents were social scientists at major universities. Their work would dominate the Western debate on development of Third World countries during the 1950s and the 1960s. Walt Rostow, Talcott Parsons, Gabriel Almond, Edward Shils, Alex Inkeles, and Lucian Pye are some of the scholars notably associated with the theory. Taken as a whole, modernization theory can be understood as an intellectual product of its proponents' confidence in the political, economic, cultural, and moral superiority of the postwar United States and, more broadly, of Western Europe. It can also be regarded as these scholars' intellectual response to the geopolitical challenge posed against the US by the Leninist alternative of Communism or, more specifically, China's and the Soviet Union's support of workers' revolution in developing countries during the 1950s and the 1960s. Because of its intellectual 'neatness' and its proponents' connections to the US government, modernization thinking became a key component of US foreign policy, especially during the 1960s and amid the Vietnam War. (Rostow himself was part of the Kennedy administration and later President Lyndon Johnson's national security advisor.) Equally, because of its intellectual 'neatness', which captivated policy makers in Washington, modernization theory was eventually unable to overcome massive criticisms of its underlying concepts, categories, and ideology, as well as to account for the historical and contemporary cases of anomaly thrown at it. To all intents and purposes, the theory had lost its predominance in the Western study of development by the mid-1970s. However, its spirit (the quest for modernization) and ideas (how to achieve modernization) would continue to shape the debate on development of developing countries inside and outside the United States.

Modernization scholars regarded the United States, England, and other capitalist, industrialized countries as 'modern societies', and developing, non-Communist countries as 'traditional societies'. They considered the achievements of modern societies as goals of transition for traditional societies. On the political front, such achievements include the establishment of a democratic political system and a welfare state; on the economic front, private ownership, progressive taxation, urbanization, and industrialization; on the cultural front, mass literacy, social levelling, and the normalization of scientific rationality and technology. This delineation of 'modern' societies reflected both belief in the theory and practice of American liberalism, which consolidated the United States' dominant place in the world after the war, and confidence that the achievements by the US were widely exportable. Although modernization scholars differed on how the transition to modernity, that is, the above conditions on different fronts, could be carried through by traditional societies, they all agreed openly or tacitly that traditional societies were inferior to modern societies, and therefore modernization was desirable. Even though the Soviet and the Chinese Communist Party embraced many of the goals of transition mentioned by modernization scholars, the latter opposed the Leninist, Communist path. They considered the Leninist alternative of 'building socialism', which suppressed individual freedom and private property and promoted class conflict and violence, a pathological way of bringing a society to modernity. Capitalist democracy was superior to what they saw as Communist totalitarianism. Their exemplar of the goodness of capitalist democracy was, once again, the stability and prosperity of mid-century America, minus its racial tensions. The Soviet Union was considered modern but illiberal. Modernization scholars also regarded fascism as a radical mass movement by and large opposed to the goals of modernity. In short, the end-point of modernization was supposed to be a society more or less resembling the United States.

For modernization scholars, the transition to modernity entails not only a reorganization of the economy of a society, but also a complete transformation of its political, social, and cultural norms. Economic and technological advance does not precede but is dependent on changes in individual attitudes and outlooks and social relations. In this respect, modernization theory is incompatible with neoliberal scholarship that privileges the role of the market. Talcott Parsons provided what would become a principal assumption of the so-called value orientations of the inhabitants of 'modern' and 'traditional' societies. Self-discipline, commitment to group values, use of universal evaluative standards, belief in meritocracy, and confining one's action, concern, or opinion to a specific sphere were taken as modern orientations. Immediate need for gratification or emotional expression, focus on personal interests, use of different standards for different people or situations, belief that personal attributes other than individual achievement are more important in deciding one's social position, and extending the significance of an object or one's action beyond its immediate sphere of relevance were regarded as prevalent value orientations in traditional societies. Modernization therefore involves moving a population from one set of value orientations to another. Within their writings, modernization scholars displayed certitude and confidence that they had unlocked the mystery of development and believed that modernization would occur rapidly when the right mix of policies was enacted in developing countries.

In practice, modernization scholars were quite ready to promote US economic aid to developing countries and to accept the state apparatuses of traditional societies as the main engine of modernization. They differed on how the state should deal with local traditions, forms of production, and organizations. Some were more respectful of local cultures; others seemed to favor a heavy-handed approach that involved destruction of local groups or even entire communities. But all envisioned that the local elite, especially those supportive of the US, would bring modern habits, values, and ethics to the general population through conscious programmes of social engineering, many of which were planned with US assistance. The dominance of modernization thinking thus led to US support of existing powers in traditional societies, while the Leninist alternative encouraged precisely the opposite, the removal of such power centres. In the end, as institutionalized democracy seemed distant to such societies after their gaining of independence from their colonial masters, but the Communist threat looked imminent, modernization scholars rationalized that the local military would serve as a modernizing force. They thus turned to supporting military dictatorship in such societies, which they believed would eventually wither away, giving way to a more democratic system of rule.

By the early 1970s, modernization theory was under heavy attack by the Left and the Right, and by academics and policy makers alike. Its intellectual 'neatness', which had helped the theory find sponsors in Washington, became its Achilles' heel. The failure of the US government to establish in the developing world 'modern', democratic societies and its violent involvement in Vietnam also drained interest from the theory. The theory's monolithic definition of 'modern' and 'traditional' societies was criticized by historians and scholars sensitive to the specificity and diversity of societies, while the theory's vision of a linear process of modernization failed to stand up to scrutiny, too. The theory was criticized for ignoring the lopsided power relation between the developed and the developing world, laying the burden of development solely on the latter and portraying the former as a benign facilitator. In short, modernization scholars were accused of being unwilling to genuinely understand other societies, but of trying to categorize and change what they saw as backward societies. On the Right, the rise of Reaganism and the faith in the market eventually replaced postwar American liberalism and the faith in a progressive welfare state, and therefore the vision that such a benign form of government could be exported to every corner of the world. But if modernization theory is no longer in vogue within Western academia, as scholars have largely abandoned the need for a grand theory of development and focused on smaller issues, the desire to expedite modernization has been a staple of scholarly thinking in developing countries. Like modernization

scholars, these scholars, seeing their own country as 'backward', have been willing to countenance or even promote authoritarian rule in the meantime in order to bring the society to modernity, to a democratic political system with all the niceties suggested by modernization theory.

Eddy U

Bibliography

Evans, P. B. and Stephens J. D. 'Development and the world economy', in Smelser N. J. (ed.) 1988. *Handbook of Sociology*. Newbury Park: Sage.

Fewsmith, J. 2001. *China Since Tiananmen: the politics of transition*. Cambridge: Cambridge University Press.

Gilman N. 2003. *Mandarin of the future: modernization theory in Cold War America*. Baltimore: Johns Hopkins University Press.

Inkeles A. 1969. 'Making men modern: on the causes and consequences of individual change in six developing countries', *American Journal of Sociology*, 75, 208–25.

Related essays

America; capitalism; class; Cold War; convergence and divergence; development and growth; developmental assistance; developmental taxonomies; governing science; industrialization; liberalism; modernity; Pax Americana; Prebisch, Raúl; socialism; taxation; technical assistance; technologies; underdevelopment; Vietnam War; welfare state; Westernization

Money

A venerated convention would define money as any good or token that functions as a means of payment, a medium of exchange, a store of value and/or a unit of account. These classic functions may be met together in one currency; or different functions may evoke different currencies; or the different functions may be differently prioritized in local economic and political theory, as shown by the many systems studied by historians, archeologists and anthropologists over the approximately 4,500 years of money use.

An anthropological approach to money necessarily encompasses the depth of its history, the breadth of its variation and the popular practices that emerge outside, or against, the mainstream practices that are centred in political and political economic accounts of money. To start a history of money in the modern era and with the rise of the nation state is valid in the sense that capitalist institutions such as state finance, banks, investment and insurance ushered in new financial powers, practices and international regimes. But it also can take attention away from deep-rooted expert and popular practices that had already created whole areas of commercial and political geography with their own borders, routes of circulation, points of authority and moral economies of exchange and payment. Some of these have only recently been studied, and Ho's (2006) study of the Indian Ocean and beyond showcases the multilingual skills and the multisite research needed to do so. We can only assume that more remain beyond the present reach of Western scholarship. In the era between the 18th century and the present, when Euro-American money politics was not only nationalist but imperialist and then internationalist, these local and regional currency practices appeared backward at best, and dangerously transgressive of imperial or collective international interests at worst. So histories of modern money that are based largely on sources from the European nations and capitalist institutions can elide the persistence and growth of past practices. They can also efface, as in Niall Ferguson's (2002) volume, the struggles that imperial policies had over controlling even the money and finance that they themselves issued in the colonies, where the formal financial institutions differed and local institutions developed further to meet local needs. It is to disjunctures and interfaces that an anthropological and transnational concern should turn, in addition to the insurgent world of finance.

With close attention to the non-European world, then, any 'grand narrative' of monetary history over the last 150 years would start with the multiple currencies and moral economies of the great trading ecumenes and move into their rapid reduction and subjugation through colonial power by the end of the 19th century. The demise of piracy on the high seas of the Caribbean and the Molucca Straits in Indonesia, and the fall in power of the trade entrepôts of the Arabian Peninsula and the Mediterranean, attest to the political and the technological success of the European state. By 1914 there were only 59 independent countries, most of them working on the gold standard centred on Britain, the world's great power of the time. A new period of monetary proliferation was inaugurated with the creation of new nations: up from 59 to 192 by 1995. This 'balkanization' is striking but it is also counteracted by two more powerful processes at the transnational level: monetary unions such as the European Community, and the invention by the financial institutions of three large categories of currency: hard, soft and commodity-based, each with quite different functions in national and international economics. The form of money remains national, and so does the theory, to a considerable degree. However, the hard currencies – of which the dollar, the euro, the yen and the pound sterling are by far the most important – can function as financial assets in the international world and exchanges. Most do so in the form of financial instruments (government bonds, other investments), in 'dollarized' market payments, and also in the form of banknotes passed from hand to hand, especially for large-ticket items. Soft currencies, by contrast, function mainly as media of exchange within their own nations because they inspire insufficient investor confidence to qualify as long-term assets. Commodity currencies lie in between, linked to the price on the international market of the key commodities their nations produce, such as minerals and agricultural staples. Of the 59 countries in the world that now have commodity currencies, 22 are in Africa, including all the mineral-based economies like Burundi and Zambia.

Popular dynamics have to be seen within this changing macro political-economic context, without however being reduced to it. The trade monies of West Africa were not strictly speaking the 'indigenous currencies' they are often depicted as in museum exhibits. They had been produced or traded in Europe for export to West Africa in the era of the slave trade, where they became the primary media for internal trade expansion and wealth denomination. Gold and silver circulated widely in many forms: as gold dust (to be weighed in transaction) in Asante; as silver coin in the Dutch East Indies; as jewellery in India; as Maria-Theresa silver thalers (or dollars) in North Africa and the Arabian

Peninsula. Gold remains a money for storage of wealth, even after all the hard currencies have gone off the gold standard, because of freedom of convertibility. This popularity of the precious metals, however, combined with their centrality in Western monetary valuation, had a serious downside for colonial governments who were otherwise relentless in their monetization of economies for purposes of development and taxation. They had to limit the convertibility of the circulating currencies in the colonies, including gold and minted money, to avoid fluctuation affecting inflation at home. But the colonial attempt to shift the colonies entirely to fiat money (based entirely on trust in the issuing power) was often either resisted or evaded, largely because precious metal and 'paleo-monies' functioned better as stores of wealth in areas where colonial money was physically unstable or insufficient, and where no modern financial institutions had been developed. Manillas and cowries were demonetized by law in Nigeria as late as 1948. The British had to mint Maria-Theresa thalers in London in order to pay for the campaigns of World War 2 in Ethiopia, and they continue to circulate in the Sahara and Yemen to this day. Precious metals, diamonds and other materials with world market value have ambiguous status in fiat money regimes. Whenever there are limits on convertibility and difficulties in storing wealth in fiat currencies, there is always likely to be a popular demand for commodities that tap into others, several of which have had money functions in the past and have their own experts, modes of accounting, expert validation, training and trade associations, and also moral backing. As with the apparent 'revival' of barter in times of great uncertainty (as in the post-Soviet world of the 1990s), the revival of old monies is not necessarily 'traditional'. Historians are still studying the fragmented sources for accounts that do justice to the power and longevity of old monies in complex regional trading zones, such as the Horn of Africa/Red Sea zone where popular expertise allowed the Maria-Theresa thaler to buffer and mediate the failures of national monies on the commodity markets throughout the 19th and much of the 20th century.

Indeed, innovation in commodity trade, evasion of state monetary institutions, the tenacity of old currencies and the invention of new 'social monies' all reflect a certain alacrity with which monetary forms are now grasped more or less throughout the world. The penetration of Western monies into social relations and local and regional markets has been theorized as originally entailing violence by a long genealogy of thinkers, from Karl Marx and Mark Twain, to Georges Dupré and Pierre-Philippe Rey, and – within anthropology – Sidney Mintz and Eric Wolf. The insertion of Western monies was either a secondary stage to conquest (as in Spanish gold and silver extraction from Latin America), an accompanying process to enslavement (as in the Caribbean), or a process that manipulated the valuation of local commodities (as in India) and subjected the terms of trade of local monies (as with soft currencies). Many of these interventions were powerful enough to eliminate any opportunity for fundamental resistance; rather people were positioned to exercise only the flexibilities open to them.

In the long run, however, the peoples of the world have embraced money as a source of income and a means of provisioning, even while suffering exclusion or chronic difficulty in accessing the optimal institutions and resources to make their own money work as an asset. Many states and their citizens struggle to stay within the current international monetary regimes imposed through structural adjustment measures. At the same time, there is transgressive monetary invention – on the part of large and small actors – on the margins. Eric Hobsbawm suggested in his The age of extremes (1994) that we now have a profusion of small states and 'interstitial economic centres' not unlike those in Europe in the late Middle Ages, which act as 'territorial enclaves' and offshore tax havens. Within some nations, the colonial distinction between the 'useful' and the 'useless' areas has been revived. In the 'useful' areas, there is work but in price regimes that put a premium on families having at least one member in a hard-currency economy, as a source of dependable remittances. Migration is one of the most powerful results of the hard/soft currency distinction. In the 'useless' areas and the microregions that cross remote international borders, such as the Chad Basin in Africa, people are regrouping themselves around monetary systems that escape in a different way the failed equivalences between money incomes, money prices and the livelihoods of a prosperous citizenry (Roitman

2005). Working for a living looks increasingly like an impossibility, or even an oxymoron, if one hoped not only to equate effort with money income but also with investment in the future. Often predatory in the acquisition of goods, those who give up on the official money regime making sense for them devote relentless shrewdness to arbitrage across currency regimes.

One overall consequence of the post-1989 globalization process has been this further retreat from any expectation or ideology of self-provisioning: of living without money or using only national monies in a local division of labour. Instead, people live within monetary regimes in which the points and terms of conversion between types of money have come closer and closer to home, through management of remittances, mediation of travel and transnational employment, purchase of goods from around the world, and participation in pilgrimages and religious movements. In view of the ubiquity of the conversion issue, there is a new scholarly interest in its history and practice, and especially in multicurrency economies of the past and present. Standard monetary theory works with unitary national monies. These turn out to be not so widespread. China in the 19th century, Italy in the Renaissance, Atlantic Africa over the era of the slave trade and many others at distinct moments in their history, all used currencies that were not denominations and had no fixed exchange rate with each other. One inference is the importance of accounting, and the concepts of nature and number that allow conversion rates to seem stable. Another is the rise of expertise in conversions, both very locally where particular transactions are made in parallel as well as official economies, and at the international and institutional level between hard, soft and commodity currencies. New studies are on the way to explore these promising directions.

Jane I. Guyer

Bibliography

Blanc J. 2006. *Exclusion et liens financiers: monnaies sociales*. Paris: Economica.

De Cecco M. 1984. *The international gold standard: money and empire*. New York: St. Martin's Press.

Ferguson N. 2002. *The cash nexus: money and power in the modern world 1700–2000*. New York: Basic Books.

Guyer J. I. 2004. *Marginal gains: monetary transactions in Atlantic Africa*. Chicago: University of Chicago Press.

Ho E. 2006. *The graves of Tarim: geneaology and mobility across the Indian Ocean*. Berkeley: University of California Press.

Hobsbawm E. 1994. *The age of extremes: a history of the world, 1914–1991*. New York: Pantheon.

Kuroda A. 2007. 'The Maria-Theresa dollar in the early twentieth century Red Sea region: a complementary interface between multiple markets', *Financial History Review*, 14, 1, 89–110.

Roitman J. 2005. *Fiscal disobedience: an anthropology of economic regulation in Central Africa*. Princeton: Princeton University Press.

Yotopoulos P. A. 2006. *Asymmetric globalization: impact on the Third World*. Working Paper 270. Stanford: Center for International Development, Stanford University.

Related essays

dollar; euromarkets; financial centres; financial markets; gold; human mobility; international migration regimes; investment; loans; oil; religious pilgrimage; remittances; slavery; Swiss banks; trade

Monsanto *See* **Pesticides**

Moon Treaty

The Moon Treaty is short for the 'Agreement on Activities of States on the Moon and other Celestial Bodies' (United Nations General Assembly Resolution 34/68). The treaty was approved on 18 December 1979 and came into force on 11 July 1984.

The Moon Treaty is one of a string of legal documents covering transnational use of outer space. The first document was a treaty between Canada, the United States, Mexico, Nigeria, South Africa, Spain, and the United Kingdom in 1960, which regulated the tracking of satellites. It was followed by the non-binding UNESCO resolution 12/5 of the same year limiting their use to education only. These agreements came in response to the Soviet satellite *Sputnik*, launched on 4 October 1957.

As there were no legal restrictions for outer space, everyone could in principle us it as they pleased. In practice the expense of launching rockets and satellites limited its use to wealthy nations using outer space to demonstrate their power, enhance their military control, or display moral or scientific superiority. The first agreement limiting such use came in 1963 with an agreement between the Soviet Union, the United Kingdom, and the United States to ban nuclear weapon tests in outer space.

This was followed by the Outer Space Treaty which was approved by the United Nations in 1963, and came into force on 10 October 1967. This treaty was inspired by the prospects of opening a new realm for human use and exploration, while it recognized the common interest in outer space being used for peaceful purposes only. It states that all space above airspace is beyond the limit of national sovereignty, a province of all humankind, and thus comprises a common heritage to be explored and use for the benefit and in the interest of all countries. While this treaty was negotiated at the United Nations, an intense race to be the first nation on the Moon took place. President Kennedy of the United States had announced in May 1961 that his nation committed itself to sending a spaceship to the Moon and to returning it safely back to the Earth. People of small and large nations around the world would follow various outer space activities carried out by the two superpowers to reach this aim, and it caused a planetary sensation when the US astronaut Neil Armstrong, on 21 July 1969, became the first human being on the Moon. The planting of the US flag was to many the very image of imperialism, while it also raised legal questions with respect to ownership of the Moon. According to the philosopher John Locke, famous for his thinking about property rights, the natural world is a common property for all only until someone appropriates it by mixing his or her labour with the land and fences it with a stake, such as a flag. The Moon could thus be seen as annexed US soil.

The Moon Treaty came in response to such worries by the international community. It declared the Moon a demilitarized zone and its resources the common heritage of all peoples. The important Article 11 states that 'the moon is not subject to national appropriation by any claim of sovereignty, by means of use or occupation, or by any other means. Neither the surface nor the subsurface of the moon, nor any part thereof or natural resources in place, shall become property of any State, international intergovernmental or non-governmental organization, national organization or non-governmental entity or of any natural person'.

The Moon Treaty's firm rejection of national as well as private ownership has not hindered various business scams in which the Moon has been divided up into property lots and sold over and over again to people all over the world dreaming of owning this ultimate piece of land.

Peder Anker

Bibliography

Beattie D. A. 2001. *Taking science to the Moon*. Baltimore: Johns Hopkins University Press.

Fawcett J. E. S. 1984. *Outer space: new challenges to law and policy*. Oxford: Clarendon Press.

McDougall W. A. 1986. *The heavens and the Earth: a political history of the space age*. New York: Basic Books.

Related essays

Abolition of Forced Labour Convention; Antarctic Treaty; Cold War; International Maritime Conference 1853; outer space; United Nations system

Museum of America (Museo de América) *See* Museums

Museums

Museums are institutions that acquire, preserve, interpret and exhibit objects and materials related to human activity and the natural world drawn from around the whole planet and spanning all of history.

National art galleries, museums of natural history, museums of ethnography and history are some examples of the variety of contents that this institution has dealt with since its inception. These contents have, however, multiplied considerably within the last decades. The appearance of museums of costumes, automobiles, and dolls shows that almost any theme or object can be part of an exhibit. Nonetheless, the first public museums – the national art galleries and the museums of natural history – became consolidated in Europe in the second half of the 19th century with a clear and determined nationalist purpose and as emblems of imperial power. Even though the museum emerged as an instrument for the creation and expansion of the nation state, it has also been functioning as a transnational device of worldwide influence that circulates ideas, representations, images and accounts of other places and cultures and remote times, as their collections summon visitors from the entire world.

Starting with the decade of the 1970s, the transnationalizing effects of the museum have brought about important changes in its function and administration. Museums, traditionally considered temples of art and knowledge and guardians of national treasures, turned into spaces of dissent and dispute, centres of activity and discussion, 'zones of contact' between representors and those represented. Economic globalization has also left its mark on the administration of museums and has exerted increasing pressure on the institutions to think of the art market, the collections and the exhibits in global terms. Moreover, state museums now compete with important private museums that have opened branches in different countries accompanying the transnationalization of the economy.

The second half of the 19th century saw the emergence of the public museum that was not only devoted to housing and classifying objects pertinent to science – as did cabinets of curiosities – or exhibiting the artistic treasures of the monarch – as was the case of royal galleries – but clearly aimed at instructing the citizenry and fomenting the common good. Two factors exerted influence on the expansion of the museum: the preoccupation regarding the chaotic situation of the growing mass of population that concentrated in the cities as a consequence of the industrializing process, and the historical demands of creating a national consciousness. In the case of England, the criticisms regarding the situation of the urban population gave way to the appearance of municipal museums whose objective was to provide instruction and entertainment to the urbanites. But the museum also became an optical instrument at the service of the nation state. As a device that creates and makes tradition visible, the museum served the nation state in the creation of a legitimizing historical tradition. Through its collections – be they artistic or historical – the museum constructed an account of the past and, thanks to a specific disposition of the objects, created an illusion of reality. The

museum was a place where identities were constructed, the relation between the citizen and the state was put into action, and the ritual of citizenship was performed. The wealth of a collection stood for the wealth of the nation. If before the appearance of the public museum the national collections had been in the hands of the king or the prince, the new host was the state. It appeared as a progressive institution that sought the spiritual well-being of its citizens, preserved the common heritage and guaranteed the free access of the public, thus showing its commitment to the principle of equality.

Between the end of the 18th century and the first decades of the 19th century the museum became ubiquitous on the five continents: the United States (Peale Museum, 1786); France (Musée Central des Arts, later Musée du Louvre, 1793); Spain (Museo del Prado, 1819); Prussia (Museumsinsel, 1830); Russia (Hermitage Museum, 1852); England (National Gallery, 1824); Indonesia (Collection of the Batavia Society of Arts and Science, 1778); India (Collection of the Asiatic Society of Bengal, 1784); South Africa (Collection of Andrew Smith, 1825); Australia (Australian Museum, 1829); Brazil (Museu Real – then Nacional – do Rio de Janeiro, 1818); and others.

The museum contributed, alongside scientific expeditions and travel writing, to the emergence of a global, historical conscience. In one of the first and most important museums of the world, the Musée du Louvre, the architecture, the ornamental details and the disposition of the pieces extolled the French State emerging from the Revolution and constructed a historical account that situated France as heir to classical civilization, legitimizing its existence and its colonial expansion. The appearance of these genealogical and evolutionary accounts became plainly evident in the museums of natural history that appeared as a novelty in the 19th century. In contrast to the cabinets of curiosities, museums of natural history made it their goal to not only exhibit exotic objects and pieces but also to explain the world, establishing hierarchies and a system of classification – of the kind inaugurated by Carl Linné's *Sistema Naturae* in 1735 – capable of structuring what was already familiar and interpreting what was different. Soon taxonomies migrated from the world of botany and zoology to anthropology, and science put itself at the service of the empires, justifying European expansion.

Museums thus became spaces for cultural recognition and comparison, and national art galleries in Europe talked of a culture that was heir to the Greco-Roman tradition, able to extend civilization to the whole planet. In these museums some halls were devoted to the art of the great non-European civilizations (China, Egypt, Mesopotamia), showing the capacity of the Old Continent for incorporating the treasures of other cultures. In the Victoria and Albert Museum (opened in 1852 as South Kensington Museum), one of the most important museums of art and design in the world, the exhibition is organized attending to the different branches of art: painting, sculpture, ceramics, architecture, etc., with the exception of the British and Asian collections that show off the national and colonial wealth. However, European metropolises also saw the proliferation of museums of anthropology and ethnography – often as part of those of natural history – where citizens could find out about the ways of life in other parts of the planet. If European civilization was represented by high culture and great men, other cultures appeared defined by primitive activities such as witchcraft or cannibalism that were perpetuated in time, and which situated those cultures at a stage removed from progress, thus justifying colonial intervention. Museums of ethnography became devices that translated other cultural modes to European codes, instruments of domination – to the extent that they placed these cultures into a hierarchical system conceived and led by Europe – as well as emblems of colonial power. Non-European cultures were not seen as alternative presents, rather as historical phases that had been surpassed by Europe, a fact that justified Europe's intervention and leadership. The capacity of the imperial metropolises to dominate their colonies was based on their adeptness at comprehending and incorporating the colonized cultures, and the museum became established as one of the places where this knowledge was displayed and made public.

The processes of decolonization after the Second World War, the appearance of new subjects and social movements and the flows of population – immigrants and tourists – have impelled the transnationalization of the museum. With the emancipation of the old colonies a new elite came into power which – having been educated in Europe or in the United States – maintained, from the very beginning, an ambiguous relation with the museum, an institution emblematic of Western culture. Postcolonial elites utilized the museum as a symbol of civilization at the same time as they denounced the metropolitan museums for the artistic and historical depredation that their countries had been subjected to during the colonial administration, and demanded the devolution of objects, human remains and works of art. An incident in 1992 almost compromised the participation of African teams in the Olympic Games in Barcelona, as the exhibition in the Museu Darder d'Història Natural in Banyoles (Catalunya, Spain) of a stuffed Bushman generated bitter polemics. The issue was only settled with the eventual repatriation of the body in 2000.

However, the new political leaders of decolonized countries were not alone in criticizing the role and the contents of the museum. In the USA and Great Britain ethnic minorities have questioned the legitimacy of the institution. In these countries museums turned into one of the most controversial spaces and, in consequence, they have contributed significantly to the development of a whole series of new models for museums. In contrast to the museums of the old European metropolises, in the USA, Canada and Australia the rupture of the hegemonic cultural models did not stem solely from the pressure that these institutions received from former colonies or from minorities of foreign origin but also from demands formulated by native peoples that had been colonized. In the United States the first group that rebelled against the old museum paradigm were the Afro-Americans in the 1960s. Native Americans followed, with the addition that some leaders thought of museums as potential instruments for the promotion of the native social and cultural rebirth.

Lastly, population movements of so far unknown proportions have caused the circulation, as never before, of the images projected by the museum. Even more importantly, the influx of tourists to the principal cities has turned the museum into a profitable enterprise, a fact that has generated significant changes in its administration and functioning. In the USA during the 1970s museums received 350 million visitors annually, while in 1988 the figures rose to 566 million. In Europe, the most traditional museums such as the British Museum, the Louvre, or the Hermitage regularly receive 3 million visits per year. This has brought about the appearance and proliferation of private museums and private entities that have begun to finance the museums. The big museums now move in a global environment and do not think in terms of their citizens or national resources any more when putting together an exhibit, but rather in terms of great itinerant collections to which numerous institutions contribute. Museums like the Guggenheim of New York have gone even further, opening up branches and projecting other new ones in countries such as Spain or Brazil, thus exemplifying clearly the transnationalizing tendencies of the museum.

These frenetic activities in connection with the museum suggests that, despite all opinions to the contrary, we are not facing the disappearance of the museum but rather the breakdown of a certain way of understanding the institution.

Marisa González de Oleaga
Fernando Monge

Bibliography

Anderson G. (ed.) 2004. *Reinventing the museum: historical and contemporary perspectives on the paradigm shift*. Walnut Creek: Alta Mira.

Carbonell, B. M. (ed.) 2004. *Museums studies: an anthology of contexts*. Oxford and Malden: Blackwell.

Clifford J. 1988. *The predicament of culture: twentieth-century ethnography, literature, and art*. Cambridge, MA: Harvard University Press.

Hudson K. 1987. *Museums of influence*. Cambridge: Cambridge University Press.

Karp I. and Levine S. D. (eds.) 1991. *Exhibiting cultures: the poetics and politics of museum display*. London: Smithsonian Institution Press.

Pratt M. L. 1992. *Imperial eyes: travel writing and transculturation*. London: Routledge.

Simpson M. G. 2001. *Making representations: museums in the post-colonial era*. London: Routledge.

Related essays

art market; civilizations; diasporas; empires and imperialism; Kessler, Harry von; libraries; modernity; Museum of America (Museo de América); nation and state; *non-lieux*; philanthropy; scientific expeditions; tourism; world heritage

Museum of America (Museo de América)

Situated in Madrid, Spain, the Museum's was founded in 1941 by decree, when the Franco government decided on constructing a museum that would extol Spain's imperial past. Even though the permanent exhibition was inaugurated as recently as 1994 – two years after the commemorations of the 500th anniversary of Columbus' expedition – it maintains certain characteristics of old-style colonial museums. It is the only Hispano-American museum that carries this name, and that pretends to represent the whole American continent, making almost no mention of its national divisions or any allusion to the different human groups that have forged the identity of those territories. It is, in fact, a museum about Spanish influence in America, stressing Spain's historical contributions, with special emphasis on religion and language. The criterion of organization – characteristic of an evolutionist view of the human and natural world – is the complexity of social and natural organisms. By structuring its contents disregarding national divisions, the Museum functions as an instrument of transnationalization, while it also serves as a device – tinged with a certain imperial nostalgia – for the national reorganization of the one-time metropolis by emphasizing the hegemonic role of Spain – both historical and cultural – on the American continent. Whereas during the last years Spanish society is becoming increasingly diverse and multicultural, with immigrants from Latin America and elsewhere clearly visible today, the Museum of America remains mostly unaltered since its reopening in 1994.

Marisa González de Oleaga
Fernando Monge

Related essays

civilizations; empires and imperialism; museums; Westernization

Music

Music is increasingly understood as an essential part of a new concept of culture, which is medial and not fixed through language. Therefore the consideration of music begins to cross the borders of music history as a discipline, and especially allows the representation of cultural identities outside territorially determined borders. Although the development of an international music industry is part of economic considerations, music as a topic in transnational historical research is not yet established.

The incorporation of music into the discussion of multimediality and cultural networking processes calls for interdisciplinary cooperations. On the one hand they should investigate the dissemination of non-lingual media, on the other contribute to the representation of globalization processes in the light of local individuality against the formation of global identity. Forays in these direction have proposed at least four stimulating hypotheses. Firstly, music relies on non-lingual semantics; its distribution across borders sheds light on the entanglements of cultures. Secondly, the fusion and transformation of cultural elements can be observed in musical globalization processes. Thirdly, the social aspect of music attributed to the respective culture and its consensus-forming or oppositional function offers important indications on the relations between culture and power. Fourthly, in the portrayal of transnationally interpreted music, conflicts between eurocentristic, seemingly universally high and international popular cultures play a vital role. Basic changes can be observed in the manner in which cultural studies include music. The discussion of jazz as an expression of Afro-American identity, as a target for totalitarian censure or, more recently, as a Cold War weapon, has been possible in the context of a traditional history of cultural-political measures. However, new developments include questions about the transcultural meaning of music, thoughts on music as intangible heritage and discussions on the existence of a global sound. An expression of global commercialization, this global sound acquires the meaning of a political statement when events such as Live Aid concerts or the foundation of a United Nations Orchestra in 1988 create a global audience, reaching far beyond the possibilities of the political institutions. Using both these older and recent developments, this entry will explore musical travels across borders in the modern age.

Medial framework

Music as a global and transnational phenomenon relies on media to transport it. Carriers of music can be musicians themselves, but also sheet music, instruments, sound recordings or video clips. Characteristics and distribution of these media depend on whether they find a market and which technologies are available. An important step was the possibility to conserve music, beginning with the invention of the phonograph in 1877. At the same time music requires recipients who perceive and interpret it. These factors and the manifold interaction enable music to cross borders and set transcultural processes in motion. As a result musical parameters like rhythm, harmony or instrumentation can be separated from their original context, and be combined in the new national and cultural one with musical elements of different origin. Thus new varieties of music can be created. These processes can be found in all phases of music history. However, since the mid 19th century the directions of musical flows have widened considerably.

The most primitive and at the same time oldest medium for the dissemination of music is human beings who either invent music themselves or reproduce what they hear. They take their music everywhere with them, and can always come into contact with other music, include it in their repertoire and vary it according to taste. The formation of musical notation systems in different cultures was apparently an important step towards the locally independent dissemination of music. But all kinds of notation (letters, numbers, syllables, symbols) require a basic musical education and they normally depend on their traditional cultural context. Therefore there is no universally valid notation system, and the spreading of a certain type of notation allows conclusions to be drawn on the monopolization of musical categorization systems. Here the greatest influence is displayed by the Western European music culture. Its notation system has spread across the world, with adaptations as for example in China, despite its idiosyncratic fit to the needs of Western classical music and its limitations concerning the applicability to various forms of non-European music. As it was free from such ontological ties to any canon of music, at least at first sight, the invention of sound recordings was the decisive step towards the diffusion of music via mass media and the increasing professionalization of musicians. The technological developments of the last 130 years have made it possible for diverse varieties of music to be perceived unchanged throughout the world.

Cultural borders, their construction, dissipation or transgression can also be proven by the study of music instruments. In the 19th century the image of a national instrument grows in importance even though the instruments do not represent local characteristics. Bagpipes, typically associated with Scotland, can also be found in Brittany and Ireland; while the alphorn, though scarcely played in the middle of the 19th century, symbolizes Switzerland. The saxophone is a striking example of the border-crossing potential of an instrument, which combines different musical traditions and cultures. Invented by the Belgian Adolphe Sax about 1840, the instrument was introduced in France in 1842. It was awarded medals at the Paris World's Fairs of 1855 and 1867 and gained international publicity. At the end of the patent protection, numerous European and US instrument makers started to supply a growing demand for the saxophone. At this time, the saxophone had not only crossed national borders, but also the limits between musical genres. It was used in military bands as well as in contemporary classical music. However, the most important step was the travel to the United States. First played on the new continent by French military bands performing at a Boston music festival in 1872, the saxophone later came in contact with an up-and-coming musical genre, jazz. Modified from a military instrument to a typical entertainment instrument, the saxophone returned to Europe and spread all over the world. Further evidence of the saxophone's global character can be seen in Caribbean music, where so-called xaphoons or bamboo saxophones appeared in the 1970s. Used in Hawai'i and Jamaica, these bamboo instruments combine the saxophone with clarinets and chalumeaux. Therefore, the saxophone can be seen as an important step in the development of a global sound.

National anthems

Music has played an important role in the Western invention of the nation as an imagined community. Since the end of the 18th century, an integral attribute of an independent state is the national anthem, which in turn became a genre with its own codes, especially relating to musical texture. The attribution of a certain piece of music to a certain nation is a construct, which usually has little to do with the musical culture of the state and rather aims at being recognizable as a national anthem. Most national anthems, with a few exceptions (for example Japan, China and Burkina Faso), can be divided into three different musical groups. The oldest type praises the sovereign in a prayer-like form, typically in a measured tempo, small ambit and steady rhythm. The most well-known example is the British national anthem 'God Save the King/Queen'. In contrast, the French national anthem represents the patriotic anthem, with its faster tempo, wider ambit, accentuated rhythms, and passionate patriotic lyrics. The third anthem type is in stark contrast: simple and in the style of popular song, it tries to express peace and the love of the homeland. Despite the differences between these three types of national anthem, their common roots lie in the Western European music culture. The existence and structure of national anthems originated on the one hand within the replication of European nation building in other countries throughout the modern age, and on the other hand in the impact of European countries on their colonies, or European migrations on their destinations. Numerous anthems of former colonial states closely imitate the military music of the respective colonial power. The British and French anthems play an important role in the development of this music in that they form the basis of countless other national anthems. Several different lyrics were based around the melody of 'God Save the King/Queen', though they ultimately praised the Danish king, the German Kaiser ('Heil dir im Siegerkranz') or the Prince of Liechtenstein. The 'Marseillaise', and especially its characteristic opening, has been adopted in many national anthems, including in non-European states like Cameroon, Nicaragua and the Philippines. The influence of migration processes is also clear. Composers of Italian origin composed several South American anthems. Their compositional techniques are reminiscent of the Italian opera of the 19th century, despite the fact it is not proven whether they drew on a certain model or simply composed in a style familiar to them. How much anthems can be similar without explicit use of the same sample is shown, amongst others, by the national anthems of Andorra, Barbados and Oman, which in addition bear a great resemblance to a German folk song.

In contrast, the number of anthems which explicitly refer to so-called folk songs is very small. Mostly Asian countries such as Japan,

Tibet or Sri Lanka represent their own music traditions in their anthems. Often the performance of these national anthems requires the use of typical traditional instruments and a specific body language that put them in a class of their own, as a testimony that the universalization of the genre of the national anthem was not synonymous with the mere borrowing of its European version.

While the UN has its own postage stamps, the institution does not yet have its own anthem. But several supranational anthems have been developed in different modern ages, in different contexts. The 'Internationale', written 1870, firstly sung to the 'Marseillaise' and since 1888 to an own tune, already accentuates in its title its border-crossing approach and was seen as the anthem of the communist movement. It was translated into numerous languages and versions around the world, often depending on a certain political situation. The 'Ode an die Freude', part of Beethoven's Ninth Symphony, and the anthem of the European Union, is the most popular example of a very different, but nearly always transnational use of an anthem. First attempts to establish the 'Ode an die Freude' as a European anthem were made in the 1920s by Richard Coudenhove-Kalergi, founder of the 'Union Paneuropéenne'. Since then, this music has a special border-crossing quality. While German nationalists loved it because of its Germanness, French republicans called it the 'Marseillaise de l'humanité' (the Marseillaise of humankind), Communists heard in it a call for a world without class distinctions, and the Catholic Church had no doubt it was the Gospel that it transmogrified. It was performed at the opening of NATO headquarters in Brussels in 1967 and again in December 1989 after the fall of the Wall in two great concerts in Berlin, conducted by Leonard Bernstein. Even outside Europe, this music enjoys a special attraction. Since the 1980s numerous professional and amateur choral groups have been formed in Japan with the sole purpose of performing the Ninth – which had been imported and firstly performed by German prisoners of war in 1914 – especially at the end of the year. It was no accident that it was in Japan, at the opening of the Winter Olympics in Nagano in 1998, that Seiji Ozawa realized a global performance of the 'Ode an die Freude' and conducted orchestras on the five continents through a satellite linkup.

National folk music

Alongside the invention of national anthems the collection and study of musical popular culture has played an important role in nation building since the end of the 18th century. Nation builders were mostly interested in lyrics, but they also drew on certain harmonic phrases or rhythms to construct a common national identity. Folk music institutions were established in numerous countries not only in Europe, but also in South America. They endeavoured to collect and conserve the local music and make it available to the general public in comprehensive editions. The research into folk music therefore belongs to the same tradition as the study of other non-lingual phenomena of popular culture, like fairy tales, traditional costumes or settlement patterns. Folk songs have thus been collected with a similar ardour in many different nation states to construct national difference.

The example of National Socialist Germany completes the picture by showing how a totalitarian regime instrumentalized the study of popular songs to justify its claim on regions which were not included within its national borders. During the Third Reich, National Socialist cultural institutions specifically supported all kinds of research on the subject of the German *Volkslied* (folk song) outside Germany's borders: in French Alsace-Lorraine, Austrian South Tyrol, and also in Poland or in Russian districts with German immigrants. The fact that music had spread with emigrating people was used to raise political claims in the respective regions or to strengthen the local German-based culture.

Global sound

The construct of a border-crossing music had already been successfully realized by a very ancient transnational organization, the Catholic Church. Since the turn of the 9th century the close cooperation between the Church and the Carolingian sovereigns allowed the establishment of the so-called *cantus romanus* in the expanding Franconian Empire. While the choral texts were mostly successfully standardized, minor regional differences in the use of music appeared again soon after these attempts at unification since it was not possible to note either exact pitch or rhythm with the notation system. However, certain chants, especially the *ordinarium missae* (Kyrie, Gloria, Credo, Sanctus and Agnus Dei), did receive a fixed and permanent position in the liturgy. On the wings of Catholic missionary zeal, this linking element of Latin liturgical music spread from the Franconian Empire across the world. It was not until the Second Vatican Council (1962–65) that church music in the vernacular was officially accepted. The 2007 decisions in favour of a re-establishment of Latin church chants were based on the argument that the reglobalization of faith calls for the need of a common mode of its expression.

The 19th century's invention of the sounding nation, a nation with its specific music, allowed at the same time the presentation of an international sound. World Fairs and expositions, an expression of a century concentrated on national competitions but already marked by global tendencies, intensified the processes of transcultural interchange. It was especially the Asian music performed on these occasions that had a strong impact on the work of contemporaneous composers, especially on Claude Debussy. In addition to Spanish and Arabian patterns, it was the music of Indonesian *gamelan* players he had heard during the Paris World Fair in 1889 that he tried to adapt into European music. However, these circulations also made it evident that the European standardization of notation impeded the precise appropriation of 'foreign' music. The European system of whole and half-tone steps offered only a very restricted range of tones and of rhythmic notation. The European notation of non-European music was only possible after a complex extension of the notation system established in Europe.

After World War I, the League of Nations Commission Internationale de Coopération Intellectuelle concentrated transnational musical approaches in many ways: it networked musicians, supported copyright protection and called for the establishment of international standards, including the determination of a sound and diapason system as well as rules for national music editions. In harmony with the League's political aims, it also supported its folk music research. Starting from the first International Congress of Folklore, which took place in Prague in 1928 and was attended by representatives from Japan, Chile, Hungary (Béla Bartók) and numerous other countries, a separate section of folklore was created, the Commission Internationale des Arts Populaires. The members of the commission hoped that the knowledge of many different kinds of popular music

would be able to offer an important contribution to international understanding. Yet, the music ethnologists met with similar problems to the composers: the Western notation system developed in the context of European classical music already showed considerable deficiencies in the notation of European folk music and either failed completely in the field of non-European music or distorted this music considerably. The new communication technologies, sound recording, radio and film, provided the missing link and gave a new input in the transnational value of music. Even the scientists had high expectations of this new technology. Relevant documentation or, ideally, a film was supposed to be added to each scientific edition of folk music in order to obtain a maximum level of authenticity and to release music from its written standardization. The League of Nations used the new possibilities of sound recording not only for such scientific purposes, but also to transmit numerous concerts of popular music via its own broadcasting station. The intention was to send music to as many countries as possible.

More generally, the distribution of music through records and radios has represented an important step towards a mass medialization and commercialization, throughout successive technological changes. Music had become independent. Once recorded, it could be reproduced as often as possible, taken everywhere in the form of vinyls, tapes, cassettes and CDs and played endlessly without alteration. This increased mobility allowed and supported the distribution of international music cultures. While in the first half of the 20th century it was mostly Western music that was recorded and sold, a change of musical flows began with the popularity of jazz, rock and pop music after World War 2, the rise of reggae, salsa and Afro-beat from the 1960s, and the establishment of the world music genre more recently. The mobility generated by recorded music triggered further musical entanglements.

One of the most important places for musical exchange has been the American border regions, contact zones between South America, North America and the Caribbean, where Latino popular music replete with African patterns has continued to flourish. Various styles have been created and established, often in relation to the different origins of the Latin American immigrants. An example of the diffusion and migration of a musical genre between different groups of emigrants and the new homeland is the circulation of *merengue* on the east coast of the US. Imported by émigrés from the Dominican Republic, where it is the most important genre, *merengue* was not only consumed by Dominicans in the United States and in Puerto Rico, but also by US Americans and Puerto Ricans. As a result the importance of the two states as *merengue* markets has continuously grown since the 1990s, and today more *merengue* music is sold there than in the Dominican Republic itself. Besides these marketing changes, Latino popular music also has a great influence on aesthetic aspects. Numerous groups, composed by musicians with US American and diverse Latin American origins, brought together their musical backgrounds and created hybrid styles based on *merengue*, salsa, rap, hip hop or Dancehall. The situation has been similar on the east coast. In the 1970s the influence of rock 'n' roll on Chicano musicians resulted in the creation of the so-called 'East Side Sound': rock 'n' roll in English with musical reminiscences of Latin-stemmed music. However, music was also used to establish a separate Chicano identity in the United States, by politicizing lyrics and referring to Mexican traditions in the bands' names. Later, in the 1980s and 1990s, global youth cultures like punk, rap and hip hop were also adapted. The re-Mexicanization of music, through a Mexican-stemmed genre called *banda*, has opened the way for other new inventions like 'rock *en español*'.

Transnational music organizations

Transnational cooperation of music producers and musicologists can be observed in analogy with the general development of cross-border networks; however, this only appeared late after the First World War. In addition, music is mentioned as a transnational linking element in a number of civil-society organizations, which do not have an explicit musical agenda. The International Friendship Association founded in 1926, for example, claims musical gatherings as part of its identity. Similarly, charity concerts often contribute to the financing of transnational activities and have been support mechanisms for humanitarian organizations well before charity benefits à la Band Aid hit the stage. Charity concerts were also suitable to the goals of the International Broadcasting Union, as it tried to air continentwide and even intercontinental concerts with a message of world peace and understanding. The Eurovision Song Contest, a show to present popular music from the member states of the European Broadcasting Union, is one of the most popular non-sportive programmes in Europe.

Musicians themselves organized across borders, to strengthen their art and also their rights. The International Concert Federation (1929) not only aimed at transnational exchange of compositions and musicians, but also attempted to establish laws supporting the rights of musicians in the member states, and contribute to worldwide dissemination of music with an organization whose members, in the interwar period, originated solely from European countries. A number of organizations were dedicated to the transnational observation of copy and performance rights. The International Bureau of Musicians (IMUSA), founded in 1926 and based in Vienna, supported both contemporary music and the realization of multilateral conventions for its protection. The transnational presence of contemporary music is a remarkable phenomenon. Supporting the exchange of music and regular world concerts, the International Society for Contemporary Music (ISCM), founded in 1922 and based in London, has had an extraordinarily global network since as early as the 1920s. In 1938 members of this organization came not only from Europe and the US, but also from Argentina, Australia, Colombia, Cuba and Palestine. The first members of the ISCM were, among others, Anton Webern, Béla Bartók, Darius Milhaud and Igor Stravinsky.

The organizational trend was not limited to musicians, but tapped all the subsections of the 'worlds of music'. Musicologists created their own organization in 1927, the International Musicological Society in Basel, to further musicological research. In a strict sense, it was a re-creation: the first International Musical Society founded in 1899 by Oskar Fleischer and Max Seiffer had ceased to exist with the outbreak of World War I in 1914. The Permanent Council for International Co-operation between Composers, founded in 1934 in Wiesbaden, also wanted to secure the moral rights of composers, while the International Federation of Dramatic and Musical Criticism founded in 1926 demanded the civic-societal right of criticism. After all these foundations, which happened in a relatively short period of time, owners of music shops soon followed suit in 1936. The International Bureau for the Exchange of Information and Cooperation between Music Publishers in Leipzig proposed to secure the international investigation of copyright breaches and bring together different syndicates to maintain business interests. Beside these organizations, focused on the musicians' rights, there are various other organizations, which aim to promote a certain instrument such as the Confédération Internationale des Accordéonistes, founded in 1935. A second phase of organization building started after World War 2 with the establishing of UNESCO. The most important of these organizations is the International Music Council (IMC), created in 1949 as a result of strong incentives from Julian Huxley, director-general of UNESCO. In addition to the 76 national committees, it includes 34 other international organizations with a wide thematic range, for example the European Festivals Organization, founded in 1952, Jeunesses Musicales International, founded in 1945, or the International Association of Music Libraries, founded in 1951.

Conclusion

In 2007, the IMC announced the second World Forum on Music in Beijing. From a historical point of view, the forum's agenda shows well-known concerns: the debate on intellectual property rights goes back to the 19th century and continues to balance national and international interests. Moreover, the adaptation of new developments in music is part of the discussion on how technological innovations produce new sounds and provide access to new publics. The aim to foster musical diversity too is part of the UNESCO programme but is based on the historical development of fostering traditional music. However, the World Forum announced a political programme where music is regarded as a specific form of literacy and the right of access to music as part of the catalogue of human rights. In this situation of dynamic change, music is of growing importance in historical research as an indicator of transnational and transcultural development. Points of interest are the analysis of musical flows, the role of music in the invention of a cultural or national identity, the border-crossing abilities of music, and the epistemological consequences of introducing music into the concepts of entangled and connected histories.

Christiane Sibille

Bibliography

Breidenbach J. and Zukrigel I. (eds) 1998. *Tanz der Kulturen: Kulturelle Identität in einer globalisierten Welt.* Munich: Kunstmann.

Burnet R. 1996. *The global jukebox: the international music industry.* London and New York: Routledge.

Eisenstadt S. N. 2006. 'Culture and power – a comparative civilizational analysis', *Erwägen, Wissen, Ethik,* 17, 1, 3–16.

Gienow-Hecht J. C. E and Schumacher F. (eds) 2003. *Culture and international history.* Oxford and New York: Berghahn.

Glaner B. 'Nationalhymnen', in Finscher L. (ed.) 1997. *Die Musik in Geschichte und Gegenwart, Sachteil Bd. 7.* Kassel: Bärenreiter; Stuttgart: Metzler, 32.

Miller K. 'Talking machine world: selling the local in the global music industry, 1900–1920', in Hopkins A. G. (ed) 2006. *Global history: interactions between the universal and the local,* Basingstoke: Palgrave Macmillan.

Pacini Hernandez D. 'Race, ethnicity and the production of Latin/o popular music', in Gebesmair A. and Smudits A. (eds) 2001. *Global repertoires: popular music within and beyond the transnational music industry,* Aldershot: Ashgate, 55–72.

Taylor D. 1997. *Global pop: world music, world markets.* London and New York: Routledge.

Related essays

1960s; antropofagia; Beatles; benefits and charity concerts; broadcasting; Cantonese opera; childhood; Christianity; classical music; Communist Manifesto; diasporas; European institutions; expositions; human mobility; humanities; intellectual property rights; intergovernmental organizations; international non-governmental organizations (INGOs); Italian opera; jazz; literature; Little Red Book; Muslim networks; nation and state; Nazism; orchestras; panisms; performing artists; prizes; radio; rock; salsa; Santería; Second Vatican Ecumenical Council; social sciences; technical standardization; theatre; war; Westernization

Muslim networks

The notion of network has had great success in characterizing the Islamic civilization since the 1950s, and particularly in the work of Ira Lapidus. Based upon a reading of the world of Ibn Battuta, and taking their cue from the notion of umma (the universal community of the faithful), many scholars have since used the network paradigm to describe the specificities of this civilization. The danger of such an approach was the reification of a topos whose rigidity could mask many factors, from the complex status of the state to the specific role of religion. What seems most difficult is to trace the 'network' theme from the medieval world to the modern one.

Islam is a universalist religion and, since the time of the Prophet, the Revelation is meant not to know borders and to spread. But since that time, too, it has had to deal with the reality of a world in which borders and empires do structure the political, cultural and territorial landscape. Therefore, the circulation of people, ideas and ideologies is crucial in the understanding of the evolution of the relationship between a religious, cultural and political conception of society and the realities of the different periods of history. The early confrontation of the new religion with borders and empires is crucial to the understanding of what happens many centuries later, in the Age of Nations. The memory, sometimes enriched by a mythical dimension, of a medieval united Islamic Empire built by conquest is instrumental in the revival and reinterpretation of old Islamic networks in a transnational perspective. But medieval Islam was built in the frame of a territorialized political reality more complex than the idea of an identity between religion and territory or state can show. Even before the rise of the national idea in the 19th century, religion was embedded in a divided world, and cross-border routes that were set up at that time are still important in the shaping of today's Islamic networks.

The most ancient and most important of all is surely the pilgrimage. In the 19th century, it acquired a new meaning, anchored in medieval traditions, themselves reinterpreted by the Ottomans: the manifestation of a distinctly Muslim political unity (or at least its rhetorical possibility) in the context of colonization, nationalisms and decline of the imperial idea. Not only did Muslims from different origins converge yearly on Mecca, but their routes connected an archipelago of cities linked by religion, trade and culture. There, the religious network merged with a commercial one. Trade, cultural contacts, political or private alliances were structured by this net of exchanges. From

city to city, notables were in touch and formed the core of a strongly interconnected social milieu. These networks stretched beyond the regional Arabic world: merchants were in close contact with Asia, Africa, the shores of the Indian Ocean and Persia. As the Iranian and Saudi examples in the last two decades of the 20th century illustrate, the pilgrimage still has a great influence on local politics in many Muslim countries. It is the occasion for encounters of Muslims from all nations, and the opportunity for the deployment of a religious rhetoric into politics.

In addition to this complex networked reality, the Muslim world was structured from medieval times by the presence of schools to which young scholars of various origins were sent. From Damascus to Baghdad and from Cairo to Kairouan, the educational networks proved for centuries a way in which a cultural unity fermented, able to transcend many of the other factors defining its identity. In the 19th century, this educational network, which extended beyond the Arab World towards the Indian Ocean, was reinforced and served as a relay for the propagation of various reform movements. It should not be seen as a network organized around a single core, even if the al-Azhar university in Cairo confirmed its prominent role, but rather as a multicentred network, as suggested by the 19th-century Southeast Asian success of the curriculum for madrasa education that had been devised in Indian Lucknow by Mullah Nizamuddin Sehalvi in the early 18th century (the Dars i Nizami). Charity networks also derive from a medieval origin. They were reinterpreted in the 19th and 20th centuries and serve in the present world as the armature of strong networks whose function is both social and political, from the Middle East to East Asia, and from migrant communities in Europe or America to Bosnia or Central Asia.

With the decline of the Ottoman Empire in the 19th century and the end of the idea of a united Muslim political structure, or at least of its imperial declension, Muslim networks had to confront the national paradigm. This notion itself was far from neutral in this region: the emergence of the notion of nation was laden with many ambiguities, resulting from European imperialism, colonialism and from new interpretations, ethnical or religious, of the identity of the self.

The meaning of cross-border contacts changed radically as nations were progressively built as territorialized entities that mirrored a perception of ethnicity, or at least as result of struggles to define some conceptions of ethnicity. As most nations of the Muslim world were not to know independence before the 20th century, even sometimes until the 1960s, transnational political networks and themes first developed in the context of oppression and occupation. At first, they did not claim to provide a supranational identity. Rather, they offered an alternative and inspiring way in the national fights for independence from foreign occupation or domination, based on a reading of the Muslim past. In Egypt, in the 1870s and 1880s, strong debates around the reform of Islam and the need to fight British domination arose, with contributions by important characters such as Al-Sayyid Jamal al-Din al-Afghani and his pupil Muhammad 'Abduh. The first was an Afghan with a long travelling record, first along the traditional routes of Muslim networks, then along the routes of Ottoman politics with a diplomatic career that took him from Paris to Munich and Russia. At the turn of the 20th century, the political fermentation became even more intense, mostly in Egypt, but also in Syria, Tunisia and Iraq, but was unable to effectively confront the ambiguities of the time. The rivalries between European powers, the national idea and universal Islam were the data of an impossible equation.

The emergence in Egypt of the Muslim Brotherhood in the 1920s both illustrates these ambiguities and traces a new path. The son of teacher in a Koranic school, Hasan al-Banna (1906–49) created the Brotherhood in 1928 as a political movement aimed at contesting the colonial influence on Egyptian society. But instead of only using the political vocabulary of nationalism, he mixed it with medieval and Koranic references. The ideology of al-Banna was based upon the revival of old Islamic principles, and, most of all, on their injection into the modern world in order to challenge domination. With al-Banna, Islam, as a religious, social and political doctrine, became the source of ferment of a national movement against the unsatisfactory developments of the nation. But it was potentially transnational, as al-Banna's principles were considered relevant for the whole Muslim world. What was new was not the Islamic references as such. They had been persistent in Egyptian society, embodied in Koranic schools, the al-Azhar University, mosques and pilgrimages. Neither was the attempt to revamp the role of Islam in modern society new; the real novelty was instead the insertion of such cultural references into the frame of modern politics. As some nationalists had socialist internationalism as a general ideological frame, the Brothers had Islamic unity. From their successes in 1940s and 1950s Egypt, and influence on characters such as Nasser and later Sadat, the Brothers developed a network of international contacts based upon both national resistance movements in occupied countries (such as Algeria and Tunisia) and more traditional educational Koranic or charitable movements. They supported the fight for independence in North Africa and the Middle East and provided support to various nationalist organizations. They also fought against other forms of nationalism, inspired by socialism, even if sometimes the common goal of fighting European imperialism made them accept alliances.

The Nasserite period in Egypt is crucial, though, to understanding the evolution of the Brotherhood. As Nasser and the Free Officers came to power in 1952 thanks to a coup supported by the Brotherhood and its social and political support networks, there were great expectations from the organization regarding his action and the reform of the state he was to promote. But after a few months, Nasser chose to develop a nationalism whose ideology was contrary to the principles of the Brothers and did not reflect their aspiration to see Islam made a general organizational principle for social and political life. Following this disagreement, massive arrests of Brothers took place in 1954. This decision inaugurated a long season of severe Nasserite repression against the Brotherhood. Brotherhood members pursued their action under cover or from exile in Jordan or other countries of the region, where they redeveloped a network focusing on political activism and on social welfare. The Cold War confronted the network with new challenges. As the socialist-nationalists were to become affiliates of Moscow, the Muslim Brotherhood tended to become instrumental in countering this presence, in a complex relationship with the United States. In the 1960s, under the influence of Sayyid Qutb, the ideology of the Brotherhood became more radical, and replete with more explicit calls for an Islamic state. First in Egypt, later in Syria and Iraq, their aim became to fight the post-Nasserite and Baathist national ideology. The Brothers were now part of global politics.

However, if contacts between the various national Brotherhoods were important, their priorities remained the overthrowing of governments in their own individual countries. The idea of an Islamic state was generally applied to or from a single national reality, even if it resorted to principles with a universal aspiration. The 1970s and 1980s were marked by this evolution: Muslim political networks continued to be used in a typical Cold War confrontation, and new networks developed in this context, with new patrons acting as buffers for the United States, such as Pakistan and Saudi Arabia. The Salafi movement in its present form of a transnational Jihadist organization, itself rooted in a tradition of extremist interpretation of religion, can be seen as a byproduct of the Cold War and its Afghan echoes, enhanced by Saudi relays, as much as a novelty in radicalization. The Muslim Brotherhood still presented itself as an alternative for nations in crisis, with a great influence in Egyptian politics, while more extreme networks, which developed an ideology of violence, turned their activism against secular countries backed by the Soviet Union, towards what was perceived as Western domination. The current state of affairs is a result of these developments. Political extremist Muslim networks now present a variety reflecting both the struggles of the previous decades and the invention of a new form in the political use of religion. Apart from terrorist networks, whose action has to be analysed in the complex context of post-Cold War international politics and domestic situations in Pakistan, Saudi Arabia, Yemen and Egypt, all entangled with the contradictory games played by US, Iranian and Libyan intelligence agencies, the Muslim world has known an important development in the last few decades. In connection with the conflicts in Afghanistan and the Balkans, Muslim charity organizations have evolved into large institutions, often tied to the foreign policy of Gulf countries. This modern reinterpretation of an old tradition has contributed, notably through the activity of charity organizations in Europe and the United States, to a redefinition of Islamic networks. All these recent developments have also contributed to limiting our understanding of the notion of Muslim network to the realm of terrorism.

But other forms of Muslim networks had an importance in the shaping of our present world, such as new Muslim educational networks. In Turkey and along the old trade routes towards the Balkans and Central Asia, the Gülen educational movement, for example, presents a challenge to the secular state inherited from the Kemalist period. The Gülen movement, one of the several groups inspired by the educational Islamic movement of Said Nursi (1876–1960), is an illustration of how Muslim networks have proposed an alternative vision of society. To date, the Gülen community claims to have created more than 500 educational institutions in Turkey, Central Asia and the Balkans, but also in Mongolia and Bangladesh, as well as in some Western cities. Its apparently paradoxical mix of Turkish nationalism, Western-style techniques and Islamic spirituality may have been a condition of this success. What is common to similar networks is an attempt to develop a Muslim vision of modernity. The diversity of their political and religious options shows that there is no single paradigm and that Muslim networks are themselves diverse. The general feature of recent culturally networked Muslim movements is their often being rooted in a specific religious tradition, reinterpreted according to the perceived challenges of the modern world. Present Sufism illustrates this trend of a medieval spirituality and sociability being reinterpreted in the context of a changing world, especially along the flows of migration. In European and American migrant communities, Sufism has proved an efficient source of fermentation of community life and of definition of the self. Sufi spirituality and activism have also created forms of transnational networking, with routes of spirituality that were traced on older routes of trade redefined by the paths of migration. The Sufi network, that linked the Arab world, Turkey, Southeast Asia and Africa until the middle of the 20th century, has been completed by branches in Europe and America in the last few decades. This expansion of the traditional Sufi catchment, and the traffic of ideas and people that took these expanding routes of spirituality, brought about new spiritual forms, often in the direction of some 'New Age Sufism'. But more classical forms of Sufism thought also had a structuring role in migrant communities. As a mirror of identity, Sufism has been a key feature in the organization and internal life of Turkish and North African communities in Europe. Among the younger generation of migrants or citizens of migrant descent, not so much attracted by the communal structures built by the previous generation around the values of nationalism, Sufism has proved a means to express a distinctive identity within European societies. The paradox is that Sufism, a form of spirituality often regarded as potentially deviant by orthodox clerics in the Muslim world, has sometimes served, outside the orthodox world, as a cultural accommodation chamber for the evolution of young zealots in the direction of radical Islamic networks.

But Muslim networks in the contemporary world must not be seen as exclusively political, spiritual or esoteric. There is also a whole aspect of cultural life, which contributes to the enrichment of the expression of a complex identity. Dance, theatre, music, painting, cinema have proved able to attract the support of a dynamic Muslim cultural network. Cinema, which contributed to the spreading of a common Arab culture and language from Egypt and Lebanon, is experiencing a strong revival as a generation of directors has taken up the exploration of the meanings of the Muslim identity, both in the Arab world and in migrant communities in Europe. With the increased access to recorded and broadcast music that started in the 1950s, the scale of diffusion of music in the Muslim world has changed, with huge consequences for cultural habits. One of the first stars of this new market, Egyptian singer Um Khalthum (1904–1975), was not only a great singer and a fervent supporter of Egyptian nationalism, but also the most prominent representative of a generation which benefited from the development of the transistor radio and microgroove record, with the result of an unprecedented fame in the whole Muslim world. Since that period, always with strong national and local peculiarities, the Muslim world has been irrigated by a rich and diverse popular music, from traditional folk music to hip hop. Muslim networks also developed in the 1990s and the 2000s along the routes of the Internet. The content of the numerous electronic Muslim networks is more complex than common wisdom might suggest. Of course, the search for alternative sources of information in a Muslim world where censorship has long dominated local medias, or the possibility of accessing a world platform for political and religious propaganda, have been key factors in the spreading of such networks. But what is most important

in the life of millions of connected Muslims is another aspect of the electronic networked society: contact, communication across the barriers of migration or the rigidity of local societies, and marriage. In societies in which the codification of marriage has long been a central feature in the life of the youth, and often remains so, electronic networks prove an efficient means to both respect the basic principles and norms suggested by tradition and religion, and enlarge horizons. The proliferation of Muslim Internet forums for marriage is a sign of this new social function of the network.

Nora Lafi

Bibliography

Allievi S. and Nielsen J. 2003. *Muslim networks and transnational communities in and across Europe*. Leiden and Boston: Brill.

Balci B. 2003. 'Les écoles néo-nurcu de Fethullah Gülen en Asie centrale', *Revue des mondes musulmans et de la Méditerranée*, 101–102, July, 305–30.

Bennison A. 'Muslim universalism and Western globalization', in Hopkins A. (ed.) 2002. *Globalization in history*, New York: Norton, 73–98.

Bianchi R. R. 2004. *Guests of God: pilgrimage and politics in the Islamic world*. Oxford: Oxford University Press.

Böttcher A. 'Sunni and Shi'i networking in the Middle-East', in Roberson B. A. (ed.) 2003. *Shaping the current Islamic reformation*, London: Routledge, 50–72.

Cooke M. and Lawrence B. B. (eds) 2005. *Muslim networks: from hajj to hip hop*. Chapel Hill: University of North Carolina Press.

Esposito J. L. and Yavuz M. H. *Turkish Islam and the secular state: the Gülen movement*. Syracuse, NY: Syracuse University Press.

Loimeier R. (ed.) 2000. *Die islamische Welt als Netzwerk*. Würzburg: Ergon.

Related essays

al-Jazeera; Cold War; diasporas; film; higher education; information economy; international non-governmental organizations (INGOs); internationalisms; Islam; Koran; marriage; music; nation and state; New Age; oil; pan-isms; religious pilgrimage; Romanticism; Shiber, Saba George; terrorism; trade; world orders

N

Nation and state

The ideas of nation and state presuppose a stubborn pluralism in the organization of global political association. They refer to units that remain persistently multiple and autonomous, although in continuing interaction and influenced by overarching transnational influences that have their own history. The hyphen (whether written in, or implicit) that sutures the term 'nation-state' (*état-nation* in French) is crucial. It testifies to the separate histories of the two overlapping concepts although the term 'national state' (*Nationalstaat* in German) is often used as an equivalent. As a conceptual entity the nation state emerged in the aftermath of the Napoleonic Wars, the composite noun reflecting what became the worldwide project during the 19th and 20th centuries of constructing or reconstructing sovereign territorial units (i.e. states) that supposedly incorporated a given people united by language or 'culture' or shared history (nation).

Sometimes emerging out of older multiethnic empires (including those of antiquity), sometimes constructed out of fragmented smaller jurisdictions, the nation state in the 19th century came to designate a territorial community that had achieved the modern aspiration of political sovereignty for a collectively defined people. The conceptual kinship of 'nation' from 'people' is more apparent in other language families with terms related to nationality developed from the noun *Volk* in German or *narod* in Russian. Accompanying these associations of ethnicity have often been powerful emotive attributions of collective gender. These have found expression through metaphoric vocabulary, e.g. 'fatherland' or *patrie*, through imagery (often maternal), or by virtue of characteristic national activity (the male soldier). What shared qualities of a given population actually determined nationality was and remains a deeply contested issue.

Despite the term's effort to separate the idea of nation and state, common usage today tends to conflate the two ideas. Over time, outside intervention or tenacious agitation and even violence at home has resulted in the extension of state-like administrative prerogatives to peoples living in a geographically defined region of a larger nation state, such as the Basque provinces and Catalonia, Québec, Belgian Flanders, and most recently contemporary Kosovo or Iraqi Kurdistan. Conversely minority peoples who seek to maintain their cultural heritage within larger nation states but without a cohesive territorial base sometimes also claim the term 'nation' as do Canadian 'first nations' or American Indian 'nations'.

Whereas nations did not have to be defined in territorial terms, territory was integral to the idea of a state. That is, states are authorities over bounded segments of the Earth's surface that recognize no more powerful encompassing political unit within their spatial jurisdiction, even if they often delegate particular powers to 'supranational' associations. States exchange ambassadors, make war, sign treaties, and exercise supreme legal authority within their borders. Confusion arises because contemporary terminology tends to refer to such sovereign units as nations, regulates some of their relationships through so-called 'international law', and labels the association that encompasses most of them as the United Nations (UN).

The emergence of 'Westphalian' statehood

The history of the nation state thus originated from two sources. 'State' has long referred to the legal institutions of territorial authority. It expresses the fact that continuity of stipulated offices and agencies exists beyond the lifetime and personal authority of given rulers or dynastic families. By the end of the 16th century, so Quentin Skinner explains, the concept of the state had become 'the most important object of analysis in European political thought' as the 'form of public power separate from both the ruler and the ruled, and constituting the supreme political authority within a certain defined territory' (Skinner 1978, 348–58). The term 'reason of state' (*raison d'état*) emerged to summarize the policies that the institutional continuity of the state might demand, often at odds (as Machiavelli had stressed) with usual Christian humanist ethics. This European-wide discourse reflected the vast transnational splintering of post-Reformation Christian authority, the intensive communication of ideas in an era of print culture, and the painful search for alternative principles of legitimacy. Late-16th- and 17th-century writers (e.g. Jean Bodin in the 1570s and Thomas Hobbes in the 1640s and

1650s) focused on the absolute authority that such sovereignty required. Without a powerful ruler, so Hobbes argued in *Leviathan* (1651), individuals within territories must live in the same insecure and violence-prone 'state of nature' as nations did in the international realm.

The international properties of statehood and sovereignty were defined most decisively with the end of the Thirty Years' War and the Treaties of Westphalia (Münster and Osnabrück) in 1648 that finally sealed that long and complex struggle. The war had begun over issues of the religious balance of power in the Holy Roman Empire, the long-standing imperial confederation that had claimed to speak for Latin Christianity and whose crown had tended to settle in the Austrian Habsburg dynastic line. It ended with the three hundred-odd cities, knights, and princes (including the ecclesiastical ones) represented in the imperial Reichstag winning the right to conclude treaties, to exchange ambassadors, and even to make war and peace (though not against the emperor). Each prince was equal in sovereignty. The idea of sovereignty thus emerged with a dual thrust. Looking 'inward', sovereignty was defined as the prince's governmental supremacy within the territorial unit – supremacy especially above any rival claims of religious authority. Looking 'outward' to the collection of states as a whole, sovereignty was defined as the international independence sanctioned by the Treaties of Westphalia or recognition by other states more generally. A sovereign state was supposedly subject to no international authority that it did not freely accept. In fact, though, the treaties devoted much attention to protecting minority religious claims within states.

By the early 20th century, following three centuries of reflection, Max Weber defined the state as 'the association enjoying a monopoly of legal violence within a given territory'. The widespread adoption of the Weberian criteria – although they raise further issues of definition and theory – itself reflected the 20th-century rise of a global social science. Precisely because these properties of statehood – a supreme legal power within a home territory and full rights vis-à-vis other states – continued to be highly theorized after 1648, we tend to refer today to the 'Westphalian' order. Nevertheless, such a vision of state sovereignty, absolute and integral, was foreign to large areas of the world. Within South Asia, for example, the Mughal

Empire and its successor, the British Raj, recognized partial sovereignty for hundreds of princes or rajahs or sultans, and claimed only what medieval European law often defined as suzerainty. Even in the early United States, the national government signed treaties with Indian nations which recognized both degrees of tribal statehood, including control of territory, as well as degrees of incorporation within the international boundaries of the North American republic. The Westphalian concepts were thus restricted in scope, but as European influence spread through trade, diplomacy, and conquest, the more absolute categories of state and nation also diffused.

Certain consequences follow from the Westphalian notions of statehood according to so-called 'realist' theorists of international relations. With no supranational authority and a state of nature on the international level, states will elevate their own interests (whether survival or expansion) above overarching communal interests. What precludes constant conflict among states are the prudential calculations arising from countervailing coalitions or the balance of power. In fact, an alternative analytical approach, sometimes identified with Hugo Grotius and represented by such contemporary historians and theorists as Akira Iriye, Dorothy Ross, the late Hedley Bull, or John Keane, has always suggested that the life of states was not so ruthless. Although insecure and competitive, states, in this view at least, still endeavour to assure a certain 'society' among themselves, elaborating international law and institutions to facilitate diplomacy, impose restraints on warfare, and to encourage commerce, medical cooperation, and cultural exchange.

Meanwhile states have grown internally as administrative apparatuses, often employing significant percentages of the working population, running military establishments, welfare systems, educational institutions, tending to infrastructure, as well as the fiscal apparatus needed to pay for these activities. Measured by the share of national output that passes through governmental hands, Western states probably attained their greatest peacetime size (roughly 30 to 55 per cent) in the 1970s, following which political efforts to limit their scope began to take effect. While liberal and conservative political theories have distinguished the state from society more generally, in practice the state has been too great a prize and retains too much power over society for powerful families or parties or interests not to seek continuing influence over control of its institutions.

The rediscovery of nations

The component 'nation' within the hyphenated term 'nation-state' remains as problematic as that of 'state'. The idea of nation had perhaps an even longer history. Deriving from the Latin word for birth, a nation was often associated with the so called '*gens*' (reflecting the original Greek root) or early component peoples of the Italian peninsula absorbed by the expanding Roman Republic. They were recognized as sharing either a common clan-like tribal ancestry, a given language, and/or long residence in a particular region. Such tribe-like bodies might not have enjoyed a state structure; indeed in some cases they had 'scattered' (a translation derived from the Greek term *diaspora*) into disparate regions far from their original homeland. The Jews were often discussed as a nation even after their own revived kingdom of Judaea had been eliminated by Roman conquerors.

The 18th-century republic of letters devoted the same attention to nations that European thinkers had given to the state a century and a half earlier. The fascination accompanied the intense focus on the progress of society and commerce alongside politics that occupied Enlightenment thinkers from one academy to another. The new enthusiasm was in line with that broader emerging movement of Romanticism, which celebrated the 'original', the 'natural', the diverse, the association filled with vital spiritual content and emotional fervour – and, conversely, downplayed the uniform, the classical, the so-called 'rational'. Among Central European German speakers this often comprised part of a reaction against supposedly French classical models that had proved so powerful in the wake of Louis XIV's hegemonic aspirations. The Prussian Johann Gottfried von Herder proposed that each national grouping had its own national spirit or *Volksgeist* expressed in certain traditional art forms, religious usages, environmental impacts, and language. Inspired by this sort of thinking, 19th- and then 20th-century enthusiasts went off to chronicle folk customs, search for ancient languages, collect fables and folk songs and fairy tales (the brothers Grimm quite notably), compile dictionaries (Noah Webster), and invent historical romances (Sir Walter Scott) and even supposed Bardic poems, such as the fraudulent 'Ossian' or Longfellow's numbingly dactylic 'Hiawatha'.

For 18th- and early-19th-century intellectuals (as for statesmen) the divergence of states and nations became a paramount issue. The deprivation or defence of statehood became an epic theme. The Ukrainian revolt under Mazeppa, and Pascal Paoli's defence of Corsican independence, which so excited British and American contemporaries, joined the earlier defence of the Dutch Republic that Friedrich Schiller celebrated. Greeks and Serbs had been conquered by the Ottoman Empire; the British and French extirpated the Celtic kingdoms on their peripheries; and most notoriously – since it happened so late and during an age that thought of itself as 'enlightened' – the Polish territories were partitioned in the late 18th century and the Polish state extinguished until 1919, although it seemed clear that a Polish nation persisted.

But just recovering or fabricating a cultural patrimony did not suffice for the early-19th-century nationalists who insisted that national identity be recognized as the basis of a sovereign state. By virtue of its long history as an insular and Protestant kingdom, Great Britain had long celebrated a national consciousness. The North American colonists from Great Britain (Canadians and West Indians excepted) had founded their own state in the 1780s, declaring they were no longer part of a monarchical British empire, but 'free and independent' Americans. In this case, since they shared a language and ancestry with the metropole they disavowed, they made rights-based claims the basis for seeking recognition by international treaty – as had the Dutch 140 years earlier. Their example had an impact on the Creole elites of Spanish America. The claim that nation states should emerge as privileged historical communities was decisively advanced by the wars of the French Revolution and Napoleon. Often welcomed initially by enthusiasts of the revolution and the French republic, the French conquests that followed soon proved exploitative and oppressive, costly in terms of resources and manpower. Against the claims of a Paris-based empire and its satellites, emerged those of the local national 'people' – whether Spanish, Tyrolean, Prussian, Italian, or Russian. Armed 'national' resistance took place as French rule flagged and British or Russian military efforts continued at the peripheries of the French empire – in Spain,

Italy, and then Russia and Central Europe. Political leaders and literati of the Prussian monarchy – Karl Freiherr vom Stein, Karl von Hardenberg, Wilhelm von Humboldt, the philosopher Johannes Fichte, the poet Ernst Moritz Arndt, among others – which had been trounced, virtually halved, and occupied by the French, defined a specifically German nationhood that was destined to achieve, so they claimed, political expression as a state. In Italy, where Napoleon himself had merged much of the northern portions of the country, intellectuals also began calling for an Italian national unit and no longer just reform of their local state which the 18th-century reformers had never really put into question. French conquests had begun in the name of the liberation of Europe's peoples. They ended by fomenting a nationalism directed against that very mission.

Successes for the nation state

These early national ideals and expressions went largely unrealized in the next decades. The statesmen at the Congress of Vienna were concerned with stabilizing the monarchical units of Europe and preventing any further eruption of French republican and imperial ambitions. Italy remained in Metternich's derisive formulation a 'geographical expression' redivided into middling and small states largely dominated by Vienna and its allies, while the German national aspirations of the Prussian reformers were fobbed off with a weak German Confederation that Austria could dominate.

Still, aspirations for national statehood were not to be entirely suppressed. When the Greeks revolted against the Porte in the early 1820s, Western European public opinion took up their cause with enthusiasm, and Metternich could not simply acquiesce in suppression of their rebellion. So too with Serbia in 1830: thus nationalism (united with Orthodox Christianity) came to the Balkans. In the Americas the Haitians of colour had secured the independence of their island republic against Napoleon's efforts at reconquest. The Spanish colonies resumed a revolt against the restored Bourbon monarchs and largely prevailed, bringing independence if not stability to Mexico and the republics of South America by the late 1820s. A second wave of post-Vienna revolutions caught up France in 1830 and ignited a period of nationalist student agitation in Germany, while in

Italy radical nationalist secret societies – the so-called Carbonari – took up the aspirations of revolutionary unification. The 25-year-old exile, Giuseppe Mazzini, began almost a half-century career of propaganda on behalf of republicanism and national unification, writing perhaps the most influential and generous-spirited tracts of the age, in which he celebrated an Italian republic as a type of association that should be in line as well with broad religious aspiration. A new generation of Prussian civil servants began to conceive that their kingdom might spearhead a wider German unification and organized a customs union (Zollverein) that spanned the German states, even as students agitated for German nationalism. Within the confines of the now reorganized Austrian Empire, Hungarians and Czechs and Croatians also called for varying degrees of secession and independence; while the Polish national cause was supported in French exile by the eloquent patriotic poet Adam Mickiewicz.

Revolutionaries in 1848 sought both constitutional government and the construction of national states. While they seemed likely to succeed in the spring, by the fall the monarchs had regrouped, many middle-class elements had grown fearful of revolutionary violence, and Austrian, Prussian, and Russian armies defeated the nationalist claimants for almost a decade. Despite the intervening reaction, however, by the late 1850s the national movement would prevail in northern Italy under the auspices of the Piedmontese gentry led by Camillo Cavour with the crucial support of French Emperor Napoleon III. Following Franco-Piedmontese military victory over Austria, and Garibaldi's ousting of the Bourbons from Sicily and Naples, the Savoy (Piedmont) monarch became King of a united Italy by 1861, with annexation of Venetia and Rome following by 1866–70. Central Europe offered a more complex outcome. German liberals in 1848 called for a national state and a new all-German parliament at Frankfurt. But their plans for a 'large Germany' that included the German domains of the Austrian Empire were frustrated by Vienna's insistence that Habsburg lands must enter in entirety or not at all. That left a 'small' German solution excluding the Habsburg lands, but the Prussian monarch was not prepared to risk Austrian hostility and after renewed uprisings in 1849 dispersed the Frankfurt assembly. As in Italy, a decade of setbacks followed, with a revival of nationalism only by the late 1850s. Meanwhile Czech and Hungarian jealousies allowed the Habsburg administrators and generals to suppress the local revolts within their domains from Italy to Bohemia and Hungary (the last in 1849 with help from Russian forces).

Despite these defeats, the 1850s and the 1860s proved to be a dynamic period of authoritarian constitutional experimentation from above and rapid development of industry. The technology of the railway, the steamship, and the telegraph encouraged ambitious visions of national consolidation and territorial expansion. The new leaders of finance, industry, and science could not simply be excluded from power. On their side, many of the German liberals were to repent of their youthful Frankfurt idealism. They proved willing to acquiesce in Bismarck's humbling of the new Prussian legislature in the 1860s over tax and army issues in return for the military successes against Denmark, Austria, and finally France. Newly popular Social Darwinist concepts seemed to lend scientific sanction to nationalism as part of a universal struggle for power. Prussian victories indicated that nation states would serve as a new crucible for war and expansion, what Bismarck saw as settlements of 'blood and iron'. Bismarck and Moltke's defeat of Austria in 1866 allowed formation of a North German confederation dominated by Prussia, and proclamation of the new German Empire crowned the decisive victory over the French in 1870–71. These triumphs constituted part of a remarkable mid-century global pattern of territorial reorganization – whether in Japan (the Meiji Restoration), British India (the formation of the Raj and displacement of the East India Company), the unification of Upper and Lower Canada, the reunification of the United States after the Civil War.

The successes of unification changed the nature of Western European nationalism after 1870. Previously nationalism had been an aspiration and ideology situated largely on the 'left', expounded by liberal intellectuals and leaders who were looking for internal liberalism (freedoms of the press and speech, a greater role for parliament) at the same time they wanted their nation to achieve self-government. It was also secular after 1848 since the Catholic Church saw liberal nationalism as an enemy to be feared – rightly so in light of the secularization of monasteries, insistence on secular education, and conquest of the 'temporal power' or Roman state. But after the unification of Italy and Austria, nationalism increasingly became an ideology taken up by conservatives and reactionaries. It offered the parties of the Right a new electoral appeal for an age of mass suffrage, as politics in the Third French Republic would clearly reveal.

Of course the national state remained just an aspiration for many after 1870. The Habsburg, Romanov, and Ottoman empires still ruled many 'nations' whose goals of independence remained unattainable until those empires collapsed. The Russo–Turkish war of 1875–78 allowed the re-emergence of Bulgaria and final recognition of Romania. Norway, which had been transferred from Denmark to Sweden in the early 19th century, seceded in 1905. With the collapse of Germany, Austria-Hungary, Tsarist Russia and the Ottoman sultanate in World War 1, the nation state was brought to Central Europe. National self-determination inspired Woodrow Wilson but was given lip service by the Germans and other powers as well. Poland was re-established as a state in 1919. A Ukrainian national state briefly re-emerged after 1917 before being reabsorbed by Bolshevik Russia, soon reorganized as the Soviet Union. The military leader Mustapha Kemal 'Atatürk' forged the Turkish core of the Ottoman territories into a new modernizing national unit, while the British and French partitioned the Middle Eastern territories into dependent national units held as Mandates under the auspices of the League of Nations. Austrian-Hungarian territory was reconfigured as Czechoslovakia and a reduced and resentful Hungarian state, while other lands comprised parts of the new Kingdom of the Serbs, Croats, and Slovenes (later Yugoslavia) and an enlarged Romania. The German speakers of the new Austrian Republic felt the pull of the larger Germany to their north.

The post-World War 1 settlement left many grievances. To use ethnicity (language above all) as a principle of establishing boundaries was difficult when so many peoples were scattered among each other. Of the approximately 100 million inhabitants of Eastern and East Central Europe, perhaps a quarter were left as discontented 'irridenta' or 'unredeemed' national minorities. Germans and Hungarians resented their territorial losses. Two of the creations of the Paris Peace

Conference–Czechoslovakia and Yugoslavia – would dissolve into smaller national components in the 1990s. Among some groups, there would be nostalgic reminiscences for the world of enforced coexistence under imperial masters.

At Versailles, Indians and Koreans presented their briefs for independence, but it took another world war to advance the formation of national states in India, Vietnam and what became the two Koreas. Decolonization by weakened and discredited Europeans brought new nations to Africa and Asia. The transition was often painful: the French fought unsuccessfully to retain a hold in Indochina and Algeria and the Dutch yielded the Indies (Indonesia) only in the face of American pressure. The British gave up some of their domains quickly but often left behind territories riven by violence. Postcolonial politics was often turbulent. India, of course, could fuse a grand tradition of its own national and imperial cultures with institutions left by the Raj. Indonesia likewise welded together an overlay of long histories. Some of the new African countries might also reclaim precolonial national experiences. But colonialism left the many of the new units in Africa with more of a statist than a national tradition. Their rulers – sometimes emerging from anti-colonial struggles, sometimes trained as military officers or administrators by the colonial powers – often inherited the traditions of the state they had served or fought, and they had to invent a nation that might fill the boundaries they had also inherited.

Perhaps the final chapter of nation-state formation occurred as the Soviet Union dissolved in 1991 allowing the re-emergence of the Baltic states (Lithuania, Latvia, Estonia) along with Ukraine, Moldova, Georgia, Armenia, Azerbaijan and the republics of Central Asia. The nation state had apparently become the universal institutional form by which the peoples of the globe sought to reconcile their aspirations for 'belonging' with their needs for administration and governance.

Cultural and religious bases

The nation state has seemed so inexorably destined to be a political entity that only in the recent decades of so-called globalization has it really been put into question. What was the basis of emerging nations, whether venerable or only recently created?

The original nationalist champions of the 19th century believed in primordial communities of language, faith, and race or consanguinity that must claim political form. Some recent social theorists, occasionally labelled 'primordialists', such as Anthony D. Smith, Ernest Gellner, and Miroslav Hroch have dropped the organic implications but have still argued that at the basis of nationalist 'revivals' there really were age-old communities of language, cultural legacies, and intensive networks of communication (this last a measure of community championed by the political scientist, Karl Deutsch). Other historical theorists, labelled 'constructivists', have stressed the linguistic mixes of territories and the 'invention' rather than the retrieval of a national tradition. Like Benedict Anderson, they see the national project as the work of intellectuals facilitated by modern mass media. Primordialist and constructivist theorists alike have stressed the process of creating national identity, which is how the Italian statesman Massimo d'Azeglio defined his new country's task after 1860: 'We have made Italy; now we must make Italians'. In light of modern nationalism, nation-state formation may have often seemed inexorable. Nevertheless, it had to overcome or at least absorb competing loyalties of class or faith. Marxist writers found it easy to identify and often denigrate national movements as a product of bourgeois liberalism, just as in 18th-century Eastern Europe, especially Poland, many intellectuals and leaders could conceive of civic national existence only for the widespread gentry.

Similar contradictions marked the relationship of the nation state to organized religion. This was fraught and complex. To be sure, populist nationalism might arise from religious loyalties, as in Napoleonic Italy and Spain, when peasant communities, local priests, and partisan leaders engaged in low-level warfare or guerrillas against the French occupiers and sometimes their local upper-class and intellectual collaborators. On the other hand, Catholic populist forces could also seek enhanced civic inclusion by peaceful means. Daniel O'Connell organized Irish Catholic voters to demand the right to sit as members of parliament. Later in the 19th century the Lithuanian peasantry achieved a linguistic and political revival against German Lutheran landlords and the Russian state. Ukrainian national ideas drew on the monastic intellectual centres of the Orthodox Church as well as 'Cossack' magnates to mobilize a peasant citizenry and provide the vigour for nationalist intellectual revival.

Despite these convergences of nationalism and religion, it seemed destined that the nation state after mid century, whether predominantly in France, Italy, and Mexico, or in Protestant Germany, must be constructed over the resistance of the Catholic Church. Not only was there a Papal 'state' or 'temporal power' within the Italian peninsula whose independence was incompatible with a national territorial programme after 1848, but also the Church defined liberalism as a doctrinal enemy and liberal nationalists felt they had to achieve their programme at the expense of religious school systems. Not all Catholics resisted the nation state. Some proposed political participation as Christian Democrats, first around 1900 and then again after World War 2. Others drew on their religious loyalties to justify nationalist authoritarianism, whether in 20th-century France, Spain, or Argentina.

Multiple possibilities also existed in Asia. Islamic revival movements from Indonesia to Egypt repeatedly rebelled against colonial occupation. Chinese anti-Manchu and anti-foreign rebellions drew on syncretic religious programmes. Hindu militants, Thai Buddhists, and state-sponsored Shinto in Japan could reinforce Asian nationalisms. With its billion adherents spread (even before the rise of the European and North American communities) over northern Africa, the Middle East, and South Asia, Islam has motivated different political orientations. If during the colonial period it served as a nationalist force, since the 1970s the spokesmen for a pan-Islamic orientation, envisaging revivalist practices and the community of the faithful, have broken with nation-state categories. In effect, the Ottoman Empire and the Persian dynasties kept major Islamic populations linked to a traditional Ulama and state-oriented version of Muslim practice. The disappearance of the Ottoman state in 1923 freed Muslims to support anti-colonial struggles, while the Iranian revolution of l978 in Iran provided the spokesmen for a Mullah-oriented transnational Shi'i Islam with a major national centre. Since the 1950s, the idea of an Arab nation underlying the diverse states of the Middle East has gathered periodic loyalties, while the claims to statehood on the part of a Palestinian nation alongside the revived Jewish national state of Israel continue to embroil global politics more broadly. It is also possible that a moderate Islamic analogue of European Christian Democracy may be set to emerge in Turkey and perhaps elsewhere. The safest summary may be to say that Islam will develop the same range of attitudes toward the nation as Christianity.

We live, at least for now, in a world of nation states. They are fated to be uneasy associations since what nationality involves, what claims it makes, what communities it encompasses remains contested and evolving. If not based on ethnicity, it must be based on history and on compact. Ernst Renan, the conservative French social thinker of the late 19th century, argued in 1882 that a nation must be a daily plebiscite. That is asking a lot. Along with family (and perhaps faith for some) the nation state exerts the largest claim on our loyalties even to the point of putting our lives at risk. It may be that in a world of increased global community – shared music and entertainment and concerns about the environment – the nation state will become less compelling a framework for orientation. For now, however, even in an age of globalization and postmodern detachment, it remains the major form that the 'peoples' of the globe exercise for authoritative political community. Paradoxically the nation state is the most transnational of our options for regulating political life.

Charles S. Maier

Bibliography

Anderson B. 1991. *Imagined communities: reflections on the origin and spread of nationalism.* London: Verso.

Breuilly J. 1994. *Nationalism and the state,* 2nd edition. Chicago: Chicago University Press.

Chatterjee P. 1986. *Nationalist thought and the colonial world: a derivative discourse.* London: Zed.

Eley G. and Suny R. G. (eds) 1996. *Becoming national: a reader.* Oxford and New York: Oxford University Press.

Skinner Q. 1978. *The foundations of modern political thought,* 2 vols. Cambridge: Cambridge University Press.

Smith A. D. (ed.) 2001. *Nationalism: theory, ideology, history.* Oxford: Polity.

Smith A. D. 2000. *The Nation in history: historiographical debates about ethnicity and nationalism*. Hanover, NH: University Press of New England.

White P. J. 'Globalization and the mythology of the "nation state"', in Hopkins A. G. (ed.) 2006. *Global history: interactions between the universal and the local*, Basingstoke: Palgrave Macmillan.

Related essays

1848; 1989; anti-Catholicism; Armenian genocide; body shopping; broadcasting; Christianity; conspiracy theories; decolonization; diasporas; empires and imperialism; ethnicity and race; European Union (EU); exile; film; governing science; higher education; historians and the nation state; humanities; indigenous networks; intellectual property rights; internationalisms; Internet; Islam; Italian opera; kindergarten; language diplomacy; language; League of Nations system; legal order; liberalism; libraries; literature; mail; Maoism; measurement; museums; music; Muslim networks; national parks; partitions; police; race-mixing; radio; regions; religion; religious pilgrimage; Romanticism; services; socialism; spatial regimes; taxation; *The Wretched of the Earth*; transnational; United Nations Educational, Scientific and Cultural Organization (UNESCO) educational programmes; United Nations system; war; Wilson, Woodrow; women's movements; world orders; Zionism

Nation state and historians *See* Historians and the nation state

National accounting systems

National accounting systems are the procedures formalized during the 20th century to calculate the dynamic macrostatistics of national economies, including most famously the statistics of gross national income and gross national product (GNP) that became defining yardsticks by which governments and international organizations attempted to manage economies during the post-World War 2 decades.

GNP (or the now more common GDP, gross domestic product) is essentially an assessment of the total annual production of goods and services in an economy, a number related to gross national income, which is the income

derived from that output (minus depreciation). The computation of these statistics is a complex process that uses an interlinked accounting framework and so-called sector tables to determine the aggregate levels of production, consumption, capital formation, and investment in an economy and the flows between components.

The modern history of national accounting began with periodic income estimates during the 19th and early 20th centuries, when global competition between nations and empires spurred interest in numerical representations of national wealth and relative levels of 'civilization'.

Estimates, however, were ad hoc, not standardized, and not part of official state practice. This began to change with a transnational statistical revolution beginning after the First World War by which economists over the following four decades reoriented their discipline toward highly quantified techniques. The aggregate empirical methodologies and Keynesian theories that arose in the contexts of the Great Depression and World War 2 emphasized macroeconomic measurement of employment, demand, and national income and supported applied forms of analysis that could help states take new responsibility for avoiding economic crises.

Interrelated developments in Great Britain and the United States during the 1930s depression resulted in regular calculations of national product and income statistics. This work was pioneered in the US by Wesley Clair Mitchell at the National Bureau of Economic Research, by the National Conference on Research in Income and Wealth and by New Deal agencies, and in Great Britain by the Economic Advisory Council. National accounting innovation also received a boost from a transnational cohort of Anglo-American economists interested in using these procedures to validate the heretical ideas of John Maynard Keynes, a British economist who had argued that stagnant economies could be jumpstarted by using government spending – even if this meant unbalanced budgets.

The American economist Simon Kuznets devised a coherent set of national accounting techniques amid such interest, and he first developed the statistic of GNP and related measures of consumption, savings, and investment to understand how to avoid high, long-term unemployment. Keynes himself was at the forefront of related innovations that yielded insights into the relation of government expenditure to national income.

In the early 1940s, economists convinced officials to apply these methodologies to war planning. By applying national accounting conventions developed by Kuznets and planners in the new British Central Statistical Office, analysts could plan war production, resource mobilization and government financing. In the US, these techniques seemed so successfully employed by the War Production Board that the postwar economist John Kenneth Galbraith declared Simon Kuznets one of the least recognized contributors to Allied victory.

Similar trends were at work in the Axis powers and other countries, but by the end of World War 2, Anglo-American-style macroeconomics stood at the centre of transnational flows of economic knowledge within the non-Marxist branches of the discipline.

This influence was reflected in successful American and British promotion of national accounting in occupied Japan and Germany and in such new multilateral institutions erected after the war to rebuild the world economy as the Organization for Economic Cooperation and Development (OECD) and the World Bank. American statisticians like Stuart Rice, chair of the United Nations Committee on Statistics, placed national accounting practices at the centre of their visions of postwar reconstruction in the ruined economies of Asia and Europe. The British economist Richard Stone, moreover, played a central role in the creation for the first time of international standards for computing national accounts (the 'System of National Accounts' or SNA), published by the United Nations in 1952. Stone's seminal contributions with the UN extended for over two decades and included work on the revisions of the SNA in 1968. By that time, however, there existed a vigorous field of research on national accounting around the world, and contributions to the evolving UN standards were increasingly multilateral.

The UN and new regional multilateral organizations after the war required formal national accounting systems of their member countries, and the 1950s and 1960s witnessed a dramatic increase in the number of nations producing official income estimates. Although many attempted to adhere to the latest UN standards, nearly half of all non-socialist-economy countries as late as the 1980s had yet to adopt them completely. The Soviet bloc countries, moreover, rejected the SNA in favor of an alternative system known as the Material Product System, which adopted a more restricted definition of national product by including in its calculation only goods and services related to the production of material goods (thus counting as irrelevant non-materials goods such as education, finance, etc.). With the fall of the Soviet Union and market liberalization in China, the great majority of nations now attempt to adhere to the current UN standards, last revised in 1993.

The resulting global regime of national accounting helped reorient policy making around the world during the postwar decades toward the ideal of rapid growth. Though a blunt instrument, GNP thus took on an outsized role in the latter half of the 20th century as one of the key numbers by which the presumed progress of nations came to be measured, a conceptual paradigm that still influences economic thinking in the early 21st century even as many continue to devise alternative accounting standards designed to provide a fuller picture of levels of social welfare than critics say can be captured by the macroeconomic methods of the SNA.

Scott O'Bryan

Bibliography

Comim F. 2001. 'Richard Stone and measurement criteria for national accounts', in Klein J. L. and Morgan M. S. (eds) 2001. *The age of economic measurement* (annual supplement to vol. 33 of History of Political Economy), Cambridge: Cambridge University Press, 213–34.

Engerman D. C. 2007. 'Bernath Lecture: American knowledge and global power', *Diplomatic History*, 31, 4, 599–622.

O'Bryan S. P. 2002. 'Economic knowledge and the science of national income in 20th-century Japan', *Japan Studies Review*, 6, 1–20.

Studenski P. 1958. *The income of nations: theory, measurement, and analysis, past and present.* New York: New York University Press.

Related essays

civilizations; convergence and divergence; development and growth; developmental taxonomies; economics; intergovernmental organizations; technical standardization; transnational; underdevelopment; United Nations system; war

National Basketball Association (NBA) See Sport

National parks

Once fiercely 'national' – as the name implies – national parks have evolved over more than a century to reflect transnational concerns about environmental conservation. A body of thinking about protected areas has developed that reflects the cross-transmission of ideas from almost all areas of the globe. During the course of its existence, the once iconic national park – a large, generally unpopulated but carefully managed recreational wilderness – has become a more flexible form of land use. The objectives of national parks have also altered. Once lauded for their preservation of landscape and wildlife and for the absence of people, national parks are now designed as well considered systems that encompass representative biomes in order to provide ecosystem services and opportunities for sustainable development (generally ecotourism), scientific research and biodiversity conservation. In addition, management of national parks as 'fortresses' that excluded local communities and indigenous knowledge has altered in favour of a broader 'community conservation' in which all sectors of the population have a stake.

In 1962 the International Union for the Conservation of Nature and National Resources (the IUCN or World Conservation Union) defined a number of protected area categories to be applied universally. National parks are Category II, that is, natural areas protecting ecological integrity, excluding inappropriate exploitation or occupation, and providing spiritual, scientific, educational and recreational opportunities as along as they are environmentally and culturally compatible. Normally, ownership of such properties is vested in the highest competent authority of the nation. They differ from strict nature reserves and from wilderness as well as from biosphere reserves, although the requirements and characteristics of each may overlap. In 2003 national parks (some 3,881 sites) comprised 23.5 per cent (4,400,000 km²) of the total global protected area.

The United States claims to have invented national parks with Congressional approval of Yellowstone in Wyoming in 1872 as a 'public park or pleasuring ground for the benefit and enjoyment of the people' in which all its geological and scenic wonders would be preserved 'in their natural condition'. In fact, the words 'national park' were first used in legislation in 1879, and applied to a public open space in Sydney, Australia, that was modelled on the urban parks of Europe. The United States' first parks, it is argued by Roderick Nash among others, were predicated on the idea of political and economic democracy, monumental spaces of which a new nation might rightly be proud and that were accessible to all citizens, unlike the parks of Europe. The foundation of the North American national parks fed on an ideology of national identity expressed through landscape. Because this had to be 'pristine nature' there was no room for the Indian American and many were removed to make way for the parks. Although the removal of Africans from national parks was also integral to Africa's early parks, this form of protected area emanated from 'game reserves' that were established by colonial governments intent on preserving desirable species of wildlife and illusions of 'the hunt' based on a European stereotype of the relationship between animals and people.

Visitor access is a core component of national parks, and this has worked to the economic benefit of many countries with significant natural beauty or bounty. While the United States spearheaded recreation and public ownership, Africa and other less developed continents imbued national parks with wildlife and ecological values. The early history of national parks demonstrates scant concern for the interests of local or indigenous people. Most often, in the United States, India and many parts of Africa, they were forcibly removed from national parks in order to make way for recreational tourism. In addition, national parks were a convenient way of administering national borders. Both these aspects of national park history are changing. Conservation strategies infused by transnational ideas of indigenous rights are becoming the norm. Moreover, national boundaries are becoming increasingly irrelevant and transboundary or transfrontier conservation areas (often called 'peace parks') are planned for many parts of the world.

Jane Carruthers

Bibliography
Chape S., Blyth S., Fish L., Fox P. and
    Spalding M. (comps) 2003. 2003 United

Nations List of Protected Areas. Gland/
    Cambridge: IUCN/UNEP-WCMC.
Mackenzie J. M. 1988. The empire of
    nature: hunting, conservation and British
    imperialism. Manchester: Manchester
    University Press.
Nash R. 1982. Wilderness and the American mind.
    3rd edition. New Haven: Yale University
    Press.

Related essays

borders and borderlands; conservation and
preservation; environmentalism; indigenous
networks; nation and state; sustainable
development; tourism; wildlife films; World
Conservation Union (IUCN) / World Wide
Fund for Nature (WWF); world heritage

Natural hazards

Contrary to widespread popular usage, there
are no such things as 'natural disasters'. There
are certainly disasters but for one to take place
two forces with their own separate trajectories have to come together at the same time and
place to create an event. On one side, there is
the hazard that can be purely natural like an
earthquake, volcanic eruption and typhoon or
increasingly more human-induced as in the
case of fire, chemical releases and ozone depletion. On the other side are human populations
whose social, economic and political organizations are largely culturally determined. The
manner in which social systems are structured leaves some people more exposed than
others. Critical to discerning the nature of
disasters, then, is an appreciation of the ways
in which human systems place people at risk
in relation to each other and to their environment, a causal relationship that can best be
understood in terms of an individual's, household's, community's or society's vulnerability.
Vulnerability is determined by a combination
of factors that include class, gender, age and
ethnicity among others. This condition, however, should not be confused with poverty.
Though the poor are much more likely to be
affected by disasters, wealth, too, generates
its own types of risks. One has only to consider how coastal locations contribute to the
exposure of expensive beachside properties or
how tourists are subject to all manner of perils. For example, the largest recorded number
of Swedes to die in a single disaster in modern
history occurred in Thailand as a result of the
Indian Ocean tsunami of 2004.

Disasters, then, have two historical
trajectories, one 'natural' and the other societal. They are 'historical' in the sense that
both forces change over time. The fact that
the nature of hazards varies over the years is
perhaps less immediately apparent than the
human element. Geophysical and climatic
conditions not only alter in the long term, over
hundreds of thousands of years, but also within
much shorter time spans that have affected
human societies within recorded history. The
variations in mean average temperatures associated with the Late Medieval Optimum (1100–
1400), Little Ice Age (1600–1800) and Modern
Optimum (since 1800) not only had effects on
agriculture, human nutrition and population
density but also have important bearing on
the intensity and frequency with which people were subject to extreme events at any given
location. More recently, scientific evidence
suggests a strong correlation between floods,
droughts and related hazards and higher temperatures, the release of heat-retaining gases
into the atmosphere, and variations in precipitation levels around the world. Even the
magnitude of hurricanes in the Caribbean and
Pacific has been linked to rising sea-surface
temperatures. Such arguments, however, are
still controversial and evidence suggests that
floods may be no higher today than in the past
and that warmer waters are only one of many
factors contributing to the generation of hurricanes. Nor are hazards purely destructive:
one only has to consider the relationship of
the annual flooding of the Nile to the prosperity of Egypt or of the typhoon season to precipitation levels in the Philippines to realize
their long term significance to human settlement and history. All in all, however, there are
now impressive data series for certain world
regions that shed light on what occurred in
the preinstrumental age. Much of this evidence has been collated into large data series
such as EURO-CLIMHIST on weather-related
events in Europe over the period 750–1850
CE or the massive Japanese compendiums on
earthquakes that chronicle such events since
the 7th century.

The historical trajectory of societies is
much more apparent to perceive. Quite evidently people and the cultures they create
have changed over time. The question in relation to natural hazards, however, is to what
extent these alterations made populations
more or less vulnerable and what if anything
they did about that vulnerability. Vulnerability

recognizes that certain people in the past may have been situated in more perilous settings than others as a result of a particular configuration of political, economic, social, ideological and environmental factors. Attempting to view the course of recorded history from this perspective requires focusing on certain key elements in any society's relationship to its environment: the number and distribution of its people, how they fed and housed themselves, and the 'appropriateness' of their technology to environmental conditions.

The accelerating pace of change has transformed the nature and degree to which societies are exposed to hazards though arguably the adoption of agriculture still remains the single biggest alteration affecting people's vulnerability. The European conquest of the Americas with its drastic reduction in indigenous populations and subversion of their cultural adaptations also left the ensuing societies far more exposed to risks that persist to this day, a process that was replicated in parts of Africa, Australasia and the Pacific. Nonetheless, there is no denying the impact of recent changes. While the Industrial Revolution increasingly had important implications for people's vulnerability after 1750, the size of the population affected was initially not large and its influence felt only indirectly outside of a local or a regional scale. Nor should the impact that traditional societies had on their environments be minimized: perhaps more forests, for example, were cleared prior to 1950 than have been felled since and flood, drought and localized climate change were very much features of the preindustrial age as they were subsequently. Clearly, however, the exponential increase in world population from approximately 1½ billion in 1900 to over 6 billion by 2000 and the increasing demands of a mass-production and consumption world market have created unprecedented environmental strains that are expressed by climate change, rising sea levels, toxins in the food chain and the generation of waste products among others. The scale of this human explosion must also be considered in conjunction with the mass migrations of peoples from one part of the world to another. More than mere numbers, the European, Chinese and African diasporas over the past five centuries involved millions of people leaving environments they were familiar with to settle in new

ones whose ecological processes they poorly understood. The ensuing encounters created their own forms of hazard: rampant species colonization such as the proliferation of rabbits in Australia or the widespread soil erosion associated with the 20th-century Dust Bowl in the midwestern US.

But, perhaps, the single most significant factor affecting global vulnerability today is urbanization with the number of people living in towns and cities rapidly exceeding those living in rural areas. There is no straight correlation, however, between increased urbanization and heightened vulnerability. The concentration of population in urban areas rather than dispersed across an extensive countryside means that people are increasingly less likely to experience a hazard but that more are adversely affected when they do. In developed countries where it is more likely that building and zoning codes are enforced, older buildings retrofitted, emergency services better equipped and early warning systems more fully developed, the number of fatalities has declined dramatically in proportion to the total population even if the material costs have increased as much as eightfold in real terms since the 1960s.

The same, however, cannot be said of developing countries where the dynamics of urban growth are putting more people at risk faster than ever before. Cities like Dhaka, Kinshasa and Lagos are approximately 40 times larger today than they were in 1950, while more than 200 million people in China alone have moved to urban centres in the last thirty years, raising the spectre of a 'planet of slums' in the not too distant future. Many of these cities are fast becoming potential disaster zones through sheer size of population, unmindful modification of the natural environment or expansion into areas unsuited for such purposes. Again, it is the poorer members of society, particularly recent rural migrants who are unduly put at risk. Not only are they forced to live in the most perilous surroundings along eroding river banks, atop unstable slopes or beneath mountains of waste, but they stand to disproportionately lose most in a disaster that may strip them of all their assets in a moment.

The past, however, also challenges our notions that contemporary and Western ways are always better. An indigenous earthquake-resistant architecture evolved in northwestern Turkey during the Ottoman Empire and in the Spanish Philippines where the style was known as 'earthquake baroque'. These were attempts to minimize loss by constructing buildings that took account of regularly occurring hazards. An alternative approach with another recurrent urban threat, that of fire, was much favoured in Qing China, Tokugawa Japan and Mughal India. Cheaply constructed 'ephemeral cities' were built, ones where people readily accepted the periodic loss of their homes and allowed for the easy removal of costly interior features that could be reused in structures of a similar nature.

This rapidly expanding and increasingly urbanized world population daily runs the risk of exceeding its food supply. While harvest failure is inherent to all forms of agriculture throughout history, more traditional farming practices favour techniques that reduced the likelihood of famine. Crop diversification and dispersed locations are important mechanisms for ensuring food security in communities as geographically and culturally distinct as the Ivatan islanders of the South China Sea or Swiss farmers on the slopes of the Alps. In societies exposed to the constant threat of hazard, such strategies make good sense from the perspective of cultivators who are mainly engaged in minimizing risk rather than maximizing surplus. Unfortunately, the wholesale commercialization of agriculture and the adoption of high-yield seed, while raising production, have adversely affected these types of adaptive strategies. Moreover, the intensification of commercial farming especially in Western nations has also put livestock more at risk over the last fifty years. As small farms have been progressively replaced by large industrialized agropastoral enterprises, the exposure of confined animals to hazards such as failed infrastructure, non-functioning automated systems, and diseases have resulted in large losses. The extent to which intensive farming practices render national food markets more vulnerable to the impact of hazards was graphically illustrated when Hurricane Floyd hit the southeastern seaboard of the USA in 1999. North Carolina, the state worst affected, is also the second largest hog producer in the country with 90 per cent of its farms located in the worst affected areas.

Technology has often been seen as the appropriate response to hazard. The extensive flood protection systems erected by the Chinese, Vietnamese and especially the Dutch over the centuries allowed agriculture and industry to flourish on hitherto marginal lands but at the cost of intensifying their exposure to hazards. The Netherlands suffered its worst disaster in 300 years when the combination of gale-force winds and a high spring-tide breached the dikes one night in 1953 drowning 1,835 people and inundating 200,000 hectares. Attempts to use science to predict such occurrences began in the second half of the 19th century with the development of meteorology and seismography. Great advances were made next century as balloons, aircraft and satellites added enormously to the quantity and quality of the data available, allowing computer-generated models to forecast both immediate and more seasonal weather conditions. A greater ability to project the onset of the 1997/98 El Niño Southern Oscillation event, the most powerful in recent history, however, did little to alleviate its adverse effects on nearly 111 million people or prevent it from causing over US$34 billion in direct losses. Even the ability to accurately predict smaller-scale phenomena remains problematic: Sydney was suddenly struck by a severe hailstorm in April 1999 that left AU$1 billion worth of damages. Most early-warning provisions, moreover, remain hazard-specific and national in character and so lack a truly comprehensive outlook, a partial exception being the Pacific Tsunami Warning System based in Hawai'i that serves 26 member states.

However, as Hurricane Katrina that devastated large parts of the southern USA in August 2005 proved, technological know-how and scientific expertise have their limits and Western developed countries may have as much to learn about disaster preparedness, management and recovery from non-Western developing countries as the latter do from the former. In fact, a country's response to natural hazard may depend more on its social and organizational practices than on any measure of its wealth and resources. With a policy of public education, annual national training exercises, a comprehensive early-warning system, an integrated civil defence structure and strong government leadership, Cuba is better able to protect its citizens than most other states. Hurricane Jeanne that cut a swath of destruction through the Caribbean in 2004 passed without loss of life over Cuba but left 3,000 dead in neighbouring Haiti. The country now serves as a best-practice model for the United Nations and has even organized special medical brigades to provide assistance to other states during disasters.

By drawing attention to the processes that put people at risk and how they deal with that consequent vulnerability over time, natural hazards provide a measure by which to assess how successful past and present societies have been in adapting to their environments. It is also important to consider disasters as more than purely destructive events in the short term and to view them as transformative agents in the longer term. In fact, disasters may be significant catalysts of change in their own right, causing political, economic and social adjustments, triggering needed adaptations in human behaviour and the built environment, as well as perhaps contributing to the overthrow of dynasties, economic systems and even civilizations.

Greg Bankoff

Bibliography

Blaikie P., Cannon T., Davis I. and Wisner B. 2004. *At risk: natural hazards, people's vulnerability and disasters*. London and New York: Routledge.

Davis M. 2006. *Planet of slums*. London and New York: Verso.

Diamond J. 2005. *Collapse: how societies chose to fail or survive*. London: Allen Lane.

Hewitt K. (ed.) 1983. *Interpretations of calamity from the viewpoint of human ecology*. Hemel Hempstead and Boston: Allen and Unwin.

Oliver-Smith A. and Hoffman S. (eds) 1999. *The angry Earth: disaster in anthropological perspectives*. New York and London: Routledge.

Quarantelli E. 1998. *What is a disaster? perspectives on the question*. London and New York: Routledge.

Related essays

agriculture; air pollution; benefits and charity concerts; climate change; human mobility

Nazism

This term is the German shorthand for National Socialism, the set of ideas promoted by the National Socialist German Workers' Party, founded in 1920, which emerged as the most powerful political force in German politics in the early 1930s, gained power in 1933 and ruled Germany until 1945. Along with fascism in Italy, National Socialism served as a model for a developmental dictatorship which could revive and secure national destiny. In the interwar period, Nazi Germany was counted among the 'young nations' which had challenged the status quo of the French and British empires. As a movement of national renewal, Nazism found admirers and emulators in Eastern and Southern Europe and in South America. And although the horrors of World War 2 have precluded all but the tiniest gatherings of neo-Nazis, the Nazis and especially Hitler remain widely consumed cultural icons throughout the world.

However, the Nazis saw the revival of Germany as rooted in a more complex aetiology which called for rooting out biological dangers through sterilization, destroying supposedly alien blood, as exemplified by Jews, and securing Germany's future by establishing a continental empire in Eastern Europe. Germany's model was not Great Britain, but the United States, where European invaders had plundered, and in large part killed indigenous people. While National Socialism identified itself politically with fascist parties throughout Europe, it rejected broader political alliances in pursuit of imperial policies that would benefit Germany. Thus the European war the Nazis sought once they had consolidated power was not simply ideological, but explicitly national. Invading Poland in 1939 and the Soviet Union in 1941, the Nazis aimed to create a Greater German Empire in which German colonists would ruthlessly exploit the labour and resources of the Slavic peoples they occupied, wipe out the vestiges of autonomous nationalities and cultures, and physically remove the Jews. After 1941, the physical removal of the Jews meant physical extermination; by 1945, the Nazis had murdered two thirds of Europe's Jewish population. As long as they were victorious, the Nazis' ambitions knew no limits and they even contemplated the conquest of the globe, an unprecedented aim. However, Germany's resources never matched either the scale of its ambitions or the resolve of its enemies.

Germany's war cost the lives of millions of civilians, who constituted three quarters of the estimated 35 million casualties in World War 2. Nazi Germany's quest for empire and living space in the years 1939–45 tore up the histories of European nations with unprecedented violence, created alliances with local collaborators, which remained long-forgotten, and produced the conditions under which the Soviet Union would occupy Eastern Europe and divide the continent in a Cold War for more than forty years. In Western Europe, an anti-fascist, anti-Nazi consensus undoubtedly strengthened the foundations of postwar democracy. World War 2 had the further effect of globalizing the power of the victorious combatants, the Soviet Union and the United States.

The political consequences of Nazi Germany's military invasion of Europe have been largely resolved with the end of Communism in 1989, but the memories of collaboration, occupation, and extermination continue to cast long shadows. Nazism remains an easily identifiable incarnation of evil around the world and in popular culture, but it also revealed how even the most audacious political movements relied on the collaboration and complicity of a much wider public of citizens. The defeat of the Nazis also strengthened a universal discourse of human rights as exemplified in the Nuremberg trials in which leading Nazis were indicted for crimes against humanity. Without the Allied victory in 1945 the Declaration of Human Rights in 1948 is not imaginable. As a result, Nazism remains a vital topic for intellectual study. However, the threat of neo-Nazism in the years since 1945 is minimal because the democratic capacities of European societies have vastly expanded and the characteristically nationalist resentments of the post-World War 1 years no longer apply.

Peter Fritzsche

Bibliography

Caplan J. (ed.) 2008. *The short Oxford history of Germany: Nazi Germany 1933–1945.* Oxford: Oxford University Press.

Fritzsche P. 2008. *Life and death in the Third Reich.* Cambridge, MA: Harvard University Press.

Klemperer V. 1998. *I will bear witness*, 2 vols. New York: Random House.

Weinberg G. L. 1994. *A world at arms: a global history of World War II.* Cambridge: Cambridge University Press.

Related essays

anarchism; animal rights; anti-racism; antisemitism; ethnicity and race; eugenics; fascism and anti-fascism; forced migrations; genocide; international non-governmental organizations (INGOs); liberalism; life and physical sciences; music; pan-isms; police; race-mixing; socialism; war crimes; world orders

Neoliberalism

Neoliberalism holds that prosperity flows from market forces. It gained influence when the high-inflation, high-unemployment traumas of the 1970s developed world proved impervious to, and indeed came to be seen as created by, Keynesian notions of macroeconomic 'demand management'. From 1980s deregulatory reforms in New Zealand and much of the developed world, with mainly domestic consequences, neoliberalism extended to an ethos for policy in the developing world, with strongly transnational implications.

Neoliberalism is distinct from institutional neoliberalism of the post-Second World War, which advocated international cooperation, and from the redistributionist liberalism of 20th-century American parlance. It is a descendant of classical liberalism, from which it differs in breadth and pragmatism: classical liberals were additionally concerned with the primacy of the individual over society.

Neoliberalism's central ambition is market flexibility in firms, their products, and their factors of production: labour and capital. Flexibility requires freedom of movement at home and across borders, making neoliberalism a major transnational force. Curiously, neoliberalism generally does not advocate transnational labour flows. This inconsistency, though pragmatic, sets it apart from classical liberalism and the latter's truer descendant, libertarianism.

Neoliberalism does advocate free international capital flows, which constitutes its greatest transnational legacy. Academia has achieved a tentative conclusion that financial liberalization promotes development. The consensus is weak because free capital flows have made the developing world's encounter with neoliberalism traumatic. Model reformers in the 'emerging markets' experienced financial crises in the 1990s, usually following economic and financial liberalisation. As a consequence, the emerging 21st-century paradigm of developing-world economic policy in some respects eschews neoliberalism. Extensive currency management, as practised in much of East Asia, is a prominent example: it recognizes that a liberal approach to currencies can allow foreign investors' exuberance to ruin the growth dynamic that attracted their capital in the first place.

Free trade is fundamental to neoliberalism. Exports allow world markets to guide the economy to its most efficient production configuration. Imports undermine domestic monopolies, enhancing market flexibility. Neoliberalism thus erodes barriers, including the barriers that define national sovereignty. Freedom of capital movement gives domestic policy makers less flexibility to pursue purely domestic-oriented policy. For example, monetary authorities cannot offset an adverse shock with an expansionary policy without seeing their exchange rate weaken or, alternatively, their foreign currency reserves diminish. Some see this loss of sovereignty as a virtue, since it provides a check on imprudent policies.

Neoliberalism is the ideological motor of current globalization. Transnational flows of products and capital, as well as skilled labour, are neoliberal objectives. As the late historian Charles Kindleberger argued, their realization requires the commitment of a hegemonic power. In this sense, the ascendancy of neoliberal ideology in the United States nourished late 20th-century globalization just as the pre-eminence of classical liberalism in Britain underpinned globalization between 1870 and the First World War. The hesitancy of any such commitment in the interwar decades may be one cause of that period's stagnation, with 'zero-sum' views on trade and capital flows. By contrast, neoliberalism sees globalization as a positive-sum game with long-term, intertemporal balancing of accounts.

The Enlightenment's emphasis on personal freedom and rational scepticism makes it a touchstone for neoliberalism. Some see globalization as pushing the Enlightenment across frontiers, explaining the rise of religious fundamentalism as a reaction to such permeation and its effect on traditions. The notion of displacement of national varieties of culture by a monolithic market culture has a rich intellectual heritage. Karl Polanyi believed that liberalism begets civilizational destruction by commoditizing humans and their environment. As market forces become unbearable for humans and wreck their environment, humanity seeks shelter in competing forms of society. According to Polanyi, fascism and Marxism were the alternatives *du jour* in the interwar period.

Neoliberal reforms bequeath legacies varied enough to provide sustenance to champions and detractors alike. The United States, Britain and Chile all boast above-average growth rates, arguably on the foundation of neoliberal policies. Yet they also exhibit above-average income disparities. Mixed success of neoliberal reforms in some of the developing world, and particularly in Latin America, has led to the ideology's repudiation in some academic circles. Like Edwardian liberalism, neoliberalism may have a finite life span. Whether the world will be a better place without it is less certain.

Scott Urban

Bibliography

Eichengreen B. 'Financial instability', in Lomborg B. (ed.) 2004. *Global crises, global solutions: priorities for a world of scarcity.* Cambridge: Cambridge University Press.

Kindleberger C. 1962. *The world in Depression, 1929–39.* Oxford: Allen Lane.

Polanyi K. 1944. *The great transformation.* New York: Farrar and Rinehart.

Related essays

1989; convergence and divergence; debt crises; debt crises (developing countries); democracy; development and growth; Economic Commission for Latin America and the Caribbean (ECLAC); financial centres; financial markets; information economy; International Monetary Fund (IMF); investment; liberalism; loans; management; money; open door and free flow; Pax Americana; public policy; trade; trade agreements; underdevelopment; Universal Postal Union (UPU); Washington Consensus; World Bank

New Age

'New Age' can best be defined by the common ground between scattered groups that share more or less the same beliefs in the arrival of a new era in human evolution, astrologically defined as the Age of Aquarius. For some of these, the special moment is on the point of happening, whereas for others it has already happened. This heterogeneous movement leads the way in aspirations to personal realization, not only on a material level, not only in the increase in leisure and free time, but also in an idiom of spiritual paths and aims. Since the 1960s, these aspirations have developed markedly in advanced industrial societies, which are not only the wealthiest but also those in which material wealth is most widely shared and where the population enjoys a minimum of economic and social security.

New Agers seek inspiration from ancient mysteries, from the secrets of ancient Egypt, from medieval alchemy, but also from the discoveries of the most recent science such as quantum physics, relativity theory and molecular biology. New Age ideology is constructed by modifying ideas from all sorts of traditions, including science. Jesus and the Buddha become spiritual guides for self-knowledge, while the mystery of the 'secret unity of all the traditions' is due to be finally revealed. By following the example of the great founders of religions, one can become one's own God. The idea of the divine for the New Age is related to individual power and interior freedom, but also to global harmony and cosmic interdependence. Some indeed prefer the term 'holism' to 'New Age'. This idea of the divine is expressed in a general cult of 'energy', a current that is both cosmic and personal, spiritual and material, and determines both individual cycles and also universal cycles – the dark or happy periods in the history of the world. All of us would possess a parcel of energy that links us to the Whole, hence the development of so-called transpersonal psychology (a clue to the incorporation of the Jungian seam of psychoanalysis).

The New Age is a machine for absorbing traditional ideas into the ideological structure I have called 'individuo-globalism', which characterizes the advanced industrial societies. It announces a return to, or advent of, the spiritual which transcends contemporary materialism, but which is not a return to outdated religious tradition. But this ideological machine does not succeed in absorbing religious traditions without reaction from them, including mixed reactions from indigenous or aboriginal traditions, which the New Age specially values as part of a reinterpretation of the relations between human beings and nature, based on the Gaia hypothesis which sees the Earth as a living organism and the Universe as a space of universal interdependence. The Vatican, too, has tried to fight this 'neopaganism' which undermines the idea of a personal God the Creator, just as certain Buddhist groups object to what they see as the reduction, according to New Age interpretations, of the idea of Nirvana to that of well-being.

Since the beginning of the 21st century, the New Age has tended to detach itself from these traditional sources and in particular from the Theosophical movement with its neo-esoteric discourse. The central idea of personal development has come to dominate instead. This trend was already present in some historical components of the New Age, such as the Holistic Health Movement which emerged at the very beginning of the 1960s, and the Human Potential Movement founded by Abraham Maslow in the mid 1960s, but was formerly suffused by an eschatological ambiance, a hope of transcending individual and social materialism. There is talk now of the Next Age to show that the idea of the Age of Aquarius has been dropped: thus the prophetic aspect of the New Age has been abandoned in favour of personal and global development, no longer anti-materialist and critical of capitalism but, on the contrary, assisting with its promotion. Consequently, the executives of big corporations are initiated into practices such as sophrology or yoga with the support of their employers, and the corporation itself makes a commitment to improving the happiness of its staff as well as to the sustainable development of the planet.

Raphaël Liogier

Bibliography

Bloom W. 2004. SOULution. London: Cygnus.

Heelas P. 1996. The New Age movement. Oxford: Blackwell.

Heelas P. and Woodhead L. 2005. The spiritual revolution: why religion is giving way to spirituality. Oxford: Blackwell.

Liogier R. 2009. La religion post-industrielle: souci de soi, conscience du monde. Paris: Flammarion.

Related essays

Buddhism; Christianity; civilizations; consumer society; feel-good culture; religion; yoga

New man

The process of globalization, ancient in its history, but contemporary in its present incarnation, requires new understanding. Much confusion surrounds the attempt. Within the discipline of history, a subfield called world history arose in Europe and America roughly after 1945 to describe the effort to see the past in a non-Eurocentric fashion. So, too, global history arose to focus on the thread of globalization running through world history, paying most attention to the period after the 15th century. More recently, new global history has arisen, emphasizing the globalizing process since World War 2. In all three of these subfields, the desire to transcend traditional boundaries, such as today the nation state, is a common characteristic. Outside the discipline of history, work in international history, international relations, sociology, anthropology, and political science takes up the same task. In this context, the terms 'international', 'transnational', and 'global' jostle uneasily for pre-eminence. The usual disciplines are in disarray. What we are witnessing is a transition from one to another, then to another, and yet to another perspective. Or to put it another way, the disciplines are to be seen as on a spectrum, though this misses the dynamism present. We can grasp one piece of what is happening by concentrating on what I am calling 'The New Man in a Global Epoch'. As I wish to present it, the topic can give us insight into how transnational history offers us greater knowledge of our present circumstances.

The new man appears first in the Bible (for example, Paul, Romans 6:6, and elsewhere). Then in the more secular 18th century, he reappears, for example, in terms of Crèvecoeur's *Letters from an American farmer*. Here we are told that the American is that individual, come from Europe, who sheds his overcivilized veneer and takes on a new identity. Such a person 'begins to feel the effect of a sort of resurrection... he now feels himself a new man'. Thus, he leaves behind him the old authority relations of the Old World and steps forward as an equal to all others, with his 'past' behind him.

We must note a few points before carrying on. One is that we are still in a patriarchal framework, stretching from Biblical days to the 18th century: the new man is gendered; there is not yet a new woman. A second point is that even in a time of Enlightenment, the language is still religious: Crèvecoeur speaks of 'resurrection'. It is a tone that hangs over the future of the term well into the 20th century. Lastly, this version of the new man predates any sort of international setting. He is an individual, at first Christian, and then American.

The shift to an international order takes place in the 19th century. And it is the Russian

thinker, N. G. Chernyshevsky, who introduces a version of the new man who can inhabit such an order. In his novel, *What is to be done?* (1864), he writes of a married couple, Vera and Lopukov, where the husband tells his wife that he is the 'first new man that you have met'. In this case, by new man he means one of advanced views. Such men believe in free love, as well as political reform. As his companion he needs a new woman. Thus, the concept has become gendered.

The new man (and woman) is an historical phenomenon of unprecedented novelty, and bound to suffer many vicissitudes. As Chernyshevsky tells us, 'It is born of an epoch; it is a sign of the times'. It is an epoch that is international in background, though none of this is stressed in our Russian thinker's novel. He stays within the confines mainly of family life, which he wishes to transfigure, and his new man is a forerunner of what can be called the revolutionary ascetic, the man who denies his feelings, leads the hard life, and is capable of becoming a revolutionary.

History moves in strange ways, and we must be prepared to follow her in her erratic course. Our next step is to focus on Nicolay Lenin (a pseudonym for Vladimir Ilyich Ulyanov), who, exiled to his family farm while still a young man, read *What is to be done?* (later, in 1902, to become the title of one of his own most significant writings). It is Chernyshevsky who supplied the character model for the future Lenin; Karl Marx supplied the philosophy and ideology for how to bring about a society fit for such an individual. As Lenin himself said, these two thinkers were the most formative influences on his life as a revolutionary.

It is now time to bring internationalism back in. It becomes, as noted, a major theme in the 19th century. With the spread of nation states as the dominant political form, their interactions are to be regulated by an international order. Only peoples who have reached the level of the civilized nations can have a role in the game, through their nation states. Japan at the end of the century is a good example of how one people adopted Western ways and was accorded entrance – a tale well told, for example, by Gerrit Gong.

Marx, who is right in the middle of the century, having been born in 1818 and dying in 1883, conceived of Marxist Communism as an international movement. His envisioned actor, however, was not the nation state, but the proletariat. This is the new man, though

Marx does not use that term, who will succeed the bourgeoisie. Marx's eyes are on the new society, which will be worldwide. 'Proletarier aller Länder, vereinigt euch!' (most often translated as 'Working men of all countries, unite!') he trumpets at the end of the Communist Manifesto. In so doing, 'They have a world to win'.

In order to accomplish this end, the workers must organize themselves in an International Working Men's Association, one which transcends national boundaries. Such an organization is correlated with the market that is being created by the bourgeoisie, a 'world-market', that 'draws all, even the most barbarian, nations into civilization'. It is extraordinary how prescient Marx (and Engels) was in delineating the future globalizing process, with capitalism at its core. Yet, it is critical to remember that he is still operating conceptually in terms of internationalism as his organizing principle.

Many threads need to be drawn together in this discussion. The new man as such seems to have faded from view. Implicitly, of course, he exists in Marxist society. Proletarian man (and Marx was quite sexist) is freed from the fetters of private property, nationalism, religion and other traditional restraints. He is not bound by the needs of division of labour and exists as a kind of free spirit, fishing in the afternoon and philosophizing in the evening. But Marx's call is mainly for an international working men's society, with less thought given to its prime inhabitant than to its transcendent character.

However, the theme of the new man returns with a vengeance with Lenin. Once the Bolsheviks have taken over the Tsarist society, they aim directly for the creation of a new man – a communist – to live in it and run it. The prototype of such a man is Lenin himself: utilitarian, efficient, unemotional, ascetic, and completely dedicated to the industrialization of Russia. Only this time it will be achieved in communist, not capitalist (as it had been at the end of the 19th century), fashion. Originally inspired by Chernyshevsky, Lenin goes on to adapt the idea of the new man in a very Benthamite form.

With Lenin's successor, Stalin, new Soviet Man loses some of its Benthamite features and takes on a more Russian and 'Asiatic' cast. For some forty years, the party fostered this creation. Cast in terms of an international movement – the Communist International takes on at least four incarnations – it is very much an assertion of a nationalism wrapped in the clothes of an empire. The motto is 'Socialism in One Country'. Translated, this means that internationalism is a means of defending and asserting Russian power.

Such is the strange mixture of elements – the new man, internationalism, and hints of globalization – that we find in Chernyshevsky, Marx, Lenin, and Stalin in the course of a century and a half. The main thread we wish to pull on here is internationalism. It is the organizing principle for both capitalist and communist societies during the entire time. It also gives rise to a field called international relations and subsequently to the study of international history. It is a forerunner of transnational history. Both still take the nation state as the centre of the story. The major difference is that internationalism retains the nation state as its prime concern, wrapping around it the notion of something larger, while transnationalism focuses on the forces involved in the wrapping, so to speak.

Internationalism, of course, persists into the present. In fact, international organizations expand exponentially. But as the processes of globalization also increase, the mindset involved in internationalism runs up more and more against issues and problems with which it can no longer deal adequately. It is supplanted and supplemented by mindsets that can be designated as transnational and global. Both accept the need to transcend the national framework that has persisted and dominated for over three hundred years. While all three perspectives – international, transnational and global history – seek to rise above Eurocentrism, it is only the last two that aspire to go further. In this aspiration, does the new man reappear in global history of a contemporary nature? Or has the idea of a new man been transposed out of all recognition in the global epoch? Let us indulge in brief speculations.

In doing so, let us focus on the role of the computer within globalization, and ask, so to speak, what is computer man? The first part of the answer is, of course, that the person sitting at the computer is non-gendered. 'It' operates the keyboard in the sense that the recipient of an e-mail, for example, does not 'know' the sex of the sender unless specifically told so, and indeed can be fooled in many cases. 'It' has no place in the usual sense, and exists in virtual space. 'It' roams the globe in a split second, and transcends ordinary communal ties and boundaries.

This 'new man', to retain the older usage, exists as part of a networked society. He has a name and an address but it is a user name and a password. Sexless as stated earlier, he has no national or ethnic identity. Social hierarchies and distinctions are meaningless in virtual space and in regard to its inhabitants. In the eyes, then, of both a transnational and global perspective, the line of discourse about a new man has come to an end. We must think in entirely different terms.

Others will speak of transnational history in detail. Here I will conclude with a few more words about global history, and particularly new global history. It exists on a spectrum with transnational history, and in practice, tackles similar problems. It is useful, however, to see it as a complementary mindset.

First and foremost, New Global History (NGH) focuses on post-World War 2 developments that foster increased interconnectedness and interdependence and the compression of space/time. It does so in terms of research into the 'factors', such as nuclear weapons, multinational corporations, non-governmental organizations, the UN, environmental dangers and suchlike that transcend national and other 'traditional' boundaries. It undertakes research into these organizations, institutions, and developments as they push us to a reappraisal of such terms as sovereignty and legitimacy.

Foregoing other specifics, let me say that NGH favours a new periodization; that is, since around 1945 we gain special insight by seeing ourselves in a global epoch, and recognize that there has been a rupture (though links, of course, still exist) between earlier globalizations and our present-day version. It also insists on viewing globalization holistically; it is not merely a matter of economics and free markets compressing the world, but of social, cultural, political, intellectual developments that both link and divide peoples in new ways. Thus, NGH claims to be a new way of thinking, a new division of the past, a new way of seeing globalization, and a particular research project.

It is, in fact, more limited, certainly temporally, than transnational history, and thus less likely to appeal to the ordinary historian, who wishes not to be restricted to the contemporary period. One consequence is that social scientists other than historians – sociologists, anthropologists, political scientists, international relations people, etc. – are equally involved in NGH research projects. Yet, with this said, NGH can provide inspiration for the historian working on pre-20th-century episodes in a transnational fashion. So, when in a recent *American Historical Review* (December 2006) 'conversation' on transnational history, Isabel Hofmehr declares that 'The key claim of any transnational approach is a central concern with movements, flows, and circulation, not simply as a theme or motif but as an analytic set of methods which define the endeavor itself', it might equally well have been said by a new global historian. When Sven Beckert in the same conversation says that transnational history is a 'way of seeing', the new global historian nods his or her head.

Acknowledging differences simply strengthens the ways in which world, transnational, and (new) global history are all responding to the challenge of trying to understand humanity at a time when boundaries are blurring more and more, and when boundaries and bonds are recognized as social constructions.

At such a time and in such a world, internationalism seems conceptually and practically to take us only so far as a way of comprehending our situation. So, too, as a concept and an aspiration, the 'new man' seems to have met 'his' demise. In his place, I am suggesting, is a 'person' of vague and shifting outlines, sitting at a computer 'somewhere', and occupied with trying to understand and live in the processes and flows that constitute the concerns of transnational and global historians. The new man as such, it seems, has disappeared in the new millennium of the 21st century. This is paradoxical, because the new man depended on millennial hopes. Instead, with internationalism no longer the preferred setting (though international institutions still flourish), humanity steps forward as the desired protagonist of transnational and global history. One of the key tasks for the transnational historian is to help in defining exactly what identity humanity has had in the past and will have in the present and the future. It is in its own way a 'millennial' task.

Bruce Mazlish

Bibliography

'AHR Conversation: On Transnational History', *American Historical Review*, 111, 5, December 2006.

Chernyshevsky N. G. 1961. *What is to be done? Tales about new people.* Tucker B. R. (trans.). New York: Vintage.

Gong G. W. 1984. The standard of 'civilization' in international society. Oxford: Clarendon.

Crèvecoeur H. St J. de 1793. Letters from an American farmer. Philadelphia: Matthew Carey.

Mazlish B. 1976. The revolutionary ascetic: evolution of a political type. New York: Basic Books.

Mazlish B. 2006. The new global history. London and New York: Routledge.

Related essays

America; Comintern and Cominform; globalization; evangelicalism; femininity; film; history; internationalisms; modernity; outer space; Pax Americana; socialism; spatial regimes; The Wretched of the Earth; transnational; worker's movements

News and press agencies

The global dissemination of news was made possible by the establishment of the first news agencies in Europe during the mid 19th century, and these still dominate news sources 150 years later. The rise of the news agency is inextricably linked with the development of the new communications technology of the telegraph. By facilitating international communication, the telegraph played a critical role in the globalization of commerce and the expansion of European empires from the second half of the 19th century to the end of the First World War, a period rightfully characterized as the golden age of telegraphy.

From 1851, when the first public telegraph service was introduced in Britain, a network of cables was rapidly laid down, so that by the end of the 19th century the telegraph allowed London to communicate directly with far-flung corners of the British Empire within minutes. British supremacy over the undersea networks was overwhelming: by 1892 the British Empire possessed more than 66 per cent of global cables, accounting for 163,619 kilometres in length. The unprecedented growth in global trade and investment required a constant source of reliable information about international trade and economic affairs. European imperial governments depended on a regular and reliable supply of news essential for maintaining political alliances and military security. Waves of emigration as a result of industrialization and empire also helped to create demand

for news from relatives at home and abroad at a time when news was increasingly being seen as a commodity. The newspaper industry played a significant role in the development of international telegraph networks, in order to exploit the rapid increase in demand for news, especially the financial information required to conduct international commerce. The establishment of the news agency was the most important development in the newspaper industry of the 19th century, altering the process of news dissemination internationally.

Increasing demand among business clients for commercial news – about businesses, stocks, currencies, commodities, harvests – ensured that news agencies would grow in power and reach. The French Havas agency (ancestor of Agence France Presse, AFP) was founded in 1835, the German agency Wolff in 1849 and the British Reuters in 1851. The news agencies signed a treaty, the 'Ring Combination', in 1870 to divide up the world market between the three of them. The cartel was dominated by the better-resourced Reuters, whose reserved territories were larger or of greater news importance than others. British control of cable lines made London itself an unrivalled centre for world news, further enhanced by Britain's wide-ranging commercial, financial and imperial activities and its influence on world opinion. The expansion of news agencies outside Europe 'was intimately associated with the territorial colonialism of the late nineteenth century' (Boyd-Barrett 1980, 23).

The global dominance of Reuters was partly based on the agency's close relationship with the British foreign and colonial administrations, which during the second half of the 19th century made Reuters function, as its official biographer noted, 'as an institution of the British Empire' (Read 1992, 40). Such proximity to the colonial establishment reflected particularly during imperial wars such as the Boer War (1899–1902), during which agency reports supported the British actions. In 1910, Reuters started an imperial news service and a year later, the agency made a secret arrangement with the British government under which it offered to circulate on its wires official speeches to every corner of the Empire, in return for an annual fee of £500 from the Colonial Office. During the First World War, Reuters launched a wartime news service by arrangement with the Foreign

Office, while the agency's managing director during the war years, George Jones, was in charge of cable and wireless propaganda for the British Department of Information. Reuters entered into another agreement with the British Foreign Office – which remained in force until the Second World War – under which the agency would circulate specific messages on its international wires, to be paid for by the government.

Since the end of the Second World War, Reuters, 'the largest financial information provider in the world', has continued to dominate production and distribution of international news. Though established in 1848, it was not until the turn of the 20th century that the US agency, Associated Press (AP), started to go international. Its global expansion – first to Latin America and then to Europe and elsewhere – paralleled political changes in Europe with the weakening of the European empires after the First World War. The ascendancy of the US after the Second World War ensured that AP became one of the most powerful news agencies in the world. From global news agencies to transnational newspapers and radio stations, from providers of television news footage, to 24-hour news and documentary channels, the US/UK-based media organizations demonstrate what has been called 'the US/UK news duopoly' (Tunstall and Machin 1999, 88). Of the three biggest international news agencies (AP, Reuters and AFP), AP is the largest, with an average daily news output of 20 million words, more than double that of its closest rival Reuters, and over three times the output of the French agency. These news agencies contribute significantly to the globalization of news and though traditionally they sold news reports and still photographs, they have diversified their operations by offering video news feeds for broadcasters and online information and financial databases. The companies which run the world's two biggest wire services also own the world's two top international television news agencies – Associated Press Television News (APTN) and Reuters Television – dominating the global trade in news footage. No credible broadcaster can manage without access to one of these two news giants, especially for coverage of international news. APTN was launched in 1998 following the acquisition from US network ABC of TV news agency Worldwide Television News (WTN) by AP, integrating it with the operations of APTV, the

London-based video news agency launched by AP in 1994. By 2007, Reuters Television (formerly Visnews) was providing, in addition to its flagship World News Service, coverage of financial news, sports, showbiz and ready-to-air packages. Acknowledging the importance of television news, AFP too launched an English-language television service, AFP TV, based in London. The US-UK news duopoly is based on professional output – a reputation for speed and accuracy in the coverage of international events. However, does their interpretation of global political and financial events reflect Western or more specifically US editorial priorities?

This issue of 'one-way flow of news' generated much controversy in the global South, where some news agencies have promoted the notion of development journalism, claimed to pursue a news agenda different from that of the mainstream media, steeped in the so-called 'coups and earthquakes' syndrome, and to investigate the process behind a story rather than merely reporting the news event itself. Distortions in the media's coverage of crises in developing countries can affect the understanding of the South in the North, it is argued, and also among the countries of the South, since most of the news flow continues to be from North to South and limited South–South news exchange takes place. In addition, in most of the developing world, the media generally cater to the requirements of the urban readership, with little contact with the villages where the majority of the population live. The acceptance of Western definitions of what constitutes news by most journalists in the South can affect the coverage of development issues directly and adversely. UNESCO-supported regional exchange mechanisms were established in the late 1970s to increase and improve South–South news and information traffic. Though regional news agencies such as Pan African News Agency (PANA), Caribbean News Agency (CANA) and Organization of Asia-Pacific News Agencies (OANA), encouraged journalists in developing countries to think in terms of regional issues, they failed to make major difference to the global, or even regional news flow.

Other governmental efforts to check the imbalance in global news, such as the Non-Aligned News Agencies Pool (NANAP, 1975), a collection of government-sponsored news agencies to improve international exchange, designed to promote news among non-aligned countries, lacked journalistic credibility and have withered into irrelevance. Global impact of other smaller agencies such as the London-based Gemini News Service, an international news features agency with an explicit development agenda, which was established in 1967 and continued to operate effectively until the end of 1990s, has been at best modest. A more enduring news agency, from a Southern perspective, is the Rome-based Inter Press Service (IPS), set up in 1964 as a journalists' cooperative by Roberto Savio, an Italian freelance journalist who served as its director-general until 1999, and Pablo Piacentini, an Argentinean political scientist. However, in the age of rapid marketization of news, organizations such as IPS play a rather minor role in a news-world dominated by transnational news agencies.

Daya Thussu

Bibliography

Boyd-Barrett O. 1980. *The international news agencies*. London: Constable.

Boyd-Barrett O. and Thussu D. 1992. *Contraflow in global news: international and regional news exchange mechanisms*. London: John Libbey.

Read D. 1992. *The power of news: the history of Reuters, 1849–1989*. Oxford: Oxford University Press.

Tunstall J. and Machin D. 1999. *The Anglo-American media connection*. Oxford: Oxford University Press.

Related essays

broadcasting; commodity trading; empires and imperialism; financial centres; financial markets; information economy; radio; regions; telephone and telegraphy; world orders

Nomads

Pastoral nomadism is connected with the maintenance of herds all year round on natural pastures which requires mobility within the boundaries of specific grazing territories, or between such territories. According to some estimates, 40 million people in the world are mobile pastoralists. They live mainly in Africa, in the extended Middle East, in Central and Inner Asia, in South Asia, and in the Far North. In some countries, such as Niger, Djibouti or Somalia, mobile pastoralists constitute the

majority of the population; in many others they constitute a significant minority.

In the ancient and medieval periods, most nomads occupied the exclusive or dominating position in the ecological zone they inhabited. In other cases, they utilized several ecological zones separating lands where people engaged in cultivation. In still other cases, nomads shared the same zones with agriculturalists. Usually, nomads' military strength and political independence prevented non-pastoralist groups from encroaching upon their territory or inhibiting their migrations. Pastoral nomadic societies began to decay at the onset of modern times, when the balance of power changed. In some parts of the world this happened earlier than in others, but eventually the process took a similar path all over the planet. The continental empires of Russia, China, and Ottoman Turkey were first to encroach upon the territories of nomads. In the 19th century, with the emergence of overseas empires, most nomads in other parts of the world also lost their political independence. Not infrequently, colonial powers confiscated some of their lands, strove to control their migratory routes, and forced them to pay taxes. Still, some exceptions notwithstanding, in general, these powers did not intentionally try to undermine the traditional way of life and social organization of the nomads.

In the postcolonial period, since 1945, many national governments demonstrate an even stronger anti-pastoralist bias. They consider nomads as insufficiently productive, and, at the same time, as a disruptive and unruly element that has to be pacified, domesticated and preferably sedentarized. Nomads are often portrayed as ignorant, irrational, backward, lazy, uncooperative, destructive to the environment, and resisting modernization. In addition, many government officials and development planners consider nomadic movements as detrimental to economic development.

Population growth, industrial development, and urbanization result in the encroachment of sedentary populations into territories occupied by the nomads. This is often encouraged by national governments. In Lesotho, Botswana, Zimbabwe, Nigeria, Mali, Cameroon, Ethiopia, Sudan, Kenya, Syria, Israel, Turkey, Iran, Central Asian countries, India, China (especially in Inner Mongolia and Xinjiang), as well as in the Scandinavian Arctic and Siberia, many pasturelands were appropriated by the state, or were simply seized by agriculturalists to be put under the plough or to industrial purposes. At the same time, nation states put a certain brake on the movements of stock and pastoralists, disrupt many traditional migratory routes of the nomads and prevent them from crossing state boundaries, although in the past these boundaries were never fixed and, thus, remain arbitrary and meaningless to nomads. No wonder nomads consider such restrictions as illegitimate and detrimental to their economic activity. As a rule, contemporary nation states remain alien to the nomads. The latter cannot escape them, as they were sometimes capable of doing in the 19th and in the early 20th centuries, but they do not benefit from the state either. When they are running away from the state, the state is running after them; and the state is much faster.

In many countries, traditional pastoral nomadism is not a viable economic option anymore. In East Africa, in the Middle East, in Central Asia, and in the Russian North the inability of many pastoralists to subsist primarily on a livestock economy has become a common theme, and their future is problematic. This is despite the fact that mobile pastoralism remains a viable economic alternative for vast desert and semi-desert territories unsuitable for cultivation.

Anatoly M. Khazanov

Bibliography

Barfield T. J. 1993. *The nomadic alternative*. Englewood Cliffs: Prentice-Hall.

Galaty J. G. and Johnson D. L. (eds) 1990. *The world of pastoralism: herding systems in comparative perspective*. New York: Guildford.

Khazanov A. M. 1994. *Nomads and the other world*. Madison: University of Wisconsin Press.

Related essays
agriculture; borders and borderlands; development and growth; empire and migration; empires and imperialism; genocide; nation and state; temporary migrations

Non-lieux

Contributing to the continuing discussions over the characteristics of postindustrial cities and landscapes, the French social anthropologist Marc Augé has put forth the term 'non-lieux', derived from the etymologically related 'utopia' – both terms mean 'non-place'. According to his 'theory of supermodernity', non-lieux are increasingly ubiquitous, urban and uniform microcosms integrated into the global economy but relatively detached from local specificity, historical references or social structures. Designed for purposes of consumption, communication or circulation and displaying a high degree of standardized, functional architecture, non-places comprise loci of commerce such as shopping malls, tourist sites and theme parks, transit areas such as subways, train stations, airports, motorways and their service areas, as well as the virtual networks of the net-world.

The French neologism 'non-lieux' emerged from a seam of discourses on the formative forces and structures of urban development in the late 20th century. Sociological literature since Durkheim and Simmel had studied the effects of industrial urbanization on the built environment and social identities. Drawing on that venerable tradition, the town and regional planner Melvin M. Webber (1920–2006) observed the rise of 'non-place communities' (1964) as a result of automobilization, instant communication, mass media, and globalizing corporate networks. Webber described the dissolution of traditional community bonds, and sketched the formation of individuals who, as a result, weakened attachments to their local 'place community' while developing networks of belonging to a 'world community'. Also in the 1960s, the German psychoanalyst Alexander Mitscherlich (1908–82) coined the phrase 'inhospitability of the city', which referred both to the continued blight of urban centres torn asunder by World War 2 and to the functional dissociation brought about by residential segregation, the design of New Towns and recurrent bouts of suburbanization. Mitscherlich maintained that the suburban single-family house represented a concept of urban irresponsibility, concluding that only the purposely designed town (as opposed to the merely agglomerated one) could be a home town, because a place one calls home required markings of identity of place. Another decade later, the social geographer Edward C. Relph elaborated the theoretical connection between one's perception of places, processes of standardization, and a loss of identity. 'Placelessness' occurred when different cities no longer look different, but instead give the impression of being one, with the help of modern modes of communication and mobility. In mass culture, Relph observed a merging of places created solely for purposes of tourism and entertainment ('Disneyfication'). Such 'merged' places detach themselves from tradition, commodify history (museumization), and pursue a common idea (futurization).

While drawing on various sociological approaches, non-lieux also relate to French philosophy and the trinity of place, space and time. One possible definition of 'place' was described by the French philosopher Henri Lefèbvre (1901–91) in his 1970 classic, *La révolution urbaine*. Consisting of discontinuous layers of space, urban communities can either be understood as isotopias, i.e. places of sameness or the same place, or heterotopias – the place of otherness or place of the others, which is at the same time both excluded and included. Between isotopias and heterotopias Lefèbvre posited 'neutral spaces' (crossroads, places of transit), that he characterized not as meaningless but as 'indifferent'. Lefèbvre's interpretation of space also conceals 'U-topia' as 'non-place', which does not take place and has no place, the place of somewhere else. In *L'invention du quotidien* (1980), the cultural philosopher Michel de Certeau (1925–86) uses an action-oriented perspective to establish a border between space and place. A place for him is a constellation of fixed points with evidence of possible stability, whereas space is a network of moving elements, filled with the movements which build up inside it. Neglecting the aspect of time, which for the post-structuralist Michel Foucault (1926–84) merely determines a possible division between the elements within space, de Certeau concentrates on the two archetypes of places: on utopias, which are placements without real places, and on heterotopias.

Marc Augé (b.1935), a student of Georges Balandier and Claude Lévi-Strauss, delivered the lexicon-establishing ethnological analysis of non-places. In *Non-lieux* (1992), he circumscribed what he considers to be emblematic locales of a globally interconnected world by employing an overarching interpretative model of 'supermodernity' – a descendant of modernity, whose most blatant feature is excess; an excess of events and of space, which, in turn, results in an individualization of references. If places are spaces symbolized by an identity, relationships and a specific history, Augé regards places without these references as non-lieux – among them places and infrastructures of transit, means of transport, places of consumption, hotels, tourist sites, homes for asylum seekers, and virtual rooms. Augé neglects the division between space and place as formulated by de Certeau and concentrates more on the type and intensity of how people regard and make use of certain places. To Augé, a non-place comes into being though the relationship of individuals to these places. This relationship is marked by (1) a solitary form of contract; (2) a reduced measure of writing and words, and a commensurate increase in the use of non-place-specific symbols and support like signposts, screens or posters; (3) a constant confrontation with the present; (4) the creation of a relative anonymity through a temporary identity, and (5) the testing of this identity beforehand or afterwards. Take the example of the credit card. Being part of a daily silent trafficking, such a card requires the acceptance of a privileged circle of users of a contractual and tested financial creditworthiness. On receipt of secret codes, users gain access to a languageless money-transaction system, together with a provisional identity for the duration of the contractual period. Whether the card is used at a supermarket, a service station or a cash machine, card holders gain entry to a group of individuals who interact with texts and signs created by other institutions. The language of non-places is thus not directed at an individual in an anthropological sense but at an average person; terms-of-use apply to all group members without discrimination. The space constructed for travellers represents the archetype of a non-place. But Augé makes no difference between employing a credit card, riding in a high-speed train, or shopping in a department store. In his view, all non-places are marked by relative anonymity and temporary identities. They transform individuals into passers-by; citizens into customers, travellers into passengers, all bound into solitude and similitude. Non-places never exist in a pure form. Augé concludes however that the non-place is the opposite of utopia as it exists but does not accommodate any kind of organic community whatsoever. Paradoxically, he admits, the anonymity of service stations, chat rooms and malls can provide liberating experiences, just like logos and brands aspire to provide reassuring landmarks in the global cosmos of consumption.

The Italian architect and architectural historian Vittorio Magnago Lampugnani (b.1951) has argued that Augé staged his non-places in a far too pushy way and that solely their interchangeability makes them an architectural emblem of globalization. Lampugnani goes on to differentiate between 'good' and 'bad' types of non-places. The 'bad' types withdraw urban energy from cities and create an urban dispositive in miniature, typified by large shopping centres at the outskirts of towns. 'Good' examples of non-places are the well known types of urban architecture that originated in the 19th century, such as way-stations of mass transportation. Taking exception to Augé's classification, Lampugnani exempts airports from the list of 'non-places', and one is inclined to agree with him when considering how, for example, New York's John F. Kennedy International Airport by Eero Saarinen, marked by its easily recognizable and identity-providing architectural code, has created a place of urban character and significant destination in its own right.

Another leitmotif of non-places was seized upon in the 1990s frenzy over the presumed digital revolution and its effects. With the benefit of hindsight, many staples of the debate about the ramifications of virtual media seem both lacking in saliency and dated. Some have taken Augé's theory of a present continually reproducing itself further by postulating, like the economist William Knoke in his *Bold new world* (1996), that the placeless community describes a world of total ubiquity for things and people. And yet, one is hard-pressed to verify the hyperbolic expectation of millenarian Internet augurs that place would no longer determine how we work, when we shop or where we live. Likewise, art exhibitions have displayed interest in the idea of placelessness, and non-places. Using videos, photography and sculpture as their media of expression, contemporary artists have found these notions a fruitful lens through which to approach modern-day built environments and their inhabitants. In her video 'Night Watch' of 2001, the artist Katrin Korfmann moved a bench in the Amsterdam Rijksmuseum into the centre of attention and transformed the museum from a place of contemplation and edification into a luxurious waiting room for various tourists in transit. In contrast to transit, Ori Gerscht focused on Sarajevo's stone housing blocks with their grid-type facades, uniform front windows and bright colours; in a photo taken in 1998 and titled 'Thin Lines', he depicted these residences as a type of building to be found anywhere in the world – with only their bullet holes and broken windows bearing witness to history of a specifically 'place-ful' form of architecture.

Augé can thus be credited with having coined an evocative concept suggesting a popular, if ambivalent discomfort with postindustrial place making. Today, more than fifteen years later, seemingly diverse sites such as airport lounges, highway ramps, or subway escalators are widely perceived as ubiquitous spatial arrangements, and as characteristic, worldwide markers of our time – i.e. as a category sui generis. Augé's model describes local sites marked by agencies of transglobal capitalism. Not surprisingly, the figures associated with non-lieux – hypermobility, 24/7 flexibility, global presence – resemble the same images projected by the very global players responsible for some of the ongoing reconfiguration of the human habitat. Critics contest this, arguing that Augé underestimates the human capacity to appropriate anonymous forces for their own ends. More, they charge, he illuminates the democratic and humanizing character of traditional places and obscures the actors shaping the presumed postmodern placelessness. Still, as a heuristic fiction, non-lieux may remain a worthwhile venue for transnational studies, not least in the fields of urban, transportation and consumer history. Augé's 'ethnography of solitude' could be put to the test by historical enquiries into specific negotiations between global orderings and local appropriation, or between the twin forces of individualization and standardization. Such theory-inspired microhistories of particular locales qualifying as non-lieux could help to illuminate processes and patterns of social change across borders, not least among these the emergence, or recurrence, of patchwork identities, community bonds and feelings of belonging in (late) modern, that is, increasingly urban, societies.

Oliver Schmidt

Bibliography

Augé M. 1992. Non-lieux: introduction à une anthropologie de la surmodernité. Paris: Seuil. Translated as Non-places: introduction to an anthropology of supermodernity (Howe J. trans.) 1995. New York: Verso.

Certeau M. de 1980. L'invention du quotidien: arts de faire. Paris: Union Générale d'Éditions. Translated as The practice of everyday life (Rendall S. trans.) 1984. Berkeley: University of California Press.

Lampugnani V. M. 2002. Verhaltene Geschwindig keit: die Zukunft der telematischen Stadt. Berlin: Wagenbach.

Lefèbvre H. 1970. La révolution urbaine. Paris: Gallimard. Translated as The urban revolution (Bononno R. trans., foreword Smith N.) 2003. Minneapolis: University of Minnesota Press.

Mitscherlich A. 1965. Die Unwirtlichkeit unserer Städte: Anstiftung zum Unfrieden. Frankfurt am Main: Suhrkamp.

Relph E. 1976. Place and placelessness. London: Pion.

Webber M. M. 1964. Explorations into urban structure. Philadelphia: University of Pennsylvania Press.

Related essays

border commuters; cities; city planning; consumer society; Internet; modernity; theme parks; urbanization; War and Peace in the Global Village

Non-violence

Non-violence refers to the principle and practice of rejecting violence and using alternative methods to promote political and social change. Principled commitment to non-violence can be unique to an individual person, and the practice of non-violent action can be limited to local and national arenas. However, the history of non-violence is transnational in the case of both the spread of ideas on the phenomenon and the cross-border mobilization that is often central to its successful application.

The modern history of non-violence has religious and ethical roots that transcend not only national boundaries but also assumed divisions between 'Eastern' and 'Western' cultures. For instance, practitioners of non-violence have been influenced inter alia by both Christian teachings, such as the Sermon on the Mount, and Hindu texts, especially the Bhagavad-Gita.

The Bhagavad-Gita was amongst the key influences on one of the pioneering Western writers on non-violence, Henry David Thoreau (1817–62), whose 1849 essay on 'Resistance to civil government' introduced and justified civil disobedience (deliberate violation of the law to challenge injustice). Thoreau's work in turn influenced later non-violent thinkers and campaigners worldwide, including Russian writer Leo Tolstoy (1828–1910) and Indian campaigner Mohandas Gandhi (1869–1948). Thoreau was a participant in the movement for the abolition of slavery in the United States, which is one of the earliest examples of a campaign that used non-violent methods transnationally. Anti-slavery activists on each side of the Atlantic shared expertise and adopted cross-border non-violent tactics such as boycotts of slave-produced goods. Some of the non-violent techniques used in the anti-slavery campaign were subsequently adopted in later transnational campaigns, including the women's suffrage movement.

The anti-slavery and women's suffrage campaigns are significant examples of 'passive resistance,' which developed in Europe and North America from the late 18th century onwards. Transnational groups such as Mennonites and Quakers practised non-violence long before then, but the social changes stimulated by the industrial revolution noticeably accelerated the growth of large-scale non-violent campaigns. Throughout Europe, 'passive resistance' was applied both in nationalist struggles, especially the Hungarian independence campaign, and in the labour movement, which developed the strike technique and organized across borders in the International Workingmen's Association (1864).

The practice of 'passive resistance' in Europe, together with non-violent actions elsewhere such as boycotts in China, influenced the central figure in the history of non-violence, Mohandas Gandhi. Gandhi was also familiar with the writings of Western authors including Thoreau and especially Tolstoy, with whom he corresponded at the start of his career. Like Tolstoy, Gandhi found inspiration in Christian teachings, but the Hindu and Jain religious traditions on which he was brought up in India were a greater influence. Gandhi's term for non-violent resistance was satyagraha, taken from the Sanskrit words for truth and firmness. This term was created to distinguish it from 'passive resistance' which implied weakness on the part of those who used it and did not imply principled commitment to the use only of non-violent methods. Gandhi's practice of satyagraha on behalf of the Indian minority in South Africa to 1914 and to promote Indian independence from the British Empire from 1920 has been of critical importance in inspiring subsequent non-violent movements, even though Gandhi was not always able to enforce non-violent discipline on his followers and the achievement of Indian independence was the product as much of geopolitical factors as of Gandhi's campaigns.

Gandhi's influence was especially substantial in the case of some of the leaders of African independence movements. Although African countries had very diverse paths towards freedom from colonial rule, a number of the most notable leaders of African independence struggles, including Kwame Nkrumah in Ghana, Kenneth Kaunda in Zambia and Julius Nyerere in Tanzania saw in Gandhi's campaigns for Indian independence a model for African liberation.

Civil rights leaders in the United States were also inspired by Gandhi's approach. Some of them, such as Bayard Rustin (1912–87), received training in non-violent methods in India and passed on these tactics to the US civil rights movement. US peace organizations also passed on Gandhian methods: in 1942 members of the Fellowship of Reconciliation established the Congress of Racial Equality (CORE), which pioneered non-violent tactics such as freedom rides. The apparent success of non-violent action in contributing towards civil rights legislation in the USA in 1964–65, combined with the charismatic promotion of Gandhian non-violence by Martin Luther King (1929–68) further popularized the notion that non-violent methods can contribute towards significant political change.

In subsequent decades, non-violent action was used, though not exclusively, to promote a wide variety of objectives worldwide, including civil rights in Northern Ireland in 1967–72, regime change in Iran in 1979, and in the 1980s abolition of apartheid in South Africa and democratization in many countries (such as the Philippines in 1986, Burma from 1988, and Central and Eastern European states in the 'velvet' revolutions of 1989).

Transnational mobilization was often central to these campaigns. For instance, in the campaign against apartheid in South Africa in the 1980s, non-violent struggle by the United Democratic Front at home was complemented by non-violent actions abroad to promote economic sanctions. However, international support is not a sufficient condition for success: the transnational campaign in support of Burma's democratization, for example, has failed to yield results. In fact, transnational mobilization has sometimes been counterproductive, as was the case with the civil rights movement in Northern Ireland in 1967–72 when cross-border interactions exported and amplified tensions.

A notable development in the post-Gandhi era is the increasing role of international non-governmental organizations in promoting non-violent action transnationally. While arguably the majority of international non-governmental organizations rely on non-violent methods to promote their objectives, some, particularly in the international peace movement, include in their objectives cross-border promotion of non-violent methods. One such organization is the International Fellowship of Reconciliation, a Christian pacifist group that is especially notable for having assisted in laying the groundwork for the 'people power' revolution in the Philippines in 1986 and in facilitating the creation in 1974 of the Latin American non-violent movement, Servicio Paz y Justicia.

Another peace organization, War Resisters International, helped in developing the technique of transnational non-violent intervention, which it practised in its 1968 'Czechoslovakia Support Actions' at the time of the Prague Spring. Transnational non-violent intervention was pioneered by British peace campaigner Maude Royden (1876–1956), who tried to assemble an unarmed 'Peace Army' in the 1930s to act as a Gandhian 'Living Wall' between Japanese and Chinese armed forces. Although Royden's plans failed, by the 1960s transnational non-violent intervention was commonly practised, including in the Sahara Protest Action of 1959–60, the San Francisco to Moscow Walk in 1960–61 and the World Peace Brigade in 1960–64. Organizations such as Peace Brigades International and Greenpeace International continue the practice of transnational non-violent intervention to this day, in the accompaniment of activists in danger and in launching non-violent actions from the Rainbow Warrior ship respectively.

One of the boldest claims in respect of the importance of international peace organizations in the history of non-violent action is their apparent role in complementing the efforts of national non-violent resistance movements in campaigning for different aspects of the changes that facilitated the end of the Cold War. It has been argued that while national non-violent resistance movements in Central and Eastern European countries were important in pressing for one aspect of the changes that facilitated the Cold War's end (the cessation of Communist rule in Central and Eastern Europe), international anti-nuclear organizations assisted by pushing for another aspect (arms control agreements).

Since the end of the Cold War, non-violent action has continued to be central to significant campaigns for political change, notably those contributing to the 'colour revolutions' in Serbia in 2000, Georgia in 2003 and Ukraine in 2004–05. The spread of ideas across borders and transnational mobilization were as important in these campaigns as they had been in earlier cases. For instance, the writings of American non-violent strategist Gene Sharp (1928–) inspired Serb non-violent resistance groups, especially the student organization Otpor, which in turn helped train non-violent activists in Georgia and Ukraine.

Until recently, the best-known cases of non-violent action focused on national rather than transnational targets. With the development of economic globalization, however, the use of non-violent tactics against transnational bodies has become increasingly prominent. Global businesses have been frequently targeted by non-violent campaigns, starting in 1977 with a transnational boycott of Nestlé in response to its infant-formula marketing methods. More recently, global economic institutions such as the World Trade Organization have become a key focus for non-violent campaigners. The history of non-violence is therefore now transnational not only in terms of the spread of ideas across borders and in transnational mobilization, but also in terms of the targets of non-violent resistance.

Thomas Richard Davies

Bibliography

Ackerman P. and DuVall J. 2000. *A force more powerful: a century of non-violent conflict.* Basingstoke and New York: Palgrave Macmillan.

Gan B. and Holmes R. (eds) 2004. *Non-violence in theory and practice,* 2nd edition. Long Grove: Waveland.

Randle M. 1994. *Civil resistance.* London: Fontana.

Sharp G. 1973. *The politics of non-violent action.* Boston: Porter Sargent.

Related essays

1989; abolitionism; African liberation; Cold War; decolonization; democracy; disarmament; empires and imperialism; Gandhi, Mohandas Karamchand; Greenpeace; international non-governmental organizations (INGOs); pacifism; women's movements; workers' movements

Gandhi, Mohandas Karamchand 1869–1948

Mohandas Karamchand Gandhi was a leader of the Indian national movement from 1919 until his death, whose writings and example have had an impact on movements against colonialism and racism throughout the world. Known as the Mahatma, or 'great soul', Gandhi is today largely remembered as an Indian figure, but his ideas were profoundly shaped by his engagement with transnational currents of thought and practice, which he in turn deeply influenced.

Gandhi was born on 2 October 1869, in the port city of Porbandar in northwest India. His father was a high-ranking official. As a child, Gandhi was influenced by his mother's intense religiosity, which emphasized non-violence, vegetarianism, and tolerance. When the time came for him to go to England to study law, he promised his mother that he would abstain from wine, meat, and women.

In 1888, Gandhi arrived in London. Initially embarrassed by his vegetarianism, Gandhi soon discovered the British vegetarian movement. This connection introduced Gandhi to the writings of thinkers such as the Russian novelist Leo Tolstoy and the American writer Henry David Thoreau (both vegetarians), who would prove a central influence on his own spiritual and political development. Gandhi threw himself into the movement with zeal, honing his organizational skills and serving on the board of the London Vegetarian Society.

Gandhi was admitted to the London Bar in 1891 and returned to India, but had little success in his attempts to establish a law practice.

In 1893, an Indian trading firm with interests in South Africa hired Gandhi to represent it there. It was in South Africa that Gandhi first encountered intense racial prejudice and became committed to political struggle. He remained in South Africa more than twenty years and gradually became a central figure in the campaign of Indians there for equality as subjects of the British Empire. There, Gandhi developed his notion of 'passive resistance' to oppression, a programme inspired by Thoreau's writing on 'civil disobedience' and Tolstoy's advocacy of non-violence. He also explored paths to the spiritual life. Inspired by the writings of the British social thinker John Ruskin, Gandhi established 'utopian socialist' agrarian communities, where members lived and ate in communal accommodation and shared both work and property. For Gandhi, struggles for political and civil rights were connected to internal struggles for purity and truth in one's own life. Gandhi called his method 'satyagraha', a Sanskrit term connoting a search for truth.

Gandhi returned to India in 1914. During the First World War he recruited Indians to fight for the Empire, as he had in South Africa during the Boer War, reasoning that if Indians wanted equal rights within the Empire they should contribute to its defence. After the war, however, the British reneged on their promises of Indian home rule, and Gandhi, realizing that racism was inherent in the edifice of empire, had a change of heart. In the spring of 1919 he initiated a satyagraha campaign against legislation designed to suppress the Indian struggle for home rule by extending the government's wartime powers of internment without trial. This campaign catapulted Gandhi into the leadership of the Indian nationalist movement, but outbreaks of violence prompted Gandhi to call off the movement and retire from political life in 1922.

Gandhi returned to lead the movement in 1928, spearheading a demand for full Indian home rule, and in 1930 he launched a massive satyagraha campaign against the salt tax. Not long after, he again retreated to his ashram to pursue his spiritual quest. During the Second World War, Gandhi declared that Indians could not fight again for the empire without full self-government, and in 1942 he led a movement calling on the British to 'quit India'. When the negotiations for Indian independence began in 1945, Gandhi was a steadfast opponent of the partition of India between Hindus and Muslims, but partition nevertheless became a reality in the summer of 1947. On 30 January 1948, he was shot and killed by a Hindu fanatic.

Erez Manela

Bibliography

Kapur S. 1992. *Raising up a prophet: the African-American encounter with Gandhi.* Boston, MA: Beacon.

Markovits C. 2003. *The un-Gandhian Gandhi: the life and afterlife of the Mahatma.* London: Anthem.

Swan M. 1985. *Gandhi: the South African experience.* Johannesburg: Raven.

Weber T. 2004. *Gandhi as disciple and mentor.* Cambridge: Cambridge University Press.

Related essays

African liberation; anti-racism; decolonization; empires and imperialism; Mandela, Nelson; non-violence; pacifism; temperance; white men's countries

North Atlantic Treaty Organization (NATO)

The North Atlantic Treaty Organization, a military and political alliance, was established by ten Western European nations as well as the United States and Canada in 1949. NATO was established at the height of Cold War confrontation as a response to a perceived threat of Soviet expansionism on the European continent following World War 2 and in the situation of virtual impotence of the United Nations Security Council, deadlocked by the Soviet veto, to deal with assaults on international peace and stability. The Organization is to be seen, along with the Marshall Plan and steps toward economic cooperation in Europe, as a part of complex efforts of European nations to overcome, by joint efforts, the damage inflicted by the war on various spheres of European life and to coordinate measures for rehabilitation and renovation of the continent. The predominant concern of governments was to organize regional security arrangements that would make such rehabilitation possible in the situation of rivalry between two leading postwar powers. Although conceived as a predominantly military alliance, however, NATO from the outset was composed of a political and a military structure. The political component includes the North Atlantic Council, consisting of ambassadors and permanent representatives of member nations, which is empowered to make all political decisions. Decisions are made only on the basis of a full consensus. NATO's senior military authority is a military committee which advises the council. The committee consists of military representatives from the member states. The military branch also includes three commands: Allied Command Atlantic, Allied Command Channel, and Allied Command Europe.

At the time of its formation NATO's objectives were limited to those of a defensive character. Members agreed that an armed attack against one should be considered an attack against them all, and that they would come to the aid of each other. The Organization's primary goal was to deter an attack from the Soviet Union and its allies against Western Europe. However, a broader mission of NATO as a vehicle of unity of European nations and their desire to coordinate their efforts in various spheres should be seen in the statement that its general aim is to 'safeguard the freedom, common heritage and civilization' of its members by promoting 'stability and well-being in the North Atlantic Area'. At the same time, member nations regard NATO as a part of a global transnational structure with the United Nations at its apex. Article One of the NATO Treaty contains an assertion that its parties would strive to settle any international disputes by peaceful means and would refrain from the threat or use of force 'in any manner inconsistent with the purposes of the United Nations'. Article Five includes a provision that signatories would report an armed attack to the UN Security Council together with the measures which they are taking to deal with it and would terminate such measures after the Security Council undertakes steps necessary to restore and maintain international peace and security. Leaders of the member nations have never ceased to reassure the world that the terms of the NATO Treaty are fundamentally consistent with the UN Charter.

In the course of its history NATO has undergone a number of transformations. Originally consisting of 12 countries, the Organization expanded to include Greece and Turkey in 1952 and West Germany in 1955. Since the end of the Cold War the Organization has admitted a number of new states – former Warsaw Pact countries, including the Czech Republic, Hungary and Poland (1999), as well as Slovenia, Slovakia, Bulgaria and Romania along with Estonia, Latvia and Lithuania (2004). Therefore, today NATO represents one of the two institutions that constitute the transnational structure of Europe (the other being the European Union). With the continuing membership in the Organization of the United States and Canada, it also serves as a bridge in the dialogue of nations across the Atlantic.

Ilya V. Gaiduk

Bibliography
Kaplan L. 1999. *The long entanglement: NATO's first fifty years*. Westport: Praeger.
Schmidt G. (ed.) 2001. *A history of NATO: the first fifty years*, 3 vols. Basingstoke: Palgrave Macmillan.

Related essays
Cold War; European institutions; Marshall Plan; Pax Americana; regional communities; United Nations system; war

Nudism

Nudism is the international movement concerned with the place, status and function of human nakedness in modern society. It developed from renewed interest 19th century Western Europeans took in ancient Greece and nudity's role in that culture.

Modern nudism took shape in the mid-1850s when intellectuals from Austria, Switzerland and Germany theorized that nudity in nature could counter the ills associated with urban living. Organized nudism (including communal nudity, vegetarianism and exercise) was practiced by the 1890s and quickly became a significant feature of German culture.

By the early 1920s, similar nudist movements had appeared in France, Switzerland and England. But the focus of English nudism eventually shifted so that simplicity and freedom – rather than physical well-being – became the central tenet. English nudism served as the basis of an Australian movement which began in the 1930s and emphasized heightened aesthetic consciousness of embodied physicality.

Nudism crossed the Atlantic to the United States in the late 1920s. A German immigrant,

Kurt Barthel, established the first American nudist organization, the American League for Physical Culture. As the movement evolved, other organizations, such as the International Nudist Conference, redefined nudism as forming the basis of alternative, self-sustaining communal living.

Although associated primarily with industrialized Western nations, organized nudism has emerged recently in Mexico, Argentina and especially Brazil. Founded in 1984, the Brazilian nudist movement is the largest in Latin America. Like its predecessors, Brazilian nudism is based on utopian ideals, in this case, of nudity as the great social equalizer in a society overrun by inequality.

M. M. Adjarian

Bibliography
Lester H. C. 1968. *Godiva Rides Again: a history of the nudist movement.* New York: Vantage.
Toepfer K. 1997. *Empire of ecstasy: nudity and movement in German body culture.* Berkeley: University of California Press.

Related essays
beauty; bodybuilding; feel-good culture

Nursing

Nursing has evolved as a professional field since the beginnings of the 20th century. Historians in the past stressed the heritage of Florence Nightingale (1820–1910) as a turning point in the birth of the profession on a global scale. Her great charismatic and personal influence was undeniable, especially in Western Europe. However, the core elements of professionalism received the strongest impulse not so much from the icon of nurse reform – the 'Lady with the Lamp' – but resulted to a great extent from continuous private relationships between nursing leaders across the Atlantic and beyond. These women imbued their followers with a sense of professional identity and were behind the major collectivist or associative movements that carved the tortuous path toward the rise of the profession. By the end of the 19th century and during a few decades well into the next century, international and national conferences, social movements and organizations brought about and constantly fuelled the interchange of nurses, touched by feminist and professional ideas, from different countries across the world.

In the 19th century, training schools in Europe and elsewhere were not yet emblems of professionalism, for they lacked a formal body of knowledge, and interaction rituals that could strengthen a fledgling occupational status and an autonomous institutional space; these characteristics would seal the *esprit de corps* of registered nurses only later in the 20th century. In 1860, Miss Nightingale's Training School, one of the first formal educational practice to appear in Europe, was based on a hospital-centred model. It stressed the need for *vocation* among young candidates and for systematic training in the wards. This dimension of professionalism soon crossed Atlantic boundaries and went as far as colonial Australia and Canada in the West, and Korea and Japan in the East, on the wings of Nightingale nursing superintendents for schools and hospitals. Around the world, the new professional nurses challenged the patriarchal structure of the recently medicalized hospitals.

The first signs of professional group and collective identity were soon to emerge from, or against, the daily experience of nursing subservience in the hospitals. One first assault on the professional powers of medicinemen was the creation of the British Nurses Association, in 1887, under the inspiration of Ethel Bedford Fenwick. It was she who was also instrumental in encouraging US Johns Hopkins University nurses Adelaide Nutting and Lavinia Dock to organize the US profession, when she met them to contribute to the Chicago 1893 international congress on social work and philanthropy. It was there, also, that there crystallized the bonds of friendship and professional solidarity that would form the sisterly network from which Fenwick created the International Council of Nurses (ICN) a few years later, after a conference of the International Council of Women (1899). For many of these women, indeed, the nurse question and the woman question were one and the same.

This crisscrossing of ideas that unfurled from the 1860s defies any simple labelling of 'national systems' (e.g., the 'British', the 'French' system, etc.) of nursing education at that time of intense ideological effervescence and collective debate about best practices and doctrines. National corporative groups were also far from merely national in their scope and geographic outreach, for they became key elements in the circulation of actors and ideas across national boundaries at the turn of the century. A turning point in the flow of conceptions about professionals originated in the world of politics, when US President Woodrow Wilson favored some of his advisors' enthusiasm with the idea of placing the Red Cross organizations under a new multinational agency tied to the projected League of Nations, in order to give some demonstration of the 'international spirit'. The Cannes April 1919 conference, organized by the allied Red Cross, resulted in specific proposals for the creation of a League of Red Cross Societies (LRCS), which demarcated an important line of activity for a specific Nursing Division. The attempts by this group to spread public health and hospital nursing training were not isolated. The Rockefeller Foundation was soon to begin its sponsorship of public health nursing and nursing education programs in the US, in Europe, and in Latin America, supporting national associations of nurses, financing schools of nursing and demonstration programmes.

The subsequent rivalries were, in fact, music to the ears of the nursing professionals, badly in need of identity-building conflicts and alliances. The ICN was, until the 1920s, little more than a club of British, North American and Northern European nurses. During the interwar years, the political skirmishes between agencies such as the LRCS and the Rockefeller Foundation triggered heated debates and intense interaction among leading professionals and currents of ideas, and the ICN benefited from this new scenario. The exchange of professional worldviews peaked during the general meetings of the International Council of Nurses – which convened in several European and American countries in the interwar period – and reflected, in turn, the widespread circulation of ideas and individual members, before and after the international conferences. The political tone of the general meetings, with their celebration of human community, owed a great deal to the agenda of other institutions such as the LRCS, the International Council of Women, and the International Labour Office. Another viewpoint – US professional imperialism as the subtext of internationalization of the nursing world – could be interpreted from another angle, as the suppression of British imperialism in international nursing affairs. But what is really at stake, here, is the politics of professionalism inside the ICN,

which pointed in the direction of increasing autonomy, increased associational life, and strengthened anti-patriarchal ideologies among nurses in the West. From this angle of analysis, it matters little whether the dominant role was played by North American or British professionals.

But, whatever progress the profession may have attained under the auspices of ICN meetings and its wide membership, the rather timid developments in Asian countries such as Japan should sound a note of caution to excessive emphasis on transnational flows of ideas and practices. Even if some diseases – such as malaria, trachoma and tuberculosis – were a common and heavy burden to societies in the West and East, the institutional responses to fight those epidemics, as well as the educational policies to meet the needs of public health professionals, varied immensely. The cultural, political – particularly the degree of state intervention – and professional milieu eventually came to model or crystallize the contours of the educational and work patterns for professionals in each country. In the case of France, for example, there were more intra-national cleavages among the leading nursing professionals and their educational proposals than the international flows of ideas of reform would suggest. In fact, each French subgroup had its foreign patrons and references which were used in the national competition to design the new French nurse.

This was also the time of the great upsurge of philanthropic foundations in the field of public health, in connection with state-run programs. Rural health was an especially strong concern in Central Europe or in Latin America during the 1920s and 1930s, when the rural populations of many countries were immersed in nation-building health campaigns, which gave unparalleled importance to public health nursing. The expanding role that public health nursing had in other parts of the Western and Eastern hemispheres before World War 2 was also due to the efforts of the Rockefeller Foundation and to the attention paid by international agencies (such as the League of Nations) to the concepts of preventive medicine and social health. The combined issues of race and gender posed problems for the opening of new educational programmes in both hemispheres. Race was a more poignant problem on a global scale. Could deeply segmented class structures – particularly in the agrarian societies of Eastern Europe, Asia, and Latin America – afford a truly democratic profession divided along racial and gender lines? In many countries, nursing leaders and health authorities considered that focusing on small elites within the profession would be a valid strategy to create a professionally legitimate territory and attract promising young students. Supposedly, these were pre-conditions for professional pride and market opportunities, which could bar the competition from the untrained, cheap labour of aux-iliaries, and establish a reasonable degree of autonomy within the medical hierarchy at the hospitals. This sometimes included the idea that colored nurses should be guided by pro-fessionals from a 'more experienced race'. In 1923, the Rockefeller Foundation's plans to send a 'colored' nurse to the faculty of the newly founded Anna Nery School, in Rio de Janeiro, were cancelled, after considering that a 'half-breed' might not be accepted by the Brazilian elites. This would have prevented the school from attracting young students of high social standing, a precondition for the creation of a 'respectable' profession advocated by nursing leaders, Rockefeller organizations and League of Red Cross nursing groups alike.

The export of professionalism on a global scale forced its protagonists to tackle con-texts of racial prejudice and social neglect for the poor among the elites in every foreign country. Such problems still loomed large during and after World War 2, when philan-thropic foundations and intergovernmental organizations (United Nations Relief and Rehabilitation Administration, the World Health Organization and others) embarked on a massive attempt to implement profes-sional nursing in Asia and Africa. The new context for community nursing in the devel-oping world, particularly the health educa-tion campaigns, faced adverse cultural, pol-itical, and economic conditions. The fight against gender and racial discrimination in nursing could not easily surpass the social atmosphere in which the profession emerged in underdeveloped countries. A related chal-lenge lay in the hierarchical cleavages within the profession, particularly in underdevel-oped and less developed countries, where the ancillaries' tasks often created or reflected insurmountable distances between the pro-fessional elite and its auxiliaries, reproducing old rituals of status dominance on behalf of medical doctors toward registered nurses. Under these circumstances, the dimension

of vocation could hardly emerge in the lower echelons of the profession. The negative con-sequences of these status differences for the profession were not, in fact, fully discussed or debated at the meetings of the ICN. A second challenge related to the declining impact of transnational organization, due to the emer-gence of segmented associations which raise, recognize, and stiffen language barriers. For example, the Federación Panamericana de Profesionales de Enfermería (Latin American Nursing Association, 1970), while strengthening the ties among Spanish- and Portuguese-speaking professionals, has at the same time weakened the intellectual and political exchange with the International Council of Nurses. Ironically, the intense political militancy of the Latin American leaders seems to neglect the fact that radical nursing politics had its inception as early as 1922, at the meeting of ICN's Grand Council in Copenhagen.

Luiz A. Castro-Santos

Bibliography
Armeny S. 1983. 'Organized nurses, women philanthropists, and the intellectual bases for cooperation among women, 1898–1920', in Lagemann E. C. (ed.) Nursing history: new perspectives, new possibilities, North Tarrytown: Rockefeller Archive Center, and New York: Teachers College Press.
Brush B. and Lynaugh J. 1999. Nurses of all nations: a history of the International Council of Nurses, 1899–1999. Philadelphia: Lippincott Williams & Wilkins.
Castro-Santos L. A. and Faria L. 2004. 'A cooperação internacional e a enfermagem de saúde pública no Rio de Janeiro e São Paulo', Horizontes, 22, 2, 123–50.
Godden J. and Helmstadter C. 2004. 'Woman's mission and professional knowledge: Nightingale nursing in Colonial Australia and Canada', Social History of Medicine, 17, 2, 157–74.
Rafferty A. M. 1995. 'Internationalising nursing education during the interwar period', in Weindling P. (ed.) International health organizations and movements, 1918–1939. Cambridge University Press.
Schultheiss K. 2001. Bodies and souls: politics and the professionalization of nursing in France. Cambridge, MA: Harvard University Press.
Takahashi A. 2002. 'The Western mode of nursing evangelized? Nursing

professionalism in the twentieth century', in Stanton J. (ed.) *Innovations in medicine and health: diffusion and resistance in the twentieth century*. London: Routledge.

Vessuri,H. 2001. 'Enfermería de salud pública, modernización y cooperación internacional: el proyecto de la Escuela Nacional de Enfermeras de Venezuela, 1936–1950', *História, ciências, saúde – Manguinhos*, 8, 3, September/December, 507–40.

Related essays

brain drain; empire and migration; engineering; executives and professionals; expositions; germs; guestworkers; health policy; human mobility; International Red Cross and Red Crescent movement; League of Nations system; nation and state; philanthropic foundations; United Nations system; women's movements

Nutrition and diet *See* Diet and nutrition

O

Oceans

Oceans, the vast expanses of salt water between the continents, make up the majority of the earth's surface and, for the most part, are not part of any nation's territory or sovereignty.

They cover about 140 million square miles, or 70 per cent of the earth's surface. Although they are the dominant geographical feature of the planet, they are so forbidding that humans know far less about them than about most of the remote pieces of land on earth, with the possible exception of Antarctica. Although the oceans might appear to be timeless and unchanging, they are constantly in flux, whether in the short term of ebbing and flowing tides and life cycles of species or the long term of shifting currents and varying sea levels. Some of this change comes from humans, who have had a noticeable impact on the oceans, especially through fishing and pollution; it may be that human-induced climate change will bring a number of major changes over the course of the next several centuries.

Oceans have served at least three major functions: resource extraction, especially fishing; transportation and migration; and the expansion of political power through warfare and exploration. The three functions are intertwined thoroughly; exploration often led to commerce or colonization, for instance, and technological breakthroughs might apply to military problems or oceanography. Because of their great value, oceans have inspired much thought about sovereignty, law, science, and human control of nature. Most important, there has been an ongoing intellectual tension between the idea that the ocean should be open to all users and the idea that powerful states should get to set rules favourable to themselves. Even in one of the seemingly most benign areas, scientific research, it is apparent that wealthier, powerful states dominate, and poorer states have access only to what the more powerful states wish to grant them. Together, science and diplomacy are tools that states can use to establish a semblance of control over the high seas, and yet it is apparent that, because there is no sovereignty on the oceans, chaos will always be a powerful force.

Searching for order on the seas

The defining moment of modern transnational history of the oceans came in 1982 with the signing of the agreements from the Third UN Conference on the Law of the Sea (UNCLOS III), which were far more comprehensive than earlier conventions signed in 1958 and 1960 at UNCLOS I and II. The conventions attempted to bring the world's governments to a rudimentary set of rules for the aforementioned major functions on the high seas. In essence, the Law of the Sea conventions recognized the seas as the common domain of humanity, beyond national sovereignties. Most of the terms were widely accepted, but not codified, before the meetings began in the 1950s, such as the right to free passage for people, naval vessels on peaceful missions, and goods. Many others, such as ownership of the sea's resources and definitions of territorial waters, had to be hammered out. The tension between power and equality has been evident in the US's response to the convention, which has been ratified by more than 150 nations. Despite supporting most of its terms, US President Reagan refused to sign it because it limited the rights of the technologically advanced nations to mine seabed minerals. The United States has since signed, but still has not ratified, the convention.

UNCLOS was the culmination of centuries of discussions about the legal status of the high seas. At the beginning of the 20th century governments generally accepted the three-mile territorial limit that Hugo Grotius had defined in 1602, and they still bore some sympathy for the idea that a government could exclude foreign commerce from that zone if it wished. Grotius' idea suggested that the high seas beyond three miles were open to everyone, but also that military might would set the rules on those seas. Ships on those seas were supposed to fly their home nation's flag to indicate whose rules they followed and whose sovereignty they represented – ships without flags, whether pirate vessels or Greenpeace protest boats, were making bold political statements. Throughout the century there were challenges to those ideas from multiple directions, whether from German submarines seeking to shut off free use of the seas, South American efforts to extend economic control to the edge of the continental shelf, or conventions to regulate the taking of marine animals like fish or whales on the high seas. After World War 2, for instance, Peru led several Latin American states in advocating a 200-mile economic exclusion zone in order to control fisheries and mineral exploration, which ultimately served as the trigger for the UNCLOS discussions. And yet even with the centuries of work, the recent rise of piracy in the western Pacific and western Indian oceans makes clear that the law of the sea is a thin veneer, with no enforcement mechanism to speak of and no sovereign power backing it up.

Just as nations have developed a law of the sea as a means to control the oceans, they have also sponsored scientific research as a way to understand it better. The majority of that science has been instigated to improve humanity's ability to extract resources from the ocean. Over the course of the 20th century, the scientific approach to the oceans changed substantially, from very basic exploration of individual physical and ecological components of the oceans to much more complex studies. Fisheries studies that began by focusing on just one species were replaced in the middle of the century by studies of species' interactions.

Scientifically, the oceans are a collection of hundreds of ecosystems with millions of species. Relatively few of those species have had value commercially or as cuisine, but taking out those species for human use can unravel an ecosystem. All ecosystems are in constant flux, whether from seasonal cycles or the ebb and flow of individual species, but the constant stress on one element of the system – a particularly valuable fish for instance – presents a different kind of flux. As an example, cod provided abundance for decades, but eventually the toll taken by fishermen from around the North Atlantic became too great, the cod stocks collapsed, and the rest of the ecosystem around the northwestern Atlantic was thrown out of kilter. Of course, species have collapsed on a regular basis throughout the Earth's history, so ecosystems eventually recalibrate as new species move in or old residents change their behaviour or density, but the impact on human communities, such as fishing villages in Newfoundland, can be disastrous.

Making a living from the sea

Fishing is one of the most basic ways in which people interact with the oceans. From necessarily primitive beginnings, fishing grew through stages from an in-shore activity to a range of approaches including lengthy transoceanic voyages in search of certain species. For most of human history, fishing was a local activity, nibbling away at the piscine (or mammalian or reptilian) abundance on the edges of the sea. Whether forced by overfishing or encouraged by more seaworthy craft, fishermen began to move further asea, so that European fishermen were far out into the Atlantic before Columbus' famous voyage of 1492, and much of the early history of Europeans in northeastern North America is based on the cod fishery.

The exploitation of the sea's fisheries expanded with improvements in technology. Spears, hooks, and nets were the most basic forms of extracting fish and whales from the seas, and they are still in use today, albeit in different forms. Whaling demonstrates both the long-term continuity of harvesting technology and the recent rapid bursts of innovation, as well as harvesters' ability to decimate species rapidly. When US whalers dominated the industry in Herman Melville's age, they were using technology that was largely unchanged from previous centuries. They found an international market for their whale oil as fuel for lamps in particular, but scarcity of whales in temperate waters and competition from the expansion of the petroleum industry left the whaling industry in decline by the late 19th century.

Then inventors around the world revitalized whaling. The new exploding harpoon, the design of a stern slipway on whaling vessels, and better refining techniques for whale oil all made it possible to catch huge Blue Whales and process them on the high seas. Whereas Captain Ahab's *Pequod* sailed alone, the modern whaling vessel, called a floating factory, sailed with a flotilla of smaller ships, requiring enormous amounts of capital and government support. Norwegians and Britons led the way in the 20th century in whaling, but they were watched closely, and sometimes imitated, by Japanese, Soviets, Germans, South Africans, Argentines, and many others. Early on, the most successful whaling ventures were those that joined British capital with Norwegian talent, particularly talent at hitting a fast-moving whale with a harpoon. Indeed, the government of Norway worked to limit the number of Norwegian harpoonmen who worked for foreign expeditions, because their knowledge was so valuable. The small number of skilled harpoonmen served as one of the best choke-points on the industry.

While whaling was largely about acquiring an edible fat, rendered into margarine, it also had political implications. Most whaling in the first decade of the century took place in the waters near Antarctica, increasing the value of specks of land like South Georgia Island. As technological developments allowed whalers to operate for months at sea, they became less dependent on those islands, hence the ability of governments to control them dropped. Attempts at regulation in the 1930s by the League of Nations, a cartel of whaling companies, and the Norwegian and British governments all failed to bring what would now be called sustainability to whaling. World War 2 brought the destruction of most of the whaling fleets, financial ruin for many whaling companies, and a desire for greater international organization to promote cooperation. Those conditions allowed for the creation of a permanent agency to manage the industry, the International Whaling Commission (IWC), in 1946. Member states granted the IWC a limited sovereignty over their citizens' actions on the oceans. Even though it turned out to be inadequate, plagued by cheating, scientific disputes, and overhunting, this new sovereignty was an important initiative in trying to work out a cooperative oceans regime.

The constant state of flux of the oceans has limited the diplomatic options to resolve unfriendly competition for resources. Those options are already constrained by limits on national sovereignty over pelagic vessels, the often ruthless economic competition among fishing nations, and the difficulty of enforcing such treaties. In addition, fish populations and whole ecosystems are constantly changing, so it is impossible to write one set of fixed rules that will work for more than a few years, even if they happened to be based on perfectly enlightened science. In addition, it appears to be human nature to work from an optimistic perspective when it comes to fishing, so regulators tend to assume that the best years are the ones upon which to base their models. When a series of bad years comes, as it inevitably will with cyclical fisheries, the regulations fixed by diplomacy fail to keep anybody happy. Because so many fisheries are transnational, they need permanent transnational bodies to regulate them, but the world's nations have not perfected such a system yet.

While fishing has been the most prominent economic activity on the oceans, and certainly the one that has generated the most diplomatic discussion, the last few decades have seen a rapid increase in mineral extraction as well. Seabed oil drilling has been both the most lucrative and controversial activity. The lucre comes from the rising demand for fossil fuels, and the controversy comes from both the political struggles for control and the risk of a major oil spill. In the 1970s, UNCLOS was delayed by deliberation over who had the right to mine manganese nodules on the ocean floor. The idea of mining manganese on the seabed would have been the stuff of science fiction in the first part of the last century – and turned out to be fundamentally infeasible anyway. But the debate over access to those resources reflected a deeper split between the view that the oceans should be the equal property of all humanity and that the rules should be set by the most powerful nations.

Studying the oceans

Part of the reason that codifying a law of the sea had been so complicated was the legacy of exploration, which naturally had been the usual domain of powerful empires. People had been using the seas to search for uncharted land and better trade routes for centuries. Such explorers had mapped most of the earth's coasts by the 20th century, so exploration in the tradition of Giovanni Caboto or Charles Wilkes was largely a thing of the past. The new trend of exploring in the 20th century, mapping undersea topography, for instance, used technology that would have been unfamiliar to the explorers of old, but it shared the old mixture of scientific curiosity and political gains as motivation. The simple desire to know what had seemed unknowable drove people to look for deep-sea fish, underwater valleys and ridges, and rare minerals. That such knowledge might be turned to military advantage in the submarine duels of the Cold War or to profit through seabed mining only helped to justify the expense and time invested.

The decline in fisheries has been a major, although not the only prominent, impetus for scientific research on the oceans. Beyond fisheries, the major subject of scientific research has been oceanography, broadly defined as the study of the physical attributes of the seas. The most important step forward for modern oceanography came with the British *Challenger* expedition of 1872, which took four years to circle the globe, gathering hydro-graphic data along the way. Other indus-trialized societies felt compelled to launch similar expeditions, simultaneously proving themselves and contributing to international understanding of the common seas. Such understanding made transportation easier, improved fishing, and contributed to the gen-eral store of knowledge to which humanity is constantly adding.

Historically, the most important proponent of combining fisheries biology with oceanog-raphy has been the International Council for the Exploration of the Sea (ICES). ICES was founded by several Northern European states in 1902 as a means to promote international scientific cooperation, and it has grown to twenty states and spawned a few regional imi-tators since then. Most of the original mem-bers had begun work on fisheries research, and their scientists had concluded that they could not separate fish, scientifically, from their physical environment. ICES reflected two key ideas: that the oceans were the com-mon heritage of humanity, and that scientific management could improve the sea's yield of fish. Relatively weak states like Denmark were on an equal footing with powerful states like Germany when it came to generating and sharing knowledge. And they collaborated in schemes such as fish stocking and regulation plans. The ICES model of cooperation broke down, not surprisingly, during times of war, but the idea was resilient enough to spring to life after the fighting stopped. Not only did ICES scientists work hard to establish the idea of cooperation on pelagic resource ques-tions, they also made numerous innovations in research techniques that became standard around the world. At the beginning of the 21st century, ICES continues to conduct path-breaking research on fisheries.

In contrast with ICES' emphasis on multi-lateral cooperation, the Cold War reinforced the idea of nationalist competition in scien-tific research. After World War 2, oceanog-raphers on both sides of the Iron Curtain tried – and failed – to fuse the peaceful idea of cooperation with the contradictory nation-alist idea that science sponsored by powerful states should reinforce their power. Pelagic research was getting even more expen-sive, and with the advent of more sophisti-cated submarines it was gaining more dir-ect military applications. Cooperation was important for oceanography even as much

of the funded research was classified at vari-ous levels of secrecy. Because of the expense and diplomatic value, the United States and the Soviet Union used marine sciences to build alliances and détente between them, even as ideology sometimes got in the way of scientific research: Soviet scientists, for instance, were long prevented from working on plate-tectonic theory because their superi-ors found it to be too idealistic, not grounded sufficiently in materialism.

Blue highways

Beyond extracting goods from the seas, peo-ple have used the seas as a means of com-merce. Trading is probably as old as fishing, and both have seen large changes in the last century. Into the 19th century, most trad-ing vessels moved by wind, assuming that the wind blew as expected (or blew at all). Transport of goods over long distances could be quite slow, and of course accidents made delivery chancy. Steam technology then made it possible to move bulk goods, not just high-value objects like precious metals, slaves, and spices, and trade boomed. By the start of the First World War, international commerce accounted for 21 per cent of the world's eco-nomic production, the highest it had been to that point. Continued improvements in naval architecture and a post-1945 commitment to knock down barriers to trade furthered the expansion of seaborne commerce. In 1959, the UN launched the International Maritime Organization to set standards for shipping. By the early 21st century, approximately 90 per cent of global trade moved by sea.

As goods have moved more easily, so too have people. The modern era has witnessed a range of migrations that have fundamentally changed the distribution of people around the globe. Europeans have moved around the world by the millions, sometimes form-ing settler societies like Australia, where the indigenous people have largely been wiped out; sometimes mixing with large numbers of indigenous peoples, such as Argentina; and sometimes leaving just a thin veneer of Western imperialism, as in Angola. Of course, in that same period millions moved unwill-ingly over the seas, as the slave trade from Africa used the oceans as its highways. Just as stream travel eased the way for enhanced com-merce, it made the migrations of people much easier in the late 1800s. The flow of migrants reshaped societies throughout the Western

Hemisphere; the additional 26 million people who came to the United States between 1870 and 1920 were emblematic of the changes throughout the former temperate colonies of the European empires.

If the early 20th century witnessed voluntary migrations, the second half of the century brought attention to seaborne refugee movements. Ironically, as shipping got better, more migrants were turning to small, flimsy vessels for political reasons, hoping to evade immigration authorities at both ends of their journeys. Beginning in 1975, hundreds of thousands fled Vietnam, introducing the term 'boat people' to the English language. In 1979, thousands fled Cuba for the United States in the Mariel boat lift, and there is an ongoing flow of migrants seeking to escape Haiti for other countries throughout the Caribbean, or crossing the Mediterranean Sea to enter the European Union. The experience of leaving via ship reflects the lawlessness and opportunities of the high seas. The state might be able to control land borders, but it cannot stop every boat slipping out of every harbour every night. On the flip side, once out at sea, boatloads of migrants are exposed to pirates, not to mention the vagaries of the weather. It is impossible to know how many people have been victims of piracy, but at least thousands of Vietnamese suffered at their hands. Refugees cast themselves to the sea to escape the sovereign power that oppressed them, but they often find that the lack of sovereignty on the high seas means that no one is there to protect them.

War and peace on the high seas
The violence committed by pirates, of course, pales beside the violence of naval warfare. The seas have been the site of battles since probably only a few minutes after the invention of the ship. Naval power has had two functions: protecting commerce from pirates and sovereign enemies as well as extending the state's power to distant shores. Many of the technological advances that have drastically changed fishing, scientific research, and commerce have had roots in naval developments or have contributed to changes in naval policies. Sonar, for instance, gained recognition for its use in anti-submarine warfare in the 1940s, and it then became useful in undersea exploration and fishing. These new technologies made it

easier for the most powerful navies to sustain a global reach.

In the last hundred years, the biggest naval development has been the rise of the submarine. In its earliest forms, the submarine was designed to fulfil the old role of commerce raider, but it could not play the role within the loose rules of war at sea developed to that point. Those rules required some protection for neutral vessels and passenger ships, compelling the seizing vessel to provide safe passage for the passengers and crews. A submarine's military value depended on stealth, so the act of seizing a vessel was inherently dangerous. If it did stop a vessel for search and seizure, it had no way to provide a prize crew or give the ship's crew safe passage. During the First World War, Germany used submarines in an effort to destroy Allied commerce as a means to win the war. Woodrow Wilson accurately saw the German tactics as an assault on larger values. As he put it, civilization had been slowly and painfully building up rules for use of the seas, but submarine warfare threatened to unravel all of it in short order. In a sense, how nations behaved on the high seas revealed something greater about the state of civilization. The same crises in the next world war only reinforced the idea that submarine warfare against neutral states was the tool of uncivilized states, and a misdemeanour to some universal laws.

Of course submarines' role changed dramatically after the Second World War. Commerce raiding was still on the agenda, but the invention of long-range missile technology allowed submarines to become an arm of nations' nuclear arsenals. The stealth that had served submarines so well in commerce warfare now made it impossible to defend against them, pre-emptively strike them, or even know where they were hiding in the vast seas. Those few nations that could build the extremely complex nuclear submarines were using the lack of sovereignty on the high seas to extend their power, and they were also tapping the scientific discoveries of oceanographers to help those submarines hide and navigate. The oceans had always been the source of a potential threat of coastal bombardment, but now they were hiding an incredibly dangerous force that could strike literally anywhere on earth.

With the rise of environmentalism around the world, new ways of thinking about the oceans appeared in the last third of the

20th century. Instead of studying the oceans to maximize production, scientific research often focused on identifying ecological problems and finding remedies for them. The decline in many fisheries alerted people to the idea that the ocean was not timeless and unchangeable, but potentially fragile. The increase in shipping led to an increase in accidents, some of them spectacular oil spills that took enormous tolls on marine life. And finally, new theories about global climate change warned that land-based activity – burning fossil fuels – had the capacity to influence sea levels, weather patterns, and even the Gulf Stream and other ocean currents. Hence, even as human efforts to control the oceans have met with limited success, they might unwittingly be causing broad changes that will make the oceans even more forbidding for them.

Kurk Dorsey

Bibliography

Glassner M. 1990. *Neptune's domain: a political geography of the sea*. London and Boston: Unwin Hyman.

Hamblin J. 2005. *Oceanographers and the Cold War: disciples of marine science*. Seattle: University of Washington Press.

Hollick A. 1981. *U.S. foreign policy and the law of the sea*. Princeton: Princeton University Press.

Kurlansky M. 1997. *Cod: a biography of the fish that changed the world*. London and New York: Penguin.

Langewiesche W. 2004. *The outlaw sea: a world of freedom, chaos, and crime*. New York: North Point.

Rozwadowski H. 2002. *The sea knows no boundaries: a century of marine science under ICES*. Copenhagen: International Council for the Exploration of the Sea.

Taylor A. 2006. 'Globalization and new comparative economic history', NBER [National Bureau of Economic Research] *Reporter: Research Summary*, Winter [online]. Available: www.nber.org/reporter/winter06/taylor.html#N_4_, accessed 9 June 2007.

Tønnessen J. N. and Johnsen A. O. 1982. *The history of modern whaling*. Berkeley: University of California Press.

Related essays

Antarctic Treaty; borders and borderlands; climate change; Cold War; containerized freight; ecology; empire and migration; environmentalism; fisheries; food; freshwater management; human mobility; intergovernmental organizations; International Maritime Conference 1853; international migration regimes; legal order; mapping; oil; refugees; regions; religious pilgrimage; scientific expeditions; steamships; trade; transportation infrastructures; war; world orders

Oil

Oil by its very nature crosses and defies political boundaries, national or otherwise. It flows underground, often in unpredictable ways and amounts. Once oil is brought to the surface through wells and pumps, a global market of exchange distributes it and a remarkable array of petroleum products across and around national borders, literally powering the international economy. The contemporary world's most essential global commodity, oil is also a resource that has historically held great meaning for specific nations – for both the evolution of their political power and their national identities – especially as oil emerged in the 20th century as the most important energy source for industrializing nations. This, combined with the fact that oil is distributed extraordinarily unevenly around the world, has put petroleum at the centre of countless wars and violent conflicts, both between and within nations.

On the one hand, only a transnational perspective can grasp the scale and scope of oil's place in the modern world. From its very birth, the oil industry viewed national boundaries as impediments to be overcome by political and economic negotiation at all stages of the process – from exploring and drilling for oil, to refining and marketing it. Indeed, very little time elapsed between the first successful drilling of an oil well in Titusville, Pennsylvania in 1859 and the emergence of a global search for and marketing of oil. Oil entrepreneur John D. Rockefeller, for instance, quickly built up a regional and even national monopoly for the most popular petroleum product – kerosene – in the United States, but he also quickly expanded his oil game to Europe. By the late 1870s, as historian Daniel Yergin notes, over 90 per cent of the kerosene exported from the United States did so through Rockefeller's Standard Oil Company – a company whose lineage would extend to present-day companies Exxon/Mobil and Chevron/Texaco. But Rockefeller and Standard Oil soon faced competition for the European market as the Nobel and Rothschild families developed – and competed with each other for – the emergent oil industry within Russia. By the 1890s, Russian kerosene was capturing over a quarter of the world's export trade.

Cheap to produce and affordable for many consumers in industrializing countries, kerosene drove the search for oil into increasingly far-flung directions from the United States, Europe, and Russia in the late 19th century. This search took a constellation of competing businessmen to the Dutch East Indies (what is now Indonesia). Out of that competition emerged a British-Dutch company, Royal Dutch/Shell, that pumped oil out of places like Borneo and Sumatra. It was suited less for kerosene and more for potential fuel. That recognition – of oil's worth as a fuel for ships and for the gasoline-powered automobile, just coming onto the market in the early 1900s – heated up the global exploration for oil before World War 1. While the United States had its own home-grown oil boom in California, Texas and Oklahoma, British oilmen struck oil in Iran. British capital and firms formed the Anglo-Iranian Oil Company (AIOC), which would later become British Petroleum, and helped launch another oil boom, along with many American oilmen, in Mexico. Meanwhile, throughout the 1920s a bevy of international oilmen struggled to negotiate a deal amenable to all of them for the petroleum riches discovered in the Kurdish region of northern Iraq.

The importance of oil to Great Britain, still the world's strongest imperial power, came in two signal governmental decisions: the first, to shift its navy fleet from coal to oil; and second, to have the government own 51 per cent of the AIOC. The nation's fortunes were thus bound to oil as a fuel and to another nation's ability to produce oil for the British market. But a similar point could be made about other industrializing countries. Although the United States was fortunate to be a locus of world oil production, the Great War underscored that no nation could become a Great Power without securing control over a long-term supply of petroleum. It was British Foreign Secretary Lord Curzon who made famous the idea that the Allies had 'floated to victory on a sea of oil' in World War 1, but such a lesson was not lost on any of the powers that emerged out of the war, and even American policy makers urged exploration abroad, in case domestic production fell off in the future. By the late 1930s, as American oil exploration teams found evidence of oil in Saudi Arabia, the governments of Japan and Germany were bent on territorial expansion that would bring them access to petroleum. Among the many different reasons that World War 2 was fought, the question of which nations would control the global flow of oil was certainly one of them.

The post-World War 2 period saw both an extension of the trends in the global oil market and some significant departures. In Saudi Arabia, a joint consortium of US companies found itself sitting on gigantic reserves of oil, while throughout the Persian Gulf and North Africa, American and European oil companies accumulated vast profits as oil powered both the reconstruction of Europe and the American consumer economy. But an ideological shift, already afoot before the war, began transforming the relationship between these multinational companies and the exporting countries in which they worked. In one petroleum country after another, political leaders and their publics began to argue that their nation's very sovereignty depended on how it controlled foreigners' access to oil.

The most dramatic instance of this political transformation came when Mexico nationalized its oil industry in 1938. Iran followed suit in 1953, only to have the British and US governments orchestrate a political coup that brought down the ruling government, imprisoned its leader, and reinstalled the British- and US-backed Shah. It would take decades before other exporting countries followed suit in a great wave of nationalization that occurred in the 1960s and 1970s. In the interim, however, the 1940s and 1950s saw exporting countries make increasing demands for a greater share of the vast profits foreign companies were accumulating.

The most important outcome of this trend came in 1960 with the formation of the Organization of Petroleum Exporting Countries (OPEC), an international cartel of countries whose national economies relied on oil production. Originally comprised mostly of Arab states and Iran, OPEC also included Venezuela and, later, Indonesia, Algeria and Nigeria. A relatively weak political organization initially, OPEC nonetheless signalled new directions in the international politics of oil. First, it brought (and would continue bringing) together geographically disparate exporting nations around the world in the belief that collective strength would afford them the chance for effective leverage against multinational oil companies, especially when it came to negotiating with the companies for a fairer share of oil profits in the form of tax revenue or equity ownership itself in the companies' properties. Indeed, with a seller's market emerging in the global oil market by the early 1970s, the time was ripe for OPEC to assert itself on the international political stage. Protesting US support for Israel in the 1973 Yom Kippur War, the Arab nations of OPEC, along with Iran, embargoed oil meant for the US market, and OPEC as a whole set in motion a series of price hikes that set off worldwide inflationary pressures for years to come in what Yergin has deemed the period of the 'OPEC imperium'.

If this 'imperium' marked the apex of OPEC's power as an international cartel, OPEC's collective assertion also helped propel another trend within the international oil industry: the nationalization of the oil industry throughout the globe. Thus, the very moment in which the organization successfully represented the interests of widely different exporting nations was also the moment in which most of the nations within OPEC nationalized their oil industries: so, for instance, the American consortium in Saudi Arabia, Aramco, become SaudiAramco; and so the panoply of independent foreign oil companies operating in Libya came under Muammar Qaddafi's rule. In our own century, most of the world's oil production now occurs through state-owned oil operations, such as those that exist in Saudi Arabia, Venezuela, and China. At the same time, American and European firms have successfully carved out new kinds of arrangements, called Production Sharing Agreements (PSAs), as the basis for operating in a number of foreign countries. While not a return to the old concession system, these agreements nonetheless indicate a trend toward renewed privatization in world oil operations. Although PSAs give states legal ownership of oil reserves, they also effectively remove foreign oil operations from national political scrutiny and lock exporting countries into long-term contracts that will deliver hefty profits to foreign companies.

By the oil embargo of 1973, the world's largest consumer of oil – the United States – was rapidly increasing its foreign oil imports, largely from countries which would nationalize their oil industries (the exception was Canada). Although imported oil represented less than 50 per cent of the oil used in America until the mid 1990s, the writing was on the wall by the 1980s that US oil production was declining and that the very place of the United States within international trade and politics depended on supporting the nation's unbounded access to oil in the global market. From the end of the 1970s onward, therefore, the United States has made its strategic interest in Persian Gulf oil – where one can find the bulk of the world's remaining oil reserves – the centrepiece of its Middle East policy. Given oil's strategic value since World War I, such an emphasis, backed by US military power, is not terribly surprising and shows no signs of lessening in importance. More curious, perhaps, is the evident paradox underlying Americans' continued embrace of such core national values as mobility and consumption. Such values in the early 21st century rest unalterably on 'a wave of oil' that originates in some other country. Cheap, foreign petroleum is the very foundation of the American way of life.

If oil circulates widely in the global market – crossing political boundaries multiple times as it is pumped from the earth, transported to refineries and petrochemical plants, and ultimately delivered to consumers in the form of fuel or other products – it nonetheless is a natural resource that originates in a specific place. In other words, the scale of the petroleum economy may showcase oil's global reach, but for people who live next to oil fields or refineries or petrochemical plants, the politics of oil is local. While many people have welcomed the entrance of the oil industry in their locales, in most places in the world, others have experienced the costs of such a transformation as greater than the potential monetary benefits. In the summer of 2002, for instance, Nigerian women successfully protested foreign companies' lax protection of and investment in the communities surrounding oil operations. Even before these protests and the wave of international environmental and human rights concern about oil production in developing countries, observers long noted the unalterable ways that the search for oil could industrialize a landscape. Novels such as Upton Sinclair's 1927 Oil!, about California, and Abdelrahman Munif's late 20th-century trilogy about the arrival of oil in Saudi Arabia have poignantly explored the environmental and human costs at the local level when outside capital brings oil drilling to an area. But the sheer ubiquity of petroleum-based products in the lives of people in developed nations makes it impossible for most consumers there to imagine a place that has produced the fuel or the objects they use. The gas in the car, the polar fleece sweater, the plastic grocery bag – these items typically have their origins in distant places that, at the end of the production process, have little bearing on the individual's act of consumption, hidden as those places are by that process.

Although cheap oil has fuelled developed and developing nations' economic growth, increasingly, the question will become not how these nations can gain access to the free flow of oil but how these nations can plan for the inevitable decline of world oil production. While experts disagree about whether this moment has already happened or will happen within the coming decades, the only way that nations can plan accurately for the decline in world oil production is through international cooperation: both private and state-owned oil companies will have to give an honest reckoning of how much oil they're pumping out of the ground and at what rate. Likewise, the only possible way out of the climate crisis that is upon us, the product of the industrial world's reliance on hydrocarbons, is through collective action globally. Climate change has little respect for national boundaries, ironically not unlike the oil industry itself, which has sought and continues to seek its quarry in every nook and cranny of the planet.

Karen Merrill

Bibliography

Brown J. C. 1985. 'Why foreign oil companies shifted their production from Mexico to Venezuela during the 1920s', *American Historical Review*, 90, 2, 362–85.

Okonta I. and Oronton D. 2003. *Where vultures feast: shell, human rights, and oil in the Niger Delta*. London: Verso.

Painter D. 1985. *Oil and the American century: the political economy of US foreign oil policy, 1941–1945*. Baltimore: Johns Hopkins University Press.

Simmons M. 2005. *Twilight in the desert: the coming Saudi oil shock and the world economy*. New York: John Wiley.

Vitalis R. 2007. *America's kingdom: mythmaking on the Saudi oil frontier*. Palo Alto: Stanford University Press.

Yergin D. 1991. *The prize: the epic quest for oil, money, and power*. New York: Free Press.

Related essays

arms sales; beauty pageants; brain drain; car culture; climate change; commodity trading; contract and indentured labourers; domestic service; Economic Commission for Latin America and the Caribbean (ECLAC); environmentalism; gold; guestworkers; Mexican Revolution; money; oceans; Organization of Petroleum Exporting Countries (OPEC); Pax Americana; philanthropic foundations; rubber; salt; scientific expeditions; trade; trade agreements; transportation infrastructures; T-shirt; war; world orders

OPEC

The Organization of Petroleum Exporting Countries was founded in Baghdad, Iraq in September 1960 by Iran, Iraq, Kuwait, Saudi Arabia and Venezuela. It currently consists of eleven member states that include the original founding members, Qatar (1961), Indonesia (1962), Libya (1962), United Arab Emirates (1967), Algeria (1962) and Nigeria (1971). Ecuador (1973–92) and Gabon (1975–94) are former members. It is headquartered in Vienna, Austria.

OPEC was founded in 1960 in response to the control of the international oil industry by a small group of multinational oil companies, the so-called Seven Sisters (British Petroleum, Exxon, Gulf Oil, Mobil, Royal Dutch/Shell, Socal and Texaco). In its early years OPEC's actions were largely defensive and aimed at the restoration of the posted price of crude oil that was unilaterally reduced by the Seven Sisters in 1959 and 1960. By 1971 the organization started promoting direct involvement in national oil industries and members were encouraged to demand a 20 per cent stake in the operations of oil companies in their countries, which stake was to increase gradually to a majority stake of 51 per cent.

OPEC is best known for its part in creating the 1973 oil crisis, an action that ensured this organization the leading role in determining world crude oil prices in the years to come. The oil crisis was brought about by OPEC's decision to unilaterally raise the posted price of crude oil by 70 per cent to US$5.11 per barrel. This price increase coincided with the Arab oil embargo that was implemented against the United States of America, the Netherlands and other 'unfriendly' states in retaliation for their support to Israel during the Yom Kippur War. The embargo ensured a global shortage of oil supplies which in turn led to drastic increases in the price of crude oil. By the end of 1973 the posted price of crude oil was US$11.65 per barrel, while prices of above US$17 were recorded at oil auctions.

With its newly acquired economic and political power, OPEC set out from 1973 onwards to maintain its role in influencing world crude oil prices and to increase its members' own roles in their national oil industries. Guided by Saudi Arabia, the organization's most powerful member, OPEC tried to maintain stable oil prizes by controlling the volume of oil offered on global markets. Daily oil production quotas for member states were later implemented but these quotas were generally ignored by most members who continued to produce above their quota levels in order to increase oil revenue. Though OPEC played a dominant role in global oil politics, the organization could not prevent the diversification of oil exploration and production outside OPEC countries which ultimately weakened its bargaining power in the long run. It was also not able to neutralize the adverse impacts of global political and economic events on crude oil prices as was the case in 1979 when the fall of the Shah in Iran sent world oil prices soaring. On the other hand, the 1986 oil price crash was largely engineered by Saudi Arabia which flooded the already weak oil market with oil in an attempt to regain market share. On those few occasions when OPEC members did unite, the organization proved its real power as was the case in 1997 when oil prices quickly recovered after a collapse triggered by the Asian financial crisis. OPEC's control over the global oil markets did not last, and the organization effectively lost control in 2004 when price speculation sent oil prices soaring above US$40 per barrel. Drastic oil price increases have continued since then, largely due to speculators, hedge funds and political instability in key production zones that have pushed the oil price above US125 per barrel. Despite the loss of control, OPEC still represents a considerable power in global oil politics with 40 per cent of global daily oil production and around two-thirds of proven oil reserves.

Phia Steyn

Bibliography
Amuzegar J. 1999. *Managing the oil wealth: OPEC's windfalls and pitfalls.* London and New York: IB Tauris.
Chalabi F. J. 1989. *OPEC: at the crossroads.* New York: Pergamon.
Energy Information Ad ministration, 'OPEC' [online]. Available: www.eia.doe.gov/emeu/security/opec.html
Organization of Petroleum Exporting Countries [online]. Available: www.opec.org/home

Related essays
commodity trading; gold; intergovernmental organizations; Islamic Scientific, Educational and Cultural Organization (ISESCO); North Atlantic Treaty Organization (NATO); oil; trade agreements

Olympic Games

The Olympic Games were the most significant world sporting competition and most popular cultural festival of the 20th century. Athletes from 13 nations participated in the first Olympic Games held in Athens, Greece in 1896. One hundred and eight years later, more than 11,000 athletes from 202 nations competed in Athens, Greece in the Olympic Games of 2004. It is commonly believed that the modern Olympic Games derive their origins from the Olympic Games in Ancient Greece held between 776 BCE and 393 AD. However, the modern Games emerged within the context of late-19th-century nation-state building, wide-scaled military organization, and projects of international exchange and competition. Greece held Olympic Games periodically during the 19th century to encourage a cultural rejuvenation which juxtaposed ancient traditions and athletic glory to a modern Greece, beset by economic and political problems. Other nations, too, utilized sport to instil competitive, militarily based masculine identities, particularly in regions that were ravaged by the Napoleonic and Franco-Prussian wars. As countries competed for territories and resources, sporting exchanges and world's fairs became venues for symbolic competition and the outcomes of such events became indices of cultural, economic, and political progress for emergent nations.

Inspired by the defeat of his country at the hands of the Germans in the Franco-Prussian wars, Baron Pierre de Coubertin sought to enhance the military and cultural status of France to counteract what he viewed as the weakness of young French men. Coubertin travelled to different parts of the world to assess formalized programmes of physical training. He was most impressed by the British model of sports and games in the public schools. The British, he suggested, adequately prepared their youth to defend and lead the nation. Coubertin was not successful in implementing physical education programmes in the schools of France and, thus, he was forced to turn his creative energies elsewhere. He was aware of the massive gymnastics competitions at the German *Turnfests*, the Scottish Highland Games, the English Olympick Games at Much Wenlock, and the Olympic Games of 19th-century Greece, among other sporting festivals of the world. The most significant influences on Coubertin's ideas, however, were the world's fairs and expositions of the late 19th century that attracted the attention of millions of visitors to various host cities. Borrowing the ideas for an international Olympic competition from the organizer and promoter of the games at Much Wenlock, Dr William Penny Brooks, Coubertin began to develop 'his' new enterprise.

In 1894, Coubertin carefully selected a group of wealthy sport leaders and enthusiasts to join him at a conference at the Sorbonne in Paris, ostensibly to discuss the issue of amateurism, a problem of some measure for the administrative bodies that controlled the rules and regulations of modern sport. By the end of the conference, however, the notion of amateurism was ignored and Coubertin had convinced the wealthy group to support an international competition of athletes modelled somewhat after the Ancient Greek festival, to be held every four years.

The first Games in 1896 were successful, even though Coubertin had little to do with their organization. The International Olympic Committee (IOC) became the administrative body devoted to the promotion of the Olympics. The Games of 1900 in Paris and in St Louis in 1904 were less successful by comparison, as both were embedded in world's fairs, with the competition schedule occurring over several months. However, the Games in London in 1908 and Stockholm in 1912 demonstrated that such competitions were gaining both interest and notoriety throughout the world as important international events. By 1912, the position of the IOC was more clearly defined and Coubertin maintained control over all organizational matters. He demonstrated a boundless energy towards the Games, ensuring that rival festivals would not challenge their eminent position and that like-minded men would be appointed to his IOC. By the 1920s, the IOC was the principal international sport body in the world.

Enticing the early-20th-century leaders of amateur sport from as many countries as possible was the strategy employed for Coubertin's success. But to him, amateurism was not nearly as significant as the growth of the festival itself. Coubertin's Games were shrouded in the language of international goodwill and broad participation; but sport had always been class-based and exclusionary. Situated within the broader sporting context of the era, the Olympic Games provided opportunities for participation for middle- and upper-class men only. Further, it reinforced the competitive values of industrial capitalism, by invoking notions of human progress through the breaking of records in sporting events, at a time when the most powerful nation states echoed common economic, military, and cultural distinction and development.

For the IOC and most sport organizations, this idea of human progress was increasingly contingent upon the quantitative measurement of the performance of trained, athletic men; it did not include women. Coubertin and his peers had long argued that athletic competitions should celebrate male achievements, whereas women were better suited to be spectators. Relegated to unofficial and 'feminine' events such as tennis, swimming, diving, and fencing, female athletes were finally granted five track and field events at the Olympics in Amsterdam in 1928. Sport had always sustained gender polarities, and the women who participated in the Olympics were expected to be feminine, ladylike, and well behaved. To ensure that women would not be 'masculinized', sport leaders and the world press encouraged them to participate in sports such as figure skating and gymnastics and to avoid the heavy throwing and exertive events.

From the outset of the Olympic Games and in other international sporting circles, all decision making was intensely political and frequently secured the self-interests of sport leaders. Olympic matters and the festival itself were ostensibly positioned above world politics; yet the very success of Coubertin's Olympics depended on the ebb and flow of international political relations. This, to a great extent, aided Coubertin in captivating the widespread interest of both national leaders and average citizens. The overt politicization of the Games was evident early on in the IOC's decision to prevent the so-called defeated nations of both World War 1 and 2 from participating in the immediate post-war Games. Both Antwerp, Belgium and London, England utilized the Games as a tool for rebuilding the damaged buildings, lives, and spirits of citizens in 1920 and in 1948, respectively. The 1936 Olympic Games in Berlin, however, are remembered for the most blatant invocation of political propaganda. Adolf Hitler went to great lengths to promote the new Germany and the physical superiority of his massive Olympic team. Hitler's invocation of Aryan supremacy was spoiled by the four-gold-medal performance of the black American Jesse Owens. In 1952, Avery Brundage became IOC president, emerging as one of the most influential sport leaders during the Cold War period. One of Brundage's most famous and often repeated beliefs was that sport and politics do not mix.

After the Second World War, the Olympic Games became one of the most significant venues in which to symbolically contest the politics of the Cold War. While direct nuclear confrontations remained unthinkable, the Soviet Union and the United States competed against one another for decades with unprecedented fervour on economic, political, cultural, and scientific levels and, perhaps most publicly, in sport.

As president, Brundage was faced with many crises and issues of considerable political weight: the Suez Canal crisis, the Soviet invasions of Hungary and Czechoslovakia, apartheid in South Africa, the slaughter of innocent people prior to the Games in Mexico in 1968, and the kidnapping and massacre of athletes in Munich in 1972. These events were all indicative of the sheer political importance that sport, indeed the Olympic Games, had come to assume within broader international relations. In addition to the major boycotts of

1980 (Moscow) and 1984 (Los Angeles), Cold War politicking between East and West gave new meaning to the IOC's Olympic credo 'Swifter, Higher, Stronger'. Systematic drug-taking programmes for both individuals and teams built 'super' athletes for the leading countries, while the IOC strategically ignored the problem. The insatiable appetite for performance, enhanced by the captivation of Cold War audiences worldwide through satellite television, necessitated quantitative improvements in human performance every four years.

The IOC concerned itself with other matters, particularly its financial strife and the sheer scale of sustaining a secure, growing international festival. The success of the Olympic Games depended on the capacity of host nations to finance them. However, television revenues in the 1960s and early 1970s began to offset some of the escalating costs. The massive deficit incurred by the 1976 Montréal Olympics became a pivotal moment for IOC planning; until then, any financial stability rested solely on television revenues. High costs began to deter cities from bidding for the Games. When Juan Antonio Samaranch assumed the presidency in 1980, a new era of financial planning, control, and politicking was ushered in. Samaranch insisted that the Olympic movement would be spread to all corners of the world and that spectators would be treated to the best athletes in the world, and not just the best amateur athletes. Although the distinction still exists for many in sport today, Samaranch's invitation to professional athletes signalled the end of amateurism in the Olympic Games. Samaranch's enlistment of transnational corporations as exclusive worldwide sponsors, and the profound increases in television revenues, placed the IOC on new levels of financial stability.

After the success of Peter Ueberroth's corporate-styled Games in Los Angeles in 1984, many cities clamoured to host the Games. Host city expenditures far exceeded the revenues provided by sponsorship and television, with major infrastructural expenditures such as light-rail transit, airport improvements, and extravagant Olympic facilities. Olympic bid leaders continued to cite the tremendous economic opportunities and world attention presented by hosting the Games. Consequently, bidding for the Olympic Games became a more hotly contested process, with increasing budgets for showcasing cities to IOC members long before the decisions took place. Currying the favor of IOC members became the main focus of bidding teams. Bid committees were only too willing to exchange elaborate gifts and services for votes. IOC members were plied with first-class plane tickets and valuable gifts. In November 1998, the Salt Lake City organizing committee was accused of bribing IOC members in exchange for their votes for the rights to host the 2002 winter Games. The bid team provided generous gifts including healthcare, employment, education, shopping sprees, luxurious accommodation, lavish hospitality, and cash.

In the midst of the bribery scandal, the IOC hosted a World Conference on Doping in Sport. In response to the growing criticism of performance-enhancing drugs in Olympic sport, the World Anti-Doping Agency (WADA) was formed in 1999. By the spring of 2001, all media attention focused on the bid for the 2008 Games and the appointment of a new IOC president, Jacques Rogge; due to a highly successful public relations campaign, the scandals were largely forgotten. The resilience of the IOC as a transnational organization is most recently evident in the popularity of the Athens and Torino Games and in the wide interest in the bidding for the Games of 2010 and 2012. In spite of endemic doping practices, bribery, judging fiascos, and a long history of corrupt practices, the IOC retains its power over international sport. After more than one hundred years, the world remains fascinated by the performances of the world's best athletes at the Olympic Games.

Kevin Wamsley

Bibliography
Guttmann A. 1984. *The games must go on: Avery Brundage and the Olympic movement.* New York: Columbia University Press.
Hoberman J. 1992. *Mortal engines: the science of performance and the dehumanization of sport.* New York: Free Press.
Roche M. 2000. *Mega-events and modernity: Olympics and expos in the growth of global culture.* London: Routledge.
Senn A. E. 1999. *Power, politics, and the Olympic Games.* Champaign: Human Kinetics.
Young D. 1996. *The Modern Olympics: a struggle for revival.* Baltimore: Johns Hopkins University Press.
Young K. and Wamsley K. B. (eds) 2005. *Global Olympics: historical and sociological studies of the modern Games.* Oxford: Elsevier.

Related essays
bodybuilding; Cold War; expositions; gender and sex; sport; world orders

Open door and free flow

Initially, 'open door policy' consisted in conferring equal commercial and industrial rights within a given territory on all nationals from different countries. The phrase was used for the first time to describe the commercial relations that were established between the United States of America and China at the end of 19th century. This entry will stick to this specific relationship to chart the history of this notion that, later, would frame US commercial foreign policy towards the rest of the planet. The context was then characterized by the imperialist expansion in Asia of Japan and major European countries. Contrary to the United States, these countries had gained spheres of influence in China and controlled its main ports. In 1899, US Secretary of State John Hay asked for an 'open door' policy that would provide the United States with access to China for trading purposes only, without any control of territory. Hay sent memoranda to France, Germany, Italy, Japan, Russia, and the United Kingdom asking for equality of treatment for trading and navigation purposes within all their spheres of influence. This policy was actually the result of the lobbying of American businessmen for the opening of foreign markets to their products. The open door at this stage was an offensive commercial policy by a country in search of new markets.

Since then, 'open door policy' has taken on a different meaning. Today, when a country adopts an open door policy, also called 'free flow policy', it opens its territory to direct foreign investment or, in some cases, to international migration. Open door policy is implemented by countries looking for international transfers of technology and competencies that cannot be found locally. The aim of this policy is to create industries that have the ability both to produce sophisticated products for the domestic market and to compete on the international markets, the overall goal being the expansion of exports. To be successful, such a policy must provide foreign investors with an attractive environment, for instance by granting subsidies or tax cuts.

Ironically, China was the first country to adopt this brand of the open door policy. In the 1970s, the main challenge for the Chinese government was to promote a new growth strategy based upon a more efficient use of resources, in contrast to China's previous development strategy based on self-sufficiency. The first step was the creation of four special economic zones in southern China (Shenzen, Zhuhai, Xiamen and Shantou). There, the corporate tax rate was cut down to 15 per cent (instead of 33.3 per cent outside the zone) and import duties on input goods were eliminated. These zones strongly benefited from this policy, though Hong Kong accounted for more than 50 per cent of foreign investment in the first ten years the measure was implemented. Gradually, the policy was applied to new territories: in 1984, foreign investors were granted access to fourteen coastal cities. Although they enjoyed the same advantages as those offered in the special economic zones, they now had to face specific constraints (balanced foreign exchange payments, greater exports than domestic sales). As more and more investors originated from the Western world, opening the country to foreign investment was a decisive step towards the market economy, and it helped promote the institutional and legal reforms, that were slowly applied to the whole economy. A quasi-autarchic country in 1978, China has now become a major world trade player, especially since its accession to the World Trade Organization in 2001, and open door policy is certainly at the root of this drastic change.

The open door policy has allowed China to gain successful access to foreign technology, but it is difficult to ascertain whether such a policy could be extended to all the less developed countries. To attract foreign investors, a country must offer some specific advantages, such as a significant internal market. Furthermore, multinational firms have now gained the capacity to compel countries to compete for direct foreign investments. Generalizations about the open door policy imply that the comparative attractiveness of countries will determine where industries will be located in the future.

Michel Rainelli

Bibliography
Clyde P. H. 1931. 'The Open-Door Policy of John Hay', *Historical Outlook*, 22, 5, 834–41.

Pomfret R. 1991. *Investing in China: ten years of the Open Door Policy*. Ames: Iowa State University Press, and London: Harvester Wheatsheaf.

Related essays
China; corporations; General Agreement on Tariffs and Trade (GATT) / World Trade Organization (WTO); investment; neoliberalism; Pax Americana; trade; trade (manufactured goods); trade agreements

Orchestras

The youngest member of the Berlin Philharmonic Orchestra's current roster was raised in a poor section of Caracas, Venezuela. At seventeen, he auditioned for and won a position in the orchestra's double bass section and after serving the mandatory two-year probationary period, became a full-fledged member of the legendary ensemble. This young musician's professional trajectory points to the way the transnational idea is enmeshed in the history of the modern symphony orchestra.

As a member of a Venezuelan youth orchestra, the bassist and his colleagues were devoted to watching the video performances of the Berlin Philharmonic under the baton of Herbert van Karajan, who had overseen the creation of a vast library of sound and video recordings. The young string player recalls sharing the experience with other youthful Venezuelans: 'We always were in touch and tried to imitate the [Berlin] orchestra's oceanic sound' (Wakin 2006, E1). Indeed, for listeners worldwide, the recorded legacy of the Karajan–Berlin partnership helped deepen their appreciation of orchestral music. Even in Venezuela – thousands of miles from the symphonic world of Haydn, Beethoven, and Brahms – people were touched by the brilliance of an ensemble whose past is woven into the history of European classical music.

The modern symphony orchestra emerged in Europe in the late 18th century, evolving from the baroque ensembles of an earlier period. By the late 19th century, as composers demanded larger instrumental resources, the orchestra had grown to resemble the organizations of today. But even as the orchestral music of Mozart, Beethoven and other celebrated composers was performed outside their native countries, the orchestra itself remained an institution that operated mainly within the confines of the nation. In the 20th century, the advent of sound recordings, the rise of celebrity conductors, and frequent international tours lent symphony orchestras a degree of influence that would extend well beyond the boundaries of their home countries. Indeed, orchestras, rather like musical ambassadors, became the global representatives of their native lands. With increasing frequency, foreign audiences would attend concerts and purchase records, CDs, and DVDs made by distinguished ensembles from Europe and the United States.

The development of sound recordings contributed to the transnational impact of the orchestra, as music lovers could listen to notable performances by esteemed ensembles. While primitive recordings had appeared before World War I, with the rapid improvement in recording technology that occurred in succeeding decades, large recording companies in the United States and Europe would devote substantial sums to the production and marketing of orchestral music. By making symphonic music accessible to listeners in many countries, this efflorescence of recorded music helped internationalize and expand the audience for the modern symphony orchestra. In the age of the recording, a family in rural America could listen to the Vienna Philharmonic play Beethoven, or youngsters in Caracas could thrill to the Berlin Philharmonic's interpretation of Brahms. (Starting in the 1930s, radio also allowed listeners to experience live orchestral performances, though such concerts were typically directed at domestic audiences.)

Two other facets of orchestral life, the celebrity conductor from abroad and the overseas tour, helped internationalize and expand the influence of symphony orchestras. In the United States, for example, legendary conductors from Germany, Italy, Hungary, Russia (and elsewhere) made possible the music making that would help shape the nation's cultural life. Indeed, the sensibilities of foreign maestros had no small impact on high culture in the United States, and these sometimes exotic figures deprovincialized American orchestras, exposing musicians and audiences to incisive interpretations of European symphonic music. With Toscanini conducting the New York Philharmonic (1929–36) and the NBC Symphony Orchestra (1937–54), Koussevitsky conducting in

Boston (1924–49), Stokowski in Philadelphia (1912–41), and Reiner in Chicago (1953–62), the American orchestra was a more musically interesting and sophisticated institution than it would otherwise have been. And elsewhere, 'foreign' conductors also brought a distinctive musical perspective to their adopted lands, whether one considers Germans leading British orchestras, Italians in Germany, or Russians in France.

Throughout the 20th century, international tours enlarged the global impact of the symphony orchestra. In transcending geographic barriers, such tours helped shape the musical sensibilities of foreign audiences and, at the same time, likely helped sow the seeds of international understanding. Consider the message printed in the Vienna Philharmonic's overseas programme notes: the Philharmonic, one learns, is an 'ambassador of peace, humanity, and reconciliation, concepts inseparably linked to the message of music itself'. Once the final notes have sounded and a foreign orchestra stands to accept the ovation of a local audience, such a notion is easy to embrace.

Jonathan Rosenberg

Bibliography

Horowitz J. 1994. *Understanding Toscanini: a social history of American concert life*. Berkeley: University of California Press.

Peyser J. 1986. *The orchestra: origins and transformations*. New York: Scribner's.

Wakin D. 2006. 'A youth movement at the Berlin Philharmonic', *New York Times*, 8 May.

Related essays

classical music; executives and professionals; Italian opera; music; performing artists; radio; rock

Organization models

If it is possible to speak of the existence of organizational models in both the 19th and the 20th centuries, it is because such models entered into circulation, within and across national spheres. The scale may be different, and frontiers cannot of course be discounted, but the two levels (of models and of their entry into circulation) are nonetheless identical. Models circulate because people travel – taking their know-how with them – journals and books get published, and machines can be moved, taking with them their human guardians, their doctrine and their instructions for use. Models cannot circulate without assuming some sort of material form or incarnation. The growth of markets (and hence of competition), along with wars and imperial and colonial rivalries, has contributed massively to this circulation.

The circulation of organizational models began in the early days of industry. The late 18th / early 19th century was a turning point. As workers and engineers became more mobile, in the wake of the industrial revolutions that affected in turn the European countries and the United States, a marked interest in manufacturing organization arose. Two works by British authors, Charles Babbage's *On the economy of machinery and manufactures* (1832) and Andrew Ure's *The philosophy of manufactures* (1835), were immediately translated into a number of European languages. One of the most effective innovations of the 18th century was the reorganization of France's artillery by Jean-Baptiste Vaquette de Gribeauval. He organized the troops into ranks based on their degree of expertise, developed rules for the deployment of armaments on the battlefield and saw to it that the manufacture of cannons was standardized so that they could be repaired even while under fire. His manufacturing principles crossed the Atlantic along with one of his principal engineers, Honoré Blanc, and engendered what was to become the American system of manufacture, one of the most important sources for the subsequent circulation of organizational models.

The 20th century saw an extraordinary expansion of this circulation, which now covered the entire industrialized and industrializing world. Outstanding personalities from the first phase include the Americans Frederick Taylor, Henry Ford and Alfred Sloan, and a Frenchman, Henri Fayol. By the 1980s this phase had come to an end, though it was unclear whether it had culminated in the triumph of Japanese models or a new wave of 'Americanization'. It would be wrong, however, to see this circulation in terms of 'diffusion'. It is true that Taylor, for one, maintained an international correspondence and taught students from all over the world: his disciples were to be found in many countries and formed a society to propagate his ideas, but the most notable outcome was the immense variety of local uses and translations to which his ideas were put.

The same is true of other pioneers. The success of their systems emerged from a nexus of research aimed at locally developing a more efficient organization of production and management. Their ideas were not slavishly imitated, either in their country of origin or in countries where attempts were made to 'apply' them. Each experiment was an amalgam: a local invention, but also a reinvention of the very model on which the new practices were based. What was done by apostles of 'Taylorism' was quite different from what Taylor had originally proposed. This can be discerned on two different levels. The first validation was at the individual firm level, where local profitability parameters dictated borrowing methods: one option, for example, was to adopt Taylor's suggested planning department and combine it with Ford's assembly-line production and a wage system invented by the international consultant Charles Bedaux, while still attaching the label 'Taylorism' to the ensuing package. National characteristics also emerged at another level. In Germany particularly, attempts were made to distinguish between the 'philosophies' of *Taylorismus* and *Fordismus*; around 1925, after a sustained attempt to import Scientific Management (*Taylorismus*), interest began to focus rather on production flows (*Fordismus*). France adopted the umbrella term 'American methods'. In the US, Taylorism was subsumed into an enormous movement dubbed 'systematic management'. Meanwhile, workers everywhere were becoming more radical, and when they denounced the conditions of their exploitation they tended to lump together all attempts at rationalization as 'Taylorism'. In the end, 'Taylorism' became the designation for an entire epoch, despite the fact that genuinely Taylorist procedures had been incorporated into amalgams whose original ingredients had become indistinguishable. In this framework, Taylorism was merely summarized by opposing the work of designing work and the execution work.

Machines, documents and human beings were all elements in this circulation. The human go-betweens might be travellers, visitors to a company, or trainees in offices, workshops or laboratories. They might be active in international contexts such as conferences or consultancies; equally, they might be stationary, not given to visiting but keen readers and networkers, dissecting machines and products, and skilled in concocting local amalgams.

The Soviet case is an appropriate window on this kind of circulation, although the Soviet political and economic system was very different from that of Western capitalist societies. This only made the characteristics of the transnational circulation of models stand out more clearly. During the 1920s the government had assumed responsibility for importing organizational models: an entire ministry was devoted to the process, or very nearly. The scale and amplitude of the project were immense, covering not only industry but also the administration of a rapidly growing governmental apparatus and of its ruling party. A number of journals were devoted to the spread of ideas, exchange of experiences, and introduction of machines such as the first Hollerith and Powers data processors. The towering figure in this saga was Alexei Gastev, a Bolshevik worker who had travelled in Western Europe and encountered some early Taylorist experiments. With Lenin's support, Gastev set up a 'Central Institute of Labour' which trained thousands of specialist organizers. Gastev's laboratories produced vast agglomerations of 'scientifically constructed' work norms which allegedly applied to any operation anywhere in the Soviet Union.

But if we look at local conditions, the outpourings of this 'proletarian bard' begin to seem rather less convincing. Workplaces broke into violent quarrels over the work norms. Their authors were besieged by alliances of workers and middle and lower managers. The norms issuing from the central laboratories were subordinated to local compromises. The first two five-year plans produced no significant improvements in productivity. In 1935 the Gastevian edifice was shattered by the advent of Stakhanovism; but the authorities were still anxious to give the impression of American-style organization of production based on huge factories, assembly-line working and mass production. On the other hand, the entire organization of industry that covered the Soviet Union from 1929 onwards was a direct imitation of the Konzern organization in German industry. China also tried to adopt this system in 1949, but rapidly reinterpreted in its own fashion.

The net result of all these imported forms was something quite new, rendering the original models unrecognizable. But that is precisely what makes the Soviet experience typical. 'The transfer of a productive model to other national environments necessarily implies a complex process of hybridization and mutual adjustment amongst the different institutional actors involved' (Pardi 2005, 111). The local (= national) political conditions governing the Soviet economy of labour (planned economy, shortage economy, total absence of civil liberty, restricted consumption) made it impossible to efficiently apply any strict time-and-motion study as Taylor proposed. The consequences affected the entire economy of socialism and its destiny.

The heyday of 'Americanization' was after the Second World War. This was the period of the 'M-form', when consultants spread worldwide the gospel of the multidivisional ('M') business organization invented in the US by Du Pont and General Motors in the 1920s. The collapse of the Fordist and Taylorist models in the 1970s and 1980s created the impression that they could profitably be replaced by a Japanese model sometimes referred to as 'Toyotism'. The notion that all roads led to Toyotism, partly based on the conviction that all previous roads had led to Fordo-Taylorism, was popularized by an MIT study that appeared in 1991 under the title The machine that changed the world: how Japan's secret weapon in the global auto wars will revolutionize Western industry.

Some of the most notable peculiarities of the 'Japanese' model are in fact derived from American solutions imported after the Second World War. The introduction of American mass production in the automobile industry led to local innovations: multifunctional machines, rapid adaptation of equipment, greater collective responsibility imposed on employees. It was through an inventive and determined engagement with Fordist methods that Toyota developed its own. These adaptations passed unnoticed under their cloak of Americanization. Later on, in the 1980s, the inventions stimulated by such efforts to Americanize came to be considered so 'Japanese' that they served as a source for 'post-Fordist' models. The same thing happened to many other components of the 'Japanese model', including 'quality circles' and hierarchical clusters of subcontractors. Two aspects call for particular comment. First, branding an organization as 'American' was so important that the local adjustments which made that imported

Americanization possible became invisible. Later on, exactly the same thing happened as 'Japanese' solutions were tried in the US and in Europe: the label on the package was more important than the contents. Models in circulation always carry labels, and it is important to look for the complex and composite practices which may be lurking beneath the label. Second, the wheel is now coming full circle. Efforts to introduce American methods into Japan triggered innovations, which have since been reimported into the US under a Japanese label. In other words, transnational influences are often not simple, one-way transfers but circulations, i.e., multidirectional processes with effects on the rebound.

Work by an international research network on the automobile industry, Gerpisa, has elicited a fact of major importance: there is no such thing as the Japanese model (Boyer et al. 1998). Or rather, there are several, each following its own logic. While Toyota concentrates on continual cost reduction, Honda relies on product innovation and flexible production. The Japanese model has been neither exported nor diffused. Moreover, whenever a model goes into circulation, it will always be drastically reconfigured to suit local conditions. This means that talk of convergence is out of date and it is time for ongoing analysis of an endless series of exceptions, any of which may, or may not, constitute the basis of a 'model' which, if it goes into circulation, will undergo the same sort of transformations as all its predecessors.

Yves Cohen

Bibliography

Beissinger M. 1988. *Scientific Management, socialist discipline, and Soviet power.* Cambridge, MA: Harvard University Press.

Boyer R., Charron E., Jürgens U. and Tolliday S. (eds) 1998. *Between imitation and innovation: the transfer and hybridization of productive models in the international automobile industry.* Oxford: Oxford University Press.

Cayet T. 2005. *Organiser le travail, organiser le monde: étude d'un milieu international d'organisateurs-rationalisateurs durant l'entre-deux-guerres.* Unpublished doctoral dissertation, European University Institute, Florence.

Fridenson P. 'La circulation internationale des modes managériales', in Bouilloud J.-P. and Lécuyer B.-P. (eds) 1994. *L'invention de la gestion: histoire et pratiques.* Paris: L'Harmattan, 81–9.

Kipping M. and Bjarnar O. (eds) 1998. *The Americanization of European business: the Marshall Plan and the transfer of US management models.* London: Routledge.

Pardi T. 2005. 'Where did it go wrong? Hybridization and crisis of Toyota Motor Manufacturing UK, 1989–2001', *International Sociology*, 20, 1, 93–118.

Zeitlin J. and Herrigel G. (eds) 2000. *Americanization and its limits: reworking US technology and management in postwar Europe and Japan.* Oxford: Oxford University Press.

Related essays

assembly line; body shopping; engineering; iron and steel; kindergarten; management; Marshall Plan; McDonald's; philanthropy; socialism; technical standardization; Toyotism; translation

Organization of the Petroleum Exporting Countries (OPEC) *See* Oil

Orientalism

Orientalism originally referred to a branch of scholarship devoted to the study of the Orient through its arts, literature, languages, philosophy, archaeology, religion, and history. During the 19th century its meaning expanded to include imaginative works (for example, novels, paintings) that represented the Orient. The word also referred to artistic styles that relied on the associations of the Orient or emulated the qualities of the arts in the Orient. It must be said immediately that the Orient itself has been vaguely and variously defined in Orientalism, incorporating at different moments all or parts of North Africa, the Middle East, South Asia, and East Asia. For example, in the late 19th century, Orientalism was particularly associated in France with the Arab world, in Britain with Arab and South Asian regions, and in the United States with China, Japan, and Korea.

Orientalism appeared as a discrete academic field in 17th-century Europe, was formally defined as a discipline in the early 19th century, and reached its peak in the late 19th and early 20th centuries. For much of this period, Orientalist scholarship prided itself in producing an ostensibly objective account of Oriental culture and society, free of ideological, ethnic, national, religious, or cultural distortions. Imaginative representations of the Orient such as novels and paintings also often used highly realistic modes of representation, particularly in the 19th century, even as they overtly included exoticizing and fantastic elements.

Orientalism as a branch of scholarship was a somewhat paradoxical phenomenon when viewed from a transnational perspective. On the one hand, it produced important transnational scholarly organizations and congresses and created significant intellectual and cultural exchanges not only within Europe and Europeanized countries, but between this world and the Orient (however defined). Orientalists also often generalized about the Orient and the West in ways that ignored national boundaries (however spurious their generalizations may have been). On the other hand, the notion that the East and the West were essentially different and inassimilable was foundational to the field, and thus it tended to reinforce many cultural and national divisions.

Following World War 2, in the midst of decolonization, important critiques of Orientalism's claims to objectivity began to appear. Most notably, Anouar Abdel-Malek and A. L. Tibawi asserted that Orientalist scholarship was deeply distorted by imperialist and Judaeo-Christian prejudices. Nothing, however, had the impact of Edward Said's *Orientalism* (1978), which fundamentally shifted the meaning of the word used as its title. Said discussed Orientalism as a 'corporate institution for dealing with the Orient – dealing with it by making statements about it, authorizing views of it, describing it, by teaching it, settling it, ruling over it: in short, Orientalism as a Western style for dominating, restructuring, and having authority over the Orient' (Said 1978, 3). Instead of characterizing Orientalism as disinterested and objective, Said asserted that it was an instrument of imperialism: it produced an Orient that was inferior to the West and defined Europe as the Orient's 'contrasting image, idea, personality, and experience' (Said 1978, 2). Whereas the West was rational, humane, developed, industrious, vital, superior, and modern, the East was irrational, barbarous, backward, indolent, fatalistic, inferior, and traditional.

Said relied heavily on two thinkers to formulate his new understanding of Orientalism. From Michel Foucault he took the notion of discourse, or an epistemic construction that allows some ways of thinking and disallows others. For Said, Orientalism was a discourse: a system of representations that produces and delimits what can be thought about a subject. Much of his analysis demonstrated that the language and cultural assumptions of Orientalism constructed certain forms of knowledge about the Orient. Said insisted that Orientalism was not a conspiracy nor a 'structure of lies or of myths' (Said 1978, 6): these may exist, but a critique of Orientalism cannot consist of going back to find a true Orient, because this misses the idea that the discourse produces the Orient. At the same time, Said was ambivalent about whether the Orient was purely a construction of Orientalists or something which did in some sense exist out there, in the world. His ambivalence is well captured in a sentence early on in his book: 'The Orient was almost a European invention' (Said 1978, 1). His analysis gave primacy to textual accounts, both scholarly and literary, of the Orient, and he sometimes suggested there was no empirical reality against which to test those accounts, and yet he often took Orientalists to task for misrepresenting the Arab world.

Said also invoked Antonio Gramsci's concept of hegemony, or the notion that within a society one group may dominate others through its moral and intellectual leadership, thus achieving consent from subordinate groups. Orientalism, according to Said, not only convinced Europe, or the West, of its own superiority, but served as well to convince the East of its own inferiority. As is often noted, he allowed little room for the possibility of counterhegemonic resistance from the oppressed Orient.

The impact of Said's book has been dramatic. It has been translated into at least 36 languages, and has fundamentally changed the nature of debates – both across the globe and within and outside of academic circles – regarding the relationship between the West and its others. Initially, numerous Orientalist scholars reacted with outrage, but their vehement and total rejection of the book only suggested the depth of its impact. The book also inspired a large number of carefully considered critiques. Among the more significant criticisms were the charges that Said posited a monolithic and unchanging West, that he neglected the agency of those in the Orient, and that he dehistoricized and decontextualised the texts he examined. Other criticisms of Said's work have led to some of the central insights of postcolonial theory. Indeed, many major postcolonial interventions have come as responses to Said's work. As Robert Young recently remarked, 'The production of a critique of Orientalism even today functions as the act or ceremony of initiation by which newcomers to the field assert their claim to take up a position of a speaking subject within the discourse of postcoloniality' (Young 2001, 384). In reaction to the binary distinctions that Said identified as separating the East and the West (for example, irrational vs rational, traditional vs modern) and in contrast to his univocal, monolithic Eastern and Western subjects, more recent thinkers have emphasized the ambivalence and heterogeneity of colonial discourse. And while Said was primarily concerned with identities and subjectivities that could be ascribed to the East or the West, recent scholarship has focused more on hybrid subjects who display forms of transcultural and transnational consciousness, even in the most oppressive colonial conditions.

The role that Said's *Orientalism* played in establishing postcolonial scholarship as an academic field far exceeded its specific interpretive insights and the debates it engendered, as great as these were. The book was in many ways the result of a conjunction, in the person of Said, between, on the one hand, an understanding and experience of imperial and colonial oppression and, on the other hand, a subtle command of poststructuralist modes of interpretation. Using some of the most recent and sophisticated interpretive methods of the academic world, Said suggested that imperial and colonial domination relied not simply on military and economic superiority, but also on a particular epistemology that academia itself helped to formulate and sustain. In other words, Said linked imperial and colonial power to a discourse that was forged and maintained partly within Western academic institutions. Of course there were many thinkers who had offered important theoretical critiques of colonialist ideology before Said, but he specifically implicated scholars and linked scholarly studies of the Orient to a wider field of other representations, including those that were manifestly fanciful. He began a remarkably fruitful debate within academia. His arguments were quickly picked up by scholars studying many other regions around the world. One sign of the breadth of their influence is the use of the word Orientalism now to describe any act of representation that allows one society to dominate, exoticize, or otherwise mischaracterize another. For example, paintings of Native Americans done during the 19th century in the western United States are now frequently described as 'Orientalist'.

Said's perspective was cosmopolitan: it grew out of his own experience as a Christian Palestinian who was born in Jerusalem, grew up in Egypt and Lebanon, attended boarding school and university in the United States, and made his professional career in the United States as well. He characterized his existence in America as an 'exile' and argued that it provided him with special insights precisely because it allowed him to see beyond a specific cultural or national point of view. In this sense, too, he was precocious, for much academic work devoted to questions of identity now privileges the perspectives of transnational or transcultural subjectivities, such as those of expatriates, immigrants, creoles, and members of diasporic communities.

David O'Brien

Bibliography

Macfie A. (ed.) 2000. *Orientalism: a reader.* New York: New York University Press.

MacKenzie J. 1995. *Orientalism: history, theory and the arts.* Manchester, Manchester University Press.

Said E. 1978. *Orientalism.* Harmondsworth: Penguin.

Young R. 2001. *Postcolonialism.* Oxford: Blackwell.

Related essays

cosmopolitanism and universalism; decolonization; diasporas; empires and imperialism; exile; higher education; history; humanities; knowledge; literature; music; regional communities; social sciences; translation; tropics; Westernization

Otlet, Paul *See* **Bibliographic classification**

Otlet, Paul 1868–1944

Paul Otlet was a key figure in many institutions, organizations and publications in the early 20th century, and for decades pursued projects for the organization of the international scientific and civic spheres.

Otlet's childhood spread over borders. His father, then a prosperous tramways and financial Belgian magnate, travelled extensively. Paul was educated in Paris and Brussels. Working in a Brussels law firm after graduation he met Henri La Fontaine, with whom he teamed up for a lifetime of international organization work. First, they launched the International Institute of Bibliography (now International Federation for Information and Documentation) in 1895, to develop Melvil Dewey's decimal classification. Subsequently, they collaborated on a complex project to establish international associations of intellectual and scientific elites. Otlet coined the word 'mondialisme' to singularize this project. They initiated, favoured or directed dozens of initiatives, institutions, publications and meetings, including the journal La Vie Internationale (1912), the Office Central des Institutions Internationales (1907, later Union of International Associations) and the Musée Mondial (1910). Resources for this vast effort came from their own funds and from the Belgian industrialist Ernest Solvay, the Carnegie Endowment for International Peace, and the Belgian government. After the First World War, Otlet found himself at odds with the League of Nations he had ardently supported. The League gradually grew hostile to his associative conception of intellectual cooperation, and the institutions he created in Brussels began to wither. Otlet died alone and bitter in 1944. He has been recently rediscovered as a precursor by documentation specialists who have compared his conception of documentation with the Internet, both being based on simultaneous access to small knowledge units no longer bounded by the printed format.

Pierre-Yves Saunier

Bibliography
Rayward W. B. 1975. *The universe of information: the Work of Paul Otlet for documentation and international organisation*. Moscow: VINITI.

Related essays
assembly line; body shopping; engineering; iron and steel; kindergarten; management; Marshall Plan; McDonald's; philanthropy; socialism; technical standardization; Toyotism; translation

Outer space

All space above 'airspace' which is beyond the limit of national sovereignty. This space in which aircrafts are unable to fly was declared as international territory free for all to use and explore by the United Nations in 1963.

The outer space has for centuries been a place in which heavenly utopias and religious figures were thought to exist. The ideals evoked by appealing to things existing in outer space have had a profound impact on ethical standards for people living on Earth. The philosopher Immanuel Kant (1724–1804), for example, saw a parallel between 'the starry heavens above me and the moral law within me'. The heavenly ideals (for example in Christian religious thinking) had a particular impact in setting moral standards for social behaviour on Earth.

The outer space continued to be a place in which to fix moral standards with the space explorations of the 1960s. The Soviet-made Sputnik was the first satellite to enter outer space. Launched on 4 October 1957 it aroused great pride among the people of the Soviet Union and their socialist allies who saw it as evidence of their moral and technological superiority. It awakened an equally intense sense of being socially behind on the other side of the Cold War divide. In the rest of the world people also reacted with hope or fear to the satellite's signals – a modest 'pip, pip, pip'. In 1961 the Russian cosmonaut Yuri Gagarin became the first person to orbit around the Earth in outer space, and he immediately turned into a transnational hero whose courage all socialist comrades were encouraged to follow. The reaction was different among people in the West, as his achievements became an opportunity to question their own nations' technological and social abilities. In May 1961 President Kennedy of the United States responded to these shocks by announcing that his nation should commit itself to sending a spaceship to the moon and to return it safely back to the Earth. In the following years a significant amount of money was used on both sides of the Iron Curtain to achieve this goal. A series of artifacts were built in the 1960s which aimed at colonizing outer space.

These included rockets carrying objects, plants, animals, and people into a foreign realm for human activities. Their methods for doing this were, and still are, extremely complicated technologically, and successful missions to outer space thus became an object of national pride. For both superpowers, the race to the moon was a way in which to prove the values of their respective social and political systems, and to strengthen their respective people's moral faith in their governments.

The language of this US-led program was partly inspired by the founder of the British Interplanetary Society, Arthur C. Clarke, who wrote a significant volume of fiction and non-fiction about the exploration of the outer space. In books such as *Interplanetary Flight* (1960), *Prelude to Mars* (1965), and *2001: A Space Odyssey* (1968), he came to fashion space exploration in the language of the British imperial tradition of 'colonizing' and 'conquering' new frontiers. Successful space colonization, Clarke argued, was a matter of human biological survival in view of environmental problems and dramatic population growth on Earth.

Many leading ecologists were involved in trying to make outer space habitable for human beings. They tried to design closed ecological systems within the astronauts' cabins and made plans for a larger moon station. To ecologists, building space cabins was a question of copying a piece of the earthly ecosystem and placing it behind walls in outer space. This 'cabin ecology' was construed to have a 'carrying capacity' of a given number of astronauts, which was the technical name signifying a spaceship's ability to maintain itself while supporting its crew members. Close management of the population dynamics of species on board would be of paramount importance for the ship's survival, and astronauts would therefore have to live in harmony with the spaceship in order to survive. A host of highly advanced technologies were developed to achieve this end. This was very much transnational research as ecologists from all over the world were involved. In South Africa, for example, the famous anti-apartheid activist and ecologist Edward Roux worked on the problem of carrying plant life to new planets and studied whether humans could support themselves by growing food there. As the programme for voyaging to the moon advanced during the 1960s, the public and scientific debates were dominated by increasingly bold suggestions for ways in which to inhabit outer space, including plans for space colonies on the moon, Mars, and beyond.

In July 1969 the US astronaut Neil Armstrong became the first human being on the moon. The success of this mission was a great boost to the self-confidence and pride in the American democratic way of life. Among the Soviets and their allies, on the other hand, the news caused self-examination and a sense of having lost the race. On the diplomatic front, especially in United Nations circles, tensions soon emerged with respect to what sort of activities and ownership should be allowed in outer space. A number of agreements and treaties were as a consequence signed in the 1970s, of which the Moon Treaty of 1979 was the most important. It declared the moon as a demilitarized zone and its resources as the common heritage of all peoples. Through these legal and political agreements the United Nations was able to post itself as a relevant institution in a period marked by the bipolar Cold War. Barbara Ward, an international economist at Columbia University, was one of those who thought that the United Nations should play a key role in outer space governance. She was no space enthusiast and believed money would be better spent solving environmental problems on Earth, and she used ideas about spaceship management and research into the carrying capacity of space cabins to generate ideas about transnational steering of *Spaceship Earth* (1966). This reasoning inspired Adlai Stevenson, the US Ambassador to the United Nations, to note that 'We travel together [as] passengers on a little spaceship.' 'Spaceship Earth' soon became a key term in United Nations vocabulary, especially after secretary-general U Thant used it in connection with Earth Day in 1970.

Around the same time the designer Richard Buckminster Fuller started using cabin ecology in his lectures as a model for understanding life on Earth. 'We are all astronauts,' he explained in his *Operating Manual for Spaceship Earth* (1969), a book which basically postulates using cabin ecological engineering manuals for living in outer space to solve environmental problems on Earth. To live in harmony with the Earth's ecosystem became in the 1970s a question of adopting technologies, analytical tools, and ways of living in outer space. Key environmentalist terminology such as 'carrying capacity', 'steady state economy' and 'life

support system' where based on the astronauts' life support systems in a spaceship. The
Gaia thesis of James Lovelock, for example,
basically postulated Earth as a giant space
cabin, complete with a self-regulating system
that maintained climate and chemical compositions comfortable for living organisms. The
emergence of a transnational ecological ethic
was based on the imagined lifestyle of the
astronaut in outer space. Understanding the
Earth in terms of a spaceship implied a new
set of technological, ethical and social tools
to guide humans towards the astronaut's way
of life. Numerous designs for such technologies can be found in the *Whole Earth catalog*,
edited by Stewart Brand, and published in
various incarnations since 1968. This ethic
postulates that humans on Earth, just like
astronauts, would have to adjust their lives to
a host of computer-driven cybernetic monitoring, control and device systems in order
to steer Spaceship Earth into ecological harmony. Humans of the future would have to let
technologies for renewable energy, solar cells,
recycling of air and water, waste processing,
sewage management, material reuse, and
other health-related technologies developed
for space stations be part of their daily lives.

Viewing the Earth as a giant space cabin in
outer space required a panoramic perspective
which came when the Apollo spaceship sent
images of the Earth from the moon late in
1968. The view inspired ecologists around the
world who also used the imagined communities of future space colonies on the moon and
on Mars to analyse the Earth. In *Environment,
Power and Society* (1971) the ecologist Howard
Odum made a book length case for understanding the earthly environment and human activity in terms of astronauts' life in outer space.
In the 1970s, 'Spaceship Earth' was often used
to address transnational ecological issues and
the urgent need for global leadership.

On the other hand, the ecological coloni-
ization of outer space was a technically and
economically viable idea according to the
physics professor at Princeton University,
Gerard K. O'Neill. His visions for space colonization caught the imagination of much
of the outer space debate of the 1970s. He
suggested building a colony in space free of
military purpose, in ecological harmony,
without atomic pollution or other suspicious
industrial activities. It should include citizens
from all over the world and contribute to the
well-being of the Earth as a whole. The idea

was to use material resources on the moon
to fabricate a grand space station located at
one of the points of gravitational equilibrium
between the moon and the Earth. The station
was to be complete with mountains, lakes,
and small-town communities. Moving heavy
manufacturing to the moon could relieve the
Earth of polluting industries, and a grand
space station could ease the population pressure. Such a space station, O'Neill argued, was
'likely to encourage self-sufficiency, small-
scale governmental units, cultural diversity
and high degree of independence'. It was
to be an Arcadian ecological community in
outer space, he argued in his widely read book
The High Frontier (1976). A space station could
solve most of the Earth's environmental ills,
he believed. It could be built as a 'steady state'
economy in harmony with the station's ecologically engineered system, and clean energy
could be sent back to Earth from solar power
satellites in outer space. Not only could space
stations benefit Earth 'by relieving Earth of
industry and of its burden of population',
but its ecosystem with species of animals,
birds and fish in danger on Earth could have
a chance of survival in outer space. The space
station was thus to be understood as a Noah's
Ark taking an intact ecosystem into space
from polluting industrialism on Earth. More
recently, the Biosphere 2 buildings in Arizona
were completed in 1991 in preparation for the
colonization of outer space. It was the most
expensive ecological experiment to that date,
and the scientific rationale was to figure out
the 'carrying capacity' of a closed ecosystem
with respect to how large a crew of astronauts an artificial biosphere could support.
Its proponents argued that successfully running a new biosphere inside a sealed building could show people what it would take to
successfully manage Biosphere 1 (the Earth).

The colonization of outer space has been
of key importance for ecological debate,
methodology, and practice. Technologies for
surviving in outer space, such as computer
simulation programs, sewage systems, air-
rinsing methodologies, energy-saving devices,
and solar cell panels, have become regular
ecological tools for biological survival on
Earth. The rationalist and managerial ideals
for measuring a spaceship's 'carrying capacity' of astronauts have became a standard
for organizing human practical as well as
moral life on board Spaceship Earth.

Peder Anker

Bibliography

Anker P. 2005. 'The ecological colonization of space,' *Environmental History*, 10, 239–68.

Beattie D. A. 2001. *Taking science to the Moon*. Baltimore: Johns Hopkins University Press.

McDougall W. A. 1986. *The heavens and the Earth: a political history of the space age*. New York: Basic Books.

McHale J. 1969. *The future of the future*. New York: George Braziller.

Oberg J. E. and A. R. 1986. *Pioneering space*. New York: McGraw-Hill.

Related essays

biodiversity; Cold War; conservation and preservation; ecology; environmental diplomacy; environmentalism; forests; freshwater management; Greenpeace; Moon Treaty; New Age; new man; oceans; scientific stations; spatial regimes; technologies; United Nations system; zero growth

Oxfam

Oxfam is best known as Britain's leading relief and development agency. Twenty years after its foundation in 1942, affiliates began to be formed in other countries, and in 1995 the Confederation of Oxfam International was founded, which today has 13 affiliates.

The Oxford Committee for Famine Relief was one of several committees set up in Britain at the height of World War 2 to allow essential supplies to be got through to occupied Greece. After the war, this committee enlarged its aims to include the relief of suffering of all kinds, and gradually became known by its telegraphic address. In the early 1950s, it raised funds for famine relief in Bihar, India, and for victims of the Korean War. It became prominent when its general secretary chaired the UK Publicity Committee for the UN World Refugee Year in 1959–60. In the 1960s, supported by experts in advertising, Oxfam pioneered new approaches to fund raising that played on complex feelings of responsibility and conscience as well as compassion, and it was one of the first NGOs to insist on informing and educating the public in the rich world in order to help poor people develop their resources through self-reliance. Its first field director was appointed in 1961, in South Africa, and in 1964 it began a programme of marketing handicrafts from the South, which was later to become the Oxfam Fair Trade Company. Water and sanitation became one of Oxfam's technical strengths.

Oxfam was also deeply involved in nearly all subsequent humanitarian crises where Western countries could provide relief. These included the Bangladesh war of independence (1971), the consequences of the Khmer Rouge regime in Cambodia (1979), the Ethiopian famine (1984) and many others.

In the 1970s, Oxfam also led the field in drawing attention to the need for government and international action towards alleviating poverty. It launched the Hungry for Change campaign in 1984 and soon joined with other charities in mass lobbying. Oxfam engaged with controversial issues such as the supply of medicines in the South and misuse of pesticides, always basing its findings on thorough research. Oxfam had run into trouble with the Charity Commissioners as early as 1963, over its right to give grants for long-term prevention of hunger overseas rather than its direct relief; but these difficulties reached a head in 1990 when the Commissioners launched an enquiry into Oxfam's campaigning for political change in Israel, southern Africa and elsewhere. Since then, British charity law has become more relaxed on the issue of campaigning for human rights.

As well as being conspicuously independent, Oxfam UK has continuously innovated in enlarging on its core agenda, whether in the launching of charity shops, staffed by 20,000 volunteers, or more recently in the field of humanitarian protection in conflict zones.

Internationalization of Oxfam had been a vision of its leaders since the 1950s, and had occupied organizational energy since the 1960s, resulting in the first overseas Oxfams, in Canada and Belgium. Tensions arose in the early 1970s when Oxfam Canada began to pursue a more radical agenda, of domestic education and political campaigning against right-wing governments, than Oxfam UK felt able to endorse. Furthermore, the Quebecois arm of Oxfam Canada broke off to form a separate Oxfam Quebec. While inspired by Oxfam UK, Oxfam America also developed with a distinctive approach.

In 1996 the Oxfam 'family' was formalized as Oxfam International. Unlike other networks which grew outwards from the centre or founder, Oxfam International affiliates – some with different names, such as the Dutch agency, Novib – have come together from separate histories around collective advocacy and campaigning. All the national Oxfams so far are members of the developed world, though attempts have been made to establish an autonomous Indian affiliate, and Oxfam Hong Kong has become increasingly Chinese. Oxfam International has also pioneered mutual peer-review and has promoted the principle of accountability among NGOs. Its policy is for the Oxfams to grow gradually closer together without cutting their national roots – a challenge made more sensitive by the high profile of the name, and by variations in political pressures from the different domestic constituencies.

Jonathan Benthall

Bibliography

Black M. 1992. *A cause for our times: Oxfam, the first 50 years*. Oxford: Oxfam and Oxford University Press.

Related essays

Greenpeace; health policy; human rights; international non-governmental organizations (INGOs); International Red Cross and Red Crescent movement; Islamic Relief Worldwide; Médecins Sans Frontières (MSF); pesticides, herbicides, insecticides; Pugwash Conferences; refugee relief; refugees; relief; Save the Children International Union; United Cities and Local Governments (UCLG); United Nations decades and years; war

P

Pacifism

'Pacifism' is used to describe a broad spectrum of positions, ranging from the absolute refusal to condone violence and force in personal, social and international relations, to the rejection of the use of force in international affairs, to more moderate demands for reforms of the international system. The term 'pacifism' was first coined, as a normative concept, by the Frenchman Émile Arnaud in 1901 in order to establish a common ideological denomination for the various bourgeois movements that campaigned across Europe for a federation of states, for disarmament, or for international arbitration. It was thus itself the product of growing transnational convergence and cooperation amongst European and North Atlantic peace movements. Ideologically speaking, the very concept of 'peace' is directly related to transcending borders and establishing some kind of 'global community', either, as in Christian (especially Methodist and Quaker), Hindu and Buddhist thinking, as part of a cosmos, however defined, or as a corollary of Enlightenment ideas of a world unified by reason.

It is, therefore, not surprising that peace movements have been amongst the most active transnational actors. Yet the transnational history of pacifism was far from straightforward. Connections beyond borders might take place at different levels: organization, direct contacts, as well as communication and observation about aims and forms of protest between countries and regions. And addressing local and national audiences might be at odds with demands for transnational cooperation.

Peace movements first emerged in Europe and North America in the early 19th century, with an increasing involvement of the bourgeois women's movement from the late 19th century onwards. The first peace societies emerged in Britain and North America in the mid-1810s in the wake of the mass experience of war following the French Revolution in 1789 and spread to continental Europe during the 1820s and 1830s. They had much in common with regard to their homogeneous bourgeois appearance, their organization and their means of communication through learned journals. Their main forms of campaigning were the advocacy of education for peace through national and international congresses and the petitioning of governments. This homogeneity contributed to transnational communications via a broad spectrum of transnational peace literature and, in the wake of the 1848 Revolutions, via international congresses (e.g. Brussels, 1848; Paris, 1849; Manchester, 1852) at which European peace movements delivered calls for a European peace order to their rulers.

The cohesion of this transnational community was further strengthened by the foundation of the International Peace Bureau in Bern (Switzerland) in 1892, which remained intact until the First World War. While some early pacifists had advocated linking social concerns to demands for a peaceful international order, this linkage remained on the sidelines of 19th-century transnational peace organizations, despite the contribution of socialists and anarchists within the International League of Peace and Liberty (founded in 1867 by the French writer Victor Hugo and the Italian nationalist Giuseppe Garibaldi, among others). Although their remit was much narrower, organizations such as the Inter-Parliamentary Union (founded in Paris in 1888) and the Conciliation International (founded in 1905) also belonged to the spectrum of transnational pacifist activities.

Well into the 20th century, what Sandi Cooper has termed 'patriotic pacifism', a combined belief in nationhood and patriotism with the expectation that nation states should fit into the international legal system, sat oddly with pacifists' transnational aims and forms of organization. This meant that many Western pacifists were often susceptible to the imperialist *zeitgeist* at the beginning of the 20th century, thus alienating the few non-Western participants at transnational peace congresses. It also meant that most of the traditional transnational peace organizations did not survive the First World War unscathed.

The period after the First World War was characterized by a breakup of the homogeneous peace movements and the rise of novel forms of transnational peace organizations. After World War I had set in motion the process of decolonization, the transnational pacifist organizations faced new challenges. They added members and national sections in Latin America, Asia, the Middle East and

Africa, yet they did not shed their Eurocentric mindset and were hesitant to accept their non-European colleagues' notion that national liberation was the precondition for a stable international order. At the same time, they continued to campaign for the strengthening of international organizations, such as the recently established League of Nations.

Prompted by the experience of mass warfare during World War I, a growing number of activists came to regard the nation state no longer as the basis of peace work. They instead began to search for alternative forms of international organization by linking proposals for domestic political reform and the reorganization of international politics in order to overcome the dilemmas of 'patriotic pacifism'.

These views formed a more solid base for transnational links. A congress of women pacifists held in The Hague in 1915 led to the foundation of the International Women's League for Peace and Freedom in Zurich in 1919. Most typical of the transnational organization of the new peace movement was the foundation of the War Resisters' International (WRI), which had been originally founded under the name of 'Paco' ('peace' in Esperanto) by the Dutch activist Kees Boeke in 1921. The WRI entertained close links with the burgeoning peace and anti-colonial movements in Africa and Asia as well as with transnational socialist and religious bodies, such as the anarchist Anti-Militarist Bureau and the Christian International Fellowship of Reconciliation (FOR).

These new transnational organizations had national, regional and local branches across the world and thus created unique transnational clearing houses for pacifist ideas and forms of action, which were discussed in the organizations' journals and during personal visits and applied in the transnational campaigns against rearmament and fascism during the 1920s and 1930s. The WRI and the FOR were crucial for acquainting European and North American pacifists with Mohandas K. Gandhi's strategy of non-violent action in the Indian struggle for independence. Gandhi's vision of a non-violent society and non-violence as a form of protest was itself the result of transnational diffusion. Engaging with the work of the American writer Henry David Thoreau and the Russian novelist Leo Tolstoy, Gandhi first linked their arguments for a non-violent life with demands for direct action in his campaign against the military draft in British-ruled South Africa in the early 1900s, building on the arguments of the Muslim spokesman Sheth Haji Habib. Gandhi modified the strategy as 'satyagraha', a non-violent personal and national battle, after his return to India in 1915 and practised it most famously in his 1930/31 salt march campaigns.

This appealed to many Western pacifists within the WRI and the FOR well into the 1950s and 1960s. Thus, while the following years saw the demise of this brand of pacifist nationalism in India, ideas of non-violent civil disobedience gained currency amongst Western radical pacifists, such as the Americans Richard Gregg, Gene Sharp and Bayard Rustin, who visited India and introduced the strategy into transnational debates in both Europe and North America. This formed the basis for Martin Luther King's civil rights campaign, beginning in Montgomery, Alabama, in 1955 and 1956, and for discussions about non-violence among European activists in the 1950s and 1960s.

In the period after World War 2, peace movements had to cope with two major challenges. First, they had to confront the threat of global destruction posed by nuclear weapons in an international system characterized by the nuclear arms race between the Soviet Union and the United States. Second, 'pacifism' had become discredited as a political ideology in the West. Many now blamed the rise of aggressive nationalism and racism in Italy, Germany and Japan on the predominance of 'pacifist' feelings during the 1930s, and the Soviet Union was converting advocacy of 'peace' into one of its main propaganda tools in the Cold War. The rifts this caused become evident when examining the decline of the Japanese World Conferences against Atomic and Hydrogen Bombs (Gensuikyō), which began to gain ground as a focal point for a non-aligned global anti-nuclear-weapons movement in 1955, but rapidly lost its transnational cachet when it appeared to be hijacked by Communists for propaganda purposes in the early 1960s.

Despite the continued significance of the WRI and the FOR for the transfer of non-violent direct action from India to Europe and North America, the relative importance of organized transnational peace efforts declined. For transnational historians, it is most helpful to analyse 'pacifism' after the Second World War not in organizational or ideological terms, but as social movements, loose networks of activists who framed the problem of armaments in peculiar ways and who campaigned for very specific issues, such as for nuclear disarmament and against the American war in Vietnam. Although such peace movements established links with pre-existing pacifist organizations and other related campaigns, such as the civil rights movement in the United States, their transnationalism was primarily character-ized by intensified mutual observation, aided by the rising importance of the mass media in the political process in both Western and non-Western societies and bolstered by their common concerns for a world community. On the one hand, these efforts were less sus-tained than those of previous transnational organizations. On the other hand, however, the movements' loose and often spontan-eous character made it much easier to trans-late global issues into local concerns and to transfer protest forms which were successful elsewhere.

The most important exceptions to this trend were the Communist-dominated World Peace Council, founded in the late 1940s as part of the Soviet Union's efforts at cultural diplomacy, and the Pugwash Conferences on Science and World Affairs which, following an initiative by the physi-cist Albert Schweitzer and the philosopher Bertrand Russell in 1955, brought together scientists across the blocs to tackle the issue of arms control from the late 1950s onwards. Pugwash played a major role in reinforcing reformist trends within the fledgling Soviet Union during the 1980s.

By contrast, the campaigns against nuclear weapons in Europe during the 1950s and 1960s and again during heightened Cold War tensions in the early 1980s rarely established transnational campaign organizations and continued to frame their demands in terms of national and even local concerns.

While direct and organized transnational contacts and protest events remained the exception from the 1960s onwards, movement activists continued to frame their campaigns more pronouncedly as ones that transcended national borders and continued to engage with the campaign strategies of non-Western movements in particular. The protests against the American intervention in Vietnam which swept the Western world and Japan from the mid-1960s to the early 1970s increasingly engaged with strategies first developed by Latin American socialists, such as Fidel Castro and Che Guevara, and with Maoism, most famously

at the Berlin International Vietnam Congress in 1968. Quite controversially, advocates of such strategies argued that violence might be necessary for the creation of a durable peace.

In the period since the 1960s, the nation lost much of its importance as an identity space for peace protesters, especially in the Western world. Thus transnational commu-nication, especially mediated through the ecumenical bodies of the Christian Churches, such as the Catholic Pax Christi and the All-Christian Peace Assemblies, helped bridge the Iron Curtain in the late 1970s and pro-vided crucial support and communication networks for the emergence of an independ-ent (that is: non-Communist) peace move-ment in Eastern Europe during the 1980s. Given the importance of Hindu, Buddhist and, more specifically, Gandhian ideas about peace and social action for Western peace movements since 1945, it is striking that indigenous transnational campaigns in non-Western settings remained rather weak, as nationalism and state-building efforts con-tinued to hamper peace campaigns there. Although transnational communications between peace activists have been greatly facilitated by the Internet and inexpen-sive airfares, dilemmas with balancing the demands for transnational campaigns with local, regional and national concerns are set to continue, especially as peace movements grapple with organizing campaigns against the 'war on terror' at the beginning of the 21st century.

Holger Nehring

Bibliography
Brock P. and Socknat T. P. (eds) 1999. *Challenge to Mars: essays on pacifism from 1918 to 1945*. Toronto: University of Toronto Press.
Chabod S. 2004. 'Framing, transnational diffusion, and African-American intellectuals in the land of Gandhi', *International Review of Social History*, 49, supplement, 19–40.
Cooper S. E. 1991. *Patriotic pacifism: waging war on war in Europe 1815–1914*. Oxford and New York: Oxford University Press.
Evangelista M. 1999. *Unarmed forces: the transnational movement to end the Cold War*. Ithaca: Cornell University Press.
Frost J. W. 2004. *A History of Christian, Jewish, Muslim, Hindu and Buddhist perspectives on war and peace*. 2 vols. New York: Edwin Mellen.

Nehring H. 2005. 'National internationalists:
   British and West German protests
   against nuclear weapons, the politics
   of transnational communications and
   the social history of the Cold War',
   Contemporary European History, 14, 4, 559–82.
Velacott J. 2001. 'Feminism as if all people
   mattered: working to end the causes of
   war, 1919–1939', *Contemporary European
   History*, 10, 3, 375–94.
Wittner L. S. 1993ff. *The struggle against the
   Bomb.* 3 vols. Stanford: Stanford University
   Press.

Related essays
1960s; abolitionism; African liberation;
anarchism; Buddhism; Christianity;
cosmopolitanism and universalism;
decolonization; disarmament; empires
and imperialism; Esperanto; Ethical
Culture; Gandhi, Mohandas Karamchand;
Greenpeace; international non-governmental
organizations (INGOs); internationalisms;
justice; League of Nations system; non-
violence; philanthropic foundations; prizes;
Pugwash Conferences; Vietnam War;
women's movements; world orders; youth
organizations

Schwimmer, Rosika 1877–1948

The Hungarian Rosika Schwimmer was a key
figure in the peace and suffrage movements
in Austria-Hungary before World War 1, in the
transnational peace and women's organizations which emerged in Europe during and
immediately after World War 1, and she was
a pioneer advocate of world federal government. Her whole life was characterized by
border crossings.

Schwimmer was born in Budapest in 1877,
and her worldview remained influenced
by her experiences with politics within the
multinational Habsburg Empire. From the
age of 20, her writing and organizing efforts
were transnational, as she gave lectures
throughout Europe as part of her women's
suffrage campaign. During World War 1,
as vice-president of the new International
Committee of Women for Permanent Peace
from 1915, she used her connections to campaign for ending the conflict through a neutral
conference which would organize continuous
mediation to the belligerents.

When Hungary gained independence
in 1918/19, Schwimmer served as head of

the Hungarian mission to Switzerland and
(unsuccessfully) continued her efforts for
mediation, as the United States, Britain
and France still regarded the newly independent state as an enemy nation. When a
Communist-nationalist regime was established in Hungary in 1920, she fled her
mother country and settled in the United
States in 1921, where her work for peace was
seen as a threat to national security. Her
efforts to gain US citizenship failed, when
the Supreme Court ruled in 1929 that her
refusal to promise to bear arms in defence
of the US Constitution would make it impossible to grant her the status of US citizen. In
1937, she established the Campaign for World
Government together with Lola Maverick
Lloyd. She died in New York in 1948, having remained without nationality since her
arrival in the United States, thus embodying
the challenges to pacifism and world government in an age of nation states.

Holger Nehring

Bibliography
Wenger B. S. 1990. 'Radical politics in
   a reactionary age: the unmaking of
   Rosika Schwimmer, 1914–1930', *Journal of
   Women's History*, 2, 1, 66–99.

Related essays
Gandhi, Mohandas Karamchand; Garvey,
Marcus Mosiah; Hammarskjöld family;
internationalisms; Kessler, Harry von;
pacifism; Williams, James Dixon; women's
movements; world federalism

Panama canal *See* Transportation infrastructures

Pan-isms

Pan-ism is a type of nationalist movement
that aims to create a large-scale union, be
it geographically, ethnically, linguistically,
culturally, or religiously bound. The basic
characteristic of this brand of solidarity movement is clear in the etymology of the Greek
prefix 'pan', meaning 'all'. Pan-ism aspires to
transcend already existing political arrangements and nation-state boundaries, thus often
ending up embracing oxymoronic 'transnational nationalist' claims. Examples of
such pan-isms are numerous, and include Pan-
Slavism, Pan-Germanism, Pan-Europeanism,

Pan-Turanism, Pan-Americanism, Pan-Asianism, Pan-Arabism, Pan-Africanism, and Pan-Islamism. While there are many differences among those pan movements in terms of their claims of uniformity of a group and of eventual goals, there are two identifiable features that are common to all pan-isms. First is the grand scale of their aspired unions, and second their desire to combine separate and already existing arrangements by appealing to a yet greater cohesive factor.

Commonly referred to as pan-nationalisms, pan-isms have also been called 'macro-nationalisms' owing to their explicit aspirations for a grand coalition, both in physical and psychological senses. Pan-movements have been defined as 'politicocultural movements seeking to enhance and promote the solidarity of peoples bound together by common or kindred languages, cultural similarities, the same historical traditions, and/or geographical proximity. They postulate the nation writ large in the world's community of nations' (Snyder 1984, 5). Such movements emerged against the background of more prevalent 19th- and 20th-century nation-state nationalisms that often compelled lesser nations to seek strength in numbers in the world of Great Power politics. Thus, pan-isms have been most prominent when the legitimacy of newly emerging nation-state boundaries was still being contested, as in the cases of the disintegration of the Ottoman and the Austro-Hungarian Empires and the decolonization of Western colonial empires in the Americas, Asia, and Africa. In the way that they challenge the existing sovereignty and geographical boundaries, pan-nationalisms resemble micronationalisms, i.e. smaller nationalist movements within a sovereign state – such as secessionism and ethnic nationalism. The instinct of micronationalisms to peel away from the existing arrangements mirrors the impulse of pan-isms to combine separate units, both guided by the notion that those who claim to share similar backgrounds and sentiments should belong together in either reduced or enlarged unions.

Historical roots

One can trace a pan-nationalist yearning for greater unity in various points of history. For instance, the Catholicism of the Middle Ages provided an ideological cement for the vast lands of Europe, creating a sort of Pan-Christendom. However, it was more the collapse of such an ecclesiastical order and the subsequent rise of modern nationalism in Europe that shaped pan-isms of the past two centuries. In the aftermath of the French Revolution and the Napoleonic Wars, national consciousness, especially the one based on a common language, culture, or ethnicity came to be celebrated as one of the basic human needs. Instrumental in this development were such German Romantics as Johann Gottfried Herder (1744–1803), Johann Gottlieb Fichte (1762–1814), and Ernst Moritz Arndt (1769–1860), all of whom provided formative influences on early German nationalism. Herder's thesis of a common language creating national consciousness was especially important. It set a benchmark not only for later linguistic and ethnic Pan-Germanism, but also for the most ancient pan-nationalist movement of the modern era, Pan-Slavism. In *Ideas on the Philosophy of the History of Mankind* (1784–91), Herder paid special attention to Slavic peoples, extolling their rural virtues and predicting their rise in the 19th century, urging Slav intellectuals to preserve their languages and historical memories.

The Moravian historian and politician František Palacký (1798–1876) was the foremost advocate of early Pan-Slavism and the key figure in the Pan-Slavic Congresses held at Prague (1848) and Moscow (1867). Pan-Slavism in its embryonic stages was primarily a cultural and intellectual movement concerned with the awakening of Slavic nationalism within the Ottoman and Hapsburg/Austro-Hungarian Empires. It gradually acquired a political character in the second half of the 19th century, as the movement's leadership increasingly came to be overtaken by Russian Slavophiles for partly expansionist, partly hegemonial ends. They transformed Pan-Slavism into a Russian-led, often militant crusade against Ottoman and Austro-Hungarian imperialism. This Russian version of Pan-Slavism became an explosive force that collided with other pan-isms on the Eurasian continent, including Pan-Ottomanism, Pan-Germanism, Pan-Islamism, Pan-Turkism, and Pan-Turanism in the late 19th and early 20th centuries.

In fact, the disintegration of the Ottoman, Austro-Hungarian, and Russian Empires all contributed to the rise of several major pan-nationalist movements. In the Ottoman Empire alone, the rise of Turkish nationalism and the Young Turk ideology was boosted by a number of pan-ist sentiments. Influential in the early days of the Young Turk movement was Pan-Ottomanism, which claimed to unite all peoples under the Caliphate, be they Turks, Arabs, Greeks, Jews, or Albanians. As Pan-Ottomanism failed to win broad-based support, two other potent movements emerged around the turn of the 20th century. One was Pan-Turanism and the other, Pan-Turkism. The former based its claim on the putative common linguistic origins of Turkish, Mongolian, Finnish, Hungarian, Japanese, and other languages, which supposedly originated in the land of Turan northeast of Persia. Pan-Turkism was a reinterpretation of Pan-Turanism, advancing that anyone, including non-Turks, who spoke Turkic languages should be considered to belong to a great Pan-Turkic nation. Both Pan-Turanism and Pan-Turkism in the end overextended their geographical claims, which led to their demise. Though appealing to intellectuals of many national groups, Pan-Turanism failed to become something more than a form of cultural internationalism not least because of its overambitious territorial coverage, which in effect cut across several disparate cultures, religions, and languages. As for Pan-Turkism, when the Ottoman Empires entered World War I on the side of the Central Powers, Pan-Turkism was dealt a body blow, alienating Turks of Turkey from Turks in the Russian sphere. But many of the arguments advanced by Pan-Turkists and Pan-Turanists, notably Ziya Gökalp (1876–1924), left indelible marks on the later development of Kemalism as a foundational ideology behind modern Turkish nationalism.

The First World War, which included a clash of different pan ideas, most dramatically of Pan-Germanism and Pan-Slavism, ended in what some saw as the demise of European civilization. Some hoped to rescue Europe and gain hope for world peace in Pan-Europeanism. Count Richard Coudenhove-Kalergi (1894–1972), born of a marriage between a Bohemian diplomat / Semitic scholar and a Japanese woman, who grew up in a household that included at least nine nationalities, was a born cosmopolitan and tireless advocate for a federalist Pan-Europa. Greatly dismayed by the failure of the League of Nations, rampant Pan-Germanist sentiments embraced by his fellow students in Vienna, as well as the growing anti-Semitism and the impending threat of Bolshevism,

Coudenhove-Kalergi came to be convinced that there could be no stable world without a united Europe. With his writings, lectures, and the networks he developed through the establishment of such an organization as the Pan-European Union, he laid much of the philosophical foundation for a united Europe that was to be realised in a more pragmatic way by Robert Schuman and Jean Monet in post-World War 2 Europe. For the time being, however, Coudenhove-Kalergi's one-man crusade did not suffice to prevent the outbreak of another world war.

The federalist option for a pan-nation was an exception rather than a norm. On the eve of World War 2, what made most pan-nationalisms stick were not so much the institutions and arrangements, advocated by Coudenhove-Kalergi, as more emotional and cultural claims of unity that overlapped nation-state nationalisms. The most notable monoethnic pan-nationalist movement that embraced features of irredentist and chauvinist nationalism was Pan-Germanism, which aimed for the goal of unifying all Germanic peoples dispersed throughout Central and Northern Europe. Like Pan-Arabism, it was a more or less unilingual movement, though Germanic languages could include High German, Flemish, and Scandinavian languages in its broader interpretations. Increasingly, the Pan-Germanist movement began to merge with a Nazi rendition of geopolitical ideas and pseudoscientific racialist views that legitimized Germany's cult of violence and unilateral right to expand its borders until the end of World War 2.

Such a racialist backbone of Pan-Germanism was adopted by advocates of Japan's Pan-Asianism in the 1930s and 1940s, who based their claims of singularity and superiority of the Japanese nation over other Asian groups, whom Japan nonetheless claimed to liberate from Western imperialism. This manifestation of Pan-Asianism, which formed the basis of Japan's wartime Pan-Asianist platforms for the occupation of China and Southeast Asia, such as the 'Asiatic Monroe Doctrine' and 'Greater East Asia Co-Prosperity Sphere', followed from a more cultural and spiritualist interpretation of Pan-Asianism popular from the late 19th century amongst Asian cultural elites. Inspired by the 'Asia is one' dictum of the art historian / philosopher Okakura Tenshin (1862–1913), some imagined the spiritual greatness of Asia to be embodied by the two giant civilizations of India and China. Others specifically regarded the nations of East Asia, which had undergone centuries of Chinese influences, as their Asia, sharpening and narrowing down the geographical limits of Pan-Asianism. Japan's rise as a modern imperialist power, affirmed by its victory over Russia in 1905, further complicated the Japanese-led Pan-Asianist discourse. Japan's growing self-confidence gave rise to yet another strand of Pan-Asianism. Japan, as Asia's self-appointed leader, occupied the central position in the community of Asians, lending their version of Asia a hierarchical and ultranationalist character that became increasingly contradictory to egalitarian, though vague, claims of earlier Pan-Asianism, making it less and less appealing to Asians other than Japanese.

Global versus hemispheric – the case of Pan-Americanism

While decidedly anti-Western, and especially anti-Anglo-American in its ideological indictment, Japan's wartime Pan-Asianism was as much influenced by the anti-Old World rhetoric of Pan-Americanism of the late 19th century and early 20th century as the more blatant geopolitical and racialist thinking of Pan-Germanism. Pan-Americanism, noted for its ever grander scale that embraced the entire Western hemisphere, and for its different, often conflicting historical and cultural ingredients, is indeed an interesting case that merits a closer look.

The ideological genesis of Pan-Americanism can be said to have derived from the drive for independence in South America in the early 19th century, led by charismatic leaders such as Simón Bolívar (1783–1830) and José de San Martín (1778–1850). The idea, though never consistently or systematically pursued, was to combine South America's Spanish-speaking states in some sort of a federal or confederal arrangement. Thus, although anti-Spain in politics, Pan-Americanism of South America much depended on its linguistic and cultural ties to its old colonial metropole. Over the course of the 19th century, there was an attempt by non-Spanish American states, such as Brazil and Haiti, to develop a cooperative relationship with Spanish-American states. Though no longer a strictly Hispanic movement, Pan-Americanism nonetheless remained heavily Latin, with close linguistic, cultural, and religious affinities preserved in its claim of Pan-American identity.

Enter North America, and the movement becomes much less coherent in its claim of unity. From the early stages of its history, the United States was conscious of the importance of safeguarding the entire Western Hemisphere from Old World threats, as was indicated in George Washington's farewell address in 1796. But it was the Monroe Doctrine (1823), and more importantly, the subsequent reinterpretations of the doctrine that shaped the later development of Pan-Americanism. The Monroe Doctrine was originally a unilateral declaration of US hemispheric hegemony intended to fend off European intervention in its neighbouring countries, stating: 'The citizens of the United States cherish sentiments the most friendly in favor of the liberty and happiness of their fellow men on that side of the Atlantic.' While pledging that the United States would not interfere in the affairs of 'the existing colonies or dependencies of any European power', it declared that if the European powers were to intervene in independent countries, the United States 'could not view any interposition ... in any other light than as the manifestation of an unfriendly disposition toward the United States'. The basic assumption behind this was that the United States would interpret and clarify the doctrine as events and situations necessitated. Bolívar's Pan-American Congress in Panama in 1826 was convoked in direct response to what its neighbours suspected to be US designs to take over Latin America.

Despite the underlying anti-Yankee sentiments and suspicions of US motives, Latin Americans for the most part of the 19th century welcomed the Doctrine as a display of neighbourly altruism. The increased US interest in Pan-Americanism by the late 19th century resulted in the convocation of a Pan-American Congress in Washington (October 1889 to April 1890), which set up the Commercial Bureau of the American Republics (the Pan-American Union after 1910) for, amongst other things, the settlement of tariff disputes. The term 'Pan-Americanism' too had by then gained some popular currency. It was not until the emergence of the Olney Corollary (1895) and, even more importantly the Roosevelt Corollary to the Monroe Doctrine (1906) that the Monroe

Doctrine became directly associated with US self-interest and commercial imperialism.

This new understanding of the Monroe Doctrine, heralding the advent of Big Stick diplomacy, was especially critical, as it transformed the original doctrine from one of fending off intervention by European powers to one of sanctioning intervention by the United States. Such a new understanding along strategic lines had a tremendous impact. For example, it reinforced the evolving Japanese conception of the aforementioned 'Asiatic Monroe Doctrine' as a doctrine authorizing the Japanese presence on the Asian mainland to fend off other imperialist powers.

More recently, the political agenda for Pan-Americanism stalled over different approaches to Fidel Castro's Cuba and the future of the Panama Canal. Economically, there have been some efforts at integrating American markets, such as the creation of Mercosur (1991) and the North American Free Trade Agreement (1992). But the idea of Pan-American integration, be it in a political or economic sense, is bound to be faced with the question of how to reconcile the realities of US hegemony with longer cultural and historical ties among Hispanic and Latin communities. Moreover, the US rise as a global hegemon in the post-World War 2 era suggests that its strategic or economic priorities no longer remain within the Western Hemisphere, delivering a dead letter to the US Pan-American ambitions of the late 19th and early 20th centuries.

Pan-isms today

Despite the fall of many a pan-nationalism by the end of World War 2, the two World Wars did not snuff out pan-nationalist aspirations as a political ideology entirely. The collapse of the old order and the subsequent decline of imperialism also meant that there would be new power contenders in other parts of the world, giving rise to pan movements that embraced strong anti-imperialist tenets, such as Pan-Africanism, Pan-Arabism, and Pan-Islamism. And though pan-national utopias as such do not exist, there are still strong echoes and resilient attachments to certain pan-nationalist sentiments in today's international politics. Despite the pushes of so-called globalization, that is supposedly drawing the world into one system, the pulls of nationalism, as well as pan-nationalism expressed in terms of regionalism, remain strong in certain cases.

Of all contemporary manifestations of pan-isms, the least problematic and most prevalent form takes place in subpolitical spheres. References to particular kinds of pan-ist cultural and social endeavours – for example, Pan-Asian food or Pan-African music – might provide familiar examples of such aggregate identities. There remain yet greater challenges with political manifestations of pan identities. In the past, hegemonic aspirations of a certain country were justified in terms of the consequential and overarching common good it would purportedly bring to the greater pan-nation. But it is often the reaction to the hegemon that has made pan-nationalisms impracticable, as was evident, for example, in Soviet Russia's Pan-Slavic overture to its Slavic satellites, in Nasserite Egypt's insistence on its Pan-Arabist leadership based on the Non-Alignment philosophy of the Cold War, and in Japan's claim of constructing a 'New East Asian Order' and a 'Co-Prosperity Sphere', and finally, too, the US determination to safeguard the entire Western Hemisphere from outside threats. And yet, paradoxically, for pan-national arrangements to function, a hegemon is perhaps needed.

In this cross-referential sense, the more concrete and institutional expression of federalist Pan-Europeanism, the European Union (EU), is noteworthy as arguably the only successful case of pan-ism to date. But even the case of the EU remains a qualified success, as debates over normative and economic integration, burden sharing, leadership, degree of institutionalization, and scope of membership continue to stifle a straightforward development. Other forms of formal pan-nationalist organizations can be seen in regional agreements and institutions such as the Association of Southeast Asian Nations (ASEAN) and the Organization of African Unity (OAU), now succeeded by the African Union (AU). But they fall far too short of qualifying as pan-national institutions that transcend the existing nation-state matrix.

But the regionalist expressions of pan-isms, no matter how slow or circuitous their development, should be welcome in the sense that they create a mechanism of interdependence and common interests through concrete institutional arrangements. This realization places another major contemporary manifestation of pan-ism in a very troubling light. Political Islam, or Pan-Islamism, derives its strength from radicalized interpretations of the Islamic religion, which is not contained within a specific geographical region. Today's most militant Pan-Islamists express their grievances and socioeconomic exclusion by resorting to tactics of terror. And ironically for those who claim to counter the evils of Western civilization and globalization, they often approach the problem of geographical dispersions by employing global technologies such as the Internet. This is certainly one of the most, if not the most, alarming metamorphosis of pan-movements to date.

Eri Hotta

Bibliography

Coudenhove-Kalergi R. N., Count. 1953. *An idea conquers the world*, with a preface by The Rt. Hon. Sir Winston S. Churchill. London: Hutchinson.

Hauner M. 1990. *What is Asia to us? Russia's Asian heartland yesterday and today*. London and Boston, MA: Unwin Hyman.

'The Monroe Doctrine', President James Monroe, Annual message to Congress, 2 December 1823 [online: scanned reproduction]. Available: www.ourdocuments.gov/doc.php?flash=true&doc=23

Okakura K. 1970 [1903]. *The ideals of the East: with special reference to the art of Japan*. Rulland: Charles E. Tuttle.

'The Roosevelt Corollary to the Monroe Doctrine', President Theodore Roosevelt, Annual message to Congress, 6 December 1904 [online: scanned reproduction]. Available: www.ourdocuments.gov/doc.php?flash=true&doc=56

Snyder L. L. 1984. *Macro-nationalisms: a history of the pan-movements*. Westport: Greenwood.

Related essays

Africa; Asia; civilizations; electricity infrastructures; ethnicity and race; European Union (EU); Garvey, Marcus Mosiah; internationalisms; Islam; language; Muslim networks; nation and state; Nazism; Pax Americana; regional communities; regions; Westernization; world orders; youth organizations

Paris Club *See* **Debt crises**

Partitions

Partition involves the territorial division of a previously unified political entity, carried out by an external party or parties. The involvement of third parties differentiates partition from secession, in which one part of a political entity withdraws itself from the whole. Historical cases of partition include Poland (which underwent multiple divisions in the late 18th century), Ireland (1920), Korea (1945), Germany (1945), India and Pakistan (1947), and Vietnam (1954). The UN approved a partition plan for the Palestine Mandate in 1947 but was unable to implement it. Many scholars regard the 1995 Dayton Accords, which divided Bosnia-Herzegovina into the Croatian-Muslim Federation and the Serbian Republic of Bosnia, as a recent example of partition, although in theory the Accords maintained the territorial integrity of Bosnia.

Partition is a controversial diplomatic tool. Its advocates maintain that it facilitates self-determination and that it can resolve conflict and increase stability by separating groups that are no longer able or willing to coexist peacefully. Critics argue that it exacerbates rather than resolves violence, thus decreasing stability. They note that partition can result in mass migration and even ethnic cleansing, as well as further fragmentation if additional groups within the resulting states demand independence.

Partition includes a number of transnational elements. It involves an external power or powers exerting influence over the internal affairs of a state, colony, or other political entity. Calls for partition may receive transnational support from co-religionists or co-ethnics. Partition can produce large-scale refugee flows across state boundaries, as seen in South Asia in 1947 and in the Palestinian exodus that accompanied the incomplete partition of 1948. It can result in cross-border violence, as in Ireland, where terrorist attacks by parties unhappy with the 1920 division continued for decades, and in Vietnam, where North Vietnam forced a reunification in 1975. After partition, social and economic networks that previously existed within a single state must cross state boundaries; such networks must adapt and may dissolve, if these boundaries separate unfriendly states. On the other hand, new transnational organizations, such as smuggling or terrorist groups, may appear along partition boundaries.

Local inhabitants feel the impact of partition most strongly, but calculations about whether to carry out a division are often based primarily on the interests of the external dividing party. These interests have included withdrawing quickly (in colonial cases) and delineating spheres of influence (in Cold War divisions). In both South Asia and the Palestine Mandate, British leaders saw partition as a means to divest themselves of holdings they could no longer maintain, and imperial unwillingness to devote additional resources to holding Ireland played a role in the Irish partition. The German, Korean, and Vietnamese divisions, by contrast, were part of a larger contest between the post-World War 2 great powers. Partition can also result from a desire for self-determination, which was one driving force behind the establishment of the Republic of Ireland. In some cases, local parties believe that partition provides the sole solution to irreconcilable national conflict; in South Asia, Muslim nationalists advocated a 'two-nation' theory, contending that subcontinental Muslims and Hindus were mutually incompatible nations.

Boundary making can be a particularly problematic element of partition. Commissions mandated to produce boundaries in Ireland in 1925 and South Asia in 1947 both resulted in lasting controversy. Post-partition borders may be the focus of tension or even outright war, in some cases producing highly militarized boundaries with elaborate physical barriers, most conspicuously in divided Berlin.

Partition has eventuated in reunification in a small number of cases, notably Germany and Vietnam. In such cases, formerly transnational networks become internal to the reunified state, but partition boundaries may leave ghostly traces. The Berlin Wall, that powerful symbol of Germany's partition, was largely destroyed in November 1989, but social and economic divisions between East and West Germany have taken longer to erase.

Lucy Chester

Bibliography

Chester L. 'Factors impeding the effectiveness of partition in South Asia and the Palestine Mandate', in Kalyvas S. N. and Masoud T. (eds) 2008. *Order, conflict and violence*, Cambridge: Cambridge University Press.

Kaufmann C. 1996. 'Possible and impossible solutions to ethnic civil wars', *International Security*, 20, 4, 136–75.

Kumar R. 1997. 'The troubled history of partition', *Foreign Affairs*, 76, 1, 22–34.

Related essays

borders and borderlands; Cold War; decolonization; empire and migration; empires and imperialism; nation and state; refugees; terrorism; war; world orders

Patents

A patent is a right granted by a government to a person to exclude others from particular uses of an invention for a limited period of time. Patents are granted for inventions that meet the criteria of novelty, utility, inventiveness, and patentable subject-matter. The latter includes products, processes, machines, objects of manufacture, compositions of matter, and in some jurisdictions, computer programs and business methods. The acquisition of a patent does not necessarily entitle the patentee to work the invention, but more importantly, empowers the patentee to exclude other persons from working, using, or selling the invention without the patentee's authorization.

The history of the origin of patents has largely been spiced with myths. Perhaps the most famous myth is that the patent system inspired the British Industrial Revolution. In fact, the Venetian law of 1474 which established Venice's patent system is the progenitor of the modern patent system. Predating the British Statute of Monopolies by over one hundred years, the Venetian law offered protection for inventions made in the city-state of Venice. The period of protection was ten years. All applicants for the Venetian patents had to undergo examinations by the General Welfare Board run by the Venetian Registry of Patents. The law also provided for punishments for infringements of patents. In essence, the Venetian statute codified all the criteria for patentability and in addition made provisions for the outlines of a modern patent system.

Indeed, contemporary patent systems have barely improved on the core of the Venetian statute. The decline of commerce in the Italian peninsula and the oppression of religious minorities by the Roman Catholic

Church were the principal impetuses for the dispersal of Italian artisans and innovators, and with them, the idea of patents, to other parts of Western Europe. Thus, six of the first nine patents in Brussels were granted to Italians (mainly Venetians). From Venice, the patent system spread to Russia in 1812, Belgium and the Netherlands in 1817, Spain in 1820, the Papal States in 1833, Sweden in 1834, Portugal in 1837. Despite their common Italian origin, patent systems in European states soon acquired peculiar national biases and preferences.

The patent system spread to North America, Africa, Australia, and Asia through a variety of processes, namely, colonization, commercial and diplomatic pressures, and in some rare cases, national volition. As a colonial project, the patent system was part of the institutions and norms which the colonizing Europeans imposed on the pre-existing indigenous peoples and cultures of the Americas, Asia, Australia, and Africa. Some countries, for example, Japan, adopted the patent system of their own volition. Many other countries such as China and Korea were largely coerced into adopting patent laws. In contemporary times, the patent system is ubiquitous.

Amidst international rivalry among European states, individual national patent laws were often tailored to serve the perceived self-interest of diverse states. Despite the terrible abuses that the patent system was subjected to in Continental Europe in the years 1560–1624, it has to be noted that the contemporary patent regimes owe significant normative and doctrinal debts to judicial and legislative initiatives that occurred in that era. For example, the contemporary requirement in patent law that every invention should have a specification is traceable to developments in the early British textile industry. Similarly, the tests of utility and industrial applicability were largely developed in the infant stages of industrialization. Further, registration of patents is a practice traceable to British textile industry regulations.

Patents hardly live in isolation from developments in the economic and political travails of states. The competing national interests of states in matters pertaining to the transfer and use of inventions often degenerated into abuses of the patent systems. For example, inventors who exhibited their innovations at international fairs often found out later that their inventions had been copied and patented by unscrupulous patent offices in various countries. The monopolies attributed to patents were linked to widespread inflation and joblessness. Rampant cases of piracy, discrimination against foreign nationals and other abuses led to a backlash in the mid-19th century against the patent system. Various states began to rethink their support of the system.

In Continental Europe, there were widespread calls for the abolition of patents. As the anti-patent wave swept across Europe, North America and some parts of Asia, the Netherlands abolished their patent system in 1869; Japan followed suit in 1873. In the United States of America in the 1860s, the Bill approved by the House of Representatives abolishing the United States Patent Office followed a narrowly failed passage in the Senate. The emulation in eliminating patents during this anti-patent moment of 1860–75 is significant for the main reason that it showcased the interconnected character and impact of patents. Ironically, transnational public outrage against the inefficiencies and abuses of the patent system in Europe inspired the first reform and globalization of the patent system. In response to the anti-patent ferment, European states began discussions on how to reform the patent system. The willingness of the patent advocates to accept the principle of compulsory licensing as part of a reformed patent system was crucial in redeeming the system. Preparatory work on a multilateral framework for the protection of patents in Paris from 1873 to 1878 gave birth to the Paris Convention in 1883. Signed by eleven states, the Paris Convention came into effect on 7 July 1884.

The Paris Convention created a union for the protection of industrial property. There are four categories of rules created by the Convention. The first deals with rules of international public law regulating rights and obligations of member states, organs of the organization, and the constitutional character of the organization. The second deals with those provisions which require or permit member states to legislate within the field of industrial property. The third deals with substantive laws in the field of industrial property regarding the rights and obligations of private parties. The fourth contains provisions on rules of substantive law regarding rights and obligations of parties. Perhaps the most important contribution to patent law jurisprudence by the Paris Convention was the introduction of the 'national treatment' principle and 'right of priority' doctrine, which created a regime of formal equality between nationals of all member states.

The Patent Cooperation Treaty (PCT) of 1970 represents the first major step following the Paris Convention towards a truly procedural internationalized patent system. Yet, neither the PCT nor any other treaty on patents creates a global patent. The PCT facilitates the granting of national and regional patents by streamlining the administrative processes involved in filing a patent application in different countries. The emergence of the PCT did not diminish the fervour for regional arrangements for patent protection.

Europe has remained at the forefront of harmonization of patent laws and procedure through the operation of certain conventions such as the 1973 Munich Convention on the European Patent, or European Patent Convention (EPC) and the 1975 Luxembourg Convention on the Community Patent, or Community Patent Convention (CPC). These are integral parts of the agreement relating to community patents, signed in 1989. The EPC facilitates patent protection in as many of the signatory states as the applicant wishes. The Community Patent introduced by the EPC is intended to bring together the bundle of protection rights resulting from the grant of a European patent and merge them into a single, unitary, and autonomous right of patent protection valid throughout the community of member states of the European Union. The 1989 agreement incorporating the two conventions has yet to take effect owing to delays in ratification by member states.

In Latin America, the Andean Pact has similar effects and provisions to comparable multilateral regional arrangements. In addition, the Mercado Común del Sur (MERCOSUR), established in 1991, seeks an elimination of trade barriers and the creation of a common market. It also pursues the project of a common regime on intellectual property rights. The North American Free Trade Agreement (NAFTA) is another regional framework on patents. It also seeks a harmonized patent regime for member states. Another regional actor in the global patent field is Asia-Pacific Economic Cooperation (APEC), which in 1995 adopted the Osaka Action Agenda on harmonization of patent laws among member states. The existence of two major continental intellectual property rights organizations in Africa reflects the colonial scars on the African landscape. The first African organization on the harmonization of patent laws and procedure is the Organisation Africaine de la Propriété Intellectuelle (OAPI). The OAPI was created for the French-speaking African countries after they obtained independence from France, its original agreement being signed in Libreville in 1962. The African Regional Industrial Property Organization (ARIPO), an Anglophone organization, was created at a diplomatic conference held at Lusaka, Zambia in December 1976.

Beyond regional organizations, there are also non-governmental organizations and international institutions whose policies and operations impact on the global regime on patents. This most important of the several international organizations with impact on patents is the World Intellectual Property Organization (WIPO). With headquarters in Geneva, WIPO was established in 1967 by a Convention that came into force in 1970. WIPO is a specialized agency of the United Nations, and the successor to the Bureaux Internationaux Réunis pour la Protection de la Propriété Industrielle (BIRPI, 1893) which resulted from the merger of the Bureaux that respectively administered the Paris Convention and the The Berne Convention for the Protection of Literary and Artistic Works. WIPO provides educational information and training services relating to the development and administration of intellectual property, especially in decolonized countries.

Prior to the emergence of the World Trade Organization (WTO), there were perceptions that the United Nations forums, especially WIPO, were influenced by the preponderant states of the global South. Consequently, the global North relocated intellectual property functions from the UN agencies and forums to the framework of the World Trade Organization (WTO) where it has effective control of the agenda and norm-making functions. The result was the Agreement on Trade-Related Aspects of Intellectual Property Rights (TRIPs).

The TRIPs agreement is probably the most radical international legal instrument providing minimum standards of patent laws across the globe. Article 27 (1) of the TRIPs Agreement provides that patents shall be available for any inventions, whether products or processes, in all fields of technology, provided that they are new, involve an inventive step and are capable of industrial application. Article 27 (2) and (3) provides some limited exceptions. The harmonized minimum standards for patentability largely remove individual states' competence to legislate on patentability at the country level. In addition, the introduction of a dispute settlement mechanism as part of the trade repertoire marks a significant step in the creation of enforceable global minimum standards for patent protection. It is generally acknowledged that the main impetus behind the TRIPs agreement is to secure enforcement of US intellectual property rights abroad. The phenomenon also evidences the influence of industrial actors and stakeholders on global patent regimes.

Ikechi Mgbeoji

Bibliography

Abbott F., Cottier T. and Gurry F. 1999. *The international intellectual property system: commentary and materials*. The Hague: Kluwer.

Blakeney M. 1996. *Trade Related Aspects of Intellectual Property Rights: a concise guide to the TRIPs Agreement*. London: Sweet & Maxwell.

Dutfield G. 2003. *Intellectual property and the life science industry: a twentieth century history*. Aldershot and Burlington: Ashgate.

Gervais D. 2003. *The TRIPS Agreement: drafting history and analysis*. London: Sweet & Maxwell.

Mgbeoji I. 2006. *Global biopiracy: patents, plants, and indigenous knowledge*. Vancouver: UBC Press.

Roughton A., Spence M. and Cook T. 2005. *The modern law of patents*. London: LexisNexis Butterworths.

Sherman B. and Bentley L. 1999. *The making of modern intellectual property law: the British experience*. Cambridge: Cambridge University Press.

Related essays

biopatents; corporations; decolonization; European Union (EU); expositions; food; General Agreement on Tariffs and Trade (GATT) / World Trade Organization (WTO); genetically modified organisms (GMOs); industrialization; information technology (IT) standardization; intellectual property rights; intergovernmental organizations; language; legal order; music; regional communities; seeds; technologies; trademarks; United Nations system

Pax Americana

The term 'Pax Americana' most commonly refers to the period of overall yet by no means uninterrupted peace during the Cold War that in the prevalent interpretation hinged on the military, political and economic predominance of the United States, which after 1945 had emerged as one of the international system's two superpowers, alongside the Soviet Union. Notions of an 'American peace' have increasingly been connected with the rise of a novel American empire during and after the Cold War. Yet it seems more illuminating to interpret the closest approximation of an actual 'Pax Americana' to date, which indeed emerged in the aftermath of the Second World War as a hegemonic – rather than imperial – and essentially liberal peace system. The novel quality of US aspirations to recast international order derived not only from their global scope but also from their comprehensive and universalist nature. In their most ambitious manifestation, they followed the premise that durable peace requires more than a functioning system of treaties and diplomatic rules between nations – that it depends on the global extension of an international and internal order on American terms. At the core, these include principles of republican and, eventually, democratic government and a liberal mode of capitalism, all connected with political, cultural and social norms that the United States exemplified.

Arguably, US aspirations of this kind have had an unprecedented transnational impact. Positively, yet also negatively, they have affected global, regional and local transformation and modernization processes, particularly those gaining momentum after 1945 – first in Western Europe and Japan, later – particularly from 1989 – in Eastern Europe and also across many parts of the developing world. US approaches not only acquired more legitimacy than any of the 20th century's alternative visions of world and domestic 'order' – from traditional European balance-of-power concepts to the authoritarian countermodels of the 1930s and the Soviet 'empire' of the Cold War. Both in terms of their global influence and their universal scope they also exceeded any previous hegemonic peace systems in modern or ancient times, notably the 'Pax Romana' and the 19th century's 'Pax Britannica'.

Yet it should be noted, too, that the more a hegemonic 'American peace' seemed to prevail in the 20th century the more its legitimacy has also been challenged. Such challenges have not only arisen due to US conduct – e.g. during the Vietnam War or the 2003 invasion of Iraq – but also from the perceived harmful effects on political, economic and social structures of the wider development known as 'globalization' – with which, rightly or wrongly, the expansion of an 'American model' has often become identified. Most harmful, though, has been a characteristic tension that came to mark the American superpower's behaviour: the tension between the self-proclaimed transnational principles of a 'Pax Americana' and the invocation of overriding national interests and necessities – particularly in the sphere of security – that often led US administrations after 1945 to disregard such principles, notably by pursuing unilateral policies, according themselves special prerogatives and supporting undemocratic client regimes across the developing world.

At the outset, it is thus both useful and imperative to distinguish between two phenomena that can be associated with the term 'Pax Americana'. On the one hand, one can focus on deliberate attempts made by successive US governments – or informal agents acting on behalf of Washington or US high finance – to establish something akin to an 'American peace', and the consequences such attempts had, ever since Wilson's quest to make the world 'safe' for US-style democracy after the First World War. On the other hand, however, the global expansion of American approaches to peace also occurred by different means: as a consequence of the less direct but no less consequential transnational influence exerted by the American example, and America's economic power, across national and imperial boundaries. In short, ever since the United States gained independence its example came to challenge all more traditional forms of international order, notably the European 'balance-of-power' system of the latter 19th century, yet also domestic modes and orders, from monarchical and imperialist to authoritarian and communist variants. In the 20th century, processes of 'Americanization' affected not only the classic domains of international politics and economics but eventually all major spheres of political, economic and social organization, popular and elite culture, collective mentalities, and values.

The origins of aspirations for an 'American peace'

Notions of a 'Pax Americana' and attempts to realize it do not originate with US postwar planning in the 1940s, nor even with Wilson's peace design. Indeed, the origins of such aspirations reach back considerably further: to US aspirations to establish a new order on the North American continent and to extend this order in the Western hemisphere.

In short, ever since its founders declared their independence from British rule in 1776, the history of America's relations with the world has been a history of attempts to develop a different approach to international relations, one that departed from Europe's 'harmful' traditions of autocratic rule and power politics. Most later conceptions of an 'American peace' remained informed by 17th-century Puritan ideas, essentially exceptionalist notions of a people 'chosen' by God to build a 'shining city on the hill' in the North American 'wilderness'. As stated in the influential *Federalist Papers* of 1788, the main aim of early US peace designs was to shield this 'shining city' from European encroachments. During the 19th century, this aspiration was extended to the wider Western hemisphere. The formative Monroe Doctrine of 1823 underpinned US claims for continental and later hemispheric supremacy. Its main author, John Quincy Adams, envisaged founding an American 'empire of liberty' distinct from the British empire, thus fulfilling America's 'manifest destiny'.

Outside the Western hemisphere, the US example soon exerted a powerful influence. In the 1830s, Tocqueville famously predicted that the American republic, as torch bearer for the global rise of democracy and 'middling' tendencies, would dominate the next century – alongside Russia. What the American founding fathers initiated could be invoked by 'progressive' forces across the world, first in revolutionary France, then during the European revolutions of 1848. Later, it also served as a template for anti-imperial and anti-colonial movements in South and East Asia, and for the reformers who – following the maxim 'Japanese spirit, Western things' – sought to learn from, yet not entirely adopt, American ways during Japan's Meiji era.

Starting with the Spanish-American War of 1898 the United States came to pursue both a formal and informal expansion of an imperialist 'American peace' in Latin America and the Pacific. In his 'corollary' to the Monroe Doctrine, advanced in 1904, Theodore Roosevelt claimed that the United States had the right to exercise 'an international police power' and to intervene in the internal affairs of countries in the Western hemisphere if they did not manifest US-style 'progress in stable and just civilization'. More broadly, what thus eventually gained predominance, first in an imperialist, then in a more internationalist guise was the conception of an 'Pax Americana' that was no longer 'exceptionalist' but rather 'exemplarist' and universal: the United States was to bring peace to, and set an example for, the rest of the world.

Wilson's quest for an American 'peace to end all wars'

It was only after the cataclysm of the First World War that Wilson could set out on the unprecedented path of actually proposing such a novel 'American peace'. In his influential 'Fourteen Points' address of 8 January 1918, Wilson asserted that peace could be fostered through a globalization of the US 'open door' policy, which was to further pacifying economic interdependence by breaking up the prewar period's closed blocs of imperial domination. Essentially, though, Wilson's 'Pax Americana' was to be founded not on economic or cultural premises but on new political foundations. He sought to create a radically altered international system to supersede European imperialism and the war-prone 'balance-of-power' system of the latter part of the 19th century. This was to be achieved by establishing a 'new world order' based on universal standards and rules of international law, collective security and national self-determination, enshrined in the Covenant of an unprecedented international institution: the League of Nations. Within the League, the 'strong' powers were to cooperate with 'weak' states on an equal footing, and they were to commit themselves to a security regime that required all League members to aid a victim of aggression. In other words, Wilson's was the first US attempt to establish not only a new international system but also in effect a distinctly American 'peace to end all wars'. This peace was to rest not merely on intergovernmental treaties and agreements. Rather, it was to be underpinned by the new supranational mechanism of the League and, essentially, the transnational power of enlightened 'world opinion'.

Wilson's 'vision' was buttressed by America's newly gained financial and political dominance. In many ways, the United States was indeed poised to establish a global hegemony after 1918. The war had turned the new world creditor into the world economic system's principal power while Wall Street superseded the City of London as the hub of the global financial order. Following the catastrophe of the Great War, which had widely discredited the 'old' imperial or autocratic modes and orders, European and global receptiveness to American ways of organizing peace had grown significantly; and so had, potentially, America's ability to influence transnational processes of peaceful change. As Wilson came to acknowledge, however, he could not simply impose his peace design on the other peacemakers assembled at Versailles or on the societies he sought to lead on the path of self-government. Negotiating commonly acceptable principles and ground-rules of postwar order with the victors and the vanquished of 1918 indeed became a critical precondition for building a legitimate 'new world order'.

Of obvious transnational import was Wilson's assertion that, through its example, the United States was entitled to take the lead in recasting the geopolitical map across Europe and the world in accordance with the principle of self-determination. Yet his aspiration to universalize self-determination of course interfered with the internal affairs of other countries to an unprecedented extent. At the same time, however, Wilson's championing of self-determination had a significant effect not just on the subject peoples of the Austro-Hungarian Empire but also on anti-colonial movements in the Middle East and South and East Asia (although many also seized on the alternative vision Lenin offered).

At Versailles, Wilson had to contend with a prevalent French approach to peace making that, under Premier Georges Clemenceau, sought to base postwar order on old-style foundations, particularly on a forceful containment of the vanquished Germany. In view of the massive problems he faced, it is not surprising that ultimately Wilson could not translate his peace design into a sustainable postwar order on American terms. As it came into existence, the Versailles Treaty system remained incomplete and unstable, particularly because it was forced on Weimar

Germany. At the same time, the fact that the peace makers could only implement self-determination in an inequitable manner particularly left Central and Eastern Europe structurally destabilized; the newly recognized nation states of Poland and Czechoslovakia came to share contested borders with Germany.

To found a universal global order, Wilson also had to find ways of extending his 'vision' of peace beyond the Euro-Atlantic sphere – especially to East Asia. Here, too, his policies inspired aspirations for shedding colonial rule, notably a Korean 'proclamation of independence'. In the longer term, Wilson also sought to pave the way for Chinese self-determination. Yet the key problem he faced in 1919 was that of integrating imperial Japan into the League system. Not only in the Japanese perception, however, did the suspicion prevail that the US espousal of self-determination was yet another 'Western' attempt to cloak in declarations of 'justice' and 'equality' what was in fact a further stage of imperialist domination over 'inferior races'. Though often tactically motivated, such perceptions point to a critical challenge for the legitimacy of all 20th-century American peace designs. Unsurprisingly, Wilson did not succeed in laying the foundations for a 'new order' of self-determination in East Asia. Under the 'deal' he struck, Japan only agreed to join the League in return for America's recognition of its imperial control over the Chinese province of Shandong. Revealingly, though, Wilson declined to support the Japanese demand for a 'racial equality' clause in the Preamble to the League's Covenant – essentially because he feared the backlash this would provoke in the United States.

Yet it was in the US Senate that Wilson's peace efforts suffered a fatal blow when he failed to gain its support for the Versailles Treaty in 1919–20. Wilson's failure throws into relief a fundamental challenge also affecting all subsequent attempts to consolidate an 'American peace' in the 20th century – essentially, a twofold problem of legitimacy. In a transnational perspective, US decision makers had to persuade other states and societies that the peace policies they proposed were indeed superior to all previous approaches. At the same time, in a still vital national sphere they had to persuade the American public, and its elected representatives, that the international commitments they envisaged were not only necessary but also in America's 'national interest'.

Wilson's defeat by no means marked the end of US ambitions to transform international relations, and the world, in the American mould. His Republican successors in the 1920s pursued their own, though more limited attempts to extend a 'Pax Americana' to Europe and in East Asia. The key protagonists of such aspirations were the American Secretary of State Charles Hughes and, subsequently, President Herbert Hoover. Hughes' quest for a new transatlantic 'community of ideals, interests and purposes' recast America's postwar role. He promoted a novel transnational approach to resolving international disputes: the depoliticization of European power struggles, essentially through financial experts. Not bound by national allegiances, these experts were to propose rational remedies, especially a solution to the key postwar problem of reparations, which they did in the so-called Dawes process of 1923–24 and the subsequent Young process of 1928–29. Hughes' engagement paved the way for two first 'real' peace settlements between the Western powers and Germany after 1918: the London reparations settlement of 1924 and the Locarno security pact of 1925. In East Asia and the Pacific, Hughes led efforts to establish a – then short-lived – 'Pax Americana' through the so-called Washington Treaty system of 1922, which had the potential to develop into a global naval arms-control regime. It also was to guarantee China's integrity; but the Chinese status quo remained brittle.

Hoover advanced his own and in many ways more ambitious vision of an 'American peace'. He envisaged it as an expanding global system of liberal-capitalist states in which especially informal and transnationally collaborating experts and financial elites, such as the banking firm J. P. Morgan and Co., were to play an even more significant role, superseding the traditional primacy of political decision makers. The American model of the New Era was to set the new global standard; peaceful economic competition was to become the main mode in which states and societies interacted. The new hegemon was also to lead the way in Americanizing – i.e., rationalizing – the governmental, economic and social structures of other countries.

US aspirations of this kind did not merely lead to unprecedented levels of US capital export, which 'penetrated' national economies, notably Weimar Germany, where they often clashed with existing political, economic and sociocultural configurations. They also spurred transnational modernization processes and a first wave of 'Americanization' in and beyond Europe. Particularly the American model of capitalism and 'Fordian' industrial mass production made inroads into Europe's war-ravaged societies. But both the interwar period's 'Pax Americana' and the spread of 'Americanization' remained incomplete. They were constrained by the refusal of US governments in this period to make, and legitimate, wider political commitments to underpin the transformation of the global and internal order they desired. As a consequence, both collapsed during the world economic crisis of 1929–32.

The globalization of a 'Pax Americana' after the Second World War

Transcending Wilson's pursuits of 1919 and US policies in the 1920s, the third, in many ways more comprehensive and successful attempt to establish a global 'Pax Americana' was made in the aftermath of the Second World War. In the 1940s, US policy makers sought to draw harder lessons from what in their eyes had made the 20th century a century of total wars. First came the formative pursuit of an 'American peace' for 'One World' under President Franklin D. Roosevelt. Building on cardinal Wilsonian maxims, yet also searching for new ways to realize them, Roosevelt envisaged a universal and integrative postwar order, premised on the 'Four Freedoms' of the 1941 Atlantic Charter. Free from fear or want, the peoples of and beyond Europe were also to be free to 'choose the form of government under which they will live'. In the international system Roosevelt mapped out, a benign American hegemon would co-operate with the Soviet Union, Britain and China as this system's 'Four Policemen' and create an effective supranational peace regime that rested on a more authoritative international organization, the United Nations. Eventually, it was to include both the victors and the vanquished of 1945, notably Germany and Japan.

Roosevelt based his vision of a 'Pax Americana' on the influential premise that the more US policy could open up avenues for integrating all states into a comparatively 'open' US-orientated international system, and the more it could promote the transnational adoption of an 'American way of life', the more even powers that, like the Soviet Union, originally adhered to a diametrically opposite ideology would over time gravitate to what he deemed the inherently more attractive US model. American internationalism of this kind made the United States into the principal power behind the United Nations. The Atlantic Charter indeed became a template for the UN Charter and its novel human rights regime, offering what has been called an American-style 'new deal' for the world. Subsequent US administrations during the Cold War pursued such aspirations further, from Kennedy's 'Alliance for Progress' in the 1960s to the Carter administration's focus on human rights in the latter part of the 1970s.

Immediately after the Second World War, the United States also led the way in establishing the novel institutions of the Bretton Woods system – chiefly, the International Monetary Fund and the World Bank. It thus made a decisive contribution to the establishment of new international mechanisms that, though later marred by tendencies to impose austerity programmes on particular countries or regions, overall created unprecedented possibilities for transnational cooperation and economic development. In the wider horizon of the 20th century, Roosevelt's approach to world order proved formative. In many ways, it gained new prominence with the revolutions of 1989.

Formative for the era of the Cold War, however, became another and more sustained bid for a post-1945 'Pax Americana'. It was advanced under the Truman administration, and was significantly conditioned by the escalating confrontation with the Soviet Union in what turned into the 20th century's Cold War. The Truman administration, and all US governments that followed it until 1991, would pursue the bid for a 'Pax Americana' under the leitmotif of containment, not integration. Containing the spread of Soviet influence in every sphere – from the 'heights' of superpower relations to the level of local politics, economics and culture – became the central US mission, whose long-term aim remained to overcome the Soviet system and globalize an 'American peace'. In what became the American sphere of influence, also known as the 'free world', the Truman government made unprecedented commitments to the collective security organization of the North Atlantic Treaty Organization (NATO), and – in contrast to the 1920s – to a transnationally organized postwar reconstruction, especially – through the Marshall Plan – in Europe, or more precisely Western Europe. Here, the United States also came to support novel efforts to achieve supranational integration. US policy also provided the most important external stimulus for the democratization and international (re)integration of what became West Germany. In East Asia, it promoted the overall successful recovery and rehabilitation of a postwar Japan 'embracing defeat'. In some ways, the expansion of US hegemony came to be seen as such an attractive alternative to previous authoritarianism and disorder that it took the form of an 'empire by invitation'.

The Second World War had catapulted the United States – alongside the Soviet Union – into a preponderant position without parallel in modern history, not just as a military and political superpower and the world's unchallenged economic hegemon but also – far more than even after 1918 – as one predominant political, economic and cultural 'model of the future'. In one interpretation, the United States became an 'empire of production' during the 'golden age' of rising Western prosperity (roughly, the period between the late 1940s and the mid 1970s) before turning into an 'empire of consumption'. Yet, as already noted, US predominance went far beyond the economic realm. Both positively and negatively, concrete US engagement and the indirect power of the American example spurred profound transnational changes: from Western European economic reform and political modernization to the emergence of a US-style consumer and popular culture, nourished by American advertising and the powerful imagery of Hollywood, all influencing not just international and domestic political norms but also and cultural and social expectations. This second and far more enduring wave of postwar 'Americanization' first affected Western Europe and Japan. After the Cold War, though, it became a key catalyst for the wider transnational development known as 'globalization'. The underlying message of the American peace offer to the Western world, and beyond it, was unequivocal: that it was in everybody's 'natural interest' to shun communist alternatives and become part of a democratic and capitalist 'Western system' under the aegis of the United States.

Challenges to the 'Pax Americana's' legitimacy

Yet ever since 1945 the legitimacy of an 'American peace' has also been exposed to corrosive tendencies. On one level, this can be attributed to the fact that US international conduct often became marked by double standards. Avowed US principles all too often clashed with what US decision makers invoked as cardinal necessities of US national security. Notably, Washington came to support not only democratic governments but also a plethora of more or less authoritarian client regimes across the globe as long as they prevented Communist 'infiltration' or helped to protect US energy interests. This occurred particularly in Latin America – where Chile's Pinochet regime furnishes the most notorious example – yet also in Africa, Southeast Asia and the Middle East, where American administrations firmly aligned themselves with, for example, the Shah regime in Iran and Saudi Arabia's ruling dynasty.

US efforts to act as an 'honest broker', as pursued specially under the Carter and Clinton administrations, have remained indispensable for achieving any progress in resolving the crucial Israeli–Palestinian conflict ever since the foundation of the Jewish state in 1948. What has often been – rightly – criticised as one-sided American support for Israel vis-à-vis the Palestinian people, however, has had a highly detrimental effect on the legitimacy of US peace policies. Yet probably nothing has ever done more damage in this respect than the US intervention in Iraq in 2003, which most observers, and most other powers, in fact deemed illegal under existing international law. The same can be said for the second Bush administration's wider neoimperial agenda of imposing its version of an 'American peace', not least through the 'democratization' of a 'Greater Middle East', to contain new forms of transnational terrorism.

In a wider 20th-century perspective, what came to be perceived, rightly or wrongly, as overbearing US 'imperialism' – or 'Americanization' – has not only intensified the search for alternative, mostly socialist or social-democratic alternatives. It has also provoked manifold political, economic, social, and cultural counterdevelopments, many of them transnational in scope. Opposition to US hegemony notably became a rallying point for pacifist and student protest movements during the Vietnam War era, protests against

the Reagan administration's nuclear armament programmes in the early 1980s, and the
'anti-globalization' movements of the early
21st century. Prone to simplified critiques,
the latter have tended to view the in their eyes
harmful effects of globalization – the novel
transnational 'dictatorship' of multinational
corporations and unrestrained capitalism – as
the outgrowth of US ambitions to expand, not
an 'American peace' but an 'American empire'.

Patrick Cohrs

Bibliography

Cohrs P. O. 2006. *The unfinished peace
after World War I: America, Britain and the
stabilization of Europe, 1919–1932.* Cambridge
and New York: Cambridge University
Press.

de Grazia V. 2005. *Irresistible empire: America's
advance through twentieth-century Europe.*
Cambridge, MA: Harvard University Press.

Hunt M. H. 2007. *The American ascendancy:
How the United States gained and wielded global
dominance.* Chapel Hill: University of North
Carolina Press.

Iriye A. 1993. *The globalizing of America,
1913–1945.* Cambridge and New York:
Cambridge University Press.

Maier C. S. 2006. *Among empires: American
ascendancy and its predecessors.* Cambridge,
MA: Harvard University Press.

Manela E. 2007. *The Wilsonian moment: self
determination and the international origins of
anticolonial nationalism.* Oxford and
New York: Oxford University Press.

Smith T. 1994. *America's mission: the United
States and the worldwide struggle for democracy
in the twentieth century.* Princeton: Princeton
University Press.

Westad O. A. 2005. *The global Cold War.*
Cambridge and New York: Cambridge
University Press.

Related essays

1848; 1989; America; capitalism; Cold
War; Commission on International
Labour Legislation; commodity trading;
consumer society; cosmopolitanism and
universalism; decolonization; democracy;
development and growth; developmental
assistance; economics; empires and
imperialism; European Union (EU);
evangelicalism; film; financial centres;
financial diplomacy; financial markets;
globalization; Green Revolution; history;
Hollywood; human rights; information
economy; intergovernmental organizations;
International Monetary Fund (IMF);
internationalisms; investment; Japan;
language diplomacy; League of Nations
system; legal order; love; Marshall Plan;
Mexican Revolution; modernization
theory; neoliberalism; new man; North
Atlantic Treaty Organization (NATO); oil;
open door and free flow; organization
models; pan-isms; partitions; reparations;
rubber; socialism; technical assistance;
technical standardization; trade
(manufactured goods); trade agreements;
underdevelopment; United Nations system;
Vietnam War; Westernization; Wilson,
Woodrow; World Bank; world orders

Wilson, Woodrow 1856–1924

President of the United States (1913–1921),
Wilson led his country into World War 1 and
emerged as the leading figure at the Paris
Peace Conference that followed the war.
Wilson's performance at this conference
has been widely viewed as a failure, both by
his contemporaries and by historians, and
the US Senate refused to ratify the resulting
Treaty of Versailles. But the principles that
Wilson articulated about the desired shape
of international society – a set of ideas often
referred to as 'Wilsonianism' – has remained
both influential and controversial to this day.

Initially, Wilson attempted to keep the
United States neutral in the war, but by 1917
he decided it must join the Allies to defeat
German militarism and gain a voice at the
peace negotiations. Wilson's plan for the
postwar world called for a peace based on
the principles of self-determination and the
equality of nations and advocated the establishment of a League of Nations that would
help preserve the peace. His soaring rhetoric
and stature as a world leader raised enormous expectations across the world for the
dawn of a new era in international relations,
and disappointment followed when the peace
treaties failed to meet these expectations.

Wilson's ideas, however, have remained
influential in US foreign policy. Broadly
speaking, Wilsonianism consists of three
interrelated notions. First, that moral considerations can and should apply to the
behaviour of states in the international
arena in the same way that they apply to
individual behaviour in society. Second,
that democratic states are inherently

more peaceful than authoritarian ones, and hence the protection and promotion of democracy are important to preserving international peace. Third, that the interconnectedness of the globe in the modern era requires international institutions, universal in scope, that can secure peace and help manage problems that transcend national boundaries.

Erez Manela

Bibliography
Manela E. 2007. *The Wilsonian moment: self-determination and the international origins of anticolonial nationalism.* Oxford and New York: Oxford University Press.

Related essays
cosmopolitanism and universalism; decolonization; empires and imperialism; internationalisms; language diplomacy; League of Nations system; nation and state; world orders

Pedlars

Pedlars – travelling salespeople – were to be met with in both town and country and were an important vector for the distribution of goods of all kinds. Some operated as part of a network, others individually. Members of pedlar networks generally came from regions that could be described as ecologically marginal: remote valleys, coasts, desert fringes. Their organization operated on two interconnected levels. The first depended on extended families that had migrated to the towns, and it was funded by a sort of family banking system where dowries and inheritances were deposited to fund the wholesale acquisition of wares. The second was made up of temporary migrants from the home village, buying their wares from the former fellow-migrant villagers, and selling them in both town and country. These networks provided both everyday necessities and new, even luxury, products (albeit frequently counterfeit or cheap copies), bringing luxuries within the reach of every purse. Not all of them were family-based: some were held together by religion, like the African Mourides to be found today in every European city.

Peddling, widespread in Europe since the Middle Ages, was severely endangered by the rise of nation states intent on controlling all people and goods within their borders.

As a result, cross-border networks were fragmented and pushed back within single regions. Between the mid-19th century and the First World War it is possible to distinguish three types of pedlars according to the nature of the guarantees they could offer to the city merchants from whom they bought their wares. The poorest had nothing but their picturesque character to offer: they made themselves into an entertainment, selling dream and fantasy. Their social backgrounds were most diverse, since they had taken to peddling as an escape from poverty. Others could boast a cart, regular suppliers, regular customers and sufficient funds to ensure their credit was good. Most of these had one or two established itineraries and kept proper accounts. The richest pedlars were able to set up shop and used the most modern sales technique; but they were always prepared to take to the road again if business was bad.

The endless political and economic upheavals of the 19th century, and the new roads and railroads that made towns more accessible, threatened to put an end to peddling unless pedlars were able to adapt. In fact, it became a career of last resort for men who were unable to find another job, or were between jobs. A few traditional pedlars survived for a few more decades by specializing in sought-after products such as spectacles and books; others made for the wide open spaces of the Americas or the East where they might be able to re-create the pedlar's original environment. But the First World War, by resealing every frontier, finally sounded the death-knell of these new, evolved pedlars in Europe.

By contrast, peddling, conducted by migrants leaving their home villages, is still very much a part of life in Asia, Latin America and Africa. Women play a major role in the cities, specializing in the resale of foodstuffs and clothes. They remain active in markets outside Europe, and some cover long distances, especially in Africa and the Caribbean. Indeed, wherever there are borders there will always be pedlars, men and women who can turn political and economic barriers to account. And there will always be poor people, too proud to beg, who will try to sell something however modest. In Europe's great cities some organized pedlars sell newspapers specially produced for them, reviving an ancient tradition whereby the circulation of information around urban environments was the prerogative of the poor.

Laurence Fontaine

Bibliography

Fontaine L. 1996. *History of pedlars in Europe.* Cambridge: Polity.

Lesser J. 1992. 'From pedlars to proprietors: Lebanese, Syrian and Jewish immigrants in Brazil', in Hourani A. and Shehadi N. (eds) *The Lebanese in the world: a century of emigration,* London and New York: I.B. Tauris and St. Martin's Press, 393–410.

Manchuelle F. 1997. *Willing migrants: Sonike labor diasporas, 1848–1960.* Athens, OH: Ohio University Press.

Markovits C. 2000. *The global world of Indian merchants, 1750–1947: traders of Sind from Bukhara to Panama.* Cambridge: Cambridge University Press.

Related essays

counterfeit goods; empire and migration; labour migrations; Labanese Diaspora; temporary migrations; trade (manufactured goods)

Performing artists

The emergence of performing artists on a global stage and the development of transnational performance cultures moved in tandem with the expansion of markets. From the child prodigy Wolfgang Amadeus Mozart, who traversed Europe as a child to perform for monarchs and nobles; to the itinerant European theatre troupes that spanned the continent, to the trans-Atlantic career of William Henry James ('Master Juba'), the black dancer of the 19th century, performing artists were tied to rapidly expanding systems of venues, markets, publicity and press coverage, through which performers and cultural products became visible to a broader public throughout the trans-Atlantic and trans-Pacific circuits of trade. With the livelihood of performers increasingly tied to the market rather than patronage, the rise of modern culture industries made it both possible and necessary for performers to travel internationally. Moreover, in bringing new forms of cultural production and self-expression to provincial audiences, performers enabled and encouraged the imaging of new forms of selfhood and social possibilities.

From as early as the 16th century, professional troupes of the actor-centred improvisational theatre, *commedia dell'arte*, toured the city states of what we now call the nation of Italy and later, performed in marketplaces and palaces throughout Europe. Through the 18th century, European performers were influenced by the importation of Shadow Puppet Theatre from Southeast Asia via Greek and Turkish trade routes. By the late 18th century, a new popular cultural form was concretized as phantasmagoria, characterized by popular public exhibitions of shadows, projected through the use of 'the magic lantern'. Known in France as *ombremanie*, it followed known performance routes to Britain and later the United States. Such circum-Atlantic lanes were firmly established by the slave trade as early as the dawn of 16th century and took striking form in the performance cultures of colonial New Orleans, where the music and dance of African slaves converged with European forms from London, Paris, and Salzburg, and the constant movement of slaves and traders throughout the Caribbean basin, to produce new and highly original forms of music and art, the best known of which is jazz.

As European troupes and conventions crossed the Atlantic, popular Shakespearean theatre, with socially diverse but male-only audiences thrived in US antebellum theatre. At the century's end, as Shakespeare 'migrated' to new elite venues such as theatres and concert halls, popular entertainments like vaudeville, musical revue, and musical comedy increasingly relied on a mobile group of performers. The French actress Sarah Bernhardt made her US debut in 1880 and helped to inaugurate a new generation of assertive women performers who turned the popular theatre into a space for the expression of women's sexuality and aspirations for social and political freedom.

Performing artists have also fostered the development of more or less transgressive counter-publics, where normative racial, gender, and sexual identities were challenged. Even black entertainers performing in stereotyped minstrel roles were able to speak directly to black audiences over the heads of whites. Through performance, such artists influenced metropolitan and colonial cultures alike through their articulations of a transnational vocabulary of self-expression.

Scholars have argued for the importance of embodied performance in producing identities, consolidating cultural memory and making political claims in literate, semi-literate and digital societies. In the rapidly shifting boundaries of European nation states in the wake of the Napoleonic Wars, within imperial borders, travelling theatres became a birthplace and tributary of nationalist theatre. A notable example is Josef Kajetán Tyl, a prominent figure in the 19th-century Czech National Revival Movement, who joined a travelling theatre as a subject of the Austrian Empire before establishing a Czech ensemble in an otherwise German theatre in Prague in the 1830s. Questioning the assumed primacy of the written word, Diane Taylor, writing of the contemporary Peruvian theatre group Yuyachkani, has argued for the importance of embodied performance as an alternative form of knowledge production. By making visible unacknowledged histories of violent conflict and collective trauma, Yuyachkani enacts interconnections between atrocity, embodied knowledge, and subjectivity. Similarly, musical performance played a critical role in creating a national culture in the new nation of Tanzania in the 1960s, allowing formerly colonized peoples to reimagine African culture and history when these cultures and histories had been mutilated and reinvented by colonial interests.

Travel and collaborations across national boundaries have been vital for performing artists who are marginalized within their own societies. This has been particularly relevant for African American artists. Scholars have long noted the greater commercial and critical appeal of African American cultural expressions such as jazz and black dance in Europe as compared to the United States. Jazz trumpeter Louis Armstrong and the pianist, composer and bandleader Duke Ellington embarked on their first European tours in the 1930s. The dancer, choreographer, and anthropologist Katherine Dunham took her company to Europe in 1948 when she could no longer afford to keep her dance school open. Her company toured Europe, South America, Asia and the Pacific for the majority of the next fifteen years. Dunham, like her contemporary, the dancer and choreographer Pearl Primus, was a trained anthropologist and their performances brought ethnographic knowledge to bear on their choreography. Dunham had done field research in Haiti and Jamaica; Primus did her research in West Africa. Both saw themselves as cultural ambassadors, bringing African and African diasporic art to audiences throughout the globe. Primus was known to provide an explanation of a ritual before dancing it. Dunham viewed her choreography as a quintessentially modern cultural fusion between European and Afro-diasporic forms. Dunham, followed by Martha Graham, led one of the first interracial dance companies in the United States.

Performing artists such as Dunham and Primus saw the arts as a site for undermining the racial hierarchies of modernism. To Dunham, her company demonstrated the universality of rhythm and the interchangeability of cultures. Yet if black performers travelled in search of the opportunities and freedom unavailable in racially segregated US society, it sometimes proved difficult to escape racial barriers. Dunham, for example, was barred from a hotel in Brazil, and dealt with racism in her company's accommodations when it performed for an extended run in London in 1948.

A sense of competition between national cultures would reach its height during the Cold War years. After the Second World War, the United States and the Soviet Union competed for the political allegiances and resources of peoples emerging from decades of colonialism. The superpowers joined such countries as Mexico and France that had long made the promotion and export of their arts a central part of their diplomacy. While the Soviets sent classical orchestras and ballet companies across the world, and also promoted folk cultural expressions, the United States responded with modern expressive cultures, sending such jazz musicians as Dizzy Gillespie, Louis Armstrong, Duke Ellington, and Dave Brubeck on world tours, and such modernist dancers and choreographers as Martha Graham, Alvin Ailey, Paul Taylor, and Jose Limon. Not to be outdone by Soviet sponsorship of classical music, the US also sent classical orchestras, often to entertain elites in Latin American dictatorships. If jazz was the pet project of the State Department for that form's salience for countering Soviet charges of US racism as well as promoting a racially integrated American modernism, state sponsorship had perhaps the most significant impact on the dance world as the fortunes of such renowned companies as those of Martha Graham and Alvin Ailey became inextricably bound with their State Department sponsorship.

These international tours brought artists to places that often would not have been commercially profitable or logistically viable. Yet, such sponsorship had multiple unintended consequences. In the case of jazz and the US State Department, musicians brought their own agendas, promoting civil rights and challenging State Department priorities. Moreover, their desire to connect with musicians in other countries and to learn new musical styles promoted a globalization of popular music that destabilized the purported distinctiveness of national cultures promoted by national government in this era. Indeed, scholars have pointed to the particular importance of transnational performance in challenging the hegemony of colonial powers, as transnational cultural exchanges provided a source of alternative cultural capital for all parties involved.

Today, with the stunning rise of digital culture, some critics have wondered if the scholarly interest in performance and performing artists is an ironic product of the diminished importance of live performance. Others, however, point to the new range of possibilities presented by the interplay of recorded and manipulated forms and live performance, suggesting that the transnational lives of performers will continue to play a critical role in our ability to imagine new selves and new possibilities in the social world.

Penny von Eschen

Bibliography

Foulkes J. L. 2002. *Modern bodies: dance and American modernism from Martha Graham to Alvin Ailey.* Chapel Hill: University of North Carolina Press.

Glenn S. A. 2000. *Female spectacle: the roots of modern feminism.* Cambridge, MA: Harvard University Press.

Roach J. 1996. *Cities of the dead: circum-Atlantic performance.* New York: Columbia University Press.

Taylor D. 2003. *The archive and the repertoire: performing cultural memory in the Americas.* Durham and London: Duke University Press.

Related essays

Beatles; Cantonese opera; classical music; Cold War; conceptualism; cultural capitals; ethnicity and race; femininity; Hollywood; Italian opera; jazz; labour migrations; language diplomacy; literature; music; orchestras; rock; salsa; theatre; world music

Periodical and book exchange See Book and periodical exchange

Pesticides, herbicides, insecticides

The term 'pesticide' refers to any substance used in the control of pests as defined by humans. Such pests include insects (hence the term insecticide), weeds (herbicides) and also fungi (fungicides). Pesticides may also be used in ways which fall short of killing pests. The term additionally covers defoliants used to strip trees and plants of their leaves, plant growth regulators and substances which deter insects from certain locations (for example, mosquito repellents) or attract them away from crops (for example through the use of pheromones). The production, distribution and use of pesticide chemicals is very much a transnational phenomenon touching upon many of the most contentious issues of contemporary globalization: food security, development, public health, pollution, free trade and the role of multinational corporations.

The systematic use of chemicals as an aid to pest control did not take off until the late 19th century, although some use was made of sulphur as a domestic insecticide prior to this. In the 1860s US entomologist Charles Riley pioneered the use of Paris Green, an arsenic-based paint pigment, as an insecticide spray against that perennial potato pest the Colorado beetle. Riley later became a central figure in the campaign to save the French wine industry from the fungal blight *phylloxera* which had been imported from US vineyards. It was this successful campaign which saw the development by French botanist Alexis Millardet of the copper-based compound Bordeaux Mixture, the first widely applied fungicide.

The next major development in pest control history occurred with the creation of synthetic organic pesticides during the Second World War. The insecticidal properties of diclorodiphenyltrichloroethane (DDT) were discovered by Swiss chemist Dr Paul Muller in 1939 and it was quickly patented. Other organochlorine chemicals were soon found to have similar properties, leading to the marketing of insecticides such as aldrin and dieldrin. A second branch of new synthetic pesticides, the organophosphorous compounds, came as a side-effect of wartime research into toxic gases by the German scientist Dr Gerhard Schrader. After the war Schrader put his research before the allied states and revealed the potential insecticidal application of the compounds. Parathion was the first major insecticide of the form to be marketed and others soon followed.

The development and subsequent proliferation of synthetic chemical pesticides since the 1940s has had profound social and political impacts around the world in a number of ways. The use of pesticides has undoubtedly helped increase crop yields in the last 60 years and they have also assisted in the struggle against diseases spread by insects, particularly in curbing the considerable death toll attributable to malaria. On the other hand, however, pesticides have also affected human and other life forms in negative ways. Field workers spraying the chemicals have been poisoned; food has been contaminated; accidental releases during production and transport have killed thousands and flora, fauna, water and the atmosphere have been polluted in many ways.

Pesticides thrived from the late 1940s to the 1960s, when yields of food soared and many tropical diseases appeared to be being brought under control through their use, but then the rise of environmentalism brought the side-effects into focus. The publication in 1962 of Silent Spring, by US marine biologist Rachel Carson, heralded a wave of opinion across North America and Western Europe concerned by evidence of pollution caused by pesticide use. Quickly the whole area of pesticide production, trade and use moved from being a relatively unchallenged and heralded technological development to a highly politicized set of issues. The rise in concern at the effects of organochlorine insecticides on wildlife since the 1960s has contributed to the banning of, or severe restrictions on, the use of DDT, dieldrin and other notorious chemicals in most developed countries. Pesticides continue to arouse a certain amount of political controversy in the domestic political arenas of the developed world but the phasing out of the most carcinogenic and polluting chemicals and their replacement with less toxic formulations, alongside the establishment of stringent consumer standards and health and safety regulations, has significantly reduced the environmental and health concerns. Since the 1960s it has been transnational issues of pesticide use, production and trade that have commanded most social, environmental and political significance. The introduction into developing countries of Western agricultural technology in the 1960s and 1970s, known commonly as the 'Green Revolution', opened up a massive southwards trade. Many pesticides withdrawn from domestic use in the developed world have continued to be marketed to the global South where regulatory standards tend to be much laxer. The response of many agrochemical firms to greater scrutiny of their produce by health and environmental groups in the North has been to redirect their goods to such less restrictive markets.

The 1984 Bhopal disaster served as a catalyst for a campaign involving numerous environmental and consumer groups to regulate the global production, trade and use of pesticides led by a purpose-built global pressure group, the Pesticides Action Network (PAN), formed two years earlier. The world's worst ever industrial accident occurred at an Indian chemical plant owned by the US multinational corporation Union Carbide. Forty tonnes of the highly toxic chemical methyl-isocyanate (MIC), used in the production of the insecticide carbaryl, was accidentally released, killing over 2,500 people in the short term and countless thousands of others in the ensuing years through a range of long-term health effects and birth defects. Crucially, self-interest as well as compassion in the global North came to favour the regulation of the pesticide trade in the 1980s and 1990s. Pesticides profitably dumped on the global South market can return to Northern consumers in their food imports from the same countries, or through long-range atmospheric pollution. Thus the powerful players in pesticide politics, the chemical companies and Northern governments, have gradually been persuaded of the need for regulation, paving the way for the development of international law in the 1990s. Contemporary global governance with regard to pesticides focuses on three areas: regulating permissible amounts of residual chemicals in traded food; regulating the export of certain pesticides, and outlawing the use and production of the most toxic chemicals.

Global standards for permissible levels of pesticide traces in traded foodstuffs emanate from the hybrid UN body the Codex Alimentarius Commission. Codex standards, from their inception in 1962 to the mid-1990s, were no more than scientific guidelines but, in the last decade, they have come to have much greater political significance since the World Trade Organization has used them as the benchmark for determining whether national food standards represent an unfair trade restriction. Countries are free to enact stricter measures than the Codex but many environmental and consumer groups are concerned that pesticide residue standards are coming to be more about trading convenience than safety.

The 1998 Rotterdam Convention on the Prior Informed Consent Procedure for Certain Hazardous Chemicals and Pesticides in International Trade constrains ratifying governments attempting to export pesticides banned in their own countries (the Prior Informed Consent procedure (PIC)). The Convention entered into force in 2004 and by 2006 was applying the PIC procedure to a list of 28 pesticides and eleven other industrial chemicals. The convention represents the culmination of 20 years of campaigning by PAN and other global pressure groups but its creation also owes much to the fact that the chemical industry itself came to support the procedure, having initially opposed even a voluntary version of the scheme in the 1980s. Agrochemical lobbyists, spearheaded by the Global Crop Protection Federation, came to throw their weight behind the scheme through fear that such a restriction on their trade was preferable to an alternative scenario of the export of toxic chemicals being prohibited in the domestic laws of producer countries. Under the Rotterdam Convention toxic chemicals like DDT can still be exported so long as the importing government is aware of what is entering their country and there is still a great demand for such chemicals even when their side-effects are appreciated.

Another PAN-led campaign, to entirely phase out the production and use of a 'dirty dozen' particularly hazardous and slow-degrading organochlorine pesticides, was endorsed by governments at the 1992 UN Conference on the Environment and Development (UNCED) and culminated in the 2001 Persistent Organic Pollutants (POPS) Treaty. To date the list of chemical covered by the Treaty has been determined principally in terms of human toxicity rather than wider environmental criteria. Hence the infamously environmentally unfriendly DDT is exempted from prohibition by many governments who declare that they require the use of the chemical to combat mosquitoes in the fight against malaria. This encapsulates the central dilemma posed by pesticides over the years.

These chemicals have proved to be a two-edged sword; an effective weapon in the fight against famine and disease but one which can also reap considerable collateral damage in the process.

Peter Hough

Bibliography

Hough P. 1998. *The global politics of pesticides.* London: Earthscan.

Ordish G. 1976. *The constant pest: a short history of pests and their control.* London: Peter Davies.

Related essays

agriculture; air pollution; corporations; environmental diplomacy; environmentalism; food safety standards; genetically modified organisms (GMOs); Green Revolution; health policy; international non-governmental organizations (INGOs); Monsanto; Oxfam; wine

Monsanto

With $7.3 billion in sales and operations in over one hundred countries in 2006, Monsanto is one of the largest transnational agribusiness corporations in the world, and the leading producer of agricultural biotechnology. Monsanto Chemical Works was originally established in Saint Louis, Missouri in 1901 as a food additives and pharmaceuticals producer. After the 1940s, the company expanded into petrochemicals, agrochemicals, and phosphates. Monsanto later became infamous as a producer of Agent Orange, the plant defoliant used during the Vietnam War that also had serious human health consequences, and polychlorinated biphenyls (PCBs), probable human cancer-causing chemicals that the company illegally dumped around its US-based plants.

In the late 1970s, with profits declining and pressure from environmentalists and litigators growing, CEO John Hanley shifted Monsanto's course, shedding its unprofitable businesses and investing in the life sciences. Monsanto has since sought to become the world's leading life sciences company, spending billions to acquire small biotechnology firms, pharmaceutical companies, seed companies, and related businesses. Monsanto built itself a powerful position at the heart of the international seed industry, especially through its trademark Roundup® and Roundup Ready® products, and spearheaded the commercial deployment of agricultural genetically modified organisms (GMOs) in the mid-1990s, both in the USA and globally. In 2000, it merged with pharmaceutical giant, Pharmacia & Upjohn, which spun Monsanto off into a specialized agricultural biotechnology and crop protection chemicals company.

Monsanto is known for its aggressive corporate culture, reflected in its acquisition of thirteen seed companies since 1997 (making Monsanto the largest seed producer in the world); its prosecution of farmers who fail to pay its 'technology fees' for purposeful or accidental use of its patented genes; and its army of lawyers and marketers, who seek to open regulatory doors and sell the company's genetically modified crops and other products around the world. The 'anti-GMO' movement has made Monsanto its chief corporate target, accusing it of trying to seize control of world agriculture through its aggressive patenting of seeds and plant genes.

Rachel Schurman

Bibliography
Monsanto. 2005. 2005 Annual Report [online]. Available: www.monsanto.com/monsanto/layout/investor/financial/annual_reports.asp, accessed 24 May 2007.

Related essays
agriculture; biopatents ; corporations; genetically modified organisms (GMOs); pesticides, herbicides, insecticides; seeds

Philanthropic foundations

Although the borderlines between philanthropic and charitable foundations are often blurred, the impetus behind establishing them was similar. Charities tended to be rooted in religious institutions or were created by individuals or local authorities in towns and villages for a faith-based alleviation of sickness and destitution among the elderly and the poor. Philanthropic foundations frequently also had religious and moral origins, but their mission was broader in terms of the causes they promoted and supported and of their worldwide scope. While religious charities also began to operate globally, the foundations grew to become genuinely transnational organizations. Certainly by the 20th century their activities stretched increasingly

beyond the regional and national, in an attempt to realize their universalist claim of working for the welfare of humanity.

Some facts and figures
It is no coincidence that the first and most powerful philanthropic organizations were created before 1914 by individual entrepreneurs in the United States, after they had accumulated enormous personal fortunes during the period of rapid industrialization and high economic growth on the North American continent. The impetus behind establishing a foundation and the potential benefits to its founder were well captured by John J. McCloy, the former US High Commissioner in West Germany and later a trustee of the Ford Foundation. In 1960, Alfried Krupp, son of the 'cannon king' in Essen and ten years earlier held in an Allied prison as a convicted war criminal, thought of creating the Krupp Foundation. It would be good, McCloy counselled, 'for human welfare and for Germany's and Krupp's name if the objectives of the Krupp Foundation were worldwide and similar to Ford's'. He added: 'When old John D. Rockefeller had first established the Rockefeller Foundation his name was anathema to Americans. Today the Rockefeller name is held in great honor and esteem' (Berghahn 2001, 198).

While initial funding capacities of these American foundations and a few that also emerged in Europe in the early 20th century were relatively limited, endowments grew considerably in subsequent decades. By 1937 the Rockefeller Foundation had assets of $184 million, rising to $648 million by 1960. The Carnegie Corporation disposed of assets to the tune of $164 million that had grown to $261 million in 1960. In that year, the Ford Foundation had assets of $3,316 million. By the beginning of the 21st century, the Bill and Melinda Gates Foundation had become the biggest philanthropic organisation in the world. In the summer of 2006, the billionaire investor Warren Buffett transferred some $30 billion of his wealth to the Gates Foundation, generating a trust with assets of over $60 billion of which an estimated $3 billion per annum is available for its programmes. This kind of spending power enabled the philanthropic organizations to play not only an important social and cultural role, but also to wield political influence.

However impressive the financial clout of the big foundations, it would be wrong to overlook some 70,000 small ones with total assets of $260 billion in the United States that support many domestic and international causes. While the US Treasury allowed gifts to be written off against taxes due, European finance ministries were for a long time very reluctant to give up revenue destined for their own coffers, especially in countries that had a developed state welfare system and where people were therefore also more reliant on public rather than private support. It was only in the 1990s that Germany, for example, changed the tax laws to facilitate more private giving. Today over 14,000 smaller foundations operate in the Federal Republic, next to the big ones, such as Volkswagen ($120 million), Bosch ($80 million), and Bertelsmann ($62 million). Similar developments occurred in other Western European nations and Japan. By the 1960s and nudged by the Americans, the Japanese began to be active in this field, and today the Japan Foundation is wielding considerable influence around the world with its projects.

From the start, philanthropic organizations also developed administrative structures to organize the receipt, scrutiny, and eventual granting of applications for funding. Their officers secure compliance with legal requirements, advise applicants, prepare dockets for approval by boards of trustees (usually the key decision-making body), and supervise the use of grants made. The big foundations in the United States and, following them, their counterparts in Europe and Japan developed large administrations. Today the foundations employ thousands of often academically trained, specialized officers and their staffs who are responsible for the smooth running of the organization. As in all large-scale organizations, whether public or private, there are inevitable conflicts over projects and resources within an overall hierarchical structure. Divisions and departments cooperate most of the time for the common objectives laid down in the charter and set by the foundation president and the board of trustees; but there have also been turf wars and inefficiencies. They all rely, often quite heavily, on external reviewers and consultants who, beyond their expertise within a special field, will advise the foundation on larger socioeconomic, cultural, scientific, and political trends and changing paradigms.

The social division of philanthropic labour

It is in this context that the basic direction of philanthropic support is formulated and discussions take place between the big foundations to arrive at a certain division of labour. There tend to be so many good causes to fund that competition tends to be replaced by agreement to develop complementarities. True to its name, the Carnegie Endowment for International Peace devoted itself to promoting ideas and institutions for the prevention and resolution of conflicts. The Rockefeller Foundation moved into the support of scientific and medical research. As early as 1907, it put the fight against the hook-worm on its agenda and later added the fight against yellow fever. During the interwar years it funded studies on demographic trends and population control. The ideal was to further a genuine scientific internationalism, but by the 1930s some of the projects in population studies and eugenics had become badly compromised by a covert and even overt racism. The Carnegie Corporation traditionally devoted a larger portion of its resources to education, while the Gates Foundation recently invested in the war on HIV/AIDS, especially in Africa.

The Ford Foundation, which became the largest in the world during the 1950s and 1960s, allocated considerable resources during those years both to generating a better understanding and to more expert training of the Americans about international politics and the role of the United States within the system of nation states and international organizations. Accordingly, it funded exchanges, conferences, and journals geared, on the one hand, to fighting the intellectual Cold War against the Soviet bloc and, on the other, to creating an Atlantic cultural community to counter Western European anti-Americanism. When the Cold War struggle shifted to winning over the hearts and minds of the peoples of the Third World, Ford gave its monies to agricultural development and anti-poverty and educational programmes in India, Africa, and Latin America. Initially, much of the money was channelled through indigenous governments. When this approach proved inefficient, mainly because of the corruption of local elites, the Foundation tried to work with the peasants by supplying them directly with agricultural technology. Thus, in the 1970s, Ford spent some $5.3 million on rural development (down from $13.8 million in the 1950s) and $49.2 million on agricultural technology.

Finally and most recently, the Soros Foundation gave its support to the emerging civic associations in East Central Europe in an effort to foster a civil society in the countries of the former Soviet bloc. Foundations with an explicitly party-political affiliation, such as the Friedrich Ebert Foundation, the Konrad Adenauer Foundation, the Friedrich Naumann Foundation and the Heinrich Boell Foundation in Germany, played important roles in encouraging dissident intellectuals and academics in East Central Europe in the 1970s and 1980s and oppositional movements in Spain and Portugal before the fall of the Franco and Salazar regimes.

Foundations and the world order

Are foundations as legal entities in private law to be considered part of civil society, or are they an arm of official policy projecting particular images and programmes into civil society at home and into other countries abroad? An answer to this question may be found by examining the changing relationship between America's philanthropic foundations and the political power centre in Washington during the 20th century.

In the early decades, the two sides kept apart and there was even a good deal of suspicion of government among the foundations. But parallel activities in the field of relief during famines or natural catastrophes before 1914 and after the devastations of World War 1 brought about some cooperation. In the 1930s, when the fascist governments began to project their nationalist and racist visions of themselves and their future quite uninhibitedly abroad, this in turn led to a rapprochement between Washington and the big foundations. Cooperation between the public and private sectors became even closer during World War 2 so that by the end of that conflict a range of relationships had developed.

It was Waldemar Nielsen who in his book *The Big Foundations* (1972) developed a useful taxonomy. Foundations, he argued, could (1) be monitors and critics of government activities at home or abroad; (2) develop their programmes unconcerned about central government and other agencies; (3) act as 'pilot fish' to official policy making; (4) make their programmes supplementary to government work; (5) turn themselves into partners and

collaborators of politicians and civil servants; (6) allow themselves to be used outright as private instruments of public policy.

During the 1950s and 1960s many foundations adopted positions (4) and (5), and some even became simple 'fronts' of mostly covert funding of social and cultural projects. The crisis of 1966/67, when it was revealed that the Congress for Cultural Freedom (CCF) and other associations had received secret funds from the US Central Intelligence Agency, caused the big foundations to retreat from their own earlier support of the CCF and to focus more firmly than ever before on the Third World. It was never an easy ride either. As long as the Second World existed, the Soviets and their allies continued their Cold War rhetoric and accused the Western philanthropic organizations of being the stooges of capitalist imperialism and its secret services. Nor did right-wing regimes such as Spain's or South Africa's look kindly upon foundation exchange programmes.

The problems did not disappear after the collapse of Communism. In 2003, the Ford Foundation came under fire from the 'Jewish Telegraph Agency' which charged it with having given 'financial support to several Palestinian nongovernmental organizations accused of anti-Zionist and anti-Semitic behavior at the United Nations World Conference against Racism in Durban' (*The Nation*, 5 June 2006, 13). Further investigations revealed that the accusations were not unjustified, leading the Ford Foundation president to express regrets that the 'grantees may have taken part in unacceptable behavior' (quoted ibid.).

It was another indirect admission that the big foundations wield considerable influence and power. They certainly do not distribute their grants haphazardly. In the social sciences and natural sciences their financial support has in the past reinforced more than one paradigm shift. The projects they underwrite are expected to make a difference, be it that they are the 'pilot fish' that lead the big government 'whale' in new directions or that they buttress existing projects through their cooperation with ministries.

Volker R. Berghahn

Bibliography

Arnove R.F. (ed.) 1982. *Philanthropy and cultural imperialism.* Bloomington: Indiana University Press

Berghahn,V. R. 2001. *America and the intellectual Cold Wars in Europe: Shepard Stone between philanthropy, academy, and diplomacy.* Princeton: Princeton University Press.

Berman E. H. 1985. *The ideology of philanthropy. the influence of the Carnegie, Ford and Rockefeller Foundations on American foreign policy.* Albany: State University of New York Press.

Curti M. 1963. *American philanthropy abroad.* New Brunswick: Transaction.

Gemelli G. (ed.) 1998, *The Ford Foundation and Europe.* Brussels: European Interuniversity Press.

McCarthy K. D. (ed.) 1984. *Philanthropy and culture.* Philadelphia: University of Pennsylvania Press.

Ninkovich F. 1981. *The diplomacy of ideas.* Cambridge and New York: Cambridge University Press.

Rosenberg E. 1982. *Spreading the American dream: American economic and cultural expansion, 1980–1945.* New York: Hill & Wang.

Related essays

1989; Acquired Immunodeficiency Syndrome (AIDS); Cold War; Congress for Cultural Freedom; developmental assistance; economics; eugenics; fellowships and grants; Ford Foundation; globalization; Green Revolution; health policy; higher education; history; human rights; humanities; international non-governmental organizations (INGOs); language diplomacy; League of Nations Economic and Financial Organization; League of Nations Health Organization; legal order; life and physical sciences; management; nursing; pacifism; Pax Americana; philanthropy; population; social sciences; technologies; transnational; underdevelopment; women's movements

Ford Foundation

Edsel Ford established the Ford Foundation in January 1936 with a small endowment and a focus on Michigan. When Henry Ford died in 1947, it received a large portfolio of Ford Motor Company stocks, valued at $417 million. The postwar economic boom increased assets to $492 million by the end of 1950, and for the next several decades it was the biggest philanthropic organization in the world. At the beginning of the 21st century, it is engaged, with the income from its $10.5 billion investment portfolio, in a wide range of current issues.

Many of its programmes were geared from the start to domestic improvement, while it took until the mid-1950s for a more permanent international programme to emerge. A major part of this programme, especially after 1956, related to exchanges of intellectuals and academics from East Central Europe. But considerable resources were also poured into exchanges, conferences, and journals in Western Europe in an attempt to foster a European-American community of values and cultural understanding.

Though initially successful, these programmes foundered in the late 1960s and early 1970s when their Atlanticist ideology was rejected by a younger generation of Americans and Western Europeans. The Foundation now shifted its focus towards Third World countries in Africa, Asia and Latin America, and the Overseas Development (OD) division became one of the most influential divisions. The initial strategy was to undertake nation building from above. Today the main emphasis is on local community and resource development, the fostering of civil society, conflict resolution and social justice. One recent move is a twelve-year fellows programme of $280 million, designed to bring some 3,300 young community leaders for up to three years to any university of the world.

Volker R. Berghahn

Bibliography

Berghahn V. R. 2001. *America and the intellectual Cold Wars in Europe: Shepard Stone between philanthropy, academy, and diplomacy.* Princeton: Princeton University Press.

Related essays

1989; birth control; Cold War; Congress for Cultural Freedom; developmental assistance; economics; fellowships and grants; Green Revolution; life and physical sciences; philanthropic foundations; population; social sciences; United Cities and Local Governments (UCLG); United Nations Educational, Scientific and Cultural Organization (UNESCO) educational programmes

Philanthropy

Throughout the 19th century, various models for the provision of social housing, healthcare, poor relief, primary and secondary education, and the support of the arts and culture emerged with the creation of large urban centres that produced social and cultural needs unknown to preindustrial societies. Philanthropy and charity were among the attempts to create a social, cultural and educational urban infrastructure in the 19th century. While in previous centuries, philanthropy and charity had been mostly individual acts of kindness, during the 19th century they turned into collective forms of caring for the common good. This entry focuses on the Atlantic world, where religious motivation, although still important, gave way to secular motives related to the creation of status and identity as well as to politically inspired motives (fear of social unrest and upheaval). Philanthropy was recognized as a social force that could stabilize a society that underwent large-scale social and economic change. Finally, 19th-century philanthropy and charity were, in contrast to earlier practices of kindness, preventative measures. In many cases, they involved the attempt at shaping society according to the visions of a single philanthropist or a group of philanthropists involved in the provision of financial, material, and immaterial (time for volunteering) resources. These features were later turned into organizational principles by the philanthropic foundations that developed in the early 20th century, and expanded the works of systematic philanthropy beyond the Atlantic world. Neither philanthropic donations, nor the process of creating a philanthropic network happened within the confines of the nation state. Philanthropists from various parts of the world entered by means of visits, exchanges of letters, the writing of travel reports and official publications of philanthropic organizations (annual reports and advertisements) into a transnational discourse about the nature, place, and goals of philanthropy in capitalist society.

From the 1820s onwards, travel became an important aspect of upper-class culture within the transatlantic community. Well-off Americans repeatedly travelled to Europe to enjoy life and to observe how European philanthropists and reformers dealt with the challenges posed by industrialization and urbanization. George Ticknor, one of Boston's most eminent citizens, occupies an important place in the beginning of the transatlantic transfer of philanthropic models. During the time he spent in Göttingen and Dresden, Ticknor was fascinated with the way libraries were organized in both cities. The Royal Saxon Library in Dresden, in particular, left a lasting impression on him. The large collections, the six out of seven days opening, and the concept of the circulation library he retained as important aspects of a modern library. After his return to Boston, Ticknor wanted to create a similar library in his home town. For years, Ticknor talked about the advantages of the Dresden library until the donation of Joshua Bates enabled him to fulfill his dream. Bates, a self-made banker, who had grown up in Boston but who had moved to London to work in the financial business, provided $50,000 for the project of a public library in Boston. Ticknor seized this opportunity and negotiated an agreement between Bates and the city government. In contrast to other famous libraries in the United States at that point, the Boston Public Library became a free circulating library. Ticknor's insistence that books should be freely circulated, and that the library should purchase 'morally valuable' books in several copies to allow multiple readers to read these books at the same time, turned the academic library model into an educational institution for the 'betterment of the lower classes'. The library's policy on book circulation, which goes back to the Royal Saxon Library in Dresden, made the Boston library the starting point of the public library movement in the United States and Europe. The interchange was completed at the end of the 19th century when the Boston Public Library was considered as a model for library reform in Germany.

In the realm of museums, a very similar pattern emerged. Throughout the 19th century, wealthy Americans and Canadians travelled to London, Paris, Rome, and Dresden to visit the art collections of the Old World. For decades, North Americans felt admiration and jealousy towards the European museums, which could boast the most eminent collections in ancient, medieval and early modern artifacts. The museums of London and Dresden, in particular, occupied a prominent place in the minds of upper-class Americans. When in 1869 a group of wealthy New Yorkers came together to consider the founding of an art museum in their city, William Cullen Bryant reminded his fellow citizens that even the tiny kingdom of Saxony, that was smaller in size and population than Massachusetts, possessed marvelous collections and museums, which had become a staple of the European grand tour. George Fisk Comfort, who had lived in Germany for some time in 1864/65, took the lead in developing organizational models for American art museums. Based on his experience with German art museums and German art associations, Comfort advocated the creation of membership associations, to collect enough financial and material support for the museum project from prosperous citizens. The Metropolitan Museum of Art was based on this financial infrastructure.

Just as much as German art associations had served as a model for the membership organization of the Metropolitan Museum of Art, this museum turned into a model for the founding of subsequent museums within the United States and in Canada. Byron E. Walker, an eminent banker from Toronto, admired the Metropolitan Museum when he spent time as an agent for the Canadian Bank of Commerce in New York during the early 1870s. Interested in every aspect of this new museum, Walker brought home the idea that a young nation also needs its museums and art galleries. Together with James Mavor, who had visited various art galleries from Stockholm to Munich and Prague in 1899, Walker in 1900 convinced several wealthy Torontonians that it was time for Toronto to follow New York's lead and create cultural institutions of its own. At the end of the 19th century, New York's membership associations in turn inspired many cultural reformers from Germany to create museum associations back home. As in the case of the circulating library, German museum reformers at the end of the 19th century did not look back into their own history and tradition but looked to the United States for inspiration, thus reimporting models Germans had developed much earlier. However, in the process of crossing the Atlantic those models had been modified and transformed in ways that allowed for viewing them as 'foreign imports'.

In the world of social housing, London occupied a central position since housing reformers in that metropolis invented the various models for housing reform which were recreated all over Europe from St Petersburg to Paris and in many North American cities during the last quarter of the 19th century.

Three individuals (George Peabody, Sir Sydney Waterlow and Octavia Hill) became the central figures in the European-North American world of social housing. In 1862, George Peabody, a successful Massachusetts merchant, decided to donate £500,000 to benefit the London poor. Peabody, who felt drawn to London because of his business interests in English-American financial relations, had moved permanently to London in 1832. During his lifetime, Peabody donated money to both American and English philanthropic causes. These included museums, universities and institutions, from the Peabody Institute at Baltimore to the Peabody Education Fund for the promotion of education in the South. His gift of £500,000 for the benefit of the London poor was used to create a housing trust, which was to provide healthy and affordable housing for working-class families in and around the British capital. This philanthropic enterprise soon received competition from Sydney Waterlow's Improved Industrial Dwellings Company, founded in 1863, which was based on the idea that affordable housing could be produced while guaranteeing a limited profit of 5 per cent.

Both concepts found admirers and imitators all over Europe and North America. Over the next three decades, housing trusts and limited dividend companies appeared in many cities within the transatlantic community. Within Germany, Herrmann Julius Meyer, the owner of the world famous publishing house Bibliographisches Institut, followed in Peabody's footsteps. Starting in 1887, he created the largest German housing trust in the city of Leipzig. Henry I. Bowditch, a wealthy Bostonian physician, introduced Waterlow's model to the United States. After he had visited London for six months in 1870, Bowditch advocated housing reform guided by the concept of 'Philanthropy and Five Percent'. In 1871, he convinced a number of wealthy Bostonians to join him in the creation of the Boston Cooperative Building Company, which was one of the first American limited dividend housing companies.

Bowditch was also the first to introduce Octavia Hill's ideas about housing management and the improvement of the conditions of the poor to an American audience. From 1864 Hill had taken over the management of several thousand apartments for lower-class tenants in London. In contrast to Peabody and Waterlow, Hill was convinced that the social housing problem was less a financial issue than an issue of proper management as well as education and guidance of lower-class renters. According to her concept of 'friendly rent collecting', renters had to pay the rent weekly in advance, and the rent was collected by upper-class women (the 19th-century version of social workers), who were expected to establish friendly relations with the tenants and who were in charge of teaching the tenants certain standards of cleanliness and orderly behaviour. This concept inspired social housing reformers in Russia, Germany, Switzerland, the United States, Canada, and even South Africa. In the case of Germany, the transfer of Hill's model was organized by Grand Duchess Alice of Hesse, the daughter of Queen Victoria. After she had met with Octavia Hill in 1874 in London and after she had taken several tours of Hill's housing projects, Alice arranged for Hill's book *Homes of the London Poor* to be translated and published by a German press in 1878. This book provided the intellectual basis for the founding of several Octavia Hill associations in Germany. The first such associations were founded in Berlin and Leipzig.

Hill's influence remained, however, not limited to the European and North American sphere. Throughout the 20th century, Hill's ideas travelled around the globe and influenced urban planning and the provision of low-income housing in Japan and South Africa. After they had observed Hill's management methods first hand in London, Mrs Harold Jones, a member of the National Council of Women of South Africa, and Sir Edward Thornton, the South African Secretary for Health, advocated in the mid 1930s the introduction of this practice for the expanding sector of government-owned apartments in South Africa's major municipalities. Guided by the hope that Hill's management system would produce 'much more desirable citizens' and forced by the necessity to create an effective management system for the vastly expanding government-funded housing, South Africa's government established a two-year training programme that introduced suitable women university graduates into Hill's friendly visiting and management system. Between 1938 and 1960, more than fifty women went through this training programme. During the 1930s, all major South African cities (Port Elizabeth, East London, Johannesburg and Pretoria)

appointed female housing managers trained in the Octavia Hill method to supervise state-funded housing in these cities.

Thomas Adam

Bibliography

Adam T. 2002. 'Transatlantic trading: the transfer of philanthropic models between European and North American cities during the 19th and early twentieth centuries', *Journal of Urban History*, 28, 3 (March), 328–51.

Adam T. 2006. 'Cultural baggage: the building of the urban community in a transatlantic world', in Adam T. and Gross R. (eds) *Traveling between worlds: German-American encounters*. College Station: Texas A&M University Press, 79–99.

Borgmann K. ' "The glue of civil society": a comparative approach to art museum philanthropy at the turn of the twentieth century', in Adam T. (ed.) 2004. *Philanthropy, patronage, and civil society: experiences from Germany, Great Britain, and North America*, Bloomington: Indiana University Press, 34–54.

Robinson J. 1998. 'Octavia Hill women housing managers in South Africa: femininity and urban government', *Journal of Historical Geography*, 24, 4, 459–81.

Spain D. 2006. 'Octavia Hill's philosophy of housing reform: from British roots to American soil', *Journal of Planning History*, 5, 2 (May), 106–25.

Related essays

Aga Khan Development Network; Ford Foundation; kindergarten; libraries; museums; organization models; philanthropic foundations; prizes; public policy; theatre; tourism; translation; urbanization

Physical and life sciences *See* Life and physical sciences

Pidgins and creoles

A pidgin is a spontaneously created language arising from trade, conquest or other form of contact between speakers of different native languages with no language in common. A creole is a pidgin that has expanded to become, over time, the native language of a speech community. Pidgins and creoles are examples of unplanned mixed languages that humans create in situations in which oral communication is necessary but no shared existing language is available. Many parts of the world have for generations had their widely distributed trading languages (Malay in Southeast Asia, Swahili in East Africa, Hausa in West Africa, and so on) – languages which shift and adapt themselves to serve the varying needs of their second-language users. Similarly, pidgins emerge in unstructured, non-institutional settings, sometimes reflecting the efforts of traders to do business, or of immigrants to communicate in a new setting; sometimes reflecting socially asymmetrical linguistic compromises between those in power and the communities whose services they need or wish to exploit. Today the expansion of educational services and the arrival of mass media have reduced the need or opportunity for the development of such communally created languages (though they still occur), but they were a common feature of interethnic communication and accommodation resulting from the dislocation and urbanization of populations during the colonial era and indeed probably have a history almost as long as human mobility itself.

Pidgins are often highly creative efforts to use limited linguistic means, with little redundancy (a feature of more highly developed languages used for more complex purposes), a tiny vocabulary, minimal grammar, and a range of functions limited to their particular purpose. While they may seem makeshift or improvised, they are in fact rule-bound linguistic systems. They often dispense with tense, number, inflection and the like, using circumlocution, reduplication, and simple juxtaposition of dependent clauses. They often have no writing systems, and they die out when no longer needed. Cases in point are Tây Bôi, the pidgin used by French colonists to communicate with their Vietnamese servants, the English Japanese pidgin used during the American occupation of Japan after World War 2, or the English Vietnamese pidgin that arose during the Vietnam War. Most of what we know about pidgins and creoles comes from the Western experience, but such languages were in use in many parts of the world long before Westerners arrived. Many standard modern languages had creole origins.

The origin of the term *pidgin* is unknown (it may mean 'business'), but the French term *créole* (Spanish *criollo*, Portuguese *croulo*) was originally used to denote people of European extraction born in the colonies (primarily those of the Americas) and, over time, adopting linguistic forms and habits different from those of the home country. In due course, it came also to denote their language itself. Given this history, it is useful to make a distinction in the American context between settler creoles (the language forms of transplanted Europeans), and plantation creoles (the languages of forcibly displaced Africans).

When slaves, often with different native languages, were transported to the Americas from Africa and forced into communication with one another and with their masters, pidgins developed spontaneously. Their lexical base was generally the prevailing colonial language – English, French, Portuguese, Spanish, Dutch (the so-called superstrate language) – but they often included grammatical elements from African languages (the so-called substrate languages). While there are exceptions, pidgins commonly draw lexicon from a single superstrate language and grammar from one or more substrate languages. Quite rapidly, these languages of slavery became creolized when the children of the imported slaves acquired them as their first languages and broadened their use into additional domains. By the 19th century such creoles were firmly established, particularly in the Caribbean: English-based creoles in Jamaica, Guiana, and elsewhere; French-based creoles in Haiti and St Lucia; and the Spanish-based Papiamentu which persisted in Aruba, Bonaire and Curaçao even after these territories became Dutch and is still spoken there today. A Dutch-based creole survived for many years in the interior of Dutch Guiana. Creoles have played an important part in the life of the Caribbean down to today and have persisted among the bulk of the population despite their relatively low prestige and the presence of standardized education and mass media. Popularly seen as non-standard forms of standard European languages, in essence they are separate languages; their populations are largely bilingual, using the creole patois at home and prestige forms in public settings such as schools and the workplace, though there are variations along that continuum. In Haiti, Haitian creole is used by the vast majority of the population and now has official standing alongside standard French. Although there are conflicting views among linguists, the widely used and disseminated American form known as African-American Vernacular English is thought by many to have originated in slave plantation creoles. Some new forms of English, such as the non-standard form used by many in Singapore today, may be regarded as creoles.

Although the trauma of slavery brought abrupt creolization, in other areas pidginized trading languages developed more slowly and in more restricted fashion. Creoles involve nativization (adoption as first language by children) – but expansion may take place among adults (leading to 'expanded pidgins' rather than nativized creoles) and through interaction of (adult) speakers of different substrate languages.

The *Lingua Franca*, or *Sabir*, the Romance-based, rudimentary language which grew up in the ports around the Mediterranean in the Middle Ages, was a typical mixed trading language; it survived until the 19th century, when the advent of steamships and the French conquest of North Africa changed patterns of commerce. Russenorsk, long used in Russian–Norwegian trade, had no more than a couple of hundred words drawn from both languages, without case, gender or inflection; it eventually died out in the late 19th century as contact between Norway and Russia intensified beyond occasional trading encounters.

Melanesian Pidgin English developed in the early 19th century on whaling ships, but it spread functionally and geographically, expanding to plantation workers and becoming a widely established trade language throughout the Pacific islands by mid-century. Tok Pisin, an English-based pidgin widely used in New Guinea as of the 19th century, expanded its domains of use so widely that it emerged as the common creolized lingua franca of Papua New Guinea with official status in that country and widespread media use. As with major trading languages, such pidgins were linguistic lifelines for many displaced and migrant workers. Such was the case with Lingala, a trade language among speakers of closely related Bantu languages along the Congo River, which gained prestige in the 20th century because it established itself among upwardly mobile Africans in the cities. The same is true of Sango, a pidginized language of west-central Africa. Bislama,

now the national language of the independent nation of Vanuatu, has its origins in the local plantation pidgin, derived in turn from Pacific Trade Pidgin.

In some areas, languages have expanded geographically to become auxiliary or vehicular languages with limited pidginized functions in their expanded use (Hausa, Swahili, and Malay fall into this category). In fact, such heteroglossia – the creation of linguistic systems out of elements of existing languages, or the extensive and sometimes systematized use of code switching between languages – is far more common, even in today's world, than is generally realized. Planned languages, such as Esperanto, can also be seen as examples of planned creolization.

Pidgins and creoles are much studied by linguists because they are good settings for examining language change and variation, language universals, and the social history of languages (by studying the rapid language changes characteristic of pidgins and creoles we can watch languages coming into being). Since most pidgins are unwritten, however, and since the written history of creoles is sparse, we have only a sketchy historical knowledge of their development. Indeed there is sharp disagreement about their specific origins. Creoles, especially, show striking structural and strategic similarities wherever they occur, suggesting several possibilities: (1) that similar social conditions produce similar linguistic adaptations (i.e. that similarities among languages are in part socially determined); (2) that humans possess specific bioprograms for languages that result in particular kinds of convergence (i.e. that similarities are genetically determined), or (3) that many or most such languages have a common ancestry. This last theory, once widely held, has retreated before the second, a hypothesis that would seem to confirm the views of Chomsky and Pinker that humans are 'hard-wired' for language and hence that there are certain language universals common to all human languages. Most scholars, however, see a combination of universals and substrate influence as responsible for the emergence of creoles.

Humphrey Tonkin

Bibliography

Harper T. N. 'Empire, diaspora, and the languages of globalism 1850–1914', in

Hopkins A. G. (ed.) 2002. *Globalization in world history*. New York and London: W. W. Norton, 141–66.

Rickford J. R. and McWhorter J. 'Language contact and language generation: pidgins and creoles', in Coulmas F. (ed.) 1997. *The handbook of sociolinguistics*. Oxford and Malden: Blackwell, 238–56.

Todd L. 1990. *Pidgins and creoles*, 2nd edition. London and New York: Routledge.

Winford D. 2003. *An introduction to contact linguistics*. Oxford and Malden: Blackwell.

Related essays

Africa; Asia; empire and migration; empires and imperialism; Esperanto; language; nation and state; race-mixing; trade; United Nations Educational, Scientific and Cultural Organization (UNESCO) educational programmes; war

Police

The history of the international dimensions of policing dates back to at least the 19th-century formation of nation states. The forms in which international policing takes place are multiple and have, over the course of history, proliferated under the influence of important cultural and structural developments related to modernity.

Among the first forms of international policing were intelligence efforts organized by autocratic regimes oriented to political opponents operating from abroad. During the earlier part of the 19th century, French and Austrian efforts stood out for their comprehensive scope to form Europewide police intelligence networks. The French police extended its functions to protect the security of the state to other regions of Europe by influencing police reforms abroad through adoption of French practices or by coerced importation as part of French occupation. During the period of Restoration after 1815, attempts to create a European police network were made under the direction of Metternich, the powerful statesman of the Austrian Empire, whose strong role in forging international relations also included efforts to control revolutionary unrest through censorship and espionage.

The suppression of the revolutions taking place across Europe in 1848 served as a catalyst for international policing activities in a number of ways. As political regimes sought to strengthen their rule, police institutions in many European nations were strengthened and reinforced and de facto harmonized in terms of strategies and goals. Police institutions of powerful European regimes also stationed agents abroad to be involved in covert intelligence-gathering activities. Moreover, international cooperation efforts were initiated among European police agencies. Cooperation took on the form of shared information exchange by establishing contacts between police officials or by means of the distribution of printed bulletins with information on wanted suspects. International police cooperation would also be endeavoured on a broader multilateral scale. Although most of these attempts failed because of concerns over sovereignty, some were consequential, albeit it on a limited scale.

In 1851, an international police organization was set up, when Prussian and Austrian authorities rallied the support of five other German-language territories to form the Police Union of German States. Active until the Seven-Weeks War of 1866, the Police Union explicitly functioned to track down political opponents by means of increasing information exchange through police meetings, the distribution of printed bulletins, and by stationing agents abroad. The Police Union worked without any formally specified legal arrangement and operated covertly. The Union could not attract the participation of police from non-German language countries in Europe, and because of its political dependency, it disbanded as soon as war broke out between its two dominant members.

During the latter half of the 19th century, there was an increasing need among police to establish an international organization with broad participation. However, in order to accomplish this goal successfully, police organizations would have to abandon their political position as an extension of state power. This development towards a position of autonomy took place under the influence of a process of bureaucratization.

Bureaucratization involves the adoption of principles of technical efficiency in terms of professionally defined enforcement objectives. Because police institutions were granted special powers by their respective national governments to police political opponents, they ironically could claim and gain a position of professional independence as expert institutions in the fight against criminality. On the basis of a professional ideal of crime expertise, police institutions across nations (in the industrialized West) could subsequently cooperate internationally to foster a shared understanding on the development and control of crime. Thus, police bureaucracies relied on their position of independence from politics to articulate joint programmes in the fight against crime, in general, and international crime, in particular.

In consequence of increasing bureaucratization, efforts to formalize international police cooperation were sharply on the rise during the late 19th and early 20th centuries. Initially, most of these efforts failed, because they tended to remain phrased in legal-political rather than police-professional terms. For instance, attempts to forge international police cooperation against the so-called White Slave trade failed because they were launched as part of a series of international legal agreements between nation states (reached in Paris in 1904 and 1910) that enjoyed no independent input from police. The First Congress of International Criminal Police, which was held in Monaco in 1914, likewise failed because of an exclusive attention on legal matters and a lack of participation by police professionals.

Following the interruption of World War 1, important initiatives to establish an international police organization were taken in the United States and in Europe. In the United States, the New York City Police directed the formation of an International Police Conference in 1922. Though set up by police and justified in terms of the suppression of international crime, the conference failed to garner much international support. In the absence of any realistic concerns over international crime at this point in time on the North American continent, the conference was oriented to the professionalization of US police rather than the fight against international crime. In Europe, however, the close proximity of multiple nation states was in the years after World War 1 readily recognized as being of special concern for the internationalization of criminal activities, especially in view of the continued development of technological means of transportation and communication. Thus, in 1923, an international meeting of police in Vienna led to the formation of the International Criminal Police Commission, the organization better known today as Interpol. The Commission was not only successful in garnering participation

of police from a multitude of nations and in steadily expanding its membership, but it also set up various systems of international information exchange, among them, most importantly, a central headquarters in Vienna through which information could be routed to the various member agencies.

World War 2 provided the next unavoidable obstacle in the development of international policing. As the headquarters of the International Criminal Police Commission were located in Vienna, they were rapidly placed under Nazi control following the annexation of Austria. The headquarters were subsequently moved to Berlin where they were aligned with the Nazi police. In 1946, an international police meeting in Brussels led to the refounding of the international police organization as the International Criminal Police Organization, with headquarters in Paris (which have since been relocated to Lyon, France). Despite its non-governmental status as an international police organization, Interpol was during the Cold War occasionally challenged for its political role, especially in being used for the suppression of political opponents by the Communist regimes of Eastern Europe. Because of such difficulties, the organization lost the support of the Federal Bureau of Investigation (FBI), which, under direction of J. Edgar Hoover, had risen to world fame and which had begun to create its own international system.

The rise of the FBI as a powerful police organization with a strong international programme indicates a shift in international police work during the second half of the 20th century towards the American continent. Under a general process of Americanization, the trend for international work was driven by the strong role of US police agencies, especially with respect to the objectives of international police work. Thus, the international war on drugs rose to the foreground of concern during the latter half of the 20th century.

More broadly, the process of Americanization in international police work indicates one of three important ways in which there is a persistence of nationality in international policing. First, police agencies will prefer to work unilaterally to fulfil their international missions, most typically by placing agents abroad through a system of legal attachés at foreign embassies. Second, national persistence is revealed by the fact that international police cooperation will typically be limited in function or scope, initiated for a specific purpose or coordinated on a limited international scale, involving as few partners as possible. Third, even when multilateral cooperation initiatives are established among police, such as in the case of Interpol and, more recently, the European Police Office or Europol, such cooperation is collaborative in nature, bringing police agencies of various nations together within an organization without the formation of a supranational force. Instead, international police organizations operate as facilitative communications networks among the police of various nations.

No contemporary discussion on international policing would be complete without contemplation of the impact of the terrorist attacks of September 11, 2001. Since 9/11, terrorism has moved centre stage in international police work. Importantly, while terrorism is also a prime mover in international political and legal affairs, international police organizations have taken up terrorism as a criminal enforcement objective on the basis of acquired professional policing criteria. A central question concerning the nature and course of international policing in the near future is how professional standards of counterterrorist policing will harmonize or clash with the conception of terrorism as an ideologically volatile and politically divisive problem.

Mathieu Deflem

Bibliography

Deflem M. 2002. *Policing world society: historical foundations of international police cooperation.* Oxford: Oxford University Press.

Liang H.-H. 1992. *The rise of the modern police and the European state system from Metternich to the Second World War.* Cambridge and New York: Cambridge University Press.

Nadelmann E. A. 1993. *Cops across borders: the internationalization of US criminal law enforcement.* University Park: Pennsylvania State University Press.

Related essays

1848; anarchism; Cold War; crime; criminology; drugs (illicit); governing science; individual identification systems; legal order; nation and state; Nazism; public policy; September 11, 2001; taxation; terrorism; White Slavery; workers' movements

Population

For a term that now appears neutral, even apolitical, 'population' has a complex history. It can designate any group with something in common, such as a religious community, a social class, or a large country. The size and composition of a population is determined by fertility, mortality, and migration. The degree to which governments are inclined to or even capable of controlling any or all of these factors has varied widely, and international and non-governmental organizations have been instrumental in advancing some of the most ambitious schemes to shape demographic trends. Population is therefore an important concept in transnational history, since it provides ways to analyse world politics without presuming that states or nations are the most salient units of analysis.

Yet the term 'population' is also common in the natural sciences, lending itself to inquiries that compare people to other species. One of the earliest theories of demographic growth, for instance, posited that world population would stabilize much like a captive population of fruit flies. Eugenists have long contrasted human reproduction with plant and animal breeding. Aggregating people as populations – rather than treating them as individuals, as families, or some other group of their own making – therefore has important political implications. It makes it possible to conceive of top-down policies and programmes that can literally remake political communities. At its most benign, this approach has reduced the incidence of disease and improved social and medical support for childrearing. At its most extreme, the pursuit of quantitative and 'qualitative' population goals has led to persecution of abortionists, coercive sterilization, and 'ethnic cleansing'.

The very terms used to designate policies and programmes intended to shape populations are hotly contested: relocation centres versus concentration camps; birth control versus population control; family-friendly versus pro-natalist. Other terms are more ambiguous still, such as human capital, or the quality of life, since they do not necessarily indicate any intent to influence the size or 'quality' of populations. The word eugenics, which in China has been invoked to underscore the importance of proper nutrition during pregnancy, is rejected as defamatory in the US even when used to describe screening out those considered too short or unintelligent to donate sperm or eggs. Conversely, while most Americans and Europeans consider 'family planning' to be a neutral way to refer to the provision of contraception, Indians prefer 'family welfare', since the older term summons to mind the mass sterilizations carried out during the Emergency Period.

Population is thus a protean concept that branches out in multiple directions and changes meaning according to context, presenting major challenges to researchers. Just locating the relevant archival records can require searching under such topics as manpower, statistics, public health, or migration. In essence, the concept of population provides a way of seeing and treating people collectively and 'objectively' that is indispensable for certain political projects. A historical definition cannot, therefore, be completely definitive. But it can indicate why purely national approaches – whether in terms of national histories of immigration, of birth control, or of public health – have often missed essential context, illuminating comparisons, and transnational connections.

The political science of population

Whatever its political uses and misuses, the concept of population has been quite productive for the social and natural sciences. The relationship between demographic growth, productivity, and wages was a major concern of the classical economists, most notably Thomas Robert Malthus (1766–1834), but also the Marquis de Condorcet (1743–94) and David Ricardo (1772–1823). Malthus' idea that population increased more rapidly than the means to support it struck Charles Darwin (1809–82) as an explanation for why different species were driven to adapt to their environment. The application of Darwinian theory to human societies inspired eugenics, though many preferred Jean-Baptiste Lamarck's (1744–1829) idea that the environment – and not just better breeding – could improve heritable characteristics. A refusal to separate humanity from other species, along with an appreciation for biodiversity, also led environmentalists such as Paul Ehrlich (1932–) and the Club of Rome to argue that people could not control their impact on the environment without controlling their own numbers. Feminists instead stressed the control of reproduction as what Margaret Sanger (1879–1966) called 'the pivot of civilization', above all as a site for either asserting or contesting

patriarchy. For Oswald Spengler (1880–1936), declines in fertility constituted an unmistakable sign of decadence.

Since John Graunt (1620–74) created the first life table in 1662, statistical analysis of defined populations has made it possible to calculate a whole range of revealing social indices. This now includes not just life expectancy, but a society's age structure, sex ratio, period and cohort fertility rates, and projected growth or decline. Historians influenced by Michel Foucault's (1926–84) concept of 'bio-power' generally associate the science of population with state building, even though 'governmentality' can encompass many non-state actors. Postcolonial theorists, in particular, have posited that imperial authorities were preoccupied with counting and categorizing their subjects.

Since population statistics are a measure of potential military manpower, it is not surprising that the spread of conscription encouraged some European states to give them more attention. Yet states were actually quite slow to respond to researchers' demands for more and better data, much less to embark on programmes to shape demographic trends. Aside from a few exceptions such as India and Algeria, demographic knowledge about most colonial possessions was particularly poor. It often amounted to rough headcounts rather than vital statistics or actual censuses. Population statistics can actually be problematic for public officials, since they permit invidious comparisons between different ethnic communities. To this day, ethnically divided countries refrain from holding censuses, as in the case of Lebanon, or refuse to gather data on the most politically sensitive questions, such as ethnic or religious identification in Nigeria and France.

The development of knowledge about population therefore depended not only – or mainly – on nation-building projects, but transnational lobbying among demographers as well as the growing demand for their work by insurance companies, social activists, and the media. The International Union for the Scientific Study of Population (IUSSP) was founded as a federation of national committees in 1927, then re-established as a body of individual members in 1947. Together with the UN Population and Statistical Divisions, it helped to train state officials in standardized techniques and encouraged them to hold decennial censuses around the start of each decade. Making the population of different societies 'legible' required not just a state's willingness to collect and publicize statistics, but also the development of an epistemic community of population experts who could agree on what to look for and what they were looking at.

Many of those who first pressed for improved methods of measuring population change were concerned not merely to build state capacity, but to reveal what they considered the deeper forces driving political change. Demographic knowledge, in turn, offered alternative ways to imagine political community, typically reflecting the ethnic and gender identity of population researchers. The IUSSP and UN technical agencies were long dominated by white men. Many were preoccupied by concerns that differential fertility might shift power relations within societies and between them.

One of the most common and persistent of these concerns was that the relative growth of Asia (the 'yellow peril') and Africa would challenge white supremacy. It was important in late-19th-century campaigns against Asian immigration in North America, Australia, and South Africa. By the 1930s, an international literature had developed on fertility declines among the European peoples. But this concern emerged even before there was any real evidence that the population of the rest of the world was growing relatively larger. It reflected not just a concern to preserve racial hierarchies, but also anxiety about women's increasing participation in politics and the workplace.

In the second half of the 20th century, fear of the relative growth of non-white peoples continued, albeit in more neutral terms. In 1952 the French demographer Alfred Sauvy (1898–1990) invented the term 'Third World', lumping together societies that appeared to share high mortality and fertility rates. For Sauvy, the term 'world population' was politically meaningless absent world government, and he feared that it would be exploited by those who wanted to use population growth to justify territorial reallocation. For the American demographers who dominated the UN Population Division, such as Frank Notestein (1902–83), counting world population and offering high, medium, and low projections into the future was instead a way to highlight the need for international development under the tutelage of industrialized states. He pioneered the idea that all societies must eventually undergo the same 'demographic transition'.

Closer study has uncovered tremendous diversity in fertility trends even within single states, belying any notion of a single demographic transition. Conscious fertility control was long common in India, Japan, and China, where population was once thought limited only by Malthusian pressures. The availability of modern forms of contraception – even mass distribution by governments – has not been a determining factor in fertility declines. Moreover, the historical pattern of celibacy or delayed marriage in Western Europe is now thought to be more aberrant than exemplary. The most important single factor explaining fertility declines worldwide has been women's increasing access to education. But the reason for the variation and fluctuation in fertility rates in countries with near-universal access to education and similar socioeconomic characteristics is unclear. In the absence of a general theory that can explain and predict fertility behaviour, we have only ad hoc explanations for each case.

Population movements: planning the global family

Despite the inadequacy of demographic knowledge, different theories about population growth and change have nonetheless been quite influential over the last two centuries, inspiring a number of political movements. They tended to be transnational in their approach as much as their ambitions. Annie Besant and Charles Bradlaugh organized the first Neo-Malthusian League in 1877 – Neo because, unlike Malthus himself, they endorsed the use of contraception. It reached out to similar groups in the Netherlands, Germany, France, Sweden, India, and Italy. They held their first International Conference in Paris in 1900, but failed to have much political impact. Aside from the Dutch, neo-Malthusians did not organize services to meet the growing demand for contraceptives, initially limiting their role to social critique.

Eugenics organizations came later, with the first founded in Germany in 1907, but spread quickly and counted far more influential adherents. They benefited from apprehension among elites about global migration and disparity in fertility rates among different social classes and ethnic groups. American eugenists such as Charles Davenport and Harry

Laughlin played a key role in lobbying for immigration restrictions that discriminated in favour of Northern Europeans. This was perhaps the first population policy that was expected to have a global impact, promoting the propagation of Anglo-Saxons while containing Asians to areas of high mortality. Eugenists also secured laws either permitting or requiring sterilization of the 'unfit' in dozens of American states, Scandinavia, and – most notoriously – Nazi Germany. But while the existence of a 'racist international' helps explain similarities in eugenic policies in different countries, especially a concern to prevent miscegenation, it also makes clear why eugenists worldwide were unable to unify. Potentially influential adherents in Japan, China, and India were left out.

Some eugenists were less beholden to racial hierarchy and more concerned about reversing fertility declines. Corrado Gini of Italy created a federation of 'Latin' eugenics organizations, which collaborated with Catholic groups in advocating large families and keeping contraception and abortion illegal. But pro-natalist policies were driven by interstate competition more than transnational coordination. In the leadup to World War 2, states such as France, Italy, Japan, Germany, and the USSR adopted policies to promote population growth, in some cases setting numerical targets, such as 60 million Italians by 1960. Pro-natalist policies typically included prosecution of abortionists, prohibition of contraception, and financial rewards for childbearing. Those accused of thwarting pro-natalist goals suffered persecution, leading to the decimation of the sexual reform movement in Nazi-occupied Europe. But there were only mixed results in reversing fertility declines.

It was not until after World War 2 that a population movement emerged with truly global reach. The concept of family planning was most fully developed by Sweden's Gunnar and Alva Myrdal as part of their vision of the welfare state. It arose from a concern about declining fertility among the European peoples that accelerated during the Great Depression, confirmation that population had begun to grow rapidly outside Europe and the US, and the need to present a flexible programme with broad political appeal. Many eugenists had become frustrated at their inability to have a wider impact, especially in terms of reducing the gap in fertility between rich and poor, both within the industrialized West and between rich and poor countries. Birth control activists, for their part, needed allies among governing elites to make contraception available to everyone.

Proponents often invoked the ideal of a 'global family', but family planning won a worldwide following because it could be applied differently in different places and did not specify who would actually do the planning – whether parents, local communities, national authorities, non-governmental or international organizations. In fact for many American and British proponents, family planning was merely a means to an end, 'population control', leading to long-running debates within new advocacy groups such as the International Planned Parenthood Federation (IPPF), founded in 1952.

In the League of Nations' last years some officials began to press for more study of demographic trends, though it proved difficult even to define research problems. The first leaders of new UN agencies like the Educational, Scientific, and Cultural Organization (UNESCO) and the World Health Organization (WHO) tried to win support from member states for an active role in shaping populations worldwide. They were supported by South Asian and Scandinavian states, but were defeated by Latin American countries, Italy, Ireland, and France. Later, Communist countries would join the opposition. The US initially offered strong support, helping to found the UN Fund for Population Activities (UNFPA) in 1969, but switched sides in 1984, when the Reagan administration withdrew funding from both the UNFPA and the IPPF.

One reason why the politics of international aid for family planning has focused on international and non-governmental organizations and featured such unconventional diplomatic coalitions is that they often arise out of transnational struggles among people who do not necessarily owe their primary allegiance to any particular government. The Vatican, which had permanent observer status on the governing bodies of UN agencies, has long coordinated opposition among Catholics worldwide. More recently, it has also worked with Christian evangelical and Muslim organizations. Anti-abortion campaigns have grown to become global in scope under the auspices of groups like Human Life International, which was founded in 1981 and has scored a number of legislative victories.

Defenders of family planning, for their part, have organized transnational networks of sympathetic parliamentarians, placed allies in official delegations to UN conferences, and used women's caucuses to coordinate a common agenda.

All along, non-governmental organizations like the IPPF, the Population Council (founded 1952), and the Ford Foundation have played crucial roles. The first countries to adopt policies to reduce population growth, such as India and Pakistan, had well-connected family planning associations affiliated with the IPPF. A major IPPF donor, Katherine McCormick, was the main backer of the development of the birth control pill in the 1950s. The Population Council underwrote the widespread adoption of the Intrauterine Device (IUD) in the 1960s. Until the end of that decade, the Ford Foundation was far and away the largest financial backer of family planning, with a budget that dwarfed what many governments were spending on their own programmes. NGOs cultivated government officials and, in cases like Tunisia and South Korea, designed national programmes. This is one reason why family-planning campaigns have often been quite similar despite the different social, cultural, and political conditions existing in different countries, leading to decidedly mixed results.

National family-planning programmes typically began with 'knowledge-attitude-practice' surveys that were intended to reveal latent demand for contraception. Where demand was thought insufficient or ill-informed, it was promoted through 'information-education-communication' programmes. Contraceptives were often distributed not through national health systems, which had different constituencies and conflicting interests, but stand-alone programs, including mobile camps and clinics. Rather than quality of care, these programmes typically stressed the achievement of time-bound performance targets. To that end, many resorted to financial incentives for sterilization or IUD use and, in some cases, penalties for non-participation. They also experimented with the use of paramedical personnel and commercial marketing, seeking to harness the profit motive to control population growth. But programmes that led to lowered medical standards, mass distribution of experimental or discredited contraceptives, and uninformed or non-consensual use created

international controversies, in some cases changing the politics of family planning in the wealthy countries that paid for them.

Beyond national programmes, population scientists and activists have long sought to promote global policies in which people would have common reproductive rights and responsibilities. A disproportionate number were advocates of world government, though the term 'global governance' – indicating a more informal constellation of transnational norms and institutions – is now favoured. For environmentalists in particular, a common duty to the planet overrode national differences.

But population movements were beset by faction fighting over strategy and leadership even among those who shared similar values. For some, containing the 'population explosion' justified crash programmes and coercive measures. Others considered cash payments for sterilization or denial of maternity and housing benefits to large families to be unethical or politically inept. Americans often tried to decide such questions, since they provided well over half of all international aid for family planning until the mid 1970s. This engendered resentment among those, like Sweden's Elise Ottesen-Jensen, who suspected it was driven by Cold War or even racist concerns. This is one reason why United Nations agencies and the World Bank played a leading role, especially in the spread of family planning programmes to Latin America and Africa in the 1970s and 80s, since US government officials sought help in areas where direct involvement might have provoked resistance.

Controversies over the ethics and safety of family-planning programmes sometimes divided feminists in rich and poor countries, as at the first UN Women's Conference in Mexico City in 1975. But more recently the cause of reproductive rights and health, as opposed to population control, has served to unify women across borders. Groups such as Development Alternatives with Women for a New Era (DAWN) and the Women's Environment and Development Organization (WEDO) worked to situate population concerns in a broader framework that addressed all the causes of poverty and powerlessness, not just lack of contraception. Although women's access to education had long been recognized as a key determinant of fertility, it was because of women's greater influence in population debates that it became a priority. This transnational networking, underwritten by foundations like Ford and the Pew Charitable Trusts, culminated with the 'Cairo Consensus' at the last UN population conference in 1994. Under the leadership of UNFPA Executive Director Nafis Sadik, and against the bitter opposition of Pope John Paul II, the 'Programme of Action' was ratified by the great majority of governments. It continues to guide most work in the field, though states have not followed through on funding commitments.

Prospects for the future

In recent years, with the slowing of overall growth and increasing disparities between high- and low-fertility countries, population is less often considered a global concern. Some environmentalists believe that the number of people on the planet already exceeds its carrying capacity. But more now focus on consumption, since the size of world population – which may begin declining within a few decades – matters less than how particular people consume resources and produce greenhouse gas emissions.

Yet if population concerns are less global, they are increasingly transnational. Many low-fertility countries, including Japan and Germany, would already have begun to decline in absolute numbers were it not for immigration. International adoption, a high-visibility form of migration, has been growing at a rapid rate. The pace and composition is often shaped by the legacies of population programmes, such as the pernicious combination of a one-child policy with son-preference in China. More generally, immigrant workers have played a growing role in caring for children in wealthy countries. This has made it possible for more educated women to enter or remain in the workforce, and their employees' remittances help sustain communities around the world. But it also leads to separation of families and working conditions some consider exploitative because of the lack of benefits and job security.

Ageing populations in Europe and North America also recruit large numbers of doctors and nurses from Africa and South Asia, further weakening already inadequate health services there. The effect can be measured in terms of persistently high and even increasing infant and maternal mortality rates. Life expectancy trends, which were converging for decades, have begun going in different directions. The average Japanese, for instance, can now expect to live more than twice as long as someone born in Zimbabwe.

Population trends – and the capacity to measure them – therefore continue both to reflect and affect socioeconomic disparities, with ramified but potentially far-reaching consequences. The spread of Acquired immunodeficiency syndrome (AIDS), in part through other transnational phenomena such as tourism, sex-work, and intravenous drug trafficking, has radically changed the age structure of many societies, hollowing out whole generations. On the other hand, it has spurred the development of a global network of activists and many thousands of NGOs. This has brought rapid growth in international health assistance and the targeting of other diseases, such as tuberculosis and malaria, although in ways that repeat many of the mistakes of family-planning campaigns of the past. Another example is prenatal ultrasound testing, promoted by international aid agencies as well as medical instruments companies. While originally expected to improve maternal health, it has led to the spread of sex-selective abortions. The governments of India and China have found it all but impossible to stop the practice, and in many areas women risk becoming a persecuted minority.

The future may bring even closer transnational linkages, leading to even more startling socioeconomic divergences both within countries and between them. The market in 'donated' eggs and sperm is now global in scope, and almost completely unregulated. Some infertile couples have begun to 'outsource' pregnancies to surrogate mothers in poor countries. And while national authorities have sought to restrict research in cloning and germ-line genetic engineering, global commercial and scientific competition continues to drive it forward. Preimplantation genetic diagnosis already makes it possible to pick and choose among embryos – usually to screen for diseases, but potentially to select genetic characteristics preferred by parents who can afford to pay for them. Rich people may therefore literally make themselves a breed apart.

Technological forecasts have a chequered past, and it has proven impossible even to project population growth more than ten or twenty years hence. When longer-term projections for world population hold true, it is usually because one erroneous assumption has balanced another, with errors for particular continents measured in the millions. But if fertility rates continue to decline and stabilize below replacement levels, there may be too few potential emigrants to prevent population decline and ageing in many areas. And if there is no effective regulation of genetic research, socioeconomic disparities may evolve into permanent biological differences between classes. It is therefore possible that population will once more become a global and not merely transnational concern, inspiring new movements to work across borders worldwide.

Matthew Connelly

Bibliography

Adams M. B. (ed.) 1990. *The wellborn science: eugenics in Germany, France, Brazil, and Russia.* Oxford and New York: Oxford University Press.

Caldwell J. and Caldwell P. 1986. *Limiting population growth and the Ford Foundation contribution.* London: Frances Pinter.

Chesler E. 1992. *Woman of valor: Margaret Sanger and the birth control movement in America.* New York: Doubleday.

Kühl S. 1997. *Die Internationale der Rassisten: Aufstieg und Niedergang der internationalen Bewegung fur Eugenik und Rassenhygiene im 20. Jahrhundert.* Frankfurt: Campus.

Symonds R. and Carder M. 1973. *The United Nations and the population question, 1945–1970.* London: Chatto & Windus for Sussex University Press.

Teitelbaum M. S. and Winter J. M. (eds) 1989. *Population and resources in Western intellectual traditions.* Cambridge and New York: Cambridge University Press.

Warwick D. P. 1982. *Bitter pills: population policies and their implementation in eight developing countries.* Cambridge: Cambridge University Press.

Related essays
birth control; commodity trading; condom; demographic transition; developmental taxonomies; ecology; epidemics; ethnicity and race; eugenics; forced migrations; Ford Foundation; gender and sex; Green Revolution; guestworkers; health policy; human mobility; intergovernmental organizations; international migration regimes; international non-governmental organizations (INGOs); labour migrations; nation and state; outer space; philanthropic foundations; public policy; seeds; underdevelopment; white men's countries; women's movements; world federalism; zero growth

Prebisch, Raul *See* ECLAC

Preservation and conservation *See* Conservation and preservation

Prizes

Prizes that honour outstanding achievements, and do so regardless of the laureates' national origins are no longer uncommon.

On the contrary, the number of institutions and endowments that extend beyond national borders in their search for accomplishment and talent deserving reward and encouragement has grown steadily, especially in the wake of the Second World War. According to rough estimates, the number of prizes awarded or available now runs into the thousands, after a steep, almost fourfold, increase in the 1940s and 1950s.

This increase in international prizes and awards is, of course, just one aspect of the constant progress in internationalization – even, more recently, 'de-nationalization' – of human activities over the last 150 years. The prizes simply attest to and valorize the existence of transnational spheres of work and concern. They would do little, indeed, to enhance the prestige of their recipients – and, for that matter, of the awarding bodies – if the accomplishments of the honourees could not be appreciated and their recognition not be shared internationally by a more or less sizeable, cognisant public. Although the possible pecuniary component these prizes often confer cannot be underestimated, their prestige remains their most powerful appeal.

Beyond their consequences for the careers of the recipients (or their development should the recipients be institutions), international prizes also tend to have a structuring effect on the areas and disciplines in which they are awarded, as the adjudication process could not do without a substantial consensus on the criteria of excellence. The practice of awarding prizes therefore provides those areas and disciplines not only with stimulus but also with sets of norms, elements of social stratification and a sense of identity that cannot but strengthen their cohesiveness and vitality.

Few awards are well-known and influential beyond a specialized public, however transnational. Winning a first prize in Belgium's Queen Elizabeth International Music Competition will no doubt enhance the individual's career prospects. The recipient of the International Mathematical Union's Field Medal will also enjoy enormous prestige among his or her fellow mathematicians (including the professional advantages that come with it). Neither event, however, might capture much attention or imagination beyond musicians or scientists. In contrast, juries' decisions at major international film festivals, for instance, concern crowds of prospective viewers, and literary prizes – language barriers notwithstanding – can always count on the attention of a broad spectrum of the reading public. In any case, all international prizes, from the obscure to the better-known, can potentially contribute in some way or another to heightening the awareness of ordinary citizens in spheres of common pursuits and accomplishments beyond national purpose and identity.

Medals and prizes had been instruments of royal patronage for centuries. Europe's national academies awarded prizes and medals in both the sciences and the humanities to honour colleagues of particular merit and so, later on, did various national learned societies. Being a foreign national did not preclude prominent scholars from receiving prestigious prizes, such as the Royal Society of London's Copley Medal (awarded since 1731), although academies, in particular, preferred to bestow such honours on individuals they had already previously appointed as a foreign member. In the sciences, the rationale underlying the prizes diversified over time. They began to be awarded increasingly for promising work in progress or to encourage research in areas considered to be unjustly neglected, to the point that prize money gradually became a source of research funding. Academies and government bodies held prize competitions soliciting work related mostly, although not exclusively, to scientific and technical questions. Most of the prize money came from private donors who often determined or, at least, influenced the topic of the competition. Even so, while medals and awards continued to be given as general tokens of esteem, one could argue that the prize system enabled the awarding institutions to practise, however piecemeal, science policy *avant la lettre*.

From the outset, differences from one country's practice to the other notwithstanding, prize competitions were generally open to contenders from all over Europe, often attracting the participation of prominent scholars. In some instances, such contests involved years of often parallel effort in different countries. The determination of longitude at sea is a case in point: set up in 1714 by the British Board of Longitude, the prize was awarded half a century later to an English clock maker and a German mathematician. The adjudication process was nevertheless firmly in the hands of the awarding institutions and – the rhetoric about the laureate's service to the whole of mankind notwithstanding – was subject to the sway of national concerns and priorities. This tradition was challenged when, in 1895, the Swedish industrialist Alfred Nobel (1833–96) willed the overwhelming part of his fortune to a foundation that was to carry his name.

Awarded since 1900, year after year (with a few wartime exceptions), for the highest achievements in physics, chemistry, medicine, literature and the promotion of international peace (economics was added on a parallel track in 1968), the Nobel Prize has become the epitome of international prizes – rationale, practice and impact. What was new was the fact that the selection of winners was no longer left exclusively in the hands of small councils or committees composed essentially of citizens from the awarding country. Instead, invitations had to be issued, potentially worldwide, to selected 'Swedish as well as foreign representatives for the field of culture in question' to submit nominations for the prizes.

This internationalization of the selection process, however partial, laid down in the statutes of the Nobel Foundation, was a highly original feature of its prize system. It gradually created a transnational constituency by engaging the communities of 'the fields of culture in question' actively in the selection process. This was all the more important in the sciences, for instance: the spectacular philanthropy of the inventor of dynamite and smokeless powder had made headlines worldwide, while the announcement of the prizes caused little excitement within the scientific community. The authority of the Foundation – and, consequently, the prestige of the prizes – being at stake, the awarding institutions – Swedish Academies, the Karolinska Institute in Stockholm and the Norwegian Parliament – were anxious to make choices that were sure to meet with the approval of the winners' peers. They did, and gradually the science prizes took off for the fame they enjoy today.

The Nobel literary award faced a much tougher challenge. Whereas their independence from cultural and national determinants was – and still is – a basic norm in the natural sciences, there was little hope of finding a transnationally accepted set of criteria to judge the outstanding worthiness of literary work. The nomination process did not help, as nominators seemed invariably to propose their own countries' illustrious writers. In effect the election of the literary laureate became a multinational rather than an international affair. It was to develop a truly transnational dimension over time, however, because – provided the works were translated – the general public was able to appreciate the Swedish Academy's decision and to discuss its merits. Over the years, and thanks to the unparalleled publicity surrounding the awards, the literary prize incited the world's reading public to become interested in the literary productions of countries other than their own. It contributed in this way to the emergence, at the turn of the 21st century, of a world literature which only a few people had imagined a hundred years earlier.

Alfred Nobel's generation had placed high hopes in international law and organization as means of conflict resolution, a confidence which explains why possible nominators for the Peace Prize were chosen among the members of the Interparliamentary Union, of institutions such as the International Court of Arbitration and more generally professors of political science, law, history and philosophy, etc. This relatively narrow transnational constituency of the early years widened considerably when the various international mechanisms and institutions for conflict resolution proved to be relative failures. Today, the identification of what constitutes a threat to peace and what could help to preserve it has since long fallen into the purview of public debate worldwide. Far from involving just a limited group, mainly of international lawyers, the selection process now extends to public opinion at large, a fact – however informal – that the Norwegian Parliament's Nobel Committee cannot fail to take into account. Year after year, even when the Committee decides to reserve the award or when its choice sets off controversy, the Peace Prize reminds the world's citizens of their common existence.

The case of the Nobel Prizes is both exceptional and exemplary. The internationalization of the adjudicating bodies seems to have become an element of credibility for any international award, although no systematic study has been undertaken to substantiate this claim. The sociology of international prizes has so far remained largely unexplored, with the notable exception of the Nobel Prizes.

Brigitte Schroeder-Gudehus

Bibliography
Crawford E. 1984. *The beginnings of the Nobel Institution: the Sciences Prizes, 1901–1915.* Cambridge: Cambridge University Press.

Related essays
beauty pageants; bodybuilding; cappuccino; economics; film; humanities; legal order; life and physical sciences; literature; mathematics; measurement; Olympic Games; pacifism; philanthropy; Pugwash Conferences

Productivity missions

As the name indicates, these technical missions were set up in 1949 within the widened framework of the European Reconstruction Programme (ERP, 'Marshall Plan') and had at the heart of their objective an increase in productivity.

Reflections on productivity existed in Europe from the very beginning of the 20th century, particularly concerning the evolutions of American industry. Private programmes for technical assistance developed during the interwar period, in particular in France, Germany and Great Britain, with study trips organized in the United States. Their objectives were the improvement of productivity through technological innovation and new methods for organizing production. The European ground was well prepared so as to be able to benefit from the productivity missions after the Second World War. Thus this method was not created by the Marshall Plan, but it brought about a true social 'revolution'.

These productivity missions were created in the context of the Marshall Plan, as a European initiative. They started in 1949–50 and were at their peak in 1951–52. The programmes declined from 1953 and ceased to exist in 1956. The financial effort which the Marshall Plan represented was enormous. The objectives of these missions were the organization of work, the method of planning production and the method of financial management of a company. This was the first ever systematic exchange circuit focused on productivity. The sixteen beneficiary countries of Marshall Aid were targeted by these missions, and Japan joined thereafter. The number of missions was very high: more than 180 for Italy, more than 200 for France, the same for Norway, nearly 300 for Japan. The number of participants in each mission being at least twelve, there were thus thousands of participants, senior executives, engineers, foremen, trade unionists and civil servants who could benefit from these exchanges. Moreover these missions generated transnational exchanges between the participating countries, each of which welcomed on its soil missions coming from the rest of Europe and even from non-European countries.

On the American side, the main actor was the US Technical Assistance and Productivity Agency (USTA&P), created in 1948 within the framework of the ERP and designed to organize and subsidize the missions. On the European side, the productivity missions were not directly managed by the governments, but by other suitable organizations. In 1950, the US Congress required of European governments that they create national centres of productivity. The majority of the missions were then organized on the basis of a partnership between these centres and the national trade unions. The Organisation for European Economic Cooperation (OEEC) also played a part in the coordination of the whole project, and this polycentric structure continued until the creation of the European Productivity Agency (EPA) in 1953.

Two periods are to be distinguished: from 1949 to 1952, the stress was laid on technology transfer and, secondarily, on managerial transfer; from 1953, the 'human' data of productivity reappeared, with a partial reorientation which privileged private initiative, considered to be more effective, and a limitation on financing from public funds. Three types of mission correspond to particular objectives. Short missions were initially deployed (one month), gathering ten to thirty people, mostly engineers. From 1950, missions of long duration (nine months) concerning experts were set up, starting with a formative programme in a business school before paying additional visits. From 1951, there was a multiplication of short missions (three weeks), whose members were, from within the same company, representatives with an equal share of directors, executives and trade unionists, in accordance with the wishes of the Americans. This last type of mission had an important impact.

The productivity missions towards the United States, thanks to the new character of their breadth, allowed a radical change in the direction of productivity in Europe. The new state of mind caused or developed by these productivity missions accelerated the passage to a competitive market economy, which is at the origin of the 'European miracle'.

Françoise Berger

Bibliography

Barjot D. (ed.) 2002. *Catching-up with America: productivity missions and diffusion of American economic end technological influence.* Paris: Presses de l'Université de Paris-Sorbonne.

Bjarnar O. and Kipping M. (eds) 1998. *The Americanisation of European business: the Marshall Plan and the transfer of US management models.* London and New York: Routledge.

Djelic M. L. 1998. *Exporting the American model: the postwar transformation of European business.* Oxford: Oxford University Press.

Related essays

America; Cold War; convergence; industrialization; iron and steel; Marshall Plan; Pax Americana; rubber; technologies

Professionals and executives See Executives and professionals

Psychoanalysis

Psychoanalysis consists in a theory about the structure and dynamics of mental life, in a related therapeutic system and in the institutional framework necessary for its action and reproduction. The term was coined by Sigmund Freud (1856–1939) in 1896 to designate what he considered to be a new conception of psychological reality and a new therapeutic approach to mental suffering. In spite of strong opposition and resistance, psychoanalysis became an important, world-wide, intellectual movement and therapeutic resource.

Freud, a citizen of the Austro-Hungarian Empire, of Jewish origin, had been trained as a physician and a researcher in neurology in the University of Vienna, under the influence of the prestigious German school of physiology. His growing interest in the clinical treatment of 'nervous diseases' led him to work for a short period with the psychiatrist Jean-Martin Charcot in Paris (winter of 1885–86), an eminent specialist in hysteria. His first two major psychoanalytic works were published by the turn of the century (The Interpretation of Dreams in 1899 and The Psychopathology of Everyday Life in 1901). A first formal circle of disciples was organized in 1902 in Vienna and the first local society was founded in 1908 (Vienna Psycho-Analytical Society), which already included an international circle of adherents. In fact another society had already been founded in Zurich in 1907 (the 'Freud Society'), around Eugen Bleuler and Carl Gustav Jung. What was to be considered as the First International Psychoanalytical Congress was held in Salzburg, in 1908, where nine papers were read to an audience of 42 people. A first official journal of the movement was founded then, the Jahrbuch für psychoanalytische und psychopathologische Forschungen. In that same year Freud went to the USA (accompanied by Sandor Ferenczi and Jung), as the result of an invitation by Stanley Hall who had studied in Germany. He gave a series of conferences at Clark University, Worcester, Massachusetts. In the audience were the most important names in American psychiatry, neurology and psychology. In 1910, the second International Congress was held, in Nuremberg; this was the occasion for the creation of a second journal (Zentralblatt für Psychoanalyse) and the foundation of the International Psychoanalytical Association (IPA), with Jung as its first president. In the same year there was founded the American Psychopathology Association, in Washington. It was followed by the creation of the New York Psychoanalytical Society (around Abraham Arden Brill) and the American Psychoanalytical Association (around Ernest Jones and James Jackson Putnam), both in 1911. In 1913, the new Internationale Zeitschrift für Psychoanalyse took the place of the Zentralblatt as the official organ of the IPA.

By that time, signs of the presence of psycho-analysis were visible all over the world: in 1904,

first reference to Freud in an article by the eminent Argentine psychiatrist José Ingenieros; in 1908, appearance of the first articles on psychoanalysis in Italy; in 1909, organization of a group of adepts in Sydney, Australia, and the founding of the journal Psychotherapia, in Moscow; in 1912, first reference to Freud in Japanese literature; in 1914, first paper on psychoanalysis presented at a meeting of the Brazilian Neurological Society. Serious theoretical divergences, institutional crises, and intellectual arguments permeated these heroic years. In 1914, Freud wrote the first 'History of the Psychoanalytic Movement'. After the First World War, he set up an independent publishing house (Internationaler Psychoanalytischer Verlag) as a vehicle for the diffusion of the movement, while in England Ernest Jones founded the 'International Psychoanalytical Library' and the still active International Journal of Psycho-Analysis, the first number of which appeared in 1920.

Freud and his first disciples and collaborators were quite skeptical about the positive reception of the new system of thought and therapy, for reasons directly related to the quality of their theoretical proposals, which seemed to challenge both conventional morality and established medical and psychiatric canons. Notwithstanding, some authors have shown that positive reception of the new theory was as immediate and widespread as were criticism and anathema. In spite of the hegemonic position of degeneracy theories in relation to 'mental diseases', there was a considerable sensibility to new therapeutic proposals, as a function of the growing extension and intensity of 'nervousness' and 'nervous diseases' in all Western countries and in all social classes. For instance, the preliminary notice on the Studies on Hysteria by Freud and Josef Breuer, where – for the first time – the hypothesis of the sexual etiology of hysteria was disclosed and the technique of the 'talking cure' was described, was published in January 1893, and earned a review by Frederick W. H. Myers, in the Proceedings of the Society for Psychical Research (Great Britain), in June of the same year. Although psychoanalysis was slowly built mostly out of the personal contribution of Freud, whose works were progressively offered to the public till his death, some of its crucial tenets were already present in the first publications, unchaining strong reactions of attraction and repulsion.

Psychoanalysis can be considered as a step forward in the process of psychologization that had been taking place for a long time in the Western tradition, as a corollary of the cultural emphasis on the autonomous condition of the individual self. The Freudian version of psychologization emphasized new aspects of that ideal. The first specificity is the pre-eminence of the unconscious dimension of psychic life to the detriment of the conscious one. The second one is the articulation of interiority and internal dynamics around sexual desire or sexuality. The third, finally, is the hypothesis of the necessary psychic cross-influence between the therapist and the patient (or analysand) developed in the theory of transfer and countertransfer. These aspects, which can traced to the influence of romanticism in Freudian work, ran counter to the more conventional representation of the self derived from rationalism and positivism.

That tension is at the root of the vicissitudes of the diffusion of psychoanalysis in the interwar period, a time of intense ideological and political dissension. Three main directions can be discerned. First, psychoanalysis was banned in some countries under authoritarian regimes (Nazi Germany, the Stalinist Soviet Union, Spain under Franco), or suffered strong criticism from medical, philosophical and political opponents even in the countries where it came to be most firmly implanted. Second, psychoanalysis became intensely familiar to the liberal intelligentsia, in the area of art and the humanities. Important movements and authors in these domains recognized a direct influence of psychoanalytical thought. Psychology and psychiatry became closely associated with psychoanalysis in many national contexts. In philosophy and the social sciences, the dialogue with psychoanalysis was acknowledged in several specific areas, being especially important to North American cultural anthropology, to British social anthropology and to French philosophy. Eventually, specific hybrid disciplines arose out of that collaboration, such as psychohistory or psychoanalytical anthropology. The third direction was that of education and religion. Some early sympathizers like the Swiss protestant pastor Oskar Pfister became important vehicles for the influence of psychoanalytical theory in educational and pastoral activities – still active today.

This pattern of diffusion allows for the perception of some of the cultural and political conditions for the successful diffusion of psychoanalysis in different countries, classes and status groups: (1) a politically liberal society, endowed with the possibility of personal social mobility, choice and change; (2) the hegemony of the ideology of individualism, with its emphasis on personal autonomy, moral liberty and political equality; (3) the co-presence of the expressive, qualitative or romantic version of individualism, with its emphasis on personal development and self-fulfillment; (4) the predominance of a lay public order, allowing for the emergence of a 'religious market' and the personal choice of a moral foundation for behaviour; (5) a conflict between a traditional moral order (formal subordination to religious and moral values, characterized by strict rules of self- and body control), increasingly considered as inadequate, and a new, 'modern' one (material subordination to values, characterized by a relaxation of body controls and by a flexible, negotiated self-construction); (6) a certain tension and contradiction among all the previous conditions.

In fact, psychoanalysis can be seen as a complex, many-sided theoretical structure coupled with a strategy for intervention upon psychic life and suffering, that can be used as a tool for the translation of some styles of symbolic life into an individualistic mould and setting under certain specific cultural and political conditions. As Mariano Plotkin puts it:

> Psychoanalysis provides security in rapidly changing societies undergoing a crisis in 'civilized morality', when traditional ways of interpreting collective experience seem inadequate. (Plotkin, 2001, 5)

In the decades after World War 2 – a period of intense social and economic change – psychoanalysis spread more intensely throughout the world, in spite of the growing complexity of its own identity, divided in several conflicting tendencies, in opposed national, political and epistemological versions. The IPA nowadays encompasses 57 local and regional institutions in 34 countries, although it has lost the monopoly of the international organization of the movement. Mostly since Jacques Lacan (1901–81), a French psychiatrist strongly trained in philosophy and considered as an influential renovator of the discipline, created the 'École Freudienne de Paris' (1964), following his expulsion from the IPA, there arose a new, more decentralized, trend in the organization of psychoanalytical societies. An important aspect of the diffusion was the pace and characteristics of the translation of psychoanalytical texts. Some of the works by Freud were quickly translated into other languages (around 30 nowadays), raising the permanent problem of the meaning of his original concepts in the German language. In 1967, the completion was announced of the prestigious *Standard Edition of Freud's Psychological Works*, in an English translation by James Strachey. Similar systematic initiatives took place for Spanish, Italian, and Japanese versions.

A peculiar aspect of psychoanalytical diffusion is the fact that the specific cultural and political conditions of its emergence in different national contexts have led to the development of different 'national traditions', in spite of the permanent transnational exchange and cross-influence that characterized that process. In some cases, these traditions came to pivot around eminent disciples or former followers of Freud, as was the case with Melanie Klein (1882–1960) in Great Britain and Lacan in France. Wilhelm Reich (1897–1957) and Herbert Marcuse (1898–1979) were most influential in the USA, contributing to the ambivalent psychoanalytical participation in the movement of counterculture, from the 1960s onward. A complex web of relations among national traditions and theoretical positions presides over the meaning and shape of each local process of institutionalization. The case of the exchanges between French, Argentinian and Brazilian psychoanalysis is a good example, because of its intensity and extension (particularly vivid since the influence of Lacan's thought began to spread).

In the 1990s the public influence and legitimacy of psychoanalysis clearly declined, as a result of the growing popularity of other therapeutic systems, either religious (New Age-style, mostly) or bodily focused. Some authors consider these developments as 'post-psychoanalytical', in the sense that they retain some crucial dimensions of the psychoanalytical worldview. At the same time, there was a revival of physical, empiricist, reductionism in psychiatry, inspired by recent developments in the neurosciences and psychopharmacology, that has defied psychoanalytical claims to the interpretation of the human mind and the intervention in suffering and delusion.

Luiz Fernando Dias Duarte

Bibliography

Decker H. c. 1977. *Freud in Germany: revolution and reaction in science*. New York: International Universities Press.

Jones E. 1955. *Sigmund Freud: life and work*. London: Hogarth.

Plotkin M. 2001. *Freud in the Pampas: the emergence and development of a psychoanalytic culture in Argentina*. Stanford: Stanford University Press.

Roudinesco E. c. 1982. *La bataille de cent ans: histoire de la psychanalyse en France*. Paris: Ramsay.

Roudinesco E. and Plon M. 1997. *Dictionnaire de la psychanalyse*. Paris: Fayard.

Related essays

1960s; Argentina and psychoanalysis; family; feel-good culture; higher education; history; humanities; intellectual elites; international non-governmental organizations (INGOs); kindergarten; life and physical sciences; mathematics; medicine; New Age; organization models; public policy; religion; Romanticism; sexology; social sciences; translation; Westernization

Psychoanalysis and Argentina *See* Argentina and psychoanalysis

Public policy

Public policy transfers are the processes by which policies and institutions formulated in one nation are adapted for and incorporated into the policy regimes of others. Although the term is recent, the phenomenon is as old as nations themselves; indeed it is older. The modern nation states of the late 18th and 19th centuries were not made in isolation but by piecing together ingredients from one another: more centralized forms of monarchy and policy formation, parliaments and other institutions of representation, written legal codes and constitutions, systems of bureaucratic administration, methods of revenue extraction and taxation, and systems of centralized military organization. All these institutions were constructed with a high consciousness of adaptive appropriation. Even the manufacture of popular nationalism, through the invention of patriotic rituals, flags, myths, and nation-centred identities, was a process rife with transnational appropriations. By disguising their own transnational origins, nationalist ideologies have often thrown a veil over the extent to which public policies have moved between nations. But transfers of public policies are not unusual: they have been part of the very fabric of modern nation states since their inception.

Modes of policy transfer

Historians of transnational policy transfers have commonly focused on cases of voluntary adoption and adaptation. But on the global stage, coercion has played at least as powerful a role as imitation. Military conquest has frequently been an occasion for the imposition of the victor's domestic policies on the vanquished. Napoleonic Europe was the first large-scale modern example. The satellite kingdoms established in the wake of the French armies' sweep through Central and Southern Europe were not the perfect clones of French institutions and ideals that they were advertised to be; but their abolition of the formal foundations of serfdom and the guilds, their sequestering of monastic property, their imposition of French-style administration and legal codes, and their reorganization of educational and military systems on French lines left a profound impact on post-1815 Europe long after Napoleon's armies had melted away.

Similarly, in the aftermath of the Second World War, public policies marched in with the occupying military forces. Within the sphere of the Russian armies, the imposition of Soviet-style economic, political, and social institutions was nearly total; their virtual normalization in the socialist republics of Central Europe from 1945 to 1989 constitutes perhaps the most sweeping incidence of coercive transnational policy transfer in modern times. In contrast, the British, French and US administrators of postwar Germany were much more cautious reformers. In the name of speedy restoration of social confidence, the class-stratified, prewar system of German social insurance was quickly restored, despite the hopes of some British officials to impose something closer to the universalism of the new Beveridge Plan. On the same grounds, the Weimar-era principle of labour–management codetermination was allowed to be revived once the basic market character of

postwar West Germany was assured, though US officials would have preferred a clone of the American system of industrial relations. In Japan between 1945 and 1947, where the US occupational authorities had fewer qualms about direct imposition, American-style disestablishment of state religion, American-derived anti-trust legislation, a labour disputes Act modelled on US practices, and, for a time, American-style decentralization of police and educational powers were all inscribed into Japanese public policy. Without stretching the point, Reconstruction in the US South after 1865 can be said to have been a parallel case, where acceptance of the victors' 'free labour' system in the place of slavery was the cost of defeat.

A second and more powerful mode of policy transfer was empire, where military occupation extended over time into permanent or quasi-permanent colonial administration. The point of the 19th- and 20th-century empires was domination and resource extraction; their very purpose mandated that social policies for the colonized should be sharply different than for citizens of the colonizing powers. In the European empires in Asia and Africa, as in the US empire in the Philippines, systems of labour discipline, law, and authority that would have been unthinkable at home were imposed as a matter of course on populations that the colonizers deemed insufficiently civilized. Labour unions were not legalized in French colonial Africa until 1946; the British mobilized commissions to investigate factory conditions in India on the model of their own reform practices, but the industrial labour codes that ensued for colonial India were never the same as those British workers enjoyed. Nevertheless, in the course of constructing these engines of differentiation and imperial advantage, aspects of the imperializers' own domestic social policy were transferred as well, many of them lodging deeply enough to survive the empires' overthrow.

The Indian civil service, once the very engine of imperial governance, now, after 1947, the main sinew of Indian national administration, was a particularly striking example of an imperial transfer that endured the upheaval of independence. In many of the new African states, even where systems of parliamentary governance, brought very late and very hesitantly into colonial governance, collapsed, systems of central bureaucratic state administration initially modelled on those of Britain or France endured, in some cases strongly enough for scholars to write of 'administrative mimesis'. The very aims of the new states were in part absorbed from the old. The late imperial policies of economic developmentalism set in motion after 1945 often flowed without a break into the grand public works ambitions (hydroelectric dams, airports, public buildings, road construction) of the postcolonial states. So did the basic template of education, albeit radically expanded after independence. The empires transferred new regimes of property rights. They transferred military systems. They left their permanent mark on the language of governance, even where, as in India, the new nationalist governments had initially been resolved to erase the linguistic stigma of colonization. The empires were a patchwork of newly invented institutions and institutions transferred from the colonizing powers; they sorted the colonized out into cultural and racial categories of 'otherness'; and yet they shaped the very understanding of the nation that many of the colonial nationalists would bring into independence.

The third mode of public policy transfer is voluntary adaptation. Legislative or administrative measures devised in one nation are appropriated by policy makers in another nation on the basis of their prestige, their record of experience, the advantages that the adaptation of prefabricated social policy brings, the hope of competing more effectively with rival nations, or a desire to harmonize policies with external norms. This is now the most familiar mode of public policy transfer and the one most closely studied by historians. The list of policies that have circulated in this way would include virtually the entire field of public policy, from labour policies to suffrage measures, tariff subsidies, poor relief, civil service systems, city designs, prohibition schemes, public libraries, taxation methods, and military conscription. Some of what circulates through the channels of transnational exchange are precise policy measures, such as the urban enterprise zone and urban development grant proposals that passed back and forth between British and US policy makers in the 1980s, or the maximum hours-of-labour statutes that were the mark of an advanced industrial society a century before. Others are policy ideas: free trade and protectionism in the 19th century;

Keynesianism and import-substitution economics in the mid 20th century; ideas of human rights and welfare minima; commitment to markets and privatization. Still, even in recent times, imposition plays a role, whether through the quid pro quos demanded by international lenders in return for loans and currency bailouts, the work of occupying armies and their proconsuls, or the bite of externally imposed trade sanctions and embargoes.

Networks and fields of exchange before 1945

The 19th and early 20th century was the great age of amateur policy makers, self-trained policy inventors like the British sanitarian Edwin Chadwick or the American school reformer Horace Mann, whose reputation, picked up by political reformers, social humanitarians, government officials and policy entrepreneurs, circled the globe. In some cases, figures like these spread their policy messages through travel; Henry George's electrifying speaking tours through England and Ireland in the 1880s on behalf of land reform were a striking case in point. More often, an amateur publicist spread the word, making a reputation out of knowledge of another nation's practices. William Dawson, the British admirer of imperial German social policy, Frederic Howe, the American enthusiast for European policies and social science, and Fukuzawa Yukichi, the highly influential Japanese editor, traveller, and conduit of westernization, were all examples of the type.

Even in the early phases of the transnational circulation of policies and policy ideas, however, social networks played a powerful role. The Anglo-American movement for the abolition of the slave trade and slavery would have foundered in its early years had it not been for the intimate transnational connections between English, Caribbean and North American Quakers. Women suffrage advocates constructed not only an international platform but an international sorority of feminists, bound together by visits, lecture tours, occasional conventions, and assiduous correspondence. The spread of public health legislation and labour regulations limiting the exploitation of women and child labourers was the work of small numbers of singularly committed sanitarians acutely conscious of each other's reports and experience.

Networks of these sorts carried not only policy measures but social ideologies that bound measures together into social policy families. Disciples of Adam Smith were to be found throughout Europe and the Americas in the 19th century, spreading liberal policies of free trade, free movement of labour, open competition, and free contract. In late 19th-century Latin America, positivism was a powerful transnational discourse, joined to a programme of expert-led, social science-infused reform. German university economists after 1870 wove together a commitment to state building, promotion of internal industries, and social welfare measures that attracted students from as far away as Asia, Russia and the Americas. Social maternalists at the turn of the 20th century constructed a broad array of policies (minimum wage statutes, family allowances, maternal health services, and women's labour union recognition) around a core of family-based health and welfare protections. Later, corporatism, fascism and socialism would all assume the power of travelling policy ideologies.

These networks became more formally institutionalized toward the close of the 19th century as wider and more densely organized systems of international policy exchange began to supplement the work of the amateurs. One of the marks was the proliferation of international conferences devoted to social welfare and social legislation. The Congrès International de Bienfaisance, organized in Brussels in 1856 as a small French-dominated forum for discussion of poverty and poor relief, was one of the first of these; it could count over 1,600 members worldwide by 1900. The 1900 Paris Exposition was host to over two dozen similar congresses devoted to work accidents and industrial insurance, consumer cooperatives, workers' protection legislation, low-cost housing, the condition and rights of women, peace, public hygiene, Sunday rest laws, and colonial sociology, among others. International forums of this sort were soon supplemented by more professionally focused gatherings of factory inspectors, city administrators, public foresters, city planners, juvenile court officials, social workers, and many others. The Paris-based Musée Social presented itself as an international clearing house for model legislative measures and legislative action across a broad social-economic domain. Legislative reference libraries, municipal research offices, and the new public bureaucracies contributed to the same end. By the early 20th century, there were not only influential university-based economists and political scientists with broadly transnational policy expertise (John Commons in the US, Paul Pic in France, or Alejandro Unsain in Argentina), but social policy associations (the Verein für Sozialpolitik in Germany, the Association for Social Policy in Japan, or the American Association for Labor Legislation in the US) designed to carry that knowledge into the public arena.

The movement of policy from these circulating fields of discussion into legislation was never certain. One conduit was through the circulation of model Bills, drawn on other nations' practices. The National Consumers' League, the National Civic Federation, and the American Association for Labor Legislation all played effectively on this mode in the early 20th-century United States. Another conduit was through the appointment of a high-level policy commission with a mandate to hear expert advice and testimony, which, at an impasse, often proved receptive to imported ideas that did not carry the baggage of already entrenched opinions and domestic interest configurations. Occasionally, a foreign expert would be recruited for the actual work of policy drafting, as was the case on parts of the Social Security Act of 1935 in the US and the Japanese civil code of 1898. At other times an appropriated policy idea would attach itself to the programme of a political party, often by moving through the informal transnational networks that bound the nation-centred political parties into larger affinities: liberal, labour, socialist, Catholic, and conservative. Haphazard as these systems were, they did a great deal of work. Paris-modelled city plans reshaped cities in the American Middle West, English-modelled factory inspectorates became the global norm, European-derived systems of indenture helped to scatter millions of Indian and Chinese labourers overseas.

Like all circuits of information and exchange, the circuits of transnational policy appropriation were bounded, both ideologically and spatially. The social insurance systems pioneered in Germany in the 1880s were quickly picked up in the neighbouring Austrian Empire; but it was another twenty years before they broke out of Central Europe or out of the profoundly anti-socialist ideological frame in which they had been devised.

Through the 1920s, Catholic Western Europe formed a distinctive social policy sphere, marked by indirect administration of social services and subvention of private charitable efforts, actively fostered by the Catholic centre parties. The nations of the South American cone formed a tightly associated social policy cluster, keenly observant of each other's actions. Transnational social policy networks are never, in the strict sense of the term, global; they cluster nations in bounded circuits of emulation and imagined comparability.

Where a nation broke out of its traditional circuit of exchange into another, it was an event of high political consequence. David Lloyd George and Winston Churchill's enthusiasm for German models of social efficiency in 1909–11, which brought the social insurance idea out of its central European orbit and grafted it onto democratic social politics, marked a major shift in British social politics. In the United States, the Progressive era was shaped in part by a new sense of affinity with other nations caught up in the processes of industrial capitalism and a new willingness to appropriate social policies from them. The New Deal, stocked with figures deeply versed in European social policy innovations, drew a critical part of its agenda and its energy from the same sources.

Prior to 1945, the most striking efforts to vault from one circuit of policy exchange to another occurred in Turkey and Japan. In both cases new regimes, turning on their pasts, undertook to compete with the great powers through programmes of wholesale policy importation. In Turkey between 1924 and 1938, Mustafa Kemal oversaw an ambitious project of defensive modernization. A new civil code was adopted from Switzerland, penal and labour codes from Italy, a commercial code from Germany, a five-year economic plan from the Soviet model; dress and the alphabet were westernized. 'The civilized world is far ahead of us', Mustafa Kemal explained in 1925. 'We have no choice but to catch up'.

The work of the Meiji oligarchs in Japan after 1870 was even more profound. The new regime literally began in a grand tour of the institutions of the US and Europe, instructing the caretaker government it left behind not to make any permanent moves until the group returned. It sent thousands of students abroad for study, and imported thousands of foreign experts to advise on the reform of its schools, its military institutions, its police and civil service, its factory and labour legislation, its systems of transportation and banking, its courts and its constitution. Eclectic in its early borrowings – Britain for its naval organization and postal system, the US (later France) for its primary schools, Paris for its police, Germany for its army and public universities – the regime ultimately systematized the methods of policy emulation with a thoroughness unmatched elsewhere. In the Meiji regime's race to modernize, insularity and hunger for international social knowledge, intense nationalism and wholesale transnational policy transfer were not antithetical. They were part and parcel of the same nation-building process.

Public policy transfers after 1945

Where the first part of the 20th century saw the formation of networks of transnational policy information and exchange, the second half of the century witnessed an explosive growth in their density, their global reach, and the number of subjects on which they touched. It also saw a radically changed environment in which they would work.

One of the most important of the new conditions was the emergence of the new global superpowers, each determined to shape the nations within its sphere of influence to its own template. Policy advisors from Washington and Moscow fanned out across the globe after 1945 with advice, transportable measures, and the soft- and hard-power means to make their ambitions count. Those efforts did not produce simple policy clones of the USSR and the US, even in regimes on the front lines of the Cold War such as North Vietnam, Cuba, Iran, and Guatemala. In India, where US Point IV agricultural agents and Ford Foundation development experts competed for influence with Russian five-year plan drafters, Nehru's government borrowed eclectically from both.

A second condition new to the post-1945 international system was the presence of much more intensively developed international organizations. The International Labour Office created in 1920 as a clearing house for information and best practices in labour legislation had been a forerunner. After 1945 agencies of this sort proliferated, particularly in the fields of health, population policies, and human rights policies – some of them organically connected with the

United Nations, others to the new agencies of European integration, or to the initiative of foundations or other non-government bodies. Outside the Soviet sphere, the period saw the growth of much denser international ties between university-based economists and social scientists. The rapid spread of Keynesian models of economic management in the 1950s and 1960s, like the counterswing toward neoliberal policies in the 1980s, were both dependent on communities of economists in Chile, New Delhi, or Mexico City trained in the same economic paradigms and, often, in the same American or British institutions.

A third major shift in the environment of policy making followed the global economic crisis of the 1970s. The International Monetary Fund, having lost its founding purpose with the advent of freely moving exchange rates, reconfigured itself as a general global lender, setting conditions of governmental economic performance as a criterion for recipients. The World Bank moved in the same direction after 1980, abandoning its earlier emphasis on project funding and instituting general structural adjustment loans, contingent on agreements on policy reforms: privatization of state enterprises, reduction of internal price subsidies, restructuring of tax revenue systems, all fields that had once been areas of high divergence and political choice. The winds of neoliberalism came to the developed European economies through ideological and political shifts rather than through loan contingencies. But as governments scrambled to deregulate and privatize, the advantages of models and forerunners were, as before, important. Édouard Balladur, who oversaw the breakup of state enterprises in late 1980s France, pitched his programme on the model of Margaret Thatcher's England; Jeffrey Sachs' 'shock treatment' scheme for post-Communist Poland was drawn straight from the playbook of anti-inflation measures in Bolivia; the World Bank's global campaign for social security privatization in the 1990s was promoted on the model of Singapore's experience.

Taken together, these post-1945 developments radically altered the balance between transnational policy supply and internal policy demand. In the 19th and early 20th century, information about other nations' policy experience was costly to accumulate; transnational policy proselytizers were relatively unorganized. When the Soviet systems in Eastern Europe and the former USSR disintegrated after 1989, by contrast, an extraordinary number of agents rushed into the void with advice, conditionalities, and prepackaged policy schemes. The Europe Union, the American Bar Foundation, the Ford and Soros Foundations, the World Bank and IMF, the German, French, and US governments were among the heaviest institutional players. The scale of policy transfers that ensued has probably never been equalled, as constitutional and administrative systems, structures of property and commercial law, human rights and social legislation were simultaneously redrawn under heavy transnational pressures. The results varied widely, but they clearly showed that by the end of the 20th century public policy export had become a major academic and government industry.

Even in these new contexts, the ways in which one nation's experience comes onto the political agenda of another retain aspects of the past. Formal policy comparisons, as Harold Wolman and others have shown, are much more rare than the kindling of a particular policy transfer idea in the minds of a few strategically placed policy entrepreneurs. Despite examples of general policy bandwagoning (the global rush toward privatization in the 1980s and 1990s, for example), policy makers typically single out only a few nations as appropriate policy sources. The persistence of the three welfare policy 'regimes' that Gøsta Esping-Andersen identified in 1990 – the 'liberal' welfare state policies of the US, Canada, and Australia, the 'corporatist' policies of Austria, France, Germany, and Italy, and the 'social-democratic' policies of the Scandinavian countries – attest to the continuing power of regionally and ideologically framed communities of emulation, norm setting and exchange. The experiments in authoritarian capitalism that emerged in the 1970s in Southeast Asia grew out of similar, regionally bounded circuits of policy exchange.

Transfer and transformation

Policy 'transfer', though a useful category, is a potentially misleading one. Like its synonyms in the policy studies literature – 'policy migration', 'policy imitation', 'cross-national lesson drawing', 'legal transplantation', and 'policy convergence' – it assumes that a measure designed in one country can be moved intact to another. Even in cases of close and conscious imitation, that is almost never the case. The very act of appropriation entails dynamics distinct from those that gave the policy its initial shape. Measures must be adjusted for different legal systems; they must be redesigned to fit within a different array of pre-existing institutions and pre-existing policy traditions; they must find advocates in civil society and within the government; the coalitions that make them possible must be remade anew. Uprooted from one context to another, they fail, they carry unexpected consequences, they flow into a myriad hybrid forms. Minimum wage proposals, introduced in the United States by early-20th-century social feminists directly inspired by their English counterparts, took a radically different form in the US than in England by the time they had moved into legislation; British feminists, in turn, had radically remade what they had borrowed from Australasia. The New Deal-leaning American officials who gave Japan a US-style labour disputes resolution Act thought a 'labour Bill of Rights', though it was the core of the US industrial relations system as far as American trade unionists were concerned, irrelevant to Japanese 'traditions'. The British National Insurance Act of 1911, designed, as its sponsors boasted, to bring a 'big slice of Bismarckianism' to England, was altered in virtually every detail from its German precedent.

Exact copying is very rare. Even where a statute or institution is transferred intact, experience quickly diverges. The real world of policy 'transfer' is made up of hybrids, adaptations, variations, pieces of pre-existing legislation grafted onto existing structures, syntheses of appropriated elements, altogether new policy vehicles attempting to produce effects admired elsewhere. It is here – not in some imagined movement of a policy parcel – that the continuous transnational circulation of models and policies, both voluntary and imposed, has done its real historical work.

Daniel T. Rodgers

Bibliography

Best J. (ed.) 2001. *How claims spread: cross-national diffusion of social problems.* New York: Aldine de Gruyter.

Jacoby W. 2000. *Imitation and politics: redesigning modern Germany.* Ithaca: Cornell University Press.

Miller J. 2003. 'A typology of legal transplants: using sociology, legal history, and Argentine examples to explain the transplant process', *American Journal of Comparative Law* 51, 4, 839–95.

Rodgers D. 1998. *Atlantic crossings: social politics in a progressive age.* Cambridge, MA: Harvard University Press.

Rose R. 1993. *Lesson-drawing in public policy.* Chatham, NJ: Chatham House.

Wedel J. 1998. *Collision and collusion: the strange case of Western aid to Eastern Europe, 1989–1998.* New York: St. Martin's Press.

Westney D. E. 1987. *Imitation and innovation: the transfer of Western organizational patterns to Meiji Japan.* Cambridge, MA: Harvard University Press.

Wolman H. 1992. 'Understanding cross national policy transfers: the case of Britain and the US', *Governance,* 5, 1, 27–45.

Related essays

1989; abolitionism; book and periodical exchange; city planning; *Code civil*; Commission on International Labour Legislation; convergence and divergence; developmental assistance; economics; empires and imperialism; epidemics; European Union (EU); fascism and anti-fascism; financial diplomacy; Ford Foundation; governance; governing science; health policy; higher education; intellectual elites; intellectual property rights; intergovernmental organizations; International Monetary Fund (IMF); international students; Japan; kindergarten; labour standards; language diplomacy; League of Nations Health Organization; League of Nations system; legal order; liberalism; medicine; modernity; museums; Muslim networks; nation and state; national accounting systems; neoliberalism; philanthropic foundations; philanthropy; police; population; Quesnay, Pierre; regions; socialism; statistics; taxation; technical assistance; trade agreements; United Nations Educational, Scientific and Cultural Organization (UNESCO) educational programmes; United Nations system; vaccination; Washington Consensus; welfare state; Westernization; women's movements; World Bank

Publishing

Publishing means to make a text public, consequently a publisher is a mediator between an author and his/her readers. This necessitates a certain amount of autonomy on the publisher's part, which explains why publishers have not always existed. If it is a well-known fact that printing processes and paper were invented in Asia, particularly in China, Korea and Japan at the beginning of the first millennium, Western countries are indebted to Gutenberg for gradually bringing to perfection the technique which was to revolutionize the communication system between people. It took more than three centuries before publishing properly speaking came into being in London, Leipzig and Paris before spreading to the colonies and throughout the world, including the Chinese Empire after 1850. In other words, it is when London became the world capital of the book at the end of the 18th century that the printer's role declined, the merchant thus leaving room for the mediator, the intermediary who would from then on introduce new talents and make the writer known by the public. This change did not take place without difficulty and Charles Dickens and Victor Hugo resisted the loss of their symbolic power, the sharing of the Holy Grail, yet did not succeed in preventing European publishers from turning their relationship with authors to their own profit.

It was still possible for Voltaire to despise his merchant-printer and for Tocqueville to be condescending to his. However, in a century in which the number of writers increased considerably and women of letters challenged their fellow-writers by confirming the right to be read and admired, the role of the publisher became essential from then on. Providing work for papermakers and printers who could not overdiversify their work because of their investments in steam machines, and having the distributors and booksellers under their control, publishers seized power at the very moment when international legislation on authors' rights was beginning to be enforced and when literary agents in Britain and in the United States, the authors' societies in France and the best-known writers in Germany endeavoured to regulate the market. The British copyright system would prevail throughout the British Empire and in the US, while the French legislation based on the distinction between inalienable property rights and untransferable perpetual moral rights was considered superior by the rest of the world. In spite of such differences, the figure of the publisher became a reality in all the developed countries. In the 19th and the 20th centuries, publishing companies and later conglomerates progressively replaced such a historical construction contemporaneous with the beginnings of European Romanticism. Here may lie the secret of the birth of publishing and the main reason for its takeoff.

In the 18th century, in London, the Stationers' Company registered and controlled the publication of books, and booksellers would gather and share the task of publishing. But around 1800, individualism prevailed, marking the beginning of publishing dynasties such as Longman, Routledge, Macmillan and others. In Germany, Brockhaus and Reclam dominated a strongly centralized publishing system, as in Italy, while in Paris, the capital of a nation state where competition between regions was limited to next to nothing, merchant printers of the Ancien Régime like Panckoucke or Didot had to accept the arrival of a completely regenerated profession represented by Curmer, Ladvocat, Gosselin, Charpentier and other Romantic publishers who allowed the consecration of poets such as Lamartine, Hugo and Vigny whose aura was similar to Byron's in his own country. At the same time, an important change took place, the novel taking precedence over poetry, storytelling over lyricism. In Britain, Walter Scott's fame soon became greater than Shelley's, causing emulation throughout Europe, in particular from young Balzac with the revolution of the serialized novel, the utmost symbol of the craze for reading – *Lesewut* in Germany – which took hold of the literate masses in European and American big cities around 1850. Continental publishers profiting largely from it could establish their power and, leaning on the prestige and even the cult surrounding Alexandre Dumas, Paul Féval, Frédéric Soulié in France, Charles Dickens and Wilkie Collins in England, and James Fenimore Cooper in the United States, they multiplied fiction series so as to bind their readers to the adventures of their heroes and transform them into wholehearted customers of their business. The success of these bestselling authors induced the increase of translations – or should we say adaptations – and allowed for a more and more international circulation of texts, in authorized or sometimes in pirated editions, though piracy was never limited to translated works and could concern all kinds of books.

Publishing houses in the 19th century

Born at the end of the 18th century and strengthened between 1800 and 1830, a publishing house has a certain number of strong characteristics. Created by the founders of the dynasty, such as W. H. Smith, Thomas Nelson, Friedrich Brockhaus, Philip Reclam, Louis Hachette or Pierre Larousse, it quickly developed before changing into a rationalized enterprise managed according to the principles of a large industrial company. Originally centred around the marketing of a leading genre, handbooks for travellers in the case of John Murray, Carl Baedeker or Adolphe Joanne, schoolbooks for Louis Hachette, Thomas Nelson or Fritz Payot, dictionaries for Friedrich Brockhaus, Pierre Larousse or Noah Webster, fiction for most of their colleagues, a publishing house progressively diversified its production in order to master the sector of general literature, school or university books and dictionaries or encyclopedias. To this end, the publisher availed himself of editors, or series managers who might be his sons or sons-in-law, according to the capitalistic system then flourishing, or of collaborators with strong symbolic capital such as academics, writers or authors of successful guidebooks like Alfred Joanne, the father of Hachette guidebooks. With the help of publishers' readers whose task was to check that the works published corresponded to what the company's trademark demanded, publishing companies soon standardized their productions so as to offer the reading public what it wanted in order to quench its thirst for reading.

Destined for circulating libraries in Britain, for *cabinets de lecture* and for *Leihbibliotheken* which lent their volumes to readers, or to bookshops which spread over the Continent and tried to reduce the price of novels so that people could have their own family libraries, books travelled more and more quickly and farther and farther away. Belonging to a specific series, books tended to become uniform, easily recognizable thanks to the cover colour and to the name of the firm, placed side by side with the author's name. Their formats, their prices, the number of pages and even the contents allowed customers to identify books even before they started reading them.

John Murray not only imposed the red colour of his handbooks for travellers as the symbol of guidebooks but established the rules of the genre. These were later on carefully imitated by the Koblenz printer Baedeker and the French Joanne before they dared to add their own personal touch to their model. Brockhaus's *Konversationslexicon* inspired numerous encyclopedias for the elite, and Alejandro Dumas, Pablo Féval and Eugenio Sue, as they were called in Spain and in Latin America, gave birth to very similar national literatures. Like Carolina Invernizio in Italy, Pérez Galdós in Spain indeed owed a lot to the French serial novelists, the publishers being originally responsible for these literary migrations, conceived at the start as investments to bring them profit.

Acting as innovating entrepreneurs is what distinguishes modern publishers from the mere booksellers or stationers of the past. To achieve this transformation, the publisher was compelled to thoroughly modify the logic inherent in the book economy and to turn the response to social demand into a strong dynamics of offer. An adept of Schumpeter's ideas before his time, always hard-working, watching out for technological or commercial innovations allowing him to be propelled ahead of his colleagues and to increase his market share, the new publisher incessantly endeavoured to be present in the life of the city. W. H. Smith was a pioneer of the diffusion of the press in the provinces thanks to the powerful locomotives he bought to carry newspapers at full speed throughout the British Isles. Yet it was his son who was to give the world the model of bookshops open to everyone, soon to become universal, when he set up the first railway bookstall at Euston Station in 1848. A new kind of series was then launched, such as numerous one-shilling Railway Libraries published by Longman, Chapman & Hall, Bentley, Routledge and other publishers of yellowbacks, to be imitated by Louis Hachette's Bibliothèque des Chemins de Fer which gave birth to other adaptations for the railway market and to the leisure industry, which itself anticipated 20th-century tourism. The appearance of literary agents is yet another sign of the evolution of publishing. When in 1858 Émile Aucante, George Sand's former secretary at Nohant, created the Agence Générale de la Littérature to serve as an intermediary between authors and publishers, he had no follower. The birth of literary agents, a permanent characteristic of English-speaking countries, actually took place in Great Britain with the first acknowledged literary agency created by A. P. Watt in 1875.

Company managers were very similar to the great captains of industry of their time. Publishers were however dual men, at once top-ranking merchants and intellectuals capable of speaking to writers as equals, turning publishing companies into houses in which to meet, to dine, to exchange ideas, information and projects. Till late in the 20th century, Macmillan's descendants boasted of this tradition, like Louis Hachette's grandsons, or Philip Reclam's, the founder in Germany of the Universal Bibliothek. Considered as respectable, even if they began to be accused of being first of all moneymakers, publishers could assume political responsibilities and aspire to the highest recognition. Ambroise Firmin-Didot was a member of Parliament in France, Paul Dupont a senator, and many of their British colleagues received prestigious decorations, ostentatiously proving to those they mixed with that they were not mere vulgar merchants. When they conceived their task as that of a schoolmaster educating the nation's masses like Thomas Nelson, they kept the horizon of expectation of their profession at a high level.

Publishing companies

After 1850, British publishing houses no longer had the lead. In Germany, though a decentralized state, the customs system known as Zollverein allowed for the constitution of a German book market that extended largely beyond the country's borders. In France, the Librairie Hachette was so dynamic that in 1919, the company made room for the Bank of Paris and the Netherlands on its board of directors, to help raise capital in order to face the challenges of the post-World War 1 period. In Germany, a similar evolution took place and in 1911 the Reclam publishing company conceived the first automatic dispensers of books. One million volumes were then sold per year through this new distribution system set up in every public place in 1913. This gives an idea of the distance then separating the mammoths of world publishing from the small structures created every year and desperately endeavouring to fight against their powerful and prosperous colleagues. In France, the Revue Blanche, the Mercure de France

and the Nouvelle Revue Française (NRF) managed to set up 'publishing counters', Gaston Gallimard taking over that of the NRF and making it the embryo of a prestigious publishing house.

Aware of their responsibilities at a time when the Berne Convention, signed in 1886, was beginning to unify authors' rights and literary property on an international scale, the major publishers decided ten years later to launch an international organization whose mission was to organize conferences and discuss how to solve the main problems of the time. A first meeting took place in Paris in June 1896, and Bergman, the chairman of the Börsenverein des Deutschen Buchhandels, Longman, the chairman of the Publishers' Association in the UK, Hetzel, the chairman of the French Cercle de la Librairie, as well as their Belgian, Dutch, Italian and Swiss counterparts, Cornélis-Lebègue, Belinfante, Vallardi and Payot, were appointed to an international commission responsible for the permanence of the Publishers' International Congress between two sessions. In 1901, a conference in Leipzig gave three professional periodicals, the Börsenblatt für den Deutschen Buchhandels for Germany, Switzerland, Austria, and Scandinavian countries, the Bibliographie de la France for France, Belgium, Italy, Spain and South America, and the Publishers' Circular for all English-speaking countries, the task of announcing the decisions of this international association. This was a way of asserting the predominance of German, French and British publishers over their colleagues throughout the world as well as ensuring the means of reinforcing the empires of the major publishing houses. When one examines the list of the delegates to these international conferences, one gets an idea of the overwhelming importance of publishing houses like Macmillan, Murray, Brockhaus or Hachette as well as the arrival in force of their American colleagues, Appleton, Harper and Putnam, the three managers of the American Publishers' Association.

For these huge English or Scottish companies selling books throughout the British Empire, for the German ones distributing their production in Northern and Eastern Europe, and for the French around the Mediterranean Sea as well as in South America, it was a far cry from the small publishing houses they originally were. Recruiting hundreds of authors in all kinds of sectors, endeavouring to have their books translated into the main languages of the world, put on the stage or adapted on the screen, these companies needed a strict management, an efficient division of labour and a high level of rationalization. If in those days as well as today, books had to be relatively speaking stereotyped, though no one could predict what kind would conquer the reading public, junior publishers and series directors had the responsibility of finding the best-adapted recipes and formulas to seduce the largest possible number of readers. With the arrival of mass culture in England, the United States and France, in the 1860s–80s, slightly later in Germany and the other developed countries on the Continent, the aim was clear: to offer workers and clerks their ration of dream and escapism which the cultural industry could provide for them in series and at a low price. Even before the arrival of paperbacks, with Penguin in London in 1935, Simon and Schuster in New York in 1939, Marabout in Verviers (Belgium) in 1949, and in France with Hachette in 1953, the number of copies printed – between 50,000 and 100,000 in the most successful series, such as Fayard's Livre Populaire launched in Paris in 1905 – marked the beginning of a new era, that of huge print runs.

The period of conglomerates

After 1960, the gigantic size of the dominant firms and oligopolies, perceived as a positive thing and not as a risk, led to the constitution of extremely powerful publishing companies in most countries throughout the world. In Scandinavia, Nordstedt, which began by publishing schoolbooks (like Hachette, Longman, Payot and Webster), dominated the market, just as in Italy, Mondadori, Einaudi and a few others were trying to become the region's leaders. On account of the need to meet regularly to exchange translation rights, the Frankfurt Book Fair soon became a major event, but the publishers on the east coast of the United States were eager to take advantage of the changes following World War 2 and to turn things to their profit. At this time the rapid movement of concentration taking place in European publishing companies further increased the power of companies like Bertelsmann, Hachette, Pearson, Reed Elsevier, Wolters Kluwer, Mondadori, Rizzoli Corriere della Sera, while in the United States, Houghton Mifflin in educational publishing, Random House in literature or the newly autonomous subsidiaries of British companies, HarperCollins or Macmillan, appeared as new major companies wishing to turn to their advantage the movement of world exchange and globalization which was then beginning despite the aloofness of Communist countries.

In the early 1960s, publishing took on a different aspect with the appearance in the world of the most profitable houses of industrial groups such as Westinghouse or Rank Xerox in the US. Taking place in a still national environment, with a few overlappings into neighbouring countries in the case of the English-Dutch groups Reed Elsevier and Wolters Kluwer, these mergings or strategic acquisitions allowed for large-scale economies which up-and-coming management controllers hoped to impose upon the newly reorganized groups. Numerous disappointments led some industrial companies to sell back their assets twenty years later, leading some financial groups, and later mutual and pension funds to enter this universe in order to modify its aspect radically. André Schiffrin's thunderous resignation from Pantheon Books and Random House in 1990 suddenly threw light on the radical mutation of international publishing. The publication of his book L'Édition sans frontières, first in French in 1999, translated into English the following year, and soon into about ten other languages, marked the beginning of a crossnational discussion about the nature of publishing and the risk of seeing it disappear.

While in the United States and in Great Britain powerful bookshop chains, Barnes & Noble, W. H. Smith, Blackwell and Waterstone's became decisive actors in the choice of books to be published, the diffusion and distribution of volumes played such an important part that for the first time in the history of publishing, these actors could influence publishers' decisions, a role assumed in the 19th century by British circulating libraries who could buy hundreds of copies of the same books as soon as they were morally acceptable and suited the taste of the reading public. Therefore compelled to think of the contents of their catalogue, of the sales of their leading series by hundreds of thousands of copies even before defining publishing policy, the publisher was induced more and more to choose the best-selling products well oiled with advertising. At the end of the last millennium, the next step taken by the media groups was to absorb the most prestigious publishing companies and made them parts of their empire, AOL Time Warner as early as 1998, Vivendi Universal two years later, News Corporation, Walt Disney, Viacom, Comcast and Bertelsmann, thus triggering off the planetary battle over educainment, a portmanteau word defining the limits of the two main markets of the 21st century, i.e. education and entertainment.

Vivendi Universal's thunderous bankruptcy in 2002 and the sale of its publishing subsidiary, Vivendi Universal Publishing, to Hachette Livre and Editis in 2004, the transfer of Warner Book Group to Hachette Livre in 2006, Bertelsmann's decision to focus on European book and press publishing and Walt Disney's difficulties led media groups to reconsider their strategies and modify their ambitions as regards book publishing. The development of online sales and the growing importance taken by the Internet deeply disrupted the prospects of the major media groups. A paradox which had so far remained invisible then appeared with greater acuity. The proportion of works originally written in English in the mass of translations grew continuously, passing from 40 per cent in 1980 to 60 per cent in 1995 in a market which was itself definitely growing throughout the world; yet at the same time the overall proportion of publications in this language, or rather in American English, fell from nearly 80 per cent to less than 40 per cent. This double inverted curve of exchanges or communication meant that the so-called peripheral languages, Mandarin Chinese, Hindi, and Arabic, were recovering the strength which was previously considered to have been definitely lost. In the face of such contradictions and unknown factors, which blur the future and forbid the building of castles in the air, conglomerates are hesitating, which probably explains the ceding of shares witnessed during the last few years to the benefit of groups more strictly concerned with book publishing like Hachette Livre, now Number One in Britain, Number Two or Three in the US and strongly present in Spanish-speaking countries; Pearson, still the world leader before Bertelsmann; Reed Elsevier, Wolters Kluwer, Mondadori, a subsidiary of Berlusconi's group, and a few others.

Today, no one can tell if the word 'publish' still means the same thing as it did between 1800 and 2000, and if the publisher is still a dual person, one foot strongly rooted in culture and intellectual life, and the other in marketing and business. As was the case for Vivendi Universal, mutual and pension funds are now controlling Pearson or Editis, Wendel Investissement's subsidiary, the strictly financial objectives imposed on the managers of their assets being not necessarily compatible with the production of prestigious catalogues demanding patience, taste, and sensibility, all the qualities which prevailed with the breakthrough of Pantheon Books, Gallimard, Faber and Faber, Feltrinelli and Rohwolt in the 20th century. The most pessimistic minds predict the death of publishing, unable to withstand this tendency which has gained further strength since 1998. Others explain that digitalizing and the Internet will in the long run provoke the disappearance of books and that e-ink and electronic paper will accelerate this decline. However, as the world undergoes such changes, there appear genuine new publishers every year who, from North to South, try to rekindle the flame, to give voice to authentic free and not formatted young authors, and this for the readers' greater happiness. Therefore it is not necessarily the end of the publisher's function, or the end of his or her historical cycle, and one can hope that professionals like Albert Wolff, Jacques Schiffrin, Gaston Gallimard, the Mondadori brothers or Giangiacomo Feltrinelli will have descendants in the 21st century.

Jean-Yves Mollier
with the assistance of Marie-Françoise Cachin

Bibliography

Barbier F. 1995. *L'empire du livre: le livre imprimé et la construction de l'Allemagne contemporaine (1815–1914)*. Paris: Cerf.

Griest G. L. 1970. *Mudie's Circulating Library and the Victorian novel*. Bloomington: Indiana University Press.

Mollier J. Y. 1999. *Louis Hachette (1800–1864): le fondateur d'un empire*. Paris: Fayard.

Olivero I. 1999. *L'invention de la collection*. Paris: IMEC.

Raven J. 'British publishing and bookselling: constraints and developments', in Michon J. and Mollier J. Y. (eds) 2001. *Les mutations du livre et de l'édition dans le monde du XVIIIe siècle à l'an 2000*. Québec: Les Presses de l'Université Laval; Paris: L'Harmattan, 19–30.

Schiffrin A. 2000. *The business of books*. London and New York: Verso.

Wilson C. 1985. *First with the news: the history of W. H. Smith, 1792–1972.* London: Jonathan Cape.

Wittman R. 1999. *Geschichte des deutschen Buchhandels.* Munich: Beck.

Related essays

Bible; children's literature; comics; corporations; cultural capitals; fashion; information economy; intellectual property rights; international non-governmental organizations (INGOs); investment; Kessler, Harry von; language; libraries; literature; management; *modernismo*; Romanticism; tourism; translation; wine

Bible

The transnational character of the Christian Bible (the Old Testament and the New Testament in its Roman Catholic, Orthodox and Protestant forms) is based on two contradictory, but at the same time complementary phenomena: on the one hand, the Christian Holy Scriptures created a worldwide cultural common ground by spreading one single creed and one single sacred narrative; on the other hand, through its translation into numerous languages, dialects and tribal tongues – not only worldwide but also within specific nations and societies – it conserved and often encouraged cultural pluralism.

The Bible is the Holy Scripture of c. 2.1 billion believers. In 1600 the Bible, or a portion of it, was translated into 45 languages; during the 19th century, its expansion became a worldwide phenomenon: early in the century, it was translated into 125 languages, in the second half the number increased to 205, in 1904 to 378. In 2003 the whole Bible existed in 405 languages, the New Testament in 1,034, and at least one book of the Scriptures in 864 languages and dialects, spoken by 97 per cent of the world's population. Moreover, it is the most circulated book in history.

The Bible was a vital instrument in the expansion of Christianity in Europe, and in shaping the nature of its different churches. In its vernacular translations of the 15th and 16th centuries, it fostered the creation and development of national languages and of national identities in Europe. Though the spread of the Bible in non-European languages began long before the heydays of European colonialism and imperialism, it was an integral part of the spread of the Christian faith as a result of the Christian missionary enterprise and the work of the various European and American Bible Societies outside Europe (for example: the British and Foreign Bible Society produced biblical texts in 700 languages and dialects and distributed over 550 millions copies all over the world; the Bible Society in China has distributed more than 300 million copies since 1823), which were driven by the zeal to spread the 'Word of God' and to convert non-European societies to Christianity. Since Christianity is essentially a Bible-centred religion, it was essential to make the book accessible – orally (through public worship, preaching, sermons and teaching) or in writing. As a result, many individuals and organized initiatives were involved during the 19th century in the (often heroic) enterprise of translating the Bible into numerous languages and dialects. Outside Europe, different societies faced various difficulties in the process of assimilating the Bible into their own vernacular and indigenous cultures and languages; in some cases – mainly in oral cultures with a spoken tongue only – the translation was the driving force behind the initiatives to create distinct letter scripts (alphabets), vocabularies and grammatical constructions, which resulted in spreading literacy and fostering a process of nation building.

With the expansion of European power and influence outside Europe from the mid 19th century, Christian missionary agencies were able to act more freely than before; this activity resulted in converting whole nations, or in creating minority communities of Christian believers. However, the transnational character of the Bible is based on more than its being a book of faith. It is par excellence a history of global diffusion and transmission, on the one hand, and on the other, of modes of reception of major religious and cultural assets. Goethe's statement that the Bible 'surpasses every other book in offering material for reflection and opportunity for meditation on human affairs', can be seen as showing a Christian and a Eurocentric sense of superiority and supremacy and as an announcement for the Bible's role as a spiritual tool in the service of the West's 'civilizing mission', i.e., imperialism. However, it also reflects the fact that a multitudinous variety of human societies accept the book and its sacred narrative not only as containing religious doctrine, dogmas, and articles of faith, but also as containing a multilateral repertoire of insights about the human condition and behaviour, moral dicta, paragons and paradigms; in other words, as both a meta-text and as a 'semantic reservoir' for perceptions of the world and for value judgments. Thus, the history of the Bible is also about the modes and ways the recipient societies encountered alien culture, absorbing it into their 'indigenous' (a process of indigenization) worldviews and value systems – or rejecting it – incorporating the meaning of biblical words, idioms, concepts and messages into their own system of values and thought. This was made possible only after the Bible had been translated into their language.

Yaacov Shavit

Bibliography
The Oxford Companion to the Bible. 1993, 763–78.
Batalden S., Cann, K. and Dean J. (eds) 2004. Sowing the world: the cultural impact of the British and Foreign Bible Society 1804–2004. Sheffield: Phoenix.
Nida E. A. (ed.) 1972. The Book of Thousand Languages. Revised edition.
London and New York: United Bible Societies.
Sanneh L. 1989. Translating the message – the missionary impact on culture. Maryknoll: Orbis.

Related essays
Christianity; Communist Manifesto; empires and imperialism; evangelicalism; Koran; language; Little Red Book; missionaries; nation and state; publishing; religion; The Wretched of the Earth; translation

Pugwash Conferences See **Disarmament**

Q

Quesnay, Pierre See **Financial diplomacy**

R

Race-mixing

Race-mixing refers to the establishment of sexual relationships that cut cross the boundaries of race and culture; historically such relationships have been formed between peoples from a wide variety of racial backgrounds, but frequently the historical and theoretical examinations of mixing have focused on the relationships formed between European men and non-European women.

One of the most notable demographic and cultural outcomes of movement of peoples across national and civilizational borders was the establishment of cross-cultural affective relationships, relationships that not only produced children of mixed cultural heritage but in many historical locations resulted in the emergence of an identifiable 'mixed race' community. Many such communities were created during the early modern period, when European empires rapidly extended and then consolidated their presence in the Americas, the Caribbean, Asia, the Pacific and southern Africa. At this stage, imperial endeavour was an overwhelming male endeavour and European men who worked in the colonies frequently established sexual relationships with local women, producing children that frequently occupied an awkward demographic and social space between the worlds of the colonizer and the colonized. The new wave of empire building in the late 19th century, which largely focused on Africa, parts of the central Pacific, and Southeast Asia, also produced new mixed-race communities which frequently complicated the cultural terrain of these emergent colonial societies. It is impossible to understand the culture and politics of interracial sexuality since 1850 without an appreciation of how these longer histories of migration and empire building shaped demography and cross-cultural perceptions in the modern age.

The emergence of mixed-race communities

Distinctive mixed-race communities were consolidated in those tropical colonies where small European populations oversaw plantations, directed trade, and implemented colonial policy. This was particularly the case in colonies established by Spain and Portugal in the Americas, where only a small cadre of Europeans, primarily men, exercised their authority over much larger populations of indigenous peoples and African slaves. Within these imperial contexts, a variety of sexual relationships connected the European, African, and indigenous populations, producing a range of mixed-race children. These children were classified into quickly developing racial typologies, typologies that were invested with considerable political, economic, and social significance. In New Spain, an elaborate *casta* (lineage) system classified the population on the basis of whether their parents were *peninsulares* (individuals born in Europe), *criollos* (people of European parentage born in the 'New World'), *indios* (indigenous people, 'Indians'), or *negros* (people of African ancestry). A child born to an *indio-peninsular* couple was defined as a *mestizo*, the children produced by a relationship between a *peninsular* and a *negro* was identified as a *mulatto*, while the offspring of a *indio-negro* couple was dubbed a *zambo*. The inequalities of the *casta* system were an important factor in the Mexican War of Independence (1810–21), but these categories have been durable, remaining culturally significant into the 20th century.

In colonial South Asia, the small population of merchants, administrators, and soldiers from various European nations also established sexual relationships and founded families with women from a variety of local communities. These cross-racial sexual relationships were very common until the close of the 18th century, when hardening religious and political ideologies encouraged Europeans to distance themselves. Unlike Spanish America, no overarching and enduring elaborate scheme of racial classification was developed. In fact, from the 17th century through to the 20th century, people of mixed-race ancestry as well as colonial authorities have debated the best name or term to be applied to this community. During the 16th century, Portuguese writers frequently used the racial language developed in the Iberian New World colonies, dubbing the mixed-race people of India *mestizo*, while for most of the 19th century the preferred term in British India was 'Eurasian', an appellation overshadowed (if not vanquished) by the rising popularity of 'Anglo-Indian' from the 1890s. This mixed-race community became increasingly self-contained, in part because both Britons and Hindus were reluctant to marry

Eurasians and in part because the community was economically successful and had fortified its identity through the establishment of its own schools, social clubs, and churches. Eurasians played a significant role in the British Raj, being over-represented in the forestry, post and telegraph, and railway departments. Similarly, in Burma, the Anglo-Burmese were a prominent part of the colonial cultural landscape, playing an especially prominent role in the commercial and political life of Rangoon and the hill-station of Maymyo.

Race-mixing was also pivotal in the dynamics of resource expropriation and settler colonialism. On the far-flung frontiers of empires, establishing relationships with local women not only enabled European traders, sealers, and whalers to gain knowledge about the availability of resources and the patterns of local tribal politics, but in many cases it was a precondition for their operation. In southern New Zealand, for example, the whaler John Howell was only able to establish a whaling station at Aparima (Riverton) once he finally assented to marrying a high-ranking local woman from the Kati Mamoe iwi (tribe) named Kohikohi. This marriage not only enabled Howell to set up his whaling operation, but also gave him access to a large amount of land in the surrounding district. At the same time, marriage incorporated Howell into the indigenous social order and meant that the children produced out of the marriage were firmly located within the genealogical relationships that defined rights and identity within the Maori world. This type of relationship was extremely common in southern New Zealand as the Kati Mamoe and Kai Tahu iwi used intermarriage to access new technologies and as a strategy to manage cross-cultural relationships. While the rate of intermarriage was very high in this particular locale, similar patterns of cross-racial sexual relationships and family formation emerged in much of the Pacific and in parts of North America as indigenous and 'half-caste' women became the key enabling intermediaries in sealing, whaling, and the fur trade. Because of their familiarity with two cultural and linguistic worlds, people of mixed ancestry frequently played a range of important roles as cultural brokers, serving as guides, sources of military and commercial intelligence, translators and diplomats on the edges of empires. In some instances, mixed-race individuals and families were able to exploit their culturally ambivalent position, gaining wealth, status and access to resources; but often their position in between cultures was fraught and they enjoyed the trust of neither cultural group to which they could claim to belong. And with time their influence within these colonial orders was eroded. This marginalization not only reflected the growing numbers of white women who ventured out to imperial frontiers during the 19th century, but also was a consequence of the growth of settler populations as a whole, the consolidation of colonial market economies, and the increasing capacity of colonial states. These forces coalesced to circumscribe and eventually close down the important economic and political spaces that mixed-race peoples had earlier operated within.

In many contexts, as colonialism progressed 'mixed people' were also increasingly identified as problematic by some colonized leaders and by nationalist movements. In the United States, during the 19th and early 20th centuries many Americans of European ancestry believed that Native American men were 'improved' and 'uplifted' if they married middle-class white women, but at the same time questioned the morality of white males who established relationships with Native American women (who were pejoratively called 'squaw men'). Indigenous men also were increasingly anxious about these cross-racial relationships established by their kinswomen. Within the matrilineal Cherokee nation, the tribal council passed a series of laws during the 19th century that increasingly restricted the marriage choices of Cherokee women in light of fears that white men were establishing relationships to access land and other resources. At the same time, the council constructed an even harsher legal and punitive regime designed to prevent sexual contact between Cherokee women and blacks, both free and unfree. In late-19th-century New Zealand, some Maori were concerned with interracial relationships and the ways in which white men who married into Maori communities were alienating traditional Maori land. A few decades later, other Maori leaders and Maori-dominated reform groups sought to prevent sexual contact between Maori women and 'Hindoos' and 'Chinese' market gardeners who were identified as a serious threat to Maori material and cultural advancement. In colonial South Asia, many local people distanced themselves from Eurasians not only because most Hindus saw marriage with Eurasians as a violation of caste-based practices but also because many South Asians were wary of the Eurasian community's loyalty to the Raj and its emotional investment in British culture. In the 20th century, the dominant strand of Indian nationalism remained firmly rooted in the language and symbols of Hinduism and, with time, the right wing of the nationalist movement also came under the sway of European fascist ideologies: just as these ideologies excluded Muslims from the imagined national community, there was also no space for people of mixed race who were seen as having little or no attachment to 'mother India'.

Debating the consequences of intermarriage

Imperial powers had long expressed anxieties over sexual relationships that crossed the lines of race and culture. The *Lusiad*, the 16th-century Portuguese epic, imagined the offspring of a marriage between an Indian woman and Portuguese man as a hideous and deformed two-headed, horned monster. At the same time, the Dutch traveller Jan Huyghen van Linschoten argued that the Portuguese men settled in Goa were physically weakened and prone to a variety of illnesses because of their sexual contact with local women. Such arguments stand at the heart of a long tradition within European thought that equated interracial sex with monstrosity, physical deterioration, and cultural decline. Yet, in certain contexts, some Europeans extolled the virtues of intermarriage and the strengths produced by hybridity. In the late 19th century, when many imperial administrators were worrying over the 'half-caste problem' at the margins of the British empire, some British intellectuals and nationalists were arguing that the mixture of Celtic, Saxon, Danish and Norman blood underpinned the strength and capacity of the British nation. In celebrating the status of Britons as 'a mongrel breed and a hybrid race', these British writers were marking their nation off from their European counterparts, especially German nationalists who were celebrating the supposedly homogeneous Teutonic heritage that underwrote the expansion of Prussian power and the consolidation of the German empire.

A particularly long-running debate over the fertility of interracial relationships emerged out of these early modern anxieties. Most importantly, from the 1840s much of the energy of the emergent discipline of anthropology focused on the question of interracial sexuality because it offered a crucial window on the fundamental question of whether humanity was a unified population (monogenism) or whether racial differences divided humanity into fundamental types or even distinct species (polygenism). Polygenists argued that interracial relationships tended not to produce viable pregnancies and in the long term resulted in population decline. Louis Agassiz, the leading Swiss-American scientist, became an influential exponent of polygenism after he settled in the United States in 1846, while similar arguments were championed by the Scottish anthropologist Robert Knox in the United Kingdom. While such contentions were ultimately undercut by demographic data that revealed that there were no significant connections between intermarriage and fertility as well as by methodological shifts within the sciences (especially anthropology), 20th-century racial science drew heavily upon this Victorian heritage. In the 1920s and 1930s, eugenic movements across the globe identified interracial relationships, along with mental illness, physical disability, and large working-class families, as major obstacles to social advancement, obstacles that states could overcome through a range of policy innovations and scientific interventions (including sterilization). These arguments found fertile soil in Germany, where there were long-standing anxieties about population decline. During the 1890s the eugenicist Alfred Ploetz had first elaborated the notion of *Rassenhygiene* (racial hygiene). Ploetz's eugenic theories were designed to arrest Germany's declining birth rate while simultaneously limiting reproduction by people who were disabled or mentally ill; while he was critical of anti-Semitism in the 1890s, his pioneering work became an important element of later Nazi understandings of race and population. Ploetz's notion was elaborated into an explicitly anti-miscegenationist form of racial science by his brother-in-law and fellow eugenicist Ernst Rüdin. Rüdin warned against the cultural effects of de-Nordicization and the culturally corrosive results of intermarriage. Such arguments underpinned the campaign against the so-called 'Rhineland Bastards', the mixed-race children produced out of the relationships between European mothers and black soldiers. In *Mein Kampf*, Adolf Hitler railed against these relationships which he saw as contaminating European blood and leading to Europe becoming 'negrified'. In 1937, under the supervision of the eugenicist Eugen Fischer, the Nazi state arrested and forcibly sterilized over 400 Germans of mixed-race parentage. By this stage, the tight connections between race and citizenship at the heart of the Nazi regime had been secured by the Nuremberg Laws that were passed in 1935, prohibiting intermarriage between pure Germans and Jews and non-Europeans. Hitler believed that it was racial mixing that had undercut all great civilizations and the 'adulteration of the blood and racial deterioration' was a great threat to Germany's future, a threat that had to be rebuffed by the formulation of a set of state practices that would defend the racial integrity of the German people. These beliefs underwrote the Nazis' genocidal campaigns to ensure the purity of Aryan Germans through the destruction of other populations that might contaminate the German body politic.

Managing mixing

The genocidal policies of Nazi Germany are the most potent demonstration that race-mixing was not just a scientific question, but a 'problem' for modern states which have sought to exercise a considerable degree of control over both the ethnic compositions of their populations and the ways in which their citizenry imagined the national community. Modern states have managed cross-racial relationships and their offspring in a wide variety of ways.

In South Asia, the end of imperial rule raised important questions about the future of mixed-race communities who had often been criticized by nationalist leaders. The independence of India was unsettling for the Eurasian or Anglo-Indian community given both its political and cultural investment in the Raj. Many people of mixed-race heritage left India in the 1940s and 1950s, settling in the United Kingdom or in British settler colonies like Australia. Conversely, Anglo-Burmans initially exhibited a strong desire to remain in Burma as that nation progressed towards independence in the mid 1940s, but the assassinations and unrest of 1948 encouraged many Anglo-Burmans to follow the path of Anglo-Indians and relocate to Britain or Australasia. Following India's independence in 1947, the Anglo-Indian leader Frank Anthony secured a guarantee from Prime Minister Jawaharlal Nehru that

the Anglo-Indian community could nominate two representatives to the Lok Sabha, the lower house of the Indian parliament. The Indian government granted the Anglo-Indian community the kinds of protections extended to other minority communities, including the right of the community to maintain their own schools and the recognition of English as the community's official language. Despite this political protection, this formerly large and culturally robust community has dwindled in both its demographic and political significance, being overshadowed by other minority groups such as native Christians and Sikhs and dwarfed by India's Muslim and Hindu populations. Demographic decline and migration have essentially resolved the 'mixed-race problem' in South Asia.

In Central and South America, however, race-mixing profoundly shaped the demographic makeup of the nation states that emerged in the wake of the revolutions that rewrote the region's political map in the early 19th century. Within the region, the building of nations as 'imagined communities' could not rest on any notion of a unified ethnic, racial or cultural heritage. The mixture of 'cultures' and 'races' did not undercut or collapse national boundaries; instead, the notion of mestizaje (mixture) has been a crucial element in the ideologies and processes of nation building. In the 1920s, the Mexican writer and politician José Vasconcelos Calderón, for example, argued that the Mexican nation was essentially mestizo, an argument that resonated throughout Latin America.

In many ways, it is Brazil that best exemplifies the complexity of Latin America's racial landscape and the ways in which race has been managed within the continent. Racial identification in 20th-century Brazil was more complicated and fluid than in any other nation state. At one level, this reflected the demographic patchwork produced out of both intermarriage and migration. From the 1870s through to the 1950s, some 5 million migrants were attracted to Brazil from Europe (especially Italy, Spain, Portugal, and Poland), the Middle East (Lebanon and Syria), and Japan. While many of these migrants married within their own ethnic group, many others married out into one or other of Brazil's established and very heterogeneous communities, adding further layers to the nation's mixedness. Within this racial landscape racial identity is primarily defined through appearance as individuals are placed on a complex spectrum of racial identity on the basis of their skin colour, hair, physique, and facial features. The Brazilian state has recognized and accommodated itself to this difference, allowing individuals to define their own racial identity through the census, a practice that has seen over a hundred different racial categories in regular use by the Brazilian state. Recent research has in fact recorded over 490 terms defining racial identity within Brazilian culture. While Brazilian popular culture celebrates mixedness as a central feature of the social order and the Brazilian state actively supported 'miscegenation' as an instrument for social and economic advancement for much of the 20th century, marked racial disparities remain. Brazilians with significant African ancestry enjoy less access to education, healthcare and sanitation, and conversely the Brazilian state privileges white migration. Recently the Brazilian state has begun to address these racial inequalities by introducing affirmative-action legislation aimed at advancing the well-being the nation's black population. These initiatives that rest on the identification of a 'black' population and the use of quotas, however, are promoting a simplification and hardening of racial categories.

The anxieties over blackness that can be found even within Brazil's 'racial democracy' have been at the heart of many states' attempts to regulate interracial sexual relationships. In the United States, for example, it is striking that there was much greater anxiety over interracial connections between whites and blacks than between whites and Native Americans. Where some whites saw Native Americans as suitable marriage partners, the possibility of sexual relationships between whites and African Americans, especially between white women and black men, caused great anxiety. In the late 19th and early 20th centuries, most American states passed laws that policed these racial boundaries, boundaries that were also shored up by racist vigilante groups such as the Ku Klux Klan and through the lynching of African American men suspected of making sexual advances to white women. From the 1960s, many of these state laws were dismantled under pressure from civil rights activists. In many contexts, however, whites remain anxious about the consequences of sexual relationships with African Americans, in part because the state's

'one drop' rule identifies the offspring of such relationships as black. Conversely, the generally inclusive response of African Americans to the offspring of mixed-race relationships echoes the one-drop rule, while at the same time maximizing the size of the African American community, which is of considerable political importance given the centrality of racial demographics within a democratic political system.

In Australia, the politics of sexual relationships between the descendants of white colonists and the indigenous peoples have been fraught, in part because Aborigines are understood as being both black and indigenous. Interracial sexual relationships were relatively common, if frequently unacknowledged, on the colonial frontier, but by the late 19th century, 'whiteness' had been consolidated as an integral element in settler self-identity and political discourse. While the white men who formed sexual relationships with Aboriginal women were viewed with suspicion by 'respectable' whites, there was also a widespread belief that 'white blood' would elevate and modernize Aborigines. By the early 20th century, a simplified three-tiered system was used by the state to define mixed-race people: they were half-caste, quadroon and octoroon. People with less than one-eighth of Aboriginal blood were considered white. This set of racial typologies suggested that indigeneity and/or blackness could ultimately be erased through intermarriage and cultural absorption of Aborigines into the dominant white population. However, this process of absorption could only succeed if Aborigines were also exposed to the features of 'modern civilization', so successive governments adopted a policy of removal. Children with some quantum of 'white blood' born to Aboriginal mothers were rehoused by the state with white families in an effort to 'civilize' them and to ultimately erase any cultural trace of their Aboriginality.

In both the United States and Australia the legislation that governed interracial sexual relationships and their outcomes has been dismantled, reflecting both a strong sense of what the limits of state power should be and a recognition that migration, urbanization, and demographic diversity have meant that interracial sexual relationships have become a common feature of the global order. Nevertheless, in some nations the politics of sexuality and cultural reproduction across the lines of ethnicity, race, and religion are still tightly regulated. Debates over sex, religion, and ethnicity have, for example, also been a notable feature of Israel's political landscape. The boundaries of Jewish cultural and religious identity have been tightly policed by the Chief Rabbinate of Israel, which insists that halakhic Jews (that is, converts to Judaism or individuals with Jewish mothers) cannot legitimately marry non-Jews or individuals who claim Jewish identity based solely on their paternal 'bloodlines'. These prohibitions are based on an individual's spiritual genealogy and not explicitly on race or ethnicity, but in effect they operate as a powerful deterrent against marriage across ethnic and racial lines. While these restrictions are unusual, they remind us of the political and cultural significance that most human communities in history have attached to sexuality, marriage and reproduction. Although many states have relaxed the policies that formally constrained interrelationships, in most societies the intersections between race and sexuality are still fraught: for many individuals and families, boundary crossing remains a risky business.

It is certainly now possible to think about interracial sexuality as an important feature of global cultures and, indeed, these relationships have become central to the ways in which scholars in the humanities and social sciences conceptualize postcolonial societies and the culture of globalization. Creolization, mestizaje, and hybridity have all been reworked into heuristic devices that are used to illuminate the processes of mixing, adaptation, and synthesis that shape language, social practice, and artistic expression in our mobile, mixed-up world.

Tony Ballantyne

Bibliography

Anderson A. 1991. *Race against time: the early Maori-Pakeha families and the development of the mixed-race population in southern New Zealand*. Dunedin: Hocken Library.

Ballantyne T. and A. Burton (eds) 2005. *Bodies in contact: rethinking colonial encounters in world history*. Durham, NC: Duke University Press.

Caplan C. 2001. *Children of colonialism: Anglo-Indians in a postcolonial world*. Oxford: Berg.

Ellinghaus K. 2002. 'Margins of acceptability: class, education, and interracial marriage in Australia and North America', *Frontiers: A Journal of Women Studies*, 23, 3, 55–75.

Hodes M. 1999. *Sex, love, race: crossing boundaries in North American history*. New York: New York University Press.

Stoler A. L. 2006. *Haunted by empire: geographies of intimacy in North American history*. Durham, NC: Duke University Press.

Van Kirk S. 1983. *Many tender ties: women in fur-trade society, 1670–1870*. Norman: University of Oklahoma Press.

Yarbrough F. 2004. 'Legislating women's sexuality: Cherokee marriage laws in the 19th century', *Journal of Social History*, 38, 2, 385–406.

Related essays
adoption; antisemitism; Chinese Diaspora; decolonization; diasporas; empire and migration; empires and imperialism; ethnicity and race; eugenics; femininity; marriage; nation and state; Nazism; pidgins and creoles; population; sexuality and migration; Westernization; white men's countries; White Slavery

Race and ethnicity See Ethnicity and race

Radio

The discovery of radiotelegraphy, the wireless transmission of signals on electromagnetic waves, gave rise to numerous inventions and innovations in the field of wireless communication usually referred to as radio. The complex and long-lasting innovation process of a technology that enabled mankind to 'speak through the ether' was shaped by ongoing scientific investigations into the nature of electromagnetic radiation, industrial patterns of production and commercialization of radio components and sets, and by various forms of political instrumentalization and creative cultural appropriation of radio as means of mass communication. This article concentrates on the crucial innovations of radio technology both on the transmitter and on the receiver side, emphasizing the role of radio as a transnational phenomenon of first importance. From the earliest experiments on wireless telegraphy and telephony to the transistor radio and podcasting, innovations in radio technology have challenged the authority of the political regimes of nation states and their attempts to control the free flow of information.

It was the British physicist James Clerk Maxwell (1831–79) who in 1873 made a theoretical prediction of the existence of invisible radiant energy similar to light. Thirteen years later, the German physicist Heinrich Hertz (1857–94) proved Maxwell's theory by generating and detecting radio waves and measuring their wavelengths. Hertz's name, abbreviated Hz, has been adopted internationally as the standard way to indicate the frequency of radio waves. Hertz's experiments launched a phase of intense research on both the physical nature and the practical use of radio waves for the transmission of sound and vision. Inventors in many countries each claimed to have been the 'inventor' of wireless transmission of information. But in fact the radical innovation called radio telegraphy was not the brainchild of a single genius, but the result of numerous parallel inventions based both on a common ground of shared scientific and on individually acquired tacit knowledge. As is the case for nearly all great innovations in communication technologies, the myth of the single inventor is the result of nationalistic narratives in search of their modernist heroes. But rather than actually explaining the complex interplay of various historical actors involved in the transnational framework of the radio innovation process, these stories point much more to the prominent role played by scientific discoveries and technical inventions in the mythical construction of the 'modern world'.

Before the invention of broadcasting after World War I, radio was designed as an interactive point-to-point communication system, enabling the wireless transmission and reception of coded information (wireless telegraphy), speech (wireless telephony) or recorded sound. It is the name of the Italian inventor-entrepreneur Guglielmo Marconi (1874–1937) that is most closely associated with the first convincing demonstration of the commercial potential of radio technology as an alternative to the telegraph system based on transnational cable links. While most of the scientists working on radio had little or no interest in the commercial possibilities of wireless, Marconi was stirred by the possibility of making wireless communication a practical reality. Till the formation of the Radio Corporation of America (RCA) in 1919, Marconi succeeded in establishing a dominant position in the young radio industry by gaining possession of many principal patents in wireless technology and improving the practical usability of wireless technology for commercial ends. Marconi concentrated on the development of wireless telegraphy for ship-to-ship and ship-to-shore communication, thereby demonstrating the practicability of long-distance radio communications for military and mercantile purposes. Although it took nearly a decade before Marconi's investments paid off, he can be portrayed as a classic 'entrepreneur'. As Rupert MacLaurin states in his fundamental study *Invention and innovation in the radio industry*: 'Marconi's contribution to the commercialization of wireless made him more important as an innovator than as an inventor' (MacLaurin 1949, 43).

Marconi was not the only one to foresee the potential of the new medium. Competition developed from different sides, especially from Germany (Telefunken) and the United States (American De Forest Wireless Telegraph Company and National Electric Signaling Company, NESCO). But it was not until the sinking of *The Republic* in 1909 and the *The Titanic* in 1912 that the practical importance of wireless communication for safety of life at sea won dramatic public attention and led to a series of laws passed in all main maritime countries requiring all ships above a certain size to carry wireless. This legislation and – to an even greater extent – the military use of wireless technology during the First World War gave radio a substantial boost. The interwar period was marked by three fundamental changes in the radio landscape: firstly, the invention of broadcasting and the rise of radio as a mass medium; secondly, the establishment of international bodies to plan and control the airwaves, which were inexorably extending around the globe; thirdly, the emergence of a small group of powerful firms, investing in large-scale research and owning the most important patents.

Already before the war, radio had become a widespread hobby, especially amongst men and boys. The fascination of receiving and sending meaningful electromagnetic signals through the air was shared by a steadily growing number of radio hams or amateurs, and the introduction of crystal detectors inaugurated a 'democratization of wireless' (Douglas 2004, 196), transforming the ether into a transnational medium for intercultural communication. With the discovery of the worldwide coverage of shortwave propagation by the mid-1920s, radio inaugurated the age of globalization in telecommunications. While the telegraph and telephone cable networks had created a transnational infrastructure linking the industrialized and colonial empires of the world, shortwave radio offered opportunities for a democratized medial participation beyond state-owned, government or industry-controlled networks. Despite the fact that radio amateurs – in the modern sense of the word – have become a diasporic user community compared to broadcast radio, they are still a very lively, globally operating group, exploring the possibilities of radio technology as an interactive medium for the promotion of mutual understanding and learning.

But shortwave radio did not only open up the possibility of peaceful uses. It became the backbone for the propagandistic instrumentalization of radio before, during, and after the Second World War. The transnational nature of shortwave made it the favourite tool for political propaganda during the Cold War. While the major broadcasting institutions established foreign or world service programs for shortwave distribution before the Second World War, the postwar era saw the installation of shortwave stations serving purely as propagandistic weapons in the ideological confrontation between the West and the East (Radio Liberty, Radio Free Europe and The Voice of America are the most prominent American examples). Despite the fact that the United Nations adopted a resolution in 1972 that declared systematic distortion (jamming) of the frequencies a violation of human rights, the jamming of Western broadcasts was the Eastern bloc's defence strategy against 'imperialistic radio aggressions'.

Parallel to the emergence of broadcasting and the rise of radio as a popular medium for the education, information and entertainment of the masses, radio developed into a strategic and commercial business. Both in the United States and in Europe, the big electrical corporations which for years had been dominating the market for telephone and telegraph equipment had to meet the public demand for cheap (mass-produced) and easy to handle radio sets. As MacLaurin (1949) and Griset (1995) have shown, a few global players such as Marconi, Telefunken, Compagnie Générale de Télégraphie Sans Fil (CSF) and RCA succeeded in building strategic coalitions and in 1921 formed the Commercial Radio International Committee, known as the AEFG Consortium (America, England, France, Germany Consortium). Based on patent cross-licensing and the allotment of spheres of exploitation, they ensured cost recovery for the large research investments in the new field of radio electronics, especially in the development of powerful transmission tubes and reception valves for the heterodyne (superhet) receiver.

While these big corporations in fact dominated the radio component market, thousands of small and medium-sized enterprises started producing radio sets while paying royalties to one of the big four. But it was these 'second movers' who had an innovative impact on the booming radio market by creating new radio designs meeting the practical needs and aesthetic norms of a domesticated technology. The step-by-step 'taming' of the radio receiver from an electrical device that only a skilled amateur could operate into a piece of domestic furniture marked the crucial transition from amateur to mass medium. From the perspective of innovation theory, design played a crucial role as the mediating interface between the hidden technical interior of the apparatus and the user-friendly cover or 'cabinet'. Central steps in this process were the embedding of previously exposed components into a cabinet, the reduction of tuning knobs and the integration of the electrodynamic loudspeaker into the cabinet. These changes in the design of radio cabinets can be read as gender scripts too, as material expressions of new means for use and consumption of radio broadcasting. The explicit aim of the radio industry from the mid-1920s on was to produce sets for everybody and – especially – every woman!

Even before the Second World War, mobile radio reception – both by detector or battery receivers and by car radio – became an attractive pastime activity. But it was the invention of the transistor in 1948 that revolutionized the classical model of domestic radio reception and launched new forms of mobile listening. Heralding the new era of electronics, the transistor marked the beginning of the end of the supremacy of the established American and European radio industries. The Japanese success in commercializing transistor technology by way of producing cheap but attractive transistor radios is an outstanding example of a successful economic innovation process based on 'architectural' innovations, that is, the creative appropriation of an existing invention and its strategic dissemination in the form of newly designed products. The 'Japanese invasion' of the American and later the European radio market had disastrous consequences for most of the small and medium-sized radio firms that had flourished since the late 1920s. But the transistor had a special cultural impact on the listening habits of especially the younger generation. Within a few years, the 'transistor' – as the set was simply called – became the central actor in a new youth culture that purported to know no boundaries, promoting ideals of individual liberty and radiating the sounds of rock 'n' roll and beat music in all private and public spaces. Together with the emergence of FM radio, stereo broadcasting and high-fidelity listening, the 1960s oversaw an innovative and socially important reinvention of radio during the resurrection of television as the new leading mass medium for domestic and family entertainment.

Television did not herald the death of radio, but created an atmosphere of innovative pressure compelling radio to continuously reinvent itself both on the technological level and in programming. This proved to be the case for the computer and the Internet too. Indeed, it seems as though as the Internet has given radio its rebirth as an amateur medium, enabling everybody to stream out their own sonic messages into the vast and unknown 'digital ether' called the Internet. With the invention of podcasting, the streaming of audioblogs for portable listening, and the successful commercialization of the iPod by Apple, radio has entered a new stage of mobile communication. The fact that Erin McKean, editor in chief of the *New Oxford American Dictionary*, declared 'podcast' the word of the year in 2005, and the fact that traditional broadcasters have been extremely quick to pick up on the podcasting format, show that radio – even without its qualities as a medium of simultaneity and liveliness – is anything but dead.

Andreas Fickers

Bibliography

Douglas S. J. 2004. *Listening in: radio and the American imagination.* Minneapolis: University of Minnesota Press.

Fickers A. 1998. *Der 'Transistor' als technisches und kulturelles Phänomen: die Transistorisierung der Radio- und Fernsehempfänger in der deutschen Rundfunkindustrie von 1955 bis 1965.* Bassum: GNT.

Griset P. 'Innovation and radio industry in Europe during the interwar period', in Caron F., Erker P. and Fischer W. (eds) 1995. *Innovations in the European economy between the wars*, Berlin and New York: Walter de Gruyter, 37–63.

MacLaurin W. R. 1949. *Invention and innovation in the radio industry.* New York: Macmillan.

Related essays

1960s; broadcasting; classical music; Cold War; consumer cooperation; design; evangelicalism; information economy; music; news and press agencies; orchestras; rock; technologies; telephone and telegraphy; war

Railways

As products of the great 19th-century era of European nation building, railways are inevitably associated with nationalism, imperialism and international warfare. Several French and German lines were built before 1914 as instruments of war. British military needs greatly influenced the growth of India's railways through to independence. Foreign powers often planned and sometimes built railways across national borders in pursuit of imperial ambitions, as with China. In the 20th century railways became increasingly associated with regional integration projects such as the European Union. Yet in the 21st century some lines still serve more ambivalent purposes, such as with China's incursion into Tibet.

Border-crossing railways require compatible physical infrastructures on both sides of national borders, trains suitable for through running, and staff capable of working within different commercial, regulatory, managerial and operating contexts. A transnational network is thus possible only when cooperation or coercion aligns the interests of a constellation of state and non-state actors. These may include individuals who developed ideas, drafted plans and organized the building or operation of railways, the various governmental and non-governmental organizations that helped or hindered this, and the many bodies involved in securing and working traffic. Important figures who have acted as system builders include the French engineer Philippe Vitali (1830–1910), the American author Hinton Rowan Helper (1829–1909) and the British-born South African businessman and politician Cecil Rhodes (1853–1902). In the mid 19th century they promoted the construction of railways across respectively Europe, America and Africa.

The internationalization of railways began in Europe during the second half of the 19th century as national administrations sought to remove hindrances to trade by adopting common standards for infrastructure and operations. Standardization did not have to be complete for cross-border flows to flourish; and present Eurostar passenger trains between London, Paris and Brussels run under national operating rules for part of their journeys. Even the track gauge does not have to be uniform, as demonstrated by long-established flows across breaks-of-gauge such as that between France and Spain. Nevertheless, physical incompatibilities increased costs by requiring transshipment or expensive rolling stock capable of working over the different tracks, and the history of gauges reveals the tensions that can arise whenever attempts are made to settle on a particular standard. The widespread adoption of a gauge of 1435mm (4 feet 8½ inches) in Europe, later to be defined as 'standard' by international organizations, facilitated the running of the first international trains. The dominance of British engineering practice in the critical early days of railway building across the continent facilitated this process. But even so, the adoption of non-uniform gauges in a number of regions around the world, particularly from the 1870s through to about 1940, shows that national or subnational factors long outweighed any inchoate consideration of international traffic. At a European level, serious efforts to standardize the remaining technical, administrative and legal obstacles to international traffic date from the last quarter of the 19th century. However it is only in the last 25 years or so that serious initiatives have been made to create a truly Europewide standard-gauge network.

Since the Second World War the development of international flows in postcolonial Africa has sometimes required the construction of new railways or the regauging of others to overcome the obstacle represented by the multitude of gauges inherited from former colonial administrations. International organizations have been crucial to the promotion of standardization. They were also usually the bodies where proposals for transnational railway networks were negotiated and, historically, they have associated railways with peace rather than war. Before the First World War, several European railways established organizations to deal with the legal, technical and administrative issues affecting their joint operations. The first association of any significance was the Union of German Railway Administrations (1846). This body mainly dealt with Central Europe; it became the Union of Railway Administrations of Central Europe in 1934. The European Timetable Conference (1891) and the International Transport Committee (1902) were other organizations set up by cooperation between individual railways. An important development between the world wars was the establishment of the International Union of Railways (1922) (often known by its French initials, UIC). Such bodies always invoked intergovernmental cooperation as many European railways were state-owned, operated or regulated. More explicitly intergovernmental bodies established in the last two decades of the 19th century include the International Conference for Promoting Technical Uniformity on Railways (1882) and the Central Office for International Railway Transport (1893).

In parallel with initiatives for European integration after 1945, intergovernmental bodies were formed to promote the creation of a political context in which transnational railway operation could flourish. These bodies included the Inland Transport Committee of the United Nations Economic Commission for Europe (UNECE, 1947), the European Conference of Transport Ministers (ECMT, 1953), the European Economic Community (1957) and its successor in the field of transport, the General Directorate for Energy and Transport of the European Commission. These organizations used railways as a means of promoting their particular visions of European integration. Thus the European Commission now seeks to establish a continentwide system, including some new lines, that will accelerate the establishment of the internal market and link 'peripheral' regions to Europe's 'core'.

Railways have long been important links in global transport networks. When goods were manhandled from ship to train, no international agreements were needed to ensure that the railways handled intermodal freight expeditiously. Before the Second World War, the few international railway organizations based outside Europe dealt with lines that were physically connected. For example, the Association of American Railroads (established in 1934) dealt with trains between the US, Canada and Mexico. But the containerization of worldwide trade since the 1950s has had implications for all railways. Long-established bodies operating on a global scale such as the International Railway Congress Association (1885), a forum for national governments and railway administrations to discuss technical railway matters, found new life looking for solutions to problems such as fitting maritime ISO containers onto railways that were built long before such things existed. But postcolonial Africa provides a good example of how railways built to serve one set of political and economic imperatives can be reworked to suit new priorities. Sometimes new construction has been needed partly to assert sovereignty in the international economy. The Great Uhuru ('Freedom') Railway, also known as the Tanzam link, was completed in 1975 over a 1,900km (1,200-mile) length to provide an outlet to the sea through Tanzania for Zambian copper exports as an alternative to the colonial-era route through minority-controlled Rhodesia. This, the first major railway in Central Africa since the First World War, was as much a product of global geopolitical rivalries as railways in the colonial era. It was built with the very considerable assistance of Chinese personnel, technology and loans.

The transnational railway may yet become the intercontinental one. The trans-Siberian railway, completed early in the last century, may be taken as the first line straddling two continents. But 19th-century imperialism had encouraged the speculative planning of railways on a still grander scale, from Europe to India and beyond. In the 21st century, with railway transport underpinning economic expansion in China and its already substantial trade with Europe, the possibility of a standard-gauge network connecting Asia and Europe across the Middle East can no longer be dismissed as the fantasies of railway promoters from an earlier era. But such projects will continue to raise questions familiar from the colonial past about where the balance of political and economic power lies. In recent years privatization has once again brought foreign capital into the railways in countries such as Brazil and Mexico. The rhetoric of commerce cloaks what some might see as a creeping strengthening of informal economic control by foreign neighbours. For example, Kansas City Southern is building an alliance of US-controlled lines reaching north-south from Mexico through the USA to Canada. Transnational railways will always be about more than making the trains run to time.

Irene Anastasiadou
Colin Divall

Bibliography

Burri, M., Elsasser K. T. and Gugerli D. (eds) 2003. *Die Internationalität der Eisenbahn 1850–1970*. Zürich: Chronos.

Davis C. B. and Wilburn K. E. Jr with Robinson R. E. (eds) 1991. *Railway imperialism*. New York, Westport and London: Greenwood.

Headrick D. R. 1988. *Tentacles of progress: technology transfer in the Age of Imperialism* Oxford and New York: Oxford University Press.

Puffert D. J. 1991. *The economics of spatial network externalities and the dynamics of railway gauge standardization*. Stanford: Stanford University Press.

Related essays

agriculture; car safety standards; containerized freight; contract and indentured labourers, guestworkers; corporations; debt crises; decolonization; empire and migration; empires and imperialism; European Union (EU); financial markets; food safety standards; human mobility; industrialization; intergovernmental organizations; international non-governmental organizations (INGOs); internationalisms; investment; mail; nation and state; *non-lieux*; religious pilgrimage; technical standardization; telephone and telegraphy; tourism; transnational; transportation infrastructures; war

Refugee relief

Refugee relief was provided by successive formal organizations since it became a major concern in the early 20th century.

After 1918, the disintegration of the Russian, Austro-Hungarian, German and Ottoman empires, followed by the rise of new national states, produced millions of stateless people. By 1926, Europe counted no less that 10 million refugees mostly located in the eastern part of the continent. A pioneering effort toward international protection of these persons emerged under the leadership of the Norwegian humanitarian Fridtjof Nansen. In 1921, the League of Nations asked Nansen to head the High Commission for Refugees, the first international agency to assist people displaced by military or political upheaval. With the rise of systematic border controls and the systematic use of passports, Nansen sought to provide refugees with accepted means of identification. The so-called 'Nansen Passport' granted legal protection to denationalized and stateless people. White Russians and Armenians became the primary beneficiaries of the Nansen system. Under the auspices of the League of Nations or the International Labor Office (from 1925 to 1929), it was enough to belong to an internationally recognized group of stateless people to be granted basic legal and humanitarian protection.

The rise of Nazism and European fascism revealed the inability of the League of Nations to secure shelters for people hounded out by totalitarian regimes. It also spurred a more political approach toward refugee protection. In the 1930s, international jurists and refugee advocates argued that persecution, more than statelessness, was the primary feature of political refugees. The advent of the Second World War dealt a definitive blow to the League of Nations' protection apparatus. Western leaders, such as Franklin D. Roosevelt, anticipated that 'when this ghastly war ends, there may be not one million but ten million or twenty million men, women and children belonging to many races ... who will enter into the wide picture – the problem of the human refugee' (*New York Times*, 18 October 1939). In 1943, the American-backed United Nations Relief and Rehabilitation Administration (UNRRA) was established to care for the displaced persons or 'DPs' to be found by liberating Allied armies – an estimated 11 millions in 1945. As opposed to the Nansen system, UNRRA did not provide legal protection. Its main priority was to organize the swift repatriation of DPs to their Eastern European home countries.

By 1946, however, the repatriation of DPs slowed to a halt. A large group refused on political grounds (and fear of anti-Semitism in the case of Jews) to return to their homeland. Despite staunch Soviet opposition, the United Nations mandated in December 1946 the International Refugee Organization (IRO) to find host countries for the 'last million' DPs in occupied Germany. This important postwar non-governmental organization was rapidly dubbed the 'largest travel agency in the world' as 'repatriation' gave way to a new policy of 'resettlement'. With the help of religious and welfare organizations, the IRO facilitated the distribution of European refugees throughout the world, especially in the United States, in Israel or in countries with manpower needs.

One direct legacy of postwar humanitarianism was the creation of several refugee relief agencies moulded on the UNRRA model. In the Middle East, the United Nations Work and Relief Agency (UNWRA, 1949) was established to support Palestinian refugees. Similarly, an agency devoted to Korean reconstruction (UNKRA, 1950) dealt with the civilian displacement incurred by the Korean War. The United Nations High Commission for Refugees (UNHCR) was initially created in 1950 to help resettle more than a million European refugees left homeless by the Second World War.

The DP experience also contributed to the rise of contemporary political asylum. During its existence, the IRO made political persecution the main criterion in the determination of refugees. This concept was codified into the still-effective 1951 Geneva Convention relating to the Status of Refugees. Despite this universal language of persecution, refugees in the early Cold War were still primarily thought of as European victims of totalitarian regimes.

Over time, UNHCR broadened its scope as refugee crises emerged around the globe. Tellingly, the United Nations inaugurated in 1959 a 'World Refugee Year', indicating that Europe was no longer the centre of attention for humanitarian agencies. In the 1960s and 1970s, UNHCR expanded its operations to countries in Africa and Asia. In charge today of more than 20 million uprooted people predominantly located outside the Western world (the European Union, for instance, hosts less than 5 per cent of the world refugee population), UNHCR seeks to secure international protection and durable solutions for refugees in the 21st century. Yet in the West, the acceptance of asylum seekers is still governed by a strict separation between 'true' political victims and 'false' economic refugees, a screening method directly inherited from the postwar European past.

G. Daniel Cohen

Bibliography

Marrus M. 1985. *European refugees in the 20th century.* Oxford: Oxford University Press.

Solomon K. 1991. *Refugees In the Cold War era.* Lund: Lund University Press.

Related essays

Armenian genocide; asylum seekers; displaced persons; exile; forced migrations; individual identification systems; League of Nations system; Oxfam; refugees; relief; United Nations decades and years; United Nations system

Refugees

Refugees are persons who are outside of their country of origin because they fear persecution. The contemporary international regime that addresses refugee flows is characterized by complex tensions between the recognized need for protection for threatened individuals and groups and the desire of governments to prevent irregular and unauthorized migration. Those tensions are inherent in the stated international policy that seeks 'durable solutions' for refugees, namely, repatriation, local integration or resettlement. Despite the stated policy, many refugees still languish for years or even generations in camps or segregated settlements.

The Office of the United Nations High Commissioner for Refugees (UNHCR) is the international agency for global refugee policy. Its focus when it was founded, in 1950, was European war refugees. In the 1960s and 1970s disruptions caused by decolonization stimulated huge refugee flows in the world's poorest regions. Refugees arrived in host countries in large groups, destitute, and in need of emergency assistance. The nature and scope of those new refugee situations forced Western powers, which had significant responsibility for the displacements, to expand UNHCR's geographical reach and make it a permanent agency.

The landscape of refugee flows shifted again in the mid-1980s as internal armed conflict became the primary cause of displacement. States, already reluctant to resettle refugees, became even less inclined to provide permanent resettlement or local integration for refugees, now perceived as potential actors rather than victims of broader geopolitical disruptions. Repatriation, voluntary or otherwise, became the favoured durable solution and restrictive international policies increased the number of refugees housed in long-term camps and segregated settlements in the midst of strife-ridden regions. Host countries justified these camps as safer for the refugees and for local communities. In reality this system resulted in protracted dependency and impoverishment for residents.

Refugee numbers have fluctuated between 8 million and 17 million since the early 1990s. Some states generate refugee flows while simultaneously receiving refugees. In 2004, for instance, 21,100 Liberians returned from Côte d'Ivoire, but 87,000 new Liberian refugees fled into Côte d'Ivoire, Ghana, Guinea and Sierra Leone, and another 22,200 refugees originating in Côte d'Ivoire fled to Liberia and Guinea.

At the end of 2006, the largest groups of refugees were Afghanis (2.1 million), Iraqis (1.5 million), Sudanese (686,000), Somalis (460,000), Congolese and Burundis (about 400,000 each). The UNHCR estimated the top refugee-hosting countries in late 2006 to be Pakistan (slightly over 1 million), Iran (more than 900,000), USA (844,000), Syrian Arab Republic (702,000), and Germany (605,000). Although the number of refugees had been declining since 2002, the 9.9 million global refugees at the end of 2006 represented an increase of 14 per cent over the previous year. The increase was largely the result of 1.2 million Iraqis who sought refuge in Jordan and the Syrian Arab Republic from the growing conflict in Iraq.

The UNHCR has identified 33 protracted refugee situations, defined as groups of 25,000 or more who have been refugees for more than five years. The vast majority of protracted refugees are found in poor and unstable regions, including East and West Africa, South Asia, Southeast Asia, the Caucasus, Central Asia and the Middle East. Sub-Saharan Africa, including Guinea, Kenya, Tanzania, Uganda and Zimbabwe, hosts the most protracted situations and the largest number of protracted refugees, approximately 1.9 million.

Persons 'warehoused' in refugee camps suffer psychologically, economically and socially. Entrenched camps are breeding grounds for crime, instability and conflict, and serve as prime recruiting grounds for armed groups. Militarization of refugee camps is a serious problem, threatening refugees and humanitarian workers and aggravating existing tensions in host countries.

In situations of severe instability, the dominant trend is short-term, short-distance repetitive dislocation, making it difficult to identify and protect displaced persons. Northern Uganda, for example, hosts 250,000 refugees from Sudan, Rwanda and the Democratic Republic of the Congo despite Uganda's own instability due to armed paramilitary resistance.

Contemporary refugee patterns belie the distinction between external refugees and internally displaced persons. Even though they have not crossed an international border, there are now almost as many internally displaced persons of particular concern to the UNHCR – because they are at risk of persecution – as refugees.

Barbara A. Frey

Bibliography
Gibney M., Loescher G. and Steiner N.
(eds) 2003. *Problems of protection: the UNHCR, refugees and human rights*. London: Routledge.

Related essays
anti-racism; asylum seekers; benefits and charity concerts; city planning; decolonization; displaced persons; empire and migration; feel-good culture; forced migrations; individual identification systems; refugee relief; relief; Save the Children International Union

Regional communities

Regional communities signify a group of people living in association with one another while sharing a sense of belonging to a particular geographical area. Broadly, a regional community consists of 'a limited number of states linked by a geographical relationship and by a degree of mutual dependence' whose common allegiances, values, interests, and principles may or may not be arranged in a formal organization (Nye 1968, vii). Examples of a formal arrangement include the North Atlantic Treaty Organization (NATO), the European Union (EU), the Organization of African Unity (OAU), and the Association of Southeast Asian Nations (ASEAN).

As is clear from the nomenclature, the regional community's collective identity must derive from some sort of geographical contiguity and proximity that binds otherwise separate groups together. However, geography in and of itself is not sufficient. Considerations ranging from history to culture, to the distribution of capabilities, to economic interests, and ideological differences have historically played a critical role in the formation and sustenance of regional communities. As those communities tend to deal with a wide array of issues embracing economic, corporate, and cultural interests, states and governments are not necessarily the only actors taking part in their development, even though they often remain the primary constitutive units. Also, contemporary phenomena with global ramifications such as transnational terrorism, politicized religions with global claims, and the spread of information technologies, all combine to complicate our understanding of regional communities.

Regional communities and the nation state

The best way to approach this complex topic of regional communities conceptually might be to understand different combinations of tensions and multiple layers of identities that constitute regional communities. They need to be understood on two related, but distinct levels, namely, the nation-state and transnational levels. First, within the traditional nation-state matrix, many a nation state, including the United States, Germany, Brazil, and most recently Iraq, has looked to federalism as a preferred way of reconciling their internal regional communities with the larger nation-state identity. But one should not forget that those nation states that opted for a stronger central government too have retained their regional characters. The idea that Sicilians or Okinawans can be said to be temperamentally different from their compatriots in Veneto or Hokkaido in Italy and Japan respectively reveals that claims to regional differences and uniqueness die hard. They can even withstand the pushes and pulls of a centralized national identity over a long period of time.

On the transnational level, regional communities make it necessary for the nation state to give up a certain measure of its identity and sovereignty in the collective interest of a regional framework. In such an arrangement, nation states become building blocks of a larger regional federation. This makes for a potential clash between nationalism and regionalism. For example, the suspicion that a stronger regional community would undermine the political powers of the member states has been at the very heart of the European debate since World War 2. Empirically, however, there is some evidence that European integration 'rescued' rather than damaged the political power of the member states. By agreeing to give up a measure of state sovereignty, they were able to concentrate on the reconstruction of their respective nation-state communities without having to take on the severe economic and strategic challenges alone. It appears that there continues to be enough convergence of nation-state and European interests to supersede the potential tension between the two. The idea that someone from Barcelona can peacefully combine Catalan, Spanish, and European identities suggests the relative success of the European project.

To be sure, the European case cannot be thought of as a representative one. What makes otherwise separate units cohere varies from region to region, and from circumstance to circumstance. Traditionally, the two main spheres of regional interaction in international politics have been in the security and economic arenas. We now turn to more specific aspects and histories of such security and economic regional communities in the modern era.

Security sphere

Security alliance is one of the oldest and most resilient sources of regional community. The ancient Greeks, for instance, formed regional confederacies comprised of city states, such as the Aetolian League and the Achaean League. In modern history, the collapse of the 19th-century Concert of Europe gave way to a more rigid and polarized security alliance system that was unable to accommodate newly emerging nationalisms from within and without, eventually leading to the outbreak of the two world wars. Each world war was followed by an attempt to create an international framework that sought to take diplomacy beyond the traditional concept of alliance. By creating a global system of collective security through the establishment of intergovernmental organizations such as the League of Nations and the United Nations, the internationalists of the interwar and post-World War 2 periods tried to break the pattern of regional alliance systems in which a potential threat was identified in advance. But the perceived failure or general ineffectiveness of collective security systems, combined with the advent of the Cold War bipolarity based on nuclear deterrence, prompted the renaissance of regional communities. Selective, rather than collective security systems formed on the regional level, with a far more focused perception of shared threat, appeared to offer a more realistic alternative in Cold War security policy.

One of the most tangible fruits of a regional alliance based on this notion of selective security during the Cold War was NATO, a.k.a. the Atlantic Alliance. It began with a treaty signed by Western European powers, Canada, and the United States, in 1949. Its primary role during the Cold War was to form a military alliance against a potential Soviet attack. The Soviet Union on its part responded to the rearming of the Federal Republic of Germany and its admission to NATO by creating its own version of regional defence alliance, called the Treaty of Friendship, Cooperation and Mutual Assistance, more commonly known as the Warsaw Pact, in 1955.

So too in the peripheral theatre of the Cold War, the Southeast Asia Treaty Organization (SEATO) came into being in 1954 under US leadership, even as the British and French empires were crumbling. It enjoyed less of a geographical contiguity and shared perception of threat than its Atlantic counterpart, as many countries in Southeast Asia itself opted not to join. Its raison d'être ceased with the winding down of conflicts in Indochina, and SEATO formally disbanded in 1977.

NATO and the Warsaw Pact were about perceived military threats coming from one another. In addition, much of the collective identity of the two regional defence organizations had depended on the ideological differences between the two blocs. With the conclusion of the Cold War, their existing meanings necessarily had to be reconsidered. The Warsaw Pact did not survive the collapse of the USSR, while NATO had to transform its traditional role – in the words of its first secretary-general Lord Ismay – of keeping 'the Soviets out, the Americans in, and the Germans down' in order to adjust to the newly emerging requirements of the post-Cold War era. By enlarging its membership to Central and Eastern Europe, and shifting its focus to ethnic conflicts in the former Soviet bloc, while remaining wary of residual Russian capabilities, NATO preserved its deterrent function as well as its role as a political tool in helping to create regional uniformity, and thus ensuring the survival of this regional community.

Economic sphere

In this sphere too, the end of World War 2 and the advent of the Cold War acted as a major catalyst for the emergence of regional communities. This is not to deny that various forms of economic regional communities had existed before. The Chinese tributary system in which the rulers of lesser states gained not only political legitimacy, but also beneficial trade relations from their regional hegemon, is but one example. The association of Baltic and Northern European merchants realized in the Hanseatic League is another. But in modern times, the waves of decolonization, and the increasingly powerful advocacy for greater social and economic prosperity coming from the coalition of Third World countries in the form of Dependency Theory, the North–South Problem, and the Non-Alignment Movement prompted a worldwide trend in the active formation of politicoeconomic regional alliances. These had an impact on all three major geographical bodies of the Americas, Africa, and Asia.

The fear of economic marginalization under the dominance of US-led free trade competition prompted import-dependent, less developed Latin American countries to seek combined strength in regional economic integration. In Central America, protectionist import substitution policies and other intraregional coordination including the establishment of a customs union and a central bank through the Central American Common Market (CACM) were favoured over the course of the 1960s. The subsequent military conflicts between the member states and the growing regional unrest caused by the Sandinistas and US military engagement in the 1970s and 80s hindered further development of economic regionalism in Central America, although it was followed by a revival from the early 1990s of the CACM as a preferred framework of the regional economy. In South America, the establishment of the Common Market of the South (MERCOSUR) in 1991, which includes the two regional giants of Argentina and Brazil, has worked to resist economic as well as political marginalization of the region. Broader groupings have also developed in the form of the 1948 Organization of American States (OAS, formerly, Pan-American Union), and more recently, the 1993 North American Free Trade Agreement (NAFTA), presenting Latin America with multiple frameworks with which to combat not only problems of poverty, but also environmental and political challenges.

In Africa and Southeast Asia, a comparable fear of political and economic marginalization gave rise to various regional groups, such as the Economic Community of West African States (ECOWAS), the Arab Maghreb Union (AMU), the Preferential Trade Area of Eastern and Southern Africa (PTA), and the South African Development Coordination Committee (SADCC), but so far with limited success. Too often, rivalries between aspiring regional leaders, as well as internal conflicts within member states have posed grave political challenges to the African economic framework. In this respect, the Organization of African Unity (OAU, now the African Union (AU)), a pan-African organization established in 1963, faces a long-standing challenge of managing internal political and social crises of its member states before economic cohesion can be addressed.

In contrast, Southeast Asia has been relatively successful in developing a sense of regional community through the establishment of the Association of Southeast Asian Nations (ASEAN). In spite of the aforementioned failure of SEATO, ASEAN, formed in 1967, has become a useful, albeit imperfect, forum for intraregional dialogue. Though there has only been gradual and limited growth in terms of ASEAN-wide economic integration, the community has become a legitimate and respected regional entity by emphasizing cooperation and dialogue with other non-ASEAN powers such as China, Taiwan, and Japan. The Asia-Pacific Economic Cooperation (APEC), founded in 1989, which encompasses 21 Pacific Rim economies including non-Asian powers such as Australia, New Zealand, and the United States, has posited other possibilities and expansion of the traditional regional economic framework primarily revolving around ASEAN.

But the most noteworthy economic integration in the post-World War 2 world remains the EU. The Eurocrats of the postwar period were faced with a pressing goal of reconstructing European economies ravaged by the war. In a parallel development to NATO, the European Coal and Steel Community (ECSC), founded in 1951, had a specific focus of facilitating coal and steel production within Europe, thereby making sure Germany and France would never go to war again over resources. The subsequent development of the ECSC into the European Economic Community (EEC) in 1957, European Community in 1967, and the EU in 1992, along with the promulgation of the common currency, the euro, in 1999 and the admission of ten new states from the former Soviet bloc to the EU in 2004, show that the EU has by now surpassed its initial role as a regional body dedicated solely to economic development.

The deepening of European integration, as reflected in its institutions, in which member states concede an increasingly large degree of state sovereignty, and the broad scope of issues which the EU tackles, ranging from diplomatic, to social, to environmental and scientific matters, has contributed much to the development of European unity. The widening of Europe through the addition of new members since the end of the Cold War has also stimulated the discussion of what exactly constitute the boundaries of Europe. Be it deepening or widening, however, the road to integration has never been, and perhaps will never be a smooth journey, given the potential tensions between nation-state nationalisms and larger regional allegiances as already noted. Moreover, Europe's divisions no longer come so much from the nationalisms of its member states as from citizens disaffected with the political elites of their own countries.

Politicized religions with global ambitions, most conspicuously political Islam, have recently added a new dimension to the debate about development of regional communities.

One might consider, for example, the case of young jihadis in Europe. An EU passport-carrying British citizen of Pakistani descent, or Dutch citizen of Moroccan descent, who discovers political Islam out of a sense of humiliation and isolation in the only society he has known, who reads the Koran in English translation on the Internet, can be persuaded to kill non-believers at home for the good of the community of believers elsewhere. This might in turn prompt the rise of defensive conservatism within Europe, making it harder than it already is for immigrants and descendants of immigrants to integrate and become more British, Dutch, French, or indeed, European. Whether the European development (i.e. the increasing tensions between 'the region versus the global' as opposed to 'the region versus the nation state') intimates a natural progression for the rest of the world is hard to tell. But with the more and more global and less and less geographically contiguous nature of security, as well as the economic threats plaguing the world, it seems that no regional communities will be left untouched.

Eri Hotta

Bibliography

Butler F. 'Regionalism and integration', in Baylis J. and Smith S. (eds) 1997. *The globalization of world politics: an introduction to international relations.* Oxford: Oxford University Press, 409–28.

Fawcett L. and Hurrell A. (eds) 1995. *Regionalism in world politics: regional organization and international order.* Oxford: Oxford University Press.

Milward A. 1992. *The European rescue of the nation-state.* Berkeley: University of California Press.

Nye J. S. 1968. *International regionalism: readings.* Boston: Little, Brown.

Related essays

Africa; Asia; convergence and divergence; development and growth; Economic Commission for Latin America and the Caribbean (ECLAC); electricity infrastructures; European institutions; European Union (EU); globalization; intergovernmental organizations; Islamic Scientific, Educational and Cultural Organization (ISESCO); nation and state; neoliberalism; news and press agencies; North Atlantic Treaty Organization (NATO); pan-isms; Pax Americana; railways; trade agreements; world federalism; world orders

Regions

The concept 'region' generally refers to a political community and/or a geographic space that coheres around natural or cultural features.

Whether the natural features are material (topographical, climatological or geographical) or human-made (cultural or economic), the idea of region naturalizes historical constructions. Regions may be originally defined from above by the state or academics (Quebec, Bible Belt), or they may emerge as a result of identification from below, but there is a fundamental difference between regions which are felt and lived as such by their inhabitants and regions which are solely bureaucratic creations designed to abstract and manage territories and people. The fact that the statistics division of the United Nations has divided the globe into hundreds of geographic, cultural and economic regions does not mean that these spaces are experienced as regions by the people who inhabit them. NAFTA may have helped link the economies of North America, but it has not resulted in a strengthened North American identity. Some regions seem to have more traction on the ground than others. People identify themselves as New Englanders, for example, in a way that people living in the so-called Rust Belt do not.

Transnational history asks us to de-emphasize the nation so that we may be able to recognize stories that spill over the boundaries of the nation. Rather than ignoring the nation, transnational history encourages us to historicize the nation, and not to assume that the nation is always the most important unit of analysis. As historians pursue the transnational turn, they have rediscovered regions. Regional history allows us to imagine alternative scales to the nation, encouraging the study of phenomena that are both too narrow and too broad for national narratives. Although historians have studied regions from the beginning of modern professional history, and even though this emphasis has periodically become fashionable, historians tend to view such work as amateurish or derisively refer to it as 'local history'. Nonetheless, at its best, the concept of 'region' may allow scholars to think about deterritorialized cultural and economic flows and connections in new transnational ways.

To the extent that transnational history seeks to move historians beyond a focus on the nation, it makes sense to look at units both larger and smaller than the nation. The realignment of global political power and the explosion of globalization discourses in the last thirty years has forced scholars to grapple with and question the categories of analysis that they have inherited from the 19th century. In this context, some commentators have rung the death knell of the nation and trumpeted the arrival of the region. As the noted German historian Hans Mommsen put it, 'the nation is dead, long live the region' (Applegate 1999, 1157). This formulation may, however, be both too pessimistic about the health of the nation and too optimistic about the ability of regional identities to supplant national ones. For all of the talk about globalization and eroding borders, nations still matter in the 21st century.

What is a region?

There is no clear definition of what comprises a region. Regions can be defined by landscape and topography such as rivers, mountains and plains (e.g. Ohio Valley, Andes, Pampas), or industries, commerce and culture (e.g. Rust Belt, Sun Belt, Bible Belt). Regions can be subnational (US Northwest, the Mexican North, Southern Italy) or supranational (sub-Saharan Africa, Latin America, East Asia) geographical spaces that share certain cultural and/or climactic characteristics. The invocation of geography (deserts, seas, etc.) in the very names of certain regions like the Sahara, the Gobi, the Mediterranean or the North Atlantic lends them a sense of being natural and not human constructions. However, the Mediterranean became 'The Mediterranean' not simply because of the natural features of the sea, a body of salty water largely surrounded by land, but because of its crucial role in the development of Western cultures. Of course, when pushed, none of these definitions of region stands up, and even if there are some ways in which particular spaces hold together at certain times, they are all the products of specific historical circumstances. The US Southwest was the Mexican North before 1848, and before 1821 it was the northern frontier of New Spain, and during all of these periods it was simultaneously the homeland for various indigenous groups. What links all of these different definitions of region is the idea of a space that shares certain identifiable characteristics, cultural, topographic, geographic, or economic.

There are other forms of identifications that are not defined by particular spaces, including communities based on religion, sexual orientation, political beliefs, and increasingly a whole host of fairly specific Internet-based communities of everything from *Star Trek* fans to Gnome collectors. Given the growing importance of these virtual, non-site-specific or multisited communities in the last thirty years, which has been facilitated by quick and cheap transportation (bus, car and plane) and communication (phone, Internet, and fax), it is worthwhile thinking about whether these kinds of non-territorialized spaces should be seen as analogous to geographic regions.

Immigrant communities that maintain ties to a homeland are good examples of these kind of non-territorialized or multisited communities. In the last twenty years, anthropologists and sociologists have been documenting immigrant communities in which people can be said to simultaneously participate in the community life of both their new and old homes by attending weddings, participating in important family decisions, and providing financial assistance to their sending communities. Anthropologist Roger Rouse has referred to this multisited space as the 'social space of postmodernism' (Rouse 1991). As historians, we can ask, how new is this space? Certain technologies in the last thirty years make communication and travel easier than it had been before, but studies of late 19th-century Chinese and Mexican immigrant communities in the US show a similar ability to participate simultaneously in communities in different countries. The most common concept of region, as a community tied to a particular geographic space, does not therefore account for the kinds of communities that are based in more than one non-contiguous locale. This serious limitation of the concept of region may be addressed by expanding the definition itself. The virtual space of Internet communities can help us think about and theorize virtual regions that tie together disparate geographic spaces, but one can argue that once you untether region from territory, region becomes an entirely different kind of animal. Imagining virtual regions may be a useful way to think about transnational history, but it may also broaden the concept of region so much as to make it analytically useless.

Limitations of regional history

For all of the promise of regional histories, they do not necessarily move us beyond national histories, nor are they incompatible with them. If regional histories are primarily concerned with the ways in which national events and phenomena play out in a particular context, they solidify the idea of the nation. Therefore, viewing regional histories as variations on a national theme bolsters the notion of national coherence. If regional histories set out to undermine the sense of national coherence by focusing on secessionist or autonomist movements, the idea of the nation is merely shifted to a different terrain. In these instances, present-day national boundaries are questioned in favour of different national configurations (Basques, Catalans, Palestinians, and Northern Irish movements for autonomy/secession/independence, to name just a few examples). In all of these cases, the notion of a national homeland with fixed geographic boundaries continues to be the central category of analysis for historians, and political aspiration for the inhabitants.

Regional histories may end up bringing us back to the national framework because scholars and lay people alike conceive of culturally based regional communities in ways similar to national communities. Part of the attraction of the notion of region is that it appears to grow organically from a connection to the land, a place, or a culture. As one book about regions and regionalism in the US put it, the ideal cultural region is a 'perfect coincidence between culture and topography, between "blood" and "land"' (Steiner and Mondale 1988, xi). The slippage from culture to blood and the overlay of a biological reference onto a territory precisely echoes 19th-century notions of nation. While scholars may accept the idea that nations are 'imagined communities', they don't often acknowledge the extent to which these communities are often imagined as culturally and biologically coherent entities. Restrictive immigration legislation and eugenics policies from the late 19th century onward were based on the idea of maintaining both a racial hierarchy as well as a particular racial mixture in the nation. While some regions invoke political economy more than culture (the Rust Belt, the Global South, for example), regions that are defined as essentialized cultural communities reproduce the problems inherent in national histories.

Intellectuals and politicians may imagine essentialized cultural communities that are larger than the nation. Supranational units such as those represented by pan-African, pan- American or pan-Asian movements invoke cultural commonalities, but they also often serve political and economic ends by creating trading blocks and political alliances (Mercosur, the European Union, FTAA, etc.). These supranational units are comprised of conglomerates of nations, and may be as much pan-nationalist as they are transnationalist. However, to the degree that pan-African movements sought to unite a transatlantic diasporic black populace, they were not strictly territorially based movements. Similarly, pan-Latin American movements since the late 19th century have resonated with Latinos living to the north of the Rio Grande. Pan-nationalist movements thus blend territorially defined nationalism with a broader appeal to cultural nationalism among diasporic people, who although they may have a vague sense of homeland, do not necessarily have the hope or intention of returning.

Regionalism, nationalism, and even supranational alliances in the Global South are often conceived of by their architects as a strategy to resist imperial capitalist exploitation. In contrast, some neoliberals hope that large-scale regional affiliations will eliminate trade and political barriers that exist between nations. Rather than invoking primordial ties as a bulwark against national imposition on locals or imperial imposition on subaltern nations, these neoliberals hope for stronger regional international markets as a way to break down protectionist national legislation. This kind of regionalism, propagated by proponents of NAFTA, the FTAA, the European Union and Mercosur, although in competition with one another, seeks to overcome national boundaries in the interest of global trade.

In contrast to the supranational coalitions, smaller subnational units hold particular charm for historians seeking to find 'authentic' identities. While nations and trading blocs seem like looming political projects defined by elites in metropolitan centres and imposed on the rest of us, regions seem, well, more natural. Nathaniel Hawthorne summed up this anti-national sentiment when he complained, 'we have so much country that we have no country at all'. Instead, Hawthorne extolled his small nation (patria chica): 'New England is quite as large a lump of this earth as my heart can really take in' (Steiner and Mondale 1988, x). The illustrious poet William Stafford echoed this reification of local experience when he stated that 'all human enhancements of events and experiences...are regional in the sense that they derive from immediate relation to felt life' (Steiner and Mondale 1988, ix). Stafford's formulation suggests that regions are real because we can feel regions in a way that we cannot feel nations. It is precisely this kind of mystification of subnational regions that has led so many historians to turn to them as a refuge from the abstraction of the nation. Regions, both big and small, can be a useful concept in the toolbox of transnational history, but only as long as regions are subject to the same kind of critical historicizing and deconstruction that we regularly apply to nations and national identities.

Regions and nations in modern professional history

Modern professional history emerged in the 19th century to justify and legitimize newly formed nation states. It should therefore not be surprising that historians have had such a difficult time in de-emphasizing the nation, even as they seek to write regional histories. Historians' secular myths about the nation replaced religious origin myths. As Eugen Weber put it, 'historians were the clerisy of the nineteenth century because it fell to them to rewrite foundation myths; and history was the theology of the nineteenth century because it provided societies cast loose from the moorings of custom and habit with new anchorage in a rediscovered – or reinvented – past' (Applegate 1999, 1159). The legacy of the 19th-century origins of the historical profession is still with us today; undergraduate history courses are largely conceived as national narratives, graduate programmes are mostly organized into national fields, and scholarship is typically categorized according to nation. Even supranational regional units like Europe, Latin America, and East Asia are built upon the foundational blocks of national histories. While journals dedicated to comparative history and historical theoretical approaches have emerged in the past forty to fifty years (i.e. *Comparative Studies in Society* and History (1958), History and Theory (1960), Journal of Social History (1967) and Journal of World History (1990)), history positions in universities, graduate training and undergraduate education are still largely conceived in national and supranational regional units (Latin America, Africa, East Asia, Middle East).

In US history, local, regional and national histories have coexisted but the former two have served the latter and the trend in the US academy has been toward national approaches, particularly after World War 2. The geopolitical pre-eminence of the US in this period may have contributed to the push for national history as a way to explain US global hegemony in a way that ignored the legacy of US neocolonial rule. The trend toward national histories of the US was also given a boost after World War 2 with the rise of modernization theory. This theory, popularized by Walt Rostow's *Five Stages of Growth*, emerging in the 1950s and 1960s in Anglo-American academia, conceived of the world in isolated national units even as it was supposed to apply to the entire globe equally. Modernization theory reinforced the primacy of national histories and predicted the elimination of regional differences as national markets and a monolithic national culture developed. For modernization theorists, regional histories would continue to be significant only as specific data points in a unilinear national trajectory. Dependency theory, which developed as a critique of modernization theory in the 1960s, emphasized colonial and neocolonial relationships between the core and periphery. Instead of a view of the world made up of individual billiard balls (nations) running along simultaneous paths and occasionally banging into one another, dependency theory presented a dynamic image of co-centric circles with lines sucking resources from the peripheral countries to the metropolis. Although dependency theory allowed for a more integrated and relational view of the world, the nation still remained the principal unit of analysis. Immanuel Wallerstein's World Systems theory allowed for a more nuanced version of dependency, and subsequent scholars have developed ever more elaborate theories to explain the regional inequalities within nations as part of what some have called 'internal colonialism'. Even though World Systems theory allows us to

theorize regional relationships rather than just national ones, it tends to see local particularities only in terms of macro global-scale phenomena.

Just as modernization theory encouraged national histories, the critique of modernization theory has led to renewed interest in studying regional rather than national phenomena. However, while trying to avoid the exclusionary pitfalls of nationalist thinking, regional studies have uncritically assumed that regions are coherent. Studies that project a protonational framework onto regions, like that of the Basques or the Catalans, do not really help us to theorize contingent and multiple-sited communities; rather, they reproduce the prejudices and silences of nations, but on a smaller scale. Scholars have been less apt to apply their deconstructionist tools to regional or ethnic autonomist and secessionist movements than they are to nations, either because of political sympathies for these movements or a sense that regionalist cultural identities invoke older 'primordial' ties to place. However, these notions of primordial ties need to be problematized and historicized as much as that of nations if we hope to move beyond a national perspective.

The US West as a region

The historiography of the US West demonstrates the wide-ranging ways in which histories of a region can be employed. Perhaps the most influential piece of historical writing ever produced in the US was an 1893 essay by Frederick Jackson Turner entitled 'The significance of the frontier in American history'. Turner, who began by referencing an 1890 census statistic suggesting that the frontier had finally closed, argued that US democracy was formed in the process of easterners heading west to the frontier, encouraging people to become self-reliant and develop new forms of self-governance. This first attempt at US Western history clearly marked the region as part of the national narrative. In fact, the western frontier became the linchpin of the national story. Turner and his disciplines emphasized the West as a frontier process less than as a place.

In the 1980s, a whole cadre of scholars began critiquing the Turnerian perspective, some arguing for studies that focused on the cultural, climactic and economic particularities of the region and others insisting that the region not be understood as a place apart from the rest of the nation or international market forces. One of the primary evangelizers of the New Western History, Patricia Nelson Limerick, argued for the importance of the West as a unique place, and criticized the old frontier model for seeing it as a stage for the unfolding of the frontier play. Much ink was spilled defending and attacking the New Western History, but in the end most historians recognized the importance of the US West as both a 'process' and a 'place'. However, the outcome of this particular debate is less interesting than the fact that these historians still posed their questions in terms of US history. Whether the West was a stage for playing out the Turnerian frontier thesis, and thereby the drama of the US, or a unique region, the explicit and implicit references of the New Western History were to the US nation. Limerick pushed for comparative histories of European conquest, making the important point that the 'American West was an important meeting ground, the point where Indian America, Latin America, Anglo-America, Afro-America, and Asia intersected' (Limerick 1987, 27). The West is a different kind of place for different people. For the Chinese arriving in San Francisco, this same space was the East, and for the Mexicans arriving in California and Texas, it was el norte. The New Western History helped historians to think outside of the Turnerian framework, and to begin deconstructing US foundational myths, but it did not provide a framework for histories to move beyond the nation both in terms of scholarship and scope.

Building on the foundation established by Chicano studies as well as the New Western History, US-Mexico borderlands history began to be reconceived in the late 1980s and early 1990s. Borderlands histories hold out the promise of allowing us to look at a particular region without overemphasizing any particular nation. The borderlands approach, whether isolating the US-Mexico border region or that of the Greek-Albanian border, attempts to understand the relations in a cultural and economic region straddling two or more countries. At their best, these histories recognize the importance of nation states in determining economic, political and cultural difference across a boundary line without overemphasizing the nation and

obscuring processes and experiences that are not determined by the nation.

The borderlands approach can just as easily reify the nation either by carving imagined 'third-spaces' from two or more nations or by using the border to highlight national distinctiveness. Herbert Eugene Bolton coined the term 'Spanish Borderlands' in 1921 in reference to his work on the northern frontier of New Spain's American empire. The relative remoteness of this frontier zone from the central economic and political centres of Spanish colonial power, along with particular institutions (principally the mission and the presidio) and climactic conditions, gave the Spanish borderlands its coherence. Even after the US-Mexico boundary line sundered this region into two nations, many of the same processes worked to unify this borderlands space. Scholars have recognized regional coherence in bi-national contiguous spaces from the Basque region of northern Spain and southwestern France to the Punjab-Bengal region dividing India from Pakistan to the US-Mexico border. Although these types of border studies desire to escape from the limited political imagining of national histories, they can easily fall back into a reification of proto-national regional identifications. Thus, the 'third-space' of border regions become a site in which to privilege the resistance of a local culture against the centralizing power of the nation state. Or, the border space becomes a way to show how nations define themselves through exclusions and displays of state power at their borders. The border can thus highlight differences between the nations rather than similarities. Imagining the border as a 'third-space' or as a site of forging national identity steps away from national history without moving us toward transnational history.

Conclusion

Conceiving of the world as regions rather than nations is a helpful exercise to move us toward transnational history. However, depending on how regions are conceived, they may reproduce the same kind of blindness and essentialized notions of community that seem so prevalent in national histories, and from which transnational historians seek to escape. Focusing on regions can help historians to write transnational histories as long as regions remain objects of study and are not assumed to be perfectly coherent transhistorical things. Reconceptualizing regions as virtual, deterritorialized spaces is an even more radical departure from national and even regional history as we know it. Mapping this virtual world is a daunting task for historians who are used to plotting their actors' movements on Cartesian grids.

The artist Yanagi Yukinori's installation entitled 'Pacific' (1996) provides an artistic articulation expression of nation and region in a way that allows us to see these spaces as continuously in flux and in the process of cross-pollination. His installation consists of a series of coloured flags representing nations, former colonial powers and indigenous groups that border the Pacific Ocean. The flag boxes are connected to the others by clear tubes, through which hundreds of ants carry colored grains of sand from one flag to the other. In the process, the ants slowly erode each flag and create new configurations of the national symbols. Yanagi's installation reminds us that both nations and regions are constantly in the process of deterioration and reconstruction, and they are never as coherent as their architects would like them to be. Focusing on the ants and the circuits through which the ants migrate allows us to see regions and nations as processes in flux and not just fixed things. Focusing on migrants as they cross borders is one way to imagine regions as a series of pathways that not only link various nations but fundamentally transform them in the process.

Elliott Young

Bibliography

Applegate C. 1999. 'A Europe of regions: reflections on the historiography of sub-national places in modern times', *American Historical Review*, 104, 4, 1157–82.

Ching L. 1991. 'Globalizing the regional, regionalizing the global: mass culture and Asianism in the age of late capital', reprinted in Appadurai A. (ed.) 2001. *Globalization*. Durham, NC: Duke University Press.

Limerick P. 1987. *The legacy of conquest: the unbroken past of the American West*. New York: Norton.

Rouse R. 1991. 'Mexican migration and the social space of postmodernism', *Diaspora* 1, 1, 8–23.

Sidway J. 2002. *Imagined regional communities: integration and sovereignty in the Global South*. London: Routledge.

Steiner M. and Mondale, C. (eds) 1988. *Region and regionalism in the United States: a sourcebook for the humanities and social sciences*. New York: Garland.

Related essays

Africa; Asia; border commuters; borders and borderlands; culture; electricity infrastructures; freshwater management; historians and the nation state; history; human mobility; language; modernization theory; nation and state; news and press agencies; oceans; pan-isms; patents; regional communities; salsa; technical standardization; trade

Relief

One of the meanings of 'relief' is assistance given to help people recover from a state of immediate need, whether resulting from natural or 'man-made' disaster. Today, in the context of international aid, it is often contrasted with 'development', or programmes designed to improve such people's life-chances over a longer term, though the distinction is increasingly blurred. The distinction between natural and man-made disasters is also blurred today, since it is realized that suffering caused by natural disasters is usually aggravated by political ill-will. The term 'humanitarian' is sometimes used as a straight synonym for 'relief', but also has a technical meaning in the context of International Humanitarian Law (Geneva law), which sets out to define the responsibilities of parties engaged in armed conflicts. Recently the term 'humanitarian space' has become popular: this refers primarily to safe zones and corridors, and by extension to the scope for action, based on impartial and independent principles, to bring relief to affected populations. More controversially, the right of 'humanitarian intervention' (*droit d'ingérence*), or armed intervention in response to grave violations of the laws of humanity, has been partially accepted by lawyers.

Relief before Dunant: continuities and differences

Modern practices of relief have historical origins that were in the first place religious – for injunctions to be charitable are common to every world faith – and subsequently philosophical, based on the recognition of a common humanity. Until recently, Western historians largely underestimated non-Western traditions such as the Islamic institution of *waqf* (charitable foundation) and the 'Confucian' paternalism that sustained the Manchu dynasty for centuries in China until its decline and collapse in 1911. Secular motivations underpin much of the organization of relief today; but less obviously, religious motivations are still prominent.

Overseas relief in Europe may be dated back at least to the period of the Crusades and the foundation of sovereign orders of knighthood with mixed military and 'hospitaller' aims. One of these, the Order of Malta, founded in Jerusalem in the 11th century, still survives with some 12,000 Roman Catholic members worldwide and extraterritorial diplomatic status. Though still wedded anachronistically to the ideal of an aristocracy of birth, the Order of Malta's extensive commitments have included some pioneering projects such as the support during the 1980s of traditional healing in refugee camps in Thailand.

One of the innovations of the Enlightenment was a recognition that neither the suffering of the wounded or defeated in battle nor natural disasters, such as the earthquake that destroyed three-quarters of Lisbon in 1755, need be accepted with fatalism. Major international relief operations were carried out from the United States, for instance in 1793 to rescue French aristocrats driven from Santo Domingo, or from France during the war of Greek Independence (1821–29), when collections of money and clothes were organized for the benefit of Greek insurgents.

Britain was an important source of overseas relief in the 19th century. At home, relief was provided in workhouses under the Poor Law, but charitable Relief Committees were also founded. Similar practices were followed by the British rulers of India. Disparaging indigenous practices of philanthropy, they initiated road-building programmes with a view to inhibiting popular violence and also to discouraging what they saw as indolence. Indians who flocked to relief camps – mainly peasants, artisans and other marginal groups – were described as 'paupers' and 'vagrants' in language that can be traced back to Elizabethan times. The government then sought to disperse those employed on relief works back to their normal work by wage reductions.

Hostile criticism was published in the Indian press, and 'the schism between the limited responsibility which the state was willing to undertake and its claims of being the ultimate source of generosity and patronage was central to the critique later put forward by Indian nationalists' (Sharma, 2001, 231).

Whereas strict press censorship during the Crimean War (1854–56) prevented the French public from knowing about the death rate in the French forces, their British ally was informed by war reporters that seven times more soldiers were being lost as a result of illness than on the battlefield, so that some remedial action was taken. Florence Nightingale established her fame as a military hospital administrator in Turkey, and later in her long career she was to despatch nurses to military hospitals in the United States and France.

The consequences when relief is withheld also recur in British modern history. For instance, the Great Famine in Ireland (1845–52) left British rule temporarily more entrenched – many poor farmers having died or emigrated – but in the long run resulted in a legacy of hatred against it. The Famine was aggravated by the *laissez-faire* policies of Ireland's English rulers, some of whom saw it as an opportunity to rid the country of an unproductive peasantry. The government intervened with substantial relief too late and too meanly to prevent massive suffering, while a significant role was played by voluntary organizations such as the Quakers.

Overseas relief also emerged in the context of imperial European-based rule. Great advances were made in tropical medicine during the 19th century under the French and British colonial systems: for instance, in the aetiology of malaria, bubonic plague and sleeping sickness. The last great exponent of 'bush medicine' was Albert Schweitzer (1875–1965), the Alsatian scholar and musician who devoted most of his life after 1913 to hospital work in the French Congo (now Gabon). Venerated towards the end of his life and awarded the Nobel Peace Prize in 1952, he was posthumously criticized as a condescending racist, but has more recently been hailed as a precursor of 'appropriate healthcare'. Medical care in the context of emergency relief is subject to the contradiction that increasingly afflicts all other branches of medicine: between what is technically possible and what is locally affordable.

These disputed issues survive into our time: the critique of relief as a form of control that reinforces domination; the endeavour by Western providers to establish monopolies; the anxiety that facilities provided for the distressed may tempt them into dependence; the importance of free media in holding authorities to account; the withholding of relief in what is now termed 'ethnic cleansing'. However, the foundation of the Red Cross Movement is rightly regarded as a turning point in the history of relief.

International aspirations and mononational achievements

History meets myth with the foundation of the International Committee of the Red Cross (ICRC) by Henry Dunant in 1864, and the ratification of the First Geneva Convention. The ICRC, still the core of the Movement, has retained a certain mystique and has influenced other agencies both to emulate it (such as Save the Children Fund) and to react against it (such as Médecins Sans Frontières, Doctors Without Frontiers). Part of its uniqueness stems from its role as guardian of International Humanitarian Law. But it is also unique in being independent yet authorized by governments, international yet mononational. Though now employing many non-Swiss staff, the ICRC remains a private Swiss institution.

Arguably the most effective international relief organizations have indeed been mononational in culture. Save the Children Fund was founded in Britain in 1919 as a result of the suffering imposed on children in Austria and Germany by the Allied governments' blockade. It grew into a major relief and development agency and has remained one of the most respected institutions in British public life, though until recently it had the closest links with British diplomacy. Oxfam, also British, was founded in similar circumstances in 1942, in the middle of the Second World War in order to bring food aid to Nazi-occupied Greece, which was also the victim of a blockade. More recently, Médecins Sans Frontières was created by French doctors and journalists in 1971. Among the leading US-based relief agencies, CARE was founded by businessmen in 1945 to send food packets to Europe, and it has grown into one of the most important aid organizations. The acronym originally stood for 'Cooperative for American Remittances to Europe' but this was changed to the (hardly ever used) 'Cooperative for Assistance and Relief Everywhere, Inc'. CARE has successfully internationalized in that most of its employees are citizens of the countries where they work. But like many large American NGOs it has accepted such extensive financial support from the US Government (43 per cent of revenue in 2005) that as a quid pro quo it has been expected, implicitly and at times with embarrassing candour, to act as a 'force-multiplier' for US foreign policy, which has sometimes been held to detract from its advocacy for the poorest and for human rights.

All these agencies have become far less mononational over the last 15 years as the importance and potential of transnational NGOs has come to be widely appreciated. However, the process of internationalization has invariably resulted in problems of management and coordination. Save the Children Fund sought to internationalize almost immediately after its launching in Britain, with the foundation in Geneva in 1920 of the Save the Children International Union. International cooperation was held up by World War 2, but gathered strength subsequently: in 1997 the International Save the Children Alliance was formed to coordinate all operations. The parent British charity has found itself on a mid-position between the large US affiliate, with its generally conservative policies, and a number of Scandinavian affiliates that have adopted radical definitions of children's rights.

The official Roman Catholic network of relief agencies is known as Caritas Internationalis, founded in 1897. Despite the Church's global reach, Caritas's national members – such as CAFOD (Catholic Fund for Overseas Development) in Britain and Secours Catholique in France – have operated as national institutions with different names. Many other Christian Third World-oriented agencies have operated all over the world, reflecting the diversity of the Christian churches but usually linked to a donor nation state. It is the religious Orders such as the Franciscans which perhaps have had most experience of integrated transnational organization.

Surprisingly few international relief NGOs have operated on the model of multinational companies. An exception is World Vision, which was founded in the USA on evangelical Christian principles in 1950 to address the needs of Korean War orphans, and has grown to be one of the largest relief agencies, with a turnover rising to US$2 billion. Though it has often been thought of as an American organization, its management and financial systems have been integrated internationally. This enabled it to become one of the first Euro-American NGOs to be able, in the early 1990s, to operate national branches in Africa with all-African staff.

The rise of international bureaucracies

At the end of World War 1, the United States President, Woodrow Wilson, proposed the foundation of the League of Nations. A key figure during this period was the Norwegian explorer Fridtjof Nansen. He lobbied for the foundation of the League, pioneered the care and repatriation of refugees and also coordinated relief on behalf of the Red Cross for millions of Russians dying in the famine of 1921–22. The new Soviet government in Russia had initially set out to dismantle the edifice of prerevolutionary philanthropy, which according to Marxist theory did nothing but alleviate the symptoms of poverty while obfuscating the causes. However, the famine's severity impelled the Communist Party leaders, despite their hatred of private charity, to appeal for help not only to the privately organized All-Russian Committee for Aid to the Starving (whose members were soon arrested) but to the American Relief Administration, the Save the Children International Union, and many other foreign organizations. The Bolshevik regime used the well publicized suffering of their people to insist on controlling the distribution of foreign aid and thus to obtain international recognition.

The end of World War 2 saw more concerted efforts to maintain world peace, with the foundation in 1945 of the United Nations. The onset of the Cold War inhibited the evolution of the UN's main political institutions. However, under the auspices of the UN a host of intergovernmental humanitarian agencies were founded and they have since continued to grow.

The first of these – actually preceding the foundation of the UN itself – was the United Nations Relief and Rehabilitation Administration (UNRRA), a huge operation that ran refugee camps, prevented epidemics, promoted social reconstruction and organized the repatriation of some 7 million refugees between 1943 and 1946. With the participation of 52 countries, UNRRA was subject to the authority of SHAEF (Supreme Headquarters of the Allied Expeditionary Force), and the US government provided nearly half its budget. It cooperated with numerous voluntary agencies, such as the American Jewish Joint Distribution Committee, which had been active in assisting Jewish populations since 1914 and now focused on the care and reintegration or resettlement of survivors of the Shoah. The incipient Cold War brought UNRRA to a close and it was succeeded by the more specialized institutions under the UN that survive today.

The coordination of disaster relief under the UN has had a chequered history, partly because it has usually been entrusted to diplomats rather than people with field experience and partly because of the bureaucratic overhead. By contrast, organizations such as the ICRC, Médecins Sans Frontières or Oxfam have short reporting lines and can react with agility. Occasionally however an outstanding personality such as the Japanese academic Mme Sadako Ogata (1927–), who was High Commissioner for Refugees between 1991 and 2000 – a period of rapid expansion and intense pressure on the agency's resources, especially in ex-Yugoslavia and central Africa – succeeded in providing dynamic, if politically contentious, leadership.

Christian organizations have long been prominent in relief activities. But they were marginal to the worldwide debate on economic development that has raged since the 1960s – for this was generally predicated on the 'secularization thesis'. Quite recently, the importance of Faith-Based Organizations on the international scene has been discovered, and these new bureaucracies may have begun to displace some of the authority of traditional religious hierarchies. However, despite the mass of research on NGOs since the early 1990s, the Islamic aid organizations that had emerged since the 1970s were largely omitted from the analysis of aid flows. These have since been accused of not sufficiently separating relief aid from religiously inspired programmes – not to mention the graver allegations that some of them have been implicated in facilitating terrorism, which were almost certainly greatly exaggerated. In fact, if we seek to apply the same criteria to Islamic charities as are generally applied to Christian charities, rather than remain content with Euro-centric prejudices, the

Islamic charities appear to have been guilty of no more than a historical time-lag: only recently giving up the ground to NGO professionals that was previously dominated by religiously motivated volunteers. While a number of Islamic charities, especially those deriving from Saudi Arabia and the Gulf, have continued to work with mixed religious and secular objectives, the pace has been set by agencies such as Islamic Relief Worldwide, which – while reflecting Islamic moral values and drawing on the Quran's rich teaching on charitable giving – have complied fully with international norms relating to non-discrimination and have begun to cooperate amicably with non-Islamic charities. Whereas some field areas in the 1980s such as Afghanistan saw intense competition between Islamic and 'Western' relief agencies, in 2006 CAFOD and Islamic Relief Worldwide were cooperating in that country with joint programmes of food distribution.

The proliferation of NGOs during the last 30 years has led to a system of 'deregulation' where many small NGOs are free to offer relief services, and the result in a zone such as post-tsunami Aceh in Indonesia has been organizational anarchy. Major relief NGOs that are both independent and genuinely transnational are relatively few in number, and have normally taken at least 20 years to become fully established. Attention has recently been paid to the organizational issues that ensue when relief NGOs expand to a global scale, and revealed some of the turbulence in 'humanitarian space'.

Turbulence in 'humanitarian space'

Though some rumblings were detectable earlier, it was not until the 1980s that relief aid began to attract a sustained critical attention that has now burgeoned into countless conferences and publications. A number of interlocking themes that began to emerge then may be identified, at the same time as an increasing expertise in the technical aspects of planning and implementing effective aid.

First, it came to be recognized that aid agencies had underestimated the capacity of 'coping mechanisms' whereby local populations responded to disasters such as food shortages. For instance, indiscriminate cereal aid can lower the price of grain and impoverish peasant farmers. An informed judgment has to be made, preferably in advance of crisis,

as to the point where the local coping mechanisms are coming under excessive strain.

Second, local 'civil society' was often underestimated by international agencies, which have tended to exaggerate their own impact. Agencies relying on expatriates and undertaking only short-term commitments can never acquire the same level of local confidence as those that engage with communities over a long period – which was often achieved by missionaries and others during the colonial years. By far the largest proportion of relief aid after a natural disaster, such as a flood or earthquake, has normally been provided by local individuals and organizations.

Third, even 'natural' disasters have a manmade component. Famines, at least in modern times, are completely preventable in principle and have in fact been prevented in countries with a free press and democratic institutions. Many regimes such as Mugabe's in Zimbabwe have used the threat of famine to subdue opposition. Disaster preparedness is a low priority in most poor countries, so that, for instance, defective construction has caused unnecessary suffering in earthquake zones. Water shortages in some arid zones have been aggravated by investment in luxury tourism. Dense populations in a country such as Bangladesh have forced many to make a living in areas highly vulnerable to flooding. Even the most apparently 'natural' disasters, such as the destruction of remote mountain villages in Pakistan as a result of the great earthquake in 2005, have clear political implications, for the effort expended on bringing relief aid to this difficult terrain was miniscule compared to the effort expended by the US and its allies on military activities in the region.

Fourth, relief aid has been widely used as a continuation of national diplomacy and economic activity by other means. The wheat farmers of the USA have survived because of their government's grain shipments to poor countries. In recent years, especially since 9/11, the link with national and global security considerations has been particularly marked. Sometimes relief agencies have gone outside their traditionally restricted humanitarian brief to call for military interventions – appeals which can have unintended consequences and even make a crisis worse. Meanwhile the military are sometimes irreplaceable in providing humanitarian relief, and have done so since the Berlin Airlift in

1948, but relationships between military and humanitarian interests have had to be renegotiated as a result of crises in Afghanistan and elsewhere.

Fifth, relief NGOs like all organizations have tended to set their sights on their own survival as a priority, and to compete by means of sophisticated marketing operations. This might be defended on the grounds that humanitarian needs are limitless, but it has been rare to see two NGOs with similar programmes merging together to cut costs. Lip-service has been paid to the principle of public accountability, but in practice NGOs have been judged more by peer assessment than through the admittedly difficult process of ascertaining the views of aid beneficiaries.

Sixth, the whole field of disaster relief has been permeated by the mass media, particularly television. A symbiotic relationship has often been negotiated between NGOs, which needed publicity, and journalists, who needed access to field areas. Elements of news have been subconsciously fitted into a folk narrative akin to the traditional fairy story, featuring a hero (the aid worker), a donor, a villain or affliction to be defeated, magical aids (modern technology), a false hero (charities that deceive the public or waste funds) and finally a princess who congratulates the hero on his return. Usually the mass media have singled out one major disaster at a time, particularly if it was out of the ordinary in some way (in the case of the Indian Ocean tsunami, because of the heavy casualties among European tourists), and have moved on to another quite soon. It is as if the same principle of relentlessly pursuing novelty applies as in the world of consumer fashion. Conscientious broadcasters and NGOs have done their best to break this narrative mould, but it has proved difficult: roving Western celebrities have become increasingly prominent in fund-raising campaigns.

Seventh, relief aid supplied with the best of intentions has in fact supported 'aid economies' that help ruthless regimes to stay in power or in some cases prolong a conflict. During the heyday of Communism, by contrast, Communist governments never allowed national disasters to be publicized and they refused relief aid from foreign countries. This changed with the Armenian earthquake in 1988, widely publicized so that foreign relief teams were allowed to complement the sluggish response of the Soviet State. In the mid 1990s, the North Korean Communist government, though one of the most reclusive in the world, allowed international aid agencies to intervene, when 5 to 10 per cent of their population, around 1 or 2 million people, were dying as a result of famine. But the aid agencies were prevented from conducting their usual tasks of needs assessment, monitoring and evaluation. A number of Western NGOs, including Médecins Sans Frontières, Action Contre la Faim and Oxfam, later decided to withdraw for ethical reasons on the grounds that they were refused access to the most vulnerable, but no doubt for more political reasons also. However, a former UN official criticized their decision, asking whether it was right to condemn Korean children to death just because they were born in North Korea; and indeed most relief programmes are conducted in non-democratic countries that disrespect human rights. In 2006 the World Food Programme was still supplying substantial food aid to North Korea, but the regime was apparently using it to discourage internal opposition.

Eighth (and only since the early 1990s), the relative immunity that used to be accorded to aid workers as supposedly neutral agents in dangerous zones has been increasingly violated. There has been an eightfold increase in major violent incidents directed against aid workers since 1996. In late 2004, a British employee of CARE in occupied Iraq, Margaret Hassan, who was married to an Iraqi and who had personally opposed the war in Iraq, was abducted and brutally murdered. In many cases the motive appears to have been more to sow indiscriminate chaos against agencies seen as promoting 'Western' interests than to single out any particular agency for its political affiliations.

In short, relief NGOs have been engaged in continuous soul searching. Some major NGOs have come to adopt a broad mandate including such tasks as political advocacy and protection of the vulnerable, as well as economic development. Others have been drawn towards a 'neo-Dunantist' or 'minimalist' role, reverting to a strict definition of 'humanitarian space', or to an ethic of 'do no harm' influenced by Quaker or Buddhist philosophies.

Jonathan Benthall

Bibliography

Benthall J. 1993. *Disasters, relief and the media.* London: IB Tauris.

Benthall J. and Bellion-Jourdan J. 2003. *The Charitable Crescent: politics of aid in the Muslim world.* London: IB Tauris.

de Waal A. 1989. *Famine that kills.* Oxford: Clarendon Press.

Duriez B., Mabille F. and Rousselet K. (eds) 2006. *Les ONG confessionnelles.* Paris: L'Harmattan.

Rufin J.-C. 1994. *L'aventure humanitaire.* Paris: Gallimard.

Ryfman Ph. 1999. *La question humanitaire: histoire, problématiques, acteurs en enjeux de l'aide humanitaire internationale.* Paris: Ellipses.

Schloms M. 2006. 'Le dilemme inévitable de l'action humanitaire', *Cultures et conflits,* 60, 85–102.

Sharma S. 2001. *Famine, philanthropy and the colonial state: North India in the early nineteenth century.* New Delhi: Oxford University Press.

Siméant J. 2005. 'What is going global? The patterns of globalizing French NGOs "without borders"'. *Review of International Political Economy,* 12, 5, 851–83.

Websites:

Humanitarian Policy Group, Overseas Development Institute: www.odi.org.uk/hpg

International NGO Training and Research Centre: www.intrac.org

Related essays

adoption; Christianity; evangelicalism; feel-good culture; information economy; intergovernmental organizations; international non-governmental organizations (INGOs); International Red Cross and Red Crescent movement; Islam; Islamic Relief Worldwide; League of Nations Health Organization; League of Nations system; Médecins Sans Frontières (MSF); natural hazards; nursing; Oxfam; philanthropy; refugee relief; refugees; Save the Children International Union; United Nations system

Religion

Religion is a notoriously hard concept to define. A definition that focused on human interaction with supernatural agents would leave out strands of Buddhism, a definition that focused on religion as an overarching worldview, or an ultimate concern, would include secular forces such as nationalism, humanism and Marxism. There is no scholarly consensus as to what constitutes a religion or whether religion as a phenomenon is truly a distinct category of human life open to analysis. Many have called the term into question and argued for its replacement. Some have gone as far as to argue that the category is solely the creation of the scholar's study, that in fact there are no data for religion.

Religion: a word and a concept

For a concept often assumed to describe a distinct and universal human experience the word is surprisingly absent from many languages and cultures. Classical Greece lacked the notion of a religion as something separate from other spheres of life; the same is true for ancient Egypt and India. Classical Hebrew has no word that signifies religion nor does classical Sanskrit.

Of what today are considered the world's major religions – Hinduism, Buddhism, Taoism, Confucianism, Judaism, Christianity and Islam – only the last has named itself. Otherwise, these religions have been named by outsiders. Religion, therefore, is not a native category; from the mid 19th century it is a term imposed by colonialists upon some part of the culture of native life. Indeed, the terms Hinduism, Buddhism, Taoism, and Confucianism emerge under the lens of European colonialism. It is not until late in the modern construction of the category of religion and its colonial export around the globe that 'religion' begins to emerge as a first-person characterization. The construction of the religion of others, moreover, is based upon the template of the religion of the colonial powers. To be a religion, foreign practices were seen to resemble yet also lacking in relation to Christianity. As we shall see, Western consciousness literally constructed religions and the category itself is transnational in its development.

Given its complexity and ambiguity as a category, it should come as no surprise that there are as many definitions for, and approaches to, religion as there are theologians, philosophers, psychologists, sociologists, anthropologists, linguists and others who have tackled the term. In modern times religion has been examined in terms of its essence (notable exponents would include Immanuel Kant, Friedrich Schleiermacher,

Ludwig Feuerbach, Karl Marx, Sigmund Freud, Albrecht Ritschl, Rudolf Otto, and John Dewey among others), its origin (Lucien Lévy-Bruhl, Max Müller, Sir James Frazer, Herbert Spencer, Edward Burnett Tylor, A. R. Radcliffe Brown and Bronislaw Malinowski), its function (Émile Durkheim, Max Weber, Talcott Parsons, Clifford Geertz, Robert Bellah, Mary Douglas, and Victor Turner), its description (Cornelius Petrus Tiele, Geraardus van der Leeuw, and Mircea Eliade), its language (Ludwig Wittgenstein, Paul Ricoeur, Carl Jung, Alfred J. Ayer, D. Z. Phillips) and comparatively between religions (Frederick Denison Maurice, Karl Rahner, Raimon Panikkar, Paul Tillich, Sarvepalli Radhakrishnan, Huston Smith, Wilfred Cantwell Smith and John Hick).

The understanding of religion which remains dominant today in the modern West is that of a special kind of belief – personal, private, unique, autonomous and irreducible to other aspects of human life. It is an understanding, however, tinged by a Protestant bias and that has a time and place of birth. The modern concept of religion is born out of the ashes of the religious wars that engulfed Europe in the 16th and 17th centuries. Our understanding of religion, therefore, is a product of the Western European Enlightenment's attempt to leave behind conflicts fuelled by religion.

Two figures and texts are central to understanding the notion of religion we inherit – John Locke's (1632–1704) *Letter Concerning Toleration* and Friedrich Schleiermacher's (1768–1834) *On Religion: Speeches to its Cultured Despisers*. Locke's *Letter Concerning Toleration* (1689) was published in the same year as the Act of Toleration and William and Mary's acceptance of the Magna Carta or Bill of Rights, which marked England's transition into a constitutional monarchy. Writing in the aftermath of religious conflict spurred by persecution of dissenters by the established church, Locke sought peace between government and religion by restricting the latter to personal belief. To do so, Locke distinguished between speculative and practical articles of faith. Speculative articles, on the one hand, did not drive believers to action; they had no societal consequences and merely needed to be believed. Practical articles, on the other hand, dealt with how life should be lived and thus could well impinge upon society. Locke allowed governments the right to restrict practical articles of faith only; speculative articles of faith were to be held freely. He thus drew a sharp distinction between the inner private realm of religion and the outer public realm of politics: the former could be governed by faith but the later had to be governed by reason. He bought tolerance at the price of the privatization of faith.

Friedrich Schleiermacher, a central figure in the German Romantic movement and the father of liberal Protestant theology, published *On Religion* in 1799. The book was both an explanation of his religious views and a critique of his Romantic (and cultured) friends' understanding of religion. According to Schleiermacher, they look at religion but see only the external husk that covers and hides its true essence. His goal, therefore, is to shed light on religion's essential nature. In the process, Schleiermacher argues that religion is neither knowledge nor ethics; it provides no information about the natural world or incentives toward action. As such, religion properly conceived no longer competes with science and is safe from accusations of violence. Instead, religion is feeling – an immediate self-consciousness, an immediate intuition of the finite self existing in and through the infinite. The feeling lies before thought, as thought requires language which shatters the immediacy of the intuition. The essence of religion, therefore, cannot be taught or analytically broken down; at best it can be indirectly evoked or awakened through literature and art. What is most significant about *On Religion*, however, is that it represents the first book to be written about 'religion' as a generic category. Rather than focusing on some part of religion or religions, the book focuses on religion as a concept distinct from all other aspects of life – religion in itself.

Empires and religion

The Enlightenment gave birth to the modern category of religion and simultaneously unleashed modern colonialism. With colonialism, this particular understanding of religion travelled beyond Western Europe as a central element of the European imperial era. As early as 1798 Napoleon invaded Egypt with a force that included scholars and scientists whose task was to examine and catalogue life in that nation. The end product was the monumental 23-volume *Description de l'Egypte* (1809–18) which became the foundation of modern research into Egypt and an early example of a pattern that would become increasingly dominant throughout the 19th century – scholars and missionaries using categories from the imperial west to catalogue the knowledge of conquered peoples and rank them on a civilizational ladder where they inevitably fell on the lower rung.

The category of religion played an important role in this process. Remember that with both Locke and Schleiermacher, what is revealed as truly important are not religion's outer manifestations, but rather its inner truth. This understanding of religion served a growing missionary enterprise into Asia, India and Africa. From this standpoint, any colonized person who insisted upon the need for local rituals or practices, outer manifestations, could be dismissed as not genuinely religious.

In 1877 the Dutch government passed the Dutch Universities Act which separated its state universities from the Dutch Reformed Church. Dogmatics and practical theology were replaced by the history of religions. The science of religion, *Religionswissenschaft*, emerged as an alternative to theology. Despite the new science's pretension to scientific neutrality, models of religion based on the Christian West shaped scholars' perception of foreign customs.

Take the notion of 'Hinduism', a category widely recognized as a fiction created in the colonial era to make sense of what, for British Protestants, was a baffling array of practices. Hinduism was constructed by Western scholars based upon a Judeo-Christian understanding of what would constitute a religion as India lay under British rule. The construction of Hinduism took place by identifying the heart of Indian religion with a body of sacred texts. Indeed, Western religious traditions are text-based – the Hebrew Bible, the Christian Bible, the Qur'an – Hinduism too had to be organized around the written word. The earliest translators of Indian texts were Christian missionaries who constructed a uniform canon from a wide assortment of materials and traditions. Missionaries were followed by politicians. The *Dharmasastras*, for example, were translated by the British ruling authority under the mistaken assumption that they represented a comprehensive Hindu law code while in fact they were a set of laws governing only the priestly *Brahmin* caste. In reality, there was no uniformity to be found. In addition, Europe's conflicted religious history, in which

doctrinal differences led to violence, fed into missionary and scholarly perceptions of the unity of Hinduism as an entity. They saw no other way to explain the peaceful coexistence among apparently rival gods; they had to belong to the same religion.

Central to the creation of the new science of religion was the accumulation of texts. Scholars needed something to study. A pivotal figure in this process was Max Müller (1823–1900), professor of comparative philology at Oxford, under whose editorship the 50-volume *The Sacred Books of the East* (1879–1910) was compiled and who previously, with the sponsorship of the East India Company, had prepared the first critical edition of the *Rig-Veda*. The establishment of a textual grounding to foreign religious practices helped establish notions of Christian, and thus Western, superiority.

Here Buddhism, another category that does not emerge until the 18th century – it is not until the eighth edition of the Encyclopedia Britannica (1853–61) that under the entry 'Japan' there is mention of 'the religion of the Buddha' – is useful as an example. In the first half of the 19th century, Buddhism was an array of practices to be found outside of Europe, in the far Orient, a location that was geographically and culturally other. The location of Buddhism, from the Orient to the Christian West, begins to shift in 1824, the year Brian Houghton Hodgson (1800–94) proclaims that the original documents of the Buddhist canon are to be found in Sanskrit in the monasteries of Nepal. These documents make their way into libraries in Calcutta, London, Oxford and Paris. By the second half of the 19th century the seat of Buddhism is no longer the Orient but rather Western libraries that collected and studied the ancient texts. Buddhism, previously only found in the Orient, was now being judged by a Western consciousness that through the possession of texts claimed to know what Buddhism truly was and should be. The West now held the key to understanding the true essence of Buddhism.

Hinduism and Buddhism, as constructed in the West, avoided monks, ritual, the vernacular, the native layperson, and focused instead on enlightenment gained through knowledge. Their ideal state was thus built around a Protestant and Enlightenment model of religion: downplaying ritual and affirming internal states of belief. When the lives of monks, the practice of rituals, the existence of shrines, the practice of everyday religion came to be defined in relation to texts interpreted by the West, these real-life expressions in the East came to be seen as signs of a degenerating and corrupt religion. This, in turn, justified the missionary zeal of a supposedly thriving Christianity and Western world over the Orient and its religions in decay.

The construction and denigration of religions outside the Christian West followed a different path in Africa. In this context African religious practices, rather than examples of degeneration, served as examples of animism, identified by E. B. Tylor (1832–1917) in his *Primitive culture: researches into the development of mythology, philosophy, religion, language, art and custom* (1871), as the primitive religion of humankind. African practices and peoples were incorporated into evolutionary theories of religion as examples of the prehistory of humankind, occupants of the lowest rung of the civilizational ladder. Once again, this categorization of a people's practices carried severe social and political implications. Witness the emergence of an apartheid comparative religion developed by figures such as Afrikaner anthropologist and administrator for Bantu affairs, W. M. Eiselen, in 20th-century South Africa. For apartheid comparative religion, Africans had not fully developed the capacity for reason, as made evident by their religious practices. Given their primitive mentality Christian education was the only way they could become useful to the nation. Until then the rational use of the land required, as the Tomlinson Commission stated in 1955, that 80 per cent of the population be relegated to 13 per cent of the land. The 'white man's burden' and the usurpation of land were thus backed up by the comparative study of religion.

One can also see this process at work in the United States at Chicago's 1893 World's Columbian Exposition, celebrating the 400th anniversary of Columbus's voyage to the New World. These international exhibits (20 per cent of the English population visited the 1851 London's Great Exhibition while Chicago's was visited by 27 million people at a time the country's population stood at 66 million) were places where the pathway of modernization was demonstrated through the cataloguing of peoples. In the United States, Native Americans were the group

used to highlight the evolution of human beings from superstition to modernity. It is no coincidence, therefore, that while other social groups organized their own exhibits, Native American cultures were displayed by American anthropologists. They were remnants of a past left behind.

The first ever World Parliament of Religions, held as part of the Columbian Exposition, included representatives from Hinduism, Buddhism, Judaism, Roman Catholicism, Eastern Orthodoxy, Protestantism, Islam, Shinto, Confucianism, Taoism, Jainism and others. One figure stood above all others, the Hindu Swami Vivekananda (1863–1902). Vivekananda argued that Hinduism was the universal religion of the human race and the answer to Western materialism. His talk met with great success and he proceeded to travel and lecture throughout the United States, opening Vedantic centres in New York and London and becoming a major influence on the Theosophical Society. Most importantly, Vivekananda takes the Western construction of Hinduism and the Western construction of religion for his own purposes. With him, the colonial definition of Hinduism as otherworldly and mystical is embraced as India's redeeming gift to humankind. The stereotypes used to paint the picture of a passive and meek Indian are instead used to highlight superiority to the West. Vivekananda, furthermore, constructs his Hinduism on what is arguably a Protestant Christian template. For him, Hinduism is empty of specific ritual practice, lacks temple worship, and instead is based upon the pursuit of inner wisdom through the practice of *yoga* (Sanskrit word meaning 'discipline'). His Hinduism avoided any kind of sectarian debate and provided a basis for Indian identity that would serve as an impetus toward the struggle for independence from British rule. The religious and cultural unity that colonial scholars had invented now served as the basis for a fusion of nation and religion in the quest for an autonomous India. Indeed, Vivekananda's take on Hinduism would later influence figures as diverse as the atheist Hindu nationalist Savarkar (1883–1966), Mahatma Gandhi (1869–1948), the mystic Sri Aurobindo (Aurobindo Ackroyd Ghose, 1872–1950) and the first prime minister of a free India, Jawaharlal Nehru (1889–1964), all of whom played a role in Indian independence.

The end of religion or religion resurrected?

International expositions at the end of the 19th century organized cultures and religions according to their supposed level of development; the exhibits themselves were architectural incarnations of social evolutionism. According to some theorists, this evolution would lead to the gradual disappearance of religion in more advanced societies. The 'secularization thesis' owes its origin to a host of different thinkers including Auguste Comte (1798–1857), who coined the term sociology, and whose four-volume *Système de politique positive* (1851–54) argued that humankind progresses from the theological to the metaphysical to the positive stage; Karl Marx (1818–83), who in early writings such as his 'Contribution to a critique of Hegel's Philosophy of Right' and 'On the Jewish Question' (1843) claimed that religion was a defect that would be overcome as society overcame capitalism; and Sigmund Freud (1856–1939) who in his *The future of an illusion* (1927) argued that it was both imperative and inevitable that society move from placing its trust in religion to placing its trust in society. Within this line of thought secularization is the inevitable outcome of modernization, and modernization is seen as necessarily harmful to religion.

The secularization thesis lies in the background of what is today perhaps the most important issue in religion – the struggle between liberal and fundamentalist worldviews. Within Christianity, this struggle has played itself out most openly in the United States. It origins lie in two developments. First, the scientific revolution brought about by the work of Copernicus, Galileo and Newton. Modern scientific beliefs were often at odds with established religious beliefs; Scripture and nature no longer mirrored each other. Second, the rise of biblical criticism in the 19th and early 20th centuries, exemplified in works such as David Friedrich Strauss's (1808–1874) *Life of Jesus* (1837), Albert Schweitzer's (1875–1965) *The quest of the historical Jesus* (1906), and Rudolf Bultmann's (1884–1976) *History of the Synoptic tradition* (1921). Once scholars approached the Bible as an object of study their conclusions were threatening to traditional Christian beliefs. Most Christians, for example, had believed that the Gospels were historically accurate pictures of Jesus. Biblical scholars, starting with Strauss, concluded that this was unequivocally not the case. But if the Gospels were not historically accurate pictures of Jesus, then what was? Where can believers go to find the historical Jesus? The assault on the Bible was particularly treacherous for Protestant Christians. For them, following Martin Luther, the Bible is the privileged anchor for right belief. How is one supposed to define right belief when its source no longer seems secure? These developments seemed to relegate religious belief to the sphere of blind faith and lent credence to the argument that as societies matured religion would gradually disappear.

Liberalism was one reaction to these developments. Liberal thinkers such as John Dewey (1859–1952) in *A common faith* (1934) and liberal theologians such as Gordon Kaufman in his *In face of mystery* (1995) embraced the conclusions of the scientific revolution and biblical criticism and rethought Christianity for a new age by getting rid of those elements that do not fit within a modern scientific worldview. Here the tendency is to update Christian ideas so they do not clash with the progress of knowledge. Fundamentalism was the other reaction. In 1910 a group of Protestant Christians wrote a pamphlet titled 'The Fundamentals'. Those who subscribed to the pamphlet's ideas came to be known as fundamentalists. Unlike liberals, they emphasized strict obedience to, and belief in, the Bible as the answer to all of life's questions. The liberal and fundamentalist position famously clashed in the 1925 Scopes 'monkey trial'. Scopes, a teacher of high-school biology in the US, was on trial for defying a state law that forbade the teaching of evolutionary theory in public schools. During the trial, the prosecution defended biblical inerrancy while the defence ridiculed biblical literalism. The Supreme Court eventually reversed Scopes' conviction.

The 20th-century Middle East has been the other main arena where the secularization thesis, and the struggle between liberalism and fundamentalism, have been played out. The conditions under which Islamic fundamentalism emerged, however, are different from its Christian counterpart. While the latter set itself up in opposition to innovation within its own culture, Islamic fundamentalism focused on innovation spread by Western imperialism.

Take as an example Turkey, the former core of the Ottoman Empire, the last remaining Islamic empire which collapsed following the Central Powers' defeat in World War I. Turkey declared its independence in 1922 under the leadership of Mustafa Kemal Atatürk (1881–1938). Atatürk followed an explicitly Western model in mapping Turkey's development and forced the adoption of Western customs and institutions. He dissolved Islamic religious order, replaced shari'a (Islamic law) with a new civil code, closed Islamic schools, banned traditional Islamic dress and enforced Western dress codes, banned the use of Arabic script and replaced it with the Latin-based alphabet, and despite the Islamic prohibition on alcoholic beverages established a state-owned industry and encouraged domestic production. Atatürk thus embarked on a programme of radical modernization part and parcel of which was the secularization of society – the forced transformation of a region according to parameters defined elsewhere as to what modern society should look like. The implicit model of religion, moreover, was that propagated by Locke and Schleiermacher, an internal state or belief with no consequences for public life. The continued influence of a European Enlightenment model of religion in the construction of Turkey as a nation state is thus evident.

The transnational spread of a privatized model of religion in the Middle East produced a strong counter-reaction among Muslims who remained committed to a society based upon Islam. This reaction intensified with the failure of these Western-inspired models to deal with the needs of their societies. In addition, the Arab defeat in the Six Day War with Israel in 1967 was seen as revealing the impotence of Muslims despite their independence from colonial rule and Israel's annexation of Jerusalem for its capital highlighted the failure of the West as an ally.

The model of society and religion upon which these developments were based was opposed by the intellectual forerunners of Islamic fundamentalism, including Mawlana Maududi (1903–79), founder of Jamaat-e-Islami, one of Pakistan's more important Islamic parties, Hassan al-Bana (1906–49), founder of the Muslim Brotherhood, and Sayyid Qutb (1906–66) who spent ten years in an Egyptian prison and whose Milestones (1964) was deemed so dangerous that anyone in possession of a copy could be tried for sedition. For all these figures Islam was the only legitimate basis for society; for them Islam's very nature was public and encompassed all spheres of existence. Governments who engaged in secular reforms, moreover, were by definition illegitimate and thus should be opposed. In fact, the weakness of Arab states stems from their adoption of Western secular ideas. The path to strength, therefore, is the rejection of an imposed model of religion and society and the return to Islam. These are the ideas that lie at the foundation of groups such as Hamas, Hezbollah and Al-Qaeda.

Across the world, from Asia to the Middle East to the United States, fundamentalist religious movements are on the rise. This rise represents a crisis of the model of privatized religion inherited from the Enlightenment. Samuel Huntington in his The clash of civilizations and the remaking of world order (1996) has argued that future wars will be based neither on ideology nor economics but on culture, religion therefore playing a central role. Huntington's thesis, however, has been criticized for making civilizations and religions monolithic blocs, thus ignoring the diversity of views present in categories such as Islam or the West. More accurate, perhaps, is to see the rise of fundamentalism as a struggle over the redefinition of religion and its place in modern life; a rebellion against the privatized faith of the Enlightenment that is being played out within different religious traditions.

Ivan Petrella

Bibliography

Almond P. C. 1988. The British discovery of Buddhism. Cambridge: Cambridge University Press.

Burris J. P. 2001. Exhibiting religion: colonialism and spectacle at international expositions 1851–1893. Charlottesville: University Press of Virginia.

Capps W. 1995. Religious studies: the making of a discipline. Minneapolis: Fortress.

Chidester D. 1996. Savage systems: colonialism and comparative religion in Southern Africa. Charlottesville: University Press of Virginia.

King R. 1999. 'Orientalism and the modern myth of "Hinduism"', Numen, 46, 2, 146–85.

Masuzawa T. 2005. The invention of world religions or, how European universalism was preserved in the language of pluralism. Chicago: Chicago University Press.

Smith J. Z. 2004. Relating religion: essays in the study of religion. Chicago: Chicago University Press.

van der Veer P. 2001. *Imperial encounters: religion and modernity in India and Britain.* Princeton: Princeton University Press.

Related essays

Buddhism; Christianity; civilizations; decolonization; empire and migration; evangelicalism; expositions; feel-good culture; Gandhi, Mohandas Karamchand; Ghose, Aurobindo Ackroyd; Islam; knowledge; liberalism; liberation theology; missionaries; modernity; religious fundamentalism; religious pilgrimage; Santería; Shi'i Islam; voodoo; Westernization; yoga

Religious fundamentalism

Religious fundamentalism describes belief systems characterized by the rejection of modern values and the embrace of scriptural literalism. Religious fundamentalism can be found in all major world religions and is often associated with political concerns of nation states. The term 'fundamentalism' was coined in 1920 to describe a movement of conservative American Protestant groups. These groups collectively published a series of brochures entitled 'The fundamentals: a testimony to truth', which promoted a literalist reading of the Bible. The Bible, according to the contributing authors, was the infallible word of God and ought to be understood literally, rather than interpretively, as proponents of liberal theology and biblical criticism advocated.

Since the 1920s, the term 'fundamentalism' has been generalized to apply also to Catholics and non-Christians in other parts of the world. In 1957 Leonard Binder, a scholar of Islam, applied the term 'fundamentalism' to describe the politicization of religion on the Indian subcontinent as a reaction to European colonialism. He found that the European colonial enterprise ironically paved the way for its own downfall by providing the texts Indian politicians would later use to forge an independent national identity. Because Protestant European scholars classified the array of ritual and belief they observed on the subcontinent as the religion of Hinduism – and all religions, they assumed, revolve around sacred text – they sought translations of narratives to function as scripture. Indian nationalists appropriated these texts to create a national mythology that supported the independence movement. With the Islamic Revolution of 1979, journalists employed the term 'fundamentalism' to describe Muslims who employed dramatic and sometimes violent means to draw attention to Western political, economic, and cultural interference in Iran. This usage shares similarities with Binder's application of fundamentalism to describe the appropriation of religion in non-Western, non-Christian contexts to protest Western imperialism.

Despite the broadening of the fundamentalist label, religious fundamentalism typically involves a shared set of distinct characteristics. Religious fundamentalists reject modern values in favour of principles found in revealed scripture. Based upon selective readings of scripture, religious fundamentalists harbour visions of a Golden Age characterized by a divine moral order. This moral order is often hierarchical, patriarchal, and rigid, with set rules for collective worship, and may be led by a visionary charismatic leader. A partial reading of scripture combined with loyalty to a scripturally inspired history inspires religious fundamentalists to agitate for changes within the present so that it may resemble a more idealized past.

Religious fundamentalists, in advocating anti-modern values, see no hypocrisy in using modern technology, such as the Internet, cell phones, and air travel, to achieve their social and political goals. Moreover, such technology has enabled local fundamentalist groups to develop into international organizations by maintaining communication across national boundaries. Fundamentalist groups are also able to communicate transnationally by taking advantage of international television coverage. Fundamentalist demonstrators in non-English-speaking countries will often display messages written in English in the knowledge that television crews will broadcast their footage around the globe. Modern technology has facilitated radical fundamentalists to observe and appropriate violent tactics from each other across national and cultural borders. The widespread use of suicide attacks by the Tamil Tigers of Sri Lanka in the 1980s was followed by a rise in suicide attacks by Palestinian groups in the 1990s. Radical religious fundamentalists view the use of such violent tactics not as criminal behaviour, but as defensive measures to reclaim or defend moral ideals.

Fundamentalist movements are transnational in distinct ways. The ultra-orthodox Jewish *haredim*, for example, attempt to live in such a way as to deny the legitimacy of national boundaries. Following the Holocaust, the *haredim* found refuge in large cities in the United States and Israel, where they were allowed to develop relatively independent communities with their own schools, hospitals, police, and other civil institutions. By living in such insular communities, the *haredim* identify themselves first and foremost as religious believers, rather than as participants in political entities. As a result, they live a tenuous existence, both living within nations and yet denying their legitimacy on religious grounds.

In contrast to the *haredim*, Roman Catholic traditionalists do not deny the legitimacy of the state and, in fact, are often recognized for their involvement in right-wing national politics. They reject *aggiornamento*, or the updating of traditions established with the Second Vatican Council of 1962–65, beginning with their defence of the Latin Tridentine liturgy. Their insistence upon continuing to perform the Latin mass in spite of the rise of national languages symbolizes a protest against the perceived decline of the Church in the face of modernity's challenges.

The transnational character of Roman Catholic traditionalism also develops out of the seminary system of education, publishing ventures, and international conferences. In order to attend a traditionalist seminary, such as the Ecône seminary (Switzerland), students often seek their education abroad, and then return to their home countries to establish traditionalist churches. The traditionalist movement is further strengthened by a number of independent publishing initiatives with international audiences. In particular, *The Remnant*, a journal published by Walter Matt of St Paul, Minnesota, is responsible for importing Roman Catholic traditionalism to the Americas from Europe. Finally, a number of popular international conferences made possible by commercial air travel enable the growth of Roman Catholic traditionalism. Drawing upon the tradition of papal visits, these conferences attract thousands of the curious faithful and are often responsible for introducing elements of traditionalism, as well as charismatic worship, to Catholic audiences around the world.

Islamic fundamentalism rose in notoriety in the late 1970s during the hostage crisis of the Iranian Revolution and gained momentum with the 1981 assassination of Egyptian President Anwar Sadat. Most recently 'Islamic fundamentalism' has referred to the Taliban of Afghanistan, Osama Bin Laden's multinational Al-Qaeda movement, and a number of suicide bombings carried out by Muslims. The roots of Islamic fundamentalism are often traced to early theological developments, which then merged with anti-imperial activism in the 19th and 20th centuries.

Islamic fundamentalism is closely associated with Wahhabism, a rigid form of Islam that emphasizes the unity of God, rejects saint veneration, and renounces changes to the early teachings and practices of Islam. Muhammad Ibn 'Abd al-Wahhab (1703–91) was himself a peripatetic scholar who studied with scholars from India and taught in various areas of the Arabian peninsula. After receiving the patronage of the Muhammad Ibn Sa'ud, Wahhab's ideas expanded with the Saudi state to conquer most of the Arabian peninsula by the early 20th century. Profits from the sale of oil then enabled the Saudi government to finance Wahhabi religious schools throughout the Muslim world, most notably in Pakistan and Southeast Asia, but also in Africa and North America. With its emphasis on maintaining a pure form of Islam, Wahhabism reinforces the notion that Western colonialism is responsible for the adulteration and demise of Muslim values. American and European economic and military presence in Muslim societies arguably strengthens the Wahhabist cause.

Fundamentalist Shi'ite Islam can be found not only in Iran, but also in Iraq and Lebanon. Although communities of Shi'is have existed outside of Iran for centuries, and Shi'is have long performed pilgrimages to major shrines located across these neighbouring regions, the rise of Shi'ism outside of Iran in the 20th century can be attributed to a number of other factors related both to anti-imperial activity and to anti-Sunni sentiment.

Although the media often use the term 'fundamentalism' to describe religious believers who employ scriptural literalism and religious reasoning to defend political activism, believers do not describe themselves as fundamentalists, especially due to the term's pejorative connotations. Hindus and Muslims find the designation inaccurate given the Christian origins of the term. With Christians and Hindus, their religious identities may further be tied to their national identities. American Christians, for example, may view patriotism and military defence of the United States as inextricably linked to their religious beliefs. Muslims, on the other hand, may find identification of their religious beliefs with a particular nation state to violate the Islamic concept of the *umma*, or community of Muslims. In addition, Muslims who aspire to reinstate a caliphate renounce the division of Muslims by national boundaries and citizenship. In viewing Muslims as a single community that transcends political borders, divisions exist predominantly along the lines of *dar al-Islam*, regions under Muslim control, and *dar al-Harb*, regions of conflict where Islam is not welcomed. Such religious believers view themselves not as fundamentalists, but as true adherents to their respective traditions.

Irene Oh

Bibliography

Juergensmeyer M. 2000. *Terror in the mind of God: the global rise of religious violence.* Berkeley: University of California Press.

Lawrence B. 1989. *Defenders of God: the fundamentalist revolt against the modern age.* Columbia, SC: University of South Carolina Press.

Riesebrodt M. 1993. *Pious passion: the emergence of modern fundamentalism in the United States and Iran.* Berkeley: University of California Press.

Marty M. and Appleby R. (eds) 1991–95. *The fundamentalism project*, Vols 1–5. Chicago: Chicago University Press.

Related essays

Bible; Buddhism; Christianity; empires and imperialism; evangelicalism; Islam; Koran; missionaries; modernity; religion; Second Vatican Ecumenical Council; Shi'i Islam

Religious pilgrimage

Pilgrimage processes, which can be defined as the voluntary and/or compulsory dislocation of individuals and groups towards a particular place that is seen as endowed with a source of sacred power, are present in supralocal or transnational religious systems. They can be found in Christianity, Islam, Judaism, Buddhism, Hinduism, Confucianism, Taoism and Shintoism. Pilgrimages connect the religious practices and beliefs of local communities with the doctrinal and ritual 'orthodoxy' that defines each particular religious system.

The pilgrim's journey engages discrete individuals and groups, who might be separated by language, culture, political boundaries and geographic distance, in the joint performance of religious and profane activities. The immersion in the sequence of ritual and devotional activities that constitutes pilgrimage creates a shared sense of belonging to what the anthropologist Victor Turner defined as a *communitas*, i.e., a group defined by an egalitarian solidarity that transcends social, cultural and national differences. Notwithstanding the broadened sense of brotherhood created by pilgrimage, it remains bounded by the normative limits of the religious system that frames it. Many people do engage in pilgrimage as members of a particular community, articulating various levels of identities in the constitution of a translocal religious system.

On the individual level, pilgrimage can be seen as a 'rite of passage', as it entices a transformation in both the social position and the religious subjectivity of the pilgrim. The process of separation from the ordinary order of everyday life and the 'liminal' character of the journey culminate with the existential experience of being in direct and, sometimes, physical contact with the aimed-for source of sacred power and truths. This process is often connected to symbols and iconic elements that shape it as a rebirth into a purified existence. The status acquired by the pilgrims makes them privileged religious actors, sometimes even religious reformers, in their communities.

The gathering of pilgrims from various cultural and social origins in the performance of pilgrimage activities also reveals the doctrinal and ritual differences that exist among the various communities connected to the same religious system. The enhanced consciousness of the local variation of the religious tradition entices the search for its 'pure' or 'original' form in order to restore the mythical unity of the community. In this sense, pilgrimage also fosters religious objectification through the detachment of religious symbols, rituals and doctrines from their local cultural contexts. This process allows the continuous re-creation of the religious tradition and the articulation of its constitutive elements in abstract normative models.

The institutional organization of authority in each religious system determines the range of possible variation and pluralism in the process of religious objectification that is unleashed by pilgrimage. In pilgrimage centres, such as Rome, Jerusalem, Mecca and Varanasi, religious authorities and entrepreneurs, such as priests, ascetics, scholars and miracle makers, compete for the power of determining the boundaries, the logic and the content of the religious tradition. Thus, pilgrims are constantly exposed to objectified forms of religious tradition through the sermons, texts and images that are produced and mobilized by the religious agents. They carry these codifications of the religious tradition back to their communities of origin as authoritative discourses and practices loaded with the holiness of the pilgrimage site.

The role of pilgrimage sites as centres for the constitution and diffusion of orthodoxies entices efforts at controlling their dynamics on the part of the institutions and power structures that frame them. Religious and political authorities often try to monitor and control the discourses and practices that take place at the pilgrimage sites and, sometimes, go as far as to select the religious and/or national groups that are allowed to visit them. For example, the Saudi government establishes quotas for pilgrims of each nationality during the period of the hajj (pilgrimage to Mecca) and, on several occasions, forbade the participation of Iranian pilgrims due to their association with Shi'i militancy and its political antagonism against the Iranian government. The Israeli policy of forbidding all Palestinians under 40 years old to enter Jerusalem also aims to erase the importance of Palestinian pilgrims in its constitution as a religious centre.

These forms of control are not implemented without resistance. For example, the joint efforts of the Syrian and Iranian government in imprinting a clear Shi'i identity on the pilgrimage shrines associated with the family and companions of Prophet Muhammad in Syria, such as the shrine of Sayda Zaynab on the outskirts of Damascus and of the mausoleums of 'Ammar bin Yasir, Uways al-Qarani and Ubay bin Ka'b in Raqqa, were met with the opposition of Sufi groups who had a devotional attachment to these sites. These Sunni Sufi groups continued to perform their pilgrimage to the shrines and in the case of Raqqa, due the small numbers of Shi'i pilgrims, they managed to regain control of the ritual dynamics of the mausoleums.

Until the mid 19th century the scope of pilgrimage was limited by the difficulties and costs of dislocation over long distances and was largely defined within conceptual and practical frameworks given by the local community. The globalization of new technologies of transportation – such as railways and the steamship – and communication – such as the printing press and telegraph – which was fostered by the imperialist expansion of the European powers, allowed the emergence of mass pilgrimage. The equilibrium between processes of localization and objectification of the religious tradition was deeply altered by this, as the circulation of people on the pilgrimage routes was carried out faster and on a larger scale. Central 'orthodoxies' circulated through mass-produced texts carried by larger numbers of pilgrims.

The number of pilgrims performing the hajj in Mecca well illustrates this trend, as there were 50,000 in 1850, 200,000 by 1890, 645,000 in 1972, more than 1 million in 1983 and 2.5 million in 2005. On the local level, the example of the construction of railroads and ports by the Dutch in Indonesia shows how the introduction of new technologies of transportation and communication enhanced the process of Islamization in rural areas of Java in the late 19th century. These technologies lessened the time and the costs of the pilgrimage to Mecca and of the production of religious texts. Therefore, the circulation of pilgrims, Muslim missionaries and Islamic texts was facilitated among the Javanese.

During the 19th century the ideological character of pilgrimage acquired further political meanings as empires and emerging nation states disputed pilgrimage centres and routes, in order to control the religious production of meanings and give a sacred character to their power. Thus, after 1860 the Ottoman sultans started to sponsor and organize the routes of pilgrimage to Mecca by favouring certain intermediary centres, such as Cairo and Damascus, from which the pilgrims should leave. This process culminated in the construction of the Hijaz Railway in 1908, linking Damascus to Medina, in order to facilitate the dislocation of larger groups of pilgrims on their way to Mecca. In the second half of the 19th century, France, Russia, Germany and England fiercely disputed the control of holy sites in

Jerusalem and Bethlehem as a way of gaining greater influence over both Christian religiosity and the internal affairs of the Ottoman Empire.

The late 19th and the early 20th centuries also saw the emergence of new pilgrimage centres in Europe, such as Lourdes in France and Fatima in Portugal. Together with older pilgrimage sites, such as the one dedicated to Our Lady of Guadalupe in Mexico, these shrines affirmed the power of the Catholic Church in defiance of secular states. Throughout Latin America the affirmation of the alliance between the Catholic Church and the nation state during the 19th and 20th centuries was made through the establishment of national pilgrimage sites, such as Luján in Argentina and Aparecida in Brazil. On the other hand, the Turkish republic affirmed its secular character in the 1920s and 1930s by closing pilgrimage sites or transforming them into museums, as happened to the tombs of Mevlana Rumi in Konya and Haci Bektash Veli in Cappadocia.

The topographic character of pilgrimage routes, which delimit a sacred territory and link dispersed communities to a symbolic centre, made them an important element in religious constructions of the nation in places such as India, Morocco and Ireland. For example, religious nationalists affirmed the 'Hindu character' of India by defining and delimiting the nation through a sacred geography of shrines, temples and holy sites connected by pilgrimage routes. On the other hand, in 1984 the Indian army battled Sikh nationalists who had occupied the Golden Temple in Amritsar in order to foster the idea of Sikh separatism. The Orthodox pilgrimage sites in Kosovo and the Catholic pilgrimage in Medjugorie, Bosnia, created sacred topographies that grounded in the landscape the territorial claims fostered by both Serbian and Croat religious nationalisms in the bloody conflicts that accompanied the breakdown of Yugoslavia in the 1990s.

Therefore, as religious nationalism became more pre-eminent in the late 20th century the dispute over the control of pilgrimage sites became also a dispute over the power of defining the political community of the nation. The destruction of the Babri Mosque in the pilgrimage town of Ayodhya, and the anti-Muslim violence that followed it, was an attempt by Hindu nationalists to control the landscape of discourses, images and memories that constitute the imaginary of the nation in India. Similarly, the destruction of the Shi'i mosque with the tomb of the Imams Ali al-Hadi and Hasan al-Askari in Samarra, in 2006, enhanced the sectarian character of the savage civil war that has ravaged Iraq since the Anglo-American invasion in 2003. The development of communication media also transformed pilgrimage centres into world-stages were competing forms of religious imagination and political power are dramatically expressed and affirmed, as was shown in the attempted murder of Pope John Paul II in St Peter's Square in 1981 and the occupation of the Great Mosque in Mecca by Islamic militants in 1979.

Another aspect of pilgrimage that was enhanced in the 20th century was its connection to market practices and processes of religious commoditization. The crowds that pilgrimage centres attract lead to the emergence of marketplaces for both religious and non-religious commodities. There is an individual and collective demand for objects and images that can evoke the experience of pilgrimage, such as travelling, performing rituals and being in contact with sacred objects and beings. The emergence of mass pilgrimage went in tandem with the industrial production of objects and images as religious souvenirs. The massified production of religious commodities, such as posters with religious figures, car-stickers with religious inscriptions or key-chains in the shape of religious objects, enhanced the circulation of the symbols and iconic images thus objectified.

Thus, in Syria and Lebanon Iranian-made posters of Ali are consumed by Sufi Sunnis and members of various Shi'i sects, articulating discrete local devotional, ritual and doctrinal traditions in a transnational religious imaginary. Also, the successful commoditization of Christian symbols and images since the 19th century has allowed the constitution of a supradenominational Christian imaginary. The commerce of religious commodities in the pilgrimage centres also articulates transnational trade routes, as a large part of the religious souvenirs sold in Lourdes, Rome, Mashad or Mecca are made in China and other Asian countries. The processes of religious commoditization unleashed by pilgrimage, as well as the experiential character of the pilgrim's quest, also allowed the resignification of some pilgrimage systems into individualized and spiritualized forms of contemporary religiosity, such as the New Age revival of the pilgrimage to Santiago de Compostela. Thus, since the 19th century pilgrimages were able to create transnational arenas through the engagement of their participants in the enactment and negotiation of their social and cultural distinctions within a framework of shared patterns of meaning and practice sanctioned by a particular religious system.

Paulo G. Pinto

Bibliography

Chiffoleau S. and Madoeuf A. 2005. *Les pélerinages au Maghreb et au Moyen Orient: espaces publics, espaces du public*. Beirut: Institut Français du Proche-Orient.

Eickelman D. and Piscatori J. 1990. *Muslim travellers: pilgrimage, migration and the religious imagination*. Berkeley: University of California Press.

Miller M.B. 2006. 'Pilgrims' progress: the business of the Hajj', *Past and Present*, 191, 189–228.

Turner V. 'Pilgrimages as social processes', in Turner, V. 1974. *Dramas, fields and metaphors: symbolic action in human society*. Ithaca: Cornell University Press.

Turner V. and Turner E. 1978. *Image and pilgrimage in Christian culture*. New York: Columbia University Press.

Related essays

Buddhism; Christianity; epidemics; Islam; literary capitals; Muslim networks; nation and state; steamships; tourism; transportation infrastructures

Remittances

To remit means to send. Remittances are the resources that migrants send to family and associates living afar. Many people move within a country or across international borders to earn higher wages, save and send remittances home. Remittances are an indicator of the strength and extent of social relations across borders. The bulk of this money goes to family members, neighbours, and friends. Thus strong social relations precede remittances. Migrants leave their family behind only geographically; for the most part migrants honour their commitments as providers and therefore send remittances consistently to cover the everyday expenses of their dependants. Remitters send a big part of what they can save from their wages abroad after they cover their own basic expenses. At home remittances are used mainly to cover basic necessities, as well as increases in food consumption, education, house construction and renovation.

Despite specific differences between cases, remittances share many commonalities across space and time. Remittances can be observed historically among English, German, Polish, Italian, and Greek migrants in the United States; Algerians, Moroccans, and sub-Saharan Africans in France; as well as Spanish, Greek, Polish, Albanian, and Turkish migrants in Germany, among many others. In 1906 remittances to Italy equalled a third of the total income from exports, thus making an important contribution to the stabilization of the balance of payments of the Italian state. The Irish government estimates that €4.4 million per annum were remitted to Ireland in the 1950s and 1960s, a major source of foreign currency. In the 1980s the global migrant population was a 100 million strong and sent US$20 billion in remittances. With a global migrant population of almost 200 million people, remittances surpassed US$200 billion in 2005. In 2007 international remittances approached the US$300 billion. Because of the size of their diasporas, Chinese, Indians, and Mexicans abroad send the largest aggregate amounts of remittances, with more than US$20 billion each in 2005. The majority of remittances are sent from the United States, Saudi Arabia, Switzerland, Germany and Spain.

Migration and remittances often arise as a result of uneven international development. Remittance flows are related to larger economic, social and political arrangements. In colonial enterprises, colonizers and bureaucrats often sent remittances to the metropolis. For example, British administrators in colonial India who did not bring their families with them would send remittances to England. Temporary labour migration from parts of England into American states was significant, for example Welsh colliers in Pennsylvania. Between 1848 and 1900 at least $260 million pounds were remitted to England from the United States and Canada. In 1913 remittances from the English-speaking world represented more than 5 per cent of the United Kingdom's GDP.

Mexicans working in mining or agriculture in the American southwest began to send remittances as early as when the new international borders were drawn following the US–Mexico War (1846–48). During the Second World War the Mexican and the United States governments signed a temporary-worker agreement called the Bracero Program (1942–64). Mexican workers enrolled in the programme were avid remittance senders, as their wives and children depended on this income to survive. More than 4.5 million contracts were signed during the duration of the programme, although many of the workers signed contracts for many years, and many others went to the United States outside of the programme. Remittances decreased after the whole family settled in the United States since many migrants stayed after their contracts ended and brought their families with them, or because many other migrants came back home and thus stopped remitting. Nonetheless, new migrant waves have kept migration and the flow of remittances in continuous increase. In the same way, temporary-working programmes in places like Japan, Israel, Spain, Germany, or the Middle East have created a large demand for workers coming from the Philippines, Turkey, Eastern Europe, Yemen, and South America to work in factories, oil fields, services, the health sector, construction and other sectors. This allows the host nations to achieve fast economic growth despite scarcity of local labour. Foreign workers enlisted in binational agreements are often banned from bringing dependants with them, so remittances are the main resources for family members left behind to subsist.

Migration and remittance patterns vary by gender. For the most part, the temporary-working agreements from Mexico to the United States and from Spain, Italy, Greece and Turkey to Germany (1955–73) initially involved mostly men; in contrast most current migrants from the Philippines and other countries are women. While members of both genders who are part of transnational households send remittances and use them to cover the household necessities, according to different surveys, overall female migrants are more likely to send remittances compared with male migrants. For example, if a father migrates, he is very likely to remit; however, if a mother is the only person to migrate, she is even more likely to remit. Female remittance recipients are also more likely to use remittances in the nutrition and education of their children than their male counterparts.

It should be stressed that remittances are not just going to poor countries from migrants settled in rich countries. Family members and neighbours may cover the migration costs as well as the first expenses of an individual abroad by remitting to them. Once the labour migrant finds a job, often through contacts with people from his/her town of origin, they will remit to pay back the debts incurred by migration. In the same way, families with children studying abroad are another example of remittance senders. Once these children access jobs abroad they may then become remittance senders themselves. Thus money, goods and people constantly move in both directions of a remittance channel.

Remittances occur also for political or collective purposes to help in reproducing and strengthening the sending communities, or helping them in their democratization or independence. Thus we see the formation of town clubs, federations, home town associations, and other organizational ties that fund certain political or ideological projects in the communities of origin. The Irish Diaspora often sent remittances to support efforts for independence. First- and second-generation Irish Americans and Irish Australians, supporting Irish independence, sent remittances to the Parnell's Land League and Redmond's home rule funds at the end of the 19th century. In the 1990s, Albanians living in Europe and the United States helped their coethnics among other ways by sending remittances during the Serbian attacks on Kosovo. While living abroad, Mexican, Jewish, Palestinian, Algerian, Kurdish, Persian and other groups contribute to political projects in their communities of origin.

Remittances could also be called repatriated wages since they represent a transfer of economic resources earned through labour or retail abroad by people who keep strong contact and a shared culture and values with family members, friends, neighbours, and business partners. We talk of collective remittances when the recipients of remittances are mutual aid organizations, religious or political organizations requesting funds for common purposes.

In the past, travelling traders exchanged valuable and scarce resources for money that would eventually reach their communities of origin and their partners in faraway lands through fellow-merchants. Remittances often travel through trusted community members who themselves travel back and forth. In the *hawala*, which means 'to change' in Arabic, a network of agents, or *hawaladars*, settle debts and distribute money to recipients far away on a system based solely on trust and reciprocity. Ancient China had a similar system called *fei qian* or 'flying money'. The *Hawala* dates from the days of the Silk Road in which trust agreements, *hundis* (debt notes) and other long-distance trading mechanisms were developed in order to avoid cash theft on the road. *Hawala* networks extend throughout the Middle East, Africa, and Asia. After 9/11 there have been efforts to destroy the *hawala* system with the argument that it can be used by terrorist networks, although there is little data supporting this assessment. *Hawala* is a cheap and efficient way that millions of migrants choose to send remittances home. In modern-day Somalia and Senegal, remittance agents may collect remittances in host communities in the US and Europe and buy goods and appliances with this capital. Once in Africa they sell the goods and distribute the remittances at very low or no commission, while making a profit from the imported merchandise.

The postal service is used by transnational communities to send letters and packages but also money in the form of cash, checks, giros or money orders. Many companies specializing in sending remittances have developed in parallel with national currencies and currency exchange mechanisms. In the UK the Money Order Office was founded in 1838 within the Royal Mail system but a reliable service between the United Kingdom and the majority of its present and former colonies was not in place until 1873. Wells Fargo's original business was the delivery of money and goods across the American West following the gold rush in the wake of the US–Mexico War. Western Union was founded in 1851 as a telegraph company which later became involved in the transmission of money orders, and today it is one of the most widespread commercial means for sending and receiving remittances across the world, controlling more than 15 per cent of the market. In 2007 Western Union executed more than 160 million consumer-to-consumer transactions and counted with more than 335,000 locations in over 200 countries. Local companies, as well as banks participation in this market has increased in the last years. The sending of remittances has historically been

an important business for intermediaries, and has interacted with new developments in transportation, telecommunications, and banking.

Remittance figures started being widely reported around 2003 when the World Bank, the International Monetary Fund, and many national central banks as well as private banks emphasized the need to quantify remittances in order to underline their importance, magnitude and possible use for profit, development and poverty alleviation. Furthermore, remittances have received a lot of attention in the past years because of the foreign currency they represent to the receiving countries, the extra resources they bring to recipients, their contagious spread among contiguous social units, and their potential to create economic development. To put remittances in perspective, the first few years of the 21st century saw the aggregate amount of these private transfers to Latin American countries surpass income received from tourism and exports, and even surpass levels of foreign aid or foreign direct investment. In some cases, remittances approach the level of revenue from oil sales abroad. Oil revenues and labour remittances are examples of capital inflows yet they have very different effects on state–society relations. In the case of Saudi Arabia the state plays a major role in the oil economy with clientele ties to trusted entrepreneurs, while remittances to Yemen have allowed for the creation of an independent entrepreneurial class that could be taxed more effectively after years of crisis. For low-income countries remittances may represent an important proportion of their GDP. Moldova, Tonga, Lebanon, Lesotho, Guyana and Haiti now receive more than 20 per cent of their GDP from remittances. This large inflow of remittances does not mean that this is free money from abroad. Remittances represent the sweat, sacrifice, and loneliness that migrants endure in order to provide their families with basic goods and a humble increase in living standards. Remittances may also increase inequality at the local level since those not receiving them are at a disadvantage. While remittances may help many households in need in the short term, the long-term perspectives depend on whether remittances can be put to uses that can support the receiving family in the future and in the absence of remittances. The evidence for such a relation between remittances and development is mixed since the results depend heavily on the context or the remittance-receiving community. Remittances do not cause development by themselves but they can be of great help when the recipients have adequate structural conditions, including access to markets and basic infrastructure, which allow them to put some of the remittances into productive activities. For example, remittances from the Indian community in the United Kingdom in the 1970s provided needed capital during the Green Revolution in India. But today some areas receiving remittances in India may lack the structural socioeconomic characteristics to put excess remittances to entrepreneurial use.

Remittances are an example of 'globalization from below' since migrants cross borders in spite of state designs, and as remittances show, they keep meaningful social connections through space. Remittances are often seen by neighbouring households that do not receive them as 'mana from heaven', creating social expectations from potential migrants that often encourage a culture of migration within small towns. Individual migration may turn into family migration through chain migration. Social networks can aid in the formation of transnational communities abroad thanks to the resources accumulated in social ties extending between the sending and receiving communities. Transnational communities exchange not only people and remittances but also food, goods, values, practices and cultural understandings – something that has been called social remittances. But at the same time, most of the wages of unskilled labour migrants are spent in the host societies, to which they contribute with they labour and where they pay for housing, transportation, food and consumer goods and which they contribute to and enrich with their food, language, music and culture in general. Remittances are the result of the strong commitments, interaction, and mutual dependence within migrant networks, towns of origin and family. Thus remittance flows change given the dispersed nature of the practice, the family trajectory and the degree of chain migration, since once most family members and associates rejoin each other remittances stop crossing borders and those resources are distributed within a consolidated household. And correspondingly, every time a meaningful social unit is spread through space, remittances may connect its different parts.

Ernesto Castañeda-Tinoco

Bibliography

Ballard R. 'Remittances and economic development in India and Pakistan', in Maimbo S. M. and Ratha D. (eds) 2005. *Remittances: development impact and future prospects*. Washington, DC: World Bank Publications, Chapter 4.

Levitt P. 2001. *The transnational villagers*. Berkeley: University of California Press.

Magee G. B. and Thompson A. S. 2006. 'The global and local: explaining migrant remittance flows in the English-speaking world, 1880–1914', *Journal of Economic History*, 66, 1, 177–202.

Massey D., Alarcón R., Durand J. and González H. 1987. *Return to Aztlán: the social process of international migration from western Mexico*. Berkeley: University of California Press.

Parreñas R. S. 2005. *Children of global migration. transnational families and gendered woes*. Stanford: Stanford University Press.

Tilly C. 2007. 'Trust networks in transnational migration', *Sociological Forum*, 22, 1, 3–24.

Zelizer V. and Tilly C. 'Relations and categories', in Markman A. and Ross B. (eds) 2006. *The psychology of learning and motivation ,Vol. 47*. Amsterdam: Elsevier, Chapter 1.

Related essays

Chinese Diaspora; contract and indentured labourers; development and growth; diasporas; domestic service; empires and migration; guestworkers; human mobility; international migration regimes; international students; mail; marriage; money; pedlars; temporary migrations; trade (manufactured goods)

Reparations

Reparations are payments made by a state to another state or to other parties as compensation for past damages or suffering that the first state caused. Though reparations can be made to individuals or groups as well as states, the payment of reparations is a political act, and is thus distinguished from compensation paid through normal judicial processes.

Looting in war has been common since time immemorial, but the practice of demanding monetary payments, known as indemnities, from the losing side in a war began in

Europe with the Thirty Years' War (1618–48). In the wake of the French Revolutionary and Napoleonic wars (1792–1815), France was required to pay a large war indemnity, and in 1871 the victorious Prussians again imposed an indemnity on France. In the 19th century, indemnities also became common in wars fought outside Europe. The British imposed an indemnity on China at the end of the First Opium War (1839–42), as did the Japanese after the Sino–Japanese war of 1894–95.

Partly because of such association with wars of imperialist expansion, the practice of imposing indemnities fell into disrepute in the early 20th century. During the First World War, US President Woodrow Wilson insisted that the Allies would not impose indemnities on the defeated powers, only 'reparations' for damages done to civilian infrastructure and populations. The new term was intended to suggest that the payments were compensatory rather than punitive, and included only civilian damages rather than the military costs of the victors. The negotiations over the size and allocation of the German payments, however, proved to be one of the most contentious issues at the Versailles peace conference of 1919. No agreement was reached on the total sum, and efforts to devise a workable plan for reparations continued without much success into the 1930s. Though the reparations clauses of the Versailles Treaty were widely considered excessively harsh, and German nationalists made much of this view in the interwar years, most of the sums demanded of Germany were in fact never paid.

During and after the Second World War, the issue of German reparations was again a contentious one among the Allies. Despite Soviet insistence, US leaders refused to set a fixed sum for reparations since they worried that American loans would have to cover what Germany could not pay. The Allies agreed instead to take reparations in kind from the industrial plant and production of occupied Germany. The Soviet Union extracted reparations worth approximately US$10 billion from their occupation zone in East Germany, and the government of West Germany also made some payments, though much smaller, to the Allies, as did Japan and other Axis powers. In addition, West Germany also paid more than US$800 million in reparations to the state of Israel as compensation for the persecution of Jews under the Third Reich.

In the first half of the 20th century, reparations were typically paid by one state to another, but the latter half of the century also saw demands for reparations to individuals or groups within states, such as the movement in the United States advocating reparations for slavery. In the 1993 Abuja Declaration, the Organization of African Unity also demanded reparations for the damages caused to Africans by slavery, as well as colonialism and neocolonialism. Other examples of reparations in recent history include the decision of the United Nations Security Council after the Gulf War of 1991 that the government of Iraq would pay 25 per cent of its oil revenues as reparations to Kuwait for damages suffered during the Iraqi occupation of that country. These payments were ended in 2003.

Erez Manela

Bibliography

Balabkins N. 1971. *West German reparations to Israel*. New Brunswick: Rutgers University Press.

Kent B. 1989. *The spoils of war: the politics, economics, and diplomacy of reparations, 1918–1932*. Oxford: Clarendon.

Kuklick B. 1972. *American policy and the division of Germany: the clash with Russia over reparations*. Ithaca: Cornell University Press.

Posner E. A. and Vermeul A. 2003. 'Reparations for slavery and other historical injustices', *Columbia Law Review*, 103, 3, 689–747.

Related essays

debt crises; financial diplomacy; financial markets; Quesnay, Pierre; slavery; war; world orders

Rock

'Rock' is a generic term that can be applied to virtually all forms of popular music with a strong back beat, often with an emphasis on the second and fourth beats, and usually in 4/4 meter. The roots of rock lie deep within the history and culture of black America. Slave songs, blues, ragtime, gospel, and jazz all provided foundations for rock music. African-American performers also defined early rock (also referred to as rock 'n' roll or rhythm 'n' blues). These include Chuck Berry, Sister Rosetta Tharpe, Little Richard, and Big Mama Thornton. Rock's early development was also influenced by white gospel and

American country and folk forms that have their roots in European musical traditions. Elvis Presley, Carl Perkins, and Wanda Jackson were especially important in these terms.

In the late 1950s, rock travelled to the United Kingdom, where British youth, often but not exclusively from working-class backgrounds, sought to emulate their American rhythm 'n' blues heroes. The results, as can be heard in early songs of The Beatles, The Rolling Stones, and The Kinks, synthesized Elizabethan lyrical and harmonic sensibilities with rock back beats. In the 1970s, English punk rockers made musical and political alliances with Caribbean and African musicians (reggae, ska, Afro-pop), cross-fertilizations facilitated by British colonial heritages.

Latin beats have also been crucial to rock's genesis and ongoing transformations. Ritchie Valens, with his massive hit 'La Bamba', Sam the Sham and the Pharoahs, with 'Woolie Bully', Question Mark and the Mysterians, with '99 Tears', and Roy Orbison's 'Pretty Woman' all exhibit either direct or indirect Latin influences. Rock in español took hold in Mexico in the 1950s and eventually travelled throughout Latin America, becoming especially important in Argentina and Chile. In the US, Latin contributions to rock became more pronounced with the success of Carlos Santana in the 1960s and Los Lobos in the 1980s. Contemporary pop phenomena, such as Ricki Martin and Shakira, have continued to synthesize rock and Latin forms in original ways.

Since its genesis, the global influences of rock have sometimes moved unexpectedly. The Plastic People of the Universe, a Czech band suppressed after the Soviet invasion of 1968, became a crucial touchstone for the Czech resistance to Soviet occupation. In the 1980s, Czechoslovakian rock bands became an important impetus to and feature of Václav Havel's 'Velvet Revolution'. The genesis of the phrase was in Havel's high regard for the 1960s underground New York art band, The Velvet Underground.

Rock was originally marketed as teen dance music, although it eventually sought and achieved recognition as a serious artistic form. Unlike its 'purer' counterparts, such as folk and bluegrass, rock has long been embedded in commercial cultures. Bob Dylan's decision to play electric guitar at the Newport Folk Festival in July 1965 was viewed by many fans as the mark of a 'sellout'. From early on, then, rock has been part of a global political economy. Large transnational corporations (for example, Columbia, Sony, BMI) have historically controlled the production and dissemination of major rock recordings and performances. As a result, the relationships between artists and business executives have often been contested. In fact, the conflict of economic and artistic imperatives is one of rock's central conundrums: the economic forces of globalization can be tracked through the commercial relationships that are central to rock's history.

Rock's simplicity and directness make it a large open text into which have been incorporated innumerable musical/cultural forms. Today rock is ubiquitous. It is impossible to imagine global popular culture without it. Played in basements, garages, auditoriums, sports fields, clubs, and gymnasiums around the world, rock is local and global, national, regional, transnational. Clearly identifiable and long-running rock traditions can be located in places as disparate as Japan, Sweden, Russia, and Mexico. New syntheses and microforms proliferate and evolve on a daily basis: Balinese punk, Korean hardcore, Canadian glam. The ease of global communication and digitalization of musical production make the infiltration of rock into local cultures easier than ever. Questions of domination are thus not far behind. Traditional musical forms must either adapt, seek cultural protection, or succumb to rock's imperial ambitions.

Thomas Shevory

Bibliography

Garofalo R. (ed.) 1991. *Rockin' the boat: mass music and mass movements*. Boston: South End Press.

Kun J. 2005. *Audiotopia: music, race, and America*. Berkeley: University of California Press.

Miller J. 2000. *Flowers in the dustbin: the rise of rock and roll, 1947–1977*. New York: Fireside Books.

Scorsese M. 2005. *Bob Dylan: No Direction Home*. DVD, Paramount.

Related essays

1960s; Beatles; benefits and charity concerts; Cantonese opera; childhood; classical music; Italian opera; jazz; music; performing artists; salsa; world music

Beatles, The

Originally The Blackjacks and then The Quarry Men, then The Silver Beetles, The Beatles began as a 'skiffle' band in Liverpool in the 1950s. Skiffle, a form of music relying upon home-made or found instruments, such as washboards and kazoos, has roots in New Orleans and Memphis jazz. John Lennon, usually considered the founder of the band, was also a fan of American rock 'n' roll. The Beatles' music was thus originally inspired by jazz, rhythm and blues, and rock forms, the roots of which can be traced to the slave societies of colonial America, and ultimately to Africa. The Beatles' musical success cannot, then, be separated from the history of British colonialism.

While the original members of the band were from Liverpool, England, they honed their sound in Hamburg, Germany, in a club owned by Bruno Koschimider. Upon return to England, the band added Ringo Starr as drummer, completing a quartet that included Lennon, Paul McCartney and George Harrison. The Beatles became the dominant force in the then emerging Mersey Sound (named for the Mersey River that runs through Liverpool), a genre of rock with a pronounced back beat, romantic lyrical themes, and strong vocal harmonies. A series of shows at Liverpool's Cavern Club, followed by appearances on the BBC, launched the band into national and then international prominence.

The Beatles led the first wave of an 'invasion' of America that followed the history of earlier British expansionism. Their arrival in the US and appearance on The Ed Sullivan Show generated an atmosphere of pandemonium, especially among adolescent girls. Beatlemania rode the wave of an emerging American youth culture fuelled by a postwar demographic bulge known as the baby boom. Some 55,000 attended a 1965 concert at Shea Stadium, the largest audience for a music show in history to that point. During the tour, the band also travelled to Tokyo and Manila for concerts. Over time, more Beatles albums would be released in Japan than in any other nation. The Beatles' international success encouraged waves of subsequent British invaders: The Rolling Stones, Herman's Hermits, The Who, Led Zeppelin, Elastica, The Spice Girls.

With the release of the breakthrough album, Rubber Soul, The Beatles became pop music's first neocolonial world-beat rock band, by incorporating Indian sitar accompaniment into the hit song 'Norwegian Wood'. George Harrison in particular, but not only he, personified the band's connections to former British colony India. In 1968, band members travelled to India, where they met and eventually declared themselves disciples of Maharishi Mahesh Yogi. The Beatles' India connections helped to spur an interest in the musical and religious cultures of the Indian subcontinent that strongly influenced 1960s European and American youth cultures. Indian cultural references fused with American psychedelia became central features of the Sergeant Pepper's Lonely Hearts Club album, considered by many critics as the band's best.

By the time of their breakup in 1969 The Beatles had reached a level of international visibility and cultural importance that no musical group had previously achieved. The impact did not disappear after the band's partnership ended. George Harrison was the primary organizer of the concert for Bangladesh, staged in 1971 at Madison Square Garden, to raise money for relief efforts for Bengalis displaced to India, the result of state persecution. Ravi Shankar and Pakistani artist Alli Akbar Khan both appeared in a show that was an organizational and musical success and which became the model for staging large rock extravaganzas as international benefit concerts. In 2000, Paul McCartney played a concert in Red Square, featuring the song 'Back in the USSR', perhaps the only song written in the US or Western Europe during the Cold War sung from the perspective of a loyal Soviet citizen.

The Beatles helped to generate the idea of a global popular culture in which rock music would have a central place. Theirs was a brief moment, but an undeniably important one. In 1997 the English band Cornershop, children of immigrants living in Northern England, released an album, When I Was Born for the 7th Time, with a cover version of the song 'Norwegian Wood', this time sung in Punjabi. Thus a circle was closed which had been drawn more than three decades earlier by one of history's most important rock bands.

Thomas Shevory

Bibliography

Beatles, The. 2000. The Beatles Anthology. San Francisco: Chronicle Books.

Beatles, The. 1993. The Beatles Complete Scores. Milwaukee: Hal Leonard Corporation.

Norman P. 1996. Shout!: The Beatles in their generation. New York: Fireside Books.

Stark S. D. 2006. Meet the Beatles: a cultural history of the band that shook *youth, gender, and the world.* New York: HarperEntertainment.

Related essays

1960s; benefits and charity concerts; music; rock; world music; yoga

Romanticism

Romanticism sometimes describes a disposition that can be found in the art of all times and places, one that is inclined to sentimentality, eroticism, and eccentricity. However, it usually expresses a style and set of values that dominated art and thought in Western Europe from roughly 1790 to 1850, a time when the circulation of ideas was facilitated by the unrelenting travels of writers and thinkers within and outside of Europe, by the profusion of translations of new and old works, and by a dramatic growth in the reading public.

Rousseau is considered the intellectual father of Romanticism. His 'romantic' works, immediately translated into many languages or read in French by foreign intellectual élites, spread inside and outside of Europe. Rousseau's books advance some of the ideas which would later constitute the core of romanticism: that humans are unique and original, that they are moved by passions, that emotions should not be obliterated for the sake of social correctness, and that contact with nature allows man to find his true Self. Especially in *Émile* (1762), under the influence of which pedagogical reforms were designed in some of the new Latin American countries, Rousseau rejected universal notions of education and advocated respect for the natural inclinations of each individual. His most important romantic works are the *Confessions* (1782–89) and more prominently his *Julie ou la nouvelle Héloïse* (1761), which enjoyed an immense popularity and was widely imitated. Fydor Emin's *Letters of Ernest and Doravra*, seen by many as the starting date of Russian romanticism, was heavily based on Rousseau's epistolary novel. The only other literary work that can compete with it in impact and readership is Goethe's *The Sorrows of the Young Werther* (1774), a novel that was rapidly translated into other languages and soon transcended European borders: only one year after its European publication, an English version appeared in the United States.

As for the propagation of romantic ideas, the role of Madame de Staël cannot be overstated both as a literary and political figure. Her *De L'Allemagne* (1810), a result of her travels in Germany and arguably the most important book in the diffusion of romanticism throughout the world, became a sort of manifesto where the new sensibility cultivated in Germany was praised and made known first to the rest of Europe and then to American lands. Banned from France, *De L'Allemagne* was published in England in 1813 both in French and English. Thanks to her considerable wealth, her numerous travels (Germany, Italy, Russia, France, and so on), and her vast network of illustrious friends throughout Europe, she connected to some of the most important intellectuals of her time. In Germany, Goethe and Schiller had their plays staged for her, while August Wilhelm von Schlegel remained in her company from 1804 until 1817. Also, her residence at Coppet – a meeting point for eminent thinkers and artists – was where major exponents of Romantic liberalism, such as Constant and Sismonde de Sismondi, developed and discussed their influential ideas. Even though she never left Europe, her works were devoured in other continents. Gertrudis Gómez de Avellaneda – a female Cuban romantic writer who translated works by Lamartine, Victor Hugo and Byron – took her as a model, as also did most of the male romantic writers in South America and the Caribbean region.

The arts came to occupy a central place in the romantic worldview. They appealed directly to the emotions, could approximate the obscure and supernatural, and were the privileged site of human expression. Accordingly, the artist – especially the poet – was now considered a superior creature radically different from the rest of men. In this sense, Byron came to represent a model to be emulated across nations: the talented poet who lived against the rules of social and moral propriety, who travelled extensively both out of curiosity and as a result of forced exile (Spain, Malta, Albania, Italy, and elsewhere), who opposed imperialism, and who in addition died young fighting for the liberation of Greece. An icon of the romantic attitude, Byron was deeply admired and enthusiastically read in many latitudes. He was also the site of controversy in Europe and other places. In Argentina – the place from where

Romanticism spread to the rest of South America – some expressed caution against the widespread enthusiasm for the new sensibility and its political implications in the turbulent Latin American context. Juan Bautista Alberdi, a liberal closely connected with the group of Argentinian romantics known as the Generation of 1837, saw Romanticism as a movement stemming from violent times in Europe, which could only encourage violence in America. He expressed this idea by imagining Byron's fascination with Juan Manuel de Rosas, the ruler whom this generation came to see as the ultimate dictator.

In aesthetic terms, Romanticism rejected the neoclassical attachment to rules, purity and decorum, advocating instead for mixture of genres, creative freedom and spontaneity, ideas that were particularly congenial to the reality of places like Latin America where a cultural break with tradition was part of the independentist enterprise and where Romanticism as aesthetics acquired importance insofar as it could contribute to a wider cultural and political project. Beauty as the central quality of the work of art was displaced by the Sublime, connected to the mysterious, the terrifying, and the grandiose. The Sublime was valued as a producer of intense emotions. Its theoretical centrality for Romanticism was later reinforced by the European expeditions to mysterious faraway lands (like the Antarctic and Arctic regions). These produced influential descriptions and images of sublime landscapes and seascapes that circulated through widely read travel narratives, with an enduring impact on the romantic imagination.

Traditional accounts of Romanticism portray it as a movement originating in Europe – mainly in Germany, Britain and later France – and subsequently spreading to many other countries in an unprecedented fashion, reaching the rest of Western Europe between the 1820s and 1830s but also – among other places – Latin America, Romania, Russia, Bulgaria, Poland, the United States, India, and Turkey, in most of these latter cases starting and fading at later dates. Many cultures, in fact, adapted romantic ideas to their specific contexts either at the very end of Romanticism's assumed heyday or even after 1850, when it had already faded in Western Europe. For example, in tight connection with nationalistic projects, most Eastern European nations turned to Romanticism around the 1848 Revolutions, and cultures under

Ottoman rule such as Bulgaria and Albania did so only after the 1860s. At the turn of the 19th century, certain Islamic thinkers such as the Iranian Sayyid Jamal ad-Din 'Al Afghani' – who travelled incessantly within the Islamic world but also to Paris, London and Russia – or his disciple Muhammad Abduh blended romantic ideas with their own philosophical and theological tradition as part of their project of modernizing Islam in the face of European domination. More recently, during the first decades of the 20th century, and probably partly due to their educational sojourns in Europe, Bengali poets who endorsed Indian independence formulated their own ideas in a productive dialogue with Romanticism, as can be seen in the literary works and public lives of Aurobindo Ackroyd Ghose or Rabindranath Tagore. Also, the Japan Romantic School – formed in 1935 and very influential for over a decade – represented one of the most powerful and controversial responses to the Japanese 'cultural crisis' in the years surrounding World War 2. Drawing on German Romanticism, the Japanese romantic intellectuals led by the prolific writer Yasuda Yojūrō sought to counter the effects of modernity and foreign cultural dominance by appealing to an ethnic Japanese identity susceptible to being recovered through poetry. Accused of complicity with fascism, it nonetheless rejected the charge by stressing its critical stance vis-à-vis the state.

Recent scholars qualify Romanticism as an originary European movement. Emphasizing the unavoidable relevance of the colonial context for the articulation of romantic ideas (both the disintegration of European domination in America and the rise of British imperialism in Asia and later Africa), they stress the centrality of the colonial peripheries in the shift of the European imagination that took place at the end of the 18th century. Romanticism was also shaped by experiences and debates connected to the European encounter with remote lands and civilizations, mostly in the American continent and India. Among them are the acquaintance with new territories and peoples through the numerous scientific expeditions sponsored by European powers in the period (such as Humboldt's and Cooke's), the interest in the study of new languages as a result of colonial economic and political ventures (for example the explosive British enthusiasm in the translation of Hindu and Muslim writings, or the teaching of Indian languages in Europe), and the abolitionist movement, deeply informed by the situation in the colonies and by events such as the slave revolution in Santo Domingo. Also, the fascination of European artists with remote landscapes and civilizations as they journeyed around the world was often connected with colonial enterprises (Coleridge's residence in Malta as secretary to the British governor) or deeply imbued with the colonial spirit (Chateaubriand's five-month stay in North America).

Romanticism arose at a decisive historical juncture, marked by the collapse of old systems and the creation of new models of collective organization. Key political events both in the New World and in Europe had an immense impact on romantic authors. The American (1776) and the French (1789) Revolutions – usually cited as major forces for the emergence of Romanticism – were embraced by many intellectuals and artists because they embodied a radical will to freedom capable of realizing a new kind of society. In addition, recent scholars have called attention to various non-European events (the indigenous rebellions in the Andes, the Latin American uprisings, the Tiradentes' rebellion in Brazil, and the slave revolution in Santo Domingo which resulted in the creation of Haiti) that were central in shaping romantic ideas. Without the political overtones it had in the rest of the New World, Romanticism affected American writers such as Cooper, Poe, Whitman, Longfellow, and Emerson. Also, European romantic painters like Caspar Friedrich or Joseph Turner were fundamental for the development of the Hudson River School.

While romanticism as a literary and artistic movement cut across national and civilization borders, it was closely connected with nationalism. Herder's view of the nation as a community united by a shared culture and language was pivotal for the emergence of nationalisms. Many of these nationalisms developed as a reaction to the Napoleonic invasions in Europe and later generalized to a resistance to any foreign rule. In Italy or in Latin America, Romanticism was immersed in the political struggle for national independence. Romantic writers such as Ugo Foscolo, Giacomo Leopardi and Alessandro Manzoni, writing from the 1810s to the 1840s, denounced foreign oppression, revived past memories and promoted linguistic unification. Giuseppe Mazzini, who started as a romantic writer and shifted to political action, was the founder of a pivotal nationalist organization called The Young Italy, emulated by patriots in other latitudes – in some cases instigated by Mazzini himself – with associations such as The Young Poland or The Young Cuba. In the 1830s, many Latin American intellectuals such as the Cuban José María Heredia and the Argentinians Domi F. Sarmiento and Esteban Echeverría embraced romantic ideas that they discovered through sojourns in Paris, or through the French literature they read (or the English literature they read in French). They embarked on the creation of national literatures, exploiting native topics and landscapes as a way to achieve cultural independence from Spain. Among many other places, Romanticism also reached Russia, Poland and Romania, where Alexander Pushkin, Adam Mickiewicz and Mihail Eminescu were respectively made 'national poets'.

Liberalism, even if usually characterized as anti-romantic because of its alleged stress on legality and material interest, was one of the responses of romantics such as Benjamin Constant and Madame de Staël to Jacobin terror and Napoleonic despotism. Unlike François Guizot and Antoine Destutt de Tracy, these romantic liberals invoked a role for the emotions within political society, both to achieve commitment and to avoid utilitarian calculation at the heart of interpersonal relationships. Similarly, John Stuart Mill developed his emblematic liberalism as a combination of Romanticism and Bentham's utilitarianism. Victor Hugo and Mazzini, as well as many thinkers in Latin America such as Juan Bautista Alberdi and Echeverría, also compounded Romanticism with classical liberalism. In places like Latin America, both circulated as part of the same intellectual mindset.

Romanticism has been identified by thinkers such as Isaiah Berlin as one of the most enduring legacies for our time. And in recent studies, various scholars have also noted the connection between postmodernism and Romanticism. Thus, it also crossed the boundaries of time.

Karina Galperin

Bibliography
Brown M. (ed.) 2000. *The Cambridge History of Literary Criticism, Volume 5: Romanticism.* Cambridge: Cambridge University Press.

Esterhammer A. (ed.) 2002. *Romantic poetry.*
   Philadelphia: John Benjamins.
Porter R. and Teich M. (eds) 1988.
   Romanticism in national context. Cambridge:
   Cambridge University Press.

Related essays

Rubber

Usually made from the latex of the Amazonian *hevea* tree, rubber was, until the development of synthetics, a tropical commodity critical for Western economies, particularly with the advent of the automobile. In 1851, at the Crystal Palace Exhibition in London, American inventor Charles Goodyear mounted a large exhibit featuring a wide array of goods he had made of rubber. In 1837 Goodyear had invented 'vulcanization', a process that combined sulphur and heated raw rubber so that rubber goods would no longer melt in the heat or become brittle in the cold. In London Goodyear was trying desperately to create a market for his products and to outpace his British rival, Thomas Hancock.

In important ways, Goodyear's exhibit foretold the divergence between the largely non-Western production and the mostly Western consumption of rubber that continued throughout the 19th and 20th centuries. While Goodyear focused on his own process and potential Western buyers, in fact the fundamental knowledge of tapping latex, heating it, and moulding it into rubber had been mastered by Meso-American Indians up to 3,000 years earlier. Yet Goodyear's exhibit focused solely on products that Europeans and Americans might purchase – that is, those made possible by European 'discovery' of rubber and Goodyear's 'invention' of vulcanization – with virtually no reference to the tropical origins of rubber or the earlier processing of it.

Rubber production and consumption remained modest until the late 19th century, when the market for bicycle and, after 1895, automobile tyres drove a rapid expansion of the market. The demand for raw rubber exploded. Although hundreds of plants produce a rubbery latex, the source of Goodyear's rubber was the *hevea brasiliensis* tree of the Amazon, much prized by Europeans and Americans for its quality. As part of the global colonial transfers of flora and fauna, in 1872 British explorer Henry Wickham successfully moved *hevea* seeds from Brazil to Kew Gardens, from which their seedlings were ultimately transferred to new concessionary plantations in British and Dutch Southeast Asian colonies. In the rubber boom of the late 19th and early 20th centuries, plantation rubber had, for Westerners, the distinct advantage of ending reliance on Brazilian middlemen. Beginning in the rubber boom years of 1890s, Western and Brazilian middlemen had put considerable pressure on indigenous tappers to seek out the isolated rubber trees in the rain forest. Labour abuses abounded. At the turn of the century, critics of the Belgian King Leopold's concession companies in the Congo Free State did for a time focus Western attention on the horrific abuses of Africans forced to gather rubber from the local *landolphia* vines (somewhat less prized in world markets than that of the *hevea* tree), but abuses in the nearby French Congo and in Brazil were largely ignored by European and American consumers. By the second decade of the 20th century, anyhow, plantation rubber production surpassed the harvesting of 'wild' rubber. It ensured a steady, cheap supply to Western factories.

Plantation owners spoke of the ways that plantation rubber represented 'progress' by reducing 'waste' and 'rationalizing' production. They 'cleared' the 'jungle', while claiming to have 'improved' the lives of workers by giving them employment. In fact, plantation workers hardly fared well. Local indigenous people in both British Malaya and the Dutch East Indies refused to work regularly on plantations, as they had other options, leading Europeans to recruit contract labourers from India, China, and Java (always referred to at the time as 'coolies') who were subsequently held by force to work until the fulfillment of their contracts. And there was no 'improvement' of the former rainforest, where light topsoil quickly eroded and where the monoculture of the rubber plantations quickly led to extensive spraying.

Demand for rubber spiked during the First World War. Although Renault taxicabs running on pneumatic rubber tyres got much of the credit for French victory in the Battle of the Marne, it was primarily the solid rubber truck tyres, such as those used on vehicles supplying French forces at Verdun in 1916, that had an impact on the ways that armies were supplied. Meanwhile Germans, cut off from natural rubber supplies by the Allied blockade, began early development of synthetic rubber.

After the First World War, when the price of raw rubber plummeted in the economic recession, British colonies produced more than half of the world's rubber, while the Americans were the predominant consumers. In an effort to speed national financial recovery, British authorities established the Stevenson restriction scheme to limit the production of rubber and thus increase the price of rubber. Americans, spurred on by manufacturer Harvey Firestone, responded with Congressionally financed studies, high-level criticisms of the British and ultimately, in Firestone's case, the leasing of more than 1 million acres in Liberia for the establishment of rubber plantations under American control. Firestone also worked closely with Commerce Secretary Herbert Hoover, who established a special office for rubber issues. Firestone and others believed that the United States, increasingly dependent on rubber, had a right to world rubber supplies, and they mobilized the language of national sovereignty in a preview of nationalistic American discussions about world oil supplies in the late 20th century.

In the late 1920s, the Stevenson scheme collapsed, in large part because indigenous smallholders in the Dutch East Indies, not bound by the policy, massively increased production on their small plots. In the 1930s, when worldwide economic recession limited demand for rubber, smallholders then simply stopped tapping, exhibiting flexibility in the face of economic conditions that plantations, with their considerable overhead and monocultural approach, could not match. In the glut of rubber in the 1930s, plantations even adapted indigenous approaches, such as ending the clean weeding around the rubber trees, thus limiting some erosion and saving labour costs.

Despite the increased importance of rubber in Western economies in the interwar years, Western consumers had little knowledge of, or interest in, the environmental or human cost of rubber production. Advertisements focused above all on prices, on the ways that automobile travel on rubber tyres would show a buyer's modernity, or his masculine identity as a father buying safe tyres or as a playboy buying performance tyres. Conditions of production were absent from the public discourse.

In the late 1920s, rubber companies began to ship liquid latex, rather than crepe sheets or smoked blocks, from Southeast Asia to their factories. Because rubber was not being formed, dissolved, and then reformed, the new liquid rubber had technical advantages. Dunlop found that latex could be whipped into foam rubber and used for both automobile and household padding in upholstered furniture. Rubber gloves could be thinner yet stronger. Elastic latex was used for swimwear and hats. Latex found its way into water-based paints. And while condoms, diaphragms and cervical caps had been made of rubber since the late 19th century, the new latex rubber was more durable: whereas condoms had been thick and had a shelf-life as short as three months, the new latex condoms had a shelf-life of five years and were thin enough to encourage regular use. In fact, latex condoms were, in most Western countries, the primary form of artificial birth control until the advent of the birth control pill. More than ever, rubber became identified in the West with modernity in the form of myriad products, discursively divorced from the conditions of tropical production in the popular imagination.

By 1939, the American economy was, by far, the most dependent on rubber. The mechanization of American society, not to mention the wide array of new rubber products, required significant quantities of rubber simply to keep trucks on the road and get automobile-dependent workers to their jobs. Rubber from Southeast Asia took on a strategic importance in US–Japanese rivalry in the Pacific. After Japanese troops occupied Southeast Asian plantations in 1942, Americans faced a shortage. As a result, a 35-mile-an-hour speed limit and gasoline ration cards – at a time when the US still had abundant oil supplies – were to limit rubber consumption. By the end of the war, the cooperation of major tyre manufacturers and support from the federal government succeeded in producing a petroleum-based synthetic rubber, ending reliance on natural rubber for many uses. In Germany, earlier success in synthetic rubber literally made the war possible. Among other locales, it was produced in one of the factories employing camp labour from Auschwitz.

For much of the period after the Second World War, roughly half of the world's rubber has come from plantations while the other half from synthetic rubber factories. Westerners maintained some control over rubber supplies even in the face of decolonization. Natural rubber, now primarily in the hands of Asians, remains crucial for certain uses, such as for sidewalls of certain tyres and for condoms.

Stephen L. Harp

Bibliography

Serier J.-B. 1993. *Histoire du caoutchouc*. Paris: Desjonquères.

Tucker R. P. 2000. *Insatiable appetite: the United States and the ecological degradation of the tropical world*. Berkeley: University of California Press.

Weinstein B. 1983. *The Amazon rubber boom, 1850–1920*. Stanford: Stanford University Press.

Related essays

acclimatization; agriculture; birth control; car culture; commodity trading; condom; contract and indentured labourers; empires and imperialism; expositions; forests; love; oil; silk; sports gear and apparel; trade agreements; tropics

Rush migrations

Rush migrations involved the rapid and often excited movement of significant numbers of people to a particular location or region in search of some scarce and hence precious commodity.

There were rush migrations before the 19th century. The mining of silver and other minerals in Central Europe and in the New World from the 12th to the 16th centuries gave rise to sudden movements of population – there were silver rushes in 15th-century Saxony, 16th-century Mexico and Bolivia, and late 17th-century Brazil. Though some historians have argued that these events were comparable with the classic rushes of the 19th century, they were essentially regional.

It is the great cycle of gold rushes in the 19th century, concentrated in recently colonized and English-speaking regions around the Pacific rim, that provides the archetype of rush migrations. Gold rushes occurred in

Georgia in the 1830s, California and southeastern Australia in the 1850s, New Zealand and British Columbia in the later 1850s and 1860s, South Dakota and South Africa in the 1880s, Western Australia in the 1890s, and Alaska and the Klondike at the turn of the 20th century. The 19th century also saw significant rush migrations provoked by other commodities – land (Oklahoma), silver (Nevada, Colorado, British Columbia, Ontario), copper (Michigan, Montana, Alaska), diamonds (South Africa) and oil (Pennsylvania, Texas), to cite only a few prominent examples.

These rushes were characterized by rapid movements of (mainly male) wealth-seeking individuals to a particular place, lured and informed by a transnational flow of information in print, letters and by word of mouth. The rushes thus saw many people move from advanced urban settings and complex economies to a simpler frontier existence where, crucially, they could work for themselves and live temporarily free from the master–servant relationship. In a deeper sense though these rushes were profoundly modern events. They presupposed an ethos that valued and prioritized individual mobility and wealth seeking over quieter and more place-based values; they were made possible by mass literacy, and by modern transport and communications technologies such as steamships and telegraphs. The discovery of a precious resource does not of itself create a rush – there needs to be both freedom of movement and a conviction that a better life might be enabled by mobility and wealth. We still know little about the myriad means of transmission of the information which provoked rushes, or about the decision making which led to people joining a rush.

Rush migrations have individually received much attention as singular and colourful events, but there is little comparative or transnational scholarship. National historiographies have often celebrated the freedoms and adventurousness of the early rush years (before for example company mining prevailed), proudly noting the development of a set of self-governing and egalitarian values that have been claimed on all sides as distinctive national traits. An obvious task of a transnational history of the rush migrations would be to investigate the development of a nascent transnational code of behaviour and even demeanour among rush migrants. A further task would be to demonstrate the patterns of exclusion and inclusion in rush migration societies. In many respects, rush societies were remarkably cosmopolitan. But uniformly, rush migrations created a crisis for indigenous populations as a frenzied invasion of their lands was triggered; around the Pacific rim the significant Chinese rush migrations were followed by at least short-term discrimination and sometimes violence.

The conditions that had made rush migrations possible began to disappear by the early 20th century, as passports, immigration restrictions, income taxes, and world wars eroded both the appeal and the possibility of moving around the globe in search of rapid wealth. 'Rushes' were reported through the 20th century – gold rushes in New Guinea in the 1920s and 1980s and in Siberia in the 1930s, diamond rushes in Venezuela in the 1960s and in northern Canada in the 1990s. But these were not dramatic transnational events; like the pre-19th-century rushes, they were at most regional. The specific circumstances that had created the possibility of the great rush migrations had passed.

David Goodman

Bibliography

Barth G. P. 1988. *Instant cities: urbanization and the rise of San Francisco and Denver*, 1st paperback ed. Albuquerque: University of New Mexico Press.

Fetherling G. 1997. *The Gold Crusades: a social history of gold rushes, 1849–1929*, revised ed. Toronto: University of Toronto Press.

Goodman D. 1994. *Gold seeking: Victoria and California in the 1850s*. Stanford: Stanford University Press.

Morrell W. P. 1940. *The gold rushes*. London: Adam & Charles Black.

Related essays

Chinese Diaspora; gold; individual identification systems; information economy; international migration regimes; modernity; oil; steamships; telephone and telegraphy; temporary migrations; universalism and cosmopolitanism

Russian Revolution

The Russian Revolution refers to the events of 1917 that replaced the Russian Empire's autocracy with the Soviet Union, a republic based on Marxist-Leninist principles. Historians differ on the precise meaning of the term.

Depending on their ideological and methodological orientation, they stress the collapse of the Romanov dynasty in March 1917, the seizure of power by Vladimir Lenin's Bolsheviks in November that year, or the sweeping social, economic, and political changes the new Soviet Union carried out over the next two decades.

The popular imagination tends to conflate these developments. To those who saw them positively, the Russian Revolution transformed a despotic, quasi-medieval backwater into a progressive industrialized power that transcended Western capitalism's inequities. By contrast, others feared the contagion of the Bolsheviks' nihilistic violence and subversion in their own societies. Whether as a secular vision of God's millennial kingdom on earth or as an apocalyptic spectre, the Russian Revolution deeply affected the 20th-century mind.

If Western public opinion at first generally greeted the event with hostility, many intellectuals were captivated by the Russian Revolution's combination of Romantic utopianism and scientific rationality (which together blended ideas imported from Europe with native Russian traditions of rebellion and egalitarianism). Leading authors during the interwar years, including George Bernard Shaw, H. G. Wells, and Lion Feuchtwanger, all reported glowingly about the Revolution's accomplishments. During the 1930s, rapid industrialization under the Soviet leader Joseph Stalin as developed economies worldwide suffered the Great Depression combined with political malaise in Western Europe and the rise of extreme right-wing governments in Germany and elsewhere to make the Russian Revolution's alternative path all the more attractive. Soviet prestige was further enhanced by its leading role in the Allied victory against the Axis powers in 1945.

The Russian Revolution's appeal to its supposed constituency, the international working class, proved less robust. As before 1917, most workers in the industrialized West found Marxism's less radical social democratic variant to be more appealing than the Leninist example. Efforts to replicate a proletarian seizure of power in Germany and Hungary shortly after World War I were quickly suppressed, and during the rest of the 20th century Communist parties in industrialized capitalist nations tended to seek power via parliamentary politics. Despite impressive gains in Italy and France during the decades after World War 2 and substantial support from Moscow, such efforts to emulate the Russian Revolution through the ballot box proved elusive in the West. The only exception, aside from Salvador Allende's short-lived coalition government in Chile of the early 1970s, was in Eastern Europe, where Soviet military occupation following Nazi Germany's defeat in 1945 ensured the success of domestic Communist parties.

The Russian Revolution found many admirers in the colonial and semicolonial nations of Asia, Africa and Latin America. Before 1917 Lenin had appealed to the nationalist sentiments of minorities within the Russian Empire to subvert tsarism, and once in power he made similar efforts to ally himself with anti-imperialist movements abroad. The latter tactic was effective in the short run, since the Russian Revolution seemed to provide an effective means to both independence and modernity. Ultimately, as the example of Mao Zedong's China demonstrates, Soviet efforts to marry their revolution with anti-colonialist nationalism globally proved to be a double-edged sword.

In the 1970s, as the regime it begat grew increasingly infirm, and its deficiencies more evident, the Russian Revolution dramatically lost its global allure. After the invasion of Czechoslovakia in 1968, followed by Alexander Solzhenitsyn's well-publicized revelations about Stalinist political repression,

even Paris's *philosophes* grew disillusioned. The Soviet Union's dissolution in 1991 would seem to have dealt a fatal blow to the Revolution as a model to emulate.

The Russian Revolution left two other important transnational legacies. The first was demographic, as some 2 million former subjects of the Tsar emigrated abroad. With many from the upper strata of pre-Revolutionary society, they immeasurably enriched the cultural and intellectual life of their new homelands. But the most devastating impact must surely be the political reaction during the 1930s in such nations as Germany, Italy and Japan, whose extreme-right regimes derived much legitimacy from their hostility to the Bolsheviks and their Revolution.

David Schimmelpenninck van der Oye

Bibliography
Fitzpatrick S. 1982. *The Russian Revolution.*
   Oxford: Oxford University Press.
Pipes R. 2001. *Communism: a history.*
   New York: Modern Library.
Raeff M. 1990. *Russia abroad.* Oxford and
   New York: Oxford University Press.

Related essays
1848; 1989; Comintern and Cominform; decolonization; diasporas; empires and imperialism; exile; fascism and anti-fascism; Mexican Revolution; millennium; Nazism; new man; social sciences; socialism

S

Salsa

Salsa is an urban popular music and dance style of the Hispanic Caribbean Basin and its diasporic communities in New York and other North American cities.

In terms of style and structure, salsa evolved primarily as a rearticulation and modernization of the Cuban *son* of the 1950s. During that decade immigrant Cuban bandleader Arsenio Rodríguez and others established a presence of the *son* among New York's Latino (then overwhelmingly Puerto Rican) community, where it circulated alongside the better-known and related mambo big-band music of Tito Puente, Machito (Frank Grillo), and others. In the mid 1960s, although Rodríguez and the mambo were in decline, bandleader Johnny Pacheco and Italian-American entrepreneur Jerry Masucci began to successfully market the music, in both modernized and *típico* (traditional, i.e., 1950s-style) modes, via their record label Fania, to a core audience of the city's 'Newyorican' community. From the early 1970s, that community, together with island-based Puerto Ricans, invigorated by a heightened sense of self-awareness and sociopolitical activism and optimism, came to adopt the modernized *son*, under Fania's marketing rubric 'salsa', as a preferred dance-music genre and an emblem of ethnic pride.

Salsa retained the basic style and structure of the Cuban *son*. However, in the salsa community the Cuban origins became largely forgotten and irrelevant, as cultural contacts with Cuba were largely cut off after the 1959 Revolution, and local dance music stagnated in Cuba itself. Stylistic innovations by trendsetters like Eddie Palmieri, Ruben Blades, and Willie Colon, and more general features such as a greater use of trombones and timbales drums gave the music a fresh sound, while lyrics about barrio life and Latino pride lent it a new social significance. In the 1980s the genre became thoroughly transnational, thriving as the preferred dance-music idiom in Venezuela and Colombia as well as in Puerto Rico and Latin New York. Leading performers in New York included not only Newyoricans but the Anglo-Americans Larry Harlow and Barry Rogers, the Dominican Johnny Pacheco, and the Panamanian Ruben Blades. Especially in the heyday of the 1970s, lyrics by Blades, Colon and others explicitly celebrated the music as an idiom that could unite all Latin Americans in an exuberant spirit of self-assertion and pride.

Although salsa is quintessentially transnational, in its diverse locales it has had varying sorts of relationships with other local and foreign genres. In Puerto Rico, for example, in the 1970s and 80s it enjoyed a special status as a quasi-national music, less through the handful of songs that incorporated iconic features of traditional island music than through the popularity of local bands, especially El Gran Combo, a veritable institution in island culture still flourishing, with renewed personnel, as of 2007. For progressive cultural nationalists resenting their island's ongoing colonial status, as well as for working-class *cocolo* audiences, salsa – although largely an apolitical dance music – served as an emblem of proud resistance to Yankee influence, which itself was embodied most conspicuously in the rock music popular among many upper-class island young people. In certain contexts, salsa's stylistic origins in Cuban music could constitute a source of awkwardness and tension, as reflected in various Puerto Rican writings on the subject.

Meanwhile, in Cuba itself, the term 'salsa' has tended to be regarded as an obscurantist label serving to deny the music's roots, but it was specifically the salsa vogue that, from the early 1980s, helped stimulate a revival of state and public interest in Cuban dance music. Since then salsa has continued to thrive, with various local ebbs and flows, throughout the Hispanic Caribbean Basin. However, its once envisioned status as the soundtrack for a pan-Latino cultural movement has been undermined by the vogue of new international Latin genres, notably the Dominican merengue and bachata, and more recently and strikingly, reggaeton, the transnational newcomer which has rapidly spread to markets in Mexico and elsewhere never substantially penetrated by salsa.

Peter Manuel

Bibliography

Manuel P. with Bilby K. and Largey M. 2006. *Caribbean currents: Caribbean music from rumba to reggae*, 2nd edition. Philadelphia: Temple University Press.

Rondón C. 1980. *El libro de la salsa: crónica de la música del caribe urbano*. Caracas: Arte.

Waxer L. (ed.) 2002. *Situating salsa: global markets and local meanings in Latin popular music.* London and New York: Routledge.

Related essays

classical music; culture; jazz; music; regions; rock; Santería; World Music

Salt

As a standard part of our daily life and food, common salt seems to be a perfect object for a transnational history: it is and has been produced and used all over the globe, often shipped around from one continent to the other, counted in statistics over a long period and has become the object of international organizations like the US-based Salt Institute, which federates salt-producing companies from numerous countries around the world. According to the US Geological Survey, world production of salt rose in 2006 to 240 million metric tons, which are not only consumed in human nutrition but also used in various kinds of chemical and pharmaceutical industries, in agriculture and in de-icing.

But what is 'salt'? The common answer to this questions given by encyclopaedias is to point to the chemical definition of sodium chloride, NaCl. But as a 'natural product' salt rarely appears in nature in a chemically pure form. It is usually the product of a technological process which has varied in history in the different corners of the world according to local knowledge and natural conditions. Chemically produced salt, coming out of large units using a highly sophisticated thermocompression distillation process (the standard method of production taken up over the course of the 20th century by most big international salt-producing companies such as Cargill, Akzo Nobel, Salins, Kali und Salz) differs highly from rock salt extracted out of mines or from sea salt produced by more or less natural evaporation. Besides technological constraints and economic considerations, consumers' and industrial users' expectations also alter the conditions in which salt is produced, and even its appearance and chemical composition.

Although the narrow chemical definition of salt has shown its practical utility (for instance in helping modern medicine to analyse the health problems caused by an excess of sodium in diet – a question heavily discussed in Western industrial countries since the spread of the health movement in the 1990s), it never became completely applicable even in the sphere of the chemical industry. Terms like 'the salt industry' indeed mask the broader fields of action of most companies in the chemical industry, varying from potash mining to pharmaceutical engineering. We have to acknowledge the instability of the category 'salt', and therefore the highly problematic status of all worldwide statistics which privilege industrial production and thus distort the picture in favour of the big industrial nations. We also have to identify its geographical variations: 'salt' might be black (in India or Hawai'i), light red (traditional salt from Peru or Mali) or grey (some sorts of sea salt, for instance in Portugal or France); it can appear in the form of small crystals or compact blocks of different size and shape; it can be mixed with other elements or condiments.

However, a general process of standardization can be observed since the second half of the 18th century due to the diffusion of chemical knowledge. This process was at first more palpable in discourse than in practice. Encyclopaedias of the 18th century like the German *Zedlers Universallexikon* already referred to a chemical conception in their definition of 'common salt', but they still used the older chemical nomenclature and had to describe at length the complex manipulations necessary for identification of the substance. In fact the authors of the 18th century, like contemporary merchants and consumers, focused on the local origins of the different salts when they tried to distinguish the specific features, forms and qualities of the product. The place of production was used like a label that helped to differentiate common 'table salts' from medical and other salts and to indicate their particular utility for specific applications, like the salting of butter or fish.

At the end of the 19th century this typology of salt had vanished from encyclopaedias and public discourse. Even experts like engineers or medical doctors would now neglect the variations in the quality of salts coming from different production sites in Europe. But the refinement of the methods of chemical analysis and the technological innovations propagated by scientifically trained engineers had incited a general trend of standardization as the chemical definition was now generally accepted as the common ideal in European industry. Normal components that used to differentiate the taste, colour or shape of the products were then considered as 'contamina-tions'. Nevertheless, even at the beginning of the 20th century most salt was still produced by hand in a traditional way so that the prac-tical knowledge of the salt maker continued to play a vital role in the actual fashioning of the product. Also, long-lasting habits of con-sumption continued to differ in the various parts of Europe: Brittany's fishermen pre-ferring coarse grey sea salt for the salting of their fish whereas the peasants of northern Germany used a white shining salt with small crystals for the preparation of their butter.

Industrial logic was another important fac-tor in standardization. From the end of the 18th century, in Europe and America, there arose a chemical industry that processed salt into soda, chlorine, and other chemicals or used it at some stage of its production process. This required more or less stable conditions for the product. The huge quantities needed in this fast developing industry favoured research into rock salt, which became the main raw material in salt-producing countries by the end of the 19th century. The introduc-tion of new automated fabrication through the vacuum distillation process was a major step in the alignment of the actual product 'salt' with its chemical definition, bringing the level of sodium chloride now up to 99 per cent An old dream of salt-work experts and experi-mented with in some places as early as in the 1850s, the distillation of brine in a vacuum environment posed considerable practical problems to the engineers. After the turn of the century, the new thermocompression dis-tillation machines were conceived in the con-text of strong international competition. In the important Cheshire industries in England the first fully automatic vacuum distiller was put to work only in the 1930s, some years after a similar machine had been installed in the Bavarian salt works of Reichenhall. But as the new machines produced a different, much finer salt, the industry first had to accommo-date the customers who were still accustomed to older and coarser salt.

This incremental standardization of the raw material was relatively independent of the changes due to the processes of concentra-tion in the salt economy. The rapidly increas-ing productivity of several salt-producing sites, like in Schönebeck in Germany or the nearby Stassfurt (mostly due to the discov-ery and exploitation of rock salt together with the opening up of the formerly well protected

national markets), reduced the varieties of salt sold in the European countries and America in the second half of the 19th century. Smaller but ineffective traditional production sites depending on closed regional markets had to shut down, or became specialized in cer-tain chemical applications – a general trend that continued during the whole 20th cen-tury and also affected an increasing number of non-European countries, with peaks in the 1950s, 70s and 90s. One of the last Western European countries to abolish the national monopoly of salt production was Austria in the 1990s, just in time to allow the new Salinen Austria AG to expand into the Eastern European market. Similar evolutions charac-terized the American salt market where the agro-alimentary group Cargill became a major player in the salt business with several acquisitions after the early 1970s.

The growing concentration of the European and American salt producers added to the older tendencies of globalization of the salt market. Salt has been a major component of trade flows between Asia, Africa and Europe for centuries, starting as early as in the 18th century when British merchants began to ship Cheshire salt from Liverpool to Africa and other regions of the world as a part of the triangular slave economy. In the second half of the 19th century, India became an import-ant market for British salt while the Prussian producers made plans to sell their salt to Germany's and France's African colonies.

The European expansion of the 19th cen-tury and the increasing economic global-ization of the 20th century challenged traditional methods of salt producing in the different parts of the world by introducing foreign salt or imposing technological innov-ation. Increasingly, the vision of the product developed by Western chemistry was incor-porated by non-Europeans, who started to condemn traditional methods of fabrication as 'improper' and 'unhealthy' as they would not produce the same white crystals as the European salt works. An Indian administra-tor in the 1930s deplored in this regard the poor quality of Madras salt and complained that 'uneducated' consumers would even pre-fer 'dark coloured salt' to the 'pure white var-iety'. Nevertheless, the introduction of new Western technologies did not trigger an auto-matic alignment of mentalities. As the anthro-pologist Philippe Geslin (1999) has shown, Susu's salt farmers in Guinea continue to produce 'male' and 'female' salt, used for very different purposes, although they accepted the new techniques introduced by French *paludiers* (salt makers) for the improvement of their fabrication methods.

An important step in the diffusion of the chemical vision of salt, however, was the international discussion on iodation that developed in the early 1920s. First propagated by French and Swiss doctors, the adding of sodium iodide and potassium iodide to table and cooking salt quickly became an accepted method worldwide to combat goitre and other forms of iodine deficiency in industrialized countries as well as elsewhere. The worldwide campaign developed by doctors, food chemists, public health officials and lobbyists for the salt industry convinced not only politicians but even reluctant consumers to accept that the chemical addition did not alter the product's quality or change its status from condiment to medicament. The overall consensus about the public use of iodation masked the fact that standards of iodation were not at all uniform and could differ from one country to another from 5mg up to 100mg per kilo. Furthermore, as recent studies on different salts sold on the German market have revealed, the quantities of iodine added might vary greatly among products. Industrial considerations can be in contradiction with clear-cut scientific definitions whose specifications are not enforced, while they are used as a marketing instrument to attract consumers.

In the last decades, at least two new trends have challenged the now classical chemical vision of salt: the promotion of salt as a 'fancy good' of modern cuisine which propelled our commodity item into the lifestyle columns of magazines worldwide; and the appearance of an orange-coloured 'Himalayan salt' on the shelves of health stores and esoteric boutiques. The latter is renowned in alternative circles for its particular healthy emanations. Perhaps the first palpable move towards an opening of the narrow chemical vision was the production of *fleur de sel* by the artisan salt makers of the Guérande coast in France in the early 1980s, in order to secure their traditional profession of *paludier* by promoting a high-quality, hand-made sea salt sold at a much higher price than the usual product. French cooks and journalists rapidly incorporated *fleur de sel* in the marketing of 'national' French cuisine and propelled it into the international market for lifestyle food. The example was taken over by inventive US entrepreneurs who revitalized the traditional salt-making industry in Hawai'i and developed new sorts of black and red salt which they sold to the gourmet restaurants and shops of the American east coast. Although nothing more than niche products, different fancy salts have acquired considerable importance for the salt-making industry as they have helped to change the old image of the banal 'table salt' into a positively connoted part of the modern cuisine and lifestyle.

Jakob Vogel

Bibliography

Adshead S. A. M. 1992. *Salt and civilization*. Basingstoke: Macmillan (now Palgrave Macmillan).

Geslin P. 1999. *L'apprentissage des mondes: une anthropologie appliquée aux transferts de technologies*. Paris: Maison des Sciences de l'Homme.

Multhauf R. P. 1978. *Neptune's gift: a history of common salt*. Baltimore: Johns Hopkins University Press.

U.S. Geological Survey 2006. *Mineral commodity summaries*, January [online]. Available: www.saltinstitute.org, accessed 30 August 2007.

Vogel J. 2007. *Ein schillerndes Kristall: eine Wissensgeschichte des Salzes zwischen Frühneuzeit und Moderne*. Cologne: Böhlau.

Related essays

commodity trading; cuisines; diet and nutrition; feel-good culture; food; gold; health policy; iron and steel; oil; rubber; silk; technologies; trade; Westernization; wine

Samsung

Samsung was founded in the Korean peninsula as a rice miller by Byung Chull Lee, during 1936, and grew as a regional exporter of food products and textiles. It was re-established in 1951, as Samsung Trading Company, and quickly acquired interests in financial services, retailing, food processing, construction, and manufacturing. Its leading technological and multinational company, Samsung Electronics, originated in 1969, and the group was central to the state-led development of heavy industry and chemicals in the 1970s. The three largest business groups (*chaebol*) accounted for nearly 45 per cent of

Korea's value-added in 1998, and Samsung evolved into the country's largest conglomerate. When Samsung, in 2004, was ranked as the world's 21st most valuable brand, it was acknowledgement of its global presence.

The creation of a South Korean state, from 1948, and the military coup of 1961 provided the leading *chaebol* with the opportunity to become large-scale, competitive businesses. General Chung-Hee Park established a strong, autocratic state, and viewed the running of the economy as a military campaign. National interests had formal priority over those of individual firms, although the government depended on the *chaebol* to transform Korea. Nonetheless, within this prominent example of state-led industrialization, firms needed good political connections as well as managerial skills. Lee had to overcome accusations of corruption and profiteering by the new Park government, plus widespread suspicion of the *chaebol*, before emerging as a chosen instrument of Korean industrialization. Strong government, nationhood and modernization were natural partners, but the modernization of a nation and therefore the emergence of a strong state also necessitated international engagement. While government policy protected the *chaebol* from foreign investment and ownership, it instilled competitiveness through export-led growth. Korea relied, too, on technological assistance, largely from Japan and the US.

To understand Samsung's contribution to Korean industrialization after 1961, we need to account for its longer transnational history and its growing transnational role. Japan had officially colonized Korea in 1910, and Lee himself was educated at Waseda University, in Japan. He incorporated his business as the Samsung Commercial Company in 1939, and subsequently established offices in Manchuria and Beijing, all part of the Japanese empire. As a trading company, Samsung acquired advantages in finance, organization and market knowledge. Imperial rule explicitly favoured Japanese economic interests, but Samsung was able to expand, and it was one of Korea's top ten companies by 1950. The Korean War of 1950–53 devastated the firm, but it did benefit as a supplier of United Nations forces, led by the US.

Samsung's diversification and growth in the 1950s reflected the previous patterns of Japanese business groups (*zaibatsu*). The Mitsubishi conglomerate emerged in the late 19th century from a trading business, but, in its turn, it had been directly influenced by the enterprises of Thomas Glover, an expatriate Scot. In this period, trading companies and business groups of European and especially British origin were central to international investment, industrialization, and multinational enterprise. So, the Japanese looked outwards for models of modernization. Mitsui, before its diversification into industry, had been a traditional merchant house, and US traders, R. W. Irwin of New York, remained an advisor and ally in its international expansion. The *zaibatsu* had similarly required the support of their government and involvement in state-directed projects; the Japanese government required their managerial expertise and international connections. Before the Second World War, the European and Japanese empires had shaped the characteristics and flows of international business. From 1945, Cold War divisions were influential, and US support for South Korea and the openness of US markets to Korean exports were critical.

The founding of Samsung Electronics in 1969 highlighted the group's participation in state-led growth, international technology transfer, and trade. Japan's Sanyo and NEC were vital partners for a while, and Samsung continued to establish joint ventures with them. Supply deals between Samsung Electronics and retailers J.C.Penney, K-Mart and Sears, in the US, brought success. In 1975, the appointment of Samsung as 'Number One' General Trading Company by the Korean government, to accelerate the country's internationalization, was a watershed for the company. International alliances with Amoco and Mitsui Petroleum facilitated entry into petrochemicals. The succession of Kun Hee Lee as chairman in 1987, the new Korean government's policies of external engagement (*segyewha*), and rising import quotas transformed Samsung into a manufacturing multinational. Many of its investments failed, yet Samsung announced its global strategic initiative in 1993, and ultimately became a world brand leader in microchips, screens, and mobile phones. Samsung Electronics sees itself as a global enterprise, whose language of business is English.

Samsung illustrates key themes in the development of multinational enterprise and in transnational history: the long-term openness of so-called 'national' business systems;

the early importance of international traders and diversified business groups; the subsequent shift towards manufacturing foreign direct investment; the replacement of colonial empires by the international relations of the Cold War, as determinants of international trade and investment; and the emergence of major transnational corporations with origins beyond the once dominant North America and Europe, and then Japan.

Robert Fitzgerald

Bibliography

Cherry J. 2001. *Korean multinationals in Europe.* London. Curzon.

Fitzgerald R. and Kim Y. C. 2005. 'Business strategy, government and globalization: policy and miscalculation in the Korean electronics industry', *Asia Pacific Business Review*, 10, 441–62.

Lee A. 1995. 'Globalization of a Korean firm: the case of Samsung', in Simon D. F. (ed.) 1997. *Corporate strategies in the Pacific Rim: global versus regional trends.* London. Routledge, 249–66.

Ungson G., Steers R. M. and Park S. 1997. *Korean enterprises: the quest for globalization.* Boston: Harvard Business School Press.

Related essays

Cold War; commodity trading; convergence and divergence; corporations; development and growth; empires and imperialism; industrialization; Japan; technical assistance; technologies; trade; trade (manufactured goods); underdevelopment

Santería

Santería is a creolized religion of Afro-Cuban (primarily Yoruba) origin, known variously as *La Regla de Ocha*, *La Regla de Ifa*, and *La Regla Lucumi*. Enslaved Africans from the Yoruba areas of contemporary Nigeria and Benin were known in colonial Cuba as Lucumi. Lucumi devotion to the Catholic saints that served as public faces or markers of Yoruba deities (orishas) was so spectacular in Cuba that outsiders often referred to Lucumi religion as Santería, 'the way of the saints'. Practitioners cultivate a lifelong relationship of service to a particular orisha guardian of the head. Although Santería draws upon many sources, its emergence and survival are owed primarily to the importation of Yoruba slaves to Cuba

during the late 18th and early 19th centuries, the formation of chartered assemblies (*cabildos*) in colonial Havana (particularly the famed Mutual Aid Society of the Lucumi Nation of Santa Barbara, founded in Havana in 1820), the transformation of the 'national' Lucumi religion in private houses (*ilés*) following the post-emancipation dissolution of the *cabildos*, and the systematic and carefully negotiated restructuring of the religion by Africans and creoles in the early 20th century.

Having emerged from the Atlantic world's long history, the religion finds Yoruba-centred New World equivalents in Brazilian Candomblé, Trinidadian Orisha religion, the Nago rites of Haitian Vodou, and has travelled everywhere that we may find Cuban exiles (especially the US mainland, Puerto Rico, and Venezuela). J. Lorand Matory has documented Afro-Brazilians' history of trade, travel, and cultural exchange with West Africa, a dialogue that has shaped Lagos as well as Bahia. Post-slavery migrants revitalized African and Afro-creole communities in Trinidad. And in Cuba and its diaspora, the growth of orisha houses has come only through similar modes of trans-Atlantic and circum-Caribbean migration and negotiation. Ritual families oriented along lines of African 'national' descent were rerouted through initiatory admission of creoles of mixed African 'nations', moving finally beyond racial, ethnic, and national boundaries. While West African initiations prepared devotees to receive a single deity, Cuban initiates receive their patron orisha as well as four to five other foundational orishas. Rites often salute a whole pantheon of orishas, condensed and miniaturized in a single indoor altar space or 'sacred grove' (most commonly inside a shelved armoire). The material culture of Cuban Catholicism and colonial life has been pressed into orisha service, including iconographies of the saints, prestige altar cloth, initiation dress and enthronement, and the use of chinaware soup tureens to house the deities' sacred stones. Santería has spread and taken on new and increasingly public faces: merging with Puerto Rican spiritism in what has come to be known as *Santerismo*, being re-Africanized in the black American Yoruba movement, and developing as a kind of Latin American lingua franca of Afro-creole spirituality (with the orishas now being served, for example, in Garifuna ceremonies in Central America and New York). In Cuba itself, state sponsorship of tourist initiations has helped spread ritual houses into Europe and Japan.

The ilé functions as a house of mutual aid. As leaders of ritual families, priests minister to the health and growth of 'godchildren' and unaffiliated outsiders who seek assistance. Music often provides a framework for opening practitioners' spiritual paths, particularly via drummings that feature the polyrhythms of the bata drums and antiphonal praise songs to the orishas. Orisha music, dance, dress, and altar making are complexly developed and provide for circulations of a ritual economy that materializes the flow of ashé (sacred force). Established on the Internet and present in almost every market penetrated by Latin migration or dance music (pioneered by many musician adherents), Santería has moved beyond its Cuban territory into ilés established throughout the world.

Keith Cartwright

Bibliography

Brown D. 2003. *Santería enthroned: art, ritual, and innovation in an Afro-Cuban Religion.* Chicago: University of Chicago Press.

Mason M. 2002. *Living Santería.* Washington, DC: Smithsonian Institution Press.

Matory J. L. 2005. *Black Atlantic religion: tradition, transnationalism, and matriarchy in the Afro-Brazilian Candomblé.* Princeton: Princeton University Press.

Murphy J. 1994. *Working the spirit: ceremonies of the African diaspora.* Boston, MA: Beacon.

Related essays

Africa; Christianity; diasporas; human mobility; music; religion; salsa; slavery; tourism; voodoo; world music

Save the Children International Union

Eglantyne Jebb and her sister Dorothy Buxton founded the Save the Children Fund in London, in 1919, to rescue the starving children of former war zones. An umbrella association, the Save the Children International Union (SCIU), founded in 1920 in Geneva, was to encourage the creation of national committees, coordinate actions, exchange information and organize representations to the various private and public international agencies based in Geneva. The patronage of the International Committee of the Red Cross, the cooperation of the international workers' organizations and of anti-slavery campaigners, the voluntary help of many of its employees, and the support of the Pope rapidly guaranteed a neutral, interdenominational and international character, obviating any reservations the initial support of the Anglican Church and of the British government might have created.

The founders trusted that an informed public opinion would abate the harsh terms of the Allied blockade of Germany. Their first initiative, the Fight the Famine Council, aimed at making representations to governments. The Council's relief committee began fieldwork in April 1919. The use of new techniques of propaganda, the unprecedented appeal to poorer classes of society, the thorough accountability of finances, the scientific nature of the knowledge it collected, the emphasis on the autonomy of local populations, were all part of a new spirit in relation to charities and internationalism.

The first campaign provided material support to the Quakers' action towards starving children of Vienna, before SCIU turned its efforts towards the famine in Russia. But this commitment to relief in wartime limited the movement's ability to survive. Relief actions towards children of other countries became more difficult as reports of acute distress were rarer, and it got harder to help countries suspected of rearming.

At the opening of the League of Nations, in 1920, SCIU officers hoped that a direct involvement of the League in the distribution of relief would strengthen their organization and help to create permanent institutions of child welfare. Instead, they received a moral acknowledgement, and an encouragement to see to the urgent epidemic of typhus in Central Europe. By 1924, after the demand for immediate relief work lowered, SCIU nevertheless convinced the General Assembly of the League that work on child welfare would provide a solid foundation to prevent future wars. The Assembly adopted the Declaration of the Rights of the Child, drafted by the SCIU, and created a Child Welfare Committee, on which SCIU received a seat.

SCIU's founders hoped to put the universalism of their Declaration into practice, its preamble promising rights 'beyond and above all considerations of race, nationality, or creed'. The 1920s were devoted to the construction of child welfare systems in Central

Europe. In the late 1920s, they turned their energies to the organization of a Conference on the African Child, which successfully took place in Geneva in 1931. It took five years, and the invasion of Ethiopia by the Italians, for the organization to be able to raise sufficient funds and open a child welfare centre in Addis Ababa. This initiative represented the first modern humanitarian initiative in Africa.

The end of the war and the start of the Spanish Civil War turned the attention of SCIU donors back to Europe, where the movement helped refugees, organized emergency relief, and coordinated international donations. The activities slowed down during the Second World War, but SCIU started planning for the relief of children after the conflict by studying needs and sending workers to work with refugees in Europe.

In 1946, SCIU merged with the International Association for the Protection of Child Welfare, which had worked on legal and medical issues, to form the International Union for Child Welfare (IUCW). The new title reflected the transition from emergency relief to general work. At the same time, the advent of UNICEF forced a redefinition of the IUCW, which emphasized independence, creativity, establishment of networks away from states, and promotion of local training. The postwar years also saw the multiplication of studies and specialized conferences, while the SCIU bulletin became the *International Child Welfare Review*. The IUCW helped in the drafting of the Geneva conventions on the protection of civilians during conflicts, and turned most of its attention to children of the developing world, by forming new national chapters, organizing conferences and helping set up child welfare institutions. It contributed significantly to the UN statements on children's rights of 1959 and 1980.

The IUCW closed in 1986, in the wake of financial irregularities. Since 1977, the International Save the Children Alliance, based in London, has assumed a similar role, with 28 national organizations, involved in 110 countries, and it continues to refer to the founders' values of neutrality, autonomy, independence, advocacy for children and large popular support.

Dominique Marshall

Bibliography
Marshall D. 'The rights of African children, the Save the Children Fund and public opinion in Europe and Ethiopia: the Centre of Child Welfare of Addis Ababa, Spring 1936', in Siegbert U. (ed.) 2006. *Proceedings of the International Conference of Ethiopian Studies*, Hamburg. Wiesbaden: Harrassowitz, 296–306.
Revue internationale de l'enfant 1970, 7, special issue on the 50th anniversary of IUCW.

Related essays
abolitionism; adoption; Africa; childhood; children's rights; Christianity; intergovernmental organizations; international non-governmental organizations (INGOs); International Red Cross and Red Crescent movement; Islamic Relief Worldwide; League of Nations system; Médecins Sans Frontières (MSF); Oxfam; Pugwash Conferences; refugee relief; relief; United Nations system; war; workers' movements

Schwimmer, Rosika *See* Pacifism

Scientific expeditions

While a thirst for learning of the world's natural properties has been a primary motivator for scientific expeditions in the modern period, it has almost always travelled in a trajectory that traced the political, economic, and cultural trends that have shaped the modern world. Science is a peculiarly Western epistemological project for creating knowledge of the natural world, and so the history of the scientific expeditions usually entails a kind of movement from the core of economic and social power based in Europe and the United States to the periphery. The embrace of Western scientific standards by emergent nations on the periphery has more recently given rise to expeditions originating from previously marginalized nations. This history is beginning to to create a more sophisticated analyses of scientific expeditions. The lion's share of historical research, however, focuses on the projection of scientific expeditions from the Western core to the periphery.

While precedents abound, the modern scientific expedition came into its most modern form during the middle of the 18th century and emerged next to the desire among *philosophes* to create an encyclopedic assemblage of knowledge. The expeditionary analogue to the *Encyclopédie* is likely the twin expeditions to Ecuador and Lapland to measure one degree of the Earth's arc. The purpose of the expeditions was to discover if the Earth was shaped like an oblate onion, as Isaac Newton had predicted, or an egg, René Descartes' hypothesis. The expeditions were commissioned by Louis XV and the French Academy of Science. Anders Celsius and Pierre Maupertuis set out for Lapland and quickly settled the dispute. The Ecuador expedition was led by Charles Marie de La Condamine and several other scientific luminaries whose 1735–39 journey is a harrowing tale.

Other geodesic expeditions had more pointed colonial ambitions. The British triangulation survey of India – a herculean task that occupied much of the first half of the 19th century – was perhaps the most explicit instance of a scientific expedition doing the work of creating an imperial archive. A fascinating counterpoint to the exacting standards of the Indian survey was Sir Robert Schomburgk's transverse survey of British Guiana (1841–44). Such scientific expeditions produced maps – shifting inscriptions of a mobile landscape – that were put to use by diplomats and colonial administrators.

Along with people and paper, scientific expeditions also led to the movement of organic and inorganic specimens across national borders. The early-modern European tradition of collecting natural 'curiosities' exploded in the 18th century as kings and aristocrats built impressive gardens, menageries and natural history museums. Gardeners such as André Thouin at the Royal Garden in Paris and Joseph Banks, a president of London's Royal Society, corresponded with hundreds of botanical enthusiasts worldwide to collect vast archives of seeds and plant specimens. Added to these repositories were boxes of natural specimens that returned both from massive expeditions, like James Cook's circumnavigations, as well as the more modest expeditions of itinerant naturalists, like Charles Darwin. Ironically, some of these organisms crossed national boundaries under the veil of intentional ignorance; the abortifacient properties of the peacock flower, common knowledge to many of the slaves of the West Indies, were unknown to many European naturalists and most women.

It is not surprising that the structures of scientific expeditions would closely follow, and sometimes lead, colonial imperatives. This imperial history helped to define expeditions in the late 19th and 20th centuries as well. There were many changes, however, the most important being the development of coal- and later oil-based transportation technology. The advent of the steamship, railroad and the automobile vastly accelerated the flow of scientists, maps and artifacts. Second, the patrons of expeditions dramatically shifted from the state to private institutions like museums and universities. Third, expeditions began to take on new purposes. More than mapping and collecting, modern expeditions were usually designed to interrogate specific questions about evolution or biodiversity, for instance. Despite these changes, expeditions continued to at least resemble and sometimes reinforce imperial processes.

It was a common practice since at least the 16th century for Western powers to establish colonial entrepôts that served as major feeders to scientific institutions in Europe. These locations multiplied during Europe's national period and became important sites that launched scientific expeditions into colonial hinterlands. These institutions were often dependent on indigenous state administration as well as the colonized people themselves. Britain excelled in the creation of colonial gardens and museums in possessions such as Ceylon, Mauritius, and notably Hong Kong and Canton. Indeed scientific expeditions to look into the flora and fauna of China played both scientific and political roles in the movement of knowledge and specimens between late-imperial China and the metropolitan core.

British scientists began actively exploring China's natural wonders shortly after the first Opium War (1839–42). With a foothold in Hong Kong, Britain continued to increase its economic, military, and scientific presence in the Celestial Kingdom. The expeditionary work by British naturalists was spurred by the commercial task of cataloging China's 'useful' plants and animals, but they were also directed by curators at Kew Gardens, the Horticultural Society of London and the British Museum to archive China's natural objects. Robert Fortune of the Horticultural Society, for instance, was one of the most successful mid-century collectors of Chinese plants. On two later expeditions, Fortune gathered specimens from China's tea districts to create tea plantations back in India. Such expeditions were actually quick jaunts of a few days' journey from a treaty port. Naturalists would often enlist the indigenous population in securing specimens. The British Museum issued forth its naturalists to hunt specimens of insects, birds, and mammals. Like Africa and India, China provided yet another environment for the genteel naturalist to engage in the manly hunt – one of the defining traits of late-Victorian natural history. A hunter's trophy on a club-house wall followed the same transnational process as a specimen in a museum diorama.

A counterpart to the slow and systematic survey, like that of British naturalists in China, was the grand expedition – an expensive and many-handed expedition with a daring leader, a team of scientists, and a small army of porters. These were the expeditions that became daily fodder in metropolitan newspapers. A famous example was the American Museum of Natural History's 'Central Asiatic Expedition' (1922–30) led by museum naturalist Roy Chapman Andrews. The effort was actually five expeditions, funded by New York's financial elite, to search for ancient human remains in Mongolia – then thought by some to be the place where humans evolved into their contemporary form. Andrews' innovation was to have the expeditionary teams travel by automobiles to provide extensive coverage of the Mongolian landscape. These were massive affairs: the 1925 expedition alone included 125 camels to portage the gasoline, oil, and spare tyres so that four cars and two trucks could carry 14 scientists and technicians, as well as Chinese cooks, Mongol interpreters, and a camp support staff.

As fragments of America's new automotive culture moved into politically tumultuous China and Mongolia, crates of paleontology artifacts crossed over to New York. The expedition failed to secure evidence of human evolution, but it did discover a trove of dinosaur fossils and, most notably, fossilized dinosaur eggs. The eggs mostly circulated through the laboratories of American paleontologists, with an exception. As a publicity ploy, Andrews sponsored a 'Great Dinosaur Egg Auction' as a fund raiser for the 1925 Asiatic expedition. Chinese officials interpreted the auction as their natural treasures entering the capitalist market – an event that resulted in major logistical problems for Andrews and his team.

Few 20th-century land-based expeditions could match the size and scale of Andrews'

Asiatic expeditions. And as the century progressed scientific expeditions became primarily the province of universities and private enterprise. The imperial nature of expeditions slipped away but was replaced by other, sometimes very similar, practices. Oil companies and interested governments, for instance, routinely employed geologists to search the world for exploitable resources. The work of Everette DeGolyer provides a case in point. DeGolyer was an American-trained geologist who, early in his career, conducted exploratory work in Mexico for a British petroleum enterprise. The financial success of the Mexican venture led to further projects and in the process, DeGolyer revolutionized the techniques for oil exploration through the use of seismographs. Then in 1943 US Secretary of the Interior Harold Ickes asked DeGolyer to assess the oil fields of the Persian Gulf region. The expedition to the oil fields of Iraq, Iran, Kuwait, Bahrain and Saudi Arabia convinced DeGolyer that the Middle East would soon play a pivotal role in petroleum production.

Expeditions on terra firma have been primarily accomplished by small and large groups of scientists from single nations. Yet certain inhospitable areas, like the ocean and outer space, call for cooperation. Both geographies played important roles in nationalistic struggles spurred by the Cold War, but from time to time scientists came together on some legion expeditions. In the 1960s, for instance, various intergovernmental organizations and international non-governmental organizations came together to coordinate the scientific exploration of the ocean. Groups like the American-led Scientific Committee on Oceanic Research and the Intergovernmental Oceanographic Commission championed the International Indian Ocean Expedition (IIOE). Between 1963 and 1965 hundreds of scientists from over 25 countries travelled on 40 oceanographic vessels to explore the biology, chemistry, and physical properties of the Indian Ocean. More than an expedition designed to solve basic oceanographic problems, IIOE scientists intended to use their work to harness the resources of the Indian Ocean for lesser developed countries. While there certainly were bumps along the way, especially the struggle between the US and the Soviet Union over primary leadership, the IIOE set an example for effective collaboration.

Scientific expeditions continue to move quickly across today's national borders. Many of them leave the metropolis to explore issues of environmental management. Since the 1970s, universities have sent out teams of scientists to keep track of the environmental health and biodiversity of the planet – many of these expeditions concentrated on the tropics of Central and South America. Such cooperation also continues today, and its problems and opportunities are probably best represented by the slow progress of the International Space Station. In one form or another, such scientific expeditions share in a long history of scientific imperialism. Whether they represent a continuation of or a distancing from imperial science is a matter of perspective.

Gary Kroll

Bibliography

Burnett G. 2000. *Masters of all they surveyed: exploration, geography, and a British El Dorado.* Chicago: University of Chicago Press.

Edney M. 1997. *Mapping an empire: the geographical construction of British India, 1765–1843.* Chicago: University of Chicago Press.

Fan F. 2004. *British naturalists in Qing China: science, empire, and cultural encounter.* Cambridge, MA: Harvard University Press.

Gallenkamp C. 2001. *Dragon hunter: Roy Chapman Andrews and the Central Asiatic expeditions.* New York: Viking.

Hamblin J. D. 2005. *Oceanographers and the Cold War: disciples of marine science.* Seattle: University of Washington Press.

Reidy M., Kroll G. and Conway E. 2006. *Exploration and science: social impact and interaction.* Santa Barbara: ABC-CLIO.

Schiebinger L. 2004. *Plants and empire: colonial bioprospecting in the Atlantic world.* Cambridge, MA: Harvard University Press.

Yergin D. 1992. *The prize: the epic quest for oil, money and power.* New York: Free Press.

Related essays

acclimatization; Antarctic Treaty; car culture; China; Chinese medicine; climate change; cosmopolitanism and universalism; drink; empires and imperialism; higher education; knowledge; life and physical sciences; mapping; measurement; medicine; museums; oceans; oil; rubber; scientific stations; steamships; wildlife films

Scientific instruments and tools

Scientific instruments can be defined as the tools which are essential for scientific research, observations and measurements, science teaching and many professional activities. They were used from antiquity in astronomy, surveying, and navigation, but only with the scientific revolution and the emergence of the 'experimental method' did their use become fundamental in every form of scientific investigation. Their number grew during the 18th century with the creation of scientific cabinets and observatories and flourished even more in the 19th century following the spectacular development of science and technology in the industrialized West. Together with specialized treatises they contributed enormously to the diffusion of scientific knowledge and practices.

By 1850 instruments firmly established themselves in laboratories, schools and universities and in the last decades of the century an increasing number of disciplines and practices (biology, medicine, human sciences, earth sciences, etc.) adopted scientific instruments. The spectacular growth of new industries (e.g. electrical and chemical) necessitated compact, direct-reading, solid and easy-to-use technical instruments designed for use in factories and power plants. Since the end of the 19th century, the discovery of X-rays, electrons, and radioactivity along with the birth of quantum mechanics and the theory of relativity opened unexpected horizons in physics and required new research tools. At the same time the rapid progresses of vacuum and cryogenics technology proved to be essential both in research and in industry. Better and faster pumps contributed to development of vacuum tubes and light bulbs, while improved cryogenic apparatus allowed researchers to liquefy hydrogen and helium and to discover superconductivity. Following the discovery of thermionic emission in 1880 (Edison effect), the first electronic tubes (diodes and triodes) appeared at the beginning of the 20th century. These made it possible to rectify electric currents, to amplify weak electric signals and to generate electrical oscillations. Electronic tubes were first profitably used in wireless communications for the production and the detection of electromagnetic waves. During World War 1 the manufacture and the performance of electronic tubes were greatly improved and in the 1920s they triggered the spectacular and rapid development of public broadcasting in the United States as well as in Europe. After the war, the introduction of new materials, the standardization of production, and the creation of 'research and development' laboratories contributed to the demise of the old-fashioned 'brass and glass' instruments. In the 1930s vacuum tubes gave birth to a new generation of sophisticated instruments such as, for example, oscilloscopes and compact pH-meters. These very successful devices, which often declared the success of a manufacturer, deeply modified (and simplified) laboratory practice and measurements.

By the 1930s progress in atomic and nuclear physics produced the first large instruments of 'big science' which were accompanied by remarkable advances in vacuum technology, cryogenics and electronics. Industrialists, electrical engineers and physicists started to collaborate in conceiving and realizing instruments, such as high-speed centrifuges, powerful X-rays apparatus or high-voltage generators, which found several applications both in the laboratories, in the hospitals and in various industrial activities. Control, testing, measurement instruments and recording apparatus became indispensable in industrial processes and in the fast-growing communication and electric networks. Instruments produced on such a large scale for equipping thousands of factories, power plants, telegraphic and telephonic systems represented large amount of money and therefore they had to be protected by patents covering all the most advanced countries.

During World War 2 many new instruments were developed for calculations (large electronic computers for ballistics and deciphering), communication, detection (radar) and avionics which after the conflict found innumerable applications in research laboratories as well as in everyday life. After the war, the United Stated was in a particularly strong technological position and their industry fully profited from the technological efforts made during the conflict. The invention of the transistor in 1947 by the Bell laboratories marked the beginning of miniaturization in electronics and the decline of the more delicate and energy-consuming vacuum tubes. The massive development of early solid-state electronics lowered the prices of 'domestic instruments' such as radios, record players and televisions, thus contributing to their capillary diffusion which led to some radical social changes. The first integrated circuits, which today contain millions of transistors in a few square millimetres, were developed in the late 1950s and were followed twenty years later by microprocessors, which made possible the advent of microcomputers. This progress completely transformed scientific instruments, thus dramatically increasing their complexity and performance. In the last decades of the 20th century, computers became the universal interface between instruments and their users, whose senses were excluded from the detection and measurement processes. Instruments produce images, data, and graphs which are independent from observers. With the birth of electronics and especially with its miniaturization, instruments became 'black boxes' whose modular and compact design hardly indicates their function or use. Thanks to miniaturization, even the commonest and apparently simplest instruments include microchips and advanced electronics whose function remains hermetic to most of their users. Today professional scientific instruments are in fact instrumental systems in which a user-friendly technology is able to conceal great complexity.

Around 1850 the production of instruments was concentrated in Great Britain, France (generally in Paris) and to a lesser extent in Germany. In the second half of the 18th century a series of favourable conditions boosted the British instrument industry, which supplied Europe with the highest-quality and most sophisticated astronomical, optical and philosophical instruments. French industry, which until the end of the *ancien régime* could not compete with British industry, developed rapidly after the Revolution of 1789. In a few decades, Parisian makers became excellent manufacturers of instruments, seriously challenging the pre-eminent position of the British. At the same time, the German precision industry, except for a few world-renowned makers of astronomical and optical instruments, did not have such an important position on the international market. But the reunification of Germany following the Franco–Prussian of 1870 war triggered the rapid growth of German industry. Combined with a very active and successful scientific and academic community, this contributed to the expansion of instrument production. Around 1900 Germany emerged as the leading producer of precision apparatus, while Great Britain retained an important position due to its large colonial market, and France gradually lost part of the international market. At the same time, the United States, after having been essentially an importer of instruments from London, Paris, Berlin or Munich, became increasingly independent from Europe. In fact, several American firms acquired international renown. Instrument makers in other European countries such as Italy, The Netherlands, Spain, Switzerland, and Scandinavian countries played a minor role on the international market and their production simply supplied part of a local market or specialized in a very particular technological niche.

Up until the last decades of 19th century, scientific instruments were produced in small workshops with a relatively small number of workers. Only the most famous makers had more than a couple of dozen workers. Around 1900 the most active and successful American and European manufacturers reorganized their production by introducing machine tools and adopting an increasingly standardized production. World War 1 forced many instrument makers to focus their production on weapons and instruments for warfare. After the war, the increasing cost of labour and raw materials, and the sometimes difficult reconversion to peacetime production, changed the landscape of the precision industry. Several century-old firms disappeared or were absorbed by much larger industrial companies. Family businesses tended to disappear and the traditional master instrument maker, who was also the inventor, scientist, engineer, mechanic and manager of his own firm, gave way to research and development laboratories and to rationalized production lines. Large corporations with various industrial activities such as Siemens, Bell, General Electric, Vickers, RCA created their own departments or subsidiaries dedicated to the development and construction of scientific instruments. The boom in atomic physics in the 1930s and the unprecedented scale of the large technological military projects of World War 2 marked the establishment of 'big science' involving large research teams, laboratories and instrumental systems, along with a complex management.

After World War 2, the United States, where a large portion of research had been stimulated by massive military expenditures, became the world's largest producer of scientific instruments. European industry, which

had been heavily destroyed by the war, slowly recovered and entered the 'big science' (and big instrument) race in 1954 with the foundation of CERN. During the years of the Cold War, the Soviet Union and its satellite countries developed their own precision industry, also profiting from the transfer of know-how and technology from a defeated Germany. Their instruments were also sold in other areas subject to Soviet influence and were sometimes retailed with a certain success because of their competitive prices. The political division of the world and the separate developments of Western and Eastern research also triggered a frantic activity of espionage centred on strategic technologies which included sophisticated instruments for military and pacific uses. But due to the isolation of the Eastern bloc, the technological gap with Western Europe grew constantly. Following the collapse of the Soviet Union and the opening of the market in Eastern Europe, most of their instrument-making industry could not compete on the international market and had to be closed or completely restructured.

During the 20th century, scientific instrument manufacturers abandoned the big cities such as London, Paris, or Berlin which had been centres of production for such a long time. The geography of instrument making changed. In the second half of the century, an economically booming Japan became an important producer of electronic instruments. Large specialized science and technology regions such as California's 'Silicon Valley' became striking examples of a remarkable concentration of university institutes, research laboratories, high-tech factories and computer companies where, following the 1970s, sophisticated instruments were conceived, tested and sometimes manufactured. Furthermore, in the last years of the 20th century, with increasing globalization, the introduction of new communication systems and production technologies, the rapid industrial and economic development of countries such as South Korea, India and China, where the cost of labour was particularly low, favoured the growth of the precision industry outside traditional Western areas of production. Today instruments are often composed of elements and parts conceived, tested, produced and assembled in different countries. On the other hand, instruments of 'big science' such as large telescopes, space stations, or high-energy accelerators came to be projected, financed, realized, managed and operated thanks to long-term international joint ventures. The complexity of contemporary scientific apparatus, therefore, seems to mirror the intricacy of its actual manufacturing and trading network and the multiplicity of its users.

Paolo Brenni

Bibliography

Brenni P. 'Physics instruments in the 20th century', in Krige J. and Pestre D. (eds) 1997. *Science in the 20th century.* Amsterdam: Harwood, 741–57.

Bud R., Cozzens S. E. and Potter R. F. (eds) 1992. *Invisible connections: instruments, institutions and science.* Bellingham: Optical Engineering Press.

Bud R. and Warner D. J. 1998. *Instruments of science: an historical encyclopedia.* New York: Garland in association with the Science Museum, London; National Museum of American History, Smithsonian Institution.

Grob B. and Hooijmaijers H. (eds) 2006. *Who needs scientific instruments?* Leiden: Museum Boerhaave.

Joerges B. and Shinn T. (eds) 2001. *Instrumentation between science, state and industry.* Dordrecht: Kluwer.

Sydenham P. H. 1979. *Measuring instruments: tools of knowledge and control.* London: Peter Peregrinus in association with the Science Museum.

Turner G. L'E. (ed.) 1991. *Gli strumenti.* Turin: Giulio Einaudi.

van Helden A. and Hankins T. L. (eds) 1994. *Instruments, Osiris, Vol. 9.* Chicago: Chicago University Press.

Related essays
life and physical sciences; mapping; measurement; patents; radio; technical standardization; war

Scientific stations

Scientific stations provide settings for scientists to make observations and perform experiments. The most famous stations have been established beyond state borders in harsh environments such as Antarctica, the ocean, or outer space. Although many stations have been national endeavours, others have drawn upon the resources of multiple countries.

An important predecessor to such scientific stations was the Belgian Antarctic Expedition of 1898, which employed citizens of five countries. This mission suffered many of the problems of multinational projects, such as the challenge of cross-cultural communication. The crew did not work well together and nearly perished. Nonetheless, later governments pursued cooperation. In 1957–58, the International Geophysical Year involved 12 countries and 40 stations near the South Pole. In 1959, a conference in Washington met to negotiate the Antarctic Treaty, and concluded that all bases there should be open for inspection and serve cooperative scientific research. One of the more ambitious projects to result from scientific cooperation at the South Pole was the International Biomedical Expedition to the Antarctic, which operated in 1980 and 1981 and included explorers from five countries. This expedition tried to handle intercultural friction by randomly pairing and shuffling tent partners.

Since the 1960s, there have been numerous efforts to create underwater habitats for scientific research. Visionary French undersea explorer Jacques-Yves Cousteau organized Conshelf II, which placed divers, including a biologist from Monaco, underwater for several weeks in 1963. Cousteau emphasized intragroup harmony, picking participants based on their social skills in addition to their diving and scientific aptitudes. Compatibility among the aquanauts was important because, while living in an isolated and dangerous environment, they found that voice communication was difficult due to increased air pressure and the high helium content of their breathing mixture, which made them sound like cartoon characters. Later underwater stations, such as the Helgoland and Chernomar projects, were more multinational. Yet despite the success and popularity of these ventures, Cousteau's conception of underwater human colonies proved unrealistic. As the space race eclipsed interest in the ocean depths, it became clear that human habitation under the sea was extremely expensive. Nonetheless, underwater exploration drew attention to the health of the marine environment and taught national space agencies useful lessons as they planned extraterrestrial investigations.

The most renowned scientific stations of recent decades have been in space. Salyut I, the first space station, was abandoned in

1971 after its original inhabitants, three Soviet cosmonauts, asphyxiated upon departure. Later Salyut stations hosted cosmonauts from countries politically friendly to the USSR. During the 1980s and 1990s, the Soviet space station Mir hosted cosmonauts from 12 countries. The cosmonauts suffered from isolation, lack of privacy, boredom, and daily life in hazardous conditions. Under these circumstances, differences of language and culture sometimes led to friction among crew members, although they also directed their irritation against those outside the station, especially ground control. Work on an International Space Station (ISS) began as an American project in the mid-1980s. The plan expanded to include participation from at least 16 countries. In 2000, it received its first resident crew, from Russia and the United States. Despite this success, the ISS suffered from spiralling costs, missed deadlines, and shifting missions. Completion was anticipated no sooner than 2010, and the scientific aspects, already dubious, were further curtailed. Space stations, even multinational ones like the ISS, originated in the quest for national political prestige. Lacking economic or scientific rationales for human space flight, governments justified the spending of vast sums by exploiting nationalism and the popularity of 'extreme' sports.

Aside from their other accomplishments, such scientific stations are of anthropological interest because they create transnational microsocieties. These missions face the challenge of achieving group cohesiveness, which is particularly acute for multinational crews because of the difficulties created by intercultural communication. Careful personnel selection and training in psychological and interpersonal coping skills may improve the crew's functioning, as do group activities and the existence of a common language.

David Paull Nickles

Bibliography
Stuster J. 1996. *Bold endeavors: lessons from polar and space exploration.* Annapolis: Naval Institute Press.

Related essays
Antarctic Treaty; life and physical sciences; outer space; scientific expeditions

Schwimmer, Rosika *See* **Pacifism**

Second Vatican Ecumenical Council

Held in Rome from 11 October 1962 to 8 December 1965, the Second Vatican Ecumenical Council had been wanted by Pope John XXIII. On 25 January 1959, he announced the decision to convene the bishops for a new Council with the aim of renewing the Catholic Church and updating her for modern times.

After three years of preparation, 2,778 Fathers, representing 79 national churches, convened in Rome: patriarchs, cardinals, bishops and general superiors of the religious orders came from every Catholic corner, including from countries beyond the Iron Curtain. Observers of the Oriental, Protestant and Anglican Churches came as well, together with two Russian Church observers, a presence that ultimately triggered other Orthodox churches to send observers to later sessions. The Churches Federations represented in Rome altogether numbered 30. During the Council's four sessions, which from 1963 took place under Paul VI's pontificate, the Fathers were called to decide the Catholic Church's theological and ecclesiological future and to promote Christian unity. Their decisions, discussions and documents influenced not only the Catholic Church, but also the Christian Church and the laity in general. Hence, the Second Vatican can be reckoned as an important turning point: besides its liturgical reform, its abolition of Latin in the rite of the Mass, and its attention to the local churches, it deliberately staged a global Church in the eyes of the world.

While it was previously personified by the Pontiff and identified with the Holy See's hegemony, the Second Vatican revealed a wider Church. If Latin American, Asian and African bishops were initially hardly able to take part in the debate (in Latin) after centuries of passive non-responsibility towards a Church stuck in the Counter-Reformation, however, the gradual progress of the proceedings proved how the bishops' whole assembly became the soul of the Council. There was an exchange and an integration between various cultures and perspectives about the way to see and live Catholicism: for example, the Fathers became more attentive to the social problems exposed by the Fathers of non-European countries such as religious freedom, mass poverty and peace.

The Fathers did not always accept the preliminary drafts proposed by the Holy See's bishops, and often went into open discussions. Furthermore, the debate took place not only during the sessions but also during informal meetings favoured and animated by the propinquity that pervaded the daily life of the Fathers for many months spread over several years. The exchange with the other Churches' observers also became decisive, affecting the Council's results. The Second Vatican Council was not only a tool for discovering an episcopal collegiate status, but it also helped in strengthening the local Churches' identities and allowed them to see and present themselves as part of one universal Church, based on their experience of encounters during the sessions.

Among all the media that attended the event, television was the one that contributed the most. It accompanied the Fathers' and Council's presence and consciousness on a planetary scale: the numerous interviews with the African and South American Fathers were an example of television's contribution to this new awareness. The Italian public television service, RAI, was at that time controlled by the Catholic party, and it covered the Council for all three years as a matter of course. The real significance of the medium was that it was in charge of giving the keys to interpreting what was happening in St Peter's as well as broadcasting images all over the world. The opening ceremony began the era of worldwide transmission: the Council's images, transmitted simultaneously in Europe, Canada and the United States, revealed a Church which had been invisible to society. It can be said that the Council's images unexpectedly disclosed the Catholic Church to the world and to Catholics themselves.

Federico Ruozzi

Bibliography
Alberigo G. and Komonchak J. A. (eds) 1995–2006. *History of Vatican II*, 5 vols. Maryknoll: Orbis; Louvain: Peeters.
Melloni A. and Fattori M. T. (eds) 1997. *L'Evento e le decisioni: Studi sulle dinamiche del concilio Vaticano II*. Bologna: Il Mulino.
Ruozzi F. 2007. For a history with the television: the II Vatican. Paper presented at the 'Rethinking television history' conference, London.
Scatena S. 2003. *La fatica della libertà: l'elaborazione della dichiarazione Dignitas humanae sulla libertà religiosa del Vaticano II*. Bologna: Il Mulino.

Related essays
antisemitism; broadcasting; Christianity; ecumenism; information society; liberation theology; music

Seeds

Seeds are the reproductive units of flowering plants, and as such are the irreducible core of the agricultural production processes upon which all human societies now depend for their survival.

Whatever the historical period, people must eat, and what they eat is ultimately derived from plant material. The alpha and the omega of farming, seeds are sown and grow into plants which, when harvested, yield grain or fruits which can either be consumed or stored as seed for the next round of production.

Once produced exclusively by farmers for their own use, seeds are now traded in a $17 billion global market dominated by a few transnational firms. Once freely exchanged as the 'common heritage of mankind', seeds and the genetic information they contain are now subject to a range of intellectual property rights, including patents. Once bred by farmers to meet local needs, seeds are now genetically engineered by corporate scientists to the specifications of a globally distributed industrial agriculture. In their dual roles as both food and means of production, seeds sit at a critical nexus where contemporary struggles over the technical, social and environmental conditions of production and consumption converge. As such, control over seeds is now at the centre of debates over globalization of the world economy.

Crop improvement is as old as agriculture itself. Out of each year's harvest farmers selected seed from those plants with the most desirable traits. Over thousands of years the slow but steady accumulation of advantageous genes resulted in more productive cultivars. As they migrated, farmers also carried seeds away from their crops' centres of origin, thus facilitating recombination with other plant populations and forcing adaptation to the exigencies of new environmental, disease, and pest challenges. The result of these complex interactions was the development by peasant farmers of thousands of locally adapted 'landraces' which are rich depositories of genetic diversity. Most crops of economic importance were subsequently spread across the world to any location suitable for their cultivation by the great 'Columbian Exchange' of people, plants, animals, and microorganisms that accompanied the European colonization of the globe after 1492.

Until 1920, farmers were still almost exclusively the principal developers of new crop cultivars. This began to change with the rediscovery in 1900 of Mendel's work illuminating the hereditary transmission of traits. The simple mass selection practised by farmers was augmented by the systematic 'crossing' of plants by scientists with the express purpose of producing new varieties with specific characteristics.

The emergence of such science-based plant breeding opened the way to the development of crop varieties that farmers could not themselves produce. Such work was at first undertaken principally by government agencies and universities rather than commercial enterprises because of a simple biological fact: seeds reproduce themselves. A new plant variety might be created by a seed company, but after purchasing seed initially, farmers could simply save harvested seed, replant it the next season, and even sell it to other farmers. Into this vacuum of private investment moved the state. In both the US and Europe, public agricultural research institutions developed a powerful presence in crop variety development and seed marketing.

In 1883, the nascent seed industry established the American Seed Trade Association as a vehicle to promote its interests. By 1900, private seed companies in both Europe and North America had become established in the vegetable sector, in which crops are grown for immature fruits rather than mature seeds. But the huge and potentially lucrative grain trade remained foreclosed to companies by farmer 'plant-back' and by the presence of public plant breeders.

This changed with the development of hybrid corn in the 1930s. Championed by US Secretary of Agriculture Henry Wallace, himself owner of a seed company, hybridization is a breeding technique that provides more productive plants but that eliminates the possibility of saving and replanting seed. Hybridization thus uncoupled seed as 'seed' from seed as 'grain' since a farmer choosing to use hybrid varieties must purchase a fresh supply of seed each year. A wide variety of seed companies (e.g., Pioneer Hi-bred

and DeKalb in the US, Limagrain in France) were established to take advantage of the rapidly growing market for hybrid seedcorn. The hybrid model was extended to additional crops (many vegetables, sugar beet, cotton, sunflower, sorghum), and by 1970, the private seed sector had become a powerful player in the transnational agribusiness constellation.

For technical reasons, many important crops such as wheat, soybeans and rice could not be effectively hybridized. There is, however, a second route to the commodification of the seed: the extension of property rights to plant germplasm. Pushed by the seed industry, during the 1960s many European countries instituted patent-like 'plant breeders' rights' (PBRs) which allowed a breeder to prevent competing companies from selling a protected plant variety. Under PBR legislation, farmers are allowed to save and replant protected seed, but not sell it to others. In 1970 the US followed the European lead by passing the Plant Variety Protection Act (PVPA). In 1980, an extension of the PVPA engendered widespread debate as to the advisability of granting proprietary rights in so fundamental a resource as plant germplasm.

Concerns over the effect of the PVPA were conditioned by growing awareness of two processes which had been unfolding since 1960: the international Green Revolution and progressive concentration in the seed sector. The Green Revolution was essentially the extension of scientific breeding techniques to the context of the Global South in the 1960s and 1970s. This involved development of a network of agricultural research institutions across the Third World under the auspices of the Consultative Group on International Agricultural Research (CGIAR). The CGIAR research centres, funded by the Rockefeller and Ford foundations and the World Bank, developed so-called 'miracle' wheat and rice varieties. The yield increases associated with these seeds enabled the emergence of a class of commercial producers, but enhanced yields were linked to use of a package of inputs (e.g., fertilizer, pesticide, machinery, irrigation) that not all farmers could afford. Thus, the Green Revolution was accompanied by regional and farm-level inequalities, accelerating mechanization, changing tenure patterns, resulting in agrichemical dependence, genetic erosion, and pest-vulnerable monocultures. Although seeds of Green Revolution varieties were made available through public institutions, the prospect of future seed and agrochemical sales to the emerging commercial sector in the Global South helped fuel a process of concentration in the seed industry that had already been stimulated by concerns regarding the need to feed a rapidly increasing world population. During the 1970s, a wave of acquisitions swept many prominent American and European seed firms into the corporate folds of multinational petrochemical and agrichemical firms such as Monsanto, Ciba Geigy, Pfizer, Upjohn, Sandoz, W.R. Grace, ARCO, and Shell.

In the 1980s, a diverse set of farm, labour, church, environmental, and social advocacy groups emerged in opposition to recent developments in the seed sector. These organizations worried that extension of PBRs would enhance economic concentration in the seed industry, facilitate non-competitive pricing, constrain the free exchange of breeding material, contribute to genetic erosion and uniformity, encourage the de-emphasis of public breeding, and force subsistence farmers into the market for seed. These concerns were reinforced as the newly multinational seed companies pressed for the globalization of PBR. Controversy over whether or not Third World farmers would benefit from the adoption of such legislation erupted in the Food and Agriculture Organization (FAO) of the United Nations in the Seed Wars of the 1980s.

The biotechnology revolution of the 1980s further reinforced developing concerns about the linkage between seeds and corporate power. The term 'biotechnology' references a set of new and uniquely powerful genetic technologies that can be applied to plant breeding. The most prominent of these is recombinant DNA (rDNA) transfer ('gene splicing', 'genetic engineering'). While conventional breeding operates on whole organisms and operates through sexual recombination, genetic engineering operates at the cellular and even the molecular level and makes it possible to move genes between completely unrelated species and thereby to create wholly novel genetically modified organisms (GMOs) such as a corn plant containing genes from a bacillus.

The proliferation of biotechnology start-ups (e.g., Genentech, Agrigenetics, Calgene, Allelix, Phytodynamics, etc.) during the 1980s was dramatic but relatively short-lived. The development of GMO seed varieties was far more difficult than scientists and venture capitalists had anticipated. With no product base and tenuous funding, the new biotechnology firms were absorbed by deep-pocket multinationals. Given the enormous technical and financial resources that need to be deployed in commercializing GMOs, concentration has continued apace. All seed companies of any significance have now been acquired by multinational companies which have themselves undergone a process of consolidation in which only five 'Gene Giants' (Monsanto, Dupont, Syngenta, Bayer, Dow) now dominate a sector that encompasses not just seeds but agrichemicals and pharmaceuticals. Even so, these Gene Giants have so far been able to commercialize only a handful of GMO varieties which incorporate only two agronomically relevant transgenic GM traits (herbicide tolerance and insecticidal action) in only four crops (soybeans, corn, cotton, canola).

The difficulty in bringing GMO seeds to market has intensified the Gene Giants' commitment to extending property rights in seeds. Realization of this goal was greatly facilitated by the 1980 US. Supreme Court's decision, in *Chakrabarty v. Diamond*, that novel life forms are patentable. Huge expanses of crop plant genomes, previously regarded as common heritage, have subsequently been patented. In addition to genetic material itself, key research methods and tools such as the gene gun and biological vectors for genetic transformation have also been patented. Further, utility patents do not allow for either a research exemption for scientists nor a farmers' exemption allowing saving and replanting of seed, as was the case under the PBR regime. Seed companies and their Gene Giant parent firms are aggressively policing the use of patented crop varieties for both research and production, and are systematically enforcing annual purchase of seed by farmers.

However, corporate biotechnologists must now deal with growing global opposition to GMOs and GMO-derived foods. This opposition has many bases. Consumers, especially in Europe, are leery of the possible health effects of the novel proteins in 'Frankenfoods'. Environmentalists worry about the unanticipated effects of biopollution as pollen from GMO varieties contaminates non-GMO crops and other plants with transgenes. Indigenous peoples and the governments of biodiverse countries object to what they term 'biopiracy' when corporate gene hunters appropriate genetic resources from their lands and patent and commercialize the resulting product without adequate compensation. Citizens from many backgrounds find corporate development of 'Terminator Technology' that genetically sterilizes seed in order to prevent plant-back by farmers to be ethically objectionable. Many social advocacy groups around the world find the concentration of economic and scientific power characteristic of the seed sector to be profoundly autocratic. They are especially concerned that farmers who depend on the ability to save and replant seed for their very survival not find themselves dependent on the Gene Giants as a result of technical or legislative fiat. In the public scientific community, there is a growing perception that the permitted scope of patenting has been stretched beyond its social utility.

Both the biological and social worlds now face a critical conjuncture. Food production must increase sufficiently to meet the needs of a human population that will likely double in the next fifty years. That production increase will have to be achieved in an ecological context of rapid climate change and considerable uncertainty. Ideally, that production increase will also be accomplished in a manner that is socially just and that preserves the capacity of the biosphere to provide for a wide range of functions and species. The manner in which we feed ourselves will be a prime determinant of how we use the earth. What characteristics we build into seeds will critically shape the quality of our own lives and the quality of the natural world in which we are embedded.

Jack R. Kloppenburg, Jr

Bibliography

Gepts P. and Hancock J. 2006. 'The future of plant breeding', Crop Science, 46, 1630–4.

Kloppenburg J., Jr 2004. First the seed: the political economy of plant biotechnology, 1492–2000. Madison: University of Wisconsin Press.

Pearse A. 1980. Seeds of plenty, seeds of want: social and economic implications of the Green Revolution. Oxford and New York: Oxford University Press.

Related essays

acclimatization; agriculture; biodiversity; biopatents; food; Ford Foundation; genetically modified organisms (GMOs); Green Revolution; indigenous knowledges; intellectual property rights; Monsanto; patents; pesticides, herbicides, insecticides; philanthropic foundations; population; Vandana Shiva Research Foundation

September 11, 2001

On the morning of September 11, 2001, terrorists hijacked four airplanes in midair on the East coast of the United States. The terrorists flew two of the airplanes into the World Trade Center in New York, killing 2,823 people and destroying the buildings completely. The third airplane struck the Pentagon, killing 125 people in the building and 64 on board the airplane. The fourth airplane crashed near Shanksville, Pennsylvania, killing all 44 people aboard.

US President George W. Bush declared that same day that the hijackings and suicides were an act of war and that the terrorists and 'those who harbor them' would be brought to justice. On 20 September, the President declared that al-Qaeda, an Islamic terrorist network, and its leader Osama bin Laden, were responsible for the attacks. According to President Bush, al-Qaeda recruited future terrorists in at least 60 countries around the world. He stated: 'Every nation, in every region, now has a decision to make. Either you are with us, or you are with the terrorists.'

Immediately after the attacks of 9/11, the United States received expressions of sympathy and support from around the world. Russian President Vladimir Putin was the first foreign leader to contact President Bush and to express his anger and indignation over the attacks. Putin compared the attacks with Russia's experiences with terrorism. Putin soon supported the presence of US troops in Central Asia for operations against international terrorism. On 9/11 China's President Jiang Zemin called President Bush as well to express his sympathy. That same month, the People's Republic sent a team of anti-terrorism experts to the United States to share intelligence on the Taliban regime in Afghanistan. The United Nations Security Council condemned the attacks in resolution 1368 and called on all states to cooperate, in order to bring the terrorists and their supporters to justice. NATO invoked, for the first time in its existence, Article 5 of its treaty, with the member states pledging support to the United

States. French newspaper Le Monde's editorial was: 'Nous sommes tous Américains' ('We are all Americans'). This international support dwindled over time, especially when the United States wanted to dispose of the Saddam Hussein regime in Iraq, while other nations, notably France and Germany, believed that the United States was moving toward war too quickly.

This War on Terror eventually led to the military invasions of Afghanistan and Iraq, resulted in an open commitment against some nations that supported terrorist groups (such as Iran and North Korea), made the United States side with, for instance, the Russian government in its fight against Chechen rebels, and led to the statement that the United States had the right to pre-emptive wars in contradiction to the Charter of the United Nations.

The emphasis the Bush administration put on a national response against other nation states denied to a large extent the transnational aspects of 9/11. Among the victims of the attacks on the World Trade Center were 209 foreigners from 36 nations. The terrorists originated from Saudi Arabia, the United Arab Emirates, Egypt, and Lebanon, and many of them lived and studied in Europe before they moved to the United States. Al-Qaeda is an organization that recruits its members around the world, while making use of the Internet to communicate. To close down the terrorist network, governments focused on international cooperation to track and block money transfers by the terrorists and share intelligence on their whereabouts (many governments also introduced laws to increase the surveillance of their own citizens, such as the Patriot Act in the United States). Another transnational consequence of these terrorist attacks was the debate in many societies about a Christian–Muslim conflict, and about immigration and the challenges of integration of, specifically, Muslims into Western societies. All these efforts did not prevent other terrorist attacks, which took place on Bali, and in Casablanca, Riyadh, Istanbul, Madrid, and London. These attacks were claimed by al-Qaeda or groups affiliated with al-Qaeda, such as the Jemaah Islamiyah on Bali or the Moroccan Islamic Combatant Group in Casablanca and Madrid. A third international upshot of the attacks was that nations like Russia and China redefined conflicts within their territory, respectively in Chechnya and Xinjiang, as part of the War on Terror, to legitimize their actions.

The United States lost more of its international standing during the War on Terror, because of the denial of the right of *habeas corpus* to alleged terrorists, the arguments in favour of torture to extract information from possible terrorists, the mistreatment of prisoners in the Iraqi Abu Ghraib prison, and the failure to establish law, order, and a stable regime in postwar Iraq.

Ruud Janssens

Bibliography

Clarke R. A. 2004. *Against all enemies: inside America's war on terror.* New York: Free Press.

Gray J. 2003. *Al Qaeda and what it means to be modern.* London: Faber and Faber.

O'Loughlin J., Ó Tuathail G. and Kolossov V. 2004. 'A "risky westward turn"? Putin's 9/11 script and ordinary Russians' [online]. Available: www.colorado.edu/IBS/PEC/johno/pub/Putin_911.pdf.

Woodward B. 2002. *Bush at war.* New York: Simon & Schuster.

Related essays

individual identification systems; Pax Americana; relief; religious fundamentalism; terrorism; war; world orders

Services

The status of service activities in economics has been much debated since Adam Smith, Ricardo and the classics, i.e., since the birth of the discipline. What is their specificity? How should their role be considered? Are they productive? A contemporary definition of services considers them as activities of an economic unit, changing the conditions of a person or of a good belonging to some other economic unit, without any transfer of property. This definition accounts for two classic characteristics of services: their immateriality, implying that they cannot be stocked, and the fact that they are somehow coproduced between users and producers. It follows that services are at the interfaces between the spheres of economic activities and domestic activities, of market and non-market activities, and are thus bound to have a highly country-specific regulatory framework. Considering transnational flows of services is thus rather puzzling.

Until the last quarter of the 20th century services tended to be considered by economists as largely untradeable. Yet services have always been exchanged internationally, even if their role in the process of internationalization has become more apparent in the last two or three decades, accompanying the rise in foreign direct investment, some two thirds of which occurred in service sectors at the turn of the 1990s.

Why is it that for so long trade in services has been quite invisible? In the first place trade in services occurs through specific kinds of transactions that are not spontaneously considered as part of trade in services, such as travel abroad or patent fees. A second reason is that some of this trade is directly linked with trade in goods such as transport and insurances expenses (trade in goods has long been valued using a cash, insurance and freight (CIF) method where all these auxiliary costs have been included). The development of large service firms, involved in international transactions such as Lloyd's insurance company (1774), or P&O (Peninsular and Oriental Steam Navigation, 1837) has thus accompanied the development of international trade. Let us notice, in passing, that both firms started dealing in information: news of deals and wrecks for Lloyd's, mail deliveries for P&O.

Attention has been brought to trade in services in the course of the process of trade liberalization. To extend it to trade in services was the main objective of the negotiations in the Uruguay Round and the creation of the World Trade Organization (WTO) General Agreement on Trade in Services (GATS) in 1994. Four modes of transaction were then distinguished. Mode 1, cross-border supply, applies when service suppliers resident in one country provide services in another country without either supplier or buyer moving to the actual location of the other. Mode 2, consumption abroad, refers to a consumer resident in one country moving to the location of the supplier to consume a service. Mode 3, commercial presence, refers to legal persons (firms) moving to the location of consumers to sell services locally through the establishment of a foreign affiliate or a branch. Mode 4, movement of natural persons, refers to a process where persons move momentarily to the country of the consumer to provide a service. International transport and finance are clear examples of mode 1,

tourism of mode 2. Mode 3, activities linked with foreign affiliates of multinationals, are not classically considered as international transactions in services (except in US national accounts where these statistics are available) but they are obviously linked with mode 4 which concerns among other things all the international transactions occurring within multinational firms, giving way to a bulk of transfer pricing. If the focus on the various forms of transaction brought about by the negotiations made this trade in services more visible, it also stressed that the country specificities of national organizations of services and the arbitrariness and fuzziness of some international transactions left the liberalization move faced with lots of invisible barriers.

Even so, in a long-term perspective the domain of trade in services is a very active one, with a lot of innovations and import substitutions, following the various phases of internationalization. The continuous reduction in transport costs for the last 150 years has fuelled the steady expansion of international trade and transport services (international transactions in mode 1). Conversely, rising wealth of populations has boosted national and international tourist activities (an international transaction in mode 2). Finally in the more recent period post-World War 2, the development of foreign direct investment, especially in the very recent period, has helped to substitute local production of foreign establishments for imports (such international transactions in mode 3 represent approximately 60 per cent of all service trade, although they are difficult to measure and thus not accounted for in most balance-of-payments calculations). The web of international transactions thus created allows some producers to travel and deliver their services abroad (mode 4 of international transactions, which represents only a small proportion of international service transactions).

The last three decades are highly illustrative of this dynamics of internal change, still with the share of service trade staying all along at a quarter of the value of a rapidly rising trade in goods. In 2005 global cross-border trade in services stood at some US$2.4 trillion (of which some US$1.3 trillion was in non-travel and non-transport categories), while trade in merchandise amounted to some US$10 trillion. Between 1990 and 2004 the share of non-travel and non-transport increased from

36 to 46 per cent of the trade in services. Much of this new trade in services has been in so-called business process outsourcing which is directly linked with the fragmentation and global production sharing which accompanies the rise in foreign direct investment, all of which has characterized the phase of internationalization of the last three decades.

But one should not be misled and consider that trade in services has been purely a complementary factor to trade in goods or to investment in industrial production. Trade in services has very often been the driving factor in shaping the forms of internationalization experienced in the long history of international economic relations. International (family) networks of merchants and bankers were clearly crucial in organizing trade in preindustrial times. Improvements in means of transportation (with the innovation that steamships represented, for instance), leading to drastic reductions in costs, played a decisive role in the development of merchandise trade in the second part of the 19th century. The development of air transport in the second half of the 20th century played a similarly crucial part, allowing among other things a globalization of production processes. Innovations in communications (such as the creation of intercontinental telephone connections) also had their impact in building up the logistics supporting trade activities. So, obviously, did the diffusion of information and communication technologies, with the paramount example of the Internet. These technological innovations helped the old merchant and bank networks (or their successors) to develop at an international level, relying more or less according to countries and practices on local associates and affiliates. In cases like that of Japan, trading houses (the *sogo soshas*) played a major role in organizing the trade relations of the country all through the 20th century.

Transport and communication improvements effectively allowed banks and distributors to be central actors in the globalization process of the last two decades of the 20th century. It is also the case that some internationalization of service trade mainly followed the internationalization of the production of goods. Thus in the 1960s and 1970s some business services in auditing or in advertising simply internationalized their activities to follow the internationalization of their customers. Still, the development of the logistics of intermediation (which includes finance, trade, transport and communication activities) is not the only driving force shaping the expansion and internal structural change of trade in services. Rises in incomes, as well as cultural changes, induced new demands for foreign services. The classic and early example is given by the development of tourism in the second half of the 19th century. The spread of Romanticism in the first part of the century paved the way for a new taste for countryside landscapes at home and abroad. Development of means of transportation as well as rises in income for an upper-middle class of wage earners and rentiers made it possible for a tourist industry to emerge at home and at international level. Dynamic entrepreneurs such as Thomas Cook helped to organize this rising industry and to enlarge its range so as to become in the 20th century a major mass industry when the rise in wages and leisure time had developed a consistent, effective demand. In the process, tourism became a major item of trade in services, and an important component of internationalization. In a similar vein demand rose for cultural services in the second half of the 20th century, leading to receipts and payments featuring in the balance of trade in services. One may also expect new demands to develop in the forthcoming decades, for example in terms of education and health services (following mixed forms of transaction, with customers moving abroad and suppliers coming to serve customers at home). Major US universities are thus setting up courses alternating teaching at home and abroad. Similarly some developing countries try to attract foreign customers for whole or part of specialized health treatments. Regarding process innovations, reduction in transportation costs as well as increasing communication potentials via the Internet will likely continue to stimulate continuous and innovative changes in the structure of service trade. Selling entertainment products or information and advice internationally is one case in point.

The liberalization of trade in services is far from complete. It is very much tied in with the liberalization of foreign direct investment. It also requires adjustments in the regulatory frameworks of services. All of which is easier to achieve within regional trading blocks. If some progress has been made in the European Union in that respect, the road map in the liberalization of trade in services is much less advanced in unions including developing countries like the MERCOSUR in Latin America or ASEAN in Southeast Asia. During the Uruguay Round, developing countries put the liberalization of financial services, telecommunications, business services, travel and transport on the agenda. No commitment was made regarding construction, engineering, distribution, education, health, recreational and cultural services. As developed economies have increased their specialization in services and delocalized much of their manufacturing activities to some developing countries, pressure is bound to increase to push further the liberalization in service trade. Also central to the international multilateral or bilateral negotiations will be the final design and enforcement of intellectual property rights. Environmental issues will most likely influence issues of technological transfers. Regulations in both domains are crucial to determining the magnitude and distribution of all the rents of innovation (fees and patents which are counted as services) attached to all intellectual productions in the entertainment or drug industries, for instance. Meanwhile the diffusion of health and education services internationally will also be an issue on the rise with the development of Internet support. A new phase of service trade is quite foreseeable with reshufflings in its components rather similar to the ones experienced in the last fifty years.

Pascal Petit

Bibliography
Hoekman B. 2006. 'Liberalising trade in services: a survey', *World Bank Policy Research Papers*, 4030, October.
Petit P. 'Transnational service corporations in the process of globalisation', in Kozul-Wright R. and Rowthorn R. (eds) 1997. *Transnational corporations and the global economy*, London: Macmillan (now Palgrave Macmillan) for WIDER, 134–63.
Petit P. 'The political economy of services in tertiary economies', in Bryson J. R. and Daniels P. W. (eds) 2007. *The handbook of service industries*, Cheltenham: Edward Elgar, 77–99.

Related essays
advertising; body shopping; commodity trading; financial centres; financial markets; General Agreement on Tariffs and Trade (GATT) / World Trade Organization (WTO); higher education; Hong Kong and Shanghai Banking Corporation (HSBC); information economy; information technology (IT) offshoring; intellectual property rights; investment; mail; marketing; patents; steamships; Swiss banks; telephone and telegraphy; tourism; trade; trade (manufactured goods)

Sex and gender *See* **Gender and sex**

Sexology

Sexology (originally sexual psychology, or even sexual psychopathology) emerged as a multidisciplinary field in the late 19th century in Europe. Its intellectual fathers (nearly all of whom were in fact men) saw it, in a way, as the victory of science over Christian religious thought and the recent penalization of non-normative sexual practices. In its beginnings, sexological texts (such as Krafft-Ebing's *Psychopathia sexualis*) circulated in professional circles, and important fractions thereof were written in Latin, to preserve lay readers from what was seen as dangerous for those not prepared to use sensitive information properly. Based on clinical case studies, this first wave of sexology would carefully develop taxonomies of sexual perversions that, through medicalization, would then be considered sexual illnesses. In tune with the positivistic project, this task, still mostly confined within Europe, was however seen as a crusade for the discovery of the sexual truth of humankind, of the sexual nature of all peoples.

Some changes took place in the early 20th century, where new thinkers started to produce sexological theories and ideas departing from the framework of psychopathology. Sex was central in Sigmund Freud's theory, and his *Three essays on the theory of sexuality* (1905) quickly crossed borders and stimulated much discussion and writing. Other key thinkers of the time were Havelock Ellis (British), whose *Studies on the psychology of sex* (1897–1928) provided a vast description of the variations of sexual expression, and Magnus Hirschfeld (German), who wrote on homosexuality. Elements contributing to this rise were the increasing diffusion of the erotic cultural legacy of the Far East, and research conducted by anthropologists like Bronislaw Malinowski and Margaret Mead in cultures distant from the European epicentre. The new writings on sexual psychology generated a significant number of exchanges initially across Europe, North America, and Australia, such as the World League for Sexual Reform which, led by Hirschfeld, promoted the World Congresses for Sexual Reform. National differences were however evident in the reactions to sexological production, with generally lower barriers to publication in Central Europe (as compared, for instance, to Britain). Ellis' *Sexual inversion*, published in Germany in 1896, was banned in England in 1897. Conversely, Hirschfeld enjoyed significant freedom to publish on homosexuality in Germany, while decades later, when he was exiled and in his last years of life, the Nazis would destroy much of his work.

A third wave for sexology came after World War 2, its epicentre being Indiana, USA. With a background in zoology, Alfred Kinsey led a positivistic enterprise aimed at quantifying sexual variations. Key books such as *Sexual behavior in the human male* (1952) and *Sexual behavior in the human female* (1957) would deeply impress 1950s North America. In this same line, in the 1960s, researchers like William Masters and Virginia Johnson explored the physiology of sex, and described the human 'sexual response', with an emphasis on a newly discovered female multiorgasmic potential. These theoretical developments reflected social processes leading to a redefinition of the relation between the sexes – notably Western feminism and the social demand of a scientific correlate to new social realities. In the late 1960s and 1970s, sexology would consolidate as a therapeutic practice, aimed at ensuring the body's sexual performance. The World Association of Sexology (WAS), formed in the late 1970s, held its first congress in Rome (1978), and regional sexological associations were formed as well. Although most sexologists of this era believed in the progressive, illuminating nature of their work, an increasing critique from social science and feminism in the 1980s and 1990s posited that sexological practice was positivistic, reinforced power structures, and was becoming increasingly commercial. In 2003, WAS changed its name to the World Association of Sexual Health, by claiming that sexual health is not a goal for clinicians only, but the crystallization of the common goal of several constituencies: sex educators, sex therapists and sex researchers. Such a move has not precluded a new development within medicine in the late 1990s, already named 'sexual medicine' by some, which appears to reinforce ideas of sexual performance but de-emphasizes the (overt) pursuit of sexual pleasure. The public image of this new development is one of family strengthening and responsibility, while the possibilities opened by the main tools of this practice (i.e. mostly drugs for erectile dysfunction and the like) have triggered a vast cross-national trade in pharmaceuticals on the Internet.

Carlos F. Cáceres

Bibliography
Tiefer L. and Giami A. 2002. 'Sexual behaviour and its medicalisation', BMJ, 325, 45.
Weeks J. 1985. *Sexuality and its discontents: meanings, myths and modern sexualities*. London and New York: Routledge & Kegan Paul.

Related essays
birth control; drugs (medical); femininity; gender and sex; love; marriage; medicine; psychoanalysis; sexuality and migration

Sex tourism and Thailand *See* Tourism

Sexuality and migration

Sexuality and international migration have always had a mutually defining relationship, but our conceptualization of that relationship has changed significantly.

The imperative to marry, for example, has an extensive history in shaping international migration. Similarly, the connections between industrialization, immigration, and the late 19th-/early 20th-century sex industry are well documented. But scholarship since the 1980s, especially in areas of lesbian, gay, bisexual, transgender, queer, feminist, racial/ethnic, and HIV/AIDS studies, has changed our understanding of sexuality, and of its role in shaping international migration. Scholars particularly highlight several key points about sexuality.

First, within Western models, sexuality has long been subsumed under gender within a normalized model of the reproductive family, and gender in turn is frequently conflated with women. This approach privileges the reproductive family; normalizes binary gender relations while lodging gender in biology rather than social relations of power; and completely erases sexuality. Second, sexuality is neither an unmediated 'natural' drive nor a private matter; rather, the state and powerful groups intervene in and deploy sexuality for varied aims including imperial projects, nation-state consolidation, and capitalist development. Third, these interventions have correlated with hierarchies of race, gender, class, and national origin. Methodologies, theories, and epistemologies must be reconfigured to address these insights – which requires challenging the heterosexual norm as a dominant paradigm that naturalizes and universalizes the 'properly' gendered, classed, and racialized male/female couple as the basis for family, community, and society (a situation that will be further addressed as 'heteronormativity'). Such a reconfiguration results not simply in 'adding' historically marginalized sexual groups to existing scholarship, but rather, in fundamentally transforming all scholarship about the connections between sexuality (in every form) and international migration. The transformations are perhaps clearest in the emergent scholarship documenting international migration by lesbian, gay, and queer (LGQ) people.

Studies of LGQ migrants raised the question of how sexuality structures all aspects of international migration. For example, scholars have debated whether and how sexuality may impel migration. They point out that global capitalism alters sexual forms and mobilizes people for migration – and that these processes may contribute to LGQ migration. The role of transnational media flows, communication technologies, product circulation, and business and tourist travel in cultivating particular sexual desires, imaginaries, and material connections that generate migration was theorized. The importance of rights discourses, sexuality-rights NGOs, and individual experiences of sexuality-based discrimination or persecution in contributing to migration was debated, especially as countries including South Africa, Australia and Canada began offering asylum to those persecuted for sexual orientation. Some scholars showed that nation states and families often unofficially encourage international migration by their sexual dissidents (as in Manuel Guzmán's concept of Puerto Rican 'sexiles'). Yet other nation states implicitly or openly disallow legal entry by LGQ immigrants.

Models of migrant settlement or incorporation, which underwent significant revision in light of transnationalism, became further complicated by focusing on LGQs. The heteronormativity of much migration

scholarship on family, community, settlement, and cultural transmission was particularly highlighted. Mainstream LGQ assumptions about identity, community, and culture were also placed in question by queer migrants. For example, scholarship showed that sexual non-conformity within migrant families and communities was often deemed not to be gender 'deviance', but rather, to be racial, ethnic, or cultural deviance/betrayal. These constructions stem not from allegedly ahistorical migrant cultures, but rather from negotiating racial, cultural, and/or ethnic hierarchies within 'receiving' societies. Lesbians become particularly oppressed by these dynamics, since the control of women's sexuality serves as a flashpoint for tensions between unequally situated groups. LGQ migrants, moreover, often faced racism, classism, sexism and cultural hierarchies within mainstream LGQ communities and institutions. Their experiences required revising conventional Western models of LGQ sexuality and identity that focused on secrecy/disclosure, gender transgression, and leaving home.

Initial scholarship on LGQ migrants was often premised on time/space binaries and developmental narratives. It suggested that LGQ migrants – such as Cuban gay men and lesbians who arrived in the United States during the 1980 Mariel boatlift – moved from one hermetically sealed national culture to another, and that that this process paralleled a shift from 'backwardness' to 'advancement' (or from 'repression' to 'liberation'). Yet these models ignored histories of imperialism, Cold War hostilities, and global capitalism that have created material links between spatially separate nation states, regions, and communities. Moreover, the models often conceptualized LGQ migration primarily in relation to sexuality, while ignoring the ways that LGQs also migrate as racialized, gendered, classed, and often neocolonized subjects. They implicitly posited a hierarchy of not only national but also queer culture, in which migrants left allegedly 'underdeveloped' queer cultures for 'progressive' queer cultures in the global North, and they presumed a single, unidirectional homogenizing process of cultural change that occurs in response to migration. New scholarship responded to these concerns, showing the emergence of multiple, hybrid sexual cultures, identities, identifications, practices and politics among LGQ migrants. These are marked by power, contestation, and creative adaptation to local, regional, national and transnational forces.

The issues raised in relation to LGQ migration have been evident in scholarship about other kinds of migration, such as that by sex workers. Scholars have theorized how the reconfiguration and dispersion of sex work, and the important role of migrants within the industry, links to the effects of global capitalism at different scales. They suggest that contemporary sex work reflects the reorganization of labor through the extension of service industries, the growing importance of affective labour, and new forms of commodification. They argue that the global sex industry draws on and rearticulates historic connections between regions and countries that are unequally situated within the global order (such as African, Asian and Latin American sex workers migrating to Western Europe and North America), and between bodies that are hierarchically positioned based on gender, culture, phenotype, and economics (such as lighter-skinned sex workers who are employed in less hazardous and more lucrative sectors than darker-skinned workers). Scholars have shown that migration renders sex workers particularly vulnerable to criminalization, exploitation, and serious abuse; theorized the connections between sex work and rights; raised questions about agency, choice, and coercion; and debated who may legitimately address these issues without replicating colonialist, racist, heterosexist and patriarchal relationships and representations. One strand of scholarship particularly examines the connections among migration, sex work, and public health issues (including HIV/AIDS) at local, national and transnational scales. The importance of questioning linear models and time/space binaries, and the centrality of issues of power and inequality at different scales, are underscored.

The focus on migrant sex workers dovetails with a growing discussion about sex tourism. Sex tourism participates in the increasing circulation of sexuality as a commodity, mediated by neocolonial linkages, global capitalism, the state, social networks and communication technologies, and it is deeply implicated in inequalities at multiple scales. Sex tourism recapitulates a long history of treating national borders as sites of sexual transgression and asymmetrical encounter, but at the same time reflects a contemporary reconfiguration of the connections between sexuality and travel. As a locus for the negotiation of unevenly situated sexual desires, practices, and identities, sex tourism has multiple ramifications, including for international migration.

A related matter that has received growing attention concerns types of marriage migration that are viewed as akin to sexual servitude. Of particular concern is Internet dating and correspondence (or 'mail-order') marriage, often between North American/Western European men and Asian or Eastern European women. Reliance on communication technologies including the postal system, photography, and telegrams has a long history in structuring male/female marriages across borders, as in early-20th-century immigration by Japanese 'picture brides'. But the role of the Internet in marriage migration raises new questions about how the circulation of sexual desires and imaginaries in a context of time/space compression and neoliberal economics may exacerbate disparities of geopolitical positioning, gender, and often class and race, sometimes with catastrophic consequences – and/or provide opportunities for renegotiation. At the same time, diasporic groups like South Asians in Canada use the Internet as one means to arrange transnational marriages for the second generation.

International marriage migration in general also receives substantial attention. Marriage migration processes are clearly gendered and sexualized, and often ethnicized, classed, and raced. They occur within a dynamic of discipline and escape within intersecting familial, community, nation-state, capitalist and global regimes of regulation, which are further mediated by individual decisions and desires. Immigrants have long used marriage as a means to migrate. For many, such as German women migrating to the US during the period 1870–1910, marriage was a practical decision; for others, like contemporary Chinese women workers in Special Economic Zones, marriage to overseas Chinese men is also tied to images of opportunity and self-fashioning.

Historically, the state and capital have played a central role in organizing configurations of sexuality, marriage and international migration. For example, as imperial powers spread their reach, officials deliberately organized the flow of administrators in ways that facilitated particular marriage arrangements. Colonial strategies in the Dutch East

Indies consistently aimed to prevent indigenous women from becoming legitimate wives, although they could serve as sexual partners to Dutch men, and this pattern was evident in other colonial systems. Many nation states' subsequent immigration control policies incorporated these kinds of logics. Thus, heterosexual and patriarchal marriage often provided privileged immigration access for preferred racial, ethnic, and class groups who conformed to patriarchy. Conversely, subordinated racial/ethnic group, low-income, lesbian, gay, and/or transgender couples often found that marriage migration was difficult or impossible (for instance, Asian immigrant marriages were disabled by US immigration policies during the first half of the 20th century). Yet state immigration marriage policies sometimes conflicted with the demands of capital for migrant labour, leading to the development of unexpected sexual and affectional formations – or 'split families' that reproduced themselves across national borders, and where sexuality assumed a complex form. Exclusionary immigration marriage policies have been periodically reconfigured in response to wider transnational processes; for example, as nations stationed troops overseas, militarized prostitution developed around many bases. The dynamics often paralleled earlier stages of imperialism, by providing men from geopolitically powerful nations with sexual access to women of less powerful nations, often across hierarchies of class, race, and culture. Yet in the 20th century, a significant volume of marriage migration resulted from these arrangements, necessitating modification to racially exclusionary immigration laws.

Since marriage has consistently served as both a metaphor and a practical means through which the state attempts to integrate selected immigrants into the dominant economic, social and cultural order, many states police against 'immigration marriage fraud' (popularly described as marriage for residency or for circumventing restrictive labour migration policies, rather than for 'love'). Sexual relations comprise an important element of the test for fraud; in the United States, marriages are evaluated through a dominant norm that associates sexuality with individual expression, intimacy within the monogamous couple, and child bearing. But immigrant marriages do not necessarily conform to these culturally and historically specific bourgeois beliefs, which contributes to social tensions, alarmist media representations, 'get tough' political campaigns – and volumes of immigration scholarship. Sexuality within marriage, however, is undeniably altered by migration. The changes cannot be mapped using a developmental model, nor treated simply as evidence of exposure to dominant norms. Instead, changing marital sexuality incorporates hybrid elements, and reflects alterations in the structures in capitalism, the uneven ways that individuals, families and communities become incorporated into global capitalism, and the impact of transnational ties.

Taken as a whole, scholarship shows that sexuality shapes all aspects of international migration, in ways that necessitate rethinking fundamental theories and methodologies. Moreover, sexuality is thoroughly implicated in hierarchies of race, class, gender, religion, and geopolitics, and in normalizing regimes of governance including the family, economy, state, and transnational. In order to theorize the connections between sexuality and international migration within the context of transnationalism, scholars must move away from methodological nationalism, linear models, and bounded social science concepts – while remaining attentive to power, inequality, agency and resistance at multiple scales.

Eithne Luibhéid

Bibliography

Brennan D. 2004. *What's love got to do with it? Transnational desire and sex tourism in the Dominican Republic*. Durham, NC: Duke University Press.

Gopinath G. 2005. *Impossible desires: queer diasporas and South Asian public cultures*. Durham, NC: Duke University Press.

Haour-Knipe M., and Rector R. (eds) 1997. *Crossing borders: migration, ethnicity, and AIDS*. London: Taylor and Francis.

Luibhéid E. 2002. *Entry denied: controlling sexuality at the border*. Minneapolis: University of Minnesota Press.

Manalansan M. F. IV 2003. *Global divas: Filipino gay men in the diaspora*. Durham, NC: Duke University Press.

Manalansan M. F. IV 2006. 'Queer intersections: sexuality and gender in migration studies', *International Migration Review*, 40, 1, 224–49.

Yue A. forthcoming. *Queer Asian migration in Australia*.

Related essays
Acquired Immunodeficiency Syndrome
(AIDS); adoption; asylum seekers; borders
and borderlands; class; empire and
migration; ethnicity and race; family
migration; femininity; gender and sex;
international migration regimes; labour
migrations; love; marriage; population;
refugees; Thailand and sex tourism; White
Slavery; women's movements

Shi'i Islam

Shi'ism is one of the two major sectarian
communities in Islam. The Shi'is are 15 per
cent of the total Muslim population in the
world. They constitute the largest religious
community in Iran, where they are 90 per cent
of the population, Iraq (60 per cent), Lebanon
(30 per cent), Bahrain and Azerbaijan.
There are also significant Shi'i minorities in
Pakistan (25 per cent), Turkey (20 per cent),
Saudi Arabia (15 per cent), Syria (15 per cent)
and India.

Religious authority in Shi'i Islam is organized in a hierarchy of specialists (mullah,
ayatollah, marja'), which has its higher ranks
educated in learning institutions (madrasa,
hawza) located in the pilgrimage centres of
Najaf, Karbala and Qom. In the second half
of the 19th century a movement of religious
reform took hold of the Shi'i communities
throughout the Middle East. The reform movement aimed to construct a public religious
identity for the Shi'is founded in shared doctrinal principles based on the Koran and in the
textual traditions related to the Imams, as well
as to eliminate practices considered to be un-
Islamic or superstitious. This movement had a
high participation of Shi'i clerics in southern
Lebanon and Syria, where it centred on the figure of the Mufti Muhsin al-Amin (1867–1952).
The construction of an abstract and general
Shi'i religious system allowed the incorporation of autonomous religious communities
that had little in common besides a strong
devotion to the figure of 'Ali and Husayn, such
as the 'Alawis, Isma'ilis, Alevis and Ja'faris,
into a transnational Shi'i identity.

Although the reform movement succeeded
in creating a shared identity and doctrinal
vocabulary among the various Shi'i communities, its effects on the actual beliefs and
practices of their members were uneven. For
example, while the 'Alawis in Syria adopted
most of the reformed Shi'i doctrines, part of
their communities continued to structure
their religious life around esoteric beliefs and
rituals. Even among the mainstream Ja'fari
Shi'is, rituals condemned by the reformers,
such as flagellation with knives and swords
during the 'Ashura, are still practised in Iraq
and south Lebanon with the approval of local
clerics.

The Iranian Revolution in 1979 consecrated
the role of clerics in the political interpretation of Shi'ism. Ayatollah Khomeini used his
prestige as marja' to gain hold and imprint an
Islamic character on the large popular mobilization against the repressive regime of the
Shah. Shi'i rituals, such as the 'Ashura, were
the occasion of mass gatherings and protest
against the secular-minded Iranian monarchy. The Islamic Republic inspired and sponsored militant and political Shi'i groups in
Lebanon, such as the Hizbollah, in their fight
against the Israeli invasion and occupation of
south Lebanon between 1982 and 2000.

Shi'i social and political organizations
also tried to foster the ideals of the Shi'i religious reform, as is shown by the opposition
of clerics linked to the Hizbollah against the
flagellation practices performed during the
'Ashura. This process is also expressed in the
missionary work sponsored by Shi'i organizations in Iran and Lebanon that aim to spread
their normative models of Shi'i religiosity
among diasporic communities. For example, since the late 1990s Shi'i missionaries
have been trying to create a public religious
identity for Shi'is in Trinidad together with
convincing them to abandon their carniva-
lesque celebration of the 'Ashura in favour
of more 'orthodox' rituals. While Shi'i missionary work has usually been used as a tool
for introducing ideals of religious reform in
pre-existing Shi'i communities, sometimes
it starts a process of proselitism and conversion. This is the case in Senegal, where
many Muslims embrace Shi'ism as a form of
expressing their discontent with local forms
of Sufi religiosity.

The Anglo-American invasion and occupation of Iraq in 2003 unleashed political and
religious processes that changed the configuration of Shi'ism. It allowed the holy cities
of Najaf and Karbala to re-emerge as major
centres of learning and pilgrimage after the
fall of Saddam Hussein's regime in 2003.
More than 2 million pilgrims, mainly Iraqis
and Iranians, but also from Pakistan, India,
Lebanon and Azerbajian, gathered there for

the celebration of the 'Ashura in 2004 and 2005. Also, the Shi'i religious authorities and political parties became major players in the Iraqi political scene, with close ties with Iran and Shi'i parties and movements in Lebanon. Therefore, at the beginning of the 21st century Shi'i Islam became a major religious force in the contemporary Middle East, connecting political and religious elites, as well as mass movements in Iran, Iraq, Syria and Lebanon.

Paulo G. Pinto

Bibliography

Adelkhah F. 2000. *Being modern in Iran.* New York: Columbia University Press.

Fischer M. 2003. *Iran: from religious dispute to revolution.* Madison: University of Wisconsin Press.

Mottahedeh R. 2000. *The mantle of the Prophet: religion and politics in Iran.* London: Oneworld.

Richard Y. 1995. *Shi'ite Islam.* Oxford: Blackwell.

Related essays

Aga Khan Development Network; Buddhism; Christianity; evangelicalism; Islam; Koran; missionaries; Muslim networks; religious pilgrimage

Shiber, Saba George 1923–68

Saba Shiber distinguished himself as an outspoken advocate for the planning of Arab cities, pushing questions of urbanism into the Arab modernizing discourse, while leading a hectic professional life as a globe-trotting planning consultant, one of the first Arabs to achieve that status.

Shiber had a rich, though brief, professional career (from the late 1940s to the late 1960s), ranging from mapping out a university in Jerusalem – his hometown – just before the creation of Israel, to participating in designing for urban renewal in the US, through post-earthquake reconstruction planning in Lebanon, consulting across the Arab world as an expert on urban matters, and finally serving as chief planner for Kuwait City in the boom years of the 1960s.

After studies in civil engineering in Beirut and in architecture in Cairo, Shiber continued his training in the US during the period 1946–48. Stranded there as a Palestinian refugee in May 1948, he combined planning

practice with teaching, while continuing his studies. (He was the second Arab to obtain a doctorate in planning in the US.) In July 1956, he moved to Beirut, which became his base for the rest of his life. After a disappointing experience working as a government official in Lebanon, he started a career as consultant in 1959, primarily in Kuwait but with brief stints in numerous other Arab cities (Aqaba, Damascus, Khobar, and elsewhere), while becoming increasingly active as proselytizer for urban planning.

His advocacy took many forms: publications (regular columns in newspapers, books), conferences and lectures worldwide, interviews, membership in international organizations. He became completely integrated into the emerging international networks of urban specialists. He had thus managed to establish himself as 'Mr. Arab Planner', as the cover of one magazine (*Middle East Business Digest*) claimed in December 1963 – a particular type of a transnational urban professional, both a local planner and a foreign expert.

Joe Nasr

Bibliography

Nasr J. 2005. 'Saba Shiber, "Mr. Arab Planner": parcours professionnel d'un urbaniste au Moyen-Orient', *Géocarrefour*, 80, 3.

Related essays

architecture; city planning; executives and professionals; Gandhi, Mohandas Karamchand; Garvey, Marcus Mosiah; international students; Muslim networks; oil; Quesnay, Pierre; regions; Schwimmer, Rosika; urbanization; Williams, James Dixon

Sign languages

Sign languages are fully fledged human languages that arise naturally in any community with a significant number of Deaf people.

There is no one universal sign language. As with all natural human languages, sign languages originate within a particular community of users. Sign languages today are largely organized along national lines, but there can be several signed languages within a single nation state. Sign languages are not pantomime or systems of gestures; they use complex grammatical rules and linguistic structures akin to those found in spoken languages. As such, it is a misnomer to consider sign languages as derivative of, or codifications for, spoken languages.

The majority of sign languages developed within and expanded outward from schools for Deaf people, which were first established on a large-scale status in 18th-century Europe (Deaf people were educated by private teachers as early as the 16th century). In the 18th and 19th centuries, deaf education was a transnational field; teachers trained in one country founded schools in other countries, and took the sign language they had learned to other nations. Whence some enduring differences that do not recoup linguistic spheres: American Sign Language (ASL) is used by Deaf people in the United States and parts of Canada. With historical roots in French Sign Language, it is mutually unintelligible vis-à-vis British Sign Language. Yet, transnational idioms also derived from these ancient circulations: the manual alphabet, representations of letters of the alphabet via distinct hand shapes, was first developed by a Franciscan monk in Spain in the 1500s and is still in use today – in a much-modified form – in many countries around the world.

There exists a form of signed communication, today called 'International Sign', that Deaf people can use to communicate with one another even without knowledge of each others' national sign languages. Unlike Esperanto, International Sign is not a planned language, but a form of cross-national signed communication which has been traced back to at least the early 19th century at a series of Parisian 'Deaf-Mute Banquets' also attended by foreign Deaf people. Throughout the 19th and 20th centuries, Deaf people met regularly in international congresses (from as early as 1873) and other forums, maintaining a transnational community which used signing as a lingua franca. International Sign is used today in a variety of settings, from informal transnational social events to the quadrennial Congresses of the World Federation of the Deaf (since 1951), and at the Deaflympics, an international Deaf sports competition enacted quadrennially since 1924.

Academic study of national sign languages has been conducted since the mid-20th century, but little research has been done on international signing. What research exists indicates International Sign is linguistically more complex than spoken language pidgins and contains grammatical structures that compare favourably with those of national signed languages. Deaf people's ability to communicate with one another across linguistic barriers may be a result of several factors, including common grammatical structures across national signed languages, a history of contact between the sign languages in question, and the visually based nature of signing used in transnational settings, somewhat akin to onomatopoeia in spoken languages.

In 1975, an attempt was made by a committee of the World Federation of the Deaf to establish a standardized lexicon of international signs in a book, *Gestuno*. This attempt was unsuccessful, reflecting the fact that International Sign is not a planned language, but a form of communication which arises naturally within a transnational community of Deaf people. While different Deaf people may attend different transnational events, a relatively stable core group of users has enabled International Sign to develop a core lexicon over time. Aside from this, the lexicon of International Sign can be said to be highly situational, shifting from event to event according to the participants' multilingual ability in various national signed languages and the geographical location of the event (local signs often predominate), among other factors. International Sign is still largely a spontaneous form of communication that takes shape whenever and wherever Deaf users of different sign languages assemble.

Joseph J. Murray

Bibliography

Supalla T. and Webb R. 'The grammar of International Sign: a new look at pidgin languages', in Emmorey K. and Reilly J. S. (eds) 1995. *Language, gesture, and space*, Hillsdale: Lawrence Erlbaum, 348–9.
Valli C. and Lucas C. 1995. *Linguistics of American Sign Language: an introduction*, 2nd ed. Washington, DC: Gallaudet University Press.

Related essays

Braille code; Esperanto; international non-governmental organizations (INGOs); language; pidgins and creoles; translation

Silk

The silk thread is secreted by an insect, *Bombyx mori*, so as to protect itself in a cocoon while transforming into a moth. The insect has to be hatched from eggs produced in the previous season, and raised by feeding on mulberry leaves until it spins cocoons ('sericulture'). In tropical areas, where mulberry leaves grow all through the year, the cycle can be repeated six or seven times a year. In temperate climates, silkworms were traditionally raised only once a year, but some technical innovations in the 19th century made it possible to repeat the cycle twice. Cocoons are too bulky to be traded over long distances and thus must be processed close to the production areas. The thread is wound up (or 'reeled') in hot water and joined with others to produce (raw) silk, which can be then woven into clothes or used to produce stockings and other silkwares.

Silkworms were first domesticated in China sometime between 2850 and 2650 BC. The secret of silk production leaked to India and Korea in 200 or 300 BC and to Japan around 300 AD. Europe had to import silk from Asia, and it is not by chance that the main land route between China and Europe is known as the Silk Road. However, around 550 AD, silkworm eggs were smuggled into the Byzantine Empire and in the next millennia silk production spread all over the northern shore of the Mediterranean. The Italian peninsula supplied the northern European countries, where silk production never developed because of the harsh climate, with silkwares and later with raw silk.

Imports from Asia resumed in the late 18th century, but they accounted for a minor share of European consumption until the 1850s, when a very serious silkworm disease, pébrine, drastically cut European production. The silk industry recovered, at least in the Italian peninsula, but Asian exports went on expanding. In fact, the silk trade boomed as the growth in income caused the demand for silk clothes, and hence for raw silk, to soar all over the Western world. From the 1870s to the late 1920s, the consumption per capita of raw silk in four major advanced countries (France, Germany, the United States and the United Kingdom) grew by 5.5 times, much more than that of any other 'natural' fibre. According to the best (but still highly uncertain) estimates, in the same years total world output grew threefold – from some 17,000 tons (a quarter from the Mediterranean) to more than 60,000 (only 7 per cent from the Mediterranean). World silk exports soared from 8,000 tons to almost 49,000 – i.e. from less than half

to more than three quarters of output. Until the 1900s, Italy, China and Japan divided the world market in roughly equal shares. However, since then, Italian production and exports have stagnated and the Chinese ones have grown slowly. As a result, on the eve of the Great Depression, Italy accounted for a mere 10 per cent of silk exports, China for 20 per cent and Japan for the rest. These changes were matched by parallel movements from the import side. Until 1890, France was the world's major importer of raw silk (on top of its small and dwindling local production) and the major exporter of silkwares. From the late 1890s, the United States overtook France as the main consumer of raw silk in the West, and from (probably) the 1900s, it replaced China as the main consumer of silk worldwide. The growth of the silk industry in Japan and that in the US were strongly related, as the medium-quality Japanese silk was especially suited to mass production of standardized goods. The introduction of 'artificial' silk (rayon) in the 1900s did not alter this picture substantially, as it was a competitor only for the low-quality natural silk for cloths.

Production of raw silk was dominated by small and medium sized companies. Although there were some big companies involved, especially in Japan, their market share was very small. The largest Japanese company in the 1920s, the Katakura, produced about 8% of the country's output. As a consequence, the world market for raw silk was a perfectly competitive one, with highly sophisticated organizations and institutions. Capital was provided by international and national banks, often on the security of silk.

The rise of silk production and trade was suddenly stopped by the Great Depression, which hit a luxury good such as silk manufactures very hard. However, unlike other luxury industries, silk did not recover after the war, as nylon, discovered in 1942, proved to be the first real substitute for natural silk for the production of stockings. Only in the 1980s did the world production of silk return to the levels of the 1920s, and that total trade is still substantially lower than it was then. Italian production never recovered and disappeared in the 1950s, and its textile industry now uses imported raw silk. The once dominant Japanese silk industry shrank and reduced itself to supplying the domestic market. In this way, China remained the main supplier of raw silk to a world market, in spite of the growing competition from new producers, in Asia (Thailand, Korea) and Latin America (Brazil).

The key factor to explain these changes in world location of the silk industry is the sluggish rate of technical progress in sericulture. Reeling, traditionally a part-time activity for peasants, who processed their own cocoons, adopted the factory system in the 19th century. The first steam-powered reeling-machine was patented in 1805 by the Frenchman Gensoul, and really effective models were developed by the 1830s. Forty years later, steam-reeling accounted for three quarters of Italian production. It produced more and better silk than the traditional techniques, and so ultimately the Asian producers had to adjust. Imported European technologies started to spread into China and Japan after the 1870s, and Japan proved capable of adapting them to its needs. Modern technology remained partially manual until the 1950s, when the first automatic machines, which could dispense with human intervention, were produced in Japan.

In contrast, the agricultural stage has not yet been mechanized. The traditional techniques for raising cocoons required a good deal of labour: the production of 12 kilograms of cocoons (the raw material for a kilogram of silk) required 80–100 hours of work. Most of this employment had to be supplied in the last days of the raising cycle, when silkworms have to be fed almost continuously. In the 19th century, farmers tried to save labour by adopting innovations – such as a reduction in the size of mulberry plants (from a tree to a bush) – and later by using tractors and lorries to transport leaves. However, all attempts to mechanize the distribution of leaves to silkworms have so far failed. Silk production, therefore, remains a labour-intensive activity, which can be economically viable only where the cost of agricultural labour during the raising period(s) is low. In fact, sericulture never took hold in the US, in spite of a suitable climate in many areas, and declined in Europe and Japan once these countries developed and wages rose. In 'advanced' countries, like 19th-century France or present-day Japan, sericulture can survive only thanks to public largesse. In other words, the disappearance of raw silk production is a sign of modern economic growth.

Giovanni Federico

Bibliography

Eng R.Y. 1986. *Economic imperialism in China: silk production and exports.* Berkeley: University of California Press.

Federico G. 1997. *An economic history of the silk industry 1830–1930.* Cambridge: Cambridge University Press.

Li L. M. 1981. *China's silk trade: traditional industry in the modern world.* Cambridge, MA: Harvard University Press.

Ma D. 2004. 'Why Japan, not China was the first to develop in Asia: lessons from sericulture', *Economic Development and Cultural Change*, 52, 2, 369–94.

Related essays

agriculture; commodity trading; dress; fashion; rubber; technologies; textiles

Skidmore, Owings & Merill *See* Architecture

Slavery

Slavery is a hereditary bundle of rights of one person over another. That sounds rather vague, but it has been the ubiquity and normalcy of slavery that have made it so difficult to challenge. Before 1800, the trade in slaves was a major organizer of transatlantic migrations. Since abolition, claims of enslavement have continued to accompany movements of low-skill and low-wage workers down to the present.

In Western Europe slavery had given way to free labour before 1500. Thus, between 1550 and 1870, Europe's colonizers of the Americas turned to Africa. From there about 11 million slaves were brought to the New World. Although the use of slaves in the European colonies was extremely profitable, the slave trade came under increasing attack by anti-slavery opponents in Europe and North America.

Many saw Western Europe's industrialization as proof that long-term economic progress was based on free labour and that unfree labour should be stamped out. By the middle of the 19th century abolition was in full swing. Many nations had outlawed the slave trade, but illegally slaves were still being shipped to the New World, notably to Brazil and Cuba, areas experiencing a new boom in sugar exports and rapidly rising slave prices.

It was not until the 1870s that international naval actions against the slave trade across the Atlantic resulted in its final demise.

The abolition of slavery itself was a more complicated process as it infringed on the property rights of the owners. In 1833 Britain had abolished slavery in its colonies by offering the slave owners financial compensation and in 1848 the abolition of colonial slavery was enacted in France and Denmark, and in the Netherlands in 1863. In 1865 slavery was abolished in the US, in 1886 in Cuba and in 1888 in Brazil. Several of the abolition acts stipulated that the ex-slaves should continue to work on the plantations for a transitional period, called apprenticeship.

No such abolitionist fervour occurred in Asia and Africa, where the slave trade continued to exist. Because few written sources exist, the volume and scope of these slave trades and populations are unknown. In the course of the 19th century, the European colonization of Asia curbed the use of slaves, as colonial legislation often outlawed slavery and prohibited owners of slaves from repossessing their slaves once they had absconded.

In Africa, the ending of the Atlantic slave trade had lowered slave prices and increased the volume of the internal slave trade and the use of slaves. European colonial administrators seemed at a loss in dealing with slavery in Africa. Force was not always the main reason for enslavement, as in some societies people offered themselves or their children as slaves in the hope that their owners would save them from starvation and protect them against violence. It is ironic that slaves made up an important section of the auxiliary troops used in establishing European colonial rule in Africa as the moral justification for this expansion was said to be the final extinction of the slave trade and of slavery.

Slavery may have been economically viable only in open resource areas, where there was free access to land. That proved to be true in some of the most flourishing export colonies in the New World with sufficient free land to allow the ex-slaves to withdraw from plantation labour as soon as they had the legal right to do so. Only in densely populated areas, where there was no land available for squatting, did the freedmen have no other option but to continue working as field hands. After the Civil War in the US, legislation enabled the freedmen to use the land of their former masters as sharecroppers. In most parts of the New World, however, employers were forced to look for labour elsewhere and this also applied to the new plantation and mining areas in South Africa, Asia, Australia and on the Pacific islands as well as to the construction of railways in the US and Uganda. Soon abolitionists were concerned that these new migrants, too, were in danger of becoming enslaved.

Indentured labour: a new system of slavery?

During the 19th century a steadily rising demand for tea, coffee, rubber, sisal and tobacco, the construction of railways and telegraph lines as well as coal and guano mining caused a dramatic increase in the demand for labour in the non-Western world. Attempts to recruit indentured labour in Europe met with limited success. During the first half of the 19th century, only the impoverished populations of the Portuguese and Spanish Atlantic islands (Madeira, Canaries, Azores) were willing to indenture themselves for service overseas, but stopped doing so as soon as economic prospects at home improved.

Again employers turned to Africa, but virtually no free African labour was forthcoming. The only 'voluntary' Africans who signed a contract of indenture for the plantation colonies were ex-slaves aboard illegal slave ships who had been liberated by the British Navy and those who had been bought as slaves (rachat préalable) by the French and then 'liberated' with no other option but to sign a contract of indenture for one of the French plantation colonies.

Abolitionist pressures against this practice forced the colonial employers to turn to Asia (British India, China, Japan, and Java) in order to obtain labour. In the Caribbean indentured labourers from Asia filled the positions the ex-slaves had left, and in some areas (Cuba, Suriname) they arrived even before the slaves had been freed and for some that made indentured labour look like a new system of slavery.

The indentured labour system was in operation between 1834 and 1939 and mainly consisted of labourers moving between tropical zones. By far the major contributor was British India sending more than 1.5 million indentured migrants to destinations such as Mauritius (452,000), British Guiana (239,000), Malaya (250,000), and Natal (152,000). China also provided about 600,000 indentured labourers, most of whom were shipped to California to build railways (300,000), to the sugar plantations on Cuba (125,000) and to the guano islands off the coast of Peru (90,000). These figures dwarf the indentured labour migration of Europeans to the Caribbean (44,000) and of 'voluntary' Africans after the ending of the slave trade (58,000 to the Caribbean and 34,000 to La Réunion).

In spite of the popular notion in Western Europe and North America that indentured labour was akin to slavery, there are many indications that the transportation and working and living conditions of indentured labourers were quite different from those of the slaves. It is true that in the ports along the Chinese coast ship captains were able to buy indentured labourers, that on Cuba these indentured migrants were auctioned to the highest bidder and that no provisions had been made for their return passage after the expiration of the contract. However, the international press exposed most of these early abuses and forced the Chinese government as well as the colonial administrations of Hong Kong and Macao in 1874 to suspend the recruitment of Chinese indentured labourers. In British India, on the other hand, the recruitment, transportation and overseas living and working conditions as well as the return voyage were carefully monitored by representatives of the British colonial administration in India, by the imperial government in London and by the various authorities in the receiving countries. Over time, the mortality rate during the voyage and the period of indenture dropped far below the death rate of those recruited for service in India itself. The rate of natural increase among the overseas Indians was high, even in areas where the slave communities had experienced a constant surplus of deaths over births. In spite of the favourable demography and the fact that the supply of recruits continued to be sufficient, the nationalists (Mahatma Gandhi among them) in India felt that the exportation of indentured labour degraded Indians and they campaigned to stop it. These pressures weighed heavily on the British colonial administration in India and during the First World War in 1916 the indentured labour

migration under government supervision was suspended and never resumed.

Are there still slaves in today's world?

Efforts by the colonial powers, the League of Nations and the United Nations to stamp out slavery and the slave trade were never completely successful, and today slaves can still be found in parts of Africa and Asia. Campaigns against the trafficking of sex workers and concerns about women working on contract as domestic servants or children working in apprenticeship arrangements continue to make claims that these workers, too, are enslaved.

Pieter Emmer

Bibliography
Eltis D. 1987. *Economic growth and the ending of the Atlantic slave trade.* Oxford: Oxford University Press.
Northrup D. 1995. *Indentured labour in the age of imperialism, 1834–1922.* Cambridge: Cambridge University Press.
Seymour D. and Engerman S. L. (eds) 1998. *A historical guide to world slavery.* Oxford: Oxford University Press.
Shlomowitz R. 1996. *Mortality and migration in the modern world.* Aldershot: Variorum.

Related essays
Abolition of Forced Labour Convention; abolitionism; contract and indentured labourers; forced migrations; League of Nations system; money; pidgins and creoles; railways; sexuality; Thailand and sex tourism; White Slavery

Smallpox

Smallpox is an acute, infectious disease that is caused by a virus and is often fatal. Before the 20th century, smallpox was endemic in many regions in Europe, Asia, and Africa. In the 20th century alone, smallpox is estimated to have caused some 300 million deaths. However, the invention and spread of vaccination in the last two hundred years, a process which culminated in a global immunization program, have made smallpox the first major human disease to be entirely eradicated. The last naturally occurring case was identified in 1977, and today the smallpox virus is known to exist only in high-security laboratories.

Smallpox was among the oldest known human diseases. It was typically transmitted through the respiratory tract, and its most characteristic symptom were the pustules that covered the body, most densely on the face and limbs. Death typically occurred in around 30 per cent of cases within two weeks of the appearance of symptoms. Survivors were left with disfiguring scars; blindness and male infertility were also common. Survivors of the disease usually acquired lifelong immunity, but smallpox remained endemic in many areas since new births constantly replenished the susceptible population. When smallpox was introduced into populations where immunity was low or absent it often produced devastating epidemics, most notably among the native populations of the Americas after the Columbian encounter.

Efforts to induce immunity to smallpox date to ancient times. One method, known as variolation, involved scratching material taken from the pustules of a smallpox sufferer into a healthy person's skin. Practised in Asia for centuries, it was introduced into Europe through the Ottoman Empire in the early 18th century. The introduction of the virus through the skin rather than the respiratory tract produced a much milder form of the disease that still conferred immunity. But variolation was a risky procedure and was never universally practised.

The discovery of the smallpox vaccine in 1796 was a crucial milestone in the efforts to control the disease. Edward Jenner, a British country doctor, discovered that inoculating healthy individuals with material taken from cowpox pustules – a bovine version of the disease – induced immunity in humans without the danger of contracting smallpox. The word 'vaccine,' from the Latin vacca, or cow, derives from this discovery. The practice of vaccination spread throughout the 19th century, first in Europe and North America and later in other regions of the world, though not without resistance. Some, including within medical establishments, argued that the procedure was ineffective and even unnatural.

By the early 20th century, however, large-scale vaccination programmes had eradicated smallpox from most of Europe and North America, and similar campaigns brought the disease under control in the Soviet Union and the People's Republic of China by mid-century. But smallpox remained endemic in many parts of the developing world, primarily in South Asia, sub-Saharan Africa, and Indonesia,

well into the 1960s. In 1967 the World Health Organization launched a global eradication programme. At the time, many doubted the feasibility of such a project, but within a decade the programme had reached its goal. After an exhaustive verification process, the WHO officially certified eradication in 1980.

Smallpox had a number of characteristics that made it especially suitable for eradication. First, there existed a dependable vaccine that, when successfully administered, provided a high degree of immunity. Second, the characteristic symptoms made the disease relatively easy to identify, and helped health workers discover outbreaks at an early stage. Third, the lack of an animal reservoir meant that once the virus was eradicated from the human population it could no longer survive in nature. Other diseases, such as malaria, which has animal vectors, or influenza, whose frequent mutations defy long-term immunity, are harder to control. Still, the success of the smallpox eradication programme has served as an inspiration to current global campaigns against other diseases, including poliomyelitis and AIDS.

Erez Manela

Bibliography

Crosby A. W. 1972. The Columbian exchange: biological and cultural consequences of 1492, new edition. Westport: Greenwood.

Fenner F., Henderson D. A., Arita I., Jezek Z. and Ladnyi I. D. 1988. Smallpox and its eradication. Geneva: World Health Organization.

Hopkins D. R. 2002. The greatest killer: smallpox in history. Chicago: Chicago University Press.

Tucker J. 2001. Scourge: the once and future threat of smallpox. New York: Grove.

Related essays
Acquired Immunodeficiency Syndrome (AIDS); animal diseases; epidemics; germs; health policy; United Nations system; vaccination

Social sciences

The social sciences have developed in a permanent tension between the aspiration to universally valid knowledge about human societies and the social sciences' dependence on nation states. Since modern systems of higher learning, research funding, and scientific publications have been predominantly organized along national lines, the social sciences have often been depicted as a plurality of national traditions. Although there are good reasons for examining national developments, historical accounts of the social sciences have too often adopted a nation-centred view. One of the paradoxical consequences of this state of affairs is that the national traditions themselves are not well understood. What is commonly called 'Austrian economics', for example, refers to a set of ideas that emerged locally, in Vienna, in a struggle that mobilized British political economy against the dominant tradition of German historical economics. Moreover, this approach became a distinct 'national school' only in exile, from the 1930s onwards. Even for a proper understanding of national schools, therefore, it is impossible to ignore the broader transnational setting. Evolving patterns of transnational mobility and exchange cut through the neat distinction between the local, the national and the international, and thus represent an essential component in the dynamics of the social sciences, as well as a fruitful perspective for rethinking their historical development.

Although remarkably few studies have taken such a view, the transnational history of the social sciences may be understood on the basis of three mechanisms which have structured the transnational flows of people and ideas: (1) the functioning of international scholarly institutions; (2) the transnational mobility of scholars, and (3) the politics of transnational exchange of non-academic institutions.

International scholarly institutions and transnational networks

Transnational connections were relatively often initiated at meetings of international social science organizations. Among these, two closely related institutions have historically provided the predominant framework: the international scientific conference and the international scientific association. Both are distinctly modern forms which have developed only since the mid 19th century. Initially covering statistics and the four basic social sciences (economics, sociology, anthropology, political science), these international organizations not only provided meeting places, offering occasions for

communication and diffusion across national borders, they have also functioned as interest groups, stimulating the international spread of knowledge and of scholarly associations in countries where they did not yet exist.

Despite the fact that international congresses and associations were above all scholarly organizations, the intellectual consequences of their modes of operation have varied enormously. In some fields, such as statistics, they played a key role in the standardization of technical and administrative tools for producing authoritative knowledge. In other cases, such as the Institut International de Sociologie, international conferences resembled a diplomatic order, with occasions for polite encounter, exchange of information and 'foreign policy', but of limited significance for actual research. In still other cases, especially after the First World War, the actual effect may have been the opposite of what was officially intended, reinforcing national rivalries and fuelling struggles for international domination. The most common pattern was undoubtedly the more or less selective adoption of ideas, methods and procedures from the leading scientific centres.

International social science organizations have developed in two distinct phases. From the mid 19th century onward, international social science organizations emerged in most fields. The process was related to the gradual institutionalization of the social sciences, and to the more general flourishing of international organizations, which were thought of as a new phase in the relations among the most advanced nation states. Actual collaboration across national borders, however, remained infrequent. Information sharing, diffusion and intellectual diplomacy were more important than transnational collaboration. The fact that the two most important sociologists around 1900, Max Weber and Émile Durkheim, never met one another and never even referred to each other's writings, illustrates the limited significance of international organizations. From the end of the Second World War to the present, new international social science organizations were founded under the auspices of the United Nations Educational, Scientific and Cultural Organization (UNESCO) and were crucial in enabling more regular transnational flows of people and ideas.

The post-1945 expansion was characterized by a tension between weakly institutionalized social science disciplines, often reflecting the specificity of national scientific cultures, and the international social sciences that seemed to offer a universal scientific language that was not context-specific. This unified conception of the social sciences lost much of its cogency and was criticized from different perspectives by the 1970s. New methodologies, critical transdisciplinary approaches (Marxism, feminism), the 'linguistic turn' in the social sciences, new forms of regional organizations, all contributed to a diversification of scientific endeavours, but also to a sense of uncertainty about the identity of the social sciences that persists to this day.

One of the first models of the international social science organizations were the international congresses of statistics, which were held from 1853 to 1876, and were founded by the Belgian astronomer and statistical entrepreneur Adolphe Quetelet. Every two or three years they brought together hundreds of participants, both academic and administrative statisticians, discussing the technical, scientific and organizational progress of their work. The proceedings of the congress represented the international state of the art. These periodic international congresses, which generally preceded the formation of international associations, led to the establishment of an International Institute of Statistics in 1885. In the anthropological sciences, including both physical and social or cultural anthropology, international congresses were held from 1865; they were more formally instituted with the founding of the International Congress of Anthropological and Ethnological Sciences (ICAES) in 1934. In political science and psychology the temporal and organizational patterns were similar, while sociology followed a slightly different path. An Institut International de Sociologie was founded in Paris as early as 1893, with its *Revue internationale de sociologie* (1893), and shortly before national sociological journals and associations emerged. More than promoting common professional standards, these early forms of transnational scientific exchange were part of a wider movement in favour of international exchange and understanding.

Despite new initiatives for international collaboration launched by the International Labour Organization (1919), the League of Nations (1920) and its Institut International de Coopération Intellectuelle (1926), or the International Bureau of Education (1925) headed by psychologist Jean Piaget, the decades after the First World War were difficult for most international associations. A major revival occurred after the Second World War, when UNESCO initiated and funded the major international associations: the International Union of Anthropological and Ethnographical Sciences (1948), the International Sociological Association (1949), the International Political Science Association (1949), and the International Economic Association (1949). Founded on the basis of a small number of national associations from the core countries, their growth was initially assured by the increasing membership of national associations. In spite of the Cold War but in line with the UNESCO policy to promote international understanding, national associations from several Communist countries in Eastern Europe also joined in the late 1950s. In the course of the 1960s and 1970s, membership increased further by allowing individuals and associate members to join, thus breaking away from the United Nations model of national representation. Among such associate members were regional organizations from Europe, Latin America and Asia. The widening geographic range of recruitment was stimulated by the process of decolonization and, after 1989, by the demise of the Communist regimes and globalization. These processes triggered global debates about the social sciences. Their diversity, the division of intellectual labour between core and peripheries, and its resulting relations of power and dependency have been discussed across national and regional borders.

The international disciplinary organizations, with their focus increasingly on ongoing research, were soon based on the functioning of specialized research groups and research committees. They organized world congresses every three to five years and launched international journals such as *Current Sociology* (1952), *Current Anthropology* (1960), and the *International Political Science Review* (1980), as well as various other regular publications (abstracts, trend reports, book series). By incorporating an increasing number of scholars and scholarly societies from an ever widening circle of countries, international organizations contributed significantly to the denationalization of the social sciences.

Intellectual migration

Different patterns of migration have shaped the development of a transnational space for the social sciences. Leaving temporary migration aside (students exchanges, travel, research missions), long-term migration has taken two forms: voluntary migration of resourceful individuals, and forced migration.

These transnational flows can have two directions. Social scientists may migrate from academic centres to a periphery in order to teach, export their skills or do research. Franz Boas, who had left Germany for the US in 1899, contributed to creating the first institutions of anthropological research in Mexico. French social scientists like psychologist Georges Dumas, anthropologist Claude Lévi-Strauss and historian Fernand Braudel had a strong impact on the development of the social sciences in Brazil through their position at the University of São Paolo during the interwar years. In the opposite direction, talented young scholars leave a peripheral position for the academic centres in order to get trained or to work with the most eminent scholars. Vienna and Prague around 1900, Berlin and Heidelberg until 1933, and Paris at least until 1940 have been such centres. Oxford and Cambridge, London, along with the most prestigious North American universities (Berkeley, Chicago, Columbia, Harvard, Yale, etc.) still are. In anthropology, Bronislaw Malinowski left Poland for London in 1910, and in 1938 the London School of Economics for Yale University. Many young psychologists visited Janet or Charcot in Paris at the end of the 19th century, or Freud in Vienna. Imperial and colonial political structures also provided a highly asymmetrical framework for voluntary migration. Some centres attract scholars on a regional scale, as is often the case with the most prestigious South African, Indian, Japanese and Mexican universities today.

The hierarchy of academic centres and national traditions is not the only factor accounting for the direction of transnational migration. Most of the scientific migration flows from Europe to North America also derive from the fact that the United States job market was relatively open to productive foreign social scientists throughout the century. The expression 'brain drain' was coined in the early 1960s to describe the rapidly increasing numbers of scientists emigrating from Europe and from Third World or 'emerging' countries to the United States. It is estimated that around 1 million students and scholars have moved from the former countries to Western centres over the past 40 years. Such a massive migration has reinforced the hegemony of American universities and research, but scientific socialization in one of the world centres has sometimes also contributed to the reinforcement of national scholarship in the migrant's country of origin. Florian Znaniecki was one of the pioneers of academic sociology in the United States but also one of the founders of sociology in his home country, Poland.

Because it often resulted in a long-lasting integration abroad, forced migration has contributed even more to the internationalization of social sciences. The numerous wars and waves of political persecution provoked intellectual exiles. Anti-Semitism under the Tsarist regime and political violence following the 1917 Bolshevik Revolution caused the emigration of 'White' Russian or Menshevik scholars (like the sociologists Pitirim Sorokin or Nikolaï Berdiaev) to Berlin, Paris and the United States. Wars outside of the Western part of the world after 1945 and the repression in the Soviet Union and its satellites also provoked the flight of social scientists abroad (like Zygmunt Bauman, Ferenc Fehér, Iván Szelényi). But the most important migration took place after 1933 with the exile of professors and researchers – a majority of them being Jewish – from Germany and occupied countries.

This scientific exodus from Europe was in part organized by transnational intellectual networks, which often pre-dated the political crises of the 1930s, like the Institute of International Education, an agency funded by the Rockefeller Foundation. The American scientific philanthropies played an important role in rescuing European scientists by channeling former beneficiaries of their grant programmes to safe countries. Ad hoc committees like the Emergency Committee in Aid of Displaced German/Foreign Scholars (1933) in New York, the Society for the Protection of Science and Learning (1936) in London, the Comité des Savants in France were created for the same purposes. Relatively new academic institutions like the New School for Social Research (1919) in New York or the London School of Economics (1895) played a specific role in securing job positions for refugees. Several hundred scholars who already were or eventually became professional social scientists emigrated between 1933 and 1942 from Europe to the United States. Due in part to the expanding system of higher education in that country, many of them were hired as fully recognized social scientists whereas only a minority of them were recognized as such before. Their intellectual impact has profoundly reshaped and 'denationalized' North American social science, and was an important factor in consolidating its global supremacy.

European refugee social scientists did more than import Continental knowledge onto foreign soil. They also developed new styles of inquiry and research programmes. Many applied their knowledge and methods to the political analysis of their countries of origin, as with the Office of Strategic Services. By taking part in the British or American war effort, they renewed hopes for social betterment by developing applied social science. Refugee scholars who remained in the United States after 1945 contributed to the intellectual climate of the Cold War era. The methodological preference for quantification, the neopositivist philosophy of science, and the hope for social progress through social research, which already characterized American social science, were reinforced by this wave of migration. The most successful refugee scholars became in turn export agents of these ways of doing social science and helped in constructing and unifying a transnational field for each of these disciplines. After the 1960s, intellectual migrations of social scientists to the United States have had more critical consequences. The new legitimacy of cultural studies, the renewed development of area studies and the current interest in transnational topics are doubtless an effect of some other transnational trajectories of prominent intellectual exiles (Arjun Appadurai, Homi Bhabha, Edward Saïd).

The politics of transnational scientific exchange

Whether for diplomatic purposes, or with a view to acquiring scientific skills, international contacts were also embedded in the international politics of individual nation states. In the late 19th and early 20th centuries, Germany stood out as the crucial purveyor of institutional and methodological models for others, eager to emulate its scientific establishment and its industrial successes. French scholars from Émile Durkheim to Raymond Aron studied in Germany in the context of the modernization of national higher education, just as their American counterparts did, from Albion Small and W. I. Thomas to Talcott Parsons. The oldest international fellowship, the Rhodes Scholarships, was established in 1902 in the United Kingdom with a view to securing and defending British rule, and also played an important role in the socialization of Anglo-American elites.

The rising nationalism of the interwar period tended to reconfigure the social sciences along national lines, and to maintain them in a subordinate position vis-à-vis the more established disciplines. The failure to create national political science associations in the major European countries before 1949 (while Canada, Sweden or Finland had established theirs in the interwar period) bears witness to the resistance of the national academic establishments, and to the strength of the humanities that were often constitutive of the national imagination.

With the European scientific infrastructure depleted by the Second World War, the United States found itself in a dominant position that ensured the hegemony of its theoretical and organizational models. New channels of scholarly exchange, such as the system of Fulbright Fellowships, increased the capacity of the country to disseminate its vision of the social sciences. This vision called for the full integration of the social sciences within the canons of modern science – a call shared by behavioral political science and Parsonian sociology – thus delivering the social sciences from any cultural attachment. The institutionalization of empirical and applied social science thus proceeded primarily against the traditional primacy of the humanistic or speculative disciplines. As a result, the institutions that acted as the receptacles of the social sciences in Europe were usually created outside and against the established universities: this is the case with the London School of Economics as well as the École des Hautes Études en Sciences Sociales in France, which stood in opposition to the faculties of Law and Letters.

Elsewhere, the redeployment of US power in a postcolonial context accounts for the success of a particular conception of the social sciences as part and parcel of the modernizing process. While they had previously emerged as fact-finding tools serving colonial administrations, in the 'behavioural era' the social sciences provided a non-ideological language for formulating and guiding national development experiences. The Americanization of some core disciplines, such as political science and sociology, was often equated with the scientific emancipation from the former colonial power – even though the rise of such subfields as 'area studies' was inseparable from American geopolitical concerns. Moreover, the behavioural sciences had a built-in international dimension to the extent that their ahistorical approach to social phenomena called for the neutralization of cultural contexts through wide-scale comparisons. But they also provided a conduit for a technocratic ethos suiting modernizing national elites on the periphery. The sociology of 'modernization', in particular, benefited from this situation to the extent that it accommodated all of its constraints: a monitoring function of social change with a focus on overall stability and a capacity for exporting the Western sequence of societal development, projected as a universal process of 'modernization'.

International power relations also implied that scientific relations between peripheral countries were mediated by the metropolitan centre, where scientific standards were established and where most transversal scientific socialization took place. By contrast, the organization of the social sciences on a regional basis was often seen as a strategy for greater autonomy. It is certainly no coincidence that the more vigorous critique of economic and scientific dependency came from Latin America, where such organizations as the Latin American Social Science Council (CLACSO, 1967) or the Latin American Social Science Faculty (FLACSO, 1958) ensured a strong level of regional scientific integration. International scientific organizations such as UNESCO paradoxically acted as conduits for this critique of the scientific metropolises, and subsequently, as reflexive and critical forums denouncing the 'relationship of dependency' in the diffusion of social scientific knowledge and calling for 'indigenization' of research and the development of autonomous regional cooperation.

If the international development of the social sciences was in large part determined by state policies and international politics, the role of private institutions and in particular of philanthropic foundations deserves a special mention. Because they were part of a constellation where a paternalistic concern for social welfare and a strong belief in modern science met a pacifist discourse inextricably intertwined with the development of mercantile designs, foundations such as the Rockefeller Foundation or the Carnegie Corporation were major forces in the transnationalization of the social sciences. While building the infrastructures of a modern social scientific establishment at home, such as the Social Science Research Council in 1923, the foundations also sought to build international networks of scholars. Just as the nascent sciences of society were supposed to ease domestic social conflict, their internationalization was supposed to foster understanding and dialogue. Cooperation on the pressing issues of the day was expected to defuse international tensions by working towards the scientific understanding of their causes. Political science, sociology and economics – all concerned with the functioning of industrial societies – benefited prominently from these efforts. The Rockefeller Foundation, in particular, promoted its reform-oriented vision throughout the 1930s by sponsoring networks of excellence made up of institutions such as the London School of Economics, Charles Rist's Institut Scientifique de Recherches Économiques et Sociales in France, the Stockholm Institute of Social and Municipal Research, or the Deutsche Hochschule für Politik in Berlin. These efforts often overlapped with public policy, and social scientific disciplines were solicited as channels for informal cultural diplomacy. Latin America, in particular, was a region where it was difficult to distinguish between scientific, philanthropic and political developments. The purpose of these early efforts was not so much the disciplinary development of the social sciences as the development of channels of communication meant to increase cooperation across borders. These 'area studies' were still an anti- or multidisciplinary endeavour, and were concerned not so much about 'normal science' as with the acquisition of regional knowledge for practical purposes. Philanthropic efforts toward disciplinary integration came later, after the Second World War, a period during which the earlier enthusiastic embrace of international liberalism was replaced by the more sober acceptance of the limits of international cooperation and the engagement of the social sciences with the defence of democracy and the Cold War. In political science, the Rockefeller Foundation played an important role in the international development of a theory of international relations. In economics, a new orthodoxy constituted around the Chicago School and the Cowles Commission rapidly became a new international standard-setting matrix. Starting in the 1950s, the Ford Foundation supported the worldwide dissemination of the 'behavioural sciences' and, in the late 1960s, targeted more specifically the Third World, after having sought to support self-sustaining regional scientific networks in Europe, such as the European Consortium for Political Research (1970).

Conclusion

Compared to the humanities and other more linguistically bound disciplines, the development of the social sciences may well appear to be a transnational project from the start. It has nevertheless remained the product of national efforts and styles of research for the major part of the last two centuries. After 1945, and more so from the 1960s onward, worldwide international exchanges have become increasingly institutionalized. But transnational disciplinary spaces of exchange remain fragile. They show a highly asymmetrical structure, where Western countries, among them the United States in the first place, hold a hegemonic position. Although contested and opposed, the recognition of work from the periphery increasingly depends on publication in Anglo-American journals. This structure has not only determined the patterns of diffusion of the social sciences, but also their very content and their fields of application, as it often supported the administrative and policy apparatus that maintained this asymmetrical world order. Yet, for the same reason, the critique of social scientific knowledge has concentrated on issues of centrality and periphery. In the last forty years, a politicized critique has questioned the dominant epistemology and the universalist underpinnings of the social sciences. Arguably, this critique has not exhausted its effects and may change the future borders of the disciplines as well as their geographical contours. But it is already clear that the social sciences cannot proceed without assimilating this critique and adopting a more historically informed reflexive stance.

Nicolas Guilhot
Johan Heilbron
Laurent Jeanpierre

Bibliography

Ash M. G. and Söllner A. (eds) 1996. *Forced migration and scientific change: émigré German-speaking scientists and scholars after 1933.* Cambridge: Cambridge University Press.

Baker F. W. G. 1992. *Forty years of the International Social Science Council: the evolution of the social sciences.* Paris: ISSC.

Charle C., Schriewer J. and Wagner P. (eds) 2004. *Transnational intellectual networks: forms of academic knowledge and the search for cultural identities.* Berlin: Campus.

Kazancigil A. and Makinson D. (eds) 1999. *World social science report.* Paris: UNESCO/ Elsevier.

Moscovici S. and Marková I. 2006. *The making of modern social psychology: the hidden story of how an international social science was created.* Cambridge: Polity.

Porter T. and Ross, D. (eds) 2003. *The modern social sciences. The Cambridge History Of Science, Volume 7.* Cambridge: Cambridge University Press.

Rasmussen A. 1995. *L'internationale scientifique (1890–1914),* 2 vols. Unpublished doctoral dissertation, École des Hautes Etudes en Sciences Sociales, Paris.

Wallerstein I. et al. 1996. *Open the social sciences: report of the Gulbenkian Commission on the Restructuring of the Social Sciences.* Stanford: Stanford University Press.

Related essays

book and periodical exchange; brain drain; class; Commission on International Labour Legislation; economics; exile; fellowships and grants; femininity; food; French theory; higher education; history; humanities; intellectual elites; intergovernmental organizations; international non-governmental organizations (INGOs); international students; knowledge; labour standards; League of Nations Economic and Financial Organization; League of Nations system; life and physical sciences; literature; mathematics; modernization theory; music; Orientalism; philanthropic foundations;

psychoanalysis; Russian Revolution; statistics; transnational; underdevelopment; women's movements

Socialism

Socialism can refer both to an established socioeconomic system and to the movement or ideology promoting that system. In contrast with capitalism, socialism entails collective control over property and the distribution of wealth, exercised by workers' councils, local communities or the state, so as to achieve social and economic equality. Although visions of socialism have varied widely, as indicated by adjectives such as 'democratic', 'guild', 'state', 'libertarian', 'Arab', 'Christian', 'scientific' and 'utopian', they share certain core principles including democracy, equality, collectivism and internationalism.

Distinctions among socialism, communism and social democracy are mainly a 20th-century phenomenon, and early proponents used these terms interchangeably. While antecedents can be traced back as far as the Diggers of 17th-century England, the term 'socialiste' first appears in 1827, when it was used by the followers of the Comte de Saint-Simon (1760–1825). 'Socialism' was first used by the English industrialist Robert Owen (1771–1858), who advocated cooperative management of industry and established model communities in Britain and the US. In the 19th century, followers of various socialist visions, including those of Owen and Charles Fourier (1772–1837), spread these European ideas to America. Much like the earlier religious migrants to the New World, these socialists engaged in social experiments based on their ideals, attempting to create harmonious and equitable societies.

Later Marxists referred to these early thinkers as 'utopian' socialists in contrast with the 'scientific' socialism advocated by Karl Marx (1818–83) and Friedrich Engels (1820–95). In this view, socialism, as the antithesis of capitalism, will emerge from the disintegration of the capitalist system, and the characteristics of socialist society will only become clear in the revolutionary process of overthrowing capitalism. For this reason, Marx himself generally refrained from defining socialism except as the negation of the capitalist system. In his influential 1917 work, State and revolution, Vladimir Lenin (1870–1924) crystallized Marx's ideas concerning socialism as a transitional stage proceeding toward communism.

An important assumption in Marxist-inspired conceptions of socialism has been the transnational nature of the capitalist system, implying that socialism too will be a transnational system, one that will ultimately overcome the nation state as the basis for organizing modern civilization. How the transition will actually be accomplished, however, is one of the most undertheorized aspects of socialist thought.

Marx played a leading role in the founding of the International Working Men's Association in 1864, later known as the First International. There remained a diversity of views, however, even within the early socialist movement. Bakunin and Proudhon's followers who espoused anarchist principles were expelled in 1872. The primary division within the 19th-century socialist movement was between advocates of gradual reform and violent revolution as alternative paths to socialism. The gradualist or reformist faction, led by Eduard Bernstein (1850–1932), dominated the inauguration of the Second International in Paris in 1889. A vocal minority of revolutionists included Lenin and Rosa Luxemburg (1871–1919), who themselves disagreed about the composition and role of the revolutionary party, as well as the nature of the future socialist state.

While there have been repeated attempts to build an international socialist movement, socialist parties have generally been established in a context of national politics. One of the first was the German Social Democratic Workers Party, established in 1869. This was followed by the Workers Party in France in 1876 and the Socialist Labor Party of the United States in 1877, with similar parties established throughout Europe by the end of the century. Japanese socialists established a party in 1901. Socialist parties exhibited the same divisions between reformist and revolutionist factions that plagued the International, except for Labour parties in Britain, Australia and New Zealand, which enjoyed relative unity.

In addition to the division between reformists and revolutionaries, the question of nationalism and internationalism similarly divided European socialists. Despite their differences, Marxists such as Karl Kautsky and Rosa Luxemburg tended to agree on the primacy of economic forces, and the independence of developmental laws from national historical circumstances. This led to both a neglect of nationalism as a political force and an undertheorization of the internationalist aspects of the socialist movement. In contrast, the Austro-Marxism that emerged in the multilingual and multiethnic context of the Austro-Hungarian Empire in the decade before World War I was forced to face squarely the national question in discussing the republican future. Whereas most contemporary Marxists considered capitalism to be a universal phenomenon, and thus assumed that socialism would naturally overcome the nation state, Austrian Marxists like Otto Bauer (1881–1938) assumed that socialism would be based on democratically organized national communities enjoying self-determination. Bauer and other Austro-Marxists put forward, as a socialist solution to ethnic separatism in the highly mixed context of the Habsburg Empire, a concept of ethnolinguistic citizenship within a multiethnic state. Although these ideas would influence Lenin's formulation of the national question in establishing the Union of Soviet Socialist Republics, they would never be as powerful as the nation state in shaping socialism in the 20th century.

With the onset of the First World War in 1914, the divisions within the world socialist movement intensified as national reformers and internationalist revolutionaries divided over whether or not to support their respective national war efforts. The decision by most socialist parties to support their governments' war efforts resulted in the demise of the Second International in 1916. The Bolshevik revolution in Russia in 1917, and the establishment of the Soviet Union, solidified this split at the same time as it created a new focus for revolutionary movements around the world. The Soviets established a Third International, the Communist International, in 1919. The Comintern remained hostile to reformist parties, which increasingly referred to themselves as social-democratic, until the rise of fascism and the promotion of a united or popular front in European politics. It was dissolved in 1943.

The Soviet Union was the world's first socialist experiment with a transnational tack. Under Lenin's leadership, the Bolsheviks attempted to transform the Russian Empire into a union of socialist republics, attempting simultaneously to address nationalist interests and internationalist aspirations. While the Bolsheviks' revolutionist doctrine anticipated that a worldwide revolution would follow the seizure of power in Russia, this failed to materialize. In an effort to make the best of a socialist revolution in a preindustrial country, Lenin's successor Joseph Stalin (1879–1953) produced the theory of 'socialism in one country', and set about transforming socialism into a program for rapid, state-led industrialization. By the 1940s, this effort had largely succeeded, but at the cost of sacrificing socialism's more democratic and egalitarian goals, as well as countless human lives. The apparent success of the Soviet Union in 'building socialism' provided a focus for socialist parties worldwide, but its shortcomings also drew criticism. During the Cold War, Communist parties in Western Europe tended to evolve into either appendages of Moscow or centrist social-democratic parties. Although the former participated in an international network, this was highly centralized and focused on defending the interests of the Soviet Union. For their part, non-Communist socialist parties and trade unions also attempted to maintain ties to similar parties in Europe and around the world.

Among socialist opponents of the Soviet Union, Leon Trotsky (1879–1940), Stalin's erstwhile ally, criticized the Soviet regime as a bureaucratic corruption of socialism. In 1938, Trotsky and his supporters established a Fourth International to compete with the Comintern. Under constant pressure, this organization split several times as competing factions claimed leadership in the 1950s and 60s. Even after his death, the international socialist movement, consistently hostile to Stalinist manifestations of socialism around the world, continued to be influenced by Trotsky's ideas concerning international revolution and the problem of bureaucratization. Mao Zedong (1893–1976), leader of the Chinese Communist Party and a dedicated follower of Stalin's vision, also criticized Soviet socialism for its bureaucratic tendencies and emphasized the need for continued class conflict under socialism. Following the split between the People's Republic of China and the Soviet Union in the late 1950s, Mao attempted to organize a 'Third World' bloc of African, Asian and Latin American countries sympathetic to socialism. Although generally unsuccessful, Maoism has inspired similar movements around the world, with active Maoist parties in numerous countries including Turkey, the Philippines and Nepal.

Numerous other socialist movements have emerged from or coexisted with the Soviet pattern. The parties comprising the Socialist International, established in 1951, descended from the gradualist and reformist factions of the early 20th century. Social democratic parties formed governments in France, Germany, Sweden and Britain, implementing policies favouring strong state intervention, public control of major resources, nationalized medicine and other forms of welfare provision and strong protections for collective bargaining and secure employment. By the end of the 20th century, these reformist programmes encountered difficulties in slow economic growth, an ageing population, high rates of unemployment, fiscal problems and resistance to further reform. Nonetheless, their earlier success indicates the potential appeal of reformist socialism in countries with strong, stable democratic institutions. Revolutionary socialism has enjoyed greater appeal in struggles for national liberation in Asia, Africa and Latin America. Socialist or Communist parties have led anti-imperialist movements throughout the colonized world, although they have not always participated successfully in establishing postcolonial states, and postcolonial nations frequently became Cold War battlegrounds.

By the 1980s, roughly 35 per cent of the world's population lived in socialist societies of one form or another. The crisis of the world socialist economy in the 1980s led to experiments with 'market socialism' in Eastern Europe and in China, leading to the wholesale restoration of capitalism by the 21st century. In the Soviet Union, political reform led to the collapse of the first socialist society and the breakup of the Soviet Union in 1991. Subsequent experiments in economic reform through 'shock therapy' produced disaster and economic crisis. The legacies of these early socialist experiments survive, however, and the world economy of the 21st century is comprised mainly of 'mixed economies' that combine free-market capitalism, foreign investment and private enterprise with public enterprise, social welfare, state-directed investment and socialist restrictions on the disposition of private assets.

As an alternative modernity and revolutionary worldview, socialism has had to reconstruct itself again in recent years. Reactions against the dominant neoliberal ideology have produced new 'sprouts of socialism' in the form of groups espousing anarchism, environmentalism, social liberties, labour rights and immigrants' rights, as well as opposition to the domination of the world economy by transnational corporations. Popular movements against war, environmental degradation and economic inequality have renewed interest in socialist ideas and prompted their adaptation to 21st-century concerns. The Social Forum, which has been held each year since 2001 and has given rise to numerous regional forums, provides a transnational focus for many of these concerns. In time, it may well be the case that the globalization of capital will finally produce its own nemesis in the form of a truly international proletariat and transnational socialist movement. It is likely, however, that any future movement will be just as prone to factionalism as the socialist movements of the past.

Robert Cliver

Bibliography

Kolakowski L. 2005. *Main currents of Marxism*, new edition, 3 vols. (Falla P. S. trans.) New York: W. W. Norton.

Lichtheim G. 1975. *A short history of socialism*. London: Fontana/Collins.

Sassoon D. 1996. *One hundred years of socialism: the West European Left in the twentieth century*. New York: New Press.

Related essays

1848; China; Comintern and Cominform; *Communist Manifesto*; consumer cooperation; development and growth; developmental assistance; empires and imperialism; Esperanto; exile; fascism and anti-fascism; higher education; industrialization; internationalisms; liberalism; literature; Little Red Book; Maoism; modernization theory; new man; organization models; public policy; Russian Revolution; surrealism; *The Wretched of the Earth*; underdevelopment; welfare state

Spatial regimes

The 'time-space compression' of the modern age signals the remaking of the earth's surface (and its vertical extension into outer space) into human-made spaces (Harvey 1989, 260). It is connected to the regional and transregional growth of transportation and communication networks such as railways and cables as well as electronic communication. The radical transformation of space is commonly associated with globalization, the ever widening, deepening and speeding up of interconnections among states, peoples, and places. This highly productive, and profoundly destructive, reassembly of natural habitat into spatial regimes – sets of rules, formal or informal, that regulate social practices – shapes the layout of the globe. Spatial regimes are finite and bounded, although they have a way of reaching, overreaching, to cover the entire world (as in empire). They articulate and imagine, 'represent', social relations in space and generate translocal commonalities (as in class or race). Spatial regimes also can be encased in representational spaces (as in World Trade Center or Makkah). Spatial regimes, in short, generate human space; they mediate and present social relations; and they represent or embody them in symbolic precincts.

'Human geography' made the expansive cultivation of space the very foundation of civilization. Cultivation, culture, and physical geography formed an inseparable bond in creating civilizations that radiated outward by virtue of the transfer and adaptation of superior technique as much as by brute force. However, 'civilized mankind', in the modern age, disentangles itself from earthspace to create a second nature in a 'revolution of space' or *Raumrevolution*, as suggested by Carl Ritter (1852), in which distant places are drawn into common spaces, while nearby locations disappear beyond the horizon. A century later, this same phenomenon was captured in the notion of the 'social production of space' by Henri Lefèbvre (1991) with its focus on economic activities that, in situating capitalism, 'energize' human-made spaces. We can think of them as transnational 'forcefields' as Charles Maier (2006) did, or as 'networks', in the words of Manuel Castells (2000). In any case, space is neither fixed nor natural, but quite literally produced and its changing makeup affects human experience and imagination.

Because space is 'made', it takes actors and actions and venues to proceed. Therefore it is useful to think of spatial regimes not simply as product, as a system of rules and regulations – institutions – and their representations, as international relations theory does. Rather, we may see them in terms of actors, whether it is colonialists, architects, the varied group of spatial planners (as in urban or infrastructural developments), or material and spiritual interlocutors such as merchants, journalists, and missionaries. We may explore the 'portals' through which they venture, and the common languages, norms and values, as well as outlooks they generate in order for each discrete 'space' to cohere around a common purpose, activity, or world picture. Last but not least, we can approach spatial regimes in terms of their separateness or incorporation, or of rejection and toleration. Spatial regimes may appear as immutable and transhistorical objects, but in fact they are cultivations that require permanent labour – the work of making connections – in order to flourish.

If this latter concept of space appears so novel, it is because the ideas both of an interactive anthropological history of humankind and of an interwoven world of hospitality, or exchange, were trumped for nearly a century by imperialist varieties of 'political geography' or 'geopolitics' that exude, as documented by Gearóid Ó Tuathail (1996), continuing fascination. Geopolitics explores the influence of geography on power. It came to focus single-mindedly on the presumed spatial needs of states, which the founding generation (Sir Halford J. Mackinder, Rudolf Kjéllen, Friedrich Ratzel) endowed with racial qualities. In order for states to survive, they had to acquire living space for self-sufficiency. Enclosure and projection of force are key to geopolitical spatial regimes. The persistence of the idea and of the quest for a world of (would-be) autonomous political spaces is all the more striking, because the main efforts to this end – Germany and Japan in their pursuit of conquest and Russia and China in their pursuit of industrial self-transformation – proved to be disastrous.

While unhelpful as an analytic tool, the rise and fall and the shifting focus of the geopolitical imaginary provide an indication of the time and space of what Carl Ritter identified as a spatial revolution in the middle of the 19th century. If the cultivation of space and its transformation into place is as common a human activity as the expansion of formal or informal control over space, the past two hundred years have seen not simply an intensification of both these processes on an unprecedented scale. Rather, the peculiarity of this modern age consists in the simultaneity and the mutual reinforcement of otherwise quite separate and separable processes – the tight assemblage of territory, authority, and rights in the homogeneous space of the nation on the one hand and the rapacious disassemblage of people, things, and ideas across spaces in circulatory regimes. The modern age, then, is an age in which the capability of making borders that incorporate or separate, with all its attending violence, is of the essence.

Contrary to geopolitics, there has always been and continues to be a multiplicity of competing and overlapping human-made spaces. No single regime, like a universal empire, has ever dominated the earth. Nor has the very multiplicity of human spaces been homogenized and synthesized into global 'empire'. What we can observe is a revolution of space – the expansion, intensification, and acceleration of interaction and the formal or informal regulation of social practices across vast distances. Some of these regimes girdle the globe (currency markets). Most of them stitch together partial spaces of global interaction (commodity chains). Many work by virtue of the transplantation of ideas and practices (such as 'property' or 'territoriality') that adhere to like principles, but prove to be diverse in their adaptation. They come about in transfers, whose changing protocols deserve attention. The multiplicity of actual spaces is usefully grouped into three distinct classes: (1) spaces of settlement; (2) spaces of unsettlement, and (3) spaces of transfer.

'Territory is the premise of state sovereignty'. Territoriality, the principle of organizing 'space with a border that allows effective control of public and political life' (Maier 2006, 34), has emerged as the single most powerful mode of producing space in the modern world. It is so successful that it has swept across the world and has produced like spatial regimes, the territorial nation, everywhere – to the degree that even failing states adhere to the, albeit empty, principle. Territoriality is a historical configuration that links constituted authority, monopolized violence, and the enforceable writ of law within an enclosed, mostly contiguous, territory. As such it is distinct from older empires, worldwide, with their patchwork of semi-sovereign political, religious, ethnic, and social entities and their porous boundaries. It is also distinct from mere territories, entities that are unable to constitute and protect an interior space of power and law. Even

when the principle of territoriality became enshrined as international law in the United Nations Charter, there was less de facto territoriality than there were de jure territorial nations. Prevailing scholarly genealogies of modern territoriality are Western, although their lineages are diverse. This is particularly the case for earlier iterations of the territorial model with its key emphasis on external boundaries, on the mastery of the interior space, and on the representation of the interior and exterior worlds through maps of the realm – the 'production of territory'. Non-Western competitors considered as a unique and fearful advantage of the Western model the ability to mobilize a territory as a whole – its natural resources, its people, its knowledge – and give this mobilization purpose and destiny, a distinct acquisitive and aggressive edge. What they admired is the shift from the 'production of territory' to the formation of 'territories of production' and, for that matter, of destruction.

Much as states aimed at enclosure, the most advantageous mobilizations of energies reached beyond the nation state. They depended on tapping and harnessing people, goods and money, as well as ideas and technologies and, in turn, produced unsettlement through the displacement of people or export of goods. Territoriality and the transterritorial mobility of people, things, and ideas are inseparable. Of course, people, things, and ideas have always moved. We might see in their mobility the very principle of human development. But mobility – the freedom to move and the violence of removal – defines the modern spatial revolution. People have overcome territorial barriers, population-politics, and settlement schemes set in their way, thus making human migration the pre-eminent space of global mobility: human settlement has extended ever deeper into a previously non-human, natural habitat. The mixing of populations – with the distinct pattern of Western outward migration being overtaken by a shift in demography and a reverse flow of people – suggests the intensity of the process. But most striking of all is the velocity of this development, which has made the city – as opposed to the countryside – the predominant space of human habitation. And while much of this development is local, it has happened on a planetary scale.

Trade and investment are the other prime motor of translocal mobility. Economists consider it a quasi-natural law that efficient economies know no boundaries, thrive on division of labour, and will expand to the ends of the world – and despite an all-too-human revulsion against marketization and globalization, the entire world has become an interconnected territory of production with three main consequences. First, the regional division of labour with its divergence of industry and agriculture – an industrial North vs an agricultural South – has given way to an uneven, but dispersed regime of mixed, global production that is accompanied by deepening social inequality. Second, if trade between nations mobilized productive energies within nations, transnational production networks have increasingly come to cut across territories. Third, the most liquid and mobile commodity, capital, has ascertained its leading role in structuring this transnational space of production. The upshot of this activity consists in the territories of production covering the globe and the shifting balance of power, favouring private finance over states, controlling the flow of capital and labour.

Other spatial regimes, primarily knowledge regimes, could be added. Suffice it here to highlight an uncanny example of the inadvertent social nature of global space. While scientific and technological knowledge claim universal validity, their application and their appropriation fall into distinct spatial regimes. The latter are no longer regionally concentrated, as if a preserve of one region or civilization. They are rather strung together across territories in tenuous networks of knowledge that not everyone shares. That is, science and technology function the same way everywhere, but neither are they equally present (as in advanced diagnostic machinery in hospitals) nor are they incorporated into regimes of social knowledge with the same effect (as in the use of this machinery to determine gender in utero). The second nature of human-made spatial regimes proves to be as highly variegated as physical space.

The only thing more liquid and more mobile than capital is knowledge and ideas. Yet, there is good reason to be cautious about pronouncements concerning the inexorable rise of a global consciousness, a homogeneous space of global imagination. To be sure, there are representations of the whole Earth, by way of satellite surveillance, that have been taken as a representational space of a globally connected world. Moreover, a functional infrastructure of transportation and communication pulls together all parts of the Earth. They are handled according to the same rules everywhere. There is, in short, globally interchangeable knowledge. However, this globality comes in the form of elaborate protocols of transfer and translation. It is the give-and-take of knowledge that 'cultivates' human-made spaces by setting boundaries of belonging. It generates the 'mental maps' (Gould and White 1986) which people use to orient themselves in an interconnected world and informs the representational spaces that set belonging in space. The paucity and embattled nature of global precincts (United Nations) and systems (capital markets) is as noteworthy as the plenitude of local things (sushi, the hamburger), representations (St Peter's, Ayodyha), or representational spaces (Chicago Futures Market) with a global reach.

Remarkable as the velocity of ideas, knowledge and images is, they settle down, albeit at different speeds, in connectives tissue across space. Saskia Sassen is most prominent in arguing that the sheer density of this tissue has raised anew 'the question of territory as a parameter for authority and rights' (Sassen 2006, 416). While it has proven impossible to isolate knowledge, ideas, and beliefs in genealogical streams that buttress territoriality, they circulate unevenly and their impact varies from one network of knowledge to another, each one of which potentially stretches the circumference of the Earth and its human population. They gain new potency in digital assemblages. Instead of a global consciousness we find neural networks of information, knowledge, images, and beliefs that make up a sense of place that is, at one and the same time, local and global, cosmopolitan and fiercely defensive of its own position in the world. The intensity of conflicts over these mental maps, as expressed in the revival of religious belief, as well as the effort to anchor them in sacred texts and to ascertain their purity, suggests that connectivity, generating mental or spiritual spaces of interaction, has become a new source of conflict every bit as creative and every bit as destructive as territorial conflicts have been in the past.

Michael Geyer

Bibliography

Castells M. 2000. *The rise of the network society.* Oxford and Malden: Blackwell.

Gould P. R. and White R. 1986. *Mental maps.* Hemel Hempstead and Boston: Allen & Unwin.

Harvey D. 1989. *The condition of postmodernity: an enquiry into the origins of cultural change.* Oxford: Basil Blackwell.

Lefèbvre H. (1991). *The production of space,* Nicholson-Smith D. (trans). Oxford and Malden: Basil Blackwell.

Maier C. S. 'Transformations of territoriality, 1600–2000', in Budde G., Conrad S. and Janz O. (eds) 2006. *Transnationale Geschichte: Themen, Tendenzen und Theorien,* Göttingen: Vandenhoeck & Ruprecht, 32–55.

Ó Tuathail G. (1996). *Critical geopolitics: the politics of writing global space.* Minneapolis: University of Minnesota Press.

Ritter C. 1852. *Einleitung zur Allgemeinen vergleichenden Geographie und Abhandlingen zur Begründung einer mehr wissenschaftlichen Behandlung der Erdkunde.* Berlin: G. Reimer.

Sassen S. 2006. *Territory, authority, rights: from medieval to global assemblages.* Princeton, Princeton University Press.

Related essays
agriculture; body shopping; borders and borderlands; Christmas and Halloween; civilizations; commodity trading; cultural capitals; empire and migration; empires and imperialism; financial centres; financial markets; food; globalization; human mobility; humanities; industrialization; information economy; information technology (IT) offshoring; intergovernmental organizations; international migration regimes; Internet; investment; life and natural sciences; literary capitals; literature; mapping; nation and state; new man; *non-lieux*; outer space; public policy; regions; social sciences; telephone and telegraphy; trade; transnational; urbanization; world orders

Sport

Few phenomena are as effective as sports in advancing globalization and transnational exchanges. Through sports, cross-border flows of ideas, cultures, personal and national aspirations, and ways of life often move successfully if not always peacefully. Sport plays an enormously important role in linking nations of different geographies, religions, power, and wealth that accept many of the same rules and standards. When the International Federation of the Football Association's (FIFA) 2006 World Cup finals kicked off in Germany, FIFA had 207 members while the membership of the United Nations was 191. The International Olympic Committee (IOC) also claims to be one of the world's largest organizations with its 203 national Olympic committees as members in 2006. Sport can have strong national characteristics – since how a country plays and enjoys sports reflects its national identity – without losing its cross-border dimensions. These are embedded in the nature of the games and in the structures of sports organizations.

Origins, organizations, and events
Although basketball was first created in the United States in the 1890s, its inventor was a Canadian by origin and the game quickly spread to the whole world. Today the National Basketball Association (NBA) consists of teams in the United States and in Canada, while NBA games are watched and enjoyed all over the world; more and more NBA players come from outside the United States. In its 2005–06 season, about 20 per cent of the NBA players were from Asia, Europe, Latin America and Africa. Since basketball games have become world games, long-term American domination of the basketball courts is being challenged. Although the brilliant performances at the Olympic Games of the so-called American 'Dream Team' in the 1990s brought both the beauty of the games and sparks of American culture to the world, the American men could only muster a bronze medal in the 2004 Olympic Games. Nevertheless, the NBA has benefited enormously from the sport's internationalization. NBA commissioner David Stern has been consciously and actively building the NBA into a global brand. To convey its international appeal and ambition, the official NBA website currently has several language versions, including a Chinese one. Moreover, a significant portion of the NBA's income comes from sales of its merchandise internationally. For the NBA officials, the world doesn't have to take over the NBA for the NBA to take over the world.

Football (soccer) too became so popular worldwide that it generated its own organizations. FIFA, the football world governing organization, promotes both football and global capitalism through its extensive partnerships with brands. Modern football originated in Britain in the 19th century. It soon became a world sport after FIFA was founded in 1904 and introduced the FIFA World Cup in 1930. Since then, almost every four years – with the exception the Second World War and its immediate aftermath – when the football World Cup finals take place, the games become the world festival and have served as a gathering ground for competitions, exchanges of different cultures, social norms and politics where national dreams can come true or crash. Called 'the beautiful game' by billions of adoring football fans throughout the world, it has become a world language that people from every corner of the world can enjoy, understand, and get excited about. The beauty and excitement of football games are also defined by their national flavour. National characteristics translate into playing styles in sports. World football fans are fascinated by the different styles of football played by different countries that reflect their individual national characteristics, such as the extremely beautiful and joyful Latin style represented by Brazil which pays attention both to style as well as substance. England's focus on winning and European teams' emphasis on both offence and defence are also distinctive.

The popularity of the World Cups can be seen from their audiences. The final match of the 1986 football World Cup drew a worldwide audience of 652 million, while the World Cup finals between Germany and Brazil in Japan in 2002 were seen by more than a billion viewers. It is estimated that the 2006 World Cup finals were viewed by 3 billion people worldwide. More interestingly, unlike the Olympics where the order of winning teams usually mirrors the real-world order of national power, the World Cup, or 'world of wonder' as Henry Kissinger described it in 2006, follows its own order in which Brazil is a dominant power but small and poor countries from Latin America and Africa can hope to become rising powers. In the wonderful world of football, the most powerful and richest countries cannot easily claim winning spots while the teams from small countries sometimes can defeat those from powerful countries in surprising ways.

Like many sports, football has now been transformed by waves of cross-border movements of both human and financial capital. A typical European football club might be coached by a Brazilian, owned by a Russian,

managed by a Swede, and have players from many different countries. Due to these developments, the differences between three major styles of play – such as Latin, English, and European – are disappearing.

Only the Olympic Games can match the popularity and influence of the football World Cups. The modern Olympic movement, like many other international sports federations, emerged in the late 19th century. Many countries played roles in reviving the modern Olympics, although a Frenchman, Pierre de Coubertin, led the campaign for the revival. Coubertin feared France had lost the Franco-Prussian War because of the physical degeneracy of the young men in the French army while the superior physical training of German youth put them at a great military advantage. Of course, the Olympic movement would have died a long time ago if the founders had focused only on nationalism. The mixing of nationalism and universalism in the modern Olympics has attracted both individuals and nation states, and eventually made it a great social force and one of the most attractive festivals in the world. The opening ceremony of the 1984 Olympic Summer Games was viewed by an estimated 522 million persons. For the 2004 Athens summer Olympic Games, a record 202 national Olympic committees took part, comprising a total of 10,500 competitors and 5,500 team officials. By the time of the closing ceremony, organizers had sold 3,589,000 tickets, although the host country has a population of only 10 million people. During the Athens Olympic Games, there were 21,500 accredited members of the media, 16,000 of whom were with broadcasting companies. About 3.9 billion people had access to programmes featuring the Athens Games, compared to 3.6 billion in Sydney in 2000. Some 35,000 hours were dedicated to the coverage in 2004, compared to 20,000 for Barcelona in 1992, 25,000 for Atlanta in 1996 and 29,600 for Sydney. Viewing performances also improved, and more people were watching the Athens Games on TV. For instance, in Spain, each individual, on average, watched more than 8 hours of the Games; in the UK, each viewer watched more than 13 hours of coverage with several peak audiences of over 10 million. In the US, NBC's coverage of the Games ranked as the top programme every night of the week during the Games. The Chinese were able to watch more than

53 hours of prime-time coverage, attracting an average audience of 85 million viewers.

Other sports which have traditionally had less cross-border appeal and little global presence and influence have tried to jump on the bandwagon. For instance, baseball, which is called America's national pastime, has only a limited presence beyond the border of the United States, in parts of Asia and Latin America, despite the fact that many major-league players have Latino backgrounds. Nevertheless, Americans have called the games among their own teams (including a few in Canada) 'The World Series'. In 2006 baseball authorities created a global tournament called the World Baseball Classic to help expand its attraction. Interestingly enough, in the 2006 baseball classic, the Americans were knocked out in the second round.

Of course, this cross-border appeal has its limitations. A clear example is the American attitude toward soccer. For billions of people in Europe, Latin America, Africa, and Asia, soccer is not only a national obsession, but even a matter of life and death, while its beauty and excitement have been enjoyed by only a very limited number of Americans. Games like cricket, which has been popular in certain countries, might never have a chance to become a world sport while Judo, Taiji and other martial arts from Asia have recently travelled to an enthusiastic reception in other parts of the world.

Sports, nations and nationalism

A nation's involvement in sports requires membership in networks of organizations that are transnational in scope, and yet sports create festivals that function as vehicles of national ambition and national identity. Sports provide a 'microcosm of society' and a reflection of its national culture, society, and even history. When athletes from around the world compete, they bring with them their ideas, ideals, and national inspirations. In other words, athletes are socialized to participate in transnational exchanges but in ways that call the attention of worldwide audiences to differences among nations as well as their shared interest in sports.

For instance, in Brazil, football gave a very diverse population a shared focus. Sports can be used as vehicles to achieve political legitimacy and international status. The gold medal count in the Olympics, the advancement in the football World Cup competition and especially the championship, are important precisely because that count and the victories involved have been displayed as a measure of a country's political legitimacy, of modernization, or world status. The motivation to win and do well in the world sports arenas and turn the victories to political advantage occurs among both developing and developed countries.

Sport can become a reaffirmation of a country and its people and it can provide a sense of national identity in major games such as the football World Cup or the Olympics. Even when a country's politics and economy are in decline or when its people experience regional segregation or rivalry, sports are expected to bring unity, identity, and hope for the future. As a matter of fact, modern sports have played significant roles in constructing identities and ideologies since their gradual emergence in the mid 19th century. In the 20th century, sports have become quite influential in a country's national identity and political system. For instance, when the Japanese authorities in 1932 decided to bid for the 1940 Olympic Games, Tokyo had to polish its international image (after occupying China's northeast). The Japanese also used the 1964 Tokyo Olympic Games as a coming-out party for a new Japan after its defeat in the Second World War.

Germans also used sports to cultivate new national identities. In 1936, Nazi Germany used the 1936 Olympic Games in Berlin to score political gains and showcase its growing power. Germany's first football World Cup victory in Switzerland in 1954 announced the beaten country's re-emergence onto the world stage. Its victory in the football World Cup at home in 1974 over the Netherlands demonstrated Germany's rising self-confidence. Another German World Cup championship (in Italy in 1990), this time against Argentina, expressed the euphoria of national reunification. Last but not least, both Spanish and Argentinian authoritarian regimes in the 1930s and 1978 respectively manipulated their countries' World Cup victories for political purposes.

Sports can even be used to promote political changes or serve as a prelude to war. The 1990 football games led to a clash between football fans of Belgrade's Red Star and Zagreb's Dynamo and eventually to the political revolution which toppled the Slobodan Milošević regime in Yugoslavia. Rioting during an El Salvador–Honduras football game in 1969 led to their 100-hour 'football war' two weeks later, with 2,000 casualties. Sport also played an important role in the Paraguayan revolution which destroyed the Alfredo Stroesssner dictatorship. When Greece defeated Portugal in the final of the European championships in July 2004, the Greeks were overjoyed. The football game seemed to unite Greeks all over the world, something politics had been unable to do. In 2006 Ivory Coast's qualification for World Cup brought together conflicting factions, and thus helped to end three years of civil war.

Because of the importance of sports competition in national politics, legitimacy, and national identity, many governments and national states have helped finance the developments of sports directly or indirectly. The fascist and Communist countries considered sports a crucial part of their national politics and financed them with state funds. In the democratic countries, sports are considered private enterprises but many governments have set up funds to promote sports activities and improve their athletes' competition skills.

Sports can start wars, make peace and shift national moods. They also bring some fun to soldiers at war. During the First World War when the British and Germans geared up to kill each other in the deadly battlefield game, the opponents could not resist the attraction of sports. They decided to have a Christmas truce in 1914 and held a 'Fritz–Tommy' match across the trenches. Germany won the game 3-2.

Sports have touched even otherwise closed societies such as Iran. In 1987 the country's spiritual and political dictator Ayatollah Ruhollah Khomeini issued a decree that women could watch football on television indoors but not watch or celebrate outside. However, when Iran's national team won the 1997 World Cup qualifying game against Australia, a sort of football revolution started when Iranian women demanded the equal right to celebrate the victory in Azadi stadium in the capital. Under strong pressure from the women, the police eventually had to monitor the women's entry into the stadium. Iran's football riots of October 2001, following its 3-1 defeat by Bahrain in the World Cup qualifying match, represented the largest mass disturbance in the country since 1979. In the 2006 World Cup finals, after the Iranian team was eliminated in the first round, both the coach and the head of the football federation were fired summarily by the Iranian government and the government even issued an apology to all Iranians for the embarrassment caused by the team. If sports events can trigger such strong actions from both government and population in a country like Iran, it might be possible for the football revolution to play larger roles elsewhere in the Middle East and other regions.

Sports and international diplomacy

Through sports, many countries articulate their national interests and ideologies, enhance cultural exchange and understanding, or project a new national image. A classic example of the role of sports in diplomacy is China's use of ping-pong diplomacy to improve its relations with the United States in 1971. Both the United States and China recognized that it was in their respective national interests to improve bilateral relations. However, due to over two decades of hostilities and mistrust, neither government knew how to offer the olive branch effectively to the other. Beijing's decision to invite the American table-tennis team to visit China in 1971 thus achieved wonders since the move helped both countries to break the diplomatic ice effectively and immediately.

In 1984 China and South Korea also played so-called 'tennis diplomacy' to symbolize a rapprochement between the two countries. This tennis match marked the first sports contact on Chinese territory between the two countries. South Korea and China had competed at international sports meetings before but had never sent their athletes to each other's territory.

During the Cold War era, small and big powers on both sides of the Iron Curtain used sports for political purposes. In the 1956 Melbourne Olympic Games, a water-polo match between Russians and Hungarians turned into a different version of the Hungarian revolution. The Hungarian team won in a brutal contest for the gold that left the pool streaked with blood.

Individuals and national governments also use sporting events to convey their political messages. Two African American Olympians gave black-power salutes by clenching their fists on the victory stand when the American national anthem was played in the 1968 Mexico Olympic Games, to symbolize black anger. At the 1972 Munich Olympic Games, 11 Israeli athletes were killed due to Palestinian terrorist actions during the Games to attract worldwide attention to their problems with Israel. From the 1960s until the early 1990s South Africa was kept out of many international sports because of its apartheid policy. In the 11th Asian Games in Beijing in 1990, the Asian countries expelled Iraq due to its invasion of Kuwait.

The United States and the Soviet Union also took turns boycotting each other's Games in Moscow (1980) and Los Angeles (1984), respectively. The American government obviously wanted to use the 1980 Games to force Moscow to withdraw its troops from Afghanistan. Moscow eventually retaliated against that American action by boycotting the 1984 Games. Because national performance is perceived to be closely correlated with global power, the results of games can be manipulated for political purposes. During the Cold War, the medal competitions in the Olympic Games between the two superpowers reflected their political confrontation. In the 2008 Beijing Olympic Games, China, with its fast-rising economic power, may try to compete with the United States for the top medal spot.

Even the United Nations uses sports to advance is agenda. In 2000, due to the disintegration of the Federal Republic of Yugoslavia and the armed conflicts that ensued, the UN Security Council included 'sport' for the first time among its sanctions. Although sports organizations, such as the IOC and the FIFA, protest political intervention in sports, they also pursue political and diplomatic purposes as well. The IOC cooperated with the UN and allowed athletes from Yugoslavia to participate in the Olympic Games on an individual basis in the 1990s and into the 21st century. The joint declaration of UN secretary-general Kofi Annan and FIFA president Joseph Blatter on 6 June 2006, prior to the opening of the World Cup finals, is also a good example of using sports for international peace and transnational harmony. In their joint message to the world, they welcomed the opening of the 2006 FIFA World Cup finals and acknowledged that football was a global language which could bridge social, cultural, and religious divides. The message indicated that the United Nations was using football as a tool mainly because it could reach more people and more communities and more effectively help build a better world in the 21st century. The United Nations also turned to football because it could help heal the emotional wounds of war among young people in refugee camps and in countries recovering from armed conflict. In 2005 at the UN world summit, all the world's governments declared that 'sports can foster peace and development, and can contribute to an atmosphere of tolerance and understanding'.

The IOC even attempted to revive the ancient Olympic truce during the Cold War era. The institution of a 'truce' was established in Ancient Greece in the 9th century BC by the signature of a treaty between several Greek city states. The treaty stipulated that during the period of the truce, the athletes, artists and their families, as well as ordinary pilgrims, could travel in total safety to participate in or attend the Olympic Games and return afterwards to their respective cities or countries. As early as 1956, the IOC expressed its desire to revive this noble Ancient Greek tradition. Obviously the call fell on deaf ears during the Cold War period. Then in 1992 the IOC adopted another resolution supporting the Olympic truce. That document was signed by members of the IOC executive board and 184 national Olympic committees. Through the efforts of the IOC, the UN General Assembly unanimously adopted a resolution at its 54th session in New York on 24 November 1999, co-sponsored by a record number of 180 member states out of 188. The resolution 'urges member states to observe the Olympic Truce, individually and collectively, during the Games of the XXVII Olympiad in Sydney and beyond'. In 2000, the IOC tried again by calling on all states (their heads, governments and assemblies) and all international and national organizations to support the Olympic truce and resort to peaceful methods to solve national or translational disputes. Although both the IOC and the world paid only lip-service to the ideal of the Olympic truce, such lip-service indicates the importance of sports in imagining real world peace. Only the unique nature of sports made it possible for the world community to discuss and embrace the ideal of an Olympic truce.

Modern sports originated in 19th-century Europe after the industrial revolution transformed traditional societies. With the rise of imperialism and European empires, sports were brought to many parts of the world through colonists, missionaries and business people. In the early 20th century, in association with the founding of the modern Olympics and FIFA and the effective work of the YMCA and YWCA, modern sports enjoyed a fast rise globally. However, modern sports suffered a substantial decline during the periods of the two world wars, not only because of the cancellation of the games in wartime but also due to the hostile environment the wars and their aftermath created, which was contrary to the spirit of modern sports. The division of the world across ideological differences during the Cold War had also affected the healthy development of modern sports. In the post-Cold War era and when the world entered the 21st century and became further integrated through the Internet, transnational enterprises, global media, and frequent moves of ideas, goods and people across borders, sport seemed to enjoy its golden age.

It is important to keep in mind that although sports have had many positive consequences for nation states and the world community, there has been a dark side to transnational sports. Corruption is one of them. In the late 1990s bribery was so rampant that it almost destroyed the IOC and forced the slow-changing organization to undertake structure reforms. Corruption in sports has also involved worldwide gambling through the Internet and by telephone. Global sports allow corruption on a global scale. Another negative side of sports was athletes' use of drugs to enhance their performance. The use of steroids could be individual or collective (as in the case of the former East Germany). International terrorism has also become a worldwide concern during Olympic Games and the soccer World Cups. What happened at the 1972 Munich Olympic Games serves as a chilling reminder of the fatal attraction of sports to terrorists. Indeed, the startling success of sports commercialization today may in the long term undermine the beauty and joy of sports and their attraction and effectiveness as an agent of internationalization and transnationalization.

Xu Guoqi

Bibliography
Bairner A. 2001. *Sport, nationalism, and globalization: European and North American perspectives*. Albany: State University of New York Press.

Guttmann A. 2002. *The Olympics: a history of the modern Games*. Urbana: University of Illinois Press.
Foer F. 2004. *How football explains the world: an unlikely theory of globalization*. New York: HarperCollins.
Houlihan B. 1994. *Sport and international politics*. New York: Harvester Wheatsheaf.
Lyberg W. 1996. *Fabulous 100 years of the IOC: facts, figures and much, much more*, Lausanne: International Olympic Committee.
Riordan J. and Kruger A. 1999. *The International politics of sport in the twentieth century*. London: E & FN Spon.
Tomlinson A. and Young C. 2006. *National identity and global sports events: culture, politics, and spectacle in the Olympics and the football World Cup*. Albany: State University of New York Press.
Young D. C. 1996. *The modern Olympics: a struggle for revival*. Baltimore: Johns Hopkins University Press.

Related essays
advertising; Asia; bodybuilding; broadcasting; corporations; cricket; National Basketball Association (NBA); Olympic Games; sports gear and apparel; World Cup; world orders

National Basketball Association (NBA)

In 1949 the Basketball Association of America and the National Basketball League merged into one league, creating the National Basketball Association (NBA). Today, the NBA is one of the world's dominating sports leagues with its games being broadcast internationally and its players being known globally.

Basketball always has been a global sport as missionaries spread it around the globe shortly after its invention by Canadian James Naismith in the late 19th century. Developments in communication technology combined with aggressive market strategies turned the NBA into a powerful symbol of the globalization of sports and its marketing opportunities. By the 1980s, the NBA – symbolized by Michael Jordan and Nike – became a vehicle of US 'soft' power and American cultural imperialism. The dark side, which remains largely unacknowledged by Jordan, Nike, and others, the fact that much of the NBA's global success is based on extensive exploitation, especially in the form of sweatshops and child labour, in those parts of the world the league also targets aggressively with its marketing.

In recent years, the NBA has more and more developed truly into a global league as an increasing number of players from around the world are drafted by its teams. Giant centre Yao Ming has opened the Chinese market for League caps, jerseys and other byproducts, while European players have received Most Valuable Player awards in recent years (the German Dirk Nowitzki and the French Tony Parker). With the arrival of those players new questions about race, ethnicity, and the culture of the League arise.

Gabriele Gottlieb

Bibliography

Veseth M. 2005. *Globaloney: unraveling the myths of globalization*. Lanham: Rowman & Littlefield.

Related essays

America; childhood; missionaries; sport; sports gear and apparel

Sports gear and apparel

The worldwide production and consumption of sports gear is closely linked to the economic, social and cultural conditions of the late 19th and early 20th centuries that facilitated the worldwide growth of organized athletics. In the 21st century, sport is arguably the world's most popular and universal form of entertainment. The manufacturing and consumption of athletic gear depends on a global body of consumers and producers and has developed transnationally over the past half century.

The international travels of 19th-century colonizers, missionaries, organizations, and individuals facilitated the widespread diffusion and adoption of sport and its attendant gear. After affluent Cubans studying in the US during the 1860s brought baseball and its equipment back to Cuba, the game's popularity in the Caribbean skyrocketed. Later, Cuban exiles fleeing their homeland after failed attempts at independence during the late 19th century introduced baseball bats and balls to the Dominican Republic. Today baseball's widespread popularity in countries as diverse as Mexico and Japan facilitates international exchanges of baseball equipment, knowledge and players.

Countries with imperial ambitions utilized sport and sports gear as religious and moral instruments of colonial power. Over time, as sports expanded beyond their original geographic locations, receiving countries selectively accepted, modified, and rejected sport and its products. The social character of sport influenced the cross-border diffusion and popularization of sports gears. For example, the British game of football remained less class-bound than cricket and therefore more easily exported to all social classes in parts of the world such as Africa, Latin America, and Asia. By contrast, cricket, with its array of exclusive regulations on dress and behaviour, experienced less widespread adoption in other countries' sporting landscape. Scholars continue to debate sport and sports gear's significance as forms of cultural imperialism, and whether recreational and sport diversity has been threatened by the export and popularization of Western sports.

The earliest entrepreneurial efforts to create and manufacture sports gear, especially footwear, reveal worldwide connections between people, ideas and sporting materials. In the late 19th century, rubber companies such as US Rubber Co. and Britain's New Liverpool Rubber Co. utilized rubber from Brazil and later Indonesia to manufacture soles for shoes, which, after being sewn to canvas tops, became some of the first athletic shoes. Bata Shoes, founded in Czechoslovakia in 1894 but later headquartered in Canada, became the world's largest shoe exporter by the 1930s, with factories all over the world. The sports manufacturing firm Adidas dominated the soccer scene after German Adolph Dassler began making shoes with three stripes out of US military scrap material from World War 2. In the early 1960s, Onitsuka Kihachirō founded the company that would become ASICS in Japan after he began successfully manufacturing and selling basketball shoes for a worldwide market.

Major international sporting events also provided key mediums through which sporting apparel and gear have been introduced to global audiences. Since the founding of the modern Olympic Games in 1896 and the FIFA World Cup in 1930, athletes wearing and using the latest gear have run to victory while acting as human billboards for sporting goods companies who manufacture the equipment. As early as the 1900 Olympic Games in Paris, US sporting-goods magnate Albert G. Spalding used his position as director of sports for the American team to showcase his athletic goods and to introduce baseball to foreign audiences.

After World War 2, the professionalization of sport, along with the general public's growing participation in athletics and exercise, transformed what had been mainly a domestic phenomenon into an international sporting marketplace characterized by high-tech designs and low-cost labour. Starting in the late 1980s, the US-based sports manufacturing firm Nike, for example, designed their Air Max Penny in the US with the help of technicians in South Korea and Taiwan. The shoe was manufactured in South Korea, Indonesia and Japan, with some 52 components arriving from five countries. The finished product, which by the end of the assembly process passed through 120 pairs of hands, sold in markets all over the world. The remarkable growth of transnational sporting goods corporations in the late 20th century have contributed dramatically to the flow of sporting products across national boundaries. Reacting to the saturated sporting-goods marketplace, companies since the 1950s have sought to enhance brand recognition through the symbolic use of images, ideas, names, and experiences. Design, advertising, and public relations have become companies' most important marketing strategy for selling sports gear and apparel.

A key branding strategy is the sponsorship of individual athletes, teams, clubs, events, and organizations to increase their brand image and to engage local and national sensibilities. The sponsoring of athletic icons such as basketball legend Michael Jordan, who signed with Nike in 1984, and Adidas' soccer superstar David Beckham, is intended to transcend national, racial, and gender lines and cultivate an international appeal. Sporting products and celebrities bear the name and logo of their manufacturers, and logos and TV advertisements are carefully crafted to appeal to global audiences.

The communications revolution starting in the 1970s has been integral to the diffusion of sports gear and the creation of an international sports culture. Although, starting in the late 19th century, sporting-goods companies advertised their wares in trade publications, rule books, and sporting journals, more recently new media such as cable TV and the Internet broadcast commercials and athletic contests that feature sporting products and their manufacturers. Today, sporting-goods companies compete with other multinational corporations to sponsor mega-sporting events; official sponsorship gives these companies the rights to employ globally recognized symbols such as the Olympic rings in their television and online advertisements.

The movement of sports gear and apparel across international boundaries has ignited cultural debates that highlight class, religion, race and gender concerns. In hopes of higher returns, sporting-goods companies in the 1970s began closing their domestic factories and relocating production overseas to countries with authoritarian governments, relaxed environmental laws, non-unionized workforces, and favourable tax abatements. In the 1990s a number of labourers, human rights organizations, and student groups began publicly protesting the exploitative conditions under which poor workers – the majority of whom were young women and children in South Korea, Taiwan, China and Vietnam – manufactured shoes, apparel, and other sporting equipment. These efforts have since encouraged some companies and governments to secure better working conditions, although sweatshop allegations continue to preoccupy transnational giants such as Nike, Reebok, Adidas, and Wilson.

The spread and popularity of branded sports gear has had unintended societal consequences as various groups appropriate sporting apparel as status symbols and as forms of cultural expression, sometimes against the desires of manufacturers. In the 1990s, critics accused various sporting-goods companies of marketing expensive shoes to the poor after newspapers articles recounted stories of young, mostly African American men killing each other over shoes and other branded apparel. In the 1980s, the Italian sporting firm Fila became popular as a hip-hop, intercity urban brand, often associated with gangs, drugs, and crime. In 1997, Nike quickly cancelled the manufacturing and selling of a specific shoe model after Muslims angrily declared that the shoe's rear logo bore a resemblance to the Arabic spelling of Allah. Sporting gear, and the behaviours and attitudes it represents, is often rejected by groups who find such products offensive to their religious, social, and political traditions.

Historically, sports gear has also operated as a contentious symbol of gender distinction and as an agent of change. Nineeenth-century dress codes and conceptions of proper gender roles kept large numbers of women from participating in public sport until the 1920s. Although male-dominated sporting organizations barred women from participating in sports, women pushed against clothing and cultural boundaries to gain access to pools and playing fields. Women in sports such as swimming, tennis, cycling and basketball have historically met fierce opposition by sports journalists, sports governing bodies, physical educators and the public who believe that competitive sports and sporting attire are immodest, unladylike, and out of synch with conventional social roles that relegate women to the domestic realm. However, women's increased presence on college and professional teams, and in global sporting events such as the Olympics and the FIFA Women's World Cup have challenged the idea that sports and sports clothing are unalterable symbols of masculinity or femininity. Today, women's sporting apparel is a lucrative business that sporting-goods companies compete to capture. Women sports celebrities such as Russian tennis star Maria Sharapova and soccer luminary Mia Hamm have international appeal and lucrative contracts with sporting-goods firms.

As women's sports gain increasing popularity on the global scene, some groups of women have objected to the abbreviated sports apparel designed and sold by most international sporting-goods firms. For example, Western-style sports clothing presents a problem for Muslim women who want to both partake in sports and adhere to religious dictates that require women to cover their bodies. This absence of sports clothing for Muslim women has opened up a market for small entrepreneurial endeavours that sell apparel specifically designed for Muslim female athletes, including a 'Hijood', a sportier-looking and closer-fitting hijab, and a full-bodied, hooded swimsuit made of lightweight, elastic fabric. This emerging international market for more modest yet fashionable clothing is one example of the way sports clothing continues to be a key social factor shaping global sporting experiences.

Elizabeth Zanoni

Bibliography

LaFeber W. 2002. *Michael Jordan and the new global capitalism*. New York: W.W. Norton.

Van Bottenburg M. 2001. *Global games*, Jackson B. (trans.). Urbana: University of Illinois Press.

Vanderbilt T 1998. *The Sneaker Book: anatomy of an industry and icon*. New York: New Press.

Related essays

advertising; beauty; benefits and charity concerts; childhood; children's rights; class; corporations; cricket; dress; fashion; femininity; gender and sex; labour standards; marketing; National Basketball Association (NBA); Olympic Games; sport; textiles

State and nation *See* **Nation and state**

Statistics

'Statistics' generally refers to quantitative data or to techniques for manipulating such data. The term statistics (*Statistik*) arose during the 18th century, when German scholars such as Gottfried Achenwall and August Ludwig von Schloezer used it to describe the comparison of information, generally non-quantitative, collected about the various political entities of the day. Quantitative social data, however, have a much older lineage than the history of the word 'statistics' would suggest. The major early collections of social statistics, from the ancient world until the early 19th century, resulted from the efforts of states to better understand, rationalize, and control the resources within their own territory. In the years since 1850, governments have further increased the scale and scope of their efforts to amass statistics, but an equally important development has been the creation and use of statistics by bodies other than national governments, whether businesses, scholars, or inter- or non-governmental organizations.

Methodologies for manipulating numerical statistics arose from many sources. Government bureaucrats, gamblers, theologians, insurers, astronomers, social scientists, and public health reformers all helped develop statistical techniques. This wide variety of progenitors illustrates the utility of statistics in many sectors of modern society. Statistical innovations flowed back and forth across international boundaries. The mathematicians Pierre Simon de Laplace, from France, and Karl Friedrich Gauss, from Germany, employed many of the most important statistical techniques by the early 19th century. Nonetheless, the application of these techniques beyond the fields of mathematics and astronomy required an enormous conceptual leap that took decades. The Belgian mathematician Adolph Quetelet traveled to Paris in 1823 to study astronomy, became fascinated by the error curve used to explain divergent observations, and saw its applicability to other phenomena, such as the characteristics of human beings. Quetelet applied probabilistic techniques for analysing the behaviour of celestial bodies to people and found surprising regularities in human conduct, even in seemingly inexplicable behaviour such as crime or suicide. His findings led him to argue for the existence of an idealized 'average man' with behaviour predictable in the aggregate (although not on an individual level), thereby raising questions about the philosophical notion of 'free will'. But statistics could emphasize differences as well as commonalities among human beings. In England, Francis Galton rejected Quetelet's focus upon the mean and the idea, from astronomy, that divergence indicated error. Instead, Galton realized that the error curve could be used to analyse variation rather than render it invisible. Galton, a cousin of Charles Darwin, was particularly intrigued by the heritability of physical and intellectual characteristics and went on to found the study of eugenics, the effort to improve human beings by scientifically directed breeding. Galton's ideas spread throughout the world and were used to defend policies based on racial Darwinism. Critics of racial Darwinism also used statistics, most notably émigré anthropologist Franz Boas when studying head circumference.

As is often true in science, the development of statistical knowledge was both a national and a transnational phenomenon. Nongovernmental statistical societies sprouted during the 1830s and 1840s as statisticians corresponded with foreign peers or read their articles in journals. Statistical organizations arose in Saxony (1831), Manchester (1833), London (1834), Boston (1839), and Dublin (1847). Meanwhile, governments were setting up their own statistical offices, as occurred in France (1831), Belgium (1831), Denmark (1834), and Norway (1837). Yet the uncoordinated collection of statistics by governments produced incompatible methodologies and made comparison across state boundaries difficult. In response, statisticians organized the first international statistical congress in 1853. One of the early scientific congresses of any kind, it occurred in Brussels under the leadership of Quetelet with attendees from 26 countries. Later statistical congresses followed in Paris (1855), Vienna (1857), London (1860), Berlin (1863), Florence (1867), The Hague (1869), St Petersburg (1872), and Budapest (1876). Governments sponsored the congresses, and sent the leaders of their statistical services as official delegates, but many other attendees lacked government affiliation. The participants addressed practical matters, such as the effort to harmonize weights and measures, while discussing social reforms such as the alleviation of poverty. While the gathering of so many statisticians facilitated networking and advanced science, nonparticipants were sometimes disturbed by the sudden concentration of so much quantitative aptitude in an enclosed area. British politician Benjamin Disraeli admitted to being disturbed by the sight of so many bald, bespectacled heads, and noted that women were shocked by the unusual appearance of the delegates.

German representatives spearheaded opposition to the creation of a permanent international commission of statisticians, apparently a position they took in alignment with the views of German Chancellor Otto von Bismarck. Nonetheless, the International Statistical Institute (ISI) was eventually founded in 1885 at The Hague with a membership drawn mainly from Europe and the United States. The ISI was a semigovernmental organization in the sense that national governments defrayed the Institute's expenses, hosted its meetings, and contributed many of the delegates and much of the data for analysis, but did not directly exercise control. In addition to the ISI, various other international gatherings of 19th-century scholars organized congresses that, while not solely devoted to statistics, made considerable use of statistical techniques, including meetings examining medicine, demography, crime, eugenics, social insurance, hygiene, geography, sociology, anthropology, and commerce. Many of the proponents of statistical thinking believed that numbers offered a unique overview of human behaviour that facilitated social reform. For example, Quetelet's research influenced Florence

Nightingale, who made ingenious use of statistical analysis in her crusades to promote public health and improve society.

The two World Wars reduced the role of the ISI as a meeting place for powerful administrative statisticians and as a coordinator of national statistics. The First World War disrupted the activities of the ISI as the organization's members found themselves on opposing sides of the conflict, but the war furthered the use of statistics by governments attempting to quantify and mobilize their resources. After the war, ISI members sought to make the Institute a special advisor to the League of Nations. The assembly of the League rejected this proposal in 1931, and the League partially displaced ISI as a collector of international statistics, although the two organizations cooperated in some matters such as the improvement of economic statistics. In September 1938, the ISI met in Prague, but abandoned the session prematurely on the second day due to the possibility of war in Europe. The German invasion of the Netherlands in May 1940 severely obstructed the workings of the ISI, which could no longer communicate with most of its members. The Institute's leadership spurned offers to relocate outside occupied Europe or to accept the German proposal of a European Statistical Institute. During the war, members from the United States, cut off from the ISI headquarters, organized an Inter American Statistical Institute. The Second World War, like the First, produced greater government support for the study of applied statistics, resulting, for example, in the first publication of figures for gross national product by the US government.

As other organizations assumed a more important role in collecting statistics, the ISI turned mainly to the discovery and popularization of mathematical techniques, although it did conduct a World Fertility Survey from 1974 until 1982. Following the Second World War, the United Nations Statistical Office (UNSO) led efforts to standardize statistical methodologies across nations and measure national accounts, trade, population, and demography. Within the United Nations umbrella, the International Labour Organization, the World Health Organization, and the World Trade Organization, among others, collected important international statistics. Other organizations challenged the UNSO for supremacy in the realm of international statistics, most notably the World Bank, the International Monetary Fund, the Organization for Economic Cooperation and Development, and the European Union. Most innovatively, 'city groups' – ad hoc, transnational gatherings – sought to circumvent the bureaucratic inertia of the existing international statistical organizations. Statisticians founded the first of these, the Voorburg group, in the Netherlands in 1987 as part of an effort to standardize statistics concerning the service sector; nearly a dozen other city groups followed. Meanwhile, various non-governmental organizations collected statistics about the environment, public health, and human rights. The use of statistics is now common when describing and analysing many transnational phenomena, such as sports, the weather, immigration, disease patterns, financial transactions, trade, and global public opinion. With the development of new techniques and more powerful computers, statistics is likely to extend its influence ever further.

David Paull Nickles

Bibliography

Desrosières A. 1998. *The politics of large numbers: a history of statistical reasoning.* Cambridge, MA: Harvard University Press.

Nixon J. 1960. *A history of the International Statistical Institute, 1885–1960.* The Hague: International Statistical Institute.

Ward M. 2004. *Quantifying the world: UN ideas and statistics.* Bloomington: Indiana University Press.

Westergaard H. 1968. *Contributions to the history of statistics.* New York: Agathon.

Related essays

criminology; eugenics; governing science; intergovernmental organizations; International Maritime Conference 1853; international non-governmental organizations (INGOs); League of Nations Economic and Financial Organization; life and physical sciences; measurement systems; nation and state; national accounting systems; population; social sciences; technical standardization

Steamships

Steamships, or steam-propelled vessels, which revolutionized ocean transport, date from the turn of the 18th into the 19th centuries and were first used in ocean crossings in the 1820s and 1830s. Their heyday was from the mid-19th century until 1914, a period during which ocean freight rates fell by half while the value of world trade increased nearly tenfold. After the First World War, they ceded pride of place to motor ships, powered by diesel engines, although these, properly speaking, represented merely an evolution in the steamship revolution. Not until containerization again revolutionized sea-borne transport in the 1960s would there be a transformation equivalent to the one introduced by the steamship.

The steamship's contribution was to introduce regular, safer, all-weather, sufficiently rapid, and increasingly lower-cost transport across great bodies of water. It brought to ocean carriage the same revolutionary possibilities that railways introduced on land at approximately the same time. Together the steamship and the railway formed a global infrastructure for the circulation of goods and people at high volumes, especially as rail lines, from the beginning, were coordinated with ports. In this regard, the steamship was indispensable to the mass migrations, imperial rule, and emergence of mass production and consumer societies that set the 19th and early 20th centuries off from their predecessors.

Two further developments, one technological, the other organizational, explain the impact steamships made upon world economies and societies. Initially, steam's advantages over sail were far from triumphant. Steamships were not hostage to winds, but early-model steam engines consumed vast quantities of coal. Fuel costs for steamships were high, whereas they were all but non-existent for ships propelled by natural power. Moreover, coal bunkers reduced considerably the space available for revenue-earning freight. At first steam's promise was limited to high-value passage, such as mail ships with first-class passengers, or expensive cargo shipments. Where routes were relatively short or with easy access to coaling stations, steamships pushed aside sail ships. But on longer routes, especially east around Africa where coaling stations were few and far between, steam offered little if any advantage over sail. The same was true of bulk shipments, for example any heavy commodity, where value per weight was low and where speed or regularity were not economically meaningful. For steam to conquer sail, it was necessary to overcome steam's disadvantages. Four

technological accomplishments brought this about. First, advances in steam engine design (from the 1850s to the 1880s) so lowered fuel consumption as to make steam transport over any distance economically practical. Second, the substitution of the screw propeller (introduced at the end of the 1830s) for the more vulnerable paddle wheel made deep water travel more reliable. Third, iron construction allowed greater cargo bays proportional to ship weight. Still more important, iron ships, theoretically, could be built as large as a ship owner desired. Sheer size, as average freighter tonnage approached six-to-eight thousand tons, and shipyards were designing passenger liners that greatly exceeded this level, made the conversion to steam irreversible. Fourth, the digging of the Suez Canal (opened 1869), a feat of technological and organizational virtuosity, erased residual advantages to sail on the long passage east.

Business organization meanwhile converted the steamship into an instrument of global interconnectedness. Shipping men quickly perceived that regular, all-season ocean transport made possible the running of regularly scheduled services along fixed routes, or what became known as liner firms as opposed to tramps. Nearly all the great liner companies before containerization (for example, Cunard, Alfred Holt, HAPAG, Norddeutscher Lloyd, Compagnie Générale Française, Messageries Maritimes, Holland-Amerika) date roughly from the age of steam. Unlike tramping companies, which simply deployed their ships to ports with available cargoes, liner companies required large, expensive organizations that, in turn, fostered greater transnational linkages. For one thing, liner companies required agents in every port of call who could arrange turnaround of ships, canvass for cargoes or passengers, and provide information on markets and competition. Consequently, liner companies established transoceanic networks across the world. While few shipping companies offered, as yet, round-the-world services, these networks, in their totality, functioned as switching mechanisms for moving anything point-to-point around the globe. For another, the high fixed costs of liner companies, the large ships they operated, and the steady volumes of flows they transported required deep-water access, state-of-the-art equipment, and rapid means of inland transport in the ports they visited. Steamships thus became not only a vehicle for transporting the world's passengers and goods, but also for investing in harbour infrastructures around the world. Port cities vying for liner calls, and thus prime insertion into the world economy, were obliged to build facilities that could handle high-volume flows while liner companies and their agents, often powerful, local trading companies, sponsored investments that would shorten their port calls and provide better liaisons with hinterland markets.

Steamships were a critical factor in the mass cross-sea migrations of the 19th century: by lowering costs, shortening transport times, regularizing travel, and stimulating the building of larger, safer, more comfortable ships and expensive, big-business shipping organizations. Three particular relationships between steamships and migration can be identified. The cost and conditions of steamship travel offered incentives for more people to move and then to reverse their migrations and return home, as many ultimately did. Steamship companies, to maximize revenues and minimize losses on regularly scheduled passenger liners sailing according to their appointed time, full or not, deployed large agent networks to recruit emigrants; in some cases they also promoted and invested in settler communities abroad. By providing the means of long-distance bulk commodity carriage for really the first time (see below), steamships encouraged the development of mines and plantations in tropical countries which in turn required the recruitment of large, cheap labour forces from countries like China and India; these migrants, too, travelled by steamship. The dynamics between steamships and migration on massive levels were thus quite complex. Steamships encouraged large-scale migration of settlers. These settlers opened new lands for production of commodities demanded by industrial and urbanized Western societies and required manufactured goods shipped in return. All three (settlers, commodities, manufactured goods) were then carried by large, reliable, and often regularly scheduled steamships at costs that made their transport feasible. Or steamships encouraged the harvesting and mining of commodities half a world away from consuming centres, which in turn drove mass migrations to work these, which in turn required more shipments of machinery, tools, and perhaps food to mining and plantation communities overseas. In either case, steamships were the triggering or indispensable ingredient.

Just as significant was the impact of steamships on commodity transport. Since the 16th century a global economy of sorts had existed, but transport of most transoceanic goods still concentrated primarily on high-value luxury products. Bigger steamships and lower costs, combined with other factors ranging from steady scheduling to port investments to technological breakthroughs like refrigerated ships, rendered high-volume carriage of bulk goods from any point of the world to another routine and economically manageable. Daily life in modern Western societies came to depend upon steady, massive flows of grain, ore, rubber, mineral and vegetable oil, meat, and practically any other commodity required for mass production or mass consumption. Steamships, along with transoceanic communication lines, made these global markets possible.

The role of steamships in transnational history is nearly boundless. Steamships, as a means of penetration, conquest, or as a line of communication, were integrally linked to the expansion and control of empire, both formal and informal. The very character of imperial societies changed once steamships encouraged greater travel by women and families to tropical settings. At the same time, steamships abetted the spread of new ideologies, such as pan-Islamic movements and later Communism, and thereby undermined imperial rule. The increase in pilgrims travelling great sea distances to Makkah, as a consequence of steamships, provides one striking example of how this new technology coordinated communities outside of the West. Steamships rearranged the hierarchy of world ports, and, like railroads, determined which cities grew as world connectors and which ones were relegated to backwater status. Steamships altered the perception of time and space. Steamships reduced the meaning of 'the remote', and created the means by which people in one part of the planet had their lives transformed by the desires or needs of people in another part thousands of miles distant. Historians today debate whether the globalized world of the early 21st century has yet to replicate the transnational conditions of world flows before 1914. Without the steamship, that debate would never take place.

Michael B. Miller

Bibliography

Fayle C. E. 1933. *A short history of the world's shipping industry.* London: Allen & Unwin.

Headrick D. R. 1981. *The tools of empire: technology and European imperialism in the nineteenth century.* Oxford and New York: Oxford University Press.

Miller M. B. 2006. 'Pilgrims' Progress: the business of the Hajj', *Past and Present*, 191, May, 189–228.

Related essays

cities; civil engineering works; commodity trading; containerized freight; diasporas; diet and nutrition; empire and migration; empires and imperialism; epidemics; family; International Maritime Conference 1853; food; human mobility; international migration regimes; labour migrations; Panama Canal; railways; religious pilgrimage; rush migrations; temporary migrations; tourism; trade; transportation infrastructures

Steel and iron *See* Iron and steel

Stockholm Conference

The 1972 United Nations Conference on the Human Environment, held in Stockholm, Sweden, ushered in the modern era of global concern for the natural environment.

The conference, proposed by the Swedish government in 1968, was a direct result of growing environmental activism in many industrialized countries. Popular concern about the effects of pollution and natural resource depletion became a new political force, as seen in the celebrations and demonstrations marking the first Earth Day in 1970. The conference also took place in the shadow of the Cold War. Notably absent were the Soviet Union and most of the Soviet bloc, protesting the decision to invite West but not East Germany.

Tensions between globalism and national sovereignty emerged as a key theme at the conference. Much in evidence was the powerful new idea of Earth as a single, integrated, ecologically fragile system, popularized by books such as *The Limits to Growth* and *Only One Earth* and the iconic image of the planet photographed from space. Conference secretary-general Maurice Strong of Canada called for 'new concepts of sovereignty, based not on the surrender of national sovereignties but on better means of exercising them collectively, and with a greater sense of responsibility for the common good' (UNEP n.d.). Many governments from the global South baulked at this framing, fearing that it would freeze in place or even worsen existing development disparities. While acknowledging the need for environmental initiatives, their clear message was that little progress could be made on the environmental agenda until the challenge of poverty had been overcome.

The conference adopted a (non-binding) Stockholm Declaration, which reaffirmed the sovereign rights of states but also asserted that states have 'the responsibility to ensure that activities within their jurisdiction or control do not cause damage to the environment of other States or of areas beyond the limits of national jurisdiction' (UNCHE 1972). The conference also led directly to the creation of a new international agency, the United Nations Environment Programme (UNEP). Although chronically underfunded and often stymied by disagreements between industrialized and less-developed countries, UNEP has been an important catalyst for global environmental action, particularly with regard to the negotiation of multilateral agreements and capacity building among less-developed countries.

Beyond the tangible products of diplomacy, Stockholm set in motion broader trends that would define global environmental politics for decades to come. The tense debate about environment and development led to the concept of 'sustainable development', defined by the World Commission on Environment and Development as development that 'meets the needs of the present without compromising the ability of future generations to meet their own needs' (WCED 1987). Sustainability would become the organizing principle of the next major environmental summit, the 1992 UN Conference on Environment and Development, held in Rio de Janeiro on the twentieth anniversary of Stockholm.

Stockholm also marked the onset of an era of explosive growth in transnational environmental activism. Among the official participants were 134 non-governmental organizations, mostly from Europe and North America. The conference included both an officially sanctioned NGO event, the Environment Forum, and an unofficial and more radicalized People's Forum that drew linkages to excluded topics: the Vietnam War, racial oppression, social injustice. This combination of official and unsanctioned NGO gatherings would become a recurring practice at future global conferences. Fuelled in part by frustration over the diplomatic impasse so evident at Stockholm, the next few decades would see a dramatic increase in the number of NGOs and social movement groups working on global environmental issues. Taking advantage of the communications revolution, many groups built linkages to foreign counterparts; a handful, such as Greenpeace, Friends of the Earth, Conservation International and the Worldwide Fund for Nature, attained a truly global scale of operation.

Viewed through the lens of intergovernmental diplomacy, the Stockholm legacy is meagre: some non-binding principles of soft international environmental law, a few international accords, and a small and inadequately funded intergovernmental organization. In transnational social terms, its legacy is more substantial. Stockholm showed the world that there is a pollution of poverty as well as a pollution of affluence, and served as an important early catalyst for the continuing development of environmentalism as a global social movement.

Ken Conca

Bibliography

United Nations Conference on the Human Environment (UNCHE) 1972. *Declaration of the United Nations Conference on the Human Environment.* 21st plenary meeting, 16 June 1972.
United Nations Environment Programme (UNEP) n.d. Stockholm 1972: *Report of the UNCHE* [online]. Available: www.unep.org/Documents.multilingual/Default.asp?DocumentID=97&ArticleID=, accessed 1 September 2006.
World Commission on Environment and Development 1987. *Our common future.* Oxford: Oxford University Press.

Related essays

air pollution; Commission on International Labour Legislation; conservation and preservation; development and growth; ecology; environmental diplomacy; environmentalism; Greenpeace; intergovernnmental organizations; International Maritime Conference 1853; outer space; sustainable development; United Nations system; United Nations Women's Conferences; World Conservation Union (IUCN) / World Wide Fund for Nature (WWF); zero growth

Surrealism

Surrealism is considered one of the most influential avant-garde movements. In its heyday in the 1930s it came to hegemonize a heterogeneous cultural scene that included many other experimental tendencies.

The origins of surrealism go back to 1919 when Romanian Dadaist artist Tristan Tzara arrived in Paris at the invitation of a circle of poets involved in publishing the review *Littérature*. In collaboration with the group that included André Breton, Louis Aragon and Philippe Soupault, Tzara launched a series of manifestos, publications and provocations that were meant to stir up the cultural environment. They proved so effective that on various occasions they actually provoked the violent reaction of the public and required police intervention. However, Tzara and Breton soon began to drift apart, and the increasing tension between them was manifested in verbal and even physical fights. Beyond a dispute for leadership, their confrontations arose from two different conceptions regarding the course the movement should take. The group led by Breton considered that the Dadaist protests began to lose their power to shock: the acts of provocation were wearing off as they became systematically utilized, while the negation of art was to eventually lead artists to a dead end. They therefore proposed leaving behind the stage of pure, nihilist destruction and move on to creating a worldview of their own. 'Leave everything. Leave Dada. Leave your wife. Leave your mistress. Leave your hopes and fears. Leave your children in the woods', Breton proclaimed in 1924 in *Les pas perdus.* Surrealism was being born. In addition to its Dadaist heritage, it also recognized other major influences such as poetic cubism (in particular Guillaume Apollinaire's calligrams from 1918), the theater of Alfred Jarry, the poetic rupture of Charles Baudelaire, Isidore-Lucien Ducasse (a.k.a. Comte de Lautréamont) and the so-called 'cursed poets'. Among its other sources it also vindicated 'savage art' or naïve art such as that of Henri Rousseau ('Le Douanier Rousseau') as well as manifestations of non-European cultures, in particular African ritual masks and collections of Australian objects.

Together with Walter Benjamin, one could say that the surrealist enterprise was motivated by a search for individual freedom (building on the concept of the Freudian unconscious) and social freedom (in connection with the political theory of Karl Marx). Surrealists questioned reason as a guide to the artistic process, and explored the boundary between the wakeful state and the dream state. Capturing the oneiric (for which they resorted to the method of automatic writing) was considered the key to the creative trove that emerges from the irruption of the unconscious. The term 'surrealism' itself is precisely related to the notion of such a widened reality, one that does not distinguish between moments of wakefulness and dreaming. As Breton defined the term in the 'First Manifesto of Surrealism' (1924): 'SURREALISM, n. Psychic automatism in its pure state, by which one proposes to express – verbally, by means of the written word, or in any other manner – the actual functioning of thought. Dictated by thought, in the absence of any control exercised by reason, exempt from any aesthetic or moral concern' (Harrison and Wood 1992, 438).

Surrealism thus aspired to be much more than a mere school or artistic trend: it wanted to radically transform the modes of apprehending the world and conceived of artistic activity as a way of obtaining knowledge. In this way, the surrealist image, whose influence can be felt in our days as well, is based on the bringing together of two different realities whose meeting provokes a meaning that is incomprehensible for Western rational logic. Chance, humour, the exaltation of love and eroticism were stepping-stones for the surrealists' poetic creation.

From the beginning, the surrealist movement extended well beyond literary production, as its members explored various other artistic languages and genres (cinema, theatre, painting, etc.) and even invented new ones. It is not possible to refer to a 'surrealist style', though, because of the formal heterogeneity that existed inside the movement. Max Ernst invented 'frottage', Man Ray made radical experiments within photography, while Antonin Artaud revolutionized theatre. Collective creation was also stimulated through procedures such as the 'cadavre exquis' and resulted in collective works such as the film Un Chien Andalou (by Luis Buñuel and Salvador Dalí). The first

explicitly political definition of the movement appeared in a declaration issued on 27 January 1925, signed by the Bureau of Surrealist Research: '3 We are determined to make a Revolution. 4 We have joined the word surrealism to the word revolution solely to show the disinterested, detached, and even entirely desperate character of this revolution. ... 8 We are specialists in Revolt. There is no means of action which we are not capable, when necessary, of employing' (Harrison and Wood 1992, 439).

In spite of some internal disagreements, Breton and other members of the group thus introduced the problem regarding the compatibility between the surrealist postulates and the necessity of a social revolution. In 1927 the polemics deepened further as Breton, Aragon, Éluard, Péret and Unik joined the French Communist Party and Pierre Naville approached Leon Trotsky, whose secretary he would later be. Two years later they launched a survey regarding the situation that arose as a consequence of the 'sentence recently applied to Leon Trotsky', the forced exile meted out by the Communist Party to the famed leader of the 1917 Russian Revolution. Breton penned the 'Second Manifesto of Surrealism' in which he decreed a series of expulsions in connection with the different political positions. This manifesto disowned even some of the literary fathers of surrealism such as Charles Baudelaire, Arthur Rimbaud, and Edgar Allan Poe, and left only Lautréamont untouched. As Giménez Frontín put it, from this document on, 'surrealism is not considered just a way of knowing, rather as that state or point of the spirit in which all contradictions of reality are abolished and in which love and revolution, poetry, subconscious and magic converge harmoniously' (Giménez Frontín 1983, 89).

A further political schism was produced in the surrealist ranks when Aragon, a veteran surrealist, returned from Moscow professing a conciliatory attitude towards the Stalinist regime. While he ended up breaking with the surrealists in 1932, the following year Breton, Éluard and René Crevel were thrown out of the French Communist Party due to their criticism of Stalin and their closeness to Trotsky. In 1938, Breton came up with the idea of founding an 'International Federation of Independent Revolutionary Art'. With this purpose in mind he travelled to Mexico to meet with the persecuted Russian leader residing there. Their meeting gave birth to the manifesto, 'Towards a Free Revolutionary Art', a declaration signed by Breton and Mexican painter Diego Rivera, though its text was authored jointly by Breton and Trotsky. The text concludes: 'Our aims: The independence of art – for the revolution. The revolution – for the complete liberation of art!' (Harrison and Wood 1992, 529).

This manifesto ought be read in together with the intention to expand the surrealist movement internationally. Hal Foster has analysed the contrast between the two surrealist maps of the world that emerged from their different manifestos: 'These two works transmit the different states of mind of the two moments: the map of 1929 denotes an imaginative appropriation of the world that rewrites it with charm according to the surrealist interests, while the horoscope-hourglass of 1937 foresees a sepulchral world whose time is completely consumed'. Without any doubt, Paris was considered the undisputed capital of this expanding surrealist movement. Nevertheless, various émigrés from the rest of the world were included in its ranks, and numerous other artistic and literary centres sprang up all around the world that bore relations to it. While this fact was in part due to the surrealists' intention to create an international movement, clearly manifested in the organization of International Exhibitions of Surrealism (the first, in 1938, called together 60 artists from 14 countries), artists from Latin American countries and peripheral or poorer parts of Europe (Southern and Eastern Europe) were also active protagonists of this process. Their relevance consists not just in what they took home from their trips to Europe and 'disseminated' in the periphery. It is equally important what these artists contributed to defining the strange character of the language and the perceptions of the metropolitan transformations. In fact, many of the integrants of the Parisian surrealist movement were from Latin America, including Peruvian artist and poet César Moro, Cuban artist Wilfredo Lam, and Chilean artist Roberto Matta, who not only extended surrealism all over the American continent but elaborated in their works a particular link between the surrealist processes and the references to prehispanic imaginaries or popular cultures. Nevertheless, although there were groups in Latin America that defined themselves as surrealist, with their own press such as the magazine Qué (edited in Buenos Aires by Aldo Pellegrini from 1928 to 1930), it is more appropriate to talk about a vast and persistent (at least, until the 1960s) influence of surrealism in Latin America than to describe it as an organic movement.

On the other hand, political events such as the fall of the Spanish Republic and the advance of fascism in Europe lead to the exile of Breton and many other members of the movement in different parts of the American continent. The surrealist exile in Mexico, Brazil, Argentina and the United States in particular was significant both in terms of what was produced in these new artistic contexts as well as for the ways local culture transformed surrealism. In the United States, for example, the beginnings of the New York School and its descendant movement, Abstract Expressionism, are closely related to the influential presence of a nucleus of surrealists in exile. Numerous artists fell beneath its spell including Jackson Pollock, Arshile Gorky, Mark Rothko, Robert Motherwell, and also John Cage, Merce Cunningham, Robert Rauschenberg and Jasper Johns. At the same time, the surrealist group in Mexico integrated Remedios Varo, Leonora Carrington, Benjamin Péret, Max Ernst, Katy and José Horna, Günther Gerzso, César Moro, Esteban Francés, and Octavio Paz among others. Sidelined from the official circle of the postrevolutionary Mexican nationalist culture, they found refuge in collective activity.

After 1946, following the end of the Second World War, Breton and most of his circle returned to Europe. Others such as Remedios Varo lived the rest of their lives in the New Continent and produced works that combined surrealist postulates with elements that their new environment opened up to them: exploiting the oneiric, arcane knowledge, magic, popular beliefs and pre-Colombian references. While the surrealist movement survived several decades longer, it could no longer be considered an avant-garde movement in the organized sense, and rather became a spring of persistent and suggestive inspirations for artists.

Ana Longoni

Bibliography
Alix J. and Sawin M. (eds) 1999. *Surrealistas en el exilio y los inicios de la Escuela de Nueva York.* Madrid: Museo Nacional Centro de Arte Reina Sofía.

Benjamin W. 1929. 'Surrealism: the last snapshot of the European intelligentsia'.

Foster H., Krauss R., Bois Y.-A. and Buchloh B. (eds) 2004. *Art since 1900: modernism, antimodernism, postmodernism*. London: Thames & Hudson.

Giménez Frontín J. L. 1983. *El surrealismo: en torno al movimiento bretoniano*. Barcelona: Montesinos.

Harrison C. and Wood P. (eds) 1992. *Art in Theory: 1900–1990: an anthology of changing ideas*. Oxford: Blackwell.

Löwy M. 2000. *L'Étoile du matin: surréalisme et marxisme*. Paris: Sillepse.

Nadeau M. 1970. *Histoire du surréalisme*. Paris: Seuil.

Pellegrini A. 1961. *Antología de la poesía surrealista*. Buenos Aires: Fabril.

Related essays

antropofagia; avant garde; conceptualism; cultural capitals; expositions; literary capitals; literature; modernismo; socialism; voodoo; wildlife films

Sustainable development

'Sustainable development' captures both old and new. While the policy agenda of sustainable development was first articulated in 1987 by the UN report, *Our Common Future*, concern over the long-run sustainability of societies has deeper roots. Recognizing those roots enriches understanding of both history and contemporary challenges.

Sustainability is a deeper attribute of societies: their ability to persist over time. *Sustainable development* is recent policy and political agenda, key elements of which include, according to UN 1992 *Agenda 21*:

- Ensuring inter- and intragenerational equity, combining concern for inequality now with safeguarding future generations' access to resources and a healthy environment.
- Valuing the role of ecological systems (climatic stability, nutrient cycles, clean air).
- Protecting non-human life forms (collectively termed *biodiversity*) for both utilitarian and innate values.
- Integrating understanding of, and improving responses to, issues spanning previously unconnected disciplines and sectors, across environment, society and economy.

- A preventative approach to environmental degradation (in legal doctrine, the *precautionary principle*).
- Internationalization of previously localized issues, through concern over equity, and understanding of global dimensions of environmental issues.
- Using new policy approaches including market mechanisms and community-based approaches.
- Ensuring community involvement in policy and management processes.

These elements have spread across cultures and time, influenced by scientific discoveries, shifts in social values, political trends (such as participatory democracy, neoliberalism), and realization of the interconnectedness of issues previously considered separately, bringing environment, society and economy onto one agenda.

A superficial understanding has modern environmentalism gaining political purchase from the 1960s, yet the roots are deeper. Ancient Greeks worried about deforestation, and classical economists (especially Malthus) worried the Old World was limited by land and food resources. The unpredicted colonization of other lands, resources and labour saw that concern abate. However, as environmental historians such as Richard Grove and William Beinart demonstrate, later concern emerged in colonized lands as much as in Europe. Simmering concern has been evident since, in George Perkins Marsh's 1864 *Man and Nature*, the writings of the Physiocrats, and renewable resource management fields such as water, fisheries and forestry. Much earlier – and only understood recently – traditional cultures evolved elaborate rules and practices structuring their interactions with nature.

The early mid-twentieth century saw the emergence of formal resource management and environmental protection advocacy, science, regulations and institutions. National and subnational governments addressed (albeit often ineffectively) blatant environmental damage and promoted 'wise use' of natural resources, and international environmental agreements and treaties proliferated. The nature of concern however shifted significantly from the 1960s, in terms of the interconnected nature of the problems (early articulations included classic essays by Kenneth Boulding and Garrett Hardin), and their apparent scale (stated vigorously in 1972 by the Club of Rome in *Limits to Growth*).

Limits, like Malthus before, was seen as disproved by events (recovery from oil shocks, newly unearthed resources, more efficient use), but concern still mounted, driven more by the effects of resource use (especially climate change) than prospects of resource scarcity. The UN World Commission on Environment and Development, in its report *Our Common Future*, brought together previous UN processes dealing with security, poverty and development, creating the environment-society-economy agenda of sustainable development. The UN Conference on Environment and Development in 1992 – the largest gathering of countries ever – detailed the scientific and policy challenges. Numerous strategies, scientific processes and international agreements followed. The consequent 2002 World Summit on Sustainable Development noted some gains, but overall it and many other reviews stressed the unfinished task of change to ensure an ecologically sustainable and humanly desirable future.

Sustainable development is a meta-policy challenge, a higher-order social goal still requiring debate, experimentation and constant effort at local, national and international scales. Seeing it as a recent, simple idea misses that point: a historical view emphasizes it. If sustainable development demands integration of issues and a long view forward, then a historical perspective can expose those constituent issues and furnish the necessary long view back.

Stephen Dovers

Bibliography

Connor R. and Dovers, S. 2004. *Institutional change for sustainable development*. Cheltenham: Edward Elgar.

Dovers S. 2000. 'On the contribution of environmental history to current debate and policy', *Environment and History*, 6, 131–60.

Related essays
biodiversity; climate change; conservation and preservation; development and growth; environmental diplomacy; environmentalism; forests; freshwater management; Greenpeace; national parks; oceans; Stockholm Conference; United Nations Educational, Scientific and Cultural Organization (UNESCO) educational programmes; United Nations system; World Conservation Union (IUCN) / World Wide Fund for Nature (WWF); zero growth

Swiss banks

Transnational banking in one country best describes both the presence and the activities of Swiss banks across the world until the last quarter of the twentieth century.

Throughout their history, Swiss banks have been deeply involved in financial activities across borders. In the 15th century, when finance was closely linked to commercial fairs, Geneva was a financial centre of the very first order. From the 16th to the 18th century, the most prominent Swiss bankers, especially in Geneva, but also in Basle, were integrated into the international economic networks formed by the Huguenot Diaspora. By the late 18th century, Geneva had become a crucial link in the financing of the French debt, a role augmented with the appointment in 1776 of the Geneva-born banker Jacques Necker as Comptroller of French finances. Private bankers (Pictet, Lombard Odier, Hentsch, or Mirabaud in Geneva; Ehinger, La Roche, Dreyfus, or Burckhardt in Basle) remained part of the European *Haute banque* throughout the 19th century, financing international trade by accepting bills of exchange, issuing foreign loans, and managing the portfolio of a highly cosmopolitan clientele.

New players emerged following the foundation of the large credit banks in the third quarter of the 19th century. By 1913, their foreign assets made up about one third of the total. Their involvement in the international economy grew stronger in the 1920s, not least as a result of the country's neutrality during the First World War. Switzerland's speciality mainly consisted in attracting foreign capital and redirecting it abroad. Germany was by far the most popular destination, attracting the bulk of the credit banks' foreign credit. They were severely hit by the German banking crisis of 1931 and the ensuing introduction of exchange controls: the assets of the eight 'big banks' halved and their profits dropped by more than two thirds between 1930 and 1935; one of them, the Schweizerische Volksbank, Bern, had to be rescued by the federal government, while another, the Banque d'Escompte Suisse, Geneva, collapsed in 1934.

However serious, this setback did not really threaten Switzerland's position as a refuge for the flight of capital. Indeed, it was during these years that the Swiss banks came to be increasingly seen in this light. A significant contributory factor was the federal banking law of 1934, whose Article 47 introduced the notorious banking secrecy. This article made those subject to it – banks' employees, managers, directors, auditors, supervisors – liable to fines or up to six months' imprisonment if they divulged business information and, above all, the names of a bank's clients. Banking secrecy undoubtedly reinforced the Swiss banks' capacity to attract foreign capital – one of their main competitive advantages. Capital inflows substantially increased from the late 1930s and even though the banks' main activity during the Second World War was financing state needs, they remained involved in transnational business, whether through credits granted to Germany or, despite severe hindrance, wealth management activities.

The end of the Second World War opened a golden age for the Swiss financial markets, increasingly embodied by the big banks. Benefiting from political and economic stability and a strong currency (the Swiss franc remained fully convertible into gold throughout the war), Switzerland was able rapidly to develop its role as a hub for accommodating and investing foreign capital. By 1975, capital inflows amounted to 40 billion francs and capital outflows to 47 billion, the 7 billion difference coming from Swiss residents' surplus savings. The top three 'big banks' (Crédit Suisse, Swiss Bank Corporation, Union Bank of Switzerland) underwent a huge expansion, with their foreign assets increasing sixfold and their foreign liabilities fivefold between 1963 and 1973, whereas national operations, on both sides of their balance sheet, increased by a factor of 2.5. Off-balance-sheet operations, including those linked to wealth management, the country's great speciality, grew even faster. In the issuing business, Switzerland kept itself apart from the Eurobond market which started up in 1963 – international issues in foreign currencies in Switzerland and the issue of loans in Swiss francs abroad were both banned by the monetary authorities. Nevertheless, Swiss banks, above all the big three, controlled the issue of foreign bonds in Swiss francs which, despite the overall success of Eurobonds, represented 11.3 per cent of the total amount of international loans by 1974. Moreover, they had a vast placing capacity in the Eurobond market

outside Switzerland, which strengthened their position in the international syndicates: in the mid 1960s, more than half of all Euro-issues were probably placed through Swiss banks.

In contrast to other European banks, not only in large economies such as Britain, France, or Germany, but also in smaller ones such as Belgium or Holland, the activities of the Swiss banks did not lead to the emergence of a few banks operating worldwide from Switzerland. Prior to 1914, the Swiss banks had very little physical presence outside their country's borders. It consisted of the Swiss Bank Corporation's two London branches (one in the City opened in 1898, followed by a 'West End' office in 1912) and the two South American subsidiaries of Crédit Suisse (the Schweizerisch-Argentinisch Hypothekenbank, established in 1910, and the Schweizerisch-Südamerikanische Bank, in 1912). Things hardly changed after World War I and it was only in 1939 that both Crédit Suisse and the Swiss Bank Corporation opened branches in New York, a reflection of the growth of financial relations between Switzerland and the United States. In 1965, despite their growing role in international finance, Swiss banks collectively had a mere eleven foreign branches. As a refuge for the flight of capital, Swiss banks were spared the effort of collecting foreign funds. Moreover, in an era when foreign branches were mainly located in developing economies, several of them under colonial rule, Swiss banks favoured other ways of carrying out their transnational activities, such as using a representative or taking a stake in a foreign bank.

A major change took place in the late 1960s and early 1970s. From eleven in 1965, the number of foreign branches of Swiss banks rose to 41 in 1975 and 79 in 1985 – and would be 167 in that year if representative offices were to be added. The rise of the Euromarkets together with vast improvements in information technology led to major changes in banking, with foreign branches increasingly located in the financial centres of the industrialized countries of Western Europe, North America and Asia. No longer content with simply placing Eurobond issues with their wealthy clientele, the 'big three' Swiss banks regularly appeared, from the 1970s, in the top ten places in the rankings of leading banks for international issues. In the 1980s and 1990s, they became major players in the world's leading financial centres, above all

London and New York, following a series of strategic mergers and acquisitions.

By the turn of turn of the 21st century, the 'big two' Swiss Banks, UBS (the result of the 1998 merger between Swiss Banking Corporation and Union Bank of Switzerland) and Crédit Suisse both ranked among the world's top ten banks, measured by market capitalization. They had also become thoroughly transnational banks, in terms of financial activities, notably global wealth management and global investment banking, and in terms of physical presence in five continents.

Youssef Cassis

Bibliography

Cassis Y. 2006. *Capitals of capital: a history of international financial centres, 1780–2005.* Cambridge: Cambridge University Press.

Cassis Y. 'Swiss international banking, 1890–1950', in Jones G. (ed.) 1990. *Banks as multinationals,* London: Routledge, 160–72.

Jung J. 2000. *Von der Schweizerischen Kreditanstalt zur Credit Suisse Group: eine Bankengeschichte.* Zürich: NZZ.

Mazbouri M. 2005. *L'émergence de la place financière suisse (1890–1913).* Lausanne: Antipodes.

Related essays
euromarkets; financial centres; financial markets; gold; Hong Kong and Shanghai Banking Corporation (HSBC); investment; loans; money

T

Taxation

Taxes are fees levied by a government on products, incomes, or economic activities. The purpose of taxation is to finance government expenditure on the local, regional and national levels, such as for street lighting, schooling, social welfare and running the military. Most historians and economists have argued that taxes have made the state, just as the state has made taxes: state sovereignty has been guaranteed through income from taxation, and taxes have normally been defined according to the territory in which they have been levied. Much more than in other areas of public policy, research on the transnational history of taxation is still in its infancy. In particular, transnational exchanges of ideas about taxation amongst subnational actors, such as municipal and regional governments, are not at all understood.

While it is true that most tax policies are almost exclusively nationally oriented, the transfer of ideas about taxation has been part and parcel of the development of national tax systems. Tax expertise was already shared within the Greek and Roman empires, and formed part of the transfers of governmental and administrative expertise across medieval Europe. With the beginning of the processes of state and nation building that began in the early 19th century and led to the establishment of sovereign nation states in Europe, in the Americas and in Asia, however, these transfers took on a distinctive quality which has characterized the transnational history of taxation to the present day.

On a structural level, we can observe a shared history of taxation. Common economic and fiscal challenges, such as revolutions, revolts, wars and major economic crises have led to common perceptions of fiscal 'crises' or 'problems'. On the level of the history of ideas, the perception of 'crises' has frequently resulted in interactions that have transcended the boundaries of governments and nation states. These exchanges have been characterized by a paradox that is key for understanding the transnational history of taxation. This paradox consists in the basic incompatibility between traditional prerogatives of sovereign governments and the smooth functioning of a liberal free-market economic system. While

state sovereignty was interpreted increasingly rigidly along territorial lines, especially from the 1880s until the 1970s, increasing economic and financial interactions across borders stood against the direct realization of this principle. From around 1800, the transnational history of taxation evolved within a complex and incremental process that unfolded through an interaction between economic and financial developments, institutional and bureaucratic factors as well as a modicum of shared ideas about what constituted 'good taxes'. From the 1970s, there was a transnational shift away from an emphasis on taxation as an instrument of social and economic management with the aim of creating social equality, towards neoliberal considerations of efficiency.

The forms of tax policy transfers varied widely. Within the British and French empires, taxation was an important tool for domination and resource extraction, and tax policies carried certain assumptions about the ways in which economy and society should be structured, often along racial lines. India, for example, bore a heavy burden of taxation that British people were not prepared to bear. British taxes on its African colonies had the purpose of financing the colonial administration and were enforced brutally. In 1907, South Africa saw a rebellion against the imposition of a poll tax for adult males, during which the British killed between 1,000 and 4,000 locals. An approach of 'empire by persuasion' was taken by the United States in Japan after World War 2 when a mission led by the Columbia University professor Carl S. Shoup attempted to introduce a novel tax system in Japan in order to aid its democratization. While the Japanese government maintained certain elements of this system, the mission as a whole was a failure. Shoup continued to be a key player in overhauling the tax systems in Cuba, Venezuela, and Liberia during the 1950s.

Ideas about taxation also crossed borders through emulation and mutual observation, although it is important to realize that none of these ideas remained unchanged during these processes; they were creatively adapted. From the late 19th century to the end of World War 2, social and academic networks were key for this process. The American reformer Henry George's campaign for 'single tax', an income tax with a single rate, was particularly popular among the rank-and-file of tax reformers around the world at the turn of the century. From the 1870s to the beginning of World War I, the ideas of German university economists, with their commitment to state building and their advocacy of socially equitable federal income taxation, influenced debates about tax reform in the United States, Imperial Japan and Tsarist Russia during the 1900s. Even after the Revolution of 1917, Russia remained for some time influenced by these transnational debates about fair taxation and state building. From the 1920s onwards, the International Fiscal Association and the American Brookings Institution's international conferences began to play an increasingly important role in transnational debates about taxation.

After 1945, international organizations began to offer the institutional contexts for transnational debates about taxation. From the 1970s onwards, the International Monetary Fund (IMF) and the World Bank have been especially important. During the 1980s, the IMF's Fiscal Affairs Department under its director Vito Tanzi became the main driving force behind the introduction of value-added taxes in developing countries in Africa and Latin America. In this context, both the model of taxation and a certain type of administrative knowledge and expertise were transferred.

From the 1980s, discussions about international 'models' of good taxation have served as vehicles for transnational observations. This has been greatly enhanced by the popularization of economic knowledge in the mass media. Thus, US President Ronald Reagan's Tax Reform Act (1986) became the rallying point for tax reformers around the world. From the mid 1990s onwards, tax reforms that established taxes with a unitary rate of tax (rather than a progressive sliding scale), similar to George's 'single tax', became the subject of transnational discussions about such 'flat taxes' since they were first introduced by Baltic states, such as Estonia.

Social networks and discussions within organizations and the wider public sphere have undergirded efforts at governmental coordination of tax policies. Despite the creation of trading zones, such as the European Union and the North American Free Trade Area, and the gradual reduction of barriers to trade within the context of the General Agreement on Tariffs and Trade (GATT) and the World Trade Organization (WTO), no multilateral tax regime has yet emerged.

Instead, governmental coordination has taken the form of bilateral agreements to avoid double taxation of persons and companies. This issue already caught governments' attention in the 19th century. But it was only with the increased intensity of transnational economic and financial interactions that policy makers began to debate transnational solutions. In 1921, the League of Nations commissioned experts to study the impact of double taxation and to draft model bilateral treaties with the purpose of avoiding double taxation.

The Organization for Economic Co-operation and Development (OECD) continued to study this problem after 1945. In 1963, the OECD drafted a Model Income Tax Convention which established two main principles for taxation: first, countries can tax income that arises from domestic sources, regardless of residence (source principle); second, and taking precedence, countries have the right to tax people who reside within their borders (residence principle). In addition, debates about common standards for taxation and about 'tax harmonization' have taken place within the European Economic Community and the European Union.

Many of these discussions have been intimately linked to the history of corporations that operated within tax systems that were based on the principle of residency. It was the problem of how to assess the tax liability of British companies whose main activities took place in the Empire that brought this issue to the fore in the late 19th century. Corporations have been able to exploit the residency principle by organizing their tax burdens according to different national fiscal regimes. This proliferation of 'transfer pricing' within large transnational corporations has led to much debate. In 2004, for example, the US tax authorities brought a court case against the pharmaceutical firm GlaxoSmithKline on the grounds that it had evaded tax on the profits of its drug Zantac. The company claimed that it had been produced by the company's British subsidiary and was therefore not liable to US taxes. The dispute was settled with an agreement under which the corporation paid some US$3.4 billion (including interest) to the US Internal Revenue Service, thus upholding the principle of territoriality.

The tension between transnational links and the assertion of the principle of territoriality continues to influence tax policies to the present day. The key paradox of the transnational history of taxation continues to be states' ability to withstand the growing integration of economic and financial markets, while at the same time creating the regulatory infrastructure that makes this integration possible.

Holger Nehring

Bibliography

Hood C. 'The tax state in the information age', in Paul T. V., Ikenberry G. J. and Hall J. A. (eds) 2003. *The nation state in question*, Princeton: Princeton University Press, 213–33.

Nehring H. and Schui F. (eds) 2007. *Global debates about taxation*. Basingstoke and New York: Palgrave Macmillan.

Steinmo S. 2003. 'The evolution of policy ideas: tax policy in the 20th century', *British Journal of Politics and International Relations*, 5, 2, 206–36.

Tanzi V. 1995. *Taxation in an integrating world*. Washington, DC: Brookings Institution.

Related essays

capitalism; convergence and divergence; corporations; developmental assistance; economics; European Union (EU); financial diplomacy; General Agreement on Tariffs and Trade (GATT) / World Trade Organization (WTO); governing science; health policy; industrialization; intergovernmental organizations; International Monetary Fund (IMF); kindergarten; measurement; modernization theory; nation and state; neoliberalism; Pax Americana; public policy; welfare state; World Bank

Technical assistance

Technical assistance is a policy and investment tool that allows developed countries the opportunity to transfer advanced capacities in various fields to developing countries, in support of improvements to their economy and society.

Technical assistance can be classified into four categories in terms of actors: (1) international organizations; (2) national governments; (3) non-governmental organizations (NGOs), and (4) private companies. Assistance typically includes not only the transfer of technology but also recommendations regarding monetary policy, fiscal policy or the social security system. Exchange and transfer projects can be pursued through trainees, sending specialists, educational grants, development planning, and dissemination of technological goods and services.

From the middle of the 19th century, advanced countries such as Britain, France and Germany transferred their ideas and production systems to developing regions by way of their colonial administration. This diffusion process was not limited to the colonial experience. For example, beginning in the mid to late 19th century, Western scholars and companies introduced new ideas and advanced technology such as railways, electronics, and banking systems to Japan, responding to both government and the private sector. Such technical and intellectual assistance promoted and accelerated Japan's rapid modernization and industrialization. From the late 19th century until World War 1, the pace of such activity increased, as did the range of world regions affected, as multinational companies and distinguished scientists such as Thomas Edison disseminated their production processes and ideas.

After World War 2, technical assistance to developing countries became formalized through such institutions as the Organization for Economic Co-operation and Development (OECD) and the United Nations Development Programme (UNDP). At the bilateral level, the Official Development Assistance (ODA) from the advanced countries has become an important diplomatic tool in relation to the developing world. The United States played a leading role in this regard in the aftermath of World War 2, and during the 1950s and 1960s. The 'Point IV Program' derived from President Truman's inauguration speech was managed by the Technical Cooperation Administration from 1950, and the US Agency for International Development (1961) would be a major player in the field later on. East and Southeast Asian countries such as Japan and South Korea could not have accomplished their rapid economic growth in the post-World War 2 period without technical assistance from the US. Since the late 1970s, the agenda of challenges confronting those countries promoting technical assistance to the developing world has expanded considerably to include environmental protection, alleviating poverty, and establishing the legal framework to support economic growth.

Technical cooperation projects and development research policy faced daunting challenges in the last quarter of the 20th century. By the late 1980s the world community had drastically changed and become more interdependent with the elimination of many barriers restricting transnational movements of goods, people, ideas and capital markets, largely due to innovations in computer and communication technology. One example of change was the adoption, in Buenos Aires, Argentina, in 1978, of an important plan to promote mutual technical cooperation between developing countries (the so-called 'Buenos Aires Plan'). Changing world conditions have shaped programmes and policies at two world institutions in particular, the United Nations and the International Monetary Fund. According to its Articles of Agreement, the IMF states that the purpose of technical assistance 'is to contribute to the development of the productive resources of member countries by enhancing the effectiveness of economic policy and financial management'. Based on this agreement, the IMF provides a wide range of technical assistance. Since the end of the Cold War, more attention has been paid to the Technical Cooperation among Developing Countries (TCDC). How to cope with the international application of the patent system, which originally protected advanced inventions, is one of the difficult problems that remain to be solved.

Finally, it should be noted that international non-governmental organizations play a growing role in providing technical assistance to the developing world, not only modelling their activities on the historical role of government, but focusing in particular on ways to assist and nurture human capital and networks independent of national ideology.

Masato Kimura

Bibliography

Agosin M. R. (ed.) 1995. *Foreign direct investment in Latin America*. Washington, DC: Inter-American Development Bank.

Davenport-Hives R. P. T. and Jones G. (eds) 1989. *British business in Asia since 1860*. Cambridge: Cambridge University Press.

International Monetary Fund 2001. 'Policy statement on IMF technical assistance', 1 April.

Jackson J. T. 2005. *The globalizers: development workers in action*. Baltimore: Johns Hopkins University Press.

Related essays

Aga Khan Development Network; civilizations; development and growth; developmental assistance; empires and imperialism; fellowships and grants; Ford Foundation; Green Revolution; International Monetary Fund (IMF); investment; League of Nations Economic and Financial Organization; League of Nations Health Organization; Maoism; modernization theory; organization models; patents; Pax Americana; philanthropic foundations; productivity missions; public policy; socialism; taxation; technologies; Toyotism; underdevelopment; United Nations system; Westernization; World Bank

Technical standardization

Standardization in the modern world refers to a form of voluntary rule setting that prescribes appropriate characteristics for artifacts or organizations so as to facilitate their reliable, orderly use and integration in wider applications, including commerce.

Standardization has accompanied the development of human culture from prehistoric times. Language depends on standardized relationships between human sounds and meanings; writing depends on similar connections between signs and either sounds or ideas; commerce and trade have always depended on standard weights and measures; and monetary economies and international trade have always required currencies calibrated to a standard measure of value, such as gold (hence 'the gold standard'). As societies have become more sophisticated, their reliance on standards has grown. The ancient Mesopotamians standardized the size of building modules (bricks and tiles), while the Romans economized on materials and labour in building their vast road network by standardizing axle lengths on their chariots to 1435 mm (the same gauge that most railway networks use today).

Transnational beginnings in the electrical world

Today's organized practice of standardization began with three 19th-century technical advances – mechanized production of artifacts with interchangeable parts (such as small arms, clocks, sewing machines and bicycles); electrical power generation, with its applications in lighting, motors and public transport; and the related development of telegraphy and telephony. In the latter half of the 19th century, mass production of standardized products with interchangeable parts made standardization a central production principle. The development of electrical supply and its applications also called for standardized measures and dimensions, starting with units of electrical current and resistance.

At first each industrialized country established its own units. But the new electrical supply industry, telegraphy, telephony and other forms of electrical transmission, and the burgeoning trade in dynamos, cables, transformers, motors and other equipment, required harmonization across national borders.

In 1865, 20 European states founded the International Telegraph Union (today's International Telecommunication Union), now the world's oldest international organization. The Union standardized equipment and protocols so as to facilitate telegraphy across national borders. It soon came to do so for telephony and radiotelephony as well, and later took charge of the radio spectrum when broadcasting began in the 1920s. It now plays a vital role in information and communication technology.

The 1875 Metric Treaty pioneered the development of shared, precise units of physical measurement (also known as 'physical standards'), which underpin all other standards except today's management standards. Six years later the first International Electrical Congress in Paris established common measures of electrical current, and thus a milestone in standardization. Though it was formally an international conference, scientists and industrialists drove the proceedings without reference to raison d'état. It set the pattern for transnational technical standardization to this day: states formally attend at the birth of international bodies, but deliberations and action proceed in their absence.

Follow-up conferences occurred every five years, until the 1904 conference decided to establish a permanent body. The founding congress of the International Electrotechnical Commission (IEC) was duly held in London in 1906. At its founding congress, the Verband Deutsche Elektrotechniker argued strongly for the exclusion of 'government' influence and met little opposition.

The IEC set a precedent, which all significant regional, global and transnational standards bodies would follow, for developing standards in international non-government organizations. Delegates referred to themselves as representing a 'movement', and even a 'brotherhood', one intended to prove a model for peaceful coexistence. Standardizers nationally and transnationally would preserve this sense of themselves well into the post-World War 2 period. True to this idea, the IEC executive was called 'the Committee of Action' (nowadays the Standardization Management Board), and an expert 'advisory committee' (later 'technical committee') came to take charge of each of the major areas of concern to the early IEC – development of a common vocabulary, common symbols, and ratings for electrical apparatus. The early emphasis on developing common units of measurement and technical terms in the IEC makes it a clear case of an epistemic community. It constantly refined the system of measurement of electrical current, and (in the interwar period) of radio frequencies. In 1938 it published its International electrotechnical vocabulary, with over 2,000 terms in English, French, German, Italian, Spanish and Esperanto. The IEC remains one of the three main transnational standardizing bodies to this day.

Along with the early national standards bodies, the IEC established today's modus operandi in legitimate standards organizations, one based on a plurality of interests represented. Committees consisted of ostensible 'experts' drawn from the different interest groups affected by the project in hand. Thus they were not 'disinterested' individuals, and only in recent times has the issue of wider and proportionate representation of all 'stakeholders' been addressed. Even so, standardizers were expected to deliberate 'transparently' and arrive at consensual decisions. In particular, this ethos informed the technical committees that developed standards and associated handbooks and guides. Each technical committee had at its disposal a secretariat that a national standards body offered free of charge. This approach underpins transnational standards work to the present time.

The first organization to commit itself to transnational standardization outside 'the electrical world' was the Swiss standards body, Verein Schweizerischer Maschinenhersteller Normalienbureau. From 1923 it invited national standard bodies from abroad to join it and cooperate in producing joint standards, mainly for mechanical engineering. Three years later the International Standards Association (ISA) was formed and took over this work. The ISA represented an early attempt to build an international standards body with a much more general mission than the IEC's: to reduce technical barriers to trade in the form of idiosyncratic, nation-specific standards. It adopted the IEC's organizational model, one centred on technical committees on which the interests of the various countries and functional groups were supposedly balanced. Once again, however, the actual composition of committees favoured those interests with sufficient resources and determination to field 'volunteers'.

The ISA had a small secretariat in Basle, and concentrated on issues relevant to Continental European countries, especially in mechanical engineering. It worked exclusively in metrics, which reduced its appeal to non-metric countries. Soon it faced the 1930s Depression, which encouraged protectionist forces with no sympathy for ISA's agenda. Though its achievements were modest, it had enrolled 21 national standards bodies by the outbreak of war in 1939, which forced it into mothballs.

The League of Nations, founded in 1920, fed off the same spirit of internationalism and peaceful coexistence in the 1920s, and undertook important standardization activities of its own, not least in the area of healthcare (for instance, in standardizing the classification of blood groups and measures for vitamin intakes). Closely aligned to it, the International Labour Organization (ILO) laid the groundwork for establishing international labour standards.

National standards bodies

As noted, standardization emerged in the 19th century as a production concept in the mass production of artifacts with interchangeable parts. Mass production of standardized goods drastically reduced unit costs and brought other benefits to consumers. Starting with the American Civil War, mass production also became a vital part of military capacity. But the gains from standardization went well beyond the sphere of production. Installation and design standards promised greater safety in buildings, their wiring and plumbing. Network standards allowed trains to move across state borders, and telegraphy and telephony to span the world. Eventually they would underpin today's interoperability of remote computers. Quality, safety and sheer doability also became part of the standardizer's *raison d'être*.

In the leading industrial countries, standardization arose spontaneously, in rational solutions to immediate production issues. In late-industrialising countries, such as the British dominions, standardization became a vital mechanism of technology transfer, such that standardizers took a leading role in economic development. In both cases, standardization was often contested, as it challenged those with a vested interest in parochialism, older technologies, or monopolies.

Resistance to standardization helped mould standardizers' self-image as a transnational 'movement' – one that, especially in the 1920s, would work alongside other movements around 'rationalization' in general, and such specific causes as 'simplified practice'. The latter promoted standardization by reducing superfluous variety in manufactured goods on the market. All these movements united under the slogan of 'rational progress', and 'propaganda' for it constituted a normal, explicit item on the early national standard bodies' agenda. Standardizers now came from much more varied disciplinary and occupational backgrounds than the electrotechnicians of the IEC, but engineers of varying specializations took the lead. As a profession, engineers gained enormous prestige from mass production; and as a professional corps, they evangelized for the socioeconomic benefits of standardization.

The earliest important national standards bodies appeared before or during World War 1 – in Britain in 1901, and in Germany and the USA in 1917. The 1920s saw their emergence in most advanced economies, even if the latter were not yet industrialized, as in the Australasian cases. Some formed spontaneously, while others were initiated by governments seeking to forge the link between science and industry as part of national development.

At first almost all national standards bodies represented an amalgam of engineers and industrialists, who came together in non-government voluntary associations, and were conscious of belonging to civil society rather than the state. They followed the British and IEC precedents in espousing democratic procedures and a plurality of interests on technical committees, even if the latter was not always achieved in practice. Above all, national standards bodies promoted the principle that the adoption of standards was voluntary. As civic organizations they have brought together large numbers of unpaid individuals from many walks of life on their technical committees – individuals who thus gain the opportunity to network, and to hone their technical and civic skills simultaneously. For instance, in 2006 a middling national standards body such as the Australian one had 8,193 experts on its 1,576 technical committees and subcommittees.

A number of factors complicated relations with governments. In many cases national standards bodies depended on government subsidies. And in spite of the voluntary principle, governments became major users of standards in regulation, starting with such basic functions as electrical wiring rules and safety requirements in building codes, which thereby became mandatory. In the booming 1920s, governments and industries also realized the trade benefits of standardization, and so worked towards a system of national standards, with conformance trademarks branded onto products. As the developers of national standards, the national standards bodies thus sought exclusive governmental recognition of their products.

In this way the latter gained prestige over proprietary and industry standards, which lack legitimacy since they are produced by individual enterprises and trade associations respectively, without the 'transparent', participatory procedures of the national standards bodies' technical committees. Governments have also had to take responsibility for national measurement systems. National standards bodies thus had to cooperate with national measurement laboratories and testing facilities, which ensure that all measuring instruments used in the wider economy are accurately calibrated in order to secure recognition in export markets. Today this private–public network, or 'national technical infrastructure', extends into forms of transnational cooperation.

In World War 2, national standards bodies became vital nodal points of the home front in wartime. Technological innovation, diffusion and transfers accelerated, in turn demanding vast numbers of war emergency standards. National standards bodies then worked intimately with many arms of their own governments and – in the case of belligerent countries – with allied national

standards bodies. But in spite of all their links to government, and their later consorting with the state-based standards institutes of developing countries in the many transnational standards forums, the older national standards bodies have always remained embedded in civil society, and thus maintain an arm's-length relationship to government.

The national standards bodies' agenda has gradually expanded from product, design, installation and network standards. The 1930s saw growing interest in quality control standards, which would lead to the widespread use of such process standards in munitions industries in World War 2, and much more generally afterwards, as well as certification and trademarking based on standards. Governments extended their use of national standards in their own purchasing routines and in detailed regulation.

The national standards bodies' expanded agenda led them to drop words like 'engineering standards association' from their names. In the 1970s they responded to a huge increase in the demand for consumer and safety standards. A decade later they began another expansion into quality management (or 'administrative') standards which replaced the older forms of quality control standards, and which have opened up a whole new field of management standards (including ones covering environmental issues, knowledge, risk, record keeping, regulatory compliance and 'social responsibility'). The arrival of information technology (IT), and technological change in telecommunications, have massively increased the field of network standards, especially to achieve interoperability in computer-based technologies, such as electronic funds transfers.

Trade, war and internationalization

As we shall see, regional, global and transnational standards forums and organizations now play a salient role in global economic regulation under the catchcry of harmonization of national standards. Development of trade and standardization arrangements in the British Empire between the wars prefigured postwar trends. The imperial government was pursuing a policy of replacing centralized control from London with a decentralized, 'federated' empire (soon to be redubbed a 'commonwealth of nations') consisting of several sovereign dominions, as well as a residue of crown colonies.

The empire, which at the time comprised a quarter of the world's population, would continue to function as a trading bloc. Harmonizing national standards was recognized as the key to the free flow of goods throughout the 'empire-preference' area. Standardizers met in separate caucuses during the five-yearly intergovernmental imperial conferences, but personal visits by leading standardizers were more frequent. The British Engineering Standards Association (from 1931 the British Standards Institution, BSI) encouraged the development of national standards bodies in the dominions, and negotiated with them flexible licensing arrangements whereby they published and sold common standards where appropriate, and mutual rights to conformance testing where they were not. Imperial national standards bodies marketed each other's standards, and maintained reference libraries with holdings of imperial and foreign standards.

In the 1930s, the BSI sought to harmonize trademarking throughout the empire: each dominion was to legislate to protect standards-compliance trademarks, and each national standards body should register its standards-conformance mark, which should then gain recognition throughout the empire. This idea sparked an early interest in process standards, which were already being used in certain firms in the US as a means to ensure that mass-produced goods conformed to the appropriate standards before they qualified for a mark. This system became a prototype for much later regional and global trading arrangements, including in today's European Union.

War brought a drastic shift in standardizers' focus from trade to technological innovation and diffusion at home, and technology transfers between allied countries. The experience of dealing with these contingencies would have a formative influence on postwar transnational standards arrangements. Even neutral industrial countries like Sweden had to switch to import-replacement manufactures, and for the first time produce goods that it had previously imported, or that had no peacetime application, such as air-raid shelters. Belligerent countries faced the same challenge, but also had to optimize armaments manufacture on the basis of rapid technology transfers from their allies. All these endeavours demanded publication of the requisite standards as a prelude to production and installation, and national standards bodies were stretched to their limits producing new, mutually compatible standards at short notice.

These issues prompted a long joint wartime project between national standards bodies that continued into the postwar period – 'ABC work' (America-Britain-Canada), that the respective bodies undertook so as to harmonize engineering-drawing and screw-thread standards, among many others. To facilitate this cooperation, Allied governments directed their national standard bodies to form a new organization, the United Nations Standards Coordination Committee (UNSCC), whose executive met for the first time in London, in June 1944. Its immediate function was to support the war effort by eradicating obstacles to technology transfers. But even at the time its spokespeople pointed to its potential to reduce technical barriers to postwar trade. For that, the UNSCC would have to develop into a far more inclusive body, and a more effective one than the ISA had been.

The first general meeting of UNSCC took place in New York in October 1945. All Allied national standards bodies attended, as well as those of Mexico and Brazil. Plans were laid for a new international body, and negotiations started with remnants of the ISA. On 14 October 1946 (which subsequently became World Standards Day), a conference – jointly hosted by UNSCC and ISA – took place in London. Delegates from 25 countries attended and formally launched the International Organization for Standardization (ISO).

In spite of Americans' taking the most visible leadership positions, the founding of ISO represented a shift away from the dominance of the English-speaking countries. The new organization based itself in Geneva; two years later the reactivated IEC – now affiliated to ISO but retaining its autonomous field of operations – moved its headquarters from London to Geneva as well. Eventually the two organizations would occupy the same building there, share some personnel and launch a number of joint technical committees. ISO's membership at the turn of the 21st century consists of 159 national standards bodies, including some 'corresponding' and 'subscribing' associate members. Only one organization from each country is admitted to membership.

The founding of ISO took its place in a flurry of diplomatic activity whereby the Allies sought to promote postwar reconstruction on the basis of trade liberalization and collective security. Alongside the UN, they founded the Bretton Woods international monetary regime, the World Bank, the International Monetary Fund, and the General Agreement on Tariff and Trade (much later replaced by the World Trade Organization). ISO was thus born to help clear away technical barriers to growing trade flows; it was to make 'recommendations' that its constituents could write into their national standards, which would thereby be 'coordinated' for trade purposes.

Transnationalizing standards development

The old rhetoric of rational progress revived in the postwar period, and with it many of the prewar transnational networks. Some of the initial ISO technical committees were in fact resuscitated ISA ones – a relationship that mirrored the UN's own takeover of a number of the League of Nations' departments, including those that had engaged in standardization during the interwar period, such as its healthcare one. But ISO soon spawned many more technical committees; after ten years it had 80 active committees, and by 2006 it had 229, many of them with attendant subcommittees and working groups. One of the formative influences on its development was Olle Sturén who eventually served a record term (1968–86) as ISO's general secretary. He raised ISO's stature above that of a 'European club', a stigma it inherited from ISA, by enrolling many national standards bodies from developing countries as active members. Today the vast majority of ISO's members represent these countries.

In 1970, as part of a watershed year that included the founding of the ISO Bulletin and the proclamation of World Standards Day, Sturén initiated a whole new category of international standards to eventually supersede the lowlier ISO 'recommendations'. In this way ISO claimed a whole new primacy for its products. Instead of being a clearinghouse for incompatibilities between national standards, international standards would ideally pre-empt the content of national standards: the latter would simply be rebadged international standards.

It was a bold move, given the degree of nationalist sentiment (not least in the US)

around standards development, and the fact that ISO's technical committees, dependent as they were on international meetings, tended to work more slowly than those of its national affiliates. In the 1990s, ISO struggled to reduce the average development time for a new standard from seven to five years. Those national standards bodies that embraced the new concept often found themselves nonetheless forced to develop provisional national standards in response to the rapid pace of technological change. In both cases standards development was a time-consuming deliberative process, such that standardizers have always faced criticism from users for not having published a suddenly urgent standard 'yesterday'. Where a national standards body published a reasonable standard in such circumstances, the relevant ISO technical committee often used it as a 'source document', and even as the first draft of an international standard, so reducing its own lead time.

As ISO's level of ambition rose, it had to face the underrepresentation of more distant and less developed countries. As John Boli has argued, INGOs such as ISO base their legitimacy on the principle of rational voluntarism, since they are neither the organs of coercive states nor able to exercise financial *force majeure*. Their representativeness and transparent, deliberative processes underpin the authority of their products. ISO has thus had to devise mechanisms whereby remote constituents could give written feedback on draft standards, and to see that their feedback was taken seriously, if they were to support the resulting standards, guides and handbooks.

Intensifying economic internationalization, however, bolstered Sturén's brainchild in at least three ways. Firstly, the General Conference on Weights and Measures, which administers the international metric system, had adopted a set of more exact units of measurement (Système international d'unités, or 'SI units') in 1960. This move precipitated a wave of national metrications in the 1970s in the previously non-metric world; today only Liberia, Burma and the US remain outside the metric system. National standards bodies in metricating countries could then recast all their dimensional standards in metrics, which boosted trade and eased cross-cultural contacts.

Secondly, the Tokyo round of GATT meetings (1973–79) worked towards its Standards Code, which would oblige signatories to remove technical barriers to trade from their standards regimes; adopting international standards would ensure compliance with it (and with its successor, WTO's Standards Code). In 1980 GATT officially adopted the Code. In 2006, 118 national standards bodies and three EU ones had acceded to the WTO Code. Today WTO enjoys a strategic partnership with the ISO, IEC and ITU, and ISO is represented on WTO's Committee on Technical Barriers to Trade.

Thirdly, firms began to do much more business with remote partners, especially with the rise of global information technologies, and could no longer rely on local business cultures to enquire whether potential partners produced quality products or services, and could be relied on to do so over time. The apparent answer to this problem came in the form of management standards, in the first instance generic quality management standards. In 1979 ISO set up its own technical committee (ISO TC 176) to develop quality management standards, and in 1987 it published its ISO 9000 series. The rate at which these standards were adopted as national standards, and sold to firms around the world, dispelled any lingering doubts about the viability of international standards. Firms and other organizations could gain certificates of compliance against ISO 9000, which became their legitimation cards on the global market. The certificate's appearance on an organization's website supposedly settled most doubts about its management, performance, reliability and probity.

In this way a new worldwide industry was born around consultant-driven implementation of ISO 9000, certification to these standards, and the accreditation of certifying bodies. Many national standards bodies have participated in this industry through for-profit subsidiaries that provide consultancy and certification services, and their participation has accorded the formally not-for-profit national standards bodies an unprecedented financial solidity. In 1994 and 2000, ISO published updated versions of the ISO 9000 series. It has also published other management standards covering such aspects of corporate life as risk management, complaints handling and regulatory compliance, as well as another major series of standards for environmental management, ISO 14000. In short, quality management standards were the major icebreakers for international standards as a whole.

In 2004, ISO braved initial controversy and committed itself to developing a standard (ISO 26000) for social responsibility in organizational life, to be published in 2008. This project raises its level of ambition still further, both in its subject matter and in the time frame it has set itself: when it subtracts time for public comment, it has only three years in which to develop this thorny concept.

In a development largely compatible with the ISO/IEC transnational standards infrastructure, regional standards bodies have grown up, starting with the European standards body, CEN (Comité Européen de Normalisation) in 1959. CEN and its electrotechnical counterpart, CENELEC (founded in 1973), led the struggle towards harmonized European standards in order to achieve a single, integrated European economy by 1992, in what is now the EU. Those aware of similar endeavours in the interwar British empire might have watched this development with a sense of déjà vu. Comparable regional standards bodies seeking to facilitate trade have been set up in the Americas (COPANT in 1961), Arab countries (AOSM in 1967), the Pacific Rim (PASC in 1973) and Africa (ARSO in 1977).

In 2006, 30,000 experts from around the world sat on ISO technical committees, while the organization itself maintains functional links with another 591 INGOs. We could see this network not only as embedded in transnational civil society, but also as a transnational technical infrastructure which – in common with most infrastructures – supports essential aspects of modern life out of sight and out of mind for the great majority of its beneficiaries.

Winton Higgins
Kristina Tamm Hallström

Bibliography

Boli J. and Thomas J. (eds) 1999. *Constructing world culture: international nongovernmental organizations since 1875.* Stanford: Stanford University Press.

Brunsson N., Jacobsson B. and associates. 2000. *A world of standards.* Oxford: Oxford University Press.

Higgins W. 2005. *Engine of change: Standards Australia since 1922.* Blackheath, NSW: Brandl & Schlesinger.

Schmidt S. and Werle R. 1998. *Coordinating technology: studies in the international standardization of telecommunications.* Cambridge, MA: MIT Press.

Tamm Hallström K. 2004. *Organizing international standardization – ISO and the IASC in quest of authority*. Cheltenham: Edward Elgar.

Related essays
broadcasting; car safety standards; engineering; European Union (EU); food safety standards; intergovernmental organizations; international non-governmental organizations (INGOs); labour standards; League of Nations Health Organization; League of Nations system; mail; measurement; music; organization models; Pax Americana; radio; railways; regions; technical assistance; technologies; telephone and telegraphy; trade; trade (manufactured goods); trademarks; United Nations decades and years; United Nations system; war

Technologies

Technology and its movement across space is a defining element of human activity. This subject stands at the centre of the European industrial revolution, for example, until recently a stable intellectual concept. But comparative studies by world historians that include other European nations and Asia have complicated explanations of Britain's technological and industrial leadership. Geographer J. M. Blaut and historian A. G. Frank have suggested that in technological terms, Asian and European civilizations after 1500 and before 1750 may not have been as far apart as once thought. No longer is it clear that Europeans possessed unique social, political, or cultural traits. Europeans drew deeply upon technologies from China and India (textiles, porcelain, and so forth) well into the 18th century, even after Europeans began to judge deficient, according to historian Michael Adas, cultures that lacked strong technological capacities.

After 1750, however, there is no dispute that British industrialists, and then others in different European nations and in North America developed technological capacities qualitatively different from those of the rest of the world. Since then, any nation aspiring to economic strength has sought to emulate Britain's first industrial economy. This essay suggests the transfer of technology between nations is pivotal to the related processes of industrialization and modernization. It also devotes attention to recent technological activities that are multinational in scope and structure, such as the protocols governing the operation of complex systems across national boundaries or consortia that undertake enormously expensive research, development and implementation efforts associated with very large projects, such as space exploration.

Diffusion and technology transfer

Technology transfer is the complicated process involved in moving technology across national, geographic, cultural, organizational, and institutional boundaries. Transfers involve technological systems and hardware, as well as knowledge, processes, people, and skills. Movements occur at the intra-organizational (e.g., knowledge management within firms) and inter-organizational (e.g., commercialization of ideas from universities or national laboratories) levels as well as spatially across national borders. The term 'technology transfer' appears problematic to some, suggesting a unidirectional effort by paternalistic experts to impose technological systems upon passive recipients. Over the past half century many social scientists have used 'diffusion' as a synonym, since sociologist Everett Rogers sketched a process characterized by innovators, early adopters, opinion leaders, change agents, late adopters, and laggards. His vocabulary and conception that individuals are vital carriers of technology across space have been extraordinarily influential. Following Rogers' lead, scholars have stressed the complexity of a process that is as much social as economic. Indeed, successful transfers demand as much creative effort by recipients as by original innovators.

The industrial revolution

While the British industrial revolution grew out of many social and economic circumstances, it was characterized by technological innovations that included the use of mineral coal to smelt and refine iron, Arkwright and Crompton's textile-spinning machinery, and Newcomen and Watt's steam engines. This is the not the place to discuss why these emerged in Britain, but we can note among the favourable conditions the natural resource base, England's political and legal system and economic and social structure, and available capital, technological skills, and entrepreneurship. Economic historian David Landes argued that this complex of factors provided the basis for self-sustaining economic growth.

As soon as British manufacturers begun to deploy these new techniques, other countries sought to acquire them, legally and otherwise. British innovators resisted, relying upon a patent system that granted inventors a twenty-year monopoly. Not all inventors secured costly patents, although James Watt's vigorous defence of his steam engine monopoly demonstrated their value. Patents might not apply to exports, but even industrial innovations not protected by patents proved difficult to transfer to Europe, as demonstrated by the lengthy struggles of French, Belgian, and other industrialists to replicate Britain's technical breakthroughs. European borrowers found they needed experience and rarely codified skills to adopt coal or steam engines. Covetous desire alone was not enough to ensure success.

Yet British textile manufacturers paradoxically discovered that it was equally difficult to prevent the spread of innovations. Cotton-spinning and later weaving machinery proved easier to transfer than coal and steam technologies, leading Parliament to prohibit the emigration of textile workers in 1774 and to impose textile machinery export restrictions. Even so, European and American mill owners regularly circumvented restrictions by offering bounties to workers, bribing customs agents, and conducting industrial espionage. Manufacturers who persevered usually could acquire English technology. Drawings and descriptions of machines and processes alone were inadequate, although after 1800 some managed to purchase machinery from manufacturers, legally or otherwise. The migration of knowledgeable people was always more important.

American acquisition of British textile technology after 1790 rested upon all of these steps, according to historian David Jeremy. Samuel Slater, who left England illegally in 1789 with knowledge of spinning machinery, launched the American industry on British lines. It was a slow process. Like early spinning mills in every country, Slater's mill in Pawtucket, Rhode Island, struggled against cheaper British imports. Tariffs helped, but American producers prospered only after Jefferson's trade embargo of 1807 and the subsequent war with Britain provided a ten-year window of protection. The best indicator of success was the Boston Manufacturing Company's

(Waltham and Lowell, Massachusetts) ability by 1820 to fabricate its own power looms. By the 1830s, American textile firms introduced innovations that British textile producers borrowed, such as automatic stops that halted looms when threads broke. In other words, the mark of success was not only *adopting* borrowed technology, but also *adapting* it to fit local circumstances.

This experience was repeated often during the 19th century by European and American industrialists acquiring techniques and machinery from Britain. Not every country could launch an iron industry, but until well into the 20th century those harbouring industrial ambitions developed British-style textile mills. Germany and Scandinavia, for example, benefited from the end of export restrictions in 1843. Many countries also borrowed British railroad technology and, not coincidentally, British capital. American railroad builders purchased locomotives and rails from England in 1830, but by 1840 were devising flexible locomotives suited to local conditions; they produced their own rails by the 1850s. Indeed, in 1843, Russian officials selected Americans to build the St Petersburg-Moscow rail line. France, Belgium, and Germany also copied the railroad technology that drove the second wave of the industrial revolution. Outside Europe, however, British and American firms built many of the world's railroads, ranging from India and South Africa to China and Latin America.

Industrializing nations during the 19th century repeatedly demonstrated the basic paradox of technology transfer: while diffusion is difficult, innovators rarely can prevent the spread of their inventions. By 1900, however, it became harder to acquire the newest industrial technologies. Backward economic, social, political, and educational conditions (compared to Europe) limited the capacity of many nations outside Western Europe and North America to adopt, much less adapt, the newest science-based technical systems.

Russia and Japan offer contrasting case studies of these later efforts to acquire industrial technology. Russia faced severe challenges in terms of capital formation, workforce skills, industrial capacity, and markets. After emerging involuntarily from self-imposed isolation in the 1850s, Meiji Japan was determined to retain independence from Europe nations and carefully controlled the process of building modern industries.

Both nations adopted multiple strategies for acquiring industrial and military technology from Europe and the United States. They bought individual machines and processes as well as entire plants and shipyards; arranged for outside experts to construct, operate and train local workers and managers; and sent technical missions abroad to learn new skills and techniques. Determined never again to be dominated by Western powers, Japan pursued industrialization with single-minded devotion and the assistance and guidance of government ministries. In 1905, the Japanese military prevailed in the Russo–Japanese War, signalling an impressive success at closing the technological gaps with Western industrial nations.

Russian transfer programmes advanced more slowly, mainly because that nation started further behind in social and economic terms. Russia's continuing economic and technical weakness was confirmed by its 1917 surrender to Germany in World War I. The new Communist regime quickly launched a determined industrialization effort in the 1920s, backed by Stalin's unprecedented ruthlessness and state-sanctioned violence. This campaign of industrialization was driven by two goals: bring the country's level of development into line with the West so Marx's economic analysis could play out, and protect the Communist regime from hostile capitalist powers. Yet even while Stalin proclaimed 'socialism in one country' – a philosophy of self-sufficiency – Soviet industrializers shared with Japan a willingness to draw upon imported technology. German and American engineers designed and oversaw construction of massive hydroelectric projects on the Dnieper River using German turbines and electrical machinery, for example. American-style tractors for collective farms emerged from Ford-style assembly lines. The Soviet government licensed aviation engines and signed technical assistance agreements in many fields of technology. And with the assistance of Western engineers and machinery producers, in 1929 the Soviet leadership launched construction of the world's largest steel mill, surpassing even the U.S. Steel Corporation's plant at Gary, Indiana. The mills at Magnitogorsk, which by 1939 produced 10 per cent of the country's steel, typified Stalin's fascination with gigantic technological systems designed to prove the Soviet Union was catching and surpassing the capitalist West. At the same time, the mill's location deep inside the Soviet Union reflected Stalin's paranoia about capitalist invasion.

Ultimately, Japan and Russia 'caught up' to Britain and other industrializing nations, but only with strenuous efforts, sacrifice, and official governmental subsidies and direction. Their experience confirmed economist Alexander Gerschenkron's analysis that late industrializers relied upon state direction to overcome relative backwardness. Clearly, technology transfer programmes remained vital for economic development during the late 19th and early 20th centuries.

The challenges of acquiring modern technology were even greater for nations that had been colonies of European powers. British rulers brought the telegraph, steam locomotives, steam ships, steam engines, and industrial manufacturing to India, for example, but often to the benefit of colonial officials. Typically, they gave Indians little say in the technologies adopted, and even less chance to become involved in their adaptation. Moreover, because few Indians received in-depth technical training, imported technologies had few spin-off effects. By the time India achieved independence, the country possessed a civil service but lacked a reservoir of workers versed in modern technologies. Into the 20th century this pattern applied to former colonies throughout Africa and Asia, as some European colonizers made few efforts to involve indigenous peoples in economic and technological activities.

Postwar economic development

Late industrializers were not, however, the only nations concerned with technology transfer during the 20th century. After World War 2, the victors hoped to acquire German advances in jet propulsion, rocketry, chemicals, and other technologies. During 1944–45, several thousand American and British teams scoured Germany for documents, machinery, and scientists and engineers. The Soviets, for their part, dismantled German factories and forcibly relocated German engineers and skilled workers. US officials later brought German rocket experts across the Atlantic. But information and technology, especially about American factory production, also flowed back to Europe during these years, under the Marshall Plan to help rebuild Europe. That programme was aptly labelled 'the most massive technology transfer in history' (Ahmad and Wilkie 1979, 79).

These activities set the stage for large-scale postwar attention to technology transfer as a mechanism for encouraging economic development. The efforts of many Western nations, however, exhibited schizophrenic tendencies. On the one hand, Western leaders hoped to close yawning economic and technological gaps faced by newly emerging nations in Asia, Africa, and Latin America by transplanting industrial technology. Yet the logic of the Cold War also spawned restrictions on technology flows to Communist nations. Neither effort proved completely successful.

Developing countries seeking to industrialize after 1945 found the Western technological systems they sought to acquire larger, more complex, and therefore more difficult to adopt than the textile, iron production, power, and railroad technologies associated with the 19th-century industrial revolution. While many economic development programmes initially emphasized agriculture, rural technologies, and basic infrastructure, Western experts and local leaders alike equated economic development with large-scale industrial technology. Foreign assistance from Western countries, philanthropic foundations such as Ford and Rockefeller, and international organizations such as the United Nations and the World Bank, favoured the latter vision. By the 1960s, however, Western experts realized they had underestimated the challenges of development and diffusion. One economist lamented, '[we] allow[ed] ourselves to believe that there was a purely technological solution – a cheap technological fix – to the problems of poverty and economic backwardness' (Rosenberg 1970, 550). Western advisors belatedly recognized that economic development required more than the diffusion of industrial facilities.

Eventually, many development experts sought to match transferred technology to local conditions and situations. They encouraged local residents to adapt imported techniques, often by starting with small projects instead of expensive show pieces. The 'appropriate technology movement' of the 1970s emphasized technically simpler and smaller systems whose skill requirements matched local capabilities. The United Nations supported solar cookers, small-scale

hydro-plants, hand water pumps, and activities related to agricultural commodities. Yet success remained elusive if leaders in developing nations favoured eye-catching high technology. Local leaders often dismissed low-tech devices as patronizing for not lessening the dependency of developing nations on the industrial West.

Yet diffusion could succeed. Upon achieving independence, India struggled during the 1950s to adopt large-scale Western industrial technology before taking enormous economic strides. One key decision involved shifting attention to local development programmes, but more important was non-alignment, that is, avoiding reliance upon either the West or the Soviet bloc. Thus India created in 1973 what later became the National Institute of Science, Technology, and Development Studies (NISTADS, 1981). Its interdisciplinary staff has studied the dynamics of diffusion, the relationship of transfer programmes to economic development, and transfers in specific high-tech fields such as biotechnology and computing. India now supports numerous transfer projects in other developing nations.

After 1950, the British industrial model finally began to be superseded as the road map for technological development. Newly industrializing countries such as Taiwan, Korea, and Brazil were influenced instead by the 'Japanese miracle' of the 1950s. Now government ministries joined with large transnational corporations to promote national policies encouraging growth first in sectors such as textiles, steel, and ship building and then in automobiles and consumer electronics. Technology transfer remained essential and, following the lead of Richard Nelson, many economists have emphasized the importance of 'national innovation systems' for growth. The term covers not only research entities, but also those institutions that move ideas into commercial marketplaces and allow adoption and adaptation of imported ideas. The ability of Japanese corporations to transform scientific breakthroughs into winning consumer products (stereos, cameras, video cassette recorders, computers, cell phones, laser disk technology, etc.) demonstrated the continued importance of technology transfer, across both national borders and organizational boundaries. For newly industrializing countries, technology transfer remained a central mechanism for development after 1980.

The Cold War

The superpower confrontation after 1945 cast a long shadow over technology transfer activities. The Cold War expanded funding for technology transfer, but both blocs often subordinated aid programmes to geopolitical considerations. Neither Western democracies nor the Soviet Union exhibited deep sensitivity to local cultural, social, and economic conditions, and military assistance often dwarfed foreign aid and economic development programmes. Both countries played politics with aid. Thus Khrushchev cut off Soviet transfer efforts in China after disputes with Mao Zedong in 1960, yet trumpeted support for Egypt's Aswan High Dam and India's Bhilai steel mill after the Americans pulled out of those projects. Through 1967 the Soviets spent $14 billion and the United States more than $100 billion on technical assistance and transfer programmes that at least in part rewarded local allies.

Yet even as Western democracies promoted technology transfers to the developing world, they also restricted technology movements to Communist nations. Both decisions reflected the Cold War logic by which technological accomplishments were a measuring stick for political/economic/social systems, as well as the source of military strength. US officials were determined to protect a technical lead over the Soviet Union. Equally determined to catch up, the USSR often relied upon another mechanism of technology transfer – industrial espionage. Since the 1920s, Soviet intelligence programmes had acquired technical knowledge in advanced industrial fields. The Soviets not only had spies inside the wartime atomic bomb project, but also sought advanced military technology through purchases and other less legal means. Attention to aviation, aerospace, and computing assumed greater priority after the war. The Soviets also mastered reverse engineering, acquiring a technical system to learn its principles and how it worked and then copying the design. Western democracies set out in 1949 with the Coordinating Committee for Multilateral Export Controls (COCOM) to restrict technology exports to the Soviet bloc and later to China. This export control regime grew more complicated until it ended in 1994, yet enjoyed mixed success because Western leaders disagreed about how restrictive COCOM should be. During the 1970s, for example, international business scholars argued the presence of American technology behind the Iron Curtain might strengthen détente, while commercial rivalries and industrial espionage allowed illegal technology movements. It was telling that Soviet Ryad computers resembled the IBM 360 and their aircraft mirrored Western designs. Quoting Lenin's aphorism that capitalists would sell the rope with which to be hanged, Western hardliners tightened controls after Ronald Regan was elected president in 1980. Yet in the end, the COCOM proved no more successful than British attempts to restrict textile machinery exports after 1775. At the same time, the Soviet Union failed to integrate and adapt the borrowed/copied/stolen technologies.

Nuclear weapons constituted a special case of technology transfer during the Cold War. Even before 1945, American officials feared the spread of atomic weapons and Congress erected barriers of secrecy around weapons labs and limited knowledge flows to British allies. The unexpected (to some) Soviet detonation of an atomic device in 1949 helped provoke a witch hunt for Communist agents. Spies certainly existed, but there were few real nuclear 'secrets'. Even so, the US government monitored the export of any technology (especially computers) that might assist the nuclear development programmes of other nations, including close allies. Yet the British (1952), French (1961), and Chinese (1964) soon joined the nuclear weapons club.

The Cuban Missile Crisis (1962) prompted diplomatic efforts to limit the spread of such weapons, culminating in the Treaty on the Non-Proliferation of Nuclear Weapons (1968). The International Atomic Energy Agency, originally organized in 1957, now monitors international compliance. Even so, India, South Africa, Pakistan, and Israel have since developed nuclear weapons. And concerns about nuclear proliferation have transcended their Cold War origins. Pakistani nuclear engineer Abdul Qadeer Khan sold uranium enrichment technology to several countries, demonstrating the continuing role of individuals as agents of diffusion. Iraqi nuclear weapons programmes figured in both Gulf Wars, and nuclear technology programmes in North Korea and Iran have roiled international relations since 2000.

Transnational technological systems

Diffusion seems inherently transnational in nature, but the technology transferred usually emerged inside national contexts. During the 20th century, however, the implementation of large-scale systems in communications and transportation required transnational management and coordination structures, that in turn prompted development of technological standards of all sorts.

The increasing scale of technological systems also fostered multinational development activities. Such projects appeared after 1950 because of the size and expense of developing large systems. Multinational business corporations earlier had carried technologies across national boundaries, but genuinely transnational research and development programmes are relatively recent. Boeing, for example, divided design responsibilities for its 777 airliner among national teams spread across the globe, thanks to interactive software on global communications networks. But it is the very largest systems, usually aerospace projects, that exceed the financial capacity of even the largest corporations and prompt new forms of transnational technological cooperation. The US space programme, for example, forced negotiations for tracking stations in Australia, South Africa, and Spain to allow continuous communication with orbiting astronauts. The Apollo Soyuz Test Project (1975) responded to US/USSR détente. More recently, the International Space Station proved feasible only after several nations agreed to share the expense. The many changes of direction in its design and disputes about funding demonstrate the political tensions inherent in such partnerships.

While the number of the genuinely international technological projects is small, many are in Europe. The formation of the European Economic Community in 1958 was the first of many cooperative economic and technological ventures. The European Space Research Organization (1962) and the related European Launcher Development Organization (1964) both had rocky starts due to the challenges of managing cooperative enterprises of this scale and visibility. Their merger to form the European Space Agency in 1973 brought together 17 member nations, as well as Canada, Hungary and the Czech Republic. Two other transnational technological enterprises are organized as quasi-business corporations. ESA spun off Arianespace in 1980 to manufacture rockets and operate the European spaceport in French Guiana. The corporation has 23 private and state partners from ten nations, and launches half of the world's satellites. The other joint technological effort is the Airbus consortium (1970), organized to compete with American aircraft producers. The manufacturing partners are Aérospatiale (France) and Deutsche Airbus (German aircraft manufacturers); CASA (Spain, 1974) and British Aerospace (1979); each contributes components for Airbus aircraft. Airbus Industrie GIE (Groupe d'Intérêt Économique) in Toulouse then handles sales, marketing and customer support. The firm has become the second leading producer of commercial aircraft in the world, with 3,915 aircraft in operation by late 2005.

Conclusion

Transnational technology interactions have taken different forms over time. Before the industrial era, the movement of technology (gunpowder from China to Europe, block printing from Asia to Europe, moveable type from Europe) was slow and cautious, driven by individual exchanges. With larger and more expensive systems, transnational entities play bigger roles in developing, financing, transferring, and/or managing technology. Moreover, efforts to create international spaces for economic and technological activities have included the British free-trade movement after 1840, the European Economic Community in the 1950s and the current European Union, and the North American Free Trade Agreement (1994). More recently, inexpensive information technology networks allow telemarketers in Indian call centres to reach the United States and take drive-through orders for McDonald's restaurants. One wonders whether national boundaries are becoming irrelevant to understanding modern technology. The question is sharpened by scholarly attention to innovation in Silicon Valley (California), Route 128 (Boston), and the Research Triangle (North Carolina). Many scholars, most notably Richard Florida and Martin Kenney, now emphasize the region as the appropriate unit of analysis for technology innovation.

Even so, national frames of reference for analysing the development and movement of technology are unlikely to disappear. National legal structures, regulations, and standards retain precedence. Tax policies, investment incentives, research funding, anti-trust, environmental, and patent policies, and educational structures are only a few of the national actions that shape the development and diffusion of technological systems. Even as cultural and social values increasingly reflect transnational influences, other factors that encourage or discourage flows of knowledge, products, and systems remain firmly rooted in nationally derived values. Perhaps the most powerful statements about the lasting influence of national structures over transnational technology movements come from economists of innovation such as Richard Nelson, an early proponent of the national innovation systems concept, which argues innovation remains a nationally bounded phenomenon. Similarly, historian Thomas Hughes stresses the importance of national styles of technological development, while technology studies scholars emphasize that local contexts can transform the same hardware into different sociotechnical systems. Clearly, national boundaries provide neither fixed analytical categories nor impermeable physical borders. But both regional and transnational analyses acquire significance at least in part by reference to the traditional national context for the development and movement of technology. Each perspective adds a layer to our understanding of technology.

Bruce E. Seely

Bibliography

Ahmad A. and Wilkie A. S. 1979. 'Technology transfer in the New International Economic Order: options, obstacles, and dilemmas', in McIntyre J. and Papp D.S. (eds) 1979. *The political economy of international technology transfer*. New York: Quorum, 77–94.

Hughes T. P. 1983. *Networks of power: electrification in Western society, 1880–1930*. Baltimore: Johns Hopkins University Press.

Inkster I. 1991. *Science and technology in history: an approach to industrial development*. New Brunswick: Rutgers University Press.

Jeremy D. J. 1981. *Transatlantic industrial revolution: the diffusion of textile technologies between Britain and America, 1790–1830s*. Cambridge, MA: MIT Press.

Kenney M. and Florida R. L. 2004. *Locating global advantage: industry dynamics in the international economy*. Stanford: Stanford University Press.

Nelson R. R. 1993. *National innovation systems: a comparative analysis*. Oxford and New York: Oxford University Press.

Rogers E. M. 1962. *Diffusion of innovations*. New York: Free Press.

Rosenberg N. 1970. 'Economic development and the transfer of technology: some historical perspectives', *Technology and Culture*, 11, 3, 550–75.

Related essays

architecture; arms trade; arms trafficking; civil engineering works; Cold War; development and growth; developmental assistance; empires and imperialism; engineering; European Union (EU); exile; expositions; fellowships and grants; genetically modified organisms (GMOs); Green Revolution; industrial espionage; industrialization; information technology (IT) offshoring; intergovernmental organizations; International Civil Aviation Organization (ICAO) and International Air Traffic Association (IATA); iron and steel; Japan; Marshall Plan; measurement; modernization theory; organization models; outer space; patents; philanthropic foundations; productivity missions; radio; railways; salt; Samsung; scientific instruments and tools; scientific stations; socialism; technical assistance; technical standardization; telephone and telegraphy; textiles; trade (manufactured goods); underdevelopment; war

Telephone and telegraphy

Telephone and telegraphy are electronic means of communication that carry messages across large distances. Telegraphy brought significant changes to diplomacy, business and journalism in the late 19th century; fibre optics revolutionized international telephone service a century later.

International communications by electric telegraph developed first in Europe and North America in the 1850s and 1860s and spread into the Middle East, Asia and Latin America in the 1870s. The first submarine cable ran under the English Channel in 1851, but the great challenge was to cross the Atlantic. Entrepreneur Cyrus Field of New York was the driving force behind this project. After several failures, Field achieved his goal of connecting Newfoundland and Ireland with

2,000 miles of submerged cable in 1866. This success encouraged British entrepreneur John Pender to lay submarine lines connecting London with India in 1870. Pender's Eastern Extension company brought China, Japan, and Australia into the global network in the early 1870s. At the same time Pender, US, French, and other British entrepreneurs connected Latin America to Europe and the United States. The system relied on submarine cables with a core of copper wire for the transmission of electric current. The copper wire was enclosed in gutta percha (a natural insulation derived from trees in Southeast Asia) and tar-coated hemp wrapped in steel wire for strength. The operator transmitted the signal by raising and lowering the telegraph key thereby breaking and completing the electrical circuit. Guglielmo Marconi, an Italian inventor working in England, introduced a new dimension to telegraphy in the early 1900s through the development of wireless transmission.

While most early submarine cables were operated by private corporations, the involvement of governments increased from the 1880s onward. The Zulus' defeat of a British force at Isandlwana in southern Africa in 1879 resulted in large government subsidies for Pender's West Africa Telegraph and other companies to connect Capetown with London. By 1887 submarine cables ran along both the east and west coasts of Africa. In 1892 the worldwide communications network relied on approximately 150,000 miles of submarine cables. This network played important roles in wars and geopolitical tensions. The Spanish-American War (1898), the Boer War (1899–1903), and the British–French confrontation at Fashoda (1898) involved the use of long-distance telegraphy. After years of indecision, Britain in 1902 spanned the Pacific with cables connecting Australia and East Asia to Canada. British expertise in telegraphic technology was a useful weapon in World War 1. The British Navy severed Germany's submarine cables, and British intelligence intercepted the Zimmermann telegram which contained Germany's unsuccessful enticement to Mexico to enter the war against the United States. The publication of this telegram helped to bring the United States into the war against Germany.

International telegraphy was too expensive for most individuals but became essential for newspapers and other businesses.

By the 1890s newspapers in major cities in Europe and North America featured coverage of events from distant lands such as Argentina, the Sudan and China, sometimes within 24 hours. Three news agencies based in Europe developed a cartel arrangement as early as the 1870s for the collection and dissemination of news. Reuters (British), Havas (French), and Wolff (German) dominated the global network. Reuters concentrated on the British Empire and Asia. Havas covered the French Empire and South America while Wolff reported on Central Europe, Scandinavia, and Russia. Businesses involved in trade and investment also made extensive use of telegraphy. The stock markets in New York, London, and other commercial centres relied on the 'stock ticker' for current prices. Bankers such as the Rothschilds and Barings, and insurance companies, especially Lloyd's of London, monitored their far-flung investments and clients. Coffee importers in the United States established a 'futures market' for that commodity based on information supplied by telegraph from Brazil and other exporting nations.

Because of the rapid expansion of international telegraphy, both governments and private companies wanted a uniform set of regulations for the new industry. The International Telegraph Union, formed in Paris in 1865, established these regulations. Negotiations took place at several conferences in the last decades of the 19th century. At the 1875 meeting in St Petersburg, Russia, delegates established regulations for the cost of sending telegrams and the security of telegram contents. Marconi's new wireless system also required groundrules. The 1906 and 1912 conferences regulated wavelengths to avoid interference. The 1912 conference adopted the easily recognizable SOS code as the universal distress signal in the aftermath of the Titanic disaster. Also, at these conferences governments and major telecommunications companies lobbied vigorously for advantages in this growing industry.

Unlike the telegraph, the telephone required large amounts of electric current to convey the human voice. Alexander Graham Bell invented the telephone in 1876, but reliable transoceanic telephonic communication became a reality only in the 1950s. Between these two dates, however, there were important developments. A telephone cable beneath the English Channel linked

London and Paris in 1891, but Europe did not develop an international telephone system until the 1920s. The technology was available, but lack of cooperation among national governments delayed progress. By the 1920s short-wave radio combined with telephone lines to make transoceanic connections. This system had a worldwide range with calls between Britain and Australia as early as 1924. These calls, however, were expensive and unreliable because of atmospheric interference. The development of high-quality submarine cables made improved transoceanic telephone conversations possible. The first transatlantic telephone cable (TAT-1) opened for business in 1956 with 36 circuits for 36 simultaneous conversations. Improved cables were soon in place. By 1983 TAT-7 carried 4,000 circuits. Altogether, the seven cables had the capacity for 11,000 conversations.

One of the most prominent lines of communication in this era was actually more telegraphic than telephonic. The United States and the Soviet Union established a 'hot line' in the 1960s to improve communications between the superpowers. The public assumed the 'hot line' was telephonic, but communications actually took place by teletype. President Richard Nixon and Premier Leonid Brezhnev used the 'hot line' to reduce international tensions during the 1973 Arab–Israeli War.

Satellite communication added another dimension to international telephony with the launch of Telstar 1 in 1962. Within two decades, 20 civilian communications satellites were in orbit. All but one of these were operated by Intelsat, a private corporation based in Washington, DC. The number of telephone circuits exceeded 50,000. This satellite system had problems, however, including the limited life span of the satellites themselves and occasionally erratic transmission.

The deployment of fibre optic cables in TAT-8 in 1988 constituted the first step in a revolution in international telephony. The tiny transparent glass fibres carried the human voice in pulses of light over large distances at great speeds. After solving initial problems including shark attacks and water seepage, the fibre optic system expanded rapidly to include over 200,000 miles of cable on the ocean floor, creating a worldwide telephone system. One large-scale project, FLAG (Fibre Optic Link Around the Globe) deployed more than 17,000 miles of cable in 1997 containing 600,000 telephone circuits. The number of telephone circuits expanded into the millions, with experimental indication that a pair of fibre optic lines had the potential to carry over 100 million telephone calls simultaneously. By 2001 overexpansion became a problem. Several fibre optic cable companies such as Global Crossing went bankrupt and others experienced financial problems, but the revolutionary worldwide telephone network remained intact.

The fibre optic system made inexpensive telephone calls available to large numbers of users. Therefore, the system supplied the personal and social needs of families and individuals. Businesses and governments, however, also made heavy use of the new system. Alongside the Internet, fibre optic telephone lines had a large impact on the day-to-day operation of corporations. Many companies headquartered in the United States established telephone call centres in India because of lower labour costs. By 2004 an estimated 200,000 English-speaking Indians handled customer calls concerning credit card accounts and computer services.

In contrast to the limited access and high cost of early telegraph services, the worldwide fibre optic system was characterized by open and easy access for users, highly competitive communications companies, and a regulatory environment that encouraged accessibility and low costs. The venerable International Telegraph Union transformed itself into the International Telecommunications Union as soon as 1934, but by the 1990s its powers were reduced when compared to the 1890s. It continued to supply a framework for negotiation and coordination in international communication (including the Internet). The actual regulation of the new global system was accomplished through the communications portion of the General Agreement on Trade in Services (GATS) sponsored by the World Trade Organization (WTO). These agreements emphasized connections between domestic telephone systems and the fibre optic network.

John A. Britton

Bibliography

Headrick D. 1991. *The invisible weapon: telecommunications and international politics,*

1851–1945. Oxford and New York: Oxford University Press.

Hecht J. 2004. *City of light: the story of fibre optics*. Oxford and New York: Oxford University Press.

Hills J. 2002. *The struggle for control of global communications: the formative century*. Urbana: University of Illinois Press.

Hugill P. 1999. *Global communications since 1844: geopolitics and technology*. Baltimore: Johns Hopkins University Press.

Winseck D., Dwayne R. and Pike R. M. 2007. *Communication and empire: media, markets, and globalization, 1860–1930*. Durham, NC: Duke University Press.

Related essays

Cold War; commodity trading; empires and imperialism; financial centres; financial markets; General Agreement on Tariffs and Trade (GATT) / World Trade Organization (WTO); information economy; Internet; mail; Mexican Revolution; news and press agencies; radio; rush migrations; spatial regimes; technologies; war

Temperance

While alcohol consumption and abuse can be found throughout human culture, organized activities to curb or eliminate the drinking of liquor are a relatively modern phenomenon. Changes in distillation processes which made alcoholic beverages much more potent coincided with new industrial and class relations which required a more disciplined labour force while religious developments, especially in Protestant Christianity, shifted the focus for Godly behaviour from institutional authority to self-regulation. Advocating an essential component of Protestant morality that was termed 'the Spirit of Capitalism' by Max Weber, transnational expansion of the temperance movement coincided with the global transactions and expansion of capitalist nations, most notably Great Britain and the United States, during the 19th and early 20th centuries. Temperance movements thrived from the 1830s through to the 1920s, at which time various and connected national efforts at government prohibition of commerce in alcohol failed and were abandoned.

Temperance movements have been strongest in Protestant countries, where millennialist theologies encouraged perfection of both the individual and of society and the values of rationality and restraint pointed away from the fleeting transcendence and permanent enslavement provided by alcohol. The United States has the most complex, well-documented national history of temperance movements. It is also the birthplace of the Order of Good Templars (New York State, 1851), the largest, most inclusive and most successful self-help fellowship of the 19th century.

In the US, the Order laid the basis both for local lodges of self-help and for political efforts at legal regulation. It also flourished later in the 19th century as an international organization, notably on sailing routes travelled by temperate sailors and captains, beginning in Canada and other Commonwealth countries, spreading from there to South America, Asia and Africa, eventually claiming over 3 million members worldwide. This success owed a lot to its flexibility to local conditions and social divides. For instance, despite a theoretical dedication to racial inclusiveness, the US Order was unable to accommodate whites and people of colour in integrated groups, and this caused a schism in the international order. Conversely, in the Cape Province of South Africa, a spin-off named the Independent Order of True Templars was a successful temperance organization conducted largely under the leadership of indigenous Africans. It was especially successful in the Nordic European countries, where its temperance concerns coincided with thriving workers' and socialist movements also disturbed about the undermining effects of drink on the labouring classes.

Temperance methods alternated between moral suasion, usually rooted in communities of drinkers, and legal coercion, directed by elites who sought to control the drinking of underclasses. The short-lived power of moral suasion crusades and the difficulty of adhering to the pledge of abstention led to the first great American experiment in government prohibition. Beginning in Maine in 1851, state after state passed laws prohibiting the production and sale of any alcoholic beverage. The rise in European immigration in the late 19th century added a new impetus to the drive for legal prohibition, as native-born Americans identified excessive drinking and its attendant social costs with rapidly expanding German, Irish and other immigrant, especially Catholic, cultures, which were relatively tolerant of alcohol consumption. The most important Catholic temperance movement began in Ireland, under the leadership of Father Theobald Mathew. Starting in the 1840s, he created a temperance ministry with decidedly nationalist, anti-British dimensions. Father Mathew eventually claimed millions of followers, as much as half the population of Ireland, and travelled to the United States, where he claimed over half a million converts, many of them Irish immigrants. The Catholic temperance tradition which he began outlasted his own ministry.

Women participated in temperance activities throughout the 19th century. Women regarded drink and drinking establishments as the antithesis of the middle-class Protestant home, in which a pure and pious wife, freed from the bread-winning task, guided the moral progress of her family. In 1874, middle-class American churchwomen, frustrated at male domination of temperance activity, started an independent organization to reflect their own interests, the Woman's Christian Temperance Union (WCTU). In the US, its base was always among the middle class and native-born. Immigrant or non-white women joined but they did so in separate, semi-autonomous chapters.

During the last quarter of the 19th century, the WCTU became the most conspicuous force not only in temperance but in organized women's activism in the United States. Under the leadership of Frances E. Willard, the WCTU skillfully employed 'Christian' and 'temperance' frameworks to shield women's social and political activism from public criticism. Willard encouraged WCTU members to participate in causes as bold as labour reform and in activities as masculine as electoral politics. The WCTU thrived in the western and midwestern US and once it went international, in other frontier situations as well. In Australia and New Zealand, for instance, women's temperance activism was opposed to bachelor worker frontier culture and supported both a respectable domesticity and women's greater roles in the public sphere. Notably temperance activists led the early and successful drives there for women's suffrage.

The WCTU was propelled by the evangelical impulse abroad. It first crossed national borders by expanding into Britain and its colonies. In Canada, for instance, the WCTU was strongest in the maritime provinces while making very little headway in Quebec. In 1884, the formation of a World's Woman's Christian Temperance Union (WWCTU) marked the start of more systematic efforts at transnational outreach. The WCTU expanded not only into Europe, but also Asia. Willard's encounter with opium dens in Chinese immigrant communities on the US Pacific coast in 1883 triggered her interest in Asia. Ian Tyrrell, historian of the WWCTU, links this westward expansion to the attraction among Asian women of both the organization's implicit 'Americanism' and the opportunities it provided for them to undertake projects of larger public significance. To build its Asian constituency, the WWCTU dispatched 'round-the-world missionaries'. Mary C. Leavitt was the first one: she began her globe-circling voyage from San Francisco in 1884, and came back in 1891. While such women spread Protestant and Anglo-American values they themselves were also made more cosmopolitan by the range of cultures and religions to which they were exposed. By 1895, there were WWCTU affiliates outside of Europe in China, Burma, Malaysia, India, Chile, Madagascar, Newfoundland, Egypt, Argentina, Brazil, Norway, Uruguay and Mexico. The WWCTU's membership reached its peak in the late 1920s.

In the United States, Australia, South Africa, and elsewhere, temperance-minded European settlers attempted to control the access to imported alcohol which ravaged, displaced and deracinated native cultures. Occasionally, as among the Iroquois in the US in the early 19th century, these missionary efforts generated strong native support. In general, however, temperance movements initiated by non-Europeans themselves have been few. In Japan, progressive men took up the cause to facilitate the participation of their nation in global capitalism and in order to become a world power. Ironically, they, rather than Japanese women, were the major native allies for the Anglo-American WWCTU female missionaries. They hoped that temperance would assist Japan to become a strong, modern nation, by enhancing both the health of the people and the industrial productivity of the economy. In 1922, in pursuit of greater military strength, Japanese temperance leaders advocated the passage of a national law to prohibit minors from drinking, the better to become physically fit soldiers and advance the Japanese empire.

By contrast, on the Subcontinent, temperance was attractive as a means to fight for and win independence from British imperial control. Influenced by scientific temperance while in England, in 1921 Gandhi initiated an Indian movement to boycott saloons, both to deny the British the income from liquor taxes and to establish a standard for self-control and upright living for citizens of a future independent India. Under his leadership, the temperance campaign built mass support for the Indian nationalist movement and popularized the image of British imperialism as morally corrupting. Although the WWCTU was temporarily successful in connecting with Gandhi's campaign, the differences between the two were ultimately determinative: nationalist vs internationalist, anti-government vs prohibitionist, Christian vs Hindu/Muslim.

From the early 20th century, prohibitory efforts became more prominent. In the US, the Anti Saloon League (ASL) surpassed the WCTU and won a nationwide ban on the sale of alcoholic beverages through a constitutional amendment. During the World War I era, other experiments in national government restriction of alcohol were attempted, for instance in pre-revolutionary Russia and in Norway. All of these ambitious attempts at government prohibition at the national level proved almost impossible to enforce and were eventually abandoned, including in the US. These failures mark the end of the classic age of temperance movements, although in their wake a new, more psychologically oriented approach to alcohol control emerged to achieve extraordinary global breath, Alcoholic Anonymous.

Ellen Carol DuBois
Rumi Yasutake

Bibliography

Blocker J. S., Fahey D. M. and Tyrrell, I. R. (eds) 2003. *Alcohol and temperance in modern society*, 2 vols. Santa Barbara: ABC-Clio.

Tyrrell I. 1991. *Woman's world/woman's empire: the Woman's Christian Temperance Union in international perspective, 1880–1930*. Chapel Hill: University of North Carolina Press.

Related essays

drink; drugs (illicit); empire and migration; evangelicalism; Gandhi, Mohandas Karamchand; international non-governmental organizations (INGOs); Japan; missionaries; women's movements

Temporary migrations

Temporary transnational migration, broadly characterized by its transitory and circular nature, is an important part of global mobility.

Seasonal migrants who leave their homes each year, entrepreneurs who spend their careers working overseas, soldiers, diplomats and students are all instrumental in creating complex global webs linking people, goods and ideas. Although scholars and policy makers have studied the costs and benefits of temporary labour in both sending and receiving countries, few have considered these workers of the world in conjunction with missionaries, soldiers, government officials as forming a distinctive system. Temporary transnational migration must be understood on its own terms by examining its impact on both sending and receiving countries and its critical role in the construction and maintenance of transnational communities.

Temporary migrants comprised a significant number of the people on the move from 1850 onwards. Nearly 80 per cent of the migrants who left the Indian subcontinent to work on the sugar, tea and rubber plantations of Southeast Asia and the Caribbean as indentured labourers between 1820 and 1920 returned to their villages. Over 80 per cent of the skilled stonemasons from the Valle Cervo region in Northern Italy who went to work in the United States, China, Panama and Egypt came home. Recent studies have shown that roughly half of all Italians who migrated to North America in the 19th century returned. Similar rates mark 19th-century Portuguese migration to Brazil. An estimated 45 per cent of European workers who migrated to the United States in the 1890s returned.

In the 20th century temporary migration continued to grow. Guest-worker programs, Cold War diplomacy and dismantlement of formal empire encouraged new forms of temporary transnational migration. Since the 1990s, developed and developing countries both report sharp increases in temporary labour migrations. Between 1998 and 2001, Japan reported a 40 per cent increase in temporary workers. Oil-producing countries in the Middle East and Western Asia have attracted over a million temporary workers from Eastern and Southern Asia. Since 1991, there has also been an increase in the deployment of troops – rarely categorized as migrants but doing temporary work nevertheless – from the US, Europe and Asia in Africa, Asia and the Middle East.

Sojourners comprise a disparate group but two types of temporary migrations predominate: labour and political. Temporary labour migration encompasses all men and women seeking work abroad. They are the largest contingent and include unskilled workers, international merchants, financiers, corporate managers, engineers. Political migration includes government officials, missionaries and soldiers and students. These transients too are workers but unlike labour migrants they are employees of institutions and organizations based in the homeland. They are part of a vast bureaucratic network that configures global economic and political power.

We can categorize both forms of temporary migration as intentional but differing over time and space. Sojourners leave with the intention to return home when they have saved enough to buy a house, land or open a business, or when their employers call them home. Although personal or political circumstances can change their plans, at the time of departure they dream of homecoming. Time defines the temporality and circularity of these migrations. Whether migrants leave for months or years, their time abroad is limited. Agricultural workers from Morocco who travel to Spain to work in the fields for a few months, like the British engineers who spend years overseeing large-scale construction projects, trace circular paths through the world. Temporary migration also collapses boundaries between villages, cities and states.

Gender distinctions mark temporary transnational migration. Until the 1970s, men dominated temporary migrations. Between 1909 and 1928, twice as many men as women emigrated. Among returners, men outnumbered women by a factor of seven. Guestworker programmes targeted single men. The *Bracero* programme, started in the 1940s to recruit Mexican workers to work in the United States, never sought women. In recent years there has been a noticeable shift in the gender composition of temporary labour migration. Since the early 1980s, women from South and Southeast Asia have outnumbered men seeking temporary work in Europe and the Middle East. Women were 65 per cent of the Indonesians working abroad in the 1980s. In the late 19th century the agents of formal imperialism – colonial administrators, soldiers and missionaries – were also mostly men. Women travelling as teachers, nurses, explorers and wives were a distinct minority. Today the diplomatic corps and armed services continue to be dominated by men. In the United States, men comprise 65 per cent of

the foreign-service officers stationed abroad and 85 per cent of all military personnel.

Global wars also shape temporary migration. Great Britain and Italy passed laws restricting migration in 1914 and 1915 respectively, and the United States followed suit with the Immigration Act of 1917. These laws sharpened distinctions between permanent and temporary migration. In the US, the Secretary of Labor quickly used his power to waive certain requirements for immigration to admit migrants from Mexico, the Bahamas and Canada for farm work. During the interwar years European countries also began to recruit temporary workers and limit permanent migration. France implemented a guest-worker programme in the early 1920s, recruiting Spaniards to work in the vineyards and farms. During World War 2, governments turned to temporary migration programmes to ease wartime labour shortages. The US expanded its labour recruitment programme in Mexico and the Caribbean. The German government instituted forced-labour programmes, drafting workers from Eastern Europe and France to work in the factories and fields. The post-1945 wars of independence brought home thousands of colonial officials, their support staff and colonial industrial elite. In 1954, 70,000 French migrants returned from Vietnam in the wake of the military defeat. The Algerian military victory in 1962 sparked a mass return of French-Algerians.

Although sharing general characteristics, labour and political migrations differ. Temporary labour migration is grounded in collective family strategies of economic and social improvement. Transient workers remain financially and emotionally enmeshed in their home communities and remain on the margins of host societies. Their transitory status is immediately visible. When Turkish men arrived in West Germany in the 1960s they found housing near their work rather than in residential areas. They saved on rent by sharing rooms with as many of their fellow countrymen as possible, even sleeping in shifts. Language and customs heightened their geographic isolation from the quotidian rhythms of German cities. At that time, few learned German or participated in local politics or culture. They came to Germany to work and save money.

Temporary migrations altered the physical appearance and social structures of the homelands. Returning migrants did not just return to their old lives but brought in new attitudes and tastes. In early-20th-century rural Italy, local gentry complained about returners who had lost their deferential attitudes and moved through the community with greater self-confidence and dignity. Returners ate the foods of the wealthy (meat and fish), and dressed in the latest urban fashions. They invested their savings in larger modern houses and filled them with new appliances. Transnational migration also redefined gender roles. In rural Sicily, male emigration enabled women to invest in houses and children's education and encouraged them to develop independent relationships with the state. In contemporary Mexico remittances enrich family budgets giving women a greater say in the allocation of money. The absence of their husbands offers women the opportunity to take on new economic roles; wives of migrants find part-time jobs or open their own businesses. The gendered nature of temporary transnational labour migration can also generate family conflict. In Kenyan families migrating husbands frequently wish to sell off a portion of the family's land to finance trips, while wives resist any such sale, seeing the land as the source of their livelihood.

Temporary political migrants are more influenced by global political economies than by familial strategies of material improvement. Underlying their diverse motives (financial concerns, personal ambition or adventure), colonial migrants contributed to a larger mission of securing markets and profits or 'civilizing' the uncivilized. Overseas, these men regulated sexual, gender, and racial systems in ways that undermined existing arrangements. In India and Africa, the British imposed their understanding of marriage as an unbreakable union between one man and one woman on cultures that rejected notions of life-long monogamy. In 1891 colonial administrators faced stiff opposition from the Hindu majority when they attempted to increase the legal age of marriage for girls from ten to twelve years of age. Colonial migrants regulated work to create a pool of dutiful, obedient wage workers, premised on the notion of the male breadwinner. These regulations excluded women from paid work. Colonial labour regulations legitimized racial hierarchies by stipulating that no European could work for a non-European, ensuring that Indians and Africans remained in the lowest-

paying jobs. Sexual and gender concerns equally shaped military migrants' relations with natives. After World War 2, the way US soldiers viewed German women, seeing them as either whores or maids, shaped notions of femininity and masculinity during Germany's reconstruction.

Two groups of political migrants have had a particularly significant impact on the sending societies: students and soldiers. In the early part of the 20th century colonized elites sent their sons to study at Oxford or the Sorbonne. Schooled in notions of Western ideas of democracy, self-government and liberty, these young men experienced daily forms of discrimination that highlighted their status as dependants. Both Gandhi and Sun Yat-Sen identified their university experiences abroad as influential in the development of their nationalist movements. The position of students among temporary migrants appears to be shifting. Increasingly students are moving as workers, feeding growing cosmopolitan networks of skilled professionals. However, they continue to influence homeland politics. Military migrations had a similar effect on sending communities. In the summer of 1944 Black Africans comprised the largest number of men in the Free French Army. Unlike in World War 1, the French recruited Africans as fellow citizens, appealing to their patriotism, and their place as citizen-soldiers. Once the war was over, they were not discharged and sent home, but placed in temporary camps. Such treatment sparked riots and protests among the veterans, undermining their sense of national allegiance. Although many soldiers continued to swear loyalty to the state that paid their pensions, the experiences of soldier migrants limited the power of the French to define Africans as political dependants and social inferiors.

From the perspective of the migrant, the differentiation of temporary from permanent migration often seems arbitrary; distinctions between sojourners and settlers are often so blurred as to become invisible. Recognizing temporary transnational migration as a distinctive system nevertheless offers new ways of understanding migrant networks. It expands the definition of migrant to include soldiers and diplomats as well as workers and makes visible the deeply gendered nature of transnational mobility. Focusing on sojourners highlights the ways migration redefines relations between global, national and local communities, fundamentally altering social and political relations.

Linda Reeder

Bibliography

Brettell C. 1986. *Men who migrate, women who wait: population and history in a Portuguese parish*. Princeton: Princeton University Press.

Chant S. (ed.) 1992. *Gender and migration in developing countries*. London: Bellhaven.

Gabaccia D. R. 2000. *Italy's many diasporas*. Seattle: University of Washington Press.

Hoerder D. 2002. *Cultures in contact: world migrations in the second millennium*. Durham, NC: Duke University Press.

Lucassen J. and Lucassen L. (eds) 1997. *Migration, migration history, history: old paradigms and new perspectives*. Bern: Peter Lang.

Page Moch L. 2003. *Moving Europeans: migration in Western Europe since 1650*, 2nd ed. Bloomington: Indiana University Press.

Reeder L. 2003. *Widows in white: gender, migration and the transformation of rural Italian women, Sicily 1880–1920*. Toronto: University of Toronto Press.

Special Issue, Winter 1986. 'Temporary worker programs: mechanisms, conditions, consequences', *International Migration Review*, 20, 4.

Related essays

agriculture; body shopping; border commuters; civil engineering works; contract and indentured labourers; decolonization; developmental assistance; diasporas; domestic service; executives and professionals; exile; family migrations; fellowships and grants; Gandhi, Mohandas Karamchand; gender and sex; guestworkers; intergovernmental organizations; international non-governmental organizations (INGOs); international schools; international students; marriage; missionaries; oil; remittances; steamships; war; wine

Terrorism

Efforts to define terrorism or identify groups or behaviours as terrorist have generated controversy and debate. Most national governments embrace a definition of terrorism like the one adopted by the US Department of State ('premeditated, politically motivated violence perpetrated against non-combatant targets by subnational groups or clandestine agents, usually intended to influence an audience') and consider such activity illegal and immoral. Political leaders sympathetic to resistance movements among dispossessed peoples, by contrast, justify violent means by revolutionary groups against imperial structures. Yet other observers define terrorism as any act or threat of violence designed to achieve a political objective, thus erasing distinctions between state and non-state actors and viewing powerful governments like the United States as leading practitioners of terrorism.

Scholars also disagree deeply about the definition of terrorism. Alex Schmid identified more than one hundred proposed definitions of terrorism, while Walter Laqueur concluded that the effort to define terrorism is of such high contention and limited intellectual utility that is should be suspended. Aiming for a practical definition, Bruce Hoffman (1998) identified signature attributes that collectively qualify behaviour as terrorism: political motivations, the use or threat of violence, the intention to gain psychological effect, and actions by a non-state, yet organized group.

Violence that might qualify as terrorism has been practised worldwide since ancient times, for domestic and international aims. According to Hoffman, the concept was popularized during the French Revolution, when a revolutionary regime practised the 'Reign of Terror' of 1793–94, a systematic use of lethal violence against domestic opponents designed to achieve psychological and political effects. In the 19th century, European nationalists embraced terrorism as a legitimate means to achieve favourable publicity and mass support of their political objectives. One Italian extremist argued that such activities constituted 'propaganda by deed'. Such a philosophy inspired a host of rebel groups, including anti-Tsarist rebels in Imperial Russia; Armenians who resisted Ottoman rule; Macedonians who sought independence from Greece, Bulgaria, and Serbia; and the Bosnians who assassinated Austro-Hungarian Archduke Franz Ferdinand in Sarajevo in 1914 and thereby triggered World War 1. Anarchist ideology that embraced violence for political purposes inspired Hungarian expatriate Leon Czolgosz to assassinate US President William McKinley in 1901. In the early 20th century, terrorism reverted to a statist technique as powerful governments used violence to suppress indigenous and subject peoples.

The modern debate over terrorism was shaped by the global dynamics of the late 20th century. Anti-colonial rebels around the world used violence to achieve political independence from Western empires, resulting in the creation of Kenya, Algeria, and many other states. In 1948, Israeli extremists assassinated United Nations mediator Folke Bernadotte to stymie a peace plan that proposed unfavourable territorial terms. By the 1970s, such rebel groups as the Irish Republican Army (IRA) and the Palestine Liberation Organization (PLO) employed violent means to achieve political aims (vis-à-vis Britain and Israel, respectively). By the 1980s, Syria, Libya, and Iran sponsored acts of terrorism by clandestine agents and subnational groups in order to achieve political objectives at the expense of nations with superior conventional forms of power. Western governments such as the United States, filtering their worldviews through the lens of the Cold War, tended to consider these violent movements as pawns or partners of the Soviet Union.

Terrorist groups lacking international political objectives also emerged in the late 20th century, from the Italian Red Brigades to the Peruvian Shining Path. Meanwhile, non-state entities involved in criminal activity, such as drug cartels in Latin America, used terrorism to resist law enforcement and other exercises of authority by national governments. In addition, the scholar Adrian Guelke (2006) notes the use of 'spoiler violence' by those who opposed peace processes in Israel-Palestine, South Africa, and Northern Ireland. Small-scale strikes among ethnic and political groups with scores to settle often appeared as terrorism even though they had limited political significance in the international context.

But even these terrorist activities displayed a transnational identity. The founder of Shining Path, for example, visited China during the Cultural Revolution and received training in Chinese ideology, propaganda, organizational tactics, and violence, even though Shining Path seemingly pursued domestic objectives. Libya's Muammar Qaddafi, moreover, reportedly supported and encouraged such terrorist groups as the PLO, the IRA, the Euskadi Ta Askatasuna (Basque Homeland and Freedom, ETA), and the Red Brigades – the last of which was also believed to have ties to France, Germany, the PLO, and Eastern European satellites of the Soviet Union. Iran was implicated in Hizbollah's taking of hostages in Lebanon in the 1980s and in an attack on a US military base in Saudi Arabia in 1996; and it financially bolstered the Islamic Resistance Movement (Hamas or 'zeal' in Arabic) after it won control of the Palestinian parliament in early 2006.

Some scholars consider the PLO as the first truly transnational terrorist group. By the 1980s, Hoffman reports, some 40 terrorist groups from around the world had sent fighters to PLO training sites in Jordan, Lebanon, and Yemen, had taken advantage of PLO weapons sources, or otherwise had collaborated with the PLO. In exchange, the PLO garnered political recognition, financial payments (including fees collected for military training), and tactical support in terrorist strikes from non-Palestinian accomplices.

Scholars have identified a complex of several factors that collectively encouraged persons to engage in terrorism in recent decades. Economic factors are crucial. Poverty and inequity breed envy and a sense of injustice that motivate acts of extremism. On a deeper level, economic change (including foundational developments such as industrialization, urbanization, and globalization) result in instability and uncertainty that undermine popular faith in governments and other traditional institutions. A mixture of a swollen, youthful population and a stagnant economy is a recipe for extremism. Economic development and globalization often raise expectations of progress which, if unfulfilled, draw attention to deprivation and trigger violent backlash. Political conditions reinforce economic factors as sparks of terrorism. Any perceived, major political injustice – ranging from colonialism to abuse of authority – might trigger a terrorist response.

Religion has also provided a powerful motive for terrorism since the 1980s. Religious terrorists are driven to action by a sense of theological or moral duty, a perception of divine calling, or a feeling of piety, and they tend to inflict more massive destruction and casualties than other terrorists. Religious terrorists found inspiration in all the world's major religions. In the late 20th century, for example, several American Christian extremists engaged in acts of terrorism against domestic institutions that offended their conservative values, such as abortion clinics. By contrast, religious terrorism became associated with Islam more than any other religion. Secular, political Islam was discredited by the disastrous Arab losses in the Arab–Israeli War of 1967 and by the failure of the PLO to achieve its goals vis-à-vis Israel. The Iranian Revolution of 1979, the assassination of Anwar Sadat in 1981, and the resistance movement against the Soviet occupation of Afghanistan in the 1980s inspired a fundamentalist ideology that gave religious sanction to political violence. Islamists preached a utopian vision of a God-centred political order that would restore righteous living and replace the repressive, secular regimes of the region. Their ideology embraced a historical view of Western repression of Muslim peoples, manifest in the Crusades and, more recently, in the West's defeat of the Ottoman Empire in World War I, capture of Ottoman territory as mandates, creation of Israel, and support of secular regimes. Propagandists readily blamed the United States and the international Jewish community for the suffering of Muslims everywhere.

In 1987–88, for example, Hamas took root among Palestinians who lost confidence in the ability of the PLO to achieve Palestinian national aspirations. Inspired by religious rhetoric and practice, Hamas organized a wave of violence against Israelis in the late 1980s intifada, the mid-1990s wave of suicide bombings that helped derail the Israeli–Palestinian peace process, and the second intifada of the early 2000s that spawned deep disharmony between Israel and the Palestinians of the occupied territories. After winning parliamentary elections in January 2006, Hamas also secured control of Gaza after battling the secular Palestine Authority. Under the hammer of Israeli military power, Hamas militants breached a wall along the Egyptian border in January 2008, to enable embattled Gazans to take brief refuge in Egypt.

Finally, some scholars suggest that a massive cultural conflict stimulated the rise of Islamic terrorism against the West in the late 20th century. Bernard Lewis and Samuel P. Huntington, for example, suggest that the expansion of modern, Western culture triggered a violent backlash among radical Muslims who feared subjugation and loss of identity in a global system dominated by the West. Many observers have interpreted this 'clash of civilizations' thesis as an explanation of the roots of modern terrorism. Yet sceptics of the Lewis-Huntington argument counter that it neglects the economic and political roots of Islamic terrorism, ignores the diversity of ideologies within the Islamic world, and overemphasizes the longevity of Western modernity. Mahmood Mamdani (2004) stresses that such secular ideologists as Muhammad Iqbal of colonial India and Sayyid Qutb of Egypt provided much of the inspiration for political Islam.

In addition to these direct causes of terrorism, certain structures of modernity enabled terrorist groups to operate across national borders more freely in recent decades than previously. For example, the Cold War left the world awash in weaponry – much of it, ironically, manufactured and exported by the United States – making it relatively easy for non-state groups to acquire effective firepower. Globalization opened borders to the relatively free transit of terrorists and their weapons. A new, global media network projected images of Western wealth and moral laxity, which bred resentment and abhorrence among conservative communities around the world. The same global media network also instantly broadcasted news of terrorist attacks, which served the psychological warfare objectives of the perpetrators. By the 1990s, the rise of electronic communications including cell phones, satellite phones, and the Internet fostered instant communication across national boundaries. Finally, Western security systems that had been shaped since 1945 to confront the Soviet adversary were unprepared to meet the threats posed by shadowy, non-state actors who defied diplomatic and legal conventions. Terrorists proved effective at finding vulnerabilities in Western embassies, business assets, and civilian airliners, striking on terms of their own choosing, and thereby neutralizing the military superiority of powerful states.

Although the number of terrorist incidents worldwide declined from the 1980s to the 1990s, the attacks that occurred tended to be more deadly, politically spectacular, religion-inspired, and related to the Middle East. Hamas developed the technique of suicide bombing against Israel, Iran backed Hizbollah fighters in Lebanon, Islamic Jihad and Jemaah Islamiya launched a campaign of terrorism against the government of Egypt that claimed 1,000 victims in 1992–97, and Islamists plotted to overthrow the secular government in

Pakistan and the pro-Western monarchy in Saudi Arabia. The Taliban seized control of Afghanistan in 1996, practised ultraconservative Islamic law, and gave sanctuary to Osama bin Laden. By the late 1990s, bin Laden essentially declared war on Saudi Arabia and the United States and called on members of his al-Qaeda network to kill Americans whenever possible. Al-Qaeda perpetrated a series of attacks on American interests, including the bombing of the World Trade Center in New York City in 1993, the bombings of the US Embassies in Kenya and Tanzania in 1998, the attack on the USS Cole in Yemen in 2000, and the notorious 9/11 attacks on New York City and Washington, DC, in 2001.

Western officials responded to Islamic terrorism in a variety of ways. Transnational responses included diplomatic policies to isolate extremists, economic sanctions against regimes cavorting with terrorism, and cooperative initiatives in law enforcement, propaganda, and public relations. After 9/11, the United States led an international coalition that occupied Afghanistan, dismantled the Taliban regime, scattered the al-Qaeda leadership, and empowered a new government. The United States also issued joint declarations with several countries that condemned terrorism as a threat to universal human values.

The United States also pursued its opposition to terrorism on more unilateral bases. In the 1990s, it launched covert operations to arrest or kill adversaries, and military reprisals against terrorist groups. After 9/11, the United States also invaded Iraq and deposed Saddam Hussein, on a flimsy pretext that his regime fostered terrorism. Several dozen states officially participated in the invasion and occupation, although the operations were clearly dominated and directed by the United States. While certain allies such as Britain showed steady support of US objectives, Spain withdrew from participation under the duress of terrorist strikes at home. Meanwhile, many other countries criticized the American decision to invade and deplored US tactics including abuse of prisoners, lengthy detention of suspects, and complicity in if not practice of torture. Such disputes among allied powers limited the transnational extent of the Western response to modern terrorism.

The US invasion of Iraq eventually sparked a resistance movement that used terrorism against US forces and the Iraqi government established under US auspices. The legacy of 9/11 and the difficulties faced in Iraq indicated the perils of dealing with the scourge of terrorism.

Peter L. Hahn

Bibliography
Guelke A. 2006. *Terrorism and global disorder: political violence in the contemporary world.* London: I.B. Tauris.
Hoffman B. 1998. *Inside terrorism.* New York: Columbia University Press.
Kepel G. 2002. *Jihad: the trail of political Islam,* Roberts A. F. (trans.). Cambridge, MA: Harvard University Press.
Mamdani M. 2004. *Good Muslim, Bad Muslim: America, the Cold War, and the roots of terror.* New York: Pantheon.
Sabasteanski A. (ed.) 2005. *Patterns of global terrorism, 1985–2004: US Department of State documents and supplementary materials.* Great Barrington: Berkshire.
Townshend C. 2002. *Terrorism: a very short introduction.* Oxford and New York: Oxford University Press.

Related essays
anarchism; arms trafficking; civilizations; Cold War; crime; empires and imperialism; information economy; Internet; Maoism; Muslim networks; nation and state; Pax Americana; religious fundamentalism; September 11, 2001; war; Westernization

Textiles

The role of textiles and clothing in transnational history is a complex story of economic forces, trade flows, political intrigue, and moral quandary. This story is ongoing, with many of the themes that arose during the industrial revolution still at the centre of discussion and debate. Since the mid 19th century, economic forces have spurred the production of textiles and apparel to seek out lower and lower wages, and these forces have led to a rapid spread of production to developing countries. However, the resulting loss of employment in rich countries has resulted in a strong political backlash that has long complicated international relations. The tension between richer and poor countries permeates the transnational history of this industry.

The world's first factories were cotton textile factories, and the industrial revolution itself is largely the story of the development of this industry. The industrial revolution was ignited by a series of technical innovations in Britain that allowed the large-scale mechanization of weaving and spinning cotton. Interestingly, although economists often argue that free trade among countries will spur innovation and productivity, it was in fact protectionism that ignited the British industrial revolution.

British consumers in the late 1700s and early 1800s were clamouring for the light and colorful cotton prints from India, and the resulting hardships for the British wool industry led the wool interests to convince the British Parliament to impose strict limits on the import of cotton cloth. The result would be the first among a long history of unintended consequences of textile and clothing trade policy: by banning imports, the Parliament did little to save the wool industry but instead inadvertently created a protected incubator for Britain to develop its own cotton textile industry.

The British cotton textile industry dominated the world market until the early 1900s. During the first half of the 19th century cotton textiles comprised nearly half of Britain's exports. In peak years, Britain supplied nearly half of the world's consumption of cotton cloth.

The economic success of the British textile industry was predicated on a variety of moral failures, however, especially in its transnational relationships. Perhaps most significantly, textiles were an important component of the 'triangular' slave trade in the 1800s, whereby Britain sold textiles to Africa in exchange for slaves, and slaves to the Americas in exchange for raw cotton, which was in turn grown primarily on slave plantations. The juxtaposition of export competitiveness with issues of human rights continues to permeate the textile and apparel trade today, as ongoing concerns about apparel 'sweatshops' make clear.

By the late 1800s, however, Britain's primacy in this industry had begun to fade as the global 'race to the bottom' accelerated. This tendency of low-end manufacturing – particularly in textiles and apparel – to seek out the lowest wages around the globe remains both pervasive and controversial. World-class cotton textile production soon emerged in Continental Europe and in New England, but soon thereafter lower wages in the American South had begun to topple these new competitors as well. By the early 1900s, Japan had emerged as the pre-eminent producer and exporter of textiles, but by the 1960s, the 'Asian tigers' (Hong Kong, Korea and Taiwan) were dominant.

Today, China and India are the world's largest and most competitive producers of textiles and clothing. However, rising costs along the east coast of China are spurring the development of the industry in newer competitor countries such as Vietnam.

By its very nature, the global race-to-the-bottom phenomenon involves the demise of the textile and apparel industries in richer countries and their emergence in poorer countries. The ongoing transnational challenges involve the loss of employment in richer countries and issues of labour exploitation in poor countries. The textile industries of most countries have developed with the benefit of well developed protectionism, and this protectionism has often been far more extensive than that afforded other industries. In general, the protection afforded the industry is the result of the significant political power of the textile interests, which is in turn the result of the geographic concentration of the industry. Though fading, for example, textile 'mill towns' continue to dot the American South, and this geographic concentration results in significant political power for the industry.

Attempts to preserve and protect these industries in richer countries have had complicated and unintended consequences in international trade and political relationships. Following World War 2, the American textile industry was successful in limiting cotton textile imports from Japan, although the import restraints were called 'voluntary'. However, rather than protect the American industry, these import limits in effect provided further impetus for the development of the industry in Hong Kong, Korea, and Taiwan. Limits were soon imposed on imports from other countries as well. Beginning in 1974, world trade in textiles and clothing was governed by the Multi Fibre Arrangement (MFA). This arrangement was a framework that allowed countries to limit the import of hundreds of textile and apparel products from dozens of countries. In effect, the MFA was used to protect the textile and apparel industries in the wealthy countries of Europe and the United States from lower-priced imports. Though the MFA was designed as a temporary measure, it was extended four times and remained in place until 1995. In 1995, during the Uruguay Round of world trade talks, the MFA was replaced by the Agreement on Textiles and Clothing (ATC), which called for quantitative limits on the imports of these goods to be phased out over a ten-year period ending in 2005. Import quotas on textile and clothing from all World Trade Organization (WTO) member countries were lifted on 1 January of that year.

Though developing countries had lobbied for the end of quotas, many began to have second thoughts as the end of the quotas neared. While the import quotas had limited poor countries' ability to sell to the US and Europe, the quotas had also kept the large and competitive producers – first Japan, then Hong Kong, Korea, and Taiwan, and finally India and China – from dominating the market. In fact, it became clear that for many small countries such as Sri Lanka and Mauritius, the textile and apparel industries were significant beneficiaries of the quota system, and perhaps had even been created by the system.

With the lifting of all quotas in early 2005, the long-feared 'China surge' materialized, with Chinese imports of many categories of textiles and apparel into both the US and Europe rising by over 100 per cent with the demise of the quotas. The political reaction in the US and Europe was swift, and quotas were quickly reimposed on China until 2007 for Europe and 2008 for the US.

Many view the textile and apparel trade policy in Europe and the US as somewhat of an embarrassment, as these policies often violate the free-trade rhetoric of the richer countries, and are also inconsistent with the broad sweeps of trade liberalization that have been in effect for most industries in the post-World War 2 era. Indeed, the textile and apparel trade regime has largely developed outside the normal channels of trade relations. As President Richard Nixon once mentioned, 'textiles are a special case'. The MFA in particular was a set of wide-ranging exceptions to both the letter and spirit of world trade rules. Although the US and Europe have since World War 2 been strong supporters of free trade, it was politically impossible for policy makers in the wealthy countries to proceed with trade liberalization without making special exceptions for the powerful textile industry. In the US and Europe, perhaps only steel and agriculture have enjoyed similar protections from the overall trend of trade liberalization.

Since the industrial revolution, the textile and apparel industries have been associated with the evils of the 'sweatshop' and these concerns continue to pervade the industry today. Whether in 18th-century England, 19th-century Massachusetts or 21st-century China, the industry's workforce has been dominated by young women from the rural areas. In each of these cases, the textile and apparel industry has not only ignited the process of industrialization, but has also ignited corollary political and labour movements geared toward protecting and expanding the rights of workers. The anti-sweatshop movement was a significant force in the protests against globalization that stymied the meetings of the World Trade Organization, the International Monetary Fund, and the World Bank during the period 1999–2003. Since the mid 1990s, most global apparel firms have instituted wide-ranging practices of monitoring and reporting to protect their international supply chains from charges of exploitative labour practices.

Pietra Rivoli

Bibliography

Kunz G. I. and Garner M. B. 2007. *Going global: the textile and apparel industry.* New York: Fairchild.

Rivoli P. 2006. *The travels of a T-shirt in the global economy.* Hoboken: Wiley.

Rose M. 2006. *Firms, networks and business values.* Cambridge: Cambridge University Press.

Rosen E. I. 2002. *Making sweatshops: the globalization of the US apparel industry.* Berkeley: University of California Press.

Related essays

childhood; children's rights; dress; fashion; General Agreement on Tariffs and Trade (GATT) / World Trade Organization (WTO); industrialization; iron and steel; labour standards; silk; sports gear and apparel; technologies; trade; trade (manufactured goods); trade agreements

Thailand and sex tourism *See* Tourism

The Wretched of the Earth *See* Decolonization

Theatre

Theatre refers to the institutionalized performance of written or improvised texts before an audience and often in a building of the same name. In the Western tradition it encompasses a wide variety of genres, which may emphasize music and singing (opera), movement (dance theatre) or the spoken word (dramatic theatre) as well as various subgenres ranging from puppetry and vaudeville to cabaret and standup comedy. Classical non-Western forms of theatre such as those found in Japan (nô, kabuki, bunraku), China (Peking opera) and India (kathakali) do not adhere to the Western divisions of sung, danced, and spoken theatre.

In all cultures, theatre is primarily a local phenomenon. It is usually made, performed and received in one place and is often subject to highly specific conventions which render transplantation across borders and cultures difficult. Theatre from a transnational perspective is therefore always a challenge to producers and receivers. Despite this local rootedness, theatre has very often travelled both on the level of production as well as on that of the texts produced by it. Greek theatre was performed in purpose-built structures from the Mediterranean to the Near East; Roman theatres were built wherever imperial rule was established. The most important European transnational theatrical phenomenon pre-1850 was the commedia dell'arte, the professional Italian troupes that performed throughout Europe between 1570 and 1750. Another important transnational export was the so-called Italian stage, the perspective-based theatre architecture developed in Italy in the 17th century and which was implemented throughout Europe and beyond in the following 150 years. Over and beyond such interconnections, there also emerged in European countries highly specific national traditions in terms of acting, writing and production which culminated in the late 18th century with the call for national theatres, a term which carried different connotations in different countries but which normally meant a combination of a building, autochthonous drama and an acting style. For ethnic groups without political sovereignty such as those in Eastern Europe, a national theatre became a political rallying cry and focalization point.

Despite the trend towards national theatres, the second half of the 19th century also saw a marked increase in transnational interconnections. The construction of railways enabled individual performers as well as whole productions to move quickly over long distances. The increasing commercialization of theatre was fostered by the abolition of the so-called 'patent system', which in France and England meant that the right to perform dramatic texts was limited to one or two theatres. This liberalization of the theatre system coupled with a rapid increase in population led to a construction boom in the metropolitan centres such as London, Paris and Berlin where the number of theatre buildings increased twentyfold between the beginning and end of the century. The genres of theatre also increased so that by the end of the century theatre had multiplied into a great number of specialist forms frequented by specific audiences. Multiethnic centres such as New York also produced audiences for theatre from different linguistic backgrounds. Up until 1918 there were dozens of thriving German, Yiddish, Italian, and Chinese-language-speaking theatres and vaudevilles in New York city. The late 19th and early 20th century saw three phenomena which were intrinsically transnational: the tours of the Meiningen Court Theatre from Germany, the art theatre movement and the reception of Japanese theatre in Europe and North America. The Meiningen tours physically transported a particular theatre style across borders while the art theatre movement provided a window on the circulation of theatrical avant-garde ideas. The Japanese example demonstrates how a theatrical form rooted in a very specific national or cultural tradition could transcend linguistic and cultural barriers and find an audience well beyond the limits of that nation.

Between 1874 and 1890 the court theatre ensemble of the small town of Meiningen in southern Germany embarked on annual tours in the course of which they visited 38 different European cities from London to Moscow. The performances were predicated on two principles: historical accuracy in scenography and an ensemble principle in acting, which meant that even star actors were relegated to smaller roles if the production demanded it. The Meiningen aesthetic was primarily a question of staging and their productions demonstrated to audiences throughout Europe what a controlling directorial vision could accomplish artistically. The tours of the Meiningen theatre are considered to be a major contributory factor in establishing staging and the director as the primary artistic forces in European theatre.

The Meiningen theatre contributed directly to the establishment of the art theatre movement throughout Europe and North America. Beginning with André Antoine's Théâtre Libre

(1887) in Paris, small highbrow theatres were set up in Berlin, Moscow, Munich, London, New York and elsewhere to (a) perform controversial plays and b) to experiment with new forms of staging. Some of these theatres such as the Moscow Art Theatre, established by Vassily Nemirovitch-Danchenko and Konstantin Stanislavsky in 1898, still exist today. These theatres and their major artists worked together closely through informal networks of shared ideas and tours. They did not always remain small. The Deutsches Theater directed by Max Reinhardt from 1905 became the basis of a commercially and artistically hugely successful theatrical concern which undertook extended tours throughout Europe and the United States. Despite evident linguistic barriers, the artistic, mainly visual, principles underlying the art theatre movement enabled considerable transnational communication. André Antoine was even invited to Turkey in 1914 to help establish a national acting school and theatre, a task which was interrupted by the outbreak of World War I.

The late 19th century also saw an upsurge of interest in the theatrical forms of non-European cultures. European imperial expansion produced a large backwash of artifacts and persons from the administered colonies. The opening of Japan after the Meiji restoration in 1868 produced a veritable craze for Japanese culture. In 1898 the Japanese actor Otojirō Kawakami together with his wife, the geisha-trained dancer Sadayakko, formed the Japanese Court Company to present Japanese theatre abroad. Arriving in San Francisco in 1899 they travelled overland via New York and London to arrive in Paris for the Exposition Universelle in 1900. Although the troupe, consisting of 20 actors, performed neither pure kabuki nor nô but new plays in 'Japanese style', they introduced to American and European spectators the conventions of Japanese theatre. Sadayakko's performances made her a major star and the troupe's performances inspired anti-naturalistic tendencies within the theatre art movement. Japanese theatre seemed to embody contemporary theatre reform ideas predicated on stylization and symbolic allusion rather than realism, the dominant convention in both European and American theatre around 1900.

The transnational exchange of ideas was not just a flow from East to West but was in fact multidirectional. Shinpa was a theatre movement begun in the 1880s as part of Japan's modernization movement after 1868. It was directed primarily at the content and staging techniques of kabuki. New plays on topical themes and more realistic representational styles were introduced. An even more radical approach was shingeki, the movement to write plays in Japanese but according to European realistic conventions, which emerged after 1900 and gradually rivalled shinpa. An equivalent to shingeki known as shinguk also emerged in Korea in the 1920s via the Japanese movement and not as a direct response to Western theatre. Japan was also the starting point for modern Chinese theatre when a group of Chinese students living in Tokyo founded the Spring Willow Dramatic Society in 1907 and performed an adaptation of Alexander Dumas's Camille in Chinese.

In India travelling British troupes visited intermittently throughout the 19th century. Around the middle of the century there emerged in different regions of India forms of commercial travelling theatre, which were far more than mere replicas of British troupes. In Bombay the Parsees, a merchant class of Persian origin, recognized the commercial potential of theatre. They built theatres and performed their plays in Gujurati. Parsee theatre was decidedly eclectic in form, drawing on a wide range of sources: Persian and Sanskrit mythology and epics, English novels, farces and plays, and medieval legends. The emphasis on varied action and spectacular stage effects indicates links to the conventions of 19th-century melodrama, which was familiar to Indian audiences via the British touring companies and which came to have a permanent influence on the production and receptive codes of commercial Indian theatre. Equivalents of Parsee theatre emerged in other regions, and it can be seen as a forerunner to contemporary Bollywood films.

The 20th century saw a steadily increasing interest in transnational theatre practices. Between the world wars Japanese nô was the theatre form that had the most profound influence in the West, especially on experimental avant-garde theatre. The list of writers and directors who studied nô reads like a Who's Who of Western modernism. Before 1945 we can name Ezra Pound, Edward Gordon Craig, W. B. Yeats, Paul

Claudel, Bertolt Brecht and Jacques Copeau. After 1945 we find Benjamin Britten, Peter Brook, Jean-Louis Barrault, Robert Wilson and Robert Lepage. There is no doubt that nô was perceived in the West as a highly complex theatre form that already embodied the more abstract, stylized theatre modernists were looking for. Although Yeats and many of his contemporaries were profoundly influenced by nô, they were fascinated by the idea of a theatre obtained by reading translations of the texts and not by actual experience of a performance. It was not until 1954 that the first Japanese troupe toured Europe and provided spectators with direct experience of nô in performance.

From the mid 1950s on a growing number of Western actors, directors, composers visited Asian countries with established theatre traditions and began to study these theatre forms at first hand. The traffic continued throughout the 1960s and 1970s as more and more Western actors came to Japan to study nô, kyōgen, butô and kabuki, kathakali in India, or the Peking opera in China. Especially in the 1960s, there was huge interest in reforming and renewing acting techniques in the West. Actors and pedagogues had become frustrated with the narrow, psychological approach associated with Stanislavsky and method acting. Asian performance genres seemed to offer a fruitful alternative.

From the 1970s a new trend towards intercultural theatre can be observed that is programmatically transnational in its very conception. The best known example is Peter Brook's work in Paris where he has experimented with a multinational troupe in search of, if not a universal theatre language, at least the possibilities of performing theatre across linguistic and cultural boundaries. His most famous (and controversial) production was a nine-hour adaptation of the Indian religious epic The Mahabharata (1985).

Since the 1980s a growing number of theatre festivals have facilitated the exchange of productions on a regular basis, which provide cosmopolitan theatre audiences with the opportunity to see work from a variety of different cultures. Major established festivals include Edinburgh, which combines an official and a fringe section, and the Adelaide festival in Australia. Since most major cities today support a performing arts festival of some kind showcasing international work,

the festival circuit has become an important new addition to national-based theatre cultures in as much as it provides an additional economy for which some theatre artists produce almost exclusively. The French-Canadian theatre director Robert Lepage, for example, works explicitly in conjunction with a number of festivals, which provide the economic backing for his productions; and there are many artists working outside subsidized theatre institutions now who make use of the same transnational networks. Advances in technology such as surtitling and a general trend towards the use of visual technologies in staging have also contributed to reducing linguistic barriers.

Christopher Balme

Bibliography

Balme C. 1999. Decolonizing the stage: theatrical syncretism and post-colonial drama. Oxford: Clarendon.

Gainor J. E. (ed.) 1995. Imperialism and theatre: essays on world theatre, drama and performance. London and New York: Routledge.

Kruger L. 1992. The national stage: theatre and cultural legitimation in England, France, and America. Chicago: Chicago University Press.

Pavis P. 1992. Theatre at the crossroads of culture, Kruger L. (trans.). London: Routledge.

Pronko L. 1967. Theater East and West: perspectives toward a total theater. Berkeley: University of California Press.

Theatre Journal 1998. Special issue on theatre and diaspora, 50, 1.

Theatre Research International. 2005. Focus issue on theatre festivals, 30, 3.

Related essays
anarchism; Cantonese opera; cultural capitals; decolonization; empire and migration; femininity; intellectual property rights; international students; Italian opera; Kessler, Harry von; kindergarten; literature; Orientalism; performing artists; surrealism

Theme parks
Theme parks are self-contained leisure spaces that charge admission and feature themed landscapes, attractions, and activities for visitors. Themes drawing on, for instance, specific historical periods, actual

or mythical places, or popular fables and legends, distinguish such parks from the broader category of amusement parks. Theme parks may be entirely contrived (e.g. Disneyland in the United States or Splendid China in China), or developed on existing sites (e.g. Colonial Williamsburg in the United States or Beamish in the UK). Similarly, they may be primarily commercial and entertaining in purpose, or educational with a focus on heritage preservation. While the origin of the modern theme park is typically attributed to the 1955 opening of Disneyland in Anaheim, earlier traces can be found in 19th- and early-20th-century World Fairs and Expositions, and – even earlier – in carnivals and market fairs.

The most commonly referenced model of theme park development is Disney, which operates five theme parks in the United States (opened in 1955 and 1971), Japan (1983), France (1992), and Hong Kong (2005). Disney's parks are arguably the most popular leisure sites on the planet, attracting over 30 million visitors each year. Disney's success beyond the United States raises questions about the transnational nature of theme park development. For visitors in France, Japan, and Hong Kong, the parks are transnational spaces of virtual travel not just to a fantasyland where 'magic' becomes real, but also to America itself. When Tokyo Disneyland was being planned, Disney's Japanese partners insisted that it be an exact replica of the Anaheim original, so that visitors could feel they had actually travelled to California. Yet the American themes of Disney parks have also been the subject of derision by defenders of national cultural heritage. Ironically, in Japan, it was the Disney Corporation itself that sought to develop more Japanese cultural themes for the park.

Still, for some observers, Disney parks represent a new form of cultural colonialism, and in this respect might be readily compared to their historical forebears: the Great Exhibitions and World Fairs which dedicated themselves to displaying the spoils of imperialism through the most advanced technology available. These earlier exhibitions paid homage to the progress of industrial civilization by inviting visitors to view the curiosities of the world with the scrutinizing gaze of the 'modern man'. Disney parks are often said to mark the postmodern extension of this imperial gaze. If the 19th-century exhibitions thrived on displaying a world 'out there',

Disney parks derive their entertainment value from dispensing with any pretence of faithfully representing the world at all. Critics of postmodernism have bemoaned this embracing of 'hyperreality', in which visitors are invited to suspend the distinction between real and fake for a few hours of amusement. And such suspension of disbelief is thought to be increasingly found beyond the theme park as one navigates the themed landscapes of the postmodern city. Indeed, Disneyland has served as a transnational model for a new generation of urban planning and community development (e.g. Seaside, Florida or 'Thames Town', China), while the EPCOT component of Disney World was originally conceived as the perfect residential community of tomorrow. In fact, Disneyland was viewed by Walt Disney himself as a utopia of sorts, an alternative world into which the visitor could escape from the alienation and unplanned growth of the postwar American city. Disneyland offered a sanitized, family-friendly answer to the vulgarity of amusement parks like Coney Island or seaside resorts like Brighton, as well as the chaos of the city more generally.

As agents of transnationalism, theme parks provide both a 'Western' model of postmodern land development and a format or platform for distinctive local and national cultural expression. A clear tension exists between the theme park as a space simultaneously of transnational desire and of national identity. In Japan and China, they serve as windows onto other lands – allowing travel abroad without leaving one's country – as well as highly scripted spaces of national culture, heritage, and identity.

Tim Oakes

Bibliography

Hendry J. 2000. *The Orient strikes back*. Oxford: Berg.

Marling K. A. 1997. *Designing Disney's theme parks*. Paris: Flammarion.

Stanley N. 1998. *Being ourselves for you*. London: Middlesex University Press.

Warren S. 'Cultural contestation at Disneyland Paris', in Crouch D. (ed.) 1999. *Tourism and leisure geographies*. London: Routledge, 109–25.

Related essays

America; city planning; jeans; empires and imperialism; expositions; Coca-Cola; comics; tourism

Tigris-Euphrates basin *See*
Freshwater management

Tourism

On an open definition, tourism can best be described as a journey, regardless of its goals and purposes, which extends beyond a duration of 24 hours and returns again to the starting point after a manageable period of time. The terms 'tourism' and 'tourist' appear to be nearly self-evident in everyday speech. In spite of this, they also evade finely adjusted analytical probing. All definitions do indeed cover a substantial part of the core of the terms, but they also lead to the conclusion that tourism is capable of great adaptability. The tremendous significance of tourism on a global scale is obvious. Its growth accelerates year after year, and its position among the largest economic sectors throughout the world is unyielding. In 2000, cross-border holiday traffic reached 700 million arrivals and achieved a turnover of $US 476 trillion. Numerous regions and entire national economies live off of tourism. Even industrial countries such as France, Italy, and Germany earn around 10 per cent of their gross domestic product from tourist activities. Today, the tourist movement is an expression of that wave of mobility which has dramatically increased with globalization. Tourism in a broader sense connotes that comprehensive process of disembedding, the release of societal groups and subjects from stable contexts of life interaction, as Anthony Giddens has so aptly described.

It has often been attempted, with plausible arguments, to establish the origin of tourism at the beginning of the modern age and to interpret tourist travel as a part of the comprehensive change in epochs beginning in 1800 as a side effect and a result of the proven breaking down of boundaries, the onset of the industrial revolution, and new consumer behaviour.

More recent research makes increasing reference to the long initial phase of tourism: the parallel history of late medieval/early modern forms of travel (out of necessity, religious and commercial motives, and as journeys with a chivalric or educational basis) and tourist voyages. The conceptual division between the everyday and vacation, which long appeared to be a criterion for the definition of tourism, has become questionable. The current reduction of vacation periods and the growing

fusion of the everyday, work, and vacation (such as with conference tourism) today frequently expose the classic figure of the tourist to be a mere construct.

The stages of the development of tourism can be clearly defined. For quite a long period, these have been anchored in Europe. A long preliminary phase of chivalric and educational travel in the 17th century was followed by a standardization of travel with the *grand tour* to Italy and with popular travel to Switzerland or the Rhine. The transition to tourism of a modern character took place around 1830, soon after the Napoleonic Wars. The revolution in communications (faster post coaches, the railway, and contact by letter and telegraph), the breakthrough at certain points of industrialization, growing economic integration, and a new understanding of the body and health all fall under the phase of the late Vormärz era (the period from the end of the Congress of Vienna in 1815 to the revolution of March 1848). They fostered the need for travel and holiday, and they were additionally strengthened by an impetus from the altered perception that was expressed by the techniques of lithography and photography. The intertwining of European areas marched on swiftly after 1830. The results of this development were expanded horizons of perception, a synoptic view of both new worlds and one's own world, and the processing of simultaneous impressions into a universalizing worldview. The 'tourist gaze' narrowed the impressions of voyages and holidays into specific characterizations and standardizations.

What was decisive for the rise in popularity of travel and tourism in the Europe of the 19th century was the social and economic advancement of a middle to upper entrepreneur class and functional elite – the bourgeoisie. For the heterogeneous middle classes that experienced and shaped the dynamics and changes of the era to an especially strong degree, travels and stays at baths and spas soon became a regular part of the canon of bourgeois existence. Much-sought-after destinations also included the sea. Ever since bathing in the sea was discovered to be invigorating and good for the health in Scarborough around 1740, the number of seaside bathing resorts grew beyond the English classics such as Brighton, Margate, and Ramsgate to include those in other countries and regions (Ostend, Bad Doberan, Dieppe) and even in

America (Newport). Bathing was concentrated upon the cool seas of the North, while the Mediterranean was for the time being still passed over since its warm waters had long been regarded as unhealthful. Although the importance of tourism around 1840 was not statistically high, a substantial growth trend could be observed everywhere. By around 1840, foreign tourists were regarded as something normal in successful health resorts such as Spa, Karlsbad, or Wiesbaden; in seaside bathing resorts such as Brighton or Blackpool; in the cities of Italy, and in Paris. Progress was helped along by tour operators such as the British firm, Thomas Cook, which began offering organized package tours in 1836 that soon encompassed all of Europe. They also contributed to the standardization both of that which was on offer and of the printed travel guide, which provided orientation and emphasized a manageable selection of sights worth seeing.

After its initial formative phase, tourism reached a new dynamic around 1860 along with an increased interweaving of its elements: railways were increasingly integrated within Europe, in Russia, and in the US, and mountain railways also gained a new vertical dimension (such as with the Jungfrau railway in Switzerland in 1873). Infrastructures such as hotels came into existence with impressive architecture and dimensions and in fascinating places, while tour organizers such as Stangen in Berlin or the aforementioned Thomas Cook operated nearly worldwide. On top of that, hiking and mountain climbing became more popular than ever, supported by the founding of the new Alpine clubs (the Alpine Club in London in 1857, the Deutscher Alpenverein in 1869, the Deutscher und Österreichischer Alpenverein in 1873, and the Club Alpino Italiano in 1873). The dramatic ascent of famous Alpine peaks (such as the Matterhorn in 1865) fascinated the international public. In addition to great improvement on the supply side, the demand also expanded. Guests came from the aristocracy and the upper-middle class. The holiday was still not yet a right that was anchored in law; rather, it remained reserved for privileged groups such as high-ranking officials. Nevertheless, it was more and more becoming a sought-after consumer good.

A decisive broadening of tourism set in after the 'heroic' decades around 1830, and the dynamic phase of interweaving took hold from around 1860 to about 1900. For the first time ever, travelling and holidays turned into a requirement of the masses. Tourism also encompassed the lower-middle classes and sometimes even labourers, who at least made use of the weekend for excursions to green spaces. Added to this, the destinations expanded. Around the Mediterranean, the Adriatic Sea including the Lido of Venice, the Italian and French Rivieras, and the Spanish coast were used as locations for seaside bathing and fresh air, and a trip to the 'Orient' was popular.

In the US, natural wonders such as Niagara Falls and the Grand Canyon drew large crowds. New forms of mobility such as the automobile revolutionized travel around 1905. The car made it possible to arrange travel and holidays with an independent time schedule, it was fascinating because of its speed, and it was a coveted status symbol that in the beginning was reserved for the upper strata of society. In parallel to the automobile, skiing, which was introduced in the Alps around the same time, became an expression of speedy, body-based mobility.

After World War 1, the new dimensions of tourism that developed around 1910 were popularized. The middle classes and labourers, who had secured the right to a holiday for the first time, took advantage of their opportunities at that time to the best of their abilities in spite of initially small budgets. In Europe, the dictatorships successfully took up the need for holidays. In Italy, through the Opera Nazionale Dopolavoro (National Recreational Organization) and in Nazi Germany, through the Kraft durch Freude ('Power through Joy') organization, members of the middle classes and labourers were led to holiday travel primarily within their own countries, and this was used to build consensus. Even though the circle of vacationers still remained manageable, popularization reached a new level.

The decade after 1945 did not yet bring any democratization of travel, but in the postwar years the felt need for holidays and relaxation grew. Beginning in 1955, with the worldwide onset of the 'economic miracle', tourism moved to the centre of the growing consumer society. In addition to access to increased household and living comforts, mobility, and media entertainment, the arranging of free time into holiday and tourism was the fourth pillar of consumer modernism.

With growing incomes that were also increasingly stable and the progressive fulfilment of important consumer needs, tourism gained in significance by leaps and bounds in Europe and the US, but also in East Asia, particularly in Japan. In Western countries, even labourers had three to four weeks of annual holiday by 1960. The threshold was crossed to the 'democratization' of travel and vacations. In addition to domestic tourism, foreign travel boomed. Particularly around the Mediterranean, first Italy and soon thereafter Spain and Greece experienced a golden age. The growing importance of air travel promoted transcontinental tourism, but mass motorization by car remained the most important means of travel and holiday transport.

The individualization of tourism and the personal arranging of travel and holidays, mostly within the framework of the family, were the great achievement of the decades up to 1970, but soon the hour of the large tour operators would also come. In Germany in 1968, when the tour companies Touropa, Scharnow, and Dr Tigges merged to form TUI, it marked the important opening of the door for standardized package travel in a vertical organization. From the travel agency to the transportation to the hotel or holiday resort, the large tourist companies provided everything from a single source, and they created the requirements for travel.

A fundamental qualitative and quantitative change in the holiday took place in connection with the weakness in the worldwide economy in the years 1973–86. Beginning in 1985, the importance of air travel, long journeys, and short holidays grew simultaneously.

The phases of foundation (1800–30), interweaving (1860–90), popularization (1900–40), and democratization (1955–70) were then followed by the phase of globalization. Nearly every destination was accessible to anyone, tour groups became more common, and they also encompassed young people, men and women, and senior citizens. Prices became extremely attractive.

Increased mobility as a result of low-cost airlines, the shortening of the holiday, and the available personal selection of destinations on the Internet made travelling and holidays more dynamic and individual to an enormous degree. The Southern hemisphere and Asia joined in as easily reachable destinations for those from the First World; Africa grew from 700,000 arrivals (1960) to 28 million (1999), and Asia increased from 900,000 to nearly 100 million in the same period. But the boom did not always have a positive effect upon the destination countries. All too often, proceeds went to the benefit of the large tour operators or local consortia, and seldom to the regional economies. Furthermore, for Southern hemisphere societies, tourism, which gobbled up resources, commonly took on postcolonial characteristics – particularly through the massive influx of sex tourists.

The rise in popularity of the destinations of Japan and China is among the most pronounced phenomena of the changes in tourism since around 1985. But as late as 1965, there were so many restrictions on foreign travel for Japanese citizens that in that year only 159,000 tourists left the country. Yet twenty years later, in 1985, their number had already grown to 5.5 million. The boom was all the more astonishing when one considers that Japanese vacation restrictions allow workers on the islands to have only 15 days of holiday per year. But the trade and foreign exchange surpluses achieved by the Japanese economy by 1985 were so massive that the government supported foreign travel to the best of its ability in order to at least symbolically approach a balanced position vis-à-vis the world economy. Added to this, travels abroad fitted very well into the Japanese family model, since travelling together fostered the close connection of small social units. And the Japanese custom of mutually exchanging gifts on a regular basis increased the interest in foreign trips on which numerous souvenirs could be acquired. As a result of the abbreviated holiday time, Japanese tourists prefer closer destinations, especially the US and the Pacific Rim. A second reason for this preference is the English language, which is not always spoken everywhere in Europe. On the other hand, there was a great interest, in Japan as well as in China, in European nature and culture, especially in the landscape and in regional customs. Japan's contribution to the opening up to tourism of neighbouring regions was of extraordinary significance. Its capital investments in Southeast Asia provided for the creation of new travel destinations in Malaysia, Thailand, Indonesia, and the Philippines. But within the country, as well, the tourist infrastructure was substantially developed.

In an even more spectacular manner, the ascent of China has also led to it reaching the level of a tourist 'great power'. In 2006, the China as a destination underwent a breathtaking growth spurt with 50 million arrivals, by far overtaking Italy (37.6 million). It will soon pass the US and will take third place in the world behind France and Spain. That is all the more astonishing when it is considered that even during the time of Mao Zedong, travel was still a rarity. But in the era of Deng Xiaoping, marked by a cautious opening to the market economy beginning in 1978, travel to China immediately met with a favourable response – on the one hand because of the accessible cost, but on the other hand thanks to the fascination that had grown over the centuries with China's culture and landscape. China-mania has been a constant of Occidental culture since as far back as the 18th century, and it revitalized itself rapidly once again. For the time being, the explosive incoming tourism on the main Asian continent has not corresponded to any boom in travel abroad to mimic that of Japan. But this will most certainly change dramatically in the years to come.

Tourism is the only economic sector that has grown without interruption for more than two centuries. It is an integral part of globalization. It follows its own waves and constantly changes them. But climate change will also dramatically change tourism in the foreseeable future. In its current form, it all too frequently has a negative effect on the climate and the environment. Tourism will continue to grow, but it will also change considerably. It remains a seismograph that reacts to change but also precedes it, and new trends aside, it also always anticipates a bit of the future.

Hans Heiss

Bibliography
Battilani P. 2001. *Vacanze di pochi, vacanze di tutti: l'evoluzione del turismo europeo.* Bologna: Il Mulino.
Hennig C. 1997. *Reiselust: Touristen, Tourismus und Urlaubskultur.* Frankfurt and Leipzig: Suhrkamp.
Spode H. 2003. *Wie die Deutschen 'Reiseweltmeister' wurden: eine Einführung in die Tourismusgeschichte.* Erfurt: Landeszentrale fur Politische Bildung Thuringen.
Urry J. 2002. *The tourist gaze.* London, Thousand Oaks and New Delhi: Sage.

Related essays
Asia; car culture; China; consumer society; cuisines; drink; expositions; feel-good culture; Japan; museums; non-lieux; Orientalism; philanthropy; publishing; railways; Santería; services; steamships; temporary migrations; Thailand and sex tourism; traffic signals; transportation infrastructures; tropics; world heritage; youth organizations

Thailand and sex tourism

In the decade following the Vietnam War, Thailand developed an array of sexual services for foreigners and became an emblem of 'sex tourism' worldwide.

Geopolitics, capital investments, and the promotion of tourism for economic development established a flow of visitors – disproportionately male – from the industrialized world, East Asia, and the Middle East. Sexual services formed a common feature of this travel. In the 1980s heyday of 'sex tourism' proper, organized tours for Europeans and Japanese men attracted notoriety for offering young Thai women's services in packaged itineraries. Yet the erotic dimensions of foreigners' relations to Thailand extend beyond formal sex tours. Go-go bars in Patpong or Pattaya have become routine tourist attractions while images of Thailand's erotic offerings circulate in global popular culture and political discourse. Thailand's infrastructure for sexual services varies somewhat by customers' nationality and is divided by sexual orientation, with child prostitution a separate and more clandestine trade. Adult services for foreigners tend not to involve the harshest conditions of bonded labour.

Opposition to sex tourism has come from Thai and international feminists, international Christian groups, and Thai voices concerned with national image. Though basic patterns continue, transnational commercial sex in Thailand has changed over time. Economic conditions (for example, the 1997 Asian economic crisis) and the HIV/AIDS epidemic modified foreign demand for sexual services. Migration or trafficking of women for sex work into and out of Thailand has increased. Reversing the paths of sex tourism, Thai women go to work in wealthier countries (Japan, Europe) while women from other countries (such as Burma, China, Russia) come to work in Thailand. Since the

1990s, public attention has turned from sex tourism to child prostitution and trafficking in women.

Ara Wilson

Bibliography
Truong T. 1990. *Sex, money, and morality: prostitution and tourism in Southeast Asia.* Atlantic Highlands: Zed.

Related essays
empire and migration; human mobility; masculinity; sexuality and migration; temporary migrations; tourism; White Slavery

Toyotism

Toyotism refers to the management culture and labour processes developed by the Toyota Motor Company (TMC), which in 2006 became the world's largest automobile manufacturer. The term designates a new dominant global industrial system of lean and flexible mass production, i.e. the capability to produce, at the lowest cost, big series of various cars. In the 1980s Toyotism was considered by management literature the 'best way', surpassing the previous Taylorist and Fordist models. But Toyotism has roots in a specific historical context and it is in constant evolution. How has Toyota adapted its production system to the changes in the automobile industry? Is the model transferrable to other national contexts and firm cultures?

TMC was created in December 1933 by Toyoda Kiichirō (1894–1952). It was a division of Toyoda Automatic Loom Works, Ltd (TALW) created in 1926 by Toyoda Sakichi (1867–1930). Three years after the founder's death, his son presented this new activity as a heritage. Actually, it was a short-term reaction. In a period of world economic crisis, TALW thus diversified and modernized its activities. The new automobile division – which became independent in 1937 – benefited from TALW's experience. Facing chronic restrictions it limited production costs, learned from foreign experiences to avoid big mistakes and buy good machines. TMC gave preference to workshop practices and to middle management rather than top-down direction. Rationalization was oriented towards efficiency rather than mass production.

The 'Toyota system of production' (TSP) was developed in the postwar period. Taïichi Ohno (1912–90) retrospectively insisted on two major components he adapted from TALW practices. 'Autonomization' was a way to have a worker take care of all the tasks of his or her post. 'Just-in-time' (*kanban*) was an attempt to reduce stocks by supplying the workshops with the exact quantity of components they needed to carry out their tasks at any given time.

The TSP relied on a specific social atmosphere. Despite a regular growth of production, Toyota underwent a financial crisis in 1949, which led to layoffs, provoked major strikes and the departure of Kiichirō Toyoda. Ishida Taizō, the new chairman (1950–62), took advantage of the Korean War to save the firm from bankruptcy and institute a culture of labour–management cooperation sealed with the tacit guarantee of life-time employment for the upper rungs of the workers. They thus participated in constant improvement activities (*kaïzen*) i.e., increase in quality, development of productivity and reduction of costs.

Toyotism achieved its culminating point in the 1980s. Toyota's phenomenal worldwide triumph encouraged management experts to select items from a successful recipe. Others argued that the model was not an addition, but a combination of five essential complementary components: mutual trust, internal competition, constant research and development, management of manufacturing costs and profit sharing. But, in this period of worldwide automobile crisis, the central component of Toyota's competitive success turned out to be the outside supplier policy. The firm concentrated on its main job – assembly – and externalized most of the peripheral activities, outsourcing even design drawings of auto parts. This subcontracting system reduced transaction costs for the firm but gave rise to fierce competition among suppliers.

By the end of the bubble economy (1987–91), Japan underwent an economic crisis, forcing Toyota to undergo a thorough reorganization (January 1992). The pursuit of cost reduction and constant growth was to be reached through six major reversals. Two are internal actions: the reintroduction of stocks and the humanization of working conditions. Two are commercial: the launching of innovative, seductive products and a bigger concern with environmental problems. The programme also advocated the development of long-term collaboration with partners and encouraged the internationalization of the firm. Rising costs and a workforce shortage in Japan led subcontracting to be moved offshore to low-wage countries in Southeast Asia. Toyota also generalized transplants, i.e. production units close to major markets. Through hybridization the Toyota methods were adapted to different national workforces. In 2002, stagnation of the Japanese economy made Toyota both lean and agile. In this process, lifetime employment has come under attack.

Toyotism is neither the stereotypical Japanese productive system nor the ultimate global production model. The success of the Toyota firm – which has known no deficit since 1952 – makes it the benchmark industrial reference.

Alain P. Michel

Bibliography

Shimizu K. 1999. Le Toyotisme. Paris: La Découverte.

Related essays

assembly line; car culture; Japan; organization models

Trade

'International trade' includes all material goods that can be traded between countries: both raw materials – from mining and agriculture – and manufactured products. It does not include services or capital movements, though it does of course relate to them in many ways. Occupying several groups of closely interdependent actors, over the 20th century it underwent profound changes which turned it into an essential element in transnational relations.

A network of interdependent actors

Some of the firms engaged in international trade in the 20th century had been so engaged for a long time: trading houses specializing in a certain type of product, often located in great ports or financial centres. Their business consists in bringing together buyers and sellers and fixing price levels; they are continually involved in risk and speculation. They abound in London and other major European trading centres such as Cologne,

Hamburg, Geneva, Antwerp and Amsterdam, but are also to be found in the US and other developed countries. They are run by agents with a profound knowledge of the workings of the market and of market trends, and their structure is comparatively loose. Their transport, warehousing and capital are often borrowed. Their operations concentrate on major primary products: metals, energy, agricultural products. Some of them are very old, going back to local or regional trading houses which have since extended their activities internationally. For example, the 'grain giant' Cargill, founded in 1865, remained within the confines of the American internal market for over a century, until the 1950s, when it began setting up subsidiaries – first in Panama, then in Geneva – to operate on the world market.

Others started life in the banking world. Some have connections with London merchant banks, or major banking houses in Continental Europe which invest in them, as Rothschild does in non-ferrous metals. Yet others were founded by ship owners, for example Louis-Dreyfus of Marseilles, which trades on the cereals and groundnut market. Such firms first flourished in colonial times, but have maintained a presence in former colonies since independence. For instance, Jardine, Matheson & Co., founded in Canton in 1832 by two Scottish adventurers who had made their fortune in the opium trade and subsequently in cottons, is now a multinational with a presence throughout the Asia-Pacific region, with wide interests in ports and airports, hotels, real estate, tourism and finance. Other great trading firms are to be found in formerly independent countries that have been drawn into the European orbit: for example, Bunge y Born of Argentina, founded in 1876 with combined Dutch and Latin American capital, which has become one of the leading players on the global foodstuffs market.

All these firms are heavily interdependent and form networks covering the entire planet. Their main activities focus on the primary product markets in London (the London Metal Exchange, the Baltic Exchange), New York (the New York Mercantile Exchange), Chicago (the Chicago Board of Trade), and also Antwerp, Rotterdam, Hamburg, Le Havre, Sydney and elsewhere. Dealers in these markets exchange contracts, i.e., financial securities representing a fixed quantity of merchandise. Because most transactions are 'forward', there are opportunities to speculate on price trends and to hedge by combining sale and purchase orders. The prices emerging from such transactions often become world reference prices for the products concerned. Thus the importance of futures markets – a traditional way of organizing international trade – has increased during recent periods of price instability. For example, since the oil shocks of 1973–74 and 1979–80, the daily prices for North Sea Brent crude on the Rotterdam spot market have been used as a database by all kinds of operators, in distinct preference to the official prices laid down by OPEC.

Thanks to their profound knowledge of the workings of these markets, the great trading firms are still indispensable cogs in the machinery of international commerce. Their success repeatedly thrusts them into the foreground, especially when the balance is disturbed and markets are jittery. For example, in the early 1970s the 'grain giants', seeking to cover the shortfall in the Soviet Union's crisis-hit wheat production, made contracts of quite unprecedented size with the Soviet procurement agency, Exportkhleb, and bought up virtually all the wheat on the market in what journalists dubbed 'the great grain robbery'. On the other hand, if the great firms are doing badly this can have a devastating and virtually uncontrollable domino effect on the world economy: in 1931 the collapse of Nordwolle, a textile trader based in Bremen, triggered the collapse of Weimar Germany's banking system and thus of its whole economy, with consequences that are now history.

However permanent a presence these firms may have in international trade, they are not immune to change. They may move away from trading into production or processing. This is what happened to the oil giant Shell, originally founded in 1897 by Marcus Samuel as a shipping company running tankers between Baku and the Far East. Similarly, none of the grain giants now derives the bulk of its turnover from actual trading. Many such firms have also relocated in response to shifts in the world's economic centre of gravity. Originally founded in Europe, they migrated to the US between the two world wars and are now gravitating towards East Asia. Their power over the world economy is considerable but it does have its limits – often imposed by governments which intervene on the markets but do not play by the rules, fixing their own prices, setting up production cartels or distorting the trade in primary products to serve their own foreign policies. This strategy has been employed more than once by the US in its relations both with the Third World and with the Socialist camp. Finally, the power of the great trading firms is largely confined to primary products. The trade in manufactures is beyond their scope because deals tend to be made directly between manufacturers and clients. This applies both to mass-produced goods and articles made to order, such as machinery. The great trading firms do not act as brokers for such goods, which pass through other channels.

Radical global change

International trade grew rapidly in the second half of the 19th century, increasing sevenfold between 1860 and 1914, despite a slight decline in the great depression of 1873–96, which was caused by a drop in the prices of primary products rather than by a contraction in the volumes of exchange. Did this expansion stimulate the growth of the European economies, or was it, as Paul Bairoch believed, merely a symptom of their own internal dynamism? Without entering into the debate here, we may at least observe that there were many factors explaining the rapid growth in worldwide trade: technical progress, from improved navigation and the coming of the railways to the transmission of news via submarine telegraph cables; a revolution in production, not only in industries such as steel and textiles but also in agriculture with increased use of fertilizers, which sucked in imports; the creation of Europe's colonial empires, which turned a number of ports into great centres for the worldwide redistribution of tropical products and minerals; the triumph of the gold standard and the spread of banking networks, enabling exporters to keep an eye on their available funds and mobilize them without difficulty; and finally, changes in trading policy: while Germany reverted to protectionism in 1879, followed by the rest of Europe (introduction of the Méline Tariff in France, 1892) with the notable exceptions of Great Britain and the Netherlands, protective customs barriers did not hamper trade; what is more, they applied only to countries that refused to sign equitable trading agreements with their partners.

All this changed in 1914. For a quarter of a century the pace was notably slower. Between

1921 and 1929, the annual growth in world trade was a mere 2.2 per cent, half what it had been before the Great War (from 1896 to 1913 it was 4 per cent). These difficulties were largely due to supranational factors. Important prewar trading powers, such as the Russian and Austro-Hungarian empires, had ceased to exist. Customs barriers proliferated across Europe. Leading currencies, with the exception of the dollar, were highly unstable until the mid 1920s. The newly created League of Nations proved incapable of brokering customs agreements that would stimulate trade. The supply of agricultural products from traditional producers was overridden by that of 'new countries' such as Canada, Argentina, Australia and New Zealand, which had stepped up production during the war, creating a glut that drove prices down. Primary producers tried to stabilize prices by destroying harvests (e.g., the Brazilian coffee harvest), or by making international agreements, as with the big American, Dutch and British firms that controlled cane sugar exports from Cuba, Java and the West Indies respectively.

During the crisis of the 1930s world trade plummeted, becoming one of the main causes of the slump which no economy could escape – a phenomenon so all-embracing that observers were flabbergasted. Prices for primary products, already in decline, crashed. Exporters of such products were unable to purchase manufactured goods, and the price of the latter dropped, though not quite so sharply. This compelled the primary producers to devalue even earlier than the industrialized countries, trampling over each other in a rush to evade the crisis – although international negotiations sometimes forced them into effective solidarity, as in 1933 when an international wheat agreement was reached thanks to the creation of a common front between the countries of Central Europe and extra-European exporters such as Argentina, Australia and Canada. However, this agreement remained in force for only a year, owing to the free-for-all that broke out as soon as prices showed signs of recovering. The state of international trade also contributed to the crisis in the industrialized countries, though in a different way. Trade contracted by two thirds in just four years, from 1929 to 1933. The deflationary spiral aggravated the effects of the slump in each country. There was a surge of protectionism,

ushered in by the US in 1930 with the Hawley-Smoot tariff, the highest in history (52 per cent by value) and followed by other countries which either reneged on existing agreements or changed the whole basis of their trading policy (thus Great Britain abandoned free exchange), or by marshalling their dependent territories into so-called 'imperial economies'. 'Proletarian' nations such as Germany, Italy and Japan, which had few or no colonies, turned to autarchy. For twenty years international trade, once a driving force, became a brake on the economy and finally brought about its collapse. On the eve of the Second World War, global trade values had sunk to mid-19th-century levels and economies were less open than they had been before 1914. France's exports, for example, dropped from 15 per cent of GNP in 1913 to 8 per cent in 1938.

A radical turnaround took place after 1945. Since the early 1950s the growth in world trade has regularly outstripped increases in production, even during the crisis of the 1970s and 1980s which, unlike that of the 1930s, did not trigger a deflationary spiral. Years in which global trade has contracted are very much the exception. In fact, there have been only four: 1958, 1975, 1982 and 2001. The trend towards increasing openness regained its pre-1914 impetus, which had ceased between the two world wars. In 2000 the percentage of world production going for export reached 25 per cent – far higher than the 15 per cent it had reached in 1973 just before the first oil shock. A number of factors contributed to this upsurge. All of them transcend the circumstances of individual economies and can justly be identified as transnational. The most important is the part played by international organizations set up to safeguard free exchange on both a worldwide and a regional basis: first the General Agreement on Tariffs and Trade (GATT) then the World Trade Organization (WTO) and, in their respective regions, the European Economic Community (EEC) and European Union (EU), Association of Southeast Asian Nations (ASEAN), North American Free Trade Agreement (NAFTA), Mercado Común del Sur (Mercosur), etc. Another decisive influence was America's attitude towards external trade, so markedly different from what it had been before World War 2. Some historians, including Britain's Alan Milward, even see this change as the principal factor in the rapid recovery from the crisis – more so than internal motors of growth within individual countries.

While that idea may require some moderation, it is undeniable that for a long time the countries with the most impressive growth rates were those most committed to international trade: witness the 'economic miracles' achieved by Germany, Italy and Japan. Similarly, the dynamic growth of France in the 1960s was largely due to its government's determination to place her in the first rank among international competitors and in the building of Europe, consciously imitating her economically mighty German neighbour. In the crisis of the 1970s, again, the economies which were most open to the outside world often recovered more quickly than those that had tried to shield themselves against international competition, even though the former had to pay a price in terms of increased vulnerability to short-term fluctuations. These positive factors were joined by others equally transnational. The stability of the international monetary system up to 1960 created a climate favourable to trade, although traders subsequently had to adjust to floating exchange rates. Geographically speaking, the scope of world trade regained its turn-of-the-century level, and even surpassed it as decolonization removed the old imperial 'preserves' – and again after 1989 owing to the collapse of the Communist bloc which allowed its former members to re-establish themselves in the market economy. International trade was further stimulated by technical progress, which revolutionized the carriage of goods by sea. The appearance of specialized giant fuel tankers and bulk carriers reduced shipping costs to an unprecedented degree as a proportion of cost prices. In the air, cargo planes made it possible to establish regular air services that firms could use to rush spare parts to their factories anywhere in the world. On land, the spread of motorway networks and the construction of large-scale infrastructure connecting islands and continents were a further spur to exchange.

As these multifarious developments proceeded, the face of international trade changed completely. Primary products as a proportion of total trade volumes fell by half within a century, from 64 per cent to 33 per cent of global value between 1913 and 2001. This was because not all prices follow the same trends: as a general rule, prices of raw materials rise more slowly than those of manufactured goods. While raw materials prices may change dramatically from time to time, often due to stockpiling at times of international tension – for example, at the beginning of the Korean War in 1950 and during the oil shocks of 1973–74 and 1979–80 – the prevailing trend is towards a relative decline in the prices of raw materials. This change is also due in part to the reduction in quantities traded. Many primary products fell victim to competition from industrial substitutes. Copper and tin, for example, can be replaced by fibreglass or aluminium; natural textiles by artificial or synthetic fibres. Demand for primary products, particularly foodstuffs, tends to be inelastic, and this has an effect on sales. Finally, the producer countries are contributing to the contraction of trade by doing the initial processing themselves. This reconfiguration of trade has been further influenced by continual shifts in the relative importance of participating continents. Just before the First World War, Europe alone accounted for four fifths of the world's manufactured goods exports, though this domination rested on internal trade among European countries rather than with the rest of the world. At present Europe accounts for only 44 per cent of these exports, and even that represents an advance on the very low levels reached just after World War 2 (31 per cent in 1948). Europe has been overtaken by other regions and other powers: the United States and Japan between the wars, and since the early 1980s the countries of Asia: both the small-scale manufacturing countries such as South Korea, Singapore, Hong Kong and Taiwan, and the great powers on a continental scale, China and India. Over the same time span, Africa's share diminished and it now accounts for only 2 per cent of world exports; the position of Latin America remains little changed, the comparative advances of Brazil and Mexico being offset by the comparative decline of other countries such as Argentina.

This triumphal picture is not, of course, entirely without its negative aspects and uncertainties. The success of international trade remains precarious, as was shown by the recession of 2001 and the difficulties the WTO is currently facing as it tries to initiate a new round of multilateral trade negotiations for services and agricultural products. People in a number of countries find protectionism a tempting answer to the alarming inequalities and tensions that come in the wake of globalization. Prices on some primary products markets are worryingly unstable – particularly for metals, as prices are being pushed up by China, which is becoming a major importer as her economy develops. Thus there are a number of factors that may undermine the status quo over the medium term and have an increasingly negative impact on the global economy. Overall, however, the vagaries of international trade tend to invigorate that economy and are conducive to prosperity.

A factor of transnational importance

International trade represents a set of important factors affecting the entire planet. Two of them seem to have been decisive in the 20th century: trade may help a country emerge from underdevelopment; and it may act as a stepping stone from one stage of the globalization process to the next.

For many years specialists in 'subordinate' economies insisted that international trade is largely responsible for underdevelopment. Their analysis, heavily drawn on by militant anti-imperialists and Third World leaders, focused on the laws of 'unfair trade'. They were fond of referring to the 'pillage' of the Third World and looked for the mechanisms of and stages in the 'long-term distortion of the terms of exchange'. Various international authorities adopted this reasoning as developed, for instance, in the theories of the Argentinean economist Raúl Prebisch. Today economists and historians take a more balanced view, while some reject the argument root and branch. As for the rulers of the countries concerned, they have performed a complete volte-face. The first meeting of UNCTAD (the United Nations Conference for Trade and Development) in 1964 adopted, among other demands, the slogan 'Trade, not aid', the idea being no longer to remain isolated from international trade but to become part of it, by insisting that the developed countries should open their markets to exports from the Third World, that primary product prices should be stabilized and that the rules by which multinationals played the trading game should be radically overhauled. Since then, certain developing countries have systematically relied on international trade to foster industrialization. This applies to small economies with limited internal resources, such as South Korea, which predicated its

industrialization on a low-cost workforce, not in order to meet its own needs but to grab a share of the world market. The strategy was notably successful and within a few years South Korea had become a model for an industrialization strategy that was becoming more and more complex. Other, larger countries with substantial resources followed suit: for example, Brazil, which exploited its mining resources to become the leading supplier to developed countries. It very soon became the leading world exporter of iron ore and non-ferrous metals, building up currency reserves that were further bolstered by massive investments on the part of multinationals, enabling the country to escape its traditional role as a single-product exporter – of raw coffee – and diversify its economy. Thus foreign trade became the core of outward-looking strategies in opposition to the strategies of solipsistic and autarchic growth originally adopted by numerous newly independent countries, some of them impressed by the Soviet socialist experiment. There have been some very abrupt about-turns: for instance, since the rise to power of Deng Xiaoping, China, whose leaders were once apostles of balanced development, refusing to favour industry at the expense of agriculture, has become a fully paid-up subscriber to the world economy without abandoning the socialist approach in political and institutional matters.

International trade can also act as a bridge from the first to the second stage of globalization. In 1914, the process of globalization was already far advanced. It profited the European economies, which monopolized two thirds of world trade, 40 per cent of which was conducted within Europe itself. There was a genuine world market, in primary products at least. The rich countries of Northwest Europe had large cash surpluses which enabled them to run trade deficits, invest in the mechanization of the United States and the 'new countries', and, secondarily, to exploit their own colonies and extract wealth from them which more than made up for their trade deficits: they were, in fact, living on unearned income. Governments scarcely intervened in this process, except to safeguard the rules. After an eclipse lasting nearly half a century, globalization resumed after 1945 and accelerated in the early 1970s. International trade still had a decisive part to play, though the cashflows at its disposal were far less than those involved in monetary speculation and capital movements. But globalization now is an entirely different thing from what it was at the beginning of the 20th century: in fact, some analysts see it as an unprecedented phenomenon, although we are really dealing with two stages in a single process. The quickening of pace around 1970 coincided with the collapse of monetary stability and unprecedented fluctuations in prices for primary products. Governments are now intervening more frequently to steer the globalization process in the direction that they think best serves the interests of their countries. Obstacles to the free circulation of goods have almost disappeared thanks to the introduction of free trade measures on both a global and a regional scale. For the first time ever it is possible to speak in terms of a unified market, not just for primary products but for almost all goods. As for the geographical balance, it is utterly different from what it was at the beginning of the 20th century. The centre of gravity of the 'world economy', which since the end of the Middle Ages had lain at the heart of Europe (from the Mediterranean to the North Sea) or just at its periphery (the North Atlantic), was still in the same place in 1914. It has now moved, apparently, towards Asia and the Pacific. The fact that Singapore has just overtaken Rotterdam as the world's biggest port is symptomatic. The change is all the more striking because it has happened so rapidly. Equally striking is the fact that the role of international trade, as a factor in transnational change, has always been decisive.

Bibliography

Chalmin P. 1983. *Négociants et chargeurs: la saga du négoce international des matières premières.* Paris: Economica.

Eichengreen B. (ed.) 1996. *The reconstruction of the international economy 1945–1960.* Cheltenham and Brookfield: Edward Elgar.

Foreman-Peck J. 1995. *A history of the world economy: international economic relations since 1850.* Hemel Hempstead: Harvester Wheatsheaf.

Jones G. (ed.) 1998. *The multinational traders.* London and New York: Routledge.

Kenwood A.G. and Lougheed A. L. 1992. *The growth of the international economy 1820–1990: an introductory text.* London and New York: Routledge.

Milward A. 1984. *The reconstruction of Western Europe 1945–1951.* London: Methuen.

Thomas M. (ed.) 1996. *The disintegration of the world economy between the world wars.* Cheltenham and Brookfield: Edward Elgar.

Related essays

arms trade; China; commodity trading; containerized freight; convergence and divergence; corporations; debt crises; development and growth; developmental assistance; drugs (illicit); drugs (medical); Economic Commission for Latin America and the Caribbean (ECLAC); empire and migration; European institutions; General Agreement on Tariffs and Trade (GATT) / World Trade Organization (WTO); globalization; Hong Kong and Shanghai Banking Corporation (HSBC); industrialization; information economy; iron and steel; League of Nations Economic and Financial Organization; modernization theory; pedlars; pidgins and creoles; railways; regional communities; rubber; salt; Samsung; steamships; technical standardization; trade (manufactured goods); trade agreements; transportation infrastructures; underdevelopment; United Fruit Company

Trade (manufactured goods)

Manufactured goods constitute a sector of international trade, to rank alongside energy, minerals and basic agricultural products. Not surprisingly, therefore, the development of this trade since the mid 19th century has followed the dominating trends of international exchange. However, its transnational impact has a number of peculiarities: a network of trade relationships that has become ever denser since the 1850s; the dominance of a small number of major exporters throughout most of the 20th century; and nowadays, the ever increasing importance of multinationals. Moreover, the trade in manufactures has contributed significantly to the trend towards global economic and social uniformity.

An ever denser network of trade relationships, 1850–1914

For diverse reasons, in the mid 19th century the trade in manufactured goods began to take the form of an ever denser network of interrelationships. Imports were organized not so much to meet a nation's needs as to facilitate the creation of new trade relationships. Technical progress contributed significantly to this development. For example, the invention of the Bessemer converter encouraged a number of steel concerns to specialize in basic products such as sheet metal or girders, which could be sold cheaply on the world market to machine manufacturers who were themselves producing for export. Similarly, the invention of the Heilmann wool comb in 1845 hugely increased the production of thread for the woollen mills, which were themselves transformed fifty years later with the introduction of the Northrop loom, substantially reducing the cost price of cloth and so facilitating exports. Naturally, the emerging world market always aimed at satisfying the final demand from both individual consumers and firms; nevertheless its development was the result of a process characterized (as traditional theorists have shown) by reciprocal specialization which was in its turn dependent on available means of production.

The rapid growth of Britain's exports – Great Britain alone accounted for 43 per cent of world exports of manufactured goods in 1860 – in itself encouraged the expansion of trade networks. This already striking phenomenon was further accentuated by twenty years of free-trade policies adopted by European governments, from France (Cobden-Chevalier Treaty, 1860) to Russia (1874). Britain herself was also a big exporter of raw materials, especially coal in which she was world leader, and agricultural products from her empire which were re-exported across the world. Her commercial might was, of course, in part an inheritance from the cotton, steel and machinery of the Industrial Revolution; and from the 1880s she faced competition from Germany and the United States, whose exports comprised mostly products of the 'second' industrial revolution such as dyes, electrical goods and high-consumption goods such as detergents, pharmaceuticals and film. Nonetheless, Britain kept its place as the leading world exporter until the outbreak of the First World War and even beyond. This supremacy depended on the enormous diversity of her manufactured exports. Thanks to the exceptionally high proportion of re-exports in her foreign trade, her vast merchant navy, her ports, brokers, banks and insurance industry, Britain was the lynchpin of commerce, the interface between Europe and the rest of the world. It should be noted, however, that 'small' countries such as Belgium, the Netherlands and Switzerland had per capita exports which were actually higher than those of Great Britain. They all contributed to the tightly woven network of trade in manufactured goods which, at this stage, worked mainly to the advantage of Europe and helped establish a domination of world trade which was to continue for many years.

The dominance of major exporting nations: 20th century

Through the 20th century the relative positions of the main exporters of manufactured goods changed constantly, though for a long time these changes were confined to a charmed circle of countries which monopolized most of world trade. This emerges clearly from the accompanying table of the world's top ten exporting nations at certain key dates.

The data are heterogeneous (manufactured exports only pre-1945, all exported goods post-1945), but they clearly show the preponderance of the major exporters through the first half of the century. Between them they accounted for nine tenths of all trade, and almost all were European countries, though joined by the US from 1880, and Japan and Canada from 1919. Their relative positions shifted over the years. Britain, in first place until just before the crisis of the 1930s, dropped to second place and then, from the 1950s, yielded both rank and market share to better-placed rivals. As Britain went down, Germany went up, irrespective of short-term fluctuations and the – actually very radical – changes in her economic policy. Just before the Second World War, despite her tyrannical form of government, she had become the world's leading exporter of manufactured goods. By the 1960s, despite her defeat and ensuing temporary eclipse, she had climbed back as far as second place; by 2003 she was at the top of the table. Few countries retained the same position in the table for very long, although France, for example, was ranked fourth over several decades before yielding that place to China in 2002.

Even setting aside Japan, which can be considered a special case, the rise of Asia is the most remarkable, as well as the most recent, shift in the balance of international trade in manufactured goods. The precocity and vigour of Japan's commercial rise is quite

Table 1 Top ten exporting countries and share of world exports (%), 1913–2005

1913		1929		1937		1951		1973		2005	
United Kingdom	30.2	United Kingdom	22.4	Germany	21.8	United States	19.7	United States	12.2	Germany	9.3
Germany	26.6	Germany	20.5	United Kingdom	20.9	United Kingdom	9.9	West Germany	11.7	United States	8.7
United States	13.0	United States	20.4	United States	19.2	France	5.3	Japan	6.4	China	7.3
France	12.1	France	10.9	Japan	6.9	Canada	5.3	France	6.3	Japan	5.7
Belgium	5.0	Belgium	5.4	Belgium	6.6	West Germany	4.5	United Kingdom	5.3	France	4.4
Italy	3.3	Japan	3.9	France	5.8	Belgium-Lux.	3.5	Canada	4.4	Netherlands	3.9
Switzerland	3.1	Italy	3.7	Canada	4.8	Netherlands	2.6	Netherlands	4.2	United Kingdom	3.6
Japan	2.3	Canada	3.5	Italy	3.5	Sweden	2.3	Belgium-Lux.	3.9	Italy	3.5
Canada	0.6	Switzerland	2.8	Switzerland	2.8	Italy	2.2	Italy	3.9	Canada	3.5
Netherlands	nd	Netherlands	2.5	Sweden	2.6	Japan	1.8	USSR	3.7	Belgium	3.2
Total top ten	96.2	Total top ten	96.0	Total top ten	94.9	Total top ten	57.1	Total top ten	62.0	Total top ten	53.1

Sources: 1913, 1929, 1937: Maizels (1963); 1951, 1973: GATT, International trade, annual reports; 2005: WTO, World trade, annual report.

exceptional: already impressive between the two world wars, it resumed with even greater force after 1945 and took the country into second place by the early 1970s. This was due entirely to sales of manufactured goods, because after the slump of the 1930s Japan ceased to rank as an exporter of raw silk or rice. The phenomenon is even more striking if we look at Japan's percentage of total world export values, which increased by a factor of 3.5 in the twenty or so years from 1951 to 1973. As far as quality is concerned, Japan was reviled in the 1930s as a peddler of shoddy imitations of Western goods, but it now leads the world in high-tech products such as electronic components and computers for both home and business use. But for many years Japan remained an isolated case. It was not until the very end of the 20th century that other Asian countries emerged among the world's great exporters of manufactured goods. In 1973 Hong Kong was still only 23rd in the world ranking. Its foreign trade, distinct from that of China (which treats the island as a 'special administrative region'), has contributed to the recent spectacular rise of China to her current third place.

Thus, whereas at one time Europe and the United States more or less divided world trade in manufactures between them, we now have a more balanced picture, or perhaps one should say a progressive dilution. In the first half of the 20th century, the top ten exporting nations accounted for 95 per cent of total manufactured trade; in 2005, for only just over half (53 per cent). If we reckon not by individual countries but by larger geographical areas, we can discern other significant trends: for example how in less than two decades part of the developing world has joined the ranks of leading vendors of manufactured goods. Thanks to the new commercial giants of the Third World – China, India, Brazil, Mexico – and to the small-scale manufacturing nations, both the first generation (South Korea, Taiwan, Hong Kong, Singapore) and the second (Indonesia, Thailand, the Philippines, Vietnam), in the 1990s the manufactured exports of these regions overtook their exports of raw materials (52.5 per cent of the total). In 1970, only 14 per cent of their total exports consisted of manufactured goods. The contrast is striking evidence of the scale and abruptness of this changeover.

Another factor is that all governments were keen to promote the export of manufactured goods. Exports had to offset imports because the developed economies could no longer count on using investment income to compensate for a trade deficit, as Britain, France and Germany – not to mention small, rich countries such as Belgium and Switzerland – had done up to the First World War. A country that imported more than it exported would inevitably drain its international cash reserves, unless – like the US – it was able to shed the weight of its own excessive consumption onto the rest of the world by increasing indebtedness. Moreover, manufactured exports were essential to economic prosperity at home: the soundness of innumerable firms, the living standards of large sections of the population, and the economic health of whole regions depended heavily on them. Various policies were tried in the attempt to maintain or restore competitiveness. Some were unsuccessful, such as the heavy pressure put on British employers between the wars to keep wages down; others worked better, such as employee participation and wage restraint which, as practised by Federal Republic of Germany after 1949, enabled her to climb rapidly back to her place among the top exporters, despite the wholesale destruction caused by the country's military defeat. Similarly, the quest for competitiveness was a key element in the French government's attempts, from the founding of the Common Market in 1959 to the signing of the Treaty of Maastricht in 1992, to curb inflationary trends, check public spending, and make the economy more structurally competitive. When this goal proved impossible to attain by traditional methods, a recourse to monetary policy became inevitable. Aggressive devaluation was part of this strategy, intended as a shot in the arm for exports which might restore a lost trade balance. Thus the United States, facing her first ever trade deficit in 1971, twice devalued the dollar and then forced the rest of the world to adopt a new international monetary system based on floating exchange rates. Thus a really major change in the transnational economic order arose from shifts in the world trade in manufactures. Third World countries that were initially reluctant to participate in the global trade in manufactures, seeing it as a token of dependence and subjection to imperialist powers, now accept it as an integral part of developmental strategies. Since the mid 1960s, a number of small Asian, Latin American and black African countries have aspired to rival South Korea by joining the enviable club of small-scale manufacturers. Whatever the method employed, by either a mature economy or a newly industrializing country, a government seeking to promote manufactured exports is unlikely to succeed in the long term unless it can count on a range of firms equipped to rise to the challenge.

A transnational actor of increasing importance: multinationals

The world trade in manufactured products, unlike that in basic commodities, has always relied more on actual manufacturers than on brokers. There are of course exceptions to this rule. Japan's *sōgō shōsha* (trade companies) will trade internationally in any product entrusted to them by an industrial firm. In the late 19th century, the European colonial powers spawned a number of export/import companies which collected basic commodities from the native population and sold them manufactured goods from the home country. French examples were the Société Commerciale de l'Ouest Africain (SCOA) and the Compagnie Française pour l'Afrique de l'Ouest (CFAO), founded by oil and soap magnates based in Marseilles; Britain had the Royal Niger Company and the British South Africa Company, both of which were long prominent in the slave trade. Some of these companies survived both the turn of the century and the dismembering of the colonial empires, but only through radical transformation. Britain's Royal Niger Company became the United Africa Company and is now a subsidiary of Unilever, which bought it at its foundation in 1929. SCOA was bought by the bank Paribas, and CFAO by the industrialist François Pinault.

More significant, as regards the structure of the world trade in manufactures, is the growing importance of a new kind of firm, the multinationals. Although a few American firms, such as Singer and Westinghouse, and some European ones like Saint-Gobain, Solvay and Siemens, had some of the characteristics of multinationals as far back as the 19th century, the phenomenon did not really take off until the second half of the 20th. There are many indicators of its importance to international trade, but its extent has aroused conflicting interpretations.

The importance of multinationals in international trade can be gauged from their share of the imports/exports of various countries. There is every indication that their impact is now considerable. Intra-group trade by multinationals organizing production among their factories across the globe probably accounts for some 30–40 per cent of the foreign trade of developing countries. Each group conducts a substantial part of its business abroad: the scale of this can be measured against a 'transnationality index', i.e. the arithmetical mean of those parts of a firm's turnover, workforce and assets which are held abroad. The figure can be very high, especially if the firm is based in a small country: in 2000 it was 85 per cent for Nestlé and 95 per cent for ABB (Asea Brown Boveri), an electrical construction group born of a merger between a Swiss firm and a Swedish firm.

Not all authors take an equally positive view of multinationals and their role, however. Some, like Robert Reich, think that multinationals, which he prefers to call 'global' or 'worldwide' firms, have emptied the term 'foreign trade' of most of its original content. They do, of course, have a registered office in some country or other – the choice is often made for tax reasons. But the notion of nationality is by definition irrelevant to their activity, whether seen in terms of jobs, capital deployment or manufactured products – which are sometimes deliberately designed to be identical, and are served by the same advertising campaigns, throughout the world. As a result, the foreign trade statistics of individual countries become virtually meaningless. Can we really talk about 'South Korean exports' when they come from a group whose registered office is in Bermuda, while its workforce is Philippine or Brazilian and its shareholders are American and Japanese pension funds? How representative are global statistics when we know that many of the results involved are from products which are not genuinely traded at all, only transferred from one factory to another within the same group? Other observers, however, think that nationality is still an important criterion; only a few industries, such as electronics, agro-alimentary, chemicals and pharmaceuticals can be called truly 'multinational'. There is indeed a lot of evidence that the 'multinationalization' of world trade has its limits. In some countries the proportion of intra-group exchange in the total of foreign trade has not increased or changed much since the early 1980s. Transnationality indexes are not much higher today than fifteen or even twenty years ago.

Whatever we may think of them, multinationals have profoundly changed the face of foreign trade in manufactured goods. This has inevitably had a substantial impact on economies and societies.

A contributor to global uniformity?

Without succumbing to the illusions of the 19th-century free-traders, who believed that the expansion of international trade would usher in an era of worldwide peace and prosperity; and equally without sinking into the pessimism of those who consider that international competition threatens to reduce entire populations to joblessness and poverty, it could well be argued that the development of the world trade in manufactures over the 20th century and into the 21st has not only spread similar lifestyles and consumer habits over the entire planet and made some areas so interdependent as to be inseparable; it has also helped to disrupt economies and weaken the fabric of societies.

The worldwide diffusion of lifestyles and consumer habits is plain to see. It often takes the form of Americanization, although the importance of the US in world change fluctuated throughout the last century. Triumphant over her European rivals in 1918, catapulted to the height of influence in 1945 by the ruin of both Europe and Japan, her supremacy was not challenged until the 1960s, and in all but a few subsequent years (when she had to yield to Germany) she retained her status as the world's greatest trading nation, and even recovered a large measure of supremacy in the early 1980s, when the international monetary system was reorganized on a basis of floating exchange rates, and again after the collapse of the Socialist bloc. America's commercial omnipotence led to worldwide adoption of American products and American lifestyles. Americanization is in fact the consequence of the worldwide expansion of trade in manufactured goods: it can be seen as a form of acculturation which was perceptible in Europe from the dawn of the 20th century and subsequently spread to other continents. But this was far from being the only form of acculturation. Within Europe, the free trade permitted by the foundation and subsequent enlargement of the European Economic Community / European Union facilitated the acquisition of consumer durables which became progressively more similar in different countries and across social boundaries, largely because such goods could be procured more abundantly and cheaply than on national markets. The same applies to the astonishing ubiquity of (for example) tape recorders made in Japan, shoes made in Brazil or Argentina, or clothes made in Tunisia or Pakistan: in each case, the expansion of the trade in manufactured goods has notably increased consumers' purchasing power, however much one may deplore the resulting trend towards uniformity.

Looking at the spatial dimension, we can see that the trade in manufactured goods has created such tight networks of interdependence that certain border regions have tended to merge: for example, the area comprising Alsace, Baden-Württemberg and the Basle region. In some parts of the world, complementary or common spaces had been part of civilization for centuries, but only now can we speak in terms of identical ways of organizing space. One example is the port-and-industry complexes that sprang up in the 1950s and 1960s on the seaboards of America, Western Europe and Japan, with their conglomeration of massive transport infrastructure, heavy industry and urbanization. It matters little whether it is located at Sparrows Point, Ijmuiden, Dunkirk, Tarento or Kobe: a specialized steel complex will work in the same way, impelled by the same need for easy access to supplies of imported iron ore and easy routes for exporting the finished products to customers abroad. Even the very means of transport will be much the same from one world's end to the other. For the carriage of goods by sea, containers, already in use before the Second World War by railway and road haulage companies for internal transportation, were from 1956 used by American ship owners on routes between continental America and Puerto Rico or Hawai'i. Ten years later they were introduced on North Atlantic and subsequently trans-Pacific routes. Now they are universal, and ports that are specially equipped to handle them have a decisive edge over the competition. Similarly, proximity to a large airport and ready access to the motorway network are often deciding factors in the location of any industrial firm that engages in foreign trade, or aspires to do so.

The resulting interdependence is now well established, though it has come about in ways that were scarcely anticipated by the early apostles of free trade. We have not seen industrialized countries becoming more complementary, each specializing in one particular kind of product to the exclusion of all others;

instead, each has continued to produce a full range of goods, and if trade with other industrialized countries has continued to expand, this does not take the form of exchanges between different industries but of exchanges within each industry. In the EU countries, for example, same-industry trade increased at varying rates in the thirty or so years from 1961 to 1992. The increase was slight in older industrialized countries such as Belgium-Luxembourg (18 per cent), but spectacular in late developers such as Ireland (86 per cent) whose initial development actually rode on the back of this kind of trade, often controlled by the multinationals.

It must nonetheless be acknowledged that the expansion of trade in manufactures has also contributed to the fragmentation and dislocation of economies and societies. This is becoming ever clearer with the progress of globalization. Relocations can destroy jobs in certain regions, especially if they have an insufficiently diversified workforce or one that is unwilling to retrain. Regions that had staked their future on international trade have turned into unemployment black spots that constitute a thorny problem for governments. In emerging countries, stark inequalities can exist between those who have a share in the new economy, open to the outside, and those who have not. In China, for example, the coastal provinces, which geographically speaking constitute only 12 per cent of the country, account for two thirds of its wealth. This is a universal phenomenon: some analysts, indeed, believe that the exponential growth of trade in manufactures is forcing the world into a more and more explosive concatenation of contrasts, polarizing societies to the benefit of a tiny minority with everyone else relegated to the ranks of the proletariat. In that case, the uniformity created by international trade would be a negative process indeed.

The whole process is hedged about with uncertainty. Nonetheless, looking back over the last century, it has to be acknowledged that the ever growing trade in manufactured goods has changed the world. It has overturned the hierarchy of nations, bringing about uniformity, imitation, and sometimes differentiation. Without it, the current world economy would undoubtedly look very different.

Jean-François Eck

Bibliography

Bairoch P. 'Globalization myths and realities: one century of external trade and foreign investment', in Boyer R. and Drache D. (eds) 1996. *States against markets: the limits of globalization.* London and New York: Routledge, 173–92.

Lorenz D. 'Newly industrialising countries in the world economy: NICs, SICs, NECs, EPZs or TEs?', in Holtfrerich C. L. (ed.) 1989. *Interactions in the world economy: perspectives from international economic history. Festschrift in honour of Wolfram Fischer.* Hemel Hempstead: Harvester Wheatsheaf, 338–66.

Maddison A. 1991. *Dynamic forces in capitalist development: a long-run comparative view.* Oxford and New York: Oxford University Press.

Maizels A. 1963. *Industrial growth and world trade.* Cambridge: Cambridge University Press.

Reich R. 1991. *The work of nations: preparing ourselves for 21st century capitalism.* New York: Knopf.

Related essays

America; car culture; commodity trading; consumer society; containerized freight; corporations; counterfeit goods; development and growth; industrialization; iron and steel; patents; Pax Americana; remittances; rubber; Samsung; steamships; technical standardization; technologies; textiles; trade; trade agreements; trademarks; transportation infrastructures; Westernization

Trade agreements

Trade agreements may be intergovernmental treaties or merely agreements between private firms; their effect is to promote trade between partner nations by, for example, reducing customs duties, fixing prices or controlling trade volumes. Some go further than this, taking the form of regional agreements which encourage more extensive cooperation among partner states, perhaps with the ultimate aim of creating a common economic area. Obviously all such agreements, whatever their nature and whoever drafts them, have transnational implications.

In the 19th century, trade agreements were the chief instrument of a government's economic policy and therefore the focus of pressure by economic interest groups. In a century of fixed exchange rates, monetary policy could have only a short-term effect on gold and capital movements, and direct government intervention in industry was limited, save in a few countries, and even then only in a few enterprises such as railways.

Agreements usually took the form of heavily protectionist bilateral treaties in the tradition of 18th-century industrialist policies. After the end of the Napoleonic Wars, Britain gained such a lead in industrial development that other countries could only industrialize through tariffs intended to protect their cotton or steel manufactures in course of modernization. This protectionism was selective, prohibiting the import of finished (cotton) goods but often – as in the German states – allowing in semi-manufactured goods such as cotton yarn, pig iron and machinery that home industries could not yet produce in sufficient quantity. Such 'educational' protectionism (the term coined by Friedrich List) was considered to be temporary: as industrialization progressed, these imports would be replaced by home-produced goods as soon as the new industries became competitive. By the mid 19th century, as industry progressed in Continental Europe, this protectionism was relaxed in a series of new agreements: either because the appetite of railway companies for rails took precedence over the interests of more expensive home steel manufacturers, or because product diversification made it possible for work to be shared out more precisely among partner states.

This liberalizing trend culminated in the Anglo–French commercial treaty of January 1860, which slashed the hitherto prohibitive customs duties on both sides – French wines and silks against English cottons. Most important, it contained a most-favoured-nation clause whereby any advantage granted thereafter to a third country would automatically be extended to the other signatory of the 1860 treaty. This liberalizing clause introduced a multilateral dimension into subsequent bilateral treaties between, for example, France and Prussia.

The revolution in agricultural markets from the 1870s, a global slowdown in economic growth which exacerbated competition, and the downward trend of product prices which eroded profits put an end to this liberal hiatus in a protectionist century. Only Britain retained her devotion to free trade, while Continental Europe through the 1870s and 1880s protected agricultural incomes by placing import duties on cheaper American corn and meat in a world market now awash

with surpluses. Industrialists, too, benefited from tariffs that gave them a monopoly over national markets. When treaties made in the 1860s expired at the end of the agreed twenty years, it was at a time of economic constraint, and negotiations for renewal were difficult and ended in the imposition of greatly increased tariffs. Sometimes the outcome was a 'customs war' as each side jacked up its tariffs: thus in the 1890s Italy and France fought it out over wine, each country trying to barricade its frontiers against imports from the other, using product standards as a lever by prohibiting certain additives or production methods. By the beginning of the 20th century, despite the rapid expansion of international trade, the world had been segmented by a network of bilateral treaties designed to protect each nation's home industries.

However, some trade agreements already had a more ambitious aim: the creation of an integrated economic area. An example is the Zollverein set up in 1834 by a group of German states to facilitate transport and trade in the northern part of what in 1871 was to become the German Reich. This economic integration, supplemented by monetary integration (only two currencies remained in use in Germany) preceded and promoted political unification. On the other hand, the proposed customs union between France and Belgium in 1837 was a failure, not only because French steel manufacturers feared competition from their more advanced Belgian counterparts but also because Great Britain, ever anxious to maintain the balance of power in Europe, refused to tolerate this joining of forces.

In the second half of the 19th century, the growing internationalization of trade encouraged international agreements to facilitate or regulate it. Great rivers such as the Rhine, Elbe and Danube became international waterways controlled by international committees; the Universal Postal Union was created to facilitate sending goods by mail; and a Railway Union was set up in 1890. By the dawn of the 20th century it was easy to assume that despite widespread protectionism, the internationalization of economic life was a fait accompli.

Although 20th-century conditions were less propitious, numerous trade agreements continued to be made, though not all were between governments. In the first half of the century big firms sought to regulate international trade by means of cartels and understandings. These may have distorted free competition and accentuated the tendency to oligopoly in some areas of industry; but they also considerably enlarged the market for the products concerned. The best-known example is the Achnacarry Agreement made in 1928 between the seven major British and American oil companies which, by stabilizing oil prices up to the early 1970s, fostered the consumption of hydrocarbons worldwide, consummated their triumph over solid fuels and ushered in a second wave of industrialization. The Aluminium Association of 1901, the Convention Internationale des Glaceries (glassmakers' convention) of 1904, the French and German potash manufacturers' agreements and the International Steel Cartel are examples showing how the trend impacted upon all branches of industry. Agriculture was also affected, though here there was a greater inclination to operate at intergovernmental level, as shown by the rubber agreements made under the aegis of colonial Britain in 1922 and the Chadbourne (sugar) Agreement of 1931, named after the American banker who brokered the deal. Then there was a plethora of agreements intended to regulate trade in basic products, either between producing countries, or between consumer countries, or between representatives of both groups. Unlike their manufacturing counterparts, however, these agreements did nothing, through the crisis years of the 1930s, either to stimulate production or to stabilize prices.

More general agreements were also signed between the two world wars. Some were as much political as economic: for example, the Franco–German agreement of 1927 was a symptom of diplomatic détente. Others enabled major controlling powers to tighten their network of influences and organize trade to their own advantage in times of crisis. Examples are the 1932 Ottawa Agreement between Britain, the dominions and India, and the fifteen or so agreements made from 1934 between the United States and other American countries under the Reciprocal Trade Agreement Act. Others genuinely sought to create common markets: bypassing the League of Nations, which proved incapable of imposing customs agreements, they progressively lowered customs barriers among signatories and abolished import embargoes. Examples are the Oslo and Ouchy agreements of 1932, the first of which united

the Scandinavian countries, and the second Belgium, the Netherlands and Luxembourg: they showed that international cooperation was still a reality, despite the then current economic crisis, and foreshadowed the regional unions that were to emerge after 1945.

After the Second World War it became difficult to make trade agreements limited to a few countries, owing to the new universal rules laid down by world organizations devoted to free trade (thus the General Agreement on Tariffs and Trade or GATT). Signatories to GATT were bound to refrain from discrimination and from according preferential treatment to partners with whom they had specific agreements. It became difficult to create regional unions or to respond positively to Third World demands for favourable treatment in international trade. In the early 1960s the first steps towards an European Economic Community, with a common external tariff and a common agricultural policy, met with fierce opposition from the United States, whose consent was forthcoming only in exchange for free access to the common market for American soya cake and other animal feeds, free of the tariffs imposed on other agricultural imports.

Despite such obstacles, regional agreements multiplied and became the commonest form of trade agreement. Some aimed to further integration among their members by creating a common customs barrier against the rest of the world, a common economic policy, and sometimes even a common currency. In other words, they were customs unions which could eventually become unified economic areas, as with the European Union. Others aimed merely at a progressive reduction of customs duties, sometimes excluding agricultural products and/or key manufactured goods. The result was no more than a free-trade area, with no unified customs tariffs and no economic union. A typical example is ASEAN (the Association of Southeast Asian Nations), formed in 1967, originally with six members and now with ten, including a number of countries specializing in small-scale manufactures. There are also intermediates between these two extremes, such as MERCOSUR (the South American Common Market), set up in 1991 by Brazil, Argentina, Uruguay and Paraguay and subsequently joined by Venezuela. While its primary purpose was to encourage internal trade, it went on to create a common external tariff – originally with numerous exceptions – that was finally unified in 2006. As a general rule, all such regional agreements were and are between countries that are either geographically or economically close to one another. They may, however, create new links of interdependence that transcend the old relationships among their members. A notable example of this is NAFTA (the North American Free Trade Agreement), signed in 1994 by the US, Canada and Mexico, which aims to spread its advantages equally among all three members, although the US has always carried vastly more weight than the other two partners, making for a somewhat unbalanced and artificial association.

These regional agreements copy from one another, as shown by the popularity of the title 'Common Market', even where the actual agreement has little in common with the one made by the six original signatories to the Treaty of Rome. It is often difficult to compare results, especially when each agreement may unite countries in very different circumstances, from leading developed economies to emerging nations. But however far (or little) advanced the integration they involve, the transnational impact of such agreements is far from negligible.

For one thing, they stimulate foreign direct investment, because companies will establish a presence in the area concerned so as to avoid its customs barriers. This phenomenon was observed in the European Union as soon as the common customs tariffs were created in 1959–68, and also thereafter, during the years when the great common market in personnel, services and capital was being developed (1986–92), in the wake of the Single European Act. Regional agreements also have the effect of speeding up internal change. They force backward sectors – such as agriculture – to modernize, even at the cost of squeezing out less competitive practitioners and forcing alignment with a dominant economic model. They create transborder regions which, thanks to the density of commercial, financial and human resources, turn into unified spaces in their own right and sometimes create their own institutional links, such as the association created in 1991 between Kent, the French region of Nord-Pas-de-Calais and the three Belgian regions of Flanders, Wallonia and Brussels, initially to prepare the infrastructure required by the Channel Tunnel, and then to develop cooperation in other matters. It is not, however, certain that such regional agreements will produce genuinely united economic areas in the image of the federated states bequeathed to us by history. The actual performance of member states, in terms of growth, employment and monetary stability, tends to show that such unions will probably not prove to be the hoped-for, or alternatively dreaded, catalyst of uniformity.

Jean-François Eck

Bibliography
Barjot D. (ed.) 1994. *International cartels revisited / Vues nouvelles sur les cartels internationaux (1880–1980)*. Caen: Lys.
Dumoulin M. (ed.) 2004. *Réseaux économiques et construction européenne / Economic networks and European integration*. Brussels: PIE / Peter Lang.
Neal L. 1979. 'The economic and finance of bilateral clearing agreements: Germany 1934–1938', *Economic History Review*, 32, 3, 391–404.
Wurm C. A. (ed.) 1989. *Internationale Kartelle und Aussenpolitik: Beiträge zur Zwischenkriegszeit*. Stuttgart: Steiner.

Related essays
agriculture; animal diseases; borders and borderlands; commodity trading; corporations; European Union (EU); food safety standards; General Agreement on Tariffs and Trade (GATT) / World Trade Organization (WTO); gold; higher education; investment; iron and steel; oil; open door and free flow; Pax Americana; regional communities; regions; rubber; services; textiles; trade; trade (manufactured goods); Washington Consensus

T-shirt

The origins of the T-shirt are normally traced to the First World War, when the light cotton garments began to be used as undershirts for soldiers. T-shirts began to be worn as outer wear by World War 2, and in the 1960s began to carry messages and pictures.

The everyday T-shirt is an illuminating example of a simple consumer product with a complex transnational life story. The journey from 'seed to shirt' involves several global industries, including cotton agriculture, textiles, and apparel. In addition, used T-shirts comprise a global industry as well. The production of a T-shirt begins with the harvesting of cotton. The raw cotton is then spun into yarn, which in turn is knitted into fabric. Finally, the fabric is cut into pieces and stitched together to form the shirt.

Today, it is common for each of these stages of the T-shirt's production to take place in a different country, as comparative advantage has led countries to specialize in certain steps links of the chain. In addition, since the mid 1980s, there has been a pronounced trend in the disintegration of the apparel industry, with supply contract relationships replacing factories owned by apparel firms. Well known sportswear firms such as Nike or Adidas rarely own the factories in which their T-shirts are produced, and instead rely on international networks of supplier factories.

Both rich and poor countries participate in the T-shirt value chain. Some of the richest and poorest countries in the world are important cotton producers. While cotton production is mechanized in rich countries such as the US, it is largely the product of manual labour in Asia and Africa. Most countries have the capability to spin yarn and knit fabric and because these processes are capital-intensive, production remains somewhat steady in wealthy countries. At the sewing stage, however, the majority of the value added is through labour, because the sewing process remains highly labour-intensive and difficult to mechanize. As a result, while cotton, yarn, and fabric are produced in both rich and poor countries, at the apparel stage the T-shirt production is likely to take place in countries with low labour costs.

China is the world's largest producer and exporter of T-shirts, with a dominant share of the market in Japan and Australia. However, as of 2007, both Europe and the United States have import limits (quotas) in place for Chinese T-shirts and other Chinese-made apparel. These import quotas are an attempt to protect the rich-country textile industries from lower-cost imports. Though little T-shirt production takes place in these wealthy countries, the textile industries continue to attempt to protect their yarn and fabric producers. In the United States, complicated trade rules result in a dominant position in the T-shirt industry for Central American producers, who stitch T-shirts together using American-made yarn, fabric and thread.

The story of the T-shirt is transnational at the level of the consumer as well as the producer. In the US and Europe, T-shirts are normally worn as informal clothing today. During the period 1995–2007, T-shirt prices dropped by approximately half, largely because of shifting production to low-wage countries. The price decline has led to higher consumption and frequent T-shirt 'giveaways' by businesses and other organizations. Many of these T-shirts end up in donation bins, and the charities collecting the T-shirts will typically sell the excess clothing to private companies, at which point the clothing enters new global industries.

Some used T-shirts are cut into squares or rectangles and sold as rags for use in factories. Others are shredded into an industrial product known as shoddy, which has numerous manufacturing uses as stuffing or padding. Most of the remaining T-shirts are exported. In quantity terms, most used European and American clothing is sold to Africa, where the T-shirts are worn by men, women and children. However, in dollar terms, the largest buyer of used T-shirts is Japan, where 'vintage' T-shirts bearing certain logos or pictures often sell for more than one hundred dollars.

Pietra Rivoli

Bibliography

Rivoli P. 2006. *The travels of a T-shirt in the global economy.* Hoboken: Wiley.

Related essays

dress; Guevara, Ernesto ('Che'); jeans; silk; sports gear and apparel; textiles

Trademarks

Trademarks can be either verbal – brand or firm names – or emblematic, in the form of manufacturers' or traders' marks or logos. They provide an indication of how goods produced by a given company are manufactured, sold and consumed. There is a difference between manufacturers' marks, which enable manufacturers to identify their products and guarantee their origin, and trademarks proper, which identify the person or organization that delivered the product to the consumer. These marks derive from complex market relationships and interactions: not only among manufacturers, dealers and consumers, but also between national and international institutions.

For many years, any problems relating to trademarks arose in a national context. As international commerce developed, industry spread and production intensified it became necessary to consider the international protection of trademarks. It was not until the latter half of the 19th century that governments began to pass specific legislation in order to combat counterfeiting, guarantee the quality of goods delivered to the consumer, and protect national manufacturing industries.

The oldest trademark law was passed in France on 23 June 1857. It stipulated that permanent ownership of a trademark could be acquired and retained through customary use. The law defined which signs could be accepted as trademarks and which products could receive such marks, along with conditions for protecting them, penalties for abuse, customs regulations, jurisdiction over trademark disputes, and foreigners' rights. Other countries passed similar, but less allembracing legislation: thus Austria-Hungary (1858), Britain (1862), Italy (1868), the US (1870–76), Germany (1874) and Switzerland (1879). These laws pursued two very different paths. In Britain and the US it was not necessary to register the trademark in advance in order to get it protected; in France, it had to be registered before use in order to safeguard it as industrial property.

Despite the existence of some 69 special conventions assuring reciprocal protection of trademarks in signatory nations, and the protection of foreign trademarks in liberal countries such as Britain, the Netherlands, Spain and Italy, the situation remained more or less anarchic and impossible to harmonize. As international trade increased, governments and traders felt it was imperative to ensure protection of trademarks in continually widening markets. It was both a key commercial requirement and a necessity for the growth of national manufactures.

The 1883 Paris Convention on the protection of industrial property covered both patents and trademarks: the eleven signatories undertook to recognize and protect trademarks registered in any member state. Such protection would require simultaneous registration of trademarks in more than one country. This was discussed at a diplomatic conference in 1890, organized by Switzerland but held in Madrid, leading to the 1891 Madrid Arrangement that was signed by five countries: France, Belgium, Spain, Switzerland and Tunisia. Centralized registration was organized by the applicant's national administration, which registered the trademark at an international office located in Bern.

These first international agreements were among countries whose national legislation depended on registration, which effectively excluded countries where industrial property rights depended on customary use. In consequence, Britain and the US held aloof from such agreements. However, the dizzying expansion of American industry at the turn of the 20th century quickened interest in trademarks among American manufacturers and diplomats: laws were passed on 20 February 1905 and in 1930, conferring ownership of a trademark on the first person to use it in foreign trade. It was not until 1946 that a federal law, the Lanham Act, harmonized the laws of various US states that had defined trademarks and regulated foreign trade practices. Nonetheless use still had to precede registration, which meant that the US could not join the Madrid Arrangement. In 1988 the Lanham Act was amended to bring it closer to Continental European legislation: it now permitted registration based on a declaration of intent to use the trademark, and proof of use was made a precondition for registration. This adjustment enabled the World Intellectual Property Organization (WIPO) to add a protocol (1990) to the Madrid Arrangement, enabling Americans to access the central registry of trademarks. The enlarged Madrid Arrangement now covers more than sixty countries, so that a single formal application can extend the protection afforded by registration in one country to a large number of others. Trademarks are also covered by agreements developed by the International Chamber of Commerce (ICC).

Meanwhile, the European Community was harmonizing internal trademark regulations. The process began in 1960, but it was not until 1988 that rules appeared in the form of a directive to approximate the laws of member states relating to trademarks. In 1996 the Office for the Harmonization of the Internal Market was set up in Spain. It operates a once-for-all registration process for Community trademarks and brands, which is binding on all member states for ten years.

The globalization of markets and the development of the Internet have stimulated the harmonization of trademark legislation by encouraging the move from national to international registration. The challenge for the 21st century will be to ensure that legislation keeps up with the accelerating pace of trade, and includes means of enforcement that will be effective in ensuring that trademark protection is effective worldwide.

Nadège Sougy

Bibliography

Beltran A., Chauveau S. and Galvez-Behar G. 2001. *Des brevets et des marques: une histoire de la propriété industrielle*. Paris: Fayard.

Le Grand F. 1926. *Les marques de fabrique au point de vue international*. Unpublished dissertation, University of Paris.

Latham D. 1992. 'Times past: early registrations in the United Kingdom', *Trade Mark World*, 51, October, 24–32.

Robert D. 1996. 'Commentary on the Lanham Trade-Mark Act', *Trademark Reporter*, July–August, 373–97.

Related essays

counterfeit goods; European Union (EU); intellectual property rights; patents; technical standardization; trade (manufactured goods)

Traffic signals

Traffic signals, notably the ubiquitous red/green lights and the octagonal stop sign, are global semiotic references, whose meaning is clearly understood across cultures. The red light means stop in New York, in Beijing, in São Paulo, in Melbourne, in Lagos, in Helsinki and in everyplace between. Strikingly a global consensus on these instruments of social control was reached in the early 20th century, an era usually associated with nationalist confrontation, rather than global collaboration.

The first red warning light was at the Flamborough Head Lighthouse in England in 1806. George Robinson, the engineer who designed the light, needed a colour other than white to allow mariners to distinguish the light from another nearby. He chose red, not for any particular cultural reason, but because tests showed that red stained glass was more transparent than any other color. The British Admiralty accepted this reasoning and decreed the use of red lanterns on the port side (where ships were not supposed to pass one another in crowded anchorages) in 1852. Since Britain dominated world trade at the time, the pattern spread across the oceans. Ships also added green on the

starboard or passing side. British engineers, the world's leading railway builders, adopted the same system (red meaning 'stop' and green meaning 'go' as customary practices). These became the international custom.

Road signals followed. The automobile-producing cities of the American Midwest experienced some of the first automotive traffic jams in 1914, the year after Henry Ford began to mass-produce Model T cars. The phrase 'traffic jam' entered the English language in 1910, a sign of the increase in traffic as automobile registration grew and generated far worse blockades than its horse-drawn predecessors. In 1917 a merchant's group, the Fifth Avenue Association, claimed gridlock was costing New York City stores US\$750,000 a day. Already 25,000 cars a day operated on that street. Chicago's trolley companies claimed automobiles slowed transit speeds by 45 per cent in the Central Business District. Initial attempts to control traffic by policemen on foot or, later, mounted in towers at the centre of intersections failed in the Midwest and elsewhere in both Europe and North America after roughly ten years of trials.

In the summer of 1914 the city of Cleveland installed the first permanent (there had been earlier, temporary installations in London and Salt Lake City) red traffic light at the corner of Euclid Ave and 105th St. Refinements followed. Cleveland added a green light shortly thereafter. Sergeant William Potts of the Detroit Police Department added a yellow caution light in 1920. Soon thereafter a system of internal lighting was adopted that allowed for green to always appear on top. Hinds-Crouse, a railway signal firm, installed the first automatic lights, allowing a steady flow of traffic, in Houston, Texas in 1922. European visitors to the US before 1920 expressed amazement at the willingness of American drivers to obey a machine but the new technology spread rapidly through the global system of cities, following the appearance of traffic. Paris adopted the first lights in Europe in 1922, Berlin followed in 1924 and London in 1931. Both Stockholm and Tokyo reported the installation of staggered automatic lights, also in 1931. Some cities too small or poor to have many cars, adopted lights as a symbol of modernity, long in advance of traffic.

Much the same diffusion was followed by stop signs after Detroit police sergeant Harry Jackson cut the corners off a square sign to create the familiar red octagonal sign in 1914. The signs stopped side street traffic from interfering with commuters on a radial boulevard bound for Detroit's upper-class suburb of Grosse Pointe. Not surprisingly neighbourhood residents objected, preferring the supposedly more democratic traffic lights (because neighbourhood cross-traffic both by car and on foot had an equal chance with the commuters). Stop signs blocked them from crossing the street while allowing affluent suburbanites to speed home.

What is most striking about this process is the pattern of uniformity that emerged. Everywhere lights were funded and installed locally. In the US the national government had no power in these matters. Certainly there was no supranational controlling body either in Europe or elsewhere. This system of technology-based social control was disseminated by a global network of municipal engineers, some of whom, by the late 1920s, had come to define themselves as traffic engineers. They were supported by the global tourism industry, which realized that familiar traffic rules would encourage motor touring.

The ideas spread in various ways. Specialized professional journals were crucial. There were hundreds of these in circulation by the late 1920s. The widely available (by 1920 the libraries at MIT, the University of Zurich, Imperial College London and the University of Karlsruhe subscribed) *Engineering Index* abstracted and offered full-text copies and translations at a reasonable price of articles from over a thousand engineering periodicals in a wide variety of languages. Engineering periodicals were not shy about borrowing from foreign counterparts. Early traffic planners also travelled to other cities looking for the best, or at least most common, practices. In 1931 *American City Magazine* reported on perhaps the first pedestrian lights, which had been installed in Stockholm.

Road engineers from a number of nations (and American states) also attended meetings of the International Roads Congress, which held sessions on traffic, beginning in 1908 in Paris, where ideas were shared formally and informally. Individual 'research trips' and consulting also spread ideas. In 1928 the Spanish Ministry of Public Works, concerned with the growth of traffic in Barcelona and Madrid, sent one of its engineers to observe control practices in both Chicago and New York. In 1931 Taiji Hirayama acknowledged

borrowing the staggered lights installed on the Ginza from American practice.

Ultimately voluntary interstate (in the US) and international bodies would play a role. In 1924 US Secretary of Commerce Herbert Hoover called a conference of 550 safety experts, mostly state and local officials, who prepared a set of uniform traffic rules (including the red/green light and octagonal stop sign). Although the results of this conference had no legal force, it cemented the national uniformity already achieved by the engineers. European nations, beginning with Britain in 1921, created their own national systems of road signs, in most cases superseding local variations and resembling the American system for at least some signs. The final step in globalization was the first League of Nations conference on uniform traffic rules in 1926. Here too the recommendation was for red/green lights and red octagonal signs. This reinforced the global standard, again already created by the engineers.

Sometimes there have been challenges to the system. In the 1920s, perceptual psychologists pointed out that colour-blind drivers could not distinguish between red and green, so other colours would be a better alternative. Some Irish nationalists wanted green displayed above red, which they associated with Britain. Some Red Guards in the 1960s proposed that red should mean go in China, but the central government blocked that. Almost every locality tried some local variation initially. Global uniformity won out each time.

Conventions held by the United Nations Economic Commission for Europe in 1949 and 1968 further standardized road signs, moving beyond the more basic stop sign and traffic light. In the early 1970s European-style, that is, totally symbolic, signs became the norm in the US and elsewhere in the world. Global tourism has reinforced this trend. The Dominican Republic, for example, borrows its system of traffic signage from the United States, which is, of course, linked to the global system. This is largely to facilitate driving for visiting Americans: the search for a road order is not connected to the needs of local traffic only.

Clay McShane

Bibliography
Barrett P. 1983. *The automobile and public transit: the formation of public policy in*

Chicago. Philadelphia: Temple University Press.

Buitter H. and Staal P. Forthcoming. 'City lights: regulated streets and the evolution of traffic lights in The Netherlands, 1920–1940', *Journal of Transport History.*

Lay M. 1992. *A history of the world's roads and the vehicles that used them.* New Brunswick: Rutgers University Press.

McShane C. 1999. 'The origins and globalization of traffic control signals', *Journal of Urban History,* 25, 3, 379–404.

Sessions G. M. 1971. *Traffic devices: historical aspects thereof.* Washington, DC: Institute of Traffic Engineers.

Related essays

car culture; car safety standards; city planning; engineering; food safety standards; information technology (IT) standardization; intergovernmental organizations; International Road Federation (IRF); League of Nations system; railways; technical standardization; tourism; transportation infrastructures; United Cities and Local Governments (UCLG)

Translation

A translation is a text that expresses in one language what was originally written in another one. To a lesser extent the term 'translation' is also applied to oral performances (e.g. the simultaneous translation of a conference) that interpret and communicate in one language what has been said in another one. It is enough to consider the multiplicity of existing languages to understand the centrality of translations in the production of cultural relations across borders. Translations make possible the understanding of languages that are not those of origin. However, their potential contribution to intercultural understanding is not self-evident.

Translation serves two purposes. In the first place it involves a *mediation*: the translation is a device that allows comprehension of a message expressed in a language that a potential receiver does not know. Unlike the interlinguistic experiences of the polyglot, translation generates indirect communication. Secondly, it is a *phenomenon of cultural selection*: not everything is translated. Decisions about what is translated reflect social and cultural rules and hierarchies.

In order to understand the power and the meaning of translation in the establishment of transnational cultural relations, it is necessary to consider it as a historical phenomenon. In societies without writing, communication is restricted to the direct interaction of the interlocutors. Cultural transmission is imprisoned in the homeostatic process of orality and memory. Although communication among different linguistic and cultural groups can be made by polyglots, the span of oral transmission is limited in terms of social space as well as in time. Writing is, foremost, accumulated material. Jack Goody and Ian Watt have demonstrated that the spread of the phonetic alphabet from Ancient Greece represented the most universal phenomenon of cultural diffusion in human history. If the famous case of the Rosetta Stone has shown the importance of translation of the written word in the constitution of bureaucratic power, the earlier emergence of technologies like papyrus, and its later composition in codex, had amplified the possibilities of intercultural transmission of thought on a large territorial scale and with long duration. Although in medieval times written culture was restricted or monopolized by the Catholic Church, and in spite of the fact that the use of Latin as a universal language limited the need for translation, towards the year 1135 there was a school of translators in Toledo which translated texts of Greek writers from Arabic into Latin.

Like many tools of the intellect that structure the current transnational cultural world, translation as we conceive it today is a product of the Renaissance. It is associated with the diffusion of the printing press and reading in vernacular languages. Although translation is, to a certain extent, ontogenic to writing, developments that took place during the Renaissance introduced a strong reformulation in its meaning. Translation became essential both for religious reforms and for the secularization of Western societies and cultures, as well as in the establishment of both cooperation and rivalry among states by way of 'printed culture'.

The process of 'civilization' that inspired the differentiation of national cultures and languages gave rise to certain structural properties in the transnational nature of translation. In the first place, it established the hierarchic structure of relations among languages, correlative to the differential power of national states and cultures. In the dawn of capitalism, French dominated the international system of communications. The philosophers of the Enlightenment who inspired the emancipation of nations were read in French. Secondly, translations were indispensable in the forging of national literatures and cultures. Once this process was completed, translation of representative authors of a national culture became instrumental to the symbolic recognition of that culture worldwide. Translation finally became a central practice in the consecration of authors, literary systems, and nations.

The deep political and cultural transformations that took place in the Western world around the mid 19th century were both cause and consequence of technological innovations such as the steam press and linotypes, technological processes that drastically reduced the costs of printing. The large-scale production of cheap printed material contributed to the emergence of massive communication systems that attracted new communities of readers formed as a result of the universalization of national educational policies. Professions and crafts associated with book production became more differentiated and interdependent. Publishing was born as an industry, a profession independent of the activities of booksellers and printers. At the same time, translation became an activity regulated in economic and legal terms.

The differences concerning the moment when different publishing crafts were institutionalized resulted from their relative power and status. In France, for instance, while a society of writers was founded in 1837 (La Société des Gens de Lettres), and one of booksellers in 1892 (Chambre Syndicale des Libraires de France), translators created their own society only in 1947 (Société Française des Traducteurs). The same can be observed in the internationalization of each profession: while the Union Internationale des Éditeurs (UIE) was founded in 1896, the Fédération Internationale des Traducteurs (FIT) appeared in 1953. Another evidence of the weak position of translation as a cultural, economical and intellectual matter is the relatively recent emergence of a theory of translation. It can be added that several institutional and theoretical innovations in the world of translation originated in countries with a subordinate position in 'the international republic of letters', such as The Netherlands, Israel, Ireland,

Québec or Catalonia. This is an additional clue that translation has long been a loosely organized space in the world of publishing.

From the 19th century the practice of translation has in fact moved between two pairs of antagonisms: one marked by the distinction between literary and technical translation; the other between the activities of occasional translators (e.g. writers and university professors) and those of full-time professionals (e.g. language specialists or translation graduates). These tensions have created the great variety of trajectories and interests that can be observed in any national or linguistic space of agents dedicated to the 'art' or to the 'profession' of translation. Translating literature is but a section in this trade and market and needs to be considered in relationship with this wider landscape.

Around the 1950s the international publishing market was reorganized, thus giving birth to some of the practices and institutions that have oriented the current production of translations and of transnational cultural relations, including international rules or legal norms for the sale of translation licences and editions. The international book fairs came to play a crucial role in the standardization of these practices. Like in a casino, the literary publishers and agents bet on the genres and authors that will set a worldwide trend. One example of this is the Frankfurt Book Fair (the worldwide centre of the book edition business) where the hierarchic structure of relations between languages, publishing markets and national cultures can be understood at first glance.

Since the end of the Second World War, and particularly since the 1980s, the domination of the English language and of American and British publishing markets have been expressed in the huge volume of publishing rights exported from these countries, and in a small percentage of translations into English. In 1978, 40 per cent of the 60,000 books published in translation worldwide were originally written in English. By the 1990s this percentage grew to 60 per cent. Nowadays, only 3 per cent of the books published in the US and 5 per cent of those published in the UK are translations from other languages. On the other hand, 13 per cent of the books published in France, 18 per cent of those published in Germany and 40 per cent of those published in The Netherlands are works in translation. These figures show that translation is, at the same time, a condition of possibility and a limitation of transnational communication and globalization.

Gustavo Sorà

Bibliography

Bourdieu P. 2002 [1990]. 'Les conditions sociales de la circulation internationale des idées', *Actes de la Recherche en Sciences Sociales*, 145, 5, 3–8.

Casanova P. 2000. *La république mondiale des lettres*. Paris: Seuil.

Heilbron J. 1999. 'Toward a sociology of translation: book translation as a cultural world-system', *European Journal of Social Theory*, 2, 4, 429–44.

Sorá G. 2003. *Traducir el Brasil: una antropología de la circulación internacional de ideas*. Buenos Aires: Libros del Zorzal.

Venuti L. 2000. *The translation studies reader*. London, Routledge.

Related essays

anti-Catholicism; antisemitism; Bible; Braille code; comics; design; diasporas; ecology; economics; environmentalism; Esperanto; European civil servants; European institutions; gender and sex; kindergarten; Koran; language; language diplomacy; literature; marketing; organization models; Orientalism; philanthropy; psychoanalysis; publishing; Romanticism; sign languages; *The Wretched of the Earth*

Transnational

Every other article in this volume begins with a short sentence defining its headword. This will not be the case here, because the purpose of this entry is to capture the historical process of defining 'transnational', 'transnationalism' and other related words. It consequently advises against a preliminary definition. From their first known uses, they have evolved in an uneven and non-linear way into buzz-words that are now ubiquitous in academic and public discussion. Though we are not familiar with the different words that have been and are used in the many languages of this planet, it seems that the American English version is now in frequent use. On the wings of the success of its lexical root ('nation'), 'transnational' has been embarked in a number of languages with only minor adaptations: 'transnasional' in Bahasa Indonesia, 'transnazionale' in Italian, 'transnacional' in Spanish, 'transnational' in French and German. Some Chinese scholars would use 'kua guo' (跨国, 'straddling countries'), others rather have 'kua wenhua' (跨文化, 'straddling cultures') – but many go for 'transnational' and use the English term as an element of a social science lingua franca. Japanese translations offer 'ekkyo' 越境 'crossing borders') and 'kokka o koeta' (国(家)を超えた, 'going beyond, or transcending, states), but some scholars would use katakana (a phonetic alphabet for words borrowed from a foreign language) to approach the English structure; then it becomes 'toransunashonaru' (トランスナショナル). However, the idea and the word are far from ubiquitous: only if hard pressed would an English Hindi speaker suggest 'paardeshi' ('transcultural') as an equivalent, stressing it is scarcely used. It is then only one section of a developing lexicological trajectory in time, space, uses and meanings, which are the object of this entry.

Where to start from?

The search for firsts is a deceptive quest, especially when it is about words. Etymological dictionaries only rely on a limited corpus, and the growth of databases makes their findings obsolete. Until now, terms from the transnational family were said to have been coined by the American Randolph Bourne (1880–1918) in 1916. Though this entry certainly does not offer an ultimate view, it is nevertheless necessary to mention earlier uses of the terms.

The German linguist Georg Curtius (1820–95) can be mentioned provisionally as the first user of the adjective 'transnational'. In his 1862 inaugural lecture at Leipzig University, where he insisted that all national languages were connected to families of languages that extended beyond contemporary national frameworks, Curtius wrote that '*Eine jede Sprache ist ihrer Grundlage nach etwas transnationales*' to point to this aspect of languages. The absence of inverted commas around *transnationales* suggests the term was not unfamiliar to German readers of his *Philologie und Sprachwissenschaft*. An anonymous author in the *Princeton Review* chose that very quote to support his views in 1868, and translated it as 'every language is fundamentally something transnational'. This is, provisionally, the first known appearance of the term in American English. Neither occurrence seems to have made much of an impression. But they firmly root the term in the 19th century, and within a mood that tried to question an 'obvious' national characteristic such as language.

Similarly, it is not merely anecdotal that 'transnational' was used regularly in the early 20th century to name the highways that made it possible for automobiles to connect distant parts of the United States. The term was then a synonym for 'transcontinental'. When US newspapers mention 'trans-national high-ways' from the 1910s, they point us to one of the possible meanings of the term, that is the idea of going through the national space from one side to the other. However grammatically incorrect, since the Latin term 'trans' means 'beyond' and not 'through', this provides evidence that the word has been empowered with a capacity to signify the act of crossing. Its first landmark use was to take a different direction.

Randolph Bourne was a character on the New York City writing scene when his 'Trans-National America' appeared in the *Atlantic Monthly* in July 1916. The director of the journal was not very happy with Bourne's lack of allegiance to the 'Anglo-Saxon ideal', but did publish the piece. In reaction to the aspirations of and anxieties over the possible conduct of the diverse strands of 'hyphenated Americans' in the context of the European war, the article was an attack on the ideal of assimilation that Bourne presented as, by and large, the purpose of the American melting pot. Bourne's suggestion was that the United States had to accept its cosmopolitan nature and make the best of the communities of different national origins that had migrated to the Great Republic. To fulfil the chances offered by the fact of being 'a unique socio-logical fabric', 'a world federation in miniature' that it owed to the privilege of being a land of migrations, America had to become the first 'international nation' and to accept its 'cosmopolitanism', said Bourne. For all his insistence on the fact that this is an American problem, 'Project and destiny', the third section of Bourne's piece, focuses on explaining how such an American achievement would be the matrix for a wider cosmopolitan enterprise, that of building the citizen of the world. This is also where he seems to thrive in terminological 'trans' invention. The first step towards a cosmopolitan horizon is to be made in the very context of the European war, Bourne suggested. Because it is 'trans-national', America can neither let European nationalisms hold sway over its destiny,

nor take shelter in Americanization and the creation of a new nationalism that would oppress its 'trans-nationals'. It needs to create something completely different, for itself and for the world, 'a trans-nationalism of ours'. 'America is coming to be, not a nationality but a transnationality, a weaving back and forth, with the other lands, of many threads of all sizes and colors' (Bourne 1916, 96). In recent times, this has led to him being hailed or accused as a precursor of multicultural-ism, though there is much more in Bourne than this: one can equally easily picture him as crusader with a belief that America has a mission to the world, that is to lead in the cosmopolitan enterprise. There are two things that are more interesting for us here. The first is that Bourne uses the preposition with its lexical meaning, which is 'beyond'. But Bourne's 'beyond' does not take place in a flat space: going beyond the national is not just stepping above it, dismissing it. Bourne's trans-national America is a transcendence of national characters and belongings, an osmosis, a further stage. Second, Bourne is putting all the current terminology on the table, its indeterminacy included. He uses 'trans-national' to describe the nature of the American population as being beyond simple national affiliation, 'trans-nationality/transnationality' to qualify the resulting situation, 'transnationalism' to coin the sense of belonging that would go beyond existing nationalisms and amount to world citizenship, and 'trans-nationals' to indicate the people with a dual sense of belonging. But, whereas others were very keen to distinguish between the meanings of, for example, 'internationalism' and 'cosmopolitanism', or to invent new terms like 'mondialité' or 'mondi-alisme' (like the Belgian Paul Otlet), Bourne did not really care, and he used the former and their derivatives as interchangeable or convergent with his 'trans' terminology. While it might have been expected that his coining of a new term would be partly a way to make for a collapsed internationalism, this was not the case. At least, Bourne was not to elaborate further on these points because of an unexpected encounter with an unhyphen-ated migrant, Spanish influenza.

In the following years, the terms seem to have been used moderately and unsystematic-ally until the early 1940s, as far as the existence of searchable databases allows us to see. But they were definitely applied to non-domestic situations. 'Transnational/trans-national' was mostly used to qualify elements that developed across national boundaries. Casual use of the terms can be encountered in major regional or national US newspapers during the 1930s: one could use the terms to speak of a 'transnational trip' to advertise a university study tour (1931); of 'trans-national affairs' to situate the agenda of a session of the annual meeting of the Institute of International Relations (1931); of the 'trans-national' character of Christianity that German bishop Galen had called upon to reject Nazi principles (1934) or of 'transnational transports' to comment on war developments in the Balkans (1941). Such random use can also be identified within the academic world: one US political scientist mentioned a 'trans-national alignment' of fascist nations in 1937, pointing to the common views and shared plans of fascist states and groups, which crossed national limits and usually disjointed nationalisms.

However, there were some significant uses of the terms that bear witness to the fact that they began to be used to present the national variable as unsatisfactory or altogether irrelevant. Of major importance is their use by German law scholars who worked in the field of international law and arbitration. The Heidelberg law professor Max Gutzwiller seems to have been the first to have imported them into the juridical vocabulary (1931). He used the terms to point to new norms and situations that 'international law' was not able to capture in a developing field, connected to such new arenas as the mixed arbitration tribunals created by the Versailles Treaty. In *Fruits of victory* (1921), the English-American journalist and peace activist Norman Angell had also taken the terms into another sphere to make his case about prewar trade, industrial and financial entanglements. He pointed to the 'trans-national' economy that bound European countries together and with other areas through the world division of labour and the connections created by economic agents. Angell deemed it 'more correct' than 'international', and used the term and its spinoffs ('trans-nationalism', 'trans-nationally') several times in his book. A similar connotation is found in *Living in a revolution* (1944) by Julian Huxley. Huxley, who would be the first director of UNESCO, has an occasional use of the terms in situations which underline the idea that national geographical and political units are, can or

ought to be superseded in the new age into which the world is being ushered. The 'transnational' industrial region of North Western Europe he describes, and the 'transnational' control of European heavy industry he hopes for, announce the forthcoming incursion of the term into the language of the political and economic world orders.

Searching for order in the postwar world

Despite its German users, despite the fact that some English writers used the terms in books initially published in England, 'transnational' does not seem to have been taken into public use in Europe. The successful career of the terms in the 1950s and 1960s mostly took place in the US. There, generic uses that have been sketched above were still operational. The phrase 'transnational highways' was used indiscriminately to name a highway that went from Austria to Greece, or the arteries planned by the federal highway programme within the US, while 'trans-national communications' or 'transnational transport' indicated that national spaces were crossed by flows that did not even stop therein. The notions of crossing and of transcendence were still both present. In addition to this, the terms gained momentum in three specific spheres.

On one hand, they were used to describe, follow and understand the economic integration of trade and of production. This does not seem to have come from the academic world. Economist Simon Kuznets' use of the term in a 1948 paper remained isolated. However, it was significant that Kuznets used the term 'trans-national economic relations' in his call to consider the study of the domestic US economy in a larger context that would include historical developments, nonmaterial exchanges (population, policies, obligations) and the 'view of the world' of a given country: the idea was to carry economic analysis beyond the national frame. This appearance in academic economics was outpaced by success in the business world. One clue is the growing favour won by the terms in firm naming during the 1950s. As witnessed by advertising blocks and business news in several US newspapers from the west to the east coasts, the first to have caught the wave seem to have been transportation companies (Trans-National Airlines), together with trade firms (Trans-National Export Co.) or travel agencies (Trans National Air Coach Inc.). The 'trans' also enjoyed favour with firms in insurance or electronics businesses, in spite of an apparent domestic orientation. But they were also deemed fit to emphasize overseas activities, as when the apparel and footwear company Genesco created a special outfit to handle its foreign operations, called Genesco Transnational Company (1964). This grass-roots success forms the background for the use of the term 'transnational corporation' that developed both in the academy and the press. From the late 1950s, it was for some a mere synonym of the phrase 'multinational corporation', a way to name a corporation that was internationally owned and controlled, while for others the 'transnational' firm was a further stage of integration, where capital, research and other aspects were managed without any regard for the company's home country interests. This use helped the terms to travel, though it remained less popular than 'multinational'. Politically, it became a minor but common cry of leftist activists to attack 'transnational capital' and 'the transnation-als' in the 1970s; geographically, it acclima-tized the term in the economic and political vocabulary abroad, as in Great Britain where it began to appear regularly in The Times from 1968, or later in France ('l'intégration capitaliste transnationale') and Germany ('Transnationale Monopole') where it began to be used to indict capitalism and its creatures.

The second sphere where 'transnational' got a grip was among those who tried to ana-lyse and explain the world political order. During the 1950s, those who commented on the current and future world order spoke of 'transnational monopoly' to describe a business whose property should be given to the community (Committee for a World Federation 1948); 'transnational cooperation' to qualify the action of the UN and its agen-cies (Walter Lippmann 1949); 'transnational groups' to label the Soviet and American blocs (William McNeill 1954); or the estab-lishment of 'trans-national communities' by scholars, scientists and others to achieve world peace (Robert Oppenheimer 1958). Law professor Myres S. McDougal used it to describe groups whose composition or activ-ities stretched across national limits, and so did political scientist Arnold Wolfers when he called corporations 'transnational actors' in world politics (1959) and decided the meaning of the terms was still open-ended: they could be used as equivalent to 'supranational' or 'international', appended to the names of

governmental, intergovernmental and civil society actors, used by those who proclaimed the end of the age of nations, or kept strictly descriptive.

The first prescriptive attempt to define what was 'transnational' in the new world order was made at the crossroads of economics and international relations. In February 1956, Philip Jessup, a professor of international law and diplomacy at Columbia University (USA) gave three lectures at Yale University Law School. A couple of months later, they were published under the title Transnational law. Though he did not acknowledge the use of the term by German-speaking law scholars in the 1930s, Jessup was capitalizing on the same kind of dissatisfaction. After having played an important role in the design and operation of several institutions of the new world order since 1943, especially in the United Nations Relief and Rehabilitation Administration, Jessup had left government service in 1953. From then on, his research work had focused on legal situations that had emerged in differ-ent fields, from United Nations law to global commons and the legal protection of foreign investments. His generic proposal, for a trans-national law to include all law that regulates actions transcending national frontiers, was a conclusion of such forays. Jessup's suggestion was to handle 'transnational situations' with reference to a corpus that did not abide by the canonical categories of law such as national/ international or private/public. Prominent in his demonstrations of the need for such a reshuffling of legal norms to fit a 'complex interrelated world community', were cases dealing with the work of UN agencies, with the development of the European institu-tions, with business and trade overseas, and with non-governmental organization activ-ities. Jessup's message was clear: there were more than relations between states in cur-rent world interactions, and many problems stretched across national borders and across the spatial and specialized categories of law. His move against the canon of international law was welcomed with a mixture of interest and resistance by law scholars, and the trans-formation of the Bulletin of the Columbia Society of International Law into the Columbia Journal Of Transnational Law in 1964 was one of the few immediate by-products of Jessup's sug-gestion. Yet he had opened a new era where the term 'transnational' would increasingly be the object of paradigmatic definitions by the academic community, with a prescriptive view to establishing new tools for a new world and an interest in achieving stability and peace through the channels of multilateral organizations.

The academic capture: the first 'transnational turn' in the social sciences

These features were all present in the late 1960s, when a group of international relations scholars defined their approach in terms of 'transnational relations' as opposed to 'international relations'. As we have seen above, the term was running loose among journalists or activists who tried to make sense of the world order. From the late 1950s, it began to surface with some regularity among the political scientists who were investigating world politics. Arnold Wolfers chose it in 1959 to identify the role of non-state corporate actors within world politics; in 1962, the Frenchman Raymond Aron spoke of a 'société transnationale' as the sphere of non-interstate relations between individuals who migrated, traded, exchanged ideas and joined with each other for celebrating, competing or protesting; the German Karl Kaiser insisted that a 'transnationale Politik' was emerging from the growing interactions between actors from different nation states. On the borderline of academy and activism, the Norwegian peace researcher Johan Galtung used 'transnational' to name the kind of loyalty that would develop in organizations that transcend national borders without comprising any nations (1967). This trend was captured and turned into a pattern in 1970/71, when Robert Keohane and Joseph Nye, two US political scientists, hosted a conference on 'Transnational Relations', the proceedings of which were published in 1971 in the journal *International Organization*. The challenge was to the realist approach in the field of international relations, and its 'state-centric view'. Focusing deliberately on 'contacts, coalitions, and interactions across state boundaries that are not controlled by the central foreign policy organs of government' (Keohane and Nye 1971, xi), they urged international relations scholars to study transnational organizations and transnational interactions (movements of money, persons, objects and ideas where 'at least one actor is not an agent of a government or an intergovernmental organization', ibid., xii) for a better understanding of contemporary world politics. Their interest in movements

across state boundaries by non-governmental actors was clearly an attempt to dislodge a theory of international relations that focused on the interactions of politically significant units contained within these state boundaries. It was also an attempt to plead for a different approach to current world policies that would diverge from the unilateralism encouraged by the realist approach. In this sense, 'transnational relations' fell in line with functionalism, neofunctionalism or linkage politics as a weapon in the anti-realist arsenal.

From these analytic and prescriptive premises, the first 'transnationalism' was born. The contributors to the Keohane and Nye volume all used this word to describe a contemporary world order marked by an abundance of transnational ties, and also to name their new approach to world politics. Only a few used it to describe a situation where national units were not relevant any more, and suggested 'transnationalism' was a further stage in the history of human societies, beyond the age of nationalism. This interest in 'transnational relations' and 'transnationalism' quickly faltered in the US, where the subfield of international relations is remarkable for its insistence on causal processes and its frequent paradigm shifts. Samuel Huntington's meticulous discussion (in *World Politics*, April 1973) of Nye and Keohane, which argued for the term to be used only when the situation met very specific conditions, and limited its 'genuineness' to the current era and to the impact of US expansion, may also have contributed to sterilizing the term. After a few years, the interest in transnational relations was taken up with more alacrity in other countries (e.g. at the French Centre d'Études des Relations Internationales) than in the United States proper. Nevertheless, this attempt to define what was transnational and what was not, with its focus on non-governmental actors, left an enduring mark on the vocabulary of other social sciences, and among some of these actors themselves. Transnationalism became 'in'.

During the 1970s, the term 'transnational corporations' featured more frequently in academic book and article titles, while the United Nations Organization created its Centre on Transnational Corporations in 1975 to monitor their behaviour. Scholars of European integration also used the term more frequently, while it spread to underline the extent of a host of non-governmental activities from terrorism to religious or political activities. Non-governmental organizations themselves found the term appealing, as they felt it stressed their difference from interstate actors much more than 'international' did. In the year 1976, the phrase 'transnational associations' made a spectacular appearance in *International Associations*, the journal published by the Union of International Associations. The journal even changed name in 1977, to become *Transnational Associations*. More generally, there were a number of activist groups, journals or think tanks, especially from the left, who began to carry the adjective 'transnational' in their names (*Agenor: Transnational Left Review* 1970, Transnational Institute 1974). This was also the moment when scholars of the European integration process regularly used the term to qualify its different dimensions, and when the spelling 'trans-national', that had lost ground during the 1960s, definitely disappeared. By and large, the 1970s made the adjective popular, and the momentary but spectacular attempt by international relations scholars to define it was one reason for this popularity.

For all their criticism of state-centric approaches to international relations, Keohane and Nye were for the most part very careful to stress they did not support or advocate the view that nation states were withering away. This ambiguity has been part and parcel of the different uses of the terms throughout the previous decades. What was defined as transnational was certainly presented as a challenge to national polities and societies, but there was no pronouncement on the result of the contest. Johan Galtung, despite his enthusiasm for such postimperialist perspectives, wrote in 1971 that the 'transnational', 'global' or 'world' phase, where international organizations would complete their shift from their national touchstones, was still hypothetical. The irrelevance of nations was to be a characteristic of the first wave of globalization discourses, and the terms from the 'transnational' family would feature prominently in this context.

The rise of transnationalism: the new condition of being in the global age

It would be of limited interest to excavate the name of the first person who used the 'transnational' family of terms to assess, explain, support or reject what began to be called

'globalization' in the 1980s. The terms were familiar enough not to have to be invented, and were used over a wide range. But it was clearly on the wings of the 'global' craze that 'transnational' and 'transnationalism' found their second wind, which is directly at the origins of the current success of the terms. In fact, a brand new range of 'trans' terms emerged at this moment: 'transmigrants', 'transurbanism' and many others. Anthropologist Arjun Appadurai may have been the most prolific inventor, with such terms as 'translocality', 'translocal' or 'transnations' that flirted along with 'transnational', 'transnationalism' or 'transnationals'.

Cultural studies and anthropology were, in fact, the major powerhouse from which emerged the renewed conceptualization and uses of 'transnational'. More exactly, one of the epicentres was the Center for Transcultural Studies in its dual embodiment at the University of Chicago and the University of Pennsylvania. The Center began to develop a programme for the internationalization of culture and communication in 1986, under the leadership of Appadurai and Carol Breckinridge. Building from the forays by British social scientists such as Stuart Hall or Paul Gilroy, among other bricks, the Center launched a Project for Transnational Cultural Studies, and established the journal *Public Culture* in 1988. It would be the platform from where an interdisciplinary group of US scholars, many with Indian origins, would investigate the new cosmopolitan cultures ushered in by the dramatic change in cultural forms and flows whose emergence they identified in the 1970s. Appadurai's writings (gathered in *Modernity at Large* in 1996) and Paul Gilroy's *Black Atlantic* were the flagships of this prolific thread that carried the 'transnational' family of terms into a large section of the US social sciences and beyond with Prasenjit Duara (history) and Gayatri Spivak (humanities). Duara was, in fact, among the few from this group to use the term to study the past, while 'transnational' was mostly used to qualify, observe, assess or prophesy a new multipolar and multicultural world in the making in the 1990s. It was not by accident that the reconnection with Randolph Bourne was explicitly made, as his 1916 plea for a transnational America had irresistible appeal for supporters of multiculturalism in the 1990s.

Another field where our terms were revamped, in parallel with the former though without apparent early connection, was the study of migration, with anthropologists and sociologists leading the march again. From the early 1980s, anthropologists Nina Glick Schiller and Georges Fouron, among others, played with the idea that contemporary migrants in the US, especially Haitians and Caribbeans, were able to endorse multiple identities that did not fit with territorialized conceptions of identity. Here again, there was the feeling that the world was criss-crossed by unprecedented flows of people and cultural artifacts (songs, images), and that this called for a reconceptualization of migrants' identities. Their statements that the migrants' identities and political activities were bounded neither by the country of origin, nor by the country of settlement, gave way to their qualification as 'transnational'. From sporadic uses in the 1970s and 1980s, 'transnational' and 'transmigrants' became a rallying cry with the volume published in 1992 by Linda Basch, Nina Glick Schiller and Cristina Szanton-Blanc (Towards a transnational perspective on migration: race, class, ethnicity, and nationalism). Sociologists of migrations joined the bandwagon with a powerful voice, and Alejandro Portes' decided endorsement of the term in 1997 was a landmark in its success on the US academic scene and beyond, together with work on Dominican entrepreneurial transnationalism by Luis Guarnizo, who attempted to theorize 'transnational social fields'. This success story still led to some discussion on the 'right' definition of the term, e.g., with the anthropologists being chagrined by what they felt was a narrowing of the term's purchase in Portes' views.

While both previous groups shared a similar fascination with the 'unprecedented' flows of people, ideas, objects and images that ran across the territorial borders of nation states, the third core of the transnational revival was focused on capital flows. British sociologist Leslie Sklair, elaborating from his research on the maquila industry and the export-processing zones in Ireland, Egypt and China, picked up where popular economics had left off, that is from the transnational corporations. For him, as he explained in 1991 (Sociology of the global system), the current global capitalist system which was recomposing the labour and production process should be approached through 'transnational practices'. At the economic level, the transnational corporation was the key actor, while the 'transnational capitalist class' was the political touchstone of the system, and the ideology of consumerism its cultural and ideological touchstone. There again, it was to capture the inner soul of globalization, here mostly economic, that 'transnational' resurfaced to qualify new developments.

There were indeed other places and fields where some kind of transnational outlook was proposed in the late 1980s and the early 1990s. Sometimes, as in history, they had no explicit or clear connections with the three cores that have been identified above. But these three have been snowballing very quickly, and were carefully looked upon from other disciplines and fields, which made them very special. Although they did not always acknowledge one another, these three pulsing cores shared a similar creed: globalization of capital, people or image flows, were making nation states irrelevant, and the social sciences had to account for this current major turn, a break in the history of the world. This purported role erred on the side of prescription and prophecy, as many of the above social scientists saw some social and political purchase in their use of the transnational family of terms. There is of course something of a paradox in the fact that, on one hand, 'transnational' was used to capture 'globalization from below', and rhymed with diasporas in pages that celebrated the agency of the new transnational identities and communities in opposing the hegemonic logic of both capital and nation states, while on the other hand it pointed to 'globalization from above' where capitalist corporations and elites were setting the pace. But this is likely what gave the terms their very wide appeal. From these premises began the current epic of the transnational family, under all its declensions ('transnationals', 'transnationality', 'transnationalism'), with a sharp rise in success after 1998.

Weeklies and dailies in most countries quickly embraced the idea of the transnationalism of migrants who were 'neither here nor there'. The transnational family began to invade the titles of social sciences dissertations and theses, first in the US, then in the other English-speaking countries, and later in Germany and Continental Europe. They also expanded far beyond anthropology, cultural studies and sociology, with an increased presence in history, geography, gender studies, religious studies and political science (most notably through the study of 'transnational civil society' and 'transnational movements'). New scholarly journals, mostly in English, endorsed the terminology (*Diaspora: A Journal of Transnational Studies* 1991, *Global Networks: A Journal of Transnational Affairs* 2001), which was also increasingly used to label research projects (e.g. the Transnational Communities Programme led by Steven Vertovec at Oxford University from 1997 or the Transnational Social Fields Network run by Ludger Pries at the Ruhr Universität Bochum in the early 2000s), teaching programmes (e.g. the MA and PhD programmes in 'transnational studies' at the University of Southampton, England, from 2003).

Gustavo Cano has rightly observed that 'transnational' was the most commonly used term in the US academic world in the late 1980s and early 1990s, before 'transnationalism' took over after 1994. One of the most salient patterns of this recent moment is that 'transnationalism' was more and more used to signify a worldview that made it tantamount to an ideology, a political project, or a way of pointing to a loose network of people with a common belief, making 'transnationalism' a social movement of some sort. The rise of 'transnationalism' was mired in a search for normative definitions: battles soon began to define what 'real' transnationalism was, or what was transnational and what was not. A cottage industry of definitions quickly developed as the label became a must-wear. Consequently, it was also criticized for lack of theorization. As early as 1994, Katherine Verdery, an anthropologist specializing in Eastern Europe, noted that the term dissolved 'when inspected more closely' and pointed to its implicit confusion between state and nation, while in 2005 migration specialists Ewa Morawska and Roger Waldinger each came to grips with the presentism and approximations that the use of the label usually included. This has not prevented projects of establishing 'transnational studies' as a new section of the social sciences. The introduction to the *Transnationalism reader: Interdisciplinary intersections and innovations* that Peggy Levitt and Sanjeev Khagram published with Routledge at the end of 2007 makes it clear that its editors believe in a paradigmatic turn taking place around the notion of 'transnationalism', whose destiny it would be to change the social sciences as we know them.

Conclusion

These evolutions in the academic world had an impact on the lay use of the transnational family of terms. While the left-wing movements pioneered the spreading use of 'transnational' in the 1960s and 1970s to pinpoint lawless and homeless corporations and capitalist practices, it is now right-wing movements that use the terms 'transnationals' or 'transnationalists' to point the finger at a group that includes academics, NGOs, activists, officers of philanthropic foundations, European Union and United Nations civil servants. They are said to be the 'transnational progressives', a global elite on the march to wash away national citizenship and democracy in favour of world government. This recent derogatory use of the terms has until now been mostly a US phenomenon. It is worth mentioning that scholars who have identified with the definition of 'transnationalism', like Alejandro Portes or Arjun Appadurai, are explicitly mentioned by these 'democracy watchers'. The latter see 'transnationalism' as the most recent version of the ideologies that have been fighting America and its values since independence. In a sense, this is a consequence of the use of 'transnationalism' that these scholars have suggested, offering it as the ideology of a world where imperial, nationalist, racial and other dominating impulses would be tamed by the multiplication of ties and links across borders. It might be a possibility that this backlash will soon expand and include other thinkers who have explicitly embraced such a view, like the German Ulrich Beck and his 'cosmopolitan perspective'. This would just confirm that, by and large, the terms of the transnational family have been entangled in scholarly and political debates since their appearance.

Pierre-Yves Saunier

Bibliography

Basch L. et al. 1992. *Towards a transnational perspective on migration: race, class, ethnicity, and nationalism.* New York: New York Academy of Sciences.

Bourne R. 1916. 'Trans-national America', *Atlantic Monthly*, 118, July, 86–97.

DeSipio L. and Cano G. 2005.
  Theoretical considerations on political
  transnationalism. Paper presented at the
  63rd Annual Conference of the Midwest
  Political Science Association, Chicago.
Fitzgerald D. and Waldinger R. 2004.
  'Transnationalism in question', American
  Journal of Sociology, 109, 5, 1177–95.
Kearney M. 1995. 'The local and the global:
  the anthropology of globalization and
  transnationalism', Annual Review of
  Anthropology, 24, 547–65.
Keohane R. O. and Nye J. S. Jr (eds) 1971.
  'Transnational relations and world
  politics', International Organization, 25, 3.
Morawska E. 'The sociology and history
  of immigration: reflections of a
  practitioner', in Bommes M. et al. (eds)
  2005. International migration research:
  constructions, omissions, and the promises of
  interdisciplinarity. Aldershot: Ashgate.
Tietje C. et al. (eds) 2006. 'Philip C. Jessup's
  Transnational law revisited on the occasion
  of the 50th anniversary of its publication',
  Essays in Transnational Economic Law, 50.

Related essays
body shopping; class; conspiracy theories;
corporations; cosmopolitanism and
universalism; democracy; diasporas;
economics; historians and the nation
state; history; human mobility; intellectual
elites; intergovernmental organizations;
international non-governmental
organizations (INGOs); internationalisms;
legal order; nation and state; new man; Otlet,
Paul; United Nations system; world orders

Transportation infrastructures

Transportation systems are actually large
sociotechnical systems that are created by
and over which individual or collective 'system builders' preside, thus shaping history
by surpassing geography and politics. Like
other infrastructures, transportation systems oscillate between the forces of nationalism and universalism, reconciling trade and
technical barriers and the spread of globalization. While infrastructures played a major
role in the integration of nation states (cf. the
unifying design of road and water networks
in 18th-century France), transportation networks were hailed one century later as the
forerunners of universal associations by Saint
Simonians. Europe was already economically
integrated at the end of the 19th century, and
European capital helped open the interiors
of the continent by funding railways. Single
nations often dominated investment within
Europe and beyond with transportation as
a key variable. By abolishing Cromwell's
restrictive Navigation Act in 1849, Britain
championed free trade and dominated world
trade until at least 1914. The mid 19th century
provided a major turning point in the long
global history of transportation: whereas
shipping had been the basis of the emerging
capitalist world system since the beginning
of the millennium, it was replaced by the
American continental version of the world
system and Germany's, based on the command of technology.

The generally accepted basic features of
globalization – compression of time and of
space – especially highlight the importance
of transportation. Since the early 1800s, the
spatial structures of economic systems have
expanded beyond national borders through
increasing global and allegedly self-regulating
markets. Fostered by colonization processes the result was a European-dominated
world of urban networks allocating worldwide resources and competencies. Transport
technologies were a condition for the development of global capitalism and have helped
shape the internationalization of trade and
the movement of peoples. Faster, reliable,
large-scale and cheap transportation allowed
a spatial division of labour leading to spatial
specializations and agglomerations that in
turn translated into a higher dependency on
networks and transportation.

During the transition from the so-called
Paleotechnic period, coal became the main
fuel operating transport vehicles, while the
later Neotechnic period brought reliance on
electricity and petroleum. This technological
shift made possible a 'transport revolution'
and the geographic expansion of transportation systems. Telegraph, railroads, then
pipelines and in the 20th century automobile
and air travel allowed faster and more flexible journeys that reduced the importance of
fixed lines of transportation. This expansion
required improvements in the synchronization and contraction of time. Synchronization
was initially introduced by railways to produce coherent timetables: Greenwich Mean
Time (GMT) was first adopted by London railways in 1847 and in 1883 by North American
ones. In the rail industry, track gauge was the

other element of standardization that allowed the expansion of the networks, but competition between private companies trying to lock others out of the market led to discontinuities of standards that are still felt today, as between France and Spain. Transcontinental railroads were nevertheless built, the 48-mile Panama Railway being the first in 1855, linking the Atlantic and Pacific oceans while the Trans-Siberian was completed in 1905. Later, rail routes were also built across Africa connecting from west to east.

Nevertheless, the sea long remained the major transcontinental carrier. Liverpool's Albert Docks (1846) symbolized the new scale of maritime trade and colonial expansion that relied on steamships (*Great Western*, 1838, built according to I. K. Brunel's plans, was the first to cross the Atlantic by steam alone). The emerging world market prompted 'venture capitalists' to imagine monumental projects of maritime canals aimed at carving isthmuses to shorten sea travel, first between the Mediterranean and the Far East (Suez Canal, 1869) by the prominent Saint Simonian system builder Ferdinand de Lesseps, then between the Atlantic and the Pacific (Panama Canal, 1914). Civil engineering climaxed in a 2,400-mile-long Seaway that opened between the Great Lakes and the St Lawrence's mouth in 1959.

Among the means of transportation characteristic of the Neotechnic era, roads stand out as the most ubiquitous. Transnational roads were nothing new, as the long history of the Silk Road proves. Still, until the 19th century roads were poor competitors against waterways and railroads because of their low speed and their limited haulage capacity. The introduction of macadam (c.1830) and above all the invention of the automobile favoured road transportation.

Further advancing the compression of time and space, air routes and airports developed in the first quarter of the 20th century. Based on earlier military usage and technology, air transportation spread to the shipping of mail in the 1920s and then to use for shipping other goods and moving passengers. As early as 1957, more passengers travelled by air than by sea on the North transatlantic route. The 1978 US Airline Deregulation Act further accelerated this trend by opening the way to an almost global air market that led to the multiplication of airlines and cheaper

travel through hub-and-spokes organization. Networks also developed underground, and the first transnational pipelines for the transportation of oil appeared at the end of the 19th century. The 522-mile-long Baku-Batumi pipeline opened in 1906 to export Russian oil at a lower price than American kerosene.

Transfers of technologies and operations between sociotechnical systems also occurred with the increasing use of new communications technologies. Modern shipyard designs developed in Europe and the USA soon spread to Asia (e.g. to Japan in 1867). Communications also made transportation systems more integrated, although decisions about their technologies and operations continued to be made on a national scale, producing geographical or technological discontinuities. Despite nation-state logics (a larger handicap in Europe than in North America), interoperability, intermodality and interconnections among systems have developed through forms of international cooperation that were typically motivated by trade. For example, common standards were introduced by professional organizations such as the Institute of Transport Engineers (New York, 1931) and the International Civil Aviation Organization (Montreal, 1947). At a regional scale, the European Conference of Transport Ministers created after 1945 planned pan-European routes for motorized transportation. Currently, the Chinese government is building a regional integrated hinterland (with the ASEAN) through investments in the Kunming-Bangkok Road and the Kunming-Singapore Railway projects.

Despite technological innovations, the geography of transnational traffic of people and goods has not changed dramatically in the past century and a half. At the beginning of the 21st century, transportation is cheaper and quicker, but flows are still concentrated on familiar maritime and inland routes with the same 'forgotten' links –notably Africa – reflecting geopolitical continuities in the global economy. Still, the Pacific has managed to achieve the same level of transoceanic movements as the Atlantic, revealing the growing share of South and East Asia in international trade. Regional geopolitics also influenced the geography of transportation systems. The collapse of the USSR created overnight new transnational routes whereas

Cambodia under the Khmer Rouge saw the destruction of links with its neighbours.

Three case studies exemplify the manipulation and juxtaposition of technical as well as non-technical elements in creating functional sociotechnical systems, despite frequent conflicts and failures. In each case, the links between transport costs, production and the international division of labour, trade regulation, nationalism, institutions, and, after 1945, regionalization processes, shaped their development.

The Panama Canal had long been envisioned, but building only began with Ferdinand de Lesseps in 1880, at a time when industrialization, wholesale trade, ports markets and fleets were being organized. Americans eventually built the Canal (it opened in 1914) thanks to their new naval power, their control of diseases, their elevated canal-with-locks solution and most importantly, their will to create an alternative trunk road from the east to the west coast to reduce the cost of shipments. Avoiding Cape Horn enabled the US to fight the Second World War on two fronts as well as controlling trade with the Caribbean and the subcontinent. Still, this fixed infrastructure threatened to become obsolete during the maritime revolution that began in the 1950s with the development of roll-on roll-off containerisation, and much bigger seagoing vessels. With more capacity needed, Panamanians in 2006 approved the building of a third navigation stream, allowing the passing of larger vessels.

State cooperation could make a difference in integrating transportation networks. If large countries saw railways as facilitating economic and political integration, the reverse was true for small or enclosed countries. The small size and central positions of Belgium and Switzerland pushed them to create transnational networks through which they might capture economic growth and trade lines. Belgium, like The Netherlands, favoured a European waterway network with common technical standards in the interest of their ports while Switzerland introduced international railway cooperation as a remedy for its own financial difficulties. Railway integration had already begun in Europe in the early 19th century with bilateral agreements between railway companies, as well as with the adoption of the 1435mm gauge,

proposed by British engineers who built railways in Belgium, Germany and Italy as early as the mid 1830s. The Swiss federal government subsequently invited European countries to the Bern Conferences (1878–86) that agreed first on the technical unity of railways then on the organization of goods transport. Their work was continued through specific bodies created by the League of Nations in Geneva. The International Union of Railways (1922) worked with the International Labour Office (1919) and the International Chamber of Commerce (1920) rail subcommittees. It had to argue with numerous other bodies until 1950, when all were assembled under the International Union of Railways umbrella (Communist countries created their own railways association, though). Full integration has still not been achieved. Until the 1950s, there was no common system providing electricity and national pride continues to express itself through different technical solutions for the construction of high-speed trains (e.g. TGV in France and ICE in Germany).

The case of intercontinental road planning reveals the tight links between politics and the economy. The Pan-American Highway envisioned by the Pan-American Road Congresses of the Organization of American States in 1925 is now almost completed but it is neither a main trade route nor a technically integrated system. Similarly, the UN Economic Commission for Asia and the Far East proposed an Asian road network in 1960 but political tensions hindered the process with frequent destruction of roads and closure of borders. In Africa as well, the UN planned a trans-Saharan route in 1962, and in 1971 a Trans-African Highway from Mombasa to Lagos to be the backbone of a future Pan-African road system. A couple of wars and economic crises later, there are still huge gaps in this road network. The European network is most advanced. Set up by the UN Economic Commission for Europe to enhance trade and to avoid a Third World War during the Cold War by building transport 'bridges', it became the early basis for the formation of a pan-European market and the integration of Europe, institutionalized much later through the Maastricht Treaty in 1993. Linked with other major projects (such as the Channel Tunnel, 1993), it is another example of the creation of a sociotechnical system by international organizations through technical, legal and political actions.

Today, transportation is even more closely linked with symbolic movements of ideas and capital through telecommunications. Together, they create hubs and nodes, and the territories that rebuild themselves around these networks profit from their positions at a number of scales from the municipal (e.g. London) to the national (e.g. Germany). With aviation, national and transnational corporations were able to match delocated headquarters and flexible production with a more centralized control. As a result, world trade continuously increases while a leisure economy encourages growth in international travel: space and time compression advances apace.

Manuel Appert
Christian Montès

Bibliography

Coilly N. and Régnier P. (eds) 2006. *Le siècle des saint-simoniens; du nouveau christianisme au canal de Suez*. Paris: BNF.

Hugill P. 1993. *World trade since 1431*. Baltimore and London: Johns Hopkins Press University Press.

Merger M., Carreras A. and Giuntini A. (eds) 1995. *Les réseaux européens transnationaux XIXe–XXe siècles, quels enjeux?* Nantes: Ouest.

Schipper F. 2006. 'All roads lead to Europe: the e-road network 1950–1975' [online]. Available: www.tie-project.nl, accessed 5 December 2006.

Schot J. and van der Vleuten E. 2005. 'Infrastructures, globalisation, and European integration: a historiographical and conceptual exploration' [online]. Available: www.tie-project.nl, accessed 5 December 2006.

Related essays

Chinese Diaspora; commodity trading; containerized freight; contract and indentured labourers; corporations; electricity infrastructures; empire and migration; financial markets; globalization; human mobility; International Civil Aviation Organization (ICAO) and International Air Transport Association (IATA); International Road Federation (IRF); investment; labour migrations; mail; non-lieux; oil; Panama Canal; railways; spatial regimes; steamships; technical standardization; telephone and telegraphy; trade; trade (manufactured goods); traffic signals; United Nations decades and years

Panama Canal

The Panama Canal is a ship canal that cuts across the Isthmus of Panama to connect the Atlantic and Pacific Oceans. The 51-mile-long route uses locks to raise and lower ships. The construction of the canal was a gigantic undertaking which involved the governments of several different nations and which mobilized a flow of humans, capital, and technology from around the globe. Its completion made commercial and military trips faster and more economical, eliminating the need for ships to traverse around Cape Horn at the tip of South America.

As early as the 16th century people began to dream of building a canal across Central America. In 1879 Ferdinand de Lesseps of France, who had overseen the building of the Suez Canal, began constructing a sea-level canal in Panama. His effort involved 19,000 labourers at its height, most of them from Jamaica. Disease, financial difficulties, and unfortunate engineering decisions prevented de Lesseps from succeeding, and his project collapsed infamously in 1889. De Lesseps was put on trial in France for fraud and found guilty, but because the statute of limitations had run out, he was never forced to serve time in prison.

After the Spanish-American War in 1898, growing interest in the US in economic and political expansionism raised anew the idea of building a canal. Alfred Thayer Mahan's *The Influence of Sea Power Upon History* was particularly persuasive in arguing that supremacy at sea would enable economic and military dominance. President Theodore Roosevelt became determined to see a canal constructed. Towards this end he gave military and political support to Panamanians seeking independence from Colombia in 1903, and then quickly negotiated the Hay-Bunau-Varilla Treaty with the new government of Panama, which gave the United States control, 'as if sovereign', in perpetuity over a ten-mile-wide strip of land across the Isthmus known as the Panama Canal Zone. The treaty also gave the US extensive rights to intervene in the Republic of Panama to improve public health or to restore order.

The number of men and women working to build the canal ranged as high as 45,000 at its height in 1913. In addition several thousand women and children accompanied their husbands and fathers to the Isthmus. Skilled labour came predominantly from the US, while unskilled labour – the bulk of the workforce – came from Barbados, Jamaica, other Caribbean islands, and, to a lesser degree, from Spain, Italy, and Greece. Under the leadership predominantly of George Washington Goethals and William C. Gorgas, the United States brought disease under control and built a vast infrastructure throughout the Zone to house, feed, and care for this large workforce. The canal was completed in 1914. During and after its completion the canal construction project encouraged continued migration of West Indians, many of whom travelled on to other sites in Central America, the Caribbean, and the United States. Many others settled permanently in the port cities of Panama.

The canal quickly became, and remains to this day, a major facilitator in the movement of people and commerce. After World War 2, Panamanians grew increasingly hostile towards the US because of its occupation of the Canal Zone. In 1964 anti-American rioting on the Isthmus led to the death of 23 Panamanians and three US Marines. Panama suspended diplomatic relations with the US over the incident, and gradually the US government determined to begin negotiations in order to transfer the canal to Panama. In 1977 the US and Panama signed the Carter-Torrijos Treaty that provided for joint operation of the canal until the year 2000, when the Panamanian government acquired full possession of the canal. In 2006 Panama announced a plan to expand the canal with a new set of locks and a new lane. Subsequently approved by popular referendum, the expansion will ultimately double the canal's capacity and be completed by 2014. It is expected to cost US$5.25 billion; higher tolls will finance the project.

Julie Greene

Bibliography
Conniff M. L. 1985. *Black labor on a white canal: Panama, 1904–1981.* Pittsburgh: University of Pittsburgh Press.
Major J. 1993. *Prize possession: the United States and the Panama Canal, 1903–1977.* Cambridge: Cambridge University Press.
McCullough, David, 1977. *The path between the seas: the creation of the Panama Canal, 1870–1914.* New York: Simon & Schuster.
Newton V. 2004. *The Silver Men: West Indian labour migration to Panama, 1850–1914.* Kingston, Jamaica: Ian Randle.

Related essays
civil engineering works; contract and indentured labourers; labour migrations; oceans; Pax Americana; transportation infrastructures

Tropics

The Greek root of the word 'tropics' means a turning, which refers both to the rotation of the spheres and the notion of limits, here both natural and moral. The intertropical zone has frequently been imagined, as it was in antiquity, as a realm of otherness, beyond the habitable human realm. Images of tropical natures and cultures have a long history and complex geography. At different moments, in different contexts, the notion of tropicality has been enrolled in a variety of philosophical, political, scientific, and aesthetic projects. In the early modern period, for instance, the theme of tropicality can be detected in the historical and philosophical reflections on human nature, and the wealth of nations. In many cases, the tropics were a 'new world' which held out to Europe the prospect of excitement and discovery, the promise of untapped wealth and exoticism. Throughout the 19th and 20th centuries, tropical difference was given institutional expression in the emergence of distinct subdisciplinary specialisms, most notably tropical medicine. However, in these fields the definition and limits of 'tropics' and the 'tropical' have been anything but settled.

After World War 2 the discourse on tropics and tropicality was further shaped by the influence of decolonization, the concept of development, global tourism, commodity advertising and environmental politics. In 1955 Claude Lévi-Strauss published his famous book *Tristes tropiques*, which picked out as a central theme the irrevocable loss of cultural variety as a result of the global spread of Western culture. The French anthropologist describes among other things the destruction of formerly 'authentic' tropical societies in Brazil. His despair of civilization combined with repugnance at growing cultural uniformity has become an important element in conceptions of the tropics during the last fifty years.

Thus the tropics were not merely a physical, but a conceptual space as well. 'Calling part of the globe "the tropics" became mostly a Western way of defining something environmentally and culturally distinct from Europe, while also perceiving a high degree of common identity between the constituent regions of the tropical world' (Arnold 1998, 2). The tropics were constructed as a world alien in terms of its climate, vegetation, diseases, and human population; they existed 'in mental and spatial juxtaposition to the perceived normality of the northern temperate zone' (loc. cit.). It was the German naturalist and great theorist of tropical geography, Alexander von Humboldt (1769–1859), who most powerfully influenced subsequent generations of naturalists and artists across Europe and the Americas in their visions of the tropics. The aesthetic depiction of landscape was an integral part of Humboldt's philosophy. For him, 'the tropical world was a privileged site, where the true variation and order of nature could be observed in all its majesty' (Driver and Martins 2005, 7). Humboldt provides a good example of the transnational character of sciences because he extends beyond particular 'national' research schools and traditions. He was a Prussian who – following his return from his travels in the Americas – spent the most productive years of his long working life in Paris and whose influence was felt across the English-speaking world and beyond, notably in Latin America.

Alongside the visions of an earthly paradise was the representation of the tropics as environmentally hazardous and disease-ridden. Behind 'the perceptual shift from paradise to pestilence' (Arnold 1998, 5) lay the massive importation of African slaves to the Americas and West Indies and the accompanying transfer of yellow fever, yaws, and other diseases from West Africa. That many of these diseases originated outside the West Indies encouraged medical writers to look beyond the confines of the Caribbean and to seek to generalize for the tropics as a whole. While much medical discussion focused on the physical effects of the tropics on Europeans, this was also a moral discourse. The climate prohibited modes of behaviour acceptable, even desirable, in Europe. There was a significant elision here between 'temperate' to describe the European climate and 'temperate' to designate forms of moderation or abstinence the tropics enjoined upon whites.

For a long time, historians regarded tropical diseases as unproblematic, as it were, and followed tropical medicine in focusing on a narrow group of specific diseases and their control. More recently it has been suggested that many so-called tropical diseases are, in fact, diseases of poverty, malnutrition, and insanitary conditions. In this context, the term 'tropical' has served an ideological function in associating the causes of these diseases with natural rather than social, economic, or political factors. The notion of tropical diseases is now widely regarded as the construction of a particular time and space, and tropical medicine is viewed as the institutionalization of a metropolitan medical perspective.

Another element closely linked to common perceptions of the tropics is the rainforest. Most basic to the Europeans' perception of the tropical rainforest was their inability to see the rainforest as another culturally defined and culturally inscribed space. Although inhabited for centuries, they insisted on calling it virgin or primeval forest, Urwald in German, 'jungle' in English. The latter is derived from the Hindustani word djanghael or jangal, meaning wasteland or uncultivated ground. This terminology negates any human encroachment on or use of the forest, and it stipulates a clear-cut dichotomy between nature and culture. Journeys to the tropical rainforests were perceived as journeys back in time, back into humanity's state of infancy, back into some sort of mythical chaos, such as the one the Old Testament evokes. Henry Morton Stanley offers a good example of images of the tropical rainforest during the 19th century (and after). In his writings, the African equatorial rainforest is imagined as some sort of primitive hell, as a chaos, as a world beyond measure and as a mirror of the darker side of 19th-century life in the urban centres of the industrialized nations, a metaphor for the Hobbesian war of all against all.

In essence, the tropics have long been a site for European fantasies of self-realization, projects of (cultural) imperialism, or the politics of human or environmental salvage. It should be emphasized, however, that artists and intellectuals working in 'the global South' have 'appropriated the language of tropicality for their own ends, and this in turn has influenced the ways in which Europeans have understood tropical nature and culture' (Driver and Martins 2005, 4). For instance, during the 1930s the Brazilian sociologist Gilberto Freyre developed the concept of Luso-tropicalism in which he stressed the ideal of the harmonious blending of racial, religious and cultural differences that, according to him, had emerged in Brazil during the colonial period. This concept was eventually taken up by Portuguese elites when discussing the future of the Asian and African colonies. Until today the tropics are both a geographical and ecological region and an 'imagined space' laden with histories, fantasies and images.

Andreas Eckert

Bibliography

Arnold D. 1998. 'India's place in the tropical world, 1770–1930', Journal of Imperial and Commonwealth History, 26, 1, 1–21.

Driver F. and Martins L. (eds) 2005. Tropical visions in an age of empire. Chicago and London: Chicago University Press.

Worboys M. 'Tropical diseases', in Bynum W. F. and Porter R. (eds) 1993. Companion encyclopedia of the history of medicine, Vol. 2, London and New York: Routledge, 512–36.

Related essays

Africa; antropofagia; Asia; civilizations; conservation and preservation; contract and indentured labourers; empires and imperialism; epidemics; forests; germs; health policy; higher education; medicine; museums; Orientalism; race-mixing; rubber; scientific expeditions; wildlife films

U

Underdevelopment

Underdevelopment refers to a range of theories focusing on the persistence of poor countries and regions within the international system.

Even though the term 'underdevelopment' seems to have been coined during the early 1940s, it rose to international prominence when Harry Truman referred to 'underdeveloped areas' in his 1949 presidential inauguration speech. Subsequently the expression and its translation into many languages such as the German *Unterentwicklung*, the Spanish *subdesarrollo* or the Chinese *butai fada* (不太发达) has been commonplace. Across a wide range of political positions 'underdevelopment' came to connote global inequality, sustained patterns of poverty and suboptimal economic performance. Indicators of underdevelopment are usually centred on economic figures such as gross domestic product, per capita income, savings rates, capacity for surplus production, and investment intensity. Yet most diagnoses of underdevelopment also consider factors ranging from life expectancies and child mortality rates to water quality, education levels, social mobility, and regional income gaps.

During the Cold War and the decolonization period, rival intellectual and ideological schools produced theories of underdevelopment, which differed profoundly in their assessments of global inequality. A very important theoretical divide emerged over issues such as whether underdevelopment was caused by endogenous or exogenous factors. A particularly polarizing problem was the question whether either institutional and political systems or economic factors needed to be seen as the root causes of underdevelopment. Usually theories of underdevelopment were not confined to national schools but tended to circulate within transnational networks of rather likeminded scholars and policy makers.

During the 1950s and early 1960s modernization theory dominated approaches to underdevelopment in the West. According to its leading theorists such as Talcott Parsons or Walt Whitman Rostow, Western societies, particularly Britain and the United States, embodied the future of the underdeveloped world. Most modernization theorists regarded domestic socioeconomic structures and not the international environment as the causes of underdevelopment. Continuing liberal Anglo-American as well as Weberian traditions of social thought, this school tended to identify precapitalistic social structures as the causes of economic stagnation. Underdevelopment was thought likely to occur in societies without professional workforces and profit-oriented domestic investors. Building on this assumption, most modernization theorists argued that underdeveloped nations would have to go through the same basic stages of development as industrialized societies had, decades if not centuries before. In that manner paving the way towards universal Westernization and modernization was defined as a strategy to counter underdevelopment. Rostow and likeminded thinkers believed that economic development had to take place in conjunction with efforts to dismantle traditional or 'backward' features of underdeveloped societies. Modernization theorists tended to argue that on a domestic level, governments could facilitate economic development by modernizing institutions such as the legal framework, the political sector or the educational system. On an international level, development aid and the inclusion in international trade patterns were deemed to be the key remedies to overcome underdevelopment.

On the other side of the Cold War divide, Soviet scholars tended to explain underdevelopment on modified Marxist, especially Leninist grounds. Theorists such as Otto Wilhelm Kuusinen and Rachik M. Avakov, for example, identified colonialism and imperialism as the main causes of underdevelopment. The depletion of resources in colonized or semi-colonized societies was seen as analogous to the exploitation of the countryside under feudalism. In many cases, theorists in the Soviet Union combined the notion of domestic feudalism and international colonialism into a comprehensive framework of analysis. Similarly to modernization theorists, Soviet analysts regarded imports of technology and know-how as well as the sudden restructuring of society as the key means to overcome underdevelopment. However, in contrast to the United States, the Soviet model typically advocated state-led patterns of industrial growth, which implied at least a high degree of central economic planning and government ownership of the means of production. Soviet observers typically argued that the root causes of underdevelopment needed to be tackled by revolutionary acts but in the wake of the decolonization period their theories became increasingly open to locally or nationally specific paths and experiences. The endorsement of more nationalist versions of socialism needs to be seen in the context of the Soviet Union supporting anti-colonial liberation movements. Soviet theorists argued that capitalist solutions to underdevelopment were bound to fail since this system put too much pressure on the masses and was inconceivable without colonial exploitation.

Some theories emerged from non-Western societies and quite explicitly contested the primacy of American and Soviet knowledge. An internationally influential alternative to the dominance of Western theories of underdevelopment, which nevertheless remained closely entangled with neo-Marxist thought, emerged in the shape of Latin American dependency theory. During the 1950s and 1960s public intellectuals in Latin America challenged development programmes and their guiding principles of underdevelopment. They drew on Marxist theories of imperialism but shifted the analytical focus away from rich and powerful nations to the underdeveloped world. Dependency theorists tended to argue that the presence of a liberal market economy and not its absence was the root cause of underdevelopment. International dependencies made it impossible for underdeveloped countries to set up functional economic circles. In Latin American societies the main objective of these explanations of underdevelopment was to gain local control over the concepts and mechanisms of development – an effort that in many national settings became an important part of identity politics. Most proposed solutions to underdevelopment revolved around ideas such as autochthonous development and dissociation from the world market.

Theories of underdevelopment related to the dependency theory movement quickly spread to other parts of the world, where they were adapted to new sociopolitical contexts. Many Third World thinkers started to argue that numerous domestic problems such as oligarchic trends, the rural–urban divide or mounting income disparities were direct consequences of a history of economic dependency and underdevelopment. In Africa, for example, critical intellectuals referred to dependency theory when questioning the prospects of national liberation

and its Western frameworks. There was a certain overlap between the prominence of these positions and the appropriation of Soviet theories by leaders of several African countries. During the 1960s many African presidents including Sékou Touré (Guinea) or Kwame Nkrumah (Ghana) were at least partly influenced by both Soviet theories and the dependency movement. Even though they positioned themselves differently vis-à-vis the West and the principle of free trade, many sub-Saharan leaders maintained that their countries' underdevelopment was the direct result of colonial exploitation.

In the Western world the spectrum of dependency theories became prominent during the 1960s, when scholars like André Gunder Frank (1929–2005) argued that underdevelopment was not a result of backwardness but the result of a hierarchical world market and massive value transfers from the now poorer world to industrialized societies. According to such theories, the world economy was characterized by the dynamics between a rich 'core' of industrialized societies and an impoverished belt of peripheral countries marked by small industrialized pockets and large backward areas. Underdevelopment is entrapped in a dynamic, in which poor countries are dependent on the export of raw materials and the import of manufactured goods. For Frank, who spent a lot of time working in Latin America and many other dependency theorists, the economic and fiscal logic of this system led to terms of trade that were progressively unfavourable to the underdeveloped world. In their eyes, one of these disadvantageous processes was higher growth rate in the demand for industrial goods than in the demand for raw materials.

World system theory, which was mainly developed during the 1970s by a circle of scholars around Immanuel Wallerstein, inherited essential elements from dependency theory but it included other scholarly approaches, most notably the Annales School. Furthermore, it added the notion of a semi-periphery to the centre–periphery dichotomy, and it assumed that single countries could rise and fall within this triadic system. Wallerstein tended to reject the categorical distinction between developed and underdeveloped societies by arguing that both needed be understood as intrinsic parts of the same capitalist world system. Departing from the main postulates of dependency theory, the Wallerstein school held that the global hierarchy could not be resolved by efforts to break away from the international system but rather required global solutions based on concerted efforts by the underprivileged. In that context, the collective self-reliance of underdeveloped societies became an increasingly prominent objective.

The failure of alternative development programmes and the quite unexpected success of many East Asian economies through world-market-oriented growth have weakened the position of dependency theory and world system theory. Since the 1980s neoliberal ideologies, which argued that free market forces and global competition would be the best remedies to underdevelopment, became politically and intellectually more influential – particularly in the United States but also in several other societies. Neoliberals tend to identify the dominance of the public sector, corruption and other distortions of the free market as the main causes for underdevelopment. Partly in response to neoliberal interpretations, more refined theories of underdevelopment have appeared, which take factors such as worldwide investment trends and strategies of multinational corporations into the picture. Furthermore, many theories start to assume that there can be divergent, locally specific solutions to underdevelopment. At present no single theory of underdevelopment has achieved the same degree of transnational prominence as dependency theory and world system theory did during the 1960s and 1970s.

In addition to the changing international economic realities, transformations in the academic landscape have weakened support for older theories of underdevelopment. For example, many economists and historians have come to argue that the intellectual parameters of underdevelopment as articulated by modernization theory, dependency theory and world system theory were too one-dimensional and abstract. On a more general level, grand master narratives, which underlie the notions of development and underdevelopment, have come to be increasingly criticized for their Eurocentric and universalistic frameworks. Partly inspired by postmodern and postcolonial movements, an increasing number of scholars have started to argue that the many older tropes of underdevelopment imply a common human teleology and hence do not allow for cultural alternatives to the Western economic system. As

part of this growing criticism large parts of movements such as the World Social Forum or Focus on the Global South Group have started to become rather influential in many parts of the world. Activists and public intellectuals like Walden Bello argue that many global institutions, most notably the World Bank or the IMF, actually perpetuate and enhance global inequalities rather than ameliorating them. The postulates of this movement, which turns against neoliberalist paradigms, include the deconcentration of international institutional power, and international decentralization at a global level, and increasing local control and self-reliance.

In recent years studies have started to include this criticism in the picture without completely abandoning the concept of underdevelopment. Today there are a growing number of studies focusing on cultural topics such as trust, social cohesion and mentalities, which are supposedly conducive to or obstructive of development. Other studies try specifically to account for the fact that some Third World societies experienced sustained levels of economic growth and rising standards of living while the conditions of other underdeveloped regions even deteriorated. For this purpose scholars are trying to develop new theories of underdevelopment, which are more locally sensitive and easier to empirically verify. Researchers such as Mitchell A. Seligson argue that the gap between the global theories and local studies of underdevelopment is too large. Future theories of underdevelopment need to address the dynamic interplay between micro- and macro-factors in order to gain wide-ranging understandings of underdevelopment that nevertheless consider the uniqueness of every single case. Concomitant with this process, environmental and other constraints have come to be more emphasized in theories of underdevelopment.

Parallel to these developments in theory, international institutions continue to set ambitious goals for leaving underdevelopment behind. For example, the UN Millennium Summit in 2000 pledged to find concrete steps to end poverty and underdevelopment in the future. The initiative also pointed to the gap between the most developed and the most underdeveloped societies, which has continually widened during the past fifty years. Declarations tend to frequently use the term 'underdevelopment' but avoid a clear definition in order to remain acceptable to different political and ideological camps.

Dominic Sachsenmaier

Bibliography

Labini P. S. 2001. *Underdevelopment: a strategy for reform*. Cambridge: Cambridge University Press.

Roxboro I. 1979. *Theories of underdevelopment*. London: Macmillan (now Palgrave Macmillan).

Seligson M. A and Passé-Smith J. T. (eds) 2001. *Development and underdevelopment: the political economy of global inequality*. Boulder and London: Lynne Rienner.

Shaffer H. G. and Prybyla J. S. 1968. *From underdevelopment to affluence: Western, Soviet and Chinese views*. New York: Appleton-Century-Crofts.

Related essays

Africa; African liberation; Asia; Cold War; convergence and divergence; debt (developing countries); development and growth; developmental assistance; Economic Commission for Latin America and the Caribbean (ECLAC); empires and imperialism; history; industrialization; investment; Maoism; millennium; modernization theory; neoliberalism; Prebisch, Raúl; Samsung; socialism; technical assistance; *The Wretched of the Earth*; trade; United Nations decades and years; United Nations Educational, Scientific and Cultural Organization (UNESCO) educational programmes; Westernization; world orders

United Cities and Local Governments (UCLG)

United Cities and Local Governments (UCLG) held its first Congress in 2004. Its creation signalled the increasing ambition of local authorities to take part in the regulation of the world order. Cross-national associations of cities have been in operation since the beginning of the 20th century, reflecting the municipalities' concern to be protagonists on the global scene. The International Union of Local Authorities (IULA), one of three groups that created UCLG, was established in 1913. Its history testifies that cities began bursting in on the international scene well before the 1990s.

The Union Internationale des Villes (UIV) was created during the 'First International Congress of Cities and Compared Exhibition of Cities' (Ghent, Belgium, 1913). Unlike several earlier attempts to organize municipalities in an international association, UIV was successful because of its solid logistical base, embedded in the socialist European networks and in the fabric of international groups created by Paul Otlet and Henri la Fontaine in Brussels. The Union's executive director, Belgian socialist senator Emile Vinck, was the man behind the Union until 1948. He kept the organization going after the First World War as a mouthpiece for self-government and a documentation network to share municipal policies and technological information. He lured in the English-speaking world's municipal organizations (hence the name IULA from 1928). But he was not able to connect effectively the Union with the League of Nations system. Organized on a national sections basis, the Union spent its early life on a knife-edge, its conferences being vital occasions to refurbish its cash flow. This changed in the mid-1930s when the German and US sections notably increased their participation. The latter, powered by Rockefeller philanthropic money and projects, wanted to use the Union as a touchstone to establish a transatlantic exchange in public administration practices. The former, imbued with the Nazi project of Neue Europa, was eager to seize power in several international associations. The (soft) clash between those two universal ambitions oriented the Union towards the discussion of technical and administrative subjects through the periodicals and conferences it had been supporting since 1913.

The Second World War, during which the Nazis seized the Union, created conditions for its revamping. Led by its Dutch and US components, the headquarters moved to The Hague (Netherlands) in 1948. The Union began to develop a worldwide strategy to expand beyond its mostly Western domain, as other municipal groups were created in Europe to foster intermunicipal links and relations (for example, the Council of European Municipalities 1951, United Towns Organization 1957), and to create strong links with the UN agencies. Steadily, IULA information work about 'best municipal practices' came to be coupled with installation, training and demonstration projects. From the 1980s, municipal autonomy and self-government recovered their importance in the Union discourse. They favourably echoed the globalization discourse of the 1990s, and espoused the increasing concern for the governance of global problems. IULA played its part in the creation of successive institutions through which local authorities were called upon to cooperate with UN agencies: the International Council for Local Environment Initiative (1990), World Associations of Cities and Local Authorities Coordination (1996), Cities Alliance Programme (1999), United Nations Committee of Local Authorities (1999). The creation of UCLG in 2004, merging IULA, United Towns Organization and the 'Metropolis' network, did not end the competition to embody the voice of local governments. Other organizations such as the Arab Towns Organisation, the Eurocities cluster and the Asian Citynet remained distinct and distinctive. But the birth of the new organization clearly points to the converging interest of local government leaders and intergovernmental organizations in bypassing national governments in fields such as environment or development.

Pierre-Yves Saunier

Bibliography

Bautz I. 1999. 'Die Auslandsbeziehungen der deutschen Kommunen vor 1945: IULA, Städtepatenschaften, Weltstädtebund', *Interregiones*, 8, 19–58.

Saunier P.-Y. 'Selling the idea of cooperation: US foundations and the European components of the Urban Internationale (1920s–1960s)', in Gemelli G. (ed.) 2001. *American Foundations and large scale research: construction and transfer of knowledge*. Bologna: Clueb, 219–46.

Saunier P.-Y. (ed.) 2002. Special Issue, 'Municipal connections: co-operation, links and transfers among European cities in the Twentieth Century', *Contemporary European History*, 11, 4.

Related essays

cities; environmentalism; global cities; governing science; intergovernmental organizations; international non-governmental organizations (INGOs); Otlet, Paul; philanthropic foundations; Pugwash Conferences; traffic signals; urbanization

United Fruit Company *See* Agriculture

United Nations (UN) decades and years

Although its founders designed the UN primarily as a collective security organization, peace enforcement and peace keeping have constituted only a fraction of the UN's activity. Unlike the UN's predecessor, the League of Nations, where most non-political activity was unanticipated and unsystematic, the UN included formal agencies to handle these tasks.

Because much of this non-political work would necessarily involve long-term commitments, some UN officials eventually proposed to address it in discrete periods ranging from years to decades. The idea of dedicated 'years' and 'decades' can be traced back to the 19th century (for example, the International Polar Years of 1882–83). When the UN took up the idea, it became subject to a majority vote of the General Assembly. For the most part, 'days' and 'weeks' were designed to commemorate or publicize issues, 'years' and 'decades' to organize remedial activity in various problem areas.

These 'UN dedications' testify to the degree to which UN officials and member governments recognized that critical global problems are transnational in character. Before 1939, only disarmament, epidemic disease, and, to a lesser extent, labour exploitation and war prevention, were routinely addressed by the League and the International Labour Office (ILO) on a transnational basis. Most other issues, including the vexing challenges regarding mandates, the treatment of minorities, and the restoration of war-ravaged economies, were left to governments acting alone.

This changed after 1945, especially after decolonization dramatically expanded the UN's membership. The General Assembly declared the first international year in December 1958, highlighting the plight of refugees. The proposal was the brainchild of four British MPs, and followed a 1957 proposal for an International Migration Year and publicity for the 1957–58 International Geophysical Year, adopted by the International Council of Scientific Unions. Two years later, the General Assembly inaugurated the first UN decade, emphasizing the importance of Third World economic development. Three additional development decades would follow, as well as decades aimed specifically at industrial development in Africa. Of the 34 decades declared by the UN between 1961 and 2006, over half have been devoted to just four subjects: economic development, transportation and communication, anti-racism, and disarmament.

Sequentially designating two, three, and even four years and/or decades to address such challenges is evidence that UN officials and member states had reconciled themselves to the need for patience. Some UN years and decades have exceeded expectations. The Year of Mobilization for Sanctions Against South Africa (1982) likely helped to accelerate the end of apartheid. The UN's Water Supply and Sanitation Decade (1981–91) witnessed notable successes in Latin America and even some African countries. The General Assembly effectively publicized small development loans when it declared 2005 as the Year of Microcredit.

Other campaigns have been less successful. Despite support voiced by industrialized countries for vague development decade goals, most governments in the developed North rejected in practice the General Assembly's recommendation to transfer 1 per cent of their wealth to the developing South. Many governments – including some in the Third World – have also sidestepped development decade attention to the interconnectivity of tariffs, domestic agricultural subsidies, and production quotas. The prosperous North ignored debt forgiveness for poor countries until the 1990s, although there has been movement in this area since then. Although the first development decades witnessed an average 4.6 per cent increase in GDP among developing countries, rapid population growth meant that real wealth, as measured on a per capita basis, has been almost non-existent for a majority of the world's poorest nations.

UN decades have occasionally generated more controversy than consensus. For instance, when the General Assembly in 1975, following a bitter debate, labelled Zionism a form of racism two years after declaring the Decade for Action to Combat Racism and Racial Discrimination (1973–83), support for the UN weakened in some capitals. Most UN years and decades have been less contentious.

Secretariat officials initially hoped to limit the number of international dedications to avoid diluting their importance. Instead, dedications proliferated. During the 1990s, the General Assembly declared eight separate calendar years as international years. Calendar year 2001 housed three UN years. The month of December 2001 contained eleven international days, ranging from drawing attention to AIDS (1 December) to Human Solidarity (20 December). Although many UN dedications had precedents, such as the 2001 Year of Mobilization against Racism, Racial Discrimination, Xenophobia, and Related Intolerance, others were innovative. Calendar year 2002 became the Year of Mountains, promoted to emphasize the importance of sustainable development in alpine regions; while 2006 became the Year of Planet Earth, actually a three-year campaign to publicize the importance of the earth sciences.

By the 21st century, specialized agencies such as ECOSOC and UNESCO had joined the General Assembly in approving such dedications. Although this might further contribute to proliferation, it has nevertheless reemphasized the transnational character of problem solving. Strictly national solutions to global problems had become as obsolete as slide-rules in a computer age.

Gary B. Ostrower

Bibliography

Drori G. S. 2005. 'United Nations dedications: a world culture in the making?', *International Sociology*, 20, 2, 175–99.

Fasulo L. 2004. *An insider's guide to the UN*. New Haven and London: Yale University Press.

Schechter M. G. 2005. *United Nations global conferences*. London and New York: Routledge.

Related essays

Acquired Immunodeficiency Syndrome (AIDS); Antarctic Treaty; biodiversity; climate change; consumer cooperation; developmental assistance; disarmament; indigenous networks; intergovernmental organizations; refugees; underdevelopment; United Nations Educational, Scientific and Cultural Organization (UNESCO) educational programmes; United Nations system; women's movements; Zionism

United Nations (UN) system

The UN Charter lists protecting mankind from the 'scourge of war' as the UN's primary goal. As with the League of Nations that emerged out of an earlier world war, collective security (the term was not invented until 1935) would be the means to do this. The primacy of maintaining peace in the UN universe would be reaffirmed by the World Court in the 1962 Expenses case (in which an advisory opinion that affirmed peacekeeping costs to be an obligation of all states no less than a charge on the UN's regular budget). Still, the objective of ensuring peace never stood alone. The Charter's preamble also obligates the UN to respect 'fundamental human rights' and human dignity, to promote social progress, and to establish the conditions that will maintain justice and respect for international law. This was an ambitious agenda. What eventually surprised most observers is that these secondary goals have become no less important – perhaps even more important – than the UN's promotion of peace.

However ambitious it seemed at the time, the early UN system was modest by contemporary standards. In 1945, the UN had 50 members. The General Assembly and Security Council flanked the UN's administrative machinery in the secretariat. The other principal organs of the UN in 1945 included the Economic and Social Council (ECOSOC), the Trusteeship Council, and the UN Educational, Scientific and Cultural Organization (UNESCO). Additional units were joined to the UN as affiliated agencies, most importantly the International Labour Organization (ILO) and the World Court (formally the Court of International Justice – ICJ). Both the ILO and the World Court dated back to the League era. Completing the system were the first UN agency, the Relief and Rehabilitation Administration (UNRRA) created in 1943 to deal with millions of wartime refugees, the Food and Agricultural Organization (FAO), and the World Health Organization (WHO). The UN system seemed complete.

It was not. By 2007, with 192 nations holding membership in the UN, the system had grown to include 47 different agencies, along with hundreds of subgroups: committees and subcommittees, functional commissions, regional commissions, funds, programmes, institutes, technical organizations, observer groups, peacekeeping operations (18 in 2007, involving over 74,000 uniformed troops, and nearly 25,000 police and civilians), advisory groups, even a university (see the accompanying chart). Added to this assembly are four related organizations, including the International Atomic Energy Agency (IAEA) and the World Trade Organization (WTO). The related organizations are not formally part of the UN, having been established by separate treaties among their member states. Nevertheless, they all complement the functional work of the UN and some even report to the General Assembly.

The task of defining such a sprawling UN system has become more challenging than eating raw eggs with a fork. Because the system grew in such an unsystematic fashion, its origins – and even its name – require some attention.

From the post-Napoleonic Congress of Vienna, influenced by the conservative desire for order and the liberal belief that reasoned cooperation would lead to progress, European conferences and unions appeared with increasing frequency after mid-century. They aimed to regulate international activity in areas like postal services, telegraphic communications, and Danube River traffic. The Hague Peace Conferences (1899 and 1907) added a more political hue to this work, culminating in the creation of the post-World War 1 League of Nations. The ILO and the World Court were created at the same time, separate from but affiliated with the League. While the League was initially more focused on collective security than would be its successor, by the 1930s League officials had established committees to address many non-political activities, including intellectual cooperation, telecommunications, health, mandates (colonial territories), refugees and slavery, and economic reconstruction.

Following the 1945 San Francisco Conference and the end of World War 2, most of these committees grew into more formal – and quasi-independent – agencies. But did they collectively constitute a 'system'? Yes, in the sense that they became much more than merely the sum of their individual parts. Together, these agencies are coordinated – albeit loosely – by increasingly well defined norms and values designed to influence the behaviour of sovereign states. Such norms and values became increasingly transnational, most notably the values of peace, self-determination, interstate cooperation, social justice, and human rights. Moreover, they have

The United Nations System

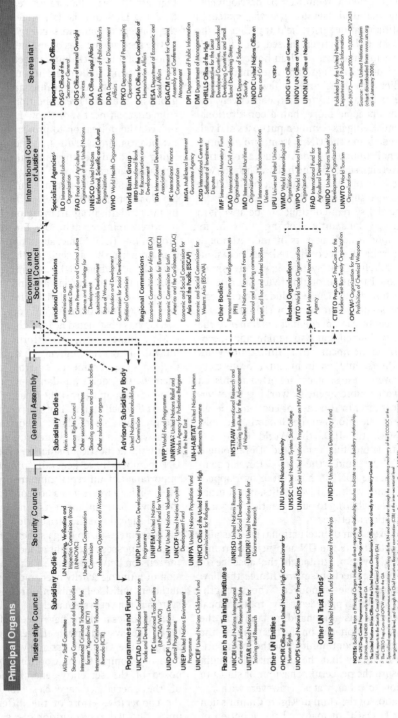

Principal Organs

Trusteeship Council · Security Council · General Assembly · Economic and Social Council · International Court of Justice · Secretariat

Trusteeship Council

Security Council

Subsidiary Bodies
Military Staff Committee
Standing Committee and ad hoc bodies
International Criminal Tribunal for the former Yugoslavia (ICTY)
International Criminal Tribunal for Rwanda (ICTR)
UN Monitoring, Verification and Inspection Commission (Iraq) (UNMOVIC)
United Nations Compensation Commission
Peacekeeping Operations and Missions

General Assembly

Subsidiary Bodies
Main committees
Human Rights Council
Other sessional committees
Standing committees and ad hoc bodies
Other subsidiary organs

Advisory Subsidiary Body
United Nations Peacebuilding Commission

Programmes and Funds
UNCTAD United Nations Conference on Trade and Development
  ITC International Trade Centre (UNCTAD/WTO)
UNDCP¹ United Nations Drug Control Programme
UNEP United Nations Environment Programme
UNICEF United Nations Children's Fund
UNDP United Nations Development Programme
  UNIFEM United Nations Development Fund for Women
  UNV United Nations Volunteers
  UNCDF United Nations Capital Development Fund
UNFPA United Nations Population Fund
UNHCR Office of the United Nations High Commissioner for Refugees
WFP World Food Programme
UNRWA² United Nations Relief and Works Agency for Palestine Refugees in the Near East
UN-HABITAT United Nations Human Settlements Programme

Research and Training Institutes
UNICRI United Nations Interregional Crime and Justice Research Institute
UNITAR United Nations Institute for Training and Research
UNRISD United Nations Research Institute for Social Development
UNIDIR² United Nations Institute for Disarmament Research
INSTRAW International Research and Training Institute for the Advancement of Women
UNU United Nations University
UNSSC United Nations System Staff College
UNAIDS Joint United Nations Programme on HIV/AIDS

Other UN Entities
OHCHR Office of the United Nations High Commissioner for Human Rights
UNOPS United Nations Office for Project Services
UNFIP United Nations Fund for International Partnerships
UNDEF United Nations Democracy Fund

Other UN Trust Funds⁷

Economic and Social Council

Functional Commissions
Commissions on:
Narcotic Drugs
Crime Prevention and Criminal Justice
Science and Technology for Development
Sustainable Development
Status of Women
Population and Development
Commission for Social Development
Statistical Commission

Regional Commissions
Economic Commission for Africa (ECA)
Economic Commission for Europe (ECE)
Economic Commission for Latin America and the Caribbean (ECLAC)
Economic and Social Commission for Asia and the Pacific (ESCAP)
Economic and Social Commission for Western Asia (ESCWA)

Other Bodies
Permanent Forum on Indigenous Issues (PFII)
United Nations Forum on Forests
Sessional and standing committees
Expert, ad hoc and related bodies

Related Organizations
WTO World Trade Organization
IAEA⁴ International Atomic Energy Agency
CTBTO Prep.Com⁵ PrepCom for the Nuclear-Test-Ban-Treaty Organization
OPCW⁵ Organization for the Prohibition of Chemical Weapons

International Court of Justice

Specialized Agencies⁶
ILO International Labour Organization
FAO Food and Agriculture Organization of the United Nations
UNESCO United Nations Educational, Scientific and Cultural Organization
WHO World Health Organization

World Bank Group
IBRD International Bank for Reconstruction and Development
IDA International Development Association
IFC International Finance Corporation
MIGA Multilateral Investment Guarantee Agency
ICSID International Centre for Settlement of Investment Disputes

IMF International Monetary Fund
ICAO International Civil Aviation Organization
IMO International Maritime Organization
ITU International Telecommunication Union
UPU Universal Postal Union
WMO World Meteorological Organization
WIPO World Intellectual Property Organization
IFAD International Fund for Agricultural Development
UNIDO United Nations Industrial Development Organization
UNWTO World Tourism Organization

Secretariat

Departments and Offices
OSG³ Office of the Secretary-General
OIOS Office of Internal Oversight Services
OLA Office of Legal Affairs
DPA Department of Political Affairs
DDA Department for Disarmament Affairs
DPKO Department of Peacekeeping Operations
OCHA Office for the Coordination of Humanitarian Affairs
DESA Department of Economic and Social Affairs
DGACM Department for General Assembly and Conference Management
DPI Department of Public Information
DM Department of Management
OHRLLS Office of the High Representative for the Least Developed Countries, Landlocked Developing Countries and Small Island Developing States
DSS Department of Safety and Security
UNODC United Nations Office on Drugs and Crime

UNOG UN Office at Geneva
UNOV UN Office at Vienna
UNON UN Office at Nairobi

Published by the United Nations Department of Public Information
06-39577—August 2006—10,000—DPI/2431

Source: The United Nations System (chart downloaded from www.un.org on 4 January 2008).

NOTES: Solid lines from a Principal Organ indicate a direct reporting relationship; dashes indicate a non-subsidiary relationship.
¹ The UN Drug Control Programme is part of the UN Office on Drugs and Crime
² UNRWA and UNIDIR report only to the GA
³ The United Nations Ethics Office and the United Nations Ombudsman's Office report directly to the Secretary-General
⁴ IAEA reports to the Security Council and the General Assembly (GA)
⁵ The CTBTO Prep.Com and OPCW report to the GA
⁶ Specialized agencies are autonomous organizations working with the UN and each other through the coordinating machinery of the ECOSOC or the intergovernmental level, and through the Chief Executives Board for coordination (CEB) at the inter-secretariat level
⁷ UNFIP is an autonomous trust fund operating under the leadership of the United Nations Deputy Secretary-General. UNDEF's advisory board recommends funding proposals for approval by the Secretary-General.

been sufficiently reinforced by developments in international law to give the system a constitutional integrity, held together by the glue of the UN Charter. Indeed, the Charter's Article 103 mandates UN authority in cases where other international agreements may conflict with the Charter. A few writers have gone so far as to argue that, collectively, the UN has become more than a constitutional system, seeing its common purposes and values redefining the UN system into an international community and not just a collection of sovereign states bound by law. The 1999 war in Kosovo and the 2003 attack on Iraq have dampened support for this point of view.

The UN system continues to be a work in progress. Constantly evolving, it is in its childhood if no longer its infancy. Although decentralized, uncoordinated, and occasionally anarchic, the system has increasingly promoted transnational activity in critically important areas. These include not only collective security (hampered by the the the right of veto held by each permanent member of the Security Council) but also human rights, economic development, arms limitation, work conditions, and environmental protection. Moreover, these subjects are often addressed by two or more agencies working together. For instance, in the case of economic development, the efforts of the General Assembly, ECOSOC, the ILO, the World Bank, the UN Institute for Trade and Development (UNITAD), and the UN Development Programme (UNDP) have often overlapped, sometimes with positive results, but at other times contributing to bureaucratic rivalry and duplication of effort.

The evolution of international law has also helped to define the UN as a genuine transnational system, although the absence of an effective mechanism to enforce this law has rarely gone unnoticed. The strengthening of legal precedents for transnational cooperation has gone hand in hand with the post-1945 emphasis on justice within the international community. For the most part, it is fair to say that the UN initially sought to ensure the peaceful behaviour of states in relation to other states. However, with the formation of the Human Rights Commission under ECOSOC in 1946 and the adoption of the Universal Declaration of Human Rights two years later, a gradual but vital change occurred. The UN – albeit haltingly and inconsistently – has established standards to regulate the way that states treat their own citizens. Thus did the UN system introduce the concept of 'human security'. Where collective security focuses on maintaining peace among nation states, human security focuses on protecting individuals (though often as members of gender, ethnic and religious groups) from abusive conditions and even from mistreatment by one's own government. Indeed, the obligation to protect individuals extends to many activities, including famine, living standards, environmental threats and human rights violations.

Here again the UN system is subject to overlap. For instance, the UNDP's efforts to raise living standards in agrarian regions have been positively reinforced by UN Environmental Programme (UNEP) measures to prevent the contamination of agricultural land. On the other hand, when UNEP recommendations concerning both agrarian and industrial pollution have threatened UNDP efforts to create jobs and to promote economic development, overlap has obstructed needed change.

More importantly, UN efforts to protect individuals against human rights abuse from their own governments or from domestic enemies (the 1994 Rwandan genocide comes to mind) run up against the Charter's Article 2, part 6 which states: 'Nothing contained in the present Charter shall authorize the UN to intervene in matters which are essentially within the domestic jurisdiction of any state'. UN members have generally promoted the importance of universal human rights only when such an interest has not conflicted with their own national interests, and most have viewed their domestic jurisdiction as central to those interests. So long as the World Court does not possess the right of judicial review, the tension between Article 2 and the expansion of human security over traditional state authority will likely remain unresolved. The system is not yet systematic.

Nevertheless, there have been efforts to make the system more efficient. As early as 1946, the General Assembly created the Advisory Committee on Coordination, composed of the secretary-general and heads of the specialized agencies, to enhance the cooperative effort of the different UN units. This led to recognition of a subsystem within the UN system – what is often called the UN Common System. It is composed of those units of the UN that share a common salary scale, pensions, and administrative transfer procedures. The 'related agencies' (e.g. IAEA and WTO) and a number of other UN units including the World Bank and the International Monetary Fund (IMF) remain outside of the Common System. A number of secretariat subcommittees, including the Consultative Committee on Administrative Questions, were assigned the task of making the Common System more efficient.

The sheer size of the UN system necessitates such efforts. The League of Nations never employed more than about 850 staff members at any one time. The UN system in 2007, including the World Bank and IMF, employed nearly 63,500 people from 175 countries, of whom 16,000 worked in the secretariat. Blue Helmet peacekeepers and support police swell this number to approximately 150,000. Nor are all UN personnel found in New York. Unlike the earlier League with its single headquarters in Geneva, the UN system has agencies headquartered in 19 cities across five continents administering over 500 duty stations.

The UN budget reflects this sprawl. In 2007, the UN's regular budget was approximately US$1.9 billion. Another US$3 billion is earmarked for peacekeeping, a critical part of UN operations unmentioned in the Charter. For the entire UN system excluding the World Bank, the IMF, and the International Fund for Agricultural Development (IFAD), the total exceeds US$15 billion. A few things are worth noting here. In real dollars, the budget for the UN, excluding peacekeeping, the IMF, IFAD and World Bank, has increased only about ten times since 1945. Considering the range of the system, some observers believe this modest increase reflects scepticism about the UN's value on the part of its most wealthy members. By minimizing UN expenses (and dues), the largest contributors have minimized the UN's reach.

The three largest contributors – the US, Japan, and Germany (the latter two without permanent seats on the Security Council) – fund over 50 per cent of the regular budget, while the poorest 48 member states collectively finance less than one half of 1 per cent of the budget. The formula used to assess annual dues gives the largest contributors disproportionate influence over UN activity, even though almost all agencies within the UN system base voting on simple majority rule. The World Bank and the IMF are exceptions, utilizing a voting formula weighted to reflect monetary contributions.

Financing of UN agencies is not confined to member-state dues. A few agencies benefit from fundraising projects such as the sale of UN International Children's Emergency Fund (UNICEF) cards and fair-deal trade products. Unlike funding for the UN's principal organs, member-state contributions to humanitarian and development agencies are voluntary, totalling about half of all UN revenues (again, excluding peacekeeping, the IMF and the World Bank). Additional funds come from private donors, such as philanthropist Ted Turner's US$1 billion 1998 gift establishing the United Nations Foundation. There are also about 150 separate trust funds within the UN system, as well as 37 separate peacekeeping accounts. Financing of the system is further complicated because of the bewildering amount of paperwork needed to track these accounts, as well as restrictions placed on the secretariat during the early 1970s that have limited the secretary-general's ability to rationalize the system.

There are two other noteworthy features of the UN system. First, non-governmental organizations (NGOs) and NGO networks have come to play an increasingly important role during the past three decades. As of 2007, thousands of NGOs were accredited to the UN, nearly 2,800 to ECOSOC alone. At least nine other UN specialized agencies accredit NGOs, which range from the International Red Cross to the National Rifle Association to the Women's International League for Peace and Freedom. The virtual explosion of NGOs since 1970 has been one of the more unanticipated features of the UN system, though NGOs have actually played a role in UN affairs since 1946. Second, while they are not formally connected to the UN, the system includes many unofficial and private support organizations. Perhaps the most important is the World Federation of UN Associations, incorporating over 100 national organizations, including the UNA-USA with 175 separate chapters and a membership exceeding 20,000. There are also many professional and business organizations supporting the UN. The UN sponsors the UN University in Tokyo and receives support from many university programmes in North America, Europe and Asia. The UN programme at Yale University is especially notable, as is the Indiana University Press which publishes the influential volumes in the UN Intellectual History Project.

In sum, the UN system almost defies description. The accompanying chart offers a sense of the whole, but no chart can adequately capture either the UN's energy or its creative disorder.

Gary B. Ostrower

Bibliography

Alger C. F. 2006. *The United Nations System: a reference handbook*. Santa Barbara, Denver and Oxford: ABC-CLIO.

Baratta J. P (ed.) 1995. *The United Nations System: a bibliography*. International Organizations Series, vol. 10. New Brunswick: Transaction.

Kennedy P. 2006. *The parliament of man: the past, present, and future of the United Nations*. New York: Random House.

MacFarlane S. N. and Foong Khong Y. 2006. *Human security and the UN: a critical history*. Bloomington and Indianapolis: Indiana University Press.

Mingst K. A. and Karns M. P. 2000. *The United Nations in the post Cold-War era*. Boulder and Oxford: Westview.

White N. D. 2002. *The United Nations System: toward international justice*. Boulder and London: Lynne Rienner.

Related essays

Acquired Immunodeficiency Syndrome (AIDS); agriculture; arms trade; arms trafficking; climate change; Cold War; democracy; developmental assistance; displaced persons; Economic Commission for Latin America and the Caribbean (ECLAC); environmental diplomacy; environmentalism; General Agreement on Tariffs and Trade (GATT) / World Trade Organization (WTO); Hammarskjöld family; health policy; human rights; International Civil Aviation Organization (ICAO) and International Air Transport Association (IATA); intellectual property rights; International Commission on Labour Legislation; International Monetary Fund (IMF); international non-governmental organizations (INGOs); International Women's Day; Islamic Scientific, Educational and Cultural Organization (ISESCO); justice; language; League of Nations system; legal order; nation and state; patents; Pax Americana; refugee relief; refugees; relief; Stockholm Conference; technical standardization; transnational; transportation infrastructures; United Nations decades and years; United Nations Educational, Scientific and Cultural Organization (UNESCO) educational programmes; United Nations Women's Conferences; Universal Postal Union; welfare state; World Bank; world orders

United Nations Educational, Scientific and Cultural Organization (UNESCO) educational programmes

Since its creation in 1945, the United Nations Educational, Scientific and Cultural Organization (UNESCO) has carried out important initiatives in education, consisting of various activities: pedagogical research, seminars and conferences, and in the field, educational projects.

Beginning in 1949, it made important efforts for the education of the Palestinian refugee children, within the framework of the United Nations Relief and Works Agency (UNRWA). The courses were first taught under tents and disused buildings and the number of students increased quickly. Despite the difficulties, the UNESCO-UNRWA programme has definitely improved the schooling of the young refugees. A number of experts and associates who worked on this project have subsequently used their experience for other educational projects, especially in Africa.

The Universal Declaration of Human Rights formulated in 1948 by the UN posited 'a right to education'. Based on this spirit, UNESCO early developed studies and reflections on adult education and promoted the notion of 'fundamental education'. It was defined by a 1950 UN interagency working group as a minimum level in general education, aiming at helping people who had never been to school to understand the problems of their living environment and to know their rights and obligations. This conception was based on the vision of a world community inspired by a common pool of knowledge and ideas. Nevertheless, the fundamental education pilot project launched by UNESCO from 1947 in the Marbial Valley (Haïti) led to disappointing if not disastrous results, as shown by correspondence between headquarters and field officers (especially the Swiss anthropologist Alfred Métraux). A failing coordination with the Haitian state, economic misery of the valley inhabitants and serious famine, conflicts about the teaching language (French or Creole) and methods, sharp religious tensions in the valley between Catholics and Protestants, slowness of communications and the mental gap between the field team and the headquarters, prevailed over the goodwill of those who committed themselves enthusiastically to the project. In order to train local teachers, UNESCO wanted to set up a world network of 12 training centres for fundamental education. Only two of them were created, both in 1950: the Regional Centre for Fundamental Education in Latin America (CREFAL, Patzcuaro, Mexico), and the Arab States Fundamental Education Centre (ASFEC, Sirsel-Layyan, Egypt). Teaching methods in these centres were supposed to be innovative, based on hands-on interaction with the locals.

From the 1950s on, the notions of 'adult education' and 'fundamental education' were increasingly criticized for implying low-standard training and also because fundamental education was associated with colonialism. Indeed, those ideas were first conceived by British colonial administrators such as John Bowers, a former administrator in Sudan, who highly influenced UNESCO conceptions and methods during the first ten years. Though it aroused tension, new notions promoted by the United Nations progressively took over at UNESCO: 'community development' and 'functional literacy'. With the first one, priority was given to the community rather than the individual. It aimed at concentrating the efforts on the training of 'leaders', who would make knowledge percolate through the community. As for functional literacy, it was essentially characterized by its economic motivations: a literate worker is more efficient and thus financially more profitable than an illiterate one. The 'Experimental World Literacy Programme' (EWLP), launched in 1965, tried to apply this idea, without real success, as shown by UNESCO archives and assessed by a 1976 report: initially conceived as a huge world campaign of mass alphabetization, the programme was reduced to 12 'adult work-oriented literacy pilot projects' of a few hundred people each, essentially in Africa and the Middle East. Based on the principle of selecting the workers to be alphabetized according to economic profitability criteria (under the influence of the World Bank Group), EWLP was soon criticized for its socially inegalitarian character and its neoliberal economic implications. It also suffered from conceptual vagueness and from

a conflict between UNESCO and the United Nations Development Programme (UNDP), as much as between UNESCO and many of the states involved. This, added to chronic delays in its realization, to the absenteeism of many 'students' and to conflicts about the choice of the alphabetization language, compromised its success.

From the 1960s on, at the insistence of the new countries which had just entered UNESCO, the latter gave absolute priority to education in its programme. The Convention against Discrimination in Education (1960) and the Recommendation concerning the Status of Teachers (1966) testified to this determination, as much as the creation of the International Institute of Educational Planning (IIEP) in Paris in 1963. This institute tried to help developing countries to conceive, plan and administer their educational systems by different means: training, research, technical assistance, creation of networks, diffusion of information. Nearly 6,000 educational planners and administrators from more than 160 countries may have benefited from its training thus far. Its first director, Philip H. Coombs, was American: a former executive director for education at the Ford Foundation, he was also Assistant Secretary of State for Educational and Cultural Affairs under President Kennedy. He then became vice-chairman of the International Council for Educational Development in New York City. Subsequent directors of the IIEP were mostly French, like Jacques Hallack, a former chief planner for education at the World Bank Group. The careers of these men reveal the intense flow of staff and ideas between UNESCO and other educational agencies, national and international. Moreover, from 1969 on, the International Education Board (IEB), created in 1925 in Geneva and directed all along by the psychologist Jean Piaget, was united with UNESCO, allowing the organization to intensify its efforts in research and documentation on education.

In conjunction with UNDP, UNESCO encouraged the training of teachers in Africa by helping to create there more than 20 teacher-training schools and 12 regional education centres. In 1963, UNESCO also established the Regional Group for Educational Planning (RGEP) in Dakar, which in 1970 became the UNESCO Regional Bureau for Educational Development in Africa (BREDA). However, these creations encountered some difficulties, and these structures have neither been able to turn out enough personnel to take over from foreign experts (mostly European) serving on Voluntary Service Overseas, nor to act always efficiently: financial problems, internal rivalries, administrative red tape, competition and duplication of efforts with other structures (like the Institute for Economic Development and Planning (IDEP), linked to the Economical Council for Africa), account for their rather disappointing results, as several UNESCO agents analyse it off the record.

All through the 1960s and the 1970s, several changes occurred at UNESCO. First of all, after first focusing on primary teaching, it also became interested in secondary and university training. Thus, between 1965 and 1970, most African countries endowed themselves with higher education systems with the help of UNESCO. Besides, the organization, originally concerned with literacy, became increasingly interested in postliteracy. Finally, it switched from quantity to quality and from number of students to content of teaching.

If Africa appeared in those years as the main field for UNESCO educational programmes, it was not the only one. Indeed, it was in South America that the organization carried out one of its most important educational achievements in the field: the Major Project to Expand Primary Teaching in Latin America (1957–66). It led to the creation of 'associate institutions' for primary teaching and for teacher training, supported by UNESCO experts. Moreover, UNESCO launched in those years ambitious projects in educational radio and television. Encouraged by the great hopes raised by audiovisual progress, most of them were bitter failures, like the Television Education Project (PETV) in Ivory Coast (1969). It aimed at compensating for the lack of local teachers and at standardizing education in the whole country. It involved up to 600,000 pupils in 1980, but was increasingly criticized by three groups of people: the African elite concerned about negritude who blamed its insufficiently African character; the French-speaking and francophile intellectuals, who resented the abandonment of the French education model; and most of the teachers, because of the decreasing role of the teacher and of technical difficulties. Launched with enthusiasm, the PETV was dropped in 1981 to the great regret of its instigators, like the Frenchman Jean-Claude Pauvert. Its results are controversial. Indeed, many children, after having fulfilled the primary television course, were not able to integrate into secondary school and became marginalized.

Around 1968, in relation to the sociocultural and ideological disruptions of the time, UNESCO opened itself to new educational trends: after a world conference on the education crisis, organized in the United States in 1967, a report entitled *Learning to be*, published in 1972, emphasized alternative educational conceptions.

From the 1980s on, UNESCO concentrated on 'life-long education', a new version of what was called in the previous years permanent education. This was actually a buzz-word, since the Council of Europe had been promoting 'continuous education' and the OECD 'recurrent education' for approximately ten years. In 1990, the World Conference on Education for All held in Jomtien (Thailand), the biggest international meeting ever organized on education issues, marked the advent of the new notion of 'education for all', which has ever since constituted UNESCO's main policy. The goal was to cut adult illiteracy rates by 50 per cent between 1990 and 2000 (781 million adults are illiterate according to the UNESCO Institute for Statistics) and to universalize primary education by 2000. In 1996, under the supervision of the Frenchman and European Union commissioner Jacques Delors, an international commission wrote a report entitled *Learning: the treasure within*. It reasserted the fact that educational systems might become a key factor for development (a major idea of functional literacy in the 1960s), and confirmed the role of governments in improving education policies, as well as the universalist range of education.

However, between 1995 and 2005, UNESCO clearly emphasized specific education types (education of disabled people, education of adults, non-formal education), and defined targets (gender equality, human rights, AIDS prevention). The education efforts of UNESCO thus became more and more segmented, breaking with the previous universalist rhetoric.

The United Nations Literacy Decade, launched in 2003, supported a definition of literacy which was not limited to basic reading, writing and counting abilities, but could develop into various forms, depending on culture, languages, and time. In order to contribute to this enterprise, UNESCO has adopted the motto 'Literacy as Freedom', and has chosen Mrs Laura Bush as an honorary ambassador. Currently, UNESCO's education policy aims at achieving Education for All by 2015, an illusory objective formulated by the Millennium for Development in September 2000. Three key areas have been selected: teacher training, by means of the Teacher Training Initiative in Sub-Saharan Africa (TTISSA) initiated in January 2006 in 46 Sub-Saharan African countries and planned for ten years; literacy, with the Literacy Initiative for Empowerment (LIFE), launched in 2006 for ten years in 35 countries that are home to 85 per cent of the world's illiterate population; and AIDS prevention education, with the Global Initiative on Education and HIV/AIDS (EDUCAIDS), led in cooperation with ten UN agencies. Finally, the organization promotes Education for Sustainable Development (ESD), in the framework of the United Nations Decade of Education for Sustainable Development (2005–14).

In the field, the results of the actions of the Education Section of UNESCO are difficult to assess. The organization does not launch huge mass literacy programmes any longer, as it did in the 1960s. As to great issues and innovative ideas concerning education in the world today, UNESCO contents itself with following and echoing them, instead of actually initiating them. Indeed, the lack of real political independence of the organization from the main countries that finance it, but also much hesitation in its conceptual choices, as well as its administrative red tape and opacity, are thought to harm the efficiency of its Education Section, that now employs about 150 people at headquarters and 250 in the field. The organization is challenged as well by other intergovernmental organizations like UNICEF or the International Development Association which works in the framework of the World Bank Group, and by many NGOs and bilateral programmes of several states or of groups of states (such as the Islamic Scientific, Educational and Cultural Organization – ISESCO).

To overcome this problem, UNESCO now favours collective projects and tries to develop partnerships with NGOs and local institutions: therefore, since 1988, UNESCO has established the UNESCO/NGO Collective Consultation on Higher Education, gathering around 60 NGOs specialized in higher education. As to the Associated Schools Project Network (ASPnet), it includes today almost 7,900 schools in 176 countries, and testifies

to the fact that UNESCO wants to play an increasing role in the coordination of educational networks in the world.

Chloé Maurel

Bibliography

Delors J. (dir.) 1996. *Learning: the treasure within*. Report to UNESCO of the International Commission on Education for the Twenty-first Century. Paris: UNESCO / Odile Jacob; London: HMSO.

Faure E. (dir.) 1972. *Learning to be: the world of education today and tomorrow*. Paris: UNESCO; London: Harrap.

Jones P. 1988. *International policies for Third World education: UNESCO, literacy and development*. London and New York: Routledge.

Maurel C. 2006. *L'UNESCO de 1945 à 1974*. Unpublished doctoral dissertation, Université de Paris 1 Panthéon-Sorbonne.

Pauvert J.-C. and Egly M. 2001. 'Le "complexe" de Bouaké, 1967–1981', *Les cahiers d'histoire*, 1. Paris: UNESCO.

United Nations Educational, Scientific and Cultural Organization 1947. *Fundamental education: common ground for all peoples*. Paris: UNESCO.

United Nations Educational, Scientific and Cultural Organization 1999. *50 années pour l'éducation*. Paris: UNESCO.

United Nations Educational, Scientific and Cultural Organization and United Nations Development Programme 1976. *The experimental world literacy programme: a critical assessment*. Paris: Expert Team on Evaluation of Experimental Functional Literacy Projects, UNESCO and UNDP, 1976.

Related essays

United Nations (UN) Women's Conferences

Starting in 1975, the United Nations convened a series of international conferences on the status of women. Although the first two of these meetings – in Mexico City in 1975 and Copenhagen in 1980 – were conflict-ridden, taken as a whole the United Nations Women's Conferences helped to ignite a new wave of feminist activism around the globe, especially in areas such as Africa, Asia and the Middle East, where international women's activism had not previously thrived.

The origins of the Mexico City World Women's Conference of 1975 reflect the context of the Cold War and the beginnings of the feminist revival of women's liberation. In 1972, the Women's International Democratic Federation (WIDF), a Soviet-sponsored international organization which was very active in Africa and Asia, had proposed a commemoration of the 25th anniversary of the founding of the United Nations Commission on the Status of Women (UNCSW). In response the General Assembly designated 1975 as International Women's Year (IWY). The UN identified three themes for the IWY, representing different geopolitical constituencies and perspectives on women's movements: legal rights (the West), economic development (the non-aligned nations) and peaceful coexistence (the Soviet bloc). These three principles were combined in what became the logo for all subsequent UN Women's Conferences, a stylized dove merged with the symbols for equality and for women. When the WIDF announced that it would sponsor an international women's conference in East Berlin, the US State Department encouraged the UN General Assembly to convene an official UN IWY meeting a few months earlier. Initially scheduled for Colombia, the conference was shifted to Mexico City in late June, 1975. The staff of the UN Secretariat planned the conference in less than six months, while a consultative committee, chaired by Princess Ashraf Pahlavi of Iran, drafted a World Plan for Action, to be debated at the conference.

The UN was in the midst of its second Decade of Development, and the final report of the Mexico City conference indicated much concern for the role of women in so-called underdeveloped nations. Conference participants voted to extend the International Women's Year to a full Decade, with the goal of improving women's status being both end in itself and a means toward national and global advancement. They also urged the UN to expand its institutional machinery for women's advancement to include a new division for research devoted to women's status (INSTRAW) and another for distributing development funds to women (UNIFEM). Each of the UN conferences featured a 'parallel' conference of interested NGO representatives. In Mexico City, the parallel conference involved many more people (6,000) than the formal conference, with women from Latin America and US particularly well represented. While the formal conference highlighted the geopolitical and ideological conflicts that stood in the way of global feminist unity, the parallel conference began the process of forging a more expansive understanding of discrimination against women, beyond formal inequalities to global structures of economic and social disparity.

The 1980 mid-Decade conference, relocated from Tehran to Copenhagen because of the Iranian Revolution of 1979, was the most rancorous of the UN Women's Conferences. Cold War antagonisms were overlaid with concerns of the nations of the Non-Aligned Movement that neoliberal economic policies were retarding the progress of the women of developing countries. The issue of Palestine stood for many of the conference conflicts. Lucille Mair of Trinidad/Tobago, General Secretary of the conference, was very much in sympathy with this agenda. Repeated references in the final conference document linking Zionism and apartheid as specific forms of colonial oppression were unacceptable to a minority at the conference, including the US delegation. The convention document was passed although not unanimously, making Copenhagen the only one of the major UN Women's Conferences which was unable to achieve consensus on its final programme.

While conflict between major geopolitical blocs took central stage at Copenhagen, one of the greatest achievements of the UN Decade of Women was occurring under the radar. This was the opening for signatures of the Convention to End All Forms of Discrimination Against Women (CEDAW). Prior to the conference, this document had been painstakingly drafted by veteran feminist diplomats from the UNCSW. CEDAW was a significant advance on the 1968 UN Declaration to End Discrimination Against Women. Not only was it legally binding on its national signatories, but it expanded the notion of gender discrimination to include cultural and social barriers as well as economic and political ones, within the private as well as the public sphere. At Copenhagen, enough member nations signed on to CEDAW to ratify it although a record number of formal objections to particular items were recorded by signatory nations. Nonetheless, the expansive wording of the document, and the requirement that signatories report regularly on their progress to a new, specialized UN committee, laid the basis for a growing international network of NGOs to press for action from their respective governments.

The UN Decade of Women concluded in 1985 in Nairobi, Kenya, at the first international women's conference ever held in Africa. Given the conflicts at Copenhagen, participants understood that the outcome of this meeting would determine whether the Decade would go down in history as a failure or a success. Margaret Kenyatta and Maureen Reagan, daughters respectively of the leaders of the host country and of the US, were especially effective conference diplomats, and the final document, 'Forward Looking Strategies for the Advancement of Women', was passed by conference consensus.

At Nairobi, the parallel conference was attended by over 8,000 women, including a record number from the global South. A 'Peace Tent' allowed for long-standing conflicts, notably between participants from Israel and Palestine, to be explored in a less politicized, more personal venue. Transnational feminist networks, built around localized NGOs, emerged to play a major role, bridging the gap between 'feminist' and 'political' concerns that had marked all previous UN Women's Conferences. As the official UN history of the Decade puts it, 'The most fundamental transformation during the Decade was the shift from a belief that development served to advance women to a new consensus that development was not possible without the full participation of women' (United Nations 1997, 37).

The perspectives and talents of this new generation of international women's NGOs remade and enlarged the global women's movement, which was on display at other UN conferences of the 1990s. In 1993, on the 45th anniversary of the adoption of the Universal Declaration of Human Rights, the UN convened a World Conference on Human Rights in Vienna. Transnational women's networks concentrated on establishing the principle that violence against women in all its forms – from child molestation to wife beating to wartime rape – constituted fundamental violations of women's human rights. The success of this campaign clarified that sexual, reproductive and other sorts of violations that women suffer because they are women are human rights abuses even though they are gender-specific. The slogan that emerged from the Vienna conference, 'Women's rights are human rights', expressed this important solution to the long-standing ghettoization of women's rights matters from general human rights concerns.

The last of the four UN Women's Conferences, in Beijing in 1995 was held to assess and accelerate progress made since the Nairobi meeting. The Platform for Action, passed at the conference by consensus (but not without numerous national reservations), added the campaign against violence against women and the achievement of sexual and reproductive freedoms to prior concerns for women's education, health, employment, public role, and cultural standing. The full achievement of two decades of UN Women's Conferences was especially clear at the parallel conference, attended by over 35,000 women, including interested individuals and numerous local NGOs as well as organizations formally registered with the UN. Chinese officials, concerned about such a large non-governmental international gathering, located the proceedings far from the formal conference, in the Huairo suburb of Beijing. Nonetheless, an estimated 5,000 Chinese women participated, inaugurating the appearance on the global feminist stage of Chinese feminism, which had not been prominent at prior UN Women's Conferences.

The UN, with a considerably expanded women's rights institutional apparatus, remains an important part of the continuing commitment declared at Beijing to raising women's status around the world. But the most profound effect of the UN women's conferences lay beyond, in the much expanded global constituency, the greatly broadened international understanding of women's rights, and the considerably deepened worldwide analysis of structural obstacles to their achievement.

Ellen Carol DuBois

Bibliography

Antrobus P. 2004. *The global women's movement: origins, issues and strategies.* Basingstoke and New York: Palgrave Macmillan.

United Nations 1997. *The United Nations and The Advancement of Women, 1945–1995.* With introduction by Boutros Boutros-Ghali, Secretary General of the United Nations. New York: United Nations.

Winslow A. (ed.) 1995. *Women, politics and the United Nations.* Westport: Greenwood.

Related essays

Abolition of Forced Labour Convention; birth control; Cold War; femininity; gender and sex; human rights; Inter-American Commission on Women; international non-governmental organizations (INGOs); International Women's Day; millennium; Stockholm Conference; underdevelopment; United Nations decades and years; United Nations system; women's movements

Universal Postal Union (UPU)

The Universal Postal Union (UPU) is the second oldest international governmental organization, overseeing a universal network for cross-border circulation of postal products. Its uninterrupted 130-year history is an outstanding example of international socio-economic collaboration.

Its development followed the nation state, which 'nationalized' postal services and created Public Post Offices (PPOs) for security and economic advantage. A maze of bilateral postal arrangements inhibited late-19th-century international commerce. Rowland Hill's reforms in England (1840) – prepaid mail at inexpensive and uniform rates – offered a conceptual underpinning for a single international postal market. This approach was adopted by 22 leading commercial nations in the Treaty of Bern (1874). The General Postal Union (renamed the Universal Postal Union in 1878) standardized the postal market and rates and created a single postal territory for the free transit and reciprocal international exchange of letters. It has been trumpeted as a paradigm for world peace and prosperity. With no enforcement authority, it created rules and regulations through consensus.

Almost exclusively European at birth, it expanded through Latin America in the late 19th century, the Commonwealth afterwards, decolonized countries following World War 2, and Africa in the 1960s to include virtually all nations. It became a United Nations agency (1948), albeit the smallest, with a staff of 150 in its International Bureau in Bern. A Congress is held every four years to set rules and regulations, but focuses on strategy since the 1980s. Operational work has devolved to the Council of Administration (a cabinet-like executive body) and the Postal Operations Council (focuses on specialist issues). The International Bureau provides administrative support and leadership on priority issues. The consensus approach allows countries to voluntarily adopt new UPU policies and products and avoid disputes. The UPU's singular achievement was creating the single postal territory, informed by principles – that international mail should be handled uniformly like domestic mail; that postal products should enjoy free transit and circulation; that postal products, rates and regulations should be standardized and simplified. It assisted technical cooperation, postal reform, and quality improvement, negotiated common standards and compatibility, and created the 'electronic post mark' for the internet. However, it never set uniform prices (a minimum/maximum range instead) and nations continuously imposed transit charges. It neglected quality of service, reflecting its lack of domestic authority.

The UPU's successful first century reflected its character as a club of postal monopolists with an apolitical focus on 'technical' matters, allowing a focused agenda and voluntaristic cooperation. Ironically, the 1970s undid this halcyon world. Falling transportation costs expanded international communications. Private (American) firms like UPS and FedEx arose to challenge the PPOs, which were 'privatized' (as in Germany, the Netherlands) or 'corporatized' when neoliberalism deregulated postal markets. The open, competitive world of private operators and competing PPOs challenged the UPU's closed, cooperative world. A metaphor for recent postal complexity is 'terminal dues'. The traditional view was that incoming and outgoing mail volumes were in balance, the sending nation alone receiving compensation. Volume asymmetries appeared as the world system expanded, developing countries bearing a particular burden. Introduced in 1969, terminal dues compensate countries that receive more mail than they send. Frustrated by this and related matters, leading postal countries formed the International Postal Corporation to manage their interests. Other international organizations draw postal attention – in international trade (the World Trade Organization and its General Agreement on Trade in Services) and international law (as in European Union regulations) – and work to private as opposed to public discourse.

The UPU experiences diminished coherence and unity, divided between the leading 15 per cent of its commercial and market-oriented members (who generate 80 per cent of traffic) and the other 160 countries that retain a public sector orientation. Outside the UPU, private operators challenge for dominance. UPU Strategic Plans focus on quality and competitive issues that threaten its members' survival, and it has created an informal Consultative Committee (2005) with private sector participation. It faces governance challenges as an intergovernmental 'public' organization in a privatized competitive world where governments no longer have a monopoly or even a predominant role in the postal market.

Robert M. Campbell

Bibliography
Campbell R. M. 2002. *The politics of postal transformation: modernizing postal systems in the electronic and global world*. Montréal and Kingston, ON: McGill-Queen's University Press.
Zacher M. W. and Sutton B. 1996. *Governing global networks: international regimes for transportation and communications*. Cambridge: Cambridge University Press.

Related essays
broadcasting; General Agreement on Tariffs and Trade (GATT) / World Trade Organization (WTO); information economy; intergovernmental organizations; International Civil Aviation Organization (ICAO) and International Air Transport Association (IATA); internationalisms; Internet; mail; nation and state; neoliberalism; services; technical standardization; telephone and telegraphy; transportation infrastructures; United Nations system

Universal Races Congress

Held between 26 and 30 July 1911, in London, the Universal Races Congress was the first international conference to bring together hundreds of representatives of more than fifty different peoples from around the world, from China, Japan, Egypt, India, Persia as well as from Europe and the United States, invited to help promote the goal of harmony between the East and West and to prevent racism from becoming a cause of global conflict and misunderstanding. The crucial geopolitical context was the sudden ascendancy of Japan in world affairs, following its crushing military victory over Russia in 1905.

The organizers on the Congress were Felix Adler, Professor of Political and Social Ethics at Columbia University and President of the International Union of Ethical Societies, and Gustave Spiller, the Union's Secretary. Together they succeeded in securing the endorsement of hundreds of statesmen, church leaders, academics and philanthropists. Papers were delivered in six sessions over three days on subjects ranging from racial science, to Japanese civilization, Indian self-government, the 'White Policy' practised by British Dominions and the Negro problem in America. Speakers included Indian politician G. K. Gokhale, Dr Wu Ting-Fang, recently Chinese Ambassador to the United States, African-American writer W. E. B. DuBois, Zionist Israel Zangwill, former president of Haiti, General Légitime, and German anthropologist Felix von Lushan, who contradicted the general spirit of the discussion by welcoming racial and national conflict as healthy and progressive.

Newspapers at the time made fun of the intellectual incoherence of the program and the irreconcilable propositions of the papers – some calling for Western scientific inquiry, others praising the spiritual traditions of Eastern cultures, some promoting universality, others asserting fundamental cultural differences – while subsequent historians have hailed this plurality as evidence of 'new cosmopolitanisms'. Further Congresses planned for Honolulu and Paris never eventuated.

Marilyn Lake

Bibliography
Fletcher I. et al. 2005. 'Forum on the Universal Races Congress', *Radical History Review*, 92, Spring.

Holton R. J. 2002. 'Cosmopolitanism or cosmopolitanisms? The Universal Races Congress of 1911', *Global Networks*, 2, 2, 153–70.

Lake M. and Reynolds H. (eds) 2008. *Drawing the global colour line: white men's countries and the international challenge of racial equality*. Cambridge: Cambridge University Press.

Related essays

anti-racism; civilizations; cosmopolitanism and universalism; Ethical Culture; ethnicity and race; internationalisms; Japan; race-mixing; white men's countries

Urbanization

Urbanization, as distinct from urban growth, reflects the proportion of the population in a given area living in towns and cities. As such, it mainly measures the movement of people between rural and urban areas. For sociologists, urbanization also refers to the accentuation of the characteristics that constitute an urban way of life. These characteristics – fleeting interactions with other humans, the rapid pace of life, anonymity, and rational behaviour managed by contract rather than custom – distinguish urban from rural life.

Studies of urbanization were central to the growth of demographic and urban history during the 20th century. They have also, more recently, contributed to growing interest in globalization and the emergence of world cities. Clearly urbanization as an empirical and conceptual device has profound implications for a history written from a transnational angle. Urbanization has been one of the most universal features throughout history, and, of course, any study must begin by focusing on the origins of cities in the ancient world. As an historic process, urbanization is concerned not merely with rates of population growth in individual cities, but equally with linkages between urban places at the national, regional and global levels, with systems and hierarchies of cities, and with creating lists of urban rank-sizes.

Questions of definition and measurement prevent unproblematic comparative studies. Variations in rates of urbanization in 19th-century Europe, for instance, mask anomalies in the differing size thresholds to define a town: 2,000 in France as against 20,000 in Italy. Historians have had to create artificial thresholds to redress this imbalance: practice

has varied widely, however, from 2,000 to 100,000. Diverging views also exist on the limits of an urban area, while reforms to local government boundaries disrupt the examination of patterns over time.

Historians have conventionally identified the urbanization of the modern developed world as a major consequence of the industrialization of Western economies during the late 18th and 19th centuries. 'Industrial urbanization', as it is known, is recognizable for its rapid pace and large-scale changes to the structure of the working environment and migration patterns. Some studies have pursued either a comparative or transnational approach. For European urbanization, rates of growth have been collected and examined in the context of the flows of capital, ideas and labour across national borders that characterized the spread of industrialization from Britain to the mainland continent. The effects of expansion in mining and textiles, combined with the liberating contribution of steam power, connected the new urban-industrial regions of the English Black Country, the Scottish Clyde, the German Ruhr valley, and the coal seams that ran from the Belgian Borinage to the French Pas-de-Calais. Manufactured goods and raw materials were shipped between ports across the world, linking cities from Glasgow to Liverpool to Hamburg to New York. Merchants and industrialists travelled the globe establishing contacts, transacting business and utilizing their knowledge to build new infrastructural networks (railways, bridges, harbours, telegraph cables) to encourage growth.

In the period 1830–1914 Europe underwent urbanization at its fastest rate, its urban population growing about sixfold between 1800 and 1910. The share of urban population in 1900 ranged between 80 per cent in England and Wales, to 40 per cent in France and 25 per cent in Italy. Excluding Russia, roughly 40 per cent of the continent was urbanized. European urbanization is best represented through Kingsley Davis' attenuated S-curve in which preindustrial cities urbanize very slowly along the bottom of the S, then accelerate through the S as they industrialize, before levelling off at the top of the S. By 1914 the developed industrialized world (excluding Japan and Russia) had effectively reached the top section of the S, which precipitated an inevitable slowdown in the rate of urbanization and the growth of urban population.

The international diffusion of 'industrial urbanization' had, by 1914, heralded a shift in power away from Britain and Europe. The extremely rapid rates of growth in North American cities from the 1840s, fuelled by industrialization, modernization and extensive immigration, especially from Europe, rewrote the urban hierarchy with New York replacing London at the zenith of the rankings, and Chicago, Philadelphia, Boston and Pittsburgh overtaking provincial cities like Birmingham, Liverpool and Glasgow. As early as 1890, some 31.8 per cent of people in the 28 largest North American cities, of 100,000 population and over, were foreign-born. With similarly rapid urbanization in Canada and Australia, transcontinental migrations – with 36–39 million Europeans emigrating overseas between 1865 and 1914 – accelerated urbanization throughout the non-European developed world and probably restrained continued urbanization within the home countries.

The effect of this transnational migration, according to Lewis Mumford, Max Weber and Louis Wirth, was most stark in the blending of hitherto diverse and varied cultures (languages, customs, cuisines and costumes). This hastened the development of a new social dynamic characterized by neighbourhood segregation. This weakened the traditional inclusivity of the city and, in so doing, typified urban life as a series of fleeting, impersonal interactions governed by the rational contract rather than social and familial networks. Ultimately, the modern city – existing as it did in a universally urban age – exhibited a homogeneous urban culture. The emergence of a mass commercial society, connected by communication networks that spanned the globe (like the telegraph and telephone), centred on urban areas. Urbanization, then, provided the built environment in which new cultural ideas could be disseminated and assimilated transnationally.

Studies of urbanization beyond the North Atlantic world have, until recently, presented a shared urban experience between Asia, Africa and Latin America. This is problematic as it overlooks the rich urban histories of these regions and individual countries like China, Egypt and India, while the transnational economic and political configuration of these regions has also differed. Attitudes from the West towards economic development and urbanization, and geopolitical constraints and cleavages have naturally affected the flow of investment, whereas religion has shaped the physical form and social relations of cities in regions like the Middle East. In advanced countries like Japan, which industrialized and urbanized later than in the West, but earlier than its regional neighbours, urbanization did not simply emulate existing trends set by 'industrial urbanization'. Latecomers learned and adapted others' experiences, yet simultaneously combined this with their own traditions to create an alternative development trajectory. In so doing, they often urbanized at a faster rate than those which preceded them.

Colonial rule in Africa, for example, was an important influence on that continent's urbanization and has been seen as a cause of many of urban Africa's problems since decolonization. Although urban areas had experienced growth prior to colonial rule, many cities such as Nairobi, Johannesburg and Harare did not exist before colonization, while others, like Abidjan, were villages. Settled during the 1880s and 1890s, these cities acted as terminals for the transportation of raw materials and goods, displacing internal trading networks (a practice similarly evident in colonial India). They also developed administrative functions to control the colonized population within the growing cities, which were teeming with an unprecedented influx of unskilled labour. The long-held view of sub-Saharan African urbanization is that it occurred without concurrent industrial development. Thus, high migration of unskilled and uneducated rural labourers into urban areas despite fewer job opportunities created a myriad of social problems that were invariably neglected by colonial authorities and, since decolonization, national administrations. The artificial reshaping of existing urbanization trends, therefore, raises questions about the benefits of transnational movements where they involve unequal power relations and the exploitation of factors of production.

The recent Chinese experience of rapid urbanization further reveals the simplicity of the Western model of 'industrial urbanization'. Since political reforms in 1978 altered China's urban administrative system, encouraged urban economies and relaxed controls over in-migration, the country's urban population has increased by around 130 million people. In a highly centralized country where the level of urbanization had not exceeded

30 per cent from 1949, socialist planning has important implications for comparative studies of urbanization, especially in terms of the importance to be attached to an urban economy and the spread of an homogeneous urban culture. The strict political controls under which Soviet-bloc cities functioned during the Cold War further illustrate the competing visions of the urban contribution to economic growth and the barriers established to resist the diffusion of alternative ideas.

In 1975 just over one-third of the world's population lived in urban areas; by 2000 this had increased to nearly half. The urbanized world has long ceased to be an exclusively Western world, then. The share of the urban population in the developed countries in 2000 was 76 per cent as against 40 per cent in the less developed countries. This masks important variations between high levels of urbanization in Latin America against relatively low levels still in Asia and Africa. Despite this, though, some of the largest-growing cities in the world are located in the developing world, with much of their growth caused by natural population increase. Between 1980 and 2000 Lagos, Dhaka, Cairo, Tianjin, Hyderabad and Lahore, among others, joined the list of the 30 largest cities in the world, displacing European industrial powers like Milan and Essen. This has in part been caused by rising levels of Western investment, with businesses attracted by low capital costs and cheap labour; but also by state policies to foster urban development, as in India and China.

In 1990 half of the world's 30 largest urban centres were Asian cities. East Asia, in particular, has experienced very rapid urbanization and dynamic economic growth, with Hong Kong, Seoul, Taipei and Jakarta rivalling Tokyo as the region's global city. Moreover, with unprecedented rates of economic growth, China's national economy has fuelled extensive urban development. In 2004 about 600 cities accommodated more than 500 million people, which is approximately 40 per cent of China's 1.29 billion population. The current global rate of urbanization is about 0.8 per cent per annum, which varies between 1.6 per cent for Africa to about 0.3 per cent for all highly industrialized countries.

Such rapid rates of urbanization have caused a myriad of social problems in the developing world, including poverty, environmental degradation and social injustice. High rural-urban migration in Africa has precipitated acute food shortages within the urban economy, underemployment and unemployment and poor health, including Acquired immunodeficiency syndrome (AIDS). This substantial labour surplus has been identified as the main cause of overurbanization. Recognizing failures in governance to tackle these problems, the United Nations hosted a major conference on human settlements in Vancouver in 1976. Known as Habitat I, the Vancouver Declaration on Human Settlements loosely committed its signatories to provide adequate shelter for everyone. In the absence of a focused mandate, however, it was two decades before the first practical recommendations for transnational cooperative action were agreed at the Habitat II conference in Istanbul (1996). Reinforced by the UN General Assembly's Millennium Declaration on Cities in 2001, and further resolutions in 2002, the UN Human Settlements Programme (UN-HABITAT) was formed to help eradicate urban poverty and promote sustainable urbanization through decentralized cooperation between cities in the developed and developing world. This shows how supranational, national and local institutions are finally starting to work towards solutions for these urban problems that reflect the varied, often chaotic, experiences of urbanization. As a determinant of transnational cooperation, the globalization of urbanization in recent decades is symptomatic of the enduring problems endemic within the rapid development of towns and cities.

Shane Ewen

Bibliography

Bairoch P. 1988. *Cities and economic development: from the dawn of history to the present.* London: Mansell.

Davis K. 1965. 'The urbanization of the human population', *Scientific American*, 60, 429–37.

Lampard E. 'The urbanizing world', in Dyos H. J. and Wolff M. (eds) 1973. *The Victorian city: images and realities*, Vol. I, London: Routledge, 3–57.

UN-HABITAT 1996. *An urbanizing world: global report on human settlements*. Oxford: Oxford University Press.

UN-HABITAT 2001. *The state of the world's cities report*. Nairobi: UN-HABITAT.

Van der Woude A., Hayami A. and de Vries J. (eds) 1990. *Urbanization in history: a process of dynamic interactions*. Oxford: Clarendon.

Related essays

cities; city planning; global cities; human mobility; industrialization; natural hazards; non-lieux; philanthropy; spatial regimes

V

Vaccination

Vaccination, synonymous with immunization, signifies a set of medical practices that are designed to stimulate the immune system to protect against disease. Vaccination operates on the principle that the controlled exposure to a disease-causing agent, be it the whole or part of a virus, bacteria, or a cancer cell, creates a lasting immune response that is rapidly mobilized against any future exposure. The idea that an infection with certain diseases can protect a person from reinfection with the same pathogen has a long history. The discovery of acquired immunity and the first artificial attempt to mimic this process were closely tied to the history of smallpox.

Smallpox, with its classic doughnut-shaped pox eruptions, was easily identifiable and common in many parts of the world by the late medieval period. The ubiquity of smallpox in medieval China and India played a key role in early medical thinking about acquired immunity and the development of the first immunizations. Scholars argue that the practice of inoculation was developed possibly as early as the 11th century with origins in India, but it is certain it was practised in China at least from the 16th century. Various forms of inoculation spread across Asia and Africa, but inoculation was not widely used in Europe and North America until the 18th century, and in areas where it was practised, such as in rural Scotland, its origins are poorly understood. In the early 18th century, physicians in Europe, England and the Americas came into contact with a Turkish method of inoculation through reports from diplomats stationed in the East. From its success in England, it spread throughout Western Europe, while physicians began to use smallpox as a model to explain the infectious character of common diseases and how infection actually worked. Thus smallpox inoculation had a marked impact on how infectious diseases were understood in the West. Italian physician Angelo Gatti, for example, argued that smallpox was caused by a specific contagion that grew in its host and that it was the relative strength of the invading virus that allowed it to thrive and reproduce in the body. Gatti argued that smallpox could be artificially bred and manipulated to make inoculation safer. The theory of attenuation (or weakening) of germs through human manipulation dominated much of the empirical research on immunization for the next century.

In 1760, Swiss scientist Daniel Bernoulli developed mathematical models to describe the epidemiology of smallpox and the protective effects of inoculation. He and others argued that universal inoculation of all children would increase life expectancy despite the fact that inoculation still posed discernable risks of injury and death. It was because of this effect that early proponents of inoculation began to call for universal access to what had become a relatively expensive practice. Some argued that if most of the populace was inoculated this would reduce the probability of smallpox encountering a susceptible person and break the cycle of infection. This was an early articulation of a key principle in vaccination science called herd immunity. Despite some initial optimism, the success of smallpox inoculation was not easily generalized to other diseases, neither in the British Isles nor on the Continent. Early attempts to use the model of inoculation to create immunity for infectious diseases like measles and rabies produced indifferent results.

It was a student of the English surgeon John Hunter, who had experimented with rabies inoculation, who moved vaccination science along by solving one of the critical problems that dogged the practice of inoculation. By substituting infectious smallpox matter with a relatively benign but seemingly related animal pox disease, the physician Edward Jenner reproduced an infection that provided the same acquired immunity as inoculation without the attendant risks of spreading smallpox. Jenner demonstrated that those inoculated with his vaccine material could not be subsequently infected with smallpox and the attenuated infection could not spread from person to person. His inoculation technique was later called 'vaccination' to distinguish it from inoculation.

Jenner's experiments with vaccination were repeated on a larger scale in smallpox hospitals in England and across Europe and his technique rapidly spread around the world. The swift penetration of Jenner's novel technique was enabled by a network of physicians, scientists, and interested lay people who maintained an extensive correspondence. Letters about vaccination reached the Near, East Asia, and Africa within a few years of Jenner's first report on vaccination. Exemplified in scientific societies, such as the Royal Society, this Republic of Letters was instrumental in the spread of vaccination technologies. Though cowpox outbreaks were relatively rare, and largely restricted to Western Europe, new sources of vaccine were soon discovered and re-engineered in various vaccine farms across the world. Vaccine material was sent both from and to England in this period as physicians debated which sources provided superior results. Jenner's vaccine material was sent to correspondents in North and South America, while Italian lymph stock became a popular source of European supplies. Numerous attempts to send preserved lymph to East Asia, Africa and Southeast Asia failed because lymph dried onto threads or plates of glass rarely survived the intense climate changes during an ocean voyage. Physicians resorted to using trade ships stocked with young children, usually orphans, who could be infected with the virus, one after another, to keep it alive for months at sea.

By the mid 19th century vaccination had largely, though not completely, supplanted traditional inoculation practices in the West. Inoculation continued to flourish in parts of India and China where its practice was long-standing; however, vaccination was also rapidly taken up in some parts of China, Japan and India. Jenner had advanced the argument that vaccination worked because all pox viruses were modified versions of the same contagion (attenuated by the leap from one species to another), and his experiments renewed the hope that it would be possible to manipulate the growth of other contagions in order to generalize the vaccination phenomenon. It was the work of French researchers Émile Roux, Charles Chamberland and Louis Pasteur who first replicated the success of vaccination with other infectious agents. Unlike his 18th-century predecessors, Pasteur successfully replicated the process of attenuation with a variety of commercially significant disease-causing agents. Using novel techniques of artificial attenuation, he developed vaccines for animal anthrax in 1881 and against human rabies in 1885.

In the last quarter of the 19th century, advances in germ theory and the laboratory science of bacteriology helped physicians identify, isolate and cultivate pure cultures of microbes responsible for a variety of diseases such as bubonic plague, human cholera, and tuberculosis. Physicians from all over the globe, keen to study the new science of bacteriology and virology, flocked to burgeoning German and French bacteriological research institutes and, through their training, transferred the techniques and skills of vaccinology back into their native lands. Cohorts of German- and French-trained bacteriologists propelled an international research agenda. In this vein, important contributions to vaccinology were made by Emil von Behring and Kitasato Shibasaburō who demonstrated that the pathogenic effects of tetanus and diphtheria came from specific soluble proteins shed by these bacteria. These toxins could be nullified if infected animals were injected with refined blood (sera) taken from animals already immune to the disease. In 1892, Paul Ehrlich showed that children already sick with diphtheria could be effectively treated with 'anti-toxin'. Diphtheria anti-toxin sera saved the lives of many children in Europe and North America. Applying tetanus serotherapy to soldiers wounded in battle also significantly decreased the number of tetanus cases among British troops during World War 1. Behring and Kitasato's discovery of bacteria toxins, and Paul Ehrlich's theory that it was a specific lock-and-key reaction between the invading agent and the cellular components that triggered immunity, provided vaccine makers with the theoretical and practical tools to produce and standardize a variety of new treatment anti-toxins and prophylactic vaccinations. These techniques led to an explosion in vaccinology in the last quarter of the 19th century. Between 1875 and 1930 vaccines were developed against typhoid, shigella, cholera, tuberculosis, plague, diphtheria, tetanus and pertussis. Many countries founded state vaccine and serum institutes with satellite labs in former Western colonies and private drug companies developed vast distribution networks for their products. Transnational trade and the military, commercial, and ethical importance of immunotherapies led international organizations such as the League of Nations to strike a committee to oversee research into the development and production of vaccines and serum therapies. International collaboration in vaccination science and manufacturing endured despite diverse vaccination practices, commercial competition, and stark differences in local policies governing the dissemination of vaccine technologies. As the burden of disease in Western countries declined after the implementation of vaccination and serum therapy, supporters of vaccination actively collected national disease statistics which became powerful weapons to spur regional governments to expand vaccine programmes.

During the 19th century, in response to smallpox epidemics, many Western countries had instituted strict compulsory infant vaccination laws in their home countries and attempted to implement similar policies in their colonies. These laws frequently sparked popular resistance to vaccination, leading to civil unrest. Historians such as Claudia Huercamp (1985), Anne Hardy (1993), Sanjoy Bhattacharya (2006) and Nadja Durbach (2005) have shown through in-depth case studies of vaccination programmes in Germany, the UK and in India, that the state's experience with universal vaccination programs often played an important role in the development of modern public health infrastructure, including birth registries, disease surveillance and legislation to support a range of regulatory powers. It was also an important example of effective modern scientific medicine which bolstered the burgeoning field of public health and helped to mobilize and delineate state-level interventions into many other areas concerning health, such as milk pasteurization and meat inspections. Vaccination thus can be seen as an important feature in constructing the bureaucratic and politic framework for many 20th- and 21st-century public health interventions. Vaccination campaigns were certainly also responsible for saving millions of lives either directly by preventing illness or indirectly by preventing the serious complications such as deafness, blindness, and lung damage that frequently accompanied natural infections of vaccine-preventable diseases.

Scientists now use a variety of strategies to target a whole host of pathogenic microorganisms including viruses, bacteria, intracellular pathogens, and prions. Significant advances were made by developing new culture techniques to grow viruses in the laboratory. These techniques led to the development of effective vaccines against many viral diseases including influenza and polio. There are also vaccines under development that can train the immune system to recognize and destroy cancer cells and clinical trials are under way to develop treatment vaccines

for breast, lung and colon cancer. Also under development are pure DNA vaccines which are designed to act like a retrovirus (which upon infection insert themselves into the host's genetic code) to produce protective immune signals that emanate from inside the host's own cells. Vaccinologists are also working on vaccines against infectious agents that have the ability to mutate very quickly (such as influenza) or those viruses (such as Human immunodeficiency virus – HIV) that quickly kill off the cell-types critical to mobilizing the immune response.

Global vaccination campaigns, in combination with a variety of other public health tools, have been remarkably successful in containing diseases that were once ubiquitous. Smallpox was declared eradicated in 1980 by the World Health Organization and polio, measles, and rubella might soon be eradicated. The possibility of eradicating these and other frightful diseases has mobilized international health organizations, such as the World Health Organization and the Global Alliance for Vaccination, to campaign for international participation and financial support. Despite the success of vaccination campaigns in industrialized countries, it is estimated that millions of children die every year in Third World countries from vaccine-preventable diseases such as tetanus, rubella, and pneumonia. International aid agencies have intensified their efforts to make children's vaccines more widely available. However, not all diseases are easily contained by immunization alone. Influenza, for example, has a range of non-human hosts that would make eradication all but impossible with current systems and technology. Newer vaccines require sophisticated manufacturing techniques that have made them extremely expensive and many countries, struggling to provide basic healthcare for their citizens, cannot absorb the costs of the new vaccines. New vaccines costs hundreds of dollars per dose and many vaccines still require refrigeration, clean needles, and aseptic administration which limit their use in remote regions. With all the promises of new vaccine technology, there are potential constraints to how effective mass vaccination campaigns can be in combating the most lethal infectious diseases suffered by the world's poorest children. In the West, vaccination was developed simultaneously with improvements to water, basic nutrition and other key social determinants of health, suggesting that vaccination programmes should not stand in stead of more holistic environmental interventions. Vaccination technologies can however provide powerful tools to enable such changes.

Jennifer Keelan

Bibliography

Bhattacharya S. 2006. *Expunging variola: the control and eradication of smallpox in India, 1947–1977.* New Delhi: Orient Longman; London: Sangam.

Durbach N. 2005. *The anti-vaccination movement in England, 1852–1907.* Durham, NC: Duke University Press

Hardy A. 1993. *The epidemic streets: infectious disease and the rise of preventive medicine 1856–1900.* Oxford: Clarendon.

Huerkamp C. 1985. 'The history of smallpox vaccination in Germany: a first step in the medicalization of the general public', *Journal of Contemporary History*, 20, 4, 617–35.

Keelan J. and Fichman M. 2007. 'Resister's logic: the anti-vaccination arguments of Alfred Russel Wallace and their role in the debates over compulsory vaccination in England, 1870–1900', *Studies in History and Philosophy of Biological and Biomedical Sciences*, 38. 3, 585–607.

Liu M. 1998. 'Vaccine developments', *Nature Medicine*, 4, 5, 515–19.

Miller G. 1957. *The adoption of inoculation for smallpox in England and France.* Philadelphia: University of Pennsylvania Press.

Plotkin S. A. 1999. 'Vaccination against the major infectious diseases', *Life Sciences*, 322, 943–51.

Related essays

Acquired Immunodeficiency Syndrome (AIDS); animal diseases; drugs (medical); epidemics; life and natural sciences; medicine; smallpox

Vandana Shiva Research Foundation for Science, Technology and Ecology *See* Biopatents

Vietnam War

The Vietnam War took place in Indochina (Vietnam, Laos and Cambodia) between the late 1950s and 1975. It was both a conflict among superpowers and an internal struggle among Indochinese groups. Though often viewed as a 'Cold War struggle', the war was also a flashpoint for ideological contests over decolonization, modernization and North–South relations.

The origins of the war lay in earlier conflicts over decolonization in Indochina. During the period 1945–54, France tried to preserve its Indochinese empire by force, but was defeated by the Viet Minh independence movement. Ho Chi Minh, the Viet Minh's charismatic founder, was the most popular nationalist in Vietnam. But he was also a Communist and many of his compatriots objected to his movement on ideological grounds. France's departure therefore failed to resolve the disputes over the postcolonial path that Vietnam and the rest of Indochina should take.

After 1954, the most obvious axis of conflict in Indochina was the rivalry between Communist-dominated North Vietnam and the anti-Communist state of South Vietnam. But the war did not result simply from the enmity between the two Vietnams. It was also shaped by disagreements among Communists and anti-Communists over contrasting visions of modernization. Ngo Dinh Diem, who ruled South Vietnam from 1954 to 1963, faced not only a North Vietnam-sponsored rural insurgency against his regime but also opposition from his fellow anti-Communists. The resistance of the latter – especially during the 'Buddhist crisis' that led to Diem's downfall in 1963 – stemmed from dissatisfaction with Diem's scheme to modernize South Vietnam along communitarian and authoritarian lines. Similarly, North Vietnam did not go to war merely in response to South Vietnamese and/ or American provocations. Hanoi's decisions were shaped by disputes between those Communist leaders who favoured a go-slow approach to reunification and those who advocated more militant means. Party chiefs disagreed not just over tactics, but over fundamental questions about the form and content of Vietnamese socialism.

Indochina's internal conflicts both exacerbated and were exacerbated by external rivalries among foreign powers. American policymakers sent huge amounts of aid (and, after 1965, huge numbers of US troops) to South Vietnam in part because they feared Communist expansion in Southeast Asia; conversely, Soviet and Chinese leaders supported North Vietnam with money, arms and soldiers partly to check US imperial designs. Still, these expenditures of blood and treasure cannot be explained by geopolitics alone. US decisions in Vietnam were driven not just by Cold War fears but also by the tenets of modernization theory, a social science doctrine which held up America itself as a model for other nations to emulate. Meanwhile, Soviet and Chinese officials competed fiercely to persuade the North Vietnamese of the virtue of their respective visions of socialism. Significantly, Vietnamese did not adopt their patrons' modernizing prescriptions wholesale, preferring instead to pick and choose from a diverse menu of discourses and traditions. For example, Ho Chi Minh drew inspiration from the French and American revolutions, as well as from the Russian and Chinese.

Perhaps the most far-reaching of the war's transnational consequences had to do with the protest movements it generated. Anti-war activism was spurred by the 'Americanization' of the war during the period 1965–68 and especially by the US bombing of North Vietnam. By the late 1960s, politically significant peace movements had emerged in South Vietnam, the United States and elsewhere. In this way, the war fuelled a global surge in expressions of popular dissent. This surge peaked in 1968, after US claims of progress in the war were undermined by the Communists' Tet Offensive. The various anti-war movements were diffuse and diverse, and their contribution to North Vietnam's eventual victory in 1975 was probably negligible, since the protests declined sharply after 1970. Yet the arguments voiced by the protestors and their critics still echo in contemporary debates about modernization, the 'global South' and the use of force in international affairs.

Edward G. Miller

Bibliography

Catton P. *Diem's final failure: prelude to America's war in Vietnam*. Lawrence: Kansas University Press.

Nguyen L. 'The War Politburo: North Vietnam's diplomatic and political road to the Tet Offensive', *Journal of Vietnamese Studies*, 1, 1–2, 4–58.

Suri J. *Power and protest: global revolution and the rise of détente*. Cambridge, MA: Harvard University Press.

Related essays

1960s; Cold War; decolonization; modernization theory; pidgins and creoles; underdevelopment; war; *War and Peace in the Global Village*

Voodoo

Voodoo refers to the historically dominant religion of Haiti, where it is generally known as *Vodou* (also *Voudou, Vodoun, Vodun*), with its creolized *Rada* rites oriented primarily to the spirits (*vodun*) of the old Fon kingdom of Dahomey in contemporary Benin. The word 'voodoo' has been used as a denigrating term of Afro-Atlantic religion in general, superficially understood and reviled as superstition, black magic, orgiastic savagery, and primitivist mumbo jumbo, particularly in Hollywood zombie films popularized after the US military occupation of Haiti (1915–34) and in the phrase 'voodoo economics' coined by George H. W. Bush in the 1980 presidential election to deprecate the 'trickle down' policies of Ronald Reagan.

The earliest print reference to Haitian Vodou was offered by Martinican traveler Moreau de St Méry in 1797 (from experiences of the 1770s), describing both the power of the '*vaudoux*' dance rites and the dangers such rites posed to colonial authority. Haitian President René Préval issued a decree in 1998 recognizing the significance of the 1791 Bois-Caiman ceremony – during which, as tradition has it, Boukman Dutty issued a call to arms and Manbo Cécile Fatiman sacrificed a black pig in the invocatory opening acts of the Haitian Revolution. Following the Revolution, Vodou traveled to Louisiana (via Cuba) and is recorded as early as 1825 in the house of Sanité Dédé, the Saint-Domingue refugee who was New Orleans' earliest Vodou priestess.

Vodou's practitioners refer to themselves as those who 'serve the spirits'. The spirits served in Vodou are known as *lwa* (or *loa*) and are divided between the 'cool' Fon-derived spirits of the Rada rites and the 'hot' spirits of the Kongo-Petwo rites. Service to the spirits has not kept *serviteurs* from attending Catholic services, and one may find the iconography of Catholic saints in Vodou ritual arenas since the *lwa* are often paired with Catholic saints whose lithographic representation and hagiographies convey something of the spirits' own attributes. At the core of Vodou lie the rites of the Fon and Nago (Yoruba) nations, agglutinated with Kongo-Angola, Catholic, and West African

Muslim rites, as well as the material culture and rituals of freemasonry, colonial opera houses, and the signs of global popular cultures.

In spite (and also because) of perceptions of its illegitimacy as a religion, Vodou has shaped and inspirited transnational histories and cultures. Having fed Haiti's revolutionary agency, Vodou offered diasporic inspiration for slave revolts across the Americas, and left lasting models of terror amongst the ruling classes of plantation societies from Virginia to Brazil. Orientations in Vodou aesthetics have proved tremendously rich for the arts. Beginning in the 1940s, outsiders' discovery and promotion of modes of 'spirit-serving' Haitian painting and sculpture opened the door to global interest in folk art, 'outsider' art, and ritual arts. Subsequent cultural pilgrimages to Haiti (linked to surrealism and the negritude movement) led to literary exploration of 'the marvellous real' as articulated by the Cuban Alejo Carpentier in 1949 after his encounters with Vodou. Earlier, and more fundamentally, the swinging ritual authority of New Orleans' multiethnic Vodou houses provided the kind of improvisational, polyrhythmic danced rites that nurtured the emergence of New Orleans jazz as the sound of modern time, a soundtrack to modernity itself.

Because Vodou is a decentralized creole religion with many initiatory lineages and a great capacity to include new ritual elements, it would be difficult to speak of a fixed theology, pantheon, or universally recognized canon. Vodou exists in plurality but does cohere around core rites and practices that enable servants of the lwa to grow in spiritual knowledge and insight (konesans) as they undergo various stages of commitment and initiation. The Vodou spirits are served in all the locations of the Haitian Diaspora, primarily the Dominican Republic, the Bahamas, the United States (especially Miami, New York City, and Boston), Montréal, and France.

Keith Cartwright

Bibliography

Bellegrade-Smith P. and Michel C. (eds) 2006. *Haitian Vodou: spirit, myth, and reality.* Bloomington: Indiana University Press.

Brown K. 2001. *Mama Lola: a Vodou priestess in Brooklyn.* Berkeley: University of California Press.

Cosentino D. (ed.) 1995. *Sacred rites of Haitian Vodou.* Los Angeles: Fowler Museum.

Related essays
Christianity; diasporas; jazz; religion; Santería; slavery; surrealism

W

War

The notion of war as a permanent feature of human life prevailed until the end of the 19th century, despite the efforts of many people – notably adherents to various peace-loving religions as well as the secular thinkers of the European Enlightenment – to devise ways to avoid or abolish it. Peace, by contrast, was regarded as an interregnum or, in the words of Sir Henry Maine, a 'modern invention'. The principal peacetime occupation for many states was to rearm for the next war. The idea of war as an abomination, a symptom of human failure or a mere shortcoming, rose to prominence only after the First World War (1914–18), and mainly in the West. War, understood therefore as a central, almost immutable, aspect of the human condition has persisted for many centuries. It has been neither aberrant nor particular but universal.

Yet the exercise of war has varied considerably over time and place. Wars have taken shape in response to the political and social environments in which they were waged, as well as being significant forces of change in their own right. The varieties of war, and of war making, have been almost as numerous and diverse as the societies which participate in them. Warfare has evolved to levels of strategic, tactical and technological sophistication that exceed the ability of most people to comprehend. But it has not done so uniformly. Small-scale tribal warfare still exists in the 21st century, even though it may employ, in some instances, modern technology: for example, the binocular, radio and shoulder-fired, surface-to-air missile.

The nature of war

Defined as the organized violence of one group against another for a set of aims and for a specific duration, war is by its very nature an international phenomenon – that is, so long as 'international' is understood broadly as predating the modern nation, referring instead to relations of one territorial authority to another. Imperial conflicts such as those between Rome and Carthage, or continental conflagrations involving a large number of sovereign entities such as the Thirty Years' War (1618–48) both followed such a definition of international war. Where such activity entails the crossing of borders, as it almost always does, it is also definably transnational. Thus war in nearly every instance may be considered a transnational event, or having transnational impact. Indeed there are few wars that escape the definition. 'Civil wars' almost always extend, in a combination of cause, execution and effect, beyond the borders of a single nation. The wars of Yugoslav succession in the 1990s, for example, involved every Balkan state, the members of the European Union, the North Atlantic Treaty Organization (NATO) and the United Nations. The October Revolution (1917) in Russia saw the intervention of any number of European nationalities and ultimately had global implications. The American Civil War (1861–65) affected the economic and political interests of, inter alia, the British (including Canadians), French, Mexicans and Russians. Indeed, the Civil War (or War Between the States, as it was known in the American South) was inspired indirectly by the Crimean War (1853–56) insofar as the latter made possible the attainment of German and Italian unification following the breakdown in the half-century-long diplomatic condominium of the British and Russian empires. Other wars of national unification (in Argentina and the United States, for example) followed the trend so that the inspiration for the wars was transnational even if the wars themselves were literally less so. Civil wars, then, are almost never exclusively civil: soldiers and materiel travel from suppliers to consumers through blockades; refugees flee battlefields; trade and prices are disrupted, creating hardship for some non-belligerents and a boon for others; neighbouring states succumb to temptations of covert or overt intervention; conflicts 'destabilize' wider regions; and are as often about some disputed border or piece of territory as they are over the contention of two or more parties to a throne. Very few can be classified as self-contained conflicts. War itself, therefore, may be defined as a kind of conflict that, in addition to being organized and directed, also involves the transgression, transfer or transformation of territorial boundaries by the use of force.

Not all violent conflicts are wars, however, and some conflicts may have transnational proportions without rising to the level of war. In spite of more contemporary, namely American, usage, the term 'war' has traditionally required two or more belligerents that are sovereign or quasi-sovereign entities, even if all parties do not fully recognize one another's legitimacy. Thus 'wars' on disease, drugs, 'terror', popular culture and the like would be known more accurately as transnational struggles, campaigns or crises than as wars, strictly speaking; whereas the various 19th-century 'wars of conquest' by the British, North Americans, Argentines, Australians and Russians against frontier populations, the early phases of the Peninsular War (c.1808–10), and the British, French and US pacification campaigns in Southeast Asia in the 1950s and 1960s all satisfy the proper definition of war, even though all did not feature fighting between equivalently matched states.

One additional genre of war – the existential – is harder to define though probably it is the most transnational of all. The Cold War of the 20th century had ideological, geopolitical, cultural and socioeconomic dimensions but it never saw a full-blown armed battle between its two contending alliances, NATO and the Warsaw Pact. It was waged instead by proxies outside Europe and by 'gamesmanship' in official and unofficial fora. That it had so many dimensions yet never ended in a single or set of battles has led to considerable debate, not least over the chronology of the Cold War itself. While most historians set its origins in 1946–47 with the impasse among the victors of the Second World War over the division of Europe, others have placed it in 1949–50 with the victory of the Chinese Communists over the Nationalists and the outbreak of the Korean War. Others have said it began with the Russian Revolution in 1917, and still others have named the French Revolution of 1789 as the starting point for the global bifurcation by idealists who would place liberty over equality versus those who would do the reverse. Consensus over the war's termination is also lacking. Did it end in 1962 with the prolonged period of 'détente' following the Cuban Missile Crisis? Or in 1971–75 with the signing of the Berlin Treaty and the Conference on Security and Cooperation in Europe? Or in 1989 with the fall of the Berlin Wall? Or, finally, in 1991 with the demise of the Soviet Union?

By the end of the 20th century, nuclear and missile know-how had spread to all parts of the world even if their deployment was not yet fully global. Should the major powers of the world ever resume anything resembling the hostility of the early 20th century, there can be little doubt that the chances for the survival of the entire world would be slim. By the early 21st century the world finds itself living in a general state of peace, albeit a precarious one, with an average of about thirty armed conflicts under way at any given time. Although nearly all of these conflicts are transnational, few, with the partial exception of those under way in the Middle East, pose a risk of acquiring a global dimension.

The transnational dimension of war will be explored here in four parts: additional types of warfare; evolution of warfare; sources, catalysts and consequences of change; attitudes toward war.

Additional types of warfare

The transnational nature of war is connected inherently to specific kinds of warfare as well as to the aims and methods of those who wage it. Although no one type of warfare is inherently more transnational than another, all comprise multinational phenomena to varying degrees. Among the most common in the modern period have been dynastic wars, wars of conquest – including imperial and colonial wars – and preventive wars. Dynastic wars are those fought over the succession to rulership, often within or between ruling families. Such conflicts very often draw on aristocratic kin networks that cross borders; therefore, dynastic wars are a variety of civil war although dynasties themselves may often be multinational. Wars of conquest, whether dynastic or not, are generally wars of aggression against weaker foes who occupy territory or resources that are coveted by a stronger power. Wars of conquest are also conducted in the name of religion or ethnicity, whereby one population seeks to destroy the livelihood, or even the existence, of another. In the 20th century the aim of such wars has been termed genocide and ethnic cleansing. In most cases, they have triggered people flows by the subjugation or mass deportation of populations, or the forced conversion of them rather than outright extermination. Imperial wars are those designed to preserve order by defending territory against invaders or by subjugating populations. In the latter respect they are related closely to wars of conquest. A common form of imperial war is the colonial war. An overseas colonial war (such as the US counterinsurgency in the Philippines from 1899 to 1902) differs from a land-based war in that it rarely involves the former aspect of border defence. By contrast, the various Russian efforts to subjugate the populations of the Caucasus in the mid 19th century never fully succeeded but nevertheless managed to defend the imperial borderlands against large-scale invasion or dissolution. Finally, preventive wars are those launched with a defensive aim in mind, although they appear aggressive to those attacked. Most are directed against a leader who is perceived to harbour greater ambitions but is momentarily vulnerable. A variation on preventive war is pre-emptive war, which is undertaken once an attack appears to be imminent. A well known example is the so-called Six Day War in 1967 when Israel attacked and defeated the combined armies of Egypt, Jordan and Syria.

Warfare is also defined by its scope and methods: conventional war, which is a war between states of relatively comparable size and strength, using uniformed combatants and taking place in battles of a clear duration (in contemporary usage, conventional war also refers to wars that do not involve nuclear weapons); unconventional war, which emphasizes deception, flexibility and uncertainty (combatants are often indistinguishable from civilians; battlefields and juridical borders are unrecognizable; battles themselves have no clear beginnings or ends). A common form of unconventional war is the guerrilla war, which is waged by small bands of roving militants who launch surprise attacks and then withdraw quickly into the forest, jungle or desert, generally with logistical support from across the border. Wars characterized by the use of guerrilla tactics include the Peninsular War (where the term originated), the War of the American Revolution (1775–83) and the Vietnam War (late 1950s to 1975). Limited war is a conflict that is terminated by either side before a full victory is achieved for fear that the war may spread to neighbouring territories or otherwise threaten larger interests. The classic case of a limited war is the Korean War (1950–53), at least from the point of view of the United States, Soviet Union and, to a lesser extent, the People's Republic of China. Another is the Gulf War (1990–91). And finally there is total war, which refers to a conflict in which all members of society – civilian and military – are drawn into the war, and in which all social, economic, political and even cultural institutions are mobilized for such effort. There have been few total wars in

history, and none which left large parts of the globe untouched. Most modern wars feature a combination of the above kinds of warfare, although there have been no wars to date that are both total and unconventional, despite the aims of 'al Qaeda' group of primarily Arab and South Asian terrorists to have initiated one against the West (c.1995–present).

Evolution of warfare

The origins of warfare are found in the fifth to the third centuries BCE during which many parts of the world witnessed territorial conflicts among warring states, the most well known having taken place in north central China and in and around the eastern Mediterranean. Most of these wars were protoimperial campaigns of political consolidation as one dominant group sought to eliminate rivals and to establish its hegemony over a particular space. Once states had combined into empires, wars became less frequent but more destructive, involving the near-extermination of urban centres and settled populations. With the eclipse of the Silk Road in the late 14th century, the locus of imperial expansion shifted westward, replacing the conquest of the Eurasian steppe and its linkage to the Mediterranean economy with the mastery of the seas, particularly the Atlantic, and the movement of people and resources to overseas colonies. Wars against indigenous populations multiplied as a function of the pre-existing political relationships among such groups, including those with a basis of coerced tribute, as in the elaborate system in place among various West African coastal populations for procuring exportable slaves from the interior. Conquerors thereby adapted their ways of warfare to exploit the greatest areas of vulnerability of indigenous populations.

As colonies became settled, the competition among European powers over routes and resources grew more intense, leading frequently to wars among them. By the final decades of the 19th century nearly all parts of the Americas and a good deal of Asia and Africa were under the colonial rule of the descendants of these conquerors, even if creole and other leaders went on to promote independence from their European sovereigns. Warfare in the West had become less frequent but more formal as the laws of war, classified distinctly since the early 17th century into those applying to European and non-European peoples, assumed universal application during this golden age of the nation state. The concepts of jus ad bellum and jus in bello, which had evolved in various forms under different names in Europe since the Middle Ages, began to merge toward the turn of the 20th century into a single doctrine of laws against war or its purported excesses – for example, the concentration camps used in the Cuban War of Independence (1895–98) and the Boer War (1899–1902). For their part, national militaries, which had once been synonymous with their dynastic houses but had become, following the French Revolution, mass organizations, now extended their reach across the world. These centralized and standardized institutions mobilized not only 'domestic' populations but also colonial ones for the greater good and glory of the 'nation'. Nation states meanwhile struck alliances with other nation-states qua empires, resulting in a complex web of intra- and extra-European alignments elaborated in principle to prevent war, but the culmination of which was the conflagration in 1914 called the Great War, or 'the war to end all war'.

The First World War, as it is known today, led to the dissolution of four Eurasian empires and, ultimately, of two additional overseas empires, but did little to stem the tide of nationalism, at least in the military field. Warfare would remain the purview of the nation state until after the Second, and even more destructive, World War (1939–45). This war ended with the surrender of Nazi Germany and Imperial Japan following a combined invasion and the explosion of two nuclear devices, respectively. The nation states that had organized the political map of the world now presided over the prospect of their own total destruction. This did not stop many from engaging in military conflict, but none would do so with the full power of weaponry known to humankind. The existential threat of war had, for the first time in human history, become truly global.

Military historians differ over whether the expanding territorial scope of warfare and its ever greater degree of technological integration has been a linear or a cyclical development. Most have divided its history into eras reflecting the dominant military technology of the time or the most emblematic warriors. Others have tended to see war as an organic process driven by different cultures in distinct ways. All seem to agree, however, on the existence of a paradox governing the long history of war: over time warfare has grown more destructive, and has put the lives of ever greater numbers of people at risk; and yet the frequency of war has declined steadily so that far fewer people, especially in the developed world, have experienced war directly. The more transnational war itself has become, the greater has been its potential for human and environmental destruction, but the less likely has been its active manifestation at any level above the subnational.

Sources, catalysts and consequences of change

The transnational causes and effects of war extend beyond the military field itself to economic, social and cultural life. The single factor most responsible for the changing nature of war is technology. Not only can a technological advantage make all the difference in a battle but it also may figure prominently in the calculation of risks at the highest levels of national leadership. Yet, technological knowledge is impossible to retain in the possession of a single state forever. It is hard to imagine gunpowder, the stirrup, crossbow, breech-loading rifle, tank or radar remaining state secrets anywhere. Such technologies travel across borders as quickly, or even more quickly, than armies or navies, especially during wartime with its immense pressures to innovate. The competitive proliferation of technology, otherwise known as the arms race, has been held responsible for starting its share of wars. Just as there has been a direct relationship between war's destructiveness and its geographic scope, there also has been a similar relationship between the latter and advances in technology. The advent of air power in the early 20th century – namely fighter aircraft, bombs and missiles – dramatically expanded the range of options open to an aggressor, and with it, the nature of modern warfare. That such a phenomenon was magnified many times over by the advent of nuclear weapons goes without saying.

The proliferation of military technology almost always continues during periods of peace. The Second World War, for example, transformed the industrial capacities of much of the world in ways that proved irreversible after 1945. What came to be called 'defence industries' assumed responsibility for entire aspects of postwar economies. That they were fuelled in large part by the Cold War in both the East and the West seems almost incidental; it is hard to imagine any national economy that had been put on a full military footing reversing course and resuming the role it had before 1939. Likewise, many governments found it difficult to resist pressures to sustain full employment once the war was over; the welfare states that proliferated around the world in the mid 20th century probably had as much to do with economic changes brought about during the war itself as they did with economic crises before and immediately after it.

The socioeconomic causes and consequences of major wars are difficult, perhaps impossible, to delimit on a national basis. The dramatic industrial boom following the American Civil War that gave that country the richest domestic economy in the world also made it the world's primary exporter of manufactured goods and, ultimately, following the First World War, the world's chief source of capital. While either war itself can hardly be said to be entirely responsible for those developments, they were nonetheless a necessary if not a sufficient causal factor. In reality, the relationship between technological innovation and war is more reciprocal than direct. Hence the telegraph and the railway, which made possible in the mid to late 19th century what Baron von der Goltz famously called the 'nation in arms', also underwrote the peacetime growth of most modern economies. While the destruction leveled by most wars has disrupted, or severed, long-standing patterns of economic and cultural interchange among peoples, the demands they have made on many societies have also contributed to their coming into greater contact with one another. One need not refer only to the transoceanic voyages of expeditionary forces made up of soldiers who otherwise would never have left their family farms; one might also note a technology such as the Internet, which was once invented by an agency of the US Defense Department for purely military use.

A similarly reciprocal, but ambivalent, relationship has existed between the modern evolution of the military profession and militarism. As militaries became more bureaucratic and complex, the cult of the warrior, and of war, has seemed to erode. Yet the reliance of leaders upon the 'military tools' at their disposal has not diminished noticeably with the professionalization of modern

militaries; indeed, it seems to have sustained the sizeable influence of such organizations in many aspects of modern life. As military services became more professional in the 19th century, military training became more transnational, either directly through officer exchange programmes, or indirectly by imitation. Thus one saw the armies of Brazil and Chile form as near-copies of the French and Prussian armies, respectively, even down to the appearance of their uniforms. To this phenomenon one must add the multinational character of nearly every modern military with the possible single exception of the Imperial Japanese Army (trained, incidentally, first by French and then by Prussian officers). By the mid 20th century there came to exist something of a global military community through the exchange – both explicit and illicit – of standards, technologies, ideas and personnel, so that even some soldiers on opposing sides of the Iron Curtain found that they had more in common with one another than with their respective civilian populations.

Attitudes toward war

Ideas and attitudes about war have also spread geographically as warfare grew more destructive and complex. The Paris Peace Conference of 1919 marked the culmination of the modern view that war is wrong, so that nine years later over sixty nations would sign a pact (the 'Kellogg-Briand Pact') that 'outlawed' war. What a contrast this poses to the 'war fever' of 1914 that saw thousands of young men rush to volunteer to fight one another for the sake of honour, God and country. The prevailing attitudes to war are never universal; there is no shortage of people, even in the early 21st century, who abjure the necessity or the desirability of military conflict. As one proponent of the United States' armed intervention against Iraq in 2003 reminded sceptics, 'It took a war to free the slaves'. Whether war is a permanent feature of human life is a question behavioural scientists will debate long into the future. Yet, while military institutions and sacrifice continue to be valued highly in many societies, war itself has come to be regarded by most people in the world as something to be avoided.

Finally, the art, science, literature and even the music of war have acquired a global dimension, in spite of fluctuations in moral attitudes toward warmongering. The network of military strategists continues to grow and deepen, becoming at once more diverse and interconnected. While military history continues to attract few students outside of war colleges, the number of institutions devoted to 'conflict studies', strategy, peacekeeping and related subjects continues to multiply around the world. There still may be no contemporary strategist who, like Sun Tzu or Clausewitz, captures the spirit of the age in conceptualizing a 'new' way of war, but the truly global society of the early 21st century is bound to produce one.

Kenneth Weisbrode

Bibliography

Brodie B. 1973. *War and politics*. London and New York: Macmillan (now Palgrave Macmillan).

Gat A. 2006. *War in human civilization*. Oxford: Oxford University Press.

Howard M. 1976. *War in European history*. Oxford: Oxford University Press.

Paret P. (ed.) 1986. *The makers of modern strategy: from Machiavelli to the nuclear age*. Princeton: Princeton University Press.

Ropp T. 1959. *War in the modern world*. Durham, NC: Duke University Press.

van Creveld M. 1991. *The transformation of war*. New York: Free Press.

Related essays

African liberation; animal diseases; arms sales; arms trafficking; art market; benefits and charity concerts; Cold War; comics; Commission on International Labour Legislation; condom; cosmetic surgery; debt crises; decolonization; diet and nutrition; displaced persons; drugs (illicit); drugs (medical); empire and migration; empires and imperialism; epidemics; exile; film; financial diplomacy; financial markets; genocide; health policy; human mobility; individual identification systems; information economy; international migration regimes; International Red Cross and Red Crescent movement; investment; jazz; League of Nations system; Mexican Revolution; music; national accounting systems; North Atlantic Treaty Organization (NATO); oceans; pacifism; partitions; public policy; radio; refugee relief; refugees; relief; reparations; Save the Children International Union; surrealism; technologies; temporary migrations; terrorism; trade; United Nations system; Vietnam War; *War and Peace in the Global Village*; war crimes; welfare state; women's movements

War and Peace in the Global Village

Marshall McLuhan's *War and Peace in the Global Village* (1968) argues that claims to sovereignty are increasingly placed in crisis by flows of electronic mediation.

In coining the term 'global village', McLuhan adverted to a concept considerably more complex than the *Oxford English Dictionary*'s definition of 'the world considered as a single community linked by telecommunications'. Rather, as the title of his volume indicates, he was identifying a dynamic notion whereby the global intensifies the experience of the local, and vice versa. The Vietnam conflict – at its height when the book was written – confirmed McLuhan's notion of the local/global dynamic in that it was the first 'television war'. The volume went further, however, arguing that, in the electronic era, borderlines of all sorts would enter into flux. 'Globes make my head spin', writes McLuhan in the epigraph; 'By the time I locate the place, they've changed the boundaries'.

Drawing on his formulation of Canada as a 'borderline case', defined not by its nationalist 'content' but by its transnational interfaces, McLuhan proposed that 'software' nations were more appropriate than 'hardware' ones in an increasingly networked culture, in which even the broadest boundaries would shift, the 'East' becoming westernized as the 'West' enters into a form of 'electrical retribalization'. Cognately, the visual (abstract) regime of print culture would recede as the acoustic (affective) space of electronic culture advances. While the attempt to adjust to such changes and yet preserve traditional identities would result in global crises, these shifts in mediation would also instigate new forms of critical awareness.

The reception of this study was itself global, with translations appearing in Paris and Montréal within two years, followed by editions in Brazil, Barcelona, Mexico, Dusseldorf (1971), Tokyo (1972), Buenos Aires, Madrid (1985), and Milan (1995), with McLuhan's central thesis living on in the work of the French writer Paul Virilio.

Richard Cavell

Bibliography

Cavell R. 2002. *McLuhan in space: a cultural geography*. Toronto: University of Toronto Press

War crimes

War crimes are violations of the laws and customs of war for which individuals may be held accountable and tried in domestic or international courts.

National borders have proved to be no barrier to the values and principles that ground individual accountability at the international level for violations of the laws and customs of war. Underlying the idea that certain acts are criminal is the assumption that human beings have basic rights that are inviolate even in wartime. Massive violations of those rights have led to the further assumption that, under certain conditions, those violations can be a concern of the international community, despite national claims to the contrary. The detailed definitions of the laws and customs of war, especially since the end of the Second World War, and an increasing emphasis on the protection of non-combatants have set the stage for the transformation of war-centred laws and customs into humanitarian law, a term now preferred by many. This has meant a shift from traditional concerns about neutrality, blockades, and other non-criminal matters, to concerns about behaviour that blatantly violates humanitarian norms and denies their validity as a set of transnational rules to regulate wartime behaviour.

One result of this shift in emphasis has been the establishment of a number of international courts with authority over violations of humanitarian norms. The authority is transnational in varying degrees, depending on the court's mandate. The International Military Tribunal in Nuremberg that tried major German leaders at the end of the Second World War was established specifically to try those whose authority and acts extended across national borders. The same was true of the Tokyo-based International Military Tribunal for the Far East, established to try major Japanese leaders accused of war crimes that transcended national borders. Criminal acts centred in a particular country during the war were to be the responsibility of that country's courts. This separation of responsibility stands at the heart of the subject of war crimes, reflecting as it does, the persistent tension between the claims of national sovereignty and the claims of a community beyond the nation state.

In each instance where an international criminal court has been established, the unwillingness or inability of state authorities to take appropriate action has been the motive to move proceedings to an international level. Thus, the two International Military Tribunals mentioned above were established by the victors in the Second World War on the grounds that the defeated powers would not prosecute their own citizens for actions that had, during the war, been part of national policies. The legal basis for the trials was the fact that some of those policies, such as the treatment of prisoners or the use of slave labour, were clear violations of the laws and customs of war. Following the trials there were hopes that their example would spark a drive to give permanence to courts with enforcement powers. But the reverse was true. Even the states that had established the Tribunals became nervous at the thought of a wider application of international accountability in other, more permanent courts.

Not until the breakup of Yugoslavia in the 1990s, with its widespread use of murder, rape, and torture for political ends, was there a move to establish a new international court. The existing International Court of Justice could not serve since it can only deal with disputes between states. The continuing carnage in Yugoslavia finally overcame national hesitations, and in 1993 the United Nations Security Council established the International Criminal Tribunal for the Former Yugoslavia. This proved to be the first of two international criminal courts with jurisdictions limited to a specific country. The second was a court for Rwanda where massacres had plunged the country into chaos. In 1994 the Security Council, at the request of the Rwandan government, established the International Criminal Tribunal for Rwanda with powers of investigation, trial, and punishment. The limited jurisdictions of these two courts suggested that international enforcement of transnational norms was going to be a cautious, country-by-country affair. But this was soon to change.

In 1998 longstanding attempts at a more comprehensive international approach to the problem of war crimes came to fruition at an international conference in Rome with the adoption of the Rome Statute for the establishment of the International Criminal Court. Despite the refusal of some countries, including the United States, to sign on to the Court, it came into existence in 2002. To address crimes committed before that date, some additional courts with limited jurisdictions were established such as the Sierra Leone Special Court, charged with investigation into events that occurred during that country's civil war. Thus it was that the 1990s and the early years of the 21st century saw an unprecedented stiffening of the international will to end impunity for the commission of war crimes. The outstanding expression of this will is the International Criminal Court. Designed as a permanent institution with jurisdiction not limited to any one country, the Court's very existence provides institutional support for transnational standards of wartime behaviour that have been long in the making and that are to apply without distinction as to location or cultural context. Four offences lie within this Court's jurisdiction: war crimes, genocide, crimes against humanity, and aggression. The drafters of the Court's statute recognized the difficulty that has marked attempts to define aggression by providing that jurisdiction over this crime would be exercised only after agreement was reached. The other crimes posed no such problem.

The precise and detailed definitions of these three other crimes in the Statute are the culmination of many years of effort to make general principles of humane behaviour the stimulus and ground for prohibiting certain specific wartime acts. There have always been some restrictions such as the rule against poisoning wells, but a concerted international effort to detail the laws of war can be traced to conferences at The Hague in 1899 and 1907. Delegates to the conferences did not envision international enforcement of the wartime rules and regulations they had agreed on. They held strictly to the prevailing concept of the primacy of the state. The Hague rules are in essence transnational, but it was understood at the time that the interpretation, application, and, if necessary, enforcement of those rules were the prerogative of the 41 countries represented at the conferences. Further, so far as the international community was concerned, a violation of the rules was a national, not an individual offence. Individual offenders were beyond international reach.

This basic position regarding the commission of war crimes changed only slowly in the years between The Hague conferences and the establishment of the International Criminal Court. Changes came about through an uneven seesaw between offence and response as ideas of transnational responsibility began to take shape. The ideas found expression in various treaties such as the 1919 Versailles Peace Treaty with its attempt to assign criminal responsibility for the First World War, and the 1928 Kellogg-Briand Pact that attempted to outlaw war altogether. Meanwhile, the nature of war was changing far more rapidly than were ideas about how to restrain and limit its violence. The Second World War, with its massive violations of even the mildly protective features of the traditional laws and customs of war, was the turning point in the history of war crimes. Flawed as the postwar trials conducted by the victorious Allies may have been, they were, in the long view, a successful assertion of a transnational interest in individual accountability for acts committed in wartime. When those acts caused widespread death and suffering among populations that the laws of war were designed to protect, they could no longer be considered the prerogative of the individual nation state to appraise, prosecute, or support, as it might choose.

The trials were followed by a burst of international rule making as members of the new United Nations, representatives of nongovernmental organizations, and private individuals rushed to fill the gaps in the laws and customs of war that had been revealed in the Second World War. In 1948 genocide was defined as an international crime in a convention ratified by many states. In 1949 four Geneva Conventions extended wartime protection to prisoners of war, members of the armed forces who were sick, wounded, or shipwrecked, and to civilians caught up in the conflict. In 1950 the crimes that had been prosecuted at Nuremberg were restated and affirmed by the UN General Assembly as crimes that were punishable under international law. Thus the Nuremberg definitions of war crimes, crimes against humanity, crimes against peace, and participation in a common plan or conspiracy to commit crimes against peace were lifted out of the specific Nuremberg context, and affirmed as applying across time and space. To make this affirmation clear, the Assembly asserted the pre-eminence of international over national law so far as war crimes were concerned. An individual could not escape responsibility for an act defined as a crime under international law by arguing that it was not a crime under national law, nor could responsibility be avoided by reason of the individual's position as head of state or other leading government official.

Only one feature was missing in this 1950s assertion of the transnational applicability of the definitions of war crimes. Lacking was an international court in which such crimes could be tried. Despite many efforts by many people in the immediate postwar period, it would be more than fifty years before such a court was established. As memories of the Second World War began to fade and attention shifted to the Cold War, there was a resurgence of national feeling that overrode assertions of the pre-eminence of a general interest over the various national interests. The Korean War (1950–53) became a test case for these different outlooks. From the perspective that had underlain the war crimes trials, the incursion of North Korean troops into South Korea was a clear case of aggression. From a Cold War perspective, the incursion was an indication of Communism's expansionist policy, to be contained or supported at all costs, depending whether the view was from the West or the East. The common ground for these different perspectives was that charges of war crimes became part of the rhetoric of conflict in this and in subsequent wars, with no serious attempt to provide international institutions that would have the power to investigate, much less prosecute the crimes that were so freely charged. This returned the primary responsibility for the enforcement of transnational standards to the nation state where it remained until the massive violations in the wars of the 1990s showed the inadequacy of that approach, and the need for the institutions discussed in this entry.

By 2002, when the International Criminal Court began operation, the gap between its treatment of the laws and customs of war and the treatment in the Hague Conventions of 1899 and 1907 was a gap of far more than years. Wartime experiences had moved nation states, however slowly and reluctantly, to delegate some authority to international courts with jurisdiction over war crimes never dreamed of by delegates at The Hague. One thing, however, had not changed in the intervening years,

and that was the desire to make 'the laws of humanity and the dictates of the public conscience', so confidently appealed to by The Hague delegates, a living presence in international affairs. The history of war crimes at the international level can be seen as an effort to make that dream a reality.

Dorothy V. Jones

Bibliography

Bass G. J. 2000. *Stay the hand of vengeance: the politics of war crimes tribunals*. Princeton: Princeton University Press.

Goldstone R. J. 2000. *For humanity: reflections of a war crimes investigator*. New Haven: Yale University Press.

Nino, C. S. 1996. *Radical evil on trial*. New Haven: Yale University Press.

Taylor T. 1992. *The anatomy of the Nuremberg trials*. Boston, MA: Little Brown.

Related essays

Abolition of Forced Labour Convention; Cold War; genocide; human rights; justice; relief; United Nations system; war

Washington Consensus

'Best practice' in Latin American economic policy by 1989 was moving from inward-oriented, state-interventionist strategies to outward-oriented, market-centred strategies. The ideas of liberal trade, non-inflationary government finance, market deregulation, privatization, and openness to foreign direct investment were gaining prominence. In the abstract, policy precepts were moving from autarchic to transnational orientation. John Williamson in 1990 called this the 'Washington Consensus'.

Latin America in the 1980s suffered an overhang of 1970s petrodollar-fuelled international bank debt, resulting in what has been known as the 'lost decade' of Latin American economic growth. In 1989, US Treasury Secretary Nicholas Brady's plan to restructure this debt encouraged participants to pursue economic reforms, providing the catalyst for Washington Consensus policies. In addition to liberal trade and the other four aforementioned policy characteristics, Williamson catalogued tax reform, financial liberalization, competitive exchange rate, secure property rights, and redirection of public expenditure toward public goods such as health, education and infrastructure.

Given its market focus, 'Washington Consensus' became inextricably linked with the transnational phenomena of neoliberalism and globalization. It became a lightning-rod for their critics, and for the implication that the IMF and World Bank had forced these on the developing world. Williamson denied this, arguing that it was '(not) a reform agenda made in Washington', and that the name 'Washington' came because it was targeting 'Washingtonians who were skeptical of whether there was a reform process under way in Latin America' (Williamson 2003, 325). Yet he also wrote that the Washington Consensus was the lowest common denominator of policy advice being addressed by the Washington-based institutions to Latin American countries as of 1989.

Whatever its origins, the Washington Consensus indeed became a flow of ideas across borders, often from the lending institutions of the developed world to the policy and 'technocratic' elite of the developing world. Its implications were distinctly transnational, aiming at an increased international flow of goods and capital. Its imputed association with neoliberalism, though nearly total, is less than accurate. The Washington Consensus as articulated by Williamson did not call for a complete opening of the capital account, which may have been one of the most fundamental sources of financial and economic disturbance in the developing world in the 1990s. Nor did it reject a role for the state as an important agent of income redistribution.

The Washington Consensus supplanted an earlier generation of development economics, including 'modernization theory', which arose after the Second World War with the study of Continental Europe's rapid industrialization in the 'long 19th century' (1800–1914). Europe's experience was thought to be applicable to the developing world, and the state was seen as vital to accelerating the process of industrialization. In rejecting these state-centred development ideas, the Washington Consensus brought neoclassical thought back to development economics. This neoclassical resurgence partly reflected neoliberal ascension in the developed world and partly stemmed from an inference of neoclassical underpinnings to East Asian postwar growth.

Whether such inference was warranted is disputed. Certainly, competition in foreign markets played a key role in the export dynamism of some East Asian 'miracle' economies; relative prices were allowed to guide the economy to a high-growth path. Yet it is not difficult to identify a state role in this process, not least in the allocation of credit and the favour granted to 'strategic' sectors. Thus the Washington Consensus may have disregarded the state's potential to play a pro-growth role, as might be argued is the case in the successes of China and, more recently, Vietnam.

Some see the latest version of the Washington Consensus – emphasizing the institutional underpinnings of functioning markets – as perpetuating the original's neglect of more fundamental barriers to growth, such as poor geography and environment. Yet even if the augmented version is a better credo for development than was its ancestor, the 'Washington Consensus' moniker is tainted beyond repair. An ethos characteristic of its times, it was an apex in the pendulum of thought emphasizing now market freedom, now market failure.

Scott Urban

Bibliography

Williamson J. 'Our agenda and the Washington Consensus', in Kuczynski P. P and Williamson J. (eds) 2003. *After the Washington Consensus*. Washington, DC: Peterson Institute for International Economics.

Williamson J. 'What Washington means by policy reform', In Williamson J. (ed.) 1990. *Latin American adjustment: how much has happened?* Washington, DC: Peterson Institute for International Economics.

Related essays

convergence and divergence; debt crises; debt crises (developing countries); development and growth; Economic Commission for Latin America and the Caribbean (ECLAC); economics; financial markets; industrialization; International Monetary Fund (IMF); investment; loans; modernization theory; neoliberalism; public policy; taxation; trade; underdevelopment; World Bank

Welfare state

A welfare state is a state in which organized power is deliberately used to modify the play of market forces and the effects of natural or man-made misfortune. Adopting various forms at different times and with varying aims and results, the primary goals of welfare provisions are to afford citizens or other persons with a certain amount of protection and equality by redistributing social risks and providing services for those in need. A minimal definition encompasses legally protected minimum standards of income, nutrition, health, housing or education; at the other extreme, the idea of comprehensive coverage and complete control from cradle to grave epitomizes the totalitarian potentials and temptations inherent in the modern state.

The welfare state is both a product and a promoter of the modern age. Its rise has been closely associated with the rise of the modern state. The welfare state has therefore primarily intensified the circulation and flows of benefits and people *within* national boundaries and thus strengthened and modified the role of the nation state. Solidarity has been shifted from smaller, sometimes self-selected circles to a national entity. Through intergenerational transfers, this community even stretches to include its still unborn members. Nevertheless, there is a second, transnational dimension to the history of the welfare state. A full explanation of the rise of the modern welfare state has to include processes of mutual perception, of learning and delimitation, in which non-state actors have often played a crucial role. Also, welfare measures have developed a tendency to transcend the boundaries of nation states and thus to form networks of transnational solidarity.

Welfare provisions – the redirecting of resources to address material hardships and social needs – had existed long before the modern nation state and the industrial era. Solidarity within families and private, cooperative and religious charity date back before the modern era. Charity, for example, is a central part of most of the world's religions. Also, it is important to note that the rise of the welfare state since the late 19th century has by no means led to a substitution or demise of these provisions. Rather, most modern welfare states are defined by a combination of independent, voluntary, mutualist and government services. From the perspective of the history of statehood, state action to ease the grievances of their peoples can also be tracked back to antiquity. However, the modern welfare state differs from previous schemes of poverty relief due to its relatively universal coverage and, of course, because of a degree of state involvement unknown to man before the 20th century. Some scholars even argue that during the second half of the 20th century the welfare aspect became the main defining criterion of modern statehood.

From the very beginning, the rise of the welfare state was embedded in transnational debates. Against the backdrop of industrialization, urbanization and the rise of the working class, many countries experimented with and instituted welfare provisions. However, this was not a story of parallel developments detached from each other. Especially within Europe, legislation passed from one country to the next. British factory legislation influenced similar provisions in France and Germany in the 1870s, and Germany's system of social security, which was put into place during the 1880s, had an impact throughout the continent. Even if interconnections within Europe were particularly strong, other parts of the world also soon became involved (predominantly areas settled by white colonizers). For example, the forefather of the New Zealand labour reforms of the 1890s, William Pember Reeves, attracted big audiences in London when lecturing about the reforms back home, and American turn-of-the-century progressives travelled from one European country to the next in search of inspiration. At the same time, Japan saw an intense debate on the German reforms beginning in the 1890s, and the interwar period brought the adoption of European-style welfare measures not only there, but also in Latin American states such as Chile, Uruguay and Cuba.

Ideas and institutions, programmes and projects, legislation and liabilities were not simply copied one to one from one country to the next, of course. Adaptations and borrowings predominated, and transnational interactions also spurred rivalling visions and countermodels. For example, Lloyd George promoted the British National Insurance Act of 1911 as the better alternative to Germany's compulsory system. Welfare measures were modelled after national styles, recalibrating and reinforcing supposedly national trajectories. Ironically, even these demarcations with respect to other national paths actually propelled the upswing of the welfare state as an inter- and transnational phenomenon. Thus, the rise of the welfare state since the late 19th century has been informed and promoted by the movement of politics, people and ideas, especially throughout the North Atlantic world that trade and capitalism had tied together.

These interactions were made possible by a specific group of transnational brokers. Many of the turn-of-the-century progressives, be they scientists or publicists, lobbyists or intellectuals, self-proclaimed experts or politicians, were not state functionaries. Often they had gained first-hand knowledge about welfare measures in other nations through study trips and visits. John Graham Brooks, the first president of the American National Consumers' League, travelled to Germany in the 1880s to investigate its accident insurance. Apart from middle-class reformers, socialist parties and trade unions with their emphasis on international solidarity also loomed large in these transnational networks. Associations such as the German Verein für Socialpolitik and the Musée Social in Paris compiled whole libraries with information about welfare measures in other countries. Travel reports and highly publicized commissions of inquiry, world fairs and conferences served as international hubs. By 1914, international research and networks covered practically all aspects of modern welfare. And even before the First World War, first steps were taken to transnationalize welfare measurements. Triggered by global migration, some welfare benefits were already made available to citizens of other countries, primarily on the basis of bilateral agreements, for example, between France and Italy and between Italy and Germany.

Exchange and interconnection continued between 1914 and 1945, even if their intensity diminished. At the same time, the First World War brought about a new level of state interventionism that was a precondition for the rise of the modern welfare state after 1945. In the interwar period, the League of Nations and especially the International Labour Organization, as the League's agency for international labour standards, was a transnational hub. Its recommendations influenced national policies, and it further promoted the transnationalization of welfare measurements. At the same time, the confrontation of system alternatives, of liberalism, fascism and Communism – as well as countless self-proclaimed 'third ways' – sharpened the contrasts and heightened the need for mutual demarcation. One of the earliest documented occurrences of the

term 'welfare state' dates back to this context: in 1939, Oxford University's Sir Alfred Zimmern defined welfare as a core element and task of modern democracies in the struggle with fascism. Thus, welfare provisions turned into ammunition in the fight between different types of regime.

This was even truer after 1945. In this era, which saw the rise of the welfare state to a level previously inconceivable in human history, the growth of the welfare state was still not an automatic matter. Rather, the relative convergence of welfare regimes, at least within the Western world, was brought about through the hard work of brokers and intermediaries. The British Beveridge Plan, proposing a uniform and universal system of social insurance, is a good example of this. Designed in 1942 as a beacon of democracy in the fight against fascism, it also shaped postwar debates. In the United States alone, some 50,000 copies of the plan were sold, and it inspired programmes in Belgium, France, West Germany, Mexico and elsewhere. During this phase, the debate about the welfare state far transcended the bounds of the North Atlantic world. Most importantly, it became a defining feature of the global confrontation between East and West. The Cold War was not least a competition between rival visions of welfare. Soviet influence thus shaped welfare provisions in the Eastern bloc, even if the grade of interference was lower in social politics than in other fields. Ironically, the relative similarities of the systems of post-1945 states such as Poland, Hungary and Czechoslovakia found their origins in the pre-1914 years and in the fact that large regions of these states had been part of the German and the Austrian empires with their early welfare provisions. The 1960s and 1970s saw the welfare state grow at a fantastic pace in most Western countries. Instead of night-watchman states, law-and-order states or instruments of authoritarian or even totalitarian rule, the production and redistribution of social well-being became the predominant occupation and the main legitimization of state action.

In the last decades, globalization has put massive pressure on the existing welfare state systems around the globe. The erosion of national sovereignty has reduced the ability of nation states to live up to the expectations many people have regarding welfare provisions. The internationalization of business and competition has thus also been a source of the crisis of the modern welfare state, even if it is by no means automatic that nations will converge at a low level of provision.

Besides the transnational interconnections between the competing, converging or conflicting paths of societies into modernity there is a second tier of transnationalization of the welfare state. International solidarity, as propagated by philanthropists, socialists and others, can involve a plea for a transnationalization of welfare measurements. During the 20th century, social security became one of the fundamental rights of humanity. The Atlantic Charter of 1941 and articles 22 to 28 of the Universal Declaration of Human Rights (adopted and proclaimed by the General Assembly of the United Nations in 1948) both grant social and cultural rights of participation. In 1966, the United Nations General Assembly adopted the International Covenant on Economic, Social and Cultural Rights under which the ratifying states committed themselves to grant a number of social rights, including the right to health. Even if many of these goals are still visions, they are more than paper tigers because of their impact on national regimes.

Western Europe is an area of especially dense transnational interactions, especially due to the European integration process. The European Union and its predecessors have been the primary site of the tendency to transnationalize welfare state regulation, although welfare has remained largely a field of activity of the nation state even here. However, the Organization for Economic Cooperation and Development, put into place as part of the Marshall Plan, was one of the early postwar centres of harmonization of social and work-related regulations, even if these exchanges of experience and processes of legal harmonization passed almost unnoticed by the broader public. All in all, the tendency for transnationalization within the EU has three dimensions. Firstly, citizens of the European Union have gained access to the welfare state of other member states. Secondly, the EU has pursued a policy of welfare measures complementing national regulations. For example, the treaties of Maastricht (1992) and Nice (2000) both contain chapters on social rights, and the EU has also instituted welfare provisions for the employees of the European Commission. Thirdly, the integration process has led to a certain degree of harmonization of the welfare systems of its member states (as well as of countries gaining access to the EU). Altogether, Europe thus serves as a good example to show that welfare states had and have a transnational dimension and that their history cannot be explained from either a strictly national perspective or simply from the vantage point of globalization.

Kiran Klaus Patel

Bibliography

Esping-Andersen G. 1990. *Three worlds of welfare capitalism*. Cambridge: Polity.

Flora P. and Heidenheimer A. J. (eds) 1981. *The development of welfare states in Europe and America*. New Brunswick: Transaction.

Kaelble H. and Schmid G. (eds) 2004. *Das europaeische Sozialmodell: auf dem Weg zum transnationalen Sozialstaat*. Berlin: Sigma.

Rodgers D. T. 1998. *Atlantic crossings: social politics in a progressive age*. Cambridge, MA: Belknap.

Related essays
body shopping; Cold War; Commission on International Labour Legislation; convergence and divergence; European Union (EU); human mobility; intellectual elites; labour standards; Marshall Plan; modernization theory; nation and state; public policy; war; workers' movements

Westernization

The idea of 'Westernization' comes from concepts of east and west, which evolved over time and were never absolute in definition. Historically, knowledge and technology moved as much from the East as they appear now to do from the West. It is a misconception that globalization, often conflated with Westernization, is something new to the contemporary era. It is equally problematic to see globalization romantically, as a continuous process, beginning in the distant past and leading up to today's world. Those who believe in the essential newness of Westernization/globalization tend to celebrate this process as the ongoing triumph of Western civilization, ignoring its composite nature and origins. However, there are also extreme counter-reactions to Westernization, which view all its processes as inherently evil and resist it as Western imperialism, potentially missing its benefits. Thus, the word

'Westernization' raises a variety of different preconceptions and problems.

The 'spectre' of composite culture, liberalism, and racial segregation

India is an excellent example of how Westernization has been conceived and resisted. India has had a long history of attempted acculturation, and other nations saw its quest to end colonial domination as an exemplar. Cultural and racial mingling was common in the early days of European presence in India. In the 17th and 18th centuries many Europeans ran two households, one Indian and the other European, partly because of the hardships involved in sailing out to India. Even in the 19th century, there are many examples of Europeans falling in love with Indians and quitting the East India Company's service, although racial attitudes were beginning to harden and make this sort of encounter taboo. The use of Indian artists to illustrate British, Dutch and French botanical collections, or artisans for the tomb of the founder of British Calcutta, Robert Clive, built by his *begum*, are examples of the continuing processes of mixture (racial, architectural and civilizational) well into the 18th century. What was West and what was East was not only blurred but also further complicated by the presence of Creoles or Eurasians: people of mixed race parentage.

As the British East India Company's rule stabilized, its Government increasingly frowned upon racial intermingling. Lord Wellesley's 'rule of morality' (Governor-General of India, 1798–1805) ushered in sharper distinctions of race, class, and behaviour. For example, by the 1820s, the Company's Government forbade Europeans to wear Indian-style clothes during office hours and in public. After 1835, Thomas Babington Macaulay's 'Anglicist' clique abolished education in the vernacular and established English as the primary language of education in India. The 'Orientalist' faction within the East India Company, closely associated with the Asiatic Society of Bengal, opposed this. They believed that knowledge could best be acquired through translations of key scientific and technological concepts into vernacular languages.

This turn towards English had profound consequences for the future of the colonized since the ruled would now have to acquire a knowledge of colonial culture (for instance, Wordsworth's poem 'Daffodils', impossible to imagine in a tropical climate which never had any daffodils) before they could understand fundamental principles of science and technology. Wherever such conditions of language were imposed, and this was quite extensive for much of the world for most colonizing European nations, it was now for the indigenous peoples a process of acquisition of knowledge at a remove; that is, the fundamental structure of debate and discourse was determined and mediated by another and foreign language; a language difficult to separate from the years of cultural and semiotic accretion that went behind it.

Thomas Babington Macaulay (Member of the Supreme Council, British India, 1835–38) claimed that education in English would provide a class of Indian followers English in habit and taste, loyal supporters of the British Government, merely different in colour. However, this liberal promise of equality never materialized: liberalism's death was written into its constitution. The 'imagined community' of the rulers strictly segregated itself both from mixed races and from indigenes. The ideals of equality, liberty, and fraternity promised by the French Revolution threatened indigenous and European elites.

There is an apocryphal story of a Bengali student of Hindu College in Kolkata (Calcutta), established in 1815 (later Presidency College), raising his top hat to an image of the Goddess Kali, addressing her as 'ma'am', and wishing her a very good day or evening; this was cited as an example of Westernization to the point of absurdity. The young Westernized Bengali mentioned above was a student of Henry Louis Vivian Derozio, a Eurasian, poet and teacher at Hindu College from 1826 to 1831, who inspired the 'Young Bengal Movement'. Its members began to acquire a reputation for rational debates on all issues, of adopting Western modes of dress, speech, drinking wine, and eating beef. This was too much for high-caste conservative and comprador Bengalis and the British to accept. British society condemned Derozio for encouraging the advances of a Bengali student towards his sister. Hindu College dismissed him on charges of 'incest' and he fell from grace and the proximity to elites, both Indian and British, which he had achieved within Calcutta's society as teacher and poet. Comprador elite Calcutta society could not bear the threat of loss of racial and Brahmanical purity and joined with British society in condemning the potential window of opportunity promised by a composite culture adhering to equality and based on rigorous rationality, not racially segregated.

Modernity versus Westernization

What came after were generations of clerks, allowed a degree, but a degree only, of Englishness in dress and speech. Of course, there were notable exceptions such as W. B. O'Shaughnessy's assistant in telegraphy, Sheeb Chandra Nandy, or Kanai Lal Dey, equally familiar with Western medicine and *Ayurveda* and an expert in chemistry, and events such as the uprisings of 1857. Historians describe the difference between the outside world of the bureaucratic office dominated by western time and dress and the domestic world where home was usually a joint family where Indian modes of dress, patriarchy and speech prevailed. They sometimes exaggerate such differences to form an artificial structuralist opposition between 'outside' and 'inside'. In fact, work and domestic life permeated one another, and one of the historically forgotten and ignored groups of victims of the 1857 uprisings were the 'baboos' or clerks who had joined the British enterprise, and who, like the British, stayed in faraway places, away from family, and were victims both 'inside' and 'outside'.

By the 1880s and 1890s, Indians and other colonized peoples were managing to enter English universities, and there they saw a different West, much more racially equal towards them. Imbued with ideas of equality they returned to find themselves without jobs, in a racially segregated context. Bayly has shown that it cannot be questioned that a form of 'modernity' was introduced over much of the world and that its vehicle was usually forms of colonial rule. Adoption of Western modes of speech and dress also involved imbibing and dialoguing with, and contributing to, ideas of the West. Not all ideas were simply 'derived' from the West nor were they unchanged, nor were 'western' ideas unchanged by this dialogue; the idea that colonial elites simply used a 'derivative discourse' simplifies intellectual history by provincializing and localizing, unable to transcend national or intellectual territoriality, or to comprehend transnational networks

and exchanges of knowledge that must sustain knowledge production and the creation of different modernities.

Indigenous populations questioned the fundamental inequalities they saw between themselves and their strictly racially segregated rulers. During Mughal rule in India, Hindu ceremonies included Muslims. Muslim ceremonies incorporated Hindu elements and motifs. Hindus, Muslims and Sikhs could gather at a Sufi shrine. British rule destroyed the sense of a shared community with its promised liberalism and strict racial segregation. Earlier uprisings or 'renovations' took two main forms: either they were millennarian uprisings seeking to put the clock back and speaking of a 'golden past' or they were religious movements such as the Wahabis in the Arab world or Chinese scholars during the rule of the Qing dynasty speaking of greater purity. The Indian Wahabis, coming a few centuries after the Arab movement, and different from it in certain fundamental aspects in terms of religious ideology, spread pan-Islamic transnational networks, and argued for a return to an idealized practice of Islam across the larger Asian landmass.

The uprisings of 1857 and many similar acts of resistance to imperialism across the globe reveal the complexity of the transition to modernity, and historians have traditionally read these events backwards from the assumed end-point of the territorial nation state and particular forms of democratic nationalisms. Modernity might have, and has, taken many forms, as a continuing process and as a transnational challenge to the territorially strictly defined nation state.

By the start of the 20th century, a generation of Indian revolutionaries took to arms and bombs, and formed secret societies, idolizing Mazzini and Garibaldi, whose biographies were secretly printed and circulated. They maintained transnational networks with Russian nihilists, Parisian socialists, and later Communists, Irish revolutionaries in Ireland and the United States, Sikh migrants in Canada and the US: importing bomb-making manuals from Paris via Pune, India, and revolutionary pamphlets and arms through French Pondicherry, India. Chinese secret societies during the revolts against the Qing dynasty in China in the late 19th century also adopted dual identities; despite their highly nativist ideology, they drew on modern concepts of republican revolution, symbolized in the person of Sun Yatsen, to give shape to their grievances against the ruling imperial house. These early revolutionaries were not initially successful but they pioneered the global move towards national independence. Some of their fears are reflected also in the change in attitude toward Westernization in the Japan of the Meiji era (1868–1912). Initially, the rush to modernization as Japan was forced open by the Western powers, leading figures such as Fukuzawa Yukichi to advocate strongly Westernized reforms, characterized by him with the term 'civilization and enlightenment' (bunmei kaika) in his Seiyō Jijō (Conditions in the West, 1867–70). By the 1880s, however, there was a deep unease among many Japanese political thinkers that some essential element of Japaneseness was being lost in the rush to Westernization, and they advocated a modernization, which did not hold itself hostage to Western assumptions and demands. In 1888, Shiga Shigetaka organized the Society for Political Education, whose journal was called Nihonjin ('The Japanese'), and whose objective was to preserve the mysterious but ill-defined 'national essence' (kokusui). Although they were in favour of technological progress and political reform, they noted, they castigated Westernizers who seemed to 'forget the excellence' of their own nation's civilization. This increasing division over the meaning of civilization would eventually lead Japan into the conflict with the West that would end with World War 2 in Asia.

The new imperialism of technology, and reaction to Westernization

Economistic explanations of the thrust for imperial expansion after 1870 have in recent decades been criticized as mechanical and Eurocentric. From the 1960s, historians of empire argued for the dynamics of the 'periphery', stressing the importance of events and processes in the locality, region, country, or the contributions of the 'man on the spot', arguing against what had up to then been a Marxist-influenced story of empire which was predominantly about metropolitan industry and capital. Yet in the telling of the story of empire in the colonized regions themselves, technology was never neutral. Though still justly arguing that a large proportion of Western imperial possessions

were an 'informal empire', Robinson later admitted that hardware or technology, such as the railroad, 'was not only the servant but also the principal generator of informal empire; in this sense imperialism was a function of the railroad' (Davis et al. 1991, 2.) The telegraph was equally powerful as a tool of empire. Cecil Rhodes, based in South Africa, claimed that his ultimate objective was to connect with the railway and telegraph system in Egypt, because he claimed the railway was his right hand and the telegraph his voice. The anxiety about the corridor to the north of Africa and Rhodes' project to take the rail and telegraph to the river Zambezi and control Bechuanaland, Matabeleland and Mashonaland shows how communication and access, especially railways and telegraphs, were an important strategic concern of the British in Africa and elsewhere: for example, the imperial race between France and England for Necker Island off the coast of Hawaii to lay a telegraph cable, an island locally dismissed as the 'little lava rock'.

The movements towards independent nation states with 'Western' ideals of social and gender equality and democracy were an idealized feature of modernity around the world, though these ideals were not a necessary condition for modernity to appear. Industrialization and forms of modernization took place under monarchy. Many authoritarian or oligarchic societies exhibiting strong traditions of egalitarianism changed through the modernizing process. Rulers were quick to agree to the construction of the telegraph and railways to exhibit, as in the case of the Ottoman Empire, ostensibly their interest in modernity and technology but in reality a desire to extend physical control over territories and peoples over which they had little power except in terms of some ill-defined claims of multilayered sovereignty. The telegraph was the means to ensure central control and penetration both for the British and the various feudatories they dealt with ranging from the Ottomans to the Sultan of Muscat. The telegraph allowed centralization in West Asia and facilitated, for a while, Ottoman and Persian subimperialism.

The advance of technology both facilitated colonialism and stimulated resistance to Westernization. European powers telegraphing to the Ottoman ruler demanded rapid responses, breaking down the traditional council and forms of political rule that had depended on counsellors and multilayered notions of sovereignty. The Wahabi pan-Islamic movement started before 1857; it argued that it was un-Islamic to be ruled by the *firinghi* (British). After the assassination of the Earl of Mayo (Viceroy of India, 1869–72), in the Andaman Islands by an alleged Wahabi fanatic, Sher Ali Afridi, of the dominant Pashtun Afridi tribe, west of the Peshawar valley (now in Pakistan), the British Government examined with urgency the transnational networks that it had lost sight of, and, ironically, facilitated with its complacency about the security of its own territories. Wahabi networks, stretching from Turkey and Persia to Patna in Bihar, India, and the Andaman Islands, were again the focus of anxiety and surveillance after letters were found addressed from Wahabis in Patna to the convict in prison.

These broader networks contrast with the Young Turk revolution of 1908, which argued for a rejuvenation of the Ottoman Empire, remodelled along the lines of a European state. By the 1880s, there was a widespread nationalist movement in Egypt, which demanded Egypt for the Egyptians. As the Ottoman Empire crumbled, peoples of northern and other parts of Africa were arguing, especially in print, for a pan-Africanism by 1900. For example, Seetsele Modiri Molema wrote *The Bantu past and present* (1920), which reveals the complex and hybrid vision that re-represented modernity for much of the still decolonizing world. However, the language in which they spoke and wrote could not be solely local in vocabulary or in thought, and intellectually was forced to engage with 'Westernization'. There were two pan-African conferences, respectively after the end of the First and Second World Wars. Pan-Africanism had several aspects: (1) the combination of black North Americans with peoples of Africa; (2) the combination with other African diasporas of the slave trade, such as the Caribbean; (3) the combination of all the peoples of Africa. However, the African peoples mirrored many of the problems facing the Indian subcontinent. Problems such as the territorial nationalism(s), tribal loyalties over the nation state, and pan-Africanism continued to be a troubled cause as leaders forged nation states.

Nelson Mandela forged a middle path, perhaps wavering between arms and ideology. He abandoned Gandhi's path of passive resistance after 1962, confessing that the brutality of apartheid suppression forced him to take up arms and amongst his many comrades were Walter Sisulu and A. M. Kathrada. On being freed after 27 years in prison Mandela famously said that he could forgive, but never forget, and the African National Congress chose the path of reconciliation rather than vengeance. Martin Luther King envisioned equality beyond race, and while upholding equality and promoting culture, was assassinated.

Following the British disaster at the Dardanelles (1915) and the German collapse during the First World War, a resurgent Turkey inspired by, amongst others, Kemal 'Ataturk', remodelled Turkey after the 'Western model'. India, China, and Myanmar retained their traditional systems of medicine alongside allopathy, whereas Japan did not: modernity and Westernization in the latter society had its price. In the present day, in decolonizing societies which have not adopted extensive land redistribution, protofeudalism exists, and is supported by international financial institutions, in many cases forcing developing economies into dangerously undiverse agriculture, producing one good such as bananas, or even illegal products such as coca leaf. Brutality often echoed modernization, whether violence towards traditions or towards 'Other' people(s) or themselves. Perceptions of Westernization differ and are imposed, accepted, rejected, and differing forms of modernisms striven after.

Reinventing identities: a failed project?

In India, Aurobindo Ghose amongst others began the movement for complete independence and the regeneration of a composite culture, which combined eastern ideas, both Muslim and Hindu, with western ones. However, because this early nationalism depended heavily on Hindu symbols and because the British government had systematically discriminated against Muslims after 1857 and then promoted them to counter this early categorical opposition to British rule, the government strategically pitched Hindus and Muslims against each other: a policy of 'divide and rule'.

Such intercommunity conflicts were present even in the 18th century but the British government, with the development of ideas of 'social science' (as practised by early anthropologists), completely transformed their scale as it demanded and created identities.

For instance, in the census of 1901, people were forced to declare whether they were Hindu or Muslim, establishing monolithic identities; nuanced categories such as Shi'a, or Kanauji pandit, or social classes, such as landlords, disappeared under this categorization. The insistence on a single identity, still demanded all over the world, has contributed to the destruction of an individual's multiple contextual identities.

Reactions to Westernization led a generation of Western-educated and -trained leaders in India to resist such categorization and reinvent themselves as national leaders. This can be seen in leaders' use of clothing. While Cambridge-educated Nehru adopted the famous Nehru jacket and the classic Congress cap, Gandhi, who was educated as a lawyer at University College London, went back to the dhoti, and Jinnah, trained in law at Lincoln's Inn, London, a secular and Westernized lawyer, was forced by circumstances ultimately to fall back exclusively on his Muslim identity and led his people into partition for the nation state of Pakistan. Therefore, through dress, speech and discourse the nationalist generation created its own identity and resisted Westernization or subordination. At a certain point, bodily practices, dress, time, and language might have achieved a semblance of homogeneity; it did not last long and modernities proliferate. This can be seen in the item that has perhaps become symbolic of Western consumer modernity: the hamburger, available in identical form around the world. Yet in India, it is not identical: adapting to local customs, fast-food burgers are made not even of lamb but usually of chicken or cottage cheese, not beef – symbolic of the way in which Westernization is adopted but also resisted.

Deep Kanta Lahiri-Choudhury

Bibliography

Bayly C. A. 2004. The birth of the modern world 1780–1914. Oxford: Blackwell.

Blacker C. 1964. The Japanese Enlightenment: a study of the writings of Fukuzawa Yukichi. Cambridge: Cambridge University Press.

Bose S. 2006. A hundred horizons: the Indian Ocean in the age of global empire. Delhi: Permanent Black.

Davis C. B. and Wilburn K. E. (eds) with Robinson R. E. 1991. Railway imperialism. London: Greenwood.

Harrison, M. 1999. Climates and constitutions: health, race, environment and British Imperialism in India 1600–1850. Delhi: Oxford University Press.

Hobson J. M. 2004. The Eastern origins of Western civilization. Cambridge: Cambridge University Press.

Karl R. and Zarrow P. (eds). 2002. Rethinking the 1898 reform period: political and cultural change in late Qing China. Cambridge, MA: Harvard University Press.

Sen A. 2002. 'How to judge globalism', The American Prospect, 13, 1, 1–14.

Starfield J. 2001. 'A dance with the Empire: Modiri Molema's Glasgow years: 1914–1921', Journal of South African Studies, special issue for Shula Marks, 27, 3, 479–503.

Related essays

1848; African liberation; antropofagia; beauty; civilizations; class; consumer society; cosmopolitanism and universalism; decolonization; democracy; dress; drugs (illicit); empires and imperialism; ethnicity and race; expositions; fashion; fast food; Gandhi, Mohandas Karamchand; Ghose, Aurobindo Ackroyd; governing science; higher education; humanities; intellectual elites; internationalisms; Islam; Japan; kindergarten; knowledge; language; liberalism; literature; Maoism; McDonald's; modernity; modernization theory; music; Muslim networks; nation and state; Orientalism; pan-isms; pidgins and creoles; race-mixing; railways; religion; Romanticism; salt; telephone and telegraphy; The Wretched of the Earth; transportation infrastructures

White men's countries

From late in the 19th century, a range of English-speaking colonies and nations in North America, South Africa and Australasia declared themselves 'white men's countries', signalling their intention to keep the 'temperate zone' for themselves to the exclusion of those deemed 'not-white', targeting in particular Chinese, Indians and Japanese, who were collectively referred to in this context as 'Asiatics'. White men's countries also rested on the imperial dispossession, displacement or destruction of Indigenous peoples, whose survivors were expected to 'die out' as evolutionary progress took its course, but who were meanwhile subject to the white man's 'protection'.

The transnational imagined community of white men was sustained by a convergence of republican and imperial discourses that supported its binary foundations: the British imperial distinction between races fit to govern themselves and those deemed not yet or not ever fit, and the republican distinction between peoples eligible for citizenship and those not. The latter distinction often referred to United States naturalization law that, from 1790, distinguished between free white persons and blacks. It also drew on the ideology of Anglo-Saxonism, that located these English-speaking self-governing communities in a much longer 'race history', harking back to the mythical glories of Hengist and Horsa. The 'white man' was the Anglo-Saxon in contemporary and colloquial mode.

White men's countries were gendered, racialized and class formations, their commitment to a masculine democracy asserted in opposition to aristocratic hereditary privilege on the one hand and servile, dependent 'coolie' labour on the other. The mid 19th century was an age when 'glorious manhood asserted its elevation', in the words of Australian republican poet Daniel Deniehy: whiteness was crucial to manhood's democratic claims. Democracy required, so its proponents such as Goldwin Smith, Charles Pearson, James Bryce and James Russel Lowell argued, a society free of all caste distinctions. When Chinese and Japanese diplomats and political campaigners invoked the equality of nations under international law, democratic white men asserted the sovereignty of the autonomous male subject. Immigration restriction became the paradigmatic expression of the sovereignty of self-governing communities, whether they be self-governing colonies or republics. The first race-based immigration restriction law was passed by the British colony of Victoria in Australia in 1855, when 'immigrant' was defined as an adult male of Chinese descent. Other British colonies and former colonies followed suit.

White men's countries drew on and were sustained by the circulation of ideas and technologies, knowledges and emotions, texts and people. American history lessons were frequently cited to demonstrate the impossibility of a multiracial democracy. Reconstruction and the enfranchisement of freed blacks after the Civil War had been presented as a disastrous mistake by James Bryce in his The American Commonwealth (1888), a 'Bible' for the nation builders of Australia and South Africa, while the celebration of the US Ku Klux Klan reached a wider popular audience with the international screening of the D. W. Griffith film Birth of a Nation.

The making of white men's countries depended on the technologies of the census (which enumerated racial groupings and their importance), the passport and the literacy or education test. Japan passed passport legislation in 1896 in an attempt to pre-empt white men's countries targeting Japanese nationals – the Japanese government would control their emigration – rather than allow them to be subjected to offensive discrimination. British governments emulated their example in attempting to persuade the Indian government to control the movement of Indians through the empire. In 1890, Mississippi pioneered the use of an education or literacy test to disenfranchise Black voters. Lobbyists for immigration restriction argued that the United States should introduce a literacy test to curb undesirable immigration from Southern and Eastern Europe. Congress passed such an Act in 1896. In the event it was vetoed by President Grover Cleveland, but not before it was copied in South Africa, where the 'American Act' became the basis of the Natal Act in 1897, which was taken up in turn by British Colonial Secretary, Joseph Chamberlain, as a model and recommended to the other British colonies.

In 1901, the new Commonwealth of Australia inaugurated the White Australia Policy with the passage of an Immigration Restriction Act, incorporating a dictation test, and the Pacific Islands Labourers Act, providing for the deportation of Islanders who had been brought to work on the sugar cane plantations of Queensland from the 1870s. In this founding act of racial expulsion, Australia followed the suggestion of many in the United States, who urged deportation to Africa as the solution to the 'Negro problem'.

The definition of who was white and not-white was, of course, always changing and always contested. Many groups of Europeans were often classified as not-white or not-quite-white-enough. The Japanese protested at the highest levels against being classified as not-white and thus lumped together with those they considered inferior or uncivilized. Indians demanded that all British subjects be treated as equals. The political achievement of white men's countries was the imposition of the binary classification itself – the division of the world into white and not-white – an imposition not successfully challenged until the 1950s and 1960s in the wake of decolonization and the enshrining of non-discrimination as a key ideal in the Universal Declaration of Human Rights in 1948, and even so its legacies remain.

Marilyn Lake

Bibliography

Huttenback R. A. 1976. *Racism and empire: white settlers and colored immigrants in the British self-governing colonies*. Ithaca: Cornell University Press.

Lake M. and Reynolds H. 2008. *Drawing the global colour line: white men's countries and the international campaign for racial equality*. Cambridge: Cambridge University Press.

White C. 1974. *The great white walls are built: restrictive immigration to North America and Australasia, 1836–1888*. Canberra: Australian Institute of International Affairs.

Related essays

anti-racism; Asia; diasporas; empire and migration; empires and imperialism; ethnicity and race; eugenics; human mobility; indentured and contract labourers; individual identification systems; internationalisms; language diplomacy; legal order; population; race-mixing

White Slavery

White Slavery, referred to at different historical junctures as wage or sexual slavery, was a term used in the 19th and early 20th century to describe, sensationalize, and mobilize against exploitation, most prominently in prostitution.

In the mid-1800s British and American labour activists such as George Henry Evans and Richard Oastler used White Slavery discourse to compare tenant or wage labour to chattel slavery. Because workingmen perceived this parallel as threatening to their masculinity, the term became associated with the labour of children and women. The latent or secondary sexual content implied in the term's use for women gradually became primary, with regard to the sexual vulnerability of workingwomen and prostitution defined as extreme coercion.

In the 1870s and 1880s critics of state-regulated prostitution, such as Britain's Josephine Butler, used White Slavery discourse to build sympathy for abolition. After Britain repealed regulated prostitution, nations like Italy, France, and Sweden, and municipalities such as Shanghai, continued regulation. Regulation critics also recirculated White Slavery discourse, as in the 1920s campaign against Buenos Aires' legalized trade. The original economic content in the term, combined with the increasingly gendered and sexualized reading of it, resurfaced in debates around the moral consequences of poor wages for women and reformers' construction of prostitution as a 'vice trust' comparable to monopoly capitalism.

Between 1890 and World War 2, White Slavery discourse framed commercial prostitution as the coercion of young women on an international scale. This was imagined to encompass traffic between Southern and Eastern Europe, the cities of Western Europe and the UK, Africa and Asia, and the Americas. Women engaged in prostitution participated in the mass migrations, and settlement conditions led a small minority of first- and second-generation immigrants to the trade. Most historians agree that a tiny percentage of prostitution entailed the extreme coercion implied in White Slavery discourse.

Nevertheless, assumptions about White Slavery generated action through international, national, and local apparatuses: International Congresses on the White Slave Traffic (1899, 1902, 1910), the International Agreement on White Slave Traffic (1904), the International Abolitionist Federation, the International Council of Women, the US White Slave Traffic Act of 1910, the League of Nations, the Asociación Nacional Argentina contra la Trata de Blancas, and films, plays, and novels in the Americas, the UK, and Europe. Jewish women played prominent roles in White Slave contention as envisioned victims, and through illustrative transnational moral protection work. The (US) National and New York Councils of Jewish Women, for example, worked against White Slavery with the Jüdischer Frauenbund and the Jewish

Association for the Protection of Girls and Women, a London organization that operated in the UK, Europe, and Buenos Aires.

In a highly racialized world, organizing against White Slavery often implied that White Slavery was worse than the enslavement of blacks. In their most hyperbolic form narratives such as Reginald Kaufman's *House of Bondage* (1910) told of dark, alien men abducting innocent white girls. In Western Europe and the Americas anti-Semitic, anti-immigrant, racist and nationalist rhetoric, and captivity narratives rooted in colonialism, informed the construction of White Slavery. Jewish, Asian, and Black men were cast as traders, while the fact that Eastern European, Black, and Asian women were more vulnerable to exploitation and vice policing was obscured. Gender, sexual, and racial hierarchies constructed this bondage: inter-ethnic or -racial sex and sex commerce were read as coercion, and the coercive elements in prostitution and capitalism were sexualized and racialized.

Although transnational, the campaign against White Slavery also generated national and local campaigns that expanded and contracted forms of citizenship, publics, and body politics. In US municipal election campaigns, for instance, native-born women's White Slavery activism translated into a political attack on immigrant men and the policing of immigrant women. Socialist deployments of the discourse reconstructed racial hierarchies among workers, moral hierarchies among women, and gendered hierarchies in working-class families.

White Slavery articulated the transnational circulation of anxieties, inequities, and changes linked with migration, racialization, industrialization, urbanization, and modern forms of capitalism and governance. In this way it parallels contemporary contention around 'sex trafficking'.

Val Marie Johnson

Bibliography
Guy D. 2000. *White Slavery and mothers alive and dead*. Lincoln, NE: University of Nebraska Press.

Related essays
antisemitism; empire and migration; forced migrations; gender and sex; human mobility; League of Nations system; marriage; police; race-mixing; slavery; white men's countries; women's movements

Wildlife films

In the spring of 2005, emperor penguins were on the move. From their home in Antarctica, they had, within a matter of months, travelled virtually to every continent on the globe. This was not some remarkable feat of biological migration. Rather, it was a triumph of technology, storytelling, and the multinational media industry. The film, *March of the Penguins*, released by Warner Independent Pictures, a subsidiary of the multimedia giant, Warner Brothers Entertainment, made movie history. The Academy Award-winning documentary film by French director Luc Jacquet captured audiences with its stunning cinematography and epic story of struggle and survival in one of the harshest landscapes and climates on Earth. Earning US$128 million in worldwide box-office returns, it also became the second-highest-grossing documentary ever to be released in North America.

Wildlife films may hardly seem the stuff of transnational history, but the production and consumption of animals on film are deeply embedded in material and cultural histories that bring issues of colonialism, political economy, environmental change, race relations, and gender into view. And, like all transnational stories, wildlife films cross boundaries, not only across political territories, but across science and art, and the animal–human divide.

In the early 20th century, hunting with the camera and the gun in quest of scientific discovery became a common test of manhood and an avocation among the patrician class of American and European society. The capture of big game on film affirmed visions of empire and a belief in the superiority of the Anglo-Saxon race. From the early days of cinema, when the famed British photographer, Cherry Kearton, accompanied former American president, conservationist, and great white hunter, Theodore Roosevelt, on African safari in 1909 and took motion pictures of his hunting exploits, film promised to benefit greatly the study of wildlife and its worldwide conservation. Until well into the 1950s, however, natural history films of Africa and Asia often portrayed the continent's indigenous people with less dignity and integrity than that reserved for the majestic species of wildlife. During the 1920s, travelogue-adventure films such as *Simba*, *Congorilla*, *Africa Speaks*, and *Ingagi*, among others, produced by large natural history museums and the emerging Hollywood studio system, attracted urban, white, middle- and upper-class audiences by playing to Hollywood conventions that dramatized the thrill and danger of safari and typecast individual Africans and tribal groups into degrading racial stereotypes. Merian Cooper and Ernest Schoedsack's 1933 blockbuster *King Kong* built upon many of the conventions that had made nature films popular in the previous decade: the mystery, intrigue, and danger of unknown lands; the violence and raw sexuality of nature waiting to be explored; the thrill and adventure of capturing and taming savage beasts; and a narrative of evolutionary and racial hierarchies that put the Anglo-Saxon race at the pinnacle of science, civilization, and modernity.

Although the camera, through an imperial gaze, helped to reinforce Western beliefs in the savagery and exoticness of non-Western people, landscapes, and wildlife, it could also reveal the unimaginable world of animal lives. Jean Painlevé (1902–89),who was active between the 1930s and the 1970s, was one film maker who marvelled at the diversity of life forms and of cinema's ability to see the unseen. Throughout his career, from his early associations with the Surrealists to his brief tenure as director of French cinema to his presidency of the International Association of Scientific Films, Painlevé found in his cinematographic explorations of undersea life the ability of nature to 'play endless tricks' upon us. Moving pictures revealed realities beyond that which the human mind, even in its wildest fantasies, could imagine or comprehend. In the witches' dance of hermaphroditic molluscs or the love life of the octopus, Painlevé treated audiences to a cinema of the unfamiliar, in which he used anthropomorphism to subvert, rather than reinforce, the centrality of humans in nature. Humans simply become one form in a myriad of divergent life forms existing within an amoral universe.

Across the Atlantic, another film maker was also experimenting with hybrid forms of science and art after World War 2 that defied conventional categories. In 1948, Walt Disney released *Beaver Valley*, the first of a series of educational entertainment nature films that the *Motion Picture Herald* placed under a new category, 'True-Life Adventures'. Ten short subjects and four feature-length films later, Disney's True-Life Adventures successfully captured and monopolized a mass market for nature on screen. Both Disney and Painlevé blurred the boundaries of art and science,

finding in music and anthropomorphism the vehicles to bring the emotive and poetic aspects of nature to the fore, but they would take the evolving genre of wildlife films in completely different directions. Whereas Painlevé found in nature the means to displace established conventions, both in cinema and in society, Disney utilized his cinematic renditions of nature to reinforce the moral values of family life, traditional gender roles, and the containment of sexuality within the home.

The financial success of Walt Disney's True Life Adventures, and the explosion of nature shows on television from the BBC, to PBS, to cable networks such as the Discovery Channel and Animal Planet, have turned wildlife into commodities for mass consumption. Animals are readily available worldwide twenty-four hours a day, seven days a week, without ever leaving the confines of home. But why look at animals?, as John Berger asks. Is it because, as cultural critic Akira Mizuta Lippit suggests, cinema has become the virtual shelter for displaced animals as they recede into the shadows of human consumption and environmental destruction? Or perhaps it reflects a desire to transcend the confines of self and species, to understand from the inside what it means to be, or even become, a non-human animal?

Transcendence of the animal–human divide has been a common trope of wildlife films since World War 2. From National Geographic's 1965 film, *Miss Goodall and the Wild Chimpanzees* to the 1988 Warner Brothers' movie *Gorillas in the Mist*, from the 1966 film adaptation of Joy Adamson's *Born Free* to the 2005 Werner Herzog film, *Grizzly Man*, the impossible but irresistible desire to become animal has resonated strongly with ethologists, amateur naturalists, and audiences alike. One touch of nature seemingly makes the whole world kin. But such a view erases the struggles and political conflicts involving people–wildlife interactions that shaped and continue to shape international relations and wildlife conservation efforts in the postcolonial period.

Throughout their history, wildlife films have championed animals as citizens of the world. When, for example, the Office of the Coordinator of Inter-American Affairs sought to promote greater cultural and economic exchange between North and South America in 1941, birds became the vehicle for doing so. In *High Over the Borders*, directed by the highly acclaimed British documentary film maker John Grierson, whose career path from the

General Post Office's film unit in Britain to the National Film Board of Canada to UNESCO embodied the transnational flows of his winged subjects, movie goers were instructed in the folly of believing in exclusive ownership of birds through a visual tour of the flyways of the Canada goose, the hummingbird, swallows, and other migratory birds that bound North and South America into a single biological, cultural, and economic region. In *Winged Migration*, the 2001 acclaimed French documentary directed by Jacques Perrin, birds similarly know 'no barriers' in their flight to the far north. And we cheer for the parrot toward the end of *Winged Migration*, as it tries to unlock the cage in which it is imprisoned, along with other animal compatriots on a boat travelling down the Amazon, snagged in the commercial net of the global pet trade. A sigh of relief comes when it succeeds in breaking free of its restraints; perhaps human domination is never complete. If true, it would be a happy ending of the wildlife film as a moral tale of our time.

Gregg Mitman

Bibliography

Bellows A. M. and McDougall M. (eds) 2000. *Science is fiction: the films of Jean Painlevé*. Cambridge, MA: MIT Press.

Bousé D. 2000. *Wildlife films*. Philadelphia: University of Pennsylvania Press.

Mitman G. 1999. *Reel nature: America's romance with wildlife on film*. Cambridge, MA: Harvard University Press.

Rony F. T. 2001. *The third eye: race, cinema, and ethnographic spectacle*. Durham, NC: Duke University Press.

Related essays
animal diseases; animal rights; biodiversity; conservation and preservation; empires and imperialism; environmentalism; ethnicity and race; film; gender and sex; Hollywood; national parks; Orientalism; tropics; William, James Dixon

Williams, James Dixon *See* Film

Wilson, Woodrow *See* Pax Americana

Wine

Wine, the fermented alcohol of a particular grape (*vitis vinifera*) of Near Eastern origin, is simultaneously a global industrial commodity and an intensely local luxury good.

Already in the 18th century, the European wine industry had become highly commercialized, with markets ranging from cheap bulk wine sold to urban labourers and more refined products destined for the continent's elite. Competition grew in the 19th century as production and distribution spread globally and as improved technology made harvests more reliable. French wine makers responded by asserting commercial distinction based on *terroir*, a term referring to the unique characteristics of particular microclimates and even the soul of the vintner. Although polemicists often contrast a traditional European approach tied to the soil with mass-produced wines from the Americas and Australasia, developments in biotechnology and marketing have brought increasing standardization to the entire industry.

Despite claims of timeless *terroir*, the French have been at the cutting edge of innovation in both production and marketing since the 18th century. Chemists Jean-Antoine Chaptal and Louis Pasteur first set oenology on a scientific footing by explaining the processes of fermentation. Firms such as Veuve Clicquot had pioneered modern techniques of industrial sparkling wine production by the 1820s, and a system of rankings (*crus*) drawn up by a syndicate of Bordeaux wine merchants for the 1855 Paris Exposition continues virtually unchanged as the global benchmark for premium wine. In the early 20th century, the French established a legal regime of *Appellation d Origine Contrôlée* (AOC) to protect wine growing regions such as 'Champagne' from competitors seeking to use their names, both within France and among neighbouring countries. The European Union eventually adopted this system, although it did not stop US firms from marketing brands such as 'Hearty Burgundy' which had no connection with the French original.

Other European producers struggled to keep up with French advances. Growers in the Mosel region of Germany, for example, began to delay the harvest as long as possible to heighten the concentration of sugar in the grapes. This method, begun in the 18th century, was systematized in the 19th century under rankings of *spätlese*, *auslese*, and *beerenaslese* wines. An 1851 tour of French wine regions by Baron Nettino Ricasoli inspired the creation of the Chianti style using sangiovese grapes supplemented by canaiolo, malvasia, and trebbiano.

European technological advances were diffused to temperate zones throughout the world in the 19th century, in many cases supplanting vineyards established in the 16th and 17th centuries by Spanish missionaries in the Americas and Dutch settlers in South Africa. Although little of this wine was shipped back to Europe in the 19th century, proletarian migrations created local demand for nascent New World wine industries. California, for example, profited from the flamboyant Hungarian exile, Agoston Haraszthy, who purchased 100,000 specimens from all over Europe in the 1860s only to lose the collection, along with his vineyards, in bankruptcy. Within a few decades, Haraszthy's successors were shipping large quantities of wine across the continent to labour migrants, particularly Italians, prompting an ethnic slur – 'dago red' – to become a generic term for cheap California wine.

New varietals and methods likewise spread to South America and Australasia in the mid-nineteenth century. Chilean wine makers were particularly avid students of the latest technological innovations, winning acclaim at the Vienna Exposition of 1873. The Argentine wine industry took off in 1885 with the opening of a railroad line from the Mendoza growing region to Buenos Aires, where Italian and Spanish migrants guzzled thirstily. European settlers in Australia and New Zealand also planted vineyards in the late 18th and early 19th centuries, but their expansion was limited by local demand and high transportation costs.

Transoceanic exchanges of vines soon threatened the nascent global wine industry with destruction. Indigenous American grapes were found to be unfit for making wine, but only after they had unleashed devastating diseases and pests. In the 1850s, a white mildew called oidium halved production in France, Italy, and Germany, until sulphur was found to be an effective means of preventing its spread. Phylloxera, an aphid native to the Mississippi Valley, began to infest both Californian and European vineyards around 1860. The louse reproduced rapidly, destroyed vine roots, and even resisted chemical insecticides. By 1890, a cure was found of grafting Old World grapes onto resistant American rootstock, but such replanting proved impossibly expensive for countless traditional growers, particularly in Italy, Spain, and Greece.

New waves of production technology and marketing techniques, along with shifting consumption trends, heralded dramatic changes in the wine industry following World War 2. Until that time, international trade remained almost completely dominated by premium European, especially French, producers. Cheaper wines were virtually all consumed in their region of production, but rapidly growing demand and improved transportation made bulk shipments of low-quality wine economically viable. Such economies of scale in turn allowed wine makers from the Americas and Australasia to seize the initiative from former market leaders in Europe.

The California wine industry had languished under Prohibition from 1920 to 1933, when almost all commercial wineries closed, although table grapes continued to be grown. For decades thereafter, producers had a reputation for excessively sweet, cheap jug wines. Beginning in the 1970s, however, select California wines began to compete for premium markets, while production expanded in the Pacific Northwest. Australian vineyards likewise improved dramatically with the help of a postwar influx of Southern European migrants. More recently, South America, South Africa, and New Zealand also began to acquire export markets, starting at the low end but rapidly increasing in quality.

Technology has contributed to the rapid rise of new wine-making regions and the increasing standardization of global production. Mechanical harvesting devices, while allowing producers to reduce labour costs, have also had consequences for taste. Some experts claim that the wider spacing of vines to accommodate the new machines has increased the sugar content of grapes and obliterated subtle mineral tastes from the wine. Even more dramatic changes have come about from increasing control over the process of fermentation. Producers now have access to a variety of technologies, including cultured yeasts, precise refrigeration controls, micro-oxygenation, and secondary fermentations. As a result, wine makers no longer needed lengthy and expensive cellar ageing to attenuate harsh acids and tannins. Indeed, one of the most controversial new techniques has been adding oak chips to stainless steel tanks rather than ageing the wines in traditional oak barrels. Meanwhile, physical labour within the vineyards has been relegated to migrants, whether North Africans and Eastern Europeans harvesting grapes in Europe or Mexicans in California.

Beginning in the 1990s, an international glut in grapes inspired a wave of industrial consolidation. The result was a series of giant conglomerates led by Australia's Southcorp, the French Pernod Ricard, and the US Constellation brands. Mergers also spread at the local level among cooperative groups and private wine growers. Thus, bankers became increasingly prominent as arbiters of the wine world. Yet despite these trends, the threat of complete homogeneity remains distant, for unlike the soft drink industry dominated by Coke and Pepsi, the two largest wine firms, Constellation and Gallo, control only 5 per cent of global sales. Moreover, boutique producers can still be tremendously profitable.

Changing production methods have inspired critical debates within an industry whose value depends heavily on tradition and mystique. National rivalries underlie many of these disputes: New World producers claim that the European AOC system acts as a break on progress by enshrining 19th-century technological innovations in law. Old World traditionalists respond by demanding that newfangled products be labelled 'industrial wine'. Nevertheless, Europeans also participate in a growing transnational consulting industry of technological specialists. French success in creating sophisticated new brands can be seen in the 'Beaujolais Nouveau', which became an international phenomenon in the 1980s. Debate has also focused on wine critics such as the American Robert Parker, whose numerical ratings can make the difference between profit and loss for vintners. Some lament that these cultural arbiters shape tastes literally as wine makers appeal to a single individual's preferences, thus homogenizing global production.

The financial stakes are extremely high as shifts in consumption habits undermine traditional markets while creating new ones. Since the 1960s, wine consumption has fallen by half among some of the highest per capita consumers including France, Italy, Spain, Argentina, and Chile. This has been offset by a tremendous boom in North American and Asian markets. The primary beneficiaries of these trends have been New World producers, whose exports have expanded by an average of 20 per cent annually since the 1990s, while European producers have grown by less than 5 per cent. As the percentage of wine traded internationally continues to grow, competition will become ever sharper.

Jeffrey M. Pilcher

Bibliography

Anderson K. (ed.) 2004. *The world's wine markets: globalization at work.* Cheltenham: Edward Elgar.

Phillips R. 2001. *A short history of wine.* New York: Ecco/HarperCollins.

Unwin T. 1991. *Wine and the vine: an historical geography of viticulture and the wine trade.* New York: Routledge.

Related essays

commodity trading; contract and indentured labourers; diasporas; drink; expositions; food; human mobility; literature; publishing; temporary migrations; trade

Women's movements

As transnational historical traditions, 'feminism' and 'women's rights' are relatively easy to define, but what about 'women's movements'? Although 'the' women's movement is often spoken of in the singular, the variety of objectives, lack of internal unity and especially differences between national traditions require that 'women's movements' be discussed in the plural. This essay will concentrate on collective efforts of women in the public sphere, particularly those that cross national boundaries. Women's public activities fall along a continuum, at one end of which is 'women's emancipation' and the other 'social reform'. These two categories are by no means mutually exclusive. But while 'emancipatory' actions tend to challenge existing gender definitions, 'social reform' often makes use of them, by elaborating women's traditional responsibility for the dependent and needy classes into a more public role. For this reason, neither female auxiliaries of organizations led by men nor mixed-sex movements with substantial female involvement without explicit programmes for female advancement will be included in this overview. Nonetheless, as efforts at social change, both types of actions altered and expanded existing understandings of women's place. Both also rely on and reinforce women's authority.

Education

Virtually everywhere, expanded formal education has been the first goal of women's movements. Individual women, especially the daughters of learned men, functioned as writers and/or scholars, but as a sex, women were virtually shut out of advanced education and thus from the intellectual and critical skills necessary for political, economic and social advancement. As the 18th-century European Enlightenment made the rational individual the standard of human development, women began to call for greater access to general, rather than sex-specific, knowledge and to base their claims to equality on equal education with men.

Inspired by the French Revolution, Mary Wollstonecraft (1759–97) placed public co-education at the centre of her hopes for the elevation of her sex. Her book, *Vindication of the rights of women* (1792), was translated into French and German. In the young United States, she also found an audience as women were brought into the nation-making project via expanded schooling, on the grounds that it would make them better 'mothers' to their young nations. Campaigns for women's higher education were linked, on the one hand, to the enhanced capacity of women for economic self-support and, on the other, to full citizenship and political rights. Campaigns for women's higher education crossed national boundaries. Russian and American women ambitious for advanced degrees enrolled in German and Swiss universities when their own countries offered them no such opportunities. Japanese female education inspired women in India and China. Christian women missionaries from the West, themselves the beneficiaries of expanded education, established schools for native women. Intended as part of their efforts at Christian uplift, these institutions nonetheless became seedbeds for the leadership of local women's movements. Ewha University, begun in Seoul in 1886 as a Methodist missionary school for girls, remains a major centre of Korean feminism to this day.

Social reform

Concerns for women's education overlapped with a wide variety of women's social reform movements in the 19th century. Groups of elite women, motivated by an expansive understanding of women's maternal and religious obligations, undertook responsibility for society's poor and dependent. In response to large-scale historical changes including industrialization, imperialism, and urbanization, such women sought modest social change, resting on religious revival and moral regeneration, rather than on legal reform or political action. In England in the 1820s, Elizabeth Fry (1780–1845) began her campaign for prison reforms such as sex-segregated jails and female matrons for women prisoners. Her initiatives were emulated and fed into by a cross-national and often Protestant-based network. In the Netherlands, her work inspired Barbara van Meerten-Schilperoort to undertake similar efforts in Gouda, while similar 'ladies' committees' for prison work were established in France, Germany, Switzerland and Denmark.

As with movements for women's education, women's social reform efforts outside of Europe drew on both European models and growing nationalist concerns. This was the case in India, with respect to the practices of child marriage and *sati* (widow immolation). British and American women travellers published accounts of women's degradation in traditional society, but a similar critique was advanced by the first generation of indigenous Indian reformers. The pioneering modern Indian women's social reformer, Pandita Ramabai (1858–1922), went to England and the US in the 1880s to raise money for and awareness of the rescue and education of victims of child marriage and young widowhood.

Temperance was a social reform with special appeal for women, drawing as it did on their resentments at male vice and irresponsibility, especially as they victimized women in their domestic roles. In the closely related social purity movement, women campaigned directly against the sexual double standard and other forms of male sexual exploitation of women. In 1864 Josephine Butler (1828–1906) began a campaign in Great Britain against the government's policy of protecting and regulating prostitution at home and in the Empire. Butler's efforts were broadly influential and inspired the formation of the International Abolitionist Federation in 1875. In the 20th century, concern with prostitution focused on the so-called 'white slave' trade, involuntary prostitution, itself a transnational phenomenon.

Early communities of women social reformers often gathered around common religious perspectives. In England and the

US, these were overwhelmingly Protestant, with Quakers playing an especially important role in fostering a transatlantic movement. In Latin America, however, the first elite women to come together around concerns for the poor and dependent, including working women, were Catholic, responding to what they regarded as the unacceptable secularism and female-excluding liberalism of their governments

The International Council of Women (ICW), founded in Washington, DC in 1888, spread moderate women's social reform movements around the world. Affiliated councils of women were often the first multipurpose women's organizations formed in their respective countries. The National Council of Argentina Women, founded in 1900, was the first in Latin America. As an international stage for women's activism, the ICW somewhat ironically rested on, indeed encouraged, national identity and pride, providing a venue for women to assert their place in a range of social projects of national uplift and promotion. This common sense of national pride along with a shared elite status among the women of the ICW allowed for a sense of international sisterhood despite the existence (and at times celebration) of national difference. ICW women were careful to avoid the taint of women's rights and other radical reforms. Although less radical than the women involved in openly emancipatory women's movements, those active in social reform efforts moved out of a confined domestic space into a more public environment, and developed expanded skills and outlooks in the process.

Emancipation

The first phase of the more explicitly emancipatory women's movement known as women's rights is usually associated with the European revolutions of 1848. The term 'emancipation' linked women's demands for legal equality with other transnational liberatory movements of the period, among wage workers, serfs, Catholics and Jews. The involvement of women on both sides of the Atlantic in the movement to end chattel slavery was particularly important in encouraging the growth of women's rights campaigns. Because of the geographic breadth of these upheavals and the networks of communication between women involved in them, historian Bonnie Anderson identifies

this as 'the first international women's movement'.

Inasmuch as democratic political rights were being claimed for the first time for European men, women emancipationists demanded equal economic and political rights for women as well. In Paris, Jeanne Deroin (1805–94)and Pauline Roland (1805–52) spearheaded a movement centred on women's rights to full political participation, followed avidly by similarly minded activists in Germany, Austria and elsewhere. A small but thriving women's rights press spread awareness of female revolutionary activism in Europe and beyond. The defeat of the mid-19th-century European revolutions resulted in political repression, explicitly excluding any overt political activity among women, which both retarded subsequent women's rights activity and spread it via the mechanism of exile. Thus Mathilde Anneke (1817–84) came from Germany to the United States, where she lent her experience to women's rights activity.

The two countries most associated with the rise of women's rights activism in the mid 19th century, the US and England, did not go through such dramatic upheavals. Nonetheless, British and US women were deeply affected by the emancipatory spirit of the age. Most of the women involved in the early US women's rights movement were veterans of the radical domestic and transatlantic campaigns to rid the United States of the taint of chattel slavery, and their concern for freedom for slaves produced a longing for self-emancipation. Led by Elizabeth Cady Stanton (1815–1902), a young mother of four, and Lucretia Mott (1793–1880), a leading Quaker abolitionist from Philadelphia, the first meeting they held, the Seneca Falls Convention, called in July 1848 for enhanced economic, educational, political and social rights. They knew about and celebrated the efforts of revolutionary women in Germany, Italy and France.

In England, Harriet Taylor (1807–58) was inspired by US events to write an article on 'The enfranchisement of women' that her soon-to-be husband John Stuart Mill elaborated in his influential book, The subjection of women (1867). Via Mill's writings, these Anglo-American liberal women's rights ideas had unprecedented impact. Translations of Mill played formative roles in women's rights movements from Sweden to Japan. Early women's rights advocacy in Asia accompanied the spread of liberal ideas and republican ambitions. In both India and China, the first exponents of women's rights ideas were men, who were committed to modernizing Hinduism and Confucianism respectively. In the 1880s in Japan, a liberal reform campaign known as the Popular Rights Movement inspired a handful of women, including Kishida Toshiko and Kusunose Kita, to agitate for their own rights.

Labour
Middle-class women active in both the female social reform and women's rights movements were concerned with the growing numbers of wage-earning women. As victims of rampant industrialization, the majority of working women suffered from low wages, sexual harassment, and severely limited job opportunities. Yet, when decently paid and trained, they represented the promise of economic independence crucial to female emancipation. As national economies became more industrialized, women workers gathered the skills and self-confidence to become, not just objects of female activism, but activists on their own behalf. Even so, well into the 20th century, women's movements disagreed as to whether working women should be removed from the inescapable inequalities of the labour force or unite to win improvement in their conditions and prospects.

Male workers traditionally tended to see women as economic competitors and/or domestic dependents, not comrades in the struggle of labour. Such opposition was particularly strong in France. Shut out from the male-dominated trade union movement, working women turned for support to middle-class women. In the US Mary Kenney O'Sullivan and Leonora O'Reilly, both women labour veterans and Irish immigrants, reached out for middle-class female allies to form an American version of the English Emma Patterson's Women's Protection and Provident League. The US Women's Trade Union League also benefited from the experience and energy of Australian Alice Henry who had been active in the labour movement in her own country. Wage-earning women who had immigrated from Eastern and Southern Europe brought their own traditions of workplace activism to these efforts.

Fearful that such movements were making headway among women wage earners, socialist parties in Europe and the US authorized the formation of an international socialist women's initiative in the 1890s. At its centre was German socialist Clara Zetkin (1857–1933). Women's socialist organizations were formed in Germany, France, Italy, the US and elsewhere. By the early 1900s it was possible to speak of a distinct Socialist Women's International. In Argentina, socialist women formed an alternative to the conventional middle-class leaders of the National Council of Women and called openly for women's political and economic rights. The socialist women's movement endorsed women's enfranchisement, which helped to generate pro-suffrage activism among working-class women. In exchange, Zetkin accepted the party's position in favour of labour regulations directed solely at working women. Zetkin argued that sex-based labour laws 'protected' working women.

By the early 20th century, middle-class women's movements were coming to share the socialist belief that sex-based labour legislation shielded working women from the ravages of capitalism. It was manifest at the ICW Conference in Berlin (1904) that middle-class advocates of women's rights, who had traditionally opposed so-called protective labour legislation exclusively for women workers, began to reconsider their position. Their approaches were 'maternalist', meaning both that they focused on the motherhood (or potential motherhood) of working women and that they positioned themselves as maternal care givers to the larger society. The principle behind the legislation they advocated was that the state had an interest in protecting women's child-bearing capacities, by shielding them from exploitative wage labour. In promoting social welfare and industrial reform legislation, they modernized the social reform tradition of an early phase of women's movements.

The American Florence Kelley (1859–1932), herself directly inspired by her youthful sojourn among European socialists and by the German model of state regulation of industrialization, was the social welfare leader par excellence, securing laws which limited the hours which women could work and established minimum wage standards. German middle-class women activists learned from Kelley to champion and reshape limits on wage labour for women workers. In countries such as Switzerland

and France, where male workers had been the most hostile to women workers, middle-class women resisted sex-based labour laws, but eventually embraced the pro-regulation position.

Suffrage

Suffrage, the demand most associated with women's movements in the early 20th century, drew on all these strands. Greater educational and economic rights prepared the way for full campaigns for equal citizenship, while temperance, socialist and social welfare activists required political tools to pursue their goals. The first successful national woman suffrage campaigns were on the outskirts of the British Empire, in New Zealand in 1893 and Australia in 1902. There the Woman's Christian Temperance Union (WCTU), a US-based organization that by the 1880s had expanded its reach across the Pacific, organized for the ballot as a weapon for women to wield to 'protect the home'. Socialist women's organizing underlay the first successful European suffrage movement, in Finland in 1906. Although focused on national citizenship, suffrage activists conceived of their efforts transnationally (more precisely transatlantically), forming the International Woman Suffrage Alliance in 1902. They celebrated each national enfranchisement as a movement victory, and took inspiration from each other's efforts.

The US campaign for woman suffrage was the longest. It began in the spirit of national rebirth and moral cleansing after the defeat of slavery in the American Civil War but over time shifted to more exclusive conceptions of women's contribution to national progress. Counterforces occasionally came from the outside, as when the African American suffragist Mary Church Terrell (1863–1954) came to the notice of Susan B. Anthony (1820–1906) at an international meeting in Germany, because there her race did not disallow appreciation for her abilities and contributions. Although its leaders, from Susan B. Anthony to Carrie Chapman Catt (1859–1947), were instigating figures in international suffragism, the American movement served as an inspiration primarily to other New World republics, rather than in Europe.

By contrast, the British suffrage movement was enormously influential internationally, both because of its spectacular tactics and because of the breadth of British imperial influence. Women's frustration at politicians' inaction produced a new and dramatic tactical repertoire ranging from mass parades to civil disobedience to prison hunger strikes in order to force parliamentary action. These English militants were known as 'suffragettes' and they were much imitated, from the US, where women were arrested and force-fed, to Nanking in 1910, where Chinese women threatened to immolate themselves to gain the vote. In 1919 in Cairo, veiled upper-class women demonstrated outside of the Egyptian parliament for the same reason. Women began to receive the parliamentary vote in England in 1918, but full and equal suffrage did not come until 1928, an irony given this worldwide notoriety.

Many European countries enfranchised women in the wake of World War I, especially in the dissolving empires of Russia and Austria-Hungary. Eurocentric assumptions notwithstanding, however, France, Italy, Belgium and Switzerland refused this trend. Meanwhile, the winds of suffrage activism were shifting in other directions. In 1935, Turkey became the first Islamic country to enfranchise women, enlivening efforts throughout the Middle East. Beginning in the 1930s, suffragists were especially successful in Latin America, which was buffered from the worst of the reactionary political developments of the period. Despite international suffragist efforts, the League of Nations refused to engage with a question it considered to be fundamentally national. Finally, in 1954, the United Nations reversed this policy and formally called for full political rights for women in all member nations. As a result, the next decade witnessed numerous enfranchisements, including in countries such as Mexico and Egypt in which women had been agitating for the vote for decades.

Peace and anti-colonialism

In addition to many suffrage victories, the World War I era brought the tradition of women's pacifism into new prominence. In 1915, in an effort to find a peaceful way out of the spreading military conflict in Europe, women from Europe and North America met in The Hague, in the Netherlands. Jane Addams (1860–1935), the distinguished American social reformer and suffragist, chaired the meeting. For her continued pacifist advocacy, she was widely maligned in her own country but was also honoured (in 1931) as a Nobel Laureate. Out of this meeting came the Women's International League for Peace and Freedom (WILPF), one of the transnational women's organizations of the period with the most international reach. It pressed for international disarmament, in a futile effort to hold back a second world war.

During these same years, an alternative framework for women's movements was becoming stronger outside of the West: anti-colonialism. Women's movements in Asia and the Middle East tended to share nationalist ambitions with male reformers and thus to cooperate with them. Even so, women's anti-colonial movements challenged hesitant male allies to support openly political roles for women and explicitly women's rights demands such as political equality and reform in marriage and family law. The Indian and Egyptian campaigns for women's enfranchisement were among the first and most influential, beginning in the wake of the First World War among elite, often educated women. Through the 1920s these movements were encouraged by European suffrage veterans, as colonial activists attended international meetings, albeit as exotic outsiders. By the 1930s, however, nationalist-suffragists were becoming more openly anti-imperialist, expanding the mass bases of their national movements, and redirecting themselves to alliances with their 'Eastern' sisters.

Feminism

The term 'feminism' first appeared during the World War 1 era in France and then rapidly spread through English and other linguistic variations. Its adherents were younger, their concerns were more individualistic, and they were the beneficiaries of gains in education, occupation, and the franchise. While earlier campaigns such as temperance addressed women's domestic discontents, feminists sought to bring the same kind of dramatic change that had transformed women's public lives to personal concerns such as marriage, sexuality and child bearing. Feminism rejected the expansive public maternalism that had brought earlier generations of women into public activism. The older generation for its part was decidedly uncomfortable with the sexual dimension of feminists' redefinition of women's rights. Instead of concentrating on service to others, feminism encouraged women to explore and elaborate their own selves; instead of focusing on the corporate power of 'womanhood', they militantly claimed 'individualism' equally for women and men. At international meetings and before the League of Nations in the 1920s and 1930s, older and younger generations clashed over political and personal style.

Feminists had their own theoreticians of women's emancipation. The Swedish writer Ellen Key (1846–1929) called for economically independent and sexually liberated mothers. Translations of Key's work made her as influential to a generation of 'new women' as Mill had been in the mid 19th century. In Japan, poet Hiratsuka Raicho (1886–1971) translated and advocated Key's ideas, and organized the Bluestockings, inspiring a similar 'new woman' movement in Korea in the 1920s. Revolutionary ideas about gender and personal life also played a major role in the 1919 'May Fourth' movement in China, dedicated to uprooting traditional Confucian hierarchy from family and personal life. Feminist writer Ding Ling (1904–86) carried May Fourth ideas into the early years of Chinese Communism.

The birth control movement, which sought not only to emancipate women from involuntary motherhood but to free female sexuality from the ever-present possibility of child bearing, was the first major activist expression of this new feminism. The birth control movement was transnational as women sought information abroad that was not available to them in their own societies. Margaret Sanger (1879–1966), who is usually identified as the founding figure of the birth control movement, learned about contraception from Aletta Jacobs (1854–1929) of the Netherlands, who in turn had learned about it in Germany. In addition to her role in breaking down legal and medical barriers to women's contraceptive ambitions in the US, Sanger introduced birth control ideas and methods internationally. Shizue Ishimoto Kato (1897–2001), a socialist and feminist, brought Sanger and her ideas to Japan in the 1920s. Australian Jesse Street (1889–1970) linked feminist activism, birth control advocacy, and sympathy with anti-colonial nationalism from this period into the post-World War 2 and early United Nations years.

The 'second wave'

Vigorous women's movements with a transnational character re-emerged in the late

1960s. While earlier women's groups tended to draw on images of maternal power, this new wave was connected to the sexual and cultural revolutions of the young, as well as to protests against US neo-imperialism, and worldwide anti-colonial and anti-racist movements. To distinguish themselves from earlier generations of women activists, the women's movements of the 1960s associated themselves with a new term, 'women's liberation'. Originating nearly simultaneously in locations as diverse as the United States and Japan, the Netherlands and Australia, this new generation of women's movements gradually spread much more broadly, in part through United Nations sponsorship of a series of worldwide women's conferences from 1975 through 1995.

Female activism in the last third of the 20th century has been called the 'second wave' of women's movements. But viewed from a transnational perspective, the gap between the two eras looks far narrower. For instance, these new women's movements built on previous birth control achievements to emphasize women's control over their reproduction, sexuality, and health, with the issue of abortion one of the flash points worldwide for women's activism and anti-feminist reaction.

As with earlier women's movements, education has remained an important issue. The form that it took in the late 20th century was the development of a specialized field of scholarship, women's studies, directed to changes in women's status and openly activist. The intellectual content of women's studies is decidedly transnational, while the institutional form that it takes varies from nation to nation, sometimes focused on helping female students to find their place in the world, sometimes on social science research to aid feminist policy makers. Women's studies scholarship has been particularly influential in the area of international development, where it has produced a major re-evaluation of the impact of modernization policies on women's status. The field of women's studies first developed in the US but now institutions and centres can be found in more than nearly 60 countries. Among other agencies, the Ford Foundation and the United Nations have encouraged internationalization of the field and links between it and area studies scholars.

Perhaps the most characteristic and influential concern of modern women's movements has been the issue of violence against women. Rape has been dramatically reconceptualized as an endemic crime, not of passion but of power, occurring not only between strangers but within marriage and among acquaintances. Awareness has dramatically increased about other forms of violence against women such as domestic assault and workplace harassment. Organized women have marched militantly through city streets to 'take back the night', pressed police agencies to take rape accusations more seriously and established their own shelters for women and children escaping violence in the home. International Women's Day was first celebrated in a mass way in India at an anti-rape demonstration in Bombay (Mumbai) in 1980. On the international stage, women activists have successfully campaigned for recognition that rape during wartime should be punished as a serious human rights abuse.

Ellen Carol DuBois

Bibliography

Anderson B. 2000. *Joyous greetings: the first international women's movement, 1830–1860.* Oxford and New York: Oxford University Press.

Dubois E. C. 'Woman suffrage around the world: three phases of woman suffrage internationalism,' in Daley C. and Nolan M. (eds) 1994. *Suffrage and beyond: international feminist perspectives,* New York: New York University Press, pp. 252–74.

Evans R. 1984. *The feminists: women's emancipation movements in Europe, America and Australasia, 1840–1920.* London: Croom Helm.

Freedman E. 2002. *No turning back: the history of feminism and the future of women.* New York: Ballantine.

Jayawardena K. 1986. *Feminism and nationalism in the Third World.* London: Zed.

Mill J. S. 1869. *The subjection of women.* London: Longman's, Green.

Rupp L. 1997. *Worlds of women: the making of an international women's movement.* Princeton: Princeton University Press.

Sklar K. K., Schuler A. and Strasser S. 1998. *Social feminists in the United States and Germany: a dialogue in documents, 1885–1933.* Ithaca: Cornell University Press.

Wieringa S. (ed.) 1988. *Women's struggles and strategies.* Aldershot: Gower.

Jacobs, Aletta 1854–1929

Aletta Jacobs was the founding mother of many aspects of Dutch feminism: higher education, suffrage, birth control, pacifism. She was born in 1854 in Groningen Province, the Netherlands, the eighth child of a liberal Jewish middle-class family. In 1892, she married her companion Carel Gerritsen, another Dutch physician and reformer; they had no children.

She was the first Dutch woman to complete formal medical education and her practice, focused on women in the slums of Amsterdam, inspired her to find a way to help women avoid unwanted pregnancies. Encouraged by British women physicians, she found her answer in 1878 in an antecedent of the vaginal diaphragm, the Mensinga pessary, developed in Germany. In 1915, Jacobs shared her knowledge with Margaret Sanger, who brought the device back to the US.

Jacobs was also an ardent suffragist. In 1883, she attempted to register to vote, in response to which Dutch law was clarified to disfranchise women explicitly. In 1894, she became president of the Dutch Woman Suffrage Association and remained so until Dutch women won the vote in 1919. Jacobs was also active in the International Woman Suffrage Association, which held its second meeting in Amsterdam, at her invitation. In 1911–12, along with Carrie Chapman Catt, president of the International Woman Suffrage Association, Jacobs went China, Indonesia, South Africa and Egypt to meet with women and discuss women's emancipation.

Last but not least, Jacobs was active in the pacifist movement. In 1915, Jacobs was the central figure in the convening of an international women's anti-war meeting in The Hague. While the meeting's efforts at encouraging negotiation failed to avert war, they resulted in a new international organization, the Women's International League for Peace and Freedom.

Ellen Carol DuBois

Bibliography
Bosch M. 2005. *Een onwrikbaar geloof in rechtvaardigheid: Aletta Jacobs, 1854–1929.* Uitgeverij: Balans.

Workers' movements

The current vogue of 'globalization', popularly used to describe a wide range of contemporary phenomena of international integration ranging from free trade to cosmopolitan cultures to current workers' movement responses, has the singular merit of directing attention to the importance of international processes in the making of workers' movements. Global interconnections are a decisive element of modernity and capitalism, and contemporary globalization is only one phase in a larger historical trend in the last four centuries. This suggests the importance of understanding popular class formation as an international process shaped by global forces, whose significance varies over time. It is useful to reconsider workers' movements from the perspective of what Marcel van der Linden calls 'transnational labour history', which questions the use of the nation state as basic unit of analysis for understanding labour history.

In relativizing and historicizing the nation state, transnational labour history directs attention towards examining workers' movements from a global perspective, stressing the role of transnational processes and interconnections in shaping labour history and the importance of comparative analysis. A national focus was characteristic of both old labour history, focused on institutions and leaders, and new labour history, which examined cultures and identities. Thus, E. P. Thompson's masterwork took the 'English working class' as its focus; it did not really examine the imperial and international context that Thompson's own material indicated was an important influence. Thus, without discounting the importance of 'national' factors in workers' movements, transnational labour history questions assumptions that workers' movements necessarily develop into national-level movements, or are primarily shaped by forces operating within the boundaries of the nation state, and thereby raises questions about the standard practices of framing labour histories as a series of national narratives. Transnational workers' movements are not, we argue, the exceptional moments of interconnection in a history of workers' movements which supposedly normally and naturally assume a national form. On the contrary, transnational workers' movements are a central, recurrent and, at times, primary feature of the history of the popular classes.

It is important, then, to situate the development of workers' movements within the context of transnational, national as well as local, dynamics and developments. Transnational labour history also raises fundamental questions about the class categories and conceptual repertoire used in understanding labour movements. A global perspective, by drawing attention to a wide variety of evolving labour processes and labour relations over the last few centuries, and in suggesting that these multiple arrangements form part of a global division of labour within an evolving capitalist system with an evolving global character, transnational labour history points to the need for a wider understanding of basic concepts like 'labour', 'workers', and the 'working class' itself. A transnational labour history for the modern period should, arguably, include the history of slaves, tenant farmers, independent artisans and peasants, as well as of wage earners, both free and unfree.

In line with these points, this entry examines transnational workers' movements from the perspective of the *longue dureé* of modernity, with particular attention to the role of transnational connections,

solidarities and organizations. It does not restrict itself to a classical Marxist understanding of the working class as simultaneously 'free' of both ownership of the means of production and extra-economic coercion. The routine use against wage labour of direct coercion, debt-bondage systems and indenture militates against such an understanding, while workers have continually overlapped with classes like peasants and independent artisans.

Linked by flows of people, ideas, models of organization and repertoires of struggle, located within evolving international and regional political economies and labour markets, transnational workers' movements have been a recurrent development, often surging forward during international crises, when pulses of revolt have swept through the popular classes and accelerated connections across the borders of provinces, colonies, empires and nation states, as well as of those of nationality and race. Our approach problematizes setting up neat binaries between so-called 'first' and 'third' worlds, or their popular classes, or assuming Eurocentric diffusion models of intellectual history. It draws attention to the importance of multiple and overlapping, yet often international, proletarian public spheres. Modifying A. G. Hopkins' schema of historical globalization, it is useful to distinguish between the protoglobalization in the 17th and 18th centuries (marked by the rise of the Atlantic economy of maritime enterprise, the plantation system and early manufacturing), the 'first' modern globalization in the late 19th and early 20th centuries (associated with industrialization and revolutions in communications and transportation), a period of relative deglobalization from the 1920s into the 1970s, and the 'second' modern globalization that followed.

Workers' movements in protoglobalization

The 'protoglobalization' of the 17th and 18th centuries was characterized by the development of an Atlantic economy centred on the slave trade in Africa, the plantation system in the Americas and elsewhere, and expanding if generally preindustrial manufacturing in Western Europe. Agricultural products like cotton, tea and tobacco were central, and there was mass migration across the Atlantic by African slaves to the Americas and the Caribbean, as well as by indentured and free Europeans, with indentured Europeans a large part of plantation labour.

Unfree labour dominated this configuration. The sailors working the Middle Passage were largely unfree, as were most Whites sent to Australia. Besides plantations worked by unfree labour, there were the *haciendas* of Latin America, supplied with labour through coercive systems like the *repartimiento*, debt bondage and various forms of tenant farming. Khoisan indentured servants, African and Asian slaves, and bonded Europeans provided the labour supply in the Dutch East Indies' Cape colony in Africa.

Slaves, unfree and free workers in Europe and the Americas, poor White peasants driven to the margins by the plantations, and the naval and military proletariat, constituted the key components of what Peter Linebaugh and Marcus Rediker call the 'Atlantic working class' in their path-breaking study. Organized around the world of maritime labour, agriculture, manufacturing and long-distance trade, this was involved in events like the English Revolution, Bacon's Rebellion, the American War of Independence, naval mutinies, the riots of the London mob, and Irish uprisings. Linebaugh and Rediker focus on the North Atlantic, but their arguments can be usefully extended to the larger world. There was, for example, a wave of slave risings across the British Empire after the slave trade was ended, in the Caribbean, Latin America and southern Africa; the successful anti-colonial revolts in Latin America can, likewise, be located within the great pulse of revolt of the late 18th and early 19th centuries.

Of great interest for this period are interracial connections, exemplified by figures like Robert Wedderburn, the former Jamaican slave active in extremist circles in early 19th-century London. C. L. R. James' study of the slave revolt in Haiti in the 1790s, for example, argued that the revolt was part of the larger moment usually labelled the 'French' Revolution, that the risings in Haiti and France radicalized one another, and contributed directly to the end of slavery in the French Empire. Linebaugh and Rediker, likewise, stress the multiracial character of the 'Atlantic working class' and its revolts. It was the circulation of ideas and activists across this world, linking struggles by sailors, slaves, soldiers, workers and peasants, and the common experience of authoritarian rule and unfree labour, that

provided the basis for this remarkable popular interracialism.

Can we speak of labour internationalism in this period? Not if we mean a formal international of unions and parties. This was a period before such organizations became common; the characteristic forms of protest were violent, insurrectionary, sometimes informal, sometimes conspiratorial. This was partly the consequence of an inability of non-proletarian groups to establish ongoing, point-of-production organizations, as well as of the routine use of coercion and terror in the structuring of class relations.

If we look, however, at other forms of organization, such as Maroon societies, cooperatives, and radical clubs and corresponding societies, and the networks between them, made by a radical press and circulation of activists, it is possible to think of informal internationalism(s) and the development of a popular public sphere spanning countries, empires and continents. In this preindustrial period, the labouring classes were multiple and overlapping: this was a period of plebeian solidarities expressed in identities like 'the people'. An important case was popular abolitionism, which in Britain (for example) found its strongest support amongst the lower classes.

Workers' movements in the first modern globalization

The industrial revolution of the late 18th century ushered in a new period of rapid global interconnection and accelerating proletarianization, culminating in the first modern globalization of the late 19th century. The 'Great Acceleration' described by C. A. Bayly, based on expanding and cheap steam and rail transport, the proliferation of telegraphs and newspapers, and of growing global flows of populations, was under way. European imperial expansion and the growth of international trade and migration laid the basis for new forms of global politics.

At the same time, the popular classes were restructured by the emergence of full-fledged, if unevenly developed, capitalism, and by changing patterns of migration. The independent artisans and peasantry (the focus of much of Thompson's study of the 'working class') were undermined by industrialization in town and country. Slavery was largely abolished by the 1880s, and wage labour – both free and unfree – assumed an ever-increasing weight worldwide. As slavery declined, so did African migration; as proletarianization increased in Europe and Asia and southern Africa, and as late industrialization took hold outside of Northern Europe, millions of Asians and Europeans migrated between, and within, the Americas, Australasia, East Europe and parts of Africa. Indentured labour from the Indian subcontinent and China was widely used throughout the world as a source of cheap labour, especially in agriculture.

Rapid proletarianization and urbanization were associated with the rise of new forms of organization, notably unions and mass political parties appropriate to the new period, and a growing proletariat. Other forms of popular organization nonetheless persisted or developed: the spread of early women's movements internationally, and the importance of rent strikes and community struggles caution against conflating working-class movements with unions and parties in this period.

Unlike the earlier period, this was a time of increasingly formal international linkages, with efforts going back to the 1830s culminating in the International Workingmen's Association (IWMA) in 1864. Within the IWMA, a critique of Marxism (which emerged in the 1840s, placing its hopes in the factory proletariat, mass parties and state power) fostered the emergence of a new 'anarchist' tradition (which elaborated revolutionary unionism, or syndicalism, sought to organize peasants, and championed self-management). Both traditions promoted universal symbols and rituals, like May Day, and were associated with new repertoires of struggle, such as strikes, petitions, sabotage, go-slows, and, where the franchise was available, class-based voting. A third tradition of moderate pro-labour reformism was also evident in the IWMA, helping lay the basis for the third major ideological strand within the workers' movement: Labourism or social democracy.

The IWMA was remarkable for uniting popular class organizations in the West with those in Latin America and North Africa, and also included affiliates that spanned countries, like the Slavic section founded by Mikhail Bakunin. The rise of unions and parties did not, however, simply supplant informal connections and linkages: on the contrary, the popular press, travelling agitators and migrant workers all played a key role in spreading the new organizational models and struggle repertoires across the globe.

Transnational networks of activists and a radical press, moving within international flows of people and ideas, were critical: Italian anarchists, for instance, linked movements in Argentina, Brazil, Egypt and Greece, while Chinese networks linked anarchism in China, France, Japan, Korea, Malaya and Vietnam.

After the IWMA collapsed, there were various moves to form a new international. The anarchists launched a short-lived Black International in 1881, followed by repeated attempts to form a stable international, finally succeeding with the formation of the syndicalist International Workers' Association / Asociación Internacional de los Trabajadores (IWA/AIT) in 1922. It was, however, largely at the level of the network that anarchism and syndicalism developed as an international movement that linked its local, national and regional organizations. The Marxists and social democrats were more successful in terms of formal internationalism, forming the Labour and Socialist International as well as the International Secretariat of National Trade Union Centres, later renamed the International Federation of Trade Unions (IFTU).

The different wings of the workers' movement in this period took an overtly formal character, yet the parties and unions were often embedded in more informal structures. Sections of the Labour and Socialist International, for example, were organized as parties, but in Germany and elsewhere, the larger parties also established significant countercultures, including neighbourhood groups, bars, sports clubs and popular libraries and schools. This development had its parallel in the anarchist and syndicalist project of developing revolutionary countercultures and counterpower, culminating in dense networks of insurgent popular associational life in the movement's great strongholds, such as Argentina and Spain.

A formal commitment to internationalism was important in this period, yet international aspirations were rarely realized in practice. The Labour and Socialist International was primarily a labour international for Greater Europe, and strikingly absent elsewhere. Anarchists and syndicalists, on the other hand, were an important force in parts of Europe and North America, played some role in the Middle East and Africa, and the dominant force on the left in East Asia and Latin America before the 1920s.

The gap between international rhetoric and sectional reality had various causes. The ideological divisions in the workers' movement of the times (like the Marxist dictum that socialism was only feasible in advanced capitalism) played a role, while rivalry between the wings of the workers' movement made it difficult to form an inclusive international.

The non-denominational Atlantic 'working class' of the protoglobalization period was fractured by the rise of nationalism and racial ideology, and by official moves to reconstitute or create specifically 'national' working classes identified with particular states. This was given a powerful impetus from above by the rise of institutions like mass schooling, by the racialization of imperial structures, as well as by the national oppression that imperialism often entailed. From below, the struggle to democratize the state also had the effect of increasing the identity of working classes as actors on a primarily national stage, while nationalism also infused large sections of the workers' movement. To the extent that national states became viewed as potential vehicles for class as well as national and racial liberation, so too did aspirations for nation states grow.

The common experience of unfree labour, which had played a role in the interracial solidarities in protoglobalization, was undermined by a growing racial division of labour (in which free labour was often White, and unfree labour was generally not), and employers pitted free against unfree labour. As proletarianization proceeded, labour market competition became sharper, providing an ongoing basis for ethnic, national and racial antagonisms within the international working class. International connections could, then, also lead workers and workers' movements to become more aware of, and more loyal to, national and other non-class identities, cultivating these as well as expressing them within international organizations as bases for particularistic claims.

In these ways, the international character of the working class, and its tendency towards a transnational workers' movement, were undermined by the pressures towards sectionalism. These developments were the backdrop for the rise of segregationist White Labourism in the British Empire and the United States of America, which combined social democracy with racial exclusion. Garveyism, with its 'race first' policies and plebeian base, could be regarded as expressing a similar tendency to combine race and class demands, although the 'Negro State' to which it aspired was never constituted. In both cases, rhetorics of labour internationalism overlapped with racial politics: in South Africa, for instance, the (White) Labour Party advocated socialism plus segregation, while in the (African and Coloured) Industrial and Commercial Workers Union, Garveyism coexisted uneasily with syndicalist ideas derived from the Industrial Workers of the World, with its vision of One Big Union of workers.

If the lived experience of transnationality helps account for the appeal of internationalist ideas amongst mobile workers in the first modern globalization, then, it does not follow that there was any simple linkage between transnational lives and internationalist politics. Nationalist networks amongst Africans, Cubans, Germans, Indians, Irish, Jews, Koreans, Poles and others also flowed within the human rivers of labour that straddled the globe; doctrines such as Garveyism, pan-Africanism, nascent pan-Islamism and White Labourism, which stressed national, racial or religious solidarities, were as common as truly internationalist outlooks. Flows of activists, people and ideas could easily spread exclusive, rather than inclusive, forms of organization.

Workers' movements and deglobalization

Starting with the First World War (1914–18), a period of deglobalization began, taking hold in the 1920s with the rise of closed national economies as well as the spread of nation states with imperial collapse after 1917 and again after the Second World War (1939–45). The world wars, which drew in millions of working-class people, also played a role in fostering national and racial antagonisms, undermining internationalism (as demonstrated by the collapse of the Labour and Socialist International in 1914), and in socializing great masses into nationalist ideology.

On the eve of the end of the first modern globalization, however, the world was rocked by a massive pulse of proletarian and colonial revolt: this started in Ireland and Mexico in 1916, surged forward with the Russian Revolution, swept around the globe, and was drowned in repression by 1924. If the Labour and Socialist International had failed the test of its formal commitments to anti-militarism and international solidarity, important new workers' internationals emerged in the postwar period: the Communist International (Comintern), the IWA/AIT, and the Communist Workers' International. The horrors of the war, the socialist hopes engendered by the Russian Revolution, and the international economic crisis, led to popular radicalism on an incredible scale, with the biggest strike wave ever, and a series of revolutionary uprisings.

When this upsurge ended deglobalization took place in earnest. Nationalist regimes imposed economic protectionism in Latin America, parts of Eastern Europe, as well as in southern Africa; fascists created authoritarian regimes stressing the virtues of nation and race; socialism became increasingly identified with the new Union of Soviet Socialist Republics, rather than with the international workers' movement; radical labour movements like those grouped in the IWA/AIT were crushed; workers' movements generally were repressed, or brought into national-level class compromises; the relatively laissez-faire immigration system was replaced with a universal passport regime.

The Great Depression, and the subsequent rise of demand-management policies in the West, accelerated the trend towards national economies, as did the collapse of the remaining empires and the rise of scores of new states, identified with nationalism or the Soviet model. As nation states spread and their power over everyday life increased, as nationalism became the dominant ideology, and as socialism became identified with loyalty to the Soviet bloc and its allied 'progressive' regimes, the space for transnational workers' movements and internationalist imaginations declined.

Deglobalization was, of course, relative: in the global boom of the 1950s and 1960s, world trade increased 800 per cent, commodity production expanded 40 times, and the modern multinational corporation first emerged. The boom entrenched the trend towards national-level class compromises, enabling rising real wages and welfare reforms in the context of a declining peasantry, rapid urbanization, and a new wave of industrialization, the latter expressed dramatically by the Newly Industrializing Countries (NICs) (including those of the Soviet bloc). There was, meanwhile, substantial if highly regulated international immigration, often into the Middle East and Greater Europe (by 1980, as Ronaldo Munck notes, there were 22 million economically active migrants not possessing citizenship in their country of employment), as well as significant migration within regions.

If the number of the world's workers grew dramatically in both absolute and relative terms, the possibilities for workers to unite across borders were undermined by the lived reality of national life and by the absence of internationalist bodies of the sort that had proliferated in the first modern globalization. The International Labour Organization (ILO), formed in 1919, acted as a forum for developing global labour standards, but it was a tripartite body, rather than a workers' international. The Comintern provided a rallying point for radical workers, and was more successful than its Marxian predecessor in drawing the popular classes of Asia and elsewhere into alliances with Western labour, but its use as an instrument of Russian foreign policy, its dissolution in 1943, and the acceptance of 'national' roads to socialism limited Communism's ability to foster internationalism and transnational organizing.

Other international bodies provided few alternatives. The IWA/AIT was in crisis and decline by the end of the 1930s, like anarchism and syndicalism more generally. The IFTU and the International Trade Secretariats (ITS) dating back to the 1890s developed as moderate bureaucratic bodies whose internationalism was generally feeble and largely diplomatic; affiliates tended to concentrate on national-level issues. The revived Labour and Socialist International was primarily a loose body of parties with a national focus. As the Cold War set in, the World Federation of Trade Unions (WFTU) formed in 1945 fractured, and the International Confederation of Free Trade Unions (ICFTU) was established on Western initiative. The bureaucracies of both internationals were deeply embroiled in the activities of rival state blocs.

Active internationalism was largely found outside of formal international structures, in the cross-border networks of migrant workers and activists pushed into exile by authoritarian regimes, in popular campaigns like anti-apartheid, and in the global diffusion of protest in 1945 and 1968. The latter took place towards the end of the great economic boom and just before the new globalization, a great pulse of struggle on both sides of the Iron Curtain in Europe, as well as in Japan, the USA, and parts of Africa and Latin America, triggering a massive strike wave into the 1970s. Overall, however, deglobalization limited space for internationalist praxis, and when the working classes of NICs like Brazil, Poland and South Africa began to organize on a large scale in the 1970s, their politics were heavily coloured by nationalism.

Globalization and labour movements today

The mediated international integration of deglobalization began to fall apart in the 1970s. Nation states played a key role in creating the new globalization, particularly through neoliberal policies, as did multinational corporations. New communications technologies and falling transport costs facilitated integration, the boom ended, national-level class compromises broke down, and international labour markets and migration expanded sharply. The economic crisis of the 1970s, followed by structural adjustment policies, hit agromineral countries especially hard, devastating many labour movements, but the retreat of the workers' movement was an international phenomenon.

The world's working class is both relatively and absolutely larger than ever before: there are more industrial workers in South Korea today, says Chris Harman, than in the entire globe when the *Communist Manifesto* was issued. However, while workers are linked through international labour markets and trade relations, wide variations in wages between regions provide the basis for serious conflicts. The omnipresence of nation states and nationalism prompts many labour movements to call for renewed protectionism and makes labour exclusion very tempting. Tied to the notion that contemporary labour must 'defend' the nation state against globalization, such policies ignore the role of nation states in promoting globalization, and undermine the prospects of workers' internationalism.

Moreover, contemporary workers' movements are characterized by the absence of definite radical alternatives, partly because of the Soviet collapse. This situation does,

however, allow for more experimentation than before 1989. One labour approach, associated with sections of Australian labour, is the 'progressive-competitive alternative', where labour consciously seeks to promote national competitiveness through pacts, skills development and active policy intervention. An alternative is represented by 'international social movement unionism', which argues for globalization-from-below through international solidarity for global labour standards and rights.

The older international structures have also attempted to reposition themselves. The ILO has tried to foster the 'governance of globalization', the WFTU has declined dramatically, while the growing ICFTU has struggled to shed its bureaucratic and Cold War past. Newer bodies like the European Trade Union Confederation have been formed, yet have tended to replicate the bureaucratic character of the ICFTU.

A different, perhaps more important, tradition of current workers' internationalism is to be found outside of these formal structures, and dates back to the 1970s: international ITS campaigns, shop-steward-to-shop-steward links in industries, campaigns for multinational collective bargaining and cross-border solidarity, and initiatives for a new type of internationalism like the Southern Initiative on Globalization and Trade Union Rights, which stresses campaign-based activism through networks in Africa, Asia and Australia. More recently, unions like the Service Employees Industrial Union of the US have initiated international organizing campaigns in multinational corporations, arguing for global unions. Meanwhile, independent union movements have revived in Africa, countries of the former Soviet bloc and elsewhere.

Significant syndicalist unions have also emerged in a number of countries since the 1970s. The Shack Dwellers' International emerged in the mid 1980s. The Seattle protests of 1999 marked a new phase for counterglobalization activity, followed by the World Social Forums and the Argentinean factory occupations. The current period has also seen the rise of rural internationalism, as in the International Peasant Movement launched in 1993, which includes the Landless Workers' Movement of Brazil. Contemporary globalization, in short, is characterized by the formation of transnational networks of activists and action, in which workers' movements have played an important role, at the same time as cleavages along ethnic, national, racial and religious lines have thrived.

Conclusions

An examination of transnational connections in modernity raises substantial questions about the definition of the 'working class' itself, as well as highlighting the point that workers' movements should not be reduced to union movements. A transnational perspective on labour history challenges the assumption that secure, waged jobs are the normal employment relationship: a wider view of workers' history shows that rather than secure, waged employment making unions possible, it is the reverse that seems true.

Our overview also raises important points about the relationship between class, nationality and race, indicating a history both of deep divisions, as well as of interracial and multinational solidarities. When Cedric Robinson posits 'black collective identity' as the negation of capitalism, or David Roediger treats White identity as equivalent to White Labourism, both ignore the wide range of ways in which racial identities are deployed and reworked in workers' movements and solidarities. Finally, globalization is not a novel challenge for workers' movements, but a recurrent feature in the development of the working class.

Philip Bonner
Jonathan Hyslop
Lucien van der Walt
with the assistance of
Andries Bezuidenhout
and Nicole Ulrich

Bibliography

Della Porta D. and Tarrow S. (eds) 2005. *Transnational protest and global activism.* Lanham and Oxford: Rowman and Littlefield.

Harman C. 1999. *A people's history of the world.* London, Chicago and Sydney: Bookmarks.

Linebaugh P. and Rediker M. 2000. *The many-headed Hydra: sailors, slaves, commoners, and the hidden history of the revolutionary Atlantic.* Boston: Beacon.

Munck R. 1988. *The new international labour studies: an introduction.* London and Atlantic Highlands: Zed.

Silver B. 2003. *Forces of labour: workers' movements and globalization since 1870.* Cambridge and New York: Cambridge University Press.

Van der Linden M. 2003. *Transnational labour history: explorations.* London: Ashgate.

Van der Linden M. and Thorpe W. (eds) 1990. *Revolutionary syndicalism: an international perspective.* Otterup/Aldershot: Scolar/Gower.

Wood A. and Baer J. A. 2006. 'Strength in numbers: urban rent strikes and political transformation in the Americas, 1904–1925', *Journal of Urban History,* 32, 6, 862–84.

Related essays

1848; 1960s; Abolition of Forced Labour Convention; abolitionism; African liberation; anarchism; anti-racism; capitalism; class; Cold War; Comintern and Cominform; Commission on International Labour Legislation; *Communist Manifesto;* consumer cooperation; contract and indentured labourers; convergence and divergence; diasporas; empire and migration; empires and imperialism; ethnicity and race; executives and professionals; exile; fascism and anti-fascism; freemasonry; Garvey, Marcus Mosiah; Ghose, Aurobindo Ackroyd; globalization; guestworkers; human mobility; individual identification systems; information economy; international migration regimes; labour standards; Little Red Book; nation and state; new man; non-violence; pan-isms; Romanticism; Russian Revolution; slavery; socialism; trade; transnational; women's movements

World Bank

The World Bank provides financial and technical assistance to developing countries as well as protection to international investors. Comprised of two main institutions – the International Bank for Reconstruction and Development (IBRD) and the International Development Association (IDA) – it is an independent, specialized agency of the United Nations. IBRD focuses on aid to middle-income nations among the poor, while IDA focuses on the poorest countries in the world; both agencies offer low-interest loans to member countries and interest-free credit and grants to non-members in order to fund social works ranging from health and education programmes to transportation and communications infrastructure projects. Its interests extend from human development, agriculture and rural services to environmental protection, electricity generation, and good governance through the development of legal institutions and anti-corruption practices. Loans and grants are often used as leverage to promote broad policy changes in the host economy. For instance, loans to microenterprises can be linked to larger banking reforms at the national level. The World Bank establishes a means for transnational aid, finance, and development entities to participate in Third World development outside of – though in cooperation with – governments around the globe.

Established under the Bretton Woods agreements of 1944, the World Bank Group, as it is called, actually consists of five agencies, all headquartered in Washington, DC. The IBRD began operations in June 1946 and approved its first loan, to France, the following year. An International Finance Corporation (IFC), designed as the private sector's investment arm within the World Bank, opened its doors in 1956 and ever since has provided loans and advice to foster development within the developing nations. The IDA began in 1960 and extends 30-year, zero-interest loans to the poorest of countries (those with a per capita income of under $500). The International Center for Settlement of Investment Disputes, founded in 1966, arbitrates disputes between member nations and individual investors. Finally, the Multilateral Investment Guarantee Agency promotes foreign direct investment in the developing world. Capitalized at over $1 billion when it began in 1988, the Agency insures private investors from political risk, disseminates information, and advises government on how to attract investments, and mediates between investors and host nations. While the IBRD has 184 members, the other agencies vary in members between 140 and 178, and nations can choose to join any of the five agencies.

The IDA and IBRD are the two agencies in which governments are directly attached. In the 1950s, it became evident that the terms of loans given by the IBRD were too rigid for the poorest of nations to meet, so the United Stated led the way in establishing the IDA as a means for the 'haves' to help the 'have nots'. The IDA would be fiscally sound, run like a bank, and thus it was placed under the World Bank's jurisdiction. Handing out its first loans in 1961, to Sudan, Honduras, Chile, and India,

the agency had provided over $161 billion in credits to 108 countries up to 2005. The terms are 'soft', or concessional, meaning loans maturities extend from 20 to 40 years, with a ten-year grace period tacked on before repayment. Thus, IDA coffers must be periodically replenished. The agency works not just with governments, but with non-governmental organizations and citizens, to foster a sense of ownership over the development process in host countries.

The IDA's successes have been many. At one level, it advocates for the countries most marginalized from globalization by seeking, on their behalf, more access to the markets of industrialized nations and encouraging regional integration. But it is at the most micro level of a nation's economy – individually owned enterprises – that the IDA has made a tremendous impact. It has done so largely through the support and cooperation of transnational non-governmental organizations. Some successes include a National AIDS Control project in India, which has trained over 52,000 doctors and 60 per cent of the nursing staffs in HIV/AIDS management, a Flood Disaster Prevention programme in Yemen that directly protects 21,000 households, a primary school textbook project throughout Africa, construction or renovation of thousands of healthcare facilities in rural Asia, and social investment programmes that generate employment in Latin America.

Yemen's efforts to provide financial and non-financial facilities to microenterprises and small businesses are another example of the IDA empowering individuals across borders. In 1998, in a nation in which 42 per cent of the population lived below the poverty line, the Yemeni government teamed with the World Bank to establish the centrepiece of the programme: a system in which non-governmental organizations would invest in the tiniest and poorest of Yemen's enterprises in order to foster employment, rising incomes, and encourage further microfinance. The IDA's Social Fund for Development Project, which harnesses the finances of the NGOs, makes possible such creative solutions to poverty through loans spread out to thousands of citizens. Thus, in Dar Seed, a 47-year-old mother of nine borrowed just $100 from an NGO to buy a billiard table which she then rented out to local kids who flocked to her front yard to play. Her family's income, before barely enough to put food on the table, rose dramatically. Another woman obtained a small loan from a microcredit agency financed by an NGO, using it to buy a sewing machine then growing into a clothing shop. From its profits, she bought a minibus to keep pace with business. She employed her sons and planned to hire non-family members as well. Roughly 25,000 other Yemenis have followed this example. Over the duration of the Project, from 2000–06, the IDA provided a credit worth $75 million, issuing an average loan of between $109 and $271 at 2 per cent interest. The success rate has been upwards of 90 per cent of the microenterprises that received loans. It is through such programmes that the IDA hopes to halve poverty in Yemen by 2015, empower women, and use the Project as a platform to expand enterprise partnerships in a global development programme.

That the World Bank Group also facilitates cross-border exchanges is evident from the work of some of its other specialized agencies. For instance, the first head of the IFC, owned by 178 nations and capitalized at over $2.45 billion, claimed that the agency was the first intergovernmental organization to have as its main objective the promotion of private enterprise. The IFC invests in enterprises which are majority-owned by the private sector. The goal is sustainable development by identifying constraints to private sector investment in infrastructure, health, and education and developing domestic financial markets through institution building and the use of innovative financial products. Some examples of its hundreds of projects were investments in the Kabul Serena Hotel in 2005 in order to encourage tourism in Afghanistan, rehabilitating and expanding shrimp production under the NOVA operation in Belize, and establishment of the Launch Tech Company of China, a firm that designs and manufactures tools and equipment in the automotive aftermarket sector. Such activities address the very nature of privately run transnational exchanges.

So does the approach of the International Center for Settlement of Investment Disputes, an autonomous agency created by and closely tied to the World Bank. Before its creation, the president of the World Bank, or the Bank itself, helped mediate investment disputes between governments and private foreign investors. From 1966 onward, officers of the Bank were relieved of this burden as the Center was designed to expand international

investments by stepping into the middle of disputes. It does not actually conduct the mediation. Rather, the Center makes its facilities available to disputants and promotes an atmosphere of confidence and trust by engaging the parties and performing administrative functions. Conciliators and arbitrators are appointed by the parties in dispute. Recourse to the Center's facilities is purely voluntary, but nations and investors have availed themselves of its services by including provisions for access to the agency in investment treaties. From the 1990s onward, the caseload of dispute arbitrations by the Center has expanded sizeably; in its 40-year existence, it has heard over 900 cases. Argentina's policies of escaping from its bilateral investment treaties in order to correct its payments imbalances and debt position after its economic collapse at the turn of the millennium have accounted for approximately one-fifth of the cases before the Center.

The Center's offices have administered the vast expansion of bilateral investment treaties since 1987, and thus have been instrumental in furthering the rights and influence of transnational investors. Ever since Germany and Pakistan signed the first bilateral investment treaty, the Center has been vested with the authority to rule on more than 1,100 bilateral investment treaties, over 800 of which were established from the late 1980s.

The example of Yemen shows that the mission of the World Bank to reduce poverty has replaced the decades-long objectives of increasing aggregate incomes, but the institution has also come under criticism. In particular, anti-globalization forces, including those seeking environmental safeguards from development and NGOs uneasy about the damage to traditional societies, have taken the World Bank Group to task. Try as it might to meet those criticisms with policies aimed at protecting individuals, the World Bank has been unable to stem the opposition. Anti-globalizationists have charged that a neoliberal and corporate 'neocolonial' mindset permeates the institution, led by the free-market United States. They claim that economic liberalization, through such enterprise-enhancing programs as those used in Yemen, destabilizes societies and removes government protections from citizens. In place of the state come NGOs and private, transnational investors who undermine local economies and do little to fight corruption, confront dictators, or promote democracy.

Politics has also intruded into World Bank affairs. In June 2005, the critics railed further at the appointment of American Paul Wolfowitz, a leader of the neoconservatives in the George W. Bush administration, to the helm of the World Bank Group. Wolfowitz had little experience with development issues but enormous influence as a proponent of cutting back government aid and favouring democratic initiatives before the eradication of poverty. Threats of street protests followed his appointment, with more moderate voices, such as economist Jeffrey Sachs, nonetheless insisting that Wolfowitz would stymie the development work of a key global institution.

The World Bank, along with the International Monetary Fund (IMF) and World Trade Organization (WTO), provoked their own transnational protest movements. After the Seattle protests against the WTO, major manifestations against the financial pillars of the capitalist system followed in Washington, DC from 2000 to 2002. The demonstrations brought the criticism of the World Bank Group into widespread public view for the first time. The IMF and World Bank protests in Washington targeted the policies of the IMF and World Bank towards developing countries. Tens of thousands marched against the supposed failed development regimes of the advanced nations, which compelled the poor countries to remain in servitude to the West. Although rather extreme in their views, they did link with environmentalists and liberals around the world to demand such changes in financial policies as debt relief, less protectionism toward the poor nations, and more generous allocations of loans and grants.

The World Bank has responded by acknowledging that the fight against corruption and poverty must escalate. Non-governmental agencies and individual investors now come under scrutiny for their participation in the continuing cycle of poverty. Regardless of the drumbeat of criticism and greater global awareness of its shortcomings, however, the five agencies of the World Bank Group still provide a staggering array of services to the poorest people on earth.

Thomas W. Zeiler

Bibliography

Harrison G. 2004. *The World Bank and Africa: the construction of governance states*. London and New York: Routledge.

Ranis G., Vreeland J. R. and Kosack S. (eds) 2006. *Globalization and the nation state: the impact of the IMF and the World Bank*. London and New York: Routledge.

Stiglitz J. 2002. *Globalization and its discontents*. New York: Norton.

The World Bank: The IBRD and IDA: working for a world free of poverty [online]. Available: www.worldbank.org, accessed 15 March 2006.

Related essays

developmental assistance; governance; intergovernmental organizations; International Monetary Fund (IMF); international non-governmental organizations (INGOs); investment; loans; neoliberalism; Pax Americana; public policy; taxation; underdevelopment; United Nations system; Washington Consensus

World Conservation Union (IUCN) / World Wide Fund for Nature (WWF)

Both the World Conservation Union (IUCN) and World Wide Fund for Nature (WWF) are products of an increasing popular concern with nature protection that arose in the West after the Second World War. Together they are undoubtedly the most powerful and best resourced global institutions working in the conservation arena and while their focuses, funding and outreach may differ in some respects, they frequently work in tandem. The intertwined history of the two institutions has mirrored changing conservation concerns in the developed world since their inception.

The IUCN was founded in 1948 and encompasses states, government agencies and non-governmental organizations. Its origins can be traced to attempts to engage the international community in transnational conservation issues from the beginning of the 20th century and to the energetic personal contributions of zoologist Dr Paul Sarasin, who convened the International Conference for the Protection of Nature in Basel in 1913, Pieter van Tienhoven's international office established in Brussels in 1928, and congresses in 1931 and 1947. The IUCN, then the International Union for the Protection of Nature, emerged under the UNESCO aegis from a further conference in Fontainebleau (1948) in the flush of postwar cooperative agreements. In 1956 the acronym 'IUCN' came into use together with the new name International Union for the Conservation of Nature and Natural Resources, and from the 1990s the organization has been referred to as the World Conservation Union.

The World Wildlife Fund – since 1986 the World Wide Fund for Nature – is a powerful transnational conservation fund-raising non-governmental organization. There is an overt link between the WWF and IUCN in that Sir Julian Huxley, nature champion and catalyst for the creation of the IUCN and first director-general of UNESCO, was also involved in forming the WWF. By the late 1950s it had become clear that the IUCN was underfunded and even likely to collapse. The WWF was founded in 1961 (with the support of IUCN) as the funding arm of the Western conservation movement, and its mission was to obtain financial support from the public directly and from big business. The money thus collected was to be used to support IUCN projects. In fact, over the years, because of its strong presence in more than one hundred countries, the WWF has prioritized projects of particular concern to the countries in which its works and raises money. The consequence has been that WWF funds many of its own projects, for example, the 'Peace Parks' (Transfrontier or Transboundary Conservation Areas) of southern Africa.

The IUCN and WWF have responded to changing conservation concerns. At first they concentrated on the preservation of endangered wildlife species (the Giant Panda [Ailuropoda melanoleuca] logo of the WWF is a case-in-point) and iconic, usually wilderness, habitats. Under pressure from the developing world, and especially after the conference in 1961 in Arusha, in newly independent Tanzania, the world bodies moved from a Western aesthetic and preservationist paradigm to a more human-centred approach linked to emerging ideas around sustainable development and poverty alleviation. Within both the IUCN and the WWF, this shift created tension and at times continues to do so because the needs and attitudes of the developing and developed world still do not converge.

Depending on the issue, various conventions and policy documents have come into existence. The WWF and IUCN engage in issues on a broad front. They have diverse initiatives that impact on international law, such as the Convention on Wetlands of International Importance especially as Waterfowl Habitat (the Ramsar Convention). The IUCN is responsible for drawing up Red Data lists of endangered species and for controlling such trade through the 1973 Convention on the International Trade in Endangered Species of Fauna and Flora (CITES). It also served as a think-tank for fresh conservation thinking, for example spearheading the Stockholm Conference in 1972 and emerging ideas around sustainable development. While, no doubt, many of these actions are beneficial, both IUCN and WWF have been characterised as 'Big Brother' because they are akin to large multinationals that set the agendas for the less powerful of the world. Since the foundation of these organizations, a wide variety of projects have had significant impacts on nature resource conservation. In moving from field work into policy and advocacy the principle has remained to transmit expertise, experience and money across national borders.

Jane Carruthers

Bibliography

Boardman R. 1981. *International organization and the conservation of nature.* Basingstoke: Macmillan (now Palgrave Macmillan).

Morphet S. and Morphet S. 1996. 'NGOs and the environment', in Willetts P. (ed.) *The conscience of the world: the influence of non-governmental organizations in the UN system.* Washington, DC: Brookings Institution.

Wolmer W. 2003. 'Transboundary conservation: the politics of ecological integrity in the Great Limpopo Transfrontier Park', *Journal of Southern African Studies*, 29, 1, 261–78.

Related essays

biodiversity; conservation and preservation; environmental diplomacy; environmentalism; intergovernmental organizations; international non-governmental organizations (INGOs); national parks; Stockholm Conference

World federalism

The concept of world federalism dates from 1625, with the publication of *On the laws of war and peace.* The work, by Dutch theorist Hugo Grotius, laid the foundation for modern international law, making the case that sovereignty for the nation state ought not to be absolute.

The world federalism movement itself, however, is very much a product of the 20th century. In the 1930s, as the League of

Nations collapsed and the Kellogg-Briand Pact to outlaw war proved a failure, some internationalists endorsed a more comprehensive critique of the nation state. In the late 1930s, federalists concentrated on a federation of Atlantic democracies, a programme outlined by Clarence Streit in his 1939 book, *Union now*. In 1945, Emery Reves expanded on the Streit programme, contending in *An anatomy of peace* that establishment of a clear plan of world law and world government would ensure peace.

In the immediate postwar years, federalists looked to the United Nations, but they soon realized that the UN would not achieve their goals of sufficiently breaking down sovereignty. In 1947, the two major federalist organizations (Americans United for World Government and World Federalists, USA) merged to form the United World Federalists (UWF). Leaders of the two organizations met in Montreux, Switzerland, to begin drafting a charter. World federalism appealed to internationalists disillusioned by the growing Cold War tensions. By 1948, UWF claimed 150,000 members of 19 nationalities.

But as they made little progress toward their ultimate goal, world federalists eventually embraced a more moderate agenda. They encouraged parliamentary meetings to enhance cultural exchange among legislators. They called for the UN to exercise sovereignty over the oceans, and focused on other environmental, and hence inherently transnational, causes. They demanded greater attention to poverty and disease in the underdeveloped world. And they championed establishment of an International Criminal Court.

Robert David Johnson

Bibliography

Heater D. B. 1996. *World citizenship and government: cosmopolitan ideas in the history of Western political thought*. London and New York: Macmillan (now Palgrave Macmillan).

Related essays
conspiracy theories; globalization; justice; legal order; League of Nations system; transnational; United Nations system; world orders

World heritage

World heritage refers broadly to the notion that certain cultural and natural resources have a special significance and deserve preservation for the benefit of all humanity. The conjunction of 'world' with 'heritage' reflects a changed understanding of ownership of and responsibility for these resources. The word 'heritage' originally referred to 'any property, and esp. land, which devolves by right of inheritance' *Oxford English Dictionary*. Over the course of the last four centuries, however, its association with individual ownership and property gave way to the idea of a cultural or natural resource belonging to a community such as the nation or, more recently, all of humanity, and whose preservation requires special oversight.

Perhaps the first official assertion of the state's responsibility as a guardian of cultural heritage occurred in a Swedish Royal Proclamation of 1666 declaring that all objects of antiquity were the property of the Crown. The great archaeological finds of the 18th century prompted further state intervention. For example, in the face of the looting of the recently discovered Herculaneum, the King of Naples decreed the buried heritage of his realm to be under the monarchy's control. It was, however, only in the 19th century that European and American (South, Central, and North) governments generally assumed strong control of ancient monuments and enacted legislation for their preservation. The same period witnessed a massive growth in popular and scholarly literature devoted to heritage and a burgeoning tourist industry centred around the physical remnants of the human past. By the turn of the century, most Western countries had established legal codes protecting their cultural heritage.

The late 18th and early 19th centuries also saw the birth of the museum. By the mid 19th century, almost every nation in the North Atlantic world possessed a museum that collected objects from a variety of civilizations and offered a narrative of history that culminated with contemporary European culture (and often the culture of the nation in which the museum was built). More recent objects (generally from the Renaissance forward) were often grouped into national schools. Most cultural traditions outside of Europe were not deemed worthy of representation in the art museum per se, and separate ethnographic museums grew up to house them, if they were deemed notable at all. Significantly, some intellectuals opposed collecting antiquities in art museums, claiming that the new institution transformed art objects into commodities and undermined a cosmopolitan view of art that transcended national boundaries. On the other hand, art museums, which have now grown to include most of the cultural traditions of the world, have become enormously important agents of cross-cultural and, indeed, transnational understanding.

Various explanations have been offered for the timing of this interest in cultural heritage. The social and political revolutions of the late 18th and 19th centuries led to feelings of separation from the past and nostalgia for earlier times, and the greater mobility and rapid changes associated with industrialization and urbanization led to a search for roots and a desire for a sense of belonging to a place or tradition. More immediately, vandalism during the French Revolution led directly to laws protecting monuments, and eventually to their classification in order of importance. Heritage also played a crucial role in the process of nation building, where it was used to invent traditions and imagine a collective past upon which national identity could be built. National and civic competition fed the growth of museums and heritage sites. It is crucial to note that heritage was primarily envisioned in this period in national terms, with the nation state being the primary guardian of the national heritage.

By the beginning of the 20th century, an interest in cultural heritage had spread across much of the globe, including the colonial world. Some colonial authorities destroyed, neglected, or dismissed the heritage of colonized peoples, while others invested considerable resources in identifying and protecting cultural monuments and artifacts in their colonial possessions. In Zimbabwe (then Southern Rhodesia), for example, the English effaced and distorted the local archaeological record, but in India they conducted an archaeological survey of the entire country and enacted a preservation campaign. The cultural and natural resources of the colonized were often vandalized, exploited for profit, or looted by the colonizers. Some colonial powers, especially Belgium, France, and England, demonstrated their power by physical appropriation of the heritage of conquered peoples. Furthermore, the concept of heritage appears in retrospect to be problematical in the colonial context: the labelling of indigenous cultural artifacts and practices as heritage often suggested that they were premodern and had to give way to the modern practices of the colonizers. For example, in North Africa the French often divided cities into old and new sections, freezing the old section in time and allowing development only in the new section.

Heritage management continues to be uneven after decolonization. Postcolonial nation states often give priority to different sites and monuments from those favoured by colonizers as they create their own national identity; looting and illegal exploitation of cultural and natural resources is endemic in many formerly colonized countries; and the cultural legacy of the colonial period tends to be neglected.

Following World War 1 various international bodies began to assert that this cultural heritage belonged to all humanity and that its preservation depended upon international cooperation and management. The Athens Charter, adopted at the First International Congress of Architects and Technicians of Historic Monuments in 1931, called for the establishment of an international organization for the restoration and preservation of monuments, historic sites, and their surrounding areas. This document referred to 'the artistic and archaeological property of mankind' as worthy of the protection of states 'acting in the spirit of the Covenant of the League of Nations'. The preamble to the Venice Charter, adopted by the International Council on Monuments and Sites (ICOMOS) in 1964, noted that 'People are becoming more and more conscious of the unity of human values and regard ancient monuments as a common heritage. The common responsibility to safeguard them for future generations is recognized'. While firm in their assertion that heritage demanded international oversight, these documents struggled with the applicability of culturally specific concepts such as authenticity and genius, and the degree to which monuments might be modified in relation to their current social or cultural purpose. The Venice Charter was formulated almost entirely by Europeans and addressed primarily European concerns.

Widespread recognition of a natural heritage came later than that of cultural heritage. Forms of soil and wildlife conservation have been practised since ancient times, but prior to the modern era, most humans were far more interested in exploiting natural resources and aggrandizing settlements than in conservation. Some new forms of conservation were promoted in Europe from the 17th to the 19th centuries, such as the preservation of forests in France, Germany, and England, but in the same period the ecology of large areas of the Americas, Africa, and Australia was radically transformed and often damaged by colonial settlements. Not until the late 19th century did nations, beginning in Europe and the United States, act in significant ways to protect wildlife, limit pollution, and preserve disappearing resources. Public pressure to preserve exceptionally beautiful natural sites as part of a national heritage first appeared in late-19th-century Europe and the United States. The United States created the first national park in 1872, and by the 1920s national parks existed on every continent. Despite some national attention to issues of conservation and the environment in the late 19th century, few international agreements protecting the environment existed before the 20th century, and initially most such accords addressed the preservation of commercially valuable animals. The increasing activity in the field of environmentalism contributed to multiplying such agreements.

Environmentalism only became a dominant issue in national politics after World War 2, when a succession of new threats began to appear: radiation from nuclear testing and power, widespread use of pesticides, unprecedented air and water pollution, acid rain, depletion of the ozone layer, carbon dioxide buildup, global warming, etc. Many nations established environmental agencies or ministries and enacted legislation to reduce some forms of pollution, yet the transnational nature of the problem limited their success. The environmental movement of the 1960s and 1970s led to a proliferation of transnational NGOs addressing environmental concerns, and ultimately to a series of international conventions addressing such issues as the preservation of wetlands and the trade in endangered species. In 1972 the United Nations established the UN Environment Programme (UNEP) to address environmental problems, and important international agreements limiting pollution continue to appear, such as the Vienna Convention for the Protection of the Ozone Layer (1985) and the Kyoto Protocol (1997), which addresses climate change and the emission of carbon dioxide and five other greenhouse gases. National governments remain reluctant, however, to cede authority to international organizations, impeding efforts to control transnational threats to the environment.

The World Heritage Convention, adopted by the General Conference of the United Nations Educational, Scientific and Cultural Organization (UNESCO) in 1972, is a watershed in the formation of a transnational conception of both cultural and natural heritage. While the Convention specifically expresses its respect of national sovereignty and existing property rights as defined by national legislation, much of its wording suggests that 'world heritage sites belong to all the peoples of the world, irrespective of the territory on which they are located' (UNESCO website). The treaty proposes that the 'deterioration or disappearance of any item of the cultural or natural heritage constitutes a harmful impoverishment of the heritage of all the nations of the world' and asserts that 'parts of the cultural or natural heritage are of outstanding interest and therefore need to be preserved as part of the world heritage of mankind as a whole'. The Convention protects monuments and sites because of their 'outstanding universal value'. States who ratify the treaty commit themselves to identify, protect, and conserve World Heritage Properties, which are placed on a World Heritage List. They gain access to the World Heritage Fund, which is particularly intended for the aid of developing countries, and to emergency assistance for urgent action to repair damage caused by human-made or natural disasters. The World Heritage Convention has been ratified by 158 countries, more than for any other UNESCO convention.

Despite the global and egalitarian ambitions of the World Heritage Convention, critics have argued that it favours the developed world, where the vast majority of sites on the World Heritage List are located. The List's predilection for large, permanent architectural monuments and urban centres, as well as sites on the international tourist itinerary, appears to reflect a Eurocentric bias, too. It is also becoming clear that natural and cultural heritage cannot be easily separated, as many landscapes and ecosystems were created by or depend upon human intervention. Finally, the decisions of the World Heritage Committee are sometimes at odds with the practices, needs, and values of the local communities that live with the heritage sites. On the other hand, inclusion on the World Heritage List generates considerable local pride, usually ensuring better preservation of sites and economic benefits from tourism.

UNESCO has changed its conception of world heritage in important ways since 1972. The existence of diverse cultural standards for the conservation of heritage was first recognized by UNESCO in 1994 in the Nara Document on Authenticity, which asserted that judgments regarding authenticity and value may vary from culture to culture. In 2003 UNESCO adopted a convention protecting intangible cultural heritage, or, as this charter defined it, 'the practice, representations, expressions, knowledge, skills – as well as the instruments, objects, artefacts, and cultural spaces associated therewith – that communities, groups, and in some cases, individuals recognize as part of their cultural heritage'. This broadened conception of the heritage was deemed a necessary response to globalization and other accelerated processes of social transformation.

Parallel to the development of UNESCO, non-governmental organizations (NGOs) have played a growing role in identifying and preserving a world heritage. Organizations such as the World Wildlife Fund for Nature (WWF), the World Conservation Union (IUCN), Greenpeace, the World Monuments Fund (WMF) and ICOMOS have functioned in important ways as advisors and watchdogs, but have had less success affecting heritage practices on the international level when unaided by governmental organizations. Interestingly, membership has been far greater in transnational NGOs devoted to environmental issues than in those devoted to cultural heritage issues, which draw far greater attention from national and local organizations. It might be argued that environmentalism is one of the strongest of the global, transnational mass movements in the contemporary world.

Efforts to identify and preserve a world heritage are currently competing with a number of other developments. Growth in tourism generates income for and interest in heritage sites, but can often degrade them as well. Looting and the licit and illicit art market increasingly threaten cultural heritage. Economic development frequently takes place at the expense of heritage preservation, and pollution continues to harm both cultural and natural heritage sites, even in remote parts of the world. Thus, the emerging understanding of heritage as a global resource shared by all humanity exists in tension with other transnational phenomena.

David O'Brien

Bibliography

Brodie N. and Tubb K.W. (eds) 2002. *Illicit antiquities: the theft of culture and the extinction of archaeology*. London: Routledge.

Cleere H. (ed.) 1989. *Archaeological heritage management in the modern world*. London: Unwin Hyman.

J. Paul Getty Trust *Cultural heritage policy documents* [online]. Available: www.getty.edu/conservation/research_resources/charters.html, accessed 30 January 2008.

Lowenthal D. 1998, 2003. *The heritage crusade and the spoils of history*. Cambridge: Cambridge University Press.

McCormick J. 1989. *The global environmental movement: reclaiming paradise*. London: Belhaven.

Related essays

civilizations; conservation and preservation; cosmopolitanism and universalism; cultural capitals; decolonization; development and growth; ecology; empires and imperialism; environmentalism; intergovernmental organizations; international non-governmental organizations (INGOs); modernity; museums; nation and state; national parks; tourism; transnational

World Music

The term 'World Music' was coined in July 1987 at a meeting of eleven representatives of British independent record companies involved in international popular music at a pub, *The Empress of Russia*, in Islington, London. It has essentially survived as a rather nebulous and highly flexible marketing term for a genre of music which is widely used in music stores, by record labels and in the music press to designate music that generally, but not exclusively, originates from non-Western sources and does not fit appropriately into the genres of reggae, jazz, blues or folk. African, Afro-Caribbean, Latin American, South Asian, Arabic, Eastern European and various indigenous musics tend to predominate in the category, which leans toward traditional and folk music, often with 'Western' beats overlaid, rather than, say, Hong

Kong Cantopop or Chinese Mandapop. The music of ethnic minorities in the first world is also strongly represented, such as that played by British South Asian and Franco-Arabic and Franco-African musicians. The equivalent US term World Beat was first used by musician Dan Del Santo in 1982.

One of the principal live performance networks for World Music is WOMAD (World of Music Arts and Dance) established in the UK in 1980 by singer Peter Gabriel, who also set up the Real World label in 1989, which has released albums by artists from all over the world, many recorded in the Real World studios in Bath, England. Their current catalogue runs to albums by some sixty artists from Australia to Finland. Another major figure in the promotion of world music is US blues guitarist Ry Cooder, whose 1994 Grammy Award-winning album Talking Timbuktu with Malian guitarist Ali Farka Toure, who died in 2006, was a major event in World Music, as was Buena Vista Social Club, the 1997 album and 1999 film (directed by Wim Wenders) which he made with Cuban musicians in Havana. A more contentious figure is US singer-songwriter Paul Simon, whose 1986 Grammy Award-winning album Graceland, made in South Africa with various local musicians, led to lengthy debates about the ethics of appropriation by first-world musicians of music by African and other third-world musicians, especially since Simon broke a cultural boycott of apartheid South Africa at the time. The extensive World Music: The Rough Guide was first published in 1994, and there is a useful series of Rough Guide compilation CDs dedicated to most countries and regions around the world, as well as individual artists such as Luambo Franco of the Congo, Indian diva Asha Bhosle and salsa star Celia Cruz, and there have been numerous other CDs, directories and publications ever since. World Music has also generated numerous debates around issues of copyright and authenticity, especially in relation to a very popular CD by Belgian producers Michel Sauchez and Eric Mouquet called Deep Forest, released in 1992, which sampled what was claimed to be UNESCO ethnographic recordings of pigmy chants over ambient-styled programmed keyboards and drum machines, but were in fact uncredited recordings of musicians from the Solomon Islands.

The term has had many detractors who have claimed it is vague, amorphous and even insulting, but it has survived as a useful shorthand music-industry term. Simon Frith has made a distinction between 'World Music from above' and 'World Music from below', the former being a music-industry-imposed term, the latter involving collaborative music by performers from different ethnic backgrounds who have exchanged musical traditions, styles and techniques in an innovative way. These two concepts roughly correspond to different viewpoints on whether World Music has contributed to the global homogenization of ethnic musics, a frequent anxiety, and the celebration of the proliferation of global musical diversity which has occurred on a grassroots level. In either case, the term has persisted, and music from increasingly remote parts of the world continues to be released to Western audiences even if power relations between musicians and record label often remain problematic.

Tony Mitchell

Bibliography

Feld S. 'Notes on World Beat', in Keil C. and Feld S. 1994. Music grooves: essays and dialogues. Chicago: Chicago University Press.

Feld S. 2000. 'A sweet lullaby for World Music', Public Culture, 12, 1, 145–71.

Frith S. 'The discourse of World Music', in Born G. and Hesmondhalgh D. (eds) 2000. Western music and its others: difference, representation, and appropriation in music. Berkeley: University of California Press, 305–22.

Mitchell T. 1996. Popular music and local identity: rock, pop and rap in Europe and Oceania. Leicester: Leicester University Press.

Related essays

dress; empires and imperialism; jazz; literature; music; performing artists; rock; salsa

World orders

'World orders' is a concept that specialists in international relations history have long used. International relations presuppose the existence of nations that interact among themselves, so that 'world orders' amount to structures of interstate affairs that nations establish. Such orders provide one framework in which transnational movements and circulations take place and connections are made, but to limit consideration of world orders just to nation states would be to ignore the fact that non-state actors can also contribute to defining and sustaining some global order. Transnational business enterprises offer one example; although they are differently defined and constituted from sovereign states, they often construct an order (sometimes called a 'regime') among themselves throughout the world. Another example would be international non-governmental organizations (INGOs) that seek to promote a global community of shared interests with regard to such issues as environmental protection and the eradication of poverty, hunger, or illiteracy in the world. Theirs is a proactive world order that does not yet exist formally but that propels so much transnational activity. There are other non-state entities such as religions, ethnic groups, and civilizations whose roles in the making (or unmaking) of world orders cannot be ignored. To discuss world orders in a transnational perspective, therefore, we must take into consideration both states and non-state actors and movements.

Geopolitics

Theories of international relations have conceptualized 'anarchy', 'hierarchy', 'balance of power', 'bipolarity', 'hegemony', and the like in order to characterize the ways in which nations behave toward one another, in the process possibly establishing some sort of stable order among themselves. One of the most influential writers on the subject, Hedley Bull (1995), posits the Hobbesian world in which all states are potentially or actually at war with each other. In such a situation, there can be no order, and only anarchy reigns. But since humankind cannot long sustain anarchy, sooner or later some mechanism emerges, a structure of governance that establishes certain arrangements for coexistence among states. Hierarchy is one such system. In interstate affairs, a pyramidal structure, with the great powers on top and weak countries at the bottom, is postulated. The great powers among themselves may constitute a state of anarchy, but sometimes they work out an arrangement among themselves to maintain some equilibrium. They do so by negotiating alliances, defensive pacts, or various modi operandi so as to combine their resources for common ends. One of the most sought-after objectives for such arrangements is some stability in international affairs. A system of stability is often built upon a balance-of-power mechanism that usually takes the form of a division

of the more powerful states into two or more groupings, among which some equilibrium is established. But if one of the groups or one power should become too preponderant and the others come to fear its hegemony, they may come together to restore the balance. International order would thus be synonymous with balance of power. When it is sustained, there may be order and stability; when it is not, conflict and war may become inevitable.

As examples of a successful interstate order, specialists usually cite such instances as the 'Vienna system' and the Bismarckian world order. The former presumably sustained a peaceful relationship among major European states for several decades after the Congress of Vienna (1815), while the latter, established in the wake of the Franco–Prussian war (1870–71), ensured stability in Europe for nearly twenty years while Bismarck was in power. On the other hand, the 'Versailles system', created after the Great War at the Paris peace conference (1919), is seen to have been a failure since it did not restore a balance of power in Europe. On the other hand, the 'Locarno system' in Europe, resulting from a conference in the Italian city (1923), may be said to have been, at least potentially, more enduring in that it brought Britain, France, and Germany together into a stable relationship, each recognizing the postwar status quo in Europe. Its Asian-Pacific counterpart was the 'Washington system', established after the naval disarmament conference held in the US capital (1921–22), which contemporary observers hailed as having brought Japan, the United States, the United Kingdom, and other powers into some sort of equilibrium, an equilibrium that lasted for about ten years. In a similar vein, the Cold War is sometimes interpreted as having produced several decades of global peace ('the long peace') through a bipolar system, in which the two superpowers equipped with nuclear weapons balanced each other.

These are all geopolitical interpretations of world order, which is seen to hinge on the disposition of power among states. 'The rise and fall of the great powers', as Paul Kennedy's popular study (1987) notes, is considered in such a perspective to have been the main story of international affairs, determining the shape of the world order at a given moment in time. There is an assumption here that world orders are produced by the great powers, and that the powers are driven by geopolitics. Because geopolitics is usually seen as a function of the economic resources and military power that a state possesses, this may be considered a power-driven definition of world order. At bottom is the conceptualization of world order as consisting of independent, sovereign states. Often referred to as the 'Westphalian system', after the Westphalian treaties that ended the Thirty Years' War in Europe (1618–48), this conception of international relations has strongly influenced both the behaviour of states and the analysis of inter-state affairs. Such a construction assumes that all states, large and small, are sovereign entities and that they are all oriented toward the preservation and augmentation of power, with the result that any order that may exist among them is by nature fragile. This sort of conceptualization, however, does not help promote a transnational understanding of world orders because, for one thing, the Westphalian framework limits its utility to Europe and its successor states such as the United States, Canada, Australia, and New Zealand. It should be recalled that in the 17th century, the region covered by the Westphalian system was rather small, especially as the Spanish and Portuguese empires in the New World as well as the French and British colonies in North America were considered to lie beyond the Westphalian system of interstate relations. Much more extensive in territory and more rooted in history than the emerging Westphalian system was the 'world order' defined by the Ottoman Empire, embracing the governance of diverse national and religious groups in the Middle East. Likewise, there was a 'Confucian world order' sustained by the Chinese Empire (then under the Qing dynasty), embracing virtually all countries and tribes in Inner Asia, Southeast Asia, and East Asia. Neither the Ottoman nor the Qing empire eschewed military power, but neither postulated an international order on the basis of independent states.

Until the late 18th century, therefore, it can be said that world order consisted of a number of regional orders, of which the Westphalian order was often the least orderly, as its constituent states continued to fight wars among themselves, thereby enhancing the relative power of some of them, which grew into great economic and military powers – and continued to engage in geopolitical pursuits of power.

Imperialism

None of these regional orders came together to form a world order until the 19th century, when the great powers of the West established control over the entire globe through colonies, semi-colonies, and spheres of influence. Thus was created a new world order, one defined by imperialism. The imperialist order was one in which there was a sharp division of the world's countries and people into two: those who ruled, and those who were ruled. The system was sustained by the superior military and economic might of the great powers, now called 'world powers', as well as by their ability to establish governance in their colonies and protectorates through the collaboration of portions of the indigenous people. What William L. Langer has called 'the diplomacy of imperialism' was a system for global governance on the basis of interimperialist agreement. This order, however, was always unstable for two reasons. First, the great powers never succeeded in agreeing on, let alone preserving, their arrangements for a global condominium. They could not refrain from disputing each other's prerogatives, as best exemplified by the 20th century's first interimperial conflict, the Russo–Japanese war (1904–05) that involved the two powers' failure to determine which of them should control Korea and southern Manchuria. The century would witness many more imperialistic conflicts, culminating in the Second World War that pitted the Japanese Empire against the Western powers' Asian colonies, and the German Reich against Soviet imperialism in Eastern Europe. Second, as the Korean and Chinese nationalist movements that developed at the very moment when Russia and Japan were at war indicated, imperialism provoked its opposite, anti-colonial and anti-imperialistic movements in many parts of the world. In East and Southeast Asia, the Middle East (in the aftermath of the demise of the Ottoman Empire following the First World War), Africa, and Central America (where the United States had established colonies and protectorates), anti-colonial struggles continued to grow and became a transnational movement by the 1940s, sharing the same language of emancipation and self-determination and linked together through the Comintern (Communist International) as well as non-communist forms of anti-imperialism such as Gandhi's peaceful protest movement. These two sources of instability doomed the world order defined by imperialism.

International organizations

Imperialism was destroyed after the end of the Second World War, and in its place nationalism was supposed to become the basis of a new world order. But the history of European interstate relations had demonstrated that independent states acting together or separately were incapable of sustaining a stable world order. There would, therefore, have to be established some supranational system to define world order. Thus, in the aftermath of the war, two parallel devices were attempted to this end: intergovernmental organizations and regional communities. One, intergovernmental organizations, had been tried before, most notably the League of Nations that in its inception was a notable experiment in interstate cooperation: to replace, as Woodrow Wilson said, balance of power by a community of nations. But the League never included all independent nations, nor did it help preserve world order when it was threatened by some of its own members (Japan, Italy). The United Nations, established in 1945, was envisaged as a more universal and, at the same time, as a more hierarchical institution than the League. It would consist of all sovereign states, but at the same time it would entrust the maintenance of international security in just five of them, the permanent members of the Security Council, who were to act under the principle of unanimity. But because unanimity was often lacking at crucial moments, the UN did not prove to be a constructive alternative to more traditional geopolitics, which was what the United States and the Soviet Union continued to engage in. Moreover, the UN was often powerless to prevent local conflicts or to mediate them once they had erupted, showing that even with the establishment of an intergovernmental organization, independent states tended to act unilaterally in pursuit of what they considered to be their national interests. It should be added, however, that in non-geopolitical areas, such as developmental assistance, environmentalism, and control of communicable diseases, the UN's various committees and affiliated agencies evidenced much cooperativeness on the part of the member states, recognizing that they could achieve far more by acting together than separately. The UN, in other words, was more successful as a mechanism for promoting world orders in non-geopolitical than in geopolitical issues. This fact indicates that the definition of world order has been vastly expanded since the end of the Second World War, as will be further discussed below.

Regional communities

Regional communities were another device tried by nations in the wake of the war. Among them the European regional community stands out as a successful example. From its inception as the European Economic Community to its ultimate growth into the European Union, the community embodied the principle of regionalism, the idea that neighbouring states should agree to share their security concerns, commercial interests, and environmental as well as other objectives. Instead of each nation pursuing its own agenda unilaterally, member states would define and seek to protect their common objectives, including regional security. The successful evolution of the European regional community has added a new dimension to conceptions of world order. Instead of an international system produced through geopolitical arrangements or through intergovernmental organizations, regionalism might provide the basis for world order. If, in addition to the European Union, other, equally successful regional schemes were developed, the world order would come to consist of several regional orders. At the beginning of the 21st century, there already existed, or were expected soon to be constructed, various regional groupings and arrangements in Southeast Asia, East Asia, North America, and South America. While not yet viable as a workable entity, African nations, on their part, have also created a regional community of their own. The list would seem to leave out only the Middle East. Whether the nations in that region would finally be able to establish something akin to a collective community would be one of the key questions that would determine the shape of a future world order.

Global economic system

It should be noted, however, that interstate arrangements, whether of geopolitical, intergovernmental, or regional variety, are all established by nations, whereas there are world orders that are not necessarily produced by them. An economically integrated world order, for instance, that emerged after around 1500 was a product as much of mercantile entrepreneurs as of states. A transnational commercial order developed in the wake of the 'discovery' of the New World, although historians disagree as to whether this 'world system' was essentially centred in Europe, as Immanuel Wallerstein (1974) has argued, or whether Asia, in particular India and China, continued to play major roles till at least the beginning of the 19th century, as André Gunder Frank (1998) has pointed out. There is little doubt, in any event, that scientific discoveries and technological inventions in the West enabled the latter to establish a closely interlinked world economic order by the second half of the 19th century. Technological and economic transformations gave rise to yet another world order, an international economic 'regime', which much later came to be referred to as 'globalization'. Globalization was clearly a type of world order, and its principal agents were merchants, bankers, trading and shipping companies, insurance businesses, labour contractors, and many others whose activities amounted to the creation of transnational networks.

Whether nations, in particular the great powers that were at that very moment establishing a world order consisting of empires, were also promoters of globalization has been debated among specialists. Many scholars, such as Niall Ferguson (2001), assume that imperialism and globalization were two sides of the same coin, that the imperialist powers by their very act of bringing their goods, capital, and technology to their colonies were promoting globalization and that, at the same time, global technologies vastly facilitated the governance of empires. As noted above, however, imperialism never worked as a system of world order. Indeed, by going to war against one another twice in 25 years, the imperialist powers severely damaged the functioning of the global economy, to such an extent that some scholars refer to the period between 1914 and 1945 as an age of economic deglobalization. Without the imperialistic rivalries that entailed armaments, patriotic excesses, and exclusionary trade policies, globalization might not have been set back for those thirty years.

In any event, globalization did re-emerge in the wake of the Second World War as a more promising means for establishing world order. In stark contrast to the failure of the two nuclear superpowers or of the United Nations to preserve world order, states and non-state actors alike contributed to the growth of an economic transnational order. Before the 1970s, this order was known as the Bretton Woods system that had been set up by the victorious nations during the war and that had tended to be dominated by one nation, the United States, which was far more successful in creating and sustaining an economic than a geopolitical world order. The momentum for globalization was so powerful that it survived the crisis of the Bretton Woods system in the early 1970s, when the dollar lost its hegemonic position in world commercial transactions and the United States began to record trade deficits, ultimately turning itself into a debtor nation. Globalization has survived not only because the European Union and other regional entities have promoted expansion of cross-national trade and investment, but also because multinational enterprises have seized the initiative and actively engaged themselves in linking all parts of the globe through goods, services, capital, and labour.

Globalization as a form of world order lacks a structure of governance comparable to national governments or to intergovernmental organizations such as the UN. But the successful continuation and expansion of economic globalization suggests that it has not 'just happened' automatically. On the contrary, governments, international bodies (such as the IMF and the World Bank), multinational enterprises, and many other bodies (including non-governmental organizations that are concerned with fighting corruption and promoting environmentalism) have often worked together to promote globalization in the belief that the reversal of the tide would be a calamity for all nations and all people. For this reason alone, economic globalization qualifies as one of the more successful world orders.

Shared values

Besides economic globalization, can there also be a world order defined by shared values? Students of globalization have been debating the question whether economic globalization will ultimately lead to the emergence of a global culture. In other words, can there be such a thing as ideological or cultural globalization? First of all, it is important to note that the European Union defines itself not simply through common commercial policies but also through shared values. All members of the regional communities are required to espouse certain principles and objectives: human rights, tolerance for diversity, environmental awareness, and many others. Some of these principles are explicitly stated as having had their origins in the Enlightenment, while others reflect more recent sensitivities. Moreover, the EU has established mechanisms for ensuring implementation of these objectives, such as the European Court of Human Rights as well as agencies that deal with common environmental, educational, and other matters. In all such regards, citizens of the member nations are supposed to consider themselves Europeans sharing certain values. It is fundamentally because of this shared ideological and moral commitment that there may be said to exist a robust regional system of governance in Europe.

Can the same things be said of other regional communities, now in existence or conceived as future possibilities? For instance, East Asia (embracing, for our purposes, China including Hong Kong, Taiwan, South Korea, and Japan) is developing as the fastest-growing area of the world economically, and these countries have entered into various bilateral and multilateral agreements, commercial, travel, and otherwise, to bind themselves even closer together. As yet, however, they have not succeeded in negotiating, let alone agreeing on, a statement of shared values. For one thing, history stands in the way. Unlike Germany and its former enemies, Japan and the victims of its colonialism and aggression (virtually all other Asian countries) have not come to a full reconciliation to the satisfaction of the latter. The problem is nationalistic history, education and propaganda in all countries, especially in Japan. It would be essential for them to understand that the past history of the region must be shared by all, that only a transnational perspective would enable them to arrive at a common understanding of that history. Even if some agreement were reached on the history issue, however, the Asian countries would still have to consider what other values they

shared (or would be able to share) in common. Unlike the European nations, they might hesitate to enshrine human rights as one such value, but without this principle, could there really be a functioning regional community? Some speak of 'Asian values' as opposed to 'Western values', but it is not clear what can be considered 'Asian'. Besides, if all regional communities were to assert their respective ideas and principles ('Asian values', 'African values', etc.), could a stable world order be built on such divergent foundations?

A moral order?

Such questions lead to a consideration of one of the fundamental conditions for the establishment of world order. Given cultural diversity, religious differences, and other divergences, can there be a moral world order embracing all people? John Boli and George W. Thomas (1999) have suggested that 'world culture', in the sense of transnational visions and objectives, has been in the process of construction primarily through the efforts of international non-governmental organizations. It may well be, as these as well as other scholars have argued, that transnational awareness of issues that all people share has been fostered more by private organizations than by governments. As non-state actors, such bodies have been freer than state agencies to cross national and regional boundaries to develop a sense of shared concern about the well-being of individuals and groups of people, regardless of where they live. With regard to human rights, for instance, various INGOs have been active in promoting the rights of refugees and minorities, while protesting against violations of the rights of prisoners, political dissidents, and many others all over the world. If non-state organizations' influence grows, it is conceivable that there may indeed emerge something akin to a global culture that might form the basis of a new world order.

Such an order, however, would not do away with existing religions, cultures, or civilizations. These are likely to stay and continue to define identities for individuals all over the world, so the question still remains as to whether religions, cultures, and civilizations may be able to come together to form some sort of global community. Over the centuries, various religious sects have tried to meet and form some sort of an ecumenical arrangement. These efforts have as yet produced little resembling a world religious order, but so long as religions exist, some such arrangements would be of critical importance to world order. Civilizations, including religions, have existed side by side since the origins of humankind, without any one of them establishing hegemony over the rest. Neither have there been 'clashes of civilizations' in modern times, contrary to repeated doomstering by fatalists. Instead, as William H. McNeill (1963), Patrick Manning (2003) and others have shown, civilizations have for centuries fed upon one another even in war as well as in peace, always transforming themselves and the global cultural landscape in the process. Nevertheless, their peaceful coexistence today and in the near future cannot simply be taken for granted but needs to be reconceptualized in terms of constructing world order. For religious intolerance or intercivilizational misunderstanding cannot be a solid foundation for any stable order. Perhaps some formula for 'dialogue among civilizations', one of the key activities undertaken by UNESCO since its inception in 1945, would have to be devised. The fact that the UN declared 2001 to be the Year for Dialogue Among Civilizations is a positive sign. Still, the continued animosity, sometimes including violence, among some religious extremists in recent years is troublesome, and serious efforts would have to continue to be made by all civilizations to aim for transcivilizational communication and understanding.

In this connection, it is relevant to note that in 19th-century European writings on international law, civilization was often equated with 'intercourse'; civilized nations were supposed to deal with each other on terms of equality, intermingling with one another at all levels and in all respects. Going a step further, we may observe that one fundamental condition of civilized behaviour is freedom of association, and association is what transnational connections entail. As people of different nations, religions, and civilizations come into closer contact with one another, are they able to establish free and equal relations among themselves? If so, there is civilization; if not, there will be no civilization despite the existence of civilizations. In some such way, we may conceptualize a world order based on the principle of civilization, one in which there are no hierarchies, no autarchies, no hegemony or discrimination, but in which transnational, transreligious, and transcivilizational connections are freely made and produce not anarchy but community, not barbarism but civilization.

Akira Iriye

Bibliography

Boli J. and Thomas G. W. 1999. *Constructing world culture: international nongovernmental organizations since 1875*. Stanford: Stanford University Press.

Bull H. 1995. *The anarchical society: a study of order in world politics*, 2nd edition. New York: Columbia University Press.

Ferguson N. 2001. *Empire: how Britain made the modern world*. London: Allen Lane.

Frank A. G. 1998. *ReOrient: global economy in the Asian age*. Berkeley: University of California Press.

Kennedy P. 1987. *The rise and fall of the great powers: economic change and military conflict from 1500 to 2000*. New York: Random House.

Manning P. 2003. *Navigating world history: a guide for researchers and teachers*. Basingstoke and New York: Palgrave Macmillan.

McNeill W. H. 1963. *The rise of the West: a history of the human community*. Chicago: Chicago University Press.

Wallerstein I. 1974. *The modern world system*, Vol. 1. New York: Academic Press.

Related essays

Africa; African liberation; America; Asia; China; civilizations; Cold War; convergence and divergence; cosmopolitanism and universalism; empires and imperialism; environmentalism; European Union (EU); financial diplomacy; financial markets; globalization; human rights; intergovernmental organizations; international migration regimes; international non-governmental organizations (INGOs); internationalisms; investment; Japan; justice; language diplomacy; League of Nations system; legal order; literature; nation and state; pan-isms; regimes; regional communities; trade; transnational; underdevelopment; United Nations system; war crimes; Westernization

WTO and GATT *See* General Agreement on Tariffs and Trade (GATT) / World Trade Organization (WTO)

Y

Yoga

Yoga has been defined in many ways, but to make any sense of its broad scope, the definition must be located within a particular historical context. The 'classical' version of yoga is that of the *Yoga Sutras* of Patanjali (probably written between 200 BCE and 200 CE), in which the eight stages of yoga begin with the practice of morality in social life: *yama, niyama* – universal and personal rules for living; followed by physical practices: *asana, pranayama* – physical poses and breathing techniques; and then move on to different states of mental attention or consciousness: *pratyahara, dharana, dhyana, samadhi* – gradual removal of external sensory input, focusing attention on a single point, uninterrupted meditative state, and – depending on the school of thought – perfect isolation or union with the Absolute.

Although there was a small contingent of scholars interested in yoga outside of India in the late 18th and early 19th centuries, the foundations for development of broader interest in yoga were set by the leaders of the neo-Hindu renaissance of the early/mid 19th century, such as Brahmo Samaj founder Rammohan Roy, Keshubchandra Sen, and Debendranath Tagore; the American Transcendentalists Emerson and Thoreau were quite taken with this approach to Hindu thought. By the 1890s, a much broader popular as well as academic audience for yoga began to develop in the United States and Western Europe. We can date a great deal of this interest to a series of public lectures that the Indian student of Sri Ramakrishna, Narendranath Datta – later known as Swami Vivekananda – gave at the Chicago World's Fair in 1893, as well as in several other American and European cities until 1897.

Vivekananda's presentation of the rich range of textual traditions that come under the heading of yoga in India was augmented substantially by his experiences in the West. Yoga, described in Vivekananda's lectures as well as printed pamphlets, became a commodity, something of value that could be acquired and circulated among the literate middle-class people of both India and the West. Swami Vivekananda presented yoga as a spiritual commodity that had an explicit exchange value for people in America and Europe. He said that India had an abundance of spiritual wealth, and that yoga was a method that could help people to achieve spiritual well-being. In return, the West – well-known for its material resources – could pay cash for the privilege of learning yoga. One of those strongly influenced by Vivekananda's teachings was Swami Sivananda of Rishikesh, India, an allopathic medical doctor from south India who left his successful career to become one of India's best-known 20th-century religious figures. Sivananda's students were sent from Rishikesh to locations throughout India and the other continents, bringing this Vivekananda-inspired approach to yogic life to middle-class people in many countries. Another of the major transnational proponents of yoga, whose focus has largely been on postures and breathing techniques, is B. K. S. Iyengar of Pune. Through these two proponents of yoga in India, extensive transnational networks of teachers and students have emerged, with surges of global popularity seen in the 1950s, 1970s, and 1990s.

For the Western audience, the appeal of yoga lay in the presentation of a universal spiritual framework that was non-exclusive, 'scientific' (testable through personal practice), and seemingly universal. For Indians, yoga was emblematic of a revered precolonial past; it offered not only ideas and practices, but also heroes and success stories, that could be applied to the rising nationalist project. No longer a set of religious ideologies and ascetic practices belonging only to a relatively small group of specialists on the Indian subcontinent, yoga has also become part of the contemporary repertoire of men and women at all life stages and in many different countries. This modern transformation represents a shift from a regional, specialized religious discourse and practice geared toward liberation of the self from the endless cycle of lives, to a transnational, secular, socially critical ideology and practice aimed at freedom to achieve personal well-being.

Sarah Strauss

Bibliography

Alter J. S. 2004. *Yoga in modern India.*
Princeton: Princeton University Press.
De Michelis E. 2005. *A history of modern yoga.*
London: Continuum.
Strauss S. 2005. *Positioning yoga.* Oxford:
Berg.

Related essays
Asia; Beatles; civilizations; commodity
trading; expositions; feel-good culture;
knowledge; New Age; Orientalism; religion;
Westernization; Zen aesthetics

Youth organizations

Youth organizations, as movements of young
people striving towards shared religious,
social, educational and political goals, have
frequently sought to build transnational
links. They wanted to proselytize, achieve
political goals, or simply help young people become acquainted with foreign lands.
Sometimes they were co-opted for the foreign policy objectives of national governments and intergovernmental agencies,
while other times they asserted themselves
as independent actors in the international
arena. Since the late 19th century, youth
organizations have been building an increasingly dense network of cross-border relationships, involving not only officials, but also
more and more grassroots members as well
as non-member youth.

Even during the founding stages, the first
youth organizations were already reaching
out internationally. The middle of the 19th
century saw the founding of the Young Men's
Christian Association (YMCA), and later
the Young Women's Christian Association
(YWCA), at first in England, and then in other
parts of Europe and in North America; their
purpose was to spread Protestant teachings
among working-class youth. In the 1890s, a
volunteer student movement emerged from
the American YMCA, sending missions to
Asia, where they set up hands-on community service projects. Similar to the Boy Scout
movement, they often established nationwide networks of local branches, engaging
youth in their hometowns. The Scouts
were first established in England in 1908
by Robert Baden-Powell as an educational
movement originally modelled on military
ideals. It quickly spread to other countries,
leading in 1920 to an international federation which would become the forerunner
of today's World Organization of the Scout
Movement.

The year 1889 saw the founding of a politically and religiously neutral organization
called the International Student Federation
(ISF/FIE), which spread to continents
beyond Europe before World War 1; with its
numerous student conventions, sports events,
and exchange programmes, it was the most
important organization in this field. Around
the year 1900, a complex middle-class youth
movement emerged in Germany and spread
across national boundaries, taking the custom of the youth grand tour (*Wanderjahr*,
Tour de France) which had become widespread among European youth since the
early 19th century, and reinterpreting it as a
cosmopolitan experience leading to a practical critique of civilization. Parallel to the
youth movement was the emergence of youth
hostels, which also began in Germany, before
spreading to other countries after 1925; these
were to offer affordable lodging to groups of
travelling youth, thus serving as central meeting points of international youth tourism.
The International Youth Hostel Federation
was established in 1932.

The end of the First World War triggered
another wave of transnational networking
among youth movements. This process was
eased by the democratization of society in
many countries, such as in Germany, where
the ban on youth political activities was
lifted. Youth had already appeared in a revolutionary role before the First World War (e.g.
circa 1830 in national youth movements such
as Giovine Italia and Junges Deutschland),
but it was only from the beginning of the
20th century that they started to see themselves as participants in a worldwide revolutionary process. Among those political youth
organizations forming immediately after
the turn of the century, it was the socialist
and Communist movements which took on
a decidedly ambitious outlook, developing
multilayered strategies of cooperation across
national borders. The socialist youth organizations, which had often been formed against
the will of the Social Democratic parties of
Europe, agreed in 1907 on the guidelines of
a common programme and established an
international office. Born in the struggle
against the military recruitment of young
men, socialist youth associations maintained their steadfast opposition throughout
World War 1, becoming radicalized around
war's end. Willi Münzenberg, the leader
of the international youth office, would
become a co-founder of Communist Youth
International in 1919. It was an activist youth
movement which wanted to help spread the
idea of world revolution, building a closely
knit network around the entire globe, and

becoming especially active in the revolutionary movements of Asia. The year 1923 saw the founding of Socialist Youth International, which was at first limited mostly to Europe; it was only after World War 2, with the formation of the International Union of Socialist Youth (IUSY) in 1946, that youth organizations particularly from 'Third World' countries also became involved. International umbrella associations of anarchist and liberal youth organizations emerged in 1928. During the heyday of nationalism following the First World War, ideas of international connectedness found considerable resonance within even the most nationalistic quarters. Movements such as *Kolonialjugend* ('colonial youth') and *Kolonialpfadfinder* ('colonial scouts') combined the idea of nationalistic expansion with romantic visions of exotic peoples and faraway lands. Already, after World War 1, organizations with continental scope were being formed in Africa, Asia, and Latin America (in part by students at European universities, such as the West African Students' Union established in London in 1925). They would frequently play a significant role in the decolonization movement. In the age of postcolonial nationalism, they ideologically as well as practically transcended the nationalist creed of postcolonial new nation states and fostered understanding and cooperation between students from different nations, for example through the Asian Student Association (formed in 1969) and the Arab Youth Union (1974).

Simultaneously, exchanges between youth associations became politically constricted, partly due to radicalizing nationalism, leading to an almost complete standstill during World War 2. The foundation of the United Nations, with its own youth department, led to a third wave of networking after 1945. It was thought that especially the young would and should advance the cause of understanding between peoples. However, this euphoria was to be limited and channelled by the Cold War, resulting in two competing currents. The World Federation of Democratic Youth (WFDY, 1945), and the International Union of Students or IUS (1946) were both originally established as organizations of the United Nations, and formed the umbrella organizations of the Communist associations and their allies. The World Assembly of Youth or WAY (1949) and the International Students' Conference (ISC, 1950) were supported by the non-Communist organizations of Western and pro-Western countries. While the ISC and WAY concentrated their activities on conferences, study trips and exchanges, the WFDY organized the 'World Festival of Youth and Students', which took place sixteen times between 1947 and 2005, attracting between 10,000 and 30,000 participants each time, with delegations from non-Communist organizations, particularly in the 1970s and 80s. Despite the divisions drawn along the fault lines of world politics, cooperation between youth organizations continued to increase significantly. They frequently coordinated campaigns to highlight global problems such as 'Third World' exploitation, environmental pollution, and racism. School and student exchanges, international work camps and youth tourism were also in part being supported and encouraged by youth organizations – frequently with the assistance of governmental agencies, which were trying to foster cultural exchange through these programmes.

The interdependence of cultural and political youth movements was stepped up by the worldwide events of '1968', which saw the culmination of various structural changes in society emerging from the 'golden years' after 1945. '1968' also signalled a change in the functioning of youth organizations, because mass consumerism, medialization, decolonization, tourism and increasing access to higher education were allowing youth to build their own relationships, individually and without the assistance of organizations. At the same time, traditional social milieus were losing their bonding powers, which meant a decreasing membership in both church and labour organizations. Around 1968, there were already signs that youth were now favouring more informal ways of getting together, while at the same time, the global character of major issues and the protest movement were becoming ever more visible. The emergence of a global youth culture from the late 1950s also affected the forms of transnational relationships. Transnational contacts became more valuable in the practical work of youth organizations; meanwhile, new international protest movements were emerging, in which numerous youths participated. They were attracted by the possibility of international engagement within a looser organizational structure. Amnesty

International (since 1961), Greenpeace (since 1979) and Attack (since 1998) are examples of global organizations that thrived on the protest branch of youth culture. Hippies, squats, and 'autonomous' left-wing radical groups represent largely unstructured youth movements combined with extensive transnational networking. As collectives of primarily young people, they represent (for now) the last wave of youth movements, finding its full vigour after the dissolution of the Soviet Union, but already beginning in the 1970s. By the wayside remain a multitude of religious, political and cultural youth organizations which are transnationally connected by mostly shrinking memberships, and which offer youth a broad frame of action.

Detlef Siegfried

Bibliography

Altbach P. G. and Uphoff N. T. 1973. The Student Internationals. Metuchen: Scarecrow.

Angel W. D. 1990. Youth movements of the world. Harlow: Longman.

Baubérot A. and Duval N. 2006. Le scoutisme entre guerre et paix au XX siècle. Paris: l'Harmattan.

Bresslein E. 1973. Drushba! Freundschaft? Von der Kommunistischen Jugendinternationale zu den Weltjugendfestspielen. Frankfurt am Main: Fischer.

Luza R. 1970. History of the International Socialist Youth Movement. Leiden: A. W. Sijthoff.

Related essays

1960s; Africa; Amnesty International (AI); anarchism; anti-racism; Asia; Christianity; Cold War; consumer society; decolonization; empires and imperialism; freemasonry; Greenpeace; higher education; international non-governmental organizations (INGOs); International Red Cross and Red Crescent movement; international students; liberalism; missionaries; pan-isms; regions; Romanticism; socialism; sport; tourism; United Nations system; women's movements; workers' movements

Z

Zen aesthetics

Zen aesthetics refers to the expressive principles of forms and objects related to Zen Buddhism, primarily in Japan, but with historical links to China and influencing the modern West. Associated with simplicity and restraint, Zen aesthetics as a form of anti-materialism has served both liberal and non-liberal politics.

The mobile history of Zen began with the transmission of the faith in the 6th century by the Indian monk Bodhidharma (Daruma) to China as Chan, where it absorbed Daoist elements before being brought to Japan by the monk Eisai (1141–1215). Zen, meaning 'meditation', is the Japanese equivalent of Chan. Current Zen aesthetics has been identified with various Japanese cultural products, including tea-drinking (imported from China by Eisai), tea-wares of various kinds, especially those characterized by imperfect shapes and blemished surfaces, and sedate architecture such as the Silver Pavilion in Kyoto. Built by Shogun Ashikaga Yoshimasa in the 15th century, the two-storey main building of the Silver Pavilion and the spartan décor of the tea-room inside a facing structure, the Tōgūdō, embodied an emergent taste for unostentatious elegance. The tea-room's diminutive size, its tatami flooring, and translucent shoji doors and window have also come to typify the Japanese-style room in subsequent ages.

Art produced by Zen monks in the Muromachi period (1336–1573), such as the kind of monochrome ink painting inspired by compositions developed in the Song (960–1279), Yuan (1260–1368), and Ming (1368–1644) dynasties, is an additional component of today's Zen aesthetic canon. Another Muromachi-period phenomenon that has been subsequently described as 'Zen' is the dry landscape garden, exemplified by Ryōanji in Kyoto.

Japanese Zen and Buddhism in general declined during the Tokugawa period (1600–1868), when the ruling warrior class adopted Neo-Confucianism as their guiding philosophy. Chinese poetry and the ritualized drinking of tea, deeply entrenched in Japanese culture by this time, persisted despite waning shogunal sponsorship of Zen Buddhism.

In the early years of the Meiji period (1868–1912) the Japanese government persecuted Buddhism as anti-scientific superstition in a movement known as haibutsu kishaku ('abolishing Buddhism and destroying Sakyamuni'), leaving many temples in a state of ruination. By the 1880s, thanks to sympathizers with traditional Japanese culture such as the American Japanophile Ernest Fenollosa (1853–1908) and his student-collaborator Okakura Kakuzō (1862–1913), Buddhism regained some footing. Zen Buddhism itself evolved into a political apparatus, due to its endorsement by nationalists such as the monk-artist Nantembō (1839–1925) and his spiritual follower General Nogi Maresuke (1849–1912), a national hero from the Sino-Japanese War (1894–95) and the Russo-Japanese War (1904–05).

Zen Buddhists' complicity in World War 2 was deep and extensive. Although Shinto and other Buddhist sects also supported Japanese imperialism, Zen's historical associations with the warrior culture made it an ideal vehicle to romanticize militarism. Books by lay persons such as Okakura and D. T. Suzuki (1870–1966) stressed the close relationship between Zen and 'the way of the samurai'; they proclaimed Zen to be the essence of Japanese culture, while largely overlooking the transnational (particularly Chinese) influences on Zen. The connection between Japanese expansive nationalism and Zen was especially clear with the Myōshin-ji School of Kyoto. The Myōshin-ji School is the largest school in Rinzai Zen, a Zen sect that emphasizes sudden enlightenment and vigorous mental exercises. In 2001, the leaders of Myōshin-ji issued a public apology, confessing the temple's wartime involvement in military fundraising and in establishing branch headquarters and missions in conquered areas.

The English editions of D. T. Suzuki's An Introduction to Zen Buddhism (1949) and of Eugen Herrigel's Zen in the Art of Archery (1953) emphasized concepts of 'emptiness' and 'no-mind', creating a reduced reading of Zen attractive to Westerners unsuspecting of the nationalist underpinnings. Among the Zen-inspired generation of Western artists who came of age in the 1950s and 1960s were the French neo-Dadaist Yves Klein, the American experimental musician John Cage, and the Japanese-American sculptor Isamu Noguchi who constructed modern versions of the dry landscape garden. The 'Zen' understanding of these individuals revolved around abstraction, humour, chance, and pure experience. After World War 2, contact with Korea, Vietnam, Laos, and Cambodia fuelled Western interest in holistic Asian ideas. Zen Buddhism became at this time a path to recovering the original purpose in art, music, or poetry, and involved the exploration of the self and the universe.

In the fashion arena of the late 20th century, Tokyo-based designers Miyake Issei (Issey), Kawakubo Rei of Comme des Garçons, and Yamamoto Yōji prompted Zen interpretations by displaying austerity in form and colour. Yamamoto showed his first collection in 1977, and his clothing has since been defined by a palette of monochromes – black, navy, and white, with occasional splashes of colour. Austerity in fashion paralleled the avant-garde's rejection of conventional ideas of finish, popular culture, and middle-class lifestyle. These Japanese designers created a new vogue that revolutionized fashion worldwide, starting in Paris. Yamamoto has been awarded the French Chevalier de l'Ordre des Arts et Lettres.

In 1998, the Chinese experimental artist, Cai Guoqiang, burned dragon-shaped patterns of exploded gunpowder onto 63 pieces of Miyake Issey's signature 'Pleats Please' garments at the Fondation Cartier pour l'Art Contemporain. Runway models paraded these white-and-sepia gowns as part of Cai's performance piece. In 2003, Cai sent large circles of fire and light into the air over New York's Central Park. These evoked the ensō, a favourite motif in Zen painting and calligraphy, as symbols of renewal and wholeness after 9/11. Such works typify the post-Orientalist moment, in which Asians deploy quasi-religious concepts, while enlisting other Asians and/or Westerners to steer ethnic marginality towards the transnational mainstream.

Aida Yuen Wong

Bibliography

Baas J. 2005. *Smile of the Buddha: Eastern philosophy and Western art from Monet to today*. Berkeley and Los Angeles: University of California Press.

Seo A. Y. with Addiss S. 1998. *The art of twentieth-century Zen*. Boston, MA: Shambhala.

Sharf R. H. 1993. 'The Zen of Japanese nationalism', *History of Religions*, 33, 1, 1–43.

Victoria B. 2006. *Zen at war*, 2nd ed. Lanham: Rowman & Littlefield.

Related essays

art market; avant garde; Buddhism; cosmopolitanism and universalism; fashion; feel-good culture; Japan; liberalism; nation and state; Orientalism; religion; Westernization; yoga

Zero growth

Broadly defined as the process of increasing activity, growth is a basic assumption of most economic theory. From the 1960s, the so-called 'zero growth' movement questioned entrenched assumptions about the desirability of growth, offering an alternative vision of sustainable equilibrium. Much debated, arguments for 'zero growth' challenged a transnational consensus about the desirability of growth and highlighted limits that might restrain humankind's development in the future.

Growth was a secular religion after World War 2, a faith that transcended divisions between East and West, North and South. The occasional naysayer, such as Mahatma Gandhi, might have condemned the cult of materialism as destructive and unsustainable, but such arguments were less appealing than the visions of affluence offered by steel mills, automobile factories, and hydroelectric dams.

Whatever else they might have disagreed on, capitalists and Communists in the Cold War concurred on the desirability of growth, as they competed to exceed each other's production targets, measured using new tools of macroeconomic analysis such as Gross Domestic Product (GDP). Within the capitalist world, 'the politics of productivity', as historian Charles Maier has described them, became a panacea for the distributional conflicts that had wrecked the prewar world. Why fight over how to divide the economic cake, asked the proponents of growth, when workers and capitalists could cooperate to make the rewards bigger for everyone? The foundation of the postwar 'miracle', growth was unchallenged for a generation, until the late 1960s when a new generation of critics began to debate the costs that it might entail.

Space exploration contributed to humankind's awareness of ecological limits. This vision of an indivisible world substantiated the arguments that a finite globe – 'Spaceship Earth' – could not support untrammelled growth and provided an essential context for the 'zero growth' movement in the early 1970s. The most influential contribution to the 'zero growth' debates – although it did not use this phrase, which was preferred by critics – was the 1972 report of The Club of Rome, an international colloquium of academics. Based upon econometric models and sophisticated computer analysis, The Club of Rome's report, The limits to growth, argued that current rates of global population and economic growth were unsustainable and, if maintained, would produce a worldwide cataclysm before the end of the 21st century. The report argued that 'negative feedback loops' – pollution and the depletion of resources – would kick in unless humankind could stabilize its own 'positive feedback loops' – growth in population and economic activity – at a 'global equilibrium'. This stable equilibrium would be a world without growth, an objective that dramatically repudiated the prevailing cult of economic expansionism.

The Club of Rome's concept of a global equilibrium depended on a theoretical model that ignored barriers between nation states; it looked at the world in terms of planetary aggregates and was thus an authentically transnational project. The report's conclusions accorded with the work of the German economist E. F. Schumacher, who inveighed against growth in the Gandhian language of sustainability and liveability.

Critics of The limits to growth took issue with the report's political assumptions and its methodological techniques. The French demographer Alfred Sauvy contended that the use of global data was inappropriate for a world that remained divided into sovereign nation states. While some nations might be approaching the limits to growth, Sauvy argued, other countries – such as Australia or Canada – still enjoyed tremendous room to expand their populations and economies.

Another complaint against The Club of Rome's agenda was that it sought to stabilize a condition of Western economic dominance. Although the report's authors insisted that redistributive justice among nations would be part of the their 'global equilibrium', critics countered that 'zero growth' was hostile to the material aspirations of the developing world. That the United States government seriously engaged with the issues raised by the 1972 report may have only reinforced suspicions elsewhere that 'global equilibrium' harboured an anti-Third World agenda.

The 'zero growth' debates of the early 1970s represented an important effort to reconcile humankind's aspirations to the physical and ecological limits of Planet Earth. Although subsequent methodological innovations have revised many of The Club of Rome's assumptions, the concept of equilibrium remains an objective for the environmentalist movement. At the same time, the growth debates of the 1970s illustrate the difficulties facing proponents of transnational objectives in a global society that, although increasingly aware of its own interdependence, remains divided into a patchwork of politically sovereign states committed to autonomous national objectives.

Daniel Sargent

Bibliography

Club of Rome 1972. The limits to growth: a report for The Club of Rome's project on the predicament of mankind. New York: Universe.

Sandbach F. 1978. 'The rise and fall of the "limits to growth" debate', Social Studies of Science, 8, 4, 495–520.

Sauvy A. 1976. Zero growth? New York: Praeger.

Schumacher E. F. 1973. Small is beautiful: a study of economics as if people mattered. London: Blond & Briggs.

Related essays

climate change; Cold War; conservation and preservation; convergence and divergence; development and growth; developmental taxonomies; ecology; economics; environmentalism; intellectual elites; national accounting systems; outer space; population; sustainable development; underdevelopment

Zionism

Zionism is a political movement intended to re-create and then maintain a Jewish state in the Holy Land, or what once was called Judaea and Palestine.

The ancient Jews or Israelites lived and mostly governed the general area of modern Israel for about thirteen hundred years, from around 1200 BC until 135 AD, during which time they suffered various conquests and exiles by the Assyrians, Babylonians, and finally Romans. After destruction of Jewish sovereignty, Jews always remained in the Holy Land but endured conquests by the Arabs, European Christian Crusaders, Tartars, Ottomans and others. Jews who lived in the Diaspora also experienced centuries of torment, and many prayed for messianic redemption and a return to Jerusalem.

A surge of romantic nationalism across Europe in the mid 19th century and a rise of racial anti-Semitism led some Jews to begin thinking seriously about taking matters into their own hands and fulfilling their dreams of restoration. Moses Hess, an assimilated German Jew, leading socialist and strong supporter of Giuseppe Mazzini's Italian nationalist movement, believed that anti-Semitism would persist and so he advocated Jewish return to Palestine in a generally unnoticed book, *Rome and Jerusalem* (1862). The pogroms of 1881–82 in Tsarist Russia, where half of the world's Jewish population lived, concentrated Jewish minds on creating Zionist organizations and settling in Palestine. These Russian Jews – who combined a devotion to various (mostly) liberal values and a spiritual bond with the soil, with a respect for their ancient religious tradition – developed a sense of nationalism, epitomized in Leo Pinsker's *Auto-Emancipation* (1882) in which he argued that anti-Semitism was virulent and deep and called Jews to establish their own state. Tens of thousands of Russian Jews moved to Palestine in the late 19th century, and they formed a majority of the Jerusalem population.

It was Theodor Herzl, a distinctly assimilated Central European Jew, who made Zionism a viable political movement and put it on the map of international politics. The anti-Semitic Dreyfus affair in allegedly liberal France galvanized Herzl into publishing *Der Judenstaat* (1896, commonly translated as *The Jewish state*), which declared that the Jews required their own state – preferably in Palestine – to avoid extinction through assimilation or, more immediately, relentless persecution. He appealed to Gentile (non-Jewish) minds and their anti-Semitic impulses, arguing that it was in Gentile self-interest for the Jews to move to (Ottoman-controlled) Palestine and establish a liberal, civilized, Western state. He convened the First Zionist Congress in Basel, Switzerland (1897), and established the organizational mechanisms for the movement. Herzl died in 1904.

Some Zionists envisioned a Jewish state as a regular state that would 'normalize' the Jewish predicament, while others conceived of a Jewish state offering additional socialist, cultural, religious, liberal and moral values. Among Gentiles, support for Zionism ranged from seeing Jewish restoration to Palestine as righting a historical wrong, offering refuge to a persecuted people, fulfilling Providential will, precipitating the Second Coming, spreading civilization, to even getting rid of Jews in their midst. And yet, many established and wealthy Jews opposed Zionism out of concern about their place and security in their native lands. Middle Eastern Arabs, particularly those in Palestine, also ardently opposed it and portrayed the movement as a Western imperialist imposition. As a radical and romantic cause that required the movement of Jews from across boundaries to return to their ancient land of sovereignty, Zionism comprised an odd mix of Jewish nationalism and internationalism, and raised almost as many questions as it attempted to answer.

Motivated by religious, humanitarian and strategic objectives, Britain, on 2 November 1917, during the First World War, issued the Balfour Declaration to world Jewry, committing the country to 'the establishment in Palestine of a national home for the Jewish people'. Britain was able to make good on the promise when it captured Palestine from the Ottomans during the war, and administered it in a postwar League of Nations mandate until 1948. The borders of Palestine, as with new Arab states, were carved out of the former Ottoman Empire with much arbitrariness, contributing to subsequent conflicts. Britain confronted the challenge of controlling an area which was majority Arab (though rising Jewish immigration changed the demographics), and eventually reneged on its commitment to the Jews, seeking to keep Palestine for itself and other Arab states. When Britain withdrew in May 1948 in the face of a United Nations vote favouring a Jewish state in Palestine, Zionists overcame attacks by neighbouring Arabs states seeking to drive them into the sea, and established the first Jewish state in more than eighteen hundred years, in one of the most dramatic political developments of the 20th century.

Since 1948, Zionism still exists as a movement, though now it essentially focuses on supporting the State of Israel, and on many of the relatively mundane challenges states normally face. But Israel is not a normal state, and it has served as a refuge and sometimes protector of Jews in persecuted lands – whether in Africa, Soviet-controlled Russia or Eastern Europe, or in Arab lands. With about 5.3 million Jews, Israel has more Jews than any other country and approximately 41% of the world's Jewish population. Its many achievements in scientific, literary, military and humanitarian spheres still inspire pride and confidence among many Jews abroad who believe a Jewish state needs to exist even if they do not live there. Still, its unresolved conflict with Palestinian Arabs – many of whom claim all the land of Israel – has weakened its international support, while it often remains a victim of long-standing religious anti-Judaism and racial anti-Semitism in Christian and Muslim lands. The Zionist movement's dream of restoration of Jewish sovereignty to the Holy Land has been fulfilled, but its hope of acceptance in the Gentile world remains elusive.

Michael Makovsky

Bibliography

Makovsky M. 2007. Churchill's Promised Land: Zionism and statecraft. New Haven: Yale University Press / New Republic Books.

Related essays

antisemitism; diasporas; empires and imperialism; Ethical Culture; Holocaust; internationalisms; kindergarten; language; literature; nation and state; Romanticism; socialism; United Nations decades and years; world orders

Name Index

Note: individuals, named organizations, cities, countries and other geographic areas are listed herein. Entries applying primarily to cities are not duplicated under countries; those to people (including heads of state) are not either. Individual buildings are listed under cities or countries as most appropriate. For countries, see also continental and other larger geographic units. Movements of thought, treaties, conventions etc. are listed in the subject index. Where authors are listed, publications generally are not; similarly, film directors are listed but generally not film titles. Organizations of primarily national scope are listed selectively, under the respective country. Most UN-sponsored organizations are listed under United Nations. Titles and positions of individuals are not given unless necessary to distinguish or identify them. Prepositions and the prefixes 'al', 'd' and 'El' are ignored in setting alphabetic order. pt: preferred term (under which entries on the subject are listed unless inappropriate).

Subject Index

Note: see the Name index for proper names of individuals, organizations and geographic units. Treaties and conventions are listed in this index. Conferences and meetings are listed selectively. pt: preferred term (under which entries on the subject are listed unless inappropriate).